UN

COMMERCIAL
CODE

FOURTEENTH EDITION

The American Law Institute

National Conference of
Commissioners on Uniform State Laws

OFFICIAL TEXT—1995

WITH COMMENTS
INCLUDING ARTICLE 2A (LEASES), REVISED ARTICLE
3 (NEGOTIABLE INSTRUMENTS), AMENDED ARTICLE
4 (BANK DEPOSITS AND COLLECTIONS), ARTICLE
4A (FUNDS TRANSFERS), REVISED ARTICLE 5 (LETTERS
OF CREDIT), REVISED ARTICLE 6 (BULK SALES),
AND REVISED (1994) ARTICLE 8
(INVESTMENT SECURITIES)
INDEX

The Executive Office
The American Law Institute
4025 Chestnut Street
Philadelphia, Pennsylvania 19104

National Conference of
Commissioners on Uniform State Laws
676 North St. Clair Street, Suite 1700
Chicago, Illinois 60611

TEXT IS PRINTED ON 10% POST CONSUMER RECYCLED PAPER

Printed with Printwise
Environmentally Advanced Water Washable Ink

PREFACE

This Pamphlet contains the text of the Uniform Commercial Code prepared under the joint sponsorship of The American Law Institute and the National Conference of Commissioners on Uniform State Laws, as last amended in 1994.

The Code is a comprehensive modernization of various statutes relating to commercial transactions including sales, leases, negotiable instruments, bank deposits and collections, funds transfers, letters of credit, bulk sales, documents of title, investment securities and secured transactions. It replaces the former Uniform Laws relating to sales, conditional sales, negotiable instruments, warehouse receipts, bills of lading, stock transfers and trust receipts.

The Code was originally approved by its sponsors and the American Bar Association in 1952, and was revised in 1958 to incorporate a number of changes that had been recommended by the New York Law Revision Commission and other agencies. Subsequent amendments that were deemed desirable in the light of experience under the Code were approved by the Permanent Editorial Board in 1962 and 1966. Article 9, Secured Transactions, was revised in 1972, and a number of conforming amendments were approved at the same time. Article 8, Investment Securities, was revised in 1977, and more conforming amendments were approved at that time. Article 2A (Leases) was approved in 1987. Article 6 (formerly Bulk Transfers, now Bulk Sales) was revised in 1989 and conforming amendments were approved at the same time. Article 4A (Funds Transfers) was approved in 1989. In 1990, substantial amendments were made to Article 2A. Further, Article 3 (formerly Commercial Paper, now Negotiable Instruments) was revised in 1990 and conforming amendments thereto were approved. In addition, conforming [to Revised Article 3] and miscellaneous amendments were made to Article 4 (Bank Deposits and Collections). A further revision of Article 8 (Investment Securities) was made in 1994. At the same time, amendments conforming to the 1994 revision of Article 8 were made to Articles 1, 4, 5, 9, and 10. Further changes in the Official Comments to some sections of the Code were made in 1995 to conform to the 1994 revision of Article 8. Article 5 (Letters of Credit) was revised in 1995 and conforming amendments thereto were made to Articles 1, 2, and 9.

OFFICIAL COMMENTS

One of the indispensable features herein consists of the Official Comments, prepared by the National Conference of Commissioners on Uniform State Laws and The American Law Institute, which appear under each section. These Comments explain the purpose and intent of the sections and the changes in the prior law that were affected by the Code.

APPENDICES RELATING TO 1972, 1977, AND 1987 CHANGES

Appendices are included containing material relating to the 1972 revision of Article 9, the 1977 revision of Article 8 and the 1987 adoption of Article 2A (Leases).

Appendix I shows the changes in Article 8, and related sections. Included under each section are statements as to the reason for change.

Appendix II shows the changes in Article 9, and related sections. Included under each section are statements as to the reasons for change. Discussions under sections of Article 11 are found in Appendix II, and treat transitional problems for those jurisdictions enacting the changes.

Appendix III contains the text of the Article 1 and Article 9 amendments conforming to new Article 2A (Leases) and the Official Comments thereto.

APPENDICES CONTAINING TEXT AND OFFICIAL COMMENTS OF PRE–REVISION ARTICLE 5, PRE–REVISION ARTICLE 6, PRE–REVISION ARTICLE 3, AND PRE–REVISION (1994) ARTICLE 8

As noted above, Article 6 was revised in 1989, Article 3 was revised in 1990, Article 8 was further revised in 1994, and Article 5 was revised in 1995. The Text and Official Comments of Article 6, Article 3, Article 8, and Article 5, as they existed prior to revision, have been retained, and may be found in Appendices IV, VII, XIII and XV, respectively.

APPENDIX CONTAINING 1990 ARTICLE 1 AMENDMENTS CONFORMING TO REVISED ARTICLE 3

In conjunction with the revision of Article 3 in 1990, conforming amendments to Article 1 were approved. These amendments may be found in Appendix VIII.

APPENDICES CONTAINING 1990 AMENDMENTS TO ARTICLE 4 WITH REASONS FOR 1990 CHANGES AND TEXT AND OFFICIAL COMMENTS OF PRE–1994 ARTICLE 4

In 1990, a substantial number of amendments were made to Article 4. Many of these were made to conform to Revised Article 3. Others were miscellaneous amendments. These amendments, together with the reasons for the 1990 changes, may all be found in Appendix IX. The text and Official Comments of Article 4 as they existed prior to amendment in 1990, have been retained, and may be found in Appendix X.

APPENDIX CONTAINING 1990 AMENDMENTS TO ARTICLE 2A

In 1990, twenty-four text amendments were made to Article 2A. In addition, the Official Comments of three sections which were not amended textually, were changed to conform to the various text amendments. All of these may be found in Appendix VI.

APPENDIX CONTAINING 1994 AND 1995 AMENDMENTS TO ARTICLES 1, 3, 4, 5, 9, AND 10 CONFORMING TO 1994 REVISION OF ARTICLE 8

In 1994 and 1995, amendments to Articles 1, 3, 4, 5, 9, and 10 were made to conform to the 1994 revision of Article 8. These amendments may be found in Appendix XII.

APPENDIX CONTAINING VARIOUS 1994 AMENDMENTS

Various amendments were made in 1994 not relating to the revision of Article 8. These amendments may be found in Appendix XI.

APPENDIX CONTAINING 1995 AMENDMENTS TO ARTICLES 1, 2, AND 9 CONFORMING TO REVISED ARTICLE 5

In 1995, amendments to Articles 1, 2, and 9 were made to conform to the revision of Article 5. These amendments may be found in Appendix XIV.

APPENDIX CONTAINING PERMANENT EDITORIAL BOARD (PEB) COMMENTARY

The Permanent Editorial Board for the Uniform Commercial Code will issue supplementary commentary on the Code from time to time. The final draft of Commentaries 1 to 14 may be found in Appendix V. These commentaries normally identify an issue, discuss the issue and come to a conclusion as to how the issue should be resolved. Often, the conclusion will result in a change in the Official Comment of one or more sections of the Code. The Official Comment, when so changed, will generally refer to the PEB Commentary which brought about the change. All changes in the Official Comments as a result of Commentaries 1 to 14 have been incorporated into this Pamphlet

SPECIAL FEATURES

The various materials in the preliminary part of this Pamphlet all contribute to a better understanding of the Code and aid in its interpretation. The Article, Part and Section analysis, beginning on page 1, provides an easy means of finding particular provisions of the Code.

TABLE OF SECTIONS OF PRIOR UNIFORM ACTS

A table has been included showing sections of the prior Uniform Acts that have been replaced by the Code and relevant sections in the Code.

PREFACE

INDEX

For this Fourteenth Edition, an expanded and up-to-date index has been prepared by the publisher's Editorial Staff.

THE PUBLISHER

March, 1996

TABLE OF CONTENTS

Uniform Commercial Code

Complete Article, Part, and Section Analysis of the Code, see page 1.

TABLE OF CONTENTS

TABLE OF CONTENTS

*

FOREWORD
TO
1987 OFFICIAL TEXT AND COMMENTS

Article 2A of the Uniform Commercial Code, along with Conforming Amendments to Articles 1 and 9, is presented, upon the recommendation of the Permanent Editorial Board for the Uniform Commercial Code, by the National Conference of Commissioners on Uniform State Laws and the American Law Institute. It represents a major development in commercial law, addressing a type of business transaction, the leasing of personal property, that has long existed. Under present law, transactions of this type are governed partly by common law principles relating to personal property, partly by principles relating to real estate leases, and partly by reference to Articles 2 and 9 of the Uniform Commercial Code, dealing with Sales and Secured Transactions respectively. The legal rules and concepts derived from these sources imperfectly fit a transaction that involves personal property rather than realty, and a lease rather than either a sale or a security interest as such. A statute directly addressing the personal property lease is therefore appropriate.

Such a statute has become especially appropriate with the exponential expansion of the number and scale of personal property lease transactions. Article 2A will apply to transactions involving billions of dollars annually. It will apply to consumer's rental of automobiles or do-it-yourself equipment, on the one hand, and to leases of such items as commercial aircraft (to the extent not preempted by federal law) and industrial machinery, on the other. The text recognizes the differences between consumer and business leasing, while resting upon concepts that apply generally to any personal property lease transactions.

The final product represents an important undertaking of the Conference and the Institute. It has proceeded, following recommendations by the Conference's Study Committee in 1981, through preparation and review by the Conference's Drafting Committee first of a proposed free-standing Uniform Personal Property Leasing Act, which was approved by the Conference, and later of Article 2A, which proceeded through the Permanent Editorial Board, the Executive Committee of the Conference, the Conference, and the Council of the Institute and the Annual Meeting of the members of the Institute. Carrying the text through these several stages has required coordination of somewhat different procedures, and continued patience and mutual forbearance At the same time, the text has been subjected to analysis and criticism from many points of view and thereby steadily improved.

The resulting product borrows from both Articles 2 and 9. These existing Articles of the Uniform Commercial Code have certain imperfections revealed by the long experience since their adoption. Article 2A cannot overcome those imperfections but seeks to minimize their significance as applied to leases. More fundamentally, there is important conceptual dissonance between Article 2 and Article 9. The formulation of Article 2A takes Articles 2 and 9 as they are for the time being and hence has required careful adjustment to this dissonance.

The drafting task has been complicated both as a matter of substance and as a matter of process. The Reporter, Ronald DeKoven, has been a master of substance and a steady and receptive principal in the process. We join with the Conference and the Institute in expressing our admiration and appreciation for his contribution to this important field of law.

GEOFFREY C. HAZARD, JR.
Chairman
Permanent Editorial Board for
the Uniform Commercial Code

October 1, 1987

FOREWORD TO 1978 OFFICIAL TEXT AND COMMENTS

Between 1958 and 1967, the Uniform Commercial Code (1958 Official Text) was enacted with but minor variations in all the states except Louisiana, as well as for the District of Columbia. Article 9 of the Code, dealing with secured transactions, was the subject of the largest variation in enactment, leading the Permanent Editorial Board, composed of representatives of the Institute and of the National Conference of Commissioners of Uniform State Laws, to initiate a "restudy in depth" of that article. This study led in turn to the recommendation by the Board of a revised Article 9 that was approved by the Institute and the Commissioners in 1971 and is still in process of enactment.

While the revision of Article 9 was under way, the enormous growth in trading in securities produced the "paperwork crunch" that threatened to engulf the industry. That emergency stimulated thought about alternative procedures that could reduce the mountains of paper generated by investment in securities. It was apparent, however, that Article 8 of the Code did not apply to a security unless it was "an instrument" (§ 8–102) and negotiable as such (§ 8–105). Any plan that would dispense with stock certificates would, therefore, be unregulated by the Code, with resultant uncertainty as to its legal implications. The problem plainly called for study and solution.

The initiative needed was taken by the Committee on Stock Certificates of the Section of Corporation, Banking and Business Law of the American Bar Association, under the chairmanship of Donald A. Scott of Philadelphia. Working with Professor Martin J. Aronstein of the Law School of the University of Pennsylvania as Reporter, the Committee's study culminated in a report issued in September 1975, proposing *inter alia* a revision of Article 8 that would adapt its norms to uncertificated investment securities. The Permanent Editorial Board had for its part designated a committee to consider the implications of electronic data processing developments for Articles 3, 4 and 8 of the Code, with Robert Haydock, Jr., of Boston, as chairman. As soon as the Scott Committee, of which Mr. Haydock also was a member, issued its report, the proposed changes in Article 8 were thoroughly reviewed by the 348 Committee. With revisions on which both committees were agreed, the proposals were then examined and to some extent revised by the Permanent Editorial Board, which in turn has recommended the text now submitted for approval by the Institute and the Commissioners. After minor revisions in which both the Institute and the Commissioners concurred, both bodies approved the text that is included in this new edition of the Code. Thus a significant improvement in the Code, adapting to important technological developments is now at hand.

1978 FOREWORD

It is well to emphasize that it is not the function of the Code to authorize or to prohibit the issuance of uncertificated securities. That is the province of the corporation laws, with which we do not deal. All that the Code does is to provide the rules to govern the respective interests in securities without certificates, as Article 8 has always governed these relationships when certificates are employed. This is the function of commercial law, to facilitate permissible transactions by articulating legal consequences that as far as possible are fair to those involved. The new provisions build imaginatively on the norms governing certificates to fill the hiatus that now obtains. Their substance is fully described in the Reporter's Introductory Comment and the explanation of the changes that appear in Appendix I and in the Official Comments.

It is appropriate that I express the special gratitude of the Permanent Editorial Board to Donald A. Scott and his American Bar Association committee, to Professor Aronstein, whose patience is exceeded only by his mastery of the commercial law, and to Charles C. Miller of Boston, who revised the Official Comments to Article 8 to take account of the Amendments.

HERBERT WECHSLER
Chairman
Permanent Editorial Board for
the Uniform Commercial Code

July 26, 1978

FOREWORD
TO
1972 OFFICIAL TEXT AND COMMENTS

The American Law Institute and the National Conference of Commissioners on Uniform State Laws present herewith the 1972 Official Text of Article 9 and related sections of the Uniform Commercial Code.

In Part I of this publication the new Official Text and Comments are set forth in full. In Part II the sections of the prior Official Draft that have been revised are set forth in a form that shows the original text and the changes now approved and recommended for uniform enactment, together with a statement of the reasons for change.*

The study that produced the new Official Text was initiated by the Permanent Editorial Board for the Uniform Commercial Code, established in 1961 by agreement of the American Law Institute and the National Conference of Commissioners on Uniform State Laws, the organizations whose joint effort had produced the Code. In its Report No. 3 of 1966, the Board, under the Chairmanship of the late General William A. Schnader of Pennsylvania said (p. x.):

> By the time the November meeting was held, 337 non-uniform, non-official amendments had been made to the various sections of Article 9. Some sections had been amended by as many as 30 jurisdictions, each jurisdiction writing its own amendment without regard to the amendments made by other jurisdictions and, of course, without regard to the Official Text. 47 of the 54 Sections of Article 9 had been non-uniformly amended.
>
> In view of this distressing situation and in view also of the fact that various practicing lawyers and law teachers have written articles or textbooks pointing out certain respects in which Article 9 might be improved, the Board decided that the time had arrived for a restudy in depth of Article 9 on Secured Transactions.

The Article 9 Review Committee was accordingly established to conduct the "restudy in depth" and report its findings to the Board. The members of the Committee were:

Joe C. Barrett, Arkansas
Carl W. Funk, Pennsylvania
Chief Judge (now Senior Judge) John S. Hastings, U.S. Court of Appeals, Seventh Circuit
Robert Haydock, Jr., Massachusetts
Ray David Henson, Michigan
Harold Marsh, Jr., California

* Part II is included as Appendix II in this pamphlet

1972 FOREWORD

William Curtis Pierce, New York
Millard H. Ruud, Texas
Judge (now Senior Judge) Sterry R. Waterman, U.S. Court of Appeals, Second Circuit
Herbert Wechsler, New York, Chairman

Professor (now Mr. Justice) Robert Braucher, Massachusetts, served as Reporter and Professor Homer Kripke, New York, as Associate Reporter. Professor Grant Gilmore, Illinois, and Peter F. Coogan, Massachusetts, were Consultants.

The Committee worked from February 1967 to October 1970 when it submitted its report to the Permanent Editorial Board. The Board approved the recommendations of the Committee, with amendments, in February 1971. A Final Report was in turn submitted by the Board to The American Law Institute in May 1971 and to the National Conference of Commissioners in August 1971 and was approved by both bodies with amendments in which the Institute, the Commissioners and the Board have all concurred.

Needless to say, the present document supersedes Preliminary Drafts Nos. 1 and 2 of the Article 9 Review Committee, published in 1968 and 1970, as well as the Final Report of the Permanent Editorial Board bearing date of April 25, 1971. Those interested in the development of the new text may find it helpful, however, to examine the explanation of the approach of the Review Committee embodied in the Final Report (pp. 195–248).

The extensive consideration of the earlier drafts produced a volume of criticism and suggestions that contributed substantially to the present work. It is appropriate that I express appreciation for this generous assistance.

It is also appropriate that I express appreciation for the indefatigable labor of the Reporters, the Consultants, the members of the Article 9 Review Committee and the counsel to the Permanent Editorial Board, Mr. Carl W. Funk of Pennsylvania, who devoted himself unremittingly to the preparation of the Official Text.

HERBERT WECHSLER
Chairman
Permanent Editorial Board for
the Uniform Commercial Code

December 17, 1971.

REPORT NO. 3

OF THE

PERMANENT EDITORIAL BOARD FOR THE UNIFORM COMMERCIAL CODE

December 15, 1966

TO THE AMERICAN LAW INSTITUTE AND THE NATIONAL CONFERENCE OF COMMISSIONERS ON UNIFORM STATE LAWS:

The last report of this Board [Report No. 2] was made on October 31, 1964, at which time 29 states and one jurisdiction (the District of Columbia) had enacted the Uniform Commercial Code. Since that time up to the date of this report, additional states and jurisdictions have enacted the Code to bring the total enactments up to 49. Only three states—Arizona, Idaho and Louisiana—have not as yet enacted the Code, and two other American jurisdictions—Guam and Puerto Rico—have its enactment under consideration.

Since 1964 our Board has had two meetings, both in Philadelphia. The first was on January 14 and 15, 1966 and the second on November 11 and 12, 1966.

At both 1966 meetings the Board received reports from Subcommittees Nos. 1, 2 and 3 to which had been assigned the task of studying and making recommendations on the many, many non-uniform amendments which had been made to the Code as it was enacted jurisdiction by jurisdiction. Three amendments were approved—amendments to Sections 2–702, 3–501 and 7–209. The first of these amendments has been adopted by California, Connecticut, Illinois, Maine, New Jersey, New Mexico and New York, the second by Iowa and the third by California. They are published herein with the amendment of the 1962 Official Comments which changes in the text require.

We also considered an amendment added as a new Section 1–209 to the New York Uniform Commercial Code.

It was the feeling of the Board that this amendment is not necessary, but that it was completely harmless and that if any states other than New York desired to add it to their Codes, they should have the blessing of the Permanent Editorial Board in doing so. Therefore, it is promulgated as a new optional section with appropriate Official Comment.

The Board also felt that Section 2–318, which has been non-uniformly amended in a number of states and entirely omitted in California and Utah, is a section not requiring uniformity throughout all American jurisdictions. Therefore, the Board is designating the present Section 2–318 as an Alternative A and is promulgating two alternatives—Alternative B and Alternative C—which states desiring warranties to have a broader impact may adopt if they choose.

Also, the Board is promulgating optional amendments to Sections 9–105 and 9–106 which will enable states having nautical contacts to amend their Codes to make it clear that a ship charter is not chattel paper but that all rights earned or unearned under a charter or other contract involving the use or hire of a vessel are contract rights and neither accounts nor general intangibles.

All of these amendments and optional amendments follow in the ensuing text.

A number of suggested amendments to Article 9 were discussed at the January meeting without definite decisions. This was due to some extent to the fact that the various people who wanted to see changes in certain sections of the Article were by no means agreed as to how the sections should be changed.

By the time the November meeting was held, 337 non-uniform, non-official amendments had been made to the various sections of Article 9. Some sections had been amended by as many as 30 jurisdictions, each jurisdiction writing its own amendment without regard to the amendments made by other jurisdictions and, of course, without regard to the Official Text. 47 of the 54 Sections of Article 9 had been non-uniformly amended.

In view of this distressing situation and in view also of the fact that various practicing lawyers and law teachers have written articles or textbooks pointing out certain respects in which Article 9 might be improved, the Board decided that the time had arrived for a restudy in depth of Article 9 on Secured Transactions.

It must be remembered that the Code has been in operation since July 1, 1954, so that a really impressive body of experience has been built up under which to make this restudy in depth.

A special Article 9 Review Committee was appointed. It consists of Professor Herbert Wechsler, Director of The American Law Institute as Chairman, Joe C. Barrett, a practicing lawyer, of Jonesboro, Arkansas, Carl W. Funk, a practicing lawyer, of Philadelphia, the Honorable John S. Hastings, Chief Judge of the United States Court of Appeals for the Seventh Circuit, Robert Haydock, Jr., a practicing lawyer, of Boston, Ray D. Henson, a practicing lawyer, of Chicago, Professor Harold Marsh, Jr. of the University of California Law School at Los Angeles, William Curtis Pierce, a practicing lawyer, of New York, Professor Millard H. Ruud of the University of Texas Law School and the Honorable Sterry R. Waterman, Judge of the United States Court of Appeals for the Second Circuit.

The Research and Reportorial Staff for the Committee will be Professor Robert Braucher of the Harvard University Law School, Reporter; Professor Homer Kripke of the New York University Law School, Associate Reporter; and Professor Soia Mentschikoff of the University of Chicago Law School, Associate Reporter ex officio.

To raise the additional funds which will be required for this work, Mr. Howard C. Petersen of Philadelphia has been appointed Chairman of a Ways and Means Committee.

REPORT NO. 3

In view of the appointment of the Article 9 Review Committee, two of the Subcommittees of the Board were relieved of their duties for the present—Subcommittee No. 3 and the Reportorial Committee. For their past services the Board expresses to them its gratitude and appreciation.

A large part of this volume [Report No. 3] is devoted to the publication of new, non-uniform amendments[1] adopted subsequent to our Report No. 2. In cases where another state has simply copied a non-uniform amendment which the Board has previously rejected, we merely refer to the page of Report No. 2 where the Board's reasons for rejection will be found. However, in cases where new, non-uniform amendments have been inserted in the Code, we are quoting the non-uniform amendment and giving our reasons for rejection.

Finally, the Board received from certain individuals and organizations suggestions for amendment of certain sections of the Code. Its Subcommittees considered these suggestions and did not find any basis for uniform amendment in any of the proposals relating to the first eight Articles of the Code. The Board approved the Subcommittees' recommendations.

As to suggestions coming to the Board for the amendment of provisions of Article 9 of the Code, all of these recommendations were referred to the special Article 9 Review Committee for study and report.

December 15, 1966

Respectfully submitted,

Wm. A. Schnader,
Pennsylvania,
Chairman

Joe C. Barrett,
Arkansas

F. M. Bird,
Georgia

James C. Dezendorf,
Oregon

Albert E. Jenner, Jr.,
Illinois

John W. MacDonald,
New York

Walter D. Malcolm,
Massachusetts

Paul A. Wolkin,
Secretary
101 North 33rd Street
Philadelphia, Pa. 19104

Consultant
Soia Mentschikoff
Illinois

1. This portion of Report No. 3 has been omitted because of space limitations.

REPORT NO. 3

Maurice H. Merrill,
Oklahoma

Alfred M. Pence,
Wyoming

George R. Richter, Jr.,
California

Herbert Wechsler,
New York

Alternates
J. Francis Ireton,
Maryland

William J. Pierce,
Michigan

REPORT NO. 2

OF THE

PERMANENT EDITORIAL BOARD FOR THE UNIFORM COMMERCIAL CODE

October 31, 1964

TO THE AMERICAN LAW INSTITUTE AND THE NATIONAL CONFERENCE OF COMMISSIONERS ON UNIFORM STATE LAWS:

The first report of this Board was made on October 31, 1962. At that time 18 states had enacted the Uniform Commercial Code.

Of the 18 states, some endeavored to adhere to the Official Text of the Code as promulgated by your two organizations which had sponsored it. For example, the Pennsylvania Code in 1962 had only one substantive departure from the Official Text and that departure was a "carry-over" from the 1952 Official Text. The 1959 Pennsylvania Act brought its Code in line with the amendments which had been officially recommended by the Editorial Board with the approval of the Executive Committees of both of your organizations.

Illinois was another state which enacted the Code almost precisely as promulgated.

However, other states made a large number of amendments and thus weakened their Codes pro tanto as uniform legislation governing in the same way the same commercial transaction wherever it occurred.

In our Report No. 1 dated October 31, 1962, we examined every unofficial amendment which had been made by any one of the 18 states and either recommended it for uniform adoption by all American jurisdictions or rejected it and gave the reasons for our action. The rejected amendments appeared at pages 65 to 135, inclusive, of our Report No. 1.[1]

Subsequent to October 31, 1962, 12 jurisdictions have enacted the Code. With the exception of Nebraska, each of these states used the 1962 Official Text of the Code as the basis for its Code bill. And the 1962 Official Text was the 1958 Official Text, plus the 1962 amendments promulgated by this Board in its Report No. 1 with the approval of the Executive Committees of both of your organizations.

We had hoped that our Report No. 1 would serve to minimize amendments to the Code by jurisdictions which would enact it subsequent to our report. While our report may have had some effect in this direction, we are sorry to say that again far too many unofficial amendments were enacted. In this report we have repeated our objections to the amendments made to Codes enacted prior to October 31, 1962, and, in addition, have examined all new, unofficial amendments made in the 30 jurisdic-

[1] These amendments have been omitted because of space limitations.

tions which have enacted the Code to date. None of the unofficial variations is such an improvement over the 1962 Official Text of the Code as to lead the Board to recommend it at this time. Therefore, for the 1965 session of legislatures the 1962 Text of the Code will continue to be the Official Text.

In the following pages we are dealing with every nonofficial amendment to the Code.[2] We are quoting the text, showing in what state or states the unofficial modification has been made and stating our objection.

We do hope that this report will serve to promote uniformity of statutory law governing commercial transactions by preventing states which have not yet enacted the Code from marring the efficiency and purpose of their Codes by making unofficial amendments, and by encouraging the jurisdictions whose Codes are not really "uniform" to clean them up by repealing the non-uniform amendments.

Lest the position of the Board be misunderstood, it may be worthwhile to say that the Board does not take the position that the 1962 Official Text is "the last word" and that the Code may not be improved as experience under its provisions develops. In due time, the Board intends to make a comprehensive examination of the Code from beginning to end. But experience has taught those interested in the uniformity of our statutory law that it has been much easier to get "uniform laws" on the books in the first instance than it has been to interest legislatures in bringing them up to date by amendment.

Uniformity of commercial law was the impelling goal of those who worked hard and long for the preparation of the Code and any future revision must, before its promulgation, be appraised from the standpoint of the likelihood of its prompt acceptance by all of the jurisdictions then operating under the Code. Amendments should be the result of experience rather than of theory. It is an interesting fact that in Pennsylvania, which stands high in commercial importance among the states, the Code has been in effect for more than ten years, with never more than one unofficial substantive amendment at any one time, and that the Permanent Editorial Board never heard of any request from any segment of business, finance or industry in Pennsylvania to amend any section of the Code.

October 31, 1964

Paul A. Wolkin,
Secretary
101 North 33rd Street
Philadelphia, Pa. 19104.

Respectfully submitted,
Wm. A. Schnader,
Pennsylvania,
Chairman

Joe C. Barrett,
Arkansas

Francis M. Bird,
Georgia

[2] This materials has been omitted because of space limitations.

REPORT NO. 2

Willoughby A. Colby,
New Hampshire

Albert E. Jenner, Jr.,
Illinois

John W. MacDonald,
New York

Walter D. Malcolm,
Massachusetts

Ross L. Malone,
New Mexico

Maurice H. Merrill,
Oklahoma

George R. Richter, Jr.,
California

Herbert Wechsler,
Pennsylvania

*

REPORT NO. 1

OF THE

PERMANENT EDITORIAL BOARD FOR THE UNIFORM COMMERCIAL CODE

October 31, 1962

TO THE AMERICAN LAW INSTITUTE AND THE NATIONAL CONFERENCE OF COMMISSIONERS ON UNIFORM STATE LAWS:

As this is the first report made by this Board, it may be worthwhile briefly to outline the history which led to the Board's establishment.

The Uniform Commercial Code was promulgated by the Conference and the Institute, with the endorsement of the American Bar Association, in the fall of 1951. It had been drafted under the supervision of an Editorial Board composed of representatives of the Conference and the Institute.

In 1953, Pennsylvania enacted the Code with no variations from the text which the Code's Editorial Board had approved.

No further enactments of the original Code ensued. The reason was that the New York Legislature, instead of enacting the Code, referred it to the New York Law Revision Commission and gave that expert body a large appropriation to enable it to make a critical line-by-line examination of the Code. When this occurred, the Code's Editorial Board was reactivated as were the subcommittees of the Board which had worked on the several articles.

In February, 1956, the New York Law Revision Commission made its report in which it approved the idea of a code of commercial law but expressed the opinion that the Code as originally drafted was unsuitable for enactment by New York.

While the Code was being studied by the New York Law Revision Commission's task forces, they were in communication with the Editorial Board's subcommittees, so that when the 1956 report was issued, its contents were no surprise to the sponsors of the Code. The Editorial Board immediately resumed intensive work. It adopted a large number of the suggestions made by the New York Commission and, late in 1956, issued a revised Code.

This revised Code was enacted by Massachusetts in September, 1957, effective on October 1, 1958, and by Kentucky in 1958, effective July 1 1960. It was published as the "1957 Official Text."

In 1958 the Code's Editorial Board promulgated certain amendments to Articles 8 and 9 of the Code, and the Code was republished as the "1958 Official Text."

Successively, Connecticut, New Hampshire, Rhode Island, Wyoming, Arkansas, New Mexico, Ohio, Oregon, Oklahoma, Illinois, New Jersey, Georgia, Alaska, New York and Michigan enacted the 1958 version of the Code. And, in 1959, Pennsylvania re-enacted the Code, substituting for the original version the 1958 Official Text.

It became apparent in 1961 that almost every state enacting the Code was making its own amendments, thus very largely imperiling the primary object of the code which is UNIFORMITY in the laws of the various states regulating commercial transactions.

In an effort to curb this tendency, the Institute applied to the Maurice and Laura Falk Foundation, (which had contributed upwards of $275,000 to the cost of preparing the original Code) for an additional grant in the amount of $125,000 to endow the work of a Permanent Editorial Board. The Falk Foundation very generously made the grant and the Board was constituted pursuant to a written agreement between the Conference and the Institute dated August 5, 1961.

This agreement provides that the Director of the Institute shall be ex officio chairman of the Board, that the Chairman of the Commercial code Committee of the Conference shall be an ex officio member, and that the Conference shall select four additional representatives and the Institute five. Not more than one elected member may come from any state and the agreement makes it clear that it is desirable, generally speaking, to have as members of the Board, lawyers who come from states which have enacted the Code.

Immediately upon the selection of the members of the Board by the Conference and the Institute, the late Judge Goodrich, who as Director of the Institute was ex officio chairman of the Board, appointed three subcommittees as follows:

Subcommittee No. 1, to consider Articles 1, 2, 6 & 7: Professor Robert Braucher, Harvard University Law School, Chairman, Bernard D. Broeker, Bethlehem, Pennsylvania, and Professor William D. Hawkland, University of Illinois Law School.

Subcommittee No. 2, to consider Articles 3, 4, 5 & 8: Walter D. Malcolm, Boston, Chairman; Robert M. Blair-Smith, Philadelphia; John J. Clarke, New York; Carl W. Funk, Philadelphia; Murdoch K. Goodwin, Philadelphia; Carlos L. Israels, New York; Arthur Littleton, Philadelphia; Soia Mentschikoff, University of Chicago Law School; and William C. Pierce, New York.

Subcommittee No. 3, to consider Article 9: J. Francis Ireton, Baltimore; Peter F. Coogan, Boston; Anthony G. Felix, Jr., Philadelphia; Grant Gilmore, Yale University Law School; Roy C. Haberkern, Jr., New York; Homer L. Kripke, New Jersey; and Durmont W. McGraw, Chicago.

Judge Goodrich also appointed Soia Mentschikoff consultant to the Board and Paul A. Wolkin of Philadelphia, as the Board's secretary.

REPORT NO. 1

The Board held its first meeting in Washington, D.C. in May, 1962, when there was a preliminary discussion of the manner in which the subcommittees and the Board would function. At this time a meeting was fixed for October 12, 13 and 14th in Philadelphia.

The subcommittees examined every amendment which had been made to the Code in the 18 Codes enacted thus far. They also examined a large number of amendments proposed in California and a somewhat smaller number proposed in Wisconsin. In both states a Code bill will probably be introduced into the legislature in 1963.

At its meeting in Philadelphia on October 12, 13 and 14th, the Board re-viewed the work of the subcommittees, and made the recommendations which follow.

We deem it appropriate in connection with this first report of the Board to print as an Appendix the agreement between The American Law Institute and the National Conference of Commissioners on Uniform State Laws dated August 5, 1961, as amended by a supplemental agreement which has just been executed by the officers of both organizations. Under Article SEVENTH of the agreement, as amended, the jurisdiction of this Board is rather limited. We certainly do not have any authority to undertake a rewriting of the Code or to make amendments merely because someone feels that a particular provision might have been drafted with greater clarity. The only justification for "clarifying amendments" must be found in clause (d) of Article SEVENTH which was added by the supplementary agreement.

Our recommendations are made in three parts.[1] Part I consists of recommendations for the amendment of the 1958 Official Text of the Code plus amendments of the Official Comments which the changes in text render necessary. Part II consists of the amendments to the Official Text made in the various states which the Board rejects, together with the reasons for rejection. Part III consists of a few amendments to the 1958 Official Comments which are deemed desirable in the light of experience under the Code.

We are not publishing our comments on the proposed California and Wisconsin amendments, but we have furnished them to the Commissioners on Uniform State Laws in those states respectively.

We understand that West Publishing Company will shortly put out a 1962 Official Text with Comments. This will contain the Text as modified by the amendments in Part I, plus the changes in Comments contained in Parts I and III.

We shall be very glad to supply copies of this Report on request.

Prior to the issuance of this Report, the amendments recommended in Part I were approved by majorities of the Executive Committees of both of the organizations to which the Report is addressed.

1. Reference is to Parts I–III of the Board's 1962 Report which, because of space limitations, could not be accommodated in this edition.

REPORT NO. 1

RESPECTFULLY SUBMITTED,

WM. A. SCHNADER,
Pennsylvania,
Acting Chairman.

October 31, 1962

JOE C. BARRETT,
Arkansas.

FRANCIS M. BIRD,
Georgia.

WILLOUGHBY A. COLBY,
New Hampshire.

ALBERT E. JENNER, JR.,
Illinois.

JOHN W. MACDONALD,
New York.

WALTER D. MALCOLM,
Massachusetts.

ROSS L. MALONE,
New Mexico.

MAURICE H. MERRILL,
Oklahoma.

GEORGE R. RICHTER, JR.,
California.

PAUL A. WOLKIN
Secretary
The American Law Institute
133 South 36th Street
Philadelphia 4, Pennsylvania

TABLE

SECTIONS OF PRIOR UNIFORM ACTS

(UNIFORM SALES ACT, NEGOTIABLE INSTRUMENTS LAW, UNIFORM BILLS OF LADING ACT, UNIFORM WAREHOUSE RECEIPTS ACT, UNIFORM STOCK TRANSFER ACT, UNIFORM CONDITIONAL SALES ACT, UNIFORM TRUST RECEIPTS ACT, UNIFORM WRITTEN OBLIGATIONS ACT, UNIFORM FIDUCIARIES ACT, WHICH ARE RESPECTIVELY ABBREVIATED AS USA, NIL, UBLA, UWRA, USTA, UCSA, UTRA, UWO AND UFA)

Showing Relevant Sections In

UNIFORM COMMERCIAL CODE

(Abbreviated as UCC)

Where there are no relevant sections in the Uniform Commercial Code, that fact is noted by the use of the abbreviation "N" for "None".

The letter "S" before a section of the Uniform Commercial Code means "See". The abbreviation "Cf." before a section means "Compare".

UNIFORM SALES ACT

U.S.A. Sec.	U.C.C. Sec.
1	2–204
	2–205
	2–206
	2–207
1(1)	2–106(1)
1(2)	2–106(1)
2	1–103
3	S. 1–201(11)
	2–203
	2–204
	2–205
	2–206
	2–207
4	1–206
	2–201
	8–319
5	S. 1–201(17)
	2–105(1) (2) (3) (4)
6	S. 1–201(17)
	2–105(1) (2) (3) (4)
7	2–613
8	2–613
9	2–305
9(1)	S. 1–205
9(2)	2–304
9(3)	2–304
10	2–305
11	S. 2–106(2)
	2–301
11 (Cont'd)	S. 2–503
	S. 2–507
	S. 2–601
12	2–313
13	2–312
14	2–313
	2–317
15	2–317
	S. 2–316
15(1)	2–315
15(2)	S. 2–104
	2–314
15(4)	2–315
15(5)	S. 1–205
	S. 2–104
	2–315
16	2–313
	2–317
16(c)	S. 2–104
17	S. 2–401
	S. 2–501
	Cf. 2–502
18	S. 2–401
	Cf. 2–502
18(2)	S. 1–205
19	S. 2–401
	S. 2–501
	Cf. 2–502
	S. 2–503
19(3)	2–326
	2–327

SECTIONS OF PRIOR UNIFORM ACTS

U.S.A. Sec.	U.C.C. Sec.
20	S. 2–401
	S. 2–503
20(2)	2–505
20(3)	2–505
20(4)	2–403
	2–505
	7–502
21	2–328
22	2–509
23	2–403
24	2–403
25	2–403
	7–502
26	2–402(1)
27	7–104
28	7–501
29	7–501
30	N.
31	7–501
32	7–501
33	7–502
	7–503
34	7–504
35	7–506
36	7–507
37	7–505
38	7–501
	7–502
39	N.
40	N.
41	2–301
	S. 2–507
	2–607(1)
42	2–310
	S. 2–507
	2–511
43(1)	2–308(a) and (b)
43(2)	S. 2–309(1)
43(3)	S. 2–503
43(4)	S. 2–503
44	S. 2–106(2)
	S. 2–601
45(1)	2–307
45(2)	S. 2–104
	2–309(1)
	2–612
46	S. 2–503
	2–504
47	S. 2–512
47(1)	S. 2–309(1)
47(2)	2–310
	2–513
47(3)	2–513
48	2–309(1)
	2–606
49	S. 2–512
	2–607(2) (3)

U.S.A Sec.	U.C.C. Sec.
50	2–602
51	S. 2–503
52(2)	2–707
53	S. 2–609
	S. 2–703
53(1) (b)	2–702(1)
54(1) (b)	S. 2–609
54(1) (c)	2–702(1)
55	S. 2–609
56	N.
57	2–702(1)
	2–705
58	2–705
59	2–705
60	2–706
61	N.
62	7–502
63	2–709
63(2)	S. 2–609
	S. 2–610
63(3)	2–701
64	2–708
	S. 2–710
64(4)	2–704
65	S. 2–610
66	N.
67(3)	2–713
68	2–716
69	S. 2–106(2)
	S. 2–507
	2–607(2) (3)
69(1)	S. 2–601
69(1) (a)	S. 2–717
69(1) (d)	2–608
69(3)	2–608
69(4)	2–608
69(5)	2–608
	2–711(3)
69(6)	2–714
69(7)	2–714
	2–715(2) (b)
70	S. 2–710
	2–715(2) (b)
71	S. 1–201(11)
	S. 1–205
	2–104
	S. 2–316
72	1–106(2)
73	1–103
74	1–102
75	2–102
76	S. 1–201(1)
	1–201(13)
	1–201(14)
	1–201(15)
	1–201(16)
	1–201(17)
	1–201(28)
	1–201(30)
	1–201(33)

SECTIONS OF PRIOR UNIFORM ACTS

U.S.A. Sec.	U.C.C. Sec.
76 (Cont'd)	1–201(34)
	1–201(44)
	S. 1–201(45)
	2–103(1)
	S. 2–107
	7–102
	7–104
76(2)	S. 1–201(19)
	2–105(1) (2) (3) (4)
76(3)	1–201(23)
77	N.
78	N.
79	N.

UNIFORM NEGOTIABLE INSTRUMENTS LAW

U.N.I.L. Sec.	U.C.C. Sec.
1	3–104
1(5)	3–102
2	3–106
3	3–105
4	3–109
5	3–104
	3–112
6	3–112
6(1)	3–114
6(4)	3–113
6(5)	1–201(24)
	3–106
	3–107
7	3–108
	3–502
8	3–110
9	3–111
9(3)	3–405
9(5)	3–204
10	3–104
11	3–114
12	3–114
13	3–115
14	3–115
	3–407
	8–206
15	3–115
	3–305
	3–407
	8–206
16	3–305
	3–306
	8–202
17	3–118
17(3)	3–109
	3–114
17(6)	3–402
18	3–401
19	3–403
20	3–403
21	3–403
22	3–207
23	3–404
	8–202
	8–205
	8–311
24	3–408
25	1–201(44)
	3–303
	3–408
26	1–201(44)
	3–303
27	1–201(44)
	3–201
	3–303
	4–209
28	3–306
	3–408
	3–415
	8–202
29	3–415
	8–201
30	3–202
	8–309
31	3–202
	8–308
32	3–202
	8–308
33	3–204
	8–308
34	3–204
	8–308
35	3–204
	8–308
36	3–204
	3–205
	3–206
	8–308
37	3–205
	3–206
	8–304
	8–308
38	3–414
39	3–205
	3–206
40	3–204
	8–310
41	3–116
42	3–117
43	3–203
44	3–414
45	3–304

SECTIONS OF PRIOR UNIFORM ACTS

U.N.I.L. Sec.	U.C.C. Sec.
46	N.
47	3–206
48	3–208
	3–605
49	3–201
	8–307
50	3–208
51	3–301
	3–603
52	3–302
	3–304
	8–301
	8–302
52(2)	8–203
	8–305
53	3–304
	8–203
	8–305
54	3–303
55	3–304
56	1–201(25)
	3–304
	8–202
	8–304
57	3–305
	8–202
	8–301
58	3–201
	3–207
	3–306
	8–301
59	3–207
	3–306
	3–307
	8–301
60	3–413
	8–201
	8–202
61	3–413
	8–201
	8–202
62	3–413
	3–418
	8–201
	8–202
63	3–402
64	3–415
	8–308
65	3–417
	8–306
	8–308
66	3–414
	8–306
	8–308
67	3–414
	8–306
	8–308
68	3–118
	3–414
	8–308
69	3–417
	8–306
	8–308
70	3–501
	3–502
	3–604
71	3–503
72	3–503
	3–504
73	3–504
74	3–505
75	3–503
76	N.
77	3–504
78	3–504
79	3–511
80	3–511
81	3–511
82	3–511
83	3–507
84	N.
85	3–503
86	3–503
87	3–121
88	3–603
89	3–501
	3–502
90	3–508
91	3–508
92	3–508
93	3–508
94	3–508
95	3–508
96	3–508
97	3–508
98	3–508
99	3–508
100	3–508
101	3–508
102	3–508
103	3–508
104	3–508
105	3–508
106	3–508
107	3–508
108	3–508
109	3–511
110	N.
111	3–511
112	3–511
113	3–511
114	3–511
115	3–511
116	3–511
117	N.
118	3–501
119	3–601
	3–603
119(3)	Cf. 1–107
	3–605

SECTIONS OF PRIOR UNIFORM ACTS

U.N.I.L. Sec.	U.C.C. Sec.
120	3–601
	3–604
	3–606
120(2)	Cf. 1–107
	3–605
121	3–208
	3–601
	3–603
122	Cf. 1–107
	3–605
123	3–605
124	3–407
	8–206
125	3–407
126	3–104
127	3–409
128	3–102
129	3–501
130	3–511
131(3)	4–503
132	3–410
133	3–410
134	3–410
135	3–410
136	3–410
	3–506
137	3–410
	3–419
138	3–410
139	3–412
140	3–412
141	3–412
142	3–412
143	3–501
144	3–501
	3–502
	3–503
145	3–503
	3–504
146	3–503
147	3–511
148	3–511
149	3–507
150	3–501
	3–502
	3–511
151	3–501
	3–511
152	3–501
	3–502
153	3–509
154	3–509
155	3–509
156	3–509
157	3–501
158	3–501

U.N.I.L. Sec.	U.C.C. Sec.
158 (Cont'd)	3–509
159	3–511
160	3–509
161	3–410
162	3–410
163	3–410
164	3–410
165	3–410
166	3–410
167	3–410
168	3–410
169	3–410
170	3–410
171	3–603
172	3–603
173	3–603
174	3–603
175	3–603
176	3–603
177	3–603
178	3–801
179	3–801
180	3–801
181	3–801
182	3–801
183	3–801
184	3–104
185	3–104
186	3–501
	3–502
	3–503
187	3–411
188	3–411
189	3–409
190	N.
191	S. 1–201(1)
	S. 1–201(4)
	S. 1–201(5)
	1–201(14)
	S. 1–201(20)
	1–201(28)
	1–201(30)
	1–201(44)
	1–201(46)
	3–102
	3–410
	8–313
192	N.
193	3–503
	Cf. 1–204
194	N.
195	N.
196	1–103
197	N.
198	N.

UNIFORM BILLS OF LADING ACT

U.B.L.A. Sec.	U.C.C. Sec.
1	S. 1–201(6)
	7–102
2	7–104
3	7–104
	7–309
4	7–104
5	7–104
6	7–304
7	7–402
8	N.
9	N.
10	N.
11	7–403
12	S. 2–705
	7–403
13	7–403
	7–404
14	S. 2–705
	7–403
15	7–403
16	7–306
17	7–601
18	N.
19	7–403
20	7–603
21	7–603
22	7–403
23	7–301
	7–401
24	7–602
25	N.
26	N.
27	N.
28	7–501
29	7–501
30	7–501
31	7–501
32	7–502
	7–503
32(b)	7–504
33	7–504
34	7–506
35	7–507
36	7–505
37	S. 2–104
38	7–501
	7–502
39	7–502
40	7–502
41	2–514
42	S. 2–705
	7–502
43	N.
44	N.
45	N.
46	N.
47	N.
48	N.
49	N.
50	N.
51	1–103
52	1–102(1)
53	S. 1–201(1)
	1–201(6)
	1–201(14)
	S. 1–201(20)
	1–201(28)
	1–201(30)
	1–201(32)
	1–201(33)
	S. 1–201(34)
	1–201(44)
	7–102
	7–104
53(2)	S. 1–201(19)
54	N.
55	N.
56	N.
57	N.

UNIFORM WAREHOUSE RECEIPTS ACT

U.W.R.A. Sec.	U.C.C. Sec.
1	1–201(45)
	7–201
2	7–104
	7–202
3	7–104
	7–204
4	7–104
5	7–104
6	7–402
7	N.
8	7–403
9	S. 2–705
	7–403
10	7–403
	7–404
11	2–705
	7–403
12	7–403

SECTIONS OF PRIOR UNIFORM ACTS

U.W.R.A. Sec.	U.C.C. Sec.
13	7–505
	7–208
14	7–505
	7–601
15	N.
16	7–505
	7–403
	7–603
17	7–505
	7–603
18	N.
19	7–505
	7–403
20	7–505
	7–203
	7–401
21	7–505
	7–204
22	7–505
	7–207
23	7–505
	7–207
24	N.
25	7–505
	7–602
26	N.
27	7–505
	7–209
	7–307
28	7–209
	7–307
29	7–209
	7–307
30	7–209
	7–307
31	7–209
	7–307
32	7–209
	7–307
33	7–210
	7–308
34	7–206
35	N.
36	N.
37	7–501
38	7–501
39	7–501
40	7–501
41	7–502
	7–503
41(b)	7–504
42	7–504
43	7–506
44	7–507
45	7–505
46	N.
47	7–501
	7–502
48	7–502
49	S. 2–705
	7–502
50	N.
51	N.
52	N.
53	N.
54	N.
55	N.
56	1–103
57	1–102(1)
58	S. 1–201(1)
	1–201(14)
	S. 1–201(17)
	S. 1–201(20)
	1–201(28)
	1–201(30)
	1–201(32)
	1–201(33)
	1–201(44)
	7–102
58(2)	S. 1–201(19)
59	7–104
60	N.
61	N.
62	N.

UNIFORM STOCK TRANSFER ACT

U.S.T.A. Sec.	U.C.C. Sec.
1	8–309
2	N.
3	8–207
4	N.
5	N.
6	N.
7	8–301
	8–315
8	N.
9	8–307
10	8–309
11	8–306
12	8–306
13	8–317
14	8–317
15	8–103
	8–204
16	8–206
17	8–405
18	1–103

SECTIONS OF PRIOR UNIFORM ACTS

U.S.T.A. Sec.	U.C.C. Sec.
19	1–102(1)
20	8–308
21	N.
22	1–201(28)
	1–201(32)
	8–313
22(1)	1–201(44)
22(2)	1–201(19)
	1–201(30)
	1–201(33)
23	N.
24	N.
25	N.
26	N.

UNIFORM CONDITIONAL SALES ACT

U.C.S.A. Sec.	U.C.C. Sec.
1	N.
2	9–206
3	N.
4	9–201
5	9–301
	9–302
6	9–401
7	S. 2–107
	9–401
	9–313
8	N.
9	2–403
	9–307
10	9–403
11	N.
12	9–404
13	N.
14	9–103(3)
15	N.
16	9–501
	9–503
17	9–501
	9–503
18	9–501
	9–506
19	9–501
	9–504
20	9–501
	9–504
21	9–501
	9–504
22	9–501
	9–504
23	9–501
	9–505
24	9–501
25	9–501
26	9–501
27 to 33 (incl.)	N.

UNIFORM TRUST RECEIPTS ACT

U.T.R.A. Sec.	U.C.C. Sec.
1	1–201(9)
	1–201(28)
	1–201(30)
	1–201(32)
	1–201(33)
	1–201(37)
	1–201(44)
2	9–203
3	9–201
	9–304
4	9–401
5	N.
6	9–501
	9–503
	9–504
7	N.
8	9–302
8(1)	9–304
8(2)	9–301
9	2–403
9(a)	9–308
	9–309
9(2)	2–403
	9–307
9(2) (b)	9–301
9(3)	9–318
10	9–306
	9–308
11	9–310
12	9–317
13(3)	9–402
	9–403
13(4)	9–402
	9–403

SECTIONS OF PRIOR UNIFORM ACTS

U.T.R.A. Sec.	U.C.C. Sec.	U.T.R.A. Sec.	U.C.C. Sec.
14 to 16 (incl.)	N.	18	1–102
17	1–103	19 to 22 (incl.)	N.

UNIFORM WRITTEN OBLIGATIONS ACT

U.W.O.A. Sec.	U.C.C. Sec.	U.W.O.A. Sec.	U.C.C. Sec.
1	Cf. 1–107 Cf. 2–209	2 to 5 (incl.)	N.

UNIFORM FIDUCIARIES ACT

U.F.A. Sec.	U.C.C. Sec.	U.F.A. Sec.	U.C.C. Sec.
1	N.	3	8–403
2	N.	4 to 16 (incl.)	N.

*

ACKNOWLEDGMENT
UNIFORM COMMERCIAL CODE
OFFICIAL TEXT AND COMMENTS

Acknowledgment is gratefully made to The American Law Institute and to the National Conference of Commissioners on Uniform State Laws for permission to reproduce the Official Text and Comments for the Uniform Commercial Code.

Section 1–102 of the Code provides that the act "shall be liberally construed and applied to promote its underlying purposes and policies" which include "to make uniform the law among the various jurisdictions".

THE PUBLISHER

March, 1996

*

UNIFORM COMMERCIAL CODE ARTICLE, PART AND SECTION ANALYSIS

ARTICLE 1. GENERAL PROVISIONS

PART 1. SHORT TITLE, CONSTRUCTION, APPLICATION AND SUBJECT MATTER OF THE ACT

PART 2. GENERAL DEFINITIONS AND PRINCIPLES OF INTERPRETATION

ARTICLE 2. SALES

PART 1. SHORT TITLE, GENERAL CONSTRUCTION AND SUBJECT MATTER

PART 2. FORM, FORMATION AND READJUSTMENT OF CONTRACT

ARTICLE, PART AND SECTION ANALYSIS

ARTICLE, PART AND SECTION ANALYSIS

Section

ARTICLE 8. INVESTMENT SECURITIES

PART 1. SHORT TITLE AND GENERAL MATTERS

PART 2. ISSUE AND ISSUER

PART 3. TRANSFER OF CERTIFICATED AND UNCERTIFICATED SECURITIES

PART 4. REGISTRATION

UNIFORM COMMERCIAL CODE

TITLE

AN ACT

To be known as the Uniform Commercial Code, Relating to Certain Commercial Transactions in or regarding Personal Property and Contracts and other Documents concerning them, including Sales, Commercial Paper, Bank Deposits and Collections, Letters of Credit, Bulk Transfers, Warehouse Receipts, Bills of Lading, other Documents of Title, Investment Securities, and Secured Transactions, including certain Sales of Accounts, Chattel Paper, and Contract Rights; Providing for Public Notice to Third Parties in Certain Circumstances; Regulating Procedure, Evidence and Damages in Certain Court Actions Involving such Transactions, Contracts or Documents; to Make Uniform the Law with Respect Thereto; and Repealing Inconsistent Legislation.

GENERAL COMMENT
of
NATIONAL CONFERENCE OF COMMISSIONERS ON UNIFORM STATE LAWS AND THE AMERICAN LAW INSTITUTE

This Comment covers the development of the Code prior to 1962. Its subsequent history leading to the 1962, 1966, 1972, 1977 and 1987 Official Text and Comment changes is contained in Reports and Forewords of the Permanent Editorial Board for the Uniform Commercial Code, which are set out, supra, this pamphlet.

Uniformity throughout American jurisdictions is one of the main objectives of this Code; and that objective cannot be obtained without substantial uniformity of construction. To aid in uniform construction of this Comment and those which follow the text of each section set forth the purpose of various provisions of this Act to promote uniformity, to aid in viewing the Act as an integrated whole, and to safeguard against misconstruction.

This Act is a revision of the original Uniform Commercial Code promulgated in 1951 and enacted in Pennsylvania in 1953, effective July 1, 1954; and these Comments are a revision of the original comments, which were before the Pennsylvania legislature at the time of its adoption of the Code. Changes from the text enacted in Pennsylvania in 1953 are clearly legitimate legislative history, but without explanation such changes may be misleading, since frequently matters have been omitted as being implicit without statement and language has been changed or added solely for clarity. Accordingly, the changes from the original text were published, under the title "1956 Recommendations of the Editorial Board for the Uniform Commercial Code," early in 1957, with reasons, and revised Comments were then prepared to restate the statutory purpose in the light of the revision of text.

The subsequent history leading to the 1962 Official Text with Comments is set out in detail in Report No. 1 of the Permanent Editorial Board for the Uniform Commercial Code. *** [See Report, supra, this pamphlet.]

Hitherto most commercial transactions have been regulated by a number of Uniform Laws prepared and promulgated by the National Conference of Commissioners on Uniform State Laws. These acts, with the dates of their promulgation by the Conference, are:

Uniform Negotiable Instruments Law 1896
Uniform Warehouse Receipts Act 1906
Uniform Sales Act 1906
Uniform Bills of Lading Act 1909
Uniform Stock Transfer Act 1909
Uniform Conditional Sales Act 1918
Uniform Trust Receipts Act 1933

Two of these acts were adopted in every American State and the remaining acts have had wide acceptance. Each of them has become a segment of the statutory law relating to commercial transactions. It has been recognized for some years that these acts needed substantial revision to keep them in step with modern commercial practices and to integrate each of them with the others.

The concept of the present Act is that "commercial transactions" is a single subject of the law, notwithstanding its many facets.

A single transaction may very well involve a contract for sale, followed by a sale, the giving of a check or draft for a part of the purchase price, and the acceptance of some form of security for the balance.

The check or draft may be negotiated and will ultimately pass through one or more banks for collection.

If the goods are shipped or stored the subject matter of the sale may be covered by a bill of lading or warehouse receipt or both.

Or it may be that the entire transaction was made pursuant to a letter of credit either domestic or foreign.

Obviously, every phase of commerce involved is but a part of one transaction, namely, the sale of and payment for goods.

If, instead of goods in the ordinary sense, the transaction involved stocks or bonds, some of the phases of the transaction would obviously be different. Others would be the same. In addition, there are certain additional formalities incident to the transfer of stocks and bonds from one owner to another.

This Act purports to deal with all the phases which may ordinarily arise in the handling of a commercial transaction, from start to finish.

Because of the close relationship of each phase of a complete transaction to every other phase, it is believed that each Article of this Act is cognate to the single broad subject "Commercial Transactions", and that this Act is valid under any constitutional provision requiring an act to deal with only one subject. See, for excellent discussions of the meaning of "single subject": House v. Creveling, 147 Tenn. 589, 250 S.W. 357 (1923) and Commonwealth v. Snyder, 279 Pa. 234, 123 A. 792 (1924).

The preparation of the Act (which Section 1–101 denominates the "Uniform Commercial Code") was begun as a joint project of The American Law Institute and the National Conference of Commissioners on Uniform State

Laws in 1942. Various drafts were considered by joint committees of both bodies and debated by the full membership of each organization at annual meetings.

In the main, the project was made possible, financially, through a large grant by The Maurice and Laura Falk Foundation of Pittsburgh, Pennsylvania, supplemented by contributions from the Beaumont Foundation of Cleveland, Ohio, and from 98 business and financial concerns and law firms. Additional funds for final revisions and study were received from the Falk Foundation and others.

The original drafting and editorial work which led to the 1952 edition of the Code was in charge of an Editorial Board of which United States Circuit Judge Herbert F. Goodrich of Philadelphia was Chairman. The other members at various times were Professor Karl N. Llewellyn of the University of Chicago Law School, Walter D. Malcolm, Esquire, of Boston, John C. Pryor, Esquire, of Burlington, Iowa, Wm. A. Schnader, Esquire, of Philadelphia, and Harrison Tweed, Esquire, of New York City. In the final stages of work on the Code, certain questions of policy were submitted for consideration to an Enlarged Editorial Board consisting at various times of the foregoing members and Howard L. Barkdull, Esquire, of Cleveland, Joe C. Barrett, Esquire, of Jonesboro, Arkansas, Robert K. Bell, Esquire, of Ocean City, N.J., Robert P. Goldman, Esquire, of Cincinnati, Dean Albert J. Harno of the University of Illinois Law School, Ben W. Heineman, Esquire, of Chicago, Carlos Israels, Esquire, of New York City, Albert E. Jenner, Esquire, of Chicago, Arthur Littleton, Esquire, of Philadelphia, Willard B. Luther, Esquire, of Boston, Kurt F. Pantzer, Esquire, of Indianapolis, Indiana, George Richter, Jr., Esquire, of Los Angeles, R. Jasper Smith, Esquire, of Springfield, Missouri, United States Circuit Judge Sterry Waterman of St. Johnsbury, Vermont, and Charles H. Willard, Esquire, of New York City.

The Chief Reporter of the Code was Professor Llewellyn, and the Associate Chief Reporter was Professor Soia Mentschikoff. Final editorial preparation of the 1952 edition was in the hands of Professor Charles Bunn of the University of Wisconsin Law School. The Coordinators for the revisions leading to this 1962 edition were Professors Robert Braucher and A.E. Sutherland of the Law School of Harvard University, Professor Braucher doing the final editorial preparation for this edition.

The actual drafting was done in some cases by practicing lawyers and in others by teachers of various law schools. The customary procedure required that before a draft was submitted for discussion to the general memberships of The American Law Institute and of the National Conference of Commissioners, it was successively approved by three groups.

The first group were the so-called "advisers", consisting of specially selected judges, practicing lawyers and law teachers. The advisers met with the draftsmen on frequent occasions to debate and iron out, not only the substance but the form and phraseology of the proposed draft.

After the draft was cleared by the advisers, it was meticulously examined by the next two groups—the Council of The American Law Institute and either the Commercial Acts Section or the Property Acts Section of the Conference of Commissioners.

When these bodies had given their approval to the draft, it came before the general membership both of the Institute and of the Conference for consideration.

In addition in the final stages leading to this 1962 edition each article was reviewed and discussed by a special Subcommittee for that article. Recommendations of the Subcommittee were reviewed and acted upon by the Enlarged Editorial Board, pursuant to authority from the sponsoring bodies.

The judges, practicing lawyers and law teachers who originally acted either as advisers or as draftsmen were:

Judges: John T. Loughran, of the New York Court of Appeals; Thomas W. Swan, United States Circuit Judge for the Second Circuit; and the late John D. Wickhem, of the Supreme Court of Wisconsin.

Practicing lawyers: Dana C. Backus, of New York, N.Y.; Howard L. Barkdull, of Cleveland, Ohio; Lawrence G. Bennett, of New York, N.Y.; Harold F. Birnbaum, of Los Angeles, California; William L. Eagleton, of Washington, D.C.; H. Vernon Eney, of Baltimore, Maryland; Fairfax Leary, Jr., of Philadelphia, Pennsylvania; Willard B. Luther, of Boston, Massachusetts; Walter D. Malcolm, of Boston, Massachusetts; Frederic M. Miller, of Des Moines, Iowa; Hiram Thomas, of New York, N.Y.; Sterry R. Waterman, of St. Johnsbury, Vermont; and Cornelius W. Wickersham, of New York, N.Y.

The law teachers were: Ralph J. Baker, of the Harvard Law School; William E. Britton, of the University of Illinois Law School; Charles Bunn, of the University of Wisconsin Law School; Arthur L. Corbin, of Yale University Law School; Allison Dunham, of Columbia University Law School; Grant Gilmore, of Yale University Law School; Albert J. Harno, of the University of Illinois Law School; Friedrich Kessler, of the Yale University Law School; Maurice H. Merrill, of the University of Oklahoma Law School; William L. Prosser, of the University of California School of Law; Louis B. Schwartz, of the University of Pennsylvania Law School; and Bruce Townsend, of the University of Indiana Law School.

The members of the Council of the Institute during the period when the Commercial Code was under consideration were: Dillon Anderson, of Houston, Texas; Fletcher R. Andrews of Cleveland Heights, Ohio; the late Walter P. Armstrong of Memphis, Tennessee; Francis M. Bird, of Atlanta, Georgia; John G. Buchanan, of Pittsburgh, Pennsylvania; Charles Bunn, of Madison, Wisconsin; Howard F. Burns, of Cleveland, Ohio; Herbert W. Clark, of San Francisco, California; R. Ammi Cutter, of Boston, Massachusetts; Norris Darrell, of New York, N.Y.; the late John W. Davis, of New York, N.Y.; Edwin D. Dickinson, of Berkeley, California; Edward J. Dimock, of New York, N.Y.; Arthur Dixon, of Chicago, Illinois; Robert G. Dodge, of Boston, Massachusetts; the late George Donworth, of Seattle, Washington; Charles E. Dunbar, Jr., of New Orleans, Louisiana; William Dean Embree, of New York, N.Y.; Frederick F. Faville, of Des Moines, Iowa; James Alger Fee, of Portland, Oregon; Gerald F. Flood, of Philadelphia, Pennsylvania; H. Eastman Hackney, of Pittsburgh, Pennsylvania; the late Augustus N. Hand, of New

York, N.Y.; Learned Hand, of New York, N.Y.; Albert J. Harno, of Urbana, Illinois; the late Earl G. Harrison, of Philadelphia, Pennsylvania; William V. Hodges, of New York, N.Y.; Joseph C. Hutcheson, Jr., of Houston, Texas; Laurence M. Hyde, of Jefferson City, Missouri; William J. Jameson, of Billings, Montana; Joseph F. Johnston, of Birmingham, Alabama; the late William H. Keller, of Lancaster, Pennsylvania; the late Daniel N. Kirby, of St. Louis, Missouri; Monte M. Lemann, of New Orleans, Louisiana; the late William Draper Lewis, of Philadelphia, Pennsylvania; the late Henry T. Lummus, of Swampscott, Massachusetts; William L. Marbury, of Baltimore, Maryland; Robert N. Miller, of Washington, D.C.; the late William D. Mitchell, of New York, N.Y.; John J. Parker, of Charlotte, North Carolina; Thomas I. Parkinson, of New York, N.Y.; George Wharton Pepper, of Philadelphia, Pennsylvania; Timothy N. Pfeiffer, of New York, N.Y.; Orie L. Phillips, of Denver, Colorado; Frederick D.G. Ribble, of Charlottesville, Virginia; William A. Schnader, of Philadelphia, Pennsylvania; Bernard G. Segal, of Philadelphia, Pennsylvania; Austin W. Scott, of Cambridge, Massachusetts; the late Harry Shulman, of New Haven, Connecticut; Henry Upson Sims, of Birmingham, Alabama; the late Sydney Smith, of Jackson, Mississippi; Eugene B. Strassburger, of Pittsburgh, Pennsylvania; Thomas W. Swan, of Guilford, Connecticut; the late Thomas Day Thacher, of New York, N.Y.; Floyd E. Thompson, of Chicago, Illinois; the late Edgar Bronson Tolman, of Chicago, Illinois; the late Robert B. Tunstall, of Norfolk, Virginia; the late Arthur J. Tuttle, of Detroit, Michigan; Harrison Tweed, of New York, N.Y.; Cornelius W. Wickersham, of New York, N.Y.; the late John D. Wickhem, of Madison, Wisconsin; Raymond S. Wilkins, of Boston, Massachusetts; Charles H. Willard, of New York, N.Y.; Laurens Williams, of Washington, D.C.; Edward L. Wright, of Little Rock, Arkansas, and Charles E. Wyzanski, Jr., of Boston, Massachusetts.

The members of the Conference's Commercial Acts Section during the same period were: Howard L. Barkdull, of Cleveland, Ohio; the late William L. Beers, of New Haven, Connecticut; Charles R. Hardin, of Newark, New Jersey; Frank E. Horack, Jr., of Bloomington, Indiana; L. Barrett Jones, of Jackson, Mississippi; Karl N. Llewellyn, now of Chicago, Illinois; Willard B. Luther, of Boston, Massachusetts; William G. McLaren, of Seattle, Washington; Frederic M. Miller, of Des Moines, Iowa; William L. Prosser, of Berkeley, California; Arthur E. Sutherland, Jr., now of Cambridge, Massachusetts; O.H. Thormodsgard, of University, North Dakota; Sterry R. Waterman, of St. Johnsbury, Vermont; and Edward L. Wright, of Little Rock, Arkansas.

The members of the Conference's Property Acts Section during the period when it cooperated in the consideration of the Code were: Joe C. Barrett, of Jonesboro, Arkansas; the late William L. Beers, of New Haven, Connecticut; Boyd M. Benson, of Huron, South Dakota; George G. Bogert, now of San Francisco, California; C. Walter Cole, of Towson, Maryland; John A. Daly, of Boston, Massachusetts; William L. Eagleton, of Washington, D.C.; H. Vernon Eney, of Baltimore, Maryland; Spencer A. Gard, of Iola, Kansas; Homer B. Harris, of Lincoln, Illinois; W.J. Jameson, of Billings, Montana; the late Sherman R. Moulton, of Burlington, Vermont; J.C. Pryor, of Burlington, Iowa; the late C.M.A. Rogers, of Mobile, Alabama; Murray M. Shoemaker, of Cincinnati, Ohio; and Greenberry Simmons, of Louisville, Kentucky.

UNIFORM COMMERCIAL CODE

The members of the Subcommittees which considered the various articles of the Code in the work leading to the 1958 Edition were:

Article 1: Charles H. Willard, Esquire, Chairman, of New York, New York; Professor Charles Bunn of the University of Wisconsin Law School, Madison, Wisconsin; Mahlon E. Lewis, Esquire, of Pittsburgh, Pennsylvania.

Article 2: Professor Robert Braucher, Chairman, of the Law School of Harvard University, Cambridge, Massachusetts; Professor Karl N. Llewellyn, of the Law School of the University of Chicago, Chicago, Illinois; Bernard D. Broeker, Esquire, of Bethlehem, Pennsylvania; Frank T. Dierson, Esquire, of New York, New York.

Article 3: Professor A.E. Sutherland, Chairman, of the Law School of Harvard University, Cambridge, Massachusetts; William R. Emblidge, Esquire, of Buffalo, New York; John J. Clarke, Esquire, of the Federal Reserve Bank of New York, New York; James V. Vergari, Esquire, of Federal Reserve Bank of Philadelphia, Philadelphia, Pennsylvania.

Article 4: Walter D. Malcolm, Esquire, Chairman, of Boston, Massachusetts; James V. Vergari, Esquire; John J. Clarke, Esquire; Henry J. Bailey, III, Esquire, of the Federal Reserve Bank of New York, New York; Rollin C. Huggins, Esquire, of Chicago, Illinois; Carl W. Funk, Esquire, of Philadelphia, Pennsylvania.

Article 5: Arthur Littleton, Esquire, Chairman, Philadelphia, Pennsylvania; Mr. Horace M. Chadsey, Vice-President of the First National Bank of Boston; Arthur F. McCarthy, Esquire, of Philadelphia, Pennsylvania; Professor Soia Mentschikoff, of the University of Chicago Law School, Chicago, Illinois. In addition, the following acted as an Advisory Committee to the Article 5 Subcommittee: Ernest A. Carlson, of the Continental Illinois National Bank and Trust Company, Chicago, Illinois; John E. Corrigan, Jr., of the First National Bank of Chicago; Guy A. Crum, of the First National Bank of Chicago; Louis F. Dempsey, of the Northern Trust Company, Chicago, Illinois; Gerard E. Keidel, of the American National Bank and Trust Company of Chicago; Robert W. Maynard, of the Harris Trust and Savings Bank, Chicago, Illinois.

Article 6: Professor Charles Bunn, Chairman; Eugene B. Strassburger, Esquire, of Pittsburgh, Pennsylvania.

Article 7: Professor Robert Braucher, Chairman; John C. Pryor, Esquire, of Burlington, Iowa.

Article 8: Carlos Israels, Esquire, Chairman, of New York, New York; Professor Soia Mentschikoff; Eliot B. Thomas, Esquire, of Philadelphia, Pennsylvania; Fred B. Lund, Esquire, of Boston, Massachusetts.

Article 9: J. Francis Ireton, Esquire, Chairman, of Baltimore, Maryland; Homer L. Kripke, Esquire, of New York, New York; Anthony G. Felix, Jr., Esquire, of Philadelphia, Pennsylvania; Peter F. Coogan, Esquire, of Boston, Massachusetts; Professor Grant Gilmore, of Yale University Law School, New Haven, Connecticut; Harold F. Birnbaum, Esquire, of Los Angeles, California; Richard R. Winters, Esquire, of Pittsburgh, Pennsylvania; Professor John Hanna, of the Law School of Columbia University, New York, New York.

In addition there were informal consultants much too numerous to mention who frequently advised those working on the Code to insure a workable set of laws. In this latter class were included practicing lawyers, hard-headed businessmen and operating bankers, who contributed generously of their time and knowledge so that, not only current business practice, but foreseeable future developments would be covered.

Committees of several Bar Associations, and in particular a committee of the Section of Corporation, Banking and Business Law of the American Bar Association, of which Mr. Walter D. Malcolm of Boston was chairman, considered the various drafts of the Code and made valuable suggestions. After final approval of the Code by the Institute and the Conference, and in accordance with the practice of the Conference, the completed Code was submitted to the American Bar Association and was approved by the House of Delegates of that Association.

* * *

ARTICLE 1
GENERAL PROVISIONS

PART 1. SHORT TITLE, CONSTRUCTION, APPLICATION AND SUBJECT MATTER OF THE ACT

PART 1

SHORT TITLE, CONSTRUCTION, APPLICATION AND SUBJECT MATTER OF THE ACT

§ 1–101. Short Title.

This Act shall be known and may be cited as Uniform Commercial Code.

Official Comment

Each Article of the Code (except this Article and Article 10) may also be cited by its own short title. See Sections 2–101, 3–101, 4–101, 5–101, 6–101, 7–101, 8–101 and 9–101.

§ 1–102. Purposes; Rules of Construction; Variation by Agreement.

(1) This Act shall be liberally construed and applied to promote its underlying purposes and policies.

(2) Underlying purposes and policies of this Act are

(a) to simplify, clarify and modernize the law governing commercial transactions;

(b) to permit the continued expansion of commercial practices through custom, usage and agreement of the parties;

(c) to make uniform the law among the various jurisdictions.

(3) The effect of provisions of this Act may be varied by agreement, except as otherwise provided in this Act and except that the obligations of good faith, diligence, reasonableness and care prescribed by this Act may not be disclaimed by agreement but the parties may by agreement determine the standards by which the performance of such obligations is to be measured if such standards are not manifestly unreasonable.

(4) The presence in certain provisions of this Act of the words "unless otherwise agreed" or words of similar import does not imply that the effect of other provisions may not be varied by agreement under subsection (3).

(5) In this Act unless the context otherwise requires

(a) words in the singular number include the plural, and in the plural include the singular;

(b) words of the masculine gender include the feminine and the neuter, and when the sense so indicates words of the neuter gender may refer to any gender.

Official Comment

Prior Uniform Statutory Provision: Section 74, Uniform Sales Act; Section 57, Uniform Warehouse Receipts Act; Section 52, Uniform Bills of Lading Act; Section 19, Uniform Stock Transfer Act; Section 18, Uniform Trust Receipts Act.

Changes: Rephrased and new material added.

Purposes of Changes:

1. Subsections (1) and (2) are intended to make it clear that:

This Act is drawn to provide flexibility so that, since it is intended to be a semi-permanent piece of legislation, it will provide its own machinery for expansion of commercial practices. It is intended to make it possible for the law embodied in this Act to be developed by the courts in the light of unforeseen and new circumstances and practices. However, the proper construction of the Act requires that its interpretation and application be limited to its reason.

Courts have been careful to keep broad acts from being hampered in their effects by later acts of limited scope. Pacific Wool Growers v. Draper & Co., 158 Or. 1, 73 P.2d 1391 (1937), and compare Section 1-104. They have recognized the policies embodied in an act as applicable in reason to subject-matter which was not expressly included in the language of the act, Commercial Nat. Bank of New Orleans v. Canal-Louisiana Bank & Trust Co., 239 U.S. 520, 36 S.Ct. 194, 60 L.Ed. 417 (1916) (bona fide purchase policy of Uniform Warehouse Receipts Act extended to case not covered but of equivalent nature). They have done the same where reason and policy so required, even where the subject-matter had been intentionally excluded from the act in general. Agar v. Orda, 264 N.Y. 248, 190 N.E. 479 (1934) (Uniform Sales Act change in seller's remedies applied to contract for sale of choses in action even though the general coverage of that Act was intentionally limited to goods "other than things in action.") They have implemented a statutory policy with liberal and useful remedies not provided in the statutory text. They have disregarded a statutory limitation of remedy where the reason of the limitation did not apply. Fiterman v. J. N. Johnson & Co., 156 Minn. 201, 194 N.W. 399 (1923) (requirement of return of the goods as a condition to rescission for breach of warranty; also, partial rescission allowed). Nothing in this Act stands in the way of the continuance of such action by the courts.

The Act should be construed in accordance with its underlying purposes and policies. The text of each section should be read in the light of the purpose and policy of the rule or principle in question, as also of the Act as a whole, and the application of the language should be construed narrowly or broadly, as the case may be, in conformity with the purposes and policies involved.

2. Subsection (3) states affirmatively at the outset that freedom of contract is a principle of the Code: "the effect" of its provisions may be varied by "agreement." The meaning of the statute itself must be found in its text, including its definitions, and in appropriate extrinsic aids; it cannot be varied by agreement. But the Code seeks to avoid the type of interference with evolutionary growth found in Manhattan Co. v. Morgan, 242 N.Y. 38, 150 N.E. 594 (1926). Thus private parties cannot make an instrument negotiable within the meaning of Article 3 except as provided in Section 3-104; nor can they change the meaning of such terms as "bona fide purchaser," "holder in due course," or "due negotiation," as used in this Act. But an agreement can change the legal consequences which would otherwise flow from the provisions of the Act. "Agreement" here includes the effect given to course of dealing, usage of trade and course of performance by Sections 1-201, 1-205 and 2-208; the effect of an agreement on the rights of third parties is left to specific provisions of this Act and to supplementary principles applicable under the next section. The rights of third parties under Section 9-301 when a security interest is unperfected, for example, cannot be destroyed by a clause in the security agreement.

This principle of freedom of contract is subject to specific exceptions found elsewhere in the Act and to the general exception stated here. The specific exceptions vary in explicitness: the statute of frauds found in Section 2-201, for example, does not explicitly preclude oral waiver of the requirement of a writing, but a fair reading denies enforcement to such a waiver as part of the "contract" made unenforceable; Section 9-501(3), on the other hand, is quite explicit. Under the exception for "the obligations of good faith, diligence, reasonableness and care prescribed by this Act," provisions of the Act prescribing such obligations are not to be disclaimed. However, the section also recognizes the prevailing practice of having agreements set forth standards by which due diligence is measured and explicitly provides that, in the absence of a showing that the standards manifestly are unreasonable, the agreement controls. In this connection, Section 1-205 incorporating into the agreement prior course of dealing and usages of trade is of particular importance.

3. Subsection (4) is intended to make it clear that, as a matter of drafting, words such as "unless otherwise agreed" have been used to avoid controversy as to whether the subject matter of a particular section does or does not fall within the exceptions to subsection (3), but absence of such words contains no negative implication since under subsection (3) the general and residual rule is that the effect of all provisions of the Act may be varied by agreement.

4. Subsection (5) is modelled on 1 U.S.C. Section 1 and New York General Construction Law Sections 22 and 35.

§ 1-103. Supplementary General Principles of Law Applicable.

Unless displaced by the particular provisions of this Act, the principles of law and equity, including the law merchant and the law relative to capacity to contract, principal and agent, estoppel, fraud, misrepresentation, duress, coercion, mistake, bankruptcy, or other validating or invalidating cause shall supplement its provisions.

Official Comment

Prior Uniform Statutory Provision: Sections 2 and 73, Uniform Sales Act; Section 196, Uniform Negotiable Instruments Act; Section 56, Uniform Warehouse Receipts Act; Section 51, Uniform Bills of Lading Act; Section 18, Uniform Stock Transfer Act; Section 17, Uniform Trust Receipts Act.

Changes: Rephrased, the reference to "estoppel" and "validating" being new.

Purposes of Changes:

1. While this section indicates the continued applicability to commercial contracts of all supplemental bodies of law except insofar as they are explicitly displaced by this Act, the principle has been stated in more detail and the phrasing enlarged to make it clear that the "validating", as well as the "invalidating" causes referred to in the prior uniform statutory provisions, are included here. "Validating" as used here in conjunction with "invalidating" is not intended as a narrow word confined to original validation, but extends to cover any factor which at any time or in any manner renders or helps to render valid any right or transaction.

2. The general law of capacity is continued by express mention to make clear that section 2 of the old Uniform Sales Act (omitted in this Act as stating no matter not contained in the general law) is also consolidated in the present section. Hence, where a statute limits the capacity of a non-complying corporation to sue, this is equally applicable to contracts of sale to which such corporation is a party.

3. The listing given in this section is merely illustrative; no listing could be exhaustive. Nor is the fact that in some sections particular circumstances have led to express reference to other fields of law intended at any time to suggest the negation of the general application of the principles of this section.

§ 1-104. Construction Against Implicit Repeal.

This Act being a general act intended as a unified coverage of its subject matter, no part of it shall be deemed to be impliedly repealed by subsequent legislation if such construction can reasonably be avoided.

Official Comment

Prior Uniform Statutory Provision: None.

Purposes:

To express the policy that no Act which bears evidence of carefully considered permanent regulative intention should lightly be regarded as impliedly repealed by subsequent legislation. This Act, carefully integrated and intended as a uniform codification of permanent character covering an entire "field" of law, is to be regarded as particularly resistant to implied repeal. See Pacific Wool Growers v. Draper & Co., 158 Or. 1, 73 P.2d 1391 (1937).

§ 1-105. Territorial Application of the Act; Parties' Power to Choose Applicable Law.

[1995 Amendment to text indicated by underline]

(1) Except as provided hereafter in this section, when a transaction bears a reasonable relation to this state and also to another state or nation the parties may agree that the law either of this state or of such other state or

nation shall govern their rights and duties. Failing such agreement this Act applies to transactions bearing an appropriate relation to this state.

(2) Where one of the following provisions of this Act specifies the applicable law, that provision governs and a contrary agreement is effective only to the extent permitted by the law (including the conflict of laws rules) so specified:

Rights of creditors against sold goods. Section 2-402.

Applicability of the Article on Leases. Sections 2A-105 and 2A-106.

Applicability of the Article on Bank Deposits and Collections. Section 4-102.

Governing law in the Article on Funds Transfers. Section 4A-507.

Letters of Credit. Section 5-116.

[*Publisher's Editorial Note: If a state adopts the repealer of Article 6—Bulk Transfers (Alternative A), there should not be any item relating to bulk transfers. If, however, a state adopts Revised Article 6—Bulk Sales (Alternative B), then the item relating to bulk sales should read as follows:*]

Bulk sales subject to the Article on Bulk Sales. Section 6-103.

Applicability of the Article on Investment Securities. Section 8-110.

Perfection provisions of the Article on Secured Transactions. Section 9-103.

As amended in 1972, 1987, 1988, 1989, 1994, and 1995.

See Appendix III for material relating to changes made in text in 1987.

For material relating to the changes made in text in 1988 and 1989, see section 2 of Alternative A (Repealer of Article 6—Bulk Transfers), Conforming Amendment to Section 1-105 following end of Alternative B (Revised Article 6—Bulk Sales), and Technical Amendment to Article 1 following end of new Article 4A—Funds Transfers.

See Appendices XII and XIV for material relating to changes made in text in 1994 and 1995, respectively.

Official Comment

Prior Uniform Statutory Provision: None.

Purposes:

1. Subsection (1) states affirmatively the right of the parties to a multi-state transaction or a transaction involving foreign trade to choose their own law. That right is subject to the firm rules stated in the five sections listed in subsection (2), and is limited to jurisdictions to which the transaction bears a "reasonable relation." In general, the test of "reasonable relation" is similar to that laid down by the Supreme Court in Seeman v. Philadelphia Warehouse Co., 274 U.S. 403, 47 S.Ct. 626, 71 L.Ed. 1123 (1927). Ordinarily the law chosen must be that of a jurisdiction where a significant enough portion of the making or performance of the contract is to occur or occurs. But an agreement as to choice of law may some-

times take effect as a shorthand expression of the intent of the parties as to matters governed by their agreement, even though the transaction has no significant contact with the jurisdiction chosen.

2. Where there is no agreement as to the governing law, the Act is applicable to any transaction having an "appropriate" relation to any state which enacts it. Of course, the Act applies to any transaction which takes place in its entirety in a state which has enacted the Act. But the mere fact that suit is brought in a state does not make it appropriate to apply the substantive law of that state. Cases where a relation to the enacting state is not "appropriate" include, for example, those where the parties have clearly contracted on the basis of some other law, as where the law of the place of contracting and the law of the place of contemplated performance are the same and are contrary to the law under the Code.

3. Where a transaction has significant contacts with a state which has enacted the Act and also with other jurisdictions, the question what relation is "appropriate" is left to judicial decision. In deciding that question, the court is not strictly bound by precedents established in other contexts. Thus a conflict-of-laws decision refusing to apply a purely local statute or rule of law to a particular multi-state transaction may not be valid precedent for refusal to apply the Code in an analogous situation. Application of the Code in such circumstances may be justified by its comprehensiveness, by the policy of uniformity, and by the fact that it is in large part a reformulation and restatement of the law merchant and of the understanding of a business community which transcends state and even national boundaries. Compare Global Commerce Corp. v. Clark-Babbitt Industries, Inc., 239 F.2d 716, 719 (2d Cir. 1956). In particular, where a transaction is governed in large part by the Code, application of another law to some detail of performance because of an accident of geography may violate the commercial understanding of the parties.

4. The Act does not attempt to prescribe choice-of-law rules for states which do not enact it, but this section does not prevent application of the Act in a court of such a state. Common-law choice of law often rests on policies of giving effect to agreements and of uniformity of result regardless of where suit is brought. To the extent that such policies prevail, the relevant considerations are similar in such a court to those outlined above.

5. Subsection (2) spells out essential limitations on the parties' right to choose the applicable law. Especially in Article 9 parties taking a security interest or asked to extend credit which may be subject to a security interest must have sure ways to find out whether and where to file and where to look for possible existing filings.

6. Section 9–103 should be consulted as to the rules for perfection of security interests and the effects of perfection and nonperfection.

§ 1–106. Remedies to Be Liberally Administered.

(1) The remedies provided by this Act shall be liberally administered to the end that the aggrieved party may be put in as good a position as if the other party had fully performed but neither consequential or special nor penal damages may be had except as specifically provided in this Act or by other rule of law.

(2) Any right or obligation declared by this Act is enforceable by action unless the provision declaring it specifies a different and limited effect.

Official Comment

Prior Uniform Statutory Provision: Subsection (1)—none; Subsection (2)—Section 72, Uniform Sales Act.

Changes: Reworded.

Purposes of Changes and New Matter: Subsection (1) is intended to effect three things:

1. First, to negate the unduly narrow or technical interpretation of some remedial provisions of prior legislation by providing that the remedies in this Act are to be liberally administered to the end stated in the section. Second, to make it clear that compensatory damages are limited to compensation. They do not include consequential or special damages, or penal damages; and the Act elsewhere makes it clear that damages must be minimized. Cf. Sections 1–203, 2–706(1), and 2–712(2). The third purpose of subsection (1) is to reject any doctrine that damages must be calculable with mathematical accuracy. Compensatory damages are often at best approximate: they have to be proved with whatever definiteness and accuracy the facts permit, but no more. Cf. Section 2–204(3).

2. Under subsection (2) any right or obligation described in this Act is enforceable by court action, even though no remedy may be expressly provided, unless a particular provision specifies a different and limited effect. Whether specific performance or other equitable relief is available is determined not by this section but by specific provisions and by supplementary principles. Cf. Sections 1–103, 2–716.

3. "Consequential" or "special" damages and "penal" damages are not defined in terms in the Code, but are used in the sense given them by the leading cases on the subject.

Cross References:

Sections 1–103, 1–203, 2–204(3), 2–701, 2–706(1), 2–712(2) and 2–716.

Definitional Cross References:

"Action". Section 1–201.
"Aggrieved party". Section 1–201.
"Party". Section 1–201.
"Remedy". Section 1–201.
"Rights". Section 1–201.

§ 1–107. Waiver or Renunciation of Claim or Right After Breach.

Any claim or right arising out of an alleged breach can be discharged in whole or in part without consideration by a written waiver or renunciation signed and delivered by the aggrieved party.

Official Comment

Prior Uniform Statutory Provision: Compare Section 1, Uniform Written Obligations Act; Sections 119(3), 120(2) and 122, Uniform Negotiable Instruments Law.

Purposes:

This section makes consideration unnecessary to the effective renunciation or waiver of rights or claims arising out of an alleged breach of a commercial contract where such renunciation is in writing and signed and delivered by the aggrieved party. Its provisions, however, must be read in conjunction with the section imposing an obligation of good faith. (Section 1–203). There may, of course, also be an oral renunciation or waiver sustained by consideration but subject to Statute of Frauds provisions and to the section of Article 2 on Sales dealing with the modification of signed writings (Section 2–209). As is made express in the latter section this Act fully recognizes the effectiveness of waiver and estoppel.

Cross References:

Sections 1–203, 2–201 and 2–209. And see Section 2–719.

Definitional Cross References:

"Aggrieved party". Section 1–201.

"Rights". Section 1–201.

"Signed". Section 1–201.

"Written". Section 1–201.

§ 1–108. Severability.

If any provision or clause of this Act or application thereof to any person or circumstances is held invalid, such invalidity shall not affect other provisions or applications of the Act which can be given effect without the invalid provision or application, and to this end the provisions of this Act are declared to be severable.

Official Comment

This is the model severability section recommended by the National Conference of Commissioners on Uniform State Laws for inclusion in all acts of extensive scope.

Definitional Cross Reference:

"Person". Section 1–201.

§ 1–109. Section Captions.

Section captions are parts of this Act.

Official Comment

Prior Uniform Statutory Provision: None.

Purposes:

To make explicit in all jurisdictions that section captions are a part of the text of this Act and not mere surplusage.

PART 2

GENERAL DEFINITIONS AND PRINCIPLES OF INTERPRETATION

§ 1–201. General Definitions.

Subject to additional definitions contained in the subsequent Articles of this Act which are applicable to specific Articles or Parts thereof, and unless the context otherwise requires, in this Act:

(1) "Action" in the sense of a judicial proceeding includes recoupment, counterclaim, set-off, suit in equity and any other proceedings in which rights are determined.

(2) "Aggrieved party" means a party entitled to resort to a remedy.

(3) "Agreement" means the bargain of the parties in fact as found in their language or by implication from other circumstances including course of dealing or usage of trade or course of performance as provided in this Act (Sections 1–205, 2–208, and 2A–207). Whether an agreement has legal consequences is determined by the provisions of this Act, if applicable; otherwise by the law of contracts (Section 1–103). (Compare "Contract".)

(4) "Bank" means any person engaged in the business of banking.

(5) "Bearer" means the person in possession of an instrument, document of title, or certificated security payable to bearer or indorsed in blank.

(6) "Bill of lading" means a document evidencing the receipt of goods for shipment issued by a person engaged in the business of transporting or forwarding goods, and includes an airbill. "Airbill" means a document serving for air transportation as a bill of lading does for marine or rail transportation, and includes an air consignment note or air waybill.

(7) "Branch" includes a separately incorporated foreign branch of a bank.

(8) "Burden of establishing" a fact means the burden of persuading the triers of fact that the existence of the fact is more probable than its non-existence.

(9) "Buyer in ordinary course of business" means a person who in good faith and without knowledge that the sale to him is in violation of the ownership rights or security interest of a third party in the goods buys in ordinary course from a person in the business of selling goods of that kind but does not include a pawnbroker. All persons who sell minerals or the like (including oil and gas) at wellhead or minehead shall be deemed to be persons in the business of selling goods of that kind. "Buying" may be for cash or by exchange of other property or on secured or unsecured credit and includes receiving goods or documents of title under a pre-existing contract for sale but does not include a transfer in bulk or as security for or in total or partial satisfaction of a money debt.

(10) "Conspicuous": A term or clause is conspicuous when it is so written that a reasonable person against whom it is to operate ought to have noticed it. A printed heading in capitals (as: NON-NEGOTIABLE BILL OF LADING) is conspicuous. Language in the body of a form is "conspicuous" if it is in larger or other contrasting type or color. But in a telegram any stated term is "conspicuous". Whether a term or clause is "conspicuous" or not is for decision by the court.

(11) "Contract" means the total legal obligation which results from the parties' agreement as affected by this Act and any other applicable rules of law. (Compare "Agreement".)

(12) "Creditor" includes a general creditor, a secured creditor, a lien creditor and any representative of creditors, including an assignee for the benefit of creditors, a trustee in bankruptcy, a receiver in equity and an executor or administrator of an insolvent debtor's or assignor's estate.

(13) "Defendant" includes a person in the position of defendant in a cross-action or counterclaim.

(14) "Delivery" with respect to instruments, documents of title, chattel paper, or certificated securities means voluntary transfer of possession.

(15) "Document of title" includes bill of lading, dock warrant, dock receipt, warehouse receipt or order for the delivery of goods, and also any other document which in the regular course of business or financing is treated as adequately evidencing that the person in possession of it is entitled to receive, hold and dispose of the document and the goods it covers. To be a

document of title a document must purport to be issued by or addressed to a bailee and purport to cover goods in the bailee's possession which are either identified or are fungible portions of an identified mass.

(16) "Fault" means wrongful act, omission or breach.

(17) "Fungible" with respect to goods or securities means goods or securities of which any unit is, by nature or usage of trade, the equivalent of any other like unit. Goods which are not fungible shall be deemed fungible for the purposes of this Act to the extent that under a particular agreement or document unlike units are treated as equivalents.

(18) "Genuine" means free of forgery or counterfeiting.

(19) "Good faith" means honesty in fact in the conduct or transaction concerned.

(20) "Holder," with respect to a negotiable instrument, means the person in possession if the instrument is payable to bearer or, in the case of an instrument payable to an identified person, if the identified person is in possession. "Holder" with respect to a document of title means the person in possession if the goods are deliverable to bearer or to the order of the person in possession.

(21) To "honor" is to pay or to accept and pay, or where a credit so engages to purchase or discount a draft complying with the terms of the credit.

(22) "Insolvency proceedings" includes any assignment for the benefit of creditors or other proceedings intended to liquidate or rehabilitate the estate of the person involved.

(23) A person is "insolvent" who either has ceased to pay his debts in the ordinary course of business or cannot pay his debts as they become due or is insolvent within the meaning of the federal bankruptcy law.

(24) "Money" means a medium of exchange authorized or adopted by a domestic or foreign government and includes a monetary unit of account established by an intergovernmental organization or by agreement between two or more nations.

(25) A person has "notice" of a fact when

(a) he has actual knowledge of it; or

(b) he has received a notice or notification of it; or

(c) from all the facts and circumstances known to him at the time in question he has reason to know that it exists.

A person "knows" or has "knowledge" of a fact when he has actual knowledge of it. "Discover" or "learn" or a word or phrase of similar import refers to knowledge rather than to reason to know. The time and circumstances under which a notice or notification may cease to be effective are not determined by this Act.

(26) A person "notifies" or "gives" a notice or notification to another by taking such steps as may be reasonably required to inform the other in

ordinary course whether or not such other actually comes to know of it. A person "receives" a notice or notification when

(a) it comes to his attention; or

(b) it is duly delivered at the place of business through which the contract was made or at any other place held out by him as the place for receipt of such communications.

(27) Notice, knowledge or a notice or notification received by an organization is effective for a particular transaction from the time when it is brought to the attention of the individual conducting that transaction, and in any event from the time when it would have been brought to his attention if the organization had exercised due diligence. An organization exercises due diligence if it maintains reasonable routines for communicating significant information to the person conducting the transaction and there is reasonable compliance with the routines. Due diligence does not require an individual acting for the organization to communicate information unless such communication is part of his regular duties or unless he has reason to know of the transaction and that the transaction would be materially affected by the information.

(28) "Organization" includes a corporation, government or governmental subdivision or agency, business trust, estate, trust, partnership or association, two or more persons having a joint or common interest, or any other legal or commercial entity.

(29) "Party", as distinct from "third party", means a person who has engaged in a transaction or made an agreement within this Act.

(30) "Person" includes an individual or an organization (See Section 1–102).

(31) "Presumption" or "presumed" means that the trier of fact must find the existence of the fact presumed unless and until evidence is introduced which would support a finding of its non-existence.

(32) "Purchase" includes taking by sale, discount, negotiation, mortgage, pledge, lien, issue or re-issue, gift or any other voluntary transaction creating an interest in property.

(33) "Purchaser" means a person who takes by purchase.

(34) "Remedy" means any remedial right to which an aggrieved party is entitled with or without resort to a tribunal.

(35) "Representative" includes an agent, an officer of a corporation or association, and a trustee, executor or administrator of an estate, or any other person empowered to act for another.

(36) "Rights" includes remedies.

(37) "Security interest" means an interest in personal property or fixtures which secures payment or performance of an obligation. The retention or reservation of title by a seller of goods notwithstanding shipment or delivery to the buyer (Section 2–401) is limited in effect to a reservation of a "security interest". The term also includes any interest of a buyer of accounts or chattel paper which is subject to Article 9. The special property

interest of a buyer of goods on identification of those goods to a contract for sale under Section 2-401 is not a "security interest", but a buyer may also acquire a "security interest" by complying with Article 9. Unless a consignment is intended as security, reservation of title thereunder is not a "security interest", but a consignment in any event is subject to the provisions on consignment sales (Section 2-326).

Whether a transaction creates a lease or security interest is determined by the facts of each case; however, a transaction creates a security interest if the consideration the lessee is to pay the lessor for the right to possession and use of the goods is an obligation for the term of the lease not subject to termination by the lessee, and

(a) the original term of the lease is equal to or greater than the remaining economic life of the goods,

(b) the lessee is bound to renew the lease for the remaining economic life of the goods or is bound to become the owner of the goods,

(c) the lessee has an option to renew the lease for the remaining economic life of the goods for no additional consideration or nominal additional consideration upon compliance with the lease agreement, or

(d) the lessee has an option to become the owner of the goods for no additional consideration or nominal additional consideration upon compliance with the lease agreement.

A transaction does not create a security interest merely because it provides that

(a) the present value of the consideration the lessee is obligated to pay the lessor for the right to possession and use of the goods is substantially equal to or is greater than the fair market value of the goods at the time the lease is entered into,

(b) the lessee assumes risk of loss of the goods, or agrees to pay taxes, insurance, filing, recording, or registration fees, or service or maintenance costs with respect to the goods,

(c) the lessee has an option to renew the lease or to become the owner of the goods,

(d) the lessee has an option to renew the lease for a fixed rent that is equal to or greater than the reasonably predictable fair market rent for the use of the goods for the term of the renewal at the time the option is to be performed, or

(e) the lessee has an option to become the owner of the goods for a fixed price that is equal to or greater than the reasonably predictable fair market value of the goods at the time the option is to be performed.

For purposes of this subsection (37):

(x) Additional consideration is not nominal if (i) when the option to renew the lease is granted to the lessee the rent is stated to be the fair market rent for the use of the goods for the term of the renewal determined at the time the option is to be performed, or (ii) when the option to become the owner of the goods is granted to the lessee the price is stated to be the fair market value of the goods determined at the time the option is to be performed. Additional consideration is nominal if it is less than the lessee's reasonably predictable cost of performing under the lease agreement if the option is not exercised;

(y) "Reasonably predictable" and "remaining economic life of the goods" are to be determined with reference to the facts and circumstances at the time the transaction is entered into; and

(z) "Present value" means the amount as of a date certain of one or more sums payable in the future, discounted to the date certain. The discount is determined by the interest rate specified by the parties if the rate is not manifestly unreasonable at the time the transaction is entered into; otherwise, the discount is determined by a commercially reasonable rate that takes into account the facts and circumstances of each case at the time the transaction was entered into.

(38) "Send" in connection with any writing or notice means to deposit in the mail or deliver for transmission by any other usual means of communication with postage or cost of transmission provided for and properly addressed and in the case of an instrument to an address specified thereon or otherwise agreed, or if there be none to any address reasonable under the circumstances. The receipt of any writing or notice within the time at which it would have arrived if properly sent has the effect of a proper sending.

(39) "Signed" includes any symbol executed or adopted by a party with present intention to authenticate a writing.

(40) "Surety" includes guarantor.

(41) "Telegram" includes a message transmitted by radio, teletype, cable, any mechanical method of transmission, or the like.

(42) "Term" means that portion of an agreement which relates to a particular matter.

(43) "Unauthorized" signature means one made without actual, implied, or apparent authority and includes a forgery.

(44) "Value". Except as otherwise provided with respect to negotiable instruments and bank collections (Sections 3–303, 4–210 and 4–211) a person gives "value" for rights if he acquires them

(a) in return for a binding commitment to extend credit or for the extension of immediately available credit whether or not drawn upon and whether or not a charge-back is provided for in the event of difficulties in collection; or

(b) as security for or in total or partial satisfaction of a pre-existing claim; or

(c) by accepting delivery pursuant to a pre-existing contract for purchase; or

(d) generally, in return for any consideration sufficient to support a simple contract.

(45) "Warehouse receipt" means a receipt issued by a person engaged in the business of storing goods for hire.

(46) "Written" or "writing" includes printing, typewriting or any other intentional reduction to tangible form.

As amended in 1962, 1972, 1977, 1987, 1990 and 1994.

See Appendices III, VIII and XI for material relating to changes made in text in 1987, 1990 and 1994.

Official Comment

Prior Uniform Statutory Provision, Changes and New Matter:

1. "Action". See similar definitions in Section 191, Uniform Negotiable Instruments Law; Section 76, Uniform Sales Act; Section 58, Uniform Warehouse Receipts Act; Section 53, Uniform Bills of Lading Act. The definition has been rephrased and enlarged.

2. "Aggrieved party". New.

3. "Agreement". New. As used in this Act the word is intended to include full recognition of usage of trade, course of dealing, course of performance and the surrounding circumstances as effective parts thereof, and of any agreement permitted under the provisions of this Act to displace a stated rule of law.

4. "Bank". See Section 191, Uniform Negotiable Instruments Law.

5. "Bearer". From Section 191, Uniform Negotiable Instruments Law. The prior definition has been broadened.

6. "Bill of Lading". See similar definitions in Section 1, Uniform Bills of Lading Act. The definition has been enlarged to include freight forwarders' bills and bills issued by contract carriers as well as those issued by common carriers. The definition of airbill is new.

7. "Branch". New.

8. "Burden of establishing a fact". New.

9. "Buyer in ordinary course of business". From Section 1, Uniform Trust Receipts Act. The definition has been expanded to make clear the type of person protected. Its major significance lies in Section 2-403 and in the Article on Secured Transactions (Article 9).

The reference to minerals and the like makes clear that a buyer in ordinary course buying minerals under the circumstances described takes free of a prior mortgage created by the sellers. See Comment to Section 9-103.

A pawnbroker cannot be a buyer in ordinary course of business because the person from whom he buys goods (or acquires ownership after foreclosing an initial pledge) is typically an ordinary user and not a person engaged in selling goods of that kind.

10. "Conspicuous". New. This is intended to indicate some of the methods of making a term attention-calling. But the test is whether attention can reasonably be expected to be called to it.

11. "Contract". New. But see Sections 3 and 71, Uniform Sales Act.

12. "Creditor". New.

13. "Defendant". From Section 76, Uniform Sales Act. Rephrased.

14. "Delivery". Section 76, Uniform Sales Act, Section 191, Uniform Negotiable Instruments Law, Section 58, Uniform Warehouse Receipts Act and Section 53, Uniform Bills of Lading Act.

15. "Document of title". From Section 76, Uniform Sales Act, but rephrased to eliminate certain ambiguities. Thus, by making it explicit that the obligation or designation of a third party as "bailee" is essential to a document of title, this definition clearly rejects any such result as obtained in Hixson v. Ward, 254 Ill. App. 505 (1929), which treated a conditional sales contract as a document of title. Also the definition is left open so that new types of documents may be included. It is unforeseeable what documents may one day serve the essential purpose now filled by warehouse receipts and bills of lading. Truck transport has

already opened up problems which do not fit the patterns of practice resting upon the assumption that a draft can move through banking channels faster than the goods themselves can reach their destination. There lie ahead air transport and such probabilities as teletype transmission of what may some day be regarded commercially as "Documents of Title". The definition is stated in terms of the function of the documents with the intention that any document which gains commercial recognition as accomplishing the desired result shall be included within its scope. Fungible goods are adequately identified within the language of the definition by identification of the mass of which they are a part.

Dock warrants were within the Sales Act definition of document of title apparently for the purpose of recognizing a valid tender by means of such paper. In current commercial practice a dock warrant or receipt is a kind of interim certificate issued by steamship companies upon delivery of the goods at the dock, entitling a designated person to have issued to him at the company's office a bill of lading. The receipt itself is invariably nonnegotiable in form although it may indicate that a negotiable bill is to be forthcoming. Such a document is not within the general compass of the definition, although trade usage may in some cases entitle such paper to be treated as a document of title. If the dock receipt actually represents a storage obligation undertaken by the shipping company, then it is a warehouse receipt within this Section regardless of the name given to the instrument.

The goods must be "described", but the description may be by marks or labels and may be qualified in such a way as to disclaim personal knowledge of the issuer regarding contents or condition. However, baggage and parcel checks and similar "tokens" of storage which identify stored goods only as those received in exchange for the token are not covered by this Article.

The definition is broad enough to include an airway bill.

16. "Fault". From Section 76, Uniform Sales Act.

17. "Fungible". See Sections 5, 6 and 76, Uniform Sales Act; Section 58, Uniform Warehouse Receipts Act. Fungibility of goods "by agreement" has been added for clarity and accuracy. ~~As to securities, see Section 8-107 and Comment.~~ *Amendment approved by the Permanent Editorial Board for Uniform Commercial Code November 4, 1995.*

18. "Genuine". New.

19. "Good faith". See Section 76(2), Uniform Sales Act; Section 58(2), Uniform Warehouse Receipts Act; Section 53(2), Uniform Bills of Lading Act; Section 22(2), Uniform Stock Transfer Act. "Good faith", whenever it is used in the Code, means at least what is here stated. In certain Articles, by specific provision, additional requirements are made applicable. See, e.g., Secs. 2–103(1)(b), 7–404. To illustrate, in the Article on Sales, Section 2–103, good faith is expressly defined as including in the case of a merchant observance of reasonable commercial standards of fair dealing in the trade, so that throughout that Article wherever a merchant appears in the case an inquiry into his observance of such standards is necessary to determine his good faith.

20. "Holder". See similar definitions in Section 191, Uniform Negotiable Instruments Law; Section 58, Uniform Warehouse Receipts Act; Section 53, Uniform Bills of Lading Act.

21. "Honor". New.

22. "Insolvency proceedings". New.

23. "Insolvent". Section 76(3), Uniform Sales Act. The three tests of insolvency—"ceased to pay his debts in the ordinary course of business," "cannot pay his debts as they become due," and "insolvent within the meaning of the federal bankruptcy law"—are expressly set up as alternative tests and must be approached from a commercial standpoint.

24. "Money". Section 6(5), Uniform Negotiable Instruments Law. The test adopted is that of sanction of government, whether by authorization before issue or

adoption afterward, which recognizes the circulating medium as a part of the official currency of that government. The narrow view that money is limited to legal tender is rejected.

25. "Notice". New. Compare N.I.L. Sec. 56. Under the definition a person has notice when he has received a notification of the fact in question. But by the last sentence the act leaves open the time and circumstances under which notice or notification may cease to be effective. Therefore such cases as Graham v. White-Phillips Co., 296 U.S. 27, 56 S.Ct. 21, 80 L.Ed. 20 (1935), are not overruled.

26. "Notifies". New. This is the word used when the essential fact is the proper dispatch of the notice, not its receipt. Compare "Send". When the essential fact is the other party's receipt of the notice, that is stated. The second sentence states when a notification is received.

27. New. This makes clear that reason to know, knowledge, or a notification, although "received" for instance by a clerk in Department A of an organization, is effective for a transaction conducted in Department B only from the time when it was or should have been communicated to the individual conducting that transaction.

28. "Organization". This is the definition of every type of entity or association, excluding an individual, acting as such. Definitions of "person" were included in Section 191, Uniform Negotiable Instruments Law; Section 76, Uniform Sales Act; Section 58, Uniform Warehouse Receipts Act; Section 53, Uniform Bills of Lading Act; Section 22, Uniform Stock Transfer Act; Section 1, Uniform Trust Receipts Act. The definition of "organization" given here includes a number of entities or associations not specifically mentioned in prior definition of "person", namely, government, governmental subdivision or agency, business trust, trust and estate.

29. "Party". New. Mention of a party includes, of course, a person acting through an agent. However, where an agent comes into opposition or contrast to his principal, particular account is taken of that situation.

30. "Person". See Comment to definition of "Organization". The reference to Section 1-102 is to subsection (5) of that section.

31. "Presumption". New.

32. "Purchase". Section 58, Uniform Warehouse Receipts Act; Section 76, Uniform Sales Act; Section 53, Uniform Bills of Lading Act; Section 22, Uniform Stock Transfer Act; Section 1, Uniform Trust Receipts Act. Rephrased.

33. "Purchaser". Section 58, Uniform Warehouse Receipts Act; Section 76, Uniform Sales Act; Section 53, Uniform Bills of Lading Act; Section 22, Uniform Stock Transfer Act; Section 1, Uniform Trust Receipts Act. Rephrased.

34. "Remedy". New. The purpose is to make it clear that both remedy and rights (as defined) include those remedial rights of "self help" which are among the most important bodies of rights under this Act, remedial rights being those to which an aggrieved party can resort on his own motion.

35. "Representative". New.

36. "Rights". New. See Comment to "Remedy".

37. "Security Interest". See Section 1, Uniform Trust Receipts Act. The present definition is elaborated, in view especially of the complete coverage of the subject in Article 9. Notice that in view of the Article the term includes the interest of certain outright buyers of certain kinds of property. Section 1-201(37) is being amended at the same time that the Article on Leases (Article 2A) is being promulgated as an amendment to this Act.

One of the reasons it was decided to codify the law with respect to leases was to resolve an issue that has created considerable confusion in the courts: what is a lease? The confusion exists, in part, due to the last two sentences of the definition of security interest in the 1978 Official Text of the Act. Section 1-

201(37). The confusion is compounded by the rather considerable change in the federal, state and local tax laws and accounting rules as they relate to leases of goods. The answer is important because the definition of lease determines not only the rights and remedies of the parties to the lease but also those of third parties. If a transaction creates a lease and not a security interest, the lessee's interest in the goods is limited to its leasehold estate; the residual interest in the goods belongs to the lessor. This has significant implications to the lessee's creditors. "On common law theory, the lessor, since he has not parted with title, is entitled to full protection against the lessee's creditors and trustee in bankruptcy ...." 1 G. Gilmore, *Security Interests in Personal Property* § 3.6, at 76 (1965).

Under pre-Act chattel security law there was generally no requirement that the lessor file the lease, a financing statement, or the like, to enforce the lease agreement against the lessee or any third party; the Article on Secured Transactions (Article 9) did not change the common law in that respect. Coogan, Leasing and the Uniform Commercial Code, in *Equipment Leasing—Leveraged Leasing* 681, 700 n.25, 729 n.80 (2d ed.1980). The Article on Leases (Article 2A) has not changed the law in that respect, except for leases of fixtures. Section 2A–309. An examination of the common law will not provide an adequate answer to the question of what is a lease. The definition of security interest in Section 1–201(37) of the 1978 Official Text of the Act provides that the Article on Secured Transactions (Article 9) governs security interests disguised as leases, *i.e.,* leases intended as security; however, the definition is vague and outmoded.

Lease is defined in Article 2A as a transfer of the right to possession and use of goods for a term, in return for consideration. Section 2A–103(1)(j). The definition continues by stating that the retention or creation of a security interest is not a lease. Thus, the task of sharpening the line between true leases and security interests disguised as leases continues to be a function of this section.

The first paragraph of this definition is a revised version of the first five sentences of the 1978 Official Text of Section 1–201(37). The changes are modest in that they make a style change in the fourth sentence and delete the reference to lease in the fifth sentence. The balance of this definition is new, although it preserves elements of the last two sentences of the prior definition. The focus of the changes was to draw a sharper line between leases and security interests disguised as leases to create greater certainty in commercial transactions.

Prior to this amendment, Section 1–201(37) provided that whether a lease was intended as security (*i.e.,* a security interest disguised as a lease) was to be determined from the facts of each case; however, (a) the inclusion of an option to purchase did not itself make the lease one intended for security, and (b) an agreement that upon compliance with the terms of the lease the lessee would become, or had the option to become, the owner of the property for no additional consideration, or for a nominal consideration, did make the lease one intended for security.

Reference to the intent of the parties to create a lease or security interest has led to unfortunate results. In discovering intent, courts have relied upon factors that were thought to be more consistent with sales or loans than leases. Most of these criteria, however, are as applicable to true leases as to security interests. Examples include the typical net lease provisions, a purported lessor's lack of storage facilities or its character as a financing party rather than a dealer in goods. Accordingly, amended Section 1–201(37) deletes all reference to the parties' intent.

The second paragraph of the new definition is taken from Section 1(2) of the Uniform Conditional Sales Act (act withdrawn 1943), modified to reflect current leasing practice. Thus, reference to the case law prior to this Act will provide a useful source of precedent. Gilmore, *Se-*

curity Law, Formalism and Article 9, 47 Neb.L.Rev. 659, 671 (1968). Whether a transaction creates a lease or a security interest continues to be determined by the facts of each case. The second paragraph further provides that a transaction creates a security interest if the lessee has an obligation to continue paying consideration for the term of the lease, if the obligation is not terminable by the lessee (thus correcting early statutory gloss, *e.g., In re Royer's Bakery, Inc.,* 1 U.C.C. Rep. Serv. (Callaghan) 342 (Bankr.E.D.Pa. 1963)) and if one of four additional tests is met. The first of these four tests, subparagraph (a), is that the original lease term is equal to or greater than the remaining economic life of the goods. The second of these tests, subparagraph (b), is that the lessee is either bound to renew the lease for the remaining economic life of the goods or to become the owner of the goods. *In re Gehrke Enters.,* 1 Bankr. 647, 651–52 (Bankr.W.D.Wis. 1979). The third of these tests, subparagraph (c), is whether the lessee has an option to renew the lease for the remaining economic life or the goods for no additional consideration or for nominal additional consideration, which is defined later in this section. *In re Celeryvale Transp.,* 44 Bankr. 1007, 1014–15 (Bankr. E.D.Tenn.1984). The fourth of these tests, subparagraph (d), is whether the lessee has an option to become the owner of the goods for no additional consideration or for nominal additional consideration. All of these tests focus on economics, not the intent of the parties. *In re Berge,* 32 Bankr. 370, 371–73 (Bankr. W.D.Wis.1983).

The focus on economics is reinforced by the next paragraph, which is new. It states that a transaction does not create a security interest merely because the transaction has certain characteristics listed therein. Subparagraph (a) has no statutory derivative; it states that a full payout lease does not *per se* create a security interest. *Rushton v. Shea,* 419 F.Supp. 1349, 1365 (D.Del.1976). Subparagraph (b) provides the same regarding the provisions of the typical net lease. *Compare All-States Leasing Co. v. Ochs,* 42 Or.App. 319, 600 P.2d 899 (Ct.App. 1979) *with In re Tillery,* 571 F.2d 1361 (5th Cir.1978). Subparagraph (c) restates and expands the provisions of former Section 1-201(37) to make clear that the option can be to buy or renew. Subparagraphs (d) and (e) treat fixed price options and provide that fair market value must be determined at the time the transaction is entered into. *Compare Arnold Mach. Co. v. Balls,* 624 P.2d 678 (Utah 1981) *with Aoki v. Shepherd Mach. Co.,* 665 F.2d 941 (9th Cir.1982).

The relationship of the second paragraph of this subsection to the third paragraph of this subsection deserves to be explored. The fixed price purchase option provides a useful example. A fixed price purchase option in a lease does not of itself create a security interest. This is particularly true if the fixed price is equal to or greater than the reasonably predictable fair market value of the goods at the time the option is to be performed. A security interest is created only if the option price is nominal and the conditions stated in the introduction to the second paragraph of this subsection are met. There is a set of purchase options whose fixed price is less than fair market value but greater than nominal that must be determined on the facts of each case to ascertain whether the transaction in which the option is included creates a lease or a security interest.

It was possible to provide for various other permutations and combinations with respect to options to purchase and renew. For example, this section could have stated a rule to govern the facts of *In re Marhoefer Packing Co.,* 674 F.2d 1139 (7th Cir.1982). This was not done because it would unnecessarily complicate the definition. Further development of this rule is left to the courts.

The fourth paragraph provides definitions and rules of construction.

38. "Send". New. Compare "notifies".

39. "Signed". New. The inclusion of authentication in the definition of

"signed" is to make clear that as the term is used in this Act a complete signature is not necessary. Authentication may be printed, stamped or written; it may be by initials or by thumbprint. It may be on any part of the document and in appropriate cases may be found in a billhead or letterhead. No catalog of possible authentications can be complete and the court must use common sense and commercial experience in passing upon these matters. The question always is whether the symbol was executed or adopted by the party with present intention to authenticate the writing.

40. "Surety". New.

41. "Telegram". New.

42. "Term". New.

43. Under the former version of § 1-201(43), it was not clear whether a reference to an "unauthorized signature" in Articles 3 and 4 applied to indorsements. The words "or indorsement" are deleted so that references to "unauthorized signature" in § 3-406 and elsewhere will unambiguously refer to any signature.

44. "Value". See Sections 25, 26, 27, 191, Uniform Negotiable Instruments Law; Section 76, Uniform Sales Act; Section 53, Uniform Bills of Lading Act; Section 58, Uniform Warehouse Receipts Act; Section 22(1), Uniform Stock Transfer Act; Section 1, Uniform Trust Receipts Act. All the Uniform Acts in the commercial law field (except the Uniform Conditional Sales Act) have carried definitions of "value". All those definitions provided that value was any consideration sufficient to support a simple contract, including the taking of property in satisfaction of or as security for a pre-existing claim. Subsections (a), (b) and (d) in substance continue the definitions of "value" in the earlier acts. Subsection (c) makes explicit that "value" is also given in a third situation: where a buyer by taking delivery under a pre-existing contract converts a contingent into a fixed obligation.

This definition is not applicable to Articles 3 and 4, but the express inclusion of immediately available credit as value follows the separate definitions in those Articles. See Sections 4-208, 4-209, 3-303. A bank or other financing agency which in good faith makes advances against property held as collateral becomes a bona fide purchaser of that property even though provision may be made for charge-back in case of trouble. Checking credit is "immediately available" within the meaning of this section if the bank would be subject to an action for slander of credit in case checks drawn against the credit were dishonored, and when a charge-back is not discretionary with the bank, but may only be made when difficulties in collection arise in connection with the specific transaction involved.

45. "Warehouse receipt". See Section 76(1), Uniform Sales Act; Section 1, Uniform Warehouse Receipts Act. Receipts issued by a field warehouse are included, provided the warehouseman and the depositor of the goods are different persons.

46. "Written" or "writing". This is a broadening of the definition contained in Section 191 of the Uniform Negotiable Instruments Law.

§ 1-202. Prima Facie Evidence by Third Party Documents.

A document in due form purporting to be a bill of lading, policy or certificate of insurance, official weigher's or inspector's certificate, consular invoice, or any other document authorized or required by the contract to be issued by a third party shall be prima facie evidence of its own authenticity and genuineness and of the facts stated in the document by the third party.

Official Comment

Prior Uniform Statutory Provision: None.

Purposes:

1. This section is designed to supply judicial recognition for documents which have traditionally been relied upon as trustworthy by commercial men.

2. This section is concerned only with documents which have been given a preferred status by the parties themselves who have required their procurement in the agreement and for this reason the applicability of the section is limited to actions arising out of the contract which authorized or required the document. The documents listed are intended to be illustrative and not all inclusive.

3. The provisions of this section go no further than establishing the documents in question as prima facie evidence and leave to the court the ultimate determination of the facts where the accuracy or authenticity of the documents is questioned. In this connection the section calls for a commercially reasonable interpretation.

Definitional Cross References:

"Bill of lading". Section 1-201.
"Contract". Section 1-201.
"Genuine". Section 1-201.

§ 1-203. Obligation of Good Faith.

Every contract or duty within this Act imposes an obligation of good faith in its performance or enforcement.

Official Comment

Prior Uniform Statutory Provision: None.

Purposes:

This section sets forth a basic principle running throughout this Act. The principle involved is that in commercial transactions good faith is required in the performance and enforcement of all agreements or duties. Particular applications of this general principle appear in specific provisions of the Act such as the option to accelerate at will (Section 1-208), the right to cure a defective delivery of goods (Section 2-508), the duty of a merchant buyer who has rejected goods to effect salvage operations (Section 2-603), substituted performance (Section 2-614), and failure of presupposed conditions (Section 2-615). The concept, however, is broader than any of these illustrations and applies generally, as stated in this section, to the performance or enforcement of every contract or duty within this Act. It is further implemented by Section 1-205 on course of dealing and usage of trade. This section does not support an independent cause of action for failure to perform or enforce in good faith. Rather, this section means that a failure to perform or enforce, in good faith, a specific duty or obligation under the contract, constitutes a breach of that contract or makes unavailable, under the particular circumstances, a remedial right or power. This distinction makes it clear that the doctrine of good faith merely directs a court towards interpreting contracts within the commercial context in which they are created, performed, and enforced, and does not create a separate duty of fairness and reasonableness which can be independently breached. See PEB Commentary No. 10, dated February 10, 1994 [Appendix V, infra].

It is to be noted that under the Sales Article definition of good faith (Section 2-103), contracts made by a merchant have incorporated in them the explicit standard not only of honesty in fact (Section 1-201), but also of observance by the merchant of reasonable commercial standards of fair dealing in the trade.

Cross References:

Sections 1-201; 1-205; 1-208; 2-103; 2-508; 2-603; 2-614; 2-615.

Definitional Cross References:

"Contract". Section 1-201.
"Good faith". Sections 1-201; 2-103.

§ 1–204. Time; Reasonable Time; "Seasonably".

(1) Whenever this Act requires any action to be taken within a reasonable time, any time which is not manifestly unreasonable may be fixed by agreement.

(2) What is a reasonable time for taking any action depends on the nature, purpose and circumstances of such action.

(3) An action is taken "seasonably" when it is taken at or within the time agreed or if no time is agreed at or within a reasonable time.

Official Comment

Prior Uniform Statutory Provision: Compare Section 193, Uniform Negotiable Instruments Law.

Purposes:

1. Subsection (1) recognizes that nothing is stronger evidence of a reasonable time than the fixing of such time by a fair agreement between the parties. However, provision is made for disregarding a clause which whether by inadvertence or overreaching fixes a time so unreasonable that it amounts to eliminating all remedy under the contract. The parties are not required to fix the most reasonable time but may fix any time which is not obviously unfair as judged by the time of contracting.

2. Under the section, the agreement which fixes the time need not be part of the main agreement, but may occur separately. Notice also that under the definition of "agreement" (Section 1–201) the circumstances of the transaction, including course of dealing or usages of trade or course of performance may be material. On the question what is a reasonable time these matters will often be important.

Definitional Cross Reference:

"Agreement". Section 1–201.

§ 1–205. Course of Dealing and Usage of Trade.

(1) A course of dealing is a sequence of previous conduct between the parties to a particular transaction which is fairly to be regarded as establishing a common basis of understanding for interpreting their expressions and other conduct.

(2) A usage of trade is any practice or method of dealing having such regularity of observance in a place, vocation or trade as to justify an expectation that it will be observed with respect to the transaction in question. The existence and scope of such a usage are to be proved as facts. If it is established that such a usage is embodied in a written trade code or similar writing the interpretation of the writing is for the court.

(3) A course of dealing between parties and any usage of trade in the vocation or trade in which they are engaged or of which they are or should be aware give particular meaning to and supplement or qualify terms of an agreement.

(4) The express terms of an agreement and an applicable course of dealing or usage of trade shall be construed wherever reasonable as consistent with each other; but when such construction is unreasonable express terms control both course of dealing and usage of trade and course of dealing controls usage of trade.

(5) An applicable usage of trade in the place where any part of performance is to occur shall be used in interpreting the agreement as to that part of the performance.

(6) Evidence of a relevant usage of trade offered by one party is not admissible unless and until he has given the other party such notice as the court finds sufficient to prevent unfair surprise to the latter.

Official Comment

Prior Uniform Statutory Provision: No such general provision but see Sections 9(1), 15(5), 18(2), and 71, Uniform Sales Act.

Purposes: This section makes it clear that:

1. This Act rejects both the "lay-dictionary" and the "conveyancer's" reading of a commercial agreement. Instead the meaning of the agreement of the parties is to be determined by the language used by them and by their action, read and interpreted in the light of commercial practices and other surrounding circumstances. The measure and background for interpretation are set by the commercial context, which may explain and supplement even the language of a formal or final writing.

2. Course of dealing under subsection (1) is restricted, literally, to a sequence of conduct between the parties previous to the agreement. However, the provisions of the Act on course of performance make it clear that a sequence of conduct after or under the agreement may have equivalent meaning. (Section 2-208.)

3. "Course of dealing" may enter the agreement either by explicit provisions of the agreement or by tacit recognition.

4. This Act deals with "usage of trade" as a factor in reaching the commercial meaning of the agreement which the parties have made. The language used is to be interpreted as meaning what it may fairly be expected to mean to parties involved in the particular commercial transaction in a given locality or in a given vocation or trade. By adopting in this context the term "usage of trade" this Act expresses its intent to reject those cases which see evidence of "custom" as representing an effort to displace or negate "established rules of law". A distinction is to be drawn between mandatory rules of law such as the Statute of Frauds provisions of Article 2 on Sales whose very office is to control and restrict the actions of the parties, and which cannot be abrogated by agreement, or by a usage of trade, and those rules of law (such as those in Part 3 of Article 2 on Sales) which fill in points which the parties have not considered and in fact agreed upon. The latter rules hold "unless otherwise agreed" but yield to the contrary agreement of the parties. Part of the agreement of the parties to which such rules yield is to be sought for in the usages of trade which furnish the background and give particular meaning to the language used, and are the framework of common understanding controlling any general rules of law which hold only when there is no such understanding.

5. A usage of trade under subsection (2) must have the "regularity of observance" specified. The ancient English tests for "custom" are abandoned in this connection. Therefore, it is not required that a usage of trade be "ancient or immemorial", "universal" or the like. Under the requirement of subsection (2) full recognition is thus available for new usages and for usages currently observed by the great majority of decent dealers, even though dissidents ready to cut corners do not agree. There is room also for proper recognition of usage agreed upon by merchants in trade codes.

6. The policy of this Act controlling explicit unconscionable contracts and clauses (Sections 1-203, 2-302) applies to implicit clauses which rest on usage of trade and carries forward the policy underlying the ancient requirement that a

custom or usage must be "reasonable". However, the emphasis is shifted. The very fact of commercial acceptance makes out a prima facie case that the usage is reasonable, and the burden is no longer on the usage to establish itself as being reasonable. But the anciently established policing of usage by the courts is continued to the extent necessary to cope with the situation arising if an unconscionable or dishonest practice should become standard.

7. Subsection (3), giving the prescribed effect to usages of which the parties "are or should be aware", reinforces the provision of subsection (2) requiring not universality but only the described "regularity of observance" of the practice or method. This subsection also reinforces the point of subsection (2) that such usages may be either general to trade or particular to a special branch of trade.

8. Although the terms in which this Act defines "agreement" include the elements of course of dealing and usage of trade, the fact that express reference is made in some sections to those elements is not to be construed as carrying a contrary intent or implication elsewhere. Compare Section 1-102(4).

9. In cases of a well established line of usage varying from the general rules of this Act where the precise amount of the variation has not been worked out into a single standard, the party relying on the usage is entitled, in any event, to the minimum variation demonstrated. The whole is not to be disregarded because no particular line of detail has been established. In case a dominant pattern has been fairly evidenced, the party relying on the usage is entitled under this section to go to the trier of fact on the question of whether such dominant pattern has been incorporated into the agreement.

10. Subsection (6) is intended to insure that this Act's liberal recognition of the needs of commerce in regard to usage of trade shall not be made into an instrument of abuse.

Cross References:

Point 1: Sections 1-203, 2-104 and 2-202.
Point 2: Section 2-208.
Point 4: Section 2-201 and Part 3 of Article 2.
Point 6: Sections 1-203 and 2-302.
Point 8: Sections 1-102 and 1-201.
Point 9: Section 2-204(3).

Definitional Cross References:

"Agreement". Section 1-201.
"Contract". Section 1-201.
"Party". Section 1-201.
"Term". Section 1-201.

§ 1-206. Statute of Frauds for Kinds of Personal Property Not Otherwise Covered.

(1) Except in the cases described in subsection (2) of this section a contract for the sale of personal property is not enforceable by way of action or defense beyond five thousand dollars in amount or value of remedy unless there is some writing which indicates that a contract for sale has been made between the parties at a defined or stated price, reasonably identifies the subject matter, and is signed by the party against whom enforcement is sought or by his authorized agent.

(2) Subsection (1) of this section does not apply to contracts for the sale of goods (Section 2-201) nor of securities (Section 8-113) nor to security agreements (Section 9-203).

As amended in 1994.

See Appendix XII for material relating to changes made in text in 1994.

Official Comment

Prior Uniform Statutory Provision: Section 4, Uniform Sales Act (which was based on Section 17 of the Statute of 29 Charles II).

Changes: Completely rewritten by this and other sections.

Purposes: To fill the gap left by the Statute of Frauds provisions for goods (Section 2-201)~~, securities (Section 8-319),~~ and security interests (Section 9-203). As to securities, see Section 8-113. The Uniform Sales Act covered the sale of "choses in action"; the principal gap relates to sale of the "general intangibles" defined in Article 9 (Section 9-106) and to transactions excluded from Article 9 by Section 9-104. Typical are the sale of bilateral contracts, royalty rights or the like. The informality normal to such transactions is recognized by lifting the limit for oral transactions to $5,000. In such transactions there is often no standard of practice by which to judge, and values can rise or drop without warning; troubling abuses are avoided when the dollar limit is exceeded by requiring that the subject-matter be reasonably identified in a signed writing which indicates that a contract for sale has been made at a defined or stated price. *Amendments approved by the Permanent Editorial Board for Uniform Commercial Code November 4, 1995.*

Definitional Cross References:

"Action". Section 1-201.
"Agreement". Section 1-201.
"Contract". Section 1-201.
"Contract for sale". Section 2-106.
"Goods". Section 2-105.
"Party". Section 1-201.
"Sale". Section 2-106.
"Signed". Section 1-201.
"Writing". Section 1-201.

§ 1-207. Performance or Acceptance Under Reservation of Rights.

(1) A party who, with explicit reservation of rights performs or promises performance or assents to performance in a manner demanded or offered by the other party does not thereby prejudice the rights reserved. Such words as "without prejudice", "under protest" or the like are sufficient.

(2) Subsection (1) does not apply to an accord and satisfaction.

As amended in 1990.

See Appendix VIII for material relating to changes made in text in 1990.

Official Comment

1. This section provides machinery for the continuation of performance along the lines contemplated by the contract despite a pending dispute, by adopting the mercantile device of going ahead with delivery, acceptance, or payment "without prejudice," "under protest," "under reserve," "with reservation of all our rights," and the like. All of these phrases completely reserve all rights within the meaning of this section. The section therefore contemplates that limited as well as general reservations and acceptance by a party may be made "subject to satisfaction of our purchaser," "subject to acceptance by our customers," or the like.

2. This section does not add any new requirement of language of reservation where not already required by law, but merely provides a specific measure on which a party can rely as that party makes or concurs in any interim adjustment in the course of performance. It does not affect or impair the provisions of this Act such as those under which the buyer's remedies for defect survive accep-

tance without being expressly claimed if notice of the defects is given within a reasonable time. Nor does it disturb the policy of those cases which restrict the effect of a waiver of a defect to reasonable limits under the circumstances, even though no such reservation is expressed.

The section is not addressed to the creation or loss of remedies in the ordinary course of performance but rather to a method of procedure where one party is claiming as of right something which the other believes to be unwarranted.

3. Judicial authority was divided on the issue of whether former Section 1–207 (present subsection (1)) applied to an accord and satisfaction. Typically the cases involved attempts to reach an accord and satisfaction by use of a check tendered in full satisfaction of a claim. Subsection (2) of revised Section 1–207 resolves this conflict by stating that Section 1–207 does not apply to an accord and satisfaction. Section 3–311 of revised Article 3 governs if an accord and satisfaction is attempted by tender of a negotiable instrument as stated in that section. If Section 3–311 does not apply, the issue of whether an accord and satisfaction has been effected is determined by the law of contract. Whether or not Section 3–311 applies, Section 1–207 has no application to an accord and satisfaction.

§ 1–208. Option to Accelerate at Will.

A term providing that one party or his successor in interest may accelerate payment or performance or require collateral or additional collateral "at will" or "when he deems himself insecure" or in words of similar import shall be construed to mean that he shall have power to do so only if he in good faith believes that the prospect of payment or performance is impaired. The burden of establishing lack of good faith is on the party against whom the power has been exercised.

Official Comment

Prior Uniform Statutory Provision: None.

Purposes:

The increased use of acceleration clauses either in the case of sales on credit or in time paper or in security transactions has led to some confusion in the cases as to the effect to be given to a clause which seemingly grants the power of an acceleration at the whim and caprice of one party. This Section is intended to make clear that despite language which can be so construed and which further might be held to make the agreement void as against public policy or to make the contract illusory or too indefinite for enforcement, the clause means that the option is to be exercised only in the good faith belief that the prospect of payment or performance is impaired.

Obviously this section has no application to demand instruments or obligations whose very nature permits call at any time with or without reason. This section applies only to an agreement or to paper which in the first instance is payable at a future date.

Definitional Cross References:

"Burden of establishing". Section 1–201.

"Good faith". Section 1–201.

"Party". Section 1–201.

"Term". Section 1–201.

§ 1–209. Subordinated Obligations.

An obligation may be issued as subordinated to payment of another obligation of the person obligated, or a creditor may subordinate his right to payment of an obligation by agreement with either the person obligated or another creditor of the person obligated. Such a subordination does not create a security interest as against either the common debtor or a subordinated creditor. This section shall be construed as declaring the law as it existed prior to the enactment of this section and not as modifying it. Added 1966.

Note: *This new section is proposed as an optional provision to make it clear that a subordination agreement does not create a security interest unless so intended.*

Official Comment

Source: New York.

Prior Uniform Statutory Provision: None.

Reason for Change: The drafting history of Article 9 makes it clear that there was no intention to cover agreements by which the rights of one unsecured creditor are subordinated to the rights of another unsecured creditor of a common debtor. Nevertheless, since in insolvency proceedings dividends otherwise payable to a subordinated creditor are turned over to the superior creditor, fears have been expressed that a subordination agreement might be treated as a "security agreement" creating a "security interest" in property of the subordinated creditor, and that inappropriate provisions of Article 9 might be applied. This optional section is intended to allay such fears by making an explicit declaration that a subordination agreement does not of itself create a security interest. Nothing in this section prevents the creation of a security interest in such a case when the parties to the agreement so intend.

Purposes:

1. Billions of dollars of subordinated debt are held by the public and by institutional investors. Commonly, the subordinated debt is subordinated on issue or acquisition and is evidenced by an investment security or by a negotiable or non-negotiable note. Debt is also sometimes subordinated after it arises, either by agreement between the subordinating creditor and the debtor, by agreement between two creditors of the same debtor, or by agreement of all three parties. The subordinated creditor may be a stockholder or other "insider" interested in the common debtor; the subordinated debt may consist of accounts or other rights to payment not evidenced by any instrument. All such cases are included in the terms "subordinated obligation," "subordination," and "subordinated creditor."

2. Subordination agreements are enforceable between the parties as contracts; and in the bankruptcy of the common debtor dividends otherwise payable to the subordinated creditor are turned over to the superior creditor. This "turnover" practice has on occasion been explained in terms of "equitable lien," "equitable assignment," or "constructive trust," but whatever the label the practice is essentially an equitable remedy and does not mean that there is a transaction "intended to create a security interest," a "sale of accounts, contract rights or chattel paper," or a "security interest created by contract," within the meaning of Section 9-102. On the other hand, nothing in this section prevents one creditor from assigning his rights to another creditor of the same debtor in such a way as to create a security interest within Article 9, where the parties so intend.

3. The last sentence of this section is intended to negate any implication that the section changes the law. It is intended to be declaratory of pre-existing law. Both the history and the text of Article 9 make it clear that it was not intended to cover subordination agreements. The provisions of Section 9-203 for signature by the "debtor" would be entirely unworkable if read to require signature by public holders of subordinated investment securities. The priorities, filing provi-

sions and remedies on default provided by Article 9 would also be largely inappropriate in many situations. The precautionary language of Section 9–316 preserving subordination of priority by agreement between secured parties points to the conclusion that similar arrangements among unsecured lenders are not covered unless otherwise within the scope of the Article.

4. The enforcement of subordination agreements is largely left to supplementary principles under Section 1–103. If the subordinated debt is evidenced by ~~an investment security, Section 8–202(1)~~ a certificated security, Section 8–202(a) authorizes enforcement against purchasers on terms stated or referred to on the security certificate. If the fact of subordination is noted on a negotiable instrument, a holder under Sections 3–302 and 3–306 is subject to the term because notice precludes him from taking free of the subordination. Sections 3–302(3)(a), 3–306 and 8–317 severely limit the rights of levying creditors of a subordinated creditor in such cases. *Amendments approved by the Permanent Editorial Board for Uniform Commercial Code November 4, 1995.*

Definitional Cross References:

"Agreement". Section 1–201.
"Creditor". Section 1–201.
"Debtor". Section 9–105.
"Person". Section 1–201.
"Rights". Section 1–201.
"Security interest". Section 1–201.

ARTICLE 2

SALES

PART 1. SHORT TITLE, GENERAL CONSTRUCTION AND SUBJECT MATTER

PART 2. FORM, FORMATION AND READJUSTMENT OF CONTRACT

PART 3. GENERAL OBLIGATION AND CONSTRUCTION OF CONTRACT

PART 7. REMEDIES

PART 1

SHORT TITLE, GENERAL CONSTRUCTION AND SUBJECT MATTER

§ 2–101. Short Title.

This Article shall be known and may be cited as Uniform Commercial Code—Sales.

Official Comment

This Article is a complete revision and modernization of the Uniform Sales Act which was promulgated by the National Conference of Commissioners on Uniform State Laws in 1906 and has been adopted in 34 states and Alaska, the District of Columbia and Hawaii.

The coverage of the present Article is much more extensive than that of the old Sales Act and extends to the various bodies of case law which have been developed both outside of and under the latter.

The arrangement of the present Article is in terms of contract for sale and the various steps of its performance. The legal consequences are stated as following directly from the contract and action taken under it without resorting to the idea of when property or title passed or was to pass as being the determining factor.

The purpose is to avoid making practical issues between practical men turn upon the location of an intangible something, the passing of which no man can prove by evidence and to substitute for such abstractions proof of words and actions of a tangible character.

§ 2-102. Scope; Certain Security and Other Transactions Excluded From This Article.

Unless the context otherwise requires, this Article applies to transactions in goods; it does not apply to any transaction which although in the form of an unconditional contract to sell or present sale is intended to operate only as a security transaction nor does this Article impair or repeal any statute regulating sales to consumers, farmers or other specified classes of buyers.

Official Comment

Prior Uniform Statutory Provision: Section 75, Uniform Sales Act.

Changes: Section 75 has been rephrased.

Purposes of Changes and New Matter: To make it clear that:

The Article leaves substantially unaffected the law relating to purchase money security such as conditional sale or chattel mortgage though it regulates the general sales aspects of such transactions. "Security transaction" is used in the same sense as in the Article on Secured Transactions (Article 9).

Cross Reference:

Article 9.

Definitional Cross References:

"Contract". Section 1-201.
"Contract for sale". Section 2-106.
"Present sale". Section 2-106.
"Sale". Section 2-106.

§ 2-103. Definitions and Index of Definitions.

(1) In this Article unless the context otherwise requires

(a) "Buyer" means a person who buys or contracts to buy goods.

(b) "Good faith" in the case of a merchant means honesty in fact and the observance of reasonable commercial standards of fair dealing in the trade.

(c) "Receipt" of goods means taking physical possession of them.

(d) "Seller" means a person who sells or contracts to sell goods.

(2) Other definitions applying to this Article or to specified Parts thereof, and the sections in which they appear are:

"Acceptance". Section 2-606.

"Banker's credit". Section 2-325.

"Between merchants". Section 2-104.

"Cancellation". Section 2-106(4).

"Commercial unit". Section 2-105.

"Confirmed credit". Section 2-325.

"Conforming to contract". Section 2-106.

"Contract for sale". Section 2-106.

"Cover". Section 2-712.

"Entrusting". Section 2-403.

"Financing agency". Section 2-104.

"Future goods". Section 2-105.

"Goods". Section 2-105.

"Identification". Section 2-501.

"Installment contract". Section 2-612.

"Letter of Credit". Section 2-325.

"Lot". Section 2-105.

"Merchant". Section 2-104.

"Overseas". Section 2-323.

"Person in position of seller". Section 2-707.

"Present sale". Section 2-106.

"Sale". Section 2-106.

"Sale on approval". Section 2-326.

"Sale or return". Section 2-326.

"Termination". Section 2-106.

(3) The following definitions in other Articles apply to this Article:

"Check". Section 3-104.

"Consignee". Section 7-102.

"Consignor". Section 7-102.

"Consumer goods". Section 9-109.

"Dishonor". Section 3-502.

"Draft". Section 3-104.

(4) In addition Article 1 contains general definitions and principles of construction and interpretation applicable throughout this Article.

As amended in 1994.

See Appendix XI for material relating to changes made in text in 1994.

Official Comment

Prior Uniform Statutory Provision: Subsection (1): Section 76, Uniform Sales Act.

Changes:

The definitions of "buyer" and "seller" have been slightly rephrased, the reference in Section 76 of the prior Act to "any legal successor in interest of such person" being omitted. The definition of "receipt" is new.

Purposes of Changes and New Matter:

1. The phrase "any legal successor in interest of such person" has been eliminated since Section 2-210 of this Article, which limits some types of delegation of performance on assignment of a sales contract, makes it clear that not every such successor can be safely included in the definition. In every ordinary case,

however, such successors are as of course included.

2. "Receipt" must be distinguished from delivery particularly in regard to the problems arising out of shipment of goods, whether or not the contract calls for making delivery by way of documents of title, since the seller may frequently fulfill his obligations to "deliver" even though the buyer may never "receive" the goods. Delivery with respect to documents of title is defined in Article 1 and requires transfer of physical delivery. Otherwise the many divergent incidents of delivery are handled incident by incident.

Cross References:

Point 1: See Section 2–210 and Comment thereon.

Point 2: Section 1–201.

Definitional Cross Reference:

"Person". Section 1–201.

§ 2–104. Definitions: "Merchant"; "Between Merchants"; "Financing Agency".

(1) "Merchant" means a person who deals in goods of the kind or otherwise by his occupation holds himself out as having knowledge or skill peculiar to the practices or goods involved in the transaction or to whom such knowledge or skill may be attributed by his employment of an agent or broker or other intermediary who by his occupation holds himself out as having such knowledge or skill.

(2) "Financing agency" means a bank, finance company or other person who in the ordinary course of business makes advances against goods or documents of title or who by arrangement with either the seller or the buyer intervenes in ordinary course to make or collect payment due or claimed under the contract for sale, as by purchasing or paying the seller's draft or making advances against it or by merely taking it for collection whether or not documents of title accompany the draft. "Financing agency" includes also a bank or other person who similarly intervenes between persons who are in the position of seller and buyer in respect to the goods (Section 2–707).

(3) "Between merchants" means in any transaction with respect to which both parties are chargeable with the knowledge or skill of merchants.

Official Comment

Prior Uniform Statutory Provision: None. But see Sections 15(2), (5), 16(c), 45(2) and 71, Uniform Sales Act, and Sections 35 and 37, Uniform Bills of Lading Act for examples of the policy expressly provided for in this Article.

Purposes:

1. This Article assumes that transactions between professionals in a given field require special and clear rules which may not apply to a casual or inexperienced seller or buyer. It thus adopts a policy of expressly stating rules applicable "between merchants" and "as against a merchant", wherever they are needed instead of making them depend upon the circumstances of each case as in the statutes cited above. This section lays the foundation of this policy by defining those who are to be regarded as professionals or "merchants" and by stating when a transaction is deemed to be "between merchants".

2. The term "merchant" as defined here roots in the "law merchant" concept of a professional in business. The professional status under the definition may be based upon specialized knowledge as to the goods, specialized knowledge as to business practices, or specialized knowledge as to both and which kind of special-

ized knowledge may be sufficient to establish the merchant status is indicated by the nature of the provisions.

The special provisions as to merchants appear only in this Article and they are of three kinds. Sections 2–201(2), 2–205, 2–207 and 2–209 dealing with the statute of frauds, firm offers, confirmatory memoranda and modification rest on normal business practices which are or ought to be typical of and familiar to any person in business. For purposes of these sections almost every person in business would, therefore, be deemed to be a "merchant" under the language "who . . . by his occupation holds himself out as having knowledge or skill peculiar to the practices . . . involved in the transaction . . ." since the practices involved in the transaction are non-specialized business practices such as answering mail. In this type of provision, banks or even universities, for example, well may be "merchants." But even these sections only apply to a merchant in his mercantile capacity; a lawyer or bank president buying fishing tackle for his own use is not a merchant.

On the other hand, in Section 2–314 on the warranty of merchantability, such warranty is implied only "if the seller is a merchant with respect to goods of that kind." Obviously this qualification restricts the implied warranty to a much smaller group than everyone who is engaged in business and requires a professional status as to particular kinds of goods. The exception in Section 2–402(2) for retention of possession by a merchant-seller falls in the same class; as does Section 2–403(2) on entrusting of possession to a merchant "who deals in goods of that kind".

A third group of sections includes 2–103(1)(b), which provides that in the case of a merchant "good faith" includes observance of reasonable commercial standards of fair dealing in the trade; 2–327(1)(c), 2–603 and 2–605, dealing with responsibilities of merchant buyers to follow seller's instructions, etc.; 2–509 on risk of loss, and 2–609 on adequate assurance of performance. This group of sections applies to persons who are merchants under either the "practices" or the "goods" aspect of the definition of merchant.

3. The "or to whom such knowledge or skill may be attributed by his employment of an agent or broker . . ." clause of the definition of merchant means that even persons such as universities, for example, can come within the definition of merchant if they have regular purchasing departments or business personnel who are familiar with business practices and who are equipped to take any action required.

Cross References:

Point 1: See Sections 1–102 and 1–203.

Point 2: See Sections 2–314, 2–315 and 2–320 to 2–325, of this Article, and Article 9.

Definitional Cross References:

"Bank". Section 1–201.
"Buyer". Section 2–103.
"Contract for sale". Section 2–106.
"Document of title". Section 1–201.
"Draft". Section 3–104.
"Goods". Section 2–105.
"Person". Section 1–201.
"Purchase". Section 1–201.
"Seller". Section 2–103.

§ 2–105. Definitions: Transferability; "Goods"; "Future" Goods; "Lot"; "Commercial Unit".

(1) "Goods" means all things (including specially manufactured goods) which are movable at the time of identification to the contract for sale other than the money in which the price is to be paid, investment securities (Article 8) and things in action. "Goods" also includes the unborn young of animals and growing crops and other identified things attached to realty as described in the section on goods to be severed from realty (Section 2–107).

(2) Goods must be both existing and identified before any interest in them can pass. Goods which are not both existing and identified are "future"

goods. A purported present sale of future goods or of any interest therein operates as a contract to sell.

(3) There may be a sale of a part interest in existing identified goods.

(4) An undivided share in an identified bulk of fungible goods is sufficiently identified to be sold although the quantity of the bulk is not determined. Any agreed proportion of such a bulk or any quantity thereof agreed upon by number, weight or other measure may to the extent of the seller's interest in the bulk be sold to the buyer who then becomes an owner in common.

(5) "Lot" means a parcel or a single article which is the subject matter of a separate sale or delivery, whether or not it is sufficient to perform the contract.

(6) "Commercial unit" means such a unit of goods as by commercial usage is a single whole for purposes of sale and division of which materially impairs its character or value on the market or in use. A commercial unit may be a single article (as a machine) or a set of articles (as a suite of furniture or an assortment of sizes) or a quantity (as a bale, gross, or carload) or any other unit treated in use or in the relevant market as a single whole.

Official Comment

Prior Uniform Statutory Provision: Subsections (1), (2), (3) and (4)—Sections 5, 6 and 76, Uniform Sales Act; Subsections (5) and (6)—none.

Changes: Rewritten.

Purposes of Changes and New Matter:

1. Subsection (1) on "goods": The phraseology of the prior uniform statutory provision has been changed so that:

The definition of goods is based on the concept of movability and the term "chattels personal" is not used. It is not intended to deal with things which are not fairly identifiable as movables before the contract is performed.

Growing crops are included within the definition of goods since they are frequently intended for sale. The concept of "industrial" growing crops has been abandoned, for under modern practices fruit, perennial hay, nursery stock and the like must be brought within the scope of this Article. The young of animals are also included expressly in this definition since they, too, are frequently intended for sale and may be contracted for before birth. The period of gestation of domestic animals is such that the provisions of the section on identification can apply as in the case of crops to be planted. The reason of this definition also leads to the inclusion of a wool crop or the like as "goods" subject to identification under this Article.

The exclusion of "money in which the price is to be paid" from the definition of goods does not mean that foreign currency which is included in the definition of money may not be the subject matter of a sales transaction. Goods is intended to cover the sale of money when money is being treated as a commodity but not to include it when money is the medium of payment.

As to contracts to sell timber, minerals, or structures to be removed from the land Section 2-107(1) (Goods to be severed from Realty: recording) controls.

The use of the word "fixtures" is avoided in view of the diversity of definitions of that term. This Article in including within its scope "things attached to realty" adds the further test that they must be capable of severance without material harm thereto. As between the parties any identified things which fall within that definition become "goods" upon the making of the contract for sale.

"Investment securities" are expressly excluded from the coverage of this Article. It is not intended by this exclusion, however, to prevent the application of a particular section of this Article by analogy to securities (as was done with the Original Sales Act in Agar v. Orda, 264 N.Y. 248, 190 N.E. 479, 99 A.L.R. 269 (1934)) when the reason of that section makes such application sensible and the situation involved is not covered by the Article of this Act dealing specifically with such securities (Article 8).

2. References to the fact that a contract for sale can extend to future or contingent goods and that ownership in common follows the sale of a part interest have been omitted here as obvious without need for expression; hence no inference to negate these principles should be drawn from their omission.

3. Subsection (4) does not touch the question of how far an appropriation of a bulk of fungible goods may or may not satisfy the contract for sale.

4. Subsections (5) and (6) on "lot" and "commercial unit" are introduced to aid in the phrasing of later sections.

5. The question of when an identification of goods takes place is determined by the provisions of Section 2-501 and all that this section says is what kinds of goods may be the subject of a sale.

Cross References:

Point 1: Sections 2-107, 2-201, 2-501 and Article 8.
Point 5: Section 2-501.
See also Section 1-201.

Definitional Cross References:

"Buyer". Section 2-103.
"Contract". Section 1-201.
"Contract for sale". Section 2-106.
"Fungible". Section 1-201.
"Money". Section 1-201.
"Present sale". Section 2-106.
"Sale". Section 2-106.
"Seller". Section 2-103.

§ 2-106. Definitions: "Contract"; "Agreement"; "Contract for Sale"; "Sale"; "Present Sale"; "Conforming" to Contract; "Termination"; "Cancellation".

(1) In this Article unless the context otherwise requires "contract" and "agreement" are limited to those relating to the present or future sale of goods. "Contract for sale" includes both a present sale of goods and a contract to sell goods at a future time. A "sale" consists in the passing of title from the seller to the buyer for a price (Section 2-401). A "present sale" means a sale which is accomplished by the making of the contract.

(2) Goods or conduct including any part of a performance are "conforming" or conform to the contract when they are in accordance with the obligations under the contract.

(3) "Termination" occurs when either party pursuant to a power created by agreement or law puts an end to the contract otherwise than for its breach. On "termination" all obligations which are still executory on both sides are discharged but any right based on prior breach or performance survives.

(4) "Cancellation" occurs when either party puts an end to the contract for breach by the other and its effect is the same as that of "termination" except that the cancelling party also retains any remedy for breach of the whole contract or any unperformed balance.

Official Comment

Prior Uniform Statutory Provision: Subsection (1)—Section 1(1) and (2), Uniform Sales Act; Subsection (2)—none, but subsection generally continues policy of Sections 11, 44 and 69, Uniform Sales Act; Subsections (3) and (4)—none.

Changes: Completely rewritten.

Purposes of Changes and New Matter:

1. Subsection (1): "Contract for sale" is used as a general concept throughout this Article, but the rights of the parties do not vary according to whether the transaction is a present sale or a contract to sell unless the Article expressly so provides.

2. Subsection (2): It is in general intended to continue the policy of requiring exact performance by the seller of his obligations as a condition to his right to require acceptance. However, the seller is in part safeguarded against surprise as a result of sudden technicality on the buyer's part by the provisions of Section 2–508 on seller's cure of improper tender or delivery. Moreover usage of trade frequently permits commercial leeways in performance and the language of the agreement itself must be read in the light of such custom or usage and also, prior course of dealing, and in a long term contract, the course of performance.

3. Subsections (3) and (4): These subsections are intended to make clear the distinction carried forward throughout this Article between termination and cancellation.

Cross References:

Point 2: Sections 1–203, 1–205, 2–208 and 2–508.

Definitional Cross References:

"Agreement". Section 1–201.
"Buyer". Section 2–103.
"Contract". Section 1–201.
"Goods". Section 2–105.
"Party". Section 1–201.
"Remedy". Section 1–201.
"Rights". Section 1–201.
"Seller". Section 2–103.

§ 2–107. Goods to Be Severed From Realty: Recording.

(1) A contract for the sale of minerals or the like (including oil and gas) or a structure or its materials to be removed from realty is a contract for the sale of goods within this Article if they are to be severed by the seller but until severance a purported present sale thereof which is not effective as a transfer of an interest in land is effective only as a contract to sell.

(2) A contract for the sale apart from the land of growing crops or other things attached to realty and capable of severance without material harm thereto but not described in subsection (1) or of timber to be cut is a contract for the sale of goods within this Article whether the subject matter is to be severed by the buyer or by the seller even though it forms part of the realty at the time of contracting, and the parties can by identification effect a present sale before severance.

(3) The provisions of this section are subject to any third party rights provided by the law relating to realty records, and the contract for sale may be executed and recorded as a document transferring an interest in land and shall then constitute notice to third parties of the buyer's rights under the contract for sale.

As amended in 1972.

Official Comment

Prior Uniform Statutory Provision: See Section 76, Uniform Sales Act on prior policy; Section 7, Uniform Conditional Sales Act.

Purposes:

1. Subsection (1). Notice that this subsection applies only if the minerals or structures "are to be severed by the seller". If the buyer is to sever, such transactions are considered contracts affecting land and all problems of the Statute of Frauds and of the recording of land rights apply to them. Therefore, the Statute of Frauds section of this Article does not apply to such contracts though they must conform to the Statute of Frauds affecting the transfer of interests in land.

2. Subsection (2). "Things attached" to the realty which can be severed without material harm are goods within this Article regardless of who is to effect the severance. The word "fixtures" has been avoided because of the diverse definitions of this term, the test of "severance without material harm" being substituted.

The provision in subsection (3) for recording such contracts is within the purview of this Article since it is a means of preserving the buyer's rights under the contract of sale.

3. The security phases of things attached to or to become attached to realty are dealt with in the Article on Secured Transactions (Article 9) and it is to be noted that the definition of goods in that Article differs from the definition of goods in this Article.

However, both Articles treat as goods growing crops and also timber to be cut under a contract of severance.

Cross References:

Point 1: Section 2-201.
Point 2: Section 2-105.
Point 3: Articles 9 and 9-105.

Definitional Cross References:

"Buyer". Section 2-103.
"Contract". Section 1-201.
"Contract for sale". Section 2-106.
"Goods". Section 2-105.
"Party". Section 1-201.
"Present sale". Section 2-106.
"Rights". Section 1-201.
"Seller". Section 2-103.

PART 2

FORM, FORMATION AND READJUSTMENT OF CONTRACT

§ 2-201. Formal Requirements; Statute of Frauds.

(1) Except as otherwise provided in this section a contract for the sale of goods for the price of $500 or more is not enforceable by way of action or defense unless there is some writing sufficient to indicate that a contract for sale has been made between the parties and signed by the party against whom enforcement is sought or by his authorized agent or broker. A writing is not insufficient because it omits or incorrectly states a term agreed upon but the contract is not enforceable under this paragraph beyond the quantity of goods shown in such writing.

(2) Between merchants if within a reasonable time a writing in confirmation of the contract and sufficient against the sender is received and the party receiving it has reason to know its contents, it satisfies the requirements of subsection (1) against such party unless written notice of objection to its contents is given within 10 days after it is received.

(3) A contract which does not satisfy the requirements of subsection (1) but which is valid in other respects is enforceable

(a) if the goods are to be specially manufactured for the buyer and are not suitable for sale to others in the ordinary course of the seller's business and the seller, before notice of repudiation is received and under circumstances which reasonably indicate that the goods are for the buyer, has made either a substantial beginning of their manufacture or commitments for their procurement; or

(b) if the party against whom enforcement is sought admits in his pleading, testimony or otherwise in court that a contract for sale was made, but the contract is not enforceable under this provision beyond the quantity of goods admitted; or

(c) with respect to goods for which payment has been made and accepted or which have been received and accepted (Sec. 2-606).

Official Comment

Prior Uniform Statutory Provision: Section 4, Uniform Sales Act (which was based on Section 17 of the Statute of 29 Charles II).

Changes: Completely rephrased; restricted to sale of goods. See also Sections 1-206, 8-319 and 9-203.

Purposes of Changes: The changed phraseology of this section is intended to make it clear that:

1. The required writing need not contain all the material terms of the contract and such material terms as are stated need not be precisely stated. All that is required is that the writing afford a basis for believing that the offered oral evidence rests on a real transaction. It may be written in lead pencil on a scratch pad. It need not indicate which party is the buyer and which the seller. The only term which must appear is the quantity term which need not be accurately stated but recovery is limited to the amount stated. The price, time and place of payment or delivery, the general quality of the goods, or any particular warranties may all be omitted.

Special emphasis must be placed on the permissibility of omitting the price term in view of the insistence of some courts on the express inclusion of this term even where the parties have contracted on the basis of a published price list. In many valid contracts for sale the parties do not mention the price in express terms, the buyer being bound to pay and the seller to accept a reasonable price which the trier of the fact may well be trusted to determine. Again, frequently the price is not mentioned since the parties have based their agreement on a price list or catalogue known to both of them and this list serves as an efficient safeguard against perjury. Finally, "market" prices and valuations that are current in the vicinity constitute a similar check. Thus if the price is not stated in the memorandum it can normally be supplied without danger of fraud. Of course if the "price" consists of goods rather than money the quantity of goods must be stated.

Only three definite and invariable requirements as to the memorandum are made by this subsection. First, it must evidence a contract for the sale of goods; second, it must be "signed", a word which includes any authentication which identifies the party to be charged; and third, it must specify a quantity.

2. "Partial performance" as a substitute for the required memorandum can validate the contract only for the goods which have been accepted or for which payment has been made and accepted.

Receipt and acceptance either of goods or of the price constitutes an unambiguous overt admission by both parties that a contract actually exists. If the court can make a just apportionment, therefore, the agreed price of any goods actually delivered can be recovered without a writing or, if the price has been paid, the seller can be forced to deliver an apportionable part of the goods. The overt actions of the parties make admissible evidence of the other terms of the contract necessary to a just apportionment. This is true even though the actions of the parties are not in themselves inconsistent with a different transaction such as a consignment for resale or a mere loan of money.

Part performance by the buyer requires the delivery of something by him that is accepted by the seller as such performance. Thus, part payment may be made by money or check, accepted by the seller. If the agreed price consists of goods or services, then they must also have been delivered and accepted.

3. Between merchants, failure to answer a written confirmation of a contract within ten days of receipt is tantamount to a writing under subsection (2) and is sufficient against both parties under subsection (1). The only effect, however, is to take away from the party who fails to answer the defense of the Statute of Frauds; the burden of persuading the trier of fact that a contract was in fact made orally prior to the written confirmation is unaffected. Compare the effect of a failure to reply under Section 2-207.

4. Failure to satisfy the requirements of this section does not render the contract void for all purposes, but merely prevents it from being judicially enforced in favor of a party to the contract. For example, a buyer who takes possession of goods as provided in an oral contract which the seller has not meanwhile repudiated, is not a trespasser. Nor would the Statute of Frauds provisions of this section be a defense to a third person who wrongfully induces a party to refuse to perform an oral contract, even though the injured party cannot maintain an action for damages against the party so refusing to perform.

5. The requirement of "signing" is discussed in the comment to Section 1-201.

6. It is not necessary that the writing be delivered to anybody. It need not be signed or authenticated by both parties but it is, of course, not sufficient against one who has not signed it. Prior to a dispute no one can determine which party's signing of the memorandum may be necessary but from the time of contracting each party should be aware that to him it is signing by the other which is important.

7. If the making of a contract is admitted in court, either in a written pleading, by stipulation or by oral statement before the court, no additional writing is necessary for protection against fraud. Under this section it is no longer possible to admit the contract in court and still treat the Statute as a defense. However, the contract is not thus conclusively established. The admission so made by a party is itself evidential against him of the truth of the facts so admitted and of nothing more; as against the other party, it is not evidential at all.

Cross References:

See Sections 1-201, 2-202, 2-207, 2-209 and 2-304.

Definitional Cross References:

"Action". Section 1-201.
"Between merchants". Section 2-104.
"Buyer". Section 2-103.
"Contract". Section 1-201.
"Contract for sale". Section 2-106.
"Goods". Section 2-105.
"Notice". Section 1-201.
"Party". Section 1-201.
"Reasonable time". Section 1-204.
"Sale". Section 2-106.
"Seller". Section 2-103.

§ 2-202. Final Written Expression: Parol or Extrinsic Evidence.

Terms with respect to which the confirmatory memoranda of the parties agree or which are otherwise set forth in a writing intended by the parties as a final expression of their agreement with respect to such terms as are included therein may not be contradicted by evidence of any prior agreement or of a contemporaneous oral agreement but may be explained or supplemented

(a) by course of dealing or usage of trade (Section 1–205) or by course of performance (Section 2–208); and

(b) by evidence of consistent additional terms unless the court finds the writing to have been intended also as a complete and exclusive statement of the terms of the agreement.

Official Comment

Prior Uniform Statutory Provisions: None.

Purposes:

1. This section definitely rejects:

(a) Any assumption that because a writing has been worked out which is final on some matters, it is to be taken as including all the matters agreed upon;

(b) The premise that the language used has the meaning attributable to such language by rules of construction existing in the law rather than the meaning which arises out of the commercial context in which it was used; and

(c) The requirement that a condition precedent to the admissibility of the type of evidence specified in paragraph (a) is an original determination by the court that the language used is ambiguous.

2. Paragraph (a) makes admissible evidence of course of dealing, usage of trade and course of performance to explain or supplement the terms of any writing stating the agreement of the parties in order that the true understanding of the parties as to the agreement may be reached. Such writings are to be read on the assumption that the course of prior dealings between the parties and the usages of trade were taken for granted when the document was phrased. Unless carefully negated they have become an element of the meaning of the words used. Similarly, the course of actual performance by the parties is considered the best indication of what they intended the writing to mean.

3. Under paragraph (b) consistent additional terms, not reduced to writing, may be proved unless the court finds that the writing was intended by both parties as a complete and exclusive statement of all the terms. If the additional terms are such that, if agreed upon, they would certainly have been included in the document in the view of the court, then evidence of their alleged making must be kept from the trier of fact.

Cross References:

Point 3: Sections 1–205, 2–207, 2–302 and 2–316.

Definitional Cross References:

"Agreed" and "agreement". Section 1–201.

"Course of dealing". Section 1–205.

"Parties". Section 1–201.

"Term". Section 1–201.

"Usage of trade". Section 1–205.

"Written" and "writing". Section 1–201.

§ 2–203. Seals Inoperative.

The affixing of a seal to a writing evidencing a contract for sale or an offer to buy or sell goods does not constitute the writing a sealed instrument and the law with respect to sealed instruments does not apply to such a contract or offer.

Official Comment

Prior Uniform Statutory Provision: Section 3, Uniform Sales Act.

Changes: Portion pertaining to "seals" rewritten.

Purposes of Changes:

1. This section makes it clear that every effect of the seal which relates to "sealed instruments" as such is wiped out insofar as contracts for sale are concerned. However, the substantial effects of a seal, except extension of the period of limitations, may be had by appropriate drafting as in the case of firm offers (see Section 2-205).

2. This section leaves untouched any aspects of a seal which relate merely to signatures or to authentication of execution and the like. Thus, a statute providing that a purported signature gives prima facie evidence of its own authenticity or that a signature gives prima facie evidence of consideration is still applicable to sales transactions even though a seal may be held to be a signature within the meaning of such a statute. Similarly, the authorized affixing of a corporate seal bearing the corporate name to a contractual writing purporting to be made by the corporation may have effect as a signature without any reference to the law of sealed instruments.

Cross Reference:

Point 1: Section 2-205.

Definitional Cross References:

"Contract for sale". Section 2-106.
"Goods". Section 2-105.
"Writing". Section 1-201.

§ 2-204. Formation in General.

(1) A contract for sale of goods may be made in any manner sufficient to show agreement, including conduct by both parties which recognizes the existence of such a contract.

(2) An agreement sufficient to constitute a contract for sale may be found even though the moment of its making is undetermined.

(3) Even though one or more terms are left open a contract for sale does not fail for indefiniteness if the parties have intended to make a contract and there is a reasonably certain basis for giving an appropriate remedy.

Official Comment

Prior Uniform Statutory Provision: Sections 1 and 3, Uniform Sales Act.

Changes: Completely rewritten by this and other sections of this Article.

Purposes of Changes:

Subsection (1) continues without change the basic policy of recognizing any manner of expression of agreement, oral, written or otherwise. The legal effect of such an agreement is, of course, qualified by other provisions of this Article.

Under subsection (1) appropriate conduct by the parties may be sufficient to establish an agreement. Subsection (2) is directed primarily to the situation where the interchanged correspondence does not disclose the exact point at which the deal was closed, but the actions of the parties indicate that a binding obligation has been undertaken.

Subsection (3) states the principle as to "open terms" underlying later sections of the Article. If the parties intend to enter into a binding agreement, this subsection recognizes that agreement as valid in law, despite missing terms, if there is any reasonably certain basis for granting a remedy. The test is not certainty as to what the parties were to do nor as to the exact amount of damages due the plaintiff. Nor is the fact that one or more terms are left to be agreed upon enough of itself to defeat an otherwise adequate agreement.

Rather, commercial standards on the point of "indefiniteness" are intended to be applied, this Act making provision elsewhere for missing terms needed for performance, open price, remedies and the like.

The more terms the parties leave open, the less likely it is that they have intended to conclude a binding agreement, but their actions may be frequently conclusive on the matter despite the omissions.

Cross References:

Subsection (1): Sections 1–103, 2–201 and 2–302.

Subsection (2): Sections 2–205 through 2–209.

Subsection (3): See Part 3.

Definitional Cross References:

"Agreement". Section 1–201.
"Contract". Section 1–201.
"Contract for sale". Section 2–106.
"Goods". Section 2–105.
"Party". Section 1–201.
"Remedy". Section 1–201.
"Term". Section 1–201.

§ 2–205. Firm Offers.

An offer by a merchant to buy or sell goods in a signed writing which by its terms gives assurance that it will be held open is not revocable, for lack of consideration, during the time stated or if no time is stated for a reasonable time, but in no event may such period of irrevocability exceed three months; but any such term of assurance on a form supplied by the offeree must be separately signed by the offeror.

Official Comment

Prior Uniform Statutory Provision: Sections 1 and 3, Uniform Sales Act.

Changes: Completely rewritten by this and other sections of this Article.

Purposes of Changes:

1. This section is intended to modify the former rule which required that "firm offers" be sustained by consideration in order to bind, and to require instead that they must merely be characterized as such and expressed in signed writings.

2. The primary purpose of this section is to give effect to the deliberate intention of a merchant to make a current firm offer binding. The deliberation is shown in the case of an individualized document by the merchant's signature to the offer, and in the case of an offer included on a form supplied by the other party to the transaction by the separate signing of the particular clause which contains the offer. "Signed" here also includes authentication but the reasonableness of the authentication herein allowed must be determined in the light of the purpose of the section. The circumstances surrounding the signing may justify something less than a formal signature or initialing but typically the kind of authentication involved here would consist of a minimum of initialing of the clause involved. A handwritten memorandum on the writer's letterhead purporting in its terms to "confirm" a firm offer already made would be enough to satisfy this section, although not subscribed, since under the circumstances it could not be considered a memorandum of mere negotiation and it would adequately show its own authenticity. Similarly, an authorized telegram will suffice, and this is true even though the original draft contained only a typewritten signature. However, despite settled courses of dealing or usages of the trade whereby firm offers are made by oral communication and relied upon without more evidence, such offers remain revocable under this Article since authentication by a writing is the essence of this section.

3. This section is intended to apply to current "firm" offers and not to long term options, and an outside time limit of

three months during which such offers remain irrevocable has been set. The three month period during which firm offers remain irrevocable under this section need not be stated by days or by date. If the offer states that it is "guaranteed" or "firm" until the happening of a contingency which will occur within the three month period, it will remain irrevocable until that event. A promise made for a longer period will operate under this section to bind the offeror only for the first three months of the period but may of course be renewed. If supported by consideration it may continue for as long as the parties specify. This section deals only with the offer which is not supported by consideration.

4. Protection is afforded against the inadvertent signing of a firm offer when contained in a form prepared by the offeree by requiring that such a clause be separately authenticated. If the offer clause is called to the offeror's attention and he separately authenticates it, he will be bound; Section 2–302 may operate, however, to prevent an unconscionable result which otherwise would flow from other terms appearing in the form.

5. Safeguards are provided to offer relief in the case of material mistake by virtue of the requirement of good faith and the general law of mistake.

Cross References:

Point 1: Section 1–102.
Point 2: Section 1–102.
Point 3: Section 2–201.
Point 5: Section 2–302.

Definitional Cross References:

"Goods". Section 2–105.
"Merchant". Section 2–104.
"Signed". Section 1–201.
"Writing". Section 1–201.

§ 2–206. Offer and Acceptance in Formation of Contract.

(1) Unless otherwise unambiguously indicated by the language or circumstances

(a) an offer to make a contract shall be construed as inviting acceptance in any manner and by any medium reasonable in the circumstances;

(b) an order or other offer to buy goods for prompt or current shipment shall be construed as inviting acceptance either by a prompt promise to ship or by the prompt or current shipment of conforming or non-conforming goods, but such a shipment of non-conforming goods does not constitute an acceptance if the seller seasonably notifies the buyer that the shipment is offered only as an accommodation to the buyer.

(2) Where the beginning of a requested performance is a reasonable mode of acceptance an offeror who is not notified of acceptance within a reasonable time may treat the offer as having lapsed before acceptance.

Official Comment

Prior Uniform Statutory Provision: Sections 1 and 3, Uniform Sales Act.

Changes: Completely rewritten in this and other sections of this Article.

Purposes of Changes: To make it clear that:

1. Any reasonable manner of acceptance is intended to be regarded as available unless the offeror has made quite clear that it will not be acceptable. Former technical rules as to acceptance, such as requiring that telegraphic offers be accepted by telegraphed acceptance, etc., are rejected and a criterion that the acceptance be "in any manner and by any medium reasonable under the circumstances," is substituted. This section is intended to remain flexible and its applicability to be enlarged as new media of

communication develop or as the more time-saving present day media come into general use.

2. Either shipment or a prompt promise to ship is made a proper means of acceptance of an offer looking to current shipment. In accordance with ordinary commercial understanding the section interprets an order looking to current shipment as allowing acceptance either by actual shipment or by a prompt promise to ship and rejects the artificial theory that only a single mode of acceptance is normally envisaged by an offer. This is true even though the language of the offer happens to be "ship at once" or the like. "Shipment" is here used in the same sense as in Section 2-504; it does not include the beginning of delivery by the seller's own truck or by messenger. But loading on the seller's own truck might be a beginning of performance under subsection (2).

3. The beginning of performance by an offeree can be effective as acceptance so as to bind the offeror only if followed within a reasonable time by notice to the offeror. Such a beginning of performance must unambiguously express the offeree's intention to engage himself. For the protection of both parties it is essential that notice follow in due course to constitute acceptance. Nothing in this section however bars the possibility that under the common law performance begun may have an intermediate effect of temporarily barring revocation of the offer, or at the offeror's option, final effect in constituting acceptance.

4. Subsection (1)(b) deals with the situation where a shipment made following an order is shown by a notification of shipment to be referable to that order but has a defect. Such a non-conforming shipment is normally to be understood as intended to close the bargain, even though it proves to have been at the same time a breach. However, the seller by stating that the shipment is non-conforming and is offered only as an accommodation to the buyer keeps the shipment or notification from operating as an acceptance.

Definitional Cross References:

"Buyer". Section 2-103.
"Conforming". Section 2-106.
"Contract". Section 1-201.
"Goods". Section 2-105.
"Notifies". Section 1-201.
"Reasonable time". Section 1-204.

§ 2-207. Additional Terms in Acceptance or Confirmation.

(1) A definite and seasonable expression of acceptance or a written confirmation which is sent within a reasonable time operates as an acceptance even though it states terms additional to or different from those offered or agreed upon, unless acceptance is expressly made conditional on assent to the additional or different terms.

(2) The additional terms are to be construed as proposals for addition to the contract. Between merchants such terms become part of the contract unless:

(a) the offer expressly limits acceptance to the terms of the offer;

(b) they materially alter it; or

(c) notification of objection to them has already been given or is given within a reasonable time after notice of them is received.

(3) Conduct by both parties which recognizes the existence of a contract is sufficient to establish a contract for sale although the writings of the parties do not otherwise establish a contract. In such case the terms of the particular contract consist of those terms on which the writings of the parties

agree, together with any supplementary terms incorporated under any other provisions of this Act.

Official Comment

Prior Uniform Statutory Provision: Sections 1 and 3, Uniform Sales Act.

Changes: Completely rewritten by this and other sections of this Article.

Purposes of Changes:

1. This section is intended to deal with two typical situations. The one is the written confirmation, where an agreement has been reached either orally or by informal correspondence between the parties and is followed by one or both of the parties sending formal memoranda embodying the terms so far as agreed upon and adding terms not discussed. The other situation is offer and acceptance, in which a wire or letter expressed and intended as an acceptance or the closing of an agreement adds further minor suggestions or proposals such as "ship by Tuesday," "rush," "ship draft against bill of lading inspection allowed," or the like. A frequent example of the second situation is the exchange of printed purchase order and acceptance (sometimes called "acknowledgment") forms. Because the forms are oriented to the thinking of the respective drafting parties, the terms contained in them often do not correspond. Often the seller's form contains terms different from or additional to those set forth in the buyer's form. Nevertheless, the parties proceed with the transaction. [Comment 1 was amended in 1966.]

2. Under this Article a proposed deal which in commercial understanding has in fact been closed is recognized as a contract. Therefore, any additional matter contained in the confirmation or in the acceptance falls within subsection (2) and must be regarded as a proposal for an added term unless the acceptance is made conditional on the acceptance of the additional or different terms. [Comment 2 was amended in 1966.]

3. Whether or not additional or different terms will become part of the agreement depends upon the provisions of subsection (2). If they are such as materially to alter the original bargain, they will not be included unless expressly agreed to by the other party. If, however, they are terms which would not so change the bargain they will be incorporated unless notice of objection to them has already been given or is given within a reasonable time.

4. Examples of typical clauses which would normally "materially alter" the contract and so result in surprise or hardship if incorporated without express awareness by the other party are: a clause negating such standard warranties as that of merchantability or fitness for a particular purpose in circumstances in which either warranty normally attaches; a clause requiring a guaranty of 90% or 100% deliveries in a case such as a contract by cannery, where the usage of the trade allows greater quantity leeways; a clause reserving to the seller the power to cancel upon the buyer's failure to meet any invoice when due; a clause requiring that complaints be made in a time materially shorter than customary or reasonable.

5. Examples of clauses which involve no element of unreasonable surprise and which therefore are to be incorporated in the contract unless notice of objection is seasonably given are: a clause setting forth and perhaps enlarging slightly upon the seller's exemption due to supervening causes beyond his control, similar to those covered by the provision of this Article on merchant's excuse by failure of presupposed conditions or a clause fixing in advance any reasonable formula of proration under such circumstances; a clause fixing a reasonable time for complaints within customary limits, or in the case of a purchase for sub-sale, providing for inspection by the sub-purchaser; a clause providing for interest on overdue invoices or fixing the seller's standard

credit terms where they are within the range of trade practice and do not limit any credit bargained for; a clause limiting the right of rejection for defects which fall within the customary trade tolerances for acceptance "with adjustment" or otherwise limiting remedy in a reasonable manner (see Sections 2–718 and 2–719).

6. If no answer is received within a reasonable time after additional terms are proposed, it is both fair and commercially sound to assume that their inclusion has been assented to. Where clauses on confirming forms sent by both parties conflict each party must be assumed to object to a clause of the other conflicting with one on the confirmation sent by himself. As a result the requirement that there be notice of objection which is found in subsection (2) is satisfied and the conflicting terms do not become a part of the contract. The contract then consists of the terms originally expressly agreed to, terms on which the confirmations agree, and terms supplied by this Act, including subsection (2). The written confirmation is also subject to Section 2–201. Under that section a failure to respond permits enforcement of a prior oral agreement; under this section a failure to respond permits additional terms to become part of the agreement. [Comment 6 was amended in 1966.]

7. In many cases, as where goods are shipped, accepted and paid for before any dispute arises, there is no question whether a contract has been made. In such cases, where the writings of the parties do not establish a contract, it is not necessary to determine which act or document constituted the offer and which the acceptance. See Section 2–204. The only question is what terms are included in the contract, and subsection (3) furnishes the governing rule. [Comment 7 was added in 1966.]

Cross References:

See generally Section 2–302.

Point 5: Sections 2–513, 2–602, 2–607, 2–609, 2–612, 2–614, 2–615, 2–616, 2–718 and 2–719.

Point 6: Sections 1–102 and 2–104.

Definitional Cross References:

"Between merchants". Section 2–104.
"Contract". Section 1–201.
"Notification". Section 1–201.
"Reasonable time". Section 1–204.
"Seasonably". Section 1–204.
"Send". Section 1–201.
"Term". Section 1–201.
"Written". Section 1–201.

§ 2–208. Course of Performance or Practical Construction.

(1) Where the contract for sale involves repeated occasions for performance by either party with knowledge of the nature of the performance and opportunity for objection to it by the other, any course of performance accepted or acquiesced in without objection shall be relevant to determine the meaning of the agreement.

(2) The express terms of the agreement and any such course of performance, as well as any course of dealing and usage of trade, shall be construed whenever reasonable as consistent with each other; but when such construction is unreasonable, express terms shall control course of performance and course of performance shall control both course of dealing and usage of trade (Section 1–205).

(3) Subject to the provisions of the next section on modification and waiver, such course of performance shall be relevant to show a waiver or modification of any term inconsistent with such course of performance.

Official Comment

Prior Uniform Statutory Provision: No such general provision but concept of this section recognized by terms such as "course of dealing", "the circumstances of the case," "the conduct of the parties," etc., in Uniform Sales Act.

Purposes:

1. The parties themselves know best what they have meant by their words of agreement and their action under that agreement is the best indication of what that meaning was. This section thus rounds out the set of factors which determines the meaning of the "agreement" and therefore also of the "unless otherwise agreed" qualification to various provisions of this Article.

2. Under this section a course of performance is always relevant to determine the meaning of the agreement. Express mention of course of performance elsewhere in this Article carries no contrary implication when there is a failure to refer to it in other sections.

3. Where it is difficult to determine whether a particular act merely sheds light on the meaning of the agreement or represents a waiver of a term of the agreement, the preference is in favor of "waiver" whenever such construction, plus the application of the provisions on the reinstatement of rights waived (see Section 2–209), is needed to preserve the flexible character of commercial contracts and to prevent surprise or other hardship.

4. A single occasion of conduct does not fall within the language of this section but other sections such as the ones on silence after acceptance and failure to specify particular defects can affect the parties' rights on a single occasion (see Sections 2–605 and 2–607).

Cross References:

Point 1: Section 1–201.

Point 2: Section 2–202.

Point 3: Sections 2–209, 2–601 and 2–607.

Point 4: Sections 2–605 and 2–607.

§ 2–209. Modification, Rescission and Waiver.

(1) An agreement modifying a contract within this Article needs no consideration to be binding.

(2) A signed agreement which excludes modification or rescission except by a signed writing cannot be otherwise modified or rescinded, but except as between merchants such a requirement on a form supplied by the merchant must be separately signed by the other party.

(3) The requirements of the statute of frauds section of this Article (Section 2–201) must be satisfied if the contract as modified is within its provisions.

(4) Although an attempt at modification or rescission does not satisfy the requirements of subsection (2) or (3) it can operate as a waiver.

(5) A party who has made a waiver affecting an executory portion of the contract may retract the waiver by reasonable notification received by the other party that strict performance will be required of any term waived, unless the retraction would be unjust in view of a material change of position in reliance on the waiver.

Official Comment

Prior Uniform Statutory Provision: Subsection (1)—Compare Section 1, Uniform Written Obligations Act; Subsections (2) to (5)—none.

Purposes of Changes and New Matter:

1. This section seeks to protect and make effective all necessary and desirable modifications of sales contracts without regard to the technicalities which at present hamper such adjustments.

2. Subsection (1) provides that an agreement modifying a sales contract needs no consideration to be binding.

However, modifications made thereunder must meet the test of good faith imposed by this Act. The effective use of bad faith to escape performance on the original contract terms is barred, and the extortion of a "modification" without legitimate commercial reason is ineffective as a violation of the duty of good faith. Nor can a mere technical consideration support a modification made in bad faith.

The test of "good faith" between merchants or as against merchants includes "observance of reasonable commercial standards of fair dealing in the trade" (Section 2–103), and may in some situations require an objectively demonstrable reason for seeking a modification. But such matters as a market shift which makes performance come to involve a loss may provide such a reason even though there is no such unforeseen difficulty as would make out a legal excuse from performance under Sections 2–615 and 2–616.

3. Subsections (2) and (3) are intended to protect against false allegations of oral modifications. "Modification or rescission" includes abandonment or other change by mutual consent, contrary to the decision in Green v. Doniger, 300 N.Y. 238, 90 N.E.2d 56 (1949); it does not include unilateral "termination" or "cancellation" as defined in Section 2–106.

The Statute of Frauds provisions of this Article are expressly applied to modifications by subsection (3). Under those provisions the "delivery and acceptance" test is limited to the goods which have been accepted, that is, to the past. "Modification" for the future cannot therefore be conjured up by oral testimony if the price involved is $500.00 or more since such modification must be shown at least by an authenticated memo. And since a memo is limited in its effect to the quantity of goods set forth in it there is safeguard against oral evidence.

Subsection (2) permits the parties in effect to make their own Statute of Frauds as regards any future modification of the contract by giving effect to a clause in a signed agreement which expressly requires any modification to be by signed writing. But note that if a consumer is to be held to such a clause on a form supplied by a merchant it must be separately signed.

4. Subsection (4) is intended, despite the provisions of subsections (2) and (3), to prevent contractual provisions excluding modification except by a signed writing from limiting in other respects the legal effect of the parties' actual later conduct. The effect of such conduct as a waiver is further regulated in subsection (5).

Cross References:

Point 1: Section 1–203.

Point 2: Sections 1–201, 1–203, 2–615 and 2–616.

Point 3: Sections 2–106, 2–201 and 2–202.

Point 4: Sections 2–202 and 2–208.

Definitional Cross References:

"Agreement". Section 1–201.
"Between merchants". Section 2–104.
"Contract". Section 1–201.
"Notification". Section 1–201.
"Signed". Section 1–201.
"Term". Section 1–201.
"Writing". Section 1–201.

§ 2–210. Delegation of Performance; Assignment of Rights.

(1) A party may perform his duty through a delegate unless otherwise agreed or unless the other party has a substantial interest in having his original promisor perform or control the acts required by the contract. No

delegation of performance relieves the party delegating of any duty to perform or any liability for breach.

(2) Unless otherwise agreed all rights of either seller or buyer can be assigned except where the assignment would materially change the duty of the other party, or increase materially the burden or risk imposed on him by his contract, or impair materially his chance of obtaining return performance. A right to damages for breach of the whole contract or a right arising out of the assignor's due performance of his entire obligation can be assigned despite agreement otherwise.

(3) Unless the circumstances indicate the contrary a prohibition of assignment of "the contract" is to be construed as barring only the delegation to the assignee of the assignor's performance.

(4) An assignment of "the contract" or of "all my rights under the contract" or an assignment in similar general terms is an assignment of rights and unless the language or the circumstances (as in an assignment for security) indicate the contrary, it is a delegation of performance of the duties of the assignor and its acceptance by the assignee constitutes a promise by him to perform those duties. This promise is enforceable by either the assignor or the other party to the original contract.

(5) The other party may treat any assignment which delegates performance as creating reasonable grounds for insecurity and may without prejudice to his rights against the assignor demand assurances from the assignee (Section 2-609).

Official Comment

Prior Uniform Statutory Provision: None.

Purposes:

1. Generally, this section recognizes both delegation of performance and assignability as normal and permissible incidents of a contract for the sale of goods.

2. Delegation of performance, either in conjunction with an assignment or otherwise, is provided for by subsection (1) where no substantial reason can be shown as to why the delegated performance will not be as satisfactory as personal performance.

3. Under subsection (2) rights which are no longer executory such as a right to damages for breach or a right to payment of an "account" as defined in the Article on Secured Transactions (Article 9) may be assigned although the agreement prohibits assignment. In such cases no question of delegation of any performance is involved. The assignment of a "contract right" as defined in the Article on Secured Transactions (Article 9) is not covered by this subsection.

4. The nature of the contract or the circumstances of the case, however, may bar assignment of the contract even where delegation of performance is not involved. This Article and this section are intended to clarify this problem, particularly in cases dealing with output requirement and exclusive dealing contracts. In the first place the section on requirements and exclusive dealing removes from the construction of the original contract most of the "personal discretion" element by substituting the reasonably objective standard of good faith operation of the plant or business to be supplied. Secondly, the section on insecurity and assurances, which is specifically referred to in subsection (5) of this section, frees the other party from the doubts and uncertainty which may afflict him under an assignment of the character in ques-

tion by permitting him to demand adequate assurance of due performance without which he may suspend his own performance. Subsection (5) is not in any way intended to limit the effect of the section on insecurity and assurances and the word "performance" includes the giving of orders under a requirements contract. Of course, in any case where a material personal discretion is sought to be transferred, effective assignment is barred by subsection (2).

5. Subsection (4) lays down a general rule of construction distinguishing between a normal commercial assignment, which substitutes the assignee for the assignor both as to rights and duties, and a financing assignment in which only the assignor's rights are transferred.

This Article takes no position on the possibility of extending some recognition or power to the original parties to work out normal commercial readjustments of the contract in the case of financing assignments even after the original obligor has been notified of the assignment. This question is dealt with in the Article on Secured Transactions (Article 9).

6. Subsection (5) recognizes that the non-assigning original party has a stake in the reliability of the person with whom he has closed the original contract, and is, therefore, entitled to due assurance that any delegated performance will be properly forthcoming.

7. This section is not intended as a complete statement of the law of delegation and assignment but is limited to clarifying a few points doubtful under the case law. Particularly, neither this section nor this Article touches directly on such questions as the need or effect of notice of the assignment, the rights of successive assignees, or any question of the form of an assignment, either as between the parties or as against any third parties. Some of these questions are dealt with in Article 9.

Cross References:

Point 3: Articles 5 and 9.
Point 4: Sections 2–306 and 2–609.
Point 5: Article 9, Sections 9–317 and 9–318.
Point 7: Article 9.

Definitional Cross References:

"Agreement". Section 1–201.
"Buyer". Section 2–103.
"Contract". Section 1–201.
"Party". Section 1–201.
"Rights". Section 1–201.
"Seller". Section 2–103.
"Term". Section 1–201.

PART 3

GENERAL OBLIGATION AND CONSTRUCTION OF CONTRACT

§ 2–301. General Obligations of Parties.

The obligation of the seller is to transfer and deliver and that of the buyer is to accept and pay in accordance with the contract.

Official Comment

Prior Uniform Statutory Provision: Sections 11 and 41, Uniform Sales Act.

Changes: Rewritten.

Purposes of Changes:

This section uses the term "obligation" in contrast to the term "duty" in order to provide for the "condition" aspects of delivery and payment insofar as they are not modified by other sections of this Article such as those on cure of tender. It thus replaces not only the general provisions of the Uniform Sales Act on the parties' duties, but also the general provisions of that Act on the effect of conditions. In order to determine what is "in accordance with the contract" under this Article usage of trade, course of dealing and performance, and the general background of circumstances must be given due consideration in conjunction with the lay meaning of the words used to define the scope of the conditions and duties.

Cross References:

Section 1-106. See also Sections 1-205, 2-208, 2-209, 2-508 and 2-612.

Definitional Cross References:

"Buyer". Section 2-103.
"Contract". Section 1-201.
"Party". Section 1-201.
"Seller". Section 2-103.

§ 2-302. Unconscionable Contract or Clause.

(1) If the court as a matter of law finds the contract or any clause of the contract to have been unconscionable at the time it was made the court may refuse to enforce the contract, or it may enforce the remainder of the contract without the unconscionable clause, or it may so limit the application of any unconscionable clause as to avoid any unconscionable result.

(2) When it is claimed or appears to the court that the contract or any clause thereof may be unconscionable the parties shall be afforded a reasonable opportunity to present evidence as to its commercial setting, purpose and effect to aid the court in making the determination.

Official Comment

Prior Uniform Statutory Provision: None.

Purposes:

1. This section is intended to make it possible for the courts to police explicitly against the contracts or clauses which they find to be unconscionable. In the past such policing has been accomplished by adverse construction of language, by manipulation of the rules of offer and acceptance or by determinations that the clause is contrary to public policy or to the dominant purpose of the contract. This section is intended to allow the court to pass directly on the unconscionability of the contract or particular clause therein and to make a conclusion of law as to its unconscionability. The basic test is whether, in the light of the general commercial background and the commercial needs of the particular trade or case, the clauses involved are so one-sided as to be unconscionable under the circumstances existing at the time of the making of the contract. Subsection (2) makes it clear that it is proper for the court to hear evidence upon these questions. The principle is one of the prevention of oppression and unfair surprise (Cf. Campbell Soup Co. v. Wentz, 172 F.2d 80, 3d Cir. 1948) and not of disturbance of allocation of risks because of superior bargaining power. The underlying basis of this section is illustrated by the results in cases such as the following:

Kansas City Wholesale Grocery Co. v. Weber Packing Corporation, 93 Utah 414, 73 P.2d 1272 (1937), where a clause limiting time for complaints was held inapplicable to latent defects in a shipment of catsup which could be discovered only by microscopic analysis; Hardy v. General Motors Acceptance Corporation, 38 Ga. App. 463, 144 S.E. 327 (1928), holding that a disclaimer of warranty clause applied only to express warranties, thus letting in a fair implied warranty; Andrews Bros. v. Singer & Co. (1934 CA) 1 K.B. 17, holding that where a car with substantial mileage was delivered instead of a "new" car, a disclaimer of warranties, including those "implied," left unaffected an "express obligation" on the description, even though the Sale of Goods Act called such an implied warranty; New Prague Flouring Mill Co. v. G. A. Spears, 194 Iowa 417, 189 N.W. 815 (1922), holding that a clause permitting the seller, upon the buyer's failure to supply shipping instructions, to cancel, ship, or allow delivery date to be indefinitely postponed 30 days at a time by the inaction, does not indefinitely postpone the date of measuring damages for the buyer's breach, to the seller's advantage; and Kansas Flour Mills Co. v. Dirks, 100 Kan. 376, 164 P. 273 (1917), where under a similar clause in a rising market the court permitted the buyer to measure his damages for non-delivery at the end of only one 30 day postponement; Green v. Arcos, Ltd. (1931 CA) 47 T.L.R. 336, where a blanket clause prohibiting rejection of shipments by the buyer was restricted to apply to shipments where discrepancies represented merely mercantile variations; Meyer v. Packard Cleveland Motor Co., 106 Ohio St. 328, 140 N.E. 118 (1922), in which the court held that a "waiver" of all agreements not specified did not preclude implied warranty of fitness of a rebuilt dump truck for ordinary use as a dump truck; Austin Co. v. J. H. Tillman Co., 104 Or. 541, 209 P. 131 (1922), where a clause limiting the buyer's remedy to return was held to be applicable only if the seller had delivered a machine needed for a construction job which reasonably met the contract description; Bekkevold v. Potts, 173 Minn. 87, 216 N.W. 790, 59 A.L.R. 1164 (1927), refusing to allow warranty of fitness for purpose imposed by law to be negated by clause excluding all warranties "made" by the seller; Robert A. Munroe & Co. v. Meyer (1930) 2 K.B. 312, holding that the warranty of description overrides a clause reading "with all faults and defects" where adulterated meat not up to the contract description was delivered.

2. Under this section the court, in its discretion, may refuse to enforce the contract as a whole if it is permeated by the unconscionability, or it may strike any single clause or group of clauses which are so tainted or which are contrary to the essential purpose of the agreement, or it may simply limit unconscionable clauses so as to avoid unconscionable results.

3. The present section is addressed to the court, and the decision is to be made by it. The commercial evidence referred to in subsection (2) is for the court's consideration, not the jury's. Only the agreement which results from the court's action on these matters is to be submitted to the general triers of the facts.

Definitional Cross Reference:

"Contract". Section 1-201.

§ 2-303. Allocation or Division of Risks.

Where this Article allocates a risk or a burden as between the parties "unless otherwise agreed", the agreement may not only shift the allocation but may also divide the risk or burden.

Official Comment

Prior Uniform Statutory Provision: None.

Purposes:

1. This section is intended to make it clear that the parties may modify or allocate "unless otherwise agreed" risks or burdens imposed by this Article as they desire, always subject, of course, to the provisions on unconscionability.

Compare Section 1-102(4).

2. The risk or burden may be divided by the express terms of the agreement or by the attending circumstances, since under the definition of "agreement" in this Act the circumstances surrounding the transaction as well as the express language used by the parties enter into the meaning and substance of the agreement.

Cross References:

Point 1: Sections 1-102, 2-302.
Point 2: Section 1-201.

Definitional Cross References:

"Party". Section 1-201.
"Agreement". Section 1-201.

§ 2-304. Price Payable in Money, Goods, Realty, or Otherwise.

(1) The price can be made payable in money or otherwise. If it is payable in whole or in part in goods each party is a seller of the goods which he is to transfer.

(2) Even though all or part of the price is payable in an interest in realty the transfer of the goods and the seller's obligations with reference to them are subject to this Article, but not the transfer of the interest in realty or the transferor's obligations in connection therewith.

Official Comment

Prior Uniform Statutory Provision: Subsections (2) and (3) of Section 9, Uniform Sales Act.

Changes: Rewritten.

Purposes of Changes:

1. This section corrects the phrasing of the Uniform Sales Act so as to avoid misconstruction and produce greater accuracy in commercial result. While it continues the essential intent and purpose of the Uniform Sales Act it rejects any purely verbalistic construction in disregard of the underlying reason of the provisions.

2. Under subsection (1) the provisions of this Article are applicable to transactions where the "price" of goods is payable in something other than money. This does not mean, however, that this whole Article applies automatically and in its entirety simply because an agreed transfer of title to goods is not a gift. The basic purposes and reasons of the Article must always be considered in determining the applicability of any of its provisions.

3. Subsection (2) lays down the general principle that when goods are to be exchanged for realty, the provisions of this Article apply only to those aspects of the transaction which concern the transfer of title to goods but do not affect the transfer of the realty since the detailed regulation of various particular contracts which fall outside the scope of this Article is left to the courts and other legislation. However, the complexities of these situations may be such that each must be analyzed in the light of the underlying reasons in order to determine the applicable principles. Local statutes dealing with realty are not to be lightly disregarded or altered by language of this Article. In contrast, this Article declares definite policies in regard to certain matters legitimately within its scope though concerned with real property situations, and in those instances the provisions of this Article control.

Cross References:

Point 1: Section 1-102.
Point 3: Sections 1-102, 1-103, 1-104 and 2-107.

Definitional Cross References:

"Goods". Section 2-105.
"Money". Section 1-201.
"Party". Section 1-201.
"Seller". Section 2-103.

§ 2-305. Open Price Term.

(1) The parties if they so intend can conclude a contract for sale even though the price is not settled. In such a case the price is a reasonable price at the time for delivery if

(a) nothing is said as to price; or

(b) the price is left to be agreed by the parties and they fail to agree; or

(c) the price is to be fixed in terms of some agreed market or other standard as set or recorded by a third person or agency and it is not so set or recorded.

(2) A price to be fixed by the seller or by the buyer means a price for him to fix in good faith.

(3) When a price left to be fixed otherwise than by agreement of the parties fails to be fixed through fault of one party the other may at his option treat the contract as cancelled or himself fix a reasonable price.

(4) Where, however, the parties intend not to be bound unless the price be fixed or agreed and it is not fixed or agreed there is no contract. In such a case the buyer must return any goods already received or if unable so to do must pay their reasonable value at the time of delivery and the seller must return any portion of the price paid on account.

Official Comment

Prior Uniform Statutory Provision: Sections 9 and 10, Uniform Sales Act.

Changes: Completely rewritten.

Purposes of Changes:

1. This section applies when the price term is left open on the making of an agreement which is nevertheless intended by the parties to be a binding agreement. This Article rejects in these instances the formula that "an agreement to agree is unenforceable" if the case falls within subsection (1) of this section, and rejects also defeating such agreements on the ground of "indefiniteness". Instead this Article recognizes the dominant intention of the parties to have the deal continue to be binding upon both. As to future performance, since this Article recognizes remedies such as cover (Section 2–712), resale (Section 2–706) and specific performance (Section 2–716) which go beyond any mere arithmetic as between contract price and market price, there is usually a "reasonably certain basis for granting an appropriate remedy for breach" so that the contract need not fail for indefiniteness.

2. Under some circumstances the postponement of agreement on price will mean that no deal has really been concluded, and this is made express in the preamble of subsection (1) ("The parties *if they so intend*") and in subsection (4). Whether or not this is so is, in most cases, a question to be determined by the trier of fact.

3. Subsection (2), dealing with the situation where the price is to be fixed by one party rejects the uncommercial idea that an agreement that the seller may fix the price means that he may fix any price he may wish by the express qualification that the price so fixed must be fixed in good faith. Good faith includes observance of reasonable commercial standards of fair dealing in the trade if the party is a merchant. (Section 2–103). But in the normal case a "posted price" or a future seller's or buyer's "given price," "price in effect," "market price," or the like satisfies the good faith requirement.

4. The section recognizes that there may be cases in which a particular person's judgment is not chosen merely as a barometer or index of a fair price but is an essential condition to the parties' intent to make any contract at all. For example, the case where a known and trusted expert is to "value" a particular painting for which there is no market standard differs sharply from the situation where a named expert is to determine the grade of cotton, and the difference would support a finding that in the one the parties did not intend to make a

binding agreement if that expert were unavailable whereas in the other they did so intend. Other circumstances would of course affect the validity of such a finding.

5. Under subsection (3), wrongful interference by one party with any agreed machinery for price fixing in the contract may be treated by the other party as a repudiation justifying cancellation, or merely as a failure to take cooperative action thus shifting to the aggrieved party the reasonable leeway in fixing the price.

6. Throughout the entire section, the purpose is to give effect to the agreement which has been made. That effect, however, is always conditioned by the requirement of good faith action which is made an inherent part of all contracts within this Act. (Section 1–203).

Cross References:

Point 1: Sections 2–204(3), 2–706, 2–712 and 2–716.

Point 3: Section 2–103.

Point 5: Sections 2–311 and 2–610.

Point 6: Section 1–203.

Definitional Cross References:

"Agreement". Section 1–201.

"Burden of establishing". Section 1–201.

"Buyer". Section 2–103.

"Cancellation". Section 2–106.

"Contract". Section 1–201.

"Contract for sale". Section 2–106.

"Fault". Section 1–201.

"Goods". Section 2–105.

"Party". Section 1–201.

"Receipt of goods". Section 2–103.

"Seller". Section 2–103.

"Term". Section 1–201.

§ 2–306. Output, Requirements and Exclusive Dealings.

(1) A term which measures the quantity by the output of the seller or the requirements of the buyer means such actual output or requirements as may occur in good faith, except that no quantity unreasonably disproportionate to any stated estimate or in the absence of a stated estimate to any normal or otherwise comparable prior output or requirements may be tendered or demanded.

(2) A lawful agreement by either the seller or the buyer for exclusive dealing in the kind of goods concerned imposes unless otherwise agreed an obligation by the seller to use best efforts to supply the goods and by the buyer to use best efforts to promote their sale.

Official Comment

Prior Uniform Statutory Provision: None.

Purposes:

1. Subsection (1) of this section, in regard to output and requirements, applies to this specific problem the general approach of this Act which requires the reading of commercial background and intent into the language of any agreement and demands good faith in the performance of that agreement. It applies to such contracts of nonproducing establishments such as dealers or distributors as well as to manufacturing concerns.

2. Under this Article, a contract for output or requirements is not too indefinite since it is held to mean the actual good faith output or requirements of the particular party. Nor does such a contract lack mutuality of obligation since, under this section, the party who will determine quantity is required to operate his plant or conduct his business in good faith and according to commercial standards of fair dealing in the trade so that his output or requirements will approximate a reasonably foreseeable figure. Reasonable elasticity in the requirements is expressly envisaged by this section and good faith variations from prior requirements are permitted even when the variation may be such as to result in discontin-

uance. A shut-down by a requirements buyer for lack of orders might be permissible when a shut-down merely to curtail losses would not. The essential test is whether the party is acting in good faith. Similarly, a sudden expansion of the plant by which requirements are to be measured would not be included within the scope of the contract as made but normal expansion undertaken in good faith would be within the scope of this section. One of the factors in an expansion situation would be whether the market price had risen greatly in a case in which the requirements contract contained a fixed price. Reasonable variation of an extreme sort is exemplified in Southwest Natural Gas Co. v. Oklahoma Portland Cement Co., 102 F.2d 630 (C.C.A.10, 1939). This Article takes no position as to whether a requirements contract is a provable claim in bankruptcy.

3. If an estimate of output or requirements is included in the agreement, no quantity unreasonably disproportionate to it may be tendered or demanded. Any minimum or maximum set by the agreement shows a clear limit on the intended elasticity. In similar fashion, the agreed estimate is to be regarded as a center around which the parties intend the variation to occur.

4. When an enterprise is sold, the question may arise whether the buyer is bound by an existing output or requirements contract. That question is outside the scope of this Article, and is to be determined on other principles of law. Assuming that the contract continues, the output or requirements in the hands of the new owner continue to be measured by the actual good faith output or requirements under the normal operation of the enterprise prior to sale. The sale itself is not grounds for sudden expansion or decrease.

5. Subsection (2), on exclusive dealing, makes explicit the commercial rule embodied in this Act under which the parties to such contracts are held to have impliedly, even when not expressly, bound themselves to use reasonable diligence as well as good faith in their performance of the contract. Under such contracts the exclusive agent is required, although no express commitment has been made, to use reasonable effort and due diligence in the expansion of the market or the promotion of the product, as the case may be. The principal is expected under such a contract to refrain from supplying any other dealer or agent within the exclusive territory. An exclusive dealing agreement brings into play all of the good faith aspects of the output and requirement problems of subsection (1). It also raises questions of insecurity and right to adequate assurance under this Article.

Cross References:

Point 4: Section 2–210.
Point 5: Sections 1–203 and 2–609.

Definitional Cross References:

"Agreement". Section 1–201.
"Buyer". Section 2–103.
"Contract for sale". Section 2–106.
"Good faith". Section 1–201.
"Goods". Section 2–105.
"Party". Section 1–201.
"Term". Section 1–201.
"Seller". Section 2–103.

§ 2–307. Delivery in Single Lot or Several Lots.

Unless otherwise agreed all goods called for by a contract for sale must be tendered in a single delivery and payment is due only on such tender but where the circumstances give either party the right to make or demand delivery in lots the price if it can be apportioned may be demanded for each lot.

Official Comment

Prior Uniform Statutory Provision: Section 45(1), Uniform Sales Act.

Changes: Rewritten and expanded.

Purposes of Changes:

1. This section applies where the parties have not specifically agreed whether delivery and payment are to be by lots and generally continues the essential intent of original Act, Section 45(1) by assuming that the parties intended delivery to be in a single lot.

2. Where the actual agreement or the circumstances do not indicate otherwise, delivery in lots is not permitted under this section and the buyer is properly entitled to reject for a deficiency in the tender, subject to any privilege in the seller to cure the tender.

3. The "but" clause of this section goes to the case in which it is not commercially feasible to deliver or to receive the goods in a single lot as for example, where a contract calls for the shipment of ten carloads of coal and only three cars are available at a given time. Similarly, in a contract involving brick necessary to build a building the buyer's storage space may be limited so that it would be impossible to receive the entire amount of brick at once, or it may be necessary to assemble the goods as in the case of cattle on the range, or to mine them.

In such cases, a partial delivery is not subject to rejection for the defect in quantity alone, if the circumstances do not indicate a repudiation or default by the seller as to the expected balance or do not give the buyer ground for suspending his performance because of insecurity under the provisions of Section 2–609. However, in such cases the undelivered balance of goods under the contract must be forthcoming within a reasonable time and in a reasonable manner according to the policy of Section 2–503 on manner of tender of delivery. This is reinforced by the express provisions of Section 2–608 that if a lot has been accepted on the reasonable assumption that its nonconformity will be cured, the acceptance may be revoked if the cure does not seasonably occur. The section rejects the rule of Kelly Construction Co. v. Hackensack Brick Co., 91 N.J.L. 585, 103 A. 417, 2 A.L.R. 685 (1918) and approves the result in Lynn M. Ranger, Inc. v. Gildersleeve, 106 Conn. 372, 138 A. 142 (1927) in which a contract was made for six carloads of coal then rolling from the mines and consigned to the seller but the seller agreed to divert the carloads to the buyer as soon as the car numbers became known to him. He arranged a diversion of two cars and then notified the buyer who then repudiated the contract. The seller was held to be entitled to his full remedy for the two cars diverted because simultaneous delivery of all of the cars was not contemplated by either party.

4. Where the circumstances indicate that a party has a right to delivery in lots, the price may be demanded for each lot if it is apportionable.

Cross References:

Point 1: Section 1–201.
Point 2: Sections 2–508 and 2–601.
Point 3: Sections 2–503, 2–608 and 2–609.

Definitional Cross References:

"Contract for sale". Section 2–106.
"Goods". Section 2–105.
"Lot". Section 2–105.
"Party". Section 1–201.
"Rights". Section 1–201.

§ 2–308. Absence of Specified Place for Delivery.

Unless otherwise agreed

(a) the place for delivery of goods is the seller's place of business or if he has none his residence; but

(b) in a contract for sale of identified goods which to the knowledge of the parties at the time of contracting are in some other place, that place is the place for their delivery; and

(c) documents of title may be delivered through customary banking channels.

Official Comment

Prior Uniform Statutory Provision: Paragraphs (a) and (b)—Section 43(1), Uniform Sales Act; Paragraph (c)—none.

Changes: Slight modification in language.

Purposes of Changes and New Matter:

1. Paragraphs (a) and (b) provide for those noncommercial sales and for those occasional commercial sales where no place or means of delivery has been agreed upon by the parties. Where delivery by carrier is "required or authorized by the agreement", the seller's duties as to delivery of the goods are governed not by this section but by Section 2-504.

2. Under paragraph (b) when the identified goods contracted for are known to both parties to be in some location other than the seller's place of business or residence, the parties are presumed to have intended that place to be the place of delivery. This paragraph also applies (unless, as would be normal, the circumstances show that delivery by way of documents is intended) to a bulk of goods in the possession of a bailee. In such a case, however, the seller has the additional obligation to procure the acknowledgment by the bailee of the buyer's right to possession.

3. Where "customary banking channels" call only for due notification by the banker that the documents are on hand, leaving the buyer himself to see to the physical receipt of the goods, tender at the buyer's address is not required under paragraph (c). But that paragraph merely eliminates the possibility of a default by the seller if "customary banking channels" have been properly used in giving notice to the buyer. Where the bank has purchased a draft accompanied by documents or has undertaken its collection on behalf of the seller, Part 5 of Article 4 spells out its duties and relations to its customer. Where the documents move forward under a letter of credit the Article on Letters of Credit spells out the duties and relations between the bank, the seller and the buyer.

4. The rules of this section apply only "unless otherwise agreed." The surrounding circumstances, usage of trade, course of dealing and course of performance, as well as the express language of the parties, may constitute an "otherwise agreement".

Cross References:

Point 1: Sections 2-504 and 2-505.
Point 2: Section 2-503.
Point 3: Section 2-512, Articles 4, Part 5, and 5.

Definitional Cross References:

"Contract for sale". Section 2-106.
"Delivery". Section 1-201.
"Document of title". Section 1-201.
"Goods". Section 2-105.
"Party". Section 1-201.
"Seller". Section 2-103.

§ 2-309. Absence of Specific Time Provisions; Notice of Termination.

(1) The time for shipment or delivery or any other action under a contract if not provided in this Article or agreed upon shall be a reasonable time.

(2) Where the contract provides for successive performances but is indefinite in duration it is valid for a reasonable time but unless otherwise agreed may be terminated at any time by either party.

(3) Termination of a contract by one party except on the happening of an agreed event requires that reasonable notification be received by the other party and an agreement dispensing with notification is invalid if its operation would be unconscionable.

Official Comment

Prior Uniform Statutory Provision: Subsection (1)—see Sections 43(2), 45(2), 47(1) and 48, Uniform Sales Act, for policy continued under this Article; Subsection (2)—none; Subsection (3)—none.

Changes: Completely different in scope.

Purposes of Changes and New Matter:

1. Subsection (1) requires that all actions taken under a sales contract must be taken within a reasonable time where no time has been agreed upon. The reasonable time under this provision turns on the criteria as to "reasonable time" and on good faith and commercial standards set forth in Sections 1–203, 1–204 and 2–103. It thus depends upon what constitutes acceptable commercial conduct in view of the nature, purpose and circumstances of the action to be taken. Agreement as to a definite time, however, may be found in a term implied from the contractual circumstances, usage of trade or course of dealing or performance as well as in an express term. Such cases fall outside of this subsection since in them the time for action is "agreed" by usage.

2. The time for payment, where not agreed upon, is related to the time for delivery; the particular problems which arise in connection with determining the appropriate time of payment and the time for any inspection before payment which is both allowed by law and demanded by the buyer are covered in Section 2–513.

3. The facts in regard to shipment and delivery differ so widely as to make detailed provision for them in the text of this Article impracticable. The applicable principles, however, make it clear that surprise is to be avoided, good faith judgment is to be protected, and notice or negotiation to reduce the uncertainty to certainty is to be favored.

4. When the time for delivery is left open, unreasonably early offers of or demands for delivery are intended to be read under this Article as expressions of desire or intention, requesting the assent or acquiescence of the other party, not as final positions which may amount without more to breach or to create breach by the other side. See Sections 2–207 and 2–609.

5. The obligation of good faith under this Act requires reasonable notification before a contract may be treated as breached because a reasonable time for delivery or demand has expired. This operates both in the case of a contract originally indefinite as to time and of one subsequently made indefinite by waiver.

When both parties let an originally reasonable time go by in silence, the course of conduct under the contract may be viewed as enlarging the reasonable time for tender or demand of performance. The contract may be terminated by abandonment.

6. Parties to a contract are not required in giving reasonable notification to fix, at peril of breach, a time which is in fact reasonable in the unforeseeable judgment of a later trier of fact. Effective communication of a proposed time limit calls for a response, so that failure to reply will make out acquiescence. Where objection is made, however, or if the demand is merely for information as to when goods will be delivered or will be ordered out, demand for assurances on the ground of insecurity may be made

under this Article pending further negotiations. Only when a party insists on undue delay or on rejection of the other party's reasonable proposal is there a question of flat breach under the present section.

7. Subsection (2) applies a commercially reasonable view to resolve the conflict which has arisen in the cases as to contracts of indefinite duration. The "reasonable time" of duration appropriate to a given arrangement is limited by the circumstances. When the arrangement has been carried on by the parties over the years, the "reasonable time" can continue indefinitely and the contract will not terminate until notice.

8. Subsection (3) recognizes that the application of principles of good faith and sound commercial practice normally call for such notification of the termination of a going contract relationship as will give the other party reasonable time to seek a substitute arrangement. An agreement dispensing with notification or limiting the time for the seeking of a substitute arrangement is, of course, valid under this subsection unless the results of putting it into operation would be the creation of an unconscionable state of affairs.

9. Justifiable cancellation for breach is a remedy for breach and is not the kind of termination covered by the present subsection.

10. The requirement of notification is dispensed with where the contract provides for termination on the happening of an "agreed event." "Event" is a term chosen here to contrast with "option" or the like.

Cross References:

Point 1: Sections 1–203, 1–204 and 2–103.
Point 2: Sections 2–320, 2–321, 2–504, and 2–511 through 2–514.
Point 5: Section 1–203.
Point 6: Section 2–609.
Point 7: Section 2–204.
Point 9: Sections 2–106, 2–318, 2–610 and 2–703.

Definitional Cross References:

"Agreement". Section 1–201.
"Contract". Section 1–201.
"Notification". Section 1–201.
"Party". Section 1–201.
"Reasonable time". Section 1–204.
"Termination". Section 2–106.

§ 2–310. Open Time for Payment or Running of Credit; Authority to Ship Under Reservation.

Unless otherwise agreed

(a) payment is due at the time and place at which the buyer is to receive the goods even though the place of shipment is the place of delivery; and

(b) if the seller is authorized to send the goods he may ship them under reservation, and may tender the documents of title, but the buyer may inspect the goods after their arrival before payment is due unless such inspection is inconsistent with the terms of the contract (Section 2–513); and

(c) if delivery is authorized and made by way of documents of title otherwise than by subsection (b) then payment is due at the time and place at which the buyer is to receive the documents regardless of where the goods are to be received; and

(d) where the seller is required or authorized to ship the goods on credit the credit period runs from the time of shipment but post-dating the invoice or delaying its dispatch will correspondingly delay the starting of the credit period.

Official Comment

Prior Uniform Statutory Provision: Sections 42 and 47(2), Uniform Sales Act.

Changes: Completely rewritten in this and other sections.

Purposes of Changes: This section is drawn to reflect modern business methods of dealing at a distance rather than face to face. Thus:

1. Paragraph (a) provides that payment is due at the time and place "the buyer is to receive the goods" rather than at the point of delivery except in documentary shipment cases (paragraph (c)). This grants an opportunity for the exercise by the buyer of his preliminary right to inspection before paying even though under the delivery term the risk of loss may have previously passed to him or the running of the credit period has already started.

2. Paragraph (b) while providing for inspection by the buyer before he pays, protects the seller. He is not required to give up possession of the goods until he has received payment, where no credit has been contemplated by the parties. The seller may collect through a bank by a sight draft against an order bill of lading "hold until arrival; inspection allowed." The obligations of the bank under such a provision are set forth in Part 5 of Article 4. In the absence of a credit term, the seller is permitted to ship under reservation and if he does payment is then due where and when the buyer is to receive the documents.

3. Unless otherwise agreed, the place for the receipt of the documents and payment is the buyer's city but the time for payment is only after arrival of the goods, since under paragraph (b), and Sections 2-512 and 2-513 the buyer is under no duty to pay prior to inspection.

4. Where the mode of shipment is such that goods must be unloaded immediately upon arrival, too rapidly to permit adequate inspection before receipt, the seller must be guided by the provisions of this Article on inspection which provide that if the seller wishes to demand payment before inspection, he must put an appropriate term into the contract. Even requiring payment against documents will not of itself have this desired result if the documents are to be held until the arrival of the goods. But under (b) and (c) if the terms are C.I.F., C.O.D., or cash against documents payment may be due before inspection.

5. Paragraph (d) states the common commercial understanding that an agreed credit period runs from the time of shipment or from that dating of the invoice which is commonly recognized as a representation of the time of shipment. The provision concerning any delay in sending forth the invoice is included because such conduct results in depriving the buyer of his full notice and warning as to when he must be prepared to pay.

Cross References:

Generally: Part 5.
Point 1: Section 2-509.
Point 2: Sections 2-505, 2-511, 2-512, 2-513 and Article 4.
Point 3: Sections 2-308(b), 2-512 and 2-513.
Point 4: Section 2-513(3)(b).

Definitional Cross References:

"Buyer". Section 2-103.
"Delivery". Section 1-201.
"Document of title". Section 1-201.
"Goods". Section 2-105.
"Receipt of goods". Section 2-103.
"Seller". Section 2-103.
"Send". Section 1-201.
"Term". Section 1-201.

§ 2-311. Options and Cooperation Respecting Performance.

(1) An agreement for sale which is otherwise sufficiently definite (subsection (3) of Section 2-204) to be a contract is not made invalid by the fact that it leaves particulars of performance to be specified by one of the parties. Any such specification must be made in good faith and within limits set by commercial reasonableness.

(2) Unless otherwise agreed specifications relating to assortment of the goods are at the buyer's option and except as otherwise provided in subsections (1)(c) and (3) of Section 2–319 specifications or arrangements relating to shipment are at the seller's option.

(3) Where such specification would materially affect the other party's performance but is not seasonably made or where one party's cooperation is necessary to the agreed performance of the other but is not seasonably forthcoming, the other party in addition to all other remedies

(a) is excused for any resulting delay in his own performance; and

(b) may also either proceed to perform in any reasonable manner or after the time for a material part of his own performance treat the failure to specify or to cooperate as a breach by failure to deliver or accept the goods.

Official Comment

Prior Uniform Statutory Provision: None.

Purposes:

1. Subsection (1) permits the parties to leave certain detailed particulars of performance to be filled in by either of them without running the risk of having the contract invalidated for indefiniteness. The party to whom the agreement gives power to specify the missing details is required to exercise good faith and to act in accordance with commercial standards so that there is no surprise and the range of permissible variation is limited by what is commercially reasonable. The "agreement" which permits one party so to specify may be found as well in a course of dealing, usage of trade, or implication from circumstances as in explicit language used by the parties.

2. Options as to assortment of goods or shipping arrangements are specifically reserved to the buyer and seller respectively under subsection (2) where no other arrangement has been made. This section rejects the test which mechanically and without regard to usage or the purpose of the option gave the option to the party "first under a duty to move" and applies instead a standard commercial interpretation to these circumstances. The "unless otherwise agreed" provision of this subsection covers not only express terms but the background and circumstances which enter into the agreement.

3. Subsection (3) applies when the exercise of an option or cooperation by one party is necessary to or materially affects the other party's performance, but it is not seasonably forthcoming; the subsection relieves the other party from the necessity for performance or excuses his delay in performance as the case may be. The contract-keeping party may at his option under this subsection proceed to perform in any commercially reasonable manner rather than wait. In addition to the special remedies provided, this subsection also reserves "all other remedies". The remedy of particular importance in this connection is that provided for insecurity. Request may also be made pursuant to the obligation of good faith for a reasonable indication of the time and manner of performance for which a party is to hold himself ready.

4. The remedy provided in subsection (3) is one which does not operate in the situation which falls within the scope of Section 2–614 on substituted performance. Where the failure to cooperate results from circumstances set forth in that Section, the other party is under a duty to proffer or demand (as the case may be) substitute performance as a condition to claiming rights against the non-cooperating party.

Cross References:

Point 1: Sections 1–201, 2–204 and 1–203.

Point 3: Sections 1–203 and 2–609.
Point 4: Section 2–614.

Definitional Cross References:

"Agreement". Section 1–201.
"Buyer". Section 2–103.
"Contract for sale". Section 2–106.
"Goods". Section 2–105.
"Party". Section 1–201.
"Remedy". Section 1–201.
"Seasonably". Section 1–204.
"Seller". Section 2–103.

§ 2–312. Warranty of Title and Against Infringement; Buyer's Obligation Against Infringement.

(1) Subject to subsection (2) there is in a contract for sale a warranty by the seller that

(a) the title conveyed shall be good, and its transfer rightful; and

(b) the goods shall be delivered free from any security interest or other lien or encumbrance of which the buyer at the time of contracting has no knowledge.

(2) A warranty under subsection (1) will be excluded or modified only by specific language or by circumstances which give the buyer reason to know that the person selling does not claim title in himself or that he is purporting to sell only such right or title as he or a third person may have.

(3) Unless otherwise agreed a seller who is a merchant regularly dealing in goods of the kind warrants that the goods shall be delivered free of the rightful claim of any third person by way of infringement or the like but a buyer who furnishes specifications to the seller must hold the seller harmless against any such claim which arises out of compliance with the specifications.

Official Comment

Prior Uniform Statutory Provision: Section 13, Uniform Sales Act.

Changes: Completely rewritten, the provisions concerning infringement being new.

Purposes of Changes:

1. Subsection (1) makes provision for a buyer's basic needs in respect to a title which he in good faith expects to acquire by his purchase, namely, that he receive a good, clean title transferred to him also in a rightful manner so that he will not be exposed to a lawsuit in order to protect it.

The warranty extends to a buyer whether or not the seller was in possession of the goods at the time the sale or contract to sell was made.

The warranty of quiet possession is abolished. Disturbance of quiet possession, although not mentioned specifically, is one way, among many, in which the breach of the warranty of title may be established.

The "knowledge" referred to in subsection 1(b) is actual knowledge as distinct from notice.

2. The provisions of this Article requiring notification to the seller within a reasonable time after the buyer's discovery of a breach apply to notice of a breach of the warranty of title, where the seller's breach was innocent. However, if the seller's breach was in bad faith he cannot be permitted to claim that he has been misled or prejudiced by the delay in giving notice. In such case the "reasonable" time for notice should receive a very liberal interpretation. Whether the breach by the seller is in good or bad faith Section 2–725 provides that the cause of action accrues when the breach occurs. Under the provisions of that section the breach of the warranty of good title occurs when tender of delivery is made

since the warranty is not one which extends to "future performance of the goods."

3. When the goods are part of the seller's normal stock and are sold in his normal course of business, it is his duty to see that no claim of infringement of a patent or trademark by a third party will mar the buyer's title. A sale by a person other than a dealer, however, raises no implication in its circumstances of such a warranty. Nor is there such an implication when the buyer orders goods to be assembled, prepared or manufactured on his own specifications. If, in such a case, the resulting product infringes a patent or trademark, the liability will run from buyer to seller. There is, under such circumstances, a tacit representation on the part of the buyer that the seller will be safe in manufacturing according to the specifications, and the buyer is under an obligation in good faith to indemnify him for any loss suffered.

4. This section rejects the cases which recognize the principle that infringements violate the warranty of title but deny the buyer a remedy unless he has been expressly prevented from using the goods. Under this Article "eviction" is not a necessary condition to the buyer's remedy since the buyer's remedy arises immediately upon receipt of notice of infringement; it is merely one way of establishing the fact of breach.

5. Subsection (2) recognizes that sales by sheriffs, executors, foreclosing lienors and persons similarly situated are so out of the ordinary commercial course that their peculiar character is immediately apparent to the buyer and therefore no personal obligation is imposed upon the seller who is purporting to sell only an unknown or limited right. This subsection does not touch upon and leaves open all questions of restitution arising in such cases, when a unique article so sold is reclaimed by a third party as the rightful owner.

6. The warranty of subsection (1) is not designated as an "implied" warranty, and hence is not subject to Section 2–316(3). Disclaimer of the warranty of title is governed instead by subsection (2), which requires either specific language or the described circumstances.

Cross References:

Point 1: Section 2–403.
Point 2: Sections 2–607 and 2–725.
Point 3: Section 1–203.
Point 4: Sections 2–609 and 2–725.
Point 6: Section 2–316.

Definitional Cross References:

"Buyer". Section 2–103.
"Contract for sale". Section 2–106.
"Goods". Section 2–105.
"Person". Section 1–201.
"Right". Section 1–201.
"Seller". Section 2–103.

§ 2–313. Express Warranties by Affirmation, Promise, Description, Sample.

(1) Express warranties by the seller are created as follows:

(a) Any affirmation of fact or promise made by the seller to the buyer which relates to the goods and becomes part of the basis of the bargain creates an express warranty that the goods shall conform to the affirmation or promise.

(b) Any description of the goods which is made part of the basis of the bargain creates an express warranty that the goods shall conform to the description.

(c) Any sample or model which is made part of the basis of the bargain creates an express warranty that the whole of the goods shall conform to the sample or model.

(2) It is not necessary to the creation of an express warranty that the seller use formal words such as "warrant" or "guarantee" or that he have a specific intention to make a warranty, but an affirmation merely of the value of the goods or a statement purporting to be merely the seller's opinion or commendation of the goods does not create a warranty.

Official Comment

Prior Uniform Statutory Provision: Sections 12, 14 and 16, Uniform Sales Act.

Changes: Rewritten.

Purposes of Changes: To consolidate and systematize basic principles with the result that:

1. "Express" warranties rest on "dickered" aspects of the individual bargain, and go so clearly to the essence of that bargain that words of disclaimer in a form are repugnant to the basic dickered terms. "Implied" warranties rest so clearly on a common factual situation or set of conditions that no particular language or action is necessary to evidence them and they will arise in such a situation unless unmistakably negated.

This section reverts to the older case law insofar as the warranties of description and sample are designated "express" rather than "implied".

2. Although this section is limited in its scope and direct purpose to warranties made by the seller to the buyer as part of a contract for sale, the warranty sections of this Article are not designed in any way to disturb those lines of case law growth which have recognized that warranties need not be confined either to sales contracts or to the direct parties to such a contract. They may arise in other appropriate circumstances such as in the case of bailments for hire, whether such bailment is itself the main contract or is merely a supplying of containers under a contract for the sale of their contents. The provisions of Section 2–318 on third party beneficiaries expressly recognize this case law development within one particular area. Beyond that, the matter is left to the case law with the intention that the policies of this Act may offer useful guidance in dealing with further cases as they arise.

3. The present section deals with affirmations of fact by the seller, descriptions of the goods or exhibitions of samples, exactly as any other part of a negotiation which ends in a contract is dealt with. No specific intention to make a warranty is necessary if any of these factors is made part of the basis of the bargain. In actual practice affirmations of fact made by the seller about the goods during a bargain are regarded as part of the description of those goods; hence no particular reliance on such statements need be shown in order to weave them into the fabric of the agreement. Rather, any fact which is to take such affirmations, once made, out of the agreement requires clear affirmative proof. The issue normally is one of fact.

4. In view of the principle that the whole purpose of the law of warranty is to determine what it is that the seller has in essence agreed to sell, the policy is adopted of those cases which refuse except in unusual circumstances to recognize a material deletion of the seller's obligation. Thus, a contract is normally a contract for a sale of something describable and described. A clause generally disclaiming "all warranties, express or implied" cannot reduce the seller's obligation with respect to such description and therefore cannot be given literal effect under Section 2–316.

This is not intended to mean that the parties, if they consciously desire, cannot make their own bargain as they wish. But in determining what they have agreed upon good faith is a factor and consideration should be given to the fact that the probability is small that a real price is intended to be exchanged for a pseudo-obligation.

5. Paragraph (1)(b) makes specific some of the principles set forth above when a description of the goods is given by the seller.

A description need not be by words. Technical specifications, blueprints and the like can afford more exact description than mere language and if made part of the basis of the bargain goods must conform with them. Past deliveries may set the description of quality, either expressly or impliedly by course of dealing. Of course, all descriptions by merchants must be read against the applicable trade usages with the general rules as to merchantability resolving any doubts.

6. The basic situation as to statements affecting the true essence of the bargain is no different when a sample or model is involved in the transaction. This section includes both a "sample" actually drawn from the bulk of goods which is the subject matter of the sale, and a "model" which is offered for inspection when the subject matter is not at hand and which has not been drawn from the bulk of the goods.

Although the underlying principles are unchanged, the facts are often ambiguous when something is shown as illustrative, rather than as a straight sample. In general, the presumption is that any sample or model just as any affirmation of fact is intended to become a basis of the bargain. But there is no escape from the question of fact. When the seller exhibits a sample purporting to be drawn from an existing bulk, good faith of course requires that the sample be fairly drawn. But in mercantile experience the mere exhibition of a "sample" does not of itself show whether it is merely intended to "suggest" or to "be" the character of the subject-matter of the contract. The question is whether the seller has so acted with reference to the sample as to make him responsible that the whole shall have at least the values shown by it. The circumstances aid in answering this question. If the sample has been drawn from an existing bulk, it must be regarded as describing values of the goods contracted for unless it is accompanied by an unmistakable denial of such responsibility. If, on the other hand, a model of merchandise not on hand is offered, the mercantile presumption that it has become a literal description of the subject matter is not so strong, and particularly so if modification on the buyer's initiative impairs any feature of the model.

7. The precise time when words of description or affirmation are made or samples are shown is not material. The sole question is whether the language or samples or models are fairly to be regarded as part of the contract. If language is used after the closing of the deal (as when the buyer when taking delivery asks and receives an additional assurance), the warranty becomes a modification, and need not be supported by consideration if it is otherwise reasonable and in order (Section 2-209).

8. Concerning affirmations of value or a seller's opinion or commendation under subsection (2), the basic question remains the same: What statements of the seller have in the circumstances and in objective judgment become part of the basis of the bargain? As indicated above, all of the statements of the seller do so unless good reason is shown to the contrary. The provisions of subsection (2) are included, however, since common experience discloses that some statements or predictions cannot fairly be viewed as entering into the bargain. Even as to false statements of value, however, the possibility is left open that a remedy may be provided by the law relating to fraud or misrepresentation.

Cross References:

Point 1: Section 2-316.
Point 2: Sections 1-102(3) and 2-318.
Point 3: Section 2-316(2)(b).
Point 4: Section 2-316.
Point 5: Sections 1-205(4) and 2-314.
Point 6: Section 2-316.
Point 7: Section 2-209.
Point 8: Section 1-103.

Definitional Cross References:

"Buyer". Section 2-103.
"Conforming". Section 2-106.

"Goods". Section 2-105.
"Seller". Section 2-103.

§ 2-314. Implied Warranty: Merchantability; Usage of Trade.

(1) Unless excluded or modified (Section 2-316), a warranty that the goods shall be merchantable is implied in a contract for their sale if the seller is a merchant with respect to goods of that kind. Under this section the serving for value of food or drink to be consumed either on the premises or elsewhere is a sale.

(2) Goods to be merchantable must be at least such as

(a) pass without objection in the trade under the contract description; and

(b) in the case of fungible goods, are of fair average quality within the description; and

(c) are fit for the ordinary purposes for which such goods are used; and

(d) run, within the variations permitted by the agreement, of even kind, quality and quantity within each unit and among all units involved; and

(e) are adequately contained, packaged, and labeled as the agreement may require; and

(f) conform to the promise or affirmations of fact made on the container or label if any.

(3) Unless excluded or modified (Section 2-316) other implied warranties may arise from course of dealing or usage of trade.

Official Comment

Prior Uniform Statutory Provision: Section 15(2), Uniform Sales Act.

Changes: Completely rewritten.

Purposes of Changes: This section, drawn in view of the steadily developing case law on the subject, is intended to make it clear that:

1. The seller's obligation applies to present sales as well as to contracts to sell subject to the effects of any examination of specific goods. (Subsection (2) of Section 2-316). Also, the warranty of merchantability applies to sales for use as well as to sales for resale.

2. The question when the warranty is imposed turns basically on the meaning of the terms of the agreement as recognized in the trade. Goods delivered under an agreement made by a merchant in a given line of trade must be of a quality comparable to that generally acceptable in that line of trade under the description or other designation of the goods used in the agreement. The responsibility imposed rests on any merchant-seller, and the absence of the words "grower or manufacturer or not" which appeared in Section 15(2) of the Uniform Sales Act does not restrict the applicability of this section.

3. A specific designation of goods by the buyer does not exclude the seller's obligation that they be fit for the general purposes appropriate to such goods. A contract for the sale of second-hand goods, however, involves only such obligation as is appropriate to such goods for that is their contract description. A person making an isolated sale of goods is not a "merchant" within the meaning of the full scope of this section and, thus, no warranty of merchantability would apply. His knowledge of any defects not appar-

ent on inspection would, however, without need for express agreement and in keeping with the underlying reason of the present section and the provisions on good faith, impose an obligation that known material but hidden defects be fully disclosed.

4. Although a seller may not be a "merchant" as to the goods in question, if he states generally that they are "guaranteed" the provisions of this section may furnish a guide to the content of the resulting express warranty. This has particular significance in the case of second-hand sales, and has further significance in limiting the effect of fine-print disclaimer clauses where their effect would be inconsistent with large-print assertions of "guarantee".

5. The second sentence of subsection (1) covers the warranty with respect to food and drink. Serving food or drink for value is a sale, whether to be consumed on the premises or elsewhere. Cases to the contrary are rejected. The principal warranty is that stated in subsections (1) and (2)(c) of this section.

6. Subsection (2) does not purport to exhaust the meaning of "merchantable" nor to negate any of its attributes not specifically mentioned in the text of the statute, but arising by usage of trade or through case law. The language used is "must be at least such as ...," and the intention is to leave open other possible attributes of merchantability.

7. Paragraphs (a) and (b) of subsection (2) are to be read together. Both refer, as indicated above, to the standards of that line of the trade which fits the transaction and the seller's business. "Fair average" is a term directly appropriate to agricultural bulk products and means goods centering around the middle belt of quality, not the least or the worst that can be understood in the particular trade by the designation, but such as can pass "without objection." Of course a fair percentage of the least is permissible but the goods are not "fair average" if they are all of the least or worst quality possible under the description. In cases of doubt as to what quality is intended, the price at which a merchant closes a contract is an excellent index of the nature and scope of his obligation under the present section.

8. Fitness for the ordinary purposes for which goods of the type are used is a fundamental concept of the present section and is covered in paragraph (c). As stated above, merchantability is also a part of the obligation owing to the purchaser for use. Correspondingly, protection, under this aspect of the warranty, of the person buying for resale to the ultimate consumer is equally necessary, and merchantable goods must therefore be "honestly" resalable in the normal course of business because they are what they purport to be.

9. Paragraph (d) on evenness of kind, quality and quantity follows case law. But precautionary language has been added as a remainder of the frequent usages of trade which permit substantial variations both with and without an allowance or an obligation to replace the varying units.

10. Paragraph (e) applies only where the nature of the goods and of the transaction require a certain type of container, package or label. Paragraph (f) applies, on the other hand, wherever there is a label or container on which representations are made, even though the original contract, either by express terms or usage of trade, may not have required either the labelling or the representation. This follows from the general obligation of good faith which requires that a buyer should not be placed in the position of reselling or using goods delivered under false representations appearing on the package or container. No problem of extra consideration arises in this connection since, under this Article, an obligation is imposed by the original contract not to deliver mislabeled articles, and the obligation is imposed where mercantile good faith so requires and without reference to the doctrine of consideration.

11. Exclusion or modification of the warranty of merchantability, or of any

part of it, is dealt with in the section to which the text of the present section makes explicit precautionary references. That section must be read with particular reference to its subsection (4) on limitation of remedies. The warranty of merchantability, wherever it is normal, is so commonly taken for granted that its exclusion from the contract is a matter threatening surprise and therefore requiring special precaution.

12. Subsection (3) is to make explicit that usage of trade and course of dealing can create warranties and that they are implied rather than express warranties and thus subject to exclusion or modification under Section 2-316. A typical instance would be the obligation to provide pedigree papers to evidence conformity of the animal to the contract in the case of a pedigreed dog or blooded bull.

13. In an action based on breach of warranty, it is of course necessary to show not only the existence of the warranty but the fact that the warranty was broken and that the breach of the warranty was the proximate cause of the loss sustained. In such an action an affirmative showing by the seller that the loss resulted from some action or event following his own delivery of the goods can operate as a defense. Equally, evidence indicating that the seller exercised care in the manufacture, processing or selection of the goods is relevant to the issue of whether the warranty was in fact broken. Action by the buyer following an examination of the goods which ought to have indicated the defect complained of can be shown as matter bearing on whether the breach itself was the cause of the injury.

Cross References:

Point 1: Section 2-316.
Point 3: Sections 1-203 and 2-104.
Point 5: Section 2-315.
Point 11: Section 2-316.
Point 12: Sections 1-201, 1-205 and 2-316.

Definitional Cross References:

"Agreement". Section 1-201.
"Contract". Section 1-201.
"Contract for sale". Section 2-106.
"Goods". Section 2-105.
"Merchant". Section 2-104.
"Seller". Section 2-103.

§ 2-315. Implied Warranty: Fitness for Particular Purpose.

Where the seller at the time of contracting has reason to know any particular purpose for which the goods are required and that the buyer is relying on the seller's skill or judgment to select or furnish suitable goods, there is unless excluded or modified under the next section an implied warranty that the goods shall be fit for such purpose.

Official Comment

Prior Uniform Statutory Provision: Section 15(1), (4), (5), Uniform Sales Act.

Changes: Rewritten.

Purposes of Changes:

1. Whether or not this warranty arises in any individual case is basically a question of fact to be determined by the circumstances of the contracting. Under this section the buyer need not bring home to the seller actual knowledge of the particular purpose for which the goods are intended or of his reliance on the seller's skill and judgment, if the circumstances are such that the seller has reason to realize the purpose intended or that the reliance exists. The buyer, of course, must actually be relying on the seller.

2. A "particular purpose" differs from the ordinary purpose for which the goods are used in that it envisages a specific use by the buyer which is peculiar to the nature of his business whereas the ordinary purposes for which goods are used are those envisaged in the concept of merchantability and go to uses which are customarily made of the goods in ques-

tion. For example, shoes are generally used for the purpose of walking upon ordinary ground, but a seller may know that a particular pair was selected to be used for climbing mountains.

A contract may of course include both a warranty of merchantability and one of fitness for a particular purpose.

The provisions of this Article on the cumulation and conflict of express and implied warranties must be considered on the question of inconsistency between or among warranties. In such a case any question of fact as to which warranty was intended by the parties to apply must be resolved in favor of the warranty of fitness for particular purpose as against all other warranties except where the buyer has taken upon himself the responsibility of furnishing the technical specifications.

3. In connection with the warranty of fitness for a particular purpose the provisions of this Article on the allocation or division of risks are particularly applicable in any transaction in which the purpose for which the goods are to be used combines requirements both as to the quality of the goods themselves and compliance with certain laws or regulations. How the risks are divided is a question of fact to be determined, where not expressly contained in the agreement, from the circumstances of contracting, usage of trade, course of performance and the like, matters which may constitute the "otherwise agreement" of the parties by which they may divide the risk or burden.

4. The absence from this section of the language used in the Uniform Sales Act in referring to the seller, "whether he be the grower or manufacturer or not," is not intended to impose any requirement that the seller be a grower or manufacturer. Although normally the warranty will arise only where the seller is a merchant with the appropriate "skill or judgment," it can arise as to non-merchants where this is justified by the particular circumstances.

5. The elimination of the "patent or other trade name" exception constitutes the major extension of the warranty of fitness which has been made by the cases and continued in this Article. Under the present section the existence of a patent or other trade name and the designation of the article by that name, or indeed in any other definite manner, is only one of the facts to be considered on the question of whether the buyer actually relied on the seller, but it is not of itself decisive of the issue. If the buyer himself is insisting on a particular brand he is not relying on the seller's skill and judgment and so no warranty results. But the mere fact that the article purchased has a particular patent or trade name is not sufficient to indicate nonreliance if the article has been recommended by the seller as adequate for the buyer's purposes.

6. The specific reference forward in the present section to the following section on exclusion or modification of warranties is to call attention to the possibility of eliminating the warranty in any given case. However it must be noted that under the following section the warranty of fitness for a particular purpose must be excluded or modified by a conspicuous writing.

Cross References:

Point 2: Sections 2-314 and 2-317.
Point 3: Section 2-303.
Point 6: Section 2-316.

Definitional Cross References:

"Buyer". Section 2-103.
"Goods". Section 2-105.
"Seller". Section 2-103.

§ 2-316. Exclusion or Modification of Warranties.

(1) Words or conduct relevant to the creation of an express warranty and words or conduct tending to negate or limit warranty shall be construed wherever reasonable as consistent with each other; but subject to the provisions of this Article on parol or extrinsic evidence (Section 2-202) negation or limitation is inoperative to the extent that such construction is unreasonable.

(2) Subject to subsection (3), to exclude or modify the implied warranty of merchantability or any part of it the language must mention merchantability and in case of a writing must be conspicuous, and to exclude or modify any implied warranty of fitness the exclusion must be by a writing and conspicuous. Language to exclude all implied warranties of fitness is sufficient if it states, for example, that "There are no warranties which extend beyond the description on the face hereof."

(3) Notwithstanding subsection (2)

(a) unless the circumstances indicate otherwise, all implied warranties are excluded by expressions like "as is", "with all faults" or other language which in common understanding calls the buyer's attention to the exclusion of warranties and makes plain that there is no implied warranty; and

(b) when the buyer before entering into the contract has examined the goods or the sample or model as fully as he desired or has refused to examine the goods there is no implied warranty with regard to defects which an examination ought in the circumstances to have revealed to him; and

(c) an implied warranty can also be excluded or modified by course of dealing or course of performance or usage of trade.

(4) Remedies for breach of warranty can be limited in accordance with the provisions of this Article on liquidation or limitation of damages and on contractual modification of remedy (Sections 2-718 and 2-719).

Official Comment

Prior Uniform Statutory Provision: None. See sections 15 and 71, Uniform Sales Act.

Purposes:

1. This section is designed principally to deal with those frequent clauses in sales contracts which seek to exclude "all warranties, express or implied." It seeks to protect a buyer from unexpected and unbargained language of disclaimer by denying effect to such language when inconsistent with language of express warranty and permitting the exclusion of implied warranties only by conspicuous language or other circumstances which protect the buyer from surprise.

2. The seller is protected under this Article against false allegations of oral warranties by its provisions on parol and extrinsic evidence and against unauthorized representations by the customary "lack of authority" clauses. This Article treats the limitation or avoidance of consequential damages as a matter of limiting remedies for breach, separate from the matter of creation of liability under a warranty. If no warranty exists, there is of course no problem of limiting remedies for breach of warranty. Under subsection (4) the question of limitation of remedy is governed by the sections referred to rather than by this section.

3. Disclaimer of the implied warranty of merchantability is permitted under subsection (2), but with the safeguard that such disclaimers must mention merchantability and in case of a writing must be conspicuous.

4. Unlike the implied warranty of merchantability, implied warranties of fitness for a particular purpose may be excluded by general language, but only if it is in writing and conspicuous.

5. Subsection (2) presupposes that the implied warranty in question exists unless excluded or modified. Whether or

not language of disclaimer satisfies the requirements of this section, such language may be relevant under other sections to the question whether the warranty was ever in fact created. Thus, unless the provisions of this Article on parol and extrinsic evidence prevent, oral language of disclaimer may raise issues of fact as to whether reliance by the buyer occurred and whether the seller had "reason to know" under the section on implied warranty of fitness for a particular purpose.

6. The exceptions to the general rule set forth in paragraphs (a), (b) and (c) of subsection (3) are common factual situations in which the circumstances surrounding the transaction are in themselves sufficient to call the buyer's attention to the fact that no implied warranties are made or that a certain implied warranty is being excluded.

7. Paragraph (a) of subsection (3) deals with general terms such as "as is," "as they stand," "with all faults," and the like. Such terms in ordinary commercial usage are understood to mean that the buyer takes the entire risk as to the quality of the goods involved. The terms covered by paragraph (a) are in fact merely a particularization of paragraph (c) which provides for exclusion or modification of implied warranties by usage of trade.

8. Under paragraph (b) of subsection (3) warranties may be excluded or modified by the circumstances where the buyer examines the goods or a sample or model of them before entering into the contract. "Examination" as used in this paragraph is not synonymous with inspection before acceptance or at any other time after the contract has been made. It goes rather to the nature of the responsibility assumed by the seller at the time of the making of the contract. Of course if the buyer discovers the defect and uses the goods anyway, or if he unreasonably fails to examine the goods before he uses them, resulting injuries may be found to result from his own action rather than proximately from a breach of warranty. See Sections 2–314 and 2–715 and comments thereto.

In order to bring the transaction within the scope of "refused to examine" in paragraph (b), it is not sufficient that the goods are available for inspection. There must in addition be a demand by the seller that the buyer examine the goods fully. The seller by the demand puts the buyer on notice that he is assuming the risk of defects which the examination ought to reveal. The language "refused to examine" in this paragraph is intended to make clear the necessity for such demand.

Application of the doctrine of "caveat emptor" in all cases where the buyer examines the goods regardless of statements made by the seller is, however, rejected by this Article. Thus, if the offer of examination is accompanied by words as to their merchantability or specific attributes and the buyer indicates clearly that he is relying on those words rather than on his examination, they give rise to an "express" warranty. In such cases the question is one of fact as to whether a warranty of merchantability has been expressly incorporated in the agreement. Disclaimer of such an express warranty is governed by subsection (1) of the present section.

The particular buyer's skill and the normal method of examining goods in the circumstances determine what defects are excluded by the examination. A failure to notice defects which are obvious cannot excuse the buyer. However, an examination under circumstances which do not permit chemical or other testing of the goods would not exclude defects which could be ascertained only by such testing. Nor can latent defects be excluded by a simple examination. A professional buyer examining a product in his field will be held to have assumed the risk as to all defects which a professional in the field ought to observe, while a nonprofessional buyer will be held to have assumed the risk only for such defects as a layman might be expected to observe.

9. The situation in which the buyer gives precise and complete specifications to the seller is not explicitly covered in

this section, but this is a frequent circumstance by which the implied warranties may be excluded. The warranty of fitness for a particular purpose would not normally arise since in such a situation there is usually no reliance on the seller by the buyer. The warranty of merchantability in such a transaction, however, must be considered in connection with the next section on the cumulation and conflict of warranties. Under paragraph (c) of that section in case of such an inconsistency the implied warranty of merchantability is displaced by the express warranty that the goods will comply with the specifications. Thus, where the buyer gives detailed specifications as to the goods, neither of the implied warranties as to quality will normally apply to the transaction unless consistent with the specifications.

Cross References:

Point 2: Sections 2-202, 2-718 and 2-719.

Point 7: Sections 1-205 and 2-208.

Definitional Cross References:

"Agreement". Section 1-201.
"Buyer". Section 2-103.
"Contract". Section 1-201.
"Course of dealing". Section 1-205.
"Goods". Section 2-105.
"Remedy". Section 1-201.
"Seller". Section 2-103.
"Usage of trade". Section 1-205.

§ 2-317. Cumulation and Conflict of Warranties Express or Implied.

Warranties whether express or implied shall be construed as consistent with each other and as cumulative, but if such construction is unreasonable the intention of the parties shall determine which warranty is dominant. In ascertaining that intention the following rules apply:

(a) Exact or technical specifications displace an inconsistent sample or model or general language of description.

(b) A sample from an existing bulk displaces inconsistent general language of description.

(c) Express warranties displace inconsistent implied warranties other than an implied warranty of fitness for a particular purpose.

Official Comment

Prior Uniform Statutory Provision: On cumulation of warranties see Sections 14, 15, and 16, Uniform Sales Act.

Changes: Completely rewritten into one section.

Purposes of Changes:

1. The present section rests on the basic policy of this Article that no warranty is created except by some conduct (either affirmative action or failure to disclose) on the part of the seller. Therefore, all warranties are made cumulative unless this construction of the contract is impossible or unreasonable.

This Article thus follows the general policy of the Uniform Sales Act except that in case of the sale of an article by its patent or trade name the elimination of the warranty of fitness depends solely on whether the buyer has relied on the seller's skill and judgment; the use of the patent or trade name is but one factor in making this determination.

2. The rules of this section are designed to aid in determining the intention of the parties as to which of inconsistent warranties which have arisen from the circumstances of their transaction shall prevail. These rules of intention are to be applied only where factors making for an equitable estoppel of the seller do not exist and where he has in perfect good faith made warranties which later turn

out to be inconsistent. To the extent that the seller has led the buyer to believe that all of the warranties can be performed, he is estopped from setting up any essential inconsistency as a defense.

3. The rules in subsections (a), (b) and (c) are designed to ascertain the intention of the parties by reference to the factor which probably claimed the attention of the parties in the first instance. These rules are not absolute but may be changed by evidence showing that the conditions which existed at the time of contracting make the construction called for by the section inconsistent or unreasonable.

Cross Reference:

Point 1: Section 2-315.

Definitional Cross Reference:

"Party". Section 1-201.

§ 2-318. Third Party Beneficiaries of Warranties Express or Implied.

Note: *If this Act is introduced in the Congress of the United States this section should be omitted. (States to select one alternative.)*

Alternative A

A seller's warranty whether express or implied extends to any natural person who is in the family or household of his buyer or who is a guest in his home if it is reasonable to expect that such person may use, consume or be affected by the goods and who is injured in person by breach of the warranty. A seller may not exclude or limit the operation of this section.

Alternative B

A seller's warranty whether express or implied extends to any natural person who may reasonably be expected to use, consume or be affected by the goods and who is injured in person by breach of the warranty. A seller may not exclude or limit the operation of this section.

Alternative C

A seller's warranty whether express or implied extends to any person who may reasonably be expected to use, consume or be affected by the goods and who is injured by breach of the warranty. A seller may not exclude or limit the operation of this section with respect to injury to the person of an individual to whom the warranty extends.

As amended in 1966.

Official Comment

Prior Uniform Statutory Provision: None.

Purposes:

1. The last sentence of this section does not mean that a seller is precluded from excluding or disclaiming a warranty which might otherwise arise in connection with the sale provided such exclusion or modification is permitted by Section 2-316. Nor does that sentence preclude the seller from limiting the remedies of his own buyer and of any beneficiaries, in any manner provided in Sections 2-718 or 2-719. To the extent that the contract of sale contains provisions under which warranties are excluded or modified, or remedies for breach are limited, such provisions are equally operative against beneficiaries of warranties under this section.

What this last sentence forbids is exclusion of liability by the seller to the persons to whom the warranties which he has made to his buyer would extend under this section.

2. The purpose of this section is to give certain beneficiaries the benefit of the same warranty which the buyer received in the contract of sale, thereby freeing any such beneficiaries from any technical rules as to "privity." It seeks to accomplish this purpose without any derogation of any right or remedy resting on negligence. It rests primarily upon the merchant-seller's warranty under this Article that the goods sold are merchantable and fit for the ordinary purposes for which such goods are used rather than the warranty of fitness for a particular purpose. Implicit in the section is that any beneficiary of a warranty may bring a direct action for breach of warranty against the seller whose warranty extends to him [As amended in 1966].

3. The first alternative expressly includes as beneficiaries within its provisions the family, household and guests of the purchaser. Beyond this, the section in this form is neutral and is not intended to enlarge or restrict the developing case law on whether the seller's warranties, given to his buyer who resells, extend to other persons in the distributive chain.

The second alternative is designed for states where the case law has already developed further and for those that desire to expand the class of beneficiaries. The third alternative goes further, following the trend of modern decisions as indicated by Restatement of Torts 2d § 402A (Tentative Draft No. 10, 1965) in extending the rule beyond injuries to the person [As amended in 1966].

Cross References:

Point 1: Sections 2-316, 2-718 and 2-719.

Point 2: Section 2-314.

Definitional Cross References:

"Buyer". Section 2-103.
"Goods". Section 2-105.
"Seller". Section 2-103.

§ 2-319. F.O.B. and F.A.S. Terms.

(1) Unless otherwise agreed the term F.O.B. (which means "free on board") at a named place, even though used only in connection with the stated price, is a delivery term under which

(a) when the term is F.O.B. the place of shipment, the seller must at that place ship the goods in the manner provided in this Article (Section 2-504) and bear the expense and risk of putting them into the possession of the carrier; or

(b) when the term is F.O.B. the place of destination, the seller must at his own expense and risk transport the goods to that place and there tender delivery of them in the manner provided in this Article (Section 2-503);

(c) when under either (a) or (b) the term is also F.O.B. vessel, car or other vehicle, the seller must in addition at his own expense and risk load the goods on board. If the term is F.O.B. vessel the buyer must name the vessel and in an appropriate case the seller must comply with the provisions of this Article on the form of bill of lading (Section 2-323).

(2) Unless otherwise agreed the term F.A.S. vessel (which means "free alongside") at a named port, even though used only in connection with the stated price, is a delivery term under which the seller must

(a) at his own expense and risk deliver the goods alongside the vessel in the manner usual in that port or on a dock designated and provided by the buyer; and

(b) obtain and tender a receipt for the goods in exchange for which the carrier is under a duty to issue a bill of lading.

(3) Unless otherwise agreed in any case falling within subsection (1)(a) or (c) or subsection (2) the buyer must seasonably give any needed instructions for making delivery, including when the term is F.A.S. or F.O.B. the loading berth of the vessel and in an appropriate case its name and sailing date. The seller may treat the failure of needed instructions as a failure of cooperation under this Article (Section 2-311). He may also at his option move the goods in any reasonable manner preparatory to delivery or shipment.

(4) Under the term F.O.B. vessel or F.A.S. unless otherwise agreed the buyer must make payment against tender of the required documents and the seller may not tender nor the buyer demand delivery of the goods in substitution for the documents.

Official Comment

Prior Uniform Statutory Provision: None.

Purposes:

1. This section is intended to negate the uncommercial line of decision which treats an "F.O.B." term as "merely a price term." The distinctions taken in subsection (1) handle most of the issues which have on occasion led to the unfortunate judicial language just referred to. Other matters which have led to sound results being based on unhappy language in regard to F.O.B. clauses are dealt with in this Act by Section 2-311(2) (seller's option re arrangements relating to shipment) and Sections 2-614 and 615 (substituted performance and seller's excuse).

2. Subsection (1)(c) not only specifies the duties of a seller who engages to deliver "F.O.B. vessel," or the like, but ought to make clear that no agreement is soundly drawn when it looks to reshipment from San Francisco or New York, but speaks merely of "F.O.B." the place.

3. The buyer's obligations stated in subsection (1)(c) and subsection (3) are, as shown in the text, obligations of cooperation. The last sentence of subsection (3) expressly, though perhaps unnecessarily, authorizes the seller, pending instructions, to go ahead with such preparatory moves as shipment from the interior to the named point of delivery. The sentence presupposes the usual case in which instructions "fail"; a prior repudiation by the buyer, giving notice that breach was intended, would remove the reason for the sentence, and would normally bring into play, instead, the second sentence of Section 2-704, which duly calls for lessening damages.

4. The treatment of "F.O.B. vessel" in conjunction with F.A.S. fits, in regard to the need for payment against documents, with standard practice and case-law; but "F.O.B. vessel" is a term which by its very language makes express the need for an "on board" document. In this respect, that term is stricter than the ordinary overseas "shipment" contract (C.I.F., etc., Section 2-320).

Cross References:

Sections 2-311(3), 2-323, 2-503 and 2-504.

Definitional Cross References:

"Agreed". Section 1-201.
"Bill of lading". Section 1-201.
"Buyer". Section 2-103.
"Goods". Section 2-105.
"Seasonably". Section 1-204.
"Seller". Section 2-103.
"Term". Section 1-201.

§ 2–320. C.I.F. and C. & F. Terms.

(1) The term C.I.F. means that the price includes in a lump sum the cost of the goods and the insurance and freight to the named destination. The term C. & F. or C.F. means that the price so includes cost and freight to the named destination.

(2) Unless otherwise agreed and even though used only in connection with the stated price and destination, the term C.I.F. destination or its equivalent requires the seller at his own expense and risk to

(a) put the goods into the possession of a carrier at the port for shipment and obtain a negotiable bill or bills of lading covering the entire transportation to the named destination; and

(b) load the goods and obtain a receipt from the carrier (which may be contained in the bill of lading) showing that the freight has been paid or provided for; and

(c) obtain a policy or certificate of insurance, including any war risk insurance, of a kind and on terms then current at the port of shipment in the usual amount, in the currency of the contract, shown to cover the same goods covered by the bill of lading and providing for payment of loss to the order of the buyer or for the account of whom it may concern; but the seller may add to the price the amount of the premium for any such war risk insurance; and

(d) prepare an invoice of the goods and procure any other documents required to effect shipment or to comply with the contract; and

(e) forward and tender with commercial promptness all the documents in due form and with any indorsement necessary to perfect the buyer's rights.

(3) Unless otherwise agreed the term C. & F. or its equivalent has the same effect and imposes upon the seller the same obligations and risks as a C.I.F. term except the obligation as to insurance.

(4) Under the term C.I.F. or C. & F. unless otherwise agreed the buyer must make payment against tender of the required documents and the seller may not tender nor the buyer demand delivery of the goods in substitution for the documents.

Official Comment

Prior Uniform Statutory Provisions: None.

Purposes: To make it clear that:

1. The C.I.F. contract is not a destination but a shipment contract with risk of subsequent loss or damage to the goods passing to the buyer upon shipment if the seller has properly performed all his obligations with respect to the goods. Delivery to the carrier is delivery to the buyer for purposes of risk and "title". Delivery of possession of the goods is accomplished by delivery of the bill of lading, and upon tender of the required documents the buyer must pay the agreed price without awaiting the arrival of the goods and if they have been lost or damaged after proper shipment he must seek his remedy

against the carrier or insurer. The buyer has no right of inspection prior to payment or acceptance of the documents.

2. The seller's obligations remain the same even though the C.I.F. term is "used only in connection with the stated price and destination".

3. The insurance stipulated by the C.I.F. term is for the buyer's benefit, to protect him against the risk of loss or damage to the goods in transit. A clause in a C.I.F. contract "insurance—for the account of sellers" should be viewed in its ordinary mercantile meaning that the sellers must pay for the insurance and not that it is intended to run to the seller's benefit.

4. A bill of lading covering the entire transportation from the port of shipment is explicitly required but the provision on this point must be read in the light of its reason to assure the buyer of as full protection as the conditions of shipment reasonably permit, remembering always that this type of contract is designed to move the goods in the channels commercially available. To enable the buyer to deal with the goods while they are afloat the bill of lading must be one that covers only the quantity of goods called for by the contract. The buyer is not required to accept his part of the goods without a bill of lading because the latter covers a larger quantity, nor is he required to accept a bill of lading for the whole quantity under a stipulation to hold the excess for the owner. Although the buyer is not compelled to accept either goods or documents under such circumstances he may of course claim his rights in any goods which have been identified to his contract.

5. The seller is given the option of paying or providing for the payment of freight. He has no option to ship "freight collect" unless the agreement so provides. The rule of the common law that the buyer need not pay the freight if the goods do not arrive is preserved.

Unless the shipment has been sent "freight collect" the buyer is entitled to receive documentary evidence that he is not obligated to pay the freight; the seller is therefore required to obtain a receipt "showing that the freight has been paid or provided for." The usual notation in the appropriate space on the bill of lading that the freight has been prepaid is a sufficient receipt, as at common law. The phrase "provided for" is intended to cover the frequent situation in which the carrier extends credit to a shipper for the freight on successive shipments and receives periodical payments of the accrued freight charges from him.

6. The requirement that unless otherwise agreed the seller must procure insurance "of a kind and on terms then current at the port for shipment in the usual amount, in the currency of the contract, sufficiently shown to cover the same goods covered by the bill of lading", applies to both marine and war risk insurance. As applied to marine insurance, it means such insurance as is usual or customary at the port for shipment with reference to the particular kind of goods involved, the character and equipment of the vessel, the route of the voyage, the port of destination and any other considerations that affect the risk. It is the substantial equivalent of the ordinary insurance in the particular trade and on the particular voyage and is subject to agreed specifications of type or extent of coverage. The language does not mean that the insurance must be adequate to cover all risks to which the goods may be subject in transit. There are some types of loss or damage that are not covered by the usual marine insurance and are excepted in bills of lading or in applicable statutes from the causes of loss or damage for which the carrier or the vessel is liable. Such risks must be borne by the buyer under this Article.

Insurance secured in compliance with a C.I.F. term must cover the entire transportation of the goods to the named destination.

7. An additional obligation is imposed upon the seller in requiring him to procure customary war risk insurance at the buyer's expense. This changes the com-

mon law on the point. The seller is not required to assume the risk of including in the C.I.F. price the cost of such insurance, since it often fluctuates rapidly, but is required to treat it simply as a necessary for the buyer's account. What war risk insurance is "current" or usual turns on the standard forms of policy or rider in common use.

8. The C.I.F. contract calls for insurance covering the value of the goods at the time and place of shipment and does not include any increase in market value during transit or any anticipated profit to the buyer on a sale by him.

The contract contemplates that before the goods arrive at their destination they may be sold again and again on C.I.F. terms and that the original policy of insurance and bill of lading will run with the interest in the goods by being transferred to each successive buyer. A buyer who becomes the seller in such an intermediate contract for sale does not thereby, if his sub-buyer knows the circumstances, undertake to insure the goods again at an increased price fixed in the new contract or to cover the increase in price by additional insurance, and his buyer may not reject the documents on the ground that the original policy does not cover such higher price. If such a sub-buyer desires additional insurance he must procure it for himself.

Where the seller exercises an option to ship "freight collect" and to credit the buyer with the freight against the C.I.F. price, the insurance need not cover the freight since the freight is not at the buyer's risk. On the other hand, where the seller prepays the freight upon shipping under a bill of lading requiring prepayment and providing that the freight shall be deemed earned and shall be retained by the carrier "ship and/or cargo lost or not lost," or using words of similar import, he must procure insurance that will cover the freight, because notwithstanding that the goods are lost in transit the buyer is bound to pay the freight as part of the C.I.F. price and will be unable to recover it back from the carrier.

9. Insurance "for the account of whom it may concern" is usual and sufficient. However, for a valid tender the policy of insurance must be one which can be disposed of together with the bill of lading and so must be "sufficiently shown to cover the same goods covered by the bill of lading". It must cover separately the quantity of goods called for by the buyer's contract and not merely insure his goods as part of a larger quantity in which others are interested, a case provided for in American mercantile practice by the use of negotiable certificates of insurance which are expressly authorized by this section. By usage these certificates are treated as the equivalent of separate policies and are good tender under C.I.F. contracts. The term "certificate of insurance", however, does not of itself include certificates or "cover notes" issued by the insurance broker and stating that the goods are covered by a policy. Their sufficiency as substitutes for policies will depend upon proof of an established usage or course of dealing. The present section rejects the English rule that not only brokers' certificates and "cover notes" but also certain forms of American insurance certificates are not the equivalent of policies and are not good tender under a C.I.F. contract.

The seller's failure to tender a proper insurance document is waived if the buyer refuses to make payment on other and untenable grounds at a time when proper insurance could have been obtained and tendered by the seller if timely objection had been made. Even a failure to insure on shipment may be cured by seasonable tender of a policy retroactive in effect; e.g., one insuring the goods "lost or not lost." The provisions of this Article on cure of improper tender and on waiver of buyer's objections by silence are applicable to insurance tenders under a C.I.F. term. Where there is no waiver by the buyer as described above, however, the fact that the goods arrive safely does not cure the seller's breach of his obligations to insure them and tender to the buyer a proper insurance document.

10. The seller's invoice of the goods shipped under a C.I.F. contract is regarded as a usual and necessary document upon which reliance may properly be placed. It is the document which evidences points of description, quality and the like which do not readily appear in other documents. This Article rejects those statements to the effect that the invoice is a usual but not a necessary document under a C.I.F. term.

11. The buyer needs all of the documents required under a C.I.F. contract, in due form and with necessary endorsements, so that before the goods arrive he may deal with them by negotiating the documents or may obtain prompt possession of the goods after their arrival. If the goods are lost or damaged in transit the documents are necessary to enable him promptly to assert his remedy against the carrier or insurer. The seller is therefore obligated to do what is mercantilely reasonable in the circumstances and should make every reasonable exertion to send forward the documents as soon as possible after the shipment. The requirement that the documents be forwarded with "commercial promptness" expresses a more urgent need for action than that suggested by the phrase "reasonable time".

12. Under a C.I.F. contract the buyer, as under the common law, must pay the price upon tender of the required documents without first inspecting the goods, but his payment in these circumstances does not constitute an acceptance of the goods nor does it impair his right of subsequent inspection or his options and remedies in the case of improper delivery. All remedies and rights for the seller's breach are reserved to him. The buyer must pay before inspection and assert his remedy against the seller afterward unless the nonconformity of the goods amounts to a real failure of consideration, since the purpose of choosing this form of contract is to give the seller protection against the buyer's unjustifiable rejection of the goods at a distant port of destination which would necessitate taking possession of the goods and suing the buyer there.

13. A valid C.I.F. contract may be made which requires part of the transportation to be made on land and part on the sea, as where the goods are to be brought by rail from an inland point to a seaport and thence transported by vessel to the named destination under a "through" or combination bill of lading issued by the railroad company. In such a case shipment by rail from the inland point within the contract period is a timely shipment notwithstanding that the loading of the goods on the vessel is delayed by causes beyond the seller's control.

14. Although subsection (2) stating the legal effects of the C.I.F. term is an "unless otherwise agreed" provision, the express language used in an agreement is frequently a precautionary, fuller statement of the normal C.I.F. terms and hence not intended as a departure or variation from them. Moreover, the dominant outlines of the C.I.F. term are so well understood commercially that any variation should, whenever reasonably possible, be read as falling within those dominant outlines rather than as destroying the whole meaning of a term which essentially indicates a contract for proper shipment rather than one for delivery at destination. Particularly careful consideration is necessary before a printed form or clause is construed to mean agreement otherwise and where a C.I.F. contract is prepared on a printed form designed for some other type of contract, the C.I.F. terms must prevail over printed clauses repugnant to them.

15. Under subsection (4) the fact that the seller knows at the time of the tender of the documents that the goods have been lost in transit does not affect his rights if he has performed his contractual obligations. Similarly, the seller cannot perform under a C.I.F. term by purchasing and tendering landed goods.

16. Under the C. & F. term, as under the C.I.F. term, title and risk of loss are intended to pass to the buyer on shipment. A stipulation in a C. & F. contract

that the seller shall effect insurance on the goods and charge the buyer with the premium (in effect that he shall act as the buyer's agent for that purpose) is entirely in keeping with the pattern. On the other hand, it often happens that the buyer is in a more advantageous position than the seller to effect insurance on the goods or that he has in force an "open" or "floating" policy covering all shipments made by him or to him, in either of which events the C. & F. term is adequate without mention of insurance.

17. It is to be remembered that in a French contract the term "C.A.F." does not mean "Cost and Freight" but has exactly the same meaning as the term "C.I.F." since it is merely the French equivalent of that term. The "A" does not stand for "and" but for "assurance" which means insurance.

Cross References:

Point 4: Section 2–323.
Point 6: Section 2–509(1)(a).
Point 9: Sections 2–508 and 2–605(1)(a).
Point 12: Sections 2–321(3), 2–512 and 2–513(3) and Article 5.

Definitional Cross References:

"Bill of lading". Section 1–201.
"Buyer". Section 2–103.
"Contract". Section 1–201.
"Goods". Section 2–105.
"Rights". Section 1–201.
"Seller". Section 2–103.
"Term". Section 1–201.

§ 2–321. C.I.F. or C. & F.: "Net Landed Weights"; "Payment on Arrival"; Warranty of Condition on Arrival.

Under a contract containing a term C.I.F. or C. & F.

(1) Where the price is based on or is to be adjusted according to "net landed weights", "delivered weights", "out turn" quantity or quality or the like, unless otherwise agreed the seller must reasonably estimate the price. The payment due on tender of the documents called for by the contract is the amount so estimated, but after final adjustment of the price a settlement must be made with commercial promptness.

(2) An agreement described in subsection (1) or any warranty of quality or condition of the goods on arrival places upon the seller the risk of ordinary deterioration, shrinkage and the like in transportation but has no effect on the place or time of identification to the contract for sale or delivery or on the passing of the risk of loss.

(3) Unless otherwise agreed where the contract provides for payment on or after arrival of the goods the seller must before payment allow such preliminary inspection as is feasible; but if the goods are lost delivery of the documents and payment are due when the goods should have arrived.

Official Comment

Prior Uniform Statutory Provision: None.

Purposes:

This section deals with two variations of the C.I.F. contract which have evolved in mercantile practice but are entirely consistent with the basic C.I.F. pattern. Subsections (1) and (2), which provide for a shift to the seller of the risk of quality and weight deterioration during shipment, are designed to conform the law to the best mercantile practice and usage without changing the legal consequences of the C.I.F. or C. & F. term as to the passing of marine risks to the buyer at the point of shipment. Subsection (3) provides that where under the contract documents are to be presented for payment after arrival of the goods, this amounts merely to a postponement of the payment under the C.I.F. contract and is not to be confused with the "no arrival, no sale" contract. If the goods are lost, delivery of the documents and payment against them are due when the goods should have arrived. The clause for payment on or after arrival is not to be construed as such a condition precedent to payment that if the goods are lost in transit the buyer need never pay and the seller must bear the loss.

Cross Reference:

Section 2-324.

Definitional Cross References:

"Agreement". Section 1-201.
"Contract". Section 1-201.
"Delivery". Section 1-201.
"Goods". Section 2-105.
"Seller". Section 2-103.
"Term". Section 1-201.

§ 2-322. Delivery "Ex-Ship".

(1) Unless otherwise agreed a term for delivery of goods "ex-ship" (which means from the carrying vessel) or in equivalent language is not restricted to a particular ship and requires delivery from a ship which has reached a place at the named port of destination where goods of the kind are usually discharged.

(2) Under such a term unless otherwise agreed

(a) the seller must discharge all liens arising out of the carriage and furnish the buyer with a direction which puts the carrier under a duty to deliver the goods; and

(b) the risk of loss does not pass to the buyer until the goods leave the ship's tackle or are otherwise properly unloaded.

Official Comment

Prior Uniform Statutory Provision: None.

Purposes:

1. The delivery term, "ex-ship", as between seller and buyer, is the reverse of the f.a.s. term covered.

2. Delivery need not be made from any particular vessel under a clause calling for delivery "ex-ship", even though a vessel on which shipment is to be made originally is named in the contract, unless the agreement by appropriate language, restricts the clause to delivery from a named vessel.

3. The appropriate place and manner of unloading at the port of destination depend upon the nature of the goods and the facilities and usages of the port.

4. A contract fixing a price "ex-ship" with payment "cash against documents" calls only for such documents as are appropriate to the contract. Tender of a delivery order and of a receipt for the freight after the arrival of the carrying vessel is adequate. The seller is not required to tender a bill of lading as a document of title nor is he required to insure the goods for the buyer's benefit, as the goods are not at the buyer's risk during the voyage.

Cross Reference:

Point 1: Section 2-319(2).

Definitional Cross References:

"Buyer". Section 2-103.
"Goods". Section 2-105.
"Seller". Section 2-103.
"Term". Section 1-201.

§ 2-323. Form of Bill of Lading Required in Overseas Shipment; "Overseas".

(1) Where the contract contemplates overseas shipment and contains a term C.I.F. or C. & F. or F.O.B. vessel, the seller unless otherwise agreed must obtain a negotiable bill of lading stating that the goods have been loaded in board or, in the case of a term C.I.F. or C. & F., received for shipment.

(2) Where in a case within subsection (1) a bill of lading has been issued in a set of parts, unless otherwise agreed if the documents are not to be sent from abroad the buyer may demand tender of the full set; otherwise only one part of the bill of lading need be tendered. Even if the agreement expressly requires a full set

(a) due tender of a single part is acceptable within the provisions of this Article on cure of improper delivery (subsection (1) of Section 2-508); and

(b) even though the full set is demanded, if the documents are sent from abroad the person tendering an incomplete set may nevertheless require payment upon furnishing an indemnity which the buyer in good faith deems adequate.

(3) A shipment by water or by air or a contract contemplating such shipment is "overseas" insofar as by usage of trade or agreement it is subject to the commercial, financing or shipping practices characteristic of international deep water commerce.

Official Comment

Prior Uniform Statutory Provision: None.

Purposes:

1. Subsection (1) follows the "American" rule that a regular bill of lading indicating delivery of the goods at the dock for shipment is sufficient, except under a term "F.O.B. vessel." See Section 2-319 and comment thereto.

2. Subsection (2) deals with the problem of bills of lading covering deep water shipments, issued not as a single bill of lading but in a set of parts, each part referring to the other parts and the entire set constituting in commercial practice and at law a single bill of lading. Commercial practice in international commerce is to accept and pay against presentation of the first part of a set if the part is sent from overseas even though the contract of the buyer requires presentation of a full set of bills of lading provided adequate indemnity for the missing parts is forthcoming.

This subsection codifies that practice as between buyer and seller. Article 5 (Section 5-113) authorizes banks presenting drafts under letters of credit to give indemnities against the missing parts, and this subsection means that the buyer must accept and act on such indemnities if he in good faith deems them adequate. But neither this subsection nor Article 5 decides whether a bank which has issued a letter of credit is similarly bound. The issuing bank's obligation under a letter of credit is independent and depends on its own terms. See Article 5.

Cross References:

Sections 2-508(2), 5-113.

Definitional Cross References:

"Bill of lading". Section 1-201.
"Buyer". Section 2-103.
"Contract". Section 1-201.
"Delivery". Section 1-201.
"Financing agency". Section 2-104.

"Person". Section 1-201.
"Seller". Section 2-103.
"Send". Section 1-201.
"Term". Section 1-201.

§ 2-324. "No Arrival, No Sale" Term.

Under a term "no arrival, no sale" or terms of like meaning, unless otherwise agreed,

(a) the seller must properly ship conforming goods and if they arrive by any means he must tender them on arrival but he assumes no obligation that the goods will arrive unless he has caused the non-arrival; and

(b) where without fault of the seller the goods are in part lost or have so deteriorated as no longer to conform to the contract or arrive after the contract time, the buyer may proceed as if there had been casualty to identified goods (Section 2-613).

Official Comment

Prior Uniform Statutory Provision: None.

Purposes:

1. The "no arrival, no sale" term in a "destination" overseas contract leaves risk of loss on the seller but gives him an exemption from liability for non-delivery. Both the nature of the case and the duty of good faith require that the seller must not interfere with the arrival of the goods in any way. If the circumstances impose upon him the responsibility for making or arranging the shipment, he must have a shipment made despite the exemption clause. Further, the shipment made must be a conforming one, for the exemption under a "no arrival, no sale" term applies only to the hazards of transportation and the goods must be proper in all other respects.

The reason of this section is that where the seller is reselling goods bought by him as shipped by another and this fact is known to the buyer, so that the seller is not under any obligation to make the shipment himself, the seller is entitled under the "no arrival, no sale" clause to exemption from payment of damages for non-delivery if the goods do not arrive or if the goods which actually arrive are non-conforming. This does not extend to sellers who arrange shipment by their own agents, in which case the clause is limited to casualty due to marine hazards. But sellers who make known that they are contracting only with respect to what will be delivered to them by parties over whom they assume no control are entitled to the full quantum of the exemption.

2. The provisions of this Article on identification must be read together with the present section in order to bring the exemption into application. Until there is some designation of the goods in a particular shipment or on a particular ship as being those to which the contract refers there can be no application of an exemption for their non-arrival.

3. The seller's duty to tender the agreed or declared goods if they do arrive is not impaired because of their delay in arrival or by their arrival after transshipment.

4. The phrase "to arrive" is often employed in the same sense as "no arrival, no sale" and may then be given the same effect. But a "to arrive" term, added to a C.I.F. or C. & F. contract, does not have the full meaning given by this section to "no arrival, no sale". Such a "to arrive" term is usually intended to operate only to the extent that the risks are not covered by the agreed insurance and the loss or casualty is due to such uncovered hazards. In some instances the "to arrive" term may be regarded as a time of payment term, or, in the case of the reselling seller discussed in point 1 above, as ne-

gating responsibility for conformity of the goods, if they arrive, to any description which was based on his good faith belief of the quality. Whether this is the intention of the parties is a question of fact based on all the circumstances surrounding the resale and in case of ambiguity the rules of Sections 2-316 and 2-317 apply to preclude dishonor.

5. Paragraph (b) applies where goods arrive impaired by damage or partial loss during transportation and makes the policy of this Article on casualty to identified goods applicable to such a situation. For the term cannot be regarded as intending to give the seller an unforeseen profit through casualty; it is intended only to protect him from loss due to causes beyond his control.

Cross References:

Point 1: Section 1-203.
Point 2: Section 2-501(a) and (c).
Point 5: Section 2-613.

Definitional Cross References:

"Buyer". Section 2-103.
"Conforming". Section 2-106.
"Contract". Section 1-201.
"Fault". Section 1-201.
"Goods". Section 2-105.
"Sale". Section 2-106.
"Seller". Section 2-103.
"Term". Section 1-201.

§ 2-325. "Letter of Credit" Term; "Confirmed Credit".

(1) Failure of the buyer seasonably to furnish an agreed letter of credit is a breach of the contract for sale.

(2) The delivery to seller of a proper letter of credit suspends the buyer's obligation to pay. If the letter of credit is dishonored, the seller may on seasonable notification to the buyer require payment directly from him.

(3) Unless otherwise agreed the term "letter of credit" or "banker's credit" in a contract for sale means an irrevocable credit issued by a financing agency of good repute and, where the shipment is overseas, of good international repute. The term "confirmed credit" means that the credit must also carry the direct obligation of such an agency which does business in the seller's financial market.

Official Comment

Prior Uniform Statutory Provision: None.

Purposes: To express the established commercial and banking understanding as to the meaning and effects of terms calling for "letters of credit" or "confirmed credit":

1. Subsection (2) follows the general policy of this Article and Article 3 (Section 3-802) on conditional payment, under which payment by check or other short-term instrument is not ordinarily final as between the parties if the recipient duly presents the instrument and honor is refused. Thus the furnishing of a letter of credit does not substitute the financing agency's obligation for the buyer's, but the seller must first give the buyer reasonable notice of his intention to demand direct payment from him.

2. Subsection (2) requires that the credit be irrevocable and be a prime credit as determined by the standing of the issuer. It is not necessary, unless otherwise agreed, that the credit be a negotiation credit; the seller can finance himself by an assignment of the proceeds under Section 5-116(2).

3. The definition of "confirmed credit" is drawn on the supposition that the credit is issued by a bank which is not doing direct business in the seller's financial market; there is no intention to require the obligation of two banks both local to the seller.

Cross References:

Sections 2-403, 2-511(3) and 3-802 and Article 5.

Definitional Cross References:

"Buyer". Section 2-103.
"Contract for sale". Section 2-106.
"Draft". Section 3-104.
"Financing agency". Section 2-104.
"Notifies". Section 1-201.
"Overseas". Section 2-323.
"Purchaser". Section 1-201.
"Seasonably". Section 1-204.
"Seller". Section 2-103.
"Term". Section 1-201.

§ 2-326. Sale on Approval and Sale or Return; Consignment Sales and Rights of Creditors.

(1) Unless otherwise agreed, if delivered goods may be returned by the buyer even though they conform to the contract, the transaction is

(a) a "sale on approval" if the goods are delivered primarily for use, and

(b) a "sale or return" if the goods are delivered primarily for resale.

(2) Except as provided in subsection (3), goods held on approval are not subject to the claims of the buyer's creditors until acceptance; goods held on sale or return are subject to such claims while in the buyer's possession.

(3) Where goods are delivered to a person for sale and such person maintains a place of business at which he deals in goods of the kind involved, under a name other than the name of the person making delivery, then with respect to claims of creditors of the person conducting the business the goods are deemed to be on sale or return. The provisions of this subsection are applicable even though an agreement purports to reserve title to the person making delivery until payment or resale or uses such words as "on consignment" or "on memorandum". However, this subsection is not applicable if the person making delivery

(a) complies with an applicable law providing for a consignor's interest or the like to be evidenced by a sign, or

(b) establishes that the person conducting the business is generally known by his creditors to be substantially engaged in selling the goods of others, or

(c) complies with the filing provisions of the Article on Secured Transactions (Article 9).

(4) Any "or return" term of a contract for sale is to be treated as a separate contract for sale within the statute of frauds section of this Article (Section 2-201) and as contradicting the sale aspect of the contract within the provisions of this Article on parol or extrinsic evidence (Section 2-202).

Official Comment

Prior Uniform Statutory Provision: Section 19(3), Uniform Sales Act.

Changes: Completely rewritten in this and the succeeding section.

Purposes of Changes: To make it clear that:

1. A "sale on approval" or "sale or return" is distinct from other types of transactions with which they have frequently been confused. The type of "sale on approval," "on trial" or "on satisfaction" dealt with involves a contract under which the seller undertakes a particular

business risk to satisfy his prospective buyer with the appearance or performance of the goods in question. The goods are delivered to the proposed purchaser but they remain the property of the seller until the buyer accepts them. The price has already been agreed. The buyer's willingness to receive and test the goods is the consideration for the seller's engagement to deliver and sell. The type of "sale or return" involved herein is a sale to a merchant whose unwillingness to buy is overcome only by the seller's engagement to take back the goods (or any commercial unit of goods) in lieu of payment if they fail to be resold. These two transactions are so strongly delineated in practice and in general understanding that every presumption runs against a delivery to a consumer being a "sale or return" and against a delivery to a merchant for resale being a "sale on approval."

The right to return the goods for failure to conform to the contract does not make the transaction a "sale on approval" or "sale or return" and has nothing to do with this and the following section. The present section is not concerned with remedies for breach of contract. It deals instead with a power given by the contract to turn back the goods even though they are wholly as warranted.

This section nevertheless presupposes that a contract for sale is contemplated by the parties although that contract may be of the peculiar character here described.

Where the buyer's obligation as a buyer is conditioned not on his personal approval but on the article's passing a described objective test, the risk of loss by casualty pending the test is properly the seller's and proper return is at his expense. On the point of "satisfaction" as meaning "reasonable satisfaction" where an industrial machine is involved, this Article takes no position.

2. Pursuant to the general policies of this Act which require good faith not only between the parties to the sales contract, but as against interested third parties, subsection (3) resolves all reasonable doubts as to the nature of the transaction in favor of the general creditors of the buyer. As against such creditors words such as "on consignment" or "on memorandum", with or without words of reservation of title in the seller, are disregarded when the buyer has a place of business at which he deals in goods of the kind involved. A necessary exception is made where the buyer is known to be engaged primarily in selling the goods of others or is selling under a relevant sign law, or the seller complies with the filing provisions of Article 9 as if his interest were a security interest. However, there is no intent in this Section to narrow the protection afforded to third parties in any jurisdiction which has a selling Factors Act. The purpose of the exception is merely to limit the effect of the present subsection itself, in the absence of any such Factors Act, to cases in which creditors of the buyer may reasonably be deemed to have been misled by the secret reservation.

3. Subsection (4) resolves a conflict in the pre-existing case law by recognition that an "or return" provision is so definitely at odds with any ordinary contract for sale of goods that where written agreements are involved it must be contained in a written memorandum. The "or return" aspect of a sales contract must be treated as a separate contract under the Statute of Frauds section and as contradicting the sale insofar as questions of parol or extrinsic evidence are concerned.

Cross References:

Point 2: Article 9.
Point 3: Sections 2-201 and 2-202.

Definitional Cross References:

"Between merchants". Section 2-104.
"Buyer". Section 2-103.
"Conform". Section 2-106.
"Contract for sale". Section 2-106.
"Creditor". Section 1-201.
"Goods". Section 2-105.
"Sale". Section 2-106.
"Seller". Section 2-103.

§ 2–327. Special Incidents of Sale on Approval and Sale or Return.

(1) Under a sale on approval unless otherwise agreed

(a) although the goods are identified to the contract the risk of loss and the title do not pass to the buyer until acceptance; and

(b) use of the goods consistent with the purpose of trial is not acceptance but failure seasonably to notify the seller of election to return the goods is acceptance, and if the goods conform to the contract acceptance of any part is acceptance of the whole; and

(c) after due notification of election to return, the return is at the seller's risk and expense but a merchant buyer must follow any reasonable instructions.

(2) Under a sale or return unless otherwise agreed

(a) the option to return extends to the whole or any commercial unit of the goods while in substantially their original condition, but must be exercised seasonably; and

(b) the return is at the buyer's risk and expense.

Official Comment

Prior Uniform Statutory Provision: Section 19(3), Uniform Sales Act.

Changes: Completely rewritten in preceding and this section.

Purposes of Changes: To make it clear that:

1. In the case of a sale on approval:

If all of the goods involved conform to the contract, the buyer's acceptance of part of the goods constitutes acceptance of the whole. Acceptance of part falls outside the normal intent of the parties in the "on approval" situation and the policy of this Article allowing partial acceptance of a defective delivery has no application here. A case where a buyer takes home two dresses to select one commonly involves two distinct contracts; if not, it is covered by the words "unless otherwise agreed".

2. In the case of a sale or return, the return of any unsold unit merely because it is unsold is the normal intent of the "sale or return" provision, and therefore the right to return for this reason alone is independent of any other action under the contract which would turn on wholly different considerations. On the other hand, where the return of goods is for breach, including return of items resold by the buyer and returned by the ultimate purchasers because of defects, the return procedure is governed not by the present section but by the provisions on the effects and revocation of acceptance.

3. In the case of a sale on approval the risk rests on the seller until acceptance of the goods by the buyer, while in a sale or return the risk remains throughout on the buyer.

4. Notice of election to return given by the buyer in a sale on approval is sufficient to relieve him of any further liability. Actual return by the buyer to the seller is required in the case of a sale or return contract. What constitutes due "giving" of notice, as required in "on approval" sales, is governed by the provisions on good faith and notice. "Seasonable" is used here as defined in Section 1–204. Nevertheless, the provisions of both this Article and of the contract on this point must be read with commercial reason and with full attention to good faith.

Cross References:

Point 1: Sections 2–501, 2–601 and 2–603.

Point 2: Sections 2-607 and 2-608.
Point 4: Sections 1-201 and 1-204.

Definitional Cross References:

"Agreed". Section 1-201.
"Buyer". Section 2-103.
"Commercial unit". Section 2-105.
"Conform". Section 2-106.
"Contract". Section 1-201.
"Goods". Section 2-105.
"Merchant". Section 2-104.
"Notifies". Section 1-201.
"Notification". Section 1-201.
"Sale on approval". Section 2-326.
"Sale or return". Section 2-326.
"Seasonably". Section 1-204.
"Seller". Section 2-103.

§ 2-328. Sale by Auction.

(1) In a sale by auction if goods are put up in lots each lot is the subject of a separate sale.

(2) A sale by auction is complete when the auctioneer so announces by the fall of the hammer or in other customary manner. Where a bid is made while the hammer is falling in acceptance of a prior bid the auctioneer may in his discretion reopen the bidding or declare the goods sold under the bid on which the hammer was falling.

(3) Such a sale is with reserve unless the goods are in explicit terms put up without reserve. In an auction with reserve the auctioneer may withdraw the goods at any time until he announces completion of the sale. In an auction without reserve, after the auctioneer calls for bids on an article or lot, that article or lot cannot be withdrawn unless no bid is made within a reasonable time. In either case a bidder may retract his bid until the auctioneer's announcement of completion of the sale, but a bidder's retraction does not revive any previous bid.

(4) If the auctioneer knowingly receives a bid on the seller's behalf or the seller makes or procures such a bid, and notice has not been given that liberty for such bidding is reserved, the buyer may at his option avoid the sale or take the goods at the price of the last good faith bid prior to the completion of the sale. This subsection shall not apply to any bid at a forced sale.

Official Comment

Prior Uniform Statutory Provision: Section 21, Uniform Sales Act.

Changes: Completely rewritten.

Purposes of Changes: To make it clear that:

1. The auctioneer may in his discretion either reopen the bidding or close the sale on the bid on which the hammer was falling when a bid is made at that moment. The recognition of a bid of this kind by the auctioneer in his discretion does not mean a closing in favor of such a bidder, but only that the bid has been accepted as a continuation of the bidding. If recognized, such a bid discharges the bid on which the hammer was falling when it was made.

2. An auction "with reserve" is the normal procedure. The crucial point, however, for determining the nature of an auction is the "putting up" of the goods. This Article accepts the view that the goods may be withdrawn before they are actually "put up," regardless of whether the auction is advertised as one without reserve, without liability on the part of the auction announcer to persons who are present. This is subject to any peculiar facts which might bring the case within the "firm offer" principle of this Article, but an offer to persons generally would require unmistakable language in order to fall within that section. The prior announcement of the nature of the auc-

tion either as with reserve or without reserve will, however, enter as an "explicit term" in the "putting up" of the goods and conduct thereafter must be governed accordingly. The present section continues the prior rule permitting withdrawal of bids in auctions both with and without reserve; and the rule is made explicit that the retraction of a bid does not revive a prior bid.

Cross Reference:

Point 2: Section 2-205.

Definitional Cross References:

"Buyer". Section 2-103.
"Good faith". Section 1-201.
"Goods". Section 2-105.
"Lot". Section 2-105.
"Notice". Section 1-201.
"Sale". Section 2-106.
"Seller". Section 2-103.

PART 4

TITLE, CREDITORS AND GOOD FAITH PURCHASERS

§ 2-401. Passing of Title; Reservation for Security; Limited Application of This Section.

Each provision of this Article with regard to the rights, obligations and remedies of the seller, the buyer, purchasers or other third parties applies irrespective of title to the goods except where the provision refers to such title. Insofar as situations are not covered by the other provisions of this Article and matters concerning title become material the following rules apply:

(1) Title to goods cannot pass under a contract for sale prior to their identification to the contract (Section 2-501), and unless otherwise explicitly agreed the buyer acquires by their identification a special property as limited by this Act. Any retention or reservation by the seller of the title (property) in goods shipped or delivered to the buyer is limited in effect to a reservation of a security interest. Subject to these provisions and to the provisions of the Article on Secured Transactions (Article 9), title to goods passes from the seller to the buyer in any manner and on any conditions explicitly agreed on by the parties.

(2) Unless otherwise explicitly agreed title passes to the buyer at the time and place at which the seller completes his performance with reference to the physical delivery of the goods, despite any reservation of a security interest and even though a document of title is to be delivered at a different time or place; and in particular and despite any reservation of a security interest by the bill of lading

(a) if the contract requires or authorizes the seller to send the goods to the buyer but does not require him to deliver them at destination, title passes to the buyer at the time and place of shipment; but

(b) if the contract requires delivery at destination, title passes on tender there.

(3) Unless otherwise explicitly agreed where delivery is to be made without moving the goods,

(a) if the seller is to deliver a document of title, title passes at the time when and the place where he delivers such documents; or

(b) if the goods are at the time of contracting already identified and no documents are to be delivered, title passes at the time and place of contracting.

(4) A rejection or other refusal by the buyer to receive or retain the goods, whether or not justified, or a justified revocation of acceptance revests title to the goods in the seller. Such revesting occurs by operation of law and is not a "sale".

Official Comment

Prior Uniform Statutory Provision: See generally, Sections 17, 18, 19 and 20, Uniform Sales Act.

Purposes: To make it clear that:

1. This Article deals with the issues between seller and buyer in terms of step by step performance or non-performance under the contract for sale and not in terms of whether or not "title" to the goods has passed. That the rules of this section in no way alter the rights of either the buyer, seller or third parties declared elsewhere in the Article is made clear by the preamble of this section. This section, however, in no way intends to indicate which line of interpretation should be followed in cases where the applicability of "public" regulation depends upon a "sale" or upon location of "title" without further definition. The basic policy of this Article that known purpose and reason should govern interpretation cannot extend beyond the scope of its own provisions. It is therefore necessary to state what a "sale" is and when title passes under this Article in case the courts deem any public regulation to incorporate the defined term of the "private" law.

2. "Future" goods cannot be the subject of a present sale. Before title can pass the goods must be identified in the manner set forth in Section 2-501. The parties, however, have full liberty to arrange by specific terms for the passing of title to goods which are existing.

3. The "special property" of the buyer in goods identified to the contract is excluded from the definition of "security interest"; its incidents are defined in provisions of this Article such as those on the rights of the seller's creditors, on good faith purchase, on the buyer's right to goods on the seller's insolvency, and on the buyer's right to specific performance or replevin.

4. The factual situations in subsections (2) and (3) upon which passage of title turn actually base the test upon the time when the seller has finally committed himself in regard to specific goods. Thus in a "shipment" contract he commits himself by the act of making the shipment. If shipment is not contemplated subsection (3) turns on the seller's final commitment, i.e. the delivery of documents or the making of the contract.

Cross References:

Point 2: Sections 2-102, 2-501 and 2-502.

Point 3: Sections 1-201, 2-402, 2-403, 2-502 and 2-716.

Definitional Cross References:

"Agreement". Section 1-201.
"Bill of lading". Section 1-201.
"Buyer". Section 2-103.
"Contract". Section 1-201.
"Contract for sale". Section 2-106.
"Delivery". Section 1-201.
"Document of title". Section 1-201.
"Good faith". Section 2-103.
"Goods". Section 2-105.
"Party". Section 1-201.
"Purchaser". Section 1-201.
"Receipt" of goods. Section 2-103.
"Remedy". Section 1-201.
"Rights". Section 1-201.
"Sale". Section 2-106.
"Security interest". Section 1-201.
"Seller". Section 2-103.
"Send". Section 1-201.

§ 2-402. Rights of Seller's Creditors Against Sold Goods.

(1) Except as provided in subsections (2) and (3), rights of unsecured creditors of the seller with respect to goods which have been identified to a contract for sale are subject to the buyer's rights to recover the goods under this Article (Sections 2-502 and 2-716).

(2) A creditor of the seller may treat a sale or an identification of goods to a contract for sale as void if as against him a retention of possession by the seller is fraudulent under any rule of law of the state where the goods are situated, except that retention of possession in good faith and current course of trade by a merchant-seller for a commercially reasonable time after a sale or identification is not fraudulent.

(3) Nothing in this Article shall be deemed to impair the rights of creditors of the seller

(a) under the provisions of the Article on Secured Transactions (Article 9); or

(b) where identification to the contract or delivery is made not in current course of trade but in satisfaction of or as security for a pre-existing claim for money, security or the like and is made under circumstances which under any rule of law of the state where the goods are situated would apart from this Article constitute the transaction a fraudulent transfer or voidable preference.

Official Comment

Prior Uniform Statutory Provision: Subsection (2)—Section 26, Uniform Sales Act; Subsections (1) and (3)—none.

Changes: Rephrased.

Purposes of Changes and New Matter: To avoid confusion on ordinary issues between current sellers and buyers and issues in the field of preference and hindrance by making it clear that:

1. Local law on questions of hindrance of creditors by the seller's retention of possession of the goods are outside the scope of this Article, but retention of possession in the current course of trade is legitimate. Transactions which fall within the law's policy against improper preferences are reserved from the protection of this Article.

2. The retention of possession of the goods by a merchant seller for a commercially reasonable time after a sale or identification in current course is exempted from attack as fraudulent. Similarly, the provisions of subsection (3) have no application to identification or delivery made in the current course of trade, as measured against general commercial understanding of what a "current" transaction is.

Definitional Cross References:

"Contract for sale". Section 2-106.
"Creditor". Section 1-201.
"Good faith". Section 2-103.
"Goods". Section 2-105.
"Merchant". Section 2-104.
"Money". Section 1-201.
"Reasonable time". Section 1-204.
"Rights". Section 1-201.
"Sale". Section 2-106.
"Seller". Section 2-103.

§ 2-403. Power to Transfer; Good Faith Purchase of Goods; "Entrusting".

(1) A purchaser of goods acquires all title which his transferor had or had power to transfer except that a purchaser of a limited interest acquires rights

only to the extent of the interest purchased. A person with voidable title has power to transfer a good title to a good faith purchaser for value. When goods have been delivered under a transaction of purchase the purchaser has such power even though

(a) the transferor was deceived as to the identity of the purchaser, or

(b) the delivery was in exchange for a check which is later dishonored, or

(c) it was agreed that the transaction was to be a "cash sale", or

(d) the delivery was procured through fraud punishable as larcenous under the criminal law.

(2) Any entrusting of possession of goods to a merchant who deals in goods of that kind gives him power to transfer all rights of the entruster to a buyer in ordinary course of business.

(3) "Entrusting" includes any delivery and any acquiescence in retention of possession regardless of any condition expressed between the parties to the delivery or acquiescence and regardless of whether the procurement of the entrusting or the possessor's disposition of the goods have been such as to be larcenous under the criminal law.

[*Publisher's Editorial Note: If a state adopts the repealer of Article 6—Bulk Transfers (Alternative A), subsec. (4) should read as follows:*]

(4) The rights of other purchasers of goods and of lien creditors are governed by the Articles on Secured Transactions (Article 9) and Documents of Title (Article 7).

[*Publisher's Editorial Note: If a state adopts Revised Article 6—Bulk Sales (Alternative B), subsec. (4) should read as follows:*]

(4) The rights of other purchasers of goods and of lien creditors are governed by the Articles on Secured Transactions (Article 9), Bulk Sales (Article 6) and Documents of Title (Article 7).

As amended in 1988.

For material relating to the changes made in text in 1988, see section 3 of Alternative A (Repealer of Article 6—Bulk Transfers) and Conforming Amendment to Section 2–403 following end of Alternative B (Revised Article 6—Bulk Sales).

Official Comment

Prior Uniform Statutory Provision: Sections 20(4), 23, 24, 25, Uniform Sales Act; Section 9, especially 9(2), Uniform Trust Receipts Act; Section 9, Uniform Conditional Sales Act.

Changes: Consolidated and rewritten.

Purposes of Changes: To gather together a series of prior uniform statutory provisions and the case-law thereunder and to state a unified and simplified policy on good faith purchase of goods.

1. The basic policy of our law allowing transfer of such title as the transferor has is generally continued and expanded under subsection (1). In this respect the provisions of the section are applicable to a person taking by any form of "purchase" as defined by this Act. Moreover the policy of this Act expressly providing

for the application of supplementary general principles of law to sales transactions wherever appropriate joins with the present section to continue unimpaired all rights acquired under the law of agency or of apparent agency or ownership or other estoppel, whether based on statutory provisions or on case law principles. The section also leaves unimpaired the powers given to selling factors under the earlier Factors Acts. In addition subsection (1) provides specifically for the protection of the good faith purchaser for value in a number of specific situations which have been troublesome under prior law.

On the other hand, the contract of purchase is of course limited by its own terms as in a case of pledge for a limited amount or of sale of a fractional interest in goods.

2. The many particular situations in which a buyer in ordinary course of business from a dealer has been protected against reservation of property or other hidden interest are gathered by subsections (2)–(4) into a single principle protecting persons who buy in ordinary course out of inventory. Consignors have no reason to complain, nor have lenders who hold a security interest in the inventory, since the very purpose of goods in inventory is to be turned into cash by sale.

The principle is extended in subsection (3) to fit with the abolition of the old law of "cash sale" by subsection (1)(c). It is also freed from any technicalities depending on the extended law of larceny; such extension of the concept of theft to include trick, particular types of fraud, and the like is for the purpose of helping conviction of the offender; it has no proper application to the long-standing policy of civil protection of buyers from persons guilty of such trick or fraud. Finally, the policy is extended, in the interest of simplicity and sense, to any entrusting by a bailor; this is in consonance with the explicit provisions of Section 7–205 on the powers of a warehouseman who is also in the business of buying and selling fungible goods of the kind he warehouses. As to entrusting by a secured party, subsection (2) is limited by the more specific provisions of Section 9–307(1), which deny protection to a person buying farm products from a person engaged in farming operations.

3. The definition of "buyer in ordinary course of business" (Section 1–201) is effective here and preserves the essence of the healthy limitations engrafted by the case-law on the older statutes. The older loose concept of good faith and wide definition of value combined to create apparent good faith purchasers in many situations in which the result outraged common sense; the court's solution was to protect the original title especially by use of "cash sale" or of over-technical construction of the enabling clauses of the statutes. But such rulings then turned into limitations on the proper protection of buyers in the ordinary market. Section 1–201(9) cuts down the category of buyer in ordinary course in such fashion as to take care of the results of the cases, but with no price either in confusion or in injustice to proper dealings in the normal market.

4. Except as provided in subsection (1), the rights of purchasers other than buyers in ordinary course are left to the Articles on Secured Transactions, Documents of Title, and Bulk Sales.

Cross References:

Point 1: Sections 1–103 and 1–201.

Point 2: Sections 1–201, 2–402, 7–205 and 9–307(1).

Points 3 and 4: Sections 1–102, 1–201, 2–104, 2–707 and Articles 6, 7 and 9.

Definitional Cross References:

"Buyer in ordinary course of business". Section 1–201.

"Good faith". Sections 1–201 and 2–103.

"Goods". Section 2–105.

"Person". Section 1–201.

"Purchaser". Section 1–201.

"Signed". Section 1–201.

"Term". Section 1–201.

"Value". Section 1–201.

PART 5

PERFORMANCE

§ 2-501. Insurable Interest in Goods; Manner of Identification of Goods.

(1) The buyer obtains a special property and an insurable interest in goods by identification of existing goods as goods to which the contract refers even though the goods so identified are non-conforming and he has an option to return or reject them. Such identification can be made at any time and in any manner explicitly agreed to by the parties. In the absence of explicit agreement identification occurs

(a) when the contract is made if it is for the sale of goods already existing and identified;

(b) if the contract is for the sale of future goods other than those described in paragraph (c), when goods are shipped, marked or otherwise designated by the seller as goods to which the contract refers;

(c) when the crops are planted or otherwise become growing crops or the young are conceived if the contract is for the sale of unborn young to be born within twelve months after contracting or for the sale of crops to be harvested within twelve months or the next normal harvest season after contracting whichever is longer.

(2) The seller retains an insurable interest in goods so long as title to or any security interest in the goods remains in him and where the identification is by the seller alone he may until default or insolvency or notification to the buyer that the identification is final substitute other goods for those identified.

(3) Nothing in this section impairs any insurable interest recognized under any other statute or rule of law.

Official Comment

Prior Uniform Statutory Provision: See Sections 17 and 19, Uniform Sales Act.

Purposes:

1. The present section deals with the manner of identifying goods to the contract so that an insurable interest in the buyer and the rights set forth in the next section will accrue. Generally speaking, identification may be made in any manner "explicitly agreed to" by the parties. The rules of paragraphs (a), (b) and (c) apply only in the absence of such "explicit agreement".

2. In the ordinary case identification of particular existing goods as goods to which the contract refers is unambiguous and may occur in one of many ways. It is possible, however, for the identification to be tentative or contingent. In view of the limited effect given to identification by this Article, the general policy is to resolve all doubts in favor of identification.

3. The provision of this section as to "explicit agreement" clarifies the present confusion in the law of sales which has arisen from the fact that under prior uniform legislation all rules of presumption with reference to the passing of title or to appropriation (which in turn depended upon identification) were regarded as subject to the contrary intention of the par-

ties or of the party appropriating. Such uncertainty is reduced to a minimum under this section by requiring "explicit agreement" of the parties before the rules of paragraphs (a), (b) and (c) are displaced—as they would be by a term giving the buyer power to select the goods. An "explicit" agreement, however, need not necessarily be found in the terms used in the particular transaction. Thus, where a usage of the trade has previously been made explicit by reduction to a standard set of "rules and regulations" currently incorporated by reference into the contracts of the parties, a relevant provision of those "rules and regulations" is "explicit" within the meaning of this section.

4. In view of the limited function of identification there is no requirement in this section that the goods be in deliverable state or that all of the seller's duties with respect to the processing of the goods be completed in order that identification occur. For example, despite identification the risk of loss remains on the seller under the risk of loss provisions until completion of his duties as to the goods and all of his remedies remain dependent upon his not defaulting under the contract.

5. Undivided shares in an identified fungible bulk, such as grain in an elevator or oil in a storage tank, can be sold. The mere making of the contract with reference to an undivided share in an identified fungible bulk is enough under subsection (a) to effect an identification if there is no explicit agreement otherwise. The seller's duty, however, to segregate and deliver according to the contract is not affected by such an identification but is controlled by other provisions of this Article.

6. Identification of crops under paragraph (c) is made upon planting only if they are to be harvested within the year or within the next normal harvest season. The phrase "next normal harvest season" fairly includes nursery stock raised for normally quick "harvest," but plainly excludes a "timber" crop to which the concept of a harvest "season" is inapplicable.

Paragraph (c) is also applicable to a crop of wool or the young of animals to be born within twelve months after contracting. The product of a lumbering, mining or fishing operation, though seasonal, is not within the concept of "growing". Identification under a contract for all or part of the output of such an operation can be effected early in the operation.

Cross References:

Point 1: Section 2-502.

Point 4: Sections 2-509, 2-510 and 2-703.

Point 5: Sections 2-105, 2-308, 2-503 and 2-509.

Point 6: Sections 2-105(1), 2-107(1) and 2-402.

Definitional Cross References:

"Agreement". Section 1-201.
"Contract". Section 1-201.
"Contract for sale". Section 2-106.
"Future goods". Section 2-105.
"Goods". Section 2-105.
"Notification". Section 1-201.
"Party". Section 1-201.
"Sale". Section 2-106.
"Security interest". Section 1-201.
"Seller". Section 2-103.

§ 2-502. Buyer's Right to Goods on Seller's Insolvency.

(1) Subject to subsection (2) and even though the goods have not been shipped a buyer who has paid a part or all of the price of goods in which he has a special property under the provisions of the immediately preceding section may on making and keeping good a tender of any unpaid portion of their price recover them from the seller if the seller becomes insolvent within ten days after receipt of the first installment on their price.

(2) If the identification creating his special property has been made by the buyer he acquires the right to recover the goods only if they conform to the contract for sale.

Official Comment

Prior Uniform Statutory Provision: Compare Sections 17, 18 and 19, Uniform Sales Act.

Purposes:

1. This section gives an additional right to the buyer as a result of identification of the goods to the contract in the manner provided in Section 2-501. The buyer is given a right to the goods on the seller's insolvency occurring within 10 days after he receives the first installment on their price.

2. The question of whether the buyer also acquires a security interest in identified goods and has rights to the goods when insolvency takes place after the ten-day period provided in this section depends upon compliance with the provisions of the Article on Secured Transactions (Article 9).

3. Subsection (2) is included to preclude the possibility of unjust enrichment which exists if the buyer were permitted to recover goods even though they were greatly superior in quality or quantity to that called for by the contract for sale.

Cross References:

Point 1: Sections 1-201 and 2-702.
Point 2: Article 9.

Definitional Cross References:

"Buyer". Section 2-103.
"Conform". Section 2-106.
"Contract for sale". Section 2-106.
"Goods". Section 2-105.
"Insolvent". Section 1-201.
"Rights". Section 1-201.
"Seller". Section 2-103.

§ 2-503. Manner of Seller's Tender of Delivery.

(1) Tender of delivery requires that the seller put and hold conforming goods at the buyer's disposition and give the buyer any notification reasonably necessary to enable him to take delivery. The manner, time and place for tender are determined by the agreement and this Article, and in particular

(a) tender must be at a reasonable hour, and if it is of goods they must be kept available for the period reasonably necessary to enable the buyer to take possession; but

(b) unless otherwise agreed the buyer must furnish facilities reasonably suited to the receipt of the goods.

(2) Where the case is within the next section respecting shipment tender requires that the seller comply with its provisions.

(3) Where the seller is required to deliver at a particular destination tender requires that he comply with subsection (1) and also in any appropriate case tender documents as described in subsections (4) and (5) of this section.

(4) Where goods are in the possession of a bailee and are to be delivered without being moved

(a) tender requires that the seller either tender a negotiable document of title covering such goods or procure acknowledgment by the bailee of the buyer's right to possession of the goods; but

(b) tender to the buyer of a non-negotiable document of title or of a written direction to the bailee to deliver is sufficient tender unless the buyer seasonably objects, and receipt by the bailee of notification of the buyer's rights fixes those rights as against the bailee and all third persons; but risk of loss of the goods and of any failure by the bailee to honor the non-negotiable document of title or to obey the direction remains on the seller until the buyer has had a reasonable time to present the document or direction, and a refusal by the bailee to honor the document or to obey the direction defeats the tender.

(5) Where the contract requires the seller to deliver documents

(a) he must tender all such documents in correct form, except as provided in this Article with respect to bills of lading in a set (subsection (2) of Section 2-323); and

(b) tender through customary banking channels is sufficient and dishonor of a draft accompanying the documents constitutes non-acceptance or rejection.

Official Comment

Prior Uniform Statutory Provision: See Sections 11, 19, 20, 43(3) and (4), 46 and 51, Uniform Sales Act.

Changes: The general policy of the above sections is continued and supplemented but subsection (3) changes the rule of prior section 19(5) as to what constitutes a "destination" contract and subsection (4) incorporates a minor correction as to tender of delivery of goods in the possession of a bailee.

Purposes of Changes:

1. The major general rules governing the manner of proper or due tender of delivery are gathered in this section. The term "tender" is used in this Article in two different senses. In one sense it refers to "due tender" which contemplates an offer coupled with a present ability to fulfill all the conditions resting on the tendering party and must be followed by actual performance if the other party shows himself ready to proceed. Unless the context unmistakably indicates otherwise this is the meaning of "tender" in this Article and the occasional addition of the word "due" is only for clarity and emphasis. At other times it is used to refer to an offer of goods or documents under a contract as if in fulfillment of its conditions even though there is a defect when measured against the contract obligation. Used in either sense, however, "tender" connotes such performance by the tendering party as puts the other party in default if he fails to proceed in some manner.

2. The seller's general duty to tender and deliver is laid down in Section 2-301 and more particularly in Section 2-507. The seller's right to a receipt if he demands one and receipts are customary is governed by Section 1-205. Subsection (1) of the present section proceeds to set forth two primary requirements of tender: first, that the seller "put and hold conforming goods at the buyer's disposition" and, second, that he "give the buyer any notice reasonably necessary to enable him to take delivery."

In cases in which payment is due and demanded upon delivery the "buyer's disposition" is qualified by the seller's right to retain control of the goods until payment by the provision of this Article on delivery on condition. However, where the seller is demanding payment on delivery he must first allow the buyer to inspect the goods in order to avoid impairing his tender unless the contract for sale is on C.I.F., C.O.D., cash against documents or similar terms negating the privilege of inspection before payment.

In the case of contracts involving documents the seller can "put and hold conforming goods at the buyer's disposition" under subsection (1) by tendering documents which give the buyer complete control of the goods under the provisions of Article 7 on due negotiation.

3. Under paragraph (a) of subsection (1) usage of the trade and the circumstances of the particular case determine

what is a reasonable hour for tender and what constitutes a reasonable period of holding the goods available.

4. The buyer must furnish reasonable facilities for the receipt of the goods tendered by the seller under subsection (1), paragraph (b). This obligation of the buyer is no part of the seller's tender.

5. For the purposes of subsections (2) and (3) there is omitted from this Article the rule under prior uniform legislation that a term requiring the seller to pay the freight or cost of transportation to the buyer is equivalent to an agreement by the seller to deliver to the buyer or at an agreed destination. This omission is with the specific intention of negating the rule, for under this Article the "shipment" contract is regarded as the normal one and the "destination" contract as the variant type. The seller is not obligated to deliver at a named destination and bear the concurrent risk of loss until arrival, unless he has specifically agreed so to deliver or the commercial understanding of the terms used by the parties contemplates such delivery.

6. Paragraph (a) of subsection (4) continues the rule of the prior uniform legislation as to acknowledgment by the bailee. Paragraph (b) of subsection (4) adopts the rule that between the buyer and the seller the risk of loss remains on the seller during a period reasonable for securing acknowledgment of the transfer from the bailee, while as against all other parties the buyer's rights are fixed as of the time the bailee receives notice of the transfer.

7. Under subsection (5) documents are never "required" except where there is an express contract term or it is plainly implicit in the peculiar circumstances of the case or in a usage of trade. Documents may, of course, be "authorized" although not required, but such cases are not within the scope of this subsection. When documents are required, there are three main requirements of this subsection: (1) "All": each required document is essential to a proper tender; (2) "Such": the documents must be the ones actually required by the contract in terms of source and substance; (3) "Correct form": All documents must be in correct form.

When a prescribed document cannot be procured, a question of fact arises under the provision of this Article on substituted performance as to whether the agreed manner of delivery is actually commercially impracticable and whether the substitute is commercially reasonable.

Cross References:

Point 2: Sections 1–205, 2–301, 2–310, 2–507 and 2–513 and Article 7.

Point 5: Sections 2–308, 2–310 and 2–509.

Point 7: Section 2–614(1).

Specific matters involving tender are covered in many additional sections of this Article. See Sections 1–205, 2–301, 2–306 to 2–319, 2–321(3), 2–504, 2–507(2), 2–511(1), 2–513, 2–612 and 2–614.

Definitional Cross References:

"Agreement". Section 1–201.
"Bill of lading". Section 1–201.
"Buyer". Section 2–103.
"Conforming". Section 2–106.
"Contract". Section 1–201.
"Delivery". Section 1–201.
"Dishonor". Section 3–508.
"Document of title". Section 1–201.
"Draft". Section 3–104.
"Goods". Section 2–105.
"Notification". Section 1–201.
"Reasonable time". Section 1–204.
"Receipt" of goods. Section 2–103.
"Rights". Section 1–201.
"Seasonably". Section 1–204.
"Seller". Section 2–103.
"Written". Section 1–201.

§ 2–504. Shipment by Seller.

Where the seller is required or authorized to send the goods to the buyer and the contract does not require him to deliver them at a particular destination, then unless otherwise agreed he must

(a) put the goods in the possession of such a carrier and make such a contract for their transportation as may be reasonable having regard to the nature of the goods and other circumstances of the case; and

(b) obtain and promptly deliver or tender in due form any document necessary to enable the buyer to obtain possession of the goods or otherwise required by the agreement or by usage of trade; and

(c) promptly notify the buyer of the shipment.

Failure to notify the buyer under paragraph (c) or to make a proper contract under paragraph (a) is a ground for rejection only if material delay or loss ensues.

Official Comment

Prior Uniform Statutory Provision: Section 46, Uniform Sales Act.

Changes: Rewritten.

Purposes of Changes: To continue the general policy of the prior uniform statutory provision while incorporating certain modifications with respect to the requirement that the contract with the carrier be made expressly on behalf of the buyer and as to the necessity of giving notice of the shipment to the buyer, so that:

1. The section is limited to "shipment" contracts as contrasted with "destination" contracts or contracts for delivery at the place where the goods are located. The general principles embodied in this section cover the special cases of F.O.B. point of shipment contracts and C.I.F. and C. & F. contracts. Under the preceding section on manner of tender of delivery, due tender by the seller requires that he comply with the requirements of this section in appropriate cases.

2. The contract to be made with the carrier under paragraph (a) must conform to all express terms of the agreement, subject to any substitution necessary because of failure of agreed facilities as provided in the later provision on substituted performance. However, under the policies of this Article on good faith and commercial standards and on buyer's rights on improper delivery, the requirements of explicit provisions must be read in terms of their commercial and not their literal meaning. This policy is made express with respect to bills of lading in a set in the provision of this Article on form of bills of lading required in overseas shipment.

3. In the absence of agreement, the provision of this Article on options and cooperation respecting performance gives the seller the choice of any reasonable carrier, routing and other arrangements. Whether or not the shipment is at the buyer's expense the seller must see to any arrangements, reasonable in the circumstances, such as refrigeration, watering of live stock, protection against cold, the sending along of any necessary help, selection of specialized cars and the like for paragraph (a) is intended to cover all necessary arrangements whether made by contract with the carrier or otherwise. There is, however, a proper relaxation of such requirements if the buyer is himself in a position to make the appropriate arrangements and the seller gives him reasonable notice of the need to do so. It is an improper contract under paragraph (a) for the seller to agree with the carrier to a limited valuation below the true value and thus cut off the buyer's opportunity to recover from the carrier in the event of loss, when the risk of shipment is placed on the buyer by his contract with the seller.

4. Both the language of paragraph (b) and the nature of the situation it concerns indicate that the requirement that the seller must obtain and deliver promptly to the buyer in due form any document necessary to enable him to obtain possession of the goods is intended to cumulate with the other duties of the

seller such as those covered in paragraph (a).

In this connection, in the case of pool car shipments a delivery order furnished by the seller on the pool car consignee, or on the carrier for delivery out of a larger quantity, satisfies the requirements of paragraph (b) unless the contract requires some other form of document.

5. This Article, unlike the prior uniform statutory provision, makes it the seller's duty to notify the buyer of shipment in all cases. The consequences of his failure to do so, however, are limited in that the buyer may reject on this ground only where material delay or loss ensues.

A standard and acceptable manner of notification in open credit shipments is the sending of an invoice and in the case of documentary contracts is the prompt forwarding of the documents as under paragraph (b) of this section. It is also usual to send on a straight bill of lading but this is not necessary to the required notification. However, should such a document prove necessary or convenient to the buyer, as in the case of loss and claim against the carrier, good faith would require the seller to send it on request.

Frequently the agreement expressly requires prompt notification as by wire or cable. Such a term may be of the essence and the final clause of paragraph (c) does not prevent the parties from making this a particular ground for rejection. To have this vital and irreparable effect upon the seller's duties, such a term should be part of the "dickered" terms written in any "form," or should otherwise be called seasonably and sharply to the seller's attention.

6. Generally, under the final sentence of the section, rejection by the buyer is justified only when the seller's dereliction as to any of the requirements of this section in fact is followed by material delay or damage. It rests on the seller, so far as concerns matters not within the peculiar knowledge of the buyer, to establish that his error has not been followed by events which justify rejection.

Cross References:

Point 1: Sections 2-319, 2-320 and 2-503(2).

Point 2: Sections 1-203, 2-323(2), 2-601 and 2-614(1).

Point 3: Section 2-311(2).

Point 5: Section 1-203.

Definitional Cross References:

"Agreement". Section 1-201.
"Buyer". Section 2-103.
"Contract". Section 1-201.
"Delivery". Section 1-201.
"Goods". Section 2-105.
"Notifies". Section 1-201.
"Seller". Section 2-103.
"Send". Section 1-201.
"Usage of trade". Section 1-205.

§ 2-505. Seller's Shipment Under Reservation.

(1) Where the seller has identified goods to the contract by or before shipment:

(a) his procurement of a negotiable bill of lading to his own order or otherwise reserves in him a security interest in the goods. His procurement of the bill to the order of a financing agency or of the buyer indicates in addition only the seller's expectation of transferring that interest to the person named.

(b) a non-negotiable bill of lading to himself or his nominee reserves possession of the goods as security but except in a case of conditional delivery (subsection (2) of Section 2-507) a non-negotiable bill of lading naming the buyer as consignee reserves no security interest even though the seller retains possession of the bill of lading.

(2) When shipment by the seller with reservation of a security interest is in violation of the contract for sale it constitutes an improper contract for transportation within the preceding section but impairs neither the rights given to the buyer by shipment and identification of the goods to the contract nor the seller's powers as a holder of a negotiable document.

Official Comment

Prior Uniform Statutory Provision: Section 20(2), (3), (4), Uniform Sales Act.

Changes: Completely rephrased, the "powers" of the parties in cases of reservation being emphasized primarily rather than the "rightfulness" of reservation.

Purposes of Changes: To continue in general the policy of the prior uniform statutory provision with certain modifications of emphasis and language, so that:

1. The security interest reserved to the seller under subsection (1) is restricted to securing payment or performance by the buyer and the seller is strictly limited in his disposition and control of the goods as against the buyer and third parties. Under this Article, the provision as to the passing of interest expressly applies "despite any reservation of security title" and also provides that the "rights, obligations and remedies" of the parties are not altered by the incidence of title generally. The security interest, therefore, must be regarded as a means given to the seller to enforce his rights against the buyer which is unaffected by and in turn does not affect the location of title generally. The rules set forth in subsection (1) are not to be altered by any apparent "contrary intent" of the parties as to passing of title, since the rights and remedies of the parties to the contract of sale, as defined in this Article, rest on the contract and its performance or breach and not on stereotyped presumptions as to the location of title.

This Article does not attempt to regulate local procedure in regard to the effective maintenance of the seller's security interest when the action is in replevin by the buyer against the carrier.

2. Every shipment of identified goods under a negotiable bill of lading reserves a security interest in the seller under subsection (1) paragraph (a).

It is frequently convenient for the seller to make the bill of lading to the order of a nominee such as his agent at destination, the financing agency to which he expects to negotiate the document or the bank issuing a credit to him. In many instances, also, the buyer is made the order party. This Article does not deal directly with the question as to whether a bill of lading made out by the seller to the order of a nominee gives the carrier notice of any rights which the nominee may have so as to limit its freedom or obligation to honor the bill of lading in the hands of the seller as the original shipper if the expected negotiation fails. This is dealt with in the Article on Documents of Title (Article 7).

3. A non-negotiable bill of lading taken to a party other than the buyer under subsection (1) paragraph (b) reserves possession of the goods as security in the seller but if he seeks to withhold the goods improperly the buyer can tender payment and recover them.

4. In the case of a shipment by non-negotiable bill of lading taken to a buyer, the seller, under subsection (1) retains no security interest or possession as against the buyer and by the shipment he *de facto* loses control as against the carrier except where he rightfully and effectively stops delivery in transit. In cases in which the contract gives the seller the right to payment against delivery, the seller, by making an immediate demand for payment, can show that his delivery is conditional, but this does not prevent the buyer's power to transfer full title to a sub-buyer in ordinary course or other purchaser under Section 2–403.

5. Under subsection (2) an improper reservation by the seller which would con-

stitute a breach in no way impairs such of the buyer's rights as result from identification of the goods. The security title reserved by the seller under subsection (1) does not protect his holding of the document or the goods for the purpose of exacting more than is due him under the contract.

Cross References:

Point 1: Section 1-201.
Point 2: Article 7.
Point 3: Sections 2-501(2) and 2-504.
Point 4: Sections 2-403, 2-507(2) and 2-705.
Point 5: Sections 2-310, 2-319(4), 2-320(4), 2-501 and 2-502 and Article 7.

Definitional Cross References:

"Bill of lading". Section 1-201.
"Buyer". Section 2-103.
"Consignee". Section 7-102.
"Contract". Section 1-201.
"Contract for sale". Section 2-106.
"Delivery". Section 1-201.
"Financing agency". Section 2-104.
"Goods". Section 2-105.
"Holder". Section 1-201.
"Person". Section 1-201.
"Security interest". Section 1-201.
"Seller". Section 2-103.

§ 2-506. Rights of Financing Agency.

(1) A financing agency by paying or purchasing for value a draft which relates to a shipment of goods acquires to the extent of the payment or purchase and in addition to its own rights under the draft and any document of title securing it any rights of the shipper in the goods including the right to stop delivery and the shipper's right to have the draft honored by the buyer.

(2) The right to reimbursement of a financing agency which has in good faith honored or purchased the draft under commitment to or authority from the buyer is not impaired by subsequent discovery of defects with reference to any relevant document which was apparently regular on its face.

Official Comment

Prior Uniform Statutory Provision: None.

Purposes:

1. "Financing agency" is broadly defined in this Article to cover every normal instance in which a party aids or intervenes in the financing of a sales transaction. The term as used in subsection (1) is not in any sense intended as a limitation and covers any other appropriate situation which may arise outside the scope of the definition.

2. "Paying" as used in subsection (1) is typified by the letter of credit, or "authority to pay" situation in which a banker, by arrangement with the buyer or other consignee, pays on his behalf a draft for the price of the goods. It is immaterial whether the draft is formally drawn on the party paying or his principal, whether it is a sight draft paid in cash or a time draft "paid" in the first instance by acceptance, or whether the payment is viewed as absolute or conditional. All of these cases constitute "payment" under this subsection. Similarly, "purchasing for value" is used to indicate the whole area of financing by the seller's banker, and the principle of subsection (1) is applicable without any niceties of distinction between "purchase," "discount," "advance against collection" or the like. But it is important to notice that the only right to have the draft honored that is acquired is that *against the buyer*; if any right against any one else is claimed it will have to be under some separate obligation of that other person. A letter of credit does not necessarily protect *purchasers* of drafts. See Article 5. And for the relations of the parties to documentary drafts see Part 5 of Article 4.

3. Subsection (1) is made applicable to payments or advances against a draft

which "relates to" a shipment of goods and this has been chosen as a term of maximum breadth. In particular the term is intended to cover the case of a draft against an invoice or against a delivery order. Further, it is unnecessary that there be an explicit assignment of the invoice attached to the draft to bring the transaction within the reason of this subsection.

4. After shipment, "the rights of the shipper in the goods" are merely security rights and are subject to the buyer's right to force delivery upon tender of the price. The rights acquired by the financing agency are similarly limited and, moreover, if the agency fails to procure any outstanding negotiable document of title, it may find its exercise of these rights hampered or even defeated by the seller's disposition of the document to a third party. This section does not attempt to create any new rights in the financing agency against the carrier which would force the latter to honor a stop order from the agency, a stranger to the shipment, or any new rights against a holder to whom a document of title has been duly negotiated under Article 7.

Cross References:

Point 1: Section 2-104(2) and Article 4.

Point 2: Part 5 of Article 4, and Article 5.

Point 4: Sections 2-501 and 2-502(1) and Article 7.

Definitional Cross References:

"Buyer". Section 2-103.
"Document of title". Section 1-201.
"Draft". Section 3-104.
"Financing agency". Section 2-104.
"Good faith". Section 2-103.
"Goods". Section 2-105.
"Honor". Section 1-201.
"Purchase". Section 1-201.
"Rights". Section 1-201.
"Value". Section 1-201.

§ 2-507. Effect of Seller's Tender; Delivery on Condition.

(1) Tender of delivery is a condition to the buyer's duty to accept the goods and, unless otherwise agreed, to his duty to pay for them. Tender entitles the seller to acceptance of the goods and to payment according to the contract.

(2) Where payment is due and demanded on the delivery to the buyer of goods or documents of title, his right as against the seller to retain or dispose of them is conditional upon his making the payment due.

Official Comment

Prior Uniform Statutory Provision: See Sections 11, 41, 42 and 69, Uniform Sales Act.

Purposes:

1. Subsection (1) continues the policies of the prior uniform statutory provisions with respect to tender and delivery by the seller. Under this Article the same rules in these matters are applied to present sales and to contracts for sale. But the provisions of this subsection must be read within the framework of the other sections of this Article which bear upon the question of delivery and payment.

2. The "unless otherwise agreed" provision of subsection (1) is directed primarily to cases in which payment in advance has been promised or a letter of credit term has been included. Payment "according to the contract" contemplates immediate payment, payment at the end of an agreed credit term, payment by a time acceptance or the like. Under this Act, "contract" means the total obligation in law which results from the parties' agreement including the effect of this Article. In this context, therefore, there must be considered the effect in law of such provisions as those on means and manner of

payment and on failure of agreed means and manner of payment.

3. Subsection (2) deals with the effect of a conditional delivery by the seller and in such a situation makes the buyer's "right as against the seller" conditional upon payment. These words are used as words of limitation to conform with the policy set forth in the bona fide purchase sections of this Article. Should the seller after making such a conditional delivery fail to follow up his rights, the condition is waived. This subsection (2) codifies the cash seller's right of reclamation which is in the nature of a lien. There is no specific time limit for a cash seller to exercise the right of reclamation. However, the right will be defeated by delay causing prejudice to the buyer, waiver, estoppel, or ratification of the buyer's right to retain possession. Common law rules and precedents governing such principles are applicable (Section 1–103). If third parties are involved, Section 2–403(1) protects good faith purchasers. See PEB Commentary No. 1, dated March 10, 1990 [Appendix V, infra].

Cross References:

Point 1: Sections 2–310, 2–503, 2–511, 2–601 and 2–711 to 2–713.

Point 2: Sections 1–201, 2–511 and 2–614.

Point 3: Sections 2–401, 2–403, and 2–702(1)(b).

Definitional Cross References:

"Buyer". Section 2–103.
"Contract". Section 1–201.
"Delivery". Section 1–201.
"Document of title". Section 1–201.
"Goods". Section 2–105.
"Rights". Section 1–201.
"Seller". Section 2–103.

§ 2–508. Cure by Seller of Improper Tender or Delivery; Replacement.

(1) Where any tender or delivery by the seller is rejected because non-conforming and the time for performance has not yet expired, the seller may seasonably notify the buyer of his intention to cure and may then within the contract time make a conforming delivery.

(2) Where the buyer rejects a non-conforming tender which the seller had reasonable grounds to believe would be acceptable with or without money allowance the seller may if he seasonably notifies the buyer have a further reasonable time to substitute a conforming tender.

Official Comment

Prior Uniform Statutory Provision: None.

Purposes:

1. Subsection (1) permits a seller who has made a non-conforming tender in any case to make a conforming delivery within the contract time upon seasonable notification to the buyer. It applies even where the seller has taken back the non-conforming goods and refunded the purchase price. He may still make a good tender within the contract period. The closer, however, it is to the contract date, the greater is the necessity for extreme promptness on the seller's part in notifying of his intention to cure, if such notification is to be "seasonable" under this subsection.

The rule of this subsection, moreover, is qualified by its underlying reasons. Thus if, after contracting for June delivery, a buyer later makes known to the seller his need for shipment early in the month and the seller ships accordingly, the "contract time" has been cut down by the supervening modification and the time for cure of tender must be referred to this modified time term.

2. Subsection (2) seeks to avoid injustice to the seller by reason of a surprise

rejection by the buyer. However, the seller is not protected unless he had "reasonable grounds to believe" that the tender would be acceptable. Such reasonable grounds can lie in prior course of dealing, course of performance or usage of trade as well as in the particular circumstances surrounding the making of the contract. The seller is charged with commercial knowledge of any factors in a particular sales situation which require him to comply strictly with his obligations under the contract as, for example, strict conformity of documents in an overseas shipment or the sale of precision parts or chemicals for use in manufacture. Further, if the buyer gives notice either implicitly, as by a prior course of dealing involving rigorous inspections, or expressly, as by the deliberate inclusion of a "no replacement" clause in the contract, the seller is to be held to rigid compliance. If the clause appears in a "form" contract evidence that it is out of line with trade usage or the prior course of dealing and was not called to the seller's attention may be sufficient to show that the seller had reasonable grounds to believe that the tender would be acceptable.

3. The words "a further reasonable time to substitute a conforming tender" are intended as words of limitation to protect the buyer. What is a "reasonable time" depends upon the attending circumstances. Compare Section 2–511 on the comparable case of a seller's surprise demand for legal tender.

4. Existing trade usages permitting variations without rejection but with price allowance enter into the agreement itself as contractual limitations of remedy and are not covered by this section.

Cross References:

Point 2: Section 2–302.
Point 3: Section 2–511.
Point 4: Sections 1–205 and 2–721.

Definitional Cross References:

"Buyer". Section 2–103.
"Conforming". Section 2–106.
"Contract". Section 1–201.
"Money". Section 1–201.
"Notifies". Section 1–201.
"Reasonable time". Section 1–204.
"Seasonably". Section 1–204.
"Seller". Section 2–103.

§ 2–509. Risk of Loss in the Absence of Breach.

(1) Where the contract requires or authorizes the seller to ship the goods by carrier

(a) if it does not require him to deliver them at a particular destination, the risk of loss passes to the buyer when the goods are duly delivered to the carrier even though the shipment is under reservation (Section 2–505); but

(b) if it does require him to deliver them at a particular destination and the goods are there duly tendered while in the possession of the carrier, the risk of loss passes to the buyer when the goods are there duly so tendered as to enable the buyer to take delivery.

(2) Where the goods are held by a bailee to be delivered without being moved, the risk of loss passes to the buyer

(a) on his receipt of a negotiable document of title covering the goods; or

(b) on acknowledgment by the bailee of the buyer's right to possession of the goods; or

(c) after his receipt of a non-negotiable document of title or other written direction to deliver, as provided in subsection (4)(b) of Section 2–503.

(3) In any case not within subsection (1) or (2), the risk of loss passes to the buyer on his receipt of the goods if the seller is a merchant; otherwise the risk passes to the buyer on tender of delivery.

(4) The provisions of this section are subject to contrary agreement of the parties and to the provisions of this Article on sale on approval (Section 2–327) and on effect of breach on risk of loss (Section 2–510).

Official Comment

Prior Uniform Statutory Provision: Section 22, Uniform Sales Act.

Changes: Rewritten, subsection (3) of this section modifying prior law.

Purposes of Changes: To make it clear that:

1. The underlying theory of these sections on risk of loss is the adoption of the contractual approach rather than an arbitrary shifting of the risk with the "property" in the goods. The scope of the present section, therefore, is limited strictly to those cases where there has been no breach by the seller. Where for any reason his delivery or tender fails to conform to the contract, the present section does not apply and the situation is governed by the provisions on effect of breach on risk of loss.

2. The provisions of subsection (1) apply where the contract "requires or authorizes" shipment of the goods. This language is intended to be construed parallel to comparable language in the section on shipment by seller. In order that the goods be "duly delivered to the carrier" under paragraph (a) a contract must be entered into with the carrier which will satisfy the requirements of the section on shipment by the seller and the delivery must be made under circumstances which will enable the seller to take any further steps necessary to a due tender. The underlying reason of this subsection does not require that the shipment be made after contracting, but where, for example, the seller buys the goods afloat and later diverts the shipment to the buyer, he must identify the goods to the contract before the risk of loss can pass. To transfer the risk it is enough that a proper shipment and a proper identification come to apply to the same goods although, aside from special agreement, the risk will not pass retroactively to the time of shipment in such a case.

3. Whether the contract involves delivery at the seller's place of business or at the situs of the goods, a merchant seller cannot transfer risk of loss and it remains upon him until actual receipt by the buyer, even though full payment has been made and the buyer has been notified that the goods are at his disposal. Protection is afforded him, in the event of breach by the buyer, under the next section.

The underlying theory of this rule is that a merchant who is to make physical delivery at his own place continues meanwhile to control the goods and can be expected to insure his interest in them. The buyer, on the other hand, has no control of the goods and it is extremely unlikely that he will carry insurance on goods not yet in his possession.

4. Where the agreement provides for delivery of the goods as between the buyer and seller without removal from the physical possession of a bailee, the provisions on manner of tender of delivery apply on the point of transfer of risk. Due delivery of a negotiable document of title covering the goods or acknowledgment by the bailee that he holds for the buyer completes the "delivery" and passes the risk.

5. The provisions of this section are made subject by subsection (4) to the "contrary agreement" of the parties. This language is intended as the equivalent of the phrase "unless otherwise agreed" used more frequently throughout this Act. "Contrary" is in no way used

as a word of limitation and the buyer and seller are left free to readjust their rights and risks as declared by this section in any manner agreeable to them. Contrary agreement can also be found in the circumstances of the case, a trade usage or practice, or a course of dealing or performance.

Cross References:

Point 1: Section 2–510(1).
Point 2: Sections 2–503 and 2–504.
Point 3: Sections 2–104, 2–503 and 2–510.
Point 4: Section 2–503(4).
Point 5: Section 1–201.

Definitional Cross References:

"Agreement". Section 1–201.
"Buyer". Section 2–103.
"Contract". Section 1–201.
"Delivery". Section 1–201.
"Document of title". Section 1–201.
"Goods". Section 2–105.
"Merchant". Section 2–104.
"Party". Section 1–201.
"Receipt" of goods. Section 2–103.
"Sale on approval". Section 2–326.
"Seller". Section 2–103.

§ 2–510. Effect of Breach on Risk of Loss.

(1) Where a tender or delivery of goods so fails to conform to the contract as to give a right of rejection the risk of their loss remains on the seller until cure or acceptance.

(2) Where the buyer rightfully revokes acceptance he may to the extent of any deficiency in his effective insurance coverage treat the risk of loss as having rested on the seller from the beginning.

(3) Where the buyer as to conforming goods already identified to the contract for sale repudiates or is otherwise in breach before risk of their loss has passed to him, the seller may to the extent of any deficiency in his effective insurance coverage treat the risk of loss as resting on the buyer for a commercially reasonable time.

Official Comment

Prior Uniform Statutory Provision: None.

Purposes: To make clear that:

1. Under subsection (1) the seller by his individual action cannot shift the risk of loss to the buyer unless his action conforms with all the conditions resting on him under the contract.

2. The "cure" of defective tenders contemplated by subsection (1) applies only to those situations in which the seller makes changes in goods already tendered, such as repair, partial substitution, sorting out from an improper mixture and the like since "cure" by repossession and new tender has no effect on the risk of loss of the goods originally tendered. The seller's privilege of cure does not shift the risk, however, until the cure is completed.

Where defective documents are involved a cure of the defect by the seller or a waiver of the defects by the buyer will operate to shift the risk under this section. However, if the goods have been destroyed prior to the cure or the buyer is unaware of their destruction at the time he waives the defect in the documents, the risk of the loss must still be borne by the seller, for the risk shifts only at the time of cure, waiver of documentary defects or acceptance of the goods.

3. In cases where there has been a breach of the contract, if the one in control of the goods is the aggrieved party, whatever loss or damage may prove to be uncovered by his insurance falls upon the contract breaker under subsections (2) and (3) rather than upon him. The word "effective" as applied to insurance cover-

age in those subsections is used to meet the case of supervening insolvency of the insurer. The "deficiency" referred to in the text means such deficiency in the insurance coverage as exists without subrogation. This section merely distributes the risk of loss as stated and is not intended to be disturbed by any subrogation of an insurer.

Cross Reference:

Section 2-509.

Definitional Cross References:

"Buyer". Section 2-103.
"Conform". Section 2-106.
"Contract for sale". Section 2-106.
"Goods". Section 2-105.
"Seller". Section 2-103.

§ 2-511. Tender of Payment by Buyer; Payment by Check.

(1) Unless otherwise agreed tender of payment is a condition to the seller's duty to tender and complete any delivery.

(2) Tender of payment is sufficient when made by any means or in any manner current in the ordinary course of business unless the seller demands payment in legal tender and gives any extension of time reasonably necessary to procure it.

(3) Subject to the provisions of this Act on the effect of an instrument on an obligation (Section 3-310), payment by check is conditional and is defeated as between the parties by dishonor of the check on due presentment.

As amended in 1994.

See Appendix XI for material relating to changes made in text in 1994.

Official Comment

Prior Uniform Statutory Provision: Section 42, Uniform Sales Act.

Changes: Rewritten by this section and Section 2-507.

Purposes of Changes:

1. The requirement of payment against delivery in subsection (1) is applicable to non-commercial sales generally and to ordinary sales at retail although it has no application to the great body of commercial contracts which carry credit terms. Subsection (1) applies also to documentary contracts in general and to contracts which look to shipment by the seller but contain no term on time and manner of payment, in which situations the payment may, in proper case, be demanded against delivery of appropriate documents.

In the case of specific transactions such as C.O.D. sales or agreements providing for payment against documents, the provisions of this subsection must be considered in conjunction with the special sections of the Article dealing with such terms. The provision that tender of payment is a condition to the seller's duty to tender and complete "any delivery" integrates this section with the language and policy of the section on delivery in several lots which call for separate payment. Finally, attention should be directed to the provision on right to adequate assurance of performance which recognizes, even before the time for tender, an obligation on the buyer not to impair the seller's expectation of receiving payment in due course.

2. Unless there is agreement otherwise the concurrence of the conditions as to tender of payment and tender of delivery requires their performance at a single place or time. This Article determines that place and time by determining in various other sections the place and time for tender of delivery under various circumstances and in particular types of transactions. The sections dealing with time and place of delivery together with

the section on right to inspection of goods answer the subsidiary question as to when payment may be demanded before inspection by the buyer.

3. The essence of the principle involved in subsection (2) is avoidance of commercial surprise at the time of performance. The section on substituted performance covers the peculiar case in which legal tender is not available to the commercial community.

4. Subsection (3) is concerned with the rights and obligations as between the parties to a sales transaction when payment is made by check. This Article recognizes that the taking of a seemingly solvent party's check is commercially normal and proper and, if due diligence is exercised in collection, is not to be penalized in any way. The conditional character of the payment under this section refers only to the effect of the transaction "as between the parties" thereto and does not purport to cut into the law of "absolute" and "conditional" payment as applied to such other problems as the discharge of sureties or the responsibilities of a drawee bank which is at the same time an agent for collection.

The phrase "by check" includes not only the buyer's own but any check which does not effect a discharge under Article 3 (Section 3–802). Similarly the reason of this subsection should apply and the same result should be reached where the buyer "pays" by sight draft on a commercial firm which is financing him.

5. Under subsection (3) payment by check is defeated if it is not honored upon due presentment. This corresponds to the provisions of article on Commercial Paper. (Section 3–802). But if the seller procures certification of the check instead of cashing it, the buyer is discharged. (Section 3–411).

6. Where the instrument offered by the buyer is not a payment but a credit instrument such as a note or a check post-dated by even one day, the seller's acceptance of the instrument insofar as third parties are concerned, amounts to a delivery on credit and his remedies are set forth in the section on buyer's insolvency. As between the buyer and the seller, however, the matter turns on the present subsection and the section on conditional delivery and subsequent dishonor of the instrument gives the seller rights on it as well as for breach of the contract for sale.

Cross References:

Point 1: Sections 2–307, 2–310, 2–320, 2–325, 2–503, 2–513 and 2–609.

Point 2: Sections 2–307, 2–310, 2–319, 2–322, 2–503, 2–504 and 2–513.

Point 3: Section 2–614.

Point 5: Article 3, esp. Sections 3–802 and 3–411.

Point 6: Sections 2–507, 2–702, and Article 3.

Definitional Cross References:

"Buyer". Section 2–103.
"Check". Section 3–104.
"Dishonor". Section 3–508.
"Party". Section 1–201.
"Reasonable time". Section 1–204.
"Seller". Section 2–103.

§ 2–512. Payment by Buyer Before Inspection.

[*1995 Amendments to text indicated by strikeout and underline*]

(1) Where the contract requires payment before inspection non-conformity of the goods does not excuse the buyer from so making payment unless

(a) the non-conformity appears without inspection; or

(b) despite tender of the required documents the circumstances would justify injunction against honor under ~~the provisions of~~ this Act (Section ~~5–114~~ 5–109(b)).

(2) Payment pursuant to subsection (1) does not constitute an acceptance of goods or impair the buyer's right to inspect or any of his remedies.

As amended in 1995.

See Appendix XIV for material relating to changes made in text in 1995.

Official Comment

Prior Uniform Statutory Provision: None, but see Sections 47 and 49, Uniform Sales Act.

Purposes:

1. Subsection (1) of the present section recognizes that the essence of a contract providing for payment before inspection is the intention of the parties to shift to the buyer the risks which would usually rest upon the seller. The basic nature of the transaction is thus preserved and the buyer is in most cases required to pay first and litigate as to any defects later.

2. "Inspection" under this section is an inspection in a manner reasonable for detecting defects in goods whose surface appearance is satisfactory.

3. Clause (a) of this subsection states an exception to the general rule based on common sense and normal commercial practice. The apparent non-conformity referred to is one which is evident in the mere process of taking delivery.

4. Clause (b) is concerned with contracts for payment against documents and incorporates the general clarification and modification of the case law contained in the section on excuse of a financing agency. Section 5-114.

5. Subsection (2) makes explicit the general policy of the Uniform Sales Act that the payment required before inspection in no way impairs the buyer's remedies or rights in the event of a default by the seller. The remedies preserved to the buyer are all of his remedies, which include as a matter of reason the remedy for total non-delivery after payment in advance.

The provision on performance or acceptance under reservation of rights does not apply to the situations contemplated here in which payment is made in due course under the contract and the buyer need not pay "under protest" or the like in order to preserve his rights as to defects discovered upon inspection.

6. This section applies to cases in which the contract requires payment before inspection either by the express agreement of the parties or by reason of the effect in law of that contract. The present section must therefore be considered in conjunction with the provision on right to inspection of goods which sets forth the instances in which the buyer is not entitled to inspection before payment.

Cross References:

Point 4: Article 5.
Point 5: Section 1-207.
Point 6: Section 2-513(3).

Definitional Cross References:

"Buyer". Section 2-103.
"Conform". Section 2-106.
"Contract". Section 1-201.
"Financing agency". Section 2-104.
"Goods". Section 2-105.
"Remedy". Section 1-201.
"Rights". Section 1-201.

§ 2-513. Buyer's Right to Inspection of Goods.

(1) Unless otherwise agreed and subject to subsection (3), where goods are tendered or delivered or identified to the contract for sale, the buyer has a right before payment or acceptance to inspect them at any reasonable place and time and in any reasonable manner. When the seller is required or authorized to send the goods to the buyer, the inspection may be after their arrival.

(2) Expenses of inspection must be borne by the buyer but may be recovered from the seller if the goods do not conform and are rejected.

(3) Unless otherwise agreed and subject to the provisions of this Article on C.I.F. contracts (subsection (3) of Section 2–321), the buyer is not entitled to inspect the goods before payment of the price when the contract provides

(a) for delivery "C.O.D." or on other like terms; or

(b) for payment against documents of title, except where such payment is due only after the goods are to become available for inspection.

(4) A place or method of inspection fixed by the parties is presumed to be exclusive but unless otherwise expressly agreed it does not postpone identification or shift the place for delivery or for passing the risk of loss. If compliance becomes impossible, inspection shall be as provided in this section unless the place or method fixed was clearly intended as an indispensable condition failure of which avoids the contract.

Official Comment

Prior Uniform Statutory Provisions: Section 47(2), (3), Uniform Sales Act.

Changes: Rewritten, Subsections (2) and (3) being new.

Purposes of Changes and New Matter: To correspond in substance with the prior uniform statutory provision and to incorporate in addition some of the results of the better case law so that:

1. The buyer is entitled to inspect goods as provided in subsection (1) unless it has been otherwise agreed by the parties. The phrase "unless otherwise agreed" is intended principally to cover such situations as those outlined in subsections (3) and (4) and those in which the agreement of the parties negates inspection before tender of delivery. However, no agreement by the parties can displace the entire right of inspection except where the contract is simply for the sale of "this thing." Even in a sale of boxed goods "as is" inspection is a right of the buyer, since if the boxes prove to contain some other merchandise altogether the price can be recovered back; nor do the limitations of the provision on effect of acceptance apply in such a case.

2. The buyer's right of inspection is available to him upon tender, delivery or appropriation of the goods with notice to him. Since inspection is available to him on tender, where payment is due against delivery he may, unless otherwise agreed, make his inspection before payment of the price. It is also available to him after receipt of the goods and so may be postponed after receipt for a reasonable time. Failure to inspect before payment does not impair the right to inspect after receipt of the goods unless the case falls within subsection (4) on agreed and exclusive inspection provisions. The right to inspect goods which have been appropriated with notice to the buyer holds whether or not the sale was by sample.

3. The buyer may exercise his right of inspection at any reasonable time or place and in any reasonable manner. It is not necessary that he select the most appropriate time, place or manner to inspect or that his selection be the customary one in the trade or locality. Any reasonable time, place or manner is available to him and the reasonableness will be determined by trade usages, past practices between the parties and the other circumstances of the case.

The last sentence of subsection (1) makes it clear that the place of arrival of shipped goods is a reasonable place for their inspection.

4. Expenses of an inspection made to satisfy the buyer of the seller's performance must be assumed by the buyer in the first instance. Since the rule pro-

vides merely for an allocation of expense there is no policy to prevent the parties from providing otherwise in the agreement. Where the buyer would normally bear the expenses of the inspection but the goods are rightly rejected because of what the inspection reveals, demonstrable and reasonable costs of the inspection are part of his incidental damage caused by the seller's breach.

5. In the case of payment against documents, subsection (3) requires payment before inspection, since shipping documents against which payment is to be made will commonly arrive and be tendered while the goods are still in transit. This Article recognizes no exception in any peculiar case in which the goods happen to arrive before the documents. However, where by the agreement payment is to await the arrival of the goods, inspection before payment becomes proper since the goods are then "available for inspection."

Where by the agreement the documents are to be held until arrival the buyer is entitled to inspect before payment since the goods are then "available for inspection". Proof of usage is not necessary to establish this right, but if inspection before payment is disputed the contrary must be established by usage or by an explicit contract term to that effect.

For the same reason, that the goods are available for inspection, a term calling for payment against storage documents or a delivery order does not normally bar the buyer's right to inspection before payment under subsection (3)(b). This result is reinforced by the buyer's right under subsection (1) to inspect goods which have been appropriated with notice to him.

6. Under subsection (4) an agreed place or method of inspection is generally held to be intended as exclusive. However, where compliance with such an agreed inspection term becomes impossible, the question is basically one of intention. If the parties clearly intend that the method of inspection named is to be a necessary condition without which the entire deal is to fail, the contract is at an end if that method becomes impossible. On the other hand, if the parties merely seek to indicate a convenient and reliable method but do not intend to give up the deal in the event of its failure, any reasonable method of inspection may be substituted under this Article.

Since the purpose of an agreed place of inspection is only to make sure at that point whether or not the goods will be thrown back, the "exclusive" feature of the named place is satisfied under this Article if the buyer's failure to inspect there is held to be an acceptance with the knowledge of such defects as inspection would have revealed within the section on waiver of buyer's objections by failure to particularize. Revocation of the acceptance is limited to the situations stated in the section pertaining to that subject. The reasonable time within which to give notice of defects within the section on notice of breach begins to run from the point of the "acceptance."

7. Clauses on time of inspection are commonly clauses which limit the time in which the buyer must inspect and give notice of defects. Such clauses are therefore governed by the section of this Article which requires that such a time limitation must be reasonable.

8. Inspection under this Article is not to be regarded as a "condition precedent to the passing of title" so that risk until inspection remains on the seller. Under subsection (4) such an approach cannot be sustained. Issues between the buyer and seller are settled in this Article almost wholly by special provisions and not by the technical determination of the locus of the title. Thus "inspection as a condition to the passing of title" becomes a concept almost without meaning. However, in peculiar circumstances inspection may still have some of the consequences hitherto sought and obtained under that concept.

9. "Inspection" under this section has to do with the buyer's check-up on whether the seller's performance is in accordance with a contract previously made

and is not to be confused with the "examination" of the goods or of a sample or model of them at the time of contracting which may affect the warranties involved in the contract.

Cross References:

Generally: Sections 2-310(b), 2-321(3) and 2-606(1)(b).

Point 1: Section 2-607.
Point 2: Sections 2-501 and 2-502.
Point 4: Section 2-715.
Point 5: Section 2-321(3).
Point 6: Sections 2-606 to 2-608.
Point 7: Section 1-204.
Point 8: Comment to Section 2-401.
Point 9: Section 2-316(3)(b).

Definitional Cross References:

"Buyer". Section 2-103.
"Conform". Section 2-106.
"Contract". Section 1-201.
"Contract for sale". Section 2-106.
"Document of title". Section 1-201.
"Goods". Section 2-105.
"Party". Section 1-201.
"Presumed". Section 1-201.
"Reasonable time". Section 1-204.
"Rights". Section 1-201.
"Seller". Section 2-103.
"Send". Section 1-201.
"Term". Section 1-201.

§ 2-514. When Documents Deliverable on Acceptance; When on Payment.

Unless otherwise agreed documents against which a draft is drawn are to be delivered to the drawee on acceptance of the draft if it is payable more than three days after presentment; otherwise, only on payment.

Official Comment

Prior Uniform Statutory Provision: Section 41, Uniform Bills of Lading Act.

Changes: Rewritten.

Purposes of Changes: To make the provision one of general application so that:

1. It covers any document against which a draft may be drawn, whatever may be the form of the document, and applies to interpret the action of a seller or consignor insofar as it may affect the rights and duties of any buyer, consignee or financing agency concerned with the paper. Supplementary or corresponding provisions are found in Sections 4-503 and 5-112.

2. An "arrival" draft is a sight draft within the purpose of this section.

Cross References:

Point 1: See Sections 2-502, 2-505(2), 2-507(2), 2-512, 2-513, 2-607 concerning protection of rights of buyer and seller, and 4-503 and 5-112 on delivery of documents.

Definitional Cross References:

"Delivery". Section 1-201.
"Draft". Section 3-104.

§ 2-515. Preserving Evidence of Goods in Dispute.

In furtherance of the adjustment of any claim or dispute

(a) either party on reasonable notification to the other and for the purpose of ascertaining the facts and preserving evidence has the right to inspect, test and sample the goods including such of them as may be in the possession or control of the other; and

(b) the parties may agree to a third party inspection or survey to determine the conformity or condition of the goods and may agree that the findings shall be binding upon them in any subsequent litigation or adjustment.

Official Comment

Prior Uniform Statutory Provision: None.

Purposes:

1. To meet certain serious problems which arise when there is a dispute as to the quality of the goods and thereby perhaps to aid the parties in reaching a settlement, and to further the use of devices which will promote certainty as to the condition of the goods, or at least aid in preserving evidence of their condition.

2. Under paragraph (a), to afford either party an opportunity for preserving evidence, whether or not agreement has been reached, and thereby to reduce uncertainty in any litigation and, in turn perhaps, to promote agreement.

Paragraph (a) does not conflict with the provisions on the seller's right to resell rejected goods or the buyer's similar right. Apparent conflict between these provisions which will be suggested in certain circumstances is to be resolved by requiring prompt action by the parties. Nor does paragraph (a) impair the effect of a term for payment before inspection. Short of such defects as amount to fraud or substantial failure of consideration, non-conformity is neither an excuse nor a defense to an action for non-acceptance of documents. Normally, therefore, until the buyer has made payment, inspected and rejected the goods, there is no occasion or use for the rights under paragraph (a).

3. Under paragraph (b), to provide for third party inspection upon the agreement of the parties, thereby opening the door to amicable adjustments based upon the findings of such third parties.

The use of the phrase "conformity or condition" makes it clear that the parties' agreement may range from a complete settlement of all aspects of the dispute by a third party to the use of a third party merely to determine and record the condition of the goods so that they can be resold or used to reduce the stake in controversy. "Conformity", at one end of the scale of possible issues, includes the whole question of interpretation of the agreement and its legal effect, the state of the goods in regard to quality and condition, whether any defects are due to factors which operate at the risk of the buyer, and the degree of non-conformity where that may be material. "Condition", at the other end of the scale, includes nothing but the degree of damage or deterioration which the goods show. Paragraph (b) is intended to reach any point in the gamut which the parties may agree upon.

The principle of the section on reservation of rights reinforces this paragraph in simplifying such adjustments as the parties wish to make in partial settlement while reserving their rights as to any further points. Paragraph (b) also suggests the use of arbitration, where desired, of any points left open, but nothing in this section is intended to repeal or amend any statute governing arbitration. Where any question arises as to the extent of the parties' agreement under the paragraph, the presumption should be that it was meant to extend only to the relation between the contract description and the goods as delivered, since that is what a craftsman in the trade would normally be expected to report upon. Finally, a written and authenticated report of inspection or tests by a third party, whether or not sampling has been practicable, is entitled to be admitted as evidence under this Act, for it is a third party document.

Cross References:

Point 2: Sections 2–513(3), 2–706 and 2–711(2) and Article 5.

Point 3: Sections 1–202 and 1–207.

Definitional Cross References:

"Conform". Section 2–106.
"Goods". Section 2–105.
"Notification". Section 1–201.
"Party". Section 1–201.

PART 6

BREACH, REPUDIATION AND EXCUSE

§ 2–601. Buyer's Rights on Improper Delivery.

Subject to the provisions of this Article on breach in installment contracts (Section 2–612) and unless otherwise agreed under the sections on contractual limitations of remedy (Sections 2–718 and 2–719), if the goods or the tender of delivery fail in any respect to conform to the contract, the buyer may

(a) reject the whole; or

(b) accept the whole; or

(c) accept any commercial unit or units and reject the rest.

Official Comment

Prior Uniform Statutory Provision: No one general equivalent provision but numerous provisions, dealing with situations of non-conformity where buyer may accept or reject, including Sections 11, 44 and 69(1), Uniform Sales Act.

Changes: Partial acceptance in good faith is recognized and the buyer's remedies on the contract for breach of warranty and the like, where the buyer has returned the goods after transfer of title, are no longer barred.

Purposes of Changes: To make it clear that:

1. A buyer accepting a non-conforming tender is not penalized by the loss of any remedy otherwise open to him. This policy extends to cover and regulate the acceptance of a part of any lot improperly tendered in any case where the price can reasonably be apportioned. Partial acceptance is permitted whether the part of the goods accepted conforms or not. The only limitation on partial acceptance is that good faith and commercial reasonableness must be used to avoid undue impairment of the value of the remaining portion of the goods. This is the reason for the insistence on the "commercial unit" in paragraph (c). In this respect, the test is not only what unit has been the basis of contract, but whether the partial acceptance produces so materially adverse an effect on the remainder as to constitute bad faith.

2. Acceptance made with the knowledge of the other party is final. An original refusal to accept may be withdrawn by a later acceptance if the seller has indicated that he is holding the tender open. However, if the buyer attempts to accept, either in whole or in part, after his original rejection has caused the seller to arrange for other disposition of the goods, the buyer must answer for any ensuing damage since the next section provides that any exercise of ownership after rejection is wrongful as against the seller. Further, he is liable even though the seller may choose to treat his action as acceptance rather than conversion, since the damage flows from the misleading notice. Such arrangements for resale or other disposition of the goods by the seller must be viewed as within the normal contemplation of a buyer who has given notice of rejection. However, the buyer's attempts in good faith to dispose of defective goods where the seller has failed to give instructions within a reasonable time are not to be regarded as an acceptance.

Cross References:

Sections 2–602(2)(a), 2–612, 2–718 and 2–719.

Definitional Cross References:

"Buyer". Section 2–103.

"Commercial unit". Section 2–105.

"Conform". Section 2–106.

"Contract". Section 1-201.
"Goods". Section 2-105.
"Installment contract". Section 2-612.
"Rights". Section 1-201.

§ 2-602. Manner and Effect of Rightful Rejection.

(1) Rejection of goods must be within a reasonable time after their delivery or tender. It is ineffective unless the buyer seasonably notifies the seller.

(2) Subject to the provisions of the two following sections on rejected goods (Sections 2-603 and 2-604),

(a) after rejection any exercise of ownership by the buyer with respect to any commercial unit is wrongful as against the seller; and

(b) if the buyer has before rejection taken physical possession of goods in which he does not have a security interest under the provisions of this Article (subsection (3) of Section 2-711), he is under a duty after rejection to hold them with reasonable care at the seller's disposition for a time sufficient to permit the seller to remove them; but

(c) the buyer has no further obligations with regard to goods rightfully rejected.

(3) The seller's rights with respect to goods wrongfully rejected are governed by the provisions of this Article on Seller's remedies in general (Section 2-703).

Official Comment

Prior Uniform Statutory Provision: Section 50, Uniform Sales Act.

Changes: Rewritten.

Purposes of Changes: To make it clear that:

1. A tender or delivery of goods made pursuant to a contract of sale, even though wholly non-conforming, requires affirmative action by the buyer to avoid acceptance. Under subsection (1), therefore, the buyer is given a reasonable time to notify the seller of his rejection, but without such seasonable notification his rejection is ineffective. The sections of this Article dealing with inspection of goods must be read in connection with the buyer's reasonable time for action under this subsection. Contract provisions limiting the time for rejection fall within the rule of the section on "Time" and are effective if the time set gives the buyer a reasonable time for discovery of defects. What constitutes a due "notifying" of rejection by the buyer to the seller is defined in Section 1-201.

2. Subsection (2) lays down the normal duties of the buyer upon rejection, which flow from the relationship of the parties. Beyond his duty to hold the goods with reasonable care for the buyer's [seller's] disposition, this section continues the policy of prior uniform legislation in generally relieving the buyer from any duties with respect to them, except when the circumstances impose the limited obligation of salvage upon him under the next section.

3. The present section applies only to rightful rejection by the buyer. If the seller has made a tender which in all respects conforms to the contract, the buyer has a positive duty to accept and his failure to do so constitutes a "wrongful rejection" which gives the seller immediate remedies for breach. Subsection (3) is included here to emphasize the sharp distinction between the rejection of an improper tender and the non-acceptance which is a breach by the buyer.

4. The provisions of this section are to be appropriately limited or modified when a negotiation is in process.

Cross References:

Point 1: Sections 1–201, 1–204(1) and (3), 2–512(2), 2–513(1) and 2–606(1)(b).

Point 2: Section 2–603(1).

Point 3: Section 2–703.

Definitional Cross References:

"Buyer". Section 2–103.

"Commercial unit". Section 2–105.

"Goods". Section 2–105.

"Merchant". Section 2–104.

"Notifies". Section 1–201.

"Reasonable time". Section 1–204.

"Remedy". Section 1–201.

"Rights". Section 1–201.

"Seasonably". Section 1–204.

"Security interest". Section 1–201.

"Seller". Section 2–103.

§ 2–603. Merchant Buyer's Duties as to Rightfully Rejected Goods.

(1) Subject to any security interest in the buyer (subsection (3) of Section 2–711), when the seller has no agent or place of business at the market of rejection a merchant buyer is under a duty after rejection of goods in his possession or control to follow any reasonable instructions received from the seller with respect to the goods and in the absence of such instructions to make reasonable efforts to sell them for the seller's account if they are perishable or threaten to decline in value speedily. Instructions are not reasonable if on demand indemnity for expenses is not forthcoming.

(2) When the buyer sells goods under subsection (1), he is entitled to reimbursement from the seller or out of the proceeds for reasonable expenses of caring for and selling them, and if the expenses include no selling commission then to such commission as is usual in the trade or if there is none to a reasonable sum not exceeding ten per cent on the gross proceeds.

(3) In complying with this section the buyer is held only to good faith and good faith conduct hereunder is neither acceptance nor conversion nor the basis of an action for damages.

Official Comment

Prior Uniform Statutory Provision: None.

Purposes:

1. This section recognizes the duty imposed upon the merchant buyer by good faith and commercial practice to follow any reasonable instructions of the seller as to reshipping, storing, delivery to a third party, reselling or the like. Subsection (1) goes further and extends the duty to include the making of reasonable efforts to effect a salvage sale where the value of the goods is threatened and the seller's instructions do not arrive in time to prevent serious loss.

2. The limitations on the buyer's duty to resell under subsection (1) are to be liberally construed. The buyer's duty to resell under this section arises from commercial necessity and thus is present only when the seller has "no agent or place of business at the market of rejection". A financing agency which is acting in behalf of the seller in handling the documents rejected by the buyer is sufficiently the seller's agent to lift the burden of salvage resale from the buyer. (See provisions of Sections 4–503 and 5–112 on bank's duties with respect to rejected documents.) The buyer's duty to resell is extended only to goods in his "possession or control", but these are intended as words of wide, rather than narrow, import. In effect, the measure of the buyer's "control" is whether he can practica-

bly effect control without undue commercial burden.

3. The explicit provisions for reimbursement and compensation to the buyer in subsection (2) are applicable and necessary only where he is not acting under instructions from the seller. As provided in subsection (1) the seller's instructions to be "reasonable" must on demand of the buyer include indemnity for expenses.

4. Since this section makes the resale of perishable goods an affirmative duty in contrast to a mere right to sell as under the case law, subsection (3) makes it clear that the buyer is liable only for the exercise of good faith in determining whether the value of the goods is sufficiently threatened to justify a quick resale or whether he has waited a sufficient length of time for instructions, or what a reasonable means and place of resale is.

5. A buyer who fails to make a salvage sale when his duty to do so under this section has arisen is subject to damages pursuant to the section on liberal administration of remedies.

Cross References:

Point 2: Sections 4-503 and 5-112.

Point 5: Section 1-106. Compare generally section 2-706.

Definitional Cross References:

"Buyer". Section 2-103.
"Good faith". Section 1-201.
"Goods". Section 2-105.
"Merchant". Section 2-104.
"Security interest". Section 1-201.
"Seller". Section 2-103.

§ 2-604. Buyer's Options as to Salvage of Rightfully Rejected Goods.

Subject to the provisions of the immediately preceding section on perishables if the seller gives no instructions within a reasonable time after notification of rejection the buyer may store the rejected goods for the seller's account or reship them to him or resell them for the seller's account with reimbursement as provided in the preceding section. Such action is not acceptance or conversion.

Official Comment

Prior Uniform Statutory Provision: None.

Purposes:

The basic purpose of this section is twofold: on the one hand it aims at reducing the stake in dispute and on the other at avoiding the pinning of a technical "acceptance" on a buyer who has taken steps towards realization on or preservation of the goods in good faith. This section is essentially a salvage section and the buyer's right to act under it is conditioned upon (1) non-conformity of the goods, (2) due notification of rejection to the seller under the section on manner of rejection, and (3) the absence of any instructions from the seller which the merchant-buyer has a duty to follow under the preceding section.

This section is designed to accord all reasonable leeway to a rightfully rejecting buyer acting in good faith. The listing of what the buyer may do in the absence of instructions from the seller is intended to be not exhaustive but merely illustrative. This is not a "merchant's" section and the options are pure options given to merchant and nonmerchant buyers alike. The merchant-buyer, however, may in some instances be under a duty rather than an option to resell under the provisions of the preceding section.

Cross References:

Sections 2-602(1), and 2-603(1) and 2-706.

Definitional Cross References:

"Buyer". Section 2-103.
"Notification". Section 1-201.

"Reasonable time". Section 1-204.
"Seller". Section 2-103.

§ 2-605. Waiver of Buyer's Objections by Failure to Particularize.

(1) The buyer's failure to state in connection with rejection a particular defect which is ascertainable by reasonable inspection precludes him from relying on the unstated defect to justify rejection or to establish breach

(a) where the seller could have cured it if stated seasonably; or

(b) between merchants when the seller has after rejection made a request in writing for a full and final written statement of all defects on which the buyer proposes to rely.

(2) Payment against documents made without reservation of rights precludes recovery of the payment for defects apparent on the face of the documents.

Official Comment

Prior Uniform Statutory Provision: None.

Purposes:

1. The present section rests upon a policy of permitting the buyer to give a quick and informal notice of defects in a tender without penalizing him for omissions in his statement, while at the same time protecting a seller who is reasonably misled by the buyer's failure to state curable defects.

2. Where the defect in a tender is one which could have been cured by the seller, a buyer who merely rejects the delivery without stating his objections to it is probably acting in commercial bad faith and seeking to get out of a deal which has become unprofitable. Subsection (1)(a), following the general policy of this Article which looks to preserving the deal wherever possible, therefore insists that the seller's right to correct his tender in such circumstances be protected.

3. When the time for cure is past, subsection (1)(b) makes it plain that a seller is entitled upon request to a final statement of objections upon which he can rely. What is needed is that he make clear to the buyer exactly what is being sought. A formal demand under paragraph (b) will be sufficient in the case of a merchant-buyer.

4. Subsection (2) applies to the particular case of documents the same principle which the section on effects of acceptance applies to the case of goods. The matter is dealt with in this section in terms of "waiver" of objections rather than of right to revoke acceptance, partly to avoid any confusion with the problems of acceptance of goods and partly because defects in documents which are not taken as grounds for rejection are generally minor ones. The only defects concerned in the present subsection are defects in the documents which are apparent on their face. Where payment is required against the documents they must be inspected before payment, and the payment then constitutes acceptance of the documents. Under the section dealing with this problem, such acceptance of the documents does not constitute an acceptance of the goods or impair any options or remedies of the buyer for their improper delivery. Where the documents are delivered without requiring such contemporary action as payment from the buyer, the reason of the next section on what constitutes acceptance of goods, applies. Their acceptance by non-objection is therefore postponed until after a reasonable time for their inspection. In either situation, however, the buyer "waives" only what is apparent on the face of the documents.

Cross References:

Point 2: Section 2-508.

Point 4: Sections 2-512(2), 2-606(1)(b), 2-607(2).

Definitional Cross References:

"Between merchants". Section 2-104.

"Buyer". Section 2-103.

"Seasonably". Section 1-204.

"Seller". Section 2-103.

"Writing" and "written". Section 1-201.

§ 2-606. What Constitutes Acceptance of Goods.

(1) Acceptance of goods occurs when the buyer

(a) after a reasonable opportunity to inspect the goods signifies to the seller that the goods are conforming or that he will take or retain them in spite of their non-conformity; or

(b) fails to make an effective rejection (subsection (1) of Section 2-602), but such acceptance does not occur until the buyer has had a reasonable opportunity to inspect them; or

(c) does any act inconsistent with the seller's ownership; but if such act is wrongful as against the seller it is an acceptance only if ratified by him.

(2) Acceptance of a part of any commercial unit is acceptance of that entire unit.

Official Comment

Prior Uniform Statutory Provision: Section 48, Uniform Sales Act.

Changes: Rewritten, the qualification in paragraph (c) and subsection (2) being new; otherwise the general policy of the prior legislation is continued.

Purposes of Changes and New Matter: To make it clear that:

1. Under this Article "acceptance" as applied to goods means that the buyer, pursuant to the contract, takes particular goods which have been appropriated to the contract as his own, whether or not he is obligated to do so, and whether he does so by words, action, or silence when it is time to speak. If the goods conform to the contract, acceptance amounts only to the performance by the buyer of one part of his legal obligation.

2. Under this Article acceptance of goods is always acceptance of identified goods which have been appropriated to the contract or are appropriated by the contract. There is no provision for "acceptance of title" apart from acceptance in general, since acceptance of title is not material under this Article to the detailed rights and duties of the parties. (See Section 2-401). The refinements of the older law between acceptance of goods and of title become unnecessary in view of the provisions of the sections on effect and revocation of acceptance, on effects of identification and on risk of loss, and those sections which free the seller's and buyer's remedies from the complications and confusions caused by the question of whether title has or has not passed to the buyer before breach.

3. Under paragraph (a), payment made after tender is always one circumstance tending to signify acceptance of the goods but in itself it can never be more than one circumstance and is not conclusive. Also, a conditional communication of acceptance always remains subject to its expressed conditions.

4. Under paragraph (c), any action taken by the buyer, which is inconsistent with his claim that he has rejected the goods, constitutes an acceptance. However, the provisions of paragraph (c) are subject to the sections dealing with rejec-

tion by the buyer which permit the buyer to take certain actions with respect to the goods pursuant to his options and duties imposed by those sections, without effecting an acceptance of the goods. The second clause of paragraph (c) modifies some of the prior case law and makes it clear that "acceptance" in law based on the wrongful act of the acceptor is acceptance only as against the wrongdoer and then only at the option of the party wronged.

In the same manner in which a buyer can bind himself, despite his insistence that he is rejecting or has rejected the goods, by an act inconsistent with the seller's ownership under paragraph (c), he can obligate himself by a communication of acceptance despite a prior rejection under paragraph (a). However, the sections on buyer's rights on improper delivery and on the effect of rightful rejection, make it clear that after he once rejects a tender, paragraph (a) does not operate in favor of the buyer unless the seller has re-tendered the goods or has taken affirmative action indicating that he is holding the tender open. See also Comment 2 to Section 2–601.

5. Subsection (2) supplements the policy of the section on buyer's rights on improper delivery, recognizing the validity of a partial acceptance but insisting that the buyer exercise this right only as to whole commercial units.

Cross References:

Point 2: Sections 2–401, 2–509, 2–510, 2–607, 2–608 and Part 7.

Point 4: Sections 2–601 through 2–604.

Point 5: Section 2–601.

Definitional Cross References:

"Buyer". Section 2–103.

"Commercial unit". Section 2–105.

"Goods". Section 2–105.

"Seller". Section 2–103.

§ 2–607. Effect of Acceptance; Notice of Breach; Burden of Establishing Breach After Acceptance; Notice of Claim or Litigation to Person Answerable Over.

(1) The buyer must pay at the contract rate for any goods accepted.

(2) Acceptance of goods by the buyer precludes rejection of the goods accepted and if made with knowledge of a non-conformity cannot be revoked because of it unless the acceptance was on the reasonable assumption that the non-conformity would be seasonably cured but acceptance does not of itself impair any other remedy provided by this Article for non-conformity.

(3) Where a tender has been accepted

(a) the buyer must within a reasonable time after he discovers or should have discovered any breach notify the seller of breach or be barred from any remedy; and

(b) if the claim is one for infringement or the like (subsection (3) of Section 2–312) and the buyer is sued as a result of such a breach he must so notify the seller within a reasonable time after he receives notice of the litigation or be barred from any remedy over for liability established by the litigation.

(4) The burden is on the buyer to establish any breach with respect to the goods accepted.

(5) Where the buyer is sued for breach of a warranty or other obligation for which his seller is answerable over

(a) he may give his seller written notice of the litigation. If the notice states that the seller may come in and defend and that if the seller does not do so he will be bound in any action against him by his buyer by any determination of fact common to the two litigations, then unless the seller after seasonable receipt of the notice does come in and defend he is so bound.

(b) if the claim is one for infringement or the like (subsection (3) of Section 2-312) the original seller may demand in writing that his buyer turn over to him control of the litigation including settlement or else be barred from any remedy over and if he also agrees to bear all expense and to satisfy any adverse judgment, then unless the buyer after seasonable receipt of the demand does turn over control the buyer is so barred.

(6) The provisions of subsections (3), (4) and (5) apply to any obligation of a buyer to hold the seller harmless against infringement or the like (subsection (3) of Section 2-312).

Official Comment

Prior Uniform Statutory Provision: Subsection (1)—Section 41, Uniform Sales Act; Subsections (2) and (3)—Sections 49 and 69, Uniform Sales Act.

Changes: Rewritten.

Purposes of Changes: To continue the prior basic policies with respect to acceptance of goods while making a number of minor though material changes in the interest of simplicity and commercial convenience so that:

1. Under subsection (1), once the buyer accepts a tender the seller acquires a right to its price on the contract terms. In cases of partial acceptance, the price of any part accepted is, if possible, to be reasonably apportioned, using the type of apportionment familiar to the courts in quantum valebant cases, to be determined in terms of "the contract rate," which is the rate determined from the bargain in fact (the agreement) after the rules and policies of this Article have been brought to bear.

2. Under subsection (2) acceptance of goods precludes their subsequent rejection. Any return of the goods thereafter must be by way of revocation of acceptance under the next section. Revocation is unavailable for a non-conformity known to the buyer at the time of acceptance, except where the buyer has accepted on the reasonable assumption that the non-conformity would be seasonably cured.

3. All other remedies of the buyer remain unimpaired under subsection (2). This is intended to include the buyer's full rights with respect to future installments despite his acceptance of any earlier non-conforming installment.

4. The time of notification is to be determined by applying commercial standards to a merchant buyer. "A reasonable time" for notification from a retail consumer is to be judged by different standards so that in his case it will be extended, for the rule of requiring notification is designed to defeat commercial bad faith, not to deprive a good faith consumer of his remedy.

The content of the notification need merely be sufficient to let the seller know that the transaction is still troublesome and must be watched. There is no reason to require that the notification which saves the buyer's rights under this section must include a clear statement of all the objections that will be relied on by the buyer, as under the section covering statements of defects upon rejection (Section 2-605). Nor is there reason for requiring the notification to be a claim for damages or of any threatened litigation or other resort to a remedy. The notification which saves the buyer's rights under this Article need only be such as informs the seller that the transaction is claimed to involve a breach, and thus opens the way for normal settlement through negotiation.

5. Under this Article various beneficiaries are given rights for injuries sustained by them because of the seller's breach of warranty. Such a beneficiary does not fall within the reason of the present section in regard to discovery of defects and the giving of notice within a reasonable time after acceptance, since he has nothing to do with acceptance. However, the reason of this section does extend to requiring the beneficiary to notify the seller that an injury has occurred. What is said above, with regard to the extended time for reasonable notification from the lay consumer after the injury is also applicable here; but even a beneficiary can be properly held to the use of good faith in notifying, once he has had time to become aware of the legal situation.

6. Subsection (4) unambiguously places the burden of proof to establish breach on the buyer after acceptance. However, this rule becomes one purely of procedure when the tender accepted was non-conforming and the buyer has given the seller notice of breach under subsection (3). For subsection (2) makes it clear that acceptance leaves unimpaired the buyer's right to be made whole, and that right can be exercised by the buyer not only by way of cross-claim for damages, but also by way of recoupment in diminution or extinction of the price.

7. Subsections (3)(b) and (5)(b) give a warrantor against infringement an opportunity to defend or compromise third-party claims or be relieved of his liability. Subsection (5)(a) codifies for all warranties the practice of voucher to defend. Compare Section 3-803. Subsection (6) makes these provisions applicable to the buyer's liability for infringement under Section 2-312.

8. All of the provisions of the present section are subject to any explicit reservation of rights.

Cross References:

Point 1: Section 1-201.
Point 2: Section 2-608.
Point 4: Sections 1-204 and 2-605.
Point 5: Section 2-318.
Point 6: Section 2-717.
Point 7: Sections 2-312 and 3-803.
Point 8: Section 1-207.

Definitional Cross References:

"Burden of establishing". Section 1-201.
"Buyer". Section 2-103.
"Conform". Section 2-106.
"Contract". Section 1-201.
"Goods". Section 2-105.
"Notifies". Section 1-201.
"Reasonable time". Section 1-204.
"Remedy". Section 1-201.
"Seasonably". Section 1-204.

§ 2-608. Revocation of Acceptance in Whole or in Part.

(1) The buyer may revoke his acceptance of a lot or commercial unit whose non-conformity substantially impairs its value to him if he has accepted it

(a) on the reasonable assumption that its non-conformity would be cured and it has not been seasonably cured; or

(b) without discovery of such non-conformity if his acceptance was reasonably induced either by the difficulty of discovery before acceptance or by the seller's assurances.

(2) Revocation of acceptance must occur within a reasonable time after the buyer discovers or should have discovered the ground for it and before any substantial change in condition of the goods which is not caused by their own defects. It is not effective until the buyer notifies the seller of it.

(3) A buyer who so revokes has the same rights and duties with regard to the goods involved as if he had rejected them.

Official Comment

Prior Uniform Statutory Provision: Section 69(1)(d), (3), (4) and (5), Uniform Sales Act.

Changes: Rewritten.

Purposes of Changes: To make it clear that:

1. Although the prior basic policy is continued, the buyer is no longer required to elect between revocation of acceptance and recovery of damages for breach. Both are now available to him. The non-alternative character of the two remedies is stressed by the terms used in the present section. The section no longer speaks of "rescission," a term capable of ambiguous application either to transfer of title to the goods or to the contract of sale and susceptible also of confusion with cancellation for cause of an executed or executory portion of the contract. The remedy under this section is instead referred to simply as "revocation of acceptance" of goods tendered under a contract for sale and involves no suggestion of "election" of any sort.

2. Revocation of acceptance is possible only where the non-conformity substantially impairs the value of the goods to the buyer. For this purpose the test is not what the seller had reason to know at the time of contracting; the question is whether the non-conformity is such as will in fact cause a substantial impairment of value to the buyer though the seller had no advance knowledge as to the buyer's particular circumstances.

3. "Assurances" by the seller under paragraph (b) of subsection (1) can rest as well in the circumstances or in the contract as in explicit language used at the time of delivery. The reason for recognizing such assurances is that they induce the buyer to delay discovery. These are the only assurances involved in paragraph (b). Explicit assurances may be made either in good faith or bad faith. In either case any remedy accorded by this Article is available to the buyer under the section on remedies for fraud.

4. Subsection (2) requires notification of revocation of acceptance within a reasonable time after discovery of the grounds for such revocation. Since this remedy will be generally resorted to only after attempts at adjustment have failed, the reasonable time period should extend in most cases beyond the time in which notification of breach must be given, beyond the time for discovery of non-conformity after acceptance and beyond the time for rejection after tender. The parties may by their agreement limit the time for notification under this section, but the same sanctions and considerations apply to such agreements as are discussed in the comment on manner and effect of rightful rejection.

5. The content of the notice under subsection (2) is to be determined in this case as in others by considerations of good faith, prevention of surprise, and reasonable adjustment. More will generally be necessary than the mere notification of breach required under the preceding section. On the other hand the requirements of the section on waiver of buyer's objections do not apply here. The fact that quick notification of trouble is desirable affords good ground for being slow to bind a buyer by his first statement. Following the general policy of this Article, the requirements of the content of notification are less stringent in the case of a non-merchant buyer.

6. Under subsection (2) the prior policy is continued of seeking substantial justice in regard to the condition of goods restored to the seller. Thus the buyer may not revoke his acceptance if the goods have materially deteriorated except by reason of their own defects. Worthless goods, however, need not be offered back and minor defects in the articles reoffered are to be disregarded.

7. The policy of the section allowing partial acceptance is carried over into the present section and the buyer may revoke his acceptance, in appropriate cases, as to the entire lot or any commercial unit thereof.

Cross References:

Point 3: Section 2-721.

Point 4: Sections 1-204, 2-602 and 2-607.

Point 5: Sections 2-605 and 2-607.

Point 7: Section 2-601.

Definitional Cross References:

"Buyer". Section 2-103.

"Commercial unit". Section 2-105.

"Conform". Section 2-106.

"Goods". Section 2-105.

"Lot". Section 2-105.

"Notifies". Section 1-201.

"Reasonable time". Section 1-204.

"Rights". Section 1-201.

"Seasonably". Section 1-204.

"Seller". Section 2-103.

§ 2-609. Right to Adequate Assurance of Performance.

(1) A contract for sale imposes an obligation on each party that the other's expectation of receiving due performance will not be impaired. When reasonable grounds for insecurity arise with respect to the performance of either party the other may in writing demand adequate assurance of due performance and until he receives such assurance may if commercially reasonable suspend any performance for which he has not already received the agreed return.

(2) Between merchants the reasonableness of grounds for insecurity and the adequacy of any assurance offered shall be determined according to commercial standards.

(3) Acceptance of any improper delivery or payment does not prejudice the aggrieved party's right to demand adequate assurance of future performance.

(4) After receipt of a justified demand failure to provide within a reasonable time not exceeding thirty days such assurance of due performance as is adequate under the circumstances of the particular case is a repudiation of the contract.

Official Comment

Prior Uniform Statutory Provision: See Sections 53, 54(1)(b), 55 and 63(2), Uniform Sales Act.

Purposes:

1. The section rests on the recognition of the fact that the essential purpose of a contract between commercial men is actual performance and they do not bargain merely for a promise, or for a promise plus the right to win a lawsuit and that a continuing sense of reliance and security that the promised performance will be forthcoming when due, is an important feature of the bargain. If either the willingness or the ability of a party to perform declines materially between the time of contracting and the time for performance, the other party is threatened with the loss of a substantial part of what he has bargained for. A seller needs protection not merely against having to deliver on credit to a shaky buyer, but also against having to procure and manufacture the goods, perhaps turning down other customers. Once he has been given reason to believe that the buyer's performance has become uncertain, it is an undue hardship to force him to continue his own performance. Similarly, a buyer who believes that the seller's deliveries have become uncertain cannot safely wait for the due date of performance when he has been buying to assure himself of materials for his current manufacturing or to replenish his stock of merchandise.

2. Three measures have been adopted to meet the needs of commercial men in such situations. First, the aggrieved party is permitted to suspend his own perfor-

mance and any preparation therefor, with excuse for any resulting necessary delay, until the situation has been clarified. "Suspend performance" under this section means to hold up performance pending the outcome of the demand, and includes also the holding up of any preparatory action. This is the same principle which governs the ancient law of stoppage and seller's lien, and also of excuse of a buyer from prepayment if the seller's actions manifest that he cannot or will not perform. (Original Act, Section 63(2).)

Secondly, the aggrieved party is given the right to require adequate assurance that the other party's performance will be duly forthcoming. This principle is reflected in the familiar clauses permitting the seller to curtail deliveries if the buyer's credit becomes impaired, which when held within the limits of reasonableness and good faith actually express no more than the fair business meaning of any commercial contract.

Third, and finally, this section provides the means by which the aggrieved party may treat the contract as broken if his reasonable grounds for insecurity are not cleared up within a reasonable time. This is the principle underlying the law of anticipatory breach, whether by way of defective part performance or by repudiation. The present section merges these three principles of law and commercial practice into a single theory of general application to all sales agreements looking to future performance.

3. Subsection (2) of the present section requires that "reasonable" grounds and "adequate" assurance as used in subsection (1) be defined by commercial rather than legal standards. The express reference to commercial standards carries no connotation that the obligation of good faith is not equally applicable here.

Under commercial standards and in accord with commercial practice, a ground for insecurity need not arise from or be directly related to the contract in question. The law as to "dependence" or "independence" of promises within a single contract does not control the application of the present section.

Thus a buyer who falls behind in "his account" with the seller, even though the items involved have to do with separate and legally distinct contracts, impairs the seller's expectation of due performance. Again, under the same test, a buyer who requires precision parts which he intends to use immediately upon delivery, may have reasonable grounds for insecurity if he discovers that his seller is making defective deliveries of such parts to other buyers with similar needs. Thus, too, in a situation such as arose in Jay Dreher Corporation v. Delco Appliance Corporation, 93 F.2d 275 (C.C.A.2, 1937), where a manufacturer gave a dealer an exclusive franchise for the sale of his product but on two or three occasions breached the exclusive dealing clause, although there was no default in orders, deliveries or payments under the separate sales contract between the parties, the aggrieved dealer would be entitled to suspend his performance of the contract for sale under the present section and to demand assurance that the exclusive dealing contract would be lived up to. There is no need for an explicit clause tying the exclusive franchise into the contract for the sale of goods since the situation itself ties the agreements together.

The nature of the sales contract enters also into the question of reasonableness. For example, a report from an apparently trustworthy source that the seller had shipped defective goods or was planning to ship them would normally give the buyer reasonable grounds for insecurity. But when the buyer has assumed the risk of payment before inspection of the goods, as in a sales contract on C.I.F. or similar cash against documents terms, that risk is not to be evaded by a demand for assurance. Therefore no ground for insecurity would exist under this section unless the report went to a ground which would excuse payment by the buyer.

4. What constitutes "adequate" assurance of due performance is subject to the same test of factual conditions. For example, where the buyer can make use of a

defective delivery, a mere promise by a seller of good repute that he is giving the matter his attention and that the defect will not be repeated, is normally sufficient. Under the same circumstances, however, a similar statement by a known corner-cutter might well be considered insufficient without the posting of a guaranty or, if so demanded by the buyer, a speedy replacement of the delivery involved. By the same token where a delivery has defects, even though easily curable, which interfere with easy use by the buyer, no verbal assurance can be deemed adequate which is not accompanied by replacement, repair, money-allowance, or other commercially reasonable cure.

A fact situation such as arose in Corn Products Refining Co. v. Fasola, 94 N.J.L. 181, 109 A. 505 (1920) offers illustration both of reasonable grounds for insecurity and "adequate" assurance. In that case a contract for the sale of oils on 30 days' credit, 2% off for payment within 10 days, provided that credit was to be extended to the buyer only if his financial responsibility was satisfactory to the seller. The buyer had been in the habit of taking advantage of the discount but at the same time that he failed to make his customary 10 day payment, the seller heard rumors, in fact false, that the buyer's financial condition was shaky. Thereupon, the seller demanded cash before shipment or security satisfactory to him. The buyer sent a good credit report from his banker, expressed willingness to make payments when due on the 30 day terms and insisted on further deliveries under the contract. Under this Article the rumors, although false, were enough to make the buyer's financial condition "unsatisfactory" to the seller under the contract clause. Moreover, the buyer's practice of taking the cash discounts is enough, apart from the contract clause, to lay a commercial foundation for suspicion when the practice is suddenly stopped. These matters, however, go only to the justification of the seller's demand for security, or his "reasonable grounds for insecurity".

The adequacy of the assurance given is not measured as in the type of "satisfaction" situation affected with intangibles, such as in personal service cases, cases involving a third party's judgment as final, or cases in which the whole contract is dependent on one party's satisfaction, as in a sale on approval. Here, the seller must exercise good faith and observe commercial standards. This Article thus approves the statement of the court in James B. Berry's Sons Co. of Illinois v. Monark Gasoline & Oil Co., Inc., 32 F.2d 74 (C.C.A.8, 1929), that the seller's satisfaction under such a clause must be based upon reason and must not be arbitrary or capricious; and rejects the purely personal "good faith" test of the Corn Products Refining Co. case, which held that in the seller's sole judgment, if for *any* reason he was dissatisfied, he was entitled to revoke the credit. In the absence of the buyer's failure to take the 2% discount as was his custom, the banker's report given in that case would have been "adequate" assurance under this Act, regardless of the language of the "satisfaction" clause. However, the seller is reasonably entitled to feel insecure at a sudden expansion of the buyer's use of a credit term, and should be entitled either to security or to a satisfactory explanation.

The entire foregoing discussion as to adequacy of assurance by way of explanation is subject to qualification when repeated occasions for the application of this section arise. This Act recognizes that repeated delinquencies must be viewed as cumulative. On the other hand, commercial sense also requires that if repeated claims for assurance are made under this section, the basis for these claims must be increasingly obvious.

5. A failure to provide adequate assurance of performance and thereby to re-establish the security of expectation, results in a breach only "by repudiation" under subsection (4). Therefore, the possibility is continued of retraction of the repudiation under the section dealing with that problem, unless the aggrieved party has acted on the breach in some manner.

The thirty day limit on the time to provide assurance is laid down to free the question of reasonable time from uncertainty in later litigation.

6. Clauses seeking to give the protected party exceedingly wide powers to cancel or readjust the contract when ground for insecurity arises must be read against the fact that good faith is a part of the obligation of the contract and not subject to modification by agreement and includes, in the case of a merchant, the reasonable observance of commercial standards of fair dealing in the trade. Such clauses can thus be effective to enlarge the protection given by the present section to a certain extent, to fix the reasonable time within which requested assurance must be given, or to define adequacy of the assurance in any commercially reasonable fashion. But any clause seeking to set up arbitrary standards for action is ineffective under this Article. Acceleration clauses are treated similarly in the Articles on Commercial Paper and Secured Transactions.

Cross References:

Point 3: Section 1-203.
Point 5: Section 2-611.
Point 6: Sections 1-203 and 1-208 and Articles 3 and 9.

Definitional Cross References:

"Aggrieved party". Section 1-201.
"Between merchants". Section 2-104.
"Contract". Section 1-201.
"Contract for sale". Section 2-106.
"Party". Section 1-201.
"Reasonable time". Section 1-204.
"Rights". Section 1-201.
"Writing". Section 1-201.

§ 2-610. Anticipatory Repudiation.

When either party repudiates the contract with respect to a performance not yet due the loss of which will substantially impair the value of the contract to the other, the aggrieved party may

(a) for a commercially reasonable time await performance by the repudiating party; or

(b) resort to any remedy for breach (Section 2-703 or Section 2-711), even though he has notified the repudiating party that he would await the latter's performance and has urged retraction; and

(c) in either case suspend his own performance or proceed in accordance with the provisions of this Article on the seller's right to identify goods to the contract notwithstanding breach or to salvage unfinished goods (Section 2-704).

Official Comment

Prior Uniform Statutory Provision: See Sections 63(2) and 65, Uniform Sales Act.

Purposes: To make it clear that:

1. With the problem of insecurity taken care of by the preceding section and with provision being made in this Article as to the effect of a defective delivery under an installment contract, anticipatory repudiation centers upon an overt communication of intention or an action which renders performance impossible or demonstrates a clear determination not to continue with performance.

Under the present section when such a repudiation substantially impairs the value of the contract, the aggrieved party may at any time resort to his remedies for breach, or he may suspend his own performance while he negotiates with, or awaits performance by, the other party. But if he awaits performance beyond a commercially reasonable time he cannot recover resulting damages which he should have avoided.

2. It is not necessary for repudiation that performance be made literally and

utterly impossible. Repudiation can result from action which reasonably indicates a rejection of the continuing obligation. And, a repudiation automatically results under the preceding section on insecurity when a party fails to provide adequate assurance of due future performance within thirty days after a justifiable demand therefor has been made. Under the language of this section, a demand by one or both parties for more than the contract calls for in the way of counter-performance is not in itself a repudiation nor does it invalidate a plain expression of desire for future performance. However, when under a fair reading it amounts to a statement of intention not to perform except on conditions which go beyond the contract, it becomes a repudiation.

3. The test chosen to justify an aggrieved party's action under this section is the same as that in the section on breach in installment contracts—namely the substantial value of the contract. The most useful test of substantial value is to determine whether material inconvenience or injustice will result if the aggrieved party is forced to wait and receive an ultimate tender minus the part or aspect repudiated.

4. After repudiation, the aggrieved party may immediately resort to any remedy he chooses provided he moves in good faith (see Section 1–203). Inaction and silence by the aggrieved party may leave the matter open but it cannot be regarded as misleading the repudiating party. Therefore the aggrieved party is left free to proceed at any time with his options under this section, unless he has taken some positive action which in good faith requires notification to the other party before the remedy is pursued.

Cross References:

Point 1: Sections 2–609 and 2–612.
Point 2: Section 2–609.
Point 3: Section 2–612.
Point 4: Section 1–203.

Definitional Cross References:

"Aggrieved party". Section 1–201.
"Contract". Section 1–201.
"Party". Section 1–201.
"Remedy". Section 1–201.

§ 2–611. Retraction of Anticipatory Repudiation.

(1) Until the repudiating party's next performance is due he can retract his repudiation unless the aggrieved party has since the repudiation cancelled or materially changed his position or otherwise indicated that he considers the repudiation final.

(2) Retraction may be by any method which clearly indicates to the aggrieved party that the repudiating party intends to perform, but must include any assurance justifiably demanded under the provisions of this Article (Section 2–609).

(3) Retraction reinstates the repudiating party's rights under the contract with due excuse and allowance to the aggrieved party for any delay occasioned by the repudiation.

Official Comment

Prior Uniform Statutory Provision: None.

Purposes: To make it clear that:

1. The repudiating party's right to reinstate the contract is entirely dependent upon the action taken by the aggrieved party. If the latter has cancelled the contract or materially changed his position at any time after the repudiation, there can be no retraction under this section.

2. Under subsection (2) an effective retraction must be accompanied by any assurances demanded under the section

dealing with right to adequate assurance. A repudiation is of course sufficient to give reasonable ground for insecurity and to warrant a request for assurance as an essential condition of the retraction. However, after a timely and unambiguous expression of retraction, a reasonable time for the assurance to be worked out should be allowed by the aggrieved party before cancellation.

Cross Reference:

Point 2: Section 2–609.

Definitional Cross References:

"Aggrieved party". Section 1–201.
"Cancellation". Section 2–106.
"Contract". Section 1–201.
"Party". Section 1–201.
"Rights". Section 1–201.

§ 2–612. "Installment Contract"; Breach.

(1) An "installment contract" is one which requires or authorizes the delivery of goods in separate lots to be separately accepted, even though the contract contains a clause "each delivery is a separate contract" or its equivalent.

(2) The buyer may reject any installment which is non-conforming if the non-conformity substantially impairs the value of that installment and cannot be cured or if the non-conformity is a defect in the required documents; but if the non-conformity does not fall within subsection (3) and the seller gives adequate assurance of its cure the buyer must accept that installment.

(3) Whenever non-conformity or default with respect to one or more installments substantially impairs the value of the whole contract there is a breach of the whole. But the aggrieved party reinstates the contract if he accepts a non-conforming installment without seasonably notifying of cancellation or if he brings an action with respect only to past installments or demands performance as to future installments.

Official Comment

Prior Uniform Statutory Provision: Section 45(2), Uniform Sales Act.

Changes: Rewritten.

Purposes of Changes: To continue prior law but to make explicit the more mercantile interpretation of many of the rules involved, so that:

1. The definition of an installment contract is phrased more broadly in this Article so as to cover installment deliveries tacitly authorized by the circumstances or by the option of either party.

2. In regard to the apportionment of the price for separate payment this Article applies the more liberal test of what can be apportioned rather than the test of what is clearly apportioned by the agreement. This Article also recognizes approximate calculation or apportionment of price subject to subsequent adjustment. A provision for separate payment for each lot delivered ordinarily means that the price is at least roughly calculable by units of quantity, but such a provision is not essential to an "installment contract." If separate acceptance of separate deliveries is contemplated, no generalized contrast between wholly "entire" and wholly "divisible" contracts has any standing under this Article.

3. This Article rejects any approach which gives clauses such as "each delivery is a separate contract" their legalistically literal effect. Such contracts nonetheless call for installment deliveries. Even where a clause speaks of "a separate contract for all purposes", a commercial reading of the language under the section on good faith and commercial standards requires that the singleness of the document and the negotiation, together with the sense of the situation, prevail

over any uncommercial and legalistic interpretation.

4. One of the requirements for rejection under subsection (2) is non-conformity substantially impairing the value of the installment in question. However, an installment agreement may require accurate conformity in quality as a condition to the right to acceptance if the need for such conformity is made clear either by express provision or by the circumstances. In such a case the effect of the agreement is to define explicitly what amounts to substantial impairment of value impossible to cure. A clause requiring accurate compliance as a condition to the right to acceptance must, however, have some basis in reason, must avoid imposing hardship by surprise and is subject to waiver or to displacement by practical construction.

Substantial impairment of the value of an installment can turn not only on the quality of the goods but also on such factors as time, quantity, assortment, and the like. It must be judged in terms of the normal or specifically known purposes of the contract. The defect in required documents refers to such matters as the absence of insurance documents under a C.I.F. contract, falsity of a bill of lading, or one failing to show shipment within the contract period or to the contract destination. Even in such cases, however, the provisions on cure of tender apply if appropriate documents are readily procurable.

5. Under subsection (2) an installment delivery must be accepted if the non-conformity is curable and the seller gives adequate assurance of cure. Cure of non-conformity of an installment in the first instance can usually be afforded by an allowance against the price, or in the case of reasonable discrepancies in quantity either by a further delivery or a partial rejection. This Article requires reasonable action by a buyer in regard to discrepant delivery and good faith requires that the buyer make any reasonable minor outlay of time or money necessary to cure an overshipment by severing out an acceptable percentage thereof. The seller must take over a cure which involves any material burden; the buyer's obligation reaches only to cooperation. Adequate assurance for purposes of subsection (2) is measured by the same standards as under the section on right to adequate assurance of performance.

6. Subsection (3) is designed to further the continuance of the contract in the absence of an overt cancellation. The question arising when an action is brought as to a single installment only is resolved by making such action waive the right to cancellation. This involves merely a defect in one or more installments, as contrasted with the situation where there is a true repudiation within the section on anticipatory repudiation. Whether the non-conformity in any given installment justifies cancellation as to the future depends, not on whether such non-conformity indicates an intent or likelihood that the future deliveries will also be defective, but whether the non-conformity substantially impairs the value of the whole contract. If only the seller's security in regard to future installments is impaired, he has the right to demand adequate assurances of proper future performance but has not an immediate right to cancel the entire contract. It is clear under this Article, however, that defects in prior installments are cumulative in effect, so that acceptance does not wash out the defect "waived." Prior policy is continued, putting the rule as to buyer's default on the same footing as that in regard to seller's default.

7. Under the requirement of seasonable notification of cancellation under subsection (3), a buyer who accepts a non-conforming installment which substantially impairs the value of the entire contract should properly be permitted to withhold his decision as to whether or not to cancel pending a response from the seller as to his claim for cure or adjustment. Similarly, a seller may withhold a delivery pending payment for prior ones, at the same time delaying his decision as to cancellation. A reasonable time for notifying of cancellation, judged by commercial standard under the section on

good faith, extends of course to include the time covered by any reasonable negotiation in good faith. However, during this period the defaulting party is entitled, on request, to know whether the contract is still in effect, before he can be required to perform further.

Cross References:

Point 2: Sections 2–307 and 2–607.
Point 3: Section 1–203.
Point 5: Sections 2–208 and 2–609.
Point 6: Section 2–610.

Definitional Cross References:

"Action". Section 1–201.
"Aggrieved party". Section 1–201.
"Buyer". Section 2–103.
"Cancellation". Section 2–106.
"Conform". Section 2–106.
"Contract". Section 1–201.
"Lot". Section 2–105.
"Notifies". Section 1–201.
"Seasonably". Section 1–204.
"Seller". Section 2–103.

§ 2–613. Casualty to Identified Goods.

Where the contract requires for its performance goods identified when the contract is made, and the goods suffer casualty without fault of either party before the risk of loss passes to the buyer, or in a proper case under a "no arrival, no sale" term (Section 2–324) then

(a) if the loss is total the contract is avoided; and

(b) if the loss is partial or the goods have so deteriorated as no longer to conform to the contract the buyer may nevertheless demand inspection and at his option either treat the contract as avoided or accept the goods with due allowance from the contract price for the deterioration or the deficiency in quantity but without further right against the seller.

Official Comment

Prior Uniform Statutory Provision: Sections 7 and 8, Uniform Sales Act.

Changes: Rewritten, the basic policy being continued but the test of a "divisible" or "indivisible" sale or contract being abandoned in favor of adjustment in business terms.

Purposes of Changes:

1. Where goods whose continued existence is presupposed by the agreement are destroyed without fault of either party, the buyer is relieved from his obligation but may at his option take the surviving goods at a fair adjustment. "Fault" is intended to include negligence and not merely wilful wrong. The buyer is expressly given the right to inspect the goods in order to determine whether he wishes to avoid the contract entirely or to take the goods with a price adjustment.

2. The section applies whether the goods were already destroyed at the time of contracting without the knowledge of either party or whether they are destroyed subsequently but before the risk of loss passes to the buyer. Where under the agreement, including of course usage of trade, the risk has passed to the buyer before the casualty, the section has no application. Beyond this, the essential question in determining whether the rules of this section are to be applied is whether the seller has or has not undertaken the responsibility for the continued existence of the goods in proper condition through the time of agreed or expected delivery.

3. The section on the term "no arrival, no sale" makes clear that delay in arrival, quite as much as physical change in the goods, gives the buyer the options set forth in this section.

Cross Reference:

Point 3: Section 2–324.

Definitional Cross References:

"Buyer". Section 2-103.
"Conform". Section 2-106.
"Contract". Section 1-201.
"Fault". Section 1-201.
"Goods". Section 2-105.
"Party". Section 1-201.
"Rights". Section 1-201.
"Seller". Section 2-103.

§ 2-614. Substituted Performance.

(1) Where without fault of either party the agreed berthing, loading, or unloading facilities fail or an agreed type of carrier becomes unavailable or the agreed manner of delivery otherwise becomes commercially impracticable but a commercially reasonable substitute is available, such substitute performance must be tendered and accepted.

(2) If the agreed means or manner of payment fails because of domestic or foreign governmental regulation, the seller may withhold or stop delivery unless the buyer provides a means or manner of payment which is commercially a substantial equivalent. If delivery has already been taken, payment by the means or in the manner provided by the regulation discharges the buyer's obligation unless the regulation is discriminatory, oppressive or predatory.

Official Comment

Prior Uniform Statutory Provision: None.

Purposes:

1. Subsection (1) requires the tender of a commercially reasonable substituted performance where agreed to facilities have failed or become commercially impracticable. Under this Article, in the absence of specific agreement, the normal or usual facilities enter into the agreement either through the circumstances, usage of trade or prior course of dealing.

This section appears between Section 2-613 on casualty to identified goods and the next section on excuse by failure of presupposed conditions, both of which deal with excuse and complete avoidance of the contract where the occurrence or non-occurrence of a contingency which was a basic assumption of the contract makes the expected performance impossible. The distinction between the present section and those sections lies in whether the failure or impossibility of performance arises in connection with an incidental matter or goes to the very heart of the agreement. The differing lines of solution are contrasted in a comparison of International Paper Co. v. Rockefeller, 161 App.Div. 180, 146 N.Y.S. 371 (1914) and Meyer v. Sullivan, 40 Cal.App. 723, 181 P. 847 (1919). In the former case a contract for the sale of spruce to be cut from a particular tract of land was involved. When a fire destroyed the trees growing on that tract the seller was held excused since performance was impossible. In the latter case the contract called for delivery of wheat "f.o.b. Kosmos Steamer at Seattle." The war led to cancellation of that line's sailing schedule after space had been duly engaged and the buyer was held entitled to demand substituted delivery at the warehouse on the line's loading dock. Under this Article, of course, the seller would also be entitled, had the market gone the other way, to make a substituted tender in that manner.

There must, however, be a true commercial impracticability to excuse the agreed to performance and justify a substituted performance. When this is the case a reasonable substituted performance tendered by either party should excuse him from strict compliance with contract terms which do not go to the essence of the agreement.

2. The substitution provided in this section as between buyer and seller does not carry over into the obligation of a financing agency under a letter of credit, since such an agency is entitled to performance which is plainly adequate on its face and without need to look into commercial evidence outside of the documents. See Article 5, especially Sections 5-102, 5-103, 5-109, 5-110, 5-114.

3. Under subsection (2) where the contract is still executory on both sides, the seller is permitted to withdraw unless the buyer can provide him with a commercially equivalent return despite the governmental regulation. Where, however, only the debt for the price remains, a larger leeway is permitted. The buyer may pay in the manner provided by the regulation even though this may not be commercially equivalent provided that the regulation is not "discriminatory, oppressive or predatory."

Cross Reference:

Point 2: Article 5.

Definitional Cross References:

"Buyer". Section 2-103.
"Fault". Section 1-201.
"Party". Section 1-201.
"Seller". Section 2-103.

§ 2-615. Excuse by Failure of Presupposed Conditions.

Except so far as a seller may have assumed a greater obligation and subject to the preceding section on substituted performance:

(a) Delay in delivery or non-delivery in whole or in part by a seller who complies with paragraphs (b) and (c) is not a breach of his duty under a contract for sale if performance as agreed has been made impracticable by the occurrence of a contingency the non-occurrence of which was a basic assumption on which the contract was made or by compliance in good faith with any applicable foreign or domestic governmental regulation or order whether or not it later proves to be invalid.

(b) Where the causes mentioned in paragraph (a) affect only a part of the seller's capacity to perform, he must allocate production and deliveries among his customers but may at his option include regular customers not then under contract as well as his own requirements for further manufacture. He may so allocate in any manner which is fair and reasonable.

(c) The seller must notify the buyer seasonably that there will be delay or non-delivery and, when allocation is required under paragraph (b), of the estimated quota thus made available for the buyer.

Official Comment

Prior Uniform Statutory Provision: None.

Purposes:

1. This section excuses a seller from timely delivery of goods contracted for, where his performance has become commercially impracticable because of unforeseen supervening circumstances not within the contemplation of the parties at the time of contracting. The destruction of specific goods and the problem of the use of substituted performance on points other than delay or quantity, treated elsewhere in this Article, must be distinguished from the matter covered by this section.

2. The present section deliberately refrains from any effort at an exhaustive expression of contingencies and is to be interpreted in all cases sought to be

brought within its scope in terms of its underlying reason and purpose.

3. The first test for excuse under this Article in terms of basic assumption is a familiar one. The additional test of commercial impracticability (as contrasted with "impossibility," "frustration of performance" or "frustration of the venture") has been adopted in order to call attention to the commercial character of the criterion chosen by this Article.

4. Increased cost alone does not excuse performance unless the rise in cost is due to some unforeseen contingency which alters the essential nature of the performance. Neither is a rise or a collapse in the market in itself a justification, for that is exactly the type of business risk which business contracts made at fixed prices are intended to cover. But a severe shortage of raw materials or of supplies due to a contingency such as war, embargo, local crop failure, unforeseen shutdown of major sources of supply or the like, which either causes a marked increase in cost or altogether prevents the seller from securing supplies necessary to his performance, is within the contemplation of this section. (See Ford & Sons, Ltd., v. Henry Leetham & Sons, Ltd., 21 Com.Cas. 55 (1915, K.B.D.).)

5. Where a particular source of supply is exclusive under the agreement and fails through casualty, the present section applies rather than the provision on destruction or deterioration of specific goods. The same holds true where a particular source of supply is shown by the circumstances to have been contemplated or assumed by the parties at the time of contracting. (See Davis Co. v. Hoffmann-LaRoche Chemical Works, 178 App.Div. 855, 166 N.Y.S. 179 (1917) and International Paper Co. v. Rockefeller, 161 App. Div. 180, 146 N.Y.S. 371 (1914).) There is no excuse under this section, however, unless the seller has employed all due measures to assure himself that his source will not fail. (See Canadian Industrial Alcohol Co., Ltd., v. Dunbar Molasses Co., 258 N.Y. 194, 179 N.E. 383, 80 A.L.R. 1173 (1932) and Washington Mfg. Co. v. Midland Lumber Co., 113 Wash. 593, 194 P. 777 (1921).)

In the case of failure of production by an agreed source for causes beyond the seller's control, the seller should, if possible, be excused since production by an agreed source is without more a basic assumption of the contract. Such excuse should not result in relieving the defaulting supplier from liability nor in dropping into the seller's lap an unearned bonus of damages over. The flexible adjustment machinery of this Article provides the solution under the provision on the obligation of good faith. A condition to his making good the claim of excuse is the turning over to the buyer of his rights against the defaulting source of supply to the extent of the buyer's contract in relation to which excuse is being claimed.

6. In situations in which neither sense nor justice is served by either answer when the issue is posed in flat terms of "excuse" or "no excuse," adjustment under the various provisions of this Article is necessary, especially the sections on good faith, on insecurity and assurance and on the reading of all provisions in the light of their purposes, and the general policy of this Act to use equitable principles in furtherance of commercial standards and good faith.

7. The failure of conditions which go to convenience or collateral values rather than to the commercial practicability of the main performance does not amount to a complete excuse. However, good faith and the reason of the present section and of the preceding one may properly be held to justify and even to require any needed delay involved in a good faith inquiry seeking a readjustment of the contract terms to meet the new conditions.

8. The provisions of this section are made subject to assumption of greater liability by agreement and such agreement is to be found not only in the expressed terms of the contract but in the circumstances surrounding the contracting, in trade usage and the like. Thus the exemptions of this section do not apply when the contingency in question is

sufficiently foreshadowed at the time of contracting to be included among the business risks which are fairly to be regarded as part of the dickered terms, either consciously or as a matter of reasonable, commercial interpretation from the circumstances. (See Madeirense Do Brasil, S.A. v. Stulman-Emrick Lumber Co., 147 F.2d 399 (C.C.A., 2 Cir., 1945).) The exemption otherwise present through usage of trade under the present section may also be expressly negated by the language of the agreement. Generally, express agreements as to exemptions designed to enlarge upon or supplant the provisions of this section are to be read in the light of mercantile sense and reason, for this section itself sets up the commercial standard for normal and reasonable interpretation and provides a minimum beyond which agreement may not go.

Agreement can also be made in regard to the consequences of exemption as laid down in paragraphs (b) and (c) and the next section on procedure on notice claiming excuse.

9. The case of a farmer who has contracted to sell crops to be grown on designated land may be regarded as falling either within the section on casualty to identified goods or this section, and he may be excused, when there is a failure of the specific crop, either on the basis of the destruction of identified goods or because of the failure of a basic assumption of the contract.

Exemption of the buyer in the case of a "requirements" contract is covered by the "Output and Requirements" section both as to assumption and allocation of the relevant risks. But when a contract by a manufacturer to buy fuel or raw material makes no specific reference to a particular venture and no such reference may be drawn from the circumstances, commercial understanding views it as a general deal in the general market and not conditioned on any assumption of the continuing operation of the buyer's plant. Even when notice is given by the buyer that the supplies are needed to fill a specific contract of a normal commercial kind, commercial understanding does not see such a supply contract as conditioned on the continuance of the buyer's further contract for outlet. On the other hand, where the buyer's contract is in reasonable commercial understanding conditioned on a definite and specific venture or assumption as, for instance, a war procurement subcontract known to be based on a prime contract which is subject to termination, or a supply contract for a particular construction venture, the reason of the present section may well apply and entitle the buyer to the exemption.

10. Following its basic policy of using commercial practicability as a test for excuse, this section recognizes as of equal significance either a foreign or domestic regulation and disregards any technical distinctions between "law," "regulation," "order" and the like. Nor does it make the present action of the seller depend upon the eventual judicial determination of the legality of the particular governmental action. The seller's good faith belief in the validity of the regulation is the test under this Article and the best evidence of his good faith is the general commercial acceptance of the regulation. However, governmental interference cannot excuse unless it truly "supervenes" in such a manner as to be beyond the seller's assumption of risk. And any action by the party claiming excuse which causes or colludes in inducing the governmental action preventing his performance would be in breach of good faith and would destroy his exemption.

11. An excused seller must fulfill his contract to the extent which the supervening contingency permits, and if the situation is such that his customers are generally affected he must take account of all in supplying one. Subsections (a) and (b), therefore, explicitly permit in any proration a fair and reasonable attention to the needs of regular customers who are probably relying on spot orders for supplies. Customers at different stages of the manufacturing process may be fairly treated by including the seller's manufacturing requirements. A fortiori, the seller may also take account of contracts later in date than the one in question.

The fact that such spot orders may be closed at an advanced price causes no difficulty, since any allocation which exceeds normal past requirements will not be reasonable. However, good faith requires, when prices have advanced, that the seller exercise real care in making his allocations, and in case of doubt his contract customers should be favored and supplies prorated evenly among them regardless of price. Save for the extra care thus required by changes in the market, this section seeks to leave every reasonable business leeway to the seller.

Cross References:

Point 1: Sections 2-613 and 2-614.
Point 2: Section 1-102.
Point 5: Sections 1-203 and 2-613.
Point 6: Sections 1-102, 1-203 and 2-609.
Point 7: Section 2-614.
Point 8: Sections 1-201, 2-302 and 2-616.
Point 9: Sections 1-102, 2-306 and 2-613.

Definitional Cross References:

"Between merchants". Section 2-104.
"Buyer". Section 2-103.
"Contract". Section 1-201.
"Contract for sale". Section 2-106.
"Good faith". Section 1-201.
"Merchant". Section 2-104.
"Notifies". Section 1-201.
"Seasonably". Section 1-201.
"Seller". Section 2-103.

§ 2-616. Procedure on Notice Claiming Excuse.

(1) Where the buyer receives notification of a material or indefinite delay or an allocation justified under the preceding section he may by written notification to the seller as to any delivery concerned, and where the prospective deficiency substantially impairs the value of the whole contract under the provisions of this Article relating to breach of installment contracts (Section 2-612), then also as to the whole,

(a) terminate and thereby discharge any unexecuted portion of the contract; or

(b) modify the contract by agreeing to take his available quota in substitution.

(2) If after receipt of such notification from the seller the buyer fails so to modify the contract within a reasonable time not exceeding thirty days the contract lapses with respect to any deliveries affected.

(3) The provisions of this section may not be negated by agreement except in so far as the seller has assumed a greater obligation under the preceding section.

Official Comment

Prior Uniform Statutory Provision: None.

Purposes:

This section seeks to establish simple and workable machinery for providing certainty as to when a supervening and excusing contingency "excuses" the delay, "discharges" the contract, or may result in a waiver of the delay by the buyer. When the seller notifies, in accordance with the preceding section, claiming excuse, the buyer may acquiesce, in which case the contract is so modified. No consideration is necessary in a case of this kind to support such a modification. If the buyer does not elect so to modify the contract, he may terminate it and under subsection (2) his silence after receiving the seller's claim of excuse operates as such a termination. Subsection (3) denies effect to any contract clause made in advance of trouble which would require the buyer to stand ready to take delivery whenever the seller is excused from delivery by unforeseen circumstances.

Cross References:

Point 1: Sections 2-209 and 2-615.

Definitional Cross References:

"Buyer". Section 2-103.

"Contract". Section 1-201.

"Installment contract". Section 2-612.

"Notification". Section 1-201.

"Reasonable time". Section 1-204.

"Seller". Section 2-103.

"Termination". Section 2-106.

"Written". Section 1-201.

PART 7

REMEDIES

§ 2-701. Remedies for Breach of Collateral Contracts Not Impaired.

Remedies for breach of any obligation or promise collateral or ancillary to a contract for sale are not impaired by the provisions of this Article.

Official Comment

Prior Uniform Statutory Provision: None.

Purposes:

Whether a claim for breach of an obligation collateral to the contract for sale requires separate trial to avoid confusion of issues is beyond the scope of this Article; but contractual arrangements which as a business matter enter vitally into the contract should be considered a part thereof in so far as cross-claims or defenses are concerned.

Definitional Cross References:

"Contract for sale". Section 2-106.

"Remedy". Section 1-201.

§ 2-702. Seller's Remedies on Discovery of Buyer's Insolvency.

(1) Where the seller discovers the buyer to be insolvent he may refuse delivery except for cash including payment for all goods theretofore delivered under the contract, and stop delivery under this Article (Section 2-705).

(2) Where the seller discovers that the buyer has received goods on credit while insolvent he may reclaim the goods upon demand made within ten days after the receipt, but if misrepresentation of solvency has been made to the particular seller in writing within three months before delivery the ten day limitation does not apply. Except as provided in this subsection the seller may not base a right to reclaim goods on the buyer's fraudulent or innocent misrepresentation of solvency or of intent to pay.

(3) The seller's right to reclaim under subsection (2) is subject to the rights of a buyer in ordinary course or other good faith purchaser under this Article (Section 2-403). Successful reclamation of goods excludes all other remedies with respect to them.

As amended in 1966.

Official Comment

Prior Uniform Statutory Provision: Subsection (1)—Sections 53(1)(b), 54(1)(c) and 57, Uniform Sales Act; Subsection (2)—none; Subsection (3)—Section 76(3), Uniform Sales Act.

Changes: Rewritten, the protection given to a seller who has sold on credit and has delivered goods to the buyer immediately preceding his insolvency being extended.

Purposes of Changes and New Matter: To make it clear that:

1. The seller's right to withhold the goods or to stop delivery except for cash when he discovers the buyer's insolvency is made explicit in subsection (1) regardless of the passage of title, and the concept of stoppage has been extended to include goods in the possession of any bailee who has not yet attorned to the buyer.

2. Subsection (2) takes as its base line the proposition that any receipt of goods on credit by an insolvent buyer amounts to a tacit business misrepresentation of solvency and therefore is fraudulent as against the particular seller. This Article makes discovery of the buyer's insolvency and demand within a ten day period a condition of the right to reclaim goods on this ground. The ten day limitation period operates from the time of receipt of the goods.

An exception to this time limitation is made when a written misrepresentation of solvency has been made to the particular seller within three months prior to the delivery. To fall within the exception the statement of solvency must be in writing, addressed to the particular seller and dated within three months of the delivery.

3. Because the right of the seller to reclaim goods under this section constitutes preferential treatment as against the buyer's other creditors, subsection (3) provides that such reclamation bars all his other remedies as to the goods involved. As amended 1966.

Cross References:

Point 1: Sections 2–401 and 2–705. Compare Section 2–502.

Definitional Cross References:

"Buyer". Section 2–103.
"Buyer in ordinary course of business". Section 1–201.
"Contract". Section 1–201.
"Good faith". Section 1–201.
"Goods". Section 2–105.
"Insolvent". Section 1–201.
"Person". Section 1–201.
"Purchaser". Section 1–201.
"Receipt" of goods. Section 2–103.
"Remedy". Section 1–201.
"Rights". Section 1–201.
"Seller". Section 2–103.
"Writing". Section 1–201.

§ 2–703. Seller's Remedies in General.

Where the buyer wrongfully rejects or revokes acceptance of goods or fails to make a payment due on or before delivery or repudiates with respect to a part or the whole, then with respect to any goods directly affected and, if the breach is of the whole contract (Section 2–612), then also with respect to the whole undelivered balance, the aggrieved seller may

(a) withhold delivery of such goods;

(b) stop delivery by any bailee as hereafter provided (Section 2–705);

(c) proceed under the next section respecting goods still unidentified to the contract;

(d) resell and recover damages as hereafter provided (Section 2–706);

(e) recover damages for non-acceptance (Section 2–708) or in a proper case the price (Section 2–709);

(f) cancel.

Official Comment

Prior Uniform Statutory Provision: No comparable index section. See Section 53, Uniform Sales Act.

Purposes:

1. This section is an index section which gathers together in one convenient place all of the various remedies open to a seller for any breach by the buyer. This Article rejects any doctrine of election of remedy as a fundamental policy and thus the remedies are essentially cumulative in nature and include all of the available remedies for breach. Whether the pursuit of one remedy bars another depends entirely on the facts of the individual case.

2. The buyer's breach which occasions the use of the remedies under this section may involve only one lot or delivery of goods, or may involve all of the goods which are the subject matter of the particular contract. The right of the seller to pursue a remedy as to all the goods when the breach is as to only one or more lots is covered by the section on breach in installment contracts. The present section deals only with the remedies available after the goods involved in the breach have been determined by that section.

3. In addition to the typical case of refusal to pay or default in payment, the language in the preamble, "fails to make a payment due," is intended to cover the dishonor of a check on due presentment, or the non-acceptance of a draft, and the failure to furnish an agreed letter of credit.

4. It should also be noted that this Act requires its remedies to be liberally administered and provides that any right or obligation which it declares is enforceable by action unless a different effect is specifically prescribed (Section 1–106).

Cross References:

Point 2: Section 2–612.
Point 3: Section 2–325.
Point 4: Section 1–106.

Definitional Cross References:

"Aggrieved party". Section 1–201.
"Buyer". Section 2–103.
"Cancellation". Section 2–106.
"Contract". Section 1–201.
"Goods". Section 2–105.
"Remedy". Section 1–201.
"Seller". Section 2–103.

§ 2–704. Seller's Right to Identify Goods to the Contract Notwithstanding Breach or to Salvage Unfinished Goods.

(1) An aggrieved seller under the preceding section may

(a) identify to the contract conforming goods not already identified if at the time he learned of the breach they are in his possession or control;

(b) treat as the subject of resale goods which have demonstrably been intended for the particular contract even though those goods are unfinished.

(2) Where the goods are unfinished an aggrieved seller may in the exercise of reasonable commercial judgment for the purposes of avoiding loss and of effective realization either complete the manufacture and wholly identify the goods to the contract or cease manufacture and resell for scrap or salvage value or proceed in any other reasonable manner.

Official Comment

Prior Uniform Statutory Provision: Sections 63(3) and 64(4), Uniform Sales Act.

Changes: Rewritten, the seller's rights being broadened.

Purposes of Changes:

1. This section gives an aggrieved seller the right at the time of breach to identify to the contract any conforming finished goods, regardless of their resalability, and to use reasonable judgment as to completing unfinished goods. It thus makes the goods available for resale under the resale section, the seller's primary remedy, and in the special case in which resale is not practicable, allows the action for the price which would then be necessary to give the seller the value of his contract.

2. Under this Article the seller is given express power to complete manufacture or procurement of goods for the contract unless the exercise of reasonable commercial judgment as to the facts as they appear at the time he learns of the breach makes it clear that such action will result in a material increase in damages. The burden is on the buyer to show the commercially unreasonable nature of the seller's action in completing manufacture.

Cross References:

Sections 2–703 and 2–706.

Definitional Cross References:

"Aggrieved party". Section 1–201.
"Conforming". Section 2–106.
"Contract". Section 1–201.
"Goods". Section 2–105.
"Rights". Section 1–201.
"Seller". Section 2–103.

§ 2–705. Seller's Stoppage of Delivery in Transit or Otherwise.

(1) The seller may stop delivery of goods in the possession of a carrier or other bailee when he discovers the buyer to be insolvent (Section 2–702) and may stop delivery of carload, truckload, planeload or larger shipments of express or freight when the buyer repudiates or fails to make a payment due before delivery or if for any other reason the seller has a right to withhold or reclaim the goods.

(2) As against such buyer the seller may stop delivery until

(a) receipt of the goods by the buyer; or

(b) acknowledgment to the buyer by any bailee of the goods except a carrier that the bailee holds the goods for the buyer; or

(c) such acknowledgment to the buyer by a carrier by reshipment or as warehouseman; or

(d) negotiation to the buyer of any negotiable document of title covering the goods.

(3)(a) To stop delivery the seller must so notify as to enable the bailee by reasonable diligence to prevent delivery of the goods.

(b) After such notification the bailee must hold and deliver the goods according to the directions of the seller but the seller is liable to the bailee for any ensuing charges or damages.

(c) If a negotiable document of title has been issued for goods the bailee is not obliged to obey a notification to stop until surrender of the document.

(d) A carrier who has issued a non-negotiable bill of lading is not obliged to obey a notification to stop received from a person other than the consignor.

Official Comment

Prior Uniform Statutory Provision: Sections 57–59, Uniform Sales Act; see also Sections 12, 14 and 42, Uniform Bills of Lading Act and Sections 9, 11 and 49, Uniform Warehouse Receipts Act.

Changes: This section continues and develops the above sections of the Uniform Sales Act in the light of the other uniform statutory provisions noted.

Purposes: To make it clear that:

1. Subsection (1) applies the stoppage principle to other bailees as well as carriers.

It also expands the remedy to cover the situations, in addition to buyer's insolvency, specified in the subsection. But since stoppage is a burden in any case to carriers, and might be a very heavy burden to them if it covered all small shipments in all these situations, the right to stop for reasons other than insolvency is limited to carload, truckload, planeload or larger shipments. The seller shipping to a buyer of doubtful credit can protect himself by shipping C.O.D.

Where stoppage occurs for insecurity it is merely a suspension of performance, and if assurances are duly forthcoming from the buyer the seller is not entitled to resell or divert.

Improper stoppage is a breach by the seller if it effectively interferes with the buyer's right to due tender under the section on manner of tender of delivery. However, if the bailee obeys an unjustified order to stop he may also be liable to the buyer. The measure of his obligation is dependent on the provisions of the Documents of Title Article (Section 7–303). Subsection 3(b) therefore gives him a right of indemnity as against the seller in such a case.

2. "Receipt by the buyer" includes receipt by the buyer's designated representative, the subpurchaser, when shipment is made direct to him and the buyer himself never receives the goods. It is entirely proper under this Article that the seller, by making such direct shipment to the sub-purchaser, be regarded as acquiescing in the latter's purchase and as thus barred from stoppage of the goods as against him.

As between the buyer and the seller, the latter's right to stop the goods at any time until they reach the place of final delivery is recognized by this section.

Under subsection (3)(c) and (d), the carrier is under no duty to recognize the stop order of a person who is a stranger to the carrier's contract. But the seller's right as against the buyer to stop delivery remains, whether or not the carrier is obligated to recognize the stop order. If the carrier does obey it, the buyer cannot complain merely because of that circumstance; and the seller becomes obligated under subsection (3)(b) to pay the carrier any ensuing damages or charges.

3. A diversion of a shipment is not a "reshipment" under subsection (2)(c) when it is merely an incident to the original contract of transportation. Nor is the procurement of "exchange bills" of lading which change only the name of the consignee to that of the buyer's local agent but do not alter the destination of a reshipment.

Acknowledgment by the carrier as a "warehouseman" within the meaning of this Article requires a contract of a truly different character from the original shipment, a contract not in extension of transit but as a warehouseman.

4. Subsection (3)(c) makes the bailee's obedience of a notification to stop conditional upon the surrender of any outstanding negotiable document.

5. Any charges or losses incurred by the carrier in following the seller's orders,

whether or not he was obligated to do so, fall to the seller's charge.

6. After an effective stoppage under this section the seller's rights in the goods are the same as if he had never made a delivery.

Cross References:

Sections 2-702 and 2-703.

Point 1: Sections 2-503 and 2-609, and Article 7.

Point 2: Section 2-103 and Article 7.

Definitional Cross References:

"Buyer". Section 2-103.
"Contract for sale". Section 2-106.
"Document of title". Section 1-201.
"Goods". Section 2-105.
"Insolvent". Section 1-201.
"Notification". Section 1-201.
"Receipt" of goods. Section 2-103.
"Rights". Section 1-201.
"Seller". Section 2-103.

§ 2-706. Seller's Resale Including Contract for Resale.

(1) Under the conditions stated in Section 2-703 on seller's remedies, the seller may resell the goods concerned or the undelivered balance thereof. Where the resale is made in good faith and in a commercially reasonable manner the seller may recover the difference between the resale price and the contract price together with any incidental damages allowed under the provisions of this Article (Section 2-710), but less expenses saved in consequence of the buyer's breach.

(2) Except as otherwise provided in subsection (3) or unless otherwise agreed resale may be at public or private sale including sale by way of one or more contracts to sell or of identification to an existing contract of the seller. Sale may be as a unit or in parcels and at any time and place and on any terms but every aspect of the sale including the method, manner, time, place and terms must be commercially reasonable. The resale must be reasonably identified as referring to the broken contract, but it is not necessary that the goods be in existence or that any or all of them have been identified to the contract before the breach.

(3) Where the resale is at private sale the seller must give the buyer reasonable notification of his intention to resell.

(4) Where the resale is at public sale

(a) only identified goods can be sold except where there is a recognized market for a public sale of futures in goods of the kind; and

(b) it must be made at a usual place or market for public sale if one is reasonably available and except in the case of goods which are perishable or threaten to decline in value speedily the seller must give the buyer reasonable notice of the time and place of the resale; and

(c) if the goods are not to be within the view of those attending the sale the notification of sale must state the place where the goods are located and provide for their reasonable inspection by prospective bidders; and

(d) the seller may buy.

(5) A purchaser who buys in good faith at a resale takes the goods free of any rights of the original buyer even though the seller fails to comply with one or more of the requirements of this section.

(6) The seller is not accountable to the buyer for any profit made on any resale. A person in the position of a seller (Section 2–707) or a buyer who has rightfully rejected or justifiably revoked acceptance must account for any excess over the amount of his security interest, as hereinafter defined (subsection (3) of Section 2–711).

Official Comment

Prior Uniform Statutory Provision: Section 60, Uniform Sales Act.

Changes: Rewritten.

Purposes of Changes: To simplify the prior statutory provision and to make it clear that:

1. The only condition precedent to the seller's right of resale under subsection (1) is a breach by the buyer within the section on the seller's remedies in general or insolvency. Other meticulous conditions and restrictions of the prior uniform statutory provision are disapproved by this Article and are replaced by standards of commercial reasonableness. Under this section the seller may resell the goods after any breach by the buyer. Thus, an anticipatory repudiation by the buyer gives rise to any of the seller's remedies for breach, and to the right of resale. This principle is supplemented by subsection (2) which authorizes a resale of goods which are not in existence or were not identified to the contract before the breach.

2. In order to recover the damages prescribed in subsection (1) the seller must act "in good faith and in a commercially reasonable manner" in making the resale. This standard is intended to be more comprehensive than that of "reasonable care and judgment" established by the prior uniform statutory provision. Failure to act properly under this section deprives the seller of the measure of damages here provided and relegates him to that provided in Section 2–708.

Under this Article the seller resells by authority of law, in his own behalf, for his own benefit and for the purpose of fixing his damages. The theory of a seller's agency is thus rejected.

3. If the seller complies with the prescribed standard of duty in making the resale, he may recover from the buyer the damages provided for in subsection (1). Evidence of market or current prices at any particular time or place is relevant only on the question of whether the seller acted in a commercially reasonable manner in making the resale.

The distinction drawn by some courts between cases where the title had not passed to the buyer and the seller had resold as owner, and cases where the title had passed and the seller had resold by virtue of his lien on the goods, is rejected.

4. Subsection (2) frees the remedy of resale from legalistic restrictions and enables the seller to resell in accordance with reasonable commercial practices so as to realize as high a price as possible in the circumstances. By "public" sale is meant a sale by auction. A "private" sale may be effected by solicitation and negotiation conducted either directly or through a broker. In choosing between a public and private sale the character of the goods must be considered and relevant trade practices and usages must be observed.

5. Subsection (2) merely clarifies the common law rule that the time for resale is a reasonable time after the buyer's breach, by using the language "commercially reasonable." What is such a reasonable time depends upon the nature of the goods, the condition of the market and the other circumstances of the case; its length cannot be measured by any legal yardstick or divided into degrees. Where a seller contemplating resale receives a demand from the buyer for inspection under the section of preserving evidence of goods in dispute, the time for resale may be appropriately lengthened.

On the question of the place for resale, subsection (2) goes to the ultimate test, the commercial reasonableness of the seller's choice as to the place for an advantageous resale. This Article rejects the theory that the seller is required to resell at the agreed place for delivery and that a resale elsewhere can be permitted only in exceptional cases.

6. The purpose of subsection (2) being to enable the seller to dispose of the goods to the best advantage, he is permitted in making the resale to depart from the terms and conditions of the original contract for sale to any extent "commercially reasonable" in the circumstances.

7. The provision of subsection (2) that the goods need not be in existence to be resold applies when the buyer is guilty of anticipatory repudiation of a contract for future goods, before the goods or some of them have come into existence. In such a case the seller may exercise the right of resale and fix his damages by "one or more contracts to sell" the quantity of conforming future goods affected by the repudiation. The companion provision of subsection (2) that resale may be made although the goods were not identified to the contract prior to the buyer's breach, likewise contemplates an anticipatory repudiation by the buyer but occurring after the goods are in existence. If the goods so identified conform to the contract, their resale will fix the seller's damages quite as satisfactorily as if they had been identified before the breach.

8. Where the resale is to be by private sale, subsection (3) requires that reasonable notification of the seller's intention to resell must be given to the buyer. The length of notification of a private sale depends upon the urgency of the matter. Notification of the time and place of this type of sale is not required.

Subsection (4)(b) requires that the seller give the buyer reasonable notice of the time and place of a public resale so that he may have an opportunity to bid or to secure the attendance of other bidders. An exception is made in the case of goods "which are perishable or threaten to decline speedily in value."

9. Since there would be no reasonable prospect of competitive bidding elsewhere, subsection (4) requires that a public resale "must be made at a usual place or market for public sale if one is reasonably available;" i.e., a place or market which prospective bidders may reasonably be expected to attend. Such a market may still be "reasonably available" under this subsection, though at a considerable distance from the place where the goods are located. In such a case the expense of transporting the goods for resale is recoverable from the buyer as part of the seller's incidental damages under subsection (1). However, the question of availability is one of commercial reasonableness in the circumstances and if such "usual" place or market is not reasonably available, a duly advertised public resale may be held at another place if it is one which prospective bidders may reasonably be expected to attend, as distinguished from a place where there is no demand whatsoever for goods of the kind.

Paragraph (a) of subsection (4) qualifies the last sentence of subsection (2) with respect to resales of unidentified and future goods at public sale. If conforming goods are in existence the seller may identify them to the contract after the buyer's breach and then resell them at public sale. If the goods have not been identified, however, he may resell them at public sale only as "future" goods and only where there is a recognized market for public sale of futures in goods of the kind.

The provisions of paragraph (c) of subsection (4) are intended to permit intelligent bidding.

The provision of paragraph (d) of subsection (4) permitting the seller to bid and, of course, to become the purchaser, benefits the original buyer by tending to increase the resale price and thus decreasing the damages he will have to pay.

10. This Article departs in subsection (5) from the prior uniform statutory provision in permitting a good faith purchaser at resale to take a good title as against the buyer even though the seller fails to

comply with the requirements of this section.

11. Under subsection (6), the seller retains profit, if any, without distinction based on whether or not he had a lien since this Article divorces the question of passage of title to the buyer from the seller's right of resale or the consequences of its exercise. On the other hand, where "a person in the position of a seller" or a buyer acting under the section on buyer's remedies, exercises his right of resale under the present section he does so only for the limited purpose of obtaining cash for his "security interest" in the goods. Once that purpose has been accomplished any excess in the resale price belongs to the seller to whom an accounting must be made as provided in the last sentence of subsection (6).

Cross References:

Point 1: Sections 2–610, 2–702 and 2–703.

Point 2: Section 1–201.

Point 3: Sections 2–708 and 2–710.

Point 4: Section 2–328.

Point 8: Section 2–104.

Point 9: Section 2–710.

Point 11: Sections 2–401, 2–707 and 2–711(3).

Definitional Cross References:

"Buyer". Section 2–103.
"Contract". Section 1–201.
"Contract for sale". Section 2–106.
"Good faith". Section 2–103.
"Goods". Section 2–105.
"Merchant". Section 2–104.
"Notification". Section 1–201.
"Person in position of seller". Section 2–707.
"Purchase". Section 1–201.
"Rights". Section 1–201.
"Sale". Section 2–106.
"Security interest". Section 1–201.
"Seller". Section 2–103.

§ 2–707. "Person in the Position of a Seller".

(1) A "person in the position of a seller" includes as against a principal an agent who has paid or become responsible for the price of goods on behalf of his principal or anyone who otherwise holds a security interest or other right in goods similar to that of a seller.

(2) A person in the position of a seller may as provided in this Article withhold or stop delivery (Section 2–705) and resell (Section 2–706) and recover incidental damages (Section 2–710).

Official Comment

Prior Uniform Statutory Provision: Section 52(2), Uniform Sales Act.

Changes: Rewritten.

Purposes of Changes: To make it clear that:

In addition to following in general the prior uniform statutory provision, the case of a financing agency which has acquired documents by honoring a letter of credit for the buyer or by discounting a draft for the seller has been included in the term "a person in the position of a seller."

Cross Reference:

Article 5, Section 2–506.

Definitional Cross References:

"Consignee". Section 7–102.
"Consignor". Section 7–102.
"Goods". Section 2–105.
"Security interest". Section 1–201.
"Seller". Section 2–103.

§ 2–708. Seller's Damages for Non-acceptance or Repudiation.

(1) Subject to subsection (2) and to the provisions of this Article with respect to proof of market price (Section 2–723), the measure of damages for

non-acceptance or repudiation by the buyer is the difference between the market price at the time and place for tender and the unpaid contract price together with any incidental damages provided in this Article (Section 2-710), but less expenses saved in consequence of the buyer's breach.

(2) If the measure of damages provided in subsection (1) is inadequate to put the seller in as good a position as performance would have done then the measure of damages is the profit (including reasonable overhead) which the seller would have made from full performance by the buyer, together with any incidental damages provided in this Article (Section 2-710), due allowance for costs reasonably incurred and due credit for payments or proceeds of resale.

Official Comment

Prior Uniform Statutory Provision: Section 64, Uniform Sales Act.

Changes: Rewritten.

Purposes of Changes: To make it clear that:

1. The prior uniform statutory provision is followed generally in setting the current market price at the time and place for tender as the standard by which damages for non-acceptance are to be determined. The time and place of tender is determined by reference to the section on manner of tender of delivery, and to the sections on the effect of such terms as FOB, FAS, CIF, C & F, Ex Ship and No Arrival, No Sale.

In the event that there is no evidence available of the current market price at the time and place of tender, proof of a substitute market may be made under the section on determination and proof of market price. Furthermore, the section on the admissibility of market quotations is intended to ease materially the problem of providing competent evidence.

2. The provision of this section permitting recovery of expected profit including reasonable overhead where the standard measure of damages is inadequate, together with the new requirement that price actions may be sustained only where resale is impractical, are designed to eliminate the unfair and economically wasteful results arising under the older law when fixed price articles were involved. This section permits the recovery of lost profits in all appropriate cases, which would include all standard priced goods. The normal measure there would be list price less cost to the dealer or list price less manufacturing cost to the manufacturer. It is not necessary to a recovery of "profit" to show a history of earnings, especially of a new venture is involved.

3. In all cases the seller may recover incidental damages.

Cross References:

Point 1: Sections 2-319 through 2-324, 2-503, 2-723 and 2-724.
Point 2: Section 2-709.
Point 3: Section 2-710.

Definitional Cross References:

"Buyer". Section 2-103.
"Contract". Section 1-201.
"Seller". Section 2-103.

§ 2-709. Action for the Price.

(1) When the buyer fails to pay the price as it becomes due the seller may recover, together with any incidental damages under the next section, the price

(a) of goods accepted or of conforming goods lost or damaged within a commercially reasonable time after risk of their loss has passed to the buyer; and

(b) of goods identified to the contract if the seller is unable after reasonable effort to resell them at a reasonable price or the circumstances reasonably indicate that such effort will be unavailing.

(2) Where the seller sues for the price he must hold for the buyer any goods which have been identified to the contract and are still in his control except that if resale becomes possible he may resell them at any time prior to the collection of the judgment. The net proceeds of any such resale must be credited to the buyer and payment of the judgment entitles him to any goods not resold.

(3) After the buyer has wrongfully rejected or revoked acceptance of the goods or has failed to make a payment due or has repudiated (Section 2-610), a seller who is held not entitled to the price under this section shall nevertheless be awarded damages for non-acceptance under the preceding section.

Official Comment

Prior Uniform Statutory Provision: Section 63, Uniform Sales Act.

Changes: Rewritten, important commercially needed changes being incorporated.

Purposes of Changes: To make it clear that:

1. Neither the passing of title to the goods nor the appointment of a day certain for payment is now material to a price action.

2. The action for the price is now generally limited to those cases where resale of the goods is impracticable except where the buyer has accepted the goods or where they have been destroyed after risk of loss has passed to the buyer.

3. This section substitutes an objective test by action for the former "not readily resalable" standard. An action for the price under subsection (1)(b) can be sustained only after a "reasonable effort to resell" the goods "at reasonable price" has actually been made or where the circumstances "reasonably indicate" that such an effort will be unavailing.

4. If a buyer is in default not with respect to the price, but on an obligation to make an advance, the seller should recover not under this section for the price as such, but for the default in the collateral (though coincident) obligation to finance the seller. If the agreement between the parties contemplates that the buyer will acquire, on making the advance, a security interest in the goods, the buyer on making the advance has such an interest as soon as the seller has rights in the agreed collateral. See Section 9-204.

5. "Goods accepted" by the buyer under subsection (1)(a) include only goods as to which there has been no justified revocation of acceptance, for such a revocation means that there has been a default by the seller which bars his rights under this section. "Goods lost or damaged" are covered by the section on risk of loss. "Goods identified to the contract" under subsection (1)(b) are covered by the section on identification and the section on identification notwithstanding breach.

6. This section is intended to be exhaustive in its enumeration of cases where an action for the price lies.

7. If the action for the price fails, the seller may nonetheless have proved a case entitling him to damages for non-acceptance. In such a situation, subsection (3) permits recovery of those damages in the same action.

Cross References:

Point 4: Section 1-106.

Point 5: Sections 2-501, 2-509, 2-510 and 2-704.

Point 7: Section 2-708.

Definitional Cross References:

"Action". Section 1-201.
"Buyer". Section 2-103.
"Conforming". Section 2-106.
"Contract". Section 1-201.
"Goods". Section 2-105.
"Seller". Section 2-103.

§ 2-710. Seller's Incidental Damages.

Incidental damages to an aggrieved seller include any commercially reasonable charges, expenses or commissions incurred in stopping delivery, in the transportation, care and custody of goods after the buyer's breach, in connection with return or resale of the goods or otherwise resulting from the breach.

Official Comment

Prior Uniform Statutory Provision: See Sections 64 and 70, Uniform Sales Act.

Purposes: To authorize reimbursement of the seller for expenses reasonably incurred by him as a result of the buyer's breach. The section sets forth the principal normal and necessary additional elements of damage flowing from the breach but intends to allow all commercially reasonable expenditures made by the seller.

Definitional Cross References:

"Aggrieved party". Section 1-201.
"Buyer". Section 2-103.
"Goods". Section 2-105.
"Seller". Section 2-103.

§ 2-711. Buyer's Remedies in General; Buyer's Security Interest in Rejected Goods.

(1) Where the seller fails to make delivery or repudiates or the buyer rightfully rejects or justifiably revokes acceptance then with respect to any goods involved, and with respect to the whole if the breach goes to the whole contract (Section 2-612), the buyer may cancel and whether or not he has done so may in addition to recovering so much of the price as has been paid

(a) "cover" and have damages under the next section as to all the goods affected whether or not they have been identified to the contract; or

(b) recover damages for non-delivery as provided in this Article (Section 2-713).

(2) Where the seller fails to deliver or repudiates the buyer may also

(a) if the goods have been identified recover them as provided in this Article (Section 2-502); or

(b) in a proper case obtain specific performance or replevy the goods as provided in this Article (Section 2-716).

(3) On rightful rejection or justifiable revocation of acceptance a buyer has a security interest in goods in his possession or control for any payments made on their price and any expenses reasonably incurred in their inspection, receipt, transportation, care and custody and may hold such goods and resell them in like manner as an aggrieved seller (Section 2-706).

Official Comment

Prior Uniform Statutory Provision: No comparable index section; Subsection (3)—Section 69(5), Uniform Sales Act.

Changes: The prior uniform statutory provision is generally continued and expanded in Subsection (3).

Purposes of Changes and New Matter:

1. To index in this section the buyer's remedies, subsection (1) covering those remedies permitting the recovery of money damages, and subsection (2) covering those which permit reaching the goods themselves. The remedies listed here are those available to a buyer who has not accepted the goods or who has justifiably revoked his acceptance. The remedies available to a buyer with regard to goods finally accepted appear in the section dealing with breach in regard to accepted goods. The buyer's right to proceed as to all goods when the breach is as to only some of the goods is determined by the section on breach in installment contracts and by the section on partial acceptance.

Despite the seller's breach, proper retender of delivery under the section on cure of improper tender or replacement can effectively preclude the buyer's remedies under this section, except for any delay involved.

2. To make it clear in subsection (3) that the buyer may hold and resell rejected goods if he has paid a part of the price or incurred expenses of the type specified. "Paid" as used here includes acceptance of a draft or other time negotiable instrument or the signing of a negotiable note. His freedom of resale is coextensive with that of a seller under this Article except that the buyer may not keep any profit resulting from the resale and is limited to retaining only the amount of the price paid and the costs involved in the inspection and handling of the goods. The buyer's security interest in the goods is intended to be limited to the items listed in subsection (3), and the buyer is not permitted to retain such funds as he might believe adequate for his damages. The buyer's right to cover, or to have damages for non-delivery, is not impaired by his exercise of his right of resale.

3. It should also be noted that this Act requires its remedies to be liberally administered and provides that any right or obligation which it declares is enforceable by action unless a different effect is specifically prescribed (Section 1–106).

Cross References:

Point 1: Sections 2–508, 2–601(c), 2–608, 2–612 and 2–714.
Point 2: Section 2–706.
Point 3: Section 1–106.

Definitional Cross References:

"Aggrieved party". Section 1–201.
"Buyer". Section 2–103.
"Cancellation". Section 2–106.
"Contract". Section 1–201.
"Cover". Section 2–712.
"Goods". Section 2–105.
"Notifies". Section 1–201.
"Receipt" of goods. Section 2–103.
"Remedy". Section 1–201.
"Security interest". Section 1–201.
"Seller". Section 2–103.

§ 2–712. "Cover"; Buyer's Procurement of Substitute Goods.

(1) After a breach within the preceding section the buyer may "cover" by making in good faith and without unreasonable delay any reasonable purchase of or contract to purchase goods in substitution for those due from the seller.

(2) The buyer may recover from the seller as damages the difference between the cost of cover and the contract price together with any incidental or consequential damages as hereinafter defined (Section 2–715), but less expenses saved in consequence of the seller's breach.

(3) Failure of the buyer to effect cover within this section does not bar him from any other remedy.

Official Comment

Prior Uniform Statutory Provision: None.

Purposes:

1. This section provides the buyer with a remedy aimed at enabling him to obtain the goods he needs thus meeting his essential need. This remedy is the buyer's equivalent of the seller's right to resell.

2. The definition of "cover" under subsection (1) envisages a series of contracts or sales, as well as a single contract or sale; goods not identical with those involved but commercially usable as reasonable substitutes under the circumstances of the particular case; and contracts on credit or delivery terms differing from the contract in breach, but again reasonable under the circumstances. The test of proper cover is whether at the time and place the buyer acted in good faith and in a reasonable manner, and it is immaterial that hindsight may later prove that the method of cover used was not the cheapest or most effective.

The requirement that the buyer must cover "without unreasonable delay" is not intended to limit the time necessary for him to look around and decide as to how he may best effect cover. The test here is similar to that generally used in this Article as to reasonable time and seasonable action.

3. Subsection (3) expresses the policy that cover is not a mandatory remedy for the buyer. The buyer is always free to choose between cover and damages for non-delivery under the next section.

However, this subsection must be read in conjunction with the section which limits the recovery of consequential damages to such as could not have been obviated by cover. Moreover, the operation of the section on specific performance of contracts for "unique" goods must be considered in this connection for availability of the goods to the particular buyer for his particular needs is the test for that remedy and inability to cover is made an express condition to the right of the buyer to replevy the goods.

4. This section does not limit cover to merchants, in the first instance. It is the vital and important remedy for the consumer buyer as well. Both are free to use cover: the domestic or non-merchant consumer is required only to act in normal good faith while the merchant buyer must also observe all reasonable commercial standards of fair dealing in the trade, since this falls within the definition of good faith on his part.

Cross References:

Point 1: Section 2–706.
Point 2: Section 1–204.
Point 3: Sections 2–713, 2–715 and 2–716.
Point 4: Section 1–203.

Definitional Cross References:

"Buyer". Section 2–103.
"Contract". Section 1–201.
"Good faith". Section 2–103.
"Goods". Section 2–105.
"Purchase". Section 1–201.
"Remedy". Section 1–201.
"Seller". Section 2–103.

§ 2–713. Buyer's Damages for Non-delivery or Repudiation.

(1) Subject to the provisions of this Article with respect to proof of market price (Section 2–723), the measure of damages for non-delivery or repudiation by the seller is the difference between the market price at the time when the buyer learned of the breach and the contract price together with any incidental and consequential damages provided in this Article (Section 2–715), but less expenses saved in consequence of the seller's breach.

(2) Market price is to be determined as of the place for tender or, in cases of rejection after arrival or revocation of acceptance, as of the place of arrival.

Official Comment

Prior Uniform Statutory Provision: Section 67(3), Uniform Sales Act.

Changes: Rewritten.

Purposes of Changes: To clarify the former rule so that:

1. The general baseline adopted in this section uses as a yardstick the market in which the buyer would have obtained cover had he sought that relief. So the place for measuring damages is the place of tender (or the place of arrival if the goods are rejected or their acceptance is revoked after reaching their destination) and the crucial time is the time at which the buyer learns of the breach.

2. The market or current price to be used in comparison with the contract price under this section is the price for goods of the same kind and in the same branch of trade.

3. When the current market price under this section is difficult to prove the section on determination and proof of market price is available to permit a showing of a comparable market price or, where no market price is available, evidence of spot sale prices is proper. Where the unavailability of a market price is caused by a scarcity of goods of the type involved, a good case is normally made for specific performance under this Article. Such scarcity conditions, moreover, indicate that the price has risen and under the section providing for liberal administration of remedies, opinion evidence as to the value of the goods would be admissible in the absence of a market price and a liberal construction of allowable consequential damages should also result.

4. This section carries forward the standard rule that the buyer must deduct from his damages any expenses saved as a result of the breach.

5. The present section provides a remedy which is completely alternative to cover under the preceding section and applies only when and to the extent that the buyer has not covered.

Cross References:

Point 3: Sections 1-106, 2-716 and 2-723.

Point 5: Section 2-712.

Definitional Cross References:

"Buyer". Section 2-103.
"Contract". Section 1-201.
"Seller". Section 2-103.

§ 2-714. Buyer's Damages for Breach in Regard to Accepted Goods.

(1) Where the buyer has accepted goods and given notification (subsection (3) of Section 2-607) he may recover as damages for any non-conformity of tender the loss resulting in the ordinary course of events from the seller's breach as determined in any manner which is reasonable.

(2) The measure of damages for breach of warranty is the difference at the time and place of acceptance between the value of the goods accepted and the value they would have had if they had been as warranted, unless special circumstances show proximate damages of a different amount.

(3) In a proper case any incidental and consequential damages under the next section may also be recovered.

Official Comment

Prior Uniform Statutory Provision: Section 69(6) and (7), Uniform Sales Act.

Changes: Rewritten.

Purposes of Changes:

1. This section deals with the remedies available to the buyer after the goods have been accepted and the time for revocation of acceptance has gone by. In general this section adopts the rule of the prior uniform statutory provision for measuring damages where there has been a breach of warranty as to goods accepted, but goes further to lay down an explicit provision as to the time and place for determining the loss.

The section on deduction of damages from price provides an additional remedy for a buyer who still owes part of the purchase price, and frequently the two remedies will be available concurrently. The buyer's failure to notify of his claim under the section on effects of acceptance, however, operates to bar his remedies under either that section or the present section.

2. The "non-conformity" referred to in subsection (1) includes not only breaches of warranties but also any failure of the seller to perform according to his obligations under the contract. In the case of such non-conformity, the buyer is permitted to recover for his loss "in any manner which is reasonable."

3. Subsection (2) describes the usual, standard and reasonable method of ascertaining damages in the case of breach of warranty but it is not intended as an exclusive measure. It departs from the measure of damages for non-delivery in utilizing the place of acceptance rather than the place of tender. In some cases the two may coincide, as where the buyer signifies his acceptance upon the tender. If, however, the non-conformity is such as would justify revocation of acceptance, the time and place of acceptance under this section is determined as of the buyer's decision not to revoke.

4. The incidental and consequential damages referred to in subsection (3), which will usually accompany an action brought under this section, are discussed in detail in the comment on the next section.

Cross References:

Point 1: Compare Section 2–711; Sections 2–607 and 2–717.
Point 2: Section 2–106.
Point 3: Sections 2–608 and 2–713.
Point 4: Section 2–715.

Definitional Cross References:

"Buyer". Section 2–103.
"Conform". Section 2–106.
"Goods". Section 1–201.
"Notification". Section 1–201.
"Seller". Section 2–103.

§ 2–715. Buyer's Incidental and Consequential Damages.

(1) Incidental damages resulting from the seller's breach include expenses reasonably incurred in inspection, receipt, transportation and care and custody of goods rightfully rejected, any commercially reasonable charges, expenses or commissions in connection with effecting cover and any other reasonable expense incident to the delay or other breach.

(2) Consequential damages resulting from the seller's breach include

(a) any loss resulting from general or particular requirements and needs of which the seller at the time of contracting had reason to know and which could not reasonably be prevented by cover or otherwise; and

(b) injury to person or property proximately resulting from any breach of warranty.

Official Comment

Prior Uniform Statutory Provisions: Subsection (2)(b)—Sections 69(7) and 70, Uniform Sales Act.

Changes: Rewritten.

Purposes of Changes and New Matter:

1. Subsection (1) is intended to provide reimbursement for the buyer who incurs reasonable expenses in connection with the handling of rightfully rejected goods or goods whose acceptance may be justifiably revoked, or in connection with effecting cover where the breach of the contract lies in non-conformity or non-delivery of the goods. The incidental damages listed are not intended to be exhaustive but are merely illustrative of the typical kinds of incidental damage.

2. Subsection (2) operates to allow the buyer, in an appropriate case, any consequential damages which are the result of the seller's breach. The "tacit agreement" test for the recovery of consequential damages is rejected. Although the older rule at common law which made the seller liable for all consequential damages of which he had "reason to know" in advance is followed, the liberality of that rule is modified by refusing to permit recovery unless the buyer could not reasonably have prevented the loss by cover or otherwise. Subparagraph (2) carries forward the provisions of the prior uniform statutory provision as to consequential damages resulting from breach of warranty, but modifies the rule by requiring first that the buyer attempt to minimize his damages in good faith, either by cover or otherwise.

3. In the absence of excuse under the section on merchant's excuse by failure of presupposed conditions, the seller is liable for consequential damages in all cases where he had reason to know of the buyer's general or particular requirements at the time of contracting. It is not necessary that there be a conscious acceptance of an insurer's liability on the seller's part, nor is his obligation for consequential damages limited to cases in which he fails to use due effort in good faith.

Particular needs of the buyer must generally be made known to the seller while general needs must rarely be made known to charge the seller with knowledge.

Any seller who does not wish to take the risk of consequential damages has available the section on contractual limitation of remedy.

4. The burden of proving the extent of loss incurred by way of consequential damage is on the buyer, but the section on liberal administration of remedies rejects any doctrine of certainty which requires almost mathematical precision in the proof of loss. Loss may be determined in any manner which is reasonable under the circumstances.

5. Subsection (2)(b) states the usual rule as to breach of warranty, allowing recovery for injuries "proximately" resulting from the breach. Where the injury involved follows the use of goods without discovery of the defect causing the damage, the question of "proximate" cause turns on whether it was reasonable for the buyer to use the goods without such inspection as would have revealed the defects. If it was not reasonable for him to do so, or if he did in fact discover the defect prior to his use, the injury would not proximately result from the breach of warranty.

6. In the case of sale of wares to one in the business of reselling them, resale is one of the requirements of which the seller has reason to know within the meaning of subsection (2)(a).

Cross References:

Point 1: Section 2-608.

Point 3: Sections 1-203, 2-615 and 2-719.

Point 4: Section 1-106.

Definitional Cross References:

"Cover". Section 2-712.

"Goods". Section 1-201.

"Person". Section 1-201.

"Receipt" of goods. Section 2-103.
"Seller". Section 2-103.

§ 2-716. Buyer's Right to Specific Performance or Replevin.

(1) Specific performance may be decreed where the goods are unique or in other proper circumstances.

(2) The decree for specific performance may include such terms and conditions as to payment of the price, damages, or other relief as the court may deem just.

(3) The buyer has a right of replevin for goods identified to the contract if after reasonable effort he is unable to effect cover for such goods or the circumstances reasonably indicate that such effort will be unavailing or if the goods have been shipped under reservation and satisfaction of the security interest in them has been made or tendered.

Official Comment

Prior Uniform Statutory Provision: Section 68, Uniform Sales Act.

Changes: Rephrased.

Purposes of Changes: To make it clear that:

1. The present section continues in general prior policy as to specific performance and injunction against breach. However, without intending to impair in any way the exercise of the court's sound discretion in the matter, this Article seeks to further a more liberal attitude than some courts have shown in connection with the specific performance of contracts of sale.

2. In view of this Article's emphasis on the commercial feasibility of replacement, a new concept of what are "unique" goods is introduced under this section. Specific performance is no longer limited to goods which are already specific or ascertained at the time of contracting. The test of uniqueness under this section must be made in terms of the total situation which characterizes the contract. Output and requirements contracts involving a particular or peculiarly available source or market present today the typical commercial specific performance situation, as contrasted with contracts for the sale of heirlooms or priceless works of art which were usually involved in the older cases. However, uniqueness is not the sole basis of the remedy under this section for the relief may also be granted "in other proper circumstances" and inability to cover is strong evidence of "other proper circumstances".

3. The legal remedy of replevin is given the buyer in cases in which cover is reasonably unavailable and goods have been identified to the contract. This is in addition to the buyer's right to recover identified goods on the seller's insolvency (Section 2-502).

4. This section is intended to give the buyer rights to the goods comparable to the seller's rights to the price.

5. If a negotiable document of title is outstanding, the buyer's right of replevin relates of course to the document not directly to the goods. See Article 7, especially Section 7-602.

Cross References:

Point 3: Section 2-502.
Point 4: Section 2-709.
Point 5: Article 7.

Definitional Cross References:

"Buyer". Section 2-103.
"Goods". Section 1-201.
"Rights". Section 1-201.

§ 2–717. Deduction of Damages From the Price.

The buyer on notifying the seller of his intention to do so may deduct all or any part of the damages resulting from any breach of the contract from any part of the price still due under the same contract.

Official Comment

Prior Uniform Statutory Provision: See Section 69(1)(a), Uniform Sales Act.

Purposes:

1. This section permits the buyer to deduct from the price damages resulting from any breach by the seller and does not limit the relief to cases of breach of warranty as did the prior uniform statutory provision. To bring this provision into application the breach involved must be of the same contract under which the price in question is claimed to have been earned.

2. The buyer, however, must give notice of his intention to withhold all or part of the price if he wishes to avoid a default within the meaning of the section on insecurity and right to assurances. In conformity with the general policies of this Article, no formality of notice is required and any language which reasonably indicates the buyer's reason for holding up his payment is sufficient.

Cross Reference:

Point 2: Section 2–609.

Definitional Cross References:

"Buyer". Section 2–103.
"Notifies". Section 1–201.

§ 2–718. Liquidation or Limitation of Damages; Deposits.

(1) Damages for breach by either party may be liquidated in the agreement but only at an amount which is reasonable in the light of the anticipated or actual harm caused by the breach, the difficulties of proof of loss, and the inconvenience or nonfeasibility of otherwise obtaining an adequate remedy. A term fixing unreasonably large liquidated damages is void as a penalty.

(2) Where the seller justifiably withholds delivery of goods because of the buyer's breach, the buyer is entitled to restitution of any amount by which the sum of his payments exceeds

(a) the amount to which the seller is entitled by virtue of terms liquidating the seller's damages in accordance with subsection (1), or

(b) in the absence of such terms, twenty per cent of the value of the total performance for which the buyer is obligated under the contract or $500, whichever is smaller.

(3) The buyer's right to restitution under subsection (2) is subject to offset to the extent that the seller establishes

(a) a right to recover damages under the provisions of this Article other than subsection (1), and

(b) the amount or value of any benefits received by the buyer directly or indirectly by reason of the contract.

(4) Where a seller has received payment in goods their reasonable value or the proceeds of their resale shall be treated as payments for the purposes of subsection (2); but if the seller has notice of the buyer's breach before reselling goods received in part performance, his resale is subject to the

conditions laid down in this Article on resale by an aggrieved seller (Section 2–706).

Official Comment

Prior Uniform Statutory Provision: None.

Purposes:

1. Under subsection (1) liquidated damage clauses are allowed where the amount involved is reasonable in the light of the circumstances of the case. The subsection sets forth explicitly the elements to be considered in determining the reasonableness of a liquidated damage clause. A term fixing unreasonably large liquidated damages is expressly made void as a penalty. An unreasonably small amount would be subject to similar criticism and might be stricken under the section on unconscionable contracts or clauses.

2. Subsection (2) refuses to recognize a forfeiture unless the amount of the payment so forfeited represents a reasonable liquidation of damages as determined under subsection (1). A special exception is made in the case of small amounts (20% of the price or $500, whichever is smaller) deposited as security. No distinction is made between cases in which the payment is to be applied on the price and those in which it is intended as security for performance. Subsection (2) is applicable to any deposit or down or part payment. In the case of a deposit or turn in of goods resold before the breach, the amount actually received on the resale is to be viewed as the deposit rather than the amount allowed the buyer for the trade in. However, if the seller knows of the breach prior to the resale of the goods turned in, he must make reasonable efforts to realize their true value, and this is assured by requiring him to comply with the conditions laid down in the section on resale by an aggrieved seller.

Cross References:

Point 1: Section 2–302.
Point 2: Section 2–706.

Definitional Cross References:

"Aggrieved party". Section 1–201.
"Agreement". Section 1–201.
"Buyer". Section 2–103.
"Goods". Section 2–105.
"Notice". Section 1–201.
"Party". Section 1–201.
"Remedy". Section 1–201.
"Seller". Section 2–103.
"Term". Section 1–201.

§ 2–719. Contractual Modification or Limitation of Remedy.

(1) Subject to the provisions of subsections (2) and (3) of this section and of the preceding section on liquidation and limitation of damages,

(a) the agreement may provide for remedies in addition to or in substitution for those provided in this Article and may limit or alter the measure of damages recoverable under this Article, as by limiting the buyer's remedies to return of the goods and repayment of the price or to repair and replacement of non-conforming goods or parts; and

(b) resort to a remedy as provided is optional unless the remedy is expressly agreed to be exclusive, in which case it is the sole remedy.

(2) Where circumstances cause an exclusive or limited remedy to fail of its essential purpose, remedy may be had as provided in this Act.

(3) Consequential damages may be limited or excluded unless the limitation or exclusion is unconscionable. Limitation of consequential damages for injury to the person in the case of consumer goods is prima facie unconscionable but limitation of damages where the loss is commercial is not.

Official Comment

Prior Uniform Statutory Provision: None.

Purposes:

1. Under this section parties are left free to shape their remedies to their particular requirements and reasonable agreements limiting or modifying remedies are to be given effect.

However, it is of the very essence of a sales contract that at least minimum adequate remedies be available. If the parties intend to conclude a contract for sale within this Article they must accept the legal consequence that there be at least a fair quantum of remedy for breach of the obligations or duties outlined in the contract. Thus any clause purporting to modify or limit the remedial provisions of this Article in an unconscionable manner is subject to deletion and in that event the remedies made available by this Article are applicable as if the stricken clause had never existed. Similarly, under subsection (2), where an apparently fair and reasonable clause because of circumstances fails in its purpose or operates to deprive either party of the substantial value of the bargain, it must give way to the general remedy provisions of this Article.

2. Subsection (1)(b) creates a presumption that clauses prescribing remedies are cumulative rather than exclusive. If the parties intend the term to describe the sole remedy under the contract, this must be clearly expressed.

3. Subsection (3) recognizes the validity of clauses limiting or excluding consequential damages but makes it clear that they may not operate in an unconscionable manner. Actually such terms are merely an allocation of unknown or undeterminable risks. The seller in all cases is free to disclaim warranties in the manner provided in Section 2–316.

Cross References:

Point 1: Section 2–302.
Point 3: Section 2–316.

Definitional Cross References:

"Agreement". Section 1–201.
"Buyer". Section 2–103.
"Conforming". Section 2–106.
"Contract". Section 1–201.
"Goods". Section 2–105.
"Remedy". Section 1–201.
"Seller". Section 2–103.

§ 2–720. Effect of "Cancellation" or "Rescission" on Claims for Antecedent Breach.

Unless the contrary intention clearly appears, expressions of "cancellation" or "rescission" of the contract or the like shall not be construed as a renunciation or discharge of any claim in damages for an antecedent breach.

Official Comment

Prior Uniform Statutory Provision: None.

Purpose:

This section is designed to safeguard a person holding a right of action from any unintentional loss of rights by the ill-advised use of such terms as "cancellation", "rescission", or the like. Once a party's rights have accrued they are not to be lightly impaired by concessions made in business decency and without intention to forego them. Therefore, unless the cancellation of a contract expressly declares that it is "without reservation of rights", or the like, it cannot be considered to be a renunciation under this section.

Cross Reference:

Section 1–107.

Definitional Cross References:

"Cancellation". Section 2–106.
"Contract". Section 1–201.

§ 2-721. Remedies for Fraud.

Remedies for material misrepresentation or fraud include all remedies available under this Article for non-fraudulent breach. Neither rescission or a claim for rescission of the contract for sale nor rejection or return of the goods shall bar or be deemed inconsistent with a claim for damages or other remedy.

Official Comment

Prior Uniform Statutory Provision: None.

Purposes: To correct the situation by which remedies for fraud have been more circumscribed than the more modern and mercantile remedies for breach of warranty. Thus the remedies for fraud are extended by this section to coincide in scope with those for non-fraudulent breach. This section thus makes it clear that neither rescission of the contract for fraud nor rejection of the goods bars other remedies unless the circumstances of the case make the remedies incompatible.

Definitional Cross References:

"Contract for sale". Section 2-106.
"Goods". Section 1-201.
"Remedy". Section 1-201.

§ 2-722. Who Can Sue Third Parties for Injury to Goods.

Where a third party so deals with goods which have been identified to a contract for sale as to cause actionable injury to a party to that contract

(a) a right of action against the third party is in either party to the contract for sale who has title to or a security interest or a special property or an insurable interest in the goods; and if the goods have been destroyed or converted a right of action is also in the party who either bore the risk of loss under the contract for sale or has since the injury assumed that risk as against the other;

(b) if at the time of the injury the party plaintiff did not bear the risk of loss as against the other party to the contract for sale and there is no arrangement between them for disposition of the recovery, his suit or settlement is, subject to his own interest, as a fiduciary for the other party to the contract;

(c) either party may with the consent of the other sue for the benefit of whom it may concern.

Official Comment

Prior Uniform Statutory Provision: None.

Purposes: To adopt and extend somewhat the principle of the statutes which provide for suit by the real party in interest. The provisions of this section apply only after identification of the goods. Prior to that time only the seller has a right of action. During the period between identification and final acceptance (except in the case of revocation of acceptance) it is possible for both parties to have the right of action. Even after final acceptance both parties may have the right of action if the seller retains possession or otherwise retains an interest.

Definitional Cross References:

"Action". Section 1-201.
"Buyer". Section 2-103.
"Contract for sale". Section 2-106.
"Goods". Section 2-105.

"Party". Section 1–201.
"Rights". Section 1–201.
"Security interest". Section 1–201.

§ 2–723. Proof of Market Price: Time and Place.

(1) If an action based on anticipatory repudiation comes to trial before the time for performance with respect to some or all of the goods, any damages based on market price (Section 2–708 or Section 2–713) shall be determined according to the price of such goods prevailing at the time when the aggrieved party learned of the repudiation.

(2) If evidence of a price prevailing at the times or places described in this Article is not readily available the price prevailing within any reasonable time before or after the time described or at any other place which in commercial judgment or under usage of trade would serve as a reasonable substitute for the one described may be used, making any proper allowance for the cost of transporting the goods to or from such other place.

(3) Evidence of a relevant price prevailing at a time or place other than the one described in this Article offered by one party is not admissible unless and until he has given the other party such notice as the court finds sufficient to prevent unfair surprise.

Official Comment

Prior Uniform Statutory Provision: None.

Purposes: To eliminate the most obvious difficulties arising in connection with the determination of market price, when that is stipulated as a measure of damages by some provision of this Article. Where the appropriate market price is not readily available the court is here granted reasonable leeway in receiving evidence of prices current in other comparable markets or at other times comparable to the one in question. In accordance with the general principle of this Article against surprise, however, a party intending to offer evidence of such a substitute price must give suitable notice to the other party.

This section is not intended to exclude the use of any other reasonable method of determining market price or of measuring damages if the circumstances of the case make this necessary.

Definitional Cross References:

"Action". Section 1–201.
"Aggrieved party". Section 1–201.
"Goods". Section 2–105.
"Notifies". Section 1–201.
"Party". Section 1–201.
"Reasonable time". Section 1–204.
"Usage of trade". Section 1–205.

§ 2–724. Admissibility of Market Quotations.

Whenever the prevailing price or value of any goods regularly bought and sold in any established commodity market is in issue, reports in official publications or trade journals or in newspapers or periodicals of general circulation published as the reports of such market shall be admissible in evidence. The circumstances of the preparation of such a report may be shown to affect its weight but not its admissibility.

Official Comment

Prior Uniform Statutory Provision: None.

Purposes: To make market quotations admissible in evidence while providing for a challenge of the material by showing the circumstances of its preparation.

No explicit provision as to the weight to be given to market quotations is contained in this section, but such quotations, in the absence of compelling challenge, offer an adequate basis for a verdict.

Market quotations are made admissible when the price or value of goods traded "in any established market" is in issue. The reason of the section does not require that the market be closely organized in the manner of a produce exchange. It is sufficient if transactions in the commodity are frequent and open enough to make a market established by usage in which one price can be expected to affect another and in which an informed report of the range and trend of prices can be assumed to be reasonably accurate.

This section does not in any way intend to limit or negate the application of similar rules of admissibility to other material, whether by action of the courts or by statute. The purpose of the present section is to assure a minimum of mercantile administration in this important situation and not to limit any liberalizing trend in modern law.

Definitional Cross Reference:

"Goods". Section 2–105.

§ 2–725. Statute of Limitations in Contracts for Sale.

(1) An action for breach of any contract for sale must be commenced within four years after the cause of action has accrued. By the original agreement the parties may reduce the period of limitation to not less than one year but may not extend it.

(2) A cause of action accrues when the breach occurs, regardless of the aggrieved party's lack of knowledge of the breach. A breach of warranty occurs when tender of delivery is made, except that where a warranty explicitly extends to future performance of the goods and discovery of the breach must await the time of such performance the cause of action accrues when the breach is or should have been discovered.

(3) Where an action commenced within the time limited by subsection (1) is so terminated as to leave available a remedy by another action for the same breach such other action may be commenced after the expiration of the time limited and within six months after the termination of the first action unless the termination resulted from voluntary discontinuance or from dismissal for failure or neglect to prosecute.

(4) This section does not alter the law on tolling of the statute of limitations nor does it apply to causes of action which have accrued before this Act becomes effective.

Official Comment

Prior Uniform Statutory Provision: None.

Purposes: To introduce a uniform statute of limitations for sales contracts, thus eliminating the jurisdictional variations and providing needed relief for concerns doing business on a nationwide scale whose contracts have heretofore been governed by several different periods of limitation depending upon the state in which the transaction occurred. This Article takes sales contracts out of the general laws limiting the time for commencing contractual actions and selects a four year period as the most appropriate to modern business practice. This is within the normal commercial record keeping period.

Subsection (1) permits the parties to reduce the period of limitation. The minimum period is set at one year. The parties may not, however, extend the statutory period.

Subsection (2), providing that the cause of action accrues when the breach occurs, states an exception where the warranty extends to future performance.

Subsection (3) states the saving provision included in many state statutes and permits an additional short period for bringing new actions, where suits begun within the four year period have been terminated so as to leave a remedy still available for the same breach.

Subsection (4) makes it clear that this Article does not purport to alter or modify in any respect the law on tolling of the Statute of Limitations as it now prevails in the various jurisdictions.

Definitional Cross References:

"Action". Section 1–201.
"Aggrieved party". Section 1–201.
"Agreement". Section 1–201.
"Contract for sale". Section 2–106.
"Goods". Section 2–105.
"Party". Section 1–201.
"Remedy". Section 1–201.
"Term". Section 1–201.
"Termination". Section 2–106.

ARTICLE 2A

LEASES

PART 1. GENERAL PROVISIONS

PART 2. FORMATION AND CONSTRUCTION OF LEASE CONTRACT

PART 3. EFFECT OF LEASE CONTRACT

See Appendix III for text of conforming amendments to other articles of the Code and official comments thereto.

National Conference of Commissioners on Uniform State Laws

REPORTER

Ronald DeKoven, New York, New York

DRAFTING COMMITTEE

CHAIRMAN

Edward I. Cutler, Tampa, Florida

MEMBERS

Marion W. Benfield, Jr., Champaign, Illinois
William E. Hogan, New York, New York
Stanley M. Johnston, Springfield, Illinois
Peter F. Langrock, Middlebury, Vermont
Morris W. Macey, Atlanta, Georgia
Frederick H. Miller, Norman, Oklahoma
Donald Osheim, Watertown, South Dakota
Howard J. Swibel, Chicago, Illinois
Phillip Carroll, Little Rock, Arkansas
President, National Conference (Member Ex Officio)
William J. Pierce, Ann Arbor, Michigan
Executive Director, National Conference
Harvey Bartle, III, Philadelphia, Pennsylvania
Chairman, Division C (Member Ex Officio)

ABA ADVISOR, SECTION OF CORPORATION, BANKING, AND BUSINESS LAW

Ronald M. Bayer, Los Angeles, California

ABA ADVISOR, SECTION OF TAXATION

William M. Toomajian, Cleveland, Ohio

FOREWORD

Article 2A of the Uniform Commercial Code, along with Conforming Amendments to Articles 1 and 9, is presented, upon the recommendation of the Permanent Editorial Board for the Uniform Commercial Code, by the National Conference of Commissioners on Uniform State Laws and the American Law Institute. It represents a major development in commercial law, addressing a type of business transaction, the leasing of personal property, that has long existed. Under present law, transactions of this type are governed partly by common law principles relating to personal property, partly by principles relating to real estate leases, and partly by reference to Articles 2 and 9 of the Uniform Commercial Code, dealing with Sales and Secured Transactions respectively. The legal rules and concepts derived from these sources imperfectly fit a transaction that involves personal property rather than realty, and a lease rather than either a sale or a security interest as such. A statute directly addressing the personal property lease is therefore appropriate.

Such a statute has become especially appropriate with the exponential expansion of the number and scale of personal property lease transactions. Article 2A will apply to transactions involving billions of dollars annually. It will apply to consumer's rental of automobiles or do-it-yourself equipment, on the one hand, and to leases of such items as commercial aircraft (to the extent not preempted by federal law) and industrial machinery, on the other. The text recognizes the differences between consumer and business leasing, while resting upon concepts that apply generally to any personal property lease transactions.

The final product represents an important undertaking of the Conference and the Institute. It has proceeded, following recommendations by the Conference's Study Committee in 1981, through preparation and review by the Conference's Drafting Committee first of a proposed free-standing Uniform Personal Property Leasing Act, which was approved by the Conference, and later of Article 2A, which proceeded through the Permanent Editorial Board, the Executive Committee of the Conference, the Conference, and the Council of the Institute and the Annual Meeting of the members of the Institute. Carrying the text through these several stages has required coordination of somewhat different procedures, and continued patience and mutual forbearance. At the same time, the text has been subjected to analysis and criticism from many points of view and thereby steadily improved.

The resulting product borrows from both Articles 2 and 9. These existing Articles of the Uniform Commercial Code have certain imperfections revealed by the long experience since their adoption. Article 2A cannot overcome those imperfections but seeks to minimize their significance as applied to leases. More fundamentally, there is important conceptual dissonance between Article 2 and Article 9. The formulation of Article 2A takes Articles 2 and 9 as they are for the time being and hence has required careful adjustment to this dissonance.

The drafting task has been complicated both as a matter of substance and as a matter of process. The Reporter, Ronald DeKoven, has been a master of substance and a steady and receptive principal in the process. We join with the Conference and the Institute in expressing our admiration and appreciation for his contribution to this important field of law.

Geoffrey C. Hazard, Jr., *Chairman*
Permanent Editorial
Board for the Uniform
Commercial Code

October 1, 1987

PART 1

GENERAL PROVISIONS

§ 2A–101. Short Title.

This Article shall be known and may be cited as the Uniform Commercial Code—Leases.

See Appendix VI [following Amendment 24 therein] for material relating to changes in the Official Comment to conform to the 1990 amendments to various sections of Article 2A.

Official Comment

Rationale for Codification:

There are several reasons for codifying the law with respect to leases of goods. An analysis of the case law as it applies to leases of goods suggests at least three significant issues to be resolved by codification. First, what is a lease? It is necessary to define lease to determine whether a transaction creates a lease or a security interest disguised as a lease. If the transaction creates a security interest disguised as a lease, the lessor will be required to file a financing statement or take other action to perfect its interest in the goods against third parties. There is no such requirement with respect to leases. Yet the distinction between a lease and a security interest disguised as a lease is not clear. Second, will the lessor be deemed to have made warranties to the lessee? If the transaction is a sale the express and implied warranties of Article 2 of the Uniform Commercial Code apply. However, the warranty law with respect to leases is uncertain. Third, what remedies are available to the lessor upon the lessee's default? If the transaction is a security interest disguised as a lease, the answer is stated in Part 5 of the Article on Secured Transactions (Article 9). There is no clear answer with respect to leases.

There are reasons to codify the law with respect to leases of goods in addition to those suggested by a review of the reported cases. The answer to this important question should not be limited to the issues raised in these cases. Is it not also proper to determine the remedies available to the lessee upon the lessor's default? It is, but that issue is not reached through a review of the reported cases. This is only one of the many issues presented in structuring, negotiating and documenting a lease of goods.

Statutory Analogue:

After it was decided to proceed with the codification project, the drafting committee of the National Conference of Commissioners on Uniform State Laws looked for a statutory analogue, gradually narrowing the focus to the Article on Sales (Article 2) and the Article on Secured Transactions (Article 9). A review of the literature with respect to the sale of goods reveals that Article 2 is predicated upon certain assumptions: Parties to the sales transaction frequently are without counsel; the agreement of the parties often is oral or evidenced by scant writings; obligations between the parties are bilateral; applicable law is influenced by the need to preserve freedom of contract. A review of the literature with respect to personal property security law reveals that Article 9 is predicated upon very different assumptions: Parties to a secured transaction regularly are represented by counsel; the agreement of the parties frequently is reduced to a writing, extensive in scope; the obligations between the parties are essentially unilateral; and applicable law seriously limits freedom of contract.

The lease is closer in spirit and form to the sale of goods than to the creation of a security interest. While parties to a lease are sometimes represented by counsel and their agreement is often reduced to a writing, the obligations of the parties are bilateral and the common law of leasing is dominated by the need to preserve freedom of contract. Thus the drafting committee concluded that Article 2 was the appropriate statutory analogue.

Issues: The drafting committee then identified and resolved several issues critical to codification:

Scope: The scope of the Article was limited to leases (Section 2A–102). There was no need to include leases intended as security, *i.e.*, security interests disguised as leases, as they are adequately treated in Article 9. Further, even if leases intended as security were included, the need to preserve the distinction would remain, as policy suggests treatment significantly different from that accorded leases.

Definition of Lease: Lease was defined to exclude leases intended as security (Section 2A–103(1)(j)). Given the litigation to date a revised definition of security interest was suggested for inclusion in the Act. (Section 1–201(37)). This revision sharpens the distinction between leases and security interests disguised as leases.

Filing: The lessor was not required to file a financing statement against the lessee or take any other action to protect the lessor's interest in the goods (Section 2A–301). The refined definition of security interest will more clearly signal the need to file to potential lessors of goods. Those lessors who are concerned will file a protective financing statement (Section 9–408).

Warranties: All of the express and implied warranties of the Article on Sales (Article 2) were included (Sections 2A–210 through 2A–216), revised to reflect differences in lease transactions. The lease of goods is sufficiently similar to the sale of goods to justify this decision. Further, many courts have reached the same decision.

Certificate of Title Laws: Many leasing transactions involve goods subject to certificate of title statutes. To avoid conflict with those statutes, this Article is subject to them (Section 2A–104(1)(a)).

Consumer Leases: Many leasing transactions involve parties subject to consumer protection statutes or decisions. To avoid conflict with those laws this Article is subject to them to the extent provided in (Section 2A–104(1)(c) and (2)). Further, certain consumer protections have been incorporated in the Article.

Finance Leases: Certain leasing transactions substitute the supplier of the goods for the lessor as the party responsible to the lessee with respect to warranties and the like. The definition of finance lease (Section 2A–103(1)(g)) was developed to describe these transactions. Various sections of the Article implement the substitution of the supplier for the lessor, including Sections 2A–209 and 2A–407. No attempt was made to fashion a special rule where the finance lessor is an affiliate of the supplier of goods; this is to be developed by the courts, case by case.

Sale and Leaseback: Sale and leaseback transactions are becoming increasingly common. A number of state statutes treat transactions where possession is retained by the seller as fraudulent *per se* or *prima facie* fraudulent. That position is not in accord with modern practice and thus is changed by the Article "if the buyer bought for value and in good faith" (Section 2A–308(3)).

Remedies: The Article has not only provided for lessor's remedies upon default by the lessee (Sections 2A–523 through 2A–531), but also for lessee's remedies upon default by the lessor (Sections 2A–508 through 2A–522). This is a significant departure from Article 9, which provides remedies only for the secured party upon default by the debtor. This difference is compelled by the bilateral nature of the obligations between the parties to a lease.

Damages: Many leasing transactions are predicated on the parties' ability to stipulate an appropriate measure of damages in the event of default. The rule with respect to sales of goods (Section 2–718) is not sufficiently flexible to accommodate this practice. Consistent with the common law emphasis upon freedom to contract, the Article has created a revised rule that allows greater flexibility with respect to leases of goods (Section 2A–504(1)).

History:

This Article is a revision of the Uniform Personal Property Leasing Act, which was approved by the National Conference of Commissioners on Uniform State Laws in August, 1985. However, it was believed that the subject matter of the Uniform Personal Property Leasing Act would be better treated as an article of this Act. Thus, although the Conference promulgated the Uniform Personal Property Leasing Act as a Uniform Law, activity was held in abeyance to allow time to restate the Uniform Personal Property Leasing Act as Article 2A.

In August, 1986 the Conference approved and recommended this Article (including conforming amendments to Article 1 and Article 9) for promulgation as an amendment to this Act. In December, 1986 the Council of the American Law Institute approved and recommended this Article (including conforming amendments to Article 1 and Article 9), with official comments, for promulgation as an amendment to this Act. In March, 1987 the Permanent Editorial Board for the Uniform Commercial Code approved and recommended this Article (including conforming amendments to Article 1 and Article 9), with official comments, for promulgation as an amendment to this Act. In May, 1987 the American Law Institute approved and recommended this Article (including conforming amendments to Article 1 and Article 9), with official comments, for promulgation as an amendment to this Act. In August, 1987 the Conference confirmed its approval of the final text of this Article.

Upon its initial promulgation, Article 2A was rapidly enacted in several states, was introduced in a number of other states, and underwent bar association, law revision commission and legislative study in still further states. In that process debate emerged, principally sparked by the study of Article 2A by the California Bar Association, California's non-uniform amendments to Article 2A, and articles appearing in a symposium on Article 2A published after its promulgation in the Alabama Law Review. The debate chiefly centered on whether Article 2A had struck the proper balance or was clear enough concerning the ability of a lessor to grant a security interest in its leasehold interest and in the residual, priority between a secured party and the lessee, and the lessor's remedy structure under Article 2A.

This debate over issues on which reasonable minds could and did differ began to affect the enactment effort for Article 2A in a deleterious manner. Consequently, the Standby Committee for Article 2A, composed predominantly of the former members of the drafting committee, reviewed the legislative actions and studies in the various states, and opened a dialogue with the principal proponents of the non-uniform amendments. Negotiations were conducted in conjunction with, and were facilitated by, a study of the uniform Article and the non-uniform Amendments by the New York Law Revision Commission. Ultimately, a consensus was reached, which has been approved by the membership of the Conference, the Permanent Editorial Board, and the Council of the Institute. Rapid and uniform enactment of Article 2A is expected as a result of the completed amendments. The Article 2A experience reaffirms the essential viability of the procedures of the Conference and the Institute for creating and updating uniform state law in the commercial law area.

Relationship of Article 2A to Other Articles:

The Article on Sales provided a useful point of reference for codifying the law of leases. Many of the provisions of that Article were carried over, changed to reflect differences in style, leasing terminology or leasing practices. Thus, the official comments to those sections of Article 2 whose provisions were carried over are incorporated by reference in Article 2A, as well; further, any case law interpreting those provisions should be viewed as persuasive but not binding on a court when deciding a similar issue with respect to leases. Any change in the sequence that has been made when carrying over a provision from Article 2 should be viewed as a matter of style, not substance. This is not to suggest that in other instances Article 2A did not also incorporate substantially revised provisions of Article 2, Article 9 or otherwise where the revision was driven by a concern over the substance; but for the lack of a mandate, the drafting committee might well have made the same or a similar change in the statutory analogue. Those sections in Article 2A include Sections 2A-104, 2A-105, 2A-106, 2A-108(2) and (4), 2A-109(2), 2A-208, 2A-214(2) and (3)(a), 2A-216, 2A-303, 2A-306, 2A-503, 2A-504(3)(b), 2A-506(2), and 2A-515. For lack of relevance or significance not all of the provisions of Article 2 were incorporated in Article 2A.

This codification was greatly influenced by the fundamental tenet of the common law as it has developed with respect to leases of goods: freedom of the parties to contract. Note that, like all other Articles of this Act, the principles of construction and interpretation contained in Article 1 are applicable throughout Article 2A (Section 2A-103(4)). These principles include the ability of the parties to vary the effect of the provisions of Article 2A, subject to certain limitations including those that relate to the obligations of good faith, diligence, reasonableness and care (Section 1-102(3)). Consistent with those principles no negative inference is to be drawn by the episodic use of the phrase "unless otherwise agreed" in certain provisions of Article 2A. Section 1-102(4). Indeed, the contrary is true, as the general rule in the Act, including this Article, is that the effect of the Act's provisions may be varied by agreement. Section 1-102(3). This conclusion follows even where the statutory analogue contains the phrase and the correlative provision in Article 2A does not.

§ 2A-102. Scope.

This Article applies to any transaction, regardless of form, that creates a lease.

Official Comment

Uniform Statutory Source: Section 9-102(1). Throughout this Article, unless otherwise stated, references to "Section" are to other sections of this Act.

Changes: Substantially revised.

Purposes: This Article governs transactions as diverse as the lease of a hand tool to an individual for a few hours and the leveraged lease of a complex line of industrial equipment to a multi-national organization for a number of years.

To achieve that end it was necessary to provide that this Article applies to any transaction, regardless of form, that creates a lease. Since lease is defined as a transfer of an interest in goods (Section 2A-103(1)(j)) and goods is defined to include fixtures (Section 2A-103(1)(h)), application is limited to the extent the transaction relates to goods, including fixtures. Further, since the definition of lease does not include a sale (Section 2-106(1)) or retention or creation of a security interest (Section 1-201(37)), application is further limited; sales and security interests are governed by other Articles of this Act.

Finally, in recognition of the diversity of the transactions to be governed, the sophistication of many of the parties to these transactions, and the common law tradition as it applies to the bailment for hire or lease, freedom of contract has been preserved. DeKoven, Proceedings After Default by the Lessee Under a True Lease of Equipment, in 1C P. Coogan, W. Hogan, D. Vagts, *Secured Transactions Under the Uniform Commercial Code*, § 29B.02[2] (1986). Thus, despite the extensive regulatory scheme established by this Article, the parties to a lease will be able to create private rules to govern their transaction. Sections 2A-103(4) and 1-102(3). However, there are special rules in this Article governing consumer leases, as well as other state and federal statutes, that may further limit freedom of contract with respect to consumer leases.

A court may apply this Article by analogy to any transaction, regardless of form, that creates a lease of personal property other than goods, taking into account the expressed intentions of the parties to the transaction and any differences between a lease of goods and a lease of other property. Such application has precedent as the provisions of the Article on Sales (Article 2) have been applied by analogy to leases of goods. *E.g.*, Hawkland, *The Impact of the Uniform Commercial Code on Equipment Leasing*, 1972 Ill.L.F. 446; Murray, *Under the Spreading Analogy of Article 2 of the Uniform Commercial Code*, 39 Fordham L.Rev. 447 (1971). Whether such application would be appropriate for other bailments of personal property, gratuitous or for hire, should be determined by the facts of each case. *See Mieske v. Bartell Drug Co.*, 92 Wash.2d 40, 46-48, 593 P.2d 1308, 1312 (1979).

Further, parties to a transaction creating a lease of personal property other than goods, or a bailment of personal property may provide by agreement that this Article applies. Upholding the parties' choice is consistent with the spirit of this Article.

Cross References:

Sections 1-102(3), 1-201(37), Article 2, esp. Section 2-106(1), and Sections 2A-103(1)(h), 2A-103(1)(j) and 2A-103(4).

Definitional Cross Reference:

"Lease". Section 2A-103(1)(j).

§ 2A-103. Definitions and Index of Definitions.

(1) In this Article unless the context otherwise requires:

(a) "Buyer in ordinary course of business" means a person who in good faith and without knowledge that the sale to him [or her] is in violation of the ownership rights or security interest or leasehold interest of a third party in the goods buys in ordinary course from a person in the business of selling goods of that kind but does not include a pawnbroker. "Buying" may be for cash or by exchange of other property or on secured or unsecured credit and includes receiving goods or documents of title under a pre-existing contract for sale but does not include a transfer in bulk or as security for or in total or partial satisfaction of a money debt.

(b) "Cancellation" occurs when either party puts an end to the lease contract for default by the other party.

(c) "Commercial unit" means such a unit of goods as by commercial usage is a single whole for purposes of lease and division of which materially impairs its character or value on the market or in use. A commercial unit may be a single article, as a machine, or a set of articles, as a suite of furniture or a line of machinery, or a quantity, as a gross or carload, or any other unit treated in use or in the relevant market as a single whole.

(d) "Conforming" goods or performance under a lease contract means goods or performance that are in accordance with the obligations under the lease contract.

(e) "Consumer lease" means a lease that a lessor regularly engaged in the business of leasing or selling makes to a lessee who is an individual and who takes under the lease primarily for a personal, family, or household purpose [, if the total payments to be made under the lease contract, excluding payments for options to renew or buy, do not exceed $_______].

(f) "Fault" means wrongful act, omission, breach, or default.

(g) "Finance lease" means a lease with respect to which:

(i) the lessor does not select, manufacture, or supply the goods;

(ii) the lessor acquires the goods or the right to possession and use of the goods in connection with the lease; and

(iii) one of the following occurs:

(A) the lessee receives a copy of the contract by which the lessor acquired the goods or the right to possession and use of the goods before signing the lease contract;

(B) the lessee's approval of the contract by which the lessor acquired the goods or the right to possession and use of the goods is a condition to effectiveness of the lease contract;

(C) the lessee, before signing the lease contract, receives an accurate and complete statement designating the promises and warranties, and any disclaimers of warranties, limitations or modifications of remedies, or liquidated damages, including those of a third party, such as the manufacturer of the goods, provided to the lessor by the person supplying the goods in connection with or as part of the contract by which the lessor acquired the goods or the right to possession and use of the goods; or

(D) if the lease is not a consumer lease, the lessor, before the lessee signs the lease contract, informs the lessee in writing (a) of the identity of the person supplying the goods to the lessor, unless the lessee has selected that person and directed the lessor to acquire the goods or the right to possession and use of the goods from that person, (b) that the lessee is entitled under this Article to the promises and warranties, including those of any third party, provided to the lessor by the person supplying the goods in connection with or as part of the contract by which the lessor acquired the goods or the right to possession and use of the goods, and (c) that the lessee may communicate with the person supplying the goods to the lessor and receive an accurate and complete statement of those promises and warranties, including any disclaimers and limitations of them or of remedies.

(h) "Goods" means all things that are movable at the time of identification to the lease contract, or are fixtures (Section 2A-309), but the term does not include money, documents, instruments, accounts, chattel paper, general intangibles, or minerals or the like, including oil and gas, before extraction. The term also includes the unborn young of animals.

(i) "Installment lease contract" means a lease contract that authorizes or requires the delivery of goods in separate lots to be separately accepted, even though the lease contract contains a clause "each delivery is a separate lease" or its equivalent.

(j) "Lease" means a transfer of the right to possession and use of goods for a term in return for consideration, but a sale, including a sale on approval or a sale or return, or retention or creation of a security interest is not a lease. Unless the context clearly indicates otherwise, the term includes a sublease.

(k) "Lease agreement" means the bargain, with respect to the lease, of the lessor and the lessee in fact as found in their language or by implication from other circumstances including course of dealing or usage of trade or course of performance as provided in this Article. Unless the context clearly indicates otherwise, the term includes a sublease agreement.

(*l*) "Lease contract" means the total legal obligation that results from the lease agreement as affected by this Article and any other applicable rules of law. Unless the context clearly indicates otherwise, the term includes a sublease contract.

(m) "Leasehold interest" means the interest of the lessor or the lessee under a lease contract.

(n) "Lessee" means a person who acquires the right to possession and use of goods under a lease. Unless the context clearly indicates otherwise, the term includes a sublessee.

(*o*) "Lessee in ordinary course of business" means a person who in good faith and without knowledge that the lease to him [or her] is in violation of the ownership rights or security interest or leasehold interest of a third party in the goods, leases in ordinary course from a person in the business of selling or leasing goods of that kind but does not include a pawnbroker. "Leasing" may be for cash or by exchange of other property or on secured or unsecured credit and includes receiving goods or documents of title under a pre-existing lease contract but does not include a transfer in bulk or as security for or in total or partial satisfaction of a money debt.

(p) "Lessor" means a person who transfers the right to possession and use of goods under a lease. Unless the context clearly indicates otherwise, the term includes a sublessor.

(q) "Lessor's residual interest" means the lessor's interest in the goods after expiration, termination, or cancellation of the lease contract.

(r) "Lien" means a charge against or interest in goods to secure payment of a debt or performance of an obligation, but the term does not include a security interest.

(s) "Lot" means a parcel or a single article that is the subject matter of a separate lease or delivery, whether or not it is sufficient to perform the lease contract.

(t) "Merchant lessee" means a lessee that is a merchant with respect to goods of the kind subject to the lease.

(u) "Present value" means the amount as of a date certain of one or more sums payable in the future, discounted to the date certain. The discount is determined by the interest rate specified by the parties if the rate was not manifestly unreasonable at the time the transaction was entered into; otherwise, the discount is determined by a commercially reasonable rate that takes into account the facts and circumstances of each case at the time the transaction was entered into.

(v) "Purchase" includes taking by sale, lease, mortgage, security interest, pledge, gift, or any other voluntary transaction creating an interest in goods.

(w) "Sublease" means a lease of goods the right to possession and use of which was acquired by the lessor as a lessee under an existing lease.

(x) "Supplier" means a person from whom a lessor buys or leases goods to be leased under a finance lease.

(y) "Supply contract" means a contract under which a lessor buys or leases goods to be leased.

(z) "Termination" occurs when either party pursuant to a power created by agreement or law puts an end to the lease contract otherwise than for default.

(2) Other definitions applying to this Article and the sections in which they appear are:

"Accessions". Section 2A–310(1).

"Construction mortgage". Section 2A–309(1)(d).

"Encumbrance". Section 2A–309(1)(e).

"Fixtures". Section 2A–309(1)(a).

"Fixture filing". Section 2A–309(1)(b).

"Purchase money lease". Section 2A–309(1)(c).

(3) The following definitions in other Articles apply to this Article:

"Account". Section 9–106.

"Between merchants". Section 2–104(3).

"Buyer". Section 2–103(1)(a).

"Chattel paper". Section 9–105(1)(b).

"Consumer goods". Section 9–109(1).

"Document". Section 9-105(1)(f).

"Entrusting". Section 2-403(3).

"General intangibles". Section 9-106.

"Good faith". Section 2-103(1)(b).

"Instrument". Section 9-105(1)(i).

"Merchant". Section 2-104(1).

"Mortgage". Section 9-105(1)(j).

"Pursuant to commitment". Section 9-105(1)(k).

"Receipt". Section 2-103(1)(c).

"Sale". Section 2-106(1).

"Sale on approval". Section 2-326.

"Sale or return". Section 2-326.

"Seller". Section 2-103(1)(d).

(4) In addition Article 1 contains general definitions and principles of construction and interpretation applicable throughout this Article.

As amended in 1990.

See Appendix VI for material relating to changes made in text in 1990.

Official Comment

(a) "Buyer in ordinary course of business". Section 1-201(9).

(b) "Cancellation". Section 2-106(4). The effect of a cancellation is provided in Section 2A-505(1).

(c) "Commercial unit". Section 2-105(6).

(d) "Conforming". Section 2-106(2).

(e) "Consumer lease". New. This Article includes a subset of rules that applies only to consumer leases. Sections 2A-106, 2A-108(2), 2A-108(4), 2A-109(2), 2A-221, 2A-309, 2A-406, 2A-407, 2A-504(3)(b), and 2A-516(3)(b).

For a transaction to qualify as a consumer lease it must first qualify as a lease. Section 2A-103(1)(j). Note that this Article regulates the transactional elements of a lease, including a consumer lease; consumer protection statutes, present and future, and existing consumer protection decisions are unaffected by this Article. Section 2A-104(1)(c) and (2). Of course, Article 2A as state law also is subject to federal consumer protection law.

This definition is modeled after the definition of consumer lease in the Consumer Leasing Act, 15 U.S.C. § 1667 (1982), and in the Unif. Consumer Credit Code § 1.301(14), 7A U.L.A. 43 (1974). However, this definition of consumer lease differs from its models in several respects: the lessor can be a person regularly engaged either in the business of leasing or of selling goods, the lease need not be for a term exceeding four months, a lease primarily for an agricultural purpose is not covered, and whether there should be a limitation by dollar amount and its amount is left up to the individual states.

This definition focuses on the parties as well as the transaction. If a lease is within this definition, the lessor must be regularly engaged in the business of leasing or selling, and the lessee must be an individual, not an organization; note that a lease to two or more individuals having a common interest through marriage or the like is not excluded as a lease to an organization under Section 1–201(28). The lessee must take the interest primarily for a personal, family or household purpose. If required by the enacting state, total payments under the lease contract, excluding payments for options to renew or buy, cannot exceed the figure designated.

(f) "Fault". Section 1–201(16).

(g) "Finance Lease". New. This Article includes a subset of rules that applies only to finance leases. Sections 2A–209, 2A–211(2), 2A–212(1), 2A–213, 2A–219(1), 2A–220(1)(a), 2A–221, 2A–405(c), 2A–407, 2A–516(2) and 2A–517(1)(a) and (2).

For a transaction to qualify as a finance lease it must first qualify as a lease. Section 2A–103(1)(j). Unless the lessor is comfortable that the transaction will qualify as a finance lease, the lease agreement should include provisions giving the lessor the benefits created by the subset of rules applicable to the transaction that qualifies as a finance lease under this Article.

A finance lease is the product of a three party transaction. The supplier manufactures or supplies the goods pursuant to the lessee's specification, perhaps even pursuant to a purchase order, sales agreement or lease agreement between the supplier and the lessee. After the prospective finance lease is negotiated, a purchase order, sales agreement, or lease agreement is entered into by the lessor (as buyer or prime lessee) or an existing order, agreement or lease is assigned by the lessee to the lessor, and the lessor and the lessee then enter into a lease or sublease of the goods. Due to the limited function usually performed by the lessor, the lessee looks almost entirely to the supplier for representations, covenants and warranties. If a manufacturer's warranty carries through, the lessee may also look to that. Yet, this definition does not restrict the lessor's function solely to the supply of funds; if the lessor undertakes or performs other functions, express warranties, covenants and the common law will protect the lessee.

This definition focuses on the transaction, not the status of the parties; to avoid confusion it is important to note that in other contexts, *e.g.*, tax and accounting, the term finance lease has been used to connote different types of lease transactions, including leases that are disguised secured transactions. M. Rice, *Equipment Financing,* 62–71 (1981). A lessor who is a merchant with respect to goods of the kind subject to the lease may be a lessor under a finance lease. Many leases that are leases back to the seller of goods (Section 2A–308(3)) will be finance leases. This conclusion is easily demonstrated by a hypothetical. Assume that B has bought goods from C pursuant to a sales contract. After delivery to and acceptance of the goods by B, B negotiates to sell the goods to A and simultaneously to lease the goods back from A, on terms and conditions that, we assume, will qualify the transaction as a lease. Section 2A–103(1)(j). In documenting the sale and lease back, B assigns the original sales contract between B, as buyer, and C, as seller, to A. A review of these facts leads to the conclusion that the lease from A to B qualifies as a finance lease, as all three conditions of the definition are satisfied. Subparagraph (i) is satisfied as A, the lessor, had nothing to do with the selection, manufacture, or supply of the equipment. Subparagraph (ii) is satisfied as A, the lessor, bought the equipment at the same time that A leased the equipment to B, which certainly is in connection with the lease. Finally, subparagraph (iii)(A) is satisfied as A entered into the sales contract with B at the same time that A leased the equipment back to B. B, the lessee, will have received a copy of the sales contract in a timely fashion.

Subsection (i) requires the lessor to remain outside the selection, manufacture and supply of the goods; that is the rationale for releasing the lessor from most of its traditional liability. The lessor is not prohibited from possession, maintenance or operation of the goods, as policy does not require such prohibition. To insure the lessee's reliance on the supplier, and not on the lessor, subsection (ii) requires that the goods (where the lessor is the buyer of the goods) or that the right to possession and use of the goods (where the lessor is the prime lessee and the sublessor of the goods) be acquired in connection with the lease (or sublease) to qualify as a finance lease. The scope of the phrase "in connection with" is to be developed by the courts, case by case. Finally, as the lessee generally relies almost entirely upon the supplier for representations and covenants, and upon the supplier or a manufacturer, or both, for warranties with respect to the goods, subsection (iii) requires that one of the following occur: (A) the lessee receive a copy of the supply contract before signing the lease contract; (B) the lessee's approval of the supply contract is a condition to the effectiveness of the lease contract; (C) the lessee receive a statement describing the promises and warranties and any limitations relevant to the lessee before signing the lease contract; or (D) before signing the lease contract and except in a consumer lease, the lessee receive a writing identifying the supplier (unless the supplier was selected and required by the lessee) and the rights of the lessee under Section 2A-209, and advising the lessee a statement of promises and warranties is available from the supplier. Thus, even where oral supply orders or computer placed supply orders are compelled by custom and usage the transaction may still qualify as a finance lease if the lessee approves the supply contract before the lease contract is effective and such approval was a condition to the effectiveness of the lease contract. Moreover, where the lessor does not want the lessee to see the entire supply contract, including price information, the lessee may be provided with a separate statement of the terms of the supply contract relevant to the lessee; promises between the supplier and the lessor that do not affect the lessee need not be included. The statement can be a restatement of those terms or a copy of portions of the supply contract with the relevant terms clearly designated. Any implied warranties need not be designated, but a disclaimer or modification of remedy must be designated. A copy of any manufacturer's warranty is sufficient if that is the warranty provided. However, a copy of any Regulation M disclosure given pursuant to 12 C.F.R. § 213.4(g) concerning warranties in itself is not sufficient since those disclosures need only briefly identify express warranties and need not include any disclaimer of warranty.

If a transaction does not qualify as a finance lease, the parties may achieve the same result by agreement; no negative implications are to be drawn if the transaction does not qualify. Further, absent the application of special rules (fraud, duress, and the like), a lease that qualifies as a finance lease and is assigned by the lessor or the lessee to a third party does not lose its status as a finance lease under this Article. Finally, this Article creates no special rule where the lessor is an affiliate of the supplier; whether the transaction qualifies as a finance lease will be determined by the facts of each case.

(h) "Goods". Section 9-105(1)(h). See Section 2A-103(3) for reference to the definition of "Account", "Chattel paper", "Document", "General intangibles" and "Instrument". See Section 2A-217 for determination of the time and manner of identification.

(i) "Installment lease contract". Section 2-612(1).

(j) "Lease". New. There are several reasons to codify the law with respect to leases of goods. An analysis of the case law as it applies to leases of goods suggests at least several significant issues to be resolved by codification. First and foremost is the definition of a lease. It is necessary to define lease to determine whether a transaction creates a lease or a security interest disguised as a lease. If the transaction creates a security interest disguised as a lease, the transaction will be governed by the Article on Secured Transactions (Article 9) and the lessor will be required to file a financing statement or take other action to perfect its interest in the goods against third parties. There is no such requirement with respect to leases under the common law and, except with respect to leases of fixtures (Section 2A–309), this Article imposes no such requirement. Yet the distinction between a lease and a security interest disguised as a lease is not clear from the case law at the time of the promulgation of this Article. DeKoven, *Leases of Equipment: Puritan Leasing Company v. August, A Dangerous Decision,* 12 U.S.F. L.Rev. 257 (1978).

At common law a lease of personal property is a bailment for hire. While there are several definitions of bailment for hire, all require a thing to be let and a price for the letting. Thus, in modern terms and as provided in this definition, a lease is created when the lessee agrees to furnish consideration for the right to the possession and use of goods over a specified period of time. Mooney, *Personal Property Leasing: A Challenge,* 36 Bus. Law. 1605, 1607 (1981). Further, a lease is neither a sale (Section 2–106(1)) nor a retention or creation of a security interest (Section 1–201(37)). Due to extensive litigation to distinguish true leases from security interests, an amendment to Section 1–201(37) has been promulgated with this Article to create a sharper distinction.

This section as well as Section 1–201(37) must be examined to determine whether the transaction in question creates a lease or a security interest. The following hypotheticals indicate the perimeters of the issue. Assume that A has purchased a number of copying machines, new, for $1,000 each; the machines have an estimated useful economic life of three years. A advertises that the machines are available to rent for a minimum of one month and that the monthly rental is $100.00. A intends to enter into leases where A provides all maintenance, without charge to the lessee. Further, the lessee will rent the machine, month to month, with no obligation to renew. At the end of the lease term the lessee will be obligated to return the machine to A's place of business. This transaction qualifies as a lease under the first half of the definition, for the transaction includes a transfer by A to a prospective lessee of possession and use of the machine for a stated term, month to month. The machines are goods (Section 2A–103(1)(h)). The lessee is obligated to pay consideration in return, $100.00 for each month of the term.

However, the second half of the definition provides that a sale or a security interest is not a lease. Since there is no passing of title, there is no sale. Sections 2A–103(3) and 2–106(1). Under pre-Act security law this transaction would have created a bailment for hire or a true lease and not a conditional sale. *Da Rocha v. Macomber*, 330 Mass. 611, 614–15, 116 N.E.2d 139, 142 (1953). Under Section 1–201(37), as amended with the promulgation of this Article, the same result would follow. While the lessee is obligated to pay rent for the one month term of the lease, one of the other four conditions of the second paragraph of Section 1–201(37) must be met and none is. The term of the lease is one month and the economic life of the machine is 36 months; thus, subparagraph (a) of Section 1–201(37) is not now satisfied. Considering the amount of the monthly rent, absent economic duress or coercion, the lessee is not bound either to renew the lease for the remaining economic life of the goods or to become the owner. If the lessee did lease the machine for 36 months, the lessee would have paid the lessor $3,600 for a machine that could have been purchased for $1,000; thus, subparagraph (b) of Section 1–201(37) is not satisfied. Finally, there are no options; thus, subparagraphs (c) and (d) of Section 1–201(37) are not satisfied. This transaction creates a lease, not a security interest. However, with each renewal of the lease the facts and circumstances at the time of each renewal must be examined to determine if that conclusion remains accurate, as it is possible that a transaction that first creates a lease, later creates a security interest.

Assume that the facts are changed and that A requires each lessee to lease the goods for 36 months, with no right to terminate. Under pre-Act security law this transaction would have created a conditional sale, and not a bailment for hire or true lease. *Hervey v. Rhode Island Locomotive Works*, 93 U.S. 664, 672–73 (1876). Under this subsection, and Section 1–201(37), as amended with the inclusion of this Article in the Act, the same result would follow. The lessee's obligation for the term is not subject to termination by the lessee and the term is equal to the economic life of the machine.

Between these extremes there are many transactions that can be created. Some of the transactions have not been properly categorized by the courts in applying the 1978 and earlier Official Texts of Section 1–201(37). This subsection, together with Section 1–201(37), as amended with the promulgation of this Article, draws a brighter line, which should create a clearer signal to the professional lessor and lessee.

(k) "Lease agreement". This definition is derived from the first sentence of Section 1–201(3). Because the definition of lease is broad enough to cover future transfers, lease agreement includes an agreement contemplating a current or subsequent transfer. Thus it was not necessary to make an express reference to an agreement for the future lease of goods (Section 2–106(1)). This concept is also incorporated in the definition of lease contract. Note that the definition of lease does not include transactions in ordinary building materials that are incorporated into an improvement on land. Section 2A–309(2).

The provisions of this Article, if applicable, determine whether a lease agreement has legal consequences; otherwise the law of bailments and other applicable law determine the same. Sections 2A–103(4) and 1–103.

(*l*) "Lease contract". This definition is derived from the definition of contract in Section 1–201(11). Note that a lease contract may be for the future lease of goods, since this notion is included in the definition of lease.

(m) "Leasehold interest". New.

(n) "Lessee". New.

(*o*) "Lessee in ordinary course of business". Section 1–201(9).

(p) "Lessor". New.

(q) "Lessor's residual interest". New.

(r) "Lien". New. This term is used in Section 2A–307 (Priority of Liens Arising by Attachment or Levy on, Security Interests in, and Other Claims to Goods).

(s) "Lot". Section 2–105(5).

(t) "Merchant lessee". New. This term is used in Section 2A–511 (Merchant Lessee's Duties as to Rightfully Rejected Goods). A person may satisfy the requirement of dealing in goods of the kind subject to the lease as lessor, lessee, seller, or buyer.

(u) "Present value". New. Authorities agree that present value should be used to determine fairly the damages payable by the lessor or the lessee on default. *E.g., Taylor v. Commercial Credit Equip. Corp.*, 170 Ga.App. 322, 316 S.E.2d 788 (1984). Present value is defined to mean an amount that represents the discounted value as of a date certain of one or more sums payable in the future. This is a function of the economic principle that a dollar today is more valuable to the holder than a dollar payable in two years. While there is no question as to the principle, reasonable people would differ as to the rate of discount to apply in determining the value of that future dollar today. To minimize litigation, this Article allows the parties to specify the discount or interest rate, if the rate was not manifestly unreasonable at the time the transaction was entered into. In all other cases, the interest rate will be a commercially reasonable rate that takes into account the facts and circumstances of each case, as of the time the transaction was entered into.

(v) "Purchase". Section 1–201(32). This definition omits the reference to lien contained in the definition of purchase in Article 1 (Section 1–201(32)). This should not be construed to exclude consensual liens from the definition of purchase in this Article; the exclusion was mandated by the scope of the definition of lien in Section 2A-103(1)(r). Further, the definition of purchaser in this Article adds a reference to lease; as purchase is defined in Section 1-201(32) to include any other voluntary transaction creating an interest in property, this addition is not substantive.

(w) "Sublease". New.

(x) "Supplier". New.

(y) "Supply contract". New.

(z) "Termination". Section 2-106(3). The effect of a termination is provided in Section 2A-505(2).

§ 2A-104. Leases Subject to Other Law.

(1) A lease, although subject to this Article, is also subject to any applicable:

(a) certificate of title statute of this State: (list any certificate of title statutes covering automobiles, trailers, mobile homes, boats, farm tractors, and the like);

(b) certificate of title statute of another jurisdiction (Section 2A-105); or

(c) consumer protection statute of this State, or final consumer protection decision of a court of this State existing on the effective date of this Article.

(2) In case of conflict between this Article, other than Sections 2A-105, 2A-304(3), and 2A-305(3), and a statute or decision referred to in subsection (1), the statute or decision controls.

(3) Failure to comply with an applicable law has only the effect specified therein.

As amended in 1990.

See Appendix VI for material relating to changes made in text in 1990.

Official Comment

Uniform Statutory Source: Sections 9-203(4) and 9-302(3)(b) and (c).

Changes: Substantially revised.

Purposes:

1. This Article creates a comprehensive scheme for the regulation of transactions that create leases. Section 2A-102. Thus, the Article supersedes all prior legislation dealing with leases, except to the extent set forth in this Section.

2. Subsection (1) states the general rule that a lease, although governed by the scheme of this Article, also may be governed by certain other applicable laws. This may occur in the case of a consumer lease. Section 2A-103(1)(e). Those laws may be state statutes existing prior to enactment of Article 2A or passed afterward. In this case, it is desirable for this Article to specify which statute controls. Or the law may be a pre-existing consumer protection decision. This Article preserves such decisions. Or the law may be a statute of the United States. Such a law controls without any statement in this Article under applicable principles of preemption.

An illustration of a statute of the United States that governs consumer leases is the Consumer Leasing Act, 15 U.S.C. §§ 1667-1667(e) (1982) and its implementing regulation, Regulation M, 12 C.F.R. § 213 (1986); the statute mandates disclosures of certain lease terms, delimits the liability of a lessee in leasing personal property, and regulates the advertising of lease terms. An illustration of a state statute that governs consumer leases and which if adopted in the enacting state prevails over this Article is the Unif. Consumer Credit Code, which includes many provisions similar to those of the Consumer Leasing Act, e.g. Unif. Consumer Credit Code §§ 3.202, 3.209, 3.401, 7A U.L.A. 108–09, 115, 125 (1974), as well as provisions in addition to those of the Consumer Leasing Act, e.g., Unif. Consumer Credit Code §§ 5.109–.111, 7A U.L.A. 171–76 (1974) (the right to cure a default). Such statutes may define consumer lease so as to govern transactions within and without the definition of consumer lease under this Article.

3. Under subsection (2), subject to certain limited exclusions, in case of conflict a statute or a decision described in subsection (1) prevails over this Article. For example, a provision like Unif. Consumer Credit Code § 5.112, 7A U.L.A. 176 (1974), limiting self-help repossession, prevails over Section 2A–525(3). A consumer protection decision rendered after the effective date of this Article may supplement its provisions. For example, in relation to Article 9 a court might conclude that an acceleration clause may not be enforced against an individual debtor after late payments have been accepted unless a prior notice of default is given. To the extent the decision establishes a general principle applicable to transactions other than secured transactions, it may supplement Section 2A–502.

4. Consumer protection in lease transactions is primarily left to other law. However, several provisions of this Article do contain special rules that may not be varied by agreement in the case of a consumer lease. *E.g.*, Sections 2A–106, 2A–108, and 2A–109(2). Were that not so, the ability of the parties to govern their relationship by agreement together with the position of the lessor in a consumer lease too often could result in a one-sided lease agreement.

5. In construing this provision the reference to statute should be deemed to include applicable regulations. A consumer protection decision is "final" on the effective date of this Article if it is not subject to appeal on that date or, if subject to appeal, is not later reversed on appeal. Of course, such a decision can be overruled by a later decision or superseded by a later statute.

Cross References:

Sections 2A–103(1)(e), 2A–106, 2A–108, 2A–109(2) and 2A–525(3).

Definitional Cross Reference:

"Lease". Section 2A–103(1)(j).

§ 2A–105. Territorial Application of Article to Goods Covered by Certificate of Title.

Subject to the provisions of Sections 2A–304(3) and 2A–305(3), with respect to goods covered by a certificate of title issued under a statute of this State or of another jurisdiction, compliance and the effect of compliance or noncompliance with a certificate of title statute are governed by the law (including the conflict of laws rules) of the jurisdiction issuing the certificate until the earlier of (a) surrender of the certificate, or (b) four months after the goods are removed from that jurisdiction and thereafter until a new certificate of title is issued by another jurisdiction.

Official Comment

Uniform Statutory Source: Section 9–103(2)(a) and (b).

Changes: Substantially revised. The provisions of the last sentence of Section 9–103(2)(b) have not been incorporated as it is superfluous in this context. The provisions of Section 9–103(2)(d) have not been incorporated because the problems dealt with are adequately addressed by this section and Sections 2A–304(3) and 305(3).

Purposes: The new certificate referred to in (b) must be permanent, not temporary. Generally, the lessor or creditor whose interest is indicated on the most recently issued certificate of title will prevail over interests indicated on certificates issued previously by other jurisdictions. This provision reflects a policy that it is reasonable to require holders of interests in goods covered by a certificate of title to police the goods or risk losing their interests when a new certificate of title is issued by another jurisdiction.

Cross References:

Sections 2A-304(3), 2A-305(3), 9-103(2)(b) and 9-103(2)(d).

Definitional Cross Reference:

"Goods". Section 2A-103(1)(h).

§ 2A-106. Limitation on Power of Parties to Consumer Lease to Choose Applicable Law and Judicial Forum.

(1) If the law chosen by the parties to a consumer lease is that of a jurisdiction other than a jurisdiction in which the lessee resides at the time the lease agreement becomes enforceable or within 30 days thereafter or in which the goods are to be used, the choice is not enforceable.

(2) If the judicial forum chosen by the parties to a consumer lease is a forum that would not otherwise have jurisdiction over the lessee, the choice is not enforceable.

Official Comment

Uniform Statutory Source: Unif. Consumer Credit Code § 1.201(8), 7A U.L.A. 36 (1974).

Changes: Substantially revised.

Purposes: There is a real danger that a lessor may induce a consumer lessee to agree that the applicable law will be a jurisdiction that has little effective consumer protection, or to agree that the applicable forum will be a forum that is inconvenient for the lessee in the event of litigation. As a result, this section invalidates these choice of law or forum clauses, except where the law chosen is that of the state of the consumer's residence or where the goods will be kept, or the forum chosen is one that otherwise would have jurisdiction over the lessee.

Subsection (1) limits potentially abusive choice of law clauses in consumer leases. The 30-day rule in subsection (1) was suggested by Section 9-103(1)(c). This section has no effect on choice of law clauses in leases that are not consumer leases. Such clauses would be governed by other law.

Subsection (2) prevents enforcement of potentially abusive jurisdictional consent clauses in consumer leases. By using the term judicial forum, this section does not limit selection of a nonjudicial forum, such as arbitration. This section has no effect on choice of forum clauses in leases that are not consumer leases; such clauses are, as a matter of current law, "prima facie valid". *The Bremen v. Zapata Off-Shore Co.*, 407 U.S. 1, 10 (1972). Such clauses would be governed by other law, including the Model Choice of Forum Act (1968).

Cross Reference:

Section 9-103(1)(c).

Definitional Cross References:

"Consumer lease". Section 2A-103(1)(e).

"Lease agreement". Section 2A-103(1)(k).

"Lessee". Section 2A-103(1)(n).

"Goods". Section 2A-103(1)(h).

"Party". Section 1-201(29).

§ 2A-107. Waiver or Renunciation of Claim or Right After Default.

Any claim or right arising out of an alleged default or breach of warranty may be discharged in whole or in part without consideration by a written waiver or renunciation signed and delivered by the aggrieved party.

Official Comment

Uniform Statutory Source: Section 1-107.

Changes: Revised to reflect leasing practices and terminology. This clause is used throughout the official comments to this Article to indicate the scope of change in the provisions of the Uniform Statutory Source included in the section; these changes range from one extreme, *e.g.*, a significant difference in practice (a warranty as to merchantability is not implied in a finance lease (Section 2A-212)) to the other extreme, *e.g.*, a modest difference in style or terminology (the transaction governed is a lease not a sale (Section ~~2A-203~~ 2A-103 *)).

Cross References:

Sections ~~2A-203~~ 2A-103 * and 2A-212.

Definitional Cross References:

"Aggrieved party". Section 1-201(2).
"Delivery". Section 1-201(14).
"Rights". Section 1-201(36).
"Signed". Section 1-201(39).
"Written". Section 1-201(46).

* *Previous incorrect cross reference corrected by Permanent Editorial Board action November 1992.*

§ 2A-108. Unconscionability.

(1) If the court as a matter of law finds a lease contract or any clause of a lease contract to have been unconscionable at the time it was made the court may refuse to enforce the lease contract, or it may enforce the remainder of the lease contract without the unconscionable clause, or it may so limit the application of any unconscionable clause as to avoid any unconscionable result.

(2) With respect to a consumer lease, if the court as a matter of law finds that a lease contract or any clause of a lease contract has been induced by unconscionable conduct or that unconscionable conduct has occurred in the collection of a claim arising from a lease contract, the court may grant appropriate relief.

(3) Before making a finding of unconscionability under subsection (1) or (2), the court, on its own motion or that of a party, shall afford the parties a reasonable opportunity to present evidence as to the setting, purpose, and effect of the lease contract or clause thereof, or of the conduct.

(4) In an action in which the lessee claims unconscionability with respect to a consumer lease:

(a) If the court finds unconscionability under subsection (1) or (2), the court shall award reasonable attorney's fees to the lessee.

(b) If the court does not find unconscionability and the lessee claiming unconscionability has brought or maintained an action he [or she] knew to be groundless, the court shall award reasonable attorney's fees to the party against whom the claim is made.

(c) In determining attorney's fees, the amount of the recovery on behalf of the claimant under subsections (1) and (2) is not controlling.

Official Comment

Uniform Statutory Source: Section 2–302 and Unif. Consumer Credit Code § 5.108, 7A U.L.A. 167–69 (1974).

Changes: Subsection (1) is taken almost verbatim from the provisions of Section 2–302(1). Subsection (2) is suggested by the provisions of Unif. Consumer Credit Code § 5.108(1), (2), 7A U.L.A. 167 (1974). Subsection (3), taken from the provisions of Section 2–302(2), has been expanded to cover unconscionable conduct. Unif. Consumer Credit Code § 5.108(3), 7A U.L.A. 167 (1974). The provision for the award of attorney's fees to consumers, subsection (4), covers unconscionability under subsection (1) as well as (2). Subsection (4) is modeled on the provisions of Unif. Consumer Credit Code § 5.108(6), 7A U.L.A. 169 (1974).

Purposes: Subsections (1) and (3) of this section apply the concept of unconscionability reflected in the provisions of Section 2–302 to leases. *See Dillman & Assocs. v. Capitol Leasing Co.*, 110 Ill. App.3d 335, 342, 442 N.E.2d 311, 316 (App.Ct.1982). Subsection (3) omits the adjective "commercial" found in subsection 2–302(2) because subsection (3) is concerned with all leases and the relevant standard of conduct is determined by the context.

The balance of the section is modeled on the provisions of Unif. Consumer Credit Code § 5.108, 7A U.L.A. 167–69 (1974). Thus subsection (2) recognizes that a consumer lease or a clause in a consumer lease may not itself be unconscionable but that the agreement would never have been entered into if unconscionable means had not been employed to induce the consumer to agree. To make a statement to induce the consumer to lease the goods, in the expectation of invoking an integration clause in the lease to exclude the statement's admissibility in a subsequent dispute, may be unconscionable. Subsection (2) also provides a consumer remedy for unconscionable conduct, such as using or threatening to use force or violence, in the collection of a claim arising from a lease contract. These provisions are not exclusive. The remedies of this section are in addition to remedies otherwise available for the same conduct under other law, for example, an action in tort for abusive debt collection or under another statute of this State for such conduct. The reference to appropriate relief in subsection (2) is intended to foster liberal administration of this remedy. Sections 2A–103(4) and 1–106(1).

Subsection (4) authorizes an award of reasonable attorney's fees if the court finds unconscionability with respect to a consumer lease under subsection (1) or (2). Provision is also made for recovery by the party against whom the claim was made if the court does not find unconscionability and does find that the consumer knew the action to be groundless. Further, subsection (4)(b) is independent of, and thus will not override, a term in the lease agreement that provides for the payment of attorney's fees.

Cross References:

Sections 1–106(1), 2–302 and 2A–103(4).

Definitional Cross References:

"Action". Section 1–201(1).

"Consumer lease". Section 2A–103(1)(e).

"Lease contract". Section 2A–103(1)(*l*).

"Lessee". Section 2A–103(1)(n).

"Party". Section 1–201(29).

§ 2A–109. Option to Accelerate at Will.

(1) A term providing that one party or his [or her] successor in interest may accelerate payment or performance or require collateral or additional collateral "at will" or "when he [or she] deems himself [or herself] insecure" or in words of similar import must be construed to mean that he [or she] has power to do so only if he [or she] in good faith believes that the prospect of payment or performance is impaired.

(2) With respect to a consumer lease, the burden of establishing good faith under subsection (1) is on the party who exercised the power; otherwise the burden of establishing lack of good faith is on the party against whom the power has been exercised.

Official Comment

Uniform Statutory Source: Section 1–208 and Unif. Consumer Credit Code § 5.109(2), 7A U.L.A. 171 (1974).

Purposes: Subsection (1) reflects modest changes in style to the provisions of the first sentence of Section 1–208.

Subsection (2), however, reflects a significant change in the provisions of the second sentence of Section 1–208 by creating a new rule with respect to a consumer lease. A lease provision allowing acceleration at the will of the lessor or when the lessor deems itself insecure is of critical importance to the lessee. In a consumer lease it is a provision that is not usually agreed to by the parties but is usually mandated by the lessor. Therefore, where its invocation depends not on specific criteria but on the discretion of the lessor, its use should be regulated to prevent abuse. Subsection (1) imposes a duty of good faith upon its exercise. Subsection (2) shifts the burden of establishing good faith to the lessor in the case of a consumer lease, but not otherwise.

Cross Reference:

Section 1–208.

Definitional Cross References:

"Burden of establishing". Section 1–201(8).

"Consumer lease". Section 2A–103(1)(e).

"Good faith". Sections 1–201(19) and 2–103(1)(b).

"Party". Section 1–201(29).

"Term". Section 1–201(42).

PART 2

FORMATION AND CONSTRUCTION OF LEASE CONTRACT

§ 2A–201. Statute of Frauds.

(1) A lease contract is not enforceable by way of action or defense unless:

(a) the total payments to be made under the lease contract, excluding payments for options to renew or buy, are less than $1,000; or

(b) there is a writing, signed by the party against whom enforcement is sought or by that party's authorized agent, sufficient to indicate that a lease contract has been made between the parties and to describe the goods leased and the lease term.

(2) Any description of leased goods or of the lease term is sufficient and satisfies subsection (1)(b), whether or not it is specific, if it reasonably identifies what is described.

(3) A writing is not insufficient because it omits or incorrectly states a term agreed upon, but the lease contract is not enforceable under subsection (1)(b) beyond the lease term and the quantity of goods shown in the writing.

(4) A lease contract that does not satisfy the requirements of subsection (1), but which is valid in other respects, is enforceable:

(a) if the goods are to be specially manufactured or obtained for the lessee and are not suitable for lease or sale to others in the ordinary course of the lessor's business, and the lessor, before notice of repudiation is received and under circumstances that reasonably indicate that the goods are for the lessee, has made either a substantial beginning of their manufacture or commitments for their procurement;

(b) if the party against whom enforcement is sought admits in that party's pleading, testimony or otherwise in court that a lease contract was made, but the lease contract is not enforceable under this provision beyond the quantity of goods admitted; or

(c) with respect to goods that have been received and accepted by the lessee.

(5) The lease term under a lease contract referred to in subsection (4) is:

(a) if there is a writing signed by the party against whom enforcement is sought or by that party's authorized agent specifying the lease term, the term so specified;

(b) if the party against whom enforcement is sought admits in that party's pleading, testimony, or otherwise in court a lease term, the term so admitted; or

(c) a reasonable lease term.

Official Comment

Uniform Statutory Source: Sections 2–201, 9–203(1) and 9–110.

Changes: This section is modeled on Section 2–201, with changes to reflect the differences between a lease contract and a contract for the sale of goods. In particular, subsection (1)(b) adds a requirement that the writing "describe the goods leased and the lease term", borrowing that concept, with revisions, from the provisions of Section 9–203(1)(a). Subsection (2), relying on the statutory analogue in Section 9–110, sets forth the minimum criterion for satisfying that requirement.

Purposes: The changes in this section conform the provisions of Section 2–201 to custom and usage in lease transactions. Section 2–201(2), stating a special rule between merchants, was not included in this section as the number of such transactions involving leases, as opposed to sales, was thought to be modest. Subsection (4) creates no exception for transactions where payment has been made and accepted. This represents a departure from the analogue, Section 2–201(3)(c). The rationale for the departure is grounded in the distinction between sales and leases. Unlike a buyer in a sales transaction, the lessee does not tender payment in full for goods delivered, but only payment of rent for one or more months. It was decided that, as a matter of policy, this act of payment is not a sufficient substitute for the required memorandum. Subsection (5) was needed to establish the criteria for supplying the lease term if it is omitted, as the lease contract may still be enforceable under subsection (4).

Cross References:

Sections 2-201, 9-110 and 9-203(1)(a).

Definitional Cross References:

"Action". Section 1-201(1).
"Agreed". Section 1-201(3).
"Buying". Section 2A-103(1)(a).
"Goods". Section 2A-103(1)(h).
"Lease". Section 2A-103(1)(j).
"Lease contract". Section 2A-103(1)(*l*).
"Lessee". Section 2A-103(1)(n).
"Lessor". Section 2A-103(1)(p).
"Notice". Section 1-201(25).
"Party". Section 1-201(29).
"Sale". Section 2-106(1).
"Signed". Section 1-201(39).
"Term". Section 1-201(42).
"Writing". Section 1-201(46).

§ 2A-202. Final Written Expression: Parol or Extrinsic Evidence.

Terms with respect to which the confirmatory memoranda of the parties agree or which are otherwise set forth in a writing intended by the parties as a final expression of their agreement with respect to such terms as are included therein may not be contradicted by evidence of any prior agreement or of a contemporaneous oral agreement but may be explained or supplemented:

(a) by course of dealing or usage of trade or by course of performance; and

(b) by evidence of consistent additional terms unless the court finds the writing to have been intended also as a complete and exclusive statement of the terms of the agreement.

Official Comment

Uniform Statutory Source: Section 2-202.

Definitional Cross References:

"Agreement". Section 1-201(3).
"Course of dealing". Section 1-205.
"Party". Section 1-201(29).
"Term". Section 1-201(42).
"Usage of trade". Section 1-205.
"Writing". Section 1-201(46).

§ 2A-203. Seals Inoperative.

The affixing of a seal to a writing evidencing a lease contract or an offer to enter into a lease contract does not render the writing a sealed instrument and the law with respect to sealed instruments does not apply to the lease contract or offer.

Official Comment

Uniform Statutory Source: Section 2-203.

Changes: Revised to reflect leasing practices and terminology.

Definitional Cross References:

"Lease contract". Section 2A-103(1)(*l*).
"Writing". Section 1-201(46).

§ 2A-204. Formation in General.

(1) A lease contract may be made in any manner sufficient to show agreement, including conduct by both parties which recognizes the existence of a lease contract.

(2) An agreement sufficient to constitute a lease contract may be found although the moment of its making is undetermined.

(3) Although one or more terms are left open, a lease contract does not fail for indefiniteness if the parties have intended to make a lease contract and there is a reasonably certain basis for giving an appropriate remedy.

Official Comment

Uniform Statutory Source: Section 2–204.

Changes: Revised to reflect leasing practices and terminology.

Definitional Cross References:

"Agreement". Section 1–201(3).

"Lease contract". Section 2A–103(1)(*l*).

"Party". Section 1–201(29).

"Remedy". Section 1–201(34).

"Term". Section 1–201(42).

§ 2A–205. Firm Offers.

An offer by a merchant to lease goods to or from another person in a signed writing that by its terms gives assurance it will be held open is not revocable, for lack of consideration, during the time stated or, if no time is stated, for a reasonable time, but in no event may the period of irrevocability exceed 3 months. Any such term of assurance on a form supplied by the offeree must be separately signed by the offeror.

Official Comment

Uniform Statutory Source: Section 2–205.

Changes: Revised to reflect leasing practices and terminology.

Definitional Cross References:

"Goods". Section 2A–103(1)(h).

"Lease". Section 2A–103(1)(j).

"Merchant". Section 2–104(1).

"Person". Section 1–201(30).

"Reasonable time". Section 1–204(1) and (2).

"Signed". Section 1–201(39).

"Term". Section 1–201(42).

"Writing". Section 1–201(46).

§ 2A–206. Offer and Acceptance in Formation of Lease Contract.

(1) Unless otherwise unambiguously indicated by the language or circumstances, an offer to make a lease contract must be construed as inviting acceptance in any manner and by any medium reasonable in the circumstances.

(2) If the beginning of a requested performance is a reasonable mode of acceptance, an offeror who is not notified of acceptance within a reasonable time may treat the offer as having lapsed before acceptance.

Official Comment

Uniform Statutory Source: Section 2–206(1)(a) and (2).

Changes: Revised to reflect leasing practices and terminology.

Definitional Cross References:

"Lease contract". Section 2A–103(1)(*l*).

"Notifies". Section 1–201(26).
"Reasonable time". Section 1–204(1) and (2).

§ 2A–207. Course of Performance or Practical Construction.

(1) If a lease contract involves repeated occasions for performance by either party with knowledge of the nature of the performance and opportunity for objection to it by the other, any course of performance accepted or acquiesced in without objection is relevant to determine the meaning of the lease agreement.

(2) The express terms of a lease agreement and any course of performance, as well as any course of dealing and usage of trade, must be construed whenever reasonable as consistent with each other; but if that construction is unreasonable, express terms control course of performance, course of performance controls both course of dealing and usage of trade, and course of dealing controls usage of trade.

(3) Subject to the provisions of Section 2A–208 on modification and waiver, course of performance is relevant to show a waiver or modification of any term inconsistent with the course of performance.

Official Comment

Uniform Statutory Source: Sections 2–208 and 1–205(4).

Changes: Revised to reflect leasing practices and terminology, except that subsection (2) was further revised to make the subsection parallel the provisions of Section 1–205(4) by adding that course of dealing controls usage of trade.

Purposes: The section should be read in conjunction with Section 2A–208. In particular, although a specific term may control over course of performance as a matter of lease construction under subsection (2), subsection (3) allows the same course of dealing to show a waiver or modification, if Section 2A–208 is satisfied.

Cross References:

Sections 1–205(4), 2–208 and 2A–208.

Definitional Cross References:

"Course of dealing". Section 1–205.
"Knowledge". Section 1–201(25).
"Lease agreement". Section 2A–103(1)(k).
"Lease contract". Section 2A–103(1)(*l*).
"Party". Section 1–201(29).
"Term". Section 1–201(42).
"Usage of trade". Section 1–205.

§ 2A–208. Modification, Rescission and Waiver.

(1) An agreement modifying a lease contract needs no consideration to be binding.

(2) A signed lease agreement that excludes modification or rescission except by a signed writing may not be otherwise modified or rescinded, but, except as between merchants, such a requirement on a form supplied by a merchant must be separately signed by the other party.

(3) Although an attempt at modification or rescission does not satisfy the requirements of subsection (2), it may operate as a waiver.

(4) A party who has made a waiver affecting an executory portion of a lease contract may retract the waiver by reasonable notification received by

the other party that strict performance will be required of any term waived, unless the retraction would be unjust in view of a material change of position in reliance on the waiver.

Official Comment

Uniform Statutory Source: Section 2–209.

Changes: Revised to reflect leasing practices and terminology, except that the provisions of subsection 2–209(3) were omitted.

Purposes: Section 2–209(3) provides that "the requirements of the statute of frauds section of this Article (Section 2–201) must be satisfied if the contract as modified is within its provisions." This provision was not incorporated as it is unfair to allow an oral modification to make the entire lease contract unenforceable, *e.g.* if the modification takes it a few dollars over the dollar limit. At the same time, the problem could not be solved by providing that the lease contract would still be enforceable in its pre-modification state (if it then satisfied the statute of frauds) since in some cases that might be worse than no enforcement at all. Resolution of the issue is left to the courts based on the facts of each case.

Cross References:

Sections 2–201 and 2–209.

Definitional Cross References:

"Agreement". Section 1–201(3).
"Between merchants". Section 2–104(3).
"Lease agreement". Section 2A–103(1)(k).
"Lease contract". Section 2A–103(1)(*l*).
"Merchant". Section 2–104(1).
"Notification". Section 1–201(26).
"Party". Section 1–201(29).
"Signed". Section 1–201(39).
"Term". Section 1–201(42).
"Writing". Section 1–201(46).

§ 2A–209. Lessee Under Finance Lease as Beneficiary of Supply Contract.

(1) The benefit of a supplier's promises to the lessor under the supply contract and of all warranties, whether express or implied, including those of any third party provided in connection with or as part of the supply contract, extends to the lessee to the extent of the lessee's leasehold interest under a finance lease related to the supply contract, but is subject to the terms of the warranty and of the supply contract and all defenses or claims arising therefrom.

(2) The extension of the benefit of a supplier's promises and of warranties to the lessee (Section 2A–209(1)) does not: (i) modify the rights and obligations of the parties to the supply contract, whether arising therefrom or otherwise, or (ii) impose any duty or liability under the supply contract on the lessee.

(3) Any modification or rescission of the supply contract by the supplier and the lessor is effective between the supplier and the lessee unless, before the modification or rescission, the supplier has received notice that the lessee has entered into a finance lease related to the supply contract. If the modification or rescission is effective between the supplier and the lessee, the lessor is deemed to have assumed, in addition to the obligations of the lessor to the lessee under the lease contract, promises of the supplier to the lessor

and warranties that were so modified or rescinded as they existed and were available to the lessee before modification or rescission.

(4) In addition to the extension of the benefit of the supplier's promises and of warranties to the lessee under subsection (1), the lessee retains all rights that the lessee may have against the supplier which arise from an agreement between the lessee and the supplier or under other law.

As amended in 1990.

See Appendix VI for material relating to changes made in text in 1990.

Official Comment

Uniform Statutory Source: None.

Changes: This section is modeled on Section 9–318, the Restatement (Second) of Contracts §§ 302–315 (1981), and leasing practices. *See Earman Oil Co. v. Burroughs Corp.*, 625 F.2d 1291, 1296–97 (5th Cir.1980).

Purposes:

1. The function performed by the lessor in a finance lease is extremely limited. Section 2A–103(1)(g). The lessee looks to the supplier of the goods for warranties and the like or, in some cases as to warranties, to the manufacturer if a warranty made by that person is passed on. That expectation is reflected in subsection (1), which is self-executing. As a matter of policy, the operation of this provision may not be excluded, modified or limited; however, an exclusion, modification, or limitation of any term of the supply contract or warranty, including any with respect to rights and remedies, and any defense or claim such as a statute of limitations, effective against the lessor as the acquiring party under the supply contract, is also effective against the lessee as the beneficiary designated under this provision. For example, the supplier is not precluded from excluding or modifying an express or implied warranty under a supply contract. Sections 2–312(2) and 2–316, or Section 2A–214. Further, the supplier is not precluded from limiting the rights and remedies of the lessor and from liquidating damages. Sections 2–718 and 2–719 or Sections 2A–503 and 2A–504. If the supply contract excludes or modifies warranties, limits remedies, or liquidates damages with respect to the lessor, such provisions are enforceable against the lessee as beneficiary. Thus, only selective discrimination against the beneficiaries designated under this section is precluded, i.e., exclusion of the supplier's liability to the lessee with respect to warranties made to the lessor. This section does not affect the development of other law with respect to products liability.

2. Enforcement of this benefit is by action. Sections 2A–103(4) and 1–106(2).

3. The benefit extended by these provisions is not without a price, as this Article also provides in the case of a finance lease that is not a consumer lease that the lessee's promises to the lessor under the lease contract become irrevocable and independent upon the lessee's acceptance of the goods. Section 2A–407.

4. Subsection (2) limits the effect of subsection (1) on the supplier and the lessor by preserving, notwithstanding the transfer of the benefits of the supply contract to the lessee, all of the supplier's and the lessor's rights and obligations with respect to each other and others; it further absolves the lessee of any duties with respect to the supply contract that might have been inferred from the extension of the benefits thereof.

5. Subsections (2) and (3) also deal with difficult issues related to modification or rescission of the supply contract. Subsection (2) states a rule that determines the impact of the statutory extension of benefit contained in subsection (1)

upon the relationship of the parties to the supply contract and, in a limited respect, upon the lessee. This statutory extension of benefit, like that contained in Sections 2A–216 and 2–318, is not a modification of the supply contract by the parties. Thus, subsection (3) states the rules that apply to a modification or rescission of the supply contract by the parties. Subsection (3) provides that a modification or rescission is not effective between the supplier and the lessee if, before the modification or rescission occurs, the supplier received notice that the lessee has entered into the finance lease. On the other hand, if the modification or rescission is effective, then to the extent of the modification or rescission of the benefit or warranty, the lessor by statutory dictate assumes an obligation to provide to the lessee that which the lessee would otherwise lose. For example, assume a reduction in an express warranty from four years to one year. No prejudice to the lessee may occur if the goods perform as agreed. If, however, there is a breach of the express warranty after one year and before four years pass, the lessor is liable. A remedy for any prejudice to the lessee because of the bifurcation of the lessee's recourse resulting from the action of the supplier and the lessor is left to resolution by the courts based on the facts of each case.

6. Subsection (4) makes it clear that the rights granted to the lessee by this section do not displace any rights the lessee otherwise may have against the supplier.

Cross References:

Sections 2A–103(1)(g), 2A–407 and 9–318.

Definitional Cross References:

"Action". Section 1–201(1).
"Finance lease". Section 2A–103(1)(g).
"Leasehold interest". Section 2A–103(1)(m).
"Lessee". Section 2A–103(1)(n).
"Lessor". Section 2A–103(1)(p).
"Notice". Section 1–201(25).
"Party". Section 1–201(29).
"Rights". Section 1–201(36).
"Supplier". Section 2A–103(1)(x).
"Supply contract". Section 2A–103(1)(y).
"Term". Section 1–201(42).

§ 2A–210. Express Warranties.

(1) Express warranties by the lessor are created as follows:

(a) Any affirmation of fact or promise made by the lessor to the lessee which relates to the goods and becomes part of the basis of the bargain creates an express warranty that the goods will conform to the affirmation or promise.

(b) Any description of the goods which is made part of the basis of the bargain creates an express warranty that the goods will conform to the description.

(c) Any sample or model that is made part of the basis of the bargain creates an express warranty that the whole of the goods will conform to the sample or model.

(2) It is not necessary to the creation of an express warranty that the lessor use formal words, such as "warrant" or "guarantee," or that the lessor have a specific intention to make a warranty, but an affirmation merely of the value of the goods or a statement purporting to be merely the lessor's opinion or commendation of the goods does not create a warranty.

Official Comment

Uniform Statutory Source: Section 2-313.

Changes: Revised to reflect leasing practices and terminology.

Purposes: All of the express and implied warranties of the Article on Sales (Article 2) are included in this Article, revised to reflect the differences between a sale of goods and a lease of goods. Sections 2A-210 through 2A-216. The lease of goods is sufficiently similar to the sale of goods to justify this decision. Hawkland, *The Impact of the Uniform Commercial Code on Equipment Leasing*, 1972 Ill.L.F. 446, 459-60. Many state and federal courts have reached the same conclusion.

Value of the goods, as used in subsection (2), includes rental value.

Cross References:

Article 2, esp. Section 2-313, and Sections 2A-210 through 2A-216.

Definitional Cross References:

"Conforming". Section 2A-103(1)(d).
"Goods". Section 2A-103(1)(h).
"Lessee". Section 2A-103(1)(n).
"Lessor". Section 2A-103(1)(p).
"Value". Section 1-201(44).

§ 2A-211. Warranties Against Interference and Against Infringement; Lessee's Obligation Against Infringement.

(1) There is in a lease contract a warranty that for the lease term no person holds a claim to or interest in the goods that arose from an act or omission of the lessor, other than a claim by way of infringement or the like, which will interfere with the lessee's enjoyment of its leasehold interest.

(2) Except in a finance lease there is in a lease contract by a lessor who is a merchant regularly dealing in goods of the kind a warranty that the goods are delivered free of the rightful claim of any person by way of infringement or the like.

(3) A lessee who furnishes specifications to a lessor or a supplier shall hold the lessor and the supplier harmless against any claim by way of infringement or the like that arises out of compliance with the specifications.

See Appendix VI [following Amendment 24 therein] for material relating to changes in the Official Comment to conform to the 1990 amendments to various sections of Article 2A.

Official Comment

Uniform Statutory Source: Section 2-312.

Changes: This section is modeled on the provisions of Section 2-312, with modifications to reflect the limited interest transferred by a lease contract and the total interest transferred by a sale. Section 2-312(2), which is omitted here, is incorporated in Section 2A-214. The warranty of quiet possession was abolished with respect to sales of goods. Section 2-312 official comment 1. Section 2A-211(1) reinstates the warranty of quiet possession with respect to leases. Inherent in the nature of the limited interest transferred by the lease—the right to possession and use of the goods—is the need of the lessee for protection greater than that afforded to the buyer. Since the scope of the protection is limited to claims or interests that arose from acts or omissions of the lessor, the lessor will be in position to evaluate the potential cost, certainly a far better position than that enjoyed by the lessee. Further, to the extent the market will allow, the lessor can attempt to pass on the anticipated additional cost to the lessee in the guise of higher rent.

Purposes: General language was chosen for subsection (1) that expresses the essence of the lessee's expectation: with an exception for infringement and the like, no person holding a claim or interest that arose from an act or omission of the lessor will be able to interfere with the lessee's use and enjoyment of the goods for the lease term. Subsection (2), like other similar provisions in later sections, excludes the finance lessor from extending this warranty; with few exceptions (Sections 2A-210 and 2A-211(1)), the lessee under a finance lease is to look to the supplier for warranties and the like or, in some cases as to warranties, to the manufacturer if a warranty made by that person is passed on. Subsections (2) and (3) are derived from Section 2-312(3). These subsections, as well as the analogue, should be construed so that applicable principles of law and equity supplement their provisions. Sections 2A-103(4) and 1-103.

Cross References:

Sections 2-312, 2-312(1), 2-312(2), 2-312 official comment 1, 2A-210, 2A-211(1) and 2A-214.

Definitional Cross References:

"Delivery". Section 1-201(14).
"Finance lease". Section 2A-103(1)(g).
"Goods". Section 2A-103(1)(h).
"Lease". Section 2A-103(1)(j).
"Lease contract". Section 2A-103(1)(*l*).
"Leasehold interest". Section 2A-103(1)(m).
"Lessee". Section 2A-103(1)(n).
"Lessor". Section 2A-103(1)(p).
"Merchant". Section 2-104(1).
"Person". Section 1-201(30).
"Supplier". Section 2A-103(1)(x).

§ 2A-212. Implied Warranty of Merchantability.

(1) Except in a finance lease, a warranty that the goods will be merchantable is implied in a lease contract if the lessor is a merchant with respect to goods of that kind.

(2) Goods to be merchantable must be at least such as

(a) pass without objection in the trade under the description in the lease agreement;

(b) in the case of fungible goods, are of fair average quality within the description;

(c) are fit for the ordinary purposes for which goods of that type are used;

(d) run, within the variation permitted by the lease agreement, of even kind, quality, and quantity within each unit and among all units involved;

(e) are adequately contained, packaged, and labeled as the lease agreement may require; and

(f) conform to any promises or affirmations of fact made on the container or label.

(3) Other implied warranties may arise from course of dealing or usage of trade.

Official Comment

Uniform Statutory Source: Section 2-314.

Changes: Revised to reflect leasing practices and terminology. *E.g., Glenn Dick Equip. Co. v. Galey Constr., Inc.*, 97 Idaho

216, 225, 541 P.2d 1184, 1193 (1975) (implied warranty of merchantability (Article 2) extends to lease transactions).

Definitional Cross References:

"Conforming". Section 2A-103(1)(d).
"Course of dealing". Section 1-205.
"Finance lease". Section 2A-103(1)(g).
"Fungible". Section 1-201(17).
"Goods". Section 2A-103(1)(h).
"Lease agreement". Section 2A-103(1)(k).
"Lease contract". Section 2A-103(1)(*l*).
"Lessor". Section 2A-103(1)(p).
"Merchant". Section 2-104(1).
"Usage of trade". Section 1-205.

§ 2A-213. Implied Warranty of Fitness for Particular Purpose.

Except in a finance lease, if the lessor at the time the lease contract is made has reason to know of any particular purpose for which the goods are required and that the lessee is relying on the lessor's skill or judgment to select or furnish suitable goods, there is in the lease contract an implied warranty that the goods will be fit for that purpose.

Official Comment

Uniform Statutory Source: Section 2-315.

Changes: Revised to reflect leasing practices and terminology. *E.g., All-States Leasing Co. v. Bass*, 96 Idaho 873, 879, 538 P.2d 1177, 1183 (1975) (implied warranty of fitness for a particular purpose (Article 2) extends to lease transactions).

Definitional Cross References:

"Finance lease". Section 2A-103(1)(g).
"Goods". Section 2A-103(1)(h).
"Knows". Section 1-201(25).
"Lease contract". Section 2A-103(1)(*l*).
"Lessee". Section 2A-103(1)(n).
"Lessor". Section 2A-103(1)(p).

§ 2A-214. Exclusion or Modification of Warranties.

(1) Words or conduct relevant to the creation of an express warranty and words or conduct tending to negate or limit a warranty must be construed wherever reasonable as consistent with each other; but, subject to the provisions of Section 2A-202 on parol or extrinsic evidence, negation or limitation is inoperative to the extent that the construction is unreasonable.

(2) Subject to subsection (3), to exclude or modify the implied warranty of merchantability or any part of it the language must mention "merchantability", be by a writing, and be conspicuous. Subject to subsection (3), to exclude or modify any implied warranty of fitness the exclusion must be by a writing and be conspicuous. Language to exclude all implied warranties of fitness is sufficient if it is in writing, is conspicuous and states, for example, "There is no warranty that the goods will be fit for a particular purpose".

(3) Notwithstanding subsection (2), but subject to subsection (4),

(a) unless the circumstances indicate otherwise, all implied warranties are excluded by expressions like "as is," or "with all faults," or by other language that in common understanding calls the lessee's attention to the exclusion of warranties and makes plain that there is no implied warranty, if in writing and conspicuous;

(b) if the lessee before entering into the lease contract has examined the goods or the sample or model as fully as desired or has refused to examine the goods, there is no implied warranty with regard to defects that an examination ought in the circumstances to have revealed; and

(c) an implied warranty may also be excluded or modified by course of dealing, course of performance, or usage of trade.

(4) To exclude or modify a warranty against interference or against infringement (Section 2A–211) or any part of it, the language must be specific, be by a writing, and be conspicuous, unless the circumstances, including course of performance, course of dealing, or usage of trade, give the lessee reason to know that the goods are being leased subject to a claim or interest of any person.

Official Comment

Uniform Statutory Source: Sections 2–316 and 2–312(2).

Changes: Subsection (2) requires that a disclaimer of the warranty of merchantability be conspicuous and in writing as is the case for a disclaimer of the warranty of fitness; this is contrary to the rule stated in Section 2–316(2) with respect to the disclaimer of the warranty of merchantability. This section also provides that to exclude or modify the implied warranty of merchantability, fitness or against interference or infringement the language must be in writing and conspicuous. There are, however, exceptions to the rule. *E.g.*, course of dealing, course of performance, or usage of trade may exclude or modify an implied warranty. Section 2A–214(3)(c). The analogue of Section 2–312(2) has been moved to subsection (4) of this section for a more unified treatment of disclaimers; there is no policy with respect to leases of goods that would justify continuing certain distinctions found in the Article on Sales (Article 2) regarding the treatment of the disclaimer of various warranties. *Compare* Sections 2–312(2) and 2–316(2). Finally, the example of a disclaimer of the implied warranty of fitness stated in subsection (2) differs from the analogue stated in Section 2–316(2); this example should promote a better understanding of the effect of the disclaimer.

Purposes: These changes were made to reflect leasing practices. *E.g., FMC Finance Corp. v. Murphree,* 632 F.2d 413, 418 (5th Cir.1980) (disclaimer of implied warranty under lease transactions must be conspicuous and in writing). The omission of the provisions of Section 2–316(4) was not substantive. Sections 2A–503 and 2A–504.

Cross References:

Article 2, esp. Sections 2–312(2) and 2–316, and Sections 2A–503 and 2A–504.

Definitional Cross References:

"Conspicuous". Section 1–201(10).
"Course of dealing". Section 1–205.
"Fault". Section 2A–103(1)(f).
"Goods". Section 2A–103(1)(h).
"Knows". Section 1–201(25).
"Lease". Section 2A–103(1)(j).
"Lease contract". Section 2A–103(1)(*l*).
"Lessee". Section 2A–103(1)(n).
"Person". Section 1–201(30).
"Usage of trade". Section 1–205.
"Writing". Section 1–201(46).

§ 2A–215. Cumulation and Conflict of Warranties Express or Implied.

Warranties, whether express or implied, must be construed as consistent with each other and as cumulative, but if that construction is unreasonable, the intention of the parties determines which warranty is dominant. In ascertaining that intention the following rules apply:

(a) Exact or technical specifications displace an inconsistent sample or model or general language of description.

(b) A sample from an existing bulk displaces inconsistent general language of description.

(c) Express warranties displace inconsistent implied warranties other than an implied warranty of fitness for a particular purpose.

Official Comment

Uniform Statutory Source: Section 2–317.

Definitional Cross Reference:

"Party". Section 1–201(29).

§ 2A–216. Third-Party Beneficiaries of Express and Implied Warranties.

ALTERNATIVE A

A warranty to or for the benefit of a lessee under this Article, whether express or implied, extends to any natural person who is in the family or household of the lessee or who is a guest in the lessee's home if it is reasonable to expect that such person may use, consume, or be affected by the goods and who is injured in person by breach of the warranty. This section does not displace principles of law and equity that extend a warranty to or for the benefit of a lessee to other persons. The operation of this section may not be excluded, modified, or limited, but an exclusion, modification, or limitation of the warranty, including any with respect to rights and remedies, effective against the lessee is also effective against any beneficiary designated under this section.

ALTERNATIVE B

A warranty to or for the benefit of a lessee under this Article, whether express or implied, extends to any natural person who may reasonably be expected to use, consume, or be affected by the goods and who is injured in person by breach of the warranty. This section does not displace principles of law and equity that extend a warranty to or for the benefit of a lessee to other persons. The operation of this section may not be excluded, modified, or limited, but an exclusion, modification, or limitation of the warranty, including any with respect to rights and remedies, effective against the lessee is also effective against the beneficiary designated under this section.

ALTERNATIVE C

A warranty to or for the benefit of a lessee under this Article, whether express or implied, extends to any person who may reasonably be expected to use, consume, or be affected by the goods and who is injured by breach of the warranty. The operation of this section may not be excluded, modified, or limited with respect to injury to the person of an individual to whom the warranty extends, but an exclusion, modification, or limitation of the warranty, including any with respect to rights and remedies, effective against the lessee is also effective against the beneficiary designated under this section.

Official Comment

Uniform Statutory Source: Section 2-318.

Changes: The provisions of Section 2-318 have been included in this section, modified in two respects: first, to reflect leasing practice, including the special practices of the lessor under a finance lease; second, to reflect and thus codify elements of the official comment to Section 2-318 with respect to the effect of disclaimers and limitations of remedies against third parties.

Purposes: Alternative A is based on the 1962 version of Section 2-318 and is least favorable to the injured person as the doctrine of privity imposed by other law is abrogated to only a limited extent. Alternatives B and C are based on later additions to Section 2-318 and are more favorable to the injured person. In determining which alternative to select, the state legislature should consider making its choice parallel to the choice it made with respect to Section 2-318, as interpreted by the courts.

The last sentence of each of Alternatives A, B and C does not preclude the lessor from excluding or modifying an express or implied warranty under a lease. Section 2A-214. Further, that sentence does not preclude the lessor from limiting the rights and remedies of the lessee and from liquidating damages. Sections 2A-503 and 2A-504. If the lease excludes or modifies warranties, limits remedies for breach, or liquidates damages with respect to the lessee, such provisions are enforceable against the beneficiaries designated under this section. However, this last sentence forbids selective discrimination against the beneficiaries designated under this section, *i.e.*, exclusion of the lessor's liability to the beneficiaries with respect to warranties made by the lessor to the lessee.

Other law, including the Article on Sales (Article 2), may apply in determining the extent to which a warranty to or for the benefit of the lessor extends to the lessee and third parties. This is in part a function of whether the lessor has bought or leased the goods.

This Article does not purport to change the development of the relationship of the common law, with respect to products liability, including strict liability in tort (as restated in Restatement (Second) of Torts, § 402A (1965)), to the provisions of this Act. *Compare Cline v. Prowler Indus. of Maryland*, 418 A.2d 968 (Del. 1980) and *Hawkins Constr. Co. v. Matthews Co.*, 190 Neb. 546, 209 N.W.2d 643 (1973) with *Dippel v. Sciano*, 37 Wis.2d 443, 155 N.W.2d 55 (1967).

Cross References:

Article 2, esp. Section 2-318, and Sections 2A-214, 2A-503 and 2A-504.

Definitional Cross References:

"Goods". Section 2A-103(1)(h).
"Lessee". Section 2A-103(1)(n).
"Person". Section 1-201(30).
"Remedy". Section 1-201(34).
"Rights". Section 1-201(36).

§ 2A-217. Identification.

Identification of goods as goods to which a lease contract refers may be made at any time and in any manner explicitly agreed to by the parties. In the absence of explicit agreement, identification occurs:

(a) when the lease contract is made if the lease contract is for a lease of goods that are existing and identified;

(b) when the goods are shipped, marked, or otherwise designated by the lessor as goods to which the lease contract refers, if the lease contract is for a lease of goods that are not existing and identified; or

(c) when the young are conceived, if the lease contract is for a lease of unborn young of animals.

Official Comment

Uniform Statutory Source: Section 2-501.

Changes: This section, together with Section 2A-218, is derived from the provisions of Section 2-501, with changes to reflect lease terminology; however, this section omits as irrelevant to leasing practice the treatment of special property.

Purposes: With respect to subsection (b) there is a certain amount of ambiguity in the reference to when goods are designated, *e.g.*, when the lessor is both selling and leasing goods to the same lessee/buyer and has marked goods for delivery but has not distinguished between those related to the lease contract and those related to the sales contract. As in Section 2-501(1)(b), this issue has been left to be resolved by the courts, case by case.

Cross References:

Sections 2-501 and 2A-218.

Definitional Cross References:

"Agreement". Section 1-201(3).
"Goods". Section 2A-103(1)(h).
"Lease". Section 2A-103(1)(j).
"Lease contract". Section 2A-103(1)(*l*).
"Lessor". Section 2A-103(1)(p).
"Party". Section 1-201(29).

§ 2A-218. Insurance and Proceeds.

(1) A lessee obtains an insurable interest when existing goods are identified to the lease contract even though the goods identified are nonconforming and the lessee has an option to reject them.

(2) If a lessee has an insurable interest only by reason of the lessor's identification of the goods, the lessor, until default or insolvency or notification to the lessee that identification is final, may substitute other goods for those identified.

(3) Notwithstanding a lessee's insurable interest under subsections (1) and (2), the lessor retains an insurable interest until an option to buy has been exercised by the lessee and risk of loss has passed to the lessee.

(4) Nothing in this section impairs any insurable interest recognized under any other statute or rule of law.

(5) The parties by agreement may determine that one or more parties have an obligation to obtain and pay for insurance covering the goods and by agreement may determine the beneficiary of the proceeds of the insurance.

Official Comment

Uniform Statutory Source: Section 2-501.

Changes: This section, together with Section 2A-217, is derived from the provisions of Section 2-501, with changes and additions to reflect leasing practices and terminology.

Purposes: Subsection (2) states a rule allowing substitution of goods by the lessor under certain circumstances, until default or insolvency of the lessor, or until notification to the lessee that identification is final. Subsection (3) states a rule regarding the lessor's insurable interest that, by virtue of the difference between a sale and a lease, necessarily is different from the rule stated in Section 2-501(2) regarding the seller's insurable interest. For this purpose the option to buy shall be deemed to have been exercised by the lessee when the resulting sale is closed, not when the lessee gives notice to the lessor. Further, subsection (5) is new and reflects the common practice of shifting the responsibility and cost of insuring the goods between the parties to the lease transaction.

Cross References:

Sections 2-501, 2-501(2) and 2A-217.

Definitional Cross References:

"Agreement". Section 1-201(3).
"Buying". Section 2A-103(1)(a).
"Conforming". Section 2A-103(1)(d).
"Goods". Section 2A-103(1)(h).
"Insolvent". Section 1-201(23).
"Lease contract". Section 2A-103(1)(*l*).
"Lessee". Section 2A-103(1)(n).
"Lessor". Section 2A-103(1)(p).
"Notification". Section 1-201(26).
"Party". Section 1-201(29).

§ 2A-219. Risk of Loss.

(1) Except in the case of a finance lease, risk of loss is retained by the lessor and does not pass to the lessee. In the case of a finance lease, risk of loss passes to the lessee.

(2) Subject to the provisions of this Article on the effect of default on risk of loss (Section 2A-220), if risk of loss is to pass to the lessee and the time of passage is not stated, the following rules apply:

(a) If the lease contract requires or authorizes the goods to be shipped by carrier

(i) and it does not require delivery at a particular destination, the risk of loss passes to the lessee when the goods are duly delivered to the carrier; but

(ii) if it does require delivery at a particular destination and the goods are there duly tendered while in the possession of the carrier, the risk of loss passes to the lessee when the goods are there duly so tendered as to enable the lessee to take delivery.

(b) If the goods are held by a bailee to be delivered without being moved, the risk of loss passes to the lessee on acknowledgment by the bailee of the lessee's right to possession of the goods.

(c) In any case not within subsection (a) or (b), the risk of loss passes to the lessee on the lessee's receipt of the goods if the lessor, or, in the case of a finance lease, the supplier, is a merchant; otherwise the risk passes to the lessee on tender of delivery.

Official Comment

Uniform Statutory Source: Section 2-509(1) through (3).

Changes: Subsection (1) is new. The introduction to subsection (2) is new, but subparagraph (a) incorporates the provisions of Section 2-509(1); subparagraph (b) incorporates the provisions of Section 2-509(2) only in part, reflecting current practice in lease transactions.

Purposes: Subsection (1) states rules related to retention or passage of risk of loss consistent with current practice in lease transactions. The provisions of subsection (4) of Section 2-509 are not incorporated as they are not necessary. This section does not deal with responsibility for loss caused by the wrongful act of either the lessor or the lessee.

Cross References:

Sections 2-509(1), 2-509(2) and 2-509(4).

Definitional Cross References:

"Delivery". Section 1-201(14).
"Finance lease". Section 2A-103(1)(g).

"Goods". Section 2A-103(1)(h).
"Lease contract". Section 2A-103(1)(*l*).
"Lessee". Section 2A-103(1)(n).
"Lessor". Section 2A-103(1)(p).
"Merchant". Section 2-104(1).
"Receipt". Section 2-103(1)(c).
"Rights". Section 1-201(36).
"Supplier". Section 2A-103(1)(x).

§ 2A-220. Effect of Default on Risk of Loss.

(1) Where risk of loss is to pass to the lessee and the time of passage is not stated:

(a) If a tender or delivery of goods so fails to conform to the lease contract as to give a right of rejection, the risk of their loss remains with the lessor, or, in the case of a finance lease, the supplier, until cure or acceptance.

(b) If the lessee rightfully revokes acceptance, he [or she], to the extent of any deficiency in his [or her] effective insurance coverage, may treat the risk of loss as having remained with the lessor from the beginning.

(2) Whether or not risk of loss is to pass to the lessee, if the lessee as to conforming goods already identified to a lease contract repudiates or is otherwise in default under the lease contract, the lessor, or, in the case of a finance lease, the supplier, to the extent of any deficiency in his [or her] effective insurance coverage may treat the risk of loss as resting on the lessee for a commercially reasonable time.

Official Comment

Uniform Statutory Source: Section 2-510.

Changes: Revised to reflect leasing practices and terminology. The rule in Section (1)(b) does not allow the lessee under a finance lease to treat the risk of loss as having remained with the supplier from the beginning. This is appropriate given the limited circumstances under which the lessee under a finance lease is allowed to revoke acceptance. Section 2A-517 and Section 2A-516 official comment.

Definitional Cross References:

"Conforming". Section 2A-103(1)(d).
"Delivery". Section 1-201(14).
"Finance lease". Section 2A-103(1)(g).
"Goods". Section 2A-103(1)(h).
"Lease contract". Section 2A-103(1)(*l*).
"Lessee". Section 2A-103(1)(n).
"Lessor". Section 2A-103(1)(p).
"Reasonable time". Section 1-204(1) and (2).
"Rights". Section 1-201(36).
"Supplier". Section 2A-103(1)(x).

§ 2A-221. Casualty to Identified Goods.

If a lease contract requires goods identified when the lease contract is made, and the goods suffer casualty without fault of the lessee, the lessor or the supplier before delivery, or the goods suffer casualty before risk of loss passes to the lessee pursuant to the lease agreement or Section 2A-219, then:

(a) if the loss is total, the lease contract is avoided; and

(b) if the loss is partial or the goods have so deteriorated as to no longer conform to the lease contract, the lessee may nevertheless demand inspection and at his [or her] option either treat the lease contract as avoided or, except in a finance lease that is not a consumer lease, accept the goods with due allowance from the rent payable for the balance of the lease term for the deterioration or the deficiency in quantity but without further right against the lessor.

Official Comment

Uniform Statutory Source: Section 2–613.

Changes: Revised to reflect leasing practices and terminology.

Purpose: Due to the vagaries of determining the amount of due allowance (Section 2–613(b)), no attempt was made in subsection (b) to treat a problem unique to lease contracts and installment sales contracts: determining how to recapture the allowance, *e.g.*, application to the first or last rent payments or allocation, *pro rata*, to all rent payments.

Cross References:

Section 2–613.

Definitional Cross References:

"Conforming". Section 2A–103(1)(d).
"Consumer lease". Section 2A–103(1)(e).
"Delivery". Section 1–201(14).
"Fault". Section 2A–103(1)(f).
"Finance lease". Section 2A–103(1)(g).
"Goods". Section 2A–103(1)(h).
"Lease". Section 2A–103(1)(j).
"Lease agreement". Section 2A–103(1)(k).
"Lease contract". Section 2A–103(1)(*l*).
"Lessee". Section 2A–103(1)(n).
"Lessor". Section 2A–103(1)(p).
"Rights". Section 1–201(36).
"Supplier". Section 2A–103(1)(x).

PART 3

EFFECT OF LEASE CONTRACT

§ 2A–301. Enforceability of Lease Contract.

Except as otherwise provided in this Article, a lease contract is effective and enforceable according to its terms between the parties, against purchasers of the goods and against creditors of the parties.

See Appendix VI [following Amendment 24 therein] for material relating to changes in the Official Comment to conform to the 1990 amendments to various sections of Article 2A.

Official Comment

Uniform Statutory Source: Section 9–201.

Changes: The first sentence of Section 9–201 was incorporated, modified to reflect leasing terminology. The second sentence of Section 9–201 was eliminated as not relevant to leasing practices.

Purposes:

1. This section establishes a general rule regarding the validity and enforceability of a lease contract. The lease contract is effective and enforceable between the parties and against third parties. Exceptions to this general rule arise where there is a specific rule to the contrary in this Article. Enforceability is, thus, dependent upon the lease contract meeting the requirements of the Statute of Frauds provisions of Section 2A–201. Enforceability is also a function of the lease contract conforming to the principles of construction and interpretation contained in the Article on General Provisions (Article 1). Section 2A–103(4).

2. The effectiveness or enforceability of the lease contract is not dependent upon the lease contract or any financing statement or the like being filed or recorded; however, the priority of the interest of a lessor of fixtures with respect to the interests of certain third parties in such fixtures is subject to the provisions of the Article on Secured Transactions (Article 9). Section 2A–309. Prior to the adoption of this Article filing or recording was not required with respect to leases, only leases intended as security. The definition of security interest, as amended concurrently with the adoption of this Article, more clearly delineates leases and leases intended as security and thus signals the need to file. Section 1–201(37). Those lessors who are concerned about whether the transaction creates a lease or a security interest will continue to file a protective financing statement. Section 9–408. Coogan, Leasing and the Uniform Commercial Code, in *Equipment Leasing-Leveraged Leasing* 681, 744–46 (2d ed. 1980).

3. **Hypothetical:**

(a) In construing this section it is important to recognize its relationship to other sections in this Article. This is best demonstrated by reference to a hypothetical. Assume that on February 1 A, a manufacturer of combines and other farm equipment, leased a fleet of six combines to B, a corporation engaged in the business of farming, for a 12 month term. Under the lease agreement between A and B, A agreed to defer B's payment of the first two months' rent to April 1. On March 1 B recognized that it would need only four combines and thus subleased two combines to C for an 11 month term.

(b) This hypothetical raises a number of issues that are answered by the sections contained in this part. Since lease is defined to include sublease (Section 2A–103(1)(j) and (w)), this section provides that the prime lease between A and B and the sublease between B and C are enforceable in accordance with their terms, except as otherwise provided in this Article; that exception, in this case, is one of considerable scope.

(c) The separation of ownership, which is in A, and possession, which is in B with respect to four combines and which is in C with respect to two combines, is not relevant. Section 2A–302. A's interest in the six combines cannot be challenged simply because A parted with possession to B, who in turn parted with possession of some of the combines to C. Yet it is important to note that by the terms of Section 2A–302 this conclusion is subject to change if otherwise provided in this Article.

(d) B's entering the sublease with C raises an issue that is treated by this part. In a dispute over the leased combines A may challenge B's right to sublease. The rule is permissive as to transfers of interests under a lease contract, including subleases. Section 2A–303(2). However, the rule has two significant qualifications. If the prime lease contract between A and B prohibits B from subleasing the combines, or makes such a sublease an event of default, Section 2A–303(2) applies; thus, while B's interest under the prime lease may be transferred under the sublease to C, A may have a remedy pursuant to Section 2A–303(5). Absent a prohibition or default provision in the prime lease contract A might be able to argue that the sublease to C materially increases A's risk; thus, while B's interest under the prime lease may be transferred under the sublease to C, A may have a remedy pursuant to Section 2A–303(5). Section 2A–303(5)(b)(ii).

(e) Resolution of this issue is also a function of the section dealing with the sublease of goods by a prime lessee (Section 2A–305). Subsection (1) of Section 2A–305, which is subject to the rules of Section 2A–303 stated above, provides that C takes subject to the interest of A under the prime lease between A and B. However, there are two exceptions. First, if B is a merchant (Sections 2A-103(3) and 2-104(1)) dealing in goods of that kind and C is a sublessee in the ordinary course of business (Sections 2A-103(1)(*o*) and 2A-103(1)(n)), C takes free of the prime lease between A and B. Second, if B has rejected the six combines under the prime lease with A, and B disposes of the goods by sublease to C, C takes free of the prime lease if C can establish good faith. Section 2A-511(4).

(f) If the facts of this hypothetical are expanded and we assume that the prime lease obligated B to maintain the combines, an additional issue may be presented. Prior to entering the sublease, B, in satisfaction of its maintenance covenant, brought the two combines that it desired to sublease to a local independent dealer of A's. The dealer did the requested work for B. C inspected the combines on the dealer's lot after the work was completed. C signed the sublease with B two days later. C, however, was prevented from taking delivery of the two combines as B refused to pay the dealer's invoice for the repairs. The dealer furnished the repair service to B in the ordinary course of the dealer's business. If under applicable law the dealer has a lien on repaired goods in the dealer's possession, the dealer's lien will take priority over B's and C's interests and also should take priority over A's interest, depending upon the terms of the lease contract and the applicable law. Section 2A-306.

(g) Now assume that C is in financial straits and one of C's creditors obtains a judgment against C. If the creditor levies on C's subleasehold interest in the two combines, who will prevail? Unless the levying creditor also holds a lien covered by Section 2A-306, discussed above, the judgment creditor will take its interest subject to B's rights under the sublease and A's rights under the prime lease. Section 2A-307(1). The hypothetical becomes more complicated if we assume that B is in financial straits and B's creditor holds the judgment. Here the judgment creditor takes subject to the sublease unless the lien attached to the two combines before the sublease contract became enforceable. Section 2A-307(2)(a). However, B's judgment creditor cannot prime A's interest in the goods because, with respect to A, the judgment creditor is a creditor of B in its capacity as lessee under the prime lease between A and B. Thus, here the judgment creditor's interest is subject to the lease between A and B. Section 2A-307(1).

(h) Finally, assume that on April 1 B is unable to pay A the deferred rent then due under the prime lease, but that C is current in its payments under the sublease from B. What effect will B's default under the prime lease between A and B have on C's rights under the sublease between B and C? Section 2A-301 provides that a lease contract is effective against the creditors of either party. Since a lease contract includes a sublease contract (Section 2A-103(1)(*l*)), the sublease contract between B and C arguably could be enforceable against A, a prime lessor who has extended unsecured credit to B, the prime lessee/sublessor, if the sublease contract meets the requirements of Section 2A-201. However, the rule stated in Section 2A-301 is subject to other provisions in this Article. Under Section 2A-305, C, as sublessee, would take subject to the prime lease contract in most cases. Thus, B's default under the prime lease will in most cases lead to A's recovery of the goods from C. Section 2A-523. A and C could provide otherwise by agreement. Section 2A-311. C's recourse will be to assert a claim for damages against B. Sections 2A-211(1) and 2A-508.

4. **Relationship Between Sections:**

(a) As the analysis of the hypothetical demonstrates, Part 3 of the Article focuses on issues that relate to the enforceability of the lease contract (Sections 2A-301, 2A-302 and 2A-303) and to the priority of various claims to the goods subject to the lease contract (Sections 2A-304, 2A-305, 2A-306, 2A-307, 2A-308, 2A-309, 2A-310, and 2A-311).

(b) This section states a general rule of enforceability, which is subject to specific rules to the contrary stated elsewhere in the Article. Section 2A-302 negates any notion that the separation of title and possession is fraudulent as a rule of law. Finally, Section 2A-303 states rules with respect to the transfer of the lessor's interest (as well as the residual interest in the goods) or the lessee's interest under the lease contract. Qualifications are imposed as a function of various issues, including whether the transfer is the creation or enforcement of a security interest or one that is material to the other party to the lease contract. In addition, a system of rules is created to deal with the rights and duties among assignor, assignee and the other party to the lease contract.

(c) Sections 2A-304 and 2A-305 are twins that deal with good faith transferees of goods subject to the lease contract. Section 2A-304 creates a set of rules with respect to transfers by the lessor of goods subject to a lease contract; the transferee considered is a subsequent lessee of the goods. The priority dispute covered here is between the subsequent lessee and the original lessee of the goods (or persons claiming through the original lessee). Section 2A-305 creates a set of rules with respect to transfers by the lessee of goods subject to a lease contract; the transferees considered are buyers of the goods or sublessees of the goods. The priority dispute covered here is between the transferee and the lessor of the goods (or persons claiming through the lessor).

(d) Section 2A-306 creates a rule with respect to priority disputes between holders of liens for services or materials furnished with respect to goods subject to a lease contract and the lessor or the lessee under that contract. Section 2A-307 creates a rule with respect to priority disputes between the lessee and creditors of the lessor and priority disputes between the lessor and creditors of the lessee.

(e) Section 2A-308 creates a series of rules relating to allegedly fraudulent transfers and preferences. The most significant rule is that set forth in subsection (3) which validates sale-leaseback transactions if the buyer-lessor can establish that he or she bought for value and in good faith.

(f) Sections 2A-309 and 2A-310 create a series of rules with respect to priority disputes between various third parties and a lessor of fixtures or accessions, respectively, with respect thereto.

(g) Finally, Section 2A-311 allows parties to alter the statutory priorities by agreement.

Cross References:

Article 1, especially Section 1-201(37), and Sections 2-104(1), 2A-103(1)(j), 2A-103(1)(*l*), 2A-103(1)(n), 2A-103(1)(*o*) and 2A-103(1)(w), 2A-103(3), 2A-103(4), 2A-201, 2A-301 through 2A-303, 2A-303(2), 2A-303(5), 2A-304 through 2A-307, 2A-307(1), 2A-307(2)(a), 2A-308 through 2A-311, 2A-508, 2A-511(4), 2A-523, Article 9, especially Sections 9-201 and 9-408.

Definitional Cross References:

"Creditor". Section 1-201(12).
"Goods". Section 2A-103(1)(h).
"Lease contract". Section 2A-103(1)(*l*).
"Party". Section 1-201(29).
"Purchaser". Section 1-201(33).
"Term". Section 1-201(42).

§ 2A-302. Title to and Possession of Goods.

Except as otherwise provided in this Article, each provision of this Article applies whether the lessor or a third party has title to the goods, and whether the lessor, the lessee, or a third party has possession of the goods, notwithstanding any statute or rule of law that possession or the absence of possession is fraudulent.

Official Comment

Uniform Statutory Source: Section 9-202.

Changes: Section 9-202 was modified to reflect leasing terminology and to clarify the law of leases with respect to fraudulent conveyances or transfers.

Purposes: The separation of ownership and possession of goods between the lessor and the lessee (or a third party) has created problems under certain fraudulent conveyance statutes. *See, e.g., In re Ludlum Enters.*, 510 F.2d 996 (5th Cir. 1975); *Suburbia Fed. Sav. & Loan Ass'n v. Bel-Air Conditioning Co.*, 385 So.2d 1151 (Fla.Dist.Ct.App.1980). This section provides, among other things, that separation of ownership and possession *per se* does not affect the enforceability of the lease contract. Sections 2A-301 and 2A-308.

Cross References:

Sections 2A-301, 2A-308 and 9-202.

Definitional Cross References:

"Goods". Section 2A-103(1)(h).
"Lessee". Section 2A-103(1)(n).
"Lessor". Section 2A-103(1)(p).

§ 2A-303. Alienability of Party's Interest Under Lease Contract or of Lessor's Residual Interest in Goods; Delegation of Performance; Transfer of Rights.

(1) As used in this section, "creation of a security interest" includes the sale of a lease contract that is subject to Article 9, Secured Transactions, by reason of Section 9-102(1)(b).

(2) Except as provided in subsections (3) and (4), a provision in a lease agreement which (i) prohibits the voluntary or involuntary transfer, including a transfer by sale, sublease, creation or enforcement of a security interest, or attachment, levy, or other judicial process, of an interest of a party under the lease contract or of the lessor's residual interest in the goods, or (ii) makes such a transfer an event of default, gives rise to the rights and remedies provided in subsection (5), but a transfer that is prohibited or is an event of default under the lease agreement is otherwise effective.

(3) A provision in a lease agreement which (i) prohibits the creation or enforcement of a security interest in an interest of a party under the lease contract or in the lessor's residual interest in the goods, or (ii) makes such a transfer an event of default, is not enforceable unless, and then only to the extent that, there is an actual transfer by the lessee of the lessee's right of possession or use of the goods in violation of the provision or an actual delegation of a material performance of either party to the lease contract in violation of the provision. Neither the granting nor the enforcement of a security interest in (i) the lessor's interest under the lease contract or (ii) the lessor's residual interest in the goods is a transfer that materially impairs the prospect of obtaining return performance by, materially changes the duty of, or materially increases the burden or risk imposed on, the lessee within the purview of subsection (5) unless, and then only to the extent that, there is an actual delegation of a material performance of the lessor.

(4) A provision in a lease agreement which (i) prohibits a transfer of a right to damages for default with respect to the whole lease contract or of a right to payment arising out of the transferor's due performance of the transferor's entire obligation, or (ii) makes such a transfer an event of default, is not enforceable, and such a transfer is not a transfer that materially impairs the prospect of obtaining return performance by, materially changes the duty of, or materially increases the burden or risk imposed on, the other party to the lease contract within the purview of subsection (5).

(5) Subject to subsections (3) and (4):

(a) if a transfer is made which is made an event of default under a lease agreement, the party to the lease contract not making the transfer, unless that party waives the default or otherwise agrees, has the rights and remedies described in Section 2A-501(2);

(b) if paragraph (a) is not applicable and if a transfer is made that (i) is prohibited under a lease agreement or (ii) materially impairs the prospect of obtaining return performance by, materially changes the duty of, or materially increases the burden or risk imposed on, the other party to the lease contract, unless the party not making the transfer agrees at any time to the transfer in the lease contract or otherwise, then, except as limited by contract, (i) the transferor is liable to the party not making the transfer for damages caused by the transfer to the extent that the damages could not reasonably be prevented by the party not making the transfer and (ii) a court having jurisdiction may grant other appropriate relief, including cancellation of the lease contract or an injunction against the transfer.

(6) A transfer of "the lease" or of "all my rights under the lease", or a transfer in similar general terms, is a transfer of rights and, unless the language or the circumstances, as in a transfer for security, indicate the contrary, the transfer is a delegation of duties by the transferor to the transferee. Acceptance by the transferee constitutes a promise by the transferee to perform those duties. The promise is enforceable by either the transferor or the other party to the lease contract.

(7) Unless otherwise agreed by the lessor and the lessee, a delegation of performance does not relieve the transferor as against the other party of any duty to perform or of any liability for default.

(8) In a consumer lease, to prohibit the transfer of an interest of a party under the lease contract or to make a transfer an event of default, the language must be specific, by a writing, and conspicuous.

As amended in 1990.

See Appendix VI for material relating to changes made in text in 1990.

Official Comment

Uniform Statutory Source: Sections 2-210 and 9-311.

Changes: The provisions of Sections 2-210 and 9-311 were incorporated in this section, with substantial modifications to reflect leasing terminology and practice and to harmonize the principles of the respective provisions, i.e. limitations on delegation of performance on the one hand and alienability of rights on the other. In addition, unlike Section 2–210 which deals only with voluntary transfers, this section deals with involuntary as well as voluntary transfers. Moreover, the principle of Section 9–318(4) denying effectiveness to contractual terms prohibiting assignments of receivables due and to become due also is implemented.

Purposes:

1. Subsection (2) states a rule, consistent with Section 9–311, that voluntary and involuntary transfers of an interest of a party under the lease contract or of the lessor's residual interest, including by way of the creation or enforcement of a security interest, are effective, notwithstanding a provision in the lease agreement prohibiting the transfer or making the transfer an event of default. Although the transfers are effective, the provision in the lease agreement is nevertheless enforceable, but only as provided in subsection (5). Under subsection (5) the prejudiced party is limited to the remedies on "default under the lease contract" in this Article and, except as limited by this Article, as provided in the lease agreement, if the transfer has been made an event of default. Section 2A–501(2). Usually, there will be a specific provision to this effect or a general provision making a breach of a covenant an event of default. In those cases where the transfer is prohibited, but not made an event of default, the prejudiced party may recover damages; or, if the damage remedy would be ineffective adequately to protect that party, the court can order cancellation of the lease contract or enjoin the transfer. This rule that such provisions generally are enforceable is subject to subsections (3) and (4), which make such provisions unenforceable in certain instances.

2. The first such instance is described in subsection (3). A provision in a lease agreement which prohibits the creation or enforcement of a security interest, including sales of lease contracts subject to Article 9 (Sections 9–102(1)(b) and 9–104(f)), or makes it an event of default is generally not enforceable, reflecting the policy of Section 9–318(4). However, that policy gives way to the doctrine stated in Section 2–210(2), which gives one party to a contract the right to protect itself against an actual delegation (but not just a provision under which delegation might later occur) of a material performance by the other party. Accordingly, such a provision in a lease agreement is enforceable when the transfer delegates a material performance. Generally, as expressly provided in subsection (6), a transfer for security is not a delegation of duties. However, inasmuch as the creation of a security interest includes the sale of a lease contract, if there are then unperformed duties on the part of the lessor/seller, there could be a delegation of duties in the sale, and, if such a delegation actually takes place and is of a material performance, a provision in a lease agreement prohibiting it or making it an event of default would be enforceable, giving rise to the rights and remedies stated in subsection (5). The statute does not define "material." The parties may set standards to determine its meaning. The term is intended to exclude delegations of matters such as accounting to a professional accountant and the performance of, as opposed to the responsibility for, maintenance duties to a person in the maintenance service industry.

3. For similar reasons, the lessor is entitled to protect its residual interest in the goods by prohibiting anyone but the lessee from possessing or using them. Accordingly, under subsection (3) if there is an actual transfer by the lessee of its right of possession or use of the goods in violation of a provision in the lease agreement, such a provision likewise is enforceable, giving rise to the rights and remedies stated in subsection (5). A transfer of the lessee's right of possession or use of the goods resulting from the enforcement of a security interest granted by the les-

see in its leasehold interest is a "transfer by the lessee" under this subsection.

4. Finally, subsection (3) protects against a claim that the creation or enforcement of a security interest in the lessor's interest under the lease contract or in the residual interest is a transfer that materially impairs the prospect of obtaining return performance by, materially changes the duty of, or materially increases the burden or risk imposed on the lessee so as to give rise to the rights and remedies stated in subsection (5), unless the transfer involves an actual delegation of a material performance of the lessor.

5. While it is not likely that a transfer by the lessor of its right to payment under the lease contract would impair at a future time the ability of the lessee to obtain the performance due the lessee under the lease contract from the lessor, if under the circumstances reasonable grounds for insecurity as to receiving that performance arise, the lessee may employ the provision of this Article for demanding adequate assurance of due performance and has the remedy provided in that circumstance. Section 2A–401.

6. Sections 9–206 and 9–318(1) through (3) also are relevant. Section 9–206 sanctions an agreement by a lessee not to assert certain types of claims or defenses against the lessor's assignee. Section 9–318(1) through (3) deal with, among other things, the other party's rights against the assignee where Section 9–206(1) does not apply. Since the definition of contract under Section 1–201(11) includes a lease agreement, the definition of account debtor under Section 9–105(1)(a) includes a lessee of goods. As a result, Section 9–206 applies to lease agreements, and there is no need to restate those sections in this Article. The reference to "defenses or claims arising out of a sale" in Section 9–318(1) should be interpreted broadly to include defenses or claims arising out of a lease inasmuch as that section codifies the common law rule with respect to contracts, including lease contracts.

7. Subsection (4) is based upon Section 2–210(2) and Section 9–318(4). It makes unenforceable a prohibition against transfers of certain rights to payment or a provision making the transfer an event of default. It also provides that such transfers do not materially impair the prospect of obtaining return performance by, materially change the duty of, or materially increase the burden or risk imposed on, the other party to the lease contract so as to give rise to the rights and remedies stated in subsection (5). Accordingly, a transfer of a right to payment cannot be prohibited or made an event of default, or be one that materially impairs performance, changes duties or increases risk, if the right is already due or will become due without further performance being required by the party to receive payment. Thus, a lessor can transfer the right to future payments under the lease contract, including by way of a grant of a security interest, and the transfer will not give rise to the rights and remedies stated in subsection (5) if the lessor has no remaining performance under the lease contract. The mere fact that the lessor is obligated to allow the lessee to remain in possession and to use the goods as long as the lessee is not in default does not mean that there is "remaining performance" on the part of the lessor. Likewise, the fact that the lessor has potential liability under a "non-operating" lease contract for breaches of warranty does not mean that there is "remaining performance." In contrast, the lessor would have "remaining performance" under a lease contract requiring the lessor to regularly maintain and service the goods or to provide "upgrades" of the equipment on a periodic basis in order to avoid obsolescence. The basic distinction is between a mere potential duty to respond which is not "remaining performance," and an affirmative duty to render stipulated performance. Although the distinction may be difficult to draw in some cases, it is instructive to focus on the difference between "operating" and "non-operating" leases as generally understood in the marketplace. Even if there is "remaining performance" under

a lease contract, a transfer for security of a right to payment that is made an event of default or that is in violation of a prohibition against transfer does not give rise to the rights and remedies under subsection (5) if it does not constitute an actual delegation of a material performance under subsection (3).

8. The application of either the rule of subsection (3) or the rule of subsection (4) to the grant by the lessor of a security interest in the lessor's right to future payment under the lease contract may produce the same result. Both subsections generally protect security transfers by the lessor in particular because the creation by the lessor of a security interest or the enforcement of that interest generally will not prejudice the lessee's rights if it does not result in a delegation of the lessor's duties. To the contrary, the receipt of loan proceeds or relief from the enforcement of an antecedent debt normally should enhance the lessor's ability to perform its duties under the lease contract. Nevertheless, there are circumstances where relief might be justified. For example, if ownership of the goods is transferred pursuant to enforcement of a security interest to a party whose ownership would prevent the lessee from continuing to possess the goods, relief might be warranted. See 49 U.S.C. § 1401(a) and (b) which places limitations on the operation of aircraft in the United States based on the citizenship or corporate qualification of the registrant.

9. Relief on the ground of material prejudice when the lease agreement does not prohibit the transfer or make it an event of default should be afforded only in extreme circumstances, considering the fact that the party asserting material prejudice did not insist upon a provision in the lease agreement that would protect against such a transfer.

10. Subsection (5) implements the rule of subsection (2). Subsection (2) provides that, even though a transfer is effective, a provision in the lease agreement prohibiting it or making it an event of default may be enforceable as provided in subsection (5). See Brummond v. First National Bank of Clovis, 656 P.2d 884, 35 U.C.C.Rep.Serv. (Callaghan) 1311 (N.Mex.1983), stating the analogous rule for Section 9-311. If the transfer prohibited by the lease agreement is made an event of default, then, under subsection 5(a), unless the default is waived or there is an agreement otherwise, the aggrieved party has the rights and remedies referred to in Section 2A-501(2), viz. those in this Article and, except as limited in the Article, those provided in the lease agreement. In the unlikely circumstance that the lease agreement prohibits the transfer without making a violation of the prohibition an event of default or, even if there is no prohibition against the transfer, and the transfer is one that materially impairs performance, changes duties, or increases risk (for example, a sublease or assignment to a party using the goods improperly or for an illegal purpose), then subsection 5(b) is applicable. In that circumstance, unless the party aggrieved by the transfer has otherwise agreed in the lease contract, such as by assenting to a particular transfer or to transfers in general, or agrees in some other manner, the aggrieved party has the right to recover damages from the transferor and a court may, in appropriate circumstances, grant other relief, such as cancellation of the lease contract or an injunction against the transfer.

11. If a transfer gives rise to the rights and remedies provided in subsection (5), the transferee as an alternative may propose, and the other party may accept, adequate cure or compensation for past defaults and adequate assurance of future due performance under the lease contract. Subsection (5) does not preclude any other relief that may be available to a party to the lease contract aggrieved by a transfer subject to an enforceable prohibition, such as an action for interference with contractual relations.

12. Subsection (8) requires that a provision in a consumer lease prohibiting a transfer, or making it an event of default, must be specific, written and conspicuous. See Section 1-201(10). This assists in

protecting a consumer lessee against surprise assertions of default.

13. Subsection (6) is taken almost verbatim from the provisions of Section 2–210(4). The subsection states a rule of construction that distinguishes a commercial assignment, which substitutes the assignee for the assignor as to rights and duties, and an assignment for security or financing assignment, which substitutes the assignee for the assignor only as to rights. Note that the assignment for security or financing assignment is a subset of all security interests. Security interest is defined to include "any interest of a buyer of . . . . chattel paper". Section 1–201(37). Chattel paper is defined to include a lease. Section 9–105(1)(b). Thus, a buyer of leases is the holder of a security interest in the leases. That conclusion should not influence this issue, as the policy is quite different. Whether a buyer of leases is the holder of a commercial assignment, or an assignment for security or financing assignment should be determined by the language of the assignment or the circumstances of the assignment.

Cross References:

Sections 1–201(11), 1–201(37), 2–210, 2A–401, 9–102(1)(b), 9–104(f), 9–105(1)(a), 9–206, and 9–318.

Definitional Cross References:

"Agreed" and "Agreement". Section 1–201(3).
"Conspicuous". Section 1–201(10).
"Goods". Section 2A–103(1)(h).
"Lease". Section 2A–103(1)(j).
"Lease contract". Section 2A–103(1)(*l*).
"Lessee". Section 2A–103(1)(n).
"Lessor". Section 2A–103(1)(p).
"Lessor's residual interest". Section 2A–103(1)(q).
"Notice". Section 1–201(25).
"Party". Section 1–201(29).
"Person". Section 1–201(30).
"Reasonable time". Section 1–204(1) and (2).
"Rights". Section 1–201(36).
"Term". Section 1–201(42).
"Writing". Section 1–201(46).

§ 2A–304. Subsequent Lease of Goods by Lessor.

(1) Subject to Section 2A–303, a subsequent lessee from a lessor of goods under an existing lease contract obtains, to the extent of the leasehold interest transferred, the leasehold interest in the goods that the lessor had or had power to transfer, and except as provided in subsection (2) and Section 2A–527(4), takes subject to the existing lease contract. A lessor with voidable title has power to transfer a good leasehold interest to a good faith subsequent lessee for value, but only to the extent set forth in the preceding sentence. If goods have been delivered under a transaction of purchase, the lessor has that power even though:

(a) the lessor's transferor was deceived as to the identity of the lessor;

(b) the delivery was in exchange for a check which is later dishonored;

(c) it was agreed that the transaction was to be a "cash sale"; or

(d) the delivery was procured through fraud punishable as larcenous under the criminal law.

(2) A subsequent lessee in the ordinary course of business from a lessor who is a merchant dealing in goods of that kind to whom the goods were entrusted by the existing lessee of that lessor before the interest of the subsequent lessee became enforceable against that lessor obtains, to the extent of the leasehold interest transferred, all of that lessor's and the existing lessee's rights to the goods, and takes free of the existing lease contract.

(3) A subsequent lessee from the lessor of goods that are subject to an existing lease contract and are covered by a certificate of title issued under a statute of this State or of another jurisdiction takes no greater rights than those provided both by this section and by the certificate of title statute.

As amended in 1990.

See Appendix VI for material relating to changes made in text in 1990.

Official Comment

Uniform Statutory Source: Section 2-403.

Changes: While Section 2-403 was used as a model for this section, the provisions of Section 2-403 were significantly revised to reflect leasing practices and to integrate this Article with certificate of title statutes.

Purposes:

1. This section must be read in conjunction with, as it is subject to, the provisions of Section 2A-303, which govern voluntary and involuntary transfers of rights and duties under a lease contract, including the lessor's residual interest in the goods.

2. This section must also be read in conjunction with Section 2-403. This section and Section 2A-305 are derived from Section 2-403, which states a unified policy on good faith purchases of goods. Given the scope of the definition of purchaser (Section 1-201(33)), a person who bought goods to lease as well as a person who bought goods subject to an existing lease from a lessor will take pursuant to Section 2-403. Further, a person who leases such goods from the person who bought them should also be protected under Section 2-403, first because the lessee's rights are derivative and second because the definition of purchaser should be interpreted to include one who takes by lease; no negative implication should be drawn from the inclusion of lease in the definition of purchase in this Article. Section 2A-103(1)(v).

3. There are hypotheticals that relate to an entrustee's unauthorized lease of entrusted goods to a third party that are outside the provisions of Sections 2-403, 2A-304 and 2A-305. Consider a sale of goods by M, a merchant, to B, a buyer. After paying for the goods B allows M to retain possession of the goods as B is short of storage. Before B calls for the goods M leases the goods to L, a lessee. This transaction is not governed by Section 2-403(2) as L is not a buyer in the ordinary course of business. Section 1-201(9). Further, this transaction is not governed by Section 2A-304(2) as B is not an existing lessee. Finally, this transaction is not governed by Section 2A-305(2) as B is not M's lessor. Section 2A-307(2) resolves the potential dispute between B, M and L. By virtue of B's entrustment of the goods to M and M's lease of the goods to L, B has a cause of action against M under the common law. Sections 2A-103(4) and 1-103. *See, e.g.,* Restatement (Second) of Torts §§ 222A-243. Thus, B is a creditor of M. Sections 2A-103(4) and 1-201(12). Section 2A-307(2) provides that B, as M's creditor, takes subject to M's lease to L. Thus, if L does not default under the lease, L's enjoyment and possession of the goods should be undisturbed. However, B is not without recourse. B's action should result in a judgment against M providing, among other things, a turnover of all proceeds arising from M's lease to L, as well as a transfer of all of M's right, title and interest as lessor under M's lease to L, including M's residual interest in the goods. Section 2A-103(1)(q).

4. Subsection (1) states a rule with respect to the leasehold interest obtained by a subsequent lessee from a lessor of goods under an existing lease contract. The interest will include such leasehold interest as the lessor has in the goods as

well as the leasehold interest that the lessor had the power to transfer. Thus, the subsequent lessee obtains unimpaired all rights acquired under the law of agency, apparent agency, ownership or other estoppel, whether based upon statutory provisions or upon case law principles. Sections 2A–103(4) and 1–103. In general, the subsequent lessee takes subject to the existing lease contract, including the existing lessee's rights thereunder. Furthermore, the subsequent lease contract is, of course, limited by its own terms, and the subsequent lessee takes only to the extent of the leasehold interest transferred thereunder.

5. Subsection (1) further provides that a lessor with voidable title has power to transfer a good leasehold interest to a good faith subsequent lessee for value. In addition, subsections (1)(a) through (d) provide specifically for the protection of the good faith subsequent lessee for value in a number of specific situations which have been troublesome under prior law.

6. The position of an existing lessee who entrusts leased goods to its lessor is not distinguishable from the position of other entrusters. Thus, subsection (2) provides that the subsequent lessee in the ordinary course of business takes free of the existing lease contract between the lessor entrustee and the lessee entruster, if the lessor is a merchant dealing in goods of that kind. Further, the subsequent lessee obtains all of the lessor entrustee's and the lessee entruster's rights to the goods, but only to the extent of the leasehold interest transferred by the lessor entrustee. Thus, the lessor entrustee retains the residual interest in the goods. Section 2A–103(1)(q). However, entrustment by the existing lessee must have occurred before the interest of the subsequent lessee became enforceable against the lessor. Entrusting is defined in Section 2–403(3) and that definition applies here. Section 2A–103(3).

7. Subsection (3) states a rule with respect to a transfer of goods from a lessor to a subsequent lessee where the goods are subject to an existing lease and covered by a certificate of title. The subsequent lessee's rights are no greater than those provided by this section and the applicable certificate of title statute, including any applicable case law construing such statute. Where the relationship between the certificate of title statute and Section 2–403, the statutory analogue to this section, has been construed by a court, that construction is incorporated here. Sections 2A–103(4) and 1–102(1) and (2). The better rule is that the certificate of title statutes are in harmony with Section 2–403 and thus would be in harmony with this section. *E.g., Atwood Chevrolet-Olds v. Aberdeen Mun. School Dist.*, 431 So.2d 926, 928 (Miss.1983); *Godfrey v. Gilsdorf*, 476 P.2d 3, 6, 86 Nev. 714, 718 (1970); *Martin v. Nager*, 192 N.J.Super. 189, 197–98, 469 A.2d 519, 523 (Super.Ct.Ch.Div.1983). Where the certificate of title statute is silent on this issue of transfer, this section will control.

Cross References:

Sections 1–102, 1–103, 1–201(33), 2–403, 2A–103(1)(v), 2A–103(3), 2A–103(4), 2A–303 and 2A–305.

Definitional Cross References:

"Agreed". Section 1–201(3).

"Delivery". Section 1–201(14).

"Entrusting". Section 2–403(3).

"Good faith". Sections 1–201(19) and 2–103(1)(b).

"Goods". Section 2A–103(1)(h).

"Lease". Section 2A–103(1)(j).

"Lease contract". Section 2A–103(1)(*l*).

"Leasehold interest". Section 2A–103(1)(m).

"Lessee". Section 2A–103(1)(n).

"Lessee in the ordinary course of business". Section 2A–103(1)(*o*).

"Lessor". Section 2A–103(1)(p).

"Merchant". Section 2–104(1).

"Purchase". Section 2A–103(1)(v).

"Rights". Section 1–201(36).

"Value". Section 1–201(44).

§ 2A–305. Sale or Sublease of Goods by Lessee.

(1) Subject to the provisions of Section 2A–303, a buyer or sublessee from the lessee of goods under an existing lease contract obtains, to the extent of

the interest transferred, the leasehold interest in the goods that the lessee had or had power to transfer, and except as provided in subsection (2) and Section 2A–511(4), takes subject to the existing lease contract. A lessee with a voidable leasehold interest has power to transfer a good leasehold interest to a good faith buyer for value or a good faith sublessee for value, but only to the extent set forth in the preceding sentence. When goods have been delivered under a transaction of lease the lessee has that power even though:

(a) the lessor was deceived as to the identity of the lessee;

(b) the delivery was in exchange for a check which is later dishonored; or

(c) the delivery was procured through fraud punishable as larcenous under the criminal law.

(2) A buyer in the ordinary course of business or a sublessee in the ordinary course of business from a lessee who is a merchant dealing in goods of that kind to whom the goods were entrusted by the lessor obtains, to the extent of the interest transferred, all of the lessor's and lessee's rights to the goods, and takes free of the existing lease contract.

(3) A buyer or sublessee from the lessee of goods that are subject to an existing lease contract and are covered by a certificate of title issued under a statute of this State or of another jurisdiction takes no greater rights than those provided both by this section and by the certificate of title statute.

Official Comment

Uniform Statutory Source: Section 2–403.

Changes: While Section 2–403 was used as a model for this section, the provisions of Section 2–403 were significantly revised to reflect leasing practice and to integrate this Article with certificate of title statutes.

Purposes: This section, a companion to Section 2A–304, states the rule with respect to the leasehold interest obtained by a buyer or sublessee from a lessee of goods under an existing lease contract. *Cf.* Section 2A–304 official comment. Note that this provision is consistent with existing case law, which prohibits the bailee's transfer of title to a good faith purchaser for value under Section 2–403(1). *Rohweder v. Aberdeen Product. Credit Ass'n*, 765 F.2d 109 (8th Cir. 1985).

Subsection (2) is also consistent with existing case law. *American Standard Credit, Inc. v. National Cement Co.*, 643 F.2d 248, 269–70 (5th Cir. 1981); *but cf. Exxon Co., U.S.A. v. TLW Computer Indus.*, 37 U.C.C.Rep.Serv. (Callaghan) 1052, 1057–58 (D.Mass.1983). Unlike Section 2A–304(2), this subsection does not contain any requirement with respect to the time that the goods were entrusted to the merchant. In Section 2A–304(2) the competition is between two customers of the merchant lessor; the time of entrusting was added as a criterion to create additional protection to the customer who was first in time: the existing lessee. In subsection (2) the equities between the competing interests were viewed as balanced.

There appears to be some overlap between Section 2–403(2) and Section 2A–305(2) with respect to a buyer in the ordinary course of business. However, an examination of this Article's definition of buyer in the ordinary course of business (Section 2A–103(1)(a)) makes clear that this reference was necessary to treat entrusting in the context of a lease.

Subsection (3) states a rule of construction with respect to a transfer of goods from a lessee to a buyer or sublessee, where the goods are subject to an existing lease and covered by a certificate of title. *Cf.* Section 2A-304 official comment.

Cross References:

Sections 2-403, 2A-103(1)(a), 2A-304 and 2A-305(2).

Definitional Cross References:

"Buyer". Section 2-103(1)(a).
"Buyer in the ordinary course of business". Section 2A-103(1)(a).
"Delivery". Section 1-201(14).
"Entrusting". Section 2-403(3).
"Good faith". Sections 1-201(19) and 2-103(1)(b).
"Goods". Section 2A-103(1)(h).
"Lease". Section 2A-103(1)(j).
"Lease contract". Section 2A-103(1)(*l*).
"Leasehold interest." Section 2A-103(1)(m).
"Lessee". Section 2A-103(1)(n).
"Lessee in the ordinary course of business". Section 2A-103(1)(*o*).
"Lessor". Section 2A-103(1)(p).
"Merchant". Section 2-104(1).
"Rights". Section 1-201(36).
"Sale". Section 2-106(1).
"Sublease". Section 2A-103(1)(w).
"Value". Section 1-201(44).

§ 2A-306. Priority of Certain Liens Arising by Operation of Law.

If a person in the ordinary course of his [or her] business furnishes services or materials with respect to goods subject to a lease contract, a lien upon those goods in the possession of that person given by statute or rule of law for those materials or services takes priority over any interest of the lessor or lessee under the lease contract or this Article unless the lien is created by statute and the statute provides otherwise or unless the lien is created by rule of law and the rule of law provides otherwise.

Official Comment

Uniform Statutory Source: Section 9-310.

Changes: The approach reflected in the provisions of Section 9-310 was included, but revised to conform to leasing terminology and to expand the exception to the special priority granted to protected liens to cover liens created by rule of law as well as those created by statute.

Purposes: This section should be interpreted to allow a qualified lessor or a qualified lessee to be the competing lienholder if the statute or rule of law so provides. The reference to statute includes applicable regulations and cases; these sources must be reviewed in resolving a priority dispute under this section.

Cross Reference:

Section 9-310.

Definitional Cross References:

"Goods". Section 2A-103(1)(h).
"Lease contract". Section 2A-103(1)(*l*).
"Lessee". Section 2A-103(1)(n).
"Lessor". Section 2A-103(1)(p).
"Lien". Section 2A-103(1)(r).
"Person". Section 1-201(30).

§ 2A-307. Priority of Liens Arising by Attachment or Levy on, Security Interests in, and Other Claims to Goods.

(1) Except as otherwise provided in Section 2A-306, a creditor of a lessee takes subject to the lease contract.

(2) Except as otherwise provided in subsections (3) and (4) and in Sections 2A-306 and 2A-308, a creditor of a lessor takes subject to the lease contract unless:

(a) the creditor holds a lien that attached to the goods before the lease contract became enforceable;

(b) the creditor holds a security interest in the goods and the lessee did not give value and receive delivery of the goods without knowledge of the security interest; or

(c) the creditor holds a security interest in the goods which was perfected (Section 9–303) before the lease contract became enforceable.

(3) A lessee in the ordinary course of business takes the leasehold interest free of a security interest in the goods created by the lessor even though the security interest is perfected (Section 9–303) and the lessee knows of its existence.

(4) A lessee other than a lessee in the ordinary course of business takes the leasehold interest free of a security interest to the extent that it secures future advances made after the secured party acquires knowledge of the lease or more than 45 days after the lease contract becomes enforceable, whichever first occurs, unless the future advances are made pursuant to a commitment entered into without knowledge of the lease and before the expiration of the 45-day period.

As amended in 1990.

See Appendix VI for material relating to changes made in text in 1990.

Official Comment

Uniform Statutory Source: None for subsection (1). Subsection (2) is derived from Section 9–301, and subsections (3) and (4) are derived from Section 9–307(1) and (3), respectively.

Changes: The provisions of Sections 9–301 and 9–307(1) and (3) were incorporated, and modified to reflect leasing terminology and the basic concepts reflected in this Article.

Purposes:

1. Subsection (1) states a general rule of priority that a creditor of the lessee takes subject to the lease contract. The term lessee (Section 2A–103(1)(n)) includes sublessee. Therefore, this subsection not only covers disputes between the prime lessor and a creditor of the prime lessee but also disputes between the prime lessor, or the sublessor, and a creditor of the sublessee. Section 2A–301 official comment 3(g). Further, by using the term creditor (Section 1–201(12)), this subsection will cover disputes with a general creditor, a secured creditor, a lien creditor and any representative of creditors. Section 2A–103(4).

2. Subsection (2) states a general rule of priority that a creditor of a lessor takes subject to the lease contract. Note the discussion above with regard to the scope of these rules. Section 2A–301 official comment 3(g). Thus, the section will not only cover disputes between the prime lessee and a creditor of the prime lessor but also disputes between the prime lessee, or the sublessee, and a creditor of the sublessor.

3. To take priority over the lease contract, and the interests derived therefrom, the creditor must come within one of three exceptions stated within the rule. First, subsection (2)(a) provides that where the creditor holds a lien (Section 2A–103(1)(r)) that attached before the lease contract became enforceable (Section 2A–301), the creditor does not take subject to the lease. Second, subsection (2)(b) provides that when the creditor holds a security interest (Section 1–

201(37)), whether or not perfected, the creditor has priority over a lessee who did not give value (Section 1-201(44)) and receive delivery of the goods without knowledge (Section 1-201(25)) of the security interest. As to other lessees, under subsection (2)(c) a secured creditor holding a perfected security interest before the time the lease contract became enforceable (Section 2A-301) does not take subject to the lease. With respect to this provision, the lessee in these circumstances is treated like a buyer so that perfection of a purchase money security interest does not relate back (Section 9-301).

4. The rules of this section operate in favor of whichever party to the lease contract may enforce it, even if one party perhaps may not, e.g., under Section 2A-201(1)(b).

5. The rules stated in subsections (2)(b) and (c), and the rule in subsection (3), are best understood by reviewing a hypothetical. Assume that a merchant engaged in the business of selling and leasing musical instruments obtained possession of a truck load of musical instruments on deferred payment terms from a supplier of musical instruments on January 6. To secure payment of such credit the merchant granted the supplier a security interest in the instruments; the security interest was perfected by filing on January 15. The merchant, as lessor, entered into a lease to an individual of one of the musical instruments supplied by the supplier; the lease became enforceable on January 10. Under subsection (2)(b) the lessee will prevail (assuming the lessee qualifies thereunder) unless subsection (c) provides otherwise. Under the rule stated in subsection (2)(c) a priority dispute between the supplier, as the lessor's secured creditor, and the lessee would be determined by ascertaining on January 10 (the day the lease became enforceable) the validity and perfected status of the security interest in the musical instrument and the enforceability of the lease contract by the lessee. Nothing more appearing, under the rule stated in subsection (2)(c), the supplier's security interest in the musical instrument would not have priority over the lease contract. Moreover, subsection (2) states that its rules are subject to the rules of subsections (3) and (4). Under this hypothetical the lessee should qualify as a "lessee in the ordinary course of business". Section 2A-103(1)(*o*). Subsection (3) also makes clear that the lessee in the ordinary course of business will win even if he or she knows of the existence of the supplier's security interest.

6. Subsections (3) and (4), which are modeled on the provisions of Section 9-307(1) and (3), respectively, state two exceptions to the priority rule stated in subsection (2) with respect to a creditor who holds a security interest. The lessee in the ordinary course of business will be treated in the same fashion as the buyer in the ordinary course of business, given a priority dispute with a secured creditor over goods subject to a lease contract.

Cross References:

Sections 1-201(12), 1-201(25), 1-201(37), 1-201(44), 2A-103(1)(n), 2A-103(1)(*o*), 2A-103(1)(r), 2A-103(4), 2A-201(1)(b), 2A-301 official comment 3(g), Article 9, especially Sections 9-301, 9-307(1) and 9-307(3).

Definitional Cross References:

"Creditor". Section 1-201(12).

"Goods". Section 2A-103(1)(h).

"Knowledge" and "Knows". Section 1-201(25).

"Lease". Section 2A-103(1)(j).

"Lease contract". Section 2A-103(1)(*l*).

"Leasehold interest". Section 2A-103(1)(m).

"Lessee". Section 2A-103(1)(n).

"Lessee in the ordinary course of business". Section 2A-103(1)(*o*).

"Lessor". Section 2A-103(1)(p).

"Lien". Section 2A-103(1)(r).

"Party". Section 1-201(29).

"Pursuant to commitment". Section 2A-103(3).

"Security interest". Section 1-201(37).

§ 2A–308. Special Rights of Creditors.

(1) A creditor of a lessor in possession of goods subject to a lease contract may treat the lease contract as void if as against the creditor retention of possession by the lessor is fraudulent under any statute or rule of law, but retention of possession in good faith and current course of trade by the lessor for a commercially reasonable time after the lease contract becomes enforceable is not fraudulent.

(2) Nothing in this Article impairs the rights of creditors of a lessor if the lease contract (a) becomes enforceable, not in current course of trade but in satisfaction of or as security for a pre-existing claim for money, security, or the like, and (b) is made under circumstances which under any statute or rule of law apart from this Article would constitute the transaction a fraudulent transfer or voidable preference.

(3) A creditor of a seller may treat a sale or an identification of goods to a contract for sale as void if as against the creditor retention of possession by the seller is fraudulent under any statute or rule of law, but retention of possession of the goods pursuant to a lease contract entered into by the seller as lessee and the buyer as lessor in connection with the sale or identification of the goods is not fraudulent if the buyer bought for value and in good faith.

Official Comment

Uniform Statutory Source: Section 2–402(2) and (3)(b).

Changes: Rephrased and new material added to conform to leasing terminology and practice.

Purposes: Subsection (1) states a general rule of avoidance where the lessor has retained possession of goods if such retention is fraudulent under any statute or rule of law. However, the subsection creates an exception under certain circumstances for retention of possession of goods for a commercially reasonable time after the lease contract becomes enforceable.

Subsection (2) also preserves the possibility of an attack on the lease by creditors of the lessor if the lease was made in satisfaction of or as security for a pre-existing claim, and would constitute a fraudulent transfer or voidable preference under other law.

Finally, subsection (3) states a new rule with respect to sale-leaseback transactions, *i.e.*, transactions where the seller sells goods to a buyer but possession of the goods is retained by the seller pursuant to a lease contract between the buyer as lessor and the seller as lessee. Notwithstanding any statute or rule of law that would treat such retention as fraud, whether *per se, prima facie,* or otherwise, the retention is not fraudulent if the buyer bought for value (Section 1–201(44)) and in good faith (Sections 1–201(19) and 2–103(1)(b)). Section 2A–103(3) and (4). This provision overrides Section 2–402(2) to the extent it would otherwise apply to a sale-leaseback transaction.

Cross References:

Sections 1–201(19), 1–201(44), 2–402(2) and 2A–103(4).

Definitional Cross References:

"Buyer". Section 2–103(1)(a).
"Contract". Section 1–201(11).
"Creditor". Section 1–201(12).
"Good faith". Sections 1–201(19) and 2–103(1)(b).
"Goods". Section 2A–103(1)(h).
"Lease contract". Section 2A–103(1)(*l*).
"Lessee". Section 2A–103(1)(n).
"Lessor". Section 2A–103(1)(p).
"Money". Section 1–201(24).

"Reasonable time". Section 1-204(1) and (2).
"Rights". Section 1-201(36).
"Sale". Section 2-106(1).
"Seller". Section 2-103(1)(d).
"Value". Section 1-201(44).

§ 2A-309. Lessor's and Lessee's Rights When Goods Become Fixtures.

(1) In this section:

(a) goods are "fixtures" when they become so related to particular real estate that an interest in them arises under real estate law;

(b) a "fixture filing" is the filing, in the office where a mortgage on the real estate would be filed or recorded, of a financing statement covering goods that are or are to become fixtures and conforming to the requirements of Section 9-402(5);

(c) a lease is a "purchase money lease" unless the lessee has possession or use of the goods or the right to possession or use of the goods before the lease agreement is enforceable;

(d) a mortgage is a "construction mortgage" to the extent it secures an obligation incurred for the construction of an improvement on land including the acquisition cost of the land, if the recorded writing so indicates; and

(e) "encumbrance" includes real estate mortgages and other liens on real estate and all other rights in real estate that are not ownership interests.

(2) Under this Article a lease may be of goods that are fixtures or may continue in goods that become fixtures, but no lease exists under this Article of ordinary building materials incorporated into an improvement on land.

(3) This Article does not prevent creation of a lease of fixtures pursuant to real estate law.

(4) The perfected interest of a lessor of fixtures has priority over a conflicting interest of an encumbrancer or owner of the real estate if:

(a) the lease is a purchase money lease, the conflicting interest of the encumbrancer or owner arises before the goods become fixtures, the interest of the lessor is perfected by a fixture filing before the goods become fixtures or within ten days thereafter, and the lessee has an interest of record in the real estate or is in possession of the real estate; or

(b) the interest of the lessor is perfected by a fixture filing before the interest of the encumbrancer or owner is of record, the lessor's interest has priority over any conflicting interest of a predecessor in title of the encumbrancer or owner, and the lessee has an interest of record in the real estate or is in possession of the real estate.

(5) The interest of a lessor of fixtures, whether or not perfected, has priority over the conflicting interest of an encumbrancer or owner of the real estate if:

(a) the fixtures are readily removable factory or office machines, readily removable equipment that is not primarily used or leased for use in the operation of the real estate, or readily removable replacements of domestic appliances that are goods subject to a consumer lease, and before the goods become fixtures the lease contract is enforceable; or

(b) the conflicting interest is a lien on the real estate obtained by legal or equitable proceedings after the lease contract is enforceable; or

(c) the encumbrancer or owner has consented in writing to the lease or has disclaimed an interest in the goods as fixtures; or

(d) the lessee has a right to remove the goods as against the encumbrancer or owner. If the lessee's right to remove terminates, the priority of the interest of the lessor continues for a reasonable time.

(6) Notwithstanding subsection (4)(a) but otherwise subject to subsections (4) and (5), the interest of a lessor of fixtures, including the lessor's residual interest, is subordinate to the conflicting interest of an encumbrancer of the real estate under a construction mortgage recorded before the goods become fixtures if the goods become fixtures before the completion of the construction. To the extent given to refinance a construction mortgage, the conflicting interest of an encumbrancer of the real estate under a mortgage has this priority to the same extent as the encumbrancer of the real estate under the construction mortgage.

(7) In cases not within the preceding subsections, priority between the interest of a lessor of fixtures, including the lessor's residual interest, and the conflicting interest of an encumbrancer or owner of the real estate who is not the lessee is determined by the priority rules governing conflicting interests in real estate.

(8) If the interest of a lessor of fixtures, including the lessor's residual interest, has priority over all conflicting interests of all owners and encumbrancers of the real estate, the lessor or the lessee may (i) on default, expiration, termination, or cancellation of the lease agreement but subject to the agreement and this Article, or (ii) if necessary to enforce other rights and remedies of the lessor or lessee under this Article, remove the goods from the real estate, free and clear of all conflicting interests of all owners and encumbrancers of the real estate, but the lessor or lessee must reimburse any encumbrancer or owner of the real estate who is not the lessee and who has not otherwise agreed for the cost of repair of any physical injury, but not for any diminution in value of the real estate caused by the absence of the goods removed or by any necessity of replacing them. A person entitled to reimbursement may refuse permission to remove until the party seeking removal gives adequate security for the performance of this obligation.

(9) Even though the lease agreement does not create a security interest, the interest of a lessor of fixtures, including the lessor's residual interest, is perfected by filing a financing statement as a fixture filing for leased goods that are or are to become fixtures in accordance with the relevant provisions of the Article on Secured Transactions (Article 9).

As amended in 1990.

See Appendix VI for material relating to changes made in text in 1990.

Official Comment

Uniform Statutory Source: Section 9–313.

Changes: Revised to reflect leasing terminology and to add new material.

Purposes:

1. While Section 9–313 provided a model for this section, certain provisions were substantially revised.

2. Section 2A–309(1)(c), which is new, defines purchase money lease to exclude leases where the lessee had possession or use of the goods or the right thereof before the lease agreement became enforceable. This term is used in subsection (4)(a) as one of the conditions that must be satisfied to obtain priority over the conflicting interest of an encumbrancer or owner of the real estate.

3. Section 2A–309(4), which states one of several priority rules found in this section, deletes reference to office machines and the like (Section 9–313(4)(c)) as well as certain liens (Section 9–313(4)(d)). However, these items are included in subsection (5), another priority rule that is more permissive than the rule found in subsection (4) as it applies whether or not the interest of the lessor is perfected. In addition, subsection (5)(a) expands the scope of the provisions of Section 9–313(4)(c) to include readily removable equipment not primarily used or leased for use in the operation of real estate; the qualifier is intended to exclude from the expanded rule equipment integral to the operation of real estate, *e.g.*, heating and air conditioning equipment.

4. The rule stated in subsection (7) is more liberal than the rule stated in Section 9–313(7) in that issues of priority not otherwise resolved in this subsection are left for resolution by the priority rules governing conflicting interests in real estate, as opposed to the Section 9–313(7) automatic subordination of the security interest in fixtures. Note that, for the purpose of this section, where the interest of an encumbrancer or owner of the real estate is paramount to the interest of the lessor, the latter term includes the residual interest of the lessor.

5. The rule stated in subsection (8) is more liberal than the rule stated in Section 9–313(8) in that the right of removal is extended to both the lessor and the lessee and the occasion for removal includes expiration, termination or cancellation of the lease agreement, and enforcement of rights and remedies under this Article, as well as default. The new language also provides that upon removal the goods are free and clear of conflicting interests of owners and encumbrancers of the real estate.

6. Finally, subsection (9) provides a mechanism for the lessor of fixtures to perfect its interest by filing a financing statement under the provisions of the Article on Secured Transactions (Article 9), even though the lease agreement does not create a security interest. Section 1–201(37). The relevant provisions of Article 9 must be interpreted permissively to give effect to this mechanism as it implicitly expands the scope of Article 9 so that its filing provisions apply to transactions that create a lease of fixtures, even though the lease agreement does not create a security interest. This mechanism is similar to that provided in Section 2–326(3)(c) for the seller of goods on consignment, even though the consignment is not "intended as security". Section 1–201(37). Given the lack of litigation with respect to the mechanism created for consignment sales, this new mechanism should prove effective.

Cross References:

Sections 1–201(37), 2A–309(1)(c), 2A–309(4), Article 9, especially Sections 9–313, 9–313(4)(c), 9–313(4)(d), 9–313(7), 9–313(8) and 9–408.

Definitional Cross References:

"Agreed". Section 1-201(3).
"Cancellation". Section 2A-103(1)(b).
"Conforming". Section 2A-103(1)(d).
"Consumer lease". Section 2A-103(1)(e).
"Goods". Section 2A-103(1)(h).
"Lease". Section 2A-103(1)(j).
"Lease agreement". Section 2A-103(1)(k).
"Lease contract". Section 2A-103(1)(*l*).
"Lessee". Section 2A-103(1)(n).
"Lessor". Section 2A-103(1)(p).
"Lien". Section 2A-103(1)(r).
"Mortgage". Section 9-105(1)(j).
"Party". Section 1-201(29).
"Person". Section 1-201(30).
"Reasonable time". Section 1-204(1) and (2).
"Remedy". Section 1-201(34).
"Rights". Section 1-201(36).
"Security interest". Section 1-201(37).
"Termination". Section 2A-103(1)(z).
"Value". Section 1-201(44).
"Writing". Section 1-201(46).

§ 2A-310. Lessor's and Lessee's Rights When Goods Become Accessions.

(1) Goods are "accessions" when they are installed in or affixed to other goods.

(2) The interest of a lessor or a lessee under a lease contract entered into before the goods became accessions is superior to all interests in the whole except as stated in subsection (4).

(3) The interest of a lessor or a lessee under a lease contract entered into at the time or after the goods became accessions is superior to all subsequently acquired interests in the whole except as stated in subsection (4) but is subordinate to interests in the whole existing at the time the lease contract was made unless the holders of such interests in the whole have in writing consented to the lease or disclaimed an interest in the goods as part of the whole.

(4) The interest of a lessor or a lessee under a lease contract described in subsection (2) or (3) is subordinate to the interest of

(a) a buyer in the ordinary course of business or a lessee in the ordinary course of business of any interest in the whole acquired after the goods became accessions; or

(b) a creditor with a security interest in the whole perfected before the lease contract was made to the extent that the creditor makes subsequent advances without knowledge of the lease contract.

(5) When under subsections (2) or (3) and (4) a lessor or a lessee of accessions holds an interest that is superior to all interests in the whole, the lessor or the lessee may (a) on default, expiration, termination, or cancellation of the lease contract by the other party but subject to the provisions of the lease contract and this Article, or (b) if necessary to enforce his [or her] other rights and remedies under this Article, remove the goods from the whole, free and clear of all interests in the whole, but he [or she] must reimburse any holder of an interest in the whole who is not the lessee and who has not otherwise agreed for the cost of repair of any physical injury but not for any diminution in value of the whole caused by the absence of the goods removed or by any necessity for replacing them. A person entitled to reimbursement

may refuse permission to remove until the party seeking removal gives adequate security for the performance of this obligation.

Official Comment

Uniform Statutory Source: Section 9–314.

Changes: Revised to reflect leasing terminology and to add new material.

Purposes: Subsections (1) and (2) restate the provisions of subsection (1) of Section 9–314 to clarify the definition of accession and to add leasing terminology to the priority rule that applies when the lease is entered into before the goods become accessions. Subsection (3) restates the provisions of subsection (2) of Section 9–314 to add leasing terminology to the priority rule that applies when the lease is entered into on or after the goods become accessions. Unlike the rule with respect to security interests, the lease is merely subordinate, not invalid.

Subsection (4) creates two exceptions to the priority rules stated in subsections (2) and (3). Subsection (4) deletes the special priority rule found in the provisions of Section 9–314(3)(b) as the interests of the lessor and lessee are entitled to greater protection.

Finally, subsection (5) is modeled on the provisions of Section 9–314(4) with respect to removal of accessions, restated to reflect the parallel changes in Section 2A–309(8).

Neither this section nor Section 9–314 governs where the accession to the goods is not subject to the interest of a lessor or a lessee under a lease contract and is not subject to the interest of a secured party under a security agreement. This issue is to be resolved by the courts, case by case.

Cross References:

Sections 2A–309(8), 9–314(1), 9–314(2), 9–314(3)(b), 9–314(4).

Definitional Cross References:

"Agreed". Section 1–201(3).
"Buyer in the ordinary course of business". Section 2A–103(1)(a).
"Cancellation". Section 2A–103(1)(b).
"Creditor". Section 1–201(12).
"Goods". Section 2A–103(1)(h).
"Holder". Section 1–201(20).
"Knowledge". Section 1–201(25).
"Lease". Section 2A–103(1)(j).
"Lease contract". Section 2A–103(1)(*l*).
"Lessee". Section 2A–103(1)(n).
"Lessee in the ordinary course of business". Section 2A–103(1)(*o*).
"Lessor". Section 2A–103(1)(p).
"Party". Section 1–201(29).
"Person". Section 1–201(30).
"Remedy". Section 1–201(34).
"Rights". Section 1–201(36).
"Security interest". Section 1–201(37).
"Termination". Section 2A–103(1)(z).
"Value". Section 1–201(44).
"Writing". Section 1–201(46).

§ 2A–311. Priority Subject to Subordination.

Nothing in this Article prevents subordination by agreement by any person entitled to priority.

As added in 1990.

See Appendix VI for material relating to the adoption of section in 1990.

Official Comment

Uniform Statutory Source: Section 9–316.

Purposes: The several preceding sections deal with questions of priority. This section is inserted to make it entirely clear that a person entitled to priority may effectively agree to subordinate the claim. Only the person entitled to priority may make such an agreement: the rights of such a person cannot be adversely affected by an agreement to which that person is not a party.

Cross References:

Sections 1-102 and 2A-304 through 2A-310.

Definitional Cross References:

"Agreement". Section 1-201(3).

"Person". Section 1-201(30).

PART 4

PERFORMANCE OF LEASE CONTRACT: REPUDIATED, SUBSTITUTED AND EXCUSED

§ 2A-401. Insecurity: Adequate Assurance of Performance.

(1) A lease contract imposes an obligation on each party that the other's expectation of receiving due performance will not be impaired.

(2) If reasonable grounds for insecurity arise with respect to the performance of either party, the insecure party may demand in writing adequate assurance of due performance. Until the insecure party receives that assurance, if commercially reasonable the insecure party may suspend any performance for which he [or she] has not already received the agreed return.

(3) A repudiation of the lease contract occurs if assurance of due performance adequate under the circumstances of the particular case is not provided to the insecure party within a reasonable time, not to exceed 30 days after receipt of a demand by the other party.

(4) Between merchants, the reasonableness of grounds for insecurity and the adequacy of any assurance offered must be determined according to commercial standards.

(5) Acceptance of any nonconforming delivery or payment does not prejudice the aggrieved party's right to demand adequate assurance of future performance.

Official Comment

Uniform Statutory Source: Section 2-609.

Changes: Revised to reflect leasing practices and terminology. Note that in the analogue to subsection (3) (Section 2-609(4)), the adjective "justified" modifies demand. The adjective was deleted here as unnecessary, implying no substantive change.

Definitional Cross References:

"Aggrieved party". Section 1-201(2).

"Agreed". Section 1-201(3).

"Between merchants". Section 2-104(3).

"Conforming". Section 2A-103(1)(d).

"Delivery". Section 1-201(14).

"Lease contract". Section 2A-103(1)(*l*).

"Party". Section 1-201(29).

"Reasonable time". Section 1-204(1) and (2).

"Receipt". Section 2-103(1)(c).

"Rights". Section 1-201(36).

"Writing". Section 1-201(46).

§ 2A–402. Anticipatory Repudiation.

If either party repudiates a lease contract with respect to a performance not yet due under the lease contract, the loss of which performance will substantially impair the value of the lease contract to the other, the aggrieved party may:

(a) for a commercially reasonable time, await retraction of repudiation and performance by the repudiating party;

(b) make demand pursuant to Section 2A–401 and await assurance of future performance adequate under the circumstances of the particular case; or

(c) resort to any right or remedy upon default under the lease contract or this Article, even though the aggrieved party has notified the repudiating party that the aggrieved party would await the repudiating party's performance and assurance and has urged retraction. In addition, whether or not the aggrieved party is pursuing one of the foregoing remedies, the aggrieved party may suspend performance or, if the aggrieved party is the lessor, proceed in accordance with the provisions of this Article on the lessor's right to identify goods to the lease contract notwithstanding default or to salvage unfinished goods (Section 2A–524).

Official Comment

Uniform Statutory Source: Section 2–610.

Changes: Revised to reflect leasing practices and terminology.

Definitional Cross References:

"Aggrieved party". Section 1–201(2).
"Goods". Section 2A–103(1)(h).
"Lease contract". Section 2A–103(1)(*l*).
"Lessor". Section 2A–103(1)(p).
"Notifies". Section 1–201(26).
"Party". Section 1–201(29).
"Reasonable time". Section 1–204(1) and (2).
"Remedy". Section 1–201(34).
"Rights". Section 1–201(36).
"Value". Section 1–201(44).

§ 2A–403. Retraction of Anticipatory Repudiation.

(1) Until the repudiating party's next performance is due, the repudiating party can retract the repudiation unless, since the repudiation, the aggrieved party has cancelled the lease contract or materially changed the aggrieved party's position or otherwise indicated that the aggrieved party considers the repudiation final.

(2) Retraction may be by any method that clearly indicates to the aggrieved party that the repudiating party intends to perform under the lease contract and includes any assurance demanded under Section 2A–401.

(3) Retraction reinstates a repudiating party's rights under a lease contract with due excuse and allowance to the aggrieved party for any delay occasioned by the repudiation.

Official Comment

Uniform Statutory Source: Section 2-611.

Changes: Revised to reflect leasing practices and terminology. Note that in the analogue to subsection (2) (Section 2-611(2)) the adjective "justifiably" modifies demanded. The adjective was deleted here (as it was in Section 2A-401) as unnecessary, implying no substantive change.

Definitional Cross References:

"Aggrieved party". Section 1-201(2).
"Cancellation". Section 2A-103(1)(b).
"Lease contract". Section 2A-103(1)(*l*).
"Party". Section 1-201(29).
"Rights". Section 1-201(36).

§ 2A-404. Substituted Performance.

(1) If without fault of the lessee, the lessor and the supplier, the agreed berthing, loading, or unloading facilities fail or the agreed type of carrier becomes unavailable or the agreed manner of delivery otherwise becomes commercially impracticable, but a commercially reasonable substitute is available, the substitute performance must be tendered and accepted.

(2) If the agreed means or manner of payment fails because of domestic or foreign governmental regulation:

(a) the lessor may withhold or stop delivery or cause the supplier to withhold or stop delivery unless the lessee provides a means or manner of payment that is commercially a substantial equivalent; and

(b) if delivery has already been taken, payment by the means or in the manner provided by the regulation discharges the lessee's obligation unless the regulation is discriminatory, oppressive, or predatory.

Official Comment

Uniform Statutory Source: Section 2-614.

Changes: Revised to reflect leasing practices and terminology.

Definitional Cross References:

"Agreed". Section 1-201(3).
"Delivery". Section 1-201(14).
"Fault". Section 2A-103(1)(f).
"Lessee". Section 2A-103(1)(n).
"Lessor". Section 2A-103(1)(p).
"Supplier". Section 2A-103(1)(x).

§ 2A-405. Excused Performance.

Subject to Section 2A-404 on substituted performance, the following rules apply:

(a) Delay in delivery or nondelivery in whole or in part by a lessor or a supplier who complies with paragraphs (b) and (c) is not a default under the lease contract if performance as agreed has been made impracticable by the occurrence of a contingency the nonoccurrence of which was a basic assumption on which the lease contract was made or by compliance in good faith with any applicable foreign or domestic governmental regulation or order, whether or not the regulation or order later proves to be invalid.

(b) If the causes mentioned in paragraph (a) affect only part of the lessor's or the supplier's capacity to perform, he [or she] shall allocate production and deliveries among his [or her] customers but at his [or her] option may include regular customers not then under contract for sale or lease as well as his [or her] own requirements for further manufacture. He [or she] may so allocate in any manner that is fair and reasonable.

(c) The lessor seasonably shall notify the lessee and in the case of a finance lease the supplier seasonably shall notify the lessor and the lessee, if known, that there will be delay or nondelivery and, if allocation is required under paragraph (b), of the estimated quota thus made available for the lessee.

Official Comment

Uniform Statutory Source: Section 2–615.

Changes: Revised to reflect leasing practices and terminology.

Definitional Cross References:

"Agreed". Section 1–201(3).
"Contract". Section 1–201(11).
"Delivery". Section 1–201(14).
"Finance lease". Section 2A–103(1)(g).
"Good faith". Sections 1–201(19) and 2–103(1)(b).
"Knows". Section 1–201(25).
"Lease". Section 2A–103(1)(j).
"Lease contract". Section 2A–103(1)(*l*).
"Lessee". Section 2A–103(1)(n).
"Lessor". Section 2A–103(1)(p).
"Notifies". Section 1–201(26).
"Sale". Section 2–106(1).
"Seasonably". Section 1–204(3).
"Supplier". Section 2A–103(1)(x).

§ 2A–406. Procedure on Excused Performance.

(1) If the lessee receives notification of a material or indefinite delay or an allocation justified under Section 2A–405, the lessee may by written notification to the lessor as to any goods involved, and with respect to all of the goods if under an installment lease contract the value of the whole lease contract is substantially impaired (Section 2A–510):

(a) terminate the lease contract (Section 2A–505(2)); or

(b) except in a finance lease that is not a consumer lease, modify the lease contract by accepting the available quota in substitution, with due allowance from the rent payable for the balance of the lease term for the deficiency but without further right against the lessor.

(2) If, after receipt of a notification from the lessor under Section 2A–405, the lessee fails so to modify the lease agreement within a reasonable time not exceeding 30 days, the lease contract lapses with respect to any deliveries affected.

Official Comment

Uniform Statutory Source: Section 2–616(1) and (2).

Changes: Revised to reflect leasing practices and terminology. Note that subsection 1(a) allows the lessee under a lease, including a finance lease, the right to terminate the lease for excused performance (Sections 2A–404 and 2A–405).

However, subsection 1(b), which allows the lessee the right to modify the lease for excused performance, excludes a finance lease that is not a consumer lease. This exclusion is compelled by the same policy that led to codification of provisions with respect to irrevocable promises. Section 2A–407.

Definitional Cross References:

"Consumer lease". Section 2A–103(1)(e).

"Delivery". Section 1–201(14).

"Finance lease". Section 2A–103(1)(g).

"Goods". Section 2A–103(1)(h).

"Installment lease contract". Section 2A–103(1)(i).

"Lease agreement". Section 2A–103(1)(k).

"Lease contract". Section 2A–103(1)(*l*).

"Lessee". Section 2A–103(1)(n).

"Lessor". Section 2A–103(1)(p).

"Notice". Section 1–201(25).

"Reasonable time". Section 1–204(1) and (2).

"Receipt". Section 2–103(1)(c).

"Rights". Section 1–201(36).

"Termination". Section 2A–103(1)(z).

"Value". Section 1–201(44).

"Written". Section 1–201(46).

§ 2A–407. Irrevocable Promises: Finance Leases.

(1) In the case of a finance lease that is not a consumer lease the lessee's promises under the lease contract become irrevocable and independent upon the lessee's acceptance of the goods.

(2) A promise that has become irrevocable and independent under subsection (1):

(a) is effective and enforceable between the parties, and by or against third parties including assignees of the parties; and

(b) is not subject to cancellation, termination, modification, repudiation, excuse, or substitution without the consent of the party to whom the promise runs.

(3) This section does not affect the validity under any other law of a covenant in any lease contract making the lessee's promises irrevocable and independent upon the lessee's acceptance of the goods.

As amended in 1990.

See Appendix VI for material relating to changes made in text in 1990.

Official Comment

Uniform Statutory Source: None.

Purposes:

1. This section extends the benefits of the classic "hell or high water" clause to a finance lease that is not a consumer lease. This section is self-executing; no special provision need be added to the contract. This section makes covenants in a finance lease irrevocable and independent due to the function of the finance lessor in a three party relationship: the lessee is looking to the supplier to perform the essential covenants and warranties. Section 2A–209. Thus, upon the lessee's acceptance of the goods the lessee's promises to the lessor under the lease contract become irrevocable and independent. The provisions of this section remain subject to the obligation of good faith (Sections 2A–103(4) and 1–203), and the lessee's revocation of acceptance (Section 2A–517).

2. The section requires the lessee to perform even if the lessor's performance after the lessee's acceptance is not in

accordance with the lease contract; the lessee may, however, have and pursue a cause of action against the lessor, e.g., breach of certain limited warranties (Sections 2A-210 and 2A-211(1)). This is appropriate because the benefit of the supplier's promises and warranties to the lessor under the supply contract and, in some cases, the warranty of a manufacturer who is not the supplier, is extended to the lessee under the finance lease. Section 2A-209. Despite this balance, this section excludes a finance lease that is a consumer lease. That a consumer be obligated to pay notwithstanding defective goods or the like is a principle that is not tenable under case law (Unico v. Owen, 50 N.J. 101, 232 A.2d 405 (1967)), state statute (Unif.Consumer Credit Code §§ 3.403-.405, 7A U.L.A. 126-31 (1974), or federal statute (15 U.S.C. § 1666i (1982)).

3. The relationship of the three parties to a transaction that qualifies as a finance lease is best demonstrated by a hypothetical. A, the potential lessor, has been contacted by B, the potential lessee, to discuss the lease of an expensive line of equipment that B has recently placed an order for with C, the manufacturer of such goods. The negotiation is completed and A, as lessor, and B, as lessee, sign a lease of the line of equipment for a 60-month term. B, as buyer, assigns the purchase order with C to A. If this transaction creates a lease (Section 2A-103(1)(j)), this transaction should qualify as a finance lease. Section 2A-103(1)(g).

4. The line of equipment is delivered by C to B's place of business. After installation by C and testing by B, B accepts the goods by signing a certificate of delivery and acceptance, a copy of which is sent by B to A and C. One year later the line of equipment malfunctions and B falls behind in its manufacturing schedule.

5. Under this Article, because the lease is a finance lease, no warranty of fitness or merchantability is extended by A to B. Sections 2A-212(1) and 2A-213. Absent an express provision in the lease agreement, application of Section 2A-210 or Section 2A-211(1), or application of the principles of law and equity, including the law with respect to fraud, duress, or the like (Sections 2A-103(4) and 1-103), B has no claim against A. B's obligation to pay rent to A continues as the obligation became irrevocable and independent when B accepted the line of equipment (Section 2A-407(1)). B has no right of set-off with respect to any part of the rent still due under the lease. Section 2A-508(6). However, B may have another remedy. Despite the lack of privity between B and C (the purchase order with C having been assigned by B to A), B may have a claim against C. Section 2A-209(1).

6. This section does not address whether a "hell or high water" clause, *i.e.*, a clause that is to the effect of this section, is enforceable if included in a finance lease that is a consumer lease or a lease that is not a finance lease. That issue will continue to be determined by the facts of each case and other law which this section does not affect. Sections 2A-104, 2A-103(4), 9-206 and 9-318. However, with respect to finance leases that are not consumer leases courts have enforced "hell or high water" clauses. *In re O.P.M. Leasing Servs.*, 21 Bankr. 993, 1006 (Bankr.S.D.N.Y.1982).

7. Subsection (2) further provides that a promise that has become irrevocable and independent under subsection (1) is enforceable not only between the parties but also against third parties. Thus, the finance lease can be transferred or assigned without disturbing enforceability. Further, subsection (2) also provides that the promise cannot, among other things, be cancelled or terminated without the consent of the lessor.

Cross References:

Sections 1-103, 1-203, 2A-103(1)(g), 2A-103(1)(j), 2A-103(4), 2A-104, 2A-209, 2A-209(1), 2A-210, 2A-211(1), 2A-212(1), 2A-213, 2A-517(1)(b), 9-206 and 9-318.

Definitional Cross References:

"Cancellation". Section 2A-103(1)(b).

"Consumer lease". Section 2A-103(1)(e).
"Finance lease". Section 2A-103(1)(g).
"Goods". Section 2A-103(1)(h).
"Lease contract". Section 2A-103(1)(*l*).
"Lessee". Section 2A-103(1)(n).
"Party". Section 1-201(29).
"Termination". Section 2A-103(1)(z).

PART 5
DEFAULT
A. IN GENERAL

§ 2A-501. Default: Procedure.

(1) Whether the lessor or the lessee is in default under a lease contract is determined by the lease agreement and this Article.

(2) If the lessor or the lessee is in default under the lease contract, the party seeking enforcement has rights and remedies as provided in this Article and, except as limited by this Article, as provided in the lease agreement.

(3) If the lessor or the lessee is in default under the lease contract, the party seeking enforcement may reduce the party's claim to judgment, or otherwise enforce the lease contract by self-help or any available judicial procedure or nonjudicial procedure, including administrative proceeding, arbitration, or the like, in accordance with this Article.

(4) Except as otherwise provided in Section 1-106(1) or this Article or the lease agreement, the rights and remedies referred to in subsections (2) and (3) are cumulative.

(5) If the lease agreement covers both real property and goods, the party seeking enforcement may proceed under this Part as to the goods, or under other applicable law as to both the real property and the goods in accordance with that party's rights and remedies in respect of the real property, in which case this Part does not apply.

As amended in 1990.

See Appendix VI for material relating to changes made in text in 1990.

Official Comment

Uniform Statutory Source: Section 9-501.

Changes: Substantially revised.

Purposes:

1. Subsection (1) is new and represents a departure from the Article on Secured Transactions (Article 9) as the subsection makes clear that whether a party to the lease agreement is in default is determined by this Article as well as the agreement. Sections 2A-508 and 2A-523. It further departs from Article 9 in recognizing the potential default of either party, a function of the bilateral nature of the obligations between the parties to the lease contract.

2. Subsection (2) is a version of the first sentence of Section 9-501(1), revised to reflect leasing terminology.

3. Subsection (3), an expansive version of the second sentence of Section 9-

501(1), lists the procedures that may be followed by the party seeking enforcement; in effect, the scope of the procedures listed in subsection (3) is consistent with the scope of the procedures available to the foreclosing secured party.

4. Subsection (4) establishes that the parties' rights and remedies are cumulative. DeKoven, *Leases of Equipment: Puritan Leasing Company v. August, A Dangerous Decision*, 12 U.S.F.L.Rev. 257, 276–80 (1978). Cumulation, and largely unrestricted selection, of remedies is allowed in furtherance of the general policy of the Commercial Code, stated in Section 1–106, that remedies be liberally administered to put the aggrieved party in as good a position as if the other party had fully performed. Therefore, cumulation of, or selection among, remedies is available to the extent necessary to put the aggrieved party in as good a position as it would have been in had there been full performance. However, cumulation of, or selection among, remedies is not available to the extent that the cumulation or selection would put the aggrieved party in a better position than it would have been in had there been full performance by the other party.

5. Section 9–501(3), which, among other things, states that certain rules, to the extent they give rights to the debtor and impose duties on the secured party, may not be waived or varied, was not incorporated in this Article. Given the significance of freedom of contract in the development of the common law as it applies to bailments for hire and the lessee's lack of an equity of redemption, there was no reason to impose that restraint.

Cross References:

Sections 1–106, 2A–508, 2A–523, Article 9, especially Sections 9–501(1) and 9–501(3).

Definitional Cross References:

"Goods". Section 2A–103(1)(h).

"Lease agreement". Section 2A–103(1)(k).

"Lease contract". Section 2A–103(1)(*l*).

"Lessee". Section 2A–103(1)(n).

"Lessor". Section 2A–103(1)(p).

"Party". Section 1–201(29).

"Remedy". Section 1–201(34).

"Rights". Section 1–201(36).

§ 2A–502. Notice After Default.

Except as otherwise provided in this Article or the lease agreement, the lessor or lessee in default under the lease contract is not entitled to notice of default or notice of enforcement from the other party to the lease agreement.

Official Comment

Uniform Statutory Source: None.

Purposes: This section makes clear that absent agreement to the contrary or provision in this Article to the contrary, *e.g.*, Section 2A–516(3)(a), the party in default is not entitled to notice of default or enforcement. While a review of Part 5 of Article 9 leads to the same conclusion with respect to giving notice of default to the debtor, it is never stated. Although Article 9 requires notice of disposition and strict foreclosure, the different scheme of lessors' and lessees' rights and remedies developed under the common law, and codified by this Article, generally does not require notice of enforcement; furthermore, such notice is not mandated by due process requirements. However, certain sections of this Article do require notice. *E.g.*, Section ~~2A–517(2)~~ 2A–517(4) *.

Cross References:

Sections 2A–516(3)(a), ~~2A–517(2)~~ 2A–517(4) *, and Article 9, esp. Part 5.

Definitional Cross References:

"Lease agreement". Section 2A–103(1)(k).

"Lease contract". Section 2A–103(1)(*l*).

"Lessee". Section 2A-103(1)(n).
"Lessor". Section 2A-103(1)(p).
"Notice". Section 1-201(25).
"Party". Section 1-201(29).

* *Previous incorrect cross reference corrected by Permanent Editorial Board action, November 1992.*

§ 2A-503. Modification or Impairment of Rights and Remedies.

(1) Except as otherwise provided in this Article, the lease agreement may include rights and remedies for default in addition to or in substitution for those provided in this Article and may limit or alter the measure of damages recoverable under this Article.

(2) Resort to a remedy provided under this Article or in the lease agreement is optional unless the remedy is expressly agreed to be exclusive. If circumstances cause an exclusive or limited remedy to fail of its essential purpose, or provision for an exclusive remedy is unconscionable, remedy may be had as provided in this Article.

(3) Consequential damages may be liquidated under Section 2A-504, or may otherwise be limited, altered, or excluded unless the limitation, alteration, or exclusion is unconscionable. Limitation, alteration, or exclusion of consequential damages for injury to the person in the case of consumer goods is prima facie unconscionable but limitation, alteration, or exclusion of damages where the loss is commercial is not prima facie unconscionable.

(4) Rights and remedies on default by the lessor or the lessee with respect to any obligation or promise collateral or ancillary to the lease contract are not impaired by this Article.

As amended in 1990.

See Appendix VI for material relating to changes made in text in 1990.

Official Comment

Uniform Statutory Source: Sections 2-719 and 2-701.

Changes: Rewritten to reflect lease terminology and to clarify the relationship between this section and Section 2A-504.

Purposes:

1. A significant purpose of this Part is to provide rights and remedies for those parties to a lease who fail to provide them by agreement or whose rights and remedies fail of their essential purpose or are unenforceable. However, it is important to note that this implies no restriction on freedom to contract. Sections 2A-103(4) and 1-102(3). Thus, subsection (1), a revised version of the provisions of Section 2-719(1), allows the parties to the lease agreement freedom to provide for rights and remedies in addition to or in substitution for those provided in this Article and to alter or limit the measure of damages recoverable under this Article. Except to the extent otherwise provided in this Article (*e.g.*, Sections 2A-105, 106 and 108(1) and (2)), this Part shall be construed neither to restrict the parties' ability to provide for rights and remedies or to limit or alter the measure of damages by agreement, nor to imply disapproval of rights and remedy schemes other than those set forth in this Part.

2. Subsection (2) makes explicit with respect to this Article what is implicit in Section 2-719 with respect to the Article on Sales (Article 2): if an exclusive reme-

dy is held to be unconscionable, remedies under this Article are available. Section 2–719 official comment 1.

3. Subsection (3), a revision of Section 2–719(3), makes clear that consequential damages may also be liquidated. Section 2A–504(1).

4. Subsection (4) is a revision of the provisions of Section 2–701. This subsection leaves the treatment of default with respect to obligations or promises collateral or ancillary to the lease contract to other law. Sections 2A–103(4) and 1–103. An example of such an obligation would be that of the lessor to the secured creditor which has provided the funds to leverage the lessor's lease transaction; an example of such a promise would be that of the lessee, as seller, to the lessor, as buyer, in a sale-leaseback transaction.

Cross References:

Sections 1–102(3), 1–103, Article 2, especially Sections 2–701, 2–719, 2–719(1), 2–719(3), 2–719 official comment 1, and Sections 2A–103(4), 2A–105, 2A–106, 2A–108(1), 2A–108(2), and 2A–504.

Definitional Cross References:

"Agreed". Section 1–201(3).
"Consumer goods". Section 9–109(1).
"Lease agreement". Section 2A–103(1)(k).
"Lease contract". Section 2A–103(1)(*l*).
"Lessee". Section 2A–103(1)(n).
"Lessor". Section 2A–103(1)(p).
"Person". Section 1–201(30).
"Remedy". Section 1–201(34).
"Rights". Section 1–201(36).

§ 2A–504. Liquidation of Damages.

(1) Damages payable by either party for default, or any other act or omission, including indemnity for loss or diminution of anticipated tax benefits or loss or damage to lessor's residual interest, may be liquidated in the lease agreement but only at an amount or by a formula that is reasonable in light of the then anticipated harm caused by the default or other act or omission.

(2) If the lease agreement provides for liquidation of damages, and such provision does not comply with subsection (1), or such provision is an exclusive or limited remedy that circumstances cause to fail of its essential purpose, remedy may be had as provided in this Article.

(3) If the lessor justifiably withholds or stops delivery of goods because of the lessee's default or insolvency (Section 2A–525 or 2A–526), the lessee is entitled to restitution of any amount by which the sum of his [or her] payments exceeds:

(a) the amount to which the lessor is entitled by virtue of terms liquidating the lessor's damages in accordance with subsection (1); or

(b) in the absence of those terms, 20 percent of the then present value of the total rent the lessee was obligated to pay for the balance of the lease term, or, in the case of a consumer lease, the lesser of such amount or $500.

(4) A lessee's right to restitution under subsection (3) is subject to offset to the extent the lessor establishes:

(a) a right to recover damages under the provisions of this Article other than subsection (1); and

(b) the amount or value of any benefits received by the lessee directly or indirectly by reason of the lease contract.

Official Comment

Uniform Statutory Source: Sections 2–718(1), (2), (3) and 2–719(2).

Changes: Substantially rewritten.

Purposes: Many leasing transactions are predicated on the parties' ability to agree to an appropriate amount of damages or formula for damages in the event of default or other act or omission. The rule with respect to sales of goods (Section 2–718) may not be sufficiently flexible to accommodate this practice. Thus, consistent with the common law emphasis upon freedom to contract with respect to bailments for hire, this section has created a revised rule that allows greater flexibility with respect to leases of goods.

Subsection (1), a significantly modified version of the provisions of Section 2–718(1), provides for liquidation of damages in the lease agreement at an amount or by a formula. Section 2–718(1) does not by its express terms include liquidation by a formula; this change was compelled by modern leasing practice. Subsection (1), in a further expansion of Section 2–718(1), provides for liquidation of damages for default as well as any other act or omission.

A liquidated damages formula that is common in leasing practice provides that the sum of lease payments past due, accelerated future lease payments, and the lessor's estimated residual interest, less the net proceeds of disposition (whether by sale or re-lease) of the leased goods is the lessor's damages. Tax indemnities, costs, interest and attorney's fees are also added to determine the lessor's damages. Another common liquidated damages formula utilizes a periodic depreciation allocation as a credit to the aforesaid amount in mitigation of a lessor's damages. A third formula provides for a fixed number of periodic payments as a means of liquidating damages. Stipulated loss or stipulated damage schedules are also common. Whether these formulae are enforceable will be determined in the context of each case by applying a standard of reasonableness in light of the harm anticipated when the formula was agreed to. Whether the inclusion of these formulae will affect the classification of the transaction as a lease or a security interest is to be determined by the facts of each case. Section 1–201(37). *E.g., In re Noack*, 44 Bankr. 172, 174–75 (Bankr.E.D.Wis. 1984).

This section does not incorporate two other tests that under sales law determine enforceability of liquidated damages, *i.e.*, difficulties of proof of loss and inconvenience or nonfeasibility of otherwise obtaining an adequate remedy. The ability to liquidate damages is critical to modern leasing practice; given the parties' freedom to contract at common law, the policy behind retaining these two additional requirements here was thought to be outweighed. Further, given the expansion of subsection (1) to enable the parties to liquidate the amount payable with respect to an indemnity for loss or diminution of anticipated tax benefits resulted in another change: the last sentence of Section 2–718(1), providing that a term fixing unreasonably large liquidated damages is void as a penalty, was also not incorporated. The impact of local, state and federal tax laws on a leasing transaction can result in an amount payable with respect to the tax indemnity many times greater than the original purchase price of the goods. By deleting the reference to unreasonably large liquidated damages the parties are free to negotiate a formula, restrained by the rule of reasonableness in this section. These changes should invite the parties to liquidate damages. Peters, *Remedies for Breach of Contracts Relating to the Sale of Goods Under the Uniform Commercial Code: A Roadmap for Article Two*, 73 Yale L.J. 199, 278 (1963).

Subsection (2), a revised version of Section 2–719(2), provides that if the liquidated damages provision is not enforceable or fails of its essential purpose, remedy may be had as provided in this Article.

Subsection (3)(b) of this section differs from subsection (2)(b) of Section 2–718;

in the absence of a valid liquidated damages amount or formula the lessor is permitted to retain 20 percent of the present value of the total rent payable under the lease. The alternative limitation of $500 contained in Section 2-718 is deleted as unrealistically low with respect to a lease other than a consumer lease.

Cross References:

Sections 1-201(37), 2-718, 2-718(1), 2-718(2)(b) and 2-719(2).

Definitional Cross References:

"Consumer lease". Section 2A-103(1)(e).
"Delivery". Section 1-201(14).
"Goods". Section 2A-103(1)(h).
"Insolvent". Section 1-201(23).
"Lease agreement". Section 2A-103(1)(k).
"Lease contract". Section 2A-103(1)(*l*).
"Lessee". Section 2A-103(1)(n).
"Lessor". Section 2A-103(1)(p).
"Lessor's residual interest". Section 2A-103(1)(q).
"Party". Section 1-201(29).
"Present value". Section 2A-103(1)(u).
"Remedy". Section 1-201(34).
"Rights". Section 1-201(36).
"Term". Section 1-201(42).
"Value". Section 1-201(44).

§ 2A-505. Cancellation and Termination and Effect of Cancellation, Termination, Rescission, or Fraud on Rights and Remedies.

(1) On cancellation of the lease contract, all obligations that are still executory on both sides are discharged, but any right based on prior default or performance survives, and the cancelling party also retains any remedy for default of the whole lease contract or any unperformed balance.

(2) On termination of the lease contract, all obligations that are still executory on both sides are discharged but any right based on prior default or performance survives.

(3) Unless the contrary intention clearly appears, expressions of "cancellation," "rescission," or the like of the lease contract may not be construed as a renunciation or discharge of any claim in damages for an antecedent default.

(4) Rights and remedies for material misrepresentation or fraud include all rights and remedies available under this Article for default.

(5) Neither rescission nor a claim for rescission of the lease contract nor rejection or return of the goods may bar or be deemed inconsistent with a claim for damages or other right or remedy.

Official Comment

Uniform Statutory Source: Sections 2-106(3) and (4), 2-720 and 2-721.

Changes: Revised to reflect leasing practices and terminology.

Definitional Cross References:

"Cancellation". Section 2A-103(1)(b).
"Goods". Section 2A-103(1)(h).
"Lease contract". Section 2A-103(1)(*l*).
"Party". Section 1-201(29).
"Remedy". Section 1-201(34).
"Rights". Section 1-201(36).
"Termination". Section 2A-103(1)(z).

§ 2A-506. Statute of Limitations.

(1) An action for default under a lease contract, including breach of warranty or indemnity, must be commenced within 4 years after the cause of

action accrued. By the original lease contract the parties may reduce the period of limitation to not less than one year.

(2) A cause of action for default accrues when the act or omission on which the default or breach of warranty is based is or should have been discovered by the aggrieved party, or when the default occurs, whichever is later. A cause of action for indemnity accrues when the act or omission on which the claim for indemnity is based is or should have been discovered by the indemnified party, whichever is later.

(3) If an action commenced within the time limited by subsection (1) is so terminated as to leave available a remedy by another action for the same default or breach of warranty or indemnity, the other action may be commenced after the expiration of the time limited and within 6 months after the termination of the first action unless the termination resulted from voluntary discontinuance or from dismissal for failure or neglect to prosecute.

(4) This section does not alter the law on tolling of the statute of limitations nor does it apply to causes of action that have accrued before this Article becomes effective.

Official Comment

Uniform Statutory Source: Section 2–725.

Changes: Substantially rewritten.

Purposes: Subsection (1) does not incorporate the limitation found in Section 2–725(1) prohibiting the parties from extending the period of limitation. Breach of warranty and indemnity claims often arise in a lease transaction; with the passage of time such claims often diminish or are eliminated. To encourage the parties to commence litigation under these circumstances makes little sense.

Subsection (2) states two rules for determining when a cause of action accrues. With respect to default, the rule of Section 2–725(2) is not incorporated in favor of a more liberal rule of the later of the date when the default occurs or when the act or omission on which it is based is or should have been discovered. With respect to indemnity, a similarly liberal rule is adopted.

Cross References:

Sections 2–725(1) and 2–725(2).

Definitional Cross References:

"Action". Section 1–201(1).
"Aggrieved party". Section 1–201(2).
"Lease contract". Section 2A–103(1)(*l*).
"Party". Section 1–201(29).
"Remedy". Section 1–201(34).
"Termination". Section 2A–103(1)(z).

§ 2A–507. Proof of Market Rent: Time and Place.

(1) Damages based on market rent (Section 2A–519 or 2A–528) are determined according to the rent for the use of the goods concerned for a lease term identical to the remaining lease term of the original lease agreement and prevailing at the times specified in Sections 2A–519 and 2A–528.

(2) If evidence of rent for the use of the goods concerned for a lease term identical to the remaining lease term of the original lease agreement and prevailing at the times or places described in this Article is not readily available, the rent prevailing within any reasonable time before or after the time described or at any other place or for a different lease term which in

commercial judgment or under usage of trade would serve as a reasonable substitute for the one described may be used, making any proper allowance for the difference, including the cost of transporting the goods to or from the other place.

(3) Evidence of a relevant rent prevailing at a time or place or for a lease term other than the one described in this Article offered by one party is not admissible unless and until he [or she] has given the other party notice the court finds sufficient to prevent unfair surprise.

(4) If the prevailing rent or value of any goods regularly leased in any established market is in issue, reports in official publications or trade journals or in newspapers or periodicals of general circulation published as the reports of that market are admissible in evidence. The circumstances of the preparation of the report may be shown to affect its weight but not its admissibility.

As amended in 1990.

See Appendix VI for material relating to changes made in text in 1990.

Official Comment

Uniform Statutory Source: Sections 2–723 and 2–724.

Changes: Revised to reflect leasing practices and terminology. Sections 2A–519 and 2A–528 specify the times as of which market rent is to be determined.

Definitional Cross References:

"Goods". Section 2A–103(1)(h).

"Lease". Section 2A–103(1)(j).

"Lease agreement". Section 2A–103(1)(k).

"Notice". Section 1–201(25).

"Party". Section 1–201(29).

"Reasonable time". Section 1–204(1) and (2).

"Usage of trade". Section 1–205.

"Value". Section 1–201(44).

B. DEFAULT BY LESSOR

§ 2A–508. Lessee's Remedies.

(1) If a lessor fails to deliver the goods in conformity to the lease contract (Section 2A–509) or repudiates the lease contract (Section 2A–402), or a lessee rightfully rejects the goods (Section 2A–509) or justifiably revokes acceptance of the goods (Section 2A–517), then with respect to any goods involved, and with respect to all of the goods if under an installment lease contract the value of the whole lease contract is substantially impaired (Section 2A–510), the lessor is in default under the lease contract and the lessee may:

(a) cancel the lease contract (Section 2A–505(1));

(b) recover so much of the rent and security as has been paid and is just under the circumstances;

(c) cover and recover damages as to all goods affected whether or not they have been identified to the lease contract (Sections 2A–518 and 2A–520), or recover damages for nondelivery (Sections 2A–519 and 2A–520);

(d) exercise any other rights or pursue any other remedies provided in the lease contract.

(2) If a lessor fails to deliver the goods in conformity to the lease contract or repudiates the lease contract, the lessee may also:

(a) if the goods have been identified, recover them (Section 2A–522); or

(b) in a proper case, obtain specific performance or replevy the goods (Section 2A–521).

(3) If a lessor is otherwise in default under a lease contract, the lessee may exercise the rights and pursue the remedies provided in the lease contract, which may include a right to cancel the lease, and in Section 2A–519(3).

(4) If a lessor has breached a warranty, whether express or implied, the lessee may recover damages (Section 2A–519(4)).

(5) On rightful rejection or justifiable revocation of acceptance, a lessee has a security interest in goods in the lessee's possession or control for any rent and security that has been paid and any expenses reasonably incurred in their inspection, receipt, transportation, and care and custody and may hold those goods and dispose of them in good faith and in a commercially reasonable manner, subject to Section 2A–527(5).

(6) Subject to the provisions of Section 2A–407, a lessee, on notifying the lessor of the lessee's intention to do so, may deduct all or any part of the damages resulting from any default under the lease contract from any part of the rent still due under the same lease contract.

As amended in 1990.

See Appendix VI for material relating to changes made in text in 1990.

Official Comment

Uniform Statutory Source: Sections 2–711 and 2–717.

Changes: Substantially rewritten.

Purposes:

1. This section is an index to Sections 2A–509 through 522 which set out the lessee's rights and remedies after the lessor's default. The lessor and the lessee can agree to modify the rights and remedies available under this Article; they can, among other things, provide that for defaults other than those specified in subsection (1) the lessee can exercise the rights and remedies referred to in subsection (1); and they can create a new scheme of rights and remedies triggered by the occurrence of the default. Sections 2A–103(4) and 1–102(3).

2. Subsection (1), a substantially rewritten version of the provisions of Section 2–711(1), lists three cumulative remedies of the lessee where the lessor has failed to deliver conforming goods or has repudiated the contract, or the lessee has rightfully rejected or justifiably revoked. Sections 2A–501(2) and (4). Subsection (1) also allows the lessee to exercise any contractual remedy. This Article rejects any general doctrine of election of remedy. To determine if one remedy bars another in a particular case is a function of whether the lessee has been put in as good a position as if the lessor had fully performed the lease agreement. Use of multiple remedies is barred only if the effect is to put the lessee in a better position than it would have been in had the lessor fully performed under the lease. Sections 2A–103(4), 2A–501(4), and 1–106(1). Subsection (1)(b), in recognition that no bright line can be created that would operate fairly in all install-

ment lease cases and in recognition of the fact that a lessee may be able to cancel the lease (revoke acceptance of the goods) after the goods have been in use for some period of time, does not require that all lease payments made by the lessee under the lease be returned upon cancellation. Rather, only such portion as is just of the rent and security payments made may be recovered. If a defect in the goods is discovered immediately upon tender to the lessee and the goods are rejected immediately, then the lessee should recover all payments made. If, however, for example, a 36–month equipment lease is terminated in the 12th month because the lessor has materially breached the contract by failing to perform its maintenance obligations, it may be just to return only a small part or none of the rental payments already made.

3. Subsection (2), a version of the provisions of Section 2–711(2) revised to reflect leasing terminology, lists two alternative remedies for the recovery of the goods by the lessee; however, each of these remedies is cumulative with respect to those listed in subsection (1).

4. Subsection (3) is new. It covers defaults which do not deprive the lessee of the goods and which are not so serious as to justify rejection or revocation of acceptance under subsection (1). It also covers defaults for which the lessee could have rejected or revoked acceptance of the goods but elects not to do so and retains the goods. In either case, a lessee which retains the goods is entitled to recover damages as stated in Section 2A–519(3). That measure of damages is "the loss resulting in the ordinary course of events from the lessor's default as determined in any manner that is reasonable together with incidental and consequential damages, less expenses saved in consequence of the lessor's breach."

5. Subsection (1)(d) and subsection (3) recognize that the lease agreement may provide rights and remedies in addition to or different from those which Article 2A provides. In particular, subsection (3) provides that the lease agreement may give the remedy of cancellation of the lease for defaults by the lessor that would not otherwise be material defaults which would justify cancellation under subsection (1). If there is a right to cancel, there is, of course, a right to reject or revoke acceptance of the goods.

6. Subsection (4) is new and merely adds to the completeness of the index by including a reference to the lessee's recovery of damages upon the lessor's breach of warranty; such breach may not rise to the level of a default by the lessor justifying revocation of acceptance. If the lessee properly rejects or revokes acceptance of the goods because of a breach of warranty, the rights and remedies are those provided in subsection (1) rather than those in Section 2A–519(4).

7. Subsection (5), a revised version of the provisions of Section 2–711(3), recognizes, on rightful rejection or justifiable revocation, the lessee's security interest in goods in its possession and control. Section 9–113, which recognized security interests arising under the Article on Sales (Article 2), was amended with the adoption of this Article to reflect the security interests arising under this Article. Pursuant to Section 2A–511(4), a purchaser who purchases goods from the lessee in good faith takes free of any rights of the lessor, or in the case of a finance lease, the supplier. Such goods, however, must have been rightfully rejected and disposed of pursuant to Section 2A–511 or 2A–512. However, Section 2A–517(5) provides that the lessee will have the same rights and duties with respect to goods where acceptance has been revoked as with respect to goods rejected. Thus, Section 2A–511(4) will apply to the lessee's disposition of such goods.

8. Pursuant to Section 2A–527(5), the lessee must account to the lessor for the excess proceeds of such disposition, after satisfaction of the claim secured by the lessee's security interest.

9. Subsection (6), a slightly revised version of the provisions of Section 2–717, sanctions a right of set-off by the lessee, subject to the rule of Section 2A–407 with respect to irrevocable promises in a fi-

nance lease that is not a consumer lease, and further subject to an enforceable "hell or high water" clause in the lease agreement. Section 2A-407 official comment. No attempt is made to state how the set-off should occur; this is to be determined by the facts of each case.

10. There is no special treatment of the finance lease in this section. Absent supplemental principles of law and equity to the contrary, in the case of most finance leases, following the lessee's acceptance of the goods, the lessee will have no rights or remedies against the lessor, because the lessor's obligations to the lessee are minimal. Sections 2A-210 and 2A-211(1). Since the lessee will look to the supplier for performance, this is appropriate. Section 2A-209.

Cross References:

Sections 1-102(3), 1-103, 1-106(1), Article 2, especially Sections 2-711, 2-717 and Sections 2A-103(4), 2A-209, 2A-210, 2A-211(1), 2A-407, 2A-501(2), 2A-501(4), 2A-509 through 2A-522, 2A-511(3), 2A-517(5), 2A-527(5) and Section 9-113.

Definitional Cross References:

"Conforming". Section 2A-103(1)(d).
"Delivery". Section 1-201(14).
"Good faith". Sections 1-201(19) and 2-103(1)(b).
"Goods". Section 2A-103(1)(h).
"Installment lease contract". Section 2A-103(1)(i).
"Lease contract". Section 2A-103(1)(*l*).
"Lessee". Section 2A-103(1)(n).
"Lessor". Section 2A-103(1)(p).
"Notifies". Section 1-201(26).
"Receipt". Section 2-103(1)(c).
"Remedy". Section 1-201(34).
"Rights". Section 1-201(36).
"Security interest". Section 1-201(37).
"Value". Section 1-201(44).

§ 2A-509. Lessee's Rights on Improper Delivery; Rightful Rejection.

(1) Subject to the provisions of Section 2A-510 on default in installment lease contracts, if the goods or the tender or delivery fail in any respect to conform to the lease contract, the lessee may reject or accept the goods or accept any commercial unit or units and reject the rest of the goods.

(2) Rejection of goods is ineffective unless it is within a reasonable time after tender or delivery of the goods and the lessee seasonably notifies the lessor.

Official Comment

Uniform Statutory Source: Sections 2-601 and 2-602(1).

Changes: Revised to reflect leasing practices and terminology.

Definitional Cross References:

"Commercial unit". Section 2A-103(1)(c).
"Conforming". Section 2A-103(1)(d).
"Delivery". Section 1-201(14).
"Goods". Section 2A-103(1)(h).
"Installment lease contract". Section 2A-103(1)(i).
"Lease contract". Section 2A-103(1)(*l*).
"Lessee". Section 2A-103(1)(n).
"Lessor". Section 2A-103(1)(p).
"Notifies". Section 1-201(26).
"Reasonable time". Section 1-204(1) and (2).
"Rights". Section 1-201(36).
"Seasonably". Section 1-204(3).

§ 2A-510. Installment Lease Contracts: Rejection and Default.

(1) Under an installment lease contract a lessee may reject any delivery that is nonconforming if the nonconformity substantially impairs the value of

that delivery and cannot be cured or the nonconformity is a defect in the required documents; but if the nonconformity does not fall within subsection (2) and the lessor or the supplier gives adequate assurance of its cure, the lessee must accept that delivery.

(2) Whenever nonconformity or default with respect to one or more deliveries substantially impairs the value of the installment lease contract as a whole there is a default with respect to the whole. But, the aggrieved party reinstates the installment lease contract as a whole if the aggrieved party accepts a nonconforming delivery without seasonably notifying of cancellation or brings an action with respect only to past deliveries or demands performance as to future deliveries.

Official Comment

Uniform Statutory Source: Section 2–612.

Changes: Revised to reflect leasing practices and terminology.

Definitional Cross References:

"Action". Section 1–201(1).
"Aggrieved party". Section 1–201(2).
"Cancellation". Section 2A–103(1)(b).
"Conforming". Section 2A–103(1)(d).
"Delivery". Section 1–201(14).
"Installment lease contract". Section 2A–103(1)(i).
"Lessee". Section 2A–103(1)(n).
"Lessor". Section 2A–103(1)(p).
"Notifies". Section 1–201(26).
"Seasonably". Section 1–204(3).
"Supplier". Section 2A–103(1)(x).
"Value". Section 1–201(44).

§ 2A–511. Merchant Lessee's Duties as to Rightfully Rejected Goods.

(1) Subject to any security interest of a lessee (Section 2A–508(5)), if a lessor or a supplier has no agent or place of business at the market of rejection, a merchant lessee, after rejection of goods in his [or her] possession or control, shall follow any reasonable instructions received from the lessor or the supplier with respect to the goods. In the absence of those instructions, a merchant lessee shall make reasonable efforts to sell, lease, or otherwise dispose of the goods for the lessor's account if they threaten to decline in value speedily. Instructions are not reasonable if on demand indemnity for expenses is not forthcoming.

(2) If a merchant lessee (subsection (1)) or any other lessee (Section 2A–512) disposes of goods, he [or she] is entitled to reimbursement either from the lessor or the supplier or out of the proceeds for reasonable expenses of caring for and disposing of the goods and, if the expenses include no disposition commission, to such commission as is usual in the trade, or if there is none, to a reasonable sum not exceeding 10 percent of the gross proceeds.

(3) In complying with this section or Section 2A–512, the lessee is held only to good faith. Good faith conduct hereunder is neither acceptance or conversion nor the basis of an action for damages.

(4) A purchaser who purchases in good faith from a lessee pursuant to this section or Section 2A–512 takes the goods free of any rights of the lessor and the supplier even though the lessee fails to comply with one or more of the requirements of this Article.

Official Comment

Uniform Statutory Source: Sections 2–603 and 2–706(5).

Changes: Revised to reflect leasing practices and terminology. This section, by its terms, applies to merchants as well as others. Thus, in construing the section it is important to note that under this Act the term good faith is defined differently for merchants (Section 2–103(1)(b)) than for others (Section 1–201(19)). Section 2A–103(3) and (4).

Definitional Cross References:

"Action". Section 1–201(1).

"Good faith". Sections 1–201(19) and 2–103(1)(b).

"Goods". Section 2A–103(1)(h).

"Lease". Section 2A–103(1)(j).

"Lessee". Section 2A–103(1)(n).

"Lessor". Section 2A–103(1)(p).

"Merchant lessee". Section 2A–103(1)(t).

"Purchaser". Section 1–201(33).

"Rights". Section 1–201(36).

"Security interest". Section 1–201(37).

"Supplier". Section 2A–103(1)(x).

"Value". Section 1–201(44).

§ 2A–512. Lessee's Duties as to Rightfully Rejected Goods.

(1) Except as otherwise provided with respect to goods that threaten to decline in value speedily (Section 2A–511) and subject to any security interest of a lessee (Section 2A–508(5)):

(a) the lessee, after rejection of goods in the lessee's possession, shall hold them with reasonable care at the lessor's or the supplier's disposition for a reasonable time after the lessee's seasonable notification of rejection;

(b) if the lessor or the supplier gives no instructions within a reasonable time after notification of rejection, the lessee may store the rejected goods for the lessor's or the supplier's account or ship them to the lessor or the supplier or dispose of them for the lessor's or the supplier's account with reimbursement in the manner provided in Section 2A–511; but

(c) the lessee has no further obligations with regard to goods rightfully rejected.

(2) Action by the lessee pursuant to subsection (1) is not acceptance or conversion.

Official Comment

Uniform Statutory Source: Sections 2–602(2)(b) and (c) and 2–604.

Changes: Substantially rewritten.

Purposes: The introduction to subsection (1) references goods that threaten to decline in value speedily and not perishables, the reference in Section 2–604, the statutory analogue. This is a change in style, not substance, as the first phrase includes the second. Subparagraphs (a) and (c) are revised versions of the provisions of Section 2–602(2)(b) and (c). Subparagraph (a) states the rule with respect to the lessee's treatment of goods in its possession following rejection; subparagraph (b) states the rule regarding such goods if the lessor or supplier then fails to give instructions to the lessee. If the lessee performs in a fashion consistent with subparagraphs (a) and (b), subparagraph (c) exonerates the lessee.

Cross References:

Sections 2–602(2)(b), 2–602(2)(c) and 2–604.

Definitional Cross References:

"Action". Section 1-201(1).
"Goods". Section 2A-103(1)(h).
"Lessee". Section 2A-103(1)(n).
"Lessor". Section 2A-103(1)(p).
"Notification". Section 1-201(26).
"Reasonable time". Section 1-204(1) and (2).
"Seasonably". Section 1-204(3).
"Security interest". Section 1-201(37).
"Supplier". Section 2A-103(1)(x).
"Value". Section 1-201(44).

§ 2A-513. Cure by Lessor of Improper Tender or Delivery; Replacement.

(1) If any tender or delivery by the lessor or the supplier is rejected because nonconforming and the time for performance has not yet expired, the lessor or the supplier may seasonably notify the lessee of the lessor's or the supplier's intention to cure and may then make a conforming delivery within the time provided in the lease contract.

(2) If the lessee rejects a nonconforming tender that the lessor or the supplier had reasonable grounds to believe would be acceptable with or without money allowance, the lessor or the supplier may have a further reasonable time to substitute a conforming tender if he [or she] seasonably notifies the lessee.

Official Comment

Uniform Statutory Source: Section 2-508.

Changes: Revised to reflect leasing practices and terminology.

Definitional Cross References:

"Conforming". Section 2A-103(1)(d).
"Delivery". Section 1-201(14).
"Lease contract". Section 2A-103(1)(*l*).
"Lessee". Section 2A-103(1)(n).
"Lessor". Section 2A-103(1)(p).
"Money". Section 1-201(24).
"Notifies". Section 1-201(26).
"Reasonable time". Section 1-204(1) and (2).
"Seasonably". Section 1-204(3).
"Supplier". Section 2A-103(1)(x).

§ 2A-514. Waiver of Lessee's Objections.

(1) In rejecting goods, a lessee's failure to state a particular defect that is ascertainable by reasonable inspection precludes the lessee from relying on the defect to justify rejection or to establish default:

(a) if, stated seasonably, the lessor or the supplier could have cured it (Section 2A-513); or

(b) between merchants if the lessor or the supplier after rejection has made a request in writing for a full and final written statement of all defects on which the lessee proposes to rely.

(2) A lessee's failure to reserve rights when paying rent or other consideration against documents precludes recovery of the payment for defects apparent on the face of the documents.

Official Comment

Uniform Statutory Source: Section 2-605.

Changes: Revised to reflect leasing practices and terminology.

Purposes: The principles applicable to the commercial practice of payment against documents (subsection 2) are explained in official comment 4 to Section 2-605, the statutory analogue to this section.

Cross Reference:

Section 2-605 official comment 4.

Definitional Cross References:

"Between merchants". Section 2-104(3).

"Goods". Section 2A-103(1)(h).

"Lessee". Section 2A-103(1)(n).

"Lessor". Section 2A-103(1)(p).

"Rights". Section 1-201(36).

"Seasonably". Section 1-204(3).

"Supplier". Section 2A-103(1)(x).

"Writing". Section 1-201(46).

§ 2A-515. Acceptance of Goods.

(1) Acceptance of goods occurs after the lessee has had a reasonable opportunity to inspect the goods and

(a) the lessee signifies or acts with respect to the goods in a manner that signifies to the lessor or the supplier that the goods are conforming or that the lessee will take or retain them in spite of their nonconformity; or

(b) the lessee fails to make an effective rejection of the goods (Section 2A-509(2)).

(2) Acceptance of a part of any commercial unit is acceptance of that entire unit.

Official Comment

Uniform Statutory Source: Section 2-606.

Changes: The provisions of Section 2-606(1)(a) were substantially rewritten to provide that the lessee's conduct may signify acceptance. Further, the provisions of Section 2-606(1)(c) were not incorporated as irrelevant given the lessee's possession and use of the leased goods.

Cross References:

Sections 2-606(1)(a) and 2-606(1)(c).

Definitional Cross References:

"Commercial unit". Section 2A-103(1)(c).

"Conforming". Section 2A-103(1)(d).

"Goods". Section 2A-103(1)(h).

"Lessee". Section 2A-103(1)(n).

"Lessor". Section 2A-103(1)(p).

"Supplier". Section 2A-103(1)(x).

§ 2A-516. Effect of Acceptance of Goods; Notice of Default; Burden of Establishing Default After Acceptance; Notice of Claim or Litigation to Person Answerable Over.

(1) A lessee must pay rent for any goods accepted in accordance with the lease contract, with due allowance for goods rightfully rejected or not delivered.

(2) A lessee's acceptance of goods precludes rejection of the goods accepted. In the case of a finance lease, if made with knowledge of a nonconformity, acceptance cannot be revoked because of it. In any other case, if made with knowledge of a nonconformity, acceptance cannot be revoked because of it unless the acceptance was on the reasonable assumption that the nonconformity would be seasonably cured. Acceptance does not of itself impair any other remedy provided by this Article or the lease agreement for nonconformity.

(3) If a tender has been accepted:

(a) within a reasonable time after the lessee discovers or should have discovered any default, the lessee shall notify the lessor and the supplier, if any, or be barred from any remedy against the party not notified;

(b) except in the case of a consumer lease, within a reasonable time after the lessee receives notice of litigation for infringement or the like (Section 2A–211) the lessee shall notify the lessor or be barred from any remedy over for liability established by the litigation; and

(c) the burden is on the lessee to establish any default.

(4) If a lessee is sued for breach of a warranty or other obligation for which a lessor or a supplier is answerable over the following apply:

(a) The lessee may give the lessor or the supplier, or both, written notice of the litigation. If the notice states that the person notified may come in and defend and that if the person notified does not do so that person will be bound in any action against that person by the lessee by any determination of fact common to the two litigations, then unless the person notified after seasonable receipt of the notice does come in and defend that person is so bound.

(b) The lessor or the supplier may demand in writing that the lessee turn over control of the litigation including settlement if the claim is one for infringement or the like (Section 2A–211) or else be barred from any remedy over. If the demand states that the lessor or the supplier agrees to bear all expense and to satisfy any adverse judgment, then unless the lessee after seasonable receipt of the demand does turn over control the lessee is so barred.

(5) Subsections (3) and (4) apply to any obligation of a lessee to hold the lessor or the supplier harmless against infringement or the like (Section 2A–211).

As amended in 1990.

See Appendix VI for material relating to changes made in text in 1990.

Official Comment

Uniform Statutory Source: Section 2–607.

Changes: Substantially revised.

Purposes:

1. Subsection (2) creates a special rule for finance leases, precluding revocation if acceptance is made with knowledge of

nonconformity with respect to the lease agreement, as opposed to the supply agreement; this is not inequitable as the lessee has a direct claim against the supplier. Section 2A-209(1). Revocation of acceptance of a finance lease is permitted if the lessee's acceptance was without discovery of the nonconformity (with respect to the lease agreement, not the supply agreement) and was reasonably induced by the lessor's assurances. Section 2A-517(1)(b). Absent exclusion or modification, the lessor under a finance lease makes certain warranties to the lessee. Sections 2A-210 and 2A-211(1). Revocation of acceptance is not prohibited even after the lessee's promise has become irrevocable and independent. Section 2A-407 official comment. Where the finance lease creates a security interest, the rule may be to the contrary. *General Elec. Credit Corp. of Tennessee v. Ger-Beck Mach. Co.*, 806 F.2d 1207 (3rd Cir. 1986).

2. Subsection (3)(a) requires the lessee to give notice of default, within a reasonable time after the lessee discovered or should have discovered the default. In a finance lease, notice may be given either to the supplier, the lessor, or both, but remedy is barred against the party not notified. In a finance lease, the lessor is usually not liable for defects in the goods and the essential notice is to the supplier. While notice to the finance lessor will often not give any additional rights to the lessee, it would be good practice to give the notice since the finance lessor has an interest in the goods. Subsection (3)(a) does not use the term finance lease, but the definition of supplier is a person from whom a lessor buys or leases goods to be leased under a finance lease. Section 2A-103(1)(x). Therefore, there can be a "supplier" only in a finance lease. Subsection (4) applies similar notice rules as to lessors and suppliers if a lessee is sued for a breach of warranty or other obligation for which a lessor or supplier is answerable over.

3. Subsection (3)(b) requires the lessee to give the lessor notice of litigation for infringement or the like. There is an exception created in the case of a consumer lease. While such an exception was considered for a finance lease, it was not created because it was not necessary—the lessor in a finance lease does not give a warranty against infringement. Section 2A-211(2). Even though not required under subsection (3)(b), the lessee who takes under a finance lease should consider giving notice of litigation for infringement or the like to the supplier, because the lessee obtains the benefit of the suppliers' promises subject to the suppliers' defenses or claims. Sections 2A-209(1) and 2-607(3)(b).

Cross References:

Sections 2-607(3)(b), 2A-103(1)(x), 2A-209(1), 2A-210, 2A-211(1), 2A-211(2), 2A-407 official comment and 2A-517(1)(b).

Definitional Cross References:

"Action". Section 1-201(1).
"Agreement". Section 1-201(3).
"Burden of establishing". Section 1-201(8).
"Conforming". Section 2A-103(1)(d).
"Consumer lease". Section 2A-103(1)(e).
"Delivery". Section 1-201(14).
"Discover". Section 1-201(25).
"Finance lease". Section 2A-103(1)(g).
"Goods". Section 2A-103(1)(h).
"Knowledge". Section 1-201(25).
"Lease agreement". Section 2A-103(1)(k).
"Lease contract". Section 2A-103(1)(*l*).
"Lessee". Section 2A-103(1)(n).
"Lessor". Section 2A-103(1)(p).
"Notice". Section 1-201(25).
"Notifies". Section 1-201(26).
"Person". Section 1-201(30).
"Reasonable time". Section 1-204(1) and (2).
"Receipt". Section 2-103(1)(c).
"Remedy". Section 1-201(34).
"Seasonably". Section 1-204(3).
"Supplier". Section 2A-103(1)(x).
"Written". Section 1-201(46).

§ 2A–517. Revocation of Acceptance of Goods.

(1) A lessee may revoke acceptance of a lot or commercial unit whose nonconformity substantially impairs its value to the lessee if the lessee has accepted it:

(a) except in the case of a finance lease, on the reasonable assumption that its nonconformity would be cured and it has not been seasonably cured; or

(b) without discovery of the nonconformity if the lessee's acceptance was reasonably induced either by the lessor's assurances or, except in the case of a finance lease, by the difficulty of discovery before acceptance.

(2) Except in the case of a finance lease that is not a consumer lease, a lessee may revoke acceptance of a lot or commercial unit if the lessor defaults under the lease contract and the default substantially impairs the value of that lot or commercial unit to the lessee.

(3) If the lease agreement so provides, the lessee may revoke acceptance of a lot or commercial unit because of other defaults by the lessor.

(4) Revocation of acceptance must occur within a reasonable time after the lessee discovers or should have discovered the ground for it and before any substantial change in condition of the goods which is not caused by the nonconformity. Revocation is not effective until the lessee notifies the lessor.

(5) A lessee who so revokes has the same rights and duties with regard to the goods involved as if the lessee had rejected them.

As amended in 1990.

See Appendix VI for material relating to changes made in text in 1990.

Official Comment

Uniform Statutory Source: Section 2–608.

Changes: Revised to reflect leasing practices and terminology. Note that in the case of a finance lease the lessee retains a limited right to revoke acceptance. Sections 2A–517(1)(b) and 2A–516 official comment. New subsections (2) and (3) added.

Purposes:

1. The section states the situations under which the lessee may return the goods to the lessor and cancel the lease. Subsection (2) recognizes that the lessor may have continuing obligations under the lease and that a default as to those obligations may be sufficiently material to justify revocation of acceptance of the leased items and cancellation of the lease by the lessee. For example, a failure by the lessor to fulfill its obligation to maintain leased equipment or to supply other goods which are necessary for the operation of the leased equipment may justify revocation of acceptance and cancellation of the lease.

2. Subsection (3) specifically provides that the lease agreement may provide that the lessee can revoke acceptance for defaults by the lessor which in the absence of such an agreement might not be considered sufficiently serious to justify revocation. That is, the parties are free to contract on the question of what defaults are so material that the lessee can cancel the lease.

Cross Reference:

Section 2A–516 official comment.

Definitional Cross References:

"Commercial unit". Section 2A–103(1)(c).

"Conforming". Section 2A–103(1)(d).

"Discover". Section 1–201(25).

"Finance lease". Section 2A–103(1)(g).

"Goods". Section 2A–103(1)(h).

"Lessee". Section 2A–103(1)(n).

"Lessor". Section 2A–103(1)(p).

"Lot". Section 2A–103(1)(s).

"Notifies". Section 1–201(26).

"Reasonable time". Section 1–204(1) and (2).

"Rights". Section 1–201(36).

"Seasonably". Section 1–204(3).

"Value". Section 1–201(44).

§ 2A–518. Cover; Substitute Goods.

(1) After a default by a lessor under the lease contract of the type described in Section 2A–508(1), or, if agreed, after other default by the lessor, the lessee may cover by making any purchase or lease of or contract to purchase or lease goods in substitution for those due from the lessor.

(2) Except as otherwise provided with respect to damages liquidated in the lease agreement (Section 2A–504) or otherwise determined pursuant to agreement of the parties (Sections 1–102(3) and 2A–503), if a lessee's cover is by a lease agreement substantially similar to the original lease agreement and the new lease agreement is made in good faith and in a commercially reasonable manner, the lessee may recover from the lessor as damages (i) the present value, as of the date of the commencement of the term of the new lease agreement, of the rent under the new lease agreement applicable to that period of the new lease term which is comparable to the then remaining term of the original lease agreement minus the present value as of the same date of the total rent for the then remaining lease term of the original lease agreement, and (ii) any incidental or consequential damages, less expenses saved in consequence of the lessor's default.

(3) If a lessee's cover is by lease agreement that for any reason does not qualify for treatment under subsection (2), or is by purchase or otherwise, the lessee may recover from the lessor as if the lessee had elected not to cover and Section 2A–519 governs.

As amended in 1990.

See Appendix VI for material relating to changes made in text in 1990.

Official Comment

Uniform Statutory Source: Section 2–712.

Changes: Substantially revised.

Purposes:

1. Subsection (1) allows the lessee to take action to fix its damages after default by the lessor. Such action may consist of the lease of goods. The decision to cover is a function of commercial judgment, not a statutory mandate replete with sanctions for failure to comply. *Cf.* Section 9–507.

2. Subsection (2) states a rule for determining the amount of lessee's damages provided that there is no agreement to the contrary. The lessee's damages will be established using the new lease agreement as a measure if the following three criteria are met: (i) the lessee's cover is by lease agreement, (ii) the lease agreement is substantially similar to the original lease agreement, and (iii) such cover

was effected in good faith, and in a commercially reasonable manner. Thus, the lessee will be entitled to recover from the lessor the present value, as of the date of commencement of the term of the new lease agreement, of the rent under the new lease agreement applicable to that period which is comparable to the then remaining term of the original lease agreement less the present value of the rent reserved for the remaining term under the original lease, together with incidental or consequential damages less expenses saved in consequence of the lessor's default. Consequential damages may include loss suffered by the lessee because of deprivation of the use of the goods during the period between the default and the acquisition of the goods under the new lease agreement. If the lessee's cover does not satisfy the criteria of subsection (2), Section 2A-519 governs.

3. Two of the three criteria to be met by the lessee are familiar, but the concept of the new lease agreement being substantially similar to the original lease agreement is not. Given the many variables facing a party who intends to lease goods and the rapidity of change in the market place, the policy decision was made not to draft with specificity. It was thought unwise to seek to establish certainty at the cost of fairness. Thus, the decision of whether the new lease agreement is substantially similar to the original will be determined case by case.

4. While the section does not draw a bright line, it is possible to describe some of the factors that should be considered in finding that a new lease agreement is substantially similar to the original. First, the goods subject to the new lease agreement should be examined. For example, in a lease of computer equipment the new lease might be for more modern equipment. However, it may be that at the time of the lessor's breach it was not possible to obtain the same type of goods in the market place. Because the lessee's remedy under Section 2A-519 is intended to place the lessee in essentially the same position as if he had covered, if goods similar to those to have been delivered under the original lease are not available, then the computer equipment in this hypothetical should qualify as a commercially reasonable substitute. *See* Section 2-712(1).

5. Second, the various elements of the new lease agreement should also be examined. Those elements include the presence or absence of options to purchase or release; the lessor's representations, warranties and covenants to the lessee, as well as those to be provided by the lessee to the lessor; and the services, if any, to be provided by the lessor or by the lessee. All of these factors allocate cost and risk between the lessor and the lessee and thus affect the amount of rent to be paid. If the differences between the original lease and the new lease can be easily valued, it would be appropriate for a court to adjust the difference in rental to take account of the difference between the two leases, find that the new lease is substantially similar to the old lease, and award cover damages under this section. If, for example, the new lease requires the lessor to insure the goods in the hands of the lessee, while the original lease required the lessee to insure, the usual cost of such insurance could be deducted from the rent due under the new lease before determining the difference in rental between the two leases.

6. Having examined the goods and the agreement, the test to be applied is whether, in light of these comparisons, the new lease agreement is substantially similar to the original lease agreement. These findings should not be made with scientific precision, as they are a function of economics, nor should they be made independently with respect to the goods and each element of the agreement, as it is important that a sense of commercial judgment pervade the finding. To establish the new lease as a proper measure of damage under subsection (2), these factors, taken as a whole, must result in a finding that the new lease agreement is substantially similar to the original.

7. A new lease can be substantially similar to the original lease even though its term extends beyond the remaining

term of the original lease, so long as both (a) the lease terms are commercially comparable (e.g., it is highly unlikely that a one-month rental and a five-year lease would reflect similar commercial realities), and (b) the court can fairly apportion a part of the rental payments under the new lease to that part of the term of the new lease which is comparable to the remaining lease term under the original lease. Also, the lease term of the new lease may be comparable to the term of the original lease even though the beginning and ending dates of the two leases are not the same. For example, a two-month lease of agricultural equipment for the months of August and September may be comparable to a two-month lease running from the 15th of August to the 15th of October if in the particular location two-month leases beginning on August 15th are basically interchangeable with two-month leases beginning August 1st. Similarly, the term of a one-year truck lease beginning on the 15th of January may be comparable to the term of a one-year truck lease beginning January 2d. If the lease terms are found to be comparable, the court may base cover damages on the entire difference between the costs under the two leases.

Cross References:

Sections 2–712(1), 2A–519 and 9–507.

Definitional Cross References:

"Agreement". Section 1–201(3).
"Contract". Section 1–201(11).
"Good faith". Sections 1–201(19) and 2–103(1)(b).
"Goods". Section 2A–103(1)(h).
"Lease". Section 2A–103(1)(j).
"Lease agreement". Section 2A–103(1)(k).
"Lease contract". Section 2A–103(1)(*l*).
"Lessee". Section 2A–103(1)(n).
"Lessor". Section 2A–103(1)(p).
"Party". Section 1–201(29).
"Present value". Section 2A–103(1)(u).
"Purchase". Section 2A–103(1)(v).

§ 2A–519. Lessee's Damages for Non-delivery, Repudiation, Default, and Breach of Warranty in Regard to Accepted Goods.

(1) Except as otherwise provided with respect to damages liquidated in the lease agreement (Section 2A–504) or otherwise determined pursuant to agreement of the parties (Sections 1–102(3) and 2A–503), if a lessee elects not to cover or a lessee elects to cover and the cover is by lease agreement that for any reason does not qualify for treatment under Section 2A–518(2), or is by purchase or otherwise, the measure of damages for non-delivery or repudiation by the lessor or for rejection or revocation of acceptance by the lessee is the present value, as of the date of the default, of the then market rent minus the present value as of the same date of the original rent, computed for the remaining lease term of the original lease agreement, together with incidental and consequential damages, less expenses saved in consequence of the lessor's default.

(2) Market rent is to be determined as of the place for tender or, in cases of rejection after arrival or revocation of acceptance, as of the place of arrival.

(3) Except as otherwise agreed, if the lessee has accepted goods and given notification (Section 2A–516(3)), the measure of damages for non-conforming tender or delivery or other default by a lessor is the loss resulting in the ordinary course of events from the lessor's default as determined in any manner that is reasonable together with incidental and consequential damages, less expenses saved in consequence of the lessor's default.

(4) Except as otherwise agreed, the measure of damages for breach of warranty is the present value at the time and place of acceptance of the difference between the value of the use of the goods accepted and the value if they had been as warranted for the lease term, unless special circumstances show proximate damages of a different amount, together with incidental and consequential damages, less expenses saved in consequence of the lessor's default or breach of warranty.

As amended in 1990.

See Appendix VI for material relating to changes made in text in 1990.

Official Comment

Uniform Statutory Source: Sections 2–713 and 2–714.

Changes: Substantially revised.

Purposes:

1. Subsection (1), a revised version of the provisions of Section 2–713(1), states the basic rule governing the measure of lessee's damages for non-delivery or repudiation by the lessor or for rightful rejection or revocation of acceptance by the lessee. This measure will apply, absent agreement to the contrary, if the lessee does not cover or if the cover does not qualify under Section 2A–518. There is no sanction for cover that does not qualify.

2. The measure of damage is the present value, as of the date of default, of the market rent for the remaining term of the lease less the present value of the original rent for the remaining term of the lease, plus incidental and consequential damages less expenses saved in consequence of the default. Note that the reference in Section 2A–519(1) is to the date of default not to the date of an event of default. An event of default under a lease agreement becomes a default under a lease agreement only after the expiration of any relevant period of grace and compliance with any notice requirements under this Article and the lease agreement. American Bar Foundation, *Commentaries on Indentures,* § 5–1, at 216–217 (1971). Section 2A–501(1). This conclusion is also a function of whether, as a matter of fact or law, the event of default has been waived, suspended or cured. Sections 2A–103(4) and 1–103.

3. Subsection (2), a revised version of the provisions of Section 2–713(2), states the rule with respect to determining market rent.

4. Subsection (3), a revised version of the provisions of Section 2–714(1) and (3), states the measure of damages where goods have been accepted and acceptance is not revoked. The subsection applies both to defaults which occur at the inception of the lease and to defaults which occur subsequently, such as failure to comply with an obligation to maintain the leased goods. The measure in essence is the loss, in the ordinary course of events, flowing from the default.

5. Subsection (4), a revised version of the provisions of Section 2–714(2), states the measure of damages for breach of warranty. The measure in essence is the present value of the difference between the value of the goods accepted and of the goods if they had been as warranted.

6. Subsections (1), (3) and (4) specifically state that the parties may by contract vary the damages rules stated in those subsections.

Cross References:

Sections 2–713(1), 2–713(2), 2–714 and Section 2A–518.

Definitional Cross References:

"Conforming". Section 2A–103(1)(d).
"Delivery". Section 1–201(14).
"Goods". Section 2A–103(1)(h).

"Lease". Section 2A-103(1)(j).
"Lease agreement". Section 2A-103(1)(k).
"Lessee". Section 2A-103(1)(n).
"Lessor". Section 2A-103(1)(p).
"Notification". Section 1-201(26).
"Present value". Section 2A-103(1)(u).
"Value". Section 1-201(44).

§ 2A-520. Lessee's Incidental and Consequential Damages.

(1) Incidental damages resulting from a lessor's default include expenses reasonably incurred in inspection, receipt, transportation, and care and custody of goods rightfully rejected or goods the acceptance of which is justifiably revoked, any commercially reasonable charges, expenses or commissions in connection with effecting cover, and any other reasonable expense incident to the default.

(2) Consequential damages resulting from a lessor's default include:

(a) any loss resulting from general or particular requirements and needs of which the lessor at the time of contracting had reason to know and which could not reasonably be prevented by cover or otherwise; and

(b) injury to person or property proximately resulting from any breach of warranty.

Official Comment

Uniform Statutory Source: Section 2-715.

Changes: Revised to reflect leasing terminology and practices.

Purposes: Subsection (1), a revised version of the provisions of Section 2-715(1), lists some examples of incidental damages resulting from a lessor's default; the list is not exhaustive. Subsection (1) makes clear that it applies not only to rightful rejection, but also to justifiable revocation.

Subsection (2), a revised version of the provisions of Section 2-715(2), lists some examples of consequential damages resulting from a lessor's default; the list is not exhaustive.

Cross References:

Section 2-715.

Definitional Cross References:

"Goods". Section 2A-103(1)(h).
"Knows". Section 1-201(25).
"Lessee". Section 2A-103(1)(n).
"Lessor". Section 2A-103(1)(p).
"Person". Section 1-201(30).
"Receipt". Section 2-103(1)(c).

§ 2A-521. Lessee's Right to Specific Performance or Replevin.

(1) Specific performance may be decreed if the goods are unique or in other proper circumstances.

(2) A decree for specific performance may include any terms and conditions as to payment of the rent, damages, or other relief that the court deems just.

(3) A lessee has a right of replevin, detinue, sequestration, claim and delivery, or the like for goods identified to the lease contract if after reasonable effort the lessee is unable to effect cover for those goods or the circumstances reasonably indicate that the effort will be unavailing.

Official Comment

Uniform Statutory Source: Section 2–716.

Changes: Revised to reflect leasing practices and terminology, and to expand the reference to the right of replevin in subsection (3) to include other similar rights of the lessee.

Definitional Cross References:

"Delivery". Section 1–201(14).

"Goods". Section 2A–103(1)(h).

"Lease contract". Section 2A–103(1)(*l*).

"Lessee". Section 2A–103(1)(n).

"Rights". Section 1–201(36).

"Term". Section 1–201(42).

§ 2A–522. Lessee's Right to Goods on Lessor's Insolvency.

(1) Subject to subsection (2) and even though the goods have not been shipped, a lessee who has paid a part or all of the rent and security for goods identified to a lease contract (Section 2A–217) on making and keeping good a tender of any unpaid portion of the rent and security due under the lease contract may recover the goods identified from the lessor if the lessor becomes insolvent within 10 days after receipt of the first installment of rent and security.

(2) A lessee acquires the right to recover goods identified to a lease contract only if they conform to the lease contract.

Official Comment

Uniform Statutory Source: Section 2–502.

Changes: Revised to reflect leasing practices and terminology.

Definitional Cross References:

"Conforming". Section 2A–103(1)(d).

"Goods". Section 2A–103(1)(h).

"Insolvent". Section 1–201(23).

"Lease contract". Section 2A–103(1)(*l*).

"Lessee". Section 2A–103(1)(n).

"Lessor". Section 2A–103(1)(p).

"Receipt". Section 2–103(1)(c).

"Rights". Section 1–201(36).

C. DEFAULT BY LESSEE

§ 2A–523. Lessor's Remedies.

(1) If a lessee wrongfully rejects or revokes acceptance of goods or fails to make a payment when due or repudiates with respect to a part or the whole, then, with respect to any goods involved, and with respect to all of the goods if under an installment lease contract the value of the whole lease contract is substantially impaired (Section 2A–510), the lessee is in default under the lease contract and the lessor may:

(a) cancel the lease contract (Section 2A–505(1));

(b) proceed respecting goods not identified to the lease contract (Section 2A–524);

(c) withhold delivery of the goods and take possession of goods previously delivered (Section 2A–525);

(d) stop delivery of the goods by any bailee (Section 2A–526);

(e) dispose of the goods and recover damages (Section 2A-527), or retain the goods and recover damages (Section 2A-528), or in a proper case recover rent (Section 2A-529);

(f) exercise any other rights or pursue any other remedies provided in the lease contract.

(2) If a lessor does not fully exercise a right or obtain a remedy to which the lessor is entitled under subsection (1), the lessor may recover the loss resulting in the ordinary course of events from the lessee's default as determined in any reasonable manner, together with incidental damages, less expenses saved in consequence of the lessee's default.

(3) If a lessee is otherwise in default under a lease contract, the lessor may exercise the rights and pursue the remedies provided in the lease contract, which may include a right to cancel the lease. In addition, unless otherwise provided in the lease contract:

(a) if the default substantially impairs the value of the lease contract to the lessor, the lessor may exercise the rights and pursue the remedies provided in subsections (1) or (2); or

(b) if the default does not substantially impair the value of the lease contract to the lessor, the lessor may recover as provided in subsection (2).

As amended in 1990.

See Appendix VI for material relating to changes made in text in 1990.

Official Comment

Uniform Statutory Source: Section 2-703.

Changes: Substantially revised.

Purposes:

1. Subsection (1) is an index to Sections 2A-524 through 2A-531 and states that the remedies provided in those sections are available for the defaults referred to in subsection (1): wrongful rejection or revocation of acceptance, failure to make a payment when due, or repudiation. In addition, remedies provided in the lease contract are available. Subsection (2) sets out a remedy if the lessor does not pursue to completion a right or actually obtain a remedy available under subsection (1), and subsection (3) sets out statutory remedies for defaults not specifically referred to in subsection (1). Subsection (3) provides that, if any default by the lessee other than those specifically referred to in subsection (1) is material, the lessor can exercise the remedies provided in subsection (1) or (2); otherwise the available remedy is as provided in subsection (3). A lessor who has brought an action seeking or has nonjudicially pursued one or more of the remedies available under subsection (1) may amend so as to claim or may nonjudicially pursue a remedy under subsection (2) unless the right or remedy first chosen has been pursued to an extent actually inconsistent with the new course of action. The intent of the provision is to reject the doctrine of election of remedies and to permit an alteration of course by the lessor unless such alteration would actually have an effect on the lessee that would be unreasonable under the circumstances. Further, the lessor may pursue remedies under both subsections (1) and (2) unless doing so would put the lessor in a better position than it would have been in had the lessee fully performed.

2. The lessor and the lessee can agree to modify the rights and remedies available under the Article; they can, among other things, provide that for defaults other than those specified in subsection (1) the lessor can exercise the rights and remedies referred to in subsection (1), whether or not the default would otherwise be held to substantially impair the value of the lease contract to the lessor; they can also create a new scheme of rights and remedies triggered by the occurrence of the default. Sections 2A–103(4) and 1–102(3).

3. Subsection (1), a substantially rewritten version of Section 2–703, lists various cumulative remedies of the lessor where the lessee wrongfully rejects or revokes acceptance, fails to make a payment when due, or repudiates. Section 2A–501(2) and (4). The subsection also allows the lessor to exercise any contractual remedy.

4. This Article rejects any general doctrine of election of remedy. Whether, in a particular case, one remedy bars another, is a function of whether lessor has been put in as good a position as if the lessee had fully performed the lease contract. Multiple remedies are barred only if the effect is to put the lessor in a better position than it would have been in had the lessee fully performed under the lease. Sections 2A–103(4), 2A–501(4), and 1–106(1).

5. **Hypothetical:** To better understand the application of subparagraphs (a) through (e), it is useful to review a hypothetical. Assume that A is a merchant in the business of selling and leasing new bicycles of various types. B is about to engage in the business of subleasing bicycles to summer residents of and visitors to an island resort. A, as lessor, has agreed to lease 60 bicycles to B. While there is one master lease, deliveries and terms are staggered. 20 bicycles are to be delivered by A to B's island location on June 1; the term of the lease of these bicycles is four months. 20 bicycles are to be delivered by A to B's island location on July 1; the term of the lease of these bicycles is three months. Finally, 20 bicycles are to be delivered by A to B's island location on August 1; the term of the lease of these bicycles is two months. B is obligated to pay rent to A on the 15th day of each month during the term for the lease. Rent is $50 per month, per bicycle. B has no option to purchase or release and must return the bicycles to A at the end of the term, in good condition, reasonable wear and tear excepted. Since the retail price of each bicycle is $400 and bicycles used in the retail rental business have a useful economic life of 36 months, this transaction creates a lease. Sections 2A–103(1)(j) and 1–201(37).

6. A's current inventory of bicycles is not large. Thus, upon signing the lease with B in February, A agreed to purchase 60 new bicycles from A's principal manufacturer, with special instructions to drop ship the bicycles to B's island location in accordance with the delivery schedule set forth in the lease.

7. The first shipment of 20 bicycles was received by B on May 21. B inspected the bicycles, accepted the same as conforming to the lease and signed a receipt of delivery and acceptance. However, due to poor weather that summer, business was terrible and B was unable to pay the rent due on June 15. Pursuant to the lease A sent B notice of default and proceeded to enforce his rights and remedies against B.

8. A's counsel first advised A that under Section 2A–510(2) and the terms of the lease B's failure to pay was a default with respect to the whole. Thus, to minimize A's continued exposure, A was advised to take possession of the bicycles. If A had possession of the goods A could refuse to deliver. Section 2A–525(1). However, the facts here are different. With respect to the bicycles in B's possession, A has the right to take possession of the bicycles, without breach of the peace. Section 2A–525(2). If B refuses to allow A access to the bicycles, A can proceed by action, including replevin or injunctive relief.

9. With respect to the 40 bicycles that have not been delivered, this Article provides various alternatives. First, assume that 20 of the remaining 40 bicycles have been manufactured and delivered by the manufacturer to a carrier for shipment to B. Given the size of the shipment, the carrier was using a small truck for the delivery and the truck had not yet reached the island ferry when the manufacturer (at the request of A) instructed the carrier to divert the shipment to A's place of business. A's right to stop delivery is recognized under these circumstances. Section 2A-526(1). Second, assume that the 20 remaining bicycles were in the process of manufacture when B defaulted. A retains the right (as between A as lessor and B as lessee) to exercise reasonable commercial judgment whether to complete manufacture or to dispose of the unfinished goods for scrap. Since A is not the manufacturer and A has a binding contract to buy the bicycles, A elected to allow the manufacturer to complete the manufacture of the bicycles, but instructed the manufacturer to deliver the completed bicycles to A's place of business. Section 2A-524(2).

10. Thus, so far A has elected to exercise the remedies referred to in subparagraphs (b) through (d) in subsection (1). None of these remedies bars any of the others because A's election and enforcement merely resulted in A's possession of the bicycles. Had B performed A would have recovered possession of the bicycles. Thus A is in the process of obtaining the benefit of his bargain. Note that A could exercise any other rights or pursue any other remedies provided in the lease contract (Section 2A-523(1)(f)), or elect to recover his loss due to the lessee's default under Section 2A-523(2).

11. A's counsel next would determine what action, if any, should be taken with respect to the goods. As stated in subparagraph (e) and as discussed fully in Section 2A-527(1) the lessor may, but has no obligation to, dispose of the goods by a substantially similar lease (indeed, the lessor has no obligation whatsoever to dispose of the goods at all) and recover damages based on that action, but lessor will not be able to recover damages which put it in a better position than performance would have done, nor will it be able to recover damages for losses which it could have reasonably avoided. In this case, since A is in the business of leasing and selling bicycles, A will probably inventory the 60 bicycles for its retail trade.

12. A's counsel then will determine which of the various means of ascertaining A's damages against B are available. Subparagraph (e) catalogues each relevant section. First, under Section 2A-527(2) the amount of A's claim is computed by comparing the original lease between A and B with any subsequent lease of the bicycles but only if the subsequent lease is substantially similar to the original lease contract. While the section does not define this term, the official comment does establish some parameters. If, however, A elects to lease the bicycles to his retail trade, it is unlikely that the resulting lease will be substantially similar to the original, as leases to retail customers are considerably different from leases to wholesale customers like B. If, however, the leases were substantially similar, the damage claim is for accrued and unpaid rent to the beginning of the new lease, plus the present value as of the same date, of the rent reserved under the original lease for the balance of its term less the present value as of the same date of the rent reserved under the replacement lease for a term comparable to the balance of the term of the original lease, together with incidental damages less expenses saved in consequence of the lessee's default.

13. If the new lease is not substantially similar or if A elects to sell the bicycles or to hold the bicycles, damages are computed under Section 2A-528 or 2A-529.

14. If A elects to pursue his claim under Section 2A-528(1) the damage rule is the same as that stated in Section 2A-528(2) except that damages are measured from default if the lessee never took possession of the goods or from the time when the lessor did or could have regained possession and that the standard

of comparison is not the rent reserved under a substantially similar lease entered into by the lessor but a market rent, as defined in Section 2A–507. Further, if the facts of this hypothetical were more elaborate A may be able to establish that the measure of damage under subsection (1) is inadequate to put him in the same position that B's performance would have, in which case A can claim the present value of his lost profits.

15. Yet another alternative for computing A's damage claim against B which will be available in some situations is recovery of the present value, as of entry of judgment, of the rent for the then remaining lease term under Section 2A–529. However, this formulation is not available if the goods have been repossessed or tendered back to A. For the 20 bicycles repossessed and the remaining 40 bicycles, A will be able to recover the present value of the rent only if A is unable to dispose of them, or circumstances indicate the effort will be unavailing. If A has prevailed in an action for the rent, at any time up to collection of a judgment by A against B, A might dispose of the bicycles. In such case A's claim for damages against B is governed by Section 2A–527 or 2A–528. Section 2A–529(3). The resulting recalculation of claim should reduce the amount recoverable by A against B and the lessor is required to cause an appropriate credit to be entered against the earlier judgment. However, the nature of the post-judgment proceedings to resolve this issue, and the sanctions for a failure to comply, if any, will be determined by other law.

16. Finally, if the lease agreement had so provided pursuant to subparagraph (f), A's claim against B would not be determined under any of these statutory formulae, but pursuant to a liquidated damages clause. Section 2A–504(1).

17. These various methods of computing A's damage claim against B are alternatives subject to Section 2A–501(4). However, the pursuit of any one of these alternatives is not a bar to, nor has it been barred by, A's earlier action to obtain possession of the 60 bicycles. These formulae, which vary as a function of an overt or implied mitigation of damage theory, focus on allowing A a recovery of the benefit of his bargain with B. Had B performed, A would have received the rent as well as the return of the 60 bicycles at the end of the term.

18. Finally, A's counsel should also advise A of his right to cancel the lease contract under subparagraph (a). Section 2A–505(1). Cancellation will discharge all existing obligations but preserve A's rights and remedies.

19. Subsection (2) recognizes that a lessor who is entitled to exercise the rights or to obtain a remedy granted by subsection (1) may choose not to do so. In such cases, the lessor can recover damages as provided in subsection (2). For example, for non-payment of rent, the lessor may decide not to take possession of the goods and cancel the lease, but rather to merely sue for the unpaid rent as it comes due plus lost interest or other damages "determined in any reasonable manner." Subsection (2) also negates any loss of alternative rights and remedies by reason of having invoked or commenced the exercise or pursuit of any one or more rights or remedies.

20. Subsection (3) allows the lessor access to a remedy scheme provided in this Article as well as that contained in the lease contract if the lessee is in default for reasons other than those stated in subsection (1). Note that the reference to this Article includes supplementary principles of law and equity, *e.g.*, fraud, misrepresentation and duress. Sections 2A–103(4) and 1–103.

21. There is no special treatment of the finance lease in this section. Absent supplementary principles of law to the contrary, in most cases the supplier will have no rights or remedies against the defaulting lessee. Section 2A–209(2)(ii). Given that the supplier will look to the lessor for payment, this is appropriate. However, there is a specific exception to this rule with respect to the right to identify goods to the lease contract. Section

2A-524(2). The parties are free to create a different result in a particular case. Sections 2A-103(4) and 1-102(3).

Cross References:

Sections 1-102(3), 1-103, 1-106(1), 1-201(37), 2-703, 2A-103(1)(j), 2A-103(4), 2A-209(2)(ii), 2A-501(4), 2A-504(1), 2A-505(1), 2A-507, 2A-510(2), 2A-524 through 2A-531, 2A-524(2), 2A-525(1), 2A-525(2), 2A-526(1), 2A-527(1), 2A-527(2), 2A-528(1) and 2A-529(3).

Definitional Cross References:

"Delivery". Section 1-201(14).
"Goods". Section 2A-103(1)(h).
"Installment lease contract". Section 2A-103(1)(i).
"Lease contract". Section 2A-103(1)(*l*).
"Lessee". Section 2A-103(1)(n).
"Lessor". Section 2A-103(1)(p).
"Remedy". Section 1-201(34).
"Rights". Section 1-201(36).
"Value". Section 1-201(44).

§ 2A-524. Lessor's Right to Identify Goods to Lease Contract.

(1) After default by the lessee under the lease contract of the type described in Section 2A-523(1) or 2A-523(3)(a) or, if agreed, after other default by the lessee, the lessor may:

(a) identify to the lease contract conforming goods not already identified if at the time the lessor learned of the default they were in the lessor's or the supplier's possession or control; and

(b) dispose of goods (Section 2A-527(1)) that demonstrably have been intended for the particular lease contract even though those goods are unfinished.

(2) If the goods are unfinished, in the exercise of reasonable commercial judgment for the purposes of avoiding loss and of effective realization, an aggrieved lessor or the supplier may either complete manufacture and wholly identify the goods to the lease contract or cease manufacture and lease, sell, or otherwise dispose of the goods for scrap or salvage value or proceed in any other reasonable manner.

As amended in 1990.

See Appendix VI for material relating to changes made in text in 1990.

Official Comment

Uniform Statutory Source: Section 2-704.

Changes: Revised to reflect leasing practices and terminology.

Purposes: The remedies provided by this section are available to the lessor (i) if there has been a default by the lessee which falls within Section 2A-523(1) or 2A-523(3)(a), or (ii) if there has been any other default for which the lease contract gives the lessor the remedies provided by this section. Under "(ii)", the lease contract may give the lessor the remedies of identification and disposition provided by this section in various ways. For example, a lease provision might specifically refer to the remedies of identification and disposition, or it might refer to this section by number (*i.e.,* 2A-524), or it might do so by a more general reference such as "all rights and remedies provided by Article 2A for default by the lessee."

Definitional Cross References:

"Aggrieved party". Section 1-201(2).
"Conforming". Section 2A-103(1)(d).
"Goods". Section 2A-103(1)(h).
"Learn". Section 1-201(25).

"Lease". Section 2A–103(1)(j).
"Lease contract". Section 2A–103(1)(*l*).
"Lessor". Section 2A–103(1)(p).
"Rights". Section 1–201(36).
"Supplier". Section 2A–103(1)(x).
"Value". Section 1–201(44).

§ 2A–525. Lessor's Right to Possession of Goods.

(1) If a lessor discovers the lessee to be insolvent, the lessor may refuse to deliver the goods.

(2) After a default by the lessee under the lease contract of the type described in Section 2A–523(1) or 2A–523(3)(a) or, if agreed, after other default by the lessee, the lessor has the right to take possession of the goods. If the lease contract so provides, the lessor may require the lessee to assemble the goods and make them available to the lessor at a place to be designated by the lessor which is reasonably convenient to both parties. Without removal, the lessor may render unusable any goods employed in trade or business, and may dispose of goods on the lessee's premises (Section 2A–527).

(3) The lessor may proceed under subsection (2) without judicial process if it can be done without breach of the peace or the lessor may proceed by action.

As amended in 1990.

See Appendix VI for material relating to changes made in text in 1990.

Official Comment

Uniform Statutory Source: Sections 2–702(1) and 9–503.

Changes: Substantially revised.

Purposes:

1. Subsection (1), a revised version of the provisions of Section 2–702(1), allows the lessor to refuse to deliver goods if the lessee is insolvent. Note that the provisions of Section 2–702(2), granting the unpaid seller certain rights of reclamation, were not incorporated in this section. Subsection (2) made this unnecessary.

2. Subsection (2), a revised version of the provisions of Section 9–503, allows the lessor, on a Section 2A–523(1) or 2A–523(3)(a) default by the lessee, the right to take possession of or reclaim the goods. Also, the lessor can contract for the right to take possession of the goods for other defaults by the lessee. Therefore, since the lessee's insolvency is an event of default in a standard lease agreement, subsection (2) is the functional equivalent of Section 2–702(2). Further, subsection (2) sanctions the classic crate and delivery clause obligating the lessee to assemble the goods and to make them available to the lessor. Finally, the lessor may leave the goods in place, render them unusable (if they are goods employed in trade or business), and dispose of them on the lessee's premises.

3. Subsection (3), a revised version of the provisions of Section 9–503, allows the lessor to proceed under subsection (2) without judicial process, absent breach of the peace, or by action. Sections 2A–501(3), 2A–103(4) and 1–201(1). In the appropriate case action includes injunctive relief. *Clark Equip. Co. v. Armstrong Equip. Co.*, 431 F.2d 54 (5th Cir. 1970), *cert. denied,* 402 U.S. 909 (1971). This Section, as well as a number of other Sections in this Part, are included in the Article to codify the lessor's common law right to protect the lessor's reversionary

interest in the goods. Section 2A-103(1)(q). These Sections are intended to supplement and not displace principles of law and equity with respect to the protection of such interest. Sections 2A-103(4) and 1-103. Such principles apply in many instances, *e.g.*, loss or damage to goods if risk of loss passes to the lessee, failure of the lessee to return goods to the lessor in the condition stipulated in the lease, and refusal of the lessee to return goods to the lessor after termination or cancellation of the lease. See also Section 2A-532.

Cross References:

Sections 1-106(2), 2-702(1), 2-702(2), 2A-103(4), 2A-501(3), 2A-532 and 9-503.

Definitional Cross References:

"Action". Section 1-201(1).
"Delivery". Section 1-201(14).
"Discover". Section 1-201(25).
"Goods". Section 2A-103(1)(h).
"Insolvent". Section 1-201(23).
"Lease contract". Section 2A-103(1)(*l*).
"Lessee". Section 2A-103(1)(n).
"Lessor". Section 2A-103(1)(p).
"Party". Section 1-201(29).
"Rights". Section 1-201(36).

§ 2A-526. Lessor's Stoppage of Delivery in Transit or Otherwise.

(1) A lessor may stop delivery of goods in the possession of a carrier or other bailee if the lessor discovers the lessee to be insolvent and may stop delivery of carload, truckload, planeload, or larger shipments of express or freight if the lessee repudiates or fails to make a payment due before delivery, whether for rent, security or otherwise under the lease contract, or for any other reason the lessor has a right to withhold or take possession of the goods.

(2) In pursuing its remedies under subsection (1), the lessor may stop delivery until

(a) receipt of the goods by the lessee;

(b) acknowledgment to the lessee by any bailee of the goods, except a carrier, that the bailee holds the goods for the lessee; or

(c) such an acknowledgment to the lessee by a carrier via reshipment or as warehouseman.

(3)(a) To stop delivery, a lessor shall so notify as to enable the bailee by reasonable diligence to prevent delivery of the goods.

(b) After notification, the bailee shall hold and deliver the goods according to the directions of the lessor, but the lessor is liable to the bailee for any ensuing charges or damages.

(c) A carrier who has issued a nonnegotiable bill of lading is not obliged to obey a notification to stop received from a person other than the consignor.

Official Comment

Uniform Statutory Source: Section 2-705.

Changes: Revised to reflect leasing practices and terminology.

Definitional Cross References:

"Bill of lading". Section 1-201(6).
"Delivery". Section 1-201(14).
"Discover". Section 1-201(25).
"Goods". Section 2A-103(1)(h).
"Insolvent". Section 1-201(23).

"Lease contract". Section 2A-103(1)(*l*).
"Lessee". Section 2A-103(1)(n).
"Lessor". Section 2A-103(1)(p).
"Notifies" and "Notification". Section 1-201(26).
"Person". Section 1-201(30).
"Receipt". Section 2-103(1)(c).
"Remedy". Section 1-201(34).
"Rights". Section 1-201(36).

§ 2A-527. Lessor's Rights to Dispose of Goods.

(1) After a default by a lessee under the lease contract of the type described in Section 2A-523(1) or 2A-523(3)(a) or after the lessor refuses to deliver or takes possession of goods (Section 2A-525 or 2A-526), or, if agreed, after other default by a lessee, the lessor may dispose of the goods concerned or the undelivered balance thereof by lease, sale, or otherwise.

(2) Except as otherwise provided with respect to damages liquidated in the lease agreement (Section 2A-504) or otherwise determined pursuant to agreement of the parties (Sections 1-102(3) and 2A-503), if the disposition is by lease agreement substantially similar to the original lease agreement and the new lease agreement is made in good faith and in a commercially reasonable manner, the lessor may recover from the lessee as damages (i) accrued and unpaid rent as of the date of the commencement of the term of the new lease agreement, (ii) the present value, as of the same date, of the total rent for the then remaining lease term of the original lease agreement minus the present value, as of the same date, of the rent under the new lease agreement applicable to that period of the new lease term which is comparable to the then remaining term of the original lease agreement, and (iii) any incidental damages allowed under Section 2A-530, less expenses saved in consequence of the lessee's default.

(3) If the lessor's disposition is by lease agreement that for any reason does not qualify for treatment under subsection (2), or is by sale or otherwise, the lessor may recover from the lessee as if the lessor had elected not to dispose of the goods and Section 2A-528 governs.

(4) A subsequent buyer or lessee who buys or leases from the lessor in good faith for value as a result of a disposition under this section takes the goods free of the original lease contract and any rights of the original lessee even though the lessor fails to comply with one or more of the requirements of this Article.

(5) The lessor is not accountable to the lessee for any profit made on any disposition. A lessee who has rightfully rejected or justifiably revoked acceptance shall account to the lessor for any excess over the amount of the lessee's security interest (Section 2A-508(5)).

As amended in 1990.

See Appendix VI for material relating to changes made in text in 1990.

Official Comment

Uniform Statutory Source: Section 2-706(1), (5) and (6).

Changes: Substantially revised.

Purposes:

1. Subsection (1), a revised version of the first sentence of subsection 2-706(1),

allows the lessor the right to dispose of goods after a statutory or other material default by the lessee (even if the goods remain in the lessee's possession—Section 2A–525(2)), after the lessor refuses to deliver or takes possession of the goods, or, if agreed, after other contractual default. The lessor's decision to exercise this right is a function of a commercial judgment, not a statutory mandate replete with sanctions for failure to comply. Cf. Section 9–507. As the owner of the goods, in the case of a lessor, or as the prime lessee of the goods, in the case of a sublessor, compulsory disposition of the goods is inconsistent with the nature of the interest held by the lessor or the sublessor and is not necessary because the interest held by the lessee or the sublessee is not protected by a right of redemption under the common law or this Article. Subsection 2A–527(5).

2. The rule for determining the measure of damages recoverable by the lessor against the lessee is a function of several variables. If the lessor has elected to effect disposition under subsection (1) and such disposition is by lease that qualifies under subsection (2), the measure of damages set forth in subsection (2) will apply, absent agreement to the contrary. Sections 2A–504, 2A–103(4) and 1–102(3).

3. The lessor's damages will be established using the new lease agreement as a measure if the following three criteria are satisfied: (i) the lessor disposed of the goods by lease, (ii) the lease agreement is substantially similar to the original lease agreement, and (iii) such disposition was in good faith, and in a commercially reasonable manner. Thus, the lessor will be entitled to recover from the lessee the accrued and unpaid rent as of the date of commencement of the term of the new lease, and the present value, as of the same date, of the rent, under the original lease for the then remaining term less the present value as of the same date of the rent under the new lease agreement applicable to the period of the new lease comparable to the remaining term under the original lease, together with incidental damages less expenses saved in consequence of the lessee's default. If the lessor's disposition does not satisfy the criteria of subsection (2), the lessor may calculate its claim against the lessee pursuant to Section 2A–528. Section 2A–523(1)(e).

4. Two of the three criteria to be met by the lessor are familiar, but the concept of the new lease agreement that is substantially similar to the original lease agreement is not. Given the many variables facing a party who intends to lease goods and the rapidity of change in the market place, the policy decision was made not to draft with specificity. It was thought unwise to seek to establish certainty at the cost of fairness. The decision of whether the new lease agreement is substantially similar to the original will be determined case by case.

5. While the section does not draw a bright line, it is possible to describe some of the factors that should be considered in a finding that a new lease agreement is substantially similar to the original. The various elements of the new lease agreement should be examined. Those elements include the options to purchase or release; the lessor's representations, warranties and covenants to the lessee as well as those to be provided by the lessee to the lessor; and the services, if any, to be provided by the lessor or by the lessee. All of these factors allocate cost and risk between the lessor and the lessee and thus affect the amount of rent to be paid. These findings should not be made with scientific precision, as they are a function of economics, nor should they be made independently, as it is important that a sense of commercial judgment pervade the finding. See Section 2A–507(2). To establish the new lease as a proper measure of damage under subsection (2), these various factors, taken as a whole, must result in a finding that the new lease agreement is substantially similar to the original. If the differences between the original lease and the new lease can be easily valued, it would be appropriate for a court to find that the new lease is substantially similar to the old lease, adjust the difference in the rent between the two leases to take account of the

differences, and award damages under this section. If, for example, the new lease requires the lessor to insure the goods in the hands of the lessee, while the original lease required the lessee to insure, the usual cost of such insurance could be deducted from rent due under the new lease before the difference in rental between the two leases is determined.

6. The following hypothetical illustrates the difficulty of providing a bright line. Assume that A buys a jumbo tractor for $1 million and then leases the tractor to B for a term of 36 months. The tractor is delivered to and is accepted by B on May 1. On June 1 B fails to pay the monthly rent to A. B returns the tractor to A, who immediately releases the tractor to C for a term identical to the term remaining under the lease between A and B. All terms and conditions under the lease between A and C are identical to those under the original lease between A and B, except that C does not provide any property damage or other insurance coverage, and B agreed to provide complete coverage. Coverage is expensive and difficult to obtain. It is a question of fact whether it is so difficult to adjust the recovery to take account of the difference between the two leases as to insurance that the second lease is not substantially similar to the original.

7. A new lease can be substantially similar to the original lease even though its term extends beyond the remaining term of the original lease, so long as both (a) the lease terms are commercially comparable (e.g., it is highly unlikely that a one-month rental and a five-year lease would reflect similar realities), and (b) the court can fairly apportion a part of the rental payments under the new lease to that part of the term of the new lease which is comparable to the remaining lease term under the original lease. Also, the lease term of the new lease may be comparable to the remaining term of the original lease even though the beginning and ending dates of the two leases are not the same. For example, a two-month lease of agricultural equipment for the months of August and September may be comparable to a two-month lease running from the 15th of August to the 15th of October if in the particular location two-month leases beginning on August 15th are basically interchangeable with two-month leases beginning August 1st. Similarly, the term of a one-year truck lease beginning on the 15th of January may be comparable to the term of a one-year truck lease beginning January 2d. If the lease terms are found to be comparable, the court may base cover damages on the entire difference between the costs under the two leases.

8. Subsection (3), which is new, provides that if the lessor's disposition is by lease that does not qualify under subsection (2), or is by sale or otherwise, Section 2A–528 governs.

9. Subsection (4), a revised version of subsection 2–706(5), applies to protect a subsequent buyer or lessee who buys or leases from the lessor in good faith and for value, pursuant to a disposition under this section. Note that by its terms, the rule in subsection 2A–304(1), which provides that the subsequent lessee takes subject to the original lease contract, is controlled by the rule stated in this subsection.

10. Subsection (5), a revised version of subsection 2–706(6), provides that the lessor is not accountable to the lessee for any profit made by the lessor on a disposition. This rule follows from the fundamental premise of the bailment for hire that the lessee under a lease of goods has no equity of redemption to protect.

Cross References:

Sections 1–102(3), 2–706(1), 2–706(5), 2–706(6), 2A–103(4), 2A–304(1), 2A–504, 2A–507(2), 2A–523(1)(e), 2A–525(2), 2A–527(5), 2A–528 and 9–507.

Definitional Cross References:

"Buyer" and "Buying". Section 2–103(1)(a).

"Delivery". Section 1–201(14).

"Good faith". Sections 1–201(19) and 2–103(1)(b).

"Goods". Section 2A-103(1)(h).
"Lease". Section 2A-103(1)(j).
"Lease contract". Section 2A-103(1)(*l*).
"Lessee". Section 2A-103(1)(n).
"Lessor". Section 2A-103(1)(p).
"Present value". Section 2A-103(1)(u).
"Rights". Section 1-201(36).
"Sale". Section 2-106(1).
"Security interest". Section 1-201(37).
"Value". Section 1-201(44).

§ 2A-528. Lessor's Damages for Non-acceptance, Failure to Pay, Repudiation, or Other Default.

(1) Except as otherwise provided with respect to damages liquidated in the lease agreement (Section 2A-504) or otherwise determined pursuant to agreement of the parties (Sections 1-102(3) and 2A-503), if a lessor elects to retain the goods or a lessor elects to dispose of the goods and the disposition is by lease agreement that for any reason does not qualify for treatment under Section 2A-527(2), or is by sale or otherwise, the lessor may recover from the lessee as damages for a default of the type described in Section 2A-523(1) or 2A-523(3)(a), or, if agreed, for other default of the lessee, (i) accrued and unpaid rent as of the date of default if the lessee has never taken possession of the goods, or, if the lessee has taken possession of the goods, as of the date the lessor repossesses the goods or an earlier date on which the lessee makes a tender of the goods to the lessor, (ii) the present value as of the date determined under clause (i) of the total rent for the then remaining lease term of the original lease agreement minus the present value as of the same date of the market rent at the place where the goods are located computed for the same lease term, and (iii) any incidental damages allowed under Section 2A-530, less expenses saved in consequence of the lessee's default.

(2) If the measure of damages provided in subsection (1) is inadequate to put a lessor in as good a position as performance would have, the measure of damages is the present value of the profit, including reasonable overhead, the lessor would have made from full performance by the lessee, together with any incidental damages allowed under Section 2A-530, due allowance for costs reasonably incurred and due credit for payments or proceeds of disposition.

As amended in 1990.

See Appendix VI for material relating to changes made in text in 1990.

Official Comment

Uniform Statutory Source: Section 2-708.

Changes: Substantially revised.

Purposes:

1. Subsection (1), a substantially revised version of Section 2-708(1), states the basic rule governing the measure of lessor's damages for a default described in Section 2A-523(1) or (3)(a), and, if agreed, for a contractual default. This measure will apply if the lessor elects to retain the goods (whether undelivered, returned by the lessee, or repossessed by the lessor after acceptance and default by the lessee) or if the lessor's disposition does not qualify under subsection 2A-527(2). Section 2A-527(3). Note that under some of these conditions, the lessor may recover damages from the lessee pursuant to the rule set forth in Section 2A-529. There is no sanction for disposition that does not qualify under subsection

2A-527(2). Application of the rule set forth in this section is subject to agreement to the contrary. Sections 2A-504, 2A-103(4) and 1-102(3).

2. If the lessee has never taken possession of the goods, the measure of damage is the accrued and unpaid rent as of the date of default together with the present value, as of the date of default, of the original rent for the remaining term of the lease less the present value as of the same date of market rent, and incidental damages, less expenses saved in consequence of the default. Note that the reference in Section 2A-528(1)(i) and (ii) is to the date of default not to the date of an event of default. An event of default under a lease agreement becomes a default under a lease agreement only after the expiration of any relevant period of grace and compliance with any notice requirements under this Article and the lease agreement. American Bar Foundation, *Commentaries on Indentures,* § 5-1, at 216-217 (1971). Section 2A-501(1). This conclusion is also a function of whether, as a matter of fact or law, the event of default has been waived, suspended or cured. Sections 2A-103(4) and 1-103. If the lessee has taken possession of the goods, the measure of damages is the accrued and unpaid rent as of the earlier of the time the lessor repossesses the goods or the time the lessee tenders the goods to the lessor plus the difference between the present value, as of the same time, of the rent under the lease for the remaining lease term and the present value, as of the same time, of the market rent.

3. Market rent will be computed pursuant to Section 2A-507.

4. Subsection (2), a somewhat revised version of the provisions of subsection 2-708(2), states a measure of damages which applies if the measure of damages in subsection (1) is inadequate to put the lessor in as good a position as performance would have. The measure of damage is the lessor's profit, including overhead, together with incidental damages, with allowance for costs reasonably incurred and credit for payments or proceeds of disposition. In determining the amount of due credit with respect to proceeds of disposition a proper value should be attributed to the lessor's residual interest in the goods. Sections 2A-103(1)(q) and 2A-507(4).

5. In calculating profit, a court should include any expected appreciation of the goods, *e.g.* the foal of a leased brood mare. Because this subsection is intended to give the lessor the benefit of the bargain, a court should consider any reasonable benefit or profit expected by the lessor from the performance of the lease agreement. *See Honeywell, Inc. v. Lithonia Lighting, Inc.*, 317 F.Supp. 406, 413 (N.D.Ga.1970); *Locks v. Wade*, 36 N.J.Super. 128, 131, 114 A.2d 875, 877 (Super.Ct.App.Div.1955). Further, in calculating profit the concept of present value must be given effect. *Taylor v. Commercial Credit Equip. Corp.*, 170 Ga.App. 322, 316 S.E.2d 788 (Ct.App.1984). *See generally* Section 2A-103(1)(u).

Cross References:

Sections 1-102(3), 2-708, 2A-103(1)(u), 2A-402, 2A-504, 2A-507, 2A-527(2) and 2A-529.

Definitional Cross References:

"Agreement". Section 1-201(3).
"Goods". Section 2A-103(1)(h).
"Lease". Section 2A-103(1)(j).
"Lease agreement". Section 2A-103(1)(k).
"Lessee". Section 2A-103(1)(n).
"Lessor". Section 2A-103(1)(p).
"Party". Section 1-201(29).
"Present value". Section 2A-103(1)(u).
"Sale". Section 2-106(1).

§ 2A-529. Lessor's Action for the Rent.

(1) After default by the lessee under the lease contract of the type described in Section 2A-523(1) or 2A-523(3)(a) or, if agreed, after other default by the lessee, if the lessor complies with subsection (2), the lessor may recover from the lessee as damages:

(a) for goods accepted by the lessee and not repossessed by or tendered to the lessor, and for conforming goods lost or damaged within a commercially reasonable time after risk of loss passes to the lessee (Section 2A–219), (i) accrued and unpaid rent as of the date of entry of judgment in favor of the lessor, (ii) the present value as of the same date of the rent for the then remaining lease term of the lease agreement, and (iii) any incidental damages allowed under Section 2A–530, less expenses saved in consequence of the lessee's default; and

(b) for goods identified to the lease contract if the lessor is unable after reasonable effort to dispose of them at a reasonable price or the circumstances reasonably indicate that effort will be unavailing, (i) accrued and unpaid rent as of the date of entry of judgment in favor of the lessor, (ii) the present value as of the same date of the rent for the then remaining lease term of the lease agreement, and (iii) any incidental damages allowed under Section 2A–530, less expenses saved in consequence of the lessee's default.

(2) Except as provided in subsection (3), the lessor shall hold for the lessee for the remaining lease term of the lease agreement any goods that have been identified to the lease contract and are in the lessor's control.

(3) The lessor may dispose of the goods at any time before collection of the judgment for damages obtained pursuant to subsection (1). If the disposition is before the end of the remaining lease term of the lease agreement, the lessor's recovery against the lessee for damages is governed by Section 2A–527 or Section 2A–528, and the lessor will cause an appropriate credit to be provided against a judgment for damages to the extent that the amount of the judgment exceeds the recovery available pursuant to Section 2A–527 or 2A–528.

(4) Payment of the judgment for damages obtained pursuant to subsection (1) entitles the lessee to the use and possession of the goods not then disposed of for the remaining lease term of and in accordance with the lease agreement.

(5) After default by the lessee under the lease contract of the type described in Section 2A–523(1) or Section 2A–523(3)(a) or, if agreed, after other default by the lessee, a lessor who is held not entitled to rent under this section must nevertheless be awarded damages for non-acceptance under Section 2A–527 or Section 2A–528.

As amended in 1990.

See Appendix VI for material relating to changes made in text in 1990.

Official Comment

Uniform Statutory Source: Section 2–709.

Changes: Substantially revised.

Purposes:

1. Absent a lease contract provision to the contrary, an action for the full unpaid rent (discounted to present value as of

the time of entry of judgment as to rent due after that time) is available as to goods not lost or damaged only if the lessee retains possession of the goods or the lessor is or apparently will be unable to dispose of them at a reasonable price after reasonable effort. There is no general right in a lessor to recover the full rent from the lessee upon holding the goods for the lessee. If the lessee tenders goods back to the lessor, and the lessor refuses to accept the tender, the lessor will be limited to the damages it would have suffered had it taken back the goods. The rule in Article 2 that the seller can recover the price of accepted goods is rejected here. In a lease, the lessor always has a residual interest in the goods which the lessor usually realizes upon at the end of a lease term by either sale or a new lease. Therefore, it is not a substantial imposition on the lessor to require it to take back and dispose of the goods if the lessee chooses to tender them back before the end of the lease term: the lessor will merely do earlier what it would have done anyway, sell or relet the goods. Further, the lessee will frequently encounter substantial difficulties if the lessee attempts to sublet the goods for the remainder of the lease term. In contrast to the buyer who owns the entire interest in goods and can easily dispose of them, the lessee is selling only the right to use the goods under the terms of the lease and the sublessee must assume a relationship with the lessor. In that situation, it is usually more efficient to eliminate the original lessee as a middleman by allowing the lessee to return the goods to the lessor who can then redispose of them.

2. In some situations even where possession of the goods is reacquired, a lessor will be able to recover as damages the present value of the full rent due, not under this section, but under 2A-528(2) which allows a lost profit recovery if necessary to put the lessor in the position it would have been in had the lessee performed. Following is an example of such a case. A is a lessor of construction equipment and maintains a substantial inventory. B leases from A a backhoe for a period of two weeks at a rental of $1,000. After three days, B returns the backhoe and refuses to pay the rent. A has five backhoes in inventory, including the one returned by B. During the next 11 days after the return by B of the backhoe, A rents no more than three backhoes at any one time and, therefore, always has two on hand. If B had kept the backhoe for the full rental period, A would have earned the full rental on that backhoe, plus the rental on the other backhoes it actually did rent during that period. Getting this backhoe back before the end of the lease term did not enable A to make any leases it would not otherwise have made. The only way to put A in the position it would have been in had the lessee fully performed is to give the lessor the full rentals. A realized no savings at all because the backhoe was returned early and might even have incurred additional expense if it was paying for parking space for equipment in inventory. A has no obligation to relet the backhoe for the benefit of B rather than leasing that backhoe or any other in inventory for its own benefit. Further, it is probably not reasonable to expect A to dispose of the backhoe by sale when it is returned in an effort to reduce damages suffered by B. Ordinarily, the loss of a two-week rental would not require A to reduce the size of its backhoe inventory. Whether A would similarly be entitled to full rentals as lost profit in a one-year lease of a backhoe is a question of fact: in any event the lessor, subject to mitigation of damages rules, is entitled to be put in as good a position as it would have been had the lessee fully performed the lease contract.

3. Under subsection (2) a lessor who is able and elects to sue for the rent due under a lease must hold goods not lost or damaged for the lessee. Subsection (3) creates an exception to the subsection (2) requirement. If the lessor disposes of those goods prior to collection of the judgment (whether as a matter of law or agreement), the lessor's recovery is governed by the measure of damages in Section 2A-527 if the disposition is by lease that is substantially similar to the original lease, or otherwise by the measure of

damages in Section 2A–528. Section 2A–523 official comment.

4. Subsection (4), which is new, further reinforces the requisites of Subsection (2). In the event the judgment for damages obtained by the lessor against the lessee pursuant to subsection (1) is satisfied, the lessee regains the right to use and possession of the remaining goods for the balance of the original lease term; a partial satisfaction of the judgment creates no right in the lessee to use and possession of the goods.

5. The relationship between subsections (2) and (4) is important to understand. Subsection (2) requires the lessor to hold for the lessee identified goods in the lessor's possession. Absent agreement to the contrary, whether in the lease or otherwise, under most circumstances the requirement that the lessor hold the goods for the lessee for the term will mean that the lessor is not allowed to use them. Sections 2A–103(4) and 1–203. Further, the lessor's use of the goods could be viewed as a disposition of the goods that would bar the lessor from recovery under this section, remitting the lessor to the two preceding sections for a determination of the lessor's claim for damages against the lessee.

6. Subsection (5), the analogue of subsection 2–709(3), further reinforces the thrust of subsection (3) by stating that a lessor who is held not entitled to rent under this section has not elected a remedy; the lessor must be awarded damages under Sections 2A–527 and 2A–528. This is a function of two significant policies of this Article—that resort to a remedy is optional, unless expressly agreed to be exclusive (Section 2A–503(2)) and that rights and remedies provided in this Article generally are cumulative. (Section 2A–501(2) and (4)).

Cross References:

Sections 1–203, 2–709, 2–709(3), 2A–103(4), 2A–501(2), 2A–501(4), 2A–503(2), 2A–504, 2A–523(1)(e), 2A–525(2), 2A–527, 2A–528 and 2A–529(2).

Definitional Cross References:

"Action". Section 1–201(1).
"Conforming". Section 2A–103(1)(d).
"Goods". Section 2A–103(1)(h).
"Lease". Section 2A–103(1)(j).
"Lease agreement". Section 2A–103(1)(k).
"Lease contract". Section 2A–103(1)(*l*).
"Lessee". Section 2A–103(1)(n).
"Lessor". Section 2A–103(1)(p).
"Present value". Section 2A–103(1)(u).
"Reasonable time". Section 1–204(1) and (2).

§ 2A–530. Lessor's Incidental Damages.

Incidental damages to an aggrieved lessor include any commercially reasonable charges, expenses, or commissions incurred in stopping delivery, in the transportation, care and custody of goods after the lessee's default, in connection with return or disposition of the goods, or otherwise resulting from the default.

Official Comment

Uniform Statutory Source: Section 2–710.

Changes: Revised to reflect leasing practices and terminology.

Definitional Cross References:

"Aggrieved party". Section 1–201(2).
"Delivery". Section 1–201(14).
"Goods". Section 2A–103(1)(h).
"Lessee". Section 2A–103(1)(n).
"Lessor". Section 2A–103(1)(p).

§ 2A–531. Standing to Sue Third Parties for Injury to Goods.

(1) If a third party so deals with goods that have been identified to a lease contract as to cause actionable injury to a party to the lease contract (a) the lessor has a right of action against the third party, and (b) the lessee also has a right of action against the third party if the lessee:

(i) has a security interest in the goods;

(ii) has an insurable interest in the goods; or

(iii) bears the risk of loss under the lease contract or has since the injury assumed that risk as against the lessor and the goods have been converted or destroyed.

(2) If at the time of the injury the party plaintiff did not bear the risk of loss as against the other party to the lease contract and there is no arrangement between them for disposition of the recovery, his [or her] suit or settlement, subject to his [or her] own interest, is as a fiduciary for the other party to the lease contract.

(3) Either party with the consent of the other may sue for the benefit of whom it may concern.

Official Comment

Uniform Statutory Source: Section 2–722.

Changes: Revised to reflect leasing practices and terminology.

Definitional Cross References:

"Action". Section 1–201(1).

"Goods". Section 2A–103(1)(h).

"Lease contract". Section 2A–103(1)(*l*).

"Lessee". Section 2A–103(1)(n).

"Lessor". Section 2A–103(1)(p).

"Party". Section 1–201(29).

"Rights". Section 1–201(36).

"Security interest". Section 1–201(37).

§ 2A–532. Lessor's Rights to Residual Interest.

In addition to any other recovery permitted by this Article or other law, the lessor may recover from the lessee an amount that will fully compensate the lessor for any loss of or damage to the lessor's residual interest in the goods caused by the default of the lessee.

As added in 1990.

See Appendix VI for material relating to adoption of section in 1990.

Official Comment

Uniform Statutory Source: None.

Purposes: This section recognizes the right of the lessor to recover under this Article (as well as under other law) from the lessee for failure to comply with the lease obligations as to the condition of leased goods when returned to the lessor, for failure to return the goods at the end of the lease, or for any other default which causes loss or injury to the lessor's residual interest in the goods.

ARTICLE 1 AND ARTICLE 9: CONFORMING AMENDMENTS

See Appendix III for text and official comments.

[REVISED] ARTICLE 3

NEGOTIABLE INSTRUMENTS

[For the Text and Official Comments of Article 3 as they existed prior to revision in 1990, see Appendix VII, infra. For the 1990 amendments to Article 1 and Article 4 conforming to Revised Article 3, see Appendices VIII and IX, respectively, infra. See new Section 3–312, adopted in August, 1991.]

PART 1. GENERAL PROVISIONS AND DEFINITIONS

PART 2. NEGOTIATION, TRANSFER, AND INDORSEMENT

PART 3. ENFORCEMENT OF INSTRUMENTS

National Conference of Commissioners on Uniform State Laws

REPORTERS

Robert L. Jordan, Los Angeles, California

William D. Warren, Los Angeles, California

DRAFTING COMMITTEE

CO-CHAIRMEN

Robert Haydock, Jr., Boston, Massachusetts

Carlyle C. Ring, Jr., Alexandria, Virginia

MEMBERS

Boris Auerbach, Cincinnati, Ohio

William M. Burke, Los Angeles, California

William E. Hogan, New York, New York

Charles W. Joiner, Ann Arbor, Michigan

Frederick H. Miller, Norman, Oklahoma

Donald J. Rapson, Livingston, New Jersey, *The American Law Institute Representative*

Lawrence J. Bugge, Madison, Wisconsin, *President (Member Ex Officio)*

Neal Ossen, Hartford, Connecticut, *Chairman, Division C (Member Ex Officio)*

REVIEW COMMITTEE

CHAIRMAN

Frank F. Jestrab, Chevy Chase, Maryland

MEMBERS

Rupert R. Bullivant, Portland, Oregon

Michael Franck, Lansing, Michigan

CONSULTANT

Fairfax Leary, Jr., Villanova, Pennsylvania

ADVISORS

Thomas C. Baxter, Jr., *Federal Reserve Bank of New York*

Roland E. Brandel, *American Bar Association*

Leon P. Ciferni, *National Westminster Bank USA*

William B. Davenport, *American Bar Association, Section of Business Law, Ad Hoc Committee on Payment Systems*

Carl Felsenfeld, *Association of the Bar of the City of New York*

Thomas J. Greco, *American Bankers Association*

Oliver I. Ireland, *Board of Governors of Federal Reserve System*

John R.H. Kimball, *Federal Reserve Bank of Boston*

John F. Lee, *New York Clearing House Association*

Norman R. Nelson, *New York Clearing House Association*

Ernest T. Patrikis, *Federal Reserve Bank of New York*

Anne B. Pope, *National Corporate Cash Management Association*

Paul S. Turner, *Occidental Petroleum Corporation* and *National Corporate Cash Management Association*

Stanley M. Walker, *Exxon Company, U.S.A.* and *National Corporate Cash Management Association*

ADDITIONAL PARTICIPANTS

Henry N. Dyhouse, *U.S. Central Credit Union*

Robert Egan, *Chemical Bank*

Paul T. Even, *National Gypsum Company*

James Foorman, *First Chicago Corporation*

J. Kevin French, *Exxon Company, U.S.A.*

Richard M. Gottlieb, *Manufacturers Hanover Trust Company*

Douglas E. Harris, *Morgan Guaranty Trust Company of New York*

Arthur L. Herold, *National Corporate Cash Management Association*

Shirley Holder, *Atlantic Richfield Company*

Paul E. Homrighausen, *Bankers Clearing House Association* and *National Automated Clearing House Association*

Gail M. Inaba, *Morgan Guaranty Trust Company of New York*

Richard P. Kessler, Jr., *Credit Union National Association*

James W. Kopp, *Shell Oil Company*

Donald R. Lawrence, *Citibank N.A.*

Robert M. MacAllister, *Chase Manhattan Bank NA*

Thomas E. Montgomery, *California Bankers Association*

W. Robert Moore, *American Bankers Association*

Samuel Newman, *Manufacturers Hanover Trust Company*

Nena Nodge, *National Corporate Cash Management Association*

Robert J. Pisapia, *Occidental Petroleum Corporation*

Deborah S. Prutzman, *Arnold & Porter*

James S. Rogers, Professor of Law, Newton, Massachusetts

Robert M. Rosenblith, *Manufacturers Hanover Trust Company*

Jamileh Soufan, *American General Corporation*

Irma Villarreal, *Aon Corporation*

PREFATORY NOTE

Revised Article 3 (with miscellaneous and conforming amendments to Articles 1 and 4) is a companion undertaking to Article 4A on funds transfers. Both efforts were undertaken for the purpose of accommodating modern technologies and practices in payment systems and with respect to negotiable instruments. Both efforts were drafted by the same committee over essentially the same period of time. The work on Article 4A was accorded priority and completed in 1989, and revised Article 3 was completed in 1990.

Revised Article 3 may, not inappropriately, be regarded as the latest effort in the progressive codification of the common law of negotiable instruments that began with the English Bills of Exchange Act enacted by Parliament in 1882. The Uniform Negotiable Instruments Law was promulgated by the Conference in 1896, and it in turn was reorganized and modernized by original Article 3—Commercial Paper as part of the Uniform Commercial Code jointly promulgated in 1952 by the Conference and the American Law Institute. Revised Article 3 in 1990 modernizes, reorganizes and clarifies the law.

Purpose of Drafting Effort

The original Articles 3 and 4 and their predecessors were based upon a paper payment system. Literally, there has been an explosion in the volume of paper to process since Articles 3 and 4 were first promulgated. In the early '50s, around 7 billion checks were processed annually. Correctly anticipating an increase in check volume as the result of a retail approach taken by bankers at that time, the American Bankers Association in 1954 placed a team on a research and development project to identify the most efficient method of processing checks mechanically. The eminently successful MICR line technology was the result. Upon its implementation, checks were processed at high rates of speed. In major part as a result of this technology, a seven-fold explosion in check volume has occurred between the '50s and 1988. In 1988, the Federal Reserve estimated check volume at 48 billion written annually. In 1987, Congress enacted the Expedited Funds Availability Act, and the Federal Reserve Board implemented it in 1988 with Regulation CC. Regulation CC covers many aspects of the forward check collection process and all aspects of the return process.

Present Articles 3 and 4, written for a paper-based system, do not adequately address the issues of responsibility and liability as they relate to modern technologies now employed and the procedures required by the current volume of checks and by the "Expedited Funds Availability Act" and Regulation CC. While agreements among parties to particular transactions have provided some relief, such stop-gap measures are no longer adequate.

In addition, practices have developed which are not easily accommodated within existing Article 3. For example, variable rate notes were unknown when Article 3 first was promulgated; they are common today. Questions about the "cash equivalency" of cashier's checks and money orders have arisen as banks have sought to raise defenses to the payment of these instruments.

The revision of Article 3 and Article 4 to update, improve and maintain the viability of it is necessary to accommodate these changing practices and modern technologies, the needs of a rapidly expanding national and international economy, the requirement for more rapid funds availability, and the need for more clarity and certainty. Absent such an update, further Federal preemption of state law may likely occur.

Uniformity is Essential

Traditionally, the legal structures for payments have been regulated by state law through the Uniform Commercial Code. In recent years, however, the Federal government has established regulations for credit and debit cards, and for the availability of funds in a way that regulates much of the check collection process.

With respect to wholesale funds transfers, on an average day two trillion dollars is transferred. Article 4A of the UCC promulgated in 1989 provides the governing comprehensive rules. In 1990, 12 states enacted Article 4A including California, New York and Illinois. In 1991, Article 4A has been introduced in the legislatures of most of the other states, and it is anticipated that most, if not all, will enact Article 4A uniformly. Within a short time, perhaps by 1992, the law of wholesale funds transfers should be uniform throughout the 50 states.

The law for payments through checks and which governs other negotiable instruments similarly should be uniform and up-to-date, either through state enactments or Federal preemption. Otherwise, checks as a viable payment system in international and national transactions will be severely hampered and the utility of other negotiable instruments impaired.

Process of Achieving Uniformity

The essence of uniform law revision is to obtain a sufficient consensus and balance among the interests of the various participants so that universal and uniform adoption by the legislatures of all 50 states may be achieved. As is the practice of the Conference, announcement of the drafting undertaking for Articles 3, 4 and 4A was widely circulated in 1985. Anyone who so requested, received notice of all meetings and was invited to attend. Upon request, names were put on a mailing list to receive copies of drafts as they progressed. In addition, the American Bar Association Ad Hoc Committee on Payments Systems closely followed the work of the Conference and widely circulated the drafts.

The Drafting Committee had 3 or 4 meetings each year and, by August 1990, had held 20 meetings. The drafting meetings began on Friday morning and ended on Sunday at noon. All the meetings were well attended, and the average attendance was 50 or more. The discussion of the drafts was open for comment by all those who attended. In addition, the reporters received a substantial amount of comment and suggestions by written and other communications between meetings of the drafting committee. The work product was read line for line at the annual meetings of the Conference three different years. In addition, the American Law Institute circulated the drafts two or three times to its entire membership. The ALI consultative group also held a meeting to comment and make suggestions on the draft. In addition, progress reports were published annually in *The Business Lawyer* from 1985 through 1990.

The consensus, balance and quality achieved in this lengthy deliberative process is a product not only of the fine work of the reporters and the drafting committee, but also the faithful and energetic participation of the advisors and participants in the drafting meetings. The advisors representing a variety of interests were:

Thomas C. Baxter, Jr., Federal Reserve Bank of New York

Roland E. Brandel, American Bar Association

Leon P. Ciferni, National Westminster Bank USA

William B. Davenport, American Bar Association, Section of Business Law, Ad Hoc Committee on Payment Systems

Carl Felsenfeld, Association of the Bar of the City of New York

Thomas J. Greco, American Bankers Association

Oliver I. Ireland, Board of Governors of Federal Reserve System

John R. H. Kimball, Federal Reserve Bank of Boston

John F. Lee, New York Clearing House Association

Norman R. Nelson, New York Clearing House Association

Ernest T. Patrikis, Federal Reserve Bank of New York

Anne B. Pope, National Corporate Cash Management Association

Paul S. Turner, Occidental Petroleum Corporation and National Corporate Cash Management Association

Stanley M. Walker, Exxon Company, U.S.A. and National Corporate Cash Management Association

Other participants who regularly attended drafting meetings were:

Henry N. Dyhouse, U.S. Central Credit Union

Robert Egan, Chemical Bank

Paul T. Even, National Gypsum Corporation

James Foorman, First Chicago Corporation

J. Kevin French, Exxon Company, U.S.A.

Richard M. Gottlieb, Manufacturers Hanover Trust Company

Douglas E. Harris, National Corporate Cash Management Association

Arthur L. Herold, National Corporate Cash Management Association

Shirley Holder, Atlantic Richfield Company

Paul E. Homrighausen, Bankers Clearing House Association

Gail M. Inaba, Morgan Guaranty Trust Company of New York

Richard P. Kessler, Jr., Credit Union National Association

James W. Kopp, Shell Oil Company

Donald R. Lawrence, Citibank, N.A.

Robert M. McAllister, Chase Manhattan Bank, N.A.

Thomas E. Montgomery, California Bankers Association

W. Robert Moore, American Bankers Association

Samuel Newman, Manufacturers Hanover Trust Company

Nena Nodge, National Corporate Cash Management Association

Robert J. Pisapia, Occidental Petroleum Corporation

Deborah S. Prutzman, Arnold & Porter

James S. Rogers, Professor of Law, Newton, Massachusetts

Robert M. Rosenblith, Manufacturers Hanover Trust Company
Jamileh Soufan, American General Corporation
Irma Villarreal, Aon Corporation

Balance Achieved

The consensus reflected in Revised Article 3 and in the conforming amendments to Articles 1 and 4 is supported by the participants from the banking community, the users, and the Federal regulators because it reflects a balance that each interest can reasonably embrace. Some of the benefits of the Revision include:

A. Benefits in the Public Interest

Certainty—Revised Articles 3 and 4 remove numerous uncertainties that exist in the current provisions and thus reduce risk to the payment system and allow appropriate planning by its users and operators.

Speed and Reliability—The Revision removes impediments to the use of automation, and better conforms to Regulation CC to expedite the availability of funds to customers and to reduce risks to banks.

Lower Costs—The Revision by providing for modern technologies, lowers costs to banks and thus to their customers.

Reduced Litigation—By clarification of troublesome issues, and by the provisions of Sections 3–404 through 3–406 which reform rules for allocation of loss from forgeries and alterations, the Revision should significantly reduce litigation.

B. Benefits to Users

"Good Faith"—The definition of good faith under Sections 3–103(a)(4) and 4–104(c) is expanded to include observance of reasonable commercial standards of fair dealing. This objective standard for good faith applies to the performance of all duties and obligations established under Articles 3 and 4.

Fiduciary Provisions—Section 3–307 protects drawers and persons owed a fiduciary responsibility by imposing stricter standards for obtaining holder in due course rights by a person dealing with the defaulting agent or fiduciary. It also spells out the circumstances under which a person receiving funds has notice of a breach of fiduciary duty, and resulting liability.

Accord and Satisfaction—Under Section 3–311 payees can avoid the unintentional accord and satisfaction by returning the funds or by giving a notice that requires checks to be sent to a particular office where such proposals can be handled. On the other hand, the drawer of a full settlement check is protected from the instrument being indorsed with protest and thus losing the money and being liable on the balance of the claim.

Cashier's Checks—Section 3–411 and related provisions considerably improve the acceptability of bank obligations like cashier's checks as cash equivalents by providing disincentives to wrongful dishonor, such as the possible recovery of consequential damages.

Indorser Liability—Section 3–415 gives more time to hold a check before the user loses indorser liability.

Reporting Forgeries—Section 4–406 increases the outside time a customer has to report forged checks or alterations to thirty days. It also requires a bank truncating checks to retain the item or the capacity to furnish legible copies for seven years.

Individual Agent and Corporate Liability—Section 3–402, as to corporate instruments signed by agents without adequate indication and representation, (except as against a holder in due course), allows a representative to show the parties did not intend individual liability. It affords full protection to the agent that signs a corporate check, even though the check does not show representative status. Also, Section 3–403(b) makes it clear that a signature of an organization is considered unauthorized if more than one signature is required and it is missing.

Direct Suits—Section 3–420 allows a person whose indorsement is forged to sue the depositary bank directly, rather than each drawee of the checks involved.

C. Benefits to the Banking Community

Certainty—Section 3–104 and related provisions clarify what types of contracts are within Article 3 and how they are to be treated, thus promoting certainty of legal rules and reducing litigation costs and risks. Checks that may omit "words of negotiability" are included as fully negotiable; confusion over travelers checks is eliminated; variable rate instruments are included; and there is clarification of the impact of the FTC "Holder" Rule, clarification of the ability of parties to an instrument that is not included in Article 3 to contract for the application of its rules to their contract; and clarification of ordinary money orders as checks rather than bank obligations.

"Ordinary Care"—In Sections 3–103(a)(7) and 4–104(c), ordinary care is defined, making clear that financial institutions taking checks for processing or for payment by automated means need not manually handle each instrument if that is consistent with the institution's procedures and the procedures used do not vary unreasonably from the general usage of banks. This clarification is designed to accommodate and facilitate efficiency, thus lowering costs and lowering expedited funds availability risks. The definition of ordinary care relates to those specific instances in the Code where the standard of ordinary care is set forth.

Statute of Limitations—Sections 3–118 and 4–111 include statutory periods of limitations which will make the law uniform rather than leaving the topic to widely varying state laws.

Employee Fraud—Section 3–405 expands a per se negligence rule to the case of an indorsement forged by an employee whose duties involve handling checks. It also covers that of a faithless employee who supplies a name and then forges the indorsement, but does not require a precise match between the name of the payee and the indorsement.

Bank Definition—The definition of bank is expanded for the purposes of Articles 3 and 4 to clearly include savings and loans and credit unions so that their checks are directly governed by the Code. Section 4–104 clarifies that checks drawn on credit lines are subject to the rules for checks drawn on deposit accounts.

Truncation—Section 4–110 authorizes electronic presentment of items and related provisions remove impediments to truncation. Truncation will reduce risks from mandated funds availability and improve the check collection process. Section 4–406 allows an institution the benefit of its provisions even though it does not return the checks due to truncation. If both the customer and the institution fail to use ordinary care, a comparative negligence standard is used rather than placing the full loss on the institution.

Table of Disposition of Sections in Former Article 3

The reference to a section in Revised Article 3 is to the section that refers to the issue addressed by the section in Former Article 3. If there is no comparable section in Revised Article 3 to a section in Former Article 3, that fact is indicated by the word "Omitted."

Former Article 3 Section	Revised Article 3 or 4 Section
3–101	3–101
3–102(1)(a)	3–105(a)
3–102(1)(b)	3–103(a)(6)
3–102(1)(c)	3–103(a)(9)
3–102(1)(d)	Omitted. See Comment 2 to 3–414.
3–102(1)(e)	3–104(b)
3–102(2)	3–103(b)
3–102(3)	3–103(c)
3–102(4)	3–103(d)
3–103(1)	3–102(a)
3–103(2)	3–102(b)
3–104(1)	3–104(a)
3–104(2)(a)	3–104(e)
3–104(2)(b)	3–104(f)
3–104(2)(c)	3–104(j)
3–104(2)(d)	3–104(e)
3–104(3)	Omitted.
3–105(1)(a)	3–106(a)
3–105(1)(b)	Omitted. See Comment 1 to 3–106.
3–105(1)(c)	Omitted. See Comment 1 to 3–106.
3–105(1)(d)	Omitted. See Comment 1 to 3–106.
3–105(1)(e)	Omitted. See Comment 1 to 3–106.
3–105(1)(f)	3–106(b)(ii)
3–105(1)(g)	3–106(b)(ii)
3–105(1)(h)	3–106(b)(ii)
3–105(2)(a)	3–106(a)(ii)
3–105(2)(b)	3–106(b)(ii)
3–106(1)	3–104(a)
3–106(2)	Omitted.
3–107(1)	Omitted. See Comment to 3–107.
3–107(2)	3–107
3–108	3–108(a)
3–109(1)	3–108(b)
3–109(2)	Omitted.
3–110(1)	3–109(b)
3–110(1)(a)	Omitted.
3–110(1)(b)	Omitted.
3–110(1)(c)	Omitted.
3–110(1)(d)	3–110(d)
3–110(1)(e)	3–110(c)(2)(i)
3–110(1)(f)	3–110(c)(2)(iv)
3–110(1)(g)	Omitted.
3–110(2)	Omitted.
3–110(3)	3–109(b)
3–111(a)	3–109(a)(1)
3–111(b)	3–109(a)(1)
3–111(c)	3–109(a)(3) and 3–205(b)

Former Article 3 Section	Revised Article 3 or 4 Section
3–112(1)(a)	Omitted.
3–112(1)(b)	3–104(a)(3)(i)
3–112(1)(c)	3–104(a)(3)(i)
3–112(1)(d)	3–104(a)(3)(ii)
3–112(1)(e)	3–104(a)(3)(iii)
3–112(1)(f)	3–311
3–112(1)(g)	Omitted.
3–112(2)	Omitted.
3–113	Omitted.
3–114(1)	Omitted. See Comment to 3–113.
3–114(2)	3–113(a)
3–114(3)	Omitted. See Comment to 3–113.
3–115	3–115
3–116(a)	3–110(d)
3–116(b)	3–110(d)
3–117(a)	3–110(c)(2)(ii)
3–117(b)	3–110(c)(2)(i)
3–117(c)	Omitted.
3–118(a)	3–104(e) and 3–103(a)(6)
3–118(b)	3–114
3–118(c)	3–114
3–118(d)	3–112
3–118(e)	3–116(a)
3–118(f)	Omitted.
3–119	3–117 and 3–106(a) and (b)
3–120	4–106(a)
3–121	4–106(b)
3–122	Omitted. See Comment 1 to 3–118.
3–201(1)	3–203(b)
3–201(2)	3–204(c)
3–201(3)	3–203(c)
3–202(1)	3–201(a)
3–202(2)	3–204(a)
3–202(3)	3–203(d)
3–202(4)	Omitted.
3–203	3–204(d)
3–204(1)	3–205(a)
3–204(2)	3–205(b)
3–204(3)	3–205(c)
3–205	Omitted.
3–206(1)	3–206(a)
3–206(2)	3–206(c)(4) and (d)
3–206(3)	3–206(b), (c), and (e)
3–206(4)	3–206(d) and (e)
3–207(1)(a)	3–202(a)(i)
3–207(1)(b)	3–202(a)(ii)
3–207(1)(c)	3–202(a)(iii)
3–207(1)(d)	3–202(a)(iii)
3–207(2)	3–202(b)
3–208	3–207
3–301	Omitted. See Comment to 3–301.
3–302(1)	3–302(a)
3–302(2)	Omitted. See Comment 4 to 3–302.
3–302(3)(a)	3–302(c)(i)
3–302(3)(b)	3–302(c)(iii)
3–302(3)(c)	3–302(c)(ii)
3–302(4)	3–302(e)
3–303(a)	3–303(a)(1) and (2)
3–303(b)	3–303(a)(3)

Former Article 3 Section	Revised Article 3 or 4 Section
3–303(c)	3–303(a)(4) and (5)
3–304(1)(a)	3–302(a)(1)
3–304(1)(b)	Omitted.
3–304(2)	3–307(b)
3–304(3)(a)	3–302(a)(2)(iii); 3–304(b)(1)
3–304(3)(b)	3–304(b)(3)
3–304(3)(c)	3–304(a)(1), (2) and (3)
3–304(4)(a)	Omitted.
3–304(4)(b)	Omitted.
3–304(4)(c)	Omitted.
3–304(4)(d)	Omitted.
3–304(4)(e)	3–307
3–304(4)(f)	3–304(c)
3–304(5)	3–302(b)
3–304(6)	Omitted.
3–305(1)	3–306
3–305(2)(a)	3–305(a)(1)(i)
3–305(2)(b)	3–305(a)(1)(ii)
3–305(2)(c)	3–305(a)(1)(iii)
3–305(2)(d)	3–305(a)(1)(iv)
3–305(2)(e)	3–601(b)
3–306(a)	3–306
3–306(b)	3–305(a)(2)
3–306(c)	3–305(a)(2); 3–303(b); 3–105(b)
3–306(d)	3–305(c)
3–307(1)(a)	3–308(a)
3–307(1)(b)	3–308(a)
3–307(2)	3–308(b)
3–307(3)	3–308(b)
3–401(1)	3–401(a)
3–401(2)	3–401(b)
3–402	3–204(a)
3–403(1)	3–402(a)
3–403(2)(a)	3–402(b)(2)
3–403(2)(b)	3–402(b)(2)
3–403(3)	3–402(b)(1)
3–404(1)	3–403(a)
3–404(2)	3–403(a)
3–405(1)(a)	3–404(a)
3–405(1)(b)	3–404(b)(i)
3–405(1)(c)	3–405
3–405(2)	3–403(c)
3–406	3–406
3–407(1)(a)	3–407(a)(i)
3–407(1)(b)	3–407(a)(ii)
3–407(1)(c)	3–407(a)(i)
3–407(2)(a)	3–407(b)
3–407(2)(b)	3–407(b)
3–407(3)	3–407(c)
3–408	3–303(b)
3–409(1)	3–408
3–409(2)	Omitted. See Comment 1 to 3–408.
3–410(1)	3–409(a)
3–410(2)	3–409(b)
3–410(3)	3–409(c)
3–411(1)	3–409(d); 3–414(c); 3–415(d)
3–411(2)	3–409(d)
3–411(3)	Omitted.
3–412(1)	3–410(a)

Former Article 3 Section	Revised Article 3 or 4 Section
3–412(2)	3–410(b)
3–412(3)	3–410(c)
3–413(1)	3–412; 3–413(a)
3–413(2)	3–414(b) and (e)
3–413(3)	Omitted.
3–414(1)	3–415(a) and (b)
3–414(2)	Omitted.
3–415(1)	3–419(a)
3–415(2)	3–419(b)
3–415(3)	Omitted. See 3–605(h)
3–415(4)	3–419(c)
3–415(5)	3–419(e)
3–416(1)	Omitted.
3–416(2)	3–419(d)
3–416(3)	Omitted.
3–416(4)	3–419(c)
3–416(5)	Omitted.
3–416(6)	Omitted.
3–417(1)	3–417
3–417(2)	3–416
3–417(3)	Omitted.
3–417(4)	Omitted.
3–418	3–418
3–419(1)	3–420(a)
3–419(2)	3–420(b)
3–419(3)	3–420(c)
3–419(4)	3–206(c)(4) and (d)
3–501(1)(a)	3–414(b); 3–502(b)(3) and (4)
3–501(1)(b)	3–415(a); 3–502(a)(1) and (2); 3–502(b), (c), (d) and (e)
3–501(1)(c)	3–414(f); 3–415(e)
3–501(2)(a)	3–503(a)
3–501(2)(b)	Omitted. See Comment 2 to 3–414.
3–501(3)	Omitted. See Comment to 3–505.
3–501(4)	Omitted.
3–502(1)(a)	3–415(e)
3–502(1)(b)	3–414(f)
3–502(2)	Omitted. See Comment to 3–505.
3–503	Omitted. See Comment to 3–502.
3–504(1)	3–501(a)
3–504(2)(a)	3–501(b)(1)
3–504(2)(b)	3–501(b)(1)
3–504(2)(c)	3–501(b)(1); 3–111
3–504(3)(a)	3–501(b)(1)
3–504(3)(b)	Omitted.
3–504(4)	3–501(b)(1)
3–504(5)	Omitted.
3–505(1)(a)	3–501(b)(2)(i)
3–505(1)(b)	3–501(b)(2)(ii)
3–505(1)(c)	Omitted.
3–505(1)(d)	3–501(b)(2)(iii)
3–505(2)	Omitted.
3–506(1)	Omitted.
3–506(2)	Omitted.
3–507(1)	3–502
3–507(2)	Omitted.
3–507(3)	3–501(b)(3)(i)
3–507(4)	Omitted.
3–508(1)	3–503(b)

Former Article 3 Section	Revised Article 3 or 4 Section
3–508(2)	3–503(c)
3–508(3)	3–503(b)
3–508(4)	Omitted.
3–508(5)	Omitted.
3–508(6)	Omitted.
3–508(7)	Omitted.
3–508(8)	3–503(b)
3–509(1)	3–505(b)
3–509(2)	3–505(b)
3–509(3)	3–505(b)
3–509(4)	Omitted.
3–509(5)	Omitted.
3–510(a)	3–505(a)(1)
3–510(b)	3–505(a)(2)
3–510(c)	3–505(a)(3)
3–511(1)	Omitted.
3–511(2)(a)	3–504(a)(iv)
3–511(2)(b)	3–504(a)(ii), (iv), and (v); 3–504(b)
3–511(2)(c)	3–504(a)(i)
3–511(3)(a)	3–504(a)(ii)
3–511(3)(b)	3–504(a)(ii)
3–511(4)	3–502(f)
3–511(5)	Omitted.
3–511(6)	Omitted.
3–601(1)	3–601(a)
3–601(2)	3–601(a)
3–601(3)	Omitted.
3–602	3–601(b)
3–603(1)	3–602(a) and (b)
3–603(1)(a)	3–602(b)(2)
3–603(1)(b)	Omitted. See 3–206(c)(3).
3–603(2)	Omitted.
3–604(1)	3–603(c)
3–604(2)	3–603(b)
3–604(3)	3–603(c)
3–605(1)(a)	3–604(a)(i)
3–605(1)(b)	3–604(a)(ii)
3–605(2)	3–604(b)
3–606(1)(a)	3–605(b) and (c)
3–606(1)(b)	3–605(e)
3–606(2)	Omitted.
3–701(1)	Omitted.
3–701(2)	Omitted.
3–701(3)	Omitted.
3–801(1)	Omitted.
3–801(2)	Omitted.
3–801(3)	Omitted.
3–801(4)	Omitted.
3–802(1)(a)	3–310(a) and (c)
3–802(1)(b)	3–310(b) and (c)
3–802(2)	Omitted.
3–803	3–119
3–804	3–309
3–805	Omitted. See Comment 2 to 3–104.

PART 1

GENERAL PROVISIONS AND DEFINITIONS

§ 3–101. Short Title.

This Article may be cited as Uniform Commercial Code—Negotiable Instruments.

§ 3–102. Subject Matter.

(a) This Article applies to negotiable instruments. It does not apply to money, to payment orders governed by Article 4A, or to securities governed by Article 8.

(b) If there is conflict between this Article and Article 4 or 9, Articles 4 and 9 govern.

(c) Regulations of the Board of Governors of the Federal Reserve System and operating circulars of the Federal Reserve Banks supersede any inconsistent provision of this Article to the extent of the inconsistency.

Official Comment

1. Former Article 3 had no provision affirmatively stating its scope. Former Section 3–103 was a limitation on scope. In revised Article 3, Section 3–102 states that Article 3 applies to "negotiable instruments," defined in Section 3–104. Section 3–104(b) also defines the term "instrument" as a synonym for "negotiable instrument." In most places Article 3 uses the shorter term "instrument." This follows the convention used in former Article 3.

2. The reference in former Section 3–103(1) to "documents of title" is omitted as superfluous because these documents contain no promise to pay money. The definition of "payment order" in Section 4A–103(a)(1)(iii) excludes drafts which are governed by Article 3. Section 3–102(a) makes clear that a payment order governed by Article 4A is not governed by Article 3. Thus, Article 3 and Article 4A are mutually exclusive.

Article 8 states in ~~Section 8–102(1)(c)~~ Section 8–103(d) that "A writing that is a ~~certificated~~ security certificate is governed by this Article and not by Article 3, even though it also meets the requirements of that Article." Section 3–102(a) conforms to this provision. With respect to some promises or orders to pay money, there may be a question whether the promise or order is an instrument under Section 3–104(a) or a certificated security under ~~Section 8–102(1)(a)~~ Section 8–102(a)(4) and (15). Whether a writing is covered by Article 3 or Article 8 has important consequences. Among other things, under Section 8–207, the issuer of a certificated security may treat the registered owner as the owner for all purposes until the presentment for registration of a transfer. The issuer of a negotiable instrument, on the other hand, may discharge its obligation to pay the instrument only by paying a person entitled to enforce under Section 3–301. There are also important consequences to an indorser. An indorser of a security does not undertake the issuer's obligation or make any warranty that the issuer will honor the underlying obligation, while an indorser of a negotiable instrument becomes secondarily liable on the underlying obligation. *Amendments approved by the Permanent Editorial Board for Uniform Commercial Code November 4, 1995.*

Ordinarily the distinction between instruments and certificated securities in non-bearer form should be relatively clear. A certificated security under Article 8 must be in registered form (~~Section 8-102(1)(a)(i)~~ Section 8-102(a)(13)) so that it can be registered on the issuer's records. By contrast, registration plays no part in Article 3. The distinction between an instrument and a certificated security in bearer form may be somewhat more difficult and will generally lie in the economic functions of the two writings. Ordinarily, negotiable instruments under Article 3 will be separate and distinct instruments, while certificated securities under Article 8 will be either one of a class or series or by their terms divisible into a class or series (~~Section 8-102(1)(a)(iii)~~ Section 8-102(a)(15)(ii)). Thus, a promissory note in bearer form could come under either Article 3 if it were simply an individual note, or under Article 8 if it were one of a series of notes or divisible into a series. An additional distinction is whether the instrument is of the type commonly dealt in on securities exchanges or markets or commonly recognized as a medium for investment (~~Section 8-102(1)(a)(ii)~~ Section 8-102(a)(15)(iii)). Thus, a check written in bearer form (i.e., a check made payable to "cash") would not be a certificated security within Article 8 of the Uniform Commercial Code. *Amendments approved by the Permanent Editorial Board for Uniform Commercial Code November 4, 1995.*

Occasionally, a particular writing may fit the definition of both a negotiable instrument under Article 3 and of an investment security under Article 8. In such cases, the instrument is subject exclusively to the requirements of Article 8. ~~Section 8-102(1)(c)~~ Section 8-103(d) and Section 3-102(a). *Amendments approved by the Permanent Editorial Board for Uniform Commercial Code November 4, 1995.*

3. Although the terms of Article 3 apply to transactions by Federal Reserve Banks, federal preemption would make ineffective any Article 3 provision that conflicts with federal law. The activities of the Federal Reserve Banks are governed by regulations of the Federal Reserve Board and by operating circulars issued by the Reserve Banks themselves. In some instances, the operating circulars are issued pursuant to a Federal Reserve Board regulation. In other cases, the Reserve Bank issues the operating circular under its own authority under the Federal Reserve Act, subject to review by the Federal Reserve Board. Section 3-102(c) states that Federal Reserve Board regulations and operating circulars of the Federal Reserve Banks supersede any inconsistent provision of Article 3 to the extent of the inconsistency. Federal Reserve Board regulations, being valid exercises of regulatory authority pursuant to a federal statute, take precedence over state law if there is an inconsistency. Childs v. Federal Reserve Bank of Dallas, 719 F.2d 812 (5th Cir.1983), reh. den. 724 F.2d 127 (5th Cir.1984). Section 3-102(c) treats operating circulars as having the same effect whether issued under the Reserve Bank's own authority or under a Federal Reserve Board regulation. Federal statutes may also preempt Article 3. For example, the Expedited Funds Availability Act, 12 U.S.C. § 4001 et seq., provides that the Act and the regulations issued pursuant to the Act supersede any inconsistent provisions of the UCC. 12 U.S.C. § 4007(b).

4. In Clearfield Trust Co. v. United States, 318 U.S. 363 (1943), the Court held that if the United States is a party to an instrument, its rights and duties are governed by federal common law in the absence of a specific federal statute or regulation. In United States v. Kimbell Foods, Inc., 440 U.S. 715 (1979), the Court stated a three-pronged test to ascertain whether the federal common-law rule should follow the state rule. In most instances courts under the *Kimbell* test have shown a willingness to adopt UCC rules in formulating federal common law on the subject. In *Kimbell* the Court adopted the priorities rules of Article 9.

5. In 1989 the United Nations Commission on International Trade Law completed a Convention on International Bills of Exchange and International Promissory Notes. If the United States becomes a party to this Convention, the Convention will preempt state law with respect to

international bills and notes governed by the Convention. Thus, an international bill of exchange or promissory note that meets the definition of instrument in Section 3–104 will not be governed by Article 3 if it is governed by the Convention.

§ 3–103. Definitions.

(a) In this Article:

(1) "Acceptor" means a drawee who has accepted a draft.

(2) "Drawee" means a person ordered in a draft to make payment.

(3) "Drawer" means a person who signs or is identified in a draft as a person ordering payment.

(4) "Good faith" means honesty in fact and the observance of reasonable commercial standards of fair dealing.

(5) "Maker" means a person who signs or is identified in a note as a person undertaking to pay.

(6) "Order" means a written instruction to pay money signed by the person giving the instruction. The instruction may be addressed to any person, including the person giving the instruction, or to one or more persons jointly or in the alternative but not in succession. An authorization to pay is not an order unless the person authorized to pay is also instructed to pay.

(7) "Ordinary care" in the case of a person engaged in business means observance of reasonable commercial standards, prevailing in the area in which the person is located, with respect to the business in which the person is engaged. In the case of a bank that takes an instrument for processing for collection or payment by automated means, reasonable commercial standards do not require the bank to examine the instrument if the failure to examine does not violate the bank's prescribed procedures and the bank's procedures do not vary unreasonably from general banking usage not disapproved by this Article or Article 4.

(8) "Party" means a party to an instrument.

(9) "Promise" means a written undertaking to pay money signed by the person undertaking to pay. An acknowledgment of an obligation by the obligor is not a promise unless the obligor also undertakes to pay the obligation.

(10) "Prove" with respect to a fact means to meet the burden of establishing the fact (Section 1–201(8)).

(11) "Remitter" means a person who purchases an instrument from its issuer if the instrument is payable to an identified person other than the purchaser.

(b) Other definitions applying to this Article and the sections in which they appear are:

"Acceptance"	Section 3–409
"Accommodated party"	Section 3–419
"Accommodation party"	Section 3–419

"Alteration"	Section 3–407
"Anomalous indorsement"	Section 3–205
"Blank indorsement"	Section 3–205
"Cashier's check"	Section 3–104
"Certificate of deposit"	Section 3–104
"Certified check"	Section 3–409
"Check"	Section 3–104
"Consideration"	Section 3–303
"Draft"	Section 3–104
"Holder in due course"	Section 3–302
"Incomplete instrument"	Section 3–115
"Indorsement"	Section 3–204
"Indorser"	Section 3–204
"Instrument"	Section 3–104
"Issue"	Section 3–105
"Issuer"	Section 3–105
"Negotiable instrument"	Section 3–104
"Negotiation"	Section 3–201
"Note"	Section 3–104
"Payable at a definite time"	Section 3–108
"Payable on demand"	Section 3–108
"Payable to bearer"	Section 3–109
"Payable to order"	Section 3–109
"Payment"	Section 3–602
"Person entitled to enforce"	Section 3–301
"Presentment"	Section 3–501
"Reacquisition"	Section 3–207
"Special indorsement"	Section 3–205
"Teller's check"	Section 3–104
"Transfer of instrument"	Section 3–203
"Traveler's check"	Section 3–104
"Value"	Section 3–303

(c) The following definitions in other Articles apply to this Article:

"Bank"	Section 4–105
"Banking day"	Section 4–104
"Clearing house"	Section 4–104
"Collecting bank"	Section 4–105
"Depositary bank"	Section 4–105
"Documentary draft"	Section 4–104
"Intermediary bank"	Section 4–105
"Item"	Section 4–104
"Payor bank"	Section 4–105
"Suspends payments"	Section 4–104

(d) In addition, Article 1 contains general definitions and principles of construction and interpretation applicable throughout this Article.

Official Comment

1. Subsection (a) defines some common terms used throughout the Article that were not defined by former Article 3 and adds the definitions of "order" and "promise" found in former Section 3–102(1)(b) and (c).

2. The definition of "order" includes an instruction given by the signer to itself. The most common example of this kind of order is a cashier's check: a draft with respect to which the drawer and drawee are the same bank or branches of the same bank. Former Section 3-118(a) treated a cashier's check as a note. It stated "a draft drawn on the drawer is effective as a note." Although it is technically more correct to treat a cashier's check as a promise by the issuing bank to pay rather than an order to pay, a cashier's check is in the form of a check and it is normally referred to as a check. Thus, revised Article 3 follows banking practice in referring to a cashier's check as both a draft and a check rather than a note. Some insurance companies also follow the practice of issuing drafts in which the drawer draws on itself and makes the draft payable at or through a bank. These instruments are also treated as drafts. The obligation of the drawer of a cashier's check or other draft drawn on the drawer is stated in Section 3-412.

An order may be addressed to more than one person as drawee either jointly or in the alternative. The authorization of alternative drawees follows former Section 3-102(1)(b) and recognizes the practice of drawers, such as corporations issuing dividend checks, who for commercial convenience name a number of drawees, usually in different parts of the country. Section 3-501(b)(1) provides that presentment may be made to any one of multiple drawees. Drawees in succession are not permitted because the holder should not be required to make more than one presentment. Dishonor by any drawee named in the draft entitles the holder to rights of recourse against the drawer or indorsers.

3. The last sentence of subsection (a)(9) is intended to make it clear that an I.O.U. or other written acknowledgment of indebtedness is not a note unless there is also an undertaking to pay the obligation.

4. Subsection (a)(4) introduces a definition of good faith to apply to Articles 3 and 4. Former Articles 3 and 4 used the definition in Section 1-201(19). The definition in subsection (a)(4) is consistent with the definitions of good faith applicable to Articles 2, 2A, 4, and 4A. The definition requires not only honesty in fact but also "observance of reasonable commercial standards of fair dealing." Although fair dealing is a broad term that must be defined in context, it is clear that it is concerned with the fairness of conduct rather than the care with which an act is performed. Failure to exercise ordinary care in conducting a transaction is an entirely different concept than failure to deal fairly in conducting the transaction. Both fair dealing and ordinary care, which is defined in Section 3-103(a)(7), are to be judged in the light of reasonable commercial standards, but those standards in each case are directed to different aspects of commercial conduct.

5. Subsection (a)(7) is a definition of ordinary care which is applicable not only to Article 3 but to Article 4 as well. See Section 4-104(c). The general rule is stated in the first sentence of subsection (a)(7) and it applies both to banks and to persons engaged in businesses other than banking. Ordinary care means observance of reasonable commercial standards of the relevant businesses prevailing in the area in which the person is located. The second sentence of subsection (a)(7) is a particular rule limited to the duty of a bank to examine an instrument taken by a bank for processing for collection or payment by automated means. This particular rule applies primarily to Section 4-406 and it is discussed in Comment 4 to that section. Nothing in Section 3-103(a)(7) is intended to prevent a customer from proving that the procedures followed by a bank are unreasonable, arbitrary, or unfair.

6. In subsection (c) reference is made to a new definition of "bank" in amended Article 4.

§ 3-104. Negotiable Instrument.

(a) Except as provided in subsections (c) and (d), "negotiable instrument" means an unconditional promise or order to pay a fixed amount of money, with or without interest or other charges described in the promise or order, if it:

(1) is payable to bearer or to order at the time it is issued or first comes into possession of a holder;

(2) is payable on demand or at a definite time; and

(3) does not state any other undertaking or instruction by the person promising or ordering payment to do any act in addition to the payment of money, but the promise or order may contain (i) an undertaking or power to give, maintain, or protect collateral to secure payment, (ii) an authorization or power to the holder to confess judgment or realize on or dispose of collateral, or (iii) a waiver of the benefit of any law intended for the advantage or protection of an obligor.

(b) "Instrument" means a negotiable instrument.

(c) An order that meets all of the requirements of subsection (a), except paragraph (1), and otherwise falls within the definition of "check" in subsection (f) is a negotiable instrument and a check.

(d) A promise or order other than a check is not an instrument if, at the time it is issued or first comes into possession of a holder, it contains a conspicuous statement, however expressed, to the effect that the promise or order is not negotiable or is not an instrument governed by this Article.

(e) An instrument is a "note" if it is a promise and is a "draft" if it is an order. If an instrument falls within the definition of both "note" and "draft," a person entitled to enforce the instrument may treat it as either.

(f) "Check" means (i) a draft, other than a documentary draft, payable on demand and drawn on a bank or (ii) a cashier's check or teller's check. An instrument may be a check even though it is described on its face by another term, such as "money order."

(g) "Cashier's check" means a draft with respect to which the drawer and drawee are the same bank or branches of the same bank.

(h) "Teller's check" means a draft drawn by a bank (i) on another bank, or (ii) payable at or through a bank.

(i) "Traveler's check" means an instrument that (i) is payable on demand, (ii) is drawn on or payable at or through a bank, (iii) is designated by the term "traveler's check" or by a substantially similar term, and (iv) requires, as a condition to payment, a countersignature by a person whose specimen signature appears on the instrument.

(j) "Certificate of deposit" means an instrument containing an acknowledgment by a bank that a sum of money has been received by the bank and a promise by the bank to repay the sum of money. A certificate of deposit is a note of the bank.

Official Comment

1. The definition of "negotiable instrument" defines the scope of Article 3 since Section 3–102 states: "This Article

applies to negotiable instruments." The definition in Section 3-104(a) incorporates other definitions in Article 3. An instrument is either a "promise," defined in Section 3-103(a)(9), or "order," defined in Section 3-103(a)(6). A promise is a written undertaking to pay money signed by the person undertaking to pay. An order is a written instruction to pay money signed by the person giving the instruction. Thus, the term "negotiable instrument" is limited to a signed writing that orders or promises payment of money. "Money" is defined in Section 1-201(24) and is not limited to United States dollars. It also includes a medium of exchange established by a foreign government or monetary units of account established by an intergovernmental organization or by agreement between two or more nations. Five other requirements are stated in Section 3-104(a): First, the promise or order must be "unconditional." The quoted term is explained in Section 3-106. Second, the amount of money must be "a fixed amount *** with or without interest or other charges described in the promise or order." Section 3-112(b) relates to "interest." Third, the promise or order must be "payable to bearer or to order." The quoted phrase is explained in Section 3-109. An exception to this requirement is stated in subsection (c). Fourth, the promise or order must be payable "on demand or at a definite time." The quoted phrase is explained in Section 3-108. Fifth, the promise or order may not state "any other undertaking or instruction by the person promising or ordering payment to do any act in addition to the payment of money" with three exceptions. The quoted phrase is based on the first sentence of N.I.L. Section 5 which is the precursor of "no other promise, order, obligation or power given by the maker or drawer" appearing in former Section 3-104(1)(b). The words "instruction" and "undertaking" are used instead of "order" and "promise" that are used in the N.I.L. formulation because the latter words are defined terms that include only orders or promises to pay money. The three exceptions stated in Section 3-104(a)(3) are based on and are intended to have the same meaning as former Section 3-112(1)(b), (c), (d), and (e), as well as N.I.L. § 5(1), (2), and (3). Subsection (b) states that "instrument" means a "negotiable instrument." This follows former Section 3-102(1)(e) which treated the two terms as synonymous.

2. Unless subsection (c) applies, the effect of subsection (a)(1) and Section 3-102(a) is to exclude from Article 3 any promise or order that is not payable to bearer or to order. There is no provision in revised Article 3 that is comparable to former Section 3-805. The comment to former Section 3-805 states that the typical example of a writing covered by that section is a check reading "Pay John Doe." Such a check was governed by former Article 3 but there could not be a holder in due course of the check. Under Section 3-104(c) such a check is governed by revised Article 3 and there can be a holder in due course of the check. But subsection (c) applies only to checks. The comment to former Section 3-805 does not state any example other than the check to illustrate that section. Subsection (c) is based on the belief that it is good policy to treat checks, which are payment instruments, as negotiable instruments whether or not they contain the words "to the order of". These words are almost always pre-printed on the check form. Occasionally the drawer of a check may strike out these words before issuing the check. In the past some credit unions used check forms that did not contain the quoted words. Such check forms may still be in use but they are no longer common. Absence of the quoted words can easily be overlooked and should not affect the rights of holders who may pay money or give credit for a check without being aware that it is not in the conventional form.

Total exclusion from Article 3 of other promises or orders that are not payable to bearer or to order serves a useful purpose. It provides a simple device to clearly exclude a writing that does not fit the pattern of typical negotiable instruments and which is not intended to be a negotiable instrument. If a writing could be an instrument despite the absence of "to order" or "to bearer" language and a dispute arises with respect to the writing, it might be argued that the writing is a negotiable instrument because the other requirements of subsection (a) are somehow met. Even if the argument is eventually found to be without merit it can be used as a litigation ploy. Words making a promise or order payable to bearer or to order are the most distinguishing feature of a negotiable instrument and such words are frequently referred to as "words of negotiability." Article 3 is not meant to apply to contracts for the sale of goods or services or the sale or lease of real property or similar writings that may contain a promise to pay money. The use of words of negotiability in such contracts would be an aberration. Absence of the words precludes any argument that such contracts might be negotiable instruments.

An order or promise that is excluded from Article 3 because of the requirements of Section 3–104(a) may nevertheless be similar to a negotiable instrument in many respects. Although such a writing cannot be made a negotiable instrument within Article 3 by contract or conduct of its parties, nothing in Section 3–104 or in Section 3–102 is intended to mean that in a particular case involving such a writing a court could not arrive at a result similar to the result that would follow if the writing were a negotiable instrument. For example, a court might find that the obligor with respect to a promise that does not fall within Section 3–104(a) is precluded from asserting a defense against a bona fide purchaser. The preclusion could be based on estoppel or ordinary principles of contract. It does not depend upon the law of negotiable instruments. An example is stated in the paragraph following Case # 2 in Comment 4 to Section 3–302.

Moreover, consistent with the principle stated in Section 1–102(2)(b), the immediate parties to an order or promise that is not an instrument may provide by agreement that one or more of the provisions of Article 3 determine their rights and obligations under the writing. Upholding the parties' choice is not inconsistent with Article 3. Such an agreement may bind a transferee of the writing if the transferee has notice of it or the agreement arises from usage of trade and the agreement does not violate other law or public policy. An example of such an agreement is a provision that a transferee of the writing has the rights of a holder in due course stated in Article 3 if the transferee took rights under the writing in good faith, for value, and without notice of a claim or defense.

Even without an agreement of the parties to an order or promise that is not an instrument, it may be appropriate, consistent with the principles stated in Section 1–102(2), for a court to apply one or more provisions of Article 3 to the writing by analogy, taking into account the expectations of the parties and the differences between the writing and an instrument governed by Article 3. Whether such application is appropriate depends upon the facts of each case.

3. Subsection (d) allows exclusion from Article 3 of a writing that would otherwise be an instrument under subsection (a) by a statement to the effect that the writing is not negotiable or is not governed by Article 3. For example, a promissory note can be stamped with the legend NOT NEGOTIABLE. The effect under subsection (d) is not only to negate the possibility of a holder in due course, but to prevent the writing from being a negotiable instrument for any purpose. Subsection (d) does not, however, apply to a check. If a writing is excluded from Article 3 by subsection (d), a court could, nevertheless, apply Article 3 principles to it by analogy as stated in Comment 2.

4. Instruments are divided into two general categories: drafts and notes. A draft is an instrument that is an order. A note is an instrument that is a promise. Section 3–104(e). The term "bill of exchange" is not used in Article 3. It is generally understood to be a synonym for the term "draft." Subsections (f) through (j) define particular instruments

that fall within the categories of draft and note. The term "draft," defined in subsection (e), includes a "check" which is defined in subsection (f). "Check" includes a share draft drawn on a credit union payable through a bank because the definition of bank (Section ~~4–104~~ 4–105 *) includes credit unions. However, a draft drawn on an insurance company payable through a bank is not a check because it is not drawn on a bank. "Money orders" are sold both by banks and non-banks. They vary in form and their form determines how they are treated in Article 3. The most common form of money order sold by banks is that of an ordinary check drawn by the purchaser except that the amount is machine impressed. That kind of money order is a check under Article 3 and is subject to a stop order by the purchaser-drawer as in the case of ordinary checks. The seller bank is the drawee and has no obligation to a holder to pay the money order. If a money order falls within the definition of a teller's check, the rules applicable to teller's checks apply. Postal money orders are subject to federal law. "Teller's check" is separately defined in subsection (h). A teller's check is always drawn by a bank and is usually drawn on another bank. In some cases a teller's check is drawn on a nonbank but is made payable at or through a bank. Article 3 treats both types of teller's check identically, and both are included in the definition of "check." A cashier's check, defined in subsection (g), is also included in the definition of "check." Traveler's checks are issued both by banks and nonbanks and may be in the form of a note or draft. Subsection (i) states the essential characteristics of a traveler's check. The requirement that the instrument be "drawn on or payable at or through a bank" may be satisfied without words on the instrument that identify a bank as drawee or paying agent so long as the instrument bears an appropriate routing number that identifies a bank as paying agent.

The definitions in Regulation CC § 229.2 of the terms "check," "cashier's check," "teller's check," and "traveler's check" are different from the definitions of those terms in Article 3.

Certificates of deposit are treated in former Article 3 as a separate type of instrument. In revised Article 3, Section 3–104(j) treats them as notes.

* *Previous incorrect cross reference corrected by Permanent Editorial Board action November 1992.*

§ 3–105. Issue of Instrument.

(a) "Issue" means the first delivery of an instrument by the maker or drawer, whether to a holder or nonholder, for the purpose of giving rights on the instrument to any person.

(b) An unissued instrument, or an unissued incomplete instrument that is completed, is binding on the maker or drawer, but nonissuance is a defense. An instrument that is conditionally issued or is issued for a special purpose is binding on the maker or drawer, but failure of the condition or special purpose to be fulfilled is a defense.

(c) "Issuer" applies to issued and unissued instruments and means a maker or drawer of an instrument.

Official Comment

1. Under former Section 3–102(1)(a) "issue" was defined as the first delivery to a "holder or a remitter" but the term "remitter" was neither defined nor otherwise used. In revised Article 3, Section 3–105(a) defines "issue" more broadly to include the first delivery to anyone by the

drawer or maker for the purpose of giving rights to anyone on the instrument. "Delivery" with respect to instruments is defined in Section 1-201(14) as meaning "voluntary transfer of possession."

2. Subsection (b) continues the rule that nonissuance, conditional issuance or issuance for a special purpose is a defense of the maker or drawer of an instrument. Thus, the defense can be asserted against a person other than a holder in due course. The same rule applies to nonissuance of an incomplete instrument later completed.

3. Subsection (c) defines "issuer" to include the signer of an unissued instrument for convenience of reference in the statute.

§ 3-106. Unconditional Promise or Order.

(a) Except as provided in this section, for the purposes of Section 3-104(a), a promise or order is unconditional unless it states (i) an express condition to payment, (ii) that the promise or order is subject to or governed by another writing, or (iii) that rights or obligations with respect to the promise or order are stated in another writing. A reference to another writing does not of itself make the promise or order conditional.

(b) A promise or order is not made conditional (i) by a reference to another writing for a statement of rights with respect to collateral, prepayment, or acceleration, or (ii) because payment is limited to resort to a particular fund or source.

(c) If a promise or order requires, as a condition to payment, a countersignature by a person whose specimen signature appears on the promise or order, the condition does not make the promise or order conditional for the purposes of Section 3-104(a). If the person whose specimen signature appears on an instrument fails to countersign the instrument, the failure to countersign is a defense to the obligation of the issuer, but the failure does not prevent a transferee of the instrument from becoming a holder of the instrument.

(d) If a promise or order at the time it is issued or first comes into possession of a holder contains a statement, required by applicable statutory or administrative law, to the effect that the rights of a holder or transferee are subject to claims or defenses that the issuer could assert against the original payee, the promise or order is not thereby made conditional for the purposes of Section 3-104(a); but if the promise or order is an instrument, there cannot be a holder in due course of the instrument.

Official Comment

1. This provision replaces former Section 3-105. Its purpose is to define when a promise or order fulfills the requirement in Section 3-104(a) that it be an "unconditional" promise or order to pay. Under Section 3-106(a) a promise or order is deemed to be unconditional unless one of the two tests of the subsection make the promise or order conditional. If the promise or order states an express condition to payment, the promise or order is not an instrument. For example, a promise states, "I promise to pay $100,000 to the order of John Doe if he conveys title to Blackacre to me." The promise is not an instrument because there is an express condition to payment. However, suppose a promise states, "In consideration of John Doe's promise to convey title to Blackacre I promise to pay $100,000 to the order of John Doe." That promise can be an instrument if Section

3–104 is otherwise satisfied. Although the recital of the executory promise of Doe to convey Blackacre might be read as an implied condition that the promise be performed, the condition is not an express condition as required by Section 3–106(a)(i). This result is consistent with former Section 3–105(1)(a) and (b). Former Section 3–105(1)(b) is not repeated in Section 3–106 because it is not necessary. It is an example of an implied condition. Former Section 3–105(1)(d), (e), and (f) and the first clause of former Section 3–105(1)(c) are other examples of implied conditions. They are not repeated in Section 3–106 because they are not necessary. The law is not changed.

Section 3–106(a)(ii) and (iii) carry forward the substance of former Section 3–105(2)(a). The only change is the use of "writing" instead of "agreement" and a broadening of the language that can result in conditionality. For example, a promissory note is not an instrument defined by Section 3–104 if it contains any of the following statements: 1. "This note is subject to a contract of sale dated April 1, 1990 between the payee and maker of this note." 2. "This note is subject to a loan and security agreement dated April 1, 1990 between the payee and maker of this note." 3. "Rights and obligations of the parties with respect to this note are stated in an agreement dated April 1, 1990 between the payee and maker of this note." It is not relevant whether any condition to payment is or is not stated in the writing to which reference is made. The rationale is that the holder of a negotiable instrument should not be required to examine another document to determine rights with respect to payment. But subsection (b)(i) permits reference to a separate writing for information with respect to collateral, prepayment, or acceleration.

Many notes issued in commercial transactions are secured by collateral, are subject to acceleration in the event of default, or are subject to prepayment. A statement of rights and obligations concerning collateral, prepayment, or acceleration does not prevent the note from being an instrument if the statement is in the note itself. See Section 3–104(a)(3) and Section 3–108(b). In some cases it may be convenient not to include a statement concerning collateral, prepayment, or acceleration in the note, but rather to refer to an accompanying loan agreement, security agreement or mortgage for that statement. Subsection (b)(i) allows a reference to the appropriate writing for a statement of these rights. For example, a note would not be made conditional by the following statement: "This note is secured by a security interest in collateral described in a security agreement dated April 1, 1990 between the payee and maker of this note. Rights and obligations with respect to the collateral are [stated in] [governed by] the security agreement." The bracketed words are alternatives, either of which complies.

Subsection (b)(ii) addresses the issues covered by former Section 3–105(1)(f), (g), and (h) and Section 3–105(2)(b). Under Section 3–106(a) a promise or order is not made conditional because payment is limited to payment from a particular source or fund. This reverses the result of former Section 3–105(2)(b). There is no cogent reason why the general credit of a legal entity must be pledged to have a negotiable instrument. Market forces determine the marketability of instruments of this kind. If potential buyers don't want promises or orders that are payable only from a particular source or fund, they won't take them, but Article 3 should apply.

2. Subsection (c) applies to traveler's checks or other instruments that may require a countersignature. Although the requirement of a countersignature is a condition to the obligation to pay, traveler's checks are treated in the commercial world as money substitutes and therefore should be governed by Article 3. The first sentence of subsection (c) allows a traveler's check to meet the definition of instrument by stating that the countersignature condition does not make it conditional for the purposes of Section 3–104. The second sentence states the effect of a failure to meet the condition. Suppose a

thief steals a traveler's check and cashes it by skillfully imitating the specimen signature so that the countersignature appears to be authentic. The countersignature is for the purpose of identification of the owner of the instrument. It is not an indorsement. Subsection (c) provides that the failure of the owner to countersign does not prevent a transferee from becoming a holder. Thus, the merchant or bank that cashed the traveler's check becomes a holder when the traveler's check is taken. The forged countersignature is a defense to the obligation of the issuer to pay the instrument, and is included in defenses under Section 3-305(a)(2). These defenses may not be asserted against a holder in due course. Whether a holder has notice of the defense is a factual question. If the countersignature is a very bad forgery, there may be notice. But if the merchant or bank cashed a traveler's check and the countersignature appeared to be similar to the specimen signature, there might not be notice that the countersignature was forged. Thus, the merchant or bank could be a holder in due course.

3. Subsection (d) concerns the effect of a statement to the effect that the rights of a holder or transferee are subject to claims and defenses that the issuer could assert against the original payee. The subsection applies only if the statement is required by statutory or administrative law. The prime example is the Federal Trade Commission Rule (16 C.F.R. Part 433) preserving consumers' claims and defenses in consumer credit sales. The intent of the FTC rule is to make it impossible for there to be a holder in due course of a note bearing the FTC legend and undoubtedly that is the result. But, under former Article 3, the legend may also have had the unintended effect of making the note conditional, thus excluding the note from former Article 3 altogether. Subsection (d) is designed to make it possible to preclude the possibility of a holder in due course without excluding the instrument from Article 3. Most of the provisions of Article 3 are not affected by the holder-in-due-course doctrine and there is no reason why Article 3 should not apply to a note bearing the FTC legend if holder-in-due-course rights are not involved. Under subsection (d) the statement does not make the note conditional. If the note otherwise meets the requirements of Section 3-104(a) it is a negotiable instrument for all purposes except that there cannot be a holder in due course of the note. No particular form of legend or statement is required by subsection (d). The form of a particular legend or statement may be determined by the other statute or administrative law. For example, the FTC legend required in a note taken by the seller in a consumer sale of goods or services is tailored to that particular transaction and therefore uses language that is somewhat different from that stated in subsection (d), but the difference in expression does not affect the essential similarity of the message conveyed. The effect of the FTC legend is to make the rights of a holder or transferee subject to claims or defenses that the issuer could assert against the original payee of the note.

§ 3-107. Instrument Payable in Foreign Money.

Unless the instrument otherwise provides, an instrument that states the amount payable in foreign money may be paid in the foreign money or in an equivalent amount in dollars calculated by using the current bank-offered spot rate at the place of payment for the purchase of dollars on the day on which the instrument is paid.

Official Comment

The definition of instrument in Section 3-104 requires that the promise or order be payable in "money." That term is defined in Section 1-201(24) and is not limited to United States dollars. Section 3–107 states than an instrument payable in foreign money may be paid in dollars if the instrument does not prohibit it. It also states a conversion rate which applies in the absence of a different conversion rate stated in the instrument. The reference in former Section 3–107(1) to instruments payable in "currency" or "current funds" has been dropped as superfluous.

§ 3–108. Payable on Demand or at Definite Time.

(a) A promise or order is "payable on demand" if it (i) states that it is payable on demand or at sight, or otherwise indicates that it is payable at the will of the holder, or (ii) does not state any time of payment.

(b) A promise or order is "payable at a definite time" if it is payable on elapse of a definite period of time after sight or acceptance or at a fixed date or dates or at a time or times readily ascertainable at the time the promise or order is issued, subject to rights of (i) prepayment, (ii) acceleration, (iii) extension at the option of the holder, or (iv) extension to a further definite time at the option of the maker or acceptor or automatically upon or after a specified act or event.

(c) If an instrument, payable at a fixed date, is also payable upon demand made before the fixed date, the instrument is payable on demand until the fixed date and, if demand for payment is not made before that date, becomes payable at a definite time on the fixed date.

Official Comment

This section is a restatement of former Section 3–108 and Section 3–109. Subsection (b) broadens former Section 3–109 somewhat by providing that a definite time includes a time readily ascertainable at the time the promise or order is issued. Subsection (b)(iii) and (iv) restates former Section 3–109(1)(d). It adopts the generally accepted rule that a clause providing for extension at the option of the holder, even without a time limit, does not affect negotiability since the holder is given only a right which the holder would have without the clause. If the extension is to be at the option of the maker or acceptor or is to be automatic, a definite time limit must be stated or the time of payment remains uncertain and the order or promise is not a negotiable instrument. If a definite time limit is stated, the effect upon certainty of time of payment is the same as if the instrument were made payable at the ultimate date with a term providing for acceleration.

§ 3–109. Payable to Bearer or to Order.

(a) A promise or order is payable to bearer if it:

(1) states that it is payable to bearer or to the order of bearer or otherwise indicates that the person in possession of the promise or order is entitled to payment;

(2) does not state a payee; or

(3) states that it is payable to or to the order of cash or otherwise indicates that it is not payable to an identified person.

(b) A promise or order that is not payable to bearer is payable to order if it is payable (i) to the order of an identified person or (ii) to an identified person or order. A promise or order that is payable to order is payable to the identified person.

(c) An instrument payable to bearer may become payable to an identified person if it is specially indorsed pursuant to Section 3–205(a). An instrument payable to an identified person may become payable to bearer if it is indorsed in blank pursuant to Section 3–205(b).

Official Comment

1. Under Section 3–104(a), a promise or order cannot be an instrument unless the instrument is payable to bearer or to order when it is issued or unless Section 3–104(c) applies. The terms "payable to bearer" and "payable to order" are defined in Section 3–109. The quoted terms are also relevant in determining how an instrument is negotiated. If the instrument is payable to bearer it can be negotiated by delivery alone. Section 3–201(b). An instrument that is payable to an identified person cannot be negotiated without the indorsement of the identified person. Section 3–201(b). An instrument payable to order is payable to an identified person. Section 3–109(b). Thus, an instrument payable to order requires the indorsement of the person to whose order the instrument is payable.

2. Subsection (a) states when an instrument is payable to bearer. An instrument is payable to bearer if it states that it is payable to bearer, but some instruments use ambiguous terms. For example, check forms usually have the words "to the order of" printed at the beginning of the line to be filled in for the name of the payee. If the drawer writes in the word "bearer" or "cash," the check reads "to the order of bearer" or "to the order of cash." In each case the check is payable to bearer. Sometimes the drawer will write the name of the payee "John Doe" but will add the words "or bearer." In that case the check is payable to bearer. Subsection (a). Under subsection (b), if an instrument is payable to bearer it can't be payable to order. This is different from former Section 3–110(3). An instrument that purports to be payable both to order and bearer states contradictory terms. A transferee of the instrument should be able to rely on the bearer term and acquire rights as a holder without obtaining the indorsement of the identified payee. An instrument is also payable to bearer if it does not state a payee. Instruments that do not state a payee are in most cases incomplete instruments. In some cases the drawer of a check may deliver or mail it to the person to be paid without filling in the line for the name of the payee. Under subsection (a) the check is payable to bearer when it is sent or delivered. It is also an incomplete instrument. This case is discussed in Comment 2 to Section 3–115. Subsection (a)(3) contains the words "otherwise indicates that it is not payable to an identified person." The quoted words are meant to cover uncommon cases in which an instrument indicates that it is not meant to be payable to a specific person. Such an instrument is treated like a check payable to "cash." The quoted words are not meant to apply to an instrument stating that it is payable to an identified person such as "ABC Corporation" if ABC Corporation is a nonexistent company. Although the holder of the check cannot be the nonexistent company, the instrument is not payable to bearer. Negotiation of such an instrument is governed by Section 3–404(b).

§ 3–110. Identification of Person to Whom Instrument Is Payable.

(a) The person to whom an instrument is initially payable is determined by the intent of the person, whether or not authorized, signing as, or in the name or behalf of, the issuer of the instrument. The instrument is payable to the person intended by the signer even if that person is identified in the instrument by a name or other identification that is not that of the intended person. If more than one person signs in the name or behalf of the issuer of an instrument and all the signers do not intend the same person as payee, the instrument is payable to any person intended by one or more of the signers.

(b) If the signature of the issuer of an instrument is made by automated means, such as a check-writing machine, the payee of the instrument is determined by the intent of the person who supplied the name or identification of the payee, whether or not authorized to do so.

(c) A person to whom an instrument is payable may be identified in any way, including by name, identifying number, office, or account number. For the purpose of determining the holder of an instrument, the following rules apply:

(1) If an instrument is payable to an account and the account is identified only by number, the instrument is payable to the person to whom the account is payable. If an instrument is payable to an account identified by number and by the name of a person, the instrument is payable to the named person, whether or not that person is the owner of the account identified by number.

(2) If an instrument is payable to:

(i) a trust, an estate, or a person described as trustee or representative of a trust or estate, the instrument is payable to the trustee, the representative, or a successor of either, whether or not the beneficiary or estate is also named;

(ii) a person described as agent or similar representative of a named or identified person, the instrument is payable to the represented person, the representative, or a successor of the representative;

(iii) a fund or organization that is not a legal entity, the instrument is payable to a representative of the members of the fund or organization; or

(iv) an office or to a person described as holding an office, the instrument is payable to the named person, the incumbent of the office, or a successor to the incumbent.

(d) If an instrument is payable to two or more persons alternatively, it is payable to any of them and may be negotiated, discharged, or enforced by any or all of them in possession of the instrument. If an instrument is payable to two or more persons not alternatively, it is payable to all of them and may be negotiated, discharged, or enforced only by all of them. If an instrument payable to two or more persons is ambiguous as to whether it is payable to the persons alternatively, the instrument is payable to the persons alternatively.

Official Comment

1. Section 3–110 states rules for determining the identity of the person to whom an instrument is initially payable if the instrument is payable to an identified

person. This issue usually arises in a dispute over the validity of an indorsement in the name of the payee. Subsection (a) states the general rule that the person to whom an instrument is payable is determined by the intent of "the person, whether or not authorized, signing as, or in the name or behalf of, the issuer of the instrument." "Issuer" means the maker or drawer of the instrument. Section 3–105(c). If X signs a check as drawer of a check on X's account, the intent of X controls. If X, as President of Corporation, signs a check as President in behalf of Corporation as drawer, the intent of X controls. If X forges Y's signature as drawer of a check, the intent of X also controls. Under Section 3–103(a)(3), Y is referred to as the drawer of the check because the signing of Y's name identifies Y as the drawer. But since Y's signature was forged Y has no liability as drawer (Section 3–403(a)) unless some other provision of Article 3 or Article 4 makes Y liable. Since X, even though unauthorized, signed in the name of Y as issuer, the intent of X determines to whom the check is payable.

In the case of a check payable to "John Smith," since there are many people in the world named "John Smith" it is not possible to identify the payee of the check unless there is some further identification or the intention of the drawer is determined. Name alone is sufficient under subsection (a), but the intention of the drawer determines which John Smith is the person to whom the check is payable. The same issue is presented in cases of misdescriptions of the payee. The drawer intends to pay a person known to the drawer as John Smith. In fact that person's name is James Smith or John Jones or some other entirely different name. If the check identifies the payee as John Smith, it is nevertheless payable to the person intended by the drawer. That person may indorse the check in either the name John Smith or the person's correct name or in both names. Section 3–204(d). The intent of the drawer is also controlling in fictitious payee cases. Section 3–404(b). The last sentence of subsection (a) refers to rare cases in which the signature of an organization requires more than one signature and the persons signing on behalf of the organization do not all intend the same person as payee. Any person intended by a signer for the organization is the payee and an indorsement by that person is an effective indorsement.

Subsection (b) recognizes the fact that in a large number of cases there is no human signer of an instrument because the instrument, usually a check, is produced by automated means such as a check-writing machine. In that case, the relevant intent is that of the person who supplied the name of the payee. In most cases that person is an employee of the drawer, but in some cases the person could be an outsider who is committing a fraud by introducing names of payees of checks into the system that produces the checks. A check-writing machine is likely to be operated by means of a computer in which is stored information as to name and address of the payee and the amount of the check. Access to the computer may allow production of fraudulent checks without knowledge of the organization that is the issuer of the check. Section 3–404(b) is also concerned with this issue. See Case # 4 in Comment 2 to Section 3–404.

2. Subsection (c) allows the payee to be identified in any way including the various ways stated. Subsection (c)(1) relates to instruments payable to bank accounts. In some cases the account might be identified by name and number, and the name and number might refer to different persons. For example, a check is payable to "X Corporation Account No. 12345 in Bank of Podunk." Under the last sentence of subsection (c)(1), this check is payable to X Corporation and can be negotiated by X Corporation even if Account No. 12345 is some other person's account or the check is not deposited in that account. In other cases the payee is identified by an account number and the name of the owner of the account is not stated. For example, Debtor pays Creditor by issuing a check drawn on Payor

Bank. The check is payable to a bank account owned by Creditor but identified only by number. Under the first sentence of subsection (c)(1) the check is payable to Creditor and, under Section 1-201(20), Creditor becomes the holder when the check is delivered. Under Section 3-201(b), further negotiation of the check requires the indorsement of Creditor. But under Section 4-205(a), if the check is taken by a depositary bank for collection, the bank may become a holder without the indorsement. Under Section 3-102(b), provisions of Article 4 prevail over those of Article 3. The depositary bank warrants that the amount of the check was credited to the payee's account.

3. Subsection (c)(2) replaces former Section 3-117 and subsection (1)(e), (f), and (g) of former Section 3-110. This provision merely determines who can deal with an instrument as a holder. It does not determine ownership of the instrument or its proceeds. Subsection (c)(2)(i) covers trusts and estates. If the instrument is payable to the trust or estate or to the trustee or representative of the trust or estate, the instrument is payable to the trustee or representative or any successor. Under subsection (c)(2)(ii), if the instrument states that it is payable to Doe, President of X Corporation, either Doe or X Corporation can be holder of the instrument. Subsection (c)(2)(iii) concerns informal organizations that are not legal entities such as unincorporated clubs and the like. Any representative of the members of the organization can act as holder. Subsection (c)(2)(iv) applies principally to instruments payable to public offices such as a check payable to County Tax Collector.

4. Subsection (d) replaces former Section 3-116. An instrument payable to X or Y is governed by the first sentence of subsection (d). An instrument payable to X and Y is governed by the second sentence of subsection (d). If an instrument is payable to X or Y, either is the payee and if either is in possession that person is the holder and the person entitled to enforce the instrument. Section 3-301. If an instrument is payable to X and Y, neither X nor Y acting alone is the person to whom the instrument is payable. Neither person, acting alone, can be the holder of the instrument. The instrument is "payable to an identified person." The "identified person" is X and Y acting jointly. Section 3-109(b) and Section 1-102(5)(a). Thus, under Section 1-201(20) X or Y, acting alone, cannot be the holder or the person entitled to enforce or negotiate the instrument because neither, acting alone, is the identified person stated in the instrument.

The third sentence of subsection (d) is directed to cases in which it is not clear whether an instrument is payable to multiple payees alternatively. In the case of ambiguity persons dealing with the instrument should be able to rely on the indorsement of a single payee. For example, an instrument payable to X and/or Y is treated like an instrument payable to X or Y.

§ 3-111. Place of Payment.

Except as otherwise provided for items in Article 4, an instrument is payable at the place of payment stated in the instrument. If no place of payment is stated, an instrument is payable at the address of the drawee or maker stated in the instrument. If no address is stated, the place of payment is the place of business of the drawee or maker. If a drawee or maker has more than one place of business, the place of payment is any place of business of the drawee or maker chosen by the person entitled to enforce the instrument. If the drawee or maker has no place of business, the place of payment is the residence of the drawee or maker.

Official Comment

If an instrument is payable at a bank in the United States, Section 3-501(b)(1) states that presentment must be made at the place of payment, i.e. the bank. The place of presentment of a check is governed by Regulation CC § 229.36.

§ 3-112. Interest.

(a) Unless otherwise provided in the instrument, (i) an instrument is not payable with interest, and (ii) interest on an interest-bearing instrument is payable from the date of the instrument.

(b) Interest may be stated in an instrument as a fixed or variable amount of money or it may be expressed as a fixed or variable rate or rates. The amount or rate of interest may be stated or described in the instrument in any manner and may require reference to information not contained in the instrument. If an instrument provides for interest, but the amount of interest payable cannot be ascertained from the description, interest is payable at the judgment rate in effect at the place of payment of the instrument and at the time interest first accrues.

Official Comment

1. Under Section 3-104(a) the requirement of a "fixed amount" applies only to principal. The amount of interest payable is that described in the instrument. If the description of interest in the instrument does not allow for the amount of interest to be ascertained, interest is payable at the judgment rate. Hence, if an instrument calls for interest, the amount of interest will always be determinable. If a variable rate of interest is prescribed, the amount of interest is ascertainable by reference to the formula or index described or referred to in the instrument. The last sentence of subsection (b) replaces subsection (d) of former Section 3-118.

2. The purpose of subsection (b) is to clarify the meaning of "interest" in the introductory clause of Section 3-104(a). It is not intended to validate a provision for interest in an instrument if that provision violates other law.

§ 3-113. Date of Instrument.

(a) An instrument may be antedated or postdated. The date stated determines the time of payment if the instrument is payable at a fixed period after date. Except as provided in Section 4-401(c), an instrument payable on demand is not payable before the date of the instrument.

(b) If an instrument is undated, its date is the date of its issue or, in the case of an unissued instrument, the date it first comes into possession of a holder.

Official Comment

This section replaces former Section 3-114. Subsections (1) and (3) of former Section 3-114 are deleted as unnecessary. Section 3-113(a) is based in part on subsection (2) of former Section 3-114. The rule that a demand instrument is not payable before the date of the instrument is subject to Section 4-401(c) which allows the payor bank to pay a postdated check unless the drawer has notified the bank of the postdating pursuant to a procedure prescribed in that subsection. With respect to an undated instrument, the date is the date of issue.

§ 3–114. Contradictory Terms of Instrument.

If an instrument contains contradictory terms, typewritten terms prevail over printed terms, handwritten terms prevail over both, and words prevail over numbers.

Official Comment

Section 3–114 replaces subsections (b) and (c) of former Section 3–118.

§ 3–115. Incomplete Instrument.

(a) "Incomplete instrument" means a signed writing, whether or not issued by the signer, the contents of which show at the time of signing that it is incomplete but that the signer intended it to be completed by the addition of words or numbers.

(b) Subject to subsection (c), if an incomplete instrument is an instrument under Section 3–104, it may be enforced according to its terms if it is not completed, or according to its terms as augmented by completion. If an incomplete instrument is not an instrument under Section 3–104, but, after completion, the requirements of Section 3–104 are met, the instrument may be enforced according to its terms as augmented by completion.

(c) If words or numbers are added to an incomplete instrument without authority of the signer, there is an alteration of the incomplete instrument under Section 3–407.

(d) The burden of establishing that words or numbers were added to an incomplete instrument without authority of the signer is on the person asserting the lack of authority.

Official Comment

1. This section generally carries forward the rules set out in former Section 3–115. The term "incomplete instrument" applies both to an "instrument," i.e. a writing meeting all the requirements of Section 3–104, and to a writing intended to be an instrument that is signed but lacks some element of an instrument. The test in both cases is whether the contents show that it is incomplete and that the signer intended that additional words or numbers be added.

2. If an incomplete instrument meets the requirements of Section 3–104 and is not completed it may be enforced in accordance with its terms. Suppose, in the following two cases, that a note delivered to the payee is incomplete solely because a space on the pre-printed note form for the due date is not filled in:

Case # 1. If the incomplete instrument is never completed, the note is payable on demand. Section 3–108(a)(ii). However, if the payee and the maker agreed to a due date, the maker may have a defense under Section 3–117 if demand for payment is made before the due date agreed to by the parties.

Case # 2. If the payee completes the note by filling in the due date agreed to by the parties, the note is payable on the due date stated. However, if the due date filled in was not the date agreed to by the parties there is an alteration of the note. Section 3–407 governs the case.

Suppose Debtor pays Creditor by giving Creditor a check on which the space for the name of the payee is left blank. The check is an instrument but it is incomplete. The check is enforceable in its incomplete form and it is payable to bearer because it does not state a payee. Section 3-109(a)(2). Thus, Creditor is a holder of the check. Normally in this kind of case Creditor would simply fill in the space with Creditor's name. When that occurs the check becomes payable to the Creditor.

3. In some cases the incomplete instrument does not meet the requirements of Section 3-104. An example is a check with the amount not filled in. The check cannot be enforced until the amount is filled in. If the payee fills in an amount authorized by the drawer the check meets the requirements of Section 3-104 and is enforceable as completed. If the payee fills in an unauthorized amount there is an alteration of the check and Section 3-407 applies.

4. Section 3-302(a)(1) also bears on the problem of incomplete instruments. Under that section a person cannot be a holder in due course of the instrument if it is so incomplete as to call into question its validity. Subsection (d) of Section 3-115 is based on the last clause of subsection (2) of former Section 3-115.

§ 3-116. Joint and Several Liability; Contribution.

(a) Except as otherwise provided in the instrument, two or more persons who have the same liability on an instrument as makers, drawers, acceptors, indorsers who indorse as joint payees, or anomalous indorsers are jointly and severally liable in the capacity in which they sign.

(b) Except as provided in Section 3-419(e) or by agreement of the affected parties, a party having joint and several liability who pays the instrument is entitled to receive from any party having the same joint and several liability contribution in accordance with applicable law.

(c) Discharge of one party having joint and several liability by a person entitled to enforce the instrument does not affect the right under subsection (b) of a party having the same joint and several liability to receive contribution from the party discharged.

Official Comment

1. Subsection (a) replaces subsection (e) of former Section 3-118. Subsection (b) states contribution rights of parties with joint and several liability by referring to applicable law. But subsection (b) is subject to Section 3-419(e). If one of the parties with joint and several liability is an accommodation party and the other is the accommodated party, Section 3-419(e) applies. Subsection (c) deals with discharge. The discharge of a jointly and severally liable obligor does not affect the right of other obligors to seek contribution from the discharged obligor.

2. Indorsers normally do not have joint and several liability. Rather, an earlier indorser has liability to a later indorser. But indorsers can have joint and several liability in two cases. If an instrument is payable to two payees jointly, both payees must indorse. The indorsement is a joint indorsement and the indorsers have joint and several liability and subsection (b) applies. The other case is that of two or more anomalous indorsers. The term is defined in Section 3-205(d). An anomalous indorsement normally indicates that the indorser signed as an accommodation party. If more than one accommodation party indorses a note as an accommodation to the maker, the indorsers have joint and several liability and subsection (b) applies.

§ 3–117. Other Agreements Affecting Instrument.

Subject to applicable law regarding exclusion of proof of contemporaneous or previous agreements, the obligation of a party to an instrument to pay the instrument may be modified, supplemented, or nullified by a separate agreement of the obligor and a person entitled to enforce the instrument, if the instrument is issued or the obligation is incurred in reliance on the agreement or as part of the same transaction giving rise to the agreement. To the extent an obligation is modified, supplemented, or nullified by an agreement under this section, the agreement is a defense to the obligation.

Official Comment

1. The separate agreement might be a security agreement or mortgage or it might be an agreement that contradicts the terms of the instrument. For example, a person may be induced to sign an instrument under an agreement that the signer will not be liable on the instrument unless certain conditions are met. Suppose X requested credit from Creditor who is willing to give the credit only if an acceptable accommodation party will sign the note of X as co-maker. Y agrees to sign as co-maker on the condition that Creditor also obtain the signature of Z as co-maker. Creditor agrees and Y signs as co-maker with X. Creditor fails to obtain the signature of Z on the note. Under Sections 3–412 and 3–419(b), Y is obliged to pay the note, but Section 3–117 applies. In this case, the agreement modifies the terms of the note by stating a condition to the obligation of Y to pay the note. This case is essentially similar to a case in which a maker of a note is induced to sign the note by fraud of the holder. Although the agreement that Y not be liable on the note unless Z also signs may not have been fraudulently made, a subsequent attempt by Creditor to require Y to pay the note in violation of the agreement is a bad faith act. Section 3–117, in treating the agreement as a defense, allows Y to assert the agreement against Creditor, but the defense would not be good against a subsequent holder in due course of the note that took it without notice of the agreement. If there cannot be a holder in due course because of Section 3–106(d), a subsequent holder that took the note in good faith, for value and without knowledge of the agreement would not be able to enforce the liability of Y. This result is consistent with the risk that a holder not in due course takes with respect to fraud in inducing issuance of an instrument.

2. The effect of merger or integration clauses to the effect that a writing is intended to be the complete and exclusive statement of the terms of the agreement or that the agreement is not subject to conditions is left to the supplementary law of the jurisdiction pursuant to Section 1–103. Thus, in the case discussed in Comment 1, whether Y is permitted to prove the condition to Y's obligation to pay the note is determined by that law. Moreover, nothing in this section is intended to validate an agreement which is fraudulent or void as against public policy, as in the case of a note given to deceive a bank examiner.

§ 3–118. Statute of Limitations.

(a) Except as provided in subsection (e), an action to enforce the obligation of a party to pay a note payable at a definite time must be commenced within six years after the due date or dates stated in the note or, if a due date is accelerated, within six years after the accelerated due date.

(b) Except as provided in subsection (d) or (e), if demand for payment is made to the maker of a note payable on demand, an action to enforce the obligation of a party to pay the note must be commenced within six years after the demand. If no demand for payment is made to the maker, an action to enforce the note is barred if neither principal nor interest on the note has been paid for a continuous period of 10 years.

(c) Except as provided in subsection (d), an action to enforce the obligation of a party to an unaccepted draft to pay the draft must be commenced within three years after dishonor of the draft or 10 years after the date of the draft, whichever period expires first.

(d) An action to enforce the obligation of the acceptor of a certified check or the issuer of a teller's check, cashier's check, or traveler's check must be commenced within three years after demand for payment is made to the acceptor or issuer, as the case may be.

(e) An action to enforce the obligation of a party to a certificate of deposit to pay the instrument must be commenced within six years after demand for payment is made to the maker, but if the instrument states a due date and the maker is not required to pay before that date, the six-year period begins when a demand for payment is in effect and the due date has passed.

(f) An action to enforce the obligation of a party to pay an accepted draft, other than a certified check, must be commenced (i) within six years after the due date or dates stated in the draft or acceptance if the obligation of the acceptor is payable at a definite time, or (ii) within six years after the date of the acceptance if the obligation of the acceptor is payable on demand.

(g) Unless governed by other law regarding claims for indemnity or contribution, an action (i) for conversion of an instrument, for money had and received, or like action based on conversion, (ii) for breach of warranty, or (iii) to enforce an obligation, duty, or right arising under this Article and not governed by this section must be commenced within three years after the [cause of action] accrues.

Official Comment

1. Section 3-118 differs from former Section 3-122, which states when a cause of action accrues on an instrument. Section 3-118 does not define when a cause of action accrues. Accrual of a cause of action is stated in other sections of Article 3 such as those that state the various obligations of parties to an instrument. The only purpose of Section 3-118 is to define the time within which an action to enforce an obligation, duty, or right arising under Article 3 must be commenced. Section 3-118 does not attempt to state all rules with respect to a statute of limitations. For example, the circumstances under which the running of a limitations period may be tolled is left to other law pursuant to Section 1-103.

2. The first six subsections apply to actions to enforce an obligation of any party to an instrument to pay the instrument. This changes present law in that indorsers who may become liable on an instrument after issue are subject to a period of limitations running from the same date as that of the maker or drawer. Subsections (a) and (b) apply to notes. If the note is payable at a definite time, a six-year limitations period starts at the due date of the note, subject to prior acceleration. If the note is payable on demand, there are two limitations periods. Although a note payable on demand could theoretically be called a day after it was issued, the normal expectation of the parties is that the note will remain outstanding until there is some reason to call

it. If the law provides that the limitations period does not start until demand is made, the cause of action to enforce it may never be barred. On the other hand, if the limitations period starts when demand for payment may be made, i.e. at any time after the note was issued, the payee of a note on which interest or portions of principal are being paid could lose the right to enforce the note even though it was treated as a continuing obligation by the parties. Some demand notes are not enforced because the payee has forgiven the debt. This is particularly true in family and other noncommercial transactions. A demand note found after the death of the payee may be presented for payment many years after it was issued. The maker may be a relative and it may be difficult to determine whether the note represents a real or a forgiven debt. Subsection (b) is designed to bar notes that no longer represent a claim to payment and to require reasonably prompt action to enforce notes on which there is default. If a demand for payment is made to the maker, a six-year limitations period starts to run when demand is made. The second sentence of subsection (b) bars an action to enforce a demand note if no demand has been made on the note and no payment of interest or principal has been made for a continuous period of 10 years. This covers the case of a note that does not bear interest or a case in which interest due on the note has not been paid. This kind of case is likely to be a family transaction in which a failure to demand payment may indicate that the holder did not intend to enforce the obligation but neglected to destroy the note. A limitations period that bars stale claims in this kind of case is appropriate if the period is relatively long.

3. Subsection (c) applies primarily to personal uncertified checks. Checks are payment instruments rather than credit instruments. The limitations period expires three years after the date of dishonor or 10 years after the date of the check, whichever is earlier. Teller's checks, cashier's checks, certified checks, and traveler's checks are treated differently under subsection (d) because they are commonly treated as cash equivalents. A great delay in presenting a cashier's check for payment in most cases will occur because the check was mislaid during that period. The person to whom traveler's checks are issued may hold them indefinitely as a safe form of cash for use in an emergency. There is no compelling reason for barring the claim of the owner of the cashier's check or traveler's check. Under subsection (d) the claim is never barred because the three-year limitations period does not start to run until demand for payment is made. The limitations period in subsection (d) in effect applies only to cases in which there is a dispute about the legitimacy of the claim of the person demanding payment.

4. Subsection (e) covers certificates of deposit. The limitations period of six years doesn't start to run until the depositor demands payment. Most certificates of deposit are payable on demand even if they state a due date. The effect of a demand for payment before maturity is usually that the bank will pay, but that a penalty will be assessed against the depositor in the form of a reduction in the amount of interest that is paid. Subsection (e) also provides for cases in which the bank has no obligation to pay until the due date. In that case the limitations period doesn't start to run until there is a demand for payment in effect and the due date has passed.

5. Subsection (f) applies to accepted drafts other than certified checks. When a draft is accepted it is in effect turned into a note of the acceptor. In almost all cases the acceptor will agree to pay at a definite time. Subsection (f) states that in that case the six-year limitations period starts to run on the due date. In the rare case in which the obligation of the acceptor is payable on demand, the six-year limitations period starts to run at the date of the acceptance.

6. Subsection (g) covers warranty and conversion cases and other actions to enforce obligations or rights arising under Article 3. A three-year period is stated and subsection (g) follows general law in

stating that the period runs from the time the cause of action accrues. Since the traditional term "cause of action" may have been replaced in some states by "claim for relief" or some equivalent term, the words "cause of action" have been bracketed to indicate that the words may be replaced by an appropriate substitute to conform to local practice.

§ 3-119. Notice of Right to Defend Action.

In an action for breach of an obligation for which a third person is answerable over pursuant to this Article or Article 4, the defendant may give the third person written notice of the litigation, and the person notified may then give similar notice to any other person who is answerable over. If the notice states (i) that the person notified may come in and defend and (ii) that failure to do so will bind the person notified in an action later brought by the person giving the notice as to any determination of fact common to the two litigations, the person notified is so bound unless after seasonable receipt of the notice the person notified does come in and defend.

Official Comment

This section is a restatement of former Section 3-803.

PART 2

NEGOTIATION, TRANSFER, AND INDORSEMENT

§ 3-201. Negotiation.

(a) "Negotiation" means a transfer of possession, whether voluntary or involuntary, of an instrument by a person other than the issuer to a person who thereby becomes its holder.

(b) Except for negotiation by a remitter, if an instrument is payable to an identified person, negotiation requires transfer of possession of the instrument and its indorsement by the holder. If an instrument is payable to bearer, it may be negotiated by transfer of possession alone.

Official Comment

1. Subsections (a) and (b) are based in part on subsection (1) of former Section 3-202. A person can become holder of an instrument when the instrument is issued to that person, or the status of holder can arise as the result of an event that occurs after issuance. "Negotiation" is the term used in Article 3 to describe this post-issuance event. Normally, negotiation occurs as the result of a voluntary transfer of possession of an instrument by a holder to another person who becomes the holder as a result of the transfer. Negotiation always requires a change in possession of the instrument because nobody can be a holder without possessing the instrument, either directly or through an agent. But in some cases the transfer of possession is involuntary and in some cases the person transferring possession is not a holder. In defining "negotiation" former Section 3-202(1) used the word "transfer," an undefined term, and "delivery," defined in Section 1-201(14) to mean voluntary change of possession. Instead, subsections (a) and (b) use the term "transfer of possession" and, subsection (a) states that negotiation can occur by an involuntary transfer of possession. For example, if an instrument is

payable to bearer and it is stolen by Thief or is found by Finder, Thief or Finder becomes the holder of the instrument when possession is obtained. In this case there is an involuntary transfer of possession that results in negotiation to Thief or Finder.

2. In most cases negotiation occurs by a transfer of possession by a holder or remitter. Remitter transactions usually involve a cashier's or teller's check. For example, Buyer buys goods from Seller and pays for them with a cashier's check of Bank that Buyer buys from Bank. The check is issued by Bank when it is delivered to Buyer, regardless of whether the check is payable to Buyer or to Seller. Section 3–105(a). If the check is payable to Buyer, negotiation to Seller is done by delivery of the check to Seller after it is indorsed by Buyer. It is more common, however, that the check when issued will be payable to Seller. In that case Buyer is referred to as the "remitter." Section 3–103(a)(11). The remitter, although not a party to the check, is the owner of the check until ownership is transferred to Seller by delivery. This transfer is a negotiation because Seller becomes the holder of the check when Seller obtains possession. In some cases Seller may have acted fraudulently in obtaining possession of the check. In those cases Buyer may be entitled to rescind the transfer to Seller because of the fraud and assert a claim of ownership to the check under Section 3–306 against Seller or a subsequent transferee of the check. Section 3–202(b) provides for rescission of negotiation, and that provision applies to rescission by a remitter as well as by a holder.

3. Other sections of Article 3 may modify the rule stated in the first sentence of subsection (b). See for example, Sections 3–404, 3–405 and 3–406.

§ 3–202. Negotiation Subject to Rescission.

(a) Negotiation is effective even if obtained (i) from an infant, a corporation exceeding its powers, or a person without capacity, (ii) by fraud, duress, or mistake, or (iii) in breach of duty or as part of an illegal transaction.

(b) To the extent permitted by other law, negotiation may be rescinded or may be subject to other remedies, but those remedies may not be asserted against a subsequent holder in due course or a person paying the instrument in good faith and without knowledge of facts that are a basis for rescission or other remedy.

Official Comment

1. This section is based on former Section 3–207. Subsection (2) of former Section 3–207 prohibited rescission of a negotiation against holders in due course. Subsection (b) of Section 3–202 extends this protection to payor banks.

2. Subsection (a) applies even though the lack of capacity or the illegality, is of a character which goes to the essence of the transaction and makes it entirely void. It is inherent in the character of negotiable instruments that any person in possession of an instrument which by its terms is payable to that person or to bearer is a holder and may be dealt with by anyone as a holder. The principle finds its most extreme application in the well settled rule that a holder in due course may take the instrument even from a thief and be protected against the claim of the rightful owner. The policy of subsection (a) is that any person to whom an instrument is negotiated is a holder until the instrument has been recovered from that person's possession. The remedy of a person with a claim to an instrument is to recover the instrument by replevin or otherwise; to impound it or to enjoin its enforcement, collection or negotiation; to recover its proceeds from the holder; or to intervene in any action brought by the holder against the obligor. As provided in Section 3–305(c), the claim

of the claimant is not a defense to the obligor unless the claimant defends the action.

3. There can be no rescission or other remedy against a holder in due course or a person who pays in good faith and without notice, even though the prior negotiation may have been fraudulent or illegal in its essence and entirely void. As against any other party the claimant may have any remedy permitted by law. This section is not intended to specify what that remedy may be, or to prevent any court from imposing conditions or limitations such as prompt action or return of the consideration received. All such questions are left to the law of the particular jurisdiction. Section 3-202 gives no right that would not otherwise exist. The section is intended to mean that any remedies afforded by other law are cut off only by a holder in due course.

§ 3-203. Transfer of Instrument; Rights Acquired by Transfer.

(a) An instrument is transferred when it is delivered by a person other than its issuer for the purpose of giving to the person receiving delivery the right to enforce the instrument.

(b) Transfer of an instrument, whether or not the transfer is a negotiation, vests in the transferee any right of the transferor to enforce the instrument, including any right as a holder in due course, but the transferee cannot acquire rights of a holder in due course by a transfer, directly or indirectly, from a holder in due course if the transferee engaged in fraud or illegality affecting the instrument.

(c) Unless otherwise agreed, if an instrument is transferred for value and the transferee does not become a holder because of lack of indorsement by the transferor, the transferee has a specifically enforceable right to the unqualified indorsement of the transferor, but negotiation of the instrument does not occur until the indorsement is made.

(d) If a transferor purports to transfer less than the entire instrument, negotiation of the instrument does not occur. The transferee obtains no rights under this Article and has only the rights of a partial assignee.

Official Comment

1. Section 3-203 is based on former Section 3-201 which stated that a transferee received such rights as the transferor had. The former section was confusing because some rights of the transferor are not vested in the transferee unless the transfer is a negotiation. For example, a transferee that did not become the holder could not negotiate the instrument, a right that the transferor had. Former Section 3-201 did not define "transfer." Subsection (a) defines transfer by limiting it to cases in which possession of the instrument is delivered for the purpose of giving to the person receiving delivery the right to enforce the instrument.

Although transfer of an instrument might mean in a particular case that title to the instrument passes to the transferee, that result does not follow in all cases. The right to enforce an instrument and ownership of the instrument are two different concepts. A thief who steals a check payable to bearer becomes the holder of the check and a person entitled to enforce it, but does not become the owner of the check. If the thief transfers the check to a purchaser the transferee obtains the right to enforce the check. If the purchaser is not a holder in due course, the owner's claim to the check may be asserted against the purchaser. Ownership rights in instruments may be determined by principles of the law of property, independent of Article 3, which do not depend upon whether the instrument was transferred under Section 3–203. Moreover, a person who has an ownership right in an instrument might not be a person entitled to enforce the instrument. For example, suppose X is the owner and holder of an instrument payable to X. X sells the instrument to Y but is unable to deliver immediate possession to Y. Instead, X signs a document conveying all of X's right, title, and interest in the instrument to Y. Although the document may be effective to give Y a claim to ownership of the instrument, Y is not a person entitled to enforce the instrument until Y obtains possession of the instrument. No transfer of the instrument occurs under Section 3–203(a) until it is delivered to Y.

An instrument is a reified right to payment. The right is represented by the instrument itself. The right to payment is transferred by delivery of possession of the instrument "by a person other than its issuer for the purpose of giving to the person receiving delivery the right to enforce the instrument." The quoted phrase excludes issue of an instrument, defined in Section 3–105, and cases in which a delivery of possession is for some purpose other than transfer of the right to enforce. For example, if a check is presented for payment by delivering the check to the drawee, no transfer of the check to the drawee occurs because there is no intent to give the drawee the right to enforce the check.

2. Subsection (b) states that transfer vests in the transferee any right of the transferor to enforce the instrument "including any right as a holder in due course." If the transferee is not a holder because the transferor did not indorse, the transferee is nevertheless a person entitled to enforce the instrument under Section 3–301 if the transferor was a holder at the time of transfer. Although the transferee is not a holder, under subsection (b) the transferee obtained the rights of the transferor as holder. Because the transferee's rights are derivative of the transferor's rights, those rights must be proved. Because the transferee is not a holder, there is no presumption under Section 3–308 that the transferee, by producing the instrument, is entitled to payment. The instrument, by its terms, is not payable to the transferee and the transferee must account for possession of the unindorsed instrument by proving the transaction through which the transferee acquired it. Proof of a transfer to the transferee by a holder is proof that the transferee has acquired the rights of a holder. At that point the transferee is entitled to the presumption under Section 3–308.

Under subsection (b) a holder in due course that transfers an instrument transfers those rights as a holder in due course to the purchaser. The policy is to assure the holder in due course a free market for the instrument. There is one exception to this rule stated in the concluding clause of subsection (b). A person who is party to fraud or illegality affecting the instrument is not permitted to wash the instrument clean by passing it into the hands of a holder in due course and then repurchasing it.

3. Subsection (c) applies only to a transfer for value. It applies only if the instrument is payable to order or specially indorsed to the transferor. The transferee acquires, in the absence of a contrary agreement, the specifically enforceable right to the indorsement of the transferor. Unless otherwise agreed, it is a right to the general indorsement of the transferor with full liability as indorser, rather than to an indorsement without recourse. The question may arise if the transferee has paid in advance and the indorsement is omitted fraudulently or through oversight. A transferor who is willing to indorse only without recourse or unwilling to indorse at all should make those intentions clear before transfer. The agreement of the transferee to take less than an unqualified indorsement need not be an express one, and the understanding may be implied from conduct, from past practice, or from the circumstances of the transaction. Subsection (c) provides that there is no negotiation of

the instrument until the indorsement by the transferor is made. Until that time the transferee does not become a holder, and if earlier notice of a defense or claim is received, the transferee does not qualify as a holder in due course under Section 3-302.

4. The operation of Section 3-203 is illustrated by the following cases. In each case Payee, by fraud, induced Maker to issue a note to Payee. The fraud is a defense to the obligation of Maker to pay the note under Section 3-305(a)(2).

Case # 1. Payee negotiated the note to X who took as a holder in due course. After the instrument became overdue X negotiated the note to Y who had notice of the fraud. Y succeeds to X's rights as a holder in due course and takes free of Maker's defense of fraud.

Case # 2. Payee negotiated the note to X who took as a holder in due course. Payee then repurchased the note from X. Payee does not succeed to X's rights as a holder in due course and is subject to Maker's defense of fraud.

Case # 3. Payee negotiated the note to X who took as a holder in due course. X sold the note to Purchaser who received possession. The note, however, was indorsed to X and X failed to indorse it. Purchaser is a person entitled to enforce the instrument under Section 3-301 and succeeds to the rights of X as holder in due course. Purchaser is not a holder, however, and under Section 3-308 Purchaser will have to prove the transaction with X under which the rights of X as holder in due course were acquired.

Case # 4. Payee sold the note to Purchaser who took for value, in good faith and without notice of the defense of Maker. Purchaser received possession of the note but Payee neglected to indorse it. Purchaser became a person entitled to enforce the instrument but did not become the holder because of the missing indorsement. If Purchaser received notice of the defense of Maker before obtaining the indorsement of Payee, Purchaser cannot become a holder in due course because at the time notice was received the note had not been negotiated to Purchaser. If indorsement by Payee was made after Purchaser received notice, Purchaser had notice of the defense when it became the holder.

5. Subsection (d) restates former Section 3-202(3). The cause of action on an instrument cannot be split. Any indorsement which purports to convey to any party less than the entire amount of the instrument is not effective for negotiation. This is true of either "Pay A one-half," or "Pay A two-thirds and B one-third." Neither A nor B becomes a holder. On the other hand an indorsement reading merely "Pay A and B" is effective, since it transfers the entire cause of action to A and B as tenants in common. An indorsement purporting to convey less than the entire instrument does, however, operate as a partial assignment of the cause of action. Subsection (d) makes no attempt to state the legal effect of such an assignment, which is left to other law. A partial assignee of an instrument has rights only to the extent the applicable law gives rights, either at law or in equity, to a partial assignee.

§ 3-204. Indorsement.

(a) "Indorsement" means a signature, other than that of a signer as maker, drawer, or acceptor, that alone or accompanied by other words is made on an instrument for the purpose of (i) negotiating the instrument, (ii) restricting payment of the instrument, or (iii) incurring indorser's liability on the instrument, but regardless of the intent of the signer, a signature and its accompanying words is an indorsement unless the accompanying words, terms of the instrument, place of the signature, or other circumstances unambiguously indicate that the signature was made for a purpose other than indorsement. For the purpose of determining whether a signature is made on an instrument, a paper affixed to the instrument is a part of the instrument.

(b) "Indorser" means a person who makes an indorsement.

(c) For the purpose of determining whether the transferee of an instrument is a holder, an indorsement that transfers a security interest in the instrument is effective as an unqualified indorsement of the instrument.

(d) If an instrument is payable to a holder under a name that is not the name of the holder, indorsement may be made by the holder in the name stated in the instrument or in the holder's name or both, but signature in both names may be required by a person paying or taking the instrument for value or collection.

Official Comment

1. Subsection (a) is a definition of "indorsement," a term which was not defined in former Article 3. Indorsement is defined in terms of the purpose of the signature. If a blank or special indorsement is made to give rights as a holder to a transferee the indorsement is made for the purpose of negotiating the instrument. Subsection (a)(i). If the holder of a check has an account in the drawee bank and wants to be sure that payment of the check will be made by credit to the holder's account, the holder can indorse the check by signing the holder's name with the accompanying words "for deposit only" before presenting the check for payment to the drawee bank. In that case the purpose of the quoted words is to restrict payment of the instrument. Subsection (a)(ii). If X wants to guarantee payment of a note signed by Y as maker, X can do so by signing X's name to the back of the note as an indorsement. This indorsement is known as an anomalous indorsement (Section 3–205(d)) and is made for the purpose of incurring indorser's liability on the note. Subsection (a)(iii). In some cases an indorsement may serve more than one purpose. For example, if the holder of a check deposits it to the holder's account in a depositary bank for collection and indorses the check by signing the holder's name with the accompanying words "for deposit only" the purpose of the indorsement is both to negotiate the check to the depositary bank and to restrict payment of the check.

The "but" clause of the first sentence of subsection (a) elaborates on former Section 3–402. In some cases it may not be clear whether a signature was meant to be that of an indorser, a party to the instrument in some other capacity such as drawer, maker or acceptor, or a person who was not signing as a party. The general rule is that a signature is an indorsement if the instrument does not indicate an unambiguous intent of the signer not to sign as an indorser. Intent may be determined by words accompanying the signature, the place of signature, or other circumstances. For example, suppose a depositary bank gives cash for a check properly indorsed by the payee. The bank requires the payee's employee to sign the back of the check as evidence that the employee received the cash. If the signature consists only of the initials of the employee it is not reasonable to assume that it was meant to be an indorsement. If there was a full signature but accompanying words indicated that it was meant as a receipt for the cash given for the check, it is not an indorsement. If the signature is not qualified in any way and appears in the place normally used for indorsements, it may be an indorsement even though the signer intended the signature to be a receipt. To take another example, suppose the drawee of a draft signs the draft on the back in the space usually used for indorsements. No words accompany the signature. Since the drawee has no reason to sign a draft unless the intent is to accept the draft, the signature is effective as an acceptance. Custom and usage may be used to determine intent. For example, by long-established custom and usage, a signature in the lower right hand corner of an instrument indicates an intent to sign as the maker of a note or the drawer of a draft. Any similar clear indication of an intent to sign in some other capacity or for some other purpose may establish that a signature is not an indorsement. For example, if the owner of a traveler's check countersigns the check in the process of negotiating it, the countersignature is not an indorsement. The countersignature is a condition to the issuer's obligation to pay and its purpose is to provide a means of verifying the identify of the person negotiating the traveler's check by allowing comparison of the specimen signature and the countersignature. The countersignature is not necessary for negotiation and the signer does not incur indorser's liability. See Comment 2 to Section 3-106.

The last sentence of subsection (a) is based on subsection (2) of former Section 3-202. An indorsement on an allonge is valid even though there is sufficient space on the instrument for an indorsement.

2. Assume that Payee indorses a note to Creditor as security for a debt. Under subsection (b) of Section 3-203 Creditor takes Payee's rights to enforce or transfer the instrument subject to the limitations imposed by Article 9. Subsection (c) of Section 3-204 makes clear that Payee's indorsement to Creditor, even though it mentions creation of a security interest, is an unqualified indorsement that gives to Creditor the right to enforce the note as its holder.

3. Subsection (d) is a restatement of former Section 3-203. Section 3-110(a) states that an instrument is payable to the person intended by the person signing as or in the name or behalf of the issuer even if that person is identified by a name that is not the true name of the person. In some cases the name used in the instrument is a misspelling of the correct name and in some cases the two names may be entirely different. The payee may indorse in the name used in the instrument, in the payee's correct name, or in both. In each case the indorsement is effective. But because an indorsement in a name different from that used in the instrument may raise a question about its validity and an indorsement in a name that is not the correct name of the payee may raise a problem of identifying the indorser, the accepted commercial practice is to indorse in both names. Subsection (d) allows a person paying or taking the instrument for value or collection to require indorsement in both names.

§ 3-205. Special Indorsement; Blank Indorsement; Anomalous Indorsement.

(a) If an indorsement is made by the holder of an instrument, whether payable to an identified person or payable to bearer, and the indorsement identifies a person to whom it makes the instrument payable, it is a "special indorsement." When specially indorsed, an instrument becomes payable to the identified person and may be negotiated only by the indorsement of that person. The principles stated in Section 3-110 apply to special indorsements.

(b) If an indorsement is made by the holder of an instrument and it is not a special indorsement, it is a "blank indorsement." When indorsed in blank, an instrument becomes payable to bearer and may be negotiated by transfer of possession alone until specially indorsed.

(c) The holder may convert a blank indorsement that consists only of a signature into a special indorsement by writing, above the signature of the indorser, words identifying the person to whom the instrument is made payable.

(d) "Anomalous indorsement" means an indorsement made by a person who is not the holder of the instrument. An anomalous indorsement does not affect the manner in which the instrument may be negotiated.

Official Comment

1. Subsection (a) is based on subsection (1) of former Section 3–204. It states the test of a special indorsement to be whether the indorsement identifies a person to whom the instrument is payable. Section 3–110 states rules for identifying the payee of an instrument. Section 3–205(a) incorporates the principles stated in Section 3–110 in identifying an indorsee. The language of Section 3–110 refers to language used by the issuer of the instrument. When that section is used with respect to an indorsement, Section 3–110 must be read as referring to the language used by the indorser.

2. Subsection (b) is based on subsection (2) of former Section 3–204. An indorsement made by the holder is either a special or blank indorsement. If the indorsement is made by a holder and is not a special indorsement, it is a blank indorsement. For example, the holder of an instrument, intending to make a special indorsement, writes the words "Pay to the order of" without completing the indorsement by writing the name of the indorsee. The holder's signature appears under the quoted words. The indorsement is not a special indorsement because it does not identify a person to whom it makes the instrument payable. Since it is not a special indorsement it is a blank indorsement and the instrument is payable to bearer. The result is analogous to that of a check in which the name of the payee is left blank by the drawer. In that case the check is payable to bearer. See the last paragraphs of Comment 2 to Section 3–115.

A blank indorsement is usually the signature of the indorser on the back of the instrument without other words. Subsection (c) is based on subsection (3) of former Section 3–204. A "restrictive indorsement" described in Section 3–206 can be either a blank indorsement or a special indorsement. "Pay to T, in trust for B" is a restrictive indorsement. It is also a special indorsement because it identifies T as the person to whom the instrument is payable. "For deposit only" followed by the signature of the payee of a check is a restrictive indorsement. It is also a blank indorsement because it does not identify the person to whom the instrument is payable.

3. The only effect of an "anomalous indorsement," defined in subsection (d), is to make the signer liable on the instrument as an indorser. Such an indorsement is normally made by an accommodation party. Section 3–419.

§ 3–206. Restrictive Indorsement.

(a) An indorsement limiting payment to a particular person or otherwise prohibiting further transfer or negotiation of the instrument is not effective to prevent further transfer or negotiation of the instrument.

(b) An indorsement stating a condition to the right of the indorsee to receive payment does not affect the right of the indorsee to enforce the instrument. A person paying the instrument or taking it for value or collection may disregard the condition, and the rights and liabilities of that person are not affected by whether the condition has been fulfilled.

(c) If an instrument bears an indorsement (i) described in Section 4–201(b), or (ii) in blank or to a particular bank using the words "for deposit," "for collection," or other words indicating a purpose of having the instrument collected by a bank for the indorser or for a particular account, the following rules apply:

(1) A person, other than a bank, who purchases the instrument when so indorsed converts the instrument unless the amount paid for the instrument is received by the indorser or applied consistently with the indorsement.

(2) A depositary bank that purchases the instrument or takes it for collection when so indorsed converts the instrument unless the amount paid by the bank with respect to the instrument is received by the indorser or applied consistently with the indorsement.

(3) A payor bank that is also the depositary bank or that takes the instrument for immediate payment over the counter from a person other than a collecting bank converts the instrument unless the proceeds of the instrument are received by the indorser or applied consistently with the indorsement.

(4) Except as otherwise provided in paragraph (3), a payor bank or intermediary bank may disregard the indorsement and is not liable if the proceeds of the instrument are not received by the indorser or applied consistently with the indorsement.

(d) Except for an indorsement covered by subsection (c), if an instrument bears an indorsement using words to the effect that payment is to be made to the indorsee as agent, trustee, or other fiduciary for the benefit of the indorser or another person, the following rules apply:

(1) Unless there is notice of breach of fiduciary duty as provided in Section 3–307, a person who purchases the instrument from the indorsee or takes the instrument from the indorsee for collection or payment may pay the proceeds of payment or the value given for the instrument to the indorsee without regard to whether the indorsee violates a fiduciary duty to the indorser.

(2) A subsequent transferee of the instrument or person who pays the instrument is neither given notice nor otherwise affected by the restriction in the indorsement unless the transferee or payor knows that the fiduciary dealt with the instrument or its proceeds in breach of fiduciary duty.

(e) The presence on an instrument of an indorsement to which this section applies does not prevent a purchaser of the instrument from becoming a holder in due course of the instrument unless the purchaser is a converter under subsection (c) or has notice or knowledge of breach of fiduciary duty as stated in subsection (d).

(f) In an action to enforce the obligation of a party to pay the instrument, the obligor has a defense if payment would violate an indorsement to which this section applies and the payment is not permitted by this section.

Official Comment

1. This section replaces former Sections 3–205 and 3–206 and clarifies the law of restrictive indorsements.

2. Subsection (a) provides that an indorsement that purports to limit further transfer or negotiation is ineffective to prevent further transfer or negotiation. If a payee indorses "Pay A only," A may negotiate the instrument to subsequent holders who may ignore the restriction on the indorsement. Subsection (b) provides that an indorsement that states a condition to the right of a holder to receive payment is ineffective to condition payment. Thus if a payee indorses "Pay A if A ships goods complying with our contract," the right of A to enforce the instrument is not affected by the condition. In the case of a note, the obligation of the maker to pay A is not affected by the indorsement. In the case of a check, the drawee can pay A without regard to the condition, and if the check is dishonored the drawer is liable to pay A. If the check was negotiated by the payee to A in return for a promise to perform a contract and the promise was not kept, the payee would have a defense or counterclaim against A if the check were dishonored and A sued the payee as indorser, but the payee would have that defense or counterclaim whether or not the condition to the right of A was expressed in the indorsement. Former Section 3–206 treated a conditional indorsement like indorsements for deposit or collection. In revised Article 3, Section 3–206(b) rejects that approach and makes the conditional indorsement ineffective with respect to parties other than the indorser and indorsee. Since the indorsements referred to in subsections (a) and (b) are not effective as restrictive indorsements, they are no longer described as restrictive indorsements.

3. The great majority of restrictive indorsements are those that fall within subsection (c) which continues previous law. The depositary bank or the payor bank, if it takes the check for immediate payment over the counter, must act consistently with the indorsement, but an intermediary bank or payor bank that takes the check from a collecting bank is not affected by the indorsement. Any other person is also bound by the indorsement. For example, suppose a check is payable to X, who indorses in blank but writes above the signature the words "For deposit only." The check is stolen and is cashed at a grocery store by the thief. The grocery store indorses the check and deposits it in Depositary Bank. The account of the grocery store is credited and the check is forwarded to Payor Bank which pays the check. Under subsection (c), the grocery store and Depositary Bank are converters of the check because X did not receive the amount paid for the check. Payor Bank and any intermediary bank in the collection process are not liable to X. This Article does not displace the law of waiver as it may apply to restrictive indorsements. The circumstances under which a restrictive indorsement may be waived by the person who made it is not determined by this Article.

4. Subsection (d) replaces subsection (4) of former Section 3–206. Suppose Payee indorses a check "Pay to T in trust for B." T indorses in blank and delivers it to (a) Holder for value; (b) Depositary Bank for collection; or (c) Payor Bank for payment. In each case these takers can safely pay T so long as they have no notice under Section 3–307 of any breach of fiduciary duty that T may be committing. For example, under subsection ~~(a)~~ (b) * of Section 3–307 these takers have notice of a breach of trust if the check was taken in any transaction known by the taker to be for T's personal benefit. Subsequent transferees of the check from Holder or Depositary Bank are not affected by the restriction unless they have knowledge that T dealt with the check in breach of trust.

5. Subsection (f) allows a restrictive indorsement to be used as a defense by a person obliged to pay the instrument if that person would be liable for paying in violation of the indorsement.

* *Previous incorrect cross reference corrected by Permanent Editorial Board action November 1992.*

§ 3-207. Reacquisition.

Reacquisition of an instrument occurs if it is transferred to a former holder, by negotiation or otherwise. A former holder who reacquires the instrument may cancel indorsements made after the reacquirer first became a holder of the instrument. If the cancellation causes the instrument to be payable to the reacquirer or to bearer, the reacquirer may negotiate the instrument. An indorser whose indorsement is canceled is discharged, and the discharge is effective against any subsequent holder.

Official Comment

Section 3-207 restates former Section 3-208. Reacquisition refers to cases in which a former holder reacquires the instrument either by negotiation from the present holder or by a transfer other than negotiation. If the reacquisition is by negotiation, the former holder reacquires the status of holder. Although Section 3-207 allows the holder to cancel all indorsements made after the holder first acquired holder status, cancellation is not necessary. Status of holder is not affected whether or not cancellation is made. But if the reacquisition is not the result of negotiation the former holder can obtain holder status only by striking the former holder's indorsement and any subsequent indorsements. The latter case is an exception to the general rule that if an instrument is payable to an identified person, the indorsement of that person is necessary to allow a subsequent transferee to obtain the status of holder. Reacquisition without indorsement by the person to whom the instrument is payable is illustrated by two examples:

Case # 1. X, a former holder, buys the instrument from Y, the present holder. Y delivers the instrument to X but fails to indorse it. Negotiation does not occur because the transfer of possession did not result in X's becoming holder. Section 3-201(a). The instrument by its terms is payable to Y, not to X. But X can obtain the status of holder by striking X's indorsement and all subsequent indorsements. When these indorsements are struck, the instrument by its terms is payable either to X or to bearer, depending upon how X originally became holder. In either case X becomes holder. Section 1-201(20).

Case # 2. X, the holder of an instrument payable to X, negotiates it to Y by special indorsement. The negotiation is part of an underlying transaction between X and Y. The underlying transaction is rescinded by agreement of X and Y, and Y returns the instrument without Y's indorsement. The analysis is the same as that in Case # 1. X can obtain holder status by cancelling X's indorsement to Y.

In Case # 1 and Case # 2, X acquired ownership of the instrument after reacquisition, but X's title was clouded because the instrument by its terms was not payable to X. Normally, X can remedy the problem by obtaining Y's indorsement, but in some cases X may not be able to conveniently obtain that indorsement. Section 3-207 is a rule of convenience which relieves X of the burden of obtaining an indorsement that serves no substantive purpose. The effect of cancellation of any indorsement under Section 3-207 is to nullify it. Thus, the person whose indorsement is canceled is relieved of indorser's liability. Since cancellation is notice of discharge, discharge is effective even with respect to the rights of a holder in due course. Sections 3-601 and 3-604.

PART 3

ENFORCEMENT OF INSTRUMENTS

§ 3–301. Person Entitled to Enforce Instrument.

"Person entitled to enforce" an instrument means (i) the holder of the instrument, (ii) a nonholder in possession of the instrument who has the rights of a holder, or (iii) a person not in possession of the instrument who is entitled to enforce the instrument pursuant to Section 3–309 or 3–418(d). A person may be a person entitled to enforce the instrument even though the person is not the owner of the instrument or is in wrongful possession of the instrument.

Official Comment

This section replaces former Section 3–301 that stated the rights of a holder. The rights stated in former Section 3–301 to transfer, negotiate, enforce, or discharge an instrument are stated in other sections of Article 3. In revised Article 3, Section 3–301 defines "person entitled to enforce" an instrument. The definition recognizes that enforcement is not limited to holders. The quoted phrase includes a person enforcing a lost or stolen instrument. Section 3–309. It also includes a person in possession of an instrument who is not a holder. A nonholder in possession of an instrument includes a person that acquired rights of a holder by subrogation or under Section 3–203(a). It also includes any other person who under applicable law is a successor to the holder or otherwise acquires the holder's rights.

§ 3–302. Holder in Due Course.

(a) Subject to subsection (c) and Section 3–106(d), "holder in due course" means the holder of an instrument if:

(1) the instrument when issued or negotiated to the holder does not bear such apparent evidence of forgery or alteration or is not otherwise so irregular or incomplete as to call into question its authenticity; and

(2) the holder took the instrument (i) for value, (ii) in good faith, (iii) without notice that the instrument is overdue or has been dishonored or that there is an uncured default with respect to payment of another instrument issued as part of the same series, (iv) without notice that the instrument contains an unauthorized signature or has been altered, (v) without notice of any claim to the instrument described in Section 3–306, and (vi) without notice that any party has a defense or claim in recoupment described in Section 3–305(a).

(b) Notice of discharge of a party, other than discharge in an insolvency proceeding, is not notice of a defense under subsection (a), but discharge is effective against a person who became a holder in due course with notice of the discharge. Public filing or recording of a document does not of itself constitute notice of a defense, claim in recoupment, or claim to the instrument.

(c) Except to the extent a transferor or predecessor in interest has rights as a holder in due course, a person does not acquire rights of a holder in due course of an instrument taken (i) by legal process or by purchase in an execution, bankruptcy, or creditor's sale or similar proceeding, (ii) by purchase as part of a bulk transaction not in ordinary course of business of the transferor, or (iii) as the successor in interest to an estate or other organization.

(d) If, under Section 3-303(a)(1), the promise of performance that is the consideration for an instrument has been partially performed, the holder may assert rights as a holder in due course of the instrument only to the fraction of the amount payable under the instrument equal to the value of the partial performance divided by the value of the promised performance.

(e) If (i) the person entitled to enforce an instrument has only a security interest in the instrument and (ii) the person obliged to pay the instrument has a defense, claim in recoupment, or claim to the instrument that may be asserted against the person who granted the security interest, the person entitled to enforce the instrument may assert rights as a holder in due course only to an amount payable under the instrument which, at the time of enforcement of the instrument, does not exceed the amount of the unpaid obligation secured.

(f) To be effective, notice must be received at a time and in a manner that gives a reasonable opportunity to act on it.

(g) This section is subject to any law limiting status as a holder in due course in particular classes of transactions.

Official Comment

1. Subsection (a)(1) is a return to the N.I.L. rule that the taker of an irregular or incomplete instrument is not a person the law should protect against defenses of the obligor or claims of prior owners. This reflects a policy choice against extending the holder in due course doctrine to an instrument that is so incomplete or irregular "as to call into question its authenticity." The term "authenticity" is used to make it clear that the irregularity or incompleteness must indicate that the instrument may not be what it purports to be. Persons who purchase or pay such instruments should do so at their own risk. Under subsection (1) of former Section 3-304, irregularity or incompleteness gave a purchaser notice of a claim or defense. But it was not clear from that provision whether the claim or defense had to be related to the irregularity or incomplete aspect of the instrument. This ambiguity is not present in subsection (a)(1).

2. Subsection (a)(2) restates subsection (1) of former Section 3-302. Section 3-305(a) makes a distinction between defenses to the obligation to pay an instrument and claims in recoupment by the maker or drawer that may be asserted to reduce the amount payable on the instrument. Because of this distinction, which was not made in former Article 3, the reference in subsection (a)(2)(vi) is to both a defense and a claim in recoupment. Notice of forgery or alteration is stated separately because forgery and alteration are not technically defenses under subsection (a) of Section 3-305.

3. Discharge is also separately treated in the first sentence of subsection (b). Except for discharge in an insolvency proceeding, which is specifically stated to be a real defense in Section 3-305(a)(1), discharge is not expressed in Article 3 as a defense and is not included in Section 3-

305(a)(2). Discharge is effective against anybody except a person having rights of a holder in due course who took the instrument without notice of the discharge. Notice of discharge does not disqualify a person from becoming a holder in due course. For example, a check certified after it is negotiated by the payee may subsequently be negotiated to a holder. If the holder had notice that the certification occurred after negotiation by the payee, the holder necessarily had notice of the discharge of the payee as indorser. Section 3–415(d). Notice of that discharge does not prevent the holder from becoming a holder in due course, but the discharge is effective against the holder. Section 3–601(b). Notice of a defense under Section 3–305(a)(1) of a maker, drawer or acceptor based on a bankruptcy discharge is different. There is no reason to give holder in due course status to a person with notice of that defense. The second sentence of subsection (b) is from former Section 3–304(5).

4. Professor Britton in his treatise Bills and Notes 309 (1961) stated: "A substantial number of decisions before the [N.I.L.] indicates that at common law there was nothing in the position of the payee as such which made it impossible for him to be a holder in due course." The courts were divided, however, about whether the payee of an instrument could be a holder in due course under the N.I.L.. Some courts read N.I.L. § 52(4) to mean that a person could be a holder in due course only if the instrument was "negotiated" to that person. N.I.L. § 30 stated that "an instrument is negotiated when it is transferred from one person to another in such manner as to constitute the transferee the holder thereof." Normally, an instrument is "issued" to the payee; it is not transferred to the payee. N.I.L. § 191 defined "issue" as the "first delivery of the instrument *** to a person who takes it as a holder." Thus, some courts concluded that the payee never could be a holder in due course. Other courts concluded that there was no evidence that the N.I.L. was intended to change the common law rule that the payee could be a holder in due course. Professor Britton states on p. 318: "The typical situations which raise the [issue] are those where the defense of a maker is interposed because of fraud by a [maker who is] principal debtor *** against a surety co-maker, or where the defense of fraud by a purchasing remitter is interposed by the drawer of the instrument against the good faith purchasing payee."

Former Section 3–302(2) stated: "A payee may be a holder in due course." This provision was intended to resolve the split of authority under the N.I.L.. It made clear that there was no intent to change the common-law rule that allowed a payee to become a holder in due course. See Comment 2 to former Section 3–302. But there was no need to put subsection (2) in former Section 3–302 because the split in authority under the N.I.L. was caused by the particular wording of N.I.L. § 52(4). The troublesome language in that section was not repeated in former Article 3 nor is it repeated in revised Article 3. Former Section 3–302(2) has been omitted in revised Article 3 because it is surplusage and may be misleading. The payee of an instrument can be a holder in due course, but use of the holder-in-due-course doctrine by the payee of an instrument is not the normal situation.

The primary importance of the concept of holder in due course is with respect to assertion of defenses or claims in recoupment (Section 3–305) and of claims to the instrument (Section 3–306). The holder-in-due-course doctrine assumes the following case as typical. Obligor issues a note or check to Obligee. Obligor is the maker of the note or drawer of the check. Obligee is the payee. Obligor has some defense to Obligor's obligation to pay the instrument. For example, Obligor issued the instrument for goods that Obligee promised to deliver. Obligee never delivered the goods. The failure of Obligee to deliver the goods is a defense. Section 3–303(b). Although Obligor has a defense against Obligee, if the instrument is negotiated to Holder and the requirements of subsection (a) are met, Holder may enforce the instrument against Obligor free of the defense. Section 3-305(b). In the typical case the holder in due course is not the payee of the instrument. Rather, the holder in due course is an immediate or remote transferee of the payee. If Obligor in our example is the only obligor on the check or note, the holder-in-due-course doctrine is irrelevant in determining rights between Obligor and Obligee with respect to the instrument.

But in a small percentage of cases it is appropriate to allow the payee of an instrument to assert rights as a holder in due course. The cases are like those referred to in the quotation from Professor Britton referred to above, or other cases in which conduct of some third party is the basis of the defense of the issuer of the instrument. The following are examples:

Case # 1. Buyer pays for goods bought from Seller by giving to Seller a cashier's check bought from Bank. Bank has a defense to its obligation to pay the check because Buyer bought the check from Bank with a check known to be drawn on an account with insufficient funds to cover the check. If Bank issued the check to Buyer as payee and Buyer indorsed it over to Seller, it is clear that Seller can be a holder in due course taking free of the defense if Seller had no notice of the defense. Seller is a transferee of the check. There is no good reason why Seller's position should be any different if Bank drew the check to the order of Seller as payee. In that case, when Buyer took delivery of the check from Bank, Buyer became the owner of the check even though Buyer was not the holder. Buyer was a remitter. Section 3-103(a)(11). At that point nobody was the holder. When Buyer delivered the check to Seller, ownership of the check was transferred to Seller who also became the holder. This is a negotiation. Section 3-201. The rights of Seller should not be affected by the fact that in one case the negotiation to Seller was by a holder and in the other case the negotiation was by a remitter. Moreover, it should be irrelevant whether Bank delivered the check to Buyer and Buyer delivered it to Seller or whether Bank delivered it directly to Seller. In either case Seller can be a holder in due course that takes free of Bank's defense.

Case # 2. X fraudulently induces Y to join X in a spurious venture to purchase a business. The purchase is to be financed by a bank loan for part of the price. Bank lends money to X and Y by deposit in a joint account of X and Y who sign a note payable to Bank for the amount of the loan. X then withdraws the money from the joint account and absconds. Bank acted in good faith and without notice of the fraud of X against Y. Bank is payee of the note executed by Y, but its right to enforce the note against Y should not be affected by the fact that Y was induced to execute the note by the fraud of X. Bank can be a holder in due course that takes free of the defense of Y. Case # 2 is similar to Case # 1. In each case the payee of the instrument has given value to the person committing the fraud in exchange for the obligation of the person against whom the fraud was committed. In each case the payee was not party to the fraud and had no notice of it.

Suppose in Case # 2 that the note does not meet the requirements of Section 3-104(a) and thus is not a negotiable instrument covered by Article 3. In that case, Bank cannot be a holder in due course but the result should be the same. Bank's rights are determined by general principles of contract law. Restatement Second, Contracts § 164(2) governs the case. If Y is induced to enter into a contract with Bank by a fraudulent misrepresentation by X, the contract is voidable by Y unless Bank "in good faith and without reason to know of the misrepresentation either gives value or relies materially on the transaction." Comment e to § 164(2) states:

"This is the same principle that protects an innocent person who purchases goods or commercial paper in good faith, without notice and for value from one who obtained them from the original owner by a misrepresentation. See Uniform Commercial Code §§ 2-403(1), 3-305. In the cases that fall within [§ 164(2)], however, the innocent person deals directly with the recipient of the misrepresentation, which is made by one not a party to the contract."

The same result follows in Case # 2 if Y had been induced to sign the note as an accommodation party (Section 3-419). If Y signs as co-maker of a note for the benefit of X, Y is a surety with respect to the obligation of X to pay the note but is liable as maker of the note to pay Bank. Section 3-419(b). If Bank is a holder in due course, the fraud of X cannot be asserted against Bank under Section 3-305(b). But the result is the same without resort to holder-in-due-course doctrine. If the note is not a negotiable instrument governed by Article 3, general rules of suretyship apply. Restatement, Security § 119 states that the surety (Y) cannot assert a defense against the creditor (Bank) based on the fraud of the principal (X) if the creditor "without knowledge of the fraud *** extended credit to the principal on the security of the surety's promise ***." The underlying principle of § 119 is the same as that of § 164(2) of Restatement Second, Contracts.

Case # 3. Corporation draws a check payable to Bank. The check is given to an officer of Corporation who is instructed to deliver it to Bank in payment of a debt owed by Corporation to Bank. Instead, the officer, intending to defraud Corporation, delivers the check to Bank in payment of the officer's personal debt, or the check is delivered to Bank for deposit to the officer's personal account. If Bank obtains payment of the check, Bank has received funds of Corporation which have been used for the personal benefit of the officer. Corporation in this case will assert a claim to the proceeds of the check against Bank. If Bank was a holder in due course of the check it took the check free of Corporation's claim. Section 3-306. The issue in this case is whether Bank had notice of the claim when it took the check. If Bank knew that the officer was a fiduciary with respect to the check, the issue is governed by Section 3-307.

Case # 4. Employer, who owed money to X, signed a blank check and delivered it to Secretary with instructions to complete the check by typing in X's name and the amount owed to X. Secretary fraudulently completed the check by typing in the name of Y, a creditor to whom Secretary owed money. Secretary then delivered the check to Y in payment of Secretary's debt. Y obtained payment of the check. This case is similar to Case # 3. Since Secretary was authorized to complete the check, Employer is bound by Secretary's act in making the check payable to Y. The drawee bank properly paid the check. Y received funds of Employer which were used for the personal benefit of Secretary. Employer asserts a claim to these funds against Y. If Y is a holder in due course, Y takes free of the claim. Whether Y is a holder in due course depends upon whether Y had notice of Employer's claim.

5. Subsection (c) is based on former Section 3-302(3). Like former Section 3-302(3), subsection (c) is intended to state existing case law. It covers a few situations in which the purchaser takes an instrument under unusual circumstances. The purchaser is treated as a successor in interest to the prior holder and can acquire no better rights. But if the prior holder was a holder in due course, the purchaser obtains rights of a holder in due course.

Subsection (c) applies to a purchaser in an execution sale or sale in bankruptcy. It applies equally to an attaching creditor or any other person who acquires the instrument by legal process or to a representative, such as an executor, administrator, receiver or assignee for the benefit of creditors, who takes the instrument as part of an estate. Subsection (c) applies to bulk purchases lying outside of the ordinary course of business of the seller.

For example, it applies to the purchase by one bank of a substantial part of the paper held by another bank which is threatened with insolvency and seeking to liquidate its assets. Subsection (c) would also apply when a new partnership takes over for value all of the assets of an old one after a new member has entered the firm, or to a reorganized or consolidated corporation taking over the assets of a predecessor.

In the absence of controlling state law to the contrary, subsection (c) applies to a sale by a state bank commissioner of the assets of an insolvent bank. However, subsection (c) may be preempted by federal law if the Federal Deposit Insurance Corporation takes over an insolvent bank. Under the governing federal law, the FDIC and similar financial institution insurers are given holder in due course status and that status is also acquired by their assignees under the shelter doctrine.

6. Subsections (d) and (e) clarify two matters not specifically addressed by former Article 3:

Case # 5. Payee negotiates a $1,000 note to Holder who agrees to pay $900 for it. After paying $500, Holder learns that Payee defrauded Maker in the transaction giving rise to the note. Under subsection (d) Holder may assert rights as a holder in due course to the extent of $555.55 ($500 ÷ $900 = .555 × $1,000 = $555.55). This formula rewards Holder with a ratable portion of the bargained for profit.

Case # 6. Payee negotiates a note of Maker for $1,000 to Holder as security for payment of Payee's debt to Holder of $600. Maker has a defense which is good against Payee but of which Holder has no notice. Subsection (e) applies. Holder may assert rights as a holder in due course only to the extent of $600. Payee does not get the benefit of the holder-in-due-course status of Holder. With respect to $400 of the note, Maker may assert any rights that Maker has against Payee. A different result follows if the payee of a note negotiated it to a person who took it as a holder in due course and that person pledged the note as security for a debt. Because the defense cannot be asserted against the pledgor, the pledgee can assert rights as a holder in due course for the full amount of the note for the benefit of both the pledgor and the pledgee.

7. There is a large body of state statutory and case law restricting the use of the holder in due course doctrine in consumer transactions as well as some business transactions that raise similar issues. Subsection (g) subordinates Article 3 to that law and any other similar law that may evolve in the future. Section 3–106(d) also relates to statutory or administrative law intended to restrict use of the holder-in-due-course doctrine. See Comment 3 to Section 3–106.

§ 3-303. Value and Consideration.

(a) An instrument is issued or transferred for value if:

(1) the instrument is issued or transferred for a promise of performance, to the extent the promise has been performed;

(2) the transferee acquires a security interest or other lien in the instrument other than a lien obtained by judicial proceeding;

(3) the instrument is issued or transferred as payment of, or as security for, an antecedent claim against any person, whether or not the claim is due;

(4) the instrument is issued or transferred in exchange for a negotiable instrument; or

(5) the instrument is issued or transferred in exchange for the incurring of an irrevocable obligation to a third party by the person taking the instrument.

(b) "Consideration" means any consideration sufficient to support a simple contract. The drawer or maker of an instrument has a defense if the instrument is issued without consideration. If an instrument is issued for a promise of performance, the issuer has a defense to the extent performance of the promise is due and the promise has not been performed. If an instrument is issued for value as stated in subsection (a), the instrument is also issued for consideration.

Official Comment

1. Subsection (a) is a restatement of former Section 3–303 and subsection (b) replaces former Section 3–408. The distinction between value and consideration in Article 3 is a very fine one. Whether an instrument is taken for value is relevant to the issue of whether a holder is a holder in due course. If an instrument is not issued for consideration the issuer has a defense to the obligation to pay the instrument. Consideration is defined in subsection (b) as "any consideration sufficient to support a simple contract." The definition of value in Section 1–201(44), which doesn't apply to Article 3, includes "any consideration sufficient to support a simple contract." Thus, outside Article 3, anything that is consideration is also value. A different rule applies in Article 3. Subsection (b) of Section 3–303 states that if an instrument is issued for value it is also issued for consideration.

Case # 1. X owes Y $1,000. The debt is not represented by a note. Later X issues a note to Y for the debt. Under subsection (a)(3) X's note is issued for value. Under subsection (b) the note is also issued for consideration whether or not, under contract law, Y is deemed to have given consideration for the note.

Case # 2. X issues a check to Y in consideration of Y's promise to perform services in the future. Although the executory promise is consideration for issuance of the check it is value only to the extent the promise is performed. Subsection (a)(1).

Case # 3. X issues a note to Y in consideration of Y's promise to perform services. If at the due date of the note Y's performance is not yet due, Y may enforce the note because it was issued for consideration. But if at the due date of the note, Y's performance is due and has not been performed, X has a defense. Subsection (b).

2. Subsection (a), which defines value, has primary importance in cases in which the issue is whether the holder of an instrument is a holder in due course and particularly to cases in which the issuer of the instrument has a defense to the instrument. Suppose Buyer and Seller signed a contract on April 1 for the sale of goods to be delivered on May 1. Payment of 50% of the price of the goods was due upon signing of the contract. On April 1 Buyer delivered to Seller a check in the amount due under the contract. The check was drawn by X to Buyer as payee and was indorsed to Seller. When the check was presented for payment to the drawee on April 2, it was dishonored because X had stopped payment. At that time Seller had not taken any action to perform the contract with Buyer. If X has a defense on the check, the defense can be asserted against Seller who is not a holder in due course because Seller did not give value for the check. Subsection (a)(1). The policy basis for subsection (a)(1) is that the holder who gives an executory promise of performance will not suffer an out-of-pocket loss to the extent the executory promise is unperformed at the time the holder learns of dishonor of the instrument. When Seller took delivery of the check on April 1, Buyer's obligation to pay 50% of the price on that date was suspended, but when the check was dishonored on April 2 the obligation revived. Section 3–310(b). If payment for goods is due at or before delivery and the buyer fails to make the payment, the

seller is excused from performing the promise to deliver the goods. Section 2-703. Thus, Seller is protected from an out-of-pocket loss even if the check is not enforceable. Holder-in-due-course status is not necessary to protect Seller.

3. Subsection (a)(2) equates value with the obtaining of a security interest or a nonjudicial lien in the instrument. The term "security interest" covers Article 9 cases in which an instrument is taken as collateral as well as bank collection cases in which a bank acquires a security interest under Section 4-210. The acquisition of a common-law or statutory banker's lien is also value under subsection (a)(2). An attaching creditor or other person who acquires a lien by judicial proceedings does not give value for the purposes of subsection (a)(2).

4. Subsection (a)(3) follows former Section 3-303(b) in providing that the holder takes for value if the instrument is taken in payment of or as security for an antecedent claim, even though there is no extension of time or other concession, and whether or not the claim is due. Subsection (a)(3) applies to any claim against any person; there is no requirement that the claim arise out of contract. In particular the provision is intended to apply to an instrument given in payment of or as security for the debt of a third person, even though no concession is made in return.

5. Subsection (a)(4) and (5) restate former Section 3-303(c). They state generally recognized exceptions to the rule that an executory promise is not value. A negotiable instrument is value because it carries the possibility of negotiation to a holder in due course, after which the party who gives it is obliged to pay. The same reasoning applies to any irrevocable commitment to a third person, such as a letter of credit issued when an instrument is taken.

§ 3-304. Overdue Instrument.

(a) An instrument payable on demand becomes overdue at the earliest of the following times:

(1) on the day after the day demand for payment is duly made;

(2) if the instrument is a check, 90 days after its date; or

(3) if the instrument is not a check, when the instrument has been outstanding for a period of time after its date which is unreasonably long under the circumstances of the particular case in light of the nature of the instrument and usage of the trade.

(b) With respect to an instrument payable at a definite time the following rules apply:

(1) If the principal is payable in installments and a due date has not been accelerated, the instrument becomes overdue upon default under the instrument for nonpayment of an installment, and the instrument remains overdue until the default is cured.

(2) If the principal is not payable in installments and the due date has not been accelerated, the instrument becomes overdue on the day after the due date.

(3) If a due date with respect to principal has been accelerated, the instrument becomes overdue on the day after the accelerated due date.

(c) Unless the due date of principal has been accelerated, an instrument does not become overdue if there is default in payment of interest but no default in payment of principal.

Official Comment

1. To be a holder in due course, one must take without notice that an instrument is overdue. Section 3-302(a)(2)(iii). Section 3-304 replaces subsection (3) of former Section 3-304. For the sake of clarity it treats demand and time instruments separately. Subsection (a) applies to demand instruments. A check becomes stale after 90 days.

Under former Section 3-304(3)(c), a holder that took a demand note had notice that it was overdue if it was taken "more than a reasonable length of time after its issue." In substitution for this test, subsection (a)(3) requires the trier of fact to look at both the circumstances of the particular case and the nature of the instrument and trade usage. Whether a demand note is stale may vary a great deal depending on the facts of the particular case.

2. Subsections (b) and (c) cover time instruments. They follow the distinction made under former Article 3 between defaults in payment of principal and interest. In subsection (b) installment instruments and single payment instruments are treated separately. If an installment is late, the instrument is overdue until the default is cured.

§ 3-305. Defenses and Claims in Recoupment.

(a) Except as stated in subsection (b), the right to enforce the obligation of a party to pay an instrument is subject to the following:

(1) a defense of the obligor based on (i) infancy of the obligor to the extent it is a defense to a simple contract, (ii) duress, lack of legal capacity, or illegality of the transaction which, under other law, nullifies the obligation of the obligor, (iii) fraud that induced the obligor to sign the instrument with neither knowledge nor reasonable opportunity to learn of its character or its essential terms, or (iv) discharge of the obligor in insolvency proceedings;

(2) a defense of the obligor stated in another section of this Article or a defense of the obligor that would be available if the person entitled to enforce the instrument were enforcing a right to payment under a simple contract; and

(3) a claim in recoupment of the obligor against the original payee of the instrument if the claim arose from the transaction that gave rise to the instrument; but the claim of the obligor may be asserted against a transferee of the instrument only to reduce the amount owing on the instrument at the time the action is brought.

(b) The right of a holder in due course to enforce the obligation of a party to pay the instrument is subject to defenses of the obligor stated in subsection (a)(1), but is not subject to defenses of the obligor stated in subsection (a)(2) or claims in recoupment stated in subsection (a)(3) against a person other than the holder.

(c) Except as stated in subsection (d), in an action to enforce the obligation of a party to pay the instrument, the obligor may not assert against the person entitled to enforce the instrument a defense, claim in recoupment, or claim to the instrument (Section 3-306) of another person, but the other person's claim to the instrument may be asserted by the obligor if the other person is joined in the action and personally asserts the claim against the person entitled to enforce the instrument. An obligor is not obliged to pay the instrument if the person seeking enforcement of the instrument does not have rights of a holder in due course and the obligor proves that the instrument is a lost or stolen instrument.

(d) In an action to enforce the obligation of an accommodation party to pay an instrument, the accommodation party may assert against the person entitled to enforce the instrument any defense or claim in recoupment under subsection (a) that the accommodated party could assert against the person entitled to enforce the instrument, except the defenses of discharge in insolvency proceedings, infancy, and lack of legal capacity.

Official Comment

1. Subsection (a) states the defenses to the obligation of a party to pay the instrument. Subsection (a)(1) states the "real defenses" that may be asserted against any person entitled to enforce the instrument.

Subsection (a)(1)(i) allows assertion of the defense of infancy against a holder in due course, even though the effect of the defense is to render the instrument voidable but not void. The policy is one of protection of the infant even at the expense of occasional loss to an innocent purchaser. No attempt is made to state when infancy is available as a defense or the conditions under which it may be asserted. In some jurisdictions it is held that an infant cannot rescind the transaction or set up the defense unless the holder is restored to the position held before the instrument was taken which, in the case of a holder in due course, is normally impossible. In other states an infant who has misrepresented age may be estopped to assert infancy. Such questions are left to other law, as an integral part of the policy of each state as to the protection of infants.

Subsection (a)(1)(ii) covers mental incompetence, guardianship, ultra vires acts or lack of corporate capacity to do business, or any other incapacity apart from infancy. Such incapacity is largely statutory. Its existence and effect is left to the law of each state. If under the state law the effect is to render the obligation of the instrument entirely null and void, the defense may be asserted against a holder in due course. If the effect is merely to render the obligation voidable at the election of the obligor, the defense is cut off.

Duress, which is also covered by subsection (a)(ii), is a matter of degree. An instrument signed at the point of a gun is void, even in the hands of a holder in due course. One signed under threat to prosecute the son of the maker for theft may be merely voidable, so that the defense is cut off. Illegality is most frequently a matter of gambling or usury, but may arise in other forms under a variety of statutes. The statutes differ in their provisions and the interpretations given them. They are primarily a matter of local concern and local policy. All such matters are therefore left to the local law. If under that law the effect of the duress or the illegality is to make the obligation entirely null and void, the defense may be asserted against a holder in due course. Otherwise it is cut off.

Subsection (a)(1)(iii) refers to "real" or "essential" fraud, sometimes called fraud in the essence or fraud in the factum, as effective against a holder in due course. The common illustration is that of the maker who is tricked into signing a note in the belief that it is merely a receipt or some other document. The theory of the defense is that the signature on the instrument is ineffective because the signer did not intend to sign such an instrument at all. Under this provision the defense extends to an instrument signed with knowledge that it is a negotiable instrument, but without knowledge of its essential terms. The test of the defense is that of excusable ignorance of the contents of the writing signed. The party must not only have been in ignorance, but must also have had no reasonable opportunity to obtain knowledge. In determining what is a reasonable opportunity all relevant factors are to be taken into account, including the intelligence, education, business experience, and ability to read or understand English of the signer. Also relevant is the nature of the representations that were made, whether the signer had good reason to rely on the representations or to have confidence in the person making them, the presence or absence of any third person who might read or explain the instrument to the signer, or any other possibility of obtaining independent information, and the apparent necessity, or lack of it, for acting without delay. Unless the misrepresentation meets this test, the defense is cut off by a holder in due course.

Subsection (a)(1)(iv) states specifically that the defense of discharge in insolvency proceedings is not cut off when the instrument is purchased by a holder in due course. "Insolvency proceedings" is defined in Section 1-201(22) and it includes bankruptcy whether or not the debtor is insolvent. Subsection (2)(e) of former Section 3-305 is omitted. The substance of that provision is stated in Section 3-601(b).

2. Subsection (a)(2) states other defenses that, pursuant to subsection (b), are cut off by a holder in due course. These defenses comprise those specifically stated in Article 3 and those based on common law contract principles. Article 3 defenses are nonissuance of the instrument, conditional issuance, and issuance for a special purpose (Section 3-105(b)); failure to countersign a traveler's check (Section 3-106(c)); modification of the obligation by a separate agreement (Section 3-117); payment that violates a restrictive indorsement (Section 3-206(f)); instruments issued without consideration or for which promised performance has not been given (Section 3-303(b)), and breach of warranty when a draft is accepted (Section 3-417(b)). The most prevalent common law defenses are fraud, misrepresentation or mistake in the issuance of the instrument. In most cases the holder in due course will be an immediate or remote transferee of the payee of the instrument. In most cases the holder-in-due-course doctrine is irrelevant if defenses are being asserted against the payee of the instrument, but in a small number of cases the payee of the instrument may be a holder in due course. Those cases are discussed in Comment 4 to Section 3-302.

Assume Buyer issues a note to Seller in payment of the price of goods that Seller fraudulently promises to deliver but which are never delivered. Seller negotiates the note to Holder who has no notice of the fraud. If Holder is a holder in due course, Holder is not subject to Buyer's defense of fraud. But in some cases an original party to the instrument is a holder in due course. For example, Buyer fraudulently induces Bank to issue a cashier's check to the order of Seller. The check is delivered by Bank to Seller, who has no notice of the fraud. Seller can be a holder in due course and can take the check free of Bank's defense of fraud. This case is discussed as Case # 1 in Comment 4 to Section 3-302. Former Section 3-305 stated that a holder in due course takes free of defenses of "any party to the instrument with whom the holder has not dealt." The meaning of this language was not at all clear and if read literally could have produced the wrong result. In the hypothetical case, it could be argued that Seller "dealt" with Bank because Bank delivered the check to Seller. But it is clear that Seller should take free of Bank's defense against Buyer regardless of whether Seller took delivery of the check from Buyer or from Bank. The quoted language is not included in Section 3-305. It is not necessary. If Buyer issues an instrument to Seller and Buyer has a defense against Seller, that defense can obviously be asserted. Buyer and Seller are the only people involved. The holder-in-due-course doctrine has no relevance. The doctrine applies only to cases in which more than two parties are involved. Its essence is that the holder in due course does not have to suffer the consequences of a defense of the obligor on the instrument that arose from an occurrence with a third party.

3. Subsection (a)(3) is concerned with claims in recoupment which can be illustrated by the following example. Buyer issues a note to the order of Seller in exchange for a promise of Seller to deliver specified equipment. If Seller fails to deliver the equipment or delivers equipment that is rightfully rejected, Buyer has a defense to the note because the performance that was the consideration for the note was not rendered. Section 3–303(b). This defense is included in Section 3–305(a)(2). That defense can always be asserted against Seller. This result is the same as that reached under former Section 3–408.

But suppose Seller delivered the promised equipment and it was accepted by Buyer. The equipment, however, was defective. Buyer retained the equipment and incurred expenses with respect to its repair. In this case, Buyer does not have a defense under Section 3–303(b). Seller delivered the equipment and the equipment was accepted. Under Article 2, Buyer is obliged to pay the price of the equipment which is represented by the note. But Buyer may have a claim against Seller for breach of warranty. If Buyer has a warranty claim, the claim may be asserted against Seller as a counterclaim or as a claim in recoupment to reduce the amount owing on the note. It is not relevant whether Seller is or is not a holder in due course of the note or whether Seller knew or had notice that Buyer had the warranty claim. It is obvious that holder-in-due-course doctrine cannot be used to allow Seller to cut off a warranty claim that Buyer has against Seller. Subsection (b) specifically covers this point by stating that a holder in due course is not subject to a "claim in recoupment *** against a person other than the holder."

Suppose Seller negotiates the note to Holder. If Holder had notice of Buyer's warranty claim at the time the note was negotiated to Holder, Holder is not a holder in due course (Section 3–302(a)(2)(iv)) and Buyer may assert the claim against Holder (Section 3–305(a)(3)) but only as a claim in recoupment, i.e. to reduce the amount owed on the note. If the warranty claim is $1,000 and the unpaid note is $10,000, Buyer owes $9,000 to Holder. If the warranty claim is more than the unpaid amount of the note, Buyer owes nothing to Holder, but Buyer cannot recover the unpaid amount of the warranty claim from Holder. If Buyer had already partially paid the note, Buyer is not entitled to recover the amounts paid. The claim can be used only as an offset to amounts owing on the note. If Holder had no notice of Buyer's claim and otherwise qualifies as a holder in due course, Buyer may not assert the claim against Holder. Section 3–305(b).

The result under Section 3–305 is consistent with the result reached under former Article 3, but the rules for reaching the result are stated differently. Under former Article 3 Buyer could assert rights against Holder only if Holder was not a holder in due course, and Holder's status depended upon whether Holder had notice of a defense by Buyer. Courts have held that Holder had that notice if Holder had notice of Buyer's warranty claim. The rationale under former Article 3 was "failure of consideration." This rationale does not distinguish between cases in which the seller fails to perform and those in which the buyer accepts the performance of seller but makes a claim against the seller because the performance is faulty. The term "failure of consideration" is subject to varying interpretations and is not used in Article 3. The use of the term "claim in recoupment" in Section 3–305(a)(3) is a more precise statement of the nature of Buyer's right against Holder. The use of the term does not change the law because the treatment of a defense under subsection (a)(2) and a claim in recoupment under subsection (a)(3) is essentially the same.

Under former Article 3, case law was divided on the issue of the extent to which an obligor on a note could assert against a transferee who is not a holder in due course a debt or other claim that the obligor had against the original payee of the instrument. Some courts limited claims to those that arose in the transaction that gave rise to the note. This is the approach taken in Section 3-305(a)(3). Other courts allowed the obligor on the note to use any debt or other claim, no matter how unrelated to the note, to offset the amount owed on the note. Under current judicial authority and non-UCC statutory law, there will be many cases in which a transferee of a note arising from a sale transaction will not qualify as a holder in due course. For example, applicable law may require the use of a note to which there cannot be a holder in due course. See Section 3-106(d) and Comment 3 to Section 3-106. It is reasonable to provide that the buyer should not be denied the right to assert claims arising out of the sale transaction. Subsection (a)(3) is based on the belief that it is not reasonable to require the transferee to bear the risk that wholly unrelated claims may also be asserted. The determination of whether a claim arose from the transaction that gave rise to the instrument is determined by law other than this Article and thus may vary as local law varies.

4. Subsection (c) concerns claims and defenses of a person other than the obligor on the instrument. It applies principally to cases in which an obligation is paid with the instrument of a third person. For example, Buyer buys goods from Seller and negotiates to Seller a cashier's check issued by Bank in payment of the price. Shortly after delivering the check to Seller, Buyer learns that Seller had defrauded Buyer in the sale transaction. Seller may enforce the check against Bank even though Seller is not a holder in due course. Bank has no defense to its obligation to pay the check and it may not assert defenses, claims in recoupment, or claims to the instrument of Buyer, except to the extent permitted by the "but" clause of the first sentence of subsection (c). Buyer may have a claim to the instrument under Section 3-306 based on a right to rescind the negotiation to Seller because of Seller's fraud. Section 3-202(b) and Comment 2 to Section 3-201. Bank cannot assert that claim unless Buyer is joined in the action in which Seller is trying to enforce payment of the check. In that case Bank may pay the amount of the check into court and the court will decide whether that amount belongs to Buyer or Seller. The last sentence of subsection (c) allows the issuer of an instrument such as a cashier's check to refuse payment in the rare case in which the issuer can prove that the instrument is a lost or stolen instrument and the person seeking enforcement does not have rights of a holder in due course.

5. Subsection (d) applies to instruments signed for accommodation (Section 3-419) and this subsection equates the obligation of the accommodation party to that of the accommodated party. The accommodation party can assert whatever defense or claim the accommodated party had against the person enforcing the instrument. The only exceptions are discharge in bankruptcy, infancy and lack of capacity. The same rule does not apply to an indorsement by a holder of the instrument in negotiating the instrument. The indorser, as transferor, makes a warranty to the indorsee, as transferee, that no defense or claim in recoupment is good against the indorser. Section 3-416(a)(4). Thus, if the indorsee sues the indorser because of dishonor of the instrument, the indorser may not assert the defense or claim in recoupment of the maker or drawer against the indorsee.

Section 3-305(d) must be read in conjunction with Section 3-605, which provides rules (usually referred to as suretyship defenses) for determining when the obligation of an accommodation party is discharged, in whole or in part, because of some act or omission of a person entitled to enforce the instrument. To the extent a rule stated in Section 3-605 is inconsistent with Section 3-305(d), the Section 3-605 rule governs. For example, under Section 3-605(b), discharge under Section 3-604 of the accommodated party does not discharge the accommodation party.

As explained in Comment 3 to Section 3–605, discharge of the accommodated party is normally part of a settlement under which the holder of a note accepts partial payment from an accommodated party who is financially unable to pay the entire amount of the note. If the holder then brings an action against the accommodation party to recover the remaining unpaid amount of the note, the accommodation party cannot use Section 3–305(d) to nullify Section 3–605(b) by asserting the discharge of the accommodated party as a defense. On the other hand, suppose the accommodated party is a buyer of goods who issued the note to the seller who took the note for the buyer's obligation to pay for the goods. Suppose the buyer has a claim for breach of warranty with respect to the goods against the seller and the warranty claim may be asserted against the holder of the note. The warranty claim is a claim in recoupment. If the holder and the accommodated party reach a settlement under which the holder accepts payment less than the amount of the note in full satisfaction of the note and the warranty claim, the accommodation party could defend an action on the note by the holder by asserting the accord and satisfaction under Section 3–305(d). There is no conflict with Section 3–605(b) because that provision is not intended to apply to settlement of disputed claims. Another example of the use of Section 3–305(d) in cases in which Section 3–605 applies is stated in Comment 4 to Section 3–605. See PEB Commentary No. 11, dated February 10, 1994 [Appendix V, infra].

§ 3–306. Claims to an Instrument.

A person taking an instrument, other than a person having rights of a holder in due course, is subject to a claim of a property or possessory right in the instrument or its proceeds, including a claim to rescind a negotiation and to recover the instrument or its proceeds. A person having rights of a holder in due course takes free of the claim to the instrument.

Official Comment

This section expands on the reference to "claims to" the instrument mentioned in former Sections 3–305 and 3–306. Claims covered by the section include not only claims to ownership but also any other claim of a property or possessory right. It includes the claim to a lien or the claim of a person in rightful possession of an instrument who was wrongfully deprived of possession. Also included is a claim based on Section 3–202(b) for rescission of a negotiation of the instrument by the claimant. Claims to an instrument under Section 3–306 are different from claims in recoupment referred to in Section 3–305(a)(3).

§ 3–307. Notice of Breach of Fiduciary Duty.

(a) In this section:

(1) "Fiduciary" means an agent, trustee, partner, corporate officer or director, or other representative owing a fiduciary duty with respect to an instrument.

(2) "Represented person" means the principal, beneficiary, partnership, corporation, or other person to whom the duty stated in paragraph (1) is owed.

(b) If (i) an instrument is taken from a fiduciary for payment or collection or for value, (ii) the taker has knowledge of the fiduciary status of the fiduciary, and (iii) the represented person makes a claim to the instrument or its proceeds on the basis that the transaction of the fiduciary is a breach of fiduciary duty, the following rules apply:

(1) Notice of breach of fiduciary duty by the fiduciary is notice of the claim of the represented person.

(2) In the case of an instrument payable to the represented person or the fiduciary as such, the taker has notice of the breach of fiduciary duty if the instrument is (i) taken in payment of or as security for a debt known by the taker to be the personal debt of the fiduciary, (ii) taken in a transaction known by the taker to be for the personal benefit of the fiduciary, or (iii) deposited to an account other than an account of the fiduciary, as such, or an account of the represented person.

(3) If an instrument is issued by the represented person or the fiduciary as such, and made payable to the fiduciary personally, the taker does not have notice of the breach of fiduciary duty unless the taker knows of the breach of fiduciary duty.

(4) If an instrument is issued by the represented person or the fiduciary as such, to the taker as payee, the taker has notice of the breach of fiduciary duty if the instrument is (i) taken in payment of or as security for a debt known by the taker to be the personal debt of the fiduciary, (ii) taken in a transaction known by the taker to be for the personal benefit of the fiduciary, or (iii) deposited to an account other than an account of the fiduciary, as such, or an account of the represented person.

Official Comment

1. This section states rules for determining when a person who has taken an instrument from a fiduciary has notice of a breach of fiduciary duty that occurs as a result of the transaction with the fiduciary. Former Section 3–304(2) and (4)(e) related to this issue, but those provisions were unclear in their meaning. Section 3–307 is intended to clarify the law by stating rules that comprehensively cover the issue of when the taker of an instrument has notice of breach of a fiduciary duty and thus notice of a claim to the instrument or its proceeds.

2. Subsection (a) defines the terms "fiduciary" and "represented person" and the introductory paragraph of subsection (b) describes the transaction to which the section applies. The basic scenario is one in which the fiduciary in effect embezzles money of the represented person by applying the proceeds of an instrument that belongs to the represented person to the personal use of the fiduciary. The person dealing with the fiduciary may be a depositary bank that takes the instrument for collection or a bank or other person that pays value for the instrument. The section also covers a transaction in which an instrument is presented for payment to a payor bank that pays the instrument by giving value to the fiduciary. Subsections (b)(2), (3), and (4) state rules for determining when the person dealing with the fiduciary has notice of breach of fiduciary duty. Subsection (b)(1) states that notice of breach of fiduciary duty is notice of the represented person's claim to the instrument or its proceeds.

Under Section 3–306, a person taking an instrument is subject to a claim to the instrument or its proceeds, unless the taker has rights of a holder in due course. Under Section 3–302(a)(2)(v), the taker cannot be a holder in due course if the instrument was taken with notice of a claim under Section 3–306. Section 3–307 applies to cases in which a represented person is asserting a claim because a breach of fiduciary duty resulted in a misapplication of the proceeds of an instrument. The claim of the represented person is a claim described in Section 3–306. Section 3–307 states rules for determining when a person taking an instrument has notice of the claim which will prevent assertion of rights as a holder in due course. It also states rules for determining when a payor bank pays an instrument with notice of breach of fiduciary duty.

Section 3–307(b) applies only if the person dealing with the fiduciary "has knowledge of the fiduciary status of the fiduciary." Notice which does not amount to knowledge is not enough to cause Section 3–307 to apply. "Knowledge" is defined in Section 1–201(25). In most cases, the "taker" referred to in Section 3–307 will be a bank or other organization. Knowledge of an organization is determined by the rules stated in Section 1–201(27). In many cases, the individual who receives and processes an instrument on behalf of the organization that is the taker of the instrument "for payment or collection or for value" is a clerk who has no knowledge of any fiduciary status of the person from whom the instrument is received. In such cases, Section 3–307 doesn't apply because, under Section 1–201(27), knowledge of the organization is determined by the knowledge of the "individual conducting that transaction," i.e. the clerk who receives and processes the instrument. Furthermore, paragraphs (2) and (4) each require that the person acting for the organization have knowledge of facts that indicate a breach of fiduciary duty. In the case of an instrument taken for deposit to an account, the knowledge is found in the fact that the deposit is made to an account other than that of the represented person or a fiduciary account for benefit of that person. In other cases the person acting for the organization must know that the instrument is taken in payment or as security for a personal debt of the fiduciary or for the personal benefit of the fiduciary. For example, if the instrument is being used to buy goods or services, the person acting for the organization must know that the goods or services are for the personal benefit of the fiduciary. The requirement that the taker have knowledge rather than notice is meant to limit Section 3–307 to relatively uncommon cases in which the person who deals with the fiduciary knows all the relevant facts: the fiduciary status and that the proceeds of the instrument are being used for the personal debt or benefit of the fiduciary or are being paid to an account that is not an account of the represented person or of the fiduciary, as such. Mere notice of these facts is not enough to put the taker on notice of the breach of fiduciary duty and does not give rise to any duty of investigation by the taker.

3. Subsection (b)(2) applies to instruments payable to the represented person or the fiduciary as such. For example, a check payable to Corporation is indorsed in the name of Corporation by Doe as its President. Doe gives the check to Bank as partial repayment of a personal loan that Bank had made to Doe. The check was indorsed either in blank or to Bank. Bank collects the check and applies the proceeds to reduce the amount owed on Doe's loan. If the person acting for Bank in the transaction knows that Doe is a fiduciary and that the check is being used to pay a personal obligation of Doe, subsection (b)(2) applies. If Corporation has a claim to the proceeds of the check because the use of the check by Doe was a breach of fiduciary duty, Bank has notice of the claim and did not take the check as a holder in due course. The same result follows if Doe had indorsed the check to himself before giving it to Bank. Subsection (b)(2) follows Uniform Fiduciaries Act § 4 in providing that if the instrument is payable to the fiduciary, as such, or to the represented person, the taker has notice of a claim if the instrument is negotiated for the fiduciary's personal debt. If fiduciary funds are deposited to a personal account of the fiduciary or to an account that is not an account of the

represented person or of the fiduciary, as such, there is a split of authority concerning whether the bank is on notice of a breach of fiduciary duty. Subsection (b)(2)(iii) states that the bank is given notice of breach of fiduciary duty because of the deposit. The Uniform Fiduciaries Act § 9 states that the bank is not on notice unless it has knowledge of facts that makes its receipt of the deposit an act of bad faith.

The rationale of subsection (b)(2) is that it is not normal for an instrument payable to the represented person or the fiduciary, as such, to be used for the personal benefit of the fiduciary. It is likely that such use reflects an unlawful use of the proceeds of the instrument. If the fiduciary is entitled to compensation from the represented person for services rendered or for expenses incurred by the fiduciary the normal mode of payment is by a check drawn on the fiduciary account to the order of the fiduciary.

4. Subsection (b)(3) is based on Uniform Fiduciaries Act § 6 and applies when the instrument is drawn by the represented person or the fiduciary as such to the fiduciary personally. The term "personally" is used as it is used in the Uniform Fiduciaries Act to mean that the instrument is payable to the payee as an individual and not as a fiduciary. For example, Doe as President of Corporation writes a check on Corporation's account to the order of Doe personally. The check is then indorsed over to Bank as in Comment 3. In this case there is no notice of breach of fiduciary duty because there is nothing unusual about the transaction. Corporation may have owed Doe money for salary, reimbursement for expenses incurred for the benefit of Corporation, or for any other reason. If Doe is authorized to write checks on behalf of Corporation to pay debts of Corporation, the check is a normal way of paying a debt owed to Doe. Bank may assume that Doe may use the instrument for his personal benefit.

5. Subsection (b)(4) can be illustrated by a hypothetical case. Corporation draws a check payable to an organization. X, an officer or employee of Corporation, delivers the check to a person acting for the organization. The person signing the check on behalf of Corporation is X or another person. If the person acting for the organization in the transaction knows that X is a fiduciary, the organization is on notice of a claim by Corporation if it takes the instrument under the same circumstances stated in subsection (b)(2). If the organization is a bank and the check is taken in repayment of a personal loan of the bank to X, the case is like the case discussed in Comment 3. It is unusual for Corporation, the represented person, to pay a personal debt of Doe by issuing a check to the bank. It is more likely that the use of the check by Doe reflects an unlawful use of the proceeds of the check. The same analysis applies if the check is made payable to an organization in payment of goods or services. If the person acting for the organization knew of the fiduciary status of X and that the goods or services were for X's personal benefit, the organization is on notice of a claim by Corporation to the proceeds of the check. See the discussion in the last paragraph of Comment 2.

§ 3-308. Proof of Signatures and Status as Holder in Due Course.

(a) In an action with respect to an instrument, the authenticity of, and authority to make, each signature on the instrument is admitted unless specifically denied in the pleadings. If the validity of a signature is denied in the pleadings, the burden of establishing validity is on the person claiming validity, but the signature is presumed to be authentic and authorized unless the action is to enforce the liability of the purported signer and the signer is dead or incompetent at the time of trial of the issue of validity of the signature. If an action to enforce the instrument is brought against a person as the undisclosed principal of a person who signed the instrument as a party to the instrument, the plaintiff has the burden of establishing that the defendant is liable on the instrument as a represented person under Section 3–402(a).

(b) If the validity of signatures is admitted or proved and there is compliance with subsection (a), a plaintiff producing the instrument is entitled to payment if the plaintiff proves entitlement to enforce the instrument under Section 3–301, unless the defendant proves a defense or claim in recoupment. If a defense or claim in recoupment is proved, the right to payment of the plaintiff is subject to the defense or claim, except to the extent the plaintiff proves that the plaintiff has rights of a holder in due course which are not subject to the defense or claim.

Official Comment

1. Section 3–308 is a modification of former Section 3–307. The first two sentences of subsection (a) are a restatement of former Section 3–307(1). The purpose of the requirement of a specific denial in the pleadings is to give the plaintiff notice of the defendant's claim of forgery or lack of authority as to the particular signature, and to afford the plaintiff an opportunity to investigate and obtain evidence. If local rules of pleading permit, the denial may be on information and belief, or it may be a denial of knowledge or information sufficient to form a belief. It need not be under oath unless the local statutes or rules require verification. In the absence of such specific denial the signature stands admitted, and is not in issue. Nothing in this section is intended, however, to prevent amendment of the pleading in a proper case.

The question of the burden of establishing the signature arises only when it has been put in issue by specific denial. "Burden of establishing" is defined in Section 1–201. The burden is on the party claiming under the signature, but the signature is presumed to be authentic and authorized except as stated in the second sentence of subsection (a). "Presumed" is defined in Section 1–201 and means that until some evidence is introduced which would support a finding that the signature is forged or unauthorized, the plaintiff is not required to prove that it is valid. The presumption rests upon the fact that in ordinary experience forged or unauthorized signatures are very uncommon, and normally any evidence is within the control of, or more accessible to, the defendant. The defendant is therefore required to make some sufficient showing of the grounds for the denial before the plaintiff is required to introduce evidence. The defendant's evidence need not be sufficient to require a directed verdict, but it must be enough to support the denial by permitting a finding in the defendant's favor. Until introduction of such evidence the presumption requires a finding for the plaintiff. Once such evidence is introduced the burden of establishing the signature by a preponderance of the total evidence is on the plaintiff. The presumption does not arise if the action is to enforce the obligation of a purported signer who has died or become incompetent before the evidence is required, and so is disabled from obtaining or introducing it. "Action" is defined in Section 1–201 and includes a claim asserted against the estate of a deceased or an incompetent.

The last sentence of subsection (a) is a new provision that is necessary to take into account Section 3–402(a) that allows an undisclosed principal to be liable on an instrument signed by an authorized representative. In that case the person enforcing the instrument must prove that the undisclosed principal is liable.

2. Subsection (b) restates former Section 3–307(2) and (3). Once signatures are proved or admitted a holder, by mere

production of the instrument, proves "entitlement to enforce the instrument" because under Section 3–301 a holder is a person entitled to enforce the instrument. Any other person in possession of an instrument may recover only if that person has the rights of a holder. Section 3–301. That person must prove a transfer giving that person such rights under Section 3–203(b) or that such rights were obtained by subrogation or succession.

If a plaintiff producing the instrument proves entitlement to enforce the instrument, either as a holder or a person with rights of a holder, the plaintiff is entitled to recovery unless the defendant proves a defense or claim in recoupment. Until proof of a defense or claim in recoupment is made, the issue as to whether the plaintiff has rights of a holder in due course does not arise. In the absence of a defense or claim in recoupment, any person entitled to enforce the instrument is entitled to recover. If a defense or claim in recoupment is proved, the plaintiff may seek to cut off the defense or claim in recoupment by proving that the plaintiff is a holder in due course or that the plaintiff has rights of a holder in due course under Section 3–203(b) or by subrogation or succession. All elements of Section 3–302(a) must be proved.

Nothing in this section is intended to say that the plaintiff must necessarily prove rights as a holder in due course. The plaintiff may elect to introduce no further evidence, in which case a verdict may be directed for the plaintiff or the defendant, or the issue of the defense or claim in recoupment may be left to the trier of fact, according to the weight and sufficiency of the defendant's evidence. The plaintiff may elect to rebut the defense or claim in recoupment by proof to the contrary, in which case a verdict may be directed for either party or the issue may be for the trier of fact. Subsection (b) means only that if the plaintiff claims the rights of a holder in due course against the defense or claim in recoupment, the plaintiff has the burden of proof on that issue.

§ 3–309. Enforcement of Lost, Destroyed, or Stolen Instrument.

(a) A person not in possession of an instrument is entitled to enforce the instrument if (i) the person was in possession of the instrument and entitled to enforce it when loss of possession occurred, (ii) the loss of possession was not the result of a transfer by the person or a lawful seizure, and (iii) the person cannot reasonably obtain possession of the instrument because the instrument was destroyed, its whereabouts cannot be determined, or it is in the wrongful possession of an unknown person or a person that cannot be found or is not amenable to service of process.

(b) A person seeking enforcement of an instrument under subsection (a) must prove the terms of the instrument and the person's right to enforce the instrument. If that proof is made, Section 3–308 applies to the case as if the person seeking enforcement had produced the instrument. The court may not enter judgment in favor of the person seeking enforcement unless it finds that the person required to pay the instrument is adequately protected against loss that might occur by reason of a claim by another person to enforce the instrument. Adequate protection may be provided by any reasonable means.

Official Comment

Section 3–309 is a modification of former Section 3–804. The rights stated are those of "a person entitled to enforce the instrument" at the time of loss rather than those of an "owner" as in former Section 3–804. Under subsection (b), judgment to enforce the instrument cannot be given unless the court finds that the defendant will be adequately protected against a claim to the instrument by a holder that may appear at some later time. The court is given discretion in determining how adequate protection is to be assured. Former Section 3-804 allowed the court to "require security indemnifying the defendant against loss." Under Section 3-309 adequate protection is a flexible concept. For example, there is substantial risk that a holder in due course may make a demand for payment if the instrument was payable to bearer when it was lost or stolen. On the other hand if the instrument was payable to the person who lost the instrument and that person did not indorse the instrument, no other person could be a holder of the instrument. In some cases there is risk of loss only if there is doubt about whether the facts alleged by the person who lost the instrument are true. Thus, the type of adequate protection that is reasonable in the circumstances may depend on the degree of certainty about the facts in the case.

§ 3-310. Effect of Instrument on Obligation for Which Taken.

(a) Unless otherwise agreed, if a certified check, cashier's check, or teller's check is taken for an obligation, the obligation is discharged to the same extent discharge would result if an amount of money equal to the amount of the instrument were taken in payment of the obligation. Discharge of the obligation does not affect any liability that the obligor may have as an indorser of the instrument.

(b) Unless otherwise agreed and except as provided in subsection (a), if a note or an uncertified check is taken for an obligation, the obligation is suspended to the same extent the obligation would be discharged if an amount of money equal to the amount of the instrument were taken, and the following rules apply:

(1) In the case of an uncertified check, suspension of the obligation continues until dishonor of the check or until it is paid or certified. Payment or certification of the check results in discharge of the obligation to the extent of the amount of the check.

(2) In the case of a note, suspension of the obligation continues until dishonor of the note or until it is paid. Payment of the note results in discharge of the obligation to the extent of the payment.

(3) Except as provided in paragraph (4), if the check or note is dishonored and the obligee of the obligation for which the instrument was taken is the person entitled to enforce the instrument, the obligee may enforce either the instrument or the obligation. In the case of an instrument of a third person which is negotiated to the obligee by the obligor, discharge of the obligor on the instrument also discharges the obligation.

(4) If the person entitled to enforce the instrument taken for an obligation is a person other than the obligee, the obligee may not enforce the obligation to the extent the obligation is suspended. If the obligee is the person entitled to enforce the instrument but no longer has possession of it because it was lost, stolen, or destroyed, the obligation may not be enforced to the extent of the amount payable on the instrument, and to that extent the obli-

gee's rights against the obligor are limited to enforcement of the instrument.

(c) If an instrument other than one described in subsection (a) or (b) is taken for an obligation, the effect is (i) that stated in subsection (a) if the instrument is one on which a bank is liable as maker or acceptor, or (ii) that stated in subsection (b) in any other case.

Official Comment

1. Section 3-310 is a modification of former Section 3-802. As a practical matter, application of former Section 3-802 was limited to cases in which a check or a note was given for an obligation. Subsections (a) and (b) of Section 3-310 are therefore stated in terms of checks and notes in the interests of clarity. Subsection (c) covers the rare cases in which some other instrument is given to pay an obligation.

2. Subsection (a) deals with the case in which a certified check, cashier's check or teller's check is given in payment of an obligation. In that case the obligation is discharged unless there is an agreement to the contrary. Subsection (a) drops the exception in former Section 3-802 for cases in which there is a right of recourse on the instrument against the obligor. Under former Section 3-802(1)(a) the obligation was not discharged if there was a right of recourse on the instrument against the obligor. Subsection (a) changes this result. The underlying obligation is discharged, but any right of recourse on the instrument is preserved.

3. Subsection (b) concerns cases in which an uncertified check or a note is taken for an obligation. The typical case is that in which a buyer pays for goods or services by giving the seller the buyer's personal check, or in which the buyer signs a note for the purchase price. Subsection (b) also applies to the uncommon cases in which a check or note of a third person is given in payment of the obligation. Subsection (b) preserves the rule under former Section 3-802(1)(b) that the buyer's obligation to pay the price is suspended, but subsection (b) spells out the effect more precisely. If the check or note is dishonored, the seller may sue on either the dishonored instrument or the contract of sale if the seller has possession of the instrument and is the person entitled to enforce it. If the right to enforce the instrument is held by somebody other than the seller, the seller can't enforce the right to payment of the price under the sales contract because that right is represented by the instrument which is enforceable by somebody else. Thus, if the seller sold the note or the check to a holder and has not reacquired it after dishonor, the only right that survives is the right to enforce the instrument.

The last sentence of subsection (b)(3) applies to cases in which an instrument of another person is indorsed over to the obligee in payment of the obligation. For example, Buyer delivers an uncertified personal check of X payable to the order of Buyer to Seller in payment of the price of goods. Buyer indorses the check over to Seller. Buyer is liable on the check as indorser. If Seller neglects to present the check for payment or to deposit it for collection within 30 days of the indorsement, Buyer's liability as indorser is discharged. Section 3-415(e). Under the last sentence of Section 3-310(b)(3) Buyer is also discharged on the obligation to pay for the goods.

4. There was uncertainty concerning the applicability of former Section 3-802 to the case in which the check given for the obligation was stolen from the payee, the payee's signature was forged, and the forger obtained payment. The last sentence of subsection (b)(4) addresses this issue. If the payor bank pays a holder, the drawer is discharged on the underlying obligation because the check was paid. Subsection (b)(1). If the payor bank pays a person not entitled to enforce the in-

strument, as in the hypothetical case, the suspension of the underlying obligation continues because the check has not been paid. Section 3-602(a). The payee's cause of action is against the depositary bank or payor bank in conversion under Section 3-420 or against the drawer under Section 3-309. In the latter case, the drawer's obligation under Section 3-414(b) is triggered by dishonor which occurs because the check is unpaid. Presentment for payment to the drawee is excused under Section 3-504(a)(i) and, under Section 3-502(e), dishonor occurs without presentment if the check is not paid. The payee cannot merely ignore the instrument and sue the drawer on the underlying contract. This would impose on the drawer the risk that the check when stolen was indorsed in blank or to bearer.

A similar analysis applies with respect to lost instruments that have not been paid. If a creditor takes a check of the debtor in payment of an obligation, the obligation is suspended under the introductory paragraph of subsection (b). If the creditor then loses the check, what are the creditor's rights? The creditor can request the debtor to issue a new check and in many cases, the debtor will issue a replacement check after stopping payment on the lost check. In that case both the debtor and creditor are protected. But the debtor is not obliged to issue a new check. If the debtor refuses to issue a replacement check, the last sentence of subsection (b)(4) applies. The creditor may not enforce the obligation of debtor for which the check was taken. The creditor may assert only rights on the check. The creditor can proceed under Section 3-309 to enforce the obligation of the debtor, as drawer, to pay the check.

5. Subsection (c) deals with rare cases in which other instruments are taken for obligations. If a bank is the obligor on the instrument, subsection (a) applies and the obligation is discharged. In any other case subsection (b) applies.

§ 3-311. Accord and Satisfaction by Use of Instrument.

(a) If a person against whom a claim is asserted proves that (i) that person in good faith tendered an instrument to the claimant as full satisfaction of the claim, (ii) the amount of the claim was unliquidated or subject to a bona fide dispute, and (iii) the claimant obtained payment of the instrument, the following subsections apply.

(b) Unless subsection (c) applies, the claim is discharged if the person against whom the claim is asserted proves that the instrument or an accompanying written communication contained a conspicuous statement to the effect that the instrument was tendered as full satisfaction of the claim.

(c) Subject to subsection (d), a claim is not discharged under subsection (b) if either of the following applies:

(1) The claimant, if an organization, proves that (i) within a reasonable time before the tender, the claimant sent a conspicuous statement to the person against whom the claim is asserted that communications concerning disputed debts, including an instrument tendered as full satisfaction of a debt, are to be sent to a designated person, office, or place, and (ii) the instrument or accompanying communication was not received by that designated person, office, or place.

(2) The claimant, whether or not an organization, proves that within 90 days after payment of the instrument, the claimant tendered repayment of the amount of the instrument to the person against

whom the claim is asserted. This paragraph does not apply if the claimant is an organization that sent a statement complying with paragraph (1)(i).

(d) A claim is discharged if the person against whom the claim is asserted proves that within a reasonable time before collection of the instrument was initiated, the claimant, or an agent of the claimant having direct responsibility with respect to the disputed obligation, knew that the instrument was tendered in full satisfaction of the claim.

Official Comment

1. This section deals with an informal method of dispute resolution carried out by use of a negotiable instrument. In the typical case there is a dispute concerning the amount that is owed on a claim.

Case # 1. The claim is for the price of goods or services sold to a consumer who asserts that he or she is not obliged to pay the full price for which the consumer was billed because of a defect or breach of warranty with respect to the goods or services.

Case # 2. A claim is made on an insurance policy. The insurance company alleges that it is not liable under the policy for the amount of the claim.

In either case the person against whom the claim is asserted may attempt an accord and satisfaction of the disputed claim by tendering a check to the claimant for some amount less than the full amount claimed by the claimant. A statement will be included on the check or in a communication accompanying the check to the effect that the check is offered as full payment or full satisfaction of the claim. Frequently, there is also a statement to the effect that obtaining payment of the check is an agreement by the claimant to a settlement of the dispute for the amount tendered. Before enactment of revised Article 3, the case law was in conflict over the question of whether obtaining payment of the check had the effect of an agreement to the settlement proposed by the debtor. This issue was governed by a common law rule, but some courts hold that the common law was modified by former Section 1-207 which they interpreted as applying to full settlement checks.

2. Comment d. to Restatement of Contracts, Section 281 discusses the full satisfaction check and the applicable common law rule. In a case like Case # 1, the buyer can propose a settlement of the disputed bill by a clear notation on the check indicating that the check is tendered as full satisfaction of the bill. Under the common law rule the seller, by obtaining payment of the check accepts the offer of compromise by the buyer. The result is the same if the seller adds a notation to the check indicating that the check is accepted under protest or in only partial satisfaction of the claim. Under the common law rule the seller can refuse the check or can accept it subject to the condition stated by the buyer, but the seller can't accept the check and refuse to be bound by the condition. The rule applies only to an unliquidated claim or a claim disputed in good faith by the buyer. The dispute in the courts was whether Section 1-207 changed the common law rule. The Restatement states that section "need not be read as changing this well-established rule."

3. As part of the revision of Article 3, Section 1-207 has been amended to add subsection (2) stating that Section 1-207 "does not apply to an accord and satisfaction." Because of that amendment and revised Article 3, Section 3-311 governs full satisfaction checks. Section 3-311 follows the common law rule with some minor variations to reflect modern business conditions. In cases covered by Section 3-311 there will often be an individual on one side of the dispute and a business organization on the other. This section is not designed to favor either the

individual or the business organization. In Case # 1 the person seeking the accord and satisfaction is an individual. In Case # 2 the person seeking the accord and satisfaction is an insurance company. Section 3-311 is based on a belief that the common law rule produces a fair result and that informal dispute resolution by full satisfaction checks should be encouraged.

4. Subsection (a) states three requirements for application of Section 3-311. "Good faith" in subsection (a)(i) is defined in Section 3-103(a)(4) as not only honesty in fact, but the observance of reasonable commercial standards of fair dealing. The meaning of "fair dealing" will depend upon the facts in the particular case. For example, suppose an insurer tenders a check in settlement of a claim for personal injury in an accident clearly covered by the insurance policy. The claimant is necessitous and the amount of the check is very small in relationship to the extent of the injury and the amount recoverable under the policy. If the trier of fact determines that the insurer was taking unfair advantage of the claimant, an accord and satisfaction would not result from payment of the check because of the absence of good faith by the insurer in making the tender. Another example of lack of good faith is found in the practice of some business debtors in routinely printing full satisfaction language on their check stocks so that all or a large part of the debts of the debtor are paid by checks bearing the full satisfaction language, whether or not there is any dispute with the creditor. Under such a practice the claimant cannot be sure whether a tender in full satisfaction is or is not being made. Use of a check on which full satisfaction language was affixed routinely pursuant to such a business practice may prevent an accord and satisfaction on the ground that the check was not tendered in good faith under subsection (a)(i).

Section 3-311 does not apply to cases in which the debt is a liquidated amount and not subject to a bona fide dispute. Subsection (a)(ii). Other law applies to cases in which a debtor is seeking discharge of such a debt by paying less than the amount owed. For the purpose of subsection (a)(iii) obtaining acceptance of a check is considered to be obtaining payment of the check.

The person seeking the accord and satisfaction must prove that the requirements of subsection (a) are met. If that person also proves that the statement required by subsection (b) was given, the claim is discharged unless subsection (c) applies. Normally the statement required by subsection (b) is written on the check. Thus, the canceled check can be used to prove the statement as well as the fact that the claimant obtained payment of the check. Subsection (b) requires a "conspicuous" statement that the instrument was tendered in full satisfaction of the claim. "Conspicuous" is defined in Section 1-201(10). The statement is conspicuous if "it is so written that a reasonable person against whom it is to operate ought to have noticed it." If the claimant can reasonably be expected to examine the check, almost any statement on the check should be noticed and is therefore conspicuous. In cases in which the claimant is an individual the claimant will receive the check and will normally indorse it. Since the statement concerning tender in full satisfaction normally will appear above the space provided for the claimant's indorsement of the check, the claimant "ought to have noticed" the statement.

5. Subsection (c)(1) is a limitation on subsection (b) in cases in which the claimant is an organization. It is designed to protect the claimant against inadvertent accord and satisfaction. If the claimant is an organization payment of the check might be obtained without notice to the personnel of the organization concerned with the disputed claim. Some business organizations have claims against very large numbers of customers. Examples are department stores, public utilities and the like. These claims are normally paid by checks sent by customers to a designated office at which clerks employed by the claimant or a bank acting for the

claimant process the checks and record the amounts paid. If the processing office is not designed to deal with communications extraneous to recording the amount of the check and the account number of the customer, payment of a full satisfaction check can easily be obtained without knowledge by the claimant of the existence of the full satisfaction statement. This is particularly true if the statement is written on the reverse side of the check in the area in which indorsements are usually written. Normally, the clerks of the claimant have no reason to look at the reverse side of checks. Indorsement by the claimant normally is done by mechanical means or there may be no indorsement at all. Section 4-205(a). Subsection (c)(1) allows the claimant to protect itself by advising customers by a conspicuous statement that communications regarding disputed debts must be sent to a particular person, office, or place. The statement must be given to the customer within a reasonable time before the tender is made. This requirement is designed to assure that the customer has reasonable notice that the full satisfaction check must be sent to a particular place. The reasonable time requirement could be satisfied by a notice on the billing statement sent to the customer. If the full satisfaction check is sent to the designated destination and the check is paid, the claim is discharged. If the claimant proves that the check was not received at the designated destination the claim is not discharged unless subsection (d) applies.

6. Subsection (c)(2) is also designed to prevent inadvertent accord and satisfaction. It can be used by a claimant other than an organization or by a claimant as an alternative to subsection (c)(1). Some organizations may be reluctant to use subsection (c)(1) because it may result in confusion of customers that causes checks to be routinely sent to the special designated person, office, or place. Thus, much of the benefit of rapid processing of checks may be lost. An organization that chooses not to send a notice complying with subsection (c)(1)(i) may prevent an inadvertent accord and satisfaction by complying with subsection (c)(2). If the claimant discovers that it has obtained payment of a full satisfaction check, it may prevent an accord and satisfaction if, within 90 days of the payment of the check, the claimant tenders repayment of the amount of the check to the person against whom the claim is asserted.

7. Subsection (c) is subject to subsection (d). If a person against whom a claim is asserted proves that the claimant obtained payment of a check known to have been tendered in full satisfaction of the claim by "the claimant or an agent of the claimant having direct responsibility with respect to the disputed obligation," the claim is discharged even if (i) the check was not sent to the person, office, or place required by a notice complying with subsection (c)(1), or (ii) the claimant tendered repayment of the amount of the check in compliance with subsection (c)(2).

A claimant knows that a check was tendered in full satisfaction of a claim when the claimant "has actual knowledge" of that fact. Section 1-201(25). Under Section 1-201(27), if the claimant is an organization, it has knowledge that a check was tendered in full satisfaction of the claim when that fact is

> "brought to the attention of the individual conducting that transaction, and in any event when it would have been brought to his attention if the organization had exercised due diligence. An organization exercises due diligence if it maintains reasonable routines for communicating significant information to the person conducting the transaction and there is reasonable compliance with the routines. Due diligence does not require an individual acting for the organization to communicate information unless such communication is part of his regular duties or unless he has reason to know of the transaction and that the transaction would be materially affected by the information."

With respect to an attempted accord and satisfaction the "individual conducting that transaction" is an employee or other agent of the organization having direct responsibility with respect to the dispute. For example, if the check and communication are received by a collection agency acting for the claimant to collect the disputed claim, obtaining payment of the check will result in an accord and satisfaction even if the claimant gave notice, pursuant to subsection (c)(1), that full satisfaction checks be sent to some other office. Similarly, if a customer asserting a claim for breach of warranty with respect to defective goods purchased in a retail outlet of a large chain store delivers the full satisfaction check to the manager of the retail outlet at which the goods were purchased, obtaining payment of the check will also result in an accord and satisfaction. On the other hand, if the check is mailed to the chief executive officer of the chain store subsection (d) would probably not be satisfied. The chief executive officer of a large corporation may have general responsibility for operations of the company, but does not normally have direct responsibility for resolving a small disputed bill to a customer. A check for a relatively small amount mailed to a high executive officer of a large organization is not likely to receive the executive's personal attention. Rather, the check would normally be routinely sent to the appropriate office for deposit and credit to the customer's account. If the check does receive the personal attention of the high executive officer and the officer is aware of the full-satisfaction language, collection of the check will result in an accord and satisfaction because subsection (d) applies. In this case the officer has assumed direct responsibility with respect to the disputed transaction.

If a full satisfaction check is sent to a lock box or other office processing checks sent to the claimant, it is irrelevant whether the clerk processing the check did or did not see the statement that the check was tendered as full satisfaction of the claim. Knowledge of the clerk is not imputed to the organization because the clerk has no responsibility with respect to an accord and satisfaction. Moreover, there is no failure of "due diligence" under Section 1–201(27) if the claimant does not require its clerks to look for full satisfaction statements on checks or accompanying communications. Nor is there any duty of the claimant to assign that duty to its clerks. Section 3–311(c) is intended to allow a claimant to avoid an inadvertent accord and satisfaction by complying with either subsection (c)(1) or (2) without burdening the check-processing operation with extraneous and wasteful additional duties.

8. In some cases the disputed claim may have been assigned to a finance company or bank as part of a financing arrangement with respect to accounts receivable. If the account debtor was notified of the assignment, the claimant is the assignee of the account receivable and the "agent of the claimant" in subsection (d) refers to an agent of the assignee.

§ 3–312. Lost, Destroyed, or Stolen Cashier's Check, Teller's Check, or Certified Check.*

(a) In this section:

(1) "Check" means a cashier's check, teller's check, or certified check.

(2) "Claimant" means a person who claims the right to receive the amount of a cashier's check, teller's check, or certified check that was lost, destroyed, or stolen.

(3) "Declaration of loss" means a written statement, made under penalty of perjury, to the effect that (i) the declarer lost posses-

* [Section 3–312 was not adopted as part of the 1990 Official Text of Revised Article 3. It was officially approved and recommended for enactment in all states in August 1991 by the National Conference of Commissioners on Uniform State Laws.]

sion of a check, (ii) the declarer is the drawer or payee of the check, in the case of a certified check, or the remitter or payee of the check, in the case of a cashier's check or teller's check, (iii) the loss of possession was not the result of a transfer by the declarer or a lawful seizure, and (iv) the declarer cannot reasonably obtain possession of the check because the check was destroyed, its whereabouts cannot be determined, or it is in the wrongful possession of an unknown person or a person that cannot be found or is not amenable to service of process.

(4) "Obligated bank" means the issuer of a cashier's check or teller's check or the acceptor of a certified check.

(b) A claimant may assert a claim to the amount of a check by a communication to the obligated bank describing the check with reasonable certainty and requesting payment of the amount of the check, if (i) the claimant is the drawer or payee of a certified check or the remitter or payee of a cashier's check or teller's check, (ii) the communication contains or is accompanied by a declaration of loss of the claimant with respect to the check, (iii) the communication is received at a time and in a manner affording the bank a reasonable time to act on it before the check is paid, and (iv) the claimant provides reasonable identification if requested by the obligated bank. Delivery of a declaration of loss is a warranty of the truth of the statements made in the declaration. If a claim is asserted in compliance with this subsection, the following rules apply:

(1) The claim becomes enforceable at the later of (i) the time the claim is asserted, or (ii) the 90th day following the date of the check, in the case of a cashier's check or teller's check, or the 90th day following the date of the acceptance, in the case of a certified check.

(2) Until the claim becomes enforceable, it has no legal effect and the obligated bank may pay the check or, in the case of a teller's check, may permit the drawee to pay the check. Payment to a person entitled to enforce the check discharges all liability of the obligated bank with respect to the check.

(3) If the claim becomes enforceable before the check is presented for payment, the obligated bank is not obliged to pay the check.

(4) When the claim becomes enforceable, the obligated bank becomes obliged to pay the amount of the check to the claimant if payment of the check has not been made to a person entitled to enforce the check. Subject to Section 4-302(a)(1), payment to the claimant discharges all liability of the obligated bank with respect to the check.

(c) If the obligated bank pays the amount of a check to a claimant under subsection (b)(4) and the check is presented for payment by a person having rights of a holder in due course, the claimant is obliged to (i) refund the payment to the obligated bank if the check is paid, or (ii) pay the amount of the check to the person having rights of a holder in due course if the check is dishonored.

(d) If a claimant has the right to assert a claim under subsection (b) and is also a person entitled to enforce a cashier's check, teller's check, or certified check which is lost, destroyed, or stolen, the claimant may assert rights with respect to the check either under this section or Section 3-309.

Added in 1991.

Official Comment

1. This section applies to cases in which a cashier's check, teller's check, or certified check is lost, destroyed, or stolen. In one typical case a customer of a bank closes his or her account and takes a cashier's check or teller's check of the bank as payment of the amount of the account. The customer may be moving to a new area and the check is to be used to open a bank account in that area. In such a case the check will normally be payable to the customer. In another typical case a cashier's check or teller's check is bought from a bank for the purpose of paying some obligation of the buyer of the check. In such a case the check may be made payable to the customer and then negotiated to the creditor by indorsement. But often, the payee of the check is the creditor. In the latter case the customer is a remitter. The section covers loss of the check by either the remitter or the payee. The section also covers loss of a certified check by either the drawer or payee.

Under Section 3-309 a person seeking to enforce a lost, destroyed, or stolen cashier's check or teller's check may be required by the court to give adequate protection to the issuing bank against loss that might occur by reason of the claim by another person to enforce the check. This might require the posting of an expensive bond for the amount of the check. Moreover, Section 3-309 applies only to a person entitled to enforce the check. It does not apply to a remitter of a cashier's check or teller's check or to the drawer of a certified check. Section 3-312 applies to both. The purpose of Section 3-312 is to offer a person who loses such a check a means of getting refund of the amount of the check within a reasonable period of time without the expense of posting a bond and with full protection of the obligated bank.

2. A claim to the amount of a lost, destroyed, or stolen cashier's check, teller's check, or certified check may be made under subsection (b) if the following requirements of that subsection are met. First, a claim may be asserted only by the drawer or payee of a certified check or the remitter or payee of a cashier's check or teller's check. An indorsee of a check is not covered because the indorsee is not an original party to the check or a remitter. Limitation to an original party or remitter gives the obligated bank the ability to determine, at the time it becomes obligated on the check, the identity of the person or persons who can assert a claim with respect to the check. The bank is not faced with having to determine the rights of some person who was not a party to the check at that time or with whom the bank had not dealt. If a cashier's check is issued to the order of the person who purchased it from the bank and that person indorses it over to a third person who loses the check, the third person may assert rights to enforce the check under Section 3-309 but has no rights under Section 3-312.

Second, the claim must be asserted by a communication to the obligated bank describing the check with reasonable certainty and requesting payment of the amount of the check. "Obligated bank" is defined in subsection (a)(4). Third, the communication must be received in time to allow the obligated bank to act on the claim before the check is paid, and the claimant must provide reasonable identification if requested. Subsections (b)(iii) and (iv). Fourth, the communication must contain or be accompanied by a declaration of loss described in subsection (b). This declaration is an affidavit or other writing made under penalty of perjury alleging the loss, destruction, or theft of the check and stating that the declarer is a person entitled to assert a claim, i.e. the drawer or payee of a certified check or the remitter or payee of a cashier's check or teller's check.

A claimant who delivers a declaration of loss makes a warranty of the truth of the statements made in the declaration. The warranty is made to the obligated bank and anybody who has a right to enforce the check. If the declaration of loss falsely alleges loss of a cashier's check that did not in fact occur, a holder of the check who was unable to obtain payment because subsection (b)(3) and (4) caused the obligated bank to dishonor the check would have a cause of action against the declarer for breach of warranty.

The obligated bank may not impose additional requirements on the claimant to assert a claim under subsection (b). For example, the obligated bank may not require the posting of a bond or other form of security. Section 3–312(b) states the procedure for asserting claims covered by the section. Thus, procedures that may be stated in other law for stating claims to property do not apply and are displaced within the meaning of Section 1–103.

3. A claim asserted under subsection (b) does not have any legal effect, however, until the date it becomes enforceable, which cannot be earlier than 90 days after the date of a cashier's check or teller's check or 90 days after the date of acceptance of a certified check. Thus, if a lost check is presented for payment within the 90–day period, the bank may pay a person entitled to enforce the check without regard to the claim and is discharged of all liability with respect to the check. This ensures the continued utility of cashier's checks, teller's checks, and certified checks as cash equivalents. Virtually all such checks are presented for payment within 90 days.

If the claim becomes enforceable and payment has not been made to a person entitled to enforce the check, the bank becomes obligated to pay the amount of the check to the claimant. Subsection (b)(4). When the bank becomes obligated to pay the amount of the check to the claimant, the bank is relieved of its obligation to pay the check. Subsection (b)(3). Thus, any person entitled to enforce the check, including even a holder in due course, loses the right to enforce the check after a claim under subsection (b) becomes enforceable.

If the obligated bank pays the claimant under subsection (b)(4), the bank is discharged of all liability with respect to the check. The only exception is the unlikely case in which the obligated bank subsequently incurs liability under Section 4–302(a)(1) with respect to the check. For example, Obligated Bank is the issuer of a cashier's check and, after a claim becomes enforceable, it pays the claimant under subsection (b)(4). Later the check is presented to Obligated Bank for payment over the counter. Under subsection (b)(3), Obligated Bank is not obliged to pay the check and may dishonor the check by returning it to the person who presented it for payment. But the normal rules of check collection are not affected by Section 3–312. If Obligated Bank retains the check beyond midnight of the day of presentment without settling for it, it becomes accountable for the amount of the check under Section 4–302(a)(1) even though it had no obligation to pay the check.

An obligated bank that pays the amount of a check to a claimant under subsection (b)(4) is discharged of all liability on the check so long as the assertion of the claim meets the requirements of subsection (b) discussed in Comment 2. This is important in cases of fraudulent declarations of loss. For example, if the claimant falsely alleges a loss that in fact did not occur, the bank, subject to Section 1–203, may rely on the declaration of loss. On the other hand, a claim may be asserted only by a person described in subsection (b)(i). Thus, the bank is discharged under subsection (a)(4) only if it pays such a person. Although it is highly unlikely, it is possible that more than one person could assert a claim under subsection (b) to the amount of a check. Such a case could occur if one of the claimants makes a false declaration of loss. The obligated bank is not required to determine whether a claimant who complies with subsection (b) is acting wrongfully. The bank may utilize procedures outside this Article, such as interpleader, under which the conflicting claims may be adjudicated.

Although it is unlikely that a lost check would be presented for payment after the claimant was paid by the bank under subsection (b)(4), it is possible for it to happen. Suppose the declaration of loss by the claimant fraudulently alleged a loss that in fact did not occur. If the claimant negotiated the check, presentment for payment would occur shortly after negotiation in almost all cases. Thus, a fraudulent declaration of loss is not likely to occur unless the check is negotiated after the 90-day period has already expired or shortly before expiration. In such a case the holder of the check, who may not have noticed the date of the check, is not entitled to payment from the obligated bank if the check is presented for payment after the claim becomes enforceable. Subsection (b)(3). The remedy of the holder who is denied payment in that case is an action against the claimant under subsection (c) if the holder is a holder in due course, or for breach of warranty under subsection (b). The holder would also have common law remedies against the claimant under the law of restitution or fraud.

4. The following cases illustrate the operation of Section 3-312:

Case # 1. Obligated Bank (OB) certified a check drawn by its customer, Drawer (D), payable to Payee (P). Two days after the check was certified, D lost the check and then asserted a claim pursuant to subsection (b). The check had not been presented for payment when D's claim became enforceable 90 days after the check was certified. Under subsection (b)(4), at the time D's claim became enforceable OB became obliged to pay D the amount of the check. If the check is later presented for payment, OB may refuse to pay the check and has no obligation to anyone to pay the check. Any obligation owed by D to P, for which the check was intended as payment, is unaffected because the check was never delivered to P.

Case # 2. Obligated Bank (OB) issued a teller's check to Remitter (R) payable to Payee (P). R delivered the check to P in payment of an obligation. P lost the check and then asserted a claim pursuant to subsection (b). To carry out P's order, OB issued an order pursuant to Section 4-403(a) to the drawee of the teller's check to stop payment of the check effective on the 90th day after the date of the teller's check. The check was not presented for payment. On the 90th day after the date of the teller's check P's claim becomes enforceable and OB becomes obliged to pay P the amount of the check. As in Case # 1, OB has no further liability with respect to the check to anyone. When R delivered the check to P, R's underlying obligation to P was discharged under Section 3-310. Thus, R suffered no loss. Since P received the amount of the check, P also suffered no loss except with respect to the delay in receiving the amount of the check.

Case # 3. Obligated Bank (OB) issued a cashier's check to its customer, Payee (P). Two days after issue, the check was stolen from P who then asserted a claim pursuant to subsection (b). Ten days after issue, the check was deposited by X in an account in Depositary Bank (DB). X had found the check and forged the indorsement of P. DB promptly presented the check to OB and obtained payment on behalf of X. On the 90th day after the date of the check P's claim becomes enforceable and P is entitled to receive the amount of the check from OB. Subsection (b)(4). Although the check was presented for payment before P's claim becomes enforceable, OB is not discharged. Because of the forged indorsement X was not a holder and neither was DB. Thus, neither is a person entitled to enforce the check (Section 3-301) and OB is not discharged under Section 3-602(a). Thus, under subsection (b)(4), because OB did not pay a person entitled to enforce the check, OB must pay P. OB's remedy is against DB for breach of warranty under Section 4-208(a)(1). As an alternative to the remedy under Section 3-312, P could recover from DB for conversion under Section 3-420(a).

Case # 4. Obligated Bank (OB) issued a cashier's check to its customer, Payee (P). P made an unrestricted blank indorsement of the check and mailed the check to P's bank for deposit to P's account. The check was never received by P's bank. When P discovered the loss, P asserted a claim pursuant to subsection (b). X found the check and deposited it in X's account in Depositary Bank (DB) after indorsing the check. DB presented the check for payment before the end of the 90-day period after its date. OB paid the check. Because of the unrestricted blank indorsement by P, X became a holder of the check. DB also became a holder. Since the check was paid before P's claim became enforceable and payment was made to a person entitled to enforce the check, OB is discharged of all liability with respect to the check. Subsection (b)(2). Thus, P is not entitled to payment from OB. Subsection (b)(4) doesn't apply.

Case # 5. Obligated Bank (OB) issued a cashier's check to its customer, Payee (P). P made an unrestricted blank indorsement of the check and mailed the check to P's bank for deposit to P's account. The check was never received by P's bank. When P discovered the loss, P asserted a claim pursuant to subsection (b). At the end of the 90-day period after the date of the check, OB paid the amount of the check to P under subsection (b)(4). X then found the check and deposited it to X's account in Depositary Bank (DB). DB presented the check to OB for payment. OB is not obliged to pay the check. Subsection (b)(4). If OB dishonors the check, DB's remedy is to charge back X's account. Section 4-214(a). Although P, as an indorser, would normally have liability to DB under Section 3-415(a) because the check was dishonored, P is released from that liability under Section 3-415(e) because collection of the check was initiated more than 30 days after the indorsement. DB has a remedy only against X. A depositary bank that takes a cashier's check that cannot be presented for payment before expiration of the 90-day period after its date is on notice that the check might not be paid because of the possibility of a claim asserted under subsection (b) which would excuse the issuer of the check from paying the check. Thus, the depositary bank cannot safely release funds with respect to the check until it has assurance that the check has been paid. DB cannot be a holder in due course of the check because it took the check when the check was overdue. Section 3-304(a)(2). Thus, DB has no action against P under subsection (c).

Case # 6. Obligated Bank (OB) issued a cashier's check payable to bearer and delivered it to its customer, Remitter (R). R held the check for 90 days and then wrongfully asserted a claim to the amount of the check under subsection (b). The declaration of loss fraudulently stated that the check was lost. R received payment from OB under subsection (b)(4). R then negotiated the check to X for value. X presented the check to OB for payment. Although OB, under subsection (b)(2), was not obliged to pay the check, OB paid X by mistake. OB's teller did not notice that the check was more than 90 days old and was not aware that OB was not obliged to pay the check. If X took the check in good faith, OB may not recover from X. Section 3-418(c). OB's remedy is to recover from R for fraud or for breach of warranty in making a false declaration of loss. Subsection (b).

PART 4

LIABILITY OF PARTIES

§ 3-401. Signature.

(a) A person is not liable on an instrument unless (i) the person signed the instrument, or (ii) the person is represented by an agent or representative who signed the instrument and the signature is binding on the represented person under Section 3-402.

(b) A signature may be made (i) manually or by means of a device or machine, and (ii) by the use of any name, including a trade or assumed name, or by a word, mark, or symbol executed or adopted by a person with present intention to authenticate a writing.

Official Comment

1. Obligation on an instrument depends on a signature that is binding on the obligor. The signature may be made by the obligor personally or by an agent authorized to act for the obligor. Signature by agents is covered by Section 3-402. It is not necessary that the name of the obligor appear on the instrument, so long as there is a signature that binds the obligor. Signature includes an indorsement.

2. A signature may be handwritten, typed, printed or made in any other manner. It need not be subscribed, and may appear in the body of the instrument, as in the case of "I, John Doe, promise to pay *** " without any other signature. It may be made by mark, or even by thumbprint. It may be made in any name, including any trade name or assumed name, however false and fictitious, which is adopted for the purpose. Parol evidence is admissible to identify the signer, and when the signer is identified the signature is effective. Indorsement in a name other than that of the indorser is governed by Section 3-204(d).

This section is not intended to affect any other law requiring a signature by mark to be witnessed, or any signature to be otherwise authenticated, or requiring any form of proof.

§ 3-402. Signature by Representative.

(a) If a person acting, or purporting to act, as a representative signs an instrument by signing either the name of the represented person or the name of the signer, the represented person is bound by the signature to the same extent the represented person would be bound if the signature were on a simple contract. If the represented person is bound, the signature of the representative is the "authorized signature of the represented person" and the represented person is liable on the instrument, whether or not identified in the instrument.

(b) If a representative signs the name of the representative to an instrument and the signature is an authorized signature of the represented person, the following rules apply:

(1) If the form of the signature shows unambiguously that the signature is made on behalf of the represented person who is identified in the instrument, the representative is not liable on the instrument.

(2) Subject to subsection (c), if (i) the form of the signature does not show unambiguously that the signature is made in a representative capacity or (ii) the represented person is not identified in the instrument, the representative is liable on the instrument to a holder in due course that took the instrument without notice that the representative was not intended to be liable on the instrument. With respect to any other person, the representative is liable on the instrument unless the representative proves that the original parties did not intend the representative to be liable on the instrument.

(c) If a representative signs the name of the representative as drawer of a check without indication of the representative status and the check is payable from an account of the represented person who is identified on the check, the signer is not liable on the check if the signature is an authorized signature of the represented person.

Official Comment

1. Subsection (a) states when the represented person is bound on an instrument if the instrument is signed by a representative. If under the law of agency the represented person would be bound by the act of the representative in signing either the name of the represented person or that of the representative, the signature is the authorized signature of the represented person. Former Section 3–401(1) stated that "no person is liable on an instrument unless his signature appears thereon." This was interpreted as meaning that an undisclosed principal is not liable on an instrument. This interpretation provided an exception to ordinary agency law that binds an undisclosed principal on a simple contract.

It is questionable whether this exception was justified by the language of former Article 3 and there is no apparent policy justification for it. The exception is rejected by subsection (a) which returns to ordinary rules of agency. If P, the principal, authorized A, the agent, to borrow money on P's behalf and A signed A's name to a note without disclosing that the signature was on behalf of P, A is liable on the instrument. But if the person entitled to enforce the note can also prove that P authorized A to sign on P's behalf, why shouldn't P also be liable on the instrument? To recognize the liability of P takes nothing away from the utility of negotiable instruments. Furthermore, imposing liability on P has the merit of making it impossible to have an instrument on which nobody is liable even though it was authorized by P. That result could occur under former Section 3–401(1) if an authorized agent signed "as agent" but the note did not identify the principal. If the dispute was between the agent and the payee of the note, the agent could escape liability on the note by proving that the agent and the payee did not intend that the agent be liable on the note when the note was issued. Former Section 3–403(2)(b). Under the prevailing interpretation of former Section 3–401(1), the principal was not liable on the note under former 3–401(1) because the principal's name did not appear on the note. Thus, nobody was liable on the note even though all parties knew that the note was signed by the agent on behalf of the principal. Under Section 3–402(a) the principal would be liable on the note.

2. Subsection (b) concerns the question of when an agent who signs an instrument on behalf of a principal is bound on the instrument. The approach followed by former Section 3–403 was to specify the form of signature that imposed or avoided liability. This approach was unsatisfactory. There are many ways in which there can be ambiguity

about a signature. It is better to state a general rule. Subsection (b)(1) states that if the form of the signature unambiguously shows that it is made on behalf of an identified represented person (for example, "P, by A, Treasurer") the agent is not liable. This is a workable standard for a court to apply. Subsection (b)(2) partly changes former Section 3–403(2). Subsection (b)(2) relates to cases in which the agent signs on behalf of a principal but the form of the signature does not fall within subsection (b)(1). The following cases are illustrative. In each case John Doe is the authorized agent of Richard Roe and John Doe signs a note on behalf of Richard Roe. In each case the intention of the original parties to the instrument is that Roe is to be liable on the instrument but Doe is not to be liable.

Case # 1. Doe signs "John Doe" without indicating in the note that Doe is signing as agent. The note does not identify Richard Roe as the represented person.

Case # 2. Doe signs "John Doe, Agent" but the note does not identify Richard Roe as the represented person.

Case # 3. The name "Richard Roe" is written on the note and immediately below that name Doe signs "John Doe" without indicating that Doe signed as agent.

In each case Doe is liable on the instrument to a holder in due course without notice that Doe was not intended to be liable. In none of the cases does Doe's signature unambiguously show that Doe was signing as agent for an identified principal. A holder in due course should be able to resolve any ambiguity against Doe.

But the situation is different if a holder in due course is not involved. In each case Roe is liable on the note. Subsection (a). If the original parties to the note did not intend that Doe also be liable, imposing liability on Doe is a windfall to the person enforcing the note. Under subsection (b)(2) Doe is prima facie liable because his signature appears on the note and the form of the signature does not unambiguously refute personal liability. But Doe can escape liability by proving that the original parties did not intend that he be liable on the note. This is a change from former Section 3–403(2)(a).

A number of cases under former Article 3 involved situations in which an agent signed the agent's name to a note, without qualification and without naming the person represented, intending to bind the principal but not the agent. The agent attempted to prove that the other party had the same intention. Some of these cases involved mistake, and in some there was evidence that the agent may have been deceived into signing in that manner. In some of the cases the court refused to allow proof of the intention of the parties and imposed liability on the agent based on former Section 3–403(2)(a) even though both parties to the instrument may have intended that the agent not be liable. Subsection (b)(2) changes the result of those cases, and is consistent with Section 3–117 which allows oral or written agreements to modify or nullify apparent obligations on the instrument.

Former Section 3–403 spoke of the represented person being "named" in the instrument. Section 3–402 speaks of the represented person being "identified" in the instrument. This change in terminology is intended to reject decisions under former Section 3–403(2) requiring that the instrument state the legal name of the represented person.

3. Subsection (c) is directed at the check cases. It states that if the check identifies the represented person the agent who signs on the signature line does not have to indicate agency status. Virtually all checks used today are in personalized form which identify the person on whose account the check is drawn. In this case, nobody is deceived into thinking that the person signing the check is meant to be liable. This subsection is meant to overrule cases decided under former Article 3 such as Griffin v. Ellinger, 538 S.W.2d 97 (Texas 1976).

§ 3-403. Unauthorized Signature.

(a) Unless otherwise provided in this Article or Article 4, an unauthorized signature is ineffective except as the signature of the unauthorized signer in favor of a person who in good faith pays the instrument or takes it for value. An unauthorized signature may be ratified for all purposes of this Article.

(b) If the signature of more than one person is required to constitute the authorized signature of an organization, the signature of the organization is unauthorized if one of the required signatures is lacking.

(c) The civil or criminal liability of a person who makes an unauthorized signature is not affected by any provision of this Article which makes the unauthorized signature effective for the purposes of this Article.

Official Comment

1. "Unauthorized" signature is defined in Section 1-201(43) as one that includes a forgery as well as a signature made by one exceeding actual or apparent authority. Former Section 3-404(1) stated that an unauthorized signature was inoperative as the signature of the person whose name was signed unless that person "is precluded from denying it." Under former Section 3-406 if negligence by the person whose name was signed contributed to an unauthorized signature, that person "is precluded from asserting the *** lack of authority." Both of these sections were applied to cases in which a forged signature appeared on an instrument and the person asserting rights on the instrument alleged that the negligence of the purported signer contributed to the forgery. Since the standards for liability between the two sections differ, the overlap between the sections caused confusion. Section 3-403(a) deals with the problem by removing the preclusion language that appeared in former Section 3-404.

2. The except clause of the first sentence of subsection (a) states the generally accepted rule that the unauthorized signature, while it is wholly inoperative as that of the person whose name is signed, is effective to impose liability upon the signer or to transfer any rights that the signer may have in the instrument. The signer's liability is not in damages for breach of warranty of authority, but is full liability on the instrument in the capacity in which the signer signed. It is, however, limited to parties who take or pay the instrument in good faith; and one who knows that the signature is unauthorized cannot recover from the signer on the instrument.

3. The last sentence of subsection (a) allows an unauthorized signature to be ratified. Ratification is a retroactive adoption of the unauthorized signature by the person whose name is signed and may be found from conduct as well as from express statements. For example, it may be found from the retention of benefits received in the transaction with knowledge of the unauthorized signature. Although the forger is not an agent, ratification is governed by the rules and principles applicable to ratification of unauthorized acts of an agent.

Ratification is effective for all purposes of this Article. The unauthorized signature becomes valid so far as its effect as a signature is concerned. Although the ratification may relieve the signer of liability on the instrument, it does not of itself relieve the signer of liability to the person whose name is signed. It does not in any way affect the criminal law. No policy of the criminal law prevents a person whose name is forged to assume liability to others on the instrument by ratifying the forgery, but the ratification cannot affect the rights of the state. While the ratification may be taken into account with other relevant facts in determining punishment, it does not relieve the signer of criminal liability.

4. Subsection (b) clarifies the meaning of "unauthorized" in cases in which an instrument contains less than all of the signatures that are required as authority to pay a check. Judicial authority was split on the issue whether the one-year notice period under former Section 4-406(4) (now Section 4-406(f)) barred a customer's suit against a payor bank that paid a check containing less than all of the signatures required by the customer to authorize payment of the check. Some cases took the view that if a customer required that a check contain the signatures of both A and B to authorize payment and only A signed, there was no unauthorized signature within the meaning of that term in former Section 4-406(4) because A's signature was neither unauthorized nor forged. The other cases correctly pointed out that it was the customer's signature at issue and not that of A; hence, the customer's signature was unauthorized if all signatures required to authorize payment of the check were not on the check. Subsection (b) follows the latter line of cases. The same analysis applies if A forged the signature of B. Because the forgery is not effective as a signature of B, the required signature of B is lacking.

Subsection (b) refers to "the authorized signature of an organization." The definition of "organization" in Section 1-201(28) is very broad. It covers not only commercial entities but also "two or more persons having a joint or common interest." Hence subsection (b) would apply when a husband and wife are both required to sign an instrument.

§ 3-404. Impostors; Fictitious Payees.

(a) If an impostor, by use of the mails or otherwise, induces the issuer of an instrument to issue the instrument to the impostor, or to a person acting in concert with the impostor, by impersonating the payee of the instrument or a person authorized to act for the payee, an indorsement of the instrument by any person in the name of the payee is effective as the indorsement of the payee in favor of a person who, in good faith, pays the instrument or takes it for value or for collection.

(b) If (i) a person whose intent determines to whom an instrument is payable (Section 3-110(a) or (b)) does not intend the person identified as payee to have any interest in the instrument, or (ii) the person identified as payee of an instrument is a fictitious person, the following rules apply until the instrument is negotiated by special indorsement:

(1) Any person in possession of the instrument is its holder.

(2) An indorsement by any person in the name of the payee stated in the instrument is effective as the indorsement of the payee in favor of a person who, in good faith, pays the instrument or takes it for value or for collection.

(c) Under subsection (a) or (b), an indorsement is made in the name of a payee if (i) it is made in a name substantially similar to that of the payee or (ii) the instrument, whether or not indorsed, is deposited in a depositary bank to an account in a name substantially similar to that of the payee.

(d) With respect to an instrument to which subsection (a) or (b) applies, if a person paying the instrument or taking it for value or for collection fails to exercise ordinary care in paying or taking the instrument and that failure substantially contributes to loss resulting from payment of the instrument, the person bearing the loss may recover from the person failing to exercise ordinary care to the extent the failure to exercise ordinary care contributed to the loss.

Official Comment

1. Under former Article 3, the impostor cases were governed by former Section 3–405(1)(a) and the fictitious payee cases were governed by Section 3–405(1)(b). Section 3–404 replaces former Section 3–405(1)(a) and (b) and modifies the previous law in some respects. Former Section 3–405 was read by some courts to require that the indorsement be in the exact name of the named payee. Revised Article 3 rejects this result. Section 3–404(c) requires only that the indorsement be made in a name "substantially similar" to that of the payee. Subsection (c) also recognizes the fact that checks may be deposited without indorsement. Section 4–205(a).

Subsection (a) changes the former law in a case in which the impostor is impersonating an agent. Under former Section 3–405(1)(a), if Impostor impersonated Smith and induced the drawer to draw a check to the order of Smith, Impostor could negotiate the check. If Impostor impersonated Smith, the president of Smith Corporation, and the check was payable to the order of Smith Corporation, the section did not apply. See the last paragraph of Comment 2 to former Section 3–405. In revised Article 3, Section 3–404(a) gives Impostor the power to negotiate the check in both cases.

2. Subsection (b) is based in part on former Section 3–405(1)(b) and in part on N.I.L. § 9(3). It covers cases in which an instrument is payable to a fictitious or nonexisting person and to cases in which the payee is a real person but the drawer or maker does not intend the payee to have any interest in the instrument. Subsection (b) applies to any instrument, but its primary importance is with respect to checks of corporations and other organizations. It also applies to forged check cases. The following cases illustrate subsection (b):

Case # 1. Treasurer is authorized to draw checks in behalf of Corporation. Treasurer fraudulently draws a check of Corporation payable to Supplier Co., a non-existent company. Subsection (b) applies because Supplier Co. is a fictitious person and because Treasurer did not intend Supplier Co. to have any interest in the check. Under subsection (b)(1) Treasurer, as the person in possession of the check, becomes the holder of the check. Treasurer indorses the check in the name "Supplier Co." and deposits it in Depositary Bank. Under subsection (b)(2) and (c)(i), the indorsement is effective to make Depositary Bank the holder and therefore a person entitled to enforce the instrument. Section 3–301.

Case # 2. Same facts as Case # 1 except that Supplier Co. is an actual company that does business with Corporation. If Treasurer intended to steal the check when the check was drawn, the result in Case # 2 is the same as the result in Case # 1. Subsection (b) applies because Treasurer did not intend Supplier Co. to have any interest in the check. It does not make any difference whether Supplier Co. was or was not a creditor of Corporation when the check was drawn. If Treasurer did not decide to steal the check until after the check was drawn, the case is covered by Section 3–405 rather than Section 3–404(b), but the result is the same. See Case # 6 in Comment 3 to Section 3–405.

Case # 3. Checks of Corporation must be signed by two officers. President and Treasurer both sign a check of Corporation payable to Supplier Co., a company that does business with Corporation from time to time but to which Corporation does not owe any money. Treasurer knows that no money is owed to Supplier Co. and does not intend that Supplier Co. have any interest in the check. President believes that money is owed to Supplier Co. Treasurer obtains possession of the check after it is signed. Subsection (b) applies because Treasurer is "a person whose intent determines to whom an instrument is payable" and Treasurer does not intend Supplier Co. to have any interest in the check. Treasurer becomes the holder of the check and may negotiate it by indorsing it in the name "Supplier Co."

Case # 4. Checks of Corporation are signed by a check-writing machine. Names of payees of checks produced by the machine are determined by information entered into the computer that operates the machine. Thief, a person who is not an employee or other agent of Corporation, obtains access to the computer and causes the check-writing machine to produce a check payable to Supplier Co., a non-existent company. Subsection (b)(ii) applies. Thief then obtains possession of the check. At that point Thief becomes the holder of the check because Thief is the person in possession of the instrument. Subsection (b)(1). Under Section 3-301 Thief, as holder, is the "person entitled to enforce the instrument" even though Thief does not have title to the check and is in wrongful possession of it. Thief indorses the check in the name "Supplier Co." and deposits it in an account in Depositary Bank which Thief opened in the name "Supplier Co." Depositary Bank takes the check in good faith and credits the "Supplier Co." account. Under subsection (b)(2) and (c)(i), the indorsement is effective. Depositary Bank becomes the holder and the person entitled to enforce the check. The check is presented to the drawee bank for payment and payment is made. Thief then withdraws the credit to the account. Although the check was issued without authority given by Corporation, the drawee bank is entitled to pay the check and charge Corporation's account if there was an agreement with Corporation allowing the bank to debit Corporation's account for payment of checks produced by the check-writing machine whether or not authorized. The indorsement is also effective if Supplier Co. is a real person. In that case subsection (b)(i) applies. Under Section 3-110(b) Thief is the person whose intent determines to whom the check is payable, and Thief did not intend Supplier Co. to have any interest in the check. When the drawee bank pays the check, there is no breach of warranty under Section 3-417(a)(1) or 4-208(a)(1) because Depositary Bank was a person entitled to enforce the check when it was forwarded for payment.

Case # 5. Thief, who is not an employee or agent of Corporation, steals check forms of Corporation. John Doe is president of Corporation and is authorized to sign checks on behalf of Corporation as drawer. Thief draws a check in the name of Corporation as drawer by forging the signature of Doe. Thief makes the check payable to the order of Supplier Co. with the intention of stealing it. Whether Supplier Co. is a fictitious person or a real person, Thief becomes the holder of the check and the person entitled to enforce it. The analysis is the same as that in Case # 4. Thief deposits the check in an account in Depositary Bank which Thief opened in the name "Supplier Co." Thief either indorses the check in a name other than "Supplier Co." or does not indorse the check at all. Under Section 4-205(a) a depositary bank may become holder of a check deposited to the account of a customer if the customer was a holder, whether or not the customer indorses. Subsection (c)(ii) treats deposit to an account in a name substantially similar to that of the payee as the equivalent of indorsement in the name of the payee. Thus, the deposit is an effective indorsement of the check. Depositary Bank becomes the holder of the check and the person entitled to enforce the check. If the check is paid by the drawee bank, there is no breach of warranty under Section 3-417(a)(1) or 4-208(a)(1) because Depositary Bank was a person entitled to enforce the check when it was forwarded for payment and, unless Depositary Bank knew about the forgery of Doe's signature, there is no breach of warranty under Section 3–417(a)(3) or 4–208(a)(3). Because the check was a forged check the drawee bank is not entitled to charge Corporation's account unless Section 3–406 or Section 4–406 applies.

3. In cases governed by subsection (a) the dispute will normally be between the drawer of the check that was obtained by the impostor and the drawee bank that paid it. The drawer is precluded from obtaining recredit of the drawer's account by arguing that the check was paid on a forged indorsement so long as the drawee bank acted in good faith in paying the check. Cases governed by subsection (b) are illustrated by Cases # 1 through # 5 in Comment 2. In Cases # 1, # 2, and # 3 there is no forgery of the check, thus the drawer of the check takes the loss if there is no lack of good faith by the banks involved. Cases # 4 and # 5 are forged check cases. Depositary Bank is entitled to retain the proceeds of the check if it didn't know about the forgery. Under Section 3–418 the drawee bank is not entitled to recover from Depositary Bank on the basis of payment by mistake because Depositary Bank took the check in good faith and gave value for the check when the credit given for the check was withdrawn. And there is no breach of warranty under Section 3–417(a)(1) or (3) or 4–208(a)(1) or (3). Unless Section 3–406 applies the loss is taken by the drawee bank if a forged check is paid, and that is the result in Case # 5. In Case # 4 the loss is taken by Corporation, the drawer, because an agreement between Corporation and the drawee bank allowed the bank to debit Corporation's account despite the unauthorized use of the check-writing machine.

If a check payable to an impostor, fictitious payee, or payee not intended to have an interest in the check is paid, the effect of subsections (a) and (b) is to place the loss on the drawer of the check rather than on the drawee or the depositary bank that took the check for collection. Cases governed by subsection (a) always involve fraud, and fraud is almost always involved in cases governed by subsection (b). The drawer is in the best position to avoid the fraud and thus should take the loss. This is true in Case # 1, Case # 2, and Case # 3. But in some cases the person taking the check might have detected the fraud and thus have prevented the loss by the exercise of ordinary care. In those cases, if that person failed to exercise ordinary care, it is reasonable that that person bear loss to the extent the failure contributed to the loss. Subsection (d) is intended to reach that result. It allows the person who suffers loss as a result of payment of the check to recover from the person who failed to exercise ordinary care. In Case # 1, Case # 2, and Case # 3, the person suffering the loss is Corporation, the drawer of the check. In each case the most likely defendant is the depositary bank that took the check and failed to exercise ordinary care. In those cases, the drawer has a cause of action against the offending bank to recover a portion of the loss. The amount of loss to be allocated to each party is left to the trier of fact. Ordinary care is defined in Section 3–103(a)(7). An example of the type of conduct by a depositary bank that could give rise to recovery under subsection (d) is discussed in Comment 4 to Section 3–405. That comment addresses the last sentence of Section 3–405(b) which is similar to Section 3–404(d).

In Case # 1, Case # 2, and Case # 3, there was no forgery of the drawer's signature. But cases involving checks payable to a fictitious payee or a payee not intended to have an interest in the check are often forged check cases as well. Examples are Case # 4 and Case # 5. Normally, the loss in forged check cases is on the drawee bank that paid the check. Case # 5 is an example. In Case # 4 the risk with respect to the forgery is shifted to the drawer because of the agreement between the drawer and the drawee bank. The doctrine that prevents a drawee bank from recovering payment with respect to a forged check if the payment was made to a person who took the check for value and in good faith is incorporated into Section 3–418 and Sections 3–417(a)(3) and 4–208(a)(3). This doctrine is based on the assumption that the depositary bank normally has no way of detecting the forgery because the drawer is not that bank's customer. On the other hand, the drawee bank, at least in some cases, may be able to detect the forgery by comparing the signature on the check with the specimen signature that the drawee has on file. But in some forged check cases the depositary bank is in a position to detect the fraud. Those cases typically involve a check payable to a fictitious payee or a payee not intended to have an interest in the check. Subsection (d) applies to those cases. If the depositary bank failed to exercise ordinary care and the failure substantially contributed to the loss, the drawer in Case # 4 or the drawee bank in Case # 5 has a cause of action against the depositary bank under subsection (d). Comment 4 to Section 3–405 can be used as a guide to the type of conduct that could give rise to recovery under Section 3–404(d).

§ 3–405. Employer's Responsibility for Fraudulent Indorsement by Employee.

(a) In this section:

(1) "Employee" includes an independent contractor and employee of an independent contractor retained by the employer.

(2) "Fraudulent indorsement" means (i) in the case of an instrument payable to the employer, a forged indorsement purporting to be that of the employer, or (ii) in the case of an instrument with respect to which the employer is the issuer, a forged indorsement purporting to be that of the person identified as payee.

(3) "Responsibility" with respect to instruments means authority (i) to sign or indorse instruments on behalf of the employer, (ii) to process instruments received by the employer for bookkeeping purposes, for deposit to an account, or for other disposition, (iii) to prepare or process instruments for issue in the name of the employer, (iv) to supply information determining the names or addresses of payees of instruments to be issued in the name of the employer, (v) to control the disposition of instruments to be issued in the name of the employer, or (vi) to act otherwise with respect to instruments in a responsible capacity. "Responsibility" does not include authority that merely allows an employee to have access to instruments or blank or incomplete instrument forms that are being stored or transported or are part of incoming or outgoing mail, or similar access.

(b) For the purpose of determining the rights and liabilities of a person who, in good faith, pays an instrument or takes it for value or for collection, if an employer entrusted an employee with responsibility with respect to the instrument and the employee or a person acting in concert with the employee makes a fraudulent indorsement of the instrument, the indorsement is effective as the indorsement of the person to whom the instrument is payable if it is made in the name of that person. If the person paying the instrument or taking it for value or for collection fails to exercise ordinary care in paying or taking the instrument and that failure substantially contributes to loss resulting from the fraud, the person bearing the loss may recover from the person failing to exercise ordinary care to the extent the failure to exercise ordinary care contributed to the loss.

(c) Under subsection (b), an indorsement is made in the name of the person to whom an instrument is payable if (i) it is made in a name substantially similar to the name of that person or (ii) the instrument, whether or not indorsed, is deposited in a depositary bank to an account in a name substantially similar to the name of that person.

Official Comment

1. Section 3–405 is addressed to fraudulent indorsements made by an employee with respect to instruments with respect to which the employer has given responsibility to the employee. It covers two categories of fraudulent indorsements: indorsements made in the name of the employer to instruments payable to the employer and indorsements made in the name of payees of instruments issued by the employer. This section applies to instruments generally but normally the instrument will be a check. Section 3–405 adopts the principle that the risk of loss for fraudulent indorsements by employees who are entrusted with responsibility with respect to checks should fall on the employer rather than the bank that takes the check or pays it, if the bank was not negligent in the transaction. Section 3–405 is based on the belief that the employer is in a far better position to avoid the loss by care in choosing employees, in supervising them, and in adopting other measures to prevent forged indorsements on instruments payable to the employer or fraud in the issuance of instruments in the name of the employer. If the bank failed to exercise ordinary care, subsection (b) allows the employer to shift loss to the bank to the extent the bank's failure to exercise ordinary care contributed to the loss. "Ordinary care" is defined in Section 3–103(a)(7). The provision applies regardless of whether the employer is negligent.

The first category of cases governed by Section 3–405 are those involving indorsements made in the name of payees of instruments issued by the employer. In this category, Section 3–405 includes cases that were covered by former Section 3–405(1)(c). The scope of Section 3–405 in revised Article 3 is, however, somewhat wider. It covers some cases not covered by former Section 3–405(1)(c) in which the entrusted employee makes a forged indorsement to a check drawn by the employer. An example is Case # 6 in Comment 3. Moreover, a larger group of employees is included in revised Section 3–405. The key provision is the definition of "responsibility" in subsection (a)(1) which identifies the kind of responsibility delegated to an employee which will cause the employer to take responsibility for the fraudulent acts of that employee. An employer can insure this risk by employee fidelity bonds.

The second category of cases governed by Section 3–405—fraudulent indorsements of the name of the employer to instruments payable to the employer—were covered in former Article 3 by Section 3–406. Under former Section 3–406, the employer took the loss only if negligence of the employer could be proved. Under revised Article 3, Section 3–406 need not be used with respect to forgeries of the employer's indorsement. Section 3–405 imposes the loss on the employer without proof of negligence.

2. With respect to cases governed by former Section 3–405(1)(c), Section 3–405 is more favorable to employers in one respect. The bank was entitled to the preclusion provided by former Section 3–405(1)(c) if it took the check in good faith. The fact that the bank acted negligently did not shift the loss to the bank so long as the bank acted in good faith. Under revised Section 3–405 the loss may be recovered from the bank to the extent the failure of the bank to exercise ordinary care contributed to the loss.

3. Section 3–404(b) and Section 3–405 both apply to cases of employee fraud. Section 3–404(b) is not limited to cases of employee fraud, but most of the cases to which it applies will be cases of employee fraud. The following cases illustrate the application of Section 3–405. In each case it is assumed that the bank that took the check acted in good faith and was not negligent.

Case # 1. Janitor, an employee of Employer, steals a check for a very large amount payable to Employer after finding it on a desk in one of Employer's offices. Janitor forges Employer's indorsement on the check and obtains payment. Since Janitor was not entrusted with "responsibility" with respect to the check, Section 3–405 does not apply. Section 3–406 might apply to this case. The issue would be whether Employer was negligent in safeguarding the check. If not, Employer could assert that the indorsement was forged and bring an action for conversion against the depositary or payor bank under Section 3–420.

Case # 2. X is Treasurer of Corporation and is authorized to write checks on behalf of Corporation by signing X's name as Treasurer. X draws a check in the name of Corporation and signs X's name as Treasurer. The check is made payable to X. X then indorses the check and obtains payment. Assume that Corporation did not owe any money to X and did not authorize X to write the check. Although the writing of the check was not authorized, Corporation is bound as drawer of the check because X had authority to sign checks on behalf of Corporation. This result follows from agency law and Section 3–402(a). Section 3–405 does not apply in this case because there is no forged indorsement. X was payee of the check so the indorsement is valid. Section 3–110(a).

Case # 3. The duties of Employee, a bookkeeper, include posting the amounts of checks payable to Employer to the accounts of the drawers of the checks. Employee steals a check payable to Employer which was entrusted to Employee and forges Employer's indorsement. The check is deposited by Employee to an account in Depositary Bank which Employee opened in the same name as Employer, and the check is honored by the drawee bank. The indorsement is effective as Employer's indorsement because Employee's duties include processing checks for bookkeeping purposes. Thus, Employee is entrusted with "responsibility" with respect to the check. Neither Depositary Bank nor the drawee bank is liable to Employer for conversion of the check. The same result follows if Employee deposited the check in the account in Depositary Bank without indorsement. Section 4–205(a). Under subsection (c) deposit in a depositary bank in an account in a name substantially similar to that of Employer is the equivalent of an indorsement in the name of Employer.

Case # 4. Employee's duties include stamping Employer's unrestricted blank indorsement on checks received by Employer and depositing them in Employer's bank account. After stamping Employer's unrestricted blank indorsement on a check, Employee steals the check and deposits it in Employee's personal bank account. Section 3–405 doesn't apply because there is no forged indorsement. Employee is authorized by Employer to indorse Employer's checks. The fraud by Employee is not the indorsement but rather the theft of the indorsed check. Whether Employer has a cause of action against the bank in which the check was deposited is determined by whether the bank had notice of the breach of fiduciary duty by Employee. The issue is determined under Section 3–307.

Case # 5. The computer that controls Employer's check-writing machine was programmed to cause a check to be issued to Supplier Co. to which money was owed by Employer. The address of Supplier Co. was included in the information in the computer. Employee is an accounts payable clerk whose duties include entering information into the computer. Employee fraudulently changed the address of Supplier Co. in the computer data bank to an address of Employee. The check was subsequently produced by the check-writing machine and mailed to the address that Employee had entered into the computer. Employee obtained possession of the check, indorsed it in the name of Supplier Co, and deposited it to an account in Depositary Bank which Employee opened in the name "Supplier Co." The check was honored by the drawee bank. The indorsement is effective under Section 3–405(b) because Employee's duties allowed Employee to supply information determining the address of the payee of the check. An employee that is entrusted with duties that enable the employee to determine the address to which a check is to be sent controls the disposition of the check and facilitates forgery of the indorsement. The employer is held responsible. The drawee may debit the account of Employer for the amount of the check. There is no breach of warranty by Depositary Bank under Section 3–417(a)(1) or 4–208(a)(1).

Case # 6. Treasurer is authorized to draw checks in behalf of Corporation. Treasurer draws a check of Corporation payable to Supplier Co., a company that sold goods to Corporation. The check was issued to pay the price of these goods. At the time the check was signed Treasurer had no intention of stealing the check. Later, Treasurer stole the check, indorsed it in the name "Supplier Co." and obtained payment by depositing it to an account in Depositary Bank which Treasurer opened in the name "Supplier Co.". The indorsement is effective under Section 3–405(b). Section 3–404(b) does not apply to this case.

Case # 7. Checks of Corporation are signed by Treasurer in behalf of Corporation as drawer. Clerk's duties include the preparation of checks for issue by Corporation. Clerk prepares a check payable to the order of Supplier Co. for Treasurer's signature. Clerk fraudulently informs Treasurer that the check is needed to pay a debt owed to Supplier Co, a company that does business with Corporation. No money is owed to Supplier Co. and Clerk intends to steal the check. Treasurer signs it and returns it to Clerk for mailing. Clerk does not indorse the check but deposits it to an account in Depositary Bank which Clerk opened in the name "Supplier Co.". The check is honored by the drawee bank. Section 3–404(b)(i) does not apply to this case because Clerk, under Section 3–110(a), is not the person whose intent determines to whom the check is payable. But Section 3–405 does apply and it treats the deposit by Clerk as an effective indorsement by Clerk because Clerk was entrusted with responsibility with respect to the check. If Supplier Co. is a fictitious person Section 3–404(b)(ii) applies. But the result is the same. Clerk's deposit is treated as an effective indorsement of the check whether Supplier Co. is a fictitious or a real person or whether money was or was not owing to Supplier Co. The drawee bank may debit the account of Corporation for the amount of the check and there is no breach of warranty by Depositary Bank under Section 3–417(1)(a).

4. The last sentence of subsection (b) is similar to subsection (d) of Section 3–404 which is discussed in Comment 3 to Section 3–404. In Case # 5, Case # 6, or Case # 7 the depositary bank may have failed to exercise ordinary care when it allowed the employee to open an account in the name "Supplier Co.," to deposit checks payable to "Supplier Co." in that account, or to withdraw funds from that account that were proceeds of checks payable to Supplier Co. Failure to exercise ordinary care is to be determined in the context of all the facts relating to the bank's conduct with respect to the bank's collection of the check. If the trier of fact finds that there was such a failure and that the failure substantially contributed to loss, it could find the depositary bank

liable to the extent the failure contributed to the loss. The last sentence of subsection (b) can be illustrated by an example. Suppose in Case # 5 that the check is not payable to an obscure "Supplier Co." but rather to a well-known national corporation. In addition, the check is for a very large amount of money. Before depositing the check, Employee opens an account in Depositary Bank in the name of the corporation and states to the person conducting the transaction for the bank that Employee is manager of a new office being opened by the corporation. Depositary Bank opens the account without requiring Employee to produce any resolutions of the corporation's board of directors or other evidence of authorization of Employee to act for the corporation. A few days later, the check is deposited, the account is credited, and the check is presented for payment. After Depositary Bank receives payment, it allows Employee to withdraw the credit by a wire transfer to an account in a bank in a foreign country. The trier of fact could find that Depositary Bank did not exercise ordinary care and that the failure to exercise ordinary care contributed to the loss suffered by Employer. The trier of fact could allow recovery by Employer from Depositary Bank for all or part of the loss suffered by Employer.

§ 3–406. Negligence Contributing to Forged Signature or Alteration of Instrument.

(a) A person whose failure to exercise ordinary care substantially contributes to an alteration of an instrument or to the making of a forged signature on an instrument is precluded from asserting the alteration or the forgery against a person who, in good faith, pays the instrument or takes it for value or for collection.

(b) Under subsection (a), if the person asserting the preclusion fails to exercise ordinary care in paying or taking the instrument and that failure substantially contributes to loss, the loss is allocated between the person precluded and the person asserting the preclusion according to the extent to which the failure of each to exercise ordinary care contributed to the loss.

(c) Under subsection (a), the burden of proving failure to exercise ordinary care is on the person asserting the preclusion. Under subsection (b), the burden of proving failure to exercise ordinary care is on the person precluded.

Official Comment

1. Section 3–406(a) is based on former Section 3–406. With respect to alteration, Section 3–406 adopts the doctrine of Young v. Grote, 4 Bing. 253 (1827), which held that a drawer who so negligently draws an instrument as to facilitate its material alteration is liable to a drawee who pays the altered instrument in good faith. Under Section 3–406 the doctrine is expanded to apply not only to drafts but to all instruments. It includes in the protected class any "person who, in good faith, pays the instrument or takes it for value or for collection." Section 3–406 rejects decisions holding that the maker of a note owes no duty of care to the holder because at the time the instrument is issued there is no contract between them. By issuing the instrument and "setting it afloat upon a sea of strangers" the maker or drawer voluntarily enters into a relation with later holders which justifies imposition of a duty of care. In this respect an instrument so negligently drawn as to facilitate alteration does not differ in principle from an instrument containing blanks which may be filled. Under Section 3–407 a person paying an altered instrument or taking it for value, in good faith and without notice of the alteration may enforce rights with respect to the instru-

ment according to its original terms. If negligence of the obligor substantially contributes to an alteration, this section gives the holder or the payor the alternative right to treat the altered instrument as though it had been issued in the altered form.

No attempt is made to define particular conduct that will constitute "failure to exercise ordinary care [that] substantially contributes to an alteration." Rather, "ordinary care" is defined in Section 3-103(a)(7) in general terms. The question is left to the court or the jury for decision in the light of the circumstances in the particular case including reasonable commercial standards that may apply.

Section 3-406 does not make the negligent party liable in tort for damages resulting from the alteration. If the negligent party is estopped from asserting the alteration the person taking the instrument is fully protected because the taker can treat the instrument as having been issued in the altered form.

2. Section 3-406 applies equally to a failure to exercise ordinary care that substantially contributes to the making of a forged signature on an instrument. Section 3-406 refers to "forged signature" rather than "unauthorized signature" that appeared in former Section 3-406 because it more accurately describes the scope of the provision. Unauthorized signature is a broader concept that includes not only forgery but also the signature of an agent which does not bind the principal under the law of agency. The agency cases are resolved independently under agency law. Section 3-406 is not necessary in those cases.

The "substantially contributes" test of former Section 3-406 is continued in this section in preference to a "direct and proximate cause" test. The "substantially contributes" test is meant to be less stringent than a "direct and proximate cause" test. Under the less stringent test the preclusion should be easier to establish. Conduct "substantially contributes" to a material alteration or forged signature if it is a contributing cause of the alteration or signature and a substantial factor in bringing it about. The analysis of "substantially contributes" in former Section 3-406 by the court in Thompson Maple Products v. Citizens National Bank of Corry, 234 A.2d 32 (Pa.Super.Ct.1967), states what is intended by the use of the same words in revised Section 3-406(b). Since Section 3-404(d) and Section 3-405(b) also use the words "substantially contributes" the analysis of these words also applies to those provisions.

3. The following cases illustrate the kind of conduct that can be the basis of a preclusion under Section 3-406(a):

Case # 1. Employer signs checks drawn on Employer's account by use of a rubber stamp of Employer's signature. Employer keeps the rubber stamp along with Employer's personalized blank check forms in an unlocked desk drawer. An unauthorized person fraudulently uses the check forms to write checks on Employer's account. The checks are signed by use of the rubber stamp. If Employer demands that Employer's account in the drawee bank be recredited because the forged check was not properly payable, the drawee bank may defend by asserting that Employer is precluded from asserting the forgery. The trier of fact could find that Employer failed to exercise ordinary care to safeguard the rubber stamp and the check forms and that the failure substantially contributed to the forgery of Employer's signature by the unauthorized use of the rubber stamp.

Case # 2. An insurance company draws a check to the order of Sarah Smith in payment of a claim of a policyholder, Sarah Smith, who lives in Alabama. The insurance company also has a policyholder with the same name who lives in Illinois. By mistake, the insurance company mails the check to the Illinois Sarah Smith who indorses the check and obtains payment. Because the payee of the check is the Alabama Sarah Smith, the indorsement by the Illinois Sarah Smith is a forged indorsement. Section 3-110(a). The trier of fact could find that the insurance company failed to exercise ordinary care when it mailed the check to the wrong person and that the failure substantially contributed to the making of the forged indorsement. In that event the insurance company could be precluded from asserting the forged indorsement against the drawee bank that honored the check.

Case # 3. A company writes a check for $10. The figure "10" and the word "ten" are typewritten in the appropriate spaces on the check form. A large blank space is left after the figure and the word. The payee of the check, using a typewriter with a typeface similar to that used on the check, writes the word "thousand" after the word "ten" and a comma and three zeros after the figure "10". The drawee bank in good faith pays $10,000 when the check is presented for payment and debits the account of the drawer in that amount. The trier of fact could find that the drawer failed to exercise ordinary care in writing the check and that the failure substantially contributed to the alteration. In that case the drawer is precluded from asserting the alteration against the drawee if the check was paid in good faith.

4. Subsection (b) differs from former Section 3–406 in that it adopts a concept of comparative negligence. If the person precluded under subsection (a) proves that the person asserting the preclusion failed to exercise ordinary care and that failure substantially contributed to the loss, the loss may be allocated between the two parties on a comparative negligence basis. In the case of a forged indorsement the litigation is usually between the payee of the check and the depositary bank that took the check for collection. An example is a case like Case # 1 of Comment 3 to Section 3–405. If the trier of fact finds that Employer failed to exercise ordinary care in safeguarding the check and that the failure substantially contributed to the making of the forged indorsement, subsection (a) of Section 3–406 applies. If Employer brings an action for conversion against the depositary bank that took the checks from the forger, the depositary bank could assert the preclusion under subsection (a). But suppose the forger opened an account in the depositary bank in a name identical to that of Employer, the payee of the check, and then deposited the check in the account. Subsection (b) may apply. There may be an issue whether the depositary bank should have been alerted to possible fraud when a new account was opened for a corporation shortly before a very large check payable to a payee with the same name is deposited. Circumstances surrounding the opening of the account may have suggested that the corporation to which the check was payable may not be the same as the corporation for which the account was opened. If the trier of fact finds that collecting the check under these circumstances was a failure to exercise ordinary care, it could allocate the loss between the depositary bank and Employer, the payee.

§ 3–407. Alteration.

(a) "Alteration" means (i) an unauthorized change in an instrument that purports to modify in any respect the obligation of a party, or (ii) an unauthorized addition of words or numbers or other change to an incomplete instrument relating to the obligation of a party.

(b) Except as provided in subsection (c), an alteration fraudulently made discharges a party whose obligation is affected by the alteration unless that party assents or is precluded from asserting the alteration. No other alteration discharges a party, and the instrument may be enforced according to its original terms.

(c) A payor bank or drawee paying a fraudulently altered instrument or a person taking it for value, in good faith and without notice of the alteration, may enforce rights with respect to the instrument (i) according to its original terms, or (ii) in the case of an incomplete instrument altered by unauthorized completion, according to its terms as completed.

Official Comment

1. This provision restates former Section 3–407. Former Section 3–407 defined a "material" alteration as any alteration that changes the contract of the parties in any respect. Revised Section 3–407 refers to such a change as an alteration. As under subsection (2) of former Section 3–407, discharge because of alteration occurs only in the case of an alteration fraudulently made. There is no discharge if a blank is filled in the honest belief that it is authorized or if a change is made with a benevolent motive such as a desire to give the obligor the benefit of a lower interest rate. Changes favorable to the obligor are unlikely to be made with any fraudulent intent, but if such an intent is found the alteration may operate as a discharge.

Discharge is a personal defense of the party whose obligation is modified and anyone whose obligation is not affected is not discharged. But if an alteration discharges a party there is also discharge of any party having a right of recourse against the discharged party because the obligation of the party with the right of recourse is affected by the alteration. Assent to the alteration given before or after it is made will prevent the party from asserting the discharge. The phrase "or is precluded from asserting the alteration" in subsection (b) recognizes the possibility of an estoppel or other ground barring the defense which does not rest on assent.

2. Under subsection (c) a person paying a fraudulently altered instrument or taking it for value, in good faith and without notice of the alteration, is not affected by a discharge under subsection (b). The person paying or taking the instrument may assert rights with respect to the instrument according to its original terms or, in the case of an incomplete instrument that is altered by unauthorized completion, according to its terms as completed. If blanks are filled or an incomplete instrument is otherwise completed, subsection (c) places the loss upon the party who left the instrument incomplete by permitting enforcement in its completed form. This result is intended even though the instrument was stolen from the issuer and completed after the theft.

§ 3–408. Drawee Not Liable on Unaccepted Draft.

A check or other draft does not of itself operate as an assignment of funds in the hands of the drawee available for its payment, and the drawee is not liable on the instrument until the drawee accepts it.

Official Comment

1. This section is a restatement of former Section 3–409(1). Subsection (2) of former Section 3–409 is deleted as misleading and superfluous. Comment 3 says of subsection (2): "It is intended to make it clear that this section does not in any way affect any liability which may arise apart from the instrument." In reality subsection (2) did not make anything clear and was a source of confusion. If all it meant was that a bank that has not certified a check may engage in other conduct that might make it liable to a holder, it stated the obvious and was superfluous. Section 1–103 is adequate to cover those cases.

2. Liability with respect to drafts may arise under other law. For example, Section 4–302 imposes liability on a payor bank for late return of an item.

§ 3–409. Acceptance of Draft; Certified Check.

(a) "Acceptance" means the drawee's signed agreement to pay a draft as presented. It must be written on the draft and may consist of the drawee's signature alone. Acceptance may be made at any time and becomes effective when notification pursuant to instructions is given or the accepted draft is delivered for the purpose of giving rights on the acceptance to any person.

(b) A draft may be accepted although it has not been signed by the drawer, is otherwise incomplete, is overdue, or has been dishonored.

(c) If a draft is payable at a fixed period after sight and the acceptor fails to date the acceptance, the holder may complete the acceptance by supplying a date in good faith.

(d) "Certified check" means a check accepted by the bank on which it is drawn. Acceptance may be made as stated in subsection (a) or by a writing on the check which indicates that the check is certified. The drawee of a check has no obligation to certify the check, and refusal to certify is not dishonor of the check.

Official Comment

1. The first three subsections of Section 3–409 are a restatement of former Section 3–410. Subsection (d) adds a definition of certified check which is a type of accepted draft.

2. Subsection (a) states the generally recognized rule that the mere signature of the drawee on the instrument is a sufficient acceptance. Customarily the signature is written vertically across the face of the instrument, but since the drawee has no reason to sign for any other purpose a signature in any other place, even on the back of the instrument, is sufficient. It need not be accompanied by such words as "Accepted," "Certified," or "Good." It must not, however, bear any words indicating an intent to refuse to honor the draft. The last sentence of subsection (a) states the generally recognized rule that an acceptance written on the draft takes effect when the drawee notifies the holder or gives notice according to instructions.

3. The purpose of subsection (c) is to provide a definite date of payment if none appears on the instrument. An undated acceptance of a draft payable "thirty days after sight" is incomplete. Unless the acceptor writes in a different date the holder is authorized to complete the acceptance according to the terms of the draft by supplying a date of acceptance. Any date supplied by the holder is effective if made in good faith.

4. The last sentence of subsection (d) states the generally recognized rule that in the absence of agreement a bank is under no obligation to certify a check. A check is a demand instrument calling for payment rather than acceptance. The bank may be liable for breach of any agreement with the drawer, the holder, or any other person by which it undertakes to certify. Its liability is not on the instrument, since the drawee is not so liable until acceptance. Section 3–408. Any liability is for breach of the separate agreement.

§ 3–410. Acceptance Varying Draft.

(a) If the terms of a drawee's acceptance vary from the terms of the draft as presented, the holder may refuse the acceptance and treat the draft as dishonored. In that case, the drawee may cancel the acceptance.

(b) The terms of a draft are not varied by an acceptance to pay at a particular bank or place in the United States, unless the acceptance states that the draft is to be paid only at that bank or place.

(c) If the holder assents to an acceptance varying the terms of a draft, the obligation of each drawer and indorser that does not expressly assent to the acceptance is discharged.

Official Comment

1. This section is a restatement of former Section 3-412. It applies to conditional acceptances, acceptances for part of the amount, acceptances to pay at a different time from that required by the draft, or to the acceptance of less than all of the drawees. It applies to any other engagement changing the essential terms of the draft. If the drawee makes a varied acceptance the holder may either reject it or assent to it. The holder may reject by insisting on acceptance of the draft as presented. Refusal by the drawee to accept the draft as presented is dishonor. In that event the drawee is not bound by the varied acceptance and is entitled to have it canceled.

If the holder assents to the varied acceptance, the drawee's obligation as acceptor is according to the terms of the varied acceptance. Under subsection (c) the effect of the holder's assent is to discharge any drawer or indorser who does not also assent. The assent of the drawer or indorser must be affirmatively expressed. Mere failure to object within a reasonable time is not assent which will prevent the discharge.

2. Under subsection (b) an acceptance does not vary from the terms of the draft if it provides for payment at any particular bank or place in the United States unless the acceptance states that the draft is to be paid only at such bank or place. Section 3-501(b)(1) states that if an instrument is payable at a bank in the United States presentment must be made at the place of payment (Section 3-111) which in this case is at the designated bank.

§ 3-411. Refusal to Pay Cashier's Checks, Teller's Checks, and Certified Checks.

(a) In this section, "obligated bank" means the acceptor of a certified check or the issuer of a cashier's check or teller's check bought from the issuer.

(b) If the obligated bank wrongfully (i) refuses to pay a cashier's check or certified check, (ii) stops payment of a teller's check, or (iii) refuses to pay a dishonored teller's check, the person asserting the right to enforce the check is entitled to compensation for expenses and loss of interest resulting from the nonpayment and may recover consequential damages if the obligated bank refuses to pay after receiving notice of particular circumstances giving rise to the damages.

(c) Expenses or consequential damages under subsection (b) are not recoverable if the refusal of the obligated bank to pay occurs because (i) the bank suspends payments, (ii) the obligated bank asserts a claim or defense of the bank that it has reasonable grounds to believe is available against the person entitled to enforce the instrument, (iii) the obligated bank has a reasonable doubt whether the person demanding payment is the person entitled to enforce the instrument, or (iv) payment is prohibited by law.

Official Comment

1. In some cases a creditor may require that the debt be paid by an obligation of a bank. The debtor may comply by obtaining certification of the debtor's check, but more frequently the debtor buys from a bank a cashier's check or teller's check payable to the creditor. The check is taken by the creditor as a cash equivalent on the assumption that the bank will pay the check. Sometimes, the debtor wants to retract payment by inducing the obligated bank not to pay. The typical case involves a dispute between the parties to the transaction in which the check is given in payment. In the case of a certified check or cashier's check, the bank can safely pay the holder of the check despite notice that there may be an adverse claim to the check (Section 3-602). It is also clear that the bank that sells a teller's check has no duty to order the bank on which it is drawn not to pay it. A debtor using any of these types of checks has no right to stop payment. Nevertheless, some banks will refuse payment as an accommodation to a customer. Section 3-411 is designed to discourage this practice.

2. The term "obligated bank" refers to the issuer of the cashier's check or teller's check and the acceptor of the certified check. If the obligated bank wrongfully refuses to pay, it is liable to pay for expenses and loss of interest resulting from the refusal to pay. There is no express provision for attorney's fees, but attorney's fees are not meant to be necessarily excluded. They could be granted because they fit within the language "expenses *** resulting from the nonpayment." In addition the bank may be liable to pay consequential damages if it has notice of the particular circumstances giving rise to the damages.

3. Subsection (c) provides that expenses or consequential damages are not recoverable if the refusal to pay is because of the reasons stated. The purpose is to limit that recovery to cases in which the bank refuses to pay even though its obligation to pay is clear and it is able to pay. Subsection (b) applies only if the refusal to honor the check is wrongful. If the bank is not obliged to pay there is no recovery. The bank may assert any claim or defense that it has, but normally the bank would not have a claim or defense. In the usual case it is a remitter that is asserting a claim to the check on the basis of a rescission of negotiation to the payee under Section 3-202. See Comment 2 to Section 3-201. The bank can assert that claim if there is compliance with Section 3-305(c), but the bank is not protected from damages under subsection (b) if the claim of the remitter is not upheld. In that case, the bank is insulated from damages only if payment is enjoined under Section 3-602(b)(1). Subsection (c)(iii) refers to cases in which the bank may have a reasonable doubt about the identity of the person demanding payment. For example, a cashier's check is payable to "Supplier Co." The person in possession of the check presents it for payment over the counter and claims to be an officer of Supplier Co. The bank may refuse payment until it has been given adequate proof that the presentment in fact is being made for Supplier Co., the person entitled to enforce the check.

§ 3-412. Obligation of Issuer of Note or Cashier's Check.

The issuer of a note or cashier's check or other draft drawn on the drawer is obliged to pay the instrument (i) according to its terms at the time it was issued or, if not issued, at the time it first came into possession of a holder, or (ii) if the issuer signed an incomplete instrument, according to its terms when completed, to the extent stated in Sections 3-115 and 3-407. The obligation is owed to a person entitled to enforce the instrument or to an indorser who paid the instrument under Section 3-415.

Official Comment

1. The obligations of the maker, acceptor, drawer, and indorser are stated in four separate sections. Section 3-412 states the obligation of the maker of a note and is consistent with former Section 3-413(1). Section 3-412 also applies to the issuer of a cashier's check or other draft drawn on the drawer. Under former Section 3-118(a), since a cashier's check or other draft drawn on the drawer was "effective as a note," the drawer was liable under former Section 3-413(1) as a maker. Under Sections 3-103(a)(6) and 3-104(f) a cashier's check or other draft drawn on the drawer is treated as a draft to reflect common commercial usage, but the liability of the drawer is stated by Section 3-412 as being the same as that of the maker of a note rather than that of the drawer of a draft. Thus, Section 3-412 does not in substance change former law.

2. Under Section 3-105(b) nonissuance of either a complete or incomplete instrument is a defense by a maker or drawer against a person that is not a holder in due course.

3. The obligation of the maker may be modified in the case of alteration if, under Section 3-406, the maker is precluded from asserting the alteration.

§ 3-413. Obligation of Acceptor.

(a) The acceptor of a draft is obliged to pay the draft (i) according to its terms at the time it was accepted, even though the acceptance states that the draft is payable "as originally drawn" or equivalent terms, (ii) if the acceptance varies the terms of the draft, according to the terms of the draft as varied, or (iii) if the acceptance is of a draft that is an incomplete instrument, according to its terms when completed, to the extent stated in Sections 3-115 and 3-407. The obligation is owed to a person entitled to enforce the draft or to the drawer or an indorser who paid the draft under Section 3-414 or 3-415.

(b) If the certification of a check or other acceptance of a draft states the amount certified or accepted, the obligation of the acceptor is that amount. If (i) the certification or acceptance does not state an amount, (ii) the amount of the instrument is subsequently raised, and (iii) the instrument is then negotiated to a holder in due course, the obligation of the acceptor is the amount of the instrument at the time it was taken by the holder in due course.

Official Comment

Subsection (a) is consistent with former Section 3-413(1). Subsection (b) has primary importance with respect to certified checks. It protects the holder in due course of a certified check that was altered after certification and before negotiation to the holder in due course. A bank can avoid liability for the altered amount by stating on the check the amount the bank agrees to pay. The subsection applies to other accepted drafts as well.

§ 3-414. Obligation of Drawer.

(a) This section does not apply to cashier's checks or other drafts drawn on the drawer.

(b) If an unaccepted draft is dishonored, the drawer is obliged to pay the draft (i) according to its terms at the time it was issued or, if not issued, at the time it first came into possession of a holder, or (ii) if the drawer signed an incomplete instrument, according to its terms when completed, to the extent stated in Sections 3–115 and 3–407. The obligation is owed to a person entitled to enforce the draft or to an indorser who paid the draft under Section 3–415.

(c) If a draft is accepted by a bank, the drawer is discharged, regardless of when or by whom acceptance was obtained.

(d) If a draft is accepted and the acceptor is not a bank, the obligation of the drawer to pay the draft if the draft is dishonored by the acceptor is the same as the obligation of an indorser under Section 3–415(a) and (c).

(e) If a draft states that it is drawn "without recourse" or otherwise disclaims liability of the drawer to pay the draft, the drawer is not liable under subsection (b) to pay the draft if the draft is not a check. A disclaimer of the liability stated in subsection (b) is not effective if the draft is a check.

(f) If (i) a check is not presented for payment or given to a depositary bank for collection within 30 days after its date, (ii) the drawee suspends payments after expiration of the 30–day period without paying the check, and (iii) because of the suspension of payments, the drawer is deprived of funds maintained with the drawee to cover payment of the check, the drawer to the extent deprived of funds may discharge its obligation to pay the check by assigning to the person entitled to enforce the check the rights of the drawer against the drawee with respect to the funds.

Official Comment

1. Subsection (a) excludes cashier's checks because the obligation of the issuer of a cashier's check is stated in Section 3–412.

2. Subsection (b) states the obligation of the drawer on an unaccepted draft. It replaces former Section 3–413(2). The requirement under former Article 3 of notice of dishonor or protest has been eliminated. Under revised Article 3, notice of dishonor is necessary only with respect to indorser's liability. The liability of the drawer of an unaccepted draft is treated as a primary liability. Under former Section 3–102(1)(d) the term "secondary party" was used to refer to a drawer or indorser. The quoted term is not used in revised Article 3. The effect of a draft drawn without recourse is stated in subsection (e).

3. Under subsection (c) the drawer is discharged of liability on a draft accepted by a bank regardless of when acceptance was obtained. This changes former Section 3–411(1) which provided that the drawer is discharged only if the holder obtains acceptance. Holders that have a bank obligation do not normally rely on the drawer to guarantee the bank's solvency. A holder can obtain protection against the insolvency of a bank acceptor by a specific guaranty of payment by the drawer or by obtaining an indorsement by the drawer. Section 3–205(d).

4. Subsection (d) states the liability of the drawer if a draft is accepted by a drawee other than a bank and the acceptor dishonors. The drawer of an unaccepted draft is the only party liable on the instrument. The drawee has no liability on the draft. Section 3–408. When the draft is accepted, the obligations change. The drawee, as acceptor, becomes primarily liable and the drawer's liability is that of a person secondarily liable as a guarantor of payment. The drawer's liability is identical to that of an indorser, and subsection (d) states the drawer's liability that way. The drawer is liable to pay the person entitled to enforce the draft or any indorser that pays pursuant to Section 3–415. The drawer in this case is dis-

charged if notice of dishonor is required by Section 3–503 and is not given in compliance with that section. A drawer that pays has a right of recourse against the acceptor. Section 3–413(a).

5. Subsection (e) does not permit the drawer of a check to avoid liability under subsection (b) by drawing the check without recourse. There is no legitimate purpose served by issuing a check on which nobody is liable. Drawing without recourse is effective to disclaim liability of the drawer if the draft is not a check. Suppose, in a documentary sale, Seller draws a draft on Buyer for the price of goods shipped to Buyer. The draft is payable upon delivery to the drawee of an order bill of lading covering the goods. Seller delivers the draft with the bill of lading to Finance Company that is named as payee of the draft. If Seller draws without recourse Finance Company takes the risk that Buyer will dishonor. If Buyer dishonors, Finance Company has no recourse against Seller but it can obtain reimbursement by selling the goods which it controls through the bill of lading.

6. Subsection (f) is derived from former Section 3–502(1)(b). It is designed to protect the drawer of a check against loss resulting from suspension of payments by the drawee bank when the holder of the check delays collection of the check. For example, X writes a check payable to Y for $1,000. The check is covered by funds in X's account in the drawee bank. Y delays initiation of collection of the check for more than 30 days after the date of the check. The drawee bank suspends payments after the 30-day period and before the check is presented for payment. If the $1,000 of funds in X's account have not been withdrawn, X has a claim for those funds against the drawee bank and, if subsection (e) were not in effect, X would be liable to Y on the check because the check was dishonored. Section 3–502(e). If the suspension of payments by the drawee bank will result in payment to X of less than the full amount of the $1,000 in the account or if there is a significant delay in payment to X, X will suffer a loss which would not have been suffered if Y had promptly initiated collection of the check. In most cases, X will not suffer any loss because of the existence of federal bank deposit insurance that covers accounts up to $100,000. Thus, subsection (e) has relatively little importance. There might be some cases, however, in which the account is not fully insured because it exceeds $100,000 or because the account doesn't qualify for deposit insurance. Subsection (f) retains the phrase "deprived of funds maintained with the drawee" appearing in former Section 3–502(1)(b). The quoted phrase applies if the suspension of payments by the drawee prevents the drawer from receiving the benefit of funds which would have paid the check if the holder had been timely in initiating collection. Thus, any significant delay in obtaining full payment of the funds is a deprivation of funds. The drawer can discharge drawer's liability by assigning rights against the drawee with respect to the funds to the holder.

§ 3–415. Obligation of Indorser.

(a) Subject to subsections (b), (c), (d), (e) and to Section 3–419(d), if an instrument is dishonored, an indorser is obliged to pay the amount due on the instrument (i) according to the terms of the instrument at the time it was indorsed, or (ii) if the indorser indorsed an incomplete instrument, according to its terms when completed, to the extent stated in Sections 3–115 and 3–407. The obligation of the indorser is owed to a person entitled to enforce the instrument or to a subsequent indorser who paid the instrument under this section.

(b) If an indorsement states that it is made "without recourse" or otherwise disclaims liability of the indorser, the indorser is not liable under subsection (a) to pay the instrument.

(c) If notice of dishonor of an instrument is required by Section 3-503 and notice of dishonor complying with that section is not given to an indorser, the liability of the indorser under subsection (a) is discharged.

(d) If a draft is accepted by a bank after an indorsement is made, the liability of the indorser under subsection (a) is discharged.

(e) If an indorser of a check is liable under subsection (a) and the check is not presented for payment, or given to a depositary bank for collection, within 30 days after the day the indorsement was made, the liability of the indorser under subsection (a) is discharged.

As amended in 1993.

Official Comment

1. Subsections (a) and (b) restate the substance of former Section 3-414(1). Subsection (2) of former Section 3-414 has been dropped because it is superfluous. Although notice of dishonor is not mentioned in subsection (a), it must be given in some cases to charge an indorser. It is covered in subsection (c). Regulation CC § 229.35(b) provides that a bank handling a check for collection or return is liable to a bank that subsequently handles the check to the extent the latter bank does not receive payment for the check. This liability applies whether or not the bank incurring the liability indorsed the check.

2. Section 3-503 states when notice of dishonor is required and how it must be given. If required notice of dishonor is not given in compliance with Section 3-503, subsection (c) of Section 3-415 states that the effect is to discharge the indorser's obligation.

3. Subsection (d) is similar in effect to Section 3-414(c) if the draft is accepted by a bank after the indorsement is made. See Comment 3 to Section 3-414. If a draft is accepted by a bank before the indorsement is made, the indorser incurs the obligation stated in subsection (a).

4. Subsection (e) modifies former Sections 3-503(2)(b) and 3-502(1)(a) by stating a 30-day rather than a seven-day period, and stating it as an absolute rather than a presumptive period.

5. As stated in subsection (a), the obligation of an indorser to pay the amount due on the instrument is generally owed not only to a person entitled to enforce the instrument but also to a subsequent indorser who paid the instrument. But if the prior indorser and the subsequent indorser are both anomalous indorsers, this rule does not apply. In that case, Section 3-116 applies. Under Section 3-116(a), the anomalous indorsers are jointly and severally liable and if either pays the instrument the indorser who pays has a right of contribution against the other. Section 3-116(b). The right to contribution in Section 3-116(b) is subject to "agreement of the affected parties." Suppose the subsequent indorser can prove an agreement with the prior indorser under which the prior indorser agreed to treat the subsequent indorser as a guarantor of the obligation of the prior indorser. Rights of the two indorsers between themselves would be governed by the agreement. Under suretyship law, the subsequent indorser under such an agreement is referred to as a sub-surety. Under the agreement, if the subsequent indorser pays the instrument there is a right to reimbursement from the prior indorser; if the prior indorser pays the instrument, there is no right of recourse against the subsequent indorser. See PEB Commentary No. 11, dated February 10, 1994 [Appendix V, infra].

§ 3–416. Transfer Warranties.

(a) A person who transfers an instrument for consideration warrants to the transferee and, if the transfer is by indorsement, to any subsequent transferee that:

(1) the warrantor is a person entitled to enforce the instrument;

(2) all signatures on the instrument are authentic and authorized;

(3) the instrument has not been altered;

(4) the instrument is not subject to a defense or claim in recoupment of any party which can be asserted against the warrantor; and

(5) the warrantor has no knowledge of any insolvency proceeding commenced with respect to the maker or acceptor or, in the case of an unaccepted draft, the drawer.

(b) A person to whom the warranties under subsection (a) are made and who took the instrument in good faith may recover from the warrantor as damages for breach of warranty an amount equal to the loss suffered as a result of the breach, but not more than the amount of the instrument plus expenses and loss of interest incurred as a result of the breach.

(c) The warranties stated in subsection (a) cannot be disclaimed with respect to checks. Unless notice of a claim for breach of warranty is given to the warrantor within 30 days after the claimant has reason to know of the breach and the identity of the warrantor, the liability of the warrantor under subsection (b) is discharged to the extent of any loss caused by the delay in giving notice of the claim.

(d) A [cause of action] for breach of warranty under this section accrues when the claimant has reason to know of the breach.

Official Comment

1. Subsection (a) is taken from subsection (2) of former Section 3–417. Subsections (3) and (4) of former Section 3–417 are deleted. Warranties under subsection (a) in favor of the immediate transferee apply to all persons who transfer an instrument for consideration whether or not the transfer is accompanied by indorsement. Any consideration sufficient to support a simple contract will support those warranties. If there is an indorsement the warranty runs with the instrument and the remote holder may sue the indorser-warrantor directly and thus avoid a multiplicity of suits.

2. Since the purpose of transfer (Section 3–203(a)) is to give the transferee the right to enforce the instrument, subsection (a)(1) is a warranty that the transferor is a person entitled to enforce the instrument (Section 3–301). Under Section 3–203(b) transfer gives the transferee any right of the transferor to enforce the instrument. Subsection (a)(1) is in effect a warranty that there are no unauthorized or missing indorsements that prevent the transferor from making the transferee a person entitled to enforce the instrument.

3. The rationale of subsection (a)(4) is that the transferee does not undertake to buy an instrument that is not enforceable in whole or in part, unless there is a contrary agreement. Even if the transferee takes as a holder in due course who takes free of the defense or claim in recoupment, the warranty gives the transferee the option of proceeding against the transferor rather than litigating with the

obligor on the instrument the issue of the holder-in-due-course status of the transferee. Subsection (3) of former Section 3-417 which limits this warranty is deleted. The rationale is that while the purpose of a "no recourse" indorsement is to avoid a guaranty of payment, the indorsement does not clearly indicate an intent to disclaim warranties.

4. Under subsection (a)(5) the transferor does not warrant against difficulties of collection, impairment of the credit of the obligor or even insolvency. The transferee is expected to determine such questions before taking the obligation. If insolvency proceedings as defined in Section 1-201(22) have been instituted against the party who is expected to pay and the transferor knows it, the concealment of that fact amounts to a fraud upon the transferee, and the warranty against knowledge of such proceedings is provided accordingly.

5. Transfer warranties may be disclaimed with respect to any instrument except a check. Between the immediate parties disclaimer may be made by agreement. In the case of an indorser, disclaimer of transferor's liability, to be effective, must appear in the indorsement with words such as "without warranties" or some other specific reference to warranties. But in the case of a check, subsection (c) of Section 3-416 provides that transfer warranties cannot be disclaimed at all. In the check collection process the banking system relies on these warranties.

6. Subsection (b) states the measure of damages for breach of warranty. There is no express provision for attorney's fees, but attorney's fees are not meant to be necessarily excluded. They could be granted because they fit within the phrase "expenses *** incurred as a result of the breach." The intention is to leave to other state law the issue as to when attorney's fees are recoverable.

7. Since the traditional term "cause of action" may have been replaced in some states by "claim for relief" or some equivalent term, the words "cause of action" in subsection (d) have been bracketed to indicate that the words may be replaced by an appropriate substitute to conform to local practice.

§ 3-417. Presentment Warranties.

(a) If an unaccepted draft is presented to the drawee for payment or acceptance and the drawee pays or accepts the draft, (i) the person obtaining payment or acceptance, at the time of presentment, and (ii) a previous transferor of the draft, at the time of transfer, warrant to the drawee making payment or accepting the draft in good faith that:

(1) the warrantor is, or was, at the time the warrantor transferred the draft, a person entitled to enforce the draft or authorized to obtain payment or acceptance of the draft on behalf of a person entitled to enforce the draft;

(2) the draft has not been altered; and

(3) the warrantor has no knowledge that the signature of the drawer of the draft is unauthorized.

(b) A drawee making payment may recover from any warrantor damages for breach of warranty equal to the amount paid by the drawee less the amount the drawee received or is entitled to receive from the drawer because of the payment. In addition, the drawee is entitled to compensation for expenses and loss of interest resulting from the breach. The right of the drawee to recover damages under this subsection is not affected by any failure of the drawee to exercise ordinary care in making payment. If the drawee accepts the draft, breach of warranty is a defense to the obligation of the acceptor. If the acceptor makes payment with respect to the draft, the acceptor is entitled to recover from any warrantor for breach of warranty the amounts stated in this subsection.

(c) If a drawee asserts a claim for breach of warranty under subsection (a) based on an unauthorized indorsement of the draft or an alteration of the draft, the warrantor may defend by proving that the indorsement is effective under Section 3–404 or 3–405 or the drawer is precluded under Section 3–406 or 4–406 from asserting against the drawee the unauthorized indorsement or alteration.

(d) If (i) a dishonored draft is presented for payment to the drawer or an indorser or (ii) any other instrument is presented for payment to a party obliged to pay the instrument, and (iii) payment is received, the following rules apply:

(1) The person obtaining payment and a prior transferor of the instrument warrant to the person making payment in good faith that the warrantor is, or was, at the time the warrantor transferred the instrument, a person entitled to enforce the instrument or authorized to obtain payment on behalf of a person entitled to enforce the instrument.

(2) The person making payment may recover from any warrantor for breach of warranty an amount equal to the amount paid plus expenses and loss of interest resulting from the breach.

(e) The warranties stated in subsections (a) and (d) cannot be disclaimed with respect to checks. Unless notice of a claim for breach of warranty is given to the warrantor within 30 days after the claimant has reason to know of the breach and the identity of the warrantor, the liability of the warrantor under subsection (b) or (d) is discharged to the extent of any loss caused by the delay in giving notice of the claim.

(f) A [cause of action] for breach of warranty under this section accrues when the claimant has reason to know of the breach.

Official Comment

1. This section replaces subsection (1) of former Section 3–417. The former provision was difficult to understand because it purported to state in one subsection all warranties given to any person paying any instrument. The result was a provision replete with exceptions that could not be readily understood except after close scrutiny of the language. In revised Section 3–417, presentment warranties made to drawees of uncertified checks and other unaccepted drafts are stated in subsection (a). All other presentment warranties are stated in subsection (d).

2. Subsection (a) states three warranties. Subsection (a)(1) in effect is a warranty that there are no unauthorized or missing indorsements. "Person entitled to enforce" is defined in Section 3–301. Subsection (a)(2) is a warranty that there is no alteration. Subsection (a)(3) is a warranty of no knowledge that there is a forged drawer's signature. Subsection (a) states that the warranties are made to the drawee and subsections (b) and (c) identify the drawee as the person entitled to recover for breach of warranty. There is no warranty made to the drawer under subsection (a) when presentment is made

to the drawee. Warranty to the drawer is governed by subsection (d) and that applies only when presentment for payment is made to the drawer with respect to a dishonored draft. In Sun 'N Sand, Inc. v. United California Bank, 582 P.2d 920 (Cal.1978), the court held that under former Section 3–417(1) a warranty was made to the drawer of a check when the check was presented to the drawee for payment. The result in that case is rejected.

3. Subsection (a)(1) retains the rule that the drawee does not admit the authenticity of indorsements and subsection (a)(3) retains the rule of Price v. Neal, 3 Burr. 1354 (1762), that the drawee takes the risk that the drawer's signature is unauthorized unless the person presenting the draft has knowledge that the drawer's signature is unauthorized. Under subsection (a)(3) the warranty of no knowledge that the drawer's signature is unauthorized is also given by prior transferors of the draft.

4. Subsection (d) applies to presentment for payment in all cases not covered by subsection (a). It applies to presentment of notes and accepted drafts to any party obliged to pay the instrument, including an indorser, and to presentment of dishonored drafts if made to the drawer or an indorser. In cases covered by subsection (d), there is only one warranty and it is the same as that stated in subsection (a)(1). There are no warranties comparable to subsections (a)(2) and (a)(3) because they are appropriate only in the case of presentment to the drawee of an unaccepted draft. With respect to presentment of an accepted draft to the acceptor, there is no warranty with respect to alteration or knowledge that the signature of the drawer is unauthorized. Those warranties were made to the drawee when the draft was presented for acceptance (Section 3–417(a)(2) and (3)) and breach of that warranty is a defense to the obligation of the drawee as acceptor to pay the draft. If the drawee pays the accepted draft the drawee may recover the payment from any warrantor who was in breach of warranty when the draft was accepted. Section 3–417(b). Thus, there is no necessity for these warranties to be repeated when the accepted draft is presented for payment. Former Section 3–417(1)(b)(iii) and (c)(iii) are not included in revised Section 3–417 because they are unnecessary. Former Section 3–417(1)(c)(iv) is not included because it is also unnecessary. The acceptor should know what the terms of the draft were at the time acceptance was made.

If presentment is made to the drawer or maker, there is no necessity for a warranty concerning the signature of that person or with respect to alteration. If presentment is made to an indorser, the indorser had itself warranted authenticity of signatures and that the instrument was not altered. Section 3–416(a)(2) and (3).

5. The measure of damages for breach of warranty under subsection (a) is stated in subsection (b). There is no express provision for attorney's fees, but attorney's fees are not meant to be necessarily excluded. They could be granted because they fit within the language "expenses *** resulting from the breach." Subsection (b) provides that the right of the drawee to recover for breach of warranty is not affected by a failure of the drawee to exercise ordinary care in paying the draft. This provision follows the result reached under former Article 3 in Hartford Accident & Indemnity Co. v. First Pennsylvania Bank, 859 F.2d 295 (3d Cir. 1988).

6. Subsection (c) applies to checks and other unaccepted drafts. It gives to the warrantor the benefit of rights that the drawee has against the drawer under Section 3–404, 3–405, 3–406, or 4–406. If the drawer's conduct contributed to a loss from forgery or alteration, the drawee should not be allowed to shift the loss from the drawer to the warrantor.

7. The first sentence of subsection (e) recognizes that checks are normally paid by automated means and that payor banks rely on warranties in making payment. Thus, it is not appropriate to allow disclaimer or warranties appearing on checks that normally will not be exam-

ined by the payor bank. The second sentence requires a breach of warranty claim to be asserted within 30 days after the drawee learns of the breach and the identity of the warrantor.

8. Since the traditional term "cause of action" may have been replaced in some states by "claim for relief" or some equivalent term, the words "cause of action" in subsection (f) have been bracketed to indicate that the words may be replaced by an appropriate substitute to conform to local practice.

§ 3-418. Payment or Acceptance by Mistake.

(a) Except as provided in subsection (c), if the drawee of a draft pays or accepts the draft and the drawee acted on the mistaken belief that (i) payment of the draft had not been stopped pursuant to Section 4-403 or (ii) the signature of the drawer of the draft was authorized, the drawee may recover the amount of the draft from the person to whom or for whose benefit payment was made or, in the case of acceptance, may revoke the acceptance. Rights of the drawee under this subsection are not affected by failure of the drawee to exercise ordinary care in paying or accepting the draft.

(b) Except as provided in subsection (c), if an instrument has been paid or accepted by mistake and the case is not covered by subsection (a), the person paying or accepting may, to the extent permitted by the law governing mistake and restitution, (i) recover the payment from the person to whom or for whose benefit payment was made or (ii) in the case of acceptance, may revoke the acceptance.

(c) The remedies provided by subsection (a) or (b) may not be asserted against a person who took the instrument in good faith and for value or who in good faith changed position in reliance on the payment or acceptance. This subsection does not limit remedies provided by Section 3-417 or 4-407.

(d) Notwithstanding Section 4-215, if an instrument is paid or accepted by mistake and the payor or acceptor recovers payment or revokes acceptance under subsection (a) or (b), the instrument is deemed not to have been paid or accepted and is treated as dishonored, and the person from whom payment is recovered has rights as a person entitled to enforce the dishonored instrument.

Official Comment

1. This section covers payment or acceptance by mistake and replaces former Section 3-418. Under former Article 3, the remedy of a drawee that paid or accepted a draft by mistake was based on the law of mistake and restitution, but that remedy was not specifically stated. It was provided by Section 1-103. Former Section 3-418 was simply a limitation on the unstated remedy under the law of mistake and restitution. Under revised Article 3, Section 3-418 specifically states the right of restitution in subsections (a) and (b). Subsection (a) allows restitution in the two most common cases in which the problem is presented: payment or acceptance of forged checks and checks on which the drawer has stopped payment. If the drawee acted under a mistaken belief that the check was not forged or had not been stopped, the drawee is entitled to recover the funds paid or to revoke the acceptance whether or not the drawee acted negligently. But in each case, by virtue of subsection (c), the drawee loses the remedy if the person receiving payment or acceptance was a person who took the check in good faith

and for value or who in good faith changed position in reliance on the payment or acceptance. Subsections (a) and (c) are consistent with former Section 3-418 and the rule of Price v. Neal. The result in the two cases covered by subsection (a) is that the drawee in most cases will not have a remedy against the person paid because there is usually a person who took the check in good faith and for value or who in good faith changed position in reliance on the payment or acceptance.

2. If a check has been paid by mistake and the payee receiving payment did not give value for the check or did not change position in reliance on the payment, the drawee bank is entitled to recover the amount of the check under subsection (a) regardless of how the check was paid. The drawee bank normally pays a check by a credit to an account of the collecting bank that presents the check for payment. The payee of the check normally receives the payment by a credit to the payee's account in the depositary bank. But in some cases the payee of the check may have received payment directly from the drawee bank by presenting the check for payment over the counter. In those cases the payee is entitled to receive cash, but the payee may prefer another form of payment such as a cashier's check or teller's check issued by the drawee bank. Suppose Seller contracted to sell goods to Buyer. The contract provided for immediate payment by Buyer and delivery of the goods 20 days after payment. Buyer paid by mailing a check for $10,000 drawn on Bank payable to Seller. The next day Buyer gave a stop payment order to Bank with respect to the check Buyer had mailed to Seller. A few days later Seller presented Buyer's check to Bank for payment over the counter and requested a cashier's check as payment. Bank issued and delivered a cashier's check for $10,000 payable to Seller. The teller failed to discover Buyer's stop order. The next day Bank discovered the mistake and immediately advised Seller of the facts. Seller refused to return the cashier's check and did not deliver any goods to Buyer.

Under Section 4-215, Buyer's check was paid by Bank at the time it delivered its cashier's check to Seller. See Comment 3 to Section 4-215. Bank is obliged to pay the cashier's check and has no defense to that obligation. The cashier's check was issued for consideration because it was issued in payment of Buyer's check. Although Bank has no defense on its cashier's check it may have a right to recover $10,000, the amount of Buyer's check, from Seller under Section 3-418(a). Bank paid Buyer's check by mistake. Seller did not give value for Buyer's check because the promise to deliver goods to Buyer was never performed. Section 3-303(a)(1). And, on these facts, Seller did not change position in reliance on the payment of Buyer's check. Thus, the first sentence of Section 3-418(c) does not apply and Seller is obliged to return $10,000 to Bank. Bank is obliged to pay the cashier's check but it has a counterclaim against Seller based on its rights under Section 3-418(a). This claim can be asserted against Seller, but it cannot be asserted against some other person with rights of a holder in due course of the cashier's check. A person without rights of a holder in due course of the cashier's check would take subject to Bank's claim against Seller because it is a claim in recoupment. Section 3-305(a)(3).

If Bank recovers from Seller under Section 3-418(a), the payment of Buyer's check is treated as unpaid and dishonored. Section 3-418(d). One consequence is that Seller may enforce Buyer's obligation as drawer to pay the check. Section 3-414. Another consequence is that Seller's rights against Buyer on the contract of sale are also preserved. Under Section 3-310(b) Buyer's obligation to pay for the goods was suspended when Seller took Buyer's check and remains suspended until the check is either dishonored or paid. Under Section ~~3-310(b)(2)~~ 3-310(b)(1) * the obligation is discharged when the check is paid. Since Section 3-418(d) treats Buyer's check as unpaid and dishonored, Buyer's obligation is not discharged and suspension of the obligation terminates. Under Section 3-310(b)(3), Seller may enforce either the contract of sale or the check subject to defenses and claims of Buyer.

If Seller had released the goods to Buyer before learning about the stop order, Bank would have no recovery against Seller under Section 3-418(a) because Seller in that case gave value for Buyer's check. Section 3-418(c). In this case Bank's sole remedy is under Section 4-407 by subrogation.

3. Subsection (b) covers cases of payment or acceptance by mistake that are not covered by subsection (a). It directs courts to deal with those cases under the law governing mistake and restitution. Perhaps the most important class of cases that falls under subsection (b), because it is not covered by subsection (a), is that of payment by the drawee bank of a check with respect to which the bank has no duty to the drawer to pay either because the drawer has no account with the bank or because available funds in the drawer's account are not sufficient to cover the amount of the check. With respect to such a case, under Restatement of Restitution § 29, if the bank paid because of a mistaken belief that there were available funds in the drawer's account sufficient to cover the amount of the check, the bank is entitled to restitution. But § 29 is subject to Restatement of Restitution § 33 which denies restitution if the holder of the check receiving payment paid value in good faith for the check and had no reason to know that the check was paid by mistake when payment was received.

The result in some cases is clear. For example, suppose Father gives Daughter a check for $10,000 as a birthday gift. The check is drawn on Bank in which both Father and Daughter have accounts. Daughter deposits the check in her account in Bank. An employee of Bank, acting under the belief that there were available funds in Father's account to cover the check, caused Daughter's account to be credited for $10,000. In fact, Father's account was overdrawn and Father did not have overdraft privileges. Since Daughter received the check gratuitously there is clear unjust enrichment if she is allowed to keep the $10,000 and Bank is unable to obtain reimbursement from Father. Thus, Bank should be permitted to reverse the credit to Daughter's account. But this case is not typical. In most cases the remedy of restitution will not be available because the person receiving payment of the check will have given value for it in good faith.

In some cases, however, it may not be clear whether a drawee bank should have a right of restitution. For example, a check-kiting scheme may involve a large number of checks drawn on a number of different banks in which the drawer's credit balances are based on uncollected funds represented by fraudulently drawn checks. No attempt is made in Section 3-418 to state rules for determining the conflicting claims of the various banks that may be victimized by such a scheme. Rather, such cases are better resolved on the basis of general principles of law and the particular facts presented in the litigation.

4. The right of the drawee to recover a payment or to revoke an acceptance under Section 3-418 is not affected by the rules under Article 4 that determine when an item is paid. Even though a payor bank may have paid an item under Section 4-215, it may have a right to recover the payment under Section 3-418. National Savings & Trust Co. v. Park Corp., 722 F.2d 1303 (6th Cir.1983), cert. denied, 466 U.S. 939 (1984), correctly states the law on the issue under former Article 3. Revised Article 3 does not change the previous law.

* *Previous incorrect cross reference corrected by Permanent Editorial Board action November 1992.*

§ 3–419. Instruments Signed for Accommodation.

(a) If an instrument is issued for value given for the benefit of a party to the instrument ("accommodated party") and another party to the instrument ("accommodation party") signs the instrument for the purpose of incurring liability on the instrument without being a direct beneficiary of the value given for the instrument, the instrument is signed by the accommodation party "for accommodation."

(b) An accommodation party may sign the instrument as maker, drawer, acceptor, or indorser and, subject to subsection (d), is obliged to pay the instrument in the capacity in which the accommodation party signs. The obligation of an accommodation party may be enforced notwithstanding any statute of frauds and whether or not the accommodation party receives consideration for the accommodation.

(c) A person signing an instrument is presumed to be an accommodation party and there is notice that the instrument is signed for accommodation if the signature is an anomalous indorsement or is accompanied by words indicating that the signer is acting as surety or guarantor with respect to the obligation of another party to the instrument. Except as provided in Section 3–605, the obligation of an accommodation party to pay the instrument is not affected by the fact that the person enforcing the obligation had notice when the instrument was taken by that person that the accommodation party signed the instrument for accommodation.

(d) If the signature of a party to an instrument is accompanied by words indicating unambiguously that the party is guaranteeing collection rather than payment of the obligation of another party to the instrument, the signer is obliged to pay the amount due on the instrument to a person entitled to enforce the instrument only if (i) execution of judgment against the other party has been returned unsatisfied, (ii) the other party is insolvent or in an insolvency proceeding, (iii) the other party cannot be served with process, or (iv) it is otherwise apparent that payment cannot be obtained from the other party.

(e) An accommodation party who pays the instrument is entitled to reimbursement from the accommodated party and is entitled to enforce the instrument against the accommodated party. An accommodated party who pays the instrument has no right of recourse against, and is not entitled to contribution from, an accommodation party.

Official Comment

1. Section 3–419 replaces former Section 3–415 and 3–416. An accommodation party is a person who signs an instrument to benefit the accommodated party either by signing at the time value is obtained by the accommodated party or later, and who is not a direct beneficiary of the value obtained. An accommodation party will usually be a co-maker or anomalous indorser. Subsection (a) distinguishes between direct and indirect benefit. For example, if X cosigns a note of Corporation that is given for a loan to Corporation, X is an accommodation party if no part of the loan was paid to X or for X's direct benefit. This is true even though X may receive indirect benefit from the loan because X is employed by Corporation or is a stockholder of Corporation, or even if X is the sole stockholder

so long as Corporation and X are recognized as separate entities.

2. It does not matter whether an accommodation party signs gratuitously either at the time the instrument is issued or after the instrument is in the possession of a holder. Subsection (b) of Section 3–419 takes the view stated in Comment 3 to former Section 3–415 that there need be no consideration running to the accommodation party: "The obligation of the accommodation party is supported by any consideration for which the instrument is taken before it is due. Subsection (2) is intended to change occasional decisions holding that there is no sufficient consideration where an accommodation party signs a note after it is in the hands of a holder who has given value. The [accommodation] party is liable to the holder in such a case even though there is no extension of time or other concession."

3. As stated in Comment 1, whether a person is an accommodation party is a question of fact. But it is almost always the case that a co-maker who signs with words of guaranty after the signature is an accommodation party. The same is true of an anomalous indorser. In either case a person taking the instrument is put on notice of the accommodation status of the co-maker or indorser. This is relevant to Section 3–605(h). But, under subsection (c), signing with words of guaranty or as an anomalous indorser also creates a presumption that the signer is an accommodation party. A party challenging accommodation party status would have to rebut this presumption by producing evidence that the signer was in fact a direct beneficiary of the value given for the instrument.

An accommodation party is always a surety. A surety who is not a party to the instrument, however, is not an accommodation party. For example, if M issues a note payable to the order of P, and S signs a separate contract in which S agrees to pay P the amount of the instrument if it is dishonored, S is a surety but is not an accommodation party. In such a case, S's rights and duties are determined under the general law of suretyship. In unusual cases two parties to an instrument may have a surety relationship that is not governed by Article 3 because the requirements of Section 3–419(a) are not met. In those cases the general law of suretyship applies to the relationship. See PEB Commentary No. 11, dated February 10, 1994 [Appendix V, infra].

4. Subsection (b) states that an accommodation party is liable on the instrument in the capacity in which the party signed the instrument. In most cases that capacity will be either that of a maker or indorser of a note. But subsection (d) provides a limitation on subsection (b). If the signature of the accommodation party is accompanied by words indicating unambiguously that the party is guaranteeing collection rather than payment of the instrument, liability is limited to that stated in subsection (d), which is based on former Section 3–416(2).

Former Article 3 was confusing because the obligation of a guarantor was covered both in Section 3–415 and in Section 3–416. The latter section suggested that a signature accompanied by words of guaranty created an obligation distinct from that of an accommodation party. Revised Article 3 eliminates that confusion by stating in Section 3–419 the obligation of a person who uses words of guaranty. Portions of former Section 3–416 are preserved. Former Section 3–416(2) is reflected in Section 3–419(d) and former Section 3–416(4) is reflected in Section 3–419(c). Words added to an anomalous indorsement indicating that payment of the instrument is guaranteed by the indorser do not change the liability of the indorser as stated in Section 3–415. This is a change from former Section 3–416(5). See PEB Commentary No. 11, supra.

5. Subsection (e) like former Section 3–415(5), provides that an accommodation party that pays the instrument is entitled to enforce the instrument against the accommodated party. Since the accommodation party that pays the instrument is entitled to enforce the instrument

against the accommodated party, the accommodation party also obtains rights to any security interest or other collateral that secures payment of the instrument. Subsection (e) also provides that an accommodation party that pays the instrument is entitled to reimbursement from the accommodated party. See PEB Commentary No. 11, supra.

6. In occasional cases, the accommodation party might pay the instrument even though the accommodated party had a defense to its obligation that was available to the accommodation party under Section 3–305(d). In such cases, the accommodation party's right to reimbursement may conflict with the accommodated party's right to raise its defense. For example, suppose the accommodation party pays the instrument without being aware of the defense. In that case the accommodation party should be entitled to reimbursement. Suppose the accommodation party paid the instrument with knowledge of the defense. In that case, to the extent of the defense, reimbursement ordinarily would not be justified, but under some circumstances reimbursement may be justified depending upon the facts of the case. The resolution of this conflict is left to the general law of suretyship. Section 1–103. See PEB Commentary No. 11, supra.

7. Section 3–419, along with Section 3–116(a) and (b), Section 3–305(d) and Section 3–605, provides rules governing the rights of accommodation parties. In addition, except to the extent that it is displaced by provisions of this Article, the general law of suretyship also applies to the rights of accommodation parties. Section 1–103. See PEB Commentary No. 11, supra.

§ 3–420. Conversion of Instrument.

(a) The law applicable to conversion of personal property applies to instruments. An instrument is also converted if it is taken by transfer, other than a negotiation, from a person not entitled to enforce the instrument or a bank makes or obtains payment with respect to the instrument for a person not entitled to enforce the instrument or receive payment. An action for conversion of an instrument may not be brought by (i) the issuer or acceptor of the instrument or (ii) a payee or indorsee who did not receive delivery of the instrument either directly or through delivery to an agent or a co-payee.

(b) In an action under subsection (a), the measure of liability is presumed to be the amount payable on the instrument, but recovery may not exceed the amount of the plaintiff's interest in the instrument.

(c) A representative, other than a depositary bank, who has in good faith dealt with an instrument or its proceeds on behalf of one who was not the person entitled to enforce the instrument is not liable in conversion to that person beyond the amount of any proceeds that it has not paid out.

Official Comment

1. Section 3–420 is a modification of former Section 3–419. The first sentence of Section 3–420(a) states a general rule that the law of conversion applicable to personal property also applies to instruments. Paragraphs (a) and (b) of former Section 3–419(1) are deleted as inappropriate in cases of noncash items that may be delivered for acceptance or payment in collection letters that contain varying instructions as to what to do in the event of nonpayment on the day of delivery. It is better to allow such cases to be governed by the general law of conversion that would address the issue of when, under the circumstances prevailing, the presenter's right to possession has been denied. The second sentence of Section 3–420(a)

states that an instrument is converted if it is taken by transfer other than a negotiation from a person not entitled to enforce the instrument or taken for collection or payment from a person not entitled to enforce the instrument or receive payment. This covers cases in which a depositary or payor bank takes an instrument bearing a forged indorsement. It also covers cases in which an instrument is payable to two persons and the two persons are not alternative payees, e.g. a check payable to John and Jane Doe. Under Section 3–110(d) the check can be negotiated or enforced only by both persons acting jointly. Thus, neither payee acting without the consent of the other, is a person entitled to enforce the instrument. If John indorses the check and Jane does not, the indorsement is not effective to allow negotiation of the check. If Depositary Bank takes the check for deposit to John's account, Depositary Bank is liable to Jane for conversion of the check if she did not consent to the transaction. John, acting alone, is not the person entitled to enforce the check because John is not the holder of the check. Section 3–110(d) and Comment 4 to Section 3–110. Depositary Bank does not get any greater rights under Section 4–205(1). If it acted for John as its customer, it did not become holder of the check under that provision because John, its customer, was not a holder.

Under former Article 3, the cases were divided on the issue of whether the drawer of a check with a forged indorsement can assert rights against a depositary bank that took the check. The last sentence of Section 3–420(a) resolves the conflict by following the rule stated in Stone & Webster Engineering Corp. v. First National Bank & Trust Co., 184 N.E.2d 358 (Mass.1962). There is no reason why a drawer should have an action in conversion. The check represents an obligation of the drawer rather than property of the drawer. The drawer has an adequate remedy against the payor bank for recredit of the drawer's account for unauthorized payment of the check.

There was also a split of authority under former Article 3 on the issue of whether a payee who never received the instrument is a proper plaintiff in a conversion action. The typical case was one in which a check was stolen from the drawer or in which the check was mailed to an address different from that of the payee and was stolen after it arrived at that address. The thief forged the indorsement of the payee and obtained payment by depositing the check to an account in a depositary bank. The issue was whether the payee could bring an action in conversion against the depositary bank or the drawee bank. In revised Article 3, under the last sentence of Section 3–420(a), the payee has no conversion action because the check was never delivered to the payee. Until delivery, the payee does not have any interest in the check. The payee never became the holder of the check nor a person entitled to enforce the check. Section 3–301. Nor is the payee injured by the fraud. Normally the drawer of a check intends to pay an obligation owed to the payee. But if the check is never delivered to the payee, the obligation owed to the payee is not affected. If the check falls into the hands of a thief who obtains payment after forging the signature of the payee as an indorsement, the obligation owed to the payee continues to exist after the thief receives payment. Since the payee's right to enforce the underlying obligation is unaffected by the fraud of the thief, there is no reason to give any additional remedy to the payee. The drawer of the check has no conversion remedy, but the drawee is not entitled to charge the drawer's account when the drawee wrongfully honored the check. The remedy of the drawee is against the depositary bank for breach of warranty under Section 3–417(a)(1) or 4–208(a)(1). The loss will fall on the person who gave value to the thief for the check.

The situation is different if the check is delivered to the payee. If the check is taken for an obligation owed to the payee, the last sentence of Section 3–310(b)(4) provides that the obligation may not be enforced to the extent of the amount of the check. The payee's rights are restricted to enforcement of the payee's rights in the instrument. In this event the payee is injured by the theft and has a cause of action for conversion.

The payee receives delivery when the check comes into the payee's possession, as for example when it is put into the payee's mailbox. Delivery to an agent is delivery to the payee. If a check is payable to more than one payee, delivery to one of the payees is deemed to be delivery to all of the payees. Occasionally, the person asserting a conversion cause of action is an indorsee rather than the original payee. If the check is stolen before the check can be delivered to the indorsee and the indorsee's indorsement is forged, the analysis is similar. For example, a check is payable to the order of A. A indorses it to B and puts it into an envelope addressed to B. The envelope is never delivered to B. Rather, Thief steals the envelope, forges B's indorsement to the check and obtains payment. Because the check was never delivered to B, the indorsee, B has no cause of action for conversion, but A does have such an action. A is the owner of the check. B never obtained rights in the check. If A intended to negotiate the check to B in payment of an obligation, that obligation was not affected by the conduct of Thief. B can enforce that obligation. Thief stole A's property not B's.

2. Subsection (2) of former Section 3-419 is amended because it is not clear why the former law distinguished between the liability of the drawee and that of other converters. Why should there be a conclusive presumption that the liability is face amount if a drawee refuses to pay or return an instrument or makes payment on a forged indorsement, while the liability of a maker who does the same thing is only presumed to be the face amount? Moreover, it was not clear under former Section 3-419(2) what face amount meant. If a note for $10,000 is payable in a year at 10% interest, it is common to refer to $10,000 as the face amount, but if the note is converted the loss to the owner also includes the loss of interest. In revised Article 3, Section 3-420(b), by referring to "amount payable on the instrument," allows the full amount due under the instrument to be recovered.

The "but" clause in subsection (b) addresses the problem of conversion actions in multiple payee checks. Section 3-110(d) states that an instrument cannot be enforced unless all payees join in the action. But an action for conversion might be brought by a payee having no interest or a limited interest in the proceeds of the check. This clause prevents such a plaintiff from receiving a windfall. An example is a check payable to a building contractor and a supplier of building material. The check is not payable to the payees alternatively. Section 3-110(d). The check is delivered to the contractor by the owner of the building. Suppose the contractor forges supplier's signature as an indorsement of the check and receives the entire proceeds of the check. The supplier should not, without qualification, be able to recover the entire amount of the check from the bank that converted the check. Depending upon the contract between the contractor and the supplier, the amount of the check may be due entirely to the contractor, in which case there should be no recovery, entirely to the supplier, in which case recovery should be for the entire amount, or part may be due to one and the rest to the other, in which case recovery should be limited to the amount due to the supplier.

3. Subsection (3) of former Section 3-419 drew criticism from the courts, that saw no reason why a depositary bank should have the defense stated in the subsection. See Knesz v. Central Jersey Bank & Trust Co., 477 A.2d 806 (N.J. 1984). The depositary bank is ultimately liable in the case of a forged indorsement check because of its warranty to the payor bank under Section 4-208(a)(1) and it

is usually the most convenient defendant in cases involving multiple checks drawn on different banks. There is no basis for requiring the owner of the check to bring multiple actions against the various payor banks and to require those banks to assert warranty rights against the depositary bank. In revised Article 3, the defense provided by Section 3-420(c) is limited to collecting banks other than the depositary bank. If suit is brought against both the payor bank and the depositary bank, the owner, of course, is entitled to but one recovery.

PART 5

DISHONOR

§ 3-501. Presentment.

(a) "Presentment" means a demand made by or on behalf of a person entitled to enforce an instrument (i) to pay the instrument made to the drawee or a party obliged to pay the instrument or, in the case of a note or accepted draft payable at a bank, to the bank, or (ii) to accept a draft made to the drawee.

(b) The following rules are subject to Article 4, agreement of the parties, and clearing-house rules and the like:

(1) Presentment may be made at the place of payment of the instrument and must be made at the place of payment if the instrument is payable at a bank in the United States; may be made by any commercially reasonable means, including an oral, written, or electronic communication; is effective when the demand for payment or acceptance is received by the person to whom presentment is made; and is effective if made to any one of two or more makers, acceptors, drawees, or other payors.

(2) Upon demand of the person to whom presentment is made, the person making presentment must (i) exhibit the instrument, (ii) give reasonable identification and, if presentment is made on behalf of another person, reasonable evidence of authority to do so, and (iii) sign a receipt on the instrument for any payment made or surrender the instrument if full payment is made.

(3) Without dishonoring the instrument, the party to whom presentment is made may (i) return the instrument for lack of a necessary indorsement, or (ii) refuse payment or acceptance for failure of the presentment to comply with the terms of the instrument, an agreement of the parties, or other applicable law or rule.

(4) The party to whom presentment is made may treat presentment as occurring on the next business day after the day of presentment if the party to whom presentment is made has established a cut-off hour not earlier than 2 p.m. for the receipt and processing of instruments presented for payment or acceptance and presentment is made after the cut-off hour.

Official Comment

Subsection (a) defines presentment. Subsection (b)(1) states the place and manner of presentment. Electronic presentment is authorized. The communication of the demand for payment or acceptance is effective when received. Subsection (b)(2) restates former Section 3-505. Subsection (b)(2)(i) allows the person to whom presentment is made to require exhibition of the instrument, unless the parties have agreed otherwise as in an electronic presentment agreement. Former Section 3-507(3) is the antecedent of subsection (b)(3)(i). Since a payor must decide whether to pay or accept on the day of presentment, subsection (b)(4) allows the payor to set a cut-off hour for receipt of instruments presented.

§ 3-502. Dishonor.

(a) Dishonor of a note is governed by the following rules:

(1) If the note is payable on demand, the note is dishonored if presentment is duly made to the maker and the note is not paid on the day of presentment.

(2) If the note is not payable on demand and is payable at or through a bank or the terms of the note require presentment, the note is dishonored if presentment is duly made and the note is not paid on the day it becomes payable or the day of presentment, whichever is later.

(3) If the note is not payable on demand and paragraph (2) does not apply, the note is dishonored if it is not paid on the day it becomes payable.

(b) Dishonor of an unaccepted draft other than a documentary draft is governed by the following rules:

(1) If a check is duly presented for payment to the payor bank otherwise than for immediate payment over the counter, the check is dishonored if the payor bank makes timely return of the check or sends timely notice of dishonor or nonpayment under Section 4-301 or 4-302, or becomes accountable for the amount of the check under Section 4-302.

(2) If a draft is payable on demand and paragraph (1) does not apply, the draft is dishonored if presentment for payment is duly made to the drawee and the draft is not paid on the day of presentment.

(3) If a draft is payable on a date stated in the draft, the draft is dishonored if (i) presentment for payment is duly made to the drawee and payment is not made on the day the draft becomes payable or the day of presentment, whichever is later, or (ii) presentment for acceptance is duly made before the day the draft becomes payable and the draft is not accepted on the day of presentment.

(4) If a draft is payable on elapse of a period of time after sight or acceptance, the draft is dishonored if presentment for acceptance is duly made and the draft is not accepted on the day of presentment.

(c) Dishonor of an unaccepted documentary draft occurs according to the rules stated in subsection (b)(2), (3), and (4), except that payment or acceptance may be delayed without dishonor until no later than the close of the third business day of the drawee following the day on which payment or acceptance is required by those paragraphs.

(d) Dishonor of an accepted draft is governed by the following rules:

(1) If the draft is payable on demand, the draft is dishonored if presentment for payment is duly made to the acceptor and the draft is not paid on the day of presentment.

(2) If the draft is not payable on demand, the draft is dishonored if presentment for payment is duly made to the acceptor and payment is not made on the day it becomes payable or the day of presentment, whichever is later.

(e) In any case in which presentment is otherwise required for dishonor under this section and presentment is excused under Section 3–504, dishonor occurs without presentment if the instrument is not duly accepted or paid.

(f) If a draft is dishonored because timely acceptance of the draft was not made and the person entitled to demand acceptance consents to a late acceptance, from the time of acceptance the draft is treated as never having been dishonored.

Official Comment

1. Section 3–415 provides that an indorser is obliged to pay an instrument if the instrument is dishonored and is discharged if the indorser is entitled to notice of dishonor and notice is not given. Under Section 3–414, the drawer is obliged to pay an unaccepted draft if it is dishonored. The drawer, however, is not entitled to notice of dishonor except to the extent required in a case governed by Section 3–414(d). Part 5 tells when an instrument is dishonored (Section 3–502) and what it means to give notice of dishonor (Section 3–503). Often dishonor does not occur until presentment (Section 3–501), and frequently presentment and notice of dishonor are excused (Section 3–504).

2. In the great majority of cases presentment and notice of dishonor are waived with respect to notes. In most cases a formal demand for payment to the maker of the note is not contemplated. Rather, the maker is expected to send payment to the holder of the note on the date or dates on which payment is due. If payment is not made when due, the holder usually makes a demand for payment, but in the normal case in which presentment is waived, demand is irrelevant and the holder can proceed against indorsers when payment is not received. Under former Article 3, in the small minority of cases in which presentment and dishonor were not waived with respect to notes, the indorser was discharged from liability (former Section 3–502(1)(a)) unless the holder made presentment to the maker on the exact day the note was due (former Section 3–503(1)(c)) and gave notice of dishonor to the indorser before midnight of the third business day after dishonor (former Section 3–508(2)). These provisions are omitted from Revised Article 3 as inconsistent with practice which seldom involves face-to-face dealings.

3. Subsection (a) applies to notes. Subsection (a)(1) applies to notes payable on demand. Dishonor requires presentment, and dishonor occurs if payment is not made on the day of presentment. There is no change from previous Article 3. Subsection (a)(2) applies to notes pay-

able at a definite time if the note is payable at or through a bank or, by its terms, presentment is required. Dishonor requires presentment, and dishonor occurs if payment is not made on the due date or the day of presentment if presentment is made after the due date. Subsection (a)(3) applies to all other notes. If the note is not paid on its due date it is dishonored. This allows holders to collect notes in ways that make sense commercially without having to be concerned about a formal presentment on a given day.

4. Subsection (b) applies to unaccepted drafts other than documentary drafts. Subsection (b)(1) applies to checks. Except for checks presented for immediate payment over the counter, which are covered by subsection (b)(2), dishonor occurs according to rules stated in Article 4. When a check is presented for payment through the check-collection system, the drawee bank normally makes settlement for the amount of the check to the presenting bank. Under Section 4–301 the drawee bank may recover this settlement if it returns the check within its midnight deadline (Section 4–104). In that case the check is not paid and dishonor occurs under Section 3–502(b)(1). If the drawee bank does not return the check or give notice of dishonor or nonpayment within the midnight deadline, the settlement becomes final payment of the check. Section 4–215. Thus, no dishonor occurs regardless of whether the check is retained or is returned after the midnight deadline. In some cases the drawee bank might not settle for the check when it is received. Under Section 4–302 if the drawee bank is not also the depositary bank and retains the check without settling for it beyond midnight of the day it is presented for payment, the bank becomes "accountable" for the amount of the check, i.e. it is obliged to pay the amount of the check. If the drawee bank is also the depositary bank, the bank is accountable for the amount of the check if the bank does not pay the check or return it or send notice of dishonor within the midnight deadline. In all cases in which the drawee bank becomes accountable, the check has not been paid and, under Section 3–502(b)(1), the check is dishonored. The fact that the bank is obliged to pay the check does not mean that the check has been paid. When a check is presented for payment, the person presenting the check is entitled to payment not just the obligation of the drawee to pay. Until that payment is made, the check is dishonored. To say that the drawee bank is obliged to pay the check necessarily means that the check has not been paid. If the check is eventually paid, the drawee bank no longer is accountable.

Subsection (b)(2) applies to demand drafts other than those governed by subsection (b)(1). It covers checks presented for immediate payment over the counter and demand drafts other than checks. Dishonor occurs if presentment for payment is made and payment is not made on the day of presentment.

Subsection (b)(3) and (4) applies to time drafts. An unaccepted time draft differs from a time note. The maker of a note knows that the note has been issued, but the drawee of a draft may not know that a draft has been drawn on it. Thus, with respect to drafts, presentment for payment or acceptance is required. Subsection (b)(3) applies to drafts payable on a date stated in the draft. Dishonor occurs if presentment for payment is made and payment is not made on the day the draft becomes payable or the day of presentment if presentment is made after the due date. The holder of an unaccepted draft payable on a stated date has the option of presenting the draft for acceptance before the day the draft becomes payable to establish whether the drawee is willing to assume liability by accepting. Under subsection (b)(3)(ii) dishonor occurs when the draft is presented and not accepted. Subsection (b)(4) applies to unaccepted drafts payable on elapse of a period of time after sight or acceptance. If the draft is payable 30 days after sight, the draft must be presented for acceptance to start the running of the 30–day period. Dishonor occurs if it is not accepted. The rules in subsection (b)(3) and (4) follow former Section 3–501(1)(a).

5. Subsection (c) gives drawees an extended period to pay documentary drafts because of the time that may be needed to examine the documents. The period prescribed is that given by Section 5–112 in cases in which a letter of credit is involved.

6. Subsection (d) governs accepted drafts. If the acceptor's obligation is to pay on demand the rule, stated in subsection (d)(1), is the same as for that of a demand note stated in subsection (a)(1). If the acceptor's obligation is to pay at a definite time the rule, stated in subsection (d)(2), is the same as that of a time note payable at a bank stated in subsection (b)(2).

7. Subsection (e) is a limitation on subsection (a)(1) and (2), subsection (b), subsection (c), and subsection (d). Each of those provisions states dishonor as occurring after presentment. If presentment is excused under Section 3–504, dishonor occurs under those provisions without presentment if the instrument is not duly accepted or paid.

8. Under subsection (b)(3)(ii) and (4) if a draft is presented for acceptance and the draft is not accepted on the day of presentment, there is dishonor. But after dishonor, the holder may consent to late acceptance. In that case, under subsection (f), the late acceptance cures the dishonor. The draft is treated as never having been dishonored. If the draft is subsequently presented for payment and payment is refused dishonor occurs at that time.

§ 3–503. Notice of Dishonor.

(a) The obligation of an indorser stated in Section 3–415(a) and the obligation of a drawer stated in Section 3–414(d) may not be enforced unless (i) the indorser or drawer is given notice of dishonor of the instrument complying with this section or (ii) notice of dishonor is excused under Section 3–504(b).

(b) Notice of dishonor may be given by any person; may be given by any commercially reasonable means, including an oral, written, or electronic communication; and is sufficient if it reasonably identifies the instrument and indicates that the instrument has been dishonored or has not been paid or accepted. Return of an instrument given to a bank for collection is sufficient notice of dishonor.

(c) Subject to Section 3–504(c), with respect to an instrument taken for collection by a collecting bank, notice of dishonor must be given (i) by the bank before midnight of the next banking day following the banking day on which the bank receives notice of dishonor of the instrument, or (ii) by any other person within 30 days following the day on which the person receives notice of dishonor. With respect to any other instrument, notice of dishonor must be given within 30 days following the day on which dishonor occurs.

Official Comment

1. Subsection (a) is consistent with former Section 3–501(2)(a), but notice of dishonor is no longer relevant to the liability of a drawer except for the case of a draft accepted by an acceptor other than a bank. Comments 2 and 4 to Section 3–414. There is no reason why drawers should be discharged on instruments they draw until payment or acceptance. They are entitled to have the instrument presented to the drawee and dishonored (Section 3–414(b)) before they are liable to pay, but no notice of dishonor need be made to them as a condition of liability.

Subsection (b), which states how notice of dishonor is given, is based on former Section 3–508(3).

2. Subsection (c) replaces former Section 3–508(2). It differs from that section in that it provides a 30–day period for a person other than a collecting bank to give notice of dishonor rather than the three-day period allowed in former Article 3. Delay in giving notice of dishonor may be excused under Section 3–504(c).

§ 3–504. Excused Presentment and Notice of Dishonor.

(a) Presentment for payment or acceptance of an instrument is excused if (i) the person entitled to present the instrument cannot with reasonable diligence make presentment, (ii) the maker or acceptor has repudiated an obligation to pay the instrument or is dead or in insolvency proceedings, (iii) by the terms of the instrument presentment is not necessary to enforce the obligation of indorsers or the drawer, (iv) the drawer or indorser whose obligation is being enforced has waived presentment or otherwise has no reason to expect or right to require that the instrument be paid or accepted, or (v) the drawer instructed the drawee not to pay or accept the draft or the drawee was not obligated to the drawer to pay the draft.

(b) Notice of dishonor is excused if (i) by the terms of the instrument notice of dishonor is not necessary to enforce the obligation of a party to pay the instrument, or (ii) the party whose obligation is being enforced waived notice of dishonor. A waiver of presentment is also a waiver of notice of dishonor.

(c) Delay in giving notice of dishonor is excused if the delay was caused by circumstances beyond the control of the person giving the notice and the person giving the notice exercised reasonable diligence after the cause of the delay ceased to operate.

Official Comment

Section 3–504 is largely a restatement of former Section 3–511. Subsection (4) of former Section 3–511 is replaced by Section 3–502(f).

§ 3–505. Evidence of Dishonor.

(a) The following are admissible as evidence and create a presumption of dishonor and of any notice of dishonor stated:

(1) a document regular in form as provided in subsection (b) which purports to be a protest;

(2) a purported stamp or writing of the drawee, payor bank, or presenting bank on or accompanying the instrument stating that acceptance or payment has been refused unless reasons for the refusal are stated and the reasons are not consistent with dishonor;

(3) a book or record of the drawee, payor bank, or collecting bank, kept in the usual course of business which shows dishonor, even if there is no evidence of who made the entry.

(b) A protest is a certificate of dishonor made by a United States consul or vice consul, or a notary public or other person authorized to administer oaths by the law of the place where dishonor occurs. It may be made upon information satisfactory to that person. The protest must identify the instrument and certify either that presentment has been made or, if not made, the reason why it was not made, and that the instrument has been dishonored by nonacceptance or nonpayment. The protest may also certify that notice of dishonor has been given to some or all parties.

Official Comment

Protest is no longer mandatory and must be requested by the holder. Even if requested, protest is not a condition to the liability of indorsers or drawers. Protest is a service provided by the banking system to establish that dishonor has occurred. Like other services provided by the banking system, it will be available if market incentives, inter-bank agreements, or governmental regulations require it, but liabilities of parties no longer rest on it. Protest may be a requirement for liability on international drafts governed by foreign law which this Article cannot affect.

PART 6

DISCHARGE AND PAYMENT

§ 3–601. Discharge and Effect of Discharge.

(a) The obligation of a party to pay the instrument is discharged as stated in this Article or by an act or agreement with the party which would discharge an obligation to pay money under a simple contract.

(b) Discharge of the obligation of a party is not effective against a person acquiring rights of a holder in due course of the instrument without notice of the discharge.

Official Comment

Subsection (a) replaces subsections (1) and (2) of former Section 3–601. Subsection (b) restates former Section 3–602. Notice of discharge is not treated as notice of a defense that prevents holder in due course status. Section 3–302(b). Discharge is effective against a holder in due course only if the holder had notice of the discharge when holder in due course status was acquired. For example, if an instrument bearing a canceled indorsement is taken by a holder, the holder has notice that the indorser has been discharged. Thus, the discharge is effective against the holder even if the holder is a holder in due course.

§ 3–602. Payment.

(a) Subject to subsection (b), an instrument is paid to the extent payment is made (i) by or on behalf of a party obliged to pay the instrument, and (ii) to a person entitled to enforce the instrument. To the extent of the payment, the obligation of the party obliged to pay the instrument is discharged even though payment is made with knowledge of a claim to the instrument under Section 3–306 by another person.

(b) The obligation of a party to pay the instrument is not discharged under subsection (a) if:

(1) a claim to the instrument under Section 3–306 is enforceable against the party receiving payment and (i) payment is made

with knowledge by the payor that payment is prohibited by injunction or similar process of a court of competent jurisdiction, or (ii) in the case of an instrument other than a cashier's check, teller's check, or certified check, the party making payment accepted, from the person having a claim to the instrument, indemnity against loss resulting from refusal to pay the person entitled to enforce the instrument; or

(2) the person making payment knows that the instrument is a stolen instrument and pays a person it knows is in wrongful possession of the instrument.

Official Comment

This section replaces former Section 3-603(1). The phrase "claim to the instrument" in subsection (a) means, by reference to Section 3-306, a claim of ownership or possession and not a claim in recoupment. Subsection (b)(1)(ii) is added to conform to Section 3-411. Section 3-411 is intended to discourage an obligated bank from refusing payment of a cashier's check, certified check or dishonored teller's check at the request of a claimant to the check who provided the bank with indemnity against loss. See Comment 1 to Section 3-411. An obligated bank that refuses payment under those circumstances not only remains liable on the check but may also be liable to the holder of the check for consequential damages. Section 3-602(b)(1)(ii) and Section 3-411, read together, change the rule of former Section 3-603(1) with respect to the obligation of the obligated bank on the check. Payment to the holder of a cashier's check, teller's check, or certified check discharges the obligation of the obligated bank on the check to both the holder and the claimant even though indemnity has been given by the person asserting the claim. If the obligated bank pays the check in violation of an agreement with the claimant in connection with the indemnity agreement, any liability that the bank may have for violation of the agreement is not governed by Article 3, but is left to other law. This section continues the rule that the obligor is not discharged on the instrument if payment is made in violation of an injunction against payment. See Section 3-411(c)(iv).

§ 3-603. Tender of Payment.

(a) If tender of payment of an obligation to pay an instrument is made to a person entitled to enforce the instrument, the effect of tender is governed by principles of law applicable to tender of payment under a simple contract.

(b) If tender of payment of an obligation to pay an instrument is made to a person entitled to enforce the instrument and the tender is refused, there is discharge, to the extent of the amount of the tender, of the obligation of an indorser or accommodation party having a right of recourse with respect to the obligation to which the tender relates.

(c) If tender of payment of an amount due on an instrument is made to a person entitled to enforce the instrument, the obligation of the obligor to pay interest after the due date on the amount tendered is discharged. If presentment is required with respect to an instrument and the obligor is able and ready to pay on the due date at every place of payment stated in the instrument, the obligor is deemed to have made tender of payment on the due date to the person entitled to enforce the instrument.

Official Comment

Section 3–603 replaces former Section 3–604. Subsection (a) generally incorporates the law of tender of payment applicable to simple contracts. Subsections (b) and (c) state particular rules. Subsection (b) replaces former Section 3–604(2). Under subsection (b) refusal of a tender of payment discharges any indorser or accommodation party having a right of recourse against the party making the tender. Subsection (c) replaces former Section 3–604(1) and (3).

§ 3–604. Discharge by Cancellation or Renunciation.

(a) A person entitled to enforce an instrument, with or without consideration, may discharge the obligation of a party to pay the instrument (i) by an intentional voluntary act, such as surrender of the instrument to the party, destruction, mutilation, or cancellation of the instrument, cancellation or striking out of the party's signature, or the addition of words to the instrument indicating discharge, or (ii) by agreeing not to sue or otherwise renouncing rights against the party by a signed writing.

(b) Cancellation or striking out of an indorsement pursuant to subsection (a) does not affect the status and rights of a party derived from the indorsement.

Official Comment

Section 3–604 replaces former Section 3–605.

§ 3–605. Discharge of Indorsers and Accommodation Parties.

(a) In this section, the term "indorser" includes a drawer having the obligation described in Section 3–414(d).

(b) Discharge, under Section 3–604, of the obligation of a party to pay an instrument does not discharge the obligation of an indorser or accommodation party having a right of recourse against the discharged party.

(c) If a person entitled to enforce an instrument agrees, with or without consideration, to an extension of the due date of the obligation of a party to pay the instrument, the extension discharges an indorser or accommodation party having a right of recourse against the party whose obligation is extended to the extent the indorser or accommodation party proves that the extension caused loss to the indorser or accommodation party with respect to the right of recourse.

(d) If a person entitled to enforce an instrument agrees, with or without consideration, to a material modification of the obligation of a party other than an extension of the due date, the modification discharges the obligation of an indorser or accommodation party having a right of recourse against the person whose obligation is modified to the extent the modification causes loss to the indorser or accommodation party with respect to the right of recourse. The loss suffered by the indorser or accommodation party as a result of the modification is equal to the amount of the right of recourse unless the person enforcing the instrument proves that no loss was caused by the modification or that the loss caused by the modification was an amount less than the amount of the right of recourse.

(e) If the obligation of a party to pay an instrument is secured by an interest in collateral and a person entitled to enforce the instrument impairs the value of the interest in collateral, the obligation of an indorser or accommodation party having a right of recourse against the obligor is discharged to the extent of the impairment. The value of an interest in collateral is impaired to the extent (i) the value of the interest is reduced to an amount less than the amount of the right of recourse of the party asserting discharge, or (ii) the reduction in value of the interest causes an increase in the amount by which the amount of the right of recourse exceeds the value of the interest. The burden of proving impairment is on the party asserting discharge.

(f) If the obligation of a party is secured by an interest in collateral not provided by an accommodation party and a person entitled to enforce the instrument impairs the value of the interest in collateral, the obligation of any party who is jointly and severally liable with respect to the secured obligation is discharged to the extent the impairment causes the party asserting discharge to pay more than that party would have been obliged to pay, taking into account rights of contribution, if impairment had not occurred. If the party asserting discharge is an accommodation party not entitled to discharge under subsection (e), the party is deemed to have a right to contribution based on joint and several liability rather than a right to reimbursement. The burden of proving impairment is on the party asserting discharge.

(g) Under subsection (e) or (f), impairing value of an interest in collateral includes (i) failure to obtain or maintain perfection or recordation of the interest in collateral, (ii) release of collateral without substitution of collateral of equal value, (iii) failure to perform a duty to preserve the value of collateral owed, under Article 9 or other law, to a debtor or surety or other person secondarily liable, or (iv) failure to comply with applicable law in disposing of collateral.

(h) An accommodation party is not discharged under subsection (c), (d), or (e) unless the person entitled to enforce the instrument knows of the accommodation or has notice under Section 3–419(c) that the instrument was signed for accommodation.

(i) A party is not discharged under this section if (i) the party asserting discharge consents to the event or conduct that is the basis of the discharge, or (ii) the instrument or a separate agreement of the party provides for waiver of discharge under this section either specifically or by general language indicating that parties waive defenses based on suretyship or impairment of collateral.

Official Comment

1. Section 3–605, which replaces former Section 3–606, can be illustrated by an example. Bank lends $10,000 to Borrower who signs a note under which Borrower is obliged to pay $10,000 to Bank on a due date stated in the note. Bank insists, however, that Accommodation Party also become liable to pay the note.

Accommodation Party can incur this liability by signing the note as a co-maker or by indorsing the note. In either case the note is signed for accommodation and Borrower is the accommodated party. Rights and obligations of Accommodation Party in this case are stated in Section 3–419. Suppose that after the note is signed, Bank agrees to a modification of the rights and obligations between Bank and Borrower. For example, Bank agrees that Borrower may pay the note at some date after the due date, or that Borrower may discharge Borrower's $10,000 obligation to pay the note by paying Bank $3,000, or that Bank releases collateral given by Borrower to secure the note. Under the law of suretyship Borrower is usually referred to as the principal debtor and Accommodation Party is referred to as the surety. Under that law, the surety can be discharged under certain circumstances if changes of this kind are made by Bank, the creditor, without the consent of Accommodation Party, the surety. Rights of the surety to discharge in such cases are commonly referred to as suretyship defenses. Section 3–605 is concerned with this kind of problem in the context of a negotiable instrument to which the principal debtor and the surety are parties. But Section 3–605 has a wider scope. It also applies to indorsers who are not accommodation parties. Unless an indorser signs without recourse, the indorser's liability under Section 3–415(a) is that of a guarantor of payment. If Bank in our hypothetical case indorsed the note and transferred it to Second Bank, Bank has rights given to an indorser under Section 3–605 if it is Second Bank that modifies rights and obligations of Borrower. Both accommodation parties and indorsers will be referred to in these Comments as sureties. The scope of Section 3–605 is also widened by subsection (e) which deals with rights of a non-accommodation party co-maker when collateral is impaired.

2. The importance of suretyship defenses is greatly diminished by the fact that they can be waived. The waiver is usually made by a provision in the note or other writing that represents the obligation of the principal debtor. It is standard practice to include a waiver of suretyship defenses in notes given to financial institutions or other commercial creditors. Section 3–605(i) allows waiver. Thus, Section 3–605 applies to the occasional case in which the creditor did not include a waiver clause in the instrument or in which the creditor did not obtain the permission of the surety to take the action that triggers the suretyship defense.

3. Subsection (b) addresses the effect of discharge under Section 3–604 of the principal debtor. In the hypothetical case stated in Comment 1, release of Borrower by Bank does not release Accommodation Party. As a practical matter, Bank will not gratuitously release Borrower. Discharge of Borrower normally would be part of a settlement with Borrower if Borrower is insolvent or in financial difficulty. If Borrower is unable to pay all creditors, it may be prudent for Bank to take partial payment, but Borrower will normally insist on a release of the obligation. If Bank takes $3,000 and releases Borrower from the $10,000 debt, Accommodation Party is not injured. To the extent of the payment Accommodation Party's obligation to Bank is reduced. The release of Borrower by Bank does not affect the right of Accommodation Party to obtain reimbursement from Borrower or to enforce the note against Borrower if Accommodation Party pays Bank. Section 3–419(e). Subsection (b) is designed to allow a creditor to settle with the principal debtor without risk of losing rights against sureties. Settlement is in the interest of sureties as well as the creditor. Subsection (b), however, is not intended to apply to a settlement of a disputed claim which discharges the obligation.

Subsection (b) changes the law stated in former Section 3–606 but the change relates largely to formalities rather than substance. Under former Section 3–606, Bank in the hypothetical case stated in Comment 1 could settle with and release Borrower without releasing Accommodation Party, but to accomplish that result

Bank had to either obtain the consent of Accommodation Party or make an express reservation of rights against Accommodation Party at the time it released Borrower. The reservation of rights was made in the agreement between Bank and Borrower by which the release of Borrower was made. There was no requirement in former Section 3–606 that any notice be given to Accommodation Party. Section 3–605 eliminates the necessity that Bank formally reserve rights against Accommodation Party in order to retain rights of recourse against Accommodation Party. See PEB Commentary No. 11, dated February 10, 1994 [Appendix V, infra].

4. Subsection (c) relates to extensions of the due date of the instrument. In most cases an extension of time to pay a note is a benefit to both the principal debtor and sureties having recourse against the principal debtor. In relatively few cases the extension may cause loss if deterioration of the financial condition of the principal debtor reduces the amount that the surety will be able to recover on its right of recourse when default occurs. Former Section 3–606(1)(a) did not take into account the presence or absence of loss to the surety. For example, suppose the instrument is an installment note and the principal debtor is temporarily short of funds to pay a monthly installment. The payee agrees to extend the due date of the installment for a month or two to allow the debtor to pay when funds are available. Under former Section 3–606 surety was discharged if consent was not given unless the payee expressly reserved rights against the surety. It did not matter that the extension of time was a trivial change in the guaranteed obligation and that there was no evidence that the surety suffered any loss because of the extension. Wilmington Trust Co. v. Gesullo, 29 U.C.C.Rep. 144 (Del.Super.Ct.1980). Under subsection (c) an extension of time results in discharge only to the extent the surety proves that the extension caused loss. For example, if the extension is for a long period the surety might be able to prove that during the period of extension the principal debtor became insolvent, thus reducing the value of the right of recourse of the surety. By putting the burden on the surety to prove loss, subsection (c) more accurately reflects what the parties would have done by agreement, and it facilitates workouts.

Under other provisions of Article 3, what is the effect of an extension agreement between the holder of a note and the maker who is an accommodated party? The question is illustrated by the following case:

Case # 1. A borrows money from Lender and issues a note payable on April 1, 1992. B signs the note for accommodation at the request of Lender. B signed the note either as co-maker or as an anomalous indorser. In either case Lender subsequently makes an agreement with A extending the due date of A's obligation to pay the note to July 1, 1992. In either case B did not agree to the extension.

What is the effect of the extension agreement on B? Could Lender enforce the note against B if the note is not paid on April 1, 1992? A's obligation to Lender to pay the note on April 1, 1992 may be modified by the agreement of Lender. If B is an anomalous indorser Lender cannot enforce the note against B unless the note has been dishonored. Section 3–415(a). Under Section 3–502(a)(3) dishonor occurs if it is not paid on the day it becomes payable. Since the agreement between A and Lender extended the due date of A's obligation to July 1, 1992 there is no dishonor because A was not obligated to pay Lender on April 1, 1992. If B is a co-maker the analysis is somewhat different. Lender has no power to amend the terms of the note without the consent of both A and B. By an agreement with A, Lender can extend the due date of A's obligation to Lender to pay the note but B's obligation is to pay the note according to the terms of the note at the time of issue. Section 3–412. However, B's obligation to pay the note is subject to a defense because B is an accommodation party. B is not obliged to pay Lender if A is not obliged to pay Lender. Under Section 3–305(d), B as an accommodation party can assert against Lender any defense of A. A has a defense based on the extension agreement. Thus, the result is that Lender could not enforce the note against B until July 1, 1992. This result is consistent with the right of B if B is an anomalous indorser.

As a practical matter an extension of the due date will normally occur when the accommodated party is unable to pay on the due date. The interest of the accommodation party normally is to defer payment to the holder rather than to pay right away and rely on an action against the accommodated party that may have little or no value. But in unusual cases the accommodation party may prefer to pay the holder on the original due date. In such cases, the accommodation party may do so. This is because the extension agreement between the accommodated party and the holder cannot bind the accommodation party to a change in its obligation without the accommodation party's consent. The effect on the recourse of the accommodation party against the accommodation party of performance by the accommodation party on the original due date is not addressed in § 3–419 and is left to the general law of suretyship.

Even though an accommodation party has the option of paying the instrument on the original due date, the accommodation party is not precluded from asserting its rights to discharge under Section 3–605(c) if it does not exercise that option. The critical issue is whether the extension caused the accommodation party a loss by increasing the difference between its cost of performing its obligation on the instrument and the amount recoverable from the accommodated party pursuant to Section 3–419(e). The decision by the accommodation party not to exercise its option to pay on the original due date may, under the circumstances, be a factor to be considered in the determination of that issue. See PEB Commentary No. 11, supra.

5. Former Section 3–606 applied to extensions of the due date of a note but not to other modifications of the obligation of the principal debtor. There was no apparent reason why former Section 3–606 did not follow general suretyship law in covering both. Under Section 3–605(d) a material modification of the obligation of the principal debtor, other than an extension of the due date, will result in discharge of the surety to the extent the modification caused loss to the surety with respect to the right of recourse. The loss caused by the modification is deemed to be the entire amount of the right of recourse unless the person seeking enforcement of the instrument proves that no loss occurred or that the loss was less than the full amount of the right of recourse. In the absence of that proof, the surety is completely discharged. The rationale for having different rules with respect to loss for extensions of the due date and other modifications is that extensions are likely to be beneficial to the surety and they are often made. Other modifications are less common and they may very well be detrimental to the surety. Modification of the obligation of the principal debtor without permission of the surety is unreasonable unless the modification is benign. Subsection (d) puts the burden on the person seeking enforcement of the instrument to prove the extent to which loss was not caused by the modification.

The following is an illustration of the kind of case to which Section 3–605(d) would apply:

Case # 2. Corporation borrows money from Lender and issues a note payable to Lender. X signs the note as an accommodation party for Corporation. The loan agreement under which the note was issued states various events of default which allow Lender to accelerate the due date of the note. Among the events of default are breach of covenants not to incur debt beyond specified limits and not to engage in any line of business substantially different from that currently carried on by Corporation. Without consent of X, Lender agrees to modify the covenants to allow Corporation to enter into a new line of business that X considers to be risky, and to incur debt beyond the limits specified in the loan agreement to finance the new venture. This modification releases X unless Lender proves that the modification did not cause loss to X or that the loss caused by the modification was less than X's right of recourse.

Sometimes there is both an extension of the due date and some other modification. In that case both subsections (c) and (d) apply. The following is an example:

Case # 3. Corporation was indebted to Lender on a note payable on April 1, 1992 and X signed the note as an accommodation party for Corporation. The interest rate on the note was 12 percent. Lender and Corporation agreed to a six-month extension of the due date of the note to October 1, 1992 and an increase in the interest rate to 14 percent after April 1, 1992. Corporation defaulted on October 1, 1992. Corporation paid no interest during the six-month extension period. Corporation is insolvent and has no assets from which unsecured creditors can be paid. Lender demanded payment from X.

Assume X is an anomalous indorser. First consider Section 3–605(c) alone. If there had been no change in the interest rate, the fact that Lender gave an extension of six months to Corporation would not result in discharge unless X could prove loss with respect to the right of recourse because of the extension. If the financial condition of Corporation on April 1, 1992 would not have allowed any recovery on the right of recourse, X can't show any loss as a result of the extension with respect to the amount due on the note on April 1, 1992. Since the note accrued interest during the six-month extension, is there a loss equal to the accrued interest? Since the interest rate was not raised, only Section 3–605(c) would apply and X probably could not prove any loss. The obligation of X includes interest on the note until the note is paid. To the extent payment was delayed X had the use of the money that X otherwise would have had to pay to Lender. X could have prevented the running of interest by paying the debt. Since X did not do so, X suffered no loss as the result of the extension.

If the interest rate was raised, Section 3–605(d) also must be considered. If X is an anomalous indorser, X's liability is to pay the note according to its terms at the time of indorsement. Section 3–415(a). Thus, X's obligation to pay interest is measured by the terms of the note (12%) rather than by the increased amount of 14 percent. The same analysis applies if X had been a co-maker. Under Section 3–412 the liability of the issuer of a note is to pay the note according to its terms at the time it was issued. Either obligation could be changed by contract and that occurred with respect to Corporation when it agreed to the increase in the interest rate, but X did not join in that agreement and is not bound by it. Thus, the most that X can be required to pay is the amount due on the note plus interest at the rate of 12 percent.

Does the modification discharge X under Section 3–605(d)? Any modification that increases the monetary obligation of X is material. An increase of the interest rate from 12 percent to 14 percent is certainly a material modification. There is a presumption that X is discharged because Section 3–605(d) creates a presumption that the modification caused a loss to X equal to the amount of the right of recourse. Thus, Lender has the burden of proving absence of loss or a loss less than the amount of the right of recourse. Since Corporation paid no interest during the six-month period, the issue is like the issue presented under Section 3–605(c) which we have just discussed. The increase in the interest rate could not have affected the right of recourse because no interest was paid by Corporation. X is in the same position as X would have been in if there had been an extension without an increase in the interest rate.

The analysis with respect to Section 3–605(c) and (d) would have been different if we change the assumptions. Suppose Corporation was not insolvent on April 1, 1992, that Corporation paid interest at the higher rate during the six-month period, and that Corporation was insolvent at the end of the six-month period. In this case it is possible that the extension and the additional burden placed on Corporation by the increased interest rate may have been detrimental to X.

There are difficulties in properly allocating burden of proof when the agreement between Lender and Corporation involves both an extension under Section 3–605(c) and a modification under Section 3–605(d). The agreement may have caused loss to X but it may be difficult to identify the extent to which the loss was caused by the extension or the other modification. If neither Lender nor X introduces evidence on the issue, the result is full discharge because Section 3–605(d) applies. Thus, Lender has the burden of overcoming the presumption in Section 3–605(d). In doing so, Lender should be entitled to a presumption that the extension of time by itself caused no loss. Section 3–605(c) is based on such a presumption and X should be required to introduce evidence on the effect of the extension on the right of recourse. Lender would have to introduce evidence on the effect of the increased interest rate. Thus both sides will have to introduce evidence. On the basis of this evidence the court will have to make a determination of the overall effect of the agreement on X's right of recourse. See PEB Commentary No. 11, supra.

6. Subsection (e) deals with discharge of sureties by impairment of collateral. It generally conforms to former Section 3–606(1)(b). Subsection (g) states common examples of what is meant by impairment. By using the term "includes," it allows a court to find impairment in other cases as well. There is extensive case law on impairment of collateral. The surety is discharged to the extent the surety proves that impairment was caused by a person entitled to enforce the instrument. For example, suppose the payee of a secured note fails to perfect the security interest. The collateral is owned by the principal debtor who subsequently files in bankruptcy. As a result of the failure to perfect, the security interest is not enforceable in bankruptcy. If the payee obtains payment from the surety, the surety is subrogated to the payee's security interest in the collateral. In this case the value of the security interest is impaired completely because the security interest is unenforceable. If the value of the collateral is as much or more than the amount of the note there is a complete discharge.

In some states a real property grantee who assumes the obligation of the grantor as maker of a note secured by the real property becomes by operation of law a principal debtor and the grantor becomes a surety. The meager case authority was split on whether former Section 3–606 applied to release the grantor if the holder released or extended the obligation of the grantee. Revised Article 3 takes no position on the effect of the release of the grantee in this case. Section 3–605(b) does not apply because the holder has not discharged the obligation of a "party," a term defined in Section 3–103(a)(8) as "party to an instrument." The assuming grantee is not a party to the instrument. The resolution of this question is governed by general principles of law, including the law of suretyship. See PEB Commentary No. 11, supra.

7. Subsection (f) is illustrated by the following case. X and Y sign a note for $1,000 as co-makers. Neither is an accommodation party. X grants a security interest in X's property to secure the note. The collateral is worth more than $1,000. Payee fails to perfect the security interest in X's property before X files in bankruptcy. As a result the security interest is not enforceable in bankruptcy. Had Payee perfected the security interest, Y could have paid the note and gained rights to X's collateral by subrogation. If the security interest had been perfected, Y could have realized on the collateral to the extent of $500 to satisfy its right of contribution against X. Payee's failure to perfect deprived Y of the benefit of the

collateral. Subsection (f) discharges Y to the extent of its loss. If there are no assets in the bankruptcy for unsecured claims, the loss is $500, the amount of Y's contribution claim against X which now has a zero value. If some amount is payable on unsecured claims, the loss is reduced by the amount receivable by Y. The same result follows if Y is an accommodation party but Payee has no knowledge of the accommodation or notice under Section 3-419(c). In that event Y is not discharged under subsection (e), but subsection (f) applies because X and Y are jointly and severally liable on the note. Under subsection (f), Y is treated as a co-maker with a right of contribution rather than an accommodation party with a right of reimbursement. Y is discharged to the extent of $500. If Y is the principal debtor and X is the accommodation party subsection (f) doesn't apply. Y, as principal debtor, is not injured by the impairment of collateral because Y would have been obliged to reimburse X for the entire $1,000 even if Payee had obtained payment from sale of the collateral.

8. Subsection (i) is a continuation of former law which allowed suretyship defenses to be waived. As the subsection provides, a party is not discharged under this section if the instrument or a separate agreement of the party waives discharge either specifically or by general language indicating that defenses based on suretyship and impairment of collateral are waived. No particular language or form of agreement is required, and the standards for enforcing such a term are the same as the standards for enforcing any other term in an instrument or agreement.

Subsection (i), however, applies only to a "discharge under this section." The right of an accommodation party to be discharged under Section 3-605(e) because of an impairment of collateral can be waived. But with respect to a note secured by personal property collateral, Article 9 also applies. If an accommodation party is a "debtor" under Section 9-105(1)(d), the accommodation party has rights under Article 9. Under Section 9-501(3)(b) rights of an Article 9 debtor under Section 9-504(3) and Section 9-505(1), which deal with disposition of collateral, cannot be waived except as provided in Article 9. These Article 9 rights are independent of rights under Section 3-605. Since Section 3-605(i) is specifically limited to discharge under Section 3-605, a waiver of rights with respect to Section 3-605 has no effect on rights under Article 9. With respect to Article 9 rights, Section 9-501(3)(b) controls. See PEB Commentary No. 11, supra.

ADDENDUM TO REVISED ARTICLE 3

Notes to Legislative Counsel

1. If revised Article 3 is adopted in your state, the reference in Section 2-511 to Section 3-802 should be changed to Section 3-310.

2. If revised Article 3 is adopted in your state and the Uniform Fiduciaries Act is also in effect in your state, you may want to consider amending Uniform Fiduciaries Act § 9 to conform to Section 3-307(b)(2)(iii) and (4)(iii). See Official Comment 3 to Section 3-307.

CONFORMING AMENDMENTS TO ARTICLES 1 AND 4

See Appendices VIII and IX.

ARTICLE 4

BANK DEPOSITS AND COLLECTIONS

Numerous conforming [to Revised Article 3] and miscellaneous amendments were made to Article 4 in 1990. The Text and Official Comments set forth below constitute Article 4 as so amended. For material relating to the amendments of 1990, see Appendix IX, infra.

For the text and Official Comments of Article 4 as they existed prior to amendment in 1990, see Appendix X, infra.

PART 1. GENERAL PROVISIONS AND DEFINITIONS

PART 2. COLLECTION OF ITEMS: DEPOSITARY AND COLLECTING BANKS

PART 1

GENERAL PROVISIONS AND DEFINITIONS

§ 4–101. Short Title.

This Article may be cited as Uniform Commercial Code—Bank Deposits and Collections.

As amended in 1990.

See Appendix IX for material relating to changes made in text in 1990.

Official Comment

1. The great number of checks handled by banks and the country-wide nature of the bank collection process require uniformity in the law of bank collections. There is needed a uniform statement of the principal rules of the bank collection process with ample provision for flexibility to meet the needs of the large volume handled and the changing needs and conditions that are bound to come with the years. This Article meets that need.

2. In 1950 at the time Article 4 was drafted, 6.7 billion checks were written annually. By the time of the 1990 revision of Article 4 annual volume was estimated by the American Bankers Associa-

tion to be about 50 billion checks. The banking system could not have coped with this increase in check volume had it not developed in the late 1950s and early 1960s an automated system for check collection based on encoding checks with machine-readable information by Magnetic Ink Character Recognition (MICR). An important goal of the 1990 revision of Article 4 is to promote the efficiency of the check collection process by making the provisions of Article 4 more compatible with the needs of an automated system and, by doing so, increase the speed and lower the cost of check collection for those who write and receive checks. An additional goal of the 1990 revision of Article 4 is to remove any statutory barriers in the Article to the ultimate adoption of programs allowing the presentment of checks to payor banks by electronic transmission of information captured from the MICR line on the checks. The potential of these programs for saving the time and expense of transporting the huge volume of checks from depositary to payor banks is evident.

3. Article 4 defines rights between parties with respect to bank deposits and collections. It is not a regulatory statute. It does not regulate the terms of the bank-customer agreement, nor does it prescribe what constraints different jurisdictions may wish to impose on that relationship in the interest of consumer protection. The revisions in Article 4 are intended to create a legal framework that accommodates automation and truncation for the benefit of all bank customers. This may raise consumer problems which enacting jurisdictions may wish to address in individual legislation. For example, with respect to Section 4-401(c), jurisdictions may wish to examine their unfair and deceptive practices laws to determine whether they are adequate to protect drawers who postdate checks from unscrupulous practices that may arise on the part of persons who induce drawers to issue postdated checks in the erroneous belief that the checks will not be immediately payable. Another example arises from the fact that under various truncation plans customers will no longer receive their cancelled checks and will no longer have the cancelled check to prove payment. Individual legislation might provide that a copy of a bank statement along with a copy of the check is prima facie evidence of payment.

§ 4-102. Applicability.

(a) To the extent that items within this Article are also within Articles 3 and 8, they are subject to those Articles. If there is conflict, this Article governs Article 3, but Article 8 governs this Article.

(b) The liability of a bank for action or non-action with respect to an item handled by it for purposes of presentment, payment, or collection is governed by the law of the place where the bank is located. In the case of action or non-action by or at a branch or separate office of a bank, its liability is governed by the law of the place where the branch or separate office is located.

As amended in 1990.

See Appendix IX for material relating to changes made in text in 1990.

Official Comment

1. The rules of Article 3 governing negotiable instruments, their transfer, and the contracts of the parties thereto apply to the items collected through banking channels wherever no specific provision is found in this Article. In the case of conflict, this Article governs. See Section 3-102(b).

Bonds and like instruments constituting investment securities under Article 8 may also be handled by banks for collection purposes. Various sections of Article 8 prescribe rules of transfer some of which (see ~~Sections 8-304 and 8-306~~ Sections 8-108 and 8-304) may conflict with provisions of this Article (Sections 4-205, 4-207, and 4-208). In the case of conflict, Article 8 governs. *Amendments approved by the Permanent Editorial Board for Uniform Commercial Code November 4, 1995.*

Section 4-210 deals specifically with overlapping problems and possible conflicts between this Article and Article 9. However, similar reconciling provisions are not necessary in the case of Articles 5 and 7. Sections 4-301 and 4-302 are consistent with Section 5-112. In the case of Article 7 documents of title frequently accompany items but they are not themselves items. See Section 4-104(a)(9).

In Clearfield Trust Co. v. United States, 318 U.S. 363 (1943), the Court held that if the United States is a party to an instrument, its rights and duties are governed by federal common law in the absence of a specific federal statute or regulation. In United States v. Kimbell Foods, Inc., 440 U.S. 715 (1979), the Court stated a three-pronged test to ascertain whether the federal common-law rule should follow the state rule. In most instances courts under the *Kimbell* test have shown a willingness to adopt UCC rules in formulating federal common law on the subject. In *Kimbell* the Court adopted the priorities rules of Article 9.

In addition, applicable federal law may supersede provisions of this Article. One federal law that does so is the Expedited Funds Availability Act, 12 U.S.C. § 4001 et seq., and its implementing Regulation CC, 12 CFR Pt. 229. In some instances this law is alluded to in the statute, e.g., Section 4-215(e) and (f). In other instances, although not referred to in this Article, the provisions of the EFAA and Regulation CC control with respect to checks. For example, except between the depositary bank and its customer, all settlements are final and not provisional (Regulation CC, Section 229.36(d)), and the midnight deadline may be extended (Regulation CC, Section 229.30(c)). The comments to this Article suggest in most instances the relevant Regulation CC provisions.

2. Subsection (b) is designed to state a workable rule for the solution of otherwise vexatious problems of the conflicts of laws:

a. The routine and mechanical nature of bank collections makes it imperative that one law govern the activities of one office of a bank. The requirement found in some cases that to hold an indorser notice must be given in accordance with the law of the place of indorsement, since that method of notice became an implied term of the indorser's contract, is more theoretical than practical.

b. Adoption of what is in essence a tort theory of the conflict of laws is consistent with the general theory of this Article that the basic duty of a collecting bank is one of good faith and the exercise of ordinary care. Justification lies in the fact that, in using an ambulatory instrument, the drawer, payee, and indorsers must know that action will be taken with respect to it in other jurisdictions. This is especially pertinent with respect to the law of the place of payment.

c. The phrase "action or non-action with respect to any item handled by it for purposes of presentment, payment, or collection" is intended to make the conflicts rule of subsection (b) apply from the inception of the collection process of an item through all phases of deposit, forwarding, presentment, payment and remittance or credit of proceeds. Specifically the subsection applies to the initial act of a depositary bank in receiving an item and to the incidents of such receipt. The conflicts rule of Weissman v. Banque De Bruxelles, 254 N.Y. 488, 173 N.E. 835 (1930), is rejected. The subsection applies to questions of possible vicarious liability of a bank for action or non-action of sub-agents (see Section 4-202(c)), and tests these questions by the law of the state of the location of the bank which uses the sub-agent. The conflicts rule of St. Nicholas Bank of New York v. State Nat. Bank, 128 N.Y. 26, 27 N.E. 849, 13 L.R.A. 241 (1891), is rejected. The subsection applies to action or non-action of a payor bank in connection with handling an item (see Sections 4-215(a), 4-301, 4-302, 4-303) as well as action or non-action of a collecting bank (Sections 4-201 through 4-216); to action or non-action of a bank which suspends payment or is affected by another bank suspending payment (Section 4-216); to action or non-action of a bank with respect to an item under the rule of Part 4 of Article 4.

d. In a case in which subsection (b) makes this Article applicable, Section 4-103(a) leaves open the possibility of an agreement with respect to applicable law. This freedom of agreement follows the general policy of Section 1-105.

§ 4-103. Variation by Agreement; Measure of Damages; Action Constituting Ordinary Care.

(a) The effect of the provisions of this Article may be varied by agreement, but the parties to the agreement cannot disclaim a bank's responsibility for its lack of good faith or failure to exercise ordinary care or limit the measure of damages for the lack or failure. However, the parties may determine by agreement the standards by which the bank's responsibility is to be measured if those standards are not manifestly unreasonable.

(b) Federal Reserve regulations and operating circulars, clearing-house rules, and the like have the effect of agreements under subsection (a), whether or not specifically assented to by all parties interested in items handled.

(c) Action or non-action approved by this Article or pursuant to Federal Reserve regulations or operating circulars is the exercise of ordinary care and, in the absence of special instructions, action or non-action consistent with clearing-house rules and the like or with a general banking usage not disapproved by this Article, is prima facie the exercise of ordinary care.

(d) The specification or approval of certain procedures by this Article is not disapproval of other procedures that may be reasonable under the circumstances.

(e) The measure of damages for failure to exercise ordinary care in handling an item is the amount of the item reduced by an amount that could not have been realized by the exercise of ordinary care. If there is also bad faith it includes any other damages the party suffered as a proximate consequence.

As amended in 1990.

See Appendix IX for material relating to changes made in text in 1990.

Official Comment

1. Section 1-102 states the general principles and rules for variation of the effect of this Act by agreement and the limitations to this power. Section 4-103 states the specific rules for variation of Article 4 by agreement and also certain standards of ordinary care. In view of the technical complexity of the field of bank collections, the enormous number of items handled by banks, the certainty that there will be variations from the

normal in each day's work in each bank, the certainty of changing conditions and the possibility of developing improved methods of collection to speed the process, it would be unwise to freeze present methods of operation by mandatory statutory rules. This section, therefore, permits within wide limits variation of the effect of provisions of the Article by agreement.

2. Subsection (a) confers blanket power to vary all provisions of the Article by agreements of the ordinary kind. The agreements may not disclaim a bank's responsibility for its own lack of good faith or failure to exercise ordinary care and may not limit the measure of damages for the lack or failure, but this subsection like Section 1-102(3) approves the practice of parties determining by agreement the standards by which the responsibility is to be measured. In the absence of a showing that the standards manifestly are unreasonable, the agreement controls. Owners of items and other interested parties are not affected by agreements under this subsection unless they are parties to the agreement or are bound by adoption, ratification, estoppel or the like.

As here used "agreement" has the meaning given to it by Section 1-201(3). The agreement may be direct, as between the owner and the depositary bank; or indirect, as in the case in which the owner authorizes a particular type of procedure and any bank in the collection chain acts pursuant to such authorization. It may be with respect to a single item; or to all items handled for a particular customer, e.g., a general agreement between the depositary bank and the customer at the time a deposit account is opened. Legends on deposit tickets, collection letters and acknowledgments of items, coupled with action by the affected party constituting acceptance, adoption, ratification, estoppel or the like, are agreements if they meet the tests of the definition of "agreement." See Section 1-201(3). First Nat. Bank of Denver v. Federal Reserve Bank, 6 F.2d 339 (8th Cir.1925) (deposit slip); Jefferson County Bldg. Ass'n v. Southern Bank & Trust Co., 225 Ala. 25, 142 So. 66 (1932) (signature card and deposit slip); Semingson v. Stock Yards Nat. Bank, 162 Minn. 424, 203 N.W. 412 (1925) (passbook); Farmers State Bank v. Union Nat. Bank, 42 N.D. 449, 454, 173 N.W. 789, 790 (1919) (acknowledgment of receipt of item).

3. Subsection (a) (subject to its limitations with respect to good faith and ordinary care) goes far to meet the requirements of flexibility. However, it does not by itself confer fully effective flexibility. Since it is recognized that banks handle a great number of items every business day and that the parties interested in each item include the owner of the item, the drawer (if it is a check), all nonbank indorsers, the payor bank and from one to five or more collecting banks, it is obvious that it is impossible, practically, to obtain direct agreements from all of these parties on all items. In total, the interested parties constitute virtually every adult person and business organization in the United States. On the other hand they may become bound to agreements on the principle that collecting banks acting as agents have authority to make binding agreements with respect to items being handled. This conclusion was assumed but was not flatly decided in Federal Reserve Bank of Richmond v. Malloy, 264 U.S. 160, at 167, 44 S.Ct. 296, at 298, 68 L.Ed. 617, 31 A.L.R. 1261 (1924).

To meet this problem subsection (b) provides that official or quasi-official rules of collection, that is Federal Reserve regulations and operating circulars, clearing-house rules, and the like, have the effect of agreements under subsection (a), whether or not specifically assented to by all parties interested in items handled. Consequently, such official or quasi-official rules may, standing by themselves but subject to the good faith and ordinary care limitations, vary the effect of the provisions of Article 4.

Federal Reserve regulations. Various sections of the Federal Reserve Act (12 U.S.C. § 221 et seq.) authorize the Board of Governors of the Federal Reserve System to direct the Federal Reserve banks to exercise bank collection functions. For example, Section 16 (12 U.S.C. § 248(*o*)) authorizes the Board to require each Federal Reserve bank to exercise the functions of a clearing house for its members and Section 13 (12 U.S.C. § 342) authorizes each Federal Reserve bank to receive deposits from nonmember banks solely for the purposes of exchange or of collection. Under this statutory authorization the Board has issued Regulation J (Subpart A—Collection of Checks and Other Items). Under the supremacy clause of the Constitution, federal regulations prevail over state statutes. Moreover, the Expedited Funds Availability Act, 12 U.S.C. Section 4007(b) provides that the Act and Regulation CC, 12 CFR 229, supersede "any provision of the law of any State, including the Uniform Commercial Code as in effect in such State, which is inconsistent with this chapter or such regulations." See Comment 1 to Section 4–102.

Federal Reserve operating circulars. The regulations of the Federal Reserve Board authorize the Federal Reserve banks to promulgate operating circulars covering operating details. Regulation J, for example, provides that "Each Reserve Bank shall receive and handle items in accordance with this subpart, and shall issue operating circulars governing the details of its handling of items and other matters deemed appropriate by the Reserve Bank." This Article recognizes that "operating circulars" issued pursuant to the regulations and concerned with operating details as appropriate may, within their proper sphere, vary the effect of the Article.

Clearing–House Rules. Local clearing houses have long issued rules governing the details of clearing; hours of clearing, media of remittance, time for return of mis-sent items and the like. The case law has recognized these rules, within their proper sphere, as binding on affected parties and as appropriate sources for the courts to look to in filling out details of bank collection law. Subsection (b) in recognizing clearing-house rules as a means of preserving flexibility continues the sensible approach indicated in the cases. Included in the term "clearing houses" are county and regional clearing houses as well as those within a single city or town. There is, of course, no intention of authorizing a local clearing house or a group of clearing houses to rewrite the basic law generally. The term "clearing-house rules" should be understood in the light of functions the clearing houses have exercised in the past.

And the like. This phrase is to be construed in the light of the foregoing. "Federal Reserve regulations and operating circulars" cover rules and regulations issued by public or quasi-public agencies under statutory authority. "Clearing-house rules" cover rules issued by a group of banks which have associated themselves to perform through a clearing house some of their collection, payment and clearing functions. Other agencies or associations of this kind may be established in the future whose rules and regulations could be appropriately looked on as constituting means of avoiding absolute statutory rigidity. The phrase "and the like" leaves open possibilities for future development. An agreement between a number of banks or even all the banks in an area simply because they are banks, would not of itself, by virtue of the phrase "and the like," meet the purposes and objectives of subsection (b).

4. Under this Article banks come under the general obligations of the use of good faith and the exercise of ordinary care. "Good faith" is defined in Section 3–103(a)(4). The term "ordinary care" is defined in Section 3–103(a)(7). These definitions are made to apply to Article 4 by Section 4–104(c). Section 4–202 states respects in which collecting banks must use ordinary care. Subsection (c) of Section 4–103 provides that action or non-action approved by the Article or pursuant to Federal Reserve regulations or operating circulars constitutes the exercise of ordinary care. Federal Reserve regulations and operating circulars constitute an affirmative standard of ordinary care

equally with the provisions of Article 4 itself.

Subsection (c) further provides that, absent special instructions, action or non-action consistent with clearing-house rules and the like or with a general banking usage not disapproved by the Article, prima facie constitutes the exercise of ordinary care. Clearing-house rules and the phrase "and the like" have the significance set forth above in these Comments. The term "general banking usage" is not defined but should be taken to mean a general usage common to banks in the area concerned. See Section 1-205(2). In a case in which the adjective "general" is used, the intention is to require a usage broader than a mere practice between two or three banks but it is not intended to require a usage broader than a mere practice between two or three banks but it is not intended to require anything as broad as a country-wide usage. A usage followed generally throughout a state, a substantial portion of a state, a metropolitan area or the like would certainly be sufficient. Consistently with the principle of Section 1-205(3), action or non-action consistent with clearing-house rules or the like or with banking usages prima facie constitutes the exercise of ordinary care. However, the phrase "in the absence of special instructions" affords owners of items an opportunity to prescribe other standards and although there may be no direct supervision or control of clearing houses or banking usages by official supervisory authorities, the confirmation of ordinary care by compliance with these standards is prima facie only, thus conferring on the courts the ultimate power to determine ordinary care in any case in which it should appear desirable to do so. The prima facie rule does, however, impose on the party contesting the standards to establish that they are unreasonable, arbitrary or unfair as used by the particular bank.

5. Subsection (d), in line with the flexible approach required for the bank collection process is designed to make clear that a novel procedure adopted by a bank is not to be considered unreasonable merely because that procedure is not specifically contemplated by this Article or by agreement, or because it has not yet been generally accepted as a bank usage. Changing conditions constantly call for new procedures and someone has to use the new procedure first. If this procedure is found to be reasonable under the circumstances, provided, of course, that it is not inconsistent with any provision of the Article or other law or agreement, the bank which has followed the new procedure should not be found to have failed in the exercise of ordinary care.

6. Subsection (e) sets forth a rule for determining the measure of damages for failure to exercise ordinary care which, under subsection (a), cannot be limited by agreement. In the absence of bad faith the maximum recovery is the amount of the item concerned. The term "bad faith" is not defined; the connotation is the absence of good faith (Section 3-103). When it is established that some part or all of the item could not have been collected even by the use of ordinary care the recovery is reduced by the amount that would have been in any event uncollectible. This limitation on recovery follows the case law. Finally, if bad faith is established the rule opens to allow the recovery of other damages, whose "proximateness" is to be tested by the ordinary rules applied in comparable cases. Of course, it continues to be as necessary under subsection (e) as it has been under ordinary common law principles that, before the damage rule of the subsection becomes operative, liability of the bank and some loss to the customer or owner must be established.

§ 4-104. Definitions and Index of Definitions.

(a) In this Article, unless the context otherwise requires:

(1) "Account" means any deposit or credit account with a bank, including a demand, time, savings, passbook, share draft, or like

account, other than an account evidenced by a certificate of deposit;

(2) "Afternoon" means the period of a day between noon and midnight;

(3) "Banking day" means the part of a day on which a bank is open to the public for carrying on substantially all of its banking functions;

(4) "Clearing house" means an association of banks or other payors regularly clearing items;

(5) "Customer" means a person having an account with a bank or for whom a bank has agreed to collect items, including a bank that maintains an account at another bank;

(6) "Documentary draft" means a draft to be presented for acceptance or payment if specified documents, certificated securities (Section 8–102) or instructions for uncertificated securities (Section 8–102), or other certificates, statements, or the like are to be received by the drawee or other payor before acceptance or payment of the draft;

(7) "Draft" means a draft as defined in Section 3–104 or an item, other than an instrument, that is an order;

(8) "Drawee" means a person ordered in a draft to make payment;

(9) "Item" means an instrument or a promise or order to pay money handled by a bank for collection or payment. The term does not include a payment order governed by Article 4A or a credit or debit card slip;

(10) "Midnight deadline" with respect to a bank is midnight on its next banking day following the banking day on which it receives the relevant item or notice or from which the time for taking action commences to run, whichever is later;

(11) "Settle" means to pay in cash, by clearing-house settlement, in a charge or credit or by remittance, or otherwise as agreed. A settlement may be either provisional or final;

(12) "Suspends payments" with respect to a bank means that it has been closed by order of the supervisory authorities, that a public officer has been appointed to take it over, or that it ceases or refuses to make payments in the ordinary course of business.

(b) Other definitions applying to this Article and the sections in which they appear are:

"Agreement for electronic presentment"	Section 4–110.
"Bank"	Section 4–105.
"Collecting bank"	Section 4–105.
"Depositary bank"	Section 4–105.
"Intermediary bank"	Section 4–105.
"Payor bank"	Section 4–105.
"Presenting bank"	Section 4–105.
"Presentment notice"	Section 4–110.

(c) The following definitions in other Articles apply to this Article:

"Acceptance"	Section 3–409.
"Alteration"	Section 3–407.
"Cashier's check"	Section 3–104.
"Certificate of deposit"	Section 3–104.
"Certified check"	Section 3–409.
"Check"	Section 3–104.
"Good faith"	Section 3–103.
"Holder in due course"	Section 3–302.
"Instrument"	Section 3–104.
"Notice of dishonor"	Section 3–503.
"Order"	Section 3–103.
"Ordinary care"	Section 3–103.
"Person entitled to enforce"	Section 3–301.
"Presentment"	Section 3–501.
"Promise"	Section 3–103.
"Prove"	Section 3–103.
"Teller's check"	Section 3–104.
"Unauthorized signature"	Section 3–403.

(d) In addition, Article 1 contains general definitions and principles of construction and interpretation applicable throughout this Article.

As amended in 1990 and 1994.

See Appendices IX and XII for material relating to changes made in text in 1990 and 1994.

Official Comment

1. Paragraph (a)(1): "Account" is defined to include both asset accounts in which a customer has deposited money and accounts from which a customer may draw on a line of credit. The limiting factor is that the account must be in a bank.

2. Paragraph (a)(3): "Banking day." Under this definition that part of a business day when a bank is open only for limited functions, e.g., to receive deposits and cash checks, but with loan, bookkeeping and other departments closed, is not part of a banking day.

3. Paragraph (a)(4): "Clearing house." Occasionally express companies, governmental agencies and other nonbanks deal directly with a clearing house; hence the definition does not limit the term to an association of banks.

4. Paragraph (a)(5): "Customer." It is to be noted that this term includes a bank carrying an account with another bank as well as the more typical nonbank customer or depositor.

5. Paragraph (a)(6): "Documentary draft" applies even though the documents do not accompany the draft but are to be received by the drawee or other payor before acceptance or payment of the draft.

6. Paragraph (a)(7): "Draft" is defined in Section 3–104 as a form of instrument. Since Article 4 applies to items that may not fall within the definition of instrument, the term is defined here to include an item that is a written order to pay money, even though the item may not qualify as an instrument. The term "order" is defined in Section 3–103.

7. Paragraph (a)(8): "Drawee" is defined in Section 3–103 in terms of an Article 3 draft which is a form of instrument. Here "drawee" is defined in terms of an Article 4 draft which includes items that may not be instruments.

8. Paragraph (a)(9): "Item" is defined broadly to include an instrument, as defined in Section 3–104, as well as prom-

ises or orders that may not be within the definition of "instrument." The terms "promise" and "order" are defined in Section 3–103. A promise is a written undertaking to pay money. An order is a written instruction to pay money. But see Section 4–110(c). Since bonds and other investment securities under Article 8 may be within the term "instrument" or "promise," they are items and when handled by banks for collection are subject to this Article. See Comment 1 to Section 4–102. The functional limitation on the meaning of this term is the willingness of the banking system to handle the instrument, undertaking or instruction for collection or payment.

9. Paragraph (a)(10): "Midnight deadline." The use of this phrase is an example of the more mechanical approach used in this Article. Midnight is selected as a termination point or time limit to obtain greater uniformity and definiteness than would be possible from other possible terminating points, such as the close of the banking day or business day.

10. Paragraph (a)(11): The term "settle" has substantial importance throughout Article 4. In the American Bankers Association Bank Collection Code, in deferred posting statutes, in Federal Reserve regulations and operating circulars, in clearing-house rules, in agreements between banks and customers and in legends on deposit tickets and collection letters, there is repeated reference to "conditional" or "provisional" credits or payments. Tied in with this concept of creditors or payments being in some way tentative, has been a related but somewhat different problem as to when an item is "paid" or "finally paid" either to determine the relative priority of the item as against attachments, stop-payment orders and the like or in insolvency situations. There has been extensive litigation in the various states on these problems. To a substantial extent the confusion, the litigation and even the resulting court decisions fail to take into account that in the collection process some debits or credits are provisional or tentative and others are final and that very many debits or credits are provisional or tentative for awhile but later become final. Similarly, some cases fail to recognize that within a single bank, particularly a payor bank, each item goes through a series of processes and that in a payor bank most of these processes are preliminary to the basic act of payment or "final payment."

The term "settle" is used as a convenient term to characterize a broad variety of conditional, provisional, tentative and also final payments of items. Such a comprehensive term is needed because it is frequently difficult or unnecessary to determine whether a particular action is tentative or final or when a particular credit shifts from the tentative class to the final class. Therefore, its use throughout the Article indicates that in that particular context it is unnecessary or unwise to determine whether the debit or the credit or the payment is tentative or final. However, if qualified by the adjective "provisional" its tentative nature is intended, and if qualified by the adjective "final" its permanent nature is intended.

Examples of the various types of settlement contemplated by the term include payments in cash; the efficient but somewhat complicated process of payment through the adjustment and offsetting of balances through clearing houses; debit or credit entries in accounts between banks; the forwarding of various types of remittance instruments, sometimes to cover a particular item but more frequently to cover an entire group of items received on a particular day.

11. Paragraph (a)(12): "Suspends payments." This term is designed to afford an objective test to determine when a bank is no longer operating as a part of the banking system.

§ 4–105. "Bank"; "Depositary Bank"; "Payor Bank"; "Intermediary Bank"; "Collecting Bank"; "Presenting Bank".

In this Article:

(1) "Bank" means a person engaged in the business of banking, including a savings bank, savings and loan association, credit union, or trust company;

(2) "Depositary bank" means the first bank to take an item even though it is also the payor bank, unless the item is presented for immediate payment over the counter;

(3) "Payor bank" means a bank that is the drawee of a draft;

(4) "Intermediary bank" means a bank to which an item is transferred in course of collection except the depositary or payor bank;

(5) "Collecting bank" means a bank handling an item for collection except the payor bank;

(6) "Presenting bank" means a bank presenting an item except a payor bank.

As amended in 1990.

See Appendix IX for material relating to changes made in text in 1990.

Official Comment

1. The definitions in general exclude a bank to which an item is issued, as this bank does not take by transfer except in the particular case covered in which the item is issued to a payee for collection, as in the case in which a corporation is transferring balances from one account to another. Thus, the definition of "depositary bank" does not include the bank to which a check is made payable if a check is given in payment of a mortgage. This bank has the status of a payee under Article 3 on Negotiable Instruments and not that of a collecting bank.

2. Paragraph (1): "Bank" is defined in Section 1–201(4) as meaning "any person engaged in the business of banking." The definition in paragraph (1) makes clear that "bank" includes savings banks, savings and loan associations, credit unions and trust companies, in addition to the commercial banks commonly denoted by use of the term "bank."

3. Paragraph (2): A bank that takes an "on us" item for collection, for application to a customer's loan, or first handles the item for other reasons is a depositary bank even though it is also the payor bank. However, if the holder presents the item for immediate payment over the counter, the payor bank is not a depositary bank.

4. Paragraph (3): The definition of "payor bank" is clarified by use of the term "drawee." That term is defined in Section 4–104 as meaning "a person ordered in a draft to make payment." An "order" is defined in Section 3–103 as meaning "a written instruction to pay money.... An authorization to pay is not an order unless the person authorized to pay is also instructed to pay." The definition of order is incorporated into Article 4 by Section 4–104(c). Thus a payor bank is one instructed to pay in the item. A bank does not become a payor bank by being merely authorized to pay or by being given an instruction to pay not contained in the item.

5. Paragraph (4): The term "intermediary bank" includes the last bank in the collection process if the drawee is not a

bank. Usually the last bank is also a presenting bank.

§ 4–106. Payable Through or Payable at Bank: Collecting Bank.

(a) If an item states that it is "payable through" a bank identified in the item, (i) the item designates the bank as a collecting bank and does not by itself authorize the bank to pay the item, and (ii) the item may be presented for payment only by or through the bank.

ALTERNATIVE A

(b) If an item states that it is "payable at" a bank identified in the item, the item is equivalent to a draft drawn on the bank.

ALTERNATIVE B

(b) If an item states that it is "payable at" a bank identified in the item, (i) the item designates the bank as a collecting bank and does not by itself authorize the bank to pay the item, and (ii) the item may be presented for payment only by or through the bank.

(c) If a draft names a nonbank drawee and it is unclear whether a bank named in the draft is a co-drawee or a collecting bank, the bank is a collecting bank.

As added in 1990.

See Appendix IX for material relating to adoption of section in 1990.

Official Comment

1. This section replaces former Sections 3–120 and 3–121. Some items are made "payable through" a particular bank. Subsection (a) states that such language makes the bank a collecting bank and not a payor bank. An item identifying a "payable through" bank can be presented for payment to the drawee only by the "payable through" bank. The item cannot be presented to the drawee over the counter for immediate payment or by a collecting bank other than the "payable through" bank.

2. Subsection (b) retains the alternative approach of the present law. Under Alternative A a note payable at a bank is the equivalent of a draft drawn on the bank and the midnight deadline provisions of Sections 4–301 and 4–302 apply. Under Alternative B a "payable at" bank is in the same position as a "payable through" bank under subsection (a).

3. Subsection (c) rejects the view of some cases that a bank named below the name of a drawee is itself a drawee. The commercial understanding is that this bank is a collecting bank and is not accountable under Section 4–302 for holding an item beyond its deadline. The liability of the bank is governed by Sections 4–202(a) and 4–103(e).

§ 4–107. Separate Office of Bank.

A branch or separate office of a bank is a separate bank for the purpose of computing the time within which and determining the place at or to which action may be taken or notices or orders shall be given under this Article and under Article 3.

As amended in 1962 and 1990.

See Appendix IX for material relating to changes made in text in 1990.

Official Comment

1. A rule with respect to the status of a branch or separate office of a bank as a part of any statute on bank collections is highly desirable if not absolutely necessary. However, practices in the operations of branches and separate offices vary substantially in the different states and it has not been possible to find any single rule that is logically correct, fair in all situations and workable under all different types of practices. The decision not to draft the section with greater specificity leaves to the courts the resolution of the issues arising under this section on the basis of the facts of each case.

2. In many states and for many purposes a branch or separate office of the bank should be treated as a separate bank. Many branches function as separate banks in the handling and payment of items and require time for doing so similar to that of a separate bank. This is particularly true if branch banking is permitted throughout a state or in different towns and cities. Similarly, if there is this separate functioning a particular branch or separate office is the only proper place for various types of action to be taken or orders or notices to be given. Examples include the drawing of a check on a particular branch by a customer whose account is carried at that branch; the presentment of that same check at that branch; the issuance of an order to the branch to stop payment on the check.

3. Section 1 of the American Bankers Association Bank Collection Code provided simply: "A branch or office of any such bank shall be deemed a bank." Although this rule appears to be brief and simple, as applied to particular sections of the ABA Code it produces illogical and, in some cases, unreasonable results. For example, under Section 11 of the ABA Code it seems anomalous for one branch of a bank to have charged an item to the account of the drawer and another branch to have the power to elect to treat the item as dishonored. Similar logical problems would flow from applying the same rule to Article 4. Warranties by one branch to another branch under Sections 4–207 and 4–208 (each considered a separate bank) do not make sense.

4. Assuming that it is not desirable to make each branch a separate bank for all purposes, this section provides that a branch or separate office is a separate bank for certain purposes. In so doing the single legal entity of the bank as a whole is preserved, thereby carrying with it the liability of the institution as a whole on such obligations as it may be under. On the other hand, in cases in which the Article provides a number of time limits for different types of action by banks, if a branch functions as a separate bank, it should have the time limits available to a separate bank. Similarly if in its relations to customers a branch functions as a separate bank, notices and orders with respect to accounts of customers of the branch should be given at the branch. For example, whether a branch has notice sufficient to affect its status as a holder in due course of an item taken by it should depend upon what notice that branch has received with respect to the item. Similarly the receipt of a stop-payment order at one branch should not be notice to another branch so as to impair the right of the second branch to be a holder in due course of the item, although in circumstances in which ordinary care requires the communication of a notice or order to the proper branch of a bank, the notice or order would be effective at the proper branch from the time it was or should have been received. See Section 1–201(27).

5. The bracketed language ("maintaining its own deposit ledger") in former Section 4–106 is deleted. Today banks

keep records on customer accounts by electronic data storage. This has led most banks with branches to centralize to some degree their record keeping. The place where records are kept has little meaning if the information is electronically stored and is instantly retrievable at all branches of the bank. Hence, the inference to be drawn from the deletion of the bracketed language is that where record keeping is done is no longer an important factor in determining whether a branch is a separate bank.

§ 4–108. Time of Receipt of Items.

(a) For the purpose of allowing time to process items, prove balances, and make the necessary entries on its books to determine its position for the day, a bank may fix an afternoon hour of 2 P.M. or later as a cutoff hour for the handling of money and items and the making of entries on its books.

(b) An item or deposit of money received on any day after a cutoff hour so fixed or after the close of the banking day may be treated as being received at the opening of the next banking day.

As amended in 1990.

See Appendix IX for material relating to changes made in text in 1990.

Official Comment

1. Each of the huge volume of checks processed each day must go through a series of accounting procedures that consume time. Many banks have found it necessary to establish a cutoff hour to allow time for these procedures to be completed within the time limits imposed by Article 4. Subsection (a) approves a cutoff hour of this type provided it is not earlier than 2 P.M. Subsection (b) provides that if such a cutoff hour is fixed, items received after the cutoff hour may be treated as being received at the opening of the next banking day. If the number of items received either through the mail or over the counter tends to taper off radically as the afternoon hours progress, a 2 P.M. cutoff hour does not involve a large portion of the items received but at the same time permits a bank using such a cutoff hour to leave its doors open later in the afternoon without forcing into the evening the completion of its settling and proving process.

2. The provision in subsection (b) that items or deposits received after the close of the banking day may be treated as received at the opening of the next banking day is important in cases in which a bank closes at twelve or one o'clock, e.g., on a Saturday, but continues to receive some items by mail or over the counter if, for example, it opens Saturday evening for the limited purpose of receiving deposits and cashing checks.

§ 4–109. Delays.

(a) Unless otherwise instructed, a collecting bank in a good faith effort to secure payment of a specific item drawn on a payor other than a bank, and with or without the approval of any person involved, may waive, modify, or extend time limits imposed or permitted by this [Act] for a period not exceeding two additional banking days without discharge of drawers or indorsers or liability to its transferor or a prior party.

(b) Delay by a collecting bank or payor bank beyond time limits prescribed or permitted by this [Act] or by instructions is excused if (i) the delay is caused by interruption of communication or computer facilities, suspension of payments by another bank, war, emergency conditions, failure of equipment, or other circumstances beyond the control of the bank, and (ii) the bank exercises such diligence as the circumstances require.

As amended in 1990.

See Appendix IX for material relating to changes made in text in 1990.

Official Comment

1. Sections 4–202(b), 4–214, 4–301, and 4–302 prescribe various time limits for the handling of items. These are the limits of time within which a bank, in fulfillment of its obligation to exercise ordinary care, must handle items entrusted to it for collection or payment. Under Section 4–103 they may be varied by agreement or by Federal Reserve regulations or operating circular, clearing-house rules, or the like. Subsection (a) permits a very limited extension of these time limits. It authorizes a collecting bank to take additional time in attempting to collect drafts drawn on nonbank payors with or without the approval of any interested party. The right of a collecting bank to waive time limits under subsection (a) does not apply to checks. The two-day extension can only be granted in a good faith effort to secure payment and only with respect to specific items. It cannot be exercised if the customer instructs otherwise. Thus limited the escape provision should afford a limited degree of flexibility in special cases but should not interfere with the overall requirement and objective of speedy collections.

2. An extension granted under subsection (a) is without discharge of drawers or indorsers. It therefore extends the times for presentment or payment as specified in Article 3.

3. Subsection (b) is another escape clause from time limits. This clause operates not only with respect to time limits imposed by the Article itself but also time limits imposed by special instructions, by agreement or by Federal regulations or operating circulars, clearing-house rules or the like. The latter time limits are "permitted" by the Code. For example, a payor bank that fails to make timely return of a dishonored item may be accountable for the amount of the item. Subsection (b) excuses a bank from this liability when its failure to meet its midnight deadline resulted from, for example, a computer breakdown that was beyond the control of the bank, so long as the bank exercised the degree of diligence that the circumstances required. In Port City State Bank v. American National Bank, 486 F.2d 196 (10th Cir.1973), the court held that a bank exercised sufficient diligence to be excused under this subsection. If delay is sought to be excused under this subsection, the bank has the burden of proof on the issue of whether it exercised "such diligence as the circumstances require." The subsection is consistent with Regulation CC, Section 229.38(e).

§ 4-110. Electronic Presentment.

(a) "Agreement for electronic presentment" means an agreement, clearing-house rule, or Federal Reserve regulation or operating circular, providing that presentment of an item may be made by transmission of an image of an item or information describing the item ("presentment notice") rather than delivery of the item itself. The agreement may provide for procedures governing retention, presentment, payment, dishonor, and other matters concerning items subject to the agreement.

(b) Presentment of an item pursuant to an agreement for presentment is made when the presentment notice is received.

(c) If presentment is made by presentment notice, a reference to "item" or "check" in this Article means the presentment notice unless the context otherwise indicates.

As added in 1990.

See Appendix IX for material relating to adoption of section in 1990.

Official Comment

1. "An agreement for electronic presentment" refers to an agreement under which presentment may be made to a payor bank by a presentment notice rather than by presentment of the item. Under imaging technology now under development, the presentment notice might be an image of the item. The electronic presentment agreement may provide that the item may be retained by a depositary bank, other collecting bank, or even a customer of the depositary bank, or it may provide that the item will follow the presentment notice. The identifying characteristic of an electronic presentment agreement is that presentment occurs when the presentment notice is received. "An agreement for electronic presentment" does not refer to the common case of retention of items by payor banks because the item itself is presented to the payor bank in these cases. Payor bank check retention is a matter of agreement between payor banks and their customers. Provisions on payor bank check retention are found in Section 4–406(b).

2. The assumptions under which the electronic presentment amendments are based are as follows: No bank will participate in an electronic presentment program without an agreement. These agreements may be either bilateral (Section 4–103(a)), under which two banks that frequently do business with each other may agree to depositary bank check retention, or multilateral (Section 4–103(b)), in which large segments of the banking industry may participate in such a program. In the latter case, federal or other uniform regulatory standards would likely supply the substance of the electronic presentment agreement, the application of which could be triggered by the use of some form of identifier on the item. Regulation CC, Section 229.36(c) authorizes truncation agreements but forbids them from extending return times or otherwise varying requirements of the part of Regulation CC governing check collection without the agreement of all parties interested in the check. For instance, an extension of return time could damage a depositary bank which must make funds available to its customers under mandatory availability schedules. The Expedited Funds Availability Act, 12 U.S.C. Section 4008(b)(2), directs the Federal Reserve Board to consider requiring that banks provide for check truncation.

3. The parties affected by an agreement for electronic presentment, with the exception of the customer, can be expected to protect themselves. For example, the payor bank can probably be expected to limit its risk of loss from drawer forgery by limiting the dollar amount of eligible items (Federal Reserve program), by reconcilement agreements (ABA Safekeeping program), by insurance (credit union share draft program), or by other means. Because agreements will exist, only minimal amendments are needed to make clear that the UCC does not prohibit electronic presentment.

§ 4–111. Statute of Limitations.

An action to enforce an obligation, duty, or right arising under this Article must be commenced within three years after the [cause of action] accrues.

As added in 1990.

See Appendix IX for material relating to adoption of section in 1990.

Official Comment

This section conforms to the period of limitations set by Section 3-118(g) for actions for breach of warranty and to enforce other obligations, duties or rights arising under Article 3. Bracketing "cause of action" recognizes that some states use a different term, such as "claim for relief."

PART 2

COLLECTION OF ITEMS: DEPOSITARY AND COLLECTING BANKS

§ 4-201. Status of Collecting Bank as Agent and Provisional Status of Credits; Applicability of Article; Item Indorsed "Pay Any Bank".

(a) Unless a contrary intent clearly appears and before the time that a settlement given by a collecting bank for an item is or becomes final, the bank, with respect to an item, is an agent or sub-agent of the owner of the item and any settlement given for the item is provisional. This provision applies regardless of the form of indorsement or lack of indorsement and even though credit given for the item is subject to immediate withdrawal as of right or is in fact withdrawn; but the continuance of ownership of an item by its owner and any rights of the owner to proceeds of the item are subject to rights of a collecting bank, such as those resulting from outstanding advances on the item and rights of recoupment or setoff. If an item is handled by banks for purposes of presentment, payment, collection, or return, the relevant provisions of this Article apply even though action of the parties clearly establishes that a particular bank has purchased the item and is the owner of it.

(b) After an item has been indorsed with the words "pay any bank" or the like, only a bank may acquire the rights of a holder until the item has been:

(1) returned to the customer initiating collection; or

(2) specially indorsed by a bank to a person who is not a bank.

As amended in 1990.

See Appendix IX for material relating to changes made in text in 1990.

Official Comment

1. This section states certain basic rules of the bank collection process. One basic rule, appearing in the last sentence of subsection (a), is that, to the extent applicable, the provisions of the Article govern without regard to whether a bank handling an item owns the item or is an agent for collection. Historically, much time has been spent and effort expended in determining or attempting to determine whether a bank was a purchaser of an item or merely an agent for collection.

See discussion of this subject and cases cited in 11 A.L.R. 1043, 16 A.L.R. 1084, 42 A.L.R. 492, 68 A.L.R. 725, 99 A.L.R. 486. See also Section 4 of the American Bankers Association Bank Collection Code. The general approach of Article 4, similar to that of other articles, is to provide, within reasonable limits, rules or answers to major problems known to exist in the bank collection process without regard to questions of status and ownership but to keep general principles such as status and ownership available to cover residual areas not covered by specific rules. In line with this approach, the last sentence of subsection (a) says in effect that Article 4 applies to practically every item moving through banks for the purpose of presentment, payment or collection.

2. Within this general rule of broad coverage, the first two sentences of subsection (a) state a rule of agency status. "Unless a contrary intent clearly appears" the status of a collecting bank is that of an agent or sub-agent for the owner of the item. Although as indicated in Comment 1 it is much less important under Article 4 to determine status than has been the case heretofore, status may have importance in some residual areas not covered by specific rules. Further, since status has been considered so important in the past, to omit all reference to it might cause confusion. The status of agency "applies regardless of the form of indorsement or lack of indorsement and even though credit given for the item is subject to immediate withdrawal as of right or is in fact withdrawn." Thus questions heretofore litigated as to whether ordinary indorsements "for deposit," "for collection" or in blank have the effect of creating an agency status or a purchase, no longer have significance in varying the prima facie rule of agency. Similarly, the nature of the credit given for an item or whether it is subject to immediate withdrawal as of right or is in fact withdrawn, does not alter the agency status. See A.L.R. references supra in Comment 1.

A contrary intent can change agency status but this must be clear. An example of a clear contrary intent would be if collateral papers established or the item bore a legend stating that the item was sold absolutely to the depositary bank.

3. The prima facie agency status of collecting banks is consistent with prevailing law and practice today. Section 2 of the American Bankers Association Bank Collection Code so provided. Legends on deposit tickets, collection letters and acknowledgments of items and Federal Reserve operating circulars consistently so provide. The status is consistent with rights of charge-back (Section 4–214 and Section 11 of the ABA Code) and risk of loss in the event of insolvency (Section 4–216 and Section 13 of the ABA Code). The right of charge-back with respect to checks is limited by Regulation CC, Section 226.36(d).

4. Affirmative statement of a prima facie agency status for collecting banks requires certain limitations and qualifications. Under current practices substantially all bank collections sooner or later merge into bank credits, at least if collection is effected. Usually, this takes place within a few days of the initiation of collection. An intermediary bank receives final collection and evidences the result of its collection by a "credit" on its books to the depositary bank. The depositary bank evidences the results of its collection by a "credit" in the account of its customer. As used in these instances the term "credit" clearly indicates a debtor-creditor relationship. At some stage in the bank collection process the agency status of a collecting bank changes to that of debtor, a debtor of its customer. Usually at about the same time it also becomes a creditor for the amount of the item, a creditor of some intermediary, payor or other bank. Thus the collection is completed, all agency aspects are terminated and the identity of the item has become completely merged in bank accounts, that of the customer with the depositary bank and that of one bank with another.

Although Section 4-215(a) provides that an item is finally paid when the payor bank takes or fails to take certain action with respect to the item, the final payment of the item may or may not result in the simultaneous final settlement for the item in the case of all prior parties. If a series of provisional debits and credits for the item have been entered in accounts between banks, the final payment of the item by the payor bank may result in the automatic firming up of all these provisional debits and credits under Section 4-215(c), and the consequent receipt of final settlement for the item by each collecting bank and the customer of the depositary bank simultaneously with such action of the payor bank. However, if the payor bank or some intermediary bank accounts for the item with a remittance draft, the next prior bank usually does not receive final settlement for the item until the remittance draft finally clears. See Section 4-213(c). The first sentence of subsection (a) provides that the agency status of a collecting bank (whether intermediary or depositary) continues until the settlement given by it for the item is or becomes final. In the case of the series of provisional credits covered by Section 4-215(c), this could be simultaneously with the final payment of the item by the payor bank. In cases in which remittance drafts are used or in straight noncash collections, this would not be until the times specified in Sections 4-213(c) and 4-215(d). With respect to checks Regulation CC Sections 229.31(c), 229.32(b) and 229.36(d) provide that all settlements between banks are final in both the forward collection and return of checks.

Under Section 4-213(a) settlements for items may be made by any means agreed to by the parties. Since it is impossible to contemplate all the kinds of settlements that will be utilized, no attempt is made in Article 4 to provide when settlement is final in all cases. The guiding principle is that settlements should be final when the presenting person has received usable funds. Section 4-213(c) and (d) and Section 4-215(c) provide when final settlement occurs with respect to certain kinds of settlement, but these provisions are not intended to be exclusive.

A number of practical results flow from the rule continuing the agency status of a collecting bank until its settlement for the item is or becomes final, some of which are specifically set forth in this Article. One is that risk of loss continues in the owner of the item rather than the agent bank. See Section 4-214. Offsetting rights favorable to the owner are that pending such final settlement, the owner has the preference rights of Section 4-216 and the direct rights of Section 4-302 against the payor bank. It also follows from this rule that the dollar limitations of Federal Deposit Insurance are measured by the claim of the owner of the item rather than that of the collecting bank. With respect to checks, rights of the parties in insolvency are determined by Regulation CC Section 229.39 and the liability of a bank handling a check to a subsequent bank that does not receive payment because of suspension of payments by another bank is stated in Regulation CC Section 229.35(b).

5. In those cases in which some period of time elapses between the final payment of the item by the payor bank and the time that the settlement of the collecting bank is or becomes final, e.g., if the payor bank or an intermediary bank accounts for the item with a remittance draft or in straight noncash collections, the continuance of the agency status of the collecting bank necessarily carries with it the continuance of the owner's status as principal. The second sentence of subsection (a) provides that whatever rights the owner has to proceeds of the item are subject to the rights of collecting banks for outstanding advances on the item and other valid rights, if any. The rule provides a sound rule to govern cases of attempted attachment of proceeds of a non-cash item in the hands of the payor bank as property of the absent owner. If a collecting bank has made an advance on an item which is still outstanding, its right to obtain reimbursement for this

advance should be superior to the rights of the owner to the proceeds or to the rights of a creditor of the owner. An intentional crediting of proceeds of an item to the account of a prior bank known to be insolvent, for the purpose of acquiring a right of setoff, would not produce a valid setoff. See 8 Zollman, Banks and Banking (1936) Sec. 5443.

6. This section and Article 4 as a whole represent an intentional abandonment of the approach to bank collection problems appearing in Section 4 of the American Bankers Association Bank Collection Code. Because the tremendous volume of items handled makes impossible the examination by all banks of all indorsements on all items and thus in fact this examination is not made, except perhaps by depositary banks, it is unrealistic to base the rights and duties of all banks in the collection chain on variations in the form of indorsements. It is anomalous to provide throughout the ABA Code that the prima facie status of collecting banks is that of agent or sub-agent but in Section 4 to provide that subsequent holders (sub-agents) shall have the right to rely on the presumption that the bank of deposit (the primary agent) is the owner of the item. It is unrealistic, particularly in this background, to base rights and duties on status of agent or owner. Thus Section 4–201 makes the pertinent provisions of Article 4 applicable to substantially all items handled by banks for presentment, payment or collection, recognizes the prima facie status of most banks as agents, and then seeks to state appropriate limits and some attributes to the general rules so expressed.

7. Subsection (b) protects the ownership rights with respect to an item indorsed "pay any bank or banker" or in similar terms of a customer initiating collection or of any bank acquiring a security interest under Section 4–210, in the event the item is subsequently acquired under improper circumstances by a person who is not a bank and transferred by that person to another person, whether or not a bank. Upon return to the customer initiating collection of an item so indorsed, the indorsement may be cancelled (Section 3–207). A bank holding an item so indorsed may transfer the item out of banking channels by special indorsement; however, under Section 4–103(e), the bank would be liable to the owner of the item for any loss resulting therefrom if the transfer had been made in bad faith or with lack of ordinary care. If briefer and more simple forms of bank indorsements are developed under Section 4–206 (e.g., the use of bank transit numbers in lieu of present lengthy forms of bank indorsements), a depositary bank having the transit number "X100" could make subsection (b) operative by indorsements such as "Pay any bank—X100." Regulation CC Section 229.35(c) states the effect of an indorsement on a check by a bank.

§ 4–202. Responsibility for Collection or Return; When Action Timely.

(a) A collecting bank must exercise ordinary care in:

(1) presenting an item or sending it for presentment;

(2) sending notice of dishonor or nonpayment or returning an item other than a documentary draft to the bank's transferor after learning that the item has not been paid or accepted, as the case may be;

(3) settling for an item when the bank receives final settlement; and

(4) notifying its transferor of any loss or delay in transit within a reasonable time after discovery thereof.

(b) A collecting bank exercises ordinary care under subsection (a) by taking proper action before its midnight deadline following receipt of an item, notice, or settlement. Taking proper action within a reasonably longer time may constitute the exercise of ordinary care, but the bank has the burden of establishing timeliness.

(c) Subject to subsection (a)(1), a bank is not liable for the insolvency, neglect, misconduct, mistake, or default of another bank or person or for loss or destruction of an item in the possession of others or in transit.

As amended in 1990.

See Appendix IX for material relating to changes made in text in 1990.

Official Comment

1. Subsection (a) states the basic responsibilities of a collecting bank. Of course, under Section 1-203 a collecting bank is subject to the standard requirement of good faith. By subsection (a) it must also use ordinary care in the exercise of its basic collection tasks. By Section 4-103(a) neither requirement may be disclaimed.

2. If the bank makes presentment itself, subsection (a)(1) requires ordinary care with respect both to the time and manner of presentment. (Sections 3-501 and 4-212.) If it forwards the item to be presented the subsection requires ordinary care with respect to routing (Section 4-204), and also in the selection of intermediary banks or other agents.

3. Subsection (a) describes types of basic action with respect to which a collecting bank must use ordinary care. Subsection (b) deals with the time for taking action. It first prescribes the general standard for timely action, namely, for items received on Monday, proper action (such as forwarding or presenting) on Monday or Tuesday is timely. Although under current "production line" operations banks customarily move items along on regular schedules substantially briefer than two days, the subsection states an outside time within which a bank may know it has taken timely action. To provide flexibility from this standard norm, the subsection further states that action within a reasonably longer time may be timely but the bank has the burden of proof. In the case of time items, action after the midnight deadline, but sufficiently in advance of maturity for proper presentation, is a clear example of a "reasonably longer time" that is timely. The standard of requiring action not later than Tuesday in the case of Monday items is also subject to possibilities of variation under the general provisions of Section 4-103, or under the special provisions regarding time of receipt of items (Section 4-108), and regarding delays (Section 4-109). This subsection (b) deals only with collecting banks. The time limits applicable to payor banks appear in Sections 4-301 and 4-302.

4. At common law the so-called New York collection rule subjected the initial collecting bank to liability for the actions of subsequent banks in the collection chain; the so-called Massachusetts rule was that each bank, subject to the duty of selecting proper intermediaries, was liable only for its own negligence. Subsection (c) adopts the Massachusetts rule. But since this is stated to be subject to subsection (a)(1) a collecting bank remains responsible for using ordinary care in selecting properly qualified intermediary banks and agents and in giving proper instructions to them. Regulation CC Section 229.36(d) states the liability of a bank during the forward collection of checks.

§ 4-203. Effect of Instructions.

Subject to Article 3 concerning conversion of instruments (Section 3-420) and restrictive indorsements (Section 3-206), only a collecting bank's transferor can give instructions that affect the bank or constitute notice to it, and a collecting bank is not liable to prior parties for any action taken pursuant to the instructions or in accordance with any agreement with its transferor.

As amended in 1990.

See Appendix IX for material relating to changes made in text in 1990.

Official Comment

This section adopts a "chain of command" theory which renders it unnecessary for an intermediary or collecting bank to determine whether its transferor is "authorized" to give the instructions. Equally the bank is not put on notice of any "revocation of authority" or "lack of authority" by notice received from any other person. The desirability of speed in the collection process and the fact that, by reason of advances made, the transferor may have the paramount interest in the item requires the rule.

The section is made subject to the provisions of Article 3 concerning conversion of instruments (Section 3–420) and restrictive indorsements (Section 3–206). Of course instructions from or an agreement with its transferor does not relieve a collecting bank of its general obligation to exercise good faith and ordinary care. See Section 4–103(a). If in any particular case a bank has exercised good faith and ordinary care and is relieved of responsibility by reason of instructions of or an agreement with its transferor, the owner of the item may still have a remedy for loss against the transferor (another bank) if such transferor has given wrongful instructions.

The rules of the section are applied only to collecting banks. Payor banks always have the problem of making proper payment of an item; whether such payment is proper should be based upon all of the rules of Articles 3 and 4 and all of the facts of any particular case, and should not be dependent exclusively upon instructions from or an agreement with a person presenting the item.

§ 4–204. Methods of Sending and Presenting; Sending Directly to Payor Bank.

(a) A collecting bank shall send items by a reasonably prompt method, taking into consideration relevant instructions, the nature of the item, the number of those items on hand, the cost of collection involved, and the method generally used by it or others to present those items.

(b) A collecting bank may send:

(1) an item directly to the payor bank;

(2) an item to a nonbank payor if authorized by its transferor; and

(3) an item other than documentary drafts to a nonbank payor, if authorized by Federal Reserve regulation or operating circular, clearing-house rule, or the like.

(c) Presentment may be made by a presenting bank at a place where the payor bank or other payor has requested that presentment be made.

As amended in 1962 and 1990.

See Appendix IX for material relating to changes made in text in 1990.

Official Comment

1. Subsection (a) prescribes the general standards applicable to proper sending or forwarding of items. Because of the many types of methods available and the desirability of preserving flexibility any attempt to prescribe limited or precise methods is avoided.

2. Subsection (b)(1) codifies the practice of direct mail, express, messenger or like presentment to payor banks. The practice is now country-wide and is justified by the need for speed, the general responsibility of banks, Federal Deposit Insurance protection and other reasons.

3. Full approval of the practice of direct sending is limited to cases in which a bank is a payor. Since nonbank drawees or payors may be of unknown responsibility, substantial risks may be attached to placing in their hands the instruments calling for payments from them. This is obviously so in the case of documentary drafts. However, in some cities practices have long existed under clearing-house procedures to forward certain types of items to certain nonbank payors. Examples include insurance loss drafts drawn by field agents on home offices. For the purpose of leaving the door open to legitimate practices of this kind, subsection (b)(3) affirmatively approves direct sending of any item other than documentary drafts to any nonbank payor, if authorized by Federal Reserve regulation or operating circular, clearing-house rule or the like.

On the other hand subsection (b)(2) approves sending any item directly to a nonbank payor if authorized by a collecting bank's transferor. This permits special instructions or agreements out of the norm and is consistent with the "chain of command" theory of Section 4–203. However, if a transferor other than the owner of the item, e.g., a prior collecting bank, authorizes a direct sending to a nonbank payor, such transferor assumes responsibility for the propriety or impropriety of such authorization.

4. Section 3–501(b) provides where presentment may be made. This provision is expressly subject to Article 4. Section 4–204(c) specifically approves presentment by a presenting bank at any place requested by the payor bank or other payor. The time when a check is received by a payor bank for presentment is governed by Regulation CC Section 229.36(b).

§ 4–205. Depositary Bank Holder of Unindorsed Item.

If a customer delivers an item to a depositary bank for collection:

(1) the depositary bank becomes a holder of the item at the time it receives the item for collection if the customer at the time of delivery was a holder of the item, whether or not the customer indorses the item, and, if the bank satisfies the other requirements of Section 3–302, it is a holder in due course; and

(2) the depositary bank warrants to collecting banks, the payor bank or other payor, and the drawer that the amount of the item was paid to the customer or deposited to the customer's account.

As amended in 1990.

See Appendix IX for material relating to changes made in text in 1990.

Official Comment

Section 3–201(b) provides that negotiation of an instrument payable to order requires indorsement by the holder. The rule of former Section 4–205(1) was that the depositary bank may supply a missing indorsement of its customer unless the item contains the words "payee's indorsement required" or the like. The cases have differed on the status of the depositary bank as a holder if it fails to supply its customer's indorsement. Marine Midland Bank, N.A. v. Price, Miller, Evans & Flowers, 446 N.Y.S.2d 797 (N.Y.App.Div. 4th Dept.1981), *rev'd,* 455 N.Y.S.2d 565 (N.Y.1982). It is common practice for depositary banks to receive unindorsed checks under so-called "lock-box" agreements from customers who receive a high volume of checks. No function would be served by requiring a depositary bank to run these items through a machine that would supply the customer's indorsement except to afford the drawer and the subsequent banks evidence that the proceeds of the item reached the customer's account. Paragraph (1) provides that the depositary bank becomes a holder when it takes the item for deposit if the depositor is a holder. Whether it supplies the customer's indorsement is immaterial. Paragraph (2) satisfies the need for a receipt of funds by the depositary bank by imposing on that bank a warranty that it paid the customer or deposited the item to the customer's account. This warranty runs not only to collecting banks and to the payor bank or nonbank drawee but also to the drawer, affording protection to these parties that the depositary bank received the item and applied it to the benefit of the holder.

§ 4–206. Transfer Between Banks.

Any agreed method that identifies the transferor bank is sufficient for the item's further transfer to another bank.

As amended in 1990.

See Appendix IX for material relating to changes made in text in 1990.

Official Comment

This section is designed to permit the simplest possible form of transfer from one bank to another, once an item gets in the bank collection chain, provided only identity of the transferor bank is preserved. This is important for tracing purposes and if recourse is necessary. However, since the responsibilities of the various banks appear in the Article it becomes unnecessary to have liability or responsibility depend on more formal indorsements. Simplicity in the form of transfer is conducive to speed. If the transfer is between banks, this section takes the place of the more formal requirements of Section 3–201.

§ 4–207. Transfer Warranties.

(a) A customer or collecting bank that transfers an item and receives a settlement or other consideration warrants to the transferee and to any subsequent collecting bank that:

(1) the warrantor is a person entitled to enforce the item;

(2) all signatures on the item are authentic and authorized;

(3) the item has not been altered;

(4) the item is not subject to a defense or claim in recoupment (Section 3–305(a)) of any party that can be asserted against the warrantor; and

(5) the warrantor has no knowledge of any insolvency proceeding commenced with respect to the maker or acceptor or, in the case of an unaccepted draft, the drawer.

(b) If an item is dishonored, a customer or collecting bank transferring the item and receiving settlement or other consideration is obliged to pay the amount due on the item (i) according to the terms of the item at the time it was transferred, or (ii) if the transfer was of an incomplete item, according to its terms when completed as stated in Sections 3–115 and 3–407. The obligation of a transferor is owed to the transferee and to any subsequent collecting bank that takes the item in good faith. A transferor cannot disclaim its obligation under this subsection by an indorsement stating that it is made "without recourse" or otherwise disclaiming liability.

(c) A person to whom the warranties under subsection (a) are made and who took the item in good faith may recover from the warrantor as damages for breach of warranty an amount equal to the loss suffered as a result of the breach, but not more than the amount of the item plus expenses and loss of interest incurred as a result of the breach.

(d) The warranties stated in subsection (a) cannot be disclaimed with respect to checks. Unless notice of a claim for breach of warranty is given to the warrantor within 30 days after the claimant has reason to know of the breach and the identity of the warrantor, the warrantor is discharged to the extent of any loss caused by the delay in giving notice of the claim.

(e) A cause of action for breach of warranty under this section accrues when the claimant has reason to know of the breach.

As added in 1990.

See Appendix IX for material relating to adoption of section in 1990.

Official Comment

Except for subsection (b), this section conforms to Section 3–416 and extends its coverage to items. The substance of this section is discussed in the Comment to Section 3–416. Subsection (b) provides that customers or collecting banks that transfer items, whether by indorsement or not, undertake to pay the item if the item is dishonored. This obligation cannot be disclaimed by a "without recourse" indorsement or otherwise. With respect to checks, Regulation CC Section 229.34 states the warranties made by paying and returning banks.

§ 4–208. Presentment Warranties.

(a) If an unaccepted draft is presented to the drawee for payment or acceptance and the drawee pays or accepts the draft, (i) the person obtaining payment or acceptance, at the time of presentment, and (ii) a previous transferor of the draft, at the time of transfer, warrant to the drawee that pays or accepts the draft in good faith that:

(1) the warrantor is, or was, at the time the warrantor transferred the draft, a person entitled to enforce the draft or authorized to obtain payment or acceptance of the draft on behalf of a person entitled to enforce the draft;

(2) the draft has not been altered; and

(3) the warrantor has no knowledge that the signature of the purported drawer of the draft is unauthorized.

(b) A drawee making payment may recover from a warrantor damages for breach of warranty equal to the amount paid by the drawee less the amount the drawee received or is entitled to receive from the drawer because of the payment. In addition, the drawee is entitled to compensation for expenses and loss of interest resulting from the breach. The right of the drawee to recover damages under this subsection is not affected by any failure of the drawee to exercise ordinary care in making payment. If the drawee accepts the draft (i) breach of warranty is a defense to the obligation of the acceptor, and (ii) if the acceptor makes payment with respect to the draft, the acceptor is entitled to recover from a warrantor for breach of warranty the amounts stated in this subsection.

(c) If a drawee asserts a claim for breach of warranty under subsection (a) based on an unauthorized indorsement of the draft or an alteration of the draft, the warrantor may defend by proving that the indorsement is effective under Section 3-404 or 3-405 or the drawer is precluded under Section 3-406 or 4-406 from asserting against the drawee the unauthorized indorsement or alteration.

(d) If (i) a dishonored draft is presented for payment to the drawer or an indorser or (ii) any other item is presented for payment to a party obliged to pay the item, and the item is paid, the person obtaining payment and a prior transferor of the item warrant to the person making payment in good faith that the warrantor is, or was, at the time the warrantor transferred the item, a person entitled to enforce the item or authorized to obtain payment on behalf of a person entitled to enforce the item. The person making payment may recover from any warrantor for breach of warranty an amount equal to the amount paid plus expenses and loss of interest resulting from the breach.

(e) The warranties stated in subsections (a) and (d) cannot be disclaimed with respect to checks. Unless notice of a claim for breach of warranty is given to the warrantor within 30 days after the claimant has reason to know of the breach and the identity of the warrantor, the warrantor is discharged to the extent of any loss caused by the delay in giving notice of the claim.

(f) A cause of action for breach of warranty under this section accrues when the claimant has reason to know of the breach.

As added in 1990.

See Appendix IX for material relating to adoption of section in 1990.

Official Comment

This section conforms to Section 3-417 and extends its coverage to items. The substance of this section is discussed in the Comment to Section 3-417. "Draft" is defined in Section 4-104 as including an item that is an order to pay so as to make clear that the term "draft" in Article 4 may include items that are not instruments within Section 3-104.

§ 4-209. Encoding and Retention Warranties.

(a) A person who encodes information on or with respect to an item after issue warrants to any subsequent collecting bank and to the payor bank or other payor that the information is correctly encoded. If the customer of a depositary bank encodes, that bank also makes the warranty.

(b) A person who undertakes to retain an item pursuant to an agreement for electronic presentment warrants to any subsequent collecting bank and to the payor bank or other payor that retention and presentment of the item comply with the agreement. If a customer of a depositary bank undertakes to retain an item, that bank also makes this warranty.

(c) A person to whom warranties are made under this section and who took the item in good faith may recover from the warrantor as damages for breach of warranty an amount equal to the loss suffered as a result of the breach, plus expenses and loss of interest incurred as a result of the breach.

As added in 1990.

See Appendix IX for material relating to adoption of section in 1990.

Official Comment

1. Encoding and retention warranties are included in Article 4 because they are unique to the bank collection process. These warranties are breached only by the person doing the encoding or retaining the item and not by subsequent banks handling the item. Encoding and check retention may be done by customers who are payees of a large volume of checks; hence, this section imposes warranties on customers as well as banks. If a customer encodes or retains, the depositary bank is also liable for any breach of this warranty.

2. A misencoding of the amount on the MICR line is not an alteration under Section 3-407(a) which defines alteration as changing the contract of the parties. If a drawer wrote a check for $2,500 and the depositary bank encoded $25,000 on the MICR line, the payor bank could debit the drawer's account for only $2,500. This subsection would allow the payor bank to hold the depositary bank liable for the amount paid out over $2,500 without first pursuing the person who received payment. Intervening collecting banks would not be liable to the payor bank for the depositary bank's error. If a drawer wrote a check for $25,000 and the depositary bank encoded $2,500, the payor bank becomes liable for the full amount of the check. The payor bank's rights against the depositary bank depend on whether the payor bank has suffered a loss. Since the payor bank can debit the drawer's account for $25,000, the payor bank has a loss only to the extent that the drawer's account is less than the full amount of the check. There is no requirement that the payor bank pursue collection against the drawer beyond the amount in the drawer's account as a condition to the payor bank's action against the depositary bank for breach of warranty. See Georgia Railroad Bank & Trust Co. v. First National Bank & Trust, 229 S.E.2d 482 (Ga.App.1976), aff'd, 235 S.E.2d 1 (Ga.1977), and First National Bank of Boston v. Fidelity Bank, National Association, 724 F.Supp. 1168 (E.D.Pa. 1989).

3. A person retaining items under an electronic presentment agreement (Section 4-110) warrants that it has complied with the terms of the agreement regarding its possession of the item and its sending a proper presentment notice. If the keeper is a customer, its depositary bank also makes this warranty.

§ 4-210. Security Interest of Collecting Bank in Items, Accompanying Documents and Proceeds.

(a) A collecting bank has a security interest in an item and any accompanying documents or the proceeds of either:

(1) in case of an item deposited in an account, to the extent to which credit given for the item has been withdrawn or applied;

(2) in case of an item for which it has given credit available for withdrawal as of right, to the extent of the credit given, whether or not the credit is drawn upon or there is a right of charge-back; or

(3) if it makes an advance on or against the item.

(b) If credit given for several items received at one time or pursuant to a single agreement is withdrawn or applied in part, the security interest remains upon all the items, any accompanying documents or the proceeds of either. For the purpose of this section, credits first given are first withdrawn.

(c) Receipt by a collecting bank of a final settlement for an item is a realization on its security interest in the item, accompanying documents, and proceeds. So long as the bank does not receive final settlement for the item or give up possession of the item or accompanying documents for purposes other than collection, the security interest continues to that extent and is subject to Article 9, but:

(1) no security agreement is necessary to make the security interest enforceable (Section 9–203(1)(a));

(2) no filing is required to perfect the security interest; and

(3) the security interest has priority over conflicting perfected security interests in the item, accompanying documents, or proceeds.

As amended in 1990.

See Appendix IX for material relating to changes made in text in 1990.

Official Comment

1. Subsection (a) states a rational rule for the interest of a bank in an item. The customer of the depositary bank is normally the owner of the item and the several collecting banks are agents of the customer (Section 4–201). A collecting agent may properly make advances on the security of paper held for collection, and acquires at common law a possessory lien for these advances. Subsection (a) applies an analogous principle to a bank in the collection chain which extends credit on items in the course of collection. The bank has a security interest to the extent stated in this section. To the extent of its security interest it is a holder for value (Sections 3–303, 4–211) and a holder in due course if it satisfies the other requirements for that status (Section 3–302). Subsection (a) does not derogate from the banker's general common law lien or right of setoff against indebtedness owing in deposit accounts. See Section 1–103. Rather subsection (a) specifically implements and extends the principle as a part of the bank collection process.

2. Subsection (b) spreads the security interest of the bank over all items in a single deposit or received under a single agreement and a single giving of credit. It also adopts the "first-in, first-out" rule.

3. Collection statistics establish that the vast majority of items handled for collection are in fact collected. The first sentence of subsection (c) reflects the fact that in the normal case the bank's security interest is self-liquidating. The remainder of the subsection correlates the security interest with the provisions of Article 9, particularly for use in the cases

of noncollection in which the security interest may be important.

§ 4-211. When Bank Gives Value for Purposes of Holder in Due Course.

For purposes of determining its status as a holder in due course, a bank has given value to the extent it has a security interest in an item, if the bank otherwise complies with the requirements of Section 3-302 on what constitutes a holder in due course.

As amended in 1990.

See Appendix IX for material relating to changes made in text in 1990.

Official Comment

The section completes the thought of the previous section and makes clear that a security interest in an item is "value" for the purpose of determining the holder's status as a holder in due course. The provision is in accord with the prior law (N.I.L. Section 27) and with Article 3 (Section 3-303). The section does not prescribe a security interest under Section 4-210 as a test of "value" generally because the meaning of "value" under other Articles is adequately defined in Section 1-201.

§ 4-212. Presentment by Notice of Item Not Payable by, Through, or at Bank; Liability of Drawer or Indorser.

(a) Unless otherwise instructed, a collecting bank may present an item not payable by, through, or at a bank by sending to the party to accept or pay a written notice that the bank holds the item for acceptance or payment. The notice must be sent in time to be received on or before the day when presentment is due and the bank must meet any requirement of the party to accept or pay under Section 3-501 by the close of the bank's next banking day after it knows of the requirement.

(b) If presentment is made by notice and payment, acceptance, or request for compliance with a requirement under Section 3-501 is not received by the close of business on the day after maturity or, in the case of demand items, by the close of business on the third banking day after notice was sent, the presenting bank may treat the item as dishonored and charge any drawer or indorser by sending it notice of the facts.

As amended in 1990.

See Appendix IX for material relating to changes made in text in 1990.

Official Comment

1. This section codifies a practice extensively followed in presentation of trade acceptances and documentary and other drafts drawn on nonbank payors. It imposes a duty on the payor to respond to the notice of the item if the item is not to be considered dishonored. Notice of such a dishonor charges drawers and indorsers.

Presentment under this section is good presentment under Article 3. See Section 3–501.

2. A drawee not receiving notice is not, of course, liable to the drawer for wrongful dishonor.

3. A bank so presenting an instrument must be sufficiently close to the drawee to be able to exhibit the instrument on the day it is requested to do so or the next business day at the latest.

§ 4–213. Medium and Time of Settlement by Bank.

(a) With respect to settlement by a bank, the medium and time of settlement may be prescribed by Federal Reserve regulations or circulars, clearing-house rules, and the like, or agreement. In the absence of such prescription:

(1) the medium of settlement is cash or credit to an account in a Federal Reserve bank of or specified by the person to receive settlement; and

(2) the time of settlement, is:

(i) with respect to tender of settlement by cash, a cashier's check, or teller's check, when the cash or check is sent or delivered;

(ii) with respect to tender of settlement by credit in an account in a Federal Reserve Bank, when the credit is made;

(iii) with respect to tender of settlement by a credit or debit to an account in a bank, when the credit or debit is made or, in the case of tender of settlement by authority to charge an account, when the authority is sent or delivered; or

(iv) with respect to tender of settlement by a funds transfer, when payment is made pursuant to Section 4A–406(a) to the person receiving settlement.

(b) If the tender of settlement is not by a medium authorized by subsection (a) or the time of settlement is not fixed by subsection (a), no settlement occurs until the tender of settlement is accepted by the person receiving settlement.

(c) If settlement for an item is made by cashier's check or teller's check and the person receiving settlement, before its midnight deadline:

(1) presents or forwards the check for collection, settlement is final when the check is finally paid; or

(2) fails to present or forward the check for collection, settlement is final at the midnight deadline of the person receiving settlement.

(d) If settlement for an item is made by giving authority to charge the account of the bank giving settlement in the bank receiving settlement, settlement is final when the charge is made by the bank receiving settlement if there are funds available in the account for the amount of the item.

As amended in 1990.

See Appendix IX for material relating to changes made in text in 1990.

Official Comment

1. Subsection (a) sets forth the medium of settlement that the person receiving settlement must accept. In nearly all cases the medium of settlement will be determined by agreement or by Federal Reserve regulations and circulars, clearing-house rules, and the like. In the absence of regulations, rules or agreement, the person receiving settlement may demand cash or credit in a Federal Reserve bank. If the person receiving settlement does not have an account in a Federal Reserve bank, it may specify the account of another bank in a Federal Reserve bank. In the unusual case in which there is no agreement on the medium of settlement and the bank making settlement tenders settlement other than cash or Federal Reserve bank credit, no settlement has occurred under subsection (b) unless the person receiving settlement accepts the settlement tendered. For example, if a payor bank, without agreement, tenders a teller's check, the bank receiving the settlement may reject the check and return it to the payor bank or it may accept the check as settlement.

2. In several provisions of Article 4 the time that a settlement occurs is relevant. Subsection (a) sets out a general rule that the time of settlement, like the means of settlement, may be prescribed by agreement. In the absence of agreement, the time of settlement for tender of the common agreed media of settlement is that set out in subsection (a)(2). The time of settlement by cash, cashier's or teller's check or authority to charge an account is the time the cash, check or authority is sent, unless presentment is over the counter in which case settlement occurs upon delivery to the presenter. If there is no agreement on the time of settlement and the tender of settlement is not made by one of the media set out in subsection (a), under subsection (b) the time of settlement is the time the settlement is accepted by the person receiving settlement.

3. Subsections (c) and (d) are special provisions for settlement by remittance drafts and authority to charge an account in the bank receiving settlement. The relationship between final settlement and final payment under Section 4-215 is addressed in subsection (b) of Section 4-215. With respect to settlement by cashier's checks or teller's checks, other than in response to over-the-counter presentment, the bank receiving settlement can keep the risk that the check will not be paid on the bank tendering the check in settlement by acting to initiate collection of the check within the midnight deadline of the bank receiving settlement. If the bank fails to initiate settlement before its midnight deadline, final settlement occurs at the midnight deadline, and the bank receiving settlement assumes the risk that the check will not be paid. If there is no agreement that permits the bank tendering settlement to tender a cashier's or teller's check, subsection (b) allows the bank receiving the check to reject it, and, if it does, no settlement occurs. However, if the bank accepts the check, settlement occurs and the time of final settlement is governed by subsection (c).

With respect to settlement by tender of authority to charge the account of the bank making settlement in the bank receiving settlement, subsection (d) provides that final settlement does not take place until the account charged has available funds to cover the amount of the item. If there is no agreement that permits the bank tendering settlement to tender an authority to charge an account as settlement, subsection (b) allows the bank receiving the tender to reject it. However, if the bank accepts the authority, settlement occurs and the time of final settlement is governed by subsection (d).

§ 4-214. Right of Charge-Back or Refund; Liability of Collecting Bank: Return of Item.

(a) If a collecting bank has made provisional settlement with its customer for an item and fails by reason of dishonor, suspension of payments by a bank, or otherwise to receive settlement for the item which is or becomes final, the bank may revoke the settlement given by it, charge back the amount of any credit given for the item to its customer's account, or obtain refund from its customer, whether or not it is able to return the item, if by its midnight deadline or within a longer reasonable time after it learns the facts it returns the item or sends notification of the facts. If the return or notice is delayed beyond the bank's midnight deadline or a longer reasonable time after it learns the facts, the bank may revoke the settlement, charge back the credit, or obtain refund from its customer, but it is liable for any loss resulting from the delay. These rights to revoke, charge back, and obtain refund terminate if and when a settlement for the item received by the bank is or becomes final.

(b) A collecting bank returns an item when it is sent or delivered to the bank's customer or transferor or pursuant to its instructions.

(c) A depositary bank that is also the payor may charge back the amount of an item to its customer's account or obtain refund in accordance with the section governing return of an item received by a payor bank for credit on its books (Section 4–301).

(d) The right to charge back is not affected by:

(1) previous use of a credit given for the item; or

(2) failure by any bank to exercise ordinary care with respect to the item, but a bank so failing remains liable.

(e) A failure to charge back or claim refund does not affect other rights of the bank against the customer or any other party.

(f) If credit is given in dollars as the equivalent of the value of an item payable in foreign money, the dollar amount of any charge-back or refund must be calculated on the basis of the bank-offered spot rate for the foreign money prevailing on the day when the person entitled to the charge-back or refund learns that it will not receive payment in ordinary course.

As amended in 1990.

See Appendix IX for material relating to changes made in text in 1990.

Official Comment

1. Under current bank practice, in a major portion of cases banks make provisional settlement for items when they are first received and then await subsequent determination of whether the item will be finally paid. This is the principal characteristic of what are referred to in banking parlance as "cash items." Statistically, this practice of settling provisionally first and then awaiting final payment is justified because the vast majority of such cash items are finally paid, with the result that in this great preponderance of cases it becomes unnecessary for the banks making the provisional settlements to make any further entries. In due course the provisional settlements become final simply with the lapse of time. However, in those cases in which the item being collected is not finally paid or if for various reasons the bank making the provisional settlement does not itself receive final payment, provision is made in subsection (a) for the reversal of the provisional settlements, charge-back of provisional credits and the right to obtain refund.

2. Various causes of a bank's not receiving final payment, with the resulting right of charge-back or refund, are stated or suggested in subsection (a). These include dishonor of the original item; dishonor of a remittance instrument given for it; reversal of a provisional credit for the item; suspension of payments by another bank. The causes stated are illustrative; the right of charge-back or refund is stated to exist whether the failure to receive final payment in ordinary course arises through one of them "or otherwise."

3. The right of charge-back or refund exists if a collecting bank has made a provisional settlement for an item with its customer but terminates if and when a settlement received by the bank for the item is or becomes final. If the bank fails to receive such a final settlement the right of charge-back or refund must be exercised promptly after the bank learns the facts. The right exists (if so promptly exercised) whether or not the bank is able to return the item. The second sentence of subsection (a) adopts the view of Appliance Buyers Credit Corp. v. Prospect National Bank, 708 F.2d 290 (7th Cir.1983), that if the midnight deadline for returning an item or giving notice is not met, a collecting bank loses its rights only to the extent of damages for any loss resulting from the delay.

4. Subsection (b) states when an item is returned by a collecting bank. Regulation CC, Section 229.31 preempts this subsection with respect to checks by allowing direct return to the depositary bank. Because a returned check may follow a different path than in forward collection, settlement given for the check is final and not provisional except as between the depositary bank and its customer. Regulation CC Section 229.36(d). See also Regulations CC Sections 229.31(c) and 229.32(b). Thus owing to the federal preemption, this subsection applies only to noncheck items.

5. The rule of subsection (d) relating to charge-back (as distinguished from claim for refund) applies irrespective of the cause of the nonpayment, and of the person ultimately liable for nonpayment. Thus charge-back is permitted even if nonpayment results from the depositary bank's own negligence. Any other rule would result in litigation based upon a claim for wrongful dishonor of other checks of the customer, with potential damages far in excess of the amount of the item. Any other rule would require a bank to determine difficult questions of fact. The customer's protection is found in the general obligation of good faith (Sections 1-203 and 4-103). If bad faith is established the customer's recovery "includes other damages, if any, suffered by the party as a proximate consequence" (Section 4-103(e); see also Section 4-402).

6. It is clear that the charge-back does not relieve the bank from any liability for failure to exercise ordinary care in handling the item. The measure of damages for such failure is stated in Section 4-103(e).

7. Subsection (f) states a rule fixing the time for determining the rate of exchange if there is a charge-back or refund of a credit given in dollars for an item payable in a foreign currency. Compare Section 3-107. Fixing such a rule is desirable to avoid disputes. If in any case the parties wish to fix a different time for determining the rate of exchange, they may do so by agreement.

§ 4-215. Final Payment of Item by Payor Bank; When Provisional Debits and Credits Become Final; When Certain Credits Become Available for Withdrawal.

(a) An item is finally paid by a payor bank when the bank has first done any of the following:

(1) paid the item in cash;

(2) settled for the item without having a right to revoke the settlement under statute, clearing-house rule, or agreement; or

(3) made a provisional settlement for the item and failed to revoke the settlement in the time and manner permitted by statute, clearing-house rule, or agreement.

(b) If provisional settlement for an item does not become final, the item is not finally paid.

(c) If provisional settlement for an item between the presenting and payor banks is made through a clearing house or by debits or credits in an account between them, then to the extent that provisional debits or credits for the item are entered in accounts between the presenting and payor banks or between the presenting and successive prior collecting banks seriatim, they become final upon final payment of the item by the payor bank.

(d) If a collecting bank receives a settlement for an item which is or becomes final, the bank is accountable to its customer for the amount of the item and any provisional credit given for the item in an account with its customer becomes final.

(e) Subject to (i) applicable law stating a time for availability of funds and (ii) any right of the bank to apply the credit to an obligation of the customer, credit given by a bank for an item in a customer's account becomes available for withdrawal as of right:

(1) if the bank has received a provisional settlement for the item, when the settlement becomes final and the bank has had a reasonable time to receive return of the item and the item has not been received within that time;

(2) if the bank is both the depositary bank and the payor bank, and the item is finally paid, at the opening of the bank's second banking day following receipt of the item.

(f) Subject to applicable law stating a time for availability of funds and any right of a bank to apply a deposit to an obligation of the depositor, a deposit of money becomes available for withdrawal as of right at the opening of the bank's next banking day after receipt of the deposit.

As amended in 1990.

See Appendix IX for material relating to changes made in text in 1990.

Official Comment

1. By the definition and use of the term "settle" (Section 4–104(a)(11)) this Article recognizes that various debits or credits, remittances, settlements or payments given for an item may be either provisional or final, that settlements sometimes are provisional and sometimes are final and sometimes are provisional for awhile but later become final. Subsection (a) defines when settlement for an item constitutes final payment.

Final payment of an item is important for a number of reasons. It is one of several factors determining the relative priorities between items and notices, stop-payment orders, legal process and setoffs (Section 4–303). It is the "end of the line" in the collection process and the "turn around" point commencing the return flow of proceeds. It is the point at which many provisional settlements become final. See Section 4–215(c). Final payment of an item by the payor bank fixes preferential rights under Section 4–216.

2. If an item being collected moves through several states, e.g., is deposited for collection in California, moves through two or three California banks to the Federal Reserve Bank of San Francisco, to the Federal Reserve Bank of Boston, to a payor bank in Maine, the collection process involves the eastward journey of the item from California to Maine and the westward journey of the proceeds from Maine to California. Subsection (a) recognizes that final payment does not take place, in this hypothetical case, on the journey of the item eastward. It also adopts the view that neither does final payment occur on the journey westward because what in fact is journeying westward are *proceeds* of the item.

3. Traditionally and under various decisions payment in cash of an item by a payor bank has been considered final payment. Subsection (a)(1) recognizes and provides that payment of an item in cash by a payor bank is final payment.

4. Section 4–104(a)(11) defines "settle" as meaning "to pay in cash, by clearing-house settlement, in a charge or credit or by remittance, or otherwise as agreed. A settlement may be either provisional or final." Subsection (a)(2) of Section 4–215 provides that an item is finally paid by a payor bank when the bank has "settled for the item without having a right to revoke the settlement under statute, clearing-house rule or agreement." Former subsection (1)(b) is modified by subsection (a)(2) to make clear that a payor bank cannot make settlement provisional by unilaterally reserving a right to revoke the settlement. The right must come from a statute (e.g., Section 4–301), clearing-house rule or other agreement. Subsection (a)(2) provides in effect that if the payor bank finally settles for an item this constitutes final payment of the item. The subsection operates if nothing has occurred and no situation exists making the settlement provisional. If under statute, clearing-house rule or agreement, a right of revocation of the settlement exists, the settlement is provisional. Conversely, if there is an absence of a right to revoke under statute, clearing-house rule or agreement, the settlement is final and such final settlement constitutes final payment of the item.

A primary example of a statutory right on the part of the payor bank to revoke a settlement is the right to revoke conferred by Section 4–301. The underlying theory and reason for deferred posting statutes (Section 4–301) is to require a settlement on the date of receipt of an item but to keep that settlement provisional with the right to revoke prior to the midnight deadline. In any case in which Section 4–301 is applicable, any settlement by the payor bank is provisional solely by virtue of the statute, subsection (a)(2) of Section 4–215 does not operate, and such provisional settlement does not constitute final payment of the item. With respect to checks, Regulation CC Section 229.36(d) provides that settlement between banks for the forward collection of checks is final. The relationship of this provision to Article 4 is discussed in the Commentary to that section.

A second important example of a right to revoke a settlement is that arising under clearing-house rules. It is very common for clearing-house rules to provide that items exchanged and settled for in a clearing (e.g., before 10:00 a.m. on Monday) may be returned and the settlements revoked up to but not later than 2:00 p.m. on the same day (Monday) or under deferred posting at some hour on the next business day (e.g., 2:00 p.m. Tuesday). Under this type of rule the Monday morning settlement is provisional and being provisional does not constitute a final payment of the item.

An example of an agreement allowing the payor bank to revoke a settlement is a case in which the payor bank is also the depositary bank and has signed a receipt or duplicate deposit ticket or has made an entry in a passbook acknowledging receipt, for credit to the account of A, of a check drawn on it by B. If the receipt, deposit ticket, passbook or other agreement with A is to the effect that any credit so entered is provisional and may be revoked pending the time required by the payor bank to process the item to determine if it is in good form and there are funds to cover it, the agreement keeps the receipt or credit provisional and avoids its being either final settlement or final payment.

The most important application of subsection (a)(2) is that in which presentment of an item has been made over the counter for immediate payment. In this case Section 4–301(a) does not apply to make the settlement provisional, and final payment has occurred unless a rule or agreement provides otherwise.

5. Former Section 4–213(1)(c) provided that final payment occurred when the payor bank completed the "process of posting." The term was defined in former Section 4–109. In the present Article, Section 4–109 has been deleted and the process-of-posting test has been abandoned in Section 4–215(a) for determining when final payment is made. Difficulties in determining when the events described in former Section 4–109 take place make the process-of-posting test unsuitable for a system of automated check collection or electronic presentment.

6. The last sentence of former Section 4–213(1) is deleted as an unnecessary source of confusion. Initially the view that payor bank may be accountable for, that is, liable for the amount of, an item that it has already paid seems incongruous. This is particularly true in the light of the language formerly found in Section 4–302 stating that the payor bank can defend against liability for accountability by showing that it has already settled for the item. But, at least with respect to former Section 4–213(1)(c), such a provision was needed because under the process-of-posting test a payor bank may have paid an item without settling for it. Now that Article 4 has abandoned the process-of-posting test, the sentence is no longer needed. If the payor bank has neither paid the item nor returned it within its midnight deadline, the payor bank is accountable under Section 4–302.

7. Subsection (a)(3) covers the situation in which the payor bank makes a provisional settlement for an item, and this settlement becomes final at a later time by reason of the failure of the payor bank to revoke it in the time and manner permitted by statute, clearing-house rule or agreement. An example of this type of situation is the clearing-house settlement referred to in Comment 4. In the illustration there given if the time limit for the return of items received in the Monday morning clearing is 2:00 p.m. on Tuesday and the provisional settlement has not been revoked at that time in a manner permitted by the clearing-house rules, the provisional settlement made on Monday morning becomes final at 2:00 p.m. on Tuesday. Subsection (a)(3) provides specifically that in this situation the item is finally paid at 2:00 p.m. Tuesday. If on the other hand a payor bank receives an item in the mail on Monday and makes some provisional settlement for the item on Monday, it has until midnight on Tuesday to return the item or give notice and revoke any settlement under Section 4–301. In this situation subsection (a)(3) of Section 4–215 provides that if the provisional settlement made on Monday is not revoked before midnight on Tuesday as permitted by Section 4–301, the item is finally paid at midnight on Tuesday. With respect to checks, Regulation CC Section 229.30(c) allows an extension of the midnight deadline under certain circumstances. If a bank does not expeditiously return a check liability may accrue under Regulation CC Section 229.38. For the relationship of that liability to responsibility under this Article, see Regulation CC Sections 229.30 and 229.38.

8. Subsection (b) relates final settlement to final payment under Section 4–215. For example, if a payor bank makes provisional settlement for an item by sending a cashier's or teller's check and that settlement fails to become final under Section 4–213(c), subsection (b) provides that final payment has not occurred. If the item is not paid, the drawer remains liable, and under Section 4–

302(a) the payor bank is accountable unless it has returned the item before its midnight deadline. In this regard, subsection (b) is an exception to subsection (a)(3). Even if the payor bank has not returned an item by its midnight deadline there is still no final payment if provisional settlement had been made and settlement failed to become final. However, if presentment of the item was over the counter for immediate payment, final payment has occurred under Section 4–215(a)(2). Subsection (b) does not apply because the settlement was not provisional. Section 4–301(a). In this case the presenting person, often the payee of the item, has the right to demand cash or the cash equivalent of federal reserve credit. If the presenting person accepts another medium of settlement such as a cashier's or teller's check, the presenting person takes the risk that the payor bank may fail to pay a cashier's check because of insolvency or that the drawee of a teller's check may dishonor it.

9. Subsection (c) states the countrywide usage that when the item is finally paid by the payor bank under subsection (a) this final payment automatically without further action "firms up" other provisional settlements made for it. However, the subsection makes clear that this "firming up" occurs only if the settlement between the presenting and payor banks was made either through a clearing house or by debits and credits in accounts between them. It does not take place if the payor bank remits for the item by sending some form of remittance instrument. Further, the "firming up" continues only to the extent that provisional debits and credits are entered seriatim in accounts between banks which are successive to the presenting bank. The automatic "firming up" is broken at any time that any collecting bank remits for the item by sending a remittance draft, because final payment to the remittee then usually depends upon final payment of the remittance draft.

10. Subsection (d) states the general rule that if a collecting bank receives settlement for an item which is or becomes final, the bank is accountable to its customer for the amount of the item. One means of accounting is to remit to its customer the amount it has received on the item. If previously it gave to its customer a provisional credit for the item in an account its receipt of final settlement for the item "firms up" this provisional credit and makes it final. When this credit given by it so becomes final, in the usual case its agency status terminates and it becomes a debtor to its customer for the amount of the item. See Section 4–201(a). If the accounting is by a remittance instrument or authorization to charge further time will usually be required to complete its accounting (Section 4–213).

11. Subsection (e) states when certain credits given by a bank to its customer become available for withdrawal as of right. Subsection (e)(1) deals with the situation in which a bank has given a credit (usually provisional) for an item to its customer and in turn has received a provisional settlement for the item from an intermediary or payor bank to which it has forwarded the item. In this situation before the provisional credit entered by the collecting bank in the account of its customer becomes available for withdrawal as of right, it is not only necessary that the provisional settlement received by the bank for the item becomes final but also that the collecting bank has a reasonable time to receive return of the item and the item has not been received within that time. How much time is "reasonable" for these purposes will of course depend on the distance the item has to travel and the number of banks through which it must pass (having in mind not only travel time by regular lines of transmission but also the successive midnight deadlines of the several banks) and other pertinent facts. Also, if the provisional settlement received is some form of a remittance instrument or authorization to charge, the "reasonable" time depends on the identity and location of the payor of the remittance instrument, the means for clearing such instrument, and other pertinent facts. With respect to checks Regu-

lation CC Sections 229.10–229.13 or similar applicable state law (Section 229.20) control. This is also time for the situation described in Comment 12.

12. Subsection (e)(2) deals with the situation of a bank that is both a depositary bank and a payor bank. The subsection recognizes that if A and B are both customers of a depositary-payor bank and A deposits B's check on the depositary-payor in A's account on Monday, time must be allowed to permit the check under the deferred posting rules of Section 4–301 to reach the bookkeeper for B's account at some time on Tuesday, and, if there are insufficient funds in B's account, to reverse or charge back the provisional credit in A's account. Consequently this provisional credit in A's account does not become available for withdrawal as of right until the opening of business on Wednesday. If it is determined on Tuesday that there are insufficient funds in B's account to pay the check, the credit to A's account can be reversed on Tuesday. On the other hand if the item is in fact paid on Tuesday, the rule of subsection (e)(2) is desirable to avoid uncertainty and possible disputes between the bank and its customer as to exactly what hour within the day the credit is available.

§ 4–216. Insolvency and Preference.

(a) If an item is in or comes into the possession of a payor or collecting bank that suspends payment and the item has not been finally paid, the item must be returned by the receiver, trustee, or agent in charge of the closed bank to the presenting bank or the closed bank's customer.

(b) If a payor bank finally pays an item and suspends payments without making a settlement for the item with its customer or the presenting bank which settlement is or becomes final, the owner of the item has a preferred claim against the payor bank.

(c) If a payor bank gives or a collecting bank gives or receives a provisional settlement for an item and thereafter suspends payments, the suspension does not prevent or interfere with the settlement's becoming final if the finality occurs automatically upon the lapse of certain time or the happening of certain events.

(d) If a collecting bank receives from subsequent parties settlement for an item, which settlement is or becomes final and the bank suspends payments without making a settlement for the item with its customer which settlement is or becomes final, the owner of the item has a preferred claim against the collecting bank.

As amended in 1990.

See Appendix IX for material relating to changes made in text in 1990.

Official Comment

1. The underlying purpose of the provisions of this section is not to confer upon banks, holders of items or anyone else preferential positions in the event of bank failures over general depositors or any other creditors of the failed banks. The purpose is to fix as definitely as possible the cut-off point of time for the completion or cessation of the collection process in the case of items that happen to be in the process at the time a particular bank suspends payments. It must be remembered that in bank collections as a whole and in the handling of items by an individual bank, items go through a whole

series of processes. It must also be remembered that at any particular point of time a particular bank (at least one of any size) is functioning as a depositary bank for some items, as an intermediary bank for others, as a presenting bank for still others and as a payor bank for still others, and that when it suspends payments it will have close to its normal load of items working through its various processes. For the convenience of receivers, owners of items, banks, and in fact substantially everyone concerned, it is recognized that at the particular moment of time that a bank suspends payment, a certain portion of the items being handled by it have progressed far enough in the bank collection process that it is preferable to permit them to continue the remaining distance, rather than to send them back and reverse the many entries that have been made or the steps that have been taken with respect to them. Therefore, having this background and these purposes in mind, the section states what items must be turned backward at the moment suspension intervenes and what items have progressed far enough that the collection process with respect to them continues, with the resulting necessary statement of rights of various parties flowing from this prescription of the cut-off time.

2. The rules stated are similar to those stated in the American Bankers Association Bank Collection Code, but with the abandonment of any theory of trust. On the other hand, some law previous to this Act may be relevant. See Note, Uniform Commercial Code: Stopping Payment of an Item Deposited with an Insolvent Depositary Bank, 40 Okla.L.Rev. 689 (1987). Although for practical purposes Federal Deposit Insurance affects materially the result of bank failures on holders of items and banks, no attempt is made to vary the rules of the section by reason of such insurance.

3. It is recognized that in view of Jennings v. United States Fidelity & Guaranty Co., 294 U.S. 216, 55 S.Ct. 394, 79 L.Ed. 869, 99 A.L.R. 1248 (1935), amendment of the National Bank Act would be necessary to have this section apply to national banks. But there is no reason why it should not apply to others. See Section 1–108.

PART 3

COLLECTION OF ITEMS: PAYOR BANKS

§ 4–301. Deferred Posting; Recovery of Payment by Return of Items; Time of Dishonor; Return of Items by Payor Bank.

(a) If a payor bank settles for a demand item other than a documentary draft presented otherwise than for immediate payment over the counter before midnight of the banking day of receipt, the payor bank may revoke the settlement and recover the settlement if, before it has made final payment and before its midnight deadline, it

(1) returns the item; or

(2) sends written notice of dishonor or nonpayment if the item is unavailable for return.

(b) If a demand item is received by a payor bank for credit on its books, it may return the item or send notice of dishonor and may revoke any credit given or recover the amount thereof withdrawn by its customer, if it acts within the time limit and in the manner specified in subsection (a).

(c) Unless previous notice of dishonor has been sent, an item is dishonored at the time when for purposes of dishonor it is returned or notice sent in accordance with this section.

(d) An item is returned:

(1) as to an item presented through a clearing house, when it is delivered to the presenting or last collecting bank or to the clearing house or is sent or delivered in accordance with clearing-house rules; or

(2) in all other cases, when it is sent or delivered to the bank's customer or transferor or pursuant to instructions.

As amended in 1990.

See Appendix IX for material relating to changes made in text in 1990.

Official Comment

1. The term "deferred posting" appears in the caption of Section 4–301. This refers to the practice permitted by statute in most of the states before the UCC under which a payor bank receives items on one day but does not post the items to the customer's account until the next day. Items dishonored were then returned after the posting on the day after receipt. Under Section 4–301 the concept of "deferred posting" merely allows a payor bank that has settled for an item on the day of receipt to return a dishonored item on the next day before its midnight deadline, without regard to when the item was actually posted. With respect to checks Regulation CC Section 229.30(c) extends the midnight deadline under the UCC under certain circumstances. See the Commentary to Regulation CC Section 229.38(d) on the relationship between the UCC and Regulation CC on settlement.

2. The function of this section is to provide the circumstances under which a payor bank that has made timely settlement for an item may return the item and revoke the settlement so that it may recover any settlement made. These circumstances are: (1) the item must be a demand item other than a documentary draft; (2) the item must be presented otherwise than for immediate payment over the counter; and (3) the payor bank must return the item (or give notice if the item is unavailable for return) before its midnight deadline and before it has paid the item. With respect to checks, see Regulation CC Section 229.31(f) on notice in lieu of return and Regulation CC Section 229.33 as to the different requirement of notice of nonpayment. An instance of when an item may be unavailable for return arises under a collecting bank check retention plan under which presentment is made by a presentment notice and the item is retained by the collecting bank. Section 4–215(a)(2) provides that final payment occurs if the payor bank has settled for an item without a right to revoke the settlement under statute, clearing-house rule or agreement. In any case in which Section 4–301(a) is applicable, the payor bank has a right to revoke the settlement by statute; therefore, Section 4–215(a)(2) is inoperable, and the settlement is provisional. Hence, if the settlement is not over the counter and the payor bank settles in a manner that does not constitute final payment, the payor bank can revoke the settlement by returning the item before its midnight deadline.

3. The relationship of Section 4–301(a) to final settlement and final payment under Section 4–215 is illustrated by the following case. Depositary Bank sends by mail an item to Payor Bank with instructions to settle by remitting a teller's check drawn on a bank in the city where Depositary Bank is located. Payor Bank sends the teller's check on the day the item was presented. Having made timely settlement, under the deferred posting provisions of Section 4–301(a), Payor Bank may revoke that settlement by returning the item before its midnight

deadline. If it fails to return the item before its midnight deadline, it has finally paid the item if the bank on which the teller's check was drawn honors the check. But if the teller's check is dishonored there has been no final settlement under Section 4–213(c) and no final payment under Section 4–215(b). Since the Payor Bank has neither paid the item nor made timely return, it is accountable for the item under Section 4–302(a).

4. The time limits for action imposed by subsection (a) are adopted by subsection (b) for cases in which the payor bank is also the depositary bank, but in this case the requirement of a settlement on the day of receipt is omitted.

5. Subsection (c) fixes a base point from which to measure the time within which notice of dishonor must be given. See Section 3–503.

6. Subsection (d) leaves banks free to agree upon the manner of returning items but establishes a precise time when an item is "returned." For definition of "sent" as used in paragraphs (1) and (2) see Section 1–201(38). Obviously the subsection assumes that the item has not been "finally paid" under Section 4–215(a). If it has been, this provision has no operation.

7. The fact that an item has been paid under proposed Section 4–215 does not preclude the payor bank from asserting rights of restitution or revocation under Section 3–418. National Savings and Trust Co. v. Park Corp., 722 F.2d 1303 (6th Cir.1983), cert. denied, 466 U.S. 939 (1984), is the correct interpretation of the present law on this issue.

§ 4–302. Payor Bank's Responsibility for Late Return of Item.

(a) If an item is presented to and received by a payor bank, the bank is accountable for the amount of:

(1) a demand item, other than a documentary draft, whether properly payable or not, if the bank, in any case in which it is not also the depositary bank, retains the item beyond midnight of the banking day of receipt without settling for it or, whether or not it is also the depositary bank, does not pay or return the item or send notice of dishonor until after its midnight deadline; or

(2) any other properly payable item unless, within the time allowed for acceptance or payment of that item, the bank either accepts or pays the item or returns it and accompanying documents.

(b) The liability of a payor bank to pay an item pursuant to subsection (a) is subject to defenses based on breach of a presentment warranty (Section 4–208) or proof that the person seeking enforcement of the liability presented or transferred the item for the purpose of defrauding the payor bank.

As amended in 1990.

See Appendix IX for material relating to changes made in text in 1990.

Official Comment

1. Subsection (a)(1) continues the former law distinguishing between cases in which the payor bank is not also the depositary bank and those in which the payor bank is also the depositary bank ("on us" items). For "on us" items the payor bank is accountable if it retains the item beyond its midnight deadline without settling for it. If the payor bank is not the depositary bank it is accountable if it retains the item beyond midnight of the banking day of receipt without set-

tling for it. It may avoid accountability either by settling for the item on the day of receipt and returning the item before its midnight deadline under Section 4–301 or by returning the item on the day of receipt. This rule is consistent with the deferred posting practice authorized by Section 4–301 which allows the payor bank to make provisional settlement for an item on the day of receipt and to revoke that settlement by returning the item on the next day. With respect to checks, Regulation CC Section 229.36(d) provides that settlements between banks for forward collection of checks are final when made. See the Commentary on that provision for its effect on the UCC.

2. If the settlement given by the payor bank does not become final, there has been no payment under Section 4–215(b), and the payor bank giving the failed settlement is accountable under subsection (a)(1) of Section 4–302. For instance, the payor bank makes provisional settlement by sending a teller's check that is dishonored. In such a case settlement is not final under Section 4–213(c) and no payment occurs under Section 4–215(b). Payor bank is accountable on the item. The general principle is that unless settlement provides the presenting bank with usable funds, settlement has failed and the payor bank is accountable for the amount of the item.

3. Subsection (b) is an elaboration of the deleted introductory language of former Section 4–302: "In the absence of a valid defense such as breach of a presentment warranty (subsection (1) of Section 4–207), settlement effected or the like...." A payor bank can defend an action against it based on accountability by showing that the item contained a forged indorsement or a fraudulent alteration. Subsection (b) drops the ambiguous "or the like" language and provides that the payor bank may also raise the defense of fraud. Decisions that hold an accountable bank's liability to be "absolute" are rejected. A payor bank that makes a late return of an item should not be liable to a defrauder operating a check kiting scheme. In Bank of Leumi Trust Co. v. Bally's Park Place Inc., 528 F.Supp. 349 (S.D.N.Y.1981), and American National Bank v. Foodbasket, 497 P.2d 546 (Wyo.1972), banks that were accountable under Section 4–302 for missing their midnight deadline were successful in defending against parties who initiated collection knowing that the check would not be paid. The "settlement effected" language is deleted as unnecessary. If a payor bank is accountable for an item it is liable to pay it. If it has made final payment for an item, it is no longer accountable for the item.

§ 4–303. When Items Subject to Notice, Stop-Payment Order, Legal Process, or Setoff; Order in Which Items May Be Charged or Certified.

(a) Any knowledge, notice, or stop-payment order received by, legal process served upon, or setoff exercised by a payor bank comes too late to terminate, suspend, or modify the bank's right or duty to pay an item or to charge its customer's account for the item if the knowledge, notice, stop-payment order, or legal process is received or served and a reasonable time for the bank to act thereon expires or the setoff is exercised after the earliest of the following:

(1) the bank accepts or certifies the item;

(2) the bank pays the item in cash;

(3) the bank settles for the item without having a right to revoke the settlement under statute, clearing-house rule, or agreement;

(4) the bank becomes accountable for the amount of the item under Section 4–302 dealing with the payor bank's responsibility for late return of items; or

(5) with respect to checks, a cutoff hour no earlier than one hour after the opening of the next banking day after the banking day on which the bank received the check and no later than the close of that next banking day or, if no cutoff hour is fixed, the close of the next banking day after the banking day on which the bank received the check.

(b) Subject to subsection (a), items may be accepted, paid, certified, or charged to the indicated account of its customer in any order.

As amended in 1990.

See Appendix IX for material relating to changes made in text in 1990.

Official Comment

1. While a payor bank is processing an item presented for payment, it may receive knowledge or a legal notice affecting the item, such as knowledge or a notice that the drawer has filed a petition in bankruptcy or made an assignment for the benefit of creditors; may receive an order of the drawer stopping payment on the item; may have served on it an attachment of the account of the drawer; or the bank itself may exercise a right of setoff against the drawer's account. Each of these events affects the account of the drawer and may eliminate or freeze all or part of whatever balance is available to pay the item. Subsection (a) states the rule for determining the relative priorities between these various legal events and the item.

2. The rule is that if any one of several things has been done to the item or if it has reached any one of several stages in its processing at the time the knowledge, notice, stop-payment order or legal process is received or served and a reasonable time for the bank to act thereon expires or the setoff is exercised, the knowledge, notice, stop-payment order, legal process or setoff comes too late, the item has priority and a charge to the customer's account may be made and is effective. With respect to the effect of the customer's bankruptcy, the bank's rights are governed by Bankruptcy Code Section 542(c) which codifies the result of Bank of Marin v. England, 385 U.S. 99 (1966). Section 4–405 applies to the death or incompetence of the customer.

3. Once a payor bank has accepted or certified an item or has paid the item in cash, the event has occurred that determines priorities between the item and the various legal events usually described as the "four legals." Paragraphs (1) and (2) of subsection (a) so provide. If a payor bank settles for an item presented over the counter for immediate payment by a cashier's check or teller's check which the presenting person agrees to accept, paragraph (3) of subsection (a) would control and the event determining priority has occurred. Because presentment was over the counter, Section 4–301(a) does not apply to give the payor bank the statutory right to revoke the settlement. Thus the requirements of paragraph (3) have been met unless a clearing-house rule or agreement of the parties provides otherwise.

4. In the usual case settlement for checks is by entries in bank accounts. Since the process-of-posting test has been abandoned as inappropriate for automated check collection, the determining event for priorities is a given hour on the day after the item is received. (Paragraph (5) of subsection (a).) The hour may be fixed by the bank no earlier than one hour after the opening on the next banking day after the bank received the check and no later than the close of that banking day. If an item is received after the payor bank's regular Section 4–108 cutoff hour, it is treated as received the next banking day. If a bank receives an item after its regular cutoff hour on Monday and an

attachment is levied at noon on Tuesday, the attachment is prior to the item if the bank had not before that hour taken the action described in paragraphs (1), (2), and (3) of subsection (a). The Commentary to Regulation CC Section 229.36(d) explains that even though settlement by a paying bank for a check is final for Regulation CC purposes, the paying bank's right to return the check before its midnight deadline under the UCC is not affected.

5. Another event conferring priority for an item and a charge to the customer's account based upon the item is stated by the language "become accountable for the amount of the item under Section 4–302 dealing with the payor bank's responsibility for late return of items." Expiration of the deadline under Section 4–302 with resulting accountability by the payor bank for the amount of the item, establishes priority of the item over notices, stop-payment orders, legal process or setoff.

6. In the case of knowledge, notice, stop-payment orders and legal process the effective time for determining whether they were received too late to affect the payment of an item and a charge to the customer's account by reason of such payment, is receipt plus a reasonable time for the bank to act on any of these communications. Usually a relatively short time is required to communicate to the accounting department advice of one of these events but certainly some time is necessary. Compare Sections 1–201(27) and 4–403. In the case of setoff the effective time is when the setoff is actually made.

7. As between one item and another no priority rule is stated. This is justified because of the impossibility of stating a rule that would be fair in all cases, having in mind the almost infinite number of combinations of large and small checks in relation to the available balance on hand in the drawer's account; the possible methods of receipt; and other variables. Further, the drawer has drawn all the checks, the drawer should have funds available to meet all of them and has no basis for urging one should be paid before another; and the holders have no direct right against the payor bank in any event, unless of course, the bank has accepted, certified or finally paid a particular item, or has become liable for it under Section 4–302. Under subsection (b) the bank has the right to pay items for which it is itself liable ahead of those for which it is not.

PART 4

RELATIONSHIP BETWEEN PAYOR BANK AND ITS CUSTOMER

§ 4–401. When Bank May Charge Customer's Account.

(a) A bank may charge against the account of a customer an item that is properly payable from the account even though the charge creates an overdraft. An item is properly payable if it is authorized by the customer and is in accordance with any agreement between the customer and bank.

(b) A customer is not liable for the amount of an overdraft if the customer neither signed the item nor benefited from the proceeds of the item.

(c) A bank may charge against the account of a customer a check that is otherwise properly payable from the account, even though payment was made before the date of the check, unless the customer has given notice to the bank of the postdating describing the check with reasonable certainty. The notice is effective for the period stated in Section 4–403(b) for stop-payment orders, and must be received at such time and in such manner as to afford the bank a reasonable opportunity to act on it before the bank takes any action with respect to the check described in Section 4-303. If a bank charges against the account of a customer a check before the date stated in the notice of postdating, the bank is liable for damages for the loss resulting from its act. The loss may include damages for dishonor of subsequent items under Section 4-402.

(d) A bank that in good faith makes payment to a holder may charge the indicated account of its customer according to:

(1) the original terms of the altered item; or

(2) the terms of the completed item, even though the bank knows the item has been completed unless the bank has notice that the completion was improper.

As amended in 1990.

See Appendix IX for material relating to changes made in text in 1990.

Official Comment

1. An item is properly payable from a customer's account if the customer has authorized the payment and the payment does not violate any agreement that may exist between the bank and its customer. For an example of a payment held to violate an agreement with a customer, see Torrance National Bank v. Enesco Federal Credit Union, 285 P.2d 737 (Cal.App. 1955). An item drawn for more than the amount of a customer's account may be properly payable. Thus under subsection (a) a bank may charge the customer's account for an item even though payment results in an overdraft. An item containing a forged drawer's signature or forged indorsement is not properly payable. Concern has arisen whether a bank may require a customer to execute a stop-payment order when the customer notifies the bank of the loss of an unindorsed or specially indorsed check. Since such a check cannot be properly payable from the customer's account, it is inappropriate for a bank to require stop-payment order in such a case.

2. Subsection (b) adopts the view of case authority holding that if there is more than one customer who can draw on an account, the nonsigning customer is not liable for an overdraft unless that person benefits from the proceeds of the item.

3. Subsection (c) is added because the automated check collection system cannot accommodate postdated checks. A check is usually paid upon presentment without respect to the date of the check. Under the former law, if a payor bank paid a postdated check before its stated date, it could not charge the customer's account because the check was not "properly payable." Hence, the bank might have been liable for wrongfully dishonoring subsequent checks of the drawer that would have been paid had the postdated check not been prematurely paid. Under subsection (c) a customer wishing to postdate a check must notify the payor bank of its postdating in time to allow the bank to act on the customer's notice before the bank has to commit itself to pay the check. If the bank fails to act on the customer's timely notice, it may be liable for damages for the resulting loss which may include damages for dishonor of subsequent items. This Act does not regulate fees that banks charge their customers for a notice of postdating or other services covered by the Act, but under principles of law such as unconscionability or good faith and fair dealing, courts have reviewed fees and the bank's exercise of a discretion to set fees. Perdue v. Crocker National Bank, 38 Cal.3d 913 (1985) (unconscionability); Best v. United Bank of Oregon, 739 P.2d 554, 562-566

(1987) (good faith and fair dealing). In addition, Section 1-203 provides that every contract or duty within this Act imposes an obligation of good faith in its performance or enforcement.

4. Section 3-407(c) states that a payor bank or drawee which pays a fraudulently altered instrument in good faith and without notice of the alteration may enforce rights with respect to the instrument according to its original terms or, in the case of an incomplete instrument altered by unauthorized completion, according to its terms as completed. Section 4-401(d) follows the rule stated in Section 3-407(c) by applying it to an altered item and allows the bank to enforce rights with respect to the altered item by charging the customer's account.

§ 4-402. Bank's Liability to Customer for Wrongful Dishonor; Time of Determining Insufficiency of Account.

(a) Except as otherwise provided in this Article, a payor bank wrongfully dishonors an item if it dishonors an item that is properly payable, but a bank may dishonor an item that would create an overdraft unless it has agreed to pay the overdraft.

(b) A payor bank is liable to its customer for damages proximately caused by the wrongful dishonor of an item. Liability is limited to actual damages proved and may include damages for an arrest or prosecution of the customer or other consequential damages. Whether any consequential damages are proximately caused by the wrongful dishonor is a question of fact to be determined in each case.

(c) A payor bank's determination of the customer's account balance on which a decision to dishonor for insufficiency of available funds is based may be made at any time between the time the item is received by the payor bank and the time that the payor bank returns the item or gives notice in lieu of return, and no more than one determination need be made. If, at the election of the payor bank, a subsequent balance determination is made for the purpose of reevaluating the bank's decision to dishonor the item, the account balance at that time is determinative of whether a dishonor for insufficiency of available funds is wrongful.

As amended in 1990.

See Appendix IX for material relating to changes made in text in 1990.

Official Comment

1. Subsection (a) states positively what has been assumed under the original Article: that if a bank fails to honor a properly payable item it may be liable to its customer for wrongful dishonor. Under subsection (b) the payor bank's wrongful dishonor of an item gives rise to a statutory cause of action. Damages may include consequential damages. Confusion has resulted from the attempts of courts to reconcile the first and second sentences of former Section 4-402. The second sentence implied that the bank was liable for some form of damages other than those proximately caused by the dishonor if the dishonor was other than by mistake. But nothing in the section described what these noncompensatory damages might be. Some courts have held that in distinguishing between mistaken dishonors and nonmistaken dishonors, the so-called "trader" rule has been retained that allowed a "merchant or trader" to recover substantial damages

for wrongful dishonor without proof of damages actually suffered. Comment 3 to former Section 4–402 indicated that this was not the intent of the drafters. White & Summers, Uniform Commercial Code, Section 18–4 (1988), states: "The negative implication is that when wrongful dishonors occur not 'through mistake' but willfully, the court may impose damages greater than 'actual damages'.... Certainly the reference to 'mistake' in the second sentence of 4–402 invites a court to adopt the relevant pre-Code distinction." Subsection (b) by deleting the reference to mistake in the second sentence precludes any inference that Section 4–402 retains the "trader" rule. Whether a bank is liable for noncompensatory damages, such as punitive damages, must be decided by Section 1–103 and Section 1–106 ("by other rule of law").

2. Wrongful dishonor is different from "failure to exercise ordinary care in handling an item," and the measure of damages is that stated in this section, not that stated in Section 4–103(e). By the same token, if a dishonor comes within this section, the measure of damages of this section applies and not another measure of damages. If the wrongful refusal of the beneficiary's bank to make funds available from a funds transfer causes the beneficiary's check to be dishonored, no specific guidance is given as to whether recovery is under this section or Article 4A. In each case this issue must be viewed in its factual context, and it was thought unwise to seek to establish certainty at the cost of fairness.

3. The second and third sentences of subsection (b) reject decisions holding that as a matter of law the dishonor of a check is not the "proximate cause" of the arrest and prosecution of the customer and leave to determination in each case as a question of fact whether the dishonor is or may be the "proximate cause."

4. Banks commonly determine whether there are sufficient funds in an account to pay an item after the close of banking hours on the day of presentment when they post debit and credit items to the account. The determination is made on the basis of credits available for withdrawal as of right or made available for withdrawal by the bank as an accommodation to its customer. When it is determined that payment of the item would overdraw the account, the item may be returned at any time before the bank's midnight deadline the following day. Before the item is returned new credits that are withdrawable as of right may have been added to the account. Subsection (c) eliminates uncertainty under Article 4 as to whether the failure to make a second determination before the item is returned on the day following presentment is a wrongful dishonor if new credits were added to the account on that day that would have covered the amount of the check.

5. Section 4–402 has been construed to preclude an action for wrongful dishonor by a plaintiff other than the bank's customer. Loucks v. Albuquerque National Bank, 418 P.2d 191 (N.Mex.1966). Some courts have allowed a plaintiff other than the customer to sue when the customer is a business entity that is one and the same with the individual or individuals operating it. Murdaugh Volkswagen, Inc. v. First National Bank, 801 F.2d 719 (4th Cir.1986) and Karsh v. American City Bank, 113 Cal.App.3d 419, 169 Cal. Rptr. 851 (1980). However, where the wrongful dishonor impugns the reputation of an operator of the business, the issue is not merely, as the court in Koger v. East First National Bank, 443 So.2d 141 (Fla.App.1983), put it, one of a literal versus a liberal interpretation of Section 4–402. Rather the issue is whether the statutory cause of action in Section 4–402 displaces, in accordance with Section 1–103, any cause of action that existed at common law in a person who is not the customer whose reputation was damaged. See Marcum v. Security Trust and Savings Co., 221 Ala. 419, 129 So. 74 (1930). While Section 4–402 should not be interpreted to displace the latter cause of action, the section itself gives no cause of action to other than a "customer," however that definition is construed, and thus confers no cause of action on the holder of

a dishonored item. First American National Bank v. Commerce Union Bank, 692 S.W.2d 642 (Tenn.App.1985).

§ 4-403. Customer's Right to Stop Payment; Burden of Proof of Loss.

(a) A customer or any person authorized to draw on the account if there is more than one person may stop payment of any item drawn on the customer's account or close the account by an order to the bank describing the item or account with reasonable certainty received at a time and in a manner that affords the bank a reasonable opportunity to act on it before any action by the bank with respect to the item described in Section 4-303. If the signature of more than one person is required to draw on an account, any of these persons may stop payment or close the account.

(b) A stop-payment order is effective for six months, but it lapses after 14 calendar days if the original order was oral and was not confirmed in writing within that period. A stop-payment order may be renewed for additional six-month periods by a writing given to the bank within a period during which the stop-payment order is effective.

(c) The burden of establishing the fact and amount of loss resulting from the payment of an item contrary to a stop-payment order or order to close an account is on the customer. The loss from payment of an item contrary to a stop-payment order may include damages for dishonor of subsequent items under Section 4-402.

As amended in 1990.

See Appendix IX for material relating to changes made in text in 1990.

Official Comment

1. The position taken by this section is that stopping payment or closing an account is a service which depositors expect and are entitled to receive from banks notwithstanding its difficulty, inconvenience and expense. The inevitable occasional losses through failure to stop or close should be borne by the banks as a cost of the business of banking.

2. Subsection (a) follows the decisions holding that a payee or indorsee has no right to stop payment. This is consistent with the provision governing payment or satisfaction. See Section 3-602. The sole exception to this rule is found in Section 4-405 on payment after notice of death, by which any person claiming an interest in the account can stop payment.

3. Payment is commonly stopped only on checks; but the right to stop payment is not limited to checks, and extends to any item payable by any bank. If the maker of a note payable at a bank is in a position analogous to that of a drawer (Section 4-106) the maker may stop payment of the note. By analogy the rule extends to drawees other than banks.

4. A cashier's check or teller's check purchased by a customer whose account is debited in payment for the check is not a check drawn on the customer's account within the meaning of subsection (a); hence, a customer purchasing a cashier's check or teller's check has no right to stop payment of such a check under subsection (a). If a bank issuing a cashier's check or teller's check refuses to pay the check as an accommodation to its customer or for other reasons, its liability on the

check is governed by Section 3–411. There is no right to stop payment after certification of a check or other acceptance of a draft, and this is true no matter who procures the certification. See Sections 3–411 and 4–303. The acceptance is the drawee's own engagement to pay, and it is not required to impair its credit by refusing payment for the convenience of the drawer.

5. Subsection (a) makes clear that if there is more than one person authorized to draw on a customer's account any one of them can stop payment of any check drawn on the account or can order the account closed. Moreover, if there is a customer, such as a corporation, that requires its checks to bear the signatures of more than one person, any of these persons may stop payment on a check. In describing the item, the customer, in the absence of a contrary agreement, must meet the standard of what information allows the bank under the technology then existing to identify the item with reasonable certainty.

6. Under subsection (b), a stop-payment order is effective after the order, whether written or oral, is received by the bank and the bank has a reasonable opportunity to act on it. If the order is written it remains in effect for six months from that time. If the order is oral it lapses after 14 days unless there is written confirmation. If there is written confirmation within the 14-day period, the six-month period dates from the giving of the oral order. A stop-payment order may be renewed any number of times by written notice given during a six-month period while a stop order is in effect. A new stop-payment order may be given after a six-month period expires, but such a notice takes effect from the date given. When a stop-payment order expires it is as though the order had never been given, and the payor bank may pay the item in good faith under Section 4–404 even though a stop-payment order had once been given.

7. A payment in violation of an effective direction to stop payment is an improper payment, even though it is made by mistake or inadvertence. Any agreement to the contrary is invalid under Section 4–103(a) if in paying the item over the stop-payment order the bank has failed to exercise ordinary care. An agreement to the contrary which is imposed upon a customer as part of a standard form contract would have to be evaluated in the light of the general obligation of good faith. Sections 1–203 and 4–104(c). The drawee is, however, entitled to subrogation to prevent unjust enrichment (Section 4–407); retains common law defenses, e.g., that by conduct in recognizing the payment the customer has ratified the bank's action in paying over a stop-payment order (Section 1–103); and retains common law rights, e.g., to recover money paid under a mistake under Section 3–418. It has sometimes been said that payment cannot be stopped against a holder in due course, but the statement is inaccurate. The payment can be stopped but the drawer remains liable on the instrument to the holder in due course (Sections 3–305, 3–414) and the drawee, if it pays, becomes subrogated to the rights of the holder in due course against the drawer. Section 4–407. The relationship between Sections 4–403 and 4–407 is discussed in the comments to Section 4–407. Any defenses available against a holder in due course remain available to the drawer, but other defenses are cut off to the same extent as if the holder were bringing the action.

§ 4–404. Bank Not Obliged to Pay Check More Than Six Months Old.

A bank is under no obligation to a customer having a checking account to pay a check, other than a certified check, which is presented more than six months after its date, but it may charge its customer's account for a payment made thereafter in good faith.

Official Comment

This section incorporates a type of statute that had been adopted in 26 jurisdictions before the Code. The time limit is set at six months because banking and commercial practice regards a check outstanding for longer than that period as stale, and a bank will normally not pay such a check without consulting the depositor. It is therefore not required to do so, but is given the option to pay because it may be in a position to know, as in the case of dividend checks, that the drawer wants payment made.

Certified checks are excluded from the section because they are the primary obligation of the certifying bank (Sections 3–409 and 3–413). The obligation runs directly to the holder of the check. The customer's account was presumably charged when the check was certified.

§ 4–405. Death or Incompetence of Customer.

(a) A payor or collecting bank's authority to accept, pay, or collect an item or to account for proceeds of its collection, if otherwise effective, is not rendered ineffective by incompetence of a customer of either bank existing at the time the item is issued or its collection is undertaken if the bank does not know of an adjudication of incompetence. Neither death nor incompetence of a customer revokes the authority to accept, pay, collect, or account until the bank knows of the fact of death or of an adjudication of incompetence and has reasonable opportunity to act on it.

(b) Even with knowledge, a bank may for 10 days after the date of death pay or certify checks drawn on or before that date unless ordered to stop payment by a person claiming an interest in the account.

As amended in 1990.

See Appendix IX for material relating to changes made in text in 1990.

Official Comment

1. Subsection (a) follows existing decisions holding that a drawee (payor) bank is not liable for the payment of a check before it has notice of the death or incompetence of the drawer. The justice and necessity of the rule are obvious. A check is an order to pay which the bank must obey under penalty of possible liability for dishonor. Further, with the tremendous volume of items handled any rule that required banks to verify the continued life and competency of drawers would be completely unworkable.

One or both of these same reasons apply to other phases of the bank collection and payment process and the rule is made wide enough to apply to these other phases. It applies to all kinds of "items"; to "customers" who own items as well as "customers" who draw or make them; to the function of collecting items as well as the function of accepting or paying them; to the carrying out of instructions to account for proceeds even though these may involve transfers to third parties; to depositary and intermediary banks as well as payor banks; and to incompetency existing at the time of the issuance of an item or the commencement of the collection or payment process as well as to incompetency occurring thereafter. Further, the requirement of actual knowledge makes inapplicable the rule of some cases that an adjudication of incompetency is constructive notice to all the world because obviously it is as impossible for banks to keep posted on such adjudications (in the absence of actual knowledge) as it is to keep posted as to death of immediate or remote customers.

2. Subsection (b) provides a limited period after death during which a bank may continue to pay checks (as distinguished from other items) even though it has notice. The purpose of the provision, as of the existing statutes, is to permit holders of checks drawn and issued shortly before death to cash them without the necessity of filing a claim in probate. The justification is that these checks normally are given in immediate payment of an obligation, that there is almost never any reason why they should not be paid, and that filing in probate is a useless formality, burdensome to the holder, the executor, the court and the bank.

This section does not prevent an executor or administrator from recovering the payment from the holder of the check. It is not intended to affect the validity of any gift causa mortis or other transfer in contemplation of death, but merely to relieve the bank of liability for the payment.

3. Any surviving relative, creditor or other person who claims an interest in the account may give a direction to the bank not to pay checks, or not to pay a particular check. Such notice has the same effect as a direction to stop payment. The bank has no responsibility to determine the validity of the claim or even whether it is "colorable." But obviously anyone who has an interest in the estate, including the person named as executor in a will, even if the will has not yet been admitted to probate, is entitled to claim an interest in the account.

§ 4–406. Customer's Duty to Discover and Report Unauthorized Signature or Alteration.

(a) A bank that sends or makes available to a customer a statement of account showing payment of items for the account shall either return or make available to the customer the items paid or provide information in the statement of account sufficient to allow the customer reasonably to identify the items paid. The statement of account provides sufficient information if the item is described by item number, amount, and date of payment.

(b) If the items are not returned to the customer, the person retaining the items shall either retain the items or, if the items are destroyed, maintain the capacity to furnish legible copies of the items until the expiration of seven years after receipt of the items. A customer may request an item from the bank that paid the item, and that bank must provide in a reasonable time either the item or, if the item has been destroyed or is not otherwise obtainable, a legible copy of the item.

(c) If a bank sends or makes available a statement of account or items pursuant to subsection (a), the customer must exercise reasonable promptness in examining the statement or the items to determine whether any payment was not authorized because of an alteration of an item or because a purported signature by or on behalf of the customer was not authorized. If, based on the statement or items provided, the customer should reasonably have discovered the unauthorized payment, the customer must promptly notify the bank of the relevant facts.

(d) If the bank proves that the customer failed, with respect to an item, to comply with the duties imposed on the customer by subsection (c), the customer is precluded from asserting against the bank:

(1) the customer's unauthorized signature or any alteration on the item, if the bank also proves that it suffered a loss by reason of the failure; and

(2) the customer's unauthorized signature or alteration by the same wrongdoer on any other item paid in good faith by the bank if the payment was made before the bank received notice from the customer of the unauthorized signature or alteration and after the customer had been afforded a reasonable period of time, not exceeding 30 days, in which to examine the item or statement of account and notify the bank.

(e) If subsection (d) applies and the customer proves that the bank failed to exercise ordinary care in paying the item and that the failure substantially contributed to loss, the loss is allocated between the customer precluded and the bank asserting the preclusion according to the extent to which the failure of the customer to comply with subsection (c) and the failure of the bank to exercise ordinary care contributed to the loss. If the customer proves that the bank did not pay the item in good faith, the preclusion under subsection (d) does not apply.

(f) Without regard to care or lack of care of either the customer or the bank, a customer who does not within one year after the statement or items are made available to the customer (subsection (a)) discover and report the customer's unauthorized signature on or any alteration on the item is precluded from asserting against the bank the unauthorized signature or alteration. If there is a preclusion under this subsection, the payor bank may not recover for breach of warranty under Section 4–208 with respect to the unauthorized signature or alteration to which the preclusion applies.

As amended in 1990.

See Appendix IX for material relating to changes made in text in 1990.

Revised Official Comment

1. Under subsection (a), if a bank that has paid a check or other item for the account of a customer makes available to the customer a statement of account showing payment of the item, the bank must either return the item to the customer or provide a description of the item sufficient to allow the customer to identify it. Under subsection (c), the customer has a duty to exercise reasonable promptness in examining the statement or the returned item to discover any unauthorized signature of the customer or any alteration and to promptly notify the bank if the customer should reasonably have discovered the unauthorized signature or alteration.

The duty stated in subsection (c) becomes operative only if the "bank sends or makes available a statement of account or items pursuant to subsection (a)." A bank is not under a duty to send a statement of account or the paid items to the customer; but, if it does not do so, the customer does not have any duties under subsection (c).

Under subsection (a), a statement of account must provide information "sufficient to allow the customer reasonably to identify the items paid." If the bank supplies its customer with an image of the paid item, it complies with this standard. But a safe harbor rule is provided. The bank complies with the standard of providing "sufficient information" if "the item is described by item number, amount, and date of payment." This means that the customer's duties under subsection (c) are triggered if the bank sends a statement of account complying with the safe harbor rule without returning the paid items. A bank does not have to return the paid items unless it has agreed with the customer to do so. Whether there is such an agreement depends upon the particular circumstances. See Section 1-201(3). If the bank elects to provide the minimum information that is "sufficient" under subsection (a) and, as a consequence, the customer could not "reasonably have discovered the unauthorized payment," there is no preclusion under subsection (d). If the customer made a record of the issued checks on the check stub or carbonized copies furnished by the bank in the checkbook, the customer should usually be able to verify the paid items shown on the statement of account and discover any unauthorized or altered checks. But there could be exceptional circumstances. For example, if a check is altered by changing the name of the payee, the customer could not normally detect the fraud unless the customer is given the paid check or the statement of account discloses the name of the payee of the altered check. If the customer could not "reasonably have discovered the unauthorized payment" under subsection (c) there would not be a preclusion under subsection (d).

The safe harbor provided by subsection (a) serves to permit a bank, based on the state of existing technology, to trigger the customer's duties under subsection (c) by providing a "statement of account showing payment of items" without having to return the paid items, in any case in which the bank has not agreed with the customer to return the paid items. The safe harbor does not, however, preclude a customer under subsection (d) from asserting its unauthorized signature or an alteration against a bank in those circumstances in which under subsection (c) the customer should not "reasonably have discovered the unauthorized payment." Whether the customer has failed to comply with its duties under subsection (c) is determined on a case-by-case basis.

The provision in subsection (a) that a statement of account contains "sufficient information if the item is described by item number, amount, and date of payment" is based upon the existing state of technology. This information was chosen because it can be obtained by the bank's computer from the check's MICR line without examination of the items involved. The other two items of information that the customer would normally want to know—the name of the payee and the date of the item—cannot currently be obtained from the MICR line. The safe harbor rule is important in determining the feasibility of payor or collecting bank check retention plans. A customer who keeps a record of checks written, e.g., on the check stubs or carbonized copies of the checks supplied by the bank in the checkbook, will usually have sufficient information to identify the items on the basis of item number, amount, and date of payment. But customers who do not utilize these record-keeping methods may not. The policy decision is that accommodating customers who do not keep adequate records is not as desirable as accommodating customers who keep more careful records. This policy results in less cost to the check collection system and thus to all customers of the system. It is expected that technological advances such as image processing may make it possible for banks to give customers more information in the future in a manner that is fully compatible with automation or truncation systems. At that time the Permanent Editorial Board may wish to make recommendations for an amendment revising the safe harbor requirements in the light of those advances.

2. Subsection (d) states the consequences of a failure by the customer to perform its duty under subsection (c) to report an alteration or the customer's unauthorized signature. Subsection (d)(1) applies to the unauthorized payment of the item to which the duty to report under subsection (c) applies. If the bank proves that the customer "should reasonably have discovered the unauthorized payment" (See Comment 1) and did not notify the bank, the customer is precluded from asserting against the bank the alteration or the customer's unauthorized signature if the bank proves that it suffered a loss as a result of the failure of

the customer to perform its subsection (c) duty. Subsection (d)(2) applies to cases in which the customer fails to report an unauthorized signature or alteration with respect to an item in breach of the subsection (c) duty (See Comment 1) and the bank subsequently pays other items of the customer with respect to which there is an alteration or unauthorized signature of the customer and the same wrongdoer is involved. If the payment of the subsequent items occurred after the customer has had a reasonable time (not exceeding 30 days) to report with respect to the first item and before the bank received notice of the unauthorized signature or alteration of the first item, the customer is precluded from asserting the alteration or unauthorized signature with respect to the subsequent items.

If the customer is precluded in a single or multiple item unauthorized payment situation under subsection (d), but the customer proves that the bank failed to exercise ordinary care in paying the item or items and that the failure substantially contributed to the loss, subsection (e) provides a comparative negligence test for allocating loss between the customer and the bank. Subsection (e) also states that, if the customer proves that the bank did not pay the item in good faith, the preclusion under subsection (d) does not apply.

Subsection (d)(2) changes former subsection (2)(b) by adopting a 30–day period in place of a 14–day period. Although the 14–day period may have been sufficient when the original version of Article 4 was drafted in the 1950s, given the much greater volume of checks at the time of the revision, a longer period was viewed as more appropriate. The rule of subsection (d)(2) follows pre-Code case law that payment of an additional item or items bearing an unauthorized signature or alteration by the same wrongdoer is a loss suffered by the bank traceable to the customer's failure to exercise reasonable care (See Comment 1) in examining the statement and notifying the bank of objections to it. One of the most serious consequences of failure of the customer to comply with the requirements of subsection (c) is the opportunity presented to the wrongdoer to repeat the misdeeds. Conversely, one of the best ways to keep down losses in this type of situation is for the customer to promptly examine the statement and notify the bank of an unauthorized signature or alteration so that the bank will be alerted to stop paying further items. Hence, the rule of subsection (d)(2) is prescribed, and to avoid dispute a specific time limit, 30 days, is designated for cases to which the subsection applies. These considerations are not present if there are no losses resulting from the payment of additional items. In these circumstances, a reasonable period for the customer to comply with its duties under subsection (c) would depend on the circumstances (Section 1–204(2)) and the subsection (d)(2) time limit should not be imported by analogy into subsection (c).

3. Subsection (b) applies if the items are not returned to the customer. Check retention plans may include a simple payor bank check retention plan or the kind of check retention plan that would be authorized by a truncation agreement in which a collecting bank or the payee may retain the items. Even after agreeing to a check retention plan, a customer may need to see one or more checks for litigation or other purposes. The customer's request for the check may always be made to the payor bank. Under subsection (b) retaining banks may destroy items but must maintain the capacity to furnish legible copies for seven years. A legible copy may include an image of an item. This Act does not define the length of the reasonable period of time for a bank to provide the check or copy of the check. What is reasonable depends on the capacity of the bank and the needs of the customer. This Act does not specify sanctions for failure to retain or furnish the items or legible copies; this is left to other laws regulating banks. See Comment 3 to Section 4–101. Moreover, this Act does not regulate fees that banks charge their customers for furnishing items or copies or other services covered by the Act, but under principles of law

such as unconscionability or good faith and fair dealing, courts have reviewed fees and the bank's exercise of a discretion to set fees. Perdue v. Crocker National Bank, 38 Cal.3d 913 (1985) (unconscionability); Best v. United Bank of Oregon, 739 P.2d 554, 562–566 (1987) (good faith and fair dealing). In addition, Section 1–203 provides that every contract or duty within this Act imposes an obligation of good faith in its performance or enforcement.

4. Subsection (e) replaces former subsection (3) and poses a modified comparative negligence test for determining liability. See the discussion on this point in the Comments to Sections 3–404, 3–405, and 3–406. The term "good faith" is defined in Section 3–103(a)(4) as including "observance of reasonable commercial standards of fair dealing." The connotation of this standard is fairness and not absence of negligence.

The term "ordinary care" used in subsection (e) is defined in Section 3–103(a)(7), made applicable to Article 4 by Section 4–104(c), to provide that sight examination by a payor bank is not required if its procedure is reasonable and is commonly followed by other comparable banks in the area. The case law is divided on this issue. The definition of "ordinary care" in Section 3–103 rejects those authorities that hold, in effect, that failure to use sight examination is negligence as a matter of law. The effect of the definition of "ordinary care" on Section 4–406 is only to provide that in the small percentage of cases in which a customer's failure to examine its statement or returned items has led to loss under subsection (d) a bank should not have to share that loss solely because it has adopted an automated collection or payment procedure in order to deal with the great volume of items at a lower cost to all customers.

5. Several changes are made in former Section 4–406(5). First, former subsection (5) is deleted and its substance is made applicable only to the one-year notice preclusion in former subsection (4) (subsection (f)). Thus if a drawer has not notified the payor bank of an unauthorized check or material alteration within the one-year period, the payor bank may not choose to recredit the drawer's account and pass the loss to the collecting banks on the theory of breach of warranty. Second, the reference in former subsection (4) to unauthorized indorsements is deleted. Section 4–406 imposes no duties on the drawer to look for unauthorized indorsements. Section 4–111 sets out a statute of limitations allowing a customer a three-year period to seek a credit to an account improperly charged by payment of an item bearing an unauthorized indorsement. Third, subsection (c) is added to Section 4–208 to assure that if a depositary bank is sued for breach of a presentment warranty, it can defend by showing that the drawer is precluded by Section 3–406 or Section 4–406(c) and (d). *Revisions approved by the Permanent Editorial Board for the Uniform Commercial Code, March 16, 1991.*

§ 4–407. Payor Bank's Right to Subrogation on Improper Payment.

If a payor bank has paid an item over the order of the drawer or maker to stop payment, or after an account has been closed, or otherwise under circumstances giving a basis for objection by the drawer or maker, to prevent unjust enrichment and only to the extent necessary to prevent loss to the bank by reason of its payment of the item, the payor bank is subrogated to the rights

(1) of any holder in due course on the item against the drawer or maker;

(2) of the payee or any other holder of the item against the drawer or maker either on the item or under the transaction out of which the item arose; and

(3) of the drawer or maker against the payee or any other holder of the item with respect to the transaction out of which the item arose.

As amended in 1990.

See Appendix IX for material relating to changes made in text in 1990.

Official Comment

1. Section 4–403 states that a stop-payment order or an order to close an account is binding on a bank. If a bank pays an item over such an order it is prima facie liable, but under subsection (c) of Section 4–403 the burden of establishing the fact and amount of loss from such payment is on the customer. A defense frequently interposed by a bank in an action against it for wrongful payment over a stop-payment order is that the drawer or maker suffered no loss because it would have been liable to a holder in due course in any event. On this argument some cases have held that payment cannot be stopped against a holder in due course. Payment can be stopped, but if it is, the drawer or maker is liable and the sound rule is that the bank is subrogated to the rights of the holder in due course. The preamble and paragraph (1) of this section state this rule.

2. Paragraph (2) also subrogates the bank to the rights of the payee or other holder against the drawer or maker either on the item or under the transaction out of which it arose. It may well be that the payee is not a holder in due course but still has good rights against the drawer. These may be on the check but also may not be as, for example, where the drawer buys goods from the payee and the goods are partially defective so that the payee is not entitled to the full price, but the goods are still worth a portion of the contract price. If the drawer retains the goods it is obligated to pay a part of the agreed price. If the bank has paid the check it should be subrogated to this claim of the payee against the drawer.

3. Paragraph (3) subrogates the bank to the rights of the drawer or maker against the payee or other holder with respect to the transaction out of which the item arose. If, for example, the payee was a fraudulent salesman inducing the drawer to issue a check for defective securities, and the bank pays the check over a stop-payment order but reimburses the drawer for such payment, the bank should have a basis for getting the money back from the fraudulent salesman.

4. The limitations of the preamble prevent the bank itself from getting any double recovery or benefits out of its subrogation rights conferred by the section.

5. The spelling out of the affirmative rights of the bank in this section does not destroy other existing rights (Section 1–103). Among others these may include the defense of a payor bank that by conduct in recognizing the payment a customer has ratified the bank's action in paying in disregard of a stop-payment order or right to recover money paid under a mistake.

PART 5

COLLECTION OF DOCUMENTARY DRAFTS

§ 4–501. Handling of Documentary Drafts; Duty to Send for Presentment and to Notify Customer of Dishonor.

A bank that takes a documentary draft for collection shall present or send the draft and accompanying documents for presentment and, upon learning that the draft has not been paid or accepted in due course, shall seasonably notify its customer of the fact even though it may have discounted or bought the draft or extended credit available for withdrawal as of right.

As amended in 1990.

See Appendix IX for material relating to changes made in text in 1990.

Official Comment

This section states the duty of a bank handling a documentary draft for a customer. "Documentary draft" is defined in Section 4–104. The duty stated exists even if the bank has bought the draft. This is because to the customer the draft normally represents an underlying commercial transaction, and if that is not going through as planned the customer should know it promptly.

§ 4–502. Presentment of "On Arrival" Drafts.

If a draft or the relevant instructions require presentment "on arrival", "when goods arrive" or the like, the collecting bank need not present until in its judgment a reasonable time for arrival of the goods has expired. Refusal to pay or accept because the goods have not arrived is not dishonor; the bank must notify its transferor of the refusal but need not present the draft again until it is instructed to do so or learns of the arrival of the goods.

As amended in 1990.

See Appendix IX for material relating to changes made in text in 1990.

Official Comment

The section is designed to establish a definite rule for "on arrival" drafts. The term includes not only drafts drawn payable "on arrival" but also drafts forwarded with instructions to present "on arrival." The term refers to the arrival of the relevant goods. Unless a bank has actual knowledge of the arrival of the goods, as for example, when it is the "notify" party on the bill of lading, the section only requires the exercise of such judgment in estimating time as a bank may be expected to have. Commonly the buyer-drawee will want the goods and will therefore call for the documents and take up the draft when they do arrive.

§ 4–503. Responsibility of Presenting Bank for Documents and Goods; Report of Reasons for Dishonor; Referee in Case of Need.

Unless otherwise instructed and except as provided in Article 5, a bank presenting a documentary draft:

(1) must deliver the documents to the drawee on acceptance of the draft if it is payable more than three days after presentment; otherwise, only on payment; and

(2) upon dishonor, either in the case of presentment for acceptance or presentment for payment, may seek and follow instructions from any referee in case of need designated in the draft or, if the presenting bank does not choose to utilize the referee's services,

it must use diligence and good faith to ascertain the reason for dishonor, must notify its transferor of the dishonor and of the results of its effort to ascertain the reasons therefor, and must request instructions.

However the presenting bank is under no obligation with respect to goods represented by the documents except to follow any reasonable instructions seasonably received; it has a right to reimbursement for any expense incurred in following instructions and to prepayment of or indemnity for those expenses.

As amended in 1990.

See Appendix IX for material relating to changes made in text in 1990.

Official Comment

1. This section states the rules governing, in the absence of instructions, the duty of the presenting bank in case either of honor or of dishonor of a documentary draft. The section should be read in connection with Section 2–514 on when documents are deliverable on acceptance, when on payment.

2. If the draft is drawn under a letter of credit, Article 5 controls. See Sections 5–109 through 5–114.

§ 4–504. Privilege of Presenting Bank to Deal With Goods; Security Interest for Expenses.

(a) A presenting bank that, following the dishonor of a documentary draft, has seasonably requested instructions but does not receive them within a reasonable time may store, sell, or otherwise deal with the goods in any reasonable manner.

(b) For its reasonable expenses incurred by action under subsection (a) the presenting bank has a lien upon the goods or their proceeds, which may be foreclosed in the same manner as an unpaid seller's lien.

As amended in 1990.

See Appendix IX for material relating to changes made in text in 1990.

Official Comment

The section gives the presenting bank, after dishonor, a privilege to deal with the goods in any commercially reasonable manner pending instructions from its transferor and, if still unable to communicate with its principal after a reasonable time, a right to realize its expenditures as if foreclosing on an unpaid seller's lien (Section 2–706). The provision includes situations in which storage of goods or other action becomes commercially necessary pending receipt of any requested instructions, even if the requested instructions are later received.

The "reasonable manner" referred to means one reasonable in the light of business factors and the judgment of a business man.

ARTICLE 4A

FUNDS TRANSFERS

This article was approved by the National Conference of Commissioners on Uniform State Laws and the American Law Institute in 1989.

PART 1. SUBJECT MATTER AND DEFINITIONS

PART 2. ISSUE AND ACCEPTANCE OF PAYMENT ORDER

PART 3. EXECUTION OF SENDER'S PAYMENT ORDER BY RECEIVING BANK

PART 4. PAYMENT

National Conference of Commissioners on Uniform State Laws

REPORTER

Robert L. Jordan, Los Angeles, California

William D. Warren, Los Angeles, California

DRAFTING COMMITTEE

CO-CHAIRMEN

Carlyle C. Ring, Jr., Alexandria, Virginia

Robert Haydock, Jr., Boston, Massachusetts

MEMBERS

Boris Auerbach, Cincinnati, Ohio

Richard F. Dole, Jr., Houston, Texas

William E. Hogan, New York, New York

Charles W. Joiner, Ann Arbor, Michigan

Frederick H. Miller, Norman, Oklahoma

Donald J. Rapson, Livingston, New Jersey, *The American Law Institute Representative*

Michael P. Sullivan, Minneapolis, Minnesota, *President, (Member Ex Officio)*

Neal Ossen, Hartford, Connecticut, *Chairman, Division C, (Member Ex Officio)*

REVIEW COMMITTEE

CHAIRMAN

Frank F. Jestrab, Chevy Chase, Maryland

MEMBERS

Rupert R. Bullivant, Portland, Oregon

Michael Franck, Lansing, Michigan

CONSULTANT

Fairfax Leary, Jr., Villanova, Pennsylvania

ADVISORS

Thomas C. Baxter, Jr., Federal Reserve Bank of New York

Roland E. Brandel, American Bar Association

Leon P. Ciferni, National Westminster Bank, U.S.A.

William B. Davenport, American Bar Association, Section of Business Law, Ad Hoc Committee on Payment Systems

Carl Felsenfeld, Association of the Bar of the City of New York

J. Kevin French, Exxon Company, U.S.A.

Thomas J. Greco, American Bankers Association

Arthur L. Herold, National Corporate Cash Management Association

John R. H. Kimball, Federal Reserve Bank of Boston

John F. Lee, New York Clearing House Association

W. Robert Moore, American Bankers Association

Ernest T. Patrikis, Federal Reserve Bank of New York

Richard B. Wagner, General Motors Corporation

ADDITIONAL PARTICIPANTS

Dean Bitner, Sears, Roebuck & Company

Henry N. Dyhouse, U.S. Central Credit Union

James Foorman, First Chicago Corporation

Richard M. Gottlieb, Manufacturers Hanover Trust Company

Shirley Holder, Atlantic Richfield Company

Paul E. Homrighausen, Bankers Clearing House Association and National Automated Clearing House Association

Gail M. Inaba, Morgan Guaranty Trust Company of New York

Oliver I. Ireland, Board of Governors of Federal Reserve System

Richard P. Kessler, Jr., Credit Union National Association

James W. Kopp, Shell Oil Company

Robert M. MacAllister, Chase Manhattan Bank NA

Thomas E. Montgomery, California Bankers Association

Norman R. Nelson, New York Clearing House Association

Samuel Newman, Manufacturers Hanover Trust Company

Nena Nodge, National Corporate Cash Management Association

Robert J. Pisapia, Occidental Petroleum Corporation

Deborah S. Prutzman, Arnold & Porter

Robert M. Rosenblith, Manufacturers Hanover Trust Company

Paul S. Turner, Occidental Petroleum Corporation

Irma Villarreal, Aon Corporation

Suzanne Weakley, Atlantic Richfield Company

PREFATORY NOTE

The National Conference of Commissioners on Uniform State laws and The American Law Institute have approved a new Article 4A to the Uniform Commercial Code. Comments that follow each of the sections of the statute are intended as official comments. They explain in detail the purpose and meaning of the various sections and the policy considerations on which they are based.

Description of transaction covered by Article 4A.

There are a number of mechanisms for making payments through the banking system. Most of these mechanisms are covered in whole or part by state or federal statutes. In terms of number of transactions, payments made by check or credit card are the most common payment methods. Payment by check is covered by Articles 3 and 4 of the UCC and some aspects of payment by credit card are covered by federal law. In recent years electronic funds transfers have been increasingly common in consumer transactions. For example, in some cases a retail customer can pay for purchases by use of an access or debit card inserted in a terminal at the retail store that allows the bank account of the customer to be instantly debited. Some aspects of these point-of-sale transactions and other consumer payments that are effected electronically are covered by a federal statute, the Electronic Fund Transfer Act (EFTA). If any part of a funds transfer is covered by EFTA, the entire funds transfer is excluded from Article 4A.

Another type of payment, commonly referred to as a wholesale wire transfer, is the primary focus of Article 4A. Payments that are covered by Article 4A are overwhelmingly between business or financial institutions. The dollar volume of payments made by wire transfer far exceeds the dollar volume of payments made by other means. The volume of payments by wire transfer over the two principal wire payment systems—the Federal Reserve wire transfer network (Fedwire) and the New York Clearing House Interbank Payments Systems (CHIPS)—exceeds one trillion dollars per day. Most payments carried out by use of automated clearing houses are consumer payments covered by EFTA and therefore not covered by Article 4A. There is, however, a significant volume of nonconsumer ACH payments that closely resemble wholesale wire transfers. These payments are also covered by Article 4A.

There is some resemblance between payments made by wire transfer and payments made by other means such as paper-based checks and credit cards or electronically-based consumer payments, but there are also many differences. Article 4A excludes from its coverage these other payment mechanisms. Article 4A follows a policy of treating the transaction that it covers—a "funds transfer"—as a unique method of payment that is governed by unique principles of law that address the operational and policy issues presented by this kind of payment.

The funds transfer that is covered by Article 4A is not a complex transaction and can be illustrated by the following example which is used throughout the Prefatory Note as a basis for discussion. X, a debtor, wants to pay an obligation owed to Y. Instead of delivering to Y a negotiable instrument such as a check or some other writing such as a credit card slip that enables Y to obtain payment from a bank, X transmits an instruction to X's bank to credit a sum of money to the bank account of Y. In most cases X's bank and Y's bank are different banks. X's bank may carry out X's instruction by instructing Y's bank to credit Y's account in the amount that X requested. The instruction that X issues to its bank is a "payment order." X is the "sender" of the payment order and X's bank is the "receiving bank" with respect to X's order. Y is the "beneficiary" of X's order. When X's bank issues an instruction to Y's bank to carry out X's payment order, X's bank "executes" X's order. The instruction of X's bank to Y's bank is also a payment order. With respect to that order, X's bank is the sender, Y's bank is the receiving bank, and Y is the beneficiary. The entire series of transactions by which X pays Y is knows as the "funds transfer." With respect to the funds transfer, X is the "originator," X's bank is the "originator's bank," Y is the "beneficiary" and Y's bank is the "beneficiary's bank." In more complex transactions there are one or more additional banks known as "intermediary banks" between X's bank and Y's bank. In the funds transfer the instruction contained in the payment order of X to its bank is carried out by a series of payment orders by each bank in the transmission chain to the next bank in the chain until Y's bank receives a payment order to make the credit to Y's account. In most cases, the payment order of each bank to the next bank in the chain is transmitted electronically, and often the payment order of X to its bank is also transmitted electronically, but the means of transmission does not have any legal significance. A payment order may be transmitted by any means, and in some cases the payment order is transmitted by a slow means such as first class mail. To reflect this fact, the broader term "funds transfer" rather than the narrower term "wire transfer" is used in Article 4A to describe the overall payment transaction.

Funds transfers are divided into two categories determined by whether the instruction to pay is given by the person making payment or the person receiving payment. If the instruction is given by the person making the payment, the transfer is commonly referred to as a "credit transfer." If the instruction is given by the person receiving payment, the transfer is commonly referred to as a "debit transfer." Article 4A governs credit transfers and excludes debit transfers.

Why is Article 4A needed?

There is no comprehensive body of law that defines the rights and obligations that arise from wire transfers. Some aspects of wire transfers are governed by rules of the principal transfer systems. Transfers made by Fedwire are governed by Federal Reserve Regulation J and transfers over CHIPS are governed by the CHIPS rules. Transfers made by means of automated clearing houses are governed by uniform rules adopted by various associations of banks in various parts of the nation or by Federal Reserve rules or operating circulars. But the various funds transfer system rules apply to only limited aspects of wire transfer transactions. The resolution of the many issues that are not covered by funds transfer system rules depends on contracts of the parties, to the extent that they exist, or principles of law applicable to other payment mechanisms that might be applied by analogy. The result is a great deal of uncertainty. There is no consensus about the juridical nature of a wire transfer and consequently of the rights and obligations that are created. Article 4A is intended to provide the comprehensive body of law that we do not have today.

Characteristics of a funds transfer.

There are a number of characteristics of funds transfers covered by Article 4A that have influenced the drafting of the statute. The typical funds transfer involves a large amount of money. Multimillion dollar transactions are commonplace. The originator of the transfer and the beneficiary are typically sophisticated business or financial organizations. High speed is another predominant characteristic. Most funds transfers are completed on the same day, even in complex transactions in which there are several intermediary banks in the transmission chain. A funds transfer is a highly efficient substitute for payments made by the delivery of paper instruments. Another characteristic is extremely low cost. A transfer that involves many millions of dollars can be made for a price of a few dollars. Price does not normally vary very much or at all with the amount of the transfer. This system of pricing may not be feasible if the bank is exposed to very large liabilities in connection with the transaction. The pricing system assumes that the price reflects primarily the cost of the mechanical operation performed by the bank, but in fact, a bank may have more or less potential liability with respect to a funds transfer depending upon the amount of the transfer. Risk of loss to banks carrying out a funds transfer may arise from a variety of causes. In some funds transfers, there may be extensions of very large amounts of credit for short periods of time by the banks that carry out a funds transfer. If a payment order is issued to the beneficiary's bank, it is normal for the bank to release funds to the beneficiary immediately. Sometimes, payment to the beneficiary's bank by the bank that issued the order to the beneficiary's bank is delayed until the end of the day. If that payment is not received because of the insolvency of the bank that is obliged to pay, the beneficiary's bank may suffer a loss. There is also risk of loss if a bank fails to execute the payment order of a customer, or if the order is executed late. There also may be an error in the payment order issued by a bank that is executing the payment order of its customer. For example, the error might relate to the amount to be paid or to the identity of the person to be paid. Because the dollar amounts involved in funds transfers are so large, the risk of loss if something goes wrong in a transaction may also be very large. A major policy issue in the drafting of Article 4A is that of determining how risk of loss is to be allocated given the price structure in the industry.

Concept of acceptance and effect of acceptance by the beneficiary's bank.

Rights and obligations under Article 4A arise as the result of "acceptance" of a payment order by the bank to which the order is addressed.

Section 4A–209. The effect of acceptance varies depending upon whether the payment order is issued to the beneficiary's bank or to a bank other than the beneficiary's bank. Acceptance by the beneficiary's bank is particularly important because it defines when the beneficiary's bank becomes obligated to the beneficiary to pay the amount of the payment order. Although Article 4A follows convention in using the term "funds transfer" to identify the payment from X to Y that is described above, no money or property right of X is actually transferred to Y. X pays Y by causing Y's bank to become indebted to Y in the amount of the payment. This debt arises when Y's bank accepts the payment order that X's bank issued to Y's bank to execute X's order. If the funds transfer was carried out by use of one or more intermediary banks between X's bank and Y's bank, Y's bank becomes indebted to Y when Y's bank accepts the payment order issued to it by an intermediary bank. The funds transfer is completed when this debt is incurred. Acceptance, the event that determines when the debt of Y's bank to Y arises, occurs (i) when Y's bank pays Y or notifies Y of receipt of the payment order, or (ii) when Y's bank receives payment from the bank that issued a payment order to Y's bank.

The only obligation of the beneficiary's bank that results from acceptance of a payment order is to pay the amount of the order to the beneficiary. No obligation is owed to either the sender of the payment order accepted by the beneficiary's bank or to the originator of the funds transfer. The obligation created by acceptance by the beneficiary's bank is for the benefit of the beneficiary. The purpose of the sender's payment order is to effect payment by the originator to the beneficiary and that purpose is achieved when the beneficiary's bank accepts the payment order. Section 4A–405 states rules for determining when the obligation of the beneficiary's bank to the beneficiary has been paid.

Acceptance by a bank other than the beneficiary's bank.

In the funds transfer described above, what is the obligation of X's bank when it receives X's payment order? Funds transfers by a bank on behalf of its customer are made pursuant to an agreement or arrangement that may or may not be reduced to a formal document signed by the parties. It is probably true that in most cases there is either no express agreement or the agreement addresses only some aspects of the transaction. Substantial risk is involved in funds transfers and a bank may not be willing to give this service to all customers, and may not be willing to offer it to any customer unless certain safeguards against loss such as security procedures are in effect. Funds transfers often involve the giving of credit by the receiving bank to the customer, and that also may involve an agreement. These considerations are reflected in Article 4A by the principle that, in the absence of a contrary agreement, a receiving bank does not incur liability with respect to a payment order until it accepts it. If X and X's bank in the hypothetical case had an agreement that obliged the bank to act on X's payment orders and the bank failed to comply with the agreement, the bank can be held liable for breach of the agreement. But apart from any obligation arising by agreement, the bank does not incur any liability with respect to X's payment order until the bank accepts the order. X's payment order is treated by Article 4A as a request by

X to the bank to take action that will cause X's payment order to be carried out. That request can be accepted by X's bank by "executing" X's payment order. Execution occurs when X's bank sends a payment order to Y's bank intended by X's bank to carry out the payment order of X. X's bank could also execute X's payment order by issuing a payment order to an intermediary bank instructing the intermediary bank to instruct Y's bank to make the credit to Y's account. In that case execution and acceptance of X's order occur when the payment order of X's bank is sent to the intermediary bank. When X's bank executes X's payment order the bank is entitled to receive payment from X and may debit an authorized account of X. If X's bank does not execute X's order and the amount of the order is covered by a withdrawable credit balance in X's authorized account, the bank must pay X interest on the money represented by X's order unless X is given prompt notice of rejection of the order. Section 4A–210(b).

Bank error in funds transfers.

If a bank, other than the beneficiary's bank, accepts a payment order, the obligations and liabilities are owed to the originator of the funds transfer. Assume in the example stated above, that X's bank executes X's payment order by issuing a payment order to an intermediary bank that executes the order of X's bank by issuing a payment order to Y's bank. The obligations of X's bank with respect to execution are owed to X. The obligations of the intermediary bank with respect to execution are also owed to X. Section 4A–302 states standards with respect to the time and manner of execution of payment orders. Section 4A–305 states the measure of damages for improper execution. It also states that a receiving bank is liable for damages if it fails to execute a payment order that it was obliged by express agreement to execute. In each case consequential damages are not recoverable unless an express agreement of the receiving bank provides for them. The policy basis for this limitation is discussed in Comment 2 to Section 4A–305.

Error in the consummation of a funds transfer is not uncommon. There may be a discrepancy in the amount that the originator orders to be paid to the beneficiary and the amount that the beneficiary's bank is ordered to pay. For example, if the originator's payment order instructs payment of $100,000 and the payment order of the originator's bank instructs payment of $1,000,000, the originator's bank is entitled to receive only $100,000 from the originator and has the burden of recovering the additional $900,000 paid to the beneficiary by mistake. In some cases the originator's bank or an intermediary bank instructs payment to a beneficiary other than the beneficiary stated in the originator's payment order. If the wrong beneficiary is paid the bank that issued the erroneous payment order is not entitled to receive payment of the payment order that it executed and has the burden of recovering the mistaken payment. The originator is not obliged to pay its payment order. Section 4A–303 and Section 4A–207 state rules for determining the rights and obligations of the various parties to the funds transfer in these cases and in other typical cases in which error is made.

Pursuant to Section 4A–402(c) the originator is excused from the obligation to pay the originator's bank if the funds transfer is not completed, i.e. payment by the originator to the beneficiary is not made. Payment by the originator to the beneficiary occurs when the beneficiary's bank accepts a payment order for the benefit of the beneficiary of the originator's payment order. Section 4A–406. If for any reason that acceptance does not occur, the originator is not required to pay the payment order that it issued or, if it already paid, is entitled to refund of the payment with interest. This "money-back guarantee" is an important protection of the originator of a funds transfer. The same rule applies to any other sender in the funds transfer. Each sender's obligation to pay is excused if the beneficiary's bank does not accept a payment order for the benefit of the beneficiary of that sender's order. There is an important exception to this rule. It is common practice for the originator of a funds transfer to designate the intermediary bank or banks through which the funds transfer is to be routed. The originator's bank is required by Section 4A–302 to follow the instruction of the originator with respect to intermediary banks. If the originator's bank sends a payment order to the intermediary bank designated in the originator's order and the intermediary bank causes the funds transfer to miscarry by failing to execute the payment order or by instructing payment to the wrong beneficiary, the originator's bank is not required to pay its payment order and if it has already paid it is entitled to recover payment from the intermediary bank. This remedy is normally adequate, but if the originator's bank already paid its order and the intermediary bank has suspended payments or is not permitted by law to refund payment, the originator's bank will suffer a loss. Since the originator required the originator's bank to use the failed intermediary bank, Section 4A–402(e) provides that in this case the originator is obliged to pay its payment order and has a claim against the intermediary bank for the amount of the order. The same principle applies to any other sender that designates a subsequent intermediary bank.

Unauthorized payment orders.

An important issue addressed in Section 4A–202 and Section 4A–203 is how the risk of loss from unauthorized payment orders is to be allocated. In a large percentage of cases, the payment order of the originator of the funds transfer is transmitted electronically to the originator's bank. In these cases it may not be possible for the bank to know whether the electronic message has been authorized by its customer. To ensure that no unauthorized person is transmitting messages to the bank, the normal practice is to establish security procedures that usually involve the use of codes or identifying numbers or words. If the bank accepts a payment order that purports to be that of its customer after verifying its authenticity by complying with a security procedure agreed to by the customer and the bank, the customer is bound to pay the order even if it was not authorized. But there is an important limitation on this rule. The bank is entitled to payment in the case of an unauthorized order only if the court finds that the security procedure was a commercially reasonable method of providing security against unauthorized payment orders. The customer can also avoid liability if it can prove that the unauthorized order was not initiated by an employee or other agent of the customer having access to confidential security information or by a person who obtained that information from a source controlled by the customer. The policy issues are discussed in the comments following Section

4A–203. If the bank accepts an unauthorized payment order without verifying it in compliance with a security procedure, the loss falls on the bank.

Security procedures are also important in cases of error in the transmission of payment orders. There may be an error by the sender in the amount of the order, or a sender may transmit a payment order and then erroneously transmit a duplicate of the order. Normally, the sender is bound by the payment order even if it is issued by mistake. But in some cases an error of this kind can be detected by a security procedure. Although the receiving bank is not obliged to provide a security procedure for the detection of error, if such a procedure is agreed to by the bank Section 4A–205 provides that if the error is not detected because the receiving bank does not comply with the procedure, any resulting loss is borne by the bank failing to comply with the security procedure.

Insolvency losses.

Some payment orders do not involve the granting of credit to the sender by the receiving bank. In those cases, the receiving bank accepts the sender's order at the same time the bank receives payment of the order. This is true of a transfer of funds by Fedwire or of cases in which the receiving bank can debit a funded account of the sender. But in some cases the granting of credit is the norm. This is true of a payment order over CHIPS. In a CHIPS transaction the receiving bank usually will accept the order before receiving payment from the sending bank. Payment is delayed until the end of the day when settlement is made through the Federal Reserve System. If the receiving bank is an intermediary bank, it will accept by issuing a payment order to another bank and the intermediary bank is obliged to pay that payment order. If the receiving bank is the beneficiary's bank, the bank usually will accept by releasing funds to the beneficiary before the bank has received payment. If a sending bank suspends payments before settling its liabilities at the end of the day, the financial stability of banks that are net creditors of the insolvent bank may also be put into jeopardy, because the dollar volume of funds transfers between the banks may be extremely large. With respect to two banks that are dealing with each other in a series of transactions in which each bank is sometimes a receiving bank and sometimes a sender, the risk of insolvency can be managed if amounts payable as a sender and amounts receivable as a receiving bank are roughly equal. But if these amounts are significantly out of balance, a net creditor bank may have a very significant credit risk during the day before settlement occurs. The Federal Reserve System and the banking community are greatly concerned with this risk, and various measures have been instituted to reduce this credit exposure. Article 4A also addresses this problem. A receiving bank can always avoid this risk by delaying acceptance of a payment order until after the bank has received payment. For example, if the beneficiary's bank credits the beneficiary's account it can avoid acceptance by not notifying the beneficiary of the receipt of the order or by notifying the beneficiary that the credit may not be withdrawn until the beneficiary's bank receives payment. But if the beneficiary's bank releases funds to the beneficiary before receiving settlement, the result in a funds transfer other than a transfer by means of an automated clearing house or similar provisional settlement system is that the beneficiary's bank may not recover the funds if it fails to receive settlement. This rule encourages the banking system to impose credit limitations on banks that issue payment orders. These limitations are already in effect. CHIPS has also proposed a loss-sharing plan to be adopted for implementation in the second half of 1990 under which CHIPS participants will be required to provide funds necessary to complete settlement of the obligations of one or more participants that are unable to meet settlement obligations. Under this plan, it will be a virtual certainty that there will be settlement on CHIPS in the event of failure by a single bank. Section 4A–403(b) and (c) are also addressed to reducing risks of insolvency. Under these provisions the amount owed by a failed bank with respect to payment orders it issued is the net amount owing after setting off amounts owed to the failed bank with respect to payment orders it received. This rule allows credit exposure to be managed by limitations on the net debit position of a bank.

International transfers.

The major international legal document dealing with the subject of electronic funds transfers is the Model Law on International Credit Transfers adopted in 1992 by the United Nations Commission on International Trade Law. It covers basically the same type of transaction as does Article 4A, although it requires the funds transferred to have an international component. The Model Law and Article 4A basically live together in harmony, but to the extent there are differences they must be recognized and, to the extent possible, avoided or adjusted by agreement. See PEB Commentary No. 13, dated February 16, 1994 [Appendix V, infra].

PART 1

SUBJECT MATTER AND DEFINITIONS

§ 4A–101. Short Title.

This Article may be cited as Uniform Commercial Code—Funds Transfers.

§ 4A–102. Subject Matter.

Except as otherwise provided in Section 4A–108, this Article applies to funds transfers defined in Section 4A–104.

Official Comment

Article 4A governs a specialized method of payment referred to in the Article as a funds transfer but also commonly referred to in the commercial community as a wholesale wire transfer. A funds transfer is made by means of one or more payment orders. The scope of Article 4A is determined by the definitions of "payment order" and "funds transfer" found in Section 4A–103 and Section 4A–104.

The funds transfer governed by Article 4A is in large part a product of recent and developing technological changes. Before this Article was drafted there was no comprehensive body of law—statutory or judicial—that defined the juridical nature of a funds transfer or the rights and obligations flowing from payment orders. Judicial authority with respect to funds transfers is sparse, undeveloped and not uniform. Judges have had to resolve disputes by referring to general principles of common law or equity, or they have sought guidance in statutes such as Article 4 which are applicable to other payment methods. But attempts to define rights and obligations in funds transfers by general principles or by analogy to rights and obligations in negotiable instrument law or the law of check collection have not been satisfactory.

In the drafting of Article 4A, a deliberate decision was made to write on a clean slate and to treat a funds transfer as a unique method of payment to be governed by unique rules that address the particular issues raised by this method of payment. A deliberate decision was also made to use precise and detailed rules to assign responsibility, define behavioral norms, allocate risks and establish limits on liability, rather than to rely on broadly stated, flexible principles. In the drafting of these rules, a critical consideration was that the various parties to funds transfers need to be able to predict risk with certainty, to insure against risk, to adjust operational and security procedures, and to price funds transfer services appropriately. This consideration is particularly important given the very large amounts of money that are involved in funds transfers.

Funds transfers involve competing interests—those of the banks that provide funds transfer services and the commercial and financial organizations that use the services, as well as the public interest. These competing interests were represented in the drafting process and they were thoroughly considered. The rules that emerged represent a careful and delicate balancing of those interests and are intended to be the exclusive means of determining the rights, duties and liabilities of the affected parties in any situation covered by particular provisions of the Article. Consequently, resort to principles of law or equity outside of Article 4A is not appropriate to create rights, duties and liabilities inconsistent with those stated in this Article.

§ 4A-103. Payment Order—Definitions.

(a) In this Article:

(1) "Payment order" means an instruction of a sender to a receiving bank, transmitted orally, electronically, or in writing, to pay, or to cause another bank to pay, a fixed or determinable amount of money to a beneficiary if:

(i) the instruction does not state a condition to payment to the beneficiary other than time of payment,

(ii) the receiving bank is to be reimbursed by debiting an account of, or otherwise receiving payment from, the sender, and

(iii) the instruction is transmitted by the sender directly to the receiving bank or to an agent, funds-transfer system, or communication system for transmittal to the receiving bank.

(2) "Beneficiary" means the person to be paid by the beneficiary's bank.

(3) "Beneficiary's bank" means the bank identified in a payment order in which an account of the beneficiary is to be credited pursuant to the order or which otherwise is to make payment to the beneficiary if the order does not provide for payment to an account.

(4) "Receiving bank" means the bank to which the sender's instruction is addressed.

(5) "Sender" means the person giving the instruction to the receiving bank.

(b) If an instruction complying with subsection (a)(1) is to make more than one payment to a beneficiary, the instruction is a separate payment order with respect to each payment.

(c) A payment order is issued when it is sent to the receiving bank.

Official Comment

This section is discussed in the Comment following Section 4A-104.

§ 4A-104. Funds Transfer—Definitions.

In this Article:

(a) "Funds transfer" means the series of transactions, beginning with the originator's payment order, made for the purpose of making payment to the beneficiary of the order. The term includes any payment order issued by the originator's bank or an intermediary bank intended to carry out the originator's payment order. A funds transfer is completed by acceptance by the beneficiary's bank of a payment order for the benefit of the beneficiary of the originator's payment order.

(b) "Intermediary bank" means a receiving bank other than the originator's bank or the beneficiary's bank.

(c) "Originator" means the sender of the first payment order in a funds transfer.

(d) "Originator's bank" means (i) the receiving bank to which the payment order of the originator is issued if the originator is not a bank, or (ii) the originator if the originator is a bank.

Official Comment

1. Article 4A governs a method of payment in which the person making payment (the "originator") directly transmits an instruction to a bank either to make payment to the person receiving payment (the "beneficiary") or to instruct some other bank to make payment to the beneficiary. The payment from the originator to the beneficiary occurs when the bank that is to pay the beneficiary becomes obligated to pay the beneficiary. There are two basic definitions: "Payment order" stated in Section 4A-103 and "Funds transfer" stated in Section 4A-104. These definitions, other related definitions, and the scope of Article 4A can best be understood in the context of specific fact situations. Consider the following cases:

Case #1. X, which has an account in Bank A, instructs that bank to pay $1,000,000 to Y's account in Bank A. Bank A carries out X's instruction by making a credit of $1,000,000 to Y's account and notifying Y that the credit is available for immediate withdrawal. The instruction by X to Bank A is a "payment order" which was issued when it was sent to Bank A. Section 4A-103(a)(1) and (c). X is the "sender" of the payment order and Bank A is the "receiving bank." Section 4A-103(a)(5) and (a)(4). Y is the "beneficiary" of the payment order and Bank A is the "beneficiary's bank." Section 4A–103(a)(2) and (a)(3). When Bank A notified Y of receipt of the payment order, Bank A "accepted" the payment order. Section 4A–209(b)(1). When Bank A accepted the order it incurred an obligation to Y to pay the amount of the order. Section 4A–404(a). When Bank A accepted X's order, X incurred an obligation to pay Bank A the amount of the order. Section 4A–402(b). Payment from X to Bank A would normally be made by a debit to X's account in Bank A. Section 4A–403(a)(3). At the time Bank A incurred the obligation to pay Y, payment of $1,000,000 by X to Y was also made. Section 4A–406(a). Bank A paid Y when it gave notice to Y of a withdrawable credit of $1,000,000 to Y's account. Section 4A–405(a). The overall transaction, which comprises the acts of X and Bank A, in which the payment by X to Y is accomplished is referred to as the "funds transfer." Section 4A–104(a). In this case only one payment order was involved in the funds transfer. A one-payment-order funds transfer is usually referred to as a "book transfer" because the payment is accomplished by the receiving bank's debiting the account of the sender and crediting the account of the beneficiary in the same bank. X, in addition to being the sender of the payment order to Bank A, is the "originator" of the funds transfer. Section 4A–104(c). Bank A is the "originator's bank" in the funds transfer as well as the beneficiary's bank. Section 4A–104(d).

Case #2. Assume the same facts as in Case #1 except that X instructs Bank A to pay $1,000,000 to Y's account in Bank B. With respect to this payment order, X is the sender, Y is the beneficiary, and Bank A is the receiving bank. Bank A carries out X's order by instructing Bank B to pay $1,000,000 to Y's account. This instruction is a payment order in which Bank A is the sender, Bank B is the receiving bank, and Y is the beneficiary. When Bank A issued its payment order to Bank B, Bank A "executed" X's order. Section 4A–301(a). In the funds transfer, X is the originator, Bank A is the originator's bank, and Bank B is the beneficiary's bank. When Bank A executed X's order, X incurred an obligation to pay Bank A the amount of the order. Section 4A–402(c). When Bank B accepts the payment order issued to it by Bank A, Bank B incurs an obligation to Y to pay the amount of the order (Section 4A–404(a)) and Bank A incurs an obligation to pay Bank B. Section 4A–402(b). Acceptance by Bank B also results in payment of $1,000,000 by X to Y. Section 4A–406(a). In this case two payment orders are involved in the funds transfer.

Case #3. Assume the same facts as in Case #2 except that Bank A does not execute X's payment order by issuing a payment order to Bank B. One bank will not normally act to carry out a funds transfer for another bank unless there is a preexisting arrangement between the banks for transmittal of payment orders and settlement of accounts. For example, if Bank B is a foreign bank with which Bank A has no relationship, Bank A can utilize a bank that is a correspondent of both Bank A and Bank B. Assume Bank A issues a payment order to Bank C to pay $1,000,000 to Y's account in Bank B. With respect to this order, Bank A is the sender, Bank C is the receiving bank, and Y is the beneficiary. Bank C will execute the payment order of Bank A by issuing a payment order to Bank B to pay $1,000,000 to Y's account in Bank B. With respect to Bank C's payment order, Bank C is the sender, Bank B is the receiving bank, and Y is the beneficiary. Payment of $1,000,000 by X to Y occurs when Bank B accepts the payment order issued to it by Bank C. In this case the funds transfer involves three payment orders. In the funds transfer, X is the originator, Bank A is the originator's bank, Bank B is the beneficiary's bank, and Bank C is an "intermediary bank." Section 4A–104(b). In some cases there may be more than one intermediary bank, and in those cases each intermediary bank is treated like Bank C in Case #3.

As the three cases demonstrate, a payment under Article 4A involves an overall transaction, the funds transfer, in which the originator, X, is making payment to the beneficiary, Y, but the funds transfer may encompass a series of payment orders that are issued in order to effect the payment initiated by the originator's payment order.

In some cases the originator and the beneficiary may be the same person. This will occur, for example, when a corporation orders a bank to transfer funds from an account of the corporation in that bank to another account of the corporation in that bank or in some other bank. In some funds transfers the first bank to issue a payment order is a bank that is executing a payment order of a customer that is not a bank. In this case the customer is the originator. In other cases, the first bank to issue a payment order is not acting for a customer, but is making a payment for its own account. In that event the first bank to issue a payment order is the originator as well as the originator's bank.

2. "Payment order" is defined in Section 4A–103(a)(1) as an instruction to a bank to pay, or to cause another bank to pay, a fixed or determinable amount of money. The bank to which the instruction is addressed is known as the "receiving bank." Section 4A–103(a)(4). "Bank" is defined in Section 4A–105(a)(2). The effect of this definition is to limit Article 4A to payments made through the banking system. A transfer of funds made by an entity outside the banking system is excluded. A transfer of funds through an entity other than a bank is usually a consumer transaction involving relatively small amounts of money and a single contract carried out by transfers of cash or a cash equivalent such as a check. Typically, the transferor delivers cash or a check to the company making the transfer, which agrees to pay a like amount to a person designated by the transferor. Transactions covered by Article 4A typically involve very large amounts of money in which several transactions involving several banks may be necessary to carry out the payment. Payments are normally made by debits or credits to bank accounts. Originators and beneficiaries are almost always business organizations and the transfers are usually made to pay obligations. Moreover, these transactions are frequently done on the basis of very short-term credit granted by the receiving bank to the sender of the payment order. Wholesale wire transfers involve policy questions that are distinct from those involved in consumer-based transactions by nonbanks.

3. Further limitations on the scope of Article 4A are found in the three requirements found in subparagraphs (i), (ii), and (iii) of Section 4A–103(a)(1). Subparagraph (i) states that the instruction to pay is a payment order only if it "does not state a condition to payment to the beneficiary other than time of payment." An instruction to pay a beneficiary sometimes is subject to a requirement that the beneficiary perform some act such as delivery of documents. For example, a New York bank may have issued a letter of credit in favor of X, a California seller of goods to be shipped to the New York bank's customer in New York. The terms of the letter of credit provide for payment to X if documents are presented to prove shipment of the goods. Instead of providing for presentment of the documents to the New York bank, the letter of credit states that they may be presented to a California bank that acts as an agent for payment. The New York bank sends an instruction to the California bank to pay X upon presentation of the required documents. The instruction is not covered by Article 4A because payment to the beneficiary is conditional upon receipt of shipping documents. The function of banks in a funds transfer under Article 4A is comparable to the role of banks in the collection and payment of checks in that it is essentially mechanical in nature. The low price and high speed that characterize funds transfers reflect this fact. Conditions to payment by the California bank other than time of payment impose responsibilities on that bank that go beyond those in Article 4A funds transfers. Although the payment by the New York

bank to X under the letter of credit is not covered by Article 4A, if X is paid by the California bank, payment of the obligation of the New York bank to reimburse the California bank could be made by an Article 4A funds transfer. In such a case there is a distinction between the payment by the New York bank to X under the letter of credit and the payment by the New York bank to the California bank. For example, if the New York bank pays its reimbursement obligation to the California bank by a Fedwire naming the California bank as beneficiary (see Comment 1 to Section 4A–107), payment is made to the California bank rather than to X. That payment is governed by Article 4A and it could be made either before or after payment by the California bank to X. The payment by the New York bank to X under the letter of credit is not governed by Article 4A and it occurs when the California bank, as agent of the New York bank, pays X. No payment order was involved in that transaction. In this example, if the New York bank had erroneously sent an instruction to the California bank unconditionally instructing payment to X, the instruction would have been an Article 4A payment order. If the payment order was accepted (Section 4A–209(b)) by the California bank, a payment by the New York bank to X would have resulted (Section 4A–406(a)). But Article 4A would not prevent recovery of funds from X on the basis that X was not entitled to retain the funds under the law of mistake and restitution, letter of credit law or other applicable law.

4. Transfers of funds made through the banking system are commonly referred to as either "credit" transfers or "debit" transfers. In a credit transfer the instruction to pay is given by the person making payment. In a debit transfer the instruction to pay is given by the person receiving payment. The purpose of subparagraph (ii) of subsection (a)(1) of Section 4A–103 is to include credit transfers in Article 4A and to exclude debit transfers. All of the instructions to pay in the three cases described in Comment 1 fall within subparagraph (ii). Take Case #2 as an example. With respect to X's instruction given to Bank A, Bank A will be reimbursed by debiting X's account or otherwise receiving payment from X. With respect to Bank A's instruction to Bank B, Bank B will be reimbursed by receiving payment from Bank A. In a debit transfer, a creditor, pursuant to authority from the debtor, is enabled to draw on the debtor's bank account by issuing an instruction to pay to the debtor's bank. If the debtor's bank pays, it will be reimbursed by the debtor rather than by the person giving the instruction. For example, the holder of an insurance policy may pay premiums by authorizing the insurance company to order the policyholder's bank to pay the insurance company. The order to pay may be in the form of a draft covered by Article 3, or it might be an instruction to pay that is not an instrument under that Article. The bank receives reimbursement by debiting the policyholder's account. Or, a subsidiary corporation may make payments to its parent by authorizing the parent to order the subsidiary's bank to pay the parent from the subsidiary's account. These transactions are not covered by Article 4A because subparagraph (2) is not satisfied. Article 4A is limited to transactions in which the account to be debited by the receiving bank is that of the person in whose name the instruction is given.

If the beneficiary of a funds transfer is the originator of the transfer, the transfer is governed by Article 4A if it is a credit transfer in form. If it is in the form of a debit transfer it is not governed by Article 4A. For example, Corporation has accounts in Bank A and Bank B. Corporation instructs Bank A to pay to Corporation's account in Bank B. The funds transfer is governed by Article 4A. Sometimes, Corporation will authorize Bank B to draw on Corporation's account in Bank A for the purpose of transferring funds into Corporation's account in Bank B. If Corporation also makes an agreement with Bank A under which Bank A is authorized to follow instructions of Bank B, as agent of Corporation, to transfer funds from Customer's account in Bank A, the instruction of Bank B is a payment order of Customer and is governed by Article 4A. This kind of transaction is known in the wire-transfer business as a "drawdown transfer." If Corporation does not make such an agreement with Bank A and Bank B instructs Bank A to make the transfer, the order is in form a debit transfer and is not governed by Article 4A. These debit transfers are normally ACH transactions in which Bank A relies on Bank B's warranties pursuant to ACH rules, including the warranty that the transfer is authorized.

5. The principal effect of subparagraph (iii) of subsection (a) of Section 4A–103 is to exclude from Article 4A payments made by check or credit card. In those cases the instruction of the debtor to the bank on which the check is drawn or to which the credit card slip is to be presented is contained in the check or credit card slip signed by the debtor. The instruction is not transmitted by the debtor directly to the debtor's bank. Rather, the instruction is delivered or otherwise transmitted by the debtor to the creditor who then presents it to the bank either directly or through bank collection channels. These payments are governed by Articles 3 and 4 and federal law. There are, however, limited instances in which the paper on which a check is printed can be used as the means of transmitting a payment order that is covered by Article 4A. Assume that Originator instructs Originator's Bank to pay $10,000 to the account of Beneficiary in Beneficiary's Bank. Since the amount of Originator's payment order is small, if Originator's Bank and Beneficiary's Bank do not have an account relationship, Originator's Bank may execute Originator's order by issuing a teller's check payable to Beneficiary's Bank for $10,000 along with instructions to credit Beneficiary's account in that amount. The instruction to Beneficiary's Bank to credit Beneficiary's account is a payment order. The check is the means by which Originator's Bank pays its obligation as sender of the payment order. The instruction of Originator's Bank to Beneficiary's Bank might be given in a letter accompanying the check or it may be written on the check itself. In either case the instruction to Beneficiary's Bank is a payment order but the check itself (which is an order to pay addressed to the drawee rather than to Beneficiary's Bank) is an instrument under Article 3 and is not a payment order. The check can be both the means by which Originator's Bank pays its obligation under § 4A–402(b) to Beneficiary's Bank and the means by which the instruction to Beneficiary's Bank is transmitted.

6. Most payments covered by Article 4A are commonly referred to as wire transfers and usually involve some kind of electronic transmission, but the applicability of Article 4A does not depend upon the means used to transmit the instruction of the sender. Transmission may be by letter or other written communication, oral communication or electronic communication. An oral communication is normally given by telephone. Frequently the message is recorded by the receiving bank to provide evidence of the transaction, but apart from problems of proof there is no need to record the oral instruction. Transmission of an instruction may be a direct communication between the sender and the receiving bank or through an intermediary such as an agent of the sender, a communication system such as international cable, or a funds transfer system such as CHIPS, SWIFT or an automated clearing house.

§ 4A–105. Other Definitions.

(a) In this Article:

(1) "Authorized account" means a deposit account of a customer in a bank designated by the customer as a source of payment of payment orders issued by the customer to the bank. If a custom-

er does not so designate an account, any account of the customer is an authorized account if payment of a payment order from that account is not inconsistent with a restriction on the use of that account.

(2) "Bank" means a person engaged in the business of banking and includes a savings bank, savings and loan association, credit union, and trust company. A branch or separate office of a bank is a separate bank for purposes of this Article.

(3) "Customer" means a person, including a bank, having an account with a bank or from whom a bank has agreed to receive payment orders.

(4) "Funds-transfer business day" of a receiving bank means the part of a day during which the receiving bank is open for the receipt, processing, and transmittal of payment orders and cancellations and amendments of payment orders.

(5) "Funds-transfer system" means a wire transfer network, automated clearing house, or other communication system of a clearing house or other association of banks through which a payment order by a bank may be transmitted to the bank to which the order is addressed.

(6) "Good faith" means honesty in fact and the observance of reasonable commercial standards of fair dealing.

(7) "Prove" with respect to a fact means to meet the burden of establishing the fact (Section 1-201(8)).

(b) Other definitions applying to this Article and the sections in which they appear are:

"Acceptance"	Section 4A-209
"Beneficiary"	Section 4A-103
"Beneficiary's bank"	Section 4A-103
"Executed"	Section 4A-301
"Execution date"	Section 4A-301
"Funds transfer"	Section 4A-104
"Funds-transfer system rule"	Section 4A-501
"Intermediary bank"	Section 4A-104
"Originator"	Section 4A-104
"Originator's bank"	Section 4A-104
"Payment by beneficiary's bank to beneficiary"	Section 4A-405
"Payment by originator to beneficiary"	Section 4A-406
"Payment by sender to receiving bank"	Section 4A-403
"Payment date"	Section 4A-401
"Payment order"	Section 4A-103
"Receiving bank"	Section 4A-103
"Security procedure"	Section 4A-201
"Sender"	Section 4A-103

(c) The following definitions in Article 4 apply to this Article:

"Clearing house"	Section 4–104
"Item"	Section 4–104
"Suspends payments"	Section 4–104

(d) In addition Article 1 contains general definitions and principles of construction and interpretation applicable throughout this Article.

Official Comment

1. The definition of "bank" in subsection (a)(2) includes some institutions that are not commercial banks. The definition reflects the fact that many financial institutions now perform functions previously restricted to commercial banks, including acting on behalf of customers in funds transfers. Since many funds transfers involve payment orders to or from foreign countries the definition also covers foreign banks. The definition also includes Federal Reserve Banks. Funds transfers carried out by Federal Reserve Banks are described in Comments 1 and 2 to Section 4A–107.

2. Funds transfer business is frequently transacted by banks outside of general banking hours. Thus, the definition of banking day in Section 4–104(1)(c) cannot be used to describe when a bank is open for funds transfer business. Subsection (a)(4) defines a new term, "funds transfer business day," which is applicable to Article 4A. The definition states, "is open for the receipt, processing, and transmittal of payment orders and cancellations and amendments of payment orders." In some cases it is possible to electronically transmit payment orders and other communications to a receiving bank at any time. If the receiving bank is not open for the processing of an order when it is received, the communication is stored in the receiving bank's computer for retrieval when the receiving bank is open for processing. The use of the conjunctive makes clear that the defined term is limited to the period during which all functions of the receiving bank can be performed, i.e., receipt, processing, and transmittal of payment orders, cancellations and amendments.

3. Subsection (a)(5) defines "funds transfer system." The term includes a system such as CHIPS which provides for transmission of a payment order as well as settlement of the obligation of the sender to pay the order. It also includes automated clearing houses, operated by a clearing house or other association of banks, which process and transmit payment orders of banks to other banks. In addition the term includes organizations that provide only transmission services such as SWIFT. The definition also includes the wire transfer network and automated clearing houses of Federal Reserve Banks. Systems of the Federal Reserve Banks, however, are treated differently from systems of other associations of banks. Funds transfer systems other than systems of the Federal Reserve Banks are treated in Article 4A as a means of communication of payment orders between participating banks. Section 4A–206. The Comment to that section and the Comment to Section 4A–107 explain how Federal Reserve Banks function under Article 4A. Funds transfer systems are also able to promulgate rules binding on participating banks that, under Section 4A–501, may supplement or in some cases may even override provisions of Article 4A.

4. Subsection (d) incorporates definitions stated in Article 1 as well as principles of construction and interpretation stated in that Article. Included is Section 1–103. The last paragraph of the Comment to Section 4A–102 is addressed to the issue of the extent to which general principles of law and equity should apply to situations covered by provisions of Article 4A.

§ 4A-106. Time Payment Order Is Received.

(a) The time of receipt of a payment order or communication cancelling or amending a payment order is determined by the rules applicable to receipt of a notice stated in Section 1-201(27). A receiving bank may fix a cut-off time or times on a funds-transfer business day for the receipt and processing of payment orders and communications cancelling or amending payment orders. Different cut-off times may apply to payment orders, cancellations, or amendments, or to different categories of payment orders, cancellations, or amendments. A cut-off time may apply to senders generally or different cut-off times may apply to different senders or categories of payment orders. If a payment order or communication cancelling or amending a payment order is received after the close of a funds-transfer business day or after the appropriate cut-off time on a funds-transfer business day, the receiving bank may treat the payment order or communication as received at the opening of the next funds-transfer business day.

(b) If this Article refers to an execution date or payment date or states a day on which a receiving bank is required to take action, and the date or day does not fall on a funds-transfer business day, the next day that is a funds-transfer business day is treated as the date or day stated, unless the contrary is stated in this Article.

Official Comment

The time that a payment order is received by a receiving bank usually defines the payment date or the execution date of a payment order. Section 4A-401 and Section 4A-301. The time of receipt of a payment order, or communication cancelling or amending a payment order is defined in subsection (a) by reference to the rules stated in Section 1-201(27). Thus, time of receipt is determined by the same rules that determine when a notice is received. Time of receipt, however, may be altered by a cut-off time.

§ 4A-107. Federal Reserve Regulations and Operating Circulars.

Regulations of the Board of Governors of the Federal Reserve System and operating circulars of the Federal Reserve Banks supersede any inconsistent provision of this Article to the extent of the inconsistency.

Official Comment

1. Funds transfers under Article 4A may be made, in whole or in part, by payment orders through a Federal Reserve Bank in what is usually referred to as a transfer by Fedwire. If Bank A, which has an account in Federal Reserve Bank X, wants to pay $1,000,000 to Bank B, which has an account in Federal Reserve Bank Y, Bank A can issue an instruction to Reserve Bank X requesting a debit of $1,000,000 to Bank A's Reserve account and an equal credit to Bank B's Reserve account. Reserve Bank X will debit Bank A's account and will credit the account of Reserve Bank Y. Reserve Bank X will issue an instruction to Reserve Bank Y requesting a debit of $1,000,000 to the account of Reserve Bank X and an equal credit to Bank B's account in Reserve Bank Y. Reserve Bank Y will make the requested debit and credit and will give Bank B an advice of credit. The definition of "bank" in Section 4A-105(a)(2) includes both Reserve

Bank X and Reserve Bank Y. Bank A's instruction to Reserve Bank X to pay money to Bank B is a payment order under Section 4A–103(a)(1). Bank A is the sender and Reserve Bank X is the receiving bank. Bank B is the beneficiary of Bank A's order and of the funds transfer. Bank A is the originator of the funds transfer and is also the originator's bank. Section 4A–104(c) and (d). Reserve Bank X, an intermediary bank under Section 4A–104(b), executes Bank A's order by sending a payment order to Reserve Bank Y instructing that bank to credit the Federal Reserve account of Bank B. Reserve Bank Y is the beneficiary's bank.

Suppose the transfer of funds from Bank A to Bank B is part of a larger transaction in which Originator, a customer of Bank A, wants to pay Beneficiary, a customer of Bank B. Originator issues a payment order to Bank A to pay $1,000,000 to the account of Beneficiary in Bank B. Bank A may execute Originator's order by means of Fedwire which simultaneously transfers $1,000,000 from Bank A to Bank B and carries a message instructing Bank B to pay $1,000,000 to the account of Y. The Fedwire transfer is carried out as described in the previous paragraph, except that the beneficiary of the funds transfer is Beneficiary rather than Bank B. Reserve Bank X and Reserve Bank Y are intermediary banks. When Reserve Bank Y advises Bank B of the credit to its Federal Reserve account it will also instruct Bank B to pay to the account of Beneficiary. The instruction is a payment order to Bank B which is the beneficiary's bank. When Reserve Bank Y advises Bank B of the credit to its Federal Reserve account Bank B receives payment of the payment order issued to it by Reserve Bank Y. Section 4A–403(a)(1). The payment order is automatically accepted by Bank B at the time it receives the payment order of Reserve Bank Y. Section 4A–209(b)(2). At the time of acceptance by Bank B payment by Originator to Beneficiary also occurs. Thus, in a Fedwire transfer, payment to the beneficiary's bank, acceptance by the beneficiary's bank and payment by the originator to the beneficiary all occur simultaneously by operation of law at the time the payment order to the beneficiary's bank is received.

If Originator orders payment to the account of Beneficiary in Bank C rather than Bank B, the analysis is somewhat modified. Bank A may not have any relationship with Bank C and may not be able to make payment directly to Bank C. In that case, Bank A could send a Fedwire instructing Bank B to instruct Bank C to pay Beneficiary. The analysis is the same as the previous case except that Bank B is an intermediary bank and Bank C is the beneficiary's bank.

2. A funds transfer can also be made through a Federal Reserve Bank in an automated clearing house transaction. In a typical case, Originator instructs Originator's Bank to pay to the account of Beneficiary in Beneficiary's Bank. Originator's instruction to pay a particular beneficiary is transmitted to Originator's Bank along with many other instructions for payment to other beneficiaries by many different beneficiary's banks. All of these instructions are contained in a magnetic tape or other electronic device. Transmission of instructions to the various beneficiary's banks requires that Originator's instructions be processed and repackaged with instructions of other originators so that all instructions to a particular beneficiary's bank are transmitted together to that bank. The repackaging is done in processing centers usually referred to as automated clearing houses. Automated clearing houses are operated either by Federal Reserve Banks or by other associations of banks. If Originator's Bank chooses to execute Originator's instructions by transmitting them to a Federal Reserve Bank for processing by the Federal Reserve Bank, the transmission to the Federal Reserve Bank results in the issuance of payment orders by Originator's Bank to the Federal Reserve Bank, which is an intermediary bank. Processing by the Federal Reserve Bank will result in the issuance of payment orders by the Federal Reserve Bank to Beneficiary's Bank as well as payment

orders to other beneficiary's banks making payments to carry out Originator's instructions.

3. Although the terms of Article 4A apply to funds transfers involving Federal Reserve Banks, federal preemption would make ineffective any Article 4A provision that conflicts with federal law. The payments activities of the Federal Reserve Banks are governed by regulations of the Federal Reserve Board and by operating circulars issued by the Reserve Banks themselves. In some instances, the operating circulars are issued pursuant to a Federal Reserve Board regulation. In other cases, the Reserve Bank issues the operating circular under its own authority under the Federal Reserve Act, subject to review by the Federal Reserve Board. Section 4A-107 states that Federal Reserve Board regulations and operating circulars of the Federal Reserve Banks supersede any inconsistent provision of Article 4A to the extent of the inconsistency. Federal Reserve Board regulations, being valid exercises of regulatory authority pursuant to a federal statute, take precedence over state law if there is an inconsistency. Childs v. Federal Reserve Bank of Dallas, 719 F.2d 812 (5th Cir.1983), reh. den. 724 F.2d 127 (5th Cir.1984). Section 4A-107 treats operating circulars as having the same effect whether issued under the Reserve Bank's own authority or under a Federal Reserve Board regulation.

§ 4A-108. Exclusion of Consumer Transactions Governed by Federal Law

This Article does not apply to a funds transfer any part of which is governed by the Electronic Fund Transfer Act of 1978 (Title XX, Public Law 95-630, 92 Stat. 3728, 15 U.S.C. § 1693 et seq.) as amended from time to time.

Official Comment

The Electronic Fund Transfer Act of 1978 is a federal statute that covers a wide variety of electronic funds transfers involving consumers. The types of transfers covered by the federal statute are essentially different from the wholesale wire transfers that are the primary focus of Article 4A. Section 4A-108 excludes a funds transfer from Article 4A if any part of the transfer is covered by the federal law. Existing procedures designed to comply with federal law will not be affected by Article 4A. The effect of Section 4A-108 is to make Article 4A and EFTA mutually exclusive. For example, if a funds transfer is to a consumer account in the beneficiary's bank and the funds transfer is made in part by use of Fedwire and in part by means of an automated clearing house, EFTA applies to the ACH part of the transfer but not to the Fedwire part. Under Section 4A-108, Article 4A does not apply to any part of the transfer. However, in the absence of any law to govern the part of the funds transfer that is not subject to EFTA, a court might apply appropriate principles from Article 4A by analogy.

PART 2

ISSUE AND ACCEPTANCE OF PAYMENT ORDER

§ 4A-201. Security Procedure.

"Security procedure" means a procedure established by agreement of a customer and a receiving bank for the purpose of (i) verifying that a payment order or communication amending or cancelling a payment order is that of the customer, or (ii) detecting error in the transmission or the content of the payment order or communication. A security procedure may require the use of algorithms or other codes, identifying words or numbers, encryption, callback procedures, or similar security devices. Comparison of a signature on a payment order or communication with an authorized specimen signature of the customer is not by itself a security procedure.

Official Comment

A large percentage of payment orders and communications amending or cancelling payment orders are transmitted electronically and it is standard practice to use security procedures that are designed to assure the authenticity of the message. Security procedures can also be used to detect error in the content of messages or to detect payment orders that are transmitted by mistake as in the case of multiple transmission of the same payment order. Security procedures might also apply to communications that are transmitted by telephone or in writing. Section 4A-201 defines these security procedures. The definition of security procedure limits the term to a procedure "established by agreement of a customer and a receiving bank." The term does not apply to procedures that the receiving bank may follow unilaterally in processing payment orders. The question of whether loss that may result from the transmission of a spurious or erroneous payment order will be borne by the receiving bank or the sender or purported sender is affected by whether a security procedure was or was not in effect and whether there was or was not compliance with the procedure. Security procedures are referred to in Sections 4A-202 and 4A-203, which deal with authorized and verified payment orders, and Section 4A-205, which deals with erroneous payment orders.

§ 4A-202. Authorized and Verified Payment Orders.

(a) A payment order received by the receiving bank is the authorized order of the person identified as sender if that person authorized the order or is otherwise bound by it under the law of agency.

(b) If a bank and its customer have agreed that the authenticity of payment orders issued to the bank in the name of the customer as sender will be verified pursuant to a security procedure, a payment order received by the receiving bank is effective as the order of the customer, whether or not authorized, if (i) the security procedure is a commercially reasonable method of providing security against unauthorized payment orders, and (ii) the bank proves that it accepted the payment order in good faith and in compliance with the security procedure and any written agreement or instruction of the customer restricting acceptance of payment orders issued in the name of the customer. The bank is not required to follow an instruction that violates a written agreement with the customer or notice of which is not received at a time and in a manner affording the bank a reasonable opportunity to act on it before the payment order is accepted.

(c) Commercial reasonableness of a security procedure is a question of law to be determined by considering the wishes of the customer expressed to the bank, the circumstances of the customer known to the bank, including the size, type, and frequency of payment orders normally issued by the customer to the bank, alternative security procedures offered to the customer, and security procedures in general use by customers and receiving banks similarly situated. A security procedure is deemed to be commercially reasonable if (i) the security procedure was chosen by the customer after the bank offered, and the customer refused, a security procedure that was commercially reasonable for that customer, and (ii) the customer expressly agreed in writing to be bound by any payment order, whether or not authorized, issued in its name and accepted by the bank in compliance with the security procedure chosen by the customer.

(d) The term "sender" in this Article includes the customer in whose name a payment order is issued if the order is the authorized order of the customer under subsection (a), or it is effective as the order of the customer under subsection (b).

(e) This section applies to amendments and cancellations of payment orders to the same extent it applies to payment orders.

(f) Except as provided in this section and in Section 4A–203(a)(1), rights and obligations arising under this section or Section 4A–203 may not be varied by agreement.

Official Comment

This section is discussed in the Comment following Section 4A–203.

§ 4A–203. Unenforceability of Certain Verified Payment Orders.

(a) If an accepted payment order is not, under Section 4A–202(a), an authorized order of a customer identified as sender, but is effective as an order of the customer pursuant to Section 4A–202(b), the following rules apply:

(1) By express written agreement, the receiving bank may limit the extent to which it is entitled to enforce or retain payment of the payment order.

(2) The receiving bank is not entitled to enforce or retain payment of the payment order if the customer proves that the order was not caused, directly or indirectly, by a person (i) entrusted at any time with duties to act for the customer with respect to payment orders or the security procedure, or (ii) who obtained access to transmitting facilities of the customer or who obtained, from a source controlled by the customer and without authority of the receiving bank, information facilitating breach of the security procedure, regardless of how the information was obtained or whether the customer was at fault. Information includes any access device, computer software, or the like.

(b) This section applies to amendments of payment orders to the same extent it applies to payment orders.

Official Comment

1. Some person will always be identified as the sender of a payment order. Acceptance of the order by the receiving bank is based on a belief by the bank that

the order was authorized by the person identified as the sender. If the receiving bank is the beneficiary's bank acceptance means that the receiving bank is obliged to pay the beneficiary. If the receiving bank is not the beneficiary's bank, acceptance means that the receiving bank has executed the sender's order and is obliged to pay the bank that accepted the order issued in execution of the sender's order. In either case the receiving bank may suffer a loss unless it is entitled to enforce payment of the payment order that it accepted. If the person identified as the sender of the order refuses to pay on the ground that the order was not authorized by that person, what are the rights of the receiving bank? In the absence of a statute or agreement that specifically addresses the issue, the question usually will be resolved by the law of agency. In some cases, the law of agency works well. For example, suppose the receiving bank executes a payment order given by means of a letter apparently written by a corporation that is a customer of the bank and apparently signed by an officer of the corporation. If the receiving bank acts solely on the basis of the letter, the corporation is not bound as the sender of the payment order unless the signature was that of the officer and the officer was authorized to act for the corporation in the issuance of payment orders, or some other agency doctrine such as apparent authority or estoppel causes the corporation to be bound. Estoppel can be illustrated by the following example. Suppose P is aware that A, who is unauthorized to act for P, has fraudulently misrepresented to T that A is authorized to act for P. T believes A and is about to rely on the misrepresentation. If P does not notify T of the true facts although P could easily do so, P may be estopped from denying A's lack of authority. A similar result could follow if the failure to notify T is the result of negligence rather than a deliberate decision. Restatement, Second, Agency § 8B. Other equitable principles such as subrogation or restitution might also allow a receiving bank to recover with respect to an unauthorized payment order that it accepted. In Gatoil (U.S.A.), Inc. v. Forest Hill State Bank, 1 U.C.C.Rep.Serv.2d 171 (D.Md.1986), a joint venturer not authorized to order payments from the account of the joint venture, ordered a funds transfer from the account. The transfer paid a bona fide debt of the joint venture. Although the transfer was unauthorized the court refused to require recredit of the account because the joint venture suffered no loss. The result can be rationalized on the basis of subrogation of the receiving bank to the right of the beneficiary of the funds transfer to receive the payment from the joint venture.

But in most cases these legal principles give the receiving bank very little protection in the case of an authorized payment order. Cases like those just discussed are not typical of the way that most payment orders are transmitted and accepted, and such cases are likely to become even less common. Given the large amount of the typical payment order, a prudent receiving bank will be unwilling to accept a payment order unless it has assurance that the order is what it purports to be. This assurance is normally provided by security procedures described in Section 4A–201.

In a very large percentage of cases covered by Article 4A, transmission of the payment order is made electronically. The receiving bank may be required to act on the basis of a message that appears on a computer screen. Common law concepts of authority of agent to bind principal are not helpful. There is no way of determining the identity or the authority of the person who caused the message to be sent. The receiving bank is not relying on the authority of any particular person to act for the purported sender. The case is not comparable to payment of a check by the drawee bank on the basis of a signature that is forged. Rather, the receiving bank relies on a security procedure pursuant to which the authenticity of the message can be "tested" by various devices which are designed to provide certainty that the message is that of the sender identified in the payment order. In the wire transfer business the concept of "authorized" is different from that found in agency law. In that business a payment order is treated as the order of the person in whose name it is issued if it is properly tested pursuant to a security procedure and the order passes the test.

Section 4A–202 reflects the reality of the wire transfer business. A person in whose name a payment order is issued is considered to be the sender of the order if the order is "authorized" as stated in subsection (a) or if the order is "verified" pursuant to a security procedure in compliance with subsection (b). If subsection (b) does not apply, the question of whether the customer is responsible for the order is determined by the law of agency. The issue is one of actual or apparent authority of the person who caused the order to be issued in the name of the customer. In some cases the law of agency might allow the customer to be bound by an unauthorized order if conduct of the customer can be used to find an estoppel against the customer to deny that the order was unauthorized. If the customer is bound by the order under any of these agency doctrines, subsection (a) treats the order as authorized and thus the customer is deemed to be the sender of the order. In most cases, however, subsection (b) will apply. In that event there is no need to make an agency law analysis to determine authority. Under Section 4A–202, the issue of liability of the purported sender of the payment order will be determined by agency law only if the receiving bank did not comply with subsection (b).

2. The scope of Section 4A–202 can be illustrated by the following cases. *Case #1.* A payment order purporting to be that of Customer is received by Receiving Bank but the order was fraudulently transmitted by a person who had no authority to act for Customer. *Case #2.* An authentic payment order was sent by Customer, but before the order was received by Receiving Bank the order was fraudulently altered by an unauthorized person to change the beneficiary. *Case #3.* An authentic payment order was received by Receiving Bank, but before the order was executed by Receiving Bank a person who had no authority to act for Customer fraudulently sent a communication purporting to amend the order by changing the beneficiary. In each case Receiving Bank acted on the fraudulent communication by accepting the payment order. These cases are all essentially similar and they are treated identically by Section 4A–202. In each case Receiving Bank acted on a communication that it thought was authorized by Customer when in fact the communication was fraudulent. No distinction is made between Case #1 in which Customer took no part at all in the transaction and Case #2 and Case #3 in which an authentic order was fraudulently altered or amended by an unauthorized person. If subsection (b) does not apply, each case is governed by subsection (a). If there are no additional facts on which an estoppel might be found, Customer is not responsible in Case #1 for the fraudulently issued payment order, in Case #2 for the fraudulent alteration or in Case #3 for the fraudulent amendment. Thus, in each case Customer is not liable to pay the order and Receiving Bank takes the loss. The only remedy of Receiving Bank is to seek recovery from the person who received payment as beneficiary of the fraudulent order. If there was verification in compliance with subsection (b), Customer will take the loss unless Section 4A–203 applies.

3. Subsection (b) of Section 4A–202 is based on the assumption that losses due to fraudulent payment orders can best be avoided by the use of commercially reasonable security procedures, and that the use of such procedures should be encouraged. The subsection is designed to protect both the customer and the receiving bank. A receiving bank needs to be able to rely on objective criteria to determine whether it can safely act on a payment order. Employees of the bank can be trained to "test" a payment order according to the various steps specified in the security procedure. The bank is responsible for the acts of these employees. Subsection (b)(ii) requires the bank to

prove that it accepted the payment order in good faith and "in compliance with the security procedure." If the fraud was not detected because the bank's employee did not perform the acts required by the security procedure, the bank has not complied. Subsection (b)(ii) also requires the bank to prove that it complied with any agreement or instruction that restricts acceptance of payment orders issued in the name of the customer. A customer may want to protect itself by imposing limitations on acceptance of payment orders by the bank. For example, the customer may prohibit the bank from accepting a payment order that is not payable from an authorized account, that exceeds the credit balance in specified accounts of the customer, or that exceeds some other amount. Another limitation may relate to the beneficiary. The customer may provide the bank with a list of authorized beneficiaries and prohibit acceptance of any payment order to a beneficiary not appearing on the list. Such limitations may be incorporated into the security procedure itself or they may be covered by a separate agreement or instruction. In either case, the bank must comply with the limitations if the conditions stated in subsection (b) are met. Normally limitations on acceptance would be incorporated into an agreement between the customer and the receiving bank, but in some cases the instruction might be unilaterally given by the customer. If standing instructions or an agreement state limitations on the ability of the receiving bank to act, provision must be made for later modification of the limitations. Normally this would be done by an agreement that specifies particular procedures to be followed. Thus, subsection (b) states that the receiving bank is not required to follow an instruction that violates a written agreement. The receiving bank is not bound by an instruction unless it has adequate notice of it. Subsections (25), (26) and (27) of Section 1-201 apply.

Subsection (b)(i) assures that the interests of the customer will be protected by providing an incentive to a bank to make available to the customer a security procedure that is commercially reasonable. If a commercially reasonable security procedure is not made available to the customer, subsection (b) does not apply. The result is that subsection (a) applies and the bank acts at its peril in accepting a payment order that may be unauthorized. Prudent banking practice may require that security procedures be utilized in virtually all cases except for those in which personal contact between the customer and the bank eliminates the possibility of an unauthorized order. The burden of making available commercially reasonable security procedures is imposed on receiving banks because they generally determine what security procedures can be used and are in the best position to evaluate the efficacy of procedures offered to customers to combat fraud. The burden on the customer is to supervise its employees to assure compliance with the security procedure and to safeguard confidential security information and access to transmitting facilities so that the security procedure cannot be breached.

4. The principal issue that is likely to arise in litigation involving subsection (b) is whether the security procedure in effect when a fraudulent payment order was accepted was commercially reasonable. The concept of what is commercially reasonable in a given case is flexible. Verification entails labor and equipment costs that can vary greatly depending upon the degree of security that is sought. A customer that transmits very large numbers of payment orders in very large amounts may desire and may reasonably expect to be provided with state-of-the-art procedures that provide maximum security. But the expense involved may make use of a state-of-the-art procedure infeasible for a customer that normally transmits payment orders infrequently or in relatively low amounts. Another variable is the type of receiving bank. It is reasonable to require large money center banks to make available state-of-the-art security procedures. On the other hand, the same requirement may not be reasonable for a small country bank. A receiving bank might have several security procedures that are designed to meet the

varying needs of different customers. The type of payment order is another variable. For example, in a wholesale wire transfer, each payment order is normally transmitted electronically and individually. A testing procedure will be individually applied to each payment order. In funds transfers to be made by means of an automated clearing house many payment orders are incorporated into an electronic device such as a magnetic tape that is physically delivered. Testing of the individual payment orders is not feasible. Thus, a different kind of security procedure must be adopted to take into account the different mode of transmission.

The issue of whether a particular security procedure is commercially reasonable is a question of law. Whether the receiving bank complied with the procedure is a question of fact. It is appropriate to make the finding concerning commercial reasonability a matter of law because security procedures are likely to be standardized in the banking industry and a question of law standard leads to more predictability concerning the level of security that a bank must offer to its customers. The purpose of subsection (b) is to encourage banks to institute reasonable safeguards against fraud but not to make them insurers against fraud. A security procedure is not commercially unreasonable simply because another procedure might have been better or because the judge deciding the question would have opted for a more stringent procedure. The standard is not whether the security procedure is the best available. Rather it is whether the procedure is reasonable for the particular customer and the particular bank, which is a lower standard. On the other hand, a security procedure that fails to meet prevailing standards of good banking practice applicable to the particular bank should not be held to be commercially reasonable. Subsection (c) states factors to be considered by the judge in making the determination of commercial reasonableness. Sometimes an informed customer refuses a security procedure that is commercially reasonable and suitable for that customer and insists on using a higher-risk procedure because it is more convenient or cheaper. In that case, under the last sentence of subsection (c), the customer has voluntarily assumed the risk of failure of the procedure and cannot shift the loss to the bank. But this result follows only if the customer expressly agrees in writing to assume that risk. It is implicit in the last sentence of subsection (c) that a bank that accedes to the wishes of its customer in this regard is not acting in bad faith by so doing so long as the customer is made aware of the risk. In all cases, however, a receiving bank cannot get the benefit of subsection (b) unless it has made available to the customer a security procedure that is commercially reasonable and suitable for use by that customer. In most cases, the mutual interest of bank and customer to protect against fraud should lead to agreement to a security procedure which is commercially reasonable.

5. The effect of Section 4a–202(b) is to place the risk of loss on the customer if an unauthorized payment order is accepted by the receiving bank after verification by the bank in compliance with a commercially reasonable security procedure. An exception to this result is provided by Section 4A–203(a)(2). The customer may avoid the loss resulting from such a payment order if the customer can prove that the fraud was not committed by a person described in that subsection. Breach of a commercially reasonable security procedure requires that the person committing the fraud have knowledge of how the procedure works and knowledge of codes, identifying devices, and the like. That person may also need access to transmitting facilities through an access device or other software in order to breach the security procedure. This confidential information must be obtained either from a source controlled by the customer or from a source controlled by the receiving bank. If the customer can prove that the person committing the fraud did not obtain the confidential information from an agent or former agent of the customer or from a source controlled by the customer, the loss is shifted to the bank. "Prove" is

defined in Section 4A-105(a)(7). Because of bank regulation requirements, in this kind of case there will always be a criminal investigation as well as an internal investigation of the bank to determine the probable explanation for the breach of security. Because a funds transfer fraud usually will involve a very large amount of money, both the criminal investigation and the internal investigation are likely to be thorough. In some cases there may be an investigation by bank examiners as well. Frequently, these investigations will develop evidence of who is at fault and the cause of the loss. The customer will have access to evidence developed in these investigations and that evidence can be used by the customer in meeting its burden of proof.

6. The effect of Section 4A-202(b) may also be changed by an agreement meeting the requirements of Section 4A-203(a)(1). Some customers may be unwilling to take all or part of the risk of loss with respect to unauthorized payment orders even if all of the requirements of Section 4A-202(b) are met. By virtue of Section 4A-203(a)(1), a receiving bank may assume all of the risk of loss with respect to unauthorized payment orders or the customer and bank may agree that losses from unauthorized payment orders are to be divided as provided in the agreement.

7. In a large majority of cases the sender of a payment order is a bank. In many cases in which there is a bank sender, both the sender and the receiving bank will be members of a funds transfer system over which the payment order is transmitted. Since Section 4A-202(f) does not prohibit a funds transfer system rule from varying rights and obligations under Section 4A-202, a rule of the funds transfer system can determine how loss due to an unauthorized payment order from a participating bank to another participating bank is to be allocated. A funds transfer system rule, however, cannot change the rights of a customer that is not a participating bank. § 4A-501(b). Section 4A-202(f) also prevents variation by agreement except to the extent stated.

§ 4A-204. Refund of Payment and Duty of Customer to Report With Respect to Unauthorized Payment Order.

(a) If a receiving bank accepts a payment order issued in the name of its customer as sender which is (i) not authorized and not effective as the order of the customer under Section 4A-202, or (ii) not enforceable, in whole or in part, against the customer under Section 4A-203, the bank shall refund any payment of the payment order received from the customer to the extent the bank is not entitled to enforce payment and shall pay interest on the refundable amount calculated from the date the bank received payment to the date of the refund. However, the customer is not entitled to interest from the bank on the amount to be refunded if the customer fails to exercise ordinary care to determine that the order was not authorized by the customer and to notify the bank of the relevant facts within a reasonable time not exceeding 90 days after the date the customer received notification from the bank that the order was accepted or that the customer's account was debited with respect to the order. The bank is not entitled to any recovery from the customer on account of a failure by the customer to give notification as stated in this section.

(b) Reasonable time under subsection (a) may be fixed by agreement as stated in Section 1-204(1), but the obligation of a receiving bank to refund payment as stated in subsection (a) may not otherwise be varied by agreement.

Official Comment

1. With respect to unauthorized payment orders, in a very large percentage of cases a commercially reasonable security procedure will be in effect. Section 4A-204 applies only to cases in which (i) no commercially reasonable security procedure is in effect, (ii) the bank did not comply with a commercially reasonable security procedure that was in effect, (iii) the sender can prove, pursuant to Section 4A-203(a)(2), that the culprit did not obtain confidential security information controlled by the customer, or (iv) the bank, pursuant to Section 4A-203(a)(1) agreed to take all or part of the loss resulting from an unauthorized payment order. In each of these cases the bank takes the risk of loss with respect to an unauthorized payment order because the bank is not entitled to payment from the customer with respect to the order. The bank normally debits the customer's account or otherwise receives payment from the customer shortly after acceptance of the payment order. Subsection (a) of Section 4A-204 states that the bank must recredit the account or refund payment to the extent the bank is not entitled to enforce payment.

2. Section 4A-204 is designed to encourage a customer to promptly notify the receiving bank that it has accepted an unauthorized payment order. Since cases of unauthorized payment orders will almost always involve fraud, the bank's remedy is normally to recover from the beneficiary of the unauthorized order if the beneficiary was party to the fraud. This remedy may not be worth very much and it may not make any difference whether or not the bank promptly learns about the fraud. But in some cases prompt notification may make it easier for the bank to recover some part of its loss from the culprit. The customer will routinely be notified of the debit to its account with respect to an unauthorized order or will otherwise be notified of acceptance of the order. The customer has a duty to exercise ordinary care to determine that the order was unauthorized after it has received notification from the bank, and to advise the bank of the relevant facts within a reasonable time not exceeding 90 days after receipt of notification. Reasonable time is not defined and it may depend on the facts of the particular case. If a payment order for $1,000,000 is wholly unauthorized, the customer should normally discover it in far less than 90 days. If a $1,000,000 payment order was authorized but the name of the beneficiary was fraudulently changed, a much longer period may be necessary to discover the fraud. But in any event, if the customer delays more than 90 days the customer's duty has not been met. The only consequence of a failure of the customer to perform this duty is a loss of interest on the refund payable by the bank. A customer that acts promptly is entitled to interest from the time the customer's account was debited or the customer otherwise made payment. The rate of interest is stated in Section 4A-506. If the customer fails to perform the duty, no interest is recoverable for any part of the period before the bank learns that it accepted an unauthorized order. But the bank is not entitled to any recovery from the customer based on negligence for failure to inform the bank. Loss of interest is in the nature of a penalty on the customer designed to provide an incentive for the customer to police its account. There is no intention to impose a duty on the customer that might result in shifting loss from the unauthorized order to the customer.

§ 4A-205. Erroneous Payment Orders.

(a) If an accepted payment order was transmitted pursuant to a security procedure for the detection of error and the payment order (i) erroneously instructed payment to a beneficiary not intended by the sender, (ii) erroneously instructed payment in an amount greater than the amount intended by the sender, or (iii) was an erroneously transmitted duplicate of a payment order previously sent by the sender, the following rules apply:

(1) If the sender proves that the sender or a person acting on behalf of the sender pursuant to Section 4A–206 complied with the security procedure and that the error would have been detected if the receiving bank had also complied, the sender is not obliged to pay the order to the extent stated in paragraphs (2) and (3).

(2) If the funds transfer is completed on the basis of an erroneous payment order described in clause (i) or (iii) of subsection (a), the sender is not obliged to pay the order and the receiving bank is entitled to recover from the beneficiary any amount paid to the beneficiary to the extent allowed by the law governing mistake and restitution.

(3) If the funds transfer is completed on the basis of a payment order described in clause (ii) of subsection (a), the sender is not obliged to pay the order to the extent the amount received by the beneficiary is greater than the amount intended by the sender. In that case, the receiving bank is entitled to recover from the beneficiary the excess amount received to the extent allowed by the law governing mistake and restitution.

(b) If (i) the sender of an erroneous payment order described in subsection (a) is not obliged to pay all or part of the order, and (ii) the sender receives notification from the receiving bank that the order was accepted by the bank or that the sender's account was debited with respect to the order, the sender has a duty to exercise ordinary care, on the basis of information available to the sender, to discover the error with respect to the order and to advise the bank of the relevant facts within a reasonable time, not exceeding 90 days, after the bank's notification was received by the sender. If the bank proves that the sender failed to perform that duty, the sender is liable to the bank for the loss the bank proves it incurred as a result of the failure, but the liability of the sender may not exceed the amount of the sender's order.

(c) This section applies to amendments to payment orders to the same extent it applies to payment orders.

Official Comment

1. This section concerns error in the content or in the transmission of payment orders. It deals with three kinds of error. *Case #1.* The order identifies a beneficiary not intended by the sender. For example, Sender intends to wire funds to a beneficiary identified only by an account number. The wrong account number is stated in the order. *Case #2.* The error is in the amount of the order. For example, Sender intends to wire $1,000 to Beneficiary. Through error, the payment order instructs payment of $1,000,000. *Case #3.* A payment order is sent to the receiving bank and then, by mistake, the same payment order is sent to the receiving bank again. In Case #3, the receiving bank may have no way of knowing whether the second order is a duplicate of the first or is another order. Similarly, in Case #1 and Case #2, the receiving bank may have no way of knowing that the error exists. In each case, if this section does not apply and the funds transfer is completed, Sender is obliged to pay the order. Section 4A–402. Sender's reme-

dy, based on payment by mistake, is to recover from the beneficiary that received payment.

Sometimes, however, transmission of payment orders of the sender to the receiving bank is made pursuant to a security procedure designed to detect one or more of the errors described above. Since "security procedure" is defined by Section 4A–201 as "a procedure established by agreement of a customer and a receiving bank for the purpose of * * * detecting error * * *," Section 4A–205 does not apply if the receiving bank and the customer did not agree to the establishment of a procedure for detecting error. A security procedure may be designed to detect an account number that is not one to which Sender normally makes payment. In that case, the security procedure may require a special verification that payment to the stated account number was intended. In the case of dollar amounts, the security procedure may require different codes for different dollar amounts. If a $1,000,000 payment order contains a code that is inappropriate for that amount, the error in amount should be detected. In the case of duplicate orders, the security procedure may require that each payment order be identified by a number or code that applies to no other order. If the number or code of each payment order received is registered in a computer base, the receiving bank can quickly identify a duplicate order. The three cases covered by this section are essentially similar. In each, if the error is not detected, some beneficiary will receive funds that the beneficiary was not intended to receive. If this section applies, the risk of loss with respect to the error of the sender is shifted to the bank which has the burden of recovering the funds from the beneficiary. The risk of loss is shifted to the bank only if the sender proves that the error would have been detected if there had been compliance with the procedure and that the sender (or an agent under Section 4A–206) complied. In the case of a duplicate order or a wrong beneficiary, the sender doesn't have to pay the order. In the case of an overpayment, the sender does not have to pay the order to the extent of the overpayment. If subsection (a)(1) applies, the position of the receiving bank is comparable to that of a receiving bank that erroneously executes a payment order as stated in Section 4A–303. However, failure of the sender to timely report the error is covered by Section 4A–205(b) rather than by Section 4A–304 which applies only to erroneous execution under Section 4A–303. A receiving bank to which the risk of loss is shifted by subsection (a)(1) or (2) is entitled to recover the amount erroneously paid to the beneficiary to the extent allowed by the law of mistake and restitution. Rights of the receiving bank against the beneficiary are similar to those of a receiving bank that erroneously executes a payment order as stated in Section 4A–303. Those rights are discussed in Comment 2 to Section 4A–303.

2. A security procedure established for the purpose of detecting error is not effective unless both sender and receiving bank comply with the procedure. Thus, the bank undertakes a duty of complying with the procedure for the benefit of the sender. This duty is recognized in subsection (a)(1). The loss with respect to the sender's error is shifted to the bank if the bank fails to comply with the procedure and the sender (or an agent under Section 4A–206) does comply. Although the customer may have been negligent in transmitting the erroneous payment order, the loss is put on the bank on a last-clear-chance theory. A similar analysis applies to subsection (b). If the loss with respect to an error is shifted to the receiving bank and the sender is notified by the bank that the erroneous payment order was accepted, the sender has a duty to exercise ordinary care to discover the error and notify the bank of the relevant facts within a reasonable time not exceeding 90 days. If the bank can prove that the sender failed in this duty it is entitled to compensation for the loss incurred as a result of the failure. Whether the bank is entitled to recover from the sender depends upon whether the failure to give timely notice would have made any difference. If the bank could not have recov-

ered from the beneficiary that received payment under the erroneous payment order even if timely notice had been given, the sender's failure to notify did not cause any loss of the bank.

3. Section 4A-205 is subject to variation by agreement under Section 4A-501. Thus, if a receiving bank and its customer have agreed to a security procedure for detection of error, the liability of the receiving bank for failing to detect an error of the customer as provided in Section 4A-205 may be varied as provided in an agreement of the bank and the customer.

§ 4A-206. Transmission of Payment Order Through Funds-Transfer or Other Communication System.

(a) If a payment order addressed to a receiving bank is transmitted to a funds-transfer system or other third-party communication system for transmittal to the bank, the system is deemed to be an agent of the sender for the purpose of transmitting the payment order to the bank. If there is a discrepancy between the terms of the payment order transmitted to the system and the terms of the payment order transmitted by the system to the bank, the terms of the payment order of the sender are those transmitted by the system. This section does not apply to a funds-transfer system of the Federal Reserve Banks.

(b) This section applies to cancellations and amendments of payment orders to the same extent it applies to payment orders.

Official Comment

1. A payment order may be issued to a receiving bank directly by delivery of a writing or electronic device or by an oral or electronic communication. If an agent of the sender is employed to transmit orders on behalf of the sender, the sender is bound by the order transmitted by the agent on the basis of agency law. Section 4A-206 is an application of that principle to cases in which a funds transfer or communication system acts as an intermediary in transmitting the sender's order to the receiving bank. The intermediary is deemed to be an agent of the sender for the purpose of transmitting payment orders and related messages for the sender. Section 4A-206 deals with error by the intermediary.

2. Transmission by an automated clearing house of an association of banks other than the Federal Reserve Banks is an example of a transaction covered by Section 4A-206. Suppose Originator orders Originator's Bank to cause a large number of payments to be made to many accounts in banks in various parts of the country. These payment orders are electronically transmitted to Originator's Bank and stored in an electronic device that is held by Originator's Bank. Or, transmission of the various payment orders is made by delivery to Originator's Bank of an electronic device containing the instruction to the bank. In either case the terms of the various payment orders by Originator are determined by the information contained in the electronic device. In order to execute the various orders, the information in the electronic device must be processed. For example, if some of the orders are for payments to accounts in Bank X and some to accounts in Bank Y, Originator's Bank will execute these orders of Originator by issuing a series of payment orders to Bank X covering all payments to accounts in that bank, and by issuing a series of payment orders to Bank Y covering all payments to accounts in that bank. The orders to Bank X may be transmitted together by means of an electronic device, and those to Bank Y may be included in another electronic device. Typically, this processing is done by an automated clearing house acting for a group of banks including Originator's

Bank. The automated clearing house is a funds transfer system. Section 4A-105(a)(5). Originator's Bank delivers Originator's electronic device or transmits the information contained in the device to the funds transfer system for processing into payment orders of Originator's Bank to the appropriate beneficiary's banks. The processing may result in an erroneous payment order. Originator's Bank, by use of Originator's electronic device, may have given information to the funds transfer system instructing payment of $100,000 to an account in Bank X, but because of human error or an equipment malfunction the processing may have converted that instruction into an instruction to Bank X to make a payment of $1,000,000. Under Section 4A-206, Originator's Bank issued a payment order for $1,000,000 to Bank X when the erroneous information was sent to Bank X. Originator's Bank is responsible for the error of the automated clearing house. The liability of the funds transfer system that made the error is not governed by Article 4A. It is left to the law of contract, a funds transfer system rule, or other applicable law.

In the hypothetical case just discussed, if the automated clearing house is operated by a Federal Reserve Bank, the analysis is different. Section 4A-206 does not apply. Originator's Bank will execute Originator's payment orders by delivery or transmission of the electronic information to the Federal Reserve Bank for processing. The result is that Originator's Bank has issued payment orders to the Federal Reserve Bank which, in this case, is acting as an intermediary bank. When the Federal Reserve Bank has processed the information given to it by Originator's Bank it will issue payment orders to the various beneficiary's banks. If the processing results in an erroneous payment order, the Federal Reserve Bank has erroneously executed the payment order of Originator's Bank and the case is governed by Section 4A-303.

§ 4A-207. Misdescription of Beneficiary.

(a) Subject to subsection (b), if, in a payment order received by the beneficiary's bank, the name, bank account number, or other identification of the beneficiary refers to a nonexistent or unidentifiable person or account, no person has rights as a beneficiary of the order and acceptance of the order cannot occur.

(b) If a payment order received by the beneficiary's bank identifies the beneficiary both by name and by an identifying or bank account number and the name and number identify different persons, the following rules apply:

(1) Except as otherwise provided in subsection (c), if the beneficiary's bank does not know that the name and number refer to different persons, it may rely on the number as the proper identification of the beneficiary of the order. The beneficiary's bank need not determine whether the name and number refer to the same person.

(2) If the beneficiary's bank pays the person identified by name or knows that the name and number identify different persons, no person has rights as beneficiary except the person paid by the beneficiary's bank if that person was entitled to receive payment from the originator of the funds transfer. If no person has rights as beneficiary, acceptance of the order cannot occur.

(c) If (i) a payment order described in subsection (b) is accepted, (ii) the originator's payment order described the beneficiary inconsistently by name and number, and (iii) the beneficiary's bank pays the person identified by number as permitted by subsection (b)(1), the following rules apply:

(1) If the originator is a bank, the originator is obliged to pay its order.

(2) If the originator is not a bank and proves that the person identified by number was not entitled to receive payment from the originator, the originator is not obliged to pay its order unless the originator's bank proves that the originator, before acceptance of the originator's order, had notice that payment of a payment order issued by the originator might be made by the beneficiary's bank on the basis of an identifying or bank account number even if it identifies a person different from the named beneficiary. Proof of notice may be made by any admissible evidence. The originator's bank satisfies the burden of proof if it proves that the originator, before the payment order was accepted, signed a writing stating the information to which the notice relates.

(d) In a case governed by subsection (b)(1), if the beneficiary's bank rightfully pays the person identified by number and that person was not entitled to receive payment from the originator, the amount paid may be recovered from that person to the extent allowed by the law governing mistake and restitution as follows:

(1) If the originator is obliged to pay its payment order as stated in subsection (c), the originator has the right to recover.

(2) If the originator is not a bank and is not obliged to pay its payment order, the originator's bank has the right to recover.

Official Comment

1. Subsection (a) deals with the problem of payment orders issued to the beneficiary's bank for payment to nonexistent or unidentifiable persons or accounts. Since it is not possible in that case for the funds transfer to be completed, subsection (a) states that the order cannot be accepted. Under Section 4A–402(c), a sender of a payment order is not obliged to pay its order unless the beneficiary's bank accepts a payment order instructing payment to the beneficiary of that sender's order. Thus, if the beneficiary of a funds transfer is nonexistent or unidentifiable, each sender in the funds transfer that has paid its payment order is entitled to get its money back.

2. Subsection (b), which takes precedence over subsection (a), deals with the problem of payment orders in which the description of the beneficiary does not allow identification of the beneficiary because the beneficiary is described by name and by an identifying number or an account number and the name and number refer to different persons. A very large percentage of payment orders issued to the beneficiary's bank by another bank are processed by automated means using machines capable of reading orders on standard formats that identify the beneficiary by an identifying number or the number of a bank account. The processing of the order by the beneficiary's bank and the crediting of the beneficiary's account are done by use of the identifying or bank account number without human reading of the payment order itself. The process is comparable to that used in automated payment of checks. The standard format, however, may also allow the

inclusion of the name of the beneficiary and other information which can be useful to the beneficiary's bank and the beneficiary but which plays no part in the process of payment. If the beneficiary's bank has both the account number and name of the beneficiary supplied by the originator of the funds transfer, it is possible for the beneficiary's bank to determine whether the name and number refer to the same person, but if a duty to make that determination is imposed on the beneficiary's bank the benefits of automated payment are lost. Manual handling of payment orders is both expensive and subject to human error. If payment orders can be handled on an automated basis there are substantial economies of operation and the possibility of clerical error is reduced. Subsection (b) allows banks to utilize automated processing by allowing banks to act on the basis of the number without regard to the name if the bank does not know that the name and number refer to different persons. "Know" is defined in Section 1–201(25) to mean actual knowledge, and Section 1–201(27) states rules for determining when an organization has knowledge of information received by the organization. The time of payment is the pertinent time at which knowledge or lack of knowledge must be determined.

Although the clear trend is for beneficiary's banks to process payment orders by automated means, Section 4A–207 is not limited to cases in which processing is done by automated means. A bank that processes by semi-automated means or even manually may rely on number as stated in Section 4A–207.

In cases covered by subsection (b) the erroneous identification would in virtually all cases be the identifying or bank account number. In the typical case the error is made by the originator of the funds transfer. The originator should know the name of the person who is to receive payment and can further identify that person by an address that would normally be known to the originator. It is not unlikely, however, that the originator may not be sure whether the identifying or account number refers to the person the originator intends to pay. Subsection (b)(1) deals with the typical case in which the beneficiary's bank pays on the basis of the account number and is not aware at the time of payment that the named beneficiary is not the holder of the account which was paid. In some cases the false number will be the result of error by the originator. In other cases fraud is involved. For example, Doe is the holder of shares in Mutual Fund. Thief, impersonating Doe, requests redemption of the shares and directs Mutual Fund to wire the redemption proceeds to Doe's account #12345 in Beneficiary's Bank. Mutual Fund originates a funds transfer by issuing a payment order to Originator's Bank to make the payment to Doe's account #12345 in Beneficiary's Bank. Originator's Bank executes the order by issuing a conforming payment order to Beneficiary's Bank which makes payment to account #12345. That account is the account of Roe rather than Doe. Roe might be a person acting in concert with Thief or Roe might be an innocent third party. Assume that Roe is a gem merchant that agreed to sell gems to Thief who agreed to wire the purchase price to Roe's account in Beneficiary's Bank. Roe believed that the credit to Roe's account was a transfer of funds from Thief and released the gems to Thief in good faith in reliance on the payment. The case law is unclear on the responsibility of a beneficiary's bank in carrying out a payment order in which the identification of the beneficiary by name and number is conflicting. See Securities Fund Services, Inc. v. American National Bank, 542 F.Supp. 323 (N.D.Ill.1982) and Bradford Trust Co. v. Texas American Bank, 790 F.2d 407 (5th Cir.1986). Section 4A–207 resolves the issue.

If Beneficiary's Bank did not know about the conflict between the name and number, subsection (b)(1) applies. Beneficiary's Bank has no duty to determine whether there is a conflict and it may rely on the number as the proper identification of the beneficiary of the order. When it accepts the order, it is entitled to payment from Originator's Bank. Section 4A–402(b). On the other hand, if Beneficiary's Bank knew about the conflict between the name and number and nevertheless paid Roe, subsection (b)(2) applies. Under that provision, acceptance of the payment order of Originator's Bank did not occur because there is no beneficiary of that order. Since acceptance did not occur Originator's Bank is not obliged to pay Beneficiary's Bank. Section 4A–402(b). Similarly, Mutual Fund is excused from its obligation to pay Originator's Bank. Section 4A–402(c). Thus, Beneficiary's Bank takes the loss. Its only cause of action is against Thief. Roe is not obliged to return the payment to the beneficiary's bank because Roe received the payment in good faith and for value. Article 4A makes irrelevant the issue of whether Mutual Fund was or was not negligent in issuing its payment order.

3. Normally, subsection (b)(1) will apply to the hypothetical case discussed in Comment 2. Beneficiary's Bank will pay on the basis of the number without knowledge of the conflict. In that case subsection (c) places the loss on either Mutual Fund or Originator's Bank. It is not unfair to assign the loss to Mutual Fund because it is the person who dealt with the imposter and it supplied the wrong account number. It could have avoided the loss if it had not used an account number that it was not sure was that of Doe. Mutual Fund, however, may not have been aware of the risk involved in giving both name and number. Subsection (c) is designed to protect the originator, Mutual Fund, in this case. Under that subsection, the originator is responsible for the inconsistent description of the beneficiary if it had notice that the order might be paid by the beneficiary's bank on the basis of the number. If the originator is a bank, the originator always has that responsibility. The rationale is that any bank should know how payment orders are processed and paid. If the originator is not a bank, the originator's bank must prove that its customer, the originator, had notice. Notice can be proved by any admissible evidence, but the bank can always prove notice by providing the customer with a written statement of the required information and obtaining the customer's signature to the statement. That statement will then apply to any payment order accepted by the bank thereafter. The information need not be supplied more than once.

In the hypothetical case if Originator's Bank made the disclosure stated in the last sentence of subsection (c)(2), Mutual Fund must pay Originator's Bank. Under subsection (d)(1), Mutual Fund has an action to recover from Roe if recovery from Roe is permitted by the law governing mistake and restitution. Under the assumed facts Roe should be entitled to keep the money as a person who took it in good faith and for value since it was taken as payment for the gems. In that case, Mutual Fund's only remedy is against Thief. If Roe was not acting in good faith, Roe has to return the money to Mutual Fund. If Originator's Bank does not prove that Mutual Fund had notice as stated in subsection (c)(2), Mutual Fund is not required to pay Originator's Bank. Thus, the risk of loss falls on Originator's Bank whose remedy is against Roe or Thief as stated above. Subsection (d)(2).

§ 4A–208. Misdescription of Intermediary Bank or Beneficiary's Bank.

(a) This subsection applies to a payment order identifying an intermediary bank or the beneficiary's bank only by an identifying number.

(1) The receiving bank may rely on the number as the proper identification of the intermediary or beneficiary's bank and need not determine whether the number identifies a bank.

(2) The sender is obliged to compensate the receiving bank for any loss and expenses incurred by the receiving bank as a result of its

reliance on the number in executing or attempting to execute the order.

(b) This subsection applies to a payment order identifying an intermediary bank or the beneficiary's bank both by name and an identifying number if the name and number identify different persons.

(1) If the sender is a bank, the receiving bank may rely on the number as the proper identification of the intermediary or beneficiary's bank if the receiving bank, when it executes the sender's order, does not know that the name and number identify different persons. The receiving bank need not determine whether the name and number refer to the same person or whether the number refers to a bank. The sender is obliged to compensate the receiving bank for any loss and expenses incurred by the receiving bank as a result of its reliance on the number in executing or attempting to execute the order.

(2) If the sender is not a bank and the receiving bank proves that the sender, before the payment order was accepted, had notice that the receiving bank might rely on the number as the proper identification of the intermediary or beneficiary's bank even if it identifies a person different from the bank identified by name, the rights and obligations of the sender and the receiving bank are governed by subsection (b)(1), as though the sender were a bank. Proof of notice may be made by any admissible evidence. The receiving bank satisfies the burden of proof if it proves that the sender, before the payment order was accepted, signed a writing stating the information to which the notice relates.

(3) Regardless of whether the sender is a bank, the receiving bank may rely on the name as the proper identification of the intermediary or beneficiary's bank if the receiving bank, at the time it executes the sender's order, does not know that the name and number identify different persons. The receiving bank need not determine whether the name and number refer to the same person.

(4) If the receiving bank knows that the name and number identify different persons, reliance on either the name or the number in executing the sender's payment order is a breach of the obligation stated in Section 4A–302(a)(1).

Official Comment

1. This section addresses an issue similar to that addressed by Section 4A–207. Because of automation in the processing of payment orders, a payment order may identify the beneficiary's bank or an intermediary bank by an identifying number. The bank identified by number might or might not also be identified by name. The following two cases illustrate Section 4A–208(a) and (b):

Case #1. Originator's payment order to Originator's Bank identifies the beneficiary's bank as Bank A and instructs payment to Account #12345 in that bank. Originator's Bank executes Originator's order by issuing a payment order to Intermediary Bank. In the payment order of Originator's Bank the beneficiary's bank is identified as Bank A but is also identified by number, #67890. The identifying number refers to Bank B rather than Bank A. If processing by Intermediary Bank of the payment order of Originator's Bank is done by automated means, Intermediary Bank, in executing the order, will rely on the identifying number and will issue a payment order to Bank B rather than Bank A. If there is an Account #12345 in Bank B, the payment order of Intermediary Bank would normally be accepted and payment would be made to a person not intended by Originator. In this case, Section 4A–208(b)(1) puts the risk of loss on Originator's Bank. Intermediary Bank may rely on the number #67890 as the proper identification of the beneficiary's bank. Intermediary Bank has properly executed the payment order of Originator's Bank. By using the wrong number to describe the beneficiary's bank, Originator's Bank has improperly executed Originator's payment order because the payment order of Originator's Bank provides for payment to the wrong beneficiary, the holder of Account #12345 in Bank B rather than the holder of Account #12345 in Bank A. Section 4A–302(a)(1) and Section 4A–303(c). Originator's Bank is not entitled to payment from Originator but is required to pay Intermediary Bank. Section 4A–303(c) and Section 4A–402(c). Intermediary Bank is also entitled to compensation for any loss and expenses resulting from the error by Originator's Bank.

If there is no Account #12345 in Bank B, the result is that there is no beneficiary of the payment order issued by Originator's Bank and the funds transfer will not be completed. Originator's Bank is not entitled to payment from Originator and Intermediary Bank is not entitled to payment from Originator's Bank. Section 4A–402(c). Since Originator's Bank improperly executed Originator's payment order it may be liable for damages under Section 4A–305. As stated above, Intermediary Bank is entitled to compensation for loss and expenses resulting from the error by Originator's Bank.

Case #2. Suppose the same payment order by Originator to Originator's Bank as in Case #1. In executing the payment order Originator's Bank issues a payment order to Intermediary Bank in which the beneficiary's bank is identified only by number, #67890. That number does not refer to Bank A. Rather, it identifies a person that is not a bank. If processing by Intermediary Bank of the payment order of Originator's Bank is done by automated means, Intermediary Bank will rely on the number #67890 to identify the beneficiary's bank. Intermediary Bank has no duty to determine whether the number identifies a bank. The funds transfer cannot be completed in this case because no bank is identified as the beneficiary's bank. Subsection (a) puts the risk of loss on Originator's Bank. Originator's Bank is not entitled to payment from Originator. Section 4A–402(c). Originator's Bank has improperly executed Originator's payment order and may be liable for damages under Section 4A–305. Originator's Bank is obliged to compensate Intermediary Bank for loss and expenses resulting from the error by Originator's Bank.

Subsection (a) also applies if #67890 identifies a bank, but the bank is not Bank A. Intermediary Bank may rely on the number as the proper identification of the beneficiary's bank. If the bank to which Intermediary Bank sends its payment order accepts the order, Intermediary Bank is entitled to payment from Originator's Bank, but Originator's Bank is not entitled to payment from Originator. The analysis is similar to that in Case #1.

2. Subsection (b)(2) of Section 4A–208 addresses cases in which an erroneous identification of a beneficiary's bank or intermediary bank by name and number is made in a payment order of a sender that is not a bank. Suppose Originator issues a payment order to Originator's Bank that instructs that bank to use an intermediary bank identified as Bank A and by an identifying number, #67890.

The identifying number refers to Bank B. Originator intended to identify Bank A as intermediary bank. If Originator's Bank relied on the number and issued a payment order to Bank B the rights of Originator's Bank depend upon whether the proof of notice stated in subsection (b)(2) is made by Originator's Bank. If proof is made, Originator's Bank's rights are governed by subsection (b)(1) of Section 4A–208. Originator's Bank is not liable for breach of Section 4A–302(a)(1) and is entitled to compensation from Originator for any loss and expenses resulting from Originator's error. If notice is not proved, Originator's Bank may not rely on the number in executing Originator's payment order. Since Originator's Bank does not get the benefit of subsection (b)(1) in that case, Originator's Bank improperly executed Originator's payment order and is in breach of the obligation stated in Section 4A–302(a)(1). If notice is not given, Originator's Bank can rely on the name if it is not aware of the conflict in name and number. Subsection (b)(3).

3. Although the principal purpose of Section 4A–208 is to accommodate automated processing of payment orders, Section 4A–208 applies regardless of whether processing is done by automation, semiautomated means or manually.

§ 4A–209. Acceptance of Payment Order.

(a) Subject to subsection (d), a receiving bank other than the beneficiary's bank accepts a payment order when it executes the order.

(b) Subject to subsections (c) and (d), a beneficiary's bank accepts a payment order at the earliest of the following times:

(1) when the bank (i) pays the beneficiary as stated in Section 4A–405(a) or 4A–405(b), or (ii) notifies the beneficiary of receipt of the order or that the account of the beneficiary has been credited with respect to the order unless the notice indicates that the bank is rejecting the order or that funds with respect to the order may not be withdrawn or used until receipt of payment from the sender of the order;

(2) when the bank receives payment of the entire amount of the sender's order pursuant to Section 4A–403(a)(1) or 4A–403(a)(2); or

(3) the opening of the next funds-transfer business day of the bank following the payment date of the order if, at that time, the amount of the sender's order is fully covered by a withdrawable credit balance in an authorized account of the sender or the bank has otherwise received full payment from the sender, unless the order was rejected before that time or is rejected within (i) one hour after that time, or (ii) one hour after the opening of the next business day of the sender following the payment date if that time is later. If notice of rejection is received by the sender after the payment date and the authorized account of the sender does not bear interest, the bank is obliged to pay interest to the sender on the amount of the order for the number of days elapsing after the payment date to the day the sender receives notice or learns that the order was not accepted, counting that day as an elapsed day. If the withdrawable credit balance during that period falls below the amount of the order, the amount of interest payable is reduced accordingly.

(c) Acceptance of a payment order cannot occur before the order is received by the receiving bank. Acceptance does not occur under subsection (b)(2) or (b)(3) if the beneficiary of the payment order does not have an account with the receiving bank, the account has been closed, or the receiving bank is not permitted by law to receive credits for the beneficiary's account.

(d) A payment order issued to the originator's bank cannot be accepted until the payment date if the bank is the beneficiary's bank, or the execution date if the bank is not the beneficiary's bank. If the originator's bank executes the originator's payment order before the execution date or pays the beneficiary of the originator's payment order before the payment date and the payment order is subsequently canceled pursuant to Section 4A-211(b), the bank may recover from the beneficiary any payment received to the extent allowed by the law governing mistake and restitution.

Official Comment

1. This section treats the sender's payment order as a request by the sender to the receiving bank to execute or pay the order and that request can be accepted or rejected by the receiving bank. Section 4A-209 defines when acceptance occurs. Section 4A-210 covers rejection. Acceptance of the payment order imposes an obligation on the receiving bank to the sender if the receiving bank is not the beneficiary's bank, or to the beneficiary if the receiving bank is the beneficiary's bank. These obligations are stated in Section 4A-302 and Section 4A-404.

2. Acceptance by a receiving bank other than the beneficiary's bank is defined in Section 4A-209(a). That subsection states the only way that a bank other than the beneficiary's bank can accept a payment order. A payment order to a bank other than the beneficiary's bank is, in effect, a request that the receiving bank execute the sender's order by issuing a payment order to the beneficiary's bank or to an intermediary bank. Normally, acceptance occurs at the time of execution, but there is an exception stated in subsection (d) and discussed in Comment 9. Execution occurs when the receiving bank "issues a payment order intended to carry out" the sender's order. Section 4A-301(a). In some cases the payment order issued by the receiving bank may not conform to the sender's order. For example, the receiving bank might make a mistake in the amount of its order, or the order might be issued to the wrong beneficiary's bank or for the benefit of the wrong beneficiary. In all of these cases there is acceptance of the sender's order by the bank when the receiving bank issues its order intended to carry out the sender's order, even though the bank's payment order does not in fact carry out the instruction of the sender. Improper execution of the sender's order may lead to liability to the sender for damages or it may mean that the sender is not obliged to pay its payment order. These matters are covered in Section 4A-303, Section 4A-305, and Section 4A-402.

3. A receiving bank has no duty to accept a payment order unless the bank makes an agreement, either before or after issuance of the payment order, to accept it, or acceptance is required by a funds transfer system rule. If the bank makes such an agreement it incurs a contractual obligation based on the agreement and may be held liable for breach of contract if a failure to execute violates the agreement. In many cases a bank will enter into an agreement with its customer to govern the rights and obligations of the parties with respect to payment orders issued to the bank by the customer or, in cases in which the sender is also a bank, there may be a funds transfer system rule that governs the obligations of a receiving bank with respect to payment orders transmitted over the system. Such agreements or rules can specify the

circumstances under which a receiving bank is obliged to execute a payment order and can define the extent of liability of the receiving bank for breach of the agreement or rule. Section 4A-305(d) states the liability for breach of an agreement to execute a payment order.

4. In the case of a payment order issued to the beneficiary's bank, acceptance is defined in Section 4A-209(b). The function of a beneficiary's bank that receives a payment order is different from that of a receiving bank that receives a payment order for execution. In the typical case, the beneficiary's bank simply receives payment from the sender of the order, credits the account of the beneficiary and notifies the beneficiary of the credit. Acceptance by the beneficiary's bank does not create any obligation to the sender. Acceptance by the beneficiary's bank means that the bank is liable to the beneficiary for the amount of the order. Section 4A-404(a). There are three ways in which the beneficiary's bank can accept a payment order which are described in the following comments.

5. Under Section 4A-209(b)(1), the beneficiary's bank can accept a payment order by paying the beneficiary. In the normal case of crediting an account of the beneficiary, payment occurs when the beneficiary is given notice of the right to withdraw the credit, the credit is applied to a debt of the beneficiary, or "funds with respect to the order" are otherwise made available to the beneficiary. Section 4A-405(a). The quoted phrase covers cases in which funds are made available to the beneficiary as a result of receipt of a payment order for the benefit of the beneficiary but the release of funds is not expressed as payment of the order. For example, the beneficiary's bank might express a release of funds equal to the amount of the order as a "loan" that will be automatically repaid when the beneficiary's bank receives payment by the sender of the order. If the release of funds is designated as a loan pursuant to a routine practice of the bank, the release is conditional payment of the order rather than a loan, particularly if normal incidents of a loan such as the signing of a loan agreement or note and the payment of interest are not present. Such a release of funds is payment to the beneficiary under Section 4A-405(a). Under Section 4A-405(c) the bank cannot recover the money from the beneficiary if the bank does not receive payment from the sender of the payment order that it accepted. Exceptions to this rule are stated in § 4A-405(d) and (e). The beneficiary's bank may also accept by notifying the beneficiary that the order has been received. "Notifies" is defined in Section 1-201(26). In some cases a beneficiary's bank will receive a payment order during the day but settlement of the sender's obligation to pay the order will not occur until the end of the day. If the beneficiary's bank wants to defer incurring liability to the beneficiary until the beneficiary's bank receives payment, it can do so. The beneficiary's bank incurs no liability to the beneficiary with respect to a payment order that it receives until it accepts the order. If the bank does not accept pursuant to subsection (b)(1), acceptance does not occur until the end of the day when the beneficiary's bank receives settlement. If the sender settles, the payment order will be accepted under subsection (b)(2) and the funds will be released to the beneficiary the next morning. If the sender doesn't settle, no acceptance occurs. In either case the beneficiary's bank suffers no loss.

6. In most cases the beneficiary's bank will receive a payment order from another bank. If the sender is a bank and the beneficiary's bank receives payment from the sender by final settlement through the Federal Reserve System or a funds transfer system (Section 4A-403(a)(1)) or, less commonly, through credit to an account of the beneficiary's bank with the sender or another bank (Section 4A-403(a)(2)), acceptance by the beneficiary's bank occurs at the time payment is made. Section 4A-209(b)(2). A minor exception to this rule is stated in Section 4A-209(c). Section 4A-209(b)(2) results in automatic acceptance of payment orders issued to a beneficiary's

bank by means of Fedwire because the Federal Reserve account of the beneficiary's bank is credited and final payment is made to that bank when the payment order is received.

Subsection (b)(2) would also apply to cases in which the beneficiary's bank mistakenly pays a person who is not the beneficiary of the payment order issued to the beneficiary's bank. For example, suppose the payment order provides for immediate payment to Account #12345. The beneficiary's bank erroneously credits Account #12346 and notifies the holder of that account of the credit. No acceptance occurs in this case under subsection (b)(1) because the beneficiary of the order has not been paid or notified. The holder of Account #12345 is the beneficiary of the order issued to the beneficiary's bank. But acceptance will normally occur if the beneficiary's bank takes no other action, because the bank will normally receive settlement with respect to the payment order. At that time the bank has accepted because the sender paid its payment order. The bank is liable to pay the holder of Account #12345. The bank has paid the holder of Account #12346 by mistake, and has a right to recover the payment if the credit is withdrawn, to the extent provided in the law governing mistake and restitution.

7. Subsection (b)(3) covers cases of inaction by the beneficiary's bank. It applies whether or not the sender is a bank and covers a case in which the sender and the beneficiary both have accounts with the receiving bank and payment will be made by debiting the account of the sender and crediting the account of the beneficiary. Subsection (b)(3) is similar to subsection (b)(2) in that it bases acceptance by the beneficiary's bank on payment by the sender. Payment by the sender is effected by a debit to the sender's account if the account balance is sufficient to cover the amount of the order. On the payment date (Section 4A-401) of the order the beneficiary's bank will normally credit the beneficiary's account and notify the beneficiary of receipt of the order if it is satisfied that the sender's account balance covers the order or is willing to give credit to the sender. In some cases, however, the bank may not be willing to give credit to the sender and it may not be possible for the bank to determine until the end of the day on the payment date whether there are sufficient good funds in the sender's account. There may be various transactions during the day involving funds going into and out of the account. Some of these transactions may occur late in the day or after the close of the banking day. To accommodate this situation, subsection (b)(3) provides that the status of the account is determined at the opening of the next funds transfer business day of the beneficiary's bank after the payment date of the order. If the sender's account balance is sufficient to cover the order, the beneficiary's bank has a source of payment and the result in almost all cases is that the bank accepts the order at that time if it did not previously accept under subsection (b)(1). In rare cases, a bank may want to avoid acceptance under subsection (b)(3) by rejecting the order as discussed in Comment 8.

8. Section 4A-209 is based on a general principle that a receiving bank is not obliged to accept a payment order unless it has agreed or is bound by a funds transfer system rule to do so. Thus, provision is made to allow the receiving bank to prevent acceptance of the order. This principle is consistently followed if the receiving bank is not the beneficiary's bank. If the receiving bank is not the beneficiary's bank, acceptance is in the control of the receiving bank because it occurs only if the order is executed. But in the case of the beneficiary's bank acceptance can occur by passive receipt of payment under subsection (b)(2) or (3). In the case of a payment made by Fedwire acceptance cannot be prevented. In other cases the beneficiary's bank can prevent acceptance by giving notice of rejection to the sender before payment occurs under Section 4A-403(a)(1) or (2). A minor exception to the ability of the beneficiary's bank to reject is stated in Section 4A-502(c)(3).

Under subsection (b)(3) acceptance occurs at the opening of the next funds transfer business day of the beneficiary's bank following the payment date unless the bank rejected the order before that time or it rejects within one hour after that time. In some cases the sender and the beneficiary's bank may not be in the same time zone or the beginning of the business day of the sender and the funds transfer business day of the beneficiary's bank may not coincide. For example, the sender may be located in California and the beneficiary's bank in New York. Since in most cases notice of rejection would be communicated electronically or by telephone, it might not be feasible for the bank to give notice before one hour after the opening of the funds transfer business day in New York because at that hour, the sender's business day may not have started in California. For that reason, there are alternative deadlines stated in subsection (b)(3). In the case stated, the bank acts in time if it gives notice within one hour after the opening of the business day of the sender. But if the notice of rejection is received by the sender after the payment date, the bank is obliged to pay interest to the sender if the sender's account does not bear interest. In that case the bank had the use of funds of the sender that the sender could reasonably assume would be used to pay the beneficiary. The rate of interest is stated in Section 4A–506. If the sender receives notice on the day after the payment date the sender is entitled to one day's interest. If receipt of notice is delayed for more than one day, the sender is entitled to interest for each additional day of delay.

9. Subsection (d) applies only to a payment order by the originator of a funds transfer to the originator's bank and it refers to the following situation. On April 1, Originator instructs Bank A to make a payment on April 15 to the account of Beneficiary in Bank B. By mistake, on April 1, Bank A executes Originator's payment order by issuing a payment order to Bank B instructing immediate payment to Beneficiary. Bank B credited Beneficiary's account and immediately released the funds to Beneficiary. Under subsection (d) no acceptance by Bank A occurred on April 1 when Originator's payment order was executed because acceptance cannot occur before the execution date which in this case would be April 15 or shortly before that date. Section 4A–301(b). Under Section 4A–402(c), Originator is not obliged to pay Bank A until the order is accepted and that can't occur until the execution date. But Bank A is required to pay Bank B when Bank B accepted Bank A's order on April 1. Unless Originator and Beneficiary are the same person, in almost all cases Originator is paying a debt owed to Beneficiary and early payment does not injure Originator because Originator does not have to pay Bank A until the execution date. Section 4A–402(c). Bank A takes the interest loss. But suppose that on April 3, Originator concludes that no debt was owed to Beneficiary or that the debt was less than the amount of the payment order. Under Section 4A–211(b) Originator can cancel its payment order if Bank A has not accepted. If early execution of Originator's payment order is acceptance, Originator can suffer a loss because cancellation after acceptance is not possible without the consent of Bank A and Bank B. Section 4A–211(c). If Originator has to pay Bank A, Originator would be required to seek recovery of the money from Beneficiary. Subsection (d) prevents this result and puts the risk of loss on Bank A by providing that the early execution does not result in acceptance until the execution date. Since on April 3 Originator's order was not yet accepted, Originator can cancel it under Section 4A–211(b). The result is that Bank A is not entitled to payment from Originator but is obliged to pay Bank B. Bank A has paid Beneficiary by mistake. If Originator's payment order is cancelled, Bank A becomes the originator of an erroneous funds transfer to Beneficiary. Bank A has the burden of recovering payment from Beneficiary on the basis of a payment by mistake. If Beneficiary received the money in good faith in payment of a debt owed to Beneficiary by

Originator, the law of mistake and restitution may allow Beneficiary to keep all or part of the money received. If Originator owed money to Beneficiary, Bank A has paid Originator's debt and, under the law of restitution, which applies pursuant to Section 1-103, Bank A is subrogated to Beneficiary's rights against Originator on the debt.

If Bank A is the Beneficiary's bank and Bank A credited Beneficiary's account and released the funds to Beneficiary on April 1, the analysis is similar. If Originator's order is cancelled, Bank A has paid Beneficiary by mistake. The right of Bank A to recover the payment from Beneficiary is similar to Bank A's rights in the preceding paragraph.

§ 4A-210. Rejection of Payment Order.

(a) A payment order is rejected by the receiving bank by a notice of rejection transmitted to the sender orally, electronically, or in writing. A notice of rejection need not use any particular words and is sufficient if it indicates that the receiving bank is rejecting the order or will not execute or pay the order. Rejection is effective when the notice is given if transmission is by a means that is reasonable in the circumstances. If notice of rejection is given by a means that is not reasonable, rejection is effective when the notice is received. If an agreement of the sender and receiving bank establishes the means to be used to reject a payment order, (i) any means complying with the agreement is reasonable and (ii) any means not complying is not reasonable unless no significant delay in receipt of the notice resulted from the use of the noncomplying means.

(b) This subsection applies if a receiving bank other than the beneficiary's bank fails to execute a payment order despite the existence on the execution date of a withdrawable credit balance in an authorized account of the sender sufficient to cover the order. If the sender does not receive notice of rejection of the order on the execution date and the authorized account of the sender does not bear interest, the bank is obliged to pay interest to the sender on the amount of the order for the number of days elapsing after the execution date to the earlier of the day the order is canceled pursuant to Section 4A-211(d) or the day the sender receives notice or learns that the order was not executed, counting the final day of the period as an elapsed day. If the withdrawable credit balance during that period falls below the amount of the order, the amount of interest is reduced accordingly.

(c) If a receiving bank suspends payments, all unaccepted payment orders issued to it are deemed rejected at the time the bank suspends payments.

(d) Acceptance of a payment order precludes a later rejection of the order. Rejection of a payment order precludes a later acceptance of the order.

Official Comment

1. With respect to payment orders issued to a receiving bank other than the beneficiary's bank, notice of rejection is not necessary to prevent acceptance of the order. Acceptance can occur only if the receiving bank executes the order. Section 4A-209(a). But notice of rejection will routinely be given by such a bank in cases in which the bank cannot or is not willing to execute the order for some reason. There are many reasons why a bank doesn't execute an order. The payment order may not clearly instruct the receiving bank because of some ambiguity in the order or an internal

inconsistency. In some cases, the receiving bank may not be able to carry out the instruction because of equipment failure, credit limitations on the receiving bank, or some other factor which makes proper execution of the order infeasible. In those cases notice of rejection is a means of informing the sender of the facts so that a corrected payment order can be transmitted or the sender can seek alternate means of completing the funds transfer. The other major reason for not executing an order is that the sender's account is insufficient to cover the order and the receiving bank is not willing to give credit to the sender. If the sender's account is sufficient to cover the order and the receiving bank chooses not to execute the order, notice of rejection is necessary to prevent liability to pay interest to the sender if the case falls within Section 4A–210(b) which is discussed in Comment 3.

2. A payment order to the beneficiary's bank can be accepted by inaction of the bank. Section 4A–209(b)(2) and (3). To prevent acceptance under those provisions it is necessary for the receiving bank to send notice of rejection before acceptance occurs. Subsection (a) of Section 4A–210 states the rule that rejection is accomplished by giving notice of rejection. This incorporates the definitions in Section 1–201(26). Rejection is effective when notice is given if it is given by a means that is reasonable in the circumstances. Otherwise, it is effective when the notice is received. The question of when rejection is effective is important only in the relatively few cases under subsection (b)(2) and (3) in which a notice of rejection is necessary to prevent acceptance. The question of whether a particular means is reasonable depends on the facts in a particular case. In a very large percentage of cases the sender and the receiving bank will be in direct electronic contact with each other and in those cases a notice of rejection can be transmitted instantaneously. Since time is of the essence in a large proportion of funds transfers, some quick means of transmission would usually be required, but this is not always the case. The parties may specify by agreement the means by which communication between the parties is to be made.

3. Subsection (b) deals with cases in which a sender does not learn until after the execution date that the sender's order has not been executed. It applies only to cases in which the receiving bank was assured of payment because the sender's account was sufficient to cover the order. Normally, the receiving bank will accept the sender's order if it is assured of payment, but there may be some cases in which the bank chooses to reject. Unless the receiving bank had obligated itself by agreement to accept, the failure to accept is not wrongful. There is no duty of the receiving bank to accept the payment order unless it is obliged to accept by express agreement. Section 4A–212. But even if the bank has not acted wrongfully, the receiving bank had the use of the sender's money that the sender could reasonably assume was to be the source of payment of the funds transfer. Until the sender learns that the order was not accepted the sender is denied the use of that money. Subsection (b) obliges the receiving bank to pay interest to the sender as restitution unless the sender receives notice of rejection on the execution date. The time of receipt of notice is determined pursuant to § 1–201(27). The rate of interest is stated in Section 4A–506. If the sender receives notice on the day after the execution date, the sender is entitled to one day's interest. If receipt of notice is delayed for more than one day, the sender is entitled to interest for each additional day of delay.

4. Subsection (d) treats acceptance and rejection as mutually exclusive. If a payment order has been accepted, rejection of that order becomes impossible. If a payment order has been rejected it cannot be accepted later by the receiving bank. Once notice of rejection has been given, the sender may have acted on the notice by making the payment through other channels. If the receiving bank wants to act on a payment order that it has rejected it has to obtain the consent

of the sender. In that case the consent of the sender would amount to the giving of a second payment order that substitutes for the rejected first order. If the receiving bank suspends payments (Section 4-104(1)(k)), subsection (c) provides that unaccepted payment orders are deemed rejected at the time suspension of payments occurs. This prevents acceptance by passage of time under Section 4A-209(b)(3).

§ 4A-211. Cancellation and Amendment of Payment Order.

(a) A communication of the sender of a payment order cancelling or amending the order may be transmitted to the receiving bank orally, electronically, or in writing. If a security procedure is in effect between the sender and the receiving bank, the communication is not effective to cancel or amend the order unless the communication is verified pursuant to the security procedure or the bank agrees to the cancellation or amendment.

(b) Subject to subsection (a), a communication by the sender cancelling or amending a payment order is effective to cancel or amend the order if notice of the communication is received at a time and in a manner affording the receiving bank a reasonable opportunity to act on the communication before the bank accepts the payment order.

(c) After a payment order has been accepted, cancellation or amendment of the order is not effective unless the receiving bank agrees or a funds-transfer system rule allows cancellation or amendment without agreement of the bank.

(1) With respect to a payment order accepted by a receiving bank other than the beneficiary's bank, cancellation or amendment is not effective unless a conforming cancellation or amendment of the payment order issued by the receiving bank is also made.

(2) With respect to a payment order accepted by the beneficiary's bank, cancellation or amendment is not effective unless the order was issued in execution of an unauthorized payment order, or because of a mistake by a sender in the funds transfer which resulted in the issuance of a payment order (i) that is a duplicate of a payment order previously issued by the sender, (ii) that orders payment to a beneficiary not entitled to receive payment from the originator, or (iii) that orders payment in an amount greater than the amount the beneficiary was entitled to receive from the originator. If the payment order is canceled or amended, the beneficiary's bank is entitled to recover from the beneficiary any amount paid to the beneficiary to the extent allowed by the law governing mistake and restitution.

(d) An unaccepted payment order is canceled by operation of law at the close of the fifth funds-transfer business day of the receiving bank after the execution date or payment date of the order.

(e) A canceled payment order cannot be accepted. If an accepted payment order is canceled, the acceptance is nullified and no person has any right or obligation based on the acceptance. Amendment of a payment order is deemed to be cancellation of the original order at the time of amendment and issue of a new payment order in the amended form at the same time.

(f) Unless otherwise provided in an agreement of the parties or in a funds-transfer system rule, if the receiving bank, after accepting a payment order, agrees to cancellation or amendment of the order by the sender or is bound by a funds-transfer system rule allowing cancellation or amendment without the bank's agreement, the sender, whether or not cancellation or amendment is effective, is liable to the bank for any loss and expenses, including reasonable attorney's fees, incurred by the bank as a result of the cancellation or amendment or attempted cancellation or amendment.

(g) A payment order is not revoked by the death or legal incapacity of the sender unless the receiving bank knows of the death or of an adjudication of incapacity by a court of competent jurisdiction and has reasonable opportunity to act before acceptance of the order.

(h) A funds-transfer system rule is not effective to the extent it conflicts with subsection (c)(2).

Official Comment

1. This section deals with cancellation and amendment of payment orders. It states the conditions under which cancellation or amendment is both effective and rightful. There is no concept of wrongful cancellation or amendment of a payment order. If the conditions stated in this section are not met the attempted cancellation or amendment is not effective. If the stated conditions are met the cancellation or amendment is effective and rightful. The sender of a payment order may want to withdraw or change the order because the sender has had a change of mind about the transaction or because the payment order was erroneously issued or for any other reason. One common situation is that of multiple transmission of the same order. The sender that mistakenly transmits the same order twice wants to correct the mistake by cancelling the duplicate order. Or, a sender may have intended to order a payment of $1,000,000 but mistakenly issued an order to pay $10,000,000. In this case the sender might try to correct the mistake by cancelling the order and issuing another order in the proper amount. Or, the mistake could be corrected by amending the order to change it to the proper amount. Whether the error is corrected by amendment or cancellation and reissue the net result is the same. This result is stated in the last sentence of subsection (e).

2. Subsection (a) allows a cancellation or amendment of a payment order to be communicated to the receiving bank "orally, electronically, or in writing." The quoted phrase is consistent with the language of Section 4A–103(a) applicable to payment orders. Cancellations and amendments are normally subject to verification pursuant to security procedures to the same extent as payment orders. Subsection (a) recognizes this fact by providing that in cases in which there is a security procedure in effect between the sender and the receiving bank the bank is not bound by a communication cancelling or amending an order unless verification has been made. This is necessary to protect the bank because under subsection (b) a cancellation or amendment can be effective by unilateral action of the sender. Without verification the bank cannot be sure whether the communication was or was not effective to cancel or amend a previously verified payment order.

3. If the receiving bank has not yet accepted the order, there is no reason why the sender should not be able to cancel or amend the order unilaterally so long as the requirements of subsections (a) and (b) are met. If the receiving bank has accepted the order, it is possible to cancel or amend but only if the requirements of subsection (c) are met.

First consider the case of a receiving bank other than the beneficiary's bank. If the bank has not yet accepted the order, the sender can unilaterally cancel or amend. The communication amending or cancelling the payment order must be received in time to allow the bank to act on it before the bank issues its payment order in execution of the sender's order. The time that the sender's communication is received is governed by Section 4a–106. If a payment order does not specify a delayed payment date or execution date, the order will normally be executed shortly after receipt. Thus, as a practical matter, the sender will have very little time in which to instruct cancellation or amendment before acceptance. In addition, a receiving bank will normally have cut-off times for receipt of such communications, and the receiving bank is not obliged to act on communications received after the cut-off hour. Cancellation by the sender after execution of the order by the receiving bank requires the agreement of the bank unless a funds transfer rule otherwise provides. Subsection (c). Although execution of the sender's order by the receiving bank does not itself impose liability on the receiving bank (under Section 4A–402 no liability is incurred by the receiving bank to pay its order until it is accepted), it would commonly be the case that acceptance follows shortly after issuance. Thus, as a practical matter, a receiving bank that has executed a payment order will incur a liability to the next bank in the chain before it would be able to act on the cancellation request of its customer. It is unreasonable to impose on the receiving bank a risk of loss with respect to a cancellation request without the consent of the receiving bank.

The statute does not state how or when the agreement of the receiving bank must be obtained for cancellation after execution. The receiving bank's consent could be obtained at the time cancellation occurs or it could be based on a preexisting agreement. Or, a funds transfer system rule could provide that cancellation can be made unilaterally by the sender. By virtue of that rule any receiving bank covered by the rule is bound. Section 4A–501. If the receiving bank has already executed the sender's order, the bank would not consent to cancellation unless the bank to which the receiving bank has issued its payment order consents to cancellation of that order. It makes no sense to allow cancellation of a payment order unless all subsequent payment orders in the funds transfer that were issued because of the cancelled payment order are also cancelled. Under subsection (c)(1), if a receiving bank consents to cancellation of the payment order after it has executed, the cancellation is not effective unless the receiving bank also cancels the payment order issued by the bank.

4. With respect to a payment order issued to the beneficiary's bank, acceptance is particularly important because it creates liability to pay the beneficiary, it defines when the originator pays its obligation to the beneficiary, and it defines when any obligation for which the payment is made is discharged. Since acceptance affects the rights of the originator and the beneficiary it is not appropriate to allow the beneficiary's bank to agree to cancellation or amendment except in unusual cases. Except as provided in subsection (c)(2), cancellation or amendment after acceptance by the beneficiary's bank is not possible unless all parties affected by the order agree. Under subsection (c)(2), cancellation or amendment is possible only in the four cases stated. The following examples illustrate subsection (c)(2):

Case #1. Originator's Bank executed a payment order issued in the name of its customer as sender. The order was not authorized by the customer and was fraudulently issued. Beneficiary's Bank accepted the payment order issued by Originator's Bank. Under subsection (c)(2) Originator's Bank can cancel the order if Beneficiary's Bank consents. It doesn't make any difference whether the payment order that Originator's Bank accepted was or was not enforceable against the customer under Section 4A–202(b).

Verification under that provision is important in determining whether Originator's Bank or the customer has the risk of loss, but it has no relevance under Section 4A–211(c)(2). Whether or not verified, the payment order was not authorized by the customer. Cancellation of the payment order to Beneficiary's Bank causes the acceptance of Beneficiary's Bank to be nullified. Subsection (e). Beneficiary's Bank is entitled to recover payment from the beneficiary to the extent allowed by the law of mistake and restitution. In this kind of case the beneficiary is usually a party to the fraud who has no right to receive or retain payment of the order.

Case #2. Originator owed Beneficiary $1,000,000 and ordered Bank A to pay that amount to the account of Beneficiary in Bank B. Bank A issued a complying order to Bank B, but by mistake issued a duplicate order as well. Bank B accepted both orders. Under subsection (c)(2)(i) cancellation of the duplicate order could be made by Bank A with the consent of Bank B. Beneficiary has no right to receive or retain payment of the duplicate payment order if only $1,000,000 was owed by Originator to Beneficiary. If Originator owed $2,000,000 to Beneficiary, the law of restitution might allow Beneficiary to retain the $1,000,000 paid by Bank B on the duplicate order. In that case Bank B is entitled to reimbursement from Bank A under subsection (f).

Case #3. Originator owed $1,000,000 to X. Intending to pay X, Originator ordered Bank A to pay $1,000,000 to Y's account in Bank B. Bank A issued a complying payment order to Bank B which Bank B accepted by releasing the $1,000,000 to Y. Under subsection (c)(2)(ii) Bank A can cancel its payment order to Bank B with the consent of Bank B if Y was not entitled to receive payment from Originator. Originator can also cancel its order to Bank A with Bank A's consent. Subsection (c)(1). Bank B may recover the $1,000,000 from Y unless the law of mistake and restitution allows Y to retain some or all of the amount paid. If no debt was owed to Y, Bank B should have a right of recovery.

Case #4. Originator owed Beneficiary $10,000. By mistake Originator ordered Bank A to pay $1,000,000 to the account of Beneficiary in Bank B. Bank A issued a complying order to Bank B which accepted by notifying Beneficiary of its right to withdraw $1,000,000. Cancellation is permitted in this case under subsection (c)(2)(iii). If Bank B paid Beneficiary it is entitled to recover the payment except to the extent the law of mistake and restitution allows Beneficiary to retain payment. In this case Beneficiary might be entitled to retain $10,000, the amount of the debt owed to Beneficiary. If Beneficiary may retain $10,000, Bank B would be entitled to $10,000 from Bank A pursuant to subsection (f). In this case Originator also cancelled its order. Thus Bank A would be entitled to $10,000 from Originator pursuant to subsection (f).

5. Unless constrained by a funds transfer system rule, a receiving bank may agree to cancellation or amendment of the payment order under subsection (c) but is not required to do so regardless of the circumstances. If the receiving bank has incurred liability as a result of its acceptance of the sender's order, there are substantial risks in agreeing to cancellation or amendment. This is particularly true for a beneficiary's bank. Cancellation or amendment after acceptance by the beneficiary's bank can be made only in the four cases stated and the beneficiary's bank may not have any way of knowing whether the requirements of subsection (c) have been met or whether it will be able to recover payment from the beneficiary that received payment. Even with indemnity the beneficiary's bank may be reluctant to alienate its customer, the beneficiary, by denying the customer the funds. Subsection (c) leaves the decision to the beneficiary's bank unless the consent of the beneficiary's bank is not required under a funds transfer system rule or other interbank agreement. If a receiving bank agrees to cancellation or amendment under subsection (c)(1) or (2), it is automatically enti-

tled to indemnification from the sender under subsection (f). The indemnification provision recognizes that a sender has no right to cancel a payment order after it is accepted by the receiving bank. If the receiving bank agrees to cancellation, it is doing so as an accommodation to the sender and it should not incur a risk of loss in doing so.

6. Acceptance by the receiving bank of a payment order issued by the sender is comparable to acceptance of an offer under the law of contracts. Under that law the death or legal incapacity of an offeror terminates the offer even though the offeree has no notice of the death or incapacity. Restatement Second, Contracts § 48. Comment a. to that section states that the "rule seems to be a relic of the obsolete view that a contract requires a 'meeting of minds,' and it is out of harmony with the modern doctrine that a manifestation of assent is effective without regard to actual mental assent." Subsection (g), which reverses the Restatement rule in the case of a payment order, is similar to Section 4–405(1) which applies to checks. Subsection (g) does not address the effect of the bankruptcy of the sender of a payment order before the order is accepted, but the principle of subsection (g) has been recognized in Bank of Marin v. England, 385 U.S. 99 (1966). Although Bankruptcy Code Section 542(c) may not have been drafted with wire transfers in mind, its language can be read to allow the receiving bank to charge the sender's account for the amount of the payment order if the receiving bank executed it in ignorance of the bankruptcy.

7. Subsection (d) deals with stale payment orders. Payment orders normally are executed on the execution date or the day after. An order issued to the beneficiary's bank is normally accepted on the payment date or the day after. If a payment order is not accepted on its execution or payment date or shortly thereafter, it is probable that there was some problem with the terms of the order or the sender did not have sufficient funds or credit to cover the amount of the order. Delayed acceptance of such an order is normally not contemplated, but the order may not have been cancelled by the sender. Subsection (d) provides for cancellation by operation of law to prevent an unexpected delayed acceptance.

8. A funds transfer system rule can govern rights and obligations between banks that are parties to payment orders transmitted over the system even if the rule conflicts with Article 4A. In some cases, however, a rule governing a transaction between two banks can affect a third party in an unacceptable way. Subsection (h) deals with such a case. A funds transfer system rule cannot allow cancellation of a payment order accepted by the beneficiary's bank if the rule conflicts with subsection (c)(2). Because rights of the beneficiary and the originator are directly affected by acceptance, subsection (c)(2) severely limits cancellation. These limitations cannot be altered by funds transfer system rule.

§ 4A–212. Liability and Duty of Receiving Bank Regarding Unaccepted Payment Order.

If a receiving bank fails to accept a payment order that it is obliged by express agreement to accept, the bank is liable for breach of the agreement to the extent provided in the agreement or in this Article, but does not otherwise have any duty to accept a payment order or, before acceptance, to take any action, or refrain from taking action, with respect to the order except as provided in this Article or by express agreement. Liability based on acceptance arises only when acceptance occurs as stated in Section 4A–209, and liability is limited to that provided in this Article. A receiving bank is not the agent of the sender or beneficiary of the payment order it accepts, or of any other party to the funds transfer, and the bank owes no duty to any party to the funds transfer except as provided in this Article or by express agreement.

Official Comment

With limited exceptions stated in this Article, the duties and obligations of receiving banks that carry out a funds transfer arise only as a result of acceptance of payment orders or of agreements made by receiving banks. Exceptions are stated in Section 4A-209(b)(3) and Section 4A-210(b). A receiving bank is not like a collecting bank under Article 4. No receiving bank, whether it be an originator's bank, an intermediary bank or a beneficiary's bank, is an agent for any other party in the funds transfer.

PART 3

EXECUTION OF SENDER'S PAYMENT ORDER BY RECEIVING BANK

§ 4A-301. Execution and Execution Date.

(a) A payment order is "executed" by the receiving bank when it issues a payment order intended to carry out the payment order received by the bank. A payment order received by the beneficiary's bank can be accepted but cannot be executed.

(b) "Execution date" of a payment order means the day on which the receiving bank may properly issue a payment order in execution of the sender's order. The execution date may be determined by instruction of the sender but cannot be earlier than the day the order is received and, unless otherwise determined, is the day the order is received. If the sender's instruction states a payment date, the execution date is the payment date or an earlier date on which execution is reasonably necessary to allow payment to the beneficiary on the payment date.

Official Comment

1. The terms "executed," "execution" and "execution date" are used only with respect to a payment order to a receiving bank other than the beneficiary's bank. The beneficiary's bank can accept the payment order that it receives, but it does not execute the order. Execution refers to the act of the receiving bank in issuing a payment order "intended to carry out" the payment order that the bank received. A receiving bank has executed an order even if the order issued by the bank does not carry out the order received by the bank. For example, the bank may have erroneously issued an order to the wrong beneficiary, or in the wrong amount or to the wrong beneficiary's bank. In each of these cases execution has occurred but the execution is erroneous. Erroneous execution is covered in Section 4A-303.

2. "Execution date" refers to the time a payment order should be executed rather than the day it is actually executed. Normally the sender will not specify an execution date, but most payment orders are meant to be executed immediately. Thus, the execution date is normally the day the order is received by the receiving bank. It is common for the sender to specify a "payment date" which is defined in Section 4A-401 as "the day on which the amount of the order is payable to the beneficiary by the beneficiary's bank." Except for automated clearing house transfers, if a funds transfer is entirely within the United States and the payment is to be carried out electronically, the execution date is the payment date unless the order is received after the payment date. If the payment is to be carried out through an automated clearing house, execution may occur before the

payment date. In an ACH transfer the beneficiary is usually paid one or two days after issue of the originator's payment order. The execution date is determined by the stated payment date and is a day before the payment date on which execution is reasonably necessary to allow payment on the payment date. A funds transfer system rule could also determine the execution date of orders received by the receiving bank if both the sender and the receiving bank are participants in the funds transfer system. The execution date can be determined by the payment order itself or by separate instructions of the sender or an agreement of the sender and the receiving bank. The second sentence of subsection (b) must be read in the light of Section 4A-106 which states that if a payment order is received after the cut-off time of the receiving bank it may be treated by the bank as received at the opening of the next funds transfer business day.

3. Execution on the execution date is timely, but the order can be executed before or after the execution date. Section 4A-209(d) and Section 4A-402(c) state the consequences of early execution and Section 4A-305(a) states the consequences of late execution.

§ 4A-302. Obligations of Receiving Bank in Execution of Payment Order.

(a) Except as provided in subsections (b) through (d), if the receiving bank accepts a payment order pursuant to Section 4A-209(a), the bank has the following obligations in executing the order:

(1) The receiving bank is obliged to issue, on the execution date, a payment order complying with the sender's order and to follow the sender's instructions concerning (i) any intermediary bank or funds-transfer system to be used in carrying out the funds transfer, or (ii) the means by which payment orders are to be transmitted in the funds transfer. If the originator's bank issues a payment order to an intermediary bank, the originator's bank is obliged to instruct the intermediary bank according to the instruction of the originator. An intermediary bank in the funds transfer is similarly bound by an instruction given to it by the sender of the payment order it accepts.

(2) If the sender's instruction states that the funds transfer is to be carried out telephonically or by wire transfer or otherwise indicates that the funds transfer is to be carried out by the most expeditious means, the receiving bank is obliged to transmit its payment order by the most expeditious available means, and to instruct any intermediary bank accordingly. If a sender's instruction states a payment date, the receiving bank is obliged to transmit its payment order at a time and by means reasonably necessary to allow payment to the beneficiary on the payment date or as soon thereafter as is feasible.

(b) Unless otherwise instructed, a receiving bank executing a payment order may (i) use any funds-transfer system if use of that system is reasonable in the circumstances, and (ii) issue a payment order to the beneficiary's bank or to an intermediary bank through which a payment order conforming to the sender's order can expeditiously be issued to the beneficiary's bank if the receiving bank exercises ordinary care in the selection of the intermediary bank. A receiving bank is not required to follow an instruction of the sender designating a funds-transfer system to be used in carrying out the funds transfer if the receiving bank, in good faith, determines that it is not feasible to follow the instruction or that following the instruction would unduly delay completion of the funds transfer.

(c) Unless subsection (a)(2) applies or the receiving bank is otherwise instructed, the bank may execute a payment order by transmitting its payment order by first class mail or by any means reasonable in the circumstances. If the receiving bank is instructed to execute the sender's order by transmitting its payment order by a particular means, the receiving bank may issue its payment order by the means stated or by any means as expeditious as the means stated.

(d) Unless instructed by the sender, (i) the receiving bank may not obtain payment of its charges for services and expenses in connection with the execution of the sender's order by issuing a payment order in an amount equal to the amount of the sender's order less the amount of the charges, and (ii) may not instruct a subsequent receiving bank to obtain payment of its charges in the same manner.

Official Comment

1. In the absence of agreement, the receiving bank is not obliged to execute an order of the sender. Section 4A–212. Section 4A–302 states the manner in which the receiving bank may execute the sender's order if execution occurs. Subsection (a)(1) states the residual rule. The payment order issued by the receiving bank must comply with the sender's order and, unless some other rule is stated in the section, the receiving bank is obliged to follow any instruction of the sender concerning which funds transfer system is to be used, which intermediary banks are to be used, and what means of transmission is to be used. The instruction of the sender may be incorporated in the payment order itself or may be given separately. For example, there may be a master agreement between the sender and receiving bank containing instructions governing payment orders to be issued from time to time by the sender to the receiving bank. In most funds transfers, speed is a paramount consideration. A sender that wants assurance that the funds transfer will be expeditiously completed can specify the means to be used. The receiving bank can follow the instructions literally or it can use an equivalent means. For example, if the sender instructs the receiving bank to transmit by telex, the receiving bank could use telephone instead. Subsection (c). In most cases the sender will not specify a particular means but will use a general term such as "by wire" or "wire transfer" or "as soon as possible." These words signify that the sender wants a same-day transfer. In these cases the receiving bank is required to use a telephonic or electronic communication to transmit its order and is also required to instruct any intermediary bank to which it issues its order to transmit by similar means. Subsection (a)(2). In other cases, such as an automated clearing house transfer, a same-day transfer is not contemplated. Normally the sender's instruction or the context in which the payment order is received makes clear the type of funds transfer that is appropriate. If the sender states a payment date with respect to the payment order, the receiving bank is obliged to execute the order at a time and in a manner to meet the payment date if that is feasible. Subsection (a)(2). This provision would apply to many ACH transfers made to pay recurring debts of the sender. In other cases, involving relatively small amounts, time may not be an important factor and cost may be a more important element. Fast means, such as telephone or electronic

transmission, are more expensive than slow means such as mailing. Subsection (c) states that in the absence of instructions the receiving bank is given discretion to decide. It may issue its payment order by first class mail or by any means reasonable in the circumstances. Section 4A–305 states the liability of a receiving bank for breach of the obligations stated in Section 4A–302.

2. Subsection (b) concerns the choice of intermediary banks to be used in completing the funds transfer, and the funds transfer system to be used. If the receiving bank is not instructed about the matter, it can issue an order directly to the beneficiary's bank or can issue an order to an intermediary bank. The receiving bank also has discretion concerning use of a funds transfer system. In some cases it may be reasonable to use either an automated clearing house system or a wire transfer system such as Fedwire or CHIPS. Normally, the receiving bank will follow the instruction of the sender in these matters, but in some cases it may be prudent for the bank not to follow instructions. The sender may have designated a funds transfer system to be used in carrying out the funds transfer, but it may not be feasible to use the designated system because of some impediment such as a computer breakdown which prevents prompt execution of the order. The receiving bank is permitted to use an alternate means of transmittal in a good faith effort to execute the order expeditiously. The same leeway is not given to the receiving bank if the sender designates an intermediary bank through which the funds transfer is to be routed. The sender's designation of that intermediary bank may mean that the beneficiary's bank is expecting to obtain a credit from that intermediary bank and may have relied on that anticipated credit. If the receiving bank uses another intermediary bank the expectations of the beneficiary's bank may not be realized. The receiving bank could choose to route the transfer to another intermediary bank and then to the designated intermediary bank if there were some reason such as a lack of a correspondent-bank relationship or a bilateral credit limitation, but the designated intermediary bank cannot be circumvented. To do so violates the sender's instructions.

3. The normal rule, under subsection (a)(1), is that the receiving bank, in executing a payment order, is required to issue a payment order that complies as to amount with that of the sender's order. In most cases the receiving bank issues an order equal to the amount of the sender's order and makes a separate charge for services and expenses in executing the sender's order. In some cases, particularly if it is an intermediary bank that is executing an order, charges are collected by deducting them from the amount of the payment order issued by the executing bank. If that is done, the amount of the payment order accepted by the beneficiary's bank will be slightly less than the amount of the originator's payment order. For example, Originator, in order to pay an obligation of $1,000,000 owed to Beneficiary, issues a payment order to Originator's Bank to pay $1,000,000 to the account of Beneficiary in Beneficiary's Bank. Originator's Bank issues a payment order to Intermediary Bank for $1,000,000 and debits Originator's account for $1,000,010. The extra $10 is the fee of Originator's Bank. Intermediary Bank executes the payment order of Originator's Bank by issuing a payment order to Beneficiary's Bank for $999,990, but under § 4A–402(c) is entitled to receive $1,000,000 from Originator's Bank. The $10 difference is the fee of Intermediary Bank. Beneficiary's Bank credits Beneficiary's account for $999,990. When Beneficiary's Bank accepts the payment order of Intermediary Bank the result is a payment of $999,990 from Originator to Beneficiary. Section 4A–406(a). If that payment discharges the $1,000,000 debt, the effect is that Beneficiary has paid the charges of Intermediary Bank and Originator has paid the charges of Originator's Bank. Subsection (d) of Section 4A–302 allows Intermediary Bank to collect its charges by deducting them from the amount of the payment order, but only if instructed to do so by Origina-

tor's Bank. Originator's Bank is not authorized to give that instruction to Intermediary Bank unless Originator authorized the instruction. Thus, Originator can control how the charges of Originator's Bank and Intermediary Bank are to be paid. Subsection (d) does not apply to charges of Beneficiary's Bank to Beneficiary.

In the case discussed in the preceding paragraph the $10 charge is trivial in relation to the amount of the payment and it may not be important to Beneficiary how the charge is paid. But it may be very important if the $1,000,000 obligation represented the price of exercising a right such as an option favorable to Originator and unfavorable to Beneficiary. Beneficiary might well argue that it was entitled to receive $1,000,000. If the option was exercised shortly before its expiration date, the result could be loss of the option benefit because the required payment of $1,000,000 was not made before the option expired. Section 4A–406(c) allows Originator to preserve the option benefit. The amount received by Beneficiary is deemed to be $1,000,000 unless Beneficiary demands the $10 and Originator does not pay it.

§ 4A–303. Erroneous Execution of Payment Order.

(a) A receiving bank that (i) executes the payment order of the sender by issuing a payment order in an amount greater than the amount of the sender's order, or (ii) issues a payment order in execution of the sender's order and then issues a duplicate order, is entitled to payment of the amount of the sender's order under Section 4A–402(c) if that subsection is otherwise satisfied. The bank is entitled to recover from the beneficiary of the erroneous order the excess payment received to the extent allowed by the law governing mistake and restitution.

(b) A receiving bank that executes the payment order of the sender by issuing a payment order in an amount less than the amount of the sender's order is entitled to payment of the amount of the sender's order under Section 4A–402(c) if (i) that subsection is otherwise satisfied and (ii) the bank corrects its mistake by issuing an additional payment order for the benefit of the beneficiary of the sender's order. If the error is not corrected, the issuer of the erroneous order is entitled to receive or retain payment from the sender of the order it accepted only to the extent of the amount of the erroneous order. This subsection does not apply if the receiving bank executes the sender's payment order by issuing a payment order in an amount less than the amount of the sender's order for the purpose of obtaining payment of its charges for services and expenses pursuant to instruction of the sender.

(c) If a receiving bank executes the payment order of the sender by issuing a payment order to a beneficiary different from the beneficiary of the sender's order and the funds transfer is completed on the basis of that error, the sender of the payment order that was erroneously executed and all previous senders in the funds transfer are not obliged to pay the payment orders they issued. The issuer of the erroneous order is entitled to recover from the beneficiary of the order the payment received to the extent allowed by the law governing mistake and restitution.

Official Comment

1. Section 4A–303 states the effect of erroneous execution of a payment order by the receiving bank. Under Section

4A-402(c) the sender of a payment order is obliged to pay the amount of the order to the receiving bank if the bank executes the order, but the obligation to pay is excused if the beneficiary's bank does not accept a payment order instructing payment to the beneficiary of the sender's order. If erroneous execution of the sender's order causes the wrong beneficiary to be paid, the sender is not required to pay. If erroneous execution causes the wrong amount to be paid the sender is not obliged to pay the receiving bank an amount in excess of the amount of the sender's order. Section 4A-303 takes precedence over Section 4A-402(c) and states the liability of the sender and the rights of the receiving bank in various cases of erroneous execution.

2. Subsections (a) and (b) deal with cases in which the receiving bank executes by issuing a payment order in the wrong amount. If Originator ordered Originator's Bank to pay $1,000,000 to the account of Beneficiary in Beneficiary's Bank, but Originator's Bank erroneously instructed Beneficiary's Bank to pay $2,000,000 to Beneficiary's account, subsection (a) applies. If Beneficiary's Bank accepts the order of Originator's Bank, Beneficiary's Bank is entitled to receive $2,000,000 from Originator's Bank, but Originator's Bank is entitled to receive only $1,000,000 from Originator. Originator's Bank is entitled to recover the overpayment from Beneficiary to the extent allowed by the law governing mistake and restitution. Originator's Bank would normally have a right to recover the overpayment from Beneficiary, but in unusual cases the law of restitution might allow Beneficiary to keep all or part of the overpayment. For example, if Originator owed $2,000,000 to Beneficiary and Beneficiary received the extra $1,000,000 in good faith in discharge of the debt, Beneficiary may be allowed to keep it. In this case Originator's Bank has paid an obligation of Originator and under the law of restitution, which applies through Section 1-103, Originator's Bank would be subrogated to Beneficiary's rights against Originator on the obligation paid by Originator's Bank.

If Originator's Bank erroneously executed Originator's order by instructing Beneficiary's Bank to pay less than $1,000,000, subsection (b) applies. If Originator's Bank corrects its error by issuing another payment order to Beneficiary's Bank that results in payment of $1,000,000 to Beneficiary, Originator's Bank is entitled to payment of $1,000,000 from Originator. If the mistake is not corrected, Originator's Bank is entitled to payment from Originator only in the amount of the order issued by Originator's Bank.

3. Subsection (a) also applies to duplicate payment orders. Assume Originator's Bank properly executes Originator's $1,000,000 payment order and then by mistake issues a second $1,000,000 payment order in execution of Originator's order. If Beneficiary's Bank accepts both orders issued by Originator's Bank, Beneficiary's Bank is entitled to receive $2,000,000 from Originator's Bank but Originator's Bank is entitled to receive only $1,000,000 from Originator. The remedy of Originator's Bank is the same as that of a receiving bank that executes by issuing an order in an amount greater than the sender's order. It may recover the overpayment from Beneficiary to the extent allowed by the law governing mistake and restitution and in a proper case as stated in Comment 2 may have subrogation rights if it is not entitled to recover from Beneficiary.

4. Suppose Originator instructs Originator's Bank to pay $1,000,000 to Account #12345 in Beneficiary's Bank. Originator's Bank erroneously instructs Beneficiary's Bank to pay $1,000,000 to Account #12346 and Beneficiary's Bank accepted. Subsection (c) covers this case. Originator is not obliged to pay its payment order, but Originator's Bank is required to pay $1,000,000 to Beneficiary's Bank. The remedy of Originator's Bank is to recover $1,000,000 from the holder of Account #12346 that received payment by mistake. Recovery based on the law of mistake and restitution is described in Comment 2.

§ 4A–304. Duty of Sender to Report Erroneously Executed Payment Order.

If the sender of a payment order that is erroneously executed as stated in Section 4A–303 receives notification from the receiving bank that the order was executed or that the sender's account was debited with respect to the order, the sender has a duty to exercise ordinary care to determine, on the basis of information available to the sender, that the order was erroneously executed and to notify the bank of the relevant facts within a reasonable time not exceeding 90 days after the notification from the bank was received by the sender. If the sender fails to perform that duty, the bank is not obliged to pay interest on any amount refundable to the sender under Section 4A–402(d) for the period before the bank learns of the execution error. The bank is not entitled to any recovery from the sender on account of a failure by the sender to perform the duty stated in this section.

Official Comment

This section is identical in effect to Section 4A–204 which applies to unauthorized orders issued in the name of a customer of the receiving bank. The rationale is stated in Comment 2 to Section 4A–204.

§ 4A–305. Liability for Late or Improper Execution or Failure to Execute Payment Order.

(a) If a funds transfer is completed but execution of a payment order by the receiving bank in breach of Section 4A–302 results in delay in payment to the beneficiary, the bank is obliged to pay interest to either the originator or the beneficiary of the funds transfer for the period of delay caused by the improper execution. Except as provided in subsection (c), additional damages are not recoverable.

(b) If execution of a payment order by a receiving bank in breach of Section 4A–302 results in (i) noncompletion of the funds transfer, (ii) failure to use an intermediary bank designated by the originator, or (iii) issuance of a payment order that does not comply with the terms of the payment order of the originator, the bank is liable to the originator for its expenses in the funds transfer and for incidental expenses and interest losses, to the extent not covered by subsection (a), resulting from the improper execution. Except as provided in subsection (c), additional damages are not recoverable.

(c) In addition to the amounts payable under subsections (a) and (b), damages, including consequential damages, are recoverable to the extent provided in an express written agreement of the receiving bank.

(d) If a receiving bank fails to execute a payment order it was obliged by express agreement to execute, the receiving bank is liable to the sender for its expenses in the transaction and for incidental expenses and interest losses resulting from the failure to execute. Additional damages, including consequential damages, are recoverable to the extent provided in an express written agreement of the receiving bank, but are not otherwise recoverable.

(e) Reasonable attorney's fees are recoverable if demand for compensation under subsection (a) or (b) is made and refused before an action is brought on the claim. If a claim is made for breach of an agreement under subsection (d) and the agreement does not provide for damages, reasonable attorney's fees are recoverable if demand for compensation under subsection (d) is made and refused before an action is brought on the claim.

(f) Except as stated in this section, the liability of a receiving bank under subsections (a) and (b) may not be varied by agreement.

Official Comment

1. Subsection (a) covers cases of delay in completion of a funds transfer resulting from an execution by a receiving bank in breach of Section 4A-302(a). The receiving bank is obliged to pay interest on the amount of the order for the period of the delay. The rate of interest is stated in Section 4A-506. With respect to wire transfers (other than ACH transactions) within the United States, the expectation is that the funds transfer will be completed the same day. In those cases, the originator can reasonably expect that the originator's account will be debited on the same day as the beneficiary's account is credited. If the funds transfer is delayed, compensation can be paid either to the originator or to the beneficiary. The normal practice is to compensate the beneficiary's bank to allow that bank to compensate the beneficiary by back-valuing the payment by the number of days of delay. Thus, the beneficiary is in the same position that it would have been in if the funds transfer had been completed on the same day. Assume on Day 1, Originator's Bank issues its payment order to Intermediary Bank which is received on that day. Intermediary Bank does not execute that order until Day 2 when it issues an order to Beneficiary's Bank which is accepted on that day. Intermediary Bank complies with subsection (a) by paying one day's interest to Beneficiary's Bank for the account of Beneficiary.

2. Subsection (b) applies to cases of breach of Section 4A-302 involving more than mere delay. In those cases the bank is liable for damages for improper execution but they are limited to compensation for interest losses and incidental expenses of the sender resulting from the breach, the expenses of the sender in the funds transfer and attorney's fees. This subsection reflects the judgment that imposition of consequential damages on a bank for commission of an error is not justified.

The leading common law case on the subject of consequential damages is Evra Corp. v. Swiss Bank Corp., 673 F.2d 951 (7th Cir.1982), in which Swiss Bank, an intermediary bank, failed to execute a payment order. Because the beneficiary did not receive timely payment the originator lost a valuable ship charter. The lower court awarded the originator $2.1 million for lost profits even though the amount of the payment order was only $27,000. The Seventh Circuit reversed, in part on the basis of the common law rule of Hadley v. Baxendale that consequential damages may not be awarded unless the defendant is put on notice of the special circumstances giving rise to them. Swiss Bank may have known that the originator was paying the shipowner for the hire of a vessel but did not know that a favorable charter would be lost if the payment was delayed. "Electronic payments are not so unusual as to automatically place a bank on notice of extraordinary consequences if such a transfer goes awry. Swiss Bank did not have enough information to infer that if it lost a $27,000 payment order it would face liability in excess of $2 million." 673 F.2d at 956.

If *Evra* means that consequential damages can be imposed if the culpable bank has notice of particular circumstances giving rise to the damages, it does not provide an acceptable solution to the problem of bank liability for consequential damages. In the typical case transmission of the payment order is made electronically. Personnel of the receiving bank that process payment orders are not the appropriate people to evaluate the risk of liability for consequential damages in relation to the price charged for the wire transfer service. Even if notice is received by higher level management personnel who could make an appropriate decision whether the risk is justified by the price, liability based on notice would require evaluation of payment orders on an individual basis. This kind of evaluation is inconsistent with the high-speed, low-price, mechanical nature of the processing system that characterizes wire transfers. Moreover, in *Evra* the culpable bank was an intermediary bank with which the originator did not deal. Notice to the originator's bank would not bind the intermediary bank, and it seems impractical for the originator's bank to convey notice of this kind to intermediary banks in the funds transfer. The success of the wholesale wire transfer industry has largely been based on its ability to effect payment at low cost and great speed. Both of these essential aspects of the modern wire transfer system would be adversely affected by a rule that imposed on banks liability for consequential damages. A banking industry amicus brief in *Evra* stated: "Whether banks can continue to make EFT services available on a widespread basis, by charging reasonable rates, depends on whether they can do so without incurring unlimited consequential risks. Certainly, no bank would handle for $3.25 a transaction entailing potential liability in the millions of dollars."

As the court in *Evra* also noted, the originator of the funds transfer is in the best position to evaluate the risk that a funds transfer will not be made on time and to manage that risk by issuing a payment order in time to allow monitoring of the transaction. The originator, by asking the beneficiary, can quickly determine if the funds transfer has been completed. If the originator has sent the payment order at a time that allows a reasonable margin for correcting error, no loss is likely to result if the transaction is monitored. The other published cases on this issue reach the *Evra* result. Central Coordinates, Inc. v. Morgan Guaranty Trust Co., 40 U.C.C.Rep.Serv. 1340 (N.Y.Sup.Ct.1985), and Gatoil (U.S.A.), Inc. v. Forest Hill State Bank, 1 U.C.C.Rep.Serv.2d 171 (D.Md.1986).

Subsection (c) allows the measure of damages in subsection (b) to be increased by an express written agreement of the receiving bank. An originator's bank might be willing to assume additional responsibilities and incur additional liability in exchange for a higher fee.

3. Subsection (d) governs cases in which a receiving bank has obligated itself by express agreement to accept payment orders of a sender. In the absence of such an agreement there is no obligation by a receiving bank to accept a payment order. Section 4A–212. The measure of damages for breach of an agreement to accept a payment order is the same as that stated in subsection (b). As in the case of subsection (b), additional damages, including consequential damages, may be recovered to the extent stated in an express written agreement of the receiving bank.

4. Reasonable attorney's fees are recoverable only in cases in which damages are limited to statutory damages stated in subsections (a), (b) and (d). If additional damages are recoverable because provided for by an express written agreement, attorney's fees are not recoverable. The rationale is that there is no need for statutory attorney's fees in the latter case, because the parties have agreed to a measure of damages which may or may not provide for attorney's fees.

5. The effect of subsection (f) is to prevent reduction of a receiving bank's liability under Section 4A–305.

PART 4

PAYMENT

§ 4A–401. Payment Date.

"Payment date" of a payment order means the day on which the amount of the order is payable to the beneficiary by the beneficiary's bank. The payment date may be determined by instruction of the sender but cannot be earlier than the day the order is received by the beneficiary's bank and, unless otherwise determined, is the day the order is received by the beneficiary's bank.

Official Comment

"Payment date" refers to the day the beneficiary's bank is to pay the beneficiary. The payment date may be expressed in various ways so long as it indicates the day the beneficiary is to receive payment. For example, in ACH transfers the payment date is the equivalent of "settlement date" or "effective date." Payment date applies to the payment order issued to the beneficiary's bank, but a payment order issued to a receiving bank other than the beneficiary's bank may also state a date for payment to the beneficiary. In the latter case, the statement of a payment date is to instruct the receiving bank concerning time of execution of the sender's order. Section 4A–301(b).

§ 4A–402. Obligation of Sender to Pay Receiving Bank.

(a) This section is subject to Sections 4A–205 and 4A–207.

(b) With respect to a payment order issued to the beneficiary's bank, acceptance of the order by the bank obliges the sender to pay the bank the amount of the order, but payment is not due until the payment date of the order.

(c) This subsection is subject to subsection (e) and to Section 4A–303. With respect to a payment order issued to a receiving bank other than the beneficiary's bank, acceptance of the order by the receiving bank obliges the sender to pay the bank the amount of the sender's order. Payment by the sender is not due until the execution date of the sender's order. The obligation of that sender to pay its payment order is excused if the funds transfer is not completed by acceptance by the beneficiary's bank of a payment order instructing payment to the beneficiary of that sender's payment order.

(d) If the sender of a payment order pays the order and was not obliged to pay all or part of the amount paid, the bank receiving payment is obliged to refund payment to the extent the sender was not obliged to pay. Except as provided in Sections 4A–204 and 4A–304, interest is payable on the refundable amount from the date of payment.

(e) If a funds transfer is not completed as stated in subsection (c) and an intermediary bank is obliged to refund payment as stated in subsection (d) but is unable to do so because not permitted by applicable law or because the bank suspends payments, a sender in the funds transfer that executed a payment order in compliance with an instruction, as stated in Section 4A–

302(a)(1), to route the funds transfer through that intermediary bank is entitled to receive or retain payment from the sender of the payment order that it accepted. The first sender in the funds transfer that issued an instruction requiring routing through that intermediary bank is subrogated to the right of the bank that paid the intermediary bank to refund as stated in subsection (d).

(f) The right of the sender of a payment order to be excused from the obligation to pay the order as stated in subsection (c) or to receive refund under subsection (d) may not be varied by agreement.

Official Comment

1. Subsection (b) states that the sender of a payment order to the beneficiary's bank must pay the order when the beneficiary's bank accepts the order. At that point the beneficiary's bank is obliged to pay the beneficiary. Section 4A-404(a). The last clause of subsection (b) covers a case of premature acceptance by the beneficiary's bank. In some funds transfers, notably automated clearing house transfers, a beneficiary's bank may receive a payment order with a payment date after the day the order is received. The beneficiary's bank might accept the order before the payment date by notifying the beneficiary of receipt of the order. Although the acceptance obliges the beneficiary's bank to pay the beneficiary, payment is not due until the payment date. The last clause of subsection (b) is consistent with that result. The beneficiary's bank is also not entitled to payment from the sender until the payment date.

2. Assume that Originator instructs Bank A to order immediate payment to the account of Beneficiary in Bank B. Execution of Originator's payment ordered by Bank A is acceptance under Section 4A-209(a). Under the second sentence of Section 4A-402(c) the acceptance creates an obligation of Originator to pay Bank A the amount of the order. The last clause of that sentence deals with attempted funds transfers that are not completed. In that event the obligation of the sender to pay its payment order is excused. Originator makes payment to Beneficiary when Bank B, the beneficiary's bank, accepts a payment order for the benefit of Beneficiary. Section 4A-406(a). If that acceptance by Bank B does not occur, the funds transfer has miscarried because Originator has not paid Beneficiary. Originator doesn't have to pay its payment order, and if it has already paid it is entitled to refund of the payment with interest. The rate of interest is stated in Section 4A-506. This "money-back guarantee" is an important protection of Originator. Originator is assured that it will not lose its money if something goes wrong in the transfer. For example, risk of loss resulting from payment to the wrong beneficiary is borne by some bank, not by Originator. The most likely reason for noncompletion is a failure to execute or an erroneous execution of a payment order by Bank A or an intermediary bank. Bank A may have issued its payment order to the wrong bank or it may have identified the wrong beneficiary in its order. The money-back guarantee is particularly important to Originator if noncompletion of the funds transfer is due to the fault of an intermediary bank rather than Bank A. In that case Bank A must refund payment to Originator, and Bank A has the burden of obtaining refund from the intermediary bank that it paid.

Subsection (c) can result in loss if an intermediary bank suspends payments. Suppose Originator instructs Bank A to pay to Beneficiary's account in Bank B and to use Bank C as an intermediary bank. Bank A executes Originator's order by issuing a payment order to Bank C. Bank A pays Bank C. Bank C fails to execute the order of Bank A and suspends payments. Under subsections (c) and (d), Originator is not obliged to pay Bank A and is entitled to refund from Bank A of any payment that it may have made. Bank A is entitled to a refund from Bank C, but Bank C is insolvent. Subsection (e) deals with this case. Bank A was required to issue its payment order to Bank C because Bank C was designated as an intermediary bank by Originator. Section 4A-302(a)(1). In this case Originator takes the risk of insolvency of Bank C. Under subsection (e), Bank A is entitled to payment from Originator and Originator is subrogated to the right of Bank A under subsection (d) to refund of payment from Bank C.

3. A payment order is not like a negotiable instrument on which the drawer or maker has liability. Acceptance of the order by the receiving bank creates an obligation of the sender to pay the receiving bank the amount of the order. That is the extent of the sender's liability to the receiving bank and no other person has any rights against the sender with respect to the sender's order.

§ 4A-403. Payment by Sender to Receiving Bank.

(a) Payment of the sender's obligation under Section 4A-402 to pay the receiving bank occurs as follows:

(1) If the sender is a bank, payment occurs when the receiving bank receives final settlement of the obligation through a Federal Reserve Bank or through a funds-transfer system.

(2) If the sender is a bank and the sender (i) credited an account of the receiving bank with the sender, or (ii) caused an account of the receiving bank in another bank to be credited, payment occurs when the credit is withdrawn or, if not withdrawn, at midnight of the day on which the credit is withdrawable and the receiving bank learns of that fact.

(3) If the receiving bank debits an account of the sender with the receiving bank, payment occurs when the debit is made to the extent the debit is covered by a withdrawable credit balance in the account.

(b) If the sender and receiving bank are members of a funds-transfer system that nets obligations multilaterally among participants, the receiving bank receives final settlement when settlement is complete in accordance with the rules of the system. The obligation of the sender to pay the amount of a payment order transmitted through the funds-transfer system may be satisfied, to the extent permitted by the rules of the system, by setting off and applying against the sender's obligation the right of the sender to receive payment from the receiving bank of the amount of any other payment order transmitted to the sender by the receiving bank through the funds-transfer system. The aggregate balance of obligations owed by each sender to each receiving bank in the funds-transfer system may be satisfied, to the extent permitted by the rules of the system, by setting off and applying against that balance the aggregate balance of obligations owed to the sender by other members of the system. The aggregate balance is determined after the right of setoff stated in the second sentence of this subsection has been exercised.

(c) If two banks transmit payment orders to each other under an agreement that settlement of the obligations of each bank to the other under Section 4A-402 will be made at the end of the day or other period, the total amount owed with respect to all orders transmitted by one bank shall be set off against the total amount owed with respect to all orders transmitted by the other bank. To the extent of the setoff, each bank has made payment to the other.

(d) In a case not covered by subsection (a), the time when payment of the sender's obligation under Section 4A–402(b) or 4A–402(c) occurs is governed by applicable principles of law that determine when an obligation is satisfied.

Official Comment

1. This section defines when a sender pays the obligation stated in Section 4A–402. If a group of two or more banks engage in funds transfers with each other, the participating banks will sometimes be senders and sometimes receiving banks. With respect to payment orders other than Fedwires, the amounts of the various payment orders may be credited and debited to accounts of one bank with another or to a clearing house account of each bank and amounts owed and amounts due are netted. Settlement is made through a Federal Reserve Bank by charges to the Federal Reserve accounts of the net debtor banks and credits to the Federal Reserve accounts of the net creditor banks. In the case of Fedwires the sender's obligation is settled by a debit to the Federal Reserve account of the sender and a credit to the Federal Reserve account of the receiving bank at the time the receiving bank receives the payment order. Both of these cases are covered by subsection (a)(1). When the Federal Reserve settlement becomes final the obligation of the sender under Section 4A–402 is paid.

2. In some cases a bank does not settle an obligation owed to another bank through a Federal Reserve Bank. This is the case if one of the banks is a foreign bank without access to the Federal Reserve payment system. In this kind of case, payment is usually made by credits or debits to accounts of the two banks with each other or to accounts of the two banks in a third bank. Suppose Bank B has an account in Bank A. Bank A advises Bank B that its account in Bank A has been credited $1,000,000 and that the credit is immediately withdrawable. Bank A also instructs Bank B to pay $1,000,000 to the account of Beneficiary in Bank B. This case is covered by subsection (a)(2). Bank B may want to immediately withdraw this credit. For example, it might do so by instructing Bank A to debit the account and pay some third party. Payment by Bank A to Bank B of Bank A's payment order occurs when the withdrawal is made. Suppose Bank B does not withdraw the credit. Since Bank B is the beneficiary's bank, one of the effects of receipt of payment by Bank B is that acceptance of Bank A's payment order automatically occurs at the time of payment. Section 4A–209(b)(2). Acceptance means that Bank B is obliged to pay $1,000,000 to Beneficiary. Section 4A–404(a). Subsection (a)(2) of Section 4A–403 states that payment does not occur until midnight if the credit is not withdrawn. This allows Bank B an opportunity to reject the order if it does not have time to withdraw the credit to its account and it is not willing to incur the liability to Beneficiary before it has use of the funds represented by the credit.

3. Subsection (a)(3) applies to a case in which the sender (bank or nonbank) has a funded account in the receiving bank. If Sender has an account in Bank and issues a payment order to Bank, Bank can obtain payment from Sender by debiting the account of Sender, which pays its Section 4A–402 obligation to Bank when the debit is made.

4. Subsection (b) deals with multilateral settlements made through a funds transfer system and is based on the CHIPS settlement system. In a funds transfer system such as CHIPS, which allows the various banks that transmit payment orders over the system to settle obligations at the end of each day, settlement is not based on individual payment

orders. Each bank using the system engages in funds transfers with many other banks using the system. Settlement for any participant is based on the net credit or debit position of that participant with all other banks using the system. Subsection (b) is designed to make clear that the obligations of any sender are paid when the net position of that sender is settled in accordance with the rules of the funds transfer system. This provision is intended to invalidate any argument, based on common-law principles, that multilateral netting is not valid because mutuality of obligation is not present. Subsection (b) dispenses with any mutuality of obligation requirements. Subsection (c) applies to cases in which two banks send payment orders to each other during the day and settle with each other at the end of the day or at the end of some other period. It is similar to subsection (b) in that it recognizes that a sender's obligation to pay a payment order is satisfied by a setoff. The obligations of each bank as sender to the other as receiving bank are obligations of the bank itself and not as representative of customers. These two sections are important in the case of insolvency of a bank. They make clear that liability under Section 4A-402 is based on the net position of the insolvent bank after setoff.

5. Subsection (d) relates to the uncommon case in which the sender doesn't have an account relationship with the receiving bank and doesn't settle through a Federal Reserve Bank. An example would be a customer that pays over the counter for a payment order that the customer issues to the receiving bank. Payment would normally be by cash, check or bank obligation. When payment occurs is determined by law outside Article 4A.

§ 4A-404. Obligation of Beneficiary's Bank to Pay and Give Notice to Beneficiary.

(a) Subject to Sections 4A-211(e), 4A-405(d), and 4A-405(e), if a beneficiary's bank accepts a payment order, the bank is obliged to pay the amount of the order to the beneficiary of the order. Payment is due on the payment date of the order, but if acceptance occurs on the payment date after the close of the funds-transfer business day of the bank, payment is due on the next funds-transfer business day. If the bank refuses to pay after demand by the beneficiary and receipt of notice of particular circumstances that will give rise to consequential damages as a result of nonpayment, the beneficiary may recover damages resulting from the refusal to pay to the extent the bank had notice of the damages, unless the bank proves that it did not pay because of a reasonable doubt concerning the right of the beneficiary to payment.

(b) If a payment order accepted by the beneficiary's bank instructs payment to an account of the beneficiary, the bank is obliged to notify the beneficiary of receipt of the order before midnight of the next funds-transfer business day following the payment date. If the payment order does not instruct payment to an account of the beneficiary, the bank is required to notify the beneficiary only if notice is required by the order. Notice may be given by first class mail or any other means reasonable in the circumstances. If the bank fails to give the required notice, the bank is obliged to pay interest to the beneficiary on the amount of the payment order from the day notice should have been given until the day the beneficiary learned of receipt of the payment order by the bank. No other damages are recoverable. Reasonable attorney's fees are also recoverable if demand for interest is made and refused before an action is brought on the claim.

(c) The right of a beneficiary to receive payment and damages as stated in subsection (a) may not be varied by agreement or a funds-transfer system rule. The right of a beneficiary to be notified as stated in subsection (b) may be varied by agreement of the beneficiary or by a funds-transfer system rule if the beneficiary is notified of the rule before initiation of the funds transfer.

Official Comment

1. The first sentence of subsection (a) states the time when the obligation of the beneficiary's bank arises. The second and third sentences state when the beneficiary's bank must make funds available to the beneficiary. They also state the measure of damages for failure, after demand, to comply. Since the Expedited Funds Availability Act, 12 U.S.C. 4001 et seq., also governs funds availability in a funds transfer, the second and third sentences of subsection (a) may be subject to preemption by that Act.

2. Subsection (a) provides that the beneficiary of an accepted payment order may recover consequential damages if the beneficiary's bank refuses to pay the order after demand by the beneficiary if the bank at that time had notice of the particular circumstances giving rise to the damages. Such damages are recoverable only to the extent the bank had "notice of the damages." The quoted phrase requires that the bank have notice of the general type or nature of the damages that will be suffered as a result of the refusal to pay and their general magnitude. There is no requirement that the bank have notice of the exact or even the approximate amount of the damages, but if the amount of damages is extraordinary the bank is entitled to notice of that fact. For example, in Evra Corp. v. Swiss Bank Corp., 673 F.2d 951 (7th Cir.1982), failure to complete a funds transfer of only $27,000 required to retain rights to a very favorable ship charter resulted in a claim for more than $2,000,000 of consequential damages. Since it is not reasonably foreseeable that a failure to make a relatively small payment will result in damages of this magnitude, notice is not sufficient if the beneficiary's bank has notice only that the $27,000 is necessary to retain rights on a ship charter. The bank is entitled to notice that an exceptional amount of damages will result as well. For example, there would be adequate notice if the bank had been made aware that damages of $1,000,000 or more might result.

3. Under the last clause of subsection (a) the beneficiary's bank is not liable for damages if its refusal to pay was "because of a reasonable doubt concerning the right of the beneficiary to payment." Normally there will not be any question about the right of the beneficiary to receive payment. Normally, the bank should be able to determine whether it has accepted the payment order and, if it has been accepted, the first sentence of subsection (a) states that the bank is obliged to pay. There may be uncommon cases, however, in which there is doubt whether acceptance occurred. For example, if acceptance is based on receipt of payment by the beneficiary's bank under Section 4A-403(a)(1) or (2), there may be cases in which the bank is not certain that payment has been received. There may also be cases in which there is doubt about whether the person demanding payment is the person identified in the payment order as beneficiary of the order.

The last clause of subsection (a) does not apply to cases in which a funds transfer is being used to pay an obligation and a dispute arises between the originator and the beneficiary concerning whether the obligation is in fact owed. For example, the originator may try to prevent payment to the beneficiary by the beneficiary's bank by alleging that the beneficiary is not entitled to payment because of fraud against the originator or a breach of contract relating to the obligation. The fraud or breach of contract claim of the originator may be grounds for recovery by the originator from the beneficiary after the beneficiary is paid, but it does not affect the obligation of the beneficiary's bank to pay the beneficiary. Unless the payment order has been cancelled pursuant to Section 4A-211(c), there is no excuse for refusing to pay the beneficiary and, in a proper case, the refusal may result in consequential damages. Except in the case of a book transfer, in which the beneficiary's bank is also the originator's bank, the originator of a funds transfer cannot cancel a payment order to the beneficiary's bank, with or without the consent of that bank, because the originator is not the sender of that order. Thus, the beneficiary's bank may safely ignore any instruction by the originator to withhold payment to the beneficiary.

4. Subsection (b) states the duty of the beneficiary's bank to notify the beneficiary of receipt of the order. If acceptance occurs under Section 4A-209(b)(1) the beneficiary is normally notified. Thus, subsection (b) applies primarily to cases in which acceptance occurs under Section 4A-209(b)(2) or (3). Notice under subsection (b) is not required if the person entitled to the notice agrees or a funds transfer system rule provides that notice is not required and the beneficiary is given notice of the rule. In ACH transactions the normal practice is not to give notice to the beneficiary unless notice is requested by the beneficiary. This practice can be continued by adoption of a funds transfer system rule. Subsection (a) is not subject to variation by agreement or by a funds transfer system rule.

§ 4A-405. Payment by Beneficiary's Bank to Beneficiary.

(a) If the beneficiary's bank credits an account of the beneficiary of a payment order, payment of the bank's obligation under Section 4A-404(a) occurs when and to the extent (i) the beneficiary is notified of the right to withdraw the credit, (ii) the bank lawfully applies the credit to a debt of the beneficiary, or (iii) funds with respect to the order are otherwise made available to the beneficiary by the bank.

(b) If the beneficiary's bank does not credit an account of the beneficiary of a payment order, the time when payment of the bank's obligation under Section 4A-404(a) occurs is governed by principles of law that determine when an obligation is satisfied.

(c) Except as stated in subsections (d) and (e), if the beneficiary's bank pays the beneficiary of a payment order under a condition to payment or agreement of the beneficiary giving the bank the right to recover payment from the beneficiary if the bank does not receive payment of the order, the condition to payment or agreement is not enforceable.

(d) A funds-transfer system rule may provide that payments made to beneficiaries of funds transfers made through the system are provisional until receipt of payment by the beneficiary's bank of the payment order it accepted. A beneficiary's bank that makes a payment that is provisional under the rule is entitled to refund from the beneficiary if (i) the rule requires that both the beneficiary and the originator be given notice of the provisional nature of the payment before the funds transfer is initiated, (ii) the beneficiary, the beneficiary's bank and the originator's bank agreed to be bound by the rule, and (iii) the beneficiary's bank did not receive payment of the payment order that it accepted. If the beneficiary is obliged to refund payment to the beneficiary's bank, acceptance of the payment order by the beneficiary's bank is nullified and no payment by the originator of the funds transfer to the beneficiary occurs under Section 4A-406.

(e) This subsection applies to a funds transfer that includes a payment order transmitted over a funds-transfer system that (i) nets obligations multilaterally among participants, and (ii) has in effect a loss-sharing agreement among participants for the purpose of providing funds necessary to complete settlement of the obligations of one or more participants that do not meet their settlement obligations. If the beneficiary's bank in the funds transfer accepts a payment order and the system fails to complete settlement pursuant to its rules with respect to any payment order in the funds transfer, (i) the acceptance by the beneficiary's bank is nullified and no person has any right or obligation based on the acceptance, (ii) the beneficiary's bank is entitled to recover payment from the beneficiary, (iii) no payment by the originator to the beneficiary occurs under Section 4A–406, and (iv) subject to Section 4A–402(e), each sender in the funds transfer is excused from its obligation to pay its payment order under Section 4A–402(c) because the funds transfer has not been completed.

Official Comment

1. This section defines when the beneficiary's bank pays the beneficiary and when the obligation of the beneficiary's bank under Section 4A–404 to pay the beneficiary is satisfied. In almost all cases the bank will credit an account of the beneficiary when it receives a payment order. In the typical case the beneficiary is paid when the beneficiary is given notice of the right to withdraw the credit. Subsection (a)(i). In some cases payment might be made to the beneficiary not by releasing funds to the beneficiary, but by applying the credit to a debt of the beneficiary. Subsection (a)(ii). In this case the beneficiary gets the benefit of the payment order because a debt of the beneficiary has been satisfied. The two principal cases in which payment will occur in this manner are setoff by the beneficiary's bank and payment of the proceeds of the payment order to a garnishing creditor of the beneficiary. These cases are discussed in Comment 2 to Section 4A–502.

2. If a beneficiary's bank releases funds to the beneficiary before it receives payment from the sender of the payment order, it assumes the risk that the sender may not pay the sender's order because of suspension of payments or other reason. Subsection (c). As stated in Comment 5 to Section 4A–209, the beneficiary's bank can protect itself against this risk by delaying acceptance. But if the bank accepts the order it is obliged to pay the beneficiary. If the beneficiary's bank has given the beneficiary notice of the right to withdraw a credit made to the beneficiary's account, the beneficiary has received payment from the bank. Once payment has been made to the beneficiary with respect to an obligation incurred by the bank under Section 4A–404(a), the payment cannot be recovered by the beneficiary's bank unless subsection (d) or (e) applies. Thus, a right to withdraw a credit cannot be revoked if the right to withdraw constituted payment of the bank's obligation. This principle applies even if funds were released as a "loan" (see Comment 5 to Section 4A–209), or were released subject to a condition that they would be repaid in the event the bank does not receive payment from the sender of the payment order, or the beneficiary agreed to return the payment if the bank did not receive payment from the sender.

3. Subsection (c) is subject to an exception stated in subsection (d) which is intended to apply to automated clearing house transfers. ACH transfers are made in batches. A beneficiary's bank will normally accept, at the same time and as part of a single batch, payment orders with respect to many different originator's banks. Comment 2 to Section 4A–206. The custom in ACH transactions is

to release funds to the beneficiary early on the payment date even though settlement to the beneficiary's bank does not occur until later in the day. The understanding is that payments to beneficiaries are provisional until the beneficiary's bank receives settlement. This practice is similar to what happens when a depositary bank releases funds with respect to a check forwarded for collection. If the check is dishonored the bank is entitled to recover the funds from the customer. ACH transfers are widely perceived as check substitutes. Section 4A–405(d) allows the funds transfer system to adopt a rule making payments to beneficiaries provisional. If such a rule is adopted, a beneficiary's bank that releases funds to the beneficiary will be able to recover the payment if it doesn't receive payment of the payment order that it accepted. There are two requirements with respect to the funds transfer system rule. The beneficiary, the beneficiary's bank and the originator's bank must all agree to be bound by the rule and the rule must require that both the beneficiary and the originator be given notice of the provisional nature of the payment before the funds transfer is initiated. There is no requirement that the notice be given with respect to a particular funds transfer. Once notice of the provisional nature of the payment has been given, the notice is effective for all subsequent payments to or from the person to whom the notice was given. Subsection (d) provides only that the funds transfer system rule must require notice to the beneficiary and the originator. The beneficiary's bank will know what the rule requires, but it has no way of knowing whether the originator's bank complied with the rule. Subsection (d) does not require proof that the originator received notice. If the originator's bank failed to give the required notice and the originator suffered as a result, the appropriate remedy is an action by the originator against the originator's bank based on that failure. But the beneficiary's bank will not be able to get the benefit of subsection (d) unless the beneficiary had notice of the provisional nature of the payment because subsection (d) requires an agreement by the beneficiary to be bound by the rule. Implicit in an agreement to be bound by a rule that makes a payment provisional is a requirement that notice be given of what the rule provides. The notice can be part of the agreement or separately given. For example, notice can be given by providing a copy of the system's operating rules.

With respect to ACH transfers made through a Federal Reserve Bank acting as an intermediary bank, the Federal Reserve Bank is obliged under Section 4A–402(b) to pay a beneficiary's bank that accepts the payment order. Unlike Fedwire transfers, under current ACH practice a Federal Reserve Bank that processes a payment order does not obligate itself to pay if the originator's bank fails to pay the Federal Reserve Bank. It is assumed that the Federal Reserve will use its right of preemption which is recognized in Section 4A–107 to disclaim the Section 4A–402(b) obligation in ACH transactions if it decides to retain the provisional payment rule.

4. Subsection (e) is another exception to subsection (c). It refers to funds transfer systems having loss-sharing rules described in the subsection. CHIPS has proposed a rule that fits the description. Under the CHIPS loss-sharing rule the CHIPS banks will have agreed to contribute funds to allow the system to settle for payment orders sent over the system during the day in the event that one or more banks are unable to meet their settlement obligations. Subsection (e) applies only if CHIPS fails to settle despite the loss-sharing rule. Since funds under the loss-sharing rule will be instantly available to CHIPS and will be in an amount sufficient to cover any failure that can be reasonably anticipated, it is extremely unlikely that CHIPS would ever fail to settle. Thus, subsection (e) addresses an event that should never occur. If that event were to occur, all payment orders made over the system would be cancelled under the CHIPS rule. Thus, no bank would receive settlement, whether or not a failed bank was involved in a particular funds transfer. Subsection (e) provides

that each funds transfer in which there is a payment order with respect to which there is a settlement failure is unwound. Acceptance by the beneficiary's bank in each funds transfer is nullified. The consequences of nullification are that the beneficiary has no right to receive or retain payment by the beneficiary's bank, no payment is made by the originator to the beneficiary and each sender in the funds transfer is, subject to Section 4A–402(e), not obliged to pay its payment order and is entitled to refund under Section 4A–402(d) if it has already paid.

§ 4A–406. Payment by Originator to Beneficiary; Discharge of Underlying Obligation.

(a) Subject to Sections 4A–211(e), 4A–405(d), and 4A–405(e), the originator of a funds transfer pays the beneficiary of the originator's payment order (i) at the time a payment order for the benefit of the beneficiary is accepted by the beneficiary's bank in the funds transfer and (ii) in an amount equal to the amount of the order accepted by the beneficiary's bank, but not more than the amount of the originator's order.

(b) If payment under subsection (a) is made to satisfy an obligation, the obligation is discharged to the same extent discharge would result from payment to the beneficiary of the same amount in money, unless (i) the payment under subsection (a) was made by a means prohibited by the contract of the beneficiary with respect to the obligation, (ii) the beneficiary, within a reasonable time after receiving notice of receipt of the order by the beneficiary's bank, notified the originator of the beneficiary's refusal of the payment, (iii) funds with respect to the order were not withdrawn by the beneficiary or applied to a debt of the beneficiary, and (iv) the beneficiary would suffer a loss that could reasonably have been avoided if payment had been made by a means complying with the contract. If payment by the originator does not result in discharge under this section, the originator is subrogated to the rights of the beneficiary to receive payment from the beneficiary's bank under Section 4A–404(a).

(c) For the purpose of determining whether discharge of an obligation occurs under subsection (b), if the beneficiary's bank accepts a payment order in an amount equal to the amount of the originator's payment order less charges of one or more receiving banks in the funds transfer, payment to the beneficiary is deemed to be in the amount of the originator's order unless upon demand by the beneficiary the originator does not pay the beneficiary the amount of the deducted charges.

(d) Rights of the originator or of the beneficiary of a funds transfer under this section may be varied only by agreement of the originator and the beneficiary.

Official Comment

1. Subsection (a) states the fundamental rule of Article 4A that payment by the originator to the beneficiary is accomplished by providing to the beneficiary the obligation of the beneficiary's bank to pay. Since this obligation arises when the beneficiary's bank accepts a payment order, the originator pays the beneficiary at the time of acceptance and in the amount of the payment order accepted.

2. In a large percentage of funds transfers, the transfer is made to pay an

obligation of the originator. Subsection (a) states that the beneficiary is paid by the originator when the beneficiary's bank accepts a payment order for the benefit of the beneficiary. When that happens the effect under subsection (b) is to substitute the obligation of the beneficiary's bank for the obligation of the originator. The effect is similar to that under Article 3 if a cashier's check payable to the beneficiary had been taken by the beneficiary. Normally, payment by funds transfer is sought by the beneficiary because it puts money into the hands of the beneficiary more quickly. As a practical matter the beneficiary and the originator will nearly always agree to the funds transfer in advance. Under subsection (b) acceptance by the beneficiary's bank will result in discharge of the obligation for which payment was made unless the beneficiary had made a contract with respect to the obligation which did not permit payment by the means used. Thus, if there is no contract of the beneficiary with respect to the means of payment of the obligation, acceptance by the beneficiary's bank of a payment order to the account of the beneficiary can result in discharge.

3. Suppose Beneficiary's contract stated that payment of an obligation owed by Originator was to be made by a cashier's check of Bank A. Instead, Originator paid by a funds transfer to Beneficiary's account in Bank B. Bank B accepted a payment order for the benefit of Beneficiary by immediately notifying Beneficiary that the funds were available for withdrawal. Before Beneficiary had a reasonable opportunity to withdraw the funds Bank B suspended payments. Under the unless clause of subsection (b) Beneficiary is not required to accept the payment as discharging the obligation owed by Originator to Beneficiary if Beneficiary's contract means that Beneficiary was not required to accept payment by wire transfer. Beneficiary could refuse the funds transfer as payment of the obligation and could resort to rights under the underlying contract to enforce the obligation. The rationale is that Originator cannot impose the risk of Bank B's insolvency on Beneficiary if Beneficiary had specified another means of payment that did not entail that risk. If Beneficiary is required to accept Originator's payment, Beneficiary would suffer a loss that would not have occurred if payment had been made by a cashier's check on Bank A, and Bank A has not suspended payments. In this case Originator will have to pay twice. It is obliged to pay the amount of its payment order to the bank that accepted it and has to pay the obligation it owes to Beneficiary which has not been discharged. Under the last sentence of subsection (b) Originator is subrogated to Beneficiary's right to receive payment from Bank B under Section 4A-404(a).

4. Suppose Beneficiary's contract called for payment by a Fedwire transfer to Bank B, but the payment order accepted by Bank B was not a Fedwire transfer. Before the funds were withdrawn by Beneficiary, Bank B suspended payments. The sender of the payment order to Bank B paid the amount of the order to Bank B. In this case the payment by Originator did not comply with Beneficiary's contract, but the noncompliance did not result in a loss to Beneficiary as required by subsection (b)(iv). A Fedwire transfer avoids the risk of insolvency of the sender of the payment order to Bank B, but it does not affect the risk that Bank B will suspend payments before withdrawal of the funds by Beneficiary. Thus, the unless clause of subsection (b) is not applicable and the obligation owed to Beneficiary is discharged.

5. Charges of receiving banks in a funds transfer normally are nominal in relationship to the amount being paid by the originator to the beneficiary. Wire transfers are normally agreed to in advance and the parties may agree concerning how these charges are to be divided between the parties. Subsection (c) states a rule that applies in the absence of agreement. In some funds transfers charges of banks that execute payment orders are collected by deducting the charges from the amount of the payment order issued by the bank, i.e. the bank

issues a payment order that is slightly less than the amount of the payment order that is being executed. The process is described in Comment 3 to Section 4A–302. The result in such a case is that the payment order accepted by the beneficiary's bank will be slightly less than the amount of the originator's order. Subsection (c) recognizes the principle that a beneficiary is entitled to full payment of a debt paid by wire transfer as a condition to discharge. On the other hand, subsection (c) prevents a beneficiary from denying the originator the benefit of the payment by asserting that discharge did not occur because deduction of bank charges resulted in less than full payment. The typical case is one in which the payment is made to exercise a valuable right such as an option which is unfavorable to the beneficiary. Subsection (c) allows discharge notwithstanding the deduction unless the originator fails to reimburse the beneficiary for the deducted charges after demand by the beneficiary.

PART 5

MISCELLANEOUS PROVISIONS

§ 4A–501. Variation by Agreement and Effect of Funds-Transfer System Rule.

(a) Except as otherwise provided in this Article, the rights and obligations of a party to a funds transfer may be varied by agreement of the affected party.

(b) "Funds-transfer system rule" means a rule of an association of banks (i) governing transmission of payment orders by means of a funds-transfer system of the association or rights and obligations with respect to those orders, or (ii) to the extent the rule governs rights and obligations between banks that are parties to a funds transfer in which a Federal Reserve Bank, acting as an intermediary bank, sends a payment order to the beneficiary's bank. Except as otherwise provided in this Article, a funds-transfer system rule governing rights and obligations between participating banks using the system may be effective even if the rule conflicts with this Article and indirectly affects another party to the funds transfer who does not consent to the rule. A funds-transfer system rule may also govern rights and obligations of parties other than participating banks using the system to the extent stated in Sections 4A–404(c), 4A–405(d), and 4A–507(c).

Official Comment

1. This section is designed to give some flexibility to Article 4A. Funds transfer system rules govern rights and obligations between banks that use the system. They may cover a wide variety of matters such as form and content of payment orders, security procedures, cancellation rights and procedures, indemnity rights, compensation rules for delays in completion of a funds transfer, time and method of settlement, credit restrictions with respect to senders of payment orders and risk allocation with respect to suspension of payments by a participating bank. Funds transfer system rules can be very effective in supplementing the provisions of Article 4A and in filling gaps that may be present in Article 4A. To the extent they do not conflict with Article 4A there is no problem with respect to their effectiveness. In that case they merely supplement Article 4A. Section 4A–501 goes further. It states that unless the contrary is stated, funds transfer system rules can override provisions of Article 4A. Thus, rights and obligations

of a sender bank and a receiving bank with respect to each other can be different from that stated in Article 4A to the extent a funds transfer system rule applies. Since funds transfer system rules are defined as those governing the relationship between participating banks, a rule can have a direct effect only on participating banks. But a rule that affects the conduct of a participating bank may indirectly affect the rights of nonparticipants such as the originator or beneficiary of a funds transfer, and such a rule can be effective even though it may affect nonparticipants without their consent. For example, a rule might prevent execution of a payment order or might allow cancellation of a payment order with the result that a funds transfer is not completed or is delayed. But a rule purporting to define rights and obligations of nonparticipants in the system would not be effective to alter Article 4A rights because the rule is not within the definition of funds transfer system rule. Rights and obligations arising under Article 4A may also be varied by agreement of the affected parties, except to the extent Article 4A otherwise provides. Rights and obligations arising under Article 4A can also be changed by Federal Reserve regulations and operating circulars of Federal Reserve Banks. Section 4A–107.

2. Subsection (b)(ii) refers to ACH transfers. Whether an ACH transfer is made through an automated clearing house of a Federal Reserve Bank or through an automated clearing house of another association of banks, the rights and obligations of the originator's bank and the beneficiary's bank are governed by uniform rules adopted by various associations of banks in various parts of the nation. With respect to transfers in which a Federal Reserve Bank acts as intermediary bank these rules may be incorporated, in whole or in part, in operating circulars of the Federal Reserve Bank. Even if not so incorporated these rules can still be binding on the association banks. If a transfer is made through a Federal Reserve Bank, the rules are effective under subsection (b)(ii). If the transfer is not made through a Federal Reserve Bank, the association rules are effective under subsection (b)(i).

§ 4A–502. Creditor Process Served on Receiving Bank; Setoff by Beneficiary's Bank.

(a) As used in this section, "creditor process" means levy, attachment, garnishment, notice of lien, sequestration, or similar process issued by or on behalf of a creditor or other claimant with respect to an account.

(b) This subsection applies to creditor process with respect to an authorized account of the sender of a payment order if the creditor process is served on the receiving bank. For the purpose of determining rights with respect to the creditor process, if the receiving bank accepts the payment order the balance in the authorized account is deemed to be reduced by the amount of the payment order to the extent the bank did not otherwise receive payment of the order, unless the creditor process is served at a time and in a manner affording the bank a reasonable opportunity to act on it before the bank accepts the payment order.

(c) If a beneficiary's bank has received a payment order for payment to the beneficiary's account in the bank, the following rules apply:

(1) The bank may credit the beneficiary's account. The amount credited may be set off against an obligation owed by the beneficiary to the bank or may be applied to satisfy creditor process served on the bank with respect to the account.

(2) The bank may credit the beneficiary's account and allow withdrawal of the amount credited unless creditor process with respect to the account is served at a time and in a manner affording the bank a reasonable opportunity to act to prevent withdrawal.

(3) If creditor process with respect to the beneficiary's account has been served and the bank has had a reasonable opportunity to act on it, the bank may not reject the payment order except for a reason unrelated to the service of process.

(d) Creditor process with respect to a payment by the originator to the beneficiary pursuant to a funds transfer may be served only on the beneficiary's bank with respect to the debt owed by that bank to the beneficiary. Any other bank served with the creditor process is not obliged to act with respect to the process.

Official Comment

1. When a receiving bank accepts a payment order, the bank normally receives payment from the sender by debiting an authorized account of the sender. In accepting the sender's order the bank may be relying on a credit balance in the account. If creditor process is served on the bank with respect to the account before the bank accepts the order but the bank employee responsible for the acceptance was not aware of the creditor process at the time the acceptance occurred, it is unjust to the bank to allow the creditor process to take the credit balance on which the bank may have relied. Subsection (b) allows the bank to obtain payment from the sender's account in this case. Under that provision, the balance in the sender's account to which the creditor process applies is deemed to be reduced by the amount of the payment order unless there was sufficient time for notice of the service of creditor process to be received by personnel of the bank responsible for the acceptance.

2. Subsection (c) deals with payment orders issued to the beneficiary's bank. The bank may credit the beneficiary's account when the order is received, but under Section 4A–404(a) the bank incurs no obligation to pay the beneficiary until the order is accepted pursuant to Section 4A–209(b). Thus, before acceptance, the credit to the beneficiary's account is provisional. But under Section 4A–209(b) acceptance occurs if the beneficiary's bank pays the beneficiary pursuant to Section 4A–405(a). Under that provision, payment occurs if the credit to the beneficiary's account is applied to a debt of the beneficiary. Subsection (c)(1) allows the bank to credit the beneficiary's account with respect to a payment order and to accept the order by setting off the credit against an obligation owed to the bank or applying the credit to creditor process with respect to the account.

Suppose a beneficiary's bank receives a payment order for the benefit of a customer. Before the bank accepts the order, the bank learns that creditor process has been served on the bank with respect to the customer's account. Normally there is no reason for a beneficiary's bank to reject a payment order, but if the beneficiary's account is garnished, the bank may be faced with a difficult choice. If it rejects the order, the garnishing creditor's potential recovery of funds of the beneficiary is frustrated. It may be faced with a claim by the creditor that the rejection was a wrong to the creditor. If the bank accepts the order, the effect is to allow the creditor to seize funds of its customer, the beneficiary. Subsection (c)(3) gives the bank no choice in this case. It provides that it may not favor its customer over the creditor by rejecting the order. The beneficiary's bank may rightfully reject only if there is an independent basis for rejection.

3. Subsection (c)(2) is similar to subsection (b). Normally the beneficiary's bank will release funds to the beneficiary shortly after acceptance or it will accept by releasing funds. Since the bank is bound by a garnishment order served before funds are released to the beneficiary, the bank might suffer a loss if funds were released without knowledge that a garnishment order had been served. Subsection (c)(2) protects the bank if it did not have adequate notice of the garnishment when the funds were released.

4. A creditor may want to reach funds involved in a funds transfer. The creditor may try to do so by serving process on the originator's bank, an intermediary bank or the beneficiary's bank. The purpose of subsection (d) is to guide the creditor and the court as to the proper method of reaching the funds involved in a funds transfer. A creditor of the originator can levy on the account of the originator in the originator's bank before the funds transfer is initiated, but that levy is subject to the limitations stated in subsection (b). The creditor of the originator cannot reach any other funds because no property of the originator is being transferred. A creditor of the beneficiary cannot levy on property of the originator and until the funds transfer is completed by acceptance by the beneficiary's bank of a payment order for the benefit of the beneficiary, the beneficiary has no property interest in the funds transfer which the beneficiary's creditor can reach. A creditor of the beneficiary that wants to reach the funds to be received by the beneficiary must serve creditor process on the beneficiary's bank to reach the obligation of the beneficiary's bank to pay the beneficiary which arises upon acceptance by the beneficiary's bank under Section 4A–404(a).

5. "Creditor process" is defined in subsection (a) to cover a variety of devices by which a creditor of the holder of a bank account or a claimant to a bank account can seize the account. Procedure and nomenclature varies widely from state to state. The term used in Section 4A–502 is a generic term.

§ 4A–503. Injunction or Restraining Order With Respect to Funds Transfer.

For proper cause and in compliance with applicable law, a court may restrain (i) a person from issuing a payment order to initiate a funds transfer, (ii) an originator's bank from executing the payment order of the originator, or (iii) the beneficiary's bank from releasing funds to the beneficiary or the beneficiary from withdrawing the funds. A court may not otherwise restrain a person from issuing a payment order, paying or receiving payment of a payment order, or otherwise acting with respect to a funds transfer.

Official Comment

This section is related to Section 4A–502(d) and to Comment 4 to Section 4A–502. It is designed to prevent interruption of a funds transfer after it has been set in motion. The initiation of a funds transfer can be prevented by enjoining the originator or the originator's bank from issuing a payment order. After the funds transfer is completed by acceptance of a payment order by the beneficiary's bank, that bank can be enjoined from releasing funds to the beneficiary or the beneficiary can be enjoined from withdrawing the funds. No other injunction is permitted. In particular, intermediary banks are protected, and injunctions against the originator and the originator's bank are limited to issuance of a payment order. Except for the beneficiary's bank, nobody can be enjoined from paying a payment order, and no receiving bank can be enjoined from receiving payment from the sender of the order that it accepted.

§ 4A-504. Order in Which Items and Payment Orders May Be Charged to Account; Order of Withdrawals From Account.

(a) If a receiving bank has received more than one payment order of the sender or one or more payment orders and other items that are payable from the sender's account, the bank may charge the sender's account with respect to the various orders and items in any sequence.

(b) In determining whether a credit to an account has been withdrawn by the holder of the account or applied to a debt of the holder of the account, credits first made to the account are first withdrawn or applied.

Official Comment

1. Subsection (a) concerns priority among various obligations that are to be paid from the same account. A customer may have written checks on its account with the receiving bank and may have issued one or more payment orders payable from the same account. If the account balance is not sufficient to cover all of the checks and payment orders, some checks may be dishonored and some payment orders may not be accepted. Although there is no concept of wrongful dishonor of a payment order in Article 4A in the absence of an agreement to honor by the receiving bank, some rights and obligations may depend on the amount in the customer's account. Section 4A-209(b)(3) and Section 4A-210(b). Whether dishonor of a check is wrongful also may depend upon the balance in the customer's account. Under subsection (a), the bank is not required to consider the competing items and payment orders in any particular order. Rather it may charge the customer's account for the various items and orders in any order. Suppose there is $12,000 in the customer's account. If a check for $5,000 is presented for payment and the bank receives a $10,000 payment order from the customer, the bank could dishonor the check and accept the payment order. Dishonor of the check is not wrongful because the account balance was less than the amount of the check after the bank charged the account $10,000 on account of the payment order. Or, the bank could pay the check and not execute the payment order because the amount of the order is not covered by the balance in the account.

2. Subsection (b) follows Section 4-208(b) in using the first-in-first-out rule for determining the order in which credits to an account are withdrawn.

§ 4A-505. Preclusion of Objection to Debit of Customer's Account.

If a receiving bank has received payment from its customer with respect to a payment order issued in the name of the customer as sender and accepted by the bank, and the customer received notification reasonably identifying the order, the customer is precluded from asserting that the bank is not entitled to retain the payment unless the customer notifies the bank of the customer's objection to the payment within one year after the notification was received by the customer.

Official Comment

This section is in the nature of a statute of repose for objecting to debits made to the customer's account. A receiving bank that executes payment orders of a customer may have received payment from the customer by debiting the customer's account with respect to a payment order that the customer was not required to pay. For example, the payment order may not have been authorized or verified pursuant to Section 4A-202 or the funds transfer may not have been completed. In either case the receiving bank is obliged to refund the payment to the customer and this obligation to refund payment cannot be varied by agreement. Section 4A-204 and Section 4A-402. Refund may also be required if the receiving bank is not entitled to payment from the customer because the bank erroneously executed a payment order. Section 4A-303. A similar analysis applies to that case. Section 4A-402(d) and (f) require refund and the obligation to refund may not be varied by agreement. Under 4A-505, however, the obligation to refund may not be asserted by the customer if the customer has not objected to the debiting of the account within one year after the customer received notification of the debit.

§ 4A-506. Rate of Interest.

(a) If, under this Article, a receiving bank is obliged to pay interest with respect to a payment order issued to the bank, the amount payable may be determined (i) by agreement of the sender and receiving bank, or (ii) by a funds-transfer system rule if the payment order is transmitted through a funds-transfer system.

(b) If the amount of interest is not determined by an agreement or rule as stated in subsection (a), the amount is calculated by multiplying the applicable Federal Funds rate by the amount on which interest is payable, and then multiplying the product by the number of days for which interest is payable. The applicable Federal Funds rate is the average of the Federal Funds rates published by the Federal Reserve Bank of New York for each of the days for which interest is payable divided by 360. The Federal Funds rate for any day on which a published rate is not available is the same as the published rate for the next preceding day for which there is a published rate. If a receiving bank that accepted a payment order is required to refund payment to the sender of the order because the funds transfer was not completed, but the failure to complete was not due to any fault by the bank, the interest payable is reduced by a percentage equal to the reserve requirement on deposits of the receiving bank.

Official Comment

1. A receiving bank is required to pay interest on the amount of a payment order received by the bank in a number of situations. Sometimes the interest is payable to the sender and in other cases it is payable to either the originator or the beneficiary of the funds transfer. The relevant provisions are Section 4A-204(a), Section 4A-209(b)(3), Section 4A-210(b), Section 4A-305(a), Section 4A-402(d) and Section 4A-404(b). The rate of interest may be governed by a funds transfer system rule or by agreement as stated in subsection (a). If subsection (a) doesn't apply, the rate is determined under subsection (b). Subsection (b) is illustrated by the following example. A bank is obliged to pay interest on $1,000,-000 for three days, July 3, July 4, and July 5. The published Fed Funds rate is .082 for July 3 and .081 for July 5. There is no published rate for July 4 because that day is not a banking day. The rate for July 3 applies to July 4. The applicable Fed Funds rate is .08167 (the average of .082, .082, and .081) divided by 360 which equals .0002268. The amount of

interest payable is $1,000,000 × .0002268 × 3 = $680.40.

2. In some cases, interest is payable in spite of the fact that there is no fault by the receiving bank. The last sentence of subsection (b) applies to those cases. For example, a funds transfer might not be completed because the beneficiary's bank rejected the payment order issued to it by the originator's bank or an intermediary bank. Section 4A–402(c) provides that the originator is not obliged to pay its payment order and Section 4A–402(d) provides that the originator's bank must refund any payment received plus interest. The requirement to pay interest in this case is not based on fault by the originator's bank. Rather, it is based on restitution. Since the originator's bank had the use of the originator's money, it is required to pay the originator for the value of that use. The value of that use is not determined by multiplying the interest rate by the refundable amount because the originator's bank is required to deposit with the Federal Reserve a percentage of the bank's deposits as a reserve requirement. Since that deposit does not bear interest, the bank had use of the refundable amount reduced by a percentage equal to the reserve requirement. If the reserve requirement is 12%, the amount of interest payable by the bank under the formula stated in subsection (b) is reduced by 12%.

§ 4A–507. Choice of Law.

(a) The following rules apply unless the affected parties otherwise agree or subsection (c) applies:

(1) The rights and obligations between the sender of a payment order and the receiving bank are governed by the law of the jurisdiction in which the receiving bank is located.

(2) The rights and obligations between the beneficiary's bank and the beneficiary are governed by the law of the jurisdiction in which the beneficiary's bank is located.

(3) The issue of when payment is made pursuant to a funds transfer by the originator to the beneficiary is governed by the law of the jurisdiction in which the beneficiary's bank is located.

(b) If the parties described in each paragraph of subsection (a) have made an agreement selecting the law of a particular jurisdiction to govern rights and obligations between each other, the law of that jurisdiction governs those rights and obligations, whether or not the payment order or the funds transfer bears a reasonable relation to that jurisdiction.

(c) A funds-transfer system rule may select the law of a particular jurisdiction to govern (i) rights and obligations between participating banks with respect to payment orders transmitted or processed through the system, or (ii) the rights and obligations of some or all parties to a funds transfer any part of which is carried out by means of the system. A choice of law made pursuant to clause (i) is binding on participating banks. A choice of law made pursuant to clause (ii) is binding on the originator, other sender, or a receiving bank having notice that the funds-transfer system might be used in the funds transfer and of the choice of law by the system when the originator, other sender, or receiving bank issued or accepted a payment order. The beneficiary of a funds transfer is bound by the choice of law if, when the funds transfer is initiated, the beneficiary has notice that the funds-transfer system might be used in the funds transfer and of the choice of law by the system.

The law of a jurisdiction selected pursuant to this subsection may govern, whether or not that law bears a reasonable relation to the matter in issue.

(d) In the event of inconsistency between an agreement under subsection (b) and a choice-of-law rule under subsection (c), the agreement under subsection (b) prevails.

(e) If a funds transfer is made by use of more than one funds-transfer system and there is inconsistency between choice-of-law rules of the systems, the matter in issue is governed by the law of the selected jurisdiction that has the most significant relationship to the matter in issue.

Official Comment

1. Funds transfers are typically interstate or international in character. If part of a funds transfer is governed by Article 4A and another part is governed by other law, the rights and obligations of parties to the funds transfer may be unclear because there is no clear consensus in various jurisdictions concerning the juridical nature of the transaction. Unless all of a funds transfer is governed by a single law it may be very difficult to predict the result if something goes wrong in the transfer. Section 4A-507 deals with this problem. Subsection (b) allows parties to a funds transfer to make a choice-of-law agreement. Subsection (c) allows a funds transfer system to select the law of a particular jurisdiction to govern funds transfers carried out by means of the system. Subsection (a) states residual rules if no choice of law has occurred under subsection (b) or subsection (c).

2. Subsection (a) deals with three sets of relationships. Rights and obligations between the sender of a payment order and the receiving bank are governed by the law of the jurisdiction in which the receiving bank is located. If the receiving bank is the beneficiary's bank the rights and obligations of the beneficiary are also governed by the law of the jurisdiction in which the receiving bank is located. Suppose Originator, located in Canada, sends a payment order to Originator's Bank located in a state in which Article 4A has been enacted. The order is for payment to an account of Beneficiary in a bank in England. Under subsection (a)(1), the rights and obligations of Originator and Originator's Bank toward each other are governed by Article 4A if an action is brought in a court in the Article 4A state. If an action is brought in a Canadian court, the conflict of laws issue will be determined by Canadian law which might or might not apply the law of the state in which Originator's Bank is located. If that law is applied, the execution of Originator's order will be governed by Article 4A, but with respect to the payment order of Originator's Bank to the English bank, Article 4A may or may not be applied with respect to the rights and obligations between the two banks. The result may depend upon whether action is brought in a court in the state in which Originator's Bank is located or in an English court. Article 4A is binding only on a court in a state that enacts it. It can have extraterritorial effect only to the extent courts of another jurisdiction are willing to apply it. Subsection (c) also bears on the issues discussed in this Comment.

Under Section 4A-406 payment by the originator to the beneficiary of the funds transfer occurs when the beneficiary's bank accepts a payment order for the benefit of the beneficiary. A jurisdiction in which Article 4A is not in effect may follow a different rule or it may not have a clear rule. Under Section 4A-507(a)(3) the issue is governed by the law of the jurisdiction in which the beneficiary's bank is located. Since the payment to the beneficiary is made through the beneficiary's bank it is reasonable that the issue of when payment occurs be governed by the law of the jurisdiction in which the bank is located. Since it is difficult in many cases to determine where a beneficiary is located, the location of the beneficiary's bank provides a more certain rule.

3. Subsection (b) deals with choice-of-law agreements and it gives maximum freedom of choice. Since the law of funds transfers is not highly developed in the case law there may be a strong incentive to choose the law of a jurisdiction in which Article 4A is in effect because it provides a greater degree of certainty with respect to the rights of various parties. With respect to commercial transactions, it is often said that "[u]niformity and predictability based upon commercial convenience are the prime considerations in making the choice of governing law ...." R. Leflar, American Conflicts Law, § 185 (1977). Subsection (b) is derived in part from recently enacted choice-of-law rules in the States of New York and California. N.Y.Gen. Obligations Law 5–1401 (McKinney's 1989 Supp.) and California Civil Code § 1646.5. This broad endorsement of freedom of contract is an enhancement of the approach taken by Restatement (Second) of Conflict of Laws § 187(b) (1971). The Restatement recognizes the basic right of freedom of contract, but the freedom granted the parties may be more limited than the freedom granted here. Under the formulation of the Restatement, if there is no substantial relationship to the jurisdiction whose law is selected and there is no "other" reasonable basis for the parties' choice, then the selection of the parties need not be honored by a court. Further, if the choice is violative of a fundamental policy of a state which has a materially greater interest than the chosen state, the selection could be disregarded by a court. Those limitations are not found in subsection (b).

4. Subsection (c) may be the most important provision in regard to creating uniformity of law in funds transfers. Most rights stated in Article 4A regard parties who are in privity of contract such as originator and beneficiary, sender and receiving bank, and beneficiary's bank and beneficiary. Since they are in privity they can make a choice of law by agreement. But that is not always the case. For example, an intermediary bank that improperly executes a payment order is not in privity with either the originator or the beneficiary. The ability of a funds transfer system to make a choice of law by rule is a convenient way of dispensing with individual agreements and to cover cases in which agreements are not feasible. It is probable that funds transfer systems will adopt a governing law to increase the certainty of commercial transactions that are effected over such systems. A system rule might adopt the law of an Article 4A state to govern transfers on the system in order to provide a consistent, unitary, law governing all transfers made on the system. To the extent such system rules develop, individual choice-of-law agreements become unnecessary.

Subsection (c) has broad application. A system choice of law applies not only to rights and obligations between banks that use the system, but may also apply to other parties to the funds transfer so long as some part of the transfer was carried out over the system. The originator and any other sender or receiving bank in the funds transfer is bound if at the time it issues or accepts a payment order it had notice that the funds transfer involved use of the system and that the system chose the law of a particular jurisdiction. Under Section 4A–107, the Federal Reserve by regulation could make a similar choice of law to govern funds transfers carried out by use of Federal Reserve Banks. Subsection (d) is a limitation on subsection (c). If parties have made a choice-of-law agreement that conflicts with a choice of law made under subsection (c), the agreement prevails.

5. Subsection (e) addresses the case in which a funds transfer involves more than one funds transfer system and the systems adopt conflicting choice-of-law rules. The rule that has the most significant relationship to the matter at issue prevails. For example, each system should be able to make a choice of law governing payment orders transmitted

over that system with regard to a choice
of law made by another system.

TECHNICAL AMENDMENT TO ARTICLE 1

A state enacting Article 4A should amend Section 1–105(2) by adding the following:

"Governing law in the Article on Funds Transfers. Section 4A–507."

[REVISED] ARTICLE 5

LETTERS OF CREDIT

[For the Text and Official Comments of Article 5 as they existed prior to revision in 1995, see Appendix XV, infra.]

[For the conforming amendments to other articles of the Code, see Appendix XIV, infra.]

John P. Burton, Santa Fe, New Mexico, *National Conference Representative and The American Law Institute Representative*

Bruce A. Coggeshall, Portland, Maine

William C. Hillman, Boston, Massachusetts

Edwin E. Huddleson, III, Washington, District of Columbia, *The American Law Institute Representative*

Jeremiah Marsh, Chicago, Illinois

Richard L. Morningstar, Washington, District of Columbia

Edwin E. Smith, Boston, Massachusetts

Sandra S. Stern, Scarsdale, New York

Richard C. Hite, Wichita, Kansas, *President (Member Ex Officio)*

Neal Ossen, Hartford, Connecticut, *Chairman, Division C (Member Ex Officio)*

REVIEW COMMITTEE

CHAIRMAN

William M. Burke, Los Angeles, California

MEMBERS

Boris Auerbach, Wyoming, Ohio

Robert J. Desiderio, Albuquerque, New Mexico

PREFATORY NOTE

Reason for Revision

When the original Article 5 was drafted 40 years ago, it was written for paper transactions and before many innovations in letters of credit. Now electronic and other media are used extensively. Since the 50's, standby letters of credit have developed and now nearly $500 billion standby letters of credit are issued annually worldwide, of which $250 billion are issued in the United States. The use of deferred payment letters of credit has also greatly increased. The customs and practices for letters of credit have evolved and are reflected in the Uniform Customs and Practice (UCP), usually incorporated into letters of credit, particularly international letters of credit, which have seen four revisions since the 1950's; the current version became effective in 1994 (UCP 500). Lastly, in a number of areas, court decisions have resulted in conflicting rules.

Prior to the appointment of a drafting committee, the ABA UCC Committee appointed a Task Force composed of knowledgeable practitioners and academics. The ABA Task Force studied the case law, evolving technologies and the changes in customs and practices. The Task Force identified a large number of issues which they discussed at some length, and made recommendations for revisions to Article 5. The Task Force stated in a foreword:

> "As a result of these increases and changes in usage, practice, players, and pressure, it comes as no surprise that there has been a sizable increase in litigation. Indeed, the approximately 62 cases report-

ed in the United States in 1987 constituted double the cumulative reported cases up to 1965....

Moreover, almost forty years of hard use have revealed weaknesses, gaps and errors in the original statute which compromise its relevance. U.C.C. Article 5 was one of the few areas of the Uniform Commercial Code which did not benefit from prior codification and it should come as no surprise that it may require some revision....

Measured in terms of these areas which are vital to any system of commercial law, the current combination of statute and case law is found wanting in major respects both as to predictability and certainty. What is at issue here are not matters of sophistry but important issues of substance which have not been resolved by the current case law/code method and which admit of little likelihood of such resolution." (45 Bus. Lawyer 1521, at 1532, 1535–6)[1]

The Drafting Committee began its deliberations with the Task Force Report in hand. The final work of the Drafting Committee varies from many of the suggestions of the Task Force.

Need for Uniformity

Letters of Credit are a major instrument in international trade, as well as domestic transactions. To facilitate its usefulness and competitiveness, it is essential that U.S. law be in harmony with international rules and practices, as well as flexible enough to accommodate changes in technology and practices that have, and are, evolving. Not only should the rules be consistent within the United States, but they need to be substantively and procedurally consistent with international practices.

Thus, the goals of the drafting effort were:

- conforming the Article 5 rules to current customs and practices;
- accommodating new forms of Letters of Credit, changes in customs and practices, and evolving technology, particularly the use of electronic media;
- maintaining Letters of Credit as an inexpensive and efficient instrument facilitating trade; and
- resolving conflicts among reported decisions.

Process of Achieving Uniformity

The essence of uniform law revision is to obtain a sufficient consensus and balance among the interests of the various participants so that universal and uniform enactment by the various States may be achieved.

1. The Task Force members were: Professor James E. Byrne (George Mason University School of Law) Chair; Professor Boris Kozolchyk (University of Arizona College of Law); Michael Evan Avidon (Moses & Singer); James G. Barnes (Baker & McKenzie); Arthur G. Lloyd (Citibank N.A.); Janis S. Penton (Rosen, Wachtell & Gilbert); Richard F. Purcell (Connell, Rice & Sugar Co.); Alan L. Bloodgood (Morgan Guaranty Trust Co.); Charles del Busto (Manufacturers Hanover Trust Co.); Vincent Maulella (Manufacturers Hanover Trust Co.).

In part this is accomplished by extensive consultation on and broad circulation of the drafts from 1990, when the project began, until approval of the final draft by the American law Institute (ALI) and the National Conference of Commissioners on Uniform State Laws (NCCUSL).

Hundreds of groups were invited to participate in the drafting process. Twenty Advisors were appointed, representing a cross-section of interested parties. In addition 20 Observers regularly attended drafting meetings and over 100 were on the mailing list to receive all drafts of the revision.

The Drafting Committee meetings were open and all those who attended were afforded full opportunity to express their views and participate in the dialogue. The Advisors and Observers were a balanced group with ten representatives of users (Beneficiaries and Applicants); five representatives of governmental agencies; five representatives of the U.S. Council on International Banking (USCIB); seven from major banks in letter of credit transactions; eight from regional banks; and seven law professors who teach and write on Letters of Credit.

Nine Drafting Committee meetings were held that began Friday morning and ended Sunday noon. In addition, the draft was twice debated in full by NCCUSL, once by the ALI Council, once considered by the ALI Consultative Group and once by an ad hoc Committee of the Council; and reviewed and discussed by the ABA Subcommittee on Letters of Credit semi-annually and by several state and city bar association committees.

The drafts were regularly reviewed and discussed in *The Business Lawyer*, *Letter of Credit Update*, and in other publications.

The consensus, balance and quality achieved in this lengthy deliberative process is a product of not only its Reporter and the Drafting Committee, but also the faithful and energetic participation of the following Advisors and active participants:

Advisors

Professor Gerald T. McLaughlin, Loyola Law School, ABA, Section of Business Law

James G. Barnes, Baker & McKenzie/U.S. Council on International Banking, Inc.

Harold S. Burman, U.S. Department of State

James E. Byrne, George Mason University, Institute of International Banking Law and Practice Inc.

Professor John Dolan, original ABA Advisor

Henry N. Dyhouse, U.S. Central Credit Union

David P. Goch, Treasury Management Association

Thomas J. Greco, American Bankers Association

Henry Harfield, Shearman & Sterling

Oliver I. Ireland, Board of Governors of Federal Reserve Board

James W. Kopp, Shell Oil Company/Treasury Management Association

Professor Boris Kozolchyk, University of Arizona/National Law Center for Inter–American Free Trade, U.S. Council on International Banking, Inc.

Vincent M. Maulella, Manufacturers Hanover Trust Co./U.S.Council on International Banking, Inc.

Robert M. Rosenblith, National Westminster Bank

Bradley K. Sabel, Federal Reserve Bank of New York

Joseph H. Sommer, Federal Reserve Bank of New York

Jamileh Soufan, American General Corporation/Treasury Management Association

Dan Taylor, U.S. Council on International Banking, Inc.

William H. Thornton, Security Pacific National Bank/California Bankers Association

Paul S. Turner, Occidental Petroleum Corporation/Treasury Management Association

Stanley M. Walker, Exxon Company U.S.A./Treasury Management Association

Active Participants

Michael E. Avidon, Moses & Singer/N.Y. State Bar Association, Banking Law Committee, Subcommittee on Letters of Credit

Walter B. Baker, ABN AMRO Bank, N.V.

Thomas C. Baxter, Jr., Federal Reserve Bank of New York

Professor Amelia H. Boss, Pennsylvania Bar Association, Section of Corporation, Banking & Business Law, Commercial Law Committee

Maria A. Chanco, Bank of America, N.T. & S.A.

Frank P. Curran, Treasury Management Association

Carol R. Dennis, Office of Federal Procurement Policy, OFMB

Albert J. Givray, Oklahoma Bar Association, Section of Banking & Commercial Law

Sidney S. Goldstein, New York State Bar Association

Professor Egon Guttman, The American University

George A. Hisert, State Bar of California, Section of Business Law, Committee on UCC, Subcommittee on Letters of Credit

Larry J. Jones, Mobil Oil Credit Corporation

Carter H. Klein, Jenner & Block

Arthur G. Lloyd, ABA, Section of Business Law, Committee on UCC, Subcommittee on Letters of Credit, Working Group on UCC Article 5 Revision

Rebecca S. McCulloch, ABN AMRO Bank, N.V.

Dennis L. Noah, First National Bank of Maryland/U.S. Council on International Banking, Inc.

James Purvis, The Bank of California

James E. Roselle, First National Bank of Chicago

R. David Whitaker, ABA, Section of Business Law, Committee on UCC, Subcommittee on ECP, Working Group on EDC

Brooke Wunnicke, ABA, Section of Business Law, Committee on UCC, Subcommittee on Letters of Credit

Balance of Benefits

Uniform laws can be enacted only if there is a consensus that the benefits achieved advance the public interest in a manner that can be embraced by all users of the law. It appears that as drafted, Revised Article 5 will enjoy substantial support by the participating interests in letter of credit transactions.

Benefits of Revised Article 5 in General

Independence Principle. Revised Article 5 clearly and forcefully states the independence of the letter of credit obligations from the underlying transactions that was unexpressed in, but was a fundamental predicate for, the original Article 5 (Sections 5–103(d) and 5–108(f)). Certainty of payment, independent of other claims, setoffs or other causes of action, is a core element of the commercial utility of letters of credit.

Clarifications. The revision authorizes the use of electronic technology (Sections 5-102(a)(14) and 5-104); expressly permits deferred payment letters of credit (Section 5-102(a)(8)) and two party letters of credit (Section 5-102(a)(10)); provides rules for unstated expiry dates (Section 5-106(c)), perpetual letters of credit (Section 5-106(d)), and non-documentary conditions (Section 5-108(g)); clarifies and establishes rules for successors by operation of law (Sections 5-102(a)(15) and 5-113); conforms to existing practice for assignment of proceeds (Section 5-114); and clarifies the rules where decisions have been in conflict (Section 5-106, Comment 1; Section 5-108, Comments 1, 3, 4, 7, and 9; Section 5-109, Comments 1 and 3; Section 5-113, Comment 1; and Section 5-117, Comment 1).

Harmonizes with International Practice

The UCP is used in most international letters of credit and in many domestic letters of credit. These international practices are well known and employed by the major issuers and users of letters of credit. Revisions have been made to Article 5 to coordinate the Article 5 rules with current international practice (e.g., deferred payment obligations, reasonable time to examine documents, preclusion, non-documentary conditions, return of documents, and irrevocable unless stated to be revocable).

Benefits of Revised Article 5 to Issuers

Consequential Damages. Section 5-111 precludes consequential and punitive damages. It, however, provides strong incentives for Issuers to honor, including provisions for attorneys fees and expenses of litigation, interest, and specific performance. If consequential and punitive damages were allowed, the cost of letters of credit could rise substantially.

Statute of Limitation. Section 5–115 establishes a one year statute of limitation from the expiration date or from accrual of the cause of action, whichever occurs later. Because it is usually obvious to all when there has been a breach, a short limitation period is fair to potential plaintiffs.

Choice of Law. Section 5–116 permits the issuer (or nominated party or adviser) to choose the law of the jurisdiction that will govern even if that law bears no relation to the transaction. Absent agreement, Section 5–116 states choice of law rules.

Assignment of Proceeds. Section 5–114 conforms more fully to existing practice and provides an orderly procedure for recording and accommodating assignments by consent of the issuer (or nominated party).

Subrogation. Section 5–117 clarifies the subrogation rights of an Issuer who has honored a letter of credit. These rights of subrogation also extend to an applicant who reimburses and a nominated party who pays or gives value.

Recognition of UCP. Section 5–116(c) expressly recognizes that if the UCP is incorporated by reference into the letter of credit, the agreement varies the provisions of Article 5 with which it may conflict except for the non-variable provisions of Article 5.

Benefits of Revised Article 5 to Applicants

Warranties. Section 5–110 specifies the warranties made by a beneficiary. It gives the applicant on a letter of credit which has been honored a direct cause of action if a drawing is fraudulent or forged or if a drawing violates any agreement augmented by a letter of credit.

Strict Compliance. Absent agreement to the contrary, the issuer must dishonor a presentation that does not strictly comply under standard practice with the terms and conditions of the letter of credit (Section 5–108).

Subrogation. New Section 5–117 clarifies the parties' rights of subrogation if the letter of credit is honored.

Limitations on General Disclaimers and Waivers. Section 5–103(c) limits the effect of general disclaimers and waivers in a letter of credit, or reimbursement or other agreement.

Benefits of Revised Article 5 to Beneficiaries

Irrevocable. A letter of credit is irrevocable unless the letter of credit expressly provides it is revocable (Section 5–106(a)).

Preclusion. Section 5–108(c) now provides that the Issuer is precluded from asserting any discrepancy not stated in its notice timely given, except for fraud, forgery or expiration.

Timely Examination. Section 5–108(b) requires examination and notice of any discrepancies within a reasonable time not to exceed the 7th business day after presentation of the documents.

Transfers by Operation of Law. New Section 5–113 allows a successor to a beneficiary by operation of law to make presentation and receive payment or acceptance.

Damages. The damages provided are expanded and clarified. They include attorneys fees and expenses of litigation and payment of the full amount of the wrongfully dishonored or repudiated demand, with interest, without an obligation of the beneficiary to mitigate damages (Section 5–111).

Revisions for Article 9 and Transition Provisions

The draft includes suggested revisions to conform Article 9 to the Article 5 changes. Article 9 itself is under revision and the interface with Revised Article 5 will be more fully examined by the Article 9 drafting committee, as well, in light of changes to Article 9. The Article 9 revisions will probably not be completed until 1998–9. Revised Article 8 (1994) also makes changes to Article 9 so care should be taken to coordinate the changes of both Revised Articles 5 and 8 within each State.

The draft also includes transition provisions and some cross reference changes in other Articles of the UCC.

Lastly, there follows a table showing the changes from the original Article 5 made by the revisions to Article 5.

Table of Disposition of Sections in Former Article 5

The reference to a section in revised Article 5 is to the section that refers to the issue addressed by the section in former Article 5. If there is no comparable section in Revised Article 5 to a section in former Article 5, that fact is indicated by the word "Omitted" and a reason is stated.

Former Article 5 Section	Revised Article 5 Section
5-101	5-101
5-102(1)	5-103(a)
5-102(2)	Omitted (inherent in 5-103(a) and definitions)
5-103(3)	(first sentence omitted) 5-103(b)
5-103(1)(a)	5-102(a)(10); 5-106(a); 5-102(a)(8)
5-103(1)(b)	5-102(a)(6)("Document"), and 5-102(a)(14)("Record"); "Documentary" draft or demand not used
5-103(1)(c)	5-102(a)(9)
5-103(1)(d)	5-102(a)(3)
5-103(1)(e)	5-102(a)(1)
5-103(1)(f)	5-102(a)(4)
5-103(1)(g)	("Applicant" rather than "Customer") 5-102(a)(2)
5-103(2)	Omitted as not applicable
5-103(3)	5-102(b)
5-103(4)	5-102(c)
5-104	5-104 and 5-102(6) and (14)
5-105	5-105
5-106(1)	5-106(a)
5-106(2)	5-106(b)
5-106(3)	5-106(b)
5-106(4)	5-106(b)
5-107(1)	5-107(c)
5-107(2)	5-107(a)
5-107(3)	5-107(c)
5-107(4)	Omitted as inadvisable default rule
5-108	Omitted (as outdated)
5-109(1)	5-108
5-109(2)	5-108
5-109(3)	Omitted (all issuers required to observe standard practices)
5-110(1)	Omitted (covered in definitions and comments)
5-110(2)	Omitted (covered in definitions and comments)
5-111(1)	5-110(a)
5-111(2)	5-110(b)
5-112(1)	5-108(b) and (c)
5-112(2)	5-108(h)
5-112(3)	5-102(a)(12)
5-113	Omitted (covered by other contract law)
5-114(1)	5-108(a)
5-114(2)(a)	5-109(a)(1)
5-114(2)(b)	5-109(a)(2)
5-114(3)	5-108(i)
5-114(4), (5)	Omitted; were optional
5-115(1)	5-111
5-115(2)	5-111
5-116(1)	5-112
5-116(2)	5-114

Former Article 5 Section	Revised Article 5 Section
5–116(3)	5–114
5–117	Omitted (covered by other law)

Table of New Provisions

(Provisions which were not included in former Article 5 and subjects not addressed in former Article 5.)

Subject	Revised Article 5 Section
"Successor to a beneficiary"	5–102(15)
Non-variable terms	5–103(c)
Independence principle	5–103(d)
Unstated expiry date	5–106(c)
Perpetual letter of credit	5–106(d)
Preclusion of unstated deficiencies	5–108(c)
Standard practice	5–108(e)
Independence of obligation	5–108(f)
Non-documentary conditions	5–108(g)
Standards for issuing injunction	5–109(b)
Transfer by operation of law	5–113
Statute of Limitation	5–115
Choice of law	5–116
Subrogation	5–117

§ 5–101. Short Title.

This article may be cited as Uniform Commercial Code—Letters of Credit.

Official Comment

The Official Comment to the original Section 5–101 was a remarkably brief inaugural address. Noting that letters of credit had not been the subject of statutory enactment and that the law concerning them had been developed in the cases, the Comment stated that Article 5 was intended "within its limited scope" to set an independent theoretical frame for the further development of letters of credit. That statement addressed accurately conditions as they existed when the statement was made, nearly half a century ago. Since Article 5 was originally drafted, the use of letters of credit has expanded and developed, and the case law concerning these developments is, in some respects, discordant.

Revision of Article 5 therefore has required reappraisal both of the statutory goals and of the extent to which particular statutory provisions further or adversely affect achievement of those goals.

The statutory goal of Article 5 was originally stated to be: (1) to set a substantive theoretical frame that describes the function and legal nature of letters of credit; and (2) to preserve procedural flexibility in order to accommodate further development of the efficient use of letters of credit. A letter of credit is an idiosyncratic form of undertaking that supports performance of an obligation incurred in a separate financial, mercantile, or other transaction or arrangement. The objectives of the original and revised Article 5 are best achieved (1) by defining the peculiar characteristics of a letter of credit that distinguish it and the legal consequences of its use from other forms of assurance such as secondary guarantees, performance bonds, and insurance policies, and from ordinary contracts, fiduciary engagements, and escrow arrangements; and (2) by preserving flexibility through variation by agreement in order to respond to and accommodate developments in custom and usage that are not inconsistent with the essential definitions and substantive mandates of the statute. No statute can, however, prescribe the manner in which such substantive rights and duties are to be enforced or imposed without risking stultification of wholesome developments in the letter of credit mechanism. Letter of credit law should remain responsive to commercial reality and in particular to the customs and expectations of the international banking and mercantile community. Courts should read the terms of this article in a manner consistent with these customs and expectations.

The subject matter in Article 5, letters of credit, may also be governed by an international convention that is now being drafted by UNCITRAL, the draft Convention on Independent Guarantees and Standby Letters of Credit. The Uniform Customs and Practice is an international body of trade practice that is commonly adopted by international and domestic letters of credit and as such is the "law of the transaction" by agreement of the parties. Article 5 is consistent with and was influenced by the rules in the existing version of the UCP. In addition to the UCP and the international convention, other bodies of law apply to letters of credit. For example, the federal bankruptcy law applies to letters of credit with respect to applicants and beneficiaries that are in bankruptcy; regulations of the Federal Reserve Board and the Comptroller of the Currency lay out requirements for banks that issue letters of credit and describe how letters of credit are to be treated for calculating asset risk and for the purpose of loan limitations. In addition there is an array of anti-boycott and other similar laws that may affect the issuance and performance of letters of credit. All of these laws are beyond the scope of Article 5, but in certain circumstances they will override Article 5.

§ 5-102. Definitions.

(a) In this article:

(1) "Adviser" means a person who, at the request of the issuer, a confirmer, or another adviser, notifies or requests another adviser to notify the beneficiary that a letter of credit has been issued, confirmed, or amended.

(2) "Applicant" means a person at whose request or for whose account a letter of credit is issued. The term includes a person who requests an issuer to issue a letter of credit on behalf of another if the person making the request undertakes an obligation to reimburse the issuer.

(3) "Beneficiary" means a person who under the terms of a letter of credit is entitled to have its complying presentation honored. The term includes a person to whom drawing rights have been transferred under a transferable letter of credit.

(4) "Confirmer" means a nominated person who undertakes, at the request or with the consent of the issuer, to honor a presentation under a letter of credit issued by another.

(5) "Dishonor" of a letter of credit means failure timely to honor or to take an interim action, such as acceptance of a draft, that may be required by the letter of credit.

(6) "Document" means a draft or other demand, document of title, investment security, certificate, invoice, or other record, statement, or representation of fact, law, right, or opinion (i) which is presented in a written or other medium permitted by the letter of credit or, unless prohibited by the letter of credit, by the standard practice referred to in Section 5-108(e) and (ii) which is capable of being examined for compliance with the terms and conditions of the letter of credit. A document may not be oral.

(7) "Good faith" means honesty in fact in the conduct or transaction concerned.

(8) "Honor" of a letter of credit means performance of the issuer's undertaking in the letter of credit to pay or deliver an item of value. Unless the letter of credit otherwise provides, "honor" occurs

(i) upon payment,

(ii) if the letter of credit provides for acceptance, upon acceptance of a draft and, at maturity, its payment, or

(iii) if the letter of credit provides for incurring a deferred obligation, upon incurring the obligation and, at maturity, its performance.

(9) "Issuer" means a bank or other person that issues a letter of credit, but does not include an individual who makes an engagement for personal, family, or household purposes.

(10) "Letter of credit" means a definite undertaking that satisfies the requirements of Section 5-104 by an issuer to a beneficiary at the

request or for the account of an applicant or, in the case of a financial institution, to itself or for its own account, to honor a documentary presentation by payment or delivery of an item of value.

(11) "Nominated person" means a person whom the issuer (i) designates or authorizes to pay, accept, negotiate, or otherwise give value under a letter of credit and (ii) undertakes by agreement or custom and practice to reimburse.

(12) "Presentation" means delivery of a document to an issuer or nominated person for honor or giving of value under a letter of credit.

(13) "Presenter" means a person making a presentation as or on behalf of a beneficiary or nominated person.

(14) "Record" means information that is inscribed on a tangible medium, or that is stored in an electronic or other medium and is retrievable in perceivable form.

(15) "Successor of a beneficiary" means a person who succeeds to substantially all of the rights of a beneficiary by operation of law, including a corporation with or into which the beneficiary has been merged or consolidated, an administrator, executor, personal representative, trustee in bankruptcy, debtor in possession, liquidator, and receiver.

(b) Definitions in other Articles applying to this article and the sections in which they appear are:

"Accept" or "Acceptance" Section 3-409

"Value" Sections 3-303, 4-211

(c) Article 1 contains certain additional general definitions and principles of construction and interpretation applicable throughout this article.

Official Comment

1. Since no one can be a confirmer unless that person is a nominated person as defined in Section 5-102(a)(11), those who agree to "confirm" without the designation or authorization of the issuer are not confirmers under Article 5. Nonetheless, the undertakings to the beneficiary of such persons may be enforceable by the beneficiary as letters of credit issued by the "confirmer" for its own account or as guarantees or contracts outside of Article 5.

2. The definition of "document" contemplates and facilitates the growing recognition of electronic and other nonpaper media as "documents," however, for the time being, data in those media constitute documents only in certain circumstances. For example, a facsimile received by an issuer would be a document only if the letter of credit explicitly permitted it, if the standard practice authorized it and the letter did not prohibit it, or the agreement of the issuer and beneficiary permitted it. The fact that data transmitted in a nonpaper (unwritten) medium can be recorded on paper by a recipient's computer printer, facsimile machine, or the like does not under current practice render the data so transmitted a "document." A facsimile or S.W.I.F.T. message received directly by the issuer is in an electronic medium when it crosses the boundary of the issuer's place of business. One wishing to make a presentation by facsimile (an electronic medium) will have

to procure the explicit agreement of the issuer (assuming that the standard practice does not authorize it). Where electronic transmissions are authorized neither by the letter of credit nor by the practice, the beneficiary may transmit the data electronically to its agent who may be able to put it in written form and make a conforming presentation.

3. "Good faith" continues in revised Article 5 to be defined as "honesty in fact." "Observance of reasonable standards of fair dealing" has not been added to the definition. The narrower definition of "honesty in fact" reinforces the "independence principle" in the treatment of "fraud," "strict compliance," "preclusion," and other tests affecting the performance of obligations that are unique to letters of credit. This narrower definition—which does not include "fair dealing"—is appropriate to the decision to honor or dishonor a presentation of documents specified in a letter of credit. The narrower definition is also appropriate for other parts of revised Article 5 where greater certainty of obligations is necessary and is consistent with the goals of speed and low cost. It is important that U.S. letters of credit have continuing vitality and competitiveness in international transactions.

For example, it would be inconsistent with the "independence" principle if any of the following occurred: (i) the beneficiary's failure to adhere to the standard of "fair dealing" in the underlying transaction or otherwise in presenting documents were to provide applicants and issuers with an "unfairness" defense to dishonor even when the documents complied with the terms of the letter of credit; (ii) the issuer's obligation to honor in "strict compliance in accordance with standard practice" were changed to "reasonable compliance" by use of the "fair dealing" standard, or (iii) the preclusion against the issuer (Section 5-108(d)) were modified under the "fair dealing" standard to enable the issuer later to raise additional deficiencies in the presentation. The rights and obligations arising from presentation, honor, dishonor and reimbursement, are independent and strict, and thus "honesty in fact" is an appropriate standard.

The contract between the applicant and beneficiary is not governed by Article 5, but by applicable contract law, such as Article 2 or the general law of contracts. "Good faith" in that contract is defined by other law, such as Section 2-103(1)(b) or Restatement of Contracts 2d, § 205, which incorporate the principle of "fair dealing" in most cases, or a State's common law or other statutory provisions that may apply to that contract.

The contract between the applicant and the issuer (sometimes called the "reimbursement" agreement) is governed in part by this article (e.g., Sections 5-108(i), 5-111(b), and 5-103(c)) and partly by other law (e.g., the general law of contracts). The definition of good faith in Section 5-102(a)(7) applies only to the extent that the reimbursement contract is governed by provisions in this article; for other purposes good faith is defined by other law.

4. Payment and acceptance are familiar modes of honor. A third mode of honor, incurring an unconditional obligation, has legal effects similar to an acceptance of a time draft but does not technically constitute an acceptance. The practice of making letters of credit available by "deferred payment undertaking" as now provided in UCP 500 has grown up in other countries and spread to the United States. The definition of "honor" will accommodate that practice.

5. The exclusion of consumers from the definition of "issuer" is to keep creditors from using a letter of credit in consumer transactions in which the consumer might be made the issuer and the creditor would be the beneficiary. If that transaction were recognized under Article 5, the effect would be to leave the consumer without defenses against the creditor. That outcome would violate the policy behind the Federal Trade Commission Rule in 16 CFR Part 433. In a consumer transaction, an individual cannot be an issuer where that person would otherwise

be either the principal debtor or a guarantor.

6. The label on a document is not conclusive; certain documents labelled "guarantees" in accordance with European (and occasionally, American) practice are letters of credit. On the other hand, even documents that are labelled "letter of credit" may not constitute letters of credit under the definition in Section 5–102(a). When a document labelled a letter of credit requires the issuer to pay not upon the presentation of documents, but upon the determination of an extrinsic fact such as applicant's failure to perform a construction contract, and where that condition appears on its face to be fundamental and would, if ignored, leave no obligation to the issuer under the document labelled letter of credit, the issuer's undertaking is not a letter of credit. It is probably some form of suretyship or other contractual arrangement and may be enforceable as such. See Sections 5–102(a)(10) and 5–103(d). Therefore, undertakings whose fundamental term requires an issuer to look beyond documents and beyond conventional reference to the clock, calendar, and practices concerning the form of various documents are not governed by Article 5. Although Section 5–108(g) recognizes that certain nondocumentary conditions can be included in a letter of credit without denying the undertaking the status of letter of credit, that section does not apply to cases where the nondocumentary condition is fundamental to the issuer's obligation. The rules in Sections 5–102(a)(10), 5–103(d), and 5–108(g) approve the conclusion in Wichita Eagle & Beacon Publishing Co. v. Pacific Nat. Bank, 493 F.2d 1285 (9th Cir.1974).

The adjective "definite" is taken from the UCP. It approves cases that deny letter of credit status to documents that are unduly vague or incomplete. See, e.g., *Transparent Products Corp. v. Paysaver Credit Union,* 864 F.2d 60 (7th Cir. 1988). Note, however, that no particular phrase or label is necessary to establish a letter of credit. It is sufficient if the undertaking of the issuer shows that it is intended to be a letter of credit. In most cases the parties' intention will be indicated by a label on the undertaking itself indicating that it is a "letter of credit," but no such language is necessary.

A financial institution may be both the issuer and the applicant or the issuer and the beneficiary. Such letters are sometimes issued by a bank in support of the bank's own lease obligations or on behalf of one of its divisions as an applicant or to one of its divisions as beneficiary, such as an overseas branch. Because wide use of letters of credit in which the issuer and the applicant or the issuer and the beneficiary are the same would endanger the unique status of letters of credit, only financial institutions are authorized to issue them.

In almost all cases the ultimate performance of the issuer under a letter of credit is the payment of money. In rare cases the issuer's obligation is to deliver stock certificates or the like. The definition of letter of credit in Section 5–102(a)(10) contemplates those cases.

7. Under the UCP any bank is a nominated bank where the letter of credit is "freely negotiable." A letter of credit might also nominate by the following: "We hereby engage with the drawer, indorsers, and bona fide holders of drafts drawn under and in compliance with the terms of this credit that the same will be duly honored on due presentation" or "available with any bank by negotiation." A restricted negotiation credit might be "available with x bank by negotiation" or the like.

Several legal consequences may attach to the status of nominated person. First, when the issuer nominates a person, it is authorizing that person to pay or give value and is authorizing the beneficiary to make presentation to that person. Unless the letter of credit provides otherwise, the beneficiary need not present the documents to the issuer before the letter of credit expires; it need only present those documents to the nominated person. Secondly, a nominated person that gives value in good faith has a right to payment from the issuer despite fraud. Section 5-109(a)(1).

8. A "record" must be in or capable of being converted to a perceivable form. For example, an electronic message recorded in a computer memory that could be printed from that memory could constitute a record. Similarly, a tape recording of an oral conversation could be a record.

9. Absent a specific agreement to the contrary, documents of a beneficiary delivered to an issuer or nominated person are considered to be presented under the letter of credit to which they refer, and any payment or value given for them is considered to be made under that letter of credit. As the court held in Alaska Textile Co. v. Chase Manhattan Bank, N.A., 982 F.2d 813, 820 (2d Cir.1992), it takes a "significant showing" to make the presentation of a beneficiary's documents for "collection only" or otherwise outside letter of credit law and practice.

10. Although a successor of a beneficiary is one who succeeds "by operation of law," some of the successions contemplated by Section 5-102(a)(15) will have resulted from voluntary action of the beneficiary such as merger of a corporation. Any merger makes the successor corporation the "successor of a beneficiary" even though the transfer occurs partly by operation of law and partly by the voluntary action of the parties. The definition excludes certain transfers, where no part of the transfer is "by operation of law"—such as the sale of assets by one company to another.

11. "Draft" in Article 5 does not have the same meaning it has in Article 3. For example, a document may be a draft under Article 5 even though it would not be a negotiable instrument, and therefore would not qualify as a draft under Section 3-104(e).

§ 5-103. Scope.

(a) This article applies to letters of credit and to certain rights and obligations arising out of transactions involving letters of credit.

(b) The statement of a rule in this article does not by itself require, imply, or negate application of the same or a different rule to a situation not provided for, or to a person not specified, in this article.

(c) With the exception of this subsection, subsections (a) and (d), Sections 5-102(a)(9) and (10), 5-106(d), and 5-114(d), and except to the extent prohibited in Sections 1-102(3) and 5-117(d), the effect of this article may be varied by agreement or by a provision stated or incorporated by reference in an undertaking. A term in an agreement or undertaking generally excusing liability or generally limiting remedies for failure to perform obligations is not sufficient to vary obligations prescribed by this article.

(d) Rights and obligations of an issuer to a beneficiary or a nominated person under a letter of credit are independent of the existence, performance, or nonperformance of a contract or arrangement out of which the letter of credit arises or which underlies it, including contracts or arrangements between the issuer and the applicant and between the applicant and the beneficiary.

Official Comment

1. Sections 5-102(a)(10) and 5-103 are the principal limits on the scope of Article 5. Many undertakings in commerce and contract are similar, but not identical to the letter of credit. Principal among those are "secondary," "accessory," or "suretyship" guarantees. Although the word "guarantee" is some-

times used to describe an independent obligation like that of the issuer of a letter of credit (most often in the case of European bank undertakings but occasionally in the case of undertakings of American banks), in the United States the word "guarantee" is more typically used to describe a suretyship transaction in which the "guarantor" is only secondarily liable and has the right to assert the underlying debtor's defenses. This article does not apply to secondary or accessory guarantees and it is important to recognize the distinction between letters of credit and those guarantees. It is often a defense to a secondary or accessory guarantor's liability that the underlying debt has been discharged or that the debtor has other defenses to the underlying liability. In letter of credit law, on the other hand, the independence principle recognized throughout Article 5 states that the issuer's liability is independent of the underlying obligation. That the beneficiary may have breached the underlying contract and thus have given a good defense on that contract to the applicant against the beneficiary is no defense for the issuer's refusal to honor. Only staunch recognition of this principle by the issuers and the courts will give letters of credit the continuing vitality that arises from the certainty and speed of payment under letters of credit. To that end, it is important that the law not carry into letter of credit transactions rules that properly apply only to secondary guarantees or to other forms of engagement.

2. Like all of the provisions of the Uniform Commercial Code, Article 5 is supplemented by Section 1–103 and, through it, by many rules of statutory and common law. Because this article is quite short and has no rules on many issues that will affect liability with respect to a letter of credit transaction, law beyond Article 5 will often determine rights and liabilities in letter of credit transactions. Even within letter of credit law, the article is far from comprehensive; it deals only with "certain" rights of the parties. Particularly with respect to the standards of performance that are set out in Section 5–108, it is appropriate for the parties and the courts to turn to customs and practice such as the Uniform Customs and Practice for Documentary Credits, currently published by the International Chamber of Commerce as I.C.C. Pub. No. 500 (hereafter UCP). Many letters of credit specifically adopt the UCP as applicable to the particular transaction. Where the UCP are adopted but conflict with Article 5 and except where variation is prohibited, the UCP terms are permissible contractual modifications under Sections 1–102(3) and 5–103(c). See Section 5–116(c). Normally Article 5 should not be considered to conflict with practice except when a rule explicitly stated in the UCP or other practice is different from a rule explicitly stated in Article 5.

Except by choosing the law of a jurisdiction that has not adopted the Uniform Commercial Code, it is not possible entirely to escape the Uniform Commercial Code. Since incorporation of the UCP avoids only "conflicting" Article 5 rules, parties who do not wish to be governed by the nonconflicting provisions of Article 5 must normally either adopt the law of a jurisdiction other than a State of the United States or state explicitly the rule that is to govern. When rules of custom and practice are incorporated by reference, they are considered to be explicit terms of the agreement or undertaking.

Neither the obligation of an issuer under Section 5–108 nor that of an adviser under Section 5–107 is an obligation of the kind that is invariable under Section 1–102(3). Section 5–103(c) and Comment 1 to Section 5–108 make it clear that the applicant and the issuer may agree to almost any provision establishing the obligations of the issuer to the applicant. The last sentence of subsection (c) limits the power of the issuer to achieve that result by a nonnegotiated disclaimer or limitation of remedy.

What the issuer could achieve by an explicit agreement with its applicant or by a term that explicitly defines its duty, it cannot accomplish by a general disclaimer. The restriction on disclaimers in the last sentence of subsection (c) is based more on procedural than on substantive unfairness. Where, for example, the reimbursement agreement provides explicitly that the issuer need not examine any documents, the applicant understands the risk it has undertaken. A term in a reimbursement agreement which states generally that an issuer will not be liable unless it has acted in "bad faith" or committed "gross negligence" is ineffective under Section 5–103(c). On the other hand, less general terms such as terms that permit issuer reliance on an oral or electronic message believed in good faith to have been received from the applicant or terms that entitle an issuer to reimbursement when it honors a "substantially" though not "strictly" complying presentation, are effective. In each case the question is whether the disclaimer or limitation is sufficiently clear and explicit in reallocating a liability or risk that is allocated differently under a variable Article 5 provision.

Of course, no term in a letter of credit, whether incorporated by reference to practice rules or stated specifically, can free an issuer from a conflicting contractual obligation to its applicant. If, for example, an issuer promised its applicant that it would pay only against an inspection certificate of a particular company but failed to require such a certificate in its letter of credit or made the requirement only a nondocumentary condition that had to be disregarded, the issuer might be obliged to pay the beneficiary even though its payment might violate its contract with its applicant.

3. Parties should generally avoid modifying the definitions in Section 5–102. The effect of such an agreement is almost inevitably unclear. To say that something is a "guarantee" in the typical domestic transaction is to say that the parties intend that particular legal rules apply to it. By acknowledging that something is a guarantee, but asserting that it is to be treated as a "letter of credit," the parties leave a court uncertain about where the rules on guarantees stop and those concerning letters of credit begin.

4. Section 5–102(2) and (3) of Article 5 are omitted as unneeded; the omission does not change the law.

§ 5–104. Formal Requirements.

A letter of credit, confirmation, advice, transfer, amendment, or cancellation may be issued in any form that is a record and is authenticated (i) by a signature or (ii) in accordance with the agreement of the parties or the standard practice referred to in Section 5–108(e).

Official Comment

1. Neither Section 5–104 nor the definition of letter of credit in Section 5–102(a)(10) requires inclusion of all the terms that are normally contained in a letter of credit in order for an undertaking to be recognized as a letter of credit under Article 5. For example, a letter of credit will typically specify the amount available, the expiration date, the place where presentation should be made, and the documents that must be presented to entitle a person to honor. Undertakings that have the formalities required by Section 5–104 and meet the conditions specified in Section 5–102(a)(10) will be recognized as letters of credit even though they omit one or more of the items usually contained in a letter of credit.

2. The authentication specified in this section is authentication only of the identity of the issuer, confirmer, or adviser.

An authentication agreement may be by system rule, by standard practice, or by direct agreement between the parties. The reference to practice is intended to incorporate future developments in the UCP and other practice rules as well as those that may arise spontaneously in commercial practice.

3. Many banking transactions, including the issuance of many letters of credit, are now conducted mostly by electronic means. For example, S.W.I.F.T. is currently used to transmit letters of credit from issuing to advising banks. The letter of credit text so transmitted may be printed at the advising bank, stamped "original" and provided to the beneficiary in that form. The printed document may then be used as a way of controlling and recording payments and of recording and authorizing assignments of proceeds or transfers of rights under the letter of credit. Nothing in this section should be construed to conflict with that practice.

To be a record sufficient to serve as a letter of credit or other undertaking under this section, data must have a durability consistent with that function. Because consideration is not required for a binding letter of credit or similar undertaking (Section 5-105) yet those undertakings are to be strictly construed (Section 5-108), parties to a letter of credit transaction are especially dependent on the continued availability of the terms and conditions of the letter of credit or other undertaking. By declining to specify any particular medium in which the letter of credit must be established or communicated, Section 5-104 leaves room for future developments.

§ 5-105. Consideration.

Consideration is not required to issue, amend, transfer, or cancel a letter of credit, advice, or confirmation.

Official Comment

It is not to be expected that any issuer will issue its letter of credit without some form of remuneration. But it is not expected that the beneficiary will know what the issuer's remuneration was or whether in fact there was any identifiable remuneration in a given case. And it might be difficult for the beneficiary to prove the issuer's remuneration. This section dispenses with this proof and is consistent with the position of Lord Mansfield in *Pillans v. Van Mierop,* 97 Eng.Rep. 1035 (K.B. 1765) in making consideration irrelevant.

§ 5-106. Issuance, Amendment, Cancellation, and Duration.

(a) A letter of credit is issued and becomes enforceable according to its terms against the issuer when the issuer sends or otherwise transmits it to the person requested to advise or to the beneficiary. A letter of credit is revocable only if it so provides.

(b) After a letter of credit is issued, rights and obligations of a beneficiary, applicant, confirmer, and issuer are not affected by an amendment or cancellation to which that person has not consented except to the extent the letter of credit provides that it is revocable or that the issuer may amend or cancel the letter of credit without that consent.

(c) If there is no stated expiration date or other provision that determines its duration, a letter of credit expires one year after its stated date of issuance or, if none is stated, after the date on which it is issued.

(d) A letter of credit that states that it is perpetual expires five years after its stated date of issuance, or if none is stated, after the date on which it is issued.

Official Comment

1. This section adopts the position taken by several courts, namely that letters of credit that are silent as to revocability are irrevocable. See, e.g., *Weyerhaeuser Co. v. First Nat. Bank,* 27 UCC Rep.Serv. 777 (S.D. Iowa 1979); West Va. Hous. Dev. Fund v. Sroka, 415 F.Supp. 1107 (W.D.Pa.1976). This is the position of the current UCP (500). Given the usual commercial understanding and purpose of letters of credit, revocable letters of credit offer unhappy possibilities for misleading the parties who deal with them.

2. A person can consent to an amendment by implication. For example, a beneficiary that tenders documents for honor that conform to an amended letter of credit but not to the original letter of credit has probably consented to the amendment. By the same token an applicant that has procured the issuance of a transferable letter of credit has consented to its transfer and to performance under the letter of credit by a person to whom the beneficiary's rights are duly transferred. If some, but not all of the persons involved in a letter of credit transaction consent to performance that does not strictly conform to the original letter of credit, those persons assume the risk that other nonconsenting persons may insist on strict compliance with the original letter of credit. Under subsection (b) those not consenting are not bound. For example, an issuer might agree to amend its letter of credit or honor documents presented after the expiration date in the belief that the applicant has consented or will consent to the amendment or will waive presentation after the original expiration date. If that belief is mistaken, the issuer is bound to the beneficiary by the terms of the letter of credit as amended or waived, even though it may be unable to recover from the applicant.

In general, the rights of a recognized transferee beneficiary cannot be altered without the transferee's consent, but the same is not true of the rights of assignees of proceeds from the beneficiary. When the beneficiary makes a complete transfer of its interest that is effective under the terms for transfer established by the issuer, adviser, or other party controlling transfers, the beneficiary no longer has an interest in the letter of credit, and the transferee steps into the shoes of the beneficiary as the one with rights under the letter of credit. Section 5-102(a)(3). When there is a partial transfer, both the original beneficiary and the transferee beneficiary have an interest in performance of the letter of credit and each expects that its rights will not be altered by amendment unless it consents.

The assignee of proceeds under a letter of credit from the beneficiary enjoys no such expectation. Notwithstanding an assignee's notice to the issuer of the assignment of proceeds, the assignee is not a person protected by subsection (b). An assignee of proceeds should understand that its rights can be changed or completely extinguished by amendment or cancellation of the letter of credit. An assignee's claim is precarious, for it depends entirely upon the continued existence of the letter of credit and upon the beneficiary's preparation and presentation of documents that would entitle the beneficiary to honor under Section 5-108.

3. The issuer's right to cancel a revocable letter of credit does not free it from a duty to reimburse a nominated person who has honored, accepted, or undertaken a deferred obligation prior to receiving notice of the amendment or cancellation. Compare UCP Article 8.

4. Although all letters of credit should specify the date on which the issuer's engagement expires, the failure to specify an expiration date does not invalidate the letter of credit, or diminish or relieve the obligation of any party with respect to the letter of credit. A letter of credit that may be revoked or terminated at the discretion of the issuer by notice to the beneficiary is not "perpetual."

§ 5-107. Confirmer, Nominated Person, and Adviser.

(a) A confirmer is directly obligated on a letter of credit and has the rights and obligations of an issuer to the extent of its confirmation. The confirmer also has rights against and obligations to the issuer as if the issuer were an applicant and the confirmer had issued the letter of credit at the request and for the account of the issuer.

(b) A nominated person who is not a confirmer is not obligated to honor or otherwise give value for a presentation.

(c) A person requested to advise may decline to act as an adviser. An adviser that is not a confirmer is not obligated to honor or give value for a presentation. An adviser undertakes to the issuer and to the beneficiary accurately to advise the terms of the letter of credit, confirmation, amendment, or advice received by that person and undertakes to the beneficiary to check the apparent authenticity of the request to advise. Even if the advice is inaccurate, the letter of credit, confirmation, or amendment is enforceable as issued.

(d) A person who notifies a transferee beneficiary of the terms of a letter of credit, confirmation, amendment, or advice has the rights and obligations of an adviser under subsection (c). The terms in the notice to the transferee beneficiary may differ from the terms in any notice to the transferor beneficiary to the extent permitted by the letter of credit, confirmation, amendment, or advice received by the person who so notifies.

Official Comment

1. A confirmer has the rights and obligations identified in Section 5-108. Accordingly, unless the context otherwise requires, the terms "confirmer" and "confirmation" should be read into this article wherever the terms "issuer" and "letter of credit" appear.

A confirmer that has paid in accordance with the terms and conditions of the letter of credit is entitled to reimbursement by the issuer even if the beneficiary committed fraud (see Section 5-109(a)(1)(ii)) and, in that sense, has greater rights against the issuer than the beneficiary has. To be entitled to reimbursement from the issuer under the typical confirmed letter of credit, the confirmer must submit conforming documents, but the confirmer's presentation to the issuer need not be made before the expiration date of the letter of credit.

A letter of credit confirmation has been analogized to a guarantee of issuer performance, to a parallel letter of credit issued by the confirmer for the account of the issuer or the letter of credit applicant or both, and to a back-to-back letter of credit in which the confirmer is a kind of beneficiary of the original issuer's letter of credit. Like letter of credit undertakings, confirmations are both unique and flexible, so that no one of these analogies is perfect, but unless otherwise indicated in the letter of credit or confirmation, a confirmer should be viewed by the letter of credit issuer and the beneficiary as an issuer of a parallel letter of credit for the account of the original letter of credit issuer. Absent a direct agreement between the applicant and a confirmer, normally the obligations of a confirmer are to the issuer not the applicant, but the applicant might have a right to injunction against a confirmer under Section 5-109 or warranty claim under Section 5-110, and either might have claims against the other under Section 5-117.

2. No one has a duty to advise until that person agrees to be an adviser or

undertakes to act in accordance with the instructions of the issuer. Except where there is a prior agreement to serve or where the silence of the adviser would be an acceptance of an offer to contract, a person's failure to respond to a request to advise a letter of credit does not in and of itself create any liability, nor does it establish a relationship of issuer and adviser between the two. Since there is no duty to advise a letter of credit in the absence of a prior agreement, there can be no duty to advise it timely or at any particular time. When the adviser manifests its agreement to advise by actually doing so (as is normally the case), the adviser cannot have violated any duty to advise in a timely way. This analysis is consistent with the result of Sound of Market Street v. Continental Bank International, 819 F.2d 384 (3d Cir.1987) which held that there is no such duty. This section takes no position on the reasoning of that case, but does not overrule the result. By advising or agreeing to advise a letter of credit, the adviser assumes a duty to the issuer and to the beneficiary accurately to report what it has received from the issuer, but, beyond determining the apparent authenticity of the letter, an adviser has no duty to investigate the accuracy of the message it has received from the issuer. "Checking" the apparent authenticity of the request to advise means only that the prospective adviser must attempt to authenticate the message (e.g., by "testing" the telex that comes from the purported issuer), and if it is unable to authenticate the message must report that fact to the issuer and, if it chooses to advise the message, to the beneficiary. By proper agreement, an adviser may disclaim its obligation under this section.

3. An issuer may issue a letter of credit which the adviser may advise with different terms. The issuer may then believe that it has undertaken a certain engagement, yet the text in the hands of the beneficiary will contain different terms, and the beneficiary would not be entitled to honor if the documents it submitted did not comply with the terms of the letter of credit as originally issued. On the other hand, if the adviser also confirmed the letter of credit, then as a confirmer it will be independently liable on the letter of credit as advised and confirmed. If in that situation the beneficiary's ultimate presentation entitled it to honor under the terms of the confirmation but not under those in the original letter of credit, the confirmer would have to honor but might not be entitled to reimbursement from the issuer.

4. When the issuer nominates another person to "pay," "negotiate," or otherwise to take up the documents and give value, there can be confusion about the legal status of the nominated person. In rare cases the person might actually be an agent of the issuer and its act might be the act of the issuer itself. In most cases the nominated person is not an agent of the issuer and has no authority to act on the issuer's behalf. Its "nomination" allows the beneficiary to present to it and earns it certain rights to payment under Section 5-109 that others do not enjoy. For example, when an issuer issues a "freely negotiable credit," it contemplates that banks or others might take up documents under that credit and advance value against them, and it is agreeing to pay those persons but only if the presentation to the issuer made by the nominated person complies with the credit. Usually there will be no agreement to pay, negotiate, or to serve in any other capacity by the nominated person, therefore the nominated person will have the right to decline to take the documents. It may return them or agree merely to act as a forwarding agent for the documents but without giving value against them or taking any responsibility for their conformity to the letter of credit.

§ 5-108. Issuer's Rights and Obligations.

(a) Except as otherwise provided in Section 5-109, an issuer shall honor a presentation that, as determined by the standard practice referred to in subsection (e), appears on its face strictly to comply with the terms and conditions of the letter of credit. Except as otherwise provided in Section 5–113 and unless otherwise agreed with the applicant, an issuer shall dishonor a presentation that does not appear so to comply.

(b) An issuer has a reasonable time after presentation, but not beyond the end of the seventh business day of the issuer after the day of its receipt of documents:

(1) to honor,

(2) if the letter of credit provides for honor to be completed more than seven business days after presentation, to accept a draft or incur a deferred obligation, or

(3) to give notice to the presenter of discrepancies in the presentation.

(c) Except as otherwise provided in subsection (d), an issuer is precluded from asserting as a basis for dishonor any discrepancy if timely notice is not given, or any discrepancy not stated in the notice if timely notice is given.

(d) Failure to give the notice specified in subsection (b) or to mention fraud, forgery, or expiration in the notice does not preclude the issuer from asserting as a basis for dishonor fraud or forgery as described in Section 5–109(a) or expiration of the letter of credit before presentation.

(e) An issuer shall observe standard practice of financial institutions that regularly issue letters of credit. Determination of the issuer's observance of the standard practice is a matter of interpretation for the court. The court shall offer the parties a reasonable opportunity to present evidence of the standard practice.

(f) An issuer is not responsible for:

(1) the performance or nonperformance of the underlying contract, arrangement, or transaction,

(2) an act or omission of others, or

(3) observance or knowledge of the usage of a particular trade other than the standard practice referred to in subsection (e).

(g) If an undertaking constituting a letter of credit under Section 5–102(a)(10) contains nondocumentary conditions, an issuer shall disregard the nondocumentary conditions and treat them as if they were not stated.

(h) An issuer that has dishonored a presentation shall return the documents or hold them at the disposal of, and send advice to that effect to, the presenter.

(i) An issuer that has honored a presentation as permitted or required by this article:

(1) is entitled to be reimbursed by the applicant in immediately available funds not later than the date of its payment of funds;

(2) takes the documents free of claims of the beneficiary or presenter;

(3) is precluded from asserting a right of recourse on a draft under Sections 3–414 and 3–415;

(4) except as otherwise provided in Sections 5–110 and 5–117, is precluded from restitution of money paid or other value given by mistake to the extent the mistake concerns discrepancies in the documents or tender which are apparent on the face of the presentation; and

(5) is discharged to the extent of its performance under the letter of credit unless the issuer honored a presentation in which a required signature of a beneficiary was forged.

Official Comment

1. This section combines some of the duties previously included in Sections 5–114 and 5–109. Because a confirmer has the rights and duties of an issuer, this section applies equally to a confirmer and an issuer. See Section 5–107(a).

The standard of strict compliance governs the issuer's obligation to the beneficiary and to the applicant. By requiring that a "presentation" appear strictly to comply, the section requires not only that the documents themselves appear on their face strictly to comply, but also that the other terms of the letter of credit such as those dealing with the time and place of presentation are strictly complied with. Typically, a letter of credit will provide that presentation is timely if made to the issuer, confirmer, or any other nominated person prior to expiration of the letter of credit. Accordingly, a nominated person that has honored a demand or otherwise given value before expiration will have a right to reimbursement from the issuer even though presentation to the issuer is made after the expiration of the letter of credit. Conversely, where the beneficiary negotiates documents to one who is not a nominated person, the beneficiary or that person acting on behalf of the beneficiary must make presentation to a nominated person, confirmer, or issuer prior to the expiration date.

This section does not impose a bifurcated standard under which an issuer's right to reimbursement might be broader than a beneficiary's right to honor. However, the explicit deference to standard practice in Section 5–108(a) and (e) and elsewhere expands issuers' rights of reimbursement where that practice so provides. Also, issuers can and often do contract with their applicants for expanded rights of reimbursement. Where that is done, the beneficiary will have to meet a more stringent standard of compliance as to the issuer than the issuer will have to meet as to the applicant. Similarly, a nominated person may have reimbursement and other rights against the issuer based on this article, the UCP, bank-to-bank reimbursement rules, or other agreement or undertaking of the issuer. These rights may allow the nominated person to recover from the issuer even when the nominated person would have no right to obtain honor under the letter of credit.

The section adopts strict compliance, rather than the standard that commentators have called "substantial compliance," the standard arguably applied in *Banco Español de Credito v. State Street Bank and Trust Company,* 385 F.2d 230 (1st Cir.1967) and *Flagship Cruises Ltd. v. New England Merchants Nat. Bank,* 569 F.2d 699 (1st Cir.1978). Strict compliance does not mean slavish conformity to the terms of the letter of credit. For example, standard practice (what issuers do) may recognize certain presentations as complying that an unschooled layman would regard as discrepant. By adopting standard practice as a way of measuring strict compliance, this article indorses the conclusion of the court in *New Braunfels Nat. Bank v. Odiorne,* 780 S.W.2d 313 (Tex.Ct.App. 1989) (beneficiary could collect when draft requested payment on 'Letter of Credit No. 86–122–5' and letter of credit specified 'Letter of Credit No. 86–122–S' holding strict compliance does not demand oppressive perfectionism). The section also indorses the result in *Tosco Corp. v. Federal Deposit Insur-*

ance Corp., 723 F.2d 1242 (6th Cir.1983). The letter of credit in that case called for "drafts Drawn under Bank of Clarksville Letter of Credit Number 105." The draft presented stated "drawn under Bank of Clarksville, Clarksville, Tennessee letter of Credit No. 105." The court correctly found that despite the change of upper case "L" to a lower case "l" and the use of the word "No." instead of "Number," and despite the addition of the words "Clarksville, Tennessee," the presentation conformed. Similarly a document addressed by a foreign person to General Motors as "Jeneral Motors" would strictly conform in the absence of other defects.

Identifying and determining compliance with standard practice are matters of interpretation for the court, not for the jury. As with similar rules in Sections 4A–202(c) and 2–302, it is hoped that there will be more consistency in the outcomes and speedier resolution of disputes if the responsibility for determining the nature and scope of standard practice is granted to the court, not to a jury. Granting the court authority to make these decisions will also encourage the salutary practice of courts' granting summary judgment in circumstances where there are no significant factual disputes. The statute encourages outcomes such as *American Coleman Co. v. Intrawest Bank,* 887 F.2d 1382 (10th Cir.1989), where summary judgment was granted.

In some circumstances standards may be established between the issuer and the applicant by agreement or by custom that would free the issuer from liability that it might otherwise have. For example, an applicant might agree that the issuer would have no duty whatsoever to examine documents on certain presentations (e.g., those below a certain dollar amount). Where the transaction depended upon the issuer's payment in a very short time period (e.g., on the same day or within a few hours of presentation), the issuer and the applicant might agree to reduce the issuer's responsibility for failure to discover discrepancies. By the same token, an agreement between the applicant and the issuer might permit the issuer to examine documents exclusively by electronic or electro-optical means. Neither those agreements nor others like them explicitly made by issuers and applicants violate the terms of Section 5–108(a) or (b) or Section 5–103(c).

2. Section 5–108(a) balances the need of the issuer for time to examine the documents against the possibility that the examiner (at the urging of the applicant or for fear that it will not be reimbursed) will take excessive time to search for defects. What is a "reasonable time" is not extended to accommodate an issuer's procuring a waiver from the applicant. See Article 14c of the UCP.

Under both the UCC and the UCP the issuer has a reasonable time to honor or give notice. The outside limit of that time is measured in business days under the UCC and in banking days under the UCP, a difference that will rarely be significant. Neither business nor banking days are defined in Article 5, but a court may find useful analogies in Regulation CC, 12 CFR 229.2, in state law outside of the Uniform Commercial Code, and in Article 4.

Examiners must note that the seven-day period is not a safe harbor. The time within which the issuer must give notice is the lesser of a reasonable time or seven business days. Where there are few documents (as, for example, with the mine run standby letter of credit), the reasonable time would be less than seven days. If more than a reasonable time is consumed in examination, no timely notice is possible. What is a "reasonable time" is to be determined by examining the behavior of those in the business of examining documents, mostly banks. Absent prior agreement of the issuer, one could not expect a bank issuer to examine documents while the beneficiary waited in the lobby if the normal practice was to give the documents to a person who had the opportunity to examine those together with many others in an orderly process. That the applicant has not yet paid the issuer or that the applicant's account with the issuer is insufficient to cover the amount of the draft is not a basis for extension of the time period.

This section does not preclude the issuer from contacting the applicant during its examination; however, the decision to honor rests with the issuer, and it has no duty to seek a waiver from the applicant or to notify the applicant of receipt of the documents. If the issuer dishonors a conforming presentation, the beneficiary will be entitled to the remedies under Section 5–111, irrespective of the applicant's views.

Even though the person to whom presentation is made cannot conduct a reasonable examination of documents within the time after presentation and before the expiration date, presentation establishes the parties' rights. The beneficiary's right to honor or the issuer's right to dishonor arises upon presentation at the place provided in the letter of credit even though it might take the person to whom presentation has been made several days to determine whether honor or dishonor is the proper course. The issuer's time for honor or giving notice of dishonor may be extended or shortened by a term in the letter of credit. The time for the issuer's performance may be otherwise modified or waived in accordance with Section 5–106.

The issuer's time to inspect runs from the time of its "receipt of documents." Documents are considered to be received only when they are received at the place specified for presentation by the issuer or other party to whom presentation is made.

Failure of the issuer to act within the time permitted by subsection (b) constitutes dishonor. Because of the preclusion in subsection (c) and the liability that the issuer may incur under Section 5–111 for wrongful dishonor, the effect of such a silent dishonor may ultimately be the same as though the issuer had honored, i.e., it may owe damages in the amount drawn but unpaid under the letter of credit.

3. The requirement that the issuer send notice of the discrepancies or be precluded from asserting discrepancies is new to Article 5. It is taken from the similar provision in the UCP and is intended to promote certainty and finality.

The section thus substitutes a strict preclusion principle for the doctrines of waiver and estoppel that might otherwise apply under Section 1–103. It rejects the reasoning in *Flagship Cruises Ltd. v. New England Merchants' Nat. Bank,* 569 F.2d 699 (1st Cir.1978) and *Wing On Bank Ltd. v. American Nat. Bank & Trust Co.,* 457 F.2d 328 (5th Cir.1972) where the issuer was held to be estopped only if the beneficiary relied on the issuer's failure to give notice.

Assume, for example, that the beneficiary presented documents to the issuer shortly before the letter of credit expired, in circumstances in which the beneficiary could not have cured any discrepancy before expiration. Under the reasoning of *Flagship* and *Wing On*, the beneficiary's inability to cure, even if it had received notice, would absolve the issuer of its failure to give notice. The virtue of the preclusion obligation adopted in this section is that it forecloses litigation about reliance and detriment.

Even though issuers typically give notice of the discrepancy of tardy presentation when presentation is made after the expiration of a credit, they are not required to give that notice and the section permits them to raise late presentation as a defect despite their failure to give that notice.

4. To act within a reasonable time, the issuer must normally give notice without delay after the examining party makes its decision. If the examiner decides to dishonor on the first day, it would be obliged to notify the beneficiary shortly thereafter, perhaps on the same business day. This rule accepts the reasoning in cases such as *Datapoint Corp. v. M & I Bank,* 665 F.Supp. 722 (W.D.Wis. 1987) and *Esso Petroleum Canada, Div. of Imperial Oil, Ltd. v. Security Pacific Bank,* 710 F.Supp. 275 (D.Or.1989).

The section deprives the examining party of the right simply to sit on a presentation that is made within seven days of expiration. The section requires the examiner to examine the documents and make a decision and, having made a decision to dishonor, to communicate promptly with the presenter. Nevertheless, a beneficiary who presents documents shortly before the expiration of a letter of credit runs the risk that it will never have the opportunity to cure any discrepancies.

5. Confirmers, other nominated persons, and collecting banks acting for beneficiaries can be presenters and, when so, are entitled to the notice provided in subsection (b). Even nominated persons who have honored or given value against an earlier presentation of the beneficiary and are themselves seeking reimbursement or honor need notice of discrepancies in the hope that they may be able to procure complying documents. The issuer has the obligations imposed by this section whether the issuer's performance is characterized as "reimbursement" of a nominated person or as "honor."

6. In many cases a letter of credit authorizes presentation by the beneficiary to someone other than the issuer. Sometimes that person is identified as a "payor" or "paying bank," or as an "acceptor" or "accepting bank," in other cases as a "negotiating bank," and in other cases there will be no specific designation. The section does not impose any duties on a person other than the issuer or confirmer, however a nominated person or other person may have liability under this article or at common law if it fails to perform an express or implied agreement with the beneficiary.

7. The issuer's obligation to honor runs not only to the beneficiary but also to the applicant. It is possible that an applicant who has made a favorable contract with the beneficiary will be injured by the issuer's wrongful dishonor. Except to the extent that the contract between the issuer and the applicant limits that liability, the issuer will have liability to the applicant for wrongful dishonor under Section 5-111 as a matter of contract law. A good faith extension of the time in Section 5-108(b) by agreement between the issuer and beneficiary binds the applicant even if the applicant is not consulted or does not consent to the extension.

The issuer's obligation to dishonor when there is no apparent compliance with the letter of credit runs only to the applicant. No other party to the transaction can complain if the applicant waives compliance with terms or conditions of the letter of credit or agrees to a less stringent standard for compliance than that supplied by this article. Except as otherwise agreed with the applicant, an issuer may dishonor a noncomplying presentation despite an applicant's waiver.

Waiver of discrepancies by an issuer or an applicant in one or more presentations does not waive similar discrepancies in a future presentation. Neither the issuer nor the beneficiary can reasonably rely upon honor over past waivers as a basis for concluding that a future defective presentation will justify honor. The reasoning of *Courtaulds of North America Inc. v. North Carolina Nat. Bank,* 528 F.2d 802 (4th Cir.1975) is accepted and that expressed in *Schweibish v. Pontchartrain State Bank,* 389 So.2d 731 (La.App.1980) and *Titanium Metals Corp. v. Space Metals, Inc.,* 529 P.2d 431 (Utah 1974) is rejected.

8. The standard practice referred to in subsection (e) includes (i) international practice set forth in or referenced by the Uniform Customs and Practice, (ii) other practice rules published by associations of financial institutions, and (iii) local and regional practice. It is possible that standard practice will vary from one place to another. Where there are conflicting practices, the parties should indicate which practice governs their rights. A practice may be overridden by agreement or course of dealing. See Section 1-205(4).

9. The responsibility of the issuer under a letter of credit is to examine documents and to make a prompt decision to honor or dishonor based upon that examination. Nondocumentary conditions have no place in this regime and are

better accommodated under contract or suretyship law and practice. In requiring that nondocumentary conditions in letters of credit be ignored as surplusage, Article 5 remains aligned with the UCP (see UCP 500 Article 13c), approves cases like *Pringle-Associated Mortgage Corp. v. Southern National Bank,* 571 F.2d 871, 874 (5th Cir.1978), and rejects the reasoning in cases such as *Sherwood & Roberts, Inc. v. First Security Bank*, 682 P.2d 149 (Mont. 1984).

Subsection (g) recognizes that letters of credit sometimes contain nondocumentary terms or conditions. Conditions such as a term prohibiting "shipment on vessels more than 15 years old," are to be disregarded and treated as surplusage. Similarly, a requirement that there be an award by a "duly appointed arbitrator" would not require the issuer to determine whether the arbitrator had been "duly appointed." Likewise a term in a standby letter of credit that provided for differing forms of certification depending upon the particular type of default does not oblige the issuer independently to determine which kind of default has occurred. These conditions must be disregarded by the issuer. Where the nondocumentary conditions are central and fundamental to the issuer's obligation (as for example a condition that would require the issuer to determine in fact whether the beneficiary had performed the underlying contract or whether the applicant had defaulted) their inclusion may remove the undertaking from the scope of Article 5 entirely. See Section 5-102(a)(10) and Comment 6 to Section 5-102.

Subsection (g) would not permit the beneficiary or the issuer to disregard terms in the letter of credit such as place, time, and mode of presentation. The rule in subsection (g) is intended to prevent an issuer from deciding or even investigating extrinsic facts, but not from consulting the clock, the calendar, the relevant law and practice, or its own general knowledge of documentation or transactions of the type underlying a particular letter of credit.

Even though nondocumentary conditions must be disregarded in determining compliance of a presentation (and thus in determining the issuer's duty to the beneficiary), an issuer that has promised its applicant that it will honor only on the occurrence of those nondocumentary conditions may have liability to its applicant for disregarding the conditions.

10. Subsection (f) condones an issuer's ignorance of "any usage of a particular trade"; that trade is the trade of the applicant, beneficiary, or others who may be involved in the underlying transaction. The issuer is expected to know usage that is commonly encountered in the course of document examination. For example, an issuer should know the common usage with respect to documents in the maritime shipping trade but would not be expected to understand synonyms used in a particular trade for product descriptions appearing in a letter of credit or an invoice.

11. Where the issuer's performance is the delivery of an item of value other than money, the applicant's reimbursement obligation would be to make the "item of value" available to the issuer.

12. An issuer is entitled to reimbursement from the applicant after honor of a forged or fraudulent drawing if honor was permitted under Section 5-109(a).

13. The last clause of Section 5-108(i)(5) deals with a special case in which the fraud is not committed by the beneficiary, but is committed by a stranger to the transaction who forges the beneficiary's signature. If the issuer pays against documents on which a required signature of the beneficiary is forged, it remains liable to the true beneficiary.

§ 5-109. Fraud and Forgery.

(a) If a presentation is made that appears on its face strictly to comply with the terms and conditions of the letter of credit, but a required document is forged or materially fraudulent, or honor of the presentation would facilitate a material fraud by the beneficiary on the issuer or applicant:

(1) the issuer shall honor the presentation, if honor is demanded by (i) a nominated person who has given value in good faith and without notice of forgery or material fraud, (ii) a confirmer who has honored its confirmation in good faith, (iii) a holder in due course of a draft drawn under the letter of credit which was taken after acceptance by the issuer or nominated person, or (iv) an assignee of the issuer's or nominated person's deferred obligation that was taken for value and without notice of forgery or material fraud after the obligation was incurred by the issuer or nominated person; and

(2) the issuer, acting in good faith, may honor or dishonor the presentation in any other case.

(b) If an applicant claims that a required document is forged or materially fraudulent or that honor of the presentation would facilitate a material fraud by the beneficiary on the issuer or applicant, a court of competent jurisdiction may temporarily or permanently enjoin the issuer from honoring a presentation or grant similar relief against the issuer or other persons only if the court finds that:

(1) the relief is not prohibited under the law applicable to an accepted draft or deferred obligation incurred by the issuer;

(2) a beneficiary, issuer, or nominated person who may be adversely affected is adequately protected against loss that it may suffer because the relief is granted;

(3) all of the conditions to entitle a person to the relief under the law of this State have been met; and

(4) on the basis of the information submitted to the court, the applicant is more likely than not to succeed under its claim of forgery or material fraud and the person demanding honor does not qualify for protection under subsection (a)(1).

Official Comment

1. This recodification makes clear that fraud must be found either in the documents or must have been committed by the beneficiary on the issuer or applicant. See *Cromwell v. Commerce & Energy Bank,* 464 So.2d 721 (La.1985).

Secondly, it makes clear that fraud must be "material." Necessarily courts must decide the breadth and width of "materiality." The use of the word requires that the fraudulent aspect of a document be material to a purchaser of that document or that the fraudulent act be significant to the participants in the underlying transaction. Assume, for example, that the beneficiary has a contract to deliver 1,000 barrels of salad oil. Knowing that it has delivered only 998, the beneficiary nevertheless submits an invoice showing 1,000 barrels. If two barrels in a 1,000 barrel shipment would be an insubstantial and immaterial breach of the underlying contract, the beneficiary's act, though possibly fraudulent, is not materially so and would not justify an injunction. Conversely, the knowing submission of those invoices upon delivery of only five barrels would be materially fraudulent. The courts must examine the underlying transaction when there is an allegation of material fraud, for only by examining that transaction can one determine whether a document is fraudulent or the beneficiary has committed fraud and, if so, whether the fraud was material.

Material fraud by the beneficiary occurs only when the beneficiary has no colorable right to expect honor and where there is no basis in fact to support such a right to honor. The section indorses articulations such as those stated in *Intraworld Indus. v. Girard Trust Bank,* 336 A.2d 316 (Pa.1975), *Roman Ceramics Corp. v. People's Nat. Bank,* 714 F.2d 1207 (3d Cir.1983), and similar decisions and embraces certain decisions under Section 5-114 that relied upon the phrase "fraud in the transaction." Some of these decisions have been summarized as follows in *Ground Air Transfer v. Westate's Airlines,* 899 F.2d 1269, 1272-73 (1st Cir.1990):

> We have said throughout that courts may not "*normally*" issue an injunction because of an important exception to the general "no injunction" rule. The exception, as we also explained in Itek, 730 F.2d at 24-25, concerns "fraud" so serious as to make it obviously pointless and unjust to permit the beneficiary to obtain the money. Where the circumstances "*plainly*" show that the underlying contract forbids the beneficiary to call a letter of credit, Itek, 730 F.2d at 24; where they show that the contract deprives the beneficiary of even a "*colorable*" right to do so, id., at 25; where the contract and circumstances reveal that the beneficiary's demand for payment has "absolutely no basis in fact," id.; see Dynamics Corp. of America, 356 F.Supp. at 999; where the beneficiary's conduct has "so vitiated the entire transaction that the legitimate purposes of the independence of the issuer's obligation would no longer be served," Itek, 730 F.2d at 25 (quoting *Roman Ceramics Corp. v. Peoples National Bank,* 714 F.2d 1207, 1212 n.12, 1215 (3d Cir.1983)(quoting Intraworld Indus., 336 A.2d at 324-25)); *then* a court may enjoin payment.

2. Subsection (a)(2) makes clear that the issuer may honor in the face of the applicant's claim of fraud. The subsection also makes clear what was not stated in former Section 5-114, that the issuer may dishonor and defend that dishonor by showing fraud or forgery of the kind stated in subsection (a). Because issuers may be liable for wrongful dishonor if they are unable to prove forgery or material fraud, presumably most issuers will choose to honor despite applicant's claims of fraud or forgery unless the applicant procures an injunction. Merely because the issuer has a right to dishonor and to defend that dishonor by showing forgery or material fraud does not mean it has a duty to the applicant to dishonor. The applicant's normal recourse is to procure an injunction, if the applicant is unable to procure an injunction, it will have a claim against the issuer only in the rare case in which it can show that the issuer did not honor in good faith.

3. Whether a beneficiary can commit fraud by presenting a draft under a clean letter of credit (one calling only for a draft and no other documents) has been much debated. Under the current formulation it would be possible but difficult for there to be fraud in such a presentation. If the applicant were able to show that the beneficiary were committing material fraud on the applicant in the underlying transaction, then payment would facilitate a material fraud by the beneficiary on the applicant and honor could be enjoined. The courts should be skeptical of claims of fraud by one who has signed a "suicide" or clean credit and thus granted a beneficiary the right to draw by mere presentation of a draft.

4. The standard for injunctive relief is high, and the burden remains on the applicant to show, by evidence and not by mere allegation, that such relief is warranted. Some courts have enjoined payments on letters of credit on insufficient showing by the applicant. For example, in *Griffin Cos. v. First Nat. Bank,* 374 N.W.2d 768 (Minn.App.1985), the court enjoined payment under a standby letter of credit, basing its decision on plaintiff's allegation, rather than competent evidence, of fraud.

There are at least two ways to prohibit injunctions against honor under this section after acceptance of a draft by the issuer. First is to define honor (see Section 5–102(a)(8)) in the particular letter of credit to occur upon acceptance and without regard to later payment of the acceptance. Second is explicitly to agree that the applicant has no right to an injunction after acceptance—whether or not the acceptance constitutes honor.

5. Although the statute deals principally with injunctions against honor, it also cautions against granting "similar relief" and the same principles apply when the applicant or issuer attempts to achieve the same legal outcome by injunction against presentation (see *Ground Air Transfer Inc. v. Westates Airlines, Inc.*, 899 F.2d 1269 (1st Cir.1990)), interpleader, declaratory judgment, or attachment. These attempts should face the same obstacles that face efforts to enjoin the issuer from paying. Expanded use of any of these devices could threaten the independence principle just as much as injunctions against honor. For that reason courts should have the same hostility to them and place the same restrictions on their use as would be applied to injunctions against honor. Courts should not allow the "sacred cow of equity to trample the tender vines of letter of credit law."

6. Section 5–109(a)(1) also protects specified third parties against the risk of fraud. By issuing a letter of credit that nominates a person to negotiate or pay, the issuer (ultimately the applicant) induces that nominated person to give value and thereby assumes the risk that a draft drawn under the letter of credit will be transferred to one with a status like that of a holder in due course who deserves to be protected against a fraud defense.

7. The "loss" to be protected against—by bond or otherwise under subsection (b)(2)—includes incidental damages. Among those are legal fees that might be incurred by the beneficiary or issuer in defending against an injunction action.

§ 5–110. Warranties.

(a) If its presentation is honored, the beneficiary warrants:

(1) to the issuer, any other person to whom presentation is made, and the applicant that there is no fraud or forgery of the kind described in Section 5–109(a); and

(2) to the applicant that the drawing does not violate any agreement between the applicant and beneficiary or any other agreement intended by them to be augmented by the letter of credit.

(b) The warranties in subsection (a) are in addition to warranties arising under Article 3, 4, 7, and 8 because of the presentation or transfer of documents covered by any of those articles.

Official Comment

1. Since the warranties in subsection (a) are not given unless a letter of credit has been honored, no breach of warranty under this subsection can be a defense to dishonor by the issuer. Any defense must be based on Section 5–108 or 5–109 and not on this section. Also, breach of the warranties by the beneficiary in subsection (a) cannot excuse the applicant's duty to reimburse.

2. The warranty in Section 5–110(a)(2) assumes that payment under the letter of credit is final. It does not run to the issuer, only to the applicant. In most cases the applicant will have a direct cause of action for breach of the underlying contract. This warranty has primary application in standby letters of credit or other circumstances where the applicant is not a party to an underlying contract with the beneficiary. It is not a

warranty that the statements made on the presentation of the documents presented are truthful nor is it a warranty that the documents strictly comply under Section 5-108(a). It is a warranty that the beneficiary has performed all the acts expressly and implicitly necessary under any underlying agreement to entitle the beneficiary to honor. If, for example, an underlying sales contract authorized the beneficiary to draw only upon "due performance" and the beneficiary drew even though it had breached the underlying contract by delivering defective goods, honor of its draw would break the warranty. By the same token, if the underlying contract authorized the beneficiary to draw only upon actual default or upon its or a third party's determination of default by the applicant and if the beneficiary drew in violation of its authorization, then upon honor of its draw the warranty would be breached. In many cases, therefore, the documents presented to the issuer will contain inaccurate statements (concerning the goods delivered or concerning default or other matters), but the breach of warranty arises not because the statements are untrue but because the beneficiary's drawing violated its express or implied obligations in the underlying transaction.

3. The damages for breach of warranty are not specified in Section 5-111. Courts may find damage analogies in Section 2-714 in Article 2 and in warranty decisions under Articles 3 and 4.

Unlike wrongful dishonor cases—where the damages usually equal the amount of the draw—the damages for breach of warranty will often be much less than the amount of the draw, sometimes zero. Assume a seller entitled to draw only on proper performance of its sales contract. Assume it breaches the sales contract in a way that gives the buyer a right to damages but no right to reject. The applicant's damages for breach of the warranty in subsection (a)(2) are limited to the damages it could recover for breach of the contract of sale. Alternatively assume an underlying agreement that authorizes a beneficiary to draw only the "amount in default." Assume a default of $200,000 and a draw of $500,000. The damages for breach of warranty would be no more than $300,000.

§ 5-111. Remedies.

(a) If an issuer wrongfully dishonors or repudiates its obligation to pay money under a letter of credit before presentation, the beneficiary, successor, or nominated person presenting on its own behalf may recover from the issuer the amount that is the subject of the dishonor or repudiation. If the issuer's obligation under the letter of credit is not for the payment of money, the claimant may obtain specific performance or, at the claimant's election, recover an amount equal to the value of performance from the issuer. In either case, the claimant may also recover incidental but not consequential damages. The claimant is not obligated to take action to avoid damages that might be due from the issuer under this subsection. If, although not obligated to do so, the claimant avoids damages, the claimant's recovery from the issuer must be reduced by the amount of damages avoided. The issuer has the burden of proving the amount of damages avoided. In the case of repudiation the claimant need not present any document.

(b) If an issuer wrongfully dishonors a draft or demand presented under a letter of credit or honors a draft or demand in breach of its obligation to the applicant, the applicant may recover damages resulting from the breach, including incidental but not consequential damages, less any amount saved as a result of the breach.

(c) If an adviser or nominated person other than a confirmer breaches an obligation under this article or an issuer breaches an obligation not covered in subsection (a) or (b), a person to whom the obligation is owed may recover damages resulting from the breach, including incidental but not consequential damages, less any amount saved as a result of the breach. To the extent of the confirmation, a confirmer has the liability of an issuer specified in this subsection and subsections (a) and (b).

(d) An issuer, nominated person, or adviser who is found liable under subsection (a), (b), or (c) shall pay interest on the amount owed thereunder from the date of wrongful dishonor or other appropriate date.

(e) Reasonable attorney's fees and other expenses of litigation must be awarded to the prevailing party in an action in which a remedy is sought under this article.

(f) Damages that would otherwise be payable by a party for breach of an obligation under this article may be liquidated by agreement or undertaking, but only in an amount or by a formula that is reasonable in light of the harm anticipated.

Official Comment

1. The right to specific performance is new. The express limitation on the duty of the beneficiary to mitigate damages adopts the position of certain courts and commentators. Because the letter of credit depends upon speed and certainty of payment, it is important that the issuer not be given an incentive to dishonor. The issuer might have an incentive to dishonor if it could rely on the burden of mitigation falling on the beneficiary, (to sell goods and sue only for the difference between the price of the goods sold and the amount due under the letter of credit). Under the scheme contemplated by Section 5–111(a), the beneficiary would present the documents to the issuer. If the issuer wrongfully dishonored, the beneficiary would have no further duty to the issuer with respect to the goods covered by documents that the issuer dishonored and returned. The issuer thus takes the risk that the beneficiary will let the goods rot or be destroyed. Of course the beneficiary may have a duty of mitigation to the applicant arising from the underlying agreement, but the issuer would not have the right to assert that duty by way of defense or setoff. See Section 5–117(d). If the beneficiary sells the goods covered by dishonored documents or if the beneficiary sells a draft after acceptance but before dishonor by the issuer, the net amount so gained should be subtracted from the amount of the beneficiary's damages—at least where the damage claim against the issuer equals or exceeds the damage suffered by the beneficiary. If, on the other hand, the beneficiary suffers damages in an underlying transaction in an amount that exceeds the amount of the wrongfully dishonored demand (e.g., where the letter of credit does not cover 100 percent of the underlying obligation), the damages avoided should not necessarily be deducted from the beneficiary's claim against the issuer. In such a case, the damages would be the lesser of (i) the amount recoverable in the absence of mitigation (that is, the amount that is subject to the dishonor or repudiation plus any incidental damages) and (ii) the damages remaining after deduction for the amount of damages actually avoided.

A beneficiary need not present documents as a condition of suit for anticipatory repudiation, but if a beneficiary could never have obtained documents necessary for a presentation conforming to the letter of credit, the beneficiary cannot recover for anticipatory repudiation of the letter of credit. *Doelger v.*

Battery Park Bank, 201 A.D. 515, 194 N.Y.S. 582 (1922) and *Decor by Nikkei Int'l, Inc. v. Federal Republic of Nigeria*, 497 F.Supp. 893 (S.D.N.Y.1980), *aff'd*, 647 F.2d 300 (2d Cir.1981), *cert. denied*, 454 U.S. 1148 (1982). The last sentence of subsection (c) does not expand the liability of a confirmer to persons to whom the confirmer would not otherwise be liable under Section 5-107.

Almost all letters of credit, including those that call for an acceptance, are "obligations to pay money" as that term is used in Section 5-111(a).

2. What damages "result" from improper honor is for the courts to decide. Even though an issuer pays a beneficiary in violation of Section 5-108(a) or of its contract with the applicant, it may have no liability to an applicant. If the underlying contract has been fully performed, the applicant may not have been damaged by the issuer's breach. Such a case would occur when *A* contracts for goods at $100 per ton, but, upon delivery, the market value of conforming goods has decreased to $25 per ton. If the issuer pays over discrepancies, there should be no recovery by *A* for the price differential if the issuer's breach did not alter the applicant's obligation under the underlying contract, i.e., to pay $100 per ton for goods now worth $25 per ton. On the other hand, if the applicant intends to resell the goods and must itself satisfy the strict compliance requirements under a second letter of credit in connection with its sale, the applicant may be damaged by the issuer's payment despite discrepancies because the applicant itself may then be unable to procure honor on the letter of credit where it is the beneficiary, and may be unable to mitigate its damages by enforcing its rights against others in the underlying transaction. Note that an issuer found liable to its applicant may have recourse under Section 5-117 by subrogation to the applicant's claim against the beneficiary or other persons.

One who inaccurately advises a letter of credit breaches its obligation to the beneficiary, but may cause no damage. If the beneficiary knows the terms of the letter of credit and understands the advice to be inaccurate, the beneficiary will have suffered no damage as a result of the adviser's breach.

3. Since the confirmer has the rights and duties of an issuer, in general it has an issuer's liability, see subsection (c). The confirmer is usually a confirming bank. A confirming bank often also plays the role of an adviser. If it breaks its obligation to the beneficiary, the confirming bank may have liability as an issuer or, depending upon the obligation that was broken, as an adviser. For example, a wrongful dishonor would give it liability as an issuer under Section 5-111(a). On the other hand a confirming bank that broke its obligation to advise the credit but did not commit wrongful dishonor would be treated under Section 5-111(c).

4. Consequential damages for breach of obligations under this article are excluded in the belief that these damages can best be avoided by the beneficiary or the applicant and out of the fear that imposing consequential damages on issuers would raise the cost of the letter of credit to a level that might render it uneconomic. *A fortiori* punitive and exemplary damages are excluded, however, this section does not bar recovery of consequential or even punitive damages for breach of statutory or common law duties arising outside of this article.

5. The section does not specify a rate of interest. It leaves the setting of the rate to the court. It would be appropriate for a court to use the rate that would normally apply in that court in other situations where interest is imposed by law.

6. The court must award attorney's fees to the prevailing party, whether that party is an applicant, a beneficiary, an issuer, a nominated person, or adviser. Since the issuer may be entitled to recover its legal fees and costs from the applicant under the reimbursement agreement, allowing the issuer to recover those fees from a losing beneficiary may also protect the applicant against undeserved losses. The party entitled to attorneys' fees has been described as the "prevailing

party." Sometimes it will be unclear which party "prevailed," for example, where there are multiple issues and one party wins on some and the other party wins on others. Determining which is the prevailing party is in the discretion of the court. Subsection (e) authorizes attorney's fees in all actions where a remedy is sought "under this article." It applies even when the remedy might be an injunction under Section 5–109 or when the claimed remedy is otherwise outside of Section 5–111. Neither an issuer nor a confirmer should be treated as a "losing" party when an injunction is granted to the applicant over the objection of the issuer or confirmer; accordingly neither should be liable for fees and expenses in that case.

"Expenses of litigation" is intended to be broader than "costs." For example, expense of litigation would include travel expenses of witnesses, fees for expert witnesses, and expenses associated with taking depositions.

7. For the purposes of Section 5–111(f) "harm anticipated" must be anticipated at the time when the agreement that includes the liquidated damage clause is executed or at the time when the undertaking that includes the clause is issued. See Section 2A–504.

§ 5–112. Transfer of Letter of Credit.

(a) Except as otherwise provided in Section 5–113, unless a letter of credit provides that it is transferable, the right of a beneficiary to draw or otherwise demand performance under a letter of credit may not be transferred.

(b) Even if a letter of credit provides that it is transferable, the issuer may refuse to recognize or carry out a transfer if:

(1) the transfer would violate applicable law; or

(2) the transferor or transferee has failed to comply with any requirement stated in the letter of credit or any other requirement relating to transfer imposed by the issuer which is within the standard practice referred to in Section 5–108(e) or is otherwise reasonable under the circumstances.

Official Comment

1. In order to protect the applicant's reliance on the designated beneficiary, letter of credit law traditionally has forbidden the beneficiary to convey to third parties its right to draw or demand payment under the letter of credit. Subsection (a) codifies that rule. The term "transfer" refers to the beneficiary's conveyance of that right. Absent incorporation of the UCP (which make elaborate provision for partial transfer of a commercial letter of credit) or similar trade practice and absent other express indication in the letter of credit that the term is used to mean something else, a term in the letter of credit indicating that the beneficiary has the right to transfer should be taken to mean that the beneficiary may convey to a third party its right to draw or demand payment. Even in that case, the issuer or other person controlling the transfer may make the beneficiary's right to transfer subject to conditions, such as timely notification, payment of a fee, delivery of the letter of credit to the issuer or other person controlling the transfer, or execution of appropriate forms to document the transfer. A nominated person who is not a confirmer has no obligation to recognize a transfer.

The power to establish "requirements" does not include the right absolutely to refuse to recognize transfers under a transferable letter of credit. An issuer who wishes to retain the right to deny all transfers should not issue transferable letters of credit or should incorporate the UCP. By stating its requirements in the letter of credit an issuer may impose any requirement without regard to its conformity to practice or reasonableness. Transfer requirements of issuers and nominated persons must be made known to potential transferors and transferees to enable those parties to comply with the requirements. A common method of making such requirements known is to use a form that indicates the information that must be provided and the instructions that must be given to enable the issuer or nominated person to comply with a request to transfer.

2. The issuance of a transferable letter of credit with the concurrence of the applicant is *ipso facto* an agreement by the issuer and applicant to permit a beneficiary to transfer its drawing right and permit a nominated person to recognize and carry out that transfer without further notice to them. In international commerce, transferable letters of credit are often issued under circumstances in which a nominated person or adviser is expected to facilitate the transfer from the original beneficiary to a transferee and to deal with that transferee. In those circumstances it is the responsibility of the nominated person or adviser to establish procedures satisfactory to protect itself against double presentation or dispute about the right to draw under the letter of credit. Commonly such a person will control the transfer by requiring that the original letter of credit be given to it or by causing a paper copy marked as an original to be issued where the original letter of credit was electronic. By keeping possession of the original letter of credit the nominated person or adviser can minimize or entirely exclude the possibility that the original beneficiary could properly procure payment from another bank. If the letter of credit requires presentation of the original letter of credit itself, no other payment could be procured. In addition to imposing whatever requirements it considers appropriate to protect itself against double payment the person that is facilitating the transfer has a right to charge an appropriate fee for its activity.

"Transfer" of a letter of credit should be distinguished from "assignment of proceeds." The former is analogous to a novation or a substitution of beneficiaries. It contemplates not merely payment to but also performance by the transferee. For example, under the typical terms of transfer for a commercial letter of credit, a transferee could comply with a letter of credit transferred to it by signing and presenting its own draft and invoice. An assignee of proceeds, on the other hand, is wholly dependent on the presentation of a draft and invoice signed by the beneficiary.

By agreeing to the issuance of a transferable letter of credit, which is not qualified or limited, the applicant may lose control over the identity of the person whose performance will earn payment under the letter of credit.

§ 5-113. Transfer by Operation of Law.

(a) A successor of a beneficiary may consent to amendments, sign and present documents, and receive payment or other items of value in the name of the beneficiary without disclosing its status as a successor.

(b) A successor of a beneficiary may consent to amendments, sign and present documents, and receive payment or other items of value in its own name as the disclosed successor of the beneficiary. Except as otherwise provided in subsection (e), an issuer shall recognize a disclosed successor of a beneficiary as beneficiary in full substitution for its predecessor upon compliance with the requirements for recognition by the issuer of a transfer of drawing rights by operation of law under the standard practice referred to in

Section 5–108(e) or, in the absence of such a practice, compliance with other reasonable procedures sufficient to protect the issuer.

(c) An issuer is not obliged to determine whether a purported successor is a successor of a beneficiary or whether the signature of a purported successor is genuine or authorized.

(d) Honor of a purported successor's apparently complying presentation under subsection (a) or (b) has the consequences specified in Section 5–108(i) even if the purported successor is not the successor of a beneficiary. Documents signed in the name of the beneficiary or of a disclosed successor by a person who is neither the beneficiary nor the successor of the beneficiary are forged documents for the purposes of Section 5–109.

(e) An issuer whose rights of reimbursement are not covered by subsection (d) or substantially similar law and any confirmer or nominated person may decline to recognize a presentation under subsection (b).

(f) A beneficiary whose name is changed after the issuance of a letter of credit has the same rights and obligations as a successor of a beneficiary under this section.

Official Comment

This section affirms the result in *Pastor v. Nat. Republic Bank of Chicago,* 76 Ill.2d 139, 390 N.E.2d 894 (Ill.1979) and *Federal Deposit Insurance Co. v. Bank of Boulder,* 911 F.2d 1466 (10th Cir.1990).

An issuer's requirements for recognition of a successor's status might include presentation of a certificate of merger, a court order appointing a bankruptcy trustee or receiver, a certificate of appointment as bankruptcy trustee, or the like. The issuer is entitled to rely upon such documents which on their face demonstrate that presentation is made by a successor of a beneficiary. It is not obliged to make an independent investigation to determine the fact of succession.

§ 5–114. Assignment of Proceeds.

(a) In this section, "proceeds of a letter of credit" means the cash, check, accepted draft, or other item of value paid or delivered upon honor or giving of value by the issuer or any nominated person under the letter of credit. The term does not include a beneficiary's drawing rights or documents presented by the beneficiary.

(b) A beneficiary may assign its right to part or all of the proceeds of a letter of credit. The beneficiary may do so before presentation as a present assignment of its right to receive proceeds contingent upon its compliance with the terms and conditions of the letter of credit.

(c) An issuer or nominated person need not recognize an assignment of proceeds of a letter of credit until it consents to the assignment.

(d) An issuer or nominated person has no obligation to give or withhold its consent to an assignment of proceeds of a letter of credit, but consent may not be unreasonably withheld if the assignee possesses and exhibits the letter of credit and presentation of the letter of credit is a condition to honor.

(e) Rights of a transferee beneficiary or nominated person are independent of the beneficiary's assignment of the proceeds of a letter of credit and are superior to the assignee's right to the proceeds.

(f) Neither the rights recognized by this section between an assignee and an issuer, transferee beneficiary, or nominated person nor the issuer's or nominated person's payment of proceeds to an assignee or a third person affect the rights between the assignee and any person other than the issuer, transferee beneficiary, or nominated person. The mode of creating and perfecting a security interest in or granting an assignment of a beneficiary's rights to proceeds is governed by Article 9 or other law. Against persons other than the issuer, transferee beneficiary, or nominated person, the rights and obligations arising upon the creation of a security interest or other assignment of a beneficiary's right to proceeds and its perfection are governed by Article 9 or other law.

Official Comment

1. Subsection (b) expressly validates the beneficiary's present assignment of letter of credit proceeds if made after the credit is established but before the proceeds are realized. This section adopts the prevailing usage—"assignment of proceeds"—to an assignee. That terminology carries with it no implication, however, that an assignee acquires no interest until the proceeds are paid by the issuer. For example, an "assignment of the right to proceeds" of a letter of credit for purposes of security that meets the requirements of Section 9-203(1) would constitute the present creation of a security interest in that right. This security interest can be perfected by possession (Section 9-305) if the letter of credit is in written form. Although subsection (a) explains the meaning of "'proceeds' of a letter of credit," it should be emphasized that those proceeds also may be Article 9 proceeds of other collateral. For example, if a seller of inventory receives a letter of credit to support the account that arises upon the sale, payments made under the letter of credit are Article 9 proceeds of the inventory, account, and any document of title covering the inventory. Thus, the secured party who had a perfected security interest in that inventory, account, or document has a perfected security interest in the proceeds collected under the letter of credit, so long as they are identifiable cash proceeds (Section 9-306(2), (3)). This perfection is continuous, regardless of whether the secured party perfected a security interest in the right to letter of credit proceeds.

2. An assignee's rights to enforce an assignment of proceeds against an issuer and the priority of the assignee's rights against a nominated person or transferee beneficiary are governed by Article 5. Those rights and that priority are stated in subsections (c), (d), and (e). Note also that Section 4-210 gives first priority to a collecting bank that has given value for a documentary draft.

3. By requiring that an issuer or nominated person consent to the assignment of proceeds of a letter of credit, subsections (c) and (d) follow more closely recognized national and international letter of credit practices than did prior law. In most circumstances, it has always been advisable for the assignee to obtain the consent of the issuer in order better to safeguard its right to the proceeds. When notice of an assignment has been received, issuers normally have required signatures on a consent form. This practice is reflected in the revision. By unconditionally consenting to such an assignment, the issuer or nominated person becomes bound, subject to the rights of the superior parties specified in subsection (e), to pay to the assignee the assigned letter of credit proceeds that the issuer or nominated person would otherwise pay to the beneficiary or another assignee.

Where the letter of credit must be presented as a condition to honor and the assignee holds and exhibits the letter of credit to the issuer or nominated person, the risk to the issuer or nominated person of having to pay twice is minimized. In such a situation, subsection (d) provides that the issuer or nominated person may not unreasonably withhold its consent to the assignment.

§ 5–115. Statute of Limitations.

An action to enforce a right or obligation arising under this article must be commenced within one year after the expiration date of the relevant letter of credit or one year after the [claim for relief] [cause of action] accrues, whichever occurs later. A [claim for relief] [cause of action] accrues when the breach occurs, regardless of the aggrieved party's lack of knowledge of the breach.

Official Comment

1. This section is based upon Sections 4–111 and 2–725(2).

2. This section applies to all claims for which there are remedies under Section 5–111 and to other claims made under this article, such as claims for breach of warranty under Section 5–110. Because it covers all claims under Section 5–111, the statute of limitations applies not only to wrongful dishonor claims against the issuer but also to claims between the issuer and the applicant arising from the reimbursement agreement. These might be for reimbursement (issuer v. applicant) or for breach of the reimbursement contract by wrongful honor (applicant v. issuer).

3. The statute of limitations, like the rest of the statute, applies only to a letter of credit issued on or after the effective date and only to transactions, events, obligations, or duties arising out of or associated with such a letter. If a letter of credit was issued before the effective date and an obligation on that letter of credit was breached after the effective date, the complaining party could bring its suit within the time that would have been permitted prior to the adoption of Section 5–115 and would not be limited by the terms of Section 5–115.

§ 5–116. Choice of Law and Forum.

(a) The liability of an issuer, nominated person, or adviser for action or omission is governed by the law of the jurisdiction chosen by an agreement in the form of a record signed or otherwise authenticated by the affected parties in the manner provided in Section 5–104 or by a provision in the person's letter of credit, confirmation, or other undertaking. The jurisdiction whose law is chosen need not bear any relation to the transaction.

(b) Unless subsection (a) applies, the liability of an issuer, nominated person, or adviser for action or omission is governed by the law of the jurisdiction in which the person is located. The person is considered to be located at the address indicated in the person's undertaking. If more than one address is indicated, the person is considered to be located at the address from which the person's undertaking was issued. For the purpose of jurisdiction, choice of law, and recognition of interbranch letters of credit, but not enforcement of a judgment, all branches of a bank are considered separate juridical entities and a bank is considered to be located at the place where its relevant branch is considered to be located under this subsection.

(c) Except as otherwise provided in this subsection, the liability of an issuer, nominated person, or adviser is governed by any rules of custom or practice, such as the Uniform Customs and Practice for Documentary Credits, to which the letter of credit, confirmation, or other undertaking is expressly made subject. If (i) this article would govern the liability of an issuer, nominated person, or adviser under subsection (a) or (b), (ii) the relevant undertaking incorporates rules of custom or practice, and (iii) there is conflict between this article and those rules as applied to that undertaking, those rules govern except to the extent of any conflict with the nonvariable provisions specified in Section 5-103(c).

(d) If there is conflict between this article and Article 3, 4, 4A, or 9, this article governs.

(e) The forum for settling disputes arising out of an undertaking within this article may be chosen in the manner and with the binding effect that governing law may be chosen in accordance with subsection (a).

Official Comment

1. Although it would be possible for the parties to agree otherwise, the law normally chosen by agreement under subsection (a) and that provided in the absence of agreement under subsection (b) is the substantive law of a particular jurisdiction not including the choice of law principles of that jurisdiction. Thus, two parties, an issuer and an applicant, both located in Oklahoma might choose the law of New York. Unless they agree otherwise, the section anticipates that they wish the substantive law of New York to apply to their transaction and they do not intend that a New York choice of law principle might direct a court to Oklahoma law. By the same token, the liability of an issuer located in New York is governed by New York substantive law—in the absence of agreement—even in circumstances in which choice of law principles found in the common law of New York might direct one to the law of another State. Subsection (b) states the relevant choice of law principles and it should not be subordinated to some other choice of law rule. Within the States of the United States *renvoi* will not be a problem once every jurisdiction has enacted Section 5-116 because every jurisdiction will then have the same choice of law rule and in a particular case all choice of law rules will point to the same substantive law.

Subsection (b) does not state a choice of law rule for the "liability of an applicant." However, subsection (b) does state a choice of law rule for the liability of an issuer, nominated person, or adviser, and since some of the issues in suits by applicants against those persons involve the "liability of an issuer, nominated person, or adviser," subsection (b) states the choice of law rule for those issues. Because an issuer may have liability to a confirmer both as an issuer (Section 5-108(a), Comment 5 to Section 5-108) and as an applicant (Section 5-107(a), Comment 1 to Section 5-107, Section 5-108(i)), subsection (b) may state the choice of law rule for some but not all of the issuer's liability in a suit by a confirmer.

2. Because the confirmer or other nominated person may choose different law from that chosen by the issuer or may be located in a different jurisdiction and fail to choose law, it is possible that a confirmer or nominated person may be obligated to pay (under their law) but will not be entitled to payment from the issuer (under its law). Similarly, the rights of an unreimbursed issuer, confirmer, or nominated person against a beneficiary under Section 5-109, 5-110, or 5-117, will not necessarily be governed by the same law that applies to the issuer's or confirmer's obligation upon presentation. Because the UCP and other practice are incorporated in most international letters of credit, disputes arising from different legal obligations to honor have not been frequent. Since Section 5-108 incorporates standard practice, these problems

should be further minimized—at least to the extent that the same practice is and continues to be widely followed.

3. This section does not permit what is now authorized by the nonuniform Section 5-102(4) in New York. Under the current law in New York a letter of credit that incorporates the UCP is not governed in any respect by Article 5. Under revised Section 5-116 letters of credit that incorporate the UCP or similar practice will still be subject to Article 5 in certain respects. First, incorporation of the UCP or other practice does not override the nonvariable terms of Article 5. Second, where there is no conflict between Article 5 and the relevant provision of the UCP or other practice, both apply. Third, practice provisions incorporated in a letter of credit will not be effective if they fail to comply with Section 5-103(c). Assume, for example, that a practice provision purported to free a party from any liability unless it were "grossly negligent" or that the practice generally limited the remedies that one party might have against another. Depending upon the circumstances, that disclaimer or limitation of liability might be ineffective because of Section 5-103(c).

Even though Article 5 is generally consistent with UCP 500, it is not necessarily consistent with other rules or with versions of the UCP that may be adopted after Article 5's revision, or with other practices that may develop. Rules of practice incorporated in the letter of credit or other undertaking are those in effect when the letter of credit or other undertaking is issued. Except in the unusual cases discussed in the immediately preceding paragraph, practice adopted in a letter of credit will override the rules of Article 5 and the parties to letter of credit transactions must be familiar with practice (such as future versions of the UCP) that is explicitly adopted in letters of credit.

4. In several ways Article 5 conflicts with and overrides similar matters governed by Articles 3 and 4. For example, "draft" is more broadly defined in letter of credit practice than under Section 3-104. The time allowed for honor and the required notification of reasons for dishonor are different in letter of credit practice than in the handling of documentary and other drafts under Articles 3 and 4.

5. Subsection (e) must be read in conjunction with existing law governing subject matter jurisdiction. If the local law restricts a court to certain subject matter jurisdiction not including letter of credit disputes, subsection (e) does not authorize parties to choose that forum. For example, the parties' agreement under Section 5-116(e) would not confer jurisdiction on a probate court to decide a letter of credit case.

If the parties choose a forum under subsection (e) and if—because of other law—that forum will not take jurisdiction, the parties' agreement or undertaking should then be construed (for the purpose of forum selection) as though it did not contain a clause choosing a particular forum. That result is necessary to avoid sentencing the parties to eternal purgatory where neither the chosen State nor the State which would have jurisdiction but for the clause will take jurisdiction—the former in disregard of the clause and the latter in honor of the clause.

§ 5-117. Subrogation of Issuer, Applicant, and Nominated Person.

(a) An issuer that honors a beneficiary's presentation is subrogated to the rights of the beneficiary to the same extent as if the issuer were a secondary obligor of the underlying obligation owed to the beneficiary and of the applicant to the same extent as if the issuer were the secondary obligor of the underlying obligation owed to the applicant.

(b) An applicant that reimburses an issuer is subrogated to the rights of the issuer against any beneficiary, presenter, or nominated person to the same extent as if the applicant were the secondary obligor of the obligations owed to the issuer and has the rights of subrogation of the issuer to the rights of the beneficiary stated in subsection (a).

(c) A nominated person who pays or gives value against a draft or demand presented under a letter of credit is subrogated to the rights of:

(1) the issuer against the applicant to the same extent as if the nominated person were a secondary obligor of the obligation owed to the issuer by the applicant;

(2) the beneficiary to the same extent as if the nominated person were a secondary obligor of the underlying obligation owed to the beneficiary; and

(3) the applicant to same extent as if the nominated person were a secondary obligor of the underlying obligation owed to the applicant.

(d) Notwithstanding any agreement or term to the contrary, the rights of subrogation stated in subsections (a) and (b) do not arise until the issuer honors the letter of credit or otherwise pays and the rights in subsection (c) do not arise until the nominated person pays or otherwise gives value. Until then, the issuer, nominated person, and the applicant do not derive under this section present or prospective rights forming the basis of a claim, defense, or excuse.

Official Comment

1. By itself this section does not grant any right of subrogation. It grants only the right that would exist if the person seeking subrogation "were a secondary obligor." (The term "secondary obligor" refers to a surety, guarantor, or other person against whom or whose property an obligee has recourse with respect to the obligation of a third party. See Restatement of the Law Third, Suretyship § 1 (1995).) If the secondary obligor would not have a right to subrogation in the circumstances in which one is claimed under this section, none is granted by this section. In effect, the section does no more than to remove an impediment that some courts have found to subrogation because they conclude that the issuer's or other claimant's rights are "independent" of the underlying obligation. If, for example, a secondary obligor would not have a subrogation right because its payment did not fully satisfy the underlying obligation, none would be available under this section. The section indorses the position of Judge Becker in *Tudor Development Group, Inc. v. United States Fidelity and Guaranty*, 968 F.2d 357 (3rd Cir.1991).

2. To preserve the independence of the letter of credit obligation and to insure that subrogation not be used as an offensive weapon by an issuer or others, the admonition in subsection (d) must be carefully observed. Only one who has completed its performance in a letter of credit transaction can have a right to subrogation. For example, an issuer may not dishonor and then defend its dishonor or assert a setoff on the ground that it is subrogated to another person's rights. Nor may the issuer complain after honor that its subrogation rights have been impaired by any good faith dealings between the beneficiary and the applicant or any other person. Assume, for example, that the beneficiary under a standby letter of credit is a mortgagee. If the mortgagee were obliged to issue a release of the mortgage upon payment of the underlying debt (by the issuer under the letter of credit), that release might impair the issuer's rights of subrogation, but the bene-

ficiary would have no liability to the issuer for having granted that release.

Transition Provisions

§ [ ]. Effective Date.

This [Act] shall become effective on ______, 199__.

§ [ ]. Repeal.

This [Act] [repeals] [amends] [insert citation to existing Article 5].

§ [ ]. Applicability.

This [Act] applies to a letter of credit that is issued on or after the effective date of this [Act]. This [Act] does not apply to a transaction, event, obligation, or duty arising out of or associated with a letter of credit that was issued before the effective date of this [Act].

§ [ ]. Savings Clause.

A transaction arising out of or associated with a letter of credit that was issued before the effective date of this [Act] and the rights, obligations, and interests flowing from that transaction are governed by any statute or other law amended or repealed by this [Act] as if repeal or amendment had not occurred and may be terminated, completed, consummated, or enforced under that statute or other law.

CONFORMING AMENDMENTS TO ARTICLES 1, 2, AND 9

See Appendix XIV, infra.

REPEALER OF ARTICLE 6
BULK TRANSFERS
and
[REVISED] ARTICLE 6
BULK SALES

(States To Select One Alternative)

[For the Text and Official Comments of Article 6 as it existed prior to revision in 1989, see Appendix IV, infra.]

ALTERNATIVE A

[END OF ALTERNATIVE A]

ALTERNATIVE B

[END OF ALTERNATIVE B]

National Conference of Commissioners on Uniform State Laws

CO–REPORTERS

Steven L. Harris, Champaign, Illinois

William D. Hawkland, Baton Rouge, Louisiana

DRAFTING COMMITTEE

CHAIRMAN

Gerald L. Bepko, Indianapolis, Indiana

MEMBERS

William C. Hillman, Providence, Rhode Island

Frederick H. Miller, Norman, Oklahoma

Raymond P. Pepe, Harrisburg, Pennsylvania

Donald J. Rapson, Livingston, New Jersey, *The American Law Institute Representative*

Curtis R. Reitz, Philadelphia, Pennsylvania

Millard H. Ruud, Austin, Texas, *Drafting Liaison*

Hiroshi Sakai, Honolulu, Hawaii

Michael P. Sullivan, Minneapolis, Minnesota, *President (Member Ex Officio)*

Neal Ossen, Hartford, Connecticut, *Chairman, Division C (Member Ex Officio)*

REVIEW COMMITTEE
CHAIRMAN

John A. Chanin, Honolulu, Hawaii

MEMBERS

Stephen E. Cicilline, Providence, Rhode Island

Morris W. Macey, Atlanta, Georgia

Robert G. Pugh, Shreveport, Louisiana

ABA ADVISOR, SECTION OF CORPORATION, BANKING, AND BUSINESS LAW

Howard Ruda, New York, New York

ADDITIONAL ADVISORS

Don L. Baker, Commercial Law League of America

William Z. Fox, National Auctioneers Association

Thomas J. Greco, American Bankers Association

Frank R. Kennedy, National Bankruptcy Conference

James E. Snider, National Association of Credit Management

Douglas H. Williams, National Commercial Finance Association

PREFATORY NOTE

Background. Bulk sale legislation originally was enacted in response to a fraud perceived to be common around the turn of the century: a merchant would acquire his stock in trade on credit, then sell his entire inventory ("in bulk") and abscond with the proceeds, leaving creditors unpaid. The creditors had a right to sue the merchant on the unpaid debts, but that right often was of little practical value. Even if the merchant-debtor was found, in personam jurisdiction over him might not have been readily available. Those creditors who succeeded in obtaining a judgment often were unable to satisfy it because the defrauding seller had spent or hidden the sale proceeds. Nor did the creditors ordinarily have recourse to the merchandise sold. The transfer of the inventory to an innocent buyer effectively immunized the goods from the reach of the seller's creditors. The creditors of a bulk seller thus might be left without a means to satisfy their claims.

To a limited extent, the law of fraudulent conveyances ameliorated the creditors' plight. When the buyer in bulk was in league with the seller or paid less than full value for the inventory, fraudulent conveyance law enabled the defrauded creditors to avoid the sale and apply the transferred inventory toward the satisfaction of their claims against the seller. But fraudulent conveyance law provided no remedy against persons who bought in good faith, without reason to know of the seller's intention to pocket the proceeds and disappear, and for adequate value. In those cases, the only remedy for the seller's creditors was to attempt to recover from the absconding seller.

State legislatures responded to this perceived "bulk sale risk" with a variety of legislative enactments. Common to these statutes was the imposition of a duty on the buyer in bulk to notify the seller's creditors of the impending sale. The buyer's failure to comply with these and any other statutory duties generally afforded the seller's creditors a remedy analogous to the remedy for fraudulent conveyances: the creditors acquired the right to set aside the sale and reach the transferred inventory in the hands of the buyer.

Like its predecessors, Article 6 (1987 Official Text) is remarkable in that it obligates buyers in bulk to incur costs to protect the interests of the seller's creditors, with whom they usually have no relationship. Even more striking is that Article 6 affords creditors a remedy against a good faith purchaser for full value without notice of any wrongdoing on the part of the seller. The Article thereby impedes normal business transactions, many of which can be expected to benefit the seller's creditors. For this reason, Article 6 has been subjected to serious criticism. See, e.g., Rapson, *U.C.C. Article 6: Should It Be Revised or "Deep-Sixed"?* 38 Bus.Law. 1753 (1983).

In the legal context in which Article 6 (1987 Official Text) and its nonuniform predecessors were enacted, the benefits to creditors appeared to justify the costs of interfering with good faith transactions. Today, however, creditors are better able than ever to make informed decisions about whether to extend credit. Changes in technology have enabled credit reporting services to provide fast, accurate, and more complete credit histories at relatively little cost. A search of the public real estate and personal property records will disclose most encumbrances on a debtor's property with little inconvenience.

In addition, changes in the law now afford creditors greater opportunities to collect their debts. The development of "minimum contacts" with the forum state as a basis for *in personam* jurisdiction and the universal promulgation of state long-arm statutes and rules have greatly improved the possibility of obtaining personal jurisdiction over a debtor who flees to another state. Widespread enactment of the Uniform Enforcement of Foreign Judgments Act has facilitated nation-wide collection of judgments. And to the extent that a bulk sale is fraudulent and the buyer is a party to fraud, aggrieved creditors have a remedy under the Uniform Fraudulent Transfer Act. Moreover, creditors of a merchant no longer face the choice of extending unsecured credit or no credit at all. Retaining an interest in inventory to secure its price has become relatively simple and inexpensive under Article 9.

Finally, there is no evidence that, in today's economy, fraudulent bulk sales are frequent enough, or engender credit losses significant enough, to require regulation of all bulk sales, including the vast majority that are conducted in good faith. Indeed, the experience of the Canadian Province of British Columbia, which repealed its Sale of Goods in Bulk Act in 1985, and of the United Kingdom, which never has enacted bulk sales legislation, suggests that regulation of bulk sales no longer is necessary.

Recommendation. The National Conference of Commissioners on Uniform State Laws and the American Law Institute believe that changes in the business and legal contexts in which sales are conducted have made regulation of bulk sales unnecessary. The Conference and the Institute therefore withdraw their support for Article 6 of the Uniform Commercial Code and encourage those states that have enacted the Article to repeal it.

The Conference and the Institute recognize that bulk sales may present a particular problem in some states and that some legislatures may wish to continue to regulate bulk sales. They believe that existing Article 6 has become inadequate for that purpose. For those states that are disinclined to repeal Article 6, they have promulgated a revised version of Article 6. The revised Article is designed to afford better protection to creditors while minimizing the impediments to good-faith transactions.

The Official Comment to Section 6–101 explains the rationale underlying the revisions and highlights the major substantive changes reflected in them. Of particular interest is Section 6–103(1)(a), which limits the application of the revised Article to bulk sales by sellers whose principal business is the sale of inventory from stock. In approving this provision, the Conference and the Institute were mindful that some states have expanded the coverage of existing Article 6 to include bulk sales conducted by sellers whose principal business is the operation of a restaurant or tavern. Expansion of the scope of revised Article 6 is inconsistent with the recommendation that Article 6 be repealed. Nevertheless, the inclusion of restaurants and taverns within the scope of the revised Article as it is enacted in particular jurisdictions would not disturb the internal logic and structure of the revised Article.

ALTERNATIVE A

Section

[§ 1. Repeal.

Article 6 and Section 9–111 of the Uniform Commercial Code are hereby repealed, effective ______.

§ 2. Amendment.

Section 1–105(2) of the Uniform Commercial Code is hereby amended to read as follows:

(2) Where one of the following provisions of this Act specifies the applicable law, that provision governs and a contrary agreement is effective only to the extent permitted by the law (including the conflict of laws rules) so specified:

Rights of creditors against sold goods. Section 2–402.

Applicability of the Article on Leases. Sections 2A–105 and 2A–106.

Applicability of the Article on Bank Deposits and Collections. Section 4–102.

~~Bulk transfers subject to the Article on Bulk Transfers. Section 6–102.~~

Applicability of the Article on Investment Securities. Section 8–106.

Perfection provisions of the Article on Secured Transactions. Section 9–103.

§ 3. Amendment.

Section 2–403(4) of the Uniform Commercial Code is hereby amended to read as follows:

(4) The rights of other purchasers of goods and of lien creditors are governed by the Articles on Secured Transactions (Article 9)~~, Bulk Transfers (Article 6)~~ and Documents of Title (Article 7).

§ 4. Savings Clause.

Rights and obligations that arose under Article 6 and Section 9–111 of the Uniform Commercial Code before their repeal remain valid and may be enforced as though those statutes had not been repealed.]

[END OF ALTERNATIVE A]

ALTERNATIVE B

Section

[§ 6–101. Short Title.

This Article shall be known and may be cited as Uniform Commercial Code—Bulk Sales.

Official Comment

Prior Uniform Statutory Provision: Section 6–101 (1987 Official Text).

Change: This Article applies only to sales, as defined in Section 2–103(1), and not to other transfers.

Purpose of Change: Transfers other than sales, *e.g.*, grants of security interests, do not present risks to creditors necessitating advance notice in accordance with the provisions of this Article. The Uniform Fraudulent Transfer Act affords a remedy to creditors who are injured by donative transfers.

Rationale for Revision of the Article:

Article 6 (1987 Official Text) imposes upon transferees in bulk several duties toward creditors of the transferor. These duties include the duty to notify the creditors of the impending bulk transfer and, in those jurisdictions that have adopted optional Section 6–106, the duty to assure that the new consideration for the transfer is applied to pay debts of the transferor.

Compliance with the provisions of Article 6 can be burdensome, particularly when the transferor has a large number of creditors. When the transferor is actively engaged in business at a number of locations, assembling a current list of creditors may not be possible. Mailing a notice to each creditor may prove costly. When the goods that are the subject of the transfer are located in several jurisdictions, the transferor may be obligated to comply with Article 6 as enacted in each jurisdiction. The widespread enactment of nonuniform amendments makes compliance with Article 6 in multiple-state transactions problematic. Moreover, the Article requires compliance even when there is no reason to believe that the transferor is conducting a fraudulent transfer, *e.g.*, when the transferor is scaling down the business but remaining available to creditors.

Article 6 imposes strict liability for noncompliance. Failure to comply with the provisions of the Article renders the transfer ineffective, even when the transferor has attempted compliance in good faith, and even when no creditor has been injured by the noncompliance. The potential liability for minor noncompliance may be high. If the transferor should enter bankruptcy before the expiration of the limitation period, Bankruptcy Code §§ 544(b), 550(a), 11 U.S.C. §§ 544(b), 550(a), may enable the transferor's bankruptcy trustee to set aside the entire transaction and recover from the noncomplying transferee all the goods transferred or their value. The trustee has this power even though the noncompliance was with respect to only a single creditor holding a small claim.

The benefits that compliance affords to creditors do not justify the substantial burdens and risks that the Article imposes upon good faith purchasers of business assets. The Article requires that notice be sent only ten days before the transferee takes possession of the goods or pays for them, whichever happens first. Given the delay between sending the notice and its receipt, creditors have scant opportunity to avail themselves of a judicial or nonjudicial remedy before the transfer has been consummated.

In some cases Article 6 may have the unintended effect of injuring, rather than aiding, creditors of the transferor. Those transferees who recognize the burdens and risks that Article 6 imposes upon them sometimes agree to purchase only at a reduced price. Others refuse to purchase at all, leaving the creditors to realize only the liquidation value, rather than the going concern value, of the business goods.

As a response to these inadequacies and others, the National Conference of Commissioners on Uniform State Laws has completely revised Article 6. This revision is designed to reduce the burdens and risks imposed upon good-faith buyers of business assets while increasing the protection afforded to creditors. Among the major changes it makes are the following:

—this Article applies only when the buyer has notice, or after reasonable inquiry would have had notice, that the seller will not continue to operate the same or a similar kind of business after the sale (Section 6–102(1)(c)).

—this Article does not apply to sales in which the value of the property otherwise available to creditors is less than $10,000 or those in which the value of the property is greater than $25,000,000 (Section 6–103(3)(*l*)).

—the choice-of-law provision (Sections 6–103(1)(b) and 6–103(2)) limits the applicable law to that of one jurisdiction.

—when the seller is indebted to a large number of persons, the buyer need neither obtain a list of those persons nor send individual notices to each person but instead may give notice by filing (Sections 6–105(2) and 6–104(2)).

—the notice period is increased from 10 days to 45 days (Section 6–105(5)), and the statute of limitations is extended from six months to one year (Section 6–110).

—the notice must include a copy of a "schedule of distribution," which sets forth how the net contract price is to be distributed (Sections 6–105(3) and 6–106(1)).

—a buyer who makes a good faith effort to comply with the requirements of this Article or to exclude the sale from the application of this Article, or who acts on the good faith belief that this Article does not apply to the sale, is not liable for noncompliance (Section 6–107(3)).

—a buyer's noncompliance does not render the sale ineffective or otherwise affect the buyer's title to the goods; rather, the liability of a noncomplying buyer is for damages caused by the noncompliance (Sections 6–107(1) and 6–107(8)).

In addition to making these and other major substantive changes, revised Article 6 resolves the ambiguities that three decades of law practice, judicial construction, and scholarly inquiry have disclosed.

§ 6–102. Definitions and Index of Definitions.

(1) In this Article, unless the context otherwise requires:

(a) "Assets" means the inventory that is the subject of a bulk sale and any tangible and intangible personal property used or held for use primarily in, or arising from, the seller's business and sold in connection with that inventory, but the term does not include:

(i) fixtures (section 9–313(1)(a)) other than readily removable factory and office machines;

(ii) the lessee's interest in a lease of real property; or

(iii) property to the extent it is generally exempt from creditor process under nonbankruptcy law.

(b) "Auctioneer" means a person whom the seller engages to direct, conduct, control, or be responsible for a sale by auction.

(c) "Bulk sale" means:

(i) in the case of a sale by auction or a sale or series of sales conducted by a liquidator on the seller's behalf, a sale or series of sales not in the ordinary course of the seller's business of more than half of the seller's inventory, as measured by value on the date of the bulk-sale agreement, if on that date the auctioneer or liquidator has notice, or after reasonable inquiry would have had notice, that the seller will not continue to operate the same or a similar kind of business after the sale or series of sales; and

(ii) in all other cases, a sale not in the ordinary course of the seller's business of more than half the seller's inventory, as measured by value on the date of the bulk-sale agreement, if on that date the buyer has notice, or after reasonable inquiry would have had notice, that the seller will not continue to operate the same or a similar kind of business after the sale.

(d) "Claim" means a right to payment from the seller, whether or not the right is reduced to judgment, liquidated, fixed, matured, disputed, secured, legal, or equitable. The term includes costs of collection and attorney's fees only to the extent that the laws of this state permit the holder of the claim to recover them in an action against the obligor.

(e) "Claimant" means a person holding a claim incurred in the seller's business other than:

(i) an unsecured and unmatured claim for employment compensation and benefits, including commissions and vacation, severance, and sick-leave pay;

(ii) a claim for injury to an individual or to property, or for breach of warranty, unless:

(A) a right of action for the claim has accrued;

(B) the claim has been asserted against the seller; and

(C) the seller knows the identity of the person asserting the claim and the basis upon which the person has asserted it; and

(States To Select One Alternative)

ALTERNATIVE A

[(iii) a claim for taxes owing to a governmental unit.]

ALTERNATIVE B

[(iii) a claim for taxes owing to a governmental unit, if:

(A) a statute governing the enforcement of the claim permits or requires notice of the bulk sale to be given to the governmental unit in a manner other than by compliance with the requirements of this Article; and

(B) notice is given in accordance with the statute.]

(f) "Creditor" means a claimant or other person holding a claim.

(g) (i) "Date of the bulk sale" means:

(A) if the sale is by auction or is conducted by a liquidator on the seller's behalf, the date on which more than ten percent of the net proceeds is paid to or for the benefit of the seller; and

(B) in all other cases, the later of the date on which:

(I) more than ten percent of the net contract price is paid to or for the benefit of the seller; or

(II) more than ten percent of the assets, as measured by value, are transferred to the buyer.

(ii) For purposes of this subsection:

(A) Delivery of a negotiable instrument (Section 3–104(1)) to or for the benefit of the seller in exchange for assets constitutes payment of the contract price pro tanto;

(B) To the extent that the contract price is deposited in an escrow, the contract price is paid to or for the benefit of the seller when the seller acquires the unconditional right to receive the deposit or when the deposit is delivered to the seller or for the benefit of the seller, whichever is earlier; and

(C) An asset is transferred when a person holding an unsecured claim can no longer obtain through judicial proceedings rights to the asset that are superior to those of the buyer arising as a result of the bulk sale. A person holding an unsecured claim can obtain those superior rights to a tangible asset at least until the buyer has an unconditional right, under the bulk-sale agreement, to possess the asset, and a person holding an unsecured claim can obtain those superior rights to an intangible asset at least until the buyer has an unconditional right, under the bulk-sale agreement, to use the asset.

(h) "Date of the bulk-sale agreement" means:

(i) in the case of a sale by auction or conducted by a liquidator (subsection (c)(i)), the date on which the seller engages the auctioneer or liquidator; and

(ii) in all other cases, the date on which a bulk-sale agreement becomes enforceable between the buyer and the seller.

(i) "Debt" means liability on a claim.

(j) "Liquidator" means a person who is regularly engaged in the business of disposing of assets for businesses contemplating liquidation or dissolution.

(k) "Net contract price" means the new consideration the buyer is obligated to pay for the assets less:

(i) the amount of any proceeds of the sale of an asset, to the extent the proceeds are applied in partial or total satisfaction of a debt secured by the asset; and

(ii) the amount of any debt to the extent it is secured by a security interest or lien that is enforceable against the asset before and after it has been sold to a buyer. If a debt is secured by an asset and other property of the seller, the amount of the debt secured by a security interest or lien that is enforceable against the asset is determined by multiplying the debt by a fraction, the numerator of which is the value of the new consideration for the asset on the date of the bulk sale and the denominator of which is the value of all property securing the debt on the date of the bulk sale.

(*l*) "Net proceeds" means the new consideration received for assets sold at a sale by auction or a sale conducted by a liquidator on the seller's behalf less:

(i) commissions and reasonable expenses of the sale;

(ii) the amount of any proceeds of the sale of an asset, to the extent the proceeds are applied in partial or total satisfaction of a debt secured by the asset; and

(iii) the amount of any debt to the extent it is secured by a security interest or lien that is enforceable against the asset before and after it has been sold to a buyer. If a debt is secured by an asset and other property of the seller, the amount of the debt secured by a security interest or lien that is enforceable against the asset is determined by multiplying the debt by a fraction, the numerator of which is the value of the new consideration for the asset on the date of the bulk sale and the denominator of which is the value of all property securing the debt on the date of the bulk sale.

(m) A sale is "in the ordinary course of the seller's business" if the sale comports with usual or customary practices in the kind of business in which the seller is engaged or with the seller's own usual or customary practices.

(n) "United States" includes its territories and possessions and the Commonwealth of Puerto Rico.

(*o*) "Value" means fair market value.

(p) "Verified" means signed and sworn to or affirmed.

(2) The following definitions in other Articles apply to this Article:

(a) "Buyer."	Section 2–103(1)(a).
(b) "Equipment."	Section 9–109(2).
(c) "Inventory."	Section 9–109(4).
(d) "Sale."	Section 2–106(1).
(e) "Seller."	Section 2–103(1)(d).

(3) In addition, Article 1 contains general definitions and principles of construction and interpretation applicable throughout this Article.

Official Comment

1. (a) "Assets". New. The term generally includes only "personal property." Whether particular property is "personal property" is to be determined by law outside this Article; however, for purposes of this Article, (i) the term includes "readily removable factory and office machines" (compare Section 9–313(4)(c)), even if they are covered by applicable real estate law and thus are "fixtures" as defined in Section 9–313(1)(a); (ii) the term does not include the lessee's interest in a lease of real property, even if that interest is considered to be personal property under other applicable law; and (iii) the term does not include property to the extent that it is "generally exempt from creditor process under nonbankruptcy law."

(b) "Auctioneer". Compare Section 6–108(3) (1987 Official Text).

(c) "Bulk Sale". Bulk sales are of two kinds. Subsection (1)(c)(i) describes bulk sales conducted by a professional intermediary (i.e., an auctioneer or liquidator), as to which sales Section 6-108 applies. If these indirect sales occur as a series of related sales, then the entire series is treated as a single "bulk sale" and the term applies to the sales in the aggregate. Sales made directly by the seller to the buyer, described in subsection (1)(c)(ii), include sales conducted by an auctioneer or liquidator for its own account.

The elements of both direct and indirect sales are the same. Some of these elements have been borrowed from the 1987 Official Text of Article 6 and restated. For example, the term includes only sales that are not "in the ordinary course of the seller's business" (subsection (1)(m)). The sale must be of "more than half of the seller's inventory, as measured by value [subsection (1)(*o*)] on the date of the bulk-sale agreement [subsection (1)(h)]." All inventory owned by the seller should be included in the calculation, regardless of where it is located. Inventory that is encumbered by a security interest or lien should be counted at its gross value, although the fact that it is encumbered may affect the applicability of this Article to the sale.

The determination whether a sale is a "bulk sale" and thus subject to this Article is not affected by whether other types of property are sold in connection with inventory. However, other provisions of this Article take account of the fact that other property may be sold in connection with inventory. For example, the availability of the exclusion in Section 6-103(3)(*l*) turns on the value of all the "assets," not just the inventory. Similarly, the notice required by Section 6-105 must describe the "assets," not just the inventory. And Section 6-107(4) measures the buyer's maximum cumulative liability for noncompliance by the value of the inventory and equipment sold in the bulk sale.

In an effort to limit its coverage to sales posing the greatest risks to creditors, this Article adds an additional element to the definition of "bulk sale." A sale is not a "bulk sale" unless the buyer, auctioneer, or liquidator has notice, or after a reasonable inquiry would have had notice, that the seller will not continue to operate the same or a similar kind of business after the sale. Whether a person has "notice" depends upon what the person knows and what the person would have known had the person conducted a reasonable inquiry. The issue of whether a transaction was a bulk sale is likely to be litigated only when the seller has absconded with the sale proceeds. This Article requires that the matters as to which the buyer, auctioneer, or liquidator had notice be determined only by reference to facts that the person knew or would have known at the date of the bulk-sale agreement. Reference to what actually occurred is inappropriate.

Whether an inquiry is "reasonable" depends on the facts and circumstances of each case. These facts and circumstances may include the identities of the buyer and seller and the type of assets being sold. In some cases, a reasonable inquiry may consist of no inquiry at all concerning the seller's future.

Not every change in business operations poses a substantial enough risk to creditors to justify the costs of compliance with this Article. Thus, in determining whether post-sale business is of a kind that is "the same" or "similar" to the business conducted before the sale, a court should consider whether, viewed from the perspective of the creditors of the seller, the change poses extraordinary risks or whether the change is a normal risk that creditors can be assumed to take. In particular, when the post-bulk sale business differs from the pre-bulk sale business only in the size of the business conducted, the seller should be considered to be continuing in the same or a similar kind of business and the sale should not be considered a bulk sale.

The seller must "continue to operate" the same or a similar kind of business as owner. If the owner sells the business assets to a buyer and continues to manage the business as an employee of the buyer, the seller is not continuing to operate the business within the meaning of this Article.

(d) "Claim". New. The first sentence derives from Bankruptcy Code § 101(4), 11 U.S.C. § 101(4). Changes, including the deletion of Section 101(4)(B), were made for stylistic purposes only.

(e) "Claimant". New. This term defines the category of claim holders who are the primary beneficiaries of the duties that this Article imposes. Compare "Creditor" (subsection (1)(f)).

States that choose not to afford taxing authorities the benefits of this Article should adopt Alternative A. Adoption of Alternative B would afford the benefits of this Article to taxing authorities except with respect to those taxes as to which there has been compliance with another statute requiring that notice of the bulk sale be given to the taxing authority.

(f) "Creditor". New. The term includes all holders of claims against the seller, even holders of claims arising from consumer transactions. Compare "Claimant" (subsection (1)(e)).

(g) "Date of the bulk sale". New. The parties are able to control the date of the bulk sale in several ways. They can keep the proceeds of the sale in escrow, thereby delaying the date of payment, or they can specifically agree that the assets remain subject to the reach of the seller's creditors, thereby delaying the date that the assets are transferred. By adjusting the time that the buyer acquires an unconditional right to possess tangible assets and the time the buyer acquires an unconditional right to use intangible assets, the parties may affect the substantive rights of creditors and thereby control the date the assets are transferred.

The connection between the time of transfer and the buyer's rights under the bulk-sale agreement appears only for purposes of sales to which this Article applies. Subsection (1)(g) does not purport to affect the rights of creditors of a seller of property for other purposes or under other circumstances.

(h) "Date of the bulk-sale agreement". New. Law outside this Article, including the provisions of Article 2, determines when an agreement for a bulk sale becomes enforceable between the buyer and the seller and when an auctioneer or liquidator is engaged.

(i) "Debt". New. This subsection is borrowed from Bankruptcy Code Section 101(11).

(j) "Liquidator". New. Although the definition of "liquidator" is quite broad, the term is used with respect to sales that are "conducted" by a liquidator on behalf of the seller. See subsection (1)(c)(i). Thus only those liquidators that "conduct" sales will be affected by this Article.

(k) "Net contract price". New. Consideration is not "new consideration" to the extent that it consists of the partial or total satisfaction of an antecedent debt owed to the buyer by the seller. When the buyer buys assets along with property other than assets, the "net contract price" is that portion of the new consideration allocable to the assets.

(*l*) "Net proceeds". New. The term appears, without definition, in Section 6-108 (1987 Official Text).

(m) "In the ordinary course of the seller's business". New.

(n) "United States". New. This subsection derives from Section 9-103(3)(c).

(*o*) "Value". New. The definition in Section 1-201(44) is not appropriate in the context of this Article.

(p) "Verified". New.

2. "Good faith". This Article adopts the definition of "good faith" in Article 1 in all cases, even when the buyer is a merchant.

Cross-References:

Point 1(a): Section 9-313.

Point 1(c): Sections 1-201 and 6-103.

Point 1(g): Article 2 generally.

Point 1(h): Section 2-201 and Article 2 generally.

§ 6-103. Applicability of Article.

(1) Except as otherwise provided in subsection (3), this Article applies to a bulk sale if:

(a) the seller's principal business is the sale of inventory from stock; and

(b) on the date of the bulk-sale agreement the seller is located in this state or, if the seller is located in a jurisdiction that is not a part of the United States, the seller's major executive office in the United States is in this state.

(2) A seller is deemed to be located at his [or her] place of business. If a seller has more than one place of business, the seller is deemed located at his [or her] chief executive office.

(3) This Article does not apply to:

(a) a transfer made to secure payment or performance of an obligation;

(b) a transfer of collateral to a secured party pursuant to Section 9-503;

(c) a sale of collateral pursuant to Section 9-504;

(d) retention of collateral pursuant to Section 9-505;

(e) a sale of an asset encumbered by a security interest or lien if (i) all the proceeds of the sale are applied in partial or total satisfaction of the debt secured by the security interest or lien or (ii) the security interest or lien is enforceable against the asset after it has been sold to the buyer and the net contract price is zero;

(f) a general assignment for the benefit of creditors or to a subsequent transfer by the assignee;

(g) a sale by an executor, administrator, receiver, trustee in bankruptcy, or any public officer under judicial process;

(h) a sale made in the course of judicial or administrative proceedings for the dissolution or reorganization of an organization;

(i) a sale to a buyer whose principal place of business is in the United States and who:

(i) not earlier than 21 days before the date of the bulk sale, (A) obtains from the seller a verified and dated list of claimants of whom the seller has notice three days before the seller sends or delivers the list to the buyer or (B) conducts a reasonable inquiry to discover the claimants;

(ii) assumes in full the debts owed to claimants of whom the buyer has knowledge on the date the buyer receives the list of claimants from the seller or on the date the buyer completes the reasonable inquiry, as the case may be;

(iii) is not insolvent after the assumption; and

(iv) gives written notice of the assumption not later than 30 days after the date of the bulk sale by sending or delivering a notice to the claimants identified in subparagraph (ii) or by filing a notice in the office of the [Secretary of State];

(j) a sale to a buyer whose principal place of business is in the United States and who:

(i) assumes in full the debts that were incurred in the seller's business before the date of the bulk sale;

(ii) is not insolvent after the assumption; and

(iii) gives written notice of the assumption not later than 30 days after the date of the bulk sale by sending or delivering a notice to each creditor whose debt is assumed or by filing a notice in the office of the [Secretary of State];

(k) a sale to a new organization that is organized to take over and continue the business of the seller and that has its principal place of business in the United States if:

(i) the buyer assumes in full the debts that were incurred in the seller's business before the date of the bulk sale;

(ii) the seller receives nothing from the sale except an interest in the new organization that is subordinate to the claims against the organization arising from the assumption; and

(iii) the buyer gives written notice of the assumption not later than 30 days after the date of the bulk sale by sending or delivering a notice to each creditor whose debt is assumed or by filing a notice in the office of the [Secretary of State];

(*l*) a sale of assets having:

(i) a value, net of liens and security interests, of less than $10,000. If a debt is secured by assets and other property of the seller, the net value of the assets is determined by subtracting from their value an amount equal to the product of the debt multiplied by a fraction, the numerator of which is the value of the assets on the date of the bulk sale and the denominator of which is the value of all property securing the debt on the date of the bulk sale; or

(ii) a value of more than $25,000,000 on the date of the bulk-sale agreement; or

(m) a sale required by, and made pursuant to, statute.

(4) The notice under subsection (3)(i)(iv) must state: (i) that a sale that may constitute a bulk sale has been or will be made; (ii) the date or prospective date of the bulk sale; (iii) the individual, partnership, or corporate names and the addresses of the seller and buyer; (iv) the address to which inquiries about the sale may be made, if different from the seller's address; and (v) that the buyer has assumed or will assume in full the debts owed to claimants of whom the buyer has knowledge on the date the buyer receives the list of claimants from the seller or completes a reasonable inquiry to discover the claimants.

(5) The notice under subsections (3)(j)(iii) and (3)(k)(iii) must state: (i) that a sale that may constitute a bulk sale has been or will be made; (ii) the date or prospective date of the bulk sale; (iii) the individual, partnership, or corporate names and the addresses of the seller and buyer; (iv) the address to which inquiries about the sale may be made, if different from the seller's address; and (v) that the buyer has assumed or will assume the debts that were incurred in the seller's business before the date of the bulk sale.

(6) For purposes of subsection (3)(*l*), the value of assets is presumed to be equal to the price the buyer agrees to pay for the assets. However, in a sale

by auction or a sale conducted by a liquidator on the seller's behalf, the value of assets is presumed to be the amount the auctioneer or liquidator reasonably estimates the assets will bring at auction or upon liquidation.

Official Comment

Prior Uniform Statutory Provision: Sections 6–102 and 6–103 (1987 Official Text).

Changes: New choice-of-law provision; exclusions from the Article clarified, revised, and expanded.

Purposes of Changes and New Matter:

1. Subsection (1)(a) follows Section 6–102(3) of the 1987 Official Text and makes Article 6 applicable only when the seller's principal business is the sale of inventory from stock. This Article does not apply to a sale by a seller whose principal business is the sale of goods other than inventory, e.g., a farmer, is the sale of inventory not from stock, e.g., a manufacturer who produces goods to order, or is the sale of services, e.g., a dry cleaner, barber, or operator of a hotel, tavern, or restaurant.

2. The choice-of-law rule in subsections (1)(b) and (2) derives from Section 9–103(3) and should be interpreted consistently with the Official Comment and case law construing that Section. Any agreement between the buyer and the seller with regard to the law governing a bulk sale does not affect the choice-of-law rule in this Article.

3. Some of the transactions excluded by subsection (3), e.g., those excluded by subsection (3)(a), may not be bulk sales. This Article nevertheless specifically excludes them in order to allay any doubts about the Article's applicability. Certain transactions, e.g., the sale of fully encumbered inventory that remains subject to a security interest, may be excluded by more than one subsection.

4. Subsections (3)(a), (b), (c), (d), and (e) derive from subsections (1) and (3) of Section 6–103 (1987 Official Text).

5. Subsections (3)(f), (g), and (h) restate subsections (2), (4), and (5) of Section 6–103 with minor changes.

6. Subsections (3)(i), (j), and (k) relate to sales in which the buyer assumes specified debts of the seller. A bulk sale does not fall within any of these subsections unless the buyer's assumption of debts is binding and irrevocable.

Subsection (3)(j) derives from subsection (6) of Section 6–103 (1987 Official Text) and is available to buyers who are not insolvent (as defined in Section 1–201(23)), assume all the seller's business debts in full, and give notice of the assumption. Subsection (3)(k) derives from subsection (7) of Section 6–103 (1987 Official Text) and excludes transactions in which the risks to creditors are minimal. Like subsection (3)(j), this subsection applies only if the buyer assumes all the seller's business debts in full and gives notice of the assumption. In addition, the buyer must be a new organization that is organized to take over and continue the seller's business, the seller must receive nothing from the sale other than an interest in the new organization, and the seller's interest must be subordinate to the claims arising from the assumption. Sales that may qualify for the exclusion include the incorporation of a partnership or sole proprietorship.

Buyers often are reluctant to assume debts of which they have no knowledge. Subsection (3)(i), which is new, permits a qualifying buyer to exclude a sale from this Article by assuming only those debts owed to claimants of whom the buyer has knowledge after the buyer either conducts a reasonable inquiry to discover claimants or obtains a list of claimants from the seller. A buyer who takes a verified list from the seller is held to have knowledge of the claimants on the list and is entitled to rely in good faith on the list without making further inquiry. The protection afforded by the assumption of these debts, while not perfect, is sufficiently great to eliminate the need for compliance with Article 6.

7. Subsection (3)(*l*) is new. Although the bulk sale of even a very small business may be of concern to some creditors, losses to creditors from sales of assets in which the seller's equity is less than $10,000 are not likely to justify the costs of complying with this Article. Sales of assets having a value of more than $25,000,000 have not presented serious risks to creditors. Publicity normally attends sales of that magnitude, and the sellers are unlikely to be able successfully to remove the proceeds from the reach of creditors. As used in this subsection, "price" includes all consideration for the assets, not only new consideration. Compare "Net contract price" (Section 6-102(1)(k)). If the auctioneer or liquidator does not make an estimation, then no presumption arises.

8. Subsection (3)(m) is new. This Article assumes that creditors are aware of statutes that may require their debtors to conduct bulk sales under specified circumstances, *e.g.*, upon the termination of a franchise or of a contract between a dealer and supplier, and are able to take account of any risk that those sales may impose.

Cross-References:

Point 1: Section 9-109.

Point 2: Sections 1-105 and 9-103.

Point 3: Section 6-102.

Point 4: Sections 9-111, 9-503, 9-504, and 9-505.

Point 6: Sections 1-201 and 1-203.

Point 7: Section 6-102.

Definitional Cross-References:

"Asset". Section 6-102.

"Auctioneer". Section 6-102.

"Bulk sale". Section 6-102.

"Buyer". Section 2-103.

"Claimant". Section 6-102.

"Collateral". Section 9-105.

"Date of the bulk sale". Section 6-102.

"Date of the bulk-sale agreement". Section 6-102.

"Debt". Section 6-102.

"Insolvent". Section 1-201.

"Inventory". Section 9-109.

"Knowledge". Section 1-201.

"Liquidator". Section 6-102.

"Net contract price". Section 6-102.

"Notice". Section 1-201.

"Organization". Section 1-201.

"Presumed". Section 1-201.

"Proceeds". Section 9-306.

"Sale". Section 2-106.

"Secured party". Section 9-105.

"Security interest". Section 1-201.

"Seller". Section 2-103.

"Send". Section 1-201.

"United States". Section 6-102.

"Value". Section 6-102.

"Verified". Section 6-102.

§ 6-104. Obligations of Buyer.

(1) In a bulk sale as defined in Section 6-102(1)(c)(ii) the buyer shall:

(a) obtain from the seller a list of all business names and addresses used by the seller within three years before the date the list is sent or delivered to the buyer;

(b) unless excused under subsection (2), obtain from the seller a verified and dated list of claimants of whom the seller has notice three days before the seller sends or delivers the list to the buyer and including, to the extent known by the seller, the address of and the amount claimed by each claimant;

(c) obtain from the seller or prepare a schedule of distribution (Section 6–106(1));

(d) give notice of the bulk sale in accordance with Section 6–105;

(e) unless excused under Section 6–106(4), distribute the net contract price in accordance with the undertakings of the buyer in the schedule of distribution; and

(f) unless excused under subsection (2), make available the list of claimants (subsection (1)(b)) by:

(i) promptly sending or delivering a copy of the list without charge to any claimant whose written request is received by the buyer no later than six months after the date of the bulk sale;

(ii) permitting any claimant to inspect and copy the list at any reasonable hour upon request received by the buyer no later than six months after the date of the bulk sale; or

(iii) filing a copy of the list in the office of the [Secretary of State] no later than the time for giving a notice of the bulk sale (Section 6–105(5)). A list filed in accordance with this subparagraph must state the individual, partnership, or corporate name and a mailing address of the seller.

(2) A buyer who gives notice in accordance with Section 6–105(2) is excused from complying with the requirements of subsections (1)(b) and (1)(f).

Official Comment

Prior Uniform Statutory Provision: Section 6–104 (1987 Official Text).

Changes: Revised and rewritten.

Purposes of Changes and New Matter:

1. Subsection (1) sets forth the buyer's duties in a bulk sale conducted by the seller. The buyer's failure to perform these duties may result in liability under Section 6–107. An auctioneer in a bulk sale by auction and a liquidator in a bulk sale that the liquidator conducts on the seller's behalf have similar duties but may face somewhat different liability. See Section 6–108(1). The buyer's duties are designed to afford the seller's claimants the opportunity to learn of the bulk sale before the seller has removed the assets from their reach and has received payment that is easily secreted.

2. Section 6–104(3) (1987 Official Text) provides that "[r]esponsibility for the completeness and accuracy of the list of creditors rests on the transferor, and the transfer is not rendered ineffective by errors or omissions therein unless the transferee is shown to have had knowledge." This sentence has been deleted as superfluous. Nothing in this Article suggests that the buyer is responsible for the completeness or accuracy of the list of claimants. The buyer's only obligations with respect to the list are to obtain it from the seller and to make it available. A buyer who sends or delivers notice of the bulk sale in accordance with Section 6–105(1) may rely in good faith on the list supplied by the seller unless, at the time the notice is sent or delivered, the buyer has knowledge of a claimant not on the list. A buyer who knows of a claimant not on the list is obligated to send notice of the bulk sale to that claimant.

3. The buyer's only obligation with respect to the net contract price is to comply with the schedule of distribution. The schedule may provide for the buyer to pay the entire net contract price to the seller. If so, the buyer complies with the requirements of Section 6-104(1)(e) by paying the entire net contract price to the seller.

4. The purpose of the list of claimants is to enable the buyer to give claimants notice of the bulk sale. If the buyer gives notice by filing in a public office (Section 6-105(2)), then the buyer need not obtain or preserve a list of the seller's claimants.

Cross-References:

Point 1: Sections 6-107 and 6-108.

Point 2: Sections 6-105 and 1-203.

Point 3: Section 6-106.

Point 4: Section 6-105.

Definitional Cross-References:

"Buyer". Section 2-103.

"Bulk sale". Section 6-102.

"Claimant". Section 6-102.

"Date of the bulk sale". Section 6-102.

"Net contract price". Section 6-102.

"Notice". Section 1-201.

"Seller". Section 2-103.

"Verified". Section 6-102.

§ 6-105. Notice to Claimants.

(1) Except as otherwise provided in subsection (2), to comply with Section 6-104(1)(d), the buyer shall send or deliver a written notice of the bulk sale to each claimant on the list of claimants (Section 6-104(1)(b)) and to any other claimant of whom the buyer has knowledge at the time the notice of the bulk sale is sent or delivered.

(2) A buyer may comply with Section 6-104(1)(d) by filing a written notice of the bulk sale in the office of the [Secretary of State] if:

(a) on the date of the bulk-sale agreement the seller has 200 or more claimants, exclusive of claimants holding secured or matured claims for employment compensation and benefits, including commissions and vacation, severance, and sick-leave pay; or

(b) the buyer has received a verified statement from the seller stating that, as of the date of the bulk-sale agreement, the number of claimants, exclusive of claimants holding secured or matured claims for employment compensation and benefits, including commissions and vacation, severance, and sick-leave pay, is 200 or more.

(3) The written notice of the bulk sale must be accompanied by a copy of the schedule of distribution (Section 6-106(1)) and state at least:

(a) that the seller and buyer have entered into an agreement for a sale that may constitute a bulk sale under the laws of the State of ______;

(b) the date of the agreement;

(c) the date on or after which more than ten percent of the assets were or will be transferred;

(d) the date on or after which more than ten percent of the net contract price was or will be paid, if the date is not stated in the schedule of distribution;

(e) the name and a mailing address of the seller;

(f) any other business name and address listed by the seller pursuant to Section 6–104(1)(a);

(g) the name of the buyer and an address of the buyer from which information concerning the sale can be obtained;

(h) a statement indicating the type of assets or describing the assets item by item;

(i) the manner in which the buyer will make available the list of claimants (Section 6–104(1)(f)), if applicable; and

(j) if the sale is in total or partial satisfaction of an antecedent debt owed by the seller, the amount of the debt to be satisfied and the name of the person to whom it is owed.

(4) For purposes of subsections (3)(e) and (3)(g), the name of a person is the person's individual, partnership, or corporate name.

(5) The buyer shall give notice of the bulk sale not less than 45 days before the date of the bulk sale and, if the buyer gives notice in accordance with subsection (1), not more than 30 days after obtaining the list of claimants.

(6) A written notice substantially complying with the requirements of subsection (3) is effective even though it contains minor errors that are not seriously misleading.

(7) A form substantially as follows is sufficient to comply with subsection (3):

Notice of Sale

(1) ______, whose address is ______, is described in this notice as the "seller."

(2) ______, whose address is ______, is described in this notice as the "buyer."

(3) The seller has disclosed to the buyer that within the past three years the seller has used other business names, operated at other addresses, or both, as follows: ______.

(4) The seller and the buyer have entered into an agreement dated ______, for a sale that may constitute a bulk sale under the laws of the state of ______.

(5) The date on or after which more than ten percent of the assets that are the subject of the sale were or will be transferred is ______, and [if not stated in the schedule of distribution] the date on or after which more than ten percent of the net contract price was or will be paid is ______.

(6) The following assets are the subject of the sale: ______.

(7) [If applicable] The buyer will make available to claimants of the seller a list of the seller's claimants in the following manner: ______.

(8) [If applicable] The sale is to satisfy $______ of an antecedent debt owed by the seller to ______.

(9) A copy of the schedule of distribution of the net contract price accompanies this notice.

[End of Notice]

Official Comment

Prior Uniform Statutory Provision: Sections 6–105 and 6–107 (1987 Official Text).

Changes: Revised, alternative method of giving notice added, and form of notice added.

Purposes of Changes and New Matter:

1. Subsection (1) sets forth the method by which the buyer may discharge the duty to notify the seller's claimants of the impending sale. The buyer "has knowledge" of a claimant only if the buyer has actual knowledge sufficient to enable the buyer to send a notice to the claimant. A buyer who knows only that the seller has other, unidentified claimants complies with this subsection by giving notice to the claimants on the seller's list.

2. Subsection (2) is new. It affords the buyer the opportunity to publish notice in cases in which the number of claimants—and thus the costs of compliance and risk of inadvertent noncompliance—are large. Although a filed notice will not inform every claimant of the impending sale, a filed notice is expected to inform a sufficient number of claimants (perhaps through credit reporting services) to enable them to stop an unfair or fraudulent transaction before it occurs.

The buyer may give notice by filing if the seller actually has 200 or more claimants or if the buyer receives a verified statement that the seller has 200 or more claimants. Claimants who hold secured or matured claims for employment compensation and benefits are not counted in determining the number of claimants for this purpose; however, they are entitled to receive notice of the bulk sale.

The duty to give notice must be performed in good faith. A buyer who receives a verified statement from the seller but knows the statement to be false does not act in good faith and thus does not comply with subsection (2)(b).

3. Subsection (3) prescribes the contents of the notice. The contents are the same regardless of whether notice is sent to each claimant or filed, except that the information in subsection (3)(i) is required only when notice is sent. The requirements of subsection (3) are the minimum; a notice that includes additional information is effective. The requirement in subsection (3)(h) for the description of assets is modeled on Section 9–402(1). Neither the identification of assets by serial number nor an item-by-item list of assets is required.

Subsection (3)(j) applies when the sale satisfies a debt owed by the seller to the buyer or to a third party. Section 6–103(3) excludes certain sales of this kind from the application of this Article.

4. Subsection (4) requires that a notice give the proper name of the seller and the buyer. A trade name is insufficient. See Official Comment 7 to UCC § 9–402. However, subsection (3)(f) requires that trade names be added when the seller has provided them to the buyer. The list need not include trade names or other names that the seller has used but not listed, even if the buyer knows of the names.

5. Subsection (5) requires that notice be given not less than 45 days before the date of the bulk sale. The period was extended from the 10 days afforded by the 1987 Official Text to provide ample time for claimants to receive or discover the notice and to take any action that the law permits to collect their claims from the seller. For example, depending upon the facts of each case and upon applicable law, claimants might seek to enjoin the sale, acquire a judicial lien on the assets or the proceeds, threaten to refuse to deal

with the buyer unless the seller's debt is paid, or file an involuntary bankruptcy petition against the seller. The "date of the bulk sale" is defined in such a way as to permit the seller to transfer the assets to the buyer or the buyer to pay the price to the seller (but not both) before or during the 45 days.

6. Subsection (6) derives from Section 9–402(8). The purpose of filing is to give notice to claimants. Whether an error in the seller's name is seriously misleading should depend upon whether a claimant searching under the seller's correct name could have found the filing. Whether an error other than in the seller's name is seriously misleading should depend upon whether the error prejudiced the ability of claimants to assert their rights.

Cross-References:

Point 1: Sections 1–201 and 6–104.

Point 2: Sections 1–203 and 6–104.

Point 3: Sections 6–102, 6–104, and 9–402.

Point 4: Sections 6–104 and 9–402.

Point 5: Sections 6–102.

Point 6: Sections 6–107 and 9–402.

Definitional Cross-References:

"Asset". Section 6–102.

"Bulk sale". Section 6–102.

"Buyer". Section 2–103.

"Claim". Section 6–102.

"Claimant". Section 6–102.

"Date of the bulk sale". Section 6–102.

"Date of the bulk-sale agreement". Section 6–102.

"Debt". Section 6–102.

"Knowledge". Section 1–201.

"Net contract price". Section 6–102.

"Seller". Section 2–103.

"Send". Section 1–201.

"Verified". Section 6–102.

"Written". Section 1–201.

§ 6–106. Schedule of Distribution.

(1) The seller and buyer shall agree on how the net contract price is to be distributed and set forth their agreement in a written schedule of distribution.

(2) The schedule of distribution may provide for distribution to any person at any time, including distribution of the entire net contract price to the seller.

(3) The buyer's undertakings in the schedule of distribution run only to the seller. However, a buyer who fails to distribute the net contract price in accordance with the buyer's undertakings in the schedule of distribution is liable to a creditor only as provided in Section 6–107(1).

(4) If the buyer undertakes in the schedule of distribution to distribute any part of the net contract price to a person other than the seller, and, after the buyer has given notice in accordance with Section 6–105, some or all of the anticipated net contract price is or becomes unavailable for distribution as a consequence of the buyer's or seller's having complied with an order of court, legal process, statute, or rule of law, the buyer is excused from any obligation arising under this Article or under any contract with the seller to distribute the net contract price in accordance with the buyer's undertakings in the schedule if the buyer:

(a) distributes the net contract price remaining available in accordance with any priorities for payment stated in the schedule of distribution and, to the extent that the price is insufficient to pay all the debts having a given priority, distributes the price pro rata among those debts shown in the schedule as having the same priority;

(b) distributes the net contract price remaining available in accordance with an order of court;

(c) commences a proceeding for interpleader in a court of competent jurisdiction and is discharged from the proceeding; or

(d) reaches a new agreement with the seller for the distribution of the net contract price remaining available, sets forth the new agreement in an amended schedule of distribution, gives notice of the amended schedule, and distributes the net contract price remaining available in accordance with the buyer's undertakings in the amended schedule.

(5) The notice under subsection (4)(d) must identify the buyer and the seller, state the filing number, if any, of the original notice, set forth the amended schedule, and be given in accordance with subsection (1) or (2) of Section 6-105, whichever is applicable, at least 14 days before the buyer distributes any part of the net contract price remaining available.

(6) If the seller undertakes in the schedule of distribution to distribute any part of the net contract price, and, after the buyer has given notice in accordance with Section 6-105, some or all of the anticipated net contract price is or becomes unavailable for distribution as a consequence of the buyer's or seller's having complied with an order of court, legal process, statute, or rule of law, the seller and any person in control of the seller are excused from any obligation arising under this Article or under any agreement with the buyer to distribute the net contract price in accordance with the seller's undertakings in the schedule if the seller:

(a) distributes the net contract price remaining available in accordance with any priorities for payment stated in the schedule of distribution and, to the extent that the price is insufficient to pay all the debts having a given priority, distributes the price pro rata among those debts shown in the schedule as having the same priority;

(b) distributes the net contract price remaining available in accordance with an order of court;

(c) commences a proceeding for interpleader in a court of competent jurisdiction and is discharged from the proceeding; or

(d) prepares a written amended schedule of distribution of the net contract price remaining available for distribution, gives notice of the amended schedule, and distributes the net contract price remaining available in accordance with the amended schedule.

(7) The notice under subsection (6)(d) must identify the buyer and the seller, state the filing number, if any, of the original notice, set forth the amended schedule, and be given in accordance with subsection (1) or (2) of Section 6-105, whichever is applicable, at least 14 days before the seller distributes any part of the net contract price remaining available.

Official Comment

Purposes:

1. A principal purpose of bulk sales legislation has been to impair the ability of a seller to liquidate inventory and abscond with the proceeds, leaving creditors unpaid. Toward this end, a significant minority of jurisdictions adopted optional Section 6-106 (1987 Official Text), which imposes upon a transferee in bulk the duty to apply the new consideration for the transfer to the debts of the transferor pro rata. When one or more of these debts is unliquidated, disputed, or allegedly secured, making a pro rata distribution may prove quite difficult and distribution of the consideration may be delayed considerably. In addition, since preferences generally are permitted under state law, the appropriateness of mandating a pro rata distribution is questionable. Accordingly, this Article does not require the buyer to apply the consideration to payment of the seller's debts.

This Article recognizes, however, that the seller's claimants have an interest in learning what will happen to the net contract price. If the contemplated distribution is objectionable, claimants should be able to avail themselves of whatever remedies state law or federal law allows to prevent the sale or tie up the price. On the other hand, if the price is to be distributed in a manner that is favorable to creditors, then advance knowledge of that fact will facilitate the sale by obviating any need for claimants to interfere with it.

To afford advance notice of the intended distribution of the contract price, Section 6-105(3) requires the buyer to include with the notice of the sale a copy of the "schedule of distribution"—i.e., of the agreement between the buyer and the seller on how the net contract price is to be distributed.

2. This Article does not require the net contract price to be applied in any particular fashion. Rather, the buyer and the seller may agree to whatever they wish. They must, however, disclose their agreement in ample time before the date of the bulk sale. See Section 6-105(5). The terms of the schedule of distribution in any given sale will be a function of the negotiations between buyer and seller as affected by any applicable non-Code law (e.g., corporate dissolution statutes) imposing distribution requirements in sales of the kind conducted.

In formulating the schedule, the parties may be well advised to consider the likely reaction of claimants to the schedule. For example, a schedule that contemplates the distribution of the entire net contract price to the seller or to a single creditor may prompt the filing of an involuntary bankruptcy petition. A schedule that contemplates paying the net contract price into an escrow established for the benefit of the seller's claimants may be more favorably received.

The seller may incur additional debt between the time the schedule is published and the time the net contract price is paid. The schedule may provide for payment of those debts from the net contract price.

3. Unless otherwise agreed, the buyer's only liability to creditors for failure to comply with his undertakings in the schedule of distribution is set forth in Section 6-107(1). A creditor named in the schedule may not rely on the creation or publication of the schedule as the basis for imposing liability against the buyer on any other theory, including that of estoppel or third-party beneficiary.

The seller may wish to undertake to pay some of the price to creditors. The seller may, but need not, include this undertaking in the schedule of distribution. The buyer is not responsible for performance of the seller's undertakings. Thus, if the seller makes an undertaking with respect to payment of the net contract price and fails to perform in accordance with it, the buyer faces no liability. However, certain persons in control of the seller may be liable under those circumstances. See Section 6-107(11).

4. In some cases, the precise amount of the net contract price may be unknown at the time that the schedule of distribution is formulated and notice of the bulk sale is given. In other cases, the net contract price may prove to be less than originally anticipated. Parties who fail to provide for these contingencies in the schedule of distribution and are unable to abide by the original schedule may be required to give a new notice with a new schedule.

The inability to abide by the schedule may be due to an external legal event, e.g., the suffering of a garnishment lien on the net contract price, the filing of a bankruptcy petition, or compliance with a corporate dissolution statute. If so, subsection (4), which applies to the extent that the net contract price is within the control of the buyer, may afford relief to the buyer, and subsection (6), which applies to the extent the net contract price is within the control of the seller, may afford relief to a person in control of the seller. Although this Article imposes no obligation on sellers with respect to distribution of the net contract price (or otherwise), a seller may incur an obligation of this kind by agreement with the buyer. Accordingly, subsection (6) provides the means by which the seller as well as a person in control of the seller may be excused from any such obligation.

Subsections (4)(a) and (6)(a) permit the buyer or seller respectively to distribute the net contract price remaining available in accordance with any priorities for payment. A schedule need not afford priority to particular debts. If the schedule contains no priorities, then the debts are treated as if they are all of the same priority, and the buyer or seller, as the case may be, may distribute the price pro rata in partial satisfaction of the debts set forth in the schedule. Law other than this Article determines whether a court order or a proceeding for interpleader is available for purposes of subsections (4)(b), (4)(c), (6)(b), and (6)(c).

Cross-References:

Point 1: Sections 6-104 and 6-105.

Point 2: Sections 6-105.

Point 3: Sections 1-102 and 6-107.

Definitional Cross-References:

"Buyer". Section 2-103.

"Contract". Section 1-201.

"Creditor". Section 1-201.

"Debt". Section 6-102.

"Net contract price". Section 6-102.

"Person". Section 1-201.

"Seller". Section 2-103.

"Written". Section 1-201.

§ 6-107. Liability for Noncompliance.

(1) Except as provided in subsection (3), and subject to the limitation in subsection (4):

(a) a buyer who fails to comply with the requirements of Section 6-104(1)(e) with respect to a creditor is liable to the creditor for damages in the amount of the claim, reduced by any amount that the creditor would not have realized if the buyer had complied; and

(b) a buyer who fails to comply with the requirements of any other subsection of Section 6-104 with respect to a claimant is liable to the claimant for damages in the amount of the claim, reduced by any amount that the claimant would not have realized if the buyer had complied.

(2) In an action under subsection (1), the creditor has the burden of establishing the validity and amount of the claim, and the buyer has the burden of establishing the amount that the creditor would not have realized if the buyer had complied.

(3) A buyer who:

(a) made a good faith and commercially reasonable effort to comply with the requirements of Section 6–104(1) or to exclude the sale from the application of this Article under Section 6–103(3); or

(b) on or after the date of the bulk-sale agreement, but before the date of the bulk sale, held a good faith and commercially reasonable belief that this Article does not apply to the particular sale is not liable to creditors for failure to comply with the requirements of Section 6–104. The buyer has the burden of establishing the good faith and commercial reasonableness of the effort or belief.

(4) In a single bulk sale the cumulative liability of the buyer for failure to comply with the requirements of Section 6–104(1) may not exceed an amount equal to:

(a) if the assets consist only of inventory and equipment, twice the net contract price, less the amount of any part of the net contract price paid to or applied for the benefit of the seller or a creditor; or

(b) if the assets include property other than inventory and equipment, twice the net value of the inventory and equipment less the amount of the portion of any part of the net contract price paid to or applied for the benefit of the seller or a creditor which is allocable to the inventory and equipment.

(5) For the purposes of subsection (4)(b), the "net value" of an asset is the value of the asset less (i) the amount of any proceeds of the sale of an asset, to the extent the proceeds are applied in partial or total satisfaction of a debt secured by the asset and (ii) the amount of any debt to the extent it is secured by a security interest or lien that is enforceable against the asset before and after it has been sold to a buyer. If a debt is secured by an asset and other property of the seller, the amount of the debt secured by a security interest or lien that is enforceable against the asset is determined by multiplying the debt by a fraction, the numerator of which is the value of the asset on the date of the bulk sale and the denominator of which is the value of all property securing the debt on the date of the bulk sale. The portion of a part of the net contract price paid to or applied for the benefit of the seller or a creditor that is "allocable to the inventory and equipment" is the portion that bears the same ratio to that part of the net contract price as the net value of the inventory and equipment bears to the net value of all of the assets.

(6) A payment made by the buyer to a person to whom the buyer is, or believes he [or she] is, liable under subsection (1) reduces pro tanto the buyer's cumulative liability under subsection (4).

(7) No action may be brought under subsection (1)(b) by or on behalf of a claimant whose claim is unliquidated or contingent.

(8) A buyer's failure to comply with the requirements of Section 6–104(1) does not (i) impair the buyer's rights in or title to the assets, (ii) render the sale ineffective, void, or voidable, (iii) entitle a creditor to more than a single satisfaction of his [or her] claim, or (iv) create liability other than as provided in this Article.

(9) Payment of the buyer's liability under subsection (1) discharges pro tanto the seller's debt to the creditor.

(10) Unless otherwise agreed, a buyer has an immediate right of reimbursement from the seller for any amount paid to a creditor in partial or total satisfaction of the buyer's liability under subsection (1).

(11) If the seller is an organization, a person who is in direct or indirect control of the seller, and who knowingly, intentionally, and without legal justification fails, or causes the seller to fail, to distribute the net contract price in accordance with the schedule of distribution is liable to any creditor to whom the seller undertook to make payment under the schedule for damages caused by the failure.

Official Comment

Prior Uniform Statutory Provision: None.

Purposes:

1. This section sets forth the consequences of noncompliance with the requirements of Section 6–104. Although other legal consequences may result from a bulk sale—*e.g.*, the buyer may be liable to the seller under Article 2 or to the seller's creditors under the Uniform Fraudulent Transfer Act—no other consequences may be imposed by reason of the buyer's failure to comply with the requirements of this Article.

The two subsections of Section 6–107(1) reflect the duties set forth in Section 6–104. The duties generally run only to claimants, but the duty to distribute the net contract price in accordance with the schedule of distribution (Section 6–104(1)(e)) may run also to certain creditors.

2. Article 6 (1987 Official Text), like many of its nonuniform predecessors, makes a noncomplying transfer ineffective against aggrieved creditors. In contrast, noncompliance with this Article neither renders the sale ineffective nor otherwise affects the buyer's rights in or title to the assets.

Liability under this Article is for breach of a statutory duty. The buyer's only liability is personal (*in personam*) liability. Aggrieved creditors may only recover money damages. *In rem* remedies, which are available upon noncompliance with Article 6 (1987 Official Text), are not available under this Article. Thus, aggrieved creditors no longer may treat the sale as if it had not occurred and use the judicial process to apply assets purchased by the buyer toward the satisfaction of their claims against the seller.

The change in the theory of liability and in the available remedy should be of particular significance if the seller enters bankruptcy after the sale is consummated. When an aggrieved creditor of the transferor has a nonbankruptcy right to avoid a transfer in whole or in part, as may be the case under Article 6 (1987 Official Text), the transferor's bankruptcy trustee may avoid the entire transfer. See Bankruptcy Code § 544(b), 11 U.S.C. § 544(b). Under this Article, a person who is aggrieved by the buyer's noncompliance may not avoid the sale. Rather, the person is entitled only to recover damages as provided in this section. Because no creditor has the right to avoid the transaction or to assert a remedy that is the functional equivalent of avoidance, the seller's bankruptcy trustee likewise should be unable to do so.

3. This Article makes explicit what is implicit in Article 6 (1987 Official Text): only those persons as to whom there has been noncompliance are entitled to a remedy. For example, if notices are sent to each claimant other than claimant A, claimant B cannot recover. Similarly, a creditor who acquires a claim after notice is given has no remedy unless the buyer undertakes in the schedule of distribution

to pay that creditor and the buyer fails to meet the obligation.

4. Unlike Article 6 (1987 Official Text), which imposes strict liability upon a noncomplying transferee, this Article imposes liability for noncompliance only when the failure to comply actually has injured a creditor and only to the extent of the injury. Each creditor's damages are measured by the injury that the particular creditor sustained as a consequence of the buyer's failure to comply. This measure is stated as the amount of the debt reduced by any amount that the person would not have realized if the buyer had complied. Compare Section 4-103(5).

5. A buyer is liable only for the buyer's own noncompliance with the requirements of Section 6-104. Under that section, the only step the buyer must take to discover the identity of the seller's claimants is to obtain a list of claimants from the seller. If the seller's list is incomplete and the buyer lacks knowledge of claimant C, then claimant C has no remedy under subsection (1)(b) of this section.

6. The creditor has the burden of establishing the validity and amount of the debt owed by the seller as well as the fact of the buyer's noncompliance. In contesting the allegation of noncompliance, the buyer may introduce evidence tending to show either that the sale was not a bulk sale or that the sale was a bulk sale to which this Article does not apply. In contesting the validity and amount of the debt, the buyer may introduce evidence tending to show that the seller had a defense to the debt. The buyer has the burden of establishing the amount that the creditor would not have realized even if the buyer had complied. Implicit in subsection (2) is that certain failures to comply with the requirements of this Article will cause no injury and thus result in no liability.

The following examples illustrate the operation of subsection (2):

Example 1: The buyer fails to give notice of the bulk sale. Claimant D, who appears on seller's list of claimants, admits to having had actual knowledge of the impending sale two months before it occurred. The buyer is likely to be able to meet the burden of establishing that even had the buyer given notice of the sale, claimant D would not have recovered any more than the claimant actually recovered.

Example 2: The buyer failed to obtain a list of seller's business names (Section 6-104(1)(a)) or to make available the list of claimants (Section 6-104(1)(f)). In many cases, the buyer may be able to meet the burden of establishing that compliance with those subsections would not have enabled claimants to recover any more than they actually recovered.

7. Subsection (3) may afford a complete defense to a noncomplying buyer. This defense is available to buyers who establish that they made a good faith effort to comply with the requirements of this Article or made a good faith effort to exclude the sale from the application of this Article (e.g., by assuming debts and attempting to comply with the notice requirements of Section 6-103(3)(i), (j), or (k)). When a buyer makes a good faith effort to comply with this Article or to exclude the transaction from its coverage, the injury caused by noncompliance is likely to be *de minimis.* In any event, the primary responsibility for satisfying claims rests with the creditors, and this Article imposes no greater duty upon buyers who attempt to comply with this Article or to exclude a sale from its application than to make a good faith effort to do so.

The defense of subsection (3) also is available to buyers who act on the good faith belief that this Article does not apply to the sale (e.g., because the sale is not a bulk sale or is excluded under Section 6-103). The good-faith-belief defense is an acknowledgement that reasonable people may disagree over whether a given transaction is or is not a bulk sale and over whether Section 6-103 excludes a particular transaction. A buyer acting in good faith should be protected from the liability that this Article otherwise would impose on buyers who may be completely innocent of wrongdoing. A buyer who is unaware of the requirements of this Article holds no belief concerning the applicability of the Article and so may not use the defense.

8. Even a buyer who completely fails to comply with this Article may not be liable in an amount equal to sum of the seller's debts. Subsection (4) limits the aggregate recovery for "any one bulk sale," which term includes a series of sales by a liquidator. The maximum cumulative liability for noncompliance with this Article parallels the maximum recovery generally available to creditors under the 1987 Official Text of Article 6. Under that Article, the noncomplying transferee may have to "pay twice" for the goods. First, the transferee may pay the purchase price to the transferor; then, the transferee may lose the goods to aggrieved creditors.

Under this Article, the maximum cumulative liability is an amount equal to twice the net contract price of the inventory and equipment (i.e., twice the amount that would be available to unsecured creditors from the inventory and equipment), less the amount of any portion of that net contract price paid to or applied for the benefit of the seller or a creditor of the seller. Unless the buyer receives credit for amounts paid to the seller (which amounts the creditors have a right to apply to payment of their claims), the buyer might wind up paying an amount equal to the net contract price three times (once to the seller and twice to aggrieved creditors). The grant of credit for amounts paid to the seller's creditors recognizes that ordinarily the seller has no obligation to pay creditors pro rata.

When the assets sold consist of only inventory and equipment, calculation of the maximum cumulative liability is relatively simple. But when the assets sold include property in addition to inventory and equipment, the calculation becomes more difficult. When inventory or equipment secures a debt that also is secured by other collateral and the aggregate value of the collateral exceeds the secured debt, a determination of the amount in clause (ii) of subsection (5) may require an allocation of the collateral to the debt in accordance with the statutory formula. In addition, one may need to determine which portion of payments of the net contract price is allocable to inventory and equipment. Subsection (5) directs that this allocation be made by multiplying the part of the net contract price paid to or applied for the benefit of the seller or a creditor by a fraction whose nominator is the net value of the inventory and equipment and whose denominator is the net value of all the assets.

Sometimes the seller may receive the net contract price and pay some or all of it to one or more creditors. In determining whether a payment to a creditor was made from the net contract price or from another source, courts are free to employ tracing rules. Amounts paid to secured parties usually are taken into account in determining the net contract price; if so, the buyer should not receive credit for them.

9. The buyer need not wait for judgment to be entered before paying a person believed to be a creditor of the seller. Indeed, the buyer is entitled to credit for amounts paid to persons who in fact may not be creditors of the seller, as long as the buyer acts with the belief that the seller is so indebted. As is the case with respect to all obligations under the Code, the buyer's belief must be held in good faith.

10. Any amounts paid by the buyer in satisfaction of the liability created by Section 6-107(1) reduce the seller's liability to the recipient pro tanto. Consequently, the buyer is entitled to immediate reimbursement of those amounts from the seller. The right of reimbursement is available only for amounts paid to actual creditors. Amounts paid to those whom the buyer incorrectly believes to be creditors ordinarily are not recoverable from the seller, although the buyer is entitled to credit for those amounts against the

aggregate liability in subsection (4). Of course, the buyer and seller may vary the seller's reimbursement obligation by agreement.

11. Because of the difficulty in valuing claims that are unliquidated or contingent, persons holding claims of that kind may not bring an action under subsection (1)(b). If the claim remains unliquidated or contingent throughout the limitation period in Section 6-110, then these creditors have no remedy for noncompliance under that subsection. They may, however, be entitled to a remedy under subsection (1)(a) of (11) for failure to distribute the net contract price in accordance with the schedule of distribution.

12. In certain circumstances, subsection (11) imposes liability on a person in direct or indirect control of a seller that is an organization. Excuse under Section 6-106(6) is a "legal justification" that prevents liability from attaching under subsection (11). No special provision applies to the seller who fails to comply with the schedule. The seller already owes the debt to the creditor, and other law governs the consequences of a debtor who fails to pay a debt when promised.

Cross-References:

Point 1: Section 6-104.

Point 4: Section 4-103.

Point 5: Sections 6-104 and 6-105.

Point 6: Sections 1-201, 6-102, 6-103, and 6-104.

Point 7: Sections 1-102, 1-201, 6-102 and 6-103.

Point 8: Section 6-102.

Point 9: Section 1-203.

Point 10: Section 1-102.

Point 11: Sections 6-102 and 6-110.

Point 12: Section 6-106.

Definitional Cross-References:

"Assets". Section 6-102.

"Bulk sale". Section 6-102.

"Burden of establishing". Section 1-201.

"Buyer". Section 2-103.

"Claim". Section 6-102.

"Claimant". Section 6-102.

"Creditor". Section 6-102.

"Date of the bulk sale". Section 6-102.

"Equipment". Section 6-102.

"Good faith". Section 6-102.

"Inventory". Section 9-109.

"Net contract price". Section 6-102.

"Organization". Section 1-201.

"Person". Section 1-201.

"Proceeds". Section 9-306.

"Security interest". Section 1-201.

"Seller". Section 2-103.

"Written". Section 1-201.

§ 6-108. Bulk Sales by Auction; Bulk Sales Conducted by Liquidator.

(1) Sections 6-104, 6-105, 6-106, and 6-107 apply to a bulk sale by auction and a bulk sale conducted by a liquidator on the seller's behalf with the following modifications:

(a) "buyer" refers to auctioneer or liquidator, as the case may be;

(b) "net contract price" refers to net proceeds of the auction or net proceeds of the sale, as the case may be;

(c) the written notice required under Section 6-105(3) must be accompanied by a copy of the schedule of distribution (Section 6-106(1)) and state at least:

(i) that the seller and the auctioneer or liquidator have entered into an agreement for auction or liquidation services that may constitute an agreement to make a bulk sale under the laws of the State of ______;

(ii) the date of the agreement;

(iii) the date on or after which the auction began or will begin or the date on or after which the liquidator began or will begin to sell assets on the seller's behalf;

(iv) the date on or after which more than ten percent of the net proceeds of the sale were or will be paid, if the date is not stated in the schedule of distribution;

(v) the name and a mailing address of the seller;

(vi) any other business name and address listed by the seller pursuant to Section 6-104(1)(a);

(vii) the name of the auctioneer or liquidator and an address of the auctioneer or liquidator from which information concerning the sale can be obtained;

(viii) a statement indicating the type of assets or describing the assets item by item;

(ix) the manner in which the auctioneer or liquidator will make available the list of claimants (Section 6-104(1)(f)), if applicable; and

(x) if the sale is in total or partial satisfaction of an antecedent debt owed by the seller, the amount of the debt to be satisfied and the name of the person to whom it is owed; and

(d) in a single bulk sale the cumulative liability of the auctioneer or liquidator for failure to comply with the requirements of this section may not exceed the amount of the net proceeds of the sale allocable to inventory and equipment sold less the amount of the portion of any part of the net proceeds paid to or applied for the benefit of a creditor which is allocable to the inventory and equipment.

(2) A payment made by the auctioneer or liquidator to a person to whom the auctioneer or liquidator is, or believes he [or she] is, liable under this section reduces pro tanto the auctioneer's or liquidator's cumulative liability under subsection (1)(d).

(3) A form substantially as follows is sufficient to comply with subsection (1)(c):

Notice of Sale

(1) ______, whose address is ______, is described in this notice as the "seller."

(2) ______, whose address is ______, is described in this notice as the "auctioneer" or "liquidator."

(3) The seller has disclosed to the auctioneer or liquidator that within the past three years the seller has used other business names, operated at other addresses, or both, as follows: ______.

(4) The seller and the auctioneer or liquidator have entered into an agreement dated ______ for auction or liquidation services that may constitute an agreement to make a bulk sale under the laws of the State of ______.

(5) The date on or after which the auction began or will begin or the date on or after which the liquidator began or will begin to sell assets on the seller's behalf is ______, and [if not stated in the schedule of distribution] the date on or after which more than ten percent of the net proceeds of the sale were or will be paid is ______.

(6) The following assets are the subject of the sale: ______.

(7) [If applicable] The auctioneer or liquidator will make available to claimants of the seller a list of the seller's claimants in the following manner: ______.

(8) [If applicable] The sale is to satisfy $______ of an antecedent debt owed by the seller to ______.

(9) A copy of the schedule of distribution of the net proceeds accompanies this notice.

[End of Notice]

(4) A person who buys at a bulk sale by auction or conducted by a liquidator need not comply with the requirements of Section 6-104(1) and is not liable for the failure of an auctioneer or liquidator to comply with the requirements of this section.

Official Comment

Prior Uniform Statutory Provision: Section 6-108.

Changes: Revised, expanded to include sales conducted by a liquidator on the seller's behalf, and form of notice added.

Purposes of Changes and New Matter:

1. This section applies only to bulk sales by auction or conducted by a liquidator on the seller's behalf, as defined in Section 6-102(1)(c). Bulk sales conducted by an auctioneer or liquidator on its own behalf are treated as ordinary bulk sales and are not subject to this section.

2. Regardless of whether the assets are sold directly from the seller to the buyer, are sold to a variety of buyers at auction, or are sold on the seller's behalf by a liquidator to one or more buyers, a going-out-of-business sale of inventory presents similar risks to claimants. Auctioneers and liquidators are likely to be in a better position to ascertain whether the sale they are conducting is, or is part of, a bulk sale than are their customers. Accordingly, buyers at auctions and from liquidators selling assets of others need not be concerned with complying with this Article. Instead, this section imposes upon auctioneers and liquidators duties and liabilities that are similar, but not always identical, to those of a buyer under Sections 6-104(1) and 6-107. Except to the extent that this section treats bulk sales by auctioneers and liquidators differently from those conducted by the seller on its own behalf, the Official Comments to Sections 6-104(1) and 6-107, as well as the Comments to Sections 6-105 and 6-106, which those sections incorporate by reference, are applicable to sales to which this section applies.

3. Subsection (1)(d) sets forth the maximum cumulative liability for auctioneers and liquidators "in any one bulk sale," which term includes a series of sales by a liquidator. This liability is to be calculated in a manner similar to that

set forth in Sections 6–107(4) and 6–107(5). The term "net proceeds of the auction or sale allocable to inventory and equipment" is analogous to the term "net value of the inventory and equipment"; however, the former takes into account the reasonable expenses of the auction or sale whereas the latter does not. Also, the latter is doubled whereas the former is not. The "amount of the portion of any part of the net proceeds paid to or applied for the benefit of a creditor which is allocable to inventory and equipment" is determined by multiplying the part of the net proceeds paid to or applied for the benefit of a creditor by a fraction whose numerator is the net proceeds of the sale allocable to inventory and equipment and whose denominator is the total net proceeds of the auction or sale. Because the amount of the net proceeds allocable to inventory and equipment is not doubled, the auctioneer or liquidator is not entitled to credit for payments made to the seller.

4. Section 6–107(3) applies to all bulk sales. Accordingly, an auctioneer or liquidator who makes a good faith effort to comply with the requirements of this Article or to exclude the sale from this Article or who acts under a good faith belief that this Article does not apply to the sale faces no liability whatsoever.

Cross-References:

Point 1: Section 6–102.

Point 2: Sections 6–102, 6–104, 6–105, 6–106, and 6–107.

Point 3: Sections 6–102 and 6–107.

Point 4: Section 6–107.

Definitional Cross-References:

"Assets". Section 6–102.

"Auctioneer". Section 6–102.

"Bulk sale". Section 6–102.

"Claimants". Section 6–102.

"Creditor". Section 6–102.

"Debt". Section 6–102.

"Equipment". Section 9–109.

"Inventory". Section 9–109.

"Liquidator". Section 6–102.

"Net proceeds". Section 6–102.

"Person". Section 1–201.

"Seller". Section 2–103.

"Written". Section 1–201.

§ 6–109. What Constitutes Filing; Duties of Filing Officer; Information From Filing Officer.

(1) Presentation of a notice or list of claimants for filing and tender of the filing fee or acceptance of the notice or list by the filing officer constitutes filing under this Article.

(2) The filing officer shall:

(a) mark each notice or list with a file number and with the date and hour of filing;

(b) hold the notice or list or a copy for public inspection;

(c) index the notice or list according to each name given for the seller and for the buyer; and

(d) note in the index the file number and the addresses of the seller and buyer given in the notice or list.

(3) If the person filing a notice or list furnishes the filing officer with a copy, the filing officer upon request shall note upon the copy the file number and date and hour of the filing of the original and send or deliver the copy to the person.

(4) The fee for filing and indexing and for stamping a copy furnished by the person filing to show the date and place of filing is $______ for the first page and $______ for each additional page. The fee for indexing each name more than two is $______.

(5) Upon request of any person, the filing officer shall issue a certificate showing whether any notice or list with respect to a particular seller or buyer is on file on the date and hour stated in the certificate. If a notice or list is on file, the certificate must give the date and hour of filing of each notice or list and the name and address of each seller, buyer, auctioneer, or liquidator. The fee for the certificate is $______ if the request for the certificate is in the standard form prescribed by the [Secretary of State] and otherwise is $______. Upon request of any person, the filing officer shall furnish a copy of any filed notice or list for a fee of $______.

(6) The filing officer shall keep each notice or list for two years after it is filed.

Official Comment

Prior Uniform Statutory Provision: None.

Purposes of New Matter:

This Article contemplates public filing of bulk sale notices and lists of claimants in a single filing office in each state. This section, which derives substantially from Sections 9-403 and 9-407, governs filing. The filing system is designed to enable one seeking information about a sale to discover any filed notices or lists by searching under either the seller's or the buyer's (but not the auctioneer's or liquidator's) individual, partnership, or corporate name.

Cross-References:

Sections 6-103, 6-105, 9-403, and 9-407.

Definitional Cross-References:

"Auctioneer". Section 6-102.

"Buyer". Section 2-103.

"Liquidator". Section 6-102.

"Person". Section 1-201.

"Seller". Section 2-103.

"Send". Section 1-201.

§ 6-110. Limitation of Actions.

(1) Except as provided in subsection (2), an action under this Article against a buyer, auctioneer, or liquidator must be commenced within one year after the date of the bulk sale.

(2) If the buyer, auctioneer, or liquidator conceals the fact that the sale has occurred, the limitation is tolled and an action under this Article may be commenced within the earlier of (i) one year after the person bringing the action discovers that the sale has occurred or (ii) one year after the person bringing the action should have discovered that the sale has occurred, but no later than two years after the date of the bulk sale. Complete noncompliance with the requirements of this Article does not of itself constitute concealment.

(3) An action under Section 6-107(11) must be commenced within one year after the alleged violation occurs.]

Official Comment

Prior Uniform Statutory Provision: Section 6–111 (1987 Official Text).

Changes: Statute of limitations extended and clarified.

Purposes of Changes and New Matter:

1. This Article imposes liability upon only those who do not make a good faith and commercially reasonable effort to comply with the requirements of the Article or to exclude the sale from the application of the Article and who do not hold a good faith and commercially reasonable belief that the Article is inapplicable to the sale. Consequently, it extends the six-month limitation period of the 1987 Official Text, which applies to good faith transferees as well as those not in good faith, to one year. The period commences with the date of the bulk sale.

2. Cases decided under the 1987 Official Text of Article 6 disagree over whether the complete failure to comply with the requirements of that Article constitutes a concealment that tolls the limitation. This Article adopts the view that noncompliance does not of itself constitute concealment.

3. This Article does not contemplate tolling the limitation for actions against a person in control of the seller who fails to distribute the net contract price in accordance with the schedule of distribution. Those actions must be commenced within one year after the alleged violation occurs.

Cross-References:

Point 1: Sections 1–201, 6–102, 6–107 and 6–108.

Point 3: Section 6–107.

Definitional Cross-References:

"Action". Section 1–201.

"Auctioneer". Section 6–102.

"Buyer". Section 2–103.

"Date of the bulk sale". Section 6–102.

"Liquidator". Section 6–102.

[End of Alternative B]

CONFORMING AMENDMENT TO SECTION 1–105

States adopting Alternative B should amend Section 1–105(2) of the Uniform Commercial Code to read as follows:

(2) Where one of the following provisions of this Act specifies the applicable law, that provision governs and a contrary agreement is effective only to the extent permitted by the law (including the conflict of laws rules) so specified:

Rights of creditors against sold goods. Section 2–402.

Applicability of the Article on Leases. Sections 2A–105 and 2A–106.

Applicability of the Article on Bank Deposits and Collections. Section 4–102.

Bulk ~~transfers~~ sales subject to the Article on Bulk ~~Transfers~~ Sales. Section ~~6–102~~ 6–103.

Applicability of the Article on Investment Securities. Section 8–106.

Perfection provisions of the Article on Secured Transactions. Section 9–103.

CONFORMING AMENDMENT TO SECTION 2–403

States adopting Alternative B should amend Section 2–403(4) of the Uniform Commercial Code to read as follows:

(4) The rights of other purchasers of goods and of lien creditors are governed by the Articles on Secured Transactions (Article 9), Bulk ~~Transfers~~ Sales (Article 6) and Documents of Title (Article 7).

ARTICLE 7

WAREHOUSE RECEIPTS, BILLS OF LADING AND OTHER DOCUMENTS OF TITLE

PART 1. GENERAL

PART 2. WAREHOUSE RECEIPTS: SPECIAL PROVISIONS

PART 3. BILLS OF LADING: SPECIAL PROVISIONS

PART 4. WAREHOUSE RECEIPTS AND BILLS OF LADING: GENERAL OBLIGATIONS

PART 5. WAREHOUSE RECEIPTS AND BILLS OF LADING: NEGOTIATION AND TRANSFER

PART 1

GENERAL

§ 7–101. Short Title.

This Article shall be known and may be cited as Uniform Commercial Code—Documents of Title.

Official Comment

This Article is a consolidation and revision of the Uniform Warehouse Receipts Act and the Uniform Bills of Lading Act, and embraces also the provisions of the Uniform Sales Act relating to negotiation of documents of title.

The only substantial omissions of material covered in the previous uniform acts are the criminal provisions found in the Warehouse Receipts and Bills of Lading acts. These criminal provisions are inappropriate to a Commercial Code, and for the most part duplicate portions of the ordinary criminal law relating to frauds.

The Article does not attempt to define the tort liability of bailees, except to hold certain classes of bailees to a minimum standard of reasonable care. For important classes of bailees, liabilities in case of loss, damage or destruction, as well as other legal questions associated with particular documents of title, are governed by federal statutes, international treaties, and in some cases regulatory state laws, which supersede the provisions of this Article in case of inconsistency. See Section 7–103.

§ 7–102. Definitions and Index of Definitions.

(1) In this Article, unless the context otherwise requires:

(a) "Bailee" means the person who by a warehouse receipt, bill of lading or other document of title acknowledges possession of goods and contracts to deliver them.

(b) "Consignee" means the person named in a bill to whom or to whose order the bill promises delivery.

(c) "Consignor" means the person named in a bill as the person from whom the goods have been received for shipment.

(d) "Delivery order" means a written order to deliver goods directed to a warehouseman, carrier or other person who in the ordinary course of business issues warehouse receipts or bills of lading.

(e) "Document" means document of title as defined in the general definitions in Article 1 (Section 1-201).

(f) "Goods" means all things which are treated as movable for the purposes of a contract of storage or transportation.

(g) "Issuer" means a bailee who issues a document except that in relation to an unaccepted delivery order it means the person who orders the possessor of goods to deliver. Issuer includes any person for whom an agent or employee purports to act in issuing a document if the agent or employee has real or apparent authority to issue documents, notwithstanding that the issuer received no goods or that the goods were misdescribed or that in any other respect the agent or employee violated his instructions.

(h) "Warehouseman" is a person engaged in the business of storing goods for hire.

(2) Other definitions applying to this Article or to specified Parts thereof, and the sections in which they appear are:

"Duly negotiate". Section 7-501.

"Person entitled under the document". Section 7-403(4).

(3) Definitions in other Articles applying to this Article and the sections in which they appear are:

"Contract for sale". Section 2-106.

"Overseas". Section 2-323.

"Receipt" of goods. Section 2-103.

(4) In addition Article 1 contains general definitions and principles of construction and interpretation applicable throughout this Article.

Official Comment

Prior Uniform Statutory Provision: Section 76, Uniform Sales Act; Section 58, Uniform Warehouse Receipts Act; Sections 1 and 53, Uniform Bills of Lading Act.

Changes: Applicable definitions from the uniform acts have been consolidated and revised; definition of delivery order is new.

Purposes of Changes and New Matter:

1. "Bailee" was not defined in the old uniform acts. It is used in this Article as a blanket term to designate carriers, warehousemen and others who normally issue documents of title on the basis of goods which they have received. The definition does not, however, require actual possession of the goods. If a bailee acknowledges possession when he does not have it he is bound by sections of this Article which declare the "bailee's" obligations. (See definition of "Issuer" in this section and Sections 7-203 and 7-301 on liability in case of non-receipt.)

2. The definition of warehouse receipt contained in the general definitions section of this Act (Section 1-201) eliminates the requirement of the Uniform Warehouse Receipts Act that the issuing warehouseman be "lawfully engaged" in busi-

ness. The warehouseman's compliance with applicable state regulations such as the filing of a bond has no bearing on the substantive issues dealt with in this Article. Certainly the issuer's violations of law should not diminish his responsibility on documents he has put in commercial circulation. The Uniform Warehouse Receipts Act requirement that the warehouseman be engaged "for profit" has also been eliminated in view of the existence of state operated and co-operative warehouses. But it is still essential that the business be storing goods "for hire" (Section 1-201 and this section). A person does not become a warehouseman by storing his own goods.

3. Delivery orders, which were included without qualification in the Uniform Sales Act definition of document of title, must be treated differently in this consolidation of provisions from the three uniform acts. When a delivery order has been accepted by the bailee it is for practical purposes indistinguishable from a warehouse receipt. Prior to such acceptance there is no basis for imposing obligations on the bailee other than the ordinary obligation of contract which the bailee may have assumed to the depositor of the goods.

Cross References:

Point 1: Sections 7-203 and 7-301.

Point 2: Sections 1-201 and 7-203.

See general comment to document of title in Section 1-201.

Definitional Cross References:

"Bill of lading". Section 1-201.

"Contract". Section 1-201.

"Contract for sale". Section 2-106.

"Delivery". Section 1-201.

"Document of title". Section 1-201.

"Person". Section 1-201.

"Purchase". Section 1-201.

"Receipt of goods". Section 2-103.

"Right". Section 1-201.

"Warehouse receipt". Section 1-201.

"Written". Section 1-201.

§ 7-103. Relation of Article to Treaty, Statute, Tariff, Classification or Regulation.

To the extent that any treaty or statute of the United States, regulatory statute of this State or tariff, classification or regulation filed or issued pursuant thereto is applicable, the provisions of this Article are subject thereto.

Official Comment

Prior Uniform Statutory Provision: None.

Purposes:

1. To make clear what would of course be true without the Section, that applicable Federal law is paramount.

2. To make clear also that *regulatory* state statutes (such as those fixing or authorizing a commission to fix rates and prescribe services, authorizing different charges for goods of different values, and limiting liability for loss to the declared value on which the charge was based) are not affected by the Article and are controlling on the matters which they cover. Notice that the reference is not only to such statutes, but to tariffs, classifications and regulations filed or issued pursuant to them.

Cross References:

Sections 7-201, 7-202, 7-204, 7-206, 7-309, 7-401, and 7-403.

Definitional Cross Reference:

"Bill of lading". Section 1-201.

§ 7-104. Negotiable and Non-negotiable Warehouse Receipt, Bill of Lading or Other Document of Title.

(1) A warehouse receipt, bill of lading or other document of title is negotiable

(a) if by its terms the goods are to be delivered to bearer or to the order of a named person; or

(b) where recognized in overseas trade, if it runs to a named person or assigns.

(2) Any other document is non-negotiable. A bill of lading in which it is stated that the goods are consigned to a named person is not made negotiable by a provision that the goods are to be delivered only against a written order signed by the same or another named person.

Official Comment

Prior Uniform Statutory Provision: Sections 27 and 76, Uniform Sales Act; Sections 2, 3, 4, and 5, Uniform Warehouse Receipts Act; Sections 2, 3, 4, 5 and 53, Uniform Bills of Lading Act.

Changes: Consolidated and rewritten.

Purposes of Changes:

This Article deals with a class of commercial paper representing commodities in storage or transportation. This "commodity paper" is to be distinguished from what might be called "money paper" dealt with in the Article of this Act on Commercial Paper (Article 3) and "investment paper" dealt with in the Article of this Act on Investment Securities (Article 8). The class of "commodity paper" is designated "document of title" following the terminology of the Uniform Sales Act Section 76. Section 1-201. The distinctions between negotiable and nonnegotiable documents in this section makes the most important subclassification employed in the Article, in that the holder of negotiable documents may acquire more rights than his transferor had (See Section 7-502).

A document of title is negotiable only if it satisfies this section. "Deliverable on proper indorsement and surrender of this receipt" will not render a document negotiable. Bailees often include such provisions as a means of insuring return of non-negotiable receipts for record purposes. Such language may be regarded as insistence by the bailee upon a particular kind of receipt in connection with delivery of the goods. Subsections (1)(a) and (2) make it clear that a document is not negotiable which provides for delivery to order or bearer only if written instructions to that effect are given by a named person.

Cross Reference:

Section 7-502.

Definitional Cross References:

"Bearer". Section 1-201.
"Bill of lading". Section 1-201.
"Delivery". Section 1-201.
"Document of title". Section 1-201.
"Overseas". Section 2-323.
"Person". Section 1-201.
"Warehouse receipt". Section 1-201.

§ 7-105. Construction Against Negative Implication.

The omission from either Part 2 or Part 3 of this Article of a provision corresponding to a provision made in the other Part does not imply that a corresponding rule of law is not applicable.

Official Comment

Prior Uniform Statutory Provision: None.

Purposes:

To avoid any impairment, for example, of any common-law right of indemnity a warehouseman may have corresponding to Section 7-301(5), or of any contractual security interest a carrier might have corresponding to Section 7-209(2).

Cross References:

Parts 2 and 3 of Article 7.

PART 2

WAREHOUSE RECEIPTS: SPECIAL PROVISIONS

§ 7-201. Who May Issue a Warehouse Receipt; Storage Under Government Bond.

(1) A warehouse receipt may be issued by any warehouseman.

(2) Where goods including distilled spirits and agricultural commodities are stored under a statute requiring a bond against withdrawal or a license for the issuance of receipts in the nature of warehouse receipts, a receipt issued for the goods has like effect as a warehouse receipt even though issued by a person who is the owner of the goods and is not a warehouseman.

Official Comment

Prior Uniform Statutory Provision: Section 1, Uniform Warehouse Receipts Act.

Changes: Provision added to cover storage under government bond or under licensing statute.

Purposes:

It is not intended by reenactment of subsection (1) to repeal any provisions of special licensing or other statutes regulating who may become a warehouseman. See Section 10-103. Subsection (2) covers receipts issued by the owner for whiskey or other goods stored in bonded warehouses under such statutes as 26 U.S.C. Chapter 26. Limitations on the transfer of the receipts and criminal sanctions for violation of such limitations are not impaired. Section 7-103. Compare Section 7-401(d) on the liability of the issuer in such cases.

Cross References:

Sections 7-103, 7-401, 10-103.

Definitional Cross References:

"Warehouse receipt". Section 1-201.
"Warehouseman". Section 7-102.

§ 7-202. Form of Warehouse Receipt; Essential Terms; Optional Terms.

(1) A warehouse receipt need not be in any particular form.

(2) Unless a warehouse receipt embodies within its written or printed terms each of the following, the warehouseman is liable for damages caused by the omission to a person injured thereby:

(a) the location of the warehouse where the goods are stored;

(b) the date of issue of the receipt;

(c) the consecutive number of the receipt;

(d) a statement whether the goods received will be delivered to the bearer, to a specified person, or to a specified person or his order;

(e) the rate of storage and handling charges, except that where goods are stored under a field warehousing arrangement a statement of that fact is sufficient on a non-negotiable receipt;

(f) a description of the goods or of the packages containing them;

(g) the signature of the warehouseman, which may be made by his authorized agent;

(h) if the receipt is issued for goods of which the warehouseman is owner, either solely or jointly or in common with others, the fact of such ownership; and

(i) a statement of the amount of advances made and of liabilities incurred for which the warehouseman claims a lien or security interest (Section 7-209). If the precise amount of such advances made or of such liabilities incurred is, at the time of the issue of the receipt, unknown to the warehouseman or to his agent who issues it, a statement of the fact that advances have been made or liabilities incurred and the purpose thereof is sufficient.

(3) A warehouseman may insert in his receipt any other terms which are not contrary to the provisions of this Act and do not impair his obligation of delivery (Section 7-403) or his duty of care (Section 7-204). Any contrary provisions shall be ineffective.

Official Comment

Prior Uniform Statutory Provision: Section 2, Uniform Warehouse Receipts Act.

Changes: Exemption for field warehouse receipts added in subsection (2)(e).

Purposes:

To make clear that the formal requirements of the Uniform Warehouse Receipts Act are continued but not to displace particular legislation requiring other or different specifications of form, see Sections 7-103 and 10-103. This section does not require that a receipt be issued but states formal requirements for those which are issued.

Cross References:

Sections 7-103 and 10-103.

Definitional Cross References:

"Bearer". Section 1-201.
"Delivery". Section 1-201.
"Goods". Section 7-102.
"Person". Section 1-201.
"Security interest". Section 1-201.
"Term". Section 1-201.
"Warehouse receipt". Section 1-201.
"Warehouseman". Section 7-102.
"Written". Section 1-201.

§ 7-203. Liability for Non-receipt or Misdescription.

A party to or purchaser for value in good faith of a document of title other than a bill of lading relying in either case upon the description therein of the goods may recover from the issuer damages caused by the non-receipt or misdescription of the goods, except to the extent that the document conspicuously indicates that the issuer does not know whether any part or all of the goods in fact were received or conform to the description, as where the description is in terms of marks or labels or kind, quantity or condition, or the receipt or description is qualified by "contents, condition and quality unknown", "said to contain" or the like, if such indication be true, or the party or purchaser otherwise has notice.

Official Comment

Prior Uniform Statutory Provision: Section 20, Uniform Warehouse Receipts Act.

Changes: New section confined to problem of non-receipt and misdescription.

Purposes of Changes and New Matter:

This section is a simplified restatement of existing law as to the method by which a bailee may avoid responsibility for the accuracy of descriptions which are made by or in reliance upon information furnished by the depositor. The issuer is liable on documents issued by an agent, contrary to instructions of his principal, without receiving goods. No disclaimer of the latter liability is permitted.

Cross References:

Sections 7-301 and 7-203.

Definitional Cross References:

"Conspicuous". Section 1-201.
"Document". Section 7-102.
"Document of title". Section 1-201.
"Goods". Section 7-102.
"Issuer". Section 7-102.
"Notice". Section 1-201.
"Party". Section 1-201.
"Purchaser". Section 1-201.
"Receipt of goods". Section 2-103.
"Value". Section 1-201.

§ 7-204. Duty of Care; Contractual Limitation of Warehouseman's Liability.

(1) A warehouseman is liable for damages for loss of or injury to the goods caused by his failure to exercise such care in regard to them as a reasonably careful man would exercise under like circumstances but unless otherwise agreed he is not liable for damages which could not have been avoided by the exercise of such care.

(2) Damages may be limited by a term in the warehouse receipt or storage agreement limiting the amount of liability in case of loss or damage, and setting forth a specific liability per article or item, or value per unit of weight, beyond which the warehouseman shall not be liable; provided, however, that such liability may on written request of the bailor at the time of signing such storage agreement or within a reasonable time after receipt of the warehouse receipt be increased on part or all of the goods thereunder, in which event increased rates may be charged based on such increased valuation, but that no such increase shall be permitted contrary to a lawful limitation of liability contained in the warehouseman's tariff, if any. No such limitation is effective with respect to the warehouseman's liability for conversion to his own use.

(3) Reasonable provisions as to the time and manner of presenting claims and instituting actions based on the bailment may be included in the warehouse receipt or tariff.

(4) This section does not impair or repeal . . .

Note: *Insert in subsection (4) a reference to any statute which imposes a higher responsibility upon the warehouseman or invalidates contractual limitations which would be permissible under this Article.*

Official Comment

Prior Uniform Statutory Provision: Sections 3 and 21, Uniform Warehouse Receipts Act.

Changes: Consolidated and rewritten; material on limitation of remedy is new.

Purposes of Changes:

The old uniform acts provided that receipts could not contain terms impairing the obligation of reasonable care. Whether this is violated by a stipulation that in case of loss the bailee's liability is limited to stated amounts has been much controverted. The section is intended to eliminate that controversy by setting forth the conditions under which liability is so limited. However, as subsection (4) makes clear, the states as well as the federal government may supplement this section with more rigid standards of responsibility for some or all bailees.

Cross References:

Sections 7-103 and 10-103.

Definitional Cross References:

"Action". Section 1-201.
"Agreed". Section 1-201.
"Goods". Section 7-102.
"Reasonable time". Section 1-204.
"Sign". Section 1-201.
"Term". Section 1-201.
"Value". Section 1-201.
"Warehouse receipt". Section 1-201.
"Warehouseman". Section 7-102.
"Written". Section 1-201.

§ 7-205. Title Under Warehouse Receipt Defeated in Certain Cases.

A buyer in the ordinary course of business of fungible goods sold and delivered by a warehouseman who is also in the business of buying and selling such goods takes free of any claim under a warehouse receipt even though it has been duly negotiated.

Official Comment

Prior Uniform Statutory Provision: None.

Purposes:

The typical case covered by this section is that of the warehouseman-dealer in grain, and the substantive question at issue is whether in case the warehouseman becomes insolvent the receipt holders shall be able to trace and recover grain shipped to farmers and other purchasers from the elevator. This was possible under the old acts, although courts were eager to find estoppels to prevent it. The practical difficulty of tracing fungible grain means that the preservation of this theoretical right adds little to the commercial acceptability of negotiable grain receipts, which really circulate on the credit of the warehouseman. Moreover, on default of the warehouseman, the receipt holders at least share in what grain remains, whereas retaking the grain from a good faith cash purchaser reduces him completely to the status of general creditor in a situation where there was very little he could do to guard against the loss. Compare 15 U.S.C. Section 714p, enacted in 1955.

Cross References:

Sections 2-403 and 9-307.

Definitional Cross References:

"Buyer in ordinary course of business". Section 1-201.
"Delivery". Section 1-201.
"Duly negotiate". Section 7-501.
"Fungible" goods. Section 1-201.
"Goods". Section 7-102.
"Value". Section 1-201.
"Warehouse receipt". Section 1-201.
"Warehouseman". Section 7-102.

§ 7-206. Termination of Storage at Warehouseman's Option.

(1) A warehouseman may on notifying the person on whose account the goods are held and any other person known to claim an interest in the goods

require payment of any charges and removal of the goods from the warehouse at the termination of the period of storage fixed by the document, or, if no period is fixed, within a stated period not less than thirty days after the notification. If the goods are not removed before the date specified in the notification, the warehouseman may sell them in accordance with the provisions of the section on enforcement of a warehouseman's lien (Section 7-210).

(2) If a warehouseman in good faith believes that the goods are about to deteriorate or decline in value to less than the amount of his lien within the time prescribed in subsection (1) for notification, advertisement and sale, the warehouseman may specify in the notification any reasonable shorter time for removal of the goods and in case the goods are not removed, may sell them at public sale held not less than one week after a single advertisement or posting.

(3) If as a result of a quality or condition of the goods of which the warehouseman had no notice at the time of deposit the goods are a hazard to other property or to the warehouse or to persons, the warehouseman may sell the goods at public or private sale without advertisement on reasonable notification to all persons known to claim an interest in the goods. If the warehouseman after a reasonable effort is unable to sell the goods he may dispose of them in any lawful manner and shall incur no liability by reason of such disposition.

(4) The warehouseman must deliver the goods to any person entitled to them under this Article upon due demand made at any time prior to sale or other disposition under this section.

(5) The warehouseman may satisfy his lien from the proceeds of any sale or disposition under this section but must hold the balance for delivery on the demand of any person to whom he would have been bound to deliver the goods.

Official Comment

Prior Uniform Statutory Provision: Section 34, Uniform Warehouse Receipts Act.

Changes: Rewritten and expanded to define the warehouseman's right to terminate the storage not only where the goods are perishable or hazardous as in Uniform Warehouse Receipts Act, Section 34, but also for any other reason including decline in value of the goods imperilling the warehouseman's security for charges.

Purposes of Changes:

1. Most warehousing is for an indefinite term, the bailor being entitled to delivery on reasonable demand. It is necessary to define the warehouseman's power to terminate the bailment, since it would be commercially intolerable to allow warehousemen to order removal of the goods on short notice. The thirty day period provided where the document does not carry its own period of termination corresponds to commercial practice of computing rates on a monthly basis. The right to terminate under subsection (1) includes a right to require payment of "any charges", but does not depend on the existence of unpaid charges.

2. In permitting expeditious disposition of perishable and hazardous goods Uniform Warehouse Receipts Act, Section 34, made no distinction between cases where the warehouseman knowingly undertook to store such goods and cases where the goods were discovered to be of that character subsequent to storage. The former situation presents no such

emergency as justifies the summary power of removal and sale. Subsections (2) and (3) distinguish between the two situations.

3. Protection of his lien is the only interest which the warehouseman has to justify summary sale of perishable goods which are not hazardous. This same interest must be recognized when the stored goods, although not perishable, decline in market value to a point which threatens the warehouseman's security.

4. The right to order removal of stored goods is subject to provisions of the public warehousing laws of some states forbidding warehousemen from discriminating among customers. Nor does the section relieve the warehouseman of any obligation under the states laws to secure the approval of a public official before disposing of deteriorating goods. Such *regulatory* statutes and the regulations under them remain in force and operative. Sections 7-103, 10-103.

Cross References:

Sections 7-103, 7-403, 10-103.

Definitional Cross References:

"Delivery". Section 1-201.
"Document". Section 7-102.
"Good faith". Section 1-201.
"Goods". Section 7-102.
"Notice". Section 1-201.
"Notification". Section 1-201.
"Person". Section 1-201.
"Reasonable time". Section 1-204.
"Value". Section 1-201.
"Warehouseman". Section 7-102.

§ 7-207. Goods Must Be Kept Separate; Fungible Goods.

(1) Unless the warehouse receipt otherwise provides, a warehouseman must keep separate the goods covered by each receipt so as to permit at all times identification and delivery of those goods except that different lots of fungible goods may be commingled.

(2) Fungible goods so commingled are owned in common by the persons entitled thereto and the warehouseman is severally liable to each owner for that owner's share. Where because of overissue a mass of fungible goods is insufficient to meet all the receipts which the warehouseman has issued against it, the persons entitled include all holders to whom overissued receipts have been duly negotiated.

Official Comment

Prior Uniform Statutory Provision: Sections 22, 23 and 24, Uniform Warehouse Receipts Act.

Changes: Consolidated and revised; holders of overissued receipts permitted to share in mass of fungible goods.

Purposes of Changes:

No change of substance is made other than the explicit statement that holders to whom overissued receipts have been duly negotiated shall share in a mass of fungible goods. Where individual ownership interests are merged into claims on a common fund, as is necessarily the case with fungible goods, there is no policy reason for discriminating between successive purchasers of similar claims.

Definitional Cross References:

"Delivery". Section 1-201.
"Duly negotiate". Section 7-501.
"Fungible" goods. Section 1-201.
"Goods". Section 7-102.
"Holder". Section 1-201.
"Person". Section 1-201.
"Warehouse receipt". Section 1-201.
"Warehouseman". Section 7-102.

§ 7-208. Altered Warehouse Receipts.

Where a blank in a negotiable warehouse receipt has been filled in without authority, a purchaser for value and without notice of the want of authority may treat the insertion as authorized. Any other unauthorized alteration leaves any receipt enforceable against the issuer according to its original tenor.

Official Comment

Prior Uniform Statutory Provision: Section 13, Uniform Warehouse Receipts Act.

Changes: Generally revised and simplified; explicit treatment of the situation where a blank in an executed document is filled without authority.

Purposes of Changes:

1. The execution of warehouse receipts in blank is a dangerous practice. As between the issuer and an innocent purchaser the risks should clearly fall on the former.

2. An unauthorized alteration whether made with or without fraudulent intent does not relieve the issuer of his liability on the warehouse receipt as originally executed. The unauthorized alteration itself is of course ineffective against the warehouseman.

Definitional Cross References:

"Issuer". Section 7-102.
"Notice". Section 1-201.
"Purchaser". Section 1-201.
"Value". Section 1-201.
"Warehouse receipt". Section 1-201.

§ 7-209. Lien of Warehouseman.

(1) A warehouseman has a lien against the bailor on the goods covered by a warehouse receipt or on the proceeds thereof in his possession for charges for storage or transportation (including demurrage and terminal charges), insurance, labor, or charges present or future in relation to the goods, and for expenses necessary for preservation of the goods or reasonably incurred in their sale pursuant to law. If the person on whose account the goods are held is liable for like charges or expenses in relation to other goods whenever deposited and it is stated in the receipt that a lien is claimed for charges and expenses in relation to other goods, the warehouseman also has a lien against him for such charges and expenses whether or not the other goods have been delivered by the warehouseman. But against a person to whom a negotiable warehouse receipt is duly negotiated a warehouseman's lien is limited to charges in an amount or at a rate specified on the receipt or if no charges are so specified then to a reasonable charge for storage of the goods covered by the receipt subsequent to the date of the receipt.

(2) The warehouseman may also reserve a security interest against the bailor for a maximum amount specified on the receipt for charges other than those specified in subsection (1), such as for money advanced and interest. Such a security interest is governed by the Article on Secured Transactions (Article 9).

(3)(a) A warehouseman's lien for charges and expenses under subsection (1) or a security interest under subsection (2) is also effective against any person who so entrusted the bailor with possession of the goods that a pledge of them by him to a good faith purchaser for value would have been valid but is not effective against a person as to whom the document confers no right in the goods covered by it under Section 7-503.

(b) A warehouseman's lien on household goods for charges and expenses in relation to the goods under subsection (1) is also effective against all persons if the depositor was the legal possessor of the goods at the time of deposit. "Household goods" means furniture, furnishings and personal effects used by the depositor in a dwelling.

(4) A warehouseman loses his lien on any goods which he voluntarily delivers or which he unjustifiably refuses to deliver.

As amended in 1966.

Official Comment

Prior Uniform Statutory Provision: Sections 27 through 32, Uniform Warehouse Receipts Act.

Changes: Rewritten.

Purposes of Changes:

1. Subsection (1) defines the warehouseman's statutory lien. A specific lien attaches automatically, without express notation on the receipt, to goods stored under a non-negotiable receipt. That lien is limited to the usual charges arising out of a storage transaction; by notation on the receipt it can be made a general lien extending to like charges in relation to other goods. The same rules apply where the receipt is negotiable, except that as against a holder by due negotiation the lien is limited to the amount or rate specified on the receipt, or, if none is specified, to a reasonable charge for storage of the specific goods after the date of the receipt.

2. Subsection (2) provides for a security interest based upon agreement. Such a security interest arises out of relations between the parties other than bailment for storage or transportation, as where the bailee assumes the role of financer or performs a manufacturing operation, extending credit in reliance upon the goods covered by the receipt. Such a security interest is not a statutory lien. Compare Sections 9–102(2) and 9–310. It is governed in all respects by Article 9, except that subsection (2) requires that the receipt specify a maximum amount and limits the security interest to the amount specified.

3. Subsections (1) and (2) validate the lien and security interest "against the bailor." As against third parties, subsection (3)(a) continues the rule under the prior uniform statutory provision that to validate the lien the owner must have entrusted the goods to the depositor, and that the circumstances must be such that a pledge by the depositor to a good faith purchaser for value would have been valid. Thus the owner's interest will not be subjected to a lien or security interest arising out of a deposit of his goods by a thief. The warehouseman may be protected because of the actual, implied or apparent authority of the depositor, because of a Factor's Act, or because of other circumstances which would protect a bona fide pledgee, unless those circumstances are denied effect under Section 7–503. Where the third party is the holder of a security interest, the rights of the warehouseman depend on the priority given to a hypothetical bona fide pledgee by Article 9, particularly Section 9–312. Thus the special priority granted to statutory liens by Section 9–310 does not apply to liens under subsection (1) of this section, since subsection (3) "expressly provides otherwise" within the meaning of Section 9–310. As to household goods, however, subsection (3)(b) makes the warehouseman's lien "for charges and expenses in relation to the goods" effective against all persons if the depositor was the legal possessor. The purpose of the exception is to permit the warehouseman to accept household goods for storage in sole reliance on the value of the goods themselves, especially in situations of family emergency. [This paragraph was amended in 1966].

4. It is unnecessary to state here, as in Uniform Warehouse Receipts Act 31, that a bailee with a valid lien need not

deliver until the lien is satisfied. Section 7–403 provides that a person demanding delivery under a document must be prepared to satisfy the bailee's lien.

5. Where goods have been stored under a non-negotiable warehouse receipt and are sold by the person to whom the receipt has been issued, frequently the goods are not withdrawn by the new owner. The obligations of the seller of the goods in this situation are set forth in Section 2–503(4) on tender of delivery and include procurement of an acknowledgment by the bailee of the buyer's right to possession of the goods. If a new receipt is requested, such an acknowledgment can be withheld until storage charges have been paid or provided for. The statutory lien for charges on the goods sold, granted by the first sentence of subsection (1), continues valid unless the bailee gives it up. But once a new receipt is issued to the buyer, the buyer becomes "the person on whose account the goods are held" under the second sentence of subsection (1); unless he undertakes liability for charges in relation to other goods stored by the seller, there is no general lien against the buyer for such charges. Of course, the bailee may preserve the general lien in such a case either by an arrangement by which the buyer "is liable for" such charges, or by reserving a security interest under subsection (2).

Cross References:

Point 2: Sections 9–102(2) and 9–310.
Point 3: Sections 7–503, 9–310 and 9–312.
Point 4: Section 7–403.
Point 5: Section 2–503.

Definitional Cross References:

"Deliver". Section 1–201.
"Document". Section 7–102.
"Goods". Section 7–102.
"Money". Section 1–201.
"Person". Section 1–201.
"Purchaser". Section 1–201.
"Right". Section 1–201.
"Security interest". Section 1–201.
"Value". Section 1–201.
"Warehouse receipt". Section 1–201.
"Warehouseman". Section 7–102.

§ 7–210. Enforcement of Warehouseman's Lien.

(1) Except as provided in subsection (2), a warehouseman's lien may be enforced by public or private sale of the goods in block or in parcels, at any time or place and on any terms which are commercially reasonable, after notifying all persons known to claim an interest in the goods. Such notification must include a statement of the amount due, the nature of the proposed sale and the time and place of any public sale. The fact that a better price could have been obtained by a sale at a different time or in a different method from that selected by the warehouseman is not of itself sufficient to establish that the sale was not made in a commercially reasonable manner. If the warehouseman either sells the goods in the usual manner in any recognized market therefor, or if he sells at the price current in such market at the time of his sale, or if he has otherwise sold in conformity with commercially reasonable practices among dealers in the type of goods sold, he has sold in a commercially reasonable manner. A sale of more goods than apparently necessary to be offered to insure satisfaction of the obligation is not commercially reasonable except in cases covered by the preceding sentence.

(2) A warehouseman's lien on goods other than goods stored by a merchant in the course of his business may be enforced only as follows:

(a) All persons known to claim an interest in the goods must be notified.

(b) The notification must be delivered in person or sent by registered or certified letter to the last known address of any person to be notified.

(c) The notification must include an itemized statement of the claim, a description of the goods subject to the lien, a demand for payment within a specified time not less than ten days after receipt of the notification, and a conspicuous statement that unless the claim is paid within that time the goods will be advertised for sale and sold by auction at a specified time and place.

(d) The sale must conform to the terms of the notification.

(e) The sale must be held at the nearest suitable place to that where the goods are held or stored.

(f) After the expiration of the time given in the notification, an advertisement of the sale must be published once a week for two weeks consecutively in a newspaper of general circulation where the sale is to be held. The advertisement must include a description of the goods, the name of the person on whose account they are being held, and the time and place of the sale. The sale must take place at least fifteen days after the first publication. If there is no newspaper of general circulation where the sale is to be held, the advertisement must be posted at least ten days before the sale in not less than six conspicuous places in the neighborhood of the proposed sale.

(3) Before any sale pursuant to this section any person claiming a right in the goods may pay the amount necessary to satisfy the lien and the reasonable expenses incurred under this section. In that event the goods must not be sold, but must be retained by the warehouseman subject to the terms of the receipt and this Article.

(4) The warehouseman may buy at any public sale pursuant to this section.

(5) A purchaser in good faith of goods sold to enforce a warehouseman's lien takes the goods free of any rights of persons against whom the lien was valid, despite noncompliance by the warehouseman with the requirements of this section.

(6) The warehouseman may satisfy his lien from the proceeds of any sale pursuant to this section but must hold the balance, if any, for delivery on demand to any person to whom he would have been bound to deliver the goods.

(7) The rights provided by this section shall be in addition to all other rights allowed by law to a creditor against his debtor.

(8) Where a lien is on goods stored by a merchant in the course of his business the lien may be enforced in accordance with either subsection (1) or (2).

(9) The warehouseman is liable for damages caused by failure to comply with the requirements for sale under this section and in case of willful violation is liable for conversion.

As amended in 1962.

Official Comment

Prior Uniform Statutory Provision: Section 33, Uniform Warehouse Receipts Act.

Changes: Rewritten; simplified foreclosure proceeding provided for all liens other than warehousemen's lien in non-commercial storage.

Purposes of Changes:

1. Subsection (1) makes "commercial reasonableness" the standard for foreclosure proceedings in all cases except non-commercial storage with a warehouseman. The latter category embraces principally storage of household goods by private owners; and for such cases the detailed provisions as to notification, publication and public sale, found in Section 33 of the Uniform Warehouse Receipts Act are retained in subsection (2). The swifter, more flexible procedure of subsection (1) is appropriate to commercial storage. Compare seller's power of resale on breach by buyer under the provisions of the Article on Sales (Section 2-706).

2. The provisions of subsections (4) and (5) permitting the bailee to bid at public sales and confirming the title of purchasers at foreclosure sales are designed to secure more bidding and better prices.

Cross Reference:

Section 7-403.

Definitional Cross References:

"Bill of lading". Section 1-201.
"Conspicuous". Section 1-201.
"Creditor". Section 1-201.
"Delivery". Section 1-201.
"Document". Section 7-102.
"Good faith". Section 1-201.
"Goods". Section 7-102.
"Notification". Section 1-201.
"Notifies". Section 1-201.
"Person". Section 1-201.
"Purchaser". Section 1-201.
"Rights". Section 1-201.
"Term". Section 1-201.
"Warehouseman". Section 7-102.

PART 3

BILLS OF LADING: SPECIAL PROVISIONS

§ 7-301. Liability for Non-receipt or Misdescription; "Said to Contain"; "Shipper's Load and Count"; Improper Handling.

(1) A consignee of a non-negotiable bill who has given value in good faith or a holder to whom a negotiable bill has been duly negotiated relying in either case upon the description therein of the goods, or upon the date therein shown, may recover from the issuer damages caused by the misdating of the bill or the non-receipt or misdescription of the goods, except to the extent that the document indicates that the issuer does not know whether any part or all of the goods in fact were received or conform to the description, as where the description is in terms of marks or labels or kind, quantity, or condition or the receipt or description is qualified by "contents or condition of contents of packages unknown", "said to contain", "shipper's weight, load and count" or the like, if such indication be true.

(2) When goods are loaded by an issuer who is a common carrier, the issuer must count the packages of goods if package freight and ascertain the kind and quantity if bulk freight. In such cases "shipper's weight, load and count" or other words indicating that the description was made by the shipper are ineffective except as to freight concealed by packages.

(3) When bulk freight is loaded by a shipper who makes available to the issuer adequate facilities for weighing such freight, an issuer who is a common carrier must ascertain the kind and quantity within a reasonable time after receiving the written request of the shipper to do so. In such cases "shipper's weight" or other words of like purport are ineffective.

(4) The issuer may by inserting in the bill the words "shipper's weight, load and count" or other words of like purport indicate that the goods were loaded by the shipper; and if such statement be true the issuer shall not be liable for damages caused by the improper loading. But their omission does not imply liability for such damages.

(5) The shipper shall be deemed to have guaranteed to the issuer the accuracy at the time of shipment of the description, marks, labels, number, kind, quantity, condition and weight, as furnished by him; and the shipper shall indemnify the issuer against damage caused by inaccuracies in such particulars. The right of the issuer to such indemnity shall in no way limit his responsibility and liability under the contract of carriage to any person other than the shipper.

Official Comment

Prior Uniform Statutory Provision: Section 23, Uniform Bills of Lading Act.

Changes: Rewritten in part.

Purposes of Changes:

1. The provision as to misdating in subsection (1) conforms to the policy of the amendment to the Federal Bills of Lading Act by 44 Stat. 1450 (1927), as amended 49 U.S.C. Section 102, after the holding in Browne v. Union Pac. R. Co., 113 Kan. 726, 216 P. 299 (1923), affirmed on other grounds 267 U.S. 255, 45 S.Ct. 315, 69 L.Ed. 601 (1925). Subsections (2) and (3) conform to the policy of the Federal Bills of Lading Act, 49 U.S.C. Sections 100, 101, and the laws of several states. See, e.g., N.Y.Pers.Prop.Law Section 209; Report of N.Y. Law Revision Commission, N.Y.Leg.Doc. (1941) No. 65(F).

2. The language of the old Uniform Act suggested that a carrier is ordinarily liable for damage caused by improper loading, but may relieve himself of liability by disclosing on the bill that shipper actually loaded. A more accurate statement of the law is that the carrier is not liable for losses caused by act or default of the shipper, which would include improper loading. There is some question whether under present law a carrier is liable even to a good faith purchaser of a negotiable bill for such losses, if the shipper's faulty loading in fact caused the loss. It is this doubtful liability which subsection (4) permits the carrier to bar by disclosure of shipper's loading. There is no implication that decisions such as Modern Tool Corp. v. Pennsylvania R. Co., 100 F.Supp. 595 (D.N.J.1951), are disapproved.

3. This section is a simplified restatement of existing law as to the method by which a bailee may avoid responsibility for the accuracy of descriptions which are made by or in reliance upon information furnished by the depositor or shipper. The issuer is liable on documents issued by an agent, contrary to instructions of his principal, without receiving goods. No disclaimer of this liability is permitted since it is not a matter either of the care of the goods or their description.

4. The shipper's erroneous report to the carrier concerning the goods may cause damage to the carrier. Subsection (5) therefore provides appropriate indemnity.

Cross References:

Sections 7-203 and 7-309.

Definitional Cross References:

"Bill of lading". Section 1-201.
"Consignee". Section 7-102.
"Document". Section 7-102.
"Duly negotiate". Section 7-501.
"Good faith". Section 1-201.
"Goods". Section 7-102.
"Holder". Section 1-201.
"Issuer". Section 7-102.
"Notice". Section 1-201.
"Party". Section 1-201.
"Purchaser". Section 1-201.
"Receipt of goods". Section 2-103.
"Value". Section 1-201.

§ 7-302. Through Bills of Lading and Similar Documents.

(1) The issuer of a through bill of lading or other document embodying an undertaking to be performed in part by persons acting as its agents or by connecting carriers is liable to anyone entitled to recover on the document for any breach by such other persons or by a connecting carrier of its obligation under the document but to the extent that the bill covers an undertaking to be performed overseas or in territory not contiguous to the continental United States or an undertaking including matters other than transportation this liability may be varied by agreement of the parties.

(2) Where goods covered by a through bill of lading or other document embodying an undertaking to be performed in part by persons other than the issuer are received by any such person, he is subject with respect to his own performance while the goods are in his possession to the obligation of the issuer. His obligation is discharged by delivery of the goods to another such person pursuant to the document, and does not include liability for breach by any other such persons or by the issuer.

(3) The issuer of such through bill of lading or other document shall be entitled to recover from the connecting carrier or such other person in possession of the goods when the breach of the obligation under the document occurred, the amount it may be required to pay to anyone entitled to recover on the document therefor, as may be evidenced by any receipt, judgment, or transcript thereof, and the amount of any expense reasonably incurred by it in defending any action brought by anyone entitled to recover on the document therefor.

Official Comment

Prior Uniform Statutory Provision: None.

Purposes:

1. The purpose of this section is to subject the initial carrier under a through bill to suit for breach of the contract of carriage by any connecting carrier and to make it clear that any such connecting carrier holds the goods on terms which are defined by the document of title even though such connecting carrier did not issue the document. Since the connecting carrier does hold on the terms of the document, it must honor a proper demand for delivery or a diversion order just as the original bailee would have to. Similarly it has the benefits of the excuses for nondelivery and limitations of liability provided for the original bailee. Unlike the original bailee-issuer, the connecting carrier's responsibility is limited to the period while the goods are in its possession. The section is patterned generally after the Interstate Commerce Act, but does not impose any obligation to issue through bills.

2. The reference to documents other than through bills looks to the possibility that multi-purpose documents may come

into use, e.g., combination warehouse receipts and bills of lading.

3. Where the obligations or standards applicable to different parties bound by a document of title are different, the initial carrier's responsibility for portions of the journey not on its own lines will be determined by the standards appropriate to the connecting carrier. Thus a land carrier issuing a through bill of lading involving water carriage at a later stage will have the benefit of the water carrier's immunity from liability for negligence of its servants in navigating the vessel, where the law provides such an immunity for water carriers and the loss occurred while the goods were in the water carrier's possession.

4. Under Subsection (1) the issuer of a through bill of lading may become liable for the fault of another person. Subsection (3) gives it appropriate rights of recourse.

Definitional Cross References:

"Agreement". Section 1-201.
"Bailee". Section 7-102.
"Bill of lading". Section 1-201.
"Delivery". Section 1-201.
"Document". Section 7-102.
"Goods". Section 7-102.
"Issuer". Section 7-102.
"Overseas". Section 2-323.
"Party". Section 1-201.
"Person". Section 1-201.

§ 7-303. Diversion; Reconsignment; Change of Instructions.

(1) Unless the bill of lading otherwise provides, the carrier may deliver the goods to a person or destination other than that stated in the bill or may otherwise dispose of the goods on instructions from

(a) the holder of a negotiable bill; or

(b) the consignor on a non-negotiable bill notwithstanding contrary instructions from the consignee; or

(c) the consignee on a non-negotiable bill in the absence of contrary instructions from the consignor, if the goods have arrived at the billed destination or if the consignee is in possession of the bill; or

(d) the consignee on a non-negotiable bill if he is entitled as against the consignor to dispose of them.

(2) Unless such instructions are noted on a negotiable bill of lading, a person to whom the bill is duly negotiated can hold the bailee according to the original terms.

Official Comment

Prior Uniform Statutory Provision: None.

Purposes:

1. The old Acts contained no reference to diversion, a very common commercial practice which defeats delivery to the consignee originally named in a bill of lading. The carrier was protected under the heading of "justified delivery" if the substituted consignee who received delivery was "a person lawfully entitled to possession of the goods." Cf. subsection (1)(d). This in turn depended on whether the person ordering the diversion was the owner of the goods or empowered to dispose of them, which again might depend upon whether under sales law title had passed from the consignor-seller to the consignee-buyer. The carrier is plainly not in a position to decide such questions when directed by the person with whom it has contracted for transportation to change the destination of the goods in transit. Carriers may as a business matter be willing to accept instructions from consignees in which case, as under the old

uniform acts, the carrier will be liable for misdelivery if the consignee was not the owner or otherwise empowered to dispose of the goods. The section imposes no duty on carriers to undertake diversion; it is of course subject to the provisions of filed tariffs. Section 7-103.

2. It should be noted that the section provides only an immunity for carriers against liability for "misdelivery." It does not, for example, defeat the title to the goods which the consignee-buyer may have acquired from the consignor-seller upon delivery of the goods to the carrier under a non-negotiable bill of lading. Thus if the carrier, upon instructions from the consignor, returns the goods to him, the consignee may recover the goods from the consignor or his insolvent estate. However, under certain circumstances, the consignee's title may be defeated by diversion of the goods in transit to a different consignee.

Cross References:

Point 2: Sections 7-403 and 7-504(3).

Definitional Cross References:

"Bailee". Section 7-102.
"Bill of lading". Section 1-201.
"Consignee". Section 7-102.
"Consignor". Section 7-102.
"Delivery". Section 1-201.
"Goods". Section 7-102.
"Holder". Section 1-201.
"Notice". Section 1-201.
"Person". Section 1-201.
"Purchaser". Section 1-201.
"Term". Section 1-201.

§ 7-304. Bills of Lading in a Set.

(1) Except where customary in overseas transportation, a bill of lading must not be issued in a set of parts. The issuer is liable for damages caused by violation of this subsection.

(2) Where a bill of lading is lawfully drawn in a set of parts, each of which is numbered and expressed to be valid only if the goods have not been delivered against any other part, the whole of the parts constitute one bill.

(3) Where a bill of lading is lawfully issued in a set of parts and different parts are negotiated to different persons, the title of the holder to whom the first due negotiation is made prevails as to both the document and the goods even though any later holder may have received the goods from the carrier in good faith and discharged the carrier's obligation by surrender of his part.

(4) Any person who negotiates or transfers a single part of a bill of lading drawn in a set is liable to holders of that part as if it were the whole set.

(5) The bailee is obliged to deliver in accordance with Part 4 of this Article against the first presented part of a bill of lading lawfully drawn in a set. Such delivery discharges the bailee's obligation on the whole bill.

Official Comment

Prior Uniform Statutory Provision: Section 6, Uniform Bills of Lading Act.

Changes: This section adds to existing legislation, which merely prohibits bills in a set in ordinary domestic trade, a statement of the legal effect of a lawfully issued set.

Purposes of Changes:

The statement of the legal effect of a lawfully issued set is in accord with existing commercial law relating to maritime and other overseas bills. This law has been codified in the Hague and Warsaw Conventions and in the Carriage of Goods by Sea Act, the provisions of which would ordinarily govern in situations where bills in a set are recognized by this Article.

Cross Reference:

Section 10-103.

Definitional Cross References:

"Bailee". Section 7-102.
"Bill of lading". Section 7-102.
"Delivery". Section 1-201.
"Document". Section 7-102.
"Duly negotiate". Section 7-501.
"Good faith". Section 1-201.
"Goods". Section 7-102.
"Holder". Section 1-201.
"Issuer". Section 7-102.
"Overseas". Section 2-323.
"Person". Section 1-201.
"Receipt of goods". Section 2-103.

§ 7-305. Destination Bills.

(1) Instead of issuing a bill of lading to the consignor at the place of shipment a carrier may at the request of the consignor procure the bill to be issued at destination or at any other place designated in the request.

(2) Upon request of anyone entitled as against the carrier to control the goods while in transit and on surrender of any outstanding bill of lading or other receipt covering such goods, the issuer may procure a substitute bill to be issued at any place designated in the request.

Official Comment

Prior Uniform Statutory Provision: None.

Purposes:

This proposal is designed to facilitate the use of order bills in connection with fast shipments. Use of order bills on high speed shipments is impeded by the fact that the goods may arrive at destination before the documents, so that no one is ready to take delivery from the carrier. This is especially inconvenient for carriers by truck and air, who do not have terminal facilities where shipments can be held to await consignee's appearance. Order bills would be useful to take advantage of bank collection. This may be preferable to C.O.D. shipment in which the carrier, e.g. a truck driver, is the collecting and remitting agent. Financing of shipments under this plan would be handled as follows: seller at San Francisco delivers the goods to an airline with instructions to issue a bill in New York to a named bank. Seller receives a receipt embodying this undertaking to issue a destination bill. Airline wires its New York freight agent to issue the bill as instructed by the seller. Seller wires the New York bank a draft on buyer. New York bank indorses the bill to buyer when he honors the draft. Normally seller would act through his own bank in San Francisco, which would extend him credit in reliance on the airline's contract to deliver a bill to the order of its New York correspondent. This section is entirely permissive; it imposes no duty to issue such bills. Whether a connecting carrier will act as issuing agent is left to agreement between carriers.

Definitional Cross References:

"Bill of lading". Section 1-201.
"Consignor". Section 7-102.
"Goods". Section 7-102.
"Issuer". Section 7-102.
"Receipt of goods". Section 2-103.

§ 7-306. Altered Bills of Lading.

An unauthorized alteration or filling in of a blank in a bill of lading leaves the bill enforceable according to its original tenor.

Official Comment

Prior Uniform Statutory Provision: Section 16, Uniform Bills of Lading Act.

Changes: Generally revised and simplified; explicit treatment of the situation where a blank in an executed document is filled without authority.

Purposes of Changes:

An unauthorized alteration whether made with or without fraudulent intent does not relieve the issuer of his liability on the document as originally executed. Uniform Warehouse Receipts Act 13 excused the issuer from any liability to a fraudulent alterer, other than the liability to deliver the goods according to the terms of the original document. It is difficult to conceive what liability the draftsman intended to excuse. Uniform Bills of Lading Act 16 contains no such excuse provision, and is followed in this respect in the present section. Uniform Bills of Lading Act 16 characterizes an unauthorized alteration as "void" but apparently nothing more was intended than that the alteration did not change the obligation of the issuer. This is sufficiently covered by the terms of this Section. Moreover cases are conceivable in which an alteration would not be "void"; for example, an alteration made by common consent of a transferor and transferee of a document might evidence an enforceable contract between them. The same rule is made applicable to the filling in of blanks, a matter on which the prior Acts were silent.

Definitional Cross References:

"Bill of lading". Section 1-201.
"Issuer". Section 7-102.

§ 7-307. Lien of Carrier.

(1) A carrier has a lien on the goods covered by a bill of lading for charges subsequent to the date of its receipt of the goods for storage or transportation (including demurrage and terminal charges) and for expenses necessary for preservation of the goods incident to their transportation or reasonably incurred in their sale pursuant to law. But against a purchaser for value of a negotiable bill of lading a carrier's lien is limited to charges stated in the bill or the applicable tariffs, or if no charges are stated then to a reasonable charge.

(2) A lien for charges and expenses under subsection (1) on goods which the carrier was required by law to receive for transportation is effective against the consignor or any person entitled to the goods unless the carrier had notice that the consignor lacked authority to subject the goods to such charges and expenses. Any other lien under subsection (1) is effective against the consignor and any person who permitted the bailor to have control or possession of the goods unless the carrier had notice that the bailor lacked such authority.

(3) A carrier loses his lien on any goods which he voluntarily delivers or which he unjustifiably refuses to deliver.

Official Comment

Prior Uniform Statutory Provision: Sections 27 through 32, Uniform Warehouse Receipts Act.

Changes: Rewritten; lien extended to carrier. Lien of common carrier validated unless carrier had notice that consignor lacked authority to subject the goods to charges and expenses. Where the carrier is not required by law to receive the goods for transportation, lien validated against anyone who permitted the bailor to have possession even if he had no real or apparent authority.

Purposes of Changes:

The section is intended to give carriers a specific statutory lien for charges and expenses similar to that given to warehousemen by the first sentence of Section

7-209. But since carriers do not commonly claim a lien for charges in relation to other goods or lend money on the security of goods in their hands, provisions for a general lien or a security interest similar to those in Section 7-209(1) and (2) are omitted. See Comment to Section 7-105. Since the lien given by this section is specific, and the storage or transportation often preserves or increases the value of the goods, subsection (2) validates the lien against anyone who permitted the bailor to have possession of the goods. Where the carrier is required to receive the goods for transportation, the owner's interest may be subjected to charges and expenses arising out of deposit of his goods by a thief. Cf. Section 9-310. The crucial mental element is the carrier's knowledge or reason to know of the bailor's lack of authority.

Cross References:

Sections 7-209, 9-102(2) and 9-310.

Definitional Cross References:

"Bill of lading". Section 1-201.
"Consignor". Section 7-102.
"Delivery". Section 1-201.
"Goods". Section 7-102.
"Person". Section 1-201.
"Purchaser". Section 1-201.
"Value". Section 1-201.

§ 7-308. Enforcement of Carrier's Lien.

(1) A carrier's lien may be enforced by public or private sale of the goods, in block or in parcels, at any time or place and on any terms which are commercially reasonable, after notifying all persons known to claim an interest in the goods. Such notification must include a statement of the amount due, the nature of the proposed sale and the time and place of any public sale. The fact that a better price could have been obtained by a sale at a different time or in a different method from that selected by the carrier is not of itself sufficient to establish that the sale was not made in a commercially reasonable manner. If the carrier either sells the goods in the usual manner in any recognized market therefor or if he sells at the price current in such market at the time of his sale or if he has otherwise sold in conformity with commercially reasonable practices among dealers in the type of goods sold he has sold in a commercially reasonable manner. A sale of more goods than apparently necessary to be offered to ensure satisfaction of the obligation is not commercially reasonable except in cases covered by the preceding sentence.

(2) Before any sale pursuant to this section any person claiming a right in the goods may pay the amount necessary to satisfy the lien and the reasonable expenses incurred under this section. In that event the goods must not be sold, but must be retained by the carrier subject to the terms of the bill and this Article.

(3) The carrier may buy at any public sale pursuant to this section.

(4) A purchaser in good faith of goods sold to enforce a carrier's lien takes the goods free of any rights of persons against whom the lien was valid, despite noncompliance by the carrier with the requirements of this section.

(5) The carrier may satisfy his lien from the proceeds of any sale pursuant to this section but must hold the balance, if any, for delivery on demand to any person to whom he would have been bound to deliver the goods.

(6) The rights provided by this section shall be in addition to all other rights allowed by law to a creditor against his debtor.

(7) A carrier's lien may be enforced in accordance with either subsection (1) or the procedure set forth in subsection (2) of Section 7-210.

(8) The carrier is liable for damages caused by failure to comply with the requirements for sale under this section and in case of willful violation is liable for conversion.

Official Comment

Prior Uniform Statutory Provision: Section 33, Uniform Warehouse Receipts Act.

Changes: Rewritten; provisions extended to carriers' liens; simplified foreclosure proceeding provided.

Purposes of Changes:

This section is intended to give the carrier an enforcement procedure of his lien coextensive with that given the warehousemen in cases other than those covering noncommercial storage by him. See Comment to Section 7-210.

Cross Reference:

Section 7-210.

Definitional Cross References:

"Bill of lading". Section 1-201.
"Creditor". Section 1-201.
"Delivery". Section 1-201.
"Good faith". Section 1-201.
"Goods". Section 7-102.
"Notification". Section 1-201.
"Notifies". Section 1-201.
"Person". Section 1-201.
"Purchaser". Section 1-201.
"Rights". Section 1-201.
"Term". Section 1-201.

§ 7-309. Duty of Care; Contractual Limitation of Carrier's Liability.

(1) A carrier who issues a bill of lading whether negotiable or non-negotiable must exercise the degree of care in relation to the goods which a reasonably careful man would exercise under like circumstances. This subsection does not repeal or change any law or rule of law which imposes liability upon a common carrier for damages not caused by its negligence.

(2) Damages may be limited by a provision that the carrier's liability shall not exceed a value stated in the document if the carrier's rates are dependent upon value and the consignor by the carrier's tariff is afforded an opportunity to declare a higher value or a value as lawfully provided in the tariff, or where no tariff is filed he is otherwise advised of such opportunity; but no such limitation is effective with respect to the carrier's liability for conversion to its own use.

(3) Reasonable provisions as to the time and manner of presenting claims and instituting actions based on the shipment may be included in a bill of lading or tariff.

Official Comment

Prior Uniform Statutory Provision: Section 3, Uniform Bills of Lading Act.

Changes: Consolidated and rewritten.

Purposes of Changes:

The old uniform act provided that bills of lading could not contain terms impairing the obligation of reasonable care. Whether this is violated by a stipulation that in case of loss the bailee's liability is limited to stated amounts has been much controverted. For interstate rail transportation the matter is settled by the Carmack Amendment to the Interstate Commerce Act (See 49 U.S.C.A. § 20(11)). The present section is a generalized version of the Interstate Commerce Act provisions. The obligation of due care is radically qualified, in the case of maritime bills and international airbills, by federal legislation and treaty. All this special legislation would remain in effect even if Congress enacts this Code, including the present Article. See Section 7-103.

Subsection (1) does not impair any rule of law imposing the liability of an insurer on a common carrier in intrastate commerce. Subsection (2), however, applies to such liability as well as to liability based on negligence. The entire section is subject under Section 7-103 to applicable provisions in filed tariffs, such as the common disclaimer of responsibility for undeclared articles of extraordinary value, hidden from view. Tariffs which lawfully provide a maximum unit value beyond which goods are not taken fall within the same principle, and are expressly covered by the words "value as lawfully provided in the tariff."

Cross Reference:

Section 7-103.

Definitional Cross References:

"Action". Section 1-201.
"Bill of lading". Section 1-201.
"Consignor". Section 7-102.
"Document". Section 7-102.
"Goods". Section 7-102.
"Value". Section 1-201.

PART 4

WAREHOUSE RECEIPTS AND BILLS OF LADING: GENERAL OBLIGATIONS

§ 7-401. Irregularities in Issue of Receipt or Bill or Conduct of Issuer.

The obligations imposed by this Article on an issuer apply to a document of title regardless of the fact that

(a) the document may not comply with the requirements of this Article or of any other law or regulation regarding its issue, form or content; or

(b) the issuer may have violated laws regulating the conduct of his business; or

(c) the goods covered by the document were owned by the bailee at the time the document was issued; or

(d) the person issuing the document does not come within the definition of warehouseman if it purports to be a warehouse receipt.

Official Comment

Prior Uniform Statutory Provision: Section 20, Uniform Warehouse Receipts Act; Section 23, Uniform Bills of Lading Act.

Changes: Most of the material is new; the uniform act sections cited deal only with non-receipt and misdescription.

Purposes of Changes and New Matter:

The bailee's liability on his document despite non-receipt or misdescription of the goods is affirmed in Sections 7-203 and 7-301. The purpose of this section is to make it clear that regardless of irregularities a document which falls within the definition of document of title imposes on the issuer the obligations stated in this Article. For example, a bailee will not be permitted to avoid his obligation to deliver the goods (Section 7-403) or his obligation of due care with respect to them (Sections 7-204 and 7-309) by taking the position that no valid "document" was issued because he failed to file a statutory bond or did not pay stamp taxes or did not disclose the place of storage in the document. Sanctions against violations of statutory or administrative duties with respect to documents should be limited to revocation of license or other measures prescribed by the regulation imposing the duty. As to the continuing vitality of regulations, in addition to those found in this Article, of documents of title, see Sections 7-103 and 10-103.

Cross References:

Sections 7-103, 7-203, 7-204, 7-301, 7-309 and 10-103.

Definitional Cross References:

"Bailee". Section 7-102.
"Document". Section 7-102.
"Document of title". Section 1-201.
"Goods". Section 7-102.
"Issuer". Section 7-102.
"Person". Section 1-201.
"Warehouse receipt". Section 1-201.
"Warehouseman". Section 7-102.

§ 7-402. Duplicate Receipt or Bill; Overissue.

Neither a duplicate nor any other document of title purporting to cover goods already represented by an outstanding document of the same issuer confers any right in the goods, except as provided in the case of bills in a set, overissue of documents for fungible goods and substitutes for lost, stolen or destroyed documents. But the issuer is liable for damages caused by his overissue or failure to identify a duplicate document as such by conspicuous notation on its face.

Official Comment

Prior Uniform Statutory Provision: Section 6, Uniform Warehouse Receipts Act; Section 7, Uniform Bills of Lading Act.

Changes: Consolidated and rewritten.

Purposes of Changes:

1. This section treats a duplicate which is not properly identified as such like any other overissue of documents: a purchaser of such a document acquires no title but only a cause of action for damages against the person who made his deception possible, except in the cases noted in the section. But parts of a bill lawfully issued in a set of parts are not "overissue" (Section 7-304). Of course, if the issuer has clearly indicated that a document is a duplicate so that no one can be deceived by it, and in fact the duplicate is a correct copy of the original, the warehouseman is not liable for preparing and delivering such a duplicate copy.

2. The section applies to nonnegotiable documents to the extent of providing an action for damages for one who acquires an unmarked duplicate from a transferor who knew the facts and would therefore himself have had no cause of action against the issuer of the duplicate. Ordinarily the transferee of a nonnegotiable document acquires only the rights of his transferor.

3. Overissue is defined so as to exclude the common situation where two valid documents of different issuers are outstanding for the same goods at the same time. Thus freight forwarders commonly issue bills of lading to their customers for small shipments to be combined into carload shipments for which the railroad will issue a bill of lading to the forwarder. So also a warehouse receipt may be outstanding against goods, and the holder of the receipt may issue delivery orders against the same goods.

In these cases dealings with the subsequently issued documents may be effective to transfer title; e.g. negotiation of a delivery order will effectively transfer title in the ordinary case where no dishonesty has occurred and the goods are available to satisfy the orders. Section 7–503 provides for cases of conflict between documents of different issuers.

Cross References:

Point 1: Sections 7–207, 7–304, and 7–601.

Point 3: Section 7–503.

Definitional Cross References:

"Bill of lading". Section 1–201.
"Conspicuous". Section 1–201.
"Document". Section 7–102.
"Document of title". Section 1–201.
"Fungible" goods. Section 1–201.
"Goods". Section 7–102.
"Issuer". Section 7–102.
"Right". Section 1–201.

§ 7–403. Obligation of Warehouseman or Carrier to Deliver; Excuse.

(1) The bailee must deliver the goods to a person entitled under the document who complies with subsections (2) and (3), unless and to the extent that the bailee establishes any of the following:

(a) delivery of the goods to a person whose receipt was rightful as against the claimant;

(b) damage to or delay, loss or destruction of the goods for which the bailee is not liable [, but the burden of establishing negligence in such cases is on the person entitled under the document];

Note: *The brackets in (1)(b) indicate that State enactments may differ on this point without serious damage to the principle of uniformity.*

(c) previous sale or other disposition of the goods in lawful enforcement of a lien or on warehouseman's lawful termination of storage;

(d) the exercise by a seller of his right to stop delivery pursuant to the provisions of the Article on Sales (Section 2–705);

(e) a diversion, reconsignment or other disposition pursuant to the provisions of this Article (Section 7–303) or tariff regulating such right;

(f) release, satisfaction or any other fact affording a personal defense against the claimant;

(g) any other lawful excuse.

(2) A person claiming goods covered by a document of title must satisfy the bailee's lien where the bailee so requests or where the bailee is prohibited by law from delivering the goods until the charges are paid.

(3) Unless the person claiming is one against whom the document confers no right under Sec. 7–503(1), he must surrender for cancellation or notation of partial deliveries any outstanding negotiable document covering the goods, and the bailee must cancel the document or conspicuously note the partial delivery thereon or be liable to any person to whom the document is duly negotiated.

(4) "Person entitled under the document" means holder in the case of a negotiable document, or the person to whom delivery is to be made by the

terms of or pursuant to written instructions under a non-negotiable document.

Official Comment

Prior Uniform Statutory Provision: Sections 8 through 12, 16 and 19, Uniform Warehouse Receipts Act; Sections 11 through 15, 19 and 22, Uniform Bills of Lading Act.

Changes: Consolidated and rewritten.

Purposes of Changes:

1. The general and primary purpose of this revision is to simplify the statement of the bailee's obligation on the document. The interrelations of the separate sections of the old uniform acts dealing with "obligation to deliver," "justification in delivering," and "liability for misdelivery" are obscure. The present section is constructed on the basis of stating what previous deliveries or other circumstances operate to excuse the bailee's normal obligation on the document. Accordingly, "justified" deliveries under the old uniform acts now find their place as "excuse" under subsection (1). Unjustified deliveries, i.e., "misdeliveries" under the old acts, are simply omitted from the list of excuses, thus permitting the normal obligation on the document to be asserted.

2. The principal case covered by subsection (1)(a) is delivery to a person whose title is paramount to the rights represented by the document. For example, if a thief deposits stolen goods in a warehouse and takes a negotiable receipt, the warehouseman is not liable on the receipt if he has surrendered the goods to the true owner, even though the receipt is held by a good faith purchaser. See Section 7-503(1). However, if the owner entrusted the goods to a person with power of disposition, and that person deposited the goods and took a negotiable document, the owner's receipt would not be rightful as against a holder to whom the negotiable document was duly negotiated, and delivery to the owner would not give the bailee a defense against such a holder. See Sections 7-502(1)(b), 7-503(1)(a).

3. Subsection (1)(b) amounts to a cross reference to all the tort law that determines the varying responsibilities and standards of care applicable to commercial bailees. A restatement of this tort law would be beyond the scope of this Act. Much of the applicable law as to responsibility of bailees for the preservation of the goods and limitation of liability in case of loss has been codified for particular classes of bailees in interstate and foreign commerce by federal legislation and treaty and for intrastate carriers and other bailees by the regulatory state laws preserved by Section 7-103. In the absence of governing legislation the common law will prevail subject to the minimum standard of reasonable care prescribed by Sections 7-204 and 7-309 of this Article. The optional language in subsection (1)(b) states the rule laid down for interstate carriers in many federal cases. State decisions are in conflict as to both carriers and warehousemen. Particular states may prefer to adopt the federal rule.

4. Subsection (2) eliminates the implication of the old uniform acts that a request for delivery must be accompanied by a formal tender of the amount of the charges due. Rather, the bailee must request payment of the amount of his lien when asked to deliver, and only in case this request is refused is he justified in declining to deliver because of nonpayment of charges. Where delivery without payment is forbidden by law, the request is treated as implicit. Such a prohibition reflects a policy of uniformity to prevent discrimination by failure to request payment in particular cases.

5. Subsection (3) states the obvious duty of a bailee to take up a negotiable document or note partial deliveries conspicuously thereon, and the result of failure in that duty. It is subject to only one exception, that stated in subsection 1(a) of this section and in Section 7-503(1). It is limited to cases of delivery to a claim-

ant; it has no application, for example, where goods held under a negotiable document are lawfully sold to enforce the bailee's lien.

Cross References:

Point 2: Sections 7–502 and 7–503.

Point 3: Sections 7–103, 7–204, 7–309 and 10–103.

Point 5: Section 7–503(1).

Definitional Cross References:

"Bailee". Section 7–102.
"Conspicuous". Section 1–201.
"Delivery". Section 1–201.
"Document". Section 7–102.
"Document of title". Section 1–201.
"Duly negotiate". Section 7–501.
"Goods". Section 7–102.
"Person". Section 1–201.
"Receipt of goods". Section 2–103.
"Right". Section 1–201.
"Terms". Section 1–201.
"Warehouseman". Section 7–102.
"Written". Section 1–201.

§ 7–404. No Liability for Good Faith Delivery Pursuant to Receipt or Bill.

A bailee who in good faith including observance of reasonable commercial standards has received goods and delivered or otherwise disposed of them according to the terms of the document of title or pursuant to this Article is not liable therefor. This rule applies even though the person from whom he received the goods had no authority to procure the document or to dispose of the goods and even though the person to whom he delivered the goods had no authority to receive them.

Official Comment

Prior Uniform Statutory Provision: Section 10, Uniform Warehouse Receipts Act; Section 13, Uniform Bills of Lading Act.

Changes: Consolidated and rewritten.

Purposes of Changes:

The generalized test of good faith and observance of reasonable commercial standards is substituted for the attempts to particularize what constitutes good faith in the cited sections of the old uniform acts. The section states explicitly what is perhaps an implication from the old acts that the common law rule of "innocent conversion" by unauthorized "intermeddling" with another's property is inapplicable to the operations of commercial carriers and warehousemen, who in good faith and with reasonable observance of commercial standards perform obligations which they have assumed and which generally they are under a legal compulsion to assume. The section applies to delivery to a fraudulent holder of a valid document as well as to delivery to the holder of an invalid document.

Definitional Cross References:

"Bailee". Section 7–102.
"Delivery". Section 1–201.
"Document of title". Section 1–201.
"Good faith". Section 1–201.
"Goods". Section 7–102.
"Person". Section 1–201.
"Receipt of goods". Section 2–103.
"Term". Section 1–201.

PART 5

WAREHOUSE RECEIPTS AND BILLS OF LADING: NEGOTIATION AND TRANSFER

§ 7-501. Form of Negotiation and Requirements of "Due Negotiation".

(1) A negotiable document of title running to the order of a named person is negotiated by his indorsement and delivery. After his indorsement in blank or to bearer any person can negotiate it by delivery alone.

(2)(a) A negotiable document of title is also negotiated by delivery alone when by its original terms it runs to bearer.

(b) When a document running to the order of a named person is delivered to him the effect is the same as if the document had been negotiated.

(3) Negotiation of a negotiable document of title after it has been indorsed to a specified person requires indorsement by the special indorsee as well as delivery.

(4) A negotiable document of title is "duly negotiated" when it is negotiated in the manner stated in this section to a holder who purchases it in good faith without notice of any defense against or claim to it on the part of any person and for value, unless it is established that the negotiation is not in the regular course of business or financing or involves receiving the document in settlement or payment of a money obligation.

(5) Indorsement of a non-negotiable document neither makes it negotiable nor adds to the transferee's rights.

(6) The naming in a negotiable bill of a person to be notified of the arrival of the goods does not limit the negotiability of the bill nor constitute notice to a purchaser thereof of any interest of such person in the goods.

Official Comment

Prior Uniform Statutory Provision: Sections 28, 29, 31, 32 and 38, Uniform Sales Act; Sections 37, 38, 39, 40 and 47, Uniform Warehouse Receipts Act; Sections 9, 28, 29, 30, 31 and 38, Uniform Bills of Lading Act.

Changes: Consolidated and rewritten.

Purposes of Changes:

1. In general this section is intended to clarify the language of the old acts and to restate the effect of the better decisions thereunder. An important new concept is added, however, in the requirement of "regular course of business or financing" to effect the "due negotiation" which will transfer greater rights than those held by the person negotiating. The foundation of the mercantile doctrine of good faith purchase for value has always been, as shown by the case situations, the furtherance and protection of the regular course of trade. The reason for allowing a person, in bad faith or in error, to convey away rights which are not his own has from the beginning been to make possible the speedy handling of that great run of commercial transactions which are patently usual and normal.

There are two aspects to the usual and normal course of mercantile dealings, namely, the person making the transfer and the nature of the transaction itself.

The first question which arises is: Is the transferor a person with whom it is reasonable to deal as having full powers? In regard to documents of title the only holder whose possession appears, commercially, to be in order is almost invariably a person in the trade. No commercial purpose is served by allowing a tramp or a professor to "duly negotiate" an order bill of lading for hides or cotton not his own, and since such a transfer is obviously not in the regular course of business, it is excluded from the scope of the protection of subsection (4).

The second question posed by the "regular course" qualification is: Is the transaction one which is normally proper to pass full rights without inquiry, even though the transferor himself may not have such rights to pass, and even though he may be acting in breach of duty? In raising this question the "regular course" criterion has the further advantage of limiting, the effective wrongful disposition to transactions whose protection will really further trade. Obviously, the snapping up of goods for quick resale at a price suspiciously below the market deserves no protection as a matter of policy: it is also clearly outside the range of regular course.

Any notice from the face of the document sufficient to put a merchant on inquiry as to the "regular course" quality of the transaction will frustrate a "due negotiation". Thus irregularity of the document on its face or unexplained staleness of a bill of lading may appropriately be recognized as negating a negotiation in "regular" course.

A pre-existing claim constitutes value, and "due negotiation" does not require "new value." A usual and ordinary transaction in which documents are received as security for credit previously extended may be in "regular" course, even though there is a demand for additional collateral because the creditor "deems himself insecure." But the matter has moved out of the regular course of financing if the debtor is thought to be insolvent, the credit previously extended is in effect cancelled, and the creditor snatches a plank in the shipwreck under the guise of a demand for additional collateral. Where a money debt is "paid" in commodity paper, any question of "regular" course disappears, as the case is explicitly excepted from "due negotiation".

2. Negotiation under this section may be made by any holder no matter how he acquired possession of the document. The present section follows in this respect the Uniform Bills of Lading Act and amendments of the original Uniform Sales Act and Uniform Warehouse Receipts Act proposed by the Commissioners on Uniform State Laws in 1922.

3. Subsection (2)(b) makes explicit a matter upon which the intent of the old acts was clear but the language somewhat obscure: a negotiation results from a delivery to a banker or buyer to whose order the document has been taken by the person making the bailment. There is no presumption of irregularity in such a negotiation; it may very well be in "regular course."

4. This Article does not contain any provision creating a presumption of due negotiation to, and full rights in, a holder of a document of title akin to that created by Sections 16, 24 and 59 of the Negotiable Instruments Law. But the reason of the provisions of this Act (Section 1-202) on the prima facie authenticity and accuracy of third party documents, joins with the reason of the present section to work such a presumption in favor of any person who has power to make a due negotiation. It would not make sense for this Act to authorize a purchaser to indulge the presumption of regularity if the courts were not also called upon to do so.

Cross References:

Point 1: Sections 7-502 and 7-503.
Point 2: Section 7-502.

Definitional Cross References:

"Bearer". Section 1-201.
"Delivery". Section 1-201.
"Document". Section 7-102.
"Document of title". Section 1-201.
"Good faith". Section 1-201.

"Holder". Section 1-201.
"Notice". Section 1-201.
"Person". Section 1-201.
"Purchase". Section 1-201.
"Rights". Section 1-201.
"Term". Section 1-201.
"Value". Section 1-201.

§ 7-502. Rights Acquired by Due Negotiation.

(1) Subject to the following section and to the provisions of Section 7-205 on fungible goods, a holder to whom a negotiable document of title has been duly negotiated acquires thereby:

(a) title to the document;

(b) title to the goods;

(c) all rights accruing under the law of agency or estoppel, including rights to goods delivered to the bailee after the document was issued; and

(d) the direct obligation of the issuer to hold or deliver the goods according to the terms of the document free of any defense or claim by him except those arising under the terms of the document or under this Article. In the case of a delivery order the bailee's obligation accrues only upon acceptance and the obligation acquired by the holder is that the issuer and any indorser will procure the acceptance of the bailee.

(2) Subject to the following section, title and rights so acquired are not defeated by any stoppage of the goods represented by the document or by surrender of such goods by the bailee, and are not impaired even though the negotiation or any prior negotiation constituted a breach of duty or even though any person has been deprived of possession of the document by misrepresentation, fraud, accident, mistake, duress, loss, theft or conversion, or even though a previous sale or other transfer of the goods or document has been made to a third person.

Official Comment

Prior Uniform Statutory Provision: Sections 20(4), 25, 33, 38 and 62, Uniform Sales Act; Sections 41, 47, 48 and 49, Uniform Warehouse Receipts Act; Sections 32, 38, 39, 40 and 42, Uniform Bills of Lading Act.

Changes: Rewritten.

Purposes of Changes:

1. The several necessary qualifications of the broad principle that the holder of a document acquired in a due negotiation is the owner of the document and the goods have been brought together in the next section.

2. Subsection (1)(c) covers the case of "feeding" of a duly negotiated document by subsequent delivery to the bailee of such goods as the document falsely purported to cover; the bailee in such case is estopped as against the holder of the document.

3. The explicit statement in subsection (1)(d) of the bailee's direct obligation to the holder precludes the defense, sometimes successfully asserted under the old acts, that the document in question was "spent" after the carrier had delivered the goods to a previous holder. But the holder is subject to such defenses as non-negligent destruction even though not apparent on the face of the document, and the bailee's obligation is of course subject to lawful provisions in filed classifications and tariffs. See Sections 7-103, 7-403.

The sentence on delivery orders applies only to delivery orders in negotiable form which have been duly negotiated. On delivery orders, see also Section 7-503(2) and Comment.

4. Subsection (2) condenses and continues the law of a number of sections of the prior acts which gave full effect to the issuance or due negotiation of a negotiable document. The subsection adds nothing to the effect of the rules stated in subsection (1), but it has been included since such explicit references were relied upon under the prior acts to preserve the rights of a purchaser by due negotiation unimpaired. The listing is not exhaustive. Only those matters have been repeated in this subsection which were explicitly reserved in the prior acts except in the case of stoppage in transit. Here, the language has been broadened to include "any stoppage" lest an inference be drawn that a stoppage of the goods before or after transit might cut off or otherwise impair the purchaser's rights.

Cross References:

Sections 7-103, 7-205, 7-403 and 7-503.

Definitional Cross References:

"Bailee". Section 7-102.
"Delivery". Section 1-201.
"Delivery order". Section 7-102.
"Document". Section 7-102.
"Document of title". Section 1-201.
"Duly negotiate". Section 7-501.
"Fungible". Section 1-201.
"Goods". Section 7-102.
"Holder". Section 1-201.
"Issuer". Section 7-102.
"Person". Section 1-201.
"Rights". Section 1-201.
"Term". Section 1-201.
"Warehouse receipt". Section 1-201.

§ 7-503. Document of Title to Goods Defeated in Certain Cases.

(1) A document of title confers no right in goods against a person who before issuance of the document had a legal interest or a perfected security interest in them and who neither

(a) delivered or entrusted them or any document of title covering them to the bailor or his nominee with actual or apparent authority to ship, store or sell or with power to obtain delivery under this Article (Section 7-403) or with power of disposition under this Act (Sections 2-403 and 9-307) or other statute or rule of law; nor

(b) acquiesced in the procurement by the bailor or his nominee of any document of title.

(2) Title to goods based upon an unaccepted delivery order is subject to the rights of anyone to whom a negotiable warehouse receipt or bill of lading covering the goods has been duly negotiated. Such a title may be defeated under the next section to the same extent as the rights of the issuer or a transferee from the issuer.

(3) Title to goods based upon a bill of lading issued to a freight forwarder is subject to the rights of anyone to whom a bill issued by the freight forwarder is duly negotiated; but delivery by the carrier in accordance with Part 4 of this Article pursuant to its own bill of lading discharges the carrier's obligation to deliver.

Official Comment

Prior Uniform Statutory Provision: Section 33, Uniform Sales Act; Section 41, Uniform Warehouse Receipts Act; Section 32, Uniform Bills of Lading Act.

Changes: Subsection (1) narrows, as compared to the cited sections, the occasions for defeating the document holder's title.

Purposes of Changes:

1. In general it may be said that the title of a purchaser by due negotiation prevails over almost any interest in the goods which existed prior to the procurement of the document of title if the possession of the goods by the person obtaining the document derived from any action by the prior claimant which introduced the goods into the stream of commerce or carried them along that stream. A thief of the goods cannot indeed by shipping or storing them to his own order acquire power to transfer them to a good faith purchaser. Nor can a tenant or mortgagor defeat any rights of a landlord or mortgagee which have been perfected under the local law merely by wrongfully shipping or storing a portion of the crop or other goods. However, "acquiescence" by the landlord or tenant does not require active consent under subsection (1)(b) and knowledge of the likelihood of storage or shipment with no objection or effort to control it is sufficient to defeat his rights as against one who takes by "due" negotiation of a negotiable document.

On the other hand, where goods are delivered to a factor for sale, even though the factor has made no advances and is limited in his duty to sell for cash, the goods are "entrusted" to him "with actual . . . authority . . . to sell" under subsection (1)(a), and if he procures a negotiable document of title he can transfer the owner's interest to a purchaser by due negotiation. Further, where the factor is in the business of selling, goods entrusted to him simply for safekeeping or storage may be entrusted under circumstances which give him "apparent authority to ship, store or sell" under subsection (1)(a), or power of disposition under Section 2–403, 7-205 or 9–307, or under a statute such as the earlier Factors Acts, or under a rule of law giving effect to apparent ownership. See Section 1–103.

Persons having an interest in goods also frequently deliver or entrust them to agents or servants other than factors for the purpose of shipping or warehousing or under circumstances reasonably contemplating such action. Rounding out the case law development under the prior Acts, this Act is clear that such persons assume full risk that the agent to whom the goods are so delivered may ship or store in breach of duty, take a document to his own order and then proceed to misappropriate it. This Act makes no distinction between possession or mere custody in such situations and finds no exception in the case of larceny by a bailee or the like. The safeguard in such situations lies in the requirement that a due negotiation can occur only "in the regular course of business or financing" and that the purchase be in good faith and without notice. See Section 7–501. Documents of title have no market among the commercially inexperienced and the commercially experienced do not take them without inquiry from persons known to be truck drivers or petty clerks even though such persons purport to be operating in their own names.

Again, where the seller allows a buyer to receive goods under a contract for sale, though as a "conditional delivery" or under "cash sale" terms and on explicit agreement for immediate payment, the buyer thereby acquires power to defeat the seller's interest by transfer of the goods to certain good faith purchasers. See Section 2–403. Both in policy and under the language of subsection (1)(a) that same power must be extended to accomplish the same result if the buyer procures a negotiable document of title to the goods and duly negotiates it.

2. Under subsection (1) a delivery order issued by a person having no right in or power over the goods is ineffective unless the owner acts as provided in subsection (1)(a) or (b). Thus the rights of a transferee of a non-negotiable warehouse receipt can be defeated by a delivery order subsequently issued by the transferor only if the transferee "delivers or entrusts" to the "person procuring" the

delivery order or "acquiesces" in his procurement. Similarly, a second delivery order issued by the same issuer for the same goods will ordinarily be subject to the first, both under this section and under Section 7–402. After a delivery order is validly issued but before it is accepted, it may nevertheless be defeated under subsection (2) in much the same way that the rights of a transferee may be defeated under Section 7–504. For example, a buyer in ordinary course from the issuer may defeat the rights of the holder of a prior delivery order if the bailee receives notification of the buyer's rights before notification of the holder's rights. Section 7–504(2)(b). But an accepted delivery order has the same effect as a document issued by the bailee.

3. Under subsection (3) a bill of lading issued to a freight forwarder is subordinated to the freight forwarder's certificate, since the bill on its face gives notice of the fact that a freight forwarder is in the picture and has in all probability issued a certificate. But the carrier is protected in following the terms of its own bill of lading.

Cross References:

Point 1: Sections 2–403, 7–205, 7–501, 9–307, and 9–309.

Point 2: Sections 7–402 and 7–504.

Point 3: Sections 7–402, 7–403 and 7–404.

Definitional Cross References:

"Bill of lading". Section 1–201.
"Contract for sale". Section 2–106.
"Delivery". Section 1–201.
"Delivery order". Section 7–102.
"Document". Section 7–102.
"Document of title". Section 1–201.
"Duly negotiate". Section 7–501.
"Goods". Section 7–102.
"Person". Section 1–201.
"Right". Section 1–201.
"Warehouse receipt". Section 1–201.

§ 7–504. Rights Acquired in the Absence of Due Negotiation; Effect of Diversion; Seller's Stoppage of Delivery.

(1) A transferee of a document, whether negotiable or non-negotiable, to whom the document has been delivered but not duly negotiated, acquires the title and rights which his transferor had or had actual authority to convey.

(2) In the case of a non-negotiable document, until but not after the bailee receives notification of the transfer, the rights of the transferee may be defeated

(a) by those creditors of the transferor who could treat the sale as void under Section 2–402; or

(b) by a buyer from the transferor in ordinary course of business if the bailee has delivered the goods to the buyer or received notification of his rights; or

(c) as against the bailee by good faith dealings of the bailee with the transferor.

(3) A diversion or other change of shipping instructions by the consignor in a non-negotiable bill of lading which causes the bailee not to deliver to the consignee defeats the consignee's title to the goods if they have been delivered to a buyer in ordinary course of business and in any event defeats the consignee's rights against the bailee.

(4) Delivery pursuant to a non-negotiable document may be stopped by a seller under Section 2–705, and subject to the requirement of due notification there provided. A bailee honoring the seller's instructions is entitled to be indemnified by the seller against any resulting loss or expense.

Official Comment

Prior Uniform Statutory Provision: Section 34, Uniform Sales Act; Sections 41(b) and 42, Uniform Warehouse Receipts Act; Sections 32(b) and 33, Uniform Bills of Lading Act.

Changes: Generally rewritten; Subsection (3) is new.

Purposes of Changes and New Matter:

1. Under the general principles controlling negotiable documents, it is clear that in the absence of due negotiation a transferor cannot convey greater rights than he himself has, even when the negotiation is formally perfect. This section recognizes the transferor's power to transfer rights which he himself has or has "actual authority to convey." Thus, where a negotiable document of title is being transferred the operation of the principle of estoppel is not recognized, as contrasted with situations involving the transfer of the goods themselves. (Compare Section 2-403 on good faith purchase of goods.)

A necessary part of the price for the protection of regular dealings with negotiable documents of title is an insistence that no dealing which is in any way irregular shall be recognized as a good faith purchase of the document or of any rights pertaining to it. So, where the transfer of a negotiable document fails as a negotiation because a requisite indorsement is forged or otherwise missing, the purchaser in good faith and for value may be in the anomalous position of having less rights, in part, than if he had purchased the goods themselves. True, his rights are not subject to defeat by attachment of the goods or surrender of them to his transferor [Contrast subsection (2)]; but on the other hand, he cannot acquire enforceable rights to control or receive the goods over the bailee's objection merely by giving notice to the bailee. Similarly, a consignee who makes payment to his consignor against a straight bill of lading can thereby acquire the position of a good faith purchaser of goods under provisions of the Article of this Act on Sales (Section 2-403), whereas the same payment made in good faith against an unindorsed order bill would not have such effect. The appropriate remedy of a purchaser in such a situation is to regularize his status by compelling indorsement of the document (see Section 7-506).

2. As in the case of transfer—as opposed to "due negotiation"—of negotiable documents, subsection (1) empowers the transferor of a nonnegotiable document to transfer only such rights as he himself has or has "actual authority" to convey. In contrast to situations involving the goods themselves the operation of estoppel or agency principles is not here recognized to enable the transferor to convey greater rights than he actually has. Subsection (2) makes it clear, however, that the transferee of a nonnegotiable document may acquire rights greater in some respects than those of his transferor by giving notice of the transfer to the bailee.

3. Subsection (3) is in part a reiteration of the carrier's immunity from liability if it honors instructions of the consignor to divert, but there is added a provision protecting the title of the substituted consignee if the latter is a buyer in ordinary course of business. A typical situation would be where a manufacturer, having shipped a lot of standardized goods to A on nonnegotiable bill of lading, diverts the goods to customer B who pays for them. Under orthodox passage-of-title-by-appropriation doctrine A might reclaim the goods from B. However, no consideration of commercial policy supports this involvement of an innocent third party in the default of the manufacturer on his contract to A; and the common commercial practice of diverting goods in transit suggests a trade understanding in accordance with this subsection.

4. Subsection (4) gives the carrier an express right to indemnity where he honors a seller's request to stop delivery.

5. Section 1-201(27) gives the bailee protection, if due diligence is exercised, similar to that found in the third paragraph of Section 33, Uniform Bills of Lading Act, where the bailee's organization has not had time to act on a notification.

Cross References:

Point 1: Sections 2-403 and 7-506.

Point 2: Section 2-403.

Point 3: Sections 7-303 and 7-403(1)(e).

Point 4: Sections 2-705 and 7-403(1)(d).

Definitional Cross References:

"Bailee". Section 7-102.

"Bill of lading". Section 1-201.

"Buyer in ordinary course of business". Section 1-201.

"Consignee". Section 7-102.

"Consignor". Section 7-102.

"Creditor". Section 1-201.

"Delivery". Section 1-201.

"Document". Section 7-102.

"Duly negotiate". Section 7-501.

"Good faith". Section 1-201.

"Goods". Section 7-102.

"Honor". Section 1-201.

"Notification". Section 1-201.

"Purchaser". Section 1-201.

"Rights". Section 1-201.

§ 7-505. Indorser Not a Guarantor for Other Parties.

The indorsement of a document of title issued by a bailee does not make the indorser liable for any default by the bailee or by previous indorsers.

Official Comment

Prior Uniform Statutory Provision: Section 37, Uniform Sales Act; Section 45, Uniform Warehouse Receipts Act; Section 36, Uniform Bills of Lading Act.

Changes: No substantial change.

Purposes of Changes:

The indorsement of a document of title is generally understood to be directed towards perfecting the transferee's rights rather than towards assuming additional obligations. The language of the present section, however, does not preclude the one case in which an indorsement given for value guarantees future action, namely, that in which the bailee has not yet become liable upon the document at the time of the indorsement. Under such circumstances the indorser, of course, engages that appropriate honor of the document by the bailee will occur. See Section 7-502(1)(d) as to negotiable delivery orders. However, even in such a case, once the bailee attorns to the transferee, the indorser's obligation has been fulfilled and the policy of this section excludes any continuing obligation on the part of the indorser for the bailee's ultimate actual performance.

Cross Reference:

Section 7-502.

Definitional Cross References:

"Bailee". Section 7-102.

"Document of title". Section 1-201.

"Party". Section 1-201.

§ 7-506. Delivery Without Indorsement: Right to Compel Indorsement.

The transferee of a negotiable document of title has a specifically enforceable right to have his transferor supply any necessary indorsement but the transfer becomes a negotiation only as of the time the indorsement is supplied.

Official Comment

Prior Uniform Statutory Provision: Section 35, Uniform Sales Act; Section 43, Uniform Warehouse Receipts Act; Section 34, Uniform Bills of Lading Act.

Changes: Consolidated and rewritten; former requirement that transfer be "for value" eliminated.

Purposes of Changes:

1. From a commercial point of view the intention to transfer a negotiable document of title which requires an indorsement for its transfer, is incompatible with an intention to withhold such indorsement and so defeat the effective use of the document. This position is sustained by the absence of any reported case applying the prior provisions in almost forty years of decisions. Further, the preceding section and the Comment thereto make it clear that an indorsement generally imposes no responsibility on the indorser.

2. Although this section provides that delivery of a document of title without the necessary indorsement is effective as a transfer, the transferee, of course, has not regularized his position until such indorsement is supplied. Until this is done he cannot claim rights under due negotiation within the requirements of this Article (subsection (4) of Section 7-501) on "due negotiation". Similarly, despite the transfer to him of his transferor's title, he cannot demand the goods from the bailee until the negotiation has been completed and the document is in proper form for surrender. See Section 7-403(3).

Cross References:

Point 1: Section 7-505.

Point 2: Sections 7-501(4) and 7-403(2).

Definitional Cross References:

"Document of title". Section 1-201.

"Rights". Section 1-201.

§ 7-507. Warranties on Negotiation or Transfer of Receipt or Bill.

Where a person negotiates or transfers a document of title for value otherwise than as a mere intermediary under the next following section, then unless otherwise agreed he warrants to his immediate purchaser only in addition to any warranty made in selling the goods

(a) that the document is genuine; and

(b) that he has no knowledge of any fact which would impair its validity or worth; and

(c) that his negotiation or transfer is rightful and fully effective with respect to the title to the document and the goods it represents.

Official Comment

Prior Uniform Statutory Provision: Section 36, Uniform Sales Act; Section 44, Uniform Warehouse Receipts Act; Section 35, Uniform Bills of Lading Act.

Changes: Consolidated and rewritten without change in policy.

Purposes of Changes:

1. This section omits provisions of the prior acts on warranties as to the goods as unnecessary and incomplete. It is unnecessary because such warranties derive from the contract of sale and not from the transfer of the documents. The fact that transfer of control occurs by way of a document of title does not limit or displace the ordinary obligations of a seller. The former provision, moreover, was incomplete because it did not expressly include all of the warranties which might rest upon a seller under such circumstances. This Act handles the problem by

means of the precautionary reference to "any warranty made in selling the goods." If the transfer of documents attends or follows the making of a contract for the sale of goods, the general obligations on warranties as to the goods (Sections 2-312 through 2-318) are brought to bear as well as the special warranties under this section.

2. The limited warranties of a delivering or collecting intermediary are stated in Section 7-508.

Cross References:

Point 1: Sections 2-312 through 2-318.
Point 2: Section 7-508.

Definitional Cross References:

"Document". Section 7-102.
"Document of title". Section 1-201.
"Genuine". Section 1-201.
"Goods". Section 7-102.
"Person". Section 1-201.
"Purchaser". Section 1-201.
"Value". Section 1-201.

§ 7-508. Warranties of Collecting Bank as to Documents.

A collecting bank or other intermediary known to be entrusted with documents on behalf of another or with collection of a draft or other claim against delivery of documents warrants by such delivery of the documents only its own good faith and authority. This rule applies even though the intermediary has purchased or made advances against the claim or draft to be collected.

Official Comment

Prior Uniform Statutory Provision: None.

Purposes:

1. To state the limited warranties given with respect to the documents accompanying a documentary draft.

2. In warranting its authority a bank only warrants its authority from its transferor. See Section 4-203. It does not warrant the genuineness or effectiveness of the document. Compare Section 7-507.

3. Other duties and rights of banks handling documentary drafts for collection are stated in Article 4, Part 5.

Cross References:

Sections 4-203 and 7-507, 4-501 through 4-504.

Definitional Cross References:

"Collecting bank". Section 4-105.
"Delivery". Section 1-201.
"Document". Section 7-102.
"Draft". Section 5-103.
"Good faith". Section 1-201.

§ 7-509. Receipt or Bill: When Adequate Compliance With Commercial Contract.

The question whether a document is adequate to fulfill the obligations of a contract for sale or the conditions of a credit is governed by the Articles on Sales (Article 2) and on Letters of Credit (Article 5).

Official Comment

Prior Uniform Statutory Provision: None.

Purposes:

To cross-refer to the Articles of this Act which deal with the substantive issues of the type of document of title required under the contract entered into by the parties.

Cross References:

Articles 2 and 5.

Definitional Cross References:

"Contract for sale". Section 2-106.
"Document". Section 7-102.

PART 6

WAREHOUSE RECEIPTS AND BILLS OF LADING: MISCELLANEOUS PROVISIONS

§ 7-601. Lost and Missing Documents.

(1) If a document has been lost, stolen or destroyed, a court may order delivery of the goods or issuance of a substitute document and the bailee may without liability to any person comply with such order. If the document was negotiable the claimant must post security approved by the court to indemnify any person who may suffer loss as a result of non-surrender of the document. If the document was not negotiable, such security may be required at the discretion of the court. The court may also in its discretion order payment of the bailee's reasonable costs and counsel fees.

(2) A bailee who without court order delivers goods to a person claiming under a missing negotiable document is liable to any person injured thereby, and if the delivery is not in good faith becomes liable for conversion. Delivery in good faith is not conversion if made in accordance with a filed classification or tariff or, where no classification or tariff is filed, if the claimant posts security with the bailee in an amount at least double the value of the goods at the time of posting to indemnify any person injured by the delivery who files a notice of claim within one year after the delivery.

Official Comment

Prior Uniform Statutory Provision: Section 14, Uniform Warehouse Receipts Act; Section 17, Uniform Bills of Lading Act.

Changes: General Revision. Principal innovations include: affirmation of bailee's privilege to deliver to claimant without resort to judicial proceedings if the bailee acts in good faith and is willing to take the full risk of loss in case the lost document turns up in the hands of an innocent purchaser; explicit authorization to the court to order bailee to issue a substitute document rather than make physical delivery of the goods; inclusion of "stolen" as well as lost documents; extension of section to non-negotiable documents.

Purposes of Changes: The purposes of the changes insofar as they are not self-evident are as follows:

1. As to bailee's privilege to deliver without court order, doubt had arisen as to the propriety of such action under Section 54 of the Uniform Warehouse Receipts Act, which made it a crime to deliver goods covered by negotiable receipts without taking up the receipts "except in the cases provided for in Section 14" (the lost receipts section). This has been interpreted by one court as exempting from criminal liability only if the judicial procedure of Section 14 was followed. Dahl v. Winter-Truesdell-Diercks Co., 61 N.D. 84, 237 N.W. 202 (1931). Although the criminal provisions are not being re-enacted in this Act (and the Uniform Bills of Lading Act never did include such a criminal provision), it seems advisable to clarify the legality of the well established commercial practice of bailees to make delivery where they are satisfied that the claimant is the person entitled under a

lost document. Since the bailee remains liable on the document in such cases, he will usually insist that the claimant provide an indemnity bond.

2. The old acts provide only for compulsory delivery of goods; this Section provides also for compulsory issuance of a substitute document. If continuance of the bailment is desirable there is no reason to require the goods to be withdrawn and redeposited in order to secure a negotiable document. The present acts would probably be so interpreted. Section 20 of the Federal Warehouse Act and some state laws expressly require issuance of a new receipt on proof of loss and posting of bond.

3. Claimants on non-negotiable instruments are permitted to avail themselves of this procedure because straight bills of lading sometimes contain provisions that the goods shall not be delivered except upon production of the bill. If the carrier should choose to insist upon production of the bill, the consignee should have some means of compelling delivery on satisfactory proof of entitlement.

Ordinarily no security would be necessary to indemnify a bailee in delivering to the person named in a non-negotiable document. But disputes as to negotiability may arise, in which case if there is a reasonable doubt on the point the bailee should be protected against the possibility that the missing document would, in the hands of an innocent purchaser for value, be held negotiable.

4. It seems unnecessary to state, as do the present acts, that the court shall act "on satisfactory proof of such loss or destruction." The right of action created by the section is conditioned on a document being lost, stolen or destroyed. Plaintiff must of course bring himself within the section. There is nothing in the language of the old acts to suggest that they intended to impose anything but the normal burden of proof on the plaintiff in such proceedings.

5. Subsection (2) makes it clear that after delivery without court order the bailee remains liable for actual damages. Liability for conversion is provided where the delivery is dishonest, but excluded where a filed classification or tariff is followed in good faith, or where the described bond is posted in good faith and no classification or tariff is filed. Liability for conversion in other cases is left to judicial decision.

Definitional Cross References:

"Bailee". Section 7-102.
"Bill of lading". Section 1-201.
"Delivery". Section 1-201.
"Document". Section 7-102.
"Good faith". Section 1-201.
"Goods". Section 7-102.
"Person". Section 1-201.
"Warehouse receipt". Section 1-201.
"Warehouseman". Section 7-102.

§ 7-602. Attachment of Goods Covered by a Negotiable Document.

Except where the document was originally issued upon delivery of the goods by a person who had no power to dispose of them, no lien attaches by virtue of any judicial process to goods in the possession of a bailee for which a negotiable document of title is outstanding unless the document be first surrendered to the bailee or its negotiation enjoined, and the bailee shall not be compelled to deliver the goods pursuant to process until the document is surrendered to him or impounded by the court. One who purchases the document for value without notice of the process or injunction takes free of the lien imposed by judicial process.

Official Comment

Prior Uniform Statutory Provisions: Section 25, Uniform Warehouse Receipts Act; Section 24, Uniform Bills of Lading Act.

Changes: Consolidated and rewritten.

Purposes of Changes:

1. The purpose of the section is to protect the bailee from conflicting claims of the document holder and the judgment creditors of the person who deposited the goods. The rights of the former prevail unless, in effect, the judgment creditors immobilize the negotiable document. However, if the document was issued upon deposit of the goods by a person who had no power to dispose of the goods so that the document is ineffective to pass title, judgment liens are valid to the extent of the debtor's interest in the goods.

2. The last sentence covers the possibility that the holder of a document who has been enjoined from negotiating it will violate the injunction by negotiating to an innocent purchaser for value. In such case the lien will be defeated.

Cross Reference:

Point 1: Section 7-503.

Definitional Cross References:

"Bailee". Section 7-102.
"Delivery". Section 1-201.
"Document". Section 7-102.
"Goods". Section 7-102.
"Notice". Section 1-201.
"Person". Section 1-201.
"Purchase". Section 1-201.
"Value". Section 1-201.

§ 7-603. Conflicting Claims; Interpleader.

If more than one person claims title or possession of the goods, the bailee is excused from delivery until he has had a reasonable time to ascertain the validity of the adverse claims or to bring an action to compel all claimants to interplead and may compel such interpleader, either in defending an action for non-delivery of the goods, or by original action, whichever is appropriate.

Official Comment

Prior Uniform Statutory Provision: Sections 16 and 17, Uniform Warehouse Receipts Act; Sections 20 and 21, Uniform Bills of Lading Act.

Changes: Consolidation without substantial change.

Purposes of Changes:

The section enables a bailee faced with conflicting claims to the goods to compel the claimants to litigate their claims with each other rather than with him.

Definitional Cross References:

"Action". Section 1-201.
"Bailee". Section 7-102.
"Delivery". Section 1-201.
"Goods". Section 7-102.
"Person". Section 1-201.
"Reasonable time". Section 1-204.

REVISED ARTICLE 8 (1994 REVISION)

INVESTMENT SECURITIES

[For the Text and Official Comments of Article 8 as they existed prior to revision in 1994, see Appendix XIII, infra.]

[For the conforming amendments to other articles of the Code, see Appendix XII, infra.]

PART 1. SHORT TITLE AND GENERAL MATTERS

PART 2. ISSUE AND ISSUER

PART 3. TRANSFER OF CERTIFICATED AND UNCERTIFICATED SECURITIES

See Appendix XII for text of conforming amendments to other articles of the Code and Official Comments thereto.

National Conference of Commissioners on Uniform State Laws

REPORTER

James Steven Rogers, Newton, Massachusetts

DRAFTING COMMITTEE

CHAIRMAN

Curtis R. Reitz, Philadelphia, Pennsylvania

MEMBERS

Ann E. Conaway Anker, Wilmington, Delaware

John Fox Arnold, St. Louis, Missouri

Robert J. Desiderio, Albuquerque, New Mexico

Egon Guttman, Washington, District of Columbia, *The American Law Institute Representative*

Howard T. Rosen, Millburn, New Jersey

Richard B. Smith, New York, New York, *The American Law Institute Representative* and *American Bar Association Advisor*

Howard J. Swibel, Chicago, Illinois

Justin L. Vigdor, Rochester, New York

Richard C. Hite, Wichita, Kansas, *President (Member Ex Officio)*

K. King Burnett, Salisbury, Maryland, *Chairman, Division A (Member Ex Officio)*

REVIEW COMMITTEE

CHAIRMAN

Michael P. Sullivan, Minneapolis, Minnesota

MEMBERS

Gerald L. Bepko, Indianapolis, Indiana

Reed L. Martineau, Salt Lake City, Utah

ADVISORS

Charles W. Mooney, Jr., *American Bar Association, Section of Business Law*

Thomas J. Greco, *American Bankers Association*

CONSULTANTS

Jonathan Kallman, *United States Securities and Exchange Commission*

Calvin Ninomiya and Cynthia E. Reese, *United States Department of the Treasury*

Lawranne Stewart, *Board of Governors, Federal Reserve System*

Debra W. Cook and MarySue Fisher, *Federal Reserve Bank of New York*

PREFATORY NOTE

The present version of Article 8 is the product of a major revision made necessary by the fact that the prior version of Article 8 did not adequately deal with the system of securities holding through securities intermediaries that has developed in the past few decades. Although the prior version of Article 8 did contain some provisions dealing with securities holding through securities intermediaries, these were engrafted onto a structure designed for securities practices of earlier times. The resulting legal uncertainties adversely affected all participants. The revision is intended to eliminate these uncertainties by providing a modern legal structure for current securities holding practices.

I. EVOLUTION OF SECURITIES HOLDING SYSTEMS

A. The Traditional Securities Holding System

The original version of Article 8, drafted in the 1940s and 1950s, was based on the assumption that possession and delivery of physical certificates are the key elements in the securities holding system. Ownership of securities was traditionally evidenced by possession of the certificates, and changes were accomplished by delivery of the certificates.

Transfer of securities in the traditional certificate-based system was a complicated, labor-intensive process. Each time securities were traded, the physical certificates had to be delivered from the seller to the buyer, and in the case of registered securities the certificates had to be surrendered to the issuer or its transfer agent for registration of transfer. As is well known, the mechanical problems of processing the paperwork for securities transfers reached crisis proportions in the late 1960s, leading to calls for the elimination of the physical certificate and development of modern electronic systems for recording ownership of securities and transfers of ownership. That was the focus of the revision effort that led to the promulgation of the 1978 amendments to Article 8 concerning uncertificated securities.

B. The Uncertificated Securities System Envisioned by the 1978 Amendments

In 1978, amendments to Article 8 were approved to establish the commercial law rules that were thought necessary to permit the evolution of a system in which issuers would no longer issue certificates. The Drafting Committee that produced the 1978 amendments was given a fairly limited charge. It was to draft the revisions that would be needed for uncertificated securities, but otherwise leave the Article 8 rules unchanged. Accordingly, the 1978 amendments primarily took the form of adding parallel provisions dealing with uncertificated securities to the existing rules of Article 8 on certificated securities.

The system of securities holding contemplated by the 1978 amendments differed from the traditional system only in that ownership of securities would not be evidenced by physical certificates. It was contemplated that changes in ownership would continue to be reflected by changes in the records of the issuer. The main difference would be that instead of surrendering an indorsed certificate for registration of transfer, an instruction would be sent to the issuer directing it to register the transfer. Although a system of the sort contemplated by the 1978 amendments may well develop in the coming decades, this has not yet happened for most categories of securities. Mutual funds shares have long been issued in uncertificated form, but virtually all other forms of publicly traded corporate securities are still issued in certificated form. Individual investors who wish to be recorded as registered owners on the issuers' books still obtain and hold physical certificates. The certificates representing the largest portion of the shares of publicly traded companies, however, are not held by the beneficial owners, but by clearing corporations. Settlement of securities trading occurs not by delivery of certificates or by registration of transfer on the records of the issuers or their transfer agents, but by computer entries in the records of clearing corporations and securities intermediaries. That is quite different from the system envisioned by the 1978 amendments.

C. Evolution of the Indirect Holding System

At the time of the "paperwork crunch" in the late 1960s, the trading volume on the New York Stock Exchange that so seriously strained the capacities of the clearance and settlement system was in the range of 10 million shares per day. Today, the system can easily handle trading volume on routine days of hundreds of millions of shares. This processing capacity could have been achieved only by the application of modern electronic information processing systems. Yet the legal rules under which the system operates are *not* the uncertificated securities provisions of Article 8. To understand why this is so, one must delve at least a bit deeper into the operations of the current system.

If one examines the shareholder records of large corporations whose shares are publicly traded on the exchanges or in the over the counter market, one would find that one entity—Cede & Co.—is listed as the shareholder of record of somewhere in the range of sixty to eighty per cent of the outstanding shares of all publicly traded companies. Cede & Co. is the nominee name used by The Depository Trust Company ("DTC"), a limited purpose trust company organized under New York law for the purpose of acting as a depository to hold securities for the benefit of its participants, some 600 or so broker-dealers and banks. Essentially all of the trading in publicly held companies is executed through the broker-dealers who are participants in DTC, and the great bulk of public securities—the sixty to eighty per cent figure noted above—are held by these broker-dealers and banks on behalf of their customers. If all of these broker-dealers and banks held physical certificates, then as trades were executed each day it would be necessary to deliver the certificates back and forth among these broker-dealers and banks. By handing all of their securities over to a common depository all of these deliveries can be eliminated. Transfers can be accomplished by adjustments to the participants' DTC accounts.

Although the use of a common depository eliminates the needs for physical deliveries, an enormous number of entries would still have to be made on DTC's books if each transaction between its participants were recorded one by one on DTC's books. Any two major broker-dealers may have executed numerous trades with each other in a given security on a single day. Significant processing efficiency has been achieved by netting all of the transactions among the participants that occur each day, so that entries need be made on the depository's books only for the net changes in the positions of each participant at the end of each day. This clearance and netting function might well be performed by the securities exchanges or by the same institution that acts as the depository, as is the case in many other securities markets around the world. In the United States, however, this clearance and netting function is carried out by a separate corporation, National Securities Clearing Corporation ("NSCC"). All that needs to be done to settle each day's trading is for NSCC to compute the net receive and deliver obligations and to instruct DTC to make the corresponding adjustments in the participants' accounts.

The broker-dealers and banks who are participants in the DTC–NSCC system in turn provide analogous clearance and settlement functions to their own customers. If Customer A buys 100 shares of XYZ Co. through Broker, and Customer B sells 100 shares of XYZ Co. through the same Broker, the trade can be settled by entries on Broker's books. Neither DTC's books showing Broker's total position in XYZ Co., nor XYZ Co.'s books showing DTC's total position in XYZ Co., need be changed to reflect the settlement of this trade. One can readily appreciate the significance of the settlement function performed at this level if one considers that a single major bank may be acting as securities custodian for hundreds or thousands of mutual funds, pension funds, and other institutional investors. On any given day, the customers of that bank may have entered into an enormous number of trades, yet it is possible that relatively little of this trading activity will result in any net change in the custodian bank's positions on the books of DTC.

Settlement of market trading in most of the major U.S. securities markets is now effected primarily through some form of netted clearance and depository system. Virtually all publicly traded corporate equity securities, corporate debt securities, and municipal debt securities are now eligible for deposit in the DTC system. Recently, DTC has implemented a similar depository settlement system for the commercial paper market, and could, but for limitations in present Article 8, handle other forms of short-term money market securities such as bankers' acceptances. For trading in mortgage-backed securities, such as Ginnie Mae's, a similar depository settlement system has been developed by Participants Trust Company. For trading in U.S. Treasury securities, a somewhat analogous book-entry system is operated under Treasury rules by the Federal Reserve System.

D. Need for Different Legal Rules for the Direct and Indirect Holding Systems

Both the traditional paper-based system, and the uncertificated system contemplated by the 1978 amendments, can be described as "direct" securities holding systems; that is, the beneficial owners of securities have a direct relationship with the issuer of the securities. For securities in bearer form, whoever has possession of the certificate thereby has a direct claim against the issuer. For registered securities, the registered owner, whether of certificated or uncertificated securities, has a direct relationship with the issuer by virtue of being recorded as the owner on the records maintained by the issuer or its transfer agent.

By contrast, the DTC depository system for corporate equity and debt securities can be described as an "indirect holding" system, that is, the issuer's records do not show the identity of all of the beneficial owners. Instead, a large portion of the outstanding securities of any given issue are recorded on the issuer's records as belonging to a depository. The depository's records in turn show the identity of the banks or brokers who are its members, and the records of those securities intermediaries show the identity of their customers.

Even after the 1978 amendments, the rules of Article 8 did not deal effectively with the indirect holding system. The rules of the 1978 version of

Article 8 were based on the assumption that changes in ownership of securities would still be effected either by delivery of physical certificates or by registration of transfer on the books of the issuer. Yet in the indirect holding system, settlement of the vast majority of securities trades does not involve either of these events. For most, if not all, of the securities held through DTC, physical certificates representing DTC's total position do exist. These "jumbo certificates," however, are never delivered from person to person. Just as nothing ever happens to these certificates, virtually nothing happens to the official registry of stockholders maintained by the issuers or their transfer agents to reflect the great bulk of the changes in ownership of shares that occur each day.

The principal mechanism through which securities trades are settled today is not delivery of certificates or registration of transfers on the issuer's books, but netted settlement arrangements and accounting entries on the books of a multi-tiered pyramid of securities intermediaries. Herein is the basic problem. Virtually all of the rules of the prior version of Article 8 specifying how changes in ownership of securities are effected, and what happens if something goes awry in the process, were keyed to the concepts of a transfer of physical certificates or registration of transfers on the books of the issuers, yet that is not how changes in ownership are actually reflected in the modern securities holding system.

II. BRIEF OVERVIEW OF REVISED ARTICLE 8

A. Drafting Approach—Neutrality Principle

One of the objectives of the revision of Article 8 is to devise a structure of commercial law rules for investment securities that will be sufficiently flexible to respond to changes in practice over the next few decades. If it were possible to predict with confidence how the securities holding and trading system would develop, one could produce a statute designed specifically for the system envisioned. Recent experience, however, shows the danger of that approach. The 1978 amendments to Article 8 were based on the assumption that the solution to the problems that plagued the paper-based securities trading system of the 1960s would be the development of uncertificated securities. Instead, the solution thus far has been the development of the indirect holding system.

If one thought that the indirect holding system would come to dominate securities holding, one might draft Article 8 rules designed primarily for the indirect holding system, giving limited attention to the traditional direct holding system of security certificates or any uncertificated version of a direct holding system that might develop in the future. It is, however, by no means clear whether the long-term evolution will be toward decreased or increased use of direct holdings. At present, investors in most equity securities can either hold their securities through brokers or request that certificates be issued in their own name. For the immediate future it seems likely that that situation will continue. One can imagine many plausible scenarios for future evolution. Direct holding might become less and less common as investors become more familiar and comfortable with book-entry systems and/or as market or regulatory pressures develop that discourage direct holding. One might note, for example, that major brokerage firms are beginning to impose fees for having certificates issued and that some observers have suggested that acceleration of the cycle for settlement of securities trades might be facilitated by discouraging customers from obtaining certificates. On the other hand, other observers feel that it is important for investors to retain the option of holding securities in certificated form, or at least in some form that gives them a direct relationship with the issuer and does not require them to hold through brokers or other securities intermediaries. Some groups within the securities industry are beginning to work on development of uncertificated systems that would preserve this option.

Revised Article 8 takes a neutral position on the evolution of securities holding practices. The revision was based on the assumption that the path of development will be determined by market and regulatory forces and that the Article 8 rules should not seek to influence that development in any specific direction. Although various drafting approaches were considered, it became apparent early in the revision process that the differences between the direct holding system and the indirect holding system are sufficiently significant that it is best to treat them as separate systems requiring different legal concepts. Accordingly, while the rules of the prior version of Article 8 have, in large measure, been retained for the direct holding system, a new Part 5 has been added, setting out the commercial law rules for the indirect securities holding system. The principle of neutrality does carry some implications for the design of specific Article 8 rules. At the very least, the Article 8 rules for all securities holding systems should be sufficiently clear and predictable that uncertainty about the governing law does not itself operate as a constraint on market developments. In addition, an effort has been made to identify and eliminate any Article 8 rules that might act as impediments to any of the foreseeable paths of development.

B. Direct Holding System

With respect to securities held directly, Revised Article 8 retains the basic conceptual structure and rules of present law. Part 2, which is largely unchanged from former law, deals with certain aspects of the obligations of issuers. The primary purpose of the rules of Part 2 is to apply to investment securities the principles of negotiable instruments law that preclude the issuers of negotiable instruments from asserting defenses against subsequent purchasers. Part 3 deals with transfer for securities held directly. One of its principal purposes is to apply to investment securities the principles of negotiable instruments law that protect purchasers of negotiable instruments against adverse claims. Part 4 deals with the process of registration of transfer by the issuer or transfer agent.

Although the basic concepts of the direct holding system rules have been retained, there are significant changes in terminology, organization, and statement of the rules. Some of the major changes are as follows:

Simplification of Part 3. The addition of the new Part 5 on the indirect holding system makes unnecessary the rather elaborate provisions of former law, such as those in Section 8–313, that sought to fit the indirect holding system into the conceptual structure of the direct holding system.

Thus, Part 3 of Revised Article 8 is, in many respects, more similar to the original version of Article 8 than to the 1978 version.

Protected purchaser. The prior version of Article 8 used the term "bona fide purchaser" to refer to those purchasers who took free from adverse claims, and it used the phrase "good faith" in stating the requirements for such status. In order to promote clarity, Revised Article 8 states the rules that protect purchasers against adverse claims without using the phrase "good faith" and uses the new term "protected purchaser" to refer to purchasers in the direct holding system who are protected against adverse claims. See Sections 8–105 and 8–303.

Certificated versus uncertificated securities. The rules of the 1978 version of Article 8 concerning uncertificated securities have been simplified considerably. The 1978 version added provisions on uncertificated securities parallel to the provisions of the original version of Article 8 dealing with securities represented by certificates. Thus, virtually every section had one set of rules on "certificated securities" and another on "uncertificated securities." The constant juxtaposition of "certificated securities" and "uncertificated securities" has probably led readers to overemphasize the differences. Revised Article 8 has a unitary definition of "security" in Section 8–102(a)(15) which refers to the underlying intangible interest or obligation. In Revised Article 8, the difference between certificated and uncertificated is treated not as an inherent attribute of the security but as a difference in the means by which ownership is evidenced. The terms "certificated" and "uncertificated" security are used in those sections where it is important to distinguish between these two means of evidencing ownership. Revised Article 8 also deletes the provisions of the 1978 version concerning "transaction statements" and "registered pledges." These changes are explained in the Revision Notes 3, 4, and 5, below.

Scope of Parts 2, 3, and 4. The rules of Parts 2, 3, and 4 deal only with the rights of persons who hold securities directly. In typical securities holding arrangements in the modern depository system, only the clearing corporation would be a direct holder of the securities. Thus, while the rules of Parts 2, 3, and 4 would apply to the relationship between the issuer and the clearing corporation, they have no application to relationships below the clearing corporation level. Under Revised Article 8, a person who holds a security through a broker or securities custodian has a security entitlement governed by the Part 5 rules but is not the direct holder of the security. Thus, the rules of Revised Section 8–303 on the rights of "protected purchasers," which are the analog of the bona fide purchaser rules of former Article 8, do not apply to persons who hold securities through brokers or securities custodians. Instead, Part 5 contains its own rules to protect investors in the indirect holding system against adverse claims. See Revised Section 8–502.

C. Indirect Holding System

Although the Revised Article 8 provisions for the indirect holding system are somewhat complex, the basic approach taken can be summarized rather briefly. Revised Article 8 abandons the attempt to describe all of the complex relationships in the indirect holding system using the simple concepts of the traditional direct holding system. Instead, new rules specifically designed for the indirect holding system are added as Part 5 of Article 8. In a nutshell, the approach is to describe the core of the package of rights of a person who holds a security through a securities intermediary and then give that package of rights a name.

The starting point of Revised Article 8's treatment of the indirect holding system is the concept of "security entitlement." The term is defined in Section 8–102(a)(17) as "the rights and property interest of an entitlement holder with respect to a financial asset specified in Part 5." Like many legal concepts, however, the meaning of "security entitlement" is to be found less in any specific definition than in the matrix of rules that use the term. In a sense, then, the entirety of Part 5 is the definition of "security entitlement" because the Part 5 rules specify the rights and property interest that comprise a security entitlement.

Part 5 begins by specifying, in Section 8–501, when an entitlement holder acquires a security entitlement. The basic rule is very simple. A person acquires a security entitlement when the securities intermediary credits the financial asset to the person's account. The remaining sections of Part 5 specify the content of the security entitlement concept. Section 8–504 provides that a securities intermediary must maintain a sufficient quantity of financial assets to satisfy the claims of all of its entitlement holders. Section 8–503 provides that these financial assets are held by the intermediary for the entitlement holders, are not the property of the securities intermediary, and are not subject to claims of the intermediary's general creditors. Thus, a security entitlement is itself a form of property interest not merely an *in personam* claim against the intermediary. The concept of a security entitlement does, however, include a package of *in personam* rights against the intermediary. Other Part 5 rules identify the core of this package of rights, subject to specification by agreement and regulatory law. See Sections 8–505 through 8–509.

To illustrate the basic features of the new rules, consider a simple example of two investors, John and Mary, each of whom owns 1000 shares of Acme, Inc., a publicly traded company. John has a certificate representing his 1000 shares and is registered on the books maintained by Acme's transfer agent as the holder of record of those 1000 shares. Accordingly, he has a direct claim against the issuer, he receives dividends and distributions directly from the issuer, and he receives proxies directly from the issuer for purposes of voting his shares. Mary has chosen to hold her securities through her broker. She does not have a certificate and is not registered on Acme's stock books as a holder of record. She enjoys the economic and corporate benefits of ownership but does so through her broker and any other intermediaries in the chain back to the issuer. John's interest in Acme common stock would be described under Revised Article 8 as a direct interest in a "security." Thus, if John grants a security interest in his investment position, the collateral would be described as a "security." Mary's interest in Acme common stock would be described under Revised Article 8 as a "security entitlement." Thus, if Mary grants a security interest in her investment position, the collateral would be described as a "security entitlement."

For many purposes, there is no need to differentiate among the various ways that an investor might hold securities. For example, for purposes of financial accounting, John and Mary would each be described as the owner of 1000 shares of Acme common stock. For those purposes it is irrelevant that John is the registered owner and has physical possession of a certificate, while Mary holds her position through an intermediary. Revised Article 8 recognizes this point in Section 8–104 which provides that acquiring a security entitlement and acquiring a security certificate are different ways of acquiring an interest in the underlying security.

D. Security Interests

Along with the revision of Article 8, significant changes have been made in the rules concerning security interests in securities. The revision returns to the pre–1978 structure in which the rules on security interests in investment securities are set out in Article 9, rather than in Article 8. The changes in Article 9 are, in part, conforming changes to adapt Article 9 to the new concept of a security entitlement. The Article 9 changes, however, go beyond that to establish a simplified structure for the creation and perfection of security interests in investment securities, whether held directly or indirectly. In order to avoid disruption of the current numbering sequence of Article 9, the new rules on security interests in investment securities are primarily set out in a new Section 9–115.

The Revised Article 9 rules continue the long-established principle that a security interest in a security represented by a certificate can be perfected by a possessory pledge. The revised rules, however, do not require that all security interests in investment securities be implemented by procedures based on the conceptual structure of the common law pledge. Under the revised Article 9 rules, a security interest in securities can be created pursuant to Section 9–203 in the same fashion as a security interest in any other form of property, that is, by agreement between the debtor and secured party. There is no requirement of a "transfer," "delivery," or any similar action, physical or metaphysical, for the creation of an effective security interest. A security interest in securities is, of course, a form of property interest, but the only requirements for creation of this form of property interest are those set out in Section 9–203.

The perfection methods for security interests in investment securities are set out in Revised Section 9–115(4). The basic rule is that a security interest may be perfected by "control." The concept of control, defined in Section 8–106, plays an important role in both Article 8 and Article 9. In general, obtaining control means taking the steps necessary to place the lender in a position where it can have the collateral sold off without the further cooperation of the debtor. Thus, for certificated securities, a lender obtains control by taking possession of the certificate with any necessary indorsement. For securities held through a securities intermediary, the lender can obtain control in two ways. First, the lender obtains control if it becomes the entitlement holder; that is, has the securities positions transferred to an account in its own name. Second, the lender obtains control if the securities intermediary agrees to act on instructions from the secured party to dispose of the positions, even though the debtor remains the entitlement holder. Such an arrangement suffices to give the lender control even though the debtor retains the right to trade and exercise other ordinary rights of an entitlement holder.

Except where the debtor is itself a securities firm, filing of an ordinary Article 9 financing statement is also a permissible alternative method of perfection. However, filing with respect to investment property does not assure the lender the same protections as for other forms of collateral, since the priority rules provide that a secured party who obtains control has priority over a secured party who does not obtain control.

The details of the new rules on security interests, as applied both to the retail level and to arrangements for secured financing of securities dealers, are explained in the Official Comments to Section 9–115.

III. SCOPE AND APPLICATION OF ARTICLE 8

A. Terminology

To understand the scope and application of the rules of Revised Article 8, and the related security interest rules of Article 9, it is necessary to understand some of the key defined terms:

Security, defined in Section 8–102(a)(15), has essentially the same meaning as under the prior version of Article 8. The difference in Revised Article 8 is that the definition of security does not determine the coverage of all of Article 8. Although the direct holding system rules in Parts 2, 3, and 4 apply only to securities, the indirect holding system rules of Part 5 apply to the broader category of "financial assets."

Financial asset, defined in Section 8–103(a)(9), is the term used to describe the forms of property to which the indirect holding system rules of Part 5 apply. The term includes not only "securities," but also other interests, obligations, or property that are held through securities accounts. The best illustration of the broader scope of the term financial asset is the treatment of money market instruments, discussed below.

Security entitlement, defined in Section 8–103(a)(17), is the term used to describe the property interest of a person who holds a security or other financial asset through a securities intermediary.

Securities intermediary, defined in Section 8–103(a)(14), is the term used for those who hold securities for others in the indirect holding system. It covers clearing corporations, banks acting as securities custodians, and brokers holding securities for their customers.

Entitlement holder, defined in Section 8–103(a)(7), is the term used for those who hold securities through intermediaries.

Securities account, defined in Section 8–501(a), describes the form of arrangement between a securities intermediary and an entitlement holder that gives rise to a security entitlement. As explained below, the definition of securities account plays a key role in setting the scope of the indirect holding system rules of Part 5.

Investment property, defined in Section 9–115(1)(f), determines the application of the new Article 9 rules for secured transactions. In addition to securities and security entitlements, the Article 9 term "investment property" is defined to include "securities account" in order to simplify the drafting of the Article 9 rules that permit debtors to grant security interests either in specific security entitlements or in an entire securities account. The other difference between the coverage of the Article 8 and Article 9 terms is that commodity futures contracts are excluded from Article 8, but are included within the Article 9 definition of "investment property." Thus, the new Article 9 rules apply to security interests in commodity futures positions as well as security interests in securities positions.

B. Notes on Scope of Article 8

Article 8 is in no sense a comprehensive codification of the law governing securities or transactions in securities. Although Article 8 deals with some aspects of the rights of securities holders against issuers, most of that relationship is governed not by Article 8, but by corporation, securities, and contract law. Although Article 8 deals with some aspects of the rights and duties of parties who transfer securities, it is not a codification of the law of contracts for the purchase or sale of securities. (The prior version of Article 8 did include a few miscellaneous rules on contracts for the sale of securities, but these have not been included in Revised Article 8). Although the new indirect holding system rules of Part 5 deal with some aspects of the relationship between brokers or other securities professionals and their customers, Article 8 is still not in any sense a comprehensive code of the law governing the relationship between broker-dealers or other securities intermediaries and their customers. Most of the law governing that relationship is the common law of contract and agency, supplemented or supplanted by regulatory law.

The distinction between the aspects of the broker-customer relationship that are and are not dealt with in this Article may be illuminated by considering the differing roles of the broker in a typical securities transaction, in which the broker acts as agent for the customer. When a customer directs a broker to buy or sell securities for the customer, and the broker executes that trade on a securities exchange or in the over the counter market, the broker is entering into a contract for the purchase or sale of the securities as agent of the customer. The rules of the exchange, practices of the market, or regulatory law will specify when and how that contract is to be performed. For example, today the terms of the standard contract for trades in most corporate securities require the seller to deliver the securities, and the buyer to pay for them, five business days after the date that the contract was made, although the SEC has recently promulgated a rule that will accelerate the cycle to require settlement in three business days. In the common speech of the industry, the transaction in which the broker enters into a contract for the purchase or sale of the securities is referred to as executing the trade, and the transaction in which the securities are delivered and paid for is referred to as settlement. Thus, the current settlement cycle is known as T+5, that is, settlement is required on the fifth business day after the date of the trade, and the new SEC rule will change it to T+3. One must be careful in moving from the jargon of the securities industry to the jargon of the legal profession. For most practical economic purposes, the trade date is the date that counts, because that is the time at which the price is set, the risk of price changes shifts, and the parties become bound to perform. For purposes of precise legal analysis, however, the securities phrase "trade" or "execute a trade" means enter into a contract for the purchase or sale of the securities. The transfer of property interests occurs not at the time the contract is made but at the time it is performed, that is, at settlement.

The distinction between trade and settlement is important in understanding the scope of Article 8. Article 8 deals with the settlement phase of securities transactions. It deals with the mechanisms by which interests in securities are transferred, and the rights and duties of those who are involved in the transfer process. It does not deal with the process of entering into contracts for the transfer of securities or regulate the rights and duties of those involved in the contracting process. To use securities parlance, Article 8 deals not with the trade, but with settlement of the trade. Indeed, Article 8 does not even deal with all aspects of settlement. In a netted clearance and settlement system such as the NSCC–DTC system, individual trades are not settled one-by-one by corresponding entries on the books of any depository. Rather, settlement of the individual trades occurs through the clearing arrangements, in accordance with the rules and agreements that govern those arrangements.

In the rules dealing with the indirect holding system, one must be particularly careful to bear in mind the distinction between trade and settlement. Under Revised Article 8, the property interest of a person who holds securities through an intermediary is described as a "security entitlement," which is defined in Revised Section 8–102(a)(17) as the package of rights and property interest of an entitlement holder specified in Part 5. Saying that the security entitlement is a package of rights against the broker does not mean that all of the customer's rights against the broker are part of the security entitlement and hence part of the subject matter of Article 8. The distinction between trade and settlement remains fundamental. The rules of this Article on the indirect holding system deal with brokers and other intermediaries as media through which investors hold their financial assets. Brokers are also media through which investors buy and sell their financial assets, but that aspect of their role is not the subject of this Article.

The principal goal of the Article 8 revision project is to provide a satisfactory framework for analysis of the indirect holding system. The technique used in Revised Article 8 is to acknowledge explicitly that the relationship between a securities intermediary and its entitlement holders is sui generis, and to state the applicable commercial law rules directly, rather than by inference from a categorization of the relationship based on legal concepts of a different era. One of the consequences of this drafting technique is that in order to provide content to the concept of security entitlement it becomes necessary to identify the core of the package of rights that make up a security entitlement. Sections 8–504 through 8–508 cover such basic matters as the duty of the securities intermediary to maintain a sufficient quantity of securities to satisfy all of its entitlement holders, the duty of the securities intermediary to pass through to entitlement holder the economic and corporate law rights of ownership of the security, and the duty of the securities intermediary to comply with authorized entitlement orders originated by the entitlement holder. These sections are best thought of as definitional; that is, a relationship which does not include these rights is not the kind of relationship that Revised Article 8 deals with. Because these sections take the form of statements of the duties of an intermediary toward its entitlement holders, one must be careful to avoid a distorted perspective on what Revised Article 8 is and is not designed to do. Revised Article 8 is not, and should not be, a comprehensive body of private law governing the relationship between brokers and their customers, nor a body of regulatory law to police against improper conduct by brokers or other intermediaries. Many, if not most, aspects of the relationship between brokers and customers are governed by the common law of contract and agency, supplemented or supplanted by federal and state regulatory law. Revised Article 8 does not take the place of this body of private and regulatory law. If there are gaps in the regulatory law, they should be dealt with as such; Article 8 is not the place to address them. Article 8 deals with how interests in securities are evidenced and how they are transferred. By way of a rough analogy, one might think of Article 8 as playing the role for the securities markets that real estate recording acts play for the real estate markets. Real estate recording acts do not regulate the conduct of parties to real estate transactions; Article 8 does not regulate the conduct of parties to securities transactions.

C. Application of Revised Articles 8 and 9 to Common Investments and Investment Arrangements

It may aid understanding to sketch briefly the treatment under Revised Articles 8 and 9 of a variety of relatively common products and arrangements.

1. Publicly traded stocks and bonds.

"Security" is defined in Revised Section 8–102(a)(15) in substantially the same terms as in the prior version of Article 8. It covers the ordinary publicly traded investment securities, such as corporate stocks and bonds. Parts 2, 3, and 4 govern the interests of persons who hold securities directly, and Part 5 governs the interest of those who hold securities indirectly.

Ordinary publicly traded securities provide a good illustration of the relationship between the direct and indirect holding system rules. The distinction between the direct and indirect holding systems is not an attribute of the securities themselves but of the way in which a particular person holds the securities. Thus, whether one looks to the direct holding system rules of Parts 2, 3, and 4 or the indirect holding system rules of Part 5 will depend on the level in the securities holding system being analyzed.

Consider, for example, corporate stock which is held through a depository, such as DTC. The clearing corporation, or its nominee, is the registered owner of all of the securities it holds on behalf of all of its participants. Thus the rules of Parts 2, 3, and 4 of Revised Article 8 apply to the relationship between the issuer and the clearing corporation. If, as is typically the case today, the securities are still represented by certificates, the clearing corporation will be the holder of the security certificate or certificates representing its total holdings. So far as Article 8 is concerned, the relationship between the issuer and the clearing corporation is no different from the relationship between the issuer and any other registered owner.

The relationship between the clearing corporation and its participants is governed by the indirect holding system rules of Part 5. At that level, the clearing corporation is the securities intermediary and the participant is the entitlement holder. If the participant is itself a securities intermediary, such as a broker holding for its customers or a bank acting as a securities custodian, the Part 5 rules apply to its relationship to its own customers. At that level the broker or bank custodian is the securities intermediary and the customer is the entitlement holder. Note that the broker or bank custodian is both an entitlement holder and a securities intermediary—but is so with respect to different security entitlements. For purposes of Article 8 analysis, the customer's security entitlement against the broker or bank custodian is a different item of property from the security entitlement of the broker or bank custodian against the clearing corporation.

For investors who hold their securities directly, it makes no difference that some other investors hold their interests indirectly. Many investors today choose to hold their securities directly, becoming the registered owners on the books of the issuer and obtaining certificates registered in their names. For such investors, the addition of the new indirect holding system rules to Article 8 is entirely irrelevant. They will continue to deal directly with the issuers, or their transfer agents, under essentially the same rules as in the prior version of Article 8.

The securities holding options available to investors in a particular form of security may depend on the terms of the security. For example, direct holding is frequently not available for new issues of state and local government bonds. At one time, state and local government bonds were commonly issued in bearer form. Today, however, new issues of state and local government bonds must be in registered form and most are issued in what is known as "book-entry only" form; that is, the issuer specifies that the only person it will directly register as the registered owner is a clearing corporation. Thus, one of the inherent terms of the security is that investors can hold only in the indirect holding system.

2. Treasury securities.

U.S. government securities fall within the definition of security in Article 8 and therefore are governed by Article 8 in the same fashion as any other publicly held debt security, except insofar as Article 8 is preempted by applicable federal law or regulation.

New Treasury securities are no longer issued in certificated form; they can be held only through the book-entry systems established by the Treasury and Federal Reserve Banks. The Treasury offers a book-entry system, known as "Treasury Direct" which enables individual investors to have their positions recorded directly on the books of a Federal Reserve Bank, in a fashion somewhat similar to the uncertificated direct holding system contemplated by the 1978 version of Article 8. The governing law for the Treasury Direct system, however, is set out in the applicable Treasury regulations. The Treasury Direct system is not designed for active trading.

The great bulk of Treasury securities are held not through the Treasury Direct system but through a multi-tiered indirect holding system. The Federal Reserve Banks, acting as fiscal agent for the Treasury, maintain records of the holdings of member banks of the Federal Reserve System, and those banks in turn maintain records showing the extent to which they are holding for themselves or their own customers, including government securities dealers, institutional investors, or smaller banks who in turn may act as custodians for investors. The indirect holding system for Treasury securities was established under federal regulations promulgated in the 1970s. In the 1980s, Treasury released the proposed TRADES regulations that would have established a more comprehensive body of federal commercial law for the Treasury holding system. During the Article 8 revision process, Treasury withdrew these regulations, anticipating that once Revised Article 8 is enacted, it will be possible to base the law for the Treasury system on the new Article 8 rules.

3. Broker-customer relationships.

Whether the relationship between a broker and its customer is governed by the Article 8 Part 5 rules depends on the nature of the services that the broker performs for the customer.

Some investors use brokers only to purchase and sell securities. These customers take delivery of certificates representing the securities they purchase and hold them in their own names. When they wish to sell, they deliver the certificates to the brokers. The Article 8 Part 5 rules would not affect such customers, because the Part 5 rules deal with arrangements in which investors hold securities through securities intermediaries. The transaction between the customer and broker might be the traditional agency arrangement in which the broker buys or sells on behalf of the customer as agent for an undisclosed principal, or it might be a dealer transaction in which the "broker" as principal buys from or sells to the customer. In either case, if the customer takes delivery and holds the securities directly, she will become the "purchaser" of a "security" whose interest therein is governed by the rules of Parts 2, 3, and 4 of Article 8. If the customer meets the other requirements of Section 8–303(a), the customer who takes delivery can qualify as a "protected purchaser" who takes free from any adverse claims under Section 8–303(b). The broker's role in such transactions is primarily governed by non-Article 8 law. There are only a few provisions of Article 8 that affect the relationship between the customer and broker in such cases. See Section 8–108 (broker makes to the customer the warranties of a transferor) and 8–115 (broker not liable in conversion if customer was acting wrongfully against a third party in selling securities).

Many investors use brokers not only to purchase and sell securities, but also as the custodians through whom they hold their securities. The indirect holding system rules of Part 5 apply to the custodial aspect of this relationship. If a customer purchases a security through a broker and directs the broker to hold the security in an account for the customer, the customer will never become a "purchaser" of a "security" whose interest therein is governed by the rules of Parts 2, 3, and 4 of Article 8. Accordingly, the customer does not become a "protected purchaser" under Section 8–303. Rather, the customer becomes an "entitlement holder" who has a "security entitlement" to the security against the broker as "securities intermediary." See Section 8–501. It would make no sense to say that the customer in such a case takes an interest in the security free from all other claims, since the nature of the relationship is that the customer has an interest in common with other customers who hold positions in the same security through the same broker. Section 8–502, however, does protect an entitlement holder against adverse claims, in the sense that once the entitlement holder has acquired the package of rights that comprise a security entitlement no one else can take that package of rights away by arguing that the transaction that resulted in the customer's acquisition of the security entitlement was the traceable product of a transfer or transaction that was wrongful as against the claimant.

4. Bank deposit accounts; brokerage asset management accounts.

An ordinary bank deposit account would not fall within the definition of "security" in Section 8–102(a)(15), so the rules of Parts 2, 3, and 4 of Article 8 do not apply to deposit accounts. Nor would the relationship between a bank and its depositors be governed by the rules of Part 5 of Article 8. The Part 5 rules apply to "security entitlements." Section 8–501(b) provides that a person has a security entitlement when a securities intermediary credits a financial asset to the person's "securities account." "Securities account" is defined in Section 8–501(a) as "an account to which a financial asset is or may be credited in accordance with an agreement under which the person maintaining the account undertakes to treat the person for whom the account is maintained as entitled to exercise the rights that comprise the financial asset." The definition of securities account plays a key role in setting the scope of Part 5 of Article 8. A person has a security entitlement governed by Part 5 only if the relationship in question falls within the definition of "securities account." The definition of securities account in Section 8–501(a) excludes deposit accounts from the Part 5 rules of Article 8. One of the basic elements of the relationship between a securities intermediary and an entitlement holder is that the securities intermediary has the duty to hold exactly the quantity of securities that it carries for the account of its customers. See Section 8–504. The assets that a securities intermediary holds for its entitlement holder are not assets that the securities intermediary can use in its own proprietary business. See Section 8–503. A deposit account is an entirely different arrangement. A bank is not required to hold in its vaults or in deposit accounts with other banks a sum of money equal to the claims of all of its depositors. Banks are permitted to use depositors' funds in their ordinary lending business; indeed, that is a primary function of banks. A deposit account, unlike a securities account, is simply a debtor-creditor relationship. Thus a bank or other financial institution maintaining deposit accounts is not covered by Part 5 of Article 8.

Today, it is common for brokers to maintain securities accounts for their customers which include arrangements for the customers to hold liquid "cash" assets in the form of money market mutual fund shares. Insofar as the broker is holding money market mutual fund shares for its customer, the customer has a security entitlement to the money market mutual fund shares. It is also common for brokers to offer their customers an arrangement in which the customer has access to those liquid assets via a deposit account with a bank, whereby shares of the money market fund are redeemed to cover checks drawn on the account. Article 8 applies only to the securities account; the linked bank account remains an account covered by other law. Thus the rights and duties of the customer and the bank are governed not by Article 8, but by the relevant payment system law, such as Article 4 or Article 4A.

5. Trusts.

The indirect holding system rules of Part 5 of Article 8 are not intended to govern all relationships in which one person holds securities "on behalf of" another. Rather, the Part 5 rules come into play only if the relationship in question falls within the definition of securities account in Section 8–501(a). The definition of securities account serves the important function of ensuring that ordinary trust arrangements are not inadvertently swept into Part 5 of Article 8. Suppose that Bank serves as trustee of a trust for the benefit of Beneficiary. The corpus of the trust is invested in securities and other financial assets. Although Bank is, in some senses, holding securities for Beneficiary, the arrangement would not fall within the definition of securities account. Bank, as trustee, has not undertaken to treat Beneficiary as entitled to exercise all of the rights that comprise the portfolio securities. For instance, although Beneficiary receives the economic benefit of the portfolio securities, Beneficiary does not have the right to direct dispositions of individual trust assets or to exercise voting or other corporate law rights with respect to the individual securities. Thus Bank's obligations to Beneficiary as trustee are governed by ordinary trust law, not by Part 5 of Article 8. Of course, if Bank, as trustee, holds the securities through an intermediary, Part 5 of Revised Article 8 would govern the relationship between Bank, as entitlement holder, and the intermediary through which Bank holds the securities. It is also possible that a different department of Bank acts as the intermediary through which Bank, as trustee, holds the securities. Bank, *qua* securities custodian, might be holding securities for a large number of customers, including Bank's own trust department. Insofar as Bank may be regarded as acting in different capacities, Part 5 of Article 8 may be relevant to the relationship between the two sides of Bank's business. However, the relationship between Bank as trustee and the beneficiaries of the trust would remain governed by trust law, not Article 8.

6. Mutual fund shares.

Shares of mutual funds are Article 8 securities, whether the fund is organized as a corporation, business trust, or other form of entity. See Sections 8–102(a)(15) and 8–103(b). Mutual funds commonly do not issue certificates. Thus, mutual fund shares are typically uncertificated securities under Article 8.

Although a mutual fund is, in a colloquial sense, holding the portfolio securities on behalf of the fund's shareholders, the indirect holding system rules of Part 5 do not apply to the relationship between the fund and its shareholders. The Part 5 rules apply to "security entitlements." Section 8–501(e) provides that issuance of a security is not establishment of a security entitlement. Thus, because mutual funds shares do fit within the Article 8 definition of security, the relationship between the fund and its shareholders is automatically excluded from the Part 5 rules.

Of course, a person might hold shares in a mutual fund through a brokerage account. Because mutual fund shares are securities, they automatically fall within the broader term "financial asset," so the Part 5 indirect holding system rules apply to mutual fund shares that are held through securities accounts. That is, a person who holds mutual fund shares through a brokerage account could have a security entitlement to the mutual fund shares, just as the person would have a security entitlement to any other security carried in the brokerage account.

7. Stock of closely held corporations.

Ordinary corporate stock falls within the Article 8 definition of security, whether or not it is publicly traded. See Sections 8–102(a)(15) and 8–103(a). There is nothing in the new indirect holding system rules of Article 8 that would preclude their application to shares of companies that are not publicly traded. The indirect holding system rules, however, would come into play only if the shares were in fact held through a securities account with a securities intermediary. Since that is typically not the case with respect to shares of closely held corporations, transactions involving those shares will continue to be governed by the traditional rules, as amended, that are set out in Parts 2, 3, and 4 of Article 8, and the corresponding provisions of Article 9. The simplification of the Article 8 rules on uncertificated securities may, however, make the alternative of dispensing with certificates more attractive for closely held corporations.

8. Partnership interests and limited liability company shares.

Interests in partnerships or shares of limited liability companies are not Article 8 securities unless they are in fact dealt in or traded on securities exchanges or in securities markets. See Section 8–103(c). The issuers, however, may if they wish explicitly "opt-in" by specifying that the interests or shares are securities governed by Article 8. Even though interests in partnerships or shares of limited liability companies do not generally fall within the category of "security" in Article 8, they would fall within the broader term "financial asset." Accordingly, if such interests are held through a securities account with a securities intermediary, the indirect holding system rules of Part 5 apply, and the interest of a person who holds them through such an account is a security entitlement.

9. Bankers' acceptances, commercial paper, and other money market instruments.

Money market instruments, such as commercial paper, bankers' acceptances, and certificates of deposit, are good examples of a form of property that may fall within the definition of "financial asset," even though they may not fall within the definition of "security." Section 8–103(d) provides that a writing that meets the definition of security certificate under Section 8–102(a)(15) is governed by Article 8, even though it also fits within the definition of "negotiable instrument" in Article 3.

Some forms of short term money market instruments may meet the requirements of an Article 8 security, while others may not. For example, the

Article 8 definition of security requires that the obligation be in registered or bearer form. Bankers' acceptances are typically payable "to order," and thus do not qualify as Article 8 securities. Thus, the obligations of the immediate parties to a bankers' acceptance are governed by Article 3, rather than Article 8. That is an entirely appropriate classification, even for those bankers' acceptance that are handled as investment media in the securities markets, because Article 8, unlike Article 3, does not contain rules specifying the standardized obligations of parties to instruments. For example, the Article 3 rules on the obligations of acceptors and drawers of drafts are necessary to specify the obligations represented by bankers' acceptances, but Article 8 contains no provisions dealing with these issues.

Immobilization through a depository system is, however, just as important for money market instruments as for traditional securities. Under the prior version of Article 8, the rules on the depository system, set out in Section 8–320, applied only to Article 8 securities. Although some forms of money market instruments could be fitted within the language of the Article 8 definition of "security," this is not true for bankers' acceptances. Accordingly, it was not thought feasible to make bankers' acceptances eligible for deposit in clearing corporations under the prior version of Article 8. Revised Article 8 solves this problem by separating the coverage of the Part 5 rules from the definition of security. Even though a bankers' acceptance or other money market instrument is an Article 3 negotiable instrument rather than an Article 8 security, it would still fall within the definition of financial asset in Section 8–102(a)(9). Accordingly, if the instrument is held through a clearing corporation or other securities intermediary, the rules of Part 5 of Article 8 apply.

10. Repurchase agreement transactions.

Repurchase agreements are an important form of transaction in the securities business, particularly in connection with government securities. Repos and reverse repos can be used for a variety of purposes. The one that is of particular concern for purposes of commercial law rules is the use of repurchase agreements as a form of financing transaction for government securities dealers. Government securities dealers typically obtain intra-day financing from their clearing banks, and then at the end of the trading day seek overnight financing from other sources to repay that day's advances from the clearing bank. Repos are the principal source of this financing. The dealer ("repo seller") sells securities to the financing source ("repo buyer") for cash, and at the same time agrees to repurchase the same or like securities the following day, or at some other brief interval. The sources of the financing include a variety of entities seeking short term investments for surplus cash, such as pension funds, business corporations, money market funds, and banks. The pricing may be computed in various ways, but in essence the price at which the dealer agrees to repurchase the securities exceeds the price paid to the dealer by an amount equivalent to interest on the funds.

The transfer of the securities from a securities dealer as repo seller to a provider of funds as repo buyer can be effected in a variety of ways. The repo buyer might be willing to allow the repo seller to keep the securities "in its hands," relying on the dealer's representation that it will hold them on behalf of the repo buyer. In the jargon of the trade, these are known as "hold-in-custody repos" or "HIC repos." At the other extreme, the repo buyer might insist that the dealer "hand over" the securities so that in the event that the dealer fails and is unable to perform its obligation to repurchase them, the repo buyer will have the securities "in its hands." The jargon for these is "delivered-out repos." A wide variety of arrangements between these two extremes might be devised, in which the securities are "handed over" to a third party with powers concerning their disposition allocated between the repo seller and repo buyer in a variety of ways.

Specification of the rights of repo buyers is complicated by the fact that the transfer of the interest in securities from the repo seller to the repo buyer might be characterized as an outright sale or as the creation of a security interest. Article 8 does not attempt to specify any categorical rules on that issue.

Article 8 sets out rules on the rights of parties who have implemented securities transactions in certain ways. It does not, however, deal with the legal characterization of the transactions that are implemented through the Article 8 mechanisms. Rather, the Article 8 rules apply without regard to the characterization of transactions for other purposes. For example, the Article 8 rules for the direct holding system provide that a person who takes delivery of a duly indorsed security certificate for value and without notice of adverse claims takes free from any adverse claims. That rule applies without regard to the character of the transaction in which the security certificate was delivered. It applies both to delivery upon original issue and to delivery upon transfer. It applies to transfers in settlement of sales and to transfers in pledge. Similarly, the Article 8 indirect holding system rules, such as the adverse claim cut-off rules in Sections 8–502 and 8–510, apply to the transactions that fall within their terms, whether those transactions were sales, secured transactions, or something else.

Repos involve transfers of interests in securities. The Article 8 rules apply to transfers of securities in repos, just as they apply to transfers of securities in any other form of transaction. The transfer of the interest in securities from the repo seller to the repo buyer might be characterized as an outright sale or as the creation of a security interest. Article 8 does not determine that question. The rules of Revised Article 8 have, however, been drafted to minimize the possibility that disputes over the characterization of the transfer in a repo would affect substantive questions that are governed by Article 8. See, e.g., Section 8–510 and Comment 4 thereto.

11. Securities lending transactions.

In a typical securities lending transaction, the owner of securities lends them to another person who needs the securities to satisfy a delivery obligation. For example, when a customer of a broker sells a security short, the broker executes an ordinary trade as seller and so must deliver the securities at settlement. The customer is "short" against the broker because the customer has an open obligation to deliver the securities to the broker, which the customer hopes to be able to satisfy by buying in the securities at a lower price. If the short seller's broker does not have the securities in its own inventory, the broker will borrow them from someone else. The securities lender delivers the securities to the borrowing broker, and the borrowing broker becomes contractually obligated to redeliver a like quantity of the same security. Securities borrowers are required to provide collateral, usually government securities, to assure performance of their redelivery obligation.

The securities lender does not retain any property interest in the securities that are delivered to the borrower. The transaction is an outright transfer in which the borrower obtains full title. The whole point of securities lending is that the borrower needs the securities to transfer them to someone else. It would make no sense to say that the lender retains any property interest in the securities it has lent. Accordingly, even if the securities borrower defaults on its redelivery obligation, the securities lender has no property interest in the original securities that could be asserted against any person to whom the securities borrower may have transferred them. One need not look to adverse claim cut-off rules to reach that result; the securities lender never had an adverse claim. The securities borrower's default is no different from any other breach of contract. The securities lender's protection is its right to foreclose on the collateral given to secure the borrower's redelivery obligation. Perhaps the best way to understand securities lending is to note that the word "loan" in securities lending transactions is used in the sense it carries in loans of money, as distinguished from loans of specific identifiable chattels. Someone who lends money does not retain any property interest in the money that is handed over to the borrower. To use civil law terminology, securities lending is *mutuum,* rather than *commodatum.* See Story on Bailments, §§ 6 and 47.

12. Traded stock options.

Stock options issued and cleared through the Options Clearing Corporation ("OCC") are a good example of a form of investment vehicle that is treated as a financial asset to which the Part 5 rules apply, but not as an Article 8 security to which Parts 2, 3, and 4 apply. OCC carries on its books the options positions of the brokerage firms which are clearing members of OCC. The clearing members in turn carry on their books the options positions of their customers. The arrangements are structurally similar to the securities depository system. In the options structure, however, there is no issuer separate from the clearing corporation. The financial assets held through the system are standardized contracts entitling the holder to purchase or sell a certain security at a set price. Rather than being an interest in or obligation of a separate issuer, an option is a contractual right against the counter-party. In order to assure performance of the options, OCC interposes itself as counter-party to each options trade. The rules of Parts 2, 3, and 4 of this Article, however, do not well describe the obligations and rights of OCC. On the other hand, the rules of Part 5, and the related Article 9 rules on security interests and priorities, do provide a workable legal framework for the commercial law analysis of the rights of the participants in the options market. Accordingly, publicly traded securities options are included within the definition of "financial asset," but not "security." See Section 8–103(e). Thus, although OCC would not be an issuer of a security for purposes of this Article, it would be a clearing corporation, against whom its clearing members have security entitlements to the options positions. Similarly, the clearing members' customers have security entitlements against the clearing members. Traded stock options are also a good illustration of the point that the classification issues under Article 8 are very different from classification under other law, such as the federal securities laws. See Section 8–102(d). Stock options are treated as securities for purposes of federal securities laws, but not for purposes of Article 8.

13. Commodity futures.

Section 8–103(f) provides that a "commodity contract" is not a security or a financial asset. Section 9–115 defines commodity contract to include commodity futures contracts, commodity options, and options on commodity futures contracts that are traded on or subject to the rules of a board of trade that has been designated as a contract market for that contract pursuant to the federal commodities laws. Thus, commodity contracts themselves are not Article 8 securities to which the rules of Parts 2, 3, and 4 apply, nor is the relationship between a customer and a commodity futures commission merchant governed by the Part 5 rules of Article 8. Commodity contracts, however, are included within the Article 9 definition of "investment property." Thus security interests in commodity positions are governed by essentially the same set of rules as security interests in security entitlements.

14. "Whatever else they have or may devise."

The classification question posed by the above-captioned category of investment products and arrangements is among the most difficult—and important—issue raised by the Article 8 revision process. Rapid innovation is perhaps the only constant characteristic of the securities and financial markets. The rules of Revised Article 8 are intended to be sufficiently flexible to accommodate new developments.

A common mechanism by which new financial instruments are devised is that a financial institution that holds some security, financial instrument, or pool thereof, creates interests in that asset or pool which are sold to others. It is not possible to answer in the abstract the question of how such interests are treated under Article 8, because the variety of such products is limited only by human imagination and current regulatory structures. At this general level, however, one can note that there are at least three possible treatments under Article 8 of the relationship between the institution which creates the interests and the persons who hold them. (Again, it must be borne in mind that the Article 8 classification issue may be different from the classification question posed by federal securities law or other regulation.) First, creation of the new interests in the underlying assets may constitute issuance of a new Article 8 security. In that case the relationship between the institution that created the interest and the persons who hold them is not governed by the Part 5 rules, but by the rules of Parts 2, 3, and 4. See Section 8–501(e). That, for example, is the structure of issuance of mutual fund shares. Second, the relationship between the entity creating the interests and those holding them may fit within the Part 5 rules, so that the persons are treating as having security entitlements against the institution with respect to the underlying assets. That, for example, is the structure used for stock options. Third, it may be that the creation of the new interests in the underlying assets does not constitute issuance of a new Article 8 security, nor does the relationship between the entity creating the interests and those holding them fit within the Part 5 rules. In that case, the relationship is governed by other law, as in the case of ordinary trusts.

The first of these three possibilities—that the creation of the new interest is issuance of a new security for Article 8 purposes—is a fairly common pattern. For example, an American depositary receipt facility does not maintain securities accounts but issues securities called ADRs in respect of foreign securities deposited in such facility. Similarly, custodians of government securities which issue receipts, certificates, or the like representing direct interests in those securities (sometimes interests split between principal and income) do not maintain securities accounts but issue securities representing those interests. Trusts holding assets, in a variety of structured and securitized transactions, which issue certificates or the like representing "pass-through" or undivided beneficial interests in the trust assets, do not maintain securities accounts but issue securities representing those interests.

In analyzing these classification questions, courts should take care to avoid mechanical jurisprudence based solely upon exegesis of the wording of definitions in Article 8. The result of classification questions is that different sets of rules come into play. In order to decide the classification question it is necessary to understand fully the commercial setting and consider which set of rules best fits the transaction. Rather than letting the choice of rules turn on interpretation of the words of the definitions, the interpretation of the words of the definitions should turn on the suitability of the application of the substantive rules.

IV. CHANGES FROM PRIOR (1978) VERSION OF ARTICLE 8

A. Table of Disposition of Sections in Prior Version

Article 8 (1978)	Revised Articles 8 and 9
8–101	8–101
8–102(1)(a)	8–102(a)(4) & (15)
8–102(1)(b)	8–102(a)(15) & (18)
8–102(1)(c)	8–102(a)(15)
8–102(1)(d)	8–102(a)(13)
8–102(1)(e)	8–102(a)(2)
8–102(2)	8–202(b)(1)
8–102(3)	8–102(a)(5)
8–102(4)	omitted, see Revision Note 1
8–102(5)	8–102(b)
8–102(6)	8–102(c)
8–103	8–209
8–104	8–210
8–105(1)	omitted, see Revision Note 8
8–105(2)	omitted, see Revision Note 4
8–105(3)	8–114
8–106	8–110
8–107	omitted, see Revision Note 8
8–108	omitted, see Revision Note 5
8–201	8–201

Article 8 (1978)	Revised Articles 8 and 9
8–202	8–202; transaction statement provisions omitted, see Revision Note 4
8–203	8–203
8–204	8–204; transaction statement provisions omitted, see Revision Note 4
8–205	8–205; transaction statement provisions omitted, see Revision Note 4
8–206	8–206; transaction statement provisions omitted, see Revision Note 4
8–207	8–207; registered pledge provisions omitted, see Revision Note 5
8–208	8–208; transaction statement provisions omitted, see Revision Note 4
8–301	8–302(a) & (b)
8–302(1)	8–303(a)
8–302(2)	8–102(a)(1)
8–302(3)	8–303(b)
8–302(4)	8–302(c)
8–303	8–102(a)(3)
8–304(1)	8–105(d)
8–304(2)	omitted, see Revision Note 4
8–304(3)	8–105(b)
8–305	8–105(c)
8–306(1)	8–108(f)
8–306(2)	8–108(a)
8–306(3)	8–108(g)
8–306(4)	8–108(h)
8–306(5)	8–108(e)
8–306(6)	8–306(h)
8–306(7)	8–108(b), 8–306(h)
8–306(8)	omitted, see Revision Note 5
8–306(9)	8–108(c)
8–306(10)	8–108(i)
8–307	8–304(d)
8–308(1)	8–102(a)(11), 8–107
8–308(2)	8–304(a)
8–308(3)	8–304(b)
8–308(4)	8–102(a)(12)
8–308(5)	8–107 & 8–305(a)
8–308(6)	8–107
8–308(7)	8–107
8–308(8)	8–107
8–308(9)	8–304(f) & 8–305(b)
8–308(10)	8–107
8–308(11)	8–107
8–309	8–304(c)
8–310	8–304(e)
8–311(a)	omitted, see 8–106(b)(2), 8–301(b)(1), 8–303
8–311(b)	8–404
8–312	8–306
8–313(1)(a)	omitted, see Revision Note 2; see also 8–301(a)(1) & (2)

Article 8 (1978)	Revised Articles 8 and 9
8–313(1)(b)	omitted, see Revision Note 2; see also 8–301(b)(1) & (2)
8–313(1)(c)	omitted, see Revision Note 2; see also 8–301(a)(3)
8–313(1)(d)	omitted, see Revision Note 2; see also 8–501(b)
8–313(1)(e)	omitted, see Revision Note 2; see also 8–301(a)(2)
8–313(1)(f)	omitted, see Revision Note 2; see also 8–301(b)(2)
8–313(1)(g)	omitted, see Revision Notes 1 & 2; see also 8–501(b), 8–111
8–313(1)(h)–(j)	omitted, see Revision Note 2; see also 9–115 & 9–203
8–313(2)	omitted, see Revision Note 2; see also 8–503
8–313(3)	omitted, see Revision Note 2
8–313(4)	8–102(a)(14)
8–314	omitted, see Revision Note 8
8–315	omitted, see Revision Note 8
8–316	8–307
8–317	8–112
8–318	8–115
8–319	omitted, see 8–113 and Revision Note 7
8–320	omitted, see Revision Note 1
8–321	omitted, see 9–115, 9–203
8–401	8–401
8–402	8–402, see Revision Note 6
8–403	8–403, see Revision Note 6
8–404	8–404
8–405(1)	8–406
8–405(2)	8–405(a)
8–405(3)	8–405(b)
8–406	8–407
8–407	omitted, see Revision Note 8
8–408	omitted, see Revision Note 4

B. Revision Notes

1. Provisions of former Article 8 on clearing corporations.

The keystone of the treatment of the indirect holding system in the prior version of Article 8 was the special provision on clearing corporations in Section 8–320. Section 8–320 was added to Article 8 in 1962, at the very end of the process that culminated in promulgation and enactment of the original version of the Code. The key concepts of the original version of Article 8 were "bona fide purchaser" and "delivery." Under Section 8–302 (1962) one could qualify as a "bona fide purchaser" only if one had taken delivery of a security, and Section 8–313 (1962) specified what counted as a delivery.

Section 8–320 was added to take account of the development of the system in which trades can be settled by netted book-entry movements at a depository without physical deliveries of certificates. Rather than reworking the basic concepts, however, Section 8–320 brought the depository system within Article 8 by definitional fiat. Subsection (a) of Section 8–320 (1962) stated that a transfer or pledge could be effected by entries on the books of a central depository, and subsection (b) stated that such an entry "has the effect of a delivery of a security in bearer form or duly indorsed in blank." In

1978, Section 8–320 was revised to conform it to the general substitution of the concept of "transfer" for "delivery," but the basic structure remained the same. Under the 1978 version of Article 8, the only book-entry transfers that qualified the transferee for bona fide purchaser rights were those made on the books of a clearing corporation. See Sections 8–302(1)(c), 8–313(1)(g), and 8–320. Thus, for practical purposes, the indirect holding system rules of the prior version of Article 8 required that the securities be held by a clearing corporation in accordance with the central depository rules of Section 8–320.

Some of the definitional provisions concerning clearing corporation in the prior version of Article 8 seem to have conflated the commercial law rules on the effect of book-entry transactions with issues about the regulation of entities that are acting as clearing corporations. For example, the Section 8–320 rules that gave effect to book-entry transfers applied only if the security was "in the custody of the clearing corporation, another clearing corporation, [or] a custodian bank." "Custodian bank" was defined in Section 8–102(4) as "a bank or trust company that is supervised and examined by state or federal authority having supervision over banks and is acting as custodian for a clearing corporation." Although this was probably inadvertent, these definitional provisions have operated as an obstacle to the development of clearing arrangements for global trading, since they effectively precluded clearing corporations from using foreign banks as custodians.

Revised Article 8 is based on the view that Article 8 is not the proper place for regulatory decisions about whether certain sorts of financial institutions should or should not be permitted to engage in a particular aspect of the securities business, such as acting as a clearing corporation, or how they should be permitted to conduct that business. Rather, Article 8 should deal only with the commercial law questions of what duties and rights flow from doing business as a clearing corporation, leaving it to other regulatory law to decide which entities should be permitted to act as clearing corporations, and to regulate their activities. Federal securities laws now establish a detailed regulatory structure for clearing corporations; there is no need for Article 8 to duplicate parts of that structure. Revised Article 8 deletes all provision of the prior version which had the effect of specifying how clearing corporations should conduct their operations. For example, Revised Article 8 deletes the definition of "custodian bank," which operated in the prior version only as a regulatory restriction on how clearing corporations could hold securities.

In general, the structure of Revised Article 8 is such that there is relatively little need for special provisions on clearing corporations. Book-entry transactions effected through clearing corporations are treated under the same rules in Part 5 as book-entry transactions effected through any other securities intermediary. Accordingly, Revised Article 8 has no direct analog of the special provisions in Section 8–320 on transfers on the books of clearing corporations.

2. Former Section 8–313—"Transfer."

Section 8–313 of the 1978 version of Article was extremely complicated, because it attempted to cover many different issues. The following account of the evolution of Section 8–313 may assist in understanding why a different approach is taken in Revised Article 8. This explanation is, however, intended not as an actual account of historical events, but as a conceptual reconstruction, devised from the perspective of, and with the benefit of, hindsight.

The original objective of Article 8 was to ensure that certificates representing investment securities would be "negotiable" in the sense that purchasers would be protected by the bona fide purchaser rules. The requirements for bona fide purchaser status were that the purchaser had to (i) take delivery of the security and (ii) give value in good faith and without notice of adverse claims. Section 8–313 specified what counted as a "delivery," and Section 8–302 specified the other requirements.

The 1978 amendments added provisions on uncertificated securities, but the basic organizational pattern was retained. Section 8–302 continued to state the requirements of value, good faith, and lack of notice for good faith purchase, and Section 8–313 stated the mechanism by which the purchase had to be implemented. Delivery as defined in the original version of Section 8–313 had a meaning similar to the concept known in colloquial securities jargon as "good delivery"; that is, physical delivery with any necessary indorsement. Although the word "delivery" has now come to be used in securities parlance in a broader sense than physical delivery, when the provisions for uncertificated securities were added it was thought preferable to use another word. Thus, the word "transfer" was substituted for "delivery" in Section 8–313.

The 1978 amendments also moved the rules governing security interests in securities from Article 9 to Article 8, though the basic conceptual structure of the common law of pledge was retained. Since a pledge required a delivery, and since the term transfer had been substituted for delivery, the 1978 amendments provided that in order to create a security interest there must be a "transfer," in the defined Article 8 sense, from the debtor to the secured party. Accordingly, provisions had to be added to Section 8–313 so that any of the steps that should suffice to create a perfected security interest would be deemed to constitute a "transfer" within the meaning of Section 8–313. Thus, the Section 8–313 rules on "transfer," which had in the previous version dealt only with what counted as a delivery that qualified one for bona fide purchaser status, became the statutory locus for all of the rules on creation and perfection of security interests in securities. Accordingly the rather elaborate rules of subsections (1)(h), (1)(i), and (1)(j) were added.

Having expanded Section 8–313 to the point that it served as the rule specifying the formal requirements for transfer of all significant forms of interests in securities, it must have seemed only logical to take the next step and make the Section 8–313 rules the exclusive means of transferring interests in securities. Thus, while the prior version had stated that "Delivery to a purchaser occurs when . . .", the 1978 version stated that "Transfer of a security or a limited interest (including a security interest) therein to a purchaser occurs *only* . . . ." Having taken that step, however, it then became necessary to ensure that anyone who should be regarded as having an interest in a security would be covered by some provision of Section 8–313. Thus, the provisions of subsection (1)(d)(ii) and (iii) were added to make it possible to say that the customers of a securities intermediary who hold interests in securities held by the intermediary in fungible bulk received "transfers."

Section 8–313(1)(d) was the key provision in the 1978 version dealing with the indirect holding system at the level below securities depositories. It operated in essentially the same fashion as Section 8–320; that is, it stated that when a broker or bank holding securities in fungible bulk makes entries on its books identifying a quantity of the fungible bulk as belonging to the customer, that action is treated as a "transfer"—in the special Section 8–313 sense—of an interest in the security from the intermediary to the customer.

Revised Article 8 has no direct analog of the 1978 version of Section 8–313. The rules on secured transactions have been returned to Article 9, so subsections of Section 8–313 (1978) dealing with security interests are deleted from Article 8. Insofar as portions of Section 8–313 (1978) were designed to specify the formal requirements for transferees to qualify for protection against adverse claims, their place is taken by Revised Section 8–301, which defines "delivery," in a fashion somewhat akin to the pre–1978 version of Section 8–313. The descendant of the provisions of Section 8–313 (1978) dealing with the indirect holding system is Revised Section 8–501 which specifies when a person acquires a security entitlement. Section 8–501, however, is based on a different analysis of the transaction in which a customer acquires a position in the indirect holding system. The transaction is not described as a "transfer" of an interest in some portion of a fungible bulk of securities held by the securities intermediary but as the creation of a security entitlement. Accordingly, just as Revised Article 8 has no direct analog of the Section 8–320 rules on clearing corporation transfers, it has no direct analog of the Section 8–313(1) rules on "transfers" of interests in securities held in fungible bulk.

3. Uncertificated securities provisions.

Given the way that securities holding practices have evolved, the sharp distinction that the 1978 version of Article 8 drew between certificated securities and uncertificated securities has become somewhat misleading. Since many provisions of the 1978 version had separate subsections dealing first with certificated securities and then with uncertificated securities, and since people intuitively realize that the volume of trading in the modern securities markets could not possibly be handled by pushing around certificates, it was only natural for a reader of the statute to conclude that the uncertificated securities provisions of Article 8 were the basis of the book-entry system. That, however, is not the case. Although physical delivery of certificates plays little role in the settlement system, most publicly traded securities are still, in legal theory, certificated securities. To use clearance and settlement jargon, the book-entry securities holding system has used "immobilization" rather than "dematerialization."

The important legal and practical difference is between the direct holding system, in which the beneficial owners have a direct relationship with the issuer, and the indirect holding system, in which securities are held through tiers of securities intermediaries. Accordingly, in Revised Article 8 the contrast between certificated securities and uncertificated securities has been minimized or eliminated as much as possible in stating the substantive provisions.

4. Transaction statements.

Although the 1978 provisions on uncertificated securities contemplated a system in which there would be no definitive certificates as reifications of the underlying interests or obligations, the 1978 amendments did not really dispense with all requirements of paper evidence of securities holding. The 1978 amendments required issuers of uncertificated securities to send paper "transaction statements" upon registration of transfer. Section 8–408 regulated the content and format of these transaction statements in considerable detail. The statements had to be in writing, include specific information, and contain a conspicuous legend stating that "This statement is merely a record of the rights of the addressee as of the time of its issuance. Delivery of this statement, of itself, confers no rights on the recipient. This statement is neither a negotiable instrument nor a security." Issuers were required to send statements when any transfer was registered (known as "initial transaction statements") and also were required to send periodic statements at least annually and also upon any security holder's reasonable request. Fees were regulated to some extent, in that Section 8–408(8) specified that if periodic statements were sent at least quarterly, the issuer could charge for statements requested by security holders at other times.

The detailed specification of reporting requirements for issuers of uncertificated securities was quite different from the treatment of securities intermediaries. Though the prior version of Article 8 did require non-clearing corporation securities intermediaries to send confirmations of transfers—a requirement deleted in Revised Article 8—it did not regulate their content or format. Article 8 has never imposed periodic reporting requirements on securities intermediaries. Thus, reporting requirements for the indirect holding system were left to agreements and regulatory authorities, while reporting requirements for a book-entry direct holding system were imposed by statute.

Securities holding systems based on transaction statements of the sort contemplated by the 1978 amendments have not yet evolved to any major extent—indeed, the statutory specification of the details of the information system may itself have acted as an impediment to the evolution of a book-entry direct system. Accordingly, Revised Article 8 drops the statutory requirements concerning transaction statements. The record keeping and reporting obligations of issuers of uncertificated securities would be left to agreement and other law, as is the case today for securities intermediaries.

In the 1978 version, the Part 2 rules concerning transfer restrictions, issuers' defenses, and the like were based on the assumption that transaction statements would be used in a fashion analogous to traditional security certificates. For example, Sections 8–202 and 8–204 specified that the terms of a security, or any restrictions on transfer imposed by the issuer, had to be noted on the transaction statement. Revised Article 8 deletes all such references to transaction statements. The terms of securities, or of restrictions of transfer, would be governed by whatever law or agreement specifies these matters, just as is the case for various other forms of business entities, such as partnerships, that have never issued certificates representing interests. Other Part 2 rules, such as Sections 8–205, 8–206, and 8–208, attempted to state rules on forgery and related matters for transactions statements. Since Revised Article 8 does not specify the format for information systems for uncertificated securities, there is no point in attempting to state rules on the consequences of wrongful information transmission in the particular format of written statements authenticated by signatures.

5. Deletion of provisions on registered pledges.

The 1978 version of Article 8 also added detailed provisions concerning "registered pledges" of uncertificated securities. Revised Article 8 adopts a new system of rules for security interests in securities, for both the direct and indirect holding systems that make it unnecessary to have special statutory provisions for registered pledges of uncertificated securities.

The reason that the 1978 version of Article 8 created this concept was that if the only means of creating security interests was the pledge, it seemed necessary to provide some substitute for the pledge in the absence of a certificate. The point of the registered pledge was, presumably, that it permitted a debtor to grant a perfected security interest in securities, yet still keep the securities in the debtor's own name for purposes of dividends, voting, and the like. The concept of registered pledge has, however, been thought troublesome by many legal commentators and securities industry participants. For example, in Massachusetts where many mutual funds have their headquarters, a non-uniform amendment was enacted to permit the issuer of an uncertificated security to refuse to register a pledge and instead issue a certificate to the owner that the owner could then pledge by ordinary means.

Under the 1978 version of Article 8, if an issuer chose to issue securities in uncertificated form, it was also required by statute to offer a registered pledge program. Revised Articles 8 and 9 take a different approach. All of the provisions dealing with registered pledges have been deleted. This does not mean, however, that issuers cannot offer such a service. The control rules of Revised Section 8–106 and the related priority provisions in Article 9 establish a structure that permits issuers to develop systems akin to the registered pledge device, without mandating that they do so, or legislating the details of the system. In essence, the registered pledge or control device amounts to a record keeping service. A debtor can always transfer securities to its lender. In a registered pledge or control agreement arrangement, the issuer keeps track of which securities the secured party holds for its own account outright, and which securities it holds in pledge from its debtors.

Under the rules of Revised Articles 8 and 9, the registered pledge issue can easily be left to resolution by the market. The concept of control is defined in such fashion that if an issuer or securities intermediary wishes to offer a service akin to the registered pledge device it can do so. The issuer or securities intermediary would offer to enter into agreements with the debtor and secured party under which it would hold the securities for the account of the debtor, but subject to instructions from the secured party. The secured party would thereby obtain control assuring perfection and priority of its lien.

Even if such arrangements are not offered by issuers, persons who hold uncertificated securities will have several options for using them as collateral for secured loans. Under the new rules, filing is a permissible method of perfection, for debtors other than securities firms. A secured party who relies on filing is, of course, exposed to the risk that the debtor will double finance and grant a later secured lender a security interest under circumstances that give that lender control and hence priority. If the lender is unwilling to run that risk, the debtor can transfer the securities outright to the lender on the books of the issuer, though between the parties the debtor would be the owner and the lender only a secured party. That, of course, requires that the debtor trust the secured party not to dispose of the collateral wrongfully, and the debtor may also need to make arrangements with the secured party to exercise benefits of ownership such as voting and receiving distributions.

It may well be that both lenders and borrowers would prefer to have some arrangement, such as the registered pledge device of current law, that permits the debtor to remain as the registered owner entitled to vote and receive dividends but gives the lender exclusive power to order their disposition. The approach taken in this revision is that if there is a genuine demand for such arrangements, it can be met by the market. The difficulty with the approach of present Article 8 is that it mandates that any issuer that wishes to issue securities in uncertificated form must also offer this record keeping service. That obligation may well have acted as a disincentive to the development of uncertificated securities. Thus, the deletion of the mandated registered pledge provisions is consistent with the principle of neutrality toward the evolution of securities holding practices.

6. Former Section 8–403—Issuer's Duty as to Adverse Claims.

Section 8–403 of the prior version of Article 8 dealt with the obligations of issuers to adverse claimants. The starting point of American law on issuers' liability in such circumstances is the old case of *Lowry v. Commercial & Farmers' Bank,* 15 F.Cas. 1040 (C.C.D.Md.1848) (No. 8551), under which issuers could be held liable for registering a transfer at the direction of a registered owner who was acting wrongfully as against a third person in making the transfer. The *Lowry* principle imposed onerous liability on issuers, particularly in the case of transfers by fiduciaries, such as executors and trustees. To protect against risk of such liability, issuers developed the practice of requiring extensive documentation for fiduciary stock transfers to assure themselves that the fiduciaries were acting rightfully. As a result, fiduciary stock transfers were cumbersome and time consuming.

In the present century, American law has gradually moved away from the *Lowry* principle. Statutes such as the Uniform Fiduciaries Act, the Model Fiduciary Stock Transfer Act, and the Uniform Act for the Simplification of Fiduciary Security Transfers sought to avoid the delays in stock transfers that could result from issuers' demands for documentation by limiting the issuer's responsibility for transfers in breach of the registered owner's duty to others. Although these statutes provided that issuers had no duty of inquiry to determine whether a fiduciary was acting rightfully, they all provided that an issuer could be liable if the issuer acted with notice of third party claims.

The prior version of Article 8 followed the same approach as the various fiduciary transfer statutes. Issuers were not required to seek out information from which they could determine whether a fiduciary was acting properly, but they were liable if they registered a transfer with notice that the fiduciary was acting improperly. Former Section 8–308(11) said that the failure of a fiduciary to comply with a controlling instrument or failure to obtain a court approval required under local law did not render the indorsement or instruction unauthorized. However, if a fiduciary was in fact acting improperly, then the beneficiary would be treated as an adverse claimant. See Section 8–302(2) (1978) and Comment 4. Former Section 8–403 specified that if written notice of an adverse claim had been sent to the issuer, the issuer "shall inquire into the adverse claim" before registering a transfer on the indorsement or instruction of the registered owner. The issuer could "discharge any duty of inquiry by any reasonable means," including by notifying the adverse claimant that the transfer would be registered unless the adverse claimant obtained a court order or gave an indemnity bond.

Revised Article 8 rejects the *Lowry* principle altogether. It provides that an issuer is not liable for wrongful registration if it acts on an effective indorsement or instruction, even though the issuer may have notice of adverse claims, so long as the issuer has not been served with legal process and is not acting in collusion with the wrongdoer in registering the transfer. See Revised Section 8–404 and Comments thereto. The provisions of prior Section 8–403 specifying that issuers had a duty to investigate adverse claims of which they had notice are deleted.

Revised Article 8 also deletes the provisions set out in Section 8–403(3) of prior law specifying that issuers did not have a duty to inquire into the rightfulness of transfers by fiduciaries. The omission of the rules formerly in Section 8–403(3) does not, of course, mean that issuers would be liable for acting on the instruction of fiduciaries in the circumstances covered by former Section 8–403(3). Former Section 8–403(3) assumed that issuers would be liable if they registered a transfer with notice of an adverse claim. Former Section 8–403(3) was necessary only to negate any inference that knowledge that a transfer was initiated by a fiduciary might give constructive notice of adverse claims. Under Section 8–404 of Revised Article 8, mere notice of adverse claims does not impose duties on the issuer. Accordingly the provisions included in former Section 8–403(3) are unnecessary.

Although the prior version of Article 8 included provisions similar or identical to those set out in the Uniform Act for the Simplification of Fiduciary Security Transfers and similar statutes, most states retained these statutes at the time the Uniform Commercial Code was adopted. These statutes are based on a premise different from Revised Article 8. The fiduciary simplification acts are predicated on the assumption that an issuer would be liable to an adverse claimant if the issuer had notice. These statutes seek only to preclude any inference that issuers have such notice when they register transfers on the instructions of a fiduciary. Revised Article 8 is based on the view that a third party should not be able to interfere with the relationship between an issuer and its registered shareholders unless the claimant obtains legal process. Since notice of an adverse claim does not impose duties on an issuer under Revised Article 8, the Uniform Act for the Simplification of Fiduciary Security Transfers, or similar statutes, should be repealed upon enactment of Revised Article 8.

7. Former Section 8–319—Statute of Frauds.

Revised Article 8 deletes the special statute of frauds provision for securities contracts that was set out in former Section 8–319. See Revised Section 8–113. Most of the litigation involving the statute of frauds rule of the prior version of Article 8 involved informal transactions, rather than transactions on the organized securities markets. Typical cases were those in which an employee or former employee of a small enterprise sued to enforce an alleged promise that he or she would receive an equity interest in the business. The usual commercial policies relating to writings in contracts for the sale of personal property are at most tangentially implicated in such cases. There was a rather large and complex body of case law dealing with the applicability of Section 8–319 to cases of this sort. It seems doubtful that the cost of litigating these issues was warranted by whatever protections the statute of frauds offered against fraudulent claims.

Subsection (c) of former Section 8–319 provided that the statute of frauds bar did not apply if a written confirmation was sent and the recipient did not seasonably send an objection. That provision, however, presumably would not have had the effect of binding a broker's customer to the terms of a trade for which confirmation had been sent though the customer had not objected within 10 days. In the first place, the relationship between a broker and customer is ordinarily that of agent and principal; thus the broker is not seeking to enforce a contract for sale of a security, but to bind its principal for action taken by the broker as agent. Former Section 8–319 did not by its terms apply to the agency relationship. Moreover, even if former Section 8–319(c) applied, it is doubtful that it, of its own force, had the effect of precluding the customer from disputing whether there was a contract or what the terms of the contract were. Former Section 8–319(c) only removed the statute of frauds as a bar to enforcement; it did not say that there was a contract or that the confirmation had the effect of excluding other evidence of its terms. Thus, deletion of former Section 8–319 does not change the law one way or the other on whether a customer who fails to object to a written confirmation is precluded from denying the trade described in the confirmation, because that issue was never governed by former Section 8–319(c).

8. Miscellaneous.

Prior Section 8–105. Revised Article 8 deletes the statement found in Section 8–105(1) of the prior version that certificated securities "are negotiable instruments." This provision was added very late in the drafting process of the original Uniform Commercial Code. Apparently the thought was that it might be useful in dealing with potential transition problems arising out of the fact that bonds were then treated as negotiable instruments under the Uniform Negotiable Instruments Law. During that era, many other statutes, such as those specifying permissible categories of investments for regulated entities, might have used such phrases as "negotiable securities" or "negotiable instruments." Section 8–105 seems to have been included in the original version of Article 8 to avoid unfortunate interpretations of those other statutes once securities were moved from the Uniform Negotiable Instruments Law to UCC Article 8. Whether or not Section 8–105 was necessary at that time, it has surely outlived its purpose. The statement that securities "are negotiable instruments" is very confusing. As used in the Uniform Commercial Code, the term "negotiable instrument" means an instrument that is governed by Article 3; yet Article 8 securities are not governed by Article 3. Courts have occasionally cited Section 8–105(1) of prior law for the proposition that the rules that are generally thought of as characteristic of negotiability, such as the rule that bona fide purchasers take free from adverse claims, apply to certificated securities. Section 8–105(1), however, is unnecessary for that purpose, since the relevant rules are set out in specific provisions of Article 8.

Prior Sections 8–107 and 8–314. Article 8 has never been, and should not be, a comprehensive codification of the law of contracts for the purchase and sale of securities. The prior version of Article 8 did contain, however, a number of provisions dealing with miscellaneous aspects of the law of contracts as applied to contracts for the sale of securities. Section 8–107 dealt with one remedy for breach, and Section 8–314 dealt with certain aspects of performance. Revised Article 8 deletes these on the theory that inclusion of a few sections on issues of contract law is likely to cause more harm than good since inferences might be drawn from the failure to cover related issues. The deletion of these sections is not, however, intended as a rejection of the rules of contract law and interpretation that they expressed.

Prior Section 8–315. It is not entirely clear what the function of Section 8–315 of prior law was. The section specified that the owner of a security could recover it from a person to whom it had been transferred, if the transferee did not qualify as a bona fide purchaser. It seems to have been intended only to recognize that securities, like any other form of personal property, are governed by the general principle of property law that an owner can recover property from a person to whom it has been transferred under circumstances that did not cut off the owner's claim. Although many other Articles of the UCC deal with cut-off rules, Article 8 was the only one that included an affirmative statement of the rights of an owner to recover her property. It seems wiser to adopt the same approach as in Articles 2, 3, 7, and 9, and leave this point to other law. Accordingly, Section 8–315 is deleted in Revised Article 8, without, of course, implying rejection of the nearly self-evident rule that it sought to express.

Prior Section 8–407. This section, entitled "Exchangeability of Securities," seemed to say that holders of securities had the right to cause issuers to convert them back and forth from certificated to uncertificated form. The provision, however, applied only if the issuer "regularly maintains a system for issuing the class of securities involved under which both certificated and uncertificated securities are regularly issued to the category of owners, which includes the person in whose name the new security is to be registered." The provision seems unnecessary, since it applied only if the issuer decided that it should. The matter can be covered by agreement or corporate charter or by-laws.

V. ACKNOWLEDGMENTS

On behalf of the National Conference of Commissioners on Uniform State Laws and the American Law Institute, the Drafting Committee and the

Reporter acknowledge with deep appreciation the dedicated and helpful assistance of a great many individuals and organizations. Among the large number of individuals who participated in the development of Revised Article 8, special mention should be made of a few whose contributions were extraordinary.

Preceding the preparation of Revised Article 8, the topic was carefully studied by the Advisory Committee on Settlement of Market Transactions of the American Bar Association Section of Business Law, under the chairmanship of Robert Haydock, Jr., of Boston, MA. Martin Aronstein, of Philadelphia, PA, reporter for the 1977 revision of Article 8, served on the Haydock Committee and continued to advise the Drafting Committee. Robert C. Mendelson, New York, NY, who also served on the Haydock Committee, is chair of the Market Transactions Advisory Committee set up by the Securities and Exchange Commission; Bob Mendelson's considerable contribution to the preparation of Revised Article 8 was most important. Other members of the Haydock Committee had continuing roles either as members of the Drafting Committee or as sources of valuable advice to that committee.

The revision of Article 8 is the culmination of a successful federal-state collaboration among the American Law Institute and the National Conference of Commissioners on Uniform State Laws, sponsors of the Uniform Commercial Code, and representatives of the United States Department of the Treasury, the Securities and Exchange Commission, the Federal Reserve System, and other federal bodies. The product reflects the assistance of many people, and particularly of Jonathan Kallman and Ari Burstein on behalf of the SEC, Calvin Ninomiya, Cynthia E. Reese, and Virginia S. Rutledge of Treasury, Lawranne Stewart of the Board of Governors of the Federal Reserve System, Debra W. Cook and MarySue Fisher of the Federal Reserve Bank of New York, and George Wilder and Carla Behnfeldt of the Commodity Futures Trading Commission.

Representatives of organizations in the securities and banking industry and their counsel gave generously of their time and knowledge. Special mention should be made of Norman R. Nelson, New York Clearing House, R. May Lee, Public Securities Association, Robert J. Woldow and Karen Saperstein, National Securities Clearing Corporation, Leopold S. Rassnick, Participants Trust Company, Robert Wittie and Patricia Louie, Investment Company Institute, Thomas A. Williams, Richard B. Nesson and Carl Urist, Depository Trust Company, Dennis A. Dutterer, Board of Trade Clearing Corporation, Evalyn Lipton Fishbein, State Street Bank and Trust Company, Robert P. DeGregorie, Chemical Bank, Gail M. Inaba, Morgan Guaranty Trust Company of New York, Anthony J. Leitner, Goldman, Sachs & Company, Robert M. MacAllister, The Chase Manhattan Bank, N.A., Kevin J. Moynihan, Merrill Lynch, Pierce, Fenner & Smith Inc., Lois J. Radisch, J.P. Morgan & Co., James J. Volpe, First Chicago Trust Company of New York, and Richard E. Smith, Securities Transfer Association.

Many lawyers and law professors contributed to the work of the Drafting Committee. Special appreciation is due to Sandra M. Rocks, New York, NY, who participated on behalf of the ABA UCC Investment Securities Subcommittee and ABA Task Force on TRADES Regulations. Others who participated included Steven Harris and James R. McDaniel, Chicago, IL, Kenneth B. Davis, Jr., Madison, WI, David M. Huggins and Bradley Y. Smith, New York, NY, David J. Schraa, Brussels, Belgium, and Randall D. Guynn, London, England. The Reporter and Drafting Committee also received assistance from the dedicated work of lawyers, not themselves experts in securities law, who reviewed and commented upon drafts and participated in the revision process through meetings of the Members Consultative Group of the American Law Institute and at various national, state, and local bar association programs.

PART 1

SHORT TITLE AND GENERAL MATTERS

§ 8–101. Short Title.

This Article may be cited as Uniform Commercial Code—Investment Securities.

§ 8–102. Definitions.

(a) In this Article:

(1) "Adverse claim" means a claim that a claimant has a property interest in a financial asset and that it is a violation of the rights of the claimant for another person to hold, transfer, or deal with the financial asset.

(2) "Bearer form," as applied to a certificated security, means a form in which the security is payable to the bearer of the security certificate according to its terms but not by reason of an indorsement.

(3) "Broker" means a person defined as a broker or dealer under the federal securities laws, but without excluding a bank acting in that capacity.

(4) "Certificated security" means a security that is represented by a certificate.

(5) "Clearing corporation" means:

(i) a person that is registered as a "clearing agency" under the federal securities laws;

(ii) a federal reserve bank; or

(iii) any other person that provides clearance or settlement services with respect to financial assets that would require it to register as a clearing agency under the federal securities laws but for an exclusion or exemption from the registration requirement, if its activities as a clearing corporation, including promulgation of rules, are subject to regulation by a federal or state governmental authority.

(6) "Communicate" means to:

(i) send a signed writing; or
(ii) transmit information by any mechanism agreed upon by the persons transmitting and receiving the information.

(7) "Entitlement holder" means a person identified in the records of a securities intermediary as the person having a security entitlement against the securities intermediary. If a person acquires a security entitlement by virtue of Section 8–501(b)(2) or (3), that person is the entitlement holder.

(8) "Entitlement order" means a notification communicated to a securities intermediary directing transfer or redemption of a financial asset to which the entitlement holder has a security entitlement.

(9) "Financial asset," except as otherwise provided in Section 8–103, means:

(i) a security;
(ii) an obligation of a person or a share, participation, or other interest in a person or in property or an enterprise of a person, which is, or is of a type, dealt in or traded on financial markets, or which is recognized in any area in which it is issued or dealt in as a medium for investment; or
(iii) any property that is held by a securities intermediary for another person in a securities account if the securities intermediary has expressly agreed with the other person that the property is to be treated as a financial asset under this Article.

As context requires, the term means either the interest itself or the means by which a person's claim to it is evidenced, including a certificated or uncertificated security, a security certificate, or a security entitlement.

(10) "Good faith," for purposes of the obligation of good faith in the performance or enforcement of contracts or duties within this Article, means honesty in fact and the observance of reasonable commercial standards of fair dealing.

(11) "Indorsement" means a signature that alone or accompanied by other words is made on a security certificate in registered form or on a separate document for the purpose of assigning, transferring, or redeeming the security or granting a power to assign, transfer, or redeem it.

(12) "Instruction" means a notification communicated to the issuer of an uncertificated security which directs that the transfer of the security be registered or that the security be redeemed.

(13) "Registered form," as applied to a certificated security, means a form in which:

(i) the security certificate specifies a person entitled to the security; and
(ii) a transfer of the security may be registered upon books maintained for that purpose by or on behalf of the issuer, or the security certificate so states.

(14) "Securities intermediary" means:

(i) a clearing corporation; or

(ii) a person, including a bank or broker, that in the ordinary course of its business maintains securities accounts for others and is acting in that capacity.

(15) "Security," except as otherwise provided in Section 8–103, means an obligation of an issuer or a share, participation, or other interest in an issuer or in property or an enterprise of an issuer:

(i) which is represented by a security certificate in bearer or registered form, or the transfer of which may be registered upon books maintained for that purpose by or on behalf of the issuer;

(ii) which is one of a class or series or by its terms is divisible into a class or series of shares, participations, interests, or obligations; and

(iii) which:

(A) is, or is of a type, dealt in or traded on securities exchanges or securities markets; or

(B) is a medium for investment and by its terms expressly provides that it is a security governed by this Article.

(16) "Security certificate" means a certificate representing a security.

(17) "Security entitlement" means the rights and property interest of an entitlement holder with respect to a financial asset specified in Part 5.

(18) "Uncertificated security" means a security that is not represented by a certificate.

(b) Other definitions applying to this Article and the sections in which they appear are:

Appropriate person	Section 8–107
Control	Section 8–106
Delivery	Section 8–301
Investment company security	Section 8–103
Issuer	Section 8–201
Overissue	Section 8–210
Protected purchaser	Section 8–303
Securities account	Section 8–501

(c) In addition, Article 1 contains general definitions and principles of construction and interpretation applicable throughout this Article.

(d) The characterization of a person, business, or transaction for purposes of this Article does not determine the characterization of the person, business, or transaction for purposes of any other law, regulation, or rule.

Official Comment

1. "Adverse claim." The definition of the term "adverse claim" has two components. First, the term refers only to property interests. Second, the term means not merely that a person has a property interest in a financial asset but that it is a violation of the claimant's property interest for the other person to hold or transfer the security or other financial asset.

The term adverse claim is not, of course, limited to ownership rights, but extends to other property interests established by other law. A security interest, for example, would be an adverse claim with respect to a transferee from the debtor since any effort by the secured party to enforce the security interest against the property would be an interference with the transferee's interest.

The definition of adverse claim in the prior version of Article 8 might have been read to suggest that any wrongful action concerning a security, even a simple breach of contract, gave rise to an adverse claim. Insofar as such cases as *Fallon v. Wall Street Clearing Corp.*, 586 N.Y.S.2d 953, 182 A.D.2d 245, (1992) and *Pentech Intl. v. Wall St. Clearing Co.*, 983 F.2d 441 (2d Cir.1993), were based on that view, they are rejected by the new definition which explicitly limits the term adverse claim to property interests. Suppose, for example, that A contracts to sell or deliver securities to B, but fails to do so and instead sells or pledges the securities to C. B, the promisee, has an action against A for breach of contract, but absent unusual circumstances the action for breach would not give rise to a property interest in the securities. Accordingly, B does not have an adverse claim. An adverse claim might, however, be based upon principles of equitable remedies that give rise to property claims. It would, for example, cover a right established by other law to rescind a transaction in which securities were transferred. Suppose, for example, that A holds securities and is induced by B's fraud to transfer them to B. Under the law of contract or restitution, A may have a right to rescind the transfer, which gives A a property claim to the securities. If so, A has an adverse claim to the securities in B's hands. By contrast, if B had committed no fraud, but had merely committed a breach of contract in connection with the transfer from A to B, A may have only a right to damages for breach, not a right to rescind. In that case, A would not have an adverse claim to the securities in B's hands.

2. "Bearer form." The definition of "bearer form" has remained substantially unchanged since the early drafts of the original version of Article 8. The requirement that the certificate be payable to bearer by its terms rather than by an indorsement has the effect of preventing instruments governed by other law, such as chattel paper or Article 3 negotiable instruments, from being inadvertently swept into the Article 8 definition of security merely by virtue of blank indorsements. Although the other elements of the definition of security in Section 8-102(a)(14) probably suffice for that purpose in any event, the language used in the prior version of Article 8 has been retained.

3. "Broker." Broker is defined by reference to the definitions of broker and dealer in the federal securities laws. The only difference is that banks, which are excluded from the federal securities law definition, are included in the Article 8 definition when they perform functions that would bring them within the federal securities law definition if it did not have the clause excluding banks. The definition covers both those who act as agents ("brokers" in securities parlance) and those who act as principals ("dealers" in securities parlance). Since the definition refers to persons "defined" as brokers or dealers under the federal securities law, rather than to persons required to "register" as brokers or dealers under the federal securities law, it covers not only registered brokers and dealers but also those exempt from the registration require-

ment, such as purely intrastate brokers. The only substantive rules that turn on the defined term broker are one provision of the section on warranties, Section 8-108(i), and the special perfection rule in Article 9 for security interests granted by brokers, Section 9-115(4)(c).

4. "Certificated security." The term "certificated security" means a security that is represented by a security certificate.

5. "Clearing corporation." The definition of clearing corporation limits its application to entities that are subject to a rigorous regulatory framework. Accordingly, the definition includes only federal reserve banks, persons who are registered as "clearing agencies" under the federal securities laws (which impose a comprehensive system of regulation of the activities and rules of clearing agencies), and other entities subject to a comparable system of regulatory oversight.

6. "Communicate." The term "communicate" assures that the Article 8 rules will be sufficiently flexible to adapt to changes in information technology. Sending a signed writing always suffices as a communication, but the parties can agree that a different means of transmitting information is to be used. Agreement is defined in Section 1-201(3) as "the bargain of the parties in fact as found in their language or by implication from other circumstances including course of dealing or usage of trade or course of performance." Thus, use of an information transmission method might be found to be authorized by agreement, even though the parties have not explicitly so specified in a formal agreement. The term communicate is used in Sections 8-102(a)(7) (definition of entitlement order), 8-102(a)(11) (definition of instruction), and 8-403 (demand that issuer not register transfer).

7. "Entitlement holder." This term designates those who hold financial assets through intermediaries in the indirect holding system. Because many of the rules of Part 5 impose duties on securities intermediaries in favor of entitlement holders, the definition of entitlement holder is, in most cases, limited to the person specifically designated as such on the records of the intermediary. The last sentence of the definition covers the relatively unusual cases where a person may acquire a security entitlement under Section 8-501 even though the person may not be specifically designated as an entitlement holder on the records of the securities intermediary.

A person may have an interest in a security entitlement, and may even have the right to give entitlement orders to the securities intermediary with respect to it, even though the person is not the entitlement holder. For example, a person who holds securities through a securities account in its own name may have given discretionary trading authority to another person, such as an investment adviser. Similarly, the control provisions in Section 8-106 and the related provisions in Article 9 are designed to facilitate transactions in which a person who holds securities through a securities account uses them as collateral in an arrangement where the securities intermediary has agreed that if the secured party so directs the intermediary will dispose of the positions. In such arrangements, the debtor remains the entitlement holder but has agreed that the secured party can initiate entitlement orders.

8. "Entitlement order." This term is defined as a notification communicated to a securities intermediary directing transfer or redemption of the financial asset to which an entitlement holder has a security entitlement. The term is used in the rules for the indirect holding system in a fashion analogous to the use of the terms "indorsement" and "instruction" in the rules for the direct holding system. If a person directly holds a certificated security in registered form and wishes to transfer it, the means of transfer is an indorsement. If a person directly holds an uncertificated security and wishes to transfer it, the means of transfer is an instruction. If a person holds a security entitlement, the means of disposition is an entitlement order. As noted in Comment 7,

an entitlement order need not be initiated by the entitlement holder in order to be effective, so long as the entitlement holder has authorized the other party to initiate entitlement orders. See Section 8-107(b).

9. "Financial asset." The definition of "financial asset," in conjunction with the definition of "securities account" in Section 8-501, sets the scope of the indirect holding system rules of Part 5 of Revised Article 8. The Part 5 rules apply not only to securities held through intermediaries, but also to other financial assets held through intermediaries. The term financial asset is defined to include not only securities but also a broader category of obligations, shares, participations, and interests.

Having separate definitions of security and financial asset makes it possible to separate the question of the proper scope of the traditional Article 8 rules from the question of the proper scope of the new indirect holding system rules. Some forms of financial assets should be covered by the indirect holding system rules of Part 5, but not by the rules of Parts 2, 3, and 4. The term financial asset is used to cover such property. Because the term security entitlement is defined in terms of financial assets rather than securities, the rules concerning security entitlements set out in Part 5 of Article 8 and in Revised Article 9 apply to the broader class of financial assets.

The fact that something does or could fall within the definition of financial asset does not, without more, trigger Article 8 coverage. The indirect holding system rules of Revised Article 8 apply only if the financial asset is in fact held in a securities account, so that the interest of the person who holds the financial asset through the securities account is a security entitlement. Thus, questions of the scope of the indirect holding system rules cannot be framed as "Is such-and-such a 'financial asset' under Article 8?" Rather, one must analyze whether the relationship between an institution and a person on whose behalf the institution holds an asset falls within the scope of the term securities account as defined in Section 8-501. That question turns in large measure on whether it makes sense to apply the Part 5 rules to the relationship.

The term financial asset is used to refer both to the underlying asset and the particular means by which ownership of that asset is evidenced. Thus, with respect to a certificated security, the term financial asset may, as context requires, refer either to the interest or obligation of the issuer or to the security certificate representing that interest or obligation. Similarly, if a person holds a security or other financial asset through a securities account, the term financial asset may, as context requires, refer either to the underlying asset or to the person's security entitlement.

10. "Good faith." Good faith is defined in Article 8 for purposes of the application to Article 8 of Section 1-203, which provides that "Every contract or duty within this Act imposes an obligation of good faith in its performance or enforcement." The sole function of the good faith definition in Revised Article 8 is to give content to the Section 1-203 obligation as it applies to contracts and duties that are governed by Article 8. The standard is one of "reasonable commercial standards of fair dealing." The reference to commercial standards makes clear that assessments of conduct are to be made in light of the commercial setting. The substantive rules of Article 8 have been drafted to take account of the commercial circumstances of the securities holding and processing system. For example, Section 8-115 provides that a securities intermediary acting on an effective entitlement order, or a broker or other agent acting as a conduit in a securities transaction, is not liable to an adverse claimant, unless the claimant obtained legal process or the intermediary acted in collusion with the wrongdoer. This, and other similar provisions, see Sections 8-404 and 8-503(e), do not depend on notice of adverse claims, because it would impair rather than advance the interest of investors in having a sound and efficient securities clearance and set-

tlement system to require intermediaries to investigate the propriety of the transactions they are processing. The good faith obligation does not supplant the standards of conduct established in provisions of this kind.

In Revised Article 8, the definition of good faith is not germane to the question whether a purchaser takes free from adverse claims. The rules on such questions as whether a purchaser who takes in suspicious circumstances is disqualified from protected purchaser status are treated not as an aspect of good faith but directly in the rules of Section 8-105 on notice of adverse claims.

11. "Indorsement" is defined as a signature made on a security certificate or separate document for purposes of transferring or redeeming the security. The definition is adapted from the language of Section 8-308(1) of the prior version and from the definition of indorsement in the Negotiable Instruments Article, see Section 3-204(a). The definition of indorsement does not include the requirement that the signature be made by an appropriate person or be authorized. Those questions are treated in the separate substantive provision on whether the indorsement is effective, rather than in the definition of indorsement. See Section 8-107.

12. "Instruction" is defined as a notification communicated to the issuer of an uncertificated security directing that transfer be registered or that the security be redeemed. Instructions are the analog for uncertificated securities of indorsements of certificated securities.

13. "Registered form." The definition of "registered form" is substantially the same as in the prior version of Article 8. Like the definition of bearer form, it serves primarily to distinguish Article 8 securities from instruments governed by other law, such as Article 3.

14. "Securities intermediary." A "securities intermediary" is a person that in the ordinary course of its business maintains securities accounts for others and is acting in that capacity. The most common examples of securities intermediaries would be clearing corporations holding securities for their participants, banks acting as securities custodians, and brokers holding securities on behalf of their customers. Clearing corporations are listed separately as a category of securities intermediary in subparagraph (i) even though in most circumstances they would fall within the general definition in subparagraph (ii). The reason is to simplify the analysis of arrangements such as the NSCC-DTC system in which NSCC performs the comparison, clearance, and netting function, while DTC acts as the depository. Because NSCC is a registered clearing agency under the federal securities laws, it is a clearing corporation and hence a securities intermediary under Article 8, regardless of whether it is at any particular time or in any particular aspect of its operations holding securities on behalf of its participants.

The terms securities intermediary and broker have different meanings. Broker means a person engaged in the business of buying and selling securities, as agent for others or as principal. Securities intermediary means a person maintaining securities accounts for others. A stockbroker, in the colloquial sense, may or may not be acting as a securities intermediary.

The definition of securities intermediary includes the requirement that the person in question is "acting in the capacity" of maintaining securities accounts for others. This is to take account of the fact that a particular entity, such as a bank, may act in many different capacities in securities transactions. A bank may act as a transfer agent for issuers, as a securities custodian for institutional investors and private investors, as a dealer in government securities, as a lender taking securities as collateral, and as a provider of general payment and collection services that might be used in connection with securities transactions. A bank that maintains securities accounts for its customers would be a securities intermediary with respect to those accounts; but if it takes a pledge of securities from a borrower to secure a loan, it is not thereby acting as a securities intermediary with respect to the pledged securities, since it holds them for its own account rather than for a customer. In other circumstances, those two functions might be combined. For example, if the bank is a government securities dealer it may maintain securities accounts for customers and also provide the customers with margin credit to purchase or carry the securities, in much the same way that brokers provide margin loans to their customers.

15. "Security." The definition of "security" has three components. First, there is the subparagraph (i) test that the interest or obligation be fully transferable, in the sense that the issuer either maintains transfer books or the obligation or interest is represented by a certificate in bearer or registered form. Second, there is the subparagraph (ii) test that the interest or obligation be divisible, that is, one of a class or series, as distinguished from individual obligations of the sort governed by ordinary contract law or by Article 3. Third, there is the subparagraph (iii) functional test, which generally turns on whether the interest or obligation is, or is of a type, dealt in or traded on securities markets or securities exchanges. There is, however, an "opt-in" provision in subparagraph (iii) which permits the issuer of any interest or obligation that is "a medium of investment" to specify that it is a security governed by Article 8.

The divisibility test of subparagraph (ii) applies to the security—that is, the underlying intangible interest—not the means by which that interest is evidenced. Thus, securities issued in book-entry only form meet the divisibility test because the underlying intangible interest is divisible via the mechanism of the indirect holding system. This is so even though the clearing corporation is the only eligible direct holder of the security.

The third component, the functional test in subparagraph (iii), provides flexibility while ensuring that the Article 8 rules do not apply to interests or obligations in circumstances so unconnected with the securities markets that parties are unlikely to have thought of the possibility that Article 8 might apply. Subparagraph (iii)(A) covers interests or obligations that either are dealt in or traded on securities exchanges or securities markets, or are of a type dealt in or traded on securities exchanges or securities markets. The "is dealt in or traded on" phrase eliminates problems in the characterization of new forms of securities which are to be traded in the markets, even though no similar type has previously been dealt in or traded in the markets. Subparagraph (iii)(B) covers the broader category of media for investment, but it applies only if the terms of the interest or obligation specify that it is an Article 8 security. This opt-in provision allows for deliberate expansion of the scope of Article 8.

Section 8-103 contains additional rules on the treatment of particular interests as securities or financial assets.

16. "Security certificate." The term "security" refers to the underlying asset, e.g., 1000 shares of common stock of Acme, Inc. The term "security certificate" refers to the paper certificates that have traditionally been used to embody the underlying intangible interest.

17. "Security entitlement" means the rights and property interest of a person who holds securities or other financial assets through a securities intermediary. A security entitlement is both a package of personal rights against the securities intermediary and an interest in the property held by the securities intermediary. A security entitlement is not, however, a specific property interest in any financial asset held by the securities intermediary or by the clearing corporation through which the securities intermediary holds the financial asset. See Sections 8-104(c) and 8-503. The formal definition of security entitlement set out in subsection (a)(16) of this section is a cross-reference to the rules of Part 5. In a sense, then, the entirety of Part 5 is the definition of security entitlement. The Part 5 rules

specify the rights and property interest that comprise a security entitlement.

18. "Uncertificated security." The term "uncertificated security" means a security that is not represented by a security certificate. For uncertificated securities, there is no need to draw any distinction between the underlying asset and the means by which a direct holder's interest in that asset is evidenced. Compare "certificated security" and "security certificate."

Definitional Cross References:

"Agreement". Section 1-201(3).
"Bank". Section 1-201(4).
"Person". Section 1-201(30).
"Send". Section 1-201(38).
"Signed". Section 1-201(39).
"Writing". Section 1-201(46).

§ 8-103. Rules for Determining Whether Certain Obligations and Interests are Securities or Financial Assets.

(a) A share or similar equity interest issued by a corporation, business trust, joint stock company, or similar entity is a security.

(b) An "investment company security" is a security. "Investment company security" means a share or similar equity interest issued by an entity that is registered as an investment company under the federal investment company laws, an interest in a unit investment trust that is so registered, or a face-amount certificate issued by a face-amount certificate company that is so registered. Investment company security does not include an insurance policy or endowment policy or annuity contract issued by an insurance company.

(c) An interest in a partnership or limited liability company is not a security unless it is dealt in or traded on securities exchanges or in securities markets, its terms expressly provide that it is a security governed by this Article, or it is an investment company security. However, an interest in a partnership or limited liability company is a financial asset if it is held in a securities account.

(d) A writing that is a security certificate is governed by this Article and not by Article 3, even though it also meets the requirements of that Article. However, a negotiable instrument governed by Article 3 is a financial asset if it is held in a securities account.

(e) An option or similar obligation issued by a clearing corporation to its participants is not a security, but is a financial asset.

(f) A commodity contract, as defined in Section 9-115, is not a security or a financial asset.

Official Comment

1. This section contains rules that supplement the definitions of "financial asset" and "security" in Section 8-102. The Section 8-102 definitions are worded in general terms, because they must be sufficiently comprehensive and flexible to cover the wide variety of investment products that now exist or may develop. The rules in this section are intended to foreclose interpretive issues concerning the application of the general definitions to several specific investment products. No implication is made about the application of the Section 8-102 definitions to investment products not covered by this section.

2. Subsection (a) establishes an unconditional rule that ordinary corporate stock is a security. That is so whether or not the particular issue is dealt in or traded on securities exchanges or in securities markets. Thus, shares of closely held corporations are Article 8 securities.

3. Subsection (b) establishes that the Article 8 term "security" includes the various forms of the investment vehicles offered to the public by investment companies registered as such under the federal Investment Company Act of 1940, as amended. This clarification is prompted principally by the fact that the typical transaction in shares of open-end investment companies is an issuance or redemption, rather than a transfer of shares from one person to another as is the case with ordinary corporate stock. For similar reasons, the definitions of indorsement, instruction, and entitlement order in Section 8-102 refer to "redemptions" as well as "transfers," to ensure that the Article 8 rules on such matters as signature guaranties, Section 8-306, assurances, Sections 8-402 and 8-507, and effectiveness, Section 8-107, apply to directions to redeem mutual fund shares. The exclusion of insurance products is needed because some insurance company separate accounts are registered under the Investment Company Act of 1940, but these are not traded under the usual Article 8 mechanics.

4. Subsection (c) is designed to foreclose interpretive questions that might otherwise be raised by the application of the "of a type" language of Section 8-102(a)(15)(iii) to partnership interests. Subsection (c) establishes the general rule that partnership interests or shares of limited liability companies are not Article 8 securities unless they are in fact dealt in or traded on securities exchanges or in securities markets. The issuer, however, may explicitly "opt-in" by specifying that the interests or shares are securities governed by Article 8. Partnership interests or shares of limited liability companies are included in the broader term "financial asset." Thus, if they are held through a securities account, the indirect holding system rules of Part 5 apply, and the interest of a person who holds them through such an account is a security entitlement.

5. Subsection (d) deals with the line between Article 3 negotiable instruments and Article 8 investment securities. It continues the rule of the prior version of Article 8 that a writing that meets the Article 8 definition is covered by Article 8 rather than Article 3, even though it also meets the definition of negotiable instrument. However, subsection (d) provides that an Article 3 negotiable instrument is a "financial asset" so that the indirect holding system rules apply if the instrument is held through a securities intermediary. This facilitates making items such as money market instruments eligible for deposit in clearing corporations.

6. Subsection (e) is included to clarify the treatment of investment products such as traded stock options, which are treated as financial assets but not securities. Thus, the indirect holding system rules of Part 5 apply, but the direct holding system rules of Parts 2, 3, and 4 do not.

7. Subsection (f) excludes commodity contracts from all of Article 8. However, the Article 9 rules on security interests in investment property do apply to security interests in commodity positions. See Section 9-115 and Comment 8 thereto. "Commodity contract" is defined in Section 9-115.

Definitional Cross References:

"Clearing corporation". Section 8-102(a)(5).

"Commodity contract". Section 9-115.

"Financial asset". Section 8-102(a)(9).

"Security". Section 8-102(a)(15).

"Security certificate". Section 8-102(a)(16).

§ 8–104. Acquisition of Security or Financial Asset or Interest Therein.

(a) A person acquires a security or an interest therein, under this Article, if:

(1) the person is a purchaser to whom a security is delivered pursuant to Section 8–301; or

(2) the person acquires a security entitlement to the security pursuant to Section 8–501.

(b) A person acquires a financial asset, other than a security, or an interest therein, under this Article, if the person acquires a security entitlement to the financial asset.

(c) A person who acquires a security entitlement to a security or other financial asset has the rights specified in Part 5, but is a purchaser of any security, security entitlement, or other financial asset held by the securities intermediary only to the extent provided in Section 8–503.

(d) Unless the context shows that a different meaning is intended, a person who is required by other law, regulation, rule, or agreement to transfer, deliver, present, surrender, exchange, or otherwise put in the possession of another person a security or financial asset satisfies that requirement by causing the other person to acquire an interest in the security or financial asset pursuant to subsection (a) or (b).

Official Comment

1. This section lists the ways in which interests in securities and other financial assets are acquired under Article 8. In that sense, it describes the scope of Article 8. Subsection (a) describes the two ways that a person may acquire a security or interest therein under this Article: (1) by delivery (Section 8–301), and (2) by acquiring a security entitlement. Each of these methods is described in detail in the relevant substantive provisions of this Article. Part 3, beginning with the definition of "delivery" in Section 8–301, describes how interests in securities are acquired in the direct holding system. Part 5, beginning with the rules of Section 8–501 on how security entitlements are acquired, describes how interests in securities are acquired in the indirect holding system.

Subsection (b) specifies how a person may acquire an interest under Article 8 in a financial asset other than a security. This Article deals with financial assets other than securities only insofar as they are held in the indirect holding system. For example, a bankers' acceptance falls within the definition of "financial asset," so if it is held through a securities account the entitlement holder's right to it is a security entitlement governed by Part 5. The bankers' acceptance itself, however, is a negotiable instrument governed by Article 3, not by Article 8. Thus, the provisions of Parts 2, 3, and 4 of this Article that deal with the rights of direct holders of securities are not applicable. Article 3, not Article 8, specifies how one acquires a direct interest in a bankers' acceptance. If a bankers' acceptance is delivered to a clearing corporation to be held for the account of the clearing corporation's participants, the clearing corporation becomes the holder of the bankers' acceptance under the Article 3 rules specifying how negotiable instruments are transferred. The rights of the clearing corporation's participants, however, are governed by Part 5 of this Article.

2. The distinction in usage in Article 8 between the term "security" (and its cor-

relatives "security certificate" and "uncertificated security") on the one hand, and "security entitlement" on the other, corresponds to the distinction between the direct and indirect holding systems. For example, with respect to certificated securities that can be held either directly or through intermediaries, obtaining possession of a security certificate and acquiring a security entitlement are both means of holding the underlying security. For many other purposes, there is no need to draw a distinction between the means of holding. For purposes of commercial law analysis, however, the form of holding may make a difference. Where an item of property can be held in different ways, the rules on how one deals with it, including how one transfers it or how one grants a security interest in it, differ depending on the form of holding.

Although a security entitlement is means of holding the underlying security or other financial asset, a person who has a security entitlement does not have any direct claim to a specific asset in the possession of the securities intermediary. Subsection (c) provides explicitly that a person who acquires a security entitlement is a "purchaser" of any security, security entitlement, or other financial asset held by the securities intermediary only in the sense that under Section 8-503 a security entitlement is treated as a *sui generis* form of property interest.

3. Subsection (d) is designed to ensure that parties will retain their expected legal rights and duties under Revised Article 8. One of the major changes made by the revision is that the rules for the indirect holding system are stated in terms of the "security entitlements" held by investors, rather than speaking of them as holding direct interests in securities. Subsection (d) is designed as a translation rule to eliminate problems of co-ordination of terminology, and facilitate the continued use of systems for the efficient handling of securities and financial assets through securities intermediaries and clearing corporations. The efficiencies of a securities intermediary or clearing corporation are, in part, dependent on the ability to transfer securities credited to securities accounts in the intermediary or clearing corporation to the account of an issuer, its agent, or other person by book entry in a manner that permits exchanges, redemptions, conversions, and other transactions (which may be governed by pre-existing or new agreements, constitutional documents, or other instruments) to occur and to avoid the need to withdraw from immobilization in an intermediary or clearing corporation physical securities in order to deliver them for such purposes. Existing corporate charters, indentures and like documents may require the "presentation," "surrender," "delivery," or "transfer" of securities or security certificates for purposes of exchange, redemption, conversion or other reason. Likewise, documents may use a wide variety of terminology to describe, in the context for example of a tender or exchange offer, the means of putting the offeror or the issuer or its agent in possession of the security. Subsection (d) takes the place of provisions of prior law which could be used to reach the legal conclusion that book-entry transfers are equivalent to physical delivery to the person to whose account the book entry is credited.

Definitional Cross References:

"Delivery". Section 8-301.

"Financial asset". Section 8-102(a)(9).

"Person". Section 1-201(30).

"Purchaser". Sections 1-201(33) & 8-116.

"Security". Section 8-102(a)(15).

"Security entitlement". Section 8-102(a)(17).

§ 8-105. Notice of Adverse Claim.

(a) A person has notice of an adverse claim if:

(1) the person knows of the adverse claim;

(2) the person is aware of facts sufficient to indicate that there is a significant probability that the adverse claim exists and deliberately

avoids information that would establish the existence of the adverse claim; or

(3) the person has a duty, imposed by statute or regulation, to investigate whether an adverse claim exists, and the investigation so required would establish the existence of the adverse claim.

(b) Having knowledge that a financial asset or interest therein is or has been transferred by a representative imposes no duty of inquiry into the rightfulness of a transaction and is not notice of an adverse claim. However, a person who knows that a representative has transferred a financial asset or interest therein in a transaction that is, or whose proceeds are being used, for the individual benefit of the representative or otherwise in breach of duty has notice of an adverse claim.

(c) An act or event that creates a right to immediate performance of the principal obligation represented by a security certificate or sets a date on or after which the certificate is to be presented or surrendered for redemption or exchange does not itself constitute notice of an adverse claim except in the case of a transfer more than:

(1) one year after a date set for presentment or surrender for redemption or exchange; or

(2) six months after a date set for payment of money against presentation or surrender of the certificate, if money was available for payment on that date.

(d) A purchaser of a certificated security has notice of an adverse claim if the security certificate:

(1) whether in bearer or registered form, has been indorsed "for collection" or "for surrender" or for some other purpose not involving transfer; or

(2) is in bearer form and has on it an unambiguous statement that it is the property of a person other than the transferor, but the mere writing of a name on the certificate is not such a statement.

(e) Filing of a financing statement under Article 9 is not notice of an adverse claim to a financial asset.

Official Comment

1. The rules specifying whether adverse claims can be asserted against persons who acquire securities or security entitlements, Sections 8–303, 8–502, and 8–510, provide that one is protected against an adverse claim only if one takes without notice of the claim. This section defines notice of an adverse claim.

The general Article 1 definition of "notice" in Section 1–201(25)—which provides that a person has notice of a fact if "from all the facts and circumstances known to him at the time in question he has reason to know that it exists"—does not apply to the interpretation of "notice of adverse claims." The Section 1–201(25) definition of "notice" does, however, apply to usages of that term and its cognates in Article 8 in contexts other than notice of adverse claims.

2. This section must be interpreted in light of the definition of "adverse claim" in Section 8–102(a)(1). "Adverse claim" does not include all circumstances in

which a third party has a property interest in securities, but only those situations where a security is transferred in violation of the claimant's property interest. Therefore, awareness that someone other than the transferor has a property interest is not notice of an adverse claim. The transferee must be aware that the transfer violates the other party's property interest. If A holds securities in which B has some form of property interest, and A transfers the securities to C, C may know that B has an interest, but infer that A is acting in accordance with A's obligations to B. The mere fact that C knew that B had a property interest does not mean that C had notice of an adverse claim. Whether C had notice of an adverse claim depends on whether C had sufficient awareness that A was acting in violation of B's property rights. The rule in subsection (b) is a particularization of this general principle.

3. Paragraph (a)(1) provides that a person has notice of an adverse claim if the person has knowledge of the adverse claim. Knowledge is defined in Section 1–201(25) as actual knowledge.

4. Paragraph (a)(2) provides that a person has notice of an adverse claim if the person is aware of a significant probability that an adverse claim exists and deliberately avoids information that might establish the existence of the adverse claim. This is intended to codify the "willful blindness" test that has been applied in such cases. See *May v. Chapman,* 16 M. & W. 355, 153 Eng.Rep. 1225 (1847); *Goodman v. Simonds,* 61 U.S. 343 (1857).

The first prong of the willful blindness test of paragraph (a)(2) turns on whether the person is aware facts sufficient to indicate that there is a significant probability that an adverse claim exists. The "awareness" aspect necessarily turns on the actor's state of mind. Whether facts known to a person make the person aware of a "significant probability" that an adverse claim exists turns on facts about the world and the conclusions that would be drawn from those facts, taking account of the experience and position of the person in question. A particular set of facts might indicate a significant probability of an adverse claim to a professional with considerable experience in the usual methods and procedures by which securities transactions are conducted, even though the same facts would not indicate a significant probability of an adverse claim to a non-professional.

The second prong of the willful blindness test of paragraph (a)(2) turns on whether the person "deliberately avoids information" that would establish the existence of the adverse claim. The test is the character of the person's response to the information the person has. The question is whether the person deliberately failed to seek further information because of concern that suspicions would be confirmed.

Application of the "deliberate avoidance" test to a transaction by an organization focuses on the knowledge and the actions of the individual or individuals conducting the transaction on behalf of the organization. Thus, an organization that purchases a security is not willfully blind to an adverse claim unless the officers or agents who conducted that purchase transaction are willfully blind to the adverse claim. Under the two prongs of the willful blindness test, the individual or individuals conducting a transaction must know of facts indicating a substantial probability that the adverse claim exists and deliberately fail to seek further information that might confirm or refute the indication. For this purpose, information known to individuals within an organization who are not conducting or aware of a transaction, but not forwarded to the individuals conducting the transaction, is not pertinent in determining whether the individuals conducting the transaction had knowledge of a substantial probability of the existence of the adverse claim. Cf. Section 1–201(27). An organization may also "deliberately avoid information" if it acts to preclude or inhibit transmission of pertinent information to those individuals responsible for the conduct of purchase transactions.

5. Paragraph (a)(3) provides that a person has notice of an adverse claim if the person would have learned of the adverse claim by conducting an investigation that is required by other statute or regulation. This rule applies only if there is some other statute or regulation that explicitly requires persons dealing with securities to conduct some investigation. The federal securities laws require that brokers and banks, in certain specified circumstances, check with a stolen securities registry to determine whether securities offered for sale or pledge have been reported as stolen. If securities that were listed as stolen in the registry are taken by an institution that failed to comply with requirement to check the registry, the institution would be held to have notice of the fact that they were stolen under paragraph (a)(3). Accordingly, the institution could not qualify as a protected purchaser under Section 8–303. The same result has been reached under the prior version of Article 8. See *First Nat'l Bank of Cicero v. Lewco Securities,* 860 F.2d 1407 (7th Cir.1988).

6. Subsection (b) provides explicitly for some situations involving purchase from one described or identifiable as a representative. Knowledge of the existence of the representative relation is not enough in itself to constitute "notice of an adverse claim" that would disqualify the purchaser from protected purchaser status. A purchaser may take a security on the inference that the representative is acting properly. Knowledge that a security is being transferred to an individual account of the representative or that the proceeds of the transaction will be paid into that account is not sufficient to constitute "notice of an adverse claim," but knowledge that the proceeds will be applied to the personal indebtedness of the representative is. See *State Bank of Binghamton v. Bache,* 162 Misc. 128, 293 N.Y.S. 667 (1937).

7. Subsection (c) specifies whether a purchaser of a "stale" security is charged with notice of adverse claims, and therefore disqualified from protected purchaser status under Section 8–303. The fact of "staleness" is viewed as notice of certain defects after the lapse of stated periods, but the maturity of the security does not operate automatically to affect holders' rights. The periods of time here stated are shorter than those appearing in the provisions of this Article on staleness as notice of defects or defenses of an issuer (Section 8–203) since a purchaser who takes a security after funds or other securities are available for its redemption has more reason to suspect claims of ownership than issuer's defenses. An owner will normally turn in a security rather than transfer it at such a time. Of itself, a default never constitutes notice of a possible adverse claim. To provide otherwise would not tend to drive defaulted securities home and would serve only to disrupt current financial markets where many defaulted securities are actively traded. Unpaid or overdue coupons attached to a bond do not bring it within the operation of this subsection, though they may be relevant under the general test of notice of adverse claims in subsection (a).

8. Subsection (d) provides the owner of a certificated security with a means of protection while a security certificate is being sent in for redemption or exchange. The owner may endorse it "for collection" or "for surrender," and this constitutes notice of the owner's claims, under subsection (d).

Definitional Cross References:

"Adverse claim". Section 8–102(a)(1).
"Bearer form". Section 8–102(a)(2).
"Certificated security". Section 8–102(a)(4).
"Financial asset". Section 8–102(a)(9).
"Knowledge". Section 1–201(25).
"Person". Section 1–201(30).
"Purchaser". Sections 1–201(33) & 8–116.
"Registered form". Section 8–102(a)(13).
"Representative". Section 1–201(35).
"Security certificate". Section 8–102(a)(16).

§ 8–106. Control.

(a) A purchaser has "control" of a certificated security in bearer form if the certificated security is delivered to the purchaser.

(b) A purchaser has "control" of a certificated security in registered form if the certificated security is delivered to the purchaser, and:

(1) the certificate is indorsed to the purchaser or in blank by an effective indorsement; or

(2) the certificate is registered in the name of the purchaser, upon original issue or registration of transfer by the issuer.

(c) A purchaser has "control" of an uncertificated security if:

(1) the uncertificated security is delivered to the purchaser; or

(2) the issuer has agreed that it will comply with instructions originated by the purchaser without further consent by the registered owner.

(d) A purchaser has "control" of a security entitlement if:

(1) the purchaser becomes the entitlement holder; or

(2) the securities intermediary has agreed that it will comply with entitlement orders originated by the purchaser without further consent by the entitlement holder.

(e) If an interest in a security entitlement is granted by the entitlement holder to the entitlement holder's own securities intermediary, the securities intermediary has control.

(f) A purchaser who has satisfied the requirements of subsection (c)(2) or (d)(2) has control even if the registered owner in the case of subsection (c)(2) or the entitlement holder in the case of subsection (d)(2) retains the right to make substitutions for the uncertificated security or security entitlement, to originate instructions or entitlement orders to the issuer or securities intermediary, or otherwise to deal with the uncertificated security or security entitlement.

(g) An issuer or a securities intermediary may not enter into an agreement of the kind described in subsection (c)(2) or (d)(2) without the consent of the registered owner or entitlement holder, but an issuer or a securities intermediary is not required to enter into such an agreement even though the registered owner or entitlement holder so directs. An issuer or securities intermediary that has entered into such an agreement is not required to confirm the existence of the agreement to another party unless requested to do so by the registered owner or entitlement holder.

Official Comment

1. The concept of "control" plays a key role in various provisions dealing with the rights of purchasers, including secured parties. See Sections 8–303 (protected purchasers); 8–503(e) (purchasers from securities intermediaries); 8–510 (purchasers of security entitlements from entitlement holders); 9–115(4) (perfection of security interests); 9–115(5) (priorities among conflicting security interests).

Obtaining "control" means that the purchaser has taken whatever steps are necessary, given the manner in which the securities are held, to place itself in a position where it can have the securities sold, without further action by the owner.

2. Subsection (a) provides that a purchaser obtains "control" with respect to a certificated security in bearer form by taking "delivery," as defined in Section 8-301. Subsection (b) provides that a purchaser obtains "control" with respect to a certificated security in registered form by taking "delivery," as defined in Section 8-301, provided that the security certificate has been indorsed to the purchaser or in blank. Section 8-301 provides that delivery of a certificated security occurs when the purchaser obtains possession of the security certificate, or when an agent for the purchaser (other than a securities intermediary) either acquires possession or acknowledges that the agent holds for the purchaser.

3. Subsection (c) specifies the means by which a purchaser can obtain control over uncertificated securities which the transferor holds directly. Two mechanisms are possible.

Under subsection (c)(1), securities can be "delivered" to a purchaser. Section 8-301(b) provides that "delivery" of an uncertificated security occurs when the purchaser becomes the registered holder. So far as the issuer is concerned, the purchaser would then be entitled to exercise all rights of ownership. See Section 8-207. As between the parties to a purchase transaction, however, the rights of the purchaser are determined by their contract. Cf. Section 9-202. Arrangements covered by this paragraph are analogous to arrangements in which bearer certificates are delivered to a secured party—so far as the issuer or any other parties are concerned, the secured party appears to be the outright owner, although it is in fact holding as collateral property that belongs to the debtor.

Under subsection (c)(2), a purchaser has control if the issuer has agreed to act on the instructions of the purchaser, even though the owner remains listed as the registered owner. The issuer, of course, would be acting wrongfully against the registered owner if it entered into such an agreement without the consent of the registered owner. Subsection (g) makes this point explicit. The subsection (c)(2) provision makes it possible for issuers to offer a service akin to the registered pledge device of the 1978 version of Article 8, without mandating that all issuers offer that service.

4. Subsection (d) specifies the means by which a purchaser can obtain control over a security entitlement. Two mechanisms are possible, analogous to those provided in subsection (c) for uncertificated securities. Under subsection (d)(1), a purchaser has control if it is the entitlement holder. This subsection would apply whether the purchaser holds through the same intermediary that the debtor used, or has the securities position transferred to its own intermediary.

Subsection (d)(2) provides that a purchaser has control if the securities intermediary has agreed to act on entitlement orders originated by the purchaser, even though the transferor remains listed as the entitlement holder. This section specifies only the minimum requirements that such an arrangement must meet to confer "control"; the details of the arrangement can be specified by agreement. The arrangement might cover all of the positions in a particular account or subaccount, or only specified positions. There is no requirement that the control party's right to give entitlement orders be exclusive. The arrangement might provide that only the control party can give entitlement orders, or that either the entitlement holder or the control party can give entitlement orders. See subsection (f).

The following examples illustrate the rules of subsection (d):

Example 1. Debtor grants Alpha Bank a security interest in 1000 shares of XYZ Co. stock that Debtor holds through an account with Able & Co. Alpha Bank also has an account with Able. Debtor instructs Able to transfer the shares to Alpha Bank, and Able does so. Alpha Bank has control of the

1000 shares under subsection (d)(1), because Alpha Bank is the entitlement holder.

Example 2. Debtor grants Alpha Bank a security interest in 1000 shares of XYZ Co. stock that Debtor holds through an account with Able & Co. Alpha Bank does not have an account with Able. Alpha Bank uses Beta Bank as its securities custodian. Debtor instructs Able to transfer the shares to Beta Bank, for the account of Alpha Bank, and Able does so. Alpha Bank has control of the 1000 shares under subsection (d)(1), because Alpha Bank is the entitlement holder.

Example 3. Debtor grants Alpha Bank a security interest in 1000 shares of XYZ Co. stock that Debtor holds through an account with Able & Co. Debtor, Able, and Alpha Bank enter into an agreement under which Debtor will continue to receive dividends and distributions, and will continue to have the right to direct dispositions, but Alpha Bank also has the right to direct dispositions. Alpha Bank has control of the 1000 shares under subsection (d)(2).

Example 4. Able & Co., a securities dealer, grants Alpha Bank a security interest in 1000 shares of XYZ Co. stock that Able holds through an account with Clearing Corporation. Able causes Clearing Corporation to transfer the shares into Alpha Bank's account at Clearing Corporation. Alpha Bank has control of the 1000 shares under subsection (d)(1).

Example 5. Able & Co., a securities dealer, grants Alpha Bank a security interest in 1000 shares of XYZ Co. stock that Able holds through an account with Clearing Corporation. Alpha Bank does not have an account with Clearing Corporation. It holds its securities through Beta Bank, which does have an account with Clearing Corporation. Able causes Clearing Corporation to transfer the shares into Beta Bank's account at Clearing Corporation. Beta Bank credits the position to Alpha Bank's account with Beta Bank. Alpha Bank has control of the 1000 shares under subsection (d)(1).

Example 6. Able & Co. a securities dealer, grants Alpha Bank a security interest in 1000 shares of XYZ Co. stock that Able holds through an account with Clearing Corporation. Able causes Clearing Corporation to transfer the shares into a pledge account, pursuant to an agreement under which Able will continue to receive dividends, distributions, and the like, but Alpha Bank has the right to direct dispositions. Alpha Bank has control of the 1000 shares under subsection (d)(2).

Example 7. Able & Co. a securities dealer, grants Alpha Bank a security interest in 1000 shares of XYZ Co. stock that Able holds through an account with Clearing Corporation. Able, Alpha, and Clearing Corporation enter into an agreement under which Clearing Corporation will act on instructions from Alpha with respect to the XYZ Co. stock carried in Able's account, but Able will continue to receive dividends, distributions, and the like, and will also have the right to direct dispositions. Alpha Bank has control of the 1000 shares under subsection (d)(2).

Example 8. Able & Co. a securities dealer, holds a wide range of securities through its account at Clearing Corporation. Able enters into an arrangement with Alpha Bank pursuant to which Alpha provides financing to Able secured by securities identified as the collateral on lists provided by Able to Alpha on a daily or other periodic basis. Able, Alpha, and Clearing Corporation enter into an agreement under which Clearing Corporation agrees that if at any time Alpha directs Clearing Corporation to do so, Clearing Corporation will transfer any securities from Able's account at Alpha's instructions. Because Clearing Corporation has agreed to act on Alpha's instructions with respect to any securities carried in Able's account, at the moment that Alpha's security interest attaches to securities listed by Able, Alpha obtains control of those securities under subsection (d)(2). There is no requirement that Clearing Corporation be informed of which securities Able has pledged to Alpha.

5. For a purchaser to have "control" under subsection (c)(2) or (d)(2), it is essential that the issuer or securities intermediary, as the case may be, actually be a party to the agreement. If a debtor gives a secured party a power of attorney authorizing the secured party to act in the name of the debtor, but the issuer or securities intermediary does not specifically agree to this arrangement, the secured party does not have "control" within the meaning of subsection (c)(2) or (d)(2) because the issuer or securities intermediary is not a party to the agreement. The secured party does not have control under subsection (c)(1) or (d)(1) because, although the power of attorney might give the secured party authority to act on the debtor's behalf as an agent, the secured party has not actually become the registered owner or entitlement holder.

6. Subsection (e) provides that if an interest in a security entitlement is granted by an entitlement holder to the securities intermediary through which the security entitlement is maintained, the securities intermediary has control. A common transaction covered by this provision is a margin loan from a broker to its customer.

7. The term "control" is used in a particular defined sense. The requirements for obtaining control are set out in this section. The concept is not to be interpreted by reference to similar concepts in other bodies of law. In particular, the requirements for "possession" derived from the common law of pledge are not to be used as a basis for interpreting subsection (c)(2) or (d)(2). Those provisions are designed to supplant the concepts of "constructive possession" and the like. A principal purpose of the "control" concept is to eliminate the uncertainty and confusion that results from attempting to apply common law possession concepts to modern securities holding practices.

The key to the control concept is that the purchaser has the present ability to have the securities sold or transferred without further action by the transferor. There is no requirement that the powers held by the purchaser be exclusive. For example, in a secured lending arrangement, if the secured party wishes, it can allow the debtor to retain the right to make substitutions, or to direct the disposition of the uncertificated security or security entitlement. Subsection (f) is included to make clear the general point stated in subsection (c) that the test of control is whether the purchaser has obtained the requisite power, not whether the debtor has retained other powers. There is no implication that retention by the debtor of powers other than those mentioned in subsection (f) is inconsistent with the purchaser having control.

Definitional Cross References:

"Bearer form". Section 8-102(a)(2).
"Certificated security". Section 8-102(a)(4).
"Delivery". Section 8-301.
"Effective". Section 8-107.
"Entitlement holder". Section 8-102(a)(7).
"Entitlement order". Section 8-102(a)(8).
"Indorsement". Section 8-102(a)(11).
"Instruction". Section 8-102(a)(12).
"Purchaser". Sections 1-201(33) & 8-116.
"Registered form". Section 8-102(a)(13).
"Securities intermediary". Section 8-102(a)(14).
"Security entitlement". Section 8-102(a)(17).
"Uncertificated security". Section 8-102(a)(18).

§ 8-107. Whether Indorsement, Instruction, or Entitlement Order is Effective.

(a) "Appropriate person" means:

(1) with respect to an indorsement, the person specified by a security certificate or by an effective special indorsement to be entitled to the security;

(2) with respect to an instruction, the registered owner of an uncertificated security;

(3) with respect to an entitlement order, the entitlement holder;

(4) if the person designated in paragraph (1), (2), or (3) is deceased, the designated person's successor taking under other law or the designated person's personal representative acting for the estate of the decedent; or

(5) if the person designated in paragraph (1), (2), or (3) lacks capacity, the designated person's guardian, conservator, or other similar representative who has power under other law to transfer the security or financial asset.

(b) An indorsement, instruction, or entitlement order is effective if:

(1) it is made by the appropriate person;

(2) it is made by a person who has power under the law of agency to transfer the security or financial asset on behalf of the appropriate person, including, in the case of an instruction or entitlement order, a person who has control under Section 8–106(c)(2) or (d)(2); or

(3) the appropriate person has ratified it or is otherwise precluded from asserting its ineffectiveness.

(c) An indorsement, instruction, or entitlement order made by a representative is effective even if:

(1) the representative has failed to comply with a controlling instrument or with the law of the State having jurisdiction of the representative relationship, including any law requiring the representative to obtain court approval of the transaction; or

(2) the representative's action in making the indorsement, instruction, or entitlement order or using the proceeds of the transaction is otherwise a breach of duty.

(d) If a security is registered in the name of or specially indorsed to a person described as a representative, or if a securities account is maintained in the name of a person described as a representative, an indorsement, instruction, or entitlement order made by the person is effective even though the person is no longer serving in the described capacity.

(e) Effectiveness of an indorsement, instruction, or entitlement order is determined as of the date the indorsement, instruction, or entitlement order is made, and an indorsement, instruction, or entitlement order does not become ineffective by reason of any later change of circumstances.

Official Comment

1. This section defines two concepts, "appropriate person" and "effective." Effectiveness is a broader concept than appropriate person. For example, if a

security or securities account is registered in the name of Mary Roe, Mary Roe is the "appropriate person," but an indorsement, instruction, or entitlement order made by John Doe is "effective" if, under agency or other law, Mary Roe is precluded from denying Doe's authority. Treating these two concepts separately facilitates statement of the rules of Article 8 that state the legal effect of an indorsement, instruction, or entitlement order. For example, a securities intermediary is protected against liability if it acts on an effective entitlement order, but has a duty to comply with an entitlement order only if it is originated by an appropriate person. See Sections 8-115 and 8-507.

One important application of the "effectiveness" concept is in the direct holding system rules on the rights of purchasers. A purchaser of a certificated security in registered form can qualify as a protected purchaser who takes free from adverse claims under Section 8-303 only if the purchaser obtains "control." Section 8-106 provides that a purchaser of a certificated security in registered form obtains control if there has been an "effective" indorsement.

2. Subsection (a) provides that the term "appropriate person" covers two categories: (1) the person who is actually designated as the person entitled to the security or security entitlement, and (2) the successor or legal representative of that person if that person has died or otherwise lacks capacity. Other law determines who has power to transfer a security on behalf of a person who lacks capacity. For example, if securities are registered in the name of more than one person and one of the designated persons dies, whether the survivor is the appropriate person depends on the form of tenancy. If the two were registered joint tenants with right of survivorship, the survivor would have that power under other law and thus would be the "appropriate person." If securities are registered in the name of an individual and the individual dies, the law of decedents' estates determines who has power to transfer the decedent's securities. That would ordinarily be the executor or administrator, but if a "small estate statute" permits a widow to transfer a decedent's securities without administration proceedings, she would be the appropriate person. If the registration of a security or a securities account contains a designation of a death beneficiary under the Uniform Transfer on Death Security Registration Act or comparable legislation, the designated beneficiary would, under that law, have power to transfer upon the person's death and so would be the appropriate person. Article 8 does not contain a list of such representatives, because any list is likely to become outdated by developments in other law.

3. Subsection (b) sets out the general rule that an indorsement, instruction, or entitlement order is effective if it is made by the appropriate person or by a person who has power to transfer under agency law or if the appropriate person is precluded from denying its effectiveness. The control rules in Section 8-106 provide for arrangements where a person who holds securities through a securities intermediary, or holds uncertificated securities directly, enters into a control agreement giving the secured party the right to initiate entitlement orders of instructions. Paragraph 2 of subsection (b) states explicitly that an entitlement order or instruction initiated by a person who has obtained such a control agreement is "effective."

Subsections (c), (d), and (e) supplement the general rule of subsection (b) on effectiveness. The term "representative," used in subsections (c) and (d), is defined in Section 1-201(35).

4. Subsection (c) provides that an indorsement, instruction, or entitlement order made by a representative is effective even though the representative's action is a violation of duties. The following example illustrates this subsection:

Example 1. Certificated securities are registered in the name of John Doe. Doe dies and Mary Roe is appointed executor. Roe indorses the security certificate and transfers it to a purchaser in a transaction that is a violation of her duties as executor.

Roe's indorsement is effective, because Roe is the appropriate person under subsection (a)(4). This is so even though Roe's transfer violated her obligations as executor. The policies of free transferability of securities that underlie Article 8 dictate that neither a purchaser to whom Roe transfers the securities nor the issuer who registers transfer should be required to investigate the terms of the will to determine whether Roe is acting properly. Although Roe's indorsement is effective under this section, her breach of duty may be such that her beneficiary has an adverse claim to the securities that Roe transferred. The question whether that adverse claim can be asserted against purchasers is governed not by this section but by Section 8-303. Under Section 8-404, the issuer has no duties to an adverse claimant unless the claimant obtains legal process enjoining the issuer from registering transfer.

5. Subsection (d) deals with cases where a security or a securities account is registered in the name of a person specifically designated as a representative. The following example illustrates this subsection:

Example 2. Certificated securities are registered in the name of "John Jones, trustee of the Smith Family Trust." John Jones is removed as trustee and Martha Moe is appointed successor trustee. The securities, however, are not reregistered, but remain registered in the name of "John Jones, trustee of the Smith Family Trust." Jones indorses the security certificate and transfers it to a purchaser.

Subsection (d) provides that an indorsement by John Jones as trustee is effective even though Jones is no longer serving in that capacity. Since the securities were registered in the name of "John Jones, trustee of the Smith Family Trust," a purchaser, or the issuer when called upon to register transfer, should be entitled to assume without further inquiry that Jones has the power to act as trustee for the Smith Family Trust.

Note that subsection (d) does not apply to a case where the security or securities account is registered in the name of principal rather than the representative as such. The following example illustrates this point:

Example 3. Certificated securities are registered in the name of John Doe. John Doe dies and Mary Roe is appointed executor. The securities are not reregistered in the name of Mary Roe as executor. Later, Mary Roe is removed as executor and Martha Moe is appointed as her successor. After being removed, Mary Roe indorses the security certificate that is registered in the name of John Doe and transfers it to a purchaser.

Mary Roe's indorsement is not made effective by subsection (d), because the securities were not registered in the name of Mary Roe as representative. A purchaser or the issuer registering transfer should be required to determine whether Roe has power to act for John Doe. Purchasers and issuers can protect themselves in such cases by requiring signature guaranties. See Section 8-306.

6. Subsection (e) provides that the effectiveness of an indorsement, instruction, or entitlement order is determined as of the date it is made. The following example illustrates this subsection:

Example 4. Certificated securities are registered in the name of John Doe. John Doe dies and Mary Roe is appointed executor. Mary Roe indorses the security certificate that is registered in the name of John Doe and transfers it to a purchaser. After the indorsement and transfer, but before the security certificate is presented to the issuer for registration of transfer, Mary Roe is removed as executor and Martha Moe is appointed as her successor.

Mary Roe's indorsement is effective, because at the time Roe indorsed she was the appropriate person under subsection (a)(4). Her later removal as executor does not render the indorsement ineffective. Accordingly, the issuer would not be liable for registering the transfer. See Section 8-404.

Definitional Cross References:

"Entitlement order". Section 8-102(a)(8).
"Financial asset". Section 8-102(a)(9).
"Indorsement". Section 8-102(a)(11).
"Instruction". Section 8-102(a)(12).
"Representative". Section 1-201(35).
"Securities account". Section 8-501.
"Security". Section 8-102(a)(15).
"Security certificate". Section 8-102(a)(16).
"Security entitlement". Section 8-102(a)(17).
"Uncertificated security". Section 8-102(a)(18).

§ 8-108. Warranties in Direct Holding.

(a) A person who transfers a certificated security to a purchaser for value warrants to the purchaser, and an indorser, if the transfer is by indorsement, warrants to any subsequent purchaser, that:

(1) the certificate is genuine and has not been materially altered;

(2) the transferor or indorser does not know of any fact that might impair the validity of the security;

(3) there is no adverse claim to the security;

(4) the transfer does not violate any restriction on transfer;

(5) if the transfer is by indorsement, the indorsement is made by an appropriate person, or if the indorsement is by an agent, the agent has actual authority to act on behalf of the appropriate person; and

(6) the transfer is otherwise effective and rightful.

(b) A person who originates an instruction for registration of transfer of an uncertificated security to a purchaser for value warrants to the purchaser that:

(1) the instruction is made by an appropriate person, or if the instruction is by an agent, the agent has actual authority to act on behalf of the appropriate person;

(2) the security is valid;

(3) there is no adverse claim to the security; and

(4) at the time the instruction is presented to the issuer:

(i) the purchaser will be entitled to the registration of transfer;
(ii) the transfer will be registered by the issuer free from all liens, security interests, restrictions, and claims other than those specified in the instruction;
(iii) the transfer will not violate any restriction on transfer; and
(iv) the requested transfer will otherwise be effective and rightful.

(c) A person who transfers an uncertificated security to a purchaser for value and does not originate an instruction in connection with the transfer warrants that:

(1) the uncertificated security is valid;

(2) there is no adverse claim to the security;

(3) the transfer does not violate any restriction on transfer; and

(4) the transfer is otherwise effective and rightful.

(d) A person who indorses a security certificate warrants to the issuer that:

(1) there is no adverse claim to the security; and

(2) the indorsement is effective.

(e) A person who originates an instruction for registration of transfer of an uncertificated security warrants to the issuer that:

(1) the instruction is effective; and

(2) at the time the instruction is presented to the issuer the purchaser will be entitled to the registration of transfer.

(f) A person who presents a certificated security for registration of transfer or for payment or exchange warrants to the issuer that the person is entitled to the registration, payment, or exchange, but a purchaser for value and without notice of adverse claims to whom transfer is registered warrants only that the person has no knowledge of any unauthorized signature in a necessary indorsement.

(g) If a person acts as agent of another in delivering a certificated security to a purchaser, the identity of the principal was known to the person to whom the certificate was delivered, and the certificate delivered by the agent was received by the agent from the principal or received by the agent from another person at the direction of the principal, the person delivering the security certificate warrants only that the delivering person has authority to act for the principal and does not know of any adverse claim to the certificated security.

(h) A secured party who redelivers a security certificate received, or after payment and on order of the debtor delivers the security certificate to another person, makes only the warranties of an agent under subsection (g).

(i) Except as otherwise provided in subsection (g), a broker acting for a customer makes to the issuer and a purchaser the warranties provided in subsections (a) through (f). A broker that delivers a security certificate to its customer, or causes its customer to be registered as the owner of an uncertificated security, makes to the customer the warranties provided in subsection (a) or (b), and has the rights and privileges of a purchaser under this section. The warranties of and in favor of the broker acting as an agent are in addition to applicable warranties given by and in favor of the customer.

Official Comment

1. Subsections (a), (b), and (c) deal with warranties by security transferors to purchasers. Subsections (d) and (e) deal with warranties by security transferors to issuers. Subsection (f) deals with presentment warranties.

2. Subsection (a) specifies the warranties made by a person who transfers a certificated security to a purchaser for value. Paragraphs (3), (4), and (5) make explicit several key points that are implicit in the general warranty of paragraph (6) that the transfer is effective and right-

ful. Subsection (b) sets forth the warranties made to a purchaser for value by one who originates an instruction. These warranties are quite similar to those made by one transferring a certificated security, subsection (a), the principal difference being the absolute warranty of validity. If upon receipt of the instruction the issuer should dispute the validity of the security, the burden of proving validity is upon the transferor. Subsection (c) provides for the limited circumstances in which an uncertificated security could be transferred without an instruction, see Section 8–301(b)(2). Subsections (d) and (e) give the issuer the benefit of the warranties of an indorser or originator on those matters not within the issuer's knowledge.

3. Subsection (f) limits the warranties made by a purchaser for value without notice whose presentation of a security certificate is defective in some way but to whom the issuer does register transfer. The effect is to deny the issuer a remedy against such a person unless at the time of presentment the person had knowledge of an unauthorized signature in a necessary indorsement. The issuer can protect itself by refusing to make the transfer or, if it registers the transfer before it discovers the defect, by pursuing its remedy against a signature guarantor.

4. Subsection (g) eliminates all substantive warranties in the relatively unusual case of a delivery of certificated security by an agent of a disclosed principal where the agent delivers the exact certificate that it received from or for the principal. Subsection (h) limits the warranties given by a secured party who redelivers a certificate. Subsection (i) specifies the warranties of brokers in the more common scenarios.

5. Under Section 1–102(3) the warranty provisions apply "unless otherwise agreed" and the parties may enter into express agreements to allocate the risks of possible defects. Usual estoppel principles apply with respect to transfers of both certificated and uncertificated securities whenever the purchaser has knowledge of the defect, and these warranties will not be breached in such a case.

Definitional Cross References:

"Adverse claim". Section 8–102(a)(1).
"Appropriate person". Section 8–107.
"Broker". Section 8–102(a)(3).
"Certificated security". Section 8–102(a)(4).
"Indorsement". Section 8–102(a)(11).
"Instruction". Section 8–102(a)(12).
"Issuer". Section 8–201.
"Person". Section 1–201(30).
"Purchaser". Sections 1–201(33) & 8–116.
"Secured party". Section 9–105(1)(m).
"Security". Section 8–102(a)(15).
"Security certificate". Section 8–102(a)(16).
"Uncertificated security". Section 8–102(a)(18).
"Value". Sections 1–201(44) & 8–116.

§ 8–109. Warranties in Indirect Holding.

(a) A person who originates an entitlement order to a securities intermediary warrants to the securities intermediary that:

(1) the entitlement order is made by an appropriate person, or if the entitlement order is by an agent, the agent has actual authority to act on behalf of the appropriate person; and

(2) there is no adverse claim to the security entitlement.

(b) A person who delivers a security certificate to a securities intermediary for credit to a securities account or originates an instruction with respect to an uncertificated security directing that the uncertificated security be credited to a securities account makes to the securities intermediary the warranties specified in Section 8–108(a) or (b).

(c) If a securities intermediary delivers a security certificate to its entitlement holder or causes its entitlement holder to be registered as the owner of an uncertificated security, the securities intermediary makes to the entitlement holder the warranties specified in Section 8–108(a) or (b).

Official Comment

1. Subsection (a) provides that a person who originates an entitlement order warrants to the securities intermediary that the order is authorized, and warrants the absence of adverse claims. Subsection (b) specifies the warranties that are given when a person who holds securities directly has the holding converted into indirect form. A person who delivers a certificate to a securities intermediary or originates an instruction for an uncertificated security gives to the securities intermediary the transfer warranties under Section 8–108. If the securities intermediary in turn delivers the certificate to a higher level securities intermediary, it gives the same warranties.

2. Subsection (c) states the warranties that a securities intermediary gives when a customer who has been holding securities in an account with the securities intermediary requests that certificates be delivered or that uncertificated securities be registered in the customer's name. The warranties are the same as those that brokers make with respect to securities that the brokers sell to or buy on behalf of the customers. See Section 8–108(i).

3. As with the Section 8–108 warranties, the warranties specified in this section may be modified by agreement under Section 1–102(3).

Definitional Cross References:

"Adverse claim". Section 8–102(a)(1).
"Appropriate person". Section 8–107.
"Entitlement holder". Section 8–102(a)(7).
"Entitlement order". Section 8–102(a)(8).
"Instruction". Section 8–102(a)(12).
"Person". Section 1–201(30).
"Securities account". Section 8–501.
"Securities intermediary". Section 8–102(a)(14).
"Security certificate". Section 8–102(a)(16).
"Uncertificated security". Section 8–102(a)(18).

§ 8–110. Applicability; Choice of Law.

(a) The local law of the issuer's jurisdiction, as specified in subsection (d), governs:

(1) the validity of a security;

(2) the rights and duties of the issuer with respect to registration of transfer;

(3) the effectiveness of registration of transfer by the issuer;

(4) whether the issuer owes any duties to an adverse claimant to a security; and

(5) whether an adverse claim can be asserted against a person to whom transfer of a certificated or uncertificated security is registered or a person who obtains control of an uncertificated security.

(b) The local law of the securities intermediary's jurisdiction, as specified in subsection (e), governs:

(1) acquisition of a security entitlement from the securities intermediary;

(2) the rights and duties of the securities intermediary and entitlement holder arising out of a security entitlement;

(3) whether the securities intermediary owes any duties to an adverse claimant to a security entitlement; and

(4) whether an adverse claim can be asserted against a person who acquires a security entitlement from the securities intermediary or a person who purchases a security entitlement or interest therein from an entitlement holder.

(c) The local law of the jurisdiction in which a security certificate is located at the time of delivery governs whether an adverse claim can be asserted against a person to whom the security certificate is delivered.

(d) "Issuer's jurisdiction" means the jurisdiction under which the issuer of the security is organized or, if permitted by the law of that jurisdiction, the law of another jurisdiction specified by the issuer. An issuer organized under the law of this State may specify the law of another jurisdiction as the law governing the matters specified in subsection (a)(2) through (5).

(e) The following rules determine a "securities intermediary's jurisdiction" for purposes of this section:

(1) If an agreement between the securities intermediary and its entitlement holder specifies that it is governed by the law of a particular jurisdiction, that jurisdiction is the securities intermediary's jurisdiction.

(2) If an agreement between the securities intermediary and its entitlement holder does not specify the governing law as provided in paragraph (1), but expressly specifies that the securities account is maintained at an office in a particular jurisdiction, that jurisdiction is the securities intermediary's jurisdiction.

(3) If an agreement between the securities intermediary and its entitlement holder does not specify a jurisdiction as provided in paragraph (1) or (2), the securities intermediary's jurisdiction is the jurisdiction in which is located the office identified in an account statement as the office serving the entitlement holder's account.

(4) If an agreement between the securities intermediary and its entitlement holder does not specify a jurisdiction as provided in paragraph (1) or (2) and an account statement does not identify an office serving the entitlement holder's account as provided in paragraph (3), the securities intermediary's jurisdiction is the jurisdiction in which is located the chief executive office of the securities intermediary.

(f) A securities intermediary's jurisdiction is not determined by the physical location of certificates representing financial assets, or by the jurisdiction in which is organized the issuer of the financial asset with respect to which an entitlement holder has a security entitlement, or by the location of facilities for data processing or other record keeping concerning the account.

Official Comment

1. This section deals with applicability and choice of law issues concerning Article 8. The distinction between the direct and indirect holding systems plays a significant role in determining the governing law. An investor in the direct holding system is registered on the books of the issuer and/or has possession of a security certificate. Accordingly, the jurisdiction of incorporation of the issuer or location of the certificate determine the applicable law. By contrast, an investor in the indirect holding system has a security entitlement, which is a bundle of rights against the securities intermediary with respect to a security, rather than a direct interest in the underlying security. Accordingly, in the rules for the indirect holding system, the jurisdiction of incorporation of the issuer of the underlying security or the location of any certificates that might be held by the intermediary or a higher tier intermediary, do not determine the applicable law.

The phrase "local law" refers to the law of a jurisdiction other than its conflict of laws rules. See Restatement (Second) of Conflict of Laws § 4.

2. Subsection (a) provides that the law of an issuer's jurisdiction governs certain issues where the substantive rules of Article 8 determine the issuer's rights and duties. Paragraph (1) of subsection (a) provides that the law of the issuer's jurisdiction governs the validity of the security. This ensures that a single body of law will govern the questions addressed in Part 2 of Article 8, concerning the circumstances in which an issuer can and cannot assert invalidity as a defense against purchasers. Similarly, paragraphs (2), (3), and (4) of subsection (a) ensure that the issuer will be able to look to a single body of law on the questions addressed in Part 4 of Article 8, concerning the issuer's duties and liabilities with respect to registration of transfer.

Paragraph (5) of subsection (a) applies the law of an issuer's jurisdiction to the question whether an adverse claim can be asserted against a purchaser to whom transfer has been registered, or who has obtained control over an uncertificated security. Although this issue deals with the rights of persons other than the issuer, the law of the issuer's jurisdiction applies because the purchasers to whom the provision applies are those whose protection against adverse claims depends on the fact that their interests have been recorded on the books of the issuer.

The principal policy reflected in the choice of law rules in subsection (a) is that an issuer and others should be able to look to a single body of law on the matters specified in subsection (a), rather than having to look to the law of all of the different jurisdictions in which security holders may reside. The choice of law policies reflected in this subsection do not require that the body of law governing all of the matters specified in subsection (a) be that of the jurisdiction in which the issuer is incorporated. Thus, subsection (d) provides that the term "issuer's jurisdiction" means the jurisdiction in which the issuer is organized, or, if permitted by that law, the law of another jurisdiction selected by the issuer. Subsection (d) also provides that issuers organized under the law of a State which adopts this Article may make such a selection, except as to the validity issue specified in paragraph (1). The question whether an issuer can assert the defense of invalidity may implicate significant policies of the issuer's jurisdiction of incorporation. See, e.g., Section 8-202 and Comments thereto.

Although subsection (a) provides that the issuer's rights and duties concerning registration of transfer are governed by the law of the issuer's jurisdiction, other matters related to registration of transfer, such as appointment of a guardian for a registered owner or the existence of agency relationships, might be governed by another jurisdiction's law. Neither this section nor Section 1-105 deals with what law governs the appointment of the administrator or executor; that question is determined under generally applicable choice of law rules.

3. Subsection (b) provides that the law of the securities intermediary's jurisdiction governs the issues concerning the indirect holding system that are dealt with in Article 8. Paragraphs (1) and (2) cover the matters dealt with in the Article 8 rules defining the concept of security entitlement and specifying the duties of securities intermediaries. Paragraph (3) provides that the law of the security intermediary's jurisdiction determines whether the intermediary owes any duties to an adverse claimant. Paragraph (4) provides that the law of the security intermediary's jurisdiction determines whether adverse claims can be asserted against entitlement holders and others.

Subsection (e) determines what is a "securities intermediary's jurisdiction." The policy of subsection (b) is to ensure that a securities intermediary and all of its entitlement holders can look to a single, readily-identifiable body of law to determine their rights and duties. Accordingly, subsection (e) sets out a sequential series of tests to facilitate identification of that body of law. Paragraph (1) of subsection (e) permits specification of the governing law by agreement. Because the policy of this section is to enable parties to determine, in advance and with certainty, what law will apply to transactions governed by this Article, the validation of selection of governing law by agreement is not conditioned upon a determination that the jurisdiction whose law is chosen bear a "reasonable relation" to the transaction. See Section 4A–507; compare Section 1–105(1). That is also true with respect to the similar provisions in subsection (d) of this section and in Section 9–103(6).

Subsection (f) makes explicit a point that is implicit in the Article 8 description of a security entitlement as a bundle of rights against the intermediary with respect to a security or other financial asset, rather than as a direct interest in the underlying security or other financial asset. The governing law for relationships in the indirect holding system is not determined by such matters as the jurisdiction of incorporation of the issuer of the securities held through the intermediary, or the location of any physical certificates held by the intermediary or a higher tier intermediary.

4. Subsection (c) provides a choice of law rule for adverse claim issues that may arise in connection with delivery of security certificates in the direct holding system. It applies the law of the place of delivery. If a certificated security issued by an Idaho corporation is sold, and the sale is settled by physical delivery of the certificate from Seller to Buyer in New York, under subsection (c), New York law determines whether Buyer takes free from adverse claims. The domicile of Seller, Buyer, and any adverse claimant is irrelevant.

5. The following examples illustrate how a court in a jurisdiction which has enacted this section would determine the governing law:

Example 1. John Doe, a resident of Kansas, maintains a securities account with Able & Co. Able is incorporated in Delaware. Its chief executive offices are located in Illinois. The office where Doe transacts business with Able is located in Missouri. The agreement between Doe and Able specifies that it is governed by Illinois law. Through the account, Doe holds securities of a Colorado corporation, which Able holds through Clearing Corporation. The rules of Clearing Corporation provide that the rights and duties of Clearing Corporation and its participants are governed by New York law. Subsection (a) specifies that a controversy concerning the rights and duties as between the issuer and Clearing Corporation is governed by Colorado law. Subsections (b) and (e) specify that a controversy concerning the rights and duties as between the Clearing Corporation and Able is governed by New York law, and that a controversy concerning the rights and duties as between Able and Doe is governed by Illinois law.

Example 2. Same facts as to Doe and Able as in Example 1. Through the account, Doe holds securities of a Senegalese corporation, which Able holds through Clearing Corporation. Clearing Corporation's operations are located in Belgium, and its rules and agreements with its participants provide that they are governed by Belgian law. Clearing Corporation holds the securities through a custodial account at the Paris branch office of Global Bank, which is organized under English law. The agreement between Clearing Corporation and Global Bank provides that it is governed by French law. Subsection (a) specifies that a controversy concerning the rights and duties as between the issuer and Global Bank is governed by Senegalese law. Subsections (b) and (e) specify that a controversy concerning the rights and duties as between Global Bank and Clearing Corporation is governed by French law, that a controversy concerning the rights and duties as between Clearing Corporation and Able is governed by Belgian law, and that a controversy concerning the rights and duties as between Able and Doe is governed by Illinois law.

6. To the extent that this section does not specify the governing law, general choice of law rules apply. For example, suppose that in either of the examples in the preceding Comment, Doe enters into an agreement with Roe, also a resident of Kansas, in which Doe agrees to transfer all of his interests in the securities held through Able to Roe. Article 8 does not deal with whether such an agreement is enforceable or whether it gives Roe some interest in Doe's security entitlement. This section specifies what jurisdiction's law governs the issues that are dealt with in Article 8. Article 8, however, does specify that securities intermediaries have only limited duties with respect to adverse claims. See Section 8–115. Subsection (b)(3) of this section provides that Illinois law governs whether Able owes any duties to an adverse claimant. Thus, if Illinois has adopted Revised Article 8, Section 8–115 as enacted in Illinois determines whether Roe has any rights against Able.

7. The choice of law provisions concerning security interests in securities and security entitlements are set out in Section 9–103(6).

Definitional Cross References:

"Adverse claim". Section 8–102(a)(1).
"Agreement". Section 1–201(3).
"Certificated security". Section 8–102(a)(4).
"Entitlement holder". Section 8–102(a)(7).
"Financial asset". Section 8–102(a)(9).
"Issuer". Section 8–201.
"Person". Section 1–201(30).
"Purchase". Section 1–201(32).
"Securities intermediary". Section 8–102(a)(14).
"Security". Section 8–102(a)(15).
"Security certificate". Section 8–102(a)(16).
"Security entitlement". Section 8–102(a)(17).
"Uncertificated security". Section 8–102(a)(18).

§ 8–111. Clearing Corporation Rules.

A rule adopted by a clearing corporation governing rights and obligations among the clearing corporation and its participants in the clearing corporation is effective even if the rule conflicts with this [Act] and affects another party who does not consent to the rule.

Official Comment

1. The experience of the past few decades shows that securities holding and settlement practices may develop rapidly, and in unforeseeable directions. Accordingly, it is desirable that the rules of

Article 8 be adaptable both to ensure that commercial law can conform to changing practices and to ensure that commercial law does not operate as an obstacle to developments in securities practice. Even if practices were unchanging, it would not be possible in a general statute to specify in detail the rules needed to provide certainty in the operations of the clearance and settlement system.

The provisions of this Article and Article 1 on the effect of agreements provide considerable flexibility in the specification of the details of the rights and obligations of participants in the securities holding system by agreement. See Sections 8-504 through 8-509, and Section 1-102(3) and (4). Given the magnitude of the exposures involved in securities transactions, however, it may not be possible for the parties in developing practices to rely solely on private agreements, particularly with respect to matters that might affect others, such as creditors. For example, in order to be fully effective, rules of clearing corporations on the finality or reversibility of securities settlements must not only bind the participants in the clearing corporation but also be effective against their creditors. Section 8-111 provides that clearing corporation rules are effective even if they indirectly affect third parties, such as creditors of a participant. This provision does not, however, permit rules to be adopted that would govern the rights and obligations of third parties other than as a consequence of rules that specify the rights and obligations of the clearing corporation and its participants.

2. The definition of clearing corporation in Section 8-102 covers only federal reserve banks, entities registered as clearing agencies under the federal securities laws, and others subject to comparable regulation. The rules of registered clearing agencies are subject to regulatory oversight under the federal securities laws.

Definitional Cross References:

"Clearing corporation". Section 8-102(a)(5).

§ 8-112. Creditor's Legal Process.

(a) The interest of a debtor in a certificated security may be reached by a creditor only by actual seizure of the security certificate by the officer making the attachment or levy, except as otherwise provided in subsection (d). However, a certificated security for which the certificate has been surrendered to the issuer may be reached by a creditor by legal process upon the issuer.

(b) The interest of a debtor in an uncertificated security may be reached by a creditor only by legal process upon the issuer at its chief executive office in the United States, except as otherwise provided in subsection (d).

(c) The interest of a debtor in a security entitlement may be reached by a creditor only by legal process upon the securities intermediary with whom the debtor's securities account is maintained, except as otherwise provided in subsection (d).

(d) The interest of a debtor in a certificated security for which the certificate is in the possession of a secured party, or in an uncertificated security registered in the name of a secured party, or a security entitlement maintained in the name of a secured party, may be reached by a creditor by legal process upon the secured party.

(e) A creditor whose debtor is the owner of a certificated security, uncertificated security, or security entitlement is entitled to aid from a court of competent jurisdiction, by injunction or otherwise, in reaching the certificated security, uncertificated security, or security entitlement or in satisfying the claim by means allowed at law or in equity in regard to property that cannot readily be reached by other legal process.

Official Comment

1. In dealing with certificated securities the instrument itself is the vital thing, and therefore a valid levy cannot be made unless all possibility of the certificate's wrongfully finding its way into a transferee's hands has been removed. This can be accomplished only when the certificate is in the possession of a public officer, the issuer, or an independent third party. A debtor who has been enjoined can still transfer the security in contempt of court. See *Overlock v. Jerome–Portland Copper Mining Co.,* 29 Ariz. 560, 243 P. 400 (1926). Therefore, although injunctive relief is provided in subsection (e) so that creditors may use this method to gain control of the certificated security, the security certificate itself must be reached to constitute a proper levy whenever the debtor has possession.

2. Subsection (b) provides that when the security is uncertificated and registered in the debtor's name, the debtor's interest can be reached only by legal process upon the issuer. The most logical place to serve the issuer would be the place where the transfer records are maintained, but that location might be difficult to identify, especially when the separate elements of a computer network might be situated in different places. The chief executive office is selected as the appropriate place by analogy to Section 9–103(3)(d). See Comment 5(c) to that section. This section indicates only how attachment is to be made, not when it is legally justified. For that reason there is no conflict between this section and *Shaffer v. Heitner,* 433 U.S. 186 (1977).

3. Subsection (c) provides that a security entitlement can be reached only by legal process upon the debtor's security intermediary. Process is effective only if directed to the debtor's own security intermediary. If Debtor holds securities through Broker, and Broker in turn holds through Clearing Corporation, Debtor's property interest is a security entitlement against Broker. Accordingly, Debtor's creditor cannot reach Debtor's interest by legal process directed to the Clearing Corporation. See also Section 8–115.

4. Subsection (d) provides that when a certificated security, an uncertificated security, or a security entitlement is controlled by a secured party, the debtor's interest can be reached by legal process upon the secured party. This section does not attempt to provide for rights as between the creditor and the secured party, as, for example, whether or when the secured party must liquidate the security.

Definitional Cross References:

"Certificated security". Section 8–102(a)(4).
"Issuer". Section 8–201.
"Secured party". Section 9–105(1)(m).
"Securities intermediary". Section 8–102(a)(14).
"Security certificate". Section 8–102(a)(16).
"Security entitlement". Section 8–102(a)(17).
"Uncertificated security". Section 8–102(a)(18).

§ 8–113. Statute of Frauds Inapplicable.

A contract or modification of a contract for the sale or purchase of a security is enforceable whether or not there is a writing signed or record authenticated by a party against whom enforcement is sought, even if the contract or modification is not capable of performance within one year of its making.

Official Comment

This section provides that the statute of frauds does not apply to contracts for the sale of securities, reversing prior law which had a special statute of frauds in Section 8-319 (1978). With the increasing use of electronic means of communication, the statute of frauds is unsuited to the realities of the securities business. For securities transactions, whatever benefits a statute of frauds may play in filtering out fraudulent claims are outweighed by the obstacles it places in the development of modern commercial practices in the securities business.

Definitional Cross References:

"Action". Section 1-201(1).
"Contract". Section 1-201(11).
"Writing". Section 1-201(46).

§ 8-114. Evidentiary Rules Concerning Certificated Securities.

The following rules apply in an action on a certificated security against the issuer:

(1) Unless specifically denied in the pleadings, each signature on a security certificate or in a necessary indorsement is admitted.

(2) If the effectiveness of a signature is put in issue, the burden of establishing effectiveness is on the party claiming under the signature, but the signature is presumed to be genuine or authorized.

(3) If signatures on a security certificate are admitted or established, production of the certificate entitles a holder to recover on it unless the defendant establishes a defense or a defect going to the validity of the security.

(4) If it is shown that a defense or defect exists, the plaintiff has the burden of establishing that the plaintiff or some person under whom the plaintiff claims is a person against whom the defense or defect cannot be asserted.

Official Comment

This section adapts the rules of negotiable instruments law concerning procedure in actions on instruments, see Section 3-308, to actions on certificated securities governed by this Article. An "action on a security" includes any action or proceeding brought against the issuer to enforce a right or interest that is part of the security, such as an action to collect principal or interest or a dividend, or to establish a right to vote or to receive a new security under an exchange offer or plan of reorganization. This section applies only to certificated securities; actions on uncertificated securities are governed by general evidentiary principles.

Definitional Cross References:

"Action". Section 1-201(1).
"Burden of establishing". Section 1-201(8).
"Certificated security". Section 8-102(a)(4).
"Indorsement". Section 8-102(a)(11).
"Issuer". Section 8-201.
"Presumed". Section 1-201(31).
"Security". Section 8-102(a)(15).
"Security certificate". Section 8-102(a)(16).

§ 8-115. Securities Intermediary and Others Not Liable to Adverse Claimant.

A securities intermediary that has transferred a financial asset pursuant to an effective entitlement order, or a broker or other agent or bailee that has dealt with a financial asset at the direction of its customer or principal, is not liable to a person having an adverse claim to the financial asset, unless the securities intermediary, or broker or other agent or bailee:

(1) took the action after it had been served with an injunction, restraining order, or other legal process enjoining it from doing so, issued by a court of competent jurisdiction, and had a reasonable opportunity to act on the injunction, restraining order, or other legal process; or

(2) acted in collusion with the wrongdoer in violating the rights of the adverse claimant; or

(3) in the case of a security certificate that has been stolen, acted with notice of the adverse claim.

Official Comment

1. Other provisions of Article 8 protect certain purchasers against adverse claims, both for the direct holding system and the indirect holding system. See Sections 8–303 and 8–502. This section deals with the related question of the possible liability of a person who acted as the "conduit" for a securities transaction. It covers both securities intermediaries—the "conduits" in the indirect holding system—and brokers or other agents or bailees—the "conduits" in the direct holding system. The following examples illustrate its operation:

Example 1. John Doe is a customer of the brokerage firm of Able & Co. Doe delivers to Able a certificate for 100 shares of XYZ Co. common stock, registered in Doe's name and properly indorsed, and asks the firm to sell it for him. Able does so. Later, John Doe's spouse Mary Doe brings an action against Able asserting that Able's action was wrongful against her because the XYZ Co. stock was marital property in which she had an interest, and John Doe was acting wrongfully against her in transferring the securities.

Example 2. Mary Roe is a customer of the brokerage firm of Baker & Co. and holds her securities through a securities account with Baker. Roe instructs Baker to sell 100 shares of XYZ Co. common stock that she carried in her account. Baker does so. Later, Mary Roe's spouse John Roe brings an action against Baker asserting that Baker's action was wrongful against him because the XYZ Co. stock was marital property in which he had an interest, and Mary Roe was acting wrongfully against him in transferring the securities.

Under common law conversion principles, Mary Doe might be able to assert that Able & Co. is liable to her in Example 1 for exercising dominion over property inconsistent with her rights in it. On that or some similar theory John Roe might assert that Baker is liable to him in Example 2. Section 8–115 protects both Able and Baker from liability.

2. The policy of this section is similar to that of many other rules of law that protect agents and bailees from liability as innocent converters. If a thief steals property and ships it by mail, express service, or carrier, to another person, the recipient of the property does not obtain good title, even though the recipient may have given value to the thief and had no notice or knowledge that the property was stolen. Accordingly, the true owner can recover the property from the recipient or obtain damages in a conversion or similar action. An action against the postal service, express company, or carrier presents entirely different policy considerations. Accordingly, general tort law protects agents or bailees who act on the instructions of their principals or bailors. See Restatement (Second) of Torts § 235. See also UCC Section 7–404.

3. Except as provided in paragraph 3, this section applies even though the securities intermediary, or the broker or other agent or bailee, had notice or knowledge that another person asserts a claim to the securities. Consider the following examples:

Example 3. Same facts as in Example 1, except that before John Doe brought the XYZ Co. security certificate to Able for sale, Mary Doe telephoned or wrote to the firm asserting that she had an interest in all of John Doe's securities and demanding that they not trade for him.

Example 4. Same facts as in Example 2, except that before Mary Roe gave an entitlement order to Baker to sell the XYZ Co. securities from her account, John Doe telephoned or wrote to the firm asserting that he had an interest in all of Mary Roe's securities and demanding that they not trade for her.

Section 8-115 protects Able and Baker from liability. The protections of Section 8-115 do not depend on the presence or absence of notice of adverse claims. It is essential to the securities settlement system that brokers and securities intermediaries be able to act promptly on the directions of their customers. Even though a firm has notice that someone asserts a claim to a customer's securities or security entitlements, the firm should not be placed in the position of having to make a legal judgment about the validity of the claim at the risk of liability either to its customer or to the third party for guessing wrong. Under this section, the broker or securities intermediary is privileged to act on the instructions of its customer or entitlement holder, unless it has been served with a restraining order or other legal process enjoining it from doing so. This is already the law in many jurisdictions. For example a section of the New York Banking Law provides that banks need not recognize any adverse claim to funds or securities on deposit with them unless they have been served with legal process. N.Y. Banking Law § 134. Other sections of the UCC embody a similar policy. See Sections 3-602, 5-114(2)(b).

Paragraph (1) of this section refers only to a court order enjoining the securities intermediary or the broker or other agent or bailee from acting at the instructions of the customer. It does not apply to cases where the adverse claimant tells the intermediary or broker that the customer has been enjoined, or shows the intermediary or broker a copy of a court order binding the customer.

Paragraph (3) takes a different approach in one limited class of cases, those where a customer sells stolen certificated securities through a securities firm. Here the policies that lead to protection of securities firms against assertions of other sorts of claims must be weighed against the desirability of having securities firms guard against the disposition of stolen securities. Accordingly, paragraph (3) denies protection to a broker, custodian, or other agent or bailee who receives a stolen security certificate from its customer, if the broker, custodian, or other agent or bailee had notice of adverse claims. The circumstances that give notice of adverse claims are specified in Section 8-105. The result is that brokers, custodians, and other agents and bailees face the same liability for selling stolen certificated securities that purchasers face for buying them.

4. As applied to securities intermediaries, this section embodies one of the fundamental principles of the Article 8 indirect holding system rules—that a securities intermediary owes duties only to its own entitlement holders. The following examples illustrate the operation of this section in the multi-tiered indirect holding system:

Example 5. Able & Co., a broker-dealer, holds 50,000 shares of XYZ Co. stock in its account at Clearing Corporation. Able acquired the XYZ shares from another firm, Baker & Co., in a transaction that Baker contends was tainted by fraud, giving Baker a right to rescind the transaction and recover the XYZ shares from Able. Baker sends notice to Clearing Corporation stating that Baker has a claim to the 50,000 shares of XYZ Co. in Able's account. Able then initiates an entitlement order directing Clearing Corporation to transfer the 50,000 shares of XYZ Co. to another firm in settlement of a trade. Under Section 8–115, Clearing Corporation is privileged to comply with Able's entitlement order, without fear of liability to Baker. This is so even though Clearing Corporation has notice of Baker's claim, unless Baker obtains a court order enjoining Clearing Corporation from acting on Able's entitlement order.

Example 6. Able & Co., a broker-dealer, holds 50,000 shares of XYZ Co. stock in its account at Clearing Corporation. Able initiates an entitlement order directing Clearing Corporation to transfer the 50,000 shares of XYZ Co. to another firm in settlement of a trade. That trade was made by Able for its own account, and the proceeds were devoted to its own use. Able becomes insolvent, and it is discovered that Able has a shortfall in the shares of XYZ Co. stock that it should have been carrying for its customers. Able's customers bring an action against Clearing Corporation asserting that Clearing Corporation acted wrongfully in transferring the XYZ shares on Able's order because those were shares that should have been held by Able for its customers. Under Section 8–115, Clearing Corporation is not liable to Able's customers, because Clearing Corporation acted on an effective entitlement order of its own entitlement holder, Able. Clearing Corporation's protection against liability does not depend on the presence or absence of notice or knowledge of the claim by Clearing Corporation.

5. If the conduct of a securities intermediary or a broker or other agent or bailee rises to a level of complicity in the wrongdoing of its customer or principal, the policies that favor protection against liability do not apply. Accordingly, paragraph (2) provides that the protections of this section do not apply if the securities intermediary or broker or other agent or bailee acted in collusion with the customer or principal in violating the rights of another person. The collusion test is intended to adopt a standard akin to the tort rules that determine whether a person is liable as an aider or abettor for the tortious conduct of a third party. See Restatement (Second) of Torts § 876.

Knowledge that the action of the customer is wrongful is a necessary but not sufficient condition of the collusion test. The aspect of the role of securities intermediaries and brokers that Article 8 deals with is the clerical or ministerial role of implementing and recording the securities transactions that their customers conduct. Faithful performance of this role consists of following the instructions of the customer. It is not the role of the record-keeper to police whether the transactions recorded are appropriate, so mere awareness that the customer may be acting wrongfully does not itself constitute collusion. That, of course, does not insulate an intermediary or broker from responsibility in egregious cases where its action goes beyond the ordinary standards of the business of implementing and recording transactions, and reaches a level of affirmative misconduct in assisting the customer in the commission of a wrong.

Definitional Cross References:

"Broker". Section 8–102(a)(3).

"Effective". Section 8–107.

"Entitlement order". Section 8–102(a)(8).

"Financial asset". Section 8–102(a)(9).

"Securities intermediary". Section 8–102(a)(14).

"Security certificate". Section 8–102(a)(16).

§ 8–116. Securities Intermediary as Purchaser For Value.

A securities intermediary that receives a financial asset and establishes a security entitlement to the financial asset in favor of an entitlement holder is a purchaser for value of the financial asset. A securities intermediary that acquires a security entitlement to a financial asset from another securities intermediary acquires the security entitlement for value if the securities intermediary acquiring the security entitlement establishes a security entitlement to the financial asset in favor of an entitlement holder.

Official Comment

1. This section is intended to make explicit two points that, while implicit in other provisions, are of sufficient importance to the operation of the indirect holding system that they warrant explicit statement. First, it makes clear that a securities intermediary that receives a financial asset and establishes a security entitlement in respect thereof in favor of an entitlement holder is a "purchaser" of the financial asset that the securities intermediary received. Second, it makes clear that by establishing a security entitlement in favor of an entitlement holder a securities intermediary gives value for any corresponding financial asset that the securities intermediary receives or acquires from another party, whether the intermediary holds directly or indirectly.

In many cases a securities intermediary that receives a financial asset will also be transferring value to the person from whom the financial asset was received. That, however, is not always the case. Payment may occur through a different system than settlement of the securities side of the transaction, or the securities might be transferred without a corresponding payment, as when a person moves an account from one securities intermediary to another. Even though the securities intermediary does not give value to the transferor, it does give value by incurring obligations to its own entitlement holder. Although the general definition of value in Section 1-201(44)(d) should be interpreted to cover the point, this section is included to make this point explicit.

2 The following examples illustrate the effect of this section:

Example 1. Buyer buys 1000 shares of XYZ Co. common stock through Buyer's broker Able & Co. to be held in Buyer's securities account. In settlement of the trade, the selling broker delivers to Able a security certificate in street name, indorsed in blank, for 1000 shares XYZ Co. stock, which Able holds in its vault. Able credits Buyer's account for securities in that amount. Section 8-116 specifies that Able is a purchaser of the XYZ Co. stock certificate, and gave value for it. Thus, Able can obtain the benefit of Section 8-303, which protects purchasers for value, if it satisfies the other requirements of that section.

Example 2. Buyer buys 1000 shares XYZ Co. common stock through Buyer's broker Able & Co. to be held in Buyer's securities account. The trade is settled by crediting 1000 shares XYZ Co. stock to Able's account at Clearing Corporation. Able credits Buyer's account for securities in that amount. When Clearing Corporation credits Able's account, Able acquires a security entitlement under Section 8-501. Section 8-116 specifies that Able acquired this security entitlement for value. Thus, Able can obtain the benefit of Section 8-502, which protects persons who acquire security entitlements for value, if it satisfies the other requirements of that section.

Example 3. Thief steals a certificated bearer bond from Owner. Thief sends the certificate to his broker Able & Co. to be held in his securities account, and Able credits Thief's account for the bond. Section 8-116 specifies that Able is a purchaser of the bond and gave value for it. Thus, Able can obtain the benefit of Section 8-303, which protects purchasers for value, if it satisfies the other requirements of that section.

Definitional Cross References:

"Financial asset". Section 8-102(a)(9).

"Securities intermediary". Section 8-102(a)(14).

"Security entitlement". Section 8-102(a)(17).

"Entitlement holder". Section 8-102(a)(7).

PART 2

ISSUE AND ISSUER

§ 8-201. Issuer.

(a) With respect to an obligation on or a defense to a security, an "issuer" includes a person that:

(1) places or authorizes the placing of its name on a security certificate, other than as authenticating trustee, registrar, transfer agent, or the like, to evidence a share, participation, or other interest in its property or in an enterprise, or to evidence its duty to perform an obligation represented by the certificate;

(2) creates a share, participation, or other interest in its property or in an enterprise, or undertakes an obligation, that is an uncertificated security;

(3) directly or indirectly creates a fractional interest in its rights or property, if the fractional interest is represented by a security certificate; or

(4) becomes responsible for, or in place of, another person described as an issuer in this section.

(b) With respect to an obligation on or defense to a security, a guarantor is an issuer to the extent of its guaranty, whether or not its obligation is noted on a security certificate.

(c) With respect to a registration of a transfer, issuer means a person on whose behalf transfer books are maintained.

Official Comment

1. The definition of "issuer" in this section functions primarily to describe the persons whose defenses may be cut off under the rules in Part 2. In large measure it simply tracks the language of the definition of security in Section 8-102(a)(15).

2. Subsection (b) distinguishes the obligations of a guarantor as issuer from those of the principal obligor. However, it does not exempt the guarantor from the impact of subsection (d) of Section 8-202. Whether or not the obligation of the guarantor is noted on the security is immaterial. Typically, guarantors are parent corporations, or stand in some similar relationship to the principal obligor. If that relationship existed at the time the security was originally issued the guaranty would probably have been noted on the security. However, if the relationship arose afterward, e.g., through a purchase of stock or properties, or through merger or consolidation, probably the notation would not have been made. Nonetheless, the holder of the security is entitled to the benefit of the obligation of the guarantor.

3. Subsection (c) narrows the definition of "issuer" for purposes of Part 4 of this Article (registration of transfer). It is supplemented by Section 8-407.

Definitional Cross References:

"Person". Section 1-201(30).
"Security". Section 8-102(a0(15).
"Security certificate". Section 8-102(a)(16).
"Uncertificated security". Section 8-102(a)(18).

§ 8-202. Issuer's Responsibility and Defenses; Notice of Defect or Defense.

(a) Even against a purchaser for value and without notice, the terms of a certificated security include terms stated on the certificate and terms made part of the security by reference on the certificate to another instrument, indenture, or document or to a constitution, statute, ordinance, rule, regulation, order, or the like, to the extent the terms referred to do not conflict with terms stated on the certificate. A reference under this subsection does not of itself charge a purchaser for value with notice of a defect going to the validity of the security, even if the certificate expressly states that a person accepting it admits notice. The terms of an uncertificated security include those stated in any instrument, indenture, or document or in a constitution, statute, ordinance, rule, regulation, order, or the like, pursuant to which the security is issued.

(b) The following rules apply if an issuer asserts that a security is not valid:

(1) A security other than one issued by a government or governmental subdivision, agency, or instrumentality, even though issued with a defect going to its validity, is valid in the hands of a purchaser for value and without notice of the particular defect unless the defect involves a violation of a constitutional provision. In that case, the security is valid in the hands of a purchaser for value and without notice of the defect, other than one who takes by original issue.

(2) Paragraph (1) applies to an issuer that is a government or governmental subdivision, agency, or instrumentality only if there has been substantial compliance with the legal requirements governing the issue or the issuer has received a substantial consideration for the issue as a whole or for the particular security and a stated purpose of the issue is one for which the issuer has power to borrow money or issue the security.

(c) Except as otherwise provided in Section 8-205, lack of genuineness of a certificated security is a complete defense, even against a purchaser for value and without notice.

(d) All other defenses of the issuer of a security, including nondelivery and conditional delivery of a certificated security, are ineffective against a purchaser for value who has taken the certificated security without notice of the particular defense.

(e) This section does not affect the right of a party to cancel a contract for a security "when, as and if issued" or "when distributed" in the event of a material change in the character of the security that is the subject of the contract or in the plan or arrangement pursuant to which the security is to be issued or distributed.

(f) If a security is held by a securities intermediary against whom an entitlement holder has a security entitlement with respect to the security, the issuer may not assert any defense that the issuer could not assert if the entitlement holder held the security directly.

Official Comment

1. In this Article the rights of the purchaser for value without notice are divided into two aspects, those against the issuer, and those against other claimants to the security. Part 2 of this Article, and especially this section, deal with rights against the issuer.

Subsection (a) states, in accordance with the prevailing case law, the right of the issuer (who prepares the text of the security) to include terms incorporated by adequate reference to an extrinsic source, so long as the terms so incorporated do not conflict with the stated terms. Thus, the standard practice of referring in a bond or debenture to the trust indenture under which it is issued without spelling out its necessarily complex and lengthy provisions is approved. Every stock certificate refers in some manner to the charter or articles of incorporation of the issuer. At least where there is more than one class of stock authorized applicable corporation codes specifically require a statement or summary as to preferences, voting powers and the like. References to constitutions, statutes, ordinances, rules, regulations or orders are not so common, except in the obligations of governments or governmental agencies or units; but where appropriate they fit into the rule here stated.

Courts have generally held that an issuer is estopped from denying representations made in the text of a security. *Delaware–New Jersey Ferry Co. v. Leeds,* 21 Del.Ch. 279, 186 A. 913 (1936). Nor is a defect in form or the invalidity of a security normally available to the issuer as a defense. *Bonini v. Family Theatre Corporation,* 327 Pa. 273, 194 A. 498 (1937); *First National Bank of Fairbanks v. Alaska Airmotive,* 119 F.2d 267 (C.C.A.Alaska 1941).

2. The rule in subsection (a) requiring that the terms of a security be noted or referred to on the certificate is based on practices and expectations in the direct holding system for certificated securities. This rule does not express a general rule or policy that the terms of a security are effective only if they are communicated to beneficial owners in some particular fashion. Rather, subsection (a) is based on the principle that a purchaser who does obtain a certificate is entitled to assume that the terms of the security have been noted or referred to on the certificate. That policy does not come into play in a securities holding system in which purchasers do not take delivery of certificates.

The provisions of subsection (a) concerning notation of terms on security certificates are necessary only because paper certificates play such an important role for certificated securities that a purchaser should be protected against assertion of any defenses or rights that are not noted on the certificate. No similar problem exists with respect to uncertificated securities. The last sentence of subsection (a) is, strictly speaking, unnecessary, since it only recognizes the fact that the terms of an uncertificated security are determined by whatever other law or agreement governs the security. It is included only to preclude any inference that uncertificated securities are subject to any requirement analogous to the requirement of notation of terms on security certificates.

The rule of subsection (a) applies to the indirect holding system only in the sense that if a certificated security has been delivered to the clearing corporation or other securities intermediary, the terms of the security should be noted or referred to on the certificate. If the security is uncertificated, that principle does not apply even at the issuer-clearing corporation level. The beneficial owners who hold securities through the clearing corporation are bound by the terms of the security, even though they do not actually see the certificate. Since entitlement holders in an indirect holding system have not taken delivery of certificates, the policy of subsection (a) does not apply.

3. The penultimate sentence of subsection (a) and all of subsection (b) embody the concept that it is the duty of the issuer, not of the purchaser, to make sure that the security complies with the law governing its issue. The penultimate sentence of subsection (a) makes clear that the issuer cannot, by incorporating a reference to a statute or other document, charge the purchaser with notice of the security's invalidity. Subsection (b) gives to a purchaser for value without notice of the defect the right to enforce the security against the issuer despite the presence of a defect that otherwise would render the security invalid. There are three circumstances in which a purchaser does not gain such rights: first, if the defect involves a violation of constitutional provisions, these rights accrue only to a subsequent purchaser, that is, one who takes other than by original issue. This Article leaves to the law of each particular State the rights of a purchaser on original issue of a security with a constitutional defect. No negative implication is intended by the explicit grant of rights to a subsequent purchaser.

Second, governmental issuers are distinguished in subsection (b) from other issuers as a matter of public policy, and additional safeguards are imposed before governmental issues are validated. Governmental issuers are estopped from asserting defenses only if there has been substantial compliance with the legal requirements governing the issue or if substantial consideration has been received and a stated purpose of the issue is one for which the issuer has power to borrow money or issue the security. The purpose of the substantial compliance requirement is to make certain that a mere technicality as, e.g., in the manner of publishing election notices, shall not be a ground for depriving an innocent purchaser of rights in the security. The policy is here adopted of such cases as *Tommie v. City of Gadsden*, 229 Ala. 521, 158 So. 763 (1935), in which minor discrepancies in the form of the election ballot used were overlooked and the bonds were declared valid since there had been substantial compliance with the statute.

A long and well established line of federal cases recognizes the principle of estoppel in favor of purchasers for value without notices where municipalities issue bonds containing recitals of compliance with governing constitutional and statutory provisions, made by the municipal authorities entrusted with determining such compliance. *Chaffee County v. Potter*, 142 U.S. 355 (1892); *Oregon v. Jennings*, 119 U.S. 74 (1886); *Gunnison County Commissioners v. Rollins*, 173 U.S. 255 (1898). This rule has been qualified, however, by requiring that the municipality have power to issue the security. *Anthony v. County of Jasper*, 101 U.S. 693 (1879); *Town of South Ottawa v. Perkins*, 94 U.S. 260 (1876). This section follows the case law trend, simplifying the rule by setting up two conditions for an estoppel against a governmental issuer: (1) substantial consideration given, and (2) power in the issuer to borrow money or issue the security for the stated purpose. As a practical matter the problem of policing governmental issuers has been alleviated by the present practice of requiring legal opinions as to the validity of the issue. The bulk of the case law on this point is nearly 100 years old and it may be assumed that the question now seldom arises.

Section 8-210, regarding overissue, provides the third exception to the rule that an innocent purchase for value takes a valid security despite the presence of a defect that would otherwise give rise to invalidity. See that section and its Comment for further explanation.

4. Subsection (e) is included to make clear that this section does not affect the presently recognized right of either party to a "when, as and if" or "when distributed" contract to cancel the contract on substantial change.

5. Subsection (f) has been added because the introduction of the security entitlement concept requires some adaptation of the Part 2 rules, particularly those that distinguish between purchasers who take by original issue and subsequent purchasers. The basic concept of Part 2 is to apply to investment securities the principle of negotiable instruments law that an obligor is precluded from asserting most defenses against purchasers for value without notice. Section 8-202 describes in some detail which defenses issuers can raise against purchasers for value and subsequent purchasers for value. Because these rules were drafted with the direct holding system in mind, some interpretive problems might be presented in applying them to the indirect holding. For example, if a municipality issues a bond in book-entry only form, the only direct "purchaser" of that bond would be the clearing corporation. The policy of precluding the issuer from asserting defenses is, however, equally applicable. Subsection (f) is designed to ensure that the defense preclusion rules developed for the direct holding system will also apply to the indirect holding system.

Definitional Cross References:

"Certificated security". Section 8-102(a)(4).

"Notice". Section 1-201(25).

"Purchaser". Sections 1-201(33) & 8-116.

"Security". Section 8-102(a)(15).

"Uncertificated security". Section 8-102(a)(18).

"Value". Sections 1-201(44) & 8-116.

§ 8-203. Staleness as Notice of Defect or Defense.

After an act or event, other than a call that has been revoked, creating a right to immediate performance of the principal obligation represented by a certificated security or setting a date on or after which the security is to be presented or surrendered for redemption or exchange, a purchaser is charged with notice of any defect in its issue or defense of the issuer, if the act or event:

(1) requires the payment of money, the delivery of a certificated security, the registration of transfer of an uncertificated security, or any of them on presentation or surrender of the security certificate, the money or security is available on the date set for payment or exchange, and the purchaser takes the security more than one year after that date; or

(2) is not covered by paragraph (1) and the purchaser takes the security more than two years after the date set for surrender or presentation or the date on which performance became due.

Official Comment

1. The problem of matured or called securities is here dealt with in terms of the effect of such events in giving notice of the issuer's defenses and not in terms of "negotiability". The substance of this section applies only to certificated securities because certificates may be transferred to a purchaser by delivery after the security has matured, been called, or become redeemable or exchangeable. It is contemplated that uncertificated securities which have matured or been called will merely be canceled on the books of the issuer and the proceeds sent to the registered owner. Uncertificated securities which have become redeemable or exchangeable, at the option of the owner, may be transferred to a purchaser, but the transfer is effectuated only by registration of transfer, thus necessitating communication with the issuer. If defects or defenses in such securities exist,

the issuer will necessarily have the opportunity to bring them to the attention of the purchaser.

2. The fact that a security certificate is in circulation long after it has been called for redemption or exchange must give rise to the question in a purchaser's mind as to why it has not been surrendered. After the lapse of a reasonable period of time a purchaser can no longer claim "no reason to know" of any defects or irregularities in its issue. Where funds are available for the redemption the security certificate is normally turned in more promptly and a shorter time is set as the "reasonable period" than is set where funds are not available.

Defaulted certificated securities may be traded on financial markets in the same manner as unmatured and undefaulted instruments and a purchaser might not be placed upon notice of irregularity by the mere fact of default. An issuer, however, should at some point be placed in a position to determine definitely its liability on an invalid or improper issue, and for this purpose a security under this section becomes "stale" two years after the default. A different rule applies when the question is notice not of issuer's defenses but of claims of ownership. Section 8-105 and Comment.

3. Nothing in this section is designed to extend the life of preferred stocks called for redemption as "shares of stock" beyond the redemption date. After such a call, the security represents only a right to the funds set aside for redemption.

Definitional Cross References:

"Certificated security". Section 8-102(a)(4).

"Notice". Section 1-201(25).

"Purchaser". Sections 1-201(33) & 8-116.

"Security". Section 8-102(a)(15).

"Security certificate". Section 8-102(a)(16).

"Uncertificated security". Section 8-102(a)(18).

§ 8-204. Effect of Issuer's Restriction on Transfer.

A restriction on transfer of a security imposed by the issuer, even if otherwise lawful, is ineffective against a person without knowledge of the restriction unless:

(1) the security is certificated and the restriction is noted conspicuously on the security certificate; or

(2) the security is uncertificated and the registered owner has been notified of the restriction.

Official Comment

1. Restrictions on transfer of securities are imposed by issuers in a variety of circumstances and for a variety of purposes, such as to retain control of a close corporation or to ensure compliance with federal securities laws. Other law determines whether such restrictions are permissible. This section deals only with the consequences of failure to note the restriction on a security certificate.

This section imposes no bar to enforcement of a restriction on transfer against a person who has actual knowledge of it.

2. A restriction on transfer of a certificated security is ineffective against a person without knowledge of the restriction unless the restriction is noted conspicuously on the certificate. The word "noted" is used to make clear that the restriction need not be set forth in full text. Refusal by an issuer to register a transfer on the basis of an unnoted restriction would be a violation of the issuer's duty to register under Section 8-401.

3. The policy of this section is the same as in Section 8-202. A purchaser who takes delivery of a certificated securi-

ty is entitled to rely on the terms stated on the certificate. That policy obviously does not apply to uncertificated securities. For uncertificated securities, this section requires only that the registered owner has been notified of the restriction. Suppose, for example, that A is the registered owner of an uncertificated security, and that the issuer has notified A of a restriction on transfer. A agrees to sell the security to B, in violation of the restriction. A completes a written instruction directing the issuer to register transfer to B, and B pays A for the security at the time A delivers the instruction to B. A does not inform B of the restriction, and B does not otherwise have notice or knowledge of it at the time B pays and receives the instruction. B presents the instruction to the issuer, but the issuer refuses to register the transfer on the grounds that it would violate the restriction. The issuer has complied with this section, because it did notify the registered owner A of the restriction. The issuer's refusal to register transfer is not wrongful. B has an action against A for breach of transfer warranty, see Section 8-108(b)(4)(iii). B's mistake was treating an uncertificated security transaction in the fashion appropriate only for a certificated security. The mechanism for transfer of uncertificated securities is registration of transfer on the books of the issuer; handing over an instruction only initiates the process. The purchaser should make arrangements to ensure that the price is not paid until it knows that the issuer has or will register transfer.

4. In the indirect holding system, investors neither take physical delivery of security certificates nor have uncertificated securities registered in their names. So long as the requirements of this section have been satisfied at the level of the relationship between the issuer and the securities intermediary that is a direct holder, this section does not preclude the issuer from enforcing a restriction on transfer. See Section 8-202(a) and Comment 2 thereto.

5. This section deals only with restrictions imposed by the issuer. Restrictions imposed by statute are not affected. See *Quiner v. Marblehead Social Co.,* 10 Mass. 476 (1813); *Madison Bank v. Price,* 79 Kan. 289, 100 P. 280 (1909); *Healey v. Steele Center Creamery Ass'n,* 115 Minn. 451, 133 N.W. 69 (1911). Nor does it deal with private agreements between stockholders containing restrictive covenants as to the sale of the security.

Definitional Cross References:

"Certificated security". Section 8-102(a)(4).
"Conspicuous". Section 1-201(10).
"Issuer". Section 8-201.
"Knowledge". Section 1-201(25).
"Notify". Section 1-201(25).
"Purchaser". Sections 1-201(33) & 8-116.
"Security". Section 8-102(a)(15).
"Security certificate". Section 8-102(a)(16).
"Uncertificated security". Section 8-102(a)(18).

§ 8-205. Effect of Unauthorized Signature on Security Certificate.

An unauthorized signature placed on a security certificate before or in the course of issue is ineffective, but the signature is effective in favor of a purchaser for value of the certificated security if the purchaser is without notice of the lack of authority and the signing has been done by:

(1) an authenticating trustee, registrar, transfer agent, or other person entrusted by the issuer with the signing of the security certificate or of similar security certificates, or the immediate preparation for signing of any of them; or

(2) an employee of the issuer, or of any of the persons listed in paragraph (1), entrusted with responsible handling of the security certificate.

Official Comment

1. The problem of forged or unauthorized signatures may arise where an employee of the issuer, transfer agent, or registrar has access to securities which the employee is required to prepare for issue by affixing the corporate seal or by adding a signature necessary for issue. This section is based upon the issuer's duty to avoid the negligent entrusting of securities to such persons. Issuers have long been held responsible for signatures placed upon securities by parties whom they have held out to the public as authorized to prepare such securities. See *Fifth Avenue Bank of New York v. The Forty–Second & Grand Street Ferry Railroad Co.,* 137 N.Y. 231, 33 N.E. 378, 19 L.R.A. 331, 33 Am.St.Rep. 712 (1893); *Jarvis v. Manhattan Beach Co.,* 148 N.Y. 652, 43 N.E. 68, 31 L.R.A. 776, 51 Am.St. Rep. 727 (1896). The "apparent authority" concept of some of the case-law, however, is here extended and this section expressly rejects the technical distinction, made by courts reluctant to recognize forged signatures, between cases where forgers sign signatures they are authorized to sign under proper circumstances and those in which they sign signatures they are never authorized to sign. *Citizens' & Southern National Bank v. Trust Co. of Georgia,* 50 Ga.App. 681, 179 S.E. 278 (1935). Normally the purchaser is not in a position to determine which signature a forger, entrusted with the preparation of securities, has "apparent authority" to sign. The issuer, on the other hand, can protect itself against such fraud by the careful selection and bonding of agents and employees, or by action over against transfer agents and registrars who in turn may bond their personnel.

2. The issuer cannot be held liable for the honesty of employees not entrusted, directly or indirectly, with the signing, preparation, or responsible handling of similar securities and whose possible commission of forgery it has no reason to anticipate. The result in such cases as *Hudson Trust Co. v. American Linseed Co.,* 232 N.Y. 350, 134 N.E. 178 (1922), and *Dollar Savings Fund & Trust Co. v. Pittsburgh Plate Glass Co.,* 213 Pa. 307, 62 A. 916, 5 Ann.Cas. 248 (1906) is here adopted.

3. This section is not concerned with forged or unauthorized indorsements, but only with unauthorized signatures of issuers, transfer agents, etc., placed upon security certificates during the course of their issue. The protection here stated is available to all purchasers for value without notice and not merely to subsequent purchasers.

Definitional Cross References:

"Certificated security". Section 8–102(a)(4).

"Issuer". Section 8–201.

"Notice". Section 1–201(25).

"Purchaser". Sections 1–201(33) & 8–116.

"Security certificate". Section 8–102(a)(14).

"Unauthorized signature". Section 1–201(43).

§ 8–206. Completion of Alteration of Security Certificate.

(a) If a security certificate contains the signatures necessary to its issue or transfer but is incomplete in any other respect:

(1) any person may complete it by filling in the blanks as authorized; and

(2) even if the blanks are incorrectly filled in, the security certificate as completed is enforceable by a purchaser who took it for value and without notice of the incorrectness.

(b) A complete security certificate that has been improperly altered, even if fraudulently, remains enforceable, but only according to its original terms.

Official Comment

1. The problem of forged or unauthorized signatures necessary for the issue or transfer of a security is not involved here, and a person in possession of a blank certificate is not, by this section, given authority to fill in blanks with such signatures. Completion of blanks left in a transfer instruction is dealt with elsewhere (Section 8–305(a)).

2. Blanks left upon issue of a security certificate are the only ones dealt with here, and a purchaser for value without notice is protected. A purchaser is not in a good position to determine whether blanks were completed by the issuer or by some person not authorized to complete them. On the other hand the issuer can protect itself by not placing its signature on the writing until the blanks are completed or, if it does sign before all blanks are completed, by carefully selecting the agents and employees to whom it entrusts the writing after authentication. With respect to a security certificate that is completed by the issuer but later is altered, the issuer has done everything it can to protect the purchaser and thus is not charged with the terms as altered. However, it is charged according to the original terms, since it is not thereby prejudiced. If the completion or alteration is obviously irregular, the purchaser may not qualify as a purchaser who took without notice under this section.

3. Only the purchaser who physically takes the certificate is directly protected. However, a transferee may receive protection indirectly through Section 8–302(a).

4. The protection granted a purchaser for value without notice under this section is modified to the extent that an overissue may result where an incorrect amount is inserted into a blank (Section 8–210).

Definitional Cross References:

"Notice". Section 1–201(25).

"Purchaser". Sections 1–201(33) & 8–116.

"Security certificate". Section 8–102(a)(16).

"Unauthorized signature". Section 1–201(43).

"Value". Sections 1–201(44) & 8–116.

§ 8–207. Rights and Duties of Issuer with Respect to Registered Owners.

(a) Before due presentment for registration of transfer of a certificated security in registered form or of an instruction requesting registration of transfer of an uncertificated security, the issuer or indenture trustee may treat the registered owner as the person exclusively entitled to vote, receive notifications, and otherwise exercise all the rights and powers of an owner.

(b) This Article does not affect the liability of the registered owner of a security for a call, assessment, or the like.

Official Comment

1. Subsection (a) states the issuer's right to treat the registered owner of a security as the person entitled to exercise all the rights of an owner. This right of the issuer is limited by the provisions of Part 4 of this article. Once there has been due presentation for registration of transfer, the issuer has a duty to register ownership in the name of the transferee. Section 8–401. Thus its right to treat the old registered owner as exclusively entitled to the rights of ownership must cease.

The issuer may under this section make distributions of money or securities to the registered owners of securities without requiring further proof of ownership, provided that such distributions are distributable to the owners of all securities of the same issue and the terms of the security do not require surrender of a security certificate as a condition of payment or exchange. Any such distribution shall constitute a defense against a claim for the same distribution by a person, even if that person is in possession of the security certificate and is a protected purchaser of the security. See PEB Commentary No. 4, dated March 10, 1990.

2. Subsection (a) is permissive and does not require that the issuer deal exclusively with the registered owner. It is free to require proof of ownership before paying out dividends or the like if it chooses to. *Barbato v. Breeze Corporation,* 128 N.J.L. 309, 26 A.2d 53 (1942).

3. This section does not operate to determine who is finally entitled to exercise voting and other rights or to receive payments and distributions. The parties are still free to incorporate their own arrangements as to these matters in seller-purchaser agreements which may be definitive as between them.

4. No change in existing state laws as to the liability of registered owners for calls and assessments is here intended; nor is anything in this section designed to estop record holders from denying ownership when assessments are levied if they are otherwise entitled to do so under state law. See *State ex rel. Squire v. Murfey, Blosson & Co.,* 131 Ohio St. 289, 2 N.E.2d 866 (1936); *Willing v. Delaplaine,* 23 F.Supp. 579 (1937).

5. No interference is intended with the common practice of closing the transfer books or taking a record date for dividend, voting, and other purposes, as provided for in by-laws, charters, and statutes.

Definitional Cross References:

"Certificated security". Section 8-102(a)(4).

"Instruction". Section 8-102(a)(12).

"Issuer". Section 8-201.

"Registered form". Section 8-102(a)(13).

"Security". Section 8-102(a)(15).

"Uncertificated security". Section 8-102(a)(18).

§ 8-208. Effect of Signature of Authenticating Trustee, Registrar, or Transfer Agent.

(a) A person signing a security certificate as authenticating trustee, registrar, transfer agent, or the like, warrants to a purchaser for value of the certificated security, if the purchaser is without notice of a particular defect, that:

(1) the certificate is genuine;

(2) the person's own participation in the issue of the security is within the person's capacity and within the scope of the authority received by the person from the issuer; and

(3) the person has reasonable grounds to believe that the certificated security is in the form and within the amount the issuer is authorized to issue.

(b) Unless otherwise agreed, a person signing under subsection (a) does not assume responsibility for the validity of the security in other respects.

Official Comment

1. The warranties here stated express the current understanding and prevailing case law as to the effect of the signatures of authenticating trustees, transfer agents, and registrars. See *Jarvis v. Manhattan Beach Co.,* 148 N.Y. 652, 43 N.E. 68, 31 L.R.A. 776, 51 Am.St.Rep. 727 (1896). Although it has generally been

regarded as the particular obligation of the transfer agent to determine whether securities are in proper form as provided by the by-laws and Articles of Incorporation, neither a registrar nor an authenticating trustee should properly place a signature upon a certificate without determining whether it is at least regular on its face. The obligations of these parties in this respect have therefore been made explicit in terms of due care. See *Feldmeier v. Mortgage Securities, Inc.*, 34 Cal.App.2d 201, 93 P.2d 593 (1939).

2. Those cases which hold that an authenticating trustee is not liable for any defect in the mortgage or property which secures the bond or for any fraudulent misrepresentations made by the issuer are not here affected since these matters do not involve the genuineness or proper form of the security. *Ainsa v. Mercantile Trust Co.*, 174 Cal. 504, 163 P. 898 (1917); *Tschetinian v. City Trust Co.*, 186 N.Y. 432, 79 N.E. 401 (1906); *Davidge v. Guardian Trust Co. of New York*, 203 N.Y. 331, 96 N.E. 751 (1911).

3. The charter or an applicable statute may affect the capacity of a bank or other corporation undertaking to act as an authenticating trustee, registrar, or transfer agent. See, for example, the Federal Reserve Act (U.S.C.A., Title 12, Banks and Banking, Section 248) under which the Board of Governors of the Federal Reserve Bank is authorized to grant special permits to National Banks permitting them to act as trustees. Such corporations are therefore held to certify as to their legal capacity to act as well as to their authority.

4. Authenticating trustees, registrars, and transfer agents have normally been held liable for an issue in excess of the authorized amount. *Jarvis v. Manhattan Beach Co.*, supra; *Mullen v. Eastern Trust & Banking Co.*, 108 Me. 498, 81 A. 948 (1911). In imposing upon these parties a duty of due care with respect to the amount they are authorized to help issue, this section does not necessarily validate the security, but merely holds persons responsible for the excess issue liable in damages for any loss suffered by the purchaser.

5. Aside from questions of genuineness and excess issue, these parties are not held to certify as to the validity of the security unless they specifically undertake to do so. The case law which has recognized a unique responsibility on the transfer agent's part to testify as to the validity of any security which it countersigns is rejected.

6. This provision does not prevent a transfer agent or issuer from agreeing with a registrar of stock to protect the registrar in respect of the genuineness and proper form of a security certificate signed by the issuer or the transfer agent or both. Nor does it interfere with proper indemnity arrangements between the issuer and trustees, transfer agents, registrars, and the like.

7. An unauthorized signature is a signature for purposes of this section if and only if it is made effective by Section 8–205.

Definitional Cross References:

"Certificated security". Section 8–102(a)(4).
"Genuine". Section 1–201(18).
"Issuer". Section 8–201.
"Notice". Section 1–201(25).
"Purchaser". Sections 1–201(33) & 8–116.
"Security". Section 8–102(a)(15).
"Security certificate". Section 8–102(a)(16).
"Uncertificated security". Section 8–102(a)(18).
"Value". Sections 1–201(44) & 8–116.

§ 8–209. Issuer's Lien.

A lien in favor of an issuer upon a certificated security is valid against a purchaser only if the right of the issuer to the lien is noted conspicuously on the security certificate.

Official Comment

This section is similar to Sections 8-202 and 8-204 which require that the terms of a certificated security and any restriction on transfer imposed by the issuer be noted on the security certificate. This section differs from those two sections in that the purchaser's knowledge of the issuer's claim is irrelevant. "Noted" makes clear that the text of the lien provisions need not be set forth in full. However, this would not override a provision of an applicable corporation code requiring statement in haec verba. This section does not apply to uncertificated securities. It applies to the indirect holding system in the same fashion as Sections 8-202 and 8-204, see Comment 2 to Section 8-202.

Definitional Cross References:

"Certificated security". Section 8-102(a)(4).

"Issuer". Section 8-201.

"Purchaser". Sections 1-201(33) & 8-116.

"Security". Section 8-102(a)(15).

"Security certificate". Section 8-102(a)(16).

§ 8-210. Overissue.

(a) In this section, "overissue" means the issue of securities in excess of the amount the issuer has corporate power to issue, but an overissue does not occur if appropriate action has cured the overissue.

(b) Except as otherwise provided in subsections (c) and (d), the provisions of this Article which validate a security or compel its issue or reissue do not apply to the extent that validation, issue, or reissue would result in overissue.

(c) If an identical security not constituting an overissue is reasonably available for purchase, a person entitled to issue or validation may compel the issuer to purchase the security and deliver it if certificated or register its transfer if uncertificated, against surrender of any security certificate the person holds.

(d) If a security is not reasonably available for purchase, a person entitled to issue or validation may recover from the issuer the price the person or the last purchaser for value paid for it with interest from the date of the person's demand.

Official Comment

1. Deeply embedded in corporation law is the conception that "corporate power" to issue securities stems from the statute, either general or special, under which the corporation is organized. Corporation codes universally require that the charter or articles of incorporation state, at least as to capital shares, maximum limits in terms of number of shares or total dollar capital. Historically, special incorporation statutes are similarly drawn and sometimes similarly limit the face amount of authorized debt securities. The theory is that issue of securities in excess of the authorized amounts is prohibited. See, for example, *McWilliams v. Geddes & Moss Undertaking Co.,* 169 So. 894 (1936, La.); *Crawford v. Twin City Oil Co.,* 216 Ala. 216, 113 So. 61 (1927); *New York and New Haven R.R. Co. v. Schuyler,* 34 N.Y. 30 (1865). This conception persists despite modern corporation codes under which, by action of directors and stockholders, additional shares can be authorized by charter amendment and thereafter issued. This section does not give a person entitled to validation, issue, or reissue of a security, the right to compel amendment of the charter to authorize additional shares.

Therefore, in a case where issue of an additional security would require charter amendment, the plaintiff is limited to the two alternate remedies set forth in subsections (c) and (d). The last clause of subsection (a), which is added in Revised Article 8, does, however, recognize that under modern conditions, overissue may be a relatively minor technical problem that can be cured by appropriate action under governing corporate law.

2. Where an identical security is reasonably available for purchase, whether because traded on an organized market, or because one or more security owners may be willing to sell at a not unreasonable price, the issuer, although unable to issue additional shares, will be able to purchase them and may be compelled to follow that procedure. *West v. Tintic Standard Mining Co.,* 71 Utah 158, 263 P. 490 (1928).

3. The right to recover damages from an issuer who has permitted an overissue to occur is well settled. *New York and New Haven R.R. Co. v. Schuyler,* 34 N.Y. 30 (1865). The measure of such damages, however, has been open to question, some courts basing them upon the value of stock at the time registration is refused; some upon the value at the time of trial; and some upon the highest value between the time of refusal and the time of trial. *Allen v. South Boston Railroad,* 150 Mass. 200, 22 N.E. 917, 5 L.R.A. 716, 15 Am.St.Rep. 185 (1889); *Commercial Bank v. Kortright,* 22 Wend. (N.Y.) 348 (1839). The purchase price of the security to the last purchaser who gave value for it is here adopted as being the fairest means of reducing the possibility of speculation by the purchaser. Interest may be recovered by the best available measure of compensation for delay.

Definitional Cross References:

"Issuer". Section 8-201.

"Security". Section 8-102(a)(15).

"Security certificate". Section 8-102(a)(16).

"Uncertificated security". Section 8-102(a)(18).

PART 3

TRANSFER OF CERTIFICATED AND UNCERTIFICATED SECURITIES

§ 8-301. Delivery.

(a) Delivery of a certificated security to a purchaser occurs when:

(1) the purchaser acquires possession of the security certificate;

(2) another person, other than a securities intermediary, either acquires possession of the security certificate on behalf of the purchaser or, having previously acquired possession of the certificate, acknowledges that it holds for the purchaser; or

(3) a securities intermediary acting on behalf of the purchaser acquires possession of the security certificate, only if the certificate is in registered form and has been specially indorsed to the purchaser by an effective indorsement.

(b) Delivery of an uncertificated security to a purchaser occurs when:

(1) the issuer registers the purchaser as the registered owner, upon original issue or registration of transfer; or

(2) another person, other than a securities intermediary, either becomes the registered owner of the uncertificated security on behalf of the

purchaser or, having previously become the registered owner, acknowledges that it holds for the purchaser.

Official Comment

1. This section specifies the requirements for "delivery" of securities. Delivery is used in Article 8 to describe the formal steps necessary for a purchaser to acquire a direct interest in a security under this Article. The concept of delivery refers to the implementation of a transaction, not the legal categorization of the transaction which is consummated by delivery. Issuance and transfer are different kinds of transaction, though both may be implemented by delivery. Sale and pledge are different kinds of transfers, but both may be implemented by delivery.

2. Subsection (a) defines delivery with respect to certificated securities. Paragraph (1) deals with simple cases where purchasers themselves acquire physical possession of certificates. Paragraphs (2) and (3) of subsection (a) specify the circumstances in which delivery to a purchaser can occur although the certificate is in the possession of a person other than the purchaser. Paragraph (2) contains the general rule that a purchaser can take delivery through another person, so long as the other person is actually acting on behalf of the purchaser or acknowledges that it is holding on behalf of the purchaser. Paragraph (2) does not apply to acquisition of possession by a securities intermediary, because a person who holds securities through a securities account acquires a security entitlement, rather than having a direct interest. See Section 8-501. Subsection (a)(3) specifies the limited circumstances in which delivery of security certificates to a securities intermediary is treated as a delivery to the customer.

3. Subsection (b) defines delivery with respect to uncertificated securities. Use of the term "delivery" with respect to uncertificated securities, does, at least on first hearing, seem a bit solecistic. The word "delivery" is, however, routinely used in the securities business in a broader sense than manual tradition. For example, settlement by entries on the books of a clearing corporation is commonly called "delivery," as in the expression "delivery versus payment." The diction of this section has the advantage of using the same term for uncertificated securities as for certificated securities, for which delivery is conventional usage. Paragraph (1) of subsection (b) provides that delivery occurs when the purchaser becomes the registered owner of an uncertificated security, either upon original issue or registration of transfer. Paragraph (2) provides for delivery of an uncertificated security through a third person, in a fashion analogous to subsection (a)(2).

Definitional Cross References:

"Certificated security". Section 8-102(a)(4).

"Effective". Section 8-107.

"Issuer". Section 8-201.

"Purchaser". Sections 1-201(33) & 8-116.

"Registered form". Section 8-102(a)(13).

"Securities intermediary". Section 8-102(a)(14).

"Security certificate". Section 8-102(a)(16).

"Special indorsement". Section 8-304(a).

"Uncertificated security". Section 8-102(a)(18).

§ 8-302. Rights of Purchaser.

(a) Except as otherwise provided in subsections (b) and (c), upon delivery of a certificated or uncertificated security to a purchaser, the purchaser acquires all rights in the security that the transferor had or had power to transfer.

(b) A purchaser of a limited interest acquires rights only to the extent of the interest purchased.

(c) A purchaser of a certificated security who as a previous holder had notice of an adverse claim does not improve its position by taking from a protected purchaser.

Official Comment

1. Subsection (a) provides that if a certificated or uncertificated security is delivered (Section 8-301) to a purchaser in a transfer, the purchaser acquires all rights that the transferor had or had power to transfer. This statement of the familiar "shelter" principle is qualified by the exceptions that a purchaser of a limited interest acquires only that interest, subsection (b), and that a person who does not qualify as a protected purchaser cannot improve its position by taking from a subsequent protected purchaser, subsection (c).

2. Although this section provides that a purchaser acquires a property interest in a certificated or uncertificated security upon "delivery," it does not state that a person can acquire an interest in a security only by delivery. Article 8 is not a comprehensive codification of all of the law governing the creation or transfer of interests in securities. For example, the grant of a security interest is a transfer of a property interest, but the formal steps necessary to effectuate such a transfer are governed by Article 9 not by Article 8. Under the Article 9 rules, a security interest in a certificated or uncertificated security can be created by execution of a security agreement under Section 9-203 and can be perfected by filing. A transfer of an Article 9 security interest can be implemented by an Article 8 delivery, but need not be.

Similarly, Article 8 does not determine whether a property interest in certificated or uncertificated security is acquired under other law, such as the law of gifts, trusts, or equitable remedies. Nor does Article 8 deal with transfers by operation of law. For example, transfers from decedent to administrator, from ward to guardian, and from bankrupt to trustee in bankruptcy are governed by other law as to both the time they occur and the substance of the transfer. The Article 8 rules do, however, determine whether the issuer is obligated to recognize the rights that a third party, such as a transferee, may acquire under other law. See Sections 8-207, 8-401, and 8-404.

Definitional Cross References:

"Certificated security". Section 8-102(a)(4).

"Notice of adverse claim". Section 8-105.

"Protected purchaser". Section 8-303.

"Purchaser". Sections 1-201(33) & 8-116.

"Uncertificated security". Section 8-102(a)(18).

"Delivery". Section 8-301.

§ 8-303. Protected Purchaser.

(a) "Protected purchaser" means a purchaser of a certificated or uncertificated security, or of an interest therein, who:

(1) gives value;

(2) does not have notice of any adverse claim to the security; and

(3) obtains control of the certificated or uncertificated security.

(b) In addition to acquiring the rights of a purchaser, a protected purchaser also acquires its interest in the security free of any adverse claim.

Official Comment

1. Subsection (a) lists the requirements that a purchaser must meet to qualify as a "protected purchaser." Subsection (b) provides that a protected purchaser takes its interest free from adverse claims. "Purchaser" is defined broadly in Section 1-201. A secured party as well as an outright buyer can qualify as a protected purchaser. Also, "purchase" includes taking by issue, so a person to whom a security is originally issued can qualify as a protected purchaser.

2. To qualify as a protected purchaser, a purchaser must give value, take without notice of any adverse claim, and obtain control. Value is used in the broad sense defined in Section 1-201(44). See also Section 8-116 (securities intermediary as purchaser for value). Adverse claim is defined in Section 8-102(a)(1). Section 8-105 specifies whether a purchaser has notice of an adverse claim. Control is defined in Section 8-106. To qualify as a protected purchaser there must be a time at which all of the requirements are satisfied. Thus if a purchaser obtains notice of an adverse claim before giving value or satisfying the requirements for control, the purchaser cannot be a protected purchaser. See also Section 8-304(d).

The requirement that a protected purchaser obtain control expresses the point that to qualify for the adverse claim cut-off rule a purchaser must take through a transaction that is implemented by the appropriate mechanism. By contrast, the rules in Part 2 provide that any purchaser for value of a security without notice of a defense may take free of the issuer's defense based on that defense. See Section 8-202.

3. The requirements for control differ depending on the form of the security. For securities represented by bearer certificates, a purchaser obtains control by delivery. See Sections 8-106(a) and 8-301(a). For securities represented by certificates in registered form, the requirements for control are: (1) delivery as defined in Section 8-301(b), plus (2) either an effective indorsement or registration of transfer by the issuer. See Section 8-106(b). Thus, a person who takes through a forged indorsement does not qualify as a protected purchaser by virtue of the delivery alone. If, however, the purchaser presents the certificate to the issuer for registration of transfer, and the issuer registers transfer over the forged indorsement, the purchaser can qualify as a protected purchaser of the new certificate. If the issuer registers transfer on a forged indorsement, the true owner will be able to recover from the issuer for wrongful registration, see Section 8-404, unless the owner's delay in notifying the issuer of a loss or theft of the certificate results in preclusion under Section 8-406.

For uncertificated securities, a purchaser can obtain control either by delivery, see Sections 8-106(c)(1) and 8-301(b), or by obtaining an agreement pursuant to which the issuer agrees to act on instructions from the purchaser without further consent from the registered owner, see Section 8-106(c)(2). The control agreement device of Section 8-106(c)(2) takes the place of the "registered pledge" concept of the 1978 version of Article 8. A secured lender who obtains a control agreement under Section 8-106(c)(2) can qualify as a protected purchaser of an uncertificated security.

4. This section states directly the rules determining whether one takes free from adverse claims without using the phrase "good faith." Whether a person who takes under suspicious circumstances is disqualified is determined by the rules of Section 8-105 on notice of adverse claims. The term "protected purchaser," which replaces the term "bona fide purchaser" used in the prior version of Article 8, is derived from the term "protected holder" used in the Convention on International Bills and Notes prepared by the United Nations Commission on International Trade Law ("UNCITRAL").

Definitional Cross References:

"Adverse claim". Section 8-102(a)(1).

"Certificated security". Section 8-102(a)(4).
"Control". Section 8-106.
"Notice of adverse claim". Section 8-105.
"Purchaser". Sections 1-201(33) & 8-116.
"Uncertificated security". Section 8-102(a)(18).
"Value". Sections 1-201(44) & 8-116.

§ 8-304. Indorsement.

(a) An indorsement may be in blank or special. An indorsement in blank includes an indorsement to bearer. A special indorsement specifies to whom a security is to be transferred or who has power to transfer it. A holder may convert a blank indorsement to a special indorsement.

(b) An indorsement purporting to be only of part of a security certificate representing units intended by the issuer to be separately transferable is effective to the extent of the indorsement.

(c) An indorsement, whether special or in blank, does not constitute a transfer until delivery of the certificate on which it appears or, if the indorsement is on a separate document, until delivery of both the document and the certificate.

(d) If a security certificate in registered form has been delivered to a purchaser without a necessary indorsement, the purchaser may become a protected purchaser only when the indorsement is supplied. However, against a transferor, a transfer is complete upon delivery and the purchaser has a specifically enforceable right to have any necessary indorsement supplied.

(e) An indorsement of a security certificate in bearer form may give notice of an adverse claim to the certificate, but it does not otherwise affect a right to registration that the holder possesses.

(f) Unless otherwise agreed, a person making an indorsement assumes only the obligations provided in Section 8-108 and not an obligation that the security will be honored by the issuer.

Official Comment

1. By virtue of the definition of indorsement in Section 8-102 and the rules of this section, the simplified method of indorsing certificated securities previously set forth in the Uniform Stock Transfer Act is continued. Although more than one special indorsement on a given security certificate is possible, the desire for dividends or interest, as the case may be, should operate to bring the certificate home for registration of transfer within a reasonable period of time. The usual form of assignment which appears on the back of a stock certificate or in a separate "power" may be filled up either in the form of an assignment, a power of attorney to transfer, or both. If it is not filled up at all but merely signed, the indorsement is in blank. If filled up either as an assignment or as a power of attorney to transfer, the indorsement is special.

2. Subsection (b) recognizes the validity of a "partial" indorsement, e.g., as to fifty shares of the one hundred represented by a single certificate. The rights of a transferee under a partial indorsement to the status of a protected purchaser are left to the case law.

3. Subsection (c) deals with the effect of an indorsement without delivery. There must be a voluntary parting with control in order to effect a valid transfer

of a certificated security as between the parties. *Levey v. Nason,* 279 Mass. 268, 181 N.E. 193 (1932), and *National Surety Co. v. Indemnity Insurance Co. of North America,* 237 App.Div. 485, 261 N.Y.S. 605 (1933). The provision in Section 10 of the Uniform Stock Transfer Act that an attempted transfer without delivery amounts to a promise to transfer is omitted. Even under that Act the effect of such a promise was left to the applicable law of contracts, and this Article by making no reference to such situations intends to achieve a similar result. With respect to delivery there is no counterpart to subsection (d) on right to compel indorsement, such as is envisaged in *Johnson v. Johnson,* 300 Mass. 24, 13 N.E.2d 788 (1938), where the transferee under a written assignment was given the right to compel a transfer of the certificate.

4. Subsection (d) deals with the effect of delivery without indorsement. As between the parties the transfer is made complete upon delivery, but the transferee cannot become a protected purchaser until indorsement is made. The indorsement does not operate retroactively, and notice may intervene between delivery and indorsement so as to prevent the transferee from becoming a protected purchaser. Although a purchaser taking without a necessary indorsement may be subject to claims of ownership, any issuer's defense of which the purchaser had no notice at the time of delivery will be cut off, since the provisions of this Article protect all purchasers for value without notice (Section 8-202).

The transferee's right to compel an indorsement where a security certificate has been delivered with intent to transfer is recognized in the case law. See *Coats v. Guaranty Bank & Trust Co.,* 170 La. 871, 129 So. 513 (1930). A proper indorsement is one of the requisites of transfer which a purchaser of a certificated security has a right to obtain (Section 8-307). A purchaser may not only compel an indorsement under that section but may also recover for any reasonable expense incurred by the transferor's failure to respond to the demand for an indorsement.

5. Subsection (e) deals with the significance of an indorsement on a security certificate in bearer form. The concept of indorsement applies only to registered securities. A purported indorsement of bearer paper is normally of no effect. An indorsement "for collection," "for surrender" or the like, charges a purchaser with notice of adverse claims (Section 8-105(d)) but does not operate beyond this to interfere with any right the holder may otherwise possess to have the security registered.

6. Subsection (f) makes clear that the indorser of a security certificate does not warrant that the issuer will honor the underlying obligation. In view of the nature of investment securities and the circumstances under which they are normally transferred, a transferor cannot be held to warrant as to the issuer's actions. As a transferor the indorser, of course, remains liable for breach of the warranties set forth in this Article (Section 8-108).

Definitional Cross References:

"Bearer form". Section 8-102(a)(2).

"Certificated security". Section 8-102(a)(4).

"Indorsement". Section 8-102(a)(11).

"Purchaser". Sections 1-201(33) & 8-116.

"Registered form". Section 8-102(a)(13).

"Security certificate". Section 8-102(a)(16).

§ 8-305. Instruction.

(a) If an instruction has been originated by an appropriate person but is incomplete in any other respect, any person may complete it as authorized and the issuer may rely on it as completed, even though it has been completed incorrectly.

(b) Unless otherwise agreed, a person initiating an instruction assumes only the obligations imposed by Section 8–108 and not an obligation that the security will be honored by the issuer.

Official Comment

1. The term instruction is defined in Section 8–102(a)(12) as a notification communicated to the issuer of an uncertificated security directing that transfer be registered. Section 8–107 specifies who may initiate an effective instruction.

Functionally, presentation of an instruction is quite similar to the presentation of an indorsed certificate for registration. Note that instruction is defined in terms of "communicate," see Section 8–102(a)(6). Thus, the instruction may be in the form of a writing signed by the registered owner or in any other form agreed upon by the issuer and the registered owner. Allowing nonwritten forms of instructions will permit the development and employment of means of transmitting instructions electronically.

When a person who originates an instruction leaves a blank and the blank later is completed, subsection (a) gives the issuer the same rights it would have had against the originating person had that person completed the blank. This is true regardless of whether the person completing the instruction had authority to complete it. Compare Section 8–206 and its Comment, dealing with blanks left upon issue.

2. Subsection (b) makes clear that the originator of an instruction, like the indorser of a security certificate, does not warrant that the issuer will honor the underlying obligation, but does make warranties as a transferor under Section 8–108.

Definitional Cross References:

"Appropriate person". Section 8–107.
"Instruction". Section 8–102(a)(12).
"Issuer". Section 8–201.

§ 8–306. Effect of Guaranteeing Signature, Indorsement, or Instruction.

(a) A person who guarantees a signature of an indorser of a security certificate warrants that at the time of signing:

(1) the signature was genuine;

(2) the signer was an appropriate person to indorse, or if the signature is by an agent, the agent had actual authority to act on behalf of the appropriate person; and

(3) the signer had legal capacity to sign.

(b) A person who guarantees a signature of the originator of an instruction warrants that at the time of signing:

(1) the signature was genuine;

(2) the signer was an appropriate person to originate the instruction, or if the signature is by an agent, the agent had actual authority to act on behalf of the appropriate person, if the person specified in the instruction as the registered owner was, in fact, the registered owner, as to which fact the signature guarantor does not make a warranty; and

(3) the signer had legal capacity to sign.

(c) A person who specially guarantees the signature of an originator of an instruction makes the warranties of a signature guarantor under subsection (b) and also warrants that at the time the instruction is presented to the issuer:

(1) the person specified in the instruction as the registered owner of the uncertificated security will be the registered owner; and

(2) the transfer of the uncertificated security requested in the instruction will be registered by the issuer free from all liens, security interests, restrictions, and claims other than those specified in the instruction.

(d) A guarantor under subsections (a) and (b) or a special guarantor under subsection (c) does not otherwise warrant the rightfulness of the transfer.

(e) A person who guarantees an indorsement of a security certificate makes the warranties of a signature guarantor under subsection (a) and also warrants the rightfulness of the transfer in all respects.

(f) A person who guarantees an instruction requesting the transfer of an uncertificated security makes the warranties of a special signature guarantor under subsection (c) and also warrants the rightfulness of the transfer in all respects.

(g) An issuer may not require a special guaranty of signature, a guaranty of indorsement, or a guaranty of instruction as a condition to registration of transfer.

(h) The warranties under this section are made to a person taking or dealing with the security in reliance on the guaranty, and the guarantor is liable to the person for loss resulting from their breach. An indorser or originator of an instruction whose signature, indorsement, or instruction has been guaranteed is liable to a guarantor for any loss suffered by the guarantor as a result of breach of the warranties of the guarantor.

Official Comment

1. Subsection (a) provides that a guarantor of the signature of the indorser of a security certificate warrants that the signature is genuine, that the signer is an appropriate person or has actual authority to indorse on behalf of the appropriate person, and that the signer has legal capacity. Subsection (b) provides similar, though not identical, warranties for the guarantor of a signature of the originator of an instruction for transfer of an uncertificated security.

Appropriate person is defined in Section 8–107(a) to include a successor or person who has power under other law to act for a person who is deceased or lacks capacity. Thus if a certificate registered in the name of Mary Roe is indorsed by Jane Doe as executor of Mary Roe, a guarantor of the signature of Jane Doe warrants that she has power to act as executor.

Although the definition of appropriate person in Section 8–107(a) does not itself include an agent, an indorsement by an agent is effective under Section 8–107(b) if the agent has authority to act for the appropriate person. Accordingly, this section provides an explicit warranty of authority for agents.

2. The rationale of the principle that a signature guarantor warrants the authority of the signer, rather than simply the genuineness of the signature, was explained in the leading case of *Jennie*

Clarkson Home for Children v. Missouri, K. & T.R. Co., 182 N.Y. 47, 74 N.E. 571, 70 A.L.R. 787 (1905), which dealt with a guaranty of the signature of a person indorsing on behalf of a corporation. "If stock is held by an individual who is executing a power of attorney for its transfer, the member of the exchange who signs as a witness thereto guaranties not only the genuineness of the signature affixed to the power of attorney, but that the person signing is the individual in whose name the stock stands. With reference to stock standing in the name of a corporation, which can only sign a power of attorney through its authorized officers or agents, a different situation is presented. If the witnessing of the signature of the corporation is only that of the signature of a person who signs for the corporation, then the guaranty is of no value, and there is nothing to protect purchasers or the companies who are called upon to issue new stock in the place of that transferred from the frauds of persons who have signed the names of corporations without authority. If such is the only effect of the guaranty, purchasers and transfer agents must first go to the corporation in whose name the stock stands and ascertain whether the individual who signed the power of attorney had authority to do so. This will require time, and in many cases will necessitate the postponement of the completion of the purchase by the payment of the money until the facts can be ascertained. The broker who is acting for the owner has an opportunity to become acquainted with his customer, and may readily before sale ascertain, in case of a corporation, the name of the officer who is authorized to execute the power of attorney. It was therefore, we think, the purpose of the rule to cast upon the broker who witnesses the signature the duty of ascertaining whether the person signing the name of the corporation had authority to do so, and making the witness a guarantor that it is the signature of the corporation in whose name the stock stands."

3. Subsection (b) sets forth the warranties that can reasonably be expected from the guarantor of the signature of the originator of an instruction, who, though familiar with the signer, does not have any evidence that the purported owner is in fact the owner of the subject uncertificated security. This is in contrast to the position of the person guaranteeing a signature on a certificate who can see a certificate in the signer's possession in the name of or indorsed to the signer or in blank. Thus, the warranty in paragraph (2) of subsection (b) is expressly conditioned on the actual registration's conforming to that represented by the originator. If the signer purports to be the owner, the guarantor under paragraph (2), warrants only the identity of the signer. If, however, the signer is acting in a representative capacity, the guarantor warrants both the signer's identity and authority to act for the purported owner. The issuer needs no warranty as to the facts of registration because those facts can be ascertained from the issuer's own records.

4. Subsection (c) sets forth a "special guaranty of signature" under which the guarantor additionally warrants both registered ownership and freedom from undisclosed defects of record. The guarantor of the signature of an indorser of a security certificate effectively makes these warranties to a purchaser for value on the evidence of a clean certificate issued in the name of the indorser, indorsed to the indorser or indorsed in blank. By specially guaranteeing under subsection (c), the guarantor warrants that the instruction will, when presented to the issuer, result in the requested registration free from defects not specified.

5. Subsection (d) makes clear that the warranties of a signature guarantor are limited to those specified in this section and do not include a general warranty of rightfulness. On the other hand subsections (e) and (f) provide that a person guaranteeing an indorsement or an instruction does warrant that the transfer is rightful in all respects.

6. Subsection (g) makes clear what can be inferred from the combination of Sections 8-401 and 8-402, that the issuer

may not require as a condition to transfer a guaranty of the indorsement or instruction nor may it require a special signature guaranty.

7. Subsection (h) specifies to whom the warranties in this section run, and also provides that a person who gives a guaranty under this section has an action against the indorser or originator for any loss suffered by the guarantor.

Definitional Cross References:

"Appropriate person". Section 8-107.
"Genuine". Section 1-201(18).
"Indorsement". Section 8-102(a)(11).
"Instruction". Section 8-102(a)(12).
"Issuer". Section 8-201.
"Security certificate". Section 8-102(a)(16).
"Uncertificated security". Section 8-102(a)(18).

§ 8-307. Purchaser's Right to Requisites for Registration of Transfer.

Unless otherwise agreed, the transferor of a security on due demand shall supply the purchaser with proof of authority to transfer or with any other requisite necessary to obtain registration of the transfer of the security, but if the transfer is not for value, a transferor need not comply unless the purchaser pays the necessary expenses. If the transferor fails within a reasonable time to comply with the demand, the purchaser may reject or rescind the transfer.

Official Comment

1. Because registration of the transfer of a security is a matter of vital importance, a purchaser is here provided with the means of obtaining such formal requirements for registration as signature guaranties, proof of authority, transfer tax stamps and the like. The transferor is the one in a position to supply most conveniently whatever documentation may be requisite for registration of transfer, and the duty to do so upon demand within a reasonable time is here stated affirmatively. If an essential item is peculiarly within the province of the transferor so that the transferor is the only one who can obtain it, the purchaser may specifically enforce the right to obtain it. Compare Section 8-304(d). If a transfer is not for value the transferor need not pay expenses.

2. If the transferor's duty is not performed the transferee may reject or rescind the contract to transfer. The transferee is not bound to do so. An action for damages for breach of contract may be preferred.

Definitional Cross References:

"Purchaser". Sections 1-201(33) & 8-116.
"Security". Section 8-102(a)(15).
"Value". Sections 1-201(44) & 8-116.

PART 4

REGISTRATION

§ 8-401. Duty of Issuer to Register Transfer.

(a) If a certificated security in registered form is presented to an issuer with a request to register transfer or an instruction is presented to an issuer with a request to register transfer of an uncertificated security, the issuer shall register the transfer as requested if:

(1) under the terms of the security the person seeking registration of transfer is eligible to have the security registered in its name;

(2) the indorsement or instruction is made by the appropriate person or by an agent who has actual authority to act on behalf of the appropriate person;

(3) reasonable assurance is given that the indorsement or instruction is genuine and authorized (Section 8–402);

(4) any applicable law relating to the collection of taxes has been complied with;

(5) the transfer does not violate any restriction on transfer imposed by the issuer in accordance with Section 8–204;

(6) a demand that the issuer not register transfer has not become effective under Section 8–403, or the issuer has complied with Section 8–403(b) but no legal process or indemnity bond is obtained as provided in Section 8–403(d); and

(7) the transfer is in fact rightful or is to a protected purchaser.

(b) If an issuer is under a duty to register a transfer of a security, the issuer is liable to a person presenting a certificated security or an instruction for registration or to the person's principal for loss resulting from unreasonable delay in registration or failure or refusal to register the transfer.

Official Comment

1. This section states the duty of the issuer to register transfers. A duty exists only if certain preconditions exist. If any of the preconditions do not exist, there is no duty to register transfer. If an indorsement on a security certificate is a forgery, there is no duty. If an instruction to transfer an uncertificated security is not originated by an appropriate person, there is no duty. If there has not been compliance with applicable tax laws, there is no duty. If a security certificate is properly indorsed but nevertheless the transfer is in fact wrongful, there is no duty unless the transfer is to a protected purchaser (and the other preconditions exist).

This section does not constitute a mandate that the issuer must establish that all preconditions are met before the issuer registers a transfer. The issuer may waive the reasonable assurances specified in paragraph (a)(3). If it has confidence in the responsibility of the persons requesting transfer, it may ignore questions of compliance with tax laws. Although an issuer has no duty if the transfer is wrongful, the issuer has no duty to inquire into adverse claims, see Section 8–404.

2. By subsection (b) the person entitled to registration may not only compel it but may hold the issuer liable in damages for unreasonable delay.

3. Section 8–201(c) provides that with respect to registration of transfer, "issuer" means the person on whose behalf transfer books are maintained. Transfer agents, registrars or the like within the scope of their respective functions have rights and duties under this Part similar to those of the issuer. See Section 8–407.

Definitional Cross References:

"Appropriate person". Section 8–107.
"Certificated security". Section 8–102(a)(4).
"Genuine". Section 1–201(18).
"Indorsement". Section 8–102(a)(11).
"Instruction". Section 8–102(a)(12).
"Issuer". Section 8–201.
"Protected purchaser". Section 8–303.
"Registered form". Section 8–102(a)(13).
"Uncertificated security". Section 8–102(a)(18).

§ 8–402. Assurance that Indorsement or Instruction is Effective.

(a) An issuer may require the following assurance that each necessary indorsement or each instruction is genuine and authorized:

(1) in all cases, a guaranty of the signature of the person making an indorsement or originating an instruction including, in the case of an instruction, reasonable assurance of identity;

(2) if the indorsement is made or the instruction is originated by an agent, appropriate assurance of actual authority to sign;

(3) if the indorsement is made or the instruction is originated by a fiduciary pursuant to Section 8–107(a)(4) or (a)(5), appropriate evidence of appointment or incumbency;

(4) if there is more than one fiduciary, reasonable assurance that all who are required to sign have done so; and

(5) if the indorsement is made or the instruction is originated by a person not covered by another provision of this subsection, assurance appropriate to the case corresponding as nearly as may be to the provisions of this subsection.

(b) An issuer may elect to require reasonable assurance beyond that specified in this section.

(c) In this section:

(1) "Guaranty of the signature" means a guaranty signed by or on behalf of a person reasonably believed by the issuer to be responsible. An issuer may adopt standards with respect to responsibility if they are not manifestly unreasonable.

(2) "Appropriate evidence of appointment or incumbency" means:

(i) in the case of a fiduciary appointed or qualified by a court, a certificate issued by or under the direction or supervision of the court or an officer thereof and dated within 60 days before the date of presentation for transfer; or

(ii) in any other case, a copy of a document showing the appointment or a certificate issued by or on behalf of a person reasonably believed by an issuer to be responsible or, in the absence of that document or certificate, other evidence the issuer reasonably considers appropriate.

Official Comment

1. An issuer is absolutely liable for wrongful registration of transfer if the indorsement or instruction is ineffective. See Section 8–404. Accordingly, an issuer is entitled to require such assurance as is reasonable under the circumstances that all necessary indorsements are effective, and thus to minimize its risk. This section establishes the requirements the issuer may make in terms of documentation which, except in the rarest of instances, should be easily furnished. Subsection (b) provides that an issuer may require additional assurances if that requirement is reasonable under the circumstances, but if the issuer demands more than reasonable assurance that the instruction or the necessary indorsements are genuine and authorized, the presenter

may refuse the demand and sue for improper refusal to register. Section 8-401(b).

2. Under subsection (a)(1), the issuer may require in all cases a guaranty of signature. See Section 8-306. When an instruction is presented the issuer always may require reasonable assurance as to the identity of the originator. Subsection (c) allows the issuer to require that the person making these guaranties be one reasonably believed to be responsible, and the issuer may adopt standards of responsibility which are not manifestly unreasonable. Regulations under the federal securities laws, however, place limits on the requirements transfer agents may impose concerning the responsibility of eligible signature guarantors. See 17 CFR 240.17Ad-15.

3. This section, by paragraphs (2) through (5) of subsection (a), permits the issuer to seek confirmation that the indorsement or instruction is genuine and authorized. The permitted methods act as a double check on matters which are within the warranties of the signature guarantor. See Section 8-306. Thus, an agent may be required to submit a power of attorney, a corporation to submit a certified resolution evidencing the authority of its signing officer to sign, an executor or administrator to submit the usual "shortform certificate," etc. But failure of a fiduciary to obtain court approval of the transfer or to comply with other requirements does not make the fiduciary's signature ineffective. Section 8-107(c). Hence court orders and other controlling instruments are omitted from subsection (a).

Subsection (a)(3) authorizes the issuer to require "appropriate evidence" of appointment or incumbency, and subsection (c) indicates what evidence will be "appropriate". In the case of a fiduciary appointed or qualified by a court that evidence will be a court certificate dated within sixty days before the date of presentation, subsection (c)(2)(i). Where the fiduciary is not appointed or qualified by a court, as in the case of a successor trustee, subsection (c)(2)(ii) applies. In that case, the issuer may require a copy of a trust instrument or other document showing the appointment, or it may require the certificate of a responsible person. In the absence of such a document or certificate, it may require other appropriate evidence. If the security is registered in the name of the fiduciary as such, the person's signature is effective even though the person is no longer serving in that capacity, see Section 8-107(d), hence no evidence of incumbency is needed.

4. Circumstances may indicate that a necessary signature was unauthorized or was not that of an appropriate person. Such circumstances would be ignored at risk of absolute liability. To minimize that risk the issuer may properly exercise the option given by subsection (b) to require assurance beyond that specified in subsection (a). On the other hand, the facts at hand may reflect only on the rightfulness of the transfer. Such facts do not create a duty of inquiry, because the issuer is not liable to an adverse claimant unless the claimant obtains legal process. See Section 8-404.

Definitional Cross References:

"Appropriate person". Section 8-107.
"Genuine". Section 1-201(18).
"Indorsement". Section 8-102(a)(11).
"Instruction". Section 8-102(a)(12).
"Issuer". Section 8-201.

§ 8-403. Demand that Issuer Not Register Transfer.

(a) A person who is an appropriate person to make an indorsement or originate an instruction may demand that the issuer not register transfer of a security by communicating to the issuer a notification that identifies the registered owner and the issue of which the security is a part and provides an address for communications directed to the person making the demand. The demand is effective only if it is received by the issuer at a time and in a manner affording the issuer reasonable opportunity to act on it.

(b) If a certificated security in registered form is presented to an issuer with a request to register transfer or an instruction is presented to an issuer with a request to register transfer of an uncertificated security after a demand that the issuer not register transfer has become effective, the issuer shall promptly communicate to (i) the person who initiated the demand at the address provided in the demand and (ii) the person who presented the security for registration of transfer or initiated the instruction requesting registration of transfer a notification stating that:

(1) the certificated security has been presented for registration of transfer or the instruction for registration of transfer of the uncertificated security has been received;

(2) a demand that the issuer not register transfer had previously been received; and

(3) the issuer will withhold registration of transfer for a period of time stated in the notification in order to provide the person who initiated the demand an opportunity to obtain legal process or an indemnity bond.

(c) The period described in subsection (b)(3) may not exceed 30 days after the date of communication of the notification. A shorter period may be specified by the issuer if it is not manifestly unreasonable.

(d) An issuer is not liable to a person who initiated a demand that the issuer not register transfer for any loss the person suffers as a result of registration of a transfer pursuant to an effective indorsement or instruction if the person who initiated the demand does not, within the time stated in the issuer's communication, either:

(1) obtain an appropriate restraining order, injunction, or other process from a court of competent jurisdiction enjoining the issuer from registering the transfer; or

(2) file with the issuer an indemnity bond, sufficient in the issuer's judgment to protect the issuer and any transfer agent, registrar, or other agent of the issuer involved from any loss it or they may suffer by refusing to register the transfer.

(e) This section does not relieve an issuer from liability for registering transfer pursuant to an indorsement or instruction that was not effective.

Official Comment

1. The general rule under this Article is that if there has been an effective indorsement or instruction, a person who contends that registration of the transfer would be wrongful should not be able to interfere with the registration process merely by sending notice of the assertion to the issuer. Rather, the claimant must obtain legal process. See Section 8-404. Section 8-403 is an exception to this general rule. It permits the registered owner—but not third parties—to demand that the issuer not register a transfer.

2. This section is intended to alleviate the problems faced by registered owners of certificated securities who lose or misplace their certificates. A registered owner who realizes that a certificate may have been lost or stolen should promptly report that fact to the issuer, lest the owner be precluded from asserting a claim for wrongful registration. See Sec-

tion 8-406. The usual practice of issuers and transfer agents is that when a certificate is reported as lost, the owner is notified that a replacement can be obtained if the owner provides an indemnity bond. See Section 8-405. If the registered owner does not plan to transfer the securities, the owner might choose not to obtain a replacement, particularly if the owner suspects that the certificate has merely been misplaced.

Under this section, the owner's notification that the certificate has been lost would constitute a demand that the issuer not register transfer. No indemnity bond or legal process is necessary. If the original certificate is presented for registration of transfer, the issuer is required to notify the registered owner of that fact, and defer registration of transfer for a stated period. In order to prevent undue delay in the process of registration, the stated period may not exceed thirty days. This gives the registered owner an opportunity to either obtain legal process or post an indemnity bond and thereby prevent the issuer from registering transfer.

3. Subsection (e) makes clear that this section does not relieve an issuer from liability for registering a transfer pursuant to an ineffective indorsement. An issuer's liability for wrongful registration in such cases does not depend on the presence or absence of notice that the indorsement was ineffective. Registered owners who are confident that they neither indorsed the certificates, nor did anything that would preclude them from denying the effectiveness of another's indorsement, see Sections 8-107(b) and 8-406, might prefer to pursue their rights against the issuer for wrongful registration rather than take advantage of the opportunity to post a bond or seek a restraining order when notified by the issuer under this section that their lost certificates have been presented for registration in apparently good order.

Definitional Cross References:

"Appropriate person". Section 8-107.
"Certificated security". Section 8-102(a)(4).
"Communicate". Section 8-102(a)(6).
"Effective". Section 8-107.
"Indorsement". Section 8-102(a)(11).
"Instruction". Section 8-102(a)(12).
"Issuer". Section 8-201.
"Registered form". Section 8-102(a)(13).
"Uncertificated security". Section 8-102(a)(18).

§ 8-404. Wrongful Registration.

(a) Except as otherwise provided in Section 8-406, an issuer is liable for wrongful registration of transfer if the issuer has registered a transfer of a security to a person not entitled to it, and the transfer was registered:

(1) pursuant to an ineffective indorsement or instruction;

(2) after a demand that the issuer not register transfer became effective under Section 8-403(a) and the issuer did not comply with Section 8-403(b);

(3) after the issuer had been served with an injunction, restraining order, or other legal process enjoining it from registering the transfer, issued by a court of competent jurisdiction, and the issuer had a reasonable opportunity to act on the injunction, restraining order, or other legal process; or

(4) by an issuer acting in collusion with the wrongdoer.

(b) An issuer that is liable for wrongful registration of transfer under subsection (a) on demand shall provide the person entitled to the security with a like certificated or uncertificated security, and any payments or distributions that the person did not receive as a result of the wrongful registration. If an overissue would result, the issuer's liability to provide the person with a like security is governed by Section 8–210.

(c) Except as otherwise provided in subsection (a) or in a law relating to the collection of taxes, an issuer is not liable to an owner or other person suffering loss as a result of the registration of a transfer of a security if registration was made pursuant to an effective indorsement or instruction.

Official Comment

1. Subsection (a)(1) provides that an issuer is liable if it registers transfer pursuant to an indorsement or instruction that was not effective. For example, an issuer that registers transfer on a forged indorsement is liable to the registered owner. The fact that the issuer had no reason to suspect that the indorsement was forged or that the issuer obtained the ordinary assurances under Section 8–402 does not relieve the issuer from liability. The reason that issuers obtain signature guaranties and other assurances is that they are liable for wrongful registration.

Subsection (b) specifies the remedy for wrongful registration. Pre–Code cases established the registered owner's right to receive a new security where the issuer had wrongfully registered a transfer, but some cases also allowed the registered owner to elect between an equitable action to compel issue of a new security and an action for damages. Cf. *Casper v. Kalt–Zimmers Mfg. Co.*, 159 Wis. 517, 149 N.W. 754 (1914). Article 8 does not allow such election. The true owner of a certificated security is required to take a new security except where an overissue would result and a similar security is not reasonably available for purchase. See Section 8–210. The true owner of an uncertificated security is entitled and required to take restoration of the records to their proper state, with a similar exception for overissue.

2. Read together, subsections (c) and (a) have the effect of providing that an issuer has no duties to an adverse claimant unless the claimant serves legal process on the issuer to enjoin registration. Issuers, or their transfer agents, perform a record-keeping function for the direct holding system that is analogous to the functions performed by clearing corporations and securities intermediaries in the indirect holding system. This section applies to the record-keepers for the direct holding system the same standard that Section 8–115 applies to the record-keepers for the indirect holding system. Thus, issuers are not liable to adverse claimants merely on the basis of notice. As in the case of the analogous rules for the indirect holding system, the policy of this section is to protect the right of investors to have their securities transfers processed without the disruption or delay that might result if the record-keepers risked liability to third parties. It would be undesirable to apply different standards to the direct and indirect holding systems, since doing so might operate as a disincentive to the development of a book-entry direct holding system.

3. This section changes prior law under which an issuer could be held liable, even though it registered transfer on an effective indorsement or instruction, if the issuer had in some fashion been notified that the transfer might be wrongful against a third party, and the issuer did not appropriately discharge its duty to inquire into the adverse claim. See Section 8–403 (1978).

The rule of former Section 8–403 was anomalous inasmuch as Section 8–207 provides that the issuer is entitled to "treat the registered owner as the person exclusively entitled to vote, receive notifications, and otherwise exercise all the rights and powers of an owner." Under Section 8–207, the fact that a third person notifies the issuer of a claim does not preclude the issuer from treating the registered owner as the person entitled to the security. See *Kerrigan v. American Orthodontics Corp.*, 960 F.2d 43 (7th Cir. 1992). The change made in the present version of Section 8–404 ensures that the rights of registered owners and the duties of issuers with respect to registration of transfer will be protected against third-party interference in the same fashion as other rights of registered ownership.

Definitional Cross References:

"Certificated security". Section 8-102(a)(4).

"Effective". Section 8-107.

"Indorsement". Section 8-102(a)(11).

"Instruction". Section 8-102(a)(12).

"Issuer". Section 8-201.

"Security". Section 8-102(a)(15).

"Uncertificated security". Section 8-102(a)(18).

§ 8-405. Replacement of Lost, Destroyed, or Wrongfully Taken Security Certificate.

(a) If an owner of a certificated security, whether in registered or bearer form, claims that the certificate has been lost, destroyed, or wrongfully taken, the issuer shall issue a new certificate if the owner:

(1) so requests before the issuer has notice that the certificate has been acquired by a protected purchaser;

(2) files with the issuer a sufficient indemnity bond; and

(3) satisfies other reasonable requirements imposed by the issuer.

(b) If, after the issue of a new security certificate, a protected purchaser of the original certificate presents it for registration of transfer, the issuer shall register the transfer unless an overissue would result. In that case, the issuer's liability is governed by Section 8-210. In addition to any rights on the indemnity bond, an issuer may recover the new certificate from a person to whom it was issued or any person taking under that person, except a protected purchaser.

Official Comment

1. This section enables the owner to obtain a replacement of a lost, destroyed or stolen certificate, provided that reasonable requirements are satisfied and a sufficient indemnity bond supplied.

2. Where an "original" security certificate has reached the hands of a protected purchaser, the registered owner—who was in the best position to prevent the loss, destruction or theft of the security certificate—is now deprived of the new security certificate issued as a replacement. This changes the pre-UCC law under which the original certificate was ineffective after the issue of a replacement except insofar as it might represent an action for damages in the hands of a purchaser for value without notice. *Keller v. Eureka Brick Mach. Mfg. Co.,* 43 Mo.App. 84, 11 L.R.A. 472 (1890). Where both the original and the new certificate have reached protected purchasers the issuer is required to honor both certificates unless an overissue would result and the security is not reasonably available for purchase. See Section 8-210. In the latter case alone, the protected purchaser of the original certificate is relegated to an action for damages. In either case, the issuer itself may recover on the indemnity bond.

Definitional Cross References:

"Bearer form". Section 8-102(a)(2).

"Certificated security". Section 8-102(a)(4).

"Issuer". Section 8-201.

"Notice". Section 1-201(25).

"Overissue". Section 8-210.

"Protected purchaser". Section 8-303.

"Registered form". Section 8-102(a)(13).

"Security certificate". Section 8-102(a)(16).

§ 8-406. Obligation to Notify Issuer of Lost, Destroyed, or Wrongfully Taken Security Certificate.

If a security certificate has been lost, apparently destroyed, or wrongfully taken, and the owner fails to notify the issuer of that fact within a reasonable time after the owner has notice of it and the issuer registers a transfer of the security before receiving notification, the owner may not assert against the issuer a claim for registering the transfer under Section 8-404 or a claim to a new security certificate under Section 8-405.

Official Comment

An owner who fails to notify the issuer within a reasonable time after the owner knows or has reason to know of the loss or theft of a security certificate is estopped from asserting the ineffectiveness of a forged or unauthorized indorsement and the wrongfulness of the registration of the transfer. If the lost certificate was indorsed by the owner, then the registration of the transfer was not wrongful under Section 8-404, unless the owner made an effective demand that the issuer not register transfer under Section 8-403.

Definitional Cross References:

"Issuer". Section 8-201.

"Notify". Section 1-201(25).

"Security certificate". Section 8-102(a)(16).

§ 8-407. Authenticating Trustee, Transfer Agent, and Registrar.

A person acting as authenticating trustee, transfer agent, registrar, or other agent for an issuer in the registration of a transfer of its securities, in the issue of new security certificates or uncertificated securities, or in the cancellation of surrendered security certificates has the same obligation to the holder or owner of a certificated or uncertificated security with regard to the particular functions performed as the issuer has in regard to those functions.

Official Comment

1. Transfer agents, registrars, and the like are here expressly held liable both to the issuer and to the owner for wrongful refusal to register a transfer as well as for wrongful registration of a transfer in any case within the scope of their respective functions where the issuer would itself be liable. Those cases which have regarded these parties solely as agents of the issuer and have therefore refused to recognize their liability to the owner for mere nonfeasance, i.e., refusal to register a transfer, are rejected. *Hulse v. Consolidated Quicksilver Mining Corp.*, 65 Idaho 768, 154 P.2d 149 (1944); *Nicholson v. Morgan*, 119 Misc. 309, 196 N.Y.Supp. 147 (1922); *Lewis v. Hargadine-McKittrick Dry Goods Co.*, 305 Mo. 396, 274 S.W. 1041 (1924).

2. The practice frequently followed by authenticating trustees of issuing certificates of indebtedness rather than authenticating duplicate certificates where securities have been lost or stolen became obsolete in view of the provisions of Section 8-405, which makes express provision for the issue of substitute securities. It is not a breach of trust or lack of due diligence for trustees to authenticate new securities. Cf. *Switzerland General Ins. Co. v. N.Y.C. & H.R.R. Co.*, 152 App.Div. 70, 136 N.Y.S. 726 (1912).

Definitional Cross References:

"Certificated security". Section 8-102(a)(4).

"Issuer". Section 8-201.

"Security". Section 8-102(a)(15).

"Security certificate". Section 8-102(a)(16).

"Uncertificated security". Section 8-102(a)(18).

PART 5

SECURITY ENTITLEMENTS

§ 8-501. Securities Account; Acquisition of Security Entitlement from Securities Intermediary.

(a) "Securities account" means an account to which a financial asset is or may be credited in accordance with an agreement under which the person maintaining the account undertakes to treat the person for whom the account is maintained as entitled to exercise the rights that comprise the financial asset.

(b) Except as otherwise provided in subsections (d) and (e), a person acquires a security entitlement if a securities intermediary:

(1) indicates by book entry that a financial asset has been credited to the person's securities account;

(2) receives a financial asset from the person or acquires a financial asset for the person and, in either case, accepts it for credit to the person's securities account; or

(3) becomes obligated under other law, regulation, or rule to credit a financial asset to the person's securities account.

(c) If a condition of subsection (b) has been met, a person has a security entitlement even though the securities intermediary does not itself hold the financial asset.

(d) If a securities intermediary holds a financial asset for another person, and the financial asset is registered in the name of, payable to the order of, or specially indorsed to the other person, and has not been indorsed to the securities intermediary or in blank, the other person is treated as holding the financial asset directly rather than as having a security entitlement with respect to the financial asset.

(e) Issuance of a security is not establishment of a security entitlement.

Official Comment

1. Part 5 rules apply to security entitlements, and Section 8-501(b) provides that a person has a security entitlement when a financial asset has been credited to a "securities account." Thus, the term "securities account" specifies the type of arrangements between institutions and their customers that are covered by Part 5. A securities account is a consensual arrangement in which the intermediary undertakes to treat the customer as entitled to exercise the rights that comprise the financial asset. The consensual aspect is covered by the requirement that the account be established pursuant to agreement. The term agreement is used in the broad sense defined in Section 1-201(3). There is no requirement that a formal or written agreement be signed.

As the securities business is presently conducted, several significant relationships clearly fall within the definition of a securities account, including the relationship between a clearing corporation and its participants, a broker and customers who leave securities with the broker, and a bank acting as securities custodian and its custodial customers. Given the enormous variety of arrangements concerning securities that exist today, and the certainty that new arrangements will evolve in the future, it is not possible to specify all of the arrangements to which the term does and does not apply.

Whether an arrangement between a firm and another person concerning a security or other financial asset is a "securities account" under this Article depends on whether the firm has undertaken to treat the other person as entitled to exercise the rights that comprise the security or other financial asset. Section 1-102, however, states the fundamental principle of interpretation that the Code provisions should be construed and applied to promote their underlying purposes and policies. Thus, the question whether a given arrangement is a securities account should be decided not by dictionary analysis of the words of the definition taken out of context, but by considering whether it promotes the objectives of Article 8 to include the arrangement within the term securities account.

The effect of concluding that an arrangement is a securities account is that the rules of Part 5 apply. Accordingly, the definition of "securities account" must be interpreted in light of the substantive provisions in Part 5, which describe the core features of the type of relationship for which the commercial law rules of Revised Article 8 concerning security entitlements were designed. There are many arrangements between institutions and other persons concerning securities or other financial assets which do not fall within the definition of "securities account" because the institutions have not undertaken to treat the other persons as entitled to exercise the ordinary rights of an entitlement holder specified in the Part 5 rules. For example, the term securities account does not cover the relationship between a bank and its depositors or the relationship between a trustee and the beneficiary of an ordinary trust, because those are not relationships in which the holder of a financial asset has undertaken to treat the other as entitled to exercise the rights that comprise the financial asset in the fashion contemplated by the Part 5 rules.

In short, the primary factor in deciding whether an arrangement is a securities account is whether application of the Part 5 rules is consistent with the expectations of the parties to the relationship. Relationships not governed by Part 5 may be governed by other parts of Article 8 if the relationship gives rise to a new security, or may be governed by other law entirely.

2. Subsection (b) of this section specifies what circumstances give rise to security entitlements. Paragraph (1) of subsection (b) sets out the most important rule. It turns on the intermediary's conduct, reflecting a basic operating assumption of the indirect holding system that once a securities intermediary has acknowledged that it is carrying a position in a financial asset for its customer or participant, the intermediary is obligated to treat the customer or participant as entitled to the financial asset. Paragraph (1) does not attempt to specify exactly what accounting, record-keeping, or information transmission steps suffice to indicate that the intermediary has credited the account. That is left to agreement, trade practice, or rule in order to provide the flexibility necessary to accommodate varying or changing accounting and information processing systems. The point of paragraph (1) is that once an intermediary has acknowledged that it is carrying a position for the customer or participant, the customer or participant has a security entitlement. The precise form in which the intermediary manifests that acknowledgment is left to private ordering.

Paragraph (2) of subsection (b) sets out a different operational test, turning not on the intermediary's accounting system but on the facts that accounting systems are supposed to represent. Under paragraph (b)(2) a person has a security entitlement if the intermediary has received and accepted a financial asset for credit to the account of its customer or participant. For example, if a customer of a broker or bank custodian delivers a security certificate in proper form to the broker or bank to be held in the customer's account, the customer acquires a security entitlement. Paragraph (b)(2) also covers circumstances in which the intermediary receives a financial asset from a third person for credit to the account of the customer or participant. Paragraph (b)(2) is not limited to circumstances in which the intermediary receives security certificates or other financial assets in physical form. Paragraph (b)(2) also covers circumstances in which the intermediary acquires a security entitlement with respect to a financial asset which is to be credited to the account of the intermediary's own customer. For example, if a customer transfers her account from Broker A to Broker B, she acquires security entitlements against Broker B once the clearing corporation has credited the positions to Broker B's account. It should be noted, however, that paragraph (b)(2) provides that a person acquires a security entitlement when the intermediary not only receives but also accepts the financial asset for credit to the account. This limitation is included to take account of the fact that there may be circumstances in which an intermediary has received a financial asset but is not willing to undertake the obligations that flow from establishing a security entitlement. For example, a security certificate which is sent to an intermediary may not be in proper form, or may represent a type of financial asset which the intermediary is not willing to carry for others. It should be noted that in all but extremely unusual cases, the circumstances covered by paragraph (2) will also be covered by paragraph (1), because the intermediary will have credited the positions to the customer's account.

Paragraph (3) of subsection (b) sets out a residual test, to avoid any implication that the failure of an intermediary to make the appropriate entries to credit a position to a customer's securities account would prevent the customer from acquiring the rights of an entitlement holder under Part 5. As is the case with the paragraph (2) test, the paragraph (3) test would not be needed for the ordinary cases, since they are covered by paragraph (1).

3. In a sense, Section 8-501(b) is analogous to the rules set out in the provisions of Sections 8-313(1)(d) and 8-320 of the prior version of Article 8 that specified what acts by a securities intermediary or clearing corporation sufficed as a transfer of securities held in fungible bulk. Unlike the prior version of Article 8, however, this section is not based on the idea that an entitlement holder acquires rights only by virtue of a "transfer" from the securities intermediary to the entitlement holder. In the indirect holding system, the significant fact is that the securities intermediary has undertaken to treat the customer as entitled to the financial asset. It is up to the securities intermediary to take the necessary steps to ensure that it will be able to perform its undertaking. It is, for example, entirely possible that a securities intermediary might make entries in a customer's account reflecting that customer's acquisition of a certain security at a time when the securities intermediary did not itself happen to hold any units of that security. The person from whom the securities intermediary bought the security might have failed to deliver and it might have taken some time to clear up the problem, or there may have been an operational gap in time between the crediting of a customer's account and the receipt of securities from another securities intermediary. The entitlement holder's rights against the securities intermediary do not depend on whether or when the securities intermediary acquired its interests. Subsection (c) is intended to make this point clear. Subsection (c) does not mean that the intermediary is free to create security entitlements without itself holding sufficient financial assets to satisfy its entitlement holders. The duty of a securities intermediary to maintain sufficient assets is governed by Section 8-504 and regulatory law. Subsection (c) is included only to make it clear the question whether a person has acquired a security entitlement does not depend on whether the intermediary has complied with that duty.

4. Part 5 of Article 8 sets out a carefully designed system of rules for the indi-

rect holding system. Persons who hold securities through brokers or custodians have security entitlements that are governed by Part 5, rather than being treated as the direct holders of securities. Subsection (d) specifies the limited circumstance in which a customer who leaves a financial asset with a broker or other securities intermediary has a direct interest in the financial asset, rather than a security entitlement.

The customer can be a direct holder only if the security certificate, or other financial asset, is registered in the name of, payable to the order of, or specially indorsed to the customer, and has not been indorsed by the customer to the securities intermediary or in blank. The distinction between those circumstances where the customer can be treated as direct owner and those where the customer has a security entitlement is essentially the same as the distinction drawn under the federal bankruptcy code between customer name securities and customer property. The distinction does not turn on any form of physical identification or segregation. A customer who delivers certificates to a broker with blank indorsements or stock powers is not a direct holder but has a security entitlement, even though the broker holds those certificates in some form of separate safe-keeping arrangement for that particular customer. The customer remains the direct holder only if there is no indorsement or stock power so that further action by the customer is required to place the certificates in a form where they can be transferred by the broker.

The rule of subsection (d) corresponds to the rule set out in Section 8-301(a)(3) specifying when acquisition of possession of a certificate by a securities intermediary counts as "delivery" to the customer.

5. Subsection (e) is intended to make clear that Part 5 does not apply to an arrangement in which a security is issued representing an interest in underlying assets, as distinguished from arrangements in which the underlying assets are carried in a securities account. A common mechanism by which new financial instruments are devised is that a financial institution that holds some security, financial instrument, or pool thereof, creates interests in that asset or pool which are sold to others. In many such cases, the interests so created will fall within the definition of "security" in Section 8-102(a)(15). If so, then by virtue of subsection (e) of Section 8-501, the relationship between the institution that creates the interests and the persons who hold them is not a security entitlement to which the Part 5 rules apply. Accordingly, an arrangement such as an American depositary receipt facility which creates freely transferable interests in underlying securities will be issuance of a security under Article 8 rather than establishment of a security entitlement to the underlying securities.

The subsection (e) rule can be regarded as an aspect of the definitional rules specifying the meaning of securities account and security entitlement. Among the key components of the definition of security in Section 8-102(a)(15) are the "transferability" and "divisibility" tests. Securities, in the Article 8 sense, are fungible interests or obligations that are intended to be tradable. The concept of security entitlement under Part 5 is quite different. A security entitlement is the package of rights that a person has against the person's own intermediary with respect to the positions carried in the person's securities account. That package of rights is not, as such, something that is traded. When a customer sells a security that she had held through a securities account, her security entitlement is terminated; when she buys a security that she will hold through her securities account, she acquires a security entitlement. In most cases, settlement of a securities trade will involve termination of one person's security entitlement and acquisition of a security entitlement by another person. That transaction, however, is not a "transfer" of the same entitlement from one person to another. That is not to say that an entitlement holder cannot transfer an interest in her security entitlement as such; granting a security interest in a security entitlement is such a transfer. On the other hand, the nature of a security entitlement is that the intermediary is undertaking duties only to the person identified as the entitlement holder.

Definitional Cross References:

"Financial asset". Section 8-102(a)(9).

"Indorsement". Section 8-102(a)(11).

"Securities intermediary". Section 8-102(a)(14).

"Security". Section 8-102(a)(15).

"Security entitlement". Section 8-102(a)(17).

§ 8-502. Assertion of Adverse Claim Against Entitlement Holder.

An action based on an adverse claim to a financial asset, whether framed in conversion, replevin, constructive trust, equitable lien, or other theory, may not be asserted against a person who acquires a security entitlement under Section 8-501 for value and without notice of the adverse claim.

Official Comment

1. The section provides investors in the indirect holding system with protection against adverse claims by specifying that no adverse claim can be asserted against a person who acquires a security entitlement under Section 8-501 for value and without notice of the adverse claim. It plays a role in the indirect holding system analogous to the rule of the direct holding system that protected purchasers take free from adverse claims (Section 8-303).

This section does not use the locution "takes free from adverse claims" because that could be confusing as applied to the indirect holding system. The nature of indirect holding system is that an entitlement holder has an interest in common with others who hold positions in the same financial asset through the same intermediary. Thus, a particular entitlement holder's interest in the financial assets held by its intermediary is necessarily "subject to" the interests of others. See Section 8-503. The rule stated in this section might have been expressed by saying that a person who acquires a security entitlement under Section 8-501 for value and without notice of adverse claims takes "that security entitlement" free from adverse claims. That formulation has not been used, however, for fear that it would be misinterpreted as suggesting that the person acquires a right to the underlying financial assets that could not be affected by the competing rights of others claiming through common or higher tier intermediaries. A security entitlement is a complex bundle of rights. This section does not deal with the question of what rights are in the bundle. Rather, this section provides that once a person has acquired the bundle, someone else cannot take it away on the basis of assertion that the transaction in which the security entitlement was created involved a violation of the claimant's rights.

2. Because securities trades are typically settled on a net basis by book-entry movements, it would ordinarily be impossible for anyone to trace the path of any particular security, no matter how the interest of parties who hold through intermediaries is described. Suppose, for example, that S has a 1000 share position in XYZ common stock through an account with a broker, Able & Co. S's identical twin impersonates S and directs Able to sell the securities. That same day, B places an order with Baker & Co., to buy 1000 shares of XYZ common stock. Later, S discovers the wrongful act and seeks to recover "her shares." Even if S can show that, at the stage of the trade, her sell order was matched with B's buy order, that would not suffice to show that "her shares" went to B. Settlement between Able and Baker occurs on a net basis for all trades in XYZ that day; indeed Able's net position may have been such that it received rather than delivered shares in XYZ through the settlement system.

In the unlikely event that this was the only trade in XYZ common stock executed in the market that day, one could follow the shares from S's account to B's account. The plaintiff in an action in conversion or similar legal action to enforce a property interest must show that the defendant has an item of property that belongs to the plaintiff. In this example, B's security entitlement is not the same item of property that formerly was held by S, it is a new package of rights that B acquired against Baker under Section 8–501. Principles of equitable remedies might, however, provide S with a basis for contending that if the position B received was the traceable product of the wrongful taking of S's property by S's twin, a constructive trust should be imposed on B's property in favor of S. See G. Palmer, The Law of Restitution § 2.14. Section 8–502 ensures that no such claims can be asserted against a person, such as B in this example, who acquires a security entitlement under Section 8–501 for value and without notice, regardless of what theory of law or equity is used to describe the basis of the assertion of the adverse claim.

In the above example, S would ordinarily have no reason to pursue B unless Able is insolvent and S's claim will not be satisfied in the insolvency proceedings. Because S did not give an entitlement order for the disposition of her security entitlement, Able must recredit her account for the 1000 shares of XYZ common stock. See Section 8–507(b).

3. The following examples illustrate the operation of Section 8–502.

Example 1. Thief steals bearer bonds from Owner. Thief delivers the bonds to Broker for credit to Thief's securities account, thereby acquiring a security entitlement under Section 8–501(b). Under other law, Owner may have a claim to have a constructive trust imposed on the security entitlement as the traceable product of the bonds that Thief misappropriated. Because Thief was himself the wrongdoer, Thief obviously had notice of Owner's adverse claim. Accordingly, Section 8–502 does not preclude Owner from asserting an adverse claim against Thief.

Example 2. Thief steals bearer bonds from Owner. Thief owes a personal debt to Creditor. Creditor has a securities account with Broker. Thief agrees to transfer the bonds to Creditor as security for or in satisfaction of his debt to Creditor. Thief does so by sending the bonds to Broker for credit to Creditor's securities account. Creditor thereby acquires a security entitlement under Section 8–501(b). Under other law, Owner may have a claim to have a constructive trust imposed on the security entitlement as the traceable product of the bonds that Thief misappropriated. Creditor acquired the security entitlement for value, since Creditor acquired it as security for or in satisfaction of Thief's debt to Creditor. See Section 1–201(44). If Creditor did not have notice of Owner's claim, Section 8–502 precludes any action by Owner against Creditor, whether framed in constructive trust or other theory. Section 8–105 specifies what counts as notice of an adverse claim.

Example 3. Father, as trustee for Son, holds XYZ Co. shares in a securities account with Able & Co. In violation of his fiduciary duties, Father sells the XYZ Co. shares and uses the proceeds for personal purposes. Father dies, and his estate is insolvent. Assume—implausibly—that Son is able to trace the XYZ Co. shares and show that the "same shares" ended up in Buyer's securities account with Baker & Co. Section 8–502 precludes any action by Son against Buyer, whether framed in constructive trust or other theory, provided that Buyer acquired the security entitlement for value and without notice of adverse claims.

Example 4. Debtor holds XYZ Co. shares in a securities account with Able & Co. As collateral for a loan from Bank, Debtor grants Bank a security interest in the security entitlement to the XYZ Co. shares. Bank perfects by a method which leaves Debtor with the ability to dispose of the shares. See Section 9–115. In violation of the security agreement, Debtor sells the XYZ Co. shares and absconds with the proceeds. Assume—implausibly—that Bank is able to trace the XYZ Co. shares and show that the "same shares" ended up in Buyer's securities account with Baker & Co. Section 8–502 precludes any action by Bank against Buyer, whether framed in constructive trust or other theory, provided that Buyer acquired the security entitlement for value and without notice of adverse claims.

Example 5. Debtor owns controlling interests in various public companies, including Acme and Ajax. Acme owns 60% of the stock of another public company, Beta. Debtor causes the Beta stock to be pledged to Lending Bank as collateral for Ajax's debt. Acme holds the Beta stock through an account with a securities custodian, C Bank, which in turn holds through Clearing Corporation. Lending Bank is also a Clearing Corporation participant. The pledge of the Beta stock is implemented by Acme instructing C Bank to instruct Clearing Corporation to debit C Bank's account and credit Lending Bank's account. Acme and Ajax both become insolvent. The Beta stock is still valuable. Acme's liquidator asserts that the pledge of the Beta stock for Ajax's debt was wrongful as against Acme and seeks to recover the Beta stock from Lending Bank. Because the pledge was implemented by an outright transfer into Lending Bank's account at Clearing Corporation, Lending Bank acquired a security entitlement to the Beta stock under Section 8–501. Lending Bank acquired the security entitlement for value, since it acquired it as security for a debt. See Section 1–201(44). If Lending Bank did not have notice of Acme's claim, Section 8–502 will preclude any action by Acme against Lending Bank, whether framed in constructive trust or other theory.

4. Although this section protects entitlement holders against adverse claims, it does not protect them against the risk that their securities intermediary will not itself have sufficient financial assets to satisfy the claims of all of its entitlement holders. Suppose that Customer A holds 1000 shares of XYZ Co. stock in an account with her broker, Able & Co. Able in turn holds 1000 shares of XYZ Co. through its account with Clearing Corporation, but has no other positions in XYZ Co. shares, either for other customers or for its own proprietary account. Customer B places an order with Able for the purchase of 1000 shares of XYZ Co. stock, and pays the purchase price. Able credits B's account with a 1000 share position in XYZ Co. stock, but Able does not itself buy any additional XYZ Co. shares. Able fails, having only 1000 shares to satisfy the claims of A and B. Unless other insolvency law establishes a different distributional rule, A and B would share the 1000 shares held by Able pro rata, without regard to the time that their respective entitlements were established. See Section 8–503(b). Section 8–502 protects entitlement holders, such as A and B, against adverse claimants. In this case, however, the problem that A and B face is not that someone is trying to take away their entitlements, but that the entitlements are not worth what they thought. The only role that Section 8–502 plays in this case is to preclude any assertion that A has some form of claim against B by virtue of the fact that Able's establishment of an entitlement in favor of B diluted A's rights to the limited assets held by Able.

Definitional Cross References:

"Adverse claim". Section 8–102(a)(1).

"Financial asset". Section 8–102(a)(9).

"Notice of adverse claim". Section 8–105.

"Security entitlement". Section 8–102(a)(17).

"Value". Sections 1–201(44) & 8–116.

§ 8–503. Property Interest of Entitlement Holder in Financial Asset Held By Securities Intermediary.

(a) To the extent necessary for a securities intermediary to satisfy all security entitlements with respect to a particular financial asset, all interests in that financial asset held by the securities intermediary are held by the securities intermediary for the entitlement holders, are not property of the securities intermediary, and are not subject to claims of creditors of the securities intermediary, except as otherwise provided in Section 8–511.

(b) An entitlement holder's property interest with respect to a particular financial asset under subsection (a) is a pro rata property interest in all interests in that financial asset held by the securities intermediary, without regard to the time the entitlement holder acquired the security entitlement or the time the securities intermediary acquired the interest in that financial asset.

(c) An entitlement holder's property interest with respect to a particular financial asset under subsection (a) may be enforced against the securities intermediary only by exercise of the entitlement holder's rights under Sections 8–505 through 8–508.

(d) An entitlement holder's property interest with respect to a particular financial asset under subsection (a) may be enforced against a purchaser of the financial asset or interest therein only if:

(1) insolvency proceedings have been initiated by or against the securities intermediary;

(2) the securities intermediary does not have sufficient interests in the financial asset to satisfy the security entitlements of all of its entitlement holders to that financial asset;

(3) the securities intermediary violated its obligations under Section 8–504 by transferring the financial asset or interest therein to the purchaser; and

(4) the purchaser is not protected under subsection (e).

The trustee or other liquidator, acting on behalf of all entitlement holders having security entitlements with respect to a particular financial asset, may recover the financial asset, or interest therein, from the purchaser. If the trustee or other liquidator elects not to pursue that right, an entitlement holder whose security entitlement remains unsatisfied has the right to recover its interest in the financial asset from the purchaser.

(e) An action based on the entitlement holder's property interest with respect to a particular financial asset under subsection (a), whether framed in conversion, replevin, constructive trust, equitable lien, or other theory, may not be asserted against any purchaser of a financial asset or interest therein who gives value, obtains control, and does not act in collusion with the securities intermediary in violating the securities intermediary's obligations under Section 8–504.

Official Comment

1. This section specifies the sense in which a security entitlement is an interest in the property held by the securities intermediary. It expresses the ordinary understanding that securities that a firm holds for its customers are not general assets of the firm subject to the claims of creditors. Since securities intermediaries generally do not segregate securities in such fashion that one could identify particular securities as the ones held for customers, it would not be realistic for this section to state that "customers' securities" are not subject to creditors' claims. Rather subsection (a) provides that to the extent necessary to satisfy all customer claims, all units of that security held by the firm are held for the entitlement holders, are not property of the securities intermediary, and are not subject to creditors' claims, except as otherwise provided in Section 8-511.

An entitlement holder's property interest under this section is an interest with respect to a specific issue of securities or financial assets. For example, customers of a firm who have positions in XYZ common stock have security entitlements with respect to the XYZ common stock held by the intermediary, while other customers who have positions in ABC common stock have security entitlements with respect to the ABC common stock held by the intermediary.

Subsection (b) makes clear that the property interest described in subsection (a) is an interest held in common by all entitlement holders who have entitlements to a particular security or other financial asset. Temporal factors are irrelevant. One entitlement holder cannot claim that its rights to the assets held by the intermediary are superior to the rights of another entitlement holder by virtue of having acquired those rights before, or after, the other entitlement holder. Nor does it matter whether the intermediary had sufficient assets to satisfy all entitlement holders' claims at one point, but no longer does. Rather, all entitlement holders have a pro rata interest in whatever positions in that financial asset the intermediary holds.

Although this section describes the property interest of entitlement holders in the assets held by the intermediary, it does not necessarily determine how property held by a failed intermediary will be distributed in insolvency proceedings. If the intermediary fails and its affairs are being administered in an insolvency proceeding, the applicable insolvency law governs how the various parties having claims against the firm are treated. For example, the distributional rules for stockbroker liquidation proceedings under the Bankruptcy Code and Securities Investor Protection Act ("SIPA") provide that all customer property is distributed pro rata among all customers in proportion to the dollar value of their total positions, rather than dividing the property on an issue by issue basis. For intermediaries that are not subject to the Bankruptcy Code and SIPA, other insolvency law would determine what distributional rule is applied.

2. Although this section recognizes that the entitlement holders of a securities intermediary have a property interest in the financial assets held by the intermediary, the incidents of this property interest are established by the rules of Article 8, not by common law property concepts. The traditional Article 8 rules on certificated securities were based on the idea that a paper certificate could be regarded as a nearly complete reification of the underlying right. The rules on transfer and the consequences of wrongful transfer could then be written using the same basic concepts as the rules for physical chattels. A person's claim of ownership of a certificated security is a right to a specific identifiable physical object, and that right can be asserted against any person who ends up in possession of that physical certificate, unless cut off by the rules protecting purchasers for value without notice. Those concepts do not work for the indirect holding system. A security entitlement is not a

claim to a specific identifiable thing; it is a package of rights and interests that a person has against the person's securities intermediary and the property held by the intermediary. The idea that discrete objects might be traced through the hands of different persons has no place in the Revised Article 8 rules for the indirect holding system. The fundamental principles of the indirect holding system rules are that an entitlement holder's own intermediary has the obligation to see to it that the entitlement holder receives all of the economic and corporate rights that comprise the financial asset, and that the entitlement holder can look only to that intermediary for performance of the obligations. The entitlement holder cannot assert rights directly against other persons, such as other intermediaries through whom the intermediary holds the positions, or third parties to whom the intermediary may have wrongfully transferred interests, except in extremely unusual circumstances where the third party was itself a participant in the wrongdoing. Subsections (c) through (e) reflect these fundamental principles.

Subsection (c) provides that an entitlement holder's property interest can be enforced against the intermediary only by exercise of the entitlement holder's rights under Sections 8–505 through 8–508. These are the provisions that set out the duty of an intermediary to see to it that the entitlement holder receives all of the economic and corporate rights that comprise the security. If the intermediary is in insolvency proceedings and can no longer perform in accordance with the ordinary Part 5 rules, the applicable insolvency law will determine how the intermediary's assets are to be distributed.

Subsections (d) and (e) specify the limited circumstances in which an entitlement holder's property interest can be asserted against a third person to whom the intermediary transferred a financial asset that was subject to the entitlement holder's claim when held by the intermediary. Subsection (d) provides that the property interest of entitlement holders cannot be asserted against any transferee except in the circumstances therein specified. So long as the intermediary is solvent, the entitlement holders must look to the intermediary to satisfy their claims. If the intermediary does not hold financial assets corresponding to the entitlement holders' claims, the intermediary has the duty to acquire them. See Section 8–504. Thus, paragraphs (1), (2), and (3) of subsection (d) specify that the only occasion in which the entitlement holders can pursue transferees is when the intermediary is unable to perform its obligation, and the transfer to the transferee was a violation of those obligations. Even in that case, a transferee who gave value and obtained control is protected by virtue of the rule in subsection (e), unless the transferee acted in collusion with the intermediary.

Subsections (d) and (e) have the effect of protecting transferees from an intermediary against adverse claims arising out of assertions by the intermediary's entitlement holders that the intermediary acted wrongfully in transferring the financial assets. These rules, however, operate in a slightly different fashion than traditional adverse claim cut-off rules. Rather than specifying that a certain class of transferee takes free from all claims, subsections (d) and (e) specify the circumstances in which this particular form of claim can be asserted against a transferee. Revised Article 8 also contains general adverse claim cut-off rules for the indirect holding system. See Sections 8–502 and 8–510. The rule of subsections (d) and (e) takes precedence over the general cut-off rules of those sections, because Section 8–503 itself defines and sets limits on the assertion of the property interest of entitlement holders. Thus, the question whether entitlement holders' property interest can be asserted as an adverse claim against a transferee from the intermediary is governed by the collusion test of Section 8–503(e), rather than by the "without notice" test of Sections 8–502 and 8–510.

3. The limitations that subsections (c) through (e) place on the ability of customers of a failed intermediary to recover

securities or other financial assets from transferees are consistent with the fundamental policies of investor protection that underlie this Article and other bodies of law governing the securities business. The commercial law rules for the securities holding and transfer system must be assessed from the forward-looking perspective of their impact on the vast number of transactions in which no wrongful conduct occurred or will occur, rather than from the *post hoc* perspective of what rule might be most advantageous to a particular class of persons in litigation that might arise out of the occasional case in which someone has acted wrongfully. Although one can devise hypothetical scenarios where particular customers might find it advantageous to be able to assert rights against someone other than the customers' own intermediary, commercial law rules that permitted customers to do so would impair rather than promote the interest of investors and the safe and efficient operation of the clearance and settlement system. Suppose, for example, that Intermediary A transfers securities to B, that Intermediary A acted wrongfully as against its customers in so doing, and that after the transaction Intermediary A did not have sufficient securities to satisfy its obligations to its entitlement holders. Viewed solely from the standpoint of the customers of Intermediary A, it would seem that permitting the property to be recovered from B, would be good for investors. That, however, is not the case. B may itself be an intermediary with its own customers, or may be some other institution through which individuals invest, such as a pension fund or investment company. There is no reason to think that rules permitting customers of an intermediary to trace and recover securities that their intermediary wrongfully transferred work to the advantage of investors in general. To the contrary, application of such rules would often merely shift losses from one set of investors to another. The uncertainties that would result from rules permitting such recoveries would work to the disadvantage of all participants in the securities markets.

The use of the collusion test in Section 8–503(e) furthers the interests of investors generally in the sound and efficient operation of the securities holding and settlement system. The effect of the choice of this standard is that customers of a failed intermediary must show that the transferee from whom they seek to recover was affirmatively engaged in wrongful conduct, rather than casting on the transferee any burden of showing that the transferee had no awareness of wrongful conduct by the failed intermediary. The rule of Section 8–503(e) is based on the long-standing policy that it is undesirable to impose upon purchasers of securities any duty to investigate whether their sellers may be acting wrongfully.

Rather than imposing duties to investigate, the general policy of the commercial law of the securities holding and transfer system has been to eliminate legal rules that might induce participants to conduct investigations of the authority of persons transferring securities on behalf of others for fear that they might be held liable for participating in a wrongful transfer. The rules in Part 4 of Article 8 concerning transfers by fiduciaries provide a good example. Under *Lowry v. Commercial & Farmers' Bank,* 15 F.Cas. 1040 (C.C.D.Md.1848) (No. 8581), an issuer could be held liable for wrongful transfer if it registered transfer of securities by a fiduciary under circumstances where it had any reason to believe that the fiduciary may have been acting improperly. In one sense that seems to be advantageous for beneficiaries who might be harmed by wrongful conduct by fiduciaries. The consequence of the *Lowry* rule, however, was that in order to protect against risk of such liability, issuers developed the practice of requiring extensive documentation for fiduciary stock transfers, making such transfers cumbersome and time consuming. Accordingly, the rules in Part 4 of Article 8, and in the prior fiduciary transfer statutes, were designed to discourage transfer agents from conducting investigations into the rightfulness of transfers by fiduciaries.

The rules of Revised Article 8 implement for the indirect holding system the same policies that the rules on protected purchasers and registration of transfer adopt for the direct holding system. A securities intermediary is, by definition, a person who is holding securities on behalf of other persons. There is nothing unusual or suspicious about a transaction in which a securities intermediary sells securities that it was holding for its customers. That is exactly what securities intermediaries are in business to do. The interests of customers of securities intermediaries would not be served by a rule that required counterparties to transfers from securities intermediaries to investigate whether the intermediary was acting wrongfully against its customers. Quite the contrary, such a rule would impair the ability of securities intermediaries to perform the function that customers want.

The rules of Section 8-503(c) through (e) apply to transferees generally, including pledgees. The reasons for treating pledgees in the same fashion as other transferees are discussed in the Comments to Section 8-511. The statement in subsection (a) that an intermediary holds financial assets for customers and not as its own property does not, of course, mean that the intermediary lacks power to transfer the financial assets to others. For example, although Article 9 provides that for a security interest to attach the debtor must have "rights" in the collateral, see Section 9-203, the fact that an intermediary is holding a financial asset in a form that permits ready transfer means that it has such rights, even if the intermediary is acting wrongfully against its entitlement holders in granting the security interest. The question whether the secured party takes subject to the entitlement holder's claim in such a case is governed by Section 8-511, which is an application to secured transactions of the general principles expressed in subsections (d) and (e) of this section.

Definitional Cross References:

"Control". Section 8-106.

"Entitlement holder". Section 8-102(a)(7).

"Financial asset". Section 8-102(a)(9).

"Insolvency proceedings". Section 1-201(22).

"Purchaser". Sections 1-201(33) & 8-116.

"Securities intermediary". Section 8-102(a)(14).

"Security entitlement". Section 8-102(a)(17).

"Value". Sections 1-201(44) & 8-116.

§ 8-504. Duty of Securities Intermediary to Maintain Financial Asset.

(a) A securities intermediary shall promptly obtain and thereafter maintain a financial asset in a quantity corresponding to the aggregate of all security entitlements it has established in favor of its entitlement holders with respect to that financial asset. The securities intermediary may maintain those financial assets directly or through one or more other securities intermediaries.

(b) Except to the extent otherwise agreed by its entitlement holder, a securities intermediary may not grant any security interests in a financial asset it is obligated to maintain pursuant to subsection (a).

(c) A securities intermediary satisfies the duty in subsection (a) if:

(1) the securities intermediary acts with respect to the duty as agreed upon by the entitlement holder and the securities intermediary; or

(2) in the absence of agreement, the securities intermediary exercises due care in accordance with reasonable commercial standards to obtain and maintain the financial asset.

(d) This section does not apply to a clearing corporation that is itself the obligor of an option or similar obligation to which its entitlement holders have security entitlements.

Official Comment

1. This section expresses one of the core elements of the relationships for which the Part 5 rules were designed, to wit, that a securities intermediary undertakes to hold financial assets corresponding to the security entitlements of its entitlement holders. The locution "shall promptly obtain and shall thereafter maintain" is taken from the corresponding regulation under federal securities law, 17 C.F.R. § 240.15c3-3. This section recognizes the reality that as the securities business is conducted today, it is not possible to identify particular securities as belonging to customers as distinguished from other particular securities that are the firm's own property. Securities firms typically keep all securities in fungible form, and may maintain their inventory of a particular security in various locations and forms, including physical securities held in vaults or in transit to transfer agents, and book entry positions at one or more clearing corporations. Accordingly, this section states that a securities intermediary shall maintain a quantity of financial assets corresponding to the aggregate of all security entitlements it has established. The last sentence of subsection (a) provides explicitly that the securities intermediary may hold directly or indirectly. That point is implicit in the use of the term "financial asset," inasmuch as Section 8-102(a)(9) provides that the term "financial asset" may refer either to the underlying asset or the means by which it is held, including both security certificates and security entitlements.

2. Subsection (b) states explicitly a point that is implicit in the notion that a securities intermediary must maintain financial assets corresponding to the security entitlements of its entitlement holders, to wit, that it is wrongful for a securities intermediary to grant security interests in positions that it needs to satisfy customers' claims, except as authorized by the customers. This statement does not determine the rights of a secured party to whom a securities intermediary wrongfully grants a security interest; that issue is governed by Sections 8-503 and 8-511.

Margin accounts are common examples of arrangements in which an entitlement holder authorizes the securities intermediary to grant security interests in the positions held for the entitlement holder. Securities firms commonly obtain the funds needed to provide margin loans to their customers by "rehypothecating" the customers' securities. In order to facilitate rehypothecation, agreements between margin customers and their brokers commonly authorize the broker to commingle securities of all margin customers for rehypothecation to the lender who provides the financing. Brokers commonly rehypothecate customer securities having a value somewhat greater than the amount of the loan made to the customer, since the lenders who provide the necessary financing to the broker need some cushion of protection against the risk of decline in the value of the rehypothecated securities. The extent and manner in which a firm may rehypothecate customers' securities are determined by the agreement between the intermediary and the entitlement holder and by applicable regulatory law. Current regulations under the federal securities laws require that brokers obtain the explicit consent of customers before pledging customer securities or commingling different customers' securities for pledge. Federal regulations also limit the extent to which a broker may rehypothecate customer securities to 110% of the aggregate amount of the borrowings of all customers.

3. The statement in this section that an intermediary must obtain and main-

tain financial assets corresponding to the aggregate of all security entitlements it has established is intended only to capture the general point that one of the key elements that distinguishes securities accounts from other relationships, such as deposit accounts, is that the intermediary undertakes to maintain a direct correspondence between the positions it holds and the claims of its customers. This section is not intended as a detailed specification of precisely how the intermediary is to perform this duty, nor whether there may be special circumstances in which an intermediary's general duty is excused. Accordingly, the general statement of the duties of a securities intermediary in this and the following sections is supplemented by two other provisions. First, each of Sections 8-504 through 8-508 contains an "agreement/due care" provision. Second, Section 8-509 sets out general qualifications on the duties stated in these sections, including the important point that compliance with corresponding regulatory provisions constitutes compliance with the Article 8 duties.

4. The "agreement/due care" provision in subsection (c) of this section is necessary to provide sufficient flexibility to accommodate the general duty stated in subsection (a) to the wide variety of circumstances that may be encountered in the modern securities holding system. For the most common forms of publicly traded securities, the modern depository-based indirect holding system has made the likelihood of an actual loss of securities remote, though correctable errors in accounting or temporary interruptions of data processing facilities may occur. Indeed, one of the reasons for the evolution of book-entry systems is to eliminate the risk of loss or destruction of physical certificates. There are, however, some forms of securities and other financial assets which must still be held in physical certificated form, with the attendant risk of loss or destruction. Risk of loss or delay may be a more significant consideration in connection with foreign securities. An American securities intermediary may well be willing to hold a foreign security in a securities account for its customer, but the intermediary may have relatively little choice of or control over foreign intermediaries through which the security must in turn be held. Accordingly, it is common for American securities intermediaries to disclaim responsibility for custodial risk of holding through foreign intermediaries.

Subsection (c)(1) provides that a securities intermediary satisfies the duty stated in subsection (a) if the intermediary acts with respect to that duty in accordance with the agreement between the intermediary and the entitlement holder. Subsection (c)(2) provides that if there is no agreement on the matter, the intermediary satisfies the subsection (a) duty if the intermediary exercises due care in accordance with reasonable commercial standards to obtain and maintain the financial asset in question. This formulation does not state that the intermediary has a universally applicable statutory duty of due care. Section 1-102(3) provides that statutory duties of due care cannot be disclaimed by agreement, but the "agreement/due care" formula contemplates that there may be particular circumstances where the parties do not wish to create a specific duty of due care, for example, with respect to foreign securities. Under subsection (c)(1), compliance with the agreement constitutes satisfaction of the subsection (a) duty, whether or not the agreement provides that the intermediary will exercise due care.

In each of the sections where the "agreement/due care" formula is used, it provides that entering into an agreement and performing in accordance with that agreement is a method by which the securities intermediary may satisfy the statutory duty stated in that section. Accordingly, the general obligation of good faith performance of statutory and contract duties, see Sections 1-203 and 8-102(a)(10), would apply to such an agreement. It would not be consistent with the obligation of good faith performance for an agreement to purport to establish the usual sort of arrangement between an intermediary and entitlement holder, yet disclaim altogether one of the basic elements that define that relationship. For example, an agreement stating that an intermediary assumes no responsibilities whatsoever for the safekeeping any of the entitlement holder's securities positions would not be consistent with good faith performance of the intermediary's duty to obtain and maintain financial assets corresponding to the entitlement holder's security entitlements.

To the extent that no agreement under subsection (c)(1) has specified the details of the intermediary's performance of the subsection (a) duty, subsection (c)(2) provides that the intermediary satisfies that duty if it exercises due care in accordance with reasonable commercial standards. The duty of care includes both care in the intermediary's own operations and care in the selection of other intermediaries through whom the intermediary holds the assets in question. The statement of the obligation of due care is meant to incorporate the principles of the common law under which the specific actions or precautions necessary to meet the obligation of care are determined by such factors as the nature and value of the property, the customs and practices of the business, and the like.

5. This section necessarily states the duty of a securities intermediary to obtain and maintain financial assets only at the very general and abstract level. For the most part, these matters are specified in great detail by regulatory law. Broker-dealers registered under the federal securities laws are subject to detailed regulation concerning the safeguarding of customer securities. See 17 C.F.R. § 240.15c3-3. Section 8-509(a) provides explicitly that if a securities intermediary complies with such regulatory law, that constitutes compliance with Section 8-503. In certain circumstances, these rules permit a firm to be in a position where it temporarily lacks a sufficient quantity of financial assets to satisfy all customer claims. For example, if another firm has failed to make a delivery to the firm in settlement of a trade, the firm is permitted a certain period of time to clear up the problem before it is obligated to obtain the necessary securities from some other source.

6. Subsection (d) is intended to recognize that there are some circumstances, where the duty to maintain a sufficient quantity of financial assets does not apply because the intermediary is not holding anything on behalf of others. For example, the Options Clearing Corporation is treated as a "securities intermediary" under this Article, although it does not itself hold options on behalf of its participants. Rather, it becomes the issuer of the options, by virtue of guaranteeing the obligations of participants in the clearing corporation who have written or purchased the options cleared through it. See Section 8-103(e). Accordingly, the general duty of an intermediary under subsection (a) does not apply, nor would other provisions of Part 5 that depend upon the existence of a requirement that the securities intermediary hold financial assets, such as Sections 8-503 and 8-508.

Definitional Cross References:

"Agreement". Section 1-201(3).

"Clearing corporation". Section 8-102(a)(5).

"Entitlement holder". Section 8-102(a)(7).

"Financial asset". Section 8-102(a)(9).

"Securities intermediary". Section 8-102(a)(14).

"Security entitlement". Section 8-102(a)(17).

§ 8-505. Duty of Securities Intermediary with Respect to Payments and Distributions.

(a) A securities intermediary shall take action to obtain a payment or distribution made by the issuer of a financial asset. A securities intermediary satisfies the duty if:

(1) the securities intermediary acts with respect to the duty as agreed upon by the entitlement holder and the securities intermediary; or

(2) in the absence of agreement, the securities intermediary exercises due care in accordance with reasonable commercial standards to attempt to obtain the payment or distribution.

(b) A securities intermediary is obligated to its entitlement holder for a payment or distribution made by the issuer of a financial asset if the payment or distribution is received by the securities intermediary.

Official Comment

1. One of the core elements of the securities account relationships for which the Part 5 rules were designed is that the securities intermediary passes through to the entitlement holders the economic benefit of ownership of the financial asset, such as payments and distributions made by the issuer. Subsection (a) expresses the ordinary understanding that a securities intermediary will take appropriate action to see to it that any payments or distributions made by the issuer are received. One of the main reasons that investors make use of securities intermediaries is to obtain the services of a professional in performing the record-keeping and other functions necessary to ensure that payments and other distributions are received.

2. Subsection (a) incorporates the same "agreement/due care" formula as the other provisions of Part 5 dealing with the duties of a securities intermediary. See Comment 4 to Section 8–504. This formulation permits the parties to specify by agreement what action, if any, the intermediary is to take with respect to the duty to obtain payments and distributions. In the absence of specification by agreement, the intermediary satisfies the duty if the intermediary exercises due care in accordance with reasonable commercial standards. The provisions of Section 8–509 also apply to the Section 8–505 duty, so that compliance with applicable regulatory requirements constitutes compliance with the Section 8–505 duty.

3. Subsection (b) provides that a securities intermediary is obligated to its entitlement holder for those payments or distributions made by the issuer that are in fact received by the intermediary. It does not deal with the details of the time and manner of payment. Moreover, as with any other monetary obligation, the obligation to pay may be subject to other rights of the obligor, by way of set-off counterclaim or the like. Section 8–509(c) makes this point explicit.

Definitional Cross References:

"Agreement". Section 1–201(3).

"Entitlement holder". Section 8–102(a)(7).

"Financial asset". Section 8–102(a)(9).

"Securities intermediary". Section 8–102(a)(14).

"Security entitlement". Section 8–102(a)(17).

§ 8–506. Duty of Securities Intermediary to Exercise Rights as Directed by Entitlement Holder.

A securities intermediary shall exercise rights with respect to a financial asset if directed to do so by an entitlement holder. A securities intermediary satisfies the duty if:

(1) the securities intermediary acts with respect to the duty as agreed upon by the entitlement holder and the securities intermediary; or

(2) in the absence of agreement, the securities intermediary either places the entitlement holder in a position to exercise the rights directly or exercises due care in accordance with reasonable commercial standards to follow the direction of the entitlement holder.

Official Comment

1. Another of the core elements of the securities account relationships for which the Part 5 rules were designed is that although the intermediary may, by virtue of the structure of the indirect holding system, be the party who has the power to exercise the corporate and other rights that come from holding the security, the intermediary exercises these powers as representative of the entitlement holder rather than at its own discretion. This characteristic is one of the things that distinguishes a securities account from other arrangements where one person holds securities "on behalf of" another, such as the relationship between a mutual fund and its shareholders or a trustee and its beneficiary.

2. The fact that the intermediary exercises the rights of security holding as representative of the entitlement holder does not, of course, preclude the entitlement holder from conferring discretionary authority upon the intermediary. Arrangements are not uncommon in which investors do not wish to have their intermediaries forward proxy materials or other information. Thus, this section provides that the intermediary shall exercise corporate and other rights "if directed to do so" by the entitlement holder. Moreover, as with the other Part 5 duties, the "agreement/due care" formulation is used in stating how the intermediary is to perform this duty. This section also provides that the intermediary satisfies the duty if it places the entitlement holder in a position to exercise the rights directly. This is to take account of the fact that some of the rights attendant upon ownership of the security, such as rights to bring derivative and other litigation, are far removed from the matters that intermediaries are expected to perform.

3. This section, and the two that follow, deal with the aspects of securities holding that are related to investment decisions. For example, one of the rights of holding a particular security that would fall within the purview of this section would be the right to exercise a conversion right for a convertible security. It is quite common for investors to confer discretionary authority upon another person, such as an investment adviser, with respect to these rights and other investment decisions. Because this section, and the other sections of Part 5, all specify that a securities intermediary satisfies the Part 5 duties if it acts in accordance with the entitlement holder's agreement, there is no inconsistency between the statement of duties of a securities intermediary and these common arrangements.

4. Section 8–509 also applies to the Section 8–506 duty, so that compliance with applicable regulatory requirements constitutes compliance with this duty. This is quite important in this context, since the federal securities laws establish a comprehensive system of regulation of the distribution of proxy materials and exercise of voting rights with respect to securities held through brokers and other intermediaries. By virtue of Section 8–509(a), compliance with such regulatory requirement constitutes compliance with the Section 8–506 duty.

Definitional Cross References:

"Agreement". Section 1–201(3).

"Entitlement holder". Section 8–102(a)(7).

"Financial asset". Section 8–102(a)(9).

"Securities intermediary". Section 8–102(a)(14).

"Security entitlement". Section 8–102(a)(17).

§ 8–507. Duty of Securities Intermediary to Comply With Entitlement Order.

(a) A securities intermediary shall comply with an entitlement order if the entitlement order is originated by the appropriate person, the securities intermediary has had reasonable opportunity to assure itself that the entitlement order is genuine and authorized, and the securities intermediary has had reasonable opportunity to comply with the entitlement order. A securities intermediary satisfies the duty if:

(1) the securities intermediary acts with respect to the duty as agreed upon by the entitlement holder and the securities intermediary; or

(2) in the absence of agreement, the securities intermediary exercises due care in accordance with reasonable commercial standards to comply with the entitlement order.

(b) If a securities intermediary transfers a financial asset pursuant to an ineffective entitlement order, the securities intermediary shall reestablish a security entitlement in favor of the person entitled to it, and pay or credit any payments or distributions that the person did not receive as a result of the wrongful transfer. If the securities intermediary does not reestablish a security entitlement, the securities intermediary is liable to the entitlement holder for damages.

Official Comment

1. Subsection (a) of this section states another aspect of duties of securities intermediaries that make up security entitlements—the securities intermediary's duty to comply with entitlement orders. One of the main reasons for holding securities through securities intermediaries is to enable rapid transfer in settlement of trades. Thus the right to have one's orders for disposition of the security entitlement honored is an inherent part of the relationship. Subsection (b) states the correlative liability of a securities intermediary for transferring a financial asset from an entitlement holder's account pursuant to an entitlement order that was not effective.

2. The duty to comply with entitlement orders is subject to several qualifications. The intermediary has a duty only with respect to an entitlement order that is in fact originated by the appropriate person. Moreover, the intermediary has a duty only if it has had reasonable opportunity to assure itself that the order is genuine and authorized, and reasonable opportunity to comply with the order. The same "agreement/due care" formula is used in this section as in the other Part 5 sections on the duties of intermediaries, and the rules of Section 8-509 apply to the Section 8-507 duty.

3. Appropriate person is defined in Section 8-107. In the usual case, the appropriate person is the entitlement holder, see Section 8-107(a)(3). Entitlement holder is defined in Section 8-102(a)(7) as the person "identified in the records of a securities intermediary as the person having a security entitlement." Thus, the general rule is that an intermediary's duty with respect to entitlement orders runs only to the person with whom the intermediary has established a relationship. One of the basic principles of the indirect holding system is that securities intermediaries owe duties only to their own customers. See also Section 8-115. The only situation in which a securities intermediary has a duty to comply with entitlement orders originated by a person other than the person with whom the intermediary established a relationship is covered by Section 8-107(a)(4) and (a)(5), which provide that the term "appropriate person" includes the successor or personal representative of a decedent, or the custodian or guardian of a person who lacks capacity. If the entitlement holder is competent, another person does not fall within the defined term "appropriate person" merely by virtue of having power to act as an agent for the entitlement holder. Thus, an intermediary is not required to determine at its peril whether a person who purports to be

authorized to act for an entitlement holder is in fact authorized to do so. If an entitlement holder wishes to be able to act through agents, the entitlement holder can establish appropriate arrangements in advance with the securities intermediary.

One important application of this principle is that if an entitlement holder grants a security interest in its security entitlements to a third-party lender, the intermediary owes no duties to the secured party, unless the intermediary has entered into a "control" agreement in which it agrees to act on entitlement orders originated by the secured party. See Section 8-106. Even though the security agreement or some other document may give the secured party authority to act as agent for the debtor, that would not make the secured party an "appropriate person" to whom the security intermediary owes duties. If the entitlement holder and securities intermediary have agreed to such a control arrangement, then the intermediary's action in following instructions from the secured party would satisfy the subsection (a) duty. Although an agent, such as the secured party in this example, is not an "appropriate person," an entitlement order is "effective" if originated by an authorized person. See Section 8-107(a) and (b). Moreover, Section 8-507(a) provides that the intermediary satisfies its duty if it acts in accordance with the entitlement holder's agreement.

4. Subsection (b) provides that an intermediary is liable for a wrongful transfer if the entitlement order was "ineffective." Section 8-107 specifies whether an entitlement order is effective. An "effective entitlement order" is different from an "entitlement order originated by an appropriate person." An entitlement order is effective under Section 8-107(b) if it is made by the appropriate person, or by a person who has power to act for the appropriate person under the law of agency, or if the appropriate person has ratified the entitlement order or is precluded from denying its effectiveness. Thus, although a securities intermediary does not have a duty to act on an entitlement order originated by the entitlement holder's agent, the intermediary is not liable for wrongful transfer if it does so.

Subsection (b), together with Section 8-107, has the effect of leaving to other law most of the questions of the sort dealt with by Article 4A for wire transfers of funds, such as allocation between the securities intermediary and the entitlement holder of the risk of fraudulent entitlement orders.

5. The term entitlement order does not cover all directions that a customer might give a broker concerning securities held through the broker. Article 8 is not a codification of all of the law of customers and stockbrokers. Article 8 deals with the settlement of securities trades, not the trades. The term entitlement order does not refer to instructions to a broker to make trades, that is, enter into contracts for the purchase or sale of securities. Rather, the entitlement order is the mechanism of transfer for securities held through intermediaries, just as indorsements and instructions are the mechanism for securities held directly. In the ordinary case the customer's direction to the broker to deliver the securities at settlement is implicit in the customer's instruction to the broker to sell. The distinction is, however, significant in that this section has no application to the relationship between the customer and broker with respect to the trade itself. For example, assertions by a customer that it was damaged by a broker's failure to execute a trading order sufficiently rapidly or in the proper manner are not governed by this Article.

Definitional Cross References:

"Agreement". Section 1-201(3).

"Appropriate person". Section 8-107.

"Effective". Section 8-107.

"Entitlement holder". Section 8-102(a)(7).

"Entitlement order". Section 8-102(a)(8).

"Financial asset". Section 8-102(a)(9).

"Securities intermediary". Section 8-102(a)(14).

"Security entitlement". Section 8–102(a)(17).

§ 8–508. Duty of Securities Intermediary to Change Entitlement Holder's Position to Other Form of Security Holding.

A securities intermediary shall act at the direction of an entitlement holder to change a security entitlement into another available form of holding for which the entitlement holder is eligible, or to cause the financial asset to be transferred to a securities account of the entitlement holder with another securities intermediary. A securities intermediary satisfies the duty if:

(1) the securities intermediary acts as agreed upon by the entitlement holder and the securities intermediary; or

(2) in the absence of agreement, the securities intermediary exercises due care in accordance with reasonable commercial standards to follow the direction of the entitlement holder.

Official Comment

1. This section states another aspect of the duties of securities intermediaries that make up security entitlements—the obligation of the securities intermediary to change an entitlement holder's position into any other form of holding for which the entitlement holder is eligible or to transfer the entitlement holder's position to an account at another intermediary. This section does not state unconditionally that the securities intermediary is obligated to turn over a certificate to the customer or to cause the customer to be registered on the books of the issuer, because the customer may not be eligible to hold the security directly. For example, municipal bonds are now commonly issued in "book-entry only" form, in which the only entity that the issuer will register on its own books is a depository.

If security certificates in registered form are issued for the security, and individuals are eligible to have the security registered in their own name, the entitlement holder can request that the intermediary deliver or cause to be delivered to the entitlement holder a certificate registered in the name of the entitlement holder or a certificate indorsed in blank or specially indorsed to the entitlement holder. If security certificates in bearer form are issued for the security, the entitlement holder can request that the intermediary deliver or cause to be delivered a certificate in bearer form. If the security can be held by individuals directly in uncertificated form, the entitlement holder can request that the security be registered in its name. The specification of this duty does not determine the pricing terms of the agreement in which the duty arises.

2. The same "agreement/due care" formula is used in this section as in the other Part 5 sections on the duties of intermediaries. So too, the rules of Section 8–509 apply to the Section 8–508 duty.

Definitional Cross References:

"Agreement". Section 1–201(3).

"Entitlement holder". Section 8–102(a)(7).

"Financial asset". Section 8–102(a)(9).

"Securities intermediary". Section 8–102(a)(14).

"Security entitlement". Section 8–102(a)(17).

§ 8–509. Specification of Duties of Securities Intermediary by Other Statute or Regulation; Manner of Performance of Duties of Securities Intermediary and Exercise of Rights of Entitlement Holder.

(a) If the substance of a duty imposed upon a securities intermediary by Sections 8–504 through 8–508 is the subject of other statute, regulation, or rule, compliance with that statute, regulation, or rule satisfies the duty.

(b) To the extent that specific standards for the performance of the duties of a securities intermediary or the exercise of the rights of an entitlement holder are not specified by other statute, regulation, or rule or by agreement between the securities intermediary and entitlement holder, the securities intermediary shall perform its duties and the entitlement holder shall exercise its rights in a commercially reasonable manner.

(c) The obligation of a securities intermediary to perform the duties imposed by Sections 8–504 through 8–508 is subject to:

(1) rights of the securities intermediary arising out of a security interest under a security agreement with the entitlement holder or otherwise; and

(2) rights of the securities intermediary under other law, regulation, rule, or agreement to withhold performance of its duties as a result of unfulfilled obligations of the entitlement holder to the securities intermediary.

(d) Sections 8–504 through 8–508 do not require a securities intermediary to take any action that is prohibited by other statute, regulation, or rule.

Official Comment

This Article is not a comprehensive statement of the law governing the relationship between broker-dealers or other securities intermediaries and their customers. Most of the law governing that relationship is the common law of contract and agency, supplemented or supplanted by regulatory law. This Article deals only with the most basic commercial/property law principles governing the relationship. Although Sections 8–504 through 8–508 specify certain duties of securities intermediaries to entitlement holders, the point of these sections is to identify what it means to have a security entitlement, not to specify the details of performance of these duties.

For many intermediaries, regulatory law specifies in great detail the intermediary's obligations on such matters as safekeeping of customer property, distribution of proxy materials, and the like. To avoid any conflict between the general statement of duties in this Article and the specific statement of intermediaries' obligations in such regulatory schemes, subsection (a) provides that compliance with applicable regulation constitutes compliance with the duties specified in Sections 8–504 through 8–508.

Definitional Cross References:

"Agreement". Section 1–201(3).

"Entitlement holder". Section 8–102(a)(7).

"Securities intermediary". Section 8–102(a)(14).

"Security agreement". Section 9–105(1)(*l*).

"Security interest". Section 1–201(37).

§ 8-510. Rights of Purchaser of Security Entitlement from Entitlement Holder.

(a) An action based on an adverse claim to a financial asset or security entitlement, whether framed in conversion, replevin, constructive trust, equitable lien, or other theory, may not be asserted against a person who purchases a security entitlement, or an interest therein, from an entitlement holder if the purchaser gives value, does not have notice of the adverse claim, and obtains control.

(b) If an adverse claim could not have been asserted against an entitlement holder under Section 8-502, the adverse claim cannot be asserted against a person who purchases a security entitlement, or an interest therein, from the entitlement holder.

(c) In a case not covered by the priority rules in Article 9, a purchaser for value of a security entitlement, or an interest therein, who obtains control has priority over a purchaser of a security entitlement, or an interest therein, who does not obtain control. Purchasers who have control rank equally, except that a securities intermediary as purchaser has priority over a conflicting purchaser who has control unless otherwise agreed by the securities intermediary.

Official Comment

1. This section specifies certain rules concerning the rights of persons who purchase interests in security entitlements from entitlement holders. The rules of this section are provided to take account of cases where the purchaser's rights are derivative from the rights of another person who is and continues to be the entitlement holder.

2. Subsection (a) provides that no adverse claim can be asserted against a purchaser of an interest in a security entitlement if the purchaser gives value, obtains control, and does not have notice of the adverse claim. The primary purpose of this rule is to give adverse claim protection to persons who take security interests in security entitlements and obtain control, but do not themselves become entitlement holders.

The following examples illustrate subsection (a):

Example 1. X steals a certificated bearer bond from Owner. X delivers the certificate to Able & Co. for credit to X's securities account. Later, X borrows from Bank and grants bank a security interest in the security entitlement. Bank obtains control under Section 8-106(d)(2) by virtue of an agreement in which Able agrees to comply with entitlement orders originated by Bank. X absconds.

Example 2. Same facts as in Example 1, except that Bank does not obtain a control agreement. Instead, Bank perfects by filing a financing statement.

In both of these examples, when X deposited the bonds X acquired a security entitlement under Section 8-501. Under other law, Owner may be able to have a constructive trust imposed on the security entitlement as the traceable product of the bonds that X misappropriated. X granted a security interest in that entitlement to Bank. Bank was a purchaser of an interest in the security entitlement from X. In Example 1, although Bank was not a person who acquired a security entitlement from the intermediary, Bank did obtain control. If Bank did not have notice of Owner's claim, Section 8-510(a) precludes Owner from asserting an adverse claim against Bank. In Example 2, Bank had a perfected security interest, but did not obtain control. Accordingly, Section 8–510(a) does not preclude Owner from asserting its adverse claim against Bank.

3. Subsection (b) applies to the indirect holding system a limited version of the "shelter principle." The following example illustrates the relatively limited class of cases for which it may be needed:

Example 3. Thief steals a certificated bearer bond from Owner. Thief delivers the certificate to Able & Co. for credit to Thief's securities account. Able forwards the certificate to a clearing corporation for credit to Able's account. Later Thief instructs Able to sell the positions in the bonds. Able sells to Baker & Co., acting as broker for Buyer. The trade is settled by book-entries in the accounts of Able and Baker at the clearing corporation, and in the accounts of Thief and Buyer at Able and Baker respectively. Owner may be able to reconstruct the trade records to show that settlement occurred in such fashion that the "same bonds" that were carried in Thief's account at Able are traceable into Buyer's account at Baker. Buyer later decides to donate the bonds to Alma Mater University and executes an assignment of its rights as entitlement holder to Alma Mater.

Buyer had a position in the bonds, which Buyer held in the form of a security entitlement against Baker. Buyer then made a gift of the position to Alma Mater. Although Alma Mater is a purchaser, Section 1–201(33), it did not give value. Thus, Alma Mater is a person who purchased a security entitlement, or an interest therein, from an entitlement holder (Buyer). Buyer was protected against Owner's adverse claim by the Section 8–502 rule. Thus, by virtue of Section 8–510(b), Owner is also precluded from asserting an adverse claim against Alma Mater.

4. Subsection (c) specifies a priority rule for cases where an entitlement holder transfers conflicting interests in the same security entitlement to different purchasers. It follows the same principle as the Article 9 priority rule for investment property, that is, control trumps non-control. Indeed, the most significant category of conflicting "purchasers" may be secured parties. Priority questions for security interests, however, are governed by the rules in Article 9. Subsection (c) applies only to cases not covered by the Article 9 rules. It is intended primarily for disputes over conflicting claims arising out of repurchase agreement transactions that are not covered by the other rules set out in Articles 8 and 9.

The following example illustrates subsection (c):

Example 4. Dealer holds securities through an account at Alpha Bank. Alpha Bank in turns holds through a clearing corporation account. Dealer transfers securities to RP1 in a "hold in custody" repo transaction. Dealer then transfers the same securities to RP2 in another repo transaction. The repo to RP2 is implemented by transferring the securities from Dealer's regular account at Alpha Bank to a special account maintained by Alpha Bank for Dealer and RP2. The agreement among Dealer, RP2, and Alpha Bank provides that Dealer can make substitutions for the securities but RP2 can direct Alpha Bank to sell any securities held in the special account. Dealer becomes insolvent. RP1 claims a prior interest in the securities transferred to RP2.

In this example Dealer remained the entitlement holder but agreed that RP2 could initiate entitlement orders to Dealer's security intermediary, Alpha Bank. If RP2 had become the entitlement holder, the adverse claim rule of Section 8–502 would apply. Even if RP2 does not become the entitlement holder, the arrangement among Dealer, Alpha Bank, and RP2 does suffice to give RP2 control. Thus, under Section 8–510(c), RP2 has priority over RP1, because RP2 is a purchaser who obtained control, and RP1 is a purchaser who did not obtain control. The same result could be reached under Section 8–510(a) which provides that RP1's earlier in time interest cannot be asserted as an adverse claim against RP2. The same result would follow under the Article 9 priority rules if the interests of RP1 and RP2 are characterized as "security interests," see Section 9–115(5)(a). The main point of the rules of Section 8–510(c) is to ensure that there will be clear rules to cover the conflicting claims of RP1 and RP2 without characterizing their interests as Article 9 security interests.

The priority rules in Article 9 for conflicting security interests also include a default rule of pro rata treatment for cases where multiple secured parties have obtained control but omitted to specify their respective rights by agreement. See Section 9–115(5)(b) and Comment 6 to Section 9–115. Because the purchaser priority rule in Section 8–510(c) is intended to track the Article 9 priority rules, it too has a pro rata rule for cases where multiple non-secured party purchasers have obtained control but omitted to specify their respective rights by agreement.

Definitional Cross References:

"Adverse claim". Section 8–102(a)(1).
"Control". Section 8–106.
"Entitlement holder". Section 8–102(a)(7).
"Notice of adverse claim". Section 8–105.
"Purchase". Section 1–201(32).
"Purchaser". Sections 1–201(33) & 8–116.
"Securities intermediary". Section 8–102(a)(14).
"Security entitlement". Section 8–102(a)(17).
"Value". Sections 1–201(44) & 8–116.

§ 8–511. Priority Among Security Interests and Entitlement Holders.

(a) Except as otherwise provided in subsections (b) and (c), if a securities intermediary does not have sufficient interests in a particular financial asset to satisfy both its obligations to entitlement holders who have security entitlements to that financial asset and its obligation to a creditor of the securities intermediary who has a security interest in that financial asset, the claims of entitlement holders, other than the creditor, have priority over the claim of the creditor.

(b) A claim of a creditor of a securities intermediary who has a security interest in a financial asset held by a securities intermediary has priority over claims of the securities intermediary's entitlement holders who have security entitlements with respect to that financial asset if the creditor has control over the financial asset.

(c) If a clearing corporation does not have sufficient financial assets to satisfy both its obligations to entitlement holders who have security entitlements with respect to a financial asset and its obligation to a creditor of the clearing corporation who has a security interest in that financial asset, the claim of the creditor has priority over the claims of entitlement holders.

Official Comment

1. This section sets out priority rules for circumstances in which a securities intermediary fails leaving an insufficient quantity of securities or other financial assets to satisfy the claims of its entitlement holders and the claims of creditors to whom it has granted security interests in financial assets held by it. Subsection (a) provides that entitlement holders' claims have priority except as otherwise provided in subsection (b), and subsection (b) provides that the secured creditor's claim has priority if the secured creditor obtains control, as defined in Section 8–

106. The following examples illustrate the operation of these rules.

Example 1. Able & Co., a broker, borrows from Alpha Bank and grants Alpha Bank a security interest pursuant to a written agreement which identifies certain securities that are to be collateral for the loan, either specifically or by category. Able holds these securities in a clearing corporation account. Able becomes insolvent and it is discovered that Able holds insufficient securities to satisfy the claims of customers who have paid for securities that they held in accounts with Able and the collateral claims of Alpha Bank. Alpha Bank's security interest in the security entitlements that Able holds through the clearing corporation account may be perfected under the automatic perfection rule of Section 9–115(4)(c), but Alpha Bank did not obtain control under Section 8–106. Thus, under Section 8–511(a) the entitlement holders' claims have priority over Alpha Bank's claim.

Example 2. Able & Co., a broker, borrows from Beta Bank and grants Beta Bank a security interest in securities that Able holds in a clearing corporation account. Pursuant to the security agreement, the securities are debited from Alpha's account and credited to Beta's account in the clearing corporation account. Able becomes insolvent and it is discovered that Able holds insufficient securities to satisfy the claims of customers who have paid for securities that they held in accounts with Able and the collateral claims of Alpha Bank. Although the transaction between Able and Beta took the form of an outright transfer on the clearing corporation's books, as between Able and Beta, Able remains the owner and Beta has a security interest. In that respect the situation is no different than if Able had delivered bearer bonds to Beta in pledge to secure a loan. Beta's security interest is perfected, and Beta obtained control. See Sections 8–106 and 9–115. Under Section 8–511(b), Beta Bank's security interest has priority over claims of Able's customers.

The result in Example 2 is an application to this particular setting of the general principle expressed in Section 8–503, and explained in the Comments thereto, that the entitlement holders of a securities intermediary cannot assert rights against third parties to whom the intermediary has wrongfully transferred interests, except in extremely unusual circumstances where the third party was itself a participant in the transferor's wrongdoing. Under subsection (b) the claim of a secured creditor of a securities intermediary has priority over the claims of entitlement holders if the secured creditor has obtained control. If, however, the secured creditor acted in collusion with the intermediary in violating the intermediary's obligation to its entitlement holders, then under Section 8–503(e), the entitlement holders, through their representative in insolvency proceedings, could recover the interest from the secured creditor, that is, set aside the security interest.

2. The risk that investors who hold through an intermediary will suffer a loss as a result of a wrongful pledge by the intermediary is no different than the risk that the intermediary might fail and not have the securities that it was supposed to be holding on behalf of its customers, either because the securities were never acquired by the intermediary or because the intermediary wrongfully sold securities that should have been kept to satisfy customers' claims. Investors are protected against that risk by the regulatory regimes under which securities intermediaries operate. Intermediaries are required to maintain custody, through clearing corporation accounts or in other approved locations, of their customers' securities and are prohibited from using customers' securities in their own business activities. Securities firms who are carrying both customer and proprietary positions are not permitted to grant blanket liens to lenders covering all securities which they hold, for their own account or for their customers. Rather, securities firms designate specifically which posi-

tions they are pledging. Under SEC Rules 8c-1 and 15c2-1, customers' securities can be pledged only to fund loans to customers, and only with the consent of the customers. Customers' securities cannot be pledged for loans for the firm's proprietary business; only proprietary positions can be pledged for proprietary loans. SEC Rule 15c3-3 implements these prohibitions in a fashion tailored to modern securities firm accounting systems by requiring brokers to maintain a sufficient inventory of securities, free from any liens, to satisfy the claims of all of their customers for fully paid and excess margin securities. Revised Article 8 mirrors that requirement, specifying in Section 8-504 that a securities intermediary must maintain a sufficient quantity of investment property to satisfy all security entitlements, and may not grant security interests in the positions it is required to hold for customers, except as authorized by the customers.

If a failed brokerage has violated the customer protection regulations and does not have sufficient securities to satisfy customers' claims, its customers are protected against loss from a shortfall by the Securities Investor Protection Act ("SIPA"). Securities firms required to register as brokers or dealers are also required to become members of the Securities Investor Protection Corporation ("SIPC"), which provides their customers with protection somewhat similar to that provided by FDIC and other deposit insurance programs for bank depositors. When a member firm fails, SIPC is authorized to initiate a liquidation proceeding under the provisions of SIPA. If the assets of the securities firm are insufficient to satisfy all customer claims, SIPA makes contributions to the estate from a fund financed by assessments on its members to protect customers against losses up to $500,000 for cash and securities held at member firms.

Article 8 is premised on the view that the important policy of protecting investors against the risk of wrongful conduct by their intermediaries is sufficiently treated by other law.

3. Subsection (c) sets out a special rule for secured financing provided to enable clearing corporations to complete settlement. The reasons that secured financing arrangements are needed in such circumstances are explained in Comment 7 to Section 9-115. In order to permit clearing corporations to establish liquidity facilities where necessary to ensure completion of settlement, subsection (c) provides a priority for secured lenders to such clearing corporations. Subsection (c) does not turn on control because the clearing corporation may be the top tier securities intermediary for the securities pledged, so that there may be no practicable method for conferring control on the lender.

Definitional Cross References:

"Clearing corporation". Section 8-102(a)(5).

"Control". Section 8-106.

"Entitlement holder". Section 8-102(a)(7).

"Financial asset". Section 8-102(a)(9).

"Securities intermediary". Section 8-102(a)(14).

"Security entitlement". Section 8-102(a)(17).

"Security interest". Section 1-201(37).

"Value". Sections 1-201(44) & 8-116.

PART 6

TRANSITION PROVISIONS FOR REVISED ARTICLE 8

§ 8-601. Effective Date.

This [Act] takes effect....

§ 8-602. Repeals.

This [Act] repeals....

Official Comment

If the State has adopted the Uniform Act for the Simplification of Fiduciary Security Transfers, or similar legislation, it should be repealed.

§ 8–603. Savings Clause.

(a) This [Act] does not affect an action or proceeding commenced before this [Act] takes effect.

(b) If a security interest in a security is perfected at the date this [Act] takes effect, and the action by which the security interest was perfected would suffice to perfect a security interest under this [Act], no further action is required to continue perfection. If a security interest in a security is perfected at the date this [Act] takes effect but the action by which the security interest was perfected would not suffice to perfect a security interest under this [Act], the security interest remains perfected for a period of four months after the effective date and continues perfected thereafter if appropriate action to perfect under this [Act] is taken within that period. If a security interest is perfected at the date this [Act] takes effect and the security interest can be perfected by filing under this [Act], a financing statement signed by the secured party instead of the debtor may be filed within that period to continue perfection or thereafter to perfect.

Official Comment

The revision of Article 8 should present few significant transition problems. Although the revision involves significant changes in terminology and analysis, the substantive rules are, in large measure, based upon the current practices and are consistent with results that could be reached, albeit at times with some struggle, by proper interpretation of the rules of present law. Thus, the new rules can be applied, without significant dislocations, to transactions and events that occurred prior to enactment.

The enacting provisions should not, whether by applicability, transition, or savings clause language, attempt to provide that old Article 8 continues to apply to "transactions," "events," "rights," "duties," "liabilities," or the like that occurred or accrued before the effective date and that new Article 8 applies to those that occur or accrue after the effective date. The reason for revising Article 8 and corresponding provisions of Article 9 is the concern that the provisions of old Article 8 could be interpreted or misinterpreted to yield results that impede the safe and efficient operation of the national system for the clearance and settlement of securities transactions. Accordingly, it is not the case that any effort should be made to preserve the applicability of old Article 8 to transactions and events that occurred before the effective date.

Only two circumstances seem to warrant continued application of rules of old Article 8. First, to avoid disruption in the conduct of litigation, it may make sense to provide for continued application of the old Article 8 rules to lawsuits pending before the effective date. Second, there are some limited circumstances in which prior law permitted perfection of security interests by methods that are not provided for in the revised version. Section 8–313(1)(h) (1978) permitted perfection of security interests in securities held through intermediaries by notice to the intermediary. Under Revised Articles 8 and 9, security interests can be perfected in such cases by control, which requires the agreement of the intermediary, or by filing. It is likely that secured parties who relied strongly on such collateral under prior law did not simply send notices but obtained agreements from the intermediaries that would suffice for control under the new rules. However, it seems appropriate to include a provision that gives a secured creditor some opportunity after the effective date to perfect in this or any other case in which there is doubt whether the method of perfection used under prior law would be sufficient under the new version.

CONFORMING AMENDMENTS TO ARTICLES 1, 3, 4, 5, 9, AND 10

See Appendix XII, infra.

ARTICLE 9

SECURED TRANSACTIONS; SALES OF ACCOUNTS AND CHATTEL PAPER

PART 1. SHORT TITLE, APPLICABILITY AND DEFINITIONS

PART 2. VALIDITY OF SECURITY AGREEMENT AND RIGHTS OF PARTIES THERETO

PART 3. RIGHTS OF THIRD PARTIES; PERFECTED AND UNPERFECTED SECURITY INTERESTS; RULES OF PRIORITY

PART 1

SHORT TITLE, APPLICABILITY AND DEFINITIONS

§ 9–101. Short Title.

This Article shall be known and may be cited as Uniform Commercial Code—Secured Transactions.

Official Comment

This Article sets out a comprehensive scheme for the regulation of security interests in personal property and fixtures. It supersedes prior legislation dealing with such security devices as chattel mortgages, conditional sales, trust receipts, factor's liens and assignments of accounts receivable (see Note to Section 9–102).

Consumer installment sales and consumer loans present special problems of a nature which makes special regulation of them inappropriate in a general commercial codification. Many states now regulate such loans and sales under small loan acts, retail installment selling acts and the like. The National Conference of Commissioners on Uniform State Laws has proposed a Uniform Consumer Credit Code dealing with this subject. While this Article applies generally to security interests in consumer goods, it is not designed to supersede such regulatory legislation (see Notes to Sections 9–102 and 9–203). Nor is this Article designed as a substitute for small loan acts or retail installment selling acts in any state which does not presently have such legislation.

Pre-Code law recognized a wide variety of security devices, which came into use at various times to make possible different types of secured financing. Differences between one device and another persisted, in formal requisites, in the secured party's rights against the debtor and third parties, in the debtor's rights against the secured party, and in filing requirements, although many of those differences no longer served any useful function. Thus an unfiled chattel mortgage was by the law of many states "void" against creditors generally; a conditional sale, often available as a substitute for the chattel mortgage, was in some states valid against all creditors without filing, and in states where filing is required was, if unfiled, void only against lien creditors. The recognition of so many separate security devices had the result that half a dozen filing systems covering chattel security devices might be maintained within a state, some on a county basis, others on a state-wide basis, each of which had to be separately checked to determine a debtor's status.

Nevertheless, despite the great number of security devices there remained gaps in the structure. In many states, for example, a security interest could not be taken in inventory or a stock in trade although there was a real need for such financing. It was often baffling to try to maintain a technically valid security interest when financing a manufacturing process, where the collateral starts out as raw materials, becomes work in process and ends as finished goods. Furthermore, it was by no means clear, even to specialists, how under pre-Code law a security interest might be taken in many kinds of intangible property—such as television or motion picture rights—which have come to be an important source of commercial collateral.

While the chattel mortgage was adaptable for use in almost any situation where goods are collateral, there were limitations, sometimes highly technical, on the use of other devices, such as the conditional sale and particularly the trust receipt. The cases are many in which a security transaction described by the parties as a conditional sale or a trust receipt was later determined by a court to be something else, usually a chattel mortgage. The consequence of such a determination was typically to void the security interest against creditors because the security agreement was not filed *as a chattel mortgage* (even though it may have been filed as a conditional sale or a trust receipt). The already mentioned difficulty of financing on the security of inventory has been got around to some extent by the device known as "field warehousing" as well as by the use of the trust receipt. After 1940 a number of states generally authorized inventory financing by enacting statutes, similar although not uniform, known as "factor's lien" acts. Also after 1940 the increasingly important business of lending against accounts receivable inspired new statutes in that field in more than thirty states.

The growing complexity of financing transactions forced legislatures to keep piling new statutory provisions on top of our inadequate and already sufficiently complicated nineteenth-century structure of security law. The results of this continuing development were increasing costs to both parties and increasing uncertainty as to their rights and the rights of third parties dealing with them.

The aim of this Article is to provide a simple and unified structure within which the immense variety of present-day secured financing transactions can go forward with less cost and with greater certainty.

Under this Article the traditional distinctions among security devices, based largely on form, are not retained; the Article applies to all transactions intended to create security interests in personal property and fixtures, and the single term "security interest" substitutes for the variety of descriptive terms which had grown up at common law and under a hundred-year accretion of statutes. This does not mean that the old forms may not be used, and Section 9–102(2) makes it clear that they may be.

This Article does not determine whether "title" to collateral is in the secured party or in the debtor and adopts neither a "title theory" nor a "lien theory" of security interests. Rights, obligations and remedies under the Article do not depend on the location of title (Section 9–202). The location of title may become important for other purposes—as, for example, in determining the incidence of taxation—and in such a case the parties are left free to contract as they will. In this connection the use of a form which has traditionally been regarded as determinative of title (e.g., the conditional sale) could reasonably be regarded as evidencing the parties' intention with respect to title to the collateral.

Under the Article distinctions based on form (except as between pledge and nonpossessory interests) are no longer controlling. For some purposes there are distinctions based on the type of property which constitutes the collateral—industrial and commercial equipment, business inventory, farm products, consumer goods, accounts receivable, documents of title and other intangibles—and, where appropriate, the Article states special rules applicable to financing transactions involving a particular type of property. Despite the statutory simplification a greater degree of flexibility in the financing transaction is allowed than is possible under existing law.

The scheme of the Article is to make distinctions, where distinctions are necessary, along functional rather than formal lines.

This has made possible a radical simplification in the formal requisites for creation of a security interest.

A more rational filing system replaces the present system of different files for each security device which is subject to filing requirements. Thus not only is the information contained in the files made more accessible but the cost of procuring credit information, and, incidentally, of maintaining the files, is greatly reduced.

The Article's flexibility and simplified formalities should make it possible for new forms of secured financing, as they develop, to fit comfortably under its provisions, thus avoiding the necessity, so apparent in recent years, of year by year passing new statutes and tinkering with the old ones to allow legitimate business transactions to go forward.

The rules set out in this Article are principally concerned with the limits of the secured party's protection against purchasers from and creditors of the debtor. Except for procedure on default, freedom of contract prevails between the immediate parties to the security transaction.

§ 9–102. Policy and Subject Matter of Article.

(1) Except as otherwise provided in Section 9–104 on excluded transactions, this Article applies

(a) to any transaction (regardless of its form) which is intended to create a security interest in personal property or fixtures including goods, documents, instruments, general intangibles, chattel paper or accounts; and also

(b) to any sale of accounts or chattel paper.

(2) This Article applies to security interests created by contract including pledge, assignment, chattel mortgage, chattel trust, trust deed, factor's lien, equipment trust, conditional sale, trust receipt, other lien or title retention contract and lease or consignment intended as security. This Article does not apply to statutory liens except as provided in Section 9–310.

(3) The application of this Article to a security interest in a secured obligation is not affected by the fact that the obligation is itself secured by a transaction or interest to which this Article does not apply.

Note: *The adoption of this Article should be accompanied by the repeal of existing statutes dealing with conditional sales, trust receipts, factor's liens where the factor is given a non-possessory lien, chattel mortgages, crop mortgages, mortgages on railroad equipment, assignment of accounts and generally statutes regulating security interests in personal property.*

Where the state has a retail installment selling act or small loan act, that legislation should be carefully examined to determine what changes in those acts are needed to conform them to this Article. This Article primarily sets out rules defining rights of a secured party against persons dealing with the debtor; it does not prescribe regulations and controls which may be necessary to curb abuses arising in the small loan business or in the financing of consumer purchases on credit. Accordingly there is no intention to repeal existing regulatory acts in those fields by enactment or re-enactment of Article 9. See Section 9–203(4) and the Note thereto.

As amended in 1972.

Official Comment

Prior Uniform Statutory Provision: None.

Purposes:

The main purpose of this Section is to bring all consensual security interests in personal property and fixtures under this Article, except for certain types of transactions excluded by Section 9–104. In addition certain sales of accounts and chattel paper are brought within this Article to avoid difficult problems of distinguishing between transactions intended for security and those not so intended. As to security interests in fixtures created under the law applicable to real estate, see Section 9–313(1).

1. Except for sales of accounts and chattel paper, the principal test whether a transaction comes under this Article is: is the transaction intended to have effect as security? For example, Section 9–104 excludes certain transactions where the se-

curity interest (such as an artisan's lien) arises under statute or common law by reason of status and not by consent of the parties. Transactions in the form of consignments or leases are subject to this Article if the understanding of the parties or the effect of the arrangement shows that a security interest was intended. (As to consignments the provisions of Sections 2-326, 9-114 and 9-408 should be consulted.) When it is found that a security interest as defined in Section 1-201(37) was intended, this Article applies regardless of the form of the transaction or the name by which the parties may have christened it. The list of traditional security devices in subsection (2) is illustrative only; other old devices, as well as any new ones which the ingenuity of lawyers may invent, are included, so long as the requisite intent is found. The controlling definition is that contained in subsection (1).

The Article does not in terms abolish existing security devices. The conditional sale or bailment-lease, for example, is not prohibited; but even though it is used, the rules of this Article govern.

2. If an obligation is to repay money lent and is not part of chattel paper, it is either an instrument or a general intangible. A sale of an instrument or general intangible is not within this Article, but a transfer intended to have effect as security for an obligation of the transferor is covered by subsection 1(a). In either case the nature of the transaction is not affected by the fact that collateral is transferred with the instrument or general intangible. Such a transfer is treated as a transfer by operation of law, whether or not it is articulated in the agreement.

An assignment of accounts or chattel paper as security for an obligation is covered by subsection (1)(a). Commercial financing on the basis of accounts and chattel paper is often so conducted that the distinction between a security transfer and a sale is blurred, and a sale of such property is therefore covered by subsection (1)(b) whether intended for security or not, unless excluded by Section 9-104. The buyer then is treated as a secured party, and his interest as a security interest. See Sections 9-105(1)(m), 1-201(37). Certain sales which have nothing to do with commercial financing transactions are excluded by Section 9-104(f); compare Spurlin v. Sloan, 368 S.W.2d 314 (Ky.1963). See also Section 9-302(1)(e), exempting from filing casual or isolated assignments, and Section 9-302(2), preserving the perfected status of a security interest against the original debtor when a secured party assigns his interest.

Neither Section 9-102 nor any other provision of Article 9 is intended to prevent the transfer of ownership of accounts or chattel paper. The determination of whether a particular transfer of accounts or chattel paper constitutes a sale or a transfer for security purposes (such as in connection with a loan) is not governed by Article 9. Article 9 applies both to sales of accounts or chattel paper and loans secured by accounts or chattel paper primarily to incorporate Article 9's perfection rules. The use of terminology such as "security interest" to include the interest of a buyer of accounts or chattel paper, "secured party" to include a buyer of accounts or chattel paper, "debtor" to include a seller of accounts or chattel paper, and "collateral" to include accounts or chattel paper that have been sold is intended solely as a drafting technique to achieve this end and is not relevant to the sale or secured transaction determination. See PEB Commentary No. 14, dated June 10, 1994 [Appendix V, infra].

3. In general, problems of choice of law in this Article as to the validity of security agreements are governed by Section 1-105. Problems of choice of law as to perfection of security interests and the effect of perfection or non-perfection thereof, including rules requiring reperfection, are governed by Section 9-103.

4. An illustration of subsection (3) is as follows:

The owner of Blackacre borrows $10,000 from his neighbor, and secures his note by a mortgage on Blackacre. This

Article is not applicable to the creation of the real estate mortgage. Nor is it applicable to a sale of the note by the mortgagee, even though the mortgage continues to secure the note. However, when the mortgagee pledges the note to secure his own obligation to X, this Article applies to the security interest thus created, which is a security interest in an instrument even though the instrument is secured by a real estate mortgage. This Article leaves to other law the question of the effect on rights under the mortgage of delivery or non-delivery of the mortgage or of recording or non-recording of an assignment of the mortgagee's interest. See Section 9–104(j). But under Section 3–304(5) recording of the assignment does not of itself prevent X from holding the note in due course.

5. While most sections of this Article apply to a security interest without regard to the nature of the collateral or its use, some sections state special rules with reference to particular types of collateral. An index of sections where such special rules are stated follows:

ACCOUNTS

Section	
9–102(1)(b)	Sale of accounts subject to Article
9–103(1)	When Article applies; conflict of laws rules
9–104(f)	Certain sales of accounts excluded from Article
9–106	Definitions
9–205	Permissible for debtor to make collections
9–206(1)	Agreement not to assert defenses against assignee
9–301(1)(d)	Unperfected security interest subordinate to certain transferees
9–302(1)(e)	What assignments need not be filed
9–306(5)	Rule when goods whose sale gave rise to an account return to seller's possession
9–318(1)	Rights of assignee subject to defenses
9–318(2)	Modification of contract after assignment of contract right
9–318(3)	When account debtor may pay assignor
9–318(4)	Term prohibiting assignment ineffective
9–401	Place of filing
9–502	Collection rights of secured party
9–504(2)	Rights on default where underlying transaction was sale of accounts or contract rights

CHATTEL PAPER

9–102(1)(b)	Sale subject to Article
9–104(f)	Certain sales excluded from Article
9–105(1)(b)	Definition
9–205	Permissible for debtor to make collections
9–206(1)	Agreement not to assert defenses against assignee
9–207(1)	Duty of secured party in possession to preserve rights against prior parties
9–301(1)(c)	Unperfected security interest subordinate to certain transferees
9–304(1)	Perfection by filing
9–305	When possession by secured party perfects security interest
9–306(5)	Rule when goods whose sale results in chattel paper return to seller's possession
9–308	When purchasers of chattel paper have priority over security interest
9–318(1)	Rights of assignee subject to defenses
9–318(3)	When account debtor may pay assignor
9–502	Collection rights of secured party
9–504(2)	Rights on default where underlying transaction was sale

Section

DOCUMENTS AND INSTRUMENTS

Section	
9-105(1)(e)	Definition of document (and see 1-201)
9-105(1)(g)	Definition of instrument
9-206(1)	Rule where buyer of goods signs both negotiable instrument and security agreement
9-207(1)	Duty of secured party in possession of instrument to preserve rights against prior parties
9-301(1)(c)	Unperfected security interest subordinate to certain transferees
9-302(1)(b) and (f)	What interests need not be filed
9-304(1)	How security interest can be perfected
9-304(2, 3)	Perfection of security interest in goods in possession of issuer of negotiable document or of other bailee
9-304(4, 5)	Perfection of security interest in instruments or negotiable documents without filing or transfer of possession
9-305	When possession by secured party perfects security interest
9-308	When purchasers of instruments have priority over security interest
9-309	When purchasers of negotiable instruments or negotiable documents have priority over security interest
9-501(1)	Rights on default when collateral is documents
9-502	Collection rights of secured party

GENERAL INTANGIBLES

9-103(2)	When Article applies; conflict of laws rules
9-105	Obligor is "account debtor"
9-106	Definition
9-301(1)(d)	Unperfected security interest subordinate to certain transferees
9-318(1)	Rights of assignee subject to defenses
9-318(3)	When account debtor may pay assignor
9-502	Collection rights of secured party

GOODS

(See also Consumer Goods, Equipment, Farm Products, Inventory)

9-103	When Article applies with regard to goods of a type normally used in more than one jurisdiction; goods covered by certificate of title; conflict of laws rules
9-105(1)(h)	Definition
9-109	Classification of goods as consumer goods, equipment, farm products and inventory
9-203	Formal requisites of security agreement covering certain types of goods (crops or timber)
9-204	Validity of after-acquired property clause covering certain types of goods (crops, consumer goods)
9-205	Permissible for debtor to accept returned goods
9-206(2)	When security agreement can limit or modify warranties on sale
9-301(1)(c)	Unperfected security interest subordinate to certain transferees
9-304(2, 3)	Perfection of security interest in goods in possession of issuer of negotiable document or of other bailee
9-304(5)	Perfection of security interest without filing or transfer of possession where goods in possession of certain bailees
9-305	When possession by secured party perfects security interest
9-306(5)	Rule when goods whose sale gave rise to account or chattel paper return to seller's possession
9-307	When buyers of goods from debtor take free of security interest
9-313	Goods which are or become fixtures
9-314	Goods affixed to other goods

Section	
9–315	Goods commingled in a product
9–401(1)	Place of filing for fixtures
9–402	Form of financing statement covering fixtures
9–504(1)	Sale of goods by secured party after default subject to Article 2 (Sales)

CONSUMER GOODS

9–109(1)	Definition
9–203(2)	Transaction, although subject to this Article, may also be subject to certain regulatory statutes
9–204(2)	Validity of after-acquired property clause
9–206(1)	Buyer's agreement not to assert defenses against an assignee subject to statute or decision which establishes rule for buyers of consumer goods
9–302(1)(d)	When filing not required
9–307(2)	When buyers from debtor take free of security interest
9–401(1)(a)	Place of filing
9–505(1)	Secured party's duty to dispose of repossessed consumer goods
9–507(1)	Secured party's liability for improper disposition of consumer goods after default

EQUIPMENT

9–103(2)	When Article applies with regard to certain types of equipment normally used in more than one jurisdiction; conflict of laws rules
9–109(2)	Definition
9–302(1)(c)	When filing not required to perfect security interest in certain farm equipment
9–307(2)	When buyers of certain farm equipment from debtor take free of security interest
9–401(1)	Place of filing for equipment used in farming operation
9–503	Secured party's right after default to remove or to render equipment unusable

FARM PRODUCTS

9–109(3)	Definition
9–203(1)(b)	Formal requisites of security agreement covering crops
9–307	When a buyer of farm products takes free of security interest
9–312(2)	Priority of secured party who gives new value to enable debtor to produce crops
9–401(1)	Place of filing
9–402(1) and (3)	Form of financing statement covering crops

INVENTORY

9–103(3)	When Article applies with regard to certain types of inventory normally used in more than one jurisdiction; conflict of laws rules
9–109(4)	Definition
9–114	Consigned goods
9–306(5)	Rule where goods whose sale gave rise to account or chattel paper return to seller's possession
9–307(1)	When buyers from debtor take free of security interest
9–312(3), 9–304(5)	When purchase money security interest takes priority over conflicting security interest
9–408	Financing statements covering consigned or leased goods

Cross References:

Sections 9-103 and 9-104.
Point 1: Section 2-326.
Point 2: Section 1-105.

Definitional Cross References:

"Account". Section 9-106.
"Chattel paper". Section 9-105.
"Contract". Section 1-201.
"Document". Section 9-105.
"General intangibles". Section 9-106.
"Goods". Section 9-105.
"Instrument". Section 9-105.
"Security interest". Section 1-201.

§ 9-103. Perfection of Security Interest in Multiple State Transactions.

[1995 Amendments to text indicated by strikeout and underline]

(1) Documents, instruments, letters of credit, and ordinary goods.

(a) This subsection applies to documents, ~~and~~ instruments, rights to proceeds of written letters of credit, and ~~to~~ goods other than those covered by a certificate of title described in subsection (2), mobile goods described in subsection (3), and minerals described in subsection (5).

(b) Except as otherwise provided in this subsection, perfection and the effect of perfection or non-perfection of a security interest in collateral are governed by the law of the jurisdiction where the collateral is when the last event occurs on which is based the assertion that the security interest is perfected or unperfected.

(c) If the parties to a transaction creating a purchase money security interest in goods in one jurisdiction understand at the time that the security interest attaches that the goods will be kept in another jurisdiction, then the law of the other jurisdiction governs the perfection and the effect of perfection or non-perfection of the security interest from the time it attaches until thirty days after the debtor receives possession of the goods and thereafter if the goods are taken to the other jurisdiction before the end of the thirty-day period.

(d) When collateral is brought into and kept in this state while subject to a security interest perfected under the law of the jurisdiction from which the collateral was removed, the security interest remains perfected, but if action is required by Part 3 of this Article to perfect the security interest,

(i) if the action is not taken before the expiration of the period of perfection in the other jurisdiction or the end of four months after the collateral is brought into this state, whichever period first expires, the security interest becomes unperfected at the end of that period and is thereafter deemed to have been unperfected as against a person who became a purchaser after removal;

(ii) if the action is taken before the expiration of the period specified in subparagraph (i), the security interest continues perfected thereafter;

(iii) for the purpose of priority over a buyer of consumer goods (subsection (2) of Section 9-307), the period of the effectiveness of a filing in the jurisdiction from which the collateral is removed is governed by the rules with respect to perfection in subparagraphs (i) and (ii).

(2) Certificate of title.

(a) This subsection applies to goods covered by a certificate of title issued under a statute of this state or of another jurisdiction under the law of which indication of a security interest on the certificate is required as a condition of perfection.

(b) Except as otherwise provided in this subsection, perfection and the effect of perfection or non-perfection of the security interest are governed by the law (including the conflict of laws rules) of the jurisdiction issuing the certificate until four months after the goods are removed from that jurisdiction and thereafter until the goods are registered in another jurisdiction, but in any event not beyond surrender of the certificate. After the expiration of that period, the goods are not covered by the certificate of title within the meaning of this section.

(c) Except with respect to the rights of a buyer described in the next paragraph, a security interest, perfected in another jurisdiction otherwise than by notation on a certificate of title, in goods brought into this state and thereafter covered by a certificate of title issued by this state is subject to the rules stated in paragraph (d) of subsection (1).

(d) If goods are brought into this state while a security interest therein is perfected in any manner under the law of the jurisdiction from which the goods are removed and a certificate of title is issued by this state and the certificate does not show that the goods are subject to the security interest or that they may be subject to security interests not shown on the certificate, the security interest is subordinate to the rights of a buyer of the goods who is not in the business of selling goods of that kind to the extent that he gives value and receives delivery of the goods after issuance of the certificate and without knowledge of the security interest.

(3) Accounts, general intangibles and mobile goods.

(a) This subsection applies to accounts (other than an account described in subsection (5) on minerals) and general intangibles (other than uncertificated securities) and to goods which are mobile and which are of a type normally used in more than one jurisdiction, such as motor vehicles, trailers, rolling stock, airplanes, shipping containers, road building and construction machinery and commercial harvesting machinery and the like, if the goods are equipment or are inventory leased or held for lease by the debtor to others, and are not covered by a certificate of title described in subsection (2).

(b) The law (including the conflict of laws rules) of the jurisdiction in which the debtor is located governs the perfection and the effect of perfection or non-perfection of the security interest.

(c) If, however, the debtor is located in a jurisdiction which is not a part of the United States, and which does not provide for perfection of the security interest by filing or recording in that jurisdiction, the law of the jurisdiction in the United States in which the debtor has its major executive office in the United States governs the perfection and the effect of perfection or non-perfection of the security interest through filing. In the alternative, if the debtor is located in a jurisdiction which is not a part of the United States or Canada and the collateral is accounts or general intangibles for money due or to become due, the security interest may be perfected by notification to the account debtor. As used in this paragraph, "United States" includes its territories and possessions and the Commonwealth of Puerto Rico.

(d) A debtor shall be deemed located at his place of business if he has one, at his chief executive office if he has more than one place of business, otherwise at his residence. If, however, the debtor is a foreign air carrier under the Federal Aviation Act of 1958, as amended, it shall be deemed located at the designated office of the agent upon whom service of process may be made on behalf of the foreign air carrier.

(e) A security interest perfected under the law of the jurisdiction of the location of the debtor is perfected until the expiration of four months after a change of the debtor's location to another jurisdiction, or until perfection would have ceased by the law of the first jurisdiction, whichever period first expires. Unless perfected in the new jurisdiction before the end of that period, it becomes unperfected thereafter and is deemed to have been unperfected as against a person who became a purchaser after the change.

(4) Chattel paper.

The rules stated for goods in subsection (1) apply to a possessory security interest in chattel paper. The rules stated for accounts in subsection (3) apply to a non-possessory security interest in chattel paper, but the security interest may not be perfected by notification to the account debtor.

(5) Minerals.

Perfection and the effect of perfection or non-perfection of a security interest which is created by a debtor who has an interest in minerals or the like (including oil and gas) before extraction and which attaches thereto as extracted, or which attaches to an account resulting from the sale thereof at the wellhead or minehead are governed by the law (including the conflict of laws rules) of the jurisdiction wherein the wellhead or minehead is located.

(6) Investment property.

(a) This subsection applies to investment property.

(b) Except as otherwise provided in paragraph (f), during the time that a security certificate is located in a jurisdiction, perfection of a security interest, the effect of perfection or non-perfection, and the priority of a security interest in the certificated security represented thereby are governed by the local law of that jurisdiction.

(c) Except as otherwise provided in paragraph (f), perfection of a security interest, the effect of perfection or non-perfection, and the priority of a security interest in an uncertificated security are governed by the local law of the issuer's jurisdiction as specified in Section 8–110(d).

(d) Except as otherwise provided in paragraph (f), perfection of a security interest, the effect of perfection or non-perfection, and the priority of a security interest in a security entitlement or securities account are governed by the local law of the securities intermediary's jurisdiction as specified in Section 8–110(e).

(e) Except as otherwise provided in paragraph (f), perfection of a security interest, the effect of perfection or non-perfection, and the priority of a security interest in a commodity contract or commodity account are governed by the local law of the commodity intermediary's jurisdiction. The following rules determine a "commodity intermediary's jurisdiction" for purposes of this paragraph:

(i) If an agreement between the commodity intermediary and commodity customer specifies that it is governed by the law of a particular jurisdiction, that jurisdiction is the commodity intermediary's jurisdiction.

(ii) If an agreement between the commodity intermediary and commodity customer does not specify the governing law as provided in subparagraph (i), but expressly specifies that the commodity account is maintained at an office in a particular jurisdiction, that jurisdiction is the commodity intermediary's jurisdiction.

(iii) If an agreement between the commodity intermediary and commodity customer does not specify a jurisdiction as provided in subparagraphs (i) or (ii), the commodity intermediary's jurisdiction is the jurisdiction in which is located the office identified in an account statement as the office serving the commodity customer's account.

(iv) If an agreement between the commodity intermediary and commodity customer does not specify a jurisdiction as provided in subparagraphs (i) or (ii) and an account statement does not identify an office serving the commodity customer's account as provided in subparagraph (iii), the commodity intermediary's jurisdiction is the jurisdiction in which is located the chief executive office of the commodity intermediary.

(f) Perfection of a security interest by filing, automatic perfection of a security interest in investment property granted by a broker or securities intermediary, and automatic perfection of a security interest in a commodity contract or commodity account granted by a commodity intermediary are governed by the local law of the jurisdiction in which the debtor is located.

As amended in 1972, 1977, 1994, and 1995.

See Appendices XII and XIV for material relating to changes made in text in 1994 and 1995.

Official Comment

Prior Uniform Statutory Provisions: Paragraph 1(d): Section 14, Uniform Conditional Sales Act.

Purposes:

1. The general rules on choice of law between the original parties in Section 1–105 apply to this Article. However, when conflicting claims to collateral arise, the question depends on *perfection* of security interests, and thus on the effect of perfection or non-perfection. These problems are dealt with in this section. The general rule (paragraph (1)(b)) is that these questions are governed by the law of the jurisdiction where the collateral is when the last event occurs on which is based the assertion that the security interest is perfected or unperfected. This event will frequently be the filing. If the last event is not filing and perfection is through filing, the filing required is in the jurisdiction where the collateral is when the last event occurs; prior filing in another jurisdiction is not effective and is not saved by the four-month rule discussed below, which applies only when the security interest was *perfected* in the jurisdiction from which the collateral was removed. If the security interest was perfected in one jurisdiction and then removed to another jurisdiction, maintenance of perfection in the latter jurisdiction or failure to do so is the "last event" to which the basic rule refers.

There are, however, exceptions to this basic rule:

2. If the parties to a transaction creating a purchase money security interest in goods understand when the security interest attaches that the collateral will be kept in another jurisdiction, the law of that jurisdiction governs perfection and the effect of perfection or non-perfection until 30 days after the debtor receives possession of the goods (paragraph (1)(c)). A filing in that jurisdiction perfects the security interest even before the goods are removed. The 30-day period is not a period of grace during which filing is unnecessary or has retroactive effect, but merely states the period during which the other jurisdiction is the place of filing. The effect of late filing is governed by other provisions, such as Sections 9–301 and 9-312.

3. If the goods reach that jurisdiction within the 30 days, the effectiveness of the filing in that jurisdiction continues without interruption. If the collateral is not kept in that jurisdiction before the end of the 30-day period, paragraph (1)(c) ceases to be applicable and thereafter the law of the jurisdiction where the collateral is controls perfection. A failure of the collateral to reach the intended destination jurisdiction before the expiration of the 30-day period because of a conflicting claim or otherwise may cause disappointment of expectations that the law of the destination jurisdiction will govern continuously, and caution may dictate filing both in that jurisdiction and in the jurisdiction where the security interest attaches.

This section uses the concepts that goods are "kept" in a state or "brought" into a state, and related terms. These concepts imply a stopping place of a permanent nature in the state, not merely transit or storage intended to be transitory.

4.(a) Where the collateral is an automobile or other goods covered by a certificate of title issued by any state and the security interest is perfected by notation on the certificate of title, perfection is controlled by the certificate of title rather than by the law of the state wherein the security interest attached (subsection (2)).

(b) It has long been hoped that "exclusive certificate of title laws" would provide a sure means of controlling property interests in goods like automobiles, which because of their nature cannot readily be controlled by local or statewide filing alone. In theory the certificate of title should control the property interests in the vehicle wherever the vehicle may be. However, two circumstances operate to prevent the perfect operation of the certificate of title device:

First, some states have never adopted certificate of title laws. This results in a problem in the issuance of a certificate of title when the vehicle moves from a non-certificate to a certificate state, because the certificate-issuing officer is in no position to conduct a complete search to ascertain the condition of the title in a state of origin which requires no filing or in which filing could be in any one or more of several localities. Also, it seems that when a vehicle moves from a certificate to a non-certificate state, the officers issuing a new registration for the vehicle are not always meticulous to notify secured parties shown on the certificate to give them a chance to perfect their security interests in the non-certificate state when a new registration is issued. Moreover, some vehicles like mobile homes are not always registered and title certificates are not always issued even in a state which may have certificate laws applicable thereto, because the certificate laws may apply only if the mobile homes use the highways. Registration plates of a mobile home having a certificate could be removed and there would be nothing visible to show that a certificate had ever been issued for it.

Second, various fraudulent devices based on allegations of loss of the certificate of title enable a dishonest person to obtain both an original and a duplicate of title; to have a security interest shown on only one thereof; and then to effect a transfer into a new state on the basis of the clean certificate, no matter how diligent the officers in the second state may be.

Given these practical problems, the choice of applicable rules of law after interstate removals of vehicles subject to certificate of title laws is most difficult. This Article provides the rules set forth below.

(c) The security interest perfected by notation on a certificate of title will be recognized without limit as to time; but, of course, perfection by this method ceases if the certificate of title is surrendered (paragraph (2)(b)). Since the secured party ordinarily holds the certificate, surrender thereof could not occur without his action in the matter in some respect. If the vehicle is reregistered in another jurisdiction while the secured party still holds the certificate, a danger of deception to third parties arises. The section provides that the certificate ceases to control after 4 months following removal if reregistration has occurred, but during the 4 months the secured party has the same protection for cases of interstate removal as is set forth in paragraph (1)(d) of the section and Comment 7, subject to additional limitation if the reregistration also involves a new "clean" certificate of title in the removal jurisdiction and a non-professional buyer buys while that new certificate is outstanding. See paragraph (2)(d) and Comment 4(e).

(d) If a vehicle not described in the preceding paragraph (i.e., not covered by a certificate of title) is removed to a certificate state and a certificate is issued therefor, the holder of a security interest has the same 4-month protection, subject to the provision discussed in the next paragraph of Comment.

(e) Where "this state" issues a certificate of title on collateral that has come from another state subject to a security interest perfected in any manner, problems will arise if this state, from whatever cause, fails to show on its certificate the security interest perfected in the other jurisdiction. This state will have every reason, nevertheless, to make its certificate of title reliable to the type of person who most needs to rely on it. Paragraph (2)(d) of the section therefore provides that the security interest perfected in the other jurisdiction is subordinate to the rights of a limited class of persons buying the goods while there is a clean certificate of title issued by this state, without knowledge of the security interest perfected in the other jurisdiction. The limited class are buyers who are non-professionals, i.e., not dealers and not secured parties, because these are ordinarily professionals. The protective rule mentioned does not apply if this state adopts a device used under some certificate of title laws, namely, stating on the certificate of title that the vehicle may be subject to security interests not shown on the certificate, where the collateral came from a non-certificate state.

In any event the security interest perfected out of state becomes unperfected unless reperfected in this state under the usual 4-month rule (paragraph (2)(d) of the section). States which place a cautionary statement on a certificate of title coming from a non-certificate state make provision to reissue the certificate without the caution after four months.

One difficulty is that no state's certificate of title law makes any provision by which a foreign security interest may be reperfected in that state, without the co-operation of the owner or other person holding the certificate in temporarily surrendering the certificate. But that cooperation is not likely to be forth-coming from an owner who wrongfully procured the issuance of a new certificate not showing the out-of-state security interest, or from a local secured party finding himself in a priority contest with the out-of-state secured party. The only solution for the out-of-state secured party under present certificate of title laws seems to be reperfect by possession, i.e., by repossessing the goods.

5. The general rules of the section based on location of the collateral could not be applied to certain types of intangible collateral which have no location in any realistic sense, or to certain movable chattels which have no permanent location.

(a) For accounts and general intangibles there is no indispensable or symbolic document which represents the underlying claim, whose endorsement or delivery is the one effectual means of transfer. There is a considerable body of case law dealing with the situs of choses in action such as these. This case law is in the highest degree confused, contradictory and uncertain: it affords no base on which to build a statutory rule.

An account arises typically out of a sale; the contract of sale may be executed in State A, the goods shipped from a warehouse in State B to buyer (account debtor) in State C. The account may then be assigned to an assignee in State D. The seller-assignor may keep his principal records in State E. Under the non-notification system of accounts financing, the seller-assignor, despite the assignment, bills and collects from the account debtor; under notification financing the account debtor makes payment to the assignee, but the bills may be prepared and sent out by either assignor or assignee. The contacts of the transaction are with many jurisdictions: to which one is it appropriate to look for the governing law? Even more complicated situations may be anticipated when the collateral consists of novel or uncommon types of personal property, which fall within the definition of general intangibles.

If we bear in mind that our principal question is where certain financing statements shall be filed, two things become clear. *First:* since the purpose of filing is to allow subsequent creditors of the *debtor-assignor* to determine the true status of his affairs, the place chosen must be one which such creditors would normally associate with the assignor; thus the place of business of the assignee and the places of business or residences of the various account debtors must be rejected in ordinary situations. *Second:* the place chosen must be one which can be determined with the least possible risk of error. The place chosen by subsection (3) is the debtor's location, which is ordinarily the location of its chief executive office. This concept is discussed below.

(b) Another class of collateral for which a special rule is stated in subsection (3) is mobile goods of types which are normally moved for use from one jurisdiction to another. Such goods are generally classified as equipment; sometimes they may be classified as inventory, for example, goods leased by a professional lessor. Subsection (3) provides that a security interest in such equipment or inventory is subject to this Article when the debtor's location, i.e., ordinarily its chief executive office, is in this state.

While automobiles are obviously mobile goods, they will in most cases be covered by subsection (2) of this section and therefore excluded from subsection (3) by paragraph (a) thereof. If an automobile is not covered by a certificate of title and is classified as equipment or as inventory under lease, it will be subject to subsection (3). Automobiles and other mobile goods which are classified as consumer goods are not subject to subsection (3).

The rule of subsection (3) applies to goods of a type "normally used" in more than one jurisdiction; there is no requirement that particular goods be in fact used out of state. Thus, if an enterprise whose chief executive office is in State X keeps in State Y goods of the type covered by subsection (3), the rule of subsection (3) requires filing in State X even though the goods never leave State Y.

(c) "Chief executive office" does not mean the place of incorporation; it means the place from which in fact the debtor manages the main part of this business operations. This is the place where persons dealing with the debtor would normally look for credit information, and is the appropriate place for filing. The term "chief executive office" is not defined in this Section or elsewhere in this Act. Doubt may arise as to which is the "chief executive office" of a multi-state enterprise, but it would be rare that there could be more than two possibilities. A secured party in such a case may easily protect himself at no great additional burden by filing in each possible place. The subsection states a rule which will be simple to apply in most cases, and which makes it possible to dispense with much burdensome and useless filing.

(d) If the location of the debtor is moved after a security interest has been perfected in another jurisdiction, the secured party has four months within which to refile, unless the perfection in the original jurisdiction would have expired earlier (paragraph (3)(e)).

(e) Under subsection (3) each state other than that of the debtor's location in effect disclaims jurisdiction over certain accounts and general intangibles which, by common law rules, might be held to be within its jurisdiction; in the same way there is a disclaimer of jurisdiction over mobile chattels, even though they may be physically located within the state much of the time. If the jurisdiction whose law controls under this rule is a United States jurisdiction or has enacted legislation permitting perfection of the security interest by filing or recording in that jurisdiction, the law of that jurisdiction will be recognized in the disclaiming jurisdiction as perfecting the security interest. The jurisdiction of the debtor's location may not, however, have such legislation. For example, mobile equipment is used in New York; the debtor's chief place of business is in a Canadian jurisdiction which will not permit or recognize filing as to property not physically located therein. Paragraph (3)(c) solves this difficulty by permitting perfection through filing in the jurisdiction in the United States in which the debtor has its major executive office in the United States. Where the debtor is not located in the United States or Canada and the collateral is accounts or general intangibles for money due or to become due, the secured party may alternatively perfect by notification to account debtors.

(f) A sentence in paragraph (3)(d) provides a special rule for security interests in airplanes owned by a foreign air carrier. Without that sentence subsection (3) might refer such a case to the law of a foreign nation whose law is difficult or impossible to ascertain. The sentence clears up such doubts by treating as the location of the carrier the office designated for service of process in the United States under the Federal Aviation Act of 1958. To the extent that it is applicable, the Convention on the International Recognition of Rights in Aircraft (Geneva Convention) supersedes state legislation on this subject, as set forth in Section 9-302(3), but some nations are not parties to that Convention.

6. Subsection (4) deals with chattel paper, a semi-intangible security interest which may be perfected either by possession or by filing (Sections 9-304(1), 9-305). As to possessory security, subsection (4) provides that chattel paper shall be subject to the same rule as goods in subsection (1). As to non-possessory security, subsection (4) provides that it shall be subject to the same rule as the intangibles under subsection (3), except that notification to the account debtor is ruled out as an optional means of perfection under paragraph (3)(c). The reason for this is that a different alternative, possession, is available for chattel paper.

7. In addition to the foregoing rules defining which jurisdiction governs perfection of a security interest in the first instance, "this state" (i.e., a destination state after removal) adds its own rules requiring reperfection following removal of collateral other than that described in subsections (2), (3), and (5). "This state" will for four months recognize perfection under the law of the jurisdiction from which the collateral came, unless the remaining period of effectiveness of the perfection in that jurisdiction was less than four months (paragraph (1)(d)). After the four month period or the remaining period of effectiveness, whichever is shorter, the secured party must comply with perfection requirements in this state. This rule differs from the former rule of Section 14 of the Uniform Conditional Sales Act. Under that section a conditional seller was required to file within 10 days after he "received notice" that the goods had been removed into this state. Apparently, under the Uniform Conditional Sales Act, if the seller never "received notice" his interest continued or became perfected in this state without filing. Paragraph (1)(d) proceeds on the theory that not only the secured party whose collateral has been removed but also creditors of and purchasers from the debtor "in this state" should be considered.

The four-month period is long enough for a secured party to discover in most cases that the collateral has been removed and refile in this state; thereafter, if he has not done so, his interest, although originally perfected in the jurisdiction from which the collateral was removed, is subject to defeat here by purchasers of the collateral. Compare the situation arising under Section 9-403(2) when a filing lapses.

It should be noted that a "purchaser" includes a secured party. Section 1-201(32) and (33). The rights of a purchaser with a security interest against an unperfected security interest are governed by Section 9-312.

In case of delay beyond the four-month period, there is no "relation back"; and this is also true where the security interest is perfected for the first time in this state.

If the removal occurs within a short period, like two weeks, before the lapse of the filing in the original state, the secured party has only that period, not the full four months, to reperfect in "this state". But ordinarily he would have filed a continuation statement in the original jurisdiction; and he may do so to avoid lapse and allow himself the full four months if he is searching for the collateral and needs more time.

Paragraph (1)(d) does not apply to the case of goods removed from one filing district to another within this state (see subsection (3) of Section 9-401), but only to property brought into this state from another jurisdiction.

8. Subsection (5) deals with problems relating to the financing of minerals (including oil and gas) as these products come from the ground. In some cases rights in oil and gas in the ground have been split into a large variety of interests. As the oil or gas issues from the ground, it may be encumbered by the group of persons having interests therein. Or the product may be sold at minehead or wellhead and the resulting accounts assigned. The question arises as to the place of filing. The usual rule of this section in subsection (2) would make the place to search for encumbrances on the accounts the locations of the respective assignors;

but the assignors might be a number of individuals located throughout the country. To avoid the difficult problems of search thus created, subsection (5) provides that the place for filing with respect to security interests in the minerals as they issue from the ground at minehead or wellhead or in the accounts arising out of the sale of the minerals at minehead or wellhead shall be in the state where the minehead or wellhead is located. Section 9-401 similarly provides that the the place to file within the state is in the real property records in the county where the minehead or wellhead is located. These rules conform to pre-Code practice and to practice which seems to have continued in the early Code period before express provision was made for these situations.

The term "at wellhead" is intended to encompass arrangements based on sale of the product as soon as it issues from the ground and is measured, without technical distinctions as to whether title passes at the "Christmas tree" or the far side of a gathering tank or at some other point. The term "at minehead" is a comparable concept.

9. Subsection (6) of Section 9-103 specifies choice of law rules for perfection of security interests in investment property. Paragraph (b) covers security interests in certificated securities. Paragraph (c) covers security interests in uncertificated securities. Paragraph (d) covers security interests in security entitlements and securities accounts. Paragraph (e) covers security interests in commodity contracts and commodity accounts. The approach of each of these paragraphs is essentially the same. They identify the jurisdiction's law that governs questions of perfection and priority on the basis of the same principles that are used in Article 8 to determine other questions concerning that form of investment property. Thus, for certificated securities, the law of the jurisdiction where the certificate is located governs. Cf. Section 8-110(c). For uncertificated securities, the law of the issuer's jurisdiction governs. Cf. Section 8-110(a). For security entitlements and securities accounts, the law of the securities intermediary's jurisdiction governs. Cf. Section 8-110(b). For commodity contracts and commodity accounts, the law of the commodity intermediary's jurisdiction governs. Since commodity contracts and commodity accounts are not governed by Article 8, paragraph (e) contains rules that specify the commodity intermediary's jurisdiction. These are analogous to the rules in Section 8-110(e) specifying a securities intermediary's jurisdiction.

Under this subsection, if litigation about perfection or priority arises in this State, the relevant choice of law rule of paragraphs (b) through (e) may point to the law of this State or to the law of another State. If the litigation were in a tribunal of a jurisdiction that has not enacted this section, it would follow its own choice of law rules. The choice of law rules prescribed here by statute conform to generally accepted principles of choice of law. The simplicity and clarity in the choice of law rules, coupled with the explicit recognition that the parties to some securities transactions may agree on a governing law, are intended to assure that there will be one clear choice of law regardless of forum.

Paragraph (f) adapts the general choice of law principles of this subsection to cases where a secured party claims perfection on the basis of filing, or by virtue of the automatic perfection rules in Section 9-115(4)(c) and (d). In such a case, the law of the debtor's jurisdiction determines whether the requirements for that form of perfection have been satisfied. The rules in Section 9-103(3) on the debtor's location ~~*can be looked to in applying subsection (f)*~~ *and effect of change of location apply to cases governed by paragraph (f)**. The main reason for the paragraph (f) rule is to specify the proper filing office. Under the substantive rules of this Act, a security interest in investment property perfected only by filing is enforceable against the debtor or lien creditors, but not against most other claimants. See Sections 9-115(5) and (6), 8-105(e), 8-303, and 8-502. Because the choice of law rules in this section may, in some circumstances, have the effect of directing a court in a jurisdiction that has adopted this Act to look to the law of another jurisdiction, it is possible that the jurisdiction so specified will be one that has not adopted rules concerning the effect of filing as a method of perfection for investment property. In such cases, or other circumstances where the governing substantive law is not this Act, the effect of filing on the rights of other parties should be interpreted in light of the role of that form of perfection under this Act; that is, the rights of a secured party in investment property as determined under this Act perfected only by filing against another secured party or any other person who purchases or otherwise deals with the investment property should be interpreted to be no greater than the rights of that secured party under this Act. **Amendments in italics approved by the Permanent Editorial Board for Uniform Commercial Code November 4, 1995.*

The following examples illustrate these rules:

Example 1. A customer residing in New Jersey maintains a securities account with Able & Co. The agreement between the customer and Able specifies that it is governed by Pennsylvania law. Through the account the customer holds securities of a Massachusetts corporation, which Able holds through a clearing corporation located in New York. The customer obtains a margin loan from Able. Subsection (6)(d) provides that Pennsylvania law—the law of the securities intermediary's jurisdiction—governs perfection and priority of the security interest.

Example 2. A customer residing in New Jersey maintains a securities account with Able & Co. The agreement between the customer and Able specifies that it is governed by Pennsylvania law. Through the account the customer holds securities of a Massachusetts corporation, which Able holds through a clearing corporation located in New York. The customer obtains a loan from a lender located in Illinois. The lender takes a security interest and perfects by obtaining an agreement among the debtor, itself, and Able, which satisfies the requirement of Section 8-106(d)(2) to give the lender control. Subsection (6)(d) provides that Pennsylvania law—the law of the securities intermediary's jurisdiction—governs perfection and priority of the security interest.

Example 3. A customer residing in New Jersey maintains a securities account with Able & Co. The agreement between the customer and Able specifies that it is governed by Pennsylvania law. Through the account, the customer holds securities of a Massachusetts corporation, which Able holds through a clearing corporation located in New York. The customer borrows from SP1, and SP1 files a financing statement in New Jersey. Later, the customer obtains a loan from SP2. SP2 takes a security interest and perfects by obtaining an agreement among the debtor, itself, and Able, which satisfies the requirement of Section 8-106(d)(2) to give the SP2 control. Subsection (6)(f) provides that perfection of SP1's security interest by filing is governed by the location of the debtor, so the filing in New Jersey was appropriate—assuming New Jersey has adopted the revisions of Article 9 permitting perfection of security interests in investment property by filing. Subsection (6)(d), however, provides that Pennsylvania law—the law of the securities intermediary's jurisdiction—governs all other questions of perfection and priority. Thus, Pennsylvania law governs perfection of SP2's security interest, and Pennsylvania law also governs the priority of the security interests of SP1 and SP2.

Cross References:

Sections 1-105, 9-302 and 9-401.

Definitional Cross References:

"Accounts". Section 9-106.
"Attaches". Section 9-203.
"Chattel Paper". Section 9-105.
"Collateral". Section 9-105.

"Consumer Goods". Section 9–109.
"Debtor". Section 9–105.
"Document". Section 9–105.
"Equipment". Section 9–109.
"General intangibles". Section 9–106.
"Goods". Section 9–105.
"Instrument". Section 9–109.
"Purchase money security interest". Section 9–107.
"Purchaser". Section 1–201(33).
"Security interest". Section 1–201(37).

§ 9–104. Transactions Excluded From Article.

[1995 Amendments to text indicated by underline]

This Article does not apply

(a) to a security interest subject to any statute of the United States, to the extent that such statute governs the rights of parties to and third parties affected by transactions in particular types of property; or

(b) to a landlord's lien; or

(c) to a lien given by statute or other rule of law for services or materials except as provided in Section 9–310 on priority of such liens; or

(d) to a transfer of a claim for wages, salary or other compensation of an employee; or

(e) to a transfer by a government or governmental subdivision or agency; or

(f) to a sale of accounts or chattel paper as part of a sale of the business out of which they arose, or an assignment of accounts or chattel paper which is for the purpose of collection only, or a transfer of a right to payment under a contract to an assignee who is also to do the performance under the contract or a transfer of a single account to an assignee in whole or partial satisfaction of a preexisting indebtedness; or

(g) to a transfer of an interest in or claim in or under any policy of insurance, except as provided with respect to proceeds (Section 9–306) and priorities in proceeds (Section 9–312); or

(h) to a right represented by a judgment (other than a judgment taken on a right to payment which was collateral); or

(i) to any right of set-off; or

(j) except to the extent that provision is made for fixtures in Section 9–313, to the creation or transfer of an interest in or lien on real estate, including a lease or rents thereunder; or

(k) to a transfer in whole or in part of any claim arising out of tort; or

(*l*) to a transfer of an interest in any deposit account (subsection (1) of Section 9–105), except as provided with respect to proceeds (Section 9–306) and priorities in proceeds (Section 9–312); or

(m) to a transfer of an interest in a letter of credit other than the rights to proceeds of a written letter of credit.

As amended in 1972 and 1995.

For material relating to changes made in text in 1995, see Appendix XIV.

Official Comment

Prior Uniform Statutory Provisions: None.

Purposes:

To exclude certain security transactions from this Article.

1. Where a federal statute regulates the incidents of security interests in particular types of property, those security interests are of course governed by the federal statute and excluded from this Article. The Ship Mortgage Act, 1920, is an example of such a federal act. The present provisions of the Federal Aviation Act of 1958 (49 U.S.C. § 1403 et seq.) call for registration of title to and liens upon aircraft with the Civil Aeronautics Administrator and such registration is recognized as equivalent to filing under this Article (Section 9–302(3)); but to the extent that the Federal Aviation Act does not regulate the rights of parties to and third parties affected by such transactions, security interests in aircraft remain subject to this Article.

Although the Federal Copyright Act contains provisions permitting the mortgage of a copyright and for the recording of an assignment of a copyright (17 U.S.C. §§ 28, 30) such a statute would not seem to contain sufficient provisions regulating the rights of the parties and third parties to exclude security interests in copyrights from the provisions of this Article. Compare Republic Pictures Corp. v. Security-First National Bank of Los Angeles, 197 F.2d 767 (9th Cir. 1952). Compare also with respect to patents, 35 U.S.C. § 47. The filing provisions under these Acts, like the filing provisions of the Federal Aviation Act, are recognized as the equivalent to filing under this Article. Section 9–302(3) and (4).

Even such a statute as the Ship Mortgage Act is far from a comprehensive regulation of all aspects of ship mortgage financing. That Act contains provisions on formal requisites, on recordation and on foreclosure but not much more. If problems arise under a ship mortgage which are not covered by the Act, the federal admiralty court must decide whether to improvise an answer under "federal law" or to follow the law of some state with which the mortgage transaction has appropriate contacts. The exclusionary language in paragraph (a) is that this Article does not apply to such security interest "to the extent" that the federal statute governs the rights of the parties. Thus if the federal statute contained no relevant provision, this Article could be looked to for an answer.

2. Except for fixtures (Section 9–313), the Article applies only to security interests in personal property. The exclusion of landlord's liens by paragraph (b) and of leases and other interests in or liens on real estate by paragraph (j) merely reiterates the limitations on coverage already made explicit in Section 9–102(3). See Comment 4 to that section.

3. In all jurisdictions liens are given suppliers of many types of services and materials either by statute or by common law. It was thought to be both inappropriate and unnecessary for this Article to attempt a general codification of that lien structure which is in considerable part determined by local conditions and which is far removed from ordinary commercial financing. Moreover, federal law may displace state law in situations such as admiralty liens. Paragraph (c) therefore excludes statutory liens from the Article. Section 9–310 states a rule for determining priorities between such liens and the consensual security interests covered by this Article.

4. In many states assignments of wage claims and the like are regulated by statute. Such assignments present important social problems whose solution should be a matter of local regulation. Paragraph (d) therefore excludes them from this Article.

5. Certain governmental borrowings include collateral in the form of assignments of water, electricity or sewer charges, rents on dormitories or industrial buildings, tools, etc. Since these assignments are usually governed by special

provisions of law, these governmental transfers are excluded from this Article.

6. In general sales as well as security transfers of accounts and chattel paper are within the Article (see Section 9-102). Paragraph (f) excludes from the Article certain transfers of such intangibles which, by their nature, have nothing to do with commercial financing transactions.

Similarly, this paragraph excludes from the Article such transactions as that involved in Lyon v. Ty-Wood Corporation, 212 Pa.Super. 69, 239 A.2d 819 (1968) and Spurlin v. Sloan, 368 S.W.2d 314 (Ky.1963).

7. Rights under life insurance and other policies, and deposit accounts, are often put up as collateral. Such transactions are often quite special, do not fit easily under a general commercial statute and are adequately covered by existing law. Paragraphs (g) and (*l*) make appropriate exclusions, but provision is made for coverage of deposit accounts and certain insurance money as proceeds.

8. The remaining exclusions go to other types of claims which do not customarily serve as commercial collateral: judgments under paragraph (h), set-offs under paragraph (i) and tort claims under paragraph (k).

Cross References:

Point 1: Section 9-302(3).
Point 2: Sections 9-102(3) and 9-313.
Point 3: Sections 9-102(2) and 9-310.
Point 6: Section 9-102.

Definitional Cross References:

"Account". Section 9-106.
"Chattel paper". Section 9-105.
"Contract". Section 1-201.
"Deposit account". Section 9-105.
"Party". Section 1-201.
"Rights". Section 1-201.
"Security interest". Section 1-201.

§ 9-105. Definitions and Index of Definitions.

[*1995 Amendments to text indicated by underline*]

(1) In this Article unless the context otherwise requires:

(a) "Account debtor" means the person who is obligated on an account, chattel paper or general intangible;

(b) "Chattel paper" means a writing or writings which evidence both a monetary obligation and a security interest in or a lease of specific goods, but a charter or other contract involving the use or hire of a vessel is not chattel paper. When a transaction is evidenced both by such a security agreement or a lease and by an instrument or a series of instruments, the group of writings taken together constitutes chattel paper;

(c) "Collateral" means the property subject to a security interest, and includes accounts and chattel paper which have been sold;

(d) "Debtor" means the person who owes payment or other performance of the obligation secured, whether or not he owns or has rights in the collateral, and includes the seller of accounts or chattel paper. Where the debtor and the owner of the collateral are not the same person, the term "debtor" means the owner of the collateral in any provision of the Article dealing with the collateral, the obligor in any provision dealing with the obligation, and may include both where the context so requires;

(e) "Deposit account" means a demand, time, savings, passbook or like account maintained with a bank, savings and loan association, credit union or like organization, other than an account evidenced by a certificate of deposit;

(f) "Document" means document of title as defined in the general definitions of Article 1 (Section 1–201), and a receipt of the kind described in subsection (2) of Section 7–201;

(g) "Encumbrance" includes real estate mortgages and other liens on real estate and all other rights in real estate that are not ownership interests;

(h) "Goods" includes all things which are movable at the time the security interest attaches or which are fixtures (Section 9–313), but does not include money, documents, instruments, investment property, accounts, chattel paper, general intangibles, or minerals or the like (including oil and gas) before extraction. "Goods" also includes standing timber which is to be cut and removed under a conveyance or contract for sale, the unborn young of animals, and growing crops;

(i) "Instrument" means a negotiable instrument (defined in Section 3–104), or any other writing which evidences a right to the payment of money and is not itself a security agreement or lease and is of a type which is in ordinary course of business transferred by delivery with any necessary indorsement or assignment. The term does not include investment property;

(j) "Mortgage" means a consensual interest created by a real estate mortgage, a trust deed on real estate, or the like;

(k) An advance is made "pursuant to commitment" if the secured party has bound himself to make it, whether or not a subsequent event of default or other event not within his control has relieved or may relieve him from his obligation;

(*l*) "Security agreement" means an agreement which creates or provides for a security interest;

(m) "Secured party" means a lender, seller or other person in whose favor there is a security interest, including a person to whom accounts or chattel paper have been sold. When the holders of obligations issued under an indenture of trust, equipment trust agreement or the like are represented by a trustee or other person, the representative is the secured party;

(n) "Transmitting utility" means any person primarily engaged in the railroad, street railway or trolley bus business, the electric or electronics communications transmission business, the transmission of goods by pipeline, or the transmission or the production and transmission of electricity, steam, gas or water, or the provision of sewer service.

(2) Other definitions applying to this Article and the sections in which they appear are:

"Account".	Section 9–106.
"Attach".	Section 9–203.
"Commodity contract".	Section 9–115.
"Commodity customer".	Section 9–115.
"Commodity intermediary".	Section 9–115.
"Construction mortgage".	Section 9–313(1).
"Consumer goods".	Section 9–109(1).
"Control".	Section 9–115.

"Equipment".	Section 9–109(2).
"Farm products".	Section 9–109(3).
"Fixture".	Section 9–313(1).
"Fixture filing".	Section 9–313(1).
"General intangibles".	Section 9–106.
"Inventory".	Section 9–109(4).
"Investment property".	Section 9–115.
"Lien creditor".	Section 9–301(3).
"Proceeds".	Section 9–306(1).
"Purchase money security interest".	Section 9–107.
"United States".	Section 9–103.

(3) The following definitions in other Articles apply to this Article:

"Broker".	Section 8–102.
"Certificated security".	Section 8–102.
"Check".	Section 3–104.
"Clearing corporation".	Section 8–102.
"Contract for sale".	Section 2–106.
"Control".	Section 8–106.
"Delivery".	Section 8–301.
"Entitlement holder".	Section 8–102.
"Financial asset".	Section 8–102.
"Holder in due course".	Section 3–302.
"Letter of credit".	Section 5–102.
"Note".	Section 3–104.
"Proceeds of a letter of credit".	Section 5–114(a).
"Sale".	Section 2–106.
"Securities intermediary".	Section 8–102.
"Security".	Section 8–102.
"Security certificate".	Section 8–102.
"Security entitlement".	Section 8–102.
"Uncertificated security".	Section 8–102.

(4) In addition Article 1 contains general definitions and principles of construction and interpretation applicable throughout this Article.

As amended in 1966, 1972, 1977, 1994 and 1995.

See Appendices XII and XIV for material relating to changes made in text in 1994 and 1995 respectively.

Official Comment

Prior Uniform Statutory Provisions: Various.

Purposes:

1. **General.** It is necessary to have a set of terms to describe the parties to a secured transaction, the agreement itself, and the property involved therein; but the selection of the set of terms applicable to any one of the existing forms (e.g., mortgagor and mortgagee) might carry to some extent the implication that the existing law referable to that form was to be used for the construction and interpretation of this Article. Since it is desired to avoid any such implication, a set of terms has been chosen which have no common law or statutory roots tying them to a particular form.

In place of such terms as "chattel mortgage," "conditional sale," "assignment of accounts receivable," "trust receipt," etc., this Article substitutes the general term "security agreement" defined in paragraph (1)(*l*). In place of "mortgagor," "mortgagee," "conditional vendee," "conditional vendor," etc., this Article substitutes "debtor", defined in paragraph (1)(d), and "secured party", defined in paragraph (1)(m). The property subject to the security agreement is "collateral", defined in paragraph (1)(c). The interest in the collateral which is conveyed by the debtor to the secured party is a "security interest", defined in Section 1-201(37).

2. **Parties.** The parties to the security agreement are the "debtor" and the "secured party."

"Debtor": In all but a few cases the person who owes the debt and the person whose property secures the debt will be the same. Occasionally, one person furnishes security for another's debt, and sometimes property is transferred subject to a secured debt of the transferor which the transferee does not assume; in such cases, under the second sentence of the definition, the term "debtor" may, depending upon the context, include either or both such persons. Section 9-112 sets out special rules which are applicable where collateral is owned by a person who does not owe a debt.

"Secured Party": The term includes any person in whose favor there is a security interest (defined in Section 1-201). The term is used equally to refer to a person who as a seller retains a lien on or title to goods sold, to a person whose interest arises initially from a loan transaction, and to an assignee of either. Note that a seller is a "secured party" in relation to his customer; the seller becomes a "debtor" if he assigns the chattel paper as collateral. This is also true of a lender who assigns the debt as collateral. With the exceptions stated in Section 9-104(f) the Article applies to any sale of accounts or chattel paper: the term "secured party" includes an assignee of such intangibles whether by sale or for security, to distinguish him from the payee of the account, for example, who becomes a "debtor" by pledging the account as security for a loan.

On the applicability of the terms "debtor" and "secured party" to consignments and leases see Section 9-408 and Comment thereto.

"Account debtor": Where the collateral is an account, chattel paper or general intangible the original obligor is called the "account debtor", defined in paragraph (1)(a).

3. **Property subject to the security agreement.** "Collateral", defined in paragraph (1)(c), is a general term for the tangible and intangible property subject to a security interest. For some purposes the Code makes distinctions between different types of collateral and therefore further classification of collateral is necessarily Collateral which consists of tangible property is "goods", defined in paragraph (1)(h); and "goods" are again subdivided in Section 9-109. For purposes of this Article all intangible collateral fits one of five categories, two of which, "accounts", and "general intangibles" are defined in the following Section 9-106; the other three, "documents", "instruments" and "chattel paper", are defined in paragraphs (1)(f), (1)(i) and (1)(b) of this section.

"Goods": the definition in paragraph (1)(h) is similar to that contained in Section 2-105 except that the Sales Article definition refers to "time of identification to the contract for sale", while this definition refers to "the time the security interest attaches".

For the treatment of fixtures, Section 9-313 should be consulted. It will be noted that the treatment of fixtures under Section 9-313 does not at all points conform to their treatment under Section 2-107 (goods to be severed from realty). Section 2-107 relates to sale of such goods; Section 9-313 to security interests in them. The discrepancies between the two sections arise from the differences in the types of interest covered. A comparable discrepancy exists as to minerals. In the case of timber, both sections treat it as goods if it is to be severed under a contract of sale, but not otherwise.

If in any state minerals before severance are deemed to be personal property, they fall outside the Article's definition of "goods" and would therefore fall in the catch-all definition, "general intangibles", in Section 9-106. The special provisions of Section 9-103(5) would not apply and those of Section 9-103(3) would apply. The resulting problems should be considered locally.

For the purpose of this Article, goods are classified as "consumer goods", "equipment", "farm products", and "inventory"; those terms are defined in Section 9-109. When the general term "goods" is used in this Article, it includes, as may be appropriate in the context, the subclasses of goods defined in Section 9-109.

"Instrument": the term as defined in paragraph (1)(i) includes not only negotiable instruments ~~and certificated securities~~ but also any other intangibles evidenced by writings which are in ordinary course of business transferred by delivery. As in the case of chattel paper "delivery" is only the minimum stated and may be accompanied by other steps. *Amendment approved by the Permanent Editorial Board for Uniform Commercial Code November 4, 1995.*

If a writing is itself a security agreement or lease with respect to specific goods it is not an instrument although it otherwise meets the term of the definition. See Comment below on "chattel paper".

The fact that an instrument is secured by collateral, whether the collateral be other instruments, documents, goods, accounts or general intangibles, does not change the character of the principal obligation as an instrument or convert the combination of instrument and collateral into a separate Code classification of personal property. The single qualification to this principle is that an instrument which is secured by chattel paper is itself part of the chattel paper, while also retaining its identity as an instrument.

"Document": See the Comments under Sections 1-201(15) and 7-201.

"Chattel paper": To secure his own financing a secured party may wish to borrow against or sell the security agreement itself along with his interest in the collateral which he has received from his debtor. Since the refinancing of paper secured by specific goods presents some problems of its own, the term "chattel paper" is used to describe this kind of collateral. The Comments under Section 9-308 further describe this concept.

Charters of vessels are excluded from the definition of chattel paper because they fit under the definition of accounts. See Comment to Section 9-106. The term "charter" as used herein and in Section 9-106 includes bareboat charters, time charters, successive voyage charters, contracts of affreightment, contracts of carriage, and all other arrangements for use of vessels.

4. The following transactions illustrate the use of the term "chattel paper" and some of the other terms defined in this section.

A dealer sells a tractor to a farmer on conditional sales contract or purchase money security interest. The conditional sales contract is a "security agreement", the farmer is the "debtor", the dealer is the "secured party" and the tractor is the type of "collateral" defined in Section 9-109 as "equipment". But now the dealer transfers the contract to his bank, either by outright sale or to secure a loan. Since the conditional sales contract is a security agreement relating to specific equipment, the conditional sales contract is now the type of collateral called "chattel paper". In this transaction between the dealer and his bank, the bank is the "secured party", the dealer is the "debtor", and the farmer is the "account debtor".

Under the definition of "security interest" in Section 1-201(37) a lease does not create a security interest unless intended as security. Whether or not the lease itself is a security agreement, it is chattel paper when transferred if it relates to specific goods. Thus, if the dealer enters into a straight lease of the tractor to the farmer (not intended as security), and then arranges to borrow money on the security of the lease, the lease is chattel paper.

Security agreements of the type formerly known as chattel mortgages and conditional sales contracts are frequently executed in connection with a negotiable note or a series of such notes. Under the definitions in paragraphs (1)(b) and (1)(i) the rules applicable to chattel paper, rather than those relating to instruments, are applicable to the group of writings (contract plus note) taken together.

5. **Miscellaneous definitions.**

"Deposit account" is a type of collateral excluded from this Article under Section 9–104(*l*), except when it constitutes proceeds of other collateral under Section 9–306.

The terms "encumbrance" and "mortgage" are defined for use in the section on fixtures, Section 9–113.

The term "transmitting utility" is defined to designate a special class of debtors for whom separate filing rules are provided in Part 4, thus obviating all local filing and particularly the several local filings that would be necessary under the usual rules of Section 9–401 for the fixture collateral of a far-flung public utility debtor. See Comments under Sections 9–401 and 9–403.

The term "pursuant to commitment" is defined for use in the rules relating to priority of future advances in Sections 9–301(4), 9–307(3), and 9–312(7).

6. Comments to the definitions indexed in subsections (2) and (3) follow the sections in which the definitions are contained.

Cross References:

Point 2: Sections 9–104(f) and 9–112.

Point 3: Sections 2–105, 2–107, 9–106, 9–109, 9–303 and 9–313.

Definitional Cross References:

"Account". Section 9–106.

"Agreement". Section 1–201.

"Document of title". Sections 1–201, 7–201.

"General intangibles". Section 9–106.

"Holder". Section 1–201.

"Money". Section 1–201.

"Negotiable instrument". Section 3–104.

"Person". Section 1–201.

"Representative". Section 1–201.

"Rights". Section 1–201.

"Security". Section 8–102.

"Security interest". Section 1–201.

"Writing". Section 1–201.

§ 9–106. Definitions: "Account"; "General Intangibles".

[1995 Amendments to text indicated by underline]

"Account" means any right to payment for goods sold or leased or for services rendered which is not evidenced by an instrument or chattel paper, whether or not it has been earned by performance. "General intangibles" means any personal property (including things in action) other than goods, accounts, chattel paper, documents, instruments, investment property, rights to proceeds of written letters of credit, and money. All rights to payment earned or unearned under a charter or other contract involving the use or hire of a vessel and all rights incident to the charter or contract are accounts.

As amended in 1966, 1972, 1994, and 1995.

See Appendices XII and XIV for material relating to changes made in text in 1994 and 1995, respectively.

Official Comment

Prior Uniform Statutory Provision: None.

Purposes:

The terms defined in this section round out the classification of intangibles: see the definitions of "document", "chattel paper" and "instrument" in Section 9-105. Those three terms cover the various categories of commercial paper which are either negotiable or to a greater or less extent dealt with as if negotiable. The term "account" covers most choses in action which may be the subject of commercial financing transactions but which are not evidenced by an indispensable writing. The term "general intangibles" brings under this Article miscellaneous types of contractual rights and other personal property which are used or may become customarily used as commercial security. Examples are goodwill, literary rights and rights to performance. Other examples are copyrights, trademarks and patents, except to the extent that they may be excluded by Section 9-104(a). This Article solves the problems of filing of security interests in these types of intangibles (Sections 9-103(3) and 9-401). Note that this catch-all definition does not apply to money or to types of intangibles which are specifically excluded from the coverage of the Article (Section 9-104) and note also that under Section 9-302 filing under a federal statute may satisfy the filing requirements of this Article.

A right to the payment of money is frequently buttressed by ancillary covenants to insure the preservation of collateral, such as covenants in a purchase agreement, note or mortgage requiring insurance on the collateral or forbidding removal of the collateral; or covenants to preserve credit-worthiness of the promisor, such as covenants restricting dividends, etc. While these miscellaneous ancillary rights might conceivably be thought to fall within the definition of "general intangibles", it is not the intention of the Code to treat them separately and require the perfection of assignment thereof by filing in the manner required for perfection of an assignment of general intangibles. Whatever perfection is required for the perfection of an assignment of the right to the payment of money will also carry these ancillary rights.

Similarly, when the right to the payment of money is not yet earned by performance, there are frequently ancillary rights designed to assure that an assignee may complete the performance and crystallize the right to payment of money. Such rights are frequently present in a "maintenance" lease where the lessor has continuing duties to perform, or in a ship charter. These ancillary rights, if considered in the abstract, might be thought to be "general intangibles", since they do not themselves involve the payment of money; but it is not the intent of the Code to split up the rights to the payment of money and its ancillary supports, and thereby multiply the problem of perfection of assignments. Therefore, all rights of the lessor in a lease are to be perfected as "chattel paper", and all rights of the owner in a ship charter are to be perfected as "accounts".

"Account" is defined as a right to payment for goods sold or leased or services rendered; the ordinary commercial account receivable. In some special cases a right to receive money not yet earned by performance crystallizes not into an account but into a general intangible, for it is a right to payment of money that is not "for goods sold or leased or for services rendered." Examples of such rights are the right to receive payment of a loan not evidenced by an instrument or chattel paper; a right to receive partial refund of purchase prices paid by reason of retroactive volume discounts; rights to receive payment under licenses of patents and copyrights, exhibition contracts, etc.

This Article rejects any lingering common law notion that only rights already earned can be assigned. In the triangular arrangement following assignment, there is reason to allow the original parties—assignor and account debtor—more flexibility in modifying the underlying contract before performance than after performance (see Section 9-318). It will, however, be found that in most situations the same rules apply to accounts both before and after performance.

Cross References:

Sections 9-103(2), 9-104, 9-302(3), 9-318 and 9-401.

Definitional Cross References:

"Chattel paper". Section 9-105.
"Contract". Section 1-201.
"Document". Section 9-105.
"Goods". Section 9-105.
"Instrument". Section 9-105.

§ 9-107. Definitions: "Purchase Money Security Interest".

A security interest is a "purchase money security interest" to the extent that it is

(a) taken or retained by the seller of the collateral to secure all or part of its price; or

(b) taken by a person who by making advances or incurring an obligation gives value to enable the debtor to acquire rights in or the use of collateral if such value is in fact so used.

Official Comment

Prior Uniform Statutory Provision: None.

Purposes:

1. Under existing rules of law and under this Article purchase money obligations often have priority over other obligations. Thus a purchase money obligation has priority over an interest acquired under an after-acquired property clause (Section 9-312(3) and (4)); where filing is required a grace period of ten days is allowed against creditors and transferees in bulk (Section 9-301(2)); and in some instances filing may not be necessary (Section 9-302(1)(d)).

Under this section a seller has a purchase money security interest if he retains a security interest in the goods; a financing agency has a purchase money security interest when it advances money to the seller, taking back an assignment of chattel paper, and also when it makes advances to the buyer (e.g., on chattel mortgage) to enable him to buy, and he uses the money for that purpose.

2. When a purchase money interest is claimed by a secured party who is not a seller, he must of course have given present consideration. This section therefore provides that the purchase money party must be one who gives value "by making advances or incurring an obligation": the quoted language excludes from the purchase money category any security interest taken as security for or in satisfaction of a preexisting claim or antecedent debt.

Cross References:

Point 1: Sections 9-301, 9-302 and 9-312.
Point 2: Section 9-108.

Definitional Cross References:

"Collateral". Section 9-105.
"Debtor". Section 9-105.
"Person". Section 1-201.
"Rights". Section 1-201.
"Security interest". Section 1-201.
"Value". Section 1-201.

§ 9-108. When After-Acquired Collateral Not Security for Antecedent Debt.

Where a secured party makes an advance, incurs an obligation, releases a perfected security interest, or otherwise gives new value which is to be secured in whole or in part by after-acquired property his security interest in the after-acquired collateral shall be deemed to be taken for new value and not as security for an antecedent debt if the debtor acquires his rights in such collateral either in the ordinary course of his business or under a contract of purchase made pursuant to the security agreement within a reasonable time after new value is given.

Official Comment

Prior Uniform Statutory Provision: None.

Purposes:

1. Many financing transactions contemplate that the collateral will include both the debtor's existing assets and also assets thereafter acquired by him in the operation of his business. This Article generally validates such after-acquired property interests (see Section 9–204 and Comment) although they may be subordinated to later purchase money interests under Section 9–312(3) and (4).

Interests in after-acquired property have never been considered as involving transfers of property for antecedent debt merely because of the after-acquired feature, nor should they be so considered. The section makes explicit what has been true under the case law: an after-acquired property interest is not, by virtue of that fact alone, security for a pre-existing claim. This rule is of importance principally in insolvency proceedings under the federal Bankruptcy Act or state statutes which make certain transfers for antecedent debt voidable as preferences. The determination of when a transfer is for antecedent debt is largely left by the Bankruptcy Act to state law.

Two tests must be met under this section for an interest in after-acquired property to be one not taken for an antecedent debt. *First:* the secured party must, at the inception of the transaction, have given new value in some form. *Second:* the after-acquired property must come in either in the ordinary course of the debtor's business or as an acquisition which is made under a contract of purchase entered into within a reasonable time after the giving of new value and pursuant to the security agreement. The reason for the first test needs no comment. The second is in line with limitations which judicial construction has placed on the operation of after-acquired property clauses. Their coverage has been in many cases restricted to subsequent ordinary course acquisitions: this Article does not go so far (see Section 9–204 and Comment), but it does deny present value status to out of ordinary course acquisitions not made pursuant to the original loan agreement. This solution gives the secured party full protection as to the collateral which he may be reasonably thought to have contracted for; it gives other creditors the possibility, under the law of preferences, of subjecting to their claims windfall or uncontemplated acquisitions shortly before bankruptcy.

2. The term "value" is defined in Section 1–201(44) and discussed in the accompanying Comment. In this section and in other sections of this Article the term "new value" is used but is left without statutory definition. The several illustrations of "new value" given in the text of this section (making an advance, incurring an obligation, releasing a perfected security interest) as well as the "purchase money security interest" definition in Section 9–107 indicate the nature of the concept. In other situations it is left to the courts to distinguish between "new" and "old" value, between present considerations and antecedent debt.

Cross References:

Point 1: Sections 9–204 and 9–312.
Point 2: Section 9–107.

Definitional Cross References:

"Collateral". Section 9–105.
"Contract". Section 1–201.
"Debtor". Section 9–105.
"Purchase". Section 1–201.
"Rights". Section 1–201.

"Secured party". Section 9–105.
"Security agreement". Section 9–105.
"Security interest". Section 1–201.
"Value". Section 1–201.

§ 9–109. Classification of Goods: "Consumer Goods"; "Equipment"; "Farm Products"; "Inventory".

Goods are

(1) "consumer goods" if they are used or bought for use primarily for personal, family or household purposes;

(2) "equipment" if they are used or bought for use primarily in business (including farming or a profession) or by a debtor who is a non-profit organization or a governmental subdivision or agency or if the goods are not included in the definitions of inventory, farm products or consumer goods;

(3) "farm products" if they are crops or livestock or supplies used or produced in farming operations or if they are products of crops or livestock in their unmanufactured states (such as ginned cotton, wool-clip, maple syrup, milk and eggs), and if they are in the possession of a debtor engaged in raising, fattening, grazing or other farming operations. If goods are farm products they are neither equipment nor inventory;

(4) "inventory" if they are held by a person who holds them for sale or lease or to be furnished under contracts of service or if he has so furnished them, or if they are raw materials, work in process or materials used or consumed in a business. Inventory of a person is not to be classified as his equipment.

Official Comment

Prior Uniform Statutory Provision: None.

Purposes:

1. This section classifies goods as consumer goods, equipment, farm products and inventory. The classification is important in many situations: it is relevant, for example, in determining the rights of persons who buy from a debtor goods subject to a security interest (Section 9–307), in certain questions of priority (Section 9–312), in determining the place of filing (Section 9–401) and in working out rights after default (Part 5). Comment 5 to Section 9–102 contains an index of the special rules applicable to different classes of collateral.

2. The classes of goods are mutually exclusive; the same property cannot at the same time and as to the same person be both equipment and inventory, for example. In borderline cases—a physician's car or a farmer's jeep which might be either consumer goods or equipment—the principal use to which the property is put should be considered as determinative. Goods can fall into different classes at different times; a radio is inventory in the hands of a dealer and consumer goods in the hands of a householder.

3. The principal test to determine whether goods are inventory is that they are held for immediate or ultimate sale. Implicit in the definition is the criterion that the prospective sale is in the ordinary course of business. Machinery used in manufacturing, for example, is equipment and not inventory even though it is the continuing policy of the enterprise to sell machinery when it becomes obsolete. Goods to be furnished under a contract of service are inventory even though the arrangement under which they are furnished is not technically a sale. When an enterprise is engaged in the business of leasing a stock of products to users (for example, the fleet of cars owned by a car

rental agency), that stock is also included within the definition of "inventory". It should be noted that one class of goods which is not held for disposition to a purchaser or user is included in inventory: "Materials used or consumed in a business". Examples of this class of inventory are fuel to be used in operations, scrap metal produced in the course of manufacture, and containers to be used to package the goods. In general it may be said that goods used in a business are equipment when they are fixed assets or have, as identifiable units, a relatively long period of use; but are inventory, even though not held for sale, if they are used up or consumed in a short period of time in the production of some end product.

4. Goods are "farm products" only if they are in the possession of a debtor engaged in farming operations. Animals in a herd of livestock are covered whether they are acquired by purchase or result from natural increase. Products of crops or livestock remain farm products so long as they are in the possession of a debtor engaged in farming operations and have not been subjected to a manufacturing process. The terms "crops", "livestock" and "farming operations" are not defined; however, it is obvious from the text that "farming operations" includes raising livestock as well as crops; similarly, since eggs are products of livestock, livestock includes fowl.

When crops or livestock or their products come into the possession of a person not engaged in farming operations they cease to be "farm products". If they come into the possession of a marketing agency for sale or distribution or of a manufacturer or processor as raw materials, they become inventory.

Products of crops or livestock, even though they remain in the possession of a person engaged in farming operations, lose their status as farm products if they are subjected to a manufacturing process. What is and what is not a manufacturing operation is not determined by this Article. At one end of the scale some processes are so closely connected with farming—such as pasteurizing milk or boiling sap to produce maple syrup or maple sugar—that they would not rank as manufacturing. On the other hand an extensive canning operation would be manufacturing. The line is one for the courts to draw. After farm products have been subjected to a manufacturing operation, they become inventory if held for sale.

Note that the buyer in ordinary course who under Section 9-307 takes free of a security interest in goods held for sale does not include one who buys farm products from a person engaged in farming operations.

5. The principal definition of equipment is a negative one: goods used in a business (including farming or a profession) which are not inventory and not farm products. Trucks, rolling stock, tools, machinery are typical. It will be noted furthermore that any goods which are not covered by one of the other definitions in this section are to be treated as equipment.

Cross References:

Point 1: Sections 9-102, 9-307, 9-312, 9-401 and Part 5.
Point 3: Section 9-307.
Point 4: Section 9-307.

Definitional Cross References:

"Contract". Section 1-201.
"Debtor". Section 9-105.
"Goods". Section 9-105.
"Organization". Section 1-201.
"Person". Section 1-201.
"Sale". Sections 2-106 and 9-105.

§ 9-110. Sufficiency of Description.

For the purposes of this Article any description of personal property or real estate is sufficient whether or not it is specific if it reasonably identifies what is described.

Official Comment

Prior Uniform Statutory Provision: None.

Purposes:

The requirement of description of collateral (see Section 9–203 and Comment thereto) is evidentiary. The test of sufficiency of a description laid down by this section is that the description do the job assigned to it—that it make possible the identification of the thing described. Under this rule courts should refuse to follow the holdings, often found in the older chattel mortgage cases, that descriptions are insufficient unless they are of the most exact and detailed nature, the so-called "serial number" test. The same test of reasonable identification applies where a description of real estate is required in a financing statement. See Section 9–402.

Cross References:

Sections 9–203 and 9–402.

§ 9–111. Applicability of Bulk Transfer Laws.

The creation of a security interest is not a bulk transfer under Article 6 (see Section 6–103).

Official Comment

Prior Uniform Statutory Provision: None.

Purposes:

The bulk transfer laws, which have been almost everywhere enacted, were designed to prevent a once prevalent type of fraud which seems to have flourished particularly in the retail field: the owner of a debt-burdened enterprise would sell it to an unwary purchaser and then remove himself, with the purchase price and his other assets, beyond the reach of process. The creditors would find themselves with no recourse unless they could establish that the purchaser assumed existing debts. The bulk transfer laws, which require advance notice of sale to all known creditors, seem to have been successful in preventing such frauds.

There has been disagreement whether the bulk transfer laws should be applied to security as well as to sale transactions. In most states security transactions have not been covered; in a few states the opposite result has been reached either by judicial construction or by express statutory provision. Whatever the reasons may be, it seems to be true that the bulk transfer type of fraud has not often made its appearance in the security field: it may be that lenders of money are more inclined to investigate a potential borrower than are purchasers of retail stores to determine the true state of their vendor's affairs. Since compliance with the bulk transfer laws is onerous and expensive, legitimate financing transactions should not be required to comply when there is no reason to believe that other creditors will be prejudiced.

This section merely reiterates the provisions of Article 6 on Bulk Transfers which provides in Section 6–103(1) that transfers "made to give security for the performance of an obligation" are not subject to that Article.

Cross Reference:

Section 6–103(1).

Definitional Cross Reference:

"Security interest". Section 1–201.

§ 9–112. Where Collateral Is Not Owned by Debtor.

Unless otherwise agreed, when a secured party knows that collateral is owned by a person who is not the debtor, the owner of the collateral is entitled to receive from the secured party any surplus under Section 9–502(2) or under Section 9–504(1), and is not liable for the debt or for any deficiency after resale, and he has the same right as the debtor

(a) to receive statements under Section 9–208;

(b) to receive notice of and to object to a secured party's proposal to retain the collateral in satisfaction of the indebtedness under Section 9–505;

(c) to redeem the collateral under Section 9–506;

(d) to obtain injunctive or other relief under Section 9–507(1); and

(e) to recover losses caused to him under Section 9–208(2).

Official Comment

Prior Uniform Statutory Provision: None.

Purposes:

Under the definition of Section 9–105, in any provisions of the Article dealing with the collateral the term "debtor" means the owner of the collateral even though he is not the person who owes payment or performance of the obligation secured. The section covers several situations in which the implications of this definition are specifically set out.

The duties which this section imposes on a secured party toward such an owner of collateral are conditioned on the secured party's knowledge of the true state of facts. Short of such knowledge he may continue to deal exclusively with the person who owes the obligation. Nor does the section suggest that the secured party is under any duty of inquiry. It does not purport to cut across the law of conversion or of ultra vires. Whether a person who does not own property has authority to encumber it for his own debts and whether a person is free to encumber his property as collateral for the debts of another, are matters to be decided under other rules of law and are not covered by this section.

The section does not purport to be an exhaustive treatment of the subject. It isolates certain problems which may be expected to arise and states rules as to them. Others will no doubt arise: their solution is left to the courts.

Cross References:

Sections 9–105, 9–208 and Part 5.

Definitional Cross References:

"Collateral". Section 9–105.
"Debtor". Section 9–105.
"Notice". Section 1–201.
"Person". Section 1–201.
"Receive notice". Section 1–201.
"Right". Section 1–201.
"Secured party". Section 9–105.

§ 9–113. Security Interests Arising Under Article on Sales or Under Article on Leases.

A security interest arising solely under the Article on Sales (Article 2) or the Article on Leases (Article 2A) is subject to the provisions of this Article except that to the extent that and so long as the debtor does not have or does not lawfully obtain possession of the goods

(a) no security agreement is necessary to make the security interest enforceable; and

(b) no filing is required to perfect the security interest; and

(c) the rights of the secured party on default by the debtor are governed (i) by the Article on Sales (Article 2) in the case of a security interest arising solely under such Article or (ii) by the Article on Leases (Article 2A) in the case of a security interest arising solely under such Article.

As amended in 1987.

See Appendix III for material relating to changes made in text in 1987.

Official Comment

Prior Uniform Statutory Provision: None.

Purposes:

1. Under the provisions of Article 2 on Sales, a seller of goods may reserve a security interest (see, e.g., Sections 2–401 and 2–505); and in certain circumstances, whether or not a security interest is reserved, the seller has rights of resale and stoppage under Sections 2–703, 2–705 and 2–706 which are similar to the rights of a secured party. Similarly, under such sections as Sections 2–506, 2–707 and 2–711, a financing agency, an agent, a buyer or another person may have a security interest or other right in goods similar to that of a seller. The use of the term "security interest" in the Sales Article is meant to bring the interests so designated within this Article. This section makes it clear, however, that such security interests are exempted from certain provisions of this Article. Compare Section 4–208(3), making similar special provisions for security interests arising in the bank collection process.

2. The security interests to which this section applies commonly arise by operation of law in the course of a sales transaction. Since the circumstances under which they arise are defined in the Sales Article, there is no need for the "security agreement" defined in Section 9–105(1)(*l*) and required by Section 9–203(1) and paragraph (a) dispenses with such requirements. The requirement of filing may be inapplicable under Sections 9–302(1)(a) and (b), 9–304 and 9–305, where the goods are in the possession of the secured party or of a bailee other than the debtor. To avoid difficulty in the residual cases, as for example where a bailee does not receive notification of the secured party's interest until after the security interest arises, paragraph (b) dispenses with any filing requirement. Finally, paragraph (c) makes inapplicable the default provisions of Part 5 of this Article, since the Sales Article contains detailed provisions governing stoppage of delivery and resale after breach. See Sections 2–705, 2–706, 2–707(2) and 2–711(3).

3. These limitations on the applicability of this Article to security interests arising under the Sales Article are appropriate only so long as the debtor does not have or lawfully obtain possession of the goods. Compare Section 56(b) of the Uniform Sales Act. A secured party who wishes to retain a security interest after the debtor lawfully obtains possession must comply fully with all the provisions of this Article and ordinarily must file a financing statement to perfect his interest. This is the effect of the "except" clause in the preamble to this section. Note that in the case of a buyer who has a security interest in rejected goods under Section 2–711(3), the buyer is the "secured party" and the seller is the "debtor".

4. This section applies only to a "security interest". The definition of "security interest" in Section 1–201(37) expressly excludes the special property interest of a buyer of goods on identification under Section 2–401(1). The seller's interest after identification and before delivery may be more than a security interest by virtue of explicit agreement under Section 2–401(1) or 2–501(1), by virtue of the provisions of Section 2–401(2), (3) or (4), or by virtue of substitution pursuant to Section 2–501(2). In such cases, Article 9

is inapplicable by the terms of Section 9-102(1)(a).

5. Where there is a "security interest", this section applies only if the security interest arises "solely" under the Sales Article. Thus Section 1-201(37) permits a buyer to acquire by agreement a security interest in goods not in his possession or control; such a security interest does not impair his rights under the Sales Article, but any rights based on the security agreement are fully subject to this Article without regard to the limitations of this section. Similarly, a seller who reserves a security interest by agreement does not lose his rights under the Sales Article, but rights other than those conferred by the Sales Article depend on full compliance with this Article.

6. This section is amended to include security interests arising under the Article on Leases (Article 2A), which is being promulgated at the same time as this amendment. Section 2A-508(5). After the effective date of the amendment to this section all references in the Act to Section 9-113 will be deemed to refer to this section, as amended. *E.g.,* Sections 9-203(1) and 9-302(1)(f).

Cross References:

Point 1: Sections 2-401, 2-505, 2-506, 2-705, 2-706, 2-707, 2-711(3), 4-208(3).

Point 2: Sections 2-705, 2-706, 2-707(2), 2-711(3), 9-203(1), 9-302(1)(a) and (b), 9-304, 9-305 and Part 5.

Point 3: Section 2-711(3).

Point 4: Sections 2-401, 2-501 and 9-102(1)(a).

Point 6: Article 2A, esp. Section 2A-508(5).

Definitional Cross References:

"Agreement". Section 1-201(3).
"Debtor". Section 9-105.
"Goods". Sections 2A-103(1)(h), 9-105.
"Lease". Section 2A-103(1)(j).
"Party". Section 1-201(29).
"Rights". Section 1-201(36).
"Sale". Section 2-106(1).
"Secured party". Section 9-105.
"Security agreement". Section 9-105.
"Security interest". Section 1-201(37).

§ 9-114. Consignment.

(1) A person who delivers goods under a consignment which is not a security interest and who would be required to file under this Article by paragraph (3)(c) of Section 2-326 has priority over a secured party who is or becomes a creditor of the consignee and who would have a perfected security interest in the goods if they were the property of the consignee, and also has priority with respect to identifiable cash proceeds received on or before delivery of the goods to a buyer, if

(a) the consignor complies with the filing provision of the Article on Sales with respect to consignments (paragraph (3)(c) of Section 2-326) before the consignee receives possession of the goods; and

(b) the consignor gives notification in writing to the holder of the security interest if the holder has filed a financing statement covering the same types of goods before the date of the filing made by the consignor; and

(c) the holder of the security interest receives the notification within five years before the consignee receives possession of the goods; and

(d) the notification states that the consignor expects to deliver goods on consignment to the consignee, describing the goods by item or type.

(2) In the case of a consignment which is not a security interest and in which the requirements of the preceding subsection have not been met, a

person who delivers goods to another is subordinate to a person who would have a perfected security interest in the goods if they were the property of the debtor.

As added in 1972.

Official Comment

Prior Uniform Statutory Provision: None.

Purposes:

1. This section requires that where goods are furnished to a merchant under the arrangement known as consignment rather than in a security transaction, the consignor must, in order to protect his position as against an inventory secured party of the consignee, give to that party the same notice and at the same time that he would give to that party if that party had filed first with respect to inventory and if the consignor were furnishing the goods under an inventory security agreement instead of under a consignment.

For the distinction between true consignment and security arrangements, see Section 1-201(37). For the assimilation of consignments under certain circumstances to goods on sale or return and the requirement of filing in the case of consignments, see Section 2-326.

The requirements of notice in this section conform closely to the concepts and the language of Section 9-312(3), which should be consulted together with the relevant Comments.

Except in the limited cases of identifiable cash proceeds received on or before delivery of the goods to a buyer, no attempt has been made to provide rules as to perfection of a claim to proceeds of consignments (compare Section 9-306) or the priority thereof (compare Section 9-312). It is believed that under many true consignments the consignor acquires a claim for an agreed amount against the consignee at the moment of sale, and does not look to the proceeds of sale. In contrast to the assumption of this Article that rights to proceeds of security interests under Section 9-306 represent the presumed intent of the parties (compare Section 9-203(3)), the Article goes on the assumption that if consignors intend to claim the proceeds of sale, they will do so by expressly contracting for them and will perfect their security interests therein.

Cross References:

Sections 2-326 and 9-312(3).

Definitional Cross References:

"Consignment". Section 1-201(37).
"Debtor". Section 9-105.
"Goods". Section 9-105.
"Notification". Section 1-201(26).
"Proceeds". Section 9-306.
"Security interest". Section 1-201(37).

§ 9-115. Investment Property.

(1) In this Article:

(a) "Commodity account" means an account maintained by a commodity intermediary in which a commodity contract is carried for a commodity customer.

(b) "Commodity contract" means a commodity futures contract, an option on a commodity futures contract, a commodity option, or other contract that, in each case, is:

(i) traded on or subject to the rules of a board of trade that has been designated as a contract market for such a contract pursuant to the federal commodities laws; or

(ii) traded on a foreign commodity board of trade, exchange, or market, and is carried on the books of a commodity intermediary for a commodity customer.

(c) "Commodity customer" means a person for whom a commodity intermediary carries a commodity contract on its books.

(d) "Commodity intermediary" means:

(i) a person who is registered as a futures commission merchant under the federal commodities laws; or

(ii) a person who in the ordinary course of its business provides clearance or settlement services for a board of trade that has been designated as a contract market pursuant to the federal commodities laws.

(e) "Control" with respect to a certificated security, uncertificated security, or security entitlement has the meaning specified in Section 8–106. A secured party has control over a commodity contract if by agreement among the commodity customer, the commodity intermediary, and the secured party, the commodity intermediary has agreed that it will apply any value distributed on account of the commodity contract as directed by the secured party without further consent by the commodity customer. If a commodity customer grants a security interest in a commodity contract to its own commodity intermediary, the commodity intermediary as secured party has control. A secured party has control over a securities account or commodity account if the secured party has control over all security entitlements or commodity contracts carried in the securities account or commodity account.

(f) "Investment property" means:

(i) a security, whether certificated or uncertificated;

(ii) a security entitlement:

(iii) a securities account:

(iv) a commodity contract; or

(v) a commodity account.

(2) Attachment or perfection of a security interest in a securities account is also attachment or perfection of a security interest in all security entitlements carried in the securities account. Attachment or perfection of a security interest in a commodity account is also attachment or perfection of a security interest in all commodity contracts carried in the commodity account.

(3) A description of collateral in a security agreement or financing statement is sufficient to create or perfect a security interest in a certificated security, uncertificated security, security entitlement, securities account, commodity contract, or commodity account whether it describes the collateral by those terms, or as investment property, or by description of the underlying security, financial asset, or commodity contract. A description of investment property collateral in a security agreement or financing statement is sufficient if it identifies the collateral by specific listing, by category, by quantity, by a

computational or allocational formula or procedure, or by any other method, if the identity of the collateral is objectively determinable.

(4) Perfection of a security interest in investment property is governed by the following rules:

(a) A security interest in investment property may be perfected by control.

(b) Except as otherwise provided in paragraphs (c) and (d), a security interest in investment property may be perfected by filing.

(c) If the debtor is a broker or securities intermediary, a security interest in investment property is perfected when it attaches. The filing of a financing statement with respect to a security interest in investment property granted by a broker or securities intermediary has no effect for purposes of perfection or priority with respect to that security interest.

(d) If a debtor is a commodity, intermediary, a security interest in a commodity contract or a commodity account is perfected when it attaches. The filing of a financing statement with respect to a security interest in a commodity contract or a commodity account granted by a commodity intermediary has no effect for purposes of perfection or priority with respect to that security interest.

(5) Priority between conflicting security interests in the same investment property is governed by the following rules:

(a) A security interest of a secured party who has control over investment property has priority over a security interest of a secured party who does not have control over the investment property.

(b) Except as otherwise provided in paragraphs (c) and (d), conflicting security interests of secured parties each of whom has control rank equally.

(c) Except as otherwise agreed by the securities intermediary, a security interest in a security entitlement or a securities account granted to the debtor's own securities intermediary has priority over any security interest granted by the debtor to another secured party.

(d) Except as otherwise agreed by the commodity intermediary, a security interest in a commodity contract or a commodity account granted to the debtor's own commodity intermediary has priority over any security interest granted by the debtor to another secured party.

(e) Conflicting security interests granted by a broker, a securities intermediary, or a commodity intermediary which are perfected without control rank equally.

(f) In all other cases, priority between conflicting security interests in investment property is governed by Section 9–312(5), (6), and (7). Section 9–312(4) does not apply to investment property.

(6) If a security certificate in registered form is delivered to a secured party pursuant to agreement, a written security agreement is not required for attachment or enforceability of the security interest, delivery suffices for

perfection of the security interest, and the security interest has priority over a conflicting security interest perfected by means other than control, even if a necessary indorsement is lacking.

Added in 1994.

See Appendix XII, infra.

Official Comment

1. **Overview.** This section sets out the principal rules on security interests in investment property. Investment property, defined in subsection (1)(f) is a new term for a category of collateral that includes securities, whether held directly or through intermediaries, and commodity futures. The term investment property is used in Article 9 as one of the general categories of collateral, such as goods or instruments. Investment property is excluded from the definitions of goods, instruments, and general intangibles. See Sections 9-105(1)(h), 9-105(1)(i), and 9-106.

This section is added as part of the revision of Article 8 on investment securities. It relies in part on terms and concepts defined in Revised Article 8. For an overview of Revised Article 8, see the Prefatory Note to that Article. Prior to the 1978 amendments to Article 8, the rules on security interests in securities were included in Article 9. The 1978 amendments moved the key rules to Article 8. The revision of Article 8 returns these matters to Article 9. In order to avoid disruption of section numbering, the new rules on security interests in investment property are collected in this section, rather than being distributed among the various sections of Article 9 dealing with corresponding issues for other categories of collateral. On matters not covered by rules set out in this section, security interests in investment property are governed by the general rules in other sections of this Article.

The distinction between the direct and indirect holding systems plays an important role in the rules on security interests in securities. Consider two investors, X and Y, each of whom owns 1000 shares of XYZ Co. common stock. X has a certificate representing 1000 shares and is registered on the books maintained by XYZ Co.'s transfer agent as the holder of record of those 1000 shares. X has a direct relationship with the issuer, and receives dividends, distributions, and proxies directly from the issuer. In Revised Article 8 terminology, X has a direct claim to a "certificated security." If X wishes to use the investment position as collateral for a loan, X would grant the lender a security interest in the "certificated security." The Article 9 rules for such transactions are explained in Comment 2. XYZ Co. might not issue certificates, but register investors such as X directly on its stockholder books. In that case, X's interest would be an "uncertificated security." The Article 9 rules for uncertificated securities are explained in Comment 3. By contrast to these direct relationships, Y holds the securities through an account with Y's broker. Y does not have a certificate and is not registered on XYZ Co.'s stock books as a holder of record. Rather, Y holds the securities through a chain of securities intermediaries. Under Revised Article 8, Y's interest in XYZ common stock is described as a "securities entitlement." If Y wishes to use the investment position as collateral for a loan, Y would grant the lender a security interest in the "securities entitlement." The Article 9 rules for security entitlements are explained in Comment 4.

A commercial setting in which security interests in investment property play a most economically significant role is the "wholesale" level, that is, finance of securities firms and security interests that support the extension of credit in the settlement system. Comments 6 and 7 deal with these transactions. The rules on security interests in investment property also apply to commodity futures. Comment 8 deals with these transactions.

The rules on security interests in investment property are based on the concept of "control," defined in Sections 8–106 and 9–115(1)(e). If the secured party has control the security interest can attach even without a written security agreement. See Section 9–203. A security interest in investment property can also be created by a written security agreement pursuant to Section 9–203. Security interests in investment property can be perfected by control. See subsection (4)(a). Although other methods of perfection are also permitted, the basic priority rule, set out in subsection (5)(a), is that a secured party who obtains control has priority over a secured party who relies on some other method of perfection. The control priority rule is explained in Comment 5.

2. Security interests in certificated securities. A security interest in a certificated security can be created by conferring control on the secured party. Section 8–106 provides that a secured party has control of a certificated security if the certificate has been delivered, see Section 8–301, and any necessary indorsement has been supplied. Section 9–203 provides that a security interest can attach, even without a written security agreement, if the secured party has control. Section 9–115(4)(a) provides that control is a permissible method of perfection.

A security interest in a certificated security can also be created by a written security agreement pursuant to Section 9–203, and can be perfected by filing, see subsection (4)(b). (The perfection by filing rule does not apply if the debtor is a broker or securities intermediary.) However, a security interest perfected only by filing is subordinate to a conflicting security interest perfected by control. See subsection (5)(a) and Comment 5. Also, perfection by filing would not give the secured party protection against other types of adverse claims, since the Article 8 adverse claim cut-off rules require control. See Section 8–510.

Section 9–115(6) deals with cases where a secured party has taken possession of an unindorsed security certificate in registered form. It provides that even though the indorsement is lacking, delivery of the certificate to the secured party suffices for attachment and perfection of the security interest in the certificated security. It also provides that such a possessory security interest has priority over a conflicting non-control security interest, such as a security interest perfected by filing. However, without the indorsement the secured party would not get the other protections against adverse claims that flow from obtaining control. See Section 8–510.

3. Security interests in uncertificated securities. The rules on security interests in uncertificated securities apply only where the debtor is the direct holder of an uncertificated security. For example, mutual funds typically do not issue certificates, but the beneficial owners of mutual funds shares commonly are the direct holders of the shares, whose interests are recorded on the books of the issuer. If such an investor grants a security interest in the mutual funds shares, the rules in this section on security interests in uncertificated securities apply. These rules are not germane to situations where a debtor holds securities through a securities intermediary. Security interests in positions held through securities intermediaries are governed by the rules on security entitlements and securities accounts, not the rules on uncertificated securities.

A security interest in an uncertificated security can be perfected either by control or by filing. See subsection (4)(a) and (b). (The filing rule does not apply if the debtor is itself a broker or securities intermediary.) Priority disputes among conflicting security interests in an uncertificated security are governed by subsection (5). Under subsection (5)(a), a secured party who obtains control has priority over a secured party who does not have control. Thus, although filing is a permissible method of perfection, a secured party who perfects by filing takes the risk that the debtor has granted or will grant a security interest in the same property to another party who obtains control. See Comment 5.

The requirements for control with respect to uncertificated securities are set out in Section 8–106(c). There are two possibilities. First, a secured party has control if the uncertificated security is transferred from debtor to secured party on the books of the issuer. See Sections 8–106(c)(1) (control by "delivery") and 8–301(b) (defining "delivery" of uncertificated security). So far as the issuer is concerned, the secured party is the registered owner entitled to all rights of ownership, though as between the debtor and secured party the debtor remains the owner and the secured party holds its interest as secured party. Second, a secured party has control over an uncertificated security if the issuer agrees that it will comply with "instructions" originated by the secured party without further consent by the registered owner. See Section 8–106(c)(2). If the debtor, secured party, and issuer agree that the secured party has the right to direct the issuer to dispose of the security without further action by the debtor, the secured party has control even though the debtor remains listed as the registered owner and continues to receive dividends and distributions. Note, though, that there is no statutory requirement that issuers of uncertificated securities offer such arrangements.

4. Security interests in security entitlements and securities accounts. This section establishes a structure for creating security interests in securities and other financial assets that a debtor holds through an account with a securities intermediary. Under Revised Article 8, the interest of a person who holds securities through a securities account with a broker or other securities intermediary is described as a security entitlement. Thus, the Article 9 rules governing the use of that person's investment position as collateral are the rules for security entitlements and securities accounts, not the rules for certificated securities or uncertificated securities.

Attachment of security interests in security entitlements and securities accounts is governed by Section 9–203 and subsections (2) and (3) of this section. Unless the secured party has control, a written security agreement is necessary for attachment. For purposes of description of the collateral in a security agreement, it is not essential that the precise Article 8 terminology be used. See subsection (3). For example, if a debtor who holds 1000 shares of XYZ Co. common stock through a securities account signs a security agreement which describes the collateral as "1000 shares of XYZ Co. common stock," that description is sufficient, even though the debtor's interest would be described under Revised Article 8 as a "security entitlement" to 1000 shares of XYZ Co. common stock.

The Article 8 term security entitlement also covers the interest of a person in a "financial asset," if the person holds that financial asset through a securities account. "Financial asset" is a broader term than "security." See Section 8–102(a)(9). For example, a bankers' acceptance is an Article 3 negotiable instrument and hence an instrument under Section 9–105(1)(i). If a person who holds a bankers' acceptance directly wishes to grant a security interest in it, the Article 9 rules for instruments apply. However, if a person holds a bankers' acceptance through a securities account, the person has a security entitlement to the bankers' acceptance. If the person wishes to grant a security interest in the security entitlement to the bankers' acceptance, the Article 9 rules for investment property apply.

Subsection (1)(f)(iii) provides that the term investment property also includes "securities account." This is intended to facilitate transactions in which a debtor wishes to grant a security interest in all of the investment positions held through a particular account rather than in particular positions carried in the account. Just as a debtor may grant a security interest either in specifically listed items of equipment or in all of the debtor's equipment, so too a debtor who holds securities or other financial assets through a securities account may grant a security interest either in specifically listed security entitlements or in all of the security entitlements held through that account. Referring to the collateral as the securities account is a simple way of describing all of the security entitlements carried in the account. Section 9-115(2) provides that attachment or perfection of a security interest in a securities account is also attachment or perfection of a security interest in all security entitlements carried in the securities account. A security interest in a securities account would also include all other rights of the debtor against the securities intermediary arising out of the securities account. For example, a security interest in a securities account would include credit balances due to the debtor from the securities intermediary, whether or not they are proceeds of a security entitlement.

A security interest in a security entitlement or securities account can be perfected either by control or by filing. See subsections (4)(a) and (4)(b). (The filing rule does not apply if the debtor is itself a broker or securities intermediary.) Priority disputes among conflicting security interests in a security entitlement or securities account are governed by subsection (5). The basic rule of subsection (5)(a) is that a secured party who obtains control has priority over a secured party who does not have control. Thus, although filing is a permissible method of perfection, a secured party who perfects by filing takes the risk that the debtor has granted or will grant a security interest in the same property to another party who obtains control. See Comment 5.

The requirements for control with respect to security entitlements and securities accounts are set out in Sections 8-106(d) and 9-115(1)(e). There are two possibilities. First, Section 8-106(d)(1) provides that a secured party has control over a security entitlement if the secured party becomes the entitlement holder, that is, the position is transferred from debtor to secured party on the books of a securities intermediary. See Examples 1 and 2 in Comment 4 to Section 8-106. Second, Section 8-106(d)(2) provides that a secured party has control over a security entitlement if the securities intermediary agrees that it will comply with entitlement orders originated by the secured party without further consent by the debtor. See Example 3 in Comment 4 to Section 8-106. If the debtor, secured party, and issuer agree that the secured party has the right to direct the securities intermediary to dispose of the collateral without further action by the debtor, the secured party has control even though the debtor remains listed as the entitlement holder and continues to receive dividends and distributions. The secured party can obtain control even though the debtor is also allowed to continue to trade. See Section 8-106(f) and Comment 7 thereto. The three-party control agreement device is based on arrangements that have already developed in the securities business. Even under prior law, some securities brokers developed standard forms of such agreements. Note though that, as is the case with respect to issuers of uncertificated securities, there is no statutory requirement that securities intermediaries offer such control agreement arrangements.

Subsection (1)(e) provides that a secured party has control over a securities account if it has control over all security entitlements carried in the account. Thus, the rules in Section 8-106(d) on control with respect to security entitlements determine whether a secured party has control over a securities account. Control with respect to a securities account is defined in terms of obtaining control over the security entitlements simply for drafting convenience. Of course, an agreement that provides that the securities intermediary will honor instructions from the secured party concerning a securities account described as such is sufficient since such an agreement necessarily implies that the secured party has control over all security entitlements carried in the account.

If a customer borrows from its own securities intermediary, e.g., to purchase securities "on margin" or for other purposes, and grants a security interest to its intermediary, the intermediary, has control. See Section 8–106(e). A securities firm could also provide control financing arrangements to its customers through a different legal entity than the securities intermediary itself, e.g., the securities trading, custody, and credit services might be provided by different corporate entities within the financial services firm's "family." So long as the agreement with the customer provides that the entity providing the custodial function (the "securities intermediary") will act on instructions received from entity providing the credit, the credit entity has control.

5. Priority Rules. Subsection (5) specifies the priority rules for conflicting security interests in the same investment property. Subsection (5)(a) states the most important general rule—that a secured party who obtains control has priority over a secured party who does not obtain control. The other priority rules, in subsections (5)(b) through (5)(e), deal with relatively unusual circumstances not covered by the control priority rule. Subsection (5)(f) provides that the general priority rules of Section 9–312 apply to cases not covered by the specific rules in subsection (5). The principal application of this residual rule is that the usual first in time of filing rule applies to conflicting security interests that are perfected only by filing. Because the control priority rule of subsection (5)(a) provides for the ordinary cases in which persons purchase securities on margin credit from their brokers, there is no need for special rules for purchase money security interests. Accordingly, subsection (5)(f) provides that the purchase money priority rule of Section 9–312(4) does not apply to investment property.

The following examples illustrate the basic priority rules of this section:

Example 1. Debtor borrows from Alpha and grants Alpha a security interest in a variety of collateral, including all of Debtor's investment property. At that time Debtor owns 1000 shares of XYZ Co. stock for which Debtor has a certificate. Alpha perfects by filing. Later, Debtor borrows from Beta and grants Beta a security interest in the 1000 shares of XYZ Co. stock. Debtor delivers the certificate, properly indorsed, to Beta, Alpha and Beta both have perfected security interests in the XYZ Co. stock. Beta has control, see Section 8–106(b)(1), and hence has priority over Alpha.

Example 2. Debtor borrows from Alpha and grants Alpha a security interest in a variety of collateral, including all of Debtor's investment property. At that time Debtor owns 1000 shares of XYZ Co. stock, held through a securities account with Able & Co. Alpha perfects by filing. Later, Debtor borrows from Beta and grants Beta a security interest in the 1000 shares of XYZ Co. stock. Debtor instructs Able to have the 1000 shares transferred through the clearing corporation to Custodian Bank, to be credited to Beta's account with Custodian Bank. Alpha and Beta both have perfected security interests in the XYZ Co. stock. Beta has control, see Section 8–106(d)(1), and hence has priority over Alpha.

Example 3. Debtor borrows from Alpha and grants Alpha a security interest in a variety of collateral, including all of Debtor's investment property. At that time Debtor owns 1000 shares of XYZ Co. stock, which is held through a securities account with Able & Co. Alpha perfects by filing. Later, Debtor borrows from Beta and grants Beta a security interest in the 1000 shares of XYZ Co. stock. Debtor, Able, and Beta enter into an agreement under which Debtor will continue to receive dividends and distributions, and will continue to have the right to direct dispositions, but Beta will also have the right to direct dispositions and receive the proceeds. Alpha and Beta both have perfected security interests in the XYZ Co. stock. Beta has control, see Section 8-106(d)(2), and hence has priority over Alpha.

Example 4. Debtor borrows from Alpha and grants Alpha a security interest in a variety of collateral, including all of Debtor's investment property. At that time Debtor owns 1000 shares of XYZ Co. stock, held through a securities account with Able & Co. Alpha perfects by filing, Debtor's agreement with Able & Co. provides that Able has a security interest in all securities carried in the account as security for any obligations of Debtor to Able. Debtor incurs obligations to Able and later defaults on the obligations to Alpha and Able. Able has control by virtue of the rule of Section 8-106(e) that if a customer grants a security interest to its own intermediary, the intermediary has control. Since Alpha does not have control, Able has priority over Alpha under the general control priority rule of subsection (5)(a).

Example 5. Debtor holds securities through a securities account with Able & Co. Debtor's agreement with Able & Co. provides that Able has a security interest in all securities carried in the account as security for any obligations of Debtor to Able. Debtor borrows from Beta and grants Beta a security interest in 1000 shares of XYZ Co. stock carried in the account. Debtor, Able, and Beta enter into an agreement under which Debtor will continue to receive dividends and distributions and will continue to have the right to direct dispositions, but Beta will also have the right to direct dispositions and receive the proceeds. Debtor incurs obligations to Able and later defaults on the obligations to Beta and Able. Both Beta and Able have control, so the general control priority rule of subsection (5)(a) does not apply. Compare Example 4. Subsection (5)(c) provides that a security interest held by a securities intermediary in positions of its own customer has priority over a conflicting security interest of an external lender, so Able has priority over Beta. (Subsection (5)(d) has a parallel rule for commodities intermediaries.) The agreement among Able, Beta, and Debtor could, of course, determine the relative priority of the security interests of Able and Beta, see Section 9-316, but the fact that the intermediary has agreed to act on the instructions of a secured party such as Beta does not itself imply any agreement by the intermediary to subordinate.

The control priority rule does not turn on either temporal sequence or awareness of conflicting security interests. Rather, it is a structural rule, based on the principle that a lender should be able to rely on the collateral without question if the lender has taken the necessary steps to assure itself that it is in a position where it can foreclose on the collateral without further action by the debtor. The control priority rule is necessary because the perfection rules provide considerable flexibility in structuring secured financing arrangements. For example, at the "retail" level, a secured lender to an investor who wants the full measure of protection can obtain control, but the creditor may be willing to accept the greater measure of risk that follows from perfection by filing. Similarly, at the "wholesale" level, a lender to securities firms can leave the collateral with the debtor and obtain a perfected security interest under the automatic perfection rule of subsection (4)(c), but a lender who wants to be entirely sure of its position will want to obtain control. The control priority rule of subsection (5)(a) is an essential part of this system of flexibility. It is feasible to provide more than one method of perfecting secured transactions only if the rules ensure that those who take the necessary steps to obtain the full measure of protection do not run the risk of subordination to those who have not taken such steps. A secured party who is unwilling to run the risk that the debtor has granted or will grant a conflicting control security interest should not make a loan without obtaining control of the collateral.

As applied to the retail level, the control priority rule means that a secured party who obtains control has priority over a conflicting security interest perfected by filing without regard to inquiry into whether the control secured party was aware of the filed security interest. Prior to enactment of this section, Article 9 did not permit perfection of security interests in securities by filing. Accordingly, parties who deal in securities have never developed a practice of searching the UCC files before conducting securities transactions. Although filing is now a permissible method of perfection, in order to avoid disruption of existing practices in this business it is necessary to give perfection by filing a different and more limited effect for securities than for some other forms of collateral. The priority rules are not based on the assumption that parties who perfect by the usual method of obtaining control will search the files. Quite the contrary, the control priority rule is intended to ensure that secured parties who do obtain control are entirely unaffected by filings. To state the point another way, perfection by filing is intended to affect only general creditors or other secured creditors who rely on filing. The rule that a security interest perfected by filing can be primed by a control security interest, without regard to awareness, is a consequence of the system of perfection and priority rules for investment property. These rules are designed to take account of the circumstances of the securities markets, where filing is not given the same effect as for some other forms of property. No implication is made about the effect of filing with respect to security interests in other forms of property, nor about other Article 9 rules, e.g., Section 9–308, which govern the circumstances in which security interests in other forms of property perfected by filing can be primed by subsequent perfected security interests.

6. Secured finance of securities firms. Modernization of the commercial law rules governing secured finance of securities dealers and security interest arrangements in the clearance and settlement system is essential to the safe and efficient functioning of the securities markets.

Secured financing arrangements for securities firms are currently implemented in various ways. In some circumstances lenders may require that the transactions be structured as "hard pledges," where the securities are transferred on the books of a clearing corporation from the debtor's account to the lender's account or to a special pledge account for the lender where they cannot be disposed of without the specific consent of the lender. In other circumstances, lenders are content with so-called "agreement to pledge" or "agreement to deliver" arrangements, where the debtor retains the positions in its own account, but reflects on its books that the positions have been hypothecated and promises that the securities will be transferred to the secured party's account on demand.

The perfection and priority rules of this section are designed to facilitate current secured financing arrangements for securities firms as well as to provide sufficient flexibility to accommodate new arrangements that develop in the future. Hard pledge arrangements are covered by the concept of control. If the lender obtains control, the security interest is perfected and has priority over a conflicting non-control security interest. For examples of control arrangements in this setting see Examples 4 through 8 in Comment 4 to Section 8–106. The secured party can obtain control even though the debtor retains the right to trade or otherwise dispose of the collateral. See Section 8–106(f) and Examples 7 and 8 in Comment 4 to Section 8–106.

Non-control secured financing arrangements for securities firms are covered by the automatic perfection rule of subsection (4)(c). Under prior law, agreement to pledge arrangements could be implemented under a provision that a security interest in securities given for new value under a written security agreement was perfected without filing or possession for a period of 21 days. Although the security interests were temporary in legal theory, the financing arrangements could, in practice, be continued indefinitely by rolling over the loans at least every 21 days.

Accordingly, a knowledgeable creditor of a securities firm realizes that the firm's securities may be subject to security interests that are not discoverable from any public records. The perfection rule of subsection (4)(c) makes it unnecessary to engage in the purely formal practice of rolling over these arrangements every 21 days.

Priority questions concerning security interests granted by brokers and securities intermediaries are governed by the general control priority rule of subsection (5)(a), as supplemented by the special rules set out in subsections (b), (c), and (e). In cases not covered by the control priority rule, conflicting security interests rank equally. The following examples illustrate the priority rules as applied to this setting. (In all cases it is assumed that the debtor retains sufficient other securities to satisfy all customers' claims. This section deals with the relative rights of secured lenders to a securities firm. Disputes between a secured lender and the firm's own customers are governed by Section 8–511.)

> *Example 6.* Able & Co., a securities dealer, enters into financing arrangements with two lenders, Alpha Bank and Beta Bank. In each case the agreements provide that the lender will have a security interest in the securities identified on lists provided to the lender on a daily basis, that the debtor will deliver the securities to the lender on demand, and that the debtor will not list as collateral any securities which the debtor has pledged to any other lender. Upon Able's insolvency it is discovered that Able has listed the same securities on the collateral lists provided to both Alpha and Beta. Alpha and Beta both have perfected security interests under the automatic perfection rule of subsection (4)(c). Neither Alpha nor Beta has control. Subsection (5)(e) provides that the security interests of Alpha and Beta rank equally, because each of them has a non-control security interest granted by a securities firm. They share pro-rata.

> *Example 7.* Able enters into financing arrangements with Alpha Bank and Beta Bank as in Example 6. At some point, however, Beta decides that it is unwilling to continue to provide financing on a non-control basis. Able directs the clearing corporation where it holds its principal inventory of securities to move specified securities into Beta's account. Upon Able's insolvency it is discovered that a list of collateral provided to Alpha includes securities that had been moved to Beta's account. Both Alpha and Beta have perfected security interests; Alpha under the automatic perfection rule of subsection (4)(c), and Beta under that rule and also the subsection (4)(a) control perfection rule. Beta has control but Alpha does not. Beta has priority over Alpha under subsection (5)(a).

> *Example 8.* Able & Co. carries its principal inventory of securities through Clearing Corporation, which offers a "shared control" facility whereby a participant securities firm can enter into an arrangement with a lender under which the securities firm will retain the power to trade and otherwise direct dispositions of securities carried in its account, but Clearing Corporation agrees that, at any time the lender so directs, Clearing Corporation will transfer any securities from the firm's account to the lender's account or otherwise dispose of them as directed by the lender. Able enters into financing arrangements with two lenders. Alpha and Beta, each of which obtains such a control agreement from Clearing Corporation. The agreement with each lender provides that Able will designate specific securities as collateral on lists provided to the lender on a daily or other periodic basis, and that it will not pledge the same securities to different lenders. Upon Able's insolvency, it is discovered that Able has listed the same securities on the collateral lists provided to both Alpha and Beta. Both Alpha and Beta have control over the disputed securities. They share pro rata under subsection (5)(b).

7. Secured financing arrangement in the settlement system. Under the rules or agreements governing the relationship between a clearing corporation and its participants, the clearing corporation may have a security interest in securities that the participants have deposited with the clearing corporation pursuant to guaranty fund arrangements or in securities that are in the process of delivery to or from a participant's account in the settlement process. The control rules protect the clearing corporation's rights as secured party in such arrangements, since the clearing corporation would have control over the collateral under the Section 8–106 rules. The control rules also protect the rights of "upper-tier" intermediaries that are not themselves clearing corporations. For example, if a securities dealer carries its inventory through a clearing bank that provides both custodial and credit services, the clearing bank as secured party would have control and hence be assured of perfection and priority over any potential conflicting security interests granted by the securities dealer.

In some circumstances, a clearing corporation may be the debtor in a secured financing arrangement. For example, a clearing corporation that settles delivery-versus-payment transactions among its participants on a net, same-day basis relies on timely payments from all participants with net obligations due to the system. If a participant that is a net debtor were to default on its payment obligation, the clearing corporation would not receive some of the funds needed to settle with participants that are net creditors to the system. To complete end-of-day settlement after a payment default by a participant, a clearing corporation that settles on a net, same-day basis may need to draw on credit lines and pledge securities of the defaulting participant or other securities pledged by participants in the clearing corporation to secure such drawings. The clearing corporation may be the top tier securities intermediary for the securities pledged, so that it would not be practical for the lender to obtain control. Even where the clearing corporation holds some types of securities through other intermediaries, however, the clearing corporation is unlikely to be able to complete the arrangements necessary to convey "control" over the securities to be pledged in time to complete settlement in a timely manner. However, the term "securities intermediary" is defined in Section 8–102(a)(14) to include clearing corporations. Thus, the perfection rule of subsection (4)(c) applies to security interests in investment property granted by clearing corporations.

In secured financing arrangements for clearing corporations and other securities intermediaries, it is sometimes necessary to specify that a secured lender will have a security interest in a certain bundle of securities that, after all the calculations necessary to complete a processing cycle are completed, turn out to be appropriate and available for pledge. At the time the security interest attaches, the necessary computations may not have been completed, though the information that ultimately will determine what positions are to be pledged has been entered. Accordingly, subsection (3) provides that the description of collateral in a security agreement may identify the collateral by means of a computational or allocational formula.

8. Security interests in commodity futures. Section 9–115 establishes rules on security interests in commodity contracts and commodity accounts that are, in general, parallel to the rules on security interests in security entitlements and securities accounts. Note, though, that commodity contracts are not "securities" or "financial assets" under Article 8. See Section 8–103(f). Thus, the relationship between commodity intermediaries and commodity customers is not governed by the indirect holding system rules of Part 5 of Article 8. For securities, the UCC establishes rules in Article 9 on security interests, and rules in Article 8 on the rights of transferees, including secured parties, on such matters as the rights of a transferee if the transfer was itself wrongful so that another party has an adverse claim. For commodity contracts, Article 9 establishes rules on security interests, but questions of the sort dealt with in Article 8 for securities are left to other law.

Subsection (1) contains the definitions of the terms used in substantive rules on security interests in commodity contracts and commodity accounts. The key term "commodity contract" is defined in subsection (1)(b). Section 8-103(f) provides that a commodity contract, as defined in Section 9-115, is not a security or a financial asset. The result is that the indirect holding system rules in Revised Article 8 Part 5 do not apply to anything that falls within the definition of commodity contract in this section. The indirect holding system rules of Article 8, however, are intended to be sufficiently flexible that they can be applied to new developments in the securities and financial markets, where that is appropriate. Accordingly, the "commodity contract" definition in this section is narrowly drafted to ensure that it does not operate as an obstacle to the application of the new Article 8 indirect holding system rules to new products. The term commodity contract covers those contracts that are traded on or subject to the rules of a designated contract market, and foreign commodity contracts that are carried on the books of American commodity intermediaries. The effect of this definition is that the category of commodity contracts that are excluded from Article 8 but governed by Article 9 is essentially the same as the category of contracts that fall within the exclusive regulatory jurisdiction of the federal Commodities Futures Trading Commission.

Commodity contracts are rather different from securities or other financial assets. A person who enters into a commodity futures contract is not buying an asset having a certain value and holding it in anticipation of increase in value. Rather the person is entering into a contract to buy or sell a commodity at set price for delivery at a future time. That contract may become advantageous or disadvantageous as the price of the commodity fluctuates during the term of the contract. The rules of the commodity exchanges require that the contracts be marked to market on a daily basis, that is the customer pays or receives any increment attributable to that day's price change. Because commodity customers may incur obligations on their contracts, they are required to provide collateral at the outset, known as "original margin," and may be required to provide additional amounts, known as "variation margin," during the term of the contract.

The most likely setting in which a person would want to take a security interest in a commodity contract is where a lender who is advancing funds to finance an inventory of a physical commodity requires the borrower to enter into a commodity contract as a hedge against the risk of decline in the value of the commodity. The lender will want to take a security interest in both the commodity itself and the hedging commodity contract. Typically, such arrangements are structured as security interests in the entire commodity account in which the borrower carries the hedging contracts, rather than in individual contracts. Section 9-115 provides a simple mechanism for implementation of such arrangements, either by granting a security interest in the commodity account, or in particular commodity contracts carried in the account. The security interest can be perfected by filing or by control. Under subsection (1)(e) the secured party can obtain control over a commodity contract or commodity account by obtaining an agreement among the commodity customer, the secured party, and the commodity intermediary in which the commodity intermediary agrees to apply any value distributed as directed by the secured party. This provides a clear and certain legal framework for practices that have already developed in the industry.

One important effect of including commodity contracts and commodity accounts in the new Article 9 rules is to provide a clearer legal structure for the analysis of the rights of commodity clearing organizations against their participants and futures commission merchants against their customers. The rules and agreements of commodity clearing organizations generally provide that the clearing organization has the right to liquidate any participant's positions in order to satisfy obligations of the participant to the clearing corporation. Similarly, agreements between futures commission merchants and their customers generally provide that the futures commission merchant has the right to liquidate a customer's positions in order to satisfy obligations of the customer to the futures commission merchant. Section 9–115 treats these rights as security interests and applies to them the same priority rules that apply to the somewhat analogous relationships between securities clearing corporations or securities intermediaries and their participants or customers. Subsection (1)(e) provides that the commodity intermediary has control, and therefore the security interest is perfected under subsection (4)(a). Subsection (5)(d) provides that the security interest of a commodity clearing organization in its participant's commodity contracts has priority over any security interest granted by the participant to a third-party lender. Similarly, an FCM's security interest would have priority over any security interest granted by its customer to a third-party lender.

The main property that a commodity intermediary holds as collateral for the obligations that the commodity customer may incur under its commodity contracts is not other commodity contracts carried by the customer but the other property that the customer has posted as margin. Typically, this property will be securities. The commodity intermediary's security interest in such securities is governed by the rules of this section on security interests in securities, not the rules on security interests in commodity contracts or commodity accounts.

Although there are significant analytic and regulatory differences between commodities and securities, the development of commodity contracts on financial products in the past few decades has resulted in a system in which the commodity markets and security markets are closely linked. The Section 9–115 rules on security interests in commodity contracts and commodity accounts provide a structure that may be essential in times of stress in the financial markets. Suppose, for example that a firm has a position in a securities market that is hedged by a position in a commodity market, so that payments that the firm is obligated to make with respect to the securities position will be covered by the receipt of funds from the commodity position. Depending upon the settlement cycles of the different markets, it is possible that the firm could find itself in a position where it is obligated to make the payment with respect to the securities position before it receives the matching funds from the commodity position. If cross-margining arrangements have not been developed between the two markets, the firm may need to borrow funds temporarily to make the earlier payment. The Section 9–115 rules would facilitate the use of positions in one market as collateral for loans needed to cover obligations in the other market.

9. Relation to other law. Section 1–103 provides that "unless displaced by particular provisions of this Act, the principles of law and equity ... shall supplement its provisions." There may be circumstances in which a secured party's action in acquiring a security interest that has priority under this section constitutes conduct that is wrongful under other law. Though the possibility of such resort to other law may provide an appropriate "escape valve" for cases of egregious conduct, care must be taken to ensure that this does not impair the certainty and predictability of the priority rules. Whether a court may appropriately look to other law to impose liability upon or estop a party from asserting its Article 9 priority depends on an assessment of the party's conduct under the standards established by such other law as well as a determination of whether the particular application of such other law is displaced by the UCC.

Some circumstances in which other law is clearly displaced by the UCC rules are readily identifiable. Common law "first in time, first in right" principles, or correlative tort liability rules such as common law conversion principles under which a purchaser may incur liability to a party with a prior property interest without regard to awareness of that claim, are necessarily displaced by the priority rules set out in this section since these rules determine the relative ranking of security interests in investment property. So too, Article 8 provides protections against adverse claims to certain purchasers of interests in investment property. In circumstances where a secured party not only has priority under Section 9-115, but also qualifies for protection against adverse claims under Section 8-303, or 8-510, resort to other law would be precluded.

In determining whether it is appropriate in a particular case to look to other law, account must also be taken of the policies that underlie the commercial law rules on securities markets and security interests in securities. A principal objective of the revision of Article 8 and corresponding provisions of Article 9 is to ensure that secured financing transactions can be implemented on a simple, timely, and certain basis. One of the circumstances that led to the revision was the concern that uncertainty in the application of the rules on secured transactions involving securities and other financial assets could contribute to systemic risk by impairing the ability of financial institutions to provide liquidity to the markets in times of stress. The control priority rule is designed to provide a clear and certain rule to ensure that lenders who have taken the necessary steps to establish control do not face a risk of subordination to other lenders who have not done so.

The control priority rule does not turn on an inquiry into the state of a party's awareness of potential conflicting claims because a rule under which a party's rights depended on that sort of after the fact inquiry could introduce an unacceptable measure of uncertainty. If an inquiry into awareness could provide a complete and satisfactory resolution of the problem in all cases, the priority rule of this section would have incorporated that test. The fact that it does not necessarily means that resort to other law based solely on that factor is precluded, though the question whether a control secured party induced or encouraged its financing arrangement with actual knowledge that the debtor would be violating the rights of another secured party may, in some circumstances, appropriately be treated as a factor in determining whether the control party's action is the kind of egregious conduct for which resort to other law is appropriate.

Definitional Cross References:

"Broker". Section 8-102(a)(3).
"Certificated security". Section 8-102(a)(4).
"Collateral". Section 9-105(1)(c).
"Control". Section 8-106.
"Debtor". Section 9-105(1)(d).
"Delivery". Section 8-301.
"Entitlement holder". Section 8-102(a)(7).
"Secured party". Section 9-105(1)(m).
"Securities account". Section 8-501.
"Securities intermediary". Section 8-102(a)(14).
"Security". Section 8-102(a)(15).
"Security agreement". Section 9-105(1)(*l*).
"Security certificate". Section 8-102(a)(16).
"Security entitlement". Section 8-102(a)(17).
"Security interest". Section 1-201(37).
"Uncertificated security". Section 8-102(a)(18).

§ 9-116. Security Interest Arising in Purchase or Delivery of Financial Asset.

(1) If a person buys a financial asset through a securities intermediary in a transaction in which the buyer is obligated to pay the purchase price to the

securities intermediary at the time of the purchase, and the securities intermediary credits the financial asset to the buyer's securities account before the buyer pays the securities intermediary, the securities intermediary has a security interest in the buyer's security entitlement securing the buyer's obligation to pay. A security agreement is not required for attachment or enforceability of the security interest, and the security interest is automatically perfected.

(2) If a certificated security, or other financial asset represented by a writing which in the ordinary course of business is transferred by delivery with any necessary indorsement or assignment is delivered pursuant to an agreement between persons in the business of dealing with such securities or financial assets and the agreement calls for delivery versus payment, the person delivering the certificate or other financial asset has a security interest in the certificated security or other financial asset securing the seller's right to receive payment. A security agreement is not required for attachment or enforceability of the security interest, and the security interest is automatically perfected.

Added in 1994.

See Appendix XII, infra.

Official Comment

1. This section establishes two special rules concerning security interests in investment property in order to provide certainty in the securities settlement system.

2. Depending upon a securities intermediary's arrangements with its entitlement holders, the securities intermediary may treat the entitlement holder as entitled to the securities in question before the entitlement holder has actually made payment for them. For example, many brokers permit retail customers to pay for securities by check. The broker may not receive final payment of the check until several days after the broker has credited the customer's securities account for the securities. Thus, the customer will have acquired a security entitlement prior to payment. Subsection (1) provides that in such circumstances the securities intermediary has a security interest in the entitlement holder's security entitlement as security for the payment obligation. This is a codification and adaptation to the indirect holding system of the so-called "broker's lien," which has long been recognized in existing law. See Restatement of Security § 12. An intermediary who has a security interest under this section will have control by virtue of Section 8–106(e). The security interest has priority over conflicting security interests granted by the entitlement holder, under Section 9–115(5)(a) and (c).

3. Subsection (2) specifies the rights of persons who deliver certificated securities or other financial assets in physical form, such as money market instruments, if the agreed payment is not received. In the typical arrangement for settlement of physical securities, the seller's securities custodian will deliver the physical certificates to the buyer's securities custodian and receive a time-stamped delivery receipt. The buyer's securities custodian will examine the certificate to ensure that it is in good order, and that the delivery matches a trade in which the buyer has instructed the seller to deliver to that custodian. If all is in order, the receiving custodian will settle with the delivering custodian through whatever funds settlement system has been agreed upon or is used by custom and usage in that market. The understanding of the trade, however, is that the delivery is conditioned upon payment, so that if payment is not made for any reason, the security will be returned to the deliverer. Subsection (2) is

intended to clarify the rights of persons making deliveries in such circumstances. It specifies that the person making delivery has a security interest in the securities or other financial assets, securing the right to receive payment. No security agreement is required for attachment, and no filing or other action is required for perfection.

Definitional Cross References:

"Certificated security". Section 8-102(a)(4).

"Financial asset". Section 8-102(a)(9).

"Securities account". Section 8-501.

"Securities intermediary". Section 8-102(a)(14).

"Security agreement". Section 9-105(1)(*l*).

"Security entitlement". Section 8-102(a)(17).

"Security interest". Section 1-201(37).

PART 2

VALIDITY OF SECURITY AGREEMENT AND RIGHTS OF PARTIES THERETO

§ 9-201. General Validity of Security Agreement.

Except as otherwise provided by this Act a security agreement is effective according to its terms between the parties, against purchasers of the collateral and against creditors. Nothing in this Article validates any charge or practice illegal under any statute or regulation thereunder governing usury, small loans, retail installment sales, or the like, or extends the application of any such statute or regulation to any transaction not otherwise subject thereto.

Official Comment

Prior Uniform Statutory Provisions: Section 4, Uniform Conditional Sales Act; Section 3, Uniform Trust Receipts Act.

Purposes:

This section states the general validity of a security agreement. In general the security agreement is effective between the parties; it is likewise effective against third parties. Exceptions to this general rule arise where there is a specific provision in any Article of this Act, for example, where Article 1 invalidates a disclaimer of the obligations of good faith, etc. (Section 1-102(3)), or this Article subordinates the security interest because it has not been perfected (Section 9-301) or for other reasons (see Section 9-312 on priorities) or defeats the security interest where certain types of claimants are involved (for example Section 9-307 on buyers of goods). As pointed out in the Note to Section 9-102, there is no intention that the enactment of this Article should repeal retail installment selling acts or small loan acts. Nor of course are the usury laws of any state repealed. These are mentioned in the text of Section 9-201 as examples of applicable laws, outside this Code entirely, which might invalidate the terms of a security agreement.

Cross References:

Sections 1-102(3), 9-301, 9-307 and 9-312.

Definitional Cross References:

"Collateral". Section 9-105.

"Creditor". Section 1-201.

"Party". Section 1-201.

"Purchaser". Section 1-201.

"Security agreement". Section 9-105.

§ 9–202. Title to Collateral Immaterial.

Each provision of this Article with regard to rights, obligations and remedies applies whether title to collateral is in the secured party or in the debtor.

Official Comment

Prior Uniform Statutory Provision: None.

Purposes:

The rights and duties of the parties to a security transaction and of third parties are stated in this Article without reference to the location of "title" to the collateral. Thus the incidents of a security interest which secures the purchase price of goods are the same under this Article whether the secured party appears to have retained title or the debtor appears to have obtained title and then conveyed it or a lien to the secured party. This Article in no way determines which line of interpretation (title theory v. lien theory or retained title v. conveyed title) should be followed in cases where the applicability of some other rule of law depends upon who has title. Thus if a revenue law imposes a tax on the "legal" owner of goods or if a corporation law makes a vote of the stockholders prerequisite to a corporation "giving" a security interest but not if it acquires property "subject" to a security interest, this Article does not attempt to define whether the secured party is a "legal" owner or whether the transaction "gives" a security interest for the purpose of such laws. Other rules of law or the agreement of the parties determine the location of "title" for such purposes.

Petitions for reclamation brought by a secured party in his debtor's insolvency proceedings have often been granted or denied on a title theory: where the secured party has title, reclamation will be granted; where he has "merely a lien", reclamation may be denied. For the treatment of such petitions under this Article, see Point 1 of Comment to Section 9–507.

Cross References:

Sections 2–401 and 2–507.

Definitional Cross References:

"Collateral". Section 9–105.
"Debtor". Section 9–105.
"Remedy". Section 1–201.
"Rights". Section 1–201.
"Secured party". Section 9–105.

§ 9–203. Attachment and Enforceability of Security Interest; Proceeds; Formal Requisites.

(1) Subject to the provisions of Section 4–210 on the security interest of a collecting bank, Sections 9–115 and 9–116 on security interests in investment property, and Section 9–113 on a security interest arising under the Articles on Sales and Leases, a security interest is not enforceable against the debtor or third parties with respect to the collateral and does not attach unless:

(a) the collateral is in the possession of the secured party pursuant to agreement, the collateral is investment property and the secured party has control pursuant to agreement, or the debtor has signed a security agreement which contains a description of the collateral and in addition, when the security interest covers crops growing or to be grown or timber to be cut, a description of the land concerned;

(b) value has been given; and

(c) the debtor has rights in the collateral.

(2) A security interest attaches when it becomes enforceable against the debtor with respect to the collateral. Attachment occurs as soon as all of the events specified in subsection (1) have taken place unless explicit agreement postpones the time of attaching.

(3) Unless otherwise agreed a security agreement gives the secured party the rights to proceeds provided by Section 9-306.

(4) A transaction, although subject to this Article, is also subject to ______ *, and in the case of conflict between the provisions of this Article and any such statute, the provisions of such statute control. Failure to comply with any applicable statute has only the effect which is specified therein.

Note: *At * in subsection (4) insert reference to any local statute regulating small loans, retail installment sales and the like.*

The foregoing subsection (4) is designed to make it clear that certain transactions, although subject to this Article, must also comply with other applicable legislation.

This Article is designed to regulate all the "security" aspects of transactions within its scope. There is, however, much regulatory legislation, particularly in the consumer field, which supplements this Article and should not be repealed by its enactment. Examples are small loan acts, retail installment selling acts and the like. Such acts may provide for licensing and rate regulation and may prescribe particular forms of contract. Such provisions should remain in force despite the enactment of this Article. On the other hand if a retail installment selling act contains provisions on filing, rights on default, etc., such provisions should be repealed as inconsistent with this Article except that inconsistent provisions as to deficiencies, penalties, etc., in the Uniform Consumer Credit Code and other recent related legislation should remain because those statutes were drafted after the substantial enactment of the Article and with the intention of modifying certain provisions of this Article as to consumer credit.

As amended in 1972, 1977 and 1994.

See Appendices XI and XII for material relating to changes made in text in 1994.

Official Comment

Prior Uniform Statutory Provision: Section 2, Uniform Trust Receipts Act.

Purposes:

1. Subsection (1) states three basic prerequisites to the existence of a security interest: agreement, value, and collateral. In addition, the agreement must be in writing unless the collateral is in the possession of the secured party (including an agent on his behalf—see Comment 2 to Section 9-305). When all of these elements exist, the security agreement becomes enforceable between the parties and is said to "attach". Perfection of a security interest (see Section 9-303) will in many cases depend on the additional step of filing a financing statement (see Section 9-302) or possession of the collateral (Sections 9-304(1) and 9-305). Section 9-301 states who will take priority over a security interest which has attached but which has not been perfected. Subsection (2) states a rule of construction under which the security interest,

unless postponed by explicit agreement, attaches automatically when the stated events have occurred.

2. As to the type of description of collateral in a written security agreement which will satisfy the requirements of this section, see Section 9-110 and Comment thereto.

In the case of crops growing or to be grown or timber to be cut the best identification is by describing the land, and subsection (1)(a) requires such a description.

3. One purpose of the formal requisites stated in subsection (1)(a) is evidentiary. The requirement of written record minimizes the possibility of future dispute as to the terms of a security agreement and as to what property stands as collateral for the obligation secured. Where the collateral is in the possession of the secured party, the evidentiary need for a written record is much less than where the collateral is in the debtor's possession; customarily, of course, as a matter of business practice the written record will be kept, but, in this Article as at common law, the writing is not a formal requisite. Subsection (1)(a), therefore, dispenses with the written agreement—and thus with signature and description—if the collateral is in the secured party's possession.

4. The definition of "security agreement" (Section 9-105) is "an agreement which creates or provides for a security interest". Under that definition the requirement of this section that the debtor sign a security agreement is not intended to reject, and does not reject, the deeply rooted doctrine that a bill of sale although absolute in form may be shown to have been in fact given as security. Under this Article as under prior law a debtor may show by parol evidence that a transfer purporting to be absolute was in fact for security and may then, on payment of the debt, assert his fundamental right to return of the collateral and execution of an acknowledgment of satisfaction.

5. The formal requisite of a writing stated in this section is not only a condition to the enforceability of a security interest against third parties, it is in the nature of a Statute of Frauds. Unless the secured party is in possession of the collateral, his security interest, absent a writing which satisfies paragraph (1)(a), is not enforceable even against the debtor, and cannot be made so on any theory of equitable mortgage or the like. If he has advanced money, he is of course a creditor and, like any creditor, is entitled after judgment to appropriate process to enforce his claim against his debtor's assets; he will not, however, have against his debtor the rights given a secured party by Part 5 of this Article on Default. The theory of equitable mortgage, insofar as it has operated to allow creditors to enforce informal security agreements against debtors, may well have developed as a necessary escape from the elaborate requirements of execution, acknowledgment and the like which the nineteenth century chattel mortgage acts vainly relied on as a deterrent to fraud. Since this Article reduces formal requisites to a minimum, the doctrine is no longer necessary or useful. More harm than good would result from allowing creditors to establish a secured status by parol evidence after they have neglected the simple formality of obtaining a signed writing.

6. Subsection (4) states that the provisions of regulatory statutes covering the field of consumer finance prevail over the provisions of this Article in case of conflict. The second sentence of the subsection is added to make clear that no doctrine of total voidness for illegality is intended: failure to comply with the applicable regulatory statute has whatever effect may be specified in that statute, but no more.

Cross References:

Sections 4-208 and 9-113.
Point 1: Section 9-110.
Point 5: Part 5.

Definitional Cross References:

"Collateral". Section 9-105.
"Debtor". Section 9-105.

"Party". Section 1-201.
"Proceeds". Section 9-306.
"Secured party". Section 9-105.
"Security agreement". Section 9-105.
"Security interest". Section 1-201.
"Signed". Section 1-201.

§ 9-204. After-Acquired Property; Future Advances.

(1) Except as provided in subsection (2), a security agreement may provide that any or all obligations covered by the security agreement are to be secured by after-acquired collateral.

(2) No security interest attaches under an after-acquired property clause to consumer goods other than accessions (Section 9-314) when given as additional security unless the debtor acquires rights in them within ten days after the secured party gives value.

(3) Obligations covered by a security agreement may include future advances or other value whether or not the advances or value are given pursuant to commitment (subsection (1) of Section 9-105).

As amended in 1972.

Official Comment

Prior Uniform Statutory Provision: None.

Purposes:

1. Subsection (1) makes clear that a security interest arising by virtue of an after-acquired property clause has equal status with a security interest in collateral in which the debtor has rights at the time value is given under the security agreement. That is to say: the security interest in after-acquired property is not merely an "equitable" interest; no further action by the secured party—such as the taking of a supplemental agreement covering the new collateral—is required. This does not however mean that the interest is proof against subordination or defeat: Section 9-108 should be consulted on when a security interest in after-acquired collateral is not security for antecedent debt, and section 9-312(3) and (4) on when such a security interest may be subordinated to a conflicting purchase money security interest in the same collateral.

2. This Article accepts the principle of a "continuing general lien". It rejects the doctrine—of which the judicial attitude toward after-acquired property interests was one expression—that there is reason to invalidate as a matter of law what has been variously called the floating charge, the free-handed mortgage and the lien on a shifting stock. This Article validates a security interest in the debtor's existing and future assets, even though (see Section 9-205) the debtor has liberty to use or dispose of collateral without being required to account for proceeds or substitute new collateral. (See further, however, Section 9-306 on Proceeds and Comment thereto.)

The widespread nineteenth century prejudice against the floating charge was based on a feeling, often inarticulate in the opinions, that a commercial borrower should not be allowed to encumber all his assets present and future, and that for the protection not only of the borrower but of his other creditors a cushion of free assets should be preserved. That inarticulate premise has much to recommend it. This Article decisively rejects it not on the ground that it was wrong in policy but on the ground that it was not effective. In pre-Code law there was a multiplication of security devices designed to avoid the policy: field warehousing, trust receipts, factor's lien acts and so on. The cushion of free assets was not preserved. In almost every state it was possible before the Code for the borrower to give a lien on everything he held or would have.

There have no doubt been sufficient economic reasons for the change. This Article, in expressly validating the floating charge, merely recognizes an existing state of things. The substantive rules of law set forth in the balance of the Article are designed to achieve the protection of the debtor and the equitable resolution of the conflicting claims of creditors which the old rules no longer give.

Notice that the question of assignment of future accounts is treated like any other case of after-acquired property: no periodic list of accounts is required by this Act. Where less than all accounts are assigned such a list may of course be necessary to permit identification of the particular accounts assigned.

3. Subsection (1) has been already referred to in connection with after-acquired property. It also serves to validate the so-called "cross-security" clause under which collateral acquired at any time may secure advances whenever made.

4. Subsection (2) limits the operation of the after-acquired property clause against consumers. No such interest can be claimed as additional security in consumer goods (defined in Section 9–109), except accessions (see Section 9–314), acquired more than ten days after the giving of value.

5. Under subsection (3) collateral may secure future as well as present advances when the security agreement so provides. At common law and under chattel mortgage statutes there seems to have been a vaguely articulated prejudice against future advance agreements comparable to the prejudice against after-acquired property interests. Although only a very few jurisdictions went to the length of invalidating interests claimed by virtue of future advances, judicial limitations severely restricted the usefulness of such arrangements. A common limitation was that an interest claimed in collateral existing at the time the security transaction was entered into for advances made thereafter was good only to the extent that the original security agreement specified the amount of such later advances and even the times at which they should be made. In line with the policy of this Article toward after-acquired property interests this subsection validates the future advance interest, provided only that the obligation be covered by the security agreement.

The effect of after-acquired property and future advance clauses in the security agreement should not be confused with the use of financing statements in notice filing. The references to after-acquired property clauses and future advance clauses in Section 9–204 are limited to security agreements. This section follows Section 9–203, the section requiring a written security agreement, and its purpose is to make clear that confirmatory agreements are not necessary where the basic agreement has the clauses mentioned. This section has no reference to the operation of financing statements. The filing of a financing statement is effective to perfect security interests as to which the other required elements for perfection exist, whether the security agreement involved is one existing at the date of filing with an after-acquired property clause or a future advance clause, or whether the applicable security agreement is executed later. Indeed, Section 9–402(1) expressly contemplates that a financing statement may be filed when there is no security agreement. There is no need to refer to after-acquired property or future advances in the financing statement.

As in the case of interests in after-acquired collateral, a security interest based on future advances may be subordinated to conflicting interests in the same collateral. See Sections 9–301(4); 9–307(3); 9–312(3), (4) and (7).

Cross References:

Point 1: Sections 9–108 and 9–312.
Point 2: Sections 9–205 and 9–306.
Point 4: Sections 9–109 and 9–314.
Point 5: Sections 9–301(4); 9–307(3); 9–312(3), (4), and (7).

Definitional Cross References:

"Account". Section 9–106.
"Agreement". Section 1–201.

"Collateral". Section 9-105.
"Consumer goods". Section 9-109.
"Contract". Section 1-201.
"Debtor". Section 9-105.
"Purchase". Section 1-201.
"Pursuant to commitment". Section 9-105.
"Rights". Section 1-201.
"Secured party". Section 9-105.
"Security agreement". Section 9-105.
"Security interest". Section 1-201.
"Value". Section 1-201.

§ 9-205. Use or Disposition of Collateral Without Accounting Permissible.

A security interest is not invalid or fraudulent against creditors by reason of liberty in the debtor to use, commingle or dispose of all or part of the collateral (including returned or repossessed goods) or to collect or compromise accounts or chattel paper, or to accept the return of goods or make repossessions, or to use, commingle or dispose of proceeds, or by reason of the failure of the secured party to require the debtor to account for proceeds or replace collateral. This section does not relax the requirements of possession where perfection of a security interest depends upon possession of the collateral by the secured party or by a bailee.

As amended in 1972.

Official Comment

Prior Uniform Statutory Provision: None.

Purposes:

1. This Article expressly validates the floating charge or lien on a shifting stock. (See Sections 9-201, 9-204, and Comment to Section 9-204.) This section provides that a security interest is not invalid or fraudulent by reason of liberty in the debtor to dispose of the collateral without being required to account for proceeds or substitute new collateral. It repeals the rule of Benedict v. Ratner, 268 U.S. 353, 45 S.Ct. 566, 69 L.Ed. 991 (1925), and other cases which held such arrangements void as a matter of law because the debtor was given unfettered dominion or control over the collateral. The principal effect of the Benedict rule has been, not to discourage or eliminate security transactions in inventory and accounts receivable—on the contrary such transactions have vastly increased in volume—but rather to force financing arrangements in this field toward a self-liquidating basis. Furthermore, several lower court cases drew implications from Justice Brandeis' opinion in Benedict v. Ratner which required lenders operating in this field to observe a number of needless and costly formalities: for example it was thought necessary for the debtor to make daily remittances to the lender of all collections received, even though the amount remitted is immediately returned to the debtor in order to keep the loan at an agreed level.

2. The Benedict rule was, in the accounts receivable field, repealed in many of the state accounts receivable statutes enacted after 1943, and, in the inventory field, by some of the factor's lien statutes. (Benedict v. Ratner purported to state the law of New York and not a rule of federal bankruptcy law. Since its acceptance is a matter of state law, it can of course be rejected by state statute.)

3. The requirement of "policing" is the substance of the Benedict rule. While this section repeals Benedict in matters of form, the filing requirements (Section 9-302) give other creditors the opportunity to ascertain from public sources whether property of their debtor or prospective debtor is subject to secured claims, and the provisions about proceeds (Section 9-306(4)) enable creditors to claim collections which were made by the

debtor more than 10 days before insolvency proceedings and commingled or deposited in a bank account before institution of the insolvency proceedings. The repeal of the Benedict rule under this section must be read in the light of these provisions.

4. Other decisions reaching results like that in the Benedict case, but relating to other aspects of dominion (of which Lee v. State Bank & Trust Co., 54 F.2d 518 (2d Cir. 1931), is an example) are likewise rejected.

5. Nothing in Section 9-205 prevents such "policing" or dominion as the secured party and the debtor may agree upon; business and not legal reasons will determine the extent to which strict accountability, segregation of collections, daily reports and the like will be employed.

6. The last sentence is added to make clear that the section does not mean that the holder of an unfiled security interest, whose perfection depends on possession of the collateral by the secured party or by a bailee (such as a field warehouseman), can allow the debtor access to and control over the goods without thereby losing his perfected interest. The common law rules on the degree and extent of possession which are necessary to perfect a pledge interest or to constitute a valid field warehouse are not relaxed by this or any other section of this Article.

Cross References:

Point 1: Sections 9-201 and 9-204.
Point 3: Sections 9-302 and 9-306(4).
Point 6: Sections 9-304 and 9-305.

Definitional Cross References:

"Account". Section 9-106.
"Chattel paper". Section 9-105.
"Collateral". Section 9-105.
"Creditor". Section 1-201.
"Debtor". Section 9-105.
"Goods". Section 9-105.
"Proceeds". Section 9-306.
"Secured party". Section 9-105.
"Security interest". Section 1-201.

§ 9-206. Agreement Not to Assert Defenses Against Assignee; Modification of Sales Warranties Where Security Agreement Exists.

(1) Subject to any statute or decision which establishes a different rule for buyers or lessees of consumer goods, an agreement by a buyer or lessee that he will not assert against an assignee any claim or defense which he may have against the seller or lessor is enforceable by an assignee who takes his assignment for value, in good faith and without notice of a claim or defense, except as to defenses of a type which may be asserted against a holder in due course of a negotiable instrument under the Article on Negotiable Instruments (Article 3). A buyer who as part of one transaction signs both a negotiable instrument and a security agreement makes such an agreement.

(2) When a seller retains a purchase money security interest in goods the Article on Sales (Article 2) governs the sale and any disclaimer, limitation or modification of the seller's warranties.

As amended in 1962 and 1994.

See Appendix XI for material relating to changes made in text in 1994.

Official Comment

Prior Uniform Statutory Provision: Section 2, Uniform Conditional Sales Act.

Purposes:

1. Clauses are frequently inserted in installment purchase contracts under

which the conditional vendee agrees not to assert defenses against an assignee of the contract. These clauses have led to litigation and their present status under the case law is in confusion. In some jurisdictions they have been held void as attempts to create negotiable instruments outside the framework of Article 3 or on grounds of public policy; in others they have been allowed to operate to cut off at least defenses based on breach of warranty. Under subsection (1) such clauses in a security agreement are validated outside the consumer field, but only as to defenses which could be cut off if a negotiable instrument were used. This limitation is important since if the clauses were allowed to have full effect as typically drafted, they would operate to cut off real as well as personal defenses. The execution of a negotiable note in connection with a security agreement is given like effect as the execution of an agreement containing a waiver of defense clause. The same rules are made applicable to leases as to security agreements, whether or not the lease is intended as security.

2. This Article takes no position on the controversial question whether a buyer of consumer goods may effectively waive defenses by contractual clause or by execution of a negotiable note. In some states such waivers have been invalidated by statute. In other states the course of judicial decision has rendered them ineffective or unreliable—courts have found that the assignee is not protected against the buyer's defense by a clause in the contract or that the holder of a note, by reason of his too close connection with the underlying transaction, does not have the rights of a holder in due course. This Article neither adopts nor rejects the approach taken in such statutes and decisions, except that the validation of waivers in subsection (1) is expressly made "subject to any statute or decision" which may restrict the waiver's effectiveness in the case of a buyer of consumer goods.

3. Subsection (2) makes clear, as did Section 2 of the Uniform Conditional Sales Act, that purchase money security transactions are sales, and warranty rules for sales are applicable. It also prevents a buyer from inadvertently abandoning his warranties by a "no warranties" term in the security agreement when warranties have already been created under the sales arrangement. Where the sales arrangement and the purchase money security transaction are evidenced by only one writing, that writing may disclaim, limit or modify warranties to the extent permitted by Article 2.

Cross References:

Point 1: Section 3–305.
Point 2: Section 9–203(2).
Point 3: Sections 2–102 and 2–316.

Definitional Cross References:

"Agreement". Section 1–201.
"Consumer goods". Section 9–109.
"Good faith". Section 1–201.
"Goods". Section 9–105.
"Holder". Section 1–201.
"Holder in due course". Sections 3–302 and 9–105.
"Negotiable instrument". Section 3–104.
"Notice". Section 1–201.
"Purchase money security interest". Section 9–107.
"Sale". Sections 2–106 and 9–105.
"Security agreement". Section 9–105.
"Security interest". Section 1–201.
"Value". Section 1–201.

§ 9–207. Rights and Duties When Collateral Is in Secured Party's Possession.

(1) A secured party must use reasonable care in the custody and preservation of collateral in his possession. In the case of an instrument or chattel paper reasonable care includes taking necessary steps to preserve rights against prior parties unless otherwise agreed.

(2) Unless otherwise agreed, when collateral is in the secured party's possession

(a) reasonable expenses (including the cost of any insurance and payment of taxes or other charges) incurred in the custody, preservation, use or operation of the collateral are chargeable to the debtor and are secured by the collateral;

(b) the risk of accidental loss or damage is on the debtor to the extent of any deficiency in any effective insurance coverage;

(c) the secured party may hold as additional security any increase or profits (except money) received from the collateral, but money so received, unless remitted to the debtor, shall be applied in reduction of the secured obligation;

(d) the secured party must keep the collateral identifiable but fungible collateral may be commingled;

(e) the secured party may repledge the collateral upon terms which do not impair the debtor's right to redeem it.

(3) A secured party is liable for any loss caused by his failure to meet any obligation imposed by the preceding subsections but does not lose his security interest.

(4) A secured party may use or operate the collateral for the purpose of preserving the collateral or its value or pursuant to the order of a court of appropriate jurisdiction or, except in the case of consumer goods, in the manner and to the extent provided in the security agreement.

Official Comment

Prior Uniform Statutory Provision: None.

Purposes:

1. Subsection (1) states the duty to preserve collateral imposed on a pledge at common law. See Restatement of Security, §§ 17, 18. In many cases a secured party having collateral in his possession may satisfy this duty by notifying the debtor of any act which must be taken and allowing the debtor to perform such act himself. If the secured party himself takes action, his reasonable expenses may be added to the secured obligation.

Under Section 1–102(3) the duty to exercise reasonable care may not be disclaimed by agreement, although under that section the parties remain free to determine by agreement, in any manner not manifestly unreasonable, what shall constitute reasonable care in a particular case.

2. Subsection (2) states rules, which follow common law precedents, and which apply, unless there is agreement otherwise, in typical situations during the period while the secured party is in possession of the collateral.

3. The right of a secured party holding instruments or documents to have them indorsed or transferred to him or his order is dealt with in the relevant sections of Articles 3 (Commercial Paper), 7 (Warehouse Receipts, Bills of Lading and Other Documents) and 8 (Investment Securities). (Sections 3–201, 7–506, ~~8–307~~ 8–304(d).) *Amendments approved by the Permanent Editorial Board for Uniform Commercial Code November 4, 1995.*

4. This section applies when the secured party has possession of the collateral before default, as a pledgee, and also when he has taken possession of the collateral after default. See Section 9–501(1) and (2). Subsection (4) permits

operation of the collateral in the circumstances stated, and subsection (2)(a) authorizes payment of or provision for expenses of such operation. Agreements providing for such operation are common in trust indentures securing corporate bonds and are particularly important when the collateral is a going business. Such an agreement cannot of course disclaim the duty of care established by subsection (1), nor can it waive or modify the rights of the debtor contrary to Section 9–501(3).

Cross References:

Point 1: Section 1–102(3).

Point 3: Sections 3–201, 7–506 and ~~8–307~~ 8–304(d). *Amendments approved by the Permanent Editorial Board for Uniform Commercial Code November 4, 1995.*

Point 4: Section 9–501(2) and Part 5.

Definitional Cross References:

"Chattel paper". Section 9–105.
"Collateral". Section 9–105.
"Debtor". Section 9–105.
"Instrument". Section 9–105.
"Money". Section 1–201.
"Party". Section 1–201.
"Secured party". Section 9–105.
"Security interest". Section 1–201.

§ 9–208. Request for Statement of Account or List of Collateral.

(1) A debtor may sign a statement indicating what he believes to be the aggregate amount of unpaid indebtedness as of a specified date and may send it to the secured party with a request that the statement be approved or corrected and returned to the debtor. When the security agreement or any other record kept by the secured party identifies the collateral a debtor may similarly request the secured party to approve or correct a list of the collateral.

(2) The secured party must comply with such a request within two weeks after receipt by sending a written correction or approval. If the secured party claims a security interest in all of a particular type of collateral owned by the debtor he may indicate that fact in his reply and need not approve or correct an itemized list of such collateral. If the secured party without reasonable excuse fails to comply he is liable for any loss caused to the debtor thereby; and if the debtor has properly included in his request a good faith statement of the obligation or a list of the collateral or both the secured party may claim a security interest only as shown in the statement against persons misled by his failure to comply. If he no longer has an interest in the obligation or collateral at the time the request is received he must disclose the name and address of any successor in interest known to him and he is liable for any loss caused to the debtor as a result of failure to disclose. A successor in interest is not subject to this section until a request is received by him.

(3) A debtor is entitled to such a statement once every six months without charge. The secured party may require payment of a charge not exceeding $10 for each additional statement furnished.

Official Comment

Prior Uniform Statutory Provision: None.

Purposes:

1. To provide a procedure whereby a debtor may obtain from the secured party a statement of the amount due on the obligation and in some cases a statement of the collateral.

2. The financing statement required to be filed under this Article (see Section

9-402) may disclose only that a secured party may have a security interest in specified types of collateral owned by the debtor. Unless a copy of the security agreement itself is filed as the financing statement third parties are told neither the amount of the obligation secured nor which particular assets are covered. Since subsequent creditors and purchasers may legitimately need more detailed information, it is necessary to provide a procedure under which the secured party will be required to make disclosure. On the other hand, the secured party should not be under a duty to disclose details of business operations to any casual inquirer or competitor who asks for them. This section gives the right to demand disclosure only to the debtor, who will typically request a statement in connection with negotiations with subsequent creditors and purchasers, or for the purpose of establishing his credit standing and proving which of his assets are free of the security interest. The secured party is further protected against onerous requests by the provisions that he need furnish a statement of collateral only when his own records identify the collateral and that if he claims all of a particular type of collateral owned by the debtor he is not required to approve an itemized list.

Cross Reference:

Point 2: Section 9-402.

Definitional Cross References:

"Collateral". Section 9-105.
"Debtor". Section 9-105.
"Good faith". Section 1-201.
"Know". Section 1-201.
"Person". Section 1-201.
"Receive". Section 1-201.
"Secured party". Section 9-105.
"Security agreement". Section 9-105.
"Security interest". Section 1-201.
"Send". Section 1-201.
"Written". Section 1-201.

PART 3

RIGHTS OF THIRD PARTIES; PERFECTED AND UNPERFECTED SECURITY INTERESTS; RULES OF PRIORITY

§ 9-301. Persons Who Take Priority Over Unperfected Security Interests; Rights of "Lien Creditor".

(1) Except as otherwise provided in subsection (2), an unperfected security interest is subordinate to the rights of

(a) persons entitled to priority under Section 9-312;

(b) a person who becomes a lien creditor before the security interest is perfected;

(c) in the case of goods, instruments, documents, and chattel paper, a person who is not a secured party and who is a transferee in bulk or other buyer not in ordinary course of business or is a buyer of farm products in ordinary course of business, to the extent that he gives value and receives delivery of the collateral without knowledge of the security interest and before it is perfected;

(d) in the case of accounts, general intangibles, and investment property, a person who is not a secured party and who is a transferee to the extent that he gives value without knowledge of the security interest and before it is perfected.

(2) If the secured party files with respect to a purchase money security interest before or within ten days after the debtor receives possession of the

collateral, he takes priority over the rights of a transferee in bulk or of a lien creditor which arise between the time the security interest attaches and the time of filing.

(3) A "lien creditor" means a creditor who has acquired a lien on the property involved by attachment, levy or the like and includes an assignee for benefit of creditors from the time of assignment, and a trustee in bankruptcy from the date of the filing of the petition or a receiver in equity from the time of appointment.

(4) A person who becomes a lien creditor while a security interest is perfected takes subject to the security interest only to the extent that it secures advances made before he becomes a lien creditor or within 45 days thereafter or made without knowledge of the lien or pursuant to a commitment entered into without knowledge of the lien.

As amended in 1972 and 1994.

See Appendix XII for material relating to changes made in text in 1994.

Official Comment

Prior Uniform Statutory Provision: Sections 8(2) and 9(2)(b), Uniform Trust Receipts Act; Section 5, Uniform Conditional Sales Act.

Purposes:

1. This section lists the classes of persons who take priority over an unperfected security interest. As in Section 60 of the Federal Bankruptcy Act, the term "perfected" is used to describe a security interest in personal property which cannot be defeated in insolvency proceedings or in general by creditors. A security interest is "perfected" when the secured party has taken whatever steps are necessary to give him such an interest. These steps are explained in the five following sections (9-302 through 9-306).

2. Section 9-312 states general rules for the determination of priorities among conflicting security interests and in addition refers to other sections which state special rules of priority in a variety of situations. The interests given priority under Section 9-312 and the other sections therein cited take such priority in general even over a perfected security interest. *A fortiori* they take priority over an unperfected security interest, and paragraph (1)(a) of this section so states.

3. Paragraph (1)(b) provides that an unperfected security interest is subordinate to the rights of lien creditors. The section rejects the rule applied in many jurisdictions in pre-Code law that an unperfected security interest is subordinated to all creditors, but requires the lien obtained by legal proceedings to attach to the collateral before the security interest is perfected. The section subordinates the unperfected security interest but does not subordinate the secured debt to the lien.

4. Paragraphs (1)(c) and (1)(d) deal with purchasers (other than secured parties) of collateral who would take subject to a perfected security interest but who are by these subsections given priority over an unperfected security interest. In the cases of goods and of intangibles of the type whose transfer is effected by physical delivery of the representative piece of paper (instruments, documents and chattel paper) the purchaser who takes priority must both give value and receive delivery of the collateral without knowledge of the existing security interest and before perfection (paragraph (1)(c)). Thus even if the purchaser gave value without knowledge and before perfection, he would take subject to the security interest if perfection occurred before

physical delivery of the collateral to him. The paragraph (1)(c) rule is obviously not appropriate where the collateral consists of intangibles and there is no representative piece of paper whose physical delivery is the only or the customary method of transfer. Therefore with respect to such intangibles (accounts and general intangibles), paragraph (1)(d) gives priority to any transferee who has given value without knowledge and before perfection of the security interest.

The term "buyer in ordinary course of business" referred to in paragraph (1)(c) is defined in Section 1-201(9).

Other secured parties are excluded from paragraphs (1)(c) and (1)(d) because their priorities are covered in Section 9-312 (see point 2 of this Comment).

5. Except to the extent provided in subsection (2), this Article does not permit a secured party to file or take possession after another interest has received priority under subsection (1) and thereby protect himself against the intervening interest.

A few chattel mortgage statutes did have grace periods, i.e., a filing within x days after the mortgage was given related back to the day the mortgage was given. The Uniform Conditional Sales Act had a ten-day period which cut off all intervening interests. The Uniform Trust Receipts Act had a thirty-day period but did not cut off the interest of a purchaser who took delivery before the filing.

Subsection (2) gives a grace period for perfection by filing as to purchase money security interests only (that term is defined in Section 9-107). The grace period runs for ten days after the debtor receives possession of the collateral but operates to cut off only the interests of intervening lien creditors or bulk purchasers.

6. Subsection (3) defines "lien creditor", following in substance the provisions of the Uniform Trust Receipts Act.

7. Subsection (4) deals with the question whether advances under an existing security interest in collateral, made after rights of lien creditors have attached to that collateral, will take precedence over rights of lien creditors. See related problems in Sections 9-307(3) and 9-312(7). In this section, because of the impact of the rule chosen on the question whether the security interest for future advances is "protected" under Sections 6323(c)(2) and (d) of the Internal Revenue Code as amended by the Federal Tax Lien Act of 1966, the priority of the security interest for future advances over a judgment lien is made absolute for 45 days regardless of knowledge of the secured party concerning the judgment lien. If, however, the advance is made after the 45 days, the advance will not have priority unless it was made or committed without knowledge of the lien obtained by legal proceedings. The importance of the rule chosen for actual conflicts between secured parties making subsequent advances and judgment lien creditors may not be great; but the rule chosen for the first 45 days is important in effectuating the intent of the Federal Tax Lien Act of 1966.

8. The word "only" in subsection (4) is limited in its effect to the lien creditor's subjection to the specified advances. It does not limit the lien creditor's subjection to whatever other rights the secured party may have by contract or law, e.g., the right to interest before or after the attachment of the judgment lien to the collateral or the right to foreclosure expenses or other collection expenses. See PEB Commentary No. 2, dated March 10, 1990 [Appendix V, infra].

9. There is no conflict between the principle of § 9-301(1) and the "shelter principle," which is applied at several points in the statute, but is most explicitly stated in § 2-403(1): "A purchaser of goods acquires all title which his transferor had. . . ."

Although § 9-301(1) fails to state the shelter principle expressly, that principle is applicable where a person who had met the conditions for prevailing over an unperfected security interest transfers his right to another person after the security interest is perfected. See PEB Commentary No. 6, dated March 10, 1990 [Appendix V, infra].

The rules for subordination of unperfected security interests have a purpose—in common with similar rules in all filing and recording systems—to impose sanctions for not adhering to filing or recording requirements. Such rules are necessary to make the system effective and enforce the policy against secret liens. The shelter principle recognizes that when a person in a protected class transfers his right after the security interest has been perfected, the right will be diminished in value unless the sanction is continued. The sanction imposed by § 9-301(1) is that members of protected classes take free of an unperfected security interest. That sanction should be continued to protect transferees from those members in order to fulfill the purpose of the section.

Cross References:

Section 9–312.

Point 1: Sections 9–302 through 9–306.

Point 7: Sections 9–204, 9–307(3) and 9–312(7).

Definitional Cross References:

"Account". Section 9–106.

"Buyer in ordinary course of business". Section 1–201.

"Chattel paper". Section 9–105.

"Collateral". Section 9–105.

"Creditor". Section 1–201.

"Delivery". Section 1–201.

"Document". Section 9–105.

"General intangibles". Section 9–106.

"Goods". Section 9–105.

"Instrument". Section 9–105.

"Knowledge". Section 1–201.

"Person". Section 1–201.

"Purchase money security interest". Section 9–107.

"Pursuant to commitment". Section 9–105.

"Representative". Section 1–201.

"Rights". Section 1–201.

"Secured party". Section 9–105.

"Security interest". Section 1–201.

"Value". Section 1–201.

§ 9–302. When Filing Is Required to Perfect Security Interest; Security Interests to Which Filing Provisions of This Article Do Not Apply.

(1) A financing statement must be filed to perfect all security interests except the following:

(a) a security interest in collateral in possession of the secured party under Section 9–305;

(b) a security interest temporarily perfected in instruments, certificated securities, or documents without delivery under Section 9–304 or in proceeds for a 10 day period under Section 9–306;

(c) a security interest created by an assignment of a beneficial interest in a trust or a decedent's estate;

(d) a purchase money security interest in consumer goods; but filing is required for a motor vehicle required to be registered; and fixture filing is required for priority over conflicting interests in fixtures to the extent provided in Section 9–313;

(e) an assignment of accounts which does not alone or in conjunction with other assignments to the same assignee transfer a significant part of the outstanding accounts of the assignor;

(f) a security interest of a collecting bank (Section 4–210) or arising under the Articles on Sales and Leases (see Section 9–113) or covered in subsection (3) of this section;

(g) an assignment for the benefit of all the creditors of the transferor, and subsequent transfers by the assignee thereunder.

(h) a security interest in investment property which is perfected without filing under Section 9-115 or Section 9-116.

(2) If a secured party assigns a perfected security interest, no filing under this Article is required in order to continue the perfected status of the security interest against creditors of and transferees from the original debtor.

(3) The filing of a financing statement otherwise required by this Article is not necessary or effective to perfect a security interest in property subject to

(a) a statute or treaty of the United States which provides for a national or international registration or a national or international certificate of title or which specifies a place of filing different from that specified in this Article for filing of the security interest; or

(b) the following statutes of this state; [list any certificate of title statute covering automobiles, trailers, mobile homes, boats, farm tractors, or the like, and any central filing statute *.]; but during any period in which collateral is inventory held for sale by a person who is in the business of selling goods of that kind, the filing provisions of this Article (Part 4) apply to a security interest in that collateral created by him as debtor; or

(c) a certificate of title statute of another jurisdiction under the law of which indication of a security interest on the certificate is required as a condition of perfection (subsection (2) of Section 9-103).

(4) Compliance with a statute or treaty described in subsection (3) is equivalent to the filing of a financing statement under this Article, and a security interest in property subject to the statute or treaty can be perfected only by compliance therewith except as provided in Section 9-103 on multiple state transactions. Duration and renewal of perfection of a security interest perfected by compliance with the statute or treaty are governed by the provisions of the statute or treaty; in other respects the security interest is subject to this Article.

* **Note:** *It is recommended that the provisions of certificate of title acts for perfection of security interests by notation on the certificates should be amended to exclude coverage of inventory held for sale.*

As amended in 1972, 1977 and 1994.

See Appendices XI and XII for material relating to changes made in text in 1994.

Official Comment

Prior Uniform Statutory Provision: Section 5, Uniform Conditional Sales Act; Section 8, Uniform Trust Receipts Act.

Purposes:

1. Subsection (1) states the general rule that to perfect a security interest under this Article a financing statement must be filed. Paragraphs (1)(a) through (1)(g) exempt from the filing requirement

the transactions described. Subsection (3) further sets out certain transactions to which the filing provisions of this Article do not apply, but it does not defer to another state statute on the filing of inventory security interests. The cases recognized are those where suitable alternative systems for giving public notice of a security interest are available. Subsection (4) states the consequences of such other form of notice.

Section 9–303 states the time when a security interest is perfected by filing or otherwise. Part 4 of the Article deals with the mechanics of filing: place of filing, form of financing statement and so on.

2. As at common law, there is no requirement of filing when the secured party has possession of the collateral in a pledge transaction (paragraph (1)(a)), Section 9–305 should be consulted on what collateral may be pledged and on the requirements of possession.

3. Under this Article, as under the Uniform Trust Receipts Act, filing is not effective to perfect a security interest in instruments. See Section 9–304(1).

4. Where goods subject to a security interest are left in the debtor's possession, the only permanent exception from the general filing requirement is that stated in paragraph (1)(d): purchase money security interests in consumer goods. For temporary exceptions, see Sections 9–304(5)(a) and 9–306.

In many jurisdictions under prior law security interests in consumer goods under conditional sale or bailment leases were not subject to filing requirements. Paragraph (1)(d) follows the policy of those jurisdictions. The paragraph changes prior law in jurisdictions where all conditional sales and bailment leases were subject to a filing requirement, except that filing is required for purchase money security interests in consumer fixtures to attain priority under Section 9–313 against real estate interests.

Although the security interests described in paragraph (1)(d) are perfected without filing, Section 9–307(2) provides that unless a financing statement is filed certain buyers may take free of the security interest even though perfected. See that section and the Comment thereto.

On filing for security interests in motor vehicles under certificate of title laws see subsection (3) of this section.

5. A financing statement must be filed to perfect a security interest in accounts except for the transactions described in paragraphs (1)(e) and (g). It should be noted that this Article applies to sales of accounts and chattel paper as well as to transfers thereof for security (Section 9–102(1)(b)); the filing requirement of this section applies both to sales and to transfers thereof for security. In this respect this Article follows many of the pre-Code statutes regulating assignments of accounts receivable.

Over forty jurisdictions had enacted accounts receivable statutes. About half of these statutes required filing to protect or perfect assignments; of the remainder, one was a so-called "book-marking" statute and the others validated assignments without filing. This Article adopts the filing requirement, on the theory that there is no valid reason why public notice is less appropriate for assignments of accounts than for any other type of nonpossessory interest. Section 9–305, furthermore, excludes accounts from the types of collateral which may be the subject of a possessory security interest: filing is thus the only means of perfection contemplated by this Article. See Section 9–306 on accounts as proceeds.

The purpose of the subsection (1)(e) exemption is to save from *ex post facto* invalidation casual or isolated assignments: some accounts receivable statutes were so broadly drafted that all assignments, whatever their character or purpose, fell within their filing provisions. Under such statutes many assignments which no one would think of filing might have been subject to invalidation. The paragraph (1)(e) exemption goes to that type of assignment. Any person who regularly takes assignments of any debtor's accounts should file. In this connection

Section 9–104(f) which excludes certain transfers of accounts from the Article should be consulted.

Assignments of interests in trusts and estates are not required to be filed because they are often not thought of as collateral comparable to the types dealt with by this Article. Assignments for the benefit of creditors are not required to be filed because they are not financing transactions and the debtor will not ordinarily be engaging in further credit transactions.

6. With respect to the paragraph (1)(f) exemptions, see the sections cited therein and Comments thereto.

7. The following example will explain the operation of subsection (2): Buyer buys goods from seller who retains a security interest in them which he perfects. Seller assigns the perfected security interest to X. The security interest, in X's hands and without further steps on his part, continues perfected against *Buyer's* transferees and creditors. If, however, the assignment from Seller to X was itself intended for security (or was a sale of accounts or chattel paper), X must take whatever steps may be required for perfection in order to be protected against *Seller's* transferees and creditors.

8. Subsection (3) exempts from the filing provisions of this Article transactions as to which an adequate system of filing, state or federal, has been set up outside this Article and subsection (4) makes clear that when such a system exists perfection of a relevant security interest can be had only through compliance with that system (i.e., filing under this Article is not a permissible alternative).

Examples of the type of federal statute referred to in paragraph (3)(a) are the provisions of 17 U.S.C. §§ 28, 30 (copyrights), 49 U.S.C. § 1403 (aircraft), 49 U.S.C. § 20(c) (railroads). The Assignment of Claims Act of 1940, as amended, provides for notice to contracting and disbursing officers and to sureties on bonds but does not establish a national filing system and therefore is not within the scope of paragraph (3)(a). An assignee of a claim against the United States, who must of course comply with the Assignment of Claims Act, must also file under this Article in order to perfect his security interest against creditors and transferees of his assignor.

Some states have enacted central filing statutes with respect to security transactions in kinds of property which are of special importance in the local economy. Subsection (3) adopts such statutes as the appropriate filing system for such property.

In addition to such central filing statutes many states have enacted certificate of title laws covering motor vehicles and the like. Subsection (3) exempts transactions covered by such laws from the filing requirements of this Article.

For a discussion of the operation of state motor vehicle certificate of title laws in interstate contexts, see Comment 4 to Section 9–103.

9. Perfection of a security interest under a state or federal statute of the type referred to in subsection (3) has all the consequences of perfection under the provisions of this Article, Subsection (4).

10. If a security interest has been perfected under the applicable certificate of title statute and is thereafter assigned, and that statute does not expressly require the assignee to take some further action with respect to the certificate of title to reflect that it has become the secured party in order to continue such perfection, § 9–302(2) is applicable and the assignee is not required to note its name on the certificate of title "in order to continue the perfected status of the security interest against creditors of and transferees from the original debtor." See PEB Commentary No. 12, dated February 10, 1994 [Appendix V, infra].

Cross References:

Point 1: Section 9–303 and Part 4.
Point 2: Section 9–305.
Point 3: Section 9–304(1).
Point 4: Section 9–307(2).

Point 5: Sections 9-102(1)(b), 9-104(f) and 9-305.

Point 6: Sections 4-208 and 9-113.

Definitional Cross References:

"Account". Section 9-106.
"Collateral". Section 9-105.
"Consumer goods". Section 9-109.
"Creditor". Section 1-201.
"Debtor". Section 9-105.
"Delivery". Section 1-201.
"Document". Section 9-105.
"Equipment". Section 9-109.
"Fixture". Section 9-313.
"Fixture filing". Section 9-313.
"Instrument". Section 9-105.
"Inventory". Section 9-109.
"Proceeds". Section 9-306.
"Purchase". Section 1-201.
"Purchase money security interest". Section 9-107.
"Sale". Sections 2-106 and 9-105.
"Secured party". Section 9-105.
"Security interest". Section 1-201.

§ 9-303. When Security Interest Is Perfected; Continuity of Perfection.

(1) A security interest is perfected when it has attached and when all of the applicable steps required for perfection have been taken. Such steps are specified in Sections 9-115, 9-302, 9-304, 9-305 and 9-306. If such steps are taken before the security interest attaches, it is perfected at the time when it attaches.

(2) If a security interest is originally perfected in any way permitted under this Article and is subsequently perfected in some other way under this Article, without an intermediate period when it was unperfected, the security interest shall be deemed to be perfected continuously for the purposes of this Article.

As amended in 1994.

See Appendix XII for material relating to changes made in text in 1994.

Official Comment

Prior Uniform Statutory Provision: None.

Purposes:

1. The term "attach" is used in this Article to describe the point at which property becomes subject to a security interest. The requisites for attachment are stated in Section 9-203. When it attaches a security interest may be either perfected or unperfected: "Perfected" means that the secured party has taken all the steps required by this Article as specified in the several sections listed in subsection (1). A perfected security interest may still be or become subordinate to other interests (see Section 9-312) but in general after perfection the secured party is protected against creditors and transferees of the debtor and in particular against any representative of creditors in insolvency proceedings instituted by or against the debtor. Subsection (1) states the truism that the time of perfection is when the security interest has attached and any necessary steps for perfection (such as taking possession or filing) have been taken. If the steps for perfection have been taken in advance (as when the secured party files a financing statement before giving value or before the debtor acquires rights in the collateral), then the interest is perfected automatically when it attaches.

2. The following example will illustrate the operation of subsection (2): A bank which has issued a letter of credit honors drafts drawn under the credit and receives possession of the negotiable bill of lading covering the goods shipped.

Under Sections 9-304(2) and 9-305 the bank now has a perfected security interest in the document and the goods. The bank releases the bill of lading to the debtor for the purpose of procuring the goods from the carrier and selling them. Under Section 9-304(5) the bank continues to have a perfected security interest in the document and goods for 21 days. The bank files before the expiration of the 21 day period. Its security interest now continues perfected for as long as the filing is good. The goods are sold by the debtor. The bank continues to have a security interest in the proceeds of the sale to the extent stated in Section 9-306.

If the successive stages of the bank's security interest succeed each other without an intervening gap, the security interest is "continuously perfected" and the date of perfection is when the interest first became perfected (i.e., in the example given, when the bank received possession of the bill of lading against honor of the drafts). If, however, there is a gap between stages—for example, if the bank does not file until after the expiration of the 21 day period specified in Section 9-304(5), the collateral still being in the debtor's possession—then, the chain being broken, the perfection is no longer continuous. The date of perfection would now be the date of filing (after expiration of the 21 day period); the bank's interest might now become subject to attack under Section 60 of the Federal Bankruptcy Act and would be subject to any interests arising during the gap period which under Section 9-301 take priority over an unperfected security interest.

The rule of subsection (2) would also apply to the case of collateral brought into this state subject to a security interest which became perfected in another state or jurisdiction. See Section 9-103(1)(d).

Cross References:

Sections 9-302, 9-304, 9-305 and 9-306.

Point 1: Sections 9-204 and 9-312.

Point 2: Sections 9-103(1)(d) and 9-301.

Definitional Cross References:

"Attach". Section 9-203.

"Security interest". Section 1-201.

§ 9-304. Perfection of Security Interest in Instruments, Documents, Proceeds of a Written Letter of Credit, and Goods Covered by Documents; Perfection by Permissive Filing; Temporary Perfection Without Filing or Transfer of Possession.

[1995 Amendments to text indicated by strikeout and underline]

(1) A security interest in chattel paper or negotiable documents may be perfected by filing. A security interest in the rights to proceeds of a written letter of credit can be perfected only by the secured party's taking possession of the letter of credit. A security interest in money or instruments (other than instruments which constitute part of chattel paper) can be perfected only by the secured party's taking possession, except as provided in subsections (4) and (5) of this section and subsections (2) and (3) of Section 9-306 on proceeds.

(2) During the period that goods are in the possession of the issuer of a negotiable document therefor, a security interest in the goods is perfected by perfecting a security interest in the document, and any security interest in the goods otherwise perfected during such period is subject thereto.

(3) A security interest in goods in the possession of a bailee other than one who has issued a negotiable document therefor is perfected by issuance of

a document in the name of the secured party or by the bailee's receipt of notification of the secured party's interest or by filing as to the goods.

(4) A security interest in instruments, certificated securities, or negotiable documents is perfected without filing or the taking of possession for a period of 21 days from the time it attaches to the extent that it arises for new value given under a written security agreement.

(5) A security interest remains perfected for a period of 21 days without filing where a secured party having a perfected security interest in an instrument, a certificated security, a negotiable document or goods in possession of a bailee other than one who has issued a negotiable document therefor

(a) makes available to the debtor the goods or documents representing the goods for the purpose of ultimate sale or exchange or for the purpose of loading, unloading, storing, shipping, transshipping, manufacturing, processing or otherwise dealing with them in a manner preliminary to their sale or exchange, but priority between conflicting security interests in the goods is subject to subsection (3) of Section 9-312; or

(b) delivers the instrument or certificated security to the debtor for the purpose of ultimate sale or exchange or of presentation, collection, renewal or registration of transfer.

(6) After the 21 day period in subsections (4) and (5) perfection depends upon compliance with applicable provisions of this Article.

Special Legislative Note: *As Sections 9-304 and 9-305 appear in the Official Text of the Conforming Amendments to Revised Article 5 (1995), they incorporate the amendments made to these sections in 1994, when Revised Article 8 was promulgated. If Revised Article 5 with Conforming Amendments, as promulgated in 1995, is adopted by any State before Revised Article 8 with Conforming Amendments of 1994 is adopted, the 1990 text for Sections 9-304 and 9-305 should be used as a basis for amendment, as follows:*

SECTION 9-304. PERFECTION OF SECURITY INTEREST IN INSTRUMENTS, DOCUMENTS, PROCEEDS OF A WRITTEN LETTER OF CREDIT, AND GOODS COVERED BY DOCUMENTS; PERFECTION BY PERMISSIVE FILING; TEMPORARY PERFECTION WITHOUT FILING OR TRANSFER OF POSSESSION.

(1) A security interest in chattel paper or negotiable documents may be perfected by filing. A security interest in the rights to proceeds of a written letter of credit can be perfected only by the secured party's taking possession of the letter of credit. A security interest in money or instruments (other than certificated securities or instruments which constitute part of chattel paper) can be perfected only by the secured party's taking possession, except as provided in subsections (4) and (5) of this section and subsections (2) and (3) of Section 9-306 on proceeds.

. . .

SECTION 9-305. WHEN POSSESSION BY SECURED PARTY PERFECTS SECURITY INTEREST WITHOUT FILING. *A security interest in ~~letters of credit and advices of credit (subsection (2)(a) of Section 5-116),~~ goods, instruments (other than certificated securities), money, negotiable documents, or chattel paper may be perfected by the security party's taking possession of the collateral. A security interest in the right to proceeds of a written letter of credit may be perfected by the secured party's taking possession of the letter of credit. If such collateral other than goods covered by a negotiable document is held by a bailee, the secured party is deemed to have possession from the time the bailee receives notification of the secured party's interest. A security interest is perfected by possession from the time possession is taken without a relation back and continues only so long as possession is retained, unless otherwise specified in this Article. The security interest may be otherwise perfected as provided in this Article before or after the period of possession by the secured party.*

Official Comment

. . .

As amended in 1972, 1977, 1994 and 1995.

See Appendices XII and XIV for material relating to changes made in text in 1994 and 1995, respectively.

Official Comment

Prior Uniform Statutory Provision: Sections 3 and 8(1), Uniform Trust Receipts Act.

Purposes:

1. For most types of property, filing and taking possession are alternative methods of perfection. For some types of intangibles (i.e., accounts and general intangibles) filing is the only available method (see Section 9-305 and point 1 of Comment thereto). With respect to instruments subsection (1) provides that, except for the cases of "temporary perfection" covered in subsections (4) and (5), taking possession is the only available method; this provision follows the Uniform Trust Receipts Act. The rule is based on the thought that where the collateral consists of instruments, it is universal practice for the secured party to take possession of them in pledge; any surrender of possession to the debtor is for a short time; therefore it would be unwise to provide the alternative of perfection for a long period by filing which, since it in no way corresponds with commercial practice, would serve no useful purpose.

For similar reasons, filing is not permitted as to money. Perfection of security interests in certificated securities, which are covered by the definition of instruments, is governed by Section 8-321 and, therefore, excluded from this section.

Subsection (1) further provides that filing is available as a method of perfection for security interests in chattel paper and negotiable documents, which also come within Section 9-305 on perfection by possession. Chattel paper is sometimes delivered to the assignee, sometimes left in the hands of the assignor for collection;

subsection (1) allows the assignee to perfect his interest by filing in the latter case. Negotiable documents may be, and usually are, delivered to the secured party; subsection (1) follows the Uniform Trust Receipts Act in allowing filing as an alternative method of perfection. Perfection of an interest in goods through a non-negotiable document is covered in subsection (3).

2. Subsection (2), following prior law and consistently with the provisions of Article 7, takes the position that, so long as a negotiable document covering goods is outstanding, title to the goods is, so to say, locked up in the document and the proper way of dealing with such goods is through the document. Perfection therefore is to be made with respect to the document and, when made, automatically carries over to the goods. Any interest perfected directly in the goods while the document is outstanding (for example, a chattel mortgage type of security interest on goods in a warehouse) is subordinated to an outstanding negotiable document.

3. Subsection (3) takes a different approach to the problem of goods covered by a non-negotiable document or otherwise in the possession of a bailee who has not issued a negotiable document. Here title to the goods is not looked on as being locked up in the document and the secured party may perfect his interest directly in the goods by filing as to them. The subsection states two other methods of perfection: issuance of the document in the secured party's name (as consignee of a straight bill of lading or the person to whom delivery would be made under a non-negotiable warehouse receipt) and receipt of notification of the secured party's interest by the bailee which, under Section 9-305, is looked on as equivalent to taking possession by the secured party.

4. Subsections (4) and (5) follow the Uniform Trust Receipts Act in giving perfected status to security interests in instruments (other than certificated securities, which are governed by Section 8-321) and documents for a short period although there has been no filing and the collateral is in the debtor's possession. The period of 21 days is chosen to conform to the provisions of Section 60 of the Federal Bankruptcy Act. There are a variety of legitimate reasons—some of them are described in subsections (5)(a) and (5)(b)—why such collateral has to be temporarily released to a debtor and no useful purpose would be served by cluttering the files with records of such exceedingly short term transactions. Under subsection (4) the 21 day perfection runs from the date of attachment; there is no limitation on the purpose for which the debtor is in possession but the secured party must have given new value under a written security agreement. Under subsection (5) the 21 day perfection runs from the date a secured party who already has a perfected security interest turns over the collateral to the debtor (an example is a bank which has acquired a bill of lading by honoring drafts drawn under a letter of credit and subsequently turns over the bill of lading to its customer); there is no new value requirement but the turn-over must be for one or more of the purposes stated in subsections (5)(a) and (5)(b). Note that while subsection (4) is restricted to instruments and *negotiable* documents, subsection (5) extends to goods covered by non-negotiable documents as well. Thus the letter of credit bank referred to in the example could make a subsection (5) turn-over without regard to the form of the bill of lading, provided that, in the case of a non-negotiable document, it had previously perfected its interest under one of the methods stated in subsection (3). But note that the discussion of subsection (5) in this Comment deals only with perfection. Priority of a security interest in inventory after surrender of the document depends on compliance with the requirements of Section 9-312(3) on notice to prior inventory financer.

Finally, it should be noted that the 21 days applies only to the documents and to the goods obtained by surrender thereof. If the goods are sold, the security interest will continue in proceeds for only 10 days under Section 9-306, unless a further perfection occurs as to the security interest in proceeds.

Cross References:

Article 7 and Sections 9-303, 9-305 and 9-312(3).

Definitional Cross References:

"Chattel paper". Section 9-105.
"Debtor". Section 9-105.
"Document". Section 9-105.
"Goods". Section 9-105.
"Instrument". Section 9-105.
"Receives" notification. Section 1-201.
"Sale". Sections 2-106 and 9-105.
"Secured party". Section 9-105.
"Security agreement". Section 9-105.
"Security interest". Section 1-201.
"Value". Section 1-201.
"Written". Section 1-201.

§ 9-305. When Possession by Secured Party Perfects Security Interest Without Filing.

[1995 Amendments to text indicated by strikeout and underline]

A security interest in ~~letters of credit and advices of credit (subsection (2)(a) of Section 5-116),~~ goods, instruments, money, negotiable documents, or chattel paper may be perfected by the secured party's taking possession of the collateral. A security interest in the right to proceeds of a written letter of credit may be perfected by the secured party's taking possession of the letter of credit. If such collateral other than goods covered by a negotiable document is held by a bailee, the secured party is deemed to have possession from the time the bailee receives notification of the secured party's interest. A security interest is perfected by possession from the time possession is taken without a relation back and continues only so long as possession is retained, unless otherwise specified in this Article. The security interest may be otherwise perfected as provided in this Article before or after the period of possession by the secured party.

Special Legislative Note: *See Special Legislative Note, Section 9-304.*

As amended in 1972, 1977, 1994, and 1995.

See Appendices XII and XIV for material relating to changes made in text in 1994 and 1995, respectively.

Official Comment

Prior Uniform Statutory Provision: None.

Purposes:

1. As under the common law of pledge, no filing is required by this Article to perfect a security interest where the secured party has possession of the collateral. Compare Section 9-302(1)(a). This section permits a security interest to be perfected by transfer of possession only when the collateral is goods, rights to proceeds of letters of credit (if written), instruments ~~*(other than certificated securities, which are governed by Section 8-321)*~~*, documents or chattel paper: that is to say, accounts and general intangibles are excluded. *As to perfection of security interests in certificated securities by possession, see the general rules on perfection of security interests in investment property in Section 9-115(4) and the special rule in Section 9-115(6) dealing with cases where a secured party takes possession of a security certificate in registered form without obtaining an indorsement.** ~~See Section 5-116 for the special case of assignments of letters and advices of credit.~~ A securi-

ty interest in accounts and general intangibles—property not ordinarily represented by any writing whose delivery operates to transfer the claim—may under this Article be perfected only by filing, and this rule would not be affected by the fact that a security agreement or other writing described the assignment of such collateral as a "pledge". Section 9-302(1)(e) exempts from filing certain assignments of accounts which are out of the ordinary course of financing: such exempted assignments are perfected when they attach under Section 9-303(1); they do not fall within this section. ***Amendments in italics approved by the Permanent Editorial Board for Uniform Commercial Code November 4, 1995.***

2. Possession may be by the secured party himself or by an agent on his behalf: it is of course clear, however, that the debtor or a person controlled by him cannot qualify as such an agent for the secured party. See also the last sentence of Section 9-205. Where the collateral (except for goods covered by a negotiable document) is held by a bailee, the time of perfection of the security interest, under the second sentence of the section, is when the bailee receives notification of the secured party's interest: this rule rejects the common law doctrine that it is necessary for the bailee to attorn to the secured party or acknowledge that he now holds on his behalf.

3. The third sentence of the section rejects the "equitable pledge" theory of relation back, under which the taking possession was deemed to relate back to the date of the original security agreement. The relation back theory has had little vitality since the 1938 revision of the Federal Bankruptcy Act, which introduced in Section 60a provisions designed to make such interests voidable as preferences in bankruptcy proceedings. This section now brings state law into conformity with the overriding federal policy: where a pledge transaction is contemplated, perfection dates only from the time possession is taken, although a security interest may attach, unperfected, before that under the rules stated in Section 9-204. The only exception to this rule is the short twenty-one day period of perfection provided in Section 9-304(4) and (5) during which a debtor may have possession of specified collateral in which there is a perfected security interest.

Cross References:

Sections 5-116, 9-204, 9-302, 9-303 and 9-304.

Definitional Cross References:

"Chattel paper". Section 9-105.
"Collateral". Section 9-105.
"Documents". Section 9-105.
"Goods". Section 9-105.
"Instruments". Section 9-105.
"Receives" notification. Section 1-201.
"Secured party". Section 9-105.
"Security interest". Section 1-201.

§ 9-306. "Proceeds"; Secured Party's Rights on Disposition of Collateral.

(1) "Proceeds" includes whatever is received upon the sale, exchange, collection or other disposition of collateral or proceeds. Insurance payable by reason of loss or damage to the collateral is proceeds, except to the extent that it is payable to a person other than a party to the security agreement. Any payments or distributions made with respect to investment property collateral are proceeds. Money, checks, deposit accounts, and the like are "cash proceeds". All other proceeds are "non-cash proceeds".

(2) Except where this Article otherwise provides, a security interest continues in collateral notwithstanding sale, exchange or other disposition thereof unless the disposition was authorized by the secured party in the security agreement or otherwise, and also continues in any identifiable proceeds including collections received by the debtor.

(3) The security interest in proceeds is a continuously perfected security interest if the interest in the original collateral was perfected but it ceases to be a perfected security interest and becomes unperfected ten days after receipt of the proceeds by the debtor unless

(a) a filed financing statement covers the original collateral and the proceeds are collateral in which a security interest may be perfected by filing in the office or offices where the financing statement has been filed and, if the proceeds are acquired with cash proceeds, the description of collateral in the financing statement indicates the types of property constituting the proceeds; or

(b) a filed financing statement covers the original collateral and the proceeds are identifiable cash proceeds;

(c) the original collateral was investment property and the proceeds are identifiable cash proceeds; or

(d) the security interest in the proceeds is perfected before the expiration of the ten day period.

Except as provided in this section, a security interest in proceeds can be perfected only by the methods or under the circumstances permitted in this Article for original collateral of the same type.

(4) In the event of insolvency proceedings instituted by or against a debtor, a secured party with a perfected security interest in proceeds has a perfected security interest only in the following proceeds:

(a) in identifiable non-cash proceeds and in separate deposit accounts containing only proceeds;

(b) in identifiable cash proceeds in the form of money which is neither commingled with other money nor deposited in a deposit account prior to the insolvency proceedings;

(c) in identifiable cash proceeds in the form of checks and the like which are not deposited in a deposit account prior to the insolvency proceedings; and

(d) in all cash and deposit accounts of the debtor in which proceeds have been commingled with other funds, but the perfected security interest under this paragraph (d) is

(i) subject to any right to set-off; and

(ii) limited to an amount not greater than the amount of any cash proceeds received by the debtor within ten days before the institution of the insolvency proceedings less the sum of (I) the payments to the secured party on account of cash proceeds received by the debtor during such period and (II) the cash proceeds received by the debtor during such period to which the secured party is entitled under paragraphs (a) through (c) of this subsection (4).

(5) If a sale of goods results in an account or chattel paper which is transferred by the seller to a secured party, and if the goods are returned to or are repossessed by the seller or the secured party, the following rules determine priorities:

(a) If the goods were collateral at the time of sale, for an indebtedness of the seller which is still unpaid, the original security interest attaches again to the goods and continues as a perfected security interest if it was perfected at the time when the goods were sold. If the security interest was originally perfected by a filing which is still effective, nothing further is required to continue the perfected status; in any other case, the secured party must take possession of the returned or repossessed goods or must file.

(b) An unpaid transferee of the chattel paper has a security interest in the goods against the transferor. Such security interest is prior to a security interest asserted under paragraph (a) to the extent that the transferee of the chattel paper was entitled to priority under Section 9–308.

(c) An unpaid transferee of the account has a security interest in the goods against the transferor. Such security interest is subordinate to a security interest asserted under paragraph (a).

(d) A security interest of an unpaid transferee asserted under paragraph (b) or (c) must be perfected for protection against creditors of the transferor and purchasers of the returned or repossessed goods.

As amended in 1972 and 1994.

See Appendix XII for material relating to changes made in text in 1994.

Official Comment

Prior Uniform Statutory Provision: Section 10, Uniform Trust Receipts Act.

Purposes:

1. This section states a secured party's right to the proceeds received by a debtor on disposition of collateral and states when his interest in such proceeds is perfected.

It makes clear that insurance proceeds from casualty loss of collateral are proceeds within the meaning of this section.

As to the proceeds of consigned goods, see Section 9–114 and the Comment thereto.

2. (a) Whether a debtor's sale of collateral was authorized or unauthorized, prior law generally gave the secured party a claim to the proceeds. Sometimes it was said that the security interest attached to the "property" received in substitution; sometimes it was said the debtor held the proceeds as "trustee" or "agent" for the secured party. Whatever the formulation of the rule, the secured party, if he could identify the proceeds, could reclaim them or their equivalent from the debtor or his trustee in bankruptcy. This section provides new rules for insolvency proceedings. Paragraphs 4(a) through (c) substitute specific rules of identification for general principles of tracing. Paragraph 4(d) limits the security interest in proceeds not within these rules to an amount of the debtor's cash and deposit accounts not greater than cash proceeds received within ten days of insolvency proceedings less the cash proceeds during this period already paid over and less the amounts for which the security interest is recognized under paragraphs 4(a) through (c).

(b) Subsections (2) and (3) make clear that the four-month period for calculating a voidable preference in bankruptcy begins with the date of the secured party's obtaining the security interest in the original collateral and not with the date of his obtaining control of the proceeds. The interest in the proceeds "continues" as a perfected interest if the original interest was perfected; but the interest ceases to be perfected after the expiration of ten days unless a filed financing statement covered the original collateral and the proceeds are collateral of a type as to which a security interest could be perfected by a filing in the same office or unless the secured party perfects his interest in the proceeds themselves—i.e., by filing a financing statement covering them or by taking possession. See Section 9–312(6) and Comment thereto for priority of rights in proceeds perfected by a filing as to original collateral.

(c) Where cash proceeds are covered into the debtor's checking account and paid out in the operation of the debtor's business, recipients of the funds of course take free of any claim which the secured party may have in them as proceeds. What has been said relates to payments and transfers in ordinary course. The law of fraudulent conveyances would no doubt in appropriate cases support recovery of proceeds by a secured party from a transferee out of ordinary course or otherwise in collusion with the debtor to defraud the secured party.

3. In most cases when a debtor makes an unauthorized disposition of collateral, the security interest, under prior law and under this Article, continues in the original collateral in the hands of the purchaser or other transferee. That is to say, since the transferee takes subject to the security interest, the secured party may repossess the collateral from him or in an appropriate case maintain an action for conversion. Subsection (2) codifies this rule. The secured party may claim both proceeds and collateral, but may of course have only one satisfaction.

In many cases a purchaser or other transferee of collateral will take free of a security interest: in such cases the secured party's only right will be to proceeds. A transferee will acquire the collateral free and clear of a preexisting security interest only if the disposition of the collateral by the debtor was authorized by the secured party free and clear of the secured party's security interest. If the disposition was not authorized by the secured party, or was authorized by the secured party subject to the secured party's security interest, the transferee will not acquire the collateral free and clear of the security interest. The authorization may be contained in the security agreement or otherwise given. The right to proceeds, either under the rules of this section or under specific mention thereof in a security agreement or financing statement does not in itself constitute an authorization of sale. PEB Commentary No. 3, dated March 10, 1990, analyzes the interplay between this Section and Section 9–402(7) [see Appendix V, infra].

Section 9–301 states when transferees take free of unperfected security interests. Sections 9–307 on goods, 9–308 on chattel paper and instruments and 9–309 on negotiable instruments, negotiable documents and securities state when purchasers of such collateral take free of a security interest even though perfected and even though the disposition was not authorized.

4. Subsection (5) states rules to determine priorities when collateral which has been sold is returned to the debtor: for example goods returned to a department store by a dissatisfied customer. The most typical problems involve sale and return of inventory, but the subsection can also apply to equipment. Under the rule of Benedict v. Ratner, failure to segregate such returned goods sometimes led to invalidation of the entire security arrangement. This Article rejects the Benedict v. Ratner line of cases (see Section 9–205 and Comment). Subsection (5)(a) of this section reinforces the rule of Section 9–205: as between secured party and debtor (and debtor's trustee in bankruptcy) the original security interest continues on the returned goods. Whether or not the security interest in the returned goods is perfected depends upon factors stated in the text.

Paragraphs (5)(b), (c) and (d) deal with a different aspect of the returned goods situation. Assume that a dealer has sold an automobile and transferred the chattel paper or the account arising on the sale to Bank X (which had not previously financed the car as inventory). Thereafter the buyer of the automobile rightfully rescinds the sale, say for breach of warranty, and the car is returned to the dealer. Paragraph (5)(b) gives the bank as transferee of the chattel paper or the account a security interest in the car against the dealer. For protection against dealer's creditors or purchasers from him (other than buyers in the ordinary course of business, see Section 9–307), Bank X as the transferee, under paragraph (5)(d), must perfect its interest by taking possession of the car or by filing as to it. Perfection of his original interest in the chattel paper or the account does not automatically carry over to the returned car, as it does under paragraph (5)(a) where the secured party originally financed the dealer's inventory.

In the situation covered by (5)(b) and (5)(c) a secured party who financed the inventory and a secured party to whom the chattel paper or the account was transferred may both claim the returned goods—the inventory financer under paragraph (5)(a), the transferee under paragraphs (5)(b) and (5)(c). With respect to chattel paper, Section 9–308 regulates the priorities. With respect to an account, paragraph (5)(c) subordinates the security interest of the transferee of the account to that of the inventory financer. However, if the inventory security interest was unperfected, the transferee's interest could become entitled to priority under the rules stated in Section 9–312(5).

In cases of repossession by the dealer and also in cases where the chattel was returned to the dealer by the voluntary act of the account debtor, the dealer's position may be that of a mere custodian; he may be an agent for resale, but without any other obligation to the holder of the chattel paper; he may be obligated to repurchase the chattel, the chattel paper or the account from the secured party or to hold it as collateral for a loan secured by a transfer of the chattel paper or the account.

If the dealer thereafter sells the chattel to a buyer in ordinary course of business in any of the foregoing cases, the buyer is fully protected under Section 2–403(2) as well as under Section 9–307(1), whichever is technically applicable.

5. "Creditors" and "purchasers" as used in paragraph (5)(d) do not include the original secured inventory financer of the seller of goods under subsection (a). If a purchaser of chattel paper generated by a sale of the goods attains priority over the seller's inventory financer under Section 9–308, the purchaser retains that priority in the event the goods covered by the chattel paper are returned to the seller, without having to further perfect against the inventory financer. This priority issue will usually arise in the context of the original inventory financer and the chattel paper purchaser both claiming the goods or the proceeds of any sale or disposition thereof by the seller. See PEB Commentary No. 5, dated March 10, 1990 [Appendix V, infra].

6. Where a debtor has granted to a secured party a security interest in goods and the debtor later leases those goods as lessor, the lease rentals constitute proceeds of the secured party's collateral consisting of the goods. See PEB Commentary No. 9, dated June 25, 1992 [Appendix V, infra].

Cross References:

Sections 9–307, 9–308 and 9–309.
Point 3: Sections 1–205 and 9–301.
Point 4: Sections 2–403(2), 9–205 and 9–312.

Definitional Cross References:

"Account". Section 9–106.
"Bank". Section 1–201.
"Chattel paper". Section 9–105.
"Check". Sections 3–104 and 9–105.
"Collateral". Section 9–105.
"Creditors". Section 1–201.
"Debtor". Section 9–105.
"Deposit account". Section 9–105.
"Goods". Section 9–105.

"Insolvency proceedings". Section 1-201.
"Money". Section 1-201.
"Purchaser". Section 1-201.
"Sale". Sections 2-106 and 9-105.
"Secured party". Section 9-105.
"Security agreement". Section 9-105.
"Security interest". Section 1-201.

§ 9-307. Protection of Buyers of Goods.

(1) A buyer in ordinary course of business (subsection (9) of Section 1-201) other than a person buying farm products from a person engaged in farming operations takes free of a security interest created by his seller even though the security interest is perfected and even though the buyer knows of its existence.

(2) In the case of consumer goods, a buyer takes free of a security interest even though perfected if he buys without knowledge of the security interest, for value and for his own personal, family or household purposes unless prior to the purchase the secured party has filed a financing statement covering such goods.

(3) A buyer other than a buyer in ordinary course of business (subsection (1) of this section) takes free of a security interest to the extent that it secures future advances made after the secured party acquires knowledge of the purchase, or more than 45 days after the purchase, whichever first occurs, unless made pursuant to a commitment entered into without knowledge of the purchase and before the expiration of the 45 day period.

As amended in 1972.

Official Comment

Prior Uniform Statutory Provision: Section 9, Uniform Conditional Sales Act; Section 9(2), Uniform Trust Receipts Act.

Purposes:

1. This section states when buyers of goods take free of a security interest even though perfected. A buyer who takes free of a perfected security interest of course takes free of an unperfected one. Section 9-301 should be consulted to determine what purchasers, in addition to the buyers covered in this section, take free of an unperfected security interest.

Article 2 (Sales) states general rules on purchase of goods from a seller with defective or voidable title (Section 2-403).

2. The definition of "buyer in ordinary course of business" in Section 1-201(9) restricts the application of subsection (1) to buyers (except pawnbrokers) "from a person in the business of selling goods of that kind": thus the subsection applies, in the terminology of this Article, primarily to inventory. Subsection (1) further excludes from its operation buyers of "farm products", defined in Section 9-109(3), from a person engaged in farming operations. The buyer in ordinary course of business is defined as one who buys "in good faith and without knowledge that the sale to him is in violation of the ownership rights or security interest of a third party." This section provides that such a buyer takes free of a security interest, even though perfected, and although he knows the security interest exists. Reading the two provisions together, it results that the buyer takes free if he merely knows that there is a security interest which covers the goods but takes subject if he knows, in addition, that the sale is in violation of some term in the security agreement not waived by the words or conduct of the secured party.

The limitations which this section imposes on the persons who may take free of a security interest apply of course only to unauthorized sales by the debtor. If the secured party has authorized the sale in the security agreement or otherwise, the buyer takes free without regard to the limitations of this section. Section 9-306 states the right of a secured party to the proceeds of a sale, authorized or unauthorized.

3. Subsection (2) deals with buyers of "consumer goods" (defined in Section 9-109). Under Section 9-301(1)(d) no filing is required to perfect a purchase money interest in consumer goods subject to this subsection except motor vehicles required to be registered; filing is required to perfect security interests in such goods other than purchase money interests and, for motor vehicles, even in the case of purchase money interests. (The special case of fixtures has added complications that are apart from the point of this discussion.)

Under subsection (2) a buyer of consumer goods takes free of a security interest even though perfected a) if he buys without knowledge of the security interest, b) for value, c) for his own personal, family, or household purposes and d) before a financing statement is filed.

As to purchase money security interests which are perfected without filing under Section 9-302(1)(d): A secured party may file a financing statement (although filing is not required for perfection). If he does file, all buyers take subject to the security interest. If he does not file, a buyer who meets the qualifications stated in the preceding paragraph takes free of the security interest.

As to security interests which can be perfected only by filing under Section 9-302: This category includes all non-purchase money interests, and all interests, whether or not purchase money, in motor vehicles, as well as interests which may be and are filed, though filing was not required for perfection under Section 9-302. (Note that under Section 9-302(3) the filing provisions of this Article do not apply when a state has enacted a certificate of title law. Thus where motor vehicles are concerned, in a state having such a certificate of title law, perfection will be under that law.) So long as the security interest remains unperfected, not only the buyers described in subsection (2) but the purchasers described in Section 9-301 will take free of the interest. After a financing statement has been filed or after compliance with the certificate of title law all subsequent buyers, under the rule of subsection (2), are subject to the security interest.

4. Although a buyer is of course subject to the Code's system of notice from filing or possession, subsection (3) makes clear that he will not be subject to future advances under a security interest after the secured party has knowledge that the buyer has purchased the collateral and in any event after 45 days after the purchase unless the advances were made pursuant to a commitment entered into before the expiration of the 45 days and without knowledge of the purchase. Of course, a buyer in ordinary course who takes free of the security interest under subsection (1) is not subject to any future advances. Compare Sections 9-301(4) and 9-312(7).

Cross References:

Point 1: Sections 2-403 and 9-301.
Point 2: Section 9-306.
Point 3: Sections 9-301 and 9-302.
Point 4: Sections 9-301(4) and 9-312(7).

Definitional Cross References:

"Buyer in ordinary course of business". Section 1-201.
"Consumer goods". Section 9-109.
"Goods". Section 9-105.
"Knows" and "Knowledge". Section 1-201.
"Person". Section 1-201.
"Purchase". Section 1-201.
"Pursuant to commitment". Section 9-105.
"Secured party". Section 9-105.
"Security interest". Section 1-201.
"Value". Section 1-201.

§ 9-308. Purchase of Chattel Paper and Instruments.

A purchaser of chattel paper or an instrument who gives new value and takes possession of it in the ordinary course of his business has priority over a security interest in the chattel paper or instrument

(a) which is perfected under Section 9-304 (permissive filing and temporary perfection) or under Section 9-306 (perfection as to proceeds) if he acts without knowledge that the specific paper or instrument is subject to a security interest; or

(b) which is claimed merely as proceeds of inventory subject to a security interest (Section 9-306) even though he knows that the specific paper or instrument is subject to the security interest.

As amended in 1972.

Official Comment

Prior Uniform Statutory Provision: Sections 9(a) and 10 of Uniform Trust Receipts Act.

Purposes:

1. Chattel paper is defined (Section 9-105) as "a writing or writings which evidence both a monetary obligation and a security interest in or a lease of specific goods". Such paper has become an important class of collateral in financing arrangements, which may—as in the automobile and some other fields—follow an earlier financing arrangement covering inventory or which may begin with the chattel paper itself.

Arrangements where the chattel paper is delivered to the secured party who then makes collections, as well as arrangements where the debtor, whether or not he is left in possession of the paper, makes the collections, are both widely used, and are known respectively as notification (or "direct collection") and non-notification (or "indirect collection") arrangements. In the automobile field, for example, when a car is sold to a consumer buyer under an installment purchase agreement and the resulting chattel paper is assigned, the assignee usually takes possession, the obligor is notified of the assignment and is directed to make payments to the assignee. In the furniture field, for an example on the other hand, the chattel paper may be left in the dealer's hands or delivered to the assignee; in either case the obligor may not be notified, and payments are made to the dealer-assignor who receives them under a duty to remit to his assignee. The widespread use of both methods of dealing with chattel paper is recognized by the provisions of this Article, which permit perfection of a chattel paper security interest either by filing or by taking possession.

2. Although perfection by filing is permitted as to chattel paper, certain purchasers of chattel paper allowed to remain in the debtor's possession take free of the security interest despite the filing.

Clause (b) of the section deals with the case where the security interest in the chattel paper is claimed merely as proceeds—i.e., on behalf of an inventory financer who has not by some new transaction with the debtor acquired a specific interest in the chattel paper. In that case a purchaser, even though he knows of the inventory financer's proceeds interest, takes priority provided he gives new value and takes possession of the paper in the ordinary course of his business.

The same basic rule applies in favor of a purchaser of other instruments who claims priority against a proceeds interest therein of which he has knowledge. Thus a purchaser of a negotiable instrument might prevail under clause (b) even though his knowledge of the conflicting proceeds claim precluded his having holder in due course status under Section 9-309.

3. Clause (a) deals with the case where the non-possessory security interest in the chattel paper is more than a mere claim to proceeds—i.e., exists in favor of a secured party who has given value against the paper, whether or not he financed the inventory whose sale gave rise to it. In this case the purchaser, to take priority, must not only give new value and take possession in the ordinary course of his business; he must also take without knowledge of the existing security interest. Thus a secured party, who has a specific interest in the chattel paper and not merely a claim to proceeds, and who wishes to leave the paper in the debtor's possession can, because of the knowledge requirement, protect himself against purchasers by stamping or noting on the paper the fact that it has been assigned to him.

A chattel paper financer who gives new value and takes possession of chattel paper in the ordinary course of his business and is without knowledge of prior security interests in the chattel paper has no duty to search for Article 9 filings against the chattel paper or to make other inquiries which might reveal perfected prior interests in the paper, even though the chattel paper financer is aware of the possibility that a prior security interest exists. Mere knowledge of an Article 9 filing against chattel paper does not give knowledge of the existence of a security interest in the chattel paper. See PEB Commentary No. 8, dated December 10, 1991 [Appendix V, infra].

4. It should be noted that under Section 9-304(1) a security interest in an instrument, negotiable or non-negotiable, cannot be perfected by filing (except where the instrument constitutes part of chattel paper). Thus the only types of perfected non-possessory security interest that can arise in an instrument are the temporary 21 day perfection provided for in Section 9-304(4) and (5) or the 10 day perfection in proceeds of Section 9-306. Where such a perfected interest exists in a non-negotiable instrument, purchasers will take free if they qualify under clause (a) of the section.

Cross References:

Point 1: Sections 9-304(1) and 9-305.
Point 2: Section 9-306.
Point 4: Sections 9-304 and 9-306.

Definitional Cross References:

"Chattel paper". Section 9-105.
"Instrument". Section 9-105.
"Inventory". Section 9-109.
"Knowledge". Section 1-201.
"Proceeds". Section 9-306.
"Purchaser". Section 1-201.
"Security interest". Section 1-201.
"Value". Section 1-201.

§ 9-309. Protection of Purchasers of Instruments, Documents, and Securities.

Nothing in this Article limits the rights of a holder in due course of a negotiable instrument (Section 3-302) or a holder to whom a negotiable document of title has been duly negotiated (Section 7-501) or a protected purchaser of a security (Section 8-303) and the holders or purchasers take priority over an earlier security interest even though perfected. Filing under this Article does not constitute notice of the security interest to such holders or purchasers.

As amended in 1977 and 1994.

See Appendix XII for material relating to changes made in text in 1994.

Official Comment

Prior Uniform Statutory Provision: Section 9(a), Uniform Trust Receipts Act.

Purposes:

1. Under this Article as at common law and under prior statutes the rights of purchasers of negotiable paper, including negotiable documents of title and investment securities, are determined by the rules of holding in due course and the like which are applicable to the type of paper concerned. (Articles 3, 7, and 8.) This section, as did Section 9(a) of the Uniform Trust Receipts Act, makes explicit the rule which was implicitly but universally recognized under the earlier statutes.

2. Under Section 9–304(1) filing is ineffective to perfect a security interest in instruments (including securities) except those instruments which are part of chattel paper, and of course is ineffective to constitute notice to subsequent purchasers. Although filing is permissible as a method of perfection for a security interest in documents, this section follows the policy of the Uniform Trust Receipts Act in providing that the filing does not constitute notice to purchasers.

3. The operation of this section can be seen when two secured parties have a perfected security interest in an account, chattel paper, or general intangible and the secured party that does not have priority receives a payment by check directly or indirectly from the account debtor. If the recipient takes the check under circumstances that give the recipient the rights of a holder in due course (Section 3–302), then the recipient's security interest in the check will take priority over the competing security interest and the recipient will be entitled to keep the payment. See PEB Commentary No. 7, dated March 10, 1990 [Appendix V, infra].

Cross References:

Articles 3, 7, and 8 and Sections 9–304(1) and 9–308.

Definitional Cross References:

"Bona fide purchaser". Section 8–302.
"Document of title". Section 1–201.
"Duly negotiated". Section 7–501.
"Holder". Section 1–201.
"Holder in due course". Sections 3–302 and 9–105.
"Negotiable instrument". Sections 3–104 and 9–105.
"Notice". Section 1–201.
"Purchaser". Section 1–201.
"Security". Sections 8–102 and 9–105.
"Security interest". Section 1–201.

§ 9–310. Priority of Certain Liens Arising by Operation of Law.

When a person in the ordinary course of his business furnishes services or materials with respect to goods subject to a security interest, a lien upon goods in the possession of such person given by statute or rule of law for such materials or services takes priority over a perfected security interest unless the lien is statutory and the statute expressly provides otherwise.

Official Comment

1. To provide that liens securing claims arising from work intended to enhance or preserve the value of the collateral take priority over an earlier security interest even though perfected.

2. Apart from the Uniform Trust Receipts Act which had a section similar to this one, there was generally no specific statutory rule as to priority between security devices and liens for services or materials. Under chattel mortgage or conditional sales law many decisions made the priority of such liens turn on whether the secured party did or did not have "title". This section changes such rules and makes the lien for services or materials prior in all cases where they are furnished in the ordinary course of the lienor's business and the goods involved are in the lienor's possession. Some of the

statutes creating such liens expressly make the lien subordinate to a prior security interest. This section does not repeal such statutory provisions. If the statute creating the lien is silent, even though it has been construed by decision to make the lien subordinate to the security interest, this section provides a rule of interpretation that the lien should take priority over the security interest.

Cross References:

Sections 9–102(2), 9–104(c) and 9–312(1).

Definitional Cross References:

"Goods". Section 9–105.
"Person". Section 1–201.
"Security interest". Section 1–201.

§ 9–311. Alienability of Debtor's Rights: Judicial Process.

The debtor's rights in collateral may be voluntarily or involuntarily transferred (by way of sale, creation of a security interest, attachment, levy, garnishment or other judicial process) notwithstanding a provision in the security agreement prohibiting any transfer or making the transfer constitute a default.

Official Comment

Prior Uniform Statutory Provision: None.

Purposes:

1. To make clear that in all security transactions under this Article, the debtor has an interest (whether legal title or an equity) which he can dispose of and which his creditors can reach.

2. Some jurisdictions have held that when a mortgagee or conditional seller has "title" to the collateral, creditors may not proceed against the mortgagor's or vendee's interest by levy, attachment or other judicial process. This section changes those rules by providing that in all security interests the debtor's interest in the collateral remains subject to claims of creditors who take appropriate action. It is left to the law of each state to determine the form of "appropriate process".

3. Where the security interest is in inventory, difficult problems arise with reference to attachment and levy. Assume that a debt of $100,000 is secured by inventory worth twice that amount. If by attachment or levy certain units of the inventory are seized, the determination of the debtor's equity in the units seized is not a simple matter. The section leaves the solution of this problem to the courts. Procedures such as marshalling may be appropriate.

Cross References:

Sections 9–301(4), 9–307(3) and 9–312(7).

Definitional Cross References:

"Collateral". Section 9–105.
"Debtor". Section 9–105.
"Rights". Section 1–201.
"Sale". Sections 2–106 and 9–105.
"Security agreement". Section 9–105.
"Security interest". Section 1–201.

§ 9–312. Priorities Among Conflicting Security Interests in the Same Collateral.

(1) The rules of priority stated in other sections of this Part and in the following sections shall govern when applicable: Section 4–210 with respect to the security interests of collecting banks in items being collected, accompanying documents and proceeds; Section 9–103 on security interests related to other jurisdictions; Section 9–114 on consignments; Section 9–115 on security interests in investment property.

(2) A perfected security interest in crops for new value given to enable the debtor to produce the crops during the production season and given not more than three months before the crops become growing crops by planting or otherwise takes priority over an earlier perfected security interest to the extent that such earlier interest secures obligations due more than six months before the crops become growing crops by planting or otherwise, even though the person giving new value had knowledge of the earlier security interest.

(3) A perfected purchase money security interest in inventory has priority over a conflicting security interest in the same inventory and also has priority in identifiable cash proceeds received on or before the delivery of the inventory to a buyer if

(a) the purchase money security interest is perfected at the time the debtor receives possession of the inventory; and

(b) the purchase money secured party gives notification in writing to the holder of the conflicting security interest if the holder had filed a financing statement covering the same types of inventory (i) before the date of the filing made by the purchase money secured party, or (ii) before the beginning of the 21 day period where the purchase money security interest is temporarily perfected without filing or possession (subsection (5) of Section 9-304); and

(c) the holder of the conflicting security interest receives the notification within five years before the debtor receives possession of the inventory; and

(d) the notification states that the person giving the notice has or expects to acquire a purchase money security interest in inventory of the debtor, describing such inventory by item or type.

(4) A purchase money security interest in collateral other than inventory has priority over a conflicting security interest in the same collateral or its proceeds if the purchase money security interest is perfected at the time the debtor receives possession of the collateral or within ten days thereafter.

(5) In all cases not governed by other rules stated in this section (including cases of purchase money security interests which do not qualify for the special priorities set forth in subsections (3) and (4) of this section), priority between conflicting security interests in the same collateral shall be determined according to the following rules:

(a) Conflicting security interests rank according to priority in time of filing or perfection. Priority dates from the time a filing is first made covering the collateral or the time the security interest is first perfected, whichever is earlier, provided that there is no period thereafter when there is neither filing nor perfection.

(b) So long as conflicting security interests are unperfected, the first to attach has priority.

(6) For the purposes of subsection (5) a date of filing or perfection as to collateral is also a date of filing or perfection as to proceeds.

(7) If future advances are made while a security interest is perfected by filing, the taking of possession, or under Section 9-115 or Section 9-116 on

investment property, the security interest has the same priority for the purposes of subsection (5) or Section 9–115(5) with respect to the future advances as it does with respect to the first advance. If a commitment is made before or while the security interest is so perfected, the security interest has the same priority with respect to advances made pursuant thereto. In other cases a perfected security interest has priority from the date the advance is made.

As amended in 1972, 1977 and 1994.

See Appendices XI and XII for material relating to changes made in text in 1994.

Official Comment

Prior Uniform Statutory Provision: None.

Purposes:

1. In a variety of situations two or more people may claim an interest in the same property. The several sections specified in subsection (1) contain rules for determining priorities between security interests and such other claims in the situations covered in those sections. For cases not covered in those sections this section states general rules of priority between conflicting security interests.

2. Subsection (2) gives priority to a new value security interest in crops based on a current crop production loan over an earlier security interest in the crop which secured obligations (such as rent, interest or mortgage principal amortization) due more than six months before the crops become growing crops. This priority is not affected by the fact that the person making the crop loan knew of the earlier security interest.

3. Subsections (3) and (4) give priority to a purchase money security interest (defined in Section 9–107) under certain conditions over non-purchase money interests, which in this context will usually be interests asserted under after-acquired property clauses. See Section 9–204 on the extent to which after-acquired property interests are validated and Section 9–108 on when a security interest in after-acquired property is deemed taken for new value.

Prior law, under one or another theory, usually contrived to protect purchase money interests over after-acquired property interests (to the extent to which the after-acquired property interest was recognized at all). For example, in the field of industrial equipment financing it was possible, by manipulation of title theory, for the purchase money financer of new equipment (under conditional sale or equipment trust) to protect himself against the claims of prior mortgagees or bondholders under an after-acquired clause in the mortgage or trust indenture: the result was arrived at on the theory that since "title" to the equipment was never in the vendee or lessee there was nothing for the lien of the mortgage to attach to. While this Article broadly validates the after-acquired property interest, it also recognizes as sound the preference which prior law gave to the purchase money interest. That policy is carried out in subsections (3) and (4).

Subsection (4) states a general rule applicable to all types of collateral except inventory: the purchase money interest takes priority if it is perfected when the debtor receives possession of the collateral or within ten days thereafter. As to the ten day grace period, compare Section 9–301(2). The perfection requirement means that the purchase money secured party either has filed a financing statement before that time or has a temporarily perfected interest in goods covered by documents under Section 9–304(4) and (5) (which is continued in a perfected status by filing before the expiration of the 21 day period specified in that section). There is no requirement that the purchase money secured party be without notice or knowledge of the other interest; he takes priority although he knows of it or it has been filed.

Under subsection (3) the same rule of priority, but without the ten day grace period for filing, applies to a purchase money security interest in inventory, with the additional requirement that the purchase money secured party give notification, as stated in subsection (3), to any other secured party who filed earlier for the same item or type of inventory. The reason for the additional requirement of notification is that typically the arrangement between an inventory secured party and his debtor will require the secured party to make periodic advances against incoming inventory or periodic releases of old inventory as new inventory is received. A fraudulent debtor may apply to the secured party for advances even though he has already given a security interest in the inventory to another secured party. The notification requirement protects the inventory financer in such a situation: if he has received notification, he will presumably not make an advance; if he has not received notification (or if the other interest does not qualify as a purchase money interest), any advance he may make will have priority. Since an arrangement for periodic advances against incoming property is unusual outside the inventory field, no notification requirement is included in subsection (4).

Where the purchase money inventory financing began by possession of a negotiable document of title by the secured party, he must in order to retain priority give the notice required by subsection (3) at or before the usual time, i.e., when the debtor gets possession of the inventory, even though his security interest remains perfected for 21 days under Section 9–304(5).

When under these rules the purchase money secured party has priority over another secured party, the question arises whether this priority extends to the proceeds of the original collateral. Under subsection (4) which deals with non-inventory collateral and where there was no ordinary expectation that the goods would be sold, the section gives an affirmative answer. In the case of inventory collateral under subsection (3), where it was expected that the goods would be sold and where financing frequently is based on the resulting accounts, chattel paper, or other proceeds, the subsection gives an answer limited to the preservation of the purchase money priority only in so far as the proceeds are cash received on or before the delivery of the inventory to a buyer, that is, without the creation of an intervening account to which conflicting rights might attach. The conflicting rights to proceeds consisting of accounts are governed by subsection (5). See Comment 8.

The foregoing rules applicable to purchase money security interests in inventory apply also to the rights in consigned merchandise. See Section 9–114.

4. Subsection (5) states a rule for determining priority between conflicting security interests in cases not covered in the sections referred to in subsection (1) or in subsections (2), (3) and (4) of this section. Note that subsection (5) applies to cases of purchase money security interests which do not qualify for the special priorities set forth in subsections (3) and (4).

There is a single priority rule based on precedence in the time as of which the competing parties either filed their security interests or perfected their security interests. The form of the claim to priority, i.e., filing or perfection, may shift from time to time, and the rank will be based on the first filing or perfection so long as there is no intervening period without filing or perfection. Filing may occur as to particular collateral before the collateral comes into existence. Under the standards of Section 9–203 perfection cannot occur as to particular collateral until the collateral itself (and not prior collateral) comes into existence and the debtor has rights therein; but under subsection (6) of this section the secured party's priority may date from his time of perfection as to the prior collateral, if perfection or filing has been continuously maintained. Subsection (6) provides that a date of filing or perfection as to original collateral is also a date of filing or perfection as to proceeds. This rule should also be read with Section 9-306, which makes it unnecessary to claim proceeds expressly in a financing statement and provides in effect that a filing as to original collateral is also a filing as to proceeds (with exceptions therein stated). Thus, if a financing statement is filed covering inventory, then (subject to the exception involving multistate problems) this filing is also a filing as to the resulting accounts and constitutes the date of filing as to the accounts.

The party who may have had a prior security interest in inventory or may have had the only such security interest does not automatically for that reason have priority as to the accounts. His claim to accounts may or may not have priority over competing filed claims to accounts. The priority is based on precedence as to the accounts under the rules stated in the preceding paragraph.

5. The operation of this section is illustrated by the examples set forth under this and the succeeding Points.

Example 1. A files against X (debtor) on February 1. B files against X on March 1. B makes a non-purchase money advance against certain collateral on April 1. A makes an advance against the same collateral on May 1. A has priority even though B's advance was made earlier and was perfected when made. It makes no difference whether or not A knew of B's interest when he made his advance.

The problem stated in the example is peculiar to a notice filing system under which filing may be made before the security interest attaches (see Section 9-402). The Uniform Trust Receipts Act, which first introduced such a filing system, contained no hint of a solution and case law under it was unpredictable. This Article follows several of the accounts receivable statutes in determining priority by order of filing. The justification for the rule lies in the necessity of protecting the filing system—that is, of allowing the secured party who has first filed to make subsequent advances without each time having, as a condition of protection, to check for filings later than his. Note, however, that his protection is not absolute: if, in the example, B's advance creates a purchase money security interest, he has priority under subsection (4), or, in the case of inventory, under subsection (3) provided he has properly notified A. (See further Example 3 below).

Example 2. A and B make non-purchase money advances against the same collateral. The collateral is in the debtor's possession and neither interest is perfected when the second advance is made. Whichever secured party first perfects his interest (by taking possession of the collateral or by filing) takes priority and it makes no difference whether or not he knows of the other interest at the time he perfects his own.

This result may be regarded as an adoption, in this type of situation, of the idea, deeply rooted at common law, of a race of diligence among creditors. Subsection (5)(b) adds the thought that so long as neither of the interests is perfected, the one which first attached (i.e., under the advance first made) has priority. The last mentioned rule may be thought to be of merely theoretical interest, since it is hard to imagine a situation where the case would come into litigation without either A or B having perfected his interest. If neither interest had been perfected at the time of the filing of a petition in bankruptcy, of course neither would be good against the trustee in bankruptcy.

Example 3. A has a temporarily perfected (21 day) security interest, unfiled, in a negotiable document in the debtor's possession under Section 9-304(4) or (5). On the fifth day B files and thus perfects a security interest in the same document. On the tenth day A files. A has priority, whether or not he knows of B's interest when he files, because he perfected first and has maintained continuous perfection or filing.

6. The application of the priority rules to after-acquired property must be considered separately for each item of collateral. Priority does not depend only on time of perfection, but may also be based on priority in filing before perfection.

Example 4. On February 1 A makes advances to X under a security agreement which covers "all the machinery in X's plant" and contains an after-acquired property clause. A promptly files his financing statement. On March 1 X acquires a new machine, B makes an advance against it and files his financing statement. On April 1 A, under the original security agreement, makes an advance against the machine acquired March 1. If B's advance creates a purchase money security interest, he has priority under subsection (4) (provided he filed before X received possession of the machine or within ten days thereafter). If B's advance, although he gave new value, did not create a purchase money interest, A has priority as to both of his advances by virtue of his priority in filing, although the parties perfected simultaneously on March 1 as to the new machine.

The application of the priority rules to proceeds presents special features discussed in Comment 8.

7. The application of the priority rules to future advances is complicated. In general, since any secured party must operate in reference to the Code's system of notice, he takes subject to future advances under a priority security interest while it is perfected through filing or possession, whether the advances are committed or non-committed, and to any advances subsequently made "pursuant to commitment" (Section 9-105) during that period. In the rare case when a future advance is made without commitment while the security interest is perfected temporarily without either filing or possession, the future advance has priority from the date it is made. These rules are more liberal toward the priority of future advances than the corresponding rules applicable to an intervening buyer (Section 9-307(3)) because of the different characteristics of the intervening party. Compare the corresponding rule applicable to an intervening judgment creditor. (Section 9-301(4)).

Example 5. On February 1 A makes an advance against machinery in the debtor's possession and files his financing statement. On March 1 B makes an advance against the same machinery and files his financing statement. On April 1 A makes a further advance, under the original security agreement, against the same machinery (which is covered by the original financing statement and thus perfected when made). A has priority over B both as to the February 1 and as to the April 1 advance and it makes no difference whether or not A knows of B's intervening advance when he makes his second advance.

A wins, as to the April 1 advance, because he first filed even though B's interest attached, and indeed was perfected, before the April 1 advance. The same rule would apply if either A or B had perfected through possession. Section 9-204(3) and the Comment thereto should be consulted for the validation of future advances.

The same result would be reached even though A's April 1 advance was not under the original security agreement, but was under a new security agreement under A's same financing statement or during the continuation of A's possession.

8. The application of the priority rules of subsections (5) and (6) to proceeds is shown by the following examples:

Example 6. A files a financing statement covering a described type of inventory then owned or thereafter acquired. B subsequently takes a purchase money security interest in certain inventory described in A's financing statement and achieves priority over A under subsection (3) as to this inventory. This inventory is then sold, producing proceeds.

If the proceeds of the inventory are instruments or chattel paper, the rights of A and B on the one hand and any adverse claimant to these proceeds on the other are governed by Sections 9-308 and 9-309. If the proceeds are cash, subsection (3) indicates that B's priority as to the inventory carries over to the cash. Proceeds which are accounts constitute different collateral and the priorities as to the original collateral do not control the priority as to the accounts. Under Sections 9-306 and 9-312(6), A's first filing as to the inventory constitutes a first filing as to the accounts, provided that the same filing office would be appropriate for filing as to accounts under the rules of Section 9-306(3). Therefore, A has priority as to the accounts.

Many parties financing inventory are quite content to protect their first security interest in the inventory itself, realizing that when inventory is sold, someone else will be financing the accounts and the priority for inventory will not run forward to the accounts. Indeed, the cash supplied by the accounts financer will be used to pay the inventory financing. In some situations, the party financing the inventory on a purchase money basis makes contractual arrangements that the proceeds of accounts financing by another be devoted to paying off the first inventory security interest.

Example 7. In the foregoing case, if B had filed directly as to accounts, the date of that filing as to accounts would be compared with the date of A's first filing as to the inventory, and the first-to-file rule would prevail.

Subsection (6) provides that a filing as to original collateral determines the date of a filing as to the proceeds thereof. This rule implies, of course, that the filing as to the original collateral is effective as to proceeds under the rule of Section 9-306(3).

Example 8. If C had filed as to accounts in Example 6 above before either A or B had filed as to inventory, C's first filing as to accounts would have priority over the filings of A and B, which would also constitute filings as to accounts under the rule just mentioned. A's and B's position as to the inventory gives them no automatic claim to the proceeds of the inventory consisting of accounts against someone who has filed earlier as to accounts. If, on the other hand, either A's or B's filings as to the inventory constituted good filings as to accounts and these filings preceded C's direct filings as to accounts, A or B would outrank C as to the accounts.

If the filings as to inventory were not effective under subsection (6) for filing as to accounts because a filing for accounts would have to be in a different filing office under Section 9-103(3), these inventory filings would nevertheless be effective for 10 days as to accounts. If the perfection of the security interest in accounts was continued within the 10 days by appropriate filings, then A and B's interests in the accounts would date from the date of filing as to inventory.

9. Under some circumstances, a secured party who does not have priority in an account, chattel paper, or general intangible may be entitled to keep a cash payment received directly or indirectly from the account debtor. See PEB Commentary No. 7, dated March 10, 1990 [Appendix V, infra].

Cross References:

Sections 9-204(1) and 9-303.

Point 1: Sections 4-208, 9-114, 9-301, 9-304, 9-306, 9-307, 9-308, 9-309, 9-310, 9-313, 9-314, 9-315 and 9-316.

Point 3: Sections 9-108, 9-204, 9-304(4) and (5).

Points 4 to 7: Sections 9-204, 9-301(4), 9-304(4) and (5), 9-306, 9-307(3) and 9-402(1).

Point 8: Sections 9-103(6) and 9-306(3).

Definitional Cross References:

"Chattel paper". Section 9-105.
"Collateral". Section 9-105.
"Collecting bank". Section 4-105.
"Debtor". Section 9-105.
"Documents". Section 9-105.
"Give notice". Section 1-201.
"Goods". Section 9-105.

"Instruments". Section 9–105.
"Inventory". Section 9–109.
"Knowledge". Section 1–201.
"Person". Section 1–201.
"Proceeds". Section 9–306.
"Purchase money security interest". Section 9–107.
"Pursuant to commitment". Section 9–105.
"Receives" notification. Section 1–201.
"Secured party". Section 9–105.
"Security". Sections 8–102 and 9–105.
"Security interest". Section 1–201.
"Value". Section 1–201.

§ 9–313. Priority of Security Interests in Fixtures.

(1) In this section and in the provisions of Part 4 of this Article referring to fixture filing, unless the context otherwise requires

(a) goods are "fixtures" when they become so related to particular real estate that an interest in them arises under real estate law

(b) a "fixture filing" is the filing in the office where a mortgage on the real estate would be filed or recorded of a financing statement covering goods which are or are to become fixtures and conforming to the requirements of subsection (5) of Section 9–402

(c) a mortgage is a "construction mortgage" to the extent that it secures an obligation incurred for the construction of an improvement on land including the acquisition cost of the land, if the recorded writing so indicates.

(2) A security interest under this Article may be created in goods which are fixtures or may continue in goods which become fixtures, but no security interest exists under this Article in ordinary building materials incorporated into an improvement on land.

(3) This Article does not prevent creation of an encumbrance upon fixtures pursuant to real estate law.

(4) A perfected security interest in fixtures has priority over the conflicting interest of an encumbrancer or owner of the real estate where

(a) the security interest is a purchase money security interest, the interest of the encumbrancer or owner arises before the goods become fixtures, the security interest is perfected by a fixture filing before the goods become fixtures or within ten days thereafter, and the debtor has an interest of record in the real estate or is in possession of the real estate; or

(b) the security interest is perfected by a fixture filing before the interest of the encumbrancer or owner is of record, the security interest has priority over any conflicting interest of a predecessor in title of the encumbrancer or owner, and the debtor has an interest of record in the real estate or is in possession of the real estate; or

(c) the fixtures are readily removable factory or office machines or readily removable replacements of domestic appliances which are consumer goods, and before the goods become fixtures the security interest is perfected by any method permitted by this Article; or

(d) the conflicting interest is a lien on the real estate obtained by legal or equitable proceedings after the security interest was perfected by any method permitted by this Article.

(5) A security interest in fixtures, whether or not perfected, has priority over the conflicting interest of an encumbrancer or owner of the real estate where

(a) the encumbrancer or owner has consented in writing to the security interest or has disclaimed an interest in the goods as fixtures; or

(b) the debtor has a right to remove the goods as against the encumbrancer or owner. If the debtor's right terminates, the priority of the security interest continues for a reasonable time.

(6) Notwithstanding paragraph (a) of subsection (4) but otherwise subject to subsections (4) and (5), a security interest in fixtures is subordinate to a construction mortgage recorded before the goods become fixtures if the goods become fixtures before the completion of the construction. To the extent that it is given to refinance a construction mortgage, a mortgage has this priority to the same extent as the construction mortgage.

(7) In cases not within the preceding subsections, a security interest in fixtures is subordinate to the conflicting interest of an encumbrancer or owner of the related real estate who is not the debtor.

(8) When the secured party has priority over all owners and encumbrancers of the real estate, he may, on default, subject to the provisions of Part 5, remove his collateral from the real estate but he must reimburse any encumbrancer or owner of the real estate who is not the debtor and who has not otherwise agreed for the cost of repair of any physical injury, but not for any diminution in value of the real estate caused by the absence of the goods removed or by any necessity of replacing them. A person entitled to reimbursement may refuse permission to remove until the secured party gives adequate security for the performance of this obligation.

As amended in 1972.

Official Comment

Prior Uniform Statutory Provision: Section 7, Uniform Conditional Sales Act.

Purposes:

1. Section 9-313 deals with the problem that certain goods which are the subject of chattel financing become so affixed or otherwise so related to real estate that they become part of the real estate, and that chattel interests would be subordinate to real estate interests except as protected by the priorities regulated by the section. These goods are called "fixtures". Some fixtures also retain their chattel nature in that a chattel financing with respect to them may exist and may continue to be recognized, if notice thereof is given to real estate interests in accordance with this section. But this concept does not apply if the goods are integrally incorporated into the real estate.

The term "fixture filing" has been introduced and defined. It emphasizes that when a filing is intended to give the priority advantages herein discussed against real estate interests, the filing must (except as stated below) be for record in the real estate records and indexed therein, so that it will be found in a real estate search.

Since the determination in advance of judicial decision of the question whether goods have become fixtures is a difficult one, no inference may be drawn from a fixture filing that the secured party concedes that the goods are or will become fixtures. The fixture filing may be merely precautionary.

2. "Fixture" is defined to include any goods which become so related to particular real estate that an interest in them arises under real estate law and therefore, goods integrally incorporated into the real estate are clearly fixtures. But under subsection (2) no security interest exists under Article 9 in ordinary building materials incorporated into an improvement on land.

Goods may be technically "ordinary building materials," e.g., window glass, but if they are incorporated into a structure which as a whole has not become an integral part of the real estate, the rules applicable to the ordinary building materials follow the rules applicable to the structure itself. The outstanding examples presenting this kind of problem are the modern "mobile homes" and the modern prefabricated steel buildings usable as warehouses, garages, factories, etc. In the case of the mobile homes, most of them are erected on leased land and the right of the debtor under a mobile home purchase contract to remove the goods as lessee will make clear that his secured party ordinarily has a similar right. See paragraph (5)(b).

In cases where mobile homes or prefabricated steel buildings are erected by a person having an ownership interest in the land, the question into which category the buildings fall is one determined by local law. In general, the governing local law will not be that applicable in determining whether goods have become real property between landlord and tenant, or between mortgagor and mortgagee, or between grantor and grantee, but rather that applicable in a three-party situation, determining whether chattel financing can survive as against parties who acquire rights through the affixation of the goods to the real estate.

The assertion that no security interest exists in ordinary building materials is only for the operation of the priority provisions of this section. It is without prejudice to any rights which the secured party may have against the debtor himself if he incorporated the goods into real estate or against any party guilty of wrongful incorporation thereof in violation of the secured party's rights.

3. Under these concepts the section recognizes three categories of goods: (1) those which retain their chattel character entirely and are not part of the real estate; (2) ordinary building materials which have become an integral part of the real estate and cannot retain their chattel character for purposes of finance; and (3) an intermediate class which has become real estate for certain purposes, but as to which chattel financing may be preserved. This third and intermediate class is the primary subject of this section. The demarcation between these classifications is not delineated by this section.

4. In considering fixture priority problems, there will always first be a preliminary question whether real estate interests per se have an interest in the goods as part of real estate. If not, it is immaterial, so far as concerns real estate parties as such, whether a chattel security interest is perfected or unperfected. In no event does a real estate party acquire an interest in a "pure" chattel just because a security interest therein is unperfected. If on the other hand real estate law gives real estate parties an interest in the goods, a conflict arises and this section states the priorities.

(a) The principal exception to the general rule of priority stated in Comment 4(b) based on time of filing or recording is a priority given in paragraph (4)(a) to purchase money security interests in fixtures as against *prior* recorded real estate interests, provided that the purchase money security interest is filed as a fixture filing in the real estate records before the goods become fixtures or within 10 days thereafter. This priority corresponds to one given in Section 9–312(4), and the 10 days of grace represents a reduction of the purchase money priority as against prior interests in the real estate under the present Section 9–313, where the purchase money priority exists even though the security interest is *never* filed.

It should be emphasized that this purchase money priority with the 10-day grace period for filing is limited to rights against *prior* real estate interests. There is no such priority with the 10-day grace period as against subsequent real estate interests. The fixture security interest can defeat subsequent real estate interests only if it is filed first and prevails under the usual conveyancing rule recognized in paragraph (4)(b).

(b) The general principle of priority announced in this section is set forth in paragraph (4)(b). It is basically that a fixture filing gives to the fixture security interest priority as against other real estate interests according to the usual priority rule of conveyancing, that is, the first to file or record prevails. An apparent limitation to this principle set forth in paragraph (4)(b), namely that the secured party must have had priority over any interest of a predecessor in title of the conflicting encumbrancer or owner, is not really a limitation, but is an expression of the usual rule that a person must be entitled to transfer what he has. Thus, if the fixture security interest is subordinate to a mortgage, it is subordinate to an interest of an assignee of the mortgage even though the assignment is a later recorded instrument. Similarly if the fixture security interest is subordinate to the rights of an owner, it is subordinate to a subsequent grantee of the owner and likewise subordinate to a subsequent mortgagee of the owner.

(c) A qualification to the rule based on priority of filing or recording is paragraph (4)(d), where priority based on precedence in filing or recording is preserved, but there is no requirement that as against a judgment lienor of the real estate, the prior filing of the fixture security interest must be in the real estate records. The fixture security interest if perfected first should prevail even though not filed or recorded in real estate records, because generally a judgment creditor is not a reliance creditor who would have searched records. Thus, even a prior filing in the chattel records protects the priority of a fixture security interest against a subsequent judgment lien.

It is hoped that this rule will have the effect of preserving a fixture security interest so filed against invalidation by a trustee in bankruptcy. That would, of course, be the result under Section 60a of the Bankruptcy Act if the time of perfection of the fixture security interest were measured by the judgment creditor test applicable to personal property. It would not be the result if the time of perfection were measured by the purchaser test applicable to real estate. Since the fixture security interest arises against the goods in their capacity as chattels, the bankruptcy courts should apply the judgment creditor test. The effectiveness of the drafting to achieve its purpose cannot be known certainly until the courts adjudicate the question or until it is settled by amendment to Section 60a of the Bankruptcy Act.

The phrase "lien by legal or equitable proceedings" is suggested by Section 70c of the Bankruptcy Act, and is intended to encompass all liens on real estate obtained by any of the creditor action therein described.

(d) A special exception to the usual rule of priority based on precedence in time is the one of paragraph (4)(c) in favor of holders of security interests in factory and office machines, and in certain replacement domestic appliances, as discussed below. This is not as broad an exception as it might seem. To repeat, a fixture conflict is not reached if the goods are held as a matter of local law not to have become part of the real estate, which will frequently be the holding for goods of these types. If the opposite is held, the rule of paragraph (4)(c) operates only if the fixture security interest is perfected before the goods become fixtures. Having been perfected, it would of course have priority over subsequent real estate interests under the rule of paragraph (4)(b). Since it would in almost all cases be a purchase money security interest, it would also have priority over other real estate interests under the purchase-money priority of paragraph (4)(a), discussed in paragraph (a) above. The rule is stated separately because the permitted perfection is by any method permitted by the Article, and not exclusively by fixture filing in the real estate records. This rule is made necessary by the confusions of the law as to whether certain machinery and appliances become fixtures.

As an additional point, in the case of machinery, the separate statement of this rule makes clear that it is not overridden by the construction mortgage priority of subsection (6) discussed in Comment 4(e) below, as would have been true if reliance had been solely on the purchase money priority. Factory and office machines are not always financed as part of a construction mortgage, and the mortgagee should be alert to conflicting chattel financing of these machines.

As to appliances, the rule stated is limited to readily removable replacements, not original installations, of appliances which are consumer goods in the hands of the debtor (Section 9–109). To facilitate financing of original appliances in new dwellings as part of the real estate financing of the dwellings, no special priority is given to chattel financing of original appliances. The section leaves to other law of the state the question whether original installations are fixtures to which the protection accorded by this section to construction mortgages would be applicable. Likewise, it is recognized that (when not supplied by tenants) appliances in commercial apartment buildings are intended as permanent improvements, and no special rule is stated for appliances in that case. The special priority rule here stated in favor of chattel financing is limited to situations where the installation of appliances may not be intended to be permanent, i.e., replacement appliances used by the debtor or his family (consumer goods). The principal effect of the rule is to make clear that a secured party financing occasional replacements of domestic appliances in noncommercial owner-occupied contexts need not concern himself with real estate descriptions or records; indeed, for a purchase-money replacement of consumer goods, perfection without any filing will be possible. (The priority of the construction mortgage has no application to replacement appliances.)

(e) The purchase money priority presents a difficult problem in relation to construction mortgages. The latter will ordinarily have been recorded even before the commencement of delivery of materials to the job, and therefore would be prior in rank to the fixture security interests were it not for the problem of the purchase money priority. Subsection (6) expressly gives priority to the construction mortgage recorded before the filing of the fixture security interest, but this priority of a construction mortgage applies only during the construction period leading to the completion of the improvement. As to additions to the building made long after completion of the improvement, the construction priority will not apply simply because the additions are financed by the real estate mortgagee under an open end clause of his construction mortgage. In such case, the applicable principles will be those of paragraphs (4)(a) and (4)(b). A refinancing of a construction mortgage has the same priority as the mortgage itself.

The phrase "an obligation incurred for the construction of an improvement" covers both optional advances and advances pursuant to commitment, and both types of advances have the same priority under the section.

5. The section makes it impossible for a fixture supplier to retain a security interest against a contractor, to the possible surprise and deception of real estate interests, unless the debtor has an interest of record in the real estate. See paragraphs (4)(a) and (b).

On the other hand, these paragraphs do recognize that fixture filing may be necessary when the debtor is in possession of the real estate (e.g., a lessee) even without an interest of record. This possibility of a filing against a debtor who is not in the real estate chain of title makes it necessary to require the furnishing of the name of a record owner in such cases.

See Sections 9–402(3), item 3; 9–402(5); 9–403(7).

6. The status of fixtures installed by tenants (as well as such persons as licensees and holders of easements) is defined by paragraph (5)(b) to the effect that if the debtor (tenant or other interest mentioned) has the right to remove the fixture as against a real estate interest, the secured party has priority over that real estate interest.

7. Real estate lenders and title companies will have little difficulty in locating relevant fixture security interests applicable to particular parcels of real estate because of the provisions as to real estate description in fixture filings, the indexing thereof, and other related provisions in Part 4 of Article 9.

8. Real estate lending is typically long-term, and is usually done by institutional investors who can afford to take a long view of the matter rather than concentrating on the results of any particular case. It is apparent that the rule which permits and encourages purchase money fixture financing, which in contrast is typically short-term, will result in the modernization and improvement of real estate rather than in its deterioration and will on balance benefit long-term real estate lenders. Because of the short-term character of the chattel financing, it will rarely produce any conflict in fact with the real estate lender. The contrary rule would chill the availability of short-term credit for modernization of real estate by installation of new fixtures and in the long run could not help real estate lenders.

9. Subsection (8) is an important departure from Section 7 of the Uniform Conditional Sales Act and from much other conditional sales legislation. Under the Uniform Conditional Sales Act a conditional vendor could not sever and remove the affixed chattel if a "material injury to the freehold" would result. The courts of various jurisdictions were in sharp disagreement on the meaning of "material injury"; some held that only physical injury was meant; others adopted the so-called "institutional theory" and denied removal whenever the "going value" of the structure would be materially diminished by the removal. Under these rules the conditional vendor either could not remove at all, or, if he could, could damage the structure on removal without becoming accountable to the real estate claimant. The situation was complicated by the fact that it became increasingly difficult to predict what types of goods the courts in a given jurisdiction would hold not subject to removal.

Subsection (8) abandons the "material injury to the freehold" rule. Instead a secured party entitled to priority may in all cases sever and remove his collateral, subject, however, to a duty to reimburse any real estate claimant (other than the debtor himself) for any physical injury caused by the removal. The right to reimbursement is implemented by the last sentence of subsection (8) which gives the real estate claimant a statutory right to security or indemnity failing which he may refuse permission to remove. The subsection (8) rule thus accomplishes two things: it puts an end to the uncertainty which has grown up under the "material injury" rule, while at the same time it protects the real estate claimant under the reimbursement provisions.

Cross References:

Sections 2–107, 9–102(1), 9–104(j) and 9–312(1), and Parts 4 and 5.

Definitional Cross References:

"Collateral". Section 9–105.
"Contract". Section 1–201.
"Creditor". Section 1–201.
"Debtor". Section 9–105.
"Encumbrance". Section 9–105.
"Goods". Section 9–105.
"Knowledge". Section 1–201.
"Mortgage". Section 9–105.
"Person". Section 1–201.
"Purchase". Section 1–201.
"Purchaser". Section 1–201.
"Secured party". Section 9–105.
"Security interest". Section 1–201.
"Value". Section 1–201.
"Writing". Section 1–201.

§ 9-314. Accessions.

(1) A security interest in goods which attaches before they are installed in or affixed to other goods takes priority as to the goods installed or affixed (called in this section "accessions") over the claims of all persons to the whole except as stated in subsection (3) and subject to Section 9-315(1).

(2) A security interest which attaches to goods after they become part of a whole is valid against all persons subsequently acquiring interests in the whole except as stated in subsection (3) but is invalid against any person with an interest in the whole at the time the security interest attaches to the goods who has not in writing consented to the security interest or disclaimed an interest in the goods as part of the whole.

(3) The security interests described in subsections (1) and (2) do not take priority over

(a) a subsequent purchaser for value of any interest in the whole; or

(b) a creditor with a lien on the whole subsequently obtained by judicial proceedings; or

(c) a creditor with a prior perfected security interest in the whole to the extent that he makes subsequent advances

if the subsequent purchase is made, the lien by judicial proceedings obtained or the subsequent advance under the prior perfected security interest is made or contracted for without knowledge of the security interest and before it is perfected. A purchaser of the whole at a foreclosure sale other than the holder of a perfected security interest purchasing at his own foreclosure sale is a subsequent purchaser within this section.

(4) When under subsections (1) or (2) and (3) a secured party has an interest in accessions which has priority over the claims of all persons who have interests in the whole, he may on default subject to the provisions of Part 5 remove his collateral from the whole but he must reimburse any encumbrancer or owner of the whole who is not the debtor and who has not otherwise agreed for the cost of repair of any physical injury but not for any diminution in value of the whole caused by the absence of the goods removed or by any necessity for replacing them. A person entitled to reimbursement may refuse permission to remove until the secured party gives adequate security for the performance of this obligation.

Official Comment

Prior Uniform Statutory Provision: None.

Purposes:

1. To state when a secured party claiming an interest in goods installed in or affixed to other goods is entitled to priority over a party with a security interest in the whole.

2. This section changes prior law in that the secured party claiming an interest in a part (e.g., a new motor in an old car) is entitled to priority and has a right to remove even though under other rules of law the part now belongs to the whole.

3. This section does not apply to goods which, for example, are so commingled in a manufacturing process that their original identity is lost. That type of situation is covered in Section 9-315. Section 9-315 should also be consulted for the

effect of a financing statement which claims both component parts and the resulting product.

Cross References:

Sections 9-203(1), 9-303 and 9-312(1) and Part 5.

Point 3: Section 9-315.

Definitional Cross References:

"Collateral". Section 9-105.
"Creditor". Section 1-201.
"Debtor". Section 9-105.
"Goods". Section 9-105.
"Knowledge". Section 1-201.
"Person". Section 1-201.
"Purchaser". Section 1-201.
"Secured party". Section 9-105.
"Security interest". Section 1-201.
"Value". Section 1-201.
"Writing". Section 1-201.

§ 9-315. Priority When Goods Are Commingled or Processed.

(1) If a security interest in goods was perfected and subsequently the goods or a part thereof have become part of a product or mass, the security interest continues in the product or mass if

(a) the goods are so manufactured, processed, assembled or commingled that their identity is lost in the product or mass; or

(b) a financing statement covering the original goods also covers the product into which the goods have been manufactured, processed or assembled.

In a case to which paragraph (b) applies, no separate security interest in that part of the original goods which has been manufactured, processed or assembled into the product may be claimed under Section 9-314.

(2) When under subsection (1) more than one security interest attaches to the product or mass, they rank equally according to the ratio that the cost of the goods to which each interest originally attached bears to the cost of the total product or mass.

Official Comment

Prior Uniform Statutory Provision: None.

Purposes:

1. To state when a secured party whose collateral contributes to a product has priority over others who have conflicting claims in the same product.

2. This section changes the law in some jurisdictions where a security interest in goods (e.g., raw materials) was lost when the goods lost their identity by being commingled or processed. Under this section the security interest continues in the resulting mass or product in the cases stated in subsection (1).

3. This section applies not only to cases where flour, sugar and eggs are commingled into cake mix or cake, but also to cases where components are assembled into a machine. In the latter case a secured party is put to an election at the time of filing, by the last sentence of subsection (1), whether to claim under this section or to claim a security interest in one component under Section 9-314.

4. Subsection (2) is new and is needed because under subsection (1) it is possible to have more than one secured party claiming an interest in a product. The rule stated treats all such interests as being of equal priority entitled to share ratably in the product.

Cross References:

Sections 9-203(1), 9-303, 9-312(1) and 9-314.

Definitional Cross References:

"Goods". Section 9-105.
"Security interest". Section 1-201.

§ 9–316. Priority Subject to Subordination.

Nothing in this Article prevents subordination by agreement by any person entitled to priority.

Official Comment

Prior Uniform Statutory Provision: None.

Purposes:

The several preceding sections deal elaborately with questions of priority. This section is inserted to make it entirely clear that a person entitled to priority may effectively agree to subordinate his claim. Only the person entitled to priority may make such an agreement: his rights cannot be adversely affected by an agreement to which he is not a party.

Cross References:

Sections 1–102 and 9–312(1).

Definitional Cross References:

"Agreement". Section 1–201.
"Person". Section 1–201.

§ 9–317. Secured Party Not Obligated on Contract of Debtor.

The mere existence of a security interest or authority given to the debtor to dispose of or use collateral does not impose contract or tort liability upon the secured party for the debtor's acts or omissions.

Official Comment

Prior Uniform Statutory Provision: Section 12, Uniform Trust Receipts Act.

Purposes:

There were a few common law decisions, mostly in cases involving trust receipts, which suggested, if they did not hold, that a secured party who gave his debtor liberty of sale might be liable (for example, for breach of warranty) on the debtor's contracts of sale. The theory was grounded on the law of agency; the debtor being regarded as selling agent for the secured party as principal. This section rejects that theory. Section 12 of the Uniform Trust Receipts Act provided that the entruster was not subject to liability, merely because of his status as entruster, on sale of the goods subject to trust receipt. This section adopts the policy of the prior act and states it in general terms.

Cross Reference:

Section 2–210(4).

Definitional Cross References:

"Collateral". Section 9–105.
"Contract". Section 1–201.
"Debtor". Section 9–105.
"Secured party". Section 9–105.
"Security interest". Section 1–201.

§ 9–318. Defenses Against Assignee; Modification of Contract After Notification of Assignment; Term Prohibiting Assignment Ineffective; Identification and Proof of Assignment.

(1) Unless an account debtor has made an enforceable agreement not to assert defenses or claims arising out of a sale as provided in Section 9–206 the rights of an assignee are subject to

(a) all the terms of the contract between the account debtor and assignor and any defense or claim arising therefrom; and

(b) any other defense or claim of the account debtor against the assignor which accrues before the account debtor receives notification of the assignment.

(2) So far as the right to payment or a part thereof under an assigned contract has not been fully earned by performance, and notwithstanding notification of the assignment, any modification of or substitution for the contract made in good faith and in accordance with reasonable commercial standards is effective against an assignee unless the account debtor has otherwise agreed but the assignee acquires corresponding rights under the modified or substituted contract. The assignment may provide that such modification or substitution is a breach by the assignor.

(3) The account debtor is authorized to pay the assignor until the account debtor receives notification that the amount due or to become due has been assigned and that payment is to be made to the assignee. A notification which does not reasonably identify the rights assigned is ineffective. If requested by the account debtor, the assignee must seasonably furnish reasonable proof that the assignment has been made and unless he does so the account debtor may pay the assignor.

(4) A term in any contract between an account debtor and an assignor is ineffective if it prohibits assignment of an account or prohibits creation of a security interest in a general intangible for money due or to become due or requires the account debtor's consent to such assignment or security interest.

As amended in 1972.

Official Comment

Prior Uniform Statutory Provision: Section 9(3), Uniform Trust Receipts Act.

Purposes:

1. Subsection (1) makes no substantial change in prior law. An assignee has traditionally been subject to defenses or set-offs existing before an account debtor is notified of the assignment. When the account debtor's defenses on an assigned claim arise from the contract between him and the assignor, it makes no difference whether the breach giving rise to the defense occurs before or after the account debtor is notified of the assignment (paragraph (1)(a)). The account debtor may also have claims against the assignor which arise independently of that contract: an assignee is subject to all such claims which accrue before, and free of all those which accrue after, the account debtor is notified (paragraph (1)(b)). The account debtor may waive his right to assert claims or defenses against an assignee to the extent provided in Section 9-206.

2. Prior law was in confusion as to whether modification of an executory contract by account debtor and assignor without the assignee's consent was possible after notification of an assignment. Subsection (2) makes good faith modifications by assignor and account debtor without the assignee's consent effective against the assignee even after notification. This rule may do some violence to accepted doctrines of contract law. Nevertheless it is a sound and indeed a necessary rule in view of the realities of large scale procurement. When for example it becomes necessary for a government agency to cut back or modify existing contracts, comparable arrangements must be made promptly in hundreds and even thousands of subcontracts lying in many tiers below the prime contract. Typically the right to payments under these subcontracts will have been assigned. The government, as sovereign, might have the

right to amend or terminate existing contracts apart from statute. This subsection gives the prime contractor (the account debtor) the right to make the required arrangements directly with his subcontractors without undertaking the task of procuring assents from the many banks to whom rights under the contracts may have been assigned. Assignees are protected by the provision which gives them automatically corresponding rights under the modified or substituted contract. Notice that subsection (2) applies only so far as the right to payment has not been earned by performance, and therefore its application ends entirely when the work is done or the goods furnished.

3. Subsection (3) clarifies the right of an account debtor to make payment to his seller-assignor in an "indirect collection" situation (see Comment to Section 9-308). So long as the assignee permits the assignor to collect claims or leaves him in possession of chattel paper which does not indicate that payment is to be made at some place other than the assignor's place of business, the account debtor may pay the assignor even though he may know of the assignment. In such a situation an assignee who wants to take over collections must notify the account debtor to make further payments to him.

4. Subsection (4) breaks sharply with the older contract doctrines by denying effectiveness to contractual terms prohibiting assignment of sums due and to become due under contracts of sale, construction contracts and the like. Under the rule as stated, an assignment would be effective even if made to an assignee who took with full knowledge that the account debtor had sought to prohibit or restrict assignment of the claims.

It is only for the past hundred years that our law has recognized the possibility of assigning choses in action. The history of this development, at law and equity, is in broad outline well known. Lingering traces of the absolute common law prohibition have survived almost to our own day.

There can be no doubt that a term prohibiting assignment of proceeds was effective against an assignee with notice through the nineteenth century and well into the twentieth. Section 151 of the Restatement of Contracts (1932) so states the law without qualification, but the changing character of the law is shown in the proposed Section 154 of the Restatement, Second, Contracts.

The original rule of law has been progressively undermined by a process of erosion which began much earlier than the cited section of the Restatement of Contracts would suggest. The cases are legion in which courts have construed the heart out of prohibitory or restrictive terms and held the assignment good. The cases are not lacking where courts have flatly held assignments valid without bothering to construe away the prohibition. See 4 Corbin on Contracts (1951) §§ 872, 873. Such cases as Allhusen v. Caristo Const. Corp., 303 N.Y. 446, 103 N.E.2d 891 (1952), are rejected by this subsection.

This gradual and largely unacknowledged shift in legal doctrine has taken place in response to economic need: as accounts and other rights under contracts have become the collateral which secures an ever increasing number of financing transactions, it has been necessary to reshape the law so that these intangibles, like negotiable instruments and negotiable documents of title, can be freely assigned.

Subsection (4) thus states a rule of law which is widely recognized in the cases and which corresponds to current business practices. It can be regarded as a revolutionary departure only by those who still cherish the hope that we may yet return to the views entertained some two hundred years ago by the Court of King's Bench.

5. The Federal Assignment of Claims Act of 1940—to which of course this section is subject—requires that assignments of claims against the United States be filed as provided in that Act. Many large business enterprises, situated like the

United States in that claims against them are held by hundreds or thousands of subcontractors or suppliers, often require in their contract or purchase order forms that assignments against them be filed in a prescribed way. Subsection (3) requires reasonable identification of the account assigned and recognizes the right of an account debtor to require reasonable proof of the making of the assignment and to that extent validates such requirements in contracts or purchase order forms. If the notification does not contain such reasonable identification or if such reasonable proof is not furnished on request, the account debtor may disregard the assignment and make payment to the assignor. What is "reasonable" is not left to the arbitrary decision of the account debtor; if there is doubt as to the adequacy either of a notification or of proof submitted after request, the account debtor may not be safe in disregarding it unless he has notified the assignee with commercial promptness as to the respects in which identification or proof is considered defective.

6. If the thing to be assigned is the beneficiary's right under a letter of credit, Section 5-116 should be consulted.

Cross References:

Point 1: Section 9-206.
Point 3: Sections 9-205 and 9-308.
Point 4: Section 2-210(2) and (3).
Point 6: Section 5-116.

Definitional Cross References:

"Account". Section 9-106.
"Account debtor". Section 9-105.
"Agreement". Section 1-201.
"Contract". Section 1-201.
"Good faith". Section 1-201.
"Party". Section 1-201.
"Receives" notification. Section 1-201.
"Rights". Section 1-201.
"Sale". Sections 2-106 and 9-105.
"Seasonably". Section 1-204.
"Term". Section 1-201.

PART 4

FILING

§ 9-401. Place of Filing; Erroneous Filing; Removal of Collateral.

First Alternative Subsection (1)

(1) The proper place to file in order to perfect a security interest is as follows:

(a) when the collateral is timber to be cut or is minerals or the like (including oil and gas) or accounts subject to subsection (5) of Section 9-103, or when the financing statement is filed as a fixture filing (Section 9-313) and the collateral is goods which are or are to become fixtures, then in the office where a mortgage on the real estate would be filed or recorded;

(b) in all other cases, in the office of the [Secretary of State].

Second Alternative Subsection (1)

(1) The proper place to file in order to perfect a security interest is as follows:

(a) when the collateral is equipment used in farming operations, or farm products, or accounts or general intangibles arising from or relating to the sale of farm products by a farmer, or consumer goods, then in the office of the ______ in the county of the debtor's residence or if the debtor is not a resident of this state then in the office of the _______ in the county where the goods are kept, and in addition when the collateral is crops growing or to be grown in the office of the _______ in the county where the land is located;

(b) when the collateral is timber to be cut or is minerals or the like (including oil and gas) or accounts subject to subsection (5) of Section 9–103, or when the financing statement is filed as a fixture filing (Section 9–313) and the collateral is goods which are or are to become fixtures, then in the office where a mortgage on the real estate would be filed or recorded;

(c) in all other cases, in the office of the [Secretary of State].

Third Alternative Subsection (1)

(1) The proper place to file in order to perfect a security interest is as follows:

(a) when the collateral is equipment used in farming operations, or farm products, or accounts or general intangibles arising from or relating to the sale of farm products by a farmer, or consumer goods, then in the office of the _______ in the county of the debtor's residence or if the debtor is not a resident of this state then in the office of the _______ in the county where the goods are kept, and in addition when the collateral is crops growing or to be grown in the office of the _______ in the county where the land is located;

(b) when the collateral is timber to be cut or is minerals or the like (including oil and gas) or accounts subject to subsection (5) of Section 9–103, or when the financing statement is filed as a fixture filing (Section 9–313) and the collateral is goods which are or are to become fixtures, then in the office where a mortgage on the real estate would be filed or recorded;

(c) in all other cases, in the office of the [Secretary of State] and in addition, if the debtor has a place of business in only one county of this state, also in the office of _______ of such county, or, if the debtor has no place of business in this state, but resides in the state, also in the office of _______ of the county in which he resides.

Note: *One of the three alternatives should be selected as subsection (1).*

(2) A filing which is made in good faith in an improper place or not in all of the places required by this section is nevertheless effective with regard to any collateral as to which the filing complied with the requirements of this Article and is also effective with regard to collateral covered by the financing statement against any person who has knowledge of the contents of such financing statement.

(3) A filing which is made in the proper place in this state continues effective even though the debtor's residence or place of business or the location of the collateral or its use, whichever controlled the original filing, is thereafter changed.

Alternative Subsection (3)

[(3) A filing which is made in the proper county continues effective for four months after a change to another county of the debtor's residence or place of business or the location of the collateral, whichever controlled the original filing. It becomes ineffective thereafter unless a copy of the financing statement signed by the secured party is filed in the new county within said period. The security interest may also be perfected in the new county after the expiration of the four-month period; in such case perfection dates from the time of perfection in the new county. A change in the use of the collateral does not impair the effectiveness of the original filing.]

(4) The rules stated in Section 9–103 determine whether filing is necessary in this state.

(5) Notwithstanding the preceding subsections, and subject to subsection (3) of Section 9–302, the proper place to file in order to perfect a security interest in collateral, including fixtures, of a transmitting utility is the office of the [Secretary of State]. This filing constitutes a fixture filing (Section 9–313) as to the collateral described therein which is or is to become fixtures.

(6) For the purposes of this section, the residence of an organization is its place of business if it has one or its chief executive office if it has more than one place of business.

Note: *Subsection (6) should be used only if the state chooses the Second or Third Alternative Subsection (1).*

As amended in 1962 and 1972.

Official Comment

Prior Uniform Statutory Provision: Section 4, Uniform Trust Receipts Act; Sections 6 and 7, Uniform Conditional Sales Act.

Purposes:

1. Under chattel mortgage acts, the Uniform Conditional Sales Act and other conditional sales legislation the geographical unit for filing or recording was local: the county or township in which the mortgagor or vendee resided or in which the goods sold or mortgaged were kept. The Uniform Trust Receipts Act used the state as the geographical filing unit: under that Act statements of trust receipt financing were filed with an official in the state capital and were not filed locally. The state-wide filing system of the Trust Receipts Act has been followed in many accounts receivable and factor's lien acts.

Both systems have their advocates and both their own advantages and drawbacks. The principal advantage of state-wide filing is ease of access to the credit information which the files exist to provide. Consider for example the national distributor who wishes to have current information about the credit standing of the thousands of persons he sells to on credit. The more completely the files are centralized on a state-wide basis, the easier and cheaper it becomes to procure credit information; the more the files are scattered in local filing units, the more burdensome and costly. On the other hand, it can be said that most credit inquiries about local businesses, farmers and consumers come from local sources; convenience is served by having the files locally available and there is not great advantage in centralized filing.

This section does not attempt to resolve the controversy between the advocates of a completely centralized state-wide filing system and those of a large degree of local autonomy. Instead the section is drafted in a series of alternatives; local considerations of policy will determine the choice to be made.

2. Fortunately there is general agreement that the proper filing place for security interests in fixtures is in the office where a mortgage on the real estate concerned would be filed or recorded, and paragraph (1)(a) in the First Alternative and paragraph (1)(b) in the Second and Third Alternatives so provide. This provision follows the Uniform Conditional Sales Act. Note that there is no requirement for an additional filing with the chattel records.

3. In states where it is felt wise to preserve local filing for transactions of essentially local interest, either the Second or Third Alternative of subsection (1) should be adopted. Paragraph (1)(a) in both alternatives provides county (township, etc.) filing for consumer goods transactions and for agricultural transactions (farm equipment, farm products, farm accounts and crops). Note that the subsection departs from Section 6 of the Uniform Conditional Sales Act and adopts instead the policy of many chattel mortgage acts in selecting the county of the debtor's residence, rather than the county where the goods are located, as the normal filing place. Where, however, the debtor is an out-of-state resident, the filing must of necessity be in the county where the goods are, and the subsection so provides. Though not expressly stated, it is evident that filing for an assignment of accounts arising from the sale of farm products by a farmer who is not a resident must be in the county where the debtor keeps his farm products. In the case of crops growing or to be grown, where the land is in one county and the debtor's residence in another, filing must be made in both counties. Neither this filing for crops in the county where the land is nor the requirements that the security agreement (Section 9-203(1)(a)) and the financing statement (Section 9-402(1) and (3)) contain a description of the real estate point to the conclusion that a financing statement for a security interest in crops must be filed in the real estate records. This Article follows pre-Code law which recognized such a financing as a chattel mortgage. The policy of the subsection is to require filing in the place or places where a creditor would normally look for information concerning interests created by the debtor.

For some incorporated farmers, reference to residence is an anomaly. Therefore subsection (6) provides that the residence of an organization is its place of business, or its chief executive office if it has more than one place of business. Compare Section 9-103(3), which reaches essentially the same concept as a definition of the "location" of a debtor.

4. It is thought that sound policy requires a state-wide filing system for all transactions except the essentially local ones covered in paragraph (1)(a) of the Second and Third Alternatives and land-related transactions covered in paragraph (1)(b) of the Second and Third Alternatives. Paragraph (1)(c) so provides in both alternatives, as does paragraph (1)(b) in the First Alternative. In a state which has adopted either the Second or Third Alternative, central filing would be required when the collateral was goods except consumer goods, farm equipment or farm products (including crops), or was documents or chattel paper or was accounts or general intangibles, unless related to a farm. Note that the filing provisions of this Article do not apply to instruments (see Section 9-304).

If the Third Alternative subsection (1) is adopted, then local filing, in addition to the central filing, is required in all the cases stated in the preceding paragraph, with respect to any debtor whose places of business within the state are all within a single county (township, etc.) or a debtor who is not engaged in business. The last event test stated in Section 9-103(1)(b) and Comment thereto applies to determine whether local filing is required under the present section, as well as to determine in which state filing is required.

In states where the arguments for a completely centralized set of files (except for fixtures) prevail, the First Alternative subsection (1) should be adopted. That alternative provides for exclusive central filing of all security interests except those in fixtures.

5. When a secured party has in good faith attempted to comply with the filing requirements but has not done so correctly, subsection (2) makes his filing effective in so far as it was proper, and also makes it good for all collateral covered by the financing statement against any person who actually knows the contents of the improperly filed statement. The subsection rejects the occasional decisions that an improperly filed record is ineffective to give notice even to a person who knows of it. But if the Third Alternative subsection (1) is adopted, the requirements of paragraph (1)(c) are not complied with unless there is filing in both offices specified; filing in only one of two required places is not effective except as against one with actual knowledge of the contents of the defective financing statement.

6. Subsection (3) deals with change of residence or place of business or the location or use of the goods *after* a proper filing has been made. The subsection is important only when local filing is required, and covers only changes between local filing units in the state. For changes of location between states see Section 9-103(1)(d).

Subsection (3) is presented in alternative forms. Under the first no new filing is required in the county to which the collateral has been removed. Under alternative subsection (3) the original filing lapses four months after the change in location; this is basically the same rule that is applied by Section 9-103(1)(d) to the case of collateral brought into the state subject to a security interest which attached elsewhere.

7. The usual filing rules do not apply well for a transmitting utility (defined in Section 9-105). Many pre-Code statutes provided special filing rules for railroads and in some cases for other public utilities to avoid the requirements for filing with legal descriptions in every county in which such debtors had property. The Code recreates and broadens these provisions by subsection (5) of this section, which provides that for transmitting utilities the filing need only be in the office of the Secretary of State. The nature of the debtor will inform persons searching the record as to where to make a search.

Cross References:

Sections 9-302, 9-304 and 9-307(2).
Point 2: Section 9-313.
Point 6: Section 9-103(3).
Point 7: Sections 9-402(5) and 9-403(6).

Definitional Cross References:

"Account". Section 9-106.
"Collateral". Section 9-105.
"Consumer goods". Section 9-109.
"Debtor". Section 9-105.
"Equipment". Section 9-109.
"Farm products". Section 9-109.
"Financing statement". Section 9-402.
"Fixture filing". Section 9-313.
"Good faith". Section 1-201.
"Goods". Section 9-105.
"Knowledge". Section 1-201.
"Person". Section 1-201.
"Secured party". Section 9-105.
"Security interest". Section 1-201.
"Signed". Section 1-201.
"Transmitting utility". Section 9-105.

§ 9-402. Formal Requisites of Financing Statement; Amendments; Mortgage as Financing Statement.

(1) A financing statement is sufficient if it gives the names of the debtor and the secured party, is signed by the debtor, gives an address of the secured party from which information concerning the security interest may be obtained, gives a mailing address of the debtor and contains a statement indicating the types, or describing the items, of collateral. A financing

statement may be filed before a security agreement is made or a security interest otherwise attaches. When the financing statement covers crops growing or to be grown, the statement must also contain a description of the real estate concerned. When the financing statement covers timber to be cut or covers minerals or the like (including oil and gas) or accounts subject to subsection (5) of Section 9–103, or when the financing statement is filed as a fixture filing (Section 9–313) and the collateral is goods which are or are to become fixtures, the statement must also comply with subsection (5). A copy of the security agreement is sufficient as a financing statement if it contains the above information and is signed by the debtor. A carbon, photographic or other reproduction of a security agreement or a financing statement is sufficient as a financing statement if the security agreement so provides or if the original has been filed in this state.

(2) A financing statement which otherwise complies with subsection (1) is sufficient when it is signed by the secured party instead of the debtor if it is filed to perfect a security interest in

(a) collateral already subject to a security interest in another jurisdiction when it is brought into this state, or when the debtor's location is changed to this state. Such a financing statement must state that the collateral was brought into this state or that the debtor's location was changed to this state under such circumstances; or

(b) proceeds under Section 9–306 if the security interest in the original collateral was perfected. Such a financing statement must describe the original collateral; or

(c) collateral as to which the filing has lapsed; or

(d) collateral acquired after a change of name, identity or corporate structure of the debtor (subsection (7)).

(3) A form substantially as follows is sufficient to comply with subsection (1):

Name of debtor (or assignor) ____________________

Address ____________________

Name of secured party (or assignee) ____________________

Address ____________________

1. This financing statement covers the following types (or items) of property:

(Describe) ____________________

2. (If collateral is crops) The above described crops are growing or are to be grown on:

(Describe Real Estate) ____________________

3. (If applicable) The above goods are to become fixtures on*

* Where appropriate substitute either "The above timber is standing on ...." or "The above minerals or the like (including oil and gas) or accounts will be financed at the well-head or minehead of the well or mine located on ...."

(Describe Real Estate) ______ and this financing statement is to be filed [for record] in the real estate records. (If the debtor does not have an interest of record) The name of a record owner is ______

4. (If products of collateral are claimed) Products of the collateral are also covered.

(use)	....
whichever)	Signature of Debtor (or Assignor)
is)	....
applicable))	Signature of Secured Party (or Assignee)

(4) A financing statement may be amended by filing a writing signed by both the debtor and the secured party. An amendment does not extend the period of effectiveness of a financing statement. If any amendment adds collateral, it is effective as to the added collateral only from the filing date of the amendment. In this Article, unless the context otherwise requires, the term "financing statement" means the original financing statement and any amendments.

(5) A financing statement covering timber to be cut or covering minerals or the like (including oil and gas) or accounts subject to subsection (5) of Section 9–103, or a financing statement filed as a fixture filing (Section 9–313) where the debtor is not a transmitting utility, must show that it covers this type of collateral, must recite that it is to be filed [for record] in the real estate records, and the financing statement must contain a description of the real estate [sufficient if it were contained in a mortgage of the real estate to give constructive notice of the mortgage under the law of this state]. If the debtor does not have an interest of record in the real estate, the financing statement must show the name of a record owner.

(6) A mortgage is effective as a financing statement filed as a fixture filing from the date of its recording if

(a) the goods are described in the mortgage by item or type; and

(b) the goods are or are to become fixtures related to the real estate described in the mortgage; and

(c) the mortgage complies with the requirements for a financing statement in this section other than a recital that it is to be filed in the real estate records; and

(d) the mortgage is duly recorded.

No fee with reference to the financing statement is required other than the regular recording and satisfaction fees with respect to the mortgage.

(7) A financing statement sufficiently shows the name of the debtor if it gives the individual, partnership or corporate name of the debtor, whether or not it adds other trade names or names of partners. Where the debtor so changes his name or in the case of an organization its name, identity or corporate structure that a filed financing statement becomes seriously misleading, the filing is not effective to perfect a security interest in collateral acquired by the debtor more than four months after the change, unless a new appropriate financing statement is filed before the expiration of that time. A

filed financing statement remains effective with respect to collateral transferred by the debtor even though the secured party knows of or consents to the transfer.

(8) A financing statement substantially complying with the requirements of this section is effective even though it contains minor errors which are not seriously misleading.

Note: *Language in brackets is optional.*

Note: *Where the state has any special recording system for real estate other than the usual grantor-grantee index (as, for instance, a tract system or a title registration or Torrens system) local adaptations of subsection (5) and Section 9-403(7) may be necessary. See Mass.Gen. Laws Chapter 106, Section 9-409.*

As amended in 1972.

Official Comment

Prior Uniform Statutory Provision: Sections 13(3), 13(4), Uniform Trust Receipts Act.

Purposes:

1. Subsection (1) sets out the simple formal requisites of a financing statement under this Article. These requirements are: (1) signature of the debtor; (2) addresses of both parties; (3) a description of the collateral by type or item.

Where the collateral is crops growing or to be grown or when the financing statement is filed as a fixture filing (Section 9-313) or when the collateral is timber to be cut or minerals or the like (including oil and gas) financed at wellhead or minehead or accounts resulting from the sale thereof, the financing statement must also contain a description of the lands concerned. On description generally, see Section 9-110 and Comment 5 to the present section. An important distinction must be drawn, however, between the function of the description of land in reference to crops and its function in the other cases mentioned. For crops it is merely part of the description of the crops concerned, and the security interest in crops is a Code security interest, like the pre-Code "crop mortgage" which was a *chattel* mortgage. In contrast, in the other cases mentioned the function of the description of land is to have the financing statement filed in the county where the land is situated and in the realty records, as distinguished from the chattel records. Subsection (3) suggests a form which complies with the statutory requirements and makes clear that for the types of collateral mentioned other than crops, the financing statement containing a description of the land concerned is to go in the realty records. Note also subsection (5) on the adequacy of the description of land where the filing is to be in the real estate records. See also Section 9-403(7) on the indexing of these filings in the real estate records.

A copy of the security agreement may be filed in place of a separate financing statement, if it contains the required information and signature.

2. This section adopts the system of "notice filing" which proved successful under the Uniform Trust Receipts Act. What is required to be filed is not, as under chattel mortgage and conditional sales acts, the security agreement itself, but only a simple notice which may be filed before the security interest attaches or thereafter. The notice itself indicates merely that the secured party who has filed may have a security interest in the collateral described. Further inquiry from the parties concerned will be necessary to disclose the complete state of affairs. Section 9-208 provides a statutory procedure under which the secured party, at the debtor's request, may be required

to make disclosure. Notice filing has proved to be of great use in financing transactions involving inventory, accounts and chattel paper, since it obviates the necessity of refiling on each of a series of transactions in a continuing arrangement where the collateral changes from day to day. Where other types of collateral are involved, the alternative procedure of filing a signed copy of the security agreement may prove to be the simplest solution. Sometimes more than one copy of a financing statement or of a security agreement used as a financing statement is needed for filing. In such a case the section permits use of a carbon copy or photographic copy of the paper, including signatures.

However, even in the case of filings that do not necessarily involve a series of transactions the financing statement is effective to encompass transactions under a security agreement not in existence and not contemplated at the time the notice was filed, if the description of collateral in the financing statement is broad enough to encompass them. Similarly, the financing statement is valid to cover after-acquired property and future advances under security agreements whether or not mentioned in the financing statement.

3. This section departs from the requirements of many pre-Code chattel mortgage statutes that the instrument filed be acknowledged or witnessed or accompanied by affidavits of good faith. Those requirements did not seem to have been successful as a deterrent to fraud; their principal effect was to penalize good faith mortgagees who had inadvertently failed to comply with the statutory niceties. They are here abandoned in the interest of a simplified and workable filing system.

4. Subsection (2) allows the secured party to file a financing statement signed only by himself where the filing is required by any of the events listed, each of which occurs after the commencement of the financing, and therefore under circumstances where the cooperation of the debtor is not certain. Section 9–401(3), alternative provision, contains similar permission on removal between counties in this state. The secured party should not be penalized for failure to make a timely filing by reason of difficulty in procuring the signature of a possibly reluctant or hostile debtor. Financing statements filed under this subsection must explain the circumstances under which they are filed with the signature of the secured party rather than that of the debtor.

In contrast to the signatures on original financing statements, an amendment to a financing statement must be signed by both parties, to preclude either from adversely affecting the interests of the other.

The reference in subsection (4) to an amendment which "adds collateral" refers to additional types of collateral. A security interest on additional units of a type of collateral already described can be created under an after-acquired property clause or a new security agreement. See Comment 5 to Section 9–204. On priorities in such cases see Section 9–312 and Comments thereto.

5. A description of real estate must be sufficient to identify it. See Section 9–110. This formulation rejects the view that the real estate description must be by metes and bounds, or otherwise conforming to traditional real estate practice in conveyancing, but of course the incorporation of such a description by reference to the recording data of a deed, mortgage or other instrument containing the description should suffice under the most stringent standards. The proper test is that a description of real estate must be sufficient so that the fixture financing statement will fit into the real estate search system and the financing statement be found by a real estate searcher. Optional language has been added by which the test of adequacy of the description is whether it would be adequate in a mortgage of the real estate. As suggested in the Note, more detail may be required if there is a tract indexing system or a land registration system.

Where the debtor does not have an interest of record in the real estate, a fixture financing statement must show the name of a record owner, and Section 9–403(7) requires the financing statement to be indexed in the name of that owner. Thus the fixture financing statement will fit into the real estate search system.

6. A real estate mortgage may provide that it constitutes a security agreement with respect to fixtures (or other goods) in conformity with this Article. Combined mortgages on real estate and chattels are common and useful for certain purposes. This section goes further and makes provision that the recording of the real estate mortgage (if it complies with the requirements of a financing statement) shall constitute the filing of a financing statement as to the fixtures (but not, of course, as to the other goods). Section 9–403(6) makes the usual five-year maximum life for financing statements inapplicable to real estate mortgages which operate as financing statements under Section 9–402(6), and they are effective for the duration of the real estate recording.

Of course, if a combined mortgage covers chattels which are not fixtures, a regular chattel filing is necessary, and subsection (6) is inapplicable to such chattels. Likewise, filing as a "fixture filing" provided in Section 9–401 does not apply to true chattels.

7. Subsection (7) undertakes to deal with some of the problems as to who is the debtor. In the case of individuals, it contemplates filing only in the individual name, not in a trade name. In the case of partnerships it contemplates filing in the partnership name, not in the names of any of the partners, and not in any other trade names. Trade names are deemed to be too uncertain and too likely not to be known to the secured party or person searching the record, to form the basis for a filing system. However, provision is made in Section 9–403(5) for indexing in a trade name if the secured party so desires.

Subsection (7) also deals with the case of a change of name of a debtor and provides some guidelines when mergers or other changes of corporate structure of the debtor occur with the result that a filed financing statement might become seriously misleading. Not all cases can be imagined and covered by statutes in advance; however, the principle sought to be achieved by the subsection is that after a change which would be seriously misleading, the old financing statement is not effective as to new collateral acquired more than four months after the change, unless a new appropriate financing statement is filed before the expiration of the four months. The old financing statement, if legally still valid under the circumstances, would continue to protect collateral acquired before the change and, if still operative under the particular circumstances, would also protect collateral acquired within the four months. Obviously, the subsection does not undertake to state whether the old security agreement continues to operate between the secured party and the party surviving the corporate change of the debtor.

8. Subsection (7) also deals with a different problem, namely whether a new filing is necessary where the collateral has been transferred from one debtor to another. This question has been much debated both in pre-Code law and under the Code. This Article now answers the question in the negative. Thus, any person searching the condition of the ownership of a debtor must make inquiry as to the debtor's source of title, and must search in the name of a former owner if circumstances seem to require it.

PEB Commentary No. 3, dated March 10, 1990 [see Appendix V, infra], explains the interplay between this Section and Section 9–306(2). As explained in this Commentary, this Section is consistent with Section 9–306(2) since Section 9–306(2) deals with the continuation or termination of a security interest in collateral following a disposition of the collateral. The last sentence of Section 9–402(7), on the other hand, deals with the continued effectiveness of a filed financing statement to perfect any security interest that continues in the collateral following its disposition.

9. Subsection (8) is in line with the policy of this Article to simplify formal requisites and filing requirements and is designed to discourage the fanatical and impossibly refined reading of such statutory requirements in which courts have occasionally indulged themselves. As an example of the sort of reasoning which this subsection rejects, see General Motors Acceptance Corporation v. Haley, 329 Mass. 559, 109 N.E.2d 143 (1952).

Cross References:

Point 1: Section 9-110.
Point 2: Section 9-208.
Point 4: Sections 9-103, 9-306 and 9-401(3).
Point 5: Section 9-110.
Point 6: Section 9-403(6).
Point 7: Section 9-403(8).
Point 8: Section 9-311.

Definitional Cross References:

"Collateral". Section 9-105.
"Debtor". Section 9-105.
"Fixture". Section 9-313.
"Fixture filing". Section 9-313.
"Goods". Section 9-105.
"Party". Section 1-201.
"Proceeds". Section 9-306.
"Secured party". Section 9-105.
"Security agreement". Section 9-105.
"Security interest". Section 1-201.
"Signed". Section 1-201.
"Transmitting utility". Section 9-105.

§ 9-403. What Constitutes Filing; Duration of Filing; Effect of Lapsed Filing; Duties of Filing Officer.

(1) Presentation for filing of a financing statement and tender of the filing fee or acceptance of the statement by the filing officer constitutes filing under this Article.

(2) Except as provided in subsection (6) a filed financing statement is effective for a period of five years from the date of filing. The effectiveness of a filed financing statement lapses on the expiration of the five year period unless a continuation statement is filed prior to the lapse. If a security interest perfected by filing exists at the time insolvency proceedings are commenced by or against the debtor, the security interest remains perfected until termination of the insolvency proceedings and thereafter for a period of sixty days or until expiration of the five year period, whichever occurs later. Upon lapse the security interest becomes unperfected, unless it is perfected without filing. If the security interest becomes unperfected upon lapse, it is deemed to have been unperfected as against a person who became a purchaser or lien creditor before lapse.

(3) A continuation statement may be filed by the secured party within six months prior to the expiration of the five year period specified in subsection (2). Any such continuation statement must be signed by the secured party, identify the original statement by file number and state that the original statement is still effective. A continuation statement signed by a person other than the secured party of record must be accompanied by a separate written statement of assignment signed by the secured party of record and complying with subsection (2) of Section 9-405, including payment of the required fee. Upon timely filing of the continuation statement, the effectiveness of the original statement is continued for five years after the last date to which the filing was effective whereupon it lapses in the same manner as provided in subsection (2) unless another continuation statement is filed prior to such lapse. Succeeding continuation statements may be filed in the same

manner to continue the effectiveness of the original statement. Unless a statute on disposition of public records provides otherwise, the filing officer may remove a lapsed statement from the files and destroy it immediately if he has retained a microfilm or other photographic record, or in other cases after one year after the lapse. The filing officer shall so arrange matters by physical annexation of financing statements to continuation statements or other related filings, or by other means, that if he physically destroys the financing statements of a period more than five years past, those which have been continued by a continuation statement or which are still effective under subsection (6) shall be retained.

(4) Except as provided in subsection (7) a filing officer shall mark each statement with a file number and with the date and hour of filing and shall hold the statement or a microfilm or other photographic copy thereof for public inspection. In addition the filing officer shall index the statement according to the name of the debtor and shall note in the index the file number and the address of the debtor given in the statement.

(5) The uniform fee for filing and indexing and for stamping a copy furnished by the secured party to show the date and place of filing for an original financing statement or for a continuation statement shall be $______ if the statement is in the standard form prescribed by the [Secretary of State] and otherwise shall be $______, plus in each case, if the financing statement is subject to subsection (5) of Section 9-402, $______. The uniform fee for each name more than one required to be indexed shall be $______. The secured party may at his option show a trade name for any person and an extra uniform indexing fee of $______ shall be paid with respect thereto.

(6) If the debtor is a transmitting utility (subsection (5) of Section 9-401) and a filed financing statement so states, it is effective until a termination statement is filed. A real estate mortgage which is effective as a fixture filing under subsection (6) of Section 9-402 remains effective as a fixture filing until the mortgage is released or satisfied of record or its effectiveness otherwise terminates as to the real estate.

(7) When a financing statement covers timber to be cut or covers minerals or the like (including oil and gas) or accounts subject to subsection (5) of Section 9-103, or is filed as a fixture filing, [it shall be filed for record and] the filing officer shall index it under the names of the debtor and any owner of record shown on the financing statement in the same fashion as if they were the mortgagors in a mortgage of the real estate described, and, to the extent that the law of this state provides for indexing of mortgages under the name of the mortgagee, under the name of the secured party as if he were the mortgagee thereunder, or where indexing is by description in the same fashion as if the financing statement were a mortgage of the real estate described.

Note: *In states in which writings will not appear in the real estate records and indices unless actually recorded the bracketed language in subsection (7) should be used.*

As amended in 1972.

Official Comment

Prior Uniform Statutory Provision: Sections 13(3), 13(4), Uniform Trust Receipts Act; Section 10, Uniform Conditional Sales Act.

Purposes:

1. Prior law was not always clear whether a mortgage filed for record gave constructive notice from the time of presentation to the filing officer or only from the time of indexing. Subsection (1) adopts the former position.

2. Prior statutes have usually limited the effectiveness of a filing to a specified period of time after which refiling is necessary. Subsection (2) follows the same policy, establishing five years as the filing period, with an exception for the cases mentioned in subsection (6). Subsection (3) provides for the filing of one or more continuation statements (which need be signed only by the secured party) if it is desired to continue the effectiveness of the original filing.

The theory of this Article is that the public files of financing statements are self-clearing, because the filing officer may automatically discard each financing statement after a period of five years plus the year after lapse required by subsection (3), unless a continuation statement is filed, or the financing statement is still effective under subsection (6). This theory materially lessens the tension that would otherwise exist to have the files cleared by termination statements under Section 9-404. Similarly, a person searching the files need not go back past this five years plus one year; and if the indices are arranged by years, he has a limited and defined search problem. The section asks the filing officer to attach financing statements whose life has been continued by continuation statements to the latter statements, so that anything contained in the files of old years can be discarded.

Subsection (6) provides certain special filing rules, namely, filings against transmitting utilities (Section 9-105), for which financing statements are filed in the office of the [Secretary of State]; and real estate mortgages which serve as fixture financing statements and which are filed in the real estate records. In both of these cases the financing statement is valid for the life of the obligations secured. No confusion as to the required scope of search should result, because of the special nature of the filings involved.

3. Under subsection (2) the security interest becomes unperfected when filing lapses. Thereafter, the interest of the secured party is subject to defeat by purchasers and lienors even though before lapse the conflicting interest may have been junior. Compare the situation arising under Section 9-103(1)(d) when a perfected security interest under the law of another jurisdiction is not perfected in this state within four months after the property is brought into this state.

Thus if A and B both make non-purchase money advances against the same collateral, and both perfect security interests by filing, A who files first is entitled to priority under Section 9-312(5). But if no continuation statement is filed, A's filing may lapse first. So long as B's interest remains perfected thereafter, he is entitled to priority over A's unperfected interest. This rule avoids the circular priority which arose under some prior statutes, under which A was subordinate to the debtor's trustee in bankruptcy, A retained priority over B, and B's interest was valid against the trustee in bankruptcy. In re Andrews, 172 F.2d 996 (7th Cir. 1949).

4. Subsection (7) makes clear that the filings in real estate records (Sections 9-401 and 9-402(3) and (5)) shall be indexed in the real estate records, where they will be found by a real estate searcher. Where the debtor is not an owner of record, the financing statement must show the name of an owner of record, and the statement is to be indexed in his name. See Sections 9-313(4)(b) and (c); 9-402(3); 9-402(5).

Cross References:

Point 3: Sections 9-103(3), 9-301 and 9-312(5).

Point 4: Sections 9-313(4)(b) and (c), 9-401(1), 9-402(3) and (5), and 9-405(2).

Definitional Cross References:

"Debtor". Section 9-105.

"Financing statement". Section 9-402.

"Fixture". Section 9-313.

"Fixture filing". Section 9-313.

"Secured party". Section 9-105.

"Security interest". Section 1-201.

"Transmitting utility". Section 9-105.

§ 9-404. Termination Statement.

(1) If a financing statement covering consumer goods is filed on or after ______, then within one month or within ten days following written demand by the debtor after there is no outstanding secured obligation and no commitment to make advances, incur obligations or otherwise give value, the secured party must file with each filing officer with whom the financing statement was filed, a termination statement to the effect that he no longer claims a security interest under the financing statement, which shall be identified by file number. In other cases whenever there is no outstanding secured obligation and no commitment to make advances, incur obligations or otherwise give value, the secured party must on written demand by the debtor send the debtor, for each filing officer with whom the financing statement was filed, a termination statement to the effect that he no longer claims a security interest under the financing statement, which shall be identified by file number. A termination statement signed by a person other than the secured party of record must be accompanied by a separate written statement of assignment signed by the secured party of record complying with subsection (2) of Section 9-405, including payment of the required fee. If the affected secured party fails to file such a termination statement as required by this subsection, or to send such a termination statement within ten days after proper demand therefor, he shall be liable to the debtor for one hundred dollars, and in addition for any loss caused to the debtor by such failure.

(2) On presentation to the filing officer of such a termination statement he must note it in the index. If he has received the termination statement in duplicate, he shall return one copy of the termination statement to the secured party stamped to show the time of receipt thereof. If the filing officer has a microfilm or other photographic record of the financing statement, and of any related continuation statement, statement of assignment and statement of release, he may remove the originals from the files at any time after receipt of the termination statement, or if he has no such record, he may remove them from the files at any time after one year after receipt of the termination statement.

(3) If the termination statement is in the standard form prescribed by the [Secretary of State], the uniform fee for filing and indexing the termination statement shall be $______, and otherwise shall be $______, plus in each case an additional fee of $______ for each name more than one against which the termination statement is required to be indexed.

Note: *The date to be inserted should be the effective date of the revised Article 9.*

As amended in 1972.

Official Comment

Prior Uniform Statutory Provision: Section 12, Uniform Conditional Sales Act.

Purposes:

1. To provide a procedure for noting discharge of the secured obligation on the records and for noting that a financing arrangement has been terminated.

Since most financing statements expire in five years unless a continuation statement is filed (Section 9–403), no compulsion is placed on the secured party to file a termination statement unless demanded by the debtor, except in the case of consumer goods. Because many consumers will not realize the importance of clearing the situation as it appears on file, an affirmative duty is put on the secured party in that case. But many purchase money security interests in consumer goods will not be filed, except for motor vehicles (Section 9–302(1)(d)); and in the case of motor vehicles a certificate of title law may control instead of the provisions of Article 9.

2. This section adds to the usual provisions one covering the problem which arises because a secured party under a notice filing system may file notice of an intention to make advances which may never be made. Under this section a debtor may require a secured party to send a termination statement when there is no outstanding obligation and no commitment to make future advances.

Cross Reference:

Point 2: Section 9–402(1).

Definitional Cross References:

"Consumer goods". Section 9–109.
"Debtor". Section 9–105.
"Financing statement". Section 9–402.
"Person". Section 1–201.
"Secured party". Section 9–105.
"Security interest". Section 1–201.
"Send". Section 1–201.
"Value". Section 1–201.
"Written". Section 1–201.

§ 9–405. Assignment of Security Interest; Duties of Filing Officer; Fees.

(1) A financing statement may disclose an assignment of a security interest in the collateral described in the financing statement by indication in the financing statement of the name and address of the assignee or by an assignment itself or a copy thereof on the face or back of the statement. On presentation to the filing officer of such a financing statement the filing officer shall mark the same as provided in Section 9–403(4). The uniform fee for filing, indexing and furnishing filing data for a financing statement so indicating an assignment shall be $______ if the statement is in the standard form prescribed by the [Secretary of State] and otherwise shall be $______, plus in each case an additional fee of $______ for each name more than one against which the financing statement is required to be indexed.

(2) A secured party may assign of record all or part of his rights under a financing statement by the filing in the place where the original financing statement was filed of a separate written statement of assignment signed by the secured party of record and setting forth the name of the secured party of record and the debtor, the file number and the date of filing of the financing statement and the name and address of the assignee and containing a description of the collateral assigned. A copy of the assignment is sufficient as a separate statement if it complies with the preceding sentence. On presentation to the filing officer of such a separate statement, the filing officer shall mark such separate statement with the date and hour of the filing. He

shall note the assignment on the index of the financing statement, or in the case of a fixture filing, or a filing covering timber to be cut, or covering minerals or the like (including oil and gas) or accounts subject to subsection (5) of Section 9-103, he shall index the assignment under the name of the assignor as grantor and, to the extent that the law of this state provides for indexing the assignment of a mortgage under the name of the assignee, he shall index the assignment of the financing statement under the name of the assignee. The uniform fee for filing, indexing and furnishing filing data about such a separate statement of assignment shall be $______ if the statement is in the standard form prescribed by the [Secretary of State] and otherwise shall be $______, plus in each case an additional fee of $______ for each name more than one against which the statement of assignment is required to be indexed. Notwithstanding the provisions of this subsection, an assignment of record of a security interest in a fixture contained in a mortgage effective as a fixture filing (subsection (6) of Section 9-402) may be made only by an assignment of the mortgage in the manner provided by the law of this state other than this Act.

(3) After the disclosure or filing of an assignment under this section, the assignee is the secured party of record.

As amended in 1972.

Official Comment

Prior Uniform Statutory Provision: None.

Purposes:

This section provides a permissive device whereby a secured party who has assigned all or part of his interest may have the assignment noted of record. Note that under Section 9-302(2) no filing of such an assignment is required as a condition of continuing the perfected status of the security interest against creditors and transferees of the original debtor. A secured party who has assigned his interest might wish to have the fact noted of record, so that inquiries concerning the transaction would be addressed not to him but to the assignee (see Point 2 of Comment to Section 9-402). After a secured party has assigned his rights of record, the assignee becomes the "secured party of record" and may file a continuation statement under Section 9-403, a termination statement under Section 9-404, or a statement of release under Section 9-406.

Where a mortgage of real estate is effective as a financing statement filed as a fixture filing (Section 9-402(6)), then an assignment of record of the security interest may be made only in the manner in which an assignment of the mortgage may be made under the local state law.

Cross References:

Sections 9-302(2) and 9-402 through 9-406.

Definitional Cross References:

"Collateral". Section 9-105.
"Debtor". Section 9-105.
"Financing statement". Section 9-402.
"Rights". Section 1-201.
"Secured party". Section 9-105.
"Signed". Section 1-201.
"Written". Section 1-201.

§ 9-406. Release of Collateral; Duties of Filing Officer; Fees.

A secured party of record may by his signed statement release all or a part of any collateral described in a filed financing statement. The statement of release is sufficient if it contains a description of the collateral being released, the name and address of the debtor, the name and address of the secured party, and the file number of the financing statement. A statement of release signed by a person other than the secured party of record must be accompanied by a separate written statement of assignment signed by the secured party of record and complying with subsection (2) of Section 9-405, including payment of the required fee. Upon presentation of such a statement of release to the filing officer he shall mark the statement with the hour and date of filing and shall note the same upon the margin of the index of the filing of the financing statement. The uniform fee for filing and noting such a statement of release shall be $______ if the statement is in the standard form prescribed by the [Secretary of State] and otherwise shall be $______, plus in each case an additional fee of $______ for each name more than one against which the statement of release is required to be indexed.

As amended in 1972.

Official Comment

Prior Uniform Statutory Provision: None.

Purposes:

Like the preceding section, this section provides a permissive device for noting of record any release of collateral. There is no requirement that such a statement be filed when collateral is released (cf. Section 9-404 on Termination Statements). It is merely a method of making the record reflect the true state of affairs so that fewer inquiries will have to be made by persons who consult the files.

If the statement of release is not signed by the secured party of record, the assignment procedure of Section 9-405(2) must be followed.

Cross Reference:

Section 9-404.

Definitional Cross References:

"Collateral". Section 9-105.
"Debtor". Section 9-105.
"Financing statement". Section 9-402.
"Secured party". Section 9-105.
"Signed". Section 1-201.

§ 9-407. Information From Filing Officer.

[(1) If the person filing any financing statement, termination statement, statement of assignment, or statement of release, furnishes the filing officer a copy thereof, the filing officer shall upon request note upon the copy the file number and date and hour of the filing of the original and deliver or send the copy to such person.]

[(2) Upon request of any person, the filing officer shall issue his certificate showing whether there is on file on the date and hour stated therein, any presently effective financing statement naming a particular debtor and any statement of assignment thereof and if there is, giving the date and hour of filing of each such statement and the names and addresses of each secured party therein. The uniform fee for such a certificate shall be $______ if the request for the certificate is in the standard form prescribed by the [Secretary of State] and otherwise shall be $______. Upon request the filing officer shall furnish a copy of any filed financing statement or statement of assignment for a uniform fee of $______ per page.]

Note: *This section is proposed as an optional provision to require filing officers to furnish certificates. Local law and practices should be consulted with regard to the advisability of adoption.*

As amended in 1972.

Official Comment

Prior Uniform Statutory Provision: None.

Purposes:

1. Subsection (1) requires the filing officer upon request to return to the secured party a copy of the financing statement on which the material data concerning the filing are noted. Receipt of such a copy will assure the secured party that the mechanics of filing have been complied with. Note, however, that under Section 9-403(1) the secured party does not bear the risk that the filing officer will not properly perform his duties: under that section the secured party has complied with the filing requirements when he presents his financing statement for filing and the filing fee has been tendered or the statement accepted by the filing officer.

2. Subsection (2) requires the filing officer on request to issue to any person who has tendered the proper fee his certificate as to what filings have been made against any particular debtor and to furnish copies of such filed financing statements. In view of the centralized filing system adopted by this Article (see Section 9-401 and Comment thereto), this provision is of obvious convenience to a person who wishes to know what the files contain but who cannot conveniently consult files located in the state capital.

Cross References:

Point 1: Section 9-403(1).
Point 2: Section 9-401.

Definitional Cross References:

"Debtor". Section 9-105.
"Financing statement". Section 9-402.
"Person". Section 1-201.
"Secured party". Section 9-105.
"Send". Section 1-201.

§ 9-408. Financing Statements Covering Consigned or Leased Goods.

A consignor or lessor of goods may file a financing statement using the terms "consignor," "consignee," "lessor," "lessee" or the like instead of the terms specified in Section 9-402. The provisions of this Part shall apply as appropriate to such a financing statement but its filing shall not of itself be a factor in determining whether or not the consignment or lease is intended as security (Section 1-201(37)). However, if it is determined for other reasons that the consignment or lease is so intended, a security interest of the consignor or lessor which attaches to the consigned or leased goods is perfected by such filing.

As added in 1972.

Official Comment

Prior Uniform Statutory Provision: None.

Purposes:

1. Where filing is required under Sections 2-326(3) and 9-114 for a consignment which is not a security interest (Section 1-201(37)), this section authorizes the appropriate adaptations of terminology.

Apart from the rules in Part 4, the rules of this article using the terms "debtor" and "secured party" will not apply to consignments if they are not security interests. Section 9-114 on consignments essentially parallels Section 9-312(3) on inventory priorities, and the latter rule therefore does not apply to consignments. Section 2-326 states the rights of creditors of a consignee who has not filed or otherwise complied with subsection (3), and Section 9-301 on unperfected security interests is therefore not applicable. Section 2-326 and the law of consignments supply rules which are provided by Section 9-311 for security interests and that section is therefore not applicable to consignments. For reasons indicated in the Comment to Section 9-114, Section 9-306 on proceeds is inapplicable to consignments. An equivalent to the protection of a buyer in ordinary course of business against a security interest under Section 9-307(1) is provided against consignments by Section 2-403(2) and (3).

2. If a lease is actually intended as security (Section 1-201(37)), this Article applies in full. But this question of intention is a doubtful one, and the lessor may choose to file for safety even while contending that the lease is a true lease for which no filing is required. This section authorizes filing with appropriate changes of terminology, and without affecting the substantive question of classification of the lease. If the lease is a true lease, none of the provisions of the Article is applicable to the lease as an interest in the chattel. Note, however, that the Article may be applicable to the lease in its aspect as chattel paper. See Section 9-105(b).

PART 5

DEFAULT

§ 9-501. Default; Procedure When Security Agreement Covers Both Real and Personal Property.

(1) When a debtor is in default under a security agreement, a secured party has the rights and remedies provided in this Part and except as limited by subsection (3) those provided in the security agreement. He may reduce his claim to judgment, foreclose or otherwise enforce the security interest by any available judicial procedure. If the collateral is documents the secured party may proceed either as to the documents or as to the goods covered thereby. A secured party in possession has the rights, remedies and duties provided in Section 9-207. The rights and remedies referred to in this subsection are cumulative.

(2) After default, the debtor has the rights and remedies provided in this Part, those provided in the security agreement and those provided in Section 9-207.

(3) To the extent that they give rights to the debtor and impose duties on the secured party, the rules stated in the subsections referred to below may not be waived or varied except as provided with respect to compulsory disposition of collateral (subsection (3) of Section 9-504 and Section 9-505) and with respect to redemption of collateral (Section 9-506) but the parties may by agreement determine the standards by which the fulfillment of these rights and duties is to be measured if such standards are not manifestly unreasonable:

(a) subsection (2) of Section 9-502 and subsection (2) of Section 9-504 insofar as they require accounting for surplus proceeds of collateral;

(b) subsection (3) of Section 9-504 and subsection (1) of Section 9-505 which deal with disposition of collateral;

(c) subsection (2) of Section 9-505 which deals with acceptance of collateral as discharge of obligation;

(d) Section 9-506 which deals with redemption of collateral; and

(e) subsection (1) of Section 9-507 which deals with the secured party's liability for failure to comply with this Part.

(4) If the security agreement covers both real and personal property, the secured party may proceed under this Part as to the personal property or he may proceed as to both the real and the personal property in accordance with his rights and remedies in respect of the real property in which case the provisions of this Part do not apply.

(5) When a secured party has reduced his claim to judgment the lien of any levy which may be made upon his collateral by virtue of any execution based upon the judgment shall relate back to the date of the perfection of the security interest in such collateral. A judicial sale, pursuant to such execution, is a foreclosure of the security interest by judicial procedure within the meaning of this section, and the secured party may purchase at the sale and thereafter hold the collateral free of any other requirements of this Article.

As amended in 1972.

Official Comment

Prior Uniform Statutory Provision: Section 6, Uniform Trust Receipts Act; Sections 16 through 26, Uniform Conditional Sales Act.

Purposes:

1. The rights of the secured party in the collateral after the debtor's default are of the essence of a security transaction. These are the rights which distinguish the secured from the unsecured lender. This section and the following six sections state those rights as well as the limitations on their free exercise which legislative policy requires for the protection not only of the defaulting debtor but of other creditors. But subsections (1) and (2) make it clear that the statement of rights and remedies in this Part does not exclude other remedies provided by agreement.

2. Following default and the taking possession of the collateral by the secured party, there is no longer any distinction between the security interest which before default was non-possessory and that which was possessory under a pledge. Therefore no general distinction is taken in this Part between the rights of a non-possessory secured party and those of a pledgee; the latter, being in possession of the collateral at default, will of course not have to avail himself of the right to take possession under Section 9-503.

3. Section 9-207 states rights, remedies and duties with respect to collateral in the secured party's possession. That section applies not only to the situation where he is in possession before default, as a pledgee, but also, by subsections (1) and (2) of this section, to the secured party in possession after default. Nevertheless the relations of the parties have been changed by default, and Section 9-207 as it applies after default must be read together with this Part. In particular, agreements permitted under Section 9-207 cannot waive or modify the rights of the debtor contrary to subsection (3) of this section.

4. Section 1-102(3) states rules to determine which provisions of this Act are mandatory and which may be varied by

agreement. In general, provisions which relate to matters which come up between immediate parties may be varied by agreement. In the area of rights after default our legal system has traditionally looked with suspicion on agreements designed to cut down the debtor's rights and free the secured party of his duties: no mortgage clause has ever been allowed to clog the equity of redemption. The default situation offers great scope for overreaching; the suspicious attitude of the courts has been grounded in common sense.

Subsection (3) of this section contains a codification of this long-standing and deeply rooted attitude: the specified rights of the debtor and duties of the secured party may not be waived or varied except as stated. Provisions not specified in subsection (3) are subject to the general rules stated in Section 1–102(3).

5. The collateral for many corporate security issues consists of both real and personal property. In the interest of simplicity and speed subsection (4) permits, although it does not require, the secured party to proceed as to both real and personal property in accordance with his rights and remedies in respect of the real property. Except for the permission so granted, this Act leaves to other state law all questions of procedure with respect to real property. For example, this Act does not determine whether the secured party can proceed against the real estate alone and later proceed in a separate action against the personal property in accordance with his rights and remedies against the real estate. By such separate actions the secured party "proceeds as to both," and this Part does not apply in either action. But subsection (4) does give him an option to proceed under this Part as to the personal property.

6. Under subsection (1) a secured party is entitled to reduce his claim to judgment or to foreclose his interest by any available procedure, outside this Article, which state law may provide. The first sentence of subsection (5) makes clear that any judgment lien which the secured party may acquire against the collateral is, so to say, a continuation of his original interest (if perfected) and not the acquisition of a new interest or a transfer of property to satisfy an antecedent debt. The judgment lien is therefore stated to relate back to the date of perfection of the security interest. The second sentence of the subsection makes clear that a judicial sale following judgment, execution and levy is one of the methods of foreclosure contemplated by subsection (1); such a sale is governed by other law and not by this Article and the restrictions which this Article imposes on the right of a secured party to buy in the collateral at a sale under Section 9–504 do not apply.

Cross References:

Point 2: Section 9–503.
Point 3: Section 9–207.
Point 4: Section 1–102(3).
Point 5: Sections 9–102(1) and 9–104(j).
Point 6: Section 9–504.

Definitional Cross References:

"Agreement". Section 1–201.
"Collateral". Section 9–105.
"Debtor". Section 9–105.
"Documents". Section 9–105.
"Goods". Section 9–105.
"Remedy". Section 1–201.
"Rights". Section 1–201.
"Secured party". Section 9–105.
"Security agreement". Section 9–105.
"Security interest". Section 1–201.

§ 9–502. Collection Rights of Secured Party.

(1) When so agreed and in any event on default the secured party is entitled to notify an account debtor or the obligor on an instrument to make payment to him whether or not the assignor was theretofore making collections on the collateral, and also to take control of any proceeds to which he is entitled under Section 9–306.

(2) A secured party who by agreement is entitled to charge back uncollected collateral or otherwise to full or limited recourse against the debtor and who undertakes to collect from the account debtors or obligors must proceed in a commercially reasonable manner and may deduct his reasonable expenses of realization from the collections. If the security agreement secures an indebtedness, the secured party must account to the debtor for any surplus, and unless otherwise agreed, the debtor is liable for any deficiency. But, if the underlying transaction was a sale of accounts or chattel paper, the debtor is entitled to any surplus or is liable for any deficiency only if the security agreement so provides.

As amended in 1972.

Official Comment

Prior Uniform Statutory Provision: None.

Purposes:

1. The assignee of accounts, chattel paper, or instruments holds as collateral property which is not only the most liquid asset of the debtor's business but also property which may be collected without any interruption of the business, assuming it to continue after default. The situation is far different from that where the collateral is inventory or equipment, whose removal may bring the business to a halt. Furthermore the problems of valuation and identification, present where the collateral is tangible chattels, do not arise so sharply on the assignment of intangibles. Considerations, similar although not identical, apply to assignments of general intangibles, which are also covered by the rule of the section. Consequently, this section recognizes the fact that financing by assignment of intangibles lacks many of the complexities which arise after default in other types of financing, and allows the assignee to liquidate in the regular course of business by collecting whatever may become due on the collateral, whether or not the method of collection contemplated by the security arrangement before default was direct (i.e., payment by the account debtor to the assignee, "notification" financing) or indirect (i.e., payment by the account debtor to the assignor, "nonnotification" financing). By agreement, of course, the secured party may have the right to give notice and to make collections before default.

2. In one form of accounts receivable financing, which is found in the "factoring" arrangements which are common in the textile industry, the assignee assumes the credit risk—that is, he buys the account under an agreement which does not provide for recourse or charge-back against the assignor in the event the account proves uncollectible. Under such an arrangement, neither the debtor nor his creditors have any legitimate concern with the disposition which the assignee makes of the accounts. Under another form of accounts receivable financing, however, the assignee does not assume the credit risk and retains a right of full or limited recourse or charge-back for uncollectible accounts. In such a case both debtor and creditors have a right that the assignee not dump the accounts, if the result will be to increase a possible deficiency claim or to reduce a possible surplus.

3. Where an assignee has a right of charge-back or a right of recourse, subsection (2) provides that liquidation must be made with due regard to the interest of the assignor and of his other creditor—"in a commercially reasonable manner" (compare Section 9-504 and see Section 9-507(2))—and the proceeds allocated to the expenses of realization and to the indebtedness. If the "charge-back" provisions of the assignment arrangement provide only for "charge-back" of bad ac-

counts against a reserve, the debtor's claim to surplus and his liability for a deficiency are limited to the amount of the reserve.

4. Financing arrangements of the type dealt with by this section are between business men. The last sentence of subsection (2) therefore preserves freedom of contract, and the subsection recognizes that there may be a true sale of accounts or chattel paper although recourse exists. The determination whether a particular assignment constitutes a sale or a transfer for security is left to the courts. Note that, under Section 9-102, this Article applies both to sales and to security transfers of such intangibles.

Cross References:

Sections 9-205 and 9-306.

Point 3: Sections 9-504 and 9-507(2).

Point 4: Sections 9-102(1)(b) and 9-104(f).

Definitional Cross References:

"Account". Section 9-106.
"Account debtor". Section 9-105.
"Agreement". Section 1-201.
"Chattel paper". Section 9-105.
"Collateral". Section 9-105.
"Debtor". Section 9-105.
"Instrument". Section 9-105.
"Notify". Section 1-201.
"Proceeds". Section 9-306.
"Secured party". Section 9-105.
"Security agreement". Section 9-105.

§ 9-503. Secured Party's Right to Take Possession After Default.

Unless otherwise agreed a secured party has on default the right to take possession of the collateral. In taking possession a secured party may proceed without judicial process if this can be done without breach of the peace or may proceed by action. If the security agreement so provides the secured party may require the debtor to assemble the collateral and make it available to the secured party at a place to be designated by the secured party which is reasonably convenient to both parties. Without removal a secured party may render equipment unusable, and may dispose of collateral on the debtor's premises under Section 9-504.

Official Comment

Prior Uniform Statutory Provision: Section 6, Uniform Trust Receipts Act; Sections 16 and 17, Uniform Conditional Sales Act.

Purposes:

Under this Article the secured party's right to possession of the collateral (if he is not already in possession as pledgee) accrues on default unless otherwise agreed in the security agreement. This Article follows the provisions of the earlier uniform legislation in allowing the secured party in most cases to take possession without the issuance of judicial process. In the case of collateral such as heavy equipment, the physical removal from the debtor's plant and the storage of the equipment pending resale may be exceedingly expensive and in some cases impractical. The section therefore provides that in lieu of removal the lender may render equipment unusable or dispose of collateral on the debtor's premises. The authorization to render equipment unusable or to dispose of collateral without removal would not justify unreasonable action by the secured party, since, under Section 9-504(3), all his actions in connection with disposition must be taken in a "commercially reasonable manner".

Cross Reference:

Section 9-504.

Definitional Cross References:

"Action". Section 1-201.
"Collateral". Section 9-105.
"Debtor". Section 9-105.

"Equipment". Section 9–109.
"Rights". Section 1–201.
"Secured party". Section 9–105.
"Security agreement". Section 9–105.

§ 9–504. Secured Party's Right to Dispose of Collateral After Default; Effect of Disposition.

(1) A secured party after default may sell, lease or otherwise dispose of any or all of the collateral in its then condition or following any commercially reasonable preparation or processing. Any sale of goods is subject to the Article on Sales (Article 2). The proceeds of disposition shall be applied in the order following to

(a) the reasonable expenses of retaking, holding, preparing for sale or lease, selling, leasing and the like and, to the extent provided for in the agreement and not prohibited by law, the reasonable attorneys' fees and legal expenses incurred by the secured party;

(b) the satisfaction of indebtedness secured by the security interest under which the disposition is made;

(c) the satisfaction of indebtedness secured by any subordinate security interest in the collateral if written notification of demand therefor is received before distribution of the proceeds is completed. If requested by the secured party, the holder of a subordinate security interest must seasonably furnish reasonable proof of his interest, and unless he does so, the secured party need not comply with his demand.

(2) If the security interest secures an indebtedness, the secured party must account to the debtor for any surplus, and, unless otherwise agreed, the debtor is liable for any deficiency. But if the underlying transaction was a sale of accounts or chattel paper, the debtor is entitled to any surplus or is liable for any deficiency only if the security agreement so provides.

(3) Disposition of the collateral may be by public or private proceedings and may be made by way of one or more contracts. Sale or other disposition may be as a unit or in parcels and at any time and place and on any terms but every aspect of the disposition including the method, manner, time, place and terms must be commercially reasonable. Unless collateral is perishable or threatens to decline speedily in value or is of a type customarily sold on a recognized market, reasonable notification of the time and place of any public sale or reasonable notification of the time after which any private sale or other intended disposition is to be made shall be sent by the secured party to the debtor, if he has not signed after default a statement renouncing or modifying his right to notification of sale. In the case of consumer goods no other notification need be sent. In other cases notification shall be sent to any other secured party from whom the secured party has received (before sending his notification to the debtor or before the debtor's renunciation of his rights) written notice of a claim of an interest in the collateral. The secured party may buy at any public sale and if the collateral is of a type customarily sold in a recognized market or is of a type which is the subject of widely distributed standard price quotations he may buy at private sale.

(4) When collateral is disposed of by a secured party after default, the disposition transfers to a purchaser for value all of the debtor's rights therein,

discharges the security interest under which it is made and any security interest or lien subordinate thereto. The purchaser takes free of all such rights and interests even though the secured party fails to comply with the requirements of this Part or of any judicial proceedings

(a) in the case of a public sale, if the purchaser has no knowledge of any defects in the sale and if he does not buy in collusion with the secured party, other bidders or the person conducting the sale; or

(b) in any other case, if the purchaser acts in good faith.

(5) A person who is liable to a secured party under a guaranty, indorsement, repurchase agreement or the like and who receives a transfer of collateral from the secured party or is subrogated to his rights has thereafter the rights and duties of the secured party. Such a transfer of collateral is not a sale or disposition of the collateral under this Article.

As amended in 1972.

Official Comment

Prior Uniform Statutory Provision: Section 6, Uniform Trust Receipts Act; Sections 19, 20, 21, and 22, Uniform Conditional Sales Act.

Purposes:

1. The Uniform Trust Receipts Act provides that an entruster in possession after default holds the collateral with the rights and duties of a pledgee, and, in particular, that he may sell such collateral at public or private sale with a right to claim deficiency and a duty to account for any surplus. The Uniform Conditional Sales Act insisted on a sale at public auction with elaborate provisions for the giving of notice of sale. This section follows the more liberal provisions of the Trust Receipts Act. Although public sale is recognized, it is hoped that private sale will be encouraged where, as is frequently the case, private sale through commercial channels will result in higher realization on collateral for the benefit of all parties. The only restriction placed on the secured party's method of disposition is that it must be commercially reasonable. In this respect this section follows the provisions of the section on resale by a seller following a buyer's rejection of goods (Section 2-706). Subsection (1) does not restrict disposition to sale: the collateral may be sold, leased, or otherwise disposed of—subject of course to the general requirement of subsection (2) that all aspects of the disposition be "commercially reasonable". Section 9-507(2) states some tests as to what is "commercially reasonable".

2. Subsection (1) in general follows prior law in its provisions for the application of proceeds and for the debtor's right to surplus and liability for deficiency. Under paragraph (1)(c) the secured party, after paying expenses of retaking and disposition and his own debt, is required to pay over remaining proceeds to the extent necessary to satisfy the holder of any junior security interest in the same collateral if the holder of the junior interest has made a written demand and furnished on request reasonable proof of his interest: this provision is necessary in view of the fact that under subsection (4) the junior interest is discharged by the disposition. Since the requirement is conditioned on written demand, it should not result in undue burden on the secured party making the disposition. It should be noted also that under Section 9-112 where the secured party knows that the collateral is owned by a person who is not the debtor, the owner of the collateral and not the debtor is entitled to any surplus.

3. In any security transaction the debtor (or the owner of the collateral if other than the debtor: see Section 9-112) is entitled to any surplus which results

from realization on the collateral; the debtor will also, unless otherwise agreed, be liable for any deficiency. Subsection (2) so provides. Since this Article covers sales of certain intangibles as well as transfers for security, the subsection also provides that apart from agreement the right to surplus or liability for deficiency does not accrue where the transaction between debtor and secured party was a sale and not a security transaction.

4. Subsection (4) provides that a purchaser for value from a secured party after default takes free of any rights of the debtor and of the holders of junior security interests and liens, even though the secured party has not complied with the requirements of this Part or of any judicial proceedings. This subsection follows a similar provision in the Uniform Trust Receipts Act and in the section of this Act on resale by a seller (Section 2–706). Where the purchaser for value has bought at a public sale he is protected under paragraph (a) if he has no knowledge of any defects in the sale and was not guilty of collusive practices. Where the purchaser for value has bought at a private sale he must, to receive the protection of paragraph (b), qualify in all respects as a purchaser in good faith. Thus while the purchaser at a private sale is required to proceed in the exercise of good faith, the purchaser at public sale is protected so long as he is not actively in bad faith, and is put under no duty to inquire into the circumstances of the sale.

5. Both the Uniform Trust Receipts Act and the Uniform Conditional Sales Act required a waiting period after repossession and before sale (five days in the Trust Receipts Act, ten days in the Conditional Sales Act). Under subsection (3), the secured party in most cases is required to give reasonable notification of disposition to the debtor unless the debtor has after default signed a statement renouncing or modifying his right to notification of sale.

The secured party must also (except for consumer goods) give notice to any other secured parties who have in writing given notice of a claim of an interest in the collateral. This latter notice must be given before the debtor renounces his rights or before the secured party gives his notification to the debtor. Compare Section 9–505(2). Except for the requirement of notification there is no statutory period during which the collateral must be held before disposition. "Reasonable notification" is not defined in this Article; at a minimum it must be sent in such time that persons entitled to receive it will have sufficient time to take appropriate steps to protect their interests by taking part in the sale or other disposition if they so desire.

6. Section 19 of the Uniform Conditional Sales Act required that sale be made not more than thirty days after possession taken by the conditional vendor. The Uniform Trust Receipts Act contained no comparable provision. Here again this Article follows the Trust Receipts Act, and no period is set within which the disposition must be made, except in the case of consumer goods which under Section 9–505(1) must in certain instances be sold within ninety days after the secured party has taken possession. The failure to prescribe a statutory period during which disposition must be made is in line with the policy adopted in this Article to encourage disposition by private sale through regular commercial channels. It may, for example, be wise not to dispose of goods when the market has collapsed, or to sell a large inventory in parcels over a period of time instead of in bulk. Note, however, that under subsection (3) every aspect of the sale or other disposition of the collateral must be commercially reasonable; this specifically includes method, manner, time, place and terms. See Section 9–507(2). Under that provision a secured party who without proceeding under Section 9–505(2) held collateral a long time without disposing of it, thus running up large storage charges against the debtor, where no reason existed for not making a prompt sale, might well be found not to have acted in a "commercially reasonable" manner. See also Section 1–203 on the general obligation of good faith.

Cross References:

Point 1: Sections 2-706 and 9-507(2).
Point 2: Section 9-112.
Point 3: Sections 9-102(1)(b) and 9-112.
Point 4: Section 2-706.
Point 6: Sections 9-505 and 9-507(2).

Definitional Cross References:

"Account". Section 9-106.
"Agreement". Section 1-201.
"Chattel paper". Section 9-105.
"Collateral". Section 9-105.
"Consumer goods". Section 9-109.
"Contract". Section 1-201.
"Debtor". Section 9-105.
"Financing statement". Section 9-402.
"Gives" notification. Section 1-201.
"Good faith". Section 1-201.
"Goods". Section 9-105.
"Knowledge". Section 1-201.
"Person". Section 1-201.
"Proceeds". Section 9-306.
"Purchaser". Section 1-201.
"Receives" notification. Section 1-201.
"Rights". Section 1-201.
"Sale". Sections 2-106 and 9-105.
"Secured party". Section 9-105.
"Security agreement". Section 9-105.
"Security interest". Section 1-201.
"Send". Section 1-201.
"Term". Section 1-201.
"Value". Section 1-201.
"Written". Section 1-201.

§ 9-505. Compulsory Disposition of Collateral; Acceptance of the Collateral as Discharge of Obligation.

(1) If the debtor has paid sixty per cent of the cash price in the case of a purchase money security interest in consumer goods or sixty per cent of the loan in the case of another security interest in consumer goods, and has not signed after default a statement renouncing or modifying his rights under this Part a secured party who has taken possession of collateral must dispose of it under Section 9-504 and if he fails to do so within ninety days after he takes possession the debtor at his option may recover in conversion or under Section 9-507(1) on secured party's liability.

(2) In any other case involving consumer goods or any other collateral a secured party in possession may, after default, propose to retain the collateral in satisfaction of the obligation. Written notice of such proposal shall be sent to the debtor if he has not signed after default a statement renouncing or modifying his rights under this subsection. In the case of consumer goods no other notice need be given. In other cases notice shall be sent to any other secured party from whom the secured party has received (before sending his notice to the debtor or before the debtor's renunciation of his rights) written notice of a claim of an interest in the collateral. If the secured party receives objection in writing from a person entitled to receive notification within twenty-one days after the notice was sent, the secured party must dispose of the collateral under Section 9-504. In the absence of such written objection the secured party may retain the collateral in satisfaction of the debtor's obligation.

As amended in 1972.

Official Comment

Prior Uniform Statutory Provision: Section 23, Uniform Conditional Sales Act.

Purposes:

1. Experience has shown that the parties are frequently better off without a resale of the collateral; hence this section sanctions an alternative arrangement. In

lieu of resale or other disposition, the secured party may propose under subsection (2) that he keep the collateral as his own, thus discharging the obligation and abandoning any claim for a deficiency. This right may not be exercised in the case of consumer goods where the debtor has paid 60% of the price or obligation and thus has a substantial equity, and may be exercised in other cases only on notification to the debtor, unless the debtor has signed after default a statement renouncing or modifying his rights under this section, and (except in the case of consumer goods) to any other secured party who has given written notice of a claim of an interest in the collateral. In the latter case, notice must be given before the secured party receives the debtor's renunciation or before he sends his notice to the debtor. The secured party may keep the goods in lieu of sale on failure of anyone receiving notification to object within twenty-one days.

2. When an objection is received by the secured party he must then proceed to dispose of the collateral in accordance with Section 9-504, and on failure to do so would incur the liabilities set out in Section 9-507. In the case of consumer goods where 60% of the price or obligation has been paid the disposition must be made within 90 days after possession taken. For failure to make the sale within the 90-day period the secured party is liable in conversion or alternatively may incur the liabilities set out in Section 9-507.

In the absence of objection the secured party is bound by his notice.

3. After default (but not before) a consumer-debtor who has paid 60% of the cash price may sign a written renunciation of his rights to require resale of the collateral.

Cross References:

Sections 9-504 and 9-507(1).

Definitional Cross References:

"Collateral". Section 9-105.
"Consumer goods". Section 9-109.
"Debtor". Section 9-105.
"Knows". Section 1-201.
"Notice". Section 1-201.
"Person". Section 1-201.
"Purchase money security interest". Section 9-107.
"Receives" notification. Section 1-201.
"Rights". Section 1-201.
"Secured party". Section 9-105.
"Security interest". Section 1-201.
"Send". Section 1-201.
"Signed". Section 1-201.
"Written". Section 1-201.

§ 9-506. Debtor's Right to Redeem Collateral.

At any time before the secured party has disposed of collateral or entered into a contract for its disposition under Section 9-504 or before the obligation has been discharged under Section 9-505(2) the debtor or any other secured party may unless otherwise agreed in writing after default redeem the collateral by tendering fulfillment of all obligations secured by the collateral as well as the expenses reasonably incurred by the secured party in retaking, holding and preparing the collateral for disposition, in arranging for the sale, and to the extent provided in the agreement and not prohibited by law, his reasonable attorneys' fees and legal expenses.

Official Comment

Prior Uniform Statutory Provision: Section 18, Uniform Conditional Sales Act.

Purposes:

Except in the case stated in Section 9-505(1) (consumer goods) the secured party is not required to dispose of collateral within any stated period of time. Under this section so long as the secured party has not disposed of collateral in his possession or contracted for its disposition, and so long as his right to retain it has not become fixed under Section 9-505(2), the debtor or another secured party may redeem. The debtor must tender fulfillment of all obligations secured, plus certain expenses: if the agreement contains a clause accelerating the entire balance due on default in one installment, the entire balance would have to be tendered. "Tendering fulfillment" obviously means more than a new promise to perform the existing promise; it requires payment in full of all monetary obligations then due and performance in full of all other obligations then matured. If unmatured obligations remain, the security interest continues to secure them as if there had been no default.

Under Section 9-504 the secured party may make successive sales of parts of the collateral in his possession. The fact that he may have sold or contracted to sell part of the collateral would not affect the debtor's right under this section to redeem what was left. In such a case, of course, in calculating the amount required to be tendered the debtor would receive credit for net proceeds of the collateral sold.

Cross References:

Sections 9-504 and 9-505.

Definitional Cross References:

"Agreement". Section 1-201.
"Collateral". Section 9-105.
"Contract". Section 1-201.
"Debtor". Section 9-105.
"Secured party". Section 9-105.
"Writing". Section 1-201.

§ 9-507. Secured Party's Liability for Failure to Comply With This Part.

(1) If it is established that the secured party is not proceeding in accordance with the provisions of this Part disposition may be ordered or restrained on appropriate terms and conditions. If the disposition has occurred the debtor or any person entitled to notification or whose security interest has been made known to the secured party prior to the disposition has a right to recover from the secured party any loss caused by a failure to comply with the provisions of this Part. If the collateral is consumer goods, the debtor has a right to recover in any event an amount not less than the credit service charge plus ten per cent of the principal amount of the debt or the time price differential plus 10 per cent of the cash price.

(2) The fact that a better price could have been obtained by a sale at a different time or in a different method from that selected by the secured party is not of itself sufficient to establish that the sale was not made in a commercially reasonable manner. If the secured party either sells the collateral in the usual manner in any recognized market therefor or if he sells at the price current in such market at the time of his sale or if he has otherwise sold in conformity with reasonable commercial practices among dealers in the type of property sold he has sold in a commercially reasonable manner. The principles stated in the two preceding sentences with respect to sales also apply as may be appropriate to other types of disposition. A disposition which has been approved in any judicial proceeding or by any bona fide creditors' committee or representative of creditors shall conclusively be deemed to be commercially reasonable, but this sentence does not indicate that any such approval must be obtained in any case nor does it indicate that any disposition not so approved is not commercially reasonable.

Official Comment

Prior Uniform Statutory Provision: None.

Purposes:

1. The principal limitation on the secured party's right to dispose of collateral is the requirement that he proceed in good faith (Section 1-203) and in a commercially reasonable manner. See Section 9-504. In the case where he proceeds, or is about to proceed, in a contrary manner, it is vital both to the debtor and other creditors to provide a remedy for the failure to comply with the statutory duty. This remedy will be of particular importance when it is applied prospectively before the unreasonable disposition has been concluded. This section therefore provides that a secured party proposing to dispose of collateral in an unreasonable manner, may, by court order, be restrained from doing so, and such an order might appropriately provide either that he proceed with the sale or other disposition under specified terms and conditions, or that the sale be made by a representative of creditors where insolvency proceedings have been instituted. The section further provides for damages where the unreasonable disposition has been concluded, and, in the case of consumer goods, states a minimum recovery.

A case may be put in which the liquidation value of an insolvent estate would be enhanced by disposing of all the debtor's property (including that subject to a security interest) in the liquidation proceeding and in which, if a secured party repossesses and sells that part of the property which he holds as collateral, the remainder will have little or no resale value. In such a case the question may arise whether a particular court has the power to control the manner of disposition, although reasonable in other respects, in order to preserve the estate for the benefit of creditors. Such a power is no doubt inherent in a Federal bankruptcy court, and perhaps also in other courts of equity administering insolvent estates. Traditionally it was not exercised where the secured party claimed under a title retention device, such as conditional sale or trust receipt. See In re Lake's Laundry, Inc., 79 F.2d 326 (2d Cir. 1935) and the remarks of Clark, J., concurring, in In re White Plains Ice Service, Inc., 109 F.2d 913 (2d Cir. 1940). It has been held that distinctions in results based on these distinctions in form have been made obsolete by this Article. In re Yale Express System, Inc., 370 F.2d 433 (2d Cir. 1966), 384 F.2d 990 (2d Cir. 1967).

2. In view of the remedies provided the debtor and other creditors in subsection (1) when a secured party does not dispose of collateral in a commercially reasonable manner, it is of great importance to make clear what types of disposition are to be considered commercially reasonable, and in an appropriate case to give the secured party means of getting, by court order or negotiation with a creditors' committee or a representative of creditors, approval of a proposed method of disposition as a commercially reasonable one. Subsection (2) states rules to assist in the determination, and provides for such advance approval in appropriate situations. One recognized method of disposing of repossessed collateral is for the secured party to sell the collateral to or through a dealer—a method which in the long run may realize better average returns since the secured party does not usually maintain his own facilities for making such sales. Such a method of sale, fairly conducted, is recognized as commercially reasonable under the second sentence of subsection (2). However, none of the specific methods of disposition set forth in subsection (2) is to be regarded as either required or exclusive, provided only that the disposition made or about to be made by the secured party is commercially reasonable.

Cross References:

Point 1: Sections 1-203, 9-202 and 9-504.

Definitional Cross References:

"Collateral". Section 9-105.

"Consumer goods". Section 9–109.
"Creditor". Section 1–201.
"Debtor". Section 9–105.
"Knows". Section 1–201.
"Notification". Section 1–201.
"Person". Section 1–201.
"Representative". Section 1–201.
"Rights". Section 1–201.
"Secured party". Section 9–105.
"Security interest". Section 1–201.

ARTICLE 10

EFFECTIVE DATE AND REPEALER

See Article 11 for Transition Provisions for those jurisdictions adopting the 1972 amendments.

---

§ 10–101. Effective Date.

This Act shall become effective at midnight on December 31st following its enactment. It applies to transactions entered into and events occurring after that date.

Official Comment

This effective date is suggested so that there may be ample time for all those who will be affected by the provisions of the Code to become familiar with them.

§ 10–102. Specific Repealer; Provision for Transition.

(1) The following acts and all other acts and parts of acts inconsistent herewith are hereby repealed:

(Here should follow the acts to be specifically repealed including the following:

Uniform Negotiable Instruments Act
Uniform Warehouse Receipts Act
Uniform Sales Act
Uniform Bills of Lading Act
Uniform Stock Transfer Act
Uniform Conditional Sales Act
Uniform Trust Receipts Act
Also any acts regulating:
Bank collections
Bulk sales
Chattel mortgages
Conditional sales
Factor's lien acts
Farm storage of grain and similar acts
Assignment of accounts receivable)

(2) Transactions validly entered into before the effective date specified in Section 10–101 and the rights, duties and interests flowing from them remain valid thereafter and may be terminated, completed, consummated or enforced as required or permitted by any statute or other law amended or repealed by this Act as though such repeal or amendment had not occurred.

Note

Subsection (1) should be separately prepared for each state. The foregoing is a list of statutes to be checked.

Official Comment

Subsection (1) provides for the repeal of present uniform and other acts superseded by this Act. Subsection (2) provides for the transition to the Code.

§ 10–103. General Repealer.

Except as provided in the following section, all acts and parts of acts inconsistent with this Act are hereby repealed.

Official Comment

This section provides for the repeal of all other legislation inconsistent with this Act.

§ 10–104. Laws Not Repealed.

[(1)] The Article on Documents of Title (Article 7) does not repeal or modify any laws prescribing the form or contents of documents of title or the services or facilities to be afforded by bailees, or otherwise regulating bailees' businesses in respects not specifically dealt with herein; but the fact that such laws are violated does not affect the status of a document of title which otherwise complies with the definition of a document of title (Section 1–201).

As amended in 1962 and 1994.

See Appendix XII for material relating to changes made in text in 1994.

Official Comment

This section subordinates the Article of this Act on Documents of Title (Article 7) to the more specialized regulations of particular classes of bailees under other legislation and international treaties. Particularly, the provisions of that Article are superseded by applicable inconsistent provisions regarding the obligation of carriers and the limitation of their liability found in federal legislation dealing with transportation by water (including the Harter Act, Act of February 13, 1893, 27 Stat. 445, and the Carriage of Goods by Sea Act, Act of April 16, 1936, 49 Stat. 1207); the Warsaw Convention on International Air Transportation, 49 Stat. 3000, and Section 20(11) of the Interstate Commerce Act, Act of February 20, 1887, 24 Stat. 386, as amended. The Documents of Title provisions of this Act supplement such legislation largely in matters other than obligation of the bailee, e.g., form and effects of negotiation, procedure in the case of lost documents, effect of overissue, possibility of rapid transmission.

Cross Reference:

Section 7–103.

ARTICLE 11

EFFECTIVE DATE AND TRANSITION PROVISIONS

This material has been numbered Article 11 to distinguish it from Article 10, the transition provision of the 1962 Code, which may still remain in effect in some states to cover transition problems from pre-Code law to the original Uniform Commercial Code. Adaptation may be necessary in particular states. The terms "[old Code]" and "[new Code]" and "[old U.C.C.]" and "[new U.C.C.]" are used herein, and should be suitably changed in each state.

This draft was prepared by the Reporters and has not been passed upon by the Review Committee, the Permanent Editorial Board, the American Law Institute, or the National Conference of Commissioners on Uniform State Laws. It is submitted as a working draft which may be adapted as appropriate in each state. The "Discussions" were written by the Reporters to assist in understanding the purpose of the drafts.

Section

---

§ 11–101. Effective Date.

This Act shall become effective at 12:01 A.M. on ______, 19__.

§ 11–102. Preservation of Old Transition Provision.

The provisions of [here insert reference to the original transition provision in the particular state] shall continue to apply to [the new U.C.C.] and for this purpose the [old U.C.C. and new U.C.C.] shall be considered one continuous statute.

§ 11–103. Transition to [New Code]—General Rule.

Transactions validly entered into after [effective date of old U.C.C.] and before [effective date of new U.C.C.], and which were subject to the provisions of [old U.C.C.] and which would be subject to this Act as amended if they had been entered into after the effective date of [new U.C.C.] and the rights, duties and interests flowing from such transactions remain valid after the latter date and may be terminated, completed, consummated or enforced as required or permitted by the [new U.C.C.]. Security interests arising out of such transactions which are perfected when [new U.C.C.] becomes effective shall remain perfected until they lapse as provided in [new U.C.C.], and may be continued as permitted by [new U.C.C.], except as stated in Section 11-105.

§ 11-104. Transition Provision on Change of Requirement of Filing.

A security interest for the perfection of which filing or the taking of possession was required under [old U.C.C.] and which attached prior to the effective date of [new U.C.C.] but was not perfected shall be deemed perfected on the effective date of [new U.C.C.] if [new U.C.C.] permits perfection without filing or authorizes filing in the office or offices where a prior ineffective filing was made.

§ 11-105. Transition Provision on Change of Place of Filing.

(1) A financing statement or continuation statement filed prior to [effective date of new U.C.C.] which shall not have lapsed prior to [the effective date of new U.C.C.] shall remain effective for the period provided in the [old Code], but not less than five years after the filing.

(2) With respect to any collateral acquired by the debtor subsequent to the effective date of [new U.C.C.], any effective financing statement or continuation statement described in this section shall apply only if the filing or filings are in the office or offices that would be appropriate to perfect the security interests in the new collateral under [new U.C.C.].

(3) The effectiveness of any financing statement or continuation statement filed prior to [effective date of new U.C.C.] may be continued by a continuation statement as permitted by [new U.C.C.], except that if [new U.C.C.] requires a filing in an office where there was no previous financing statement, a new financing statement conforming to Section 11-106 shall be filed in that office.

(4) If the record of a mortgage of real estate would have been effective as a fixture filing of goods described therein if [new U.C.C.] had been in effect on the date of recording the mortgage, the mortgage shall be deemed effective as a fixture filing as to such goods under subsection (6) of Section 9-402 of the [new U.C.C.] on the effective date of [new U.C.C.].

§ 11-106. Required Refilings.

(1) If a security interest is perfected or has priority when this Act takes effect as to all persons or as to certain persons without any filing or recording, and if the filing of a financing statement would be required for the perfection or priority of the security interest against those persons under [new U.C.C.], the perfection and priority rights of the security interest continue until 3 years after the effective date of [new U.C.C.]. The perfection will then lapse unless a financing statement is filed as provided in subsection (4) or unless the security interest is perfected otherwise than by filing.

(2) If a security interest is perfected when [new U.C.C.] takes effect under a law other than [U.C.C.] which requires no further filing, refiling or recording to continue its perfection, perfection continues until and will lapse 3 years after [new U.C.C.] takes effect, unless a financing statement is filed as provided in subsection (4) or unless the security interest is perfected otherwise than by filing, or unless under subsection (3) of Section 9-302 the other law continues to govern filing.

(3) If a security interest is perfected by a filing, refiling or recording under a law repealed by this Act which required further filing, refiling or recording to continue its perfection, perfection continues and will lapse on the date provided by the law so repealed for such further filing, refiling or recording unless a financing statement is filed as provided in subsection (4) or unless the security interest is perfected otherwise than by filing.

(4) A financing statement may be filed within six months before the perfection of a security interest would otherwise lapse. Any such financing statement may be signed by either the debtor or the secured party. It must identify the security agreement, statement or notice (however denominated in any statute or other law repealed or modified by this Act), state the office where and the date when the last filing, refiling or recording, if any, was made with respect thereto, and the filing number, if any, or book and page, if any, of recording and further state that the security agreement, statement or notice, however denominated, in another filing office under the [U.C.C.] or under any statute or other law repealed or modified by this Act is still effective. Section 9-401 and Section 9-103 determine the proper place to file such a financing statement. Except as specified in this subsection, the provisions of Section 9-403(3) for continuation statements apply to such a financing statement.

§ 11-107. Transition Provisions as to Priorities.

Except as otherwise provided in [Article 11], [old U.C.C.] shall apply to any questions of priority if the positions of the parties were fixed prior to the effective date of [new U.C.C.]. In other cases questions of priority shall be determined by [new U.C.C.].

§ 11-108. Presumption That Rule of Law Continues Unchanged.

Unless a change in law has clearly been made, the provisions of [new U.C.C.] shall be deemed declaratory of the meaning of the [old U.C.C.].

APPENDIX I

1977 OFFICIAL TEXT SHOWING CHANGES MADE IN FORMER TEXT OF ARTICLE 8, INVESTMENT SECURITIES AND OF RELATED SECTIONS AND REASONS FOR CHANGES

REPORTER'S INTRODUCTORY COMMENT

This proposed revision of Article 8 of the Uniform Commercial Code is an outgrowth of the work of the Committee on Stock Certificates of the Section of Corporation, Banking and Business Law of the American Bar Association. That committee, formed in 1971 in response to the "Paperwork Crunch" in the securities markets during the late 1960's, was charged with determining what legislation, if any, would be advisable to facilitate the elimination, or reduction in the use, of stock certificates and with drafting such legislation as was proposed. The committee's report, issued on September 15, 1975, contained two principal recommendations: 1) that the Model Business Corporation Act be amended in order to permit the issuance of corporate stock in uncertificated form and 2) that Article 8 of the Uniform Commercial Code (and related sections of other Articles) be revised to provide rules to regulate the rights, duties and obligations of the issuers of, and persons dealing with, uncertificated investment securities. Appendix B of the report was a suggested revision of Article 8.

The suggested revision of Article 8 was submitted by the committee to the Permanent Editorial Board for the Uniform Commercial Code which, in turn, referred it to its 348 Committee for review and comment. The revision, with changes suggested by the 348 Committee, was subsequently reviewed by the Permanent Editorial Board and further drafts were presented before the 1976 meeting of the National Conference of Commissioners on Uniform State Laws, the Council of the American Law Institute and the 1977 Annual Meeting of the American Law Institute. At its 1977 meeting, the NCCUSL approved the substance of the revision and referred it to its Committee on Style. That committee made a number of stylistic changes in wording, punctuation and the like, and its product is presented herewith.

In this introductory comment, section references are to the revised Article unless preceded by the word "present". Detailed "Reasons for 1977 Change" follow almost every section of the revision, but the pattern is summarized in this introductory comment in the hope that it will be helpful to an understanding of the general scheme of the revision.

Scope

Perhaps the best approach to describing the scope of the revision is first to state what it does *not* do. The revision does not compel the issuance of uncertificated securities by any issuer. Furthermore, the revision does not authorize the issuance of uncertificated securities, a function of the state corporation laws. What the revision is intended to accomplish is to set forth a coherent group of rules for the issuers, buyers, sellers and other persons dealing with uncertificated securities, to the same extent that present Article 8 deals with these matters with respect to certificated securities. Although the primary focus of inquiry regarding the possible elimination of certificates has been on corporate stock, the revision is broad enough to cover uncertificated debt securities, should such be issued in the future. It might be noted that the most significant uncertificated system now in operation is that conducted by the Federal Reserve Banks for United States Government Bonds. It is possible, and, indeed, probable, that particular issues of securities may, temporarily or even permanently, be partly certificated and partly uncertificated. If such be the case, the choice of form will lie with the owner and provisions are made for exchangeability at the owner's option [8–407].

The present definition of "security" [present 8–102(1)(a)] is restated, in somewhat changed form but without intended change of substance, as the definition of "certificated security" [8–102(1)(a)]. A parallel definition of "uncertificated security" is then provided, differing in that it does not require representation by an instrument and somewhat narrower in scope to eliminate the inclusion of some interests, *e.g.,* bank accounts, that a broad construction might otherwise include [8–102(1)(b)]. It is not intended that either definition coincide with the definition of "security" for other purposes, *e.g.,* the federal securities laws. See Comment 3 to Section 8–102.

Approach

There has been a conscious attempt to disturb present Article 8 as little as possible. First, the subject-matter content and order of the forty-one numbered sections of the present statute have been preserved. Only four sections have been added. Three of these have no application to wholly certificated systems [8–108, 8–407 & 8–408].

Secondly, with the exception of only two present sections [8–313 & 8–317] and the other new section [8–321], there has been no attempt to change the law with respect to certificated securities. In some instances, where there seemed to be compelling reasons to do so, certain wording and structure have been changed, but without any intention to change the substance. In most instances, the language of the present Article, as it applies to certificated securities, has been preserved with minor stylistic changes.

Finally, the rules governing uncertificated securities have been formulated to conform as closely as possible to the rules for certificated securities, consistent, of course, with such changes as are demanded by the absence of an indispensable instrument. For example, the rights of secured parties [8–207], the "appropriate person" to initiate requests for registration of transfer [8–308] and the assurances an issuer may require as a condition to complying with such requests [8–402] have been structured in a way to produce a minimum of disparity of results and procedures whether certificated or uncertificated securities are involved.

Transfer

The essential difference between a certificated and an uncertificated security, and that from which the principal difficulties arise, is that the former is represented by an instrument, which may be treated as the property it represents, and the latter is not. Under present Article 8, transfer of a certificated security by purchase, a term which includes all voluntary transfers whether or not for value [present 1–201(32)], is accomplished by delivery of the certificated security to the purchaser [present 8–301(1)] or by some other method deemed to constitute delivery to the purchaser [present 8–313(1)]. Obviously, when a security is uncertificated, there is no instrument to deliver.

In the revised Article, the transfer rules are collected in a single subsection [8–313(1)] and are expressly made exclusive. The basic rule for certificated securities, transfer by delivery, is restated [8–313(1)(a)] and a coordinate rule for uncertificated securities, transfer by registration, is added [8–313(1)(b)]. The present rule, that delivery to the purchaser's broker of a certificated security issued in the name of or specially indorsed to the purchaser constitutes transfer to the purchaser, is preserved [8–313(1)(c)], but is expanded to cover such delivery not only to the purchaser's broker but to any financial intermediary acting for the purchaser. A "financial intermediary" is defined to include (in addition to brokers) banks, clearing corporations and other entities which regularly maintain security accounts for their customers [8–313(4)].

The remaining subparagraphs recognize current security-holding practices and provide explicitly for the transfer of ownership of both certificated and uncertificated securities controlled by third parties. Thus, when the controlling party is a clearing corporation [8–102(3)], transfer is effected merely by book entry [8–313(1)(g)]. When the controlling party is a financial intermediary, but not a clearing corporation, transfer is effected by confirmation to the purchaser accompanied by book entry [8–313(1)(d)]. When the controlling party is not a financial intermediary, transfer is effected by acknowledgment to the purchaser [8–313(1)(e) & (f)]. Three provisions apply only to the creation and release of security interests [8–313(1)(h), (i) & (j)].

Registration of Transfer

Registration of transfer of a certificated security is requested by presenting the security itself, duly indorsed, to the issuer [8–401(1)]. With uncertificated securities that procedure is unavailable, and the request for registration of transfer is made by an "instruction" [8–308(4)] which normally will be a signed writing [8–308(5)(a)] but which may, under the terms of a written agreement, be in other than written form [8–308(5)(b)]. To be effective, an instruction must be originated by an "appropriate person" who, for an unencumbered security, is the registered owner or his representative [8–308(7)(a) & (8)].

Upon receipt of an instruction, the issuer is under a duty to effect a duly requested registration [8–401(1)], liable for delay or failure to comply [8–401(2)], entitled to certain assurances [8–402], and liable for improper registration [8–404(3)] in much the same manner applicable to requests for registration of transfer of a certificated security.

Within two business days after registration of transfer of an uncertificated security, the issuer must send a written statement confirming the registration to both the transferor [8–408(5)] and the transferee [8–408(1)]. The statement sent to the transferor will alert him to take appropriate action if the transfer was unauthorized or otherwise improper. The statement sent to the transferee will assure him that the transfer has been properly registered and will also serve as notice to him of any liens [8–103(b)], restrictions [8–204(b)] or claims [8–304(2)] to which the uncertificated security may be subject. Unless a transferee for value is relying on a third party, *e.g.*, his broker, it is anticipated that he may withhold his consideration, in escrow or otherwise, until he receives an appropriate statement from the issuer.

Creation of Security Interests

A security interest in a certificated security is normally created by delivery (pledge) of the security, duly indorsed, to the secured party (pledgee). The physical procedure is indistinguishable from an outright transfer. The pledgee may elect to leave the security registered in the name of the debtor or to cause the registration of transfer to himself or his nominee.

A security interest in an uncertificated security may be created by registration of transfer to the secured party, a procedure which involves no concepts distinct from those involved in any outright transfer of an uncertificated security. The secured party will be in essentially the same position as the pledgee of a certificated security who obtains registration of transfer to himself.

This revision provides an additional method for evidencing a security interest in an uncertificated security—registration of pledge [8–108]. This is intended to create a situation analogous to that when the pledgee of a certificated security leaves the security registered in the debtor's name. Registration of pledge is effected by submission of an instruction [8–308(4)] to the issuer, originated by the registered owner or his representative [8–308(7)(a) & (8)]. The procedure for registration follows that established for registration of transfer. The issuer is obligated to send confirmatory statements to the pledgee and owner immediately following registration [8–408(2)] and the pledgee, like the buyer, may choose to await receipt of the statement before advancing the loan.

Once a pledge has been registered, the registered owner continues to enjoy all the rights of an owner (dividends, voting rights, notices, etc.) [8–207(2)] except one—the power to order transfer. That power passes exclusively to the registered pledgee [8–207(3)] and only the pledgee or his representative is an appropriate person to originate a transfer instruction [8–308(7)(b) & (8)]. This is substantially the situation that exists when a certificated security is pledged. The still registered owner is recognized as such by the issuer [8–207(1)], but the pledgee's possession of the duly indorsed certificate achieves the dual purpose of depriving the debtor of his power to transfer and conferring that power on the pledgee. The registered pledgee of an uncertificated security may exercise his transfer power in three ways: by outright transfer free of his pledge [8–207(4)(a)]; by transfer of ownership subject to his pledge [8–207(4)(b)]; or by transfer of his security interest to another secured party [8–207(4)(c)].

There is one area of disparity between the pledge of a certificated security and the registered pledge of an uncertificated security. When a certificated security is held by a pledgee without registration of transfer, additional securities distributed with respect to the pledged security, *e.g.*, stock dividends, will necessarily be delivered to the registered owner, since the issuer is unaware of the pledgee's interest. When an uncertificated security is subject to a registered pledge, such additional securities will, if uncertificated, be registered subject to the pledge [8–207(6)(a)] or, if certificated, will be delivered to the pledgee [8–207(6)(b)]. This appears to be a desirable result which is impractical to obtain under the pledge of a certificated security. Similarly, securities issued or money paid in exchange for an uncertificated security will be subject to the pledgee's control [8–207(6)].

Under the revised Article, the transfer rules are exclusive and expressly include the transfer of security interests [8–313(1)]. Thus, the creation of security interests is conditioned upon the use of an effective means of transfer [8–321(1)]. The transfer rules include the physical delivery of a certificated security [8–313(1)(a)] and the registration of either pledge or transfer of an uncertificated security [8–313(1)(b)]. They also include provisions when securities are controlled by third parties. When the controlling party is a clearing corporation [8–102(3)], transfer is effected by book entry [8–313(1)(g)]. When the controlling party is a financial intermediary [8–313(4)], but not a clearing corporation, transfer is effected by confirmation to the secured party accompanied by a book entry [8–313(1)(d)]. When the controlling party is not a financial intermediary, *e.g.*, a prior pledgee, transfer is effected by acknowledgment to the secured party [8–313(1)(e) & (f)]. Security interests created by any of these methods are enforceable even without a written agreement signed by the debtor [8–321(2)] since they involve either possession by the secured party or the functional equivalent thereof.

In addition, three methods of transfer, applicable only to the creation of security interests, are provided [8–313(1)(h), (i) & (j)]. These methods do require a written security agreement signed by the debtor and are included to permit the continuation of practices which result in perfected non-possessory security interests under present Article 9 [present 9–304(4) & 9–305] and to document the creation of a security interest in securities already held in the debtor's account by a financial intermediary.

Perfection of Security Interests

The security interest of the pledgee of a certificated security is both created [present 9–203(1)(a)] and perfected [present 9–304(1)] by the secured party's possession. Possessory security interests are expressly exempted from the normal filing requirements of Article 9 [9–302(1)(a)]. A non-possessory security interest may be perfected by notice to a bailee [present 9–305] or, under certain conditions and for temporary periods, automatically [present 9–304(4) & (5)].

Under the revised Article, a security interest which is effectively created is also perfected [8–321(2)]. If the security interest is created under the provision which corresponds to the present provision of Article 9 for temporary automatic perfection [8–313(1)(i)], perfection expires at the end of the 21 day period unless other steps are timely taken [8–321(2)]. Security interests in securities are expressly excluded from the perfection provisions of Article 9 [9–302(1)(f), 9–304(1) & (4) and 9–305].

Termination of Security Interests

The security interest of a pledgee of a certificated security is normally released by redelivery of the security to the debtor. Similarly, the security interest in an uncertificated security created by registration of transfer to the secured party is released by registration of transfer back to the debtor. A security interest in an uncertificated security created by registration of pledge is released by registration of release [8–108]. Registration of release is effected by submission of an instruction [8–308(4)] to the issuer, originated by the registered pledgee or his representative [8–308(7)(b) & (8)]. The procedure for registration follows that established for registration of transfer or pledge. The issuer is obligated to send confirmatory statements to the pledgee and the owner immediately following registration [8–408(3)] and the owner may choose to make arrangements to withhold his repayment until he has received an appropriate statement.

A security interest in securities controlled by a third party would normally be terminated by a transfer back to the debtor under the same method employed for its creation [8–313(1)(d), (e), (f), (g) or (h)]. Unless the parties otherwise agree, any such transfer will terminate the security interest. Provision is made for temporary continuation of perfection in the case where a certificated security is redelivered to the debtor for limited purposes [8–321(4)], analogous to similar provisions in Article 9 [present 9–304(5)].

The Initial Transaction Statement

When a security is certificated, the security itself, if genuine, is prima facie evidence of the holder's rights [8–105(3)(c)]. When a security is uncertificated, a similar, but distinctly more limited, function is served by the initial transaction statement (hereinafter "ITS"). The ITS is a signed statement sent by the issuer of an uncertificated security upon registration of transfer, pledge or release to the transferee, pledgee or owner, respectively [8–408(4)]. Like certificated securities, an ITS acts as an estoppel statement against the issuer. But unlike certificated securities, an ITS runs in favor of only the addressee and speaks only as of the time of its issuance [8–105(3)(d)]. Consequently, parties other than the addressee, particularly subsequent purchasers, cannot justifiably rely on what an ITS does or does not contain. The statute requires a warning legend to that effect [8–408(9)].

The purchaser of an uncertificated security is charged with notice of the issuer's right to a lien [8–103(b)], terms of a security [8–202(1)], restrictions on transfer [8–204(b)] and adverse claims [8–304(2)] which appear or are referred to in the ITS sent to him. Conversely, the purchaser for value without notice who receives an ITS which does not refer to defects or defenses is normally entitled to assume that none exists. Furthermore, the purchaser for value without notice who receives an ITS is generally entitled to assume that the uncertificated security referred to therein is valid [8–202(2)(a)], that, in many cases, it has been properly signed, even when it has not [8–205], that it has been properly completed, even when it has not [8–206(3)(b)] and receives the benefit of certain warranties of third party signatories [8–208(1)]. Finally, the purchaser for value without notice who receives an ITS enjoys a limitation in the warranties he has made in connection with the presentation of a certificated security to the issuer [8–306(1)] and is shielded from liability to a former owner or pledgee [8–311(a)]. In these respects, the ITS serves substantially the same function for the addressee as does a certificated security.

Under the shelter principle, the purchaser of a security acquires the rights of his transferor [8–301(1)]. If *A* had purchased an uncertificated security without knowledge of a restriction to which it was subject and had received an ITS which failed to note the restriction, he would take free of the restriction [8–204(b)]. Any purchaser from *A* would acquire the security free of the restriction and could, relying on *A*'s rights, demand a clean ITS from the issuer. If, however, *A* had knowledge of the restriction when he purchased, *A* would be subject to the restriction even if, by error, the ITS sent to him had failed to note its existence. In that event, notwithstanding *A*'s clean ITS, the rights of a purchaser from *A* would rise no higher than *A*'s, and the purchaser would take subject to the restriction. The purchaser would take free of the restriction only if he purchased without knowledge *and* if the ITS *sent to him* failed to note the restriction. In contrast, if *A* had purchased a certificated security with knowledge of a restriction not noted thereon, a purchaser from *A* without knowledge would take free of the restriction [8–204(a)] even though *A* could not have.

There is a much more significant difference. A purchaser may normally assume that the holder (registered owner, indorsee or bearer) of a certificated security is the owner and entitled to transfer it. An ITS, however, merely evidences the facts at the time of its issuance [8–105(3)(d)]. The fact that *A* exhibits an ITS showing that *A* had become the owner of an uncertificated security at some prior date gives a potential purchaser absolutely no assurance that *A* has any rights in that security now. Since the time of the ITS's issuance, *A* might have pledged, otherwise encumbered or transferred the security. While, in some cases, the purchaser may be willing to rely on *A*'s representations or on those of a third-party guarantor, he cannot justifiably rely on any rights against the issuer until he receives his own ITS.

Rights and Obligations of Buyers and Sellers

All securities of the same issue, both certificated and uncertificated, are treated as fungible. Thus, when an issue of securities is comprised of both certificated and uncertificated securities, a person obligated to transfer securities of that issue may perform either by delivering duly registered or indorsed certificated securities to his obligee or by causing the registration of transfer of equivalent uncertificated securities to his obligee [8–107(1)]. Similarly, the buyer of securities becomes obligated to pay the price whether the securities transferred to him are certificated or uncertificated [8–107(2)].

In an exchange or brokerage transaction, the selling customer may complete his obligation by delivering certificated securities to his broker [8–314(1)(a)(i)], by causing the registration of transfer of uncertificated securities to his broker [8–314(1)(a)(ii)] or, if requested, by causing a third party to acknowledge that he holds a security for the broker [8–314(1)(a)(iii)]. In addition, the selling customer can conditionally fulfill his obligation by delivering to his broker a transfer instruction for an uncertificated security, but his obligation is not completed if the instruction is presented to the issuer within thirty days *and* the issuer refuses to register the requested transfer [8–314(1)(a)(iv)]. This final alternative is also available to the selling broker in fulfilling his obligation to the buying broker, with the same condition attaching [8–314(1)(b)(iii)]. In a transaction not on an exchange or through brokers, the transferor's duty is not fulfilled, even conditionally, by the delivery of an instruction [8–314(2)].

If the issuer of an uncertificated security demands proof of authority or other evidence which is necessary to obtain registration of transfer, pledge or release of the security, the transferor, pledgor or pledgee, as the case may be, is obligated to provide such evidence, but, if the transfer, pledge or release is not for value, only if he is reimbursed for any expense involved [8–316].

The performance exception to the statute of frauds includes, in addition to the acceptance of delivery of a certificated security, the acceptance of a transfer instruction and the situation where the transfer of an uncertificated security has been registered to the alleged buyer and the alleged buyer does not object in writing to the issuer within ten days after receiving the statement confirming the registration of transfer [8–319(b)].

Warranties

The person who requests an issuer to register the transfer of a certificated security, by presenting a duly indorsed certificated security, warrants to the issuer that he has the power to do so, or, in effect, that the chain of indorsements is genuine and complete [8–306(1)]. In making that warranty, the presenter, who, in the typical case, is, or acts for, the transferee, has before him, as evidence, the security, the indorsements and signature guarantees. On the other hand, the person who requests an issuer to register the transfer (or pledge or release) of an uncertificated security does so by presenting an instruction, which is not even presumptive evidence that the originator is the registered owner or pledgee of the security involved. Hence, the presenter, as such, warrants nothing to the issuer. Rather, the originator of the instruction, who is responsible for its creation, warrants to the issuer that he will be, at the time of presentation, an appropriate person to originate the instruction and entitled to the requested registration—facts which he, and perhaps no one else, knows [8–306(5)].

The transferor of a certificated security warrants to a purchaser for value the effectiveness and rightfulness of the transfer and the genuineness of the security [8–306(2)]. In effect, he undertakes that the issuer will recognize the purchaser as the owner of the intangible interest represented by the security free from any defects not noted thereon. The warranties made by the originator of an instruction to a purchaser for value are intended to produce substantially the same obligation and include, therefore, a warranty of absence of defects—a fact which the purchaser of a certificated security can himself ascertain from the security itself [8–306(7)] but of which the purchaser of an uncertificated security cannot have knowledge until he receives his initial transaction statement from the issuer.

The warranties made by secured parties who originate instructions with respect to uncertificated securities are limited [8–306(8)] consistent with similar limitations of the warranties of secured parties who deliver certificated securities they hold in pledge [8–306(4)].

Guarantees

The signature guarantee, which is an essential element of the transfer process for widely-held securities, presents a special problem. The signature guarantor of the indorsement of a certificated security warrants that the indorser is an appropriate person, *i.e.,* that he is, or acts for, the owner [8–312(1)(b)]. To make a similar undertaking with respect to the originator of an instruction to transfer (or pledge or release) an uncertificated security, the signature guarantor, without a certificated security, prior indorsements and signature guarantees before him, would have to warrant a fact of which he has no evidence—that the originator is, or acts for, the registered owner or pledgee. That fact, however, will be known to the issuer and since the issuer is the only person who must act on the instruction, there is no need to require the signature guarantor's warranty. Hence, the warranties of the signature guarantor of an instruction are limited to genuineness, capacity and the fact that the signer is, or acts for, the *purported* owner or pledgee [8–312(2)]. The originator himself warrants to the issuer that he is an appropriate person [8–306(5)].

A special guarantee of signature is also provided by which the guarantor warrants, in effect, that the instruction will result in the requested transfer, free from defects [8–312(3)]. Although the issuer cannot require a special guarantee [8–312(7)], it is anticipated that it will be used in brokerage transactions in which the broker will specially guarantee the signature of his own customer. When a special guarantee of signature is made, the originator makes equivalent warranties to the guarantor [8–306(6)].

Finally, there is a guarantee of instruction which entails a warranty of rightfulness in all respects [8–312(6)], analogous to the guarantee of indorsement of a certificated security [8–312(5)]. This guarantee cannot be required by the issuer [8–312(7)], but when it is made, the originator makes equivalent warranties to the guarantor [8–306(7)].

Bona Fide Purchase

The concept of bona fide purchase applies to both certificated and uncertificated securities [8–302(1)]. The difference is that the purchaser of a certificated security is charged with notice only of what appears when he or a person acting in his behalf takes delivery of the security while the purchaser of an uncertificated security is charged with notice of what appears in the initial transaction statement sent to him. Thus, the purchaser of a certificated security without notice takes free of liens [8–103(a)], terms of a security which may be defenses [8–202(1)] and restrictions [8–204(a)] not noted on the security. He may also take free of any adverse claim [8–302(3)] unless the nature of the claim is such that it would be disclosed by the security itself [8–304(1)]. The purchaser of an uncertificated security without notice, however, is charged with notice of liens [8–103(b)], defenses [8–202(1)] and restrictions [8–204(b)] noted in the initial transaction statement sent to him. He is also charged with notice of adverse claims shown in the initial transaction statement [8–304(2)]. Only when he has received a clean initial transaction statement can he be sure that he enjoys bona fide purchaser status [8–302(1)(b)].

The above-described difference is of limited practical significance. As has already been noted, the purchaser of an uncertificated security cannot be sure that he has received anything (whether or not defective) until he receives his initial transaction statement. Therefore, unless he chooses to rely on the warranties of his seller or a third party guarantor, he will not release his consideration unless and until he receives a clean initial transaction statement to give him the assurance that he has, indeed, received what he bargained for. The wide-spread use of wholly certificateless systems will necessarily involve the development of escrow arrangements or other mechanisms by means of which the parties will obtain satisfactory assurances.

Adverse Claims

The treatment of adverse claims presented a very special kind of problem. With certificated securities they are communicated by mere written notification to the issuer [8–403(1)]. They do not normally constitute a serious problem because they can be so easily defeated by transfer of the security to a purchaser without knowledge [8–302(3)]. The rules for certificated securities have, therefore, been preserved [8–403(1), (2) & (3)].

With uncertificated securities, however, the rules become unworkable because transfer is accomplished only by communication with the issuer [8–313(1)(b)] and the purchaser is charged with notice of whatever appears in the initial transaction statement sent to him [8–304(2)]. Consequently, new rules have been developed for uncertificated securities. They require that a third party claim be embodied in legal process in order to make it cognizable by the issuer [8–403(4)(a)]. They also permit, under certain circumstances, the registration of transfer or pledge subject to an adverse claim [8–403(5)]. Finally, they provide protection to a registered pledgee who attained bona fide purchaser status prior to the time that notice of a cognizable adverse claim reached the issuer [8–403(6)].

Creditors' Rights

The general rule of present Article 8, that no judicial lien on a debtor's interest in a security is valid until the security is actually seized [present 8–317(1)] is wholly inapplicable to uncertificated securities and, in the light of wide-spread nominee registration, depository systems and the like, has become inadequate even with respect to certificated securities. That rule is retained only for certificated securities in the debtor's control [8–317(1)]. Uncertificated securities registered in the debtor's name may be reached only by service upon the issuer [8–317(2)]. The interest of a debtor in either certificated or uncertificated securities under the control of secured parties or financial intermediaries is reached by service upon the controlling party [8–317(3) & (4)]. When a debtor's interest in securities controlled by a third party is subject to a judicial lien, provisions are made for the transfer of such securities, free of the lien, and the shifting of the lien to the proceeds in the hands of the third party [8–317(5)].

Nominee Registration

The increasing incidence of nominee registration in brokerage accounts, bank custody accounts, security depositories and otherwise has led to new and expanded provisions regarding the rights of creditors [8–317]. The same phenomenon has also led to a revision of the general transfer rules by substituting the broader category of "financial intermediary" [8–313(4)] where only "broker" formerly appeared [8–313(1)(c) & (d), (2) & (3)].

ARTICLE 8

INVESTMENT SECURITIES

PART 1

SHORT TITLE AND GENERAL MATTERS

§ 8–101. Short Title.

This Article shall be known and may be cited as Uniform Commercial Code—Investment Securities.

Reasons for 1977 Change

Although the title of the Article has not been changed, its coverage has been broadened, by amendment to Section 8–102, to include both securities which are reified, i.e., represented by certificates or other instruments, and those which are not. The former are defined as "certificated securities" and constitute the entire subject matter of present Article 8. The latter are defined as "uncertificated securities" and are not now expressly covered by the Uniform Commercial Code. The revised Article is intended to govern the relationships, rights and duties of the issuers of and the parties that deal with both certificated and uncertificated securities to the same extent that present Article 8 governs such relationships, rights and duties with respect to certificated securities alone.

This Article does not purport to determine whether a particular issue of securities should be represented by certificates, in whole or in part. It is contemplated that such determination will be made by the issuer under appropriate state or federal law. It is further contemplated that a particular issue of securities may be partly certificated and partly uncertificated, in which event the determination will be at the option of the owner to the extent that the issuer permits.

The form of the Article has been disturbed as little as possible and each numbered section deals with the subject matter of the similarly numbered section of the present Article. Only four new sections, 8–108, 8–321, 8–407 and 8–408, have been added.

§ 8–102. Definitions and Index of Definitions.

(1) In this Article, unless the context otherwise requires:

[(a) A "security" is an instrument which

(i) is issued in bearer or registered form; and

(ii) is of a type commonly dealt in upon securities exchanges or markets or commonly recognized in any area in which it is issued or dealt in as a medium for investment; and

(iii) is either one of a class or series or by its terms is divisible into a class or series of instruments; and

(iv) evidences a share, participation or other interest in property or in an enterprise or evidences an obligation of the issuer.]

(a) A "certificated security" is a share, participation, or other interest in property of or an enterprise of the issuer or an obligation of the issuer which is

(i) represented by an instrument issued in bearer or registered form;

(ii) of a type commonly dealt in on securities exchanges or markets or commonly recognized in any area in which it is issued or dealt in as a medium for investment; and

(iii) either one of a class or series or by its terms divisible into a class or series of shares, participations, interests, or obligations.

(b) An "uncertificated security" is a share, participation, or other interest in property or an enterprise of the issuer or an obligation of the issuer which is

(i) not represented by an instrument and the transfer of which is registered upon books maintained for that purpose by or on behalf of the issuer;

(ii) of a type commonly dealt in on securities exchanges or markets; and

(iii) either one of a class or series or by its terms divisible into a class or series of shares, participations, interests, or obligations.

(c) [(b)] A "security" is either a certificated or an uncertificated security. If a security is certificated, the terms "security" and "certificated security" may mean either the intangible interest, the instrument representing that interest, or both, as the context requires. A writing [which] that is a certificated security is governed by this Article and not by [Uniform Commercial Code—Commercial Paper] Article 3, even though it also meets the requirements of that Article. This Article does not apply to money. If a certificated security has been retained by or surrendered to the issuer or its transfer agent for reasons other than registration of transfer, other temporary purpose, payment, exchange, or acquisition by the issuer, that security shall be treated as an uncertificated security for purposes of this Article.

(d) [(c)] A certificated security is in "registered form" [when] if

(i) it specifies a person entitled to the security or the rights it [evidences] represents, and [when]

(ii) its transfer may be registered upon books maintained for that purpose by or on behalf of [an] the issuer, or the security so states.

(e) [(d)] A certificated security is in "bearer form" [when] if it runs to bearer according to its terms and not by reason of any indorsement.

(2) A "subsequent purchaser" is a person who takes other than by original issue.

(3) A "clearing corporation" is a corporation registered as a "clearing agency" under the federal securities laws or a corporation:

(a) at least [ninety] 90 percent of [the] whose capital stock [of which] is held by or for one or more [persons (other than individuals)] organizations, none of which, other than a national securities exchange or association, holds in excess of 20 percent of the capital stock of the corporation, and each of [whom] which is

(i) [is] subject to supervision or regulation pursuant to the provisions of federal or state banking laws or state insurance laws, [or]

(ii) [is] a broker or dealer or investment company registered under the [Securities Exchange Act of 1934 or the Investment Company Act of 1940] federal securities laws, or

(iii) [is] a national securities exchange or association registered under [a statute of the United States such as the Securities Exchange Act of 1934,] the federal securities laws; and [none of whom, other than a national securities exchange or association, holds in excess of twenty per cent of the capital stock of such corporation; and]

(b) any remaining capital stock of which is held by individuals who have purchased [such capital stock] it at or prior to the time of their taking office as directors of [such] the corporation and who have purchased only so much of the capital stock as [may be] is necessary to permit them to qualify as [such] directors.

(4) A "custodian bank" is [any] a bank or trust company [which] that is supervised and examined by state or federal authority having supervision over banks and [which] is acting as custodian for a clearing corporation.

(5) Other definitions applying to this Article or to specified Parts thereof and the sections in which they appear are:

"Adverse claim".	Section [8-301] 8-302.
"Bona fide purchaser".	Section 8-302.
"Broker".	Section 8-303.
"Debtor".	Section 9-105.
"Financial intermediary".	Section 8-313.
"Guarantee of the signature".	Section 8-402.
"Initial transaction statement".	Section 8-408.
"Instruction".	Section 8-308.
"Intermediary Bank".	Section 4-105.
"Issuer".	Section 8-201.
"Overissue".	Section 8-104.
"Secured Party".	Section 9-105.
"Security Agreement".	Section 9-105.

(6) In addition Article 1 contains general definitions and principles of construction and interpretation applicable throughout this Article.

Reasons for 1977 Change

New paragraph (1)(a) defines "certificated security" in essentially the same terms as present paragraph (1)(a) defines "security". The definition is rearranged in order to permit a parallel definition of "uncertificated security" in new paragraph (1)(b). Two minor changes have been made. The phrase "of the issuer" has been repeated in order to make clear that it modifies "property" and "enterprise" as well as "obligation". It is understood that this was intended in the present statute. The word "represented" has been substituted for "evidenced" as more accurately conveying the notion that a certificated security is, in many ways, treated as if it were the property itself, e.g., ownership is transferred by delivery. Compare the definition of "instrument" in Section 9-105(1)(i).

This terminology, which is used throughout the revised Article, conforms to that of Section 23 of the Model Business Corporation Act and avoids confusion since there will be pieces of paper, statements and the like that will "evidence" uncertificated securities.

The definition of "uncertificated security" in paragraph (1)(b) differs from the definition of certificated security in two respects. The first change is in subparagraph (i) which provides that it is not represented by an instrument and is always registered. The second change is the omission from subparagraph (ii) of the phrase "or commonly recognized in any area in which it is issued or dealt in as a medium for investment". It was thought that where there was no requirement of representation by an instrument a great many interests which might be regarded as media for investment would be classified as securities under the umbrella of the omitted phrase. Although the official comment to the present section calls attention to the possible difference in coverage of Article 8 and other securities laws, the definition has been narrowed in order to minimize, if not eliminate, the need for strained distinctions. The remaining language of subparagraph (ii) is intended to cover such interests as the stock of closely-held corporations which, although not in fact dealt in on exchanges or markets, is "of a type" that is. Interests like bank accounts are intended to be excluded by the omission of the medium for investment language.

Paragraph (1)(c) defines "security" as either a certificated security or an uncertificated security, defined in the two preceding paragraphs. The second sentence of (1)(c) is intended to eliminate confusion arising from the fact that certificated securities (all securities under the present statute) are alternatively viewed as the actual pieces of paper and the interests they represent. See, e.g., present Section 8–103, which provides "A lien upon a security [the intangible interest] ... is valid ... only if ... noted conspicuously on the security [the piece of paper]." The final sentence of (1)(c) is to recognize that an issuer which nominally issues certificated securities but does not normally send the certificates to the owners is functionally identical to the issuer of uncertificated securities and should be guided by the same rules.

Subsection (3), which represents a change from the 1972 Official Text of the present statute, is, with limited exceptions, not part of this proposed revision. Rather, it is a revision proposed by the Banking and Securities Industry Committee to facilitate the development of the securities depository system. It has been previously approved by the Permanent Editorial Board for the Uniform Commercial Code and has been adopted by more than forty states. The changes made by this revision include the addition of "a corporation registered as a 'clearing agency' under the federal securities laws" in the opening sentence, the substitution of "organizations" for "persons (other than individuals)" and the substitution of "federal securities laws" for the specific statutory references in subparagraphs (a)(ii) and (iii).

In subsection (5) the section reference to the definition of "Adverse claim" has been changed and three new terms have been added to the list of definitions. Three terms, defined in Section 9–105, have also been included.

§ 8–103. Issuer's Lien.

A lien upon a security in favor of an issuer thereof is valid against a purchaser only if:

(a) the security is certificated and the right of the issuer to [such] the lien is noted conspicuously [on the security] thereon; or

(b) the security is uncertificated and a notation of the right of the issuer to the lien is contained in the initial transaction statement sent to the purchaser or, if his interest is transferred to him other than by registration of transfer, pledge, or release, the initial transaction statement sent to the registered owner or the registered pledgee.

Reasons for 1977 Change

The substance of the present section has been preserved in paragraph (a) which deals with certificated securities. An analogous rule for uncertificated securities is set forth in paragraph (b) which conditions the validity of an issuer's lien on a notation in the statement which must be sent to a purchaser upon registration of transfer, pledge or release under Section 8-408. When transfer is not effected by registration, see Section 8-313(1)(d), (f), (g), (h), (i) or (j), the notation must appear in the statement sent to the registered owner or pledgee who "holds" for the purchaser. Compare Sections 8-202 and 8-204 which deal, respectively, with issuers' defenses and restrictions imposed by issuers.

§ 8-104. Effect of Overissue; "Overissue".

(1) The provisions of this Article which validate a security or compel its issue or reissue do not apply to the extent that validation, issue, or reissue would result in overissue; but if:

(a) [if] an identical security which does not constitute an overissue is reasonably available for purchase, the person entitled to issue or validation may compel the issuer to purchase [and deliver such a] the security [to] for him and either to deliver a certificated security or to register the transfer of an uncertificated security to him, against surrender of [the] any certificated security [, if any, which] he holds; or

(b) [if] a security is not so available for purchase, the person entitled to issue or validation may recover from the issuer the price he or the last purchaser for value paid for it with interest from the date of his demand.

(2) "Overissue" means the issue of securities in excess of the amount [which] the issuer has corporate power to issue.

Reasons for 1977 Change

The language added to subparagraph (1)(a) gives the issuer obligated to transfer a security the alternatives of delivering a certificated security or registering the transfer of an uncertificated security to the person entitled. As a practical matter, the alternatives will be available only when the securities of the particular issue involved are partly certificated and partly uncertificated. In that event, either the registered owner or the registered pledgee will have the right, under Section 8-407, to exchange one form of security for the other, thus giving that person the ultimate choice.

§ 8-105. Certificated Securities Negotiable; Statements and Instructions Not Negotiable; Presumptions.

(1) Certificated securities governed by this Article are negotiable instruments.

(2) Statements (Section 8-408), notices, or the like, sent by the issuer of uncertificated securities and instructions (Section 8-308) are neither negotiable instruments nor certificated securities.

(3) [(2)] In any action on a security:

(a) unless specifically denied in the pleadings, each signature on [the] a certificated security [or], in a necessary indorsement, on an initial transaction statement, or on an instruction, is admitted;

(b) [when] if the effectiveness of a signature is put in issue, the burden of establishing it is on the party claiming under the signature, but the signature is presumed to be genuine or authorized;

(c) [when] if signatures on a certificated security are admitted or established, production of the [instrument] security entitles a holder to recover on it unless the defendant establishes a defense or a defect going to the validity of the security; [and]

(d) if signatures on an initial transaction statement are admitted or established, the facts stated in the statement are presumed to be true as of the time of its issuance; and

(e) [(d)] after it is shown that a defense or defect exists, the plaintiff has the burden of establishing that he or some person under whom he claims is a person against whom the defense or defect is ineffective (Section 8–202).

Reasons for 1977 Change

This section is substantially unchanged with respect to certificated securities. Subsection (2) has been added, through an abundance of caution, to make it clear that neither the various writings which must or may be sent by the issuers of uncertificated securities nor instructions, which are orders to the issuer requesting registration, are to be regarded as negotiable instruments or certificated securities. Section 8–408(9) requires an appropriate warning legend on the statements that issuers must send.

Language has been added to paragraph (3)(a) to extend the presumption of validity to signatures on initial transaction statements, sent by the issuers of uncertificated securities, and on instructions, originated by owners and pledgees of uncertificated securities. Paragraph (3)(d) has been added to give the same evidentiary value to a genuine initial transaction statement that paragraph (3)(c) accords to a genuine certificated security. It should be noted that the representations typically contained in a certificated security are of a continuing nature while the initial transaction statement speaks only as of the time of its issuance.

§ 8–106. Applicability.

The law (including the conflict of laws rules) of the jurisdiction of organization of the issuer governs the validity of a security, the effectiveness of registration by the issuer, and the rights and duties of the issuer with respect to:

(a) registration of transfer of a certificated security;

(b) registration of transfer, pledge, or release of an uncertificated security; and

(c) sending of statements of uncertificated securities.

[are governed by the law (including the conflict of laws rules) of the jurisdiction of organization of the issuer.]

Reasons for 1977 Change

No change is intended in the coverage of this section with respect to certificated securities. The transfer of certificated securities, effected by delivery, will continue to be governed by present conflict of laws rules, not included in this Article. The transfer of uncertificated securities is, under Section 8-313, generally effected by registration on the books of the issuer. Hence, the effectiveness of such registration is included in the section's coverage.

Section 8-321 provides that certain security interests in uncertificated securities can be created and released by registration. Section 8-408 obligates the issuer of uncertificated securities to send certain statements. Both these matters are brought within the coverage of this section by the addition of subparagraphs (b) and (c). The pledge and release of certificated securities is not intended to be covered by this section and continues to be governed by other conflict of laws rules, e.g., Section 9-103.

§ 8-107. Securities [Deliverable] Transferable; Action for Price.

(1) Unless otherwise agreed and subject to any applicable law or regulation respecting short sales, a person obligated to [deliver] transfer securities may [deliver] transfer any certificated security of the specified issue in bearer form or registered in the name of the transferee, or indorsed to him or in blank, or he may transfer an equivalent uncertificated security to the transferee or a person designated by the transferee.

(2) [When] If the buyer fails to pay the price as it comes due under a contract of sale, the seller may recover the price of:

(a) [of] certificated securities accepted by the buyer; [and]

(b) uncertificated securities that have been transferred to the buyer or a person designated by the buyer; and

(c) [(b) of] other securities if efforts at their resale would be unduly burdensome or if there is no readily available market for their resale.

Reasons for 1977 Change

In order to make this section equally applicable to all securities, the words "Deliverable" in the title and "deliver" in subsection (1) have been changed to "Transferable" and "transfer", respectively. Since certificated securities continue to be transferred by delivery, there is no change of substance with respect to certificated securities.

Present subsection (1) states the rule that all certificated securities of the same issue are to be regarded as fungible. New subsection (1) extends that concept to uncertificated securities of the same issue. Thus, a seller's obligation may normally be satisfied not only by the transfer of any certificated security of the same issue but also by the transfer of an uncertificated security of that issue.

Paragraph (2)(b) has been added so that the transfer of an uncertificated security to the buyer or his designee, which is the functional equivalent of the delivery of a certificated security, results in the same obligation to pay.

§ 8-108. Registration of Pledge and Release of Uncertificated Securities.

A security interest in an uncertificated security may be evidenced by the registration of pledge to the secured party or a person designated by him.

There can be no more than one registered pledge of an uncertificated security at any time. The registered owner of an uncertificated security is the person in whose name the security is registered, even if the security is subject to a registered pledge. The rights of a registered pledgee of an uncertificated security under this Article are terminated by the registration of release.

Reasons for 1977 Change

This is an entirely new section which introduces the concept of the registered pledge of uncertificated securities. The term "pledge" is used, notwithstanding the absence of physical delivery, because it reflects common terminology employed in connection with security interests in investment securities. Note that the same term has been used in present Section 8-320 to describe the security interest created by book entry by a securities depository. The rights of a registered pledgee, set forth in other sections (particularly Section 8-207), are intended to resemble, as closely as possible, the rights of the pledgee of a certificated security who retains possession of the pledged security without re-registration. Although the registration of pledge requires communication to the issuer, no details of the security agreement between the debtor and the secured party need be disclosed.

There is no provision for the registration of more than one pledge at a time. This limits the burden on issuers and insulates them from problems of conflicting priorities and the like. The registration of pledge is only one among several methods of creating security interests under Section 8-313(1) and other methods can be effectively employed to create security interests junior to that of the registered pledgee or even first security interests if, for some reason, the use of the registered pledge mechanism is inadvisable. See new Section 8-321 which deals comprehensively with security interests and incorporates the transfer rules of Section 8-313(1) by reference.

The third sentence makes it clear that the registered owner, and not the registered pledgee, is the person in whose name an uncertificated security is registered as, for example, to determine how an unsecured creditor may reach his debtor's interest under Section 8-317(2). The registration of release, in effect, nullifies the registration of pledge, and is functionally equivalent to the redelivery of a pledged certificated security to the pledgor.

PART 2

ISSUE—ISSUER

§ 8-201. "Issuer".

(1) With respect to obligations on or defenses to a security, "issuer" includes a person who:

(a) places or authorizes the placing of his name on a certificated security (otherwise than as authenticating trustee, registrar, transfer agent, or the like) to evidence that it represents a share, participation, or other interest in his property or in an enterprise, or to evidence his duty to perform an obligation [evidenced] represented by the certificated security; [or]

(b) creates shares, participations or other interests in his property or in an enterprise or undertakes obligations, which shares, participations, interests, or obligations are uncertificated securities;

(c) [(b)] directly or indirectly creates fractional interests in his rights or property, which fractional interests are [evidenced] represented by certificated securities; or

(d) [(c)] becomes responsible for or in place of any other person described as an issuer in this section.

(2) With respect to obligations on or defenses to a security, a guarantor is an issuer to the extent of his guaranty, whether or not his obligation is noted on [the] a certificated security or on statements of uncertificated securities sent pursuant to Section 8-408.

(3) With respect to registration of transfer, pledge, or release (Part 4 of this Article), "issuer" means a person on whose behalf transfer books are maintained.

Reasons for 1977 Change

The definition of "issuer" has been broadened to include persons who create either certificated securities, uncertificated securities or both. Because the first two paragraphs of present subsection (1) apply, by their terms, only to securities represented by instruments, a new paragraph (b) has been inserted which deals with uncertificated securities.

The definition of "uncertificated security" in Section 8-102 and the definition of "issuer" in this section contemplate that uncertificated securities may be either equity or debt securities. Current thinking about uncertificated securities has focused primarily on equities and the difference in the relationship between a shareholder and a corporation in contrast to that between a creditor and his debtor may militate in favor of retaining instruments to represent debt securities. It should be noted, however, that the Federal Reserve Banks, as transfer agents for the United States, have a well-developed uncertificated transfer system for United States government bonds.

Language has been added to subsection (2) to refer to the statements which issuers of uncertificated securities are obligated to send. Language has been added to subsection (3) to include the registration of pledge and release, in addition to transfer.

§ 8-202. Issuer's Responsibility and Defenses; Notice of Defect or Defense.

(1) Even against a purchaser for value and without notice, the terms of a security include:

(a) if the security is certificated, those stated on the security;

(b) if the security is uncertificated, those contained in the initial transaction statement sent to such purchaser, or if his interest is transferred to him other than by registration of transfer, pledge, or release, the initial transaction statement sent to the registered owner or registered pledgee; and

(c) those made part of the security by reference, on the certificated security or in the initial transaction statement, to another instrument, indenture, or document or to a constitution, statute, ordinance, rule, regulation, order or the like, to the extent that the terms [so] referred to do not conflict with the [stated] terms stated on the certificated security or contained in the statement. [Such] A reference under this paragraph does not of itself charge a purchaser for value with notice of a defect going to the validity of the security, even though the certificated security or statement expressly states that a person accepting it admits [such] notice.

(2) [(a)] A certificated security in the hands of a purchaser for value or an uncertificated security as to which an initial transaction statement has been sent to a purchaser for value, other than [one] a security issued by a government or governmental agency or unit, even though issued with a defect going to its validity, is valid [in the hands of a] with respect to the purchaser [for value and] if he is without notice of the particular defect unless the defect involves a violation of constitutional provisions, in which case the security is valid [in the hands of] with respect to a subsequent purchaser for value and without notice of the defect. [(b)] The rule of subparagraph (a)] This subsection applies to an issuer [which] that is a government or governmental agency or unit only if either there has been substantial compliance with the legal requirements governing the issue or the issuer has received a substantial consideration for the issue as a whole or for the particular security and a stated purpose of the issue is one for which the issuer has power to borrow money or issue the security.

(3) Except as [otherwise] provided in the case of certain unauthorized signatures [on issue] (Section 8-205), lack of genuineness of a certificated security or an initial transaction statement is a complete defense, even against a purchaser for value and without notice.

(4) All other defenses of the issuer of a certificated or uncertificated security, including nondelivery and conditional delivery of [the] a certificated security, are ineffective against a purchaser for value who has taken without notice of the particular defense.

(5) Nothing in this section shall be construed to affect the right of a party to a "when, as and if issued" or a "when distributed" contract to cancel the contract in the event of a material change in the character of the security [which] that is the subject of the contract or in the plan or arrangement pursuant to which [such] the security is to be issued or distributed.

Reasons for 1977 Change

Subsection (1) has been broadened to provide that not only the terms noted or referred to on a certificated security but also the terms noted or referred to in the initial transaction statement sent to the purchaser of an uncertificated security (or one who "holds" for the purchaser) will constitute constructive notice to persons who deal with the security.

The rule of subsection (2), which estops the issuer of a certificated security from asserting its invalidity against a purchaser for value without notice has been extended to afford the same protection to the purchaser of an uncertificated security for value and without notice to whom an initial transaction statement has been sent.

The defense of lack of genuineness which is accorded to the alleged issuer of a certificated security by present subsection (3) is similarly accorded to the alleged sender of an initial transaction statement by the added language. The exception of Section 8-205 similarly applies.

Subsection (4) applies to both certificated and uncertificated securities and language has been added to make that clear. Note that a purchaser may be chargeable with notice of an issuer's defense from another source, even in the absence of a notation on a certificated security or an initial transaction statement. Compare Section 8-103 with respect to issuer's liens.

§ 8-203. Staleness as Notice of Defects or Defenses.

(1) After an act or event [which creates] creating a right to immediate performance of the principal obligation [evidenced] represented by [the] a certificated security or [which] that sets a date on or after which the security is to be presented or surrendered for redemption or exchange, a purchaser is charged with notice of any defect in its issue or defense of the issuer if:

(a) [if] the act or event is one requiring the payment of money [or], the delivery of certificated securities, the registration of transfer of uncertificated securities, or [both] any of these on presentation or surrender of the certificated security [and such], the funds or securities are available on the date set for payment or exchange, and he takes the security more than one year after that date; and

(b) [if] the act or event is not covered by paragraph (a) and he takes the security more than [two] 2 years after the date set for surrender or presentation or the date on which [such] performance became due.

(2) A call [which] that has been revoked is not within subsection (1).

Reasons for 1977 Change

The substance of this section applies only to certificated securities because such securities may be transferred to a purchaser by delivery after they have matured, been called or become redeemable or exchangeable. It is contemplated that uncertificated securities which have matured or been called will merely be cancelled on the books of the issuer and the proceeds sent to the registered owner or registered pledgee, as the case may be. Uncertificated securities which have become redeemable or exchangeable, at the option of the owner, may be transferred to a purchaser, but the transfer is effectuated only by registration of transfer, thus necessitating communication with the issuer. If defects or defenses in such securities exist, the issuer will necessarily have the opportunity to bring them to the attention of the purchaser in the initial transaction statement sent to him.

§ 8-204. Effect of Issuer's Restrictions on Transfer.

[Unless noted conspicuously on the security a] A restriction on transfer of a security imposed by the issuer, even though otherwise lawful, is ineffective [except] against [a] any person [with] without actual knowledge of it[.] unless:

(a) the security is certificated and the restriction is noted conspicuously thereon; or

(b) the security is uncertificated and a notation of the restriction is contained in the initial transaction statement sent to the person or, if his interest is transferred to him other than by registration of transfer, pledge, or release, the initial transaction statement sent to the registered owner or the registered pledgee.

Reasons for 1977 Change

The present section provides that an issuer's restriction on transfer is valid against persons with actual knowledge and that a notation on the certificate constitutes constructive knowledge. The revised section preserves these rules with respect to certificated securities and sets forth a coordinate rule that a notation on an initial transaction statement sent with respect to an uncertificated security similarly constitutes constructive knowledge. A prospective transferee of an uncertificated security must communicate with the issuer in order to effectuate transfer by registration.

Registration of transfer by the issuer will negate the existence of restrictions on that particular transfer. Restrictions on further transfer, to be effective against a purchaser without actual knowledge, must be noted in the initial transaction statement sent to the purchaser or one who "holds" for the purchaser. Such restrictions may constitute a breach of the transferor's warranty under Section 8-306. Compare Section 8-103 which precludes the issuer from asserting a lien against a purchaser unless appropriate notations were contained in the initial transaction statement.

§ 8-205. Effect of Unauthorized Signature on [Issue] Certificated Security or Initial Transaction Statement.

An unauthorized signature placed on a certificated security prior to or in the course of issue or placed on an initial transaction statement is ineffective, [except that] but the signature is effective in favor of a purchaser for value of the certificated security or a purchaser for value of an uncertificated security to whom such initial transaction statement has been sent, if the purchaser is [and] without notice of the lack of authority and [if] the signing has been done by:

(a) an authenticating trustee, registrar, transfer agent, or other person entrusted by the issuer with the signing of the security [or], of similar securities, or of initial transaction statements or [their] the immediate preparation for signing of any of them; or

(b) an employee of the issuer, or of any of the foregoing, entrusted with responsible handling of the security or initial transaction statement.

Reasons for 1977 Change

It is contemplated that purchasers, including pledgees, of uncertificated securities should be able to and will rely on the initial transaction statements sent to them when a transfer, pledge or release is registered. In order to insure the genuineness of such statements, Section 8-408(4) requires that they be signed. Note that "signed" is a term defined by Section 1-201(39) and does not necessarily involve a manual signature.

The rule of this section with respect to the ineffectiveness of unauthorized signatures, and, more importantly, the exception to that rule in favor of purchasers for value, has been broadened to include signatures on initial transaction statements. Note that the exception, with respect to initial transaction statements, runs in favor of only the purchaser to whom the statement has been sent. Thus, a subsequent purchaser from the addressee of an initial transaction statement on which the signature was unauthorized but was done by a person described in paragraph (a) or (b) cannot rely on the exception of the section if the addressee had notice of the lack of authority.

§ 8-206. Completion or Alteration of [Instrument] Certificated Security or Initial Transaction Statement.

(1) [Where] If a certificated security contains the signatures necessary to its issue or transfer but is incomplete in any other respect:

(a) any person may complete it by filling in the blanks as authorized; and

(b) even though the blanks are incorrectly filled in, the security as completed is enforceable by a purchaser who took it for value and without notice of [such] the incorrectness.

(2) A complete certificated security [which] that has been improperly altered, even though fraudulently, remains enforceable, but only according to its original terms.

(3) If an initial transaction statement contains the signatures necessary to its validity, but is incomplete in any other respect:

(a) any person may complete it by filling in the blanks as authorized; and

(b) even though the blanks are incorrectly filled in, the statement as completed is effective in favor of the person to whom it is sent if he purchased the security referred to therein for value and without notice of the incorrectness.

(4) A complete initial transaction statement that has been improperly altered, even though fraudulently, is effective in favor of a purchaser to whom it has been sent, but only according to its original terms.

Reasons for 1977 Change

The rules of the present section with respect to certificated securities are restated in subsections (1) and (2). These rules are extended to the completion or alteration of initial transaction statements by new subsections (3) and (4).

Note that the protection of paragraph (3)(b) extends only to the addressee of the initial transaction statement. If, for example, a properly signed initial transaction statement indicated, in the space for notations of liens, the word "None", which had been incorrectly inserted, and the addressee of that statement had actual knowledge that a lien existed, a subsequent purchaser from the addressee would not take free of the lien, despite the incorrect insertion. If, however, the subsequent purchaser then received an initial transaction statement showing no liens, he would then have the protection of Section 8-103 and this section.

§ 8-207. Rights and Duties of Issuer With Respect to Registered Owners and Registered Pledgees.

(1) Prior to due presentment for registration of transfer of a certificated security in registered form, the issuer or indenture trustee may treat the registered owner as the person exclusively entitled to vote, to receive notifications, and otherwise to exercise all the rights and powers of an owner.

(2) Subject to the provisions of subsections (3), (4), and (6), the issuer or indenture trustee may treat the registered owner of an uncertificated security as the person exclusively entitled to vote, to receive notifications, and otherwise to exercise all the rights and powers of an owner.

(3) The registered owner of an uncertificated security that is subject to a registered pledge is not entitled to registration of transfer prior to the due presentment to the issuer of a release instruction. The exercise of conversion rights with respect to a convertible uncertificated security is a transfer within the meaning of this section.

(4) Upon due presentment of a transfer instruction from the registered pledgee of an uncertificated security, the issuer shall:

(a) register the transfer of the security to the new owner free of pledge, if the instruction specifies a new owner (who may be the registered pledgee) and does not specify a pledgee;

(b) register the transfer of the security to the new owner subject to the interest of the existing pledgee, if the instruction specifies a new owner and the existing pledgee; or

(c) register the release of the security from the existing pledge and register the pledge of the security to the other pledgee, if the instruction specifies the existing owner and another pledgee.

(5) Continuity of perfection of a security interest is not broken by registration of transfer under subsection (4)(b) or by registration of release and pledge under subsection (4)(c), if the security interest is assigned.

(6) If an uncertificated security is subject to a registered pledge:

(a) any uncertificated securities issued in exchange for or distributed with respect to the pledged security shall be registered subject to the pledge;

(b) any certificated securities issued in exchange for or distributed with respect to the pledged security shall be delivered to the registered pledgee; and

(c) any money paid in exchange for or in redemption of part or all of the security shall be paid to the registered pledgee.

(7) [(2)] Nothing in this Article shall be construed to affect the liability of the registered owner of a security for calls, assessments, or the like.

Reasons for 1977 Change

Under present subsection (1), the issuer of a certificated security may and, in the absence of conclusive evidence that the security has been transferred, presumably will rely on the registry to establish the identity of those entitled to ownership rights. New subsection (2) establishes the same rule for the issuer of uncertificated securities, subject, however, to the rights of registered pledgees which are set forth in subsections (3), (4) and (6). It should be noted that an uncertificated security can normally be transferred only by registration of transfer.

Under subsection (3), the owner of an uncertificated security subject to a registered pledge cannot transfer his interest until the pledge has been released by the registered pledgee. Although this requirement appears to conflict with the free alienability of the debtor's interest under Section 9-311, it does so no more than the current practice of delivery of a certificated security to the pledgee, which, in effect, deprives the owner of the power to transfer an interest without the pledgee's cooperation.

The final sentence of subsection (3) makes clear that when a convertible uncertificated security is subject to a registered pledge, it is the pledgee, and not the owner, who has the exclusive power to exercise the conversion rights. Since the exercise of conversion rights for a certificated security generally requires delivery of the security to the issuer, the cooperation of the secured party is similarly required. Note that the proceeds of the conversion are subject to the pledgee's interest or delivered to the pledgee under subsection (6).

Subsection (4) obliges the issuer to comply with the transfer instruction of the registered pledgee of an uncertificated security, thus placing such pledgee in the same position as the pledgee of a certificated security to whom the security has been delivered with all necessary indorsements. The three subparagraphs of subsection (4) provide respectively for (a) the outright transfer of the security, free of the pledgee's interest, to a buyer or any other person, including the pledgee; (b) the transfer of the owner's equity to a third person with the pledgee's interest continuing; and (c) the substitution of a new pledgee for the existing pledgee with ownership continuing undisturbed. Subsection (5) provides for continuity of perfection for purposes of priority under Article 9, the Bankruptcy Act and other statutes.

Subsection (6) protects the pledgee's interest in the proceeds of conversion, exchange or redemption of uncertificated securities, since no instrument need be surrendered to effectuate such transactions. Subsection (6) also provides that additional securities, certificated or uncertificated, issued in connection with stock splits or stock dividends will continue under the control of the registered pledgee. This contrasts with the situation when certificated securities are pledged and dividend certificates are customarily sent to the registered owner—the only party shown on the issuer's records. In that event, the pledgee must obtain the dividend certificates from the pledgor, exposing them, in the interim, to wrongful transfer.

§ 8-208. Effect of Signature of Authenticating Trustee, Registrar, or Transfer Agent.

(1) A person placing his signature upon a certificated security or an initial transaction statement as authenticating trustee, registrar, transfer agent, or the like, warrants to a purchaser for value of the certificated security or a purchaser for value of an uncertificated security to whom the initial transaction statement has been sent, if the purchaser is without notice of the particular defect, that:

(a) the certificated security or initial transaction statement is genuine; [and]

(b) his own participation in the issue or registration of the transfer, pledge, or release of the security is within his capacity and within the scope of the [authorization] authority received by him from the issuer; and

(c) he has reasonable grounds to believe that the security is in the form and within the amount the issuer is authorized to issue.

(2) Unless otherwise agreed, a person by so placing his signature does not assume responsibility for the validity of the security in other respects.

Reasons for 1977 Change

Language has been added to this section to extend the warranties of a signing authenticating trustee, registrar, transfer agent or the like to the addressees of initial transaction statements. It should be noted that this warranty extends only to the addressee. Compare Sections 8-205 and 8-206 and the explanation of changes thereunder.

PART 3

[PURCHASE] TRANSFER

§ 8-301. Rights Acquired by Purchaser [; "Adverse Claim"; Title Acquired by Bona Fide Purchaser].

(1) Upon [delivery] transfer of a security to a purchaser (Section 8-313), the purchaser acquires the rights in the security which his transferor had or had actual authority to convey unless the purchaser's rights are limited by Section 8-302(4). [except that a purchaser who has himself been a party to any fraud or illegality affecting the security or who as a prior holder had notice of an adverse claim cannot improve his position by taking from a later bona fide purchaser. "Adverse claim" includes a claim that a transfer was or would be wrongful or that a particular adverse person is the owner of or has an interest in the security.]

[(2) A bona fide purchaser in addition to acquiring the rights of a purchaser also acquires the security free of any adverse claim.]

(2) [(3)] A [purchaser] transferee of a limited interest acquires rights only to the extent of the interest [purchased] transferred. The creation or release of a security interest in a security is the transfer of a limited interest in that security.

Reasons for 1977 Change

Although the definition of "Purchase" in Section 1-201 (32) includes any "voluntary transaction", with or without consideration, the title of Part 3 has been changed to "Transfer" as a more natural description of the material covered therein. Similar changes have been made in the statutory text, where appropriate.

Transfers by operation of law, i.e., not to purchasers, are not intended to be covered by Part 3 of either the present or revised Article. Such transfers are effective upon the occurrence of the motivating event (death, bankruptcy or the like) and subsequent delivery and registration are merely confirmatory of what has already happened.

Subsection (1) states the basic rule of the present statute including the so-called shelter principle. The word "transfer" has been substituted for "delivery" in order that appropriate methods for the transfer of uncertificated securities can be included.

The balance of subsection (1) and all of present subsection (2) have been deleted from this Section but are now included in Section 8-302 which is intended to deal completely with the concept of bona fide purchase.

A sentence has been added to former subsection (3) to make clear that the creation and release of security interests are included in the statute's coverage.

§ 8-302. "Bona Fide Purchaser"; "Adverse Claim"; Title Acquired by Bona Fide Purchaser.

(1) A "bona fide purchaser" is a purchaser for value in good faith and without notice of any adverse claim:

(a) who takes delivery of a certificated security in bearer form or [of one] in registered form, issued [to him] or indorsed to him or in blank;

(b) to whom the transfer, pledge or release of an uncertificated security is registered on the books of the issuer; or

(c) to whom a security is transferred under the provisions of paragraph (c), (d)(i), or (g) of Section 8-313(1).

(2) "Adverse claim" includes a claim that a transfer was or would be wrongful or that a particular adverse person is the owner of or has an interest in the security.

(3) A bona fide purchaser in addition to acquiring the rights of a purchaser (Section 8-301) also acquires his interest in the security free of any adverse claim.

(4) Notwithstanding Section 8-301(1), the transferee of a particular certificated security who has been a party to any fraud or illegality affecting the security, or who as a prior holder of that certificated security had notice of an adverse claim, cannot improve his position by taking from a bona fide purchaser.

Reasons for 1977 Change

The definition of bona fide purchaser of a certificated security is preserved in subparagraph (1)(a). A coordinate rule for the purchaser of an uncertificated security is stated in subparagraph (1)(b). The relevant time for testing the knowledge or constructive knowledge of a purchaser is the time of delivery in the case of a certificated security and the time of registration in the case of an uncertificated security. Note that the purchaser of an uncertificated security is charged with knowledge of adverse claims noted in the initial transaction statement sent to him as provided in Section 8-304.

In the present statute, Section 8-313 equates certain events with delivery and subsection (2) thereof provides that a purchaser who is deemed to have taken delivery through his broker under certain of the procedures in subsection (1) can be a "holder." It was thought advisable to add subparagraph (1)(c) to this section in order to identify expressly those provisions of revised Section 8-313(1) that will confer "holder" status on a purchaser and thus enable him to be a bona fide purchaser under this section.

The definition of adverse claim, the description of the title of a bona fide purchaser and the exception to the shelter principle, all of which are included in Section 8-301 of the present statute, are set forth as subsections (2), (3) and (4) respectively. Language has been added to subsection (4) to make clear that it is limited to the holder of a particular certificated security.

§ 8-303. "Broker".

"Broker" means a person engaged for all or part of his time in the business of buying and selling securities, who in the transaction concerned acts for, [or] buys a security from, or sells a security to, a customer. Nothing in this Article determines the capacity in which a person acts for purposes of any other statute or rule to which [such] the person is subject.

§ 8–304. Notice to Purchaser of Adverse Claims.

(1) A purchaser (including a broker for the seller or buyer, but excluding an intermediary bank) of a certificated security is charged with notice of adverse claims if:

(a) the security, whether in bearer or registered form, has been indorsed "for collection" or "for surrender" or for some other purpose not involving transfer; or

(b) the security is in bearer form and has on it an unambiguous statement that it is the property of a person other than the transferor. The mere writing of a name on a security is not such a statement.

(2) A purchaser (including a broker for the seller or buyer, but excluding an intermediary bank) to whom the transfer, pledge, or release of an uncertificated security is registered is charged with notice of adverse claims as to which the issuer has a duty under Section 8–403(4) at the time of registration and which are noted in the initial transaction statement sent to the purchaser or, if his interest is transferred to him other than by registration of transfer, pledge, or release, the initial transaction statement sent to the registered owner or the registered pledgee.

(3) [(2)] The fact that the purchaser (including a broker for the seller or buyer) of a certificated or uncertificated security has notice that the security is held for a third person or is registered in the name of or indorsed by a fiduciary does not create a duty of inquiry into the rightfulness of the transfer or constitute constructive notice of adverse claims. [If,] However, if the purchaser (excluding an intermediary bank) has knowledge that the proceeds are being used or [that] the transaction is for the individual benefit of the fiduciary or otherwise in breach of duty, the purchaser is charged with notice of adverse claims.

Reasons for 1977 Change

Subsection (1), which deals with notice arising from what appears on a certificated security is applicable only to the purchaser of a certificated security. New subsection (2) provides that the purchaser of an uncertificated security is subject to those adverse claims that are noted on the initial transaction statement sent to him (or one who "holds" for him) confirming the transfer, pledge or release which has been registered. Subsection (3) is equally applicable to the purchasers of certificated and uncertificated securities and language has been added to make that clear.

§ 8–305. Staleness as Notice of Adverse Claims.

An act or event [which] that creates a right to immediate performance of the principal obligation [evidenced] represented by [the] a certificated security or [which] sets a date on or after which [the] a certificated security is to be presented or surrendered for redemption or exchange does not [of] itself constitute any notice of adverse claims except in the case of a [purchase] transfer:

(a) after one year from any date set for [such] presentment or surrender for redemption or exchange; or

(b) after [six] 6 months from any date set for payment of money against presentation or surrender of the security if funds are available for payment on that date.

Reasons for 1977 Change

The substance of this section applies only to certificated securities for the same reasons as Section 8-203. It is not contemplated that uncertificated securities which have been called or have matured will be traded. With uncertificated securities which have become redeemable or exchangeable, effective transfer requires communication with the issuer and, therefore, presents the opportunity for the issuer to give the prospective transferee effective notice of such claims as have been lodged with it.

§ 8-306. Warranties on Presentment and Transfer of Certificated Securities; Warranties of Originators of Instructions.

(1) A person who presents a certificated security for registration of transfer or for payment or exchange warrants to the issuer that he is entitled to the registration, payment, or exchange. But, a purchaser for value and without notice of adverse claims who receives a new, reissued, or re-registered certificated security on registration of transfer or receives an initial transaction statement confirming the registration of transfer of an equivalent uncertificated security to him warrants only that he has no knowledge of any unauthorized signature (Section 8-311) in a necessary indorsement.

(2) A person by transferring a certificated security to a purchaser for value warrants only that:

(a) his transfer is effective and rightful; [and]

(b) the security is genuine and has not been materially altered; and

(c) he knows of no fact which might impair the validity of the security.

(3) [Where] If a certificated security is delivered by an intermediary known to be entrusted with delivery of the security on behalf of another or with collection of a draft or other claim against [such] delivery, the intermediary by [such] delivery warrants only his own good faith and authority, even though he has purchased or made advances against the claim to be collected against the delivery.

(4) A pledgee or other holder for security who redelivers [the] a certificated security received, or after payment and on order of the debtor delivers that security to a third person, makes only the warranties of an intermediary under subsection (3).

(5) A person who originates an instruction warrants to the issuer that:

(a) he is an appropriate person to originate the instruction; and

(b) at the time the instruction is presented to the issuer he will be entitled to the registration of transfer, pledge, or release.

(6) A person who originates an instruction warrants to any person specially guaranteeing his signature (subsection 8-312(3)) that:

(a) he is an appropriate person to originate the instruction; and

(b) at the time the instruction is presented to the issuer

(i) he will be entitled to the registration of transfer, pledge, or release; and

(ii) the transfer, pledge, or release requested in the instruction will be registered by the issuer free from all liens, security interests, restrictions, and claims other than those specified in the instruction.

(7) A person who originates an instruction warrants to a purchaser for value and to any person guaranteeing the instruction (Section 8-312(6)) that:

(a) he is an appropriate person to originate the instruction;

(b) the uncertificated security referred to therein is valid; and

(c) at the time the instruction is presented to the issuer

(i) the transferor will be entitled to the registration of transfer, pledge, or release;

(ii) the transfer, pledge, or release requested in the instruction will be registered by the issuer free from all liens, security interests, restrictions, and claims other than those specified in the instruction; and

(iii) the requested transfer, pledge, or release will be rightful.

(8) If a secured party is the registered pledgee or the registered owner of an uncertificated security, a person who originates an instruction of release or transfer to the debtor or, after payment and on order of the debtor, a transfer instruction to a third person, warrants to the debtor or the third person only that he is an appropriate person to originate the instruction and at the time the instruction is presented to the issuer, the transferor will be entitled to the registration of release or transfer. If a transfer instruction to a third person who is a purchaser for value is originated on order of the debtor, the debtor makes to the purchaser the warranties of paragraphs (b), (c)(ii) and (c)(iii) of subsection (7).

(9) A person who transfers an uncertificated security to a purchaser for value and does not originate an instruction in connection with the transfer warrants only that:

(a) his transfer is effective and rightful; and

(b) the uncertificated security is valid.

(10) [(5)] A broker gives to his customer and to the issuer and a purchaser the applicable warranties provided in this section and has the rights and privileges of a purchaser under this section. The warranties of and in favor of the broker acting as an agent are in addition to applicable warranties given by and in favor of his customer.

Reasons for 1977 Change

The substance of the present section, with respect to certificated securities, has been preserved in the first four subsections. The section title and these subsections have been changed only to make clear that application only to certificated securities is intended. Because the registration of transfer of an uncertificated security to the transferee is functionally equivalent to the delivery of a certificated security to the transferee by the issuer, language has been added to subsection (1) to equate the position of purchasers for value without notice of adverse claims whether the security they "receive" from the issuer is certificated or uncertificated.

Subsection (5) establishes the warranty made to the issuer by the originator of an instruction, which is an order to the issuer and is defined in Section 8-308(4). These warranties are designed to protect issuers who rely on instructions which may be forged, fraudulent or otherwise improper against the persons who are responsible for the creation of such instructions. If, for example, an issuer should improperly transfer shares out of the name of a shareholder on the basis of a forged instruction, and transfer those shares to a bona fide purchaser to whom a valid initial transaction statement is sent, the issuer would be subject to liability to the purported transferor under Section 8-404(3).

Subsection (6) sets forth the warranty made by the originator of an instruction to a special signature guarantor. It adds to the two warranties of subsection (5) a warranty that the instruction will result in the registration of a "clean" transfer, pledge, or release and is consistent with the warranty made by a special signature guarantor under Section 8-312(3)(b).

Subsection (7) sets forth the warranty made by the originator of an instruction to both a purchaser for value and an instruction guarantor. It adds to the warranties in subsections (5) and (6) additional warranties of rightfulness and validity and is essentially identical to the warranty of the transferor of a certificated security under subsection (2). The absolute warranty of validity, rather than the mere denial of knowledge of invalidity, is appropriate because the instruction must be communicated to the issuer in order to complete the transfer. If, upon receipt of the instruction, the issuer should dispute the validity of the security, it seems proper to place the burden of proving validity on the transferor. It is contemplated that purchasers of uncertificated securities will not normally part with their consideration unless and until they are satisfied that the transaction has been duly registered and acknowledged to be free from defects by the issuer, except when they are relying on their brokers or other third parties.

Because the guarantor of an instruction makes an absolute warranty of rightfulness under Section 8-312(6), he is given the benefit of the originator's warranty under subsection (7).

Subsection (8) limits the warranties of the originator of an instruction when the uncertificated security is subject to a security interest and the originator is or acts for either the registered pledgee or registered owner who is the secured party. In such cases, when the instruction is for release, transfer to the debtor or transfer, after payment, to a third person on the debtor's order, the originator's warranties are limited in substantially the same way that subsection (4) limits the warranties of the pledgee of a certificated security acting under similar circumstances.

When the transferor of an uncertificated security is neither the registered owner nor the registered pledgee, the transferor will have no occasion to originate an instruction in connection with the transfer. In such cases, the transferor warrants the rightfulness of the transfer and the validity of the security to a purchaser for value, as provided in subsection (9).

§ 8–307. Effect of Delivery Without Indorsement; Right to Compel Indorsement.

[Where] If a certificated security in registered form has been delivered to a purchaser without a necessary indorsement he may become a bona fide purchaser only as of the time the indorsement is supplied[,]; but against the transferor, the transfer is complete upon delivery and the purchaser has a specifically enforceable right to have any necessary indorsement supplied.

§ 8–308. [Indorsement, How Made; Special Indorsement; Indorser Not a Guarantor; Partial Assignment] Indorsements; Instructions.

(1) An indorsement of a certificated security in registered form is made when an appropriate person signs on it or on a separate document an assignment or transfer of the security or a power to assign or transfer it or [when the] his signature [of such person] is written without more upon the back of the security.

(2) An indorsement may be in blank or special. An indorsement in blank includes an indorsement to bearer. A special indorsement specifies [the person] to whom the security is to be transferred, or who has power to transfer it. A holder may convert a blank indorsement into a special indorsement.

(3) [(5)] An indorsement purporting to be only of part of a certificated security representing units intended by the issuer to be separately transferable is effective to the extent of the indorsement.

(4) An "instruction" is an order to the issuer of an uncertificated security requesting that the transfer, pledge, or release from pledge of the uncertificated security specified therein be registered.

(5) An instruction originated by an appropriate person is:

(a) a writing signed by an appropriate person; or

(b) a communication to the issuer in any form agreed upon in a writing signed by the issuer and an appropriate person.

If an instruction has been originated by an appropriate person but is incomplete in any other respect, any person may complete it as authorized and the issuer may rely on it as completed even though it has been completed incorrectly.

(6) [(3)] "An appropriate person" in subsection (1) means [(a)] the person specified by the certificated security or by special indorsement to be entitled to the security [; or].

(7) "An appropriate person" in subsection (5) means:

(a) for an instruction to transfer or pledge an uncertificated security which is then not subject to a registered pledge, the registered owner; or

(b) for an instruction to transfer or release an uncertificated security which is then subject to a registered pledge, the registered pledgee.

(8) In addition to the persons designated in subsections (6) and (7), "an appropriate person" in subsections (1) and (5) includes:

(a) [(b) where] if the person [so specified] designated is described as a fiduciary but is no longer serving in the described capacity, [—] either that person or his successor; [or]

(b) [(c) where] if the [security or indorsement so specifies] persons designated are described as more than one person as fiduciaries and one or more are no longer serving in the described capacity, [—] the remaining fiduciary or fiduciaries, whether or not a successor has been appointed or qualified; [or]

(c) [(d) where] if the person [so specified] designated is an individual and is without capacity to act by virtue of death, incompetence, infancy, or otherwise, [—] his executor, administrator, guardian, or like fiduciary; [or]

(d) [(e) where] if the [security or indorsement so specifies] persons designated are described as more than one person as tenants by the entirety or with right of survivorship and by reason of death all cannot sign, [—] the survivor or survivors; [or]

(e) [(f)] a person having power to sign under applicable law or controlling instrument; [or] and

(f) [(g)] to the extent that the person designated or any of the foregoing persons may act through an agent, [—] his authorized agent.

(9) [(4)] Unless otherwise agreed, the indorser of a certificated security by his indorsement or the originator of an instruction by his origination assumes no obligation that the security will be honored by the issuer but only the obligations provided in Section 8–306.

(10) [(6)] Whether the person signing is appropriate is determined as of the date of signing and an indorsement made by or an instruction originated by [such a person] him does not become unauthorized for the purposes of this Article by virtue of any subsequent change of circumstances.

(11) [(7)] Failure of a fiduciary to comply with a controlling instrument or with the law of the state having jurisdiction of the fiduciary relationship, including any law requiring the fiduciary to obtain court approval of the transfer, pledge, or release, does not render his indorsement or an instruction originated by him unauthorized for the purposes of this Article.

Reasons for 1977 Change

The substance of the present section has been preserved, insofar as it applies to certificated securities, in subsections (1), (2), (3), (6), (8), (9), (10) and (11). Subsections (4), (5) and (7) deal solely with uncertificated securities. Present paragraph (3)(a) has been incorporated in new subsection (6). The remainder of present subsection (3) is incorporated in new subsection (8). Present subsections (4), (6) and (7) have been broadened to cover both forms of securities and are set forth in new subsections (9), (10) and (11). An attempt has been made to integrate the rules in order that issuers can rely on precisely the same documentation and evidence in connection with registration with respect to both certificated and uncertificated securities.

An order for the registration of transfer of a certificated security is the security itself, duly indorsed and presented to the issuer. Because uncertificated securities are not represented by instruments, a separate order, in some form, written or otherwise, is demanded. Subsection (4) defines an "instruction" as that order and further provides that not only registration of transfer, but also registration of pledge and release, can be requested thereby.

Subsection (5) provides that an instruction may be an appropriately signed writing, and it is contemplated that, in most cases, it will be. It further provides, however, that instructions may be other than signed writings when both parties, the issuer on the one hand and the registered owner or registered pledgee on the other, have agreed, in a signed writing, that some other procedure is mutually acceptable. Thus, paragraph (5)(b) is intended to facilitate the registration of transfers, pledges and releases on the authority of electronic, telegraphic or even oral instructions when the relevant parties are assured that the means selected will provide adequate safeguards against the execution of unauthorized transactions.

Subsection (7) designates the primary party appropriate to originate an instruction. When the uncertificated security is not subject to a registered pledge, the registered owner is that party and may properly originate an instruction to register either a transfer or pledge. When the uncertificated security is subject to a registered pledge, however, only the registered pledgee may properly originate an instruction to register either transfer or release. There is no provision to register a pledge other than that of a single registered pledgee. See Section 8-108.

The final phrase of subsection (9) has been inserted because of a possible ambiguity concerning the word "honored." Under the terms of Section 8-306 the transferor of a certificated security and the originator of an instruction do warrant, in effect, that the issuer will honor their respective orders to register the appropriate transaction. They do not, unless otherwise agreed, become sureties of the obligations of the issuer beyond the duty to register, as, for example, the issuer's obligations to pay interest and principal on a security which is an indebtedness of the issuer.

§ 8-309. Effect of Indorsement Without Delivery.

An indorsement of a certificated security, whether special or in blank, does not constitute a transfer until delivery of the certificated security on which it appears or, if the indorsement is on a separate document, until delivery of both the document and the certificated security.

§ 8-310. Indorsement of Certificated Security in Bearer Form.

An indorsement of a certificated security in bearer form may give notice of adverse claims (Section 8-304) but does not otherwise affect any right to registration the holder [may possess] possesses.

§ 8-311. Effect of Unauthorized Indorsement or Instruction.

Unless the owner or pledgee has ratified an unauthorized indorsement or instruction or is otherwise precluded from asserting its ineffectiveness:

(a) he may assert its ineffectiveness against the issuer or any purchaser, other than a purchaser for value and without notice of adverse claims, who has in good faith received a new, reissued, or re-registered certificated security on registration of transfer or received an initial transaction statement confirming the registration of transfer, pledge, or release of an equivalent uncertificated security to him; and

(b) an issuer who registers the transfer of a certificated security upon the unauthorized indorsement or who registers the transfer, pledge, or release of an uncertificated security upon the unauthorized instruction is subject to liability for improper registration (Section 8-404).

Reasons for 1977 Change

This section is broadened to give the same effect to an unauthorized instruction as the present statute gives to an unauthorized indorsement of a certificated security. Thus, the protection which paragraph (a) accords to a bona fide purchaser who receives a certificated security from the issuer is also accorded to a bona fide purchaser who receives an initial transaction statement with respect to an uncertificated security. Similarly, the liability of the issuer for improper registration set forth in paragraph (b) extends to improper registration pursuant to an unauthorized instruction.

§ 8-312. Effect of Guaranteeing Signature, [or] Indorsement or Instruction.

(1) Any person guaranteeing a signature of an indorser of a certificated security warrants that at the time of signing:

(a) the signature was genuine; [and]

(b) the signer was an appropriate person to indorse (Section 8-308); and

(c) the signer had legal capacity to sign.

[But the guarantor does not otherwise warrant the rightfulness of the particular transfer.]

(2) Any person guaranteeing a signature of the originator of an instruction warrants that at the time of signing:

(a) the signature was genuine;

(b) the signer was an appropriate person to originate the instruction (Section 8-308) if the person specified in the instruction as the registered owner or registered pledgee of the uncertificated security was, in fact, the registered owner or registered pledgee of such security, as to which fact the signature guarantor makes no warranty;

(c) the signer had legal capacity to sign; and

(d) the taxpayer identification number, if any, appearing on the instruction as that of the registered owner or registered pledgee was the taxpayer identification number of the signer or of the owner or pledgee for whom the signer was acting.

(3) Any person specially guaranteeing the signature of the originator of an instruction makes not only the warranties of a signature guarantor (subsection (2)) but also warrants that at the time the instruction is presented to the issuer:

(a) the person specified in the instruction as the registered owner or registered pledgee of the uncertificated security will be the registered owner or registered pledgee; and

(b) the transfer, pledge, or release of the uncertificated security requested in the instruction will be registered by the issuer free from all liens, security interests, restrictions, and claims other than those specified in the instruction.

(4) [But] The guarantor under subsections (1) and (2) or the special guarantor under subsection (3) does not otherwise warrant the rightfulness of the particular transfer, pledge, or release.

(5) [(2)] Any person [may guarantee] guaranteeing an indorsement of a certificated security [and by so doing warrants not only the signature (subsection 1)] makes not only the warranties of a signature guarantor under subsection (1) but also warrants the rightfulness of the particular transfer in all respects. [But no issuer may require a guarantee of indorsement as a condition to registration of transfer.]

(6) Any person guaranteeing an instruction requesting the transfer, pledge, or release of an uncertificated security makes not only the warranties of a special signature guarantor under subsection (3) but also warrants the rightfulness of the particular transfer, pledge, or release in all respects.

(7) [But] No issuer may require a special guarantee of signature (subsection (3)), a guarantee of indorsement (subsection (5)), or a guarantee of instruction (subsection (6)) as a condition to registration of transfer, pledge, or release.

(8) [(3)] The foregoing warranties are made to any person taking or dealing with the security in reliance on the guarantee, and the guarantor is liable to [such] the person for any loss resulting from breach of the warranties.

Reasons for 1977 Change

The substance of the present section has been preserved, insofar as it applies to certificated securities, in subsections (1), (4), (5), (7) and (8). Some of the language has been changed and restructured in order to integrate the material concerning uncertificated securities, but no change of substance is intended.

Subsection (2) sets forth the warranties that can reasonably be expected from the guarantor of the signature on an instruction, who, though familiar with the signer, does not have before him any evidence that the purported owner or pledgee is, in fact, the owner or pledgee of the subject uncertificated security. This is in distinct contrast to the position of the person guaranteeing a signature on a certificate who can see a certificate in the signer's possession in the name of or indorsed to the signer or in blank.

Thus, the warranty of appropriateness in clause (b) is expressly conditioned on the actual registration conforming to that represented by the originator. If the signer purports to be the owner or pledgee, the guarantor under clause (b), warrants only his identity. If, however, the signer is acting in a representative capacity, the guarantor warrants both his identity and his authority to act for the purported owner or pledgee. The additional warranty of clause (d) as to the taxpayer identification number is intended to prevent error or fraud resulting from identical or similar names. The warranties of subsection (2) are intended to provide satisfactory assurance to the issuer who needs no warranty as to the facts of registration because he can ascertain those facts from his own records.

Subsection (3) sets forth a "special guarantee of signature" under which the guarantor additionally warrants both registered ownership or pledge and freedom from undisclosed defects of record. The guarantor of the signature of an indorser of a certificated security effectively makes these warranties to a purchaser for value on the evidence of a clean certificate issued in the name of the indorser, indorsed to the indorser or indorsed in blank. By specially guaranteeing under subsection (3), the guarantor warrants that the instruction will, when presented to the issuer, result in the requested registration free from defects not specified. It is contemplated that the special guarantee of signature will be used principally in brokerage transactions where the broker will be specially guaranteeing the signature on an instruction originated by his own customer. The broker's risk will be no greater than that of a broker who now commonly executes the sale of a security for his customer without the absolute assurance that his customer will deliver a clean certificate at settlement.

§ 8-313. When [Delivery] Transfer to [the] Purchaser Occurs: [; Purchaser's Broker] Financial Intermediary as [Holder] Bona Fide Purchaser; "Financial Intermediary".

(1) [Delivery] Transfer of a security or a limited interest (including a security interest) therein to a purchaser occurs only [when]:

(a) at the time he or a person designated by him acquires possession of a certificated security; [or]

(b) at the time the transfer, pledge, or release of an uncertificated security is registered to him or a person designated by him;

(c) [(b)] at the time his [broker] financial intermediary acquires possession of a certificated security specially indorsed to or issued in the name of the purchaser; [or]

(d) [(c)] at the time [his broker] a financial intermediary, not a clearing corporation, sends him confirmation of the purchase and also by book entry or otherwise identifies [a specific security in the broker's possession] as belonging to the purchaser[; or]

(i) a specific certificated security in the financial intermediary's possession;

(ii) a quantity of securities that constitute or are part of a fungible bulk of certificated securities in the financial intermediary's possession or of uncertificated securities registered in the name of the financial intermediary; or

(iii) a quantity of securities that constitute or are part of a fungible bulk of securities shown on the account of the financial intermediary on the books of another financial intermediary;

(e) [(d)] with respect to an identified certificated security to be delivered while still in the possession of a third person, not a financial intermediary, [when] at the time that person acknowledges that he holds for the purchaser; [or]

(f) with respect to a specific uncertificated security the pledge or transfer of which has been registered to a third person, not a financial intermediary, at the time that person acknowledges that he holds for the purchaser;

(g) [(e)] at the time appropriate entries to the account of the purchaser or a person designated by him on the books of a clearing corporation are made under Section 8–320[.];

(h) with respect to the transfer of a security interest where the debtor has signed a security agreement containing a description of the security, at the time a written notification, which, in the case of the creation of the security interest, is signed by the debtor (which may be a copy of the security agreement) or which, in the case of the release or assignment of the security interest created pursuant to this paragraph, is signed by the secured party, is received by

(i) a financial intermediary on whose books the interest of the transferor in the security appears;

(ii) a third person, not a financial intermediary, in possession of the security, if it is certificated;

(iii) a third person, not a financial intermediary, who is the registered owner of the security, if it is uncertificated and not subject to a registered pledge; or

(iv) a third person, not a financial intermediary, who is the registered pledgee of the security, if it is uncertificated and subject to a registered pledge;

(i) with respect to the transfer of a security interest where the transferor has signed a security agreement containing a description of the security, at the time new value is given by the secured party; or

(j) with respect to the transfer of a security interest where the secured party is a financial intermediary and the security has already been transferred to the financial intermediary under paragraphs (a), (b), (c), (d), or (g), at the time the transferor has signed a security agreement containing a description of the security and value is given by the secured party.

(2) The purchaser is the owner of a security held for him by [his broker] a financial intermediary, but [is not the holder] cannot be a bona fide purchaser of a security so held except [as] in the circumstances specified in [subparagraphs] paragraphs [(b)] (c), (d)(i), and [(e)] (g) of subsection (1). [Where] If a security so held is part of a fungible bulk, as in the circumstances specified in paragraphs (d)(ii) and (d)(iii) of subsection (1), the purchaser is the owner of a proportionate property interest in the fungible bulk.

(3) Notice of an adverse claim received by the [broker] financial intermediary or by the purchaser after the [broker] financial intermediary takes delivery of a certificated security as a holder for value or after the transfer, pledge, or release of an uncertificated security has been registered free of the claim to a financial intermediary who has given value is not effective either as to the [broker] financial intermediary or as to the purchaser. However, as between the [broker] financial intermediary and the purchaser the purchaser may demand [delivery] transfer of an equivalent security as to which no notice of [an] adverse claim has been received.

(4) A "financial intermediary" is a bank, broker, clearing corporation or other person (or the nominee of any of them) which in the ordinary course of its business maintains security accounts for its customers and is acting in that

capacity. A financial intermediary may have a security interest in securities held in account for its customer.

Reasons for 1977 Change

The title of this section has been changed and its content broadened in order to identify the time when both certificated and uncertificated securities are transferred to purchasers. The content has been further extended to recognize that many transactions are conducted through financial intermediaries, a term defined in subsection (4) to include all entities, and not merely brokers, that maintain security accounts for their customers. It is one of the three sections in this revision in which it is intended to extend the coverage of Article 8 as to certificated securities. Sections 8–317 and 8–321 are the others.

Subsection (1) is expressly made applicable to limited interests, including security interests, as well as entire interests. Compare Section 8–301(2). The addition of the word "only" in the first sentence is intended to provide that the methods of transfer listed are exclusive and that compliance with one of them is essential to a valid transfer. Transfers by operation of law are excepted because they are not transfers to a "purchaser".

The rules of the present statute as they apply to certificated securities are preserved in subparagraphs (a), (c), (d)(i), (e) and (g). The coverage of (c) and (d)(i), however, is extended to situations where any financial intermediary, except a clearing corporation, is involved and the coverage of (e) is limited to third persons who are not financial intermediaries.

Subparagraph (b) is the basic rule for uncertificated securities and provides that a transfer (including a pledge or release, which are transfers of security interests) occurs when it is registered. Subparagraph (f) is the analogue of (e) and applies when an uncertificated security is controlled by a third person. In both (e) and (f), acknowledgement by the third person is the critical event.

Subparagraphs (d)(ii) and (d)(iii) have no counterpart in the present statute but are considered desirable express statements in the light of modern security holding practices of both brokers and banks. The final sentence of present subsection (2) implies this result without stating it expressly. Once the "fungible bulk" principle is established, it is immaterial whether the underlying securities are certificated, uncertificated or held in a clearing corporation account.

Entire subparagraph (d) is applicable to all financial intermediaries except clearing corporations and requires, as conditions of transfer, both a confirmation to the purchaser and a book entry. In contrast, subparagraph (g) applies only to clearing corporations and requires only the appropriate book entry. The difference results from the fact that clearing corporations will normally control only securities belonging to their customers while other financial intermediaries may themselves be the beneficial owners or pledgees of securities not held in account for their customers. In the event of the insolvency of either the financial intermediary or the customer, it appears desirable to have some objective evidence of a transfer in addition to an internal book entry. This distinction preserves the similar distinction between subparagraphs (c) and (e) of the present statute.

Under the present statute, the rules of Section 8–313(1) are neither expressly applicable to security interests nor are they expressly made exclusive. On the other hand, when value has been given and the debtor has rights in the collateral, present Section 9–203(1) permits the creation of an enforceable security interest when either the secured party has possession of the collateral *or* the debtor has signed a written security agreement. Under present Article 9, a security interest created by signed agreement, although enforceable, would, with limited exceptions, be unperfected.

Under this revision, new Section 8-321 requires a transfer under Section 8-313(1) to create an enforceable security interest and Section 9-203(1) is expressly made subject to Section 8-321. As a result, it will not be possible to create a security interest in securities by mere written agreement. It is not considered necessary to continue to provide for the creation of unperfected security interests. It is considered desirable, however, to provide for the creation of security interests, unaccompanied by possession, which can be perfected under present Article 9.

Subparagraph (h), limited to the transfer of a security interest, deals with the situation where a security interest, pursuant to written agreement, is perfected by notice to a bailee under Section 9-305. Unlike a transfer under subparagraph (d), (e) or (f) of subsection (1), Section 9-305 does not require confirmation or acknowledgement by the controlling party, but only the receipt of notice. Subparagraph (h) provides that a transfer is effective when notice is received and further identifies the party to be notified. Subparagraph (h) is applicable to both certificated and uncertificated securities and, even when certificated securities are involved, eliminates speculation as to who is the bailee and, indeed, whether there is an instrument. Unlike Section 9-305, which merely requires notification, subsection (h) requires that the notification be signed by the transferor, thereby reducing the possibility of interference by fraudulent claimants. By this revision, securities are expressly excluded from the coverage of Section 9-305.

Subparagraph (i), also limited to the transfer of a security interest, deals with the situation where a security interest, pursuant to written agreement, for new value is automatically perfected for a period of 21 days under Section 9-304(4). Under subparagraph (i), such a security interest is effectively transferred when the new value is given. Section 8-321(2) provides for the expiration of perfection after 21 days. By this revision, securities are expressly excluded from the coverage of Section 9-304(4).

Subparagraph (j) is addressed to the situation where a financial intermediary holds securities in account for a customer and also acquires a security interest in those securities for its own account, *e.g.*, a margin account with a broker or a bank lending on the collateral of its borrower's custody account. In such cases, the financial intermediary's control of the securities is in a dual capacity, and a written agreement signed by the debtor was thought to be a desirable protection.

Present subsection (2) denies holder status to a broker's customer except in cases where the broker is holding a specific certificated security for the customer's account. The effect of this is to prevent the customer from becoming a bona fide purchaser when all he has is an interest in a fungible bulk of securities. Revised subsection (2) deals with the problem expressly in terms of who can or cannot become a bona fide purchaser. Note that in neither the present nor the revised statute can the purchaser who becomes such by acknowledgment by a third party bailee or agent attain bona fide purchaser status. Subsection (2) should be compared with Section 8-302(1)(c).

Subsection (3) states the principle that once a financial intermediary has become a bona fide purchaser subsequent notice of claims to either him or his customer are ineffective, and extends the coverage to uncertificated securities. The final sentence, now applicable to all financial intermediaries, gives the customer the right to obtain a "clean" security from his broker or bank.

New subsection (4) defines the term "financial intermediary" as an entity which maintains security accounts for its customers. Note that the definition applies only when the entity is acting in that capacity. Thus, a bank is a financial intermediary in transactions involving its custody accounts but is not a financial intermediary with respect to securities it holds as a pledgee or for its own account.

§ 8-314. Duty to [Deliver] Transfer, When Completed.

(1) Unless otherwise agreed, [where] if a sale of a security is made on an exchange or otherwise through brokers:

(a) the selling customer fulfills his duty to [deliver when] transfer at the time he:

(i) [he] places [such] a certificated security in the possession of the selling broker or of a person designated by the broker; [or if requested causes an acknowledgment to be made to the selling broker that it is held for him; and]

(ii) causes an uncertificated security to be registered in the name of the selling broker or a person designated by the broker;

(iii) if requested, causes an acknowledgment to be made to the selling broker that [it] a certificated or uncertificated security is held for [him; and] the broker; or

(iv) places in the possession of the selling broker or of a person designated by the broker a transfer instruction for an uncertificated security, providing the issuer does not refuse to register the requested transfer if the instruction is presented to the issuer for registration within 30 days thereafter; and

(b) the selling broker, including a correspondent broker acting for a selling customer, fulfills his duty to [deliver] transfer at the time he:

(i) [by placing the] places a certificated security [or a like security] in the possession of the buying broker or a person designated by [him or] the buying broker;

(ii) causes an uncertificated security to be registered in the name of the buying broker or a person designated by the buying broker;

(iii) places in the possession of the buying broker or of a person designated by the buying broker a transfer instruction for an uncertificated security, providing the issuer does not refuse to register the requested transfer if the instruction is presented to the issuer for registration within 30 days thereafter; or

(iv) [by effecting] effects clearance of the sale in accordance with the rules of the exchange on which the transaction took place.

(2) Except as [otherwise] provided in this section and unless otherwise agreed, a transferor's duty to [deliver] transfer a security under a contract of purchase is not fulfilled until he:

(a) [he] places [the] a certificated security in form to be negotiated by the purchaser in the possession of the purchaser or of a person designated by the purchaser; [him or at the purchaser's request causes an acknowledgment to be made to the purchaser that it is held for him.]

(b) causes an uncertificated security to be registered in the name of the purchaser or a person designated by the purchaser; or

(c) [at the purchaser's request] if the purchaser requests, causes an acknowledgment to be made to the purchaser that [it] a certificated or uncertificated security is held for [him] the purchaser.

(3) Unless made on an exchange, a sale to a broker purchasing for his own account is within [this] subsection (2) and not within subsection (1).

Reasons for 1977 Change

This section presently provides that a transferor's duty is fulfilled by physical delivery of a certificated security. This rule is preserved in subparagraphs (1)(a)(i), (1)(b)(i) and (2)(a). New subparagraphs (1)(a)(ii), (1)(b)(ii) and (2)(b) permit the transferor also to perform by causing the registration of transfer of an uncertificated security to the transferee or his designee. Another alternative, causing a third party holder to acknowledge that he holds for the transferee if the transferee so requests, is provided in the present section and is explicitly stated in new subparagraphs (1)(a)(iii) and (2)(c). A selling broker may also fulfill his duty by effecting clearance pursuant to exchange rules. This is stated in new subparagraph (i)(b)(iv).

In brokerage transactions only, subparagraphs (1)(a)(iv) and (1)(b)(iii) permit yet another alternative. Under these, the transferor may conditionally satisfy his duty by the delivery of an instruction. Such delivery does not constitute complete performance if the instruction is timely presented for registration and the issuer refuses to comply with its request. The burden of timely presentment is placed on the recipient of the instruction and it is not intended that instructions so given will circulate in the manner in which certificated securities now commonly circulate by indorsement. It is contemplated that this method of performance will be commonly employed in transactions settled through brokers, with, in many cases, the selling broker specially guaranteeing the signature of the originator of the instruction pursuant to Section 8-312(3).

§ 8-315. Action Against [Purchaser] Transferee Based Upon Wrongful Transfer.

(1) Any person against whom the transfer of a security is wrongful for any reason, including his incapacity, [may] as against anyone except a bona fide purchaser, may:

(a) reclaim possession of the certificated security wrongfully transferred; [or]

(b) obtain possession of any new certificated security [evidencing] representing all or part of the same rights; [or]

(c) compel the origination of an instruction to transfer to him or a person designated by him an uncertificated security constituting all or part of the same rights; or

(d) have damages.

(2) If the transfer is wrongful because of an unauthorized indorsement of a certificated security, the owner may also reclaim or obtain possession of the security or a new certificated security, even from a bona fide purchaser, if the ineffectiveness of the purported indorsement can be asserted against him under the provisions of this Article on unauthorized indorsements (Section 8-311).

(3) The right to obtain or reclaim possession of a certificated security or to compel the origination of a transfer instruction may be specifically enforced and [its] the transfer of a certificated or uncertificated security enjoined and [the] a certificated security impounded pending the litigation.

Reasons for 1977 Change

The coverage of this section is broadened to include remedies for the wrongful transfer of both certificated and uncertificated securities. Subparagraph (c) is added to subsection (1) to establish the alternative remedy of compelling the origination of an instruction to transfer an equivalent uncertificated security which is the functional equivalent of subparagraph (b).

Subsection (2) is applicable only to certificated securities and language is added to make that clear. The right to specific enforcement provided in subsection (3) is extended to the origination of a transfer instruction and the right to enjoin transfer is made applicable to both certificated and uncertificated securities.

§ 8-316. Purchaser's Right to Requisites for Registration of Transfer, Pledge, or Release on Books.

Unless otherwise agreed, the transferor of a certificated security or the transferor, pledgor, or pledgee of an uncertificated security [must] on due demand must supply his purchaser with any proof of his authority to transfer, pledge, or release or with any other requisite [which may be] necessary to obtain registration of the transfer, pledge, or release of the security; but if the transfer, pledge, or release is not for value, a transferor, pledgor, or pledgee need not do so unless the purchaser furnishes the necessary expenses. Failure within a reasonable time to comply with a demand made [within a reasonable time] gives the purchaser the right to reject or rescind the transfer, pledge, or release.

Reasons for 1977 Change

Language has been added to this section in order to broaden its coverage to both certificated and uncertificated securities. Because uncertificated securities are not only transferred, but also can be pledged and released by registration, language has been added to include such transactions.

§ 8-317. [Attachment or Levy Upon Security] Creditors' Rights.

(1) Subject to the exceptions in subsections (3) and (4), no attachment or levy upon a certificated security or any share or other interest [evidenced] represented thereby which is outstanding [shall be] is valid until the security is actually seized by the officer making the attachment or levy, but a certificated security which has been surrendered to the issuer may be [attached or levied upon at the source] reached by a creditor by legal process at the issuer's chief executive office in the United States.

(2) An uncertificated security registered in the name of the debtor may not be reached by a creditor except by legal process at the issuer's chief executive office in the United States.

(3) The interest of a debtor in a certificated security that is in the possession of a secured party not a financial intermediary or in an uncertificated security registered in the name of a secured party not a financial intermediary (or in the name of a nominee of the secured party) may be reached by a creditor by legal process upon the secured party.

(4) The interest of a debtor in a certificated security that is in the possession of or registered in the name of a financial intermediary or in an

uncertificated security registered in the name of a financial intermediary may be reached by a creditor by legal process upon the financial intermediary on whose books the interest of the debtor appears.

(5) Unless otherwise provided by law, a creditor's lien upon the interest of a debtor in a security obtained pursuant to subsection (3) or (4) is not a restraint on the transfer of the security, free of the lien, to a third party for new value; but in the event of a transfer, the lien applies to the proceeds of the transfer in the hands of the secured party or financial intermediary, subject to any claims having priority.

(6) [(2)] A creditor whose debtor is the owner of a security [shall be] is entitled to [such] aid from courts of appropriate jurisdiction, by injunction or otherwise, in reaching [such] the security or in satisfying the claim by means [thereof as is] allowed at law or in equity in regard to property [which] that cannot readily be [attached or levied upon] reached by ordinary legal process.

Reasons for 1977 Change

This section has been substantially rewritten and expanded, not only to provide for the rights of creditors of the owners of uncertificated securities, but also to provide expressly for remedies against the interest of debtors in certificated securities which are not within the debtor's control. It is one of the three sections in this revision in which it is intended to extend the coverage of Article 8 as to certificated securities. Sections 8-313 and 8-321 are the others.

Subsection (1) states the rule of the present statute for certificated securities which provides that a creditor's lien upon a certificated security is not valid until actual seizure. The chief justification for this rule is the protection of purchasers from the debtor. The rule is entirely appropriate when the security is within the debtor's control. When the debtor does not have such control, the rule has no function.

The present statute recognizes a single exception to the rule where the security has been surrendered to the issuer. New subsection (1) includes this exception and expressly provides that such a security can be reached by serving the issuer at its chief executive office, replacing the cryptic phrase "at the source." The most logical place to serve the issuer would be the place where the transfer records are maintained, but that location might be difficult to identify, especially when the separate elements of a computer network might be situated in different places. The chief executive office is selected as the appropriate place by analogy to Section 9-103(3)(d).

Subsection (2) provides that process upon the issuer is the only method for a creditor to reach an uncertificated security registered in the name of the debtor. This conclusion was reached with some reluctance since it requires a creditor to institute legal action and/or a debtor to defend that action in a jurisdiction which may have no relationship to either of the parties or the dispute other than the happenstance that the debtor owns a security of the particular issuer. Nevertheless, attempts to formulate a procedure by which even a judgment creditor could effectively reach his debtor's uncertificated securities without such legal action resulted in what seemed to be an intolerable burden for issuers.

Subsection (3) provides a second exception to the seizure rule when a certificated security is in the possession of a secured party. In such a case, an effective lien can be established by service on the secured party without depriving him of his possession. This section does not attempt to provide for rights as between the creditor and the secured party, as, for example, whether or when the secured party must liquidate the security. For essentially the same reasons, subsection (3) also covers the case where an uncertificated security has been transferred into the name of a secured party either at the inception of the loan or thereafter.

Subsection (4) recognizes that certificated securities are frequently held in account for customers by banks or brokers and that such securities may be registered not only in the name of the debtor but, more commonly, in street or other nominee name. Additionally, in such cases, the securities may have been commingled, repledged or deposited so that no particular security could be identified as that of the debtor. The subsection provides that the debtor's account can be reached by process upon the entity upon whose books the interest of the debtor appears. This appears to be the most effective way of preventing the transfer of the debtor's interest and thus protecting the creditor. It is only that entity that is aware of the debtor's interest, irrespective of where the securities are located or in what name they happen to be registered. For the same reason, subsection (4) also covers the case where uncertificated securities are registered in street name.

Subsection (5) expressly provides that securities in which the debtor's interest is reached pursuant to subsections (3) or (4) may be transferred for new value, free of the creditor's lien, but, when and if they are, that the lien will be transferred to the proceeds. Nothing in subsection (5) is intended to validate any transfer that would otherwise constitute a fraudulent conveyance. Furthermore, subsection (5) is expressly subject to the procedural laws of the states and no attempt has been made to prescribe the consequences of obtaining such a lien or the procedures for its enforcement.

Particular terms to describe creditor's process have been avoided in this section. This section is not intended to have any effect on the availability of garnishment or similar third-party process as a prejudgment or post-judgment remedy. Such matters are a proper concern of the procedural rules of the states, subject, of course, to constitutional limitations.

§ 8-318. No Conversion by Good Faith [Delivery] Conduct.

An agent or bailee who in good faith (including observance of reasonable commercial standards if he is in the business of buying, selling, or otherwise dealing with securities) has received certificated securities and sold, pledged, or delivered them or has sold or caused the transfer or pledge of uncertificated securities over which he had control according to the instructions of his principal, is not liable for conversion or for participation in breach of fiduciary duty although the principal [has] had no right [to dispose of them] so to deal with the securities.

Reasons for 1977 Change

The section which exonerates the agent or bailee who has made a good faith sale, pledge or delivery of certificated securities has been broadened to provide similar protection for similar parties engaging in similar activities with respect to uncertificated securities.

§ 8-319. Statute of Frauds.

A contract for the sale of securities is not enforceable by way of action or defense unless:

(a) there is some writing signed by the party against whom enforcement is sought or by his authorized agent or broker, sufficient to indicate that a contract has been made for sale of a stated quantity of described securities at a defined or stated price; [or]

(b) delivery of [the] a certificated security or transfer instruction has been accepted, or transfer of an uncertificated security has been registered and the transferee has failed to send written objection to the issuer within 10 days after receipt of the initial transaction statement confirming the registration, or payment has been made, but the contract is enforceable under this provision only to the extent of [such] the delivery, registration, or payment; [or]

(c) within a reasonable time a writing in confirmation of the sale or purchase and sufficient against the sender under paragraph (a) has been received by the party against whom enforcement is sought and he has failed to send written objection to its contents within [ten] 10 days after its receipt; or

(d) the party against whom enforcement is sought admits in his pleading, testimony, or otherwise in court that a contract was made for the sale of a stated quantity of described securities at a defined or stated price.

Reasons for 1977 Change

This section extends the coverage of the statute of frauds to contracts for the sale of both certificated and uncertificated securities. The performance exceptions of paragraph (b) now include the acceptance of a transfer instruction by the alleged transferee and the registration of transfer of an uncertificated security to which registration the alleged transferee has not objected in writing within ten days after receiving the initial transaction statement confirming such registration. These additions, while necessary to enforcement against the alleged transferee, are unnecessary with respect to the transferor since each will almost certainly involve a writing signed by the transferor and thus will be within paragraph (a).

§ 8-320. Transfer or Pledge Within [a] Central Depository System.

(1) In addition to other methods, a transfer, pledge, or release of a security or any interest therein may be effected by the making of appropriate entries on the books of a clearing corporation reducing the account of the transferor, pledgor, or pledgee and increasing the account of the transferee, pledgee, or pledgor by the amount of the obligation, or the number of shares or rights transferred, pledged, or released, if the security is shown on the account of a transferor, pledgor, or pledgee on the books of the clearing corporation; is subject to the control of the clearing corporation; and

(a) [(1)] if [a security] certificated,

(i) [(a)] is in the custody of [a] the clearing corporation, another clearing corporation, [or of] a custodian bank or a nominee of [either subject to the instructions of the clearing corporation] any of them; and

(ii) [(b)] is in bearer form or indorsed in blank by an appropriate person or registered in the name of the clearing corporation, [or] a custodian bank, or a nominee of [either] any of them; or [and]

(b) if uncertificated, is registered in the name of the clearing corporation, another clearing corporation, a custodian bank, or a nominee of any of them;

[(c) is shown on the account of a transferor or pledgor on the books of the clearing corporation;

then, in addition to other methods, a transfer or pledge of the security or any interest therein may be effected by the making of appropriate entries on the books of the clearing corporation reducing the account of the transferor or pledgor and increasing the account of the transferee or pledgee by the amount of the obligation or the number of shares or rights transferred or pledged.]

(2) Under this section entries may be made with respect to like securities or interests therein as a part of a fungible bulk and may refer merely to a quantity of a particular security without reference to the name of the registered owner, certificate or bond number, or the like, and, in appropriate cases, may be on a net basis taking into account other transfer, [or] pledges, or releases of the same security.

(3) A transfer [or pledge] under this section [has the effect of a delivery of a security in bearer form or duly indorsed in blank (Section 8–301) representing the amount of the obligation or the number of shares or rights transferred or pledged] is effective (Section 8–313) and the purchaser acquires the rights of the transferor (Section 8–301). A pledge or release under this section is the transfer of a limited interest. If a pledge or the creation of a security interest is intended, [the making of entries has the effect of a taking of delivery by the pledgee or a secured party (Section 9–304 and 9–305)] the security interest is perfected at the time when both value is given by the pledgee and the appropriate entries are made (Section 8–321). A transferee or pledgee under this section [is a holder] may be a bona fide purchaser (Section 8–302).

(4) A transfer or pledge under this section [does] is not [constitute] a registration of transfer under Part 4 [of this Article].

(5) That entries made on the books of the clearing corporation as provided in subsection (1) are not appropriate does not affect the validity or effect of the entries [nor] or the liabilities or obligations of the clearing corporation to any person adversely affected thereby.

Reasons for 1977 Change

Changes have been made in this section to make it applicable to certificated and uncertificated securities. This will affect the operation of securities depositories in three ways. First, it will enable participants to add to their accounts with the depository by the registration of transfer of uncertificated securities to the depository or its nominee in addition to the current method of delivering certificated securities in negotiable form. Secondly, it will permit the depository to maintain its holdings of securities in uncertificated form, thus reducing custodial problems. Finally, it will permit the depository to transfer uncertificated securities out to its participants by causing the registration of transfer, as an alternative to the current method of maintaining an inventory of certificated securities for that purpose.

Subsection (1) has been restructured to make it clear that it covers securities that clearing corporation A may control through its account in clearing corporation B. The growing system of interfacing depositories makes such clarification desirable.

Subsection (3) has been rewritten to address certain consequences directly, rather than merely by analogy to the physical delivery of certificated securities.

§ 8-321. Enforceability, Attachment, Perfection and Termination of Security Interests.

(1) A security interest in a security is enforceable and can attach only if it is transferred to the secured party or a person designated by him pursuant to a provision of Section 8-313(1).

(2) A security interest so transferred pursuant to agreement by a transferor who has rights in the security to a transferee who has given value is a perfected security interest, but a security interest that has been transferred solely under paragraph (i) of Section 8-313(1) becomes unperfected after 21 days unless, within that time, the requirements for transfer under any other provision of Section 8-313(1) are satisfied.

(3) A security interest in a security is subject to the provisions of Article 9, but:

(a) no filing is required to perfect the security interest; and

(b) no written security agreement signed by the debtor is necessary to make the security interest enforceable, except as otherwise provided in paragraph (h), (i), or (j) of Section 8-313(1).

The secured party has the rights and duties provided under Section 9-207, to the extent they are applicable, whether or not the security is certificated, and, if certificated, whether or not it is in his possession.

(4) Unless otherwise agreed, a security interest in a security is terminated by transfer to the debtor or a person designated by him pursuant to a provision of Section 8-313(1). If a security is thus transferred, the security interest, if not terminated, becomes unperfected unless the security is certificated and is delivered to the debtor for the purpose of ultimate sale or exchange or presentation, collection, renewal, or registration of transfer. In that case, the security interest becomes unperfected after 21 days unless, within that time, the security (or securities for which it has been exchanged) is transferred to the secured party or a person designated by him pursuant to a provision of Section 8-313(1).

Reasons for 1977 Change

This is an entirely new section and is intended to govern the creation, perfection and termination of security interests in all securities, certificated and uncertificated. It is one of three sections in this revision in which it is intended to extend to coverage of Article 8 as to certificated securities. Sections 8-313 and 8-317 are the others. Several sections of Article 9 are made subject to or are affected by this section.

Subsection (1) provides that an effective transfer under Section 8-313(1) is an essential element to the creation of an enforceable security interest. Under present Section 9-203(1), an enforceable security interest can be created without possession if there is a written security agreement signed by the debtor. Under this revision, Section 9-203(1) is expressly made subject to this section.

Subsection (2) provides that when value has been given and the debtor has rights in the collateral, an appropriate transfer will result not only in an enforceable security interest but also in one that is perfected. Under this revision, an unperfected security interest in a security cannot be created. A security interest created by transfer under Section 8-313(1)(i), however, may become unperfected if, within 21 days, the requirements of another method of effective transfer are not satisfied. This produces the same result as present Section 9-304(4). Securities are expressly excluded from the coverage of Section 9-304(4).

Subsection (3) expressly makes a security interest in securities subject to the provisions of Article 9 except those provisions dealing with the creation and perfection of security interests. Those matters are governed by this section. In addition, the provisions of Section 9-207, which govern the rights and duties of the pledgee of a certificated security, are extended, to the extent they are applicable, to all secured parties, whether or not the possession of a certificated security is involved. Thus, in the absence of agreement to the contrary, the secured party, who might be the registered owner of an uncertificated security, would have the duty to remit dividends he received to the debtor or to apply them in reduction of the obligation under Section 9-207(2)(c).

Subsection (4) provides that a security interest is terminated by re-transfer to the debtor unless the parties otherwise agree. Even when the parties agree that the security interest is to continue, it will become unperfected unless there is delivery of a certificated security for the limited purposes described in the second sentence. This provision is intended to produce the same result as present Section 9-304(5) from the coverage of which securities are expressly excluded. The final sentence limits the continued perfection to a 21 day period, as does Section 9-304(5), and requires re-transfer to the secured party, in a manner analogous to Section 9-304(6), as a condition of continued or renewed perfection.

PART 4

REGISTRATION

§ 8-401. Duty of Issuer to Register Transfer, Pledge, or Release.

(1) [Where] If a certificated security in registered form is presented to the issuer with a request to register transfer[,] or an instruction is presented to the issuer with a request to register transfer, pledge, or release, the issuer [is under a duty to] shall register the transfer, pledge, or release as requested if:

(a) the security is indorsed or the instruction was originated by the appropriate person or persons (Section 8-308); [and]

(b) reasonable assurance is given that those indorsements or instructions are genuine and effective (Section 8-402); [and]

(c) the issuer has no duty [to inquire into] as to adverse claims or has discharged [any such] the duty (Section 8-403); [and]

(d) any applicable law relating to the collection of taxes has been complied with; and

(e) the transfer, pledge, or release is in fact rightful or is to a bona fide purchaser.

(2) [Where] If an issuer is under a duty to register a transfer, pledge, or release of a security, the issuer is also liable to the person presenting a certificated security or an instruction [it] for registration or his principal for

loss resulting from any unreasonable delay in registration or from failure or refusal to register the transfer, pledge, or release.

Reasons for 1977 Change

Subsection (1) states the duty of the issuer to honor instructions to register the transfer, pledge or release of uncertificated securities in the same terms and with the same conditions that the present statute imposes with respect to the registration of transfer of certificated securities.

The issuer's liability under subsection (2) is extended to cover losses resulting from failure to take timely action with respect to instructions to transfer, pledge or release uncertificated securities.

§ 8-402. Assurance that Indorsements and Instructions Are Effective.

(1) The issuer may require the following assurance that each necessary indorsement of a certificated security or each instruction (Section 8-308) is genuine and effective:

(a) in all cases, a guarantee of the signature ([subsection (1) of] Section 8-312(1) or (2)) of the person indorsing a certificated security or originating an instruction including, in the case of an instruction, a warranty of the taxpayer identification number or, in the absence thereof, other reasonable assurance of identity; [and]

(b) [where] if the indorsement is made or the instruction is originated by an agent, appropriate assurance of authority to sign;

(c) [where] if the indorsement is made or the instruction is originated by a fiduciary, appropriate evidence of appointment or incumbency;

(d) [where] if there is more than one fiduciary, reasonable assurance that all who are required to sign have done so; and

(e) [where] if the indorsement is made or the instruction is originated by a person not covered by any of the foregoing, assurance appropriate to the case corresponding as nearly as may be to the foregoing.

(2) A "guarantee of the signature" in subsection (1) means a guarantee signed by or on behalf of a person reasonably believed by the issuer to be responsible. The issuer may adopt standards with respect to responsibility [provided such standards] if they are not manifestly unreasonable.

(3) "Appropriate evidence of appointment or incumbency" in subsection (1) means:

(a) in the case of a fiduciary appointed or qualified by a court, a certificate issued by or under the direction or supervision of that court or an officer thereof and dated within [sixty] 60 days before the date of presentation for transfer, pledge, or release; or

(b) in any other case, a copy of a document showing the appointment or a certificate issued by or on behalf of a person reasonably believed by the issuer to be responsible or, in the absence of [such a] that document or certificate, other evidence reasonably deemed by the issuer to be appropriate. The issuer may adopt standards with respect to [such] the evidence [provided such standards] if they are not manifestly unreasonable. The issuer is not charged with notice of the contents of any document obtained pursuant to this paragraph (b) except to the extent that the contents relate directly to the appointment or incumbency.

(4) The issuer may elect to require reasonable assurance beyond that specified in this section, but if it does so and, for a purpose other than that specified in subsection (3)(b), both requires and obtains a copy of a will, trust, indenture, articles of co-partnership, by-laws, or other controlling instrument, it is charged with notice of all matters contained therein affecting the transfer, pledge, or release.

Reasons for 1977 Change

This section has been modified so as to permit the issuer to require, as a condition of honoring an instruction, precisely the same assurances and supplementary documentation as the present section permits the issuer to require as a condition of registering the transfer of a certificated security. In addition, under the last phrase of subparagraph (1)(a) the issuer may require either a warranty of the taxpayer identification number on an instruction as provided in Section 8-312(2)(d) or other evidence of identity.

§ 8-403. [Limited Duty of Inquiry] Issuer's Duty as to Adverse Claims.

(1) An issuer to whom a certificated security is presented for registration [is under a duty to] shall inquire into adverse claims if:

(a) a written notification of an adverse claim is received at a time and in a manner [which affords] affording the issuer a reasonable opportunity to act on it prior to the issuance of a new, reissued, or re-registered certificated security, and the notification identifies the claimant, the registered owner, and the issue of which the security is a part, and provides an address for communications directed to the claimant; or

(b) the issuer is charged with notice of an adverse claim from a controlling instrument [which] it has elected to require under [subsection (4) of] Section 8-402(4).

(2) The issuer may discharge any duty of inquiry by any reasonable means, including notifying an adverse claimant by registered or certified mail at the address furnished by him or, if there be no such address, at his residence or regular place of business that the certificated security has been presented for registration of transfer by a named person, and that the transfer will be registered unless within [thirty] 30 days from the date of mailing the notification, either:

(a) an appropriate restraining order, injunction, or other process issues from a court of competent jurisdiction; or

(b) there is filed with the issuer an indemnity bond, sufficient in the issuer's judgment to protect the issuer and any transfer agent, registrar, or other agent of the issuer involved[,] from any loss [which] it or they may suffer by complying with the adverse claim [is filed with the issuer].

(3) Unless an issuer is charged with notice of an adverse claim from a controlling instrument which it has elected to require under [subsection (4) of] Section 8–402(4) or receives notification of an adverse claim under subsection (1) [of this section, where], if a certificated security presented for registration is indorsed by the appropriate person or persons the issuer is under no duty to inquire into adverse claims. In particular:

(a) an issuer registering a certificated security in the name of a person who is a fiduciary or who is described as a fiduciary is not bound to inquire into the existence, extent, or correct description of the fiduciary relationship; and thereafter the issuer may assume without inquiry that the newly registered owner continues to be the fiduciary until the issuer receives written notice that the fiduciary is no longer acting as such with respect to the particular security;

(b) an issuer registering transfer on an indorsement by a fiduciary is not bound to inquire whether the transfer is made in compliance with a controlling instrument or with the law of the state having jurisdiction of the fiduciary relationship, including any law requiring the fiduciary to obtain court approval of the transfer; and

(c) the issuer is not charged with notice of the contents of any court record or file or other recorded or unrecorded document even though the document is in its possession and even though the transfer is made on the indorsement of a fiduciary to the fiduciary himself or to his nominee.

(4) An issuer is under no duty as to adverse claims with respect to an uncertificated security except:

(a) claims embodied in a restraining order, injunction, or other legal process served upon the issuer if the process was served at a time and in a manner affording the issuer a reasonable opportunity to act on it in accordance with the requirements of subsection (5);

(b) claims of which the issuer has received a written notification from the registered owner or the registered pledgee if the notification was received at a time and in a manner affording the issuer a reasonable opportunity to act on it in accordance with the requirements of subsection (5);

(c) claims (including restrictions on transfer not imposed by the issuer) to which the registration of transfer to the present registered owner was subject and were so noted in the initial transaction statement sent to him; and

(d) claims as to which an issuer is charged with notice from a controlling instrument it has elected to require under Section 8–402(4).

(5) If the issuer of an uncertificated security is under a duty as to an adverse claim, he discharges that duty by:

(a) including a notation of the claim in any statements sent with respect to the security under Sections 8–408(3), (6), and (7); and

(b) refusing to register the transfer or pledge of the security unless the nature of the claim does not preclude transfer or pledge subject thereto.

(6) If the transfer or pledge of the security is registered subject to an adverse claim, a notation of the claim must be included in the initial transaction statement and all subsequent statements sent to the transferee and pledgee under Section 8-408.

(7) Notwithstanding subsections (4) and (5), if an uncertificated security was subject to a registered pledge at the time the issuer first came under a duty as to a particular adverse claim, the issuer has no duty as to that claim if transfer of the security is requested by the registered pledgee or an appropriate person acting for the registered pledgee unless:

(a) the claim was embodied in legal process which expressly provides otherwise;

(b) the claim was asserted in a written notification from the registered pledgee;

(c) the claim was one as to which the issuer was charged with notice from a controlling instrument it required under Section 8-402(4) in connection with the pledgee's request for transfer; or

(d) the transfer requested is to the registered owner.

Reasons for 1977 Change

The present law permits an adverse claimant to delay the registration of transfer of a certificated security by thirty days merely by sending a timely written notification to the issuer identifying the claimant, registered owner and issue and giving an address for communications. This rather loose procedure has not constituted a serious problem for two reasons. First, the transfer of a certificated security is effected by delivery and the rights of the parties are established before the security is presented to the issuer for registration. More significantly, the bona fide purchaser of a security takes free of adverse claims and claims known to the issuer need not be known to him.

The present system enables the claimant to assert his rights in court before the issuer lets a new certificated security loose which might find its way into the hands of a bona fide purchaser. He can effectively do so, of course, only when the rights of a bona fide purchaser have not already intervened, but, in that minority of instances, he does receive protection. Conversely, the ease with which a claimant can register his claim with the issuer is not a great burden on the owner since the clean certificate in his hands gives him the power to transfer to a bona fide purchaser free of the adverse claim. Thus, the present statute requires no notice to the owner when a claim is filed with the issuer and the claim has no effect on transactions until the certificate is presented for registration of transfer. By then, the effect is usually limited to mere delay.

With uncertificated securities, however, transfer does not take place until registration so that any mandated delay seriously impairs an owner's ability to sell or pledge his security. Since a prudent purchaser may not pay until he receives a clean initial transaction statement, the effect of a mere letter notifying the issuer of an adverse claim, however frivolous, would be disastrous. Because of this important difference, the rules of the present section, in subsections (1), (2) and (3) have been restated, unchanged, but limited to situations involving only certificated securities. New rules, applying only to uncertificated securities, are set forth in subsections (4), (5) and (6) and are intended to accommodate the interests of owners, purchasers, issuers and adverse claimants.

Subsection (4) states that an issuer has no duty as to adverse claims except in four described situations. Mere written notifications result in a duty only when they come from existing owners and pledgees and are analogous to stop payment orders on checks. There is a duty as to claims to which the security was subject when it was purchased by the present owner, a situation with which the owner is already familiar. There is a duty as to claims arising from the issuer's request for documentation under Section 8-402.

The significant difference is that claims asserted by third parties, in order to impose a duty on the issuer, must be supported by legal process. This will constitute assurance that the claim is not merely frivolous and that its assertion is more than harassment. In most cases the owner will have been notified and have had the opportunity to be heard. While claims thus asserted may ultimately be adjudged invalid, the owner will not be tied up by a bare written communication from the claimant. On the other hand, while a more substantial burden is imposed on the claimant, there is a channel through which he can assert his claim before the rights of a bona fide purchaser intervene.

Once it is established that the claim imposes a duty on the issuer, notations of the claim must be contained in all statements sent with respect to the security and registration of transfer or pledge must be refused unless the nature of the claim is consistent with transfer or pledge subject to the claim. When transfer or pledge is registered subject to the claim, the final sentence of subsection (5) requires that the claim be noted in all statements sent to the transferee or pledgee.

Subsection (7) deals with the situation where an uncertificated security is already subject to a registered pledge when the issuer first learns of an adverse claim as to which he has a duty. In that event, the registered pledgee who became such without notice of the claim may be a bona fide purchaser with the right to transfer the security free of the claim. That right cannot be curtailed by the claim of a third party (including the registered owner) unless legal process embodying the claim expressly deals with the pledgee's interest. There is obviously no curtailment of the pledgee's right when the claim is asserted by the pledgee himself. It should be curtailed if the pledgee's right to obtain registration of transfer is called into question by a controlling instrument which the issuer elects to require before acting on the pledgee's request. Since the transfer to the registered owner is the equivalent of a release of the pledge, such a transfer should not terminate the issuer's duty as to the claim.

§ 8-404. Liability and Non-Liability for Registration.

(1) Except as [otherwise] provided in any law relating to the collection of taxes, the issuer is not liable to the owner, pledgee, or any other person suffering loss as a result of the registration of a transfer, pledge, or release of a security if:

(a) there were on or with [the] a certificated security the necessary indorsements or the issuer had received an instruction originated by an appropriate person (Section 8-308); and

(b) the issuer had no duty [to inquire into] as to adverse claims or has discharged [any such] the duty (Section 8-403).

(2) [Where] If an issuer has registered a transfer of a certificated security to a person not entitled to it, the issuer on demand [must] shall deliver a like security to the true owner unless:

(a) the registration was pursuant to subsection (1); [or]

(b) the owner is precluded from asserting any claim for registering the transfer under [subsection (1) of the following section] Section 8-405(1); or

(c) [such] the delivery would result in overissue, in which case the issuer's liability is governed by Section 8-104.

(3) If an issuer has improperly registered a transfer, pledge, or release of an uncertificated security, the issuer on demand from the injured party shall restore the records as to the injured party to the condition that would have obtained if the improper registration had not been made unless:

(a) the registration was pursuant to subsection (1); or

(b) the registration would result in overissue, in which case the issuer's liability is governed by Section 8-104.

Reasons for 1977 Change

Subsection (1) exonerates the issuer from liability to any person arising from registration of transfer, pledge or release of an uncertificated security under the same conditions that the present statute provides with respect to the registration of transfer of a certificated security.

The remedy for improper registration under subsection (2), i.e., the delivery of a like security to the true owner, is inapplicable to uncertificated securities. Thus, subsection (3) provides an analogous remedy for uncertificated securities, the restoration of the records to their proper condition. The same exception is made in the event of overissue. The exception of paragraph (2)(b) is inapplicable to uncertificated securities which, by definition, cannot be lost, destroyed or stolen, and is omitted from subsection (3).

§ 8-405. Lost, Destroyed, and Stolen Certificated Securities.

(1) [Where] If a certificated security has been lost, apparently destroyed, or wrongfully taken, and the owner fails to notify the issuer of that fact within a reasonable time after he has notice of it and the issuer registers a transfer of the security before receiving [such a] notification, the owner is precluded from asserting against the issuer any claim for registering the transfer under [the preceding section] Section 8-404 or any claim to a new security under this section.

(2) [Where] If the owner of [the] a certificated security claims that the security has been lost, destroyed, or wrongfully taken, the issuer [must] shall issue a new certificated security or, at the option of the issuer, an equivalent uncertificated security in place of the original security if the owner:

(a) so requests before the issuer has notice that the security has been acquired by a bona fide purchaser; [and]

(b) files with the issuer a sufficient indemnity bond; and

(c) satisfies any other reasonable requirements imposed by the issuer.

(3) If, after the issue of [the] a new certificated or uncertificated security, a bona fide purchaser of the original certificated security presents it for registration of transfer, the issuer [must] shall register the transfer unless registration would result in overissue, in which event the issuer's liability is

governed by Section 8-104. In addition to any rights on the indemnity bond, the issuer may recover the new certificated security from the person to whom it was issued or any person taking under him except a bona fide purchaser or may cancel the uncertificated security unless a bona fide purchaser or any person taking under a bona fide purchaser is then the registered owner or registered pledgee thereof.

Reasons for 1977 Change

Subsection (1) is applicable only to certificated securities, since only they can be lost, destroyed or stolen.

Subsection (2) permits the issuer to satisfy his obligation to replace a lost, destroyed or stolen certificated security by issuing a replacement in either certificated or uncertificated form. Such alternatives exist only when the particular issue is partly certificated and partly uncertificated. In that event, the owner may have the privilege of exchanging one for the other under Section 8-407, thus placing the ultimate option with him. Compare explanation of changes under Section 8-104.

§ 8-406. Duty of Authenticating Trustee, Transfer Agent, or Registrar.

(1) [Where] If a person acts as authenticating trustee, transfer agent, registrar, or other agent for an issuer in the registration of transfers of its certificated securities or in the registration of transfers, pledges, and releases of its uncertificated securities, [or] in the issue of new securities, or in the cancellation of surrendered securities:

(a) he is under a duty to the issuer to exercise good faith and due diligence in performing his functions; and

(b) [he has] with regard to the particular functions he performs, he has the same obligation to the holder or owner of [the] a certificated security or to the owner or pledgee of an uncertificated security and has the same rights and privileges as the issuer has in regard to those functions.

(2) Notice to an authenticating trustee, transfer agent, registrar or other [such] agent is notice to the issuer with respect to the functions performed by the agent.

Reasons for 1977 Change

The coverage of this section is broadened to include the agents of the issuers of both certificated and uncertificated securities.

§ 8-407. Exchangeability of Securities.

(1) No issuer is subject to the requirements of this section unless it regularly maintains a system for issuing the class of securities involved under which both certificated and uncertificated securities are regularly issued to the category of owners, which includes the person in whose name the new security is to be registered.

(2) Upon surrender of a certificated security with all necessary indorsements and presentation of a written request by the person surrendering the

security, the issuer, if he has no duty as to adverse claims or has discharged the duty (Section 8–403), shall issue to the person or a person designated by him an equivalent uncertificated security subject to all liens, restrictions, and claims that were noted on the certificated security.

(3) Upon receipt of a transfer instruction originated by an appropriate person who so requests, the issuer of an uncertificated security shall cancel the uncertificated security and issue an equivalent certificated security on which must be noted conspicuously any liens and restrictions of the issuer and any adverse claims (as to which the issuer has a duty under Section 8–403(4)) to which the uncertificated security was subject. The certificated security shall be registered in the name of and delivered to:

(a) the registered owner, if the uncertificated security was not subject to a registered pledge; or

(b) the registered pledgee, if the uncertificated security was subject to a registered pledge.

Reasons for 1977 Change

This is an entirely new section which deals with the right of the holder of a certificated security to exchange it for an equivalent uncertificated security and the right of the registered owner or registered pledgee of an uncertificated security to obtain a certificated security in exchange for it. This section is applicable only in those situations where both certificated and uncertificated securities exist within the same issue and either form is available to the particular owner. Subsection (1) so limits its applicability.

Neither this nor any other section of this Article is intended to mandate the establishment or continuance of a dual system of registration. It is contemplated that some issuers may provide for both forms of securities on a more or less indefinite basis. Issuers of existing issues which are necessarily wholly certificated may make uncertificated securities available with the intention to phase out the certificated securities over a period of time. Some issuers, if permitted by relevant law, may restrict the availability of uncertificated securities to particular categories of owners, e.g., brokers, banks and institutions.

Subsections (2) and (3) establish the mechanism for exchange. When a certificated security is surrendered for exchange and the issuer has a duty as to adverse claims, that duty must be discharged before an equivalent uncertificated security can be issued. When an instruction requests the issuance of a certificated security in exchange for an uncertificated security, adverse claims as to which the issuer has a duty are to be noted conspicuously thereon. In either case, the existence of the issuer's duty is determined by the provisions of Section 8–403.

§ 8–408. Statements of Uncertificated Securities.

(1) Within 2 business days after the transfer of an uncertificated security has been registered, the issuer shall send to the new registered owner and, if the security has been transferred subject to a registered pledge, to the registered pledgee a written statement containing:

(a) a description of the issue of which the uncertificated security is a part;

(b) the number of shares or units transferred;

(c) the name and address and any taxpayer identification number of the new registered owner and, if the security has been transferred subject to a registered pledge, the name and address and any taxpayer identification number of the registered pledgee;

(d) a notation of any liens and restrictions of the issuer and any adverse claims (as to which the issuer has a duty under Section 8–403(4)) to which the uncertificated security is or may be subject at the time of registration or a statement that there are none of those liens, restrictions, or adverse claims; and

(e) the date the transfer was registered.

(2) Within 2 business days after the pledge of an uncertificated security has been registered, the issuer shall send to the registered owner and the registered pledgee a written statement containing:

(a) a description of the issue of which the uncertificated security is a part;

(b) the number of shares or units pledged;

(c) the name and address and any taxpayer identification number of the registered owner and the registered pledgee;

(d) a notation of any liens and restrictions of the issuer and any adverse claims (as to which the issuer has a duty under Section 8–403(4)) to which the uncertificated security is or may be subject at the time of registration or a statement that there are none of those liens, restrictions, or adverse claims; and

(e) the date the pledge was registered.

(3) Within 2 business days after the release from pledge of an uncertificated security has been registered, the issuer shall send to the registered owner and the pledgee whose interest was released a written statement containing:

(a) a description of the issue of which the uncertificated security is a part;

(b) the number of shares or units released from pledge;

(c) the name and address and any taxpayer identification number of the registered owner and the pledgee whose interest was released;

(d) a notation of any liens and restrictions of the issuer and any adverse claims (as to which the issuer has a duty under Section 8–403(4)) to which the uncertificated security is or may be subject at the time of registration or a statement that there are none of those liens, restrictions or adverse claims; and

(e) the date the release was registered.

(4) An "initial transaction statement" is the statement sent to:

(a) the new registered owner and, if applicable, to the registered pledgee pursuant to subsection (1);

(b) the registered pledgee pursuant to subsection (2); or

(c) the registered owner pursuant to subsection (3).

Each initial transaction statement shall be signed by or on behalf of the issuer and must be identified as "Initial Transaction Statement".

(5) Within 2 business days after the transfer of an uncertificated security has been registered, the issuer shall send to the former registered owner and the former registered pledgee, if any, a written statement containing:

(a) a description of the issue of which the uncertificated security is a part;

(b) the number of shares or units transferred;

(c) the name and address and any taxpayer identification number of the former registered owner and of any former registered pledgee; and

(d) the date the transfer was registered.

(6) At periodic intervals no less frequent than annually and at any time upon the reasonable written request of the registered owner, the issuer shall send to the registered owner of each uncertificated security a dated written statement containing:

(a) a description of the issue of which the uncertificated security is a part;

(b) the name and address and any taxpayer identification number of the registered owner;

(c) the number of shares or units of the uncertificated security registered in the name of the registered owner on the date of the statement;

(d) the name and address and any taxpayer identification number of any registered pledgee and the number of shares or units subject to the pledge; and

(e) a notation of any liens and restrictions of the issuer and any adverse claims (as to which the issuer has a duty under Section 8-403(4)) to which the uncertificated security is or may be subject or a statement that there are none of those liens, restrictions, or adverse claims.

(7) At periodic intervals no less frequent than annually and at any time upon the reasonable written request of the registered pledgee, the issuer shall send to the registered pledgee of each uncertificated security a dated written statement containing:

(a) a description of the issue of which the uncertificated security is a part;

(b) the name and address and any taxpayer identification number of the registered owner;

(c) the name and address and any taxpayer identification number of the registered pledgee;

(d) the number of shares or units subject to the pledge; and

(e) a notation of any liens and restrictions of the issuer and any adverse claims (as to which the issuer has a duty under Section 8-403(4)) to which the uncertificated security is or may be subject or a statement that there are none of those liens, restrictions, or adverse claims.

(8) If the issuer sends the statements described in subsections (6) and (7) at periodic intervals no less frequent than quarterly, the issuer is not obliged to send additional statements upon request unless the owner or pledgee requesting them pays to the issuer the reasonable cost of furnishing them.

(9) Each statement sent pursuant to this section must bear a conspicuous legend reading substantially as follows: "This statement is merely a record of the rights of the addressee as of the time of its issuance. Delivery of this statement, of itself, confers no rights on the recipient. This statement is neither a negotiable instrument nor a security."

Reasons for 1977 Change

This is an entirely new section which obliges the issuer of uncertificated securities to send certain statements. The required statements are of two types. Transaction statements, required by subsections (1), (2), (3) and (5), are analogous to debit and credit advices and the periodic statements can be reconciled from them. Periodic statements, required by subsections (6) and (7) are analogous to bank statements and will advise owners and pledgees of their positions at given points in time.

The transaction statements, which are mandated upon the registration of transfer, pledge or release, must be sent within two days after the relevant registration, but it is contemplated that such statements will be prepared virtually simultaneously with the actual registration and sent immediately thereafter.

The transaction statements are intended to serve two functions. They are notice to the transferor (the owner in the case of a transfer or pledge or the pledgee in the case of a release or the transfer of a security subject to a pledge) that his interest has been reduced. In the event of fraudulent, unauthorized or otherwise improper registration, the transaction statement will serve as notice that timely action should be taken.

More importantly, these statements are notice to the transferee (new owner in the case of a transfer, pledgee in the case of a pledge, present owner in the case of a release) that the increase of his interest has, in fact, been registered. Furthermore, since all statements except those required by subsection (5) must include a notation of defects or an express statement that there are none, these statements will give the transferee the assurance equivalent to that afforded by a "clean" certificated security and create an estoppel against the issuer.

It is contemplated that transferees will and should be able to rely on these statements and, in many cases, will not part with their consideration until they receive them. In order that they will have the desired effect of establishing rights for the transferee against the issuer, subsection (4) requires that the copy of each transaction statement sent to the transferee, called an "initial transaction statement," be signed. Note that Section 1-201(39) does not require a manual signature for compliance with this requirement. Compare also Sections 8-103(b), 8-105(3)(d), 8-202, 8-204(b), 8-205, 8-206, 8-208, 8-304 and 8-313(3) for the effects of initial transaction statements.

The frequency of one year, with which periodic statements must be sent to owners and pledgees, is intended to be a minimum requirement for all issuers, including closely held corporations. Owners and pledgees are entitled to request additional statements of position at any time. It is contemplated, however, that publicly held issuers will adopt the practice of sending quarterly statements conforming to the common practice of sending quarterly reports and dividend checks. For those that do, subsection (8) eliminates the obligation to furnish additional statements of position on request unless the issuer is reimbursed for the additional cost.

Subsection (9) requires a conspicuous legend to be borne by each statement as a protection against unjustified reliance on statements of uncertificated securities by persons who might deal with them. Other than the aforesaid legend, the form of the statements required by this section is not prescribed. Perhaps the forms now used by the transfer agents of mutual funds to confirm acquisitions, dispositions, reinvestment of dividends, periodic liquidations and statements of position might serve as a model.

Amendments to Article 9 (1972 Official Text)

§ 9-103. Perfection of Security Interests in Multiple State Transactions.

. . .

(3) Accounts, general intangibles and mobile goods.

(a) This subsection applies to accounts (other than an account described in subsection (5) on minerals) and general intangibles <u>(other than uncertificated securities)</u> and to goods....

. . .

<u>(6) Uncertificated securities.</u>

<u>The law (including the conflict of laws rules) of the jurisdiction of organization of the issuer governs the perfection and the effect of perfection or non-perfection of a security interest in uncertificated securities.</u>

Reasons for 1977 Change

Uncertificated securities are included in the definition of "General intangibles" under Section 9-106. Since the perfection of a security interest in an uncertificated security is normally accomplished by registration of pledge or transfer under Article 8, uncertificated securities are excluded from the coverage of subsection (3) under which the location of the debtor would govern. New subsection (6) prescribes the law of the issuer's jurisdiction of organization as the governing law, consistent with Section 8-106.

§ 9-105. Definitions and Index of Definitions.

(1) In this Article unless the context otherwise requires:

. . .

(i) "Instrument" means a negotiable instrument (defined in Section 3-104), or a *certificated* security (defined in Section 8-102) or ...

. . .

Reasons for 1977 Change

Because Section 8-102 now defines "security" as either a certificated or an uncertificated security, the word "certificated" is inserted to limit the definition only to those securities which are represented by instruments.

§ 9-203. Attachment and Enforceability of Security Interest; Proceeds; Formal Requisites.

(1) Subject to the provisions of Section 4-208 on the security interest of a collecting bank, Section 8-321 on security interests in securities and Section 9-113 on a security interest arising under the Article on Sales, a security interest is not enforceable against the debtor or third parties with respect to the collateral and does not attach unless:

(a) the collateral is in the possession of the secured party pursuant to agreement, or the debtor has signed a security agreement which contains a description of the collateral and in addition, when the security interest covers crops growing or to be grown or timber to be cut, a description of the land concerned; [and]

(b) value has been given; and

(c) the debtor has rights in the collateral.

. . .

Reasons for 1977 Change

The added language in subsection (1) expressly makes this section subject to Section 8-321. Section 8-321(1) provides that an enforceable security interest in a security can be created only by a transfer which complies with Section 8-313(1).

It should be noted that both subsection (1) of this section and Section 8-321(2) contain the requirements that value be given and that the debtor have rights in the collateral. Subparagraph (1)(a) of this section, however, requires either possession by the secured party or a security agreement signed by the debtor. Of the various provisions of Section 8-313(1), some require possession by the secured party, some require a signed security agreement and the rest require procedures which are functionally equivalent to possession.

It is intended that compliance with some provision of Section 8-313(1) is essential to the creation of an enforceable security interest in a security and, conversely, that compliance with the requirements of subsection (1) of this section will not, of itself, suffice.

§ 9-302. When Filing is Required to Perfect Security Interest; Security Interests to Which Filing Provisions of This Article Do Not Apply.

(1) A financing statement must be filed to perfect all security interest[s] except the following:

. . .

(f) a security interest of a collecting bank (Section 4-208) or in securities (Section 8-321) or arising under the Article on Sales (see Section 9-113) or covered in subsection (3) of this section;

. . .

Reasons for 1977 Change

Section 8-321(2) provides that security interests in securities created in accordance with its provisions are perfected. Since none of its provisions, including the provisions of Section 8-313(1) incorporated therein, require filing, security interests in securities are excepted from the normal filing requirements of Article 9 by the language added to subparagraph (1)(f) of this section. Note that most of the requirements of Section 8-313(1) involve either possession or its functional equivalent.

§ 9-304. Perfection of Security Interest in Instruments, Documents, and Goods Covered by Documents; Perfection by Permissive Filing; Temporary Perfection Without Filing or Transfer of Possession.

(1) A security interest in chattel paper or negotiable documents may be perfected by filing. A security interest in money or instruments (other than certificated securities or instruments which constitute part of chattel paper) can be perfected only by the secured party's taking possession, except as provided in subsections (4) and (5) of this section and subsections (2) and (3) of Section 9-306 on proceeds.

. . .

(4) A security interest in instruments (other than certificated securities) or negotiable documents is perfected without filing or the taking of possession for a period of 21 days from the time it attaches to the extent that it arises for new value given under a written security agreement.

(5) A security interest remains perfected for a period of 21 days without filing where a secured party having a perfected security interest in an instrument (other than a certificated security), a negotiable document or goods in possession of a bailee other than one who has issued a negotiable document therefor:

. . .

(b) delivers the instrument to the debtor for the purpose of ultimate sale or exchange or of presentation, collection, renewal, or registration of transfer.

(6) After the 21 day period in subsections (4) and (5) perfection depends upon compliance with applicable provisions of this Article.

Reasons for 1977 Change

The definition of "instrument" in Section 9-105(1)(i) includes a certificated security and the perfection of security interests in all securities is governed by Section 8-321. Hence, certificated securities are expressly excluded from this section.

Note that a perfected security interest under Section 8-321 must be created by a transfer under Section 8-313(1) which, when certificated securities are involved, requires possession or a functional equivalent thereof. The 21 day initial grace period of subsection (4) is reflected in Section 8-313(1)(i) and the reference thereto in Section 8-321(2). The 21 day grace period of subsection (5) is reflected in Section 8-321(4).

§ 9-305. When Possession by Secured Party Perfects Security Interest Without Filing.

A security interest in letters of credit and advices of credit (subsection (2)(a) of Section 5-116), goods, instruments (other than certificated securities), money, negotiable documents, or chattel paper may be perfected by the secured party's taking possession of the collateral. If such collateral other than goods covered by a negotiable document is held by a bailee, the secured party is deemed to have possession from the time the bailee receives notification of the secured party's interest. A security interest is perfected by possession from the time possession is taken without relation back and continues only so long as possession is retained, unless otherwise specified in this Article. The security interest may be otherwise perfected as provided in this Article before or after the period of possession by the secured party.

Reasons for 1977 Change

The definition of "instrument" in Section 9-105(1)(i) includes a certificated security and the perfection of security interests in all securities is governed by Section 8-321. Hence, certificated securities are expressly excluded from this section.

The typical pledge of a certificated security is unaffected by this change since Section 8-313(1)(a) provides for transfer by delivery and Section 8-321(2) provides that a security interest thus transferred is perfected. Section 9-305 has been relied on to perfect security interests in securities in the hands of third parties (first pledgees, brokers, custodian banks, etc.) by notifying such third parties and assuming that they are bailees of certificated securities. When certificated securities have been repledged, held in nominee name or deposited in a securities depository, there is some doubt as to the identity of the bailee or, indeed, whether there is even an instrument that can be identified as the subject matter of the security interest.

The transfer rules of Section 8-313(1), which are incorporated in Section 8-321, are intended to settle such questions with respect to both certificated securities and uncertificated securities, which, by definition, cannot be "possessed." Note that Section 8-313(1)(h) deals explicitly with the problem of perfection by notice, provides that the notice be signed by the debtor-transferor and identifies the proper party to be notified.

§ 9-309. Protection of Purchasers of Instruments [and], Documents and Securities.

Nothing in this Article limits the rights of a holder in due course of a negotiable instrument (Section 3-302) or a holder to whom negotiable document of title has been duly negotiated (Section 7-501) or a bona fide purchaser of a security (Section [8-301] 8-302) and such holders or purchasers take priority over an earlier security interest even though perfected. Filing under this Article does not constitute notice of the security interest to such holders or purchasers.

Reasons for 1977 Change

This section presently resolves the conflict which may result when a financial intermediary or secured party wrongfully transfers a certificated security he controls. Since the term "security" now includes, under revised Section 8-102, uncertificated securities, this section will also cover the situation where a financial intermediary or secured party who is the registered owner or registered pledgee of an uncertificated security wrongfully causes the registration of transfer or pledge. In either case, a bona fide purchaser (including a pledgee) from the financial intermediary or secured party will prevail over a secured creditor of the beneficial owner who has created and perfected his security interest by notice to or acknowledgment from the wrongful transferor under Section 8-321.

§ 9-312. Priorities Among Conflicting Security Interests in the Same Collateral.

. . .

(7) If future advances are made while a security interest is perfected by filing [or], the taking of possession, or under Section 8-321 on securities, the security interest has the same priority for the purposes of subsection (5) with respect to the future advances as it does with respect to the first advance. If a commitment is made before or while the security interest is so perfected, the security interest has the same priority with respect to advances made pursuant thereto. In other cases a perfected security interest has priority from the date the advance is made.

. . .

Reasons for 1977 Change

The insertion in subsection (7) protects the future advances of a secured party who has perfected his security interest in securities under Section 8-321 even if the method did not involve his taking possession of the collateral.

Changes in Articles 1 and 5

§ 1-201. General Definitions.

Subject to additional definitions contained in the subsequent Articles of this Act which are applicable to specific Articles or Parts thereof, and unless the context otherwise requires, in this Act:

. . .

(5) "Bearer" means the person in possession of an instrument, document of title, or certificated security payable to bearer or indorsed in blank.

. . .

(14) "Delivery" with respect to instruments, documents of title, chattel paper, or certificated securities means voluntary transfer of possession.

. . .

(20) "Holder" means a person who is in possession of a document of title or an instrument or [an] a certificated investment security drawn, issued, or indorsed to him or his order or to bearer or in blank.

. . .

§ 5–114. Issuer's Duty and Privilege to Honor; Right to Reimbursement.

. . .

(2) Unless otherwise agreed when documents appear on their face to comply with the terms of a credit but a required document does not in fact conform to the warranties made on negotiation or transfer of a document of title (Section 7–507) or of a certificated security (Section 8–306) or is forged or fraudulent or there is fraud in the transaction:

(a) the issuer must honor the draft on demand for payment if honor is demanded by a negotiating bank or other holder of the draft or demand which has taken the draft or demand under the credit and under circumstances which would make it a holder in due course (Section 3–302) and in an appropriate case would make it a person to whom a document of title has been duly negotiated (Section 7–502) or a bona fide purchaser of a certificated security (Section 8–302); and

. . .

Reasons for 1977 Change

The foregoing insertions of the word "certificated" in two sections of Articles other than Article 8 and 9 are made in order to conform to the new definitions in Section 8–102. Without modification, the term "security" would include uncertificated securities as well as certificated securities.

APPENDIX II

1972 OFFICIAL TEXT SHOWING CHANGES MADE IN FORMER TEXT OF ARTICLE 9, SECURED TRANSACTIONS, AND OF RELATED SECTIONS AND REASONS FOR CHANGES

GENERAL COMMENT ON THE APPROACH OF THE REVIEW COMMITTEE FOR ARTICLE 9 *

Article 9 of the Uniform Commercial Code was the first integration of the badly fragmented field of chattel security. It was, therefore, the most innovative of the articles of the Code, and many persons have indicated their belief that it is the Code's most valuable article.

Nevertheless, the fact that it was a first integration of complex problems led to some imperfection of the drafting. The Reporters have reported to the Committee many instances in which the drafting could be improved for clarity or to answer questions that can be posed that are not now clearly answered. Yet the outstanding result of Article 9 in practice has been that it has been gratifyingly successful; that no errors with serious consequences have been disclosed; and that the demands for change have been in relatively narrow areas. The Committee has therefore felt that it is not its responsibility, consistent with the terms of creation of the Permanent Editorial Board, to seek perfection where the Code appears to be working satisfactorily without significant problems in practice, for to do so would run the risk of opening up still further problems.

The Committee has in mind that at a minimum the changes finally adopted by it, the Permanent Editorial Board and the sponsoring organizations will take several years to enact in the 51 jurisdictions which have now adopted the Code, and that it would be a great mistake to introduce serious non-uniformity into any fundamental aspect of operations under Article 9. The Code must remain uniform in its day-to-day impact and operation even if there should be a significant period which may elapse before the Committee's ultimate proposals are adopted in all enacting jurisdictions. Thus the proposed changes must be compatible in operation with the existing Code, and the Committee has eschewed amendment merely for the sake of theoretical improvement where there was no pressing problem illustrated by non-uniform amendment or by substantial demand for change.

* The Review Committee for Article 9 prepared the following document to aid understanding of its recommendations. The discussion is by topics rather than by section as in the Reasons for Change and in the Comments. This document has not been approved by the Permanent Editorial Board for the Uniform Commercial Code or by the Council of the American Law Institute. This document is in the form approved at the last meeting of the Committee in October, 1970. Where the Permanent Editorial Board recommended changes in the statutory text which are inconsistent with the Committee's discussion, that fact is noted in footnotes.

The proposed changes have been limited to Article 9 except in a few instances where an individual section of Article 1, 2 or 5 had to be changed to correspond with the changes in Article 9.

The Review Committee has not sought herein to follow the Permanent Editorial Board's past practice of commenting individually on non-uniform amendments, but has proposed a revision in depth of Article 9 to take into account the amendments and also criticisms that might lead to non-uniform amendments. To the extent that the Committee has not incorporated amendments in its proposals in exact words or in substance, they should be deemed disapproved as merely stylistic or mere matters of detail, or because the problem was handled in some other fashion, or because the Committee disagreed as a matter of policy.

There will be Reasons for Change and revised Comments to the sections changed. In addition, because the proposed changes in any given section may be related to several different problems, and the solution to one problem involves changes in more than one section, there is set forth below a Description of Proposed Changes from the 1962 Text, with Reasons Therefor, arranged by topic.[1]

The topics discussed are the following:

A. Fixtures

B. Crops and Farm Products

C. Timber

D. Oil, Gas and Minerals

E. Intangibles, Proceeds and Priorities

F. Conflict of Laws

G. Motor Vehicles and Related Problems of Perfection

1. The Committee has had a difficult judgmental task in determining the length and the amount of detail in this Statement. To outline the problems considered in full detail with discussion of arguments pro and con and other possible solutions would have expanded this Statement to the length of a treatise. The Committee has sought to find an appropriate middle ground in succinct statements of the difficulties of the existing Code and the intended operation of suggested solutions. These should be understandable to persons basically familiar with the concepts of Article 9. There is an extensive literature in which the reader can find most of the problems discussed in more detail. It would not be possible in this Statement to cite all of the worthwhile discussions, but mention may be made of Gilmore, Security Interests in Personal Property (2 volumes, 1965); Coogan, Hogan and Vagts, Secured Transactions under the Uniform Commercial Code (2 volumes, 1963); Hawkland, A Transactional Guide to the Uniform Commercial Code (ALI–ABA Joint Committee on Continuing Legal Education, 2 volumes, 1964, (hereinafter referred to as ALI–ABA Joint Committee)); Spivack, Secured Transactions (ALI–ABA Joint Committee, 1960); Davenport and Henson, Secured Transactions—ii, (ALI–ABA Joint Committee, 1966); and Uniform Commercial Code Handbook, (American Bar Ass'n, 1964). There have been published transcripts of three discussions in which various members of the Committee, Reporters, Consultants and other specialists have discussed in depth some of the problems here considered: A Practical Approach to Article 9 of the Uniform Commercial Code, 19 Bus.Law. 20 (1963); Advanced ALI–ABA Course of Study on Banking and Secured Transactions Under The Uniform Commercial Code (ALI–ABA Joint Committee, 1968); Problems of Lenders, Borrowers and Sellers Under the Uniform Commercial Code (1968). The extensive and valuable discussions of some of these problems in periodic legal literature may be located through the usual indices and also through Ezer, Uniform Commercial Code Bibliography and Supplements (ALI–ABA Joint Committee, 1966, 1967 and 1969).

H. Matters of Scope

I. Filing

J. Default

A. Fixtures

A–1. Section 9–313 deals with the problem that certain goods which are the subject of chattel financing become so affixed or otherwise so related to real estate that they become part of the real estate, and the chattel interests would be subordinate to real estate interests except as protected by the priorities regulated by the section. Such goods are called "fixtures." Some fixtures also retain their chattel nature in that a chattel financing with respect to them may exist and may continue to be recognized. But this concept does not apply if the goods are integrally incorporated into the real estate.

A–2. Existing Section 9–313 states that the rules of the Section do not apply to goods incorporated in the structure in the manner of lumber, etc. This formulation of the problem would lead to the conclusion that these goods integrally incorporated into real estate are not fixtures. In contrast, the Committee's proposal defines "fixture" to include any goods which become so related to particular real estate that an interest in them arises under real estate law and therefore, goods integrally incorporated into the real estate are clearly fixtures. This usage, in the Committee's opinion, conforms more clearly to pre–Code usage in most states than does the existing Section 9–313, and therefore permits a less confusing reference to pre–Code cases. There is no practical difference, however, because the Committee's proposal, like the existing Section 9–313, provides in substance that no security interest exists under Article 9 in ordinary building materials incorporated into an improvement on land.

A–3. Thus both the existing section and the Committee proposal recognize three categories of goods: (1) those which retain their chattel character entirely and are not part of the real estate; (2) ordinary building materials which have become an integral part of the real estate and cannot retain their chattel character for purposes of finance; and (3) the intermediate class which has become real estate for certain purposes, but as to which chattel financing may be preserved. This third and intermediate class is the primary subject of Section 9–313. The demarcation between these classifications is not delineated by this section.

A–4. Goods may be technically "ordinary building materials," e.g., window glass, but if they are incorporated into a structure which as a whole has not become an integral part of the real estate, the rules applicable to the ordinary building materials follow the rules applicable to the structure itself. The outstanding examples presenting this kind of problem are the modern "mobile homes" and the modern prefabricated steel buildings usable as warehouses, garages, factories, etc. In the case of the mobile homes, most of them are erected on leased land and the right of the debtor under a mobile home purchase contract to remove the goods as lessee will make clear that his secured party ordinarily has a similar right. See proposed paragraph (5)(b) of Section 9–313. In cases where mobile homes or prefabricated steel buildings are erected by a person having an ownership interest in the land, the question into which category the buildings fall is one determined by local law. In general, the governing local law will not be that applicable in determining whether goods have become real property between landlord and tenant, or between mortgagor and mortgagee, or between grantor and grantee, but rather that applicable in a three-party situation, determining whether chattel financing can survive as against parties who acquire rights through the affixation of the goods to the real estate.

A–5. The assertion that no security interest exists in ordinary building materials is only for the operation of the priority provisions of this section. It is without prejudice to any rights which the secured party may have against the debtor himself if he incorporated the goods into real estate or against any party guilty of wrongful incorporation thereof in violation of the secured party's rights.

A–6. In considering fixture priority problems, there will always first be a preliminary question whether real estate interests per se have an interest in the goods as part of real estate. If not, it is immaterial, so far as concerns real estate parties, as such, whether a chattel security interest is perfected or unperfected. In no event does a real estate party acquire an interest in a "pure" chattel just because a security interest therein is unperfected. If on the other hand real estate law gives real estate parties an interest in the goods, a conflict arises and this section states the priorities.

A–7. The general principle of priority announced in the proposed Section 9–313 is set forth in paragraph (4)(b). It is basically that a fixture filing gives to the fixture security interest priority as against other real estate interests according to the usual priority rule of conveyancing, that is, the first to file or record prevails. An apparent limitation to this principle set forth in paragraph (4)(b), namely that the secured party must have had priority over any interest of a predecessor in title of the conflicting encumbrancer or owner, is not really a limitation, but is an expression of the usual rule that a person must be entitled to transfer what he has. Thus, if the fixture security interest is subordinate to a mortgage, it is subordinate to an interest of an assignee of the mortgage even though the assignment is a later recorded instrument. Similarly if the fixture security interest is subordinate to the rights of an owner, it is subordinate to a subsequent grantee of the owner and likewise subordinate to a subsequent mortgagee of the owner.

A–8. A qualification of the rule based on priority of filing or recording is paragraph (4)(d), where rules of priority in filing or recording are preserved, but there is no requirement that as against a judgment lienor of the real estate, the prior filing of the fixture security interest must be in the real estate records. The Committee thought that the fixture security interest if perfected first should prevail even though not filed or recorded in real estate records, because a judgment creditor is not [2] a reliance creditor who would have searched records. Thus, even a prior filing in the chattel records should protect the priority of a fixture security interest against a subsequent judgment lien.

2. It has since been pointed out that in Pennsylvania, because of the use of the confession of judgment to obtain a real estate lien, the judgment creditor may be a reliance creditor.

It is hoped that this rule will also have the effect of preserving a fixture security interest against invalidation by a trustee in bankruptcy. That would, of course, be the result under Section 60a of the Bankruptcy Act if the time of perfection of the fixture security interest were measured by the judgment creditor test applicable to personal property. It would not be the result if the time of perfection were measured by the purchaser test applicable to real estate. It is hoped that since the fixture security interest arises against the goods in their capacity as chattels, the bankruptcy courts will apply the judgment creditor test. But the effectiveness of the Committee's drafting to achieve its purpose cannot be known certainly until the courts adjudicate the question or until it is settled by amendment to Section 60a of the Bankruptcy Act.

The phrase "lien by legal or equitable proceedings" is taken from Section 70c of the Bankruptcy Act, and is intended to encompass all of the three ways in which judgment liens are there described.

It has been suggested that a fixture security interest perfected against lien creditors but subordinate to other real estate interests might be vulnerable to attack under Section 70e of the Bankruptcy Act. The interpretation involved is in dispute among bankruptcy scholars. In any event, those concerned with the question can avoid the issue by not taking advantage of the proposed statutory sanction of a filing in other than the real estate records.

It was also suggested that paragraph (4)(d) should provide for a 10–day grace period like those in Sections 9–301(2) and 9–312(4). But the Committee thought the practical need for such a provision was slight and did not justify the resulting complexities.

A–9. A special exception to the usual rule of priority based on time is the one of paragraph (4)(c) in favor of holders of security interests in factory and office machines, and in certain replacement domestic appliances, as discussed below. This is not as broad an exception as it might seem. To repeat, a fixture conflict is reached only if the goods are held as a matter of local law to have become part of the real estate. If so, the rule of paragraph (4)(c) operates only if the fixture security interest is perfected before the goods become fixtures. Having been perfected, it would of course have priority over subsequent real estate interests under the rule of paragraph (4)(b). Since it would in almost all cases be a purchase money security interest, it would also have priority over other real estate interests under the purchase-money priority of paragraph (4)(a), to be discussed in paragraph A–11. The rule is stated separately because the permitted perfection is by any method permitted by the article, and not exclusively by fixture filing in the real estate records. This rule is made necessary by the confusions of the law as to whether certain machinery and appliances become fixtures.

As an additional point, in the case of machinery, the separate statement of this rule makes clear that it is not overridden by the construction mortgage priority of subsection (6), as would have been true if reliance had been solely on the purchase money priority. The Committee considers that factory and office machines are not always financed as part of a construction mortgage, and that it is reasonable to expect the mortgagee to be alert to conflicting chattel financing of these machines.

A-10. As to appliances, the rule stated is limited to readily removable replacements, not original installations of appliances. To facilitate financing of original appliances in new dwellings as part of the real estate financing of the dwellings, no special priority is given to chattel financing of the appliances. The section leaves to other law of the state the question whether original installations are fixtures to which the protection accorded by this section to construction mortgages would be applicable. Likewise, it is recognized that (when not supplied by tenants) appliances in commercial apartment buildings are intended as permanent improvements, and no special rule is stated for appliances in that case. The special priority rule here stated in favor of chattel financing is limited to situations where the installation of appliances may not be intended to be permanent, i.e., replacement appliances in apartment units that are likely to be owner-occupied—those with not more than four family units.[3] The principal effect of the rule is to make clear that a secured party financing occasional replacements of domestic appliances in dwellings, duplexes or similar units need not concern himself with real estate descriptions or records but may perfect by ordinary chattel filing; indeed, a purchase-money replacement in the buyer's own dwelling will be consumer goods, and perfection without filing will be possible. (The priority against the construction mortgage has no application to replacement appliances.)

A-11. The principal exception to the rule of priority based on time of filing or recording is a priority given in paragraph (4)(a) to purchase money security interests in fixtures as against *prior* recorded real estate interests, provided that the purchase money security interest is filed as a fixture filing in the real estate records before the goods become fixtures or within 10 days thereafter. This priority corresponds to one given in Section 9-312(4), and the 10 days of grace represents a reduction of the purchase money priority as against prior interests in the real estate under the present Section 9-313, where the purchase money priority exists even though the security interest is *never* filed.

It should be emphasized that this purchase money priority with the 10-day grace period for filing is limited to rights against *prior* real estate interests. There is no such priority with the 10-day grace period as against subsequent real estate interests. The fixture security interest can defeat subsequent real estate interests only if it is filed first and prevails under the usual conveyancing rule recognized in paragraph (4)(b).

A-12. The purchase money priority presents a difficult problem in relation to construction mortgages. The latter will ordinarily have been recorded even before the commencement of delivery of materials to the job, and therefor will be "prior" as against the fixture security interests. Present Section 9-313(4) seeks to work this out by treating each advance under a construction mortgage as a separate subsequent loan, but then gets into difficulties of language as to the times of actual advance and the times of commitment. The Committee's proposal is far more favorable to real estate interests,

3. The Permanent Editorial Board revised the Committee's draft to limit this rule, so far as it concerns replacement appliances, to consumer goods, i.e., those used for the buyer's personal or family purposes. The reference to buildings of four units or less was eliminated.

because it provides that the purchase money priority does not apply as against construction mortgages. The latter will ordinarily be recorded before the filing of the fixture security interest, and therefore will have priority over the latter under the basic rule of paragraph (4)(b), and subsection (6) expressly states this subordination. It is the Committee's intention that the priority of a construction mortgage shall apply only during the construction period leading to the completion of the improvement; and that as to additions to the building made long after completion of the improvement, the construction priority will not apply simply because the additions are financed by the real estate mortgagee under an open end clause of his construction mortgage. In such case, the applicable principles will be those of paragraphs (4)(a) and (4)(b). The Committee has further provided that a refinancing of a construction mortgage has the same priority as the mortgage itself. The phrase "an obligation incurred for the construction of an improvement" is intended to cover both optional advances and advances pursuant to commitment, and to include advances for incidental expenses such as financing and title costs.[4]

A–13. The term "fixture filing" has been introduced and defined. It helps to emphasize a point that was intended but not clearly set forth in the existing Code—that when a filing is intended to give the priority advantages herein discussed against real estate interests, the filing must be for record in the real estate records and indexed therein, so that it will be found in a real estate search (except as stated in paragraphs A–8 to A–10).

A–14. The prior uniform provisions seemed to make it possible for a fixture supplier to retain a security interest against a contractor, to the possible surprise and deception of real estate interests. Proposed Section 9–313(4)(a) and (b) preclude such retention by a fixture supplier by denying priority to the security interest unless the debtor has an interest of record in the real estate.

A–15. The status of fixtures installed by tenants (as well as such persons as licensees and holders of easements) is unclear under the present Code. The Committee's proposal in paragraph (5)(b) is that if the debtor (tenant or other interest mentioned) has the right to remove the fixture as against a real estate interest, the secured party has priority over that real estate interest.

A–16. The Committee proposes a change in Section 9–302(1)(d) so that there will be no exception of fixtures from the rule that a purchase money security interest in consumer goods is perfected without filing, and thus good against lien creditors and the trustee in bankruptcy. See paragraph A–8. The fixture security interest would no longer have to be filed in all cases, but only in cases (for goods other than replacement appliances) in which priority against real estate parties is desired.

A–17. In summary, effort has been made by a fresh approach to provide substantive rules that should satisfy the legitimate interests of all parties. In the Committee's opinion, there remains a necessity to preserve the possibility of purchase money fixture financing notwithstanding the existence of mortgages on the real property. Real estate lending is typically long-term, and is

4. The Permanent Editorial Board changed the text of Section 9–313(1)(c) to make clear that the term "construction mortgage" may cover land acquisition costs.

usually done by institutional investors who can afford to take a long view of the matter rather than concentrating on the results of any particular case.

It is apparent that a rule which permits and encourages purchase money fixture financing, which in contrast is typically short term, will result in the modernization and improvement of real estate rather than in its deterioration and will on balance benefit long-term real estate lenders. Because of the short-term character of the chattel financing, it will rarely produce any conflict in fact with the real estate lender. The contrary rule would chill the availability of short-term credit for modernization of real estate by installation of new fixtures and in the long run could not help real estate lenders.

The reported difficulty in locating relevant fixture security interests applicable to particular parcels of real estate has been cured by new provisions as to real estate description in fixture filings, the indexing thereof, and other related provisions in Part 4 of Article 9.

The weightiest objection to present Section 9–313 was to the possibility that fixtures constituting material portions of the value of a building might come into the building subject to fixture security interests which might have priority over the rights of a construction mortgagee. The proposed treatment reverses the position of the existing Code and accords priority to the construction mortgagee.

The draft does not go as far as some of the non-uniform amendments, which would subject fixture filing to the burden of obtaining full "legal descriptions" of real estate and would deny fixture security interests priority against existing real estate parties who had not consented thereto, thus negating the purchase money concept. The Committee's changes move very substantially toward the views which gave rise to such amendments, but do not go all the way.

B. Crops and Farm Products

B–1. In contrast with dissatisfaction with the Code's classification of timber, discussed in Section C, no difficulty seems to have arisen with respect to the recognition in Section 2–107 and in the definition of goods in Section 9–105(1) that growing crops are goods and therefore chattels. This still leaves a possibility that real estate parties such as mortgagees or grantees may have some interest in them. Section 2–107(3) recognizes that a contract for sale of growing crops may have to be recorded in realty records for protection of the buyer against real estate rights, and the Committee has found no indication that this provision declaratory of the pre–Code law has caused any difficulty. Thus no change is proposed.

B–2. The assumption that crops are chattels was carried through in pre–Code law by the treatment of crop mortgages as chattel mortgages. In some states description of the land was required, not for the purpose of placing the crop mortgages into the real estate records, but primarily for identification.

B–3. The Code carries through this treatment. It treats an encumbrance of growing crops as a Code security interest for which a financing statement is required for perfection. A description of the land in the security agreement is required in Section 9–203(1)(a) and a requirement of description of the land in the financing statement is set forth in Section 9–402(1) and (3). Alternatives (2) and (3) of Section 9–401(1) add to the usual rule that a filing for farm products be at the residence of the debtor an additional rule that there be a filing on growing crops in the county where the land is situated, but these provisions do not indicate that the filing in the latter county should be in the real estate records. This is clear from two circumstances: The name of the applicable office is left blank in these two Alternatives of Section 9–401(1) rather than being specified (as is true for fixtures) as the office where a mortgage on the real estate concerned would be filed or recorded. Also, Alternative (1) for Section 9–401(1) contemplates filing for crops only in the office of the Secretary of State, and this could not be intended as a real estate filing.

B–4. Several states have departed from the Official Text by making it clear that the filing of a crop mortgage should be treated as a real estate filing and there is logic to this. But the Official Text seems to have worked satisfactorily without extensive criticism in other states, and the Committee has determined not to make so extensive a change in theory and practice as to require crop mortgages to be filed or recorded in the real estate records. To have made the change would have required the real estate on which crops are growing to be described with a particularity suitable for real estate records, as set forth in proposed Section 9–402(5). But practice in crop mortgages has never been to require particularity in describing land on which crops are growing, and a substantial change in practice would have been required.

B–5. There may nevertheless be rights of real property mortgagees or grantees in growing crops if Code security interests in the crops have not been properly filed, comparable to the rights referred to in Section 2–107(3). The Committee has not thought it possible in the Uniform Code to deal with the diversity of existing state law on the interrelation of chattel security interests in growing crops and real estate interests.

B–6. Existing Section 9–204(4)(a) provides that no security interest in crops attaches under an after-acquired property clause to crops which become such more than one year after the security agreement, unless the agreement involves certain real estate transactions. The obvious purpose of this provision was to protect a necessitous farmer from encumbering his crops for many years in the future. The provision does not work because there is no corresponding limit on the scope of a *financing statement* covering crops, and under the Code's notice-filing rules the priority position of a security arrangement covering successive crops would be as effectively protected by the filing of a first financing statement whether the granting clause as to successive crops was in one security agreement with an after-acquired property clause or in a succession of security agreements. On the other hand the section does require an annual security agreement for crops even when the encumbrance on crops is agreed to as part of a long-term financing covering farm machinery and other assets. The provision thus appears to be meaningless in operation except to cause unnecessary paperwork, but it does introduce some element of uncertainty as to its purpose. The Committee proposes to eliminate it. See also the next paragraph.

B–7. The priority provision of Section 9–312(2) seems related to the same thinking as discussed in the preceding paragraph, and was intended perhaps to permit enabling crop financing, notwithstanding the existence of prior crop financing. However, subsection (2) is severely limited by a provision that the priority granted to current enabling financing applies only as against earlier interests which are six months or more in default. In the absence of any demand therefor, it would be inappropriate to attempt to create a revolutionary change in crop financing with a broad enabling priority to finance current crops. Such an attempt would probably be ineffectual in any event because lenders on machinery and real estate who claim crops could readily provide that it would be an event of default for the debtor to finance under the proposed enabling priority. The Committee has determined therefore to leave subsection (2) unchanged, even while recognizing that it is of little practical effect.

B–8. Several states have indicated their dissatisfaction with existing Section 9–302(1)(c), which provides a non-filing rule for purchase money security interests in farm equipment having a purchase price of $2500 or less, by reducing the amount. Authors on farm problems have suggested that the section is disadvantageous rather than advantageous to a farmer, because it in effect makes his farm machinery useless as collateral in view of prospective lenders' fear that there may be unfiled perfected security interests. The $2500 amount cannot be dismissed by lenders as immaterial, because substantial aggregates of collateral could have been financed by separate purchase money transactions each of which was no greater than $2500.

The Committee proposes that Section 9–302(1)(c) be eliminated. This makes unnecessary the reference to farm equipment in Section 9–307(2), which deals with the rights of certain buyers against perfected but unfiled security interests.

B–9. A comparable problem exists with respect to the provision of Section 9–307(1) which makes inapplicable to farm products the usual rule of that section protecting a buyer in ordinary course of trade who buys goods from a person engaged in selling goods of that kind and permitting him to take free of any security interest created by his seller. The existing section reflects pre-Code practice in distinguishing between a farmer's inventory and inventory of any other kind of businessman, but it must be seriously questioned whether the pre-Code practice is still sound under modern conditions. Feelings run strong on this issue, as evidenced by the fact that the New Mexico legislature amended other sections of the Code to make sure that waiver would not nullify the rule excluding farm products from Section 9–307(1), as had been held in Clovis National Bank v. Thomas, 425 P.2d 776 (N.M.1967). The federal government, an important farm lender, likewise insists on the preservation of its security interest on farm products as against buyers or auctioneers, in reliance on a federal rule independent of the state rule embodied in Section 9–307(1). See U.S. v. McCleskey Mills, Inc., 409 F.2d 1216 (5th Cir.1969). On the other hand, strong representations have been made to the Committee by food processers and by authors who have written on farm problems under the Code that the inapplicability of Section 9–307(1) to farm products is anomalous and unfair. Georgia has amended the section to protect auctioneers of livestock. Recognizing that the Committee's recommendation is unlikely to induce the removal of the exception for farm products from Section 9–307(1) in all enacting jurisdictions, the Committee nevertheless recommends it as an optional amendment.[5] The Committee considered various possibilities, such as distinguishing between the first buyer and sub-buyers or between a buyer of an entire annual crop and multiple buyers of milk, eggs and the like. But no solution was found. Differences of opinion on basic policy seem to be so sharp that they are unlikely to be resolved by an appeal to the goal of uniformity.

B–10. There has been criticism of the unreality of the present Code's requiring filing against farmers at the "residence". This concept is most unsatisfactory for the reality of the modern corporate farm. The Committee proposes a new Section 9–401(6) to the effect that the residence of an organization is its place of business if it has one, or its chief executive office if it has more than one place of business. The rule is thus very similar in result to the rule as to the location of a debtor in proposed Section 9–103(3), although the latter rule starts as a matter of form with the assumption that the debtor has a place of business, with resort to residence as an exception, while the rule in Section 9–401(6) starts with residence, with the place of business as an exception for the corporate case. See paragraphs F–11 and F–12.

C. Timber

C–1. In contrast with its treatment of growing crops as chattels (paragraphs B–1 to 4 of this Statement), the present Code treats timber as real estate until cut. Section 2–107; note the omission of timber from the definition of "goods" in Section 9–105(1). This treatment has proved to be unsatisfactory, and many of the important timber-cutting states have changed it to provide that timber to be cut under a conveyance or contract for sale is "goods". One reason for this is to facilitate loans by banks on timber to be cut without complying with restrictions relating to real estate mortgages.

C–2. The Committee has decided to recommend adoption of this view. See proposed changes in Section 2–107 and the definition of "goods" in Section 9–105(1). The assertion in Section 9–204(2) that the debtor has no rights in timber until it is cut is proposed to be deleted together with the remainder of that subsection. See paragraph E–18 of this Statement.

C–3. Corresponding changes have been made in Section 9–401(1) and in Section 9–402(1) and (3) to recognize a Code filing as to timber before it is cut, to require that filing to be in the real estate records of the county wherein is the land on which the timber is growing, and a new provision (Section 9–403(7)) requires the indexing thereof in real estate records. These requirements conform to the requirements for fixture filing (paragraph A–10 of this Statement). In contrast to growing crops (paragraph B–3 of this Statement), the Committee considers that standing timber has been tradition-

5. The Permanent Editorial Board deleted the committee's optional recommendation. For states that are determined to change the present policy, it is recommended that this be done by deleting the words in Section 9–307(1): "other than a person buying farm products from a person engaged in farming operations."

ally a part of the real estate and it could not be assumed that it would normally be cut at any specific time of maturity. Therefore, the filing of security interests thereon has to be in real estate records. This filing will conform to the practice of recording timber deeds in real estate records.

D. Oil, Gas and Minerals

D–1. In general, the existing Code treats oil, gas and minerals as part of the real estate until they have been extracted from the land. See Section 2–107 and the definition of "goods" in Section 9–105(1). There is no provision for filing a security interest against minerals to be effective prior to their extraction from the land, because the Code does not recognize such a security interest and therefore there is no provision for a description of the land in a financing statement covering minerals.

In contrast, the Code requires a description of the land in a security agreement covering minerals to be extracted (Section 9–203(1)(b)). Though this has caused no particular difficulty, it is incongruous and the Committee proposes to delete it.

D–2. Various requests have been made that the Committee clarify the question whether well-drilling equipment is on the one hand fixtures or on the other hand mobile equipment of the kind referred to in Section 9–103. The Committee has sought to avoid encumbering the Code with details in response to inquiries of this nature. It seems fairly clear that well casings and related material that are removable are neither fixtures nor mobile equipment.

D–3. The most significant problems in reference to minerals relate to the split ownership characteristic of oil and gas drilling and the practice of selling the product at wellhead, with the proceeds of the resulting receivable being distributed pursuant to a division order and the proceeds being sometimes repledged to the holder of the oil and gas mortgage. Since the holders of fractional interests in a well or of production payments with respect thereto may be investors living anywhere, the problem of search to determine whether they have encumbered the receivables under the "chief place of business" rule of present Section 9–103(1) or "location" rule of proposed Section 9–103(3) is a cumbersome one. It is proposed that all filings with respect to these receivables be authorized and required in the county where the well is, thus conforming to much pre-Code practice which assumed that everything related to sales at wellhead should be filed (if at all) in the real estate records in the county where the well is located. See proposed Sections 9–103(5) and 9–401(1).

The term "at wellhead" is intended to encompass all arrangements intended to cover sale of the product when it issues from the ground and is measured, without technical distinctions as to whether title passes at the "Christmas tree" or the far side of a gathering tank or some other point. "At minehead" is a comparable concept.

It is essential to note that this special rule is applicable only to security interests created by persons who have interests in the production from the well which attach when the mineral is extracted, not to buyers of the production who may have an underlying security interest on their inventory which may happen to attach to the mineral as inventory or at the wellhead or minehead when that is where the buyer acquires rights therein.

D–4. A related problem is whether, where the form of contract of sale at wellhead results in the minerals being sold by the persons who had the fractional interests, the purchaser of the product is protected from any encumbrances of the product, pursuant to Section 9–307(1) protecting buyers in ordinary course of business. The Committee has proposed in Section 1–201(9) to clarify the fact that buyers of minerals at wellhead or minehead are buyers in ordinary course of business because all persons who regularly sell the product under those circumstances are deemed to be engaged in selling goods of that kind, even though realistically the sellers may merely be investors.

E. Intangibles, Proceeds and Priorities

The Code has six classifications of intangibles, of which three are semi-intangibles embodied in pieces of paper, namely, documents, instruments and chattel paper (all defined in Section 9–105).

There are also three classifications of completely intangible rights, namely, accounts, contract rights and general intangibles (all defined in Section 9–106).

Proposals as to Semi–Intangibles

E–1. As to the classifications of semi-intangibles, experience has been generally satisfactory and few specific changes are proposed by the Committee.

E–2. A new rule is proposed in Section 9–103(4) as to the jurisdiction in which to file a financing statement relating to chattel paper, thus curing an omission in the present Code. See paragraphs F–14–15 of this Statement.

E–3. Another problem is the classification of money, which is frequently proceeds of original collateral and in some types of financing is itself original collateral. In the absence of an express specification, it could be argued that money is a general intangible, which would permit filing for a security interest therein. While this result would be so obviously unsound that it is doubted that a court would reach that result under the existing Code, it has been thought wise to provide expressly in Section 9–106 that the term "general intangibles" does not include money.

E–4. Sections 9–304(1) and 9–305 have been amended to state specifically that money may be pledged.

E–5. Section 9–304(1) makes clear that as to negotiable instruments, a non-possessory perfection of a security interest is not permitted except for temporary periods without either filing or possession under Sections 9–304(4) and (5). No doubt the failure of Section 9–304(1) to refer to temporary perfection for 10 days under the proceeds provisions of Sections 9–306(2) and (3) is a mere inadvertence of the present Code which the Committee proposes to correct, since this temporary perfection is also clearly contemplated. However, the present Section 9—306(2) and (3) go further and seemingly would permit perfection by filing continued indefinitely as to negotiable instruments which constitute proceeds of original collateral in which a security interest had been perfected by a filed financing statement which also claimed proceeds. The Committee considers this to be an error of the present Code and proposes to rectify it by providing in Section 9–306(3) that a security interest in proceeds does not persist beyond 10 days unless the security interest could have been directly filed against the proceeds as independent collateral. See also paragraphs E–22–23 of this Statement for other applications of this proposal.

E–6. The foregoing discussion should not apply to negotiable instruments which are essentially cash payment, i.e., money and checks. The proceeds security interest should apply to these cash proceeds so long as they are identifiable, and the proposed revision of Section 9–306(3) so provides.

E–7. The Committee considers that another anomaly exists between Sections 9–308 and 9–309. Under the present Code, a purchaser of negotiable instruments prevails against a conflicting proceeds claim thereto only if the purchaser is a holder in due course, which means that he cannot have notice of the conflicting claim to the instrument as proceeds of prior collateral. In contrast, the purchaser of chattel paper may under the second sentence of Section 9–308 defeat a claim to the chattel paper as proceeds of prior collateral even though the purchaser of the chattel paper knows that the specific paper is subject to the proceeds security interest. Thus, the holder of a negotiable note which is not part of chattel paper is governed by less favorable rules than the holder of an equally negotiable note which is part of chattel paper, or than the holder of non-negotiable chattel paper. The Committee has sought to remedy this by rewriting Section 9–308 so that the rights therein conferred on holders of chattel paper and non-negotiable instruments also apply to holders of negotiable instruments. Thus, holders of negotiable instruments which are proceeds may be protected under Section 9–309 if they are holders in due course, and if they do not qualify as holders in due course, they may nevertheless have the rights provided in clause (b) of Section 9–308. Section 9–308 has also been reorganized for clarity.

Proposals as to Intangibles

E–8. As to pure intangibles, i.e., intangibles not embodied in a piece of paper, the Committee considered the question whether three categories are necessary. The Committee concluded that the category "contract rights" is not necessary and proposes to eliminate the definition thereof from Section 9–106 and the references thereto in other sections. The Committee proposes to broaden the term "accounts" to include rights which under the present Code would be "contract rights" since there had not yet been complete performance by the person to whom the monetary obligation is owing.

The elimination of the term "contract rights" avoids the risk of inadvertent error where a financing statement is filed as to "accounts" and the designation turns out to be inapplicable because performance has not been completed, so that the collateral is at the stage of "contract rights."

E–9. This elimination also avoids proceeds problems and possible resulting priority questions where collateral was originally a "contract right" and after performance it became an "account." As a conforming change the Committee proposes to eliminate the statement in Section 9–306(1) that an account is proceeds of a contract right.

E–10. The only place in the 1962 Code where the concept of "contract right" was used to contrast with the concept of "account" was in Section 9–318(2). The Committee proposes to rewrite this subsection to draw the distinction between a right to money not yet completed by performance and a right so completed, without having to preserve the term "contract right" just for this purpose.

E–11. As to the substantive standard of Section 9–318(2) respecting the power of the debtor and assignor to modify a contract before performance to the prejudice of the assignee, the Committee has given consideration to the non-uniform New York amendment which limited the rights of the original parties so to do to cases where the assignee was not materially prejudiced. The Permanent Editorial Board in its Report No. 2 took the position that this New York change merely articulates a condition already included in the requirement of good faith contained in the Official Text. The Committee has considered Professor Gilmore's view that the change goes beyond articulation of the meaning implied in the term "good faith" (2 Gilmore, Security Interests in Personal Property, 1117–21 (1965) and his view disapproving the New York change on substantive grounds. The Committee adheres to the views expressed by the Permanent Editorial Board that the term "good faith" so limits the extent of the permissible change as not to make desirable adoption of the New York amendment.

E–12. The elimination of the term "contract right" requires the re-editing of the 1966 change approved by the Permanent Editorial Board in Section 9–106. The purpose of this change was to choose a single classification of intangibles for ship charters and all related rights. The classification chosen was "contract rights." With the elimination of this term, Section 9–106 has to be re-written to place all these rights in the category "accounts."

E–13. The term "account debtor" is defined in Section 9–105(1)(a) as a person who is obligated not merely on an account but also on chattel paper, general intangibles (and under the present Code, contract rights). Present Section 9–318(3) speaks of account debtors and, therefore, would apply to the debtors under all of these types of intangibles, but its scope in protecting an account debtor who pays without notice that his obligation has been assigned is limited by the phrase "that the *account* has been assigned." The Committee proposes changes in Section 9–318(3) to afford the intended protection to all account debtors without limitation by the term "account."

E–14. The Committee considered the suggestion that there is not reason for distinguishing between "accounts" and "general intangibles," both of which are defined in Section 9–106. To eliminate the two separate terms would cause great drafting difficulty in preserving Article 9's present useful distinction in the inclusion in its scope of the sale of monetary obligations represented by accounts, contract rights and chattel paper and in the exclusion from its scope of the sale of non-monetary rights known as general intangibles. Therefore, the Committee proposes to retain the two terms.

E–15. A more limited suggestion is to rectify the definitions of "accounts" and "general intangibles." It has been pointed out that some obligations for payment of money are not accounts, but are general intangibles, because the definition of "account" is limited to rights to payment for goods sold or leased or for services rendered. Thus, rights to payments constituting royalties for use of patents, copyrights, etc., or for exhibition rights to moving pictures and television, seemingly constitute general intangibles rather than accounts. A potential source of error by inadvertence thus arises. The Committee nevertheless concluded that it would be undesirable to broaden the definition of accounts to include all rights for the payment of money, because too many standard forms of agreement use the term "accounts" and reflect intention of the parties to include only traditional accounts arising from the sale of goods or services, and not miscellaneous rights for the payment of money.

Attachment and Perfection

E–16. The Code has two important concepts, attachment of security interests and perfection thereof. Attachment is in a sense defined in present Section 9–204. In general, it means the time when a security interest becomes enforceable between the primary parties because there is agreement, value has been furnished, and the debtor has rights in the collateral to which the agreement can apply.

The term "perfection" is not defined by the Code. In general, it means the point at which a security interest becomes good against third parties when there is also attachment. The additional requirements for perfection beyond the requirements for attachment are set forth in Sections 9–302 to 9–305. It would be unwise to attempt a formal definition of perfection, because of the subtlety of the problems involved in rights against many groups of third persons.

E–17. The Committee deemed the existing treatment of the concept of attachment in Section 9–203 and Section 9–204 (which also affects perfection, as indicated) to be unsatisfactory. Section 9–203 contains a statute of frauds which must be satisfied in order that the security interest be enforceable against the debtor or third parties, yet the combined treatments of attachment and perfection indicate that there could be perfection without compliance with the statute of frauds. This obvious anomaly would be corrected by proposed revisions of these sections. The three elements of attachment have been transferred to Section 9–203 from Section 9–204 and there combined with the requirement of a writing (except when the secured party is in possession), which thus becomes part of the concept of attachment.

E–18. The Committee proposes to eliminate from Section 9–204 existing subsection (2) which states various times at which the debtor acquires right in certain kinds of collateral. Some of these statements, notably the statement in paragraph (d) that the debtor has no rights in an account until it comes into existence, have played an unfortunate part in confusing the application of bankruptcy law to Code security interests. None of them seems to serve any purpose.

Proceeds

E-19. Existing Section 9-203 provides that the word "proceeds" is a sufficient description in a security agreement of collateral constituting proceeds. This seems to imply that a claim to proceeds must be based on a term in a security agreement. Yet Section 9-306(2) contemplates that the secured party will have a right in proceeds following sale of original collateral, and this right is not made dependent on the existence of a term in the security agreement. The Committee proposes to resolve this apparent inconsistency by deleting the provision in Section 9-203 and substituting proposed Section 9-203(3) to the effect that a reference to proceeds is not necessary in the security agreement to give the secured party the automatic rights provided by Section 9-306.

The Committee does not consider that this converts the security interest in proceeds into a non-contractual or statutory lien presenting problems under the Bankruptcy Act, for the security interest is still an aspect of the basically contractual security interest under the security agreement.[6]

E-20. Another anomaly appears in the provisions of present Section 9-306(3)(a) that the 10-day right to proceeds recognized by subsection (3) may be continued without further perfection if the filed financing statement covering the original collateral also covers proceeds. The form of financing statement set forth in Section 9-402(3) makes provision for a claim to proceeds, and the forms prescribed by most state filing officials contain a box by which a claim to proceeds may be made simply by checking the box. The claim is almost universally made in the case of inventory which is to be sold or receivables which are to be collected, thus producing proceeds; and the claim is very frequently made routinely in the cases of other collateral. There was deleted from Section 9-306 in the prior history of the Code a statement that a claim to proceeds constituted permission to sell, and a court has recently held that such a claim does not constitute permission to sell. Vermilion County Production Credit v. Izzard, 111 Ill.App.2d 190 (1969).

E-21. Since the claim to proceeds is routinely made, there seems to be no reason that it be required to be made in the financing statement in order to continue the perfection of the security interest in proceeds. If there is a claim to proceeds as presumed intent of the security agreement, notice of the claim comes from the claim to the original collateral claimed in the financing statement, and nothing is accomplished by the routine checking of a box. Many privately printed forms have the box checked in the print itself. The Committee therefore proposes in Section 9-306(3) to eliminate any requirement for claiming proceeds specifically.

E-22. A problem appears as to whether perfection by filing as to original collateral automatically perfects as to *all types* of proceeds. One such problem has already been discussed, namely whether the claim to proceeds perfected by filing as to original collateral negates the basic provision of the Code that one cannot file as to instruments. See paragraph E-5 of this Statement. A

6. The Permanent Editorial Board amended the text of Section 9-203(3) to make it clear that the assertion thereof is a matter of presumed intent and is "unless otherwise agreed."

provision has been added to Section 9–306(3) making it clear that the proceeds claim does not permit filing as to instruments.

E–23. A similar problem arises when the appropriate place for filing as to accounts resulting from sale of inventory collateral under Section 9–103 is in another state where the debtor is located. The revision of Section 9–306(3) makes it clear that the perfection of the security interest in the accounts as proceeds will not last more than 10 days unless there is a filing as to the accounts in the appropriate jurisdiction.

E–24. Another problem is whether the extension to proceeds of the filed security interest in original collateral (perfected by checking a box as in the existing Code or automatically perfected as in the Committee's proposal, paragraph E–21 of this Statement) really serves the intended function of public notice of the security interest. Under the existing Section 9–306 the security interest in proceeds extends without limit through cash in the debtor's hand to repeated cycles of the business so long as the proceeds can be traced, unless sometimes terminated by priority rules like those in Sections 9–308 and 9–309 or by receipt of the cash by the secured party. See In re Platt, 58 Berks Co.L.J., 275, 6 UCC Rep. 275, 281 (Referee, E.D.Pa.1966), aff'd 257 F.Supp. 478 (E.D.Pa.1966). Thus a financing statement on automobiles could theoretically operate to perfect a security interest in an oil painting traded in for an automobile or bought with the cash proceeds thereof. Several possibilities of limiting the notice as to a security interest in proceeds resulting from a filing as to original collateral present themselves. The Committee has determined not to limit the proceeds claim applicable to direct trade-ins, but to limit the claim to proceeds which have been acquired through cash proceeds to cases where the description of collateral in the financing statement indicates the types of property constituting these remote proceeds. See the proposed revision of Section 9–306(3).

E–25. Several cases have held that the proceeds of insurance on destroyed or damaged collateral are not proceeds of the collateral within the meaning of Section 9–306(1). The Committee considers the result of these cases to be unsatisfactory and proposes to revise Section 9–306(1) to make clear that insurance proceeds are proceeds. But a possibility exists that, under a contract with an insurer through a co-insurance clause or a loss payable clause, a junior secured party will be entitled to receive the insurance proceeds, and the revision has been so drafted that the Code's proceeds rules will not operate to disturb contractual arrangements.

E–26. Proceeds frequently find their way to bank or deposit accounts, and Section 9–306(4)(b) expressly contemplates that the secured party will have a security interest in the proceeds so deposited. But existing Section 9–104(k) provides that Article 9 does not apply to deposit accounts and similar accounts. The Committee proposes to amend the treatment in Section 9–104 so that it is not inconsistent with the recognition of proceeds security interests in these accounts, and to add in Section 9–105 a new definition of "deposit account" to cover all the types of accounts intended to be covered by these provisions.

E–27. Section 9–306(4) deals with cash proceeds, and is intended to substitute for difficult problems of tracing a provision that the secured party has a perfected security interest in cash proceeds (and deposit accounts derived therefrom) received within ten days before the institution of insolvency proceedings by or against the debtor, less the cash proceeds paid over to the debtor within the ten days. In the study of this subsection in connection with adoption of the Code in California, certain imperfections in the drafting were pointed out, and California amended the provision. The Committee recommends adoption of a clarifying amendment based on the California amendment. No significant change of substance is intended.

Priorities between Security Interests

E–28. In many ways Article 9 facilitates the perfection of security interests. This ease of perfection brings to the fore numerous problems of priority between security interests, or between secured parties and other persons. Each proposed change may affect priority problems by affecting the time or the method by which perfection is achieved, as in the proposed limitations of perfection as to proceeds, paragraphs E–5, 22, 23 of this Statement. Certain priority problems are discussed elsewhere in this statement—in Part A as to Fixtures; in Part E as to Sections 9–308 and 9–309; and in Part I as to the effect of lapse.

Some of the major problems of priorities are discussed in the following paragraphs.

A number of problems relate to the purchase money priority as to inventory in Section 9–312(3).

E–29. The existing Section 9–312(3) does not state how often the notification by the purchase-money financer to earlier financers of record must be given. The Committee's revision will make the notice effective for five years, by analogy to the duration of a financing statement.

E–30. The existing subsection requires notice to any secured party known to the purchase money secured party, regardless of perfection by the former. This emphasis on knowledge is inconsistent with the general disregard of knowledge as an operative fact in priority issues between secured parties in Article 9. It is also an ineffective provision, because if the purchase money secured party fails to give the necessary notice to obtain priority over the earlier unperfected secured party under subsection (3), the purchase money secured party will nevertheless obtain priority under Section 9–312(5) as the first to file or perfect. Finally, the existing subsection might be read to deny the contemplated priority to the purchase money secured party against another secured party to whom he has given proper notice unless he also gave notice to all other persons entitled to notice. The Committee proposes a revised Section 9–312(3) to rectify these points.

E–31. Under the existing Code there is uncertainty as to the relationship of Section 9–312(3) to the period of temporary perfection for 21 days of an interest in inventory without either filing or possession under Section 9–304(5), typically coming through release of a document of title to the debtor following a documentary draft or letter of credit transaction. One could conceivably take the view that the security interest under Section 9–304(5) has priority against an earlier filed security interest during the 21 days. If so, one would then have to decide either (a) that the security interest, if filed before the end of the 21 days, continued to have priority without a notice; or (b) that the notice under Section 9–312(3) had to be given before the end of the 21 days; or (c) that the priority reversed after the 21 days. None of these results seems consistent with the obvious purpose of Section 9–312(3) to permit a first-filed inventory financer to rely on his priority in making advances unless he receives notice of a competing purchase money security interest before the debtor receives the inventory. Accordingly, the Committee's proposed revision of Sections 9–304(5) and 9–312(3) requires the notice to be given before the debtor receives the inventory, and if this is done, the purchase money security interest obtains a priority and retains it so long as the interest remains perfected. The Committee's inquiry to several leading banks engaged in foreign trade indicated that this rule would not seriously inconvenience them, and the rule will certainly clarify the position of these banks and all other lenders when acting as general inventory financers.

E–32. The existing Code leaves it uncertain whether the filing required of a consignor under Section 2–326(3) includes a required notice to prior inventory financers of the consignees under Section 9–312(3). An underlying inventory financer assured of his first-filed position could as readily be deceived by consigned merchandise as he could by new inventory subject to the purchase money inventory financing priority, in the absence of notice. Accordingly, the Committee proposes a new Section 9–114 to require the consignor to give the same notices as a purchase money secured party, to attain priority against earlier-filed security interests in inventory of the debtor. These provisions are limited to true consignments. The usual rules apply to consignments that are deemed to be security interests. See Section 1–201(37).

E–33. Another group of priority problems relates to the basic priority rules of Section 9–312(5). This subsection contains two principal rules. Paragraph (a) is a first-to-file rule where both competing security interests are perfected by filing. Paragraph (b) is a first-to-perfect rule when either of the security interests is or both of them are perfected otherwise than by filing. A traffic rule is provided by existing Section 9–312(6) to the effect that a continuously perfected security interest shall be treated for the purpose of the foregoing rules as if at all times perfected in the manner it was first perfected. The problems raised have been the subject of an enormous legal literature. They are complicated by the unforeseeable effect of the temporary perfection of security interests in proceeds under Section 9–306 without filing, and by speculation as to whether a secured party could claim that his security interest was originally perfected without filing under this rule even though the security interest in proceeds was claimed in his filing as to the original collateral. They are further complicated by the question whether different rules would apply when a financing statement was drawn to cover, e.g., inventory and its proceeds (which would include accounts) and when it was drawn to cover inventory and accounts.

E–34. The Committee is convinced that to settle these questions the present paragraphs (a) and (b) of Section 9–312(5) must be replaced by a single rule. The Committee proposes a revised Section 9–312(5) and the elimination of existing Section 9–312(6). Together with this treatment should be noted the fact that an interest in proceeds automatically arises from a filed security interest in original collateral under the proposed revision of Section 9–306(3), subject to the limitations therein stated and discussed in paragraphs E–5, 22, 23 of this Statement. New proposed Section 9–312(6) makes it clear that subject to these limitations the filing as to original collateral constitutes a filing as to proceeds.

E–35. The new rule ranks conflicting perfected security interests by their priority in time, dating back to the respective times when without interruption the security interests were either perfected or were the subjects of appropriate filings.

E–36. Perhaps the most debated subject under Article 9 has been the question whether between conflicting security interests a priority as to original collateral confers a priority as to proceeds. On this topic the discussions as to proceeds (paragraphs E–19–21, E–24, of this Statement) and as to rules of Sections 9–312(5) and (6) (paragraphs E–33–34) are relevant. See also the following paragraphs E–37–38.

E–37. In the case of collateral other than inventory, e.g., equipment, assume that A has a prior purchase money security interest and B, although he was the first to file, has a junior security interest. If the equipment was sold and proceeds resulted, it seems clear that the policy favoring the purchase money secured party in Section 9–312(4) should give A the first claim to the proceeds. This is so even though the security interests will have been perfected simultaneously when the proceeds arose and the debtor acquired rights therein. The present Code does not provide for this result clearly, if at all, and the Committee proposes an amendment to Section 9–312(4) to accomplish it.

E–38. Proper policy is much less clear when the collateral involved is inventory and proceeds consisting of accounts. (Policy as to other types of receivables as proceeds is expressed in Sections 9–308 and 9–309. See paragraph E–7 of this Statement.) Accounts may be financed by some financers without prior involvement in the inventory, and some have argued that one who provides financing at the early inventory stage of the cycle of a business, which involves greater risk, is certainly to be preferred to one who provides financing only at the later stage of the cycle, and that a prior or only claim to inventory must therefore carry through to accounts as proceeds. But others feel that accounts financing is overall more important than inventory financing, and the desirable rule is one which makes accounts financing certain as to its legal position. Even if both competing financers are involved in the inventory, a purchase money priority in inventory may not represent the order of priority in time on accounts, which may be far more important than inventory financing in the particular case. A suggestion that the purchase money priority carry through to accounts if the notice provided by Section 9–312(3) has been given to accounts financers has seeming merit, but in the Committee's view it has two major difficulties: (a) The purchase-money priority as to inventory would be difficult to trace into accounts if the affected inventory was only part of the goods sold. (b) Accounts financing is intricate, and not easily or safely terminated on receipt of an inventory purchase-money notice. Prevailing practice seems to be for accounts financers to require covenants against competitive inventory financing, and to declare a default unless any inventory financier giving a purchase-money notice agrees not to assert a claim to the accounts. The Committee believes that where a financing statement as to accounts financing is filed first (with or without related inventory financing), the security interest in accounts should not be defeated by any subsequent claim to accounts as proceeds of an inventory security interest which was filed later. This result is accomplished by the absence in Section 9–312(3) of any priority rule carrying forward the purchase-money priority to proceeds which are accounts in contrast to the proposed addition to Section 9–312(4) (paragraph E–37); by the revised priority rule in Section 9–312(5); and by proposed Section 9–312(6) to the effect that a date of filing as to original collateral also defines the date of filing as to proceeds. Correspondingly, a financing statement as to inventory (carrying with it a claim to proceeds) which is filed first will under the same provisions have priority over a later-filed security interest in accounts.

Priority of Future Advances

E–39. Certain recent cases in lower courts raised the question whether a single financing statement would be effective to perfect more than one advance on the collateral described, when the later advances were not under a future advance clause of a single security agreement but were under later security agreements and were not contemplated at the time of the original agreement. Some of the reasoning makes the matter depend on whether the original debt was fully paid off or was still in existence at the time of the later advances. Coin–O–Matic Service Co. v. Rhode Island Hospital Trust Co., 3 UCC Rep. 1112 (Super.Ct.R.I.1966); In re Merriman, 4 UCC Rep. 234 (Referee, S.D.Ohio 1967). In another case, in which the point was not directly involved, Safe Deposit Bank & Trust Co. v. Berman, 393 F.2d 401 (1st Cir.1968), the court cited In re Rivet, 4 CCH Instal. Credit Guide Par. 97,858, 4 UCC Rep. 1087 (Referee, E.D.Mich.1967), which was in harmony with the first two cases cited but was subsequently reversed (see paragraph E–40). The Committee disapproves this line of cases, and believes that an appropriate financing statement may perfect security interests securing advances made under agreements not contemplated at the time of the filing of the financing statement, even if the advances then contemplated have been fully paid in the interim. Under the notice-filing procedures of the Code, the filing of a financing statement is effective to perfect security interests as to which the other required elements for perfection exist, whether the security agreement involved is one existing at the date of the filing with an after-acquired property clause or a future advance clause, or whether the applicable security agreement is executed later. Indeed, Section 9–402(1) expressly contemplates that a financing statement may be filed when there is no security agreement. In the Committee's opinion, the references to after-acquired property clauses and future advance clauses in Section 9–204 are limited to security agreements. This section follows Section 9–203, the section requiring a written security agreement, and its purpose is to make clear that confirmatory agreements are not necessary where the basic agreement has the clauses mentioned. The section has no reference to the operation of *financing statements* under the Code's notice filing system.

E–40. The Committee considered drafting a provision emphasizing its disagreement with the *Coin-O-Matic* line of cases, but concluded that the existing Code is clear enough, and should not be disturbed just to overrule some lower court cases. The *Rivet* case, cited by the First Circuit, has since been reversed by In re Rivet, 6 UCC Rep. 460 (E.D.Mich.1969).

E–41. The priority of future advances against an intervening party has been the subject of much discussion and disagreement.

E–42. Where both interests are filed security interests, the first-to-file rule of present Section 9–312(5)(a) or the corresponding proposed revision is clearly applicable.

E–43. While, under the existing Code, the position of an intervening pledge in reference to a subsequent advance by an earlier-filed secured party is debatable, the proposed unified priority rule of Section 9–312(5)(a) (paragraph E–35 of this Statement) would indicate that the subsequent advances by the first-filed party have priority, and subsequent advances under a security interest perfected by possession likewise have priority over an intervening filed security interest. These priority rules are expressly stated in proposed Section 9–312(7). That proposal also deals with the rare case of the priority position of a subsequent advance made by a secured party whose security interest is temporarily perfected without either filing or possession, against an intervening secured party. Since there is no notice by the usual methods of filing or possession of the existence of the security interest, the subsequent advances rank only from the actual date of making unless made pursuant to commitment.

E–44. In the Committee's view different problems exist with reference to the status of subsequent advances when the intervening party is a judgment creditor. He is not directly part of the Code's system of priorities. There should be a limit on the power of a debtor and secured party to squeeze out a judgment creditor who has successfully levied on a valuable equity subject to a security interest, through later enlargement of the security interest by an additional advance, unless that advance was committed in advance. Accordingly, the Committee proposes to clarify the present uncertain state of the law by a new Section 9–301(4) providing that a lien creditor does not take subject to a future advance made more than 45 days after he becomes a lien creditor unless it is made "pursuant to commitment." [7] A definition of the quoted phrase is proposed in Section 9–105(1). The 45–day period corresponds to a similar protection of advances made after the filing of tax liens in the Federal Tax Lien Act of 1966.

E–45. A similar problem arises where the intervening party is a buyer of the collateral subject to the security interest. While buyers must necessarily take subject to rights of secured parties, the Committee feels that the buyer should take subject to future advances only to the extent that they are given pursuant to commitment or within the period of 45 days after the purchase but not later than the time that the secured party acquires knowledge of the purchase. The Committee has so proposed in Section 9–307(3).

7. The Permanent Editorial Board amended Section 9–301(4) to continue the priority of the subsequent advances beyond the 45 days and until the secured party acquires knowledge of the judgment lien.

Effect of Knowledge on Priorities of Lien Creditors and Buyers

E–46. Although knowledge of unperfected security interests does not in general affect the rights of other secured parties, knowledge of unperfected security interests does under Section 9–301 preclude the attainment of priority by lien creditors and buyers (other than buyers in ordinary course of trade protected by Section 9–307(1)).

E–47. This result as to judgment creditors was severely criticized in California, which totally eliminated the element of knowledge, and gave priority to a person who became a lien creditor before the security interest was perfected, subject to a 10–day grace period. The Committee recommends the California change in Section 9–301(1)(b) but without the grace period, and a conforming change in Section 9–301(3). The Committee considered an intermediate position, making the decisive time for the existence of knowledge the point at which the creditor gave credit, not the point at which he became a lien creditor. But that position was severely criticized as inappropriate for tort creditors and as encouraging a race of diligence.

E–48. Similar considerations might be argued to be applicable to buyers referred to in Section 9–301(1)(c) and (d). However, there seems to be no criticism of these provisions or demand for change, and the Committee has concluded not to recommend any change.

Circular Priority

E–49. The elimination of the element of knowledge from Section 9–301(1)(b) (paragraph E–47) removes one possibility of circular priority. Other such possibilities are resolved by the proposals as to lapse (paragraphs F–23 and I–7). But circular priority can still arise in other situations. The Committee considered a general provision on the subject, but decided that the situations were too infrequent and diverse and the proper solutions too unclear.

F. Conflict of Laws

F–1. Section 9–103 dealing with interstate problems of perfection has occasioned much discussion, and the relationship between subsections (3) and (4) has been criticized as unclear by several courts. The committee has been aided by discussion with Professor Willis L.M. Reese, the Reporter of the Restatement Second of Conflict of Laws, who recently completed his work on cognate material. The Committee proposes a complete revision of Section 9–103, and related changes in Sections 1–105 and 9–102.

F–2. Section 9–103 was drafted in the light of the uncertainty whether the Code would be widely adopted, and the emphasis was on conflicting rules of law and a desire to make the Code rules applicable where such a result was justified under general principles. Today, when 51 jurisdictions have adopted the Code, situations of actual conflict in rules of law within the ambit of the Code will be few, and the emphasis may shift to the question of certainty as to where to file in order to perfect security interests.

Scheme of the Section

F–3. Section 9–102(1), basically intended as a scope provision on the coverage of Article 9, seems to deal with conflict of laws matters by its phrase "so far as concerns any personal property and fixtures within the jurisdiction of this state." The Committee proposes to delete this phrase and a related cross-reference, thus making Section 9–102 silent on conflicts of laws problems.

F–4. The Committee proposes to delete references to "validity" of a security interest appearing sometimes but not consistently in existing Section 9–103.

F–5. The effect of the foregoing changes will be to have questions as to the creation and validity of security interests determined according to the conflict of laws rules in Section 1–105. The cross-reference in that section to Article 9 should be amended to exclude the reference to Section 9–102. Questions as to perfection and the effect of perfection or non-perfection of security interests—i.e., questions as to the rights of third parties—will be determined by Section 9–103.

F–6. The basic rule of proposed Section 9–103, expressed in paragraph (1)(b), is believed to be that intended but not articulated in the existing section, namely, that perfection and the effect of perfection or non-perfection of a security interest are governed by the law (including the conflict of law rules) of the jurisdiction where the collateral is when a conflicting claim comes into existence.[8] That state will ordinarily look for this purpose to the law of the state where the collateral was when the events claimed to constitute perfection occurred, but the section provides special rules in the cases discussed in the next ten paragraphs.

Special Rules as to Jurisdiction Controlling Perfection The 10–Day[9] *Rule*

F–7. The relationship of the 30–day removal period in existing Section 9–103(3) to the four month removal period in that subsection is imperfectly stated. Paragraph (1)(c) of the revision limits the provision to purchase money security interests in goods and changes the 30 days to 10 days after the debtor receives possession, conforming to Sections 9–301(2) and 9–312(4).[9] The revision also makes clear that the function of the period is to have perfection controlled by the law of the state into which the parties intend to remove the collateral within that period, rather than the law of the state where the collateral is when the security interest attaches. The four month period discussed below is irrelevant to this purpose, and is placed in paragraph (1)(d). During the 10–day period,[9] perfection is fully governed by the law of the state to which the parties intend to remove the collateral, whether or not it is removed to that state within the 10 days.[9] If it is so taken, then perfection continues to be governed by the law of that state. If it is not so taken, the question of perfection reverts at the end of the 10 days[9] to the state where the collateral then is.

Paragraph (1)(c) described in this paragraph does not apply to the cases described in the next two paragraphs.

8. The text being submitted in the present printing changes this formulation to refer to the law of the jurisdiction where the collateral is when the last event occurs on which is based the assertion that the security interest is perfected.

9. The Permanent Editorial Board changed the 10 days back to 30 days.

Motor Vehicles

F–8. Paragraph (2)(b), which to some extent covers the same ground as the existing subsection (4), excludes from the general rule of paragraph (1)(b) collateral covered by a certificate of title. Paragraph (2)(d) is a partial limitation on paragraph (2)(b). These paragraphs are discussed in the treatment of motor vehicles, Part G of this Statement.

Intangibles and Mobile Goods

F–9. Subsection (3) covers essentially the same ground as existing subsections (1) and (2). They are intended to determine the jurisdiction whose law governs perfection in the case of intangibles which have no location in fact, and mobile chattels which have no permanent location. Several substantial changes have been made therein as described in paragraphs F–10 to F–16 below.

F–10. The existing subsection (1) provides that a financing statement covering accounts shall be filed in the jurisdiction where the assignor keeps his records concerning them. Existing subsection (2) provides that a financing statement covering general intangibles shall be filed in the jurisdiction of the chief place of business of the debtor. The use of separate tests for accounts and general intangibles has been criticized, because many groups of receivables may include items falling into both categories. See paragraph E–15 of this Statement. Moreover, in the type of accounts financing known as factoring, the assignment is without recourse and the debtor may keep no records concerning the accounts after transfer. A debtor's place of business may be objectively more ascertainable than the place where he keeps accounts, and will not be confused by questions on the latter test arising from remote access computer operations. Accordingly, the Committee proposes to combine the two tests into the place of business test applicable to general intangibles. See also the next paragraph.

F–11. The Committee recommends that the place of business used where there is more than one be redesignated "chief executive office" instead of "chief place of business." This will emphasize that what is intended is the executive office rather than either a statutory office or the site of the largest plant. While occasional situations of uncertainty could still arise, it is doubtful that there could be more than two possibilities in any case, and it would be easy to play safe by filing in both. See proposed paragraph (3)(d).

F–12. Provision has also been added to paragraph (3)(d) covering cases where the debtor is an individual or otherwise has no place of business, in which case his location is deemed to be his residence.

F–13. The coverage of the proposed subsection (3) would be extended to cover containers used on vehicles. The coverage would extend to inventory held for lease as well as inventory out on lease, thus accepting a California amendment designed to achieve consistency with the definition of inventory in Section 9–109(4).

F–14. The coverage of subsection (3) would be extended by proposed subsection (4) to cover perfection of non-possessory security interests in chattel paper. The existing Code has no express provision as to the jurisdiction within which to file for chattel paper, thus presumably referring the matter to the phrase in existing Section 9–102: "... this Article applies so far as concerns any ... property ... within the jurisdiction of this state...." But location is an unsatisfactory test for a filing as to chattel paper, because the paper's location is not visible to a prospective searcher for filings, it is readily transportable, and there may be more than one executed copy of the chattel paper.

F–15. The Committee considered whether proposed subsection (3) should govern the state of perfection of security interests in chattel paper completely, as it does in the case of general intangibles and accounts, but concluded to draw a distinction between the conflict of laws rule for non-possessory perfection of a security interest in chattel paper (to which Section 9–103(3) is proposed to be made applicable) and the rule for pledge or possessory perfection thereof (which is left to the general principles of subsection (1), which prescribes the law of the state where the chattel paper is in fact). The basis for the distinction was the fact that in a non-possessory perfection the problem is essentially similar to that applicable to accounts and general intangibles, but with a possessory perfection there are frequently local transactions between a local unit of a debtor and a local financer, and in that event the governing considerations should not be referred to the law of a possibly remote jurisdiction where the chief executive office of the debtor might be.

F–16. The coverage of subsection (3) on its face applies even to foreign airplanes, in contradiction to the rules provided by the Geneva Convention, to which the United States and many important foreign countries are parties. This contradiction is recognized in existing Comment 6. The textual problem would be avoided by the Committee proposal to create an exemption from the Code's filing rules for matters controlled by treaty. See paragraph G–4 of this Statement.

F–17. Since the place of filing under subsection (3) is independent of the location of the collateral, it is not affected by the 10–day rule [9] (paragraph F–7, supra) or the four-month rule (paragraph F–19, infra). The only occasion for refiling in cases subject to subsection (3) would be in cases of removal of the debtor's location, for which the Committee proposes a new paragraph (3)(e) providing for refiling within four months after removal, in keeping with the comparable rule applicable to removal of collateral (paragraph F–19, infra). The Committee reaffirms the Permanent Editorial Board's rejection in Report No. 2 of the New York subsection (6) denying the need to refile on removal of the chief place of business.[10]

F–18. Proposed paragraph (3)(c) covers the ground of existing optional subsection (5) and the third sentence of existing subsection (2). It covers the case where the jurisdiction of the location of the debtor is not a domestic jurisdiction and does not provide for filing as to the collateral. In that case, perfection by filing "in this state" is authorized if this state bears an appropriate relation to the transaction.[11] Perfection by notification to the

10. The provision of New York's subsection (6) dealing with removal of the place where the records of accounts are kept becomes unnecessary under the Committee's proposal to eliminate this rule as to the place of filing for accounts.

11. The Permanent Editorial Board changed Section 9-103(3)(c) to provide for fil-

account debtor is also authorized, except in a case of chattel paper covered by subsection (4). The Committee reaffirms the Permanent Editorial Board's rejection in Report No. 2 of the New York amendment proposing perfection without filing or notification.

The Four Months Rule on Removals

F–19. To the rules which indicate the jurisdiction whose law governs perfection and the effect of perfection or non-perfection in the first instance (paragraphs F–3 to F–16, supra) the state whose law governs under paragraphs (1)(b) and (2)(b) (paragraph F–6, supra) adds its own local rule requiring refiling within a stated period. A provision of this kind appears in existing subsection (3) and the Committee proposes refinements thereof in proposed paragraphs (1)(a) and (2)(c). The 10–day rule (formerly 30 days) [12] has been removed from these provisions and placed in paragraph (1)(c), paragraph F–7, supra, to avoid any possible reading that the two provisions are somehow interconnected. The debated question under the existing section as to the relationship between the four months rule of existing subsection (3) and the certificate of title provisions of existing subsection (4) is answered by provisions that proposed subsection (1) does not apply to goods covered by subsection (2). On subsection (2) see paragraphs G–10 to G–15 of this statement.

F–20. The state whose law controls the conflict and adds its local rule of refiling is referred to in the draft as "this state." If the litigation were to arise in a forum in another jurisdiction which recognized that the law of the state where the conflict arose controlled, it would read the Code as if it were situated in "this state."

F–21. Proposed paragraph (1)(d) refines the rule requiring refiling within four months of removal into "this state" to cover the case where the existing filing in another jurisdiction would remain effective for less than four months. The period allowed within which to refile in "this state" is the shorter of the remaining period of effectiveness in the original jurisdiction or four months, whichever period first expires. If the secured party could not locate the removed collateral in time to refile in the new jurisdiction in a shortened period, he could file a continuation statement in the original jurisdiction, thus giving himself the full four months to locate the collateral and refile in the removal jurisdiction.

F–22. Existing subsection (3) has been construed by some to require some affirmative act of reperfection in the removal state, even though the original security interest was perfected without filing (e.g., a purchase money security interest in consumer goods under Section 9–302(1)). The proposed revision makes clear that no affirmative act of perfection is needed under such circumstances. On the other hand, existing subsection (3) fails to deal with filing which achieves a status beyond perfection under Section 9–307(2) for purchase money security interests in consumer goods, and the proposed

ing against a foreign debtor on this set of facts in the jurisdiction where its major executive office in the United States is located.

12. The Permanent Editorial Board changed the 10 days back to 30 days.

paragraph (1)(d)(iii) treats this point expressly in a manner comparable to the rules described in the preceding paragraph.

F–23. The effect of lapse after four months of a security interest perfected without local filing on rights arising within the four months is not specifically covered in the present Code, but is referred to in existing Comment 7 to Section 9–103. Subparagraph (1)(d)(i) of the proposed revision makes clear that after lapse the security interest is deemed unperfected as against a person who became a purchaser after the removal. First National Bank of Bay Shore v. Stamper, 93 N.J.Super. 150, 225 A.2d 162 (1966) held in substance that a buyer during the four month period was a converter of the car, at the suit of a bank whose security interest was perfected in the state from which the car was removed. The case entirely fails to consider the effect of the subsequent lapse of the security interest of the bank for failure to reperfect after the four months. While technically the conversion was complete at the moment of purchase, it is to be hoped that the proposed clarification of the effect of lapse will cause similar cases to be analyzed in the future in terms of priority, not of conversion. (Other aspects of the *Stamper* case are discussed in paragraph G–15 of this Statement).

F–24. Terms like "removed" and "kept" in Section 9–103 imply an idea of permanence, not just passing through the jurisdiction. They thus embody the same concept as the phrase "kept in this state" in present Section 9–103(3).

F–25. New subsection (5) relating to oil, gas and mineral financing, is discussed in paragraph D–4 of this Statement.

G. Motor Vehicles and Related Problems of Perfection

The integration of the provisions of Section 9–302 as to motor vehicles and related types of collateral has been much criticized, and has led to numerous non-uniform amendments.

G–1. Paragraphs (c) and (d) of Section 9–302(1) provide that filing is required for motor vehicles required to be licensed, notwithstanding the absence of a filing requirement for purchase-money security interests in consumer goods. (The Committee proposes to omit paragraph (c) relating to farm equipment. See paragraph B–8 of this Statement.) The term "required to be licensed" is not as clear as it might be and the Committee proposes to change it to "required to be registered."

G–2. The Committee considered changing the word "motor vehicle" to "vehicle" or "collateral," but concluded to leave this to the developing policy of individual states. Over-the-road commercial trailers and semi-trailers are not involved, because the paragraph applies only to consumer goods; but public policy and administration by motor vehicle commissioners may vary as to such items as boat trailers and mobile homes. Public policy as to mobile homes ought not now to be frozen in a uniform Code. As they get larger, they cease to be mobile and are not regularly moved over the highways; thus it is not clear that registration like other trailers is the appropriate legal scheme.

G–3. The present formal inconsistency between the required filing for motor vehicles in subsection (1) and the declared inapplicability of the Code's filing requirements to certificated vehicles in subsection (3)(b) would be resolved in proposed revised subsection (3), which makes it clear that it overrides filing requirements of subsection (1).

G–4. The existing and the proposed revised subsection (3) recognize other state and federal schemes for filed public notice in lieu of Code filing. The Committee proposes an additional category of a filing scheme adopted under a treaty to which the United States is a party, which is intended to refer particularly to the Convention on the International Recognition of Rights in Aircraft (Geneva Convention). (See paragraph F–16 of this Statement.)

G–5. Existing subsection (3) provides two alternatives. Alternative A was intended to refer to "complete" certificate of title laws for motor vehicles or the like. Alternative B was intended to apply to certificate of title laws which were not mandatory but permissive at least in part, and to convert them into mandatory laws by force of the Code (except as to inventory security interests, see the next paragraphs). Neither form of drafting has proved to be satisfactory. Many states have chosen to make express references to their statutes intended to be described, instead of leaving the matter to the Code's effort at a universal description. Moreover, permissive certificate of title laws have been replaced in general by "complete" laws, and the device of Alternative B is no longer necessary. The Committee therefore submits a revision of subsection (3) which recognizes that each state will list its own statutes intended to be covered. There will be great diversity because of the existence of central filing statutes in some states for cattle and the like; and because there is considerable variation as to the applicability of the certificate of title device to boats and boat trailers, mobile homes, farm tractors, construction machinery and the like.

G–6. The Committee has revised subsection (4), partly for clarity, into new subsections (3) and (4).

G–7. The revision also covers a point which is dealt with in the existing section only in Alternative B for subsection (3), namely, that Code filing should be required for security interests in inventory, because there is no reason that the Code's carefully worked out provisions for inventory to protect buyers in Section 9–307(1) and as to rights to proceeds in Section 9–306 should be confused by perfection under a certificate of title or other non-Code system. While the Code's sponsoring organizations cannot amend certificate of title laws, it is to be hoped that certificate of title laws will be amended or construed so that the Code filing system for inventory will be exclusive and will not be duplicated by the certificate of title system. There are indications in recent case law that the courts are already so construing certificate of title laws.

G–8. The requirement in proposed paragraph (3)(b) for Code filing for security interests in inventory is limited to inventory situations controlled by state law. It is to be hoped that a state will avoid double filing by avoiding any requirement that inventory security interests created by dealers be shown on certificates of title. The Code cannot change the provisions of the Federal Aviation Act requiring all security interests in aircraft (including inventory security interests) to be filed under the federal system and making that system exclusive. Fortunately, it has been held that Section 9–307(1) of the

Code should apply to the rights of buyers in ordinary course of airplane inventory, although the federal system lacks a provision comparable to that section. Northern Illinois Corp. v. Bishop Distributing Co., 284 F.Supp. 121 (W.D.Mich.1969).

G–9. The proposed revisions of subsections (3) and (4) of Section 9–302, like the existing subsections, apply only to "property subject to" the statutes referred to. Hence the substitute forms of public notice recognized in subsection (3) do not apply to the perfection of security interests in proceeds other than such property. Such security interests must be perfected under Code rules. Compare the proposed revision of Section 9–306(3), discussed in paragraphs E–5, 22, 23 of this Statement.

G–10. The above discussion of Section 9–302 does not deal with the conflict of law problems arising from the use of certificates of title. These problems are covered by existing Sections 9–103(3) and (4), the interrelationship of which has caused much confusion and criticism; and by revisions proposed in new Section 9–103(2).

G–11. Proposed paragraph (2)(b) deals with collateral covered by a certificate of title. In general, a security interest perfected by notation on a certificate of title continues perfected so long as the certificate is outstanding or until the collateral is registered in another jurisdiction, notwithstanding removing the collateral into another state and keeping it there for more than four months. The Committee thus affirms In re White, 266 F.Supp. 863 (N.D.N.Y.1967), and later cases in their interpretation of the relationship between the certificate of title provision of existing subsection (4) and the four months rule of existing subsection (3).

G–12. If, however, reregistration occurs in another jurisdiction to which the collateral is removed while a certificate of title is left outstanding the security interest perfected by notation on the certificate of title remains perfected for four months after removal under Section 9–103(2)(c). This provision adopts the four months of proposed Section 9–103(1)(c), discussed in paragraphs F–19–21 of this Statement, for there is no reason why rights on removal of collateral perfected on a certificate of title should receive less favorable treatment than rights in collateral otherwise perfected.

G–13. Under the Uniform Certificate of Title Act and the Uniform Vehicle Code the four month period of continued perfection after removal commences from the time the first certificate of title is issued in the state to which the collateral is removed, not from the time of removal. The Committee has chosen to commence the four months with removal, to keep the periods of Sections 9–103(1)(d) and 9–103(2) consistent. It is hoped that if the Committee's recommendations are approved, the National Conference of Commissioners on Uniform State Laws will conform its Uniform Act, and that the National Committee on Uniform Traffic Laws and Ordinance will conform its Uniform Vehicle Code.

G–14. Possibilities exist that a certificate of title may be issued in a state to which collateral is removed, and that because of fraudulent affidavits or other fraudulent devices the certificate will fail to disclose a security interest perfected in another state, whether that state does or does not have a certificate of title law. Suppose under these circumstances that rights of a third party arise in reliance on the "clean" local certificate of title. What protection should the issuing state give to rights which arose in reliance on its own certificate of title as against rights which were perfected elsewhere but not shown thereon? The Committee treats this problem in proposed Section 9–103(2)(d).

G–15. The Committee believes that more protection should be given to the local "clean" certificate of title than was accorded in First National Bank of Bay Shore v. Stamper, 93 N.J.Super. 150, 225 A.2d 162 (1966). The court there felt that it was required to recognize a security interest perfected in New York for four months after removal of the car into New Jersey, even though a New Jersey buyer had innocently bought the car within the period in reliance on a New Jersey certificate of title not showing the security interest. The court gave weight to the four month provision of existing Section 9–103(3) rather than to the condition of the New Jersey title under existing Section 9–103(4). It reasoned that Section 9–103(4) provides that perfection is governed by the law of the jurisdiction which issued the certificate, and that New Jersey recognizes foreign security interests after removal within the limits set by Section 9–103(3). This reasoning gives no scope to the introduction to Section 9–103(4): "Notwithstanding subsections (2) and (3)." (The lapse aspect of the *Stamper* case is discussed in paragraph F–23 of this Statement.)

The Committee's structure in its proposed Section 9–103(2)(b) follows the structure of existing Section 9–103(4) and thus would not in itself preclude the *Stamper* reading. But the Committee believes that consumer buyers who give value and take delivery without knowledge of the security interest in situations like *Stamper* should be protected in their reliance on local clean certificates of title. Its proposed Section 9–103(2)(d) so provides.

G–16. The Committee's proposed treatment does not apply to rights acquired while a distinctive certificate of title is outstanding as described in this paragraph.

The Uniform Certificate of Title Act and Uniform Vehicle Code provide that where the vehicle comes from a state which did not require that security interests be noted on a certificate of title, the local certificate first issued shall be distinctive and shall contain the legend: "This vehicle may be subject to an undisclosed lien." If the Department receives no notice of a security interest within four months after issuance of such a certificate of title, such a certificate may be reissued without the legend. Other certificate of title laws contain comparable provisions.

H. Scope Questions

H–1. Several questions have been raised as to the status of security interests in beneficial interests in trusts and estates. These are typically not commercial collateral, and a requirement of filing with respect thereto seems inappropriate and might act as an entrapment of secured parties who would fail to analyze the collateral as a general intangible. It would be possible to exclude this kind of collateral from Article 9 by a provision in Section 9–104, but the Committee recommends leaving this collateral subject to the general rules of security law provided by Article 9 but with an exclusion from filing by a provision in Section 9–302(1).

H–2. Certain receipts issued by large grain dealers do not literally qualify as "documents" under Article 9, because the definition in Section 9–105(1) refers back to the definition of "document of title" in Section 1–201 (which requires issuance by a bailee) rather than to the provision in Section 7–201(2) which makes receipts issued by owners under specified conditions substantially the equivalent of warehouse receipts. The Committee proposes to clarify this by amendment of the definition in Section 9–105(1) to refer to both earlier sections.

H–3. When the Code was drafted, railway equipment trusts were excluded from Article 9 by Section 9–104(e) in response to the argument that they were extremely specialized securities and the market in them should not be disturbed by new rules of law. The exclusion has subsequently been criticized as unsound. Opinion among railway authorities whom the Committee consulted was divided, but few of those suggesting retention had any specific reason therefor. The Committee proposes to delete the exclusion. The effect will be that railway equipment trusts will become subject to the general rules of security law provided by Article 9. It should be noted, however, that these rules are almost always subject to agreement of the parties. Ordinarily filing under Article 9 will not be required by reason of Section 9–302(3), because filing is controlled by Section 20(c) of the Interstate Commerce Act.

I. Filing Problems

Substantial changes have been made in Part 4 of Article 9 dealing with filing. The purpose of some of these appears in the discussions of Fixtures, Timber and Oil, Gas and Minerals in Parts A, C and D of this Statement.

I–1. Far-flung railroad and other public utility corporations may have signalling systems or other chattels strung along their rights of way, and the chattels may be encumbered with a combined real estate and chattel indenture on the whole utility plant. Where the chattels are non-fixtures, the Code would require one or at most two chattel filings. But where the chattels may be fixtures, the Code would require filing in each county where the chattels exist, and with a fixture filing including real estate descriptions. This is clearly unduly onerous. Numerous states have attempted to relieve against the burden by a variety of non-uniform amendments to various sections. The Committee has accepted from some of these amendments the concept of "transmitting utility," for which it proposes a definition in Section 9–105. It proposes a Section 9–401(5) making all filings for transmitting utilities in the office of the Secretary of State. This filing constitutes a fixture filing (id.) but need not contain a description of the real estate (Proposed Section 9–402(5)).

I–2. There has been much criticism of the provision in Section 9–403(2) which terminates the effectiveness of a financing statement which states a maturity date 60 days after the stated maturity date. There seems to be no reason why a stated maturity date should terminate the effectiveness any sooner than a financing statement which does not state the date. Even though the transaction has a maturity date, the application of this provision can be avoided simply by not stating the maturity date in the financing statement. The requirement of a financing statement and the form in Section 9–401(1) and (3) do not require the maturity date to be stated even if there is one. The Committee therefore proposes to eliminate the special rule in Section 9–403(2) applicable when a maturity date is stated, and to leave all financing statements operative for five years.

I–3. There has been some objection to the five year period, on the theory that where the duration of a transaction is longer than five years, the financing statement should be good for the duration of the transaction. The Committee has accepted this view in the cases of real estate mortgages which constitute fixture security interests and transmitting utilities (Proposed Section 9–403(6)).

I–4. The Committee has chosen, however, not to recommend this change generally, or in accordance with suggestions that it be made for all combined real estate and chattel mortgages, or all combined mortgages of corporations, or of listed corporations. The burden of chattel filing, even fixture filing, is not too great in other than transmitting utility situations. The theory of the provisions for effectiveness of financing statements under the present Code is that (except for the two cases just mentioned which involve filing in offices other than the usual offices), they last for five years unless continuation statements are filed, and that the files are therefore self-clearing. A filing officer who arranges his filings by years can clear the filings of any year automatically after five years. This would not be possible if there were exceptional cases running more than five years. Moreover, searchers would have to go back to the effective date of the Code if there could be valid long-term filings.

I–5. This operating scheme raises operating questions when effectiveness of the financing statement has been extended by continuation statements, and the Committee has proposed in Section 9–403(3) that the filing officer should work out a physical annexation of the financing statement to the continuation statement to insure the preservation of those from an earlier year whose vitality has been continued.

I–6. Other detailed suggestions have been made in Section 9–403 designed to permit preservation of microfilm instead of the actual financing statements, and on the other hand to preserve the record of filings beyond the point where termination statements have been filed. Evidence of a perfection of a security interest in the past may be necessary for some time after the termination because of litigation involving bankruptcy preferences, fraudulent conveyances, or other related types of issues.

I–7. The Code's provisions as to the effect of lapse have occasioned debate. Existing Section 9–403(2) provides that upon lapse the security interest becomes unperfected, but this statement does not explicitly indicate the result when there was a right junior to the lapsed security interest. It has been argued that since the junior party was charged with notice of the lapsed security interest, he should remain junior. Comment 3 to Section 9–403 and a corresponding Comment to Section 9–103 take the position, however, that the holder of a junior security interest defeats the holder of a lapsed security interest (see also paragraph F–23 of this Statement), but neither Comment deals with the position of a buyer who bought before the lapse. The

Committee proposes in Sections 9–103(1)(d)(i) and 9–403(2) to make clear that after the lapse purchasers—i.e., buyers and secured parties—have priority over the lapsed security interest. The negative inference is that judgment lienors remain subordinate.[13]

I–8. To avoid the question whether a financing statement may lapse during a bankruptcy or other insolvency proceeding, the Committee has proposed in Section 9–403(2) that the financing statement does not lapse during the proceeding and that the secured party has a minimum of 60 days after termination of the proceeding within which to refile under Article 9. Refiling, however, requires a new financing statement signed by the debtor; to avoid this, the secured party may file a continuation statement before the end of the five-year period.

I–9. A perpetual question has existed whether in filing against sole proprietorships or partnership debtors one may use a trade name, or whether the individual name of a proprietor is required, and whether the names of partners are required to be shown as debtors. There is substantial lack of uniformity in state instructions to filing officers with respect to these matters. The Committee hopes to clarify these issues by its proposed Section 9–402(7) that one files against a partnership by the name in which it is known and that one files against an individual by his individual name. Neither the names of partners nor a trade name for individuals or partnerships need be shown. The Committee has considered the California provision that a trade name should be shown, but it seems to create too great a risk of insufficient filing, because a secured party may not know of a trade name sometimes informally used by a debtor. Trade name statutes vary so widely in scope and in the effects of compliance or non-compliance that it has not seemed feasible to tie any requirements as to trade names to the existence of such statutes.

I–10. There is presently much difference in view as to whether a secured party is under a duty to refile where he knows of and particularly where he has consented to a debtor's transfer of the property to a new debtor. The Committee has sought to standardize practices in these respects by proposing in Section 9–402(7) that no refiling is necessary following a transfer of the collateral by the debtor. This provision is, of course, limited to the continued perfection of the security interest as to collateral transferred by the original debtor. If additional collateral is assigned after the transfer, even though the mechanism is an after-acquired property clause under a security agreement which the new debtor has assumed, it seems clear that a secured party could not be safe without a filing against the new debtor.

I–11. A similar question arises with respect to the debtor's change of name. The Committee has sought to settle the matter by proposing in Section 9–402(7) that the filing is not effective as to new collateral after four months after the change of name unless the financing statement is refiled. The provision is so drafted that it will also apply to certain corporate readjustments.

13. In the case of Section 9–403(2), the Permanent Editorial Board extended this rule to judgment lienors.

I–12. As to all of these problems of filing, the Committee is desirous of avoiding loss of security interests on mere technicalities. Accordingly, the Committee proposes to take existing Section 9–402(5) as to minor errors that are not seriously misleading, move it to the end of Section 9–402 as subsection (8), and to make it clearly applicable to all provisions of that section.

I–13. Title companies have complained with some justice that practices are too loose in the use of the term "fixture" in financing statements as a catchall phrase as in descriptions like "all machinery, equipment, tools and fixtures situated at 14 Digby Road, Chicago." This leads to a question whether a fixture filing is intended and whether a possible objection to the title to the real estate mentioned should be noted. This complaint, coupled with the fact that the Committee's proposals make clear that a fixture filing should be indexed in the real estate records, has induced the Committee to propose blanks in the sample form in Section 9–402(3) for designating unmistakably when a financing statement is intended to be filed as a fixture filing, and to require a statement to that effect in filings covered by Section 9–402(5).

I–14. After considering developing practice and the needs of filing officers for uniformity, the Committee proposes adoption of a non-uniform amendment made in some states which differentiates in the filing fees between financing statements in a form prescribed by the state filing officer and filing statements in other forms. Section 9–403(5). See also Section 9–404(3).

I–15. It is proposed to amend subsection (1) of Section 9–402 so that only the debtor need sign a financing statement. However, subsection (4) would be amended to require both parties to sign an amendment to a financing statement, thus precluding the possibility that either party could unilaterally prejudice the secured party's rights under a filed financing statement.

J. Default

J–1. Existing Section 9–501(3)(c) permits variation of the provisions of Section 9–505(1) with respect to compulsory disposition of collateral, but not the provisions of Section 9–505(2) or 9–504(3). This could be construed to mean that where the secured party proposes to retain the collateral in satisfaction of the obligation under Section 9–505(2), or fixes a time of sale under Section 9–504(3), a debtor who acquiesces cannot waive the thirty day waiting period of Section 9–505(2) or the reasonable notification of Section 9–504(3). Such a result could not be justified. Accordingly, the Committee proposes to amend Section 9–501(3)(c) to extend the authorization of waivers to all of section 9–505 and to Section 9–504(3).

J–2. In the Committee's opinion the secured party's thirty day wait under Section 9–505(2) before he can retain the collateral in satisfaction of the obligation is too long. Moreover, an extra time is involved because of the secured party's uncertainty as to when the debtor "receives notification." These circumstances, coupled with the fact that the waiting period may be wasted if objection is received from the debtor or other party entitled to receive notification, probably defeat the intended purpose of the scheme, which is (at least in part) to avoid the creation of a deficiency. It takes longer to clear title by taking the goods in satisfaction of the obligation than it does to sell. In the process of sale, a deficiency is frequently established. If the program of Section 9–505(2) were made expeditious, deficiencies might sometimes be avoided. Accordingly, the Committee proposes that the waiting period be cut down to twenty-one days after the mailing of the notice.

J–3. A related difficulty in Section 9–505(2) on accepting collateral in satisfaction of the obligation in lieu of sale and in Section 9–504(3) on sale, is the persons entitled to receive notice. Both sections now require notice (except in the case of consumer goods) not only to every other secured party who has filed a financing statement "in this state" but also to every other secured party known to the secured party giving the notice. These requirements put on the secured party the necessity of searching the record in every case and of keeping a record of every telephone call by a person claiming an interest, and determining whether such person is entitled to notice. In the Committee's opinion, this burden simply is not justified in the light of the few cases in which there will be junior security interests on file and even fewer cases in which there will be an equity for the junior party to be protected. The Committee proposes instead that the only persons (other than the debtor) who need be given notice under each section are those who have given the secured party written notice of their claims of interests in the collateral.

Amendments to Article 1

§ 1–105. Territorial Application of the Act; Parties' Power to Choose Applicable Law.

(1) Except as provided hereafter in this section, when a transaction bears a reasonable relation to this state and also to another state or nation the parties may agree that the law either of this state or of such other state or nation shall govern their rights and duties. Failing such agreement this Act applies to transactions bearing an appropriate relation to this state.

(2) Where one of the following provisions of this Act specifies the applicable law, that provision governs and a contrary agreement is effective only to the extent permitted by the law (including the conflict of laws rules) so specified:

Rights of creditors against sold goods. Section 2–402.

Applicability of the Article on Bank Deposits and Collections. Section 4–102.

Bulk transfers subject to the Article on Bulk Transfers. Section 6–102.

Applicability of the Article on Investment Securities. Section 8–106.

[Policy and scope of the Article on Secured Transactions. Sections 9–102 and 9–103.]

Perfection provisions of the Article on Secured Transactions, Section 9–103.

Reasons for 1972 Change

The reference to Section 9–102 has been deleted and a change made in Section 9–102 deleting any reference therein to conflict of law problems, because there is no reason why the general principles of the present section should not be applicable to the choice of law problems within its scope. Section 9–103 continues to govern choice of law questions as to perfection of security interests and the effect of perfection and non-perfection thereof. The usual rule is that perfection is governed by the law of the jurisdiction in which the collateral is when the last event occurs on which is based the assertion that the security interest is perfected or unperfected. Section 9–103 contains special rules for the cases of intangibles which have no situs, certain types of movable goods, goods which the parties intended at the inception of the transaction to be kept in another jurisdiction, goods subject to certificate of title laws, and certain other cases. Section 9–103 also contains local law rules as to reperfection of security interests when collateral is moved from one jurisdiction to another.

§ 1–201. General Definitions [Unchanged except for definitions (9) and (37)].

(9) "Buyer in ordinary course of business" means a person who in good faith and without knowledge that the sale to him is in violation of the ownership rights or security interest of a third party in the goods buys in ordinary course from a person in the business of selling goods of that kind but does not include a pawnbroker. <u>All persons who sell minerals or the like (including oil and gas) at wellhead or minehead shall be deemed to be persons in the business of selling goods of that kind.</u> "Buying" may be for cash or by exchange of other property or on secured or unsecured credit and includes receiving goods or documents of title under a pre-existing contract for sale but does not include a transfer in bulk or as security for or in total or partial satisfaction of a money debt.

(37) "Security interest" means an interest in personal property or fixtures which secures payment or performance of an obligation. The retention or reservation of title by a seller of goods notwithstanding shipment or delivery to the buyer (Section 2–401) is limited in effect to a reservation of a "security interest". The term also includes any interest of a buyer of accounts[,] or chattel paper[, or contract rights] which is subject to Article 9. The special property interest of a buyer of goods on identification of such goods to a contract for sale under Section 2–401 is not a "security interest", but a buyer may also acquire a "security interest" by complying with Article 9. Unless a lease or consignment is intended as security, reservation of title thereunder is not a "security interest" but a consignment is in any event subject to the provisions on consignment sales (Section 2–326). Whether a lease is intended as security is to be determined by the facts of each case; however, (a) the inclusion of an option to purchase does not of itself make the lease one intended for security, and (b) an agreement that upon compliance with the terms of the lease the lessee shall become or has the option to become the owner of the property for no additional consideration or for a nominal consideration does make the lease one intended for security.

Reasons for 1972 Change of Definitions (9) and (37)

(9) The new language fits in with changes as to minerals in Section 9–103 which are explained in the references to minerals in the Reasons for Change and Comments to that section.

(37) The omission of the term "contract rights" conforms to the elimination of that term from Article 9. See Reasons for Change under Section 9-106.

Amendment to Article 2

§ 2-107. Goods to Be Severed From Realty: Recording.

(1) A contract for the sale of [timber,] minerals or the like (including oil and gas) or a structure or its materials to be removed from realty is a contract for the sale of goods within this Article if they are to be severed by the seller but until severance a purported present sale thereof which is not effective as a transfer of an interest in land is effective only as a contract to sell.

(2) A contract for the sale apart from the land of growing crops or other things attached to realty and capable of severance without material harm thereto but not described in subsection (1) or of timber to be cut is a contract for the sale of goods within this Article whether the subject matter is to be severed by the buyer or by the seller even though it forms part of the realty at the time of contracting, and the parties can by identification effect a present sale before severance.

(3) The provisions of this section are subject to any third party rights provided by the law relating to realty records, and the contract for sale may be executed and recorded as a document transferring an interest in land and shall then constitute notice to third parties of the buyer's rights under the contract for sale.

Reasons for 1972 Change

Several timber-growing states have changed the 1962 Code to make timber to be cut under a contract of severance goods, regardless of the question who is to sever them. The section is revised to adopt this change. Financing of the transaction is facilitated if the timber is treated as goods instead of real estate. A similar change is made in the definition of "goods" in Section 9-105. To protect persons dealing with timberlands, filing on timber to be cut is required in Part 4 of Article 9 to be made in real estate records in a manner comparable to fixture filing.

Amendment to Article 5

§ 5-116. Transfer and Assignment.

(1) The right to draw under a credit can be transferred or assigned only when the credit is expressly designated as transferable or assignable.

(2) Even though the credit specifically states that it is nontransferable or nonassignable the beneficiary may before performance of the conditions of the credit assign his right to proceeds. Such an assignment is an assignment of [a contract right] an account under Article 9 on Secured Transactions and is governed by that Article except that

(a) the assignment is ineffective until the letter of credit or advice of credit is delivered to the assignee which delivery constitutes perfection of the security interest under Article 9; and

(b) the issuer may honor drafts or demands for payment drawn under the credit until it receives a notification of the assignment signed by the beneficiary which reasonably identifies the credit involved in the assignment and contains a request to pay the assignee; and

(c) after what reasonably appears to be such a notification has been received the issuer may without dishonor refuse to accept or pay even to a person otherwise entitled to honor until the letter of credit or advice of credit is exhibited to the issuer.

(3) Except where the beneficiary has effectively assigned his right to draw or his right to proceeds, nothing in this section limits his right to transfer or negotiate drafts or demands drawn under the credit.

Reasons for 1972 Change

The change conforms to the deletion of the defined term "contract right" from Article 9.

ARTICLE 9

SECURED TRANSACTIONS; SALES OF ACCOUNTS [, CONTRACT RIGHTS] AND CHATTEL PAPER

PART 1

SHORT TITLE, APPLICABILITY AND DEFINITIONS

§ 9–102. Policy and [Scope] Subject Matter of Article.

(1) Except as otherwise provided [in Section 9–103 on multiple state transactions and] in Section 9–104 on excluded transactions, this Article applies [so far as concerns any personal property and fixtures within the jurisdiction of this state]

(a) to any transaction (regardless of its form) which is intended to create a security interest in personal property or fixtures including goods, documents, instruments, general intangibles, chattel paper or accounts [or contract rights]; and also

(b) to any sale of accounts [contract rights] or chattel paper.

(2) This Article applies to security interests created by contract including pledge, assignment, chattel mortgage, chattel trust, trust deed, factor's lien, equipment trust, conditional sale, trust receipt, other lien or title retention contract and lease or consignment intended as security. This Article does not apply to statutory liens except as provided in Section 9–310.

(3) The application of this Article to a security interest in a secured obligation is not affected by the fact that the obligation is itself secured by a transaction or interest to which this Article does not apply.

Note: *The adoption of this Article should be accompanied by the repeal of existing statutes dealing with conditional sales, trust receipts, factor's liens where the factor is given a non-possessory lien, chattel mortgages, crop mortgages, mortgages on railroad equipment, assignment of accounts and generally statutes regulating security interests in personal property.*

Where the state has a retail installment selling act or small loan act, that legislation should be carefully examined to determine what changes in those acts are needed to conform them to this Article. This Article primarily sets out rules defining rights of a secured party against persons dealing with the debtor; it does not prescribe regulations and controls which may be necessary to curb abuses arising in the small loan business or in the financing of consumer purchases on credit. Accordingly there is no intention to repeal existing regulatory acts in those fields [.] by enactment or re-enactment of Article 9. See Section 9–203(4) and the Note thereto.

Reasons for 1972 Change

The omissions in the first paragraph of subsection (1) make applicable the general choice of law principles of Section 1–105 (except for special rules stated in Section 9–103), instead of an incomplete statement in this section.

The omission in clause (1)(b) conforms to the elimination of the term "contract rights" from the Article. See Reasons for Change under Section 9–106.

[§ 9–103. Accounts, Contract Rights, General Intangibles and Equipment Relating to Another Jurisdiction; and Incoming Goods Already Subject to a Security Interest].

[(1) If the office where the assignor of accounts or contract rights keeps his record concerning them is in this state, the validity and perfection of a security interest therein and the possibility and effect of proper filing is governed by this Article; otherwise by the law (including the conflict of laws rules) of the jurisdiction where such office is located.]

[(2) If the chief place of business of a debtor is in this state, this Article governs the validity and perfection of a security interest and the possibility and effect of proper filing with regard to general intangibles or with regard to goods of a type which are normally used in more than one jurisdiction (such as automotive equipment, rolling stock, airplanes, road building equipment, commercial harvesting equipment, construction machinery and the like) if such goods are classified as inventory by reason of their being leased by the debtor to others. Otherwise, the law (including the conflict of laws rules) of the jurisdiction where such chief place of business is located shall govern. If the chief place of business is located in a jurisdiction which does not provide for perfection of the security interest by filing or recording in that jurisdiction, then the security interest may be perfected by filing in this state. [For the purpose of determining the validity and perfection of a security interest in an airplane, the chief place of business of a debtor who is a foreign air carrier under the Federal Aviation Act of 1958, as amended, is the designated office of the agent upon whom service of process may be made on behalf of the debtor.]]

[(3) If personal property other than that governed by subsections (1) and (2) is already subject to a security interest when it is brought into this state, the validity of the security interest in this state is to be determined by the law (including the conflict of laws rules) of the jurisdiction where the property was when the security interest attached. However, if the parties to the transaction understood at the time that the security interest attached that the property would be kept in this state and it was brought into this state within 30 days after the security interest attached for purposes other than transportation through this state, then the validity of the security interest in this state is to be determined by the law of this state. If the security interest was already perfected under the law of the jurisdiction where the property was when the security interest attached and before being brought into this state, the security interest continues perfected in this state for four months and also thereafter if within the four month period it is perfected in this state. The security interest may also be perfected in this state after the expiration of the four month period; in such case perfection dates from the time of perfection in this state. If the security interest was not perfected under the law of the jurisdiction where the property was when the security interest attached and before being brought into this state, it may be perfected in this state; in such case perfection dates from the time of perfection in this state.]

[(4) Notwithstanding subsections (2) and (3), if personal property is covered by a certificate of title issued under a statute of this state or any other jurisdiction which requires indication on a certificate of title of any security interest in the property as a condition of perfection, then the perfection is governed by the law of the jurisdiction which issued the certificate.]

[[(5) Notwithstanding subsection (1) and Section 9–302, if the office where the assignor of accounts or contract rights keeps his records concerning them is not located in a jurisdiction which is a part of the United States, its territories or possessions, and the accounts or contract rights are within the jurisdiction of this state or the transaction which creates the security interest otherwise bears an appropriate relation to this state, this Article governs the validity and perfection of the security interest and the security interest may only be perfected by notification to the account debtor.]]

§ 9–103. Perfection of Security Interests in Multiple State Transactions.

(1) Documents, instruments and ordinary goods.

(a) This subsection applies to documents and instruments and to goods other than those covered by a certificate of title described in subsection (2), mobile goods described in subsection (3), and minerals described in subsection (5).

(b) Except as otherwise provided in this subsection, perfection and the effect of perfection or non-perfection of a security interest in collateral are governed by the law of the jurisdiction where the collateral is when the last event occurs on which is based the assertion that the security interest is perfected or unperfected.

(c) If the parties to a transaction creating a purchase money security interest in goods in one jurisdiction understand at the time that the security interest attaches that the goods will be kept in another jurisdiction, then the law of the other jurisdiction governs the perfection and the effect of perfection or non-perfection of the security interest from the time it attaches until thirty days after the debtor receives possession of the goods and thereafter if the goods are taken to the other jurisdiction before the end of the thirty-day period.

(d) When collateral is brought into and kept in this state while subject to a security interest perfected under the law of the jurisdiction from which the collateral was removed, the security interest remains perfected, but if action is required by Part 3 of this Article to perfect the security interest,

(i) if the action is not taken before the expiration of the period of perfection in the other jurisdiction or the end of four months after the collateral is brought into this state, whichever period first expires, the security interest becomes unperfected at the end of that period and is thereafter deemed to have been unperfected as against a person who became a purchaser after removal;

(ii) if the action is taken before the expiration of the period specified in subparagraph (i), the security interest continues perfected thereafter;

(iii) for the purpose of priority over a buyer of consumer goods (subsection (2) of Section 9–307), the period of the effectiveness of a filing in the jurisdiction from which the collateral is removed is governed by the rules with respect to perfection in subparagraphs (i) and (ii).

(2) Certificate of title.

(a) This subsection applies to goods covered by a certificate of title issued under a statute of this state or of another jurisdiction under the law of which indication of a security interest on the certificate is required as a condition of perfection.

(b) Except as otherwise provided in this subsection, perfection and the effect of perfection or non-perfection of the security interest are governed by the law (including the conflict of laws rules) of the jurisdiction issuing the certificate until four months after the goods are removed from that jurisdiction and thereafter until the goods are registered in another jurisdiction, but in any event not beyond surrender of the certificate. After the expiration of that period, the goods are not covered by the certificate of title within the meaning of this section.

(c) Except with respect to the rights of a buyer described in the next paragraph, a security interest, perfected in another jurisdiction otherwise than by notation on a certificate of title, in goods brought into this state and thereafter covered by a certificate of title issued by this state is subject to the rules stated in paragraph (d) of subsection (1).

(d) If goods are brought into this state while a security interest therein is perfected in any manner under the law of the jurisdiction from which the goods are removed and a certificate of title is issued by this state and the certificate does not show that the goods are subject to the security interest or that they may be subject to security interests not shown on the certificate, the security interest is subordinate to the rights of a buyer of the goods who is not in the business of selling goods of that kind to the extent that he gives value and receives delivery of the goods after issuance of the certificate and without knowledge of the security interest.

(3) Accounts, general intangibles and mobile goods.

(a) This subsection applies to accounts (other than an account described in subsection (5) on minerals) and general intangibles and to goods which are mobile and which are of a type normally used in more than one jurisdiction, such as motor vehicles, trailers, rolling stock, airplanes, shipping containers, road building and construction machinery and commercial harvesting machinery and the like, if the goods are equipment or are inventory leased or held for lease by the debtor to others, and are not covered by a certificate of title described in subsection (2).

(b) The law (including the conflict of laws rules) of the jurisdiction in which the debtor is located governs the perfection and the effect of perfection or non-perfection of the security interest.

(c) If, however, the debtor is located in a jurisdiction which is not a part of the United States, and which does not provide for perfection of the security interest by filing or recording in that jurisdiction, the law of the jurisdiction in the United States in which the debtor has its major executive office in the United States governs the perfection and the effect of perfection or non-perfection of the security interest through filing. In the alternative, if the debtor is located in a jurisdiction which is not a part of the United States or Canada and the collateral is accounts or general intangibles for money due or to become due, the security interest may be perfected by notification to the account debtor. As used in this paragraph, "United States" includes its territories and possessions and the Commonwealth of Puerto Rico.

(d) A debtor shall be deemed located at his place of business if he has one, at his chief executive office if he has more than one place of business, otherwise at his residence. If, however, the debtor is a foreign air carrier under the Federal Aviation Act of 1958, as amended, it shall be deemed located at the designated office of the agent upon whom service of process may be made on behalf of the foreign air carrier.

(e) A security interest perfected under the law of the jurisdiction of the location of the debtor is perfected until the expiration of four months after a change of the debtor's location to another jurisdiction, or until perfection would have ceased by the law of the first jurisdiction, whichever period first expires. Unless perfected in the new jurisdiction before the end of that period, it becomes unperfected thereafter and is deemed to have been unperfected as against a person who became a purchaser after the change.

(4) Chattel paper.

The rules stated for goods in subsection (1) apply to a possessory security interest in chattel paper. The rules stated for accounts in subsection (3) apply to a non-possessory security interest in chattel paper, but the security interest may not be perfected by notification to the account debtor.

(5) Minerals.

Perfection and the effect of perfection or non-perfection of a security interest which is created by a debtor who has an interest in minerals or the like (including oil and gas) before extraction and which attaches thereto as extracted, or which attaches to an account resulting from the sale thereof at the wellhead or minehead are governed by the law (including the conflict of laws rules) of the jurisdiction wherein the wellhead or minehead is located.

Reasons for 1972 Change

The section has been completely rewritten to clarify the relationship of its several provisions to each other and to other sections defining the applicable law. Now that the Code has been adopted in all states but Louisiana and also adopted in the District of Columbia and the Virgin Islands, the emphasis in the revision has been to make clear where perfection of a security interest must take place, rather than on problems of actual conflicts of rules of law.

1. The section now concerns itself exclusively with perfection of security interests and the effect of perfection or non-perfection thereof. The 1962 Code has several references to the "validity" of a security agreement, and these have been deleted. Likewise, a deletion has been made from Section 9-102 of the language which went beyond that section's basic function of defining the scope of Article 9 and purported to state a choice of law rule. These two changes make it clear that Article 9 does not govern problems of choice of law between the original parties, and that this question is governed by the general choice of law provision in Section 1-105.

2. While most of the substantive materials of the section are in the 1962 Text, the statement thereof and their relationship to each other were not clear. In the revision they are clarified according to the following structure:

The basic rule of this section is that the controlling law, as to perfection of the security interests and the effect of perfection or non-perfection, is the law of the jurisdiction where the collateral is when the last event occurs on which is based the assertion that the security interest is perfected or unperfected (paragraph (1)(b)). There are certain exceptions: (i) In the case of a purchase money security interest in goods, where the parties intended to remove the collateral to another jurisdiction within 30 days after the debtor received possession of the goods, the law of the latter jurisdiction will govern the initial perfection until the expiration of the 30-day period, and thereafter if the goods are removed to the other jurisdiction before the end of the period (paragraph (1)(c)). (ii) Where the collateral is covered by a certificate of title, perfection will be governed by the law of the issuing jurisdiction (subsection (2)). (iii) If the collateral is certain mobile goods or certain intangibles, perfection will be governed by the law of the jurisdiction wherein is located the debtor (subsection (3)).

Where the collateral has been removed from the jurisdiction whose law first governed, the jurisdiction into which it is removed (i.e., "this state") adds a local requirement of re-perfection to the requirements of the state from which the collateral was removed—i.e., refiling is required within 4 months after removal, or within any lesser period during which perfection would have continued in the other jurisdiction (paragraphs (1)(d) and (2)(c)).

3. The two former rules for determining place of perfection as to intangibles (namely, for accounts, the office where the records were kept concerning the accounts; and for general intangibles, the chief place of business of the debtor) have been consolidated into the rule that the filing is at the debtor's location. That location will ordinarily be the office designated in the 1962 Text as "chief place of business," now redesignated as "chief executive office." A new provision (paragraph (3)(e)) has been added to cover the case where that office moves from one jurisdiction to another.

A principal objection to the original rule that the place for filing as to accounts was the place where the debtor kept his records with respect to them was that persons seeking to search records might not know where this place might be, in the case of a far-flung debtor or of multicorporate enterprises with central accounting. Where the debtor assigned his accounts without recourse, as in factoring, he might keep few records with respect to them. Moreover, it was thought undesirable to have one rule for accounts and another rule for general intangibles, because in many financing situations both types of receivables may be involved. See discussion in Reasons for Change to Section 9-106. Therefore, it was decided to adopt for both types of intangibles the rule heretofore applicable to general intangibles.

§ 9-104. Transactions Excluded From Article.

This Article does not apply

(a) to a security interest subject to any statute of the United States [such as the Ship Mortgage Act, 1920,] to the extent that such statute governs the rights of parties to and third parties affected by transactions in particular types of property; or

(b) to a landlord's lien; or

(c) to a lien given by statute or other rule of law for services or materials except as provided in Section 9-310 on priority of such liens; or

(d) to a transfer of a claim for wages, salary or other compensation of an employee; or

[(e) to an equipment trust covering railway rolling stock; or]

(e) to a transfer by a government or governmental subdivision or agency; or

(f) to a sale of accounts [, contract rights] or chattel paper as part of a sale of the business out of which they arose, or an assignment of accounts [, contract rights] or chattel paper which is for the purpose of collection only, or a transfer of a [contract] right to payment under a contract to an assignee who is also to do the performance under the contract or a transfer of a single account to an assignee in whole or partial satisfaction of a preexisting indebtedness; or

(g) to a transfer of an interest in or claim in or under any policy of insurance, except as provided with respect to proceeds (Section 9-306) and priorities in proceeds (Section 9-312); or

(h) to a right represented by a judgment (other than a judgment taken on a right to payment which was collateral); or

(i) to any right of set-off; or

(j) except to the extent that provision is made for fixtures in Section 9-313, to the creation or transfer of an interest in or lien on real estate, including a lease or rents thereunder; or

(k) to a transfer in whole or in part of [any of the following:] any claim arising out of tort; [any deposit, savings, passbook or like account maintained with a bank, savings and loan association, credit union or like organization.]; or

(*l*) to a transfer of an interest in any deposit account (subsection (1) of Section 9-105), except as provided with respect to proceeds (Section 9-306) and priorities in proceeds (Section 9-312).

Reasons for 1972 Change

Former paragraph (e), excluding railway equipment trusts from the coverage of Article 9, has been deleted. The whole thrust of Article 9 is to eliminate differences based on the form of a transaction, and the equipment trust serves the same function as other purchase money forms of financing. In fact, a form known as the "New York equipment trust" comes closer to a conditional sale contract then it does to a Pennsylvania equipment trust, and thus the former exclusion left substantial uncertainty. Railway financing on rolling stock will continue to be exempt from the filing provisions of Article 9 by virtue of Section 9–302(3) and (4). Thus, the principal purpose of the former exclusion will be retained. There is, however, no reason why the other provisions of Article 9 as to the rights of parties, manner of foreclosure, etc., should not be available to the parties to railway financing, since these problems are not adequately covered in any other statutes.

A new paragraph (e) has been added to make clear that this Article does not apply to security interests created by governmental debtors.

Other changes reflect the elimination of the term "contract rights" and the fact that, while transfers of claims under insurance policies and deposit accounts are in general excluded from the Article by this section, proceeds claims thereto are subject to Section 9–306.

§ 9–105. Definitions and Index of Definitions.

(1) In this Article unless the context otherwise requires:

(a) "Account debtor" means the person who is obligated on an account, chattel paper[, contract right] or general intangible;

(b) "Chattel paper" means a writing or writings which evidence both a monetary obligation and a security interest in or a lease of specific goods, but a charter or other contract involving the use or hire of a vessel is not chattel paper. When a transaction is evidenced both by such a security agreement or a lease and by an instrument or a series of instruments, the group of writings taken together constitutes chattel paper;

(c) "Collateral" means the property subject to a security interest, and includes accounts[, contract rights] and chattel paper which have been sold;

(d) "Debtor" means the person who owes payment or other performance of the obligation secured, whether or not he owns or has rights in the collateral, and includes the seller of accounts[, contract rights] or chattel paper. Where the debtor and the owner of the collateral are not the same person, the term "debtor" means the owner of the collateral in any provision of the Article dealing with the collateral, the obligor in any provision dealing with the obligation, and may include both where the context so requires;

(e) "Deposit account" means a demand, time, savings, passbook or like account maintained with a bank, savings and loan association, credit union or like organization, other than an account evidenced by a certificate of deposit;

(f) [(e)] "Document" means document of title as defined in the general definitions of Article 1 (Section 1–201) [;], and a receipt of the kind described in subsection (2) of Section 7–201;

(g) "Encumbrance" includes real estate mortgages and other liens on real estate and all other rights in real estate that are not ownership interests;

(h) [(f)] "Goods" includes all things which are movable at the time the security interest attaches or which are fixtures (Section 9-313), but does not include money, documents, instruments, accounts, chattel paper, general intangibles, [contract rights and other things in action,] or minerals or the like (including oil and gas) before extraction. "Goods" also includes standing timber which is to be cut and removed under a conveyance or contract for sale, the unborn young of animals, and growing crops;

(i) [(g)] "Instrument" means a negotiable instrument (defined in Section 3-104), or a security (defined in Section 8-102) or any other writing which evidences a right to the payment of money and is not itself a security agreement or lease and is of a type which is in ordinary course of business transferred by delivery with any necessary indorsement or assignment;

(j) "Mortgage" means a consensual interest created by a real estate mortgage, a trust deed on real estate, or the like;

(k) An advance is made "pursuant to commitment" if the secured party has bound himself to make it, whether or not a subsequent event of default or other event not within his control has relieved or may relieve him from his obligation;

(*l*) [(h)] "Security agreement" means an agreement which creates or provides for a security interest;

(m) [(i)] "Secured party" means a lender, seller or other person in whose favor there is a security interest, including a person to whom accounts[, contract rights] or chattel paper have been sold. When the holders of obligations issued under an indenture of trust, equipment trust agreement or the like are represented by a trustee or other person, the representative is the secured party;

(n) "Transmitting utility" means any person primarily engaged in the railroad, street railway or trolley bus business, the electric or electronics communications transmission business, the transmission of goods by pipeline, or the transmission or the production and transmission of electricity, steam, gas or water, or the provision of sewer service.

(2) Other definitions applying to this Article and the sections in which they appear are:

"Account". Section 9-106.

"Attach". Section 9-203.

"Construction mortgage". Section 9-313(1).

"Consumer goods". Section 9-109(1).

["Contract right". Section 9-106.]

"Equipment". Section 9-109(2).

"Farm products". Section 9-109(3).

"Fixture". Section 9-313.

"Fixture filing". Section 9-313.

"General intangibles". Section 9-106.

"Inventory". Section 9-109(4).

"Lien creditor". Section 9-301(3).

"Proceeds". Section 9-306(1).

"Purchase money security interest". Section 9-107.

"United States". Section 9-103.

(3) The following definitions in other Articles apply to this Article:

"Check". Section 3-104.

"Contract for sale". Section 2-106.

"Holder in due course". Section 3-302.

"Note". Section 3-104.

"Sale". Section 2-106.

(4) In addition Article 1 contains general definitions and principles of construction and interpretation applicable throughout this Article.

Reasons for 1972 Change

A definition of "transmitting utility" has been added to identify a class of debtor with special filing problems on farflung properties, for which special filing rules are stated in Part 4.

A definition of "deposit account" has been added to facilitate references to such accounts in the section on proceeds (Section 9-306).

A definition of "pursuant to commitment" has been added as the basis for use of this concept in Sections 9-301, 9-307, and 9-312.

Definitions of "encumbrance" and "mortgage" have been added as the basis for the use thereof in Section 9-313.

The definition of "document" has been amended to include therein the kind of receipt issued by a person who is not technically a warehouseman, as described in Section 7-201(2).

The exclusion of "other things in action" from the definition of "goods" has been deleted as unnecessary. "General intangibles", which under Section 9-106 includes "things in action", are themselves excluded from the definition of goods.

Other minor changes reflect the elimination of the classification "contract right" in Section 9-106.

§ 9-106. Definitions: "Account"; ["Contract Right";] "General Intangibles".

"Account" means any right to payment for goods sold or leased or for services rendered which is not evidenced by an instrument or chattel paper[.], whether or not it has been earned by performance. ["Contract right" means any right to payment under a contract not yet earned by performance and not evidenced by an instrument or chattel paper.] "General intangibles" means any personal property (including things in action) other than goods, accounts, [contract rights,] chattel paper, documents, [and] instruments, and money. All rights to payment earned or unearned under a charter or other contract involving the use or hire of a vessel and all rights incident to the charter or contract are [contract rights and neither] accounts [nor general intangibles].

Reasons for 1972 Change

The term "contract right" has been eliminated as unnecessary. As indicated by a sentence now being eliminated from Section 9-306(1), "contract right" was thought of as an "account" before the right to payment became unconditional by performance by the creditor. But the distinction between "account" and "contract right" was not used in the Article except in subsection (2) to Section 9-318 on the right of original parties to modify an assigned contract, and that subsection has been redrafted to preserve the distinction without needing the term "contract right". The term has been troublesome in creating a "proceeds" problem where a contract right becomes an "account" by performance; in the Code's former denial that there could be any right in an account until it came into existence (former Section 9-204(2)(d)), notwithstanding a security interest in the preexisting contract right; and in the danger of inadequate description in financing statements by claiming "accounts" or "general intangibles" when before performance they should have been described as "contract rights"; and in other respects.

"Money" is expressly excluded from the catch-all definition, "general intangible", to preclude any possible reading that a security interest in money may be perfected by filing.

The other changes are conforming changes.

§ 9-114. Consignment.

(1) A person who delivers goods under a consignment which is not a security interest and who would be required to file under this Article by paragraph (3)(c) of Section 2-326 has priority over a secured party who is or becomes a creditor of the consignee and who would have a perfected security interest in the goods if they were the property of the consignee, and also has priority with respect to identifiable cash proceeds received on or before delivery of the goods to a buyer, if

(a) the consignor complies with the filing provision of the Article on Sales with respect to consignments (paragraph (3)(c) of Section 2-326) before the consignee receives possession of the goods; and

(b) the consignor gives notification in writing to the holder of the security interest if the holder has filed a financing statement covering the same types of goods before the date of the filing made by the consignor; and

(c) the holder of the security interest receives the notification within five years before the consignee receives possession of the goods; and

(d) the notification states that the consignor expects to deliver goods on consignment to the consignee, describing the goods by item or type.

(2) In the case of a consignment which is not a security interest and in which the requirements of the preceding subsection have not been met, a person who delivers goods to another is subordinate to a person who would have a perfected security interest in the goods if they were the property of the debtor.

Reasons for 1972 Adoption of New Section

An uncertainty has existed under the 1962 Code whether the filing rule in Section 2-326(3) applicable to true consignments requires only filing under Part 4 of Article 9 or also requires notice to prior inventory secured parties of the debtor under Section 9-312(3). The new Section 9-114 accepts the latter view, and provides in substance that, in order to protect his ownership of the consigned goods, the consignor must give the same notice to an inventory secured party of the debtor that he would have to give if his transaction with the consignee was in the form of a security transaction instead of in the form of a consignment. This new section follows closely the language of Section 9-312(3).

PART 2

VALIDITY OF SECURITY AGREEMENT AND RIGHTS OF PARTIES THERETO

§ 9-203. Attachment and Enforceability of Security Interest; Proceeds; Formal Requisites.

[(1) Subject to the provisions of Section 4-208 on the security interest of a collecting bank and Section 9-113 on a security interest arising under the Article on Sales, a security interest is not enforceable against the debtor or third parties unless

(a) the collateral is in the possession of the secured party; or

(b) the debtor has signed a security agreement which contains a description of the collateral and in addition, when the security interest covers crops or oil, gas or minerals to be extracted or timber to be cut, a description of the land concerned. In describing collateral, the word "proceeds" is sufficient without further description to cover proceeds of any character.]

(1) Subject to the provisions of Section 4-208 on the security interest of a collecting bank and Section 9-113 on a security interest arising under the Article on Sales, a security interest is not enforceable against the debtor or third parties with respect to the collateral and does not attach unless

(a) the collateral is in the possession of the secured party pursuant to agreement, or the debtor has signed a security agreement which contains a description of the collateral and in addition, when the security interest covers crops growing or to be grown or timber to be cut, a description of the land concerned; and

(b) value has been given; and

(c) the debtor has rights in the collateral.

(2) A security interest attaches when it becomes enforceable against the debtor with respect to the collateral. Attachment occurs as soon as all of the events specified in subsection (1) have taken place unless explicit agreement postpones the time of attaching.

(3) Unless otherwise agreed a security agreement gives the secured party the rights to proceeds provided by Section 9-306.

(4) [(2)] A transaction, although subject to this Article, is also subject to ______ *, and in the case of conflict between the provisions of this Article and any such statute, the provisions of such statute control. Failure to comply with any applicable statute has only the effect which is specified therein.

Note: *At * in subsection (4) insert reference to any local statute regulating small loans, retail installment sales and the like.*

The foregoing subsection (4) is designed to make it clear that certain transactions, although subject to this Article, must also comply with other applicable legislation.

This Article is designed to regulate all the "security" aspects of transactions within its scope. There is, however, much regulatory legislation, particularly in the consumer field, which supplements this Article and should not be repealed by its enactment. Examples are small loan acts, retail installment selling acts and the like. Such acts may provide for licensing and rate regulation and may prescribe particular forms of contract. Such provisions should remain in force despite the enactment of this Article. On the other hand if a retail installment selling act contains provisions on filing, rights on default, etc., such provisions should be repealed as inconsistent with this Article[.] except that inconsistent provisions as to deficiencies, penalties, etc., in the Uniform Consumer Credit Code and other recent related legislation should remain because those statutes were drafted after the substantial enactment of the Article and with the intention of modifying certain provisions of this Article as to consumer credit.

Reasons for 1972 Change

Subsection (1) has been revised to incorporate into the concept of enforceability of a security interest the elements of agreement, value, and rights in the collateral, which formerly were stated in Section 9–204. These are combined with the requirement of written agreement (unless the security interest is evidenced by possession of the collateral by the secured party), and the security interest is said to "attach" when all of the events specified have occurred. This drafting cures the former anomaly that a security interest could attach and be perfected, and yet be unenforceable against anyone for lack of a written security agreement.

The requirement that a security agreement covering oil, gas or minerals to be extracted contain a description of the land concerned has been eliminated since the Article does not recognize a security interest in such collateral until it has been extracted from the land.

The former reference to proceeds in subsection (1) has been eliminated and new subsection (3) added to make clear that claims to proceeds under Section 9–306 do not require a statement in the security agreement, for it is assumed that the parties so intend unless otherwise agreed.

§ 9–204. [When Security Interest Attaches;] After-Acquired Property; Future Advances.

[(1) A security interest cannot attach until there is agreement (subsection (3) of Section 1–201) that it attach and value is given and the debtor has rights in the collateral. It attaches as soon as all of the events in the preceding sentence have taken place unless explicit agreement postpones the time of attaching.]

[(2) For the purposes of this section the debtor has no rights

(a) in crops until they are planted or otherwise become growing crops, in the young of livestock until they are conceived;

(b) in fish until caught, in oil, gas or minerals until they are extracted, in timber until it is cut;

(c) in a contract right until the contract has been made;

(d) in an account until it comes into existence.]

[(3) Except as provided in subsection (4) a security agreement may provide that collateral, whenever acquired, shall secure all obligations covered by the security agreement.]

[(4) No security interest attaches under an after-acquired property clause

(a) to crops which become such more than one year after the security agreement is executed except that a security interest in crops which is given in conjunction with a lease or a land purchase or improvement transaction evidenced by a contract, mortgage or deed of trust may if so agreed attach to crops to be grown on the land concerned during the period of such real estate transaction;

(b) to consumer goods other than accessions (Section 9–314) when given as additional security unless the debtor acquires rights in them within ten days after the secured party gives value.]

(1) Except as provided in subsection (2), a security agreement may provide that any or all obligations covered by the security agreement are to be secured by after-acquired collateral.

(2) No security interest attaches under an after-acquired property clause to consumer goods other than accessions (Section 9–314) when given as additional security unless the debtor acquires rights in them within ten days after the secured party gives value.

(3) [(5)] Obligations covered by a security agreement may include future advances or other value whether or not the advances or value are given pursuant to commitment (subsection (1) of Section 9–105).

Reasons for 1972 Change

Former subsection (1) has been eliminated. The term "attach" has been moved to Section 9–203 and related to the concept of enforceability of the security interest between the parties to the security agreement contained in that section.

Former subsection (2) has been eliminated as unnecessary and in some cases confusing. Its operation appeared to be arbitrary, and it is believed that the questions considered are best left to the courts.

Former subsections (3) and (5), now subsections (1) and (3), have been rewritten for clarity.

Former subsection (4) is redesignated (2), and clause (a) thereof relating to crops eliminated. That clause provided that no security interest in crops attaches under an after-acquired property clause to crops which become such more than one year after the security agreement, unless the agreement involved certain real estate transactions. The obvious purpose of this provision was to protect a necessitous farmer from encumbering his crops for many years in the future. The provision did not work because there was no corresponding limit on the scope of a financing statement covering crops, and under the Code's notice-filing rules the priority position of a security arrangement covering successive crops would be as effectively protected by the filing of a first financing statement whether the granting clause as to successive crops was in one security agreement with an after-acquired property clause or in a succession of security agreements. On the other hand the clause did require an annual security agreement for crops even when the encumbrance on crops was agreed to as part of a long-term financing covering farm machinery and other assets. The provision thus appeared to be meaningless in operation except to cause unnecessary paperwork, but it did introduce some element of uncertainty as to its purpose.

§ 9-205. Use or Disposition of Collateral Without Accounting Permissible.

A security interest is not invalid or fraudulent against creditors by reason of liberty in the debtor to use, commingle or dispose of all or part of the collateral (including returned or repossessed goods) or to collect or compromise accounts [contract rights] or chattel paper, or to accept the return of goods or make repossessions, or to use, commingle or dispose of proceeds, or by reason of the failure of the secured party to require the debtor to account for proceeds or replace collateral. This section does not relax the requirements of possession where perfection of a security interest depends upon possession of the collateral by the secured party or by a bailee.

Reasons for 1972 Change

The change reflects the deletion of the defined term "contract right" from the Article.

PART 3

RIGHTS OF THIRD PARTIES; PERFECTED AND UNPERFECTED SECURITY INTERESTS; RULES OF PRIORITY

§ 9-301. Persons Who Take Priority Over Unperfected Security Interests; Right of "Lien Creditor".

(1) Except as otherwise provided in subsection (2), an unperfected security interest is subordinate to the rights of

(a) persons entitled to priority under Section 9-312;

(b) a person who becomes a lien creditor [without knowledge of the security interest and] before [it] the security interest is perfected;

(c) in the case of goods, instruments, documents, and chattel paper, a person who is not a secured party and who is a transferee in bulk or other buyer not in ordinary course of business, or is a buyer of farm products in ordinary course of business, to the extent that he gives value and receives delivery of the collateral without knowledge of the security interest and before it is perfected;

(d) in the case of accounts [, contract rights,] and general intangibles, a person who is not a secured party and who is a transferee to the extent that he gives value without knowledge of the security interest and before it is perfected.

(2) If the secured party files with respect to a purchase money security interest before or within ten days after the debtor receives possession of the collateral [comes into possession of the debtor], he takes priority over the rights of a transferee in bulk or of a lien creditor which arise between the time the security interest attaches and the time of filing.

(3) A "lien creditor" means a creditor who has acquired a lien on the property involved by attachment, levy or the like and includes an assignee for benefit of creditors from the time of assignment, and a trustee in bankruptcy from the date of the filing of the petition or a receiver in equity from the time of appointment. [Unless all the creditors represented had knowledge of the security interest such a representative of creditors is a lien creditor without knowledge even though he personally has knowledge of the security interest.]

(4) A person who becomes a lien creditor while a security interest is perfected takes subject to the security interest only to the extent that it secures advances made before he becomes a lien creditor or within 45 days thereafter or made without knowledge of the lien or pursuant to a commitment entered into without knowledge of the lien.

Reasons for 1972 Change

Paragraph (1)(b) has been amended to eliminate the element of knowledge in the conditions under which a lien creditor may defeat an unperfected security interest. Knowledge of the security interest will no longer subordinate the lien creditor to the unfiled security interest. The former section denied the lien creditor priority even though he had no knowledge when he got involved by extending credit, if he acquired knowledge while attempting to extricate himself. It was completely inconsistent in spirit with the rules of priority between security interests, where knowledge plays a very minor role.

The change in subsection (2) is made to conform the language to that of the related provision in Section 9-312(4).

The second sentence of subsection (3) is deleted because the question of knowledge has been eliminated from paragraph (1)(b).

New subsection (4) deals with the question of the extent to which advances made under a perfected security interest after the rights of a lien creditor have attached to the collateral will come ahead of the position of the lien creditor. This subsection should be read with Section 9-307(3) (which deals with the same problem in the case of an intervening buyer) and Section 9-312(7) (which deals with the same problem in the case of a secured party), and paragraph (5) of Reasons for Change under Section 9-312.

In the case of the lien creditors dealt with by this subsection, the rule chosen is crucial to the priority of the security interest for advances over a federal tax lien for 45 days after the tax lien has been filed, as contemplated under section 6323(c)(2) and (d) of the Internal Revenue Code of 1954 as amended by the Federal Tax Lien Act of 1966. The actual importance of the priority rule chosen between a secured party and possible lien creditors during the 45 days is believed to be slight; but the rule chosen is essential to give the secured party the protection against Federal tax liens believed to have been intended by the Federal Tax Lien Act of 1966, the operation of which is made to depend on state law. The rule of state law was not certain before this revision. Accordingly, the priority of the security interest for future advances over the judgment lien has to be absolute for the 45 days, without regard to any knowledge of the secured party that the judgment lien exists. After the 45 days the priority of the security interest depends on the secured party's lack of knowledge of the lien at the time he makes the subsequent advance or commits to do so.

§ 9-302. When Filing Is Required to Perfect Security Interest; Security Interests to Which Filing Provisions of This Article Do Not Apply.

(1) A financing statement must be filed to perfect all security interests except the following:

(a) a security interest in collateral in possession of the secured party under Section 9-305;

(b) a security interest temporarily perfected in instruments or documents without delivery under Section 9-304 or in proceeds for a 10 day period under Section 9-306;

[(c) a purchase money security interest in farm equipment having a purchase price not in excess of $2500; but filing is required for a fixture under Section 9-313 or for a motor vehicle required to be licensed;]

(c) a security interest created by an assignment of a beneficial interest in a trust or a decedent's estate;

(d) a purchase money security interest in consumer goods; but filing is required [for a fixture under Section 9-313 or for a motor vehicle required to be licensed;] for a motor vehicle required to be registered; and fixture filing is required for priority over conflicting interests in fixtures to the extent provided in Section 9-313;

(e) an assignment of accounts [or contract rights] which does not alone or in conjunction with other assignments to the same assignee transfer a significant part of the outstanding accounts [or contract rights] of the assignor;

(f) a security interest of a collecting bank (Section 4-208) or arising under the Article on Sales (see Section 9-113) or covered in subsection (3) of this section;

(g) an assignment for the benefit of all the creditors of the transferor, and subsequent transfers by the assignee thereunder.

(2) If a secured party assigns a perfected security interest, no filing under this Article is required in order to continue the perfected status of the security interest against creditors of and transferees from the original debtor.

[(3) The filing provisions of this Article do not apply to a security interest in property subject to a statute

(a) of the United States which provides for a national registration or filing of all security interests in such property; or

Note: *States to select either Alternative A or Alternative B.*

Alternative A—

(b) of this state which provides for central filing of, or which requires indication on a certificate of title of, such security interests in such property.

Alternative B—

(b) of this state which provides for central filing of security interests in such property, or in a motor vehicle which is not inventory held for sale for which a certificate of title is required under the statutes of this state if a notation of such a security interest can be indicated by a public official on a certificate or a duplicate thereof.]

[(4) A security interest in property covered by a statute described in subsection (3) can be perfected only by registration or filing under that statute or by indication of the security interest on a certificate of title or duplicate thereof by a public official.]

(3) The filing of a financing statement otherwise required by this Article is not necessary or effective to perfect a security interest in property subject to

(a) a statute or treaty of the United States which provides for a national or international registration or a national or international certificate of title or which specifies a place of filing different from that specified in this Article for filing of the security interest; or

(b) the following statutes of this state; [[list any certificate of title statute covering automobiles, trailers, mobile homes, boats, farm tractors, or the like, and any central filing statute *.]]; but during any period in which collateral is inventory held for sale by a person who is in the business of selling goods of that kind, the filing provisions of this Article (Part 4) apply to a security interest in that collateral created by him as debtor; or

(c) a certificate of title statute of another jurisdiction under the law of which indication of a security interest on the certificate is required as a condition of perfection (subsection (2) of Section 9–103).

(4) Compliance with a statute or treaty described in subsection (3) is equivalent to the filing of a financing statement under this Article, and a security interest in property subject to the statute or treaty can be perfected only by compliance therewith except as provided in Section 9–103 on multiple state transactions. Duration and renewal of perfection of a security interest perfected by compliance with the statute or treaty are governed by the provisions of the statute or treaty; in other respects the security interest is subject to this Article.

* **Note:** *It is recommended that the provisions of certificate of title acts for perfection of security interests by notation on the certificates should be amended to exclude coverage of inventory held for sale.*

Reasons for 1972 Change

Former paragraph (1)(c), which created a nonfiling rule for purchase money security interests in certain farm equipment, has been eliminated. The analogy drawn in the 1962 Code of farm equipment to consumer goods (for which a similar non-filing rule is provided in paragraph (1)(d)) is believed to be inappropriate. The effect of the rule was to make farmers' equipment unavailable to them as collateral for loans from some lenders.

A new paragraph (1)(c) exempts from filing rules security interests created by assignments of beneficial interests in trusts and estates, because these assignments are not ordinarily thought of as subject to this Article, and a filing rule might operate to defeat many assignments.

The requirement of filing for purchase-money security interests in consumer goods which are fixtures has been made applicable only for priority against real estate interests (Section 9-313).

A new paragraph (1)(g) has been added exempting from filing assignments for the benefit of creditors because they are not financing transactions.

Former subsections (3) and (4) have been rewritten into new subsections (3) and (4). The alternatives of former subsection (3) had proved unacceptable formulations in many states. The states adopted non-uniform amendments to use language more closely geared to their certificate of title laws than the uniform alternatives. It is believed that the simplest thing is to have each state specify its statutes intended to be applicable as it adopts the revised Article 9.

Former Alternative B to subsection (3) has been abandoned as no longer serving any purpose: it had been an attempt to convert obsolete non-mandatory certificate of title laws into laws under which notation on the certificate of title was the necessary method of perfection of a security interest.

Subsection (3) continues to carry the thought that was formerly only in Alternative B—namely, that the certificate of title procedure does not control the perfection of inventory or "floor plan" security interests, but instead normal Code filing rules are applicable. Non-uniform variations to the contrary under some state laws are believed to increase operating burdens and it is hoped that the states will abandon them.

References to federal statutes have been broadened to include treaties.

§ 9-304. Perfection of Security Interest in Instruments, Documents, and Goods Covered by Documents; Perfection by Permissive Filing; Temporary Perfection Without Filing or Transfer of Possession.

(1) A security interest in chattel paper or negotiable documents may be perfected by filing. A security interest in money or instruments (other than instruments which constitute part of chattel paper) can be perfected only by the secured party's taking possession, except as provided in subsections (4) and (5) of this section and subsections (2) and (3) of Section 9-306 on proceeds.

(2) During the period that goods are in the possession of the issuer of a negotiable document therefor, a security interest in the goods is perfected by perfecting a security interest in the document, and any security interest in the goods otherwise perfected during such period is subject thereto.

(3) A security interest in goods in the possession of a bailee other than one who has issued a negotiable document therefor is perfected by issuance of a document in the name of the secured party or by the bailee's receipt of notification of the secured party's interest or by filing as to the goods.

(4) A security interest in instruments or negotiable documents is perfected without filing or the taking of possession for a period of 21 days from the

time it attaches to the extent that it arises for new value given under a written security agreement.

(5) A security interest remains perfected for a period of 21 days without filing where a secured party having a perfected security interest in an instrument, a negotiable document or goods in possession of a bailee other than one who has issued a negotiable document therefor

(a) makes available to the debtor the goods or documents representing the goods for the purpose of ultimate sale or exchange or for the purpose of loading, unloading, storing, shipping, transshipping, manufacturing, processing or otherwise dealing with them in a manner preliminary to their sale or exchange, [; or] but priority between conflicting security interests in the goods is subject to subsection (3) of Section 9–312; or

(b) delivers the instrument to the debtor for the purpose of ultimate sale or exchange or of presentation, collection, renewal or registration of transfer.

(6) After the 21 day period in subsections (4) and (5) perfection depends upon compliance with applicable provisions of this Article.

Reasons for 1972 Change

The change in subsection (1) corrects an inadvertent omission in the 1962 Text, and makes clear that a security interest in money cannot be perfected by filing.

A provision has been added to subsection (5) making it clear that the 21-day period referred to therein deals only with perfection, but that there must be compliance with the notice provisions of Section 9–312(3) in order to achieve priority over earlier inventory financers. Corresponding clarifying changes have been made in Section 9–312(3).

§ 9–305. When Possession by Secured Party Perfects Security Interest Without Filing.

A security interest in letters of credit and advices of credit (subsection (2)(a) of Section 5–116), goods, instruments, money, negotiable documents or chattel paper may be perfected by the secured party's taking possession of the collateral. If such collateral other than goods covered by a negotiable document is held by a bailee, the secured party is deemed to have possession from the time the bailee receives notification of the secured party's interest. A security interest is perfected by possession from the time possession is taken without relation back and continues only so long as possession is retained, unless otherwise specified in this Article. The security interest may be otherwise perfected as provided in this Article before or after the period of possession by the secured party.

Reasons for 1972 Change

The change corresponds to the change in Section 9–304 to clarify the special position of money.

§ 9-306. "Proceeds"; Secured Party's Rights on Disposition of Collateral.

(1) ["Proceeds" includes whatever is received when collateral or proceeds is sold, exchanged, collected or otherwise disposed of. The term also includes the account arising when the right to payment is earned under a contract right.]

"Proceeds" includes whatever is received upon the sale, exchange, collection or other disposition of collateral or proceeds. Insurance payable by reason of loss or damage to the collateral is proceeds, except to the extent that it is payable to a person other than a party to the security agreement. Money, checks, deposit accounts, and the like are "cash proceeds". All other proceeds are "non-cash proceeds".

(2) Except where this Article otherwise provides, a security interest continues in collateral notwithstanding sale, exchange or other disposition thereof [by the debtor] unless [his action was] the disposition was authorized by the secured party in the security agreement or otherwise, and also continues in any identifiable proceeds including collections received by the debtor.

(3) The security interest in proceeds is a continuously perfected security interest if the interest in the original collateral was perfected but it ceases to be a perfected security interest and becomes unperfected ten days after receipt of the proceeds by the debtor unless

[(a) a filed financing statement covering the original collateral also covers proceeds; or]

(a) a filed financing statement covers the original collateral and the proceeds are collateral in which a security interest may be perfected by filing in the office or offices where the financing statement has been filed and, if the proceeds are acquired with cash proceeds, the description of collateral in the financing statement indicates the types of property constituting the proceeds; or

(b) a filed financing statement covers the original collateral and the proceeds are identifiable cash proceeds; or

(c) [(b)] the security interest in the proceeds is perfected before the expiration of the ten day period.

Except as provided in this section, a security interest in proceeds can be perfected only by the methods or under the circumstances permitted in this Article for original collateral of the same type.

(4) In the event of insolvency proceedings instituted by or against a debtor, a secured party with a perfected security interest in proceeds has a perfected security interest only in the following proceeds:

(a) in identifiable non-cash proceeds[;] and in separate deposit accounts containing only proceeds;

(b) in identifiable cash proceeds in the form of money which is [not] neither commingled with other money [or] nor deposited in a [bank] deposit account prior to the insolvency proceedings;

(c) in identifiable cash proceeds in the form of checks and the like which are not deposited in a [bank] deposit account prior to the insolvency proceedings; and

(d) in all cash and [bank] deposit accounts of the debtor [if other cash] in which proceeds have been commingled with other funds, [or deposited in a bank account,] but the perfected security interest under this paragraph (d) is

(i) subject to any right of set-off; and

(ii) limited to an amount not greater than the amount of any cash proceeds received by the debtor within ten days before the institution of the insolvency proceedings [and commingled or deposited in a bank account prior to the insolvency proceedings less the amount of cash proceeds received by the debtor and paid over to the secured party during the ten day period,] less the sum of (I) the payments to the secured party on account of cash proceeds received by the debtor during such period and (II) the cash proceeds received by the debtor during such period to which the secured party is entitled under paragraphs (a) through (c) of this subsection (4).

(5) If a sale of goods results in an account or chattel paper which is transferred by the seller to a secured party, and if the goods are returned to or are repossessed by the seller or the secured party, the following rules determine priorities:

(a) If the goods were collateral at the time of sale, for an indebtedness of the seller which is still unpaid, the original security interest attaches again to the goods and continues as a perfected security interest if it was perfected at the time when the goods were sold. If the security interest was originally perfected by a filing which is still effective, nothing further is required to continue the perfected status; in any other case, the secured party must take possession of the returned or repossessed goods or must file.

(b) An unpaid transferee of the chattel paper has a security interest in the goods against the transferor. Such security interest is prior to a security interest asserted under paragraph (a) to the extent that the transferee of the chattel paper was entitled to priority under Section 9-308.

(c) An unpaid transferee of the account has a security interest in the goods against the transferor. Such security interest is subordinate to a security interest asserted under paragraph (a).

(d) A security interest of an unpaid transferee asserted under paragraph (b) or (c) must be perfected for protection against creditors of the transferor and purchasers of the returned or repossessed goods.

Reasons for 1972 Change

The first sentence of subsection (1) is rewritten for clarity.

The former second sentence of subsection (1) is omitted consistently with the abandonment of the term "contract right" in Section 9-106.

The new second sentence of subsection (1) is intended to overrule various cases to the effect that proceeds of insurance on collateral are not proceeds of the collateral. The "except" clause is intended to say that if the insurance contract specifies the person to whom the insurance is payable, the concept of "proceeds" will not interfere with performance of the contract.

Heretofore an apparent inconsistency and ambiguity has existed between the last sentence of Section 9-203(1)(b) of the 1962 Code, which indicated that a claim to proceeds had to be an express term of a security agreement, and Section 9-306(2), which indicated that a right to proceeds was automatic without reference to a term of a security agreement. This ambiguity has been clarified in favor of an automatic right to proceeds, on the theory that this is the intent of the parties, unless otherwise agreed. Further, there has been eliminated the requirement of claiming proceeds in a financing statement, which had resulted in a checking of a box on each financing statement in order to claim proceeds. Instead, the filed claim to the original collateral is treated as constituting automatically a filing as to proceeds. To this principle, a limitation has been stated: Where the filing as to the original collateral is an inappropriate means of perfection as to proceeds of certain types, or is made at a place that is inappropriate as to such proceeds, the filed claim to the original collateral perfects the claim to proceeds for only 10 days. One example of this is negotiable instruments as proceeds, as to which filing is inappropriate under Section 9-304(1). Another example is the case of accounts as proceeds of inventory, as to which under the rules of Section 9-103 the state of filing for the accounts might be different from the state of filing for the inventory.

The revised subsection (4) is a clarification based on the California revision. It makes clear that the claim to cash allowed in insolvency is exclusive of any other claim based on tracing.

§ 9-307. Protection of Buyers of Goods.

(1) A buyer in ordinary course of business (subsection (9) of Section 1-201) other than a person buying farm products from a person engaged in farming operations takes free of a security interest created by his seller even though the security interest is perfected and even though the buyer knows of its existence.

(2) In the case of consumer goods [and in the case of farm equipment having an original purchase price not in excess of $2500 (other than fixtures, see Section 9-313)], a buyer takes free of a security interest even though perfected if he buys without knowledge of the security interest, for value and for his own personal, family or household purposes [or his own farming operations] unless prior to the purchase the secured party has filed a financing statement covering such goods.

<u>(3) A buyer other than a buyer in ordinary course of business (subsection (1) of this section) takes free of a security interest to the extent that it secures future advances made after the secured party acquires knowledge of the purchase, or more than 45 days after the purchase, whichever first occurs, unless made pursuant to a commitment entered into without knowledge of the purchase and before the expiration of the 45 day period.</u>

Reasons for 1972 Change

The change in subsection (2) is a conforming change made necessary by the deletion of Section 9-302(1)(c) of the 1962 Code, which provided in substance that a purchase money security interest in farm equipment having an original purchase price not in excess of $2500 need not be filed. The omission of that provision in Subsection 9-302(1) makes any corresponding reference unnecessary in the present section.

Subsection (3) is one of three new provisions clarifying the extent to which future advances under a security interest may outrank an intervening right. See Sections 9-301(4) and 9-312(7) and paragraph (5) of Reasons for Change under Section 9-312.

§ 9-308. Purchase of Chattel Paper and [Non-Negotiable] Instruments.

[A purchaser of chattel paper or a non-negotiable instrument who gives new value and takes possession of it in the ordinary course of his business and without knowledge that the specific paper or instrument is subject to a security interest has priority over a security interest which is perfected under Section 9-304 (permissive filing and temporary perfection). A purchaser of chattel paper who gives new value and takes possession of it in the ordinary course of his business has priority over a security interest in chattel paper which is claimed merely as proceeds of inventory subject to a security interest (Section 9-306), even though he knows that the specific paper is subject to the security interest.]

A purchaser of chattel paper or an instrument who gives new value and takes possession of it in the ordinary course of his business has priority over a security interest in the chattel paper or instrument

(a) which is perfected under Section 9-304 (permissive filing and temporary perfection) or under Section 9-306 (perfection as to proceeds) if he acts without knowledge that the specific paper or instrument is subject to a security interest; or

(b) which is claimed merely as proceeds of inventory subject to a security interest (Section 9-306) even though he knows that the specific paper or instrument is subject to the security interest.

Reasons for 1972 Change

The section has been rewritten for clarity.

Another purpose of the changes is to make the rules of this section applicable to negotiable instruments. Heretofore, the holder of a negotiable instrument was under some circumstances in a less protected position against competing claims than the holder of chattel paper. The holder of a negotiable instrument had protection only if he achieved the holder in due course status referred to in Section 9-309, which status would not be achieved if the holder had knowledge of a conflicting proceeds claim. In contrast, the holder of chattel paper who met the stated conditions was protected under the second sentence of Section 9-308 of the 1962 Code even if he had knowledge of the conflicting proceeds claim. Under the changes, the holder of a negotiable instrument who may not qualify as holder in due course may nevertheless qualify for the protections of this section.

§ 9-312. Priorities Among Conflicting Security Interests in the Same Collateral.

[(1) The rules of priority stated in the following sections shall govern where applicable: Section 4-208 with respect to the security interest of collecting banks in items being collected, accompanying documents and proceeds; Section 9-301 on certain priorities; Section 9-304 on goods covered by documents; Section 9-306 on proceeds and repossessions; Section 9-307 on buyers of goods; Section 9-308 on possessory against non-possessory interests in chattel paper or non-negotiable instruments; Section 9-309 on security interests in negotiable instruments, documents or securities; Section 9-310 on priorities between perfected security interests and liens by operation of law; Section 9-313 on security interests in fixtures as against interests in real estate; Section 9-314 on security interests in accessions as against interest in goods; Section 9-315 on conflicting security interests where goods lose their identity or become part of a product; and Section 9-316 on contractual subordination.]

(1) The rules of priority stated in other sections of this Part and in the following sections shall govern when applicable: Section 4-208 with respect to the security interests of collecting banks in items being collected, accompanying documents and proceeds; Section 9-103 on security interests related to other jurisdictions; Section 9-114 on consignments.

(2) A perfected security interest in crops for new value given to enable the debtor to produce the crops during the production season and given not more than three months before the crops become growing crops by planting or otherwise takes priority over an earlier perfected security interest to the extent that such earlier interest secures obligations due more than six months before the crops become growing crops by planting or otherwise, even though the person giving new value had knowledge of the earlier security interest.

[(3) A purchase money security interest in inventory collateral has priority over a conflicting security interest in the same collateral if

(a) the purchase money security interest is perfected at the time the debtor receives possession of the collateral; and

(b) any secured party whose security interest is known to the holder of the purchase money security interest or who, prior to the date of the filing made by the holder of the purchase money security interest, had filed a financing statement covering the same items or type of inventory, has received notification of the purchase money security interest before the debtor receives possession of the collateral covered by the purchase money security interest; and

(c) such notification states that the person giving the notice has or expects to acquire a purchase money security interest in inventory of the debtor, describing such inventory by item or type.]

(3) A perfected purchase money security interest in inventory has priority over a conflicting security interest in the same inventory and also has priority in identifiable cash proceeds received on or before the delivery of the inventory to a buyer if

(a) the purchase money security interest is perfected at the time the debtor receives possession of the inventory; and

(b) the purchase money secured party gives notification in writing to the holder of the conflicting security interest if the holder had filed a financing statement covering the same types of inventory (i) before the date of the filing made by the purchase money secured party, or (ii) before the beginning of the 21 day period where the purchase money security interest is temporarily perfected without filing or possession (subsection (5) of Section 9-304); and

(c) the holder of the conflicting security interest receives the notification within five years before the debtor receives possession of the inventory; and

(d) the notification states that the person giving the notice has or expects to acquire a purchase money security interest in inventory of the debtor, describing such inventory by item or type.

(4) A purchase money security interest in collateral other than inventory has priority over a conflicting security interest in the same collateral or its proceeds if the purchase money security interest is perfected at the time the debtor receives possession of the collateral or within ten days thereafter.

(5) In all cases not governed by other rules stated in this section (including cases of purchase money security interests which do not qualify for the special priorities set forth in subsections (3) and (4) of this section), priority between conflicting security interests in the same collateral shall be determined [as follows:

(a) in the order of filing if both are perfected by filing, regardless of which security interest attached first under Section 9-204(1) and whether it attached before or after filing;

(b) in the order of perfection unless both are perfected by filing, regardless of which security interest attached first under Section 9-204(1) and, in the case of a filed security interest, whether it attached before or after filing; and

(c) in the order of attachment under Section 9-204(1) so long as neither is perfected.]

according to the following rules:

(a) Conflicting security interests rank according to priority in time of filing or perfection. Priority dates from the time a filing is first made covering the collateral or the time the security interest is first perfected, whichever is earlier, provided that there is no period thereafter when there is neither filing nor perfection.

(b) So long as conflicting security interests are unperfected, the first to attach has priority.

[(6) For the purpose of the priority rules of the immediately preceding subsection, a continuously perfected security interest shall be treated at all times as if perfected by filing if it was originally so perfected and it shall be treated at all times as if perfected otherwise than by filing if it was originally perfected otherwise than by filing.]

(6) For the purposes of subsection (5) a date of filing or perfection as to collateral is also a date of filing or perfection as to proceeds.

(7) If future advances are made while a security interest is perfected by filing or the taking of possession, the security interest has the same priority for the purposes of subsection (5) with respect to the future advances as it does with respect to the first advance. If a commitment is made before or while the security interest is so perfected, the security interest has the same priority with respect to advances made pursuant thereto. In other cases a perfected security interest has priority from the date the advance is made.

Reasons for 1972 Change

(1) The change in subsection (1) is primarily a simplification of statement.

(2) Changes have been made in subsection (3) to answer unresolved questions under the 1962 Code.

(a) One change answers the question how often a notice must be given under that subsection. The period of five years has been chosen by analogy to the duration of a financing statement.

(b) Another change answers the question of the priority status of the security interest in inventory temporarily perfected for 21 days without filing or perfection in a situation which begins with release of a pledged document under Section 9-304(5). The answer provided is the usual rule that the purchase-money claimant to preserve his priority resulting from the document must give the required notice before the debtor receives possession of the inventory. If the secured party fails to give timely notice, he loses his priority under this subsection.

(c) One of the most widely discussed questions under the 1962 Code was the question of the priority between a person claiming accounts as proceeds of inventory and a person claiming the accounts by direct filing with respect thereto. One issue was whether the special position of an inventory financer as a purchase money financer or as the first financer in the business cycle of the debtor gave him any special position as to accounts resulting from the inventory. In general, as revised, a negative answer has been given, and a prior right to inventory does not confer a prior right to any proceeds except identifiable cash proceeds received on or before the delivery of the inventory (i.e., without the intervention of an account). Other aspects of this issue are discussed under subsection (5) of this section.

(3) A different answer has been given in subsection (4) relating to purchase money security interests in collateral other than inventory. Here, where it is not ordinarily expected that the collateral will be sold and that proceeds will result, it seems appropriate to give the party having a purchase money security interest in the original collateral an equivalent priority in its proceeds. The 1962 Code was unclear on this point.

(4) Existing subsection (5) contains two principal rules. Paragraph (a) is a first-to-file rule where both competing security interests are perfected by filing. Paragraph (b) is a first-to-perfect rule when either of the security interests is or both of them are perfected otherwise than by filing. A traffic rule is provided by existing subsection (6) to the effect that a continuously perfected security interest shall be treated for the purpose of the foregoing rules as if at all times perfected in the manner it was first perfected. The problems raised have been the subject of an enormous legal literature. They are complicated by the unforeseeable effect of the temporary perfection of security interest in proceeds without filing under

Section 9–306, and by speculation as to whether a secured party could claim that his security interest was originally perfected without filing under this rule even though the security interest in proceeds was claimed in his filing as to the original collateral. They are further complicated by the question whether different rules would apply when a financing statement was drawn to cover, e.g., inventory and its proceeds (which would include accounts) and when it was drawn to cover inventory and accounts.

To settle these questions it is proposed to replace the present paragraphs (a) and (b) of subsection (5) by a single rule, subsection (5), and to eliminate existing subsection (6). Together with this treatment should be noted the fact that a filing as to proceeds automatically arises from a filed security interest in original collateral under the proposed revision of Section 9–306(3), subject to limitations therein discussed. New proposed subsection (6) makes it clear that subject to these limitations the time of filing or perfection as to original collateral is the time of filing or perfection as to proceeds.

The rule of proposed subsection (5) ranks conflicting perfected security interests by their priority in time, dating back to the respective times when without interruption the security interests were either perfected or were the subjects of appropriate filings.

Perhaps the most debated subject under Article 9 has been the question whether between conflicting security interests a priority as to original collateral confers a priority as to proceeds. As indicated above, in the case of collateral other than inventory, e.g., equipment, it seems clear that the policy favoring the purchase money secured party in Section 9–312(4) should give him the first claim to the proceeds. This is so even though the security interests will have been perfected simultaneously when the proceeds arise and the debtor acquires rights therein.

Proper policy is much less clear when the collateral involved is inventory and proceeds consisting of accounts. (Policy as to other types of receivables as proceeds is expressed in Sections 9–308 and 9–309). Accounts financing is more important in the economy than the financing of the kinds of inventory that produce accounts, and the desirable rule is one which makes accounts financing certain as to its legal position. Therefore, the rule proposed is that where a financing statement as to accounts is filed first (with or without related inventory financing), the security interest in accounts should not be defeated by any subsequent claim to accounts as proceeds of a security interest in inventory filed later. There is therefore no provision in Section 9–312(3) carrying forward to accounts any priority right in inventory, and proposed subsections (5) and (6) adhere firmly to the principle that a date of filing as to original collateral also defines the date of filing as to proceeds. Correspondingly, a financing statement as to inventory (carrying with it a claim to proceeds) which is filed first will under the same provisions have priority over a later-filed security interest in accounts.

(5) The priority of future advances against an intervening party has been the subject of much discussion and disagreement. Where both interests are filed security interests, the first-to-file rule of present Section 9–312(5)(a) or the corresponding proposed revision is clearly applicable. Under the 1962 Code, the position of an intervening pledgee in reference to a subsequent advance by an earlier-filed secured party is debatable. The proposed unified priority rule of subsection 9–312(5) would indicate that subsequent advances by the first-filed party have priority, and subsequent advances under a security interest perfected by possession likewise have priority over an intervening filed security interest. These priority rules are expressly stated in proposed subsection (7). That proposal also deals with the rare case of the priority position of a subsequent advance made by a secured party whose security interest is temporarily perfected without either filing or possession, against an intervening secured party. Since there is no notice by the usual methods of filing or possession

of the existence of the security interest, the subsequent advances rank only from the actual date of making unless made pursuant to commitment.

Different but related problems exist with reference to the status of subsequent advances when the intervening party is a judgment creditor. He is not directly part of the Code's system of priorities. It seems unfair to make it possible for a debtor and secured party with knowledge of the judgment lien to squeeze out a judgment creditor who has successfully levied on a valuable equity subject to a security interest, by permitting later enlargement of the security interest by an additional advance, unless that advance was committed in advance without such knowledge. Proposed Section 9-301(4) provides that a lien creditor does not take subject to a subsequent advance unless it is given or committed without knowledge, but there is an exception protecting future advances within 45 days after the levy regardless of knowledge. The 45-day period corresponds to a provision on protection of advances made after the filing of tax liens in the Federal Tax Lien Act of 1966.

A similar problem arises where the intervening party is a buyer of the collateral subject to the security interest. While buyers must necessarily take subject to rights of secured parties, the buyer should take subject to subsequent advances only to the extent that they are given "pursuant to commitment" or within the period of 45 days after the purchase but not later than the time that the secured party acquires knowledge of the purchase. It is so proposed in Section 9-307(3). A definition of the quoted phrase appears in Section 9-105.

§ 9-313. Priority of Security Interests in Fixtures.

[(1) The rules of this section do not apply to goods incorporated into a structure in the manner of lumber, bricks, tile, cement, glass, metal work and the like and no security interest in them exists under this Article unless the structure remains personal property under applicable law. The law of this state other than this Act determines whether and when other goods become fixtures. This Act does not prevent creation of an encumbrance upon fixtures or real estate pursuant to the law applicable to real estate.]

[(2) A security interest which attaches to goods before they become fixtures takes priority as to the goods over the claims of all persons who have an interest in the real estate except as stated in subsection (4).]

[(3) A security interest which attaches to goods after they become fixtures is valid against all persons subsequently acquiring interests in the real estate except as stated in subsection (4) but is invalid against any person with an interest in the real estate at the time the security interest attaches to the goods who has not in writing consented to the security interest or disclaimed an interest in the goods as fixtures.]

[(4) The security interests described in subsections (2) and (3) do not take priority over

(a) a subsequent purchaser for value of any interest in the real estate; or

(b) a creditor with a lien on the real estate subsequently obtained by judicial proceedings; or

(c) a creditor with a prior encumbrance of record on the real estate to the extent that he makes subsequent advances

if the subsequent purchase is made, the lien by judicial proceedings is obtained, or the subsequent advance under the prior encumbrance is made or contracted for without knowledge of the security interest and before it is perfected. A purchaser of the real estate at a foreclosure sale other than an encumbrancer purchasing at his own foreclosure sale is a subsequent purchaser within this section.]

(1) In this section and in the provisions of Part 4 of this Article referring to fixture filing, unless the context otherwise requires

(a) goods are "fixtures" when they become so related to particular real estate that an interest in them arises under real estate law

(b) a "fixture filing" is the filing in the office where a mortgage on the real estate would be filed or recorded of a financing statement covering goods which are or are to become fixtures and conforming to the requirements of subsection (5) of Section 9–402

(c) a mortgage is a "construction mortgage" to the extent that it secures an obligation incurred for the construction of an improvement on land including the acquisition cost of the land, if the recorded writing so indicates.

(2) A security interest under this Article may be created in goods which are fixtures or may continue in goods which become fixtures, but no security interest exists under this Article in ordinary building materials incorporated into an improvement on land.

(3) This Article does not prevent creation of an encumbrance upon fixtures pursuant to real estate law.

(4) A perfected security interest in fixtures has priority over the conflicting interest of an encumbrancer or owner of the real estate where

(a) the security interest is a purchase money security interest, the interest of the encumbrancer or owner arises before the goods become fixtures, the security interest is perfected by a fixture filing before the goods become fixtures or within ten days thereafter, and the debtor has an interest of record in the real estate or is in possession of the real estate; or

(b) the security interest is perfected by a fixture filing before the interest of the encumbrancer or owner is of record, the security interest has priority over any conflicting interest of a predecessor in title of the encumbrancer or owner, and the debtor has an interest of record in the real estate or is in possession of the real estate; or

(c) the fixtures are readily removable factory or office machines or readily removable replacements of domestic appliances which are consumer goods, and before the goods become fixtures the security interest is perfected by any method permitted by this Article; or

(d) the conflicting interest is a lien on the real estate obtained by legal or equitable proceedings after the security interest was perfected by any method permitted by this Article.

(5) A security interest in fixtures, whether or not perfected, has priority over the conflicting interest of an encumbrancer or owner of the real estate where

(a) the encumbrancer or owner has consented in writing to the security interest or has disclaimed an interest in the goods as fixtures; or

(b) the debtor has a right to remove the goods as against the encumbrancer or owner. If the debtor's right terminates, the priority of the security interest continues for a reasonable time.

(6) Notwithstanding paragraph (a) of subsection (4) but otherwise subject to subsections (4) and (5), a security interest in fixtures is subordinate to a construction mortgage recorded before the goods become fixtures if the goods become fixtures before the completion of the construction. To the extent that it is given to refinance a construction mortgage, a mortgage has this priority to the same extent as the construction mortgage.

(7) In cases not within the preceding subsections, a security interest in fixtures is subordinate to the conflicting interest of an encumbrancer or owner of the related real estate who is not the debtor.

(8) [(5)] When [under subsections (2) or (3) or (4) a] the secured party has priority over [the claims of all persons who have interests in] all owners and encumbrancers of the real estate, he may, on default, subject to the provisions of Part 5, remove his collateral from the real estate but he must reimburse any encumbrancer or owner of the real estate who is not the debtor and who has not otherwise agreed for the cost of repair of any physical injury, but not for any diminution in value of the real estate caused by the absence of the goods removed or by any necessity of replacing them. A person entitled to reimbursement may refuse permission to remove until the secured party gives adequate security for the performance of this obligation.

Reasons for 1972 Change

As the Code came to be widely enacted, the real estate bar came to realize the impact of the fixture provisions on real estate financing and real estate titles. They apparently had not fully appreciated the impact of these provisions of Article 9 on real estate matters during the enactment of the Code, because of the commonly-held assumption that Article 9 was concerned only with chattel security matters.

The treatment of fixtures in pre-Code law had varied widely from state to state. The treatment in Article 9 was based generally on prior treatment in the Uniform Conditional Sales Act, which, however, had been enacted in only a dozen states. In other states the word "fixture" had come to mean that a former chattel had become real estate for all purposes and that any chattel rights therein were lost. For lawyers trained in such states the Code provisions seemed to be extreme. Some sections of the real estate bar began attempting with some success to have Section 9-313 amended to bring it closer to the pre-Code law in their states. In some states, such as California and Iowa, Section 9-313 simply was not enacted.

Even supporters of Article 9 and of its fixture provisions came to recognize that there were some ambiguities in Section 9-313, particularly in its application to construction mortgages, and also in its failure to make it clear that filing of fixture security interests was to be in real estate records where they could be found by a standard real estate search.

Section 9-313 and related provisions of Part 4 have been redrafted to meet the legitimate criticisms and to make a substantial shift in the law in favor of construction mortgages. The specific changes are described in the 1972 Comments to Section 9-313, and the Comments to the several sections of Part 4.

§ 9-318. Defenses Against Assignee; Modification of Contract After Notification of Assignment; Term Prohibiting Assignment Ineffective; Identification and Proof of Assignment.

(1) Unless an account debtor has made an enforceable agreement not to assert defenses or claims arising out of a sale as provided in Section 9-206 the rights of an assignee are subject to

(a) all the terms of the contract between the account debtor and assignor and any defense or claim arising therefrom; and

(b) any other defense or claim of the account debtor against the assignor which accrues before the account debtor receives notification of the assignment.

(2) So far as the right to payment or a part thereof under an assigned contract has not been fully earned by performance, [right has not already become an account,] and notwithstanding notification of the assignment, any modification of or substitution for the contract made in good faith and in accordance with reasonable commercial standards is effective against an assignee unless the account debtor has otherwise agreed but the assignee acquires corresponding rights under the modified or substituted contract. The assignment may provide that such modification or substitution is a breach by the assignor.

(3) The account debtor is authorized to pay the assignor until the account debtor receives notification that the [account] amount due or to become due has been assigned and that payment is to be made to the assignee. A notification which does not reasonably identify the rights assigned is ineffective. If requested by the account debtor, the assignee must seasonably furnish reasonable proof that the assignment has been made and unless he does so the account debtor may pay the assignor.

(4) A term in any contract between an account debtor and an assignor [which] is ineffective if it prohibits assignment of an account [or contract right to which they are parties is ineffective] or prohibits creation of a security interest in a general intangible for money due or to become due or requires the account debtor's consent to such assignment or security interest.

Reasons for 1972 Change

The principal changes conform to the elimination of the term "contract right" in Section 9-106.

Minor changes in subsections (3) and (4) eliminate technical difficulties in the 1962 Code which arose out of the fact that the term "account debtor" used in these subsections is defined to include debtors under general intangibles and chattel paper, and is therefore broader than the term "account" heretofore used in these subsections. Subsection (4) is broadened to apply to general intangibles for money due as well as to accounts.

PART 4

FILING

§ 9-401. Place of Filing; Erroneous Filing; Removal of Collateral.

First Alternative Subsection (1)

(1) The proper place to file in order to perfect a security interest is as follows:

(a) when the collateral is timber to be cut or is minerals or the like (including oil and gas) or accounts subject to subsection (5) of Section 9-103, or when the financing statement is filed as a fixture filing (Section 9-313) and the collateral is goods which [at the time the security interest attaches] are or are to become fixtures, then in the office where a mortgage on the real estate [concerned] would be filed or recorded;

(b) in all other cases, in the office of the [[Secretary of State]].

Second Alternative Subsection (1)

(1) The proper place to file in order to perfect a security interest is as follows:

(a) when the collateral is equipment used in farming operations, or farm products, or accounts [, contract rights] or general intangibles arising from or relating to the sale of farm products by a farmer, or consumer goods, then in the office of the ______ in the county of the debtor's residence or if the debtor is not a resident of this state then in the office of the ______ in the county where the goods are kept, and in addition when the collateral is crops growing or to be grown in the office of the ______ in the county where the land [on which the crops are growing or to be grown] is located;

(b) when the collateral is [goods which at the time the security interest attaches are or are to become fixtures] timber to be cut or is minerals or the like (including oil and gas) or accounts subject to subsection (5) of Section 9-103, or when the financing statement is filed as a fixture filing (Section 9-313) and the collateral is goods which are or are to be become fixtures, then in the office where a mortgage on the real estate [concerned] would be filed or recorded;

(c) in all other cases, in the office of the [[Secretary of State]].

Third Alternative Subsection (1)

(1) The proper place to file in order to perfect a security interest is as follows:

(a) when the collateral is equipment used in farming operations, or farm products, or accounts [, contract rights] or general intangibles arising from or relating to the sale of farm products by a farmer, or consumer goods, then in the office of the ______ in the county of the debtor's residence or if the debtor is not a resident of this state then in the office of the ______ in the county where the goods are kept, and in addition when the collateral is crops growing or to be grown in the office of the ______ in the county where the land [on which the crops are growing or to be grown] is located;

(b) when the collateral is [goods which at the time the security interest attaches are or are to become fixtures] timber to be cut or is minerals or the like (including oil and gas) or accounts subject to subsection (5) of Section 9-103, or when the financing statement is filed as a fixture filing (Section 9-313) and the collateral is goods which are or are to become fixtures, then in the office where a mortgage on the real estate [concerned] would be filed or recorded;

(c) in all other cases, in the office of the [[Secretary of State]] and in addition, if the debtor has a place of business in only one county of this state, also in the office of ______ of such county, or, if the debtor has no place of business in this state, but resides in the state, also in the office of ______ of the county in which he resides.

Note: *One of the three alternatives should be selected as subsection (1).*

(2) A filing which is made in good faith in an improper place or not in all of the places required by this section is nevertheless effective with regard to any collateral as to which the filing complied with the requirements of this Article and is also effective with regard to collateral covered by the financing statement against any person who has knowledge of the contents of such financing statement.

(3) A filing which is made in the proper place in this state continues effective even though the debtor's residence or place of business or the location of the collateral or its use, whichever controlled the original filing, is thereafter changed.

Language in double brackets is Alternative Subsection (3)

[[(3) A filing which is made in the proper county continues effective for four months after a change to another county of the debtor's residence or place of business or the location of the collateral, whichever controlled the original filing. It becomes ineffective thereafter unless a copy of the financing statement signed by the secured party is filed in the new county within said period. The security interest may also be perfected in the new county after the expiration of the four-month period; in such case perfected dates from the time of perfection in the new county. A change in the use of the collateral does not impair the effectiveness of the original filing.]]

(4) [If collateral is brought into this state from another jurisdiction, the] The rules stated in Section 9-103 determine whether filing is necessary in this state.

(5) Notwithstanding the preceding subsections, and subject to subsection (3) of Section 9-302, the proper place to file in order to perfect a security interest in collateral, including fixtures, of a transmitting utility is the office

of the [[Secretary of State]]. This filing constitutes a fixture filing (Section 9–313) as to the collateral described therein which is or is to become fixtures.

(6) For the purposes of this section, the residence of an organization is its place of business if it has one or its chief executive office if it has more than one place of business.

Note: *Subsection (6) should be used only if the state chooses the Second or Third Alternative Subsection (1).*

Reasons for 1972 Change

The several alternatives for subsection (1) have been rewritten to provide for filing in the real estate records of security interests intended to give a priority as a "fixture filing" under Section 9–313.

This requirement for filing in real estate records applies only if the priority advantages of Section 9–313 are desired. If the secured party is not concerned about priority against real estate parties, he can file for a fixture as for an ordinary chattel, in the chattel records, omitting the filing in the real estate records, and he will have a security interest perfected against everyone but real estate parties. In the case of a purchase money security interest in consumer goods, he need not file at all. See Section 9–313(1)(d). For the question of the effect of the regular chattel filing in lieu of fixture filing in the event of the debtor's bankruptcy, see Comment 4(c) to Section 9–313.

This requirement for filing in real estate records applies also to timber to be cut and to minerals or the like (including oil and gas) financed at the wellhead or minehead or accounts resulting from the sale thereof.

This filing is not merely in the *office* where a mortgage of real estate would be recorded, but it is intended that it be filed *in the real estate records.* This is made clear by the model form in Section 9–402(3) which recites that the financing statement is to be filed for record in the real estate records, the required recital in Section 9–402(5), and the provision of Section 9–403(7) requiring the indexing thereof in the real estate records. Thus, it is intended that these filings will be readily disclosed on any real estate search and they can be treated like any real estate encumbrance so disclosed.

A new subsection (5) makes clear that a financing statement filed against a "transmitting utility" (Section 9–105) need be filed only in the office of the [Secretary of State] and not locally. Special provision had to be made for filing where these far-flung utilities were debtors. If the problem were only on non-fixtures, not more than one local filing would have been necessary under any of the alternative versions of subsection (1), but the problem was more difficult in the case of fixtures, where the standard rule would require filing with real estate descriptions in every county where there were fixtures.

There has been some difficulty in the concept that one files against farmers at their residences, in view of the number of incorporated farms. A new subsection (6) is therefore added to define the residence of an organization. Subsection (6) is also needed if the provision of the Third Alternative Subsection (1) for double filing against local business debtors is adopted.

§ 9–402. Formal Requisites of Financing Statement; Amendments; Mortgage as Financing Statement.

(1) A financing statement is sufficient if it gives the names of the debtor and the secured party, is signed by the debtor [and the secured party], gives an address of the secured party from which information concerning the security interest may be obtained, gives a mailing address of the debtor and

contains a statement indicating the types, or describing the items, of collateral. A financing statement may be filed before a security agreement is made or a security interest otherwise attaches. When the financing statement covers crops growing or to be grown [or goods which are or are to become fixtures], the statement must also contain a description of the real estate concerned. When the financing statement covers timber to be cut or covers minerals or the like (including oil and gas) or accounts subject to subsection (5) of Section 9–103, or when the financing statement is filed as a fixture filing (Section 9–313) and the collateral is goods which are or are to become fixtures, the statement must also comply with subsection (5). A copy of the security agreement is sufficient as a financing statement if it contains the above information and is signed by [both parties.] the debtor. A carbon, photographic or other reproduction of a security agreement or a financing statement is sufficient as a financing statement if the security agreement so provides or if the original has been filed in this state.

(2) A financing statement which otherwise complies with subsection (1) is sufficient [although] when it is signed [only] by the secured party instead of the debtor if it is filed to perfect a security interest in

(a) collateral already subject to a security interest in another jurisdiction when it is brought into this state, or when the debtor's location is changed to this state. Such a financing statement must state that the collateral was brought into this state or that the debtor's location was changed to this state under such circumstances; or

(b) proceeds under Section 9–306 if the security interest in the original collateral was perfected. Such a financing statement must describe the original collateral; or

(c) collateral as to which the filing has lapsed; or

(d) collateral acquired after a change of name, identity or corporate structure of the debtor (subsection (7)).

(3) A form substantially as follows is sufficient to comply with subsection (1):

Name of debtor (or assignor) ______________________________

Address ______________________________

Name of secured party (or assignee) ______________________________

Address ______________________________

1. This financing statement covers the following types (or items) of property:

   (Describe) ______________________________

2. (If collateral is crops) The above described crops are growing or are to be grown on:

   (Describe Real Estate) ______________________________

[3. (If collateral is goods which are or are to become fixtures) The above described goods are affixed or to be affixed to:

(Describe Real Estate) ______________________]

3. (If applicable) The above goods are to become fixtures on *

(Describe Real Estate) ______ and this financing statement is to be filed [[for record]] in the real estate records. (If the debtor does not have an interest of record) The name of a record owner is ______

4. (If [proceeds or] products of collateral are claimed) [Proceeds—] Products of the collateral are also covered.

(use	(	______________________
whichever	(	Signature of Debtor (or Assignor)
is	(	______________________
applicable)	(	Signature of Secured Party (or Assignee)

(4) A financing statement may be amended by filing a writing signed by both the debtor and the secured party. An amendment does not extend the period of effectiveness of a financing statement. [The term "financing statement" as used in this Article means the original financing statement and any amendments but if] If any amendment adds collateral, it is effective as to the added collateral only from the filing date of the amendment. In this Article, unless the context otherwise requires, the term "financing statement" means the original financing statement and any amendments.

(5) A financing statement covering timber to be cut or covering minerals or the like (including oil and gas) or accounts subject to subsection (5) of Section 9-103, or a financing statement filed as a fixture filing (Section 9-313) where the debtor is not a transmitting utility, must show that it covers this type of collateral, must recite that it is to be filed [[for record]] in the real estate records, and the financing statement must contain a description of the real estate [[sufficient if it were contained in a mortgage of the real estate to give constructive notice of the mortgage under the law of this state]]. If the debtor does not have an interest of record in the real estate, the financing statement must show the name of a record owner.

(6) A mortgage is effective as a financing statement filed as a fixture filing from the date of its recording if (a) the goods are described in the mortgage by item or type, (b) the goods are or are to become fixtures related to the real estate described in the mortgage, (c) the mortgage complies with the requirements for a financing statement in this section other than a recital that it is to be filed in the real estate records, and (d) the mortgage is duly recorded. No fee with reference to the financing statement is required other than the regular recording and satisfaction fees with respect to the mortgage.

(7) A financing statement sufficiently shows the name of the debtor if it gives the individual, partnership or corporate name of the debtor, whether or not it adds other trade names or the names of partners. Where the debtor so changes his name or in the case of an organization its name, identity or

* Where appropriate substitute either "The above timber is standing on ...." or "The above minerals or the like (including oil and gas) or accounts will be financed at the wellhead or minehead of the well or mine located on ...."

corporate structure that a filed financing statement becomes seriously misleading, the filing is not effective to perfect a security interest in collateral acquired by the debtor more than four months after the change, unless a new appropriate financing statement is filed before the expiration of that time. A filed financing statement remains effective with respect to collateral transferred by the debtor even though the secured party knows of or consents to the transfer.

(8) [(5)] A financing statement substantially complying with the requirements of this section is effective even though it contains minor errors which are not seriously misleading.

Note: *Language in double brackets is optional.*

Note: *Where the state has any special recording system for real estate other than the usual grantor-grantee index (as, for instance, a tract system or a title registration or Torrens system) local adaptations of subsection (5) and Section 9–403(7) may be necessary. See Mass.Gen. Laws Chapter 106, Section 9–409.*

Reasons for 1972 Change

Certain changes are conforming changes to new requirements of Section 9–401 that certain financing statements covering such collateral as timber and minerals be filed in the real estate records. Persons interested in real estate have complained with some justice that the provisions of the 1962 Code failed in several ways to tie the fixture filings to the real estate search system. Among these was the absence of clear specification that the fixture security interest was to be indexed in the real estate records. On this point, a responsive change has been made in Section 9–403. Other objections related to the adequacy of the real estate description and to the fact that the debtor might not be an owner of an interest of record in the real estate. The optional language in subsection (5) is designed to meet the objection as to real estate descriptions but without imposing on a fixture-secured party the duty of obtaining a "legal description" unless the state's recording system requires it. While no doubt a full "legal description" is proper practice in conveyancing, it is believed that something significantly less, like a street address, would be adequate in most states, and would frequently be a guide to a recorded map. Where a state has a tract index system or other special system not dependent on a grantor-grantee index, special adaptations may be required and no attempt is made in the Code to deal with all such situations.

Another objection of real estate parties has been that the name of the debtor might not be in the real estate chain of title and there have been numerous non-uniform amendments to Sections 9–401, 9–402, or 9–403 designed to require the showing of the name of the record owners of the real estate in the financing statement. Since Section 9–313(4)(a) and (b) permit fixture filing against persons in possession of the real estate who do not have interests of record, Section 9–402 requires the naming of an owner of record of the real estate in such cases, and Section 9–403(7) requires indexing the fixture filing against the name.

Subsection (6) makes it possible for a real estate mortgage to serve as a financing statement, and a related change in Section 9–403(6) makes it unnecessary to file continuation statements for such a financing statement.

Subsection (1) has been changed to require only the signature of the debtor rather than that of the secured party. The requirement of signatures of secured parties has sometimes misled secured parties, who are accustomed to pre-Code practice and real estate practice under which only the debtor, not the secured party, need sign such instruments as chattel mortgages and real estate mortgages. Thus, when the security agreement was used as the financing statement, it might have been defective under the 1962 Code for failure to have the signature of the secured party. This change also fits in with the provisions of Section 9–403(6), under which a real estate mortgage (customarily signed only by the debtor) may be effective as a financing statement.

Changes in the form of financing statement in subsection (3) conform to the foregoing and are also intended to have the secured party make clear when a financing statement is intended to be filed in real estate records. This had been a matter of some concern when the parties used the term "fixture" loosely in their description of goods.

Certain of the changes in Section 9–402 are not related to real estate filings. The changes in paragraph (2)(a) conform to Section 9–103(3), which requires refiling when the debtor's location changes. Additions in subsections (2)(d) and (7) relating to the problem of the name of the debtor against which a filing should be made and the effect of transfer are discussed in the related Comments.

§ 9–403. What Constitutes Filing; Duration of Filing; Effect of Lapsed Filing; Duties of Filing Officer.

(1) Presentation for filing of a financing statement and tender of the filing fee or acceptance of the statement by the filing officer constitutes filing under this Article.

(2) Except as provided in subsection (6)a [(2)A] filed financing statement [which states a maturity date of the obligation secured of five years or less is effective until such maturity date and thereafter for a period of sixty days. Any other filed financing statement] is effective for a period of five years from the date of filing. The effectiveness of a filed financing statement lapses [on the expiration of such sixty day period after a stated maturity date or] on the expiration of [such five] the five year period [, as the case may be] unless a continuation statement is filed prior to the lapse. If a security interest perfected by filing exists at the time insolvency proceedings are commenced by or against the debtor, the security interest remains perfected until termination of the insolvency proceedings and thereafter for a period of sixty days or until expiration of the five year period, whichever occurs later. Upon [such] lapse the security interest becomes unperfected, unless it is perfected without filing. If the security interest becomes unperfected upon lapse, it is deemed to have been unperfected as against a person who became a purchaser or lien creditor before lapse. [A filed financing statement which states that the obligation secured is payable on demand is effective for five years from the date of filing.]

(3) A continuation statement may be filed by the secured party [(i) within six months before and sixty days after a stated maturity date of five years or less, and (ii) otherwise] within six months prior to the expiration of the five year period specified in subsection (2). Any such continuation statement must be signed by the secured party, identify the original statement by file number and state that the original statement is still effective. A continuation statement signed by a person other than the secured party of record must be accompanied by a separate written statement of assignment signed by the secured party of record and complying with subsection (2) of

Section 9-405, including payment of the required fee. Upon timely filing of the continuation statement, the effectiveness of the original statement is continued for five years after the last date to which the filing was effective whereupon it lapses in the same manner as provided in subsection (2) unless another continuation statement is filed prior to such lapse. Succeeding continuation statements may be filed in the same manner to continue the effectiveness of the original statement. Unless a statute on disposition of public records provides otherwise, the filing officer may remove a lapsed statement from the files and destroy it[.] immediately if he has retained a microfilm or other photographic record, or in other cases after one year after the lapse. The filing officer shall so arrange matters by physical annexation of financing statements to continuation statements or other related filings, or by other means, that if he physically destroys the financing statements of a period more than five years past, those which have been continued by a continuation statement or which are still effective under subsection (6) shall be retained.

(4) Except as provided in subsection (7) a [(4) A] filing officer shall mark each statement with a [consecutive] file number and with the date and hour of filing and shall hold the statement or a microfilm or other photographic copy thereof for public inspection. In addition the filing officer shall index the statements according to the name of the debtor and shall note in the index the file number and the address of the debtor given in the statement.

[(5) The uniform fee for filing, indexing and furnishing filing data for an original or a continuation statement shall be $______]

(5) The uniform fee for filing and indexing and for stamping a copy furnished by the secured party to show the date and place of filing for an original financing statement or for a continuation statement shall be $______ if the statement is in the standard form prescribed by the [[Secretary of State]] and otherwise shall be $______, plus in each case, if the financing statement is subject to subsection (5) of Section 9-402, $______. The uniform fee for each name more than one required to be indexed shall be $______. The secured party may at his option show a trade name for any person and an extra uniform indexing fee of $______ shall be paid with respect thereto.

(6) If the debtor is a transmitting utility (subsection (5) of Section 9-401) and a filed financing statement so states, it is effective until a termination statement is filed. A real estate mortgage which is effective as a fixture filing under subsection (6) of Section 9-402 remains effective as a fixture filing until the mortgage is released or satisfied of record or its effectiveness otherwise terminates as to the real estate.

(7) When a financing statement covers timber to be cut or covers minerals or the like (including oil and gas) or accounts subject to subsection (5) of Section 9-103, or is filed as a fixture filing, [[it shall be filed for record and]] the filing officer shall index it under the names of the debtor and any owner of record shown on the financing statement in the same fashion as if they were the mortgagors in a mortgage of the real estate described, and, to the extent that the law of this state provides for indexing of mortgages under the name of the mortgagee, under the name of the secured party as if he were the

mortgagee thereunder, or where indexing is by description in the same fashion as if the financing statement were a mortgage of the real estate described.

Note: *In states in which writings will not appear in the real estate records and indices unless actually recorded the bracketed language in subsection (7) should be used.*

Reasons for 1972 Change

The change in subsection (2) makes every financing statement (except those described in subsection (6)), effective for a full five years, thus changing the rule of the 1962 Code that a financing statement which showed a maturity less than 5 years was effective only for the period until maturity plus 60 days. This limitation could have been easily evaded simply by not showing a maturity, even though there was one. The change facilitates renewals or extensions up to a maximum combined duration of five years, without the danger of the financing statement ceasing to be effective.

Subsection (2) also recognizes that financing statements might expire during an insolvency proceeding. While the prevailing line of decisions is to the effect that the situation is frozen at the moment of bankruptcy without an obligation to refile, there are contrary decisions, and this situation might prove an inadvertent trap to a secured party who failed to refile or file a continuation statement during a bankruptcy. The change continues the validity of the financing statement until the end of the insolvency proceedings and for 60 days thereafter, or until the expiration of the five-year period, whichever is later. Ordinarily, if the secured party expects that the secured debt may continue in existence after the end of the insolvency proceedings, he should file a continuation statement on the normal schedule, to preserve the filing for use at the end of the insolvency proceeding and to preclude any discontinuity of the filings.

Subsection (2) also clarifies the effect of lapse, a matter on which there has been some dispute among writers on the subject. Compare also Section 9–103(1)(d).

Subsection (5) is intended to adopt non-uniform amendments made in some states giving the filing officer authority to charge extra fees if the financing statement does not conform to a uniform prescribed size and content. It also permits the secured party to show a trade name at his option and to have it indexed for an extra fee.

New subsection (6) deals with transmitting utilities (Sections 9–105 and 9–401(5)) and also with real estate mortgages which are effective as financing statements under Section 9–402(6). In these special cases a financing statement is good indefinitely and its validity is not limited to five years. The filing in real estate records of a financing statement which is also a real estate mortgage will give notice to persons searching the record as to this continuing validity and will not interfere with the purpose of the Code's standard rule of five-year validity for financing statements. The name of a transmitting utility should give equivalent notice in filings against that kind of company.

The purpose of the standard rule is to permit the files to be self-clearing, so that whether or not termination statements have been filed, the filing officer can clear the files after a suitable period after the five-year validity expires, unless the duration of the financing statement has been continued by a continuation statement.

Various technical changes in this section are designed to facilitate the handling of financing statements by filing officers in reference to the use of microfilm, etc., and to carry out the principle of the self-clearing nature of the files after five years.

New subsection (7) deals with a point in reference to fixtures on which the 1962

Code was properly subject to criticism, namely, that it was not explicitly stated that the fixture filing in the county where a real estate mortgage would be recorded was intended to be made and be indexed in the real estate records. This principle is now stated and is also made applicable to timber to be cut and to minerals and the like (including oil and gas) financed at the wellhead or minehead or accounts resulting from the sale thereof.

The other minor changes coordinate with the addition of subsection (7) to Section 9–402.

§ 9–404. Termination Statement.

(1) If a financing statement covering consumer goods is filed on or after ______, then within one month or within ten days following written demand by the debtor after there is no outstanding secured obligation and no commitment to make advances, incur obligations or otherwise give value, the secured party must file with each filing officer with whom the financing statement was filed, a termination statement to the effect that he no longer claims a security interest under the financing statement, which shall be identified by file number. In other cases whenever [Whenever] there is no outstanding secured obligation and no commitment to make advances, incur obligations or otherwise give value, the secured party must on written demand by the debtor send the debtor, for each filing officer with whom the financing statement was filed, a termination statement to the effect that he no longer claims a security interest under the financing statement, which shall be identified by file number. A termination statement signed by a person other than the secured party of record must [include or] be accompanied by [the assignment or] a separate written statement of assignment signed by the secured party of record [that he has assigned the security interest to the signer of the termination statement. and] complying with subsection (2) of Section 9–405, including payment of the required fee. [The uniform fee for filing and indexing such an assignment or statement thereof shall be $______.] If the affected secured party fails to file such a termination statement as required by this subsection, or to send such a termination statement within ten days after proper demand therefor he shall be liable to the debtor for one hundred dollars, and in addition for any loss caused to the debtor by such failure.

(2) On presentation to the filing officer of such a termination statement he must note it in the index. [The filing officer shall remove from the files, mark "terminated" and send or deliver to the secured party the financing statement and any continuation statement, statement of assignment or statement of release pertaining thereto.] If he has received the termination statement in duplicate, he shall return one copy of the termination statement to the secured party stamped to show the time of receipt thereof. If the filing officer has a microfilm or other photographic record of the financing statement, and of any related continuation statement, statement of assignment and statement of release, he may remove the originals from the files at any time after receipt of the termination statement, or if he has no such record, he may remove them from the files at any time after one year after receipt of the termination statement.

(3) If the termination statement is in the standard form prescribed by the [[Secretary of State]], the uniform fee for filing and indexing [a] the termination statement [including sending or delivering the financing statement]

shall be $______, and otherwise shall be $______, plus in each case an additional fee of $______ for each name more than one against which the termination statement is required to be indexed.

Note: *The date to be inserted should be the effective date of the revised Article 9.*

Reasons for 1972 Change

The additions to subsection (1) require the filing of termination statements in the case of consumer goods even without a demand by the consumer. It is believed that consumers will frequently not understand the importance of making demand in order to clear the files. The scope of the change is not as great as might first appear, because (1) filing is not required for purchase money security interests in consumer goods, except in the case of motor vehicles (Section 9–302(1)(d)); and (2) perfection of security interests in most motor vehicles is governed by certificate of title laws, not by the provisions of Article 9.

The other changes are purely formal and tie in with corresponding changes in filing mechanics in other sections.

§ 9–405. Assignment of Security Interest; Duties of Filing Officer; Fees.

(1) A financing statement may disclose an assignment of a security interest in the collateral described in the financing statement by indication in the financing statement of the name and address of the assignee or by an assignment itself or a copy thereof on the face or back of the statement. [Either the original secured party or the assignee may sign this statement as the secured party.] On presentation to the filing officer of such a financing statement the filing officer shall mark the same as provided in Section 9–403(4). The uniform fee for filing, indexing and furnishing filing data for a financing statement so indicating an assignment shall be $______ if the statement is in the standard form prescribed by the [[Secretary of State]] and otherwise shall be $______, plus in each case an additional fee of $______ for each name more than one against which the financing statement is required to be indexed.

(2) A secured party may assign of record all or part of his rights under a financing statement by the filing in the place where the original financing statement was filed of a separate written statement of assignment signed by the secured party of record and setting forth the name of the secured party of record and the debtor, the file number and the date of filing of the financing statement and the name and address of the assignee and containing a description of the collateral assigned. A copy of the assignment is sufficient as a separate statement if it complies with the preceding sentence. On presentation to the filing officer of such a separate statement, the filing officer shall mark such separate statement with the date and hour of the filing. He shall note the assignment on the index of the financing statement, or in the case of a fixture filing, or a filing covering timber to be cut, or covering minerals or the like (including oil and gas) or accounts subject to subsection (5) of Section 9–103, he shall index the assignment under the name of the assignor as grantor and, to the extent that the law of this state provides for indexing the assignment of a mortgage under the name of the assignee, he

shall index the assignment of the financing statement under the name of the assignee. The uniform fee for filing, indexing and furnishing filing data about such a separate statement of assignment shall be $______ if the statement is in the standard form prescribed by the [[Secretary of State]] and otherwise shall be $______, plus in each case an additional fee of $______ for each name more than one against which the statement of assignment is required to be indexed. Notwithstanding the provisions of this subsection, an assignment of record of a security interest in a fixture contained in a mortgage effective as a fixture filing (subsection (6) of Section 9-402) may be made only by an assignment of the mortgage in the manner provided by the law of this state other than this Act.

(3) After the disclosure or filing of an assignment under this section, the assignee is the secured party of record.

Reasons for 1972 Change

The changes are all conforming changes connecting with changes in mechanics in other sections of Part 4; with the addition of timber and minerals or the like (including oil and gas) at wellhead or minehead and accounts resulting from the sale thereof to the groups of collateral which must be filed and indexed in the real estate records; and with the provision (Section 9-402(6)) that a mortgage of real estate may act as a financing statement of fixtures.

§ 9-406. Release of Collateral; Duties of Filing Officer; Fees.

A secured party of record may by his signed statement release all or a part of any collateral described in a filed financing statement. The statement of release is sufficient if it contains a description of the collateral being released, the name and address of the debtor, the name and address of the secured party, and the file number of the financing statement. A statement of release signed by a person other than the secured party of record must be accompanied by a separate written statement of assignment signed by the secured party of record and complying with subsection (2) of Section 9-405, including payment of the required fee. Upon presentation of such a statement of release to the filing officer he shall mark the statement with the hour and date of filing and shall note the same upon the margin of the index of the filing of the financing statement. The uniform fee for filing and noting such a statement of release shall be $______ if the statement is in the standard form prescribed by the [[Secretary of State]] and otherwise shall be $______, plus in each case an additional fee of $______ for each name more than one against which the statement of release is required to be indexed.

Reasons for 1972 Change

The changes are merely conforming changes to changes in other sections.

[[§ 9-407. Information From Filing Officer]].

[[(1) If the person filing any financing statement, termination statement, statement of assignment, or statement of release, furnishes the filing officer a copy thereof, the filing officer shall upon request note upon the copy the file number and date and hour of the filing of the original and deliver or send the copy to such person.]]

[[(2) Upon request of any person, the filing officer shall issue his certificate showing whether there is on file on the date and hour stated therein, any presently effective financing statement naming a particular debtor and any statement of assignment thereof and if there is, giving the date and hour of filing of each such statement and the names and addresses of each secured party therein. The uniform fee for such a certificate shall be $______ [plus $______ for each financing statement and for each statement of assignment reported therein.] if the request for the certificate is in the standard form prescribed by the [[Secretary of State]] and otherwise shall be $______ [plus $______ for each financing statement and for each statement of assignment reported therein.] Upon request the filing officer shall furnish a copy of any filed financing statement or statement of assignment for a uniform fee of $______ per page.]]

Reasons for 1972 Change

The change in this optional section is merely a conforming change to the changes in other sections.

Note: *This section is proposed as an optional provision to require filing officers to furnish certificates. Local law and practices should be consulted with regard to the advisability of adoption.*

§ 9-408. Financing Statements Covering Consigned or Leased Goods.

A consignor or lessor of goods may file a financing statement using the terms "consignor," "consignee," "lessor," "lessee" or the like instead of the terms specified in Section 9-402. The provisions of this Part shall apply as appropriate to such a financing statement but its filing shall not of itself be a factor in determining whether or not the consignment or lease is intended as security (Section 1-201(37)). However, if it is determined for other reasons that the consignment or lease is so intended, a security interest of the consignor or lessor which attaches to the consigned or leased goods is perfected by such filing.

Reasons for 1972 Adoption of New Section

This new section adapts the filing system of the Article to consignments and leases. Filing of consignments is required under certain conditions (Sections 2-326(3), 9-114). Filing of true leases which are not security interests (Section 1-201(37)) is not required; but because the question whether a lease is a true lease may be a close one, filing is permitted for leases.

PART 5

DEFAULT

§ 9–501. Default; Procedure When Security Agreement Covers Both Real and Personal Property.

(1) When a debtor is in default under a security agreement, a secured party has the rights and remedies provided in this Part and except as limited by subsection (3) those provided in the security agreement. He may reduce his claim to judgment, foreclose or otherwise enforce the security interest by any available judicial procedure. If the collateral is documents the secured party may proceed either as to the documents or as to the goods covered thereby. A secured party in possession has the rights, remedies and duties provided in Section 9–207. The rights and remedies referred to in this subsection are cumulative.

(2) After default, the debtor has the rights and remedies provided in this Part, those provided in the security agreement and those provided in Section 9–207.

(3) To the extent that they give rights to the debtor and impose duties on the secured party, the rules stated in the subsections referred to below may not be waived or varied except as provided with respect to compulsory disposition of collateral (subsection (3) of Section 9–504 and [(subsection (1) of] Section 9–505) and with respect to redemption of collateral (Section 9–506) but the parties may by agreement determine the standards by which the fulfillment of these rights and duties is to be measured if such standards are not manifestly unreasonable:

(a) subsection (2) of Section 9–502 and subsection (2) of Section 9–504 insofar as they require accounting for surplus proceeds of collateral;

(b) subsection (3) of Section 9–504 and subsection (1) of Section 9–505 which deal with disposition of collateral;

(c) subsection (2) of Section 9–505 which deals with acceptance of collateral as discharge of obligation;

(d) Section 9–506 which deals with redemption of collateral; and

(e) subsection (1) of Section 9–507 which deals with the secured party's liability for failure to comply with this Part.

(4) If the security agreement covers both real and personal property, the secured party may proceed under this Part as to the personal property or he may proceed as to both the real and the personal property in accordance with his rights and remedies in respect of the real property in which case the provisions of this Part do not apply.

(5) When a secured party has reduced his claim to judgment the lien of any levy which may be made upon his collateral by virtue of any execution based upon the judgment shall relate back to the date of the perfection of the security interest in such collateral. A judicial sale, pursuant to such execution, is a foreclosure of the security interest by judicial procedure within the

meaning of this section, and the secured party may purchase at the sale and thereafter hold the collateral free of any other requirements of this Article.

Reasons for 1972 Change

The change is purely technical, to clear up an ambiguity as to whether a debtor could after default agree on the time within which a sale might be held or the time after which a secured party might keep the goods in lieu of a sale.

§ 9-502. Collection Rights of Secured Party.

(1) When so agreed and in any event on default the secured party is entitled to notify an account debtor or the obligor on an instrument to make payment to him whether or not the assignor was theretofore making collections on the collateral, and also to take control of any proceeds to which he is entitled under Section 9-306.

(2) A secured party who by agreement is entitled to charge back uncollected collateral or otherwise to full or limited recourse against the debtor and who undertakes to collect from the account debtors or obligors must proceed in a commercially reasonable manner and may deduct his reasonable expenses of realization from the collections. If the security agreement secures an indebtedness, the secured party must account to the debtor for any surplus, and unless otherwise agreed, the debtor is liable for any deficiency. But, if the underlying transaction was a sale of accounts [, contract rights,] or chattel paper, the debtor is entitled to any surplus or is liable for any deficiency only if the security agreement so provides.

Reasons for 1972 Change

The change is only the deletion of the term "contract rights", which is being eliminated as a defined term under the Article.

§ 9-504. Secured Party's Right to Dispose of Collateral After Default; Effect of Disposition.

(1) A secured party after default may sell, lease or otherwise dispose of any or all of the collateral in its then condition or following any commercially reasonable preparation or processing. Any sale of goods is subject to the Article on Sales (Article 2). The proceeds of disposition shall be applied in the order following to

(a) the reasonable expenses of retaking, holding, preparing for sale <u>or lease,</u> selling, <u>leasing</u> and the like and, to the extent provided for in the agreement and not prohibited by law, the reasonable attorneys' fees and legal expenses incurred by the secured party;

(b) the satisfaction of indebtedness secured by the security interest under which the disposition is made;

(c) the satisfaction of indebtedness secured by any subordinate security interest in the collateral if written notification of demand therefor is received before distribution of the proceeds is completed. If requested by the secured party, the holder of a subordinate security interest must seasonably furnish reasonable proof of his interest, and unless he does so, the secured party need not comply with his demand.

(2) If the security interest secures an indebtedness, the secured party must account to the debtor for any surplus, and, unless otherwise agreed, the debtor is liable for any deficiency. But if the underlying transaction was a sale of accounts [, contract rights,] or chattel paper, the debtor is entitled to any surplus or is liable for any deficiency only if the security agreement so provides.

(3) Disposition of the collateral may be by public or private proceedings and may be made by way of one or more contracts. Sale or other disposition may be as a unit or in parcels and at any time and place and on any terms but every aspect of the disposition including the method, manner, time, place and terms must be commercially reasonable. Unless collateral is perishable or threatens to decline speedily in value or is of a type customarily sold on a recognized market, reasonable notification of the time and place of any public sale or reasonable notification of the time after which any private sale or other intended disposition is to be made shall be sent by the secured party to the debtor, if he has not signed after default a statement renouncing or modifying his right to notification of sale. In the case of consumer goods no other notification need be sent. In other cases notification shall be sent to any other secured party from whom the secured party has received (before sending his notification to the debtor or before the debtor's renunciation of his rights) written notice of a claim of an interest in the collateral [and except in the case of consumer goods to any other person who has a security interest in the collateral and who has duly filed a financing statement indexed in the name of the debtor in this state or who is known by the secured party to have a security interest in the collateral]. The secured party may buy at any public sale and if the collateral is of a type customarily sold in a recognized market or is of a type which is the subject of widely distributed standard price quotations he may buy at private sale.

(4) When collateral is disposed of by a secured party after default, the disposition transfers to a purchaser for value all of the debtor's rights therein, discharges the security interest under which it is made and any security interest or lien subordinate thereto. The purchaser takes free of all such rights and interests even though the secured party fails to comply with the requirements of this Part or of any judicial proceedings

(a) in the case of a public sale, if the purchaser has no knowledge of any defects in the sale and if he does not buy in collusion with the secured party, other bidders or the person conducting the sale; or

(b) in any other case, if the purchaser acts in good faith.

(5) A person who is liable to a secured party under a guaranty, indorsement, repurchase agreement or the like and who receives a transfer of collateral from the secured party or is subrogated to his rights has thereafter the rights and duties of the secured party. Such a transfer of collateral is not a sale or disposition of the collateral under this Article.

Reasons for 1972 Change

Under the 1962 Code the secured party giving notice of sale had to notify (except in the case of consumer goods) not only every other person who had duly filed a financing statement indexed in the name of the debtor in the state and who still had a security interest in the collateral, but also any other person known by the secured party to have an interest in the collateral. This meant that the secured party had to search the records in every case of notice of sale, to ascertain whether there were any other secured parties with financing statements that might be deemed to cover the collateral in question. Moreover, he ran the risk that some informal communication by letter, or even orally, might be deemed to have given him knowledge of the interest of that other party. These burdens of searching the record and of checking the secured party's files were greater than the circumstances called for because as a practical matter there would seldom be a junior secured party who really had an interest needing protection in the case of a foreclosure sale. Therefore, a change is made requiring notice to persons other than the debtor only if such persons had notified the secured party in writing of their claim of an interest in the collateral before he sent his notification to the debtor or before the debtor's renunciation of his rights. Express provision is made to recognize the right of a debtor to renounce or modify his right to notice after, but not before, default. A corresponding change is made in Section 9-505.

§ 9-505. Compulsory Disposition of Collateral; Acceptance of the Collateral as Discharge of Obligation.

(1) If the debtor has paid sixty per cent of the cash price in the case of a purchase money security interest in consumer goods or sixty per cent of the loan in the case of another security interest in consumer goods, and has not signed after default a statement renouncing or modifying his rights under this Part a secured party who has taken possession of collateral must dispose of it under Section 9-504 and if he fails to do so within ninety days after he takes possession the debtor at his option may recover in conversion or under Section 9-507(1) on secured party's liability.

(2) In any other case involving consumer goods or any other collateral a secured party in possession may, after default, propose to retain the collateral in satisfaction of the obligation. Written notice of such proposal shall be sent to the debtor [and except in the case of consumer goods to any other secured party who has a security interest in the collateral and who has duly filed a financing statement indexed in the name of the debtor in this state or is known by the secured party in possession to have a security interest in it. If the debtor or other person entitled to receive notification objects in writing within thirty days from the receipt of the notification or if any other secured party objects in writing thirty days after the secured party obtains possession the secured party must dispose of the collateral under Section 9-504.] <u>if he has not signed after default a statement renouncing or modifying his rights under this subsection. In the case of consumer goods no other notice need be given. In other cases notice shall be sent to any other secured party from whom the secured party has received (before sending his notice to the debtor or before the debtor's renunciation of his rights) written notice of a claim of an interest in the collateral. If the secured party receives objection in writing from a person entitled to receive notification within twenty-one days after the notice was sent, the secured party must dispose of the collateral under Section</u>

9–504. *In the absence of such written objection the secured party may retain the collateral in satisfaction of the debtor's obligation.*

Reasons for 1972 Change

Under subsection (2) of this section the secured party may in lieu of sale give notice to the debtor and certain other persons that he proposes to retain the collateral in lieu of sale. Under the 1962 Code the other persons were the same as those who were entitled to notice of sale under Section 9–504(3), and such other persons are limited by the change in the same fashion as they were limited in Section 9–504(3) and for the same reasons. See the Reasons for Change under Section 9–504.

ARTICLE 11

EFFECTIVE DATE AND TRANSITION PROVISIONS

Notes: *This material has been numbered Article 11 to distinguish it from Article 10, the transition provision of the 1962 Code, which may still remain in effect in some states to cover transition problems from pre-Code law to the original Uniform Commercial Code. Adaptation may be necessary in particular states. The terms "[old Code]" and "[new Code]" and "[old U.C.C.]" and "[new U.C.C.]" are used herein, and should be suitably changed in each state.*

This draft was prepared by the Reporters and has not been passed upon by the Review Committee, the Permanent Editorial Board, the American Law Institute, or the National Conference of Commissioners on Uniform State Laws. It is submitted as a working draft which may be adapted as appropriate in each state. The "Discussions" were written by the Reporters to assist in understanding the purpose of the drafts.

§ 11–101. Effective Date.

This Act shall become effective at 12:01 A.M. on ______, 19__.

Discussion

An effective date substantially after enactment is advisable to allow ample time for refilings as required.

§ 11–102. Preservation of Old Transition Provision.

The provisions of [here insert reference to the original transition provision in the particular state] shall continue to apply to [the new U.C.C.] and for this purpose the [old U.C.C. and new U.C.C.] shall be considered one continuous statute.

Discussion

This section may be necessary in states in which the U.C.C. has only recently been effective. It preserves the principle of Section 10–102(2) of the 1962 Code that pre-Code transactions continue to be governed by pre-Code law. A different principle is set forth in this Article 11 for transition problems between the [old Code] and the [new Code], because the changes are not nearly as great. That principle is that the [new Code] governs (with minor exceptions).

§ 11–103. Transition to [New Code]—General Rule.

Transactions validly entered into after [effective date of old U.C.C.] and before [effective date of new U.C.C.], and which were subject to the provisions of [old U.C.C.] and which would be subject to this Act as amended if they had been entered into after the effective date of [new U.C.C.] and the rights, duties and interests flowing from such transactions remain valid after the latter date and may be terminated, completed, consummated or enforced as required or permitted by the [new U.C.C.]. Security interests arising out of such transactions which are perfected when [new U.C.C.] becomes effective shall remain perfected until they lapse as provided in [new U.C.C.], and may be continued as permitted by [new U.C.C.], except as stated in Section 11–105.

Discussion

This makes the [new Code] applicable to existing security interests, e.g., the revised notice provisions of Part 5 will apply to existing security interests. This would be so even if a 30–day notice period concerning retention of the collateral in lieu of sale were running on the effective date of the [new Code].

Suppose that a security interest attached in State A and the secured party filed in State B and assumed that he had 30 days to have the goods reach State B, in a non-purchase money case, under Section 9–103(3) of the [old Code]. Section 9–103(1)(c) of the [new Code] limits the 30–day provision on intended removals to purchase money cases. So long as an ample period of waiting and familiarization is allowed under Section 11–101, this should cause no practical problem.

The "except" clause at the end is necessary because of the possibility that new financing statements would have to be filed in different offices.

§ 11–104. Transition Provision on Change of Requirement of Filing.

A security interest for the perfection of which filing or the taking of possession was required under [old U.C.C.] and which attached prior to the effective date of [new U.C.C.] but was not perfected shall be deemed perfected on the effective date of [new U.C.C.] if [new U.C.C.] permits perfection without filing or authorizes filing in the office or offices where a prior ineffective filing was made.

Discussion

This covers the case of a purchase money security interest in consumer goods, which would not have had to be filed under the original Code if the goods had not been fixtures. Under the [new Code] the security interest will be perfected without filing, subject to the rights of real estate parties. Section 9–301(1)(d).

This also covers the case of factory or office machinery or replacement consumer goods appliances where the filing of a financing statement under the original Code in the regular chattel files was invalid because the goods were fixtures, but under the [new Code] that filing would be proper.

Under the [old Code] the status of assignments of revenues and similar collateral for governmental obligations was unclear. Section 9–104(e) of the [new Code] will make clear that Article 9 does not apply to these transfers. Section 11–108 of this draft may apply on the theory that the changes made by the [new Code] are considered to be merely declaratory. If this does not dispose of the matter, and if it might sometime be held that an assignment by a municipality had been ineffective for lack of filing, this provision would then apply from the effective date of the [new Code].

§ 11-105. Transition Provision on Change of Place of Filing.

(1) A financing statement or continuation statement filed prior to [effective date of new U.C.C.] which shall not have lapsed prior to [the effective date of new U.C.C.] shall remain effective for the period provided in the [old Code], but not less than five years after the filing.

(2) With respect to any collateral acquired by the debtor subsequent to the effective date of [new U.C.C.], any effective financing statement or continuation statement described in this section shall apply only if the filing or filings are in the office or offices that would be appropriate to perfect the security interests in the new collateral under [new U.C.C.].

(3) The effectiveness of any financing statement or continuation statement filed prior to [effective date of new U.C.C.] may be continued by a continuation statement as permitted by [new U.C.C.], except that if [new U.C.C.] requires a filing in an office where there was no previous financing statement, a new financing statement conforming to Section 11-106 shall be filed in that office.

(4) If the record of a mortgage of real estate would have been effective as a fixture filing of goods described therein if [new U.C.C.] had been in effect on the date of recording the mortgage, the mortgage shall be deemed effective as a fixture filing as to such goods under subsection (6) of Section 9-402 of the [new U.C.C.] on the effective date of [new U.C.C.].

Discussion

Subsection (1): All existing financing statements with a duration of less than 5 years are extended to the full 5 years. In the case of transmitting utilities for which a special rule of longer validity had been provided, the special rule will be continued.

Subsection (2) makes clear that all existing financing statements and continuations on the effective date remain valid for the remainder of the five years *as to existing collateral,* even though the appropriate place for filing may have changed under the new rules for accounts, general intangibles, etc. The existing filings also apply to new collateral acquired after the effective date, unless the appropriate filing place is different under the new rules. In that case there will have to be a new filing on the effective date to catch new collateral.

Subsection (3): A continuation statement may be filed after the effective date, but if the appropriate places under the new rules are different, the filing should be a financing statement.

Subsection (4) retroactively validates real estate mortgage recording as fixture filing.

§ 11-106. Required Refilings.

(1) If a security interest is perfected or has priority when this Act takes effect as to all persons or as to certain persons without any filing or recording, and if the filing of a financing statement would be required for the perfection or priority of the security interest against those persons under [new U.C.C.], the perfection and priority rights of the security interest continue until 3 years after the effective date of [new U.C.C.]. The perfection will then lapse unless a financing statement is filed as provided in subsection (4) or unless the security interest is perfected otherwise than by filing.

(2) If a security interest is perfected when [new U.C.C.] takes effect under a law other than [U.C.C.] which requires no further filing, refiling or recording to continue its perfection, perfection continues until and will lapse 3 years after [new U.C.C.] takes effect, unless a financing statement is filed as provided in subsection (4) or unless the security interest is perfected otherwise than by filing, or unless under subsection (3) of Section 9–302 the other law continues to govern filing.

(3) If a security interest is perfected by a filing, refiling or recording under a law repealed by this Act which required further filing, refiling or recording to continue its perfection, perfection continues and will lapse on the date provided by the law so repealed for such further filing, refiling or recording unless a financing statement is filed as provided in subsection (4) or unless the security interest is perfected otherwise than by filing.

(4) A financing statement may be filed within six months before the perfection of a security interest would otherwise lapse. Any such financing statement may be signed by either the debtor or the secured party. It must identify the security agreement, statement or notice (however denominated in any statute or other law repealed or modified by this Act), state the office where and the date when the last filing, refiling or recording, if any, was made with respect thereto, and the filing number, if any, or book and page, if any, of recording and further state that the security agreement, statement or notice, however denominated, in another filing office under the [U.C.C.] or under any statute or other law repealed or modified by this Act is still effective. Section 9–401 and Section 9–103 determine the proper place to file such a financing statement. Except as specified in this subsection, the provisions of Section 9–403(3) for continuation statements apply to such a financing statement.

Discussion

Subsection (1) covers farm equipment perfected without filing. The three-year period ought to cover most existing transactions. It also applies to equipment trusts, and would appear to allow three years for filing. But generally filing under Article 9 for equipment trusts is excluded by Section 9–302(3), and the old pre-amendment filing under the Interstate Commerce Act will continue to serve the purpose.

Subsection (2) covers transmitting utility statutes and the like which were *outside the Code,* and provided for indefinite duration. It allows three years for refiling. But perfection under a certificate of title law or the like continues to be effective.

Some states dealt with transmitting utilities by *internal amendment* of the Code to permit filing which was good indefinitely. Section 11–105(1) operates to validate those filings indefinitely even though they may not have been in the Secretary of State's office.

Similarly, Section 11–105(1) would preserve the effect of Ohio's present Section 9–403(2), which in effect makes financing statements related to combined real estate and chattel mortgages good for the duration of the real estate mortgage, whether or not the chattels are fixtures.

Subsection (3) covers the case (if any) where a prior transmitting utility provision outside the Code had a filing of limited duration.

Subsection (4) covers a case where an ordinary continuation statement cannot be filed because the original filing was a non-Code filing or was a Code filing in a different filing office. It was thought advisable to use the concept of financing statement rather than the concept of continuation statement for these fact situations.

§ 11–107. Transition Provisions as to Priorities.

Except as otherwise provided in [Article 11], [old U.C.C.] shall apply to any questions of priority if the positions of the parties were fixed prior to the effective date of [new U.C.C.]. In other cases questions of priority shall be determined by [new U.C.C.].

Discussion

Most questions of priority can be broken down to questions between two parties, and the rule is that the [new Code] applies unless the rights of both parties were fixed under the [old Code].

If a creditor acquires knowledge of an unfiled security interest before the effective date of the [new Code], but gets his judgment after the effective date, the rule of the [new Code] governs, since he has no rights until after judgment and levy.

§ 11–108. Presumption that Rule of Law Continues Unchanged.

Unless a change in law has clearly been made, the provisions of [new U.C.C.] shall be deemed declaratory of the meaning of the [old U.C.C.].

Discussion

This asserts that the new Code is declaratory, except where a change is clearly intended. This is an effort to minimize transitional problems.

APPENDIX III

ARTICLE 1 AND ARTICLE 9: 1987 CONFORMING AMENDMENTS [CONFORMING TO ARTICLE 2A]

§ 1–105. Territorial Application of the Act; Parties' Power to Choose Applicable Law.

(1) Except as provided hereafter in this section, when a transaction bears a reasonable relation to this state and also to another state or nation the parties may agree that the law either of this state or of such other state or nation shall govern their rights and duties. Failing such agreement this Act applies to transactions bearing an appropriate relation to this state.

(2) Where one of the following provisions of this Act specifies the applicable law, that provision governs and a contrary agreement is effective only to the extent permitted by the law (including the conflict of laws rules) so specified:

Rights of creditors against sold goods. Section 2–402.

Applicability of the Article on Leases. Sections 2A–105 and 2A–106.

Applicability of the Article on Bank Deposits and Collections. Section 4–102.

Bulk transfers subject to the Article on Bulk Transfers. Section 6–102.

Applicability of the Article on Investment Securities. Section 8–106.

Perfection provisions of the Article on Secured Transactions. Section 9–103.

Official Comment

Uniform Statutory Source: Section 1–105, 1978 Official Text of the Act.

Changes: Subsection (2) is amended to reference two sections of the Article on Leases (Article 2A), which is being promulgated at the same time as this amendment.

§ 1–201(37). General Definitions: "Security Interest".

(37) "Security interest" means an interest in personal property or fixtures which secures payment or performance of an obligation. The retention or reservation of title by a seller of goods notwithstanding shipment or delivery to the buyer (Section 2–401) is limited in effect to a reservation of a "security interest". The term also includes any interest of a buyer of accounts or chattel paper which is subject to Article 9. The special property interest of a buyer of goods on identification of ~~such~~ those goods to a contract for sale under Section 2–401 is not a "security interest", but a buyer may also acquire a "security interest" by complying with Article 9. Unless a ~~lease or~~ consignment is intended as security, reservation of title thereunder is not a

"security interest", but a consignment ~~is~~ in any event is subject to the provisions on consignment sales (Section 2–326). ~~Whether a lease is intended as security is to be determined by the facts of each case; however, (a) the inclusion of an option to purchase does not of itself make the lease one intended for security, and (b) an agreement that upon compliance with the terms of the lease the lessee shall become or has the option to become the owner of the property for no additional consideration or for a nominal consideration does make the lease one intended for security.~~

Whether a transaction creates a lease or security interest is determined by the facts of each case; however, a transaction creates a security interest if the consideration the lessee is to pay the lessor for the right to possession and use of the goods is an obligation for the term of the lease not subject to termination by the lessee, and

(a) the original term of the lease is equal to or greater than the remaining economic life of the goods,

(b) the lessee is bound to renew the lease for the remaining economic life of the goods or is bound to become the owner of the goods,

(c) the lessee has an option to renew the lease for the remaining economic life of the goods for no additional consideration or nominal additional consideration upon compliance with the lease agreement, or

(d) the lessee has an option to become the owner of the goods for no additional consideration or nominal additional consideration upon compliance with the lease agreement.

A transaction does not create a security interest merely because it provides that

(a) the present value of the consideration the lessee is obligated to pay the lessor for the right to possession and use of the goods is substantially equal to or is greater than the fair market value of the goods at the time the lease is entered into,

(b) the lessee assumes risk of loss of the goods, or agrees to pay taxes, insurance, filing, recording, or registration fees, or service or maintenance costs with respect to the goods,

(c) the lessee has an option to renew the lease or to become the owner of the goods,

(d) the lessee has an option to renew the lease for a fixed rent that is equal to or greater than the reasonably predictable fair market rent for the use of the goods for the term of the renewal at the time the option is to be performed, or

(e) the lessee has an option to become the owner of the goods for a fixed price that is equal to or greater than the reasonably predictable fair market value of the goods at the time the option is to be performed.

For purposes of this subsection (37):

(x) Additional consideration is not nominal if (i) when the option to renew the lease is granted to the lessee the rent is stated to be the fair market rent for the use of the goods for the term of the renewal determined at the time the option is to be performed, or (ii) when the option to become the owner of the goods is granted to the lessee the price is stated to be the fair market value of the goods determined at the time the option is to be performed. Additional consideration is nominal if it is less than the lessee's reasonably predictable cost of performing under the lease agreement if the option is not exercised;

(y) "Reasonably predictable" and "remaining economic life of the goods" are to be determined with reference to the facts and circumstances at the time the transaction is entered into; and

(z) "Present value" means the amount as of a date certain of one or more sums payable in the future, discounted to the date certain. The discount is determined by the interest rate specified by the parties if the rate is not manifestly unreasonable at the time the transaction is entered into; otherwise, the discount is determined by a commercially reasonable rate that takes into account the facts and circumstances of each case at the time the transaction was entered into.

Official Comment

Uniform Statutory Source: Section 1–201(37), 1978 Official Text of the Act.

Changes: Substantially revised.

Purpose: This amendment to Section 1–201(37) is being promulgated at the same time that the Article on Leases (Article 2A) is being promulgated as an amendment to this Act.

One of the reasons it was decided to codify the law with respect to leases was to resolve an issue that has created considerable confusion in the courts: what is a lease? The confusion exists, in part, due to the last two sentences of the definition of security interest in the 1978 Official Text of the Act. Section 1–201(37). The confusion is compounded by the rather considerable change in the federal, state and local tax laws and accounting rules as they relate to leases of goods. The answer is important because the definition of lease determines not only the rights and remedies of the parties to the lease but also those of third parties. If a transaction creates a lease and not a security interest, the lessee's interest in the goods is limited to its leasehold estate; the residual interest in the goods belongs to the lessor. This has significant implications to the lessee's creditors. "On common law theory, the lessor, since he has not parted with title, is entitled to full protection against the lessee's creditors and trustee in bankruptcy. . . ." 1 G. Gilmore, *Security Interests in Personal Property* § 3.6, at 76 (1965).

Under pre-Act chattel security law there was generally no requirement that the lessor file the lease, a financing statement, or the like, to enforce the lease agreement against the lessee or any third party; the Article on Secured Transactions (Article 9) did not change the common law in that respect. Coogan, Leasing and the Uniform Commercial Code, in *Equipment Leasing—Leveraged Leasing* 681, 700 n. 25, 729 n. 80 (2d ed.1980). The Article on Leases (Article 2A) has not changed the law in that respect, except for leases of fixtures. Section 2A–309. An examination of the common law will not provide an adequate answer to the question of what is a lease. The definition of security interest in Section 1–201(37) of the 1978 Official Text of the Act provides that the Article on Secured Transactions (Article 9) governs security interests disguised as leases, *i.e.*, leases intended as security; however, the definition is vague and outmoded.

Lease is defined in Article 2A as a transfer of the right to possession and use of goods for a term, in return for consideration. Section 2A–103(1)(j). The definition continues by stating that the retention or creation of a security interest is not a lease. Thus, the task of sharpening the line between true leases and security interests disguised as leases continues to be a function of this section.

The first paragraph of this definition is a revised version of the first five sentences of the 1978 Official Text of Section 1–201(37). The changes are modest in that they make a style change in the fourth sentence and delete the reference to lease in the fifth sentence. The balance of this definition is new, although it preserves elements of the last two sentences of the prior definition. The focus of the changes was to draw a sharper line between leases and security interests disguised as leases to create greater certainty in commercial transactions.

Prior to this amendment, Section 1–201(37) provided that whether a lease was intended as security (*i.e.*, a security interest disguised as a lease) was to be determined from the facts of each cases; however, (a) the inclusion of an option to purchase did not itself make the lease one intended for security, and (b) an agreement that upon compliance with the terms of the lease the lessee would become, or had the option to become, the owner of the property for no additional consideration, or for a nominal consideration, did make the lease one intended for security.

Reference to the intent of the parties to create a lease or security interest has led to unfortunate results. In discovering intent, courts have relied upon factors that were thought to be more consistent with sales or loans than leases. Most of these criteria, however, are as applicable to true leases as to security interests. Examples include the typical net lease provisions, a purported lessor's lack of storage facilities or its character as a financing party rather than a dealer in goods. Accordingly, amended Section 1–201(37) deletes all reference to the parties' intent.

The second paragraph of the new definition is taken from Section 1(2) of the Uniform Conditional Sales Act (act withdrawn 1943), modified to reflect current leasing practice. Thus, reference to the case law prior to this Act will provide a useful source of precedent. Gilmore, *Security Law, Formalism and Article 9*, 47 Neb. L. Rev. 659, 671 (1968). Whether a transaction creates a lease or a security interest continues to be determined by the facts of each case. The second paragraph further provides that a transaction creates a security interest if the lessee has an obligation to continue paying consideration for the term of the lease, if the obligation is not terminable by the lessee (thus correcting early statutory gloss, *e.g. In re Royer's Bakery, Inc.*, 1 U.C.C. Rep. Serv. (Callaghan) 342 (Bankr. E.D. Pa. 1963)) and if one of four additional tests is met. The first of these four tests, subparagraph (a), is that the original lease term is equal to or greater than the remaining economic life of the goods. The second of these tests, subparagraph (b), is that the lessee is either bound to renew the lease for the remaining economic life of the goods or to become the owner of the goods. *In re Gehrke Enters.*, 1 Bankr. 647, 651–52 (Bankr.W.D.Wis. 1979). The third of these tests, subparagraph (c), is whether the lessee has an option to renew the lease for the remaining economic life of the goods for no additional consideration or for nominal additional consideration, which is defined later in this section. *In re Celeryvale Transp.*, 44 Bankr. 1007, 1014–15 (Bankr. E.D. Tenn. 1984). The fourth of these tests, subparagraph (d), is whether the lessee has an option to become the owner of the goods for no additional consideration or for nominal additional consideration. All of these tests focus on economics, not the intent of the parties. *In re Berge*, 32 Bankr. 370, 371–73 (Bankr. W.D.Wis.1983).

The focus on economics is reinforced by the next paragraph, which is new. It states that a transaction does not create a security interest merely because the transaction has certain characteristics listed therein. Subparagraph (a) has no statutory derivative; it states that a full payout lease does not *per se* create a security interest. *Rushton v. Shea*, 419

F.Supp. 1349, 1365 (D. Del. 1976). Subparagraph (b) provides the same regarding the provisions of the typical net lease. *Compare All-States Leasing Co. v. Ochs*, 42 Or. App. 319, 600 P.2d 899 (Ct. App. 1979) *with In re Tillery*, 571 F.2d 1361 (5th Cir.1978). Subparagraph (c) restates and expands the provisions of former Section 1-201(37) to make clear that the option can be to buy or renew. Subparagraphs (d) and (e) treat fixed price options and provide that fair market value must be determined at the time the transaction is entered into. *Compare Arnold Mach. Co. v. Balls*, 624 P.2d 678 (Utah 1981) *with Aoki v. Shepherd Mach. Co.*, 665 F.2d 941 (9th Cir. 1982).

The relationship of the second paragraph of this subsection to the third paragraph of this subsection deserves to be explored. The fixed price purchase option provides a useful example. A fixed price purchase option in a lease does not of itself create a security interest. This is particularly true if the fixed price is equal to or greater than the reasonably predictable fair market value of the goods at the time the option is to be performed. A security interest is created only if the option price is nominal and the conditions stated in the introduction to the second paragraph of this subsection are met. There is a set of purchase options whose fixed price is less than fair market value but greater than nominal that must be determined on the facts of each case to ascertain whether the transaction in which the option is included creates a lease or a security interest.

It was possible to provide for various other permutations and combinations with respect to options to purchase and renew. For example, this section could have stated a rule to govern the facts of *In re Marhoefer Packing Co.*, 674 F.2d 1139 (7th Cir. 1982). This was not done because it would unnecessarily complicate the definition. Further development of this rule is left to the courts.

The fourth paragraph provides definitions and rules of construction.

§ 9-113. Security Interests Arising Under Article on Sales or Under Article on Leases.

A security interest arising solely under the Article on Sales (Article 2) or the Article on Leases (Article 2A) is subject to the provisions of this Article except that to the extent that and so long as the debtor does not have or does not lawfully obtain possession of the goods

(a) no security agreement is necessary to make the security interest enforceable; and

(b) no filing is required to perfect the security interest; and

(c) the rights of the secured party on default by the debtor are governed (i) by the Article on Sales (Article 2) in the case of a security interest arising solely under such Article or (ii) by the Article on Leases (Article 2A) in the case of a security interest arising solely under such Article.

Official Comment

Uniform Statutory Source: Section 9-113, 1978 Official Text of the Act.

Changes: This section is amended to include security interests arising under the Article on Leases (Article 2A), which is being promulgated at the same time as this amendment. Section 2A-508(5). After the effective date of the amendment to this section all references in the Act to Section 9-113 will be deemed to refer to this section, as amended. *E.g.*, Sections 9-203(1) and 9-302(1)(f).

Cross Reference:

Article 2A, esp. Section 2A–508(5).

Definitional Cross References:

"Agreement". Section 1–201(3).
"Goods". Section 2A–103(1)(h).
"Lease". Section 2A–103(1)(j).
"Party". Section 1–201(29).
"Rights". Section 1–201(36).
"Sale". Section 2–106(1).
"Security interest". Section 1–201(37).

APPENDIX IV

PRE-REVISION ARTICLE 6

Set forth below are the Text and Official Comments of Article 6 as they existed prior to revision in 1989.

ARTICLE 6

BULK TRANSFERS

---

§ 6–101. Short Title.

This Article shall be known and may be cited as Uniform Commercial Code—Bulk Transfers.

Official Comment

Prior Uniform Statutory Provision: None.

Purposes:

1. This Article attempts to simplify and make uniform the bulk sales laws of the states that adopt this Act.

2. Many states have bulk sales laws, of varying type and coverage. Their central purpose is to deal with two common forms of commercial fraud, namely:

(a) The merchant, owing debts, who sells out his stock in trade to a friend for less than it is worth, pays his creditors less than he owes them, and hopes to come back into the business through the back door some time in the future.

(b) The merchant, owing debts, who sells out his stock in trade to anyone for any price, pockets the proceeds, and disappears leaving his creditors unpaid.

3. The first is one form of fraudulent conveyance. The substantive law concerning it has been codified by the Commissioners in the Uniform Fraudulent Conveyance Act. No change in that Act is proposed. The contribution of the bulk sales laws to the problem is in the requirement that creditors receive advance notice of bulk sales. Having such notice, they can investigate the price and other

circumstances of the sale before it occurs, and determine then instead of later whether they should try to stop it. This is a valuable policing measure, and is continued. To be effective, it requires a longer notice than five days. This Article therefore follows in this respect those laws which require a longer notice (Sections 6-105, 6-108).

4. The second form of fraud suggested above represents the major bulk sales risk, and its prevention is the central purpose of the existing bulk sales laws and of this Article. Advance notice to the seller's creditors of the impending sale is an important protection against it, since with notice the creditors can take steps to impound the proceeds if they think it necessary. In many states, typified for instance by New York, such notice is substantially the only protection which bulk sales statutes give. Other states, typified for instance by Pennsylvania, give additional protection by imposing on the buyer an obligation to ensure that the money that he pays to his indebted seller is in fact applied to pay the seller's debts. This Article requires notice to creditors (Section 6-105) and if bracketed Section 6-106 is enacted it imposes the other obligation also.

5. These are the affirmative reasons for a law such as this Article. The objections are chiefly delay and red tape on legitimate transactions, and the possibility of a trap for the unwary buyer. It is hard to avoid the latter danger. But to minimize both it and the former the transactions subject to the Article are identified as clearly as possible and are limited to those which carry the dangers to be guarded against (Sections 6-102 and 6-103), and the sanctions are such as to permit honest and solvent buyers and sellers to put through transactions promptly without undue risk. Sections 6-104 through 6-108.

Cross References:

Point 3: Sections 6-105 and 6-108.
Point 4: Sections 6-105 and 6-106.
Point 5: Sections 6-102, 6-103, 6-104 through 6-108.

§ 6-102. "Bulk Transfers"; Transfers of Equipment; Enterprises Subject to This Article; Bulk Transfers Subject to This Article.

(1) A "bulk transfer" is any transfer in bulk and not in the ordinary course of the transferor's business of a major part of the materials, supplies, merchandise or other inventory (Section 9-109) of an enterprise subject to this Article.

(2) A transfer of a substantial part of the equipment (Section 9-109) of such an enterprise is a bulk transfer if it is made in connection with a bulk transfer of inventory, but not otherwise.

(3) The enterprises subject to this Article are all those whose principal business is the sale of merchandise from stock, including those who manufacture what they sell.

(4) Except as limited by the following section all bulk transfers of goods located within this state are subject to this Article.

Official Comment

Prior Uniform Statutory Provision: None.

Purposes:

1. Much of the litigation under the existing laws has dealt with the kinds of businesses and the kinds of transfers covered. This section defines these matters.

2. The businesses covered are defined in subsection (3). Notice that they do not include farming nor contracting nor professional services, nor such things as cleaning shops, barber shops, pool halls, hotels, restaurants, and the like whose principal business is the sale not of merchandise but of services. While some bulk sales risk exists in the excluded businesses, they have in common the fact that unsecured credit is not commonly extended on the faith of a stock of merchandise.

3. The transfers included are of "materials, supplies, merchandise or other inventory" that is, of goods. Transfers of investment securities are not covered by the Article, nor are transfers of money, accounts receivable, chattel paper, contract rights, negotiable instruments, nor things in action generally. Such transfers are dealt with in other Articles, and are not believed to carry any major bulk sales risk.

4. The kinds of transfers covered are identified in paragraph (1). They are believed to be those that carry the major bulk sales risks. They are further limited by the section following.

Cross References:

Point 3: Articles 3, 4, 8 and 9.
Point 4: Section 6-103.

§ 6-103. Transfers Excepted From This Article.

The following transfers are not subject to this Article:

(1) Those made to give security for the performance of an obligation;

(2) General assignments for the benefit of all the creditors of the transferor, and subsequent transfers by the assignee thereunder;

(3) Transfers in settlement or realization of a lien or other security interests;

(4) Sales by executors, administrators, receivers, trustees in bankruptcy, or any public officer under judicial process;

(5) Sales made in the course of judicial or administrative proceedings for the dissolution or reorganization of a corporation and of which notice is sent to the creditors of the corporation pursuant to order of the court or administrative agency;

(6) Transfers to a person maintaining a known place of business in this State who becomes bound to pay the debts of the transferor in full and gives public notice of that fact, and who is solvent after becoming so bound;

(7) A transfer to a new business enterprise organized to take over and continue the business, if public notice of the transaction is given and the new enterprise assumes the debts of the transferor and he receives nothing from the transaction except an interest in the new enterprise junior to the claims of creditors;

(8) Transfers of property which is exempt from execution.

Public notice under subsection (6) or subsection (7) may be given by publishing once a week for two consecutive weeks in a newspaper of general circulation where the transferor had its principal place of business in this state an advertisement including the names and addresses of the transferor and transferee and the effective date of the transfer.

As amended in 1962.

Official Comment

Prior Uniform Statutory Provision: None.

Purposes:

1. The section defines the transfers which although within the general definition of the previous section ought not to be subjected to the requirements of this Article.

2. Some of the existing Bulk Sales laws cover "bulk mortgages" as well as outright sales. In this Code security interests of all kinds in personal property are regulated by Article 9, Secured Transactions. Subsection (1) of this section therefore excludes all transfers for security from the operation of this Article. See also Sec. 9–111.

3. The exclusions described in subsections (2), (3), (4), (5) and (8) are believed to explain themselves.

4. Subsection (6) will exclude a great many transactions from the requirements of this Article. It is believed the exclusion is justified, and that it removes many of the objections to a law of this character. The transactions excluded are outright sales, since that is the only kind of a transaction in which the transferee is likely to bind himself to pay the transferor's debts. The purpose of this Article on outright sales is to give the seller's creditors a reasonable chance to collect their debts. (See Sections 6–104 through 6–108). If the buyer is willing to assume personal liability for those debts, and is himself solvent after such assumption, there is no reason to subject the transaction to the delay and red tape which this Article imposes.

5. Subsection (7) deals with certain changes in the ownership of a business, as by incorporation, change of membership of a firm, or transfer from a sole proprietor to a firm. The exclusion is believed to be justified within the limits stated in the subsection. Notice that in all the transactions to which the subsection applies (a) both the original debtor and the new enterprise are personally bound to pay the debts, (b) the property subject to the debts before the transfer is still subject to them, and (c) the original debtor has taken nothing out of the transaction except an interest (shares in a corporation, an interest in a firm, or a subordinated obligation) which is junior to the debts.

Cross References:

Point 1: Section 6–102.

Point 2: Section 9–111 and Article 9 generally.

Point 4: Sections 6–104 through 6–108.

Definitional Cross References:

"Creditor". Sections 1–201 and 6–109.

"Person". Section 1–201.

§ 6–104. Schedule of Property, List of Creditors.

(1) Except as provided with respect to auction sales (Section 6–108), a bulk transfer subject to this Article is ineffective against any creditor of the transferor unless:

(a) The transferee requires the transferor to furnish a list of his existing creditors prepared as stated in this section; and

(b) The parties prepare a schedule of the property transferred sufficient to identify it; and

(c) The transferee preserves the list and schedule for six months next following the transfer and permits inspection of either or both and copying therefrom at all reasonable hours by any creditor of the transferor, or files the list and schedule in (a public office to be here identified).

(2) The list of creditors must be signed and sworn to or affirmed by the transferor or his agent. It must contain the names and business addresses of all creditors of the transferor, with the amounts when known, and also the names of all persons who are known to the transferor to assert claims against him even though such claims are disputed. If the transferor is the obligor of an outstanding issue of bonds, debentures or the like as to which there is an indenture trustee, the list of creditors need include only the name and address of the indenture trustee and the aggregate outstanding principal amount of the issue.

(3) Responsibility for the completeness and accuracy of the list of creditors rests on the transferor, and the transfer is not rendered ineffective by errors or omissions therein unless the transferee is shown to have had knowledge.

As amended in 1962.

Official Comment

Prior Uniform Statutory Provision: None.

Purposes:

1. The section describes the information that must be compiled and kept available to creditors on all bulk transfers subject to this Article except those made by sale at auction. Additional requirements for particular kinds of transfers are stated in the succeeding Sections (6–105 through 6–107). The section on auction sales (Section 6–108) imposes similar requirements, but on different people and with a different sanction.

2. Except for the accuracy of the list of creditors, the sanction for non-compliance with the present section is that the transfer is ineffective against creditors of the transferor. The creditors referred to are those holding claims based on transactions or events occurring before the transfer (Section 6–109). Any such creditor or creditors may therefore disregard the transfer and levy on the goods as still belonging to the transferor, or a receiver representing them can take them by whatever procedure the local law provides. But it follows also that if the debts of the transferor are paid as they mature disregard of the requirements of the section creates no liability. And a defect can always be cured by paying off the unpaid creditors.

3. The sanction for the accuracy of the list of creditors is the criminal law of the state relative to false swearing, made applicable by subsection (2).

Cross References:

Point 1: Sections 6–105 through 6–108.
Point 2: Section 6–109.

Definitional Cross References:

"Bulk transfer". Section 6–102.
"Creditor". Sections 1–201 and 6–109.
"Party". Section 1–201.
"Person". Section 1–201.
"Signed". Section 1–201.

§ 6–105. Notice to Creditors.

In addition to the requirements of the preceding section, any bulk transfer subject to this Article except one made by auction sale (Section 6–108) is ineffective against any creditor of the transferor unless at least ten days before he takes possession of the goods or pays for them, whichever happens first, the transferee gives notice of the transfer in the manner and to the persons hereafter provided (Section 6–107).

Official Comment

Prior Uniform Statutory Provision: None.

Purposes:

1. This section is the heart of the Article. It requires notice to creditors of all bulk transfers subject to the Article, except those made by auction sale. The contents of the notice, the persons to whom it must be given, and the manner of giving it are stated in Section 6–107. The section on auction sales (6–108) also calls for notice, but by a different person and with a different sanction.

2. The notice in all cases must be given ten days in advance. See Points 3 and 4 to Section 6–101.

3. The sanction for noncompliance with the section is that the transfer is ineffective against creditors. Comment 2 to Section 6–104 applies.

Cross References:

Point 1: Sections 6–107 and 6–108.

Point 2: Points 3 and 4 to Section 6–101.

Point 3: Comment 2 to Section 6–104.

Definitional Cross References:

"Bulk transfer". Section 6–102.

"Creditor". Sections 1–201 and 6–109.

[§ 6–106. Application of the Proceeds].

In addition to the requirements of the two preceding sections:

(1) Upon every bulk transfer subject to this Article for which new consideration becomes payable except those made by sale at auction it is the duty of the transferee to assure that such consideration is applied so far as necessary to pay those debts of the transferor which are either shown on the list furnished by the transferor (Section 6–104) or filed in writing in the place stated in the notice (Section 6–107) within thirty days after the mailing of such notice. This duty of the transferee runs to all the holders of such debts, and may be enforced by any of them for the benefit of all.

(2) If any of said debts are in dispute the necessary sum may be withheld from distribution until the dispute is settled or adjudicated.

(3) If the consideration payable is not enough to pay all of the said debts in full distribution shall be made pro rata.]

Note: *This section is bracketed to indicate division of opinion as to whether or not it is a wise provision, and to suggest that this is a point on which State enactments may differ without serious damage to the principle of uniformity.*

In any State where this section is omitted, the following parts of sections, also bracketed in the text, should also be omitted, namely:

Section 6–107(2)(e).
6–108(3)(c).
6–109(2).

In any State where this section is enacted, these other provisions should be also.

Optional Subsection (4)

[(4) The transferee may within ten days after he takes possession of the goods pay the consideration into the (specify court) in the county where the transferor had its principal place of business in this state and thereafter may discharge his duty under this section by giving notice by registered or certified mail to all the persons to whom the duty runs that the consideration has been paid into that court and that they should file their claims there. On motion of any interested party, the court may order the distribution of the consideration to the persons entitled to it.]

> **Note:** *Optional subsection (4) is recommended for those states which do not have a general statute providing for payment of money into court.*

As amended in 1962.

Official Comment

Prior Uniform Statutory Provision: None.

Purposes:

1. This section applies only to transfers "for which new consideration becomes payable". It applies only if something, which of course need not be money, becomes payable in consideration of the transfer. The purpose of the section is to give the transferor's creditors direct protection against improper dissipation by the transferor of the consideration which he receives for the transfer. See Comment 4 to Section 6–101.

2. Subsections (6) and (7) of Section 6–103 remove many outright transfers from the operation of this Article and therefore of course of this section. In addition it is clear from the section itself that in any case in which the seller's debts are to be paid as they mature the buyer can disregard the section without danger of added liability except that his seller will disappoint him. And in case of trouble the buyer is entitled under Section 6–109(2) to credit for sums honestly paid to particular creditors.

3. The methods by which the buyer may perform the duty stated in the section are various. He may, for instance, by agreement with the seller hold the consideration in his own hands until the debts are ascertained, or deposit it in an account subject to checks bearing his counter-signature, or deposit it in escrow with an independent agency. If the affairs of the seller are so involved that nothing else is practical the buyer will no doubt pay the consideration into the registry of an appropriate court and interplead the seller's creditors. If optional subsection (4) is enacted, specific provision is made for such a procedure. But notice that the transferee's obligation runs, not to all possible creditors of the transferor who may appear at any time in the future, but only to existing creditors whom the transferee has a chance to identify in one of the ways provided in subsection (1). [This paragraph was amended in 1962].

Cross References:

Point 1: Section 6–108, Comment 4 to Section 6–101.

Point 2: Sections 6–103(6) and (7), 6–109(2).

Point 3: Section 6–109.

Definitional Cross References:

"Bulk transfer". Section 6–102.

"Creditor". Section 6–109.

"Writing". Section 1–201.

§ 6–107. The Notice.

(1) The notice to creditors (Section 6–105) shall state:

(a) that a bulk transfer is about to be made; and

(b) the names and business addresses of the transferor and transferee, and all other business names and addresses used by the transferor within three years last past so far as known to the transferee; and

(c) whether or not all the debts of the transferor are to be paid in full as they fall due as a result of the transaction, and if so, the address to which creditors should send their bills.

(2) If the debts of the transferor are not to be paid in full as they fall due or if the transferee is in doubt on that point then the notice shall state further:

(a) the location and general description of the property to be transferred and the estimated total of the transferor's debts;
(b) the address where the schedule of property and list of creditors (Section 6–104) may be inspected;
(c) whether the transfer is to pay existing debts and if so the amount of such debts and to whom owing;
(d) whether the transfer is for new consideration and if so the amount of such consideration and the time and place of payment; [and]
[(e) if for new consideration the time and place where creditors of the transferor are to file their claims.]

(3) The notice in any case shall be delivered personally or sent by registered or certified mail to all the persons shown on the list of creditors furnished by the transferor (Section 6–104) and to all other persons who are known to the transferee to hold or assert claims against the transferor.

Note: *The words in brackets are optional. See Note under § 6–106.*

As amended in 1962.

Official Comment

Prior Uniform Statutory Provision: None.

Purposes:

1. This section specifies the contents of the notice to be given on all the transfers covered by Section 6–105 (that is, all transfers subject to the Article except those made by auction sale) and the manner in which it is to be given.

2. Under the section, if the debts of the transferor are to be paid in full as they fall due, a short form of notice is provided. This facilitates honest and solvent transactions.

3. If the transfer is by auction sale Section 6–108 applies.

4. Subsection (2)(e) is a corollary of Section 6–106 and should be omitted if that section is. See note to Section 6–106.

Cross References:

Point 1: Section 6–105.
Point 3: Section 6–108.
Point 4: Note to Section 6–106.

Definitional Cross References:

"Bulk transfer". Section 6–102.
"Creditor". Sections 1–201 and 6–109.
"Person". Section 1–201.

§ 6–108. Auction Sales; "Auctioneer".

(1) A bulk transfer is subject to this Article even though it is by sale at auction, but only in the manner and with the results stated in this section.

(2) The transferor shall furnish a list of his creditors and assist in the preparation of a schedule of the property to be sold, both prepared as before stated (Section 6–104).

(3) The person or persons other than the transferor who direct, control or are responsible for the auction are collectively called the "auctioneer". The auctioneer shall:

(a) receive and retain the list of creditors and prepare and retain the schedule of property for the period stated in this Article (Section 6-104);

(b) give notice of the auction personally or by registered or certified mail at least ten days before it occurs to all persons shown on the list of creditors and to all other persons who are known to him to hold or assert claims against the transferor; [and]

[(c) assure that the net proceeds of the auction are applied as provided in this Article (Section 6-106).]

(4) Failure of the auctioneer to perform any of these duties does not affect the validity of the sale or the title of the purchasers, but if the auctioneer knows that the auction constitutes a bulk transfer such failure renders the auctioneer liable to the creditors of the transferor as a class for the sums owing to them from the transferor up to but not exceeding the net proceeds of the auction. If the auctioneer consists of several persons their liability is joint and several.

Note: *The words in brackets are optional. See Note under § 6-106.*

As amended in 1962.

Official Comment

Prior Uniform Statutory Provision: None.

Purposes:

1. The section is intended to make appropriate application of the requirements of this Article to auction sales. It is clear that the provisions of the four previous sections in their literal form cannot be applied directly to an auction, since neither the price nor the identity of the purchaser or purchasers can be known until the sale occurs. But it is equally clear that if auctions were excluded entirely from the transfers covered by this Article the way would be open to a debtor to carry out a bulk transfer of his property without notice to his creditors and without any duty upon anyone to see to the application of the proceeds. The section attempts to meet this situation by imposing the obligations stated in the section upon the persons there described.

2. Since the obligation to give advance notice, etc., cannot rest upon bidders at an auction it is clear that the sale must be effective so far as they are concerned whether or not the section is complied with. Subsection (4) therefore states a sanction which does not affect the purchasers. Notice that the sanction applies only "if the auctioneer knows that the auction constitutes a bulk transfer." No doubt in some cases, as for instance when goods are simply received on consignment for sale, he may not know.

3. Subsection (3)(c) is a corollary of Section 6-106 and should be omitted if that section is. See note to that section.

Cross References:

Point 1: Sections 6-104 through 6-107.
Point 2: Sections 6-104 through 6-107.
Point 3: Section 6-106 and Note thereto.

Definitional Cross References:

"Bulk transfer". Section 6-102.
"Creditor". Sections 1-201 and 6-109.
"Person". Section 1-201.
"Purchaser". Section 1-201.

§ 6–109. What Creditors Protected; [Credit for Payment to Particular Creditors].

(1) The creditors of the transferor mentioned in this Article are those holding claims based on transactions or events occurring before the bulk transfer, but creditors who become such after notice to creditors is given (Sections 6–105 and 6–107) are not entitled to notice.

[(2) Against the aggregate obligation imposed by the provisions of this Article concerning the application of the proceeds (Section 6–106 and subsection (3)(c) of 6–108) the transferee or auctioneer is entitled to credit for sums paid to particular creditors of the transferor, not exceeding the sums believed in good faith at the time of the payment to be properly payable to such creditors.]

Note: *The words in brackets are optional. See Note under § 6–106.*

Official Comment

Prior Uniform Statutory Provision: None.

Purposes:

1. Subsection (1) identifies the creditors who may have rights under the various provisions of this Article. The claims referred to of course include unliquidated claims.

2. Subsection (2) gives the transferee or auctioneer appropriate credit for honest payments to particular creditors. If Section 6–106 is omitted this subsection should be also. See note to that section.

Cross References:

Point 1: Sections 6–104 through 6–108.

Point 2: Section 6–106 and Note thereto.

Definitional Cross References:

"Auctioneer". Section 6–108.
"Bulk transfer". Section 6–102.
"Creditor". Section 1–201.
"Good faith". Section 1–201.

§ 6–110. Subsequent Transfers.

When the title of a transferee to property is subject to a defect by reason of his non-compliance with the requirements of this Article, then:

(1) a purchaser of any of such property from such transferee who pays no value or who takes with notice of such non-compliance takes subject to such defect, but

(2) a purchaser for value in good faith and without such notice takes free of such defect.

Official Comment

Prior Uniform Statutory Provision: None.

Purposes:

1. The section deals with subsequent transfers by the transferee.

2. The second transfer may of course itself be a "bulk transfer" subject to this Article. Whether it is or not will depend on its own character under Sections 6–102 and 6–103.

Cross References:

Point 2: Sections 6–102 and 6–103.

Definitional Cross References:

"Good faith". Section 1–201.
"Notice". Section 1–201.

"Purchaser". Section 1-201.
"Value". Section 1-201.

§ 6-111. Limitation of Actions and Levies.

No action under this Article shall be brought nor levy made more than six months after the date on which the transferee took possession of the goods unless the transfer has been concealed. If the transfer has been concealed, actions may be brought or levies made within six months after its discovery.

Official Comment

Prior Uniform Statutory Provision: None.

Purposes:

1. This Article imposes unusual obligations on buyers of property. A short statute of limitations is therefore appropriate.

2. The main sanction for non-compliance with the Article is that the transfer "is ineffective against any creditor of the transferor." Sections 6-104, 6-105. This means, e.g., that a judgment creditor of the transferor may levy execution on the property. See Comment 2 to Section 6-104.

In such a case, which may be expected to be frequent, no "action under this Article" will be necessary. The action will have been brought and prosecuted to judgment on whatever the claim was. The only thing done "under this Article" will be the levy and resulting sale.

The short statute of limitations is therefore made applicable to levies as well as actions. "Levy", which is not a defined term in the Code, should be read broadly as including not only levies of execution proper but also attachment, garnishment, trustee process, receivership, or whatever proceeding, under the state's practice, is used to apply a debtor's property to payment of his debts.

Definitional Cross Reference:

"Action". Section 1-201.

Note to Article 6: *Section 6-106 is bracketed to indicate division of opinion as to whether or not it is a wise provision, and to suggest that this is a point on which State enactments may differ without serious damage to the principle of uniformity.*

In any State where Section 6-106 is not enacted, the following parts of sections, also bracketed in the text, should also be omitted, namely:

Sec. 6-107(2)(e).
6-108(3)(c).
6-109(2).

In any State where Section 6-106 is enacted, these other provisions should be also.

APPENDIX V

PEB COMMENTARY ON THE UNIFORM COMMERCIAL CODE

COMMENTARIES 1–7
FINAL DRAFT

(March 10, 1990)

COMMENTARY 8
FINAL DRAFT
(December 10, 1991)

COMMENTARY 9
FINAL DRAFT
(June 25, 1992)

COMMENTARY 10
FINAL DRAFT
(February 10, 1994)

COMMENTARY 11
FINAL DRAFT
(February 10, 1994)

COMMENTARY 12
FINAL DRAFT
(February 10, 1994)

COMMENTARY 13
FINAL DRAFT
(February 16, 1994)

COMMENTARY 14
SECTION 9–102(1)(b)
FINAL DRAFT
(June 10, 1994)

COMMENTARIES 1–7
FINAL DRAFT

(March 10, 1990)

Permanent Editorial Board for the Uniform Commercial Code, 4025 Chestnut Street, Philadelphia, Pennsylvania 19104.

APPENDIX V

CONTENTS

PEB RESOLUTION ON PURPOSES, STANDARDS AND PROCEDURES FOR PEB COMMENTARY TO THE UCC

1. The Permanent Editorial Board (PEB), in accordance with the standards and procedures set out in this resolution of March 14, 1987, and the authority given in the agreement between the American Law Institute and the National Conference of Commissioners on Uniform State Laws dated July 31, 1986, will issue supplemental commentary on the Uniform Commercial Code (UCC) from time to time.

a. The supplemental commentary of the PEB generally will be known as *PEB Commentary,* to distinguish it from the Official Comments to the UCC, and will be preserved separately from the Official Comments.

b. The underlying purposes and policies of the *PEB Commentary* are those specified in UCC § 1–102(2). A *PEB Commentary* should come within one or more of the following specific purposes, which should be made apparent at the inception of the Commentary: (1) to resolve an ambiguity in the UCC by restating more clearly what the PEB considers to be the legal rule; (2) to state a preferred resolution of an issue on which judicial opinion or scholarly writing diverges; (3) to elaborate on the application of the UCC where the statute and/or the Official Comment leaves doubt as to inclusion or exclusion of, or application to, particular circumstances or transactions; (4) consistent with UCC § 1–102(2)(b), to apply the principles of the UCC to new or changed circumstances; (5) to clarify or elaborate upon the operation of the UCC as it relates to other statutes (such as the Bankruptcy Code and various federal and state consumer protection statutes) and general principles of law and equity pursuant to UCC § 1–103; or (6) to otherwise improve the operation of the UCC.

c. The format of the *PEB Commentary* normally will consist of an identification of the issue, a discussion concerning the possible resolutions of the issue to be addressed, and a statement of the view of the PEB as to how the issue should be resolved. On a carefully selected basis supplemental commentary may be issued as an identified supplement to the Official Comments, in which case it generally should take the form of a brief exposition modeled substantially on the form and style of the Official Comments.

d. Topics for *PEB Commentary* will be selected periodically by the PEB from suggestions, accompanied by supporting reasons, made by PEB members and by other persons. *PEB Commentary* may be issued whether or not a perceived issue has been litigated or is in litigation, and whether or not the position taken by the PEB accords with the weight of authority on the issue. The number of topics and topics that are chosen at any given time will be determined by the PEB weighing criteria appropriate under the circumstances, which may include the practical importance of the issue, the absence of other means of resolution, the time and effort to be involved in the preparation of the *PEB Commentary,* the extent to which the *PEB Commentary* is likely to be successful in addressing an issue, whether it is known to the PEB that the topic of the *PEB Commentary* is in specific litigation and, if so, the probable impact upon that litigation, and the availability of resources. However, normally no *PEB Commentary* should be begun with respect to a UCC Article that is undergoing amendment or initial promulgation except upon consultation with and concurrence of the study or drafting committee for such amendment or initial promulgation. Moreover, except in extraordinary cases and in the case of *PEB Commentary* identified as specific supplements to Official Comments, an Official Comment, as opposed to the text of the UCC, should not be the specific subject of *PEB Commentary.*

e. For a variety of reasons, topics initially identified by the PEB for *PEB Commentary* and advisors' drafts of *PEB Commentary* (discussed in paragraph 2 below) may not result in the final approval of *PEB Commentary.* Such reasons might include the failure of a consensus to emerge on the substance of an issue or a conclusion that the issue would better be treated by a change in the UCC Official Text. No inference should be drawn from, and no weight should be accorded to, any withdrawal of an advisor's draft or any failure to proceed with a *PEB Commentary* on any particular topic.

2. The process by which *PEB Commentary* is prepared and issued by the PEB should be flexible, but usually should include:

a. periodic publication of the topics under consideration by the PEB with a request for comment by interested persons by a stated date as to whether any listed topic should be deleted or a related topic added and as to the appropriate resolution of the issues presented by the topics under consideration;

b. selection of one or more appropriate advisers, who are not members of the PEB, to review any comments submitted by interested persons and other relevant materials and to prepare a tentative adviser's draft of the proposed *PEB Commentary;*

c. publication of the adviser's draft of the *PEB Commentary,* after supervisory review of the PEB, soliciting comments by interested persons by a stated date on the substance and style of the work;

d. approval by the PEB of the substance and style of the *PEB Commentary* as finally submitted by the adviser(s) and comments submitted by interested persons or, when warranted, the withdrawal of the proposal with the reasons for withdrawal stated; and

e. periodic publication of such *PEB Commentary* as is approved by the PEB on a regular schedule.

Approval by the PEB of *PEB Commentary* shall be by three quarters of the members of the PEB voting on the *Commentary.* The manner of publication of *PEB Commentary* by the PEB will be in accordance with procedures formulated under a resolution related to that subject generally.

PEB COMMENTARY NO. 1
SECTION 2–507(2)

ISSUE

A cash seller has the right to be paid upon delivery of goods and, if not paid, to reclaim the goods. This right is codified by § 2–507(2). Payment may be made by a check, but such payment is conditional and defeated by dishonor of the check giving rise to the seller's right of reclamation. Comment 3 to § 2–507(2) states:

> "Subsection (2) deals with the effect of a conditional delivery by the seller and in such a situation makes the buyer's 'right as against the seller' conditional upon payment. These words are used as words of limitation to conform with the policy set forth in the bona fide purchase sections of this Article. Should the seller after making such a conditional delivery fail to follow up his rights, the condition is waived. *The provision of this Article for a ten day limit within which the seller may reclaim goods delivered on credit to an insolvent buyer is also applicable here.*" (emphasis supplied)

If the payment is tendered by check, the seller payee will only learn that the check has been or will be dishonored *after* the goods are delivered. The seller will gain this information either by learning from the bank where the check was deposited that it had been dishonored by the payor bank; or, sometimes by inquiring directly of the payor bank and being told that there is no such account or there is an account but with insufficient funds to cover the check. Oftentimes, the seller may not learn of the dishonor or anticipated dishonor until more than ten days after delivery of the goods.[1] Does the reference in the Comment to the requirement of § 2–702(2) requiring a credit seller to demand reclamation of the goods "within ten days after the receipt" mean that the cash seller also loses the right of reclamation where demand is made more than ten days after delivery of the goods, even though the seller did not learn of the dishonor before then?

DISCUSSION

The cash seller's right of reclamation was a common law remedy in the nature of a lien. "The ground upon which an unpaid seller is allowed a lien and kindred remedies is the inherent injustice of depriving him of goods with which he has not finally parted where it is evident that he has not been paid or will not be paid the price for them when it is due." Williston, *Sales,* 99 (1948).

The "cash sale" is expressly mentioned in the voidable title provision of § 2–403(1)(c) (along with payment by check (§ 2–403(1)(b)), but the right of reclamation is not specifically mentioned. Instead, it is implicit in § 2–507(2) and § 2–511(3). As noted by the First Circuit in Szabo v. Vinton Motors, 630 F.2d 1, 3, 29 UCC Rep.Serv. (Callaghan) 737 (1st Cir.1980):

> "Although the right of such a cash seller to reclaim goods sold in a 'bad check' transaction is not specifically set forth in the Code provisions, [footnote

1. This problem should become less significant under Federal Reserve Board Regulation CC, 12 CFR Part 229, issued pursuant to the Expedited Funds Availability Act, 12 USC Section 4001 et seq. Under Section 229.30, the payor bank has a duty to effect an "expeditious return" of the check and if the check is for $2,500 or more, Section 229.33 requires that it provide notice of non-payment that is received by the depositary bank by 4:00 P.M. on the second business day following the banking day on which the check was presented; and that the depositary bank send notice to its customer by midnight of the banking day following its receipt of the notice or within a reasonable longer time.

> omitted] such a reclamation right is inherent in 2–507(2) and 2–511(3) of the Code, Mass. Gen. Laws ch. 106, §§ 2–507(2), 2–511(3). In re Mort Co., 208 F.Supp. 309, 310 [1 UCC Rep. 166] (ED Pa.1962); In re Helms Veneer Corp., 287 F.Supp. 840, 845–46 [5 UCC Rep. 977, 983–4] (WD Va.1968). See generally Mann & Phillips, The Cash Seller Under the Uniform Commercial Code, 20 B.C.L.Rev. 370, 375–84 (1979). Section 2–507(2) makes a buyer's 'right as against the seller to retain or dispose of [the goods] . . . conditional upon his making the payment due.' Section 2–511(3), in turn, provides that 'payment by check is conditional and is defeated as between the parties by dishonor of the check on due presentment.' Taking these two Code provisions together, the clear implication is that a buyer cannot retain and, conversely, a seller has the right to reclaim goods sold in a cash transaction if the buyer's check is dishonored.
>
> "The existence of the cash seller's right to reclaim is further supported, and limited, by Comment 3 to section 2–507:
>
> "[quotation omitted]
>
> "The reference in the last sentence of Comment 3 is to the limitation contained in § 2–702(2) requiring a credit seller to reclaim goods within ten days of receipt. See note 1 supra. Based on this reference, courts have invariably held that a cash seller must make a demand for the return of the goods within ten days after the goods are received by the buyer. E.g., In re Samuels & Co., 526 F.2d 1238, 1245 (5th Cir.) (en banc), cert. denied 429 U.S. 834 (1976); In re Helms Veneer Corp., supra, at 846 *** [footnote omitted]."

See also Dugan, *Cash Sellers Under Articles 2 and 9 of the UCC,* 8 UCC L.J. 330, 345–349 (1976).

Szabo, which represents the majority view by reason of the Comment, went on to hold that the seller's right of reclamation is lost if demand is made more than ten days after delivery of the goods:

> "Appellee urges us to disregard the limitation contained in Comment 3 on the ground that it directly contradicts the language of the Code. Although official Code Comments do not have the force of law, they are helpful in explaining the Code provisions and their purpose is to promote uniformity in construction. Mass.Gen. Laws ch. 106, Comment to Title; Thompson v. United States, 408 F.2d 1075, 1084 n. 15 (8th Cir.1969). See generally Skilton, Some Comments on the Comments to the Uniform Commercial Code, 1966 Wisc. L.Rev. 597. It has been stated that the Official Comments 'are powerful dicta.' In re Yale Express System, Inc., 370 F.2d 433, 437 (2d Cir.1966). Nevertheless, it is the Code provisions and not the Comments which control. We do not, however, accept appellee's argument that there is a direct conflict between the cash sale provisions of the Code and Comment 3 to § 2–507. As noted above, Comment 3 supports a reclamation right which is only implicit in §§ 2–507(2) and 2–511(3), and limits that right by reference to another Code provision, § 2–702(2), dealing with credit sales. Comment 3 does not contradict, but merely complements and explains the Code. We decline to disregard it." (630 F.2d at 3–4).

The Eighth Circuit, however, rejected *Szabo* in Burk v. Emmick, 637 F.2d 1172, 29 UCC Rep.Serv. (Callaghan) 1489 (8th Cir.1980):

> "We reject this reasoning. In our view, it would tend to coerce the cash seller who reasonably expects the buyer to tender payment at delivery to go through the cautious motions of a credit seller dealing with an economically unstable buyer. This we are not prepared to do. . . ." (637 F.2d at 1175 n. 6).

> "Our holding is quite limited. We determine that as between the seller and the buyer, where a cash seller reclaims goods sold to a breaching buyer, the only limitation imposed upon the seller's right is a reasonableness requirement...." (637 F.2d at 1176).

There is nothing in the language of § 2–507(2) supporting the imposition of the "ten day limit" mentioned in Comment 3. At common law, there was no specific time limitation. Rather, an attempt to reclaim after excessive delay would be defeated by doctrines such as waiver, estoppel, or ratification of the buyer's property interest. See, e.g., Frech v. Lewis, 218 Pa. 141, 67 A. 45 (1907). Under § 1–103, common law principles supplement Code provisions, unless "displaced by the particular provisions." Proper implementation of this doctrine compels the conclusion that the codification of the "cash sale" concept implicit in § 2–507(2), without any mention of a time limit, means that common law rules governing enforcement are still applicable. Indeed, the third sentence of Comment 3 is consistent with this interpretation in referring to waiver where a seller fails "to follow up his rights." The cases which, even though they rely on Comment 3, impose a ten day limit, must be considered to have reached an improper result. There is no need to impose a specific time limitation for enforcement of a cash seller's right of reclamation. The common law rules defeating the right where there is delay resulting in prejudice to the buyer adequately cover instances where only the seller and buyer are involved: If the rights of third parties are implicated § 2–403(1)(b) and (c) protect good faith purchasers.

CONCLUSION

There is no justification for barring the cash seller's right or remedy of reclamation before discovery of non-payment. There is no specific time limit for a cash seller to exercise the right of reclamation. The right may be exercised as long as there has not been an excessive delay causing inequitable prejudice to the buyer. Common law rules and precedents governing such circumstances are applicable.

The last sentence of Official Comment 3 to § 2–507 is deleted as inappropriate and replaced by the following:

> ... This subsection (2) codifies the cash seller's right of reclamation which is in the nature of a lien. There is no specific time limit for a cash seller to exercise the right of reclamation. However, the right will be defeated by delay causing prejudice to the buyer, waiver, estoppel, or ratification of the buyer's right to retain possession. Common law rules and precedents governing such principles are applicable (Section 1–103). If third parties are involved, Section 2–403(1) protects good faith purchasers. See PEB Commentary No. 1, dated March 10, 1990.

PEB COMMENTARY NO. 2
SECTION 9–301(4)

ISSUE

Section 9–301(4) provides: "A person who becomes a lien creditor while a security interest is perfected takes subject to the security interest only to the extent that it secures advances made before he becomes a lien creditor or within 45 days thereafter or made without knowledge of the lien or pursuant to a commitment entered into without knowledge of the lien." Does the phrase "only to the extent that it secures advances" limit the priority of the security interest to advances, as distinguished from, e.g., accruing interest, collection expenses, and similar ancillary rights (all herein called "non-advances")?

DISCUSSION

An example to illustrate the issue is the question whether non-advances, e.g., interest on advances accruing either before or after the lien arises, or expenses of foreclosure of the security interest arising after the lien arises, are excluded from the priority of pre-lien advances under the security interest by the language quoted above.

If § 9–301(4) were read in an exclusionary fashion as suggested in the issue above, it would put on the priority of a security interest a limitation which does not have any pre-Code precedents in chattel security law or similar real estate mortgage law. Even if the language were to be read as excluding only interest and expenses incurred after the creditor's lien arose, the limitation is believed to be without precedent except for some situations in which accruing interest and expenses were considered to be "inchoate" as that concept developed in federal law concerned with rights of the United States against secured parties under the Federal Preference Act, R.S. 3166, now 31 USC 3713, and under the Federal Tax Lien Act, 26 USC 6321–6323.

Section 9–301(4) was one of three sections (the others being §§ 9–307(3) and 9–312(7)) adopted by the 1972 amendments to Article 9 to solve the much debated question of the priority of future advances against intermediate security interests or buyers of the collateral or creditors having non-consensual liens on the collateral. See the 1972 General Comments of the Review Committee for Article 9, paragraphs E–39 to –45 (republished in West's Uniform Commercial Code, 1987 Official Text with Comments, pp. 910–912), which neither by their heading nor by their text offered any suggestion that the priority considered related to anything other than the future advances themselves, as distinguished from non-advances. To the same effect, the "Reasons for 1972 Change" to §§ 9–301(4) (Rights of Lien Creditors), 9–307(3) (Rights of Buyers) and 9–312(7) (Rights of Intervening Secured Parties) do not contain any suggestion that the sections undertake to affect the priorities of non-advances. The three sections are *in pari materia,* although they use somewhat different combinations of the same elements to reach varying results in three situations.

Sections 9–301(4) and 9–307(3) provide nearly identical rules as to the priority of subsequent advances against lien creditors and buyers respectively. Section 9–307(3) reads: "A buyer ... takes free of a security interest to the extent that it secures future advances made after the secured party acquires knowledge of the purchase, or more than 45 days after the purchase, whichever first occurs, unless made pursuant to a commitment entered into without knowledge of the purchase and before the expiration of the 45 day period." The only substantive difference between this and § 9–301(4), quoted at the beginning of the Commentary, is that in § 9–307(3) the effect of knowledge of the intervening rights is to shorten the specified 45-day period during which advances may be made with the same priority as the original advance, while in § 9–301(4) absence of knowledge is a factor which can extend beyond the 45 days the right to make post-lien advances with the same priority as the original advance.

The language in § 9–307(3) sets forth the rule for future advances without suggesting that it is exclusive and excludes any priority for non-advances, while § 9–301(4) is so phrased with the word "only" that on its face it excludes any right to non-advances. It is believed that this phraseology in § 9–301(4) was just an accident of draftmanship as the draftsmen concentrated on the problem discussed in the last paragraph of the "Reasons for 1972 Change" for § 9–301(4), namely, the effect of the rule chosen on priority of the security interest as against the Federal Tax Lien under the Federal Tax Lien Act of 1966.

CONCLUSION

Section 9–301(4) should not be read as excluding or limiting interest on advances or expenses made in their collection and enforcement, or other non-advances ancillary to advances having priority against the lien creditor.

This issue was presented in Dick Warner Cargo Handling Corp. v. Aetna Business Credit, Inc., 746 F.2d 126, 39 UCC Rep.Serv. (Callaghan) 762 (2d Cir.1984), and the Court held in accordance with this conclusion.

The Official Comment to § 9–301 is amended by adding the following:

8. The word "only" in subsection (4) is limited in its effect to the lien creditor's subjection to the specified advances. It does not limit the lien creditor's subjection to whatever other rights the secured party may have by contract or law, e.g., the right to interest before or after the attachment of the judgment lien to the collateral or the right to foreclosure expenses or other collection expenses. See PEB Commentary No. 2, dated March 10, 1990.

PEB COMMENTARY NO. 3
SECTIONS 9–306(2) AND 9–402(7)

ISSUE

Is there a conflict between UCC § 9–306(2), which terminates a security interest upon any disposition of the collateral that has been authorized by the secured party, and the last sentence of UCC § 9–402(7), which continues the effectiveness of a financing statement with respect to collateral that has been transferred even though the secured party knows of and consents to the transfer?

The issue can be described by the following hypothetical: Debtor ("D") has granted to Secured Party ("SP") a security interest in collateral consisting of equipment. The security interest is perfected by the filing of a financing statement naming D as the debtor. D disposes of the collateral to Transferee ("T") who assumes D's obligations under the security agreement. SP is aware of and consents to the disposition but only on the conditions that D remain liable on the secured indebtedness and that T make all payments and perform all obligations under the security agreement in a timely manner.

DISCUSSION

1. Section 9–306(2)

Section 9–306(2) (1972 Official Text) provides:

"Except where this Article otherwise provides, a security interest continues in collateral notwithstanding sale, exchange or other disposition thereof unless the disposition was authorized by the secured party in the security agreement or otherwise, and also continues in any identifiable proceeds including collections received by the debtor."

Section 9–306(2) treats only the issue of whether a security interest continues in collateral following disposition of the collateral. Assuming the security interest continues in the collateral after disposition, this Section does not deal with the issue of whether the secured party must take further action to continue the perfected status of its security interest in the collateral. Section 9–306(2) states the general rule that a security interest in collateral is not terminated upon a disposition of the collateral and can be enforced against the collateral in the hands of the transferee. *See* Official Comment No. 3 to UCC § 9–306(2).

Section 9–306(2), however, sets forth an exception to this rule if the secured party has authorized the disposition of the collateral in the security agreement or otherwise. The intent underlying this exception is to permit a disposition of the collateral free and clear of the security interest when the secured party has authorized the disposition free and clear of its security interest in the security agreement or otherwise. In the case of such an authorized disposition, the general rule of survivability of the security interest set forth in § 9–306(2) will not apply and the security interest will terminate upon the disposition. However, this exception to the rule of survivability only applies if the secured party has authorized the disposition, by agreement or otherwise, *free and clear of the security interest.* The exception will not apply if the secured party did not authorize the disposition of the collateral or if the secured party authorized the disposition subject to its security interest. This authorization issue presents a factual question. The questions of what facts will constitute an effective express or implied authorization for purposes of this Section and what standard of proof is applicable to this determination are not addressed in the Code but are instead left to other law.

If the disposition of the collateral has been authorized by the secured party free and clear of the security interest, the security interest will terminate upon the disposition and there will be no need to determine whether the secured party must take further action to continue the perfected status of the security interest in the collateral following its disposition. On the other hand, if the security interest in the collateral survives the disposition, the secured party must then determine whether further action is necessary to continue the perfected status of its security interest following the disposition. This is a perfection issue which is not governed by § 9–306(2). This perfection issue is governed by § 9–402(7).

2. Section 9–402(7)

The last sentence of § 9–402(7) provides that "a filed financing statement remains effective with respect to collateral transferred by the debtor even though the secured party knows of or consents to the transfer."

This sentence, which was added in the 1972 Official Text, was intended to resolve an ambiguity in the 1962 Code as to whether a secured party is required to file an amended or new financing statement when the collateral is transferred. Substantial policy arguments can be made on both sides of this issue. Those favoring a refiling obligation when collateral is transferred argue that, absent refiling in the name of the transferee, secured creditors searching in the name of the transferee could be misled since they would not discover a financing statement filed in the name of the transferor. Allowing a filing against the transferor to be effective against creditors of the transferee would thus promote hidden liens in violation of the public notice purposes of Article 9. Those who argue against a refiling obligation as to collateral transferred by the debtor point to the enormous policing responsibility that a refiling duty would impose on secured creditors of the transferor, most of whom have no continuing contact with the transferor after the secured transaction other than to receive installment payments on the secured indebtedness. A refiling obligation linked to the secured creditor's "notice" or "knowledge" of the transfer would create difficult problems of proof and would foster litigation with all of its resultant costs and uncertainties. Secured creditors of the transferee can protect themselves against filings in the name of prior owners of the collateral by tracing ownership of the collateral and searching in the names of prior owners. This tracing obligation, it is argued, is not an unreasonable burden to place on creditors of the transferee since they would have this responsibility anyway in order to insure that their debtor (the transferee) has rights in the collateral sufficient to grant a security interest.

Balancing these competing policy concerns, the National Conference of Commissioners on Uniform State Laws and the American Law Institute, in adopting § 9–402(7), opted in favor of the no refiling rule as to collateral transferred by the debtor. Thus, the last sentence of § 9–402(7) makes it clear that the secured party has no refiling obligation even if the secured party knows that the collateral has been transferred or even authorized or consented to the transfer. Official Comment 8 to § 9–402(7) explains the purpose of the last sentence in § 9–402(7):

> "Subsection (7) also deals with a different problem, namely whether a new filing is necessary where the collateral has been transferred from one debtor to another. This question has been much debated both in pre-Code law and under the Code. This Article now answers the questions in the negative. Thus, any person searching the condition of the ownership of a debtor must make inquiry as to the debtor's source of title, and must search in the name of a former owner if circumstances seem to require it."

3. Harmonizing Sections 9–306(2) and 9–402(7)

Read together, §§ 9–306(2) and 9–402(7) lead to the following results when collateral is disposed of:

> If the secured party does not authorize the disposition or if the secured party authorizes the disposition subject to the security interest, the security interest will continue in the collateral following the disposition (§ 9–306(2)) and no new financing statement or amendment to the existing financing statement will be required in order to continue the perfected status of the security interest in the collateral following the disposition (§ 9–402(7)).
>
> If the secured party, in the security agreement or otherwise, authorizes the disposition free and clear of the security interest, the security interest will terminate the disposition (§ 9–306(2)) and there will be no need to be concerned with perfection issues under § 9–402(7).

Returning to the hypothetical, this analysis yields the following results: D's disposition of the collateral to T will not terminate SP's security interest under § 9–306(2) since SP did not authorize the disposition free and clear of its security interest. The disposition of the collateral was authorized by SP but subject to T's recognition of SP's security interest in the collateral. Thus, under § 9–306(2), SP's security interest continues in the collateral following the disposition. Under § 9–402(7), SP's filed financing statement remains effective following the disposition of the collateral by D to T even though SP was aware of and consented to the disposition. Therefore, SP need not file a new financing statement in the names of D or T or take any other action to continue the perfected status of its security interest in the collateral. This Commentary does not imply that the secured creditor need not take filing action if required by other Sections of the Code (e.g., Sections 9–103(1), 9–103(3) or 9–401(3)) based upon a change in location of the collateral or a change in the debtor's location following the transfer of the collateral by the debtor.

CONCLUSION

There is no conflict between § 9–306(2) and the last sentence of § 9–402(7). Section 9–306(2) deals with the effect of a disposition of the collateral upon a security interest in the collateral and sets forth a general rule of survivability which applies unless the secured party authorizes the disposition free and clear of the security interest. The last sentence of § 9–402(7) only has operative effect if the security interest survives the disposition under § 9–306(2). In this instance, the last sentence of § 9–402(7) continues the perfected status of the security interest in the transferred collateral even though the secured party may have authorized or consented to the disposition. Cases reaching this conclusion as to the interplay between UCC §§ 9–306(2) and 9–402(7) include In re Southern Properties, Inc., 44 B.R. 838, 40 UCC Rep.Serv. (Callaghan) 1089 (Bkcy.E.D.Va.1989); Loeb v. Franchise Distributors, Inc. (In re Franchise Systems, Inc.), 46 B.R. 158, 40 UCC Rep.Serv. (Callaghan) 689 (Bkcy.N.D.Ga.1985); and Matto's Inc. v. Olde Colonie Place (In re Matto's Inc.), 30 UCC Rep.Serv. (Callaghan) 1750 (Bkcy.E.D.Mich.1981).

The second paragraph of Official Comment 3 to UCC § 9–306 is supplemented as follows:

> In many cases a purchaser or other transferee of collateral will take free of a security interest: in such cases the secured party's only right will be to proceeds. A transferee will acquire the collateral free and clear of a preexisting security interest only if the disposition of the collateral by the debtor was authorized by the secured party free and clear of the secured party's security interest. If the disposition was not authorized by the secured party, or was

authorized by the secured party subject to the secured party's security interest, the transferee will not acquire the collateral free and clear of the security interest. The authorization may be contained in the security agreement or otherwise given. The right to proceeds, either under the rules of this section or under specific mention thereof in a security agreement or financing statement does not in itself constitute an authorization of sale. PEB Commentary No. 3, dated March 10, 1990, analyzes the interplay between this Section and Section 9–402(7).

Official Comment 8 to UCC § 9–402 is amended to add the following paragraph at the end of the Comment:

PEB Commentary No. 3, dated March 10, 1990, explains the interplay between this Section and Section 9–306(2). As explained in this Commentary, this Section is consistent with Section 9–306(2) since Section 9–306(2) deals with the continuation or termination of a security interest in collateral following a disposition of the collateral. The last sentence of Section 9–402(7), on the other hand, deals with the continued effectiveness of a filed financing statement to perfect any security interest that continues in the collateral following its disposition.

PEB COMMENTARY NO. 4
SECTION 8–207(1)

ISSUE

Section 8–207(1) provides that

> (1) Prior to due presentment for registration of transfer of a certificated security in registered form, the issuer or indenture trustee may treat the registered owner as the person exclusively entitled to vote, to receive notifications, and otherwise to exercise all the rights and powers of an owner.

This section has been part of the UCC since its inception, the only change made by the 1977 amendments being the addition of the word "certificated."

Under what circumstances will a distribution of money or other property to the registered owner of a certificated security provide the issuer with a defense against a claim to that distribution asserted by a pledgee who was a bona fide purchaser and in possession of that security at the time of such distribution?

DISCUSSION

1. The Statutory Scheme

As between the parties, the rights of the owner of a registered certificated security are transferred to a purchaser when the security is delivered to the purchaser. § 8–313(1)(a). The issuer is required to register that transfer when the security is presented to it with an appropriate request. § 8–401(1). Thus, between the time of delivery and presentment, the registered owner and the person ultimately entitled to the rights of ownership will be different parties. The objective of § 8–207(1) is to protect the issuer by express authorization to treat the original registered owner of a security, during this "gap" period, as the person entitled to the rights of ownership, including the right to receive distributions with respect thereto. Such protection is clearly necessary, since, in the vast majority of cases, the issuer would have no knowledge that a transfer had been made or know the identity of the purchaser. Inherent in this scheme is that a distribution to the registered owner will relieve the issuer from any liability to the purchaser for the same distribution. Without that protection, no issuer could safely make any distribution without requiring the surrender, or exhibition, of the security by the distributee—a patently impractical requirement.

In the context of outright sales of securities, the rule of § 8–207(1) does not constitute a serious problem. In such transactions, the period of incongruity between registered and actual ownership will be of limited duration, since the purchaser will normally present the security for registration of transfer as promptly as possible. The nature, amount, and record date of any imminent distributions can usually be ascertained and can be reflected in the price or otherwise adjusted between the parties.

In the context of pledges of securities, however, the pledgee, in most cases, takes delivery of the security, duly endorsed for transfer, but does not present it to the issuer for registration of transfer. Possession of the security by the pledgee effectively prevents the pledgor from transferring it to another purchaser and places the pledgee in the position where registration of transfer can be obtained in the event of the pledgor's default. When the loan is repaid, as most loans are, the securities, still registered in the pledgor's name, are returned to the pledgor. This procedure avoids two unnecessary registrations of transfer—pledgor to pledgee and, then, pledgee back to pledgor.

Furthermore, while the loan is outstanding, the pledgor, who remains the registered owner, continues to receive reports, proxy materials, and periodic dividend or interest payments, directly from the issuer and without inconvenience to the pledgee. This is precisely the result normally intended by the parties to the pledge transaction. See § 9–207(2)(c). Hence, even in the pledge context, the rule of § 8–207(1), notwithstanding the existence of dual interests in the security, generally produces results that are both efficient and fair.

2. The Problem

Section 8–207(1) does not define or limit the phrase "all the rights and powers of an owner." If that phrase is construed, as it logically might be, to include the right to receive *all* distributions, the issuer may, with impunity, distribute, to the registered owner, not only regular cash dividends and interest payments, but also extraordinary cash dividends, negotiable securities in connection with stock dividends, stock splits and spin-offs and, indeed, cash in complete liquidation of stock or partial or complete redemption of debt or redeemable equity securities.

Thus, the pledgee that fails to present its collateral for registration of transfer subjects itself to the continuing risk that the issuer will distribute cash and/or negotiable securities to the pledgor, which, if not turned over to the pledgee as the pledge agreement would normally require, will have the effect of substantially reducing or eliminating the value of the collateral in its possession. For example, the distribution of stock to the pledgor, in connection with a two-for-one split, would leave the pledgee with collateral worth only half its pre-split value, and the distribution of cash to the pledgor, as a final liquidating dividend, would render the pledgee's collateral worthless.

The pledgee, of course, is not without power to avoid these dire consequences. It could, routinely, present its collateral for registration of transfer in every pledge transaction, but only with the attendant extra expense, which would ultimately be borne by all borrowers. Alternatively, it can evaluate the risk in any particular transaction, taking into account such factors as the financial strength and integrity of the pledgor, the identity of the issuers and the likelihood that any contemplated extraordinary distributions will receive advance public notice, the extent to which the pledged securities are diversified, and the magnitude of any collateral "cushion." The fact remains, however, that part of the price paid for the protection afforded the issuer by § 8–207(1) is the risk borne by the pledgee who does not register the transfer.

3. The Cases

It is encouraging to note that only two reported cases have raised the question of the scope of issuer protection for distributions made to registered owners pursuant to § 8–207(1). Because of the aberrational fact situations involved, neither case directly addressed the issue as stated.

In New England Merchants Bank of Boston v. Old Colony Trust Co., 385 Mass. 24, 429 N.E.2d 1143, 32 UCC Rep.Serv. (Callaghan) 1592 (Mass.1982), affirming 11 Mass.App. 539, 417 N.E.2d 471, 30 UCC Rep.Serv. (Callaghan) 1661 (Mass.App.1981), the issuer, in paying a liquidating dividend, did not rely on § 8–207(1), which permits, but does not require, an issuer to recognize the registered owner, without further proof, as the person entitled to receive distributions. Rather, with an abundance of prudence, it required surrender of the stock certificates as a condition of payment. The certificates that were surrendered had been issued to the registered owner, five years earlier, to replace the original certificates which the owner had asserted were lost. Pursuant to § 8–405(2), the issuer had obtained a lost securities indemnity bond.

The claimant was the administrator of an intestate estate who had found the original certificates among the decedent's papers. Apparently, they had been delivered to the decedent, endorsed in blank, almost thirty years before, and no attempt had been made to have the transfer registered on the books of the issuer. Upon surrender of the certificates to the issuer, the claimant demanded payment of the liquidating dividend.

In denying the claim, the court stated: (1) that payment to the registered owner, pursuant to § 8–207(1) constitutes a defense against the possessor of the certificates; (2) that § 8–207(1) makes no distinction between ordinary and liquidating dividends; and (3) that the plaintiff had not established that he was a bona fide purchaser, implying that the result might have been different if he had so established. The question of bona fide purchase is relevant to the case, but only under the provisions of § 8–405(3), which deals with the rights of the holder of a security that has been reported lost and has previously been replaced.

In Bank of Honolulu v. Hawaii Corp., 829 F.2d 813, 4 UCC Rep.Serv.2d (Callaghan) 837 (9th Cir.1987), reversing 59 B.R. 410, 42 UCC Rep.Serv. (Callaghan) 1736 (Bkcy.D.Haw.1986), the claimant, a pledgee bank that had received stock certificates as collateral for a loan to the issuer's president, was unquestionably a bona fide purchaser. Subsequently, the issuer entered a Chapter X bankruptcy proceeding. The issuer's Trustee brought suit against the pledgor which was ultimately settled. As part of the settlement, the pledgor released the Trustee from "all claims ... or interests." When it later developed that there would be a distribution to stockholders, the bank filed a Proof of Stock Interest, based on the pledged stock.

The Trustee refused to honor the bank's Proof on the ground that § 8–207(1) permitted the issuer to treat the pledgor, who remained the registered owner, as the person who could "exercise all the rights and powers of an owner." In his view, these included the right to dispose of the stock, free of the pledgee's interest, in what was, essentially, a privately negotiated transaction. The trial court agreed.

The Ninth Circuit reversed, ordering entry of judgment for the bank. In so holding, however, the court stated: (1) that payment, even pursuant to § 8–207(1), does not constitute "a defense ... going to the validity of the security," which, in the court's view, is required under § 8–105(2)(c); (2) "that § 8–207 is meant to apply [only] in what might be called the normal case ... the payment of dividends in the normal course of business"; and (3) that "negotiability is negated when the transferror retains rights which ... will frustrate the exercise of rights by the transferee."

While the results in both these cases are probably correct under their own peculiar facts, the gratuitous statements of the respective courts, supporting their holdings, are in conflict with each other and tend to confuse, rather than clarify, the proper construction of the intent, scope, and limitations of § 8–207(1).

CONCLUSION

In light of this confusion, and in an effort to promote a reasonable and uniform construction of § 8–207(1), the Board offers the following guidelines:

(1) *A distribution to the registered owner of a security is protected under § 8–207(1) only if it is distributable to the owners of all securities of the same issue.* This rule would prevent an issuer from acquiring a security, free of claims, in a negotiated transaction with the registered owner without requiring surrender of the security. In such a transaction, which is, in effect, a purchase rather than a distribution by the issuer, requiring delivery of the security imposes no burden on the issuer that is not borne by any purchaser. It supports the result in the *Hawaii* case.

(2) *If the terms of a security require its surrender as a condition of payment or exchange, a distribution to the registered owner in payment or exchange is not protected under § 8–207(1) unless the security is surrendered.* The requirement of surrender is commonly included in the terms of debt securities, redeemable equity securities, and convertible securities. Since the outstanding security is rendered worthless by the redemption or exchange, it is clearly in the interest of all concerned to get it out of circulation. Even if surrender is not required by the terms of the security, issuers may, and, as a matter of prudence, frequently do, as did the issuer in the *New England Merchants* case, require surrender as a condition of payment of a liquidating dividend.

(3) *Distributions to all the registered owners of a security, the terms of which do not require the surrender thereof, are protected under § 8–207(1), regardless of the regularity, amount, or nature of such distributions.* This rule rejects the suggestion that only regular dividend and interest payments can be safely distributed to the registered owners. The issuer's lack of knowledge of unregistered transfers, which requires protection for regular payments to the registered owners, also demands similar protection for the distributions in stock dividends, stock splits, spin-offs, and other extraordinary distributions, even though they may substantially impair the value of the outstanding securities.

(4) *A distribution to the registered owner that is protected under § 8–207(1) constitutes a defense against a claim to such distribution by a person in possession of the security, even if such person is a bona fide purchaser.* The entire purpose of § 8–207(1) would be vitiated if a distribution protected by it could *not* be successfully asserted against a claim by a person in possession of the security, who, in most cases, will be a bona fide purchaser. This result can be justified by charging the transferee who elects not to register a transfer with knowledge of § 8–207(1) and notice that any distributions protected under that section will be made directly to the registered owner.

The Board believes that these guidelines strike a proper balance between the right of an issuer to rely solely on its registration records in making distributions and the ability of a pledgee to rely on its possession of a security to protect it against diminutions of value that cannot be reasonably anticipated.

The Official Comment to § 8–207 is supplemented by the addition of the following paragraph, immediately following the first paragraph of Official Comment 1:

> The issuer may, under this section, make distributions of money or securities to the registered owners of certificated securities without requiring further proof of ownership, provided that such distributions are distributable to the owners of all securities of the same issue and the terms of the security do not require its surrender as a condition of payment or exchange. Any such distribution shall constitute a defense against a claim for the same distribution by a person, even if that person is in possession of the security and is a bona fide purchaser of the security. See PEB Commentary No. 4, dated March 10, 1990.

PEB COMMENTARY NO. 5
SECTION 9–306(5)

ISSUE

Section 9–306(5)(b) gives a purchaser of a conditional sales contract or other chattel paper ("chattel paper financer") a security interest in the goods covered by the chattel paper against the seller of the goods (and of the chattel paper) if the chattel paper financer is "unpaid" and the goods are "returned to or are repossessed by the seller or the secured party." If the chattel paper financer had obtained priority in the chattel paper pursuant to § 9–308 over a secured party with a security interest in the seller's goods ("inventory financer"), does § 9–306(5)(b) enable the chattel paper financer to retain that priority without having to further perfect "for protection" under § 9–306(5)(d) against the inventory financer?

DISCUSSION

The issue will usually arise in the context of the following fact situation: (I) Secured Party #1 ("inventory financer") has a perfected security interest in all the inventory of a dealer in goods ("Dealer"); (II) Dealer sells some of its inventory to a buyer in the ordinary course of business ("BIOCOB") pursuant to a conditional sales contract ("chattel paper"); and (III) Secured Party #2 ("chattel paper financer") purchases the chattel paper from Dealer and takes possession of the paper in the ordinary course of its business.

Secured Party #1's security interest in the sold goods terminates under § 9–307(1) when they are sold to BIOCOB. However, Secured Party #1's security interest continues in the chattel paper as proceeds. If the goods are thereafter returned to Dealer, § 9–306(5)(a) provides that "if the goods were collateral at the time of sale for an indebtedness of the seller which is still unpaid," Secured Party #1's security interest in the goods "attaches again to the goods and continues as a perfected security interest." In effect, the returned goods are proceeds of the chattel paper.

Section 9–306(5)(b) also gives Secured Party #2 a security interest in the same returned goods against Dealer and states that this security interest is "prior to a security interest under [§ 9–306(5)(a)] to the extent that the [chattel paper financer] was entitled to priority under Section 9–308." This interplay between § 9–306(5)(a) and (b) arises in the following two circumstances.

First, when BIOCOB's obligation is terminated because the goods are returned to Dealer pursuant to an agreement with Dealer or because BIOCOB had a right to rescind the sale, e.g., revoke acceptance under § 2–608. See Official Comment 4 to § 9–306(5). In that circumstance, the goods once again become part of Dealer's inventory and are subject to Secured Party #1's security interest. However, because Secured Party #2 has not been paid pursuant to the chattel paper, § 9–306(5)(b) gives Secured Party #2, as an "unpaid transferee" of the chattel paper, a security interest in the goods against Dealer to secure the amount remaining unpaid under the chattel paper at the time BIOCOB's obligation was terminated.[1]

1. Dealer's sale of the chattel paper is usually accompanied by a warranty that the chattel paper is genuine, valid and enforceable according to its term. Inasmuch as BIOCOB's obligation has been terminated, Secured Party has lost the benefit of the bargain it made in purchasing the chattel paper from Dealer, i.e., the right to receive all payments required thereunder. Dealer, who has reacquired the goods, either by agreement or because BIOCOB had the right to revoke acceptance, is,

Second, when the goods are repossessed because BIOCOB has defaulted under the chattel paper and are returned to Dealer whereat Secured Party #2 then sells the goods pursuant to § 9–504. In that circumstance, if the goods are purchased at the foreclosure sale either (a) by Dealer or (b) by Secured Party #2 who then conveys the goods to Dealer pursuant to an agreement by Dealer to repurchase the goods, § 9–306(5) is applicable if Dealer does not then pay Secured Party #2 the purchase price.[2] In both of these instances, the goods once again become part of Dealer's inventory and are subject to Secured Party #1's security interest. However, because Dealer has not paid Secured Party #2 the purchase price for the goods, § 9–306(5)(b) gives Secured Party #2, as an unpaid transferee, a security interest in the goods against Dealer to secure Dealer's obligation to pay the purchase price, i.e. the successful bid price at the foreclosure sale[3] or the amount due under the repurchase agreement,[4] as the case may be.

This security interest of Secured Party #2 in the goods against Dealer is separate and distinct from the security interest evidenced by the chattel paper itself in which BIOCOB is the debtor. It attaches to the goods when returned to Dealer, whether voluntarily or through revocation of acceptance or repossession, and upon Dealer acquiring "rights in the collateral" by reason of the (i) revocation of acceptance or (ii) agreement with BIOCOB or (iii) purchase of the goods at the foreclosure sale or (iv) repurchase agreement. § 9–203(1)(c). In essence, Secured Party #2 has a security interest against Dealer in the returned goods as the proceeds of the secured transaction represented by the purchase of the chattel paper from the Dealer. In both instances, Secured Party #2 is the secured party and Dealer is the debtor. ". . . When the underlying goods are returned or repossessed, the chattel paper interest automatically shifts to the goods. . . ." 2 Gilmore, *Security Interests in Personal Property,* § 27.5.

Under § 9–306(5)(b), Secured Party #2's security interest in the returned goods against Dealer is

> ". . . prior to a security interest under paragraph (a) [i.e. that of Secured Party #1] to the extent that the transferee of the chattel paper [Secured Party #2] was entitled to priority under Section 9–308."

In the above circumstances, Secured Party #2 had priority in the chattel paper at the time it purchased the chattel paper for new value from Dealer over Secured Party #1's claim to the chattel paper as proceeds of the inventory. § 9–308(b). Accordingly, § 9–306(5)(b) gives Secured Party #2 priority over Secured Party #1 in the returned goods. This result is consistent with the policy of encouraging the purchase of chattel

therefore, liable to Secured Party #2 for those remaining payments.

2. Frequently, there will be an agreement that Dealer need not pay the purchase price until it is able to re-sell the goods.

3. When the sale or disposition to enforce the security interest in the goods is made, the proceeds are applied to BIOCOB's indebtedness under the chattel paper and BIOCOB is entitled to any surplus and liable for any deficiency. § 9–504(1) and (2). The amount due from Dealer on the sale is usually the same as the amount due under the chattel paper, but might be a different amount. Secured Party #2's security interest against Dealer terminates upon payment of that amount to Secured Party #2, but if that amount is less than that due under the chattel paper, BIOCOB remains liable to Secured Party #2 for that deficiency.

4. Instead of an agreement for Dealer to repurchase the goods, there could be an agreement to repurchase the chattel paper. That repurchase is not a sale or disposition under § 9–504(5). Upon that repurchase, Dealer becomes the secured party. If Dealer then sells the goods under § 9–504 and buys them at the sale, the same analysis applies. That is, the goods are once again part of Dealer's inventory and subject to Secured Party #1's security interest; but, if Dealer has not paid the repurchase price to Secured Party #2, § 9–306(5)(b) likewise gives Secured Party #2, as an unpaid transferee, a security interest in the goods against Dealer to secure Dealer's obligation to pay that repurchase price.

paper reflected by § 9–308. Furthermore, it is not unfair to Secured Party #1 because Secured Party #1 is entitled to receive the money paid to Dealer by Secured Party #2 upon purchase of the chattel paper as proceeds of its security interest in the goods sold to BIOCOB.[5]

The interpretative problem is presented by § 9–306(5)(d):

> "A security interest of an unpaid transferee [Secured Party #2] asserted under paragraph (b) . . . must be perfected for protection against creditors of the transferor [Dealer] and purchasers of the returned or repossessed goods."

Does this negate § 9–306(5)(b) and mean that Secured Party #2 does not have priority over Secured Party #1 in the returned goods under § 9–306(5)(b) unless Secured Party #2's security interest in the goods is perfected against Dealer? Stated differently, is Secured Party #1 a "creditor" of Dealer or a "purchaser" of the returned or repossessed goods within the purview of § 9–306(5)(d)?[6] Furthermore, assuming Secured Party #1 is such a "creditor" or "purchaser," does the requirement that Secured Party #2's security interest be "perfected for protection" against Secured Party #1 mean that Secured Party #2 must acquire priority under § 9–312? If Secured Party #1's position was prior in time under § 9–312(5)(a), must Secured Party #2 somehow follow a procedure sufficient to give it a purchase money super-priority over Secured Party #1? This priority issue will be significant in the event Secured Party #1 and Secured Party #2 both claim the goods or the proceeds of any sale or disposition thereof by Dealer.

J.I. Case v. Borg-Warner, 669 S.W.2d 543, 37 UCC Rep.Serv. (Callaghan) 1025 (Ky.App.1984), and Northwest Accept. Corp. v. Lynnwood Equipment, Inc., 1 UCC Rep.Serv.2d (Callaghan) 980, motion for reconsideration denied, 1 UCC Rep.Serv.2d (Callaghan) 171 (D.W.D.Wash.1986), both held that the chattel paper financer had priority without having to take further action to perfect with respect to the inventory financer. The courts held that in the context of § 9–306(5) the definitions of "creditor" and "purchaser" in § 1–201 are not applicable to Secured Party #1. Since Secured Party #1 is neither a "creditor" nor "purchaser" as used in § 9–306(5)(d), Secured Party #2 has priority under § 9–306(5)(b). These decisions are consistent with the intent of §§ 9–306(5)(b) and 9–308. See 2 Gilmore, Security Interests in Personal Property, § 27.5; Smith, Annual Survey: Secured Transactions, 40 The Business Lawyer 1487, 1505–1508 (1985). Cf. the opposite treatment of a transferee of accounts under § 9–306(5)(c). To conclude otherwise (i.e. that Secured Party #1 is a "creditor" or "purchaser") would nullify the intent of § 9–306(5)(b). Crocker Nat. Bank v. Clark, 724 F.2d 696, 37 UCC Rep.Serv. (Callaghan) 673 (8th Cir.1984), holding that the inventory financer was a "creditor" is not consistent with this analysis.

The drafting history to § 9–306(5) demonstrates that the inventory financer (Secured Party #1) is neither a "creditor" nor a "purchaser" within the purview of § 9–306(5)(d). In the 1952 Official Draft of the UCC, § 9–306(5) read as follows:

> "(5) If collateral which has been sold is returned to the debtor, the following rules determine the priorities:
>
> (a) As between the debtor and a secured party to whom the indebtedness originally secured by the collateral has not been paid, the original security interest continues;

5. If Secured Party #2 had purchased accounts instead of chattel paper, § 9–306(5)(c) subordinates Secured Party #2 to Secured Party #1's rights in the returned goods. This Commentary does not undertake to explore this different treatment for purchasers of accounts—or the reasons for this difference.

6. A secured creditor is included within both the definitions of "creditor" in § 1–201(12) and "purchaser" in § 1–201(32), (33), "unless the context otherwise requires."

(b) As between the debtor and an unpaid transferee of the chattel paper arising from the sale, the transferee shall have a security interest in the property returned, but such security interest must be perfected for protection against third parties;

(c) The security interest of an unpaid transferee under (b) shall have priority over a security interest claimed under (a)."

This section was redrafted to its present form pursuant to the 1956 Recommendations of the Editorial Board. The revision covered repossessions in addition to returns and added present subsection (c) which affords subordinate priority status to the purchaser of an account. The rule of former subsection (c) which affords first priority to the chattel paper purchaser was carried over to present subsection (b).

Present § 9–306(5)(d) states the rule that both the chattel paper purchaser and the account purchaser must be "perfected for protection against creditors of the transferor and purchasers of the returned or repossessed goods." The 1952 Draft, which had dealt only with the priority of the chattel paper purchaser, had set forth the same rule in then § 9–306(5)(b):

> "As between the debtor and an unpaid transferee of the chattel paper arising from the sale, the transferee shall have a security interest in the property returned, but such security interest must be perfected for protection against *third parties.*" (emphasis supplied)

It is evident from that 1952 Draft that "third parties" as used in subsection (b) did not include "a security interest claimed under (a)," because that interest was expressly covered in subsection (c). Rather, "third parties" could have referred only to "creditors of the transferor and purchasers of the returned or repossessed goods," namely, the parties more particularly identified in the reformulation of the same rule now set forth in § 9–306(5)(d). That is, "third parties" meant "creditors of the transferor" and "purchasers of the returned or repossessed goods" *other than* the inventory financer.

Accordingly, the meaning and intent of "perfected for protection" in § 9–306(5)(d) is that by reason of the goods being in the possession of Dealer, Secured Party #2 must give constructive notice of its security interest in those goods by filing a financing statement against Dealer in order to be perfected against those creditors and purchasers of Dealer (other than Secured Party #1) as to whom an unperfected security interest would otherwise be subordinate under § 9–301. Secured Party #2 should file a signed financing statement covering those returned goods either at the time it first purchases the chattel paper or prior to returning the repossessed goods to Dealer. Note, however, that filing the financing statement does not affect Secured Party #2's rights against Secured Party #1 under § 9–306(5) and will not protect Secured Party #2 against the risk that the goods may be sold by Dealer to buyers in the ordinary course of business who will take free of that security interest. § 2–403(2); § 9–307(1); see the fifth paragraph of Official Comment 4 to § 9–306.

If Secured Party #2 fails to perfect against Dealer, it will retain its priority against Secured Party #1 but may become subordinate to others under § 9–301. This may result in a circular priority, the resolution of which is beyond the scope of this Commentary. See 2 Gilmore, *Security Interests in Personal Property*, § 27.5.

CONCLUSION

"Creditors" and "purchasers" as used in § 9–306(5)(d) do not include the original secured inventory financer of the seller of goods under subsection (a). Accordingly, a purchaser of chattel paper generated by a sale of the goods by that seller, attaining priority over the inventory financer under § 9–308, retains that priority in the event the goods covered by that chattel paper are returned to the seller, without having to further perfect against that inventory financer.

The Official Comment to § 9–306 is amended by adding the following:

5. "Creditors" and "purchasers" as used in paragraph (5)(d) do not include the original secured inventory financer of the seller of goods under subsection (a). If a purchaser of chattel paper generated by a sale of the goods attains priority over the seller's inventory financer under Section 9–308, the purchaser retains that priority in the event the goods covered by the chattel paper are returned to the seller, without having to further perfect against the inventory financer. This priority issue will usually arise in the context of the original inventory financer and the chattel paper purchaser both claiming the goods or the proceeds of any sale or disposition thereof by the seller. See PEB Commentary No. 5, dated March 10, 1990.

PEB COMMENTARY NO. 6
SECTION 9–301(1)

ISSUE

Section 9–301(1) provides (with an exception that is not relevant here) that a security interest is subordinate to members of various specified classes (herein called "the protected classes") who acquired their interests while the security interest was unperfected, subject to conditions set forth for each specified class.

When a security interest is subordinated under this rule in favor of a member of a protected class, does the security interest continue subordinated under the "shelter principle" to an assignee of that protected person, although the assignee does not fit the specific requirements for a member of the protected class because he acquired his interest after the security interest was perfected? In other words, does the protected status of an assignor "shelter" the position of an assignee who by himself would not meet the standards for protection?

DISCUSSION

A right of ownership of personal property ordinarily consists in part of the right to transfer it to others in the same form and with the same attributes, e.g., freedom from competing ownership interests or defenses or security interests that are not valid against the transferring owner. This right is known as the "shelter principle."

Section 2–403(1) states the shelter principle: "A purchaser of goods acquires all title which his transferor had...." As Official Comment 1 states: "The *basic principle of our law is generally continued and expanded* under subsection (1)." [emphasis added]. Since the principle existed before the Code, it is not dependent on its codification in § 2–403(1). Examples of its use appear in four Articles of the Code:

(a) Sections 3–201(1) and Official Comment 3, 3–305 and Official Comment, and 3–306 and Official Comment 1 illustrate the concept. These provisions set forth the ability of a holder in due course of a negotiable instrument to transfer the instrument free of the defenses and claims which the transferor's status as holder in due course has cut off. It is clear that the transferor's status as holder in due course and the value of his ownership of the instrument would be impaired if he could not transfer the instrument and confer the same status upon his transferee without the transferee qualifying on his own as a holder in due course (when the transfer was a gift or because the instrument had matured or because the transferee had knowledge of a defect). To protect the holder in due course fully, the law must protect the holder's transferee.

(b) Similar shelter provisions are found in connection with equivalent negotiability rules in §§ 8–301(1) and 8–302(4) and Official Comment 5 to the latter.

(c) Similar shelter provisions are found in connection with equivalent negotiability rules in §§ 7–504(1) and 7–502(1).

(d) A similar shelter provision in respect to property rights other than those resting on negotiability is found in Article 9, § 9–313(4)(b). Under specified circumstances this provision gives the holder of a security interest in a fixture priority over the interest of an owner or an incumbrancer of the realty; but this rule is expressly subject to the condition that a real estate interest is not subordinated to the fixture security interest if the real estate interest's predecessor in title was not subject to defeat by the fixture security interest, thus applying the shelter principle. For variation of the shelter principle, see also § 9–313(6), which shelters refinancings of a superior interest from a subordinate interest which would otherwise have priority over the later refinancing.

The case of Aircraft Trading and Services, Inc. v. Braniff, Inc., 819 F.2d 1227, 3 UCC Rep.Serv.2d (Callaghan) 1297 (2d Cir.1987), first called attention to the absence of express shelter provisions in § 9–301(1). Simplifying the facts, A sold an aircraft engine to B and took back a purchase-money mortgage (security interest), which for a time A failed to record as required by federal law. B sold the engine to C, who searched the record and ascertained that there was no recorded mortgage. Thus A's mortgage was subordinate to C's interest, under § 9–301(1)(c), which provides that an unperfected security interest is subordinate to a buyer like C to the extent that he gives value and receives delivery of the collateral without knowledge of the security interest and before it is perfected. Thereafter the mortgage was recorded, thus perfecting the security interest, and still later C sold the engine to D. (D had actual knowledge of the recording, but the Court's opinion did not rest on that fact.)

The Court of Appeals held that since D did not acquire his interest while the security interest was unperfected, D's interest was subject to the security interest. The Court identified the shelter principle with § 2–403(1), then rejected its application in reliance on § 2–402(3), which reads: "Nothing in this Article should be deemed to impair the rights of creditors of the seller (a) under the provisions of the Article on Secured Transactions (Article 9)...." This Commentary does not adhere to that interpretation. Application of the shelter principle of § 2–403(1) in favor of a buyer from one who has obtained senior status under § 9–301(1) does not "impair the rights of creditors." The rights of the unperfected secured creditor have *already* been impaired by the operation of § 9–301(1). The shelter principle should be applied to protect D. Otherwise the value of C's status, as one taking free of the security interest, is unjustifiably impaired if he cannot confer that status upon his transferee. Section 2–402(3)(a) does not compel a different result. Article 2 does not apply the shelter principle, although the principle is stated in § 2–403(1) as an introduction to rules stating when the purchaser can receive *more* than the transferor had.

Once a protected party achieves such senior rights, § 9–301(1) should not be construed to interfere with those rights and the shelter principle should be deemed applicable. The Code is a "complex and interrelated statutory scheme." Bank of Honolulu v. Hawaii Corp., 829 F.2d 813, 815, 4 UCC Rep.Serv.2d (Callaghan) 837, 841 (9th Cir.1987). The Code should be interpreted to produce equivalent results in situations comparable to the four cited above. This broad approach is supported by § 1–102 and its Official Comment 1.

CONCLUSION

Underlying principles of fairness require a broad reading and a broad application of the shelter concept, even when not expressly stated. The importance of shelter is too great in the Code's scheme to support a narrow reading of the Code. Section 9–301(1) should be interpreted and applied in this circumstance to incorporate the shelter principle so that a member of a protected class who prevails thereunder can transfer what he has, even though the security interest which was unperfected when the transferor acquired his rights has since been perfected. The shelter principle also should operate even though the transferee from the protected party has knowledge of the earlier subordinated security interest. The Official Comment to § 9–301 is amended by adding the following:

9. There is no conflict between the principle of § 9–301(1) and the "shelter principle," which is applied at several points in the statute, but is most explicitly stated in § 2–403(1): "A purchaser of goods acquires all title which his transferor had...."

Although § 9–301(1) fails to state the shelter principle expressly, that principle is applicable where a person who had met the conditions for prevailing over an unperfected security interest transfers his right to another person after the security interest is perfected. See PEB Commentary No. 6, dated March 10, 1990.

The rules for subordination of unperfected security interests have a purpose—in common with similar rules in all filing and recording systems—to impose sanctions for not adhering to filing or recording requirements. Such rules are necessary to make the system effective and enforce the policy against secret liens. The shelter principle recognizes that when a person in a protected class transfers his right after the security interest has been perfected, the right will be diminished in value unless the sanction is continued. The sanction imposed by § 9–301(1) is that members of protected classes take free of an unperfected security interest. That sanction should be continued to protect transferees from those members in order to fulfill the purpose of the section.

PEB COMMENTARY NO. 7
THE RELATIVE PRIORITIES OF SECURITY INTERESTS IN THE CASH PROCEEDS OF ACCOUNTS, CHATTEL PAPER, AND GENERAL INTANGIBLES

ISSUE

Secured party A and secured party B each has a perfected security interest in the same account, chattel paper, or general intangible, with A having priority over B. If the account debtor makes payment to secured party B, directly or through the debtor, may A recover the payment from B?

DISCUSSION

The issue under discussion arises when two secured parties have a perfected security interest in an account, chattel paper, or general intangible and the secured party that does not have priority (B) receives a payment from the account debtor. The debtor, having received the payment from the account debtor, may remit it to B, or B may receive payment directly from the account debtor. See § 9–502(2) (secured parties' right to notify account debtor to make payment to the secured party); § 9–318(3) (account debtor may discharge obligation by paying assignee after receiving notification that right to receive payment has been assigned and that payment is to be made to assignee). Under these circumstances, may A, the secured party having priority in the account, chattel paper, or general intangible, recover the payment from B?

A. Payment by Check

Article 9 determines the relative priorities of security interests in accounts, chattel paper, and general intangibles. See § 9–312(5) (general rule); § 9–308 (special rule with respect to chattel paper). The Article also determines the relative priorities of security interests in payments made by the account debtor, which payments are the proceeds of the original collateral. See § 9–312(6); § 9–306(1).

When the account debtor pays B by check, or when the debtor indorses and delivers to B a check drawn by the account debtor to the order of the debtor, B will be a holder of the check. If B takes the check under the circumstances described in § 3–302(1), B will be a holder in due course. See § 3–302(1) and (2). A's filed financing statement does not constitute notice to B of A's claim to the check and does not preclude B from being a holder in due course. See § 3–305(1). Specifically, B takes priority over A's earlier, perfected security interest in the check and is entitled to keep the funds received when the check is paid. See § 9–309; Dallas Bank & Trust Co. v. Frigiking, Inc., 692 S.W.2d 163, 41 UCC Rep.Serv. (Callaghan) 1334 (Tex.Ct.App. 1985); Thorp Commercial Corp. v. Northgate Industries, Inc., 490 F.Supp. 197, 203–04, 29 UCC Rep.Serv. (Callaghan) 297, 306–307 (D.Minn.1980) (alternate holding), rev'd on other grounds, 654 F.2d 1245, 31 UCC Rep.Serv. (Callaghan) 801 (8th Cir.1981). Contra Bank of the West v. Commercial Credit Financial Services, Inc., 655 F.Supp. 807, 819–20, 3 UCC Rep.Serv.2d (Callaghan) 240, 258–259 (N.D.Cal.1987), rev'd on other grounds, 852 F.2d 1162, 6 UCC Rep.Serv.2d (Callaghan) 602 (9th Cir.1988).

Even if B is not a holder in due course, § 9–308 may give priority to B's security interest in the check. But if B takes the check under circumstances that preclude B from being a holder in due course (e.g., if a notation on the check gives B reason to know that the check constitutes A's proceeds) and from taking priority under § 9–308, then B would take the check subject to A's security interest. See § 3–306(a).

B. Payment in Cash

The Code does not specifically address the right of B to retain a cash payment from the account debtor. Accordingly, resort must be had to the principles of law and equity. See § 1–103. Under those principles, when a person assigns the same claim to two persons and the assignee without priority (B) receives payment from the obligor, the assignee receiving payment owes a duty of restitution to the assignee having priority (A). But if B gave value for the assignment (as B must have, see § 9–203(1)(b)) and obtained the payment in good faith and without knowledge or reason to know of the prior assignment, then B may retain the payment. See Restatement, Second, Contracts § 342(b), Comment *e* & Illustration 3; see also Restatement of Restitution § 126, Comment *f* & Illustration 8. Cf. § 9–306 Comment 2(c) (recipients of cash proceeds paid from the debtor's checking account in the operation of the debtor's business take free of a security interest in the proceeds). In determining whether B had reason to know of A's security interest, courts should apply § 9–309 by analogy. Otherwise, cash would be rendered less negotiable than a check.

CONCLUSION

Whether B will be entitled to keep a cash payment from an account debtor or will be under a duty of restitution to A depends on whether B received the payment in good faith and without knowledge or reason to know of A's security interest. Whether B will be entitled to keep a payment made by a check drawn by the account debtor depends on whether B is a holder in due course of the check or is entitled to priority under § 9–308. A's filed financing statement should not constitute notice to B of A's security interest in either case.

The Official Comment to § 9–309 is amended by adding the following:

3. The operation of this section can be seen when two secured parties have a perfected security interest in an account, chattel paper, or general intangible and the secured party that does not have priority receives a payment by check directly or indirectly from the account debtor. If the recipient takes the check under circumstances that give the recipient the rights of a holder in due course (Section 3–302), then the recipient's security interest in the check will take priority over the competing security interest and the recipient will be entitled to keep the payment. See Commentary No. 7, dated March 10, 1990.

The Official Comment to § 9–312 is amended by adding the following:

9. Under some circumstances, a secured party, who does not have priority in an account, chattel paper, or general intangible may be entitled to keep a cash payment received directly or indirectly from the account debtor. See PEB Commentary No. 7, dated March 10, 1990.

COMMENTARY NO. 8
FINAL DRAFT

(December 10, 1991)

Permanent Editorial Board for the Uniform Commercial Code, 4025 Chestnut Street, Philadelphia, Pennsylvania 19104.

PEB COMMENTARY NO. 8

ABA SECTION OF BUSINESS LAW LIAISON

Amelia H. Boss, Philadelphia, Pennsylvania

PREFACE TO PEB COMMENTARY

The Permanent Editorial Board (PEB) for the Uniform Commercial Code (UCC) acts under the authority of The American Law Institute and the National Conference of Commissioners on Uniform State Laws. In March, 1987, the PEB resolved to issue from time to time supplementary commentary on the UCC to be known as *PEB Commentary.* These PEB Commentaries seek to further the underlying policies of the UCC by affording guidance in interpreting and resolving issues raised by the UCC and/or the Official Comments. The Resolution states that:

> "*A PEB Commentary* should come within one or more of the following specific purposes, which should be made apparent at the inception of the Commentary: (1) to resolve an ambiguity in the UCC by restating more clearly what the PEB considers to be the legal rule; (2) to state a preferred resolution of an issue on which judicial opinion or scholarly writing diverges; (3) to elaborate on the application of the UCC where the statute and/or the Official Comment leaves doubt as to inclusion or exclusion of, or application to, particular circumstances or transactions; (4) consistent with UCC § 1–102(2)(b), to apply the principles of the UCC to new or changed circumstances; (5) to clarify or elaborate upon the operation of the UCC as it relates to other statutes (such as the Bankruptcy Code and various federal and state consumer protection statutes) and general principles of law and equity pursuant to UCC § 1–103; or (6) to otherwise improve the operation of the UCC."

The full Resolution appears in the 1990 Edition of the UCC.

PEB COMMENTARY NO. 8
SECTION 9–308

ISSUES

Section 9–308 provides special priority rules for purchasers of chattel paper who give new value and take possession of the paper in the ordinary course of their business. Under clause (a) such a purchaser takes priority over a prior perfected interest if the purchaser is without knowledge that the "specific paper" is subject to a security interest. Under clause (b) such a purchaser takes priority over a prior perfected interest "which is claimed merely as proceeds of inventory subject to a security interest (§ 9–306) even though he knows that the specific paper . . . is subject to the security interest."

This Commentary addresses two issues which arise under § 9–308. (1) When is an interest in chattel paper "claimed merely as proceeds of inventory subject to a security interest" so that the subsequent chattel paper financer who meets the other requirements of § 9–308 takes free even though it knows that the specific paper is subject to a security interest? (2) If the prior interest is more than a mere proceeds interest so that the chattel paper financer has priority only if it is without knowledge of the prior interest, does the chattel paper financer have any obligation to make a filing search or other inquiries which might lead to knowledge of the prior interest?

INTRODUCTORY DISCUSSION

Most chattel paper is generated by dealers in automobiles, trucks, machinery, and other durable goods of substantial value. Such dealers frequently sell their chattel paper or use it as collateral for loans. Buyers of chattel paper usually take possession of the paper and collect from the debtors thereon themselves. Also, some lenders on chattel paper will take possession and handle collections. (Financers with a security interest in chattel paper covering smaller appliances, television sets, etc., frequently do not take possession of the paper.)

Under the ordinary priority rules of the Code (first to file or perfect has priority) the buyer of, or lender on, chattel paper would have to make a filing search before the transaction to determine whether a prior party has filed a financing statement covering chattel paper or inventory of which the chattel paper might be proceeds. (If a security interest in inventory is perfected by filing, there is also an automatically perfected proceeds security interest in chattel paper which is generated when inventory subject to the security interest is sold.[1]) A filing search requirement before each transaction would entail substantial delays and significant expense even if the search revealed no prior filed financing statement. In the many cases in which there is a prior filed financing statement covering chattel paper or inventory, or both, the application of the general § 9–312(5) priority rules would always give the first filer priority. Such a system would make it difficult for any buyer or lender other than the first filed secured party to purchase or lend on the security of chattel paper and would make it particularly difficult for a dealer to deal as to chattel paper with anyone other than the inventory financer. Prior filings would have to be limited to specific chattel paper or subordination agreements or releases would have to be secured from prior

1. Perfection by filing for inventory is in the jurisdiction in which the inventory is located (§ 9–103(1)). Perfection by filing as to chattel paper is in the jurisdiction in which the debtor is located (§ 9–103(4)). Therefore, in cases in which the two locations are different, the inventory filing would not perfect as to the resulting chattel paper for more than 10 days (§ 9–306(3)) unless there was also a filing in the jurisdiction in which the debtor is located.

filed inventory or chattel paper financers each time items of chattel paper are transferred to a different financer.

At the time the Code was drafted, some financers of chattel paper left it with the dealer who had generated it and others took possession of the paper. The drafters of the Code did not want to disrupt those practices. Therefore, the problem presented to the drafters was how to structure priority rules so that both forms of financing could continue efficiently and safely. The Code drafters might have encouraged the practice of purchasing and taking possession of chattel paper by treating chattel paper like instruments and providing that a security interest in chattel paper could be perfected only by taking possession. That rule, however, would have denied perfected status to security interests in chattel paper left with the debtor and would have disrupted that widely used form of financing. Requiring possession for perfection of chattel paper would also have meant that an inventory financer's proceeds interest in chattel paper would be lost after 10 days unless the financer took possession of the paper. On the other hand, as already noted, applying the ordinary Code priority rules to chattel paper would have imposed substantial impediments to the widespread business of buying and taking possession of chattel paper. The drafters, therefore, in § 9–308 struck a compromise between the interests of non-possessory financers of chattel paper and inventory financers with a non-possessory proceeds interest in the paper on the one hand, and, on the other hand, competing chattel paper financers who take possession of the paper.

Under that compromise a secured party can have a non-possessory security interest in chattel paper perfected through filing (including a proceeds interest therein) which will be good against subsequent non-possessory security interests and judgment creditors including the trustee in bankruptcy, but, under § 9–308, that security interest will frequently be junior to a chattel paper purchaser who gives new value and takes possession of the paper in the ordinary course of its business.

The above discussion has reviewed the basic reason for the adoption of the rules set out in § 9–308. The discussion now turns to the two specific issues arising under § 9–308 which this Commentary addresses.

ISSUE I

When is a security interest in chattel paper claimed "merely as proceeds of inventory subject to a security interest" so that a chattel paper financer that gives new value and takes possession of the paper in the ordinary course of its business has priority even though it knows of the prior interest?

DISCUSSION OF ISSUE I

Preliminarily, it should be noted that this issue may be of limited importance since, even if the security interest is more than a mere proceeds interest, the § 9–308 chattel paper financer will take free of the interest unless it has knowledge that the *specific paper* is subject to that prior security interest. As the discussion of Issue II will show, knowledge is unlikely to be present unless the specific chattel paper has been stamped or otherwise marked to show the prior interest. The following discussion should be read with this caveat in mind.

A brief description of two common types of inventory secured financing will help put the discussion of the meaning of a "mere proceeds interest" in its business context.

(a) The first type, which will be called "type A," is inventory financing of automobiles and large items of equipment in which the financing is primarily item by item (each item of inventory secures a precise amount loaned against that item even though there may be a cross-security provision), with a requirement that the associated inventory debt be paid off when the item is sold, or after a maximum period (usually 90 days subject to renewal), whichever first occurs.

(b) The second ("type B") is a general floating loan secured by inventory and receivables (sometimes called an "availability loan") under which the debtor is entitled to borrow from the secured party such amounts as the debtor may desire, subject to a maximum availability determined by a formula, e.g., 50% of cost of saleable inventory plus 80% of the amount of receivables not in default more than 30 days. This type of financing is usually used in situations involving smaller items of inventory as to which it would be too burdensome to account on an individual basis and in which the receivables are accounts rather than chattel paper so that § 9–308 issues do not arise. However, such financing arrangements may sometimes involve larger, more expensive items of inventory which are frequently sold on credit generating chattel paper.

For the reasons stated below, the Board believes that a type A inventory financer will frequently have only a "mere proceeds interest" in chattel paper which is generated when items of inventory subject to its security interest are sold. On the other hand, as noted below, the Board believes that a type B financer has more than a mere proceeds interest in any chattel paper generated on sale of the inventory.

While Article 9 does not define "mere proceeds interest," Comments 2 and 3 to § 9–308 do indicate the intended meaning of the phrase. The pertinent sentence in Comment 2 reads: "Clause (b) of the section deals with the case where the security interest in the chattel paper is claimed merely as proceeds—i.e., on behalf of an inventory financer who has not by some new transaction with the debtor acquired a specific interest in the chattel paper." Comment 3 reads in part: "Clause (a) deals with the case where the non-possessory security interest in the chattel paper is more than a mere claim to proceeds—i.e., exists in favor of a secured party who has given value against the paper, whether or not he financed the inventory whose sale gave rise to it."

The language in Comment 2 just quoted seems to be specifically adapted to the type A transaction above and contemplates that the type A inventory financer having a proceeds claim to the chattel paper must do something more than rest on that proceeds claim in order to prevail against the person described in the preamble to § 9–308, namely, a person who "gives new value and takes possession of [chattel paper] in the ordinary course of his business." According to the Comments, such an inventory financer takes the chattel paper out of the "mere proceeds" category only by giving value against it in some new transaction. Such a lender gives new value, as it commonly will, by purchasing the chattel paper (or, in some types of transactions, making a specific loan against it). Whether the type A inventory financer will be willing to give value against the chattel paper instead of merely resting on its proceeds claim until payment will depend on the quality of the paper. That quality depends upon such factors as the credit worthiness of the buyer who is the principal obligor on the chattel paper, the amount of the buyer's down payment and hence the amount of the chattel paper debt as compared to the value of the collateral (the former inventory), and the terms under which the dealer (the former inventory debtor) is willing to assume full or limited recourse to support the buyer's obligation under the chattel paper. Not infrequently the financer and the dealer will negotiate a package purchase of several items of chattel paper in which the total price is determined by the quality of the paper, the extent of the recourse, and so on. When the financer buys, or lends against, chattel paper in the way just outlined, there is a "new transaction" by which the financer has acquired an interest in the specific chattel paper which is more than a "mere proceeds interest."

If, however, the type A inventory financer does not by some new transaction give value against specific chattel paper, the fact that the inventory debt is unpaid and that the security agreement specifically claims the chattel paper proceeds as additional collateral does not give the financer more than a mere proceeds interest. Further, while no doubt much inventory financing is carried out with nominal profit to the financer in anticipation that it will be given the opportunity to acquire the chattel paper, in the Board's opinion this anticipation of receiving the chattel paper does not take the case out of the "mere proceeds" phrase of the statute.

As pointed out above, the Board believes that the type B financer at all times has more than a mere proceeds interest in the chattel paper on hand whether or not at any specific time there is sufficient inventory on hand to secure the amount of the loan outstanding at that time. The structure of the deal is such that the chattel paper is part of the primary collateral for the debt. That interest extends to any chattel paper subsequently generated by a sale of inventory whether or not at any particular time the existing inventory is adequate security for the debt actually outstanding.

A number of reported cases have involved priority conflicts between inventory financers and purchasers of chattel paper who took possession, gave new value, and acted in the ordinary course of their business. In those cases, the courts have applied the "mere proceeds" rules of § 9–308, and the chattel paper financer has always won.[2] The courts have not always carefully reported the facts, but it is clear that in at least one of the cases, the security agreement did specifically claim an interest in chattel paper and the court did not treat that fact as significant.[3] In most of the cases, the court did not carefully consider whether the chattel paper financer had knowledge of the prior interest in the chattel paper, but in several cases the court either assumed that the chattel paper financer had knowledge or the findings of fact show that the chattel paper financer did have knowledge.[4] The results in all those cases are consistent with the position taken in this Commentary.

CONCLUSION AS TO ISSUE I

If a financer loans or extends credit for the cost of specific items of inventory and expects to be paid upon the sale of the items, the financer's security interest in chattel paper generated when the items are sold is a mere proceeds interest unless the financer in a new transaction gives value against the specific paper. On the other hand, a lender who agrees to lend up to a specified percentage of the cost of inventory and of receivables has more than a mere proceeds interest in chattel paper which is a part of the receivables covered by the security agreement. In inventory financing transactions which do not fall within the above two categories, whether the financer has more than a mere proceeds interest in chattel paper generated when inventory subject to its secured interest is sold must be determined from an examination of all the facts of the case.

2. See e.g. Aetna Finance Corp. v. Massey–Ferguson, Inc., 626 F.Supp. 482, 42 UCC Rep. Serv. (Callaghan) 1501 (S.D.Ind.1985); Northwest Acceptance Corp. v. Lynnwood Equipment, Inc., 1 UCC Rep.Serv.2d (Callaghan) 980, 1710 (W.D.Wash.1986); Rex Financial Corp. v. Great Western Bank & Trust, 23 Ariz.App. 286, 532 P.2d 558, 16 UCC Rep.Serv. (Callaghan) 1155 (Ariz.App.1975); Commercial Credit Corp. v. National Credit Corp., 251 Ark. 541, 473 S.W.2d 876, 10 UCC Rep.Serv. (Callaghan) 232 (Ark.1971); American State Bank v. Avco Financial Services of the United States, Inc., 71 Cal.App.3d 774, 139 Cal.Rptr. 658, 22 UCC Rep.Serv. (Callaghan) 235 (Cal.App. 1977); Home Savings Ass'n v. General Electric Credit Corp., 101 Nev. 595, 708 P.2d 280, 42 UCC Rep.Serv. (Callaghan) 1489 (Nev.1985); Chrysler Credit Corp. v. Sharp, 56 Misc.2d 261, 288 N.Y.S.2d 525, 5 UCC Rep.Serv. (Callaghan) 226 (N.Y.Sup.Ct.1968); Bank of Beulah v. Chase, 231 N.W.2d 738, 17 UCC Rep.Serv. (Callaghan) 259 (N.D.1975); Associates Discount Corp. v. Old Freeport Bank, 421 Pa. 609, 220 A.2d 621, 3 UCC Rep.Serv. (Callaghan) 481 (Pa.1966); Borg–Warner Acceptance Corp. v. C.I.T. Corp., 679 S.W.2d 140, 39 UCC Rep. Serv. (Callaghan) 1864 (Tex.Ct.App.1984).

3. *Home Savings Ass'n, supra* note 2.

4. *American State Bank, Rex Financial Corp.,* both *supra* note 2.

ISSUE II

Does a chattel paper financer who otherwise complies with the requisites of § 9–308 for obtaining priority over an earlier interest in chattel paper which is more than a mere proceeds interest have a duty to make inquiries, including a UCC filing search, which might produce knowledge of a prior security interest in the specific paper?

DISCUSSION OF ISSUE II

As already noted, § 9–308 gives priority to a chattel paper financer over a prior perfected direct interest in chattel paper if the chattel paper financer gives new value and takes possession of the chattel paper in the ordinary course of its business *without knowledge that the specific paper is subject to a security interest.* The Code, in § 1–201(25), carefully distinguishes between "knowledge" and "notice." "Knowledge" means "actual knowledge"; "notice" means "actual knowledge" or from "the facts and circumstances" having "reason to know." Therefore, "constructive knowledge" of what the public record might show (a common law concept frequently referred to in real estate recording cases) is not "knowledge" under § 9–308. Similarly, the use of the term "knowledge" rather than "notice" shows that § 9–308 does not adopt the view that the chattel paper financer "knows" whatever facts it has reason to know. The statute, on its face, therefore, indicates that there is no duty to make inquiries which might produce "knowledge."

However, there is a possible argument that a secured party intending to rely on the § 9–308(a) priority, if it is aware of facts which indicate that it is highly likely that there is a prior perfected security interest in the chattel paper, has an obligation to make reasonable inquiries to determine whether a prior security interest exists. For example, a prospective transferee of an appliance dealer's chattel paper may know that the dealer has been borrowing money on the security of chattel paper which the dealer has been holding and collecting, but may not know whether that lender has been paid in full nor whether it currently has a security interest in the dealer's chattel paper. Or a prospective transferee of the chattel paper may know that a UCC form 1 covering chattel paper has just been filed against the transferor. In cases like the two just described, it might be argued that there is an obligation to make inquiries even though the prospective chattel paper transferee has no "knowledge" of the prior interest.

However, imposing a duty of inquiry on transferees under § 9–308(a) is not consistent with the policies as to priority adopted in Article 9. In contrast to real estate recording and priority rules in most states, the basic priority rule in Article 9 is that the first secured party to file has priority even though that party has actual knowledge of a prior interest and files with the specific intent of gaining priority over the prior interest. See § 9–312(5). The policy reason for this pure race rule is simple: it provides clear and certain answers in practically all cases where there is a dispute as to relative priority. A rule which gives priority over prior interests only if the subsequent party does not have "knowledge" is more uncertain, and a rule that a subsequent party has priority only if he has made proper inquiries creates even greater uncertainty.

Although the basic Article 9 priority rule is pure race, in some situations, of which § 9–308(a) is one, lack of knowledge on the part of the subsequent party is required if that party is to take free of certain prior interests. Under § 9–301 buyers not in ordinary course and buyers of accounts and general intangibles lose to unperfected security interests if they have knowledge of them. Also under § 9–301 a prior perfected secured party's power to make advances which have priority over the rights of a lien creditor is cut off by knowledge of the lien creditor's interest.[5] Under § 9–

5. An advance made within 45 days after attachment of the lien takes priority over the rights of the lien creditor even though the secured party knows of the attachment of the lien.

307(3) a prior perfected secured party's power to make future advances which take priority over buyers not in ordinary course is cut off when the secured party acquires knowledge of the sale.[6]

While there are no reported cases involving a claimed duty of inquiry under § 9–308(a) or § 9–307(3), a number of cases have arisen under § 9–301 in which a prior unperfected secured party has argued that a lien creditor (under the pre–1972 version of Article 9) or a buyer not in ordinary course did not take free of its interest because the lien creditor or buyer had "notice" of the unperfected interest or was not in good faith because it had reason to know of the prior interest and made no inquiries. In some cases the prior party argued only that the "knowledge" requirement of § 9–301 includes "having reason to know"; in other cases it was argued that under the particular facts there was a good faith obligation to make inquiries. In all the cases the court found that the subsequent party without knowledge took priority and that there was no additional "without notice" or "good faith" requirement.[7] No contrary cases have been found. Those cases under § 9–301 correctly applied the knowledge rules in § 9–301 and should be followed as to the meaning of the "without knowledge" requirement of § 9–308(a).

The Comments to § 9–308 also indicate that the drafting intent was not to impose a duty of inquiry. Comment 3 notes that a prior secured party with a security interest in chattel paper can protect itself against the § 9–308(a) priority of a subsequent secured party by stamping or noting on the paper the fact that it has been assigned to it. There is no indication at all that filing itself might be sufficient, in spite of the fact that in most cases covered by § 9–308(a) the prior party will have perfected by filing. The implication is clear that the intention was that unless the chattel paper financer described in § 9–308(a) has actual knowledge of the prior interest in the specific paper, as would be the case if the paper were marked, the financer, without the burden of further inquiry, can deal with the paper free of the claims of any prior party.

There are good reasons for not imposing a duty to inquire under § 9–308(a). In the chattel paper case, if in certain cases where a prior interest is highly likely there is a duty to make inquiry, then the subsequent chattel paper transferee could never be sure when the court would hold that inquiry was necessary. Lending on the security of general assets including chattel paper is so common that a judge or jury might well conclude that in every case where a transferee purchases from a dealer the chance of a prior interest is so high that inquiries should be made. Therefore, the uncertainties which would be created by imposition of a duty to inquire are so great that the special priority which § 9–308(a) gives to chattel paper financers would be so unreliable as to be essentially worthless. The secured party who leaves the chattel paper with the debtor usually is running the risk that the debtor will collect from the obligor and fail to remit. He can fairly also run the similar risk that the debtor will not turn over to

6. The right to make advances which take priority over the rights of the buyer terminates 45 days after the sale, even if the secured party does not know of the sale.

7. The cases are: Southland Corporation v. Emerald Oil Co., 789 F.2d 1441, 2 UCC Rep. Serv.2d (Callaghan) 289 (9th Cir.1986); Broadway Nat'l Bank v. G & L Athletic Supplies, Inc., 10 Kan.App.2d 43, 691 P.2d 400, 39 UCC Rep.Serv. (Callaghan) 1492 (Kan.App.1984); Victory Nat'l Bank of Nowata v. Stewart, 6 Kan.App.2d 847, 636 P.2d 788, 32 UCC Rep. Serv. (Callaghan) 956 (Kan.App.1981); Kibbe v. Rohde, 285 Pa.Super. 379, 427 A.2d 1163, 31 UCC Rep.Serv. (Callaghan) 701 (Pa.Super.1980); Clark Oil & Refining Co. v. Liddicoat, 65 Wis.2d 612, 223 N.W.2d 530, 15 UCC Rep.Serv. (Callaghan) 1145 (Wis.1974) (lien creditor under version of § 9–301 which required lien creditor to be without knowledge of prior unperfected interest); Whitmire v. Keylon, 12 UCC Rep.Serv. (Callaghan) 1203 (Tenn. App.1973); Bloom v. Hilty, 427 Pa. 463, 234 A.2d 860, 4 UCC Rep.Serv. (Callaghan) 821 (Pa.1967).

him new value received when the debtor transfers the paper to another secured party who takes possession without knowledge of the prior interest.

Of course, under § 9–308(a) if a prospective chattel paper financer actually knows of a prior perfected security interest in the specific paper it cannot take free of it. That knowledge might come from marked paper, or from a statement by the debtor, the secured party, or third parties. However, an Article 9 filing which merely indicates that there may be a security interest in chattel paper does not give knowledge that "specific paper is subject to a security interest." Further, knowledge of a UCC form 1 filing covering chattel paper does not impose any obligation upon the chattel paper financer to make inquiries.

CONCLUSION AS TO ISSUE II

A chattel paper financer who gives new value and takes possession of chattel paper in the ordinary course of his business and is without knowledge of prior security interests in the chattel paper has no duty to search for Article 9 filings against the chattel paper or to make other inquiries which might reveal perfected prior interests in the specific chattel paper, even if the chattel paper financer is aware of the possibility that a prior security interest exists. Knowledge of a UCC form 1 filing covering chattel paper does not impose any obligation upon the chattel paper financer to make inquiries.

The Official Comment to § 9–308 is amended by adding the following to the end of Comment 3:

> A chattel paper financer who gives new value and takes possession of chattel paper in the ordinary course of his business and is without knowledge of prior security interests in the chattel paper has no duty to search for Article 9 filings against the chattel paper or to make other inquiries which might reveal perfected prior interests in the paper, even though the chattel paper financer is aware of the possibility that a prior security interest exists. Mere knowledge of an Article 9 filing against chattel paper does not give knowledge of the existence of a security interest in the chattel paper. See PEB Commentary No. 8, dated December 10, 1991.

COMMENTARY NO. 9
FINAL DRAFT

(June 25, 1992)

Permanent Editorial Board for the Uniform Commercial Code, 4025 Chestnut Street, Philadelphia, Pennsylvania 19104–3099.

APPENDIX V

ABA SECTION OF BUSINESS LAW LIAISON

AMELIA H. BOSS, Philadelphia, Pennsylvania

Preface to PEB Commentary

The Permanent Editorial Board (PEB) for the Uniform Commercial Code (UCC) acts under the authority of The American Law Institute and the National Conference of Commissioners on Uniform State Laws. In March, 1987, the PEB resolved to issue from time to time supplementary commentary on the UCC to be known as *PEB Commentary.* These PEB Commentaries seek to further the underlying policies of the UCC by affording guidance in interpreting and resolving issues raised by the UCC and/or the Official Comments. The Resolution states that:

> "A *PEB Commentary* should come within one or more of the following specific purposes, which should be made apparent at the inception of the Commentary: (1) to resolve an ambiguity in the UCC by restating more clearly what the PEB considers to be the legal rule; (2) to state a preferred resolution of an issue on which judicial opinion or scholarly writing diverges; (3) to elaborate on the application of the UCC where the statute and/or the Official Comment leaves doubt as to inclusion or exclusion of, or application to, particular circumstances or transactions; (4) consistent with UCC § 1–102(2)(b), to apply the principles of the UCC to new or changed circumstances; (5) to clarify or elaborate upon the operation of the UCC as it relates to other statutes (such as the Bankruptcy Code and various federal and state consumer protection statutes) and general principles of law and equity pursuant to UCC § 1–103; or (6) to otherwise improve the operation of the UCC."

The full Resolution appears in the 1990 Edition of the UCC.

PEB COMMENTARY NO. 9
SECTION 9–306(1)

ISSUE

Section 9–306(1) provides: " 'Proceeds' includes whatever is received upon the sale, exchange, collection or other disposition of collateral or proceeds." Where a debtor has granted to a secured party a security interest in goods and the debtor later leases those goods as lessor, do the lease rentals constitute proceeds of the secured party's collateral?

DISCUSSION

Where a debtor has granted to a secured party a security interest in goods that the debtor later leases as lessor, the lease rentals would constitute proceeds of the secured party's collateral for the reason that the debtor's conveyance of a leasehold interest in the goods constitutes a disposition of the goods for purposes of § 9–306(1).

This would certainly be the case where the lease creates a security interest under § 1–201(37). In that instance the lease is nothing more than a disguised sale of the goods, and the secured party would be entitled to a security interest in any chattel paper or payments on that chattel paper, all as proceeds resulting from that sales transaction. The following examples illustrate this conclusion:

Example 1. Debtor grants to Secured Party a security interest in Debtor's drill press. Debtor sells the drill press to Buyer who pays for the drill press by issuing to Debtor Buyer's five-year promissory note secured by a security interest in the drill press. The promissory note and security interest together constitute chattel paper under § 9–105(1)(b), and, since the chattel paper was received by Debtor upon the sale of the drill press, the chattel paper constitutes proceeds of Secured Party's collateral. When payments are made by Buyer on the promissory note, those payments, arising upon the "collection" of "proceeds," also constitute proceeds of Secured Party's collateral.

Example 2. Debtor grants to Secured Party a security interest in Debtor's drill press. Debtor leases the drill press to Lessee for a fixed term of five years not subject to termination by Lessee. The drill press is predicted to have exhausted its useful life at the end of that five-year term, and Lessee will then be entitled to purchase the drill press for the cash sum of $10. The lease constitutes chattel paper under § 9–105(1)(b). Since the chattel paper was received by Debtor upon the granting to Lessee of a leasehold interest for the entire useful life of the drill press and Lessee can become the owner of the drill press at the end of the nonterminable lease term by paying a nominal consideration, the transaction will be viewed as creating a security interest under § 1–201(37) and will be treated for Article 9 purposes as a disguised sale. Just as the chattel paper arising upon the sale of the drill press in Example 1 constituted proceeds of Secured Party's collateral, so does the chattel paper arising upon the granting of a security lease constitute proceeds of Secured Party's collateral in this example; the two transactions have precisely the same economic effect although labeled by the parties as a "sale" in Example 1 and a "lease" in this example. Similarly, when rental payments are made by Lessee on the security lease, those payments, arising upon the "collection" of "proceeds," also constitute proceeds of Secured Party's collateral.

In both Example 1 and Example 2 it is irrelevant to the payments to Debtor being treated as proceeds whether the sale or lease was authorized by Secured Party or whether the drill press constituted equipment or inventory in the hands of Debtor. This is because under § 9–306(2) Secured Party's security interest will continue "in any identifiable proceeds including collections received by the debtor" even when the disposition of the collateral was authorized by the Secured Party or where the collateral subject to the disposition was transferred to a buyer in the ordinary course as contemplated by § 9–307(1).

Lease rentals would also constitute proceeds of a secured party's collateral consisting of goods where the subsequent lease of those goods creates a "true" lease governed by Article 2A. Consider the following example:

> *Example 3.* Debtor grants to Secured Party a security interest in Debtor's drill press which then has a predicted useful life of five years. Debtor leases the drill press to Lessee for a fixed term, not subject to termination by Lessee, of two years with no purchase option. The lease would appear to be a "true" lease governed by Article 2A. See §§ 1–201(37), 2A–102, and 2A–103(1)(j). Once again, the lease constitutes chattel paper under § 9–105(1)(b). The chattel paper was received by Debtor upon the granting of a leasehold interest in the drill press for a non-terminable period of two years out of a predicted useful life of the drill press of five years. Debtor has remaining to it a residual interest in the drill press, i.e., a right to the drill press arising only at the end of the two-year lease term. See § 2A–103(1)(q) (defining "lessor's residual interest"). But an interest in the drill press constituting a right by Lessee to use the drill press for a two-year period out of the drill press's predicted five-year useful life was conveyed by Debtor to Lessee. The granting of the leasehold interest constitutes a disposition of a portion of Debtor's interest in the drill press, and the chattel paper arising upon that disposition constitutes proceeds of Secured Party's collateral. When rental payments are made by Lessee on the true lease, those payments, arising upon the "collection" of "proceeds," also constitute proceeds of Secured Party's collateral.

The foregoing analysis in Example 3, by concluding that the granting of a true leasehold interest in goods constitutes a "disposition" of the goods for purposes of § 9–306(1), is consistent with the common law rule that the granting of a real estate leasehold interest constitutes a disposition of a portion of the lessor's ownership interest in the leased estate. See, e.g., *Hueschen v. Stalie,* 98 N.M. 696, 652 P.2d 246 (1982) (real estate lease is a conveyance of an estate for a limited term with conditions); Powell, *Law of Real Property,* § 221 (1990). It is also consistent with Article 9 cases which treat the totality of a debtor's interest in goods as comprising the debtor's leasehold interest as lessor plus the debtor's residual interest in the leased goods as owner, with the necessity of a secured party's security interest in the leasehold being perfected in one manner (e.g., possession or filing as to the chattel paper) and its security interest in the lessor's residual interest being perfected in another manner (e.g., filing as to the goods). See, e.g., *In re Leasing Consultants, Inc.,* 486 F.2d 367, 13 UCC Rep.Serv. (Callaghan) 189 (2d Cir.1973). Furthermore, this analysis is consistent with Article 2A's definition of a lease being a "transfer" of a right to possession and use of the leased goods even without being a "sale" of the goods. See §§ 2–106(1) and 2A–103(1)(j). Cf. *Feldman v. Philadelphia Nat. Bank,* 408 F.Supp. 24, 37–38, 18 UCC Rep.Serv. (Callaghan) 776, 786–788 (E.D.Pa.1976) (while the court referred to chattel paper as "proceeds" of a security interest in underlying goods, the reference may be viewed as dicta since the secured party had in any event taken possession of the chattel paper). Cases such as *General Electric Credit Corp. v. Cleary Brothers Construction Co., Inc. (In re Cleary Brothers Construc-*

tion Co., Inc.), 9 B.R. 40, 30 UCC Rep.Serv. (Callaghan) 1444 (Bkrtcy.S.D.Fla.1980), and *In re A.E.I. Corp.,* 11 B.R. 97, 31 UCC Rep.Serv. (Callaghan) 1467 (Bkrtcy.E.D.Pa. 1981), to the extent that they hold that a subsequent lease of goods or payments thereon cannot constitute proceeds of a secured party's pre-existing collateral consisting of the goods, are not consistent with this analysis.

Lease rentals would constitute proceeds of a secured party's collateral consisting of goods even where the subsequent lease of the goods is for a term which is of a short duration in relation to the useful life of the goods. Where the goods have a limited useful life, any transfer of the use and possession of the goods in return for a consideration constitutes a disposition, however small, of the debtor's interest in the goods. If that consideration consists of chattel paper, that chattel paper and the payments thereon constitute proceeds of the secured party's collateral. For a case reaching an analogous conclusion in the context of a real estate mortgage, see *Old Stone Bank v. Tycon I Building Limited Partnership,* 946 F.2d 271 (4th Cir.1991) (forfeited earnest money deposit under a sales contract for mortgaged real estate constituted "proceeds" to which undersecured mortgagee is entitled under its mortgage since the deposit resulted from a disposition of valuable "lock up" rights to the collateral while the sales contract was in effect).

The foregoing analysis is intended to clarify the treatment of rental payments as proceeds of a secured party's collateral consisting of goods subsequently leased. It is not intended to address transactions where the goods become subject to the secured party's security interest at a time when the goods are already under lease by the debtor as lessor. See § 2A–307; *In re Leasing Consultants, Inc.,* 486 F.2d 367, 13 UCC Rep.Serv. (Callaghan) 189 (2d Cir.1973). Nor is it intended to address transactions where the goods, although subject to a secured party's pre-existing security interest, are not subsequently leased by the debtor as lessor. For example, the foregoing analysis is not intended to suggest that income generated from the debtor's own use and possession of goods should constitute proceeds of a secured party's pre-existing collateral consisting of the goods. Similarly, it is not intended to address other transactions where no disposition of the goods by security lease, determined by reference to § 1–201(37), or true lease, governed by Article 2A, has taken place. Cf. *In re S & J Holding Corp.,* 42 B.R. 249, 39 UCC Rep.Serv. (Callaghan) 668 (Bkrtcy. S.D.Fla.1984) (payments for playing video games on game machines).

Moreover, the foregoing analysis is not intended to suggest that, as a matter of federal bankruptcy law, a secured party is necessarily entitled to "adequate protection" compensation for the debtor's use of rental payments made under a post-petition lease by the debtor as lessor of goods in which a secured party held a perfected and unavoidable pre-petition security interest. Factors such as the term of the lease in relation to the useful life of the leased goods and the provision by the debtor of post-petition services associated with the post-petition lease of the goods may well affect the secured party's entitlement to such "adequate protection" compensation, without, however, affecting the status of the lease or the rental payments thereon as proceeds of the secured party's pre-existing collateral as a matter of state law. See 11 U.S.C. §§ 361, 363(e), and 552(b); cf. *General Electric Credit Corp. v. Cleary Brothers Construction Co., Inc. (In re Cleary Brothers Construction Co., Inc.),* 9 B.R. 40, 30 UCC Rep.Serv. (Callaghan) 1444 (Bkrtcy.S.D.Fla.1980) (instead of holding that the secured party could not claim, as proceeds of its pre-petition security interest in a crane, the rentals under a post-petition lease of the crane for a 10–day period, the court could have reached the same result by concluding that, although the rentals were proceeds of the secured party's collateral, the secured party was adequately protected).

CONCLUSION

Where a debtor has granted to a secured party a security interest in goods and the debtor later leases those goods as lessor, the lease rentals will constitute proceeds of the secured party's collateral consisting of the goods.

The Official Comment to § 9–306 is amended by adding the following:

> 6. Where a debtor has granted to a secured party a security interest in goods and the debtor later leases those goods as lessor, the lease rentals constitute proceeds of the secured party's collateral consisting of the goods. See PEB Commentary No. 9, dated June 25, 1992.

COMMENTARY NO. 10
(SECTION 1-203) FINAL DRAFT

(February 10, 1994)

Permanent Editorial Board for the Uniform Commercial Code, 4025 Chestnut Street, Philadelphia, Pennsylvania 19104-3099.

APPENDIX V

COUNSELLOR EMERITUS

MARTIN J. ARONSTEIN, Philadelphia, Pennsylvania

ABA LIAISON

LINDA C. HAYMAN, New York, New York

ABA SECTION OF BUSINESS LAW LIAISON

GEORGE A. HISERT, San Francisco, California

PREFACE TO PEB COMMENTARY

The Permanent Editorial Board (PEB) for the Uniform Commercial Code (UCC) acts under the authority of The American Law Institute and the National Conference of Commissioners on Uniform State Laws. In March, 1987, the PEB resolved to issue from time to time supplementary commentary on the UCC to be known as PEB Commentary. These PEB Commentaries seek to further the underlying policies of the UCC by affording guidance in interpreting and resolving issues raised by the UCC and/or the Official Comments. The Resolution states that:

> "A PEB Commentary should come within one or more of the following specific purposes, which should be made apparent at the inception of the Commentary: (1) to resolve an ambiguity in the UCC by restating more clearly what the PEB considers to be the legal rule; (2) to state a preferred resolution of an issue on which judicial opinion or scholarly writing diverges; (3) to elaborate on the application of the UCC where the statute and/or the Official Comment leaves doubt as to inclusion or exclusion of, or application to, particular circumstances or transactions; (4) consistent with UCC § 1-102(2)(b), to apply the principles of the UCC to new or changed circumstances; (5) to clarify or elaborate upon the operation of the UCC as it relates to other statutes (such as the Bankruptcy Code and various federal and state consumer protection statutes) and general principles of law and equity pursuant to UCC § 1-103; or (6) to otherwise improve the operation of the UCC."

The full Resolution appears in the 1990 Edition of the UCC.

PEB COMMENTARY NO. 10
SECTION 1–203

ISSUE

Section 1–203 provides that "Every contract or duty within this Act imposes an obligation of good faith in its performance or enforcement." [1] While this concept applies generally to every contract, it finds particular expression throughout the Code. For example, out of over 400 Code provisions, more than 50 sections make specific reference to "good faith." [2]

The meaning of "good faith" varies with the context. Sometimes the context is as a standard of performance or enforcement; other times the context is that of good faith purchase.[3] This Commentary deals only with good faith performance or enforcement of a right or duty under a contract that is within the Code.

In the context in which the obligation of good faith functions as the standard of contract performance or enforcement, can the failure to meet this standard support a cause of action where no other basis for a cause of action exists? This Commentary examines this question in order to promote a uniform understanding of what it means to say that a general obligation of good faith is imposed on every contracting party. In so doing, several principles are discussed.

DISCUSSION

1. Good Faith, Commercial Expectations, and the Concept of Agreement

Section 1–201(19) defines good faith as "honesty in fact in the conduct or transaction concerned." [4] Commentators have said that this general requirement of good faith sets a "subjective" standard,[5] while the particularized definitions elsewhere also create an additional "objective" standard of the observance of reasonable commercial standards of fair dealing. This Commentary applies with equal force to both standards of good faith.

1. This does not mean that the obligation of good faith as defined in the Code will necessarily apply to all aspects of the same transaction. As written, the scope of § 1–203 is co-extensive with the Code's coverage. For example, if a loan agreement that provides for an Article 9 security interest also contains financial covenants which are not governed by the Code, § 1–203 would apply to the former and the general law of contracts would apply to the latter. See, e.g., Restatement, Second, Contracts § 205 (1981).

2. Farnsworth, *Good Faith Performance and Commercial Reasonableness Under the Uniform Commercial Code,* 30 U.Chi.L.Rev. 666, 667 (1963).

3. See, e.g., UCC §§ 2–403 (good faith purchaser); 3–302 (holder in due course); 9–307 (buyer in the ordinary course of business). On the distinction between the doctrines of good faith performance and good faith purchase, see generally id.

4. This sparse definition found in Article 1 is expanded elsewhere in the Code for purposes of particular Articles. See, e.g., §§ 2–103(1)(b); 2A–103(2); 3–103(a)(4); 4–104(c); 4A–105(a)(6). This expanded definition "is concerned with the fairness of conduct rather than the care with which an act is performed." UCC § 3–103, Comment 4.

5. See Aronstein, *Good Faith Performance of Security Agreements: The Liability of Corporate Managers,* 120 U.Pa.L.Rev. 1, 31 (1971) ("Good faith [as] defined in § 1–201(19) . . . [has] been historically construed as applying only to the actor's subjective state of mind."); Braucher, *The Legislative History of the Uniform Commercial Code,* 58 Colum.L.Rev. 798, 812 (1958) (describing the test of good faith in § 1–201(19) as a "subjective" test, sometimes known as the rule of "the pure heart and empty head"); Lawrence, *The Prematurely Reported Demise of the Perfect Tender Rule,* 35 U.Kan.L.Rev. 557, 571 (1987) ("Good faith is a subjective term meaning 'honesty in fact in the contract or transaction concerned.' ").

The principal author of the Code, Karl Llewellyn, recognized that parties develop expectations over time against the background of commercial practices and that if commercial law fails to account for those practices, it will cut against the parties' actual expectations. In an unpublished commentary on the Proposed Final Draft of the Uniform Revised Sales Act, Llewellyn had this to say about good faith:

> No inconsistency of language and background exists merely because the words used mean something different to an outsider than they do to the merchants who used that language in the light of the commercial background against which they contracted. This is the necessary result of applying commercial standards and principles of good faith to the agreement.... Moreover, where the commercial background normally gives to a term in question some breadth of meaning so that it describes a range of acceptable tolerances rather than a sharp-edged single line of action, any attempted narrowing of this meaning by one party is so unusual as not likely to be expected or perceived by the other. Therefore, attention must be called to a desire to contract at material variance from the accepted commercial pattern of contract or use of language. Thus, this Act rejects any "surprise" variation from the fair and normal meaning of the agreement.[6]

Explaining the doctrine of good faith in such terms is thus a recognition that, as expressed in the Code, it serves as a directive to protect the reasonable expectations of the contracting parties. The general imperative that the reasonable expectations of the parties are the measure of the good faith of each suggests that good faith is a concept with conceptual content related to that of agreement.

The Code definition of "Agreement" reads:

> "Agreement" means the bargain of the parties in fact as found in their language or by implication from other circumstances including course of dealing or usage of trade or course of performance as provided in this Act (Sections 1-205 and 2-208).[7]

The agreement of the parties consists of more than their language alone. In elaborating on this theme, Comment 3 to § 1-201 emphasizes that "the word [agreement] is intended to include full recognition of usage of trade, course of dealing, *course of performance* and the surrounding circumstances as effective parts thereof...." (emphasis added).[8]

6. The Karl Llewellyn Papers, The University of Chicago Law Library, File J.X.2.K. 1, 9, *reprinted in* D. Patterson, *Good Faith and Lender Liability* 217 (1990).

7. UCC § 1-201(3). Furthermore, Comment 1 to § 1-205 ("Course of Dealing and Usage of Trade") reinforces this definition by stating:

> This Act rejects both the "lay-dictionary" and the "conveyancer's" reading of a commercial agreement. Instead the meaning of the agreement of the parties is to be determined by the language used by them and by their action, read and interpreted in the light of commercial practices and other surrounding circumstances. The measure and background for interpretation are set by the commercial context, which may explain and supplement even the language of a formal or final writing.

8. This Commentary recognizes the fact that course of performance is defined in Articles 2 and 2A and was originally not a part of the general definition of "Agreement" in Article 1. The concept is included here as an element of the agreement of the parties because there exists no plausible justification for excluding it. This view is strongly supported by Comments 1 and 2 to § 2-208. Comment 2, in particular, emphasizes that "a course of performance is always relevant to determine the meaning of the agreement." See also Westinghouse Credit Corp. v. Shelton, 645 F.2d 869, 31 UCC Rep.Serv. (Callaghan) 410 (10th Cir.1981) (course of performance may also be used for discerning the meaning of "Agreement" in Article 9).

The Restatement, Second, of Contracts does not reflect the Code's isolation of course of performance in Articles 2 and 2A. The Restatement provides that all four elements—express terms, course of dealing, course of performance, and usage of trade—are all elements of the meaning of "contract." See Restate-

"Course of dealing" is defined as follows:

> A course of dealing is a sequence of previous conduct between the parties to a particular transaction which is fairly to be regarded as establishing a common basis of understanding for interpreting their expressions and other conduct.[9]

"Usage of trade" is defined as follows:

> A usage of trade is any practice or method of dealing having such regularity of observance in a place, vocation or trade as to justify an expectation that it will be observed with respect to the transaction in question. The existence and scope of such a usage are to be proved as facts. If it is established that such a usage is embodied in a written trade code or similar writing the interpretation of the writing is for the court.[10]

"Course of performance" is defined as follows:

> Where the contract for sale involves repeated occasions for performance by either party with knowledge of the nature of the performance and opportunity for objection to it by the other, any course of performance accepted or acquiesced in without objection shall be relevant to determine the meaning of the agreement.[11]

In addition to two definitional sections, § 1–205 contains two additional methodological sections which direct how express terms, course of dealing, and usage of trade are to be synthesized:

> (3) A course of dealing between parties and any usage of trade in the vocation or trade in which they are engaged or of which they are or should be aware give particular meaning to and supplement or qualify terms of an agreement.
>
> (4) The express terms of an agreement and an applicable course of dealing or usage of trade shall be construed wherever reasonable as consistent with each other; but when such construction is unreasonable express terms control both course of dealing and usage of trade and course of dealing controls usage of trade.[12]

At this juncture it is important to recognize that one acts in good faith relative to the agreement of the parties. To decide the question whether a party has acted in good faith, a court must first ascertain the substance of the parties' agreement.

The performance and enforcement of agreements in a manner consistent with the reasonable expectations of the parties is in keeping with the broadest understanding of contract doctrine.[13] The Code is consistent with this tradition of thought. However,

ment, Second, Contracts § 203. In fact, § 202(4) states that "any course of performance accepted or acquiesced in without objection is given great weight in the interpretation of the agreement."

9. UCC § 1–205(1).

10. UCC § 1–205(2).

11. UCC § 2–208(1). This definition is duplicated in § 2A–207(1).

12. UCC § 1–205(3)–(4). The connection between § 1–205 and good faith is made explicit in the Comment to § 1–203, wherein it is stated that the obligation of good faith "is further implemented by Section 1–205 on course of dealing and usage of trade."

The interpretational priorities set forth in § 1–205 are, with the added inclusion of course of performance, duplicated in § 2–208(2). That section states as follows:

> The express terms of the agreement and any such course of performance, as well as any course of dealing and usage of trade, shall be construed whenever reasonable as consistent with each other; but when such construction is unreasonable, express terms shall control course of performance and course of performance shall control both course of dealing and usage of trade (Section 1–205).

See also UCC § 2A–207(2).

13. See 3 A. Corbin, *Corbin on Contracts* § 570 (West Supp.1993).

If the purpose of contract law is to enforce the reasonable expectations of parties induced by promises, then at some point it

the Code's concept of agreement broadens the sources for determining the meaning of the parties' agreement. The concept of agreement is not limited to the terms of the parties' writing: it includes a variety of elements, all of which must be synthesized.

Under § 1–205(4), the initial interpretive effort is to read all the terms as consistent with one another. Only when this is impossible does the interpreter then move to a lexical ordering of the terms, with express terms at the head of the list. Cases which make no attempt to reconcile the various terms before according priority to express terms in the construction of the parties' agreement must be considered to have proceeded improperly.[14] The better application of § 1–205(4), and the issues of interpretation which are central to it, is illustrated in cases like *Nanakuli Paving & Rock Co. v. Shell Oil Co.,* 664 F.2d 772, 32 UCC Rep.Serv. (Callaghan) 1025 (9th Cir.1981) (upholding a finding that the written price term in an asphalt supply contract was qualified by a trade practice requiring suppliers to delay price increases for jobs on which buyers have already bid). Accordingly, in order to answer the question, "Has a party performed or enforced a contractual right or duty in good faith?", the content of the parties' agreement must first be determined.[15]

2. UCC § 1–203 Does Not Create an Independent Cause of Action

The inherent flaw in the view that § 1–203 supports an independent cause of action is the belief that the obligation of good faith has an existence which is conceptually separate from the underlying agreement. As the above discussion demonstrates, however, this is an incorrect view of the duty. "A party cannot simply 'act in good faith.' One acts in good faith relative to the agreement of the parties. Thus the real question is 'What is the Agreement of the parties?' " [16] Put differently, good

> becomes necessary for courts to look to the substance rather than to the form of the agreement, and to hold that substance controls over form. What courts are doing here, whether calling the process "implication" of promises, or interpreting the requirements of "good faith," as the current fashion may be, is but a recognition that the parties occasionally have understandings or expectations that were so fundamental that they did not need to negotiate about those expectations. When the court "implies a promise" or holds that "good faith" requires a party not to violate those expectations, it is recognizing that sometimes silence says more than words, and it is understanding its duty to the spirit of the bargain is higher than its duty to the technicalities of the language.

Id. Reiter & Swan, Contracts and the Protection of Reasonable Expectations, in *Studies in Contract Law* 1, 11 (B. Reiter & J. Swan eds. 1980) ("[T]hroughout the law of contract, a striving to protect reasonable expectations is visible. . . .").

14. See, e.g., Southern Concrete Servs. v. Mableton Contractors, Inc., 407 F.Supp. 581, 19 UCC Rep.Serv. (Callaghan) 79 (N.D.Ga. 1975), *aff'd mem.,* 569 F.2d 1154 (5th Cir. 1978); Division of Triple T Serv. v. Mobil Oil Corp., 304 N.Y.S.2d 191, 6 UCC Rep.Serv. (Callaghan) 1011 (Sup.Ct.1969).

15. For a non-Code decision which is consistent with this approach, see Southwest Savings and Loan Association v. Sunamp Systems, Inc., 838 P.2d 1314 (Ariz.App.1992) (holding that inquiry does not stop with recognition that lender had general authority in written loan agreement to take the particular action, but inquiry extends to whether lender exercised that authority "for a reason beyond the risks" assumed by borrower in loan agreement, or beyond borrower's "justified expectations," in the context of how a reasonable lender might act).

16. Patterson, *supra,* at 143. Good faith is sometimes the basis of an implied term to fill a gap or deal with an omitted case, e.g., the duty of cooperation frequently imposed on a party whose cooperation is essential and not unreasonably burdensome; or, the duty to give notice within a reasonable time of some important fact of which the other party would otherwise be unaware. See § 2–309(3) and Comment 8; 2 Farnsworth on Contracts §§ 7.17, 7.17a (1990). A breach of such duties gives rise to a cause of action for breach of the contract of which the implied term becomes a part. Although such a cause of action arguably has the same practical content as a cause of action based upon a purported breach of § 1–203, there is an important methodological difference in that this Commentary requires, in the case of contracts within the Code, that the focus be upon the Agreement of the parties and their reasonable expectations.

faith merely directs attention to the parties' reasonable expectations; it is not an independent source from which rights and duties evolve.[17] The language of § 1–203 itself makes this quite clear by providing that the obligation to perform or enforce in good faith extends only to the rights and duties resulting from the parties' contract. The term "contract" is, in turn, defined as "the total legal obligation which results from the parties' *agreement....*" [18] Consequently, resort to principles of law or equity outside the Code are not appropriate to create rights, duties, and liabilities inconsistent with those stated in the Code.[19] For example, a breach of a contract or duty within the Code arising from a failure to act in good faith does not give rise to a claim for punitive damages unless specifically permitted.[20]

CONCLUSION

Section 1–203 does not support a cause of action where no other basis for a cause of action exists.

The concept of Agreement permeates the entirety of the Code. For example, § 9–105(1)(*l*) incorporates the Article 1 concept of Agreement directly into Article 9. The "agreement of the parties" cannot be read off the face of a document, but must be discerned against the background of actual commercial practice. Not only does the Code recognize "the reasonable practices and standards of the commercial community ... [as] an appropriate source of legal obligation," [21] but it also rejects the "premise that the language used [by the parties] has the meaning attributable to [it] by rules of construction existing in the law rather than the meaning which arises out of the commercial context in which it was used." [22] The correct perspective on the meaning of good faith performance and enforcement is the Agreement of the parties. The critical question is, "Has 'X' acted in good faith with respect to the performance or enforcement of some right or duty under the terms of the Agreement?" It is therefore wrong to conclude that as long as the agreement allows a party to do something, it is under all terms and conditions permissible. Such a conclusion overlooks completely the distinction between merely performing or enforcing a right or duty under an agreement on the one hand and, on the other hand, doing so in a way that recognizes that the agreement should be interpreted in a manner consistent with the reasonable expectations of the parties in the light of the commercial conditions existing in the context under scrutiny. The latter is the correct approach. Examples are: (1) Is it reasonable for a buyer in a particular locale or trade to expect that an express quantity term in a contract is "not really" a quantity term, but a mere projection to be adjusted according to market forces? [23]; (2) Does a party to a sales contract that permits discretionary termination have the right to expect that the decision whether to terminate will be made on the basis of sound business criteria?

The Official Comment to § 1–203 is amended by adding the following language at the end of the first paragraph:

17. Cases reaching this conclusion include Management Assistance, Inc. v. Computer Dimensions, Inc., 546 F.Supp. 666 (N.D.Ga.1982), *aff'd* 747 F.2d 708 (11th Cir.1984), and Chandler v. Hunter, 340 So.2d 818, 21 UCC Rep. Serv. (Callaghan) 484 (Ala.Civ.App.1976). A contrary conclusion was reached in Reid v. Key Bank of Southern Maine, Inc., 821 F.2d 9, 3 UCC Rep.Serv.2d (Callaghan) 1665 (1st Cir. 1987).

18. UCC § 1–201(11) (emphasis supplied).

19. See UCC § 1–103.

20. See UCC § 1–106(1).

21. Kastely, *Stock Equipment for the Bargain in Fact: Trade Usage, "Express Terms," and Consistency Under Section 1–205 of the Uniform Commercial Code,* 64 N.C.L.Rev. 777, 780 (1986).

22. UCC § 2–202, Comment 1.

23. See Columbia Nitrogen Corp. v. Royster Co., 451 F.2d 3, 9 UCC Rep.Serv. (Callaghan) 977 (4th Cir.1971).

This section does not support an independent cause of action for failure to perform or enforce in good faith. Rather, this section means that a failure to perform or enforce, in good faith, a specific duty or obligation under the contract, constitutes a breach of that contract or makes unavailable, under the particular circumstances, a remedial right or power. This distinction makes it clear that the doctrine of good faith merely directs a court towards interpreting contracts within the commercial context in which they are created, performed, and enforced, and does not create a separate duty of fairness and reasonableness which can be independently breached. See PEB Commentary No. 10, dated February 10, 1994.

COMMENTARY NO. 11
(SURETYSHIP ISSUES UNDER SECTIONS 3–116, 3–305, 3–415, 3–419, AND 3–605)
FINAL DRAFT

(February 10, 1994)

Permanent Editorial Board for the Uniform Commercial Code, 4025 Chestnut Street, Philadelphia, Pennsylvania 19104–3099.

COMMITTEES

PERMANENT EDITORIAL BOARD FOR THE UNIFORM COMMERCIAL CODE

APPENDIX V

SECRETARY EMERITUS

PAUL A. WOLKIN, Philadelphia, Pennsylvania

COUNSELLOR EMERITUS

MARTIN J. ARONSTEIN, Philadelphia, Pennsylvania

ABA LIAISON

LINDA C. HAYMAN, New York, New York

ABA SECTION OF BUSINESS LAW LIAISON

GEORGE A. HISERT, San Francisco, California

PREFACE TO PROPOSED PEB COMMENTARY

The Permanent Editorial Board (PEB) for the Uniform Commercial Code (UCC) acts under the authority of The American Law Institute and the National Conference of Commissioners on Uniform State Laws. In March, 1987, the PEB resolved to issue from time to time supplementary commentary on the UCC to be known as PEB Commentary. These PEB Commentaries seek to further the underlying policies of the UCC by affording guidance in interpreting and resolving issues raised by the UCC and/or the Official Comments. The Resolution states that:

> "A PEB Commentary should come within one or more of the following specific purposes, which should be made apparent at the inception of the Commentary: (1) to resolve an ambiguity in the UCC by restating more clearly what the PEB considers to be the legal rule; (2) to state a preferred resolution of an issue on which judicial opinion or scholarly writing diverges; (3) to elaborate on the application of the UCC where the statute and/or the Official Comment leaves doubt as to inclusion or exclusion of, or application to, particular circumstances or transactions; (4) consistent with UCC § 1–102(2)(b) to apply the principles of the UCC to new or changed circumstances; (5) to clarify or elaborate upon the operation of the UCC as it relates to other statutes (such as the Bankruptcy Code and various federal and state consumer protection statutes) and general principles of law and equity pursuant to UCC § 1–103; or (6) to otherwise improve the operation of the UCC."

The full Resolution appears in the 1990 Edition of the UCC.

PEB COMMENTARY NO. 11
SURETYSHIP ISSUES UNDER SECTIONS 3–116, 3–305, 3–415, 3–419, AND 3–605

INTRODUCTION

The promulgation of revised Article 3 of the Uniform Commercial Code has given rise to a number of questions concerning the provisions in that Article governing the rights and duties of accommodation parties. This heightened level of interest results from many factors. In particular, the provisions in revised Article 3 concerning accommodation parties differ significantly from those in former Article 3 in ways that are complex and not always obvious. Application of these rules often raises issues that were not pertinent under prior law. In addition, the ongoing project of The American Law Institute to publish a Restatement of Suretyship has generated greater interest in the rights and duties of sureties, including, of course, accommodation parties.

As a result of this heightened interest, the suretyship rules in Article 3 have been the subject of a great deal of scrutiny, which has resulted in a recognition that the treatment of some suretyship issues in revised Article 3 should be clarified. It is the purpose of this Commentary to answer several questions that have arisen concerning the rights and duties of accommodation parties. This Commentary concludes with a series of revisions and additions to the Comments to various sections in Article 3 that govern suretyship issues.

ISSUE 1

If another person agrees to be liable for the obligation of the maker of a note, are the rights and duties of that person determined by the provisions of Article 3 governing accommodation parties, by the general law of suretyship, or both?

DISCUSSION

A person who agrees to be liable for the debt of another is clearly a surety. See Restatement of the Law Third, Suretyship § 1 (Tent. Draft No. 1, 1992). If the person effectuates the agreement by becoming a party (i.e., a co-maker or indorser) to the same instrument that creates the obligation, the surety is also an accommodation party. In such a case, the rules in §§ 3–116, 3–305, 3–415, 3–419, and 3–605 concerning accommodation parties are applicable. Of course, these sections will not resolve all possible issues concerning the rights and duties of the surety. In the event that a situation is presented that is not resolved by those sections, the resolution may be provided by the general law of suretyship because, pursuant to § 1–103, that law is applicable unless displaced by provisions of this Act. If the surety does not effectuate the obligation by becoming a party to the note, the surety is not an accommodation party. In that case, the surety's rights and duties are determined by the general law of suretyship.

In unusual cases, two parties to an instrument may have a surety relationship that is not governed by Article 3 because the requirements of § 3–419(a) are not fulfilled. For example, assume that the payee of an instrument would like to sell it, but the potential buyer will agree to buy the instrument only if, in the event that the instrument is dishonored, the buyer has recourse not only against the issuer and the payee but also against someone more creditworthy. Accordingly, the payee produces a creditworthy person who agrees to stand behind the payee's obligations with respect to the instrument. The transfer to the buyer is then made after both the payee and the creditworthy person indorse the instrument. The creditworthy person is a party to the instrument as an indorser and is an accommodation party for the issuer who is the accommodated party. The creditworthy person is also a surety with respect to the obligation of both the issuer and the payee as indorser. The creditworthy person, however, is not an accommodation party for the payee and the payee is not an accommodated party under § 3–419(a) inasmuch as the instrument was not issued for value given for the benefit of the payee. Therefore, the general law of suretyship, and not the provisions in Article 3 concerning accommodation parties, provides the rules that govern the suretyship relationship between the creditworthy person and the payee.[1]

ISSUE 2

What are the differences between the rights of an accommodation party with respect to the accommodated party under revised Article 3 and former Article 3?

DISCUSSION

Under the general law of suretyship, as between the principal obligor and the secondary obligor, it is the principal obligor who ought to bear the cost of performance. Restatement of the Law Third, Suretyship § 1 (Tent. Draft No. 1, 1992). Suretyship law provides three mechanisms to effectuate that cost allocation. First, if the principal obligor is charged with notice of the secondary obligation, the principal obligor owes the secondary obligor a duty of performance; this duty of performance can be enforced by the secondary obligor through the mechanism commonly known as exoneration. Restatement of the Law Third, Suretyship § 17 (Tent. Draft No. 1, 1992). Second, a secondary obligor who performs may be subrogated to the rights of the obligee against the principal obligor (regardless of whether the principal obligor was charged with notice of the secondary obligation). Restatement of the Law Third, Suretyship § 23 (Tent. Draft No. 2, 1993). Third, if the principal obligor is charged with notice of the secondary obligation, the principal obligor must reimburse a secondary obligor who performs the obligation. Restatement of the Law Third, Suretyship § 18 (Tent. Draft No. 2, 1993). If the principal obligor is not charged with notice of the secondary obligation, a secondary obligor who performs is nonetheless entitled to restitution from the principal obligor. Restatement of the Law Third, Suretyship § 22 (Tent. Draft No. 2, 1993).

An accommodation party is always a surety. Former Article 3 explicitly provided in § 3–415(5) that an accommodation party who paid the instrument was entitled to enforce the instrument against the accommodated party. This right essentially codified the surety's right of subrogation. Other rights of the accommodation party against the accommodated party were left to the general law of suretyship through § 1–103. In § 3–419(e), revised Article 3 also in effect sets forth subrogation rights of accommodation parties by providing that such parties are "entitled to enforce the instrument against the accommodated party." That section also codifies the accommodation party's right to be reimbursed by the accommodated party. Unlike the general law of suretyship, however, that right is not limited to situations in which the accommodated party was charged with notice of the accommodation party's obligation. Thus, it need not be determined whether the accommodated party is charged with notice of the accommodation party's obligation, and the right of restitution that is present in the general law of suretyship is superfluous. Revised Article 3, like former Article 3, leaves the accommodated party's duty of performance and the accommoda-

1. The revisions to Comment 3 to § 3–419 and Comment 6 to § 3–605 reflect this discussion. See Appendix, par. 3 and par. 10.

tion party's concomitant right of exoneration to the general law of suretyship through § 1–103.[2]

ISSUE 3

Is an accommodation party entitled to reimbursement if the accommodated party had a defense to its obligation that could have been raised by the accommodation party against the person entitled to enforce the instrument?

DISCUSSION

The juxtaposition of the accommodated party's duty to reimburse the accommodation party (§ 3–419(e)) with the accommodated party's right to raise defenses (§ 3–305(b)) raises important policy issues. If a duty to reimburse exists even when the accommodated party had a defense, that duty could be said to obviate the value of the defense. On the other hand, if no duty to reimburse exists in such circumstances, the cost of performance will be borne ultimately by the accommodation party rather than the accommodated party.

There are a number of different contexts in which the situation may arise. Generally speaking, the accommodation party may raise as a defense to its obligation the defenses of the accommodated party to *its* obligation. See § 3–305(d). There are three exceptions. The accommodated party's defenses of discharge in insolvency proceedings, infancy, and lack of legal capacity are not available to the accommodation party. If the accommodation party pays the instrument when the accommodated party had one of these defenses, the accommodated party has no duty to reimburse the accommodation party. The accommodation party has, in a sense, assumed the risk that such defenses will exist.

Occasionally, an accommodation party will pay an instrument even though the accommodated party has a defense that is available to the accommodation party. In such cases, the existence of the duty to reimburse may depend on whether the accommodation party was aware of the defense at the time it paid the instrument. If the accommodation party was unaware of the defense, there is a duty to reimburse. Thus, there is an incentive for the accommodated party to make the accommodation party aware of any defenses it may have. If the accommodation party pays the instrument while aware of a defense of the accommodated party, however, reimbursement would ordinarily not be justified but might be justified in some circumstances. Resolution of this issue is left to the general law of suretyship through § 1–103.[3]

ISSUE 4

Section 3–415(a) provides that an indorser's obligation to pay the instrument upon dishonor is owed, *inter alia,* to a subsequent indorser who pays the instrument. What if both the prior indorser and subsequent indorser are anomalous indorsers?

DISCUSSION

In the general law of suretyship, when there are two secondary obligors for the same underlying obligation, the relationship between those two secondary obligors may be that of co-suretyship or sub-suretyship. In a co-suretyship situation, the two secondary obligors are jointly and severally liable and, as between themselves, have a right of contribution against each other. In a sub-suretyship situation, on the other hand, the second secondary obligor is, in a sense, a surety for the obligation of the first secondary obligor. Thus, as between the two secondary obligors, the first obligor occupies the

2. The revision to Comment 5 to § 3–419 reflects this discussion. See Appendix, par. 5.

3. The addition of Comments 6 and 7 to § 3–419 reflect this discussion. See Appendix, par. 6.

position of a principal obligor while the later one occupies the position of a secondary obligor. It is often difficult to determine whether the two secondary obligors are co-sureties or sub-sureties, especially in the context of negotiable instruments when the obligations of those parties may be created by a signature alone, unaccompanied by words of explanation.

Article 3 treats successive anomalous indorsers as having joint and several liability on the instrument. See § 3–116(a). If one of the anomalous indorsers pays the instrument, that indorser has a right to receive contribution from the other indorser. See § 3–116(b). Accordingly, the general rule of § 3–415(a), that a subsequent indorser who pays the instrument may recover the full amount of the instrument from a prior indorser, does not apply in such cases. Section 3–116(b) does not recognize a distinction between a co-surety and a sub-surety, but in providing for a right to contribution, § 3–116(b) has the effect of treating anomalous indorsers as though they were co-sureties. Section 3–116(b), however, is subject to "agreement of the affected parties." If the subsequent indorser can prove an agreement with the prior indorser giving the subsequent indorser rights as a sub-surety, that agreement changes the rule of § 3–116(b). If the subsequent indorser pays the instrument and has rights under the agreement as a sub-surety, the subsequent indorser has a right of recourse against the prior indorser for the amount of the payment rather than only a right to contribution; if the prior indorser pays the instrument, there is no right of recourse against the subsequent indorser.[4]

ISSUE 5

What effect do words of guaranty have on the obligation of an indorser to a person entitled to enforce an instrument?

DISCUSSION

Under former § 3–416, the obligation of an indorser who added the words "payment guaranteed" or "collection guaranteed" to the indorsement was different than that of an indorser who did not add those words. The addition of the words "payment guaranteed" (or their equivalent) meant that if the instrument was not paid when due the indorser would pay it without resort to any other party. Thus, an indorser who guaranteed payment could be said to have waived presentment, notice of dishonor, and protest, as well as all demand upon the maker or drawee. In contrast, the addition of the words "collection guaranteed" (or their equivalent) meant that the indorser was required to pay only after the holder reduced its claim against the maker or acceptor to judgment or it was shown that such a proceeding would be useless.

Section 3–419(d) preserves the concept of a guaranty of collection, but no provision is made for a guaranty of payment. Moreover, the preferred treatment given to a guarantor of collection is only applicable when the words accompanying the indorsement indicate "unambiguously that the party is guaranteeing collection rather than payment of the obligation of another party to the instrument." Thus, an indorser who adds the words "payment guaranteed," or the like, to the indorsement has the same liability as an indorser who added no special words to the indorsement. Such an indorser may be entitled, *inter alia,* to notice of dishonor pursuant to § 3–503.[5]

ISSUE 6

May a person entitled to enforce an instrument avoid discharge of an accommodation party pursuant to § 3–605 by "reserving rights" against that party in conjunction with a release, extension, or other modification of the duty of the accommodated party?

4. The addition of Comment 5 to § 3–415 reflects this discussion. See Appendix, par. 2.

5. The revision to Comment 4 to § 3–419 reflects this discussion. See Appendix, par. 4.

DISCUSSION

Under former UCC § 3–606(1)(a), a release, extension, or other modification of the accommodated party's duty accompanied by an express "reservation of rights" against the accommodation party would not discharge that party. This provision paralleled the general law of suretyship in many jurisdictions.

Article 3 rejects the reservation of rights doctrine. The effects of a release, extension, or other modification of the accommodated party's duty cannot be changed by the incantation of a "reservation of rights." Pursuant to § 3–605(b), a release of the accommodated party does not discharge the accommodation party, so there is no need for the person entitled to enforce the instrument to take any action, such as a reservation of rights, to preserve recourse against the accommodation party. Pursuant to § 3–605(c)–(d), an extension or modification of the accommodated party's duty discharges the accommodation party to the extent that the extension or modification would otherwise cause the accommodation party a loss. This discharge cannot be avoided by a "reservation of rights" by the person entitled to enforce the instrument.[6]

ISSUE 7

If a person entitled to enforce an instrument agrees to extend the due date of the accommodated party's performance and, pursuant to § 3–605(c), the extension does not discharge the accommodation party, what is the effect of the extension on the obligation of the accommodation party? In particular, is the due date for the accommodation party's performance extended correspondingly? May the accommodation party perform on the original due date?

DISCUSSION

The person entitled to enforce the instrument will not be able to enforce the instrument against the accommodation party until the extended due date. If the accommodation party is an indorser, this is because an indorser is not liable until dishonor of the instrument, which, under these circumstances, cannot occur until it is unpaid on the extended due date. If the accommodation party is a co-maker, this is because, under § 3–305(d), until the extended due date the accommodation party will be able to assert the accommodated party's defense that, pursuant to the extension agreement, performance is not yet due.

The accommodation party may, however, perform on the original due date. The accommodation party is bound in accordance with the terms of its original engagement. The agreement between the accommodated party and the person entitled to enforce the instrument cannot bind the accommodation party to a change in its obligation without the accommodation party's consent. The effect on the recourse of the accommodation party against the accommodated party of performance by the accommodation party on the original due date is not addressed in § 3–419 and is left to the general law of suretyship.

Even though the accommodation party has the option of paying the instrument on the original due date, the accommodation party is not precluded from asserting its rights to discharge under § 3–605(c) if it does not exercise that option. The critical issue is whether the extension caused the accommodation party a loss by increasing the difference between the accommodation party's cost of performing its obligation on the instrument and the amount recoverable from the accommodated party pursuant to § 3–419(e). The decision by the accommodation party not to exercise its option to pay

6. The revision to Comment 3 to § 3–605 reflects this discussion. See Appendix, par. 7.

on the original due date may, under the circumstances, be a factor to be considered in the determination of that issue.[7]

ISSUE 8

What if the person entitled to enforce the instrument agrees, in one transaction, to both an extension of time for the accommodated party's performance and another modification of the accommodation party's obligation? What if there is a dispute as to whether, as a result of these changes, the accommodation party has suffered a loss?

DISCUSSION

This question highlights the difficulties in properly allocating the burden of persuasion when the agreement between the person entitled to enforce the instrument and the accommodated party involves both an extension governed by § 3–605(c) and a modification governed by § 3–605(d). The accommodation party has the burden of demonstrating loss from an extension, but the person entitled to enforce the instrument has the burden of overcoming a presumption of loss from other modifications.

If neither party introduces evidence as to loss causation, the result is full discharge of the accommodation party because § 3–605(d) applies. If the person entitled to enforce the instrument seeks to overcome the presumption of loss from the modification, it is entitled to a presumption that the extension alone caused no loss. Thus, the accommodation party will have to introduce evidence as to the effect of the extension, while the person entitled to enforce the instrument will have to introduce evidence as to the effect of the modification. On the basis of this evidence, the court will make an overall determination of the effect of the changes on the accommodation party's right of recourse against the accommodated party.[8]

ISSUE 9

How can § 3–305(d), which provides that the accommodation party can raise defenses of the accommodated party, be reconciled with § 3–605(b), which provides that a release of the accommodated party does not discharge the accommodation party?

DISCUSSION

While § 3–305(d) provides that an accommodation party can raise most defenses of the accommodated party, that section must be read in conjunction with § 3–605, which governs the effect on the obligation of the accommodation party of an act or omission of the person entitled to enforce the instrument. Section 3–605(b) provides that a release of the accommodated party does not discharge the accommodation party. Thus, while examined in isolation, § 3–305(d) might seem to allow the accommodation party to raise, as a defense to *its* obligation, a release of the accommodated party granted by the person entitled to enforce the instrument, the applicability of that section to such a release must be considered in light of § 3–605(b). If the release of the accommodated party is part of a settlement pursuant to which the person entitled to enforce the instrument accepts partial payment from an accommodated party who is financially unable to pay the entire amount of the note, the transaction falls within the scope of § 3–605(b) and the accommodation party cannot escape liability by asserting § 3–305(d) essentially to nullify § 3–605(b). If, on the other hand, the release of the accommodated party is part of an accord and satisfaction settling a dispute as to the obligation of the accommodated party, the accommodation party may utilize § 3–

7. The revision to Comment 4 to § 3–605 reflects this discussion. See Appendix, par. 8.

8. The revision to Comment 5 to § 3–605 reflects this discussion. See Appendix, par. 9.

305(d) to assert that release as a defense to its obligation because § 3–605(b) is not intended to apply to settlement of disputed claims.[9]

ISSUE 10

What sort of language is sufficient to waive discharge under § 3–605?

DISCUSSION

Section 3–605(i) provides that a party is not discharged under that section if the instrument or a separate agreement of the party waives such discharge "either specifically or by general language indicating that parties waive defenses based on suretyship or impairment of collateral." Thus, no particular language or form of agreement is required, and the standards for enforcing such a term are the same as the standards for enforcing any other term in an instrument or agreement. There is no requirement of particularity in referring to the four grounds for discharge established by § 3–605 so long as the language used indicates that suretyship defenses are waived. By allowing the use of general language, the rule recognizes that the use of lengthy provisions containing detailed waivers or even separate identification of each ground for discharge does not necessarily promote greater understanding of an instrument's terms. Yet, the requirement that the language indicate that defenses are being waived assures that a diligent indorser or accommodation party will, at the least, not be unjustly surprised when it is asserted that the terms of the instrument or agreement delete protections that would otherwise be available. In adopting this course, § 3–605 is consistent with the general law of suretyship. See Restatement of the Law Third, Suretyship § 42 (Tent.Draft No. 2, 1993).[10]

ISSUE 11

As a result of § 3–605(i), may an accommodation party waive whatever protections it may have pursuant to Part 5 of Article 9?

DISCUSSION

Section 3–605(e) provides that impairment of an interest in collateral for the obligation of the accommodated party may discharge the accommodation party. Section 3–605(g) defines impairment of an interest in collateral as including, *inter alia,* failure to comply with applicable law in disposing of collateral. In the case of personal property or fixtures, applicable law includes, of course, Article 9. Thus, failure to comply with the rules in Part 5 of Article 9 concerning disposition of collateral constitutes impairment of an interest in collateral. In addition, under Article 9, an accommodation party may qualify as a debtor. See § 9–105. In some jurisdictions, the limits placed by § 9–501 on the power of a debtor to waive the protections of §§ 9–504 and 9–505 have been interpreted so as to limit the power of an accommodation party to waive those protections. Section 3–605(i), on the other hand, provides that an accommodation party may waive discharge under this section (including discharge for impairment of an interest in collateral pursuant to § 3–605(e)). This does not mean that the accommodation party may waive *all* protections it may have concerning disposition of collateral; rather, it provides for the waiver of protections created by § 3–605. To the extent that Article 9 also provides the accommodation party similar protections, waiver of those protections is governed by Article 9 as interpreted in each jurisdiction.[11]

9. The revision to Comment 5 to § 3–305 reflects this discussion. See Appendix, par. 1.

10. The revision to Comment 8 to § 3–605 reflects this discussion. See Appendix, par. 11.

11. The revision to Comment 8 to § 3–605 reflects this discussion. See Appendix, par. 11.

APPENDIX

1. Comment 5 to § 3–305 is amended by adding an unnumbered paragraph as follows:

Section 3–305(d) must be read in conjunction with Section 3–605, which provides rules (usually referred to as suretyship defenses) for determining when the obligation of an accommodation party is discharged, in whole or in part, because of some act or omission of a person entitled to enforce the instrument. To the extent a rule stated in Section 3–605 is inconsistent with Section 3–305(d), the Section 3–605 rule governs. For example, under Section 3–605(b), discharge under Section 3–604 of the accommodated party does not discharge the accommodation party. As explained in Comment 3 to Section 3–605, discharge of the accommodated party is normally part of a settlement under which the holder of a note accepts partial payment from an accommodated party who is financially unable to pay the entire amount of the note. If the holder then brings an action against the accommodation party to recover the remaining unpaid amount of the note, the accommodation party cannot use Section 3–305(d) to nullify Section 3–605(b) by asserting the discharge of the accommodated party as a defense. On the other hand, suppose the accommodated party is a buyer of goods who issued the note to the seller who took the note for the buyer's obligation to pay for the goods. Suppose the buyer has a claim for breach of warranty with respect to the goods against the seller and the warranty claim may be asserted against the holder of the note. The warranty claim is a claim in recoupment. If the holder and the accommodated party reach a settlement under which the holder accepts payment less than the amount of the note in full satisfaction of the note and the warranty claim, the accommodation party could defend an action on the note by the holder by asserting the accord and satisfaction under Section 3–305(d). There is no conflict with Section 3–605(b) because that provision is not intended to apply to settlement of disputed claims. Another example of the use of Section 3–305(d) in cases in which Section 3–605 applies is stated in Comment 4 to Section 3–605. See PEB Commentary No. 11, dated February 10, 1994.

2. A new Comment 5 to § 3–415 is added as follows:

5. As stated in subsection (a), the obligation of an indorser to pay the amount due on the instrument is generally owed not only to a person entitled to enforce the instrument but also to a subsequent indorser who paid the instrument. But if the prior indorser and the subsequent indorser are both anomalous indorsers, this rule does not apply. In that case, Section 3–116 applies. Under Section 3–116(a), the anomalous indorsers are jointly and severally liable and if either pays the instrument the indorser who pays has a right of contribution against the other. Section 3–116(b). The right to contribution in Section 3–116(b) is subject to "agreement of the affected parties." Suppose the subsequent indorser can prove an agreement with the prior indorser under which the prior indorser agreed to treat the subsequent indorser as a guarantor of the obligation of the prior indorser. Rights of the two indorsers between themselves would be governed by the agreement. Under suretyship law, the subsequent indorser under such an agreement is referred to as a sub-surety. Under the agreement, if the subsequent indorser pays the instrument there is a right to reimbursement from the prior indorser; if the prior indorser pays the instrument, there is no right of recourse against the subsequent indorser. See PEB Commentary No. 11, dated February 10, 1994.

3. Comment 3 to § 3–419 is amended by adding an unnumbered paragraph as follows:

An accommodation party is always a surety. A surety who is not a party to the instrument, however, is not an accommodation party. For example, if M issues a note payable to the order of P, and S signs a separate contract in which S agrees to pay P the amount of the instrument if it is dishonored, S is a surety but is not an accommodation party. In such a case, S's rights and duties are determined under the general law of suretyship. In unusual cases two parties to an instrument may have a surety relationship that is not governed by Article 3 because the requirements of Section 3–419(a) are not met. In those cases the general law of suretyship applies to the relationship. See PEB Commentary No. 11, dated February 10, 1994.

4. Comment 4 to § 3–419 is amended by adding the following sentences:

Words added to an anomalous indorsement indicating that payment of the instrument is guaranteed by the indorser do not change the liability of the indorser as stated in Section 3–415. This is a change from former Section 3–416(5). See PEB Commentary No. 11, supra.

5. Comment 5 to § 3–419 is amended by deleting the struck-out words and adding the underlined words as follows:

5. Subsection (e) ~~restates subsection (5) of present Section 3–415~~ like former Section 3–415(5), provides that an accommodation party that pays the instrument is entitled to enforce the instrument against the accommodated party. Since the accommodation party that pays the instrument is entitled to enforce the instrument against the accommodated party, the accommodation party also obtains rights to any security interest or other collateral that secures payment of the instrument. Subsection (e) also provides that an accommodation party that pays the instrument is entitled to reimbursement from the accommodated party. See PEB Commentary No. 11, supra.

6. A new Comment 6 and a new Comment 7 to § 3–419 are added as follows:

6. In occasional cases, the accommodation party might pay the instrument even though the accommodated party had a defense to its obligation that was available to the accommodation party under Section 3–305(d). In such cases, the accommodation party's right to reimbursement may conflict with the accommodated party's right to raise its defense. For example, suppose the accommodation party pays the instrument without being aware of the defense. In that case the accommodation party should be entitled to reimbursement. Suppose the accommodation party paid the instrument with knowledge of the defense. In that case, to the extent of the defense, reimbursement ordinarily would not be justified, but under some circumstances reimbursement may be justified depending upon the facts of the case. The resolution of this conflict is left to the general law of suretyship. Section 1–103. See PEB Commentary No. 11, supra.

7. Section 3–419, along with Section 3–116(a) and (b), Section 3–305(d) and Section 3–605, provides rules governing the rights of accommodation parties. In addition, except to the extent that it is displaced by provisions of this Article, the general law of suretyship also applies to the rights of accommodation parties. Section 1–103. See PEB Commentary No. 11, supra.

7. Comment 3 to § 3–605 is amended by dividing it into two paragraphs, deleting the struck-out words, and adding the underlined words as follows:

3. Subsection (b) addresses the effect of discharge under Section 3–604 of the principal debtor. In the hypothetical case stated in Comment 1, release of Borrower by Bank does not release Accommodation Party. As a practical matter, Bank will not gratuitously release Borrower. Discharge of Borrower normally would be part of a settlement with Borrower if Borrower is insolvent or in financial difficulty. If Borrower is unable to pay all creditors, it may be prudent for Bank to take partial payment, but Borrower will normally insist on a release of the obligation. If Bank takes $3,000 and releases Borrower from the $10,000 debt, Accommodation Party is not injured. To the extent of the payment Accommodation Party's obligation to Bank is reduced. The release of Borrower by Bank does not affect the right of Accommodation Party to obtain reimbursement from Borrower or to enforce the note against Borrower if Accommodation Party pays Bank. Section 3–419(e). Subsection (b) is designed to allow a creditor to settle with the principal debtor without risk of losing rights against sureties. Settlement is in the interest of sureties as well as the creditor. Subsection (b), however, is not intended to apply to a settlement of a disputed claim which discharges the obligation.

Subsection (b) changes the law stated in former Section 3–606 but the change relates largely to formalities rather than substance. Under former Section 3–606, Bank in the hypothetical case stated in Comment 1 could settle with and release Borrower without releasing Accommodation Party, but to accomplish that result Bank had to either obtain the consent of Accommodation Party or make an express reservation of rights against Accommodation Party at the time it released Borrower. The reservation of rights was made in the agreement between Bank and Borrower by which the release of Borrower was made. There was no requirement in former Section 3–606 that any notice be given to Accommodation Party. ~~The reservation of rights doctrine is abolished in~~ Section 3–605 ~~with respect to rights on instruments~~ eliminates the necessity that Bank formally reserve rights against Accommodation Party in order to retain rights of recourse against Accommodation Party. See PEB Commentary No. 11, dated February 10, 1994.

8. Comment 4 to § 3–605 is amended by adding four unnumbered paragraphs as follows:

Under other provisions of Article 3, what is the effect of an extension agreement between the holder of a note and the maker who is an accommodated party? The question is illustrated by the following case:

Case #1. A borrows money from Lender and issues a note payable on April 1, 1992. B signs the note for accommodation at the request of Lender. B signed the note either as co-maker or as an anomalous indorser. In either case Lender subsequently makes an agreement with A extending the due date of A's obligation to pay the note to July 1, 1992. In either case B did not agree to the extension.

What is the effect of the extension agreement on B? Could Lender enforce the note against B if the note is not paid on April 1, 1992? A's obligation to Lender to pay the note on April 1, 1992 may be modified by the agreement of Lender. If B is an anomalous indorser Lender cannot enforce the note against B unless the note has been dishonored. Section 3–415(a). Under Section 3–502(a)(3) dishonor occurs if it is not paid on the day it becomes payable. Since the agreement between A and Lender extended the due date of A's obligation to July 1, 1992 there is no dishonor because A was not obligated to pay Lender on April 1, 1992. If B is a co-maker the analysis is somewhat different. Lender has no power to amend the terms of the note without the consent of both A and B. By an agreement with A, Lender can extend the due date of A's obligation to Lender to pay the note but B's obligation is to pay the note according to the terms of the note at the time of issue. Section 3–412. However, B's obligation to pay the note is subject to a defense because B is an accommodation party. B is not obliged to pay Lender if A is not obliged to pay Lender. Under Section 3–305(d), B as an accommodation party can assert against Lender any defense of A. A has a defense based on the extension agreement. Thus, the result is that Lender could not enforce the note against B until July 1, 1992. This result is consistent with the right of B if B is an anomalous indorser.

As a practical matter an extension of the due date will normally occur when the accommodated party is unable to pay on the due date. The interest of the accommodation party normally is to defer payment to the holder rather than to pay right away and rely on an action against the accommodated party that may have little or no value. But in unusual cases the accommodation party may prefer to pay the holder on the original due date. In such cases, the accommodation party may do so. This is because the extension agreement between the accommodated party and the holder cannot bind the accommodation party to a change in its obligation without the accommodation party's consent. The effect on the recourse of the accommodation party against the accommodated party of performance by the accommodation party on the original due date is not addressed in § 3–419 and is left to the general law of suretyship.

Even though an accommodation party has the option of paying the instrument on the original due date, the accommodation party is not precluded from asserting its rights to discharge under Section 3–605(c) if it does not exercise that option. The critical issue is whether the extension caused the accommodation party a loss by increasing the difference between its cost of performing its obligation on the instrument and the amount recoverable from the accommodated party pursuant to Section 3–419(e). The decision by the accommodation party not to exercise its option to pay on the original due date may, under the circumstances, be a factor to be considered in the determination of that issue. See PEB Commentary No. 11, supra.

9. Comment 5 to § 3–605 is amended by adding seven unnumbered paragraphs as follows:

The following is an illustration of the kind of case to which Section 3-605(d) would apply:

Case #2. Corporation borrows money from Lender and issues a note payable to Lender. X signs the note as an accommodation party for Corporation. The loan agreement under which the note was issued states various events of default which allow Lender to accelerate the due date of the note. Among the events of default are breach of covenants not to incur debt beyond specified limits and not to engage in any line of business substantially different from that currently carried on by Corporation. Without consent of X, Lender agrees to modify the covenants to allow Corporation to enter into a new line of business that X considers to be risky, and to incur debt beyond the limits specified in the loan agreement to finance the new venture. This modification releases X unless Lender proves that the modification did not cause loss to X or that the loss caused by the modification was less than X's right of recourse.

Sometimes there is both an extension of the due date and some other modification. In that case both subsections (c) and (d) apply. The following is an example:

Case #3. Corporation was indebted to Lender on a note payable on April 1, 1992 and X signed the note as an accommodation party for Corporation. The interest rate on the note was 12 percent. Lender and Corporation agreed to a six-month extension of the due date of the note to October 1, 1992 and an increase in the interest rate to 14 percent after April 1, 1992. Corporation defaulted on October 1, 1992. Corporation paid no interest during the six-month extension period. Corporation is insolvent and has no assets from which unsecured creditors can be paid. Lender demanded payment from X.

Assume X is an anomalous indorser. First consider Section 3–605(c) alone. If there had been no change in the interest rate, the fact that Lender gave an extension of six months to Corporation would not result in discharge unless X could prove loss with respect to the right of recourse because of the extension. If the financial condition of Corporation on April 1, 1992 would not have allowed any recovery on the right of recourse, X can't show any loss as a result of the extension with respect to the amount due on the note on April 1, 1992. Since the note accrued interest during the six-month extension, is there a loss equal to the accrued interest? Since the interest rate was not raised, only Section 3–605(c) would apply and X probably could not prove any loss. The obligation of X includes interest on the note until the note is paid. To the extent payment was delayed X had the use of the money that X otherwise would have had to pay to Lender. X could have prevented the running of interest by paying the debt. Since X did not do so, X suffered no loss as the result of the extension.

If the interest rate was raised, Section 3–605(d) also must be considered. If X is an anomalous indorser, X's liability is to pay the note according to its terms at the time of indorsement. Section 3–415(a). Thus, X's obligation to pay interest is measured by the terms of the note (12%) rather than by the increased amount of 14 percent. The same analysis applies if X had been a co-maker. Under Section 3–412 the liability of the issuer of a note is to pay the note according to its terms at the time it was issued. Either obligation could be changed by contract and that occurred with respect to Corporation when it agreed to the increase in the interest rate, but X did not join in that agreement and is not bound by it. Thus, the most that X can be required to pay is the amount due on the note plus interest at the rate of 12 percent.

Does the modification discharge X under Section 3–605(d)? Any modification that increases the monetary obligation of X is material. An increase of the interest rate from 12 percent to 14 percent is certainly a material modification. There is a presumption that X is discharged because Section 3–605(d) creates a presumption that the modification caused a loss to X equal to the amount of the right of recourse. Thus, Lender has the burden of proving absence of loss or a loss less than the amount of the right of recourse. Since Corporation paid no interest during the six-month period, the issue is like the issue presented under Section 3–605(c) which we have just discussed. The increase in the interest rate could not have affected the right of recourse because no interest was paid by Corporation. X is in the same position as X would have been in if there had been an extension without an increase in the interest rate.

The analysis with respect to Section 3–605(c) and (d) would have been different if we change the assumptions. Suppose Corporation was not insolvent on April 1, 1992, that Corporation paid interest at the higher rate during the six-month period, and that Corporation was insolvent at the end of the six-month period. In this case it is possible that the extension and the additional burden placed on Corporation by the increased interest rate may have been detrimental to X.

There are difficulties in properly allocating burden of proof when the agreement between Lender and Corporation involves both an extension under Section 3–605(c) and a modification under Section 3–605(d). The agreement may have caused loss to X but it may be difficult to identify the extent to which the loss was caused by the extension or the other modification. If neither Lender nor X introduces evidence on the issue, the result is full discharge because Section 3–605(d) applies. Thus, Lender has the burden of overcoming the presumption in Section 3–605(d). In doing so, Lender should be entitled to a presumption that the extension of time by itself caused no loss. Section 3–605(c) is based on such a presumption and X should be required to introduce evidence on the effect of the extension on the right of recourse. Lender would have to introduce evidence on the effect of the increased interest rate. Thus both sides will have to introduce evidence. On the basis of this evidence the court will have to make a determination of the overall effect of the agreement on X's right of recourse. See PEB Commentary No. 11, supra.

10. The second paragraph of Comment 6 to § 3–605 is amended to read as follows:

In some states a real property grantee who assumes the obligation of the grantor as maker of a note secured by the real property becomes by operation of law a principal debtor and the grantor becomes a surety. The meager case authority was split on whether former Section 3–606 applied to release the grantor if the holder released or extended the obligation of the grantee. Revised Article 3 takes no position on the effect of the release of the grantee in this case. Section 3–605(b) does not apply because the holder has not discharged the obligation of a "party," a term defined in Section 3–103(a)(8) as "party to an instrument." The assuming grantee is not a party to the instrument. The resolution of this question is governed by general principles of law, including the law of suretyship. See PEB Commentary No. 11, supra.

11. Comment 8 to § 3–605 is amended by adding the underlined words as follows:

8. Subsection (i) is a continuation of former law which allowed suretyship defenses to be waived. <u>As the subsection provides, a party is not discharged under this section if the instrument or a separate agreement of the party waives discharge either specifically or by general language indicating that defenses based on suretyship and impairment of collateral are waived. No particular language or form of agreement is required, and the standards for enforcing such a term are the same as the standards for enforcing any other term in an instrument or agreement.</u>

<u>Subsection (i), however, applies only to a "discharge under this section." The right of an accommodation party to be discharged under Section 3–605(e) because of an impairment of collateral can be waived. But with respect to a note secured by personal property collateral, Article 9 also applies. If an accommodation party is a "debtor" under Section 9–105(1)(d), the accommodation party has rights under Article 9. Under Section 9–501(3)(b) rights of</u>

an Article 9 debtor under Section 9-504(3) and Section 9-505(1), which deal with disposition of collateral, cannot be waived except as provided in Article 9. These Article 9 rights are independent of rights under Section 3-605. Since Section 3-605(i) is specifically limited to discharge under Section 3-605, a waiver of rights with respect to Section 3-605 has no effect on rights under Article 9. With respect to Article 9 rights, Section 9-501(3)(b) controls. See PEB Commentary No. 11, supra.

COMMENTARY NO. 12
(SECTION 9–302) FINAL DRAFT

(February 10, 1994)

Permanent Editorial Board for the Uniform Commercial Code, 4025 Chestnut Street, Philadelphia, Pennsylvania 19104–3099.

APPENDIX V

COUNSELLOR EMERITUS

MARTIN J. ARONSTEIN, Philadelphia, Pennsylvania

ABA LIAISON

LINDA C. HAYMAN, New York, New York

ABA SECTION OF BUSINESS LAW LIAISON

GEORGE A. HISERT, San Francisco, California

PREFACE TO PEB COMMENTARY

The Permanent Editorial Board (PEB) for the Uniform Commercial Code (UCC) acts under the authority of The American Law Institute and the National Conference of Commissioners on Uniform State Laws. In March, 1987, the PEB resolved to issue from time to time supplementary commentary on the UCC to be known as PEB Commentary. These PEB Commentaries seek to further the underlying policies of the UCC by affording guidance in interpreting and resolving issues raised by the UCC and/or the Official Comments. The Resolution states that:

> "A PEB Commentary should come within one or more of the following specific purposes, which should be made apparent at the inception of the Commentary: (1) to resolve an ambiguity in the UCC by restating more clearly what the PEB considers to be the legal rule; (2) to state a preferred resolution of an issue on which judicial opinion or scholarly writing diverges; (3) to elaborate on the application of the UCC where the statute and/or the Official Comment leaves doubt as to inclusion or exclusion of, or application to, particular circumstances or transactions; (4) consistent with UCC § 1–102(2)(b), to apply the principles of the UCC to new or changed circumstances; (5) to clarify or elaborate upon the operation of the UCC as it relates to other statutes (such as the Bankruptcy Code and various federal and state consumer protection statutes) and general principles of law and equity pursuant to UCC § 1–103; or (6) to otherwise improve the operation of the UCC."

The full Resolution appears in the 1990 Edition of the UCC.

PEB COMMENTARY NO. 12
SECTION 9–302

ISSUE

Section 9–302(3) provides that the filing requirements of Article 9 are not applicable to the perfection of a security interest in goods covered by a certificate of title statute. In that circumstance, perfection of a relevant security interest can be had only through compliance with the certificate of title statute. If the secured party perfects its security interest pursuant to such a statute and then assigns the security interest, must the assignee take some further action to reflect that it has become the secured party in order to continue such perfection, for example, having the certificate of title endorsed or reissued to name itself as the secured party or lienholder? Or is § 9–302(2), which provides that if a secured party assigns a perfected security interest, "no filing under this Article is required in order to continue the perfected status of the security interest against creditors of and transferees from the original debtor," applicable in this instance so that the assignee need not take any further action?

DISCUSSION

Section 9–302(1) states the general rule that in order to perfect a security interest under Article 9, a financing statement must be filed, except for certain specified transactions. See Comment 1. Section 9–302(3) provides for an additional exception: "The filing of a financing statement *otherwise required by this Article* is not necessary or effective to *perfect* a security interest in property" (emphasis supplied) that is subject to a filing system set up outside the UCC, including specifically, the certificate of title statute "of this state" (subsection (b)) or "a certificate of title statute of another jurisdiction under the law of which indication of a security interest on the certificate is required as a condition of perfection (subsection (2) of Section 9–103)" (subsection (c)).[1]

Inasmuch as every jurisdiction that has enacted Article 9 has also enacted a certificate of title (or ownership) statute, the effect of these provisions is that perfection of Article 9 security interests in property covered by certificate of title laws must always be accomplished by compliance with those laws. In essence, § 9–302(3) substitutes compliance with the requirements of the applicable certificate of title statute for filing a financing statement under Article 9 as the means for perfecting a security interest in the affected property. (A major exception to this rule is that the filing provisions of Article 9 remain applicable where the collateral is inventory held for sale by a person who is in the business of selling goods of that kind, for example, an automobile dealer. Section 9–302(3)(b).)

Section 9–302(2) states a corollary rule to § 9–302(1)'s general rule on perfection, which is that the perfected security interest can be assigned by the secured party to another person without the need for a further filing under Article 9 and that the security interest of the assignee continues to be perfected, without further action,

1. Although some certificate of title statutes condition perfection on a physical notation being placed on the certificate and are clearly covered by § 9–302(3)(c) and the conflict provisions of § 9–103(2), others, while contemplating notation, provide that perfection is achieved by delivery of designated documents to a state official and could, therefore, arguably fall outside of the provisions of § 9–302(3)(c) and § 9–103(2). The Alabama Supreme Court in *Lightfoot v. Harris Trust & Savings Bank,* 357 So.2d 654, 23 UCC Rep.Serv. (Callaghan) 750 (Ala.1978), dismissed the argument and held that Article 9 applies to goods covered by a certificate of title issued under either kind of statute. This Commentary supports the position taken in *Lightfoot.*

against the creditors of and transferees from the original debtor. The security interest created in favor of the secured party is transferred by the assignment to the assignee; [2] it is the same security interest and not a new security interest. Accordingly, neither a new financing statement nor a statement of assignment is required to continue the perfection of the assignee's security interest in the property. Section 9–405 permits, but does not require, the assignee to file a statement of assignment against the original debtor. By not filing, the assignee may encounter certain risks with adverse business and legal consequences, and therefore, the assignee may opt to file a statement of assignment even though not required to do so. Some risks an assignee may encounter if the statement of assignment is not filed are: the assignor might fraudulently or inadvertently release or terminate the security interest; the assignor might assign the security interest to an innocent third party who might then file a statement of assignment and become the secured party of record; or the assignor might go out of business or disappear and make it difficult or impossible for the assignee to be able to respond to inquiries from third parties concerning the status of the security interest. The decision whether to file or not file a statement of assignment is essentially a business decision for the assignee to make, taking into account these various risk factors, as well as the cost, administrative convenience, and the like.

Inasmuch as the purpose of § 9–302(3) and (4) is to substitute compliance with the perfection requirements of the applicable certificate of title statute for filing under Article 9, § 9–302(4) makes it clear that it is only with regard to such perfection requirements that Article 9 is displaced by the certificate of title statute: "in all other respects the security interest is subject to" Article 9. Therefore, in order to determine whether § 9–302(2) is applicable to security interests perfected under § 9–302(3) and (4), it is first necessary to ascertain whether the certificate of title statute applicable to the particular transaction contains provisions concerning an assignment of a security interest and, if so, whether such provisions relate to perfection.

Even though all jurisdictions have enacted certificate of title statutes, there is a wide variation among those statutes. The Uniform Motor Vehicle Certificate of Title and Anti–Theft Act (the "Uniform Act") has been enacted in 11 jurisdictions. 11 Uniform Laws Annotated 250 (1993 Supp.). In a jurisdiction that has enacted the Uniform Act, it is clear from the provisions thereof concerning the assignment of a security interest that such provisions do not affect the perfected status of the assigned security interest. Section 22(b) of the Uniform Act expressly provides that the "assignee may, *but need not to perfect the assignment,* have the certificate of title endorsed or issued with the assignee named as lienholder, upon delivering to the Department [of Motor Vehicles] the certificate and an assignment by the lienholder named in the certificate in the form the Department prescribes." (Emphasis supplied.)

2. The assignment of that security interest, whether a grant of a security interest in the underlying security agreement (chattel paper) between the assignor-secured party and the original debtor, or a sale of that chattel paper (§ 9–102(1)(b)), is a separate and distinct secured transaction and involves different considerations. The validity and perfection of the assignee's security interest against *the creditors of and transferees from the assignor-secured party* is governed entirely by Article 9 and a jurisdiction's certificate of title statute has no applicability. Perfection would be accomplished by the assignee either taking possession of the chattel paper (§ 9–305) or by filing a financing statement against the assignor-secured party (§ 9–304(1)). Comment 7 to § 9–302 makes it clear that the rules set forth in § 9–302(1) and (2) do not apply to the perfection of the assignee's interest in the security agreement when viewed in relation to the creditors of and transferees from the assignor-secured party. Section 9–302(2) only obviates the need to take further steps in order to continue perfection of the security interest in the underlying vehicle against *the creditors of and transferees from the original debtor.*

In other jurisdictions, however, the certificate of title statute contains provisions concerning the assignment of a security interest, but the statute is not clear whether such provisions relate to perfection. In that circumstance, the guiding principle is that "[t]he certificate of title statutes, when applied as lien perfection statutes, should be construed in harmony with the general U.C.C. scheme for perfection of security interests." *In re Little-john,* 519 F.2d 356, 358, 17 UCC Rep.Serv. (Callaghan) 254, 257 (10th Cir.1975). Accord, *General Motors Acceptance Corp. v. Rupp,* 951 F.2d 283, 16 UCC Rep.Serv.2d (Callaghan) 510 (10th Cir.1991); *In re Circus Time, Inc.,* 641 F.2d 39, 30 UCC Rep.Serv. (Callaghan) 1475 (1st Cir.1981). In so construing the statutes, the courts have recognized that the primary purposes of the certificate of title statutes are to facilitate the identification of motor vehicles or boats, the ascertainment of their owners, and the prevention of theft or fraud in their transfer; to provide the state with a convenient and accessible record of title for tax purposes; and to lend stability to the business climate surrounding the sale of motor vehicles and like goods. As observed by the court in *In re Circus Time, Inc.:*

> Absolute compliance with the requirements of the Certificate of Title Acts is not necessary to perfect a security interest in a vehicle. Courts have properly interpreted such acts in light of the perfection provisions of the Uniform Commercial Code, which recognize as effective to perfect a security interest any filing that 'substantially compl[ies] with the requirements of [the Code] . . . even though it contains minor errors which are not seriously misleading.' U.C.C. § 9–402(8); [other citations omitted]. . . .

641 F.2d at 42, 30 UCC Rep.Serv. at 1479. To the extent that § 9–302(2) and the certificate of title statutes can be construed as consistent with each other, the Code's underlying purpose and policy of making "uniform the law among the various jurisdictions" (§ 1–102(2)(c)) will, of course, be better served. See *In re Hollis,* 301 F.Supp. 1, 3 (D.Conn.1969) ("[I]t is the duty of a court construing the [Certificate of Title] Act to create a uniform national interpretation.").

The corollary of the foregoing principle is that a strict and literal construction of a certificate of title statute should be avoided if it produces a result that unnecessarily conflicts with the Uniform Commercial Code. Additionally, courts have refused to apply a highly refined and technical interpretation to a certificate of title statute to defeat the perfection of a security interest. See *In re Williams,* 608 F.2d 1015 (5th Cir.1979) and *Janney v. Bell,* 111 F.2d 103 (4th Cir.1940). By way of analogy, the overwhelming majority of courts have upheld the rights of a buyer in ordinary course of business under § 2–403 even though the buyer did not obtain certificate of title. See, e.g., *Dugdale of Nebraska, Inc. v. First State Bank,* 420 N.W.2d 273, 277, 6 UCC Rep.Serv.2d (Callaghan) 111, 116–17 (Neb.1988) and Comment 7 to § 2A–304, approving this line of cases; see also *Associates Discount Corp. v. Rattan Chevrolet, Inc.,* 462 S.W.2d 546, 8 UCC Rep.Serv. (Callaghan) 117 (Tex.1970) and *Sterling Acceptance Co. v. Grimes,* 168 A.2d 600, 1 UCC Rep.Serv. (Callaghan) 487 (Pa.Super.1961), applying the same rationale to § 9–307. This same rationale should be applied to the question of whether an assignee must do something under a certificate of title statute to continue the perfected status of an assigned security interest when the statute contains provisions on assignments but does not specifically mandate any action by the assignee for perfection, or makes no or only isolated references to assignments, or is ambiguous as to what action an assignee must take and makes no mention of the consequence of the assignee's failure to take action with respect to the issue of perfection.

A number of other jurisdictions have incorporated parts of § 22 of the Uniform Act into their certificate of title statutes, but most of these states did not include the phrase "but need not to perfect the assignment" in their versions of § 22. See, e.g.,

Code of Alabama § 32–8–63. Even without the quoted phrase, it would be consistent with § 9–302(2) to view these statutes as permitting but not requiring the assignment to be noted on the certificate of title. This would also be consistent with § 9–405, which provides a permissive device for noting assignments in the public records. Those certificate of title statutes that do not specifically require, as a condition of perfection, that an assignee have the certificate of title endorsed or reissued to name itself as lienholder, but instead contain phrases like: "the title officer *shall* file each assignment received," or "*upon* receiving a certificate," or other words of similar import, may be construed consistently with § 9–302(2) as being merely permissive on this issue and as not requiring further action in order to continue perfection.

Section 9–302(2) can also be construed consistently with the certificate of title statutes in those jurisdictions where the latter is either silent as to assignments, e.g., Arizona Revised Statutes Annotated § 28–325 (Liens and encumbrances), or where there is an isolated reference to an assignee but no mention of perfection. For example, New Jersey Statutes Annotated § 39:10–9 states that "the name and the business or residence address of the secured party or his assignee shall be noted on the certificate of ownership," but makes no reference to the assignee having to note its name on the certificate in place of a secured party whose name is already noted or taking any other action such as filing a notice or document with the Division of Motor Vehicles. In those circumstances, § 9–302(3) and (4) do not have the effect of substituting the requirements of the certificate of title statute relating to perfection for "filing under this Article," inasmuch as the certificate of title statute does not state, within the purview of those UCC provisions, any requirement that the assignment of the security interest be noted on the certificate of title. As a result, § 9–302(2) remains applicable.

Some jurisdictions have certificate of title statutes that are ambiguous about what an assignee must do or whether the assignee must act in a particular way, but do not, within the meaning of § 9–302(2), relate such required action by the assignee to the continued perfection of the security interest. Pennsylvania is an example of a jurisdiction having such a statute. Section 1134(b) of Pennsylvania Consolidated Statutes Annotated, 75 Pa.C.S.A. § 1134(b), is an assignment section in the certificate of title statute which provides that the "assignee shall deliver to the department the certificate of title and an assignment by the lienholder. . . ." The certificate of title statute does not specify either a time period within which such action is to be performed or the consequences of the assignee's failure to act with respect to perfection. Id. The only consequence specified in the statute for the assignee's failure to act is contained in § 1134(a) which says, "any person without notice of the assignment is protected in dealing with the lienholder as the holder of the security interest and the lienholder remains liable for any obligations as lienholder until the assignee is named as lienholder on the certificate." 75 Pa.C.S.A. § 1134(a). That language is identical to that in § 22(a) of the Uniform Act. Section 9–302(2) and these statutes may be construed consistently with each other as not requiring the security interest to become unperfected because of the assignee's failure to have its name noted on the certificate of title. In view of the express provision in § 22(b) obviating the need for the assignee to take any action "to perfect the assignment" (see pages 3–4), the language in § 22(a), viewed in that context, does not appear to relate to perfection. The language merely restates the other potential risks and adverse business and legal consequences discussed above that might result from the failure of the assignee to have its name noted on the certificate. (See page 3.)

In summary, § 9–302(2) and certificate of title statutes that do not specifically address perfection in connection with the assignment of a security interest can be construed consistently. As a result, in accordance with the mandate of § 9–302(4) that "in all other respects the security interest is subject to" Article 9, § 9–302(2) remains applicable. In order to interpret and apply § 9–302(2) in a manner that is harmonious with the various certificate of title statutes and to simplify, clarify, and modernize the law applicable to the assignment of security interests, "no filing under this Article" as used in § 9–302(2) should be liberally and broadly construed to include "no notation of a security interest on a certificate of title" when not expressly required as a condition for perfection by the applicable certificate of title statute. See § 1–102. This interpretation is consistent with the basic function of certificate of title statutes in that the continued notation of the security interest on the certificate gives notice to creditors of and transferees from the original debtor of the existence of the security interest in the property covered by the certificate of title.

CONCLUSION

If a security interest has been perfected under the applicable certificate of title statute and is thereafter assigned, and that statute does not expressly require the assignee to take some further action with respect to the certificate of title to reflect that it has become the secured party in order to continue such perfection, § 9–302(2) is applicable and the assignee is not required to place its name on the certificate of title "in order to continue the perfected status of the security interest against creditors of and transferees from the original debtor." If the assignee, nevertheless, wishes to have the assignment noted on the certificate of title, its right to do so and the procedure therefor are governed by the applicable certificate of title statute.

The Official Comment to § 9–302 is amended by adding the following:

> 10. If a security interest has been perfected under the applicable certificate of title statute and is thereafter assigned, and that statute does not expressly require the assignee to take some further action with respect to the certificate of title to reflect that it has become the secured party in order to continue such perfection, § 9–302(2) is applicable and the assignee is not required to note its name on the certificate of title "in order to continue the perfected status of the security interest against creditors of and transferees from the original debtor." See PEB Commentary No. 12, dated February 10, 1994.

COMMENTARY NO. 13
(THE PLACE OF ARTICLE 4A IN A WORLD OF ELECTRONIC FUNDS TRANSFERS)
FINAL DRAFT

(February 16, 1994)

Permanent Editorial Board for the Uniform Commercial Code, 4025 Chestnut Street, Philadelphia, Pennsylvania 19104–3099.

PREFACE TO PEB COMMENTARY

The Permanent Editorial Board (PEB) for the Uniform Commercial Code (UCC) acts under the authority of The American Law Institute and the National Conference of Commissioners on Uniform State Laws. In March, 1987, the PEB resolved to issue from time to time supplementary commentary on the UCC to be known as PEB Commentary. These PEB Commentaries seek to further the underlying policies of the UCC by affording guidance in interpreting and resolving issues raised by the UCC and/or the Official Comments. The Resolution states that:

> "A PEB Commentary should come within one or more of the following specific purposes, which should be made apparent at the inception of the Commentary: (1) to resolve an ambiguity in the UCC by restating more clearly what the PEB considers to be the legal rule; (2) to state a preferred resolution of an issue on which judicial opinion or scholarly writing diverges; (3) to elaborate on the application of the UCC where the statute and/or the Official Comment leaves doubt as to inclusion or exclusion of, or application to, particular circumstances or transactions; (4) consistent with UCC § 1–102(2)(b), to apply the principles of the UCC to new or changed circumstances; (5) to clarify or elaborate upon the operation of the UCC as it relates to other statutes (such as the Bankruptcy Code and various federal and state consumer protection statutes) and general principles of law and equity pursuant to UCC § 1–103; or (6) to otherwise improve the operation of the UCC."

The full Resolution appears in the 1990 Edition of the UCC.

PEB COMMENTARY NO. 13
THE PLACE OF ARTICLE 4A IN A WORLD OF ELECTRONIC FUNDS TRANSFERS

ISSUE

Article 4A of the UCC deals primarily with electronic funds transfers made through the banking system.[1] Adopted by the ALI and the National Conference of Commissioners on Uniform State Laws in 1989, Article 4A has had a substantial measure of success. At this time it is law in all but a few states, has been incorporated into Regulation J of the Federal Reserve System [2] and, through their incorporation of New York State law, has been written into the Rules of CHIPS [3] and NACHA.[4]

For a transfer of funds to be governed by Article 4A, an instruction must be given to a bank ("Bank I" in this scenario) either to make payment to the person who is the ultimate recipient of the funds or to instruct some other bank ("Bank II") to make the payment.[5] If the instruction is that Bank I make payment to the ultimate recipient, the bank is dealing with its own depositor or someone who has a direct customer relationship with the bank. That relationship, while occasionally dealt with by Article 4A, is largely outside the coverage of the statute.[6]

Article 4A concentrates principally upon the relationship of one bank with another bank. Assuming that the instruction given to Bank I is that Bank I instruct Bank II to make the payment,[7] Bank II can as easily be located abroad as in the United States. For this reason, it is desirable that Article 4A find compatibility with such international law as exists in this area.

The major international legal document dealing with the subject of electronic funds transfers is the Model Law on International Credit Transfers ("Model Law") adopted in 1992 by the United Nations Commission on International Trade Law ("UNCITRAL"). It covers basically the same type of transaction as does Article 4A, although it requires the funds transferred to have an international component.[8]

No foreign State has, to date, adopted the Model Law as its own local law. Nevertheless, in examining international payments, this Commentary assumes that the United States is subject to Article 4A and that the remainder of the world, because

1. While Article 4A was clearly drafted with electronic funds transfers in mind and while its present effect will be upon such transfers, it is not limited to electronic transfers and applies by its terms to all transfers among banks outside the checking system. This concept is elaborated upon in Comment 6 to § 4A–104.

2. 12 C.F.R. Part 210, Appendix B (1993).

3. New York Clearing House Interbank Payments Systems, CHIPS Rule 3.

4. National Automatic Clearing House Association, ACH Rule 1.7.

5. We need not deal with who gives the instruction to Bank I. It might be a company or an individual originating a funds transfer; it might be another bank which is moving along an instruction that had been given to it.

6. Provisions of Article 4A that do deal with the relationship of beneficiary's bank and beneficiary are §§ 4A–404 and 4A–405.

7. Bank II can, having received the instruction from Bank I, in turn instruct another bank to make the payment. In this way, a series of banks can be involved in one transfer of funds from the party originating the transfer (called the "Originator") to the party ultimately receiving it (called the "Beneficiary").

8. Model Law, Article 1(1) requires that "any sending bank and its receiving bank (be) in different States." Henceforth, references to Article numbers will refer to the Model Law; references to sections beginning with "4A" will refer to the UCC.

of the lack of development in the law otherwise, has adopted the Model Law now offered to it by the United Nations.[9]

DISCUSSION

We will hypothesize two funds transfers. One is sent by a New York bank to San Francisco ("NY–SF") and the other to London ("NY–L").[10]

We may correctly assume that a New York bank will have both business reason and technical capacity to send funds with equal ease to both San Francisco and London. Administratively, it will normally make little if any difference to the bank whether the transfer goes east or west. For the two transfers to be subject to different legal regimes can, however, create problems. For example, if New York imposes a different level of responsibility upon the bank for completion of the funds transfer depending upon where it goes, the bank's fee structure might vary between the two. Similarly, if there are different requirements, depending upon the location of the receiving bank, of persons who must receive notices or duties as to correcting a transfer made in error, different expectations will be created for the bank's systems. The banking system was clear in its reactions to Article 4A and the Model Law through its drafting that it would find it both difficult and expensive to administer electronic funds transfers subject to conflicting legal systems.

In its final form, the Model Law is close to Article 4A both in its overall structure and in its details, but is not the same.

A. Conflicts of Laws

The conflicts of law provisions of Article 4A and the Model Law tell us what law will apply to these transfers. In this respect, the two statutes are essentially harmonious: § 4A–507(a)(1) and an optional Article Y[11] in the Model Law both prescribe that, for most issues, the law of the receiving bank will govern.[12] Thus, Article 4A will generally govern for NY–SF, and the Model Law for NY–L.[13]

B. Working of the Two Laws

Some examples will illustrate differences between Article 4A and the Model Law:

9. Full uniformity would of course occur if the United States adopted the Model Law. It is unlikely in the extreme that this will occur. See the Conclusion to this Commentary.

10. We need not deal with funds transfers made to New York from different sending banks. The UCC and the Model Law generally base their choice of law provisions on the law of the receiving bank. Thus, all funds transfers received in New York would be dealt with by New York law and there would be no problem of inconsistencies. See the discussion, *infra,* under A. Conflicts of Laws.

11. UNCITRAL was unable to agree whether a conflicts of law article belonged in the Model Law and, consequently, created an optional provision.

12. Details of both Article 4A and the Model Law introduce complexities. For example, both permit the parties to select the applicable law. In an Article 4A transaction, the relationship between a beneficiary (that is, the party who will ultimately receive the money being transferred) and its bank are governed pursuant to § 4A–507(a)(2) by the law of the jurisdiction where the bank is located. Article 4A also contains rules that will govern when the funds transfer is made through a funds-transfer system (see text *infra,* at Notes 22–24), and that system has its own choice of law rules. This Commentary does not deal with such variations.

13. One cannot exhaust the potential conflicts problems that arise even within this simple structure. For example, when the originator of the funds transfer instructs its New York bank to send funds to San Francisco or to London, the relationship of originator and bank is governed by the law of the receiving bank—New York. A funds transfer may also pass through several jurisdictions and raise additional issues. For the NY–SF and the NY–L transfers, however, the rule is that the law of California and of England will, respectively, apply.

1. Consumer Transactions

Both Article 4A and the Model Law were written without a focus on consumer-related transactions and, therefore, without the particular protections that typically accompany laws written for the benefit of consumers. In Article 4A, this is evidenced by an exclusion through § 4A–108 of transactions covered by the federal Electronic Fund Transfer Act of 1978 ("EFTA"), which is tailored for the consumer funds transfer. In the Model Law, a footnote to Article 1 provides that the Law "does not deal with issues related to the protection of consumers." [14]

This surface harmony leads, however, to problems. For example, the EFTA does not deal with the number of issues treated by Article 4A. It does not, for example, define the time when the originator of a consumer funds transfer has made payment to the beneficiary, a question answered by both Article 4A and the Model Law. If the NY–L and the NY–SF funds transfers were consumer in nature and this question arose, it would be answered for NY–L and not for NY–SF (since the latter would be governed by the EFTA).[15]

2. Variation by Agreement

Both Article 4A [16] and the Model Law [17] generally permit the parties to vary their statutory obligations by agreement except as may be specifically prohibited. Areas of specific prohibition vary, however, between the two laws.

For example, the obligation of a receiving bank that is also the beneficiary's bank to pay the amount of an order that it has accepted to the beneficiary may not be varied by agreement under § 4A–404(c). It may be varied under Article 10 of the Model Law. If our New York bank were to enter into agreements with its receiving banks defining circumstances under which an accepted order should not thereupon be paid to the beneficiary, the agreements would be effective for the NY–L transfer and not for the NY–SF transfer.[18]

3. Use of a Funds–Transfer System

Most electronic funds transfers are executed through funds-transfer systems.[19] Section 4A–206(a) provides that a funds–transfer system is the agent of the sender.

14. The Model Law does not present the sharp distinction between consumer and business transactions represented by the positioning of Article 4A and EFTA. The quoted language reflects the philosophy behind the Model Law—that its design is really for large, commercially oriented funds transfers—and justifies the positions taken on various issues. The Model Law on its face governs both consumer and commercial funds transfers and it was left to individual states to decide how their consumers would be treated.

15. Presumably a court would look to analogies in other laws to see how the question should be answered in the NY–SF context. Presumably, the closest law for this purpose would be Article 4A and the court would use the Article 4A solution.

A limited number of consumer transactions—those handled through the FedWire system and a few others such as unplanned telephone transfers—are excluded from the EFTA by Federal Reserve Regulation E and returned to coverage under Article 4A. See 12 C.F.R. § 205.3(b) (1992).

16. Section 4A–501(a).

17. Article 4.

18. One might imagine a New York bank agreeing with certain of its correspondents that they would not pay money to certain named beneficiaries without checking first with New York. That such an agreement would be effective for foreign banks but not for American banks was not the subject of detailed discussion, but one might imagine that foreign spokesmen could have wanted to support greater freedom for their banking system than the United States believes should be tolerated.

19. A "funds-transfer system" is defined under § 4A–105(a)(5) as a "wire transfer network, automated clearing house, or other communication system of a clearing house or other association of banks through which a payment order by a bank may be transmitted to the bank to which the order is addressed." Well-known domestic funds-transfer systems include the FedWire system of the Federal Reserve Banks, the CHIPS system of the New York Clearing House Association, and the sys-

Errors made by a funds-transfer system are, therefore, the errors of the bank that sent the funds through the system. (For this purpose, however, the FedWire system is excluded, and the Federal Reserve bank operating FedWire is deemed to be just another bank.) The Model Law is silent on this subject.

Thus, if, in a NY–SF transfer, the New York bank gives a payment order of $100,000 to the CHIPS system and CHIPS mistakenly transmits $1,000,000, the error is that of the New York bank, which is considered to have sent $1,000,000.[20] In a NY–L transfer, one cannot be certain. It appears, however, that the error is that of CHIPS.[21]

Under Article 4A,[22] funds-transfer system rules are given legal effect and may bind even parties who are not members of the system. Under the Model Law, the effect of a systems rule upon nonparties is not prescribed and, therefore, will be determined according to the law of contracts.[23] Generally, under American contract law, those who are not parties to a contract are not bound by its terms. If a funds-transfer system with its own rules is part of the two described funds transfers, the law applicable to the NY–L and the NY–SF transfers can be different.

4. Authentication Procedures

For the protection of the banking system and bank customers, both Article 4A and the Model Law establish procedures for the authentication of messages. The two systems work in similar manners.[24] Both protect a receiving bank if it properly authenticates a message, even if the message was sent without the sender's proper authority.[25] Both also relieve the sender of responsibility if it can prove that the message was sent by someone outside the sender's influence.[26] The Model Law [27] reimposes responsibility on the sender if the receiver can prove that the sender was responsible. Article 4A does not contain the reimposition responsibility, although this is implicit since the receiving bank will attempt to disclaim its liability by proving that the sender was responsible.

The effect of agreements varying the terms of the law again varies between Article 4A and the Model Law. Article 4A holds that (subject to certain limited and restricted exceptions) the parties may not vary its statutory authentication rights and liabilities by agreement.[28] The Model Law has no such prescription and the parties may alter their legal authentication relationships by agreement.[29] Thus, if the New York bank in our hypothetical agrees with its customers for a result other than as provided by the statutes, it will be effective for the NY–L transfer, but not for the NY–SF transfer.

tems of the National Automated Clearing House Association. Foreign systems include the Society of Worldwide Interbank Financial Telecommunication ("SWIFT"), the United Kingdom Clearing House Automated Payments System ("CHAPS"), and the Japanese BOJ-NET system.

20. See Comment 2 to § 4A–206.

21. This sort of event and its consequences are typically covered in the rules of a funds-transfer system. As discussed above, both Article 4A, § 4A–501, and the Model Law, Article 4, authorize agreements varying their provisions. Rules of a funds-transfer system would probably be considered agreements under the Model Law and are agreements specifically under § 4A–501.

22. Section 4A–501(b).

23. *Report of UNCITRAL,* U.N. Doc. A/46/17 (1991), par. 98.

24. The relevant sections are §§ 4A–201, 4A–202, and 4A–203 for Article 4A, and Article 5 for the Model Law.

25. Section 4A–202(b); Article 5(2).

26. Section 4A–203(a)(2); Article 5(4).

27. Article 5(4).

28. Section 4A–202(f).

29. Article 5(3) does provide that for the parties to agree that a sending bank will be bound by an authenticated message, the authentication must be reasonable. Section 4A–202(b) has a similar requirement.

5. Acceptance and Rejection

Under both Article 4A and the Model Law, a receiving bank is given the essentially unrestricted power to accept or reject an order sent to it. An order may be rejected by a notice sent to the sender.[30]

a. Receiving Banks Other Than the Beneficiary's Bank

If a bank (other than the beneficiary's bank) does not send a rejection notice, the legal consequences vary between the two laws; on the other hand, they resolve themselves, as the following discussion illustrates, without undue tension between them.

Under Article 4A, an order may be accepted by a bank other than the beneficiary's bank only by that bank executing a new order in favor of the next bank in line.[31] Failure to give a notice of rejection does not cause the bank to incur a penalty; neither does it result in acceptance. If the bank does not move, or "execute," the order, it is not deemed to have accepted the order, and the order is automatically canceled by operation of law in five days.[32] If the receiving bank has received actual funds covering the order, it must return the funds and pay interest to the sending bank until cancellation.[33]

Under the Model Law, a receiving bank that executes a new order is deemed to have accepted the order sent to it as under Article 4A.[34] An order that is neither executed nor rejected is deemed—unlike the Article 4A approach—to be accepted if funds covering the order have been paid to the receiving bank.[35] The receiving bank then is obligated to issue a new order in accordance with the responsibilities put by the Model Law upon the acceptor of an order. Similar to Article 4A, the payment order ceases to have effect after five days.[36] If the transfer is not completed, however, the bank must return any payment received by it plus interest to the date of payment [37] and does not suffer any further liability for its failure to execute the accepted order.

In the instant situation, still assuming that the San Francisco and the London banks are receiving banks that are not the beneficiary's bank, if an order is neither accepted nor rejected and if funds have been advanced to that bank (that is, if the order is "covered"), there would not be any duty upon the San Francisco bank to accept (that is, to execute the order in favor of the next bank in line) and the funds paid would bear interest for five days; for the NY–L transfer, the payment order would be accepted by the London bank, there would be a duty—albeit for a brief time—to move the funds, the acceptance would cease after five days, and the payment (the "cover") would bear interest until returned. The financial differences do not appear consequential since the receiving bank has the use of the funds until they are returned. Under the general structure of both laws not to impose more than interest penalties for failure to reject, the receiving bank in London would not incur other penalties for failing to honor its responsibility to move the funds.

b. The Beneficiary's Bank as a Receiving Bank

The ability of the beneficiary's bank to accept or reject payment orders is handled with essential comparability under the two laws. Under Article 4A, there are three

30. Section 4A–210(a) and Model Law Articles 7 and 9.

31. Section 4A–209(a).

32. Section 4A–211(d).

33. Section 4A–210(b) and §§ 4A–402(c) and 4A–402(d).

34. Article 7(2)(c).

35. While there is also a five-day cancellation provision, it is applicable only if the order is neither accepted nor rejected and we are dealing here with a deemed acceptance. Article 7(2), 7(3), and 7(4).

36. Article 7(4).

37. Article 14(1). This differs from Article 4A, which requires interest only for the five days.

events that trigger such a bank's acceptance, including rules based upon the relationship between the bank and the beneficiary, "cover" of the order to the bank, and the passage of time.[38] The Model Law contains eight events signifying acceptance by the beneficiary's bank.[39] One does not anticipate significant variations in practice between the two laws.

6. Time for Execution

Although their approaches to the question of when a receiving bank must take action upon an accepted payment order differ in the two laws, they have an essential similarity. For example, both Article 4A [40] and the Model Law [41] basically require that an order be executed on the day it is received. The Model Law, however, permits the order to be sent on the next day. In the event that occurs, however, the receiver must "execute for value as of" the prior day (that is, must give the next bank in line interest for the day that execution was delayed).

7. Cancellation

Both statutes provide the mechanism for a payment order to be canceled. Under Article 4A, if there is a security procedure between sender and receiver guarding the authenticity of the original order, "the" (that is, the same) procedure must be followed for cancellations.[42] If the original order was not subject to a security procedure, the cancellation order need not be authenticated. Under the Model Law, it is necessary that every cancellation be subject to some security procedure, not necessarily the same one originally used and even if no security procedure was originally used.[43] If the cancellation order is not authenticated, it is ineffective.

In addition, under the Model Law, it appears that every cancellation order must be authenticated. Under Article 4A, the cancellation must be authenticated only if there was an authentication procedure applicable to the original order.

The Article 4A approach is applicable in the NY–SF transfer; the Model Law governs the NY–L transfer.

8. The "Money–Back Guarantee"

As part of their underlying philosophy that the originator's funds will be transferred by the banking system, both Article 4A and the Model Law contain a so-called "money-back guarantee." This provides that, if the total transfer of money is not completed, the originator (who, under the model we have been following, either gave an order to the New York bank or was someone who gave an order at an earlier stage in the total funds transfer that was transmitted by another bank to the New York bank) will obtain a refund plus accumulated interest and certain other charges.[44] The provisions of the two laws are consistent in major respects. Neither permits variation by agreement. The Model Law, however, relieves receiving banks from the guarantee if they can demonstrate that they accepted the transfer despite what had been perceived as "a significant risk." [45]

38. Section 4A–209(b).

39. Article 9(1).

40. Section 4A–301(b).

41. Article 11(1).

42. Section 4A–211(a).

43. Article 12(4).

44. Section 4A–402 and Model Law Article 14.

45. A "prudent" originator's bank may agree with the originator that the money-back guarantee will not apply to a funds transfer if the bank accepted the transfer despite what it perceived as a "significant risk" that the transfer might not be completed. The example frequently given for this situation is where the transfer is to pass through areas involved in armed conflict.

9. Underpayments and the Recovery of Overpayments

Both laws contain essentially comparable provisions requiring sending banks who sent orders in amounts less than the amounts sent to them to send the differences and to permit banks who sent excessive payments to recover the excess.[46]

10. Consequential Damages

In general, the measure of damages provided by both laws for violations of their standards is the payment of interest for moneys held for the times beyond which the law allows. Occasionally, additional charges incident to the transfer will be included.[47]

Probably the single most controversial issue underlying the drafting of Article 4A was whether banks should have liability for consequential damages resulting from their negligence or failure to comply with the requirements of the statute. The banks argued that, given the traditionally low fees that they charged to transfer funds electronically, they could not at the same time subject themselves to the risk of immense and unquantifiable consequential damage recoveries. Business users of electronic funds-transfer systems asserted that consequential damages were an appropriate result of the banks' transfer responsibilities. Consequential damages were ultimately eliminated from Article 4A.[48]

Consequential damages may, however, be imposed against a bank under the Model Law. In view of the intense opposition of some national banking systems and their representatives in the United Nations to this concept, however, they were reduced in scope to where they will be imposed only where a bank has acted "(a) with the specific intent to cause loss, or (b) recklessly and with actual knowledge that loss would be likely to result." [49]

Thus, the NY–L transfer by a New York bank involves greater risk than does the NY–SF transfer.

11. Request for Assistance

Article 13 of the Model Law "requests" a bank that receives a payment order to assist the originator and each prior bank and to seek the assistance of the next receiving bank "in completing the banking procedures of the credit transfer." Article 4A has no equivalent. In the NY–L transfer, the New York bank is subject to the request; in the NY–SF transfer, it is not. There is no penalty for failing to abide by the request.[50]

The absence of penalty may suggest that a bank need have no concern about the requirement. On the other hand, the presence of a law does impose an obligation to comply. In addition, assuming that there are bank regulators enforcing compliance, the regulators in London could bring an action against the New York bank for specific performance of its obligation to assist under Article 13; United States regulators could not.

46. Section 4A–303(a) and § 4A–303(b), and Model Law Articles 15 and 16.

47. See §§ 4A–303(b) and 4A–305(b).

48. This result was ultimately agreed to by the major business interests in exchange for the consent by the banks to the "money-back guarantee" discussed in paragraph 8 above. Consequential damages were, however, authorized in favor of an ultimate beneficiary of a funds transfer against its bank that refuses to pay it after being notified of the particular circumstances giving rise to such damages. Section 4A–404(a). Consequential damages may also be provided for by express written agreement with a receiving bank. Section 4A–305(c).

49. Article 18. The terms used within the quotation marks have established meanings under United States tort law with the exception of "actual knowledge that loss would be likely to result."

50. Banks normally engage in this type of assistance even without statutory direction.

CONCLUSION

The Model Law was drafted for world-wide enactment. It is, however, unlikely in the extreme that it will be enacted in the United States in the foreseeable future.[51] It was generally accepted by the foreign states in UNCITRAL that there would be no movement to repeal Article 4A in the United States and adopt the Model Law in its stead. The two laws basically live together in harmony, but to the extent there are differences they must be recognized and, to the extent possible, avoided or adjusted by agreement.

The PREFATORY NOTE to Article 4A is amended by adding the following paragraph at the end of the PREFATORY NOTE:

International transfers.

The major international legal document dealing with the subject of electronic funds transfers is the Model Law on International Credit Transfers adopted in 1992 by the United Nations Commission on International Trade Law. It covers basically the same type of transaction as does Article 4A, although it requires the funds transferred to have an international component. The Model Law and Article 4A basically live together in harmony, but to the extent there are differences they must be recognized and, to the extent possible, avoided or adjusted by agreement. See PEB Commentary No. 13, dated February 16, 1994.

51. For further material on the subject of this Commentary, see Bhala, Rakesh K., *Paying for the Deal,* 42 Kan.L.Rev. No. 3 (1993), in which Professor Bhala uses micro-economic and banking concepts to evaluate the utility of both Article 4A and the UNCITRAL Model Law.

COMMENTARY NO. 14
(SECTION 9–102(1)(b))
FINAL DRAFT

(June 10, 1994)

Permanent Editorial Board for the Uniform Commercial Code, 4025 Chestnut Street, Philadelphia, Pennsylvania 19104–3099.

APPENDIX V

PREFACE TO PEB COMMENTARY

The Permanent Editorial Board (PEB) for the Uniform Commercial Code (UCC) acts under the authority of The American Law Institute and the National Conference of Commissioners on Uniform State Laws. In March, 1987, the PEB resolved to issue from time to time supplementary commentary on the UCC to be known as PEB Commentary. These PEB Commentaries seek to further the underlying policies of the UCC by affording guidance in interpreting and resolving issues raised by the UCC and/or the Official Comments. The Resolution states that:

> "A PEB Commentary should come within one or more of the following specific purposes, which should be made apparent at the inception of the Commentary: (1) to resolve an ambiguity in the UCC by restating more clearly what the PEB considers to be the legal rule; (2) to state a preferred resolution of an issue on which judicial opinion or scholarly writing diverges; (3) to elaborate on the application of the UCC where the statute and/or the Official Comment leaves doubt as to inclusion or exclusion of, or application to, particular circumstances or transactions; (4) consistent with UCC § 1–102(2)(b), to apply the principles of the UCC to new or changed circumstances; (5) to clarify or elaborate upon the operation of the UCC as it relates to other statutes (such as the Bankruptcy Code and various federal and state consumer protection statutes) and general principles of law and equity pursuant to UCC § 1–103; or (6) to otherwise improve the operation of the UCC."

The full Resolution appears in the 1990 Edition of the UCC.

PEB COMMENTARY NO. 14
SECTION 9–102(1)(b)

ISSUE

Does the application of Article 9 to the sale of accounts and chattel paper prevent the transfer of ownership of accounts or chattel paper?

DISCUSSION

Section 9–102(1)(b) provides, subject to certain exceptions,[1] that Article 9 applies "to any sale of accounts or chattel paper." [2] Comment 2 to § 9–102 explains that "a sale of [accounts or chattel paper is] covered by subsection (1)(b) whether intended for security or not.... The buyer then is treated as a secured party, and his interest as a security interest." [3] This Commentary examines whether that application means that ownership of receivables may not be transferred or that a buyer's interest in receivables is limited to one of security.

It is a fundamental principle of law that an owner of property may transfer ownership to another person.[4] Were a statute intended to take away that right, it would do so explicitly and such a significant curtailment of rights would be supported by substantial reason. No such reason is expressed or implied in the Code or the Official Comments. Indeed, the sale of receivables long antedates adoption of the Code, and it cannot be supposed that either the drafters of the Code or the legislatures that enacted it intended to work so drastic a change in existing law without clearly saying so. Moreover, a close reading of the text of Article 9 and its Comments, particularly in the context of the pre-Code history, compels the conclusion that Article 9 does not prevent the transfer of ownership.

Article 9 contemplates that sales of receivables may exist, and that the consequences of a sale differ from those of a transfer for security. For example, § 9–502(2) recognizes a distinction in the consequences under Article 9 between sales of receivables and transactions secured by receivables. It provides that, "[i]f the security agreement secures an indebtedness, the secured party must account to the debtor for any surplus.... But, if the underlying transaction was a sale of accounts or chattel paper, the debtor [as seller of the receivables] is entitled to any surplus [from collections of the sold receivables] ... *only if* the security agreement so provides." (Emphasis added.) Section 9–504(2) has virtually identical language. Furthermore, Comment 4 to § 9–502, after acknowledging that "there may be a true sale of accounts

1. See § 9–104(f).

2. For ease of reference, this Commentary refers to accounts and chattel paper collectively as "receivables."

3. This drafting technique is implemented by conforming definitions. Section 1–201(37), for example, states that the term "security interest" includes "any interest of a buyer of accounts or chattel paper which is subject to Article 9." Section 9–105(1)(m) provides that the term "secured party" includes "a person to whom accounts or chattel paper have been sold." Section 9–105(1)(d) provides that the term "debtor" includes "the seller of accounts or chattel paper." Section 9–105(1)(c) provides that the term "collateral" includes "accounts and chattel paper which have been sold." That such inclusion was simply a drafting technique was long ago freely acknowledged by Homer Kripke in paragraph 2 of his Practice Commentary to § 9–502 of the New York UCC, Cons.Laws N.Y.Annot.Book 62½, Part 3 (McKinney 1964): "Subsection (2) of [§ 9–502] recognizes throughout the fact that this article [9] includes within its coverage not only true security transactions in which accounts are collateral, but also sales of accounts ... which are included by artificial definitions."

4. See, e.g., Comment 1 to § 2–403.

or chattel paper," clarifies that "[t]he determination whether a particular assignment constitutes a sale or a transfer for security is left to the courts." [5]

Why, then, was Article 9 made "applicable" to the sale of receivables? The introductory Comment and Comment 2 to § 9–102 explain that Article 9 applies to both sales and security transfers of receivables to avoid the need to distinguish between such transfers for Article 9 purposes:

> [C]ertain sales of accounts and chattel paper are brought within this Article [9] to avoid difficult problems of distinguishing between transactions intended for security and those not so intended.
>
> * * *
>
> 2. * * *
>
> Commercial financing on the basis of accounts and chattel paper is often so conducted that the distinction between a security transfer and a sale is blurred, and a sale of such property is therefore covered by subsection (1)(b) whether intended for security or not....

The reason for subjecting both sales and secured transactions to Article 9 was to inform third parties of existing interests in a debtor's receivables and to provide protection for all types of assignments of receivables:

> There was an obvious reason for the inclusion of sales: it was necessary to *protect* [transferees] not only [in] straight accounts receivable financing but also [in] arrangements of the factoring type. [Emphasis added.] Article 9 merely follows the pre-Code accounts receivable statutes [covering sales of accounts and chattel paper as well as security transfers].[6]

This is not to say, however, that Article 9 has no impact upon a buyer's ownership rights regarding the purchased receivables. For example, a failure to perfect as required by Article 9 may leave the transferee's ownership of the receivables subject to the claims of third parties, such as the seller's lien creditors or trustee in bankruptcy.[7]

5. This Commentary likewise does not discuss what factors a court should look to in determining whether a particular transfer of receivables constitutes a sale or a secured loan. It addresses only whether Article 9 negates sale treatment even though a court viewing those factors would, but for Article 9, determine that the transfer was a sale. For a discussion of factors that courts have found relevant in determining whether a given transfer of receivables constitutes a sale or a secured loan, see Steven L. Schwarcz, *Structured Finance, A Guide to The Principles of Asset Securitization,* at 28–35 (2d ed. 1993).

6. 1 Gilmore, *Security Interests in Personal Property* § 8.7, at 275; § 10.5, at 308 (Little Brown & Co. 1965). Indeed, § 1–201(37) of the 1952 Official Draft of the UCC referred to a "financing buyer" of receivables and § 9–102(1)(b) referred to a "financing sale" of receivables. The word "financing" was deleted from both sections in Supplement No. 1 to the 1952 Official Draft, January 1955, pursuant to the 1954 Recommendations of the Editorial Board, for the reason that the phrases "financing buyer" and "financing sale" were perceived as "undefined concepts" and it was thought better to include all sales of receivables, subject to the exclusion provisions of § 9–104. The exclusion in § 9–104(f) was correspondingly broadened to exclude from Article 9 certain types of sales of receivables that, "by their nature, have nothing to do with commercial financing transactions." See Comment 6 to § 9–104.

7. Section 9–301(1). Just as Article 9's perfection requirement may impact upon the rights of a buyer of receivables without negating that a sale has occurred, so too does the requirement of § 9–502(2) that a buyer of receivables with a right of recourse against the seller "must proceed in a commercially reasonable manner...." Section 9–502(2) does not, however, articulate an ownership principle but rather is an abbreviated codification of the rule that would be applicable in any event under common law and § 1–103, whether the recourse right is characterized as one of suretyship or contract. Assuming perfection, the sold receivables are beyond the reach of the seller's creditors or purported transferees from the seller not earlier filed or perfected. The buyer does not have to account in any way to the seller or its creditors, and the seller has no

This perfection requirement, however, does not by its terms or by implication affect the transfer of ownership as between the seller and buyer.[8]

At least two Circuit Court opinions interpret the Code consistently with this Commentary. In *Major's Furniture Mart v. Castle Credit Corp.,*[9] the Third Circuit considered whether a transfer of a company's receivables should be construed as a sale or a secured loan. By considering that question, the court started from the premise that a transaction that Article 9 calls a security interest could nonetheless be a sale. If the transaction was a sale, the transferee would be entitled to surplus collections of the receivables. If the transaction was only for security, then the transferor would be entitled to the surplus collections. The court followed Comment 4 to § 9-502 and looked to non-UCC law to determine whether the transaction was a sale.

In *In re Contractors Equipment Supply Co.,*[10] the Ninth Circuit affirmed a lower court decision by looking to non-UCC law to determine that the transfer of receivables in question was a loan. The court stated that had there been a sale, the transferor would *not* be entitled to any surplus because "[a] sale entails the passage of title." [11]

In *Octagon Gas Systems, Inc. v. Rimmer,*[12] however, the Tenth Circuit, after stating that a purchased royalty interest in a natural gas system was an account, erroneously stated that "[t]he impact of applying Article 9 to [the buyer's] account is that Article 9's treatment of accounts sold as collateral would place [the buyer's] account within the property of [the seller's] bankruptcy estate." [13] The court reached this determination despite the transfer of the royalty interest purporting to be an outright sale of all the seller's interest. To the extent the court relied on Article 9 in reaching its determination, this Commentary adopts a contrary position.

CONCLUSION

Article 9's application to sales of receivables does not prevent the transfer of ownership. Official Comment 2 to § 9-102 therefore is amended by adding the following paragraph:

> Neither Section 9-102 nor any other provision of Article 9 is intended to prevent the transfer of ownership of accounts or chattel paper. The determination of whether a particular transfer of accounts or chattel paper constitutes a sale or a transfer for security purposes (such as in connection with a loan) is not governed by Article 9. Article 9 applies both to sales of accounts or chattel paper and loans secured by accounts or chattel paper primarily to incorporate Article 9's perfection rules. The use of terminology such as "security interest" to include the interest of a buyer of accounts or chattel

right of redemption or other legal or equitable interests in the receivables. These absolute ownership rights can exist in the buyer even if the purchase of the receivables is "with recourse." See Comment 4 to § 9-502.

8. Provisions of Article 9 that deal with matters other than perfection and priority likewise are not intended to give a seller any legal or equitable interests in receivables that have been sold. For example, the debtor's right under § 9-506 to redeem collateral prior to consummation of foreclosure by a secured party applies only where the transfer of the collateral was intended for security because it is only there that the debtor has retained rights that must be foreclosed.

9. 602 F.2d 538, 26 UCC Rep.Serv. (Callaghan) 1319 (3d Cir.1979).

10. 861 F.2d 241, 7 UCC Rep.Serv.2d (Callaghan) 583 (9th Cir.1988).

11. 861 F.2d at 245, 7 UCC Rep.Serv.2d at 587 (referring to § 9-502). Also see 861 F.2d at 245 n. 8, 7 UCC Rep.Serv.2d at 587-88 n. 8: "If the present case involved a true [sale], under basic contract law principles, the notification would have taken the account receivable out of the estate."

12. 995 F.2d 948, 20 UCC Rep.Serv.2d (Callaghan) 1330 (10th Cir.1993), cert. denied, ___ U.S. ___, 114 S.Ct. 554, 126 L.Ed.2d 455 (1993).

13. 995 F.2d at 955, 20 UCC Rep.Serv.2d at 1338.

paper, "secured party" to include a buyer of accounts or chattel paper, "debtor" to include a seller of accounts or chattel paper, and "collateral" to include accounts or chattel paper that have been sold is intended solely as a drafting technique to achieve this end and is not relevant to the sale or secured transaction determination. See PEB Commentary No. 14, dated June 10, 1994.

APPENDIX VI

1990 AMENDMENTS TO ARTICLE 2A (LEASES)

Note that following Amendment 24 there are three sections which do not have any text changes, but which have changes in their Official Comments in order to conform them to the various 1990 amendments to Article 2A.

Amendment 1

Section 2A–103 of the Article is amended to read:

§ 2A–103. Definitions and Index of Definitions.

(1) In this Article unless the context otherwise requires:

(a) "Buyer in ordinary course of business" means a person who in good faith and without knowledge that the sale to him [or her] is in violation of the ownership rights or security interest or leasehold interest of a third party in the goods, buys in ordinary course from a person in the business of selling goods of that kind but does not include a pawnbroker. "Buying" may be for cash or by exchange of other property or on secured or unsecured credit and includes receiving goods or documents of title under a pre-existing contract for sale but does not include a transfer in bulk or as security for or in total or partial satisfaction of a money debt.

(b) "Cancellation" occurs when either party puts an end to the lease contract for default by the other party.

(c) "Commercial unit" means such a unit of goods as by commercial usage is a single whole for purposes of lease and division of which materially impairs its character or value on the market or in use. A commercial unit may be a single article, as a machine, or a set of articles, as a suite of furniture or a line of machinery, or a quantity, as a gross or carload, or any other unit treated in use or in the relevant market as a single whole.

(d) "Conforming" goods or performance under a lease contract means goods or performance that are in accordance with the obligations under the lease contract.

(e) "Consumer lease" means a lease that a lessor regularly engaged in the business of leasing or selling makes to a lessee~~, except an organization,~~ who is an individual and who takes under the lease primarily for a personal, family, or household purpose[, if the total payments to be made under the lease contract, excluding payments for options to renew or buy, do not exceed ~~$25,000~~ $________].

(f) "Fault" means wrongful act, omission, breach, or default.

(g) "Finance lease" means a lease ~~in~~ with respect to which:

(i) the lessor does not select, manufacture, or supply the goods~~,~~;

(ii) the lessor acquires the goods or the right to possession and use of the goods in connection with the lease~~,~~; and

(iii) ~~either~~ one of the following occurs:

(A) the lessee receives a copy of the contract ~~evidencing the lessor's purchase~~ by which the lessor acquired the goods or the right to possession and use of the goods ~~on or~~ before signing the lease contract~~, or~~;

(B) the lessee's approval of the contract ~~evidencing the lessor's purchase~~ by which the lessor acquired the goods or the right to possession and use of the goods is a condition to effectiveness of the lease contract;

(C) the lessee, before signing the lease contract, receives an accurate and complete statement designating the promises and warranties, and any disclaimers of warranties, limitations or modifications of remedies, or liquidated damages, including those of a third party, such as the manufacturer of the goods, provided to the lessor by the person supplying the goods in connection with or as part of the contract by which the lessor acquired the goods or the right to possession and use of the goods; or

(D) if the lease is not a consumer lease, the lessor, before the lessee signs the lease contract, informs the lessee in writing (a) of the identity of the person supplying the goods to the lessor, unless the lessee has selected that person and directed the lessor to acquire the goods or the right to possession and use of the goods from that person, (b) that the lessee is entitled under this Article to the promises and warranties, including those of any third party, provided to the lessor by the person supplying the goods in connection with or as part of the contract by which the lessor acquired the goods or the right to possession and use of the goods, and (c) that the lessee may communicate with the person supplying the goods to the lessor and receive an accurate and complete statement of those promises and warranties, including any disclaimers and limitations of them or of remedies.

(h) "Goods" means all things that are movable at the time of identification to the lease contract, or are fixtures (Section 2A–309), but the term does not include money, documents, instruments, accounts, chattel paper, general intangibles, or minerals or the like, including oil and gas, before extraction. The term also includes the unborn young of animals.

(i) "Installment lease contract" means a lease contract that authorizes or requires the delivery of goods in separate lots to be separately accepted, even though the lease contract contains a clause "each delivery is a separate lease" or its equivalent.

(j) "Lease" means a transfer of the right to possession and use of goods for a term in return for consideration, but a sale, including a sale on approval or a sale or return, or retention or creation of a security interest is not a lease. Unless the context clearly indicates otherwise, the term includes a sublease.

(k) "Lease agreement" means the bargain, with respect to the lease, of the lessor and the lessee in fact as found in their language or by implication from other circumstances including course of dealing or usage of trade or course of performance as provided in this Article. Unless the context clearly indicates otherwise, the term includes a sublease agreement.

(*l*) "Lease contract" means the total legal obligation that results from the lease agreement as affected by this Article and any other applicable rules of law. Unless the context clearly indicates otherwise, the term includes a sublease contract.

(m) "Leasehold interest" means the interest of the lessor or the lessee under a lease contract.

(n) "Lessee" means a person who acquires the right to possession and use of goods under a lease. Unless the context clearly indicates otherwise, the term includes a sublessee.

(*o*) "Lessee in ordinary course of business" means a person who in good faith and without knowledge that the lease to him [or her] is in violation of the ownership rights or security interest or leasehold interest of a third party in the goods leases in ordinary course from a person in the business of selling or leasing goods of that kind but does not include a pawnbroker. "Leasing" may be for cash or by exchange of other property or on secured or unsecured credit and includes receiving goods or documents of title under a pre-existing lease contract but does not include a transfer in bulk or as security for or in total or partial satisfaction of a money debt.

(p) "Lessor" means a person who transfers the right to possession and use of goods under a lease. Unless the context clearly indicates otherwise, the term includes a sublessor.

(q) "Lessor's residual interest" means the lessor's interest in the goods after expiration, termination, or cancellation of the lease contract.

(r) "Lien" means a charge against or interest in goods to secure payment of a debt or performance of an obligation, but the term does not include a security interest.

(s) "Lot" means a parcel or a single article that is the subject matter of a separate lease or delivery, whether or not it is sufficient to perform the lease contract.

(t) "Merchant lessee" means a lessee that is a merchant with respect to goods of the kind subject to the lease.

(u) "Present value" means the amount as of a date certain of one or more sums payable in the future, discounted to the date certain. The discount is determined by the interest rate specified by the parties if the rate was not manifestly unreasonable at the time the transaction was entered into; otherwise, the discount is determined by a commercially reasonable rate that takes into account the facts and circumstances of each case at the time the transaction was entered into.

(v) "Purchase" includes taking by sale, lease, mortgage, security interest, pledge, gift, or any other voluntary transaction creating an interest in goods.

(w) "Sublease" means a lease of goods the right to possession and use of which was acquired by the lessor as a lessee under an existing lease.

(x) "Supplier" means a person from whom a lessor buys or leases goods to be leased under a finance lease.

(y) "Supply contract" means a contract under which a lessor buys or leases goods to be leased.

(z) "Termination" occurs when either party pursuant to a power created by agreement or law puts an end to the lease contract otherwise than for default.

(2) Other definitions applying to this Article and the sections in which they appear are:

"Accessions". Section 2A-310(1).

"Construction mortgage". Section 2A-309(1)(d).

"Encumbrance". Section 2A-309(1)(e).

"Fixtures". Section 2A-309(1)(a).

"Fixture filing". Section 2A-309(1)(b).

"Purchase money lease". Section 2A-309(1)(c).

(3) The following definitions in other Articles apply to this Article:

"~~Accounts~~ Account". Section 9-106.

"Between merchants". Section 2-104(3).

"Buyer". Section 2-103(1)(a).

"Chattel paper". Section 9-105(1)(b).

"Consumer goods". Section 9-109(1).

"~~Documents~~ Document". Section 9-105(1)(f).

"Entrusting". Section 2-403(3).

"General intangibles". Section 9-106.

"Good faith". Section 2-103(1)(b).

"~~Instruments~~ Instrument". Section 9-105(1)(i).

"Merchant". Section 2-104(1).

"Mortgage". Section 9-105(1)(j).

"Pursuant to commitment". Section 9-105(1)(k).

"Receipt". Section 2-103(1)(c).

"Sale". Section 2-106(1).

"Sale on ~~Approval~~ approval". Section 2-326.

"Sale or ~~Return~~ return". Section 2-326.

"Seller". Section 2-103(1)(d).

(4) In addition, Article 1 contains general definitions and principles of construction and interpretation applicable throughout this Article.

Official Comment

(a) "Buyer in ordinary course of business". Section 1-201(9).

(b) "Cancellation". Section 2-106(4). The effect of a cancellation is provided in Section 2A-505(1).

(c) "Commercial unit". Section 2-105(6).

(d) "Conforming". Section 2-106(2).

(e) "Consumer lease". New. This Article includes a subset of rules that applies only to consumer leases. Sections 2A-106, 2A-108(2), 2A-108(4), 2A-109(2), 2A-221, 2A-309, 2A-406, 2A-407, 2A-504(3)(b), and 2A-516(3)(b).

For a transaction to qualify as a consumer lease it must first qualify as a lease. Section 2A-103(1)(j). Note that this Article regulates the transactional elements of a lease, including a consumer lease; consumer protection statutes—, present and future—, and existing consumer protection decisions are unaffected by this Article. ~~Section 2A-104(1)(a) and (d)~~ Section 2A-104(1)(c) and (2). Of course, Article 2A as state law also is subject to federal consumer protection law.

This definition is modeled after the definition of consumer lease in the Consumer Leasing Act, 15 U.S.C. § 1667 (1982), and in the Unif.Consumer Credit Code § 1.301(14), 7A U.L.A. 43 (1974). However, this definition of consumer lease differs from its models in several respects: the lessor can be a person regularly engaged either in the business of leasing or of selling goods, the lease need not be for a term exceeding four months, a lease primarily for an agricultural purpose is not covered, and ~~the limitation of $25,000 is not subject to adjustment as the Consumer Price Index changes~~ whether there should be a limitation by dollar amount and its amount is left up to the individual states.

This definition focuses on the parties as well as the transaction. If a lease is within this definition, the lessor must be regularly engaged in the business of leasing or selling, and the lessee must be an individual not an organization; note that a lease to two or more individuals having a common interest through marriage or the like ~~should not be considered~~ is not excluded as a lease to an organization under Section 1-201(28). The lessee must take the interest primarily for a personal, family or household purpose. ~~Further~~ If required by the enacting state, total payments under the lease contract, excluding payments for options to renew or buy, cannot exceed ~~$25,000~~ the figure designated.

(f) "Fault". Section 1-201(16).

(g) "Finance Lease". New. This Article includes a subset of rules that applies only to finance leases. Sections 2A-209, 2A-211(2), 2A-212(1), 2A-213, 2A-219(1), 2A-220(1)(a), 2A-221, 2A-405(c), 2A-407, 2A-516(2) and 2A-517(1)(a) and (2).

For a transaction to qualify as a finance lease it must first qualify as a lease. Section 2A-103(1)(j). Unless the lessor is comfortable that the transaction will qualify as a finance lease, the lease agreement should include provisions giving the lessor the benefits created by the subset of rules applicable to the transaction that qualifies as a finance lease under this Article.

A finance lease is the product of a three party transaction. The supplier manufactures or supplies the goods pursuant to the lessee's specification, perhaps even pursuant to a purchase order, sales agreement or lease agreement between the supplier and the lessee. After the prospective finance lease is negotiated, a purchase order, sales agreement, or lease agreement is entered into by the lessor (as buyer or prime lessee) or an existing order, agreement or lease is assigned by the lessee to the lessor, and the lessor and the lessee then enter into a lease or sublease of the goods. Due to the limited function usually performed by the lessor, the lessee looks almost entirely to the supplier for representations, covenants and warranties. If a manufacturer's warranty carries through, the lessee may also look to that. Yet, this definition does not restrict the lessor's function solely to the supply of funds; if the lessor undertakes or performs other functions, express warranties, covenants and the common law will protect the lessee.

This definition focuses on the transaction, not the status of the parties; to avoid confusion it is important to note that in other contexts, e.g., tax and accounting, the term finance lease has been used to connote different types of lease transactions, including leases that are disguised secured transactions. M. Rice, *Equipment Financing*, 62–71 (1981). A lessor who is a merchant with respect to goods of the kind subject to the lease may be a lessor under a finance lease. Many leases that are leases back to the seller of goods (Section 2A–308(3)) will be finance leases. This conclusion is easily demonstrated by a hypothetical. Assume that B has bought goods from C pursuant to a sales contract. After delivery to and acceptance of the goods by B, B negotiates to sell the goods to A and simultaneously to lease the goods back from A, on terms and conditions that, we assume, will qualify the transaction as a lease. Section 2A–103(1)(j). In documenting the sale and lease back, B assigns the original sales contract between B, as buyer, and C, as seller, to A. A review of these facts leads to the conclusion that the lease from A to B qualifies as a finance lease, as all three conditions of the definition are satisfied. Subparagraph (i) is satisfied as A, the lessor, had nothing to do with the selection, manufacture, or supply of the equipment. Subparagraph (ii) is satisfied as A, the lessor, bought the equipment at the same time that A leased the equipment to B, which certainly is in connection with the lease. Finally, subparagraph (iii) (A) is satisfied as A entered into the sales contract with B at the same time that A leased the equipment back to B. B, the lessee, will have received a copy of the sales contract in a timely fashion.

Subsection (i) requires the lessor to remain outside the selection, manufacture and supply of the goods; that is the rationale for releasing the lessor from most of its traditional liability. The lessor is not prohibited from possession, maintenance or operation of the goods, as policy does not require such prohibition. To insure the lessee's reliance on the supplier, and not on the lessor, subsection (ii) requires that the goods (where the lessor is the buyer of the goods) or that the right to possession and use of the goods (where the lessor is the prime lessee and the sublessor of the goods) be acquired in connection with the lease (or sublease) to qualify as a finance lease. The scope of the phrase "in connection with" is to be developed by the courts, case by case. Finally, as the lessee generally relies almost entirely upon the supplier for representations~~,~~ and covenants, and upon the supplier or a manufacturer, or both, for warranties with respect to the goods, subsection (iii) requires that one of the following occur: (A) the lessee receive a copy of the supply contract ~~on or~~ before signing the lease contract ~~or that~~; (B) the lessee's approval of the supply contract is a condition to the effectiveness of the lease contract; (C) the lessee receive a statement describing the promises and warranties and any limitations relevant to the lessee before signing the lease contract; or (D) before signing the lease contract and except in a consumer lease, the lessee receive a writing identifying the supplier (unless the supplier was selected and required by the lessee) and the rights of the lessee under Section 2A–209, and advising the lessee a statement of promises and warranties is available from the supplier. Thus, even where oral supply orders or computer placed supply orders are compelled by custom and usage the transaction may still qualify as a finance lease if the lessee approves the supply contract before the lease contract is effective and such approval was a condition to the effectiveness of the lease contract. Moreover, where the lessor does not want the lessee to see the entire supply contract, including price information, the lessee may be provided with a separate statement of the terms of the supply contract relevant to the lessee; promises between the supplier and the lessor that do not affect the lessee need not be included. The statement can be a restatement of those terms or a copy of portions of the supply contract with the relevant terms clearly designated. Any implied warranties need not be designated, but a disclaimer or modification of remedy must be designated. A copy of any manufacturer's warranty is sufficient if that is the warranty provided. However, a copy of any Regulation M disclosure given pursuant to 12 C.F.R. § 213.4(g) concerning warranties in itself is not sufficient since those disclosures need only briefly identify express warranties and need not include any disclaimer of warranty.

If a transaction does not qualify as a finance lease, the parties may achieve the same result by agreement; no negative implications are to be drawn if the transaction does not qualify. Further, absent the application of special rules (fraud, duress, and the like), a lease that qualifies as a finance lease and is assigned by the lessor or the lessee to a third party does not lose its status as a finance lease under this Article. Finally, this Article creates no special rule where the lessor is an affiliate of the supplier; whether the transaction qualifies as a finance lease will be determined by the facts of each case.

(h) "Goods". Section 9–105(1)(h). See Section 2A–103(3) for reference to the definition of "~~Accounts~~ Account", "Chattel paper", "~~Documents~~ Document", "General intangibles" and "~~Instruments~~ Instrument". See Section 2A–217 for determination of the time and manner of identification.

(i) "Installment lease contract". Section 2–612(1).

(j) "Lease". New. There are several reasons to codify the law with respect to leases of goods. An analysis of the case law as it applies to leases of goods suggests at least several significant issues to be resolved by codification. First and foremost is the definition of a lease. It is necessary to define lease to determine whether a transaction creates a lease or a security interest disguised as a lease. If the transaction creates a security interest disguised as a lease, the transaction will be governed by the Article on Secured Transactions (Article 9) and the lessor will be required to file a financing statement or take other action to perfect its interest in the goods against third parties. There is no such requirement with respect to leases under the common law and, except with respect to leases of fixtures (Section 2A–309), this Article imposes no such requirement. Yet the distinction between a lease and a security interest disguised as a lease is not clear from the case law at the time of the promulgation of this Article. DeKoven, *Leases of Equipment: Puritan Leasing Company v. August, A Dangerous Decision*, 12 U.S.F.L.Rev. 257 (1978).

At common law a lease of personal property is a bailment for hire. While there are several definitions of bailment for hire, all require a thing to be let and a price for the letting. Thus, in modern terms and as provided in this definition, a lease is created when the lessee agrees to furnish consideration for the right to the possession and use of goods over a specified period of time. Mooney, *Personal Property Leasing: A Challenge*, 36 Bus. Law. 1605, 1607 (1981). Further, a lease is neither a sale (Section 2–106(1)) nor a retention or creation of a security interest (Section 1–201(37)). Due to extensive litigation to distinguish true leases from security interests, an amendment to Section 1–201(37) has been promulgated with this Article to create a sharper distinction.

This section as well as Section 1–201(37) must be examined to determine whether the transaction in question creates a lease or a security interest. The following hypotheticals indicate the perimeters of the issue. Assume that A has purchased a number of copying machines, new, for $1,000 each; the machines have an estimated useful economic life of three years. A advertises that the machines are available to rent for a minimum of one month and that the monthly rental is $100.00. A intends to enter into leases where A provides all maintenance, without charge to the lessee. Further, the lessee will rent the machine, month to month, with no obligation to renew. At the end of the lease term the lessee will be obligated to return the machine to A's place of business. This transaction qualifies as a lease under the first half of the definition, for the transaction includes a transfer by A to a prospective lessee of possession and use of the machine for a stated term, month to month. The machines are goods (Section 2A-103(1)(h)). The lessee is obligated to pay consideration in return, $100.00 for each month of the term.

However, the second half of the definition provides that a sale or a security interest is not a lease. Since there is no passing of title, there is no sale. Sections 2A-103(3) and 2-106(1). Under pre-Act security law this transaction would have created a bailment for hire or a true lease and not a conditional sale. *Da Rocha v. Macomber*, 330 Mass. 611, 614-15, 116 N.E.2d 139, 142 (1953). Under Section 1-201(37), as amended with the promulgation of this Article, the same result would follow. While the lessee is obligated to pay rent for the one month term of the lease, one of the other four conditions of the second paragraph of Section 1-201(37) must be met and none is. The term of the lease is one month and the economic life of the machine is 36 months; thus, subparagraph (a) of Section 1-201(37) is not now satisfied. Considering the amount of the monthly rent, absent economic duress or coercion, the lessee is not bound either to renew the lease for the remaining economic life of the goods or to become the owner. If the lessee did lease the machine for 36 months, the lessee would have paid the lessor $3,600 for a machine that could have been purchased for $1,000; thus, subparagraph (b) of Section 1-201(37) is not satisfied. Finally, there are no options; thus, subparagraphs (c) and (d) of Section 1-201(37) are not satisfied. This transaction creates a lease, not a security interest. However, with each renewal of the lease the facts and circumstances at the time of each renewal must be examined to determine if that conclusion remains accurate, as it is possible that a transaction that first creates a lease, later creates a security interest.

Assume that the facts are changed and that A requires each lessee to lease the goods for 36 months, with no right to terminate. Under pre-Act security law this transaction would have created a conditional sale, and not a bailment for hire or true lease. *Hervey v. Rhode Island Locomotive Works*, 93 U.S. (3 Otto) 664, 672-73, 23 L.Ed. 1003 (1876). Under this subsection, and Section 1-201(37), as amended with the inclusion of this Article in the Act, the same result would follow. The lessee's obligation for the term is not subject to termination by the lessee and the term is equal to the economic life of the machine.

Between these extremes there are many transactions that can be created. Some of the transactions have not been properly categorized by the courts in applying the 1978 and earlier Official Texts of Section 1-201(37). This subsection, together with Section 1-201(37), as amended with the promulgation of this Article, draws a brighter line, which should create a clearer signal to the professional lessor and lessee.

(k) "Lease agreement". This definition is derived from the first sentence of Section 1-201(3). Because the definition of lease is broad enough to cover future transfers, lease agreement includes an agreement contemplating a current or subsequent transfer. Thus it was not necessary to make an express reference to an agreement for the future lease of goods (Section 2-106(1)). This concept is also incorporated in the definition of lease contract. Note that the definition of lease does not include transactions in ordinary building materials that are incorporated into an improvement on land. Section 2A-309(2).

The provisions of this Article, if applicable, determine whether a lease agreement has legal consequences; otherwise the law of bailments and other applicable law determine the same. Sections 2A-103(4) and 1-103.

(*l*) "Lease contract". This definition is derived from the definition of contract in Section 1-201(11). Note that a lease contract may be for the future lease of goods, since this notion is included in the definition of lease.

(m) "Leasehold interest". New.

(n) "Lessee". New.

(*o*) "Lessee in ordinary course of business". Section 1–201(9).

(p) "Lessor". New.

(q) "Lessor's residual interest". New.

(r) "Lien". New. This term is used in Section 2A–307 (Priority of Liens Arising by Attachment or Levy on, Security Interests in, and Other Claims to Goods).

(s) "Lot". Section 2–105(5).

(t) "Merchant lessee". New. This term is used in Section 2A–511 (Merchant Lessee's Duties as to Rightfully Rejected Goods). A person may satisfy the requirement of dealing in goods of the kind subject to the lease as lessor, lessee, seller, or buyer.

(u) "Present value". New. Authorities agree that present value should be used to determine fairly the damages payable by the lessor or the lessee on default. *E.g., Taylor v. Commercial Credit Equip. Corp.*, 170 Ga.App. 322, 316 S.E.2d 788 (1984). Present value is defined to mean an amount that represents the discounted value as of a date certain of one or more sums payable in the future. This is a function of the economic principle that a dollar today is more valuable to the holder than a dollar payable in two years. While there is no question as to the principle, reasonable people would differ as to the rate of discount to apply in determining the value of that future dollar today. To minimize litigation, this Article allows the parties to specify the discount or interest rate, if the rate was not manifestly unreasonable at the time the transaction was entered into. In all other cases, the interest rate will be a commercially reasonable rate that takes into account the facts and circumstances of each case, as of the time the transaction was entered into.

(v) "Purchase". Section 1–201(32). This definition omits the reference to lien contained in the definition of purchase in Article 1 (Section 1–201(32)). This should not be construed to exclude consensual liens from the definition of purchase in this Article; the exclusion was mandated by the scope of the definition of lien in Section 2A–103(1)(r). Further, the definition of purchaser in this Article adds a reference to lease; as purchase is defined in Section 1–201(32) to include any other voluntary transaction creating an interest in property, this addition is not substantive.

(w) "Sublease". New.

(x) "Supplier". New.

(y) "Supply contract". New.

(z) "Termination". Section 2–106(3). The effect of a termination is provided in Section 2A–505(2).

Amendment 2

Section 2A–104 of the Article is amended to read:

§ 2A–104. Leases Subject to Other ~~Statutes~~ Law.

(1) A lease, although subject to this Article, is also subject to any applicable:

(a) ~~statute of the United States;~~

~~(b)~~ certificate of title statute of this State:

(list any certificate of title statutes covering automobiles, trailers, mobile homes, boats, farm tractors, and the like);

~~(c)~~(b) certificate of title statute of another jurisdiction (Section 2A–105); or

~~(d)~~(c) consumer protection statute of this State, or final consumer protection decision of a court of this State existing on the effective date of this Article.

(2) In case of conflict between ~~the provisions of~~ this Article, other than Sections 2A-105, 2A-304(3), and 2A-305(3), and ~~any~~ a statute or decision referred to in subsection (1), the ~~provisions of that~~ statute or decision ~~control~~ controls.

(3) Failure to comply with ~~any~~ an applicable ~~statute~~ law has only the effect specified therein.

Official Comment

Uniform Statutory Source: Sections 9-203(4) and 9-302(3)(b) and (c).

Changes: Substantially revised.

Purposes:

1. This Article creates a comprehensive scheme for the regulation of transactions that create leases. Section 2A-102. Thus, the Article supersedes all prior legislation dealing with leases, except to the extent set forth in this Section.

2. Subsection (1) states the general rule that a lease, although governed by the scheme of this Article, ~~is~~ also may be governed by certain other applicable ~~statutes~~ laws. This may occur in the case of a consumer lease. Section 2A-103(1)(e). Those laws may be state statutes existing prior to enactment of Article 2A or passed afterward. In this case, it is desirable for this Article to specify which statute controls. Or the law may be a pre-existing consumer protection decision. This Article preserves such decisions. Or the law may be a statute of the United States. Such a law controls without any statement in this Article under applicable principles of preemption.

An illustration of a statute of the United States that governs consumer leases is the Consumer Leasing Act, 15 U.S.C.A. §§ 1667-1667(e) (1982) and its implementing regulation, Regulation M, 12 C.F.R. § 213 (1986); the statute mandates disclosures of certain lease terms, delimits the liability of a lessee in leasing personal property, and regulates the advertising of lease terms. An illustration of a state statute that governs consumer leases and which if adopted in the enacting state prevails over this Article is the Unif. Consumer Credit Code, which includes many provisions similar to those of the Consumer Leasing Act, *e.g.*, Unif. Consumer Credit Code §§ 3.202, 3.209, 3.401, 7A U.L.A. 108-09, 115, 125 (1974), as well as provisions in addition to those of the Consumer Leasing Act, *e.g.*, Unif. Consumer Credit Code §§ 5.109-.111, 7A U.L.A. 171-76 (1974) (the right to cure a default). Such statutes may define consumer lease so as to govern transactions within and without the definition of consumer lease under this Article.

3. Under subsection (2), subject to certain limited exclusions, in case of conflict ~~the provisions of such~~ a statute ~~prevail~~ or a decision described in subsection (1) prevails over ~~the provisions of~~ this Article. For example, a provision like Unif. Consumer Credit Code § 5.112, 7A U.L.A. 176 (1974), limiting self-help repossession, prevails over Section 2A-525(3). A consumer protection decision rendered after the effective date of this Article may supplement its provisions. For example, in relation to Article 9 a court might conclude that an acceleration clause may not be enforced against an individual debtor after late payments have been accepted unless a prior notice of default is given. To the extent the decision establishes a general principle applicable to transactions other than secured transactions, it may supplement Section 2A-502.

4. Consumer protection in lease transactions is primarily left to other law. However, several provisions of this Article do contain special rules that may not be varied by agreement in the case of a consumer lease. *E.g.*, Sections 2A-106, 2A-108, and 2A-109(2). Were that not so, the ability of the parties to govern their relationship by agreement together with the position of the lessor in a consumer

lease too often could result in a one-sided lease agreement.

5. In construing this provision the reference to statute should be deemed to include applicable regulations. A consumer protection decision is "final" on the effective date of this Article if it is not subject to appeal on that date or, if subject to appeal, is not later reversed on appeal. Of course, such a decision can be overruled by a later decision or superseded by a later statute.

Cross References:

Sections 2A–103(1)(e), 2A–106, 2A–108, 2A–109(2) and 2A–525(3).

Definitional Cross Reference:

"Lease". Section 2A–103(1)(j).

Amendment 3

Section 2A–209 of the Article is amended to read:

§ 2A–209. Lessee Under Finance Lease as Beneficiary of Supply Contract.

(1) The benefit of ~~the~~ a supplier's promises to the lessor under the supply contract and of all warranties, whether express or implied, ~~under~~ including those of any third party provided in connection with or as part of the supply contract, extends to the lessee to the extent of the lessee's leasehold interest under a finance lease related to the supply contract, but is subject to the terms of the warranty and of the supply contract and all ~~of the supplier's~~ defenses or claims arising therefrom.

(2) The extension of the benefit of ~~the~~ a supplier's promises and of warranties to the lessee (Section 2A–209(1)) does not: ~~(a)~~ (i) modify the rights and obligations of the parties to the supply contract, whether arising therefrom or otherwise, or ~~(b)~~ (ii) impose any duty or liability under the supply contract on the lessee.

(3) Any modification or rescission of the supply contract by the supplier and the lessor is effective ~~against~~ between the supplier and the lessee unless, ~~prior to~~ before the modification or rescission, the supplier has received notice that the lessee has entered into a finance lease related to the supply contract. ~~If the supply contract is modified or rescinded after the lessee enters the finance lease, the lessee has a cause of action against the lessor, and against the supplier if the supplier has notice of the lessee's entering the finance lease when the supply contract is modified or rescinded. The lessee's recovery from such action shall put the lessee in as good a position as if the modification or rescission had not occurred.~~ If the modification or rescission is effective between the supplier and the lessee, the lessor is deemed to have assumed, in addition to the obligations of the lessor to the lessee under the lease contract, promises of the supplier to the lessor and warranties that were so modified or rescinded as they existed and were available to the lessee before modification or rescission.

(4) In addition to the extension of the benefit of the supplier's promises and of warranties to the lessee under subsection (1), the lessee retains all rights that the lessee may have against the supplier which arise from an agreement between the lessee and the supplier or under other law.

Official Comment

Uniform Statutory Source: None.

Changes: This section is modeled on Section 9–318, the Restatement (Second) of Contracts §§ 302–315 (1981), and leasing practices. *See Earman Oil Co. v. Burroughs Corp.*, 625 F.2d 1291, 1296–97 (5th Cir.1980).

Purposes:

1. The function performed by the lessor in a finance lease is extremely limited. Section 2A–103(1)(g). The lessee looks to the supplier of the goods for warranties and the like or, in some cases as to warranties, to the manufacturer if a warranty made by that person is passed on. That expectation is reflected in subsection (1), which is self-executing. As a matter of policy, the operation of this provision may not be excluded, modified or limited; however, an exclusion, modification, or limitation of any term of the supply contract or warranty, including any with respect to rights and remedies, and any defense or claim such as a statute of limitations, effective against the lessor as ~~buyer~~ the acquiring party under the supply contract, is also effective against the lessee as the beneficiary designated under this provision. ~~The~~ For example, the supplier is not precluded from excluding or modifying an express or implied warranty under a supply contract. Sections 2–312(2) and 2–316, or Section 2A–214. Further, the supplier is not precluded from limiting the rights and remedies of the lessor~~, as buyer,~~ and from liquidating damages. Sections 2–718 and 2–719 or Sections 2A–503 and 2A–504. If the supply contract excludes or modifies warranties, limits remedies ~~for breach~~, or liquidates damages with respect to the lessor, such provisions are enforceable against the lessee as beneficiary. Thus, only selective discrimination against the beneficiaries designated under this section is precluded, *i.e.*, exclusion of the supplier's liability to the lessee with respect to warranties made to the lessor. This section does not affect the development of other law with respect to products liability.

2. Enforcement of this benefit is by action. Sections 2A–103(4) and 1–106(2).

3. The benefit extended by these provisions is not without a price, as this Article also provides in the case of a finance lease that is not a consumer lease that the lessee's promises to the lessor under the lease contract become irrevocable and independent upon the lessee's acceptance of the goods. Section 2A–407.

4. Subsection (2) limits the effect of subsection (1) on the supplier and the lessor by preserving, notwithstanding the transfer of the benefits of the supply contract to the lessee, all of the supplier's and the lessor's rights and obligations with respect to each other and others; it further absolves the lessee of any duties with respect to the supply contract that might have been inferred from the extension of the benefits thereof.

5. Subsections (2) and (3) also deal with difficult issues related to modification or rescission of the supply contract. Subsection (2) states a rule that determines the impact of the statutory extension of benefit contained in subsection (1) upon the relationship of the parties to the supply contract and, in a limited respect, upon the lessee. This statutory extension of benefit, like that contained in Sections 2A–216 and 2–318, is not a modification of the supply contract by the parties. Thus, subsection (3) states the rules that apply to a modification or rescission of the supply contract by the parties. Subsection (3) ~~recognizes the lessee's potential causes of action against the lessor and the supplier arising from modification or rescission of the supply contract. The existence and extent of a cause of action by the supplier against the lessor is left to resolution by the courts based on the facts of each case.~~ provides that a modification or rescission is not effective between the supplier and the lessee if, before the modification or rescission occurs, the supplier received notice that the lessee has entered into the finance lease. On the other hand, if the modification or rescission is effective, then to the extent

of the modification or rescission of the benefit or warranty, the lessor by statutory dictate assumes an obligation to provide to the lessee that which the lessee would otherwise lose. For example, assume a reduction in an express warranty from four years to one year. No prejudice to the lessee may occur if the goods perform as agreed. If, however, there is a breach of the express warranty after one year and before four years pass, the lessor is liable. A remedy for any prejudice to the lessee because of the bifurcation of the lessee's recourse resulting from the action of the supplier and the lessor is left to resolution by the courts based on the facts of each case.

6. Subsection (4) makes it clear that the rights granted to the lessee by this section do not displace any rights the lessee otherwise may have against the supplier.

Cross References:

Sections ~~2A–103(g)~~ 2A–103(1)(g), 2A–407 and 9–318.

Definitional Cross References:

"Action". Section 1–201(1).

"Finance lease". Section 2A–103(1)(g).

"Leasehold interest". Section 2A–103(1)(m).

"Lessee". Section 2A–103(1)(n).

"Lessor". Section 2A–103(1)(p).

"Notice". Section 1–201(25).

"Party". Section 1–201(29).

"Rights". Section 1–201(36).

"Supplier". Section 2A–103(1)(x).

"Supply contract". Section 2A–103(1)(y).

"Term". Section 1–201(42).

Amendment 4

Section 2A–303 of the Article is amended to read:

§ 2A–303. Alienability of Party's Interest Under Lease Contract or of Lessor's Residual Interest in Goods; Delegation of Performance; ~~Assignment~~ Transfer of Rights.

~~(1) Any interest of a party under a lease contract and the lessor's residual interest in the goods may be transferred unless~~

~~(a) the transfer is voluntary and the lease contract prohibits the transfer; or~~

~~(b) the transfer materially changes the duty of or materially increases the burden or risk imposed on the other party to the lease contract, and within a reasonable time after notice of the transfer the other party demands that the transferee comply with subsection (2) and the transferee fails to comply.~~

~~(2) Within a reasonable time after demand pursuant to subsection (1)(b), the transferee shall:~~

~~(a) cure or provide adequate assurance that he [or she] will promptly cure any default other than one arising from the transfer;~~

~~(b) compensate or provide adequate assurance that he [or she] will promptly compensate the other party to the lease contract and any other person holding an interest in the lease contract, except the party whose interest is being transferred, for any loss to that party resulting from the transfer;~~

~~(c) provide adequate assurance of future due performance under the lease contract; and~~

~~(d) assume the lease contract.~~

~~(3) Demand pursuant to subsection (1)(b) is without prejudice to the other party's rights against the transferee and the party whose interest is transferred.~~

(1) As used in this section, "creation of a security interest" includes the sale of a lease contract that is subject to Article 9, Secured Transactions, by reason of Section 9–102(1)(b).

(2) Except as provided in subsections (3) and (4), a provision in a lease agreement which (i) prohibits the voluntary or involuntary transfer, including a transfer by sale, sublease, creation or enforcement of a security interest, or attachment, levy, or other judicial process, of an interest of a party under the lease contract or of the lessor's residual interest in the goods, or (ii) makes such a transfer an event of default, gives rise to the rights and remedies provided in subsection (5), but a transfer that is prohibited or is an event of default under the lease agreement is otherwise effective.

(3) A provision in a lease agreement which (i) prohibits the creation or enforcement of a security interest in an interest of a party under the lease contract or in the lessor's residual interest in the goods, or (ii) makes such a transfer an event of default, is not enforceable unless, and then only to the extent that, there is an actual transfer by the lessee of the lessee's right of possession or use of the goods in violation of the provision or an actual delegation of a material performance of either party to the lease contract in violation of the provision. Neither the granting nor the enforcement of a security interest in (i) the lessor's interest under the lease contract or (ii) the lessor's residual interest in the goods is a transfer that materially impairs the prospect of obtaining return performance by, materially changes the duty of, or materially increases the burden or risk imposed on, the lessee within the purview of subsection (5) unless, and then only to the extent that, there is an actual delegation of a material performance of the lessor.

~~(6)~~ (4) A provision in a lease agreement which (i) prohibits a transfer of a right to damages for default with respect to the whole lease contract or of a right to payment arising out of the ~~assignor's~~ transferor's due performance of ~~his [or her]~~ the transferor's entire obligation ~~can be assigned despite agreement otherwise~~, or (ii) makes such a transfer an event of default, is not enforceable, and such a transfer is not a transfer that materially impairs the prospect of obtaining return performance by, materially changes the duty of, or materially increases the burden or risk imposed on, the other party to the lease contract within the purview of subsection (5).

(5) Subject to subsections (3) and (4):

(a) if a transfer is made which is made an event of default under a lease agreement, the party to the lease contract not making the transfer, unless that party waives the default or otherwise agrees, has the rights and remedies described in Section 2A–501(2);

(b) if paragraph (a) is not applicable and if a transfer is made that (i) is prohibited under a lease agreement or (ii) materially impairs the prospect of obtaining return performance by, materially changes the duty of, or materially increases the burden or risk imposed on, the other party to the lease contract, unless the party not making the transfer agrees at any time to the transfer in the lease contract or otherwise, then, except as limited by contract, (i) the transferor is liable to the party not making the transfer for damages caused by the transfer to the extent that the damages could not reasonably be prevented by the party not making the transfer and (ii) a court having jurisdiction may grant other appropriate relief, including cancellation of the lease contract or an injunction against the transfer.

~~(4)~~ (6) ~~An assignment~~ A transfer of "the lease" or of "all my rights under the lease", or ~~an assignment~~ a transfer in similar general terms, is a transfer of rights~~,~~ and, unless the language or the circumstances, as in ~~an assignment~~ a transfer for security, indicate the contrary, the ~~assignment~~ transfer is a delegation of duties by the ~~assignor to the assignee and acceptance~~ transferor to the transferee. Acceptance by the ~~assignee~~ transferee constitutes a promise by ~~him [or her]~~ the transferee to perform those duties. ~~This~~ The promise is enforceable by either the ~~assignor~~ transferor or the other party to the lease contract.

~~(5)~~ (7) Unless otherwise agreed by the lessor and the lessee, ~~no~~ a delegation of performance ~~relieves~~ does not relieve the ~~assignor~~ transferor as against the other party of any duty to perform or of any liability for default.

~~(7)~~ (8) ~~To~~ In a consumer lease, to prohibit the transfer of an interest of a party under ~~a~~ the lease contract or to make a transfer an event of default, the language ~~of prohibition~~ must be specific, by a writing, and conspicuous.

Official Comment

Uniform Statutory Source: ~~Section~~ Sections 2-210 and 9-311.

Changes: ~~The provisions of Section 2-210 were incorporated in this Article, with substantial modifications to reflect leasing terminology and practice, as well as certain developments of the law with respect to creditors' rights.~~ The provisions of Sections 2-210 and 9-311 were incorporated in this section, with substantial modifications to reflect leasing terminology and practice and to harmonize the principles of the respective provisions, *i.e.* limitations on delegation of performance on the one hand and alienability of rights on the other. In addition, unlike Section 2-210 which deals only with voluntary transfers, this section deals with involuntary as well as voluntary transfers. Moreover, the principle of Section 9-318(4) denying effectiveness to contractual terms prohibiting assignments of receivables due and to become due also is implemented.

Purposes: ~~Unlike Section 2-210, which deals with voluntary transfers of rights and duties under a sales contract, this section deals with involuntary as well as voluntary transfers of rights and duties under a lease contract. Voluntary transfers are permitted unless prohibited by the lease contract or, as is also the case for involuntary transfers, there is a material change in the duty of, or a material increase in the burden or risk to, the other party to the lease contract and the transferee fails to comply with the conditions in subsection (2) within a reasonable time after a demand, which need not be in writing, has been made for such compliance.~~

~~Subsection (2) establishes four criteria that must be satisfied by the transferee after a demand has been made. These criteria are modeled on the requirements contained in the Bankruptcy Reform Act of 1978, as amended, 11 U.S.C. § 365 (1982 & Supp. II 1984), governing the assumption and assignment of an unexpired lease or executory contract by a trustee in bankruptcy. Section 2–210(5) resolves this issue for sales by allowing the other party to demand assurances from the transferee (Section 2–609). Section 365 of the Bankruptcy Code, a modern version of the provisions of Section 2–609, provided a better model for resolving this issue for leases.~~

~~Sections 9–206 and 9–318 are also relevant in this context. Section 9–206 sanctions an agreement by a lessee not to assert certain types of claims or defenses against the lessor's assignee. Section 9–318 deals with, among other things, the other party's rights against the assignee where Section 9–206(1) does not apply. Since the definition of contract under Section 1–201(11) includes a lease agreement, the definition of account debtor under Section 9–105(1)(a) includes a lessee of goods and Section 9–206 applies to lease agreements; thus, there is no need to restate those sections in this Article. However, the reference to "defenses or claims arising out of a sale" in Section 9–318(1) should be interpreted broadly to include defenses or claims arising out of a lease. This should follow as Section 9–318(1) codifies the common law rule with respect to contracts, including contracts of sale and contracts of lease. Further, Section 9–318(4) should be interpreted to allow the rule of this section to control with respect to transfers of leases.~~

1. Subsection (2) states a rule, consistent with Section 9–311, that voluntary and involuntary transfers of an interest of a party under the lease contract or of the lessor's residual interest, including by way of the creation or enforcement of a security interest, are effective, notwithstanding a provision in the lease agreement prohibiting the transfer or making the transfer an event of default. Although the transfers are effective, the provision in the lease agreement is nevertheless enforceable, but only as provided in subsection (5). Under subsection (5) the prejudiced party is limited to the remedies on "default under the lease contract" in this Article and, except as limited by this Article, as provided in the lease agreement, if the transfer has been made an event of default. Section 2A–501(2). Usually, there will be a specific provision to this effect or a general provision making a breach of a covenant an event of default. In those cases where the transfer is prohibited, but not made an event of default, the prejudiced party may recover damages; or, if the damage remedy would be ineffective adequately to protect that party, the court can order cancellation of the lease contract or enjoin the transfer. This rule that such provisions generally are enforceable is subject to subsections (3) and (4), which make such provisions unenforceable in certain instances.

2. The first such instance is described in subsection (3). A provision in a lease agreement which prohibits the creation or enforcement of a security interest, including sales of lease contracts subject to Article 9 (Sections 9–102(1)(b) and 9–104(f)), or makes it an event of default is generally not enforceable, reflecting the policy of Section 9–318(4). However, that policy gives way to the doctrine stated in Section 2–210(2), which gives one party to a contract the right to protect itself against an actual delegation (but not just a provision under which delegation might later occur) of a material performance by the other party. Accordingly, such a provision in a lease agreement is enforceable when the transfer delegates a material performance. Generally, as expressly provided in subsection (6), a transfer for security is not a delegation of duties. However, inasmuch as the creation of a security interest includes the sale of a lease contract, if there are then unperformed duties on the part of the lessor/seller, there could be a delegation of duties in the sale, and, if such a delegation actually takes place and is of a mate-

rial performance, a provision in a lease agreement prohibiting it or making it an event of default would be enforceable, giving rise to the rights and remedies stated in subsection (5). The statute does not define "material." The parties may set standards to determine its meaning. The term is intended to exclude delegations of matters such as accounting to a professional accountant and the performance of, as opposed to the responsibility for, maintenance duties to a person in the maintenance service industry.

3. For similar reasons, the lessor is entitled to protect its residual interest in the goods by prohibiting anyone but the lessee from possessing or using them. Accordingly, under subsection (3) if there is an actual transfer by the lessee of its right of possession or use of the goods in violation of a provision in the lease agreement, such a provision likewise is enforceable, giving rise to the rights and remedies stated in subsection (5). A transfer of the lessee's right of possession or use of the goods resulting from the enforcement of a security interest granted by the lessee in its leasehold interest is a "transfer by the lessee" under this subsection.

4. Finally, subsection (3) protects against a claim that the creation or enforcement of a security interest in the lessor's interest under the lease contract or in the residual interest is a transfer that materially impairs the prospect of obtaining return performance by, materially changes the duty of, or materially increases the burden or risk imposed on the lessee so as to give rise to the rights and remedies stated in subsection (5), unless the transfer involves an actual delegation of a material performance of the lessor.

5. While it is not likely that a transfer by the lessor of its right to payment under the lease contract would impair at a future time the ability of the lessee to obtain the performance due the lessee under the lease contract from the lessor, if under the circumstances reasonable grounds for insecurity as to receiving that performance arise, the lessee may employ the provision of this Article for demanding adequate assurance of due performance and has the remedy provided in that circumstance. Section 2A-401.

6. Sections 9-206 and 9-318(1) through (3) also are relevant. Section 9-206 sanctions an agreement by a lessee not to assert certain types of claims or defenses against the lessor's assignee. Section 9-318(1) through (3) deal with, among other things, the other party's rights against the assignee where Section 9-206(1) does not apply. Since the definition of contract under Section 1-201(11) includes a lease agreement, the definition of account debtor under Section 9-105(1)(a) includes a lessee of goods. As a result, Section 9-206 applies to lease agreements, and there is no need to restate those sections in this Article. The reference to "defenses or claims arising out of a sale" in Section 9-318(1) should be interpreted broadly to include defenses or claims arising out of a lease inasmuch as that section codifies the common law rule with respect to contracts, including lease contracts.

7. Subsection (4) is based upon Section 2-210(2) and Section 9-318(4). It makes unenforceable a prohibition against transfers of certain rights to payment or a provision making the transfer an event of default. It also provides that such transfers do not materially impair the prospect of obtaining return performance by, materially change the duty of, or materially increase the burden or risk imposed on, the other party to the lease contract so as to give rise to the rights and remedies stated in subsection (5). Accordingly, a transfer of a right to payment cannot be prohibited or made an event of default, or be one that materially impairs performance, changes duties or increases risk, if the right is already due or will become due without further performance being required by the party to receive payment. Thus, a lessor can transfer the right to future payments under the lease contract, including by way of a grant of a security interest, and the transfer will not give rise to the rights and remedies stated in subsection (5) if the lessor has no remaining performance

under the lease contract. The mere fact that the lessor is obligated to allow the lessee to remain in possession and to use the goods as long as the lessee is not in default does not mean that there is "remaining performance" on the part of the lessor. Likewise, the fact that the lessor has potential liability under a "non-operating" lease contract for breaches of warranty does not mean that there is "remaining performance." In contrast, the lessor would have "remaining performance" under a lease contract requiring the lessor to regularly maintain and service the goods or to provide "upgrades" of the equipment on a periodic basis in order to avoid obsolescence. The basic distinction is between a mere potential duty to respond which is not "remaining performance," and an affirmative duty to render stipulated performance. Although the distinction may be difficult to draw in some cases, it is instructive to focus on the difference between "operating" and "non-operating" leases as generally understood in the marketplace. Even if there is "remaining performance" under a lease contract, a transfer for security of a right to payment that is made an event of default or that is in violation of a prohibition against transfer does not give rise to the rights and remedies under subsection (5) if it does not constitute an actual delegation of a material performance under subsection (3).

8. The application of either the rule of subsection (3) or the rule of subsection (4) to the grant by the lessor of a security interest in the lessor's right to future payment under the lease contract may produce the same result. Both subsections generally protect security transfers by the lessor in particular because the creation by the lessor of a security interest or the enforcement of that interest generally will not prejudice the lessee's rights if it does not result in a delegation of the lessor's duties. To the contrary, the receipt of loan proceeds or relief from the enforcement of an antecedent debt normally should enhance the lessor's ability to perform its duties under the lease contract. Nevertheless, there are circumstances where relief might be justified. For example, if ownership of the goods is transferred pursuant to enforcement of a security interest to a party whose ownership would prevent the lessee from continuing to possess the goods, relief might be warranted. *See* 49 U.S.C.A. § 1401(a) and (b) which places limitations on the operation of aircraft in the United States based on the citizenship or corporate qualification of the registrant.

9. Relief on the ground of material prejudice when the lease agreement does not prohibit the transfer or make it an event of default should be afforded only in extreme circumstances, considering the fact that the party asserting material prejudice did not insist upon a provision in the lease agreement that would protect against such a transfer.

10. Subsection (5) implements the rule of subsection (2). Subsection (2) provides that, even though a transfer is effective, a provision in the lease agreement prohibiting it or making it an event of default may be enforceable as provided in subsection (5). *See Brummond v. First National Bank of Clovis*, 99 N.M. 221, 656 P.2d 884, 35 U.C.C.Rep.Serv. (Callaghan) 1311 (1983), stating the analogous rule for Section 9–311. If the transfer prohibited by the lease agreement is made an event of default, then, under subsection 5(a), unless the default is waived or there is an agreement otherwise, the aggrieved party has the rights and remedies referred to in Section 2A–501(2), *viz.* those in this Article and, except as limited in the Article, those provided in the lease agreement. In the unlikely circumstance that the lease agreement prohibits the transfer without making a violation of the prohibition an event of default or, even if there is no prohibition against the transfer, and the transfer is one that materially impairs performance, changes duties, or increases risk (for example, a sublease or assignment to a party using the goods improperly or for an illegal purpose), then subsection 5(b) is applicable. In that circumstance, unless the party aggrieved by the transfer has otherwise agreed in the lease

contract, such as by assenting to a particular transfer or to transfers in general, or agrees in some other manner, the aggrieved party has the right to recover damages from the transferor and a court may, in appropriate circumstances, grant other relief, such as cancellation of the lease contract or an injunction against the transfer.

11. If a transfer gives rise to the rights and remedies provided in subsection (5), the transferee as an alternative may propose, and the other party may accept, adequate cure or compensation for past defaults and adequate assurance of future due performance under the lease contract. Subsection (5) does not preclude any other relief that may be available to a party to the lease contract aggrieved by a transfer subject to an enforceable prohibition, such as an action for interference with contractual relations.

12. Subsection (8) requires that a provision in a consumer lease prohibiting a transfer, or making it an event of default, must be specific, written and conspicuous. *See* Section 1–201(10). This assists in protecting a consumer lessee against surprise assertions of default.

13. Subsection ~~(4)~~ (6) is taken almost verbatim from the provisions of Section 2–210(4). The subsection states a rule of construction that distinguishes a commercial assignment, which substitutes the assignee for the assignor as to rights and duties, and an assignment for security or financing assignment, which substitutes the assignee for the assignor only as to rights. Note that the assignment for security or financing assignment is a subset of all security interests. Security interest is defined to include "any interest of a buyer of . . . chattel paper". Section 1–201(37). Chattel paper is defined to include a lease. Section 9–105(1)(b). Thus, a buyer of leases is the holder of a security interest in the leases. That conclusion should not influence this issue, as the policy is quite different. Whether a buyer of leases is the holder of a commercial assignment, or an assignment for security or financing assignment should be determined by the language of the assignment or the circumstances of the assignment.

~~While it is recognized that a lease contract may impose restrictions on the transfer of an interest of a party under a lease, such restrictions are not generally favored in law. Subsection (7) balances these competing interests and ensures that both parties knowingly impose prohibitions on transfer, by providing that the language of prohibition be specific, by a writing, and conspicuous.~~

Cross References:

Sections 1–201(11), 1–201(37), 2–210, ~~2–609~~ 2A–401, 9–102(1)(b), 9–104(f), 9–105(1)(a), 9–206, and 9–318.

Definitional Cross References:

"Agreed" and "Agreement". Section 1–201(3).

"Conspicuous". Section 1–201(10).

"Goods". Section 2A–103(1)(h).

"Lease". Section 2A–103(1)(j).

"Lease contract". Section 2A–103(1)(*l*).

"Lessee". Section 2A–103(1)(n).

"Lessor". Section 2A–103(1)(p).

"Lessor's residual interest". Section 2A–103(1)(q).

"Notice". Section 1–201(25).

"Party". Section 1–201(29).

"Person". Section 1–201(30).

"Reasonable time". Section 1–204(1) and (2).

"Rights". Section 1–201(36).

"Term". Section 1–201(42).

"Writing". Section 1–201(46).

Amendment 5

Section 2A–304 of the Article is amended to read:

§ 2A–304. Subsequent Lease of Goods by Lessor.

(1) Subject to ~~the provisions of~~ Section 2A–303, a subsequent lessee from a lessor of goods under an existing lease contract obtains, to the extent of the leasehold interest transferred, the leasehold interest in the goods that the lessor had or had power to transfer, and except as provided in subsection (2) and Section 2A–527(4), takes subject to the existing lease contract. A lessor with voidable title has power to transfer a good leasehold interest to a good faith subsequent lessee for value, but only to the extent set forth in the preceding sentence. ~~When~~ If goods have been delivered under a transaction of purchase, the lessor has that power even though:

(a) the lessor's transferor was deceived as to the identity of the lessor;

(b) the delivery was in exchange for a check which is later dishonored;

(c) it was agreed that the transaction was to be a "cash sale"; or

(d) the delivery was procured through fraud punishable as larcenous under the criminal law.

(2) A subsequent lessee in the ordinary course of business from a lessor who is a merchant dealing in goods of that kind to whom the goods were entrusted by the existing lessee of that lessor before the interest of the subsequent lessee became enforceable against ~~the~~ that lessor obtains, to the extent of the leasehold interest transferred, all of ~~the~~ that lessor's and the existing lessee's rights to the goods, and takes free of the existing lease contract.

(3) A subsequent lessee from the lessor of goods that are subject to an existing lease contract and are covered by a certificate of title issued under a statute of this State or of another jurisdiction takes no greater rights than those provided both by this section and by the certificate of title statute.

Official Comment

Uniform Statutory Source: Section 2–403.

Changes: While Section 2–403 was used as a model for this section, the provisions of Section 2–403 were significantly revised to reflect leasing practices and to integrate this Article with certificate of title statutes.

Purposes:

1. This section must be read in conjunction with, as it is subject to, the provisions of Section 2A–303, which govern voluntary and involuntary transfers of rights and duties under a lease contract, including the lessor's residual interest in the goods.

2. This section must also be read in conjunction with Section 2–403. This section and Section 2A–305 are derived from Section 2–403, which states a unified policy on good faith purchases of goods. Given the scope of the definition of purchaser (Section 1–201(33)), a person who bought goods to lease as well as a person who bought goods subject to an existing lease from a lessor will take pursuant to Section 2–403. Further, a person who leases such goods from the person who bought them should also be pro-

tected under Section 2-403, first because the lessee's rights are derivative and second because the definition of purchaser should be interpreted to include one who takes by lease; no negative implication should be drawn from the inclusion of lease in the definition of purchase in this Article. Section 2A-103(1)(v).

3. There are hypotheticals that relate to an entrustee's unauthorized lease of entrusted goods to a third party that are outside the provisions of Sections 2-403, 2A-304 and 2A-305. Consider a sale of goods by M, a merchant, to B, a buyer. After paying for the goods B allows M to retain possession of the goods as B is short of storage. Before B calls for the goods M leases the goods to L, a lessee. This transaction is not governed by Section 2-403(2) as L is not a buyer in the ordinary course of business. Section 1-201(9). Further, this transaction is not governed by Section 2A-304(2) as B is not an existing lessee. Finally, this transaction is not governed by Section 2A-305(2) as B is not M's lessor. Section 2A-307(2) resolves the potential dispute between B, M and L. By virtue of B's entrustment of the goods to M and M's lease of the goods to L, B has a cause of action against M under the common law. Sections 2A-103(4) and 1-103. *See, e.g.*, Restatement (Second) of Torts §§ 222A-243. Thus, B is a creditor of M. Sections 2A-103(4) and 1-201(12). Section 2A-307(2) provides that B, as M's creditor, takes subject to M's lease to L. Thus, if L does not default under the lease, L's enjoyment and possession of the goods should be undisturbed. However, B is not without recourse. B's action should result in a judgment against M providing, among other things, a turnover of all proceeds arising from M's lease to L, as well as a transfer of all of M's right, title and interest as lessor under M's lease to L, including M's residual interest in the goods. Section 2A-103(1)(q).

4. Subsection (1) states a rule with respect to the leasehold interest obtained by a subsequent lessee from a lessor of goods under an existing lease contract. The interest will include such leasehold interest as the lessor has in the goods as well as the leasehold interest that the lessor had the power to transfer. Thus, the subsequent lessee obtains unimpaired all rights acquired under the law of agency, apparent agency, ownership or other estoppel, whether based upon statutory provisions or upon case law principles. Sections 2A-103(4) and 1-103. In general, the subsequent lessee takes subject to the existing lease contract, including the existing lessee's rights thereunder. Furthermore, the subsequent lease contract is, of course, limited by its own terms, and the subsequent lessee takes only to the extent of the leasehold interest transferred thereunder.

5. Subsection (1) further provides that a lessor with voidable title has power to transfer a good leasehold interest to a good faith subsequent lessee for value. In addition, subsections (1)(a) through (d) provide specifically for the protection of the good faith subsequent lessee for value in a number of specific situations which have been troublesome under prior law.

6. The position of an existing lessee who entrusts leased goods to its lessor is not distinguishable from the position of other entrusters. Thus, subsection (2) provides that the subsequent lessee in the ordinary course of business takes free of the existing lease contract between the lessor entrustee and the lessee entruster, if the lessor is a merchant dealing in goods of that kind. Further, the subsequent lessee obtains all of the lessor entrustee's and the lessee entruster's rights to the goods, but only to the extent of the leasehold interest transferred by the lessor entrustee. Thus, the lessor entrustee retains the residual interest in the goods. Section 2A-103(1)(q). However, entrustment by the existing lessee must have occurred before the interest of the subsequent lessee became enforceable against the lessor. Entrusting is defined in Section 2-403(3) and that definition applies here. Section 2A-103(3).

7. Subsection (3) states a rule with respect to a transfer of goods from a lessor to a subsequent lessee where the goods are subject to an existing lease and

covered by a certificate of title. The subsequent lessee's rights are no greater than those provided by this section and the applicable certificate of title statute, including any applicable case law construing such statute. Where the relationship between the certificate of title statute and Section 2–403, the statutory analogue to this section, has been construed by a court, that construction is incorporated here. Sections 2A–103(4) and 1–102(1) and (2). The better rule is that the certificate of title statutes are in harmony with Section 2–403 and thus would be in harmony with this section. *E.g., Atwood Chevrolet-Olds v. Aberdeen Mun. School Dist.,* 431 So.2d 926, 928 (Miss.1983); *Godfrey v. Gilsdorf,* 86 Nev. 714, 718, 476 P.2d 3, 6 (1970); *Martin v. Nager,* 192 N.J.Super. 189, 197–98, 469 A.2d 519, 523 (Ch.Div.1983). Where the certificate of title statute is silent on this issue of transfer, this section will control.

Cross References:

Sections 1–102, 1–103, 1–201(33), 2–403, 2A–103(1)(v), 2A–103(3), 2A–103(4), 2A–303 and 2A–305.

Definitional Cross References:

"Agreed". Section 1–201(3).

"Delivery". Section 1–201(14).

"Entrusting". Section 2–403(3).

"Good faith". Sections 1–201(19) and 2–103(1)(b).

"Goods". Section 2A–103(1)(h).

"Lease". Section 2A–103(1)(j).

"Lease contract". Section 2A–103(1)(*l*).

"Leasehold interest". Section 2A–103(1)(m).

"Lessee". Section 2A–103(1)(n).

"Lessee in the ordinary course of business". Section 2A–103(1)(*o*).

"Lessor". Section 2A–103(1)(p).

"Merchant". Section 2–104(1).

"Purchase". Section 2A–103(1)(v).

"Rights". Section 1–201(36).

"Value". Section 1–201(44).

Amendment 6

Section 2A–307 of the Article is amended to read:

§ 2A–307. Priority of Liens Arising by Attachment or Levy on, Security Interests in, and Other Claims to Goods.

(1) Except as otherwise provided in Section 2A–306, a creditor of a lessee takes subject to the lease contract.

(2) Except as otherwise provided in subsections (3) and (4) ~~of this section~~ and in Sections 2A–306 and 2A–308, a creditor of a lessor takes subject to the lease contract <u>unless</u>:

(a) ~~unless~~ the creditor holds a lien that attached to the goods before the lease contract became enforceable, ~~or~~

(b) ~~unless~~ the creditor holds a security interest in the goods ~~that under the Article on Secured Transactions (Article 9) would have priority over any other security interest in the goods perfected by a filing covering the goods and made at the time the lease contract became enforceable, whether or not any other security interest existed.~~ <u>and the lessee did not give value and receive delivery of the goods without knowledge of the security interest; or</u>

<u>(c) the creditor holds a security interest in the goods which was perfected (Section 9–303) before the lease contract became enforceable.</u>

(3) A lessee in the ordinary course of business takes the leasehold interest free of a security interest in the goods created by the lessor even though the security interest is perfected (Section 9–303) and the lessee knows of its existence.

(4) A lessee other than a lessee in the ordinary course of business takes the leasehold interest free of a security interest to the extent that it secures future advances made after the secured party acquires knowledge of the lease or more than 45 days after the lease contract becomes enforceable, whichever first occurs, unless the future advances are made pursuant to a commitment entered into without knowledge of the lease and before the expiration of the 45–day period.

Official Comment

Uniform Statutory Source: None for ~~subsections~~ subsection (1) ~~and (2)~~. ~~Subsections~~ Subsection (2) is derived from Section 9–301, and subsections (3) and (4) are derived from ~~the provisions of~~ Section 9–307(1) and (3), respectively.

Changes: The provisions of ~~Section~~ Sections 9–301 and 9–307(1) and (3) were incorporated, and modified to reflect leasing terminology and the basic concepts reflected in this Article.

Purposes:

1. Subsection (1) states a general rule of priority that a creditor of the lessee takes subject to the lease contract. The term lessee (Section 2A–103(1)(n)) includes sublessee. Therefore, this subsection not only covers disputes between the prime lessor and a creditor of the prime lessee but also disputes between the prime lessor, or the sublessor, and a creditor of the sublessee. Section 2A–301 official comment 3(g). Further, by using the term creditor (Section 1–201(12)), this subsection will cover disputes with a general creditor, a secured creditor, a lien creditor and any representative of creditors. Section 2A–103(4).

2. Subsection (2) states a general rule of priority that a creditor of a lessor takes subject to the lease contract. Note the discussion above with regard to the scope of these rules. Section 2A–301 official comment 3(g). Thus, the section will not only cover disputes between the prime lessee and a creditor of the prime lessor but also disputes between the prime lessee, or the sublessee, and a creditor of the sublessor.

3. To take priority over the lease contract, and the interests derived therefrom, the creditor must come within one of ~~two~~ three exceptions stated within the rule. First, subsection (2)(a) provides that where the creditor holds a lien (Section 2A–103(1)(r)) that attached before the lease contract became enforceable (Section 2A–301), the creditor does not take subject to the lease. Second, subsection (2)(b) provides that when the creditor holds a security interest (Section 1–201(37)) ~~that would have~~, whether or not perfected, the creditor has priority over a ~~hypothetical~~ lessee who did not give value (Section 1–201(44)) and receive delivery of the goods without knowledge (Section 1–201(25)) of the security interest. As to other lessees, under subsection (2)(c) a secured creditor holding a perfected security interest ~~perfected by a filing made at~~ before the time the lease contract became enforceable (Section 2A–301)~~, the creditor~~ does not take subject to the lease. With respect to this provision ~~the hypothetical secured creditor is not the holder of a purchase money security interest entitled to special priority: first, the facts and circumstances relating to the security interest described in Section 2A–307(2)(b) would not create a purchase money security interest as defined in Section 9–107, and second, assuming *arguendo* that it did create a purchase money security interest, the facts and circumstances relating to the security interest described in~~

~~Section 2A–307(2)(b) would not create a special priority under the provisions of Section 9–312(3) or (4). Thus, the priority rules of Section 9–312(5) govern the security interest held by the hypothetical secured creditor. The use of a hypothetical creditor as a statutory means to resolve disputes between competing interests is not without precedent. The Bankruptcy Reform Act of 1978, as amended, 11 U.S.C. § 544(a) (1982 & Supp. II 1984)~~, the lessee in these circumstances is treated like a buyer so that perfection of a purchase money security interest does not relate back (Section 9–301).

4. The rules of this section operate in favor of whichever party to the lease contract may enforce it, even if one party perhaps may not, *e.g.*, under Section 2A–201(1)(b).

5. The ~~rule~~ rules stated in ~~subsection~~ subsections (2)(b) and (c), and the rule in subsection (3), ~~is~~ are best understood by reviewing a hypothetical. Assume that a merchant engaged in the business of selling and leasing musical instruments obtained possession of a truck load of musical instruments on deferred payment terms from a supplier of musical instruments on January 6. To secure payment of such credit the merchant granted the supplier a security interest in the instruments; the security interest was perfected by filing on January 15. The merchant, as lessor, entered into a lease to an individual of one of the musical instruments supplied by the supplier; the lease became enforceable on ~~March 1~~ January 10. Under subsection (2)(b) the lessee will prevail (assuming the lessee qualifies thereunder) unless subsection (c) provides otherwise. Under the rule stated in subsection ~~(2)(b)~~ (2)(c) a priority dispute between the supplier, as the lessor's secured creditor, and the lessee would be determined by ~~assuming that~~ ascertaining on ~~March 1~~ January 10 (the day the lease became enforceable) ~~the merchant had granted a~~ the validity and perfected status of the security interest in ~~such~~ the musical ~~instruments to a hypothetical secured creditor and the hypothetical secured creditor perfected such security interest by filing on March 1. Under the priority rules of the Article on Secured Transactions (Article 9) the hypothetical secured creditor would lose in a priority dispute with the supplier. Section 9–312(5)(a). Thus~~ instrument and the enforceability of the lease contract by the lessee. Nothing more appearing, under the rule stated in subsection ~~(2)(b)~~ (2)(c), the supplier's security interest in the musical instrument would not have priority over the lease contract. ~~However~~ Moreover, subsection ~~(2)(b)~~ (2) states that its ~~rule is~~ rules are subject to the rules of subsections (3) and (4). Under this hypothetical the lessee should qualify as a "lessee in the ordinary course of business". Section 2A–103(1)(*o*). Subsection (3) also makes clear that the lessee in the ordinary course of business will win even if he or she knows of the existence of the supplier's security interest.

6. Subsections (3) and (4), which are modeled on the provisions of Section 9–307(1) and (3), respectively, state two exceptions to the priority rule stated in subsection (2) with respect to a creditor who holds a security interest. The lessee in the ordinary course of business will be treated in the same fashion as the buyer in the ordinary course of business, given a priority dispute with a secured creditor over goods subject to a lease contract.

Cross References:

Sections 1–201(12), 1–201(25), 1–201(37), 1–201(44), 2A–103(1)(n), 2A–103(1)(*o*), 2A–103(1)(r), 2A–103(4), 2A–201(1)(b), 2A–301 official comment 3(g), Article 9, ~~esp.~~ especially Sections 9–301, 9–307(1)~~,~~ and 9–307(3) ~~and 9–312(5)(a)~~.

Definitional Cross References:

"Creditor". Section 1–201(12).

"Goods". Section 2A–103(1)(h).

"Knowledge" and "Knows". Section 1–201(25).

"Lease". Section 2A–103(1)(j).

"Lease contract". Section 2A–103(1)(*l*).

"Leasehold interest". Section 2A–103(1)(m).

"Lessee". Section 2A–103(1)(n).

"Lessee in the ordinary course of business". Section 2A–103(1)(*o*).

"Lessor". Section 2A–103(1)(p).

"Lien". Section 2A–103(1)(r).

"Party". Section 1–201(29).

"Pursuant to commitment". Section 2A–103(3).

"Security interest". Section 1–201(37).

Amendment 7

Section 2A–309 of the Article is amended to read:

§ 2A–309. Lessor's and Lessee's Rights When Goods Become Fixtures.

(1) In this section:

(a) goods are "fixtures" when they become so related to particular real estate that an interest in them arises under real estate law;

(b) a "fixture filing" is the filing, in the office where a mortgage on the real estate would be filed or recorded ~~or registered~~, of a financing statement ~~concerning~~ covering goods that are or are to become fixtures and conforming to the requirements ~~of subsection (5)~~ of Section ~~9–402~~ 9–402(5);

(c) a lease is a "purchase money lease" unless the lessee has possession or use of the goods or the right to possession or use of the goods before the lease agreement is enforceable;

(d) a mortgage is a "construction mortgage" to the extent it secures an obligation incurred for the construction of an improvement on land including the acquisition cost of the land, if the recorded writing so indicates; and

(e) "encumbrance" includes real estate mortgages and other liens on real estate and all other rights in real estate that are not ownership interests.

(2) Under this Article a lease may be of goods that are fixtures or may continue in goods that become fixtures, but no lease exists under this Article of ordinary building materials incorporated into an improvement on land.

(3) This Article does not prevent creation of a lease of fixtures pursuant to real estate law.

(4) The perfected interest of a lessor of fixtures has priority over a conflicting interest of an encumbrancer or owner of the real estate if:

(a) the lease is a purchase money lease, the conflicting interest of the encumbrancer or owner arises before the goods become fixtures, the interest of the lessor is perfected by a fixture filing before the goods become fixtures or within ten days thereafter, and the lessee has an interest of record in the real estate or is in possession of the real estate; or

(b) the interest of the lessor is perfected by a fixture filing before the interest of the encumbrancer or owner is of record, the lessor's interest has priority over any conflicting interest of a predecessor in title of the encumbrancer or owner, and the lessee has an interest of record in the real estate or is in possession of the real estate.

(5) The interest of a lessor of fixtures, whether or not perfected, has priority over the conflicting interest of an encumbrancer or owner of the real estate if:

(a) the fixtures are readily removable factory or office machines, readily removable equipment that is not primarily used or leased for use in the operation of the real estate, or readily removable replacements of domestic appliances that are goods subject to a consumer lease, and before the goods become fixtures the lease contract is enforceable; or

(b) the conflicting interest is a lien on the real estate obtained by legal or equitable proceedings after the lease contract is enforceable; or

(c) the encumbrancer or owner has consented in writing to the lease or has disclaimed an interest in the goods as fixtures; or

(d) the lessee has a right to remove the goods as against the encumbrancer or owner. If the lessee's right to remove terminates, the priority of the interest of the lessor continues for a reasonable time.

(6) Notwithstanding ~~paragraph (a) of~~ subsection ~~(4)~~ (4)(a) but otherwise subject to subsections (4) and (5), the interest of a lessor of fixtures, including the lessor's residual interest, is subordinate to the conflicting interest of an encumbrancer of the real estate under a construction mortgage recorded before the goods become fixtures if the goods become fixtures before the completion of the construction. To the extent given to refinance a construction mortgage, the conflicting interest of an encumbrancer of the real estate under a mortgage has this priority to the same extent as the encumbrancer of the real estate under the construction mortgage.

(7) In cases not within the preceding subsections, priority between the interest of a lessor of fixtures, including the lessor's residual interest, and the conflicting interest of an encumbrancer or owner of the real estate who is not the lessee is determined by the priority rules governing conflicting interests in real estate.

(8) If the interest of a lessor of fixtures, including the lessor's residual interest, has priority over all conflicting interests of all owners and encumbrancers of the real estate, the lessor or the lessee may ~~(a)~~ (i) on default, expiration, termination, or cancellation of the lease agreement ~~by the other party~~ but subject to the ~~provisions of the~~ lease agreement and this Article, or ~~(b)~~ (ii) if necessary to enforce ~~his [or her]~~ other rights and remedies of the lessor or lessee under this Article, remove the goods from the real estate, free and clear of all conflicting interests of all owners and encumbrancers of the real estate, but ~~he [or she]~~ the lessor or lessee must reimburse any encumbrancer or owner of the real estate who is not the lessee and who has not otherwise agreed for the cost of repair of any physical injury, but not for any diminution in value of the real estate caused by the absence of the goods removed or by any necessity of replacing them. A person entitled to reimbursement may refuse permission to remove until the party seeking removal gives adequate security for the performance of this obligation.

(9) Even though the lease agreement does not create a security interest, the interest of a lessor of fixtures, including the lessor's residual interest, is perfected by filing a financing statement as a fixture filing for leased goods

that are or are to become fixtures in accordance with the relevant provisions of the Article on Secured Transactions (Article 9).

Official Comment

Uniform Statutory Source: Section 9–313.

Changes: Revised to reflect leasing terminology and to add new material.

Purposes:

1. While Section 9–313 provided a model for this section, certain provisions were substantially revised.

2. Section 2A–309(1)(c), which is new, defines purchase money lease to exclude leases where the lessee had possession or use of the goods or the right thereof before the lease agreement became enforceable. This term is used in subsection (4)(a) as one of the conditions that must be satisfied to obtain priority over the conflicting interest of an encumbrancer or owner of the real estate.

3. Section 2A–309(4), which states one of several priority rules found in this section, deletes reference to office machines and the like (Section 9–313(4)(c)) as well as certain liens (Section 9–313(4)(d)). However, these items are included in subsection (5), another priority rule that is more permissive than the rule found in subsection (4) as it applies whether or not the interest of the lessor is perfected. In addition, subsection (5)(a) expands the scope of the provisions of Section 9–313(4)(c) to include readily removable equipment not primarily used or leased for use in the operation of real estate; the qualifier is intended to exclude from the expanded rule equipment integral to the operation of real estate, *e.g.*, heating and air conditioning equipment.

4. The rule stated in subsection (7) is more liberal than the rule stated in Section 9–313(7) in that issues of priority not otherwise resolved in this subsection are left for resolution by the priority rules governing conflicting interests in real estate, as opposed to the Section 9–313(7) automatic subordination of the security interest in fixtures. Note that, for the purpose of this section, where the interest of an encumbrancer or owner of the real estate is paramount to the interest of the lessor, the latter term includes the residual interest of the lessor.

5. The rule stated in subsection (8) is more liberal than the rule stated in Section 9–313(8) in that the right of removal is extended to both the lessor and the lessee and the occasion for removal includes expiration, termination or cancellation of the lease agreement, and enforcement of rights and remedies under this Article, as well as default. The new language also provides that upon removal the goods are free and clear of conflicting interests of owners and encumbrancers of the real estate.

6. Finally, subsection (9) provides a mechanism for the lessor of fixtures to perfect its interest by filing a financing statement under the provisions of the Article on Secured Transactions (Article 9), even though the lease agreement does not create a security interest. Section 1–201(37). The relevant provisions of Article 9 must be interpreted permissively to give effect to this mechanism as it implicitly expands the scope~~, perfection and priority provisions~~ of Article 9 so that its filing provisions apply to ~~govern~~ transactions that create a lease of fixtures, even though the lease agreement does not create a security interest. This mechanism is similar to that provided in Section 2–326(3)(c) for the seller of goods on consignment, even though the consignment is not "intended as security". Section 1–201(37). Given the lack of litigation with respect to the mechanism created for consignment sales, this new mechanism should prove effective. ~~Note, however, that this is a more pervasive change in Article 9 than that wrought by expanding the filing system to accommodate permissive filing for leases. U.C.C. § 9–408 app. II (West 1983) (Reasons for 1972 Adoption of New Section).~~

Cross References:

Sections 1-201(37), 2A-309(1)(c), 2A-309(4), Article 9, ~~esp.~~ especially Sections 9-313, 9-313(4)(c), 9-313(4)(d), 9-313(7), 9-313(8) and 9-408.

Definitional Cross References:

"Agreed". Section 1-201(3).

"Cancellation". Section 2A-103(1)(b).

"Conforming". Section 2A-103(1)(d).

"Consumer lease". Section 2A-103(1)(e).

"Goods". Section 2A-103(1)(h).

"Lease". Section 2A-103(1)(j).

"Lease agreement". Section 2A-103(1)(k).

"Lease contract". Section 2A-103(1)(*l*).

"Lessee". Section 2A-103(1)(n).

"Lessor". Section 2A-103(1)(p).

"Lien". Section 2A-103(1)(r).

"Mortgage". Section 9-105(1)(j).

"Party". Section 1-201(29).

"Person". Section 1-201(30).

"Reasonable time". Section 1-204(1) and (2).

"Remedy". Section 1-201(34).

"Rights". Section 1-201(36).

"Security interest". Section 1-201(37).

"Termination". Section 2A-103(1)(z).

"Value". Section 1-201(44).

"Writing". Section 1-201(46).

Amendment 8

Section 2A-311 of the Article is added to read:

§ 2A-311. Priority Subject to Subordination.

Nothing in this Article prevents subordination by agreement by any person entitled to priority.

Official Comment

Uniform Statutory Source: Section 9-316.

Purposes: The several preceding sections deal with questions of priority. This section is inserted to make it entirely clear that a person entitled to priority may effectively agree to subordinate the claim. Only the person entitled to priority may make such an agreement: the rights of such a person cannot be adversely affected by an agreement to which that person is not a party.

Cross References:

Sections 1-102 and 2A-304 through 2A-310.

Definitional Cross References:

"Agreement". Section 1-201(3).

"Person". Section 1-201(30).

Amendment 9

Section 2A-407 of the Article is amended to read:

§ 2A-407. Irrevocable Promises: Finance Leases.

(1) In the case of a finance lease that is not a consumer lease the lessee's promises under the lease contract become irrevocable and independent upon the lessee's acceptance of the goods.

(2) A promise that has become irrevocable and independent under subsection (1):

(a) is effective and enforceable between the parties, and by or against third parties including assignees of the parties~~,~~; and

(b) is not subject to cancellation, termination, modification, repudiation, excuse, or substitution without the consent of the party to whom the promise runs.

(3) This section does not affect the validity under any other law of a covenant in any lease contract making the lessee's promises irrevocable and independent upon the lessee's acceptance of the goods.

Official Comment

Uniform Statutory Source: None.

Purposes:

1. This section extends the benefits of the classic "hell or high water" clause to a finance lease that is not a consumer lease. This section is self-executing; no special provision need be added to the contract. This section makes covenants in a finance lease irrevocable and independent due to the function of the finance lessor in a three party relationship: the lessee is looking to the supplier to perform the essential covenants and warranties. Section 2A–209. Thus, upon the lessee's acceptance of the goods the lessee's promises to the lessor under the lease contract become irrevocable and independent. The provisions of this section remain subject to the obligation of good faith (Sections 2A–103(4) and 1–203), and the lessee's revocation of acceptance (Section 2A–517).

2. The section requires the lessee to perform even if the lessor's performance after the lessee's acceptance is not in accordance with the lease contract; the lessee may, however, have and pursue a cause of action against the lessor, *e.g.*, breach of certain limited warranties (Sections 2A–210 and ~~211(1)~~ 2A–211(1)). This is appropriate because the benefit of the supplier's promises and warranties to the lessor under the supply contract and, in some cases, the warranty of a manufacturer who is not the supplier, is extended to the lessee under the finance lease. Section 2A–209. Despite this balance, this section excludes a finance lease that is a consumer lease. That a consumer be obligated to pay notwithstanding defective goods or the like is a principle that is not tenable under case law (*Unico v. Owen*, 50 N.J. 101, 232 A.2d 405 (1967)), state statute (Unif. Consumer Credit Code §§ 3.403–3.405, 7A U.L.A. 126–31 (1974), or federal statute (15 U.S.C.A. § 1666i (1982)).

3. The relationship of the three parties to a transaction that qualifies as a finance lease is best demonstrated by a hypothetical. A, the potential lessor, has been contacted by B, the potential lessee, to discuss the lease of an expensive line of equipment that B has recently placed an order for with C, the manufacturer of such goods. The negotiation is completed and A, as lessor, and B, as lessee, sign a lease of the line of equipment for a 60–month term. B, as buyer, assigns the purchase order with C to A. If this transaction creates a lease (Section 2A–103(1)(j)), this transaction should qualify as a finance lease. Section 2A–103(1)(g).

4. The line of equipment is delivered by C to B's place of business. After installation by C and testing by B, B accepts the goods by signing a certificate of delivery and acceptance, a copy of which is sent by B to A and C. One year later the line of equipment malfunctions and B falls behind in its manufacturing schedule.

5. Under this Article, because the lease is a finance lease, no warranty of fitness or merchantability is extended by A to B. Sections 2A–212(1) and 2A–213. Absent an express provision in the lease agreement, application of Section 2A–210 or Section 2A–211(1), or application of the principles of law and equity, including

the law with respect to fraud, duress, or the like (Sections 2A–103(4) and 1–103), B has no claim against A. B's obligation to pay rent to A continues as the obligation became irrevocable and independent when B accepted the line of equipment (Section 2A–407(1)). B has no right of set-off with respect to any part of the rent still due under the lease. Section 2A–508(6). However, B may have another remedy. Despite the lack of privity between B and C (the purchase order with C having been assigned by B to A), B may have a claim against C. Section 2A–209(1).

6. This section ~~is silent as to~~ does not address whether a "hell or high water" clause, *i.e.*, a clause that is to the effect of this section, is enforceable if included in a finance lease that is a consumer lease or a lease that is not a finance lease. That issue will continue to be determined by the facts of each case and other law which this section does not affect. Sections 2A–104, 2A–103(4), 9–206 and 9–318. However, with respect to finance leases that are not consumer leases courts have enforced "hell or high water" clauses. *In re O.P.M. Leasing Servs.*, 21 B.R. 993, 1006 (Bkrtcy.N.Y.1982).

7. Subsection (2) further provides that a promise that has become irrevocable and independent under subsection (1) is enforceable not only between the parties but also against third parties. Thus, the finance lease can be transferred or assigned without disturbing enforceability. Further, subsection (2) also provides that the promise cannot, among other things, be cancelled or terminated without the consent of the lessor.

Cross References:

Sections 1–103, 1–203, 2A–103(1)(g), 2A–103(1)(j), 2A–103(4), 2A–104, 2A–209, 2A–209(1), 2A–210, 2A–211(1), 2A–212(1), 2A–213, 2A–517(1)(b), 9–206 and 9–318.

Definitional Cross References:

"Cancellation". Section 2A–103(1)(b).

"Consumer lease". Section 2A–103(1)(e).

"Finance lease". Section 2A–103(1)(g).

"Goods". Section 2A–103(1)(h).

"Lease contract". Section 2A–103(1)(*l*).

"Lessee". Section 2A–103(1)(n).

"Party". Section 1–201(29).

"Termination". Section 2A–103(1)(z).

Amendment 10

Section 2A–501 of the Article is amended to read:

§ 2A–501. Default: Procedure.

(1) Whether the lessor or the lessee is in default under a lease contract is determined by the lease agreement and this Article.

(2) If the lessor or the lessee is in default under the lease contract, the party seeking enforcement has rights and remedies as provided in this Article and, except as limited by this Article, as provided in the lease agreement.

(3) If the lessor or the lessee is in default under the lease contract, the party seeking enforcement may reduce the party's claim to judgment, or otherwise enforce the lease contract by self-help or any available judicial procedure or nonjudicial procedure, including administrative proceeding, arbitration, or the like, in accordance with this Article.

(4) Except as otherwise provided in Section 1–106(1) or this Article or the lease agreement, the rights and remedies referred to in subsections (2) and (3) are cumulative.

(5) If the lease agreement covers both real property and goods, the party seeking enforcement may proceed under this Part as to the goods, or under other applicable law as to both the real property and the goods in accordance with ~~his [or her]~~ that party's rights and remedies in respect of the real property, in which case this Part does not apply.

Official Comment

Uniform Statutory Source: Section 9–501.

Changes: Substantially revised.

Purposes:

1. Subsection (1) is new and represents a departure from the Article on Secured Transactions (Article 9) as the subsection makes clear that whether a party to the lease agreement is in default is determined by ~~the agreement as well as~~ this Article as well as the agreement. Sections 2A–508 and 2A–523. It further departs from Article 9 in recognizing the potential default of either party, a function of the bilateral nature of the obligations between the parties to the lease contract.

2. Subsection (2) is a version of the first sentence of Section 9–501(1), revised to reflect leasing terminology.

3. Subsection (3), an expansive version of the second sentence of Section 9–501(1), lists the procedures that may be followed by the party seeking enforcement; in effect, the scope of the procedures listed in subsection (3) is consistent with the scope of the procedures available to the foreclosing secured party.

4. Subsection (4) establishes that the parties' rights and remedies are cumulative. DeKoven, *Leases of Equipment: Puritan Leasing Company v. August, A Dangerous Decision*, 12 U.S.F.L.Rev. 257, 276–80 (1978). Cumulation, and largely unrestricted selection, of remedies is allowed in furtherance of the general policy of the Commercial Code, stated in Section 1–106, that remedies be liberally administered to put the aggrieved party in as good a position as if the other party had fully performed. Therefore, cumulation of, or selection among, remedies is available to the extent necessary to put the aggrieved party in as good a position as it would have been in had there been full performance. However, cumulation of, or selection among, remedies is not available to the extent that the cumulation or selection would put the aggrieved party in a better position than it would have been in had there been full performance by the other party.

5. Section 9–501(3), which, among other things, states that certain rules, to the extent they give rights to the debtor and impose duties on the secured party, may not be waived or varied, was not incorporated in this Article. Given the significance of freedom of contract in the development of the common law as it applies to bailments for hire and the lessee's lack of an equity of redemption, there was no reason to impose that restraint.

Cross References:

Sections 1–106, 2A–508, 2A–523, Article 9, ~~esp.~~ especially Sections 9–501(1) and 9–501(3).

Definitional Cross References:

"Goods". Section 2A–103(1)(h).

"Lease agreement". Section 2A–103(1)(k).

"Lease contract". Section 2A–103(1)(*l*).

"Lessee". Section 2A–103(1)(n).

"Lessor". Section 2A–103(1)(p).

"Party". Section 1–201(29).

"Remedy". Section 1–201(34).

"Rights". Section 1–201(36).

Amendment 11

Section 2A–503 of the Article is amended to read:

§ 2A–503. Modification or Impairment of Rights and Remedies.

(1) Except as otherwise provided in this Article, the lease agreement may include rights and remedies for default in addition to or in substitution for those provided in this Article and may limit or alter the measure of damages recoverable under this Article.

(2) Resort to a remedy provided under this Article or in the lease agreement is optional unless the remedy is expressly agreed to be exclusive. If circumstances cause an exclusive or limited remedy to fail of its essential purpose, or provision for an exclusive remedy is unconscionable, remedy may be had as provided in this Article.

(3) Consequential damages may be liquidated under Section 2A–504, or may otherwise be limited, altered, or excluded unless the limitation, alteration, or exclusion is unconscionable. Limitation, alteration, or exclusion of consequential damages for injury to the person in the case of consumer goods is prima facie unconscionable but limitation, alteration, or exclusion of damages where the loss is commercial is not prima facie unconscionable.

(4) Rights and remedies on default by the lessor or the lessee with respect to any obligation or promise collateral or ancillary to the lease contract are not impaired by this Article.

Official Comment

Uniform Statutory Source: Sections 2–719 and 2–701.

Changes: Rewritten to reflect lease terminology and to clarify the relationship between this section and Section 2A–504.

Purposes:

1. A significant purpose of this Part is to provide rights and remedies for those parties to a lease who fail to provide them by agreement or whose rights and remedies fail of their essential purpose or are unenforceable. However, it is important to note that this implies no restriction on freedom to contract. Sections 2A–103(4) and 1–102(3). Thus, subsection (1), a revised version of the provisions of Section 2–719(1), allows the parties to the lease agreement freedom to provide for rights and remedies in addition to or in substitution for those provided in this Article and to alter or limit the measure of damages recoverable under this Article. Except to the extent otherwise provided in this Article (*e.g.*, Sections 2A–105, 106 and 108(1) and (2)), this Part shall be construed neither to restrict the parties' ability to provide for rights and remedies or to limit or alter the measure of damages by agreement, nor to imply disapproval of rights and remedy schemes other than those set forth in this Part.

2. Subsection (2) makes explicit with respect to this Article what is implicit in Section 2–719 with respect to the Article on Sales (Article 2): if an exclusive remedy is held to be unconscionable, remedies under this Article are available. Section 2–719 official comment 1.

3. Subsection (3), a revision of Section 2–719(3), makes clear that consequential damages may also be liquidated. Section 2A–504(1).

4. Subsection (4) is a revision of the provisions of Section 2–701. This subsec-

tion leaves the treatment of default with respect to obligations or promises collateral or ancillary to the lease contract to other law. Sections 2A-103(4) and 1-103. An example of such an obligation would be that of the lessor to the secured creditor which has provided the funds to leverage the lessor's lease transaction; an example of such a promise would be that of the lessee, as seller, to the lessor, as buyer, in a sale-leaseback transaction.

Cross References:

Sections 1-102(3), 1-103, Article 2, ~~esp.~~ especially Sections 2-701, 2-719, 2-719(1), 2-719(3), 2-719 official comment 1, and Sections 2A-103(4), 2A-105, 2A-106, 2A-108(1), 2A-108(2), and 2A-504 ~~and 2A-504(1)~~.

Definitional Cross References:

"Agreed". Section 1-201(3).

"Consumer goods". Section 9-109(1).

"Lease agreement". Section 2A-103(1)(k).

"Lease contract". Section 2A-103(1)(*l*).

"Lessee". Section 2A-103(1)(n).

"Lessor". Section 2A-103(1)(p).

"Person". Section 1-201(30).

"Remedy". Section 1-201(34).

"Rights". Section 1-201(36).

Amendment 12

Section 2A-507 of the Article is amended to read:

§ 2A-507. Proof of Market Rent: Time and Place.

(1) Damages based on market rent (Section 2A-519 or 2A-528) are determined according to the rent for the use of the goods concerned for a lease term identical to the remaining lease term of the original lease agreement and prevailing at the ~~time of the default~~ times specified in Sections 2A-519 and 2A-528.

(2) If evidence of rent for the use of the goods concerned for a lease term identical to the remaining lease term of the original lease agreement and prevailing at the times or places described in this Article is not readily available, the rent prevailing within any reasonable time before or after the time described or at any other place or for a different lease term which in commercial judgment or under usage of trade would serve as a reasonable substitute for the one described may be used, making any proper allowance for the difference, including the cost of transporting the goods to or from the other place.

(3) Evidence of a relevant rent prevailing at a time or place or for a lease term other than the one described in this Article offered by one party is not admissible unless and until he [or she] has given the other party notice the court finds sufficient to prevent unfair surprise.

(4) If the prevailing rent or value of any goods regularly leased in any established market is in issue, reports in official publications or trade journals or in newspapers or periodicals of general circulation published as the reports of that market are admissible in evidence. The circumstances of the preparation of the report may be shown to affect its weight but not its admissibility.

Official Comment

Uniform Statutory Source: Sections 2–723 and 2–724.

Changes: Revised to reflect leasing practices and terminology. ~~Section 2A–519(2) provides an example of one of the several times this Article refers to a determination of market rent prevailing at a given time or place. Section 2A–507(2).~~ Sections 2A–519 and 2A–528 specify the times as of which market rent is to be determined.

Definitional Cross References:

"Goods". Section 2A–103(1)(h).

"Lease". Section 2A–103(1)(j).

"Lease agreement". Section 2A–103(1)(k).

"Notice". Section 1–201(25).

"Party". Section 1–201(29).

"Reasonable time". Section 1–204(1) and (2).

"Usage of trade". Section 1–205.

"Value". Section 1–201(44).

Amendment 13

Section 2A–508 of the Article is amended to read:

§ 2A–508. Lessee's Remedies.

(1) If a lessor fails to deliver the goods in conformity to the lease contract (Section 2A–509) or repudiates the lease contract (Section 2A–402), or a lessee rightfully rejects the goods (Section 2A–509) or justifiably revokes acceptance of the goods (Section 2A–517), then with respect to any goods involved, and with respect to all of the goods if under an installment lease contract the value of the whole lease contract is substantially impaired (Section 2A–510), the lessor is in default under the lease contract and the lessee may:

(a) cancel the lease contract (Section 2A–505(1));

(b) recover so much of the rent and security as has been paid~~, but in the case of an installment lease contract the recovery is that which~~ and is just under the circumstances;

(c) cover and recover damages as to all goods affected whether or not they have been identified to the lease contract (Sections 2A–518 and 2A–520), or recover damages for nondelivery (Sections 2A–519 and 2A–520)~~.~~;

(d) exercise any other rights or pursue any other remedies provided in the lease contract.

(2) If a lessor fails to deliver the goods in conformity to the lease contract or repudiates the lease contract, the lessee may also:

(a) if the goods have been identified, recover them (Section 2A–522); or

(b) in a proper case, obtain specific performance or replevy the goods (Section 2A–521).

(3) If a lessor is otherwise in default under a lease contract, the lessee may exercise the rights and pursue the remedies provided in the lease contract, which may include a right to cancel the lease, and ~~this Article~~ in Section 2A–519(3).

(4) If a lessor has breached a warranty, whether express or implied, the lessee may recover damages (Section 2A-519(4)).

(5) On rightful rejection or justifiable revocation of acceptance, a lessee has a security interest in goods in the lessee's possession or control for any rent and security that has been paid and any expenses reasonably incurred in their inspection, receipt, transportation, and care and custody and may hold those goods and dispose of them in good faith and in a commercially reasonable manner, subject to ~~the provisions of~~ Section 2A-527(5).

(6) Subject to the provisions of Section 2A-407, a lessee, on notifying the lessor of the lessee's intention to do so, may deduct all or any part of the damages resulting from any default under the lease contract from any part of the rent still due under the same lease contract.

Official Comment

Uniform Statutory Source: Sections 2-711 and 2-717.

Changes: Substantially rewritten.

Purposes:

1. This section is an index to Sections 2A-509 through 522 ~~and their effect on~~ which set out the lessee's rights and remedies after the lessor's default. The lessor and the lessee can ~~otherwise~~ agree to modify the rights and remedies available under this Article; ~~thus, the parties~~ they can, among other things, ~~raise or lower the threshold of events that give rise to a lessor's default or~~ provide that for defaults other than those specified in subsection (1) the lessee can exercise the rights and remedies referred to in subsection (1); and they can create a new scheme of rights and remedies triggered by the occurrence of the default. Sections 2A-103(4) and 1-102(3).

2. Subsection (1), a substantially rewritten version of the provisions of Section 2-711(1), lists three cumulative remedies of the lessee where the lessor has failed to deliver conforming goods or has repudiated the contract, or the lessee has rightfully rejected or justifiably revoked. Sections 2A-501(2) and (4). Subsection (1) also allows the lessee to exercise any contractual remedy. This Article rejects any general doctrine of election of remedy. To determine if one remedy bars another in a particular case is a function of whether the lessee has been put in as good a position as if the lessor had fully performed the lease agreement. Use of multiple remedies is barred only if the effect is to put the lessee in a better position than it would have been in had the lessor fully performed under the lease. Sections 2A-103(4), 2A-501(4), and 1-106(1). ~~Note that a special rule has been created regarding the lessee's recovery of rent and security that have been paid in the case of an installment lease—recovery is limited to that which is just under the circumstances. With the various different types of installment leases, no bright line can be created that would operate fairly in all cases; in addition, this provision should further encourage the parties to establish their own rules by agreement.~~ Subsection (1)(b), in recognition that no bright line can be created that would operate fairly in all installment lease cases and in recognition of the fact that a lessee may be able to cancel the lease (revoke acceptance of the goods) after the goods have been in use for some period of time, does not require that all lease payments made by the lessee under the lease be returned upon cancellation. Rather, only such portion as is just of the rent and security payments made may be recovered. If a defect in the goods is discovered immediately upon tender to the lessee and the goods are rejected immediately, then the lessee should recover all payments made. If, however, for example, a 36-month equipment lease is terminated in the 12th

month because the lessor has materially breached the contract by failing to perform its maintenance obligations, it may be just to return only a small part or none of the rental payments already made.

3. Subsection (2), a version of the provisions of Section 2-711(2) revised to reflect leasing terminology, lists two alternative remedies for the recovery of the goods by the lessee; however, each of these remedies is cumulative with respect to those listed in subsection (1).

4. Subsection (3) is new~~ and allows the lessee access to the remedy scheme of this Article as well as the lease contract if the lessor is in default for reasons other than those stated in subsection (1). Note that the reference to this Article includes supplemental principles of law and equity. Sections 2A-103(4) and 1-103~~. It covers defaults which do not deprive the lessee of the goods and which are not so serious as to justify rejection or revocation of acceptance under subsection (1). It also covers defaults for which the lessee could have rejected or revoked acceptance of the goods but elects not to do so and retains the goods. In either case, a lessee which retains the goods is entitled to recover damages as stated in Section 2A-519(3). That measure of damages is "the loss resulting in the ordinary course of events from the lessor's default as determined in any manner that is reasonable together with incidental and consequential damages, less expenses saved in consequence of the lessor's breach."

5. Subsection (1)(d) and subsection (3) recognize that the lease agreement may provide rights and remedies in addition to or different from those which Article 2A provides. In particular, subsection (3) provides that the lease agreement may give the remedy of cancellation of the lease for defaults by the lessor that would not otherwise be material defaults which would justify cancellation under subsection (1). If there is a right to cancel, there is, of course, a right to reject or revoke acceptance of the goods.

6. Subsection (4) is new and merely adds to the completeness of the index by including a reference to the lessee's recovery of damages upon the lessor's breach of warranty; such breach may not rise to the level of a default by the lessor ~~(*e.g.* breach of an express warranty that the goods subject to the lease conform to description where the non conformity is such that when measured by objective criteria it reflects a minimal deviation from description) unless the breach is material or unless so provided by the lease agreement~~ justifying revocation of acceptance. If the lessee properly rejects or revokes acceptance of the goods because of a breach of warranty, the rights and remedies are those provided in subsection (1) rather than those in Section 2A-519(4).

7. Subsection (5), a revised version of the provisions of Section 2-711(3), recognizes, on rightful rejection or justifiable revocation, the lessee's security interest in goods in its possession and control. Section 9-113, which recognized security interests arising under the Article on Sales (Article 2), was amended with the adoption of this Article to reflect the security interests arising under this Article. Pursuant to Section 2A-511(4), a purchaser who purchases goods from the lessee in good faith takes free of any rights of the lessor, or in the case of a finance lease the supplier. Such goods, however, must have been rightfully rejected and disposed of pursuant to Section 2A-511 or 2A-512. However, Section ~~2A-517(3)~~ 2A-517(5) provides that the lessee will have the same rights and duties with respect to goods where acceptance has been revoked as with respect to goods rejected. Thus, Section 2A-511(4) will apply to the lessee's disposition of such goods.

8. Pursuant to Section 2A-527(5), the lessee must account to the lessor for the excess proceeds of such disposition, after satisfaction of the claim secured by the lessee's security interest.

9. Subsection (6), a slightly revised version of the provisions of Section 2-717, sanctions a right of set-off by the lessee,

subject to the rule of Section 2A-407 with respect to irrevocable promises in a finance lease that is not a consumer lease, and further subject to an enforceable "hell or high water" clause in the lease agreement. Section 2A-407 official comment. No attempt is made to state how the set-off should occur; this is to be determined by the facts of each case.

10. There is no special treatment of the finance lease in this section. Absent supplemental principles of law and equity to the contrary, in the case of most finance leases, following the lessee's acceptance of the goods the lessee will have no rights or remedies against the lessor, because the lessor's obligations to the lessee are minimal. Sections 2A-210 and 2A-211(1). Since the lessee will look to the supplier for performance, this is appropriate. Section 2A-209.

Cross References:

Sections 1-102(3), 1-103, 1-106(1), Article 2, ~~esp.~~ especially Sections 2-711, 2-717 and Sections 2A-103(4), 2A-209, 2A-210, 2A-211(1), 2A-407, 2A-501(2), 2A-501(4), 2A-509 through 2A-522, 2A-511(3), ~~2A-517(3)~~ 2A-517(5), 2A-527(5) and Section 9-113.

Definitional Cross References:

"Conforming". Section 2A-103(1)(d).

"Delivery". Section 1-201(14).

"Good faith". Sections 1-201(19) and 2-103(1)(b).

"Goods". Section 2A-103(1)(h).

"Installment lease contract". Section 2A-103(1)(i).

"Lease contract". Section 2A-103(1)(*l*).

"Lessee". Section 2A-103(1)(n).

"Lessor". Section 2A-103(1)(p).

"Notifies". Section 1-201(26).

"Receipt". Section 2-103(1)(c).

"Remedy". Section 1-201(34).

"Rights". Section 1-201(36).

"Security interest". Section 1-201(37).

"Value". Section 1-201(44).

Amendment 14

Section 2A-516 of the Article is amended to read:

§ 2A-516. Effect of Acceptance of Goods; Notice of Default; Burden of Establishing Default After Acceptance; Notice of Claim or Litigation to Person Answerable Over.

(1) A lessee must pay rent for any goods accepted in accordance with the lease contract, with due allowance for goods rightfully rejected or not delivered.

(2) A lessee's acceptance of goods precludes rejection of the goods accepted. In the case of a finance lease, if made with knowledge of a nonconformity, acceptance cannot be revoked because of it. In any other case, if made with knowledge of a nonconformity, acceptance cannot be revoked because of it unless the acceptance was on the reasonable assumption that the nonconformity would be seasonably cured. Acceptance does not of itself impair any other remedy provided by this Article or the lease agreement for nonconformity.

(3) If a tender has been accepted:

(a) within a reasonable time after the lessee discovers or should have discovered any default, the lessee shall notify the lessor and the supplier, if any, or be barred from any remedy against the party not notified;

(b) except in the case of a consumer lease, within a reasonable time after the lessee receives notice of litigation for infringement or the like (Section 2A–211) the lessee shall notify the lessor or be barred from any remedy over for liability established by the litigation; and

(c) the burden is on the lessee to establish any default.

(4) If a lessee is sued for breach of a warranty or other obligation for which a lessor or a supplier is answerable over the following apply:

(a) The lessee may give the lessor or the supplier, or both, written notice of the litigation. If the notice states that the ~~lessor or the supplier~~ person notified may come in and defend and that if the ~~lessor or the supplier~~ person notified does not do so ~~he [or she]~~ that person will be bound in any action against ~~him [or her]~~ that person by the lessee by any determination of fact common to the two litigations, then unless the ~~lessor or the supplier~~ person notified after seasonable receipt of the notice does come in and defend ~~he [or she]~~ that person is so bound.

(b) The lessor or the supplier may demand in writing that the lessee turn over control of the litigation including settlement if the claim is one for infringement or the like (Section 2A–211) or else be barred from any remedy over. If the demand states that the lessor or the supplier agrees to bear all expense and to satisfy any adverse judgment, then unless the lessee after seasonable receipt of the demand does turn over control the lessee is so barred.

(5) ~~The provisions of subsections~~ Subsections (3) and (4) apply to any obligation of a lessee to hold the lessor or the supplier harmless against infringement or the like (Section 2A–211).

Official Comment

Uniform Statutory Source: Section 2–607.

Changes: Substantially revised.

Purposes:

1. Subsection (2) creates a special rule for finance leases, precluding revocation if acceptance is made with knowledge of nonconformity with respect to the lease agreement, as opposed to the supply agreement; this is not inequitable as the lessee has a direct claim against the supplier. Section 2A–209(1). Revocation of acceptance of a finance lease is permitted if the lessee's acceptance was without discovery of the nonconformity (with respect to the lease agreement, not the supply agreement) and was reasonably induced by the lessor's assurances. Section 2A–517(1)(b). Absent exclusion or modification, the lessor under a finance lease makes certain warranties to the lessee. Sections 2A–210 and 2A–211(1). Revocation of acceptance is not prohibited even after the lessee's promise has become irrevocable and independent. Section 2A–407 official comment. Where the finance lease creates a security interest, the rule may be to the contrary. *General Elec. Credit Corp. of Tennessee v. Ger–Beck Mach. Co.*, 806 F.2d 1207 (3d Cir.1986).

2. Subsection (3)(a) requires the lessee to give notice of default, within a reasonable time after the lessee discovered or should have discovered the default. ~~In all cases, notice of default must be given to the lessor. In the case of a finance lease, notice of default must be given to the lessor and the supplier. The~~ In a finance lease, notice may be given either to the supplier, the lessor, or both, but remedy is barred against the party not notified. In a finance lease, the les-

sor is usually not liable for defects in the goods and the essential notice is to the supplier. While notice to the finance lessor will often not give any additional rights to the lessee, it would be good practice to give the notice since the finance lessor has an interest in the goods. Subsection (3)(a) does not use the term finance lease, but the definition of supplier is a person from whom a lessor buys or leases goods to be leased under a finance lease. Section 2A-103(1)(x). ~~Thus, not all sellers or lessors of goods to be leased are included within the set of persons to be given notice of default, as suppliers.~~ Therefore, there can be a "supplier" only in a finance lease. Subsection (4) applies similar notice rules as to lessors and suppliers if a lessee is sued for a breach of warranty or other obligation for which a lessor or supplier is answerable over.

3. Subsection (3)(b) requires the lessee to give the lessor notice of litigation for infringement or the like. There is an exception created in the case of a consumer lease. While such an exception was considered for a finance lease, it was not created because it was not necessary—the lessor in a finance lease does not give a warranty against infringement. Section 2A-211(2). Even though not required under subsection (3)(b), the lessee who takes under a finance lease should consider giving notice of litigation for infringement or the like to the supplier, because the lessee obtains the benefit of the suppliers' promises subject to the suppliers' defenses or claims. Sections 2A-209(1) and 2-607(3)(b).

Cross References:

Sections 2-607(3)(b), 2A-103(1)(x), 2A-209(1), 2A-210, 2A-211(1), 2A-211(2), 2A-407 official comment and 2A-517(1)(b).

Definitional Cross References:

"Action". Section 1-201(1).

"Agreement". Section 1-201(3).

"Burden of establishing". Section 1-201(8).

"Conforming". Section 2A-103(1)(d).

"Consumer lease". Section 2A-103(1)(e).

"Delivery". Section 1-201(14).

"Discover". Section 1-201(25).

"Finance lease". Section 2A-103(1)(g).

"Goods". Section 2A-103(1)(h).

"Knowledge". Section 1-201(25).

"Lease agreement". Section 2A-103(1)(k).

"Lease contract". Section 2A-103(1)(*l*).

"Lessee". Section 2A-103(1)(n).

"Lessor". Section 2A-103(1)(p).

"Notice". Section 1-201(25).

"Notifies". Section 1-201(26).

"Person". Section 1-201(30).

"Reasonable time". Section 1-204(1) and (2).

"Receipt". Section 2-103(1)(c).

"Remedy". Section 1-201(34).

"Seasonably". Section 1-204(3).

"Supplier". Section 2A-103(1)(x).

"Written". Section 1-201(46).

Amendment 15

Section 2A-517 of the Article is amended to read:

§ 2A-517. Revocation of Acceptance of Goods.

(1) A lessee may revoke acceptance of a lot or commercial unit whose nonconformity substantially impairs its value to the lessee if ~~he [or she]~~ the lessee has accepted it:

(a) except in the case of a finance lease, on the reasonable assumption that its nonconformity would be cured and it has not been seasonably cured; or

(b) without discovery of the nonconformity if the lessee's acceptance was reasonably induced either by the lessor's assurances or, except in the case of a finance lease, by the difficulty of discovery before acceptance.

(2) Except in the case of a finance lease that is not a consumer lease, a lessee may revoke acceptance of a lot or commercial unit if the lessor defaults under the lease contract and the default substantially impairs the value of that lot or commercial unit to the lessee.

(3) If the lease agreement so provides, the lessee may revoke acceptance of a lot or commercial unit because of other defaults by the lessor.

~~(2)~~(4) Revocation of acceptance must occur within a reasonable time after the lessee discovers or should have discovered the ground for it and before any substantial change in condition of the goods which is not caused by the nonconformity. Revocation is not effective until the lessee notifies the lessor.

~~(3)~~(5) A lessee who so revokes has the same rights and duties with regard to the goods involved as if the lessee had rejected them.

Official Comment

Uniform Statutory Source: Section 2–608.

Changes: Revised to reflect leasing practices and terminology. Note that in the case of a finance lease the lessee retains a limited right to revoke acceptance. Sections 2A–517(1)(b) and 2A–516 official comment. New subsections (2) and (3) added.

Purposes:

1. The section states the situations under which the lessee may return the goods to the lessor and cancel the lease. Subsection (2) recognizes that the lessor may have continuing obligations under the lease and that a default as to those obligations may be sufficiently material to justify revocation of acceptance of the leased items and cancellation of the lease by the lessee. For example, a failure by the lessor to fulfill its obligation to maintain leased equipment or to supply other goods which are necessary for the operation of the leased equipment may justify revocation of acceptance and cancellation of the lease.

2. Subsection (3) specifically provides that the lease agreement may provide that the lessee can revoke acceptance for defaults by the lessor which in the absence of such an agreement might not be considered sufficiently serious to justify revocation. That is, the parties are free to contract on the question of what defaults are so material that the lessee can cancel the lease.

Cross References:

~~Sections~~ Section 2A–516 official comment ~~and 2A–517(1)(b)~~.

Definitional Cross References:

"Commercial unit". Section 2A–103(1)(c).

"Conforming". Section 2A–103(1)(d).

"Discover". Section 1–201(25).

"Finance lease". Section 2A–103(1)(g).

"Goods". Section 2A–103(1)(h).

"Lessee". Section 2A–103(1)(n).

"Lessor". Section 2A–103(1)(p).

"Lot". Section 2A–103(1)(s).

"Notifies". Section 1–201(26).

"Reasonable time". Section 1–204(1) and (2).

"Rights". Section 1–201(36).

"Seasonably". Section 1–204(3).

"Value". Section 1–201(44).

Amendment 16

Section 2A–518 of the Article is amended to read:

§ 2A–518. Cover; Substitute Goods.

(1) After a default by a lessor under the lease contract of the type described in ~~(~~Section 2A–508(1)~~)~~, or, if agreed, after other default by the lessor, the lessee may cover by making any purchase or lease of or contract to purchase or lease goods in substitution for those due from the lessor.

(2) Except as otherwise provided with respect to damages liquidated in the lease agreement (Section 2A–504) or otherwise determined ~~by~~ pursuant to agreement of the parties (~~Section~~ Sections 1–102(3) and 2A–503), if a lessee's cover is by a lease agreement substantially similar to the original lease agreement and the new lease agreement is made in good faith and in a commercially reasonable manner, the lessee may recover from the lessor as damages ~~(a)~~ (i) the present value, as of the date of ~~default~~ the commencement of the term of the new lease agreement, of ~~the difference between~~ the ~~total~~ rent ~~for the lease term of~~ under the new lease agreement ~~and~~ applicable to that period of the new lease term which is comparable to the then remaining term of the original lease agreement minus the present value as of the same date of the total rent for the then remaining lease term of the original lease agreement, and ~~(b)~~ (ii) any incidental or consequential damages, less expenses saved in consequence of the lessor's default.

(3) If a lessee's cover is by lease agreement that for any reason does not qualify for treatment under subsection (2), or is by purchase or otherwise, the lessee may recover from the lessor as if the lessee had elected not to cover and Section 2A–519 governs.

Official Comment

Uniform Statutory Source: Section 2–712.

Changes: Substantially revised.

Purposes: 1. Subsection (1) allows the lessee to take action to fix its damages after default by the lessor. Such action may consist of the ~~purchase or~~ lease of goods. The decision to cover is a function of commercial judgment, not a statutory mandate replete with sanctions for failure to comply. *Cf.* Section 9–507.

2. Subsection (2) states a rule for determining the amount of lessee's damages provided that there is no agreement to the contrary. The lessee's damages will be established using the new lease agreement as a measure if the following three criteria are met: (i) the lessee's cover is by lease agreement, (ii) the lease agreement is substantially similar to the original lease agreement, and (iii) such cover was effected in good faith, and in a commercially reasonable manner. Thus, the lessee will be entitled to recover from the lessor the present value, as of the date of ~~default~~ commencement of the term of the new lease agreement, of the ~~difference between~~ rent under the new lease agreement applicable to that period which is comparable to the then remaining term of the original lease agreement less the present value of the rent reserved for the remaining term under ~~the new lease and~~ the original lease, together with incidental or consequential damages less expenses saved in consequence of the lessor's default. ~~Note that the reference in Section 2A–518(2)(a) is to the date of default not to the date of an event of default. An event of default under a~~

~~lease agreement becomes a default under a lease agreement only after the expiration of any relevant period of grace and compliance with any notice requirements under this Article and the lease agreement. American Bar Foundation,~~ *Commentaries on Indentures*, § 5–1, at 216–217 (1971). Section 2A–501(1). This conclusion is also a function of whether, as a matter of fact or law, the event of default has been waived, suspended or cured. Sections 2A–103(4) and 1–103. ~~Consequential damages may include loss suffered by the lessee because of deprivation of the use of the goods during the period between the default and the acquisition of the goods under the new lease agreement. If the lessee's cover does not satisfy the criteria of subsection (2), Section 2A–519 governs.~~

3. Two of the three criteria to be met by the lessee are familiar, but the concept of the new lease agreement being substantially similar to the original lease agreement is not. Given the many variables facing a party who intends to lease goods and the rapidity of change in the market place, the policy decision was made not to draft with specificity. It was thought unwise to seek to establish certainty at the cost of fairness. Thus, the decision of whether the new lease agreement is substantially similar to the original will be determined case by case.

4. While the section does not draw a bright line, it is possible to describe some of the factors that should be considered in finding that a new lease agreement is substantially similar to the original. First, the goods subject to the new lease agreement should be examined. For example, in a lease of computer equipment the new lease might be for more modern equipment. However, it may be that at the time of the lessor's breach it was not possible to obtain the same type of goods in the market place. Because the lessee's remedy under Section 2A–519 is intended to place the lessee in essentially the same position as if he had covered, if goods similar to those to have been delivered under the original lease are not available, then the computer equipment in this hypothetical should qualify as a commercially reasonable substitute. *See* Section 2–712(1).

5. Second, the various elements of the new lease agreement should also be examined. Those elements include ~~the term of the new lease (because the damages are calculated under subsection (2) as the difference between the total rent payable for the entire term of the new lease agreement and the remaining term of the original lease);~~ the presence or absence of options to purchase or release; the lessor's representations, warranties and covenants to the lessee, as well as those to be provided by the lessee to the lessor; and the services, if any, to be provided by the lessor or by the lessee. All of these factors allocate cost and risk between the lessor and the lessee and thus affect the amount of rent to be paid. If the differences between the original lease and the new lease can be easily valued, it would be appropriate for a court to adjust the difference in rental to take account of the difference between the two leases, find that the new lease is substantially similar to the old lease, and award cover damages under this section. If, for example, the new lease requires the lessor to insure the goods in the hands of the lessee, while the original lease required the lessee to insure, the usual cost of such insurance could be deducted from the rent due under the new lease before determining the difference in rental between the two leases.

6. Having examined the goods and the agreement, the test to be applied is whether, in light of these comparisons, the new lease agreement is substantially similar to the original lease agreement. These findings should not be made with scientific precision, as they are a function of economics, nor should they be made independently with respect to the goods and each element of the agreement, as it is important that a sense of commercial judgment pervade the finding. To establish the new lease as a proper measure of damage under subsection (2), these factors, taken as a whole, must result in a

finding that the new lease agreement is substantially similar to the original.

7. A new lease can be substantially similar to the original lease even though its term extends beyond the remaining term of the original lease, so long as both (a) the lease terms are commercially comparable (e.g., it is highly unlikely that a one-month rental and a five-year lease would reflect similar commercial realities), and (b) the court can fairly apportion a part of the rental payments under the new lease to that part of the term of the new lease which is comparable to the remaining lease term under the original lease. Also, the lease term of the new lease may be comparable to the term of the original lease even though the beginning and ending dates of the two leases are not the same. For example, a two-month lease of agricultural equipment for the months of August and September may be comparable to a two-month lease running from the 15th of August to the 15th of October if in the particular location two-month leases beginning on August 15th are basically interchangeable with two-month leases beginning August 1st. Similarly, the term of a one-year truck lease beginning on the 15th of January may be comparable to the term of a one-year truck lease beginning January 2d. If the lease terms are found to be comparable, the court may base cover damages on the entire difference between the costs under the two leases.

Cross References:

Sections 2–712(1), 2A–519 and 9–507.

Definitional Cross References:

"Agreement". Section 1–201(3).

"Contract". Section 1–201(11).

"Good faith". Sections 1–201(19) and 2–103(1)(b).

"Goods". Section 2A–103(1)(h).

"Lease". Section 2A–103(1)(j).

"Lease agreement". Section 2A–103(1)(k).

"Lease contract". Section 2A–103(1)(*l*).

"Lessee". Section 2A–103(1)(n).

"Lessor". Section 2A–103(1)(p).

"Party". Section 1–201(29).

"Present value". Section 2A–103(1)(u).

"Purchase". Section 2A–103(1)(v).

Amendment 17

Section 2A–519 of the Article is amended to read:

§ 2A–519. Lessee's Damages for Non-Delivery, Repudiation, Default, and Breach of Warranty in Regard to Accepted Goods.

(1) Except as otherwise provided with respect to damages liquidated in the lease agreement (Section 2A–504) or otherwise determined ~~by~~ pursuant to agreement of the parties (~~Section~~ Sections 1–102(3) and 2A–503), if a lessee elects not to cover or a lessee elects to cover and the cover is by lease agreement that for any reason does not qualify for treatment under Section 2A–518(2), or is by purchase or otherwise, the measure of damages for non-delivery or repudiation by the lessor or for rejection or revocation of acceptance by the lessee is the present value, as of the date of the default, of the ~~difference between the~~ then market rent ~~and~~ minus the present value as of the same date of the original rent, computed for the remaining lease term of the original lease agreement, together with incidental and consequential damages, less expenses saved in consequence of the lessor's default.

(2) Market rent is to be determined as of the place for tender or, in cases of rejection after arrival or revocation of acceptance, as of the place of arrival.

(3) ~~If~~ Except as otherwise agreed, if the lessee has accepted goods and given notification (Section 2A–516(3)), the measure of damages for non-conforming tender or delivery or other default by a lessor is the loss resulting in the ordinary course of events from the lessor's default as determined in any manner that is reasonable together with incidental and consequential damages, less expenses saved in consequence of the lessor's default.

(4) ~~The~~ Except as otherwise agreed, the measure of damages for breach of warranty is the present value at the time and place of acceptance of the difference between the value of the use of the goods accepted and the value if they had been as warranted for the lease term, unless special circumstances show proximate damages of a different amount, together with incidental and consequential damages, less expenses saved in consequence of the lessor's default or breach of warranty.

Official Comment

Uniform Statutory Source: Sections 2–713 and 2–714.

Changes: Substantially revised.

Purposes:

1. Subsection (1), a revised version of the provisions of Section 2–713(1), states the basic rule governing the measure of lessee's damages for non-delivery or repudiation by the lessor or for rightful rejection or revocation of acceptance by the lessee. This measure will apply, absent agreement to the contrary, if the lessee does not cover or if the cover does not qualify under Section 2A–518. There is no sanction for cover that does not qualify.

2. The measure of damage is the present value, as of the date of default, of the ~~difference between~~ market rent ~~and~~ for the remaining term of the lease less the present value of the original rent for the remaining term of the lease, plus incidental and consequential damages less expenses saved in consequence of the default. Note that the reference in Section 2A–519(1) is to the date of default not to the date of an event of default. An event of default under a lease agreement becomes a default under a lease agreement only after the expiration of any relevant period of grace and compliance with any notice requirements under this Article and the lease agreement. American Bar Foundation, *Commentaries on Indentures*, § 5–1, at 216–217 (1971). Section 2A–501(1). This conclusion is also a function of whether, as a matter of fact or law, the event of default has been waived, suspended or cured. Sections 2A–103(4) and 1–103.

3. Subsection (2), a revised version of the provisions of Section 2–713(2), states the rule with respect to determining market rent.

4. Subsection (3), a revised version of the provisions of Section 2–714(1) and (3), states the measure of damages where goods have been accepted and acceptance is not revoked. The subsection applies both to defaults which occur at the inception of the lease and to defaults which occur subsequently, such as failure to comply with an obligation to maintain the leased goods. The measure in essence is the loss, in the ordinary course of events, flowing from the default.

5. Subsection (4), a revised version of the provisions of Section 2–714(2), states the measure of damages for breach of warranty. The measure in essence is the present value of the difference between the value of the goods accepted and of the goods if they had been as warranted.

6. Subsections (1), (3) and (4) specifically state that the parties may by contract vary the damages rules stated in those subsections.

Cross References:

Sections 2-713(1), 2-713(2), 2-714 and Section 2A-518.

Definitional Cross References:

"Conforming". Section 2A-103(1)(d).

"Delivery". Section 1-201(14).

"Goods". Section 2A-103(1)(h).

"Lease". Section 2A-103(1)(j).

"Lease agreement". Section 2A-103(1)(k).

"Lessee". Section 2A-103(1)(n).

"Lessor". Section 2A-103(1)(p).

"Notification". Section 1-201(26).

"Present value". Section 2A-103(1)(u).

"Value". Section 1-201(44).

Amendment 18

Section 2A-523 of the Article is amended to read:

§ 2A-523. Lessor's Remedies.

(1) If a lessee wrongfully rejects or revokes acceptance of goods or fails to make a payment when due or repudiates with respect to a part or the whole, then, with respect to any goods involved, and with respect to all of the goods if under an installment lease contract the value of the whole lease contract is substantially impaired (Section 2A-510), the lessee is in default under the lease contract and the lessor may:

(a) cancel the lease contract (Section 2A-505(1));

(b) proceed respecting goods not identified to the lease contract (Section 2A-524);

(c) withhold delivery of the goods and take possession of goods previously delivered (Section 2A-525);

(d) stop delivery of the goods by any bailee (Section 2A-526);

(e) dispose of the goods and recover damages (Section 2A-527), or retain the goods and recover damages (Section 2A-528), or in a proper case recover rent (Section 2A-529).;

(f) exercise any other rights or pursue any other remedies provided in the lease contract.

(2) If a lessor does not fully exercise a right or obtain a remedy to which the lessor is entitled under subsection (1), the lessor may recover the loss resulting in the ordinary course of events from the lessee's default as determined in any reasonable manner, together with incidental damages, less expenses saved in consequence of the lessee's default.

~~(2)~~(3) If a lessee is otherwise in default under a lease contract, the lessor may exercise the rights and pursue the remedies provided in the lease contract ~~and this Article~~, which may include a right to cancel the lease. In addition, unless otherwise provided in the lease contract:

(a) if the default substantially impairs the value of the lease contract to the lessor, the lessor may exercise the rights and pursue the remedies provided in subsections (1) or (2); or

(b) if the default does not substantially impair the value of the lease contract to the lessor, the lessor may recover as provided in subsection (2).

Official Comment

Uniform Statutory Source: Section 2-703.

Changes: Substantially revised.

Purposes:

1. ~~This section~~ Subsection (1) is an index to Sections 2A-524 through 2A-531 and ~~their effect on the lessor's rights and remedies upon the lessee's default~~ states that the remedies provided in those sections are available for the defaults referred to in subsection (1): wrongful rejection or revocation of acceptance, failure to make a payment when due, or repudiation. In addition, remedies provided in the lease contract are available. Subsection (2) sets out a remedy if the lessor does not pursue to completion a right or actually obtain a remedy available under subsection (1), and subsection (3) sets out statutory remedies for defaults not specifically referred to in subsection (1). Subsection (3) provides that, if any default by the lessee other than those specifically referred to in subsection (1) is material, the lessor can exercise the remedies provided in subsection (1) or (2); otherwise the available remedy is as provided in subsection (3). A lessor who has brought an action seeking or has nonjudicially pursued one or more of the remedies available under subsection (1) may amend so as to claim or may nonjudicially pursue a remedy under subsection (2) unless the right or remedy first chosen has been pursued to an extent actually inconsistent with the new course of action. The intent of the provision is to reject the doctrine of election of remedies and to permit an alteration of course by the lessor unless such alteration would actually have an effect on the lessee that would be unreasonable under the circumstances. Further, the lessor may pursue remedies under both subsections (1) and (2) unless doing so would put the lessor in a better position than it would have been in had the lessee fully performed.

2. The lessor and the lessee can agree ~~otherwise~~ to modify the rights and remedies available under the Article; ~~thus, the parties~~ they can, among other things, ~~raise or lower the threshold that gives rise to lessee's default or~~ provide that for defaults other than those specified in subsection (1) the lessor can exercise the rights and remedies referred to in subsection (1), whether or not the default would otherwise be held to substantially impair the value of the lease contract to the lessor; they can also create a new scheme of rights and remedies triggered by the occurrence of the default. Sections 2A-103(4) and 1-102(3).

3. Subsection (1), a substantially rewritten version of Section 2-703, lists various cumulative remedies of the lessor where the lessee wrongfully rejects or revokes acceptance, fails to make a payment when due, or repudiates. Section ~~2A-501(4)~~ 2A-501(2) and (4). The subsection also allows the lessor to exercise any contractual remedy.

4. This Article rejects ~~the~~ any general doctrine of election of remedy. Whether, in a particular case, one remedy bars another, is a function of whether lessor has been put in as good a position as if the lessee had fully performed the lease contract. Multiple remedies are barred only if the effect is to put the lessor in a better position than it would have been in had the lessee fully performed under the lease. Sections 2A-103(4), 2A-501(4), and 1-106(1).

5. Hypothetical: ~~1.~~ To better understand the application of subparagraphs (a) through (e), it is useful to review a hypothetical. Assume that A is a merchant in the business of selling and leasing new bicycles of various types. B is about to engage in the business of subleasing bicycles to summer residents of and visitors to an island resort. A, as lessor, has agreed to lease 60 bicycles to B. While there is one master lease, deliv-

eries and terms are staggered. 20 bicycles are to be delivered by A to B's island location on June 1; the term of the lease of these bicycles is four months. 20 bicycles are to be delivered by A to B's island location on July 1; the term of the lease of these bicycles is three months. Finally, 20 bicycles are to be delivered by A to B's island location on August 1; the term of the lease of these bicycles is two months. B is obligated to pay rent to A on the 15th day of each month during the term for the lease. Rent is $50 per month, per bicycle. B has no option to purchase or release and must return the bicycles to A at the end of the term, in good condition, reasonable wear and tear excepted. Since the retail price of each bicycle is $400 and bicycles used in the retail rental business have a useful economic life of 36 months, this transaction creates a lease. Sections 2A–103(1)(j) and 1–201(37).

~~2.~~6. A's current inventory of bicycles is not large. Thus, upon signing the lease with B in February, A agreed to purchase 60 new bicycles from A's principal manufacturer, with special instructions to drop ship the bicycles to B's island location in accordance with the delivery schedule set forth in the lease.

~~3.~~7. The first shipment of 20 bicycles was received by B on May 21. B inspected the bicycles, accepted the same as conforming to the lease and signed a receipt of delivery and acceptance. However, due to poor weather that summer, business was terrible and B was unable to pay the rent due on June 15. Pursuant to the lease A sent B notice of default and proceeded to enforce his rights and remedies against B.

~~4.~~8. A's counsel first advised A that under Section 2A–510(2) and the terms of the lease B's failure to pay was a default with respect to the whole. Thus, to minimize A's continued exposure, A was advised to take possession of the bicycles. If A had possession of the goods A could refuse to deliver. Section 2A–525(1). However, the facts here are different. With respect to the bicycles in B's possession, A has the right to take possession of the bicycles, without breach of the peace. Section 2A–525(2). If B refuses to allow A access to the bicycles, A can proceed by action, including replevin or injunctive relief.

~~5.~~9. With respect to the 40 bicycles that have not been delivered, this Article provides various alternatives. First, assume that 20 of the remaining 40 bicycles have been manufactured and delivered by the manufacturer to a carrier for shipment to B. Given the size of the shipment, the carrier was using a small truck for the delivery and the truck had not yet reached the island ferry when the manufacturer (at the request of A) instructed the carrier to divert the shipment to A's place of business. A's right to stop delivery is recognized under these circumstances. Section 2A–526(1). Second, assume that the 20 remaining bicycles were in the process of manufacture when B defaulted. A retains the right (as between A as lessor and B as lessee) to exercise reasonable commercial judgment whether to complete manufacture or to dispose of the unfinished goods for scrap. Since A is not the manufacturer and A has a binding contract to buy the bicycles, A elected to allow the manufacturer to complete the manufacture of the bicycles, but instructed the manufacturer to deliver the completed bicycles to A's place of business. Section 2A–524(2).

~~6.~~10. Thus, so far A has elected to exercise the remedies referred to in subparagraphs (b) through (d) in subsection (1). None of these remedies bars any of the others because A's election and enforcement merely resulted in A's possession of the bicycles. Had B performed A would have recovered possession of the bicycles. Thus A is in the process of obtaining the benefit of his bargain. Note that A could exercise any other rights or pursue any other remedies provided in the lease contract (Section 2A–523(1)(f)), or elect to recover his loss due to the lessee's default under Section 2A–523(2).

~~7.~~11. A's counsel next would determine what action, if any, should be taken with respect to the goods. As stated in subparagraph (e) and as discussed fully in Section 2A–527(1) the lessor may, but has no obligation to, dispose of the goods by ~~lease, sale or otherwise~~ a substantially similar lease (indeed, the lessor has no obligation whatsoever to dispose of the goods at all) and recover damages based on that action, but lessor will not be able to recover damages which put it in a better position than performance would have done, nor will it be able to recover damages for losses which it could have reasonably avoided. In this case, since A is in the business of leasing and selling bicycles, A will probably inventory the 60 bicycles for its retail trade.

~~8.~~12. A's counsel then will determine which of the various~~, alternate~~ means of ascertaining A's ~~claim for~~ damages against B ~~will be computed~~ are available. Subparagraph (e) catalogues each relevant section. First, under Section 2A–527(2) the amount of A's claim ~~will be~~ is computed by comparing the original lease between A and B with any subsequent lease of the bicycles but only if the subsequent lease is substantially similar to the original lease contract. While the section does not define this term, the official comment does establish some parameters. If, however, A elects to lease the bicycles to his retail trade, it is unlikely that the resulting lease will be substantially similar to the original, as leases to retail customers are considerably different from leases to wholesale customers like B. If, however, the leases were substantially similar, the damage claim is for accrued and unpaid rent to the beginning of the new lease, plus the present value as of the same date, of the ~~difference between the~~ rent reserved under ~~both leases for the balance of their terms~~ the original lease for the balance of its term less the present value as of the same date of the rent reserved under the replacement lease for a term comparable to the balance of the term of the original lease, together with incidental damages less expenses saved in consequence of the lessee's default.

~~9.~~13. If the new lease is not substantially similar or if A elects to sell the bicycles or to hold the bicycles, damages are computed under Section 2A–528 or 2A–529.

~~10.~~14. If A elects to pursue his claim under Section 2A–528(1) the damage rule is the same as that stated in Section 2A–527(2) except that damages are measured from default if the lessee never took possession of the goods or from the time when the lessor did or could have regained possession and that the standard of comparison is not the rent reserved under a substantially similar lease entered into by the lessor but a market rent, as defined in Section 2A–507. Further, if the facts of this hypothetical were more elaborate A may be able to establish that the measure of damage under subsection (1) is inadequate to put him in the same position that B's performance would have, in which case A can claim the present value of his lost profits.

~~11.~~15. Yet another alternative for computing A's damage claim against B which will be available in some situations is ~~prescribed by~~ recovery of the present value, as of entry of judgment, of the rent for the then remaining lease term under Section 2A–529. However, ~~to use this formula A must, among other things, hold the bicycles identified in the lease contract for B. Since this would include all 60 bicycles and A is a merchant, it is unlikely to occur. Further, subsection (1)(a), which in essence allows A to receive the present value of the rent reserved under the lease, would in this case apply only to the 20 bicycles accepted by B in May. With respect to~~ this formulation is not available if the goods have been repossessed or tendered back to A. For the 20 bicycles repossessed and the remaining 40 bicycles, ~~subsection 1(b) will apply~~ A will be able to recover the present value of the rent only if A is unable to dispose of them, or circumstances indicate the effort will be unavailing~~, in which case the damage formula identical to the one set forth in (1)(a) will apply~~. ~~At~~ If A has prevailed in an action for the rent, at any time up to collection of a judgment by A against B, A ~~may~~ might dispose of the bicycles. In such case A's claim for damages against B is governed by Section 2A–527 or 2A–528. Section 2A–529(3). The resulting recalculation of claim should reduce the amount recoverable by A against B and the lessor is required to cause an appropriate credit to be entered against the earlier judgment. However, the nature of the post-judgment proceedings to resolve this issue, and the sanctions for ~~abuse~~ a failure to comply, if any, will be determined by other law.

~~12.~~16. Finally, if the lease agreement had so provided pursuant to subparagraph (f), A's claim against B would not be determined under any of these statutory formulae, but pursuant to a liquidated damages clause. Section 2A–504(1).

~~13.~~17. These various methods of computing A's damage claim against B are alternatives subject to Section 2A–501(4). However, the pursuit of any one of these alternatives is not a bar to, nor has it been barred by, A's earlier action to obtain possession of the 60 bicycles. These formulae, which vary as a function of an overt or implied mitigation of damage theory, focus on allowing A a recovery of the benefit of his bargain with B. Had B performed, A would have received the rent as well as the return of the 60 bicycles at the end of the term.

~~14.~~18. Finally, A's counsel should also advise A of his right to cancel the lease contract under subparagraph (a). Section 2A–505(1). Cancellation will discharge all existing obligations but preserve A's rights and remedies.

19. Subsection (2) recognizes that a lessor who is entitled to exercise the rights or to obtain a remedy granted by subsection (1) may choose not to do so. In such cases, the lessor can recover damages as provided in subsection (2). For example, for nonpayment of rent, the lessor may decide not to take possession of the goods and cancel the lease, but rather to merely sue for the unpaid rent as it comes due plus lost interest or other damages "determined in any reasonable manner." Subsection (2) also negates any loss of alternative rights and remedies by reason of having invoked or commenced the exercise or pursuit of any one or more rights or remedies.

~~15.~~20. Subsection ~~(2) is new and~~ (3) allows the lessor access to ~~the~~ a remedy scheme ~~of~~ provided in this Article as well as that contained in the lease contract if the lessee is in default for reasons other than those stated in subsection (1). Note that the reference to this Article includes supplementary principles of law and equity, *e.g.*, fraud, misrepresentation and duress. Sections 2A–103(4) and 1–103.

~~16.~~21. There is no special treatment of the finance lease in this section. Absent supplementary principles of law to the contrary, in most cases the supplier will have no rights or remedies against the defaulting lessee. Section ~~2A–209(2)(b)~~ 2A–209(2)(ii). Given that the supplier will look to the lessor for payment, this is appropriate. However, there is a specific exception to this rule with respect to the right to identify goods to the lease contract. Section 2A–524(2). The parties are free to create a different result in a particular case. Sections 2A–103(4) and 1–102(3).

Cross References:

Sections 1–102(3), 1–103, 1–106(1), 1–201(37), 2–703, 2A–103(1)(j), 2A–103(4), ~~2A–209(2)(b)~~ 2A–209(2)(ii), 2A–501(4), 2A–504(1), 2A–505(1), 2A–507, 2A–510(2), 2A–524 through 2A–531, 2A–524(2), 2A–525(1), 2A–525(2), 2A–526(1), 2A–527(1), 2A–527(2), 2A–528(1) and 2A–529(3).

Definitional Cross References:

"Delivery". Section 1–201(14).

"Goods". Section 2A–103(1)(h).

"Installment lease contract". Section 2A–103(1)(i).

"Lease contract". Section 2A–103(1)(*l*).

"Lessee". Section 2A–103(1)(n).

"Lessor". Section 2A–103(1)(p).

"Remedy". Section 1–201(34).

"Rights". Section 1–201(36).

"Value". Section 1–201(44).

Amendment 19

Section 2A-524 of the Article is amended to read:

§ 2A-524. Lessor's Right to Identify Goods to Lease Contract.

(1) ~~A lessor aggrieved under Section 2A-523(1)~~ After default by the lessee under the lease contract of the type described in Section 2A-523(1) or 2A-523(3)(a) or, if agreed, after other default by the lessee, the lessor may:

(a) identify to the lease contract conforming goods not already identified if at the time the lessor learned of the default they were in the lessor's or the supplier's possession or control; and

(b) dispose of goods (Section 2A-527(1)) that demonstrably have been intended for the particular lease contract even though those goods are unfinished.

(2) If the goods are unfinished, in the exercise of reasonable commercial judgment for the purposes of avoiding loss and of effective realization, an aggrieved lessor or the supplier may either complete manufacture and wholly identify the goods to the lease contract or cease manufacture and lease, sell, or otherwise dispose of the goods for scrap or salvage value or proceed in any other reasonable manner.

Official Comment

Uniform Statutory Source: Section 2-704.

Changes: Revised to reflect leasing practices and terminology.

Purposes: The remedies provided by this section are available to the lessor (i) if there has been a default by the lessee which falls within Section 2A-523(1) or 2A-523(3)(a), or (ii) if there has been any other default for which the lease contract gives the lessor the remedies provided by this section. Under "(ii)", the lease contract may give the lessor the remedies of identification and disposition provided by this section in various ways. For example, a lease provision might specifically refer to the remedies of identification and disposition, or it might refer to this section by number (*i.e.,* 2A-524), or it might do so by a more general reference such as "all rights and remedies provided by Article 2A for default by the lessee."

Definitional Cross References:

"Aggrieved party". Section 1-201(2).

"Conforming". Section 2A-103(1)(d).

"Goods". Section 2A-103(1)(h).

"Learn". Section 1-201(25).

"Lease". Section 2A-103(1)(j).

"Lease contract". Section 2A-103(1)(*l*).

"Lessor". Section 2A-103(1)(p).

"Rights". Section 1-201(36).

"Supplier". Section 2A-103(1)(x).

"Value". Section 1-201(44).

Amendment 20

Section 2A-525 of the Article is amended to read:

§ 2A-525. Lessor's Right to Possession of Goods.

(1) If a lessor discovers the lessee to be insolvent, the lessor may refuse to deliver the goods.

(2) ~~The lessor has on~~ After a default by the lessee under the lease contract of the type described in Section 2A–523(1) or 2A–523(3)(a) or, if agreed, after other default by the lessee, the lessor has the right to take possession of the goods. If the lease contract so provides, the lessor may require the lessee to assemble the goods and make them available to the lessor at a place to be designated by the lessor which is reasonably convenient to both parties. Without removal, the lessor may render unusable any goods employed in trade or business, and may dispose of goods on the lessee's premises (Section 2A–527).

(3) The lessor may proceed under subsection (2) without judicial process if ~~that~~ it can be done without breach of the peace or the lessor may proceed by action.

Official Comment

Uniform Statutory Source: ~~Section~~ Sections 2–702(1) and 9–503.

Changes: Substantially revised.

Purposes:

1. Subsection (1), a revised version of the provisions of Section 2–702(1), allows the lessor to refuse to deliver goods if the lessee is insolvent. Note that the provisions of Section 2–702(2), granting the unpaid seller certain rights of reclamation, were not incorporated in this section. Subsection (2) made this unnecessary.

2. Subsection (2), a revised version of the provisions of Section 9–503, allows the lessor, on a Section 2A–523(1) or 2A–523(3)(a) default by the lessee, the right to take possession of or reclaim the goods~~;~~. Also, the lessor can contract for the right to take possession of the goods for other defaults by the lessee. Therefore, since the lessee's insolvency is an event of default in a standard lease agreement, subsection (2) is the functional equivalent of Section 2–702(2). Further, subsection (2) sanctions the classic crate and delivery clause obligating the lessee to assemble the goods and to make them available to the lessor. Finally, the lessor may leave the goods in place, render them unusable (if they are goods employed in trade or business), and dispose of them on the lessee's premises.

3. Subsection (3), a revised version of the provisions of Section 9–503, allows the lessor to proceed under subsection (2) without judicial process, absent breach of the peace, or by action. Sections 2A–501(3), 2A–103(4) and 1–201(1). In the appropriate case action includes injunctive relief. *Clark Equip. Co. v. Armstrong Equip. Co.,* 431 F.2d 54 (5th Cir. 1970), *cert. denied,* 402 U.S. 909, 91 S.Ct. 1382, 28 L.Ed.2d 650 (1971). This Section, as well as a number of other Sections in this Part, are included in the Article to codify the lessor's common law right to protect the lessor's reversionary interest in the goods. Section 2A–103(1)(q). These Sections are intended to supplement and not displace principles of law and equity with respect to the protection of such interest. Sections 2A–103(4) and 1–103. Such principles apply in many instances, *e.g.,* loss or damage to goods if risk of loss passes to the lessee, failure of the lessee to return goods to the lessor in the condition stipulated in the lease, and refusal of the lessee to return goods to the lessor after termination or cancellation of the lease. See also Section 2A–532.

Cross References:

Sections 1–106(2), 2–702(1), 2–702(2), 2A–103(4), 2A–501(3), 2A–532 and 9–503.

Definitional Cross References:

"Action". Section 1–201(1).

"Delivery". Section 1–201(14).

"Discover". Section 1–201(25).

"Goods". Section 2A–103(1)(h).

"Insolvent". Section 1–201(23).

"Lease contract". Section 2A–103(1)(*l*).

"Lessee". Section 2A–103(1)(n).

"Lessor". Section 2A–103(1)(p).

"Party". Section 1–201(29).

"Rights". Section 1–201(36).

Amendment 21

Section 2A–527 of the Article is amended to read:

§ 2A–527. Lessor's Rights to Dispose of Goods.

(1) After a default by a lessee under the lease contract of the type described in ~~(~~Section 2A–523(1)~~)~~ or 2A–523(3)(a) or after the lessor refuses to deliver or takes possession of goods (Section 2A–525 or 2A–526), or, if agreed, after other default by a lessee, the lessor may dispose of the goods concerned or the undelivered balance thereof by lease, sale, or otherwise.

(2) Except as otherwise provided with respect to damages liquidated in the lease agreement (Section 2A–504) or otherwise determined ~~by~~ pursuant to agreement of the parties (~~Section~~ Sections 1–102(3) and 2A–503), if the disposition is by lease agreement substantially similar to the original lease agreement and the new lease agreement is made in good faith and in a commercially reasonable manner, the lessor may recover from the lessee as damages ~~(a)~~ (i) accrued and unpaid rent as of the date of ~~default~~ the commencement of the term of the new lease agreement, ~~(b)~~ (ii) the present value, as of the same date, ~~of default~~ of the ~~difference between the~~ total rent for the then remaining lease term of the original lease agreement ~~and the total rent for the lease term~~ minus the present value, as of the same date, of the rent under the new lease agreement applicable to that period of the new lease term which is comparable to the then remaining term of the original lease agreement, and ~~(c)~~ (iii) any incidental damages allowed under Section 2A–530, less expenses saved in consequence of the lessee's default.

(3) If the lessor's disposition is by lease agreement that for any reason does not qualify for treatment under subsection (2), or is by sale or otherwise, the lessor may recover from the lessee as if the lessor had elected not to dispose of the goods and Section 2A–528 governs.

(4) A subsequent buyer or lessee who buys or leases from the lessor in good faith for value as a result of a disposition under this section takes the goods free of the original lease contract and any rights of the original lessee even though the lessor fails to comply with one or more of the requirements of this Article.

(5) The lessor is not accountable to the lessee for any profit made on any disposition. A lessee who has rightfully rejected or justifiably revoked acceptance shall account to the lessor for any excess over the amount of the lessee's security interest (Section 2A–508(5)).

Official Comment

Uniform Statutory Source: Section 2–706(1), (5) and (6).

Changes: Substantially revised.

Purposes:

1. Subsection (1), a revised version of the first sentence of subsection 2–706(1),

allows the lessor the right to dispose of goods after a statutory or other material default by the lessee (even if the goods remain in the lessee's possession—Section 2A–525(2)), ~~or~~ after the lessor refuses to deliver or takes possession of the goods, or, if agreed, after other contractual default. The lessor's decision to exercise this right is a function of a commercial judgment, not a statutory mandate replete with sanctions for failure to comply. Cf. Section 9–507. As the owner of the goods, in the case of a lessor, or as the prime lessee of the goods, in the case of a sublessor, compulsory disposition of the goods is inconsistent with the nature of the interest held by the lessor or the sublessor and is not necessary because the interest held by the lessee or the sublessee is not protected by a right of redemption under the common law or this Article. Subsection 2A–527(5).

2. The rule for determining the measure of damages recoverable by the lessor against the lessee is a function of several variables. If the lessor has elected to effect disposition under subsection (1) and such disposition is by lease that qualifies under subsection (2), the measure of damages set forth in subsection (2) will apply, absent agreement to the contrary. Sections 2A–504, 2A–103(4) and 1–102(3).

3. The lessor's damages will be established using the new lease agreement as a measure if the following three criteria are satisfied: (i) the lessor disposed of the goods by lease, (ii) the lease agreement is substantially similar to the original lease agreement, and (iii) such disposition was in good faith, and in a commercially reasonable manner. Thus, the lessor will be entitled to recover from the lessee the accrued and unpaid rent as of the date of ~~default~~ commencement of the term of the new lease, and the present value, as of the same date ~~of default~~, of the ~~difference between the~~ rent ~~reserved~~ under ~~the new lease and~~ the original lease for the then remaining term less the present value as of the same date of the rent under the new lease agreement applicable to the period of the new lease comparable to the remaining term under the original lease, together with incidental damages less expenses saved in consequence of the lessee's default. If the lessor's disposition does not satisfy the criteria of subsection (2), the lessor may calculate its claim against the lessee pursuant to Section 2A–528. Section 2A–523(1)(e). ~~Note that the reference in Section 2A–527(2)(a) and (b) is to the date of default not to the date of an event of default. An event of default under a lease agreement becomes a default under a lease agreement only after the expiration of any relevant period of grace and compliance with any notice requirements under this Article and the lease agreement. American Bar Foundation,~~ *Commentaries on Indentures*, § 5–1, at 216–217 (1971). Section 2A–501(1). This conclusion is also a function of whether, as a matter of fact or law, the event of default has been waived, suspended or cured. Sections 2A–103(4) and 1–103.

4. Two of the three criteria to be met by the lessor are familiar, but the concept of the new lease agreement that is substantially similar to the original lease agreement is not. Given the many variables facing a party who intends to lease goods and the rapidity of change in the market place, the policy decision was made not to draft with specificity. It was thought unwise to seek to establish certainty at the cost of fairness. The decision of whether the new lease agreement is substantially similar to the original will be determined case by case.

5. While the section does not draw a bright line, it is possible to describe some of the factors that should be considered in a finding that a new lease agreement is substantially similar to the original. The various elements of the new lease agreement should be examined. Those elements include ~~the term of the new lease (because the damages are calculated under subsection (2) as the difference between the total rent payable for the entire term of the new lease agreement and the remaining lease term of the original lease);~~ the options to purchase or release; the lessor's representations, warranties and covenants to the lessee as well as

those to be provided by the lessee to the lessor; and the services, if any, to be provided by the lessor or by the lessee. All of these factors allocate cost and risk between the lessor and the lessee and thus affect the amount of rent to be paid. These findings should not be made with scientific precision, as they are a function of economics, nor should they be made independently, as it is important that a sense of commercial judgment pervade the finding. *See* Section 2A–507(2). To establish the new lease as a proper measure of damage under subsection (2), these various factors, taken as a whole, must result in a finding that the new lease agreement is substantially similar to the original. If the differences between the original lease and the new lease can be easily valued, it would be appropriate for a court to find that the new lease is substantially similar to the old lease, adjust the difference in the rent between the two leases to take account of the differences, and award damages under this section. If, for example, the new lease requires the lessor to insure the goods in the hands of the lessee, while the original lease required the lessee to insure, the usual cost of such insurance could be deducted from rent due under the new lease before the difference in rental between the two leases is determined.

6. The following hypothetical illustrates the difficulty of providing a bright line. Assume that A buys a jumbo tractor for $1 million and then leases the tractor to B for a term of 36 months. The tractor is delivered to and is accepted by B on May 1. On June 1 B fails to pay the monthly rent to A. B returns the tractor to A, who immediately releases the tractor to C for a term identical to the term remaining under the lease between A and B. All terms and conditions under the lease between A and C are identical to those under the original lease between A and B, except that C does not provide any property damage or other insurance coverage, and B agreed to provide complete coverage. Coverage is expensive and difficult to obtain. ~~The new lease should be viewed as not substantially similar to the original. However, if the lessor seeks a recovery under Section 2A–528 the new lease can be introduced into evidence to establish market rent (Section 2A–507), with a proper allowance for the lessor's cost of replacing the lost insurance coverage~~ It is a question of fact whether it is so difficult to adjust the recovery to take account of the difference between the two leases as to insurance that the second lease is not substantially similar to the original.

7. A new lease can be substantially similar to the original lease even though its term extends beyond the remaining term of the original lease, so long as both (a) the lease terms are commercially comparable (e.g., it is highly unlikely that a one-month rental and a five-year lease would reflect similar realities), and (b) the court can fairly apportion a part of the rental payments under the new lease to that part of the term of the new lease which is comparable to the remaining lease term under the original lease. Also, the lease term of the new lease may be comparable to the remaining term of the original lease even though the beginning and ending dates of the two leases are not the same. For example, a two-month lease of agricultural equipment for the months of August and September may be comparable to a two-month lease running from the 15th of August to the 15th of October if in the particular location two-month leases beginning on August 15th are basically interchangeable with two-month leases beginning August 1st. Similarly, the term of a one-year truck lease beginning on the 15th of January may be comparable to the term of a one-year truck lease beginning January 2d. If the lease terms are found to be comparable, the court may base cover damages on the entire difference between the costs under the two leases.

8. Subsection (3), which is new, provides that if the lessor's disposition is by lease that does not qualify under subsection (2), or is by sale or otherwise, Section 2A–528 governs.

9. Subsection (4), a revised version of subsection 2-706(5), applies to protect a subsequent buyer or lessee who buys or leases from the lessor in good faith and for value, pursuant to a disposition under this section. Note that by its terms, the rule in subsection 2A-304(1), which provides that the subsequent lessee takes subject to the original lease contract, is controlled by the rule stated in this subsection.

10. Subsection (5), a revised version of subsection 2-706(6), provides that the lessor is not accountable to the lessee for any profit made by the lessor on a disposition. This rule follows from the fundamental premise of the bailment for hire that the lessee under a lease of goods has no equity of redemption to protect.

Cross References:

Sections 1-102(3), 2-706(1), 2-706(5), 2-706(6), 2A-103(4), 2A-304(1), 2A-504, 2A-507(2), 2A-523(1)(e), 2A-525(2), 2A-527(5), 2A-528 and 9-507.

Definitional Cross References:

"Buyer" and "Buying". Section 2-103(1)(a).

"Delivery". Section 1-201(14).

"Good faith". Sections 1-201(19) and 2-103(1)(b).

"Goods". Section 2A-103(1)(h).

"Lease". Section 2A-103(1)(j).

"Lease contract". Section 2A-103(1)(*l*).

"Lessee". Section 2A-103(1)(n).

"Lessor". Section 2A-103(1)(p).

"Present value". Section 2A-103(1)(u).

"Rights". Section 1-201(36).

"Sale". Section 2-106(1).

"Security interest". Section 1-201(37).

"Value". Section 1-201(44).

Amendment 22

Section 2A-528 of the Article is amended to read:

§ 2A-528. Lessor's Damages For Non-acceptance ~~or~~, Failure to Pay, Repudiation, or Other Default.

(1) Except as otherwise provided with respect to damages liquidated in the lease agreement (Section 2A-504) or otherwise determined ~~by~~ pursuant to agreement of the parties (~~Section~~ Sections 1-102(3) and 2A-503), if a lessor elects to retain the goods or a lessor elects to dispose of the goods and the disposition is by lease agreement that for any reason does not qualify for treatment under Section 2A-527(2), or is by sale or otherwise, the lessor may recover from the lessee as damages for ~~non-acceptance or repudiation by~~ a default of the type described in Section 2A-523(1) or 2A-523(3)(a), or, if agreed, for other default of the lessee, ~~(a)~~ (i) accrued and unpaid rent as of the date of default if the lessee has never taken possession of the goods, or, if the lessee has taken possession of the goods, as of the date the lessor repossesses the goods or an earlier date on which the lessee makes a tender of the goods to the lessor, ~~(b)~~ (ii) the present value as of the date ~~of default~~ determined under clause (i) of the ~~difference between the~~ total rent for the then remaining lease term of the original lease agreement ~~and~~ minus the present value as of the same date of the market rent at the ~~time and~~ place ~~for tender~~ where the goods are located computed for the same lease term, and ~~(c)~~ (iii) any incidental damages allowed under Section 2A-530, less expenses saved in consequence of the lessee's default.

(2) If the measure of damages provided in subsection (1) is inadequate to put a lessor in as good a position as performance would have, the measure of damages is the present value of the profit, including reasonable overhead, the lessor would have made from full performance by the lessee, together with any incidental damages allowed under Section 2A–530, due allowance for costs reasonably incurred and due credit for payments or proceeds of disposition.

Official Comment

Uniform Statutory Source: Section 2–708.

Changes: Substantially revised.

Purposes:

1. Subsection (1), a substantially revised version of Section 2–708(1), states the basic rule governing the measure of lessor's damages for ~~non-acceptance or repudiation by the lessee; repudiation is defined (Section 2A–402) to include the lessee's post acceptance default for failure to pay rent and the like.~~ a default described in Section 2A–523(1) or (3)(a), and, if agreed, for a contractual default. This measure will apply if the lessor elects to retain the goods (whether undelivered, returned by the lessee, or repossessed by the lessor after acceptance and default by the lessee) or if the lessor's disposition does not qualify under subsection 2A–527(2). Section 2A–527(3). Note that under some of these conditions, the lessor may recover damages from the lessee pursuant to the rule set forth in Section 2A–529. There is no sanction for disposition that does not qualify under subsection 2A–527(2). Application of the rule set forth in this section is subject to agreement to the contrary. Sections 2A–504, 2A–103(4) and 1–102(3).

2. ~~The~~ If the lessee has never taken possession of the goods, the measure of damage is the accrued and unpaid rent as of the date of default together with the present value, as of the date of default, of the ~~difference between market rent and the~~ original rent for the remaining term of the lease less the present value as of the same date of market rent, and incidental damages, less expenses saved in consequence of the default. Note that the reference in Section ~~2A–528(1)(a) and (b)~~ 2A–528(1)(i) and (ii) is to the date of default not to the date of an event of default. An event of default under a lease agreement becomes a default under a lease agreement only after the expiration of any relevant period of grace and compliance with any notice requirements under this Article and the lease agreement. American Bar Foundation, *Commentaries on Indentures,* § 5–1, at 216–217 (1971). Section 2A–501(1). This conclusion is also a function of whether, as a matter of fact or law, the event of default has been waived, suspended or cured. Sections 2A–103(4) and 1–103. If the lessee has taken possession of the goods, the measure of damages is the accrued and unpaid rent as of the earlier of the time the lessor repossesses the goods or the time the lessee tenders the goods to the lessor plus the difference between the present value, as of the same time, of the rent under the lease for the remaining lease term and the present value, as of the same time, of the market rent.

3. Market rent will be computed pursuant to Section 2A–507. ~~In the case of a default by the lessee, the time for tender should be interpreted as the date of the default. If, as of the date of default, the lessor has attempted and failed to obtain possession of the goods, the lessor has, among various additional rights and remedies, a cause of action against the lessee for damages due to loss of use of possession of the goods between the date of default and the date the lessor obtains possession of the goods. Sections 2A–525(3), 2A–103(4), 1–201(1). *See also* Section 2A–530. This conclusion is critical to an important policy decision to protect the lessor's residual interest in the goods. Section 2A–103(1)(q).~~

4. Subsection (2), a somewhat revised version of the provisions of subsection 2–708(2), states a measure of damages which applies ~~in each case that subsection (1) applies but~~ if the measure of damages in subsection (1) is inadequate to put the lessor in as good a position as performance would have. The measure of damage is the lessor's profit, including overhead, together with incidental damages, with allowance for costs reasonably incurred and credit for payments or proceeds of disposition. In determining the amount of due credit with respect to proceeds of disposition a proper value should be attributed to the lessor's residual interest in the goods. Sections 2A–103(1)(q) and 2A–507(4).

5. In calculating profit, a court should include any expected appreciation of the goods, *e.g.* the foal of a leased brood mare. Because this subsection is intended to give the lessor the benefit of the bargain, a court should consider any reasonable benefit or profit expected by the lessor from the performance of the lease agreement. *See Honeywell, Inc. v. Lithonia Lighting, Inc.,* 317 F.Supp. 406, 413 (N.D.Ga.1970); *Locks v. Wade,* 36 N.J.Super. 128, 131, 114 A.2d 875, 877 (App.Div. 1955). Further, in calculating profit the concept of present value ~~should~~ must be given effect. *Taylor v. Commercial Credit Equip. Corp.,* 170 Ga.App. 322, 316 S.E.2d 788 (1984). *See generally* Section 2A–103(1)(u).

Cross References:

Sections 1–102(3), 2–708, 2A–103(1)(u), 2A–402, 2A–504, 2A–507, 2A–527(2) and 2A–529.

Definitional Cross References:

"Agreement". Section 1–201(3).

"Goods". Section 2A–103(1)(h).

"Lease". Section 2A–103(1)(j).

"Lease agreement". Section 2A–103(1)(k).

"Lessee". Section 2A–103(1)(n).

"Lessor". Section 2A–103(1)(p).

"Party". Section 1–201(29).

"Present value". Section 2A–103(1)(u).

"Sale". Section 2–106(1).

Amendment 23

Section 2A–529 of the Article is amended to read:

§ 2A–529. Lessor's Action for the Rent.

(1) After default by the lessee under the lease contract of the type described in ~~(Section 2A–523(1))~~ or 2A–523(3)(a) or, if agreed, after other default by the lessee, if the lessor complies with subsection (2), the lessor may recover from the lessee as damages:

(a) for goods accepted by the lessee and not repossessed by or tendered to the lessor, and for conforming goods lost or damaged within a commercially reasonable time after risk of loss passes to the lessee (Section 2A–219), (i) accrued and unpaid rent as of the date of ~~default~~ entry of judgment in favor of the lessor, (ii) the present value as of the same date ~~of default~~ of the rent for the then remaining lease term of the lease agreement, and (iii) any incidental damages allowed under Section 2A–530, less expenses saved in consequence of the lessee's default; and

(b) for goods identified to the lease contract if the lessor is unable after reasonable effort to dispose of them at a reasonable price or the circumstances reasonably indicate that effort will be unavailing, (i) accrued and unpaid rent as of the date of ~~default~~ entry of judgment in favor of the lessor, (ii) the present value as of the same date of ~~default of~~ the rent for the then remaining lease term of the lease agreement, and (iii) any incidental damages allowed under Section 2A–530, less expenses saved in consequence of the lessee's default.

(2) Except as provided in subsection (3), the lessor shall hold for the lessee for the remaining lease term of the lease agreement any goods that have been identified to the lease contract and are in the lessor's control.

(3) The lessor may dispose of the goods at any time before collection of the judgment for damages obtained pursuant to subsection (1). If the disposition is before the end of the remaining lease term of the lease agreement, the lessor's recovery against the lessee for damages ~~will be~~ is governed by Section 2A–527 or Section 2A–528, and the lessor will cause an appropriate credit to be provided against a judgment for damages to the extent that the amount of the judgment exceeds the recovery available pursuant to Section 2A–527 or 2A–528.

(4) Payment of the judgment for damages obtained pursuant to subsection (1) entitles the lessee to the use and possession of the goods not then disposed of for the remaining lease term of and in accordance with the lease agreement.

(5) After ~~a~~ default by the lessee ~~has wrongfully rejected or revoked acceptance of goods, has failed to pay rent then due, or has repudiated (Section 2A–402)~~ under the lease contract of the type described in Section 2A–523(1) or Section 2A–523(3)(a) or, if agreed, after other default by the lessee, a lessor who is held not entitled to rent under this section must nevertheless be awarded damages for non-acceptance under ~~Sections 2A–527 and~~ Section 2A–527 or Section 2A–528.

Official Comment

Uniform Statutory Source: Section 2–709.

Changes: Substantially revised.

Purposes: ~~Subsection (1) provides another method of determining the measure of lessor's damages after default by the lessee. Absent agreement to the contrary (Section 2A–504), this Article provides the lessor, in this section and the two preceding sections, three alternate methods of computing damages recoverable from the defaulting lessee (Section 2A–523(1)(e)). This section, as well as the two preceding sections, applies to goods subject to the lease, even if such goods have been repossessed from the lessee or otherwise (Section 2A–525(2)). This is a departure from Section 2–709, the statutory analogue. The departure is not surprising given the essential difference between a sale and a lease.~~

~~Absent the right to repossess the goods, the recovery stated in subsection (1)(a) would not compensate the lessor for his or her loss. Consider a lease of a carpet cleaner by A to B, for a term of two days. A purchased the carpet cleaner for $500.00. The rent for the two day term is $75.00. If B defaulted by not paying the rent and refusing to return the carpet cleaner and A was not allowed to repossess the carpet cleaner, the measure of damage stated in this section would allow a recovery of not more than $75.00, together with incidental damages. The rule stated in this Article, which allows the lessor the right to repossess the goods from the lessee and to recover damages, is consistent with the lessor's ownership of the goods. DeKoven, Proceedings After Default by the Lessee Under a True Lease of Equipment, in 1C P. Coogan, W.~~

~~Hogan, D. Vagts, *Secured Transactions Under the Uniform Commercial Code*,, § 29B.06[4] (1986). The statutory analogue, Section 2-709, only provides an action for the price of the goods sold, which is consistent with the seller's agreement to dispose of all of his or her right, title and interest in the goods to the buyer. That measure of damage would not have been appropriate here as the lessor's agreement is to dispose of possession and use of the goods for a term; the bargain includes the return of the goods at the end of the term. It would be anomalous to allow the lessee to improve on the bargain, i.e. retain the goods, solely by virtue of his or her default, even if that had been balanced by allowing the lessor to sue to recover the price or value of the goods.~~

~~The measure of the lessor's damages under this section is a function of a two-part rule. First, subparagraph (1)(a) establishes a rule of recovery with respect to goods accepted by the lessee (even if repossessed by the lessor) and with respect to conforming goods lost or damaged within a commercially reasonable time after risk of loss passed to the lessee. Thus, reading subsections (1), (2) and (3) together, if accepted goods are repossessed by the lessor and the lessor holds the goods for the lessee for the balance of the term, lessor's damages will be calculated pursuant to subsection (1)(a); if the lessor leases, sells or otherwise disposes of the goods, subsection (1)(a) is inapplicable and the lessor's damages will be calculated pursuant to Section 2A-528, unless the lessor's disposition was by a substantially similar lease, in which case Section 2A-527(2) applies. Second, subparagraph (1)(b) establishes a rule of recovery with respect to goods identified to the lease contract (but not accepted by the lessee—see subparagraph (1)(a)) only if the lessor is unable, after reasonable effort, to dispose of them at a reasonable price, or if circumstances indicate the effort would be unavailing.~~

~~As a condition to the lessor's election to employ the method to measure the lessor's claim against the lessee set forth in subsection (1), the lessor must comply with subsection (2), which provides that, with one exception, goods identified to the lease contract and in the lessor's control (whether as a result of repossession or otherwise) must be held for the lessee for the balance of the lease term. This eliminates the possibility of a double recovery by the lessor and preserves the value of the leasehold estate to the lessee.~~

1. Absent a lease contract provision to the contrary, an action for the full unpaid rent (discounted to present value as of the time of entry of judgment as to rent due after that time) is available as to goods not lost or damaged only if the lessee retains possession of the goods or the lessor is or apparently will be unable to dispose of them at a reasonable price after reasonable effort. There is no general right in a lessor to recover the full rent from the lessee upon holding the goods for the lessee. If the lessee tenders goods back to the lessor, and the lessor refuses to accept the tender, the lessor will be limited to the damages it would have suffered had it taken back the goods. The rule in Article 2 that the seller can recover the price of accepted goods is rejected here. In a lease, the lessor always has a residual interest in the goods which the lessor usually realizes upon at the end of a lease term by either sale or a new lease. Therefore, it is not a substantial imposition on the lessor to require it to take back and dispose of the goods if the lessee chooses to tender them back before the end of the lease term: the lessor will merely do earlier what it would have done anyway, sell or relet the goods. Further, the lessee will frequently encounter substantial difficulties if the lessee attempts to sublet the goods for the remainder of the lease term. In contrast to the buyer who owns the entire interest in goods and can easily dispose of them, the lessee is selling only the right to use the goods under the terms of the lease and the sublessee must assume a relationship with the lessor. In that situation, it is usually more efficient to eliminate the original lessee as a middleman by allow-

ing the lessee to return the goods to the lessor who can then redispose of them.

2. In some situations even where possession of the goods is reacquired, a lessor will be able to recover as damages the present value of the full rent due, not under this section, but under 2A–528(2) which allows a lost profit recovery if necessary to put the lessor in the position it would have been in had the lessee performed. Following is an example of such a case. A is a lessor of construction equipment and maintains a substantial inventory. B leases from A a backhoe for a period of two weeks at a rental of $1,000. After three days, B returns the backhoe and refuses to pay the rent. A has five backhoes in inventory, including the one returned by B. During the next 11 days after the return by B of the backhoe, A rents no more than three backhoes at any one time and, therefore, always has two on hand. If B had kept the backhoe for the full rental period, A would have earned the full rental on that backhoe, plus the rental on the other backhoes it actually did rent during that period. Getting this backhoe back before the end of the lease term did not enable A to make any leases it would not otherwise have made. The only way to put A in the position it would have been in had the lessee fully performed is to give the lessor the full rentals. A realized no savings at all because the backhoe was returned early and might even have incurred additional expense if it was paying for parking space for equipment in inventory. A has no obligation to relet the backhoe for the benefit of B rather than leasing that backhoe or any other in inventory for its own benefit. Further, it is probably not reasonable to expect A to dispose of the backhoe by sale when it is returned in an effort to reduce damages suffered by B. Ordinarily, the loss of a two-week rental would not require A to reduce the size of its backhoe inventory. Whether A would similarly be entitled to full rentals as lost profit in a one-year lease of a backhoe is a question of fact: in any event the lessor, subject to mitigation of damages rules, is entitled to be put in as good a position as it would have been had the lessee fully performed the lease contract.

3. Under subsection (2) a lessor who is able and elects to sue for the rent due under a lease must hold goods not lost or damaged for the lessee. Subsection (3) creates an exception to the subsection (2) requirement ~~set forth as a condition to subsection (1), that goods identified to the contract and in the lessor's control be held by the lessor. (Section 2A–529(2))~~. If the lessor disposes of those goods prior to collection of the judgment (whether as a matter of law or agreement), the lessor's recovery is governed by the measure of damages in Section 2A–527 if the disposition is by lease that is substantially similar to the original lease, or otherwise by the measure of damages in Section 2A–528. Section 2A–523 official comment ~~Number 11~~.

~~The relationship between subsections (2) and (3) is best stated by examining a hypothetical. Assume the lease is for a term of two years and after default by the lessee the lessor recovers the goods from the lessee and obtains judgment against the lessee for damages pursuant to subsection (1). If the lessor holds the goods so recovered until the end of the two year term, any subsequent disposition will have no effect on the lessor's judgment. If, however, the lessor determines that the lessee is judgment proof, the lessor might be wise to dispose of the goods before the end of the remaining lease term, even though the amount that the lessor then will be allowed to recover from the lessee, as determined by the provisions of Section 2A–527 or 2A–528, is less than the judgment. Subsection (3) allows the lessor to make this election at any time before collection of the judgment.~~

4. Subsection (4), which is new, further reinforces the requisites of Subsection (2). In the event the judgment for damages obtained by the lessor against the lessee pursuant to subsection (1) is satisfied, the lessee regains the right to use and possession of the remaining goods for the balance of the original lease term; a partial satisfaction of the judgment cre-

ates no right in the lessee to use and possession of the goods.

5. The relationship between subsections (2) and (4) is important to understand. Subsection (2) requires the lessor to hold for the lessee identified goods in the lessor's possession. Absent agreement to the contrary, whether in the lease or otherwise, under most circumstances the requirement that the lessor hold the goods for the lessee for the term will mean that the lessor is not allowed to use them. Sections 2A–103(4) and 1–203. Further, the lessor's use of the goods could be viewed as a disposition of the goods that would bar the lessor from recovery under this section, remitting the lessor to the two preceding sections for a determination of the lessor's claim for damages against the lessee.

6. Subsection (5), the analogue of subsection 2–709(3), further reinforces the thrust of subsection (3) by stating that a lessor who is held not entitled to rent under this section has not elected a remedy; the lessor must be awarded damages under Sections 2A–527 and 2A–528. This is a function of two significant policies of this Article—that resort to a remedy is optional, unless expressly agreed to be exclusive (Section 2A–503(2)) and that rights and remedies provided in this Article generally are cumulative. (Section 2A–501(2) and (4)).

Cross References:

Sections 1–203, 2–709, 2–709(3), 2A–103(4), 2A–501(2), 2A–501(4), 2A–503(2), 2A–504, 2A–523(1)(e), 2A–525(2), 2A–527, 2A–528 and 2A–529(2).

Definitional Cross References:

"Action". Section 1–201(1).

"Conforming". Section 2A–103(1)(d).

"Goods". Section 2A–103(1)(h).

"Lease". Section 2A–103(1)(j).

"Lease agreement". Section 2A–103(1)(k).

"Lease contract". Section 2A–103(1)(*l*).

"Lessee". Section 2A–103(1)(n).

"Lessor". Section 2A–103(1)(p).

"Present value". Section 2A–103(1)(u).

"Reasonable time". Section 1–204(1) and (2).

Amendment 24

Section 2A–532 of the Article is added to read:

§ 2A–532. Lessor's Rights to Residual Interest.

In addition to any other recovery permitted by this Article or other law, the lessor may recover from the lessee an amount that will fully compensate the lessor for any loss of or damage to the lessor's residual interest in the goods caused by the default of the lessee.

Official Comment

Uniform Statutory Source: None.

Purposes: This section recognizes the right of the lessor to recover under this Article (as well as under other law) from the lessee for failure to comply with the lease obligations as to the condition of leased goods when returned to the lessor, for failure to return the goods at the end of the lease, or for any other default which causes loss or injury to the lessor's residual interest in the goods.

APPENDIX TO 1990 ARTICLE 2A AMENDMENTS

The three sections that follow have some changes in their Official Comments in order to conform them to the preceding 1990 Amendments to Uniform Commercial Code Article 2A:

§ 2A–101. Short Title.

This Article shall be known and may be cited as the Uniform Commercial Code—Leases.

Official Comment

Rationale for Codification:

There are several reasons for codifying the law with respect to leases of goods. An analysis of the case law as it applies to leases of goods suggests at least three significant issues to be resolved by codification. First, what is a lease? It is necessary to define lease to determine whether a transaction creates a lease or a security interest disguised as a lease. If the transaction creates a security interest disguised as a lease, the lessor will be required to file a financing statement or take other action to perfect its interest in the goods against third parties. There is no such requirement with respect to leases. Yet the distinction between a lease and a security interest disguised as a lease is not clear. Second, will the lessor be deemed to have made warranties to the lessee? If the transaction is a sale the express and implied warranties of Article 2 of the Uniform Commercial Code apply. However, the warranty law with respect to leases is uncertain. Third, what remedies are available to the lessor upon the lessee's default? If the transaction is a security interest disguised as a lease, the answer is stated in Part 5 of the Article on Secured Transactions (Article 9). There is no clear answer with respect to leases.

There are reasons to codify the law with respect to leases of goods in addition to those suggested by a review of the reported cases. The answer to this important question should not be limited to the issues raised in these cases. Is it not also proper to determine the remedies available to the lessee upon the lessor's default? It is, but that issue is not reached through a review of the reported cases. This is only one of the many issues presented in structuring, negotiating and documenting a lease of goods.

Statutory Analogue:

After it was decided to proceed with the codification project, the drafting committee of the National Conference of Commissioners on Uniform State Laws looked for a statutory analogue, gradually narrowing the focus to the Article on Sales (Article 2) and the Article on Secured Transactions (Article 9). A review of the literature with respect to the sale of goods reveals that Article 2 is predicated upon certain assumptions: Parties to the sales transaction frequently are without counsel; the agreement of the parties often is oral or evidenced by scant writings; obligations between the parties are bilateral; applicable law is influenced by the need to preserve freedom of contract. A review of the literature with respect to personal property security law reveals that Article 9 is predicated upon very different assumptions: Parties to a secured transaction regularly are represented by counsel; the agreement of the parties frequently is reduced to a writing, extensive in scope; the obligations between the parties are essentially unilateral; and applicable law seriously limits freedom of contract.

The lease is closer in spirit and form to the sale of goods than to the creation of a security interest. While parties to a lease are sometimes represented by counsel and their agreement is often reduced to a writing, the obligations of the parties are bilateral and the common law of leasing is dominated by the need to preserve freedom of contract. Thus the drafting committee concluded that Article 2 was the appropriate statutory analogue.

Issues: The drafting committee then identified and resolved several issues critical to codification:

Scope: The scope of the Article was limited to leases (Section 2A–102). There was no need to include leases intended as security, *i.e.*, security interests disguised as leases, as they are adequately treated in Article 9. Further, even if leases intended as security were included, the need to preserve the distinction would remain, as policy suggests treatment significantly different from that accorded leases.

Definition of Lease: Lease was defined to exclude leases intended as security (Section 2A–103(1)(j)). Given the litigation to date a revised definition of security interest was suggested for inclusion in the Act. (Section 1–201(37)). This revision sharpens the distinction between leases and security interests disguised as leases.

Filing: The lessor was not required to file a financing statement against the lessee or take any other action to protect the lessor's interest in the goods (Section 2A–301). The refined definition of security interest will more clearly signal the need to file to potential lessors of goods. Those lessors who are concerned will file a protective financing statement (Section 9–408).

Warranties: All of the express and implied warranties of the Article on Sales (Article 2) were included (Sections 2A–210 through 2A–216), revised to reflect differences in lease transactions. The lease of goods is sufficiently similar to the sale of goods to justify this decision. Further, many courts have reached the same decision.

Certificate of Title Laws: Many leasing transactions involve goods subject to certificate of title statutes. To avoid conflict with those statutes, this Article is subject to them (~~Section 2A–104(1)(b)~~ Section 2A–104(1)(a)).

Consumer Leases: Many leasing transactions involve parties subject to consumer protection statutes or decisions. To avoid conflict with those ~~statutes~~ laws this Article is subject to them to the extent provided in (~~Section 2A–104(1)(a) and (d)~~ Section 2A–104(1)(c) and (2)). Further, certain consumer protections have been incorporated in the Article.

Finance Leases: Certain leasing transactions substitute the ~~seller~~ supplier of the goods for the lessor as the party responsible to the lessee with respect to warranties and the like. The definition of finance lease (Section 2A–103(1)(g)) was developed to describe these transactions. Various sections of the Article implement the substitution of the ~~seller~~ supplier for the lessor, including Sections 2A–209 and 2A–407. No attempt was made to fashion a special rule where the finance lessor is an affiliate of the ~~seller~~ supplier of goods; this is to be developed by the courts, case by case.

Sale and Leaseback: Sale and leaseback transactions are becoming increasingly common. A number of state statutes treat transactions where possession is retained by the seller as fraudulent *per se* or *prima facie* fraudulent. That position is not ~~balanced~~ in accord with modern practice and thus is changed by the Article "if the buyer bought for value and in good faith" (Section 2A–308(3)).

Remedies: The Article has not only provided for lessor's remedies upon default by the lessee (Sections 2A–523 through 2A–531), but also for lessee's remedies upon default by the lessor (Sections 2A–508 through 2A–522). This is a significant departure from Article 9, which provides remedies only for the secured party upon default by the debtor. This difference is compelled by the bilateral nature of the obligations between the parties to a lease.

Damages: Many leasing transactions are predicated on the parties' ability to stipulate an appropriate measure of damages in the event of default. The rule with respect to sales of goods (Section 2–718) is not sufficiently flexible to accommodate this practice. Consistent with the common law emphasis upon freedom to contract, the Article has created a revised rule that allows greater flexibility with respect to leases of goods (Section 2A–504(1)).

History:

This Article is a revision of the Uniform Personal Property Leasing Act, which was approved by the National Conference of Commissioners on Uniform State Laws in August, 1985. However, it was believed that the subject matter of the Uniform Personal Property Leasing Act would be better treated as an article of this Act. Thus, although the Conference promulgated the Uniform Personal Property Leasing Act as a Uniform Law, activity was ~~modest~~ held in abeyance to allow time to restate the Uniform Personal Property Leasing Act as Article 2A.

In August, 1986 the Conference approved and recommended this Article (including conforming amendments to Article 1 and Article 9) for promulgation as an amendment to this Act. In December, 1986 the Council of the American Law Institute approved and recommended this Article (including conforming amendments to Article 1 and Article 9), with official comments, for promulgation as an amendment to this Act. In March, 1987 the Permanent Editorial Board for the Uniform Commercial Code approved and recommended this Article (including conforming amendments to Article 1 and Article 9), with official comments, for promulgation as an amendment to this Act. In May, 1987 the American Law Institute approved and recommended this Article (including conforming amendments to Article 1 and Article 9), with official comments, for promulgation as an amendment to this Act. In August, 1987 the Conference confirmed its approval of the final text of this Article.

Upon its initial promulgation, Article 2A was rapidly enacted in several states, was introduced in a number of other states, and underwent bar association, law revision commission and legislative study in still further states. In that process debate emerged, principally sparked by the study of Article 2A by the California Bar Association, California's non-uniform amendments to Article 2A, and articles appearing in a symposium on Article 2A published after its promulgation in the Alabama Law Review. The debate chiefly centered on whether Article 2A had struck the proper balance or was clear enough concerning the ability of a lessor to grant a security interest in its leasehold interest and in the residual, priority between a secured party and the lessee, and the lessor's remedy structure under Article 2A.

This debate over issues on which reasonable minds could and did differ began to affect the enactment effort for Article 2A in a deleterious manner. Consequently, the Standby Committee for Article 2A, composed predominantly of the former members of the drafting committee, reviewed the legislative actions and studies in the various states, and opened a dialogue with the principal proponents of the non-uniform amendments. Negotiations were conducted in conjunction with, and were facilitated by, a study of the uniform Article and the non-uniform Amendments by the New York Law Revision Commission. Ultimately, a consensus was reached, which has been approved by the membership of the Conference, the Permanent Editorial Board, and the Council of the Institute. Rapid and uniform enactment of Article 2A is expected as a result of the completed amendments. The Article 2A experience reaffirms the essential viability of the procedures of the Conference and the Institute for creating and updating uniform state law in the commercial law area.

Relationship of Article 2A to Other Articles:

The Article on Sales provided a useful point of reference for codifying the law of leases. Many of the provisions of that

Article were carried over, changed to reflect differences in style, leasing terminology or leasing practices. Thus, the official comments to those sections of Article 2 whose provisions were carried over are incorporated by reference in Article 2A, as well; further, any case law interpreting those provisions should be viewed as persuasive but not binding on a court when deciding a similar issue with respect to leases. Any change in the sequence that has been made when carrying over a provision from Article 2 should be viewed as a matter of style, not substance. This is not to suggest that in other instances Article 2A did not also incorporate substantially revised provisions of Article 2, Article 9 or otherwise where the revision was driven by a concern over the substance; but for the lack of a mandate, the drafting committee ~~would~~ might well have made the same or a similar change in the statutory analogue. Those sections in Article 2A include Sections 2A–104, 2A–105, 2A–106, 2A–108(2) and (4), 2A–109(2), 2A–208, 2A–214(2) and (3)(a), 2A–216, 2A–303, 2A–306, 2A–503, 2A–504(3)(b), 2A–506(2), and 2A–515. For lack of relevance or significance not all of the provisions of Article 2 were incorporated in Article 2A.

This codification was greatly influenced by the fundamental tenet of the common law as it has developed with respect to leases of goods: freedom of the parties to contract. Note that, like all other Articles of this Act, the principles of construction and interpretation contained in Article 1 are applicable throughout Article 2A (Section 2A–103(4)). These principles include the ability of the parties to vary the effect of the provisions of Article 2A, subject to certain limitations including those that relate to the obligations of good faith, diligence, reasonableness and care (Section 1–102(3)). Consistent with those principles no negative inference is to be drawn by the episodic use of the phrase "unless otherwise agreed" in certain provisions of Article 2A. Section 1–102(4). Indeed, the contrary is true, as the general rule in the Act, including this Article, is that the effect of the Act's provisions may be varied by agreement. Section 1–102(3). This conclusion follows even where the statutory analogue contains the phrase and the correlative provision in Article 2A does not.

§ 2A–211. Warranties Against Interference and Against Infringement; Lessee's Obligation Against Infringement.

(1) There is in a lease contract a warranty that for the lease term no person holds a claim to or interest in the goods that arose from an act or omission of the lessor, other than a claim by way of infringement or the like, which will interfere with the lessee's enjoyment of its leasehold interest.

(2) Except in a finance lease there is in a lease contract by a lessor who is a merchant regularly dealing in goods of the kind a warranty that the goods are delivered free of the rightful claim of any person by way of infringement or the like.

(3) A lessee who furnishes specifications to a lessor or a supplier shall hold the lessor and the supplier harmless against any claim by way of infringement or the like that arises out of compliance with the specifications.

Official Comment

Uniform Statutory Source: Section 2–312.

Changes: This section is modeled on the provisions of Section 2–312, with modifications to reflect the limited interest transferred by a lease contract and the total interest transferred by a sale. Section 2–312(2), which is omitted here, is incorporated in Section 2A–214. The warranty of quiet possession was abolished with respect to sales of goods. Section 2–312 official comment 1. Section 2A–211(1) reinstates the warranty of quiet possession with respect to leases. Inherent in the nature of the limited interest transferred by the lease—the right to possession and use of the goods—is the need of the lessee for protection greater than that afforded to the buyer. Since the scope of the protection is limited to claims or interests that arose from acts or omissions of the lessor, the lessor will be in position to evaluate the potential cost, certainly a far better position than that enjoyed by the lessee. Further, to the extent the market will allow, the lessor can attempt to pass on the anticipated additional cost to the lessee in the guise of higher rent.

Purposes: General language was chosen for subsection (1) that expresses the essence of the lessee's expectation: with an exception for infringement and the like, no person holding a claim or interest that arose from an act or omission of the lessor will be able to interfere with the lessee's use and enjoyment of the goods for the lease term. Subsection (2), like other similar provisions in later sections, excludes the finance lessor from extending this warranty; with few exceptions (Sections 2A–210 and 2A–211(1)), the lessee under a finance lease is to look to the supplier for warranties and the like or, in some cases as to warranties, to the manufacturer if a warranty made by that person is passed on. Subsections (2) and (3) are derived from Section 2–312(3). These subsections, as well as the analogue, should be construed so that applicable principles of law and equity supplement their provisions. Sections 2A–103(4) and 1–103.

Cross References:

Sections 2–312, 2–312(1), 2–312(2), 2–312 official comment 1, 2A–210, 2A–211(1) and 2A–214.

Definitional Cross References:

"Delivery". Section 1–201(14).
"Finance lease". Section 2A–103(1)(g).
"Goods". Section 2A–103(1)(h).
"Lease". Section 2A–103(1)(j).
"Lease contract". Section 2A–103(1)(*l*).
"Leasehold interest". Section 2A–103(1)(m).
"Lessee". Section 2A–103(1)(n).
"Lessor". Section 2A–103(1)(p).
"Merchant". Section 2–104(1).
"Person". Section 1–201(30).
"Supplier". Section 2A–103(1)(x).

§ 2A–301. Enforceability of Lease Contract.

Except as otherwise provided in this Article, a lease contract is effective and enforceable according to its terms between the parties, against purchasers of the goods and against creditors of the parties.

Official Comment

Uniform Statutory Source: Section 9–201.

Changes: The first sentence of Section 9–201 was incorporated, modified to reflect leasing terminology. The second sentence of Section 9–201 was eliminated as not relevant to leasing practices.

Purposes:

1. This section establishes a general rule regarding the validity and enforceability of a lease contract. The lease contract is effective and enforceable between the parties and against third parties. Exceptions to this general rule arise where there is a specific rule to the contrary in this Article. Enforceability is, thus, dependent upon the lease contract meeting the requirements of the Statute of Frauds provisions of Section 2A–201. Enforceability is also a function of the lease contract conforming to the principles of construction and interpretation contained in the Article on General Provisions (Article 1). Section 2A–103(4).

2. The effectiveness or enforceability of the lease contract is not dependent upon the lease contract or any financing statement or the like being filed or recorded; however, the priority of the interest of a lessor of fixtures with respect to the interests of certain third parties in such fixtures is subject to the provisions of the Article on Secured Transactions (Article 9). Section 2A–309. Prior to the adoption of this Article filing or recording was not required with respect to leases, only leases intended as security. The definition of security interest, as amended concurrently with the adoption of this Article, more clearly delineates leases and leases intended as security and thus signals the need to file. Section 1–201(37). Those lessors who are concerned about whether the transaction creates a lease or a security interest will continue to file a protective financing statement. Section 9–408. Coogan, Leasing and the Uniform Commercial Code, in *Equipment Leasing—Leveraged Leasing* 681, 744–46 (2d ed. 1980).

3. **Hypothetical:**

~~1.~~ (a) In construing this section it is important to recognize its relationship to other sections in this Article. This is best demonstrated by reference to a hypothetical. Assume that on February 1 A, a manufacturer of combines and other farm equipment, leased a fleet of six combines to B, a corporation engaged in the business of farming, for a 12 month term. Under the lease agreement between A and B, A agreed to defer B's payment of the first two months' rent to April 1. On March 1 B recognized that it would need only four combines and thus subleased two combines to C for an 11 month term.

~~2.~~ (b) This hypothetical raises a number of issues that are answered by the sections contained in this part. Since lease is defined to include sublease (Section 2A–103(i)(j) and (w)), this section provides that the prime lease between A and B and the sublease between B and C are enforceable in accordance with their terms, except as otherwise provided in this Article; that exception, in this case, is one of considerable scope.

~~3.~~ (c) The separation of ownership, which is in A, and possession, which is in B with respect to four combines and which is in C with respect to two combines, is not relevant. Section 2A-302. A's interest in the six combines cannot be challenged simply because A parted with possession to B, who in turn parted with possession of some of the combines to C. Yet it is important to note that by the terms of Section 2A–302 this conclusion is subject to change if otherwise provided in this Article.

~~4.~~ (d) B's entering the sublease with C raises an issue that is treated by this part. In a dispute over the leased combines A may challenge B's right to sublease. The ~~general~~ rule is permissive as to transfers of interests under a lease contract, including subleases. ~~Section 2A–303(1)~~ Section 2A–303(2). However, the rule ~~creates~~ has two significant ~~exceptions~~ qualifications. If the prime lease contract between A and B prohibits B from subleasing the combines, ~~Section 2A–303(1)(a)~~ or makes such a sublease an event of default, Section 2A–303(2) applies~~, as the transfer is voluntary and prohibited~~; thus, while B's interest under the prime lease may ~~not~~ be transferred under the sublease to C, A may have a remedy pursuant to Section 2A–303(5). Absent a prohibition or default provision in the prime lease contract A might be able to argue that the sublease to C materially increases A's risk; thus, while B's interest under the prime lease may ~~not~~ be transferred under the sublease to C, ~~if after demand by A, C fails to provide the assurances required by Section 2A-303(2)~~ A may have a remedy pursuant to Section 2A–303(5). ~~Section 2A-303(1)(b)~~ Section 2A–303(5)(b)(ii).

~~5.~~ (e) Resolution of this issue is also a function of the section dealing with the sublease of goods by a prime lessee (Section 2A–305). Subsection (1) of Section 2A–305, which is subject to the ~~rule~~ rules of Section 2A–303 stated above, provides that C takes subject to the interest of A under the prime lease between A and B. However, there are two exceptions. First, if B is a merchant (Sections 2A–103(3) and 2–104(1)) dealing in goods of that kind and C is a sublessee in the ordinary course of business (Sections 2A–103(1)(*o*) and 2A–103(1)(n)), C takes free of the prime lease between A and B. Second, if B has rejected the six combines under the prime lease with A, and B disposes of the goods by sublease to C, C takes free of the prime lease if C can establish good faith. Section 2A–511(4).

~~6.~~ (f) If the facts of this hypothetical are expanded and we assume that the prime lease obligated B to maintain the combines, an additional issue may be presented. Prior to entering the sublease B, in satisfaction of its maintenance covenant, brought the two combines that it desired to sublease to a local independent dealer of A's. The dealer did the requested work for B. C inspected the combines on the dealer's lot after the work was completed. C signed the sublease with B two days later. C, however, was prevented from taking delivery of the two combines as B refused to pay the dealer's invoice for the repairs. The dealer furnished the repair service to B in the ordinary course of the dealer's business. If under applicable law the dealer has a lien on repaired goods in the dealer's possession, the dealer's lien will take priority over ~~A's,~~ B's and C's interests, and also should take priority over A's interest, depending upon the terms of the lease contract and the applicable law. Section 2A–306.

~~7.~~ (g) Now assume that C is in financial straits and one of C's creditors obtains a judgment against C. If the creditor levies on C's subleasehold interest in the two combines, who will prevail? Unless the levying creditor also holds a lien covered by Section 2A–306, discussed above, the judgment creditor will take its interest subject to B's rights under the sublease and A's rights under the prime lease. Section 2A–307(1). the hypothetical becomes more complicated if we assume that B is in financial straits and B's creditor holds the judgment. Here the judgment creditor takes subject to the sublease unless the lien attached to the two combines before the sublease contract became enforceable. Section 2A–307(2)(a). However, B's judgment creditor cannot prime A's interest in the goods because, with respect to A, the judgment creditor is a creditor of B in its capacity as lessee under the prime lease between A and B. Thus, here the judgment creditor's interest is subject to the lease between A and B. Section 2A–307(1).

~~8.~~ (h) Finally, assume that on April 1 B is unable to pay A the deferred rent then due under the prime lease, but that C is current in its payments under the sublease from B. What effect will B's default under the prime lease between A and B have on C's rights under the sublease between B and C? Section 2A–301 provides that a lease contract is effective against the creditors of either party. Since a lease contract includes a sublease contract (Section 2A–103(1)(*l*)), the sublease contract between B and C arguably could be enforceable against A, a prime lessor who has extended unsecured credit to B, the prime lessee/sublessor, if the sublease contract meets the requirements of Section 2A–201. However, the rule stated in Section 2A–301 is subject to other provisions in this Article. Under Section 2A–305, C, as sublessee, would take subject to the prime lease contract in most cases. Thus, B's default under the prime lease will in most cases lead to A's recovery of the goods from C. Section 2A–523. A and C could provide otherwise by agreement. Section 2A–311. C's recourse will be to assert a claim for damages against B. ~~Section~~ Sections 2A–211(1) and 2A–508.

4. Relationship Between Sections:

~~1.~~ (a) As the analysis of the hypothetical demonstrates, Part 3 of the Article focuses on issues that relate to the enforceability of the lease contract (Sections 2A-301, 2A-302 and 2A-303) and to the priority of various claims to the goods subject to the lease contract (Sections 2A-304, 2A-305, 2A-306, 2A-307, 2A-308, 2A-309, ~~and~~ 2A-310, and 2A-311).

~~2.~~ (b) This section states a general rule of enforceability, which is subject to specific rules to the contrary stated elsewhere in the Article. Section 2A-302 negates any notion that the separation of title and possession is fraudulent as a rule of law. Finally, Section 2A-303 states ~~a permissive rule~~ rules with respect to the transfer of the lessor's interest (as well as the residual interest in the goods) or the lessee's interest under the lease contract. ~~Conditions~~ Qualifications are imposed as a function of various issues, including whether the transfer is ~~voluntary or involuntary~~ the creation or enforcement of a security interest or one that is material to the other party to the lease contract. In addition, a system of rules is created to deal with the rights and duties among assignor, assignee and the other party to the lease contract.

~~3.~~ (c) Sections 2A-304 and 2A-305 are twins that deal with good faith transferees of goods subject to the lease contract. Section 2A-304 creates a set of rules with respect to transfers by the lessor of goods subject to a lease contract; the transferee considered is a subsequent lessee of the goods. The priority dispute covered here is between the subsequent lessee and the original lessee of the goods (or persons claiming through the original lessee). Section 2A-305 creates a set of rules with respect to transfers by the lessee of goods subject to a lease contract; the transferees considered are buyers of the goods or sublessees of the goods. The priority dispute covered here is between the transferee and the lessor of the goods (or persons claiming through the lessor).

~~4.~~ (d) Section 2A-306 creates a rule with respect to priority disputes between holders of liens for services or materials furnished with respect to goods subject to a lease contract and the lessor or the lessee under that contract. Section 2A-307 creates a rule with respect to priority disputes between the lessee and creditors of the lessor and priority disputes between the lessor and creditors of the lessee.

~~5.~~ (e) Section 2A-308 creates a series of rules relating to allegedly fraudulent transfers and preferences. The most significant rule is that set forth in subsection (3) which validates sale-leaseback transactions if the buyer-lessor can establish that he or she bought for value and in good faith.

~~6.~~ (f) ~~Finally,~~ Sections 2A-309 and 2A-310 create a series of rules with respect to priority disputes between various third parties and a lessor of fixtures or accessions, respectively, with respect thereto.

(g) Finally, Section 2A-311 allows parties to alter the statutory priorities by agreement.

Cross References:

Article 1, ~~esp.~~ especially Section 1-201(37), and Sections 2-104(1), 2A-103(1)(j), 2A-103(1)(*l*), 2A-103(1)(n), 2A-103(1)(*o*) and 2A-103(1)(w), 2A-103(3), 2A-103(4), 2A-201, 2A-301 through 2A-303, ~~2A-303(1), 2A-303(1)(a), 2A-303(1)(b)~~ 2A-303(2), 2A-303(5), 2A-304 through 2A-307, 2A-307(1), 2A-307(2)(a), 2A-308 through ~~2A-310~~ 2A-311, 2A-508, 2A-511(4), 2A-523, Article 9, ~~esp.~~ especially Sections 9-201 and 9-408.

Definitional Cross References:

"Creditor". Section 1-201(12).
"Goods". Section 2A-103(1)(h).
"Lease contract". Section 2A-103(1)(*l*).
"Party". Section 1-201(29).
"Purchaser". Section 1-201(33).
"Term". Section 1-201(42).

APPENDIX VII

PRE-REVISION ARTICLE 3

Set forth below are the Text and Official Comments of Article 3 as they existed prior to revision in 1990.

ARTICLE 3

COMMERCIAL PAPER

PART 1. SHORT TITLE, FORM AND INTERPRETATION

PART 2. TRANSFER AND NEGOTIATION

PART 1

SHORT TITLE, FORM AND INTERPRETATION

§ 3–101. Short Title.

This Article shall be known and may be cited as Uniform Commercial Code—Commercial Paper.

Official Comment

This Article represents a complete revision and modernization of the Uniform Negotiable Instruments Law.

The Comments which follow will point out the respects in which this Article changes the Negotiable Instruments Law, which was promulgated by the National Conference of Commissioners on Uniform State Laws in 1896, and was subsequently enacted in every American jurisdiction. Needless to say, in the 50 odd years of the history of that statute, there have been vast changes in commercial practices relating to the handling of negotiable instruments. The need for revision of this important statute was felt for some years before the present project was undertaken.

It should be noted especially that this Article does not apply in any way to the handling of securities. Article 8 deals with that subject. See Sec. 3–103.

§ 3–102. Definitions and Index of Definitions.

(1) In this Article unless the context otherwise requires

(a) "Issue" means the first delivery of an instrument to a holder or a remitter.

(b) An "order" is a direction to pay and must be more than an authorization or request. It must identify the person to pay with reasonable certainty. It may be addressed to one or more such persons jointly or in the alternative but not in succession.

(c) A "promise" is an undertaking to pay and must be more than an acknowledgment of an obligation.

(d) "Secondary party" means a drawer or endorser.

(e) "Instrument" means a negotiable instrument.

(2) Other definitions applying to this Article and the sections in which they appear are:

"Acceptance". Section 3-410.

"Accommodation party". Section 3-415.

"Alteration". Section 3-407.

"Certificate of deposit". Section 3-104.

"Certification". Section 3-411.

"Check". Section 3-104.

"Definite time". Section 3-109.

"Dishonor". Section 3-507.

"Draft". Section 3-104.

"Holder in due course". Section 3-302.

"Negotiation". Section 3-202.

"Note". Section 3-104.

"Notice of dishonor". Section 3-508.

"On demand". Section 3-108.

"Presentment". Section 3-504.

"Protest". Section 3-509.

"Restrictive Indorsement". Section 3-205.

"Signature". Section 3-401.

(3) The following definitions in other Articles apply to this Article:

"Account". Section 4-104.

"Banking Day". Section 4-104.

"Clearing house". Section 4-104.

"Collecting bank". Section 4-105.

"Customer". Section 4-104.

"Depositary Bank". Section 4-105.

"Documentary Draft". Section 4-104.

"Intermediary Bank". Section 4-105.

"Item". Section 4-104.

"Midnight deadline". Section 4-104.

"Payor bank". Section 4-105.

(4) In addition Article 1 contains general definitions and principles of construction and interpretation applicable throughout this Article.

Official Comment

Prior Uniform Statutory Provision: Sections 1(5), 128 and 191, Uniform Negotiable Instruments Law.

Changes: See below.

Purposes of Changes:

1. The definition of "issue" in Section 191 of the original act has been clarified in two respects. The Section 191 defini-

tion required that the instrument delivered be "complete in form" inconsistently with the provisions of Sections 14 and 15 (relating to incomplete instruments) of the original act. The "complete in form" language has therefore been deleted. Furthermore the Section 191 definition required that the delivery be "to a person who takes as a holder", thus raising difficulties in the case of the remitter (see Comment 3 to Sec. 3-302) who may not be a party to the instrument and thus not a holder. The definition in subsection (1)(a) of this Section thus provides that the delivery may be to a holder or to a remitter.

2. The definitions of "order" [subsection (b)] and "promise" [subsection (c)] are new, but state principles clearly recognized by the courts. In the case of orders the dividing line between "a direction to pay" and "an authorization or request" may not be self-evident in the occasional unusual, and therefore non-commercial, case. The prefixing of words of courtesy to the direction—as "please pay" or "kindly pay"—should not lead to a holding that the direction has degenerated into a mere request. On the other hand informal language—such as "I wish you would pay"—would not qualify as an order and such an instrument would be non-negotiable. The definition of "promise" is intended to make it clear that a mere I.O.U. is not a negotiable instrument, and to change the result in occasional cases which have held that "Due Currier & Barker seventeen dollars and fourteen cents, value received," and "I borrowed from P. Shemonia the sum of five hundred dollars with four per cent interest; the borrowed money ought to be paid within four months from the above date" were promises sufficient to make the instruments into notes.

3. The last sentence of subsection (1)(b) ("order") permits the order to be addressed to one or more persons (as drawees) in the alternative, recognizing the practice of corporations issuing dividend checks and of other drawers who for commercial convenience name a number of drawees, usually in different parts of the country. The section on presentment provides that presentment may be made to any one of such drawees. Drawees in succession are not permitted because the holder should not be required to make more than one presentment, and upon the first dishonor should have his recourse against the drawer and indorsers.

4. Comments on the definitions indexed follow the sections in which the definitions are contained.

Cross Reference:

Point 3: Section 3-504(3)(a).

Definitional Cross References:

"Bank". Section 1-201.
"Delivery". Section 1-201.
"Holder". Section 1-201.
"Money". Section 1-201.
"Person". Section 1-201.

§ 3-103. Limitations on Scope of Article.

(1) This Article does not apply to money, documents of title or investment securities.

(2) The provisions of this Article are subject to the provisions of the Article on Bank Deposits and Collections (Article 4) and Secured Transactions (Article 9).

Official Comment

Prior Uniform Statutory Provision: None.

Purposes:

1. This Article is restricted to commercial paper—that is to say, to drafts, checks, certificates of deposit and notes as defined in Section 3-104(2). Subsection

(1) expressly excludes any money, as defined in this Act (Section 1-201), even though the money may be in the form of a bank note which meets all the requirements of Section 3-104(1). Money is of course negotiable at common law or under separate statutes, but no provision of this Article is applicable to it. Subsection (1) also expressly excludes documents of title and investment securities which fall within Articles 7 and 8, respectively. To this extent the section follows decisions which held that interim certificates calling for the delivery of securities were not negotiable instruments under the original statute. Such paper is now covered under Article 8, but is not within any section of this Article. Likewise, bills of lading, warehouse receipts and other documents of title which fall within Article 7 may be negotiable under the provision of that Article, but are not covered by any section of this Article.

2. Instruments which fall within the scope of this Article may also be subject to other Articles of the Code. Many items in course of bank collection will of course be negotiable instruments, and the same may be true of collateral pledged as security for a debt. In such cases this Article, which is general, is, in case of conflicting provisions, subject to the Articles which deal specifically with the type of transaction or instrument involved: Article 4 (Bank Deposits and Collections) and Article 9 (Secured Transactions). In the case of a negotiable instrument which is subject to Article 4 because it is in course of collection or to Article 9 because it is used as collateral, the provisions of this Article continue to be applicable except insofar as there may be conflicting provisions in the Bank Collection or Secured Transactions Article.

An instrument which qualifies as "negotiable" under this Article may also qualify as a "security" under Article 8. It will be noted that the formal requisites of negotiability (Section 3-104) go to matters of form exclusively; the definition of "security" on the other hand (Section 8-102) looks principally to the manner in which an instrument is used ("commonly dealt in upon securities exchanges ... or commonly recognized ... as a medium for investment"). If an instrument negotiable in form under Section 3-104 is, because of the manner of its use, a "security" under Section 8-102, Article 8 and not this Article applies. See subsection (1) of this Section and Section 8-102(1)(b).

Cross References:

Point 1: Articles 7 and 8; Sections 1-201, 3-104(1) and (2), 3-107.

Point 2: Articles 4 and 9; Sections 3-104 and 8-102.

Definitional Cross References:

"Document of title". Section 1-201.

"Money". Section 1-201.

§ 3-104. Form of Negotiable Instruments; "Draft"; "Check"; "Certificate of Deposit"; "Note".

(1) Any writing to be a negotiable instrument within this Article must

(a) be signed by the maker or drawer; and

(b) contain an unconditional promise or order to pay a sum certain in money and no other promise, order, obligation or power given by the maker or drawer except as authorized by this Article; and

(c) be payable on demand or at a definite time; and

(d) be payable to order or to bearer.

(2) A writing which complies with the requirements of this section is

(a) a "draft" ("bill of exchange") if it is an order;

(b) a "check" if it is a draft drawn on a bank and payable on demand;

(c) a "certificate of deposit" if it is an acknowledgment by a bank of receipt of money with an engagement to repay it;

(d) a "note" if it is a promise other than a certificate of deposit.

(3) As used in other Articles of this Act, and as the context may require, the terms "draft", "check", "certificate of deposit" and "note" may refer to instruments which are not negotiable within this Article as well as to instruments which are so negotiable.

Official Comment

Prior Uniform Statutory Provision: Sections 1, 5, 10, 126, 184 and 185, Uniform Negotiable Instruments Law.

Changes: Parts of original sections combined and reworded; new provisions; original Section 10 omitted.

Purposes of Changes and New Matter: The changes are intended to bring together in one section related provisions and definitions formerly widely separated.

1. Under subsection (1)(b) any writing, to be a negotiable instrument within this Article, must be payable in money. In a few states there are special statutes, enacted at an early date when currency was less sound and barter was prevalent, which make promises to pay in commodities negotiable. Even under these statutes commodity notes are now little used and have no general circulation. This Article makes no attempt to provide for such paper, as it is a matter of purely local concern. Even if retention of the old statutes is regarded in any state as important, amendment of this section may not be necessary, since "within this Article" in subsection (1) leaves open the possibility that some writings may be made negotiable by other statutes or by judicial decision. The same is true as to any new type of paper which commercial practice may develop in the future.

2. While a writing cannot be made a negotiable instrument within this Article by contract or by conduct, nothing in this section is intended to mean that in a particular case a court may not arrive at a result similar to that of negotiability by finding that the obligor is estopped by his conduct from asserting a defense against a bona fide purchaser. Such an estoppel rests upon ordinary principles of the law of simple contract; it does not depend upon negotiability, and it does not make the writing negotiable for any other purpose. But a contract to build a house or to employ a workman, or equally a security agreement does not become a negotiable instrument by the mere insertion of a clause agreeing that it shall be one.

3. The words "no other promise, order, obligation or power" in subsection (1)(b) are an expansion of the first sentence of the original Section 5. Section 3-112 permits an instrument to carry certain limited obligations or powers in addition to the simple promise or order to pay money. Subsection (1) of this Section is intended to say that it cannot carry others.

4. Any writing which meets the requirements of subsection (1) and is not excluded under Section 3-103 is a negotiable instrument, and all sections of this Article apply to it, even though it may contain additional language beyond that contemplated by this section. Such an instrument is a draft, a check, a certificate of deposit or a note as defined in subsection (2). Traveler's checks in the usual form, for instance, are negotiable instruments under this Article when they have been completed by the identifying signature.

5. This Article omits the original Section 10, which provided that the instrument need not follow the language of the act if it "clearly indicates an intention to conform" to it. The provision has served no useful purpose, and it has been an encouragement to bad drafting and to liberality in holding questionable paper to be negotiable. The omission is not intended to mean that the instrument must

follow the language of this section, or that one term may not be recognized as clearly the equivalent of another, as in the case of "I undertake" instead of "I promise," or "Pay to holder" instead of "Pay to bearer." It does mean that either the language of the section or a clear equivalent must be found, and that in doubtful cases the decision should be against negotiability.

6. Subsection (3) is intended to make clear the same policy expressed in Section 3-805.

Cross References:

Sections 3-105 through 3-112, 3-401, 3-402 and 3-403.

Point 1: Section 3-107.
Point 3: Section 3-112.
Point 4: Sections 3-103 and 3-805.
Point 6: Section 3-805.

Definitional Cross References:

"Bank". Section 1-201.
"Bearer". Section 1-201.
"Definite time". Section 3-109.
"Money". Section 1-201.
"On demand". Section 3-108.
"Order". Section 3-102.
"Promise". Section 3-102.
"Signed". Section 1-201.
"Term". Section 1-201.
"Writing". Section 1-201.

§ 3-105. When Promise or Order Unconditional.

(1) A promise or order otherwise unconditional is not made conditional by the fact that the instrument

(a) is subject to implied or constructive conditions; or

(b) states its consideration, whether performed or promised, or the transaction which gave rise to the instrument, or that the promise or order is made or the instrument matures in accordance with or "as per" such transaction; or

(c) refers to or states that it arises out of a separate agreement or refers to a separate agreement for rights as to prepayment or acceleration; or

(d) states that it is drawn under a letter of credit; or

(e) states that it is secured, whether by mortgage, reservation of title or otherwise; or

(f) indicates a particular account to be debited or any other fund or source from which reimbursement is expected; or

(g) is limited to payment out of a particular fund or the proceeds of a particular source, if the instrument is issued by a government or governmental agency or unit; or

(h) is limited to payment out of the entire assets of a partnership, unincorporated association, trust or estate by or on behalf of which the instrument is issued.

(2) A promise or order is not unconditional if the instrument

(a) states that it is subject to or governed by any other agreement; or

(b) states that it is to be paid only out of a particular fund or source except as provided in this section.

As amended in 1962.

Official Comment

Prior Uniform Statutory Provision: Section 3, Uniform Negotiable Instruments Law.

Changes: Completely revised.

Purposes of Changes: The section is intended to make it clear that, so far as negotiability is affected, the conditional or unconditional character of the promise or order is to be determined by what is expressed in the instrument itself; and to permit certain specific limitations upon the terms of payment.

1. Paragraph (a) of subsection (1) rejects the theory of decisions which have held that a recital in an instrument that it is given in return for an executory promise gives rise to an implied condition that the instrument is not to be paid if the promise is not performed, and that this condition destroys negotiability. Nothing in the section is intended to imply that language may not be fairly construed to mean what it says, but implications, whether of law or fact, are not to be considered in determining negotiability.

2. Paragraph (b) of subsection (1) is an amplification of Section 3(2) of the original act. The final clause is intended to resolve a conflict in the decisions over the effect of such language as "This note is given for payment as per contract for the purchase of goods of even date, maturity being in conformity with the terms of such contract." It adopts the general commercial understanding that such language is intended as a mere recital of the origin of the instrument and a reference to the transaction for information, but is not meant to condition payment according to the terms of any other agreement.

3. Paragraph (c) of subsection (1) likewise is intended to resolve a conflict, and to reject cases in which a reference to a separate agreement was held to mean that payment of the instrument must be limited in accordance with the terms of the agreement, and hence was conditioned by it. Such a reference normally is inserted for the purpose of making a record or giving information to anyone who may be interested, and in the absence of any express statement to that effect is not intended to limit the terms of payment. Inasmuch as rights as to prepayment or acceleration has to do with a "speed-up" in payment and since notes frequently refer to separate agreements for a statement of these rights, such reference does not destroy negotiability even though it has mild aspects of incorporation by reference. The general reasoning with respect to subparagraph (c) also applies to a draft which on its face states that it is drawn under a letter of credit (subparagraph (d)). Paragraphs (c) and (d) therefore adopt the position that negotiability is not affected. If the reference goes further and provides that payment must be made according to the terms of the agreement, it falls under paragraph (a) of subsection (2) [As amended 1962].

4. Paragraph (e) of subsection (1) is intended to settle another conflict in the decisions, over the effect of "title security notes" and other instruments which recite the security given. It rejects cases which have held that the mere statement that the instrument is secured, by reservation of title or otherwise, carries the implied condition that payment is to be made only if the security agreement is fully performed. Again such a recital normally is included only for the purpose of making a record or giving information, and is not intended to condition payment in any way. The provision adopts the position of the great majority of the courts.

5. Paragraph (f) of subsection (1) is a rewording of Section 3(1) of the original act.

6. Paragraph (g) of subsection (1) is new. It is intended to permit municipal corporations or other governments or governmental agencies to draw checks or to issue other short-term commercial paper in which payment is limited to a particular fund or to the proceeds of particular taxes or other sources of revenue. The provision will permit some municipal

warrants to be negotiable if they are in proper form. Normally such warrants lack the words "order" or "bearer," or are marked "Not Negotiable," or are payable only in serial order, which makes them conditional.

7. Paragraph (h) of subsection (1) is new. It adopts the policy of decisions holding that an instrument issued by an unincorporated association is negotiable although its payment is expressly limited to the assets of the association, excluding the liability of individual members; and recognizing as negotiable an instrument issued by a trust estate without personal liability of the trustee. The policy is extended to a partnership and to any estate. The provision affects only the negotiability of the instrument, and is not intended to change the law of any state as to the liability of a partner, trustee, executor, administrator, or any other person on such an instrument.

8. Paragraph (a) of subsection (2) retains the generally accepted rule that where an instrument contains such language as "subject to terms of contract between maker and payee of this date," its payment is conditioned according to the terms of the agreement and the instrument is not negotiable. The distinction is between a mere recital of the existence of the separate agreement or a reference to it for information, which under paragraph (c) of subsection (1) will not affect negotiability, and any language which, fairly construed, requires the holder to look to the other agreement for the terms of payment. The intent of the provision is that an instrument is not negotiable unless the holder can ascertain all of its essential terms from its face. In the specific instance of rights as to prepayment or acceleration, however, there may be a reference to a separate agreement without destroying negotiability [As amended 1962].

9. Paragraph (b) of subsection (2) restates the last sentence of Section 3 of the original act. As noted above, exceptions are made by paragraphs (g) and (h) of subsection (1) in favor of instruments issued by governments or governmental agencies, or by a partnership, unincorporated association, trust or estate.

Cross Reference:

Section 3-104.

Definitional Cross References:

"Account". Section 4-104.
"Agreement". Section 1-201.
"Instrument". Section 3-102.
"Issue". Section 3-102.
"Order". Section 3-102.
"Promise". Section 3-102.

§ 3-106. Sum Certain.

(1) The sum payable is a sum certain even though it is to be paid

(a) with stated interest or by stated installments; or

(b) with stated different rates of interest before and after default or a specified date; or

(c) with a stated discount or addition if paid before or after the date fixed for payment; or

(d) with exchange or less exchange, whether at a fixed rate or at the current rate; or

(e) with costs of collection or an attorney's fee or both upon default.

(2) Nothing in this section shall validate any term which is otherwise illegal.

Official Comment

Prior Uniform Statutory Provision: Sections 2 and 6(5), Uniform Negotiable Instruments Law.

Changes: Reworded.

Purposes of Changes: The new language is intended to clarify doubts arising under the original section as to interest, discounts or additions, exchange, costs and attorney's fees, and acceleration or extension.

1. The section rejects decisions which have denied negotiability to a note with a term providing for a discount for early payment on the ground that at the time of issue the amount payable was not certain. It is sufficient that at any time of payment the holder is able to determine the amount then payable from the instrument itself with any necessary computation. Thus a demand note bearing interest at six per cent is negotiable. A stated discount or addition for early or late payment does not affect the certainty of the sum so long as the computation can be made, nor do different rates of interest before and after default or a specified date. The computation must be one which can be made from the instrument itself without reference to any outside source, and this section does not make negotiable a note payable with interest "at the current rate."

2. Paragraph (d) recognizes the occasional practice of making the instrument payable with exchange deducted rather than added.

3. In paragraph (e) "upon default" is substituted for the language of the original Section 2(5) in order to include any default in payment of interest or installments.

4. The section contains no specific language relating to the effect of acceleration clauses on the certainty of the sum payable. Section 2(3) of the original act contained a saving clause for provisions accelerating principal on default in payment of an installment or of interest, which led to doubt as to the effect of other accelerating provisions. This Article (Section 3-109, Definite Time) broadly validates acceleration clauses; it is not necessary to state the matter in this section as well. The disappearance of the language referred to in old Section 2(3) means merely that it was regarded as surplusage.

5. Most states have usury laws prohibiting excessive rates of interest. In some states there are statutes or rules of law invalidating a term providing for increased interest after maturity, or for costs and attorney's fees. Subsection (2) is intended to make it clear that this section is concerned only with the effect of such terms upon negotiability, and is not meant to change the law of any state as to the validity of the term itself.

Cross References:

Section 3-104.
Point 4: Section 3-109.

Definitional Cross Reference:

"Term". Section 1-201.

§ 3-107. Money.

(1) An instrument is payable in money if the medium of exchange in which it is payable is money at the time the instrument is made. An instrument payable in "currency" or "current funds" is payable in money.

(2) A promise or order to pay a sum stated in a foreign currency is for a sum certain in money and, unless a different medium of payment is specified in the instrument, may be satisfied by payment of that number of dollars which the stated foreign currency will purchase at the buying sight rate for that currency on the day on which the instrument is payable or, if payable on demand, on the day of demand. If such an instrument specifies a foreign

currency as the medium of payment the instrument is payable in that currency.

Official Comment

Prior Uniform Statutory Provision: Section 6(5), Uniform Negotiable Instruments Law.

Changes: Completely rewritten.

Purposes of Changes and New Matter: To make clear when an instrument is payable in money and to state rules applicable to instruments drawn payable in a foreign currency.

1. The term "money" is defined in Section 1–201 as "a medium of exchange authorized or adopted by a domestic or foreign government as a part of its currency". That definition rejects the narrow view of some early cases that "money" is limited to legal tender. Legal tender acts do no more than designate a particular kind of money which the obligee will be required to accept in discharge of an obligation. It rejects also the contention sometimes advanced that "money" includes any medium of exchange current and accepted in the particular community whether it be gold dust, beaver pelts, or cigarettes in occupied Germany. Such unusual "currency" is necessarily of uncertain and fluctuating value, and an instrument intended to pass generally in commerce as negotiable may not be made payable therein.

The test adopted is that of the sanction of government, which recognizes the circulating medium as a part of the official currency of that government. In particular the provision adopts the position that an instrument expressing the amount to be paid in sterling, francs, lire or other recognized currency of a foreign government is negotiable even though payable in the United States.

2. The provision on "currency" or "current funds" accepts the view of the great majority of the decisions, that "currency" or "current funds" means that the instrument is payable in money.

3. Either the amount to be paid or the medium of payment may be expressed in terms of a particular kind of money. A draft passing between Toronto and Buffalo may, according to the desire and convenience of the parties, call for payment of 100 United States dollars or of 100 Canadian dollars; and it may require either sum to be paid in either currency. Under this section an instrument in any of these forms is negotiable, whether payable in Toronto or in Buffalo.

4. As stated in the preceding paragraph the intention of the parties in making an instrument payable in a foreign currency may be that the medium of payment shall be either dollars measured by the foreign currency or the foreign currency in which the instrument is drawn. Under subsection (2) the presumption is, unless the instrument otherwise specifies, that the obligation may be satisfied by payment in dollars in an amount determined by the buying sight rate for the foreign currency on the day the instrument becomes payable. Inasmuch as the buying sight rate will fluctuate from day to day, it might be argued that an instrument expressed in a foreign currency but actually payable in dollars is not for a "sum certain". Subsection (2) makes it clear that for the purposes of negotiability under this Article such an instrument, despite exchange fluctuations, is for a sum certain.

Cross References:

Section 3–104.
Point 1: Section 1–201.
Point 4: Section 4–212(6).

Definitional Cross References:

"Instrument". Section 3–102.
"Money". Section 1–201.
"Order". Section 3–102.
"Promise". Section 3–102.
"Purchase". Section 1–201.

§ 3-108. Payable on Demand.

Instruments payable on demand include those payable at sight or on presentation and those in which no time for payment is stated.

Official Comment

Prior Uniform Statutory Provision: Section 7, Uniform Negotiable Instruments Law.

Changes: Reworded, final sentence of original section omitted.

Purposes of Changes: Except for the omission of the final sentence this section restates the substance of original Section 7. The final sentence dealt with the status of a person issuing, accepting or indorsing an instrument after maturity and provided that as to such a person the instrument was payable on demand. That language implied that the ordinary rules relating to demand instruments as to due course, holding, presentment, notice of dishonor and so on were applicable. This Article abandons that concept which served no special purpose except to trap the unwary. Under Section 3-302 (Holder in Due Course) and in view of the deletion from this section of the final sentence of original Section 7 there is no longer the possibility that one taking time paper after maturity may acquire due course rights against a post-maturity indorser. Section 3-501(4), however, provides that the indorser after maturity is not entitled to presentment, notice of dishonor or protest.

Cross References:

Sections 3-104, 3-302 and 3-501(4).

Definitional Cross Reference:

"Instrument". Section 3-102.

§ 3-109. Definite Time.

(1) An instrument is payable at a definite time if by its terms it is payable

(a) on or before a stated date or at a fixed period after a stated date; or

(b) at a fixed period after sight; or

(c) at a definite time subject to any acceleration; or

(d) at a definite time subject to extension at the option of the holder, or to extension to a further definite time at the option of the maker or acceptor or automatically upon or after a specified act or event.

(2) An instrument which by its terms is otherwise payable only upon an act or event uncertain as to time of occurrence is not payable at a definite time even though the act or event has occurred.

Official Comment

Prior Uniform Statutory Provision: Sections 4 and 17(3), Uniform Negotiable Instruments Law.

Changes: Reworded; new provisions; rule of original Section 4(3) reversed.

Purposes of Changes and New Matter: To remove uncertainties arising under the original section, and to eliminate commercially unacceptable instruments.

1. Subsection (2) reverses the rule of the original Section 4(3) as to instruments payable after events certain to happen but uncertain as to time. Almost the only use of such instruments has been in the anticipation of inheritance or future interests by borrowing on post-obituary notes. These have been much more common in England than in the United States. They are at best questionable

paper, not acceptable in general commerce, with no good reason for according them free circulation as negotiable instruments. As in the case of the occasional note payable "one year after the war" or at a similar uncertain date, they are likely to be made under unusual circumstances suggesting good reason for preserving defenses of the maker. They are accordingly eliminated.

2. With this change "definite time" is substituted for "fixed or determinable future time." The time of payment is definite if it can be determined from the face of the instrument.

3. An undated instrument payable "thirty days after date" is not payable at a definite time, since the time of payment cannot be determined on its face. It is, however, an incomplete instrument within the provisions of Section 3–115 dealing with such instruments and may be completed by dating it. It is then payable at a definite time.

4. Paragraph (c) of subsection (1) resolves a conflict in the decisions on the negotiability of instruments containing acceleration clauses as to the meaning and effect of "on or before a fixed or determinable future time" in the original Section 4(2). (Instruments expressly stated to be payable "on or before" a given date are dealt with in subsection (1)(a)). So far as certainty of time of payment is concerned a note payable at a definite time but subject to acceleration is no less certain than a note payable on demand, whose negotiability never has been questioned. It is in fact more certain, since it at least states a definite time beyond which the instrument cannot run. Objections to the acceleration clause must be based rather on the possibility of abuse by the holder, which has nothing to do with negotiability and is not limited to negotiable instruments. That problem is now covered by Section 1–208.

Subsection (1)(c) is intended to mean that the certainty of time of payment or the negotiability of the instrument is not affected by any acceleration clause, whether acceleration be at the option of the maker or the holder, or automatic upon the occurrence of some event, and whether it be conditional or unrestricted. If the acceleration term itself is uncertain it may fail on ordinary contract principles, but the instrument then remains negotiable and is payable at the definite time.

The effect of acceleration clauses upon a holder in due course is covered by the new definition of the holder in due course (Section 3–302) and by the section on notice to purchaser (subsection (3) of Section 3–304). If the purchaser is not aware of any acceleration, his delay in making presentment may be excused under the section dealing with excused presentment (subsection (1) of Section 3–511).

5. Paragraph (d) of subsection (1) is new. It adopts the generally accepted rule that a clause providing for extension at the option of the holder, even without a time limit, does not affect negotiability since the holder is given only a right which he would have without the clause. If the extension is to be at the option of the maker or acceptor or is to be automatic, a definite time limit must be stated or the time of payment remains uncertain and the instrument is not negotiable. Where such a limit is stated, the effect upon certainty of time of payment is the same as if the instrument were made payable at the ultimate date with a term providing for acceleration.

The construction and effect of extension clauses is covered by paragraph (f) of Section 3–118 on ambiguous terms and rules of construction, to which reference should be made.

Cross References:

Section 3–104.
Point 3: Section 3–115.
Point 4: Sections 1–208, 3–118(f), 3–304(3), and 3–511(1).
Point 5: Section 3–118(f).

Definitional Cross References:

"Holder". Section 1–201.
"Instrument". Section 3–102.
"Term". Section 1–201.

§ 3-110. Payable to Order.

(1) An instrument is payable to order when by its terms it is payable to the order or assigns of any person therein specified with reasonable certainty, or to him or his order, or when it is conspicuously designated on its face as "exchange" or the like and names a payee. It may be payable to the order of

(a) the maker or drawer; or

(b) the drawee; or

(c) a payee who is not maker, drawer or drawee; or

(d) two or more payees together or in the alternative; or

(e) an estate, trust or fund, in which case it is payable to the order of the representative of such estate, trust or fund or his successors; or

(f) an office, or an officer by his title as such in which case it is payable to the principal but the incumbent of the office or his successors may act as if he or they were the holder; or

(g) a partnership or unincorporated association, in which case it is payable to the partnership or association and may be indorsed or transferred by any person thereto authorized.

(2) An instrument not payable to order is not made so payable by such words as "payable upon return of this instrument properly indorsed."

(3) An instrument made payable both to order and to bearer is payable to order unless the bearer words are handwritten or typewritten.

Official Comment

Prior Uniform Statutory Provision: Section 8, Uniform Negotiable Instruments Law.

Changes: Reworded, new provisions.

Purposes of Changes and New Matter: The changes are intended to remove uncertainties arising under the original section.

1. Paragraph (d) of subsection (1) replaces the original subsections (4) and (5). It eliminates the word "jointly," which has carried a possible implication of a right of survivorship. Normally an instrument payable to "A and B" is intended to be payable to the two parties as tenants in common, and there is no survivorship in the absence of express language to that effect. The instrument may be payable to "A or B," in which case it is payable to either A or B individually. It may even be made payable to "A and/or B," in which case it is payable either to A or to B singly, or to the two together. The negotiation, enforcement and discharge of the instrument in all such cases are covered by the section on instruments payable to two or more persons (Sec. 3-116).

2. Paragraph (e) of subsection (1) is intended to change the result of decisions which have held that an instrument payable to the order of the estate of a decedent was payable to bearer, on the ground that the name of the payee did not purport to be that of any person. The intent in such cases is obviously not to make the instrument payable to bearer, but to the order of the representative of the estate. The provision extends the same principle to an instrument payable to the order of "Tilden Trust," or "Community Fund". So long as the payee can be identified, it is not necessary that it be a legal entity; and in each case the instrument is treated as payable to the order of the appropriate representative or his successor.

3. Under paragraph (f) of subsection (1) an instrument may be made payable

to the office itself ("Swedish Consulate") or to the officer by his title as such ("Treasurer of City Club"). In either case it runs to the incumbent of the office and his successors. The effect of instruments in such a form is covered by the section on instruments payable with words of description (Sec. 3-117).

4. Vestigial theories relating to the lack of "legal entity" of partnerships and various forms of unincorporated associations—such as labor unions and business trusts—make it the part of wisdom to specify that instruments made payable to such groups are order paper payable as designated and not bearer paper (subsection (1)(g)). As in the case of incorporated associations, any person having authority from the partnership or association to whose order the instrument is payable may indorse or otherwise deal with the instrument.

5. Subsection (2) is intended to change the result of cases holding that "payable upon return of this certificate properly indorsed" indicated an intention to make the instrument payable to any indorsee and so must be construed as the equivalent of "Pay to order." Ordinarily the purpose of such language is only to insure return of the instrument with indorsement in lieu of a receipt, and the word "order" is omitted with the intention that the instrument shall not be negotiable.

6. Subsection (3) is directed at occasional instruments reading "Pay to the order of John Doe or bearer." Such language usually is found only where the drawer has filled in the name of the payee on a printed form, without intending the ambiguity or noticing the word "bearer." Under such circumstances the name of the specified payee indicates an intent that the order words shall control. If the word "bearer" is handwritten or typewritten, there is sufficient indication of an intent that the instrument shall be payable to bearer. Instruments payable to "order of bearer" are covered not by this section but by the following Section 3-111.

Cross References:

Sections 3-104 and 3-111.
Point 1: Section 3-116.
Points 2, 3 and 4: Section 3-117.

Definitional Cross References:

"Bearer". Section 1-201.
"Conspicuous". Section 1-201.
"Instrument". Section 3-102.
"Negotiation". Section 3-202.
"Person". Section 1-201.
"Term". Section 1-201.

§ 3-111. Payable to Bearer.

An instrument is payable to bearer when by its terms it is payable to

(a) bearer or the order of bearer; or

(b) a specified person or bearer; or

(c) "cash" or the order of "cash", or any other indication which does not purport to designate a specific payee.

Official Comment

Prior Uniform Statutory Provision: Section 9, Uniform Negotiable Instruments Law.

Changes: Reworded; original subsections (3) and (5) omitted here but covered by Sections on impostors and signature in name of payee (Section 3-405) and on special and blank indorsements (Section 3-204).

Purposes of Changes: The rewording is intended to remove uncertainties.

1. Language such as "order of bearer" usually results when a printed form is used and the word "bearer" is filled in. Subsection (a) rejects the view that the

instrument is payable to order, and adopts the position that "bearer" is the unusual word and should control. Compare Comment 6 to Section 3-110.

2. Paragraph (c) is reworded to remove any possible implication that "Pay to the order of ______" makes the instrument payable to bearer. It is an incomplete order instrument, and falls under Section 3-115. Likewise "Pay Treasurer of X Corporation" does not mean pay bearer, even though there may be no such officer. Instruments payable to the order of an estate, trust, fund, partnership, unincorporated association or office are covered by the preceding section. This subsection applies only to such language as "Pay Cash," "Pay to the order of cash," "Pay bills payable," "Pay to the order of one keg of nails," or other words which do not purport to designate any specific payee.

3. Under Section 40 of the original Act an instrument payable to bearer on its face remained bearer paper negotiable by delivery although subsequently specially indorsed. It should be noted that Section 3-204 on special indorsement reverses this rule and allows the special indorsement to control.

Cross References:

Sections 3-104, 3-405 and 3-204.

Point 2: Sections 3-110(1)(a) and (f) and 3-115.

Point 3: Section 3-204.

Definitional Cross References:

"Bearer". Section 1-201.

"Instrument". Section 3-102.

"Person". Section 1-201.

"Term". Section 1-201.

§ 3-112. Terms and Omissions Not Affecting Negotiability.

(1) The negotiability of an instrument is not affected by

(a) the omission of a statement of any consideration or of the place where the instrument is drawn or payable; or

(b) a statement that collateral has been given to secure obligations either on the instrument or otherwise of an obligor on the instrument or that in case of default on those obligations the holder may realize on or dispose of the collateral; or

(c) a promise or power to maintain or protect collateral or to give additional collateral; or

(d) a term authorizing a confession of judgment on the instrument if it is not paid when due; or

(e) a term purporting to waive the benefit of any law intended for the advantage or protection of any obligor; or

(f) a term in a draft providing that the payee by indorsing or cashing it acknowledges full satisfaction of an obligation of the drawer; or

(g) A statement in a draft drawn in a set of parts (Section 3-801) to the effect that the order is effective only if no other part has been honored.

(2) Nothing in this section shall validate any term which is otherwise illegal.

As amended in 1962.

Official Comment

Prior Uniform Statutory Provision: Sections 5 and 6, Uniform Negotiable Instruments Law.

Changes: Reworded; new provisions; Subsection (4) of original Section 5 omitted. Subsection (4) of the original Section 6 is now covered by Section 3–113, and Subsection (5) by Section 3–107.

Purposes of Changes and New Matter: The changes are intended to remove uncertainties arising under the original sections. Subsection (4) of the original Section 5 is omitted because it has been important only in connection with bonds and other investment securities now covered by Article 8 of this Act. An option to require something to be done in lieu of payment of money is uncommon and not desirable in commercial paper.

This section permits the insertion of certain obligations and powers in addition to the simple promise or order to pay money. Under Section 3–104, dealing with form of negotiable instruments, the instrument may not contain any other promise, order, obligation or power.

1. Paragraph (b) of subsection (1) permits a clause authorizing the sale or disposition of collateral given to secure obligations either on the instrument or otherwise of an obligor on the instrument upon any default in those obligations, including a default in payment of an installment or of interest. It is not limited, as was the original Section 5(1), to default at maturity. The reference to obligations of an obligor on the instrument is intended to recognize so-called cross collateral provisions that appear in collateral note forms used by banks and others throughout the United States and to permit the use of these provisions without destroying negotiability. Paragraph (c) is new. It permits a clause, apparently not within the original section, containing a promise or power to maintain or protect collateral or to give additional collateral, whether on demand or on some other condition. Such terms frequently are accompanied by a provision for acceleration if the collateral is not given, which is now permitted by the section on what constitutes a definite time. Section 1–208 should be consulted as to the construction to be given such clauses under this Act.

2. As under the original Section 5(2), paragraph (d) is intended to mean that a confession of judgment may be authorized only if the instrument is not paid when due, and that otherwise negotiability is affected. The use of judgment notes is confined to two or three states, and in others the judgment clauses are made illegal or ineffective either by special statutes or by decision. Subsection (2) is intended to say that any such local rule remains unchanged, and that the clause itself may be invalid, although the negotiability of the instrument is not affected.

3. As in the case of the original Section 5(3), paragraph (e) applies not only to any waiver of the benefits of this Article, such as presentment, notice of dishonor or protest, but also to a waiver of the benefits of any other law such as a homestead exemption. Again subsection (2) is intended to mean that any rule which invalidates the waiver itself is not changed, and that while negotiability is not affected, a waiver of the statute of limitations contained in an instrument may be invalid.

This paragraph is to be read together with subsection (1) of Section 3–104 on form of negotiable instruments. A waiver cannot make the instrument negotiable within this Article where it does not comply with the requirements of that section.

4. Paragraph (f) is new. The effect of a clause of acknowledgment of satisfaction upon negotiability has been uncertain under the original section.

5. Paragraph (g) is intended to insure that a condition arising from the statement in question will not adversely affect negotiability.

Cross References:

Sections 3–104 and 3–105.

Point 1: Sections 1-208 and 3-109(1)(c).

Point 3: Section 3-104.

Definitional Cross References:

"Draft". Section 3-104.

"Instrument". Section 3-102.

"On demand". Section 3-108.

"Promise". Section 3-102.

"Term". Section 1-201.

§ 3-113. Seal.

An instrument otherwise negotiable is within this Article even though it is under a seal.

Official Comment

Prior Uniform Statutory Provision: Section 6(4), Uniform Negotiable Instruments Law.

Changes: Reworded.

Purposes of Changes: The revised wording is intended to change the result of decisions holding that while a seal does not affect the negotiability of an instrument it may affect it in other respects falling within the statute, such as the conclusiveness of consideration. The section is intended to place sealed instruments on the same footing as any other instruments so far as all sections of this Article are concerned. It does not affect any other statutes or rules of law relating to sealed instruments except insofar as, in the case of negotiable instruments, they are inconsistent with this Article. Thus a sealed instrument which is within this Article may still be subject to a longer statute of limitations than negotiable instruments not under seal, or to such local rules of procedure as that it may be enforced by an action of special assumpsit.

Cross Reference:

Section 3-104.

Definitional Cross Reference:

"Instrument". Section 3-102.

§ 3-114. Date, Antedating, Postdating.

(1) The negotiability of an instrument is not affected by the fact that it is undated, antedated or postdated.

(2) Where an instrument is antedated or postdated the time when it is payable is determined by the stated date if the instrument is payable on demand or at a fixed period after date.

(3) Where the instrument or any signature thereon is dated, the date is presumed to be correct.

Official Comment

Prior Uniform Statutory Provision: Sections 6(1), 11, 12 and 17(3), Uniform Negotiable Instruments Law.

Changes: Reworded; new provision; parts of original section 12 omitted.

Purposes of Changes and New Matter: The rewording is intended to remove uncertainties arising under the original sections.

1. The reference to an "illegal or fraudulent purpose" in the original Section 12 is omitted as inaccurate and misleading. Any fraud or illegality connected with the date of an instrument does not affect its negotiability, but is merely a defense under Sections 3-306 and 3-307 to the same extent as any other fraud or illegality. The provision in the same section as to acquisition of title upon delivery is also omitted, as obvious and unnecessary.

2. Subsection (2) is new. An undated instrument payable "thirty days after date" is uncertain as to time of payment, and does not fall within Section 3-109(1)(a) on definite time. It is, however, an incomplete instrument, and the date may be inserted as provided in the section dealing with such instruments (Section 3-115). When the instrument has been dated, this subsection follows decisions under the original Act in providing that the time of payment is to be determined from the stated date, even though the instrument is antedated or postdated. An antedated instrument may thus be due before it is issued. As to the liability of indorsers in such a case, see Section 3-501(4), on indorsement after maturity.

3. Subsection (3) extends the original Section 11 to any signature on an instrument. As to the meaning of "presumed," see Section 1-201.

Cross References:

Point 1: Sections 3-306 and 3-307.

Point 2: Sections 3-109(1)(a), 3-115 and 3-501(4).

Point 3: Section 1-201.

Definitional Cross References:

"Instrument". Section 3-102.
"Issue". Section 3-102.
"On demand". Section 3-108.
"Presumed". Section 1-201.
"Signature". Section 3-401.

§ 3-115. Incomplete Instruments.

(1) When a paper whose contents at the time of signing show that it is intended to become an instrument is signed while still incomplete in any necessary respect it cannot be enforced until completed, but when it is completed in accordance with authority given it is effective as completed.

(2) If the completion is unauthorized the rules as to material alteration apply (Section 3-407), even though the paper was not delivered by the maker or drawer; but the burden of establishing that any completion is unauthorized is on the party so asserting.

Official Comment

Prior Uniform Statutory Provision: Sections 13, 14 and 15, Uniform Negotiable Instruments Law.

Changes: Condensed and reworded; original Section 13 and parts of Section 14 omitted; rule of Section 15 reversed.

Purposes of Changes:

1. The original sections were lengthy and confusing. Section 13 is eliminated because it has suggested some uncertain distinction between undated instruments and those incomplete in other respects, and has carried the inference that only a holder may fill in the date. An instrument lacking in an essential date is merely one kind of incomplete instrument, to be treated like any other. The third sentence of Section 14, providing that the instrument must be filled up strictly in accordance with the authority given and within a reasonable time, is eliminated as entirely superfluous, since any authority must always be exercised in accordance with its limitations, and expires within a reasonable time unless a time limit is fixed.

2. The language "signed while still incomplete in any necessary respect" in subsection (1) is substituted for "wanting in any material particular" in the original Section 14, in order to make it entirely clear that a complete writing which lacks an essential element of an instrument and contains no blanks or spaces or anything else to indicate that what is missing is to be supplied, does not fall within the section. "Necessary" means necessary to a complete instrument. It will always include the promise or order, the designation of the payee, and the amount payable. It may include the time of payment where a blank is left for that time to be

filled in; but where it is clear that no time is intended to be stated the instrument is complete, and is payable on demand under Section 3-108. It does not include the date of issue, which under Section 3-114(1) is not essential, unless the instrument is made payable at a fixed period after that date.

3. This section omits the second sentence of the original Section 14, providing that "a signature on a blank paper delivered by the person making the signature in order that the paper may be converted into a negotiable instrument operates as a prima facie authority to fill it up as such for any amount." This had utility only in connection with the ancient practice of signing blank paper to be filled in later as an acceptance, at a time when communications were slow and difficult. The practice has been obsolete for nearly a century. It affords obvious opportunity for fraud, and should not be encouraged by express sanction in the statute. The omission is not intended, however, to mean that any person may not be authorized to write in an instrument over a signature either before or after delivery.

4. Subsection (2) states the rule generally recognized by the courts, that any unauthorized completion is an alteration of the instrument which stands on the same footing as any other alteration. Reference is therefore made to Section 3-407 where the effect of alteration is stated. Subsection (3) of that section provides that a subsequent holder in due course may in all cases enforce the instrument as completed, and replaces the final sentence of the original Section 14.

5. The language "even though the paper was not delivered" reverses the rule of the original Section 15, which provides that where an incomplete instrument has not been delivered it will not, if completed, be a valid contract in the hands of any holder as against any person whose signature was placed thereon before delivery. Since under this Article (Sections 3-305 and 3-407) neither non-delivery nor unauthorized completion is a defense against a holder in due course, it has always been illogical that the two together should invalidate the instrument in his hands. A holder in due course sees and takes the same paper, whether it was complete when stolen or completed afterward by the thief, and in each case he relies in good faith on the maker's signature. The loss should fall upon the party whose conduct in signing blank paper has made the fraud possible, rather than upon the innocent purchaser. The result is consistent with the theory of decisions holding the drawer of a check stolen and afterwards filled in to be estopped from setting up the non-delivery against an innocent party.

A similar provision protecting a depositary bank which pays an item in good faith is contained in Section 4-401. The policy of that Section should apply in favor of drawees other than banks.

6. The language on burden of establishing unauthorized completion is substituted for the "prima facie authority" of the original section 14. It follows the generally accepted rule that the full burden of proof by a preponderance of the evidence is upon the party attacking the completed instrument. "Burden of establishing" is defined in Section 1-201.

Cross References:

Point 2: Sections 3-108 and 3-114(1).

Point 4: Section 3-407.

Point 5: Sections 3-305(2), 3-407(3) and 4-401.

Point 6: Section 1-201.

Definitional Cross References:

"Alteration". Section 3-407.

"Burden of establishing". Section 1-201.

"Delivery". Section 1-201.

"Instrument". Section 3-102.

"Party". Section 1-201.

"Signed". Section 1-201.

§ 3-116. Instruments Payable to Two or More Persons.

An instrument payable to the order of two or more persons

(a) if in the alternative is payable to any one of them and may be negotiated, discharged or enforced by any of them who has possession of it;

(b) if not in the alternative is payable to all of them and may be negotiated, discharged or enforced only by all of them.

Official Comment

Prior Uniform Statutory Provision: Section 41, Uniform Negotiable Instruments Law.

Changes: Revised in wording and substance.

Purposes of Changes: The changes are intended to make clear the distinction between an instrument payable to "A or B" and one payable to "A and B." The first names either A or B as payee, so that either of them who is in possession becomes a holder as that term is defined in Section 1-201 and may negotiate, enforce or discharge the instrument. The second is payable only to A and B together, and as provided in the original section both must indorse in order to negotiate the instrument, although one may of course be authorized to sign for the other. Likewise both must join in any action to enforce the instrument, and the rights of one are not discharged without his consent by the act of the other.

If the instrument is payable to "A and/or B," it is payable in the alternative to A, or to B, or to A and B together, and it may be negotiated, enforced or discharged accordingly.

Cross Reference:

Section 1-201.

Definitional Cross References:

"Instrument". Section 3-102.
"Person". Section 1-201.

§ 3-117. Instruments Payable With Words of Description.

An instrument made payable to a named person with the addition of words describing him

(a) as agent or officer of a specified person is payable to his principal but the agent or officer may act as if he were the holder;

(b) as any other fiduciary for a specified person or purpose is payable to the payee and may be negotiated, discharged or enforced by him;

(c) in any other manner is payable to the payee unconditionally and the additional words are without effect on subsequent parties.

Official Comment

Prior Uniform Statutory Provision: Section 42, Uniform Negotiable Instruments Law.

Changes: Revised and extended.

Purposes of Changes:

1. Subsection (a) extends the policy of the original Section 42, which covered only cashiers and fiscal officers of banks and corporations, to any case where a payee is named with words describing him as agent or officer of another named person. The intent is to include all such descriptions as "John Doe, Treasurer of Town of Framingham," "John Doe, President Home Telephone Co.," "John Doe, Secretary of City Club," or "John Doe, agent of Richard Roe." In all such cases it is commercial understanding that the description is not added for mere identification but for the purpose of making the instrument payable to the principal, and that the agent or officer is named as payee only for convenience in enabling him to cash the check.

2. Subsection (b) covers such descriptions as "John Doe, Trustee of Smithers Trust," "John Doe, Administrator of the Estate of Richard Roe," or "John Doe, Executor under Will of Richard Roe." In such cases the instrument is payable to the individual named, and he may negotiate it, enforce it or discharge it, but he remains subject to any liability for breach of his obligation as a fiduciary. Any subsequent holder of the instrument is put on notice of the fiduciary position, and under the section on notice to purchaser (Section 3-304) is not a holder in due course if he takes with notice that John Doe has negotiated the instrument in payment of or as security for his own debt or in any transaction for his own benefit, or otherwise in breach of duty.

3. Any other words of description, such as "John Doe, 1121 Main Street," "John Doe, Attorney," or "Jane Doe, unremarried widow," are to be treated as mere identification, and not in any respect as a condition of payment. The same is true of any description of the payee as "Treasurer," "President," "Agent," "Trustee," "Executor," or "Administrator," which does not name the principal or beneficiary. In all such cases the person named may negotiate, enforce or discharge the instrument if he is otherwise identified, even though he does not meet the description. Any subsequent party dealing with the instrument may disregard the description and treat the paper as payable unconditionally to the individual, and is fully protected in the absence of independent notice of other facts sufficient to affect his position.

Cross Reference:

Point 2: Section 3-304(2).

Definitional Cross References:

"Holder". Section 1-201.
"Instrument". Section 3-102.
"Party". Section 1-201.
"Person". Section 1-201.

§ 3-118. Ambiguous Terms and Rules of Construction.

The following rules apply to every instrument:

(a) Where there is doubt whether the instrument is a draft or a note the holder may treat it as either. A draft drawn on the drawer is effective as a note.

(b) Handwritten terms control typewritten and printed terms, and typewritten control printed.

(c) Words control figures except that if the words are ambiguous figures control.

(d) Unless otherwise specified a provision for interest means interest at the judgment rate at the place of payment from the date of the instrument, or if it is undated from the date of issue.

(e) Unless the instrument otherwise specifies two or more persons who sign as maker, acceptor or drawer or indorser and as a part of the same transaction are jointly and severally liable even though the instrument contains such words as "I promise to pay."

(f) Unless otherwise specified consent to extension authorizes a single extension for not longer than the original period. A consent to extension, expressed in the instrument, is binding on secondary parties and accommodation makers. A holder may not exercise his option to extend an instrument over the objection of a maker or acceptor or other party who in accordance with Section 3-604 tenders full payment when the instrument is due.

Official Comment

Prior Uniform Statutory Provision: Sections 17 and 68, Uniform Negotiable Instruments Law.

Changes: Reworded; new provisions; original subsections (3) and (6) of Section 17 omitted. The original Section 17(3) is covered, so far as the question can arise, by Sections 3–109(1)(a) and 3–114 of this Article. The original Section 17(6) is now covered by Section 3–402.

Purposes of Changes and New Matter:

1. The purpose of this section is to protect holders and to encourage the free circulation of negotiable paper by stating rules of law which will preclude a resort to parol evidence for any purpose except reformation of the instrument. Except as to such reformation, these rules cannot be varied by any proof that any party intended the contrary.

2. Subsection (a): The language of the original Section 17(5) is changed to make it clear that the provision is not limited to ambiguities of phrasing, but extends to any case where the form of the instrument leaves its character as a draft or a note in doubt.

3. Subsection (b): The original Section 17(4) is revised to cover typewriting because of its frequent use in instruments, particularly in promissory notes.

4. Subsection (c): The rewording of the original Section 17(1) is intended to make it clear that figures control only where the words are ambiguous and the figures are not.

5. Subsection (d): The revision of the original Section 17(2) is intended to make it clear that where the instrument provides for payment "with interest" without specifying the rate, the judgment rate of interest of the place of payment is to be taken as intended.

6. Subsection (e): This subsection combines and revises the original Section 17(7) and the last sentence of the original Section 68. The rule applies to any two or more persons who sign in the same capacity, whether as makers, drawers, acceptors or indorsers. It applies only where such parties sign as a part of the same transaction; successive indorsers are, of course, liable severally but not jointly.

7. Subsection (f): This provision is new. It has reference to such clauses as "The makers and indorsers of this note consent that it may be extended without notice to them." Such terms usually are inserted to obtain the consent of the indorsers and any accommodation maker to extension which might otherwise discharge them under Section 3–606 dealing with impairment of recourse or collateral. An extension in accord with these terms binds secondary parties. The holder may not force an extension on a maker or acceptor who makes due tender; the holder is not free to refuse payment and keep interest running on a good note or other instrument by extending it over the objection of a maker or acceptor or other party who in accordance with Section 3–604 tenders full payment when the instrument is due. Where consent to extension has been given, the subsection provides that unless otherwise specified the consent is to be construed as authorizing only one extension for not longer than the original period of the note.

Cross References:

Sections 3–109, 3–114, 3–402 and 3–606.

Point 7: Sections 3–604 and 3–606.

Definitional Cross References:

"Draft". Section 3–104.
"Holder". Section 1–201.
"Instrument". Section 3–102.
"Issue". Section 3–102.
"Note". Section 3–104.
"Person". Section 1–201.
"Promise". Section 3–102.
"Signed". Section 1–201.
"Term". Section 1–201.

§ 3-119. Other Writings Affecting Instrument.

(1) As between the obligor and his immediate obligee or any transferee the terms of an instrument may be modified or affected by any other written agreement executed as a part of the same transaction, except that a holder in due course is not affected by any limitation of his rights arising out of the separate written agreement if he had no notice of the limitation when he took the instrument.

(2) A separate agreement does not affect the negotiability of an instrument.

Official Comment

Prior Uniform Statutory Provision: None.

Purposes: This section is new. It is intended to resolve conflicts as to the effect of a separate writing upon a negotiable instrument.

1. This Article does not attempt to state general rules as to when an instrument may be varied or affected by parol evidence, except to the extent indicated by the comment to the preceding section. This section is limited to the effect of a separate written agreement executed as a part of the same transaction. The separate writing is most commonly an agreement creating or providing for a security interest such as a mortgage, chattel mortgage, conditional sale or pledge. It may, however, be any type of contract, including an agreement that upon certain conditions the instrument shall be discharged or is not to be paid, or even an agreement that it is a sham and not to be enforced at all. Nothing in this section is intended to validate any such agreement which is fraudulent or void as against public policy, as in the case of a note given to deceive a bank examiner.

2. Other parties, such as an accommodation indorser, are not affected by the separate writing unless they were also parties to it as a part of the transaction by which they became bound on the instrument.

3. The section applies to negotiable instruments the ordinary rule that writings executed as a part of the same transaction are to be read together as a single agreement. As between the immediate parties a negotiable instrument is merely a contract, and is no exception to the principle that the courts will look to the entire contract in writing. Accordingly a note may be affected by an acceleration clause, a clause providing for discharge under certain conditions, or any other relevant term in the separate writing. "May be modified or affected" does not mean that the separate agreement must necessarily be given effect. There is still room for construction of the writing as not intended to affect the instrument at all, or as intended to affect it only for a limited purpose such as foreclosure or other realization of collateral. If there is outright contradiction between the two, as where the note is for $1,000 but the accompanying mortgage recites that it is for $2,000, the note may be held to stand on its own feet and not to be affected by the contradiction.

4. Under this Article a purchaser of the instrument may become a holder in due course although he takes it with knowledge that it was accompanied by a separate agreement, if he has no notice of any defense or claim arising from the terms of the agreement. If any limitation in the separate writing in itself amounts to a defense or claim, as in the case of an agreement that the note is a sham and cannot be enforced, a purchaser with notice of it cannot be a holder in due course. The section also covers limitations which do not in themselves give notice of any present defense or claim, such as conditions providing that under certain conditions the note shall be extended for one

year. A purchaser with notice of such limitations may be a holder in due course, but he takes the instrument subject to the limitation. If he is without such notice, he is not affected by such a limiting clause in the separate writing.

5. Subsection (2) rejects decisions which have carried the rule that contemporaneous writings must be read together to the length of holding that a clause in a mortgage affecting a note destroyed the negotiability of the note. The negotiability of an instrument is always to be determined by what appears on the face of the instrument alone, and if it is negotiable in itself a purchaser without notice of a separate writing is in no way affected by it. If the instrument itself states that it is subject to or governed by any other agreement, it is not negotiable under this Article; but if it merely refers to a separate agreement or states that it arises out of such an agreement, it is negotiable.

Cross References:

Point 1: Section 3-119.
Point 4: Section 3-304(4)(b).
Point 5: Section 3-105(2)(a) and (1)(c).

Definitional Cross References:

"Agreement". Section 1-201.
"Holder in due course". Section 3-302.
"Instrument". Section 3-102.
"Notice". Section 1-201.
"Rights". Section 1-201.
"Term". Section 1-201.
"Written" and "writing". Section 1-201.

§ 3-120. Instruments "Payable Through" Bank.

An instrument which states that it is "payable through" a bank or the like designates that bank as a collecting bank to make presentment but does not of itself authorize the bank to pay the instrument.

Official Comment

Prior Uniform Statutory Provision: None.

Purposes: Insurance, dividend or payroll checks, and occasionally other types of instruments, are sometimes made payable "through" a particular bank. This section states the commercial understanding as to the effect of such language. The bank is not named as drawee, and it is not ordered or even authorized to pay the instrument out of the drawer's account or any other funds of the drawer in its hands. Neither is it required to take the instrument for collection in the absence of special agreement to that effect. It is merely designated as a collecting bank through which presentment is properly made to the drawee.

Definitional Cross References:

"Bank". Section 1-201.
"Collecting bank". Section 4-105.
"Instrument". Section 3-102.
"Presentment". Section 3-504.

§ 3-121. Instruments Payable at Bank.

Note: *If this Act is introduced in the Congress of the United States this section should be omitted.*

(States to select either alternative)

Alternative A—

A note or acceptance which states that it is payable at a bank is the equivalent of a draft drawn on the bank payable when it falls due out of any funds of the maker or acceptor in current account or otherwise available for such payment.

Alternative B—

A note or acceptance which states that it is payable at a bank is not of itself an order or authorization to the bank to pay it.

Official Comment

Prior Uniform Statutory Provision: Section 87, Uniform Negotiable Instruments Law.

Changes: Alternative sections offered.

Purposes of Changes: The original section 87 has been amended so extensively that no uniformity has been achieved; and in many parts of the country it has been consistently disregarded in practice.

The original section represents the commercial and banking practice of New York and the surrounding states, according to which a note or acceptance made payable at a bank is treated as the equivalent of a draft drawn on the bank. The bank is not only authorized but ordered to make payment out of the account of the maker or acceptor when the instrument falls due, and it is expected to do so without consulting him. In the western and southern states a contrary understanding prevails. The note or acceptance payable at a bank is treated as merely designating a place of payment, as if the instrument were made payable at the office of an attorney. The bank's only function is to notify the maker or acceptor that the instrument has been presented and to ask for his instructions; and in the absence of specific instructions it is not regarded as required or even authorized to pay. Notwithstanding the original section western and southern banks have consistently followed the practice of asking for instructions and treating a direction not to pay as a revocation, equivalent to a direction to stop payment.

Both practices are well established, and the division is along geographical lines. A change in either practice might lead to undesirable consequences for holders, banks or depositors. The instruments involved are chiefly promissory notes, which infrequently cross state lines. There is no great need for uniformity. This section therefore offers alternative provisions, the first of which states the New York commercial understanding, and the second that of the south and west.

Cross Reference:

Section 3-502.

Definitional Cross References:

"Acceptance". Section 3-410.
"Account". Section 4-104.
"Bank". Section 1-201.
"Draft". Section 3-104.
"Instrument". Section 3-102.
"Note". Section 3-104.
"Order". Section 3-102.

§ 3-122. Accrual of Cause of Action.

(1) A cause of action against a maker or an acceptor accrues

(a) in the case of a time instrument on the day after maturity;

(b) in the case of a demand instrument upon its date or, if no date is stated, on the date of issue.

(2) A cause of action against the obligor of a demand or time certificate of deposit accrues upon demand, but demand on a time certificate may not be made until on or after the date of maturity.

(3) A cause of action against a drawer of a draft or an indorser of any instrument accrues upon demand following dishonor of the instrument. Notice of dishonor is a demand.

(4) Unless an instrument provides otherwise, interest runs at the rate provided by law for a judgment

(a) in the case of a maker, acceptor or other primary obligor of a demand instrument, from the date of demand;

(b) in all other cases from the date of accrual of the cause of action.

As amended in 1962.

Official Comment

Prior Uniform Statutory Provision: None.

Purpose:

1. This section is new. It follows the generally accepted rule that action may be brought on a demand note immediately upon issue, without demand, since presentment is not required to charge the maker under the original Act or under this Article. An exception is made in the case of certificates of deposit for the reason that banking custom and expectation is that demand will be made before any liability is incurred by the bank, and the additional reason that such certificates are issued with the understanding that they will be held for a considerable length of time, which in many instances exceeds the period of the statute of limitations. As to makers and acceptors of time instruments generally, the cause of action accrues on the day after maturity. As to drawers of drafts (including checks) and all indorsers, the cause of action accrues, in conformity with their underlying contract on the instrument (Sections 3–413 and 3–414), only upon demand made, typically in the form of a notice of dishonor, after the instrument has been presented to and dishonored by the person designated on the instrument to pay it.

2. Closely related to the accrual of a cause of action is the question of when interest begins to run where the instrument is blank on the point. A term in the instrument providing for interest controls. (See Section 3–118(d) for the construction of a term which provides for interest but does not specify the rate or the time from which it runs.) In the absence of such a term and except in the case of a maker, acceptor or other primary obligor of a demand instrument subsection (4) states the rule that interest at the judgment rate runs from the date the cause of action accrues. In the case of a primary obligor of a demand instrument, interest runs from the date of demand although the cause of action (subsection (1)(a)) accrues on the stated date of the instrument or on issue. There has been a conflict in the decisions as to when "legal" interest begins to run on a demand note. Some courts have taken the view that, since the note is due when issued without demand, it should follow that interest runs from the same date. On the other hand it is clear that there is no default until after demand by the holder and thus no reason for the imposition of the penalty on the maker. Subsection (4), therefore, adopts the position of the majority of the courts that on a demand note interest runs only from demand. This same rule is applied to acceptors and other primary obligors on a demand instrument.

Cross References:

Point 1: Sections 3–501, 3–413 and 3–414.

Point 2: Section 3–118(d).

Definitional Cross References:

"Action". Section 1–201.

"Certificate of deposit". Section 3–102.

"Dishonor". Section 3–507.

"Draft". Section 3–104.

"Instrument". Section 3–102.

"Note". Section 3–104.

"Notice of dishonor". Section 3–508.

"On demand". Section 3–108.

PART 2

TRANSFER AND NEGOTIATION

§ 3–201. Transfer: Right to Indorsement.

(1) Transfer of an instrument vests in the transferee such rights as the transferor has therein, except that a transferee who has himself been a party to any fraud or illegality affecting the instrument or who as a prior holder had notice of a defense or claim against it cannot improve his position by taking from a later holder in due course.

(2) A transfer of a security interest in an instrument vests the foregoing rights in the transferee to the extent of the interest transferred.

(3) Unless otherwise agreed any transfer for value of an instrument not then payable to bearer gives the transferee the specifically enforceable right to have the unqualified indorsement of the transferor. Negotiation takes effect only when the indorsement is made and until that time there is no presumption that the transferee is the owner.

Official Comment

Prior Uniform Statutory Provision: Sections 27, 49 and 58, Uniform Negotiable Instruments Law.

Changes: Combined and reworded; new provisions.

Purposes of Changes and New Matter: To make it clear that:

1. The section applies to any transfer, whether by a holder or not. Any person who transfers an instrument transfers whatever rights he has in it. The transferee acquires those rights even though they do not amount to "title."

2. The transfer of rights is not limited to transfers for value. An instrument may be transferred as a gift, and the donee acquires whatever rights the donor had.

3. A holder in due course may transfer his rights as such. The "shelter" provision of the last sentence of the original Section 58 is merely one illustration of the rule that anyone may transfer what he has. Its policy is to assure the holder in due course a free market for the paper, and that policy is continued in this section. The provision is not intended and should not be used to permit any holder who has himself been a party to any fraud or illegality affecting the instrument, or who has received notice of any defense or claim against it, to wash the paper clean by passing it into the hands of a holder in due course and then repurchasing it. The operation of the provision is illustrated by the following examples:

(a) A induces M by fraud to make an instrument payable to A, A negotiates it to B, who takes as a holder in due course. After the instrument is overdue B gives it to C, who has notice of the fraud. C succeeds to B's rights as a holder in due course, cutting off the defense.

(b) A induces M by fraud to make an instrument payable to A, A negotiates it to B, who takes as a holder in due course. A then repurchases the instrument from B. A does not succeed to B's rights as a holder in due course, and remains subject to the defense of fraud.

(c) A induces M by fraud to make an instrument payable to A, A negotiates it to B, who takes with notice of the fraud. B negotiates it to C, a holder in due course, and then repurchases the instrument from C. B does not succeed to C's rights as a holder in due course, and remains subject to the defense of fraud.

(d) The same facts as (c), except that B had no notice of the fraud when he first acquired the instrument, but learned of it while he was a holder and with such knowledge negotiated to C. B does not succeed to C's rights as a holder in due course, and his position is not improved by the negotiation and repurchase.

4. The rights of a transferee with respect to collateral for the instrument are determined by Article 9 (Secured Transactions).

5. Subsection (2) restates original Section 27 and is intended to make it clear that a transfer of a limited interest in the instrument passes the rights of the transferor to the extent of the interest given. Thus a transferee for security acquires all such rights subject of course to the provisions of Article 9 (Secured Transactions).

6. Subsection (3) applies only to the transfer for value of an instrument payable to order or specially indorsed. It has no application to a gift, or to an instrument payable or indorsed to bearer or indorsed in blank. The transferee acquires, in the absence of any agreement to the contrary, the right to have the indorsement of the transferor. This right is now made enforceable by an action for specific performance. Unless otherwise agreed, it is a right to the general indorsement of the transferor with full liability as indorser, rather than to an indorsement without recourse. The question commonly arises where the purchaser has paid in advance and the indorsement is omitted fraudulently or through oversight; a transferor who is willing to indorse only without recourse or unwilling to indorse at all should make his intentions clear. The agreement for the transferee to take less than an unqualified indorsement need not be an express one, and the understanding may be implied from conduct, from past practice, or from the circumstances of the transaction.

7. Subsection (3) follows the second sentence of the original Section 49 in providing that there is no effective negotiation until the indorsement is made. Until that time the purchaser does not become a holder, and if he receives earlier notice of defense against or claim to the instrument he does not qualify as a holder in due course under Section 3-302(1)(c).

8. The final clause of subsection (3), which is new, is intended to make it clear that the transferee without indorsement of an order instrument is not a holder and so is not aided by the presumption that he is entitled to recover on the instrument provided in Section 3-307(2). The terms of the obligation do not run to him, and he must account for his possession of the unindorsed paper by proving the transaction through which he acquired it. Proof of a transfer to him by a holder is proof that he has acquired the rights of a holder and that he is entitled to the presumption.

Cross References:

Sections 3-202 and 3-416.
Point 5: Article 9.
Point 7: Section 3-302(1)(c).
Point 8: Section 3-307(2).

Definitional Cross References:

"Bearer". Section 1-201.
"Holder". Section 1-201.
"Holder in due course". Section 3-302.
"Instrument". Section 3-102.
"Negotiation". Section 3-202.
"Notice". Section 1-201.
"Party". Section 1-201.
"Presumption". Section 1-201.
"Rights". Section 1-201.
"Security interest". Section 1-201.

§ 3-202. Negotiation.

(1) Negotiation is the transfer of an instrument in such form that the transferee becomes a holder. If the instrument is payable to order it is negotiated by delivery with any necessary indorsement; if payable to bearer it is negotiated by delivery.

(2) An indorsement must be written by or on behalf of the holder and on the instrument or on a paper so firmly affixed thereto as to become a part thereof.

(3) An indorsement is effective for negotiation only when it conveys the entire instrument or any unpaid residue. If it purports to be of less it operates only as a partial assignment.

(4) Words of assignment, condition, waiver, guaranty, limitation or disclaimer of liability and the like accompanying an indorsement do not affect its character as an indorsement.

Official Comment

Prior Uniform Statutory Provision: Sections 30, 31 and 32, Uniform Negotiable Instruments Law.

Changes: Combined and reworded; new provisions.

Purposes of Changes and New Matter: To make it clear that:

1. Negotiation is merely a special form of transfer, the importance of which lies entirely in the fact that it makes the transferee a holder as defined in Section 1-201. Any negotiation carries a transfer of rights as provided in the section on transfer (subsections (1) and (2) of Section 3-201).

2. Any instrument which has been specially indorsed can be negotiated only with the indorsement of the special indorsee as provided in Section 3-204 on special indorsement. An instrument indorsed in blank may be negotiated by delivery alone, provided that it bears the indorsement of all prior special indorsees.

3. Subsection (2) follows decisions holding that a purported indorsement on a mortgage or other separate paper pinned or clipped to an instrument is not sufficient for negotiation. The indorsement must be on the instrument itself or on a paper intended for the purpose which is so firmly affixed to the instrument as to become an extension or part of it. Such a paper is called an allonge.

4. The cause of action on an instrument cannot be split. Any indorsement which purports to convey to any party less than the entire amount of the instrument is not effective for negotiation. This is true of either "Pay A one-half," or "Pay A two-thirds and B one-third," and neither A nor B becomes a holder. On the other hand an indorsement reading merely "Pay A and B" is effective, since it transfers the entire cause of action to A and B as tenants in common.

The partial indorsement does, however, operate as a partial assignment of the cause of action. The provision makes no attempt to state the legal effect of such an assignment, which is left to the local law. In a jurisdiction in which a partial assignee has any rights, either at law or in equity, the partial indorsee has such rights; and in any jurisdiction where a partial assignee has no rights the partial indorsee has none.

5. Subsection (4) is intended to reject decisions holding that the addition of such words as "I hereby assign all my right, title and interest in the within note" prevents the signature from operating as an indorsement. Such words usually are added by laymen out of an excess of caution and a desire to indicate formally that the instrument is conveyed, rather than with any intent to limit the effect of the signature.

6. Subsection (4) is also intended to reject decisions which have held that the addition of "I guarantee payment" indicates an intention not to indorse but merely to guarantee. Any signature with such added words is an indorsement, and if it is made by a holder is effective for negotiation; but the liability of the indorser may be affected by the words of guarantee as provided in the section on the contract of a guarantor. (Section 3-416.)

Cross References:

Section 3–417.

Point 1: Sections 1–201 and 3–201(1) and (2).

Point 2: Section 3–204.

Point 6: Section 3–416.

Definitional Cross References:

"Bearer". Section 1–201.
"Delivery". Section 1–201.
"Holder". Section 1–201.
"Instrument". Section 3–102.
"Written". Section 1–201.

§ 3–203. Wrong or Misspelled Name.

Where an instrument is made payable to a person under a misspelled name or one other than his own he may indorse in that name or his own or both; but signature in both names may be required by a person paying or giving value for the instrument.

Official Comment

Prior Uniform Statutory Provision: Section 43, Uniform Negotiable Instruments Law.

Changes: Reworded.

Purposes of Changes: To make it clear that:

1. The party whose name is wrongly designated or misspelled may make an indorsement effective for negotiation by signing in his true name only. This is not commercially satisfactory, since any subsequent purchaser may be left in doubt as to the state of the title; but whether it is done intentionally or through oversight, the party transfers his rights and is liable on his indorsement, and there is a negotiation if identity exists.

2. He may make an effective indorsement in the wrongly designated or misspelled name only. This again is not commercially satisfactory, since his liability as an indorser may require proof of identity.

3. He may indorse in both names. This is the proper and desirable form of indorsement, and any person called upon to pay an instrument or under contract to purchase it may protect his interest by demanding indorsement in both names, and is not in default if such demand is refused.

Cross Reference:

Section 3–401(2).

Definitional Cross References:

"Instrument". Section 3–102.
"Person". Section 1–201.
"Signature". Section 3–401.

§ 3–204. Special Indorsement; Blank Indorsement.

(1) A special indorsement specifies the person to whom or to whose order it makes the instrument payable. Any instrument specially indorsed becomes payable to the order of the special indorsee and may be further negotiated only by his indorsement.

(2) An indorsement in blank specifies no particular indorsee and may consist of a mere signature. An instrument payable to order and indorsed in blank becomes payable to bearer and may be negotiated by delivery alone until specially indorsed.

(3) The holder may convert a blank indorsement into a special indorsement by writing over the signature of the indorser in blank any contract consistent with the character of the indorsement.

Official Comment

Prior Uniform Statutory Provision: Sections 9(5), 33, 34, 35, 36, and 40, Uniform Negotiable Instruments Law.

Changes: Combined and reworded; rule of Section 40 reversed.

Purposes of Changes:

The last sentence of subsection (1) reverses the rule of the original Section 40, under which an instrument drawn payable to bearer and specially indorsed could be further negotiated by delivery alone. The principle here adopted is that the special indorser, as the owner even of a bearer instrument, has the right to direct the payment and to require the indorsement of his indorsee as evidence of the satisfaction of his own obligation. The special indorsee may of course make it payable to bearer again by himself indorsing in blank.

Cross Reference:

Section 3-202.

Definitional Cross References:

"Bearer". Section 1-201.
"Delivery". Section 1-201.
"Instrument". Section 3-102.
"Person". Section 1-201.
"Signature". Section 3-401.

§ 3-205. Restrictive Indorsements.

An indorsement is restrictive which either

(a) is conditional; or

(b) purports to prohibit further transfer of the instrument; or

(c) includes the words "for collection", "for deposit", "pay any bank", or like terms signifying a purpose of deposit or collection; or

(d) otherwise states that it is for the benefit or use of the indorser or of another person.

Official Comment

Prior Uniform Statutory Provision: Sections 36 and 39, Uniform Negotiable Instruments Law.

Changes: Combined and reworded; new provisions.

Purposes of Changes and New Matter:

1. This section is intended to provide a definition of restrictive indorsements which will include the varieties of indorsement described in original Sections 36 and 39. The separate mention of conditional indorsements, those prohibiting transfer, indorsements in the bank deposit or collection process, and other indorsements to a fiduciary, permits separate treatment in subsequent sections where policy so requires.

2. This is part of a series of changes of the prior uniform statutory provisions effected by Sections 3-102, 3-205, 3-206, 3-304, 3-419, 3-603, and in Article 4, Sections 4-203 and 4-205. The purpose of the changes is generally to require a taker or payor under restrictive indorsement to apply or pay value given consistently with the indorsement, but to provide certain exceptions applying to banks in the collection process (other than depositary banks), and to some other takers and payors.

Cross References:

Sections 3-102, 3-202(2), 3-205, 3-206, 3-304, 3-419, 3-603, 4-203 and 4-205.

Definitional Cross References:

"Instrument". Section 3-102.
"Person". Section 1-201.

§ 3-206. Effect of Restrictive Indorsement.

(1) No restrictive indorsement prevents further transfer or negotiation of the instrument.

(2) An intermediary bank, or a payor bank which is not the depositary bank, is neither given notice nor otherwise affected by a restrictive indorsement of any person except the bank's immediate transferor or the person presenting for payment.

(3) Except for an intermediary bank, any transferee under an indorsement which is conditional or includes the words "for collection", "for deposit", "pay any bank", or like terms (subparagraphs (a) and (c) of Section 3-205) must pay or apply any value given by him for or on the security of the instrument consistently with the indorsement and to the extent that he does so he becomes a holder for value. In addition such transferee is a holder in due course if he otherwise complies with the requirements of Section 3-302 on what constitutes a holder in due course.

(4) The first taker under an indorsement for the benefit of the indorser or another person (subparagraph (d) of Section 3-205) must pay or apply any value given by him for or on the security of the instrument consistently with the indorsement and to the extent that he does so he becomes a holder for value. In addition such taker is a holder in due course if he otherwise complies with the requirements of Section 3-302 on what constitutes a holder in due course. A later holder for value is neither given notice nor otherwise affected by such restrictive indorsement unless he has knowledge that a fiduciary or other person has negotiated the instrument in any transaction for his own benefit or otherwise in breach of duty (subsection (2) of Section 3-304).

Official Comment

Prior Uniform Statutory Provision: Sections 36, 37, 39 and 47, Uniform Negotiable Instruments Law.

Changes: Completely revised.

Purposes of Changes:

1. Subsections (1) and (2) apply to all four classes of restrictive indorsements defined in Section 3-205. Conditional indorsements and indorsements for deposit or collection, defined in paragraphs (a) and (c) of Section 3-205, are also subject to subsection (3); and trust indorsements as defined in paragraph (d) of Section 3-205 are subject to subsection (4). This section negates the implication which has sometimes been found in the original Sections 37 and 47, that under a restrictive indorsement neither the indorsee nor any subsequent taker from him could become a holder in due course. By omitting the original Section 47, this Article also avoids any implication that a discharge is effective against a holder in due course. See Section 3-602.

2. Under subsection (1) an indorsement reading "Pay A only," or any other indorsement purporting to prohibit further transfer, is without effect for that purpose. Such indorsements have rarely appeared in reported American cases. Ordinarily further negotiation will be contemplated by the indorser, if only for bank collection. The indorsee becomes a holder, and the indorsement does not of itself give notice to subsequent parties of any defense or claim of the indorser. Hence this section gives such an indorsement the same effect as an unrestricted indorsement.

3. Subsection (2) permits an intermediary bank (Sections 3-102(3) and 4-105)

or a payor bank which is not a depositary bank (Sections 3–102(3) and 4–105) to disregard any restrictive indorsement except that of the bank's immediate transferor. Such banks ordinarily handle instruments, especially checks, in bulk and have no practicable opportunity to consider the effect of restrictive indorsements. Subsection (2) does not affect the rights of the restrictive indorser against parties outside the bank collection process or against the first bank in the collection process; such rights are governed by subsections (3) and (4) and Section 3–603.

4. Conditional indorsements are treated by this section like indorsements for deposit or collection. Under subsection (3) any transferee under such an indorsement except an intermediary bank becomes a holder for value to the extent that he acts consistently with the indorsement in paying or applying any value given by him for or on the security of the instrument. Contrary to the original Section 39, subsection (3) permits a transferee under a conditional indorsement to become a holder in due course free of the conditional indorser's claim.

5. Of the indorsements covered by this section those "for collection", "for deposit" and "pay any bank" are overwhelmingly the most frequent. Indorsements "for collection" or "for deposit" may be either special or blank; indorsements "pay any bank" are governed by Section 4–201(2). Instruments so indorsed are almost invariably destined to be lodged in a bank for collection. Subsection (3) requires any transferee other than an intermediary bank to act consistently with the purpose of collection, and Section 3–603 lays down a similar rule for payors not covered by subsection (2).

6. Subsection (4), applying to trust indorsements other than those for deposit or collection (paragraph (d) of Section 3–205) is similar to subsection (3); but in subsection (4) the duty to act consistently with the indorsement is limited to the first taker under it. If an instrument is indorsed "Pay T in trust for B" or "Pay T for B" or "Pay T for account of B" or "Pay T as agent for B," whether B is the indorser or a third person, T is of course subject to liability for any breach of his obligation as fiduciary. But trustees commonly and legitimately sell trust assets in transactions entirely outside the bank collection process; the trustee therefore has power to negotiate the instrument and make his transferee a holder in due course. Whether transferees from T have notice of a breach of trust such as to deny them the status of holders in due course is governed by the section on notice to purchasers (Section 3–304); the trust indorsement does not of itself give such notice. Payors are immunized either by subsection (2) of this section or by Section 3–603: payment to the trustee or to a purchaser from the trustee is "consistent with the terms" of the trust indorsement under Section 3–603(1)(b).

7. Several sections of Article 3 and Article 4 are explicitly made subject to the rules stated in this section. See Sections 3–306, 3–419, 4–203 and 4–205.

Cross References:

Point 1: Sections 3–205 and 3–602.

Point 2: Section 3–205(b).

Point 3: Sections 3–102(3), 3–419(4), 3–603, 4–105, 4–205(2).

Point 4: Section 3–205(a).

Point 5: Sections 3–205, 3–603 and 4–201.

Point 6: Sections 3–205, 3–304 and 3–603.

Point 7: Sections 3–306, 3–419, 4–203 and 4–205.

Definitional Cross References:

"Bank". Section 1–201.

"Depositary bank". Sections 3–102(3) and 4–105.

"Holder in due course". Section 3–302.

"Intermediary bank". Sections 3–102(3) and 4–105.

"Negotiation". Sections 3–102(2) and 3–202.

"Payor bank". Sections 3–102(3) and 4–105.

"Restrictive indorsement". Section 3–205.

"Transfer". Section 3–201.

§ 3–207. Negotiation Effective Although It May Be Rescinded.

(1) Negotiation is effective to transfer the instrument although the negotiation is

(a) made by an infant, a corporation exceeding its powers, or any other person without capacity; or

(b) obtained by fraud, duress or mistake of any kind; or

(c) part of an illegal transaction; or

(d) made in breach of duty.

(2) Except as against a subsequent holder in due course such negotiation is in an appropriate case subject to rescission, the declaration of a constructive trust or any other remedy permitted by law.

Official Comment

Prior Uniform Statutory Provision: Sections 22, 58 and 59, Uniform Negotiable Instruments Law.

Changes: Completely revised.

Purposes of Changes: To make it clear that:

1. The original Section 22, which covered only negotiation by an infant or a corporation, is extended by this section to include other negotiations which may be rescinded. The provision applies even though the party's lack of capacity, or the illegality, is of a character which goes to the essence of the transaction and makes it entirely void, and even though the party negotiating has incurred no liability and is entitled to recover the instrument and have his indorsement cancelled.

2. It is inherent in the character of negotiable paper that any person in possession of an instrument which by its terms runs to him is a holder, and that anyone may deal with him as a holder. The principle finds its most extreme application in the well settled rule that a holder in due course may take the paper even from a thief and be protected against the claim of the rightful owner. Where there is actual negotiation, even in an entirely void transaction, it is no less effective. The policy of this provision, as well as of the last sentence of the original Section 59, is that any person to whom an instrument is negotiated is a holder until the instrument has been recovered from his possession; and that any person who negotiates an instrument thereby parts with all his rights in it until such recovery. The remedy of any such claimant is to recover the paper by replevin or otherwise; to impound it or to enjoin its enforcement, collection or negotiation; to recover its proceeds from the holder; or to intervene in any action brought by the holder against the obligor. As provided in the section on the rights of one not a holder in due course (Section 3–306) his claim is not a defense to the obligor unless he himself defends the action.

3. Negotiation under this Article always includes delivery. (Section 3–202, and see Section 1–201(14)). Acquisition of possession by a thief can therefore never be negotiation under this section. But delivery by the thief to another person may be.

4. Nothing in this section is intended to impose any liability on the party negotiating. He may assert any defense available to him under Sections 3–305, 3–306 and 3–307.

5. A holder in due course takes the instrument free from all claims to it on the part of any person (Section 3–305(1)). Against him there can be no rescission or other remedy, even though the prior negotiation may have been fraudulent or

illegal in its essence and entirely void. As against any other party the claimant may have any remedy permitted by law. This section is not intended to specify what that remedy may be, or to prevent any court from imposing conditions or limitations such as prompt action or return of the consideration received. All such questions are left to the law of the particular jurisdiction. Subsection (2) of Section 3-207 gives no right where it would not otherwise exist. The section is intended to mean that any remedies afforded by the local law are cut off only by a holder in due course, and that other parties, such as a bona fide purchaser with notice that the instrument is overdue, take it subject to the claim as provided in paragraph (a) of the section on the rights of one not a holder in due course (Section 3-306).

Cross References:

Point 2: Sections 1-201 and 3-306(d).
Point 3: Sections 1-201 and 3-202.
Point 4: Sections 3-305, 3-306 and 3-307.
Point 5: Sections 3-305(1) and 3-306(a).

Definitional Cross References:

"Holder in due course". Section 3-302.
"Instrument". Section 3-102.
"Negotiation". Section 3-202.
"Person". Section 1-201.
"Remedy". Section 1-201.

§ 3-208. Reacquisition.

Where an instrument is returned to or reacquired by a prior party he may cancel any indorsement which is not necessary to his title and reissue or further negotiate the instrument, but any intervening party is discharged as against the reacquiring party and subsequent holders not in due course and if his indorsement has been cancelled is discharged as against subsequent holders in due course as well.

Official Comment

Prior Uniform Statutory Provision: Sections 48, 50 and 121, Uniform Negotiable Instruments Law.

Changes: Parts of original sections combined and rephrased.

Purposes of Changes: No change in the substance of the law is intended. "Returned to or reacquired by" is substituted for "negotiated back to" in the original Section 50 in order to make it clear that the section applies to a return by an indorsee who does not himself indorse. "Discharged" is substituted for the original language to make it clear that the discharge of the intervening party is included within the rule of the section on effect of discharge against a holder in due course (Section 3-602) and is not effective against a subsequent holder in due course who takes without notice of it.

The reacquirer may keep the instrument himself or he may further negotiate it. On further negotiation he may or may not cancel intervening indorsements. In any case intervening indorsers are discharged as to the reacquirer, since if he attempted to enforce it against them they would have an action back against him. Where the reacquirer negotiates without cancelling the intervening indorsements, the section provides that such indorsers are discharged except against subsequent holders in due course. The intervening indorser whose indorsement is stricken is, in conformity with Section 3-605, discharged even as against subsequent holders in due course.

Cross References:

Sections 3-602, 3-603(2) and 3-605.

Definitional Cross References:

"Holder in due course". Section 3-302.
"Instrument". Section 3-102.
"Party". Section 1-201.

PART 3

RIGHTS OF A HOLDER

§ 3-301. Rights of a Holder.

The holder of an instrument whether or not he is the owner may transfer or negotiate it and, except as otherwise provided in Section 3-603 on payment or satisfaction, discharge it or enforce payment in his own name.

Official Comment

Prior Uniform Statutory Provision: Section 51, Uniform Negotiable Instruments Law.

Changes: Reworded. The provision in the original Section 51 as to discharge by payment is now covered by Section 3-603(1).

Purposes of Changes: The section is revised to state in one provision all the rights of a holder, and to make it clear that every holder has such rights. The only limitations are those found in Section 3-603 on payment or satisfaction. That section provides (with stated exceptions) that payment to a holder discharges the liability of the party paying even though made with knowledge of a claim of another person to the instrument, unless the adverse claimant posts indemnity or procures the issuance of appropriate legal process restraining the payment. Thus payment to a holder in an adverse claim situation would not give discharge if the adverse claimant had followed either of the procedures provided for in the "unless" clause of Section 3-603; nor would a discharge result from payment in two other specific situations described in Section 3-603.

Cross References:

Sections 1-201, 3-307 and 3-603(1).

Definitional Cross References:

"Holder". Section 1-201.
"Instrument". Section 3-102.
"Rights". Section 1-201.

§ 3-302. Holder in Due Course.

(1) A holder in due course is a holder who takes the instrument

(a) for value; and

(b) in good faith; and

(c) without notice that it is overdue or has been dishonored or of any defense against or claim to it on the part of any person.

(2) A payee may be a holder in due course.

(3) A holder does not become a holder in due course of an instrument:

(a) by purchase of it at judicial sale or by taking it under legal process; or

(b) by acquiring it in taking over an estate; or

(c) by purchasing it as part of a bulk transaction not in regular course of business of the transferor.

(4) A purchaser of a limited interest can be a holder in due course only to the extent of the interest purchased.

Official Comment

Prior Uniform Statutory Provision: Section 52, Uniform Negotiable Instruments Law.

Changes: Reworded; new provisions.

Purposes of Changes and New Matter: The changes are intended to remove uncertainties arising under the original section.

1. The language "without notice that it is overdue" is substituted for that of the original subsection (2) in order to make it clear that the purchaser of an instrument which is in fact overdue may be a holder in due course if he takes it without notice that it is overdue. Such notice is covered by the section on notice to purchaser (Section 3-304).

2. Subsection (2) is intended to settle the long continued conflict over the status of the payee as a holder in due course. This conflict has turned very largely upon the word "negotiated" in the original Section 52(4), which is now eliminated. The position here taken is that the payee may become a holder in due course to the same extent and under the same circumstances as any other holder. This is true whether he takes the instrument by purchase from a third person or directly from the obligor. All that is necessary is that the payee meet the requirements of this section. In the following cases, among others, the payee is a holder in due course:

a. A remitter, purchasing goods from P, obtains a bank draft payable to P and forwards it to P, who takes it for value, in good faith and without notice as required by this section.

b. The remitter buys the bank draft payable to P, but it is forwarded by the bank directly to P, who takes it in good faith and without notice in payment of the remitter's obligation to him.

c. A and B sign a note as comakers. A induces B to sign by fraud, and without authority from B delivers the note to P, who takes it for value, in good faith and without notice.

d. A defrauds the maker into signing an instrument payable to P. P pays A for it in good faith and without notice, and the maker delivers the instrument directly to P.

e. D draws a check payable to P and gives it to his agent to be delivered to P in payment of D's debt. The agent delivers it to P, who takes it in good faith and without notice in payment of the agent's debt to P. But as to this case see Section 3-304(2), which may apply.

f. D draws a check payable to P but blank as to the amount, and gives it to his agent to be delivered to P. The agent fills in the check with an excessive amount, and P takes it for value, in good faith and without notice.

g. D draws a check blank as to the name of the payee, and gives it to his agent to be filled in with the name of A and delivered to A. The agent fills in the name of P, and P takes the check in good faith, for value and without notice.

3. Subsection (3) is intended to state existing case law. It covers a few situations in which the purchaser takes the instrument under unusual circumstances which indicate that he is merely a successor in interest to the prior holder and can acquire no better rights. (If such prior holder was himself a holder in due course, the purchaser succeeds to that status under Section 3-201 on Transfer.) The provision applies to a purchaser at an execution sale, a sale in bankruptcy or a sale by a state bank commissioner of the assets of an insolvent bank. It applies equally to an attaching creditor or any other person who acquires the instrument by legal process, even under an antecedent claim; and equally to a representative, such as an executor, administrator, receiver or assignee for the benefit of creditors, who takes over the instrument as part of an estate, even though he is representing antecedent creditors.

Subsection (3)(c) applies to bulk purchases lying outside of the ordinary course of business of the seller. It applies, for example, when a new partnership takes over for value all of the assets of an old one after a new member has entered the firm, or to a reorganized or consolidated corporation taking over in bulk the assets of a predecessor. It has particular application to the purchase by one bank of a substantial part of the paper held by another bank which is threatened with insolvency and seeking to liquidate its assets.

4. A purchaser of a limited interest—as a pledgee in a security transaction—may become a holder in due course, but he may enforce the instrument over defenses only to the extent of his interest, and defenses good against the pledgor remain available insofar as the pledgor retains an equity in the instrument. This is merely a special application of the general rule (Section 1-201) that a purchaser of a limited interest acquires rights only to the extent of the interest purchased. Section 27 of the original Act contained a similar provision.

Cross References:

Sections 1-201, 3-303, 3-305 and 3-306.

Point 1: Section 3-304(5).
Point 3: Section 3-201.
Point 4: Section 1-201.

Definitional Cross References:

"Good faith". Section 1-201.
"Holder". Section 1-201.
"Instrument". Section 3-102.
"Notice". Section 1-201.
"Notice of dishonor". Section 3-508.
"Person". Section 1-201.
"Purchase". Section 1-201.
"Purchaser". Section 1-201.
"Value". Section 3-303.

§ 3-303. Taking for Value.

A holder takes the instrument for value

(a) to the extent that the agreed consideration has been performed or that he acquires a security interest in or a lien on the instrument otherwise than by legal process; or

(b) when he takes the instrument in payment of or as security for an antecedent claim against any person whether or not the claim is due; or

(c) when he gives a negotiable instrument for it or makes an irrevocable commitment to a third person.

Official Comment

Prior Uniform Statutory Provision: Sections 25, 26, 27 and 54, Uniform Negotiable Instruments Law.

Changes: Combined and reworded; original Section 26 omitted.

Purposes of Changes: The changes are intended to remove uncertainties arising under the original Act.

1. The original Section 26 which had reference to the liability of accommodation parties is omitted as erroneous and misleading, since a holder who does not himself give value cannot qualify as a holder in due course in his own right merely because value has previously been given for the instrument.

2. In this Article value is divorced from consideration (Section 3-408). The latter is important only on the question of whether the obligation of a party can be enforced against him; while value is important only on the question of whether the holder who has acquired that obligation qualifies as a particular kind of holder.

3. Paragraph (a) resolves an apparent conflict between the original Section 54 and the first sentence of the original Section 25, by requiring that the agreed con-

sideration shall actually have been given. An executory promise to give value is not itself value, except as provided in paragraph (c). The underlying reason of policy is that when the purchaser learns of a defense against the instrument or of a defect in the title he is not required to enforce the instrument, but is free to rescind the transaction for breach of the transferor's warranty (Section 3–417). There is thus not the same necessity for giving him the status of a holder in due course, cutting off claims and defenses, as where he has actually paid value. A common illustration is the bank credit not drawn upon, which can be and is revoked when a claim or defense appears.

4. Paragraph (a) limits the language of the original Section 27, eliminating the attaching creditor or any other person who acquires a lien by legal process. Any such lienor has been uniformly held not to be a holder in due course.

5. Paragraph (b) restates the last sentence of the original Section 25. It adopts the generally accepted rule that the holder takes for value when he takes the instrument as security for an antecedent debt, even though there is no extension of time or other concession, and whether or not the debt is due. The provision extends the same rule to any claim against any person; there is no requirement that the claim arise out of contract. In particular the provision is intended to apply to an instrument given in payment of or as security for the debt of a third person, even though no concession is made in return.

6. Paragraph (c) is new, but states generally recognized exceptions to the rule that an executory promise is not value. A negotiable instrument is value because it carries the possibility of negotiation to a holder in due course, after which the party who gives it cannot refuse to pay. The same reasoning applies to any irrevocable commitment to a third person, such as a letter of credit issued when an instrument is taken.

Cross References:

Sections 3–302 and 3–415.
Point 1: Section 3–415.
Point 2: Section 3–408.
Point 3: Section 3–417.

Definitional Cross References:

"Holder". Section 1–201.
"Instrument". Section 3–102.
"Person". Section 1–201.
"Security interest". Section 1–201.

§ 3–304. Notice to Purchaser.

(1) The purchaser has notice of a claim or defense if

(a) the instrument is so incomplete, bears such visible evidence of forgery or alteration, or is otherwise so irregular as to call into question its validity, terms or ownership or to create an ambiguity as to the party to pay; or

(b) the purchaser has notice that the obligation of any party is voidable in whole or in part, or that all parties have been discharged.

(2) The purchaser has notice of a claim against the instrument when he has knowledge that a fiduciary has negotiated the instrument in payment of or as security for his own debt or in any transaction for his own benefit or otherwise in breach of duty.

(3) The purchaser has notice that an instrument is overdue if he has reason to know

(a) that any part of the principal amount is overdue or that there is an uncured default in payment of another instrument of the same series; or

(b) that acceleration of the instrument has been made; or

(c) that he is taking a demand instrument after demand has been made or more than a reasonable length of time after its issue. A reasonable time for a check drawn and payable within the states and territories of the United States and the District of Columbia is presumed to be thirty days.

(4) Knowledge of the following facts does not of itself give the purchaser notice of a defense or claim

(a) that the instrument is antedated or postdated;

(b) that it was issued or negotiated in return for an executory promise or accompanied by a separate agreement, unless the purchaser has notice that a defense or claim has arisen from the terms thereof;

(c) that any party has signed for accommodation;

(d) that an incomplete instrument has been completed, unless the purchaser has notice of any improper completion;

(e) that any person negotiating the instrument is or was a fiduciary;

(f) that there has been default in payment of interest on the instrument or in payment of any other instrument, except one of the same series.

(5) The filing or recording of a document does not of itself constitute notice within the provisions of this Article to a person who would otherwise be a holder in due course.

(6) To be effective notice must be received at such time and in such manner as to give a reasonable opportunity to act on it.

Official Comment

Prior Uniform Statutory Provision: Sections 45, 52, 53, 55 and 56, Uniform Negotiable Instruments Law.

Changes: Combined and reworded; new provisions.

Purposes of Changes and New Matter: The original sections are expanded, with the addition of specific provisions intended to remove uncertainties in the existing law.

1. "Notice" is defined in Section 1–201.

2. Paragraph (a) of subsection (1) replaces the provision in the original Section 52(1) requiring that the instrument be "complete and regular on its face." An instrument may be blank as to some unnecessary particular, may contain minor erasures, or even have an obvious change in the date, as where "January 2, 1948" is changed to "January 2, 1949", without even exciting suspicion. Irregularity is properly a question of notice to the purchaser of something wrong, and is so treated here.

3. "Voidable" obligation in paragraph (b) of subsection (1) is intended to limit the provision to notice of defense which will permit any party to avoid his original obligation on the instrument, as distinguished from a set-off or counterclaim.

4. Notice that one party has been discharged is not notice to the purchaser of an infirmity in the obligation of other parties who remain liable on the instrument. A purchaser with notice that an indorser is discharged takes subject to that discharge as provided in the section on effect of discharge against a holder in due course (Section 3–602) but is not prevented from taking the obligation of the maker in due course. If he has notice

that all parties are discharged he cannot be a holder in due course.

5. Subsection (2) follows the policy of Section 6 of the Uniform Fiduciaries Act, and specifies the same elements as notice of improper conduct of a fiduciary. Under paragraph (e) of subsection (4) mere notice of the existence of the fiduciary relation is not enough in itself to prevent the holder from taking in due course, and he is free to take the instrument on the assumption that the fiduciary is acting properly. The purchaser may pay cash into the hands of the fiduciary without notice of any breach of the obligation. Section 3-206 should be consulted for the effect of a restrictive indorsement.

6. Subsection (3) removes an uncertainty in the original Act by providing that reason to know of an overdue installment or other part of the principal amount is notice that the instrument is overdue and thus prevents the purchaser from taking in due course. On the other hand subsection (4)(f) makes notice that interest is overdue insufficient, on the basis of banking and commercial practice, the decisions under the original Act, and the frequency with which interest payments are in fact delayed. Notice of default in payment of any other instrument, except an uncured default in another instrument of the same series, is likewise insufficient.

7. Subsection (3) departs from the original Section 52(2) by providing that the purchaser may take accelerated paper, or a demand instrument on which demand has in fact been made, as a holder in due course if he takes without notice of the acceleration or demand. With this change the original Section 45 is eliminated, as the presumption that any negotiation has taken place before the instrument was in fact overdue is of importance only in aid of a holder in due course. Under this section it is not conclusive that the instrument was in fact overdue when it was negotiated, if the holder takes without notice of that fact.

The "reasonable time after issue" is retained from the original Section 53, but paragraph (c) adds a presumption, as that term is defined in this Act (Section 1-201), that a domestic check is stale after thirty days.

8. Paragraph (a) of subsection (4) rejects decisions holding that an instrument known to be antedated or postdated is not "regular." Such knowledge does not prevent a holder from taking in due course.

9. Paragraph (b) of subsection (4) is to be read together with the provisions of this Article as to when a promise or order is unconditional and as to other writings affecting the instrument (Sections 3-105 and 3-119). Mere notice of the existence of an executory promise or a separate agreement does not prevent the holder from taking in due course, and such notice may even appear in the instrument itself. If the purchaser has notice of any default in the promise or agreement which gives rise to a defense or claim against the instrument, he is on notice to the same extent as in the case of any other information as to the existence of a defense or claim.

10. Paragraph (d) of subsection (4) follows the policy of the original Section 14, under which any person in possession of an instrument has prima facie authority to fill blanks. It is intended to mean that the holder may take in due course even though a blank is filled in his presence, if he is without notice that the filling is improper. Section 3-407 on alteration should be consulted as to the rights of subsequent holders following such an alteration.

11. Subsection (5) is new. It removes an uncertainty arising under the original Act as to the effect of "constructive notice" through public filing or recording.

12. Subsection (6) is new. It means that notice must be received with a sufficient margin of time to afford a reasonable opportunity to act on it, and that a notice received by the president of a bank one minute before the bank's teller cashes a check is not effective to prevent the bank from becoming a holder in due course. See in this connection the provi-

sion on notice to an organization, Sec. 1-201(27).

Cross References:

Sections 3-201 and 3-302.
Point 1: Section 1-201.
Point 4: Section 3-602.
Point 5: Section 3-206.
Point 7: Section 1-201.
Point 9: Sections 3-105(1)(b) and (c) and 3-119.
Point 10: Section 3-407.
Point 12: Section 1-201.

Definitional Cross References:

"Accommodation party". Section 3-415.
"Agreement". Section 1-201.
"Alteration". Section 3-407.
"Bank". Section 1-201.
"Check". Section 3-104.
"Holder in due course". Section 3-302.
"Instrument". Section 3-102.
"Issue". Section 3-102.
"Negotiation". Section 3-202.
"Notice". Section 1-201.
"Party". Section 1-201.
"Person". Section 1-201.
"Presumed". Section 1-201.
"Promise". Section 3-102.
"Purchaser". Section 1-201.
"Reasonable time". Section 1-204.
"Signed". Section 1-201.
"Term". Section 1-201.

§ 3-305. Rights of a Holder in Due Course.

To the extent that a holder is a holder in due course he takes the instrument free from

(1) all claims to it on the part of any person; and

(2) all defenses of any party to the instrument with whom the holder has not dealt except

(a) infancy, to the extent that it is a defense to a simple contract; and

(b) such other incapacity, or duress, or illegality of the transaction, as renders the obligation of the party a nullity; and

(c) such misrepresentation as has induced the party to sign the instrument with neither knowledge nor reasonable opportunity to obtain knowledge of its character or its essential terms; and

(d) discharge in insolvency proceedings; and

(e) any other discharge of which the holder has notice when he takes the instrument.

Official Comment

Prior Uniform Statutory Provision: Sections 15, 16 and 57, Uniform Negotiable Instruments Law.

Changes: Combined and reworded; new provisions; rule of original Section 15 reversed.

Purposes of Changes and New Matter:

1. The section applies to any person who is himself a holder in due course, and equally to any transferee who acquires the rights of one (Section 3-201). "Takes" is substituted for "holds" in the original Section 57 because a holder in due course may still be subject to any claims or defenses which arise against him after he has taken the instrument.

2. The language "all claims to it on the part of any person" is substituted for "any defect of title of prior parties" in the original Section 57 in order to make it clear that the holder in due course takes the instrument free not only from any claim of legal title but also from all liens, equities or claims of any other kind. This

includes any claim for rescission of a prior negotiation, in accordance with the provisions of the section on reacquisition (Section 3-208).

3. "All defenses" includes nondelivery, conditional delivery or delivery for a special purpose. Under this Article such nondelivery or qualified delivery is a defense (Sections 3-306 and 3-307) and the defendant has the full burden of establishing it. Accordingly the "conclusive presumption" of the third sentence of the original Section 16 is abrogated in favor of a rule of law cutting off the defense.

The effect of this section, together with the sections dealing with incomplete instruments (Section 3-115) and alteration (Section 3-407) is to cut off the defense of nondelivery of an incomplete instrument against a holder in due course, and to change the rule of the original Section 15.

4. Paragraph (a) of subsection (2) is new. It follows the decisions under the original Act in providing that the defense of infancy may be asserted against a holder in due course, even though its effect is to render the instrument voidable but not void. The policy is one of protection of the infant against those who take advantage of him, even at the expense of occasional loss to an innocent purchaser. No attempt is made to state when infancy is available as a defense or the conditions under which it may be asserted. In some jurisdictions it is held that an infant cannot rescind the transaction or set up the defense unless he restores the holder to his former position, which in the case of a holder in due course is normally impossible. In other states an infant who has misrepresented his age may be estopped to assert his infancy. Such questions are left to the local law, as an integral part of the policy of each state as to the protection of infants.

5. Paragraph (b) of subsection (2) is new. It covers mental incompetence, guardianship, ultra vires acts or lack of corporate capacity to do business, any remaining incapacity of married women, or any other incapacity apart from infancy. Such incapacity is largely statutory. Its existence and effect is left to the law of each state. If under the local law the effect is to render the obligation of the instrument entirely null and void, the defense may be asserted against a holder in due course. If the effect is merely to render the obligation voidable at the election of the obligor, the defense is cut off.

6. Duress is a matter of degree. An instrument signed at the point of a gun is void, even in the hands of a holder in due course. One signed under threat to prosecute the son of the maker for theft may be merely voidable, so that the defense is cut off. Illegality is most frequently a matter of gambling or usury, but may arise in many other forms under a great variety of statutes. The statutes differ greatly in their provisions and the interpretations given them. They are primarily a matter of local concern and local policy. All such matters are therefore left to the local law. If under that law the effect of the duress or the illegality is to make the obligation entirely null and void, the defense may be asserted against a holder in due course. Otherwise it is cut off.

7. Paragraph (c) of subsection (2) is new. It follows the great majority of the decisions under the original Act in recognizing the defense of "real" or "essential" fraud, sometimes called fraud in the essence or fraud in the factum, as effective against a holder in due course. The common illustration is that of the maker who is tricked into signing a note in the belief that it is merely a receipt or some other document. The theory of the defense is that his signature on the instrument is ineffective because he did not intend to sign such an instrument at all. Under this provision the defense extends to an instrument signed with knowledge that it is a negotiable instrument, but without knowledge of its essential terms.

The test of the defense here stated is that of excusable ignorance of the contents of the writing signed. The party must not only have been in ignorance, but must also have had no reasonable opportunity to obtain knowledge. In determining what is a reasonable opportunity all relevant factors are to be taken into account, including the age and sex of the party, his intelligence, education and business experience; his ability to read or to understand English, the representations made to him and his reason to rely on them or to have confidence in the person making them; the presence or absence of any third person who might read or explain the instrument to him, or any other possibility of obtaining independent information; and the apparent necessity, or lack of it, for acting without delay.

Unless the misrepresentation meets this test, the defense is cut off by a holder in due course.

8. Paragraph (d) is also new. It is inserted to make it clear that any discharge in bankruptcy or other insolvency proceedings, as defined in this Article, is not cut off when the instrument is purchased by a holder in due course.

9. Paragraph (e) of subsection (2) is also new. Under the notice to purchaser section of this Article (Section 3-304), notice of any discharge which leaves other parties liable on the instrument does not prevent the purchaser from becoming a holder in due course. The obvious case is that of the cancellation of an indorsement, which leaves the maker and prior indorsers liable. As to such parties the purchaser may be a holder in due course, but he takes the instrument subject to the discharge of which he has notice. If he is without such notice, the discharge is not effective against him (Section 3-602).

Cross References:

Point 1: Section 3-201(1).

Point 2: Section 3-208.

Point 3: Sections 3-115(2), 3-306(c), 3-307(2) and 3-407(3).

Point 9: Sections 3-304(1)(b) and 3-602.

Definitional Cross References:

"Contract". Section 1-201.

"Holder in due course". Section 3-302.

"Insolvency proceedings". Section 1-201.

"Instrument". Section 3-102.

"Notice". Section 1-201.

"Party". Section 1-201.

"Person". Section 1-201.

"Term". Section 1-201.

§ 3-306. Rights of One Not Holder in Due Course.

Unless he has the rights of a holder in due course any person takes the instrument subject to

(a) all valid claims to it on the part of any person; and

(b) all defenses of any party which would be available in an action on a simple contract; and

(c) the defenses of want or failure of consideration, non-performance of any condition precedent, non-delivery, or delivery for a special purpose (Section 3-408); and

(d) the defense that he or a person through whom he holds the instrument acquired it by theft, or that payment or satisfaction to such holder would be inconsistent with the terms of a restrictive indorsement. The claim of any third person to the instrument is not otherwise available as a defense to any party liable thereon unless the third person himself defends the action for such party.

Official Comment

Prior Uniform Statutory Provision: Sections 16, 28, 58 and 59, Uniform Negotiable Instruments Law.

Changes: Combined, condensed and reworded.

Purposes of Changes: The changes are intended to remove the following uncertainties arising under the original sections:

1. Any transferee who acquires the rights of a holder in due course under the transfer section of this Article (Section 3-201) is included within the provisions of the preceding Section 305. This section covers any person who neither qualifies in his own right as a holder in due course nor has acquired the rights of one by transfer. In particular the section applies to a bona fide purchaser with notice that the instrument is overdue.

2. "All valid claims to it on the part of any person" includes not only claims of legal title, but all liens, equities, or other claims of right against the instrument or its proceeds. It includes claims to rescind a prior negotiation and to recover the instrument or its proceeds.

3. Paragraph (b) restates the first sentence of the original Section 58.

4. Paragraph (c) condenses the original Sections 16 and 28. Want or failure of consideration is specifically mentioned, as in the original Section 28, in order to make it clear that either is a defense which the defendant has the burden of establishing under the following section of this Article. The language as to an "ascertained or liquidated amount or otherwise" in the original Section 28 is omitted because it is believed to be superfluous. The third sentence of Section 16 is now covered by the preceding section. The fourth sentence is omitted in favor of the rule stated in the following section, which places the full burden of establishing the defense of non-delivery, conditional delivery or delivery for a special purpose upon the defendant, and makes any presumption unnecessary.

5. Paragraph (d) is substituted for the last sentence of the original Section 59, as a more detailed and explicit statement of the same policy, which is also found in the original Section 22. The contract of the obligor is to pay the holder of the instrument, and the claims of other persons against the holder are generally not his concern. He is not required to set up such a claim as a defense, since he usually will have no satisfactory evidence of his own on the issue; and the provision that he may not do so is intended as much for his protection as for that of the holder. The claimant who has lost possession of an instrument so payable or indorsed that another may become a holder has lost his rights on the instrument, which by its terms no longer runs to him. The provision includes all claims for rescission of a negotiation, whether based in incapacity, fraud, duress, mistake, illegality, breach of trust or duty or any other reason. It includes claims based on conditional delivery or delivery for a special purpose. It includes claims of legal title, lien, constructive trust or other equity against the instrument or its proceeds. The exception made in the case of theft is based on the policy which refuses to aid a proved thief to recover, and refuses to aid him indirectly by permitting his transferee to recover unless the transferee is a holder in due course. The exception concerning restrictive indorsements is intended to achieve consistency with Section 3-603 and related sections.

Nothing in this section is intended to prevent the claimant from intervening in the holder's action against the obligor or defending the action for the latter, and asserting his claim in the course of such intervention or defense. Nothing here stated is intended to prevent any interpleader, deposit in court or other available procedure under which the defendant may bring the claimant into court or be discharged without himself litigating the claim as a defense. Compare Section 3-803 on vouching in other parties alleged to be liable.

Cross References:

Section 3-302.

Point 1: Sections 3-201(1) and 3-305.

Point 2: Section 3-207.

Point 3: Section 3-307(2).

Point 4: Sections 3-305 and 3-307(2).

Point 5: Section 3-803.

Definitional Cross References:

"Action". Section 1-201.

"Contract". Section 1-201.

"Delivery". Section 1-201.

"Holder in due course". Section 3-302.

"Instrument". Section 3-102.

"Party". Section 1-201.

"Person". Section 1-201.

"Rights". Section 1-201.

§ 3-307. Burden of Establishing Signatures, Defenses and Due Course.

(1) Unless specifically denied in the pleadings each signature on an instrument is admitted. When the effectiveness of a signature is put in issue

(a) the burden of establishing it is on the party claiming under the signature; but

(b) the signature is presumed to be genuine or authorized except where the action is to enforce the obligation of a purported signer who has died or become incompetent before proof is required.

(2) When signatures are admitted or established, production of the instrument entitles a holder to recover on it unless the defendant establishes a defense.

(3) After it is shown that a defense exists a person claiming the rights of a holder in due course has the burden of establishing that he or some person under whom he claims is in all respects a holder in due course.

Official Comment

Prior Uniform Statutory Provision: Section 59, Uniform Negotiable Instruments Law.

Changes: Reworded; new provisions.

Purposes of Changes and New Matter:

1. Subsection (1) is new, although similar provisions are found in a number of states. The purpose of the requirement of a specific denial in the pleadings is to give the plaintiff notice that he must meet a claim of forgery or lack of authority as to the particular signature, and to afford him an opportunity to investigate and obtain evidence. Where local rules of pleading permit, the denial may be on information and belief, or it may be a denial of knowledge or information sufficient to form a belief. It need not be under oath unless the local statutes or rules require verification. In the absence of such specific denial the signature stands admitted, and is not in issue. Nothing in this section is intended, however, to prevent amendment of the pleading in a proper case.

The question of the burden of establishing the signature arises only when it has been put in issue by specific denial. "Burden of establishing" is defined in the definitions section of this Act (Section 1-201). The burden is on the party claiming under the signature, but he is aided by the presumption that it is genuine or authorized [as] stated in paragraph (b). "Presumption" is also defined in this Act (Section 1-201). It means that until some evidence is introduced which would support a finding that the signature is forged or unauthorized the plaintiff is not required to prove that it is authentic. The presumption rests upon the fact that in ordinary experience forged or unauthorized signatures are very uncommon, and normally any evidence is within the control of the defendant or more accessible to him. He is therefore required to make some sufficient showing of the grounds for his denial before the plaintiff is put to his proof. His evidence need not be sufficient to require a directed verdict in his favor, but it must be enough to support his denial by permitting a finding in his favor. Until he introduces such evidence the presumption requires a finding for the plaintiff. Once such evidence is introduced the burden of establishing the signature by a preponderance of the total evidence is on the plaintiff.

Under paragraph (b) this presumption does not arise where the action is to enforce the obligation of a purported signer who has died or become incompetent before the evidence is required, and so is disabled from obtaining or introducing it. "Action" of course includes a claim asserted against the estate of a deceased or an incompetent.

2. Subsection (2) is substituted for the first clause of the original Section 59. Once signatures are proved or admitted, a holder makes out his case by mere production of the instrument, and is entitled to recover in the absence of any further evidence. The defendant has the burden of establishing any and all defenses, not only in the first instance but by a preponderance of the total evidence. The provision applies only to a holder, as defined in this Act (Section 1–201). Any other person in possession of an instrument must prove his right to it and account for the absence of any necessary indorsement. If he establishes a transfer which gives him the rights of a holder (Section 3–201), this provision becomes applicable, and he is then entitled to recover unless the defendant establishes a defense.

3. Subsection (3) rephrases the last clause of the first sentence of the original Section 59. Until it is shown that a defense exists the issue as to whether the holder is a holder in due course does not arise. In the absence of a defense any holder is entitled to recover and there is no occasion to say that he is deemed prima facie to be a holder in due course. When it is shown that a defense exists the plaintiff may, if he so elects, seek to cut off the defense by establishing that he is himself a holder in due course, or that he has acquired the rights of a prior holder in due course (Section 3–201). On this issue he has the full burden of proof by a preponderance of the total evidence. "In all respects" means that he must sustain this burden by affirmative proof that the instrument was taken for value, that it was taken in good faith, and that it was taken without notice (Section 3–302).

Nothing in this section is intended to say that the plaintiff must necessarily prove that he is a holder in due course. He may elect to introduce no further evidence, in which case a verdict may be directed for the plaintiff or the defendant, or the issue of the defense may be left to the jury, according to the weight and sufficiency of the defendant's evidence. He may elect to rebut the defense itself by proof to the contrary, in which case again a verdict may be directed for either party or the issue may be for the jury. This subsection means only that if the plaintiff claims the rights of a holder in due course against the defense he has the burden of proof upon that issue.

Cross References:

Sections 3–305, 3–306, 3–401, 3–403 and 3–404.

Point 1: Section 1–201.

Point 2: Sections 1–201 and 3–201(1).

Point 3: Sections 3–201(1) and 3–302.

Definitional Cross References:

"Action". Section 1–201.

"Burden of establishing". Section 1–201.

"Defendant". Section 1–201.

"Genuine". Section 1–201.

"Holder". Section 1–201.

"Holder in due course". Section 3–302.

"Instrument". Section 3–102.

"Party". Section 1–201.

"Person". Section 1–201.

"Presumed". Section 1–201.

"Rights". Section 1–201.

"Signature". Section 3–401.

PART 4

LIABILITY OF PARTIES

§ 3-401. Signature.

(1) No person is liable on an instrument unless his signature appears thereon.

(2) A signature is made by use of any name, including any trade or assumed name, upon an instrument, or by any word or mark used in lieu of a written signature.

Official Comment

Prior Uniform Statutory Provision: Section 18, Uniform Negotiable Instruments Law.

Changes: Reworded.

Purposes of Changes: To make it clear that:

1. No one is liable on an instrument unless and until he has signed it. The chief application of the rule has been in cases holding that a principal whose name does not appear on an instrument signed by his agent is not liable on the instrument even though the payee knew when it was issued that it was intended to be the obligation of one who did not sign. The exceptions made as to collateral and virtual acceptances by the original Sections 134 and 135 are now abrogated by the definition of an acceptance and the rules governing its operation. An allonge is part of the instrument to which it is affixed. Section 3-202(2).

Nothing in this section is intended to prevent any liability arising apart from the instrument itself. The party who does not sign may still be liable on the original obligation for which the instrument was given, or for breach of any agreement to sign, or in tort for misrepresentation, or even on an oral guaranty of payment where the statute of frauds is satisfied. He may of course be liable under any separate writing. The provision is not intended to prevent an estoppel to deny that the party has signed, as where the instrument is purchased in good faith reliance upon his assurance that a forged signature is genuine.

2. A signature may be handwritten, typed, printed or made in any other manner. It need not be subscribed, and may appear in the body of the instrument, as in the case of "I, John Doe, promise to pay—" without any other signature. It may be made by mark, or even by thumbprint. It may be made in any name, including any trade name or assumed name, however false and fictitious, which is adopted for the purpose. Parol evidence is admissible to identify the signer, and when he is identified the signature is effective.

This section is not intended to affect any local statute or rule of law requiring a signature by mark to be witnessed, or any signature to be otherwise authenticated, or requiring any form of proof. It is to be read together with the provision under which a person paying or giving value for the instrument may require indorsement in both the right name and the wrong one; and with the provision that the absence of an indorsement in the right name may make an instrument so irregular as to call its ownership into question and put a purchaser upon notice which will prevent his taking as a holder in due course.

Cross References:

Sections 3-202(2), 3-402 through 3-406.

Point 1: Section 3-410.
Point 2: Section 3-203.

Definitional Cross References:

"Person". Section 1-201.
"Instrument". Section 3-102.
"Signed". Section 1-201.
"Written". Section 1-201.

§ 3-402. Signature in Ambiguous Capacity.

Unless the instrument clearly indicates that a signature is made in some other capacity it is an indorsement.

Official Comment

Prior Uniform Statutory Provision: Sections 17(6) and 63, Uniform Negotiable Instruments Law.

Changes: Combined and reworded.

Purposes of Changes: The revised language is intended to say that any ambiguity as to the capacity in which a signature is made must be resolved by a rule of law that it is an indorsement. Parol evidence is not admissible to show any other capacity, except for the purpose of reformation of the instrument as it may be permitted under the rules of the particular jurisdiction. The question is to be determined from the face of the instrument alone, and unless the instrument itself makes it clear that he has signed in some other capacity the signer must be treated as an indorser.

The indication that the signature is made in another capacity must be clear without reference to anything but the instrument. It may be found in the language used. Thus if John Doe signs after "I, John Doe, promise to pay," he is clearly a maker; and "John Doe, witness" is not liable at all. The capacity may be found in any clearly evidenced purpose of the signature, as where a drawee signing in an unusual place on the paper has no visible reason to sign at all unless he is an acceptor. It may be found in usage or custom. Thus by long established practice judicially noticed or otherwise established a signature in the lower right hand corner of an instrument indicates an intent to sign as the maker of a note or the drawer of a draft. Any similar clear indication of an intent to sign in some other capacity may be enough to remove the signature from the application of this section.

Cross Reference:

Section 3-401.

Definitional Cross References:

"Instrument". Section 3-102.
"Signature". Section 3-401.

§ 3-403. Signature by Authorized Representative.

(1) A signature may be made by an agent or other representative, and his authority to make it may be established as in other cases of representation. No particular form of appointment is necessary to establish such authority.

(2) An authorized representative who signs his own name to an instrument

(a) is personally obligated if the instrument neither names the person represented nor shows that the representative signed in a representative capacity;

(b) except as otherwise established between the immediate parties, is personally obligated if the instrument names the person represented but does not show that the representative signed in a representative capacity, or if the instrument does not name the person represented but does show that the representative signed in a representative capacity.

(3) Except as otherwise established the name of an organization preceded or followed by the name and office of an authorized individual is a signature made in a representative capacity.

Official Comment

Prior Uniform Statutory Provision: Sections 19, 20 and 21, Uniform Negotiable Instruments Law.

Changes: Combined and reworded; original Section 21 omitted.

Purposes of Changes:

1. The definition of "representative" in this Act (Section 1–201) includes an officer of a corporation or association, a trustee, an executor or administrator of an estate, or any person empowered to act for another. It is not intended to mean that a trust or an estate is necessarily a legal entity with the capacity to issue negotiable instruments, but merely that if it can issue them they may be signed by the representative.

The power to sign for another may be an express authority, or it may be implied in law or in fact, or it may rest merely upon apparent authority. It may be established as in other cases of representation, and when relevant parol evidence is admissible to prove or to deny it.

2. Subsection (2) applies only to the signature of a representative whose authority to sign for another is established. If he is not authorized his signature has the effect of an unauthorized signature (Section 3–404). Even though he is authorized the principal is not liable on the instrument, under the provisions (Section 3–401) relating to signatures, unless the instrument names him and clearly shows that the signature is made on his behalf.

3. Assuming that Peter Pringle is a principal and Arthur Adams is his agent, an instrument might, for example, bear the following signatures affixed by the agent—

(a) "Peter Pringle", or

(b) "Arthur Adams", or

(c) "Peter Pringle by Arthur Adams, Agent", or

(d) "Arthur Adams, Agent", or

(e) "Peter Pringle Arthur Adams".

A signature in form (a) does not bind Adams if authorized (Sections 3–401 and 3–404).

A signature as in (b) personally obligates the agent and parol evidence is inadmissible under subsection (2)(a) to disestablish his obligation.

The unambiguous way to make the representation clear is to sign as in (c). Any other definite indication is sufficient, as where the instrument reads "Peter Pringle promises to pay" and it is signed "Arthur Adams, Agent." Adams is not bound if he is authorized (Section 3–404).

Subsection 2(b) adopts the New York (minority) rule of Megowan v. Peterson, 173 N.Y. 1 (1902), in such a case as (d); and adopts the majority rule in such a case as (e). In both cases the section admits parol evidence in litigation between the immediate parties to prove signature by the agent in his representative capacity. [Paragraph 3 was amended in 1966].

4. The original Section 21, covering signatures by "procuration," is omitted. It was based on English practice under which the words "per procuration" added to any signature are understood to mean that the signer is acting under a power of attorney which the holder is free to examine. The holder is thus put on notice of the limited authority, and there can be no apparent authority extending beyond the power of attorney. This meaning of "per procuration" is almost unknown in the United States, and the words are understood by the ordinary banker or attorney to be merely the equivalent of "by." The

omission is not intended to suggest that a signature "by procuration" can no longer have the effect which it had under the original Section 21, in any case where a party chooses to use the expression.

Cross References:

Point 1: Section 1-201.

Point 2: Sections 3-401(1), 3-404 and 3-405.

Definitional Cross References:

"Instrument". Section 3-102.
"Person". Section 1-201.
"Representative". Section 1-201.
"Signature". Section 3-401.

§ 3-404. Unauthorized Signatures.

(1) Any unauthorized signature is wholly inoperative as that of the person whose name is signed unless he ratifies it or is precluded from denying it; but it operates as the signature of the unauthorized signer in favor of any person who in good faith pays the instrument or takes it for value.

(2) Any unauthorized signature may be ratified for all purposes of this Article. Such ratification does not of itself affect any rights of the person ratifying against the actual signer.

Official Comment

Prior Uniform Statutory Provision: Section 23, Uniform Negotiable Instruments Law.

Changes: Reworded; new provisions.

Purpose of Changes and New Matter: The changes are intended to remove uncertainties arising under the original section:

1. "Unauthorized signature" is a defined term (Section 1-201). It includes both a forgery and a signature made by an agent exceeding his actual or apparent authority.

2. The final clause of subsection (1) is new. It states the generally accepted rule that the unauthorized signature, while it is wholly inoperative as that of the person whose name is signed, is effective to impose liability upon the actual signer or to transfer any rights that he may have in the instrument. His liability is not in damages for breach of a warranty of his authority, but is full liability on the instrument in the capacity in which he has signed. It is, however, limited to parties who take or pay the instrument in good faith; and one who knows that the signature is unauthorized cannot recover from the signer on the instrument.

3. Subsection (2) is new. It settles the conflict which has existed in the decisions as to whether a forgery may be ratified. A forged signature may at least be adopted; and the word "ratified" is used in order to make it clear that the adoption is retroactive, and that it may be found from conduct as well as from express statements. Thus it may be found from the retention of benefits received in the transaction with knowledge of the unauthorized signature; and although the forger is not an agent, the ratification is governed by the same rules and principles as if he were.

This provision makes ratification effective only for the purposes of this Article. The unauthorized signature becomes valid so far as its effect as a signature is concerned. The ratification relieves the actual signer from liability on the signature. It does not of itself relieve him from liability to the person whose name is signed. It does not in any way affect the criminal law. No policy of the criminal law requires that the person whose name is forged shall not assume liability to others on the instrument; but he cannot affect the rights of the state. While the ratification may be taken into account with other relevant facts in determining punishment, it does not relieve the signer of criminal liability.

4. The words "or is precluded from denying it" are retained in subsection (1) to recognize the possibility of an estoppel against the person whose name is signed, as where he expressly or tacitly represents to an innocent purchaser that the signature is genuine; and to recognize the negligence which precludes a denial of the signature.

Cross References:

Sections 3–307, 3–401, 3–403 and 3–405.

Point 1: Section 1–201.
Point 4: Section 3–406.

Definitional Cross References:

"Good faith". Section 1–201.
"Instrument". Section 3–102.
"Person". Section 1–201.
"Rights". Section 1–201.
"Signature". Section 3–401.
"Signed". Section 1–201.
"Unauthorized signature". Section 1–201.
"Value". Section 3–303.

§ 3–405. Impostors; Signature in Name of Payee.

(1) An indorsement by any person in the name of a named payee is effective if

(a) an impostor by use of the mails or otherwise has induced the maker or drawer to issue the instrument to him or his confederate in the name of the payee; or

(b) a person signing as or on behalf of a maker or drawer intends the payee to have no interest in the instrument; or

(c) an agent or employee of the maker or drawer has supplied him with the name of the payee intending the latter to have no such interest.

(2) Nothing in this section shall affect the criminal or civil liability of the person so indorsing.

Official Comment

Prior Uniform Statutory Provision: Section 9(3), Uniform Negotiable Instruments Law.

Changes: Reworded; new provisions.

Purposes of Changes and New Matter:

1. This section enlarges the original subsection to include additional situations which it has not been held to cover. The words "fictitious or nonexisting person" have been eliminated as misleading, since the existence or nonexistence of the named payee is not decisive and is important only as it may bear on the intent that he shall have no interest in the instrument. The instrument is not made payable to bearer and indorsements are still necessary to negotiation. The section however recognizes as effective indorsement of the types of paper covered no matter by whom made. This solution is thought preferable to making such instruments bearer paper; on the face of things they are payable to order and a subsequent taker should require what purports to be a regular chain of indorsements. On the other hand it is thought to be unduly restrictive to require that the actual indorsement be made by the impostor or other fraudulent actor. In most cases the person whose fraud procured the instrument to be issued will himself indorse; when some other third person indorses it will most probably be a case of theft or a second independent fraud superimposed upon the original fraud. In neither case does there seem to be sufficient reason to reverse the rule of the section. To recapitulate: the instrument does not become bearer paper, a purportedly regular chain in indorsements is required, but any person—first thief, second impostor or third murder-

er—can effectively indorse in the name of the payee.

2. Subsection (1)(a) is new. It rejects decisions which distinguish between face-to-face imposture and imposture by mail and hold that where the parties deal by mail the dominant intent of the drawer is to deal with the name rather than with the person so that the resulting instrument may be negotiated only by indorsement of the payee whose name has been taken in vain. The result of the distinction has been under some prior law, to throw the loss in the mail imposture forward to a subsequent holder or to the drawee. Since the maker or drawer believes the two to be one and the same, the two intentions cannot be separated, and the "dominant intent" is a fiction. The position here taken is that the loss, regardless of the type of fraud which the particular impostor has committed, should fall upon the maker or drawer.

"Impostor" refers to impersonation, and does not extend to a false representation that the party is the authorized agent of the payee. The maker or drawer who takes the precaution of making the instrument payable to the principal is entitled to have his indorsement.

3. Subsection (1)(b) restates the substance of the original subsection 9(3). The test stated is not whether the named payee is "fictitious," but whether the signer intends that he shall have no interest in the instrument. The following situations illustrate the application of the subsection.

a. The drawer of a check, for his own reasons, makes it payable to P knowing that P does not exist.

b. The drawer makes the check payable in the name of P. A person named P exists, but the drawer does not know it.

c. The drawer makes the check payable to P, an existing person whom he knows, intending to receive the money himself and that P shall have no interest in the check.

d. The treasurer of a corporation draws its check payable to P, who to the knowledge of the treasurer does not exist.

e. The treasurer of a corporation draws its check payable to P. P exists but the treasurer has fraudulently added his name to the payroll intending that he shall not receive the check.

f. The president and the treasurer of a corporation both sign its check payable to P. P does not exist. The treasurer knows it but the president does not.

g. The same facts as f, except that P exists and the treasurer knows it, but intends that P shall have no interest in the check.

In all the cases stated an indorsement by any person in the name of P is effective.

4. Paragraph (c) is new. It extends the rule of the original Subsection 9(3) to include the padded payroll cases, where the drawer's agent or employee prepares the check for signature or otherwise furnishes the signing officer with the name of the payee. The principle followed is that the loss should fall upon the employer as a risk of his business enterprise rather than upon the subsequent holder or drawee. The reasons are that the employer is normally in a better position to prevent such forgeries by reasonable care in the selection or supervision of his employees, or, if he is not, is at least in a better position to cover the loss by fidelity insurance; and that the cost of such insurance is properly an expense of his business rather than of the business of the holder or drawee.

The provision applies only to the agent or employee of the drawer, and only to the agent or employee who supplies him with the name of the payee. The following situations illustrate its application.

a. An employee of a corporation prepares a padded payroll for its treasurer, which includes the name of P. P does not exist, and the employee knows it, but the treasurer does not. The treasurer draws the corporation's check payable to P.

b. The same facts as a, except that P exists and the employee knows it but intends him to have no interest in the check. In both cases an indorsement by any person in the name of P is effective and the loss falls on the corporation.

5. The section is not intended to affect criminal liability for forgery or any other crime, or civil liability to the drawer or to any other person. It is to be read together with the section under which an unauthorized signer is personally liable on the signature to any person who takes the instrument in good faith (3-404(1)).

Cross References:

Sections 3-401, 3-403, 3-404 and 3-406.

Point 5: Section 3-404(1).

Definitional Cross References:

"Instrument". Section 3-102.
"Issue". Section 3-102.
"Person". Section 1-201.
"Signature". Section 3-401.

§ 3-406. Negligence Contributing to Alteration or Unauthorized Signature.

Any person who by his negligence substantially contributes to a material alteration of the instrument or to the making of an unauthorized signature is precluded from asserting the alteration or lack of authority against a holder in due course or against a drawee or other payor who pays the instrument in good faith and in accordance with the reasonable commercial standards of the drawee's or payor's business.

Official Comment

Prior Uniform Statutory Provision: None.

Purposes:

1. This section is new. It adopts the doctrine of Young v. Grote, 4 Bing. 253 (1827), which held that a drawer who so negligently draws an instrument as to facilitate its material alteration is liable to a drawee who pays the altered instrument in good faith. It should be noted that the rule as stated in the section requires that the negligence "substantially" contribute to the alteration.

2. The section extends the above principle to the protection of a holder in due course and of payors who may not technically be drawees. It rejects decisions which have held that the maker of a note owes no duty of care to the holder because at the time the instrument is drawn there is no contract between them. By drawing the instrument and "setting it afloat upon a sea of strangers" the maker or drawer voluntarily enters into a relation with later holders which justifies his responsibility. In this respect an instrument so negligently drawn as to facilitate alteration does not differ in principle from an instrument containing blanks which may be filled.

The holder in due course under the rules governing alteration (Section 3-407) may enforce the altered instrument according to its original tenor. Where negligence of the obligor has substantially contributed to the alteration, this section gives the holder the alternative right to enforce the instrument as altered.

3. No attempt is made to define negligence which will contribute to an alteration. The question is left to the court or the jury upon the circumstances of the particular cases. Negligence usually has been found where spaces are left in the body of the instrument in which words or figures may be inserted. No unusual precautions are required, and the section is not intended to change decisions holding that the drawer of a bill is under no duty to use sensitized paper, indelible ink or a protectograph; or that it is not negligence to leave spaces between the lines or at the end of the instrument in which a provision for interest or the like can be written.

4. The section applies only where the negligence contributes to the alteration. It must afford an opportunity of which advantage is in fact taken. The section approves decisions which have refused to hold the drawer responsible where he has left spaces in a check but the payee erased all the writing with chemicals and wrote in an entirely new check.

5. This section does not make the negligent party liable in tort for damages resulting from the alteration. Instead it estops him from asserting it against the holder in due course or drawee. The reason is that in the usual case the extent of the loss, which involves the possibility of ultimate recovery from the wrongdoer, cannot be determined at the time of litigation, and the decision would have to be made on the unsatisfactory basis of burden of proof. The holder or drawee is protected by an estoppel, and the task of pursuing the wrongdoer is left to the negligent party. Any amount in fact recovered from the wrongdoer must be held for the benefit of the negligent party under ordinary principles of equity.

6. The section protects parties who act not only in good faith, (Section 1–201) but also in observance of the reasonable standards of their business. Thus any bank which takes or pays an altered check which ordinary banking standards would require it to refuse cannot take advantage of the estoppel.

7. The section applies the same rule to negligence which contributes to a forgery or other unauthorized signature, as defined in this Act (Section 1–201). The most obvious case is that of the drawer who makes use of a signature stamp or other automatic signing device and is negligent in looking after it. The section extends, however, to cases where the party has notice that forgeries of his signature have occurred and is negligent in failing to prevent further forgeries by the same person. It extends to negligence which contributes to a forgery of the signature of another, as in the case where a check is negligently mailed to the wrong person having the same name as the payee. As in the case of alteration, no attempt is made to specify what is negligence, and the question is one for the court or the jury on the facts of the particular case.

Cross References:

Sections 3–401 and 3–404.
Point 2: Section 3–407(3).
Point 6: Section 1–201.
Point 7: Section 1–201.

Definitional Cross References:

"Alteration". Section 3–407.
"Good faith". Section 1–201.
"Holder in due course". Section 3–302.
"Instrument". Section 3–102.
"Person". Section 1–201.
"Unauthorized signature". Section 1–201.

§ 3–407. Alteration.

(1) Any alteration of an instrument is material which changes the contract of any party thereto in any respect, including any such change in

(a) the number or relations of the parties; or

(b) an incomplete instrument, by completing it otherwise than as authorized; or

(c) the writing as signed, by adding to it or by removing any part of it.

(2) As against any person other than a subsequent holder in due course.

(a) alteration by the holder which is both fraudulent and material discharges any party whose contract is thereby changed unless that party assents or is precluded from asserting the defense;

(b) no other alteration discharges any party and the instrument may be enforced according to its original tenor, or as to incomplete instruments according to the authority given.

(3) A subsequent holder in due course may in all cases enforce the instrument according to its original tenor, and when an incomplete instrument has been completed, he may enforce it as completed.

Official Comment

Prior Uniform Statutory Provision: Sections 14, 15, 124 and 125, Uniform Negotiable Instruments Law.

Changes: Combined and reworded; new provisions; rule of original Section 15 reversed.

Purposes of Changes and New Matter: The changes are intended to remove uncertainties arising under the original sections, and to modify the rules as to discharge:

1. Subsection (1) substitutes a general definition for the list of illustrations in the original Section 125. Any alteration is material only as it may change the contract of a party to the instrument; and the addition or deletion of words which do not in any way affect the contract of any previous signer is not material. But any change in the contract of a party, however slight, is a material alteration; and the addition of one cent to the amount payable, or an advance of one day in the date of payment, will operate as a discharge if it is fraudulent.

Specific mention is made of a change in the number or relations of the parties in order to make it clear that any such change is material only if it changes the contract of one who has signed. The addition of a co-maker or a surety does not change in most jurisdictions the contract of one who has already signed as maker and should not be held material as to him. The addition of the name of an alternative payee is material, since it changes his obligation. Paragraph (c) makes special mention of a change in the writing signed in order to cover occasional cases of addition of sticker clauses, scissoring or perforating instruments where the separation is not authorized.

2. Paragraph (b) of subsection (1) is to be read together with Section 3-115 on incomplete instruments. Where an instrument contains blanks or is otherwise incomplete, it may be completed in accordance with the authority given and is then valid and effective as completed. If the completion is unauthorized and has the effect of changing the contract of any previous signer, this provision follows the generally accepted rule in treating it as a material alteration which may operate as a discharge.

3. Subsection (2) modifies the very rigorous rule of the original Section 124. The changes made are as follows:

a. A material alteration does not discharge any party unless it is made by the holder. Spoliation by any meddling stranger does not affect the rights of the holder. It is of course intended that the acts of the holder's authorized agent or employee, or of his confederates, are to be attributed to him.

b. A material alteration does not discharge any party unless it is made for a fraudulent purpose. There is no discharge where a blank is filled in the honest belief that it is as authorized; or where a change is made with a benevolent motive such as a desire to give the obligor the benefit of a lower interest rate. Changes favorable to the obligor are unlikely to be made with any fraudulent intent; but if such an intent is found the alteration may operate as a discharge.

c. The discharge is a personal defense of the party whose contract is changed by the alteration, and anyone whose contract is not affected cannot assert it. The contract of any party is necessarily affected, however, by the discharge of any party against whom he has a right of recourse on the instrument. Assent to the alteration given before or after it is made will prevent the party from asserting the discharge. "Or is precluded from asserting the defense" is added in paragraph (a) to recognize the possibility of an estoppel or other ground barring the defense which does not rest on assent.

d. If the alteration is not material or if it is not made for a fraudulent purpose there is no discharge, and the instrument may be enforced according to its original tenor. Where blanks are filled or an incomplete instrument is otherwise completed there is no original tenor, but the instrument may be enforced according to the authority in fact given.

4. Subsection (3) combines the final sentences of the original Sections 14 and 124, and provides that a subsequent holder in due course takes free of the discharge in all cases. The provision is merely one form of the general rule governing the effect of discharge against a holder in due course (Section 3-602). The holder in due course may enforce the instrument according to its original tenor. In this connection reference should be made to the section giving the holder in due course the right, where the maker's or drawer's negligence has substantially contributed to the alteration, to enforce the instrument in its altered form (Section 3-406). Reference should also be made to Section 4-401 covering a bank's right to charge its customer's account in the case of altered instruments.

Where blanks are filled or an incomplete instrument is otherwise completed, this subsection follows the original Section 14 in placing the loss upon the party who left the instrument incomplete and permitting the holder to enforce it in its completed form. As indicated in the comment to Section 3-115 on incomplete instruments, this result is intended even though the instrument was stolen from the maker or drawer and completed after the theft; and the effect of this subsection, together with the section on incomplete instruments is to reverse the rule of the original Section 15.

There is no inconsistency between subsection (3) and paragraph (b) of subsection (2). The holder in due course may elect to enforce the instrument either as provided in that paragraph or as provided in subsection (3).

It should be noted that a purchaser who takes the instrument with notice of any material alteration, including the unauthorized completion of an incomplete instrument, takes with notice of a claim or defense and cannot be a holder in due course (Section 3-304).

Cross References:

Sections 3-305, 3-306 and 3-307.

Point 2: Section 3-115.

Point 4: Sections 3-115, 3-304(2), 3-602 and 4-401.

Definitional Cross References:

"Contract". Section 1-201.

"Holder". Section 1-201.

"Holder in due course". Section 3-302.

"Instrument". Section 3-102.

"Party". Section 1-201.

"Person". Section 1-201.

"Signed". Section 1-201.

"Writing". Section 1-201.

§ 3-408. Consideration.

Want or failure of consideration is a defense as against any person not having the rights of a holder in due course (Section 3-305), except that no consideration is necessary for an instrument or obligation thereon given in payment of or as security for an antecedent obligation of any kind. Nothing in this section shall be taken to displace any statute outside this Act under which a promise is enforceable notwithstanding lack or failure of consideration. Partial failure of consideration is a defense pro tanto whether or not the failure is in an ascertained or liquidated amount.

Official Comment

Prior Uniform Statutory Provision: Sections 24, 25 and 28, Uniform Negotiable Instruments Law.

Changes: Combined and reworded.

Purposes of Changes:

1. "Consideration" is distinguished from "value" throughout this Article. "Consideration" refers to what the obligor has received for his obligation, and is important only on the question of whether his obligation can be enforced against him.

2. The "except" clause is intended to remove the difficulties which have arisen where a note or a draft, or an indorsement of either, is given as payment or as security for a debt already owed by the party giving it, or by a third person. The provision is intended to change the result of decisions holding that where no extension of time or other concession is given by the creditor the new obligation fails for lack of legal consideration. It is intended also to mean that an instrument given for more or less than the amount of a liquidated obligation does not fail by reason of the common law rule that an obligation for a lesser liquidated amount cannot be consideration for the surrender of a greater.

3. With respect to the necessity or sufficiency of consideration other obligations on an instrument are subject to the ordinary rules of contract law relating to contracts not under seal. Promissory estoppel or any other equivalent or substitute for consideration is to be recognized as in other contract cases. The provision of the original Section 28 as to absence or failure of consideration is now covered by the section dealing with the rights of one not a holder in due course; and the "presumption" of consideration in the original Section 24 is replaced by the provision relating to the burden of establishing defenses.

Cross References:

Point 1: Section 3-303.

Point 3: Sections 3-306(c) and 3-307(2).

Definitional Cross References:

"Holder in due course". Section 3-302.

"Instrument". Section 3-102.

"Person". Section 1-201.

"Rights". Section 1-201.

§ 3-409. Draft Not an Assignment.

(1) A check or other draft does not of itself operate as an assignment of any funds in the hands of the drawee available for its payment, and the drawee is not liable on the instrument until he accepts it.

(2) Nothing in this section shall affect any liability in contract, tort or otherwise arising from any letter of credit or other obligation or representation which is not an acceptance.

Official Comment

Prior Uniform Statutory Provision: Sections 127 and 189, Uniform Negotiable Instruments Law.

Changes: Combined and reworded; new provisions.

Purposes of Changes and New Matter:

The two original sections are combined, brought forward to appear in connection with acceptance, and reworded to remove uncertainties.

1. As under the original sections, a check or other draft does not of itself operate as an assignment in law or equity. The assignment may, however, appear from other facts, and particularly from other agreements, express or implied; and when the intent to assign is

clear the check may be the means by which the assignment is effected.

2. The language of the original Section 189, that the drawee is not liable "to the holder", is changed as inaccurate and not intended. The drawee is not liable on the instrument until he accepts; but he remains subject to any other liability to the holder. In this connection reference should be made to Section 4-302 on the payor bank's liability for late return. Such a bank if it does not either make prompt settlement or return on an item received by it will become liable to a holder of the item.

3. Subsection (2) is new. It is intended to make it clear that this section does not in any way affect any liability which may arise apart from the instrument itself. The drawee who fails to accept may be liable to the drawer or to the holder for breach of the terms of a letter of credit or any other agreement by which he is obligated to accept. He may be liable in tort or upon any other basis because of his representation that he has accepted, or that he intends to accept. The section leaves unaffected any liability of any kind apart from the instrument.

Cross References:

Sections 3-410, 3-411, 3-412 and 3-415.

Point 2: Section 4-302.

Definitional Cross References:

"Acceptance". Section 3-410.
"Check". Section 3-104.
"Contract". Section 1-201.
"Draft". Section 3-104.
"Instrument". Section 3-102.
"Letter of credit". Section 5-104.

§ 3-410. Definition and Operation of Acceptance.

(1) Acceptance is the drawee's signed engagement to honor the draft as presented. It must be written on the draft, and may consist of his signature alone. It becomes operative when completed by delivery or notification.

(2) A draft may be accepted although it has not been signed by the drawer or is otherwise incomplete or is overdue or has been dishonored.

(3) Where the draft is payable at a fixed period after sight and the acceptor fails to date his acceptance the holder may complete it by supplying a date in good faith.

Official Comment

Prior Uniform Statutory Provision: Sections 132, 133, 134, 135, 136, 137, 138, 161-170, and 191, Uniform Negotiable Instruments Law.

Changes: Combined, reworded; original Sections 134, 135, 137 and 161-170 eliminated.

Purposes of Changes:

1. The original Sections 161-170 providing for acceptance for honor are omitted from this Article. This ancient practice developed at a time when communications were slow, and particularly in overseas transactions there might be a delay of several months before the drawer could be notified of dishonor by nonacceptance and take steps to protect his credit. The need for intervention by a third party has passed with the development of the cable transfer, the letter of credit, and numerous other devices by which a substitute arrangement is promptly made. The practice has been obsolete for many years, and the sections are therefore eliminated.

2. Under Section 3-417 a person obtaining acceptance gives a warranty against alteration of the instrument before acceptance.

3. Subsection (1) adopts the rule of Section 17 of the English Bills of Exchange Act that the acceptance must be written on the draft. It eliminates the original Sections 134 and 135, providing

for "virtual" acceptance by a written promise to accept drafts to be drawn, and "collateral" acceptance by a separate writing. Both have been anomalous exceptions to the policy that no person is liable on an instrument unless his signature appears on it. Both are derived from a line of early American cases decided at a time when difficulties of communication, particularly overseas, might leave the holder in doubt for a long period whether the draft was accepted. Such conditions have long since ceased to exist, and the "virtual" or "collateral" acceptance is now almost entirely obsolete. Good commercial and banking practice does not sanction acceptance by any separate writing because of the dangers and uncertainties arising when it becomes separated from the draft. The instrument is now forwarded to the drawee for his acceptance upon it, or reliance is placed upon the obligation of the separate writing itself, as in the case of a letter of credit.

Nothing in this section is intended to eliminate any liability of the drawee in contract, tort or otherwise arising from the separate writing or any other obligation or representation, as provided in Section 3-409.

Subsection (1) likewise eliminates the original section 137, providing for acceptance by delay or refusal to return the instrument but the drawee may be liable for a conversion of the instrument under Section 3-419.

4. Subsection (1) states the generally recognized rule that the mere signature of the drawee on the instrument is a sufficient acceptance. Customarily the signature is written vertically across the face of the instrument; but since the drawee has no reason to sign for any other purpose his signature in any other place, even on the back of the instrument, is sufficient. It need not be accompanied by such words as "Accepted," "Certified," or "Good." It must not, however, bear any words indicating an intent to refuse to honor the bill; and nothing in this provision is intended to change such decisions as Norton v. Knapp, 64 Iowa 112, 19 N.W. 867 (1884), holding that the drawee's signature accompanied by the words "Kiss my foot" is not an acceptance.

5. The final sentence of subsection (1) expressly states the generally recognized rule, implied in the definition of acceptance in the original Section 191, that an acceptance written on the draft takes effect when the drawee notifies the holder or gives notice according to his instructions. Acceptance is thus an exception to the usual rule that no obligation on an instrument is effective until delivery.

6. Subsection (3) changes the last sentence of the original Section 138. The purpose of the provision is to provide a definite date of payment where none appears on the instrument. An undated acceptance of a draft payable "thirty days after sight" is incomplete; and unless the acceptor himself writes in a different date the holder is authorized to complete the acceptance according to the terms of the draft by supplying a date of presentment. Any date which the holder chooses to write in is effective providing his choice of date is made in good faith. Any different agreement not written on the draft is not effective, and parol evidence is not admissible to show it.

Cross References:

Sections 3-411, 3-412 and 3-418.
Point 2: Section 3-417.
Point 3: Sections 3-401(1), 3-409(2) and 3-419.
Point 6: Section 3-412.

Definitional Cross References:

"Delivery". Section 1-201.
"Dishonor". Section 3-507.
"Draft". Section 3-104.
"Good faith". Section 1-201.
"Holder". Section 1-201.
"Honor". Section 1-201.
"Notification". Section 1-201.
"Presentment". Section 3-504.
"Signature". Section 3-401.
"Signed". Section 1-201.
"Written". Section 1-201.

§ 3-411. Certification of a Check.

(1) Certification of a check is acceptance. Where a holder procures certification the drawer and all prior indorsers are discharged.

(2) Unless otherwise agreed a bank has no obligation to certify a check.

(3) A bank may certify a check before returning it for lack of proper indorsement. If it does so the drawer is discharged.

Official Comment

Prior Uniform Statutory Provision: Sections 187 and 188, Uniform Negotiable Instruments Law.

Changes: Combined and reworded; new provisions.

Purposes of Changes and New Matter:

1. The second sentence of subsection (1) continues the rule of original Section 188 that, while certification procured by a holder discharges the drawer and other prior parties, certification procured by the drawer leaves him liable. Under this provision any certification procured by a holder discharges the drawer and prior indorsers. Any indorsement made after a certification so procured remains effective; and where it is intended that any indorser shall remain liable notwithstanding certification, he may indorse with the words "after certification" to make his liability clear.

2. Subsection (2) is new. It states the generally recognized rule that in the absence of agreement a bank is under no obligation to certify a check, because it is a demand instrument calling for payment rather than acceptance. The bank may be liable for breach of any agreement with the drawer, the holder, or any other person by which it undertakes to certify. Its liability is not on the instrument, since the drawee is not so liable until acceptance (Section 3-409(1)). Any liability is for breach of the separate agreement.

3. Subsection (3) is new. It recognizes the banking practice of certifying a check which is returned for proper indorsement in order to protect the drawer against a longer contingent liability. It is consistent with the provision of Section 3-410(2) permitting certification although the check has not been signed or is otherwise incomplete.

Cross References:

Sections 3-412, 3-413, 3-417 and 3-418.

Point 2: Section 3-409(1).

Point 3: Section 3-410(2).

Definitional Cross References:

"Acceptance". Section 3-410.

"Bank". Section 1-201.

"Check". Section 3-104.

"Holder". Section 1-201.

§ 3-412. Acceptance Varying Draft.

(1) Where the drawee's proffered acceptance in any manner varies the draft as presented the holder may refuse the acceptance and treat the draft as dishonored in which case the drawee is entitled to have his acceptance cancelled.

(2) The terms of the draft are not varied by an acceptance to pay at any particular bank or place in the United States, unless the acceptance states that the draft is to be paid only at such bank or place.

(3) Where the holder assents to an acceptance varying the terms of the draft each drawer and indorser who does not affirmatively assent is discharged.

As amended in 1962.

Official Comment

Prior Uniform Statutory Provision: Sections 139, 140, 141 and 142, Uniform Negotiable Instruments Law.

Changes: Combined and reworded; law changed as to qualified acceptances.

Purposes of Changes:

1. The section applies to conditional acceptances, acceptances for part of the amount, acceptances to pay at a different time from that required by the draft, or to the acceptance of less than all of the drawees, all of which are covered by the original Section 141. It applies to any other engagement changing the essential terms of the draft.

2. Where the drawee offers such a varied engagement the holder has an election. He may reject the offer, insist on acceptance of the draft as presented, and treat the refusal to give it as a dishonor. In that event the drawee is not bound by his engagement, and is entitled to have it cancelled. After any necessary notice of dishonor and protest the holder may have his recourse against the drawer and indorsers.

If the holder elects to accept the offer, this section does not invalidate the drawee's varied engagement. It remains his effective obligation, which the holder may enforce against him. By his assent, however, the holder discharges any drawer or indorser who does not also assent. The rule of the original Section 142 is changed to require that the assent of the drawer or indorser be affirmatively expressed. Mere failure to object within a reasonable time is not assent which will prevent the discharge.

3. The rule of original Section 140 that an acceptance to pay at a particular place is an unqualified acceptance is modified by the provision of subsection (2) that the terms of the draft are not varied by an acceptance to pay at any particular bank or place in the United States unless the acceptance states that the draft is to be paid only at such bank or place. Section 3-504(4) provides that a draft accepted payable at a bank in the United States must be presented at the bank designated [As amended 1962].

Cross References:

Sections 3-410 and 3-413.
Point 3: Section 3-504(4).

Definitional Cross References:

"Acceptance". Section 3-410.
"Bank". Section 1-201.
"Dishonor". Section 3-507.
"Draft". Section 3-104.
"Holder". Section 1-201.
"Term". Section 1-201.
"Written". Section 1-201.

§ 3-413. Contract of Maker, Drawer and Acceptor.

(1) The maker or acceptor engages that he will pay the instrument according to its tenor at the time of his engagement or as completed pursuant to Section 3-115 on incomplete instruments.

(2) The drawer engages that upon dishonor of the draft and any necessary notice of dishonor or protest he will pay the amount of the draft to the holder or to any indorser who takes it up. The drawer may disclaim this liability by drawing without recourse.

(3) By making, drawing or accepting the party admits as against all subsequent parties including the drawee the existence of the payee and his then capacity to indorse.

Official Comment

Prior Uniform Statutory Provision: Sections 60, 61 and 62, Uniform Negotiable Instruments Law.

Changes: Combined and reworded.

Purposes of Changes:

The original sections are combined for convenience and condensed to avoid duplication of language. This section should be read in connection with the sections on incomplete instruments (3–115), negligence contributing to alteration or unauthorized signature (3–406), alteration (3–407), acceptances varying a draft (3–412) and finality of payment or acceptance (3–418). Thus a maker who signs an incomplete note engages under this section to pay it according to its tenor at the time he signs it, but by virtue of Sections 3–115 and 3–407 the note may thereafter be completed and enforced against him. In the same way, if the maker's negligence substantially contributes to alteration of the instrument, he will become liable on his note as altered under Section 3–406. When a holder assents to an acceptance varying a draft (Section 3–412) he can of course hold the acceptor only according to the form of acceptance to which the holder agreed. Section 3–418 applies the rule of Price v. Neal both to acceptance and payment; thus an acceptor may not, after acceptance, assert that the drawer's signature is unauthorized.

Subsection (1) applies to all drafts (including checks) the rule that the acceptance relates to the instrument as it was at the time of its acceptance and not (in case of alteration before acceptance) to its original tenor. The cases on this point under the original act (all of which involved checks) have been in conflict. It should be noted that under Section 3–417 a person who obtains acceptance warrants to the acceptor that the instrument has not been materially altered.

Except as indicated in the foregoing comment the section makes no change in substance from the provision of the original act.

Cross References:

Sections 3–115, 3–406, 3–407, 3–412, 3–417 and 3–418.

Definitional Cross References:

"Contract". Section 1–201.
"Dishonor". Section 3–507.
"Draft". Section 3–104.
"Holder". Section 1–201.
"Instrument". Section 3–102.
"Notice of dishonor". Section 3–508.
"Party". Section 1–201.
"Protest". Section 3–509.

§ 3–414. Contract of Indorser; Order of Liability.

(1) Unless the indorsement otherwise specifies (as by such words as "without recourse") every indorser engages that upon dishonor and any necessary notice of dishonor and protest he will pay the instrument according to its tenor at the time of his indorsement to the holder or to any subsequent indorser who takes it up, even though the indorser who takes it up was not obligated to do so.

(2) Unless they otherwise agree indorsers are liable to one another in the order in which they indorse, which is presumed to be the order in which their signatures appear on the instrument.

Official Comment

Prior Uniform Statutory Provision: Sections 38, 44, 66, 67 and 68, Uniform Negotiable Instruments Law.

Changes: Combined and reworded.

Purposes of Changes:

1. Subsection (1) states the contract of indorsement—that if the instrument is dishonored and any protest or notice of dishonor which may be necessary under Section 3-501 is given, the indorser will pay the instrument. The indorser's engagement runs to any holder (whether or not for value) and to any indorser subsequent to him who has taken the instrument up. An indorser may disclaim his liability on the contract of indorsement, but only if the indorsement itself so specifies. Since the disclaimer varies the written contract of indorsement, the disclaimer itself must be written on the instrument and cannot be proved by parol. The customary manner of disclaiming the indorser's liability under this section is to indorse "without recourse". Apart from such a disclaimer all indorsers incur this liability, without regard to whether or not the indorser transferred the instrument for value or received consideration for his indorsement.

Original Section 44, permitting a representative to indorse in such terms as to exclude personal liability, is omitted as unnecessary and included in the broader right to disclaim any liability. No change in the law is intended by this omission.

2. In addition to his liability on the contract of indorsement, an indorser, if a transferor, gives the warranties stated in Section 3-417.

3. As in the case of acceptor's liability (Section 3-413), this section conditions the indorser's liability on the tenor of the instrument at the time of his indorsement. Thus if a person indorses an altered instrument he assumes liability as indorser on the instrument as altered.

4. Subsection (2) is intended to clarify existing law under original Section 68.

The section states two presumptions: One is that the indorsers are liable to one another in the order in which they have in fact indorsed. The other is that they have in fact indorsed in the order in which their names appear. Parol evidence is admissible to show that they have indorsed in another order, or that they have otherwise agreed as to their liability to one another.

The last sentence of the original Section 68 is now covered by Section 3-118(e) (Ambiguous Terms and Rules of Construction).

Cross References:

Point 1: Section 3-501.
Point 2: Section 3-417.
Point 3: Section 3-413.
Point 4: Section 3-118(e).

Definitional Cross References:

"Contract". Section 1-201.
"Dishonor". Section 3-507.
"Holder". Section 1-201.
"Instrument". Section 3-102.
"Notice of dishonor". Section 3-508.
"Presumed". Section 1-201.
"Protest". Section 3-509.
"Signature". Section 3-401.

§ 3-415. Contract of Accommodation Party.

(1) An accommodation party is one who signs the instrument in any capacity for the purpose of lending his name to another party to it.

(2) When the instrument has been taken for value before it is due the accommodation party is liable in the capacity in which he has signed even though the taker knows of the accommodation.

(3) As against a holder in due course and without notice of the accommodation oral proof of the accommodation is not admissible to give the accommodation party the benefit of discharges dependent on his character as such. In other cases the accommodation character may be shown by oral proof.

(4) An indorsement which shows that it is not in the chain of title is notice of its accommodation character.

(5) An accommodation party is not liable to the party accommodated, and if he pays the instrument has a right of recourse on the instrument against such party.

Official Comment

Prior Uniform Statutory Provision: Sections 28, 29 and 64, Uniform Negotiable Instruments Law.

Changes: Combined and reworded; new provisions.

Purposes of Changes and New Matter: To make it clear that:

1. Subsection (1) recognizes that an accommodation party is always a surety (which includes a guarantor), and it is his only distinguishing feature. He differs from other sureties only in that his liability is on the instrument and he is a surety for another party to it. His obligation is therefore determined by the capacity in which he signs. An accommodation maker or acceptor is bound on the instrument without any resort to his principal, while an accommodation indorser may be liable only after presentment, notice of dishonor and protest. The subsection recognizes the defenses of a surety in accordance with the provisions subjecting one not a holder in due course to all simple contract defenses, as well as his rights against his principal after payment. Under subsection (3) except as against a holder in due course without notice of the accommodation, parol evidence is admissible to prove that the party has signed for accommodation. In any case, however, under subsection (4) an indorsement which is not in the chain of title (the irregular or anomalous indorsement) is notice to all subsequent takers of the instrument of the accommodation character of the indorsement.

2. Subsection (1) eliminates the language of the old Section 29 requiring that the accommodation party sign the instrument "without receiving value therefor." The essential characteristic is that the accommodation party is a surety, and not that he has signed gratuitously. He may be a paid surety, or receive other compensation from the party accommodated. He may even receive it from the payee, as where A and B buy goods and it is understood that A is to pay for all of them and that B is to sign a note only as a surety for A.

3. The obligation of the accommodation party is supported by any consideration for which the instrument is taken before it is due. Subsection (2) is intended to change occasional decisions holding that there is no sufficient consideration where an accommodation party signs a note after it is in the hands of a holder who has given value. The party is liable to the holder in such a case even though there is no extension of time or other concession. This is consistent with the provision as to antecedent obligations as consideration (Section 3-408). The limitation to "before it is due" is one of suretyship law, by which the obligation of the surety is terminated at the time limit unless in the meantime the obligation of the principal has become effective.

4. As a surety the accommodation party is not liable to the party accommodated; but he is otherwise liable on the instrument in the capacity in which he has signed. This general statement of the rule makes unnecessary the detailed provisions of the original Section 64, which is therefore eliminated, without any change in substance.

5. Subsection (5) is intended to change the result of such decisions as Quimby v. Varnum, 190 Mass. 211, 76 N.E. 671 (1906), which held that an accommodation indorser who paid the instrument could not maintain an action on it against the accommodated party since he had no "former rights" to which he was remitted. Under ordinary principles of suretyship the accommodation party who pays is subrogated to the rights of the holder paid, and should have his recourse on the instrument.

Cross References:

Sections 3-305, 3-408, 3-603, 3-604 and 3-606.

Point 1: Section 3-306(b).

Point 3: Section 3-408.

Definitional Cross References:

"Holder in due course". Section 3-302.

"Instrument". Section 3-102.

"Notice". Section 1-201.

"Party". Section 1-201.

"Presentment". Section 3-504.

"Signed". Section 1-201.

"Writing". Section 1-201.

§ 3-416. Contract of Guarantor.

(1) "Payment guaranteed" or equivalent words added to a signature mean that the signer engages that if the instrument is not paid when due he will pay it according to its tenor without resort by the holder to any other party.

(2) "Collection guaranteed" or equivalent words added to a signature mean that the signer engages that if the instrument is not paid when due he will pay it according to its tenor, but only after the holder has reduced his claim against the maker or acceptor to judgment and execution has been returned unsatisfied, or after the maker or acceptor has become insolvent or it is otherwise apparent that it is useless to proceed against him.

(3) Words of guaranty which do not otherwise specify guarantee payment.

(4) No words of guaranty added to the signature of a sole maker or acceptor affect his liability on the instrument. Such words added to the signature of one of two or more makers or acceptors create a presumption that the signature is for the accommodation of the others.

(5) When words of guaranty are used presentment, notice of dishonor and protest are not necessary to charge the user.

(6) Any guaranty written on the instrument is enforcible notwithstanding any statute of frauds.

Official Comment

Prior Uniform Statutory Provision: None.

Purposes: The section is new. It states the commercial understanding as to the meaning and effect of words of guaranty added to a signature.

An indorser who guarantees payment waives not only presentment, notice of dishonor and protest, but also all demand upon the maker or drawee. Words of guaranty do not affect the character of the indorsement as an indorsement (Section 3-202(4)); but the liability of the indorser becomes indistinguishable from that of a co-maker. A guaranty of collection likewise waives formal presentment, notice of dishonor and protest, but requires that the holder first proceed against the maker or acceptor by suit and execution, or show that such proceeding would be useless.

Subsection (6) is concerned chiefly with the type of statute of frauds which provides that no promise to answer for the debt, default or miscarriage of another is enforceable unless it is evidenced by a writing which states the consideration for the promise. It is unusual to state any consideration when a guaranty is added to a signature on a negotiable instrument, which in itself sufficiently shows the nature of the transaction; and such statutes have commonly been held not to apply to such guaranties.

Cross References:

Sections 3-202(4) and 3-415.

Definitional Cross References:

"Holder". Section 1-201.
"Insolvent". Section 1-201.
"Instrument". Section 3-102.
"Notice of dishonor". Section 3-508.
"Party". Section 1-201.
"Presumption". Section 1-201.
"Protest". Section 3-509.
"Signature". Section 3-401.
"Written". Section 1-201.

§ 3-417. Warranties on Presentment and Transfer.

(1) Any person who obtains payment or acceptance and any prior transferor warrants to a person who in good faith pays or accepts that

(a) he has a good title to the instrument or is authorized to obtain payment or acceptance on behalf of one who has a good title; and
(b) he has no knowledge that the signature of the maker or drawer is unauthorized, except that this warranty is not given by a holder in due course acting in good faith
  (i) to a maker with respect to the maker's own signature; or
  (ii) to a drawer with respect to the drawer's own signature, whether or not the drawer is also the drawee; or
  (iii) to an acceptor of a draft if the holder in due course took the draft after the acceptance or obtained the acceptance without knowledge that the drawer's signature was unauthorized; and
(c) the instrument has not been materially altered, except that this warranty is not given by a holder in due course acting in good faith
  (i) to the maker of a note; or
  (ii) to the drawer of a draft whether or not the drawer is also the drawee; or
  (iii) to the acceptor of a draft with respect to an alteration made prior to the acceptance if the holder in due course took the draft after the acceptance, even though the acceptance provided "payable as originally drawn" or equivalent terms; or
  (iv) to the acceptor of a draft with respect to an alteration made after the acceptance.

(2) Any person who transfers an instrument and receives consideration warrants to his transferee and if the transfer is by indorsement to any subsequent holder who takes the instrument in good faith that

(a) he has a good title to the instrument or is authorized to obtain payment or acceptance on behalf of one who has a good title and the transfer is otherwise rightful; and
(b) all signatures are genuine or authorized; and
(c) the instrument has not been materially altered; and
(d) no defense of any party is good against him; and
(e) he has no knowledge of any insolvency proceeding instituted with respect to the maker or acceptor or the drawer of an unaccepted instrument.

(3) By transferring "without recourse" the transferor limits the obligation stated in subsection (2)(d) to a warranty that he has no knowledge of such a defense.

(4) A selling agent or broker who does not disclose the fact that he is acting only as such gives the warranties provided in this section, but if he makes such disclosure warrants only his good faith and authority.

Official Comment

Prior Uniform Statutory Provision: Sections 65 and 69, Uniform Negotiable Instruments Law.

Changes: Combined and reworded; new provisions added.

Purposes of Changes and New Matter:

1. The obligations imposed by this section are stated in terms of warranty. Warranty terms, which are not limited to sale transactions, are used with the intention of bringing in all the usual rules of law applicable to warranties, and in particular the necessity of reliance in good faith and the availability of all remedies for breach of warranty, such as rescission of the transaction or an action for damages. Like other warranties, those stated in this section may be disclaimed by agreement between the immediate parties. In the case of an indorser, disclaimer of his liability as a transferor, to be effective, must appear in the form of the indorsement, and no parol proof of "agreement otherwise" is admissible. For corresponding warranties in the case of items in the bank collection process, Section 4-207 should be consulted.

2. Subsection (1) is new. It is intended to state the undertaking to a party who accepts or pays of one who obtains payment or acceptance or of any prior transferor. It is closely connected with the following section on the finality of acceptance or payment (Section 3-418), and should be read together with it.

3. Subsection (1)(a) retains the generally accepted rule that the party who accepts or pays does not "admit" the genuineness of indorsements, and may recover from the person presenting the instrument when they turn out to be forged. The justification for the distinction between forgery of the signature of the drawer and forgery of an indorsement is that the drawee is in a position to verify the drawer's signature by comparison with one in his hands, but has ordinarily no opportunity to verify an indorsement.

4. Subsection (1)(b) recognizes and deals with competing equities of parties accepting or paying instruments bearing unauthorized maker's or drawer's signatures and those obtaining acceptances or receiving payment. The warranties prescribed and exceptions thereto follow closely principles established at common law, particularly, those under Price v. Neal, 3 Burr. 1354 (1762).

The basic warranty that the person obtaining payment or acceptance and any prior transferor warrants that he has no knowledge that the signature of the maker or drawer is unauthorized stems from the general principle that one who presents an instrument knowing that the signature of the maker or drawer is forged or unauthorized commits an obvious fraud upon the party to whom presentment is made. However, few cases present this simple fact situation. If the signature of a maker or drawer has been forged, the parties include the dishonest forger himself and usually one or more innocent holders taking from him. Frequently, the state of knowledge of a holder is difficult to determine and sometimes a holder takes such a forged instrument in perfect good faith but subsequently learns of the forgery. Since in different fact situations holders have equities of varying strength, it is necessary to have some exceptions to the basic warranty.

The exceptions apply only in favor of a holder in due course and, within the provisions of Section 3-201, to all subsequent transferees from a holder in due course. Since a condition of the status of a holder in due course under Section 3-302(1)(a) is that the holder takes the instrument without notice of any defense against it, this condition presupposes that at the time of taking such a holder had no knowledge of the unauthorized signature. Consequently, the warranty of subsection (1)(b) is pertinent in the case of a holder in due course only in the relatively few cases where he acquires knowledge of the forgery after the taking but before the presentment. In this situation the holder in due course must continue to act in good faith to be exempted from the basic warranty.

The first exemption from the warranty by such a holder, made by subparagraph (i), is that the warranty does not run to a maker of a note with respect to the maker's own signature. This codifies the rule of Price v. Neal, and related cases. Since a maker of a note is presumed to know his own signature, if he fails to detect a forgery of his own signature and pays the note, under the Price v. Neal principle he should not be permitted to recover such payment from a holder in due course acting in good faith. Similarly, under subparagraph (ii) a drawer of a draft is presumed to know his own signature and if he fails to detect a forgery of his signature and pays a draft he may not recover that payment from a holder in due course acting in good faith. This rule applies if the drawer pays the instrument as drawer and also if he pays the instrument as drawee in a case where he is both drawer and drawee.

Under the principle of Price v. Neal a drawee of a draft is presumed to know the signature of his customer, the drawer. However, under subsection (1)(b) and subparagraph (iii) of this subsection this presumption is not strong enough to deprive such a drawee (either in accepting or paying an instrument) of the warranty of no knowledge of the unauthorized drawer's signature, unless the holder in due course took the instrument and became such a holder after the drawee's acceptance; or obtained the acceptance without knowledge that the drawer's signature was unauthorized. In the former case, the holder taking after and thereby presumably in reliance on the acceptance should be protected as against the drawee who accepted without detecting the unauthorized signature. In the latter case the holder, having no knowledge of the unauthorized signature at the time of the drawee's acceptance, would not be charged with this warranty and would be entitled to enforce such acceptance under Section 3-418, even if thereafter he acquired knowledge of the unauthorized signature prior to enforcement of the acceptance. Such right of the holder to enforce the acceptance would be valueless if immediately upon enforcing it and obtaining payment the holder became obligated to return the payment by reason of breach of the warranty of no knowledge at the time of payment.

5. Subsection (1)(c) retains the common law rule, followed by several decisions under the original Act, which has permitted a party paying a materially altered instrument in good faith to recover, and a party who accepts such an instrument to avoid such acceptance. As in the case of subsection (1)(b) this warranty is not imposed against a holder in due course acting in good faith in favor of a maker of a note or a drawer of a draft on the ground that such maker or drawer should know the form and amount of the note or draft which he has signed. The exception made by subparagraph (iii) in the case of a holder in due course of a draft accepted after the alteration follows the decisions in National City Bank of Chicago v. National Bank of Republic of Chicago, 300 Ill. 103, 132 N.E. 832, 22 A.L.R. 1153 (1921), and Wells Fargo Bank & Union Trust Company v. Bank of Italy, 214 Cal. 156, 4 P.2d 781 (1931), and is based on the principle that an acceptance is an undertaking relied upon in good faith by an innocent party. The attempt to avoid this result by certifying checks "payable as originally drawn" leaves the subsequent purchaser in uncertainty as to the amount for which the instrument is certified, and so defeats the entire purpose of certification, which is to obtain the definite obligation of the bank to honor a definite instrument. Subparagraph (iii) accordingly provides that such language is not sufficient to impose on the holder in due course the warranty of no material alteration where the holder took

the draft after the acceptance and presumably in reliance on it.

Subparagraph (iv) of subsection (1)(c) exempts a holder in due course from the warranty of no material alteration to the acceptor of a draft with respect to an alteration made after the acceptance. A drawee accepting a draft has an opportunity of ascertaining the form and particularly the amount of the draft accepted. If, thereafter, the draft is materially altered and is thereupon presented for payment to the acceptor, the acceptor has the necessary information in its records to verify the form and particularly the amount of the draft. If in spite of this available information it pays the draft, there is as much reason to leave the responsibility for such payment upon the acceptor (as against a holder in due course acting in good faith) as there is in the case of a maker or drawer paying a materially altered note or draft.

6. Under Section 3–201 parties taking from or holding under a holder in due course, within the limits of that section, will have the same rights under Section 3–417(1) as a holder in due course. Of course such parties claiming under a holder in due course must act in good faith and be free from fraud, illegality and notice as provided in Section 3–201.

7. The liabilities imposed by subsection (2) in favor of the immediate transferee apply to all persons who transfer an instrument for consideration whether or not the transfer is accompanied by indorsement. Any consideration sufficient to support a simple contract will support those warranties.

8. Subsection (2) changes the original Section 65 to extend the warranties of any *indorser* beyond the immediate transferee in all cases. Where there is an indorsement the warranty runs with the instrument and the remote holder may sue the indorser-warrantor directly and thus avoid a multiplicity of suits which might be interrupted by the insolvency of an intermediate transferor. The language of subsections (2)(b) and (2)(c) is substituted for "genuine and what it purports to be" in the original Section 65(1). The language of subsection (2)(a) is substituted for that of Section 65(2) in order to cover the case of the agent who transfers for another.

9. Subsection (2)(d) resolves a conflict in the decisions as to whether the transferor warrants that there are no defenses to the instrument good against him. The position taken is that the buyer does not undertake to buy an instrument incapable of enforcement, and that in the absence of contrary understanding the warranty is implied. Even where the buyer takes as a holder in due course who will cut off the defense, he still does not undertake to buy a lawsuit with the necessity of proving his status. Subsection (3) however provides that an indorsement "without recourse" limits the (2)(d) warranty to one that the indorser has no knowledge of such defenses. With this exception the liabilities of a "without recourse" indorser under this section are the same as those of any other transferor. Under Section 3–414 "without recourse" in an indorsement is effective to disclaim the general contract of the indorser stated in that section.

10. Subsection (2)(e) is substituted for Section 65(4). The transferor does not warrant against difficulties of collection, apart from defenses, or against impairment of the credit of the obligor or even his insolvency in the commercial sense. The buyer is expected to determine such questions for himself before he takes the obligation. If insolvency proceedings as defined in this Act (Section 1–201) have been instituted against the party who is expected to pay and the transferor knows it, the concealment of that fact amounts to a fraud upon the buyer, and the warranty against knowledge of such proceedings is provided accordingly.

11. Subsection (4) is substituted for Section 69 of the original Act. It applies only to a selling agent, as distinguished from an agent for collection. It follows the rule generally accepted that an agent who makes the disclosure warrants his good faith and authority and may not by contract assume a lesser warranty.

Cross References:

Sections 3-404, 3-405, 3-406, 3-414 and 4-207.

Point 1: Section 4-207.

Point 2: Section 3-418.

Point 4: Sections 3-201, 3-302 and 3-418.

Point 9: Section 3-414.

Point 10: Section 1-201.

Definitional Cross References:

"Acceptance". Section 3-410.

"Alteration". Section 3-407.

"Bank". Section 1-201.

"Draft". Section 3-104.

"Genuine". Section 1-201.

"Good faith". Section 1-201.

"Holder in due course". Section 3-302.

"Instrument". Section 3-102.

"Note". Section 3-104.

"Party". Section 1-201.

"Person". Section 1-201.

"Signature". Section 3-401.

"Term". Section 1-201.

§ 3-418. Finality of Payment or Acceptance.

Except for recovery of bank payments as provided in the Article on Bank Deposits and Collections (Article 4) and except for liability for breach of warranty on presentment under the preceding section, payment or acceptance of any instrument is final in favor of a holder in due course, or a person who has in good faith changed his position in reliance on the payment.

Official Comment

Prior Uniform Statutory Provision: Section 62, Uniform Negotiable Instruments Law.

Changes: Completely restated.

Purposes of Changes:

The rewording is intended to remove a number of uncertainties arising under the original section.

1. The section follows the rule of Price v. Neal, 3 Burr. 1354 (1762), under which a drawee who accepts or pays an instrument on which the signature of the drawer is forged is bound on his acceptance and cannot recover back his payment. Although the original Act is silent as to payment, the common law rule has been applied to it by all but a very few jurisdictions. The traditional justification for the result is that the drawee is in a superior position to detect a forgery because he has the maker's signature and is expected to know and compare it; a less fictional rationalization is that it is highly desirable to end the transaction on an instrument when it is paid rather than reopen and upset a series of commercial transactions at a later date when the forgery is discovered.

The rule as stated in the section is not limited to drawees, but applies equally to the maker of a note or to any other party who pays an instrument.

2. The section follows the decisions under the original Act applying the rule of Price v. Neal to the payment of overdrafts, or any other payment made in error as to the state of the drawer's account. The same argument for finality applies, with the additional reason that the drawee is responsible for knowing the state of the account before he accepts or pays.

3. The section follows decisions under the original Act, in making payment or acceptance final only in favor of a holder in due course, or a transferee who has the rights of a holder in due course under the shelter principle. If no value has been given for the instrument the holder loses nothing by the recovery of the payment or the avoidance of the acceptance, and is not entitled to profit at the expense of the drawee; and if he has given only an executory promise or credit he is not compelled to perform it after the forgery or other reason for recovery is discovered. If he has taken the instrument in bad

faith or with notice he has no equities as against the drawee.

4. The section rejects decisions under the original Act permitting recovery on the basis of mere negligence of the holder in taking the instrument. If such negligence amounts to a lack of good faith as defined in this Act (Section 1-201) or to notice under the rules (Section 3-304) relating to notice to a purchaser of an instrument, the holder is not a holder in due course and is not protected; but otherwise the holder's negligence does not affect the finality of the payment or acceptance.

5. This section is to be read together with the preceding section, which states the warranties given by the person obtaining acceptance or payment. It is also limited by the bank collection provision (Section 4-301) permitting a payor bank to recover a payment improperly paid if it returns the item or sends notice of dishonor within the limited time provided in that section. But notice that the latter right is sharply limited in time, and terminates in any case when the bank has made final payment, as defined in Section 4-213.

Cross References:

Sections 3-302, 3-303 and 3-417.
Point 2: Section 3-201(1).
Point 4: Sections 1-201, 3-302 and 3-304.
Point 5: Sections 3-417, 4-213 and 4-301.

Definitional Cross References:

"Acceptance". Section 3-410.
"Account". Section 4-104.
"Bank". Section 1-201.
"Holder in due course". Section 3-302.
"Instrument". Section 3-102.
"Presentment". Section 3-504.

§ 3-419. Conversion of Instrument; Innocent Representative.

(1) An instrument is converted when

(a) a drawee to whom it is delivered for acceptance refuses to return it on demand; or

(b) any person to whom it is delivered for payment refuses on demand either to pay or to return it; or

(c) it is paid on a forged indorsement.

(2) In an action against a drawee under subsection (1) the measure of the drawee's liability is the face amount of the instrument. In any other action under subsection (1) the measure of liability is presumed to be the face amount of the instrument.

(3) Subject to the provisions of this Act concerning restrictive indorsements a representative, including a depositary or collecting bank, who has in good faith and in accordance with the reasonable commercial standards applicable to the business of such representative dealt with an instrument or its proceeds on behalf of one who was not the true owner is not liable in conversion or otherwise to the true owner beyond the amount of any proceeds remaining in his hands.

(4) An intermediary bank or payor bank which is not a depositary bank is not liable in conversion solely by reason of the fact that proceeds of an item indorsed restrictively (Sections 3-205 and 3-206) are not paid or applied consistently with the restrictive indorsement of an indorser other than its immediate transferor.

Official Comment

Prior Uniform Statutory Provision: Section 137, Uniform Negotiable Instruments Law.

Changes: Rule changed; new provisions.

Purposes of Changes and New Matter: To remove difficulties arising under the original section, and to cover additional situations:

1. The provision of the original Section 137 that refusal to return a bill presented for acceptance is deemed to be acceptance has led to difficulties. If the bill is accepted it is not dishonored, and the holder is left without recourse against the drawer and indorsers when he has most need for immediate recourse. The drawee does not in fact accept and does everything he can to display an intention not to accept; and the "acceptance" is useless to the holder for any purpose other than an action against the drawee, since he has nothing that he can negotiate. The original rule has therefore been changed (see Section 3-410).

2. A negotiable instrument is the property of the holder. It is a mercantile specialty which embodies rights against other parties, and a thing of value. This section adopts the generally recognized rule that a refusal to return it on demand is a conversion. The provision is not limited to drafts presented for acceptance, but extends to any instrument presented for payment, including a note presented to the maker. The action is not on the instrument, but in tort for its conversion.

The detention of an instrument voluntarily delivered is not wrongful unless and until there is demand for its return. Demand for a return at a particular time may, however, be made at the time of delivery; or it may be implied under the circumstances or understood as a matter of custom. If the holder is to call for the instrument and fails to do so, he is to be regarded as extending the time. "Refuses" is meant to cover any intentional failure to return the instrument, including its intentional destruction. It does not cover a negligent loss or destruction, or any other unintentional failure to return. In such a case the party may be liable in tort for any damage sustained as a result of his negligence, but he is not liable as a converter under this section.

3. Subsection (1)(c) is new. It adopts the prevailing view of decisions holding that payment on a forged indorsement is not an acceptance, but that even though made in good faith it is an exercise of dominion and control over the instrument inconsistent with the rights of the owner, and results in liability for conversion.

4. Subsection (2) is new. It adopts the rule generally applied to the conversion of negotiable instruments, that the obligation of any party on the instrument is presumed, in the sense that the term is defined in this Act (Section 1-201), to be worth its face value. Evidence is admissible to show that for any reason such as insolvency or the existence of a defense the obligation is in fact worth less, or even that it is without value. In the case of the drawee, however, the presumption is replaced by a rule of absolute liability.

5. Subsection (3), which is new, is intended to adopt the rule of decisions which has held that a representative, such as a broker or depositary bank, who deals with a negotiable instrument for his principal in good faith is not liable to the true owner for conversion of the instrument or otherwise, except that he may be compelled to turn over to the true owner the instrument itself or any proceeds of the instrument remaining in his hands. The provisions of subsection (3) are, however, subject to the provisions of this Act concerning restrictive indorsements (Sections 3-205, 3-206 and related sections).

6. The provisions of this section are not intended to eliminate any liability on warranties of presentment and transfer (Section 3-417). Thus a collecting bank might be liable to a drawee bank which had been subject to liability under this section, even though the collecting bank might not be liable directly to the owner of the instrument.

Cross References:

Sections 3-409, 3-410, 3-411 and 3-603.

Point 4: Section 1-201.

Point 5: Sections 1-201, 3-205 and 3-206.

Point 6: Section 3-417.

Definitional Cross References:

"Acceptance". Section 3-410.
"Action". Section 1-201.
"Bank". Section 1-201.
"Collecting bank". Sections 3-102 and 4-105.
"Depositary bank". Sections 3-102 and 4-105.
"Good faith". Section 1-201.
"Instrument". Section 3-102.
"Intermediary bank". Sections 3-102 and 4-105.
"On demand". Section 3-108.
"Person". Section 1-201.
"Presumed". Section 1-201.
"Representative". Section 1-201.

PART 5

PRESENTMENT, NOTICE OF DISHONOR AND PROTEST

§ 3-501. When Presentment, Notice of Dishonor, and Protest Necessary or Permissible.

(1) Unless excused (Section 3-511) presentment is necessary to charge secondary parties as follows:

(a) presentment for acceptance is necessary to charge the drawer and indorsers of a draft where the draft so provides, or is payable elsewhere than at the residence or place of business of the drawee, or its date of payment depends upon such presentment. The holder may at his option present for acceptance any other draft payable at a stated date;

(b) presentment for payment is necessary to charge any indorser;

(c) in the case of any drawer, the acceptor of a draft payable at a bank or the maker of a note payable at a bank, presentment for payment is necessary, but failure to make presentment discharges such drawer, acceptor or maker only as stated in Section 3-502(1)(b).

(2) Unless excused (Section 3-511)

(a) notice of any dishonor is necessary to charge any indorser;

(b) in the case of any drawer, the acceptor of a draft payable at a bank or the maker of a note payable at a bank, notice of any dishonor is necessary, but failure to give such notice discharges such drawer, acceptor or maker only as stated in Section 3-502(1)(b).

(3) Unless excused (Section 3-511) protest of any dishonor is necessary to charge the drawer and indorsers of any draft which on its face appears to be drawn or payable outside of the states, territories, dependencies and possessions of the United States, the District of Columbia and the Commonwealth of Puerto Rico. The holder may at his option make protest of any dishonor of any other instrument and in the case of a foreign draft may on insolvency of the acceptor before maturity make protest for better security.

(4) Notwithstanding any provision of this section, neither presentment nor notice of dishonor nor protest is necessary to charge an indorser who has indorsed an instrument after maturity.

As amended in 1966.

Official Comment

Prior Uniform Statutory Provision: Sections 70, 89, 118, 129, 143, 144, 150, 151, 152, 157, 158 and 186, Uniform Negotiable Instruments Law.

Changes: Combined and simplified.

Purposes of Changes:

1. Part 5 simplifies the requirements of the original Act as to presentment for acceptance or payment, notice of dishonor and protest. This section assembles in one place all provisions as to when any such proceeding is necessary. It eliminates some of the requirements and simplifies others. The effect of unexcused delay in any such proceeding as a discharge is covered by the next section, and the sections following prescribe the details of the proceedings.

2. The words "Necessary to charge" are retained from the original Act. They mean that the necessary proceeding is a condition precedent to any right of action against the drawer or indorser. He is not liable and cannot be sued without the proceedings however long delayed. Under some circumstances delay is excused. If it is not excused it may operate as a discharge under the next section. Under some circumstances the proceeding may be entirely excused and the drawer or indorser is then liable as if the proceeding had been duly taken. Section 3-511 states the circumstances under which delay may be excused or the proceeding entirely excused.

3. Subsection (1)(a) retains the substance of the original Sections 143, 144 and 150. The last sentence of the subsection states the rule of the decisions both at common law and under the original Act, that the holder may at his option present any time draft for acceptance, and is not required to wait until the due date to know whether the drawee will accept it; but that if he does make presentment and acceptance is refused he must give notice of dishonor. There is no similar right to present for acceptance a draft payable on demand, since a demand draft entitles the holder to immediate payment but not to acceptance.

4. Subsections (1)(b) and (1)(c) on presentment for payment follow Section 70 of the original Act with one important change. Under the original Act and under this section ((1)(b)) presentment for payment is necessary (unless excused) to charge any drawer. Under the original Act drawers of drafts other than checks were wholly discharged by a failure to make due presentment but drawers of checks (Section 70 in conjunction with Section 186) were discharged only "to the extent of the loss caused by the delay"—that is to say, when insolvency of the drawee bank occurred after the time when presentment was due. The check rule of the original Act (somewhat modified—see Section 3-502(1)(b) and Comment thereto) is by subsection (1)(c) extended to all drawers, and also to the acceptors and makers of domiciled—"payable at a bank"—drafts and notes. Thus drawers of drafts other than checks are not, as they were under Section 70, wholly discharged by failure to make due presentment but, like drawers of checks, are discharged only as they may have suffered loss as provided in Section 3-502(1)(b). As to domiciled paper original Section 70 provided that ability and willingness to pay at the place named at maturity were "equivalent to a tender of payment"—that is to say would stop the running of interest, but had no other effect. Accordingly cases have held that makers and acceptors of domiciled paper were not discharged to any extent by the holder's failure to make presentment even when the obligor had funds available in the paying bank on the date for presentment and the bank subsequently failed. Subsection (1)(c) applies the check rule to such makers and acceptors; the "tender" language of Section 70 is eliminated; and the result in the cases referred to in the preceding sentence is reversed. Under this section as under

the original act presentment for payment is not necessary to charge primary parties (makers and acceptors of undomiciled paper).

5. Under subsection (2) the rules as to necessity of notice of dishonor run parallel with the rules as to necessity of presentment stated in subsection (1).

6. Under the original Sections 129 and 152 protest is required in the case of every "foreign draft", defined as a draft which on its face is not both drawn and payable "within this state." The result has been that upon dishonor in New York a check which appears on its face to be drawn in Jersey City must be protested in order to sue the drawer or any indorser. This has led to great inconvenience and expense of protest fees. The only function of protest is that of proof of dishonor, and it adds nothing to notice of dishonor as such.

Subsection (3) eliminates the requirement of protest except upon dishonor of a draft which on its face appears to be either drawn or payable outside of the states, territories, dependencies and possessions of the United States, the District of Columbia and the Commonwealth of Puerto Rico. The requirement is left as to such international drafts because it is generally required by foreign law, which this Article cannot affect. The formalities of protest are covered by Section 3-509 on protest, and substitutes for protest as proof of dishonor are provided for in Section 3-510 on evidence of dishonor and of notice. [This paragraph was amended in 1966].

This provision retains from the original Section 118 the rule permitting the holder at his option to make protest of any dishonor of any other instrument. Even where not required protest may have definite convenience where process does not run to another state and the taking of depositions is a slow and expensive matter. Even where the instrument is drawn and payable entirely within a state there may be convenience in saving the trip of a witness from Buffalo to New York to testify to dishonor, where the substitute evidence of dishonor and notice of dishonor cannot be relied on. Either required or optional protest is presumptive evidence of dishonor. (Section 3-510.)

7. The permissible "protest for better security" of original Section 158 is retained in the case of a foreign draft, as the practice is common in certain foreign countries.

8. Under the final sentence of Section 7 of the original Act an instrument indorsed when overdue became payable on demand as to the indorser. That language has been deleted from this Article—see Section 3-108 and Comment. It meant, among other things and in view of the provisions of the original Act as to demand paper, that such an indorser was discharged unless the instrument was presented for payment within a reasonable time after his indorsement. Presentment of overdue paper for the purpose of charging an indorser is unusual and not an expected commercial practice; the rule has been little more than a trap for those not familiar with the Act. Subsection (4), reversing the original Act, provides that as to indorsers after maturity neither presentment nor notice of dishonor nor protest is necessary; like primary parties therefore they will remain liable on the instrument for the period of the applicable statute of limitations.

Cross References:

Point 1: Sections 3-502 through 3-508.
Point 2: Sections 3-413, 3-414 and 3-511.
Point 3: Sections 3-413, 3-414 and 3-511.
Point 4: Section 3-502.
Point 6: Sections 3-413, 3-414, 3-509, 3-510 and 3-511.
Point 8: Section 3-108.

Definitional Cross References:

"Acceptance". Section 3-410.
"Bank". Section 1-201.
"Certificate of deposit". Section 3-104.
"Dishonor". Section 3-507.
"Draft". Section 3-104.
"Holder". Section 1-201.

"Instrument". Section 3-102.
"Note". Section 3-104.
"Notice of dishonor". Section 3-508.
"Party". Section 1-201.
"Presentment". Section 3-504.
"Protest". Section 3-509.
"Secondary party". Section 3-102.
"Signature". Section 3-401.

§ 3-502. Unexcused Delay; Discharge.

(1) Where without excuse any necessary presentment or notice of dishonor is delayed beyond the time when it is due

(a) any indorser is discharged; and

(b) any drawer or the acceptor of a draft payable at a bank or the maker of a note payable at a bank who because the drawee or payor bank becomes insolvent during the delay is deprived of funds maintained with the drawee or payor bank to cover the instrument may discharge his liability by written assignment to the holder of his rights against the drawee or payor bank in respect of such funds, but such drawer, acceptor or maker is not otherwise discharged.

(2) Where without excuse a necessary protest is delayed beyond the time when it is due any drawer or indorser is discharged.

Official Comment

Prior Uniform Statutory Provision: Sections 7, 70, 89, 144, 150, 152 and 186, Uniform Negotiable Instruments Law.

Changes: Combined and simplified.

Purposes of Changes:

This section is the complement of the preceding section. It covers in one section widely scattered provisions of the original Act:

1. The circumstances under which presentment or notice of dishonor or protest or delay therein are excused are stated in Section 3-511. When not excused delay operates as a discharge as provided in this section.

2. Subsection (1)(b) applies to any drawer, as well as to the makers and acceptors of drafts and notes payable at a bank, the rule of the original Section 186 providing for discharge only where the drawer of a check has sustained loss through the delay. This section expressly limits the rule to loss sustained through insolvency of the drawee or payor which was the only type of loss to which the Section 186 rule has ever been applied in the cases arising under it.

The purpose of the rule is to avoid hardship upon the holder through complete discharge, and unjust enrichment of the drawer or other party who normally has received goods or other consideration for the issue of the instrument. He is "deprived of funds" in any case where bank failure or other insolvency of the drawee or payor has prevented him from receiving the benefit of funds which would have paid the instrument if it had been duly presented.

The original language discharging the drawer "to the extent of the loss caused by the delay" has not worked out satisfactorily in the decided cases, since the amount of the loss caused by the failure of a bank is almost never ascertainable at the time of suit and may not be ascertained until some years later. The decisions have turned upon burden of proof, and the drawer has seldom succeeded in proving his discharge. Subsection (1)(b) therefore substitutes a right to discharge liability by written assignment to the holder of rights against the drawee or payor as to the funds which cover the particular instrument. The assignment is intended to give the holder an effective right to claim against the drawee or payor.

3. Subsection (2) retains the rule of the original Section 152, that any unexcused delay of a required protest is a complete discharge of all drawers and indorsers.

Cross References:

Point 1: Section 3-511(1).
Point 2: Section 3-501.
Point 3: Section 3-509.

Definitional Cross References:

"Bank". Section 1-201.
"Draft". Section 3-104.
"Holder". Section 1-201.
"Insolvent". Section 1-201.
"Instrument". Section 3-102.
"Note". Section 3-104.
"Notice of dishonor". Section 3-508.
"Payor bank". Section 4-105.
"Presentment". Section 3-504.
"Protest". Section 3-509.
"Rights". Section 1-201.
"Signature". Section 3-401.
"Written". Section 1-201.

§ 3-503. Time of Presentment.

(1) Unless a different time is expressed in the instrument the time for any presentment is determined as follows:

(a) where an instrument is payable at or a fixed period after a stated date any presentment for acceptance must be made on or before the date it is payable;

(b) where an instrument is payable after sight it must either be presented for acceptance or negotiated within a reasonable time after date or issue whichever is later;

(c) where an instrument shows the date on which it is payable presentment for payment is due on that date;

(d) where an instrument is accelerated presentment for payment is due within a reasonable time after the acceleration;

(e) with respect to the liability of any secondary party presentment for acceptance or payment of any other instrument is due within a reasonable time after such party becomes liable thereon.

(2) A reasonable time for presentment is determined by the nature of the instrument, any usage of banking or trade and the facts of the particular case. In the case of an uncertified check which is drawn and payable within the United States and which is not a draft drawn by a bank the following are presumed to be reasonable periods within which to present for payment or to initiate bank collection:

(a) with respect to the liability of the drawer, thirty days after date or issue whichever is later; and

(b) with respect to the liability of an indorser, seven days after his indorsement.

(3) Where any presentment is due on a day which is not a full business day for either the person making presentment or the party to pay or accept, presentment is due on the next following day which is a full business day for both parties.

(4) Presentment to be sufficient must be made at a reasonable hour, and if at a bank during its banking day.

Official Comment

Prior Uniform Statutory Provision: Sections 71, 72, 75, 85, 86, 144, 145, 146, 186 and 193, Uniform Negotiable Instruments Law.

Changes: Combined and simplified; new provisions.

Purposes of Changes and New Matter:

1. This section states in one place all of the rules applicable to the time of presentment. Excused delay is covered by Section 3–511 on waiver and excuse, and the effect of unexcused delay by Section 3–502 on discharge.

The original Section 86, as to the determination of the time of payment by calculation from the day the time is to run, is omitted as superfluous. It states a rule universally applied to all time calculations in the law of contracts, and has no special application to negotiable instruments. No change in the law is intended.

2. Subsection (1) contains new provisions stating the commercial understanding as to the presentment of instruments payable after sight, and of accelerated paper.

3. Subsection (2) retains the substance of the original Section 193 as to the determination of a reasonable time. It provides specific time limits which are presumed, as that term is defined in this Act (Section 1–201), to be reasonable for uncertified checks drawn and payable within the continental limits of the United States. The court-made time limit of one day after the receipt of the instrument found in decisions under the original Act has proved to be too short a time for some holders, such as the department store or other large business clearing many checks through its books shortly after the first of the month, as well as the farmer or other individual at a distance from a bank.

The time limit provided differs as to drawer and indorser. The drawer, who has himself issued the check and normally expects to have it paid and charged to his account is reasonably required to stand behind it for a longer period, especially in view of the protection now provided by Federal Deposit Insurance. The thirty days specified coincides with the time after which a purchaser has notice that a check has become stale (Section 3–304(3)(c)). The indorser, who has normally merely received the check and passed it on, and does not expect to have to pay it, is entitled to know more promptly whether it is to be dishonored, in order that he may have recourse against the person with whom he has dealt.

4. Subsection (3) replaces the original Sections 85 and 146. It is intended to make allowance for the increasing practice of closing banks or businesses on Saturday or other days of the week. It is not intended to mean that any drawee or obligor can avoid dishonor of instruments by extended closing.

5. Subsection (4) eliminates the provision of the original Section 75 permitting presentment "at any hour before the bank is closed" if the drawer has no funds in the bank. The change is made to avoid inconvenience to the bank.

"Banking day" is defined in Section 4–104.

Cross References:

Point 1: Sections 3–501, 3–502, 3–505, 3–506 and 3–511.
Point 3: Sections 1–201 and 3–304(3)(c).
Point 5: Section 4–104.

Definitional Cross References:

"Acceptance". Section 3–410.
"Bank". Section 1–201.
"Banking day". Section 4–104.
"Check". Section 3–104.
"Draft". Section 3–104.
"Instrument". Section 3–102.
"Issue". Section 3–102.
"Party". Section 1–201.
"Person". Section 1–201.
"Presentment". Section 3–504.
"Presumed". Section 1–201.

"Reasonable time". Section 1-204.
"Secondary party". Section 3-102.
"Usage of trade". Section 1-205.

§ 3-504. How Presentment Made.

(1) Presentment is a demand for acceptance or payment made upon the maker, acceptor, drawee or other payor by or on behalf of the holder.

(2) Presentment may be made

(a) by mail, in which event the time of presentment is determined by the time of receipt of the mail; or

(b) through a clearing house; or

(c) at the place of acceptance or payment specified in the instrument or if there be none at the place of business or residence of the party to accept or pay. If neither the party to accept or pay nor anyone authorized to act for him is present or accessible at such place presentment is excused.

(3) It may be made

(a) to any one of two or more makers, acceptors, drawees or other payors; or

(b) to any person who has authority to make or refuse the acceptance or payment.

(4) A draft accepted or a note made payable at a bank in the United States must be presented at such bank.

(5) In the cases described in Section 4-210 presentment may be made in the manner and with the result stated in that section.

As amended in 1962.

Official Comment

Prior Uniform Statutory Provision: Sections 72, 73, 77, 78 and 145, Uniform Negotiable Instruments Law.

Changes: Combined and simplified.

Purposes of Changes:

1. This section is intended to simplify the rules as to how presentment is made and to make it clear that any demand upon the party to pay is a presentment no matter where or how. Former technical requirements of exhibition of the instrument and the like are not required unless insisted upon by the party to pay (Section 3-505).

2. Paragraph (a) of subsection (2) authorizes presentment by mail directly to the obligor. The presentment is sufficient and the instrument is dishonored by non-acceptance or nonpayment even though the party making presentment may be liable for improper collection methods. "Through a clearing-house" means that presentment is not made when the demand reaches the clearing-house, but when it reaches the obligor. Section 4-210 should also be consulted for the methods of presenting which may properly be employed by a collecting bank. Subsection (5) of this section makes it clear that presentment made under Section 4-210 is proper presentment.

3. Paragraph (a) of subsection (3) eliminates the requirement of the original Sections 78 and 145(1) that presentment be made to each of two or more makers,

acceptors or drawees unless they are partners or one has authority to act for the others. The holder is entitled to expect that any one of the named parties will pay or accept, and should not be required to go to the trouble and expense of making separate presentment to a number of them.

4. Section 3-412 provides that an acceptance made payable at a bank in the United States does not vary the draft. Subsection (4) of this section makes it clear that a draft so accepted must be presented at the bank so designated. The same rule is applied to notes made payable at a bank. The rule of the subsection is in conformity with the provisions of Section 3-501 on presentment and Section 3-502 on the effect of failure to make presentment with reference to domiciled paper [This paragraph was amended in 1962].

Cross References:

Point 1: Sections 3-501, 3-502, 3-505 and 3-511.

Point 2: Section 4-210.

Point 5: Sections 3-412, 3-501 and 3-502.

Definitional Cross References:

"Acceptance". Section 3-410.
"Bank". Section 1-201.
"Clearing house". Section 4-104.
"Draft". Section 3-104.
"Holder". Section 1-201.
"Instrument". Section 3-102.
"Note". Section 3-104.
"Party". Section 1-201.
"Person". Section 1-201.

§ 3-505. Rights of Party to Whom Presentment Is Made.

(1) The party to whom presentment is made may without dishonor require

(a) exhibition of the instrument; and

(b) reasonable identification of the person making presentment and evidence of his authority to make it if made for another; and

(c) that the instrument be produced for acceptance or payment at a place specified in it, or if there be none at any place reasonable in the circumstances; and

(d) a signed receipt on the instrument for any partial or full payment and its surrender upon full payment.

(2) Failure to comply with any such requirement invalidates the presentment but the person presenting has a reasonable time in which to comply and the time for acceptance or payment runs from the time of compliance.

Official Comment

Prior Uniform Statutory Provision: Section 74, Uniform Negotiable Instruments Law.

Changes: Expanded and modified.

Purposes of Changes: To supplement the provisions as to how presentment is made, by permitting the party to whom it is made to insist on additional requirements:

1. In the first instance a mere demand for acceptance or payment is sufficient presentment, and if the payment is unqualifiedly refused nothing more is required. The party to whom presentment is made may, however, require exhibition of the instrument, its production at the proper place, identification of the party making presentment, and a signed receipt on the instrument, or its surrender on full payment. Failure to comply with any such requirement invalidates the presentment and means that the instrument is not dishonored. The time for present-

ment is, however, extended to give the person presenting a reasonable opportunity to comply with the requirements.

2. "Reasonable identification" means identification reasonable under all the circumstances. If the party on whom demand is made knows the person making presentment, no requirement of identification is reasonable, while if the circumstances are suspicious a great deal may be required. The requirement applies whether the instrument presented is payable to order or to bearer.

Cross References:

Point 1: Sections 3–504 and 3–506.

Definitional Cross References:

"Acceptance". Section 3–410.
"Dishonor". Section 3–507.
"Instrument". Section 3–102.
"Party". Section 1–201.
"Person". Section 1–201.
"Presentment". Section 3–504.
"Reasonable time". Section 1–204.
"Signed". Section 1–201.

§ 3–506. Time Allowed for Acceptance or Payment.

(1) Acceptance may be deferred without dishonor until the close of the next business day following presentment. The holder may also in a good faith effort to obtain acceptance and without either dishonor of the instrument or discharge of secondary parties allow postponement of acceptance for an additional business day.

(2) Except as a longer time is allowed in the case of documentary drafts drawn under a letter of credit, and unless an earlier time is agreed to by the party to pay, payment of an instrument may be deferred without dishonor pending reasonable examination to determine whether it is properly payable, but payment must be made in any event before the close of business on the day of presentment.

Official Comment

Prior Uniform Statutory Provision: Section 136, Uniform Negotiable Instruments Law.

Changes: Expanded.

Purposes of Changes: The original section covered only the time allowed to the drawee on presentment for acceptance. This section also covers the time allowed on presentment fcr payment.

Section 5–112 (Time Allowed for Honor) states the time, longer than here provided, during which a bank to which drafts are presented under a letter of credit may defer payment or acceptance without dishonor of the drafts. As to drafts drawn under a letter of credit Section 5–112 of course controls.

Section 4–301 on deferred posting should be consulted for the right of a payor bank to recover tentative settlements made by it on the day an item is received. That right does not survive final payment (Section 4–213).

Cross References:

Sections 4–301 and 5–112.

Definitional Cross References:

"Acceptance". Section 3–410.
"Dishonor". Section 3–507.
"Documentary draft". Sections 3–102 and 4–104.
"Instrument". Section 3–102.
"Letter of credit". Section 5–103.
"Party". Section 1–201.
"Presentment". Section 3–504.

§ 3–507. Dishonor; Holder's Right of Recourse; Term Allowing Re-presentment.

(1) An instrument is dishonored when

(a) a necessary or optional presentment is duly made and due acceptance or payment is refused or cannot be obtained within the prescribed time or in case of bank collections the instrument is seasonably returned by the midnight deadline (Section 4-301); or

(b) presentment is excused and the instrument is not duly accepted or paid.

(2) Subject to any necessary notice of dishonor and protest, the holder has upon dishonor an immediate right of recourse against the drawers and indorsers.

(3) Return of an instrument for lack of proper indorsement is not dishonor.

(4) A term in a draft or an indorsement thereof allowing a stated time for re-presentment in the event of any dishonor of the draft by nonacceptance if a time draft or by nonpayment if a sight draft gives the holder as against any secondary party bound by the term an option to waive the dishonor without affecting the liability of the secondary party and he may present again up to the end of the stated time.

Official Comment

Prior Uniform Statutory Provision: Sections 83 and 149, Uniform Negotiable Instruments Law.

Changes: Reworded.

Purposes of Changes:

1. The language of the section is changed in accordance with the provisions of the preceding section as to the time allowed for acceptance or payment.

2. Subsection (3) is new. It states general banking and commercial understanding. The time within which a payor bank must return items, and the methods of returning, are stated in Section 4-301. Under Section 3-411(3) a bank may certify an item so returned.

Cross References:

Point 1: Sections 3-503, 3-504, 3-505, 3-508 and 4-301.

Point 2: Sections 3-411(3), 4-301.

Definitional Cross References:

"Acceptance". Section 3-410.
"Bank". Section 1-201.
"Draft". Section 3-104.
"Holder". Section 1-201.
"Instrument". Section 3-102.
"Midnight deadline". Section 4-104.
"Notice of dishonor". Section 3-508.
"Presentment". Section 3-504.
"Protest". Section 3-509.
"Right". Section 1-201.
"Seasonably". Section 1-204.
"Secondary party". Section 3-102.
"Term". Section 1-201.

§ 3-508. Notice of Dishonor.

(1) Notice of dishonor may be given to any person who may be liable on the instrument by or on behalf of the holder or any party who has himself received notice, or any other party who can be compelled to pay the instrument. In addition an agent or bank in whose hands the instrument is dishonored may give notice to his principal or customer or to another agent or bank from which the instrument was received.

(2) Any necessary notice must be given by a bank before its midnight deadline and by any other person before midnight of the third business day after dishonor or receipt of notice of dishonor.

(3) Notice may be given in any reasonable manner. It may be oral or written and in any terms which identify the instrument and state that it has been dishonored. A misdescription which does not mislead the party notified does not vitiate the notice. Sending the instrument bearing a stamp, ticket or writing stating that acceptance or payment has been refused or sending a notice of debit with respect to the instrument is sufficient.

(4) Written notice is given when sent although it is not received.

(5) Notice to one partner is notice to each although the firm has been dissolved.

(6) When any party is in insolvency proceedings instituted after the issue of the instrument notice may be given either to the party or to the representative of his estate.

(7) When any party is dead or incompetent notice may be sent to his last known address or given to his personal representative.

(8) Notice operates for the benefit of all parties who have rights on the instrument against the party notified.

Official Comment

Prior Uniform Statutory Provision: Sections 90 through 108, Uniform Negotiable Instruments Law.

Changes: Combined and simplified.

Purposes of Changes: To simplify notice of dishonor and eliminate many of the detailed requirements of the original Act:

1. Notice is normally given by the holder or by an indorser who has himself received notice. Subsection (1) is intended to encourage and facilitate notice of dishonor by permitting any party who may be compelled to pay the instrument to notify any party who may be liable on it. Thus an indorser may notify another indorser who is not liable to the one who gives notice, even when the latter has not received notice from any other party to the instrument.

2. Except as to collecting banks, as to whom Section 4-212 controls, the time within which necessary notice must be given is extended to three days after dishonor or receipt of notice from another party. In the case of individuals the one-day time limit of the original Act has proved too short in many cases. It is extended to give the party a margin of time within which to ascertain what is required of him and get out an ordinary business letter. This time leeway eliminates the elaborate provisions as to the time of mailing in the original Sections 103 and 104.

3. Subsection (3) retains the substance of the original Sections 95 and 96. The provision approves the bank practice of returning the instrument bearing a stamp, ticket or other writing, or a notice of debit of the account, as sufficient notice. Subsection (4) retains the substance of the original Section 105.

4. Subsection (7) permits notice to be sent to the last known address of a party who is dead or incompetent rather than to his personal representative. The provision is intended to save time, as the name of the personal representative often cannot easily be ascertained, and mail addressed to the original party will reach the representative.

Cross References:

Sections 3-501, 3-507 and 3-511.

Point 2: Section 4-212.

Definitional Cross References:

"Acceptance". Section 3-410.
"Bank". Section 1-201.
"Customer". Section 4-104.
"Dishonor". Section 3-507.
"Holder". Section 1-201.
"Insolvency proceedings". Section 1-201.
"Instrument". Section 3-102.
"Issue". Section 3-102.
"Midnight deadline". Section 4-104.
"Notifies". Section 1-201.
"Party". Section 1-201.
"Person". Section 1-201.
"Representative". Section 1-201.
"Rights". Section 1-201.
"Send". Section 1-201.
"Written" and "writing". Section 1-201.

§ 3-509. Protest; Noting for Protest.

(1) A protest is a certificate of dishonor made under the hand and seal of a United States consul or vice consul or a notary public or other person authorized to certify dishonor by the law of the place where dishonor occurs. It may be made upon information satisfactory to such person.

(2) The protest must identify the instrument and certify either that due presentment has been made or the reason why it is excused and that the instrument has been dishonored by non-acceptance or nonpayment.

(3) The protest may also certify that notice of dishonor has been given to all parties or to specified parties.

(4) Subject to subsection (5) any necessary protest is due by the time that notice of dishonor is due.

(5) If, before protest is due, an instrument has been noted for protest by the officer to make protest, the protest may be made at any time thereafter as of the date of the noting.

Official Comment

Prior Uniform Statutory Provision: Sections 153, 154, 155, 156, 158 and 160, Uniform Negotiable Instruments Law.

Changes: Combined and simplified.

Purposes of Changes:

1. Protest is not necessary except on drafts drawn or payable outside of the United States. Section 3-501(3) which also permits the holder at his option to make protest on dishonor of any other instrument. This section is intended to simplify either necessary or optional protest when it is made.

2. "Protest" has been used to mean the act of making protest, and sometimes loosely to refer to the entire process of presentment, notice of dishonor and protest. In this Article it is given its original, technical meaning, that of the official certificate of dishonor.

3. Subsection (1) adds to the notary public the United States consul or vice consul, and any other person authorized to certify dishonor by the law of the place where dishonor occurs. It eliminates the requirement of the original Section 156 that protest must be made at the place of dishonor. It eliminates also the provision of the original Section 154 permitting protest by "any respectable resident of the place where the bill is dishonored, in the presence of two or more credible witnesses." This has at least left uncertainty as to the identity and credibility of the persons certifying, and has almost never been used. Any necessary delay in finding the proper officer to make protest is excused under Section 3-511.

4. "Information satisfactory to such person" does away with the requirement occasionally stated, that the person mak-

ing protest must certify as of his own knowledge. The requirement has been more honored in the breach than in the observance, and in practice protest has been made upon hearsay which the officer regards as reliable, upon the admission of the person who has dishonored, or at most upon re-presentment, which is only indirect proof of the original dishonor. There is seldom any possible motive for false protest, and the basis on which it is made is never questioned. Subsection (1) leaves to the certifying officer the responsibility for determining whether he has satisfactory information. The provision is not intended to affect any personal liability of the officer for making a false certificate.

5. The protest need not be in any particular form, so long as it certifies the matters stated in Subsection (2). It need not be annexed to the instrument, and may be forwarded separately; but annexation may identify the instrument. If the instrument is lost, destroyed, or wrongfully withheld, protest is still sufficient if it identifies the instrument; but the owner must prove his rights as in any action under this Article on a lost, destroyed or stolen instrument (Section 3–804).

6. Subsection (3) recognizes the practice of including in the protest a certification that notice of dishonor has been given to all parties or to specified parties. The next section makes such a certification presumptive evidence that the notice has been given.

7. Protest is normally forwarded with notice of dishonor. Subsection (4) extends the time for making a necessary protest to coincide with the time for giving notice of dishonor. Any delay due to circumstances beyond the holder's control is excused under Section 3–511 on waiver or excuse. Any protest which is not necessary but merely optional with the holder may be made at any time before it is used as evidence.

8. Subsection (5) retains from the original Section 155 the provision permitting the officer to note the protest and extend it formally later.

Cross References:

Point 1: Sections 3–501(3) and 3–511.
Point 3: Section 3–511(1).
Point 5: Section 3–804.
Point 6: Section 3–510(a).
Point 7: Sections 3–508(2) and 3–511(1).

Definitional Cross References:

"Dishonor". Section 3–507.
"Instrument". Section 3–102.
"Notice of dishonor". Section 3–508.
"Party". Section 1–201.
"Person". Section 1–201.
"Presentment". Section 3–504.

§ 3–510. Evidence of Dishonor and Notice of Dishonor.

The following are admissible as evidence and create a presumption of dishonor and of any notice of dishonor therein shown:

(a) a document regular in form as provided in the preceding section which purports to be a protest;

(b) the purported stamp or writing of the drawee, payor bank or presenting bank on the instrument or accompanying it stating that acceptance or payment has been refused for reasons consistent with dishonor;

(c) any book or record of the drawee, payor bank, or any collecting bank kept in the usual course of business which shows dishonor, even though there is no evidence of who made the entry.

Official Comment

Prior Uniform Statutory Provision: None.

Purposes: This section is new. It states the effect of protest as evidence, and provides two substitutes for protest as proof of dishonor:

1. Paragraph (a) states the generally accepted rule that a protest is not only admissible as evidence, but creates a presumption, as that term is defined in this Act (Section 1-201), of the dishonor which it certifies. The rule is extended to include the giving of any notice of dishonor certified by the protest. The provision also relieves the holder of the necessity of proving that a document regular in form which purports to be a protest is authentic, or that the person making it was qualified. Nothing in the provision is intended to prevent the obligor from overthrowing the presumption by evidence that there was in fact no dishonor, that notice was not given, or that the protest is not authentic or not made by a proper officer.

2. Paragraph (b) recognizes as the full equivalent of protest the stamp, ticket or other writing of the drawee, payor or presenting bank. The drawee's statement that payment is refused on account of insufficient funds always has been commercially acceptable as full proof of dishonor. It should be satisfactory evidence in any court. It is therefore made admissible, and creates a presumption of dishonor. The provision applies only where the stamp or writing states reasons for refusal which are consistent with dishonor. Thus the following reasons for refusal are not evidence of dishonor, but of justifiable refusal to pay or accept:

Indorsement missing

Signature missing

Signature illegible

Forgery

Payee altered

Date altered

Post dated

Not on us

On the other hand the following reasons are satisfactory evidence of dishonor, consistent with due presentment, and are within this provision:

Not sufficient funds

Account garnisheed

No account

Payment stopped

3. Paragraph (c) recognizes as the full equivalent of protest any books or records of the drawee, payor bank or any collecting bank kept in its usual course of business, even though there is no evidence of who made the entries. The provision, as well as that of paragraph (b), rests upon the inherent improbability that bank records, or those of the drawee, will show any dishonor which has not in fact occurred, or that the holder will attempt to proceed on the basis of dishonor if he could in fact have obtained payment.

Cross References:

Sections 3-501 and 3-508.
Point 1: Section 1-201.

Definitional Cross References:

"Acceptance". Section 3-410.
"Collecting bank". Section 4-105.
"Dishonor". Section 3-507.
"Instrument". Section 3-102.
"Notice of dishonor". Section 3-508.
"Payor bank". Section 4-105.
"Presumption". Section 1-201.
"Protest." Section 3-509.
"Writing". Section 1-201.

§ 3-511. Waived or Excused Presentment, Protest or Notice of Dishonor or Delay Therein.

(1) Delay in presentment, protest or notice of dishonor is excused when the party is without notice that it is due or when the delay is caused by circumstances beyond his control and he exercises reasonable diligence after the cause of the delay ceases to operate.

(2) Presentment or notice or protest as the case may be is entirely excused when

(a) the party to be charged has waived it expressly or by implication either before or after it is due; or

(b) such party has himself dishonored the instrument or has countermanded payment or otherwise has no reason to expect or right to require that the instrument be accepted or paid; or

(c) by reasonable diligence the presentment or protest cannot be made or the notice given.

(3) Presentment is also entirely excused when

(a) the maker, acceptor or drawee of any instrument except a documentary draft is dead or in insolvency proceedings instituted after the issue of the instrument; or

(b) acceptance or payment is refused but not for want of proper presentment.

(4) Where a draft has been dishonored by nonacceptance a later presentment for payment and any notice of dishonor and protest for nonpayment are excused unless in the meantime the instrument has been accepted.

(5) A waiver of protest is also a waiver of presentment and of notice of dishonor even though protest is not required.

(6) Where a waiver of presentment or notice or protest is embodied in the instrument itself it is binding upon all parties; but where it is written above the signature of an indorser it binds him only.

Official Comment

Prior Uniform Statutory Provision: Sections 79, 80, 81, 82, 109, 111, 112, 113, 114, 115, 116, 130, 147, 148, 150, 151, 159, Uniform Negotiable Instruments Law.

Changes: Combined and simplified.

Purposes of Changes: This section combines widely scattered sections of the original act, and is intended to simplify the rules as to when presentment, notice or protest is excused:

1. The single term "excused" is substituted for "excused," "dispensed with," "not necessary," "not required," as used variously in the original act. No change in meaning is intended.

2. Subsection (1) combines provisions found in the original Sections 81, 113, 147 and 159. Delay in making presentment either for payment or for acceptance, in giving notice of dishonor or in making protest is excused when the party has acted with reasonable diligence and the delay is not his fault. This is true where an instrument has been accelerated without his knowledge, or demand has been made by a prior holder immediately before his purchase. It is true under any other circumstances where the delay is beyond his control. The words "not imputable to his default, misconduct or negligence" found in the original Sections 81, 113 and 159 are omitted as superfluous, but no change in substance is intended.

3. Any waived presentment, notice or protest is excused, as under the original Sections 82, 109, 110 and 111. The waiver may be express or implied, oral or written, and before or after the proceeding waived is due. It may be, and often is, a term of the instrument when it is issued. Subsection (5) retains as standard commercial usage the meaning at-

tached by the original Section 111 to "protest waived."

4. Paragraph (b) of subsection (2) combines the substance of provisions found in the original Sections 79, 80, 114, 115 and 130. A party who has no right to require or reason to expect that the instrument will be honored is not entitled to presentment, notice or protest. This is of course true where he has himself dishonored the instrument or has countermanded payment. It is equally true, for example, where he is an accommodated party and has himself broken the accommodation agreement.

5. Paragraph (c) of subsection (2) combines provisions found in the original Sections 82(1), 112 and 159. The excuse is established only by proof that reasonable diligence has been exercised without success, or that reasonable diligence would in any case have been unsuccessful.

6. Paragraph (a) of subsection (3) is new. It excuses presentment in situations where immediate payment or acceptance is impossible or so unlikely that the holder cannot reasonably be expected to make presentment. He is permitted instead to have his immediate recourse upon the drawer or indorser, and let the latter file any necessary claim in probate or insolvency proceedings. The exception for the documentary draft is to preserve any profit on the resale of goods for the creditors of the drawee if his representative can find the funds to pay.

7. Paragraph (b) of subsection (3) extends the original Section 148(3) to include any case where payment or acceptance is definitely refused and the refusal is not on the ground that there has been no proper presentment. The purpose of presentment is to determine whether or not the maker, acceptor or drawee will pay or accept; and when that question is clearly determined the holder is not required to go through a useless ceremony. The provision applies to a definite refusal stating no reasons.

8. Subsection (4) retains the rule of the original Sections 116 and 151.

9. Subsection (6) retains the rule of original Section 110.

Cross References:

Sections 3-501, 3-502, 3-503, 3-507 and 3-509.

Definitional Cross References:

"Acceptance". Section 3-410.
"Dishonor". Section 3-507.
"Documentary draft". Section 4-104
"Draft". Section 3-104.
"Insolvency proceedings". Section 1-201.
"Instrument". Section 3-102.
"Issue". Section 3-102.
"Notice of dishonor". Section 3-508.
"Party". Section 1-201.
"Presentment". Section 3-504.
"Protest". Section 3-509.
"Right". Section 1-201.

PART 6

DISCHARGE

§ 3-601. Discharge of Parties.

(1) The extent of the discharge of any party from liability on an instrument is governed by the sections on

(a) payment or satisfaction (Section 3-603); or

(b) tender of payment (Section 3-604); or

(c) cancellation or renunciation (Section 3-605); or

(d) impairment of right of recourse or of collateral (Section 3-606); or

(e) reacquisition of the instrument by a prior party (Section 3-208); or

(f) fraudulent and material alteration (Section 3-407); or

(g) certification of a check (Section 3-411); or

(h) acceptance varying a draft (Section 3-412); or

(i) unexcused delay in presentment or notice of dishonor or protest (Section 3-502).

(2) Any party is also discharged from his liability on an instrument to another party by any other act or agreement with such party which would discharge his simple contract for the payment of money.

(3) The liability of all parties is discharged when any party who has himself no right of action or recourse on the instrument

(a) reacquires the instrument in his own right; or

(b) is discharged under any provision of this Article, except as otherwise provided with respect to discharge for impairment of recourse or of collateral (Section 3-606).

Official Comment

Prior Uniform Statutory Provision: Sections 119, 120 and 121, Uniform Negotiable Instruments Law.

Changes: Portions of original sections combined and reworded; new provisions.

Purposes of Changes:

1. Subsection (1) contains an index referring to all of the sections of this Article which provide for the discharge of any party. The list is exclusive so far as the provisions of this Article are concerned, but it is not intended to prevent or affect any discharge arising apart from this statute, as for example a discharge in bankruptcy or a statutory provision for discharge if the instrument is negotiated in a gaming transaction.

2. A negotiable instrument is in itself merely a piece of paper bearing a writing, and strictly speaking is incapable of being discharged. The parties are rather discharged from liability on their contracts on the instrument. The language of the original Section 119 as to discharge of the instrument itself has left uncertainties as to the effect of the discharge upon the rights of a subsequent holder in due course. It is therefore eliminated, and this section now distinguishes instead between the discharge of a single party and the discharge of all parties.

So far as the discharge of any one party is concerned a negotiable instrument differs from any other contract only in the special rules arising out of its character to which paragraphs (a) to (i) of subsection (1) are an index, and in the effect of the discharge against a subsequent holder in due course (Section 3-602). Subsection (2) therefore retains from the original Section 119(4) the provision for discharge by "any other act which will discharge a simple contract for the payment of money," and specifically recognizes the possibility of a discharge by agreement.

The discharge of any party is a defense available to that party as provided in sections on rights of those who are and are not holders in due course (Sections 3-305 and 3-306). He has the burden of establishing the defense (Section 3-307).

3. Subsection (3) substitutes for the "discharge of the instrument" the discharge of all parties from liability on their contracts on the instrument. It covers a part of the substance of the original Section 119(1), (2) and (5), the original Section 120(1) and (3), and the original Section 121(1) and (2). It states a general principle in lieu of the original detailed provisions. The principle is that all parties to an instrument are discharged when no party is left with rights against any other party on the paper.

When any party reacquires the instrument in his own right his own liability is discharged; and any intervening party to whom he was liable is also discharged as provided in Section 3–208 on reacquisition. When he is left with no right of action against an intervening party and no right of recourse against any prior party, all parties are obviously discharged. The instrument itself is not necessarily extinct, since it may be reissued or renegotiated with a new and further liability; and if it subsequently reaches the hands of a holder in due course without notice of the discharge he may still enforce it as provided in Section 3–602 on effect of discharge against a holder in due course.

Under Section 3–606 on impairment of recourse or collateral, the discharge of any party discharges those who have a right of recourse against him, except in the case of a release with reservation of rights or a failure to give notice of dishonor. A discharge of one who has himself no right of action or recourse on the instrument may thus discharge all parties. Again the instrument itself is not necessarily extinct, and if it is negotiated to a subsequent holder in due course without notice of the discharge he may enforce it as provided in Section 3–602 on effect of discharge against a holder in due course.

4. The language "any party who has himself no right of action or recourse on the instrument" is substituted for "principal debtor," which is not defined by the original Act and has been misleading. This Article also omits the original Section 192, defining the "person primarily liable." Under Section 3–415 on accommodation parties an accommodation maker or acceptor, although he is primarily liable on the instrument in the sense that he is obligated to pay it without recourse upon another, has himself a right of recourse against the accommodated payee; and his reacquisition or discharge leaves the accommodated party liable to him. The accommodated payee, although he is not primarily liable to others, has no right of action or recourse against the accommodation maker, and his reacquisition or discharge may discharge all parties.

Cross References:

Sections 3–406, 3–411, 3–412, 3–509, 3–603, 3–604 and 3–605.

Point 2: Sections 3–305, 3–306, 3–307 and 3–602.

Point 3: Sections 3–208, 3–602 and 3–606.

Point 4: Section 3–415.

Definitional Cross References:

"Action". Section 1–201.
"Agreement". Section 1–201.
"Alteration". Section 3–407.
"Certification". Section 3–411.
"Check". Section 3–104.
"Contract". Section 1–201.
"Draft". Section 3–104.
"Instrument". Section 3–102.
"Money". Section 1–201.
"Notice of dishonor". Section 3–508.
"Party". Section 1–201.
"Presentment". Section 3–504.
"Rights". Section 1–201.

§ 3–602. Effect of Discharge Against Holder in Due Course.

No discharge of any party provided by this Article is effective against a subsequent holder in due course unless he has notice thereof when he takes the instrument.

Official Comment

Prior Uniform Statutory Provision: None.

Purposes:

The section is intended to remove an uncertainty as to which the original Act is silent. It rests on the principle that any discharge of a party provided under any section of this Article is a personal defense of the party, which is cut off when a subsequent holder in due course takes the instrument without notice of the defense. Thus where an instrument is paid without surrender such a subsequent purchase cuts off the defense. This section applies only to discharges arising under the provisions of this Article, and it has no application to any discharge arising apart from it, such as a discharge in bankruptcy.

Under Section 3–304(1)(b) on notice to purchaser it is possible for a holder to take the instrument in due course even though he has notice that one or more parties have been discharged, so long as any party remains undischarged. Thus he may take with notice that an indorser of a note has been released, and still be a holder in due course as to the liability of the maker. In that event, the holder in due course is subject to the defense of the discharge of which he had notice when he took the instrument.

Cross References:

Sections 3–302, 3–304, 3–305 and 3–601.

Definitional Cross References:

"Holder in due course". Section 3–302.
"Instrument". Section 3–102.
"Notice". Section 1–201.
"Party". Section 1–201.

§ 3–603. Payment or Satisfaction.

(1) The liability of any party is discharged to the extent of his payment or satisfaction to the holder even though it is made with knowledge of a claim of another person to the instrument unless prior to such payment or satisfaction the person making the claim either supplies indemnity deemed adequate by the party seeking the discharge or enjoins payment or satisfaction by order of a court of competent jurisdiction in an action in which the adverse claimant and the holder are parties. This subsection does not, however, result in the discharge of the liability

(a) of a party who in bad faith pays or satisfies a holder who acquired the instrument by theft or who (unless having the rights of a holder in due course) holds through one who so acquired it; or

(b) of a party (other than an intermediary bank or a payor bank which is not a depositary bank) who pays or satisfies the holder of an instrument which has been restrictively indorsed in a manner not consistent with the terms of such restrictive indorsement.

(2) Payment or satisfaction may be made with the consent of the holder by any person including a stranger to the instrument. Surrender of the instrument to such a person gives him the rights of a transferee (Section 3–201).

Official Comment

Prior Uniform Statutory Provision: Sections 51, 88, 119, 121 and 171–177, Uniform Negotiable Instruments Law.

Changes: Parts of original sections combined and reworded; law changed.

Purposes of Changes: This section changes the law as follows:

1. It eliminates the "payment in due course" found in the original Sections 51, 88 and 119. "Payment in due course" discharged all parties where it was made by one who has no right of recourse on the instrument; but this is true of any other discharge of such a party, and is now covered by Section 3–601(3) on discharge of parties. Such payment was effective as a discharge against a subsequent purchaser; but since it is made at or after maturity of the instrument a

purchaser with notice of that fact cannot be a holder in due course, and one who takes without notice of the payment and the maturity should be protected against failure to take up the instrument. The matter is now covered by Section 3-602.

2. The original Sections 171-177 provide for payment of a draft "for honor" after protest. The practice originated at a time when communications were slow and difficult, and in overseas transactions there might be a delay of several months before the drawer could act upon any dishonor. It provided a method by which a third party might intervene to protect the credit of the drawer and at the same time preserve his own rights. Cable, telegraph and telephone have made the practice obsolete for nearly a century, and it is today almost entirely unknown. It has been replaced by the cable transfer, the letter of credit and numerous other devices by which a substitute arrangement is promptly made. "Payment for honor" is therefore eliminated; and subsection (2) now provides that any person may pay with the consent of the holder.

3. Payment to the holder discharges the party who makes it from his own liability on the instrument, and a part payment discharges him pro tanto. The same is true of any other satisfaction. Subsection (1) changes the law by eliminating the requirement of the original Section 88 that the payment be made in good faith and without notice that the title of the holder is defective. It adopts as a general principle the position that a payor is not required to obey an order to stop payment received from an indorser. However, this general principle is qualified by the provisions of subsection (1)(a) and (b) respecting persons who acquire an instrument by theft, or through a restrictive indorsement (Section 3-205). These provisions are thus consistent with Section 3-306 covering the rights of one not a holder in due course.

When the party to pay is notified of an adverse claim to the instrument he has normally no means of knowing whether the assertion is true. The "unless" clause of subsection (1) follows statutes which have been passed in many states on adverse claims to bank deposits. The paying party may pay despite notification of the adverse claim unless the adverse claimant supplies indemnity deemed adequate by the paying party or procures the issuance of process restraining payment in an action in which the adverse claimant and the holder of the instrument are both parties. If the paying party chooses to refuse payment and stand suit, even though not indemnified or enjoined, he is free to do so, although, under Section 3-306(d) on the rights of one not a holder in due course, except where theft or taking through a restrictive indorsement is alleged the payor must rely on the third party claimant to litigate the issue and may not himself defend on such a ground. His contract is to pay the holder of the instrument, and he performs it by making such payment. Except in cases of theft or restrictive indorsement there is no good reason to put him to inconvenience because of a dispute between two other parties unless he is indemnified or served with appropriate process.

4. With the elimination of "payment for honor", subsection (2) provides that with the consent of the holder payment may be made by anyone, including a stranger. The subsection omits the provision of the original Section 121 by which the payor is "remitted to his former rights". It rejects such decisions as Quimby v. Varnum, 190 Mass. 211, 76 N.E. 671 (1906), holding that an irregular indorser who makes payment cannot recover on the instrument. The same result is reached under Section 3-415(5) on accommodation parties. Upon payment and surrender of the paper the payor succeeds to the rights of the holder, subject to the limitation found in Section 3-201 on transfer that one who has himself been a party to any fraud or illegality affecting the instrument or who as a prior holder had notice of a defense or claim against it cannot improve his position by taking from a later holder in due course.

5. Payment discharges the liability of the person making it. It discharges the liability of other parties only as

a. The discharge of the payor discharges others who have a right of recourse against him under Section 3-606; or

b. Reacquisition of the instrument discharges intervening parties under Section 3-208 on reacquisition; or

c. The discharge of one who has himself no right of recourse on the instrument discharges all parties under Section 3-601 on discharge of parties.

Cross References:

Sections 3-604 and 3-606.
Point 1: Section 3-601(3).
Point 3: Sections 3-205 and 3-306(d).
Point 4: Sections 3-201 and 3-415(5).
Point 5: Sections 3-606, 3-208, 3-601.

Definitional Cross References:

"Action". Section 1-201.
"Holder". Section 1-201.
"Instrument". Section 3-102.
"Order". Section 3-102.
"Party". Section 1-201.
"Person". Section 1-201.
"Rights". Section 1-201.

§ 3-604. Tender of Payment.

(1) Any party making tender of full payment to a holder when or after it is due is discharged to the extent of all subsequent liability for interest, costs and attorney's fees.

(2) The holder's refusal of such tender wholly discharges any party who has a right of recourse against the party making the tender.

(3) Where the maker or acceptor of an instrument payable otherwise than on demand is able and ready to pay at every place of payment specified in the instrument when it is due, it is equivalent to tender.

Official Comment

Prior Uniform Statutory Provision: Sections 70 and 120, Uniform Negotiable Instruments Law.

Changes: Parts of original sections combined and reworded; new provisions.

Purposes of Changes and New Matter:

1. Subsection (1) is new. It states the generally accepted rule as to the effect of tender.

2. Subsection (2) rewords the original subsection 120(4). The party discharged is one who has a right of recourse against the party making tender, whether the latter be a prior party or a subsequent one who has been accommodated.

3. Subsection (3) rewords the final clause of the first sentence of the original Section 70. Where the instrument is payable at any one of two or more specified places, the maker or acceptor must be able and ready to pay at each of them. The language in original Section 70 was taken to mean that makers and acceptors of notes and drafts payable at a bank were not discharged by failure of a holder to make due presentment of such paper at the designated bank. This Article reverses that rule. See Sections 3-501 on necessity of presentment, 3-504 on how presentment is made, and 3-502 on effect of delay in presentment.

Cross References:

Section 3-601.
Point 3: Sections 3-501, 3-502 and 3-504.

Definitional Cross References:

"Holder". Section 1-201.
"Instrument". Section 3-102.
"On demand". Section 3-108.
"Party". Section 1-201.
"Right". Section 1-201.

§ 3–605. Cancellation and Renunciation.

(1) The holder of an instrument may even without consideration discharge any party

(a) in any manner apparent on the face of the instrument or the indorsement, as by intentionally cancelling the instrument or the party's signature by destruction or mutilation, or by striking out the party's signature; or

(b) by renouncing his rights by a writing signed and delivered or by surrender of the instrument to the party to be discharged.

(2) Neither cancellation nor renunciation without surrender of the instrument affects the title thereto.

Official Comment

Prior Uniform Statutory Provision: Sections 48, 119(3), 120(2), 122 and 123, Uniform Negotiable Instruments Law.

Changes: Combined and reworded.

Purposes of Changes:

1. The original Act does not state how cancellation is to be effected, except as to striking indorsements under the original Section 48. It must be done in such a manner as to be apparent on the face of the instrument, and the methods stated, which are supported by the decisions, are exclusive.

2. Subsection (1)(b) restates the original Section 122. The provision as to "discharge of the instrument" is now covered by discharge, Section 3–601(3); that as to subsequent holders in due course by Section 3–602 on effect of discharge against a holder in due course.

3. Subsection (2) is new. It is intended to make it clear that the striking of an indorsement, or any other cancellation or renunciation, does not affect the title.

Cross References:

Point 2: Sections 3–601 and 3–602.

Definitional Cross References:

"Holder". Section 1–201.
"Instrument". Section 3–102.
"Party". Section 1–201.
"Rights". Section 1–201.
"Signature". Section 3–401.
"Signed". Section 1–201.
"Writing". Section 1–201.

§ 3–606. Impairment of Recourse or of Collateral.

(1) The holder discharges any party to the instrument to the extent that without such party's consent the holder

(a) without express reservation of rights releases or agrees not to sue any person against whom the party has to the knowledge of the holder a right of recourse or agrees to suspend the right to enforce against such person the instrument or collateral or otherwise discharges such person, except that failure or delay in effecting any required presentment, protest or notice of dishonor with respect to any such person does not discharge any party as to whom presentment, protest or notice of dishonor is effective or unnecessary; or

(b) unjustifiably impairs any collateral for the instrument given by or on behalf of the party or any person against whom he has a right of recourse.

(2) By express reservation of rights against a party with a right of recourse the holder preserves

(a) all his rights against such party as of the time when the instrument was originally due; and

(b) the right of the party to pay the instrument as of that time; and

(c) all rights of such party to recourse against others.

Official Comment

Prior Uniform Statutory Provision: Section 120, Uniform Negotiable Instruments Law.

Changes: Reworded; new provisions.

Purposes of Changes and New Matter: To make it clear that:

1. The words "any party to the instrument" remove an uncertainty arising under the original section. The suretyship defenses here provided are not limited to parties who are "secondarily liable," but are available to any party who is in the position of a surety, having a right of recourse either on the instrument or dehors it, including an accommodation maker or acceptor known to the holder to be so.

2. Consent may be given in advance, and is commonly incorporated in the instrument; or it may be given afterward. It requires no consideration, and operates as a waiver of the consenting party's right to claim his own discharge.

3. The words "to the knowledge of the holder" exclude the latent surety, as for example the accommodation maker where there is nothing on the instrument to show that he has signed for accommodation and the holder is ignorant of that fact. In such a case the holder is entitled to proceed according to what is shown by the face of the paper or what he otherwise knows, and does not discharge the surety when he acts in ignorance of the relation.

4. This section retains the right of the holder to release one party, or to postpone his time of payment, while expressly reserving rights against others. Subsection (2), which is new, states the generally accepted rule as to the effect of such an express reservation of rights. [Comment 4 was amended in 1966].

5. Paragraph (b) of subsection (1) is new. The suretyship defense stated has been generally recognized as available to indorsers or accommodation parties. As to when a holder's actions in dealing with collateral may be "unjustifiable", the section on rights and duties with respect to collateral in the possession of a secured party (Section 9-207) should be consulted.

Cross Reference:

Point 5: Section 9-207.

Definitional Cross References:

"Agreement". Section 1-201.
"Holder". Section 1-201.
"Instrument". Section 3-102.
"Notice of dishonor". Section 3-508.
"Party". Section 1-201.
"Person". Section 1-201.
"Rights". Section 1-201.

PART 7

ADVICE OF INTERNATIONAL SIGHT DRAFT

§ 3-701. Letter of Advice of International Sight Draft.

(1) A "letter of advice" is a drawer's communication to the drawee that a described draft has been drawn.

(2) Unless otherwise agreed when a bank receives from another bank a letter of advice of an international sight draft the drawee bank may immediately debit the drawer's account and stop the running of interest pro tanto.

Such a debit and any resulting credit to any account covering outstanding drafts leaves in the drawer full power to stop payment or otherwise dispose of the amount and creates no trust or interest in favor of the holder.

(3) Unless otherwise agreed and except where a draft is drawn under a credit issued by the drawee, the drawee of an international sight draft owes the drawer no duty to pay an unadvised draft but if it does so and the draft is genuine, may appropriately debit the drawer's account.

Official Comment

Prior Uniform Statutory Provision: None.

Purposes: To recognize and clarify, in law, certain established practices of international banking.

1. Checks drawn by one international bank on the account it carries (in a currency foreign to itself) in another international bank are still handled under practices which reflect older conditions, but which have a real, continuing reason in the typical, European rule that a bank paying a check in good faith and in ordinary course can charge its depositor's account notwithstanding forgery of a necessary indorsement. To decrease the risk that forgery will prove successful, the practice is to send a letter of advice that a draft has been drawn and will be forthcoming. Subsection 3 recognizes that a drawer who sends no such letter forfeits any rights for improper dishonor, while still permitting the drawee to protect his delinquent drawer's credit.

2. Subsection (2) clears up for American courts, the meaning of another international practice: that of charging the drawer's account on receipt of the letter of advice. This practice involves no conception of trust or the like and the rule of Section 3–409(1) (Draft not an assignment) still applies. The debit has to do with the payment of interest only. The section recognizes the fact.

Cross Reference:

Point 2: Section 3–409(1).

Definitional Cross References:

"Account". Section 4–104.
"Bank". Section 1–201.
"Credit". Section 5–103.
"Draft". Section 3–104.
"Genuine". Section 1–201.
"Holder". Section 1–201.

PART 8

MISCELLANEOUS

§ 3–801. Drafts in a Set.

(1) Where a draft is drawn in a set of parts, each of which is numbered and expressed to be an order only if no other part has been honored, the whole of the parts constitutes one draft but a taker of any part may become a holder in due course of the draft.

(2) Any person who negotiates, indorses or accepts a single part of a draft drawn in a set thereby becomes liable to any holder in due course of that part as if it were the whole set, but as between different holders in due course to whom different parts have been negotiated the holder whose title first accrues has all rights to the draft and its proceeds.

(3) As against the drawee the first presented part of a draft drawn in a set is the part entitled to payment, or if a time draft to acceptance and payment. Acceptance of any subsequently presented part renders the drawee

liable thereon under subsection (2). With respect both to a holder and to the drawer payment of a subsequently presented part of a draft payable at sight has the same effect as payment of a check notwithstanding an effective stop order (Section 4-407).

(4) Except as otherwise provided in this section, where any part of a draft in a set is discharged by payment or otherwise the whole draft is discharged.

Official Comment

Prior Uniform Statutory Provision: Sections 178-183, Uniform Negotiable Instruments Law.

Changes: Combined and reworded.

Purposes of Changes:

The revised language makes no important change in substance, and is intended only as a clarification and supplementation of the original sections:

1. Drafts in a set customarily contain such language as "Pay ______ this first of exchange (second unpaid)," with equivalent language in the second part. Today a part also commonly bears conspicuous indication of its number. At least the first factor is necessary to notify the holder of his rights, and is therefore necessary in order to make this section apply. Subsection (1) so provides, thus stating in the statute a matter left previously to a commercial practice long uniform but expensive to establish in court.

2. The final sentence of subsection (3) is new. Payment of the part of the draft subsequently presented is improper and the drawee may not charge it to the account of the drawer, but some one has probably been unjustly enriched on the total transaction, at the expense of the drawee. So the drawee is like a bank which has paid a check over an effective stop payment order, and is subrogated as provided in that situation. Section 4-407.

3. A statement in a draft drawn in a set of parts to the effect that the order is effective only if no other part has been honored does not render the draft nonnegotiable as conditional. See Section 3-112(1)(g).

Cross References:

Point 2: Section 4-407.
Point 3: Section 3-112.

Definitional Cross References:

"Acceptance". Section 3-410.
"Check". Section 3-104.
"Draft". Section 3-104.
"Holder". Section 1-201.
"Holder in due course". Section 3-302.
"Honor". Section 1-201.
"Person". Section 1-201.
"Rights". Section 1-201.

§ 3-802. Effect of Instrument on Obligation for Which It Is Given.

(1) Unless otherwise agreed where an instrument is taken for an underlying obligation

(a) the obligation is pro tanto discharged if a bank is drawer, maker or acceptor of the instrument and there is no recourse on the instrument against the underlying obligor; and

(b) in any other case the obligation is suspended pro tanto until the instrument is due or if it is payable on demand until its presentment. If the instrument is dishonored action may be maintained on either the instrument or the obligation; discharge of the underlying obligor on the instrument also discharges him on the obligation.

(2) The taking in good faith of a check which is not post-dated does not of itself so extend the time on the original obligation as to discharge a surety.

Official Comment

Prior Uniform Statutory Provision: None.

Purposes:

1. The section is new. It is intended to settle conflicts as to the effect of an instrument as payment of the obligation for which it is given.

2. Where a holder procures certification of a check the drawer is discharged under Section 3-411 on check certification. Thereafter the original obligation is regarded as paid, and the holder must look to the certifying bank. The circumstances may indicate a similar intent in other transactions, and the question may be one of fact for the jury. Subsection (1)(a) states a rule discharging the obligation pro tanto when the instrument taken carries the obligation of a bank as drawer, maker or acceptor and there is no recourse on the instrument against the underlying obligor.

3. It is commonly said that a check or other negotiable instrument is "conditional payment." By this it is normally meant that taking the instrument is a surrender of the right to sue on the obligation until the instrument is due, but if the instrument is not paid on due presentment the right to sue on the obligation is "revived." Subsection (1)(b) states this result in terms of suspension of the obligation, which is intended to include suspension of the running of the statute of limitations. On dishonor of the instrument the holder is given his option to sue either on the instrument or on the underlying obligation. If, however, the original obligor has been discharged on the instrument (see Section 3-601) he is also discharged on the original obligation.

4. Subsection (2) is intended to remove any implication that a check given in payment of an obligation discharges a surety. The check is taken as a means of immediate payment; the thirty day period for presentment specified in Section 3-503 does not affect the surety's liability.

Cross References:

Point 2: Sections 1-201, 3-411 and 3-601.

Point 4: Section 3-503.

Definitional Cross References:

"Action". Section 1-201.
"Bank". Section 1-201.
"Check". Section 3-104.
"Dishonor". Section 3-507.
"Good faith". Section 1-201.
"Instrument". Section 3-102.
"On demand". Section 3-108.
"Presentment". Section 3-504.

§ 3-803. Notice to Third Party.

Where a defendant is sued for breach of an obligation for which a third person is answerable over under this Article he may give the third person written notice of the litigation, and the person notified may then give similar notice to any other person who is answerable over to him under this Article. If the notice states that the person notified may come in and defend and that if the person notified does not do so he will in any action against him by the person giving the notice be bound by any determination of fact common to the two litigations, then unless after seasonable receipt of the notice the person notified does come in and defend he is so bound.

Official Comment

Prior Uniform Statutory Provisions: None.

Purposes:

The section is new. It is intended to supplement, not to displace existing procedures for interpleader or joinder of parties.

The section conforms to the analogous provision in Section 2-607. It extends to such liabilities as those arising from forged indorsements even though not "on the instrument," and is intended to make it clear that the notification is not effective until received. In Hartford Accident & Indemnity Co. v. First Nat. Bank & Trust Co., 281 N.Y. 162, 22 N.E.2d 324, 123 A.L.R. 1149 (1939), the common-law doctrine of "vouching in" was held inapplicable where the party notified had no direct liability to the party giving the notice. In that case the drawer of a check, sued by the payee whose indorsement had been forged, gave notice to a collecting bank. In a second action the drawee was held liable to the drawer; but in an action by the drawee for judgment over against the collecting bank the determinations of fact in the first action were held not conclusive. This section does not disturb this result; the section is limited to cases where the person notified is "answerable over" to the person giving the notice.

Cross Reference:

Section 2-607.

Definitional Cross References:

"Action". Section 1-201.
"Defendant". Section 1-201.
"Instrument". Section 3-102.
"Notifies". Section 1-201.
"Person". Section 1-201.
"Right". Section 1-201.
"Seasonably". Section 1-204.
"Written". Section 1-201.

§ 3-804. Lost, Destroyed or Stolen Instruments.

The owner of an instrument which is lost, whether by destruction, theft or otherwise, may maintain an action in his own name and recover from any party liable thereon upon due proof of his ownership, the facts which prevent his production of the instrument and its terms. The court may require security indemnifying the defendant against loss by reason of further claims on the instrument.

Official Comment

Prior Uniform Statutory Provision: None.

Purposes:

This section is new. It is intended to provide a method of recovery on instruments which are lost, destroyed or stolen. The plaintiff who claims to be the owner of such an instrument is not a holder as that term is defined in this Act, since he is not in possession of the paper, and he does not have the holder's prima facie right to recover under the section on the burden of establishing signatures. He must prove his case. He must establish the terms of the instrument and his ownership, and must account for its absence.

If the claimant testifies falsely, or if the instrument subsequently turns up in the hands of a holder in due course, the obligor may be subjected to double liability. The court is therefore authorized to require security indemnifying the obligor against loss by reason of such possibilities. There may be cases in which so much time has elapsed, or there is so little possible doubt as to the destruction of the instrument and its ownership that there is no good reason to require the security. The requirement is therefore not an absolute one, and the matter is left to the discretion of the court.

Cross References:

Sections 1-201 and 3-307.

Definitional Cross References:

"Action". Section 1-201.

"Defendant". Section 1-201.

"Instrument". Section 3-102.

"Party". Section 1-201.

"Term". Section 1-201.

§ 3-805. Instruments Not Payable to Order or to Bearer.

This Article applies to any instrument whose terms do not preclude transfer and which is otherwise negotiable within this Article but which is not payable to order or to bearer, except that there can be no holder in due course of such an instrument.

Official Comment

Prior Uniform Statutory Provision: None.

Purposes:

This section covers the "non-negotiable instrument." As it has been used by most courts, this term has been a technical one of art. It does not refer to a writing, such as a note containing an express condition, which is not negotiable and is entirely outside of the scope of this Article and to be treated as a simple contract. It refers to a particular type of instrument which meets all requirements as to form of a negotiable instrument except that it is not payable to order or to bearer. The typical example is the check reading merely "Pay John Doe."

Such a check is not a negotiable instrument under this Article. At the same time it is still a check, a mercantile specialty which differs in many respects from a simple contract. Commercial and banking practice treats it as a check, and a long line of decisions before and after the original Act have made it clear that it is subject to the law merchant as distinguished from ordinary contract law. Although the Negotiable Instruments Law has been held by its terms not to apply to such "non-negotiable instruments" it has been recognized as a codification and restatement of the law merchant, and has in fact been applied to them by analogy.

Thus the holder of the check reading "Pay A" establishes his case by production of the instrument and proof of signatures; and the burden of proving want of consideration or any other defense is upon the obligor. Such a check passes by indorsement and delivery without words of assignment, and the indorser undertakes greater liabilities than those of an assignor. This section resolves a conflict in the decisions as to the extent of that undertaking by providing in effect that the indorser of such an instrument is not distinguished from any indorser of a negotiable instrument. The indorser is entitled to presentment, notice of dishonor and protest, and the procedure and liabilities in bank collection are the same. The rules as to alteration, the filling of blanks, accommodation parties, the liability of signing agents, discharge, and the like are those applied to negotiable instruments.

In short, the "non-negotiable instrument" is treated as a negotiable instrument, so far as its form permits. Since it lacks words of negotiability there can be no holder in due course of such an instrument, and any provision of any section of this Article peculiar to a holder in due course cannot apply to it. With this exception, such instruments are covered by all sections of this Article.

Cross Reference:

Section 3-104.

Definitional Cross References:

"Bearer". Section 1-201.

"Holder in due course". Section 3-302.

"Instrument". Section 3-102.

"Term". Section 1-201.

APPENDIX VIII

1990 ARTICLE 1 AMENDMENTS CONFORMING TO REVISED ARTICLE 3

ARTICLE 1

GENERAL PROVISIONS

§ 1–201. General Definitions.

(20) "Holder," ~~means a person who is in possession of a document of title or an instrument or a certificated investment security drawn, issued, or indorsed to him or his order or to bearer or in blank~~ with respect to a negotiable instrument, means the person in possession if the instrument is payable to bearer or, in the case of an instrument payable to an identified person, if the identified person is in possession. "Holder" with respect to a document of title means the person in possession if the goods are deliverable to bearer or to the order of the person in possession.

(24) "Money" means a medium of exchange authorized or adopted by a domestic or foreign government ~~as a part of its currency~~ and includes a monetary unit of account established by an intergovernmental organization or by agreement between two or more nations.

(43) "Unauthorized" signature ~~or indorsement~~ means one made without actual, implied, or apparent authority and includes a forgery.

Official Comment

43. Under the former version of § 1–201(43), it was not clear whether a reference to an "unauthorized signature" in Articles 3 and 4 applied to indorsements. The words "or indorsement" are deleted so that references to "unauthorized signature" in § 3–406 and elsewhere will unambiguously refer to any signature.

§ 1–207. Performance or Acceptance Under Reservation of Rights.

(1) A party who, with explicit reservation of rights, performs or promises performance or assents to performance in a manner demanded or offered by the other party does not thereby prejudice the rights reserved. Such words as "without prejudice", "under protest" or the like are sufficient.

(2) Subsection (1) does not apply to an accord and satisfaction.

Official Comment

1. This section provides machinery for the continuation of performance along the lines contemplated by the contract despite a pending dispute, by adopting the mer-

cantile device of going ahead with delivery, acceptance, or payment "without prejudice," "under protest," "under reserve," "with reservation of all our rights," and the like. All of these phrases completely reserve all rights within the meaning of this section. The section therefore contemplates that limited as well as general reservations and acceptance by a party may be made "subject to satisfaction of our purchaser," "subject to acceptance by our customers," or the like.

2. This section does not add any new requirement of language of reservation where not already required by law, but merely provides a specific measure on which a party can rely as that party makes or concurs in any interim adjustment in the course of performance. It does not affect or impair the provisions of this Act such as those under which the buyer's remedies for defect survive acceptance without being expressly claimed if notice of the defects is given within a reasonable time. Nor does it disturb the policy of those cases which restrict the effect of a waiver of a defect to reasonable limits under the circumstances, even though no such reservation is expressed.

The section is not addressed to the creation or loss of remedies in the ordinary course of performance but rather to a method of procedure where one party is claiming as of right something which the other believes to be unwarranted.

3. Judicial authority was divided on the issue of whether former Section 1-207 (present subsection (1)) applied to an accord and satisfaction. Typically the cases involved attempts to reach an accord and satisfaction by use of a check tendered in full satisfaction of a claim. Subsection (2) of revised Section 1-207 resolves this conflict by stating that Section 1-207 does not apply to an accord and satisfaction. Section 3-311 of revised Article 3 governs if an accord and satisfaction is attempted by tender of a negotiable instrument as stated in that section. If Section 3-311 does not apply, the issue of whether an accord and satisfaction has been effected is determined by the law of contract. Whether or not Section 3-311 applies, Section 1-207 has no application to an accord and satisfaction.

APPENDIX IX

1990 CONFORMING [TO REVISED ARTICLE 3] AND MISCELLANEOUS AMENDMENTS TO ARTICLE 4

ARTICLE 4

BANK DEPOSITS AND COLLECTIONS

§ 4–101. Short Title.

This Article ~~shall be known and~~ may be cited as Uniform Commercial Code—Bank Deposits and Collections.

Reason for 1990 Change

Modified to conform with current drafting practices; no intent to change substance.

§ 4–102. Applicability.

~~(1)~~(a) To the extent that items within this Article are also within ~~the scope of~~ Articles 3 and 8, they are subject to ~~the provisions of~~ those Articles. ~~In the event of~~ If there is conflict, ~~the provisions of~~ this Article governs ~~those of~~ Article 3, but ~~the provisions of~~ Article 8 governs ~~those of~~ this Article.

~~(2)~~(b) The liability of a bank for action or non-action with respect to ~~any~~ an item handled by it for purposes of presentment, payment, or collection is governed by the law of the place where the bank is located. In the case of action or non-action by or at a branch or separate office of a bank, its liability is governed by the law of the place where the branch or separate office is located.

Reason for 1990 Change

Modified to conform with current drafting practices; no intent to change substance.

§ 4–103. Variation by Agreement; Measure of Damages; ~~Certain~~ Action Constituting Ordinary Care.

~~(1)~~(a) The effect of the provisions of this Article may be varied by agreement ~~except that no agreement can~~, but the parties to the agreement cannot disclaim a bank's responsibility for its ~~own~~ lack of good faith or failure to exercise ordinary care or ~~can~~ limit the measure of damages for ~~such~~ the lack or failure~~;~~. However, ~~but~~ the parties may determine by agreement

~~determine~~ the standards by which ~~such~~ the bank's responsibility is to be measured if ~~such~~ those standards are not manifestly unreasonable.

~~(2)~~(b) Federal Reserve regulations and operating ~~letters~~ circulars, ~~clearing house~~ clearing-house rules, and the like~~,~~ have the effect of agreements under subsection ~~(1)~~ (a), whether or not specifically assented to by all parties interested in items handled.

~~(3)~~(c) Action or non-action approved by this Article or pursuant to Federal Reserve regulations or operating ~~letters~~ circulars ~~constitutes~~ is the exercise of ordinary care and, in the absence of special instructions, action or non-action consistent with ~~clearing house~~ clearing-house rules and the like or with a general banking usage not disapproved by this Article, is prima facie ~~constitutes~~ the exercise of ordinary care.

~~(4)~~(d) The specification or approval of certain procedures by this Article ~~does not constitute~~ is not disapproval of other procedures ~~which~~ that may be reasonable under the circumstances.

~~(5)~~(e) The measure of damages for failure to exercise ordinary care in handling an item is the amount of the item reduced by an amount ~~which~~ that could not have been realized by the ~~use~~ exercise of ordinary care~~, and where~~. If there is also bad faith it includes any other damages~~, if any, suffered by~~ the party suffered as a proximate consequence.

Reason for 1990 Change

Modified to conform with current drafting practices; no intent to change substance.

§ 4–104. Definitions and Index of Definitions.

~~(1)~~(a) In this Article, unless the context otherwise requires:

~~(a)~~ (1) "Account" means any deposit or credit account with a bank ~~and includes~~, including a ~~checking, time, interest or savings account~~ demand, time, savings, passbook, share draft, or like account, other than an account evidenced by a certificate of deposit;

~~(b)~~ (2) "Afternoon" means the period of a day between noon and midnight;

~~(c)~~ (3) "Banking day" means ~~that~~ the part of ~~any~~ a day on which a bank is open to the public for carrying on substantially all of its banking functions;

~~(d)~~ (4) "Clearing house" means ~~any~~ an association of banks or other payors regularly clearing items;

~~(e)~~ (5) "Customer" means ~~any~~ a person having an account with a bank or for whom a bank has agreed to collect items ~~and includes~~, including a bank ~~carrying~~ that maintains an account ~~with~~ at another bank;

~~(f)~~ (6) "Documentary draft" means ~~any negotiable or non negotiable draft with accompanying documents, securities or other papers to be delivered against honor of the draft~~ a draft to be presented for acceptance or payment if specified documents, certificated securities (Section 8–102) or instructions for uncertificated securities (Section 8–308), or other certificates, statements, or the like are to be received by the drawee or other payor before acceptance or payment of the draft;

(7) "Draft" means a draft as defined in Section 3–104 or an item, other than an instrument, that is an order;

(8) "Drawee" means a person ordered in a draft to make payment;

~~(g)~~ (9) "Item" means ~~any instrument for the payment of money even though it is not negotiable but does not include money~~ an instrument or a promise or order to pay money handled by a bank for collection or payment. The term does not include a payment order governed by Article 4A or a credit or debit card slip;

~~(h)~~ (10) "Midnight deadline" with respect to a bank is midnight on its next banking day following the banking day on which it receives the relevant item or notice or from which the time for taking action commences to run, whichever is later;

~~(i) "Properly payable" includes the availability of funds for payment at the time of decision to pay or dishonor;~~

~~(j)~~ (11) "Settle" means to pay in cash, by ~~clearing house~~ clearing-house settlement, in a charge or credit or by remittance, or otherwise as ~~instructed~~ agreed. A settlement may be either provisional or final.

~~(k)~~ (12) "Suspends payments" with respect to a bank means that it has been closed by order of the supervisory authorities, that a public officer has been appointed to take it over, or that it ceases or refuses to make payments in the ordinary course of business.

~~(2)~~(b) Other definitions applying to this Article and the sections in which they appear are:

"Agreement for electronic presentment"	Section 4–110.
"Bank"	Section 4–105.
"Collecting bank"	Section 4–105.
"Depositary bank"	Section 4–105.
"Intermediary bank"	Section 4–105.
"Payor bank"	Section 4–105.
"Presenting bank"	Section 4–105.
"Presentment notice"	Section 4–110.
~~"Remitting bank"~~	~~Section 4–105.~~

~~(3)~~(c) The following definitions in other Articles apply to this Article:

"Acceptance"	Section ~~3–410~~ 3–409.
"Alteration"	Section 3–407.
"Cashier's check"	Section 3–104.
"Certificate of deposit"	Section 3–104.
~~"Certification"~~	~~Section 3–411.~~

"Certified check"	Section 3–409.
"Check"	Section 3–104.
"Good faith"	Section 3–103.
"Holder in due course"	Section 3–302.
"Instrument"	Section 3–104.
"Notice of dishonor"	Section ~~3–508~~ 3–503.
"Order"	Section 3–103.
"Ordinary care"	Section 3–103.
"Person entitled to enforce"	Section 3–301.
"Presentment"	Section ~~3–504~~ 3–501.
"Promise"	Section 3–103.
~~"Protest"~~	~~Section 3–509.~~
"Prove"	Section 3–103.
~~"Secondary party"~~	~~Section 3–102.~~
"Teller's check"	Section 3–104.
"Unauthorized signature"	Section 3–403.

~~(4)~~(d) In addition, Article 1 contains general definitions and principles of construction and interpretation applicable throughout this Article.

Reason for 1990 Change

The definition of "account" is amended to make clear that it includes both asset accounts in which a customer has deposited money and accounts from which a customer may draw on a line of credit. The remainder of the definition is amended to bring it more into conformity with the definition of "deposit account" in Section 9–105(1)(e).

The definition of "documentary draft" is amended to recognize the existence of uncertificated securities. The reference to "accompanying documents" is deleted as obsolete. It is enough that the documents are to be received by the drawee or other payor before acceptance or payment of the draft.

The definition of "draft" is new and is explained in the Official Comment.

The definition of "drawee" is new and is explained in the Official Comment.

The definition of "item" is amended because the term "instrument" as defined in Section 3–104 and as used in Article 4 is narrower than the term "item." See the Official Comment.

The definition of "properly payable" is deleted. In former Article 4 there is no affirmative definition of the term "properly payable." Former Section 4–104(1)(i) merely implies that if the customer's account is insufficient to pay the item the item is not properly payable. The phrase is defined in proposed Section 4–401(1) in terms of the items authorized by the customer and in accordance with the bank-customer agreement. This is done to give meaning to "properly payable" in Sections 4–401(1) and 4–402(1). The latter provision makes clear that a bank that fails to pay an overdraft has not wrongfully dishonored unless it had agreed to pay the overdraft.

The definition of "settle" is amended in changing "instructed" to "agreed" to conform to Section 4–213.

The terms "remitting bank," "protest," and "second party" are deleted because they are not used in Article 4.

The other modifications are made to conform with current legislative drafting practices, with no intent to change substance.

§ 4-105. "Bank"; "Depositary Bank"; "Payor Bank"; "Intermediary Bank"; "Collecting Bank"; "Presenting Bank"~~; "Remitting Bank"~~.

In this Article ~~unless the context otherwise requires~~:

(1) "Bank" means a person engaged in the business of banking, including a savings bank, savings and loan association, credit union, or trust company.

~~(a)~~(2) "Depositary bank" means the first bank to ~~which~~ take an item ~~is transferred for collection~~ even though it is also the payor bank, unless the item is presented for immediate payment over the counter;

~~(b)~~(3) "Payor bank" means a bank ~~by which an item is payable as drawn or accepted~~ that is the drawee of a draft;

~~(c)~~(4) "Intermediary bank" means ~~any~~ a bank to which an item is transferred in course of collection except the depositary or payor bank;

~~(d)~~(5) "Collecting bank" means ~~any~~ a bank handling ~~the~~ an item for collection except the payor bank;

~~(e)~~(6) "Presenting bank" means ~~any~~ a bank presenting an item except a payor bank~~;~~.

~~(f) "Remitting bank" means any payor or intermediary bank remitting for an item.~~

Reason for 1990 Change

The definition of "bank" is added and is in conformity with that found in Section 4A-105(a)(2). See the Official Comment.

The definition of "depositary bank" is amended. The term "transferred for collection" is too limiting as the purpose for which the item is taken. The amendment makes clear that a payor bank is not also a depositary bank with respect to an item presented for immediate payment over the counter.

The definition of "payor bank" is amended to require that in order for a bank to be a payor bank it must be instructed rather than authorized to pay and that the instruction must be contained in the item. As explained in the Official Comment, this result follows from the use of the defined terms "drawee" and "draft."

The definition of "remitting bank" is deleted because the term is not used in Article 4.

The other modifications are made to conform with current legislative drafting practices, with no intent to change substance.

§ 4-106. Payable Through or Payable at Bank; Collecting Bank.

(a) If an item states that it is "payable through" a bank identified in the item, (i) the item designates the bank as a collecting bank and does not by itself authorize the bank to pay the item, and (ii) the item may be presented for payment only by or through the bank.

Alternative A

(b) If an item states that it is "payable at" a bank identified in the item, the item is equivalent to a draft drawn on the bank.

Alternative B

(b) If an item states that it is "payable at" a bank identified in the item, (i) the item designates the bank as a collecting bank and does not by itself authorize the bank to pay the item, and (ii) the item may be presented for payment only by or through the bank.

(c) If a draft names a nonbank drawee and it is unclear whether a bank named in the draft is a co-drawee or a collecting bank, the bank is a collecting bank.

Reason for 1990 Change

New section. See the Official Comment.

§ ~~4–106~~ 4–107. Separate Office of Bank.

A branch or separate office of a bank ~~[maintaining its own deposit ledgers]~~ is a separate bank for the purpose of computing the time within which and determining the place at or to which action may be taken or notice or orders ~~shall~~ must be given under this Article and under Article 3.

Reason for 1990 Change

The bracketed language in former Section 4–106 is deleted. Today banks keep records on customer accounts by electronic data storage. This has led most banks with branches to centralize to some degree their record keeping. The place where records are kept has little meaning if the information is electronically stored and is instantly retrievable at all branches of the bank. Hence, the inference to be drawn from the deletion of the bracketed language is that where record keeping is done is no longer an important factor in determining whether a branch is a separate bank.

§ ~~4–107~~ 4–108. Time of Receipt of Items.

~~(1)~~(a) For the purpose of allowing time to process items, prove balances, and make the necessary entries on its books to determine its position for the day, a bank may fix an afternoon hour of 2 P.M. or later as a ~~cut-off~~ cutoff hour for the handling of money and items and the making of entries on its books.

~~(2)~~(b) ~~Any~~ An item or deposit of money received on any day after a ~~cut-off~~ cutoff hour so fixed or after the close of the banking day may be treated as being received at the opening of the next banking day.

Reason for 1990 Change

Modified to conform with current drafting practices; no intent to change substance.

§ ~~4–108~~ 4–109. Delays.

~~(1)~~(a) Unless otherwise instructed, a collecting bank in a good faith effort to secure payment ~~may, in the case~~ of a specific ~~items~~ item drawn on a payor other than a bank, and with or without the approval of any person involved, may waive, modify, or extend time limits imposed or permitted by this [Act] for a period not ~~in excess of an~~ exceeding two additional banking ~~day~~ days without discharge of ~~secondary parties and without~~ drawers or indorsers or liability to its transferor or ~~any~~ a prior party.

~~(2)~~(b) Delay by a collecting bank or payor bank beyond time limits prescribed or permitted by this [Act] or by instructions is excused if (i) the delay is caused by interruption of communication or computer facilities, suspension of payments by another bank, war, emergency conditions, failure of equipment, or other circumstances beyond the control of the bank ~~provided it~~, and (ii) the bank exercises such diligence as the circumstances require.

Reason for 1990 Change

Subsection (a) is amended to exclude checks and other items drawn on banks from its application so that the provision will not impede the speedy collection of these items. The amended subsection authorizes a collecting bank to take additional time, not in excess of two days, in a good faith effort to collect drafts drawn on nonbank payors with or without the approval of any interested party. The term "secondary parties" is deleted because it is no longer used in Articles 3 and 4. Subsection (b) is amended to make clear that the delay is excused for one of the reasons stated only if the bank exercises such diligence as the circumstances require. With the addition of references to the interruption of computer facilities and the failure of equipment, the permissible reasons for delay enumerated are made to conform to those stated in Regulation CC Section 229.38(e). The other modifications are made to conform with current legislative drafting practices, with no intent to change substance.

~~§ 4–109. Process of Posting.~~

~~The "process of posting" means the usual procedure followed by a payor bank in determining to pay an item and in recording the payment including one or more of the following or other steps as determined by the bank:~~

~~(a) verification of any signature;~~

~~(b) ascertaining that sufficient funds are available;~~

~~(c) affixing a "paid" or other stamp;~~

~~(d) entering a charge or entry to a customer's account;~~

~~(e) correcting or reversing an entry or erroneous action with respect to the item.~~

Reason for 1990 Change

This section is deleted. In the former Article the process-of-posting test was a factor in determining when final payment of an item is made (former Section 4–213(1)) and the priority of the "four legals" (former Section 4–303(1)). Difficulties in determining when the events described in former Section 4–109 take place have led California, Nevada, and Texas to reject the process-of-posting test for these purposes. Abolition of the process-of-posting test in favor of more easily determinable time limits is more attuned to a system of automated check collection or electronic presentment.

§ 4-110. Electronic Presentment.

(a) "Agreement for electronic presentment" means an agreement, clearing-house rule, or Federal Reserve regulation or operating circular, providing that presentment of an item may be made by transmission of an image of an item or information describing the item ("presentment notice") rather than delivery of the item itself. The agreement may provide for procedures governing retention, presentment, payment, dishonor, and other matters concerning items subject to the agreement.

(b) Presentment of an item pursuant to an agreement for presentment is made when the presentment notice is received.

(c) If presentment is made by presentment notice, a reference to "item" or "check" in this Article means the presentment notice unless the context otherwise indicates.

Reason for 1990 Change

New section. See Official Comment.

§ 4-111. Statute of Limitations.

An action to enforce an obligation, duty, or right arising under this Article must be commenced within three years after the [cause of action] accrues.

Reason for 1990 Change

New section. See Official Comment.

§ 4-201. ~~Presumption and Duration of Agency~~ Status of Collecting Banks as Agent and Provisional Status of Credits; Applicability of Article; Item Indorsed "Pay Any Bank".

~~(1)~~(a) Unless a contrary intent clearly appears and ~~prior to~~ before the time that a settlement given by a collecting bank for an item is or becomes final, ~~(subsection (3) of Section 4-211 and Sections 4-212 and 4-213)~~ the bank, with respect to the item, is an agent or sub-agent of the owner of the item and any settlement given for the item is provisional. This provision applies regardless of the form of indorsement or lack of indorsement and even though credit given for the item is subject to immediate withdrawal as of right or is in fact withdrawn; but the continuance of ownership of an item by its owner and any rights of the owner to proceeds of the item are subject to rights of a collecting bank, such as those resulting from outstanding advances on the item and ~~valid~~ rights of recoupment or setoff. ~~When~~ If an item is handled by banks for purposes of presentment, payment ~~and~~, collection, or return, the relevant provisions of this Article apply even though action of the parties clearly establishes that a particular bank has purchased the item and is the owner of it.

~~(2)~~(b) After an item has been indorsed with the words "pay any bank" or the like, only a bank may acquire the rights of a holder until the item has been:

~~(a)~~(1) ~~until the item has been~~ returned to the customer initiating collection; or

~~(b)~~(2) ~~until the item has been~~ specially indorsed by a bank to a person who is not a bank.

Reason for 1990 Change

Subsection (a) is amended to delete the cross references to former Sections 4–211, 4–212 and 4–213. The reason for the deletion is to remove any implication that final settlement is determined only by these provisions. Sections 4–213(c) and (d) and 4–215(c) provide when final settlement occurs with respect to certain kinds of settlements, but these provisions are not intended to be exclusive. Since it is impossible to contemplate all the kinds of settlements that will be utilized, no attempt is made in Article 4 to provide when settlement is final in all cases. "Recoupment" is added to the second sentence to clarify the collecting bank's rights against the item or its proceeds. Terms like "valid" or "binding" have been deleted entirely from Article 4 as superfluous. "Or return" is added to the third sentence to make clear that the effect of the provision is not restricted to the forward collection activities of banks but also extends to their acts in returning items. The other modifications are made to conform with current legislative drafting practices, with no intent to change substance.

§ 4–202. Responsibility for Collection or Return; When Action ~~Seasonable~~ Timely.

~~(1)~~(a) A collecting bank must ~~use~~ exercise ordinary care in:

~~(a)~~(1) presenting an item or sending it for presentment; ~~and~~

~~(b)~~(2) sending notice of dishonor or nonpayment or returning an item other than a documentary draft to the bank's transferor ~~[or directly to the depositary bank under subsection (2) of Section 4–212] (see note to Section 4–212)~~ after learning that the item has not been paid or accepted, as the case may be; ~~and~~

~~(c)~~(3) settling for an item when the bank receives final settlement; and

~~(d) making or providing for any necessary protest; and~~

~~(e)~~(4) notifying its transferor of any loss or delay in transit within a reasonable time after discovery thereof.

~~(2) A collecting bank taking proper action before its midnight deadline following receipt of an item, notice or payment acts seasonably; taking proper action within a reasonably longer time may be seasonable but the bank has the burden of so establishing.~~

(b) A collecting bank exercises ordinary care under subsection (a) by taking proper action before its midnight deadline following receipt of an item, notice, or settlement. Taking proper action within a reasonably longer time may constitute the exercise of ordinary care, but the bank has the burden of establishing timeliness.

~~(3)~~(c) Subject to subsection ~~(1)(a)~~ (a)(1), a bank is not liable for the insolvency, neglect, misconduct, mistake, or default of another bank or person or for loss or destruction of an item in the possession of others or in transit ~~or in the possession of others~~.

Reason for 1990 Change

The term "timely" is substituted for "seasonable" throughout the section. The bracketed material in paragraph (2) of subsection (a) is deleted because the provision to which it refers in former Section 4–212 is deleted. Paragraph (d) of former subsection (1) is deleted because Article 4 has no requirement of protest. Subsection (b) is a restatement of former subsection (2). The other modifications are made to conform with current legislative drafting practices, with no intent to change substance.

§ 4–203. Effect of Instructions.

Subject to ~~the provisions of~~ Article 3 concerning conversion of instruments (Section ~~3–419~~ 3–420) and ~~the provisions of both Article 3 and this Article concerning~~ restrictive indorsements (Section 3–206), only a collecting bank's transferor can give instructions ~~which~~ that affect the bank or constitute notice to it, and a collecting bank is not liable to prior parties for any action taken pursuant to ~~such~~ the instructions or in accordance with any agreement with its transferor.

Reason for 1990 Change

Article 4 no longer has provisions on restrictive indorsements; hence, the reference to "this Article" is deleted. The other modifications are made to conform with current legislative drafting practices, with no intent to change substance.

§ 4–204. Methods of Sending and Presenting; Sending ~~Direct~~ Directly to Payor Bank.

~~(1)~~ (a) A collecting bank ~~must~~ shall send items by a reasonably prompt method, taking into consideration ~~any~~ relevant instructions, the nature of the item, the number of ~~such~~ those items on hand, ~~and~~ the cost of collection involved, and the method generally used by it or others to present ~~such~~ those items.

~~(2)~~(b) A collecting bank may send:

~~(a)~~(1) ~~any~~ an item ~~direct~~ directly to the payor bank;

~~(b)~~(2) ~~any~~ an item to ~~any~~ a nonbank payor if authorized by its transferor; and

~~(c)~~(3) ~~any~~ an item other than documentary drafts to ~~any~~ a nonbank payor, if authorized by Federal Reserve regulation or operating ~~letter~~ circular, ~~clearing house~~ clearing-house rule, or the like.

~~(3)~~(c) Presentment may be made by a presenting bank at a place where the payor bank or other payor has requested that presentment be made.

Reason for 1990 Change

Subsection (c) is amended to allow nonbank payors to request a place of payment. The other modifications are made to conform with current legislative drafting practices, with no intent to change substance.

§ 4–205. ~~Supplying Missing Indorsement; No Notice from Prior Indorsement~~ Depositary Bank Holder of Unindorsed Item.

If a customer delivers an item to a depositary bank for collection:

(1) the depositary bank becomes a holder of the item at the time it receives the item for collection if the customer at the time of delivery was a holder of the item, whether or not the customer indorses the item, and, if the bank satisfies the other requirements of Section 3–302, it is a holder in due course; and

(2) the depositary bank warrants to collecting banks, the payor bank or other payor, and the drawer that the amount of the item was paid to the customer or deposited to the customer's account.

~~(1) A depositary bank which has taken an item for collection may supply any indorsement of the customer which is necessary to title unless the item contains the words "payee's indorsement required" or the like. In the absence of such a requirement a statement placed on the item by the depositary bank to the effect that the item was deposited by a customer or credited to his account is effective as the customer's indorsement.~~

~~(2) An intermediary bank, or payor bank which is not a depositary bank, is neither given notice nor otherwise affected by a restrictive indorsement of any person except the bank's immediate transferor.~~

Reason for 1990 Change

New section. See Official Comment.

§ 4–206. Transfer Between Banks.

Any agreed method ~~which~~ that identifies the transferor bank is sufficient for the item's further transfer to another bank.

Reason for 1990 Change

Modified to conform with current drafting practices; no intent to change substance.

~~§ 4–207. Warranties of Customer and Collecting Bank on Transfer or Presentment of Items; Time for Claims.~~

~~(1) Each customer or collecting bank who obtains payment or acceptance of an item and each prior customer and collecting bank warrants to the payor bank or other payor who in good faith pays or accepts the item that~~

~~(a) he has a good title to the item or is authorized to obtain payment or acceptance on behalf of one who has a good title; and~~

~~(b) he has no knowledge that the signature of the maker or drawer is unauthorized, except that this warranty is not given by any customer or collecting bank that is a holder in due course and acts in good faith~~

~~(i) to a maker with respect to the maker's own signature; or~~

~~(ii) to a drawer with respect to the drawer's own signature, whether or not the drawer is also the drawee; or~~

(iii) to an acceptor of an item if the holder in due course took the item after the acceptance or obtained the acceptance without knowledge that the drawer's signature was unauthorized; and

(c) the item has not been materially altered, except that this warranty is not given by any customer or collecting bank that is a holder in due course and acts in good faith

(i) to the maker of a note; or

(ii) to the drawer of a draft whether or not the drawer is also the drawee; or

(iii) to the acceptor of an item with respect to an alteration made prior to the acceptance if the holder in due course took the item after the acceptance, even though the acceptance provided "payable as originally drawn" or equivalent terms; or

(iv) to the acceptor of an item with respect to an alteration made after the acceptance.

(2) Each customer and collecting bank who transfers an item and receives a settlement or other consideration for it warrants to his transferee and to any subsequent collecting bank who takes the item in good faith that

(a) he has a good title to the item or is authorized to obtain payment or acceptance on behalf of one who has a good title and the transfer is otherwise rightful; and

(b) all signatures are genuine or authorized; and

(c) the item has not been materially altered; and

(d) no defense of any party is good against him; and

(e) he has no knowledge of any insolvency proceeding instituted with respect to the maker or acceptor or the drawer of an unaccepted item.

In addition each customer and collecting bank so transferring an item and receiving a settlement or other consideration engages that upon dishonor and any necessary notice of dishonor and protest he will take up the item.

(3) The warranties and the engagement to honor set forth in the two preceding subsections arise notwithstanding the absence of indorsement or words of guaranty or warranty in the transfer or presentment and a collecting bank remains liable for their breach despite remittance to its transferor. Damages for breach of such warranties or engagement to honor shall not exceed the consideration received by the customer or collecting bank responsible plus finance charges and expenses related to the item, if any.

(4) Unless a claim for breach of warranty under this section is made within a reasonable time after the person claiming learns of the breach, the person liable is discharged to the extent of any loss caused by the delay in making claim.

Reason for 1990 Change

The section is replaced by Sections 4-207 (transfer warranties) and 4-208 (presentment warranties).

§ 4–207. Transfer Warranties.

(a) A customer or collecting bank that transfers an item and receives a settlement or other consideration warrants to the transferee and to any subsequent collecting bank that:

(1) the warrantor is a person entitled to enforce the item;

(2) all signatures on the item are authentic and authorized;

(3) the item has not been altered;

(4) the item is not subject to a defense or claim in recoupment (Section 3–305(a)) of any party that can be asserted against the warrantor; and

(5) the warrantor has no knowledge of any insolvency proceeding commenced with respect to the maker or acceptor or, in the case of an unaccepted draft, the drawer.

(b) If an item is dishonored, a customer or collecting bank transferring the item and receiving settlement or other consideration is obliged to pay the amount due on the item (i) according to the terms of the item at the time it was transferred, or (ii) if the transfer was of an incomplete item, according to its terms when completed as stated in Sections 3–115 and 3–407. The obligation of a transferor is owed to the transferee and to any subsequent collecting bank that takes the item in good faith. A transferor cannot disclaim its obligation under this subsection by an indorsement stating that it is made "without recourse" or otherwise disclaiming liability.

(c) A person to whom the warranties under subsection (a) are made and who took the item in good faith may recover from the warrantor as damages for breach of warranty an amount equal to the loss suffered as a result of the breach, but not more than the amount of the item plus expenses and loss of interest incurred as a result of the breach.

(d) The warranties stated in subsection (a) cannot be disclaimed with respect to checks. Unless notice of a claim for breach of warranty is given to the warrantor within 30 days after the claimant has reason to know of the breach and the identity of the warrantor, the warrantor is discharged to the extent of any loss caused by the delay in giving notice of the claim.

(e) A cause of action for breach of warranty under this section accrues when the claimant has reason to know of the breach.

Reason for 1990 Change

New section. See Official Comment.

§ 4–208. Presentment Warranties.

(a) If an unaccepted draft is presented to the drawee for payment or acceptance and the drawee pays or accepts the draft, (i) the person obtaining payment or acceptance, at the time of presentment, and (ii) a previous transferor of the draft, at the time of transfer, warrant to the drawee that pays or accepts the draft in good faith that:

(1) the warrantor is, or was, at the time the warrantor transferred the draft, a person entitled to enforce the draft or authorized to obtain

payment or acceptance of the draft on behalf of a person entitled to enforce the draft;

(2) the draft has not been altered; and

(3) the warrantor has no knowledge that the signature of the purported drawer of the draft is unauthorized.

(b) A drawee making payment may recover from a warrantor damages for breach of warranty equal to the amount paid by the drawee less the amount the drawee received or is entitled to receive from the drawer because of the payment. In addition, the drawee is entitled to compensation for expenses and loss of interest resulting from the breach. The right of the drawee to recover damages under this subsection is not affected by any failure of the drawee to exercise ordinary care in making payment. If the drawee accepts the draft (i) breach of warranty is a defense to the obligation of the acceptor, and (ii) if the acceptor makes payment with respect to the draft, the acceptor is entitled to recover from a warrantor for breach of warranty the amounts stated in this subsection.

(c) If a drawee asserts a claim for breach of warranty under subsection (a) based on an unauthorized indorsement of the draft or an alteration of the draft, the warrantor may defend by proving that the indorsement is effective under Section 3-404 or 3-405 or the drawer is precluded under Section 3-406 or 4-406 from asserting against the drawee the unauthorized indorsement or alteration.

(d) If (i) a dishonored draft is presented for payment to the drawer or an indorser or (ii) any other item is presented for payment to a party obliged to pay the item, and the item is paid, the person obtaining payment and a prior transferor of the item warrant to the person making payment in good faith that the warrantor is, or was, at the time the warrantor transferred the item, a person entitled to enforce the item or authorized to obtain payment on behalf of a person entitled to enforce the item. The person making payment may recover from any warrantor for breach of warranty an amount equal to the amount paid plus expenses and loss of interest resulting from the breach.

(e) The warranties stated in subsections (a) and (d) cannot be disclaimed with respect to checks. Unless notice of a claim for breach of warranty is given to the warrantor within 30 days after the claimant has reason to know of the breach and the identity of the warrantor, the warrantor is discharged to the extent of any loss caused by the delay in giving notice of the claim.

(f) A cause of action for breach of warranty under this section accrues when the claimant has reason to know of the breach.

Reason for 1990 Change

New section. See Official Comment.

§ 4-209. Encoding and Retention Warranties.

(a) A person who encodes information on or with respect to an item after issue warrants to any subsequent collecting bank and to the payor bank or other payor that the information is correctly encoded. If the customer of a depositary bank encodes, that bank also makes the warranty.

(b) A person who undertakes to retain an item pursuant to an agreement for electronic presentment warrants to any subsequent collecting bank and to the payor bank or other payor that retention and presentment of the item comply with the agreement. If a customer of a depositary bank undertakes to retain an item, that bank also makes this warranty.

(c) A person to whom warranties are made under this section and who took the item in good faith may recover from the warrantor as damages for breach of warranty an amount equal to the loss suffered as a result of the breach, plus expenses and loss of interest incurred as a result of the breach.

Reason for 1990 Change

New section. See Official Comment.

§ ~~4–208~~ 4–210. Security Interest of Collecting Bank in Items, Accompanying Documents and Proceeds.

~~(1)~~(a) A collecting bank has a security interest in an item and any accompanying documents or the proceeds of either:

~~(a)~~(1) in case of an item deposited in an account, to the extent to which credit given for the item has been withdrawn or applied;

~~(b)~~(2) in case of an item for which it has given credit available for withdrawal as of right, to the extent of the credit given, whether or not the credit is drawn upon ~~and whether~~ or ~~not~~ there is a right of charge-back; or

~~(c)~~(3) if it makes an advance on or against the item.

~~(2)~~(b) ~~When~~ If credit ~~which has been~~ given for several items received at one time or pursuant to a single agreement is withdrawn or applied in part, the security interest remains upon all the items, any accompanying documents or the proceeds of either. For the purpose of this section, credits first given are first withdrawn.

~~(3)~~(c) Receipt by a collecting bank of a final settlement for an item is a realization on its security interest in the item, accompanying documents, and proceeds. ~~To the extent and so~~ So long as the bank does not receive final settlement for the item or give up possession of the item or accompanying documents for purposes other than collection, the security interest continues to that extent and is subject to ~~the provisions of~~ Article 9, ~~except that~~ but:

~~(a)~~(1) no security agreement is necessary to make the security interest enforceable (~~subsection (1)(a) of~~ Section 9–203(1)(a)); ~~and~~

~~(b)~~(2) no filing is required to perfect the security interest; and

~~(c)~~(3) the security interest has priority over conflicting perfected security interests in the item, accompanying documents~~,~~ or proceeds.

Reason for 1990 Change

The addition of "collecting" in subsection (a) is a clarification. The other modifications are made to conform with current legislative drafting practices, with no intent to change substance.

§ ~~4-209~~ 4-211. When Bank Gives Value for Purposes of Holder in Due Course.

For purposes of determining its status as a holder in due course, ~~the~~ a bank has given value to the extent ~~that~~ it has a security interest in an item, ~~provided that~~ if the bank otherwise complies with the requirements of Section 3-302 on what constitutes a holder in due course.

Reason for 1990 Change

Modified to conform with current drafting practices; no intent to change substance.

§ ~~4-210~~ 4-212. Presentment by Notice of Item Not Payable By, Through, or at Bank; Liability of ~~Secondary Parties~~ Drawer or Indorser.

~~(1)~~(a) Unless otherwise instructed, a collecting bank may present an item not payable by, through, or at a bank by sending to the party to accept or pay a written notice that the bank holds the item for acceptance or payment. The notice must be sent in time to be received on or before the day when presentment is due and the bank must meet any requirement of the party to accept or pay under Section ~~3-505~~ 3-501 by the close of the bank's next banking day after it knows of the requirement.

~~(2)~~(b) ~~Where~~ If presentment is made by notice and ~~neither honor~~ payment, acceptance, ~~nor~~ or request for compliance with a requirement under Section ~~3-505~~ 3-501 is not received by the close of business on the day after maturity or, in the case of demand items, by the close of business on the third banking day after notice was sent, the presenting bank may treat the item as dishonored and charge any ~~secondary party~~ drawer or indorser by sending ~~him~~ it notice of the facts.

Reason for 1990 Change

The term "secondary party" is no longer used in Articles 3 and 4. The other modifications are made to conform with current legislative drafting practices, with no intent to change substance.

§ ~~4-211~~ 4-213. ~~Media of Remittance; Provisional and Final Settlement in Remittance Cases~~ Medium and Time of Settlement by Bank.

~~(1) A collecting bank may take in settlement of an item~~

~~(a) a check of the remitting bank or of another bank on any bank except the remitting bank; or~~

~~(b) a cashier's check or similar primary obligation of a remitting bank which is a member of or clears through a member of the same clearing house or group as the collecting bank; or~~

~~(c) appropriate authority to charge an account of the remitting bank or of another bank with the collecting bank; or~~

~~(d) if the item is drawn upon or payable by a person other than a bank, a cashier's check, certified check or other bank check or obligation.~~

~~(2) If before its midnight deadline the collecting bank properly dishonors a remittance check or authorization to charge on itself or presents or forwards for collection a remittance instrument of or on another bank which is of a kind approved by subsection (1) or has not been authorized by it, the collecting bank is not liable to prior parties in the event of the dishonor of such check, instrument or authorization.~~

~~(3) A settlement for an item by means of a remittance instrument or authorization to charge is or becomes a final settlement as to both the person making and the person receiving the settlement~~

~~(a) if the remittance instrument or authorization to charge is of a kind approved by subsection (1) or has not been authorized by the person receiving the settlement and in either case the person receiving the settlement acts seasonably before its midnight deadline in presenting, forwarding for collection or paying the instrument or authorization, at the time the remittance instrument or authorization is finally paid by the payer by which it is payable;~~

~~(b) if the person receiving the settlement has authorized remittance by a non-bank check or obligation or by a cashier's check or similar primary obligation of or a check upon the payor or other remitting bank which is not of a kind approved by subsection (1)(b),—at the time of the receipt of such remittance check or obligation; or~~

~~(c) if in a case not covered by sub-paragraphs (a) or (b) the person receiving the settlement fails to seasonably present, forward for collection, pay or return a remittance instrument or authorization to it to charge before its midnight deadline,—at such midnight deadline.~~

(a) With respect to settlement by a bank, the medium and time of settlement may be prescribed by Federal Reserve regulations or circulars, clearing-house rules, and the like, or agreement. In the absence of such prescription:

(1) the medium of settlement is cash or credit to an account in a Federal Reserve bank of or specified by the person to receive settlement; and

(2) the time of settlement, is;

(i) with respect to tender of settlement by cash, a cashier's check, or teller's check, when the cash or check is sent or delivered;

(ii) with respect to tender of settlement by credit in an account in a Federal Reserve Bank, when the credit is made:

(iii) with respect to tender of settlement by a credit or debit to an account in a bank, when the credit or debit is made or, in the case of tender of settlement by authority to charge an account, when the authority is sent or delivered; or

(iv) with respect to tender of settlement by a funds transfer, when payment is made pursuant to Section 4A–406(a) to the person receiving settlement.

(b) If the tender of settlement is not by a medium authorized by subsection (a) or the time of settlement is not fixed by subsection (a), no settlement occurs until the tender of settlement is accepted by the person receiving settlement.

(c) If settlement for an item is made by cashier's check or teller's check and the person receiving settlement, before its midnight deadline:

(1) presents or forwards the check for collection, settlement is final when the check is finally paid; or

(2) fails to present or forward the check for collection, settlement is final at the midnight deadline of the person receiving settlement.

(d) If settlement for an item is made by giving authority to charge the account of the bank giving settlement in the bank receiving settlement, settlement is final when the charge is made by the bank receiving settlement if there are funds available in the account for the amount of the item.

Reason for 1990 Change

New section. See the Official Comment. Former Section 4-211 applied only to settlements by remittance instruments and authorities to charge which could be received in settlement by a collecting bank without the collecting bank's being responsible if the remittance wasn't paid. The new section is much broader in stating general rules for all types of settlements with respect to the time settlement is made and the medium which the person receiving settlement must accept. Subsections (c) and (d) apply to the issues treated in former Section 4-211.

§ ~~4-212~~ 4-214. Right of Charge-Back or Refund; Liability of Collecting Bank; Return of Item.

~~(1)~~(a) If a collecting bank has made provisional settlement with its customer for an item and ~~itself~~ fails by reason of dishonor, suspension of payments by a bank, or otherwise to receive ~~a~~ settlement for the item which is or becomes final, the bank may revoke the settlement given by it, charge back the amount of any credit given for the item to its customer's account, or obtain refund from its customer, whether or not it is able to return the item~~s~~, if by its midnight deadline or within a longer reasonable time after it learns the facts it returns the item or sends notification of the facts. If the return or notice is delayed beyond the bank's midnight deadline or a longer reasonable time after it learns the facts, the bank may revoke the settlement, charge back the credit, or obtain refund from its customer, but it is liable for any loss resulting from the delay. These rights to revoke, charge back, and obtain refund terminate if and when a settlement for the item received by the bank is or becomes final ~~(subsection (3) of Section 4-211 and subsections (2) and (3) of Section 4-213)~~.

~~[(2) Within the time and manner prescribed by this section and Section 4-301, an intermediary or payor bank, as the case may be, may return an unpaid item directly to the depositary bank and may send for collection a draft on the depositary bank and obtain reimbursement. In such case, if the depositary bank has received provisional settlement for the item, it must~~

~~reimburse the bank drawing the draft and any provisional credits for the item between banks shall become and remain final.]~~

(b) A collecting bank returns an item when it is sent or delivered to the bank's customer or transferor or pursuant to its instructions.

~~(3)~~(c) A depositary bank ~~which~~ that is also the payor may charge back the amount of an item to its customer's account or obtain refund in accordance with the section governing return of an item received by a payor bank for credit on its books (Section 4–301).

~~(4)~~(d) The right to charge back is not affected by:

~~(a)~~ (1) ~~prior~~ previous use of ~~the~~ a credit given for the item; or

~~(b)~~ (2) failure by any bank to exercise ordinary care with respect to the item, but ~~any~~ a bank so failing remains liable.

~~(5)~~(e) A failure to charge back or claim refund does not affect other rights of the bank against the customer or any other party.

~~(6)~~(f) If credit is given in dollars as the equivalent of the value of an item payable in ~~a~~ foreign ~~currency~~ money, the dollar amount of any charge-back or refund ~~shall~~ must be calculated on the basis of the ~~buying sight~~ bank-offered spot rate for the foreign ~~currency~~ money prevailing on the day when the person entitled to the charge-back or refund learns that it will not receive payment in ordinary course.

Reason for 1990 Change

Subsection (a) is amended by the addition of the second sentence which adopts the view of Appliance Buyers Credit Corp. v. Prospect National Bank, 708 F.2d 290 (7th Cir.1983), that if the midnight deadline for returning an item or giving notice is not met, a collecting bank loses its rights only to the extent of damages for any loss resulting from the delay. The cross references to former Sections 4–211 and 4–213 are deleted. The reason for the deletion is to remove any implication that final settlement is determined by only these provisions. See Reasons for 1990 Change for Section 4–201.

Former subsection (2) is replaced by subsection (b). Former subsection (2) broadly allowed for direct return of all types of unpaid items. The purpose of the amendment is to limit the right of direct return with respect to noncheck items. This purpose is accomplished by subsection (b) when read against the background of Regulation CC Section 229.31 which allows for the direct return of checks but does not apply to noncheck items. Since Regulation CC preempts subsection (b) with respect to checks, the result is that the limitation on direct return found in subsection (b) applies only to noncheck items.

Subsection (f) is amended to conform to the terminology ("bank-offered spot rate") used in Section 3–107.

The other modifications are made to conform with current legislative drafting practices, with no intent to change substance.

§ ~~4–213~~ 4–215. Final Payment of Item by Payor Bank; When Provisional Debits and Credits Become Final; When Certain Credits Become Available For Withdrawal.

~~(1)~~(a) An item is finally paid by a payor bank when the bank has first done any of the following~~, whichever happens first:~~

~~(a)~~(1) paid the item in cash; ~~or~~

~~(b)~~(2) settled for the item without ~~reserving~~ having a right to revoke the settlement ~~and without having such right~~ under statute, ~~clearing house~~ clearing-house rule, or agreement; or

~~(c) completed the process of posting the item to the indicated account of the drawer, maker or other person to be charged therewith; or~~

~~(d)~~(3) made a provisional settlement for the item and failed to revoke the settlement in the time and manner permitted by statute, ~~clearing house~~ clearing-house rule, or agreement. ~~Upon a final payment under subparagraph (b), (c) or (d) the payor bank shall be accountable for the amount of the item.~~

(b) If provisional settlement for an item does not become final, the item is not finally paid.

~~(2)~~(c) If provisional settlement for an item between the presenting and payor banks is made through a clearing house or by debits or credits in an account between them, then to the extent that provisional debits or credits for the item are entered in accounts between the presenting and payor banks or between the presenting and successive prior collecting banks seriatim, they become final upon final payment of the items by the payor bank.

~~(3)~~(d) If a collecting bank receives a settlement for an item which is or becomes final, ~~(subsection (3) of Section 4-211, subsection (2) of Section 4-213)~~ the bank is accountable to its customer for the amount of the item and any provisional credit given for the item in an account with its customer becomes final.

~~(4)~~(e) Subject to (i) applicable law stating a time for availability of funds and (ii) any right of the bank to apply the credit to an obligation of the customer, credit given by a bank for an item in ~~an account with its customer~~ a customer's account becomes available for withdrawal as of right;

~~(a)~~(1) ~~in any case where~~ if the bank has received a provisional settlement for the item, when ~~such~~ the settlement becomes final and the bank has had a reasonable time to ~~learn that the settlement is final~~ receive return of the item and the item has not been received within that time;

~~(b)~~(2) ~~in any case where~~ if the bank is both ~~a~~ the depositary bank and ~~a~~ the payor bank, and the item is finally paid, at the opening of the bank's second banking day following receipt of the item.

~~(5)~~(f) ~~A deposit of money in a bank is final when made but, subject~~ Subject to applicable law stating a time for availability of funds and any right of ~~the~~ a bank to apply ~~the~~ a deposit to an obligation of the ~~customer~~ depositor, ~~the~~ a deposit of money becomes available for withdrawal as of right at the opening of the bank's next banking day ~~following~~ after receipt of the deposit.

Reason for 1990 Change

Subsection (a)(2) is amended to provide that a payor bank cannot make settlement provisional by unilaterally reserving a right to revoke the settlement. The right to revoke must come from a statute (e.g., Section 4-301), clearing-house rule or other agreement. Former subsection (1)(c) is deleted for the reason stated in the Reason for 1990 Change for former Section 4–109. Subsection (a)(3) is amended to remove the final sentence as an unnecessary source of confusion. Initially the view that payor bank may be accountable for, that is, liable for the amount of, an item that it has already paid seems incongruous. This is particularly true in the light of the language formerly found in former Section 4–302 stating that the payor bank can defend against liability for accountability by showing that it has already settled for the item. But, at least with respect to former Section 4–213(1)(c), such a provision was needed because under the process-of-posting test a payor bank may have paid an item without settling for it. Now that Article 4 has abandoned the process-of-posting test, the sentence is no longer needed. If the payor bank has neither paid the item not returned it within its midnight deadline, the payor bank is accountable under Section 4–302.

Subsection (b) was added to clarify the relationship of final settlement to final payment under Section 4–215. For example, if a payor bank makes provisional settlement for an item by sending a cashier's or teller's check and that settlement fails to become final under Section 4–213(c), subsection (b) provides that final payment has not occurred. Under Section 4–302(a) the payor bank is accountable unless it has returned the item before its midnight deadline. In this regard, subsection (b) is an exception to subsection (a)(3). Even if the payor bank has not returned an item by its midnight deadline there is still no final payment if provisional settlement had been made and settlement failed to become final. However, if presentment of the item was over the counter for immediate payment, final payment has occurred under Section 4–215(a)(2). Subsection (b) does not apply because the settlement was not provisional. Section 4–301(a). In this case the presenting person, often the payee of the item, has the right to demand cash or the cash equivalent of federal reserve credit. If the presenting person accepts another medium of settlement such as a cashier's or teller's check, the presenting person takes the risk that the payor bank may fail to pay a cashier's check because of insolvency or that the drawee of a teller's check may dishonor it.

Subsection (d) is amended to delete the cross references to former Sections 4–211 and 4–213. The reason for the deletion is to remove any implication that final settlement is determined by only those provisions. See Reasons for 1990 Change for Section 4–201.

The preamble to subsection (e), as well as subsection (f), is amended to recognize that Regulation CC Sections 229.10–229.13 and the laws of several states (Regulation CC Section 229.20) prescribe times for availability of a depositor's funds. Subsections (e) and (f) are expressly made subject to these funds availability laws. Paragraph (1) of subsection (e) is amended to delete the test that a customer may withdraw funds after the bank has had a reasonable time to "learn that the settlement is final." The depositary bank may never affirmatively learn that a settlement is final. The substituted test is that the bank may delay making funds available to a customer until it has had a reasonable time to receive return of the item and the item has not been returned. The other modifications are made to conform with current legislative drafting practices, with no intent to change substance.

§ ~~4–214~~ 4–216. Insolvency and Preference.

~~(1)~~(a) ~~Any~~ If an item is in or ~~coming~~ comes into the possession of a payor or collecting bank ~~which~~ that suspends payment and ~~which~~ the item ~~is~~ has not been finally paid, the item ~~shall~~ must be returned by the receiver, trustee, or agent in charge of the closed bank to the presenting bank or the closed bank's customer.

(2)(b) If a payor bank finally pays an item and suspends payments without making a settlement for the item with its customer or the presenting bank which settlement is or becomes final, the owner of the item has a preferred claim against the payor bank.

(3)(c) If a payor bank gives or a collecting bank gives or receives a provisional settlement for an item and thereafter suspends payments, the suspension does not prevent or interfere with the settlement's becoming final if such the finality occurs automatically upon the lapse of certain time or the happening of certain events (subsection (3) of Section 4-211, subsections (1)(d), (2) and (3) of Section 4-213).

(4)(d) If a collecting bank receives from subsequent parties settlement for an item, which settlement is or becomes final and the bank suspends payments without making a settlement for the item with its customer which settlement is or becomes final, the owner of the item has a preferred claim against such the collecting bank.

Reason for 1990 Change

Subsection (c) is amended to delete the cross references to former Sections 4-211 and 4-213. The reason for the deletion is to remove any implication that final settlement is determined by only those provisions. See Reasons for 1990 Change for Section 4-201. The other modifications are made to conform with current legislative drafting practices, with no intent to change substance.

§ 4-301. Deferred Posting; Recovery of Payment by Return of Items; Time of Dishonor; Return of Items by Payor Bank.

(1)(a) Where an authorized settlement If a payor bank settles for a demand item (other than a documentary draft) received by a payor bank presented otherwise than for immediate payment over the counter has been made before midnight of the banking day of receipt, the payor bank may revoke the settlement and recover any payment the settlement if, before it has made final payment (subsection (1) of Section 4-213) and before its midnight deadline, it

(a)(1) returns the item; or

(b)(2) sends written notice of dishonor or non-payment if the item is held for protest or is otherwise unavailable for return.

(2)(b) If a demand item is received by a payor bank for credit on its books, it may return such the item or send notice of dishonor and may revoke any credit given or recover the amount thereof withdrawn by its customer, if it acts within the time limit and in the manner specified in the preceding subsection (a).

(3)(c) Unless previous notice of dishonor has been sent, an item is dishonored at the time when for purposes of dishonor it is returned or notice sent in accordance with this section.

(4)(d) An item is returned:

~~(a)~~(1) as to an item ~~received~~ presented through a clearing house, when it is delivered to the presenting or last collecting bank or to the clearing house or is sent or delivered in accordance with clearing-house rules; or

~~(b)~~(2) in all other cases, when it is sent or delivered to the bank's customer or transferor or pursuant to ~~his~~ instructions.

Reason for 1990 Change

The term "authorized settlement" is deleted in subsection (a) because Section 4–213 makes the term superfluous. That section prescribes the medium of settlement that a bank must accept. References to settlement throughout Article 4 assume that settlement was made by tender of the proper medium; hence, the word "settles" in subsection (a) means an authorized settlement. Substitution of "settlement" for "payment" in subsection (a) is consistent with the usage throughout Article 4 in distinguishing the act of settlement from the issue of whether the settlement constitutes final payment. The cross reference to former Section 4–213 is deleted. The reason for the deletion is to remove any implication that final settlement is determined only by that provision. See Reason for 1990 Change for Section 4–201. The reference to protest is deleted in paragraph (2) of subsection (a) because Article 4 no longer deals with protest. The other modifications are made to conform with current legislative drafting practices, with no intent to change substance.

§ 4–302. Payor Bank's Responsibility for Late Return of Item.

~~In the absence of a valid defense such as breach of a presentment warranty (subsection (1) of Section 4–207), settlement effected or the like; if~~

(a) If an item is presented to ~~on~~ and received by a payor bank, the bank is accountable for the amount of:

~~(a)~~(1) a demand item, other than a documentary draft, whether properly payable or not, if the bank, in any case ~~where~~ in which it is not also the depositary bank, retains the item beyond midnight of the banking day of receipt without settling for it or, ~~regardless of~~ whether or not it is also the depositary bank, does not pay or return the item or send notice of dishonor until after its midnight deadline; or

~~(b)~~(2) any other properly payable item unless, within the time allowed for acceptance or payment of that item, the bank either accepts or pays the item or returns it and accompanying documents.

(b) The liability of a payor bank to pay an item pursuant to subsection (a) is subject to defenses based on breach of a presentment warranty (Section 4–208) or proof that the person seeking enforcement of the liability presented or transferred the item for the purpose of defrauding the payor bank.

Reason for 1990 Change

Subsection (b) is added to clarify the deleted introductory language of former Section 4–302: "In the absence of a valid defense such as breach of a presentment warranty (subsection (1) of Section 4–207), settlement effected or the like. . . ." A payor bank can defend an action against it based on accountability by showing that the item contained a forged indorsement or a fraudulent alteration. Section 4-208. Proposed subsection (b) drops the ambiguous "or the like" language and provides that the payor bank may also raise the defense of fraud. Decisions that hold an accountable bank's liability to be "absolute" are rejected. A payor bank that makes a late return of an item should not be liable to a defrauder operating a check kiting scheme. In Bank Leumi Trust Co. v. Balley's Park Place Inc., 528 F.Supp. 349 (S.D.N.Y. 1981), and American National Bank v. Foodbasket, 497 P.2d 546 (Wyo.1972), banks that were accountable under Section 4-302 for missing their midnight deadline were successful in defending against parties who initiated collection knowing that the check would not be paid. The "settlement effected" language is deleted as unnecessary. If a payor bank is accountable for an item it is liable to pay it. If it has made final payment for an item, it is no longer accountable for the item. The other modifications are made to conform with current legislative drafting practices, with no intent to change substance.

§ 4-303. When Items Subject to Notice, ~~Stop Order~~ Stop-Payment Order, Legal Process, or Setoff; Order in Which Items May be Charged or Certified.

~~(1)~~(a) Any knowledge, notice, or ~~stop order~~ stop-payment order received by, legal process served upon, or setoff exercised by a payor bank~~, whether or not effective under other rules of law~~ comes too late to terminate, suspend, or modify the bank's right or duty to pay an item or to charge its customer's account for the item~~, comes too late to so terminate, suspend or modify such right or duty~~ if the knowledge, notice, ~~stop order~~ stop-payment order, or legal process is received or served and a reasonable time for the bank to act thereon expires or the setoff is exercised after the ~~bank has done any~~ earliest of the following:

~~(a)~~(1) ~~accepted or certified~~ the bank accepts or certifies the item;

~~(b)~~(2) ~~paid~~ the bank pays the item in cash;

~~(c)~~(3) the bank settles ~~settled~~ for the item without ~~reserving~~ having a right to revoke the settlement ~~and without having such right~~ under statute, ~~clearing house~~ clearing-house rule, or agreement;

~~(d) completed the process of posting the item to the indicated account of the drawer, maker or other person to be charged therewith or otherwise has evidenced by examination of such indicated account and by action its decision to pay the item; or~~

~~(e)~~(4) ~~become~~ the bank becomes accountable for the amount of the item under ~~subsection (1)(d) of Section 4-213 and~~ Section 4-302 dealing with the payor bank's responsibility for late return of items~~.~~; or

(5) with respect to checks, a cutoff hour no earlier than one hour after the opening of the next banking day after the banking day on which the bank received the check and no later than the close of that next banking day or, if no cutoff hour is fixed, the close of the next banking day after the banking day on which the bank received the check.

~~(2)~~(b) Subject to ~~the provisions of~~ subsection ~~(1)~~ (a), items may be accepted, paid, certified, or charged to the indicated account of its customer in any order ~~convenient to the bank~~.

Reason for 1990 Change

The preamble of subsection (a) is restated in order to improve comprehension. Paragraphs (1)–(4) of subsection (a) are restated to accommodate the addition of paragraph (5) which is stated in terms of the reaching of a cutoff hour rather than the doing of an act. Subsection (a)(3) is amended to conform to Section 4–215(a)(2) which provides that a payor bank cannot make settlement provisional by unilaterally reserving a right to revoke the settlement. The right to revoke must come from a statute (e.g. Section 4–301), a clearing-house rule or other agreement. Former subsection (1)(d) is deleted for the reason stated in the Reason for 1990 Change for former Section 4–109. The reference to former Section 4–213 is deleted from subsection (a)(4) because the reference to accountability in former Section 4–213 is deleted from what is now Section 4–215.

Subsection (a)(5) is added to allow payor banks, under time pressure to return checks to meet Regulation CC deadlines, to fix a cutoff hour earlier than the close of the next banking day after the banking day on which the checks are received. Banks must have time after receiving an attachment or effecting a setoff to return a check if the attachment or setoff renders the customer's account insufficient to pay the check. Since banks are now returning checks earlier during the next banking day after the banking day of receipt owing to Regulation CC, they need a cutoff hour earlier than the close of the banking day after that of receipt because they may be returning their checks before the close of that banking day.

Subsection (b) is amended to delete "convenient to the bank" as being superfluous. The other modifications are made to conform with current legislative drafting practices, with no intent to change substance.

§ 4–401. When Bank May Charge Customer's Account.

~~(1)~~(a) ~~As against its customer, a~~ A bank may charge against ~~his~~ the account ~~any~~ of a customer an item ~~which~~ that is ~~otherwise~~ properly payable from that account even though the charge creates an overdraft. An item is properly payable if it is authorized by the customer and is in accordance with any agreement between the customer and bank.

(b) A customer is not liable for the amount of an overdraft if the customer neither signed the item nor benefited from the proceeds of the item.

(c) A bank may charge against the account of a customer a check that is otherwise properly payable from the account, even though payment was made before the date of the check, unless the customer has given notice to the bank of the postdating describing the check with reasonable certainty. The notice is effective for the period stated in Section 4–403(b) for stop-payment orders, and must be received at such time and in such manner as to afford the bank a reasonable opportunity to act on it before the bank takes any action with respect to the check described in Section 4–303. If a bank charges against the account of a customer a check before the date stated in the notice of postdating, the bank is liable for damages for the loss resulting from its act. The loss may include damages for dishonor of subsequent items under Section 4–402.

~~(2)~~(d) A bank ~~which~~ that in good faith makes payment to a holder may charge the indicated account of its customer according to:

~~(a)~~(1) the original ~~tenor~~ terms of ~~his~~ the altered item; or

~~(b)~~(2) the ~~tenor~~ terms of ~~his~~ the completed item, even though the bank knows the item has been completed unless the bank has notice that the completion was improper.

Reason for 1990 Change

Subsection (a) is amended by the addition of the second sentence which provides a more general definition of "properly payable" than the narrow definition that was contained in former Section 4-104(1)(i). An item is properly payable from a customer's account if the customer has authorized the payment and the payment does not violate the customer-bank agreement concerning the account. An item drawn for more than the balance of the customer's account may be properly payable.

Subsection (b) is added to adopt the view of case authority holding that if there is more than one customer who can draw on an account, the nonsigning customer is not liable for an overdraft unless that person benefits from the proceeds of the item.

Subsection (c) is added because the automated check collection system cannot accommodate postdated checks. A check is usually paid upon presentment without respect to the date of the check. Under the former law, if a payor bank paid a postdated check before its stated date, it could not charge the customer's account because the check was not "properly payable." Hence, the bank might have been liable for wrongfully dishonoring subsequent checks of the drawer that would have been paid had the postdated check not been prematurely paid. Under subsection (c) a customer wishing to postdate a check must notify the payor bank of its post-dating in time to allow the bank to act on the customer's notice before the bank has to commit itself to pay the check. If the bank fails to act on the customer's timely notice, it may be liable for damages for the resulting loss which may include damages for dishonor of subsequent items.

The other modifications are made to conform with current legislative drafting practices, with no intent to change substance.

§ 4-402. Bank's Liability to Customer for Wrongful Dishonor; Time of Determining Insufficiency of Account.

(a) Except as otherwise provided in this Article, a payor bank wrongfully dishonors an item if it dishonors an item that is properly payable, but a bank may dishonor an item that would create an overdraft unless it has agreed to pay the overdraft.

(b) A payor bank is liable to its customer for damages proximately caused by the wrongful dishonor of an item. ~~When the dishonor occurs through mistake liability~~ Liability is limited to actual damages proved~~. If so proximately caused and proved damages~~ and may include damages for an arrest or prosecution of the customer or other consequential damages. Whether any consequential damages are proximately caused by the wrongful dishonor is a question of fact to be determined in each case.

(c) A payor bank's determination of the customer's account balance on which a decision to dishonor for insufficiency of available funds is based may be made at any time between the time the item is received by the payor bank and the time that the payor bank returns the item or gives notice in lieu of return, and no more than one determination need be made. If, at the election of the payor bank, a subsequent balance determination is made for the purpose of reevaluating the bank's decision to dishonor the item, the account balance at that time is determinative of whether a dishonor for insufficiency of available funds is wrongful.

Reason for 1990 Change

Subsection (a) is added for the purpose of stating positively what has been assumed under the original Article: that if a bank fails to honor a properly payable item it may be liable to its customer for wrongful dishonor. Subsection (b) is amended for clarification. Under this subsection the payor bank's wrongful dishonor of an item gives rise to a statutory cause of action. Damages may include consequential damages. Confusion has resulted from the attempts of courts to reconcile the first and second sentences of former Section 4–402. The second sentence implied that the bank was liable for some form of damages other than those proximately caused by the dishonor if the dishonor was other than by mistake. But nothing in the section described what these noncompensatory damages might be. Some courts have held that in distinguishing between mistaken dishonors and nonmistaken dishonors, the so-called "trader" rule has been retained that allowed a "merchant or trader" to recover substantial damages for wrongful dishonor without proof of damages actually suffered. Comment 3 to former Section 4–402 indicated that this was not the intent of the drafters. White & Summers, Uniform Commercial Code, Section 18–4 (1988), states: "The negative implication is that when wrongful dishonors occur not 'through mistake' but willfully, the court may impose damages greater than 'actual damages' .... Certainly the reference to 'mistake' in the second sentence of 4–402 invites a court to adopt the relevant pre-Code distinction." Subsection (b) by deleting the reference to mistake in the second sentence precludes any inference that Section 4–402 retains the "trader" rule. Whether a bank is liable for noncompensatory damages, such as punitive damages, must be decided by Section 1–103 and Section 1–106 ("by other rule of law").

Subsection (c) is added for clarification. Banks commonly determine whether there are sufficient funds in an account to pay an item after the close of banking hours on the day of presentment when they post debit and credit items to the account. The determination is made on the basis of credits available for withdrawal as of right or made available for withdrawal by the bank as an accommodation to its customer. When it is determined that payment of the item would overdraw the account, the item may be returned at any time before the bank's midnight deadline the following day. Before the item is returned new credits that are withdrawable as of right may have been added to the account. Subsection (c) eliminates uncertainty under Article 4 as to whether the failure to make a second determination before the item is returned on the day following presentment is a wrongful dishonor if new credits were added to the account on that day that would have covered the amount of the check.

§ 4–403. Customer's Right to Stop Payment; Burden of Proof of Loss.

~~(1)~~(a) A customer ~~may by order to his bank stop payment of any item payable for his account but the order must be~~ or any person authorized to draw on the account if there is more than one person may stop payment of any item drawn on the customer's account or close the account by an order to the bank describing the item or account with reasonable certainty received at ~~such~~ a time and in ~~such~~ a manner ~~as to~~ that affords the bank a reasonable opportunity to act on it ~~prior to~~ before any action by the bank with respect to the item described in Section 4–303. If the signature of more than one person is required to draw on an account, any of these persons may stop payment or close the account.

~~(2) An oral order is binding upon the bank only for fourteen calendar days unless confirmed in writing within that period. A written order is effective for only six months unless renewed in writing.~~

(b) A stop-payment order is effective for six months, but it lapses after 14 calendar days if the original order was oral and was not confirmed in writing within that period. A stop-payment order may be renewed for additional six-month periods by a writing given to the bank within a period during which the stop-payment order is effective.

~~(3)~~(c) The burden of establishing the fact and amount of loss resulting from the payment of an item contrary to a ~~binding stop payment~~ stop-payment order or order to close an account is on the customer. The loss from payment of an item contrary to a stop-payment order may include damages for dishonor of subsequent items under Section 4–402.

Reason for 1990 Change

Subsection (a) removes any ambiguity that may have been present under former subsection (1) by making clear that if there is more than one person authorized to draw on a customer's account any one of them can stop payment of any check drawn on the account or can order the account closed. Moreover, if there is a customer, such as a corporation, that requires its checks to bear the signatures of more than one person, any of these persons may stop payment on a check. In describing the item, the customer, in the absence of a contrary agreement, must meet the standard of what information allows the bank under the technology then existing to identify the item with reasonable certainty. An order to close an account is assimilated to an order to stop payment in this section and in Section 4–407.

Subsection (b) restates and clarifies former subsection (2). Subsection (c) is amended by the addition of the last sentence to provide expressly for what was only assumed under the former section: that a customer's damages for payment contrary to a stop-payment order may include damages for wrongful dishonor of subsequent items. The word "binding" is deleted as superfluous.

The other modifications are made to conform with current legislative drafting practices, with no intent to change substance.

§ 4–405. Death or Incompetence of Customer.

~~(1)~~(a) A payor or collecting bank's authority to accept, pay, or collect an item or to account for proceeds of its collection, if otherwise effective, is not rendered ineffective by incompetence of a customer of either bank existing at the time the item is issued or its collection is undertaken if the bank does not know of an adjudication of incompetence. Neither death nor incompetence of a customer revokes ~~such~~ the authority to accept, pay, collect, or account until the bank knows of the fact of death or of an adjudication of incompetence and has reasonable opportunity to act on it.

~~(2)~~(b) Even with knowledge, a bank may for 10 days after the date of death pay or certify checks drawn on or ~~prior to~~ before that date unless ordered to stop payment by a person claiming an interest in the account.

Reason for 1990 Change

Modified to conform with current drafting practices; no intent to change substance.

§ 4–406. Customer's Duty to Discover and Report Unauthorized Signature or Alteration.

~~(1) When a bank sends to its customer a statement of account accompanied by items paid in good faith in support of the debit entries or holds the statement and items pursuant to a request for instructions of its customer or otherwise in a reasonable manner makes the statement and items available to the customer, the customer must exercise reasonable care and promptness to examine the statement and items to discover his unauthorized signature or any alteration on an item and must notify the bank promptly after discovery thereof.~~

(a) A bank that sends or makes available to a customer a statement of account showing payment of items for the account shall either return or make available to the customer the items paid or provide information in the statement of account sufficient to allow the customer reasonably to identify the items paid. The statement of account provides sufficient information if the item is described by item number, amount, and date of payment.

(b) If the items are not returned to the customer, the person retaining the items shall either retain the items or, if the items are destroyed, maintain the capacity to furnish legible copies of the items until the expiration of seven years after receipt of the items. A customer may request an item from the bank that paid the item, and that bank must provide in a reasonable time either the item or, if the item has been destroyed or is not otherwise obtainable, a legible copy of the item.

(c) If a bank sends or makes available a statement of account or items pursuant to subsection (a), the customer must exercise reasonable promptness in examining the statement or the items to determine whether any payment was not authorized because of an alteration of an item or because a purported signature by or on behalf of the customer was not authorized. If, based on the statement or items provided, the customer should reasonably have discovered the unauthorized payment, the customer must promptly notify the bank of the relevant facts.

~~(2)~~(d) If the bank ~~establishes~~ proves that the customer failed, with respect to an item, to comply with the duties imposed on the customer by subsection ~~(1)~~ (c), the customer is precluded from asserting against the bank;

~~(a)~~(1) ~~his~~ the customer's unauthorized signature or any alteration on the item, if the bank also ~~establishes~~ proves that it suffered a loss by reason of ~~such~~ the failure; and

~~(b)~~(2) ~~an~~ the customer's unauthorized signature or alteration by the same wrongdoer on any other item paid in good faith by the bank ~~after the first item and statement was available to the customer for a reasonable period not exceeding fourteen calendar days and before the bank receives notification from the customer of any~~

~~such unauthorized signature or alteration~~ if the payment was made before the bank received notice from the customer of the unauthorized signature or alteration and after the customer had been afforded a reasonable period of time, not exceeding 30 days, in which to examine the item or statement of account and notify the bank.

~~(3) The preclusion under subsection (2) does not apply if the customer establishes lack of ordinary care on the part of the bank in paying the item(s).~~

(e) If subsection (d) applies and the customer proves that the bank failed to exercise ordinary care in paying the item and that the failure substantially contributed to loss, the loss is allocated between the customer precluded and the bank asserting the preclusion according to the extent to which the failure of the customer to comply with subsection (c) and the failure of the bank to exercise ordinary care contributed to the loss. If the customer proves that the bank did not pay the item in good faith, the preclusion under subsection (d) does not apply.

~~(4)~~(f) Without regard to care or lack of care of either the customer or the bank, a customer who does not within one year ~~from the time~~ after the statement ~~and~~ or items are made available to the customer (subsection ~~(1)~~ (a)) discover and report ~~his~~ the customer's unauthorized signature on or any alteration ~~on the face or back of the item or does not within 3 years from that time discover and report any unauthorized indorsement~~ on the item is precluded from asserting against the bank ~~such~~ the unauthorized signature ~~or indorsement~~ or ~~such~~ alteration. If there is a preclusion under this subsection, the payor bank may not recover for breach or warranty under Section 4–208 with respect to the unauthorized signature or alteration to which the preclusion applies.

~~(5) If under this section a payor bank has a valid defense against a claim of a customer upon or resulting from payment of an item and waives or fails upon request to assert the defense the bank may not assert against any collecting bank or other prior party presenting or transferring the item a claim based upon the unauthorized signature or alteration giving rise to the customer's claim.~~

Reason for 1990 Change

Subsections (a), (b) and (c) restate and enlarge on former subsection (1). Subsection (a) recognizes that the parties may agree that the payor, a collecting bank or other person may retain the items drawn on the customer's account. In these cases the payor bank must provide sufficient information in a statement of account to allow the customer to reasonably identify the items paid. A safe harbor rule is stated that provides that the payor bank has satisfied its obligation if the item is described by item number, amount and the date of payment. This information is selected because it can be captured by the payor bank by automation without manual processing of the item.

Subsection (b) allows the bank retaining the item to destroy the item so long as it maintains the capacity to furnish legible copies for seven years. During this period the customer is entitled to demand from its payor bank the item or a copy of it. If the item is being retained by a collecting bank or other person, the payor bank must obtain the item or copy from that bank for its customer.

Subsection (c) continues the rule of former subsection (1) of requiring the customer to exercise reasonable promptness in examining the statement or items for an unauthorized signature of the customer or an alteration and to notify the bank promptly.

Subsection (d)(2) restates the conditions of the customer's preclusion and extends the 14–day period under former subsection (2) to a 30–day period. Although the 14–day period may have been sufficient when the original version of Article 4 was drafted, given the huge increase in the volume of checks, a longer period is viewed as more appropriate today.

Subsection (e) replaces former subsection (3) and poses a modified comparative negligence test for determining liability. See the discussion on this point in the Official Comments to Sections 3–404, 3–405 and 3–406. The term "good faith" is defined in Section 3–103(a)(4) as including "observance of reasonable commercial standards of fair dealing." The connotation of this standard is fairness and not absence of negligence. The term "ordinary care" used in subsection (e) is defined in Section 3–103(a)(7) to provide that sight examination by a payor bank is not required if its procedure is reasonable and is commonly followed by other comparable banks in the area. The case law is divided on this issue. The definition of "ordinary care" in Section 3–103 rejects those authorities that hold, in effect, that failure to use sight examination is negligence as a matter of law.

Subsection (f) amends former subsection (4) to delete the reference to a three-year period to discover an unauthorized indorsement. Section 4–406 imposes no duty on a customer to discover a forged indorsement. Section 4–111 sets out a statute of limitations allowing a customer a three-year period to seek a credit to an account improperly charged by payment of an item bearing an unauthorized indorsement. The final sentence added to subsection (f) incorporates the substance of former subsection (5).

The other modifications are made to conform with current legislative drafting practices, with no intent to change substance.

§ 4–407. Payor Bank's Right to Subrogation on Improper Payment.

If a payor bank has paid an item over the ~~stop payment~~ order of the drawer or maker to stop payment, or after an account has been closed, or otherwise under circumstances giving a basis for objection by the drawer or maker, to prevent unjust enrichment and only to the extent necessary to prevent loss to the bank by reason of its payment of the item, the payor bank ~~shall be~~ is subrogated to the rights

~~(a)~~(1) of any holder in due course on the item against the drawer or maker; ~~and~~

~~(b)~~(2) of the payee or any other holder of the item against the drawer or maker either on the item or under the transaction out of which the item arose; and

~~(c)~~(3) of the drawer or maker against the payee or any other holder of the item with respect to the transaction out of which the item arose.

Reason for 1990 Change

An order to close an account is assimilated to an order to stop payment in this section and in Section 4–403. The other modifications are made to conform with current legislative drafting practices, with no intent to change substance.

§ 4-501. Handling of Documentary Drafts; Duty to Send for Presentment and to Notify Customer of Dishonor.

A bank ~~which~~ that takes a documentary draft for collection ~~must~~ shall present or send the draft and accompanying documents for presentment and, upon learning that the draft has not been paid or accepted in due course, ~~must~~ shall seasonably notify its customer of ~~such~~ the fact even though it may have discounted or bought the draft or extended credit available for withdrawal as of right.

Reason for 1990 Change

Modified to conform with current drafting practices; no intent to change substance.

§ 4-502. Presentment of "On Arrival" Drafts.

~~When~~ If a draft or the relevant instructions require presentment "on arrival", "when goods arrive" or the like, the collecting bank need not present until in its judgment a reasonable time for arrival of the goods has expired. Refusal to pay or accept because the goods have not arrived is not dishonor; the bank must notify its transferor of ~~such~~ the refusal but need not present the draft again until it is instructed to do so or learns of the arrival of the goods.

Reason for 1990 Change

Modified to conform with current drafting practices; no intent to change substance.

§ 4-503. Responsibility of Presenting Bank for Documents and Goods; Report of Reasons for Dishonor; Referee in Case of Need.

Unless otherwise instructed and except as provided in Article 5, a bank presenting a documentary draft:

~~(a)~~(1) must deliver the documents to the drawee on acceptance of the draft if it is payable more than three days after presentment; otherwise, only on payment; and

~~(b)~~(2) upon dishonor, either in the case of presentment for acceptance or presentment for payment, may seek and follow instructions from any referee in case of need designated in the draft or, if the presenting bank does not choose to utilize ~~his~~ the referee's services, it must use diligence and good faith to ascertain the reason for dishonor, must notify its transferor of the dishonor and of the results of its effort to ascertain the reasons therefor, and must request instructions.

~~But~~ However the presenting bank is under no obligation with respect to goods represented by the documents except to follow any reasonable instructions seasonably received; it has a right to reimbursement for any expense incurred in following instructions and to prepayment of or indemnity for ~~such~~ those expenses.

Reason for 1990 Change

Modified to conform with current drafting practices; no intent to change substance.

§ 4–504. Privilege of Presenting Bank to Deal with Goods; Security Interest for Expenses.

~~(1)~~(a) A presenting bank ~~which~~ that, following the dishonor of a documentary draft, has seasonably requested instructions but does not receive them within a reasonable time may store, sell, or otherwise deal with the goods in any reasonable manner.

~~(2)~~(b) For its reasonable expenses incurred by action under subsection ~~(1)~~(a), the presenting bank has a lien upon the goods or their proceeds, which may be foreclosed in the same manner as an unpaid seller's lien.

Reason for 1990 Change

Modified to conform with current drafting practices; no intent to change substance.

APPENDIX X

PRE–AMENDMENT (1990) ARTICLE 4

Set forth below are the Text and Official Comments of Article 4 as they existed prior to amendment in 1990.

ARTICLE 4

BANK DEPOSITS AND COLLECTIONS

PART 1. GENERAL PROVISIONS AND DEFINITIONS

PART 1

GENERAL PROVISIONS AND DEFINITIONS

§ 4-101. Short Title.

This Article shall be known and may be cited as Uniform Commercial Code—Bank Deposits and Collections.

Official Comment

The tremendous number of checks handled by banks and the country-wide nature of the bank collection process require uniformity in the law of bank collections. Individual Federal Reserve banks process as many as 1,000,000 items a day; large metropolitan banks average 300,000 a day; banks with less than $5,000,000 on deposit handle from 1,000 to 2,000 daily. There is needed a uniform statement of the principal rules of the bank collection process with ample provision for flexibility to meet the needs of the large volume handled and the changing needs and conditions that are bound to come with the years.

The American Bankers Association Bank Collection Code, enacted in eighteen states, has stated many of the bank collection rules that have developed, and more recently Deferred Posting statutes have developed and varied further rules. With items flowing in great volume not only in and around metropolitan and smaller centers but also continuously across state lines and back and forth across the entire country, a proper situation exists for uniform rules that will state in modern concepts at least some of the rights of the parties and in addition aid this flow and not interfere with its progress.

This Article adopts many of the rules of the American Bankers Association Code that are still in current operation, the principles and rules of the Deferred Posting and other statutes, codifies some rules established by court decisions and in addition states certain patterns and procedures that exist even though not heretofore covered by statute.

§ 4-102. Applicability.

(1) To the extent that items within this Article are also within the scope of Articles 3 and 8, they are subject to the provisions of those Articles. In the event of conflict the provisions of this Article govern those of Article 3 but the provisions of Article 8 govern those of this Article.

(2) The liability of a bank for action or non-action with respect to any item handled by it for purposes of presentment, payment or collection is governed by the law of the place where the bank is located. In the case of action or non-action by or at a branch or separate office of a bank, its liability is governed by the law of the place where the branch or separate office is located.

Official Comment

Prior Uniform Statutory Provision: None.

Purposes:

1. The rules governing negotiable instruments, their transfer, and the contracts of the parties thereto apply to the items collected through banking channels wherever no specific provision is found in this Article. In the case of conflict, this Article governs. See Section 3-103(2).

Bonds and like instruments constituting investment securities under Article 8 may also be handled by banks for collection purposes. Various sections of Article 8 prescribe rules of transfer some of which (see Sections 8-304 and 8-306) may conflict with provisions of this Article (Sections 4-205 and 4-207). In the case of conflict, Article 8 governs.

Section 4-208 deals specifically with overlapping problems and possible conflicts between this Article and Article 9. However, similar reconciling provisions are not necessary in the case of Articles 5 and 7. Sections 4-301 and 4-302 are consistent with Section 5-112. In the case of Article 7 documents of title frequently accompany items but they are not themselves items. See Section 4-104(g).

2. Subsection (2) is designed to state a workable rule for the solution of otherwise vexatious problems of the conflicts of laws:

a. The routine and mechanical nature of bank collections makes it imperative that one law govern the activities of one office of a bank. The requirement found in some cases that to hold an indorser notice must be given in accordance with the law of the place of indorsement, since that method of notice became an implied term of the indorser's contract, is more theoretical than practical.

b. Adoption of what is in essence a tort theory of the conflict of laws is consistent with the general theory of this Article that the basic duty of a collecting bank is one of good faith and the exercise of ordinary care. Justification lies in the fact that, in using an ambulatory instrument, the drawer, payee, and indorsers must know that action will be taken with respect to it in other jurisdictions. This is especially pertinent with respect to the law of the place of payment.

c. The phrase "action or non-action with respect to any item handled by it for purposes of presentment, payment or collection" is intended to make the conflicts rule of subsection (2) apply from the inception of the collection process of an item through all phases of deposit, forwarding, presentment, payment and remittance or credit of proceeds. Specifically the subsection applies to the initial act of a depositary bank in receiving an item and to the incidents of such receipt. The conflicts rule of Weissman v. Banque de Bruxelles, 254 N.Y. 488, 173 N.E. 835 (1930), is rejected. The subsection applies to questions of possible vicarious liability of a bank for action or non-action of sub-agents (see Section 4–202(3)) and tests these questions by the law of the state of the location of the bank which uses the sub-agent. The conflicts rule of St. Nicholas Bank of New York v. State Nat. Bank, 128 N.Y. 26, 27 N.E. 849, 13 L.R.A. 241 (1891), is rejected. The subsection applies to action or non-action of a payor bank in connection with handling an item (see Sections 4–213(1), 4–301, 4–302, 4–303) as well as action or non-action of a collecting bank (Sections 4–201 through 4–214); to action or non-action of a bank which suspends payment or is affected by another bank suspending payment (Section 4–214); to action or non-action of a bank with respect to an item under the rule of Part 4 of Article 4.

d. Where subsection (2) makes this Article applicable, Section 4–103(1) leaves open the possibility of an agreement with respect to applicable law. Such freedom of agreement follows the general policy of Section 1–105.

Cross References:

Sections 1–105; 3–103(2) and Article 3; all sections of Article 4; 5–112; Article 7; 8–304 and 8–306; Article 9.

Definitional Cross References:

"Bank". Section 1–201.
"Branch". Section 1–201.
"Item". Section 4–104.

§ 4–103. Variation by Agreement; Measure of Damages; Certain Action Constituting Ordinary Care.

(1) The effect of the provisions of this Article may be varied by agreement except that no agreement can disclaim a bank's responsibility for its own lack of good faith or failure to exercise ordinary care or can limit the measure of damages for such lack or failure; but the parties may by agreement determine the standards by which such responsibility is to be measured if such standards are not manifestly unreasonable.

(2) Federal Reserve regulations and operating letters, clearing house rules, and the like, have the effect of agreements under subsection (1), whether or not specifically assented to by all parties interested in items handled.

(3) Action or non-action approved by this Article or pursuant to Federal Reserve regulations or operating letters constitutes the exercise of ordinary care and, in the absence of special instructions, action or non-action consistent with clearing house rules and the like or with a general banking usage not disapproved by this Article, prima facie constitutes the exercise of ordinary care.

(4) The specification or approval of certain procedures by this Article does not constitute disapproval of other procedures which may be reasonable under the circumstances.

(5) The measure of damages for failure to exercise ordinary care in handling an item is the amount of the item reduced by an amount which

could not have been realized by the use of ordinary care, and where there is bad faith it includes other damages, if any, suffered by the party as a proximate consequence.

Official Comment

Prior Uniform Statutory Provision: None; but see Sections 5 and 6 of the American Bankers Association Bank Collection Code.

Purposes:

1. Section 1-102 states the general principles and rules for variation of the effect of this Act by agreement and the limitations to this power. Section 4-103 states the specific rules for variation of Article 4 by agreement and also certain standards of ordinary care. In view of the technical complexity of the field of bank collections, the enormous number of items handled by banks, the certainty that there will be variations from the normal in each day's work in each bank, the certainty of changing conditions and the possibility of developing improved methods of collection to speed the process, it would be unwise to freeze present methods of operation by mandatory statutory rules. This section, therefore, permits within wide limits variation of provisions of the Article by agreement.

2. Subsection (1) confers blanket power to vary all provisions of the Article by agreements of the ordinary kind. The agreements may not disclaim a bank's responsibility for its own lack of good faith or failure to exercise ordinary care and may not limit the measure of damages for such lack or failure, but this subsection like Section 1-102(3) approves the practice of parties determining by agreement the standards by which such responsibility is to be measured. In the absence of a showing that the standards manifestly are unreasonable, the agreement controls. Owners of items and other interested parties are not affected by agreements under this subsection unless they are parties to the agreement or are bound by adoption, ratification, estoppel or the like.

As here used "agreement" has the meaning given to it by Section 1-201(3). The agreement may be direct, as between the owner and the depositary bank; or indirect, as where the owner authorizes a particular type of procedure and any bank in the collection chain acts pursuant to such authorization. It may be with respect to a single item; or to all items handled for a particular customer, e.g., a general agreement between the depositary bank and the customer at the time a deposit account is opened. Legends on deposit tickets, collection letters and acknowledgments of items, coupled with action by the affected party constituting acceptance, adoption, ratification, estoppel or the like, are agreements if they meet the tests of the definition of "agreement". See Section 1-201(3). First Nat. Bank of Denver v. Federal Reserve Bank, 6 F.2d 339 (8th Cir. 1925) (deposit slip); Jefferson County Bldg. Ass'n v. Southern Bank & Trust Co., 225 Ala. 25, 142 So. 66 (1932) (signature card and deposit slip); Semingson v. Stock Yards Nat. Bank, 162 Minn. 424, 203 N.W. 412 (1925) (passbook); Farmers State Bank v. Union Nat. Bank, 42 N.D. 449, 454, 173 N.W. 789, 790 (1919) (acknowledgment of receipt of item).

3. Subsection (1) (subject to its limitations with respect to good faith and ordinary care) goes far to meet the requirements of flexibility. However, it does not by itself confer fully effective flexibility. When it is recognized that banks handle probably 25,000,000 items every business day and that the parties interested in each item include the owner of the item, the drawer (if it is a check), all non-bank indorsers, the payor bank and from one to five or more collecting banks, it is obvious that it is impossible, practically, to obtain direct agreements from all of these parties on all items. *En masse*, the interested parties constitute virtually every adult person and business organization in the United States. On the other hand they

may become bound to agreements on the principle that collecting banks acting as agents have authority to make binding agreements with respect to items being handled. This conclusion was assumed but was not flatly decided in Federal Reserve Bank of Richmond v. Malloy, 264 U.S. 160, at 167, 44 S.Ct. 296, at 298, 68 L.Ed. 617, 31 A.L.R. 1261 (1924).

To meet this problem subsection (2) provides that official or quasi-official rules of collection, that is Federal Reserve regulations and operating letters, clearing house rules, and the like, have the effect of agreements under subsection (1), whether or not specifically assented to by all parties interested in items handled. Consequently, such official or quasi-official rules may, standing by themselves but subject to the good faith and ordinary care limitations, vary the effect of the provisions of Article 4.

Federal Reserve regulations. Various sections of the Federal Reserve Act (12 U.S.C.A. § 221 et seq.) authorize the Board of Governors of the Federal Reserve System to direct the Federal Reserve banks to exercise bank collection functions. For example, Section 16 (12 U.S.C.A. § 248(*o*)) authorizes the Board to require each Federal Reserve bank to exercise the functions of a clearing house for its members and Section 13 (12 U.S.C.A. § 342) authorizes each Federal Reserve bank to receive deposits from non-member banks solely for the purposes of exchange or of collection. Under this statutory authorization the Board has issued Regulation J (Check Clearing and Collection), which has been infrequently amended over the many years during which it has been in force. (Regulation G, issued under comparable statutory authority, covers the handling of "non-cash items"). Where regulations issued by the Board in pursuance of its statutory mandate may be said to have some force of law and constitute an effective means of maintaining flexibility, it is appropriate to provide that such regulations may vary this Article even though not specifically assented to by all parties interested in items handled.

Federal Reserve operating letters. The regulations of the Federal Reserve Board authorize the Federal Reserve banks to promulgate rules covering operating details. Regulation J, for example, provides that each bank may promulgate rules "not inconsistent with the terms of the law or of this regulation governing the sorting, listing, packaging and transmission of items and other details of its check clearing and collection operation. Such rules ... shall be set forth ... in ... letters of instructions to ... member and non-member clearing banks." The term "operating letters" means these "letters of instructions", sometimes called "operating circulars", issued by the Federal Reserve banks under appropriate regulation of the Board. This Article recognizes such "operating letters" issued pursuant to the regulations and concerned with operating details as appropriate means, within their proper sphere, to vary the effect of the Article.

Clearing House Rules. Local clearing houses have long issued rules governing the details of clearing; hours of clearing, media of remittance, time for return of mis-sent items and the like. The case law has recognized such rules, within their proper sphere, as binding on affected parties and as appropriate sources for the courts to look to in filling out details of bank collection law. Subsection (2) in recognizing clearing house rules as a means of preserving flexibility continues the sensible approach indicated in the cases. Included in the term "clearing houses" are county and regional clearing houses as well as those within a single city or town. There is, of course, no intention of authorizing a local clearing house or a group of clearing houses to rewrite the basic law generally. The term "clearing house rules" should be understood in the light of functions the clearing houses have exercised in the past.

And the like. This phrase is to be construed in the light of the foregoing. "Federal Reserve regulations and operating letters" cover rules and regulations issued by public or quasi-public agencies under statutory authority. "Clearing house rules" cover rules issued by a group of banks which have associated themselves to perform through a clearing house some of their collection, payment and clearing functions. Other such agencies or associations may be established in the future whose rules and regulations could be appropriately looked on as constituting means of avoiding absolute statutory rigidity. The phrase "and the like" leaves open such possibilities of future development. An agreement between a number of banks or even all the banks in an area simply because they are banks, would not of itself, by virtue of the phrase "and the like," meet the purposes and objectives of subsection (2).

4. Under this Article banks come under the general obligations of the use of good faith and the exercise of ordinary care. "Good faith" is defined in this Act (Section 1–201(19)) as "honesty in fact in the conduct or transaction concerned." The term "ordinary care" is not defined and is here used with its normal tort meaning and not in any special sense relating to bank collections. No attempt is made in the Article to define *in toto* what constitutes ordinary care or lack of it. Section 4–202 states respects in which collecting banks must use ordinary care. Subsection (3) of 4–103 provides that action or non-action approved by the Article or pursuant to Federal Reserve regulations or operating letters constitutes the exercise of ordinary care. Where Federal Reserve regulations and operating letters are issued pursuant to statutory mandate as indicated above, they constitute an affirmative standard of ordinary care equally with the provisions of Article 4 itself.

Subsection (3) further provides that, absent special instructions, action or non-action consistent with clearing house rules and the like or with a general banking usage not disapproved by the Article, prima facie constitutes the exercise of ordinary care. Clearing house rules and the phrase "and the like" have the significance set forth above in these Comments. The term "general banking usage" is not defined but should be taken to mean a general usage common to banks in the area concerned. See Section 1–205(2). Where the adjective "general" is used, the intention is to require a usage broader than a mere practice between two or three banks but it is not intended to require anything as broad as a country-wide usage. A usage followed generally throughout a state, a substantial portion of a state, a metropolitan area or the like would certainly be sufficient. Consistently with the principle of Section 1–205(3), action or nonaction consistent with clearing house rules or the like or with such banking usages prima facie constitutes the exercise of ordinary care. However, the phrase "in the absence of special instructions" affords owners of items an opportunity to prescribe other standards and where there may be no direct supervision or control of clearing houses or banking usages by official supervisory authorities, the confirmation of ordinary care by compliance with these standards is *prima facie* only, thus conferring on the courts the ultimate power to determine ordinary care in any case where it should appear desirable to do so. The *prima facie* rule does, however, impose on the party contesting the standards to establish that they are unreasonable, arbitrary or unfair.

5. Subsection (4), in line with the flexible approach required for the bank collection process is designed to make clear that a novel procedure adopted by a bank is not to be considered unreasonable merely because that procedure is not specifically contemplated by this Article or by agreement, or because it has not yet been generally accepted as a bank usage. Changing conditions constantly call for new procedures and someone has to use the new procedure first. If such a procedure when called in question is found to be reasonable under the circumstances, provided, of course, that it is not inconsistent with any provision of the Article or other law or agreement, the bank which has followed the new procedure should not be found to have failed in the exercise of ordinary care.

6. Subsection (5) sets forth a rule for determining the measure of damages which, under subsection (1), cannot be limited by agreement. In the absence of bad faith the maximum recovery is the amount of the item concerned. When it is established that some part or all of the item could not have been collected even by the use of ordinary care the recovery is reduced by the amount which would have been in any event uncollectible. This limitation on recovery follows the case law. Finally, when bad faith is established the rule opens to allow the recovery of other damages, whose "proximateness" is to be tested by the ordinary rules applied in comparable cases. Of course, it continues to be as necessary under subsection (5) as it has been under ordinary common law principles that, before the damage rule of the subsection becomes operative, liability of the bank and some loss to the customer or owner must be established.

Cross References:

Sections 1-102(3), 1-203, 1-205 and 4-202.

Definitional Cross References:

"Bank". Section 1-201.
"Good faith". Section 1-201.
"Item". Section 4-104.
"Usage". Section 1-205.

§ 4-104. Definitions and Index of Definitions.

(1) In this Article unless the context otherwise requires

(a) "Account" means any account with a bank and includes a checking, time, interest or savings account;

(b) "Afternoon" means the period of a day between noon and midnight;

(c) "Banking day" means that part of any day on which a bank is open to the public for carrying on substantially all of its banking functions;

(d) "Clearing house" means any association of banks or other payors regularly clearing items;

(e) "Customer" means any person having an account with a bank or for whom a bank has agreed to collect items and includes a bank carrying an account with another bank;

(f) "Documentary draft" means any negotiable or non-negotiable draft with accompanying documents, securities or other papers to be delivered against honor of the draft;

(g) "Item" means any instrument for the payment of money even though it is not negotiable but does not include money;

(h) "Midnight deadline" with respect to a bank is midnight on its next banking day following the banking day on which it receives the relevant item or notice or from which the time for taking action commences to run, whichever is later;

(i) "Properly payable" includes the availability of funds for payment at the time of decision to pay or dishonor;

(j) "Settle" means to pay in cash, by clearing house settlement, in a charge or credit or by remittance, or otherwise as instructed. A settlement may be either provisional or final;

(k) "Suspends payments" with respect to a bank means that it has been closed by order of the supervisory authorities, that a public officer has been appointed to take it over or that it ceases or refuses to make payments in the ordinary course of business.

(2) Other definitions applying to this Article and the sections in which they appear are:

"Collecting bank"	Section 4–105.
"Depositary bank"	Section 4–105.
"Intermediary bank"	Section 4–105.
"Payor bank"	Section 4–105.
"Presenting bank"	Section 4–105.
"Remitting bank"	Section 4–105.

(3) The following definitions in other Articles apply to this Article:

"Acceptance"	Section 3–410.
"Certificate of deposit"	Section 3–104.
"Certification"	Section 3–411.
"Check"	Section 3–104.
"Draft"	Section 3–104.
"Holder in due course"	Section 3–302.
"Notice of dishonor"	Section 3–508.
"Presentment"	Section 3–504.
"Protest"	Section 3–509.
"Secondary party"	Section 3–102.

(4) In addition Article 1 contains general definitions and principles of construction and interpretation applicable throughout this Article.

Official Comment

Prior Uniform Statutory Provision: None.

Purposes:

1. Subsection (1)(c): "Banking Day". Under this definition that part of a business day when a bank is open only for limited functions, e.g., on Saturday evenings to receive deposits and cash checks, but with loan, bookkeeping and other departments closed, is not part of a banking day.

2. Subsection (1)(d): "Clearing House". Occasionally express companies, governmental agencies and other non-banks deal directly with a clearing house; hence the definition does not limit the term to an association of banks.

3. Subsection (1)(e): "Customer". It is to be noted that this term includes a bank carrying an account with another bank as well as the more typical non-bank customer or depositor.

4. Subsection (1)(g): The word "item" is chosen because it is "banking language" and includes non-negotiable as well as negotiable paper calling for money and also similar paper governed by the Article on Investment Securities (Article 8) as well as that governed by the Article on Commercial Paper (Article 3).

5. Subsection (1)(h): "Midnight Deadline". The use of this phrase is an example of the more mechanical approach used in this Article. Midnight is selected as a termination point or time limit to obtain greater uniformity and definiteness than would be possible from other possible termination points, such as the close of the banking day or business day.

6. Subsection (1)(j): The term "settle" is a new term in bank collection language that has substantial importance throughout Article 4. In the American Bankers Association Bank Collection

Code, in deferred posting statutes, in Federal Reserve regulations and operating letters, in clearing house rules, in agreements between banks and customers and in legends on deposit tickets and collection letters, there is repeated reference to "conditional" or "provisional" credits or payments. Tied in with this concept of credits or payments being in some way tentative, has been a related but somewhat different problem as to when an item is "paid" or "finally paid" either to determine the relative priority of the item as against attachments, stop payment orders and the like or in insolvency situations. There has been extensive litigation in the various states on these problems. To a substantial extent the confusion, the litigation and even the resulting court decisions fail to take into account that in the collection process some debits or credits are provisional or tentative and others are final and that very many debits or credits are provisional or tentative for awhile but later become final. Similarly, some cases fail to recognize that within a single bank, particularly a payor bank, each item goes through a series of processes and that in a payor bank most of these processes are preliminary to the basic act of payment or "final payment".

The term "settle" is used as a convenient term to characterize a broad variety of conditional, provisional, tentative and also final payments of items. Such a comprehensive term is needed because it is frequently difficult or unnecessary to determine whether a particular action is tentative or final or when a particular credit shifts from the tentative class to the final class. Therefore, its use throughout the Article indicates that in that particular context it is unnecessary or unwise to determine whether the debit or the credit or the payment is tentative or final. However, when qualified by the adjective "provisional" its tentative nature is intended, and when qualified by the adjective "final" its permanent nature is intended.

Examples of the various types of settlement contemplated by the term include payments in cash; the efficient but somewhat complicated process of payment through the adjustment and offsetting of balances through clearing houses; debit or credit entries in accounts between banks; the forwarding of various types of remittance instruments, sometimes to cover a particular item but more frequently to cover an entire group of items received on a particular day.

7. Subsection (1)(k): "Suspends payments". This term is designed to afford an objective test to determine when a bank is no longer operating as a part of the banking system.

Definitional Cross References:

"Bank". Section 1-201.
"Documents". Section 1-201.
"Money". Section 1-201.
"Negotiable". Section 3-104.
"Notice". Section 1-201.
"Person". Section 1-201.
"Securities". Section 8-102.

§ 4-105. "Depositary Bank"; "Intermediary Bank"; "Collecting Bank"; "Payor Bank"; "Presenting Bank"; "Remitting Bank".

In this Article unless the context otherwise requires:

(a) "Depositary bank" means the first bank to which an item is transferred for collection even though it is also the payor bank;

(b) "Payor bank" means a bank by which an item is payable as drawn or accepted;

(c) "Intermediary bank" means any bank to which an item is transferred in course of collection except the depositary or payor bank;

(d) "Collecting bank" means any bank handling the item for collection except the payor bank;

(e) "Presenting bank" means any bank presenting an item except a payor bank;

(f) "Remitting bank" means any payor or intermediary bank remitting for an item.

Official Comment

Prior Uniform Statutory Provision: None.

Purposes:

1. The definitions in general exclude a bank to which an item is issued, as such bank does not take by transfer except in the particular case covered where the item is issued to a payee for collection, as where a corporation is transferring balances from one account to another. Thus, the definition of "depositary bank" does not include the bank to which a check is made payable where a check is given in payment of a mortgage. Such a bank has the status of a payee under Article 3 on Commercial Paper and not that of a collecting bank.

2. The term payor bank includes a drawee bank and also a bank at which an item is payable if the item constitutes an order on the bank to pay, for it is then "payable by" the bank. If the "at" item is not an order in the particular state (See Section 3-121), then the bank is not a payor, but will be a presenting or collecting bank.

3. Items are sometimes drawn or accepted "payable through" a particular bank. Under this Section and Section 3-120 the "payable through" bank (if it in fact handles the item) will be a collecting (and often a presenting) bank; it is not a "payor bank."

4. The term intermediary bank includes the last bank in the collection process where the payor is not a bank. Usually the last bank is also a presenting bank.

Cross References:

Article 3, especially Sections 3-120 and 3-121.

Definitional Cross References:

"Bank". Section 1-201.
"Customer". Section 4-104.
"Item". Section 4-104.

§ 4-106. Separate Office of a Bank.

A branch or separate office of a bank [maintaining its own deposit ledgers] is a separate bank for the purpose of computing the time within which and determining the place at or to which action may be taken or notices or orders shall be given under this Article and under Article 3.

As amended 1962.

Note: *The brackets are to make it optional with the several states whether to require a branch to maintain its own deposit ledgers in order to be considered to be a separate bank for certain purposes under Article 4. In some states "maintaining its own deposit ledgers" is a satisfactory test. In others branch banking practices are such that this test would not be suitable.*

Official Comment

Prior Uniform Statutory Provision: None; but see Section 1, American Bankers Association Bank Collection Code.

Purposes:

1. A rule with respect to the status of a branch or separate office of a bank as a

part of any statute on bank collections is highly desirable if not absolutely necessary. However, practices in the operations of branches and separate offices vary substantially in the different states and it has not been possible to find any single rule that is logically correct, fair in all situations and workable under all different types of practices.

2. In many states and for many purposes a branch or separate office of the bank needs to be treated as a separate bank. Many branches function as separate banks in the handling and payment of items and require time for doing so similar to that of a separate bank. This is particularly true where branch banking is permitted throughout a state or in different towns and cities. Similarly, where there is this separate functioning a particular branch or separate office is the only proper place for various types of action to be taken or orders or notices to be given. Examples include the drawing of a check on a particular branch by a customer whose account is carried at that branch; the presentment of that same check at that branch; the issuance of an order to the branch to stop payment on the check.

3. Section 1 of the American Bankers Association Bank Collection Code provides simply: "A branch or office of any such bank shall be deemed a bank." Although this rule appears to be brief and simple, as applied to particular sections of the ABA Code it produces illogical and, in some cases, unreasonable results. For example, under Section 11 of the ABA Code it seems anomalous for one branch of a bank to have charged an item to the account of the drawer and another branch to have the power to elect to treat the item as dishonored. Similar logical problems would flow from applying the same rule to Article 4. Warranties by one branch to another branch under Section 4-207 (each considered a separate bank) do not make sense.

4. Assuming that it is not desirable to make each branch a separate bank for all purposes, this Section provides that a branch or separate office is a separate bank for certain purposes. In so doing the single legal entity of the bank as a whole is preserved, thereby carrying with it the liability of the institution as a whole on such obligations as it may be under. On the other hand, where the Article provides a number of time limits for different types of action by banks, if a branch functions as a separate bank, it should have the time limits available to a separate bank. Similarly if in its relations to customers a branch functions as a separate bank, notices and orders with respect to accounts of customers of the branch should be given at the branch. For example, whether a branch has notice sufficient to affect its status as a holder in due course of an item taken by it should depend upon what notice that branch has received with respect to the item. Similarly the receipt of a stop payment order at one branch should not be notice to another branch so as to impair the right of the second branch to be a holder in due course of the item, although in circumstances in which ordinary care requires the communication of a notice or order to the proper branch of a bank, such notice or order would be effective at such proper branch from the time it was or should have been received. See Section 1-201(27).

5. Whether a branch functions as a separate bank may vary depending upon the type of activity taking place and upon practices in the different states. If the activity is that of a payor bank paying items, a branch will usually function as a separate bank if it maintains its own deposit ledgers. Similarly whether a branch functions as a separate bank in the collection of items usually depends also on whether it maintains its own deposit ledgers. Conversely, if a particular bank having branches does all of its bookkeeping at its head office, the branches of that bank do not usually function as separate banks either in the payment or collection of items.

On the other hand, in its relations to customers a branch may function as a separate bank regardless of whether it maintains its own deposit ledgers. Checks may be drawn on a particular branch and notices and stop orders delivered to that branch even though all the bookkeeping is done at the head office or another branch.

Where the words "maintaining its own deposit ledgers" are bracketed, the option is given to each state enacting the Code to include these words as a test of separateness. In those states where the maintenance by a branch of its own deposit ledgers will serve as a satisfactory standard, the bracketed words should be retained. In those states where these words will cause more problems than benefits, they may be deleted. Insofar as this latter rule allows extra time to banks maintaining branches where such extra time is not needed, it is not ideal. However, it has not been found possible to find a rule that will meet this problem and will work in all cases. Further, it is highly unlikely that large banks maintaining branches will needlessly take advantage of extra time under this rule.

Cross References:

Sections 3–504, 4–102(2).

Definitional Cross References:

"Bank". Section 1–201.
"Branch". Section 1–201.

§ 4–107. Time of Receipt of Items.

(1) For the purpose of allowing time to process items, prove balances and make the necessary entries on its books to determine its position for the day, a bank may fix an afternoon hour of 2 P.M. or later as a cut-off hour for the handling of money and items and the making of entries on its books.

(2) Any item or deposit of money received on any day after a cut-off hour so fixed or after the close of the banking day may be treated as being received at the opening of the next banking day.

Official Comment

Prior Uniform Statutory Provision: None.

Purposes:

1. After an item has been received by a bank it goes through a series of processes varying with the type of item that it is. It moves from the teller's window, branch office, or mail desk at which it is received through settlement and proving departments until it is forwarded or presented to a clearing house or another bank, if it is a transit item, or until it reaches the bookkeeping department, if the bank receiving it is the payor bank. In addition, in order that the books of the bank always remain in balance while items are moving through it, the amount of each item is included in lists or proofs of debits or credits several times as it progresses through the bank. The running of proofs, the making of debit and credit entries in subsidiary and general ledgers and the striking of a general balance for each day requires a considerable amount of time. If these processes are to be completed on any particular day during normal working hours without the employment of night forces, a number of banks have found it necessary to establish a "cut-off hour" to allow time to obtain final figures to be incorporated into the bank's position for the day. Subsection (1) approves a cut-off hour of this type provided it is not earlier than 2 P.M. Subsection (2) provides that if such a cut-off hour is fixed, items received after the cut-off hour may be treated as being received at the opening of the next banking day. Where the number of items received either through the mail or over the counter tends to taper off radically as the afternoon hours progress, a 2 P.M. cut-off hour does not involve a large portion of the items received but at the same time permits a bank using such a cut-off hour to leave its doors open later in the afternoon without forcing into the evening the completion of its settling and proving process.

2. The alternative provision in Subsection (2) that items or deposits received after the close of the banking day may be treated as received at the opening of the next banking day is important in cases where a bank closes at twelve or one o'clock, e.g., on a Saturday, but continues to receive some items by mail or over the counter if, for example, it opens Saturday evening for the limited purpose of receiving deposits and cashing checks.

Definitional Cross References:

"Afternoon". Section 4-104.
"Bank". Section 1-201.
"Banking day". Section 4-104.
"Item". Section 4-104.
"Money". Section 1-201.

§ 4-108. Delays.

(1) Unless otherwise instructed, a collecting bank in a good faith effort to secure payment may, in the case of specific items and with or without the approval of any person involved, waive, modify or extend time limits imposed or permitted by this Act for a period not in excess of an additional banking day without discharge of secondary parties and without liability to its transferor or any prior party.

(2) Delay by a collecting bank or payor bank beyond time limits prescribed or permitted by this Act or by instructions is excused if caused by interruption of communication facilities, suspension of payments by another bank, war, emergency conditions or other circumstances beyond the control of the bank provided it exercises such diligence as the circumstances require.

Official Comment

Prior Uniform Statutory Provision: None.

Purposes:

1. Sections 4-202(2), 4-212, 4-301 and 4-302 prescribe various time limits for the handling of items. These are the limits of time within which a bank, in fulfillment of its obligation to exercise ordinary care, must handle items entrusted to it for collection or payment. Under Section 4-103 they may be varied by agreement or by Federal Reserve regulations or operating letters, clearing house rules, or the like.

2. Subsection (1) of this section permits a limited extension of these time limits in special cases. It permits collecting banks to grant, within a rather narrow field, an additional banking day and to do so with or without the approval of any interested party. Such one-day extension can only be granted in a good faith effort to secure payment and only with respect to specific items. It cannot be exercised if the customer instructs otherwise. Thus limited the escape provision should afford a limited degree of flexibility in special cases but should not interfere with the overall requirement and objective of speedy collections.

3. Notice that an extension granted under Subsection (1) is "without discharge of secondary parties". It therefore extends also the times for presentment or payment, as the case may be, specified in Article 3. See Sections 3-503 and 3-506. Where this Article and Article 3 conflict, this Article controls. See Sections 3-103(2) and 4-102(1).

4. Subsection (2) is another escape clause from time limits. This clause operates not only with respect to time limits imposed by the article itself but also time limits imposed by special instructions, by agreement or by Federal Reserve regulations or operating letters, clearing house rules or the like. The latter time limits are "permitted" by the Code. This clause operates, however, only in the types of situation specified. Examples of these situations include blizzards, floods,

or hurricanes, and other "Act of God" events or conditions, and wrecks or disasters, interfering with mails; suspension of payments by another bank; abnormal operating conditions such as substantial increased volume or substantial shortage of personnel during war or emergency situations. When delay is sought to be excused under this subsection the bank must "exercise such diligence as the circumstances require" and it has the burden of proof. See Section 4–202(2).

Cross References:

Sections 3–103(2), 3–503, 3–506, 4–102(1), 4–103, 4–104, 4–202(2), 4–212, 4–213, 4–301, 4–302.

Definitional Cross References:

"Bank". Section 1–201.
"Banking day". Section 4–104.
"Collecting bank". Section 4–105.
"Good faith". Section 1–201.
"Item". Section 4–104.
"Party". Section 1–201.

§ 4–109. Process of Posting.

The "process of posting" means the usual procedure followed by a payor bank in determining to pay an item and in recording the payment including one or more of the following or other steps as determined by the bank:

(a) verification of any signature;

(b) ascertaining that sufficient funds are available;

(c) affixing a "paid" or other stamp;

(d) entering a charge or entry to a customer's account;

(e) correcting or reversing an entry or erroneous action with respect to the item.

As added in 1962.

Official Comment

Prior Uniform Statutory Provisions: None.

Purposes:

Completion of the "process of posting" is one of the measuring points for determining when an item is finally paid (subsection (1)(c) of Section 4–213) and when knowledge, notice, stop order, legal process and set-off come too late to affect a payor bank's right or duty to pay an item (subsection (1)(d) of Section 4–303). This Section defines what is meant by the "process of posting". It is the "usual procedure followed by a payor bank in determining to pay an item and in recording the payment ...". It involves the two basic elements of some decision to pay and some recording of the payment with a listing of some of the typical steps that might be involved. Procedures followed by banks in determining to pay an item and in recording the payment vary. Examples of some of these procedures will illustrate what is meant by completion of the "process of posting".

Example 1. A payor bank receives an item through the clearing on Monday morning. It is sorted under the name of the customer on Monday and under deferred posting routines (Section 4–301) reaches the bookkeeper for that customer on Tuesday morning. The bookkeeper examines the signature, verifies there are sufficient funds and decides at 11 a.m. on Tuesday to pay the item. A debit entry for or including the amount of the item is entered in the customer's account at 12 noon on Tuesday. The process of posting is completed at 12 noon on Tuesday.

Example 2. A payor bank with branches receives an item through the clearing on Monday morning. One branch does all the bookkeeping for itself and nine other branches. The item is sent to that branch and a provisional debit is entered to the customer's account for the amount of the item on Monday. After this entry is made the item is sent to the branch where the customer transacts business and at this branch a clerk verifies the signature on Tuesday, e.g. at 12 noon. If the clerk determines the signature is valid and makes a decision to pay, the process of posting is completed at 12 noon on Tuesday because there has been both a charge to the customer's account and a determination to pay. If, however, the clerk determines the signature is not valid or that the item should not be paid for some other reason, the item is then returned to the presenting bank through the clearing house and an offsetting credit entry is made in the customer's account by the bookkeeping branch. In this case there has been no determination to pay the item, no completion of the process of posting and no payment of the item.

Example 3. A payor bank receives in the mail on Monday an item drawn upon it. The item is sorted and otherwise processed on Monday and during Monday night is provisionally recorded on tape by an electronic computer as charged to the customer's account. On Tuesday a clerk examines the signature on the item and makes other checks to determine finally whether the item should be paid. If the clerk determines the signature is valid and makes a decision to pay and all processing of this item is complete, e.g., at 12 noon on Tuesday, the "process of posting" is completed at that time. If, however, the clerk determines the signature is not valid or that the item should not be paid for some other reason, the item is returned to the presenting bank and in the regular Tuesday night run of the computer the debit to the customer's account for the item is reversed or an offsetting credit entry is made. In this case, as in Example 2, there has been no determination to pay the item, no completion of the process of posting and no payment of the item.

Cross References:

Sections 4-213(1)(c), 4-303(1)(d).

Definitional Cross References:

"Account". Section 4-104(1)(a).
"Customer". Section 4-104(1)(e).
"Item". Section 4-104(1)(g).
"Payor bank". Section 4-105(b).

PART 2

COLLECTION OF ITEMS: DEPOSITARY AND COLLECTING BANKS

§ 4-201. Presumption and Duration of Agency Status of Collecting Banks and Provisional Status of Credits; Applicability of Article; Item Indorsed "Pay Any Bank".

(1) Unless a contrary intent clearly appears and prior to the time that a settlement given by a collecting bank for an item is or becomes final (subsection (3) of Section 4-211 and Sections 4-212 and 4-213) the bank is an agent or sub-agent of the owner of the item and any settlement given for the item is provisional. This provision applies regardless of the form of indorsement or lack of indorsement and even though credit given for the item is subject to immediate withdrawal as of right or is in fact withdrawn; but the continuance of ownership of an item by its owner and any rights of the owner to proceeds of the item are subject to rights of a collecting bank such as those resulting from outstanding advances on the item and valid rights of setoff. When an item is handled by banks for purposes of presentment, payment and collection, the relevant provisions of this Article apply even though action of parties clearly establishes that a particular bank has purchased the item and is the owner of it.

(2) After an item has been indorsed with the words "pay any bank" or the like, only a bank may acquire the rights of a holder

(a) until the item has been returned to the customer initiating collection; or

(b) until the item has been specially indorsed by a bank to a person who is not a bank.

Official Comment

Prior Uniform Statutory Provision: None; but see Sections 2 and 4 of the American Bankers Association Bank Collection Code.

Purposes:

1. This section states certain basic rules and presumptions of the bank collection process. One basic rule, appearing in the last sentence of subsection (1), is that, to the extent applicable, the provisions of the Article govern without regard to whether a bank handling an item owns the item or is an agent for collection. Historically, much time has been spent and effort expended in determining or attempting to determine whether a bank was a purchaser of an item or merely an agent for collection. See discussion of this subject and cases cited in 11 A.L.R. 1043, 16 A.L.R. 1084, 42 A.L.R. 492, 68 A.L.R. 725, 99 A.L.R. 486. See also Section 4 of the American Bankers Association Bank Collection Code. The general approach of Article 4, similar to that of other articles, is to provide, within reasonable limits, rules or answers to major problems known to exist in the bank collection process without regard to questions of status and ownership but to keep general principles such as status and ownership available to cover residual areas not covered by specific rules. In line with this approach, the last sentence of subsection (1) says in effect that Article 4 applies to practically every item moving through banks for the purpose of presentment, payment or collection.

2. Within this general rule of broad coverage, the first two sentences of subsection (1) state a rule of status in terms of a strong presumption. "Unless a contrary intent clearly appears" the status of a collecting bank is that of an agent or sub-agent for the owner of the item. Although as indicated in Comment 1 it is much less important under Article 4 to determine status than has been the case heretofore, such status may have importance in some residual areas not covered by specific rules. Further, where status has been considered so important in the past, to omit all reference to it might cause confusion. The presumption of agency "applies regardless of the form of indorsement or lack of indorsement and even though credit given for the item is subject to immediate withdrawal as of right or is in fact withdrawn". Thus questions heretofore litigated as to whether ordinary indorsements "for deposit", "for collection" or in blank have the effect of creating an agency status or a purchase, no longer have significance in varying the prima facie rule of agency. Similarly, the nature of the credit given for an item or whether it is subject to immediate withdrawal as of right or is in fact withdrawn, do not rebut the general presumption. See A.L.R. references supra in Comment 1.

A contrary intent can rebut the presumption but this must be clear. An example of a clear contrary intent would be if collateral papers established or the item bore a legend stating that the item was sold absolutely to the depositary bank.

3. The prima facie agency status of collecting banks is consistent with prevailing law and practice today. Section 2 of the American Bankers Association Bank Collection Code so provides. Legends on deposit tickets, collection letters and acknowledgments of items and Federal Reserve operating letters consistently so provide. The status is consistent with

rights of chargeback (Section 4-212 and Section 11 of the ABA Code) and risk of loss in the event of insolvency (Section 4-214 and Section 13 of the ABA Code).

4. Affirmative statement of a prima facie agency status for collecting banks requires certain limitations and qualifications. Under current practices substantially all bank collections sooner or later merge into bank credits, at least if collection is effected. Usually, this takes place within a few days of the initiation of collection. An intermediary bank receives final collection and evidences the result of its collection by a "credit" on its books to the depositary bank. The depositary bank evidences the results of its collection by a "credit" in the account of its customer. As used in these instances the term "credit" clearly indicates a debtor-creditor relationship. At some stage in the bank collection process the agency status of a collecting bank changes to that of debtor, a debtor of its customer. Usually at about the same time it also becomes a creditor for the amount of the item, a creditor of some intermediary, payor or other bank. Thus the collection is completed, all agency aspects are terminated and the identity of the item has become completely merged in bank accounts, that of the customer with the depositary bank and that of one bank with another.

Although Section 4-213(1) provides that an item is finally paid when the payor bank takes certain action with respect to the item such final payment of the item may or may not result in the simultaneous *final settlement* for the item in the case of all prior parties. If a series of provisional debits and credits for the item have been entered in accounts between banks, the final payment of the item by the payor bank may result in the automatic firming up of all these provisional debits and credits under Section 4-213(2), and the consequent receipt of final settlement for the item by each collecting bank and the customer of the depositary bank simultaneously with such action of the payor bank. However, if the payor bank or some intermediary bank accounts for the item with a remittance draft, the next prior bank usually does not receive final settlement for the item until such remittance draft finally clears. See Section 4-211(3)(a). The first sentence of subsection (1) provides that the agency status of a collecting bank (whether intermediary or depositary) continues until the settlement *given by it for the item* is or becomes final, referring to Sections 4-211(3), 4-212, and 4-213. In the case of the series of provisional credits covered by Section 4-213(2), this could be simultaneously with the final payment of the item by the payor bank. In cases where remittance drafts are used or in straight non-cash collections, this would not be until the times specified in Sections 4-211(3) and 4-213(3).

A number of practical results flow from this rule continuing the agency status of a collecting bank until its settlement for the item is or becomes final, some of which are specifically set forth in this Article. One is that risk of loss continues in the owner of the item rather than the agent bank. See Section 4-212. Offsetting rights favorable to the owner are that pending such final settlement, the owner has the preference rights of Section 4-214 and the direct rights of Section 4-302 against the payor bank. It also follows from this rule that the dollar limitations of Federal Deposit Insurance are measured by the claim of the owner of the item rather than that of the collecting bank.

5. In those cases where some period of time elapses between the final payment of the item by the payor bank and the time that the settlement of the collecting bank is or becomes final, e.g., where the payor bank or an intermediary bank accounts for the item with a remittance draft or in straight non-cash collections, the continuance of the agency status of the collecting bank necessarily carries with it the continuance of the owner's status as principal. The second sentence of subsection (1) provides that whatever rights the owner has to proceeds of the item are subject to the rights of collecting banks for outstanding advances on the item and

other valid rights, if any. The rule provides a sound rule to govern cases of attempted attachment of proceeds of a non-cash item in the hands of the payor bank as property of the absent owner. If a collecting bank has made an advance on an item which is still outstanding, its right to obtain reimbursement for this advance should be superior to the rights of the owner to the proceeds or to the rights of a creditor of the owner. The phrase "other valid rights, if any" is broad enough to cover legitimate rights of set-off of accounts between banks without attempting to provide that all set-offs may be valid. An intentional crediting of proceeds of an item to the account of a prior bank known to be insolvent, for the purpose of acquiring a right of set-off, would not produce a valid set-off. See 8 Zollman, Banks and Banking (1936) Sec. 5443.

6. This section and Article 4 as a whole represent an intentional abandonment of the approach to bank collection problems appearing in Section 4 of the American Bankers Association Bank Collection Code. Where the tremendous volume of items handled makes impossible the examination by all banks of all indorsements on all items and where in fact this examination is not made, except perhaps by depositary banks, it is unrealistic to base the rights and duties of all banks in the collection chain on variations in the form of indorsements. It is anomalous to provide throughout the ABA Code that the prima facie status of collecting banks is that of agent or sub-agent but in Section 4 to provide that subsequent holders (sub-agents) shall have the right to rely on the presumption that the bank of deposit (the primary agent) is the owner of the item. It is unrealistic, particularly in this background, to base rights and duties on status of agent or owner. This Section 4-201 makes the pertinent provisions of Article 4 applicable to substantially all items handled by banks for presentment, payment or collection, recognizes the prima facie status of most banks as agents, and then seeks to state appropriate limits and some attributes to the general rules and presumptions so expressed.

7. Subsection (2) protects the ownership rights with respect to an item indorsed "pay any bank or banker" or in similar terms of a customer initiating collection or of any bank acquiring a security interest under Section 4-208, in the event the item is subsequently acquired under improper circumstances by a person who is not a bank and transferred by that person to another person, whether or not a bank. Upon return to the customer initiating collection of an item so indorsed, the indorsement may be cancelled (Section 3-208). A bank holding an item so indorsed may transfer the item out of banking channels by special indorsement; however, under Section 4-103(5), such bank would be liable to the owner of the item for any loss resulting therefrom if the transfer had been made in bad faith or with lack of ordinary care. If briefer and more simple forms of bank indorsements are developed under Section 4-206 (e.g., the use of bank transit numbers in lieu of present lengthy forms of bank indorsements), a depositary bank having the transit number "X100" could make subsection (2) operative by indorsements such as "Pay any bank—X100".

Cross References:

Sections 3-206, 3-208, 4-103, 4-206, 4-208, 4-212, 4-213, 4-214 and 4-302.

Definitional Cross References:

"Bank". Section 1-201.
"Collecting bank". Section 4-105.
"Customer". Section 4-104.
"Depositary bank". Section 4-105.
"Holder". Section 1-201.
"Item". Section 4-104.
"Indorsements". Sections 3-202, 3-204, 3-205 and 3-206.
"Person". Section 1-201.
"Settle". Section 4-104.

§ 4-202. Responsibility for Collection; When Action Seasonable.

(1) A collecting bank must use ordinary care in

(a) presenting an item or sending it for presentment; and

(b) sending notice of dishonor or non-payment or returning an item other than a documentary draft to the bank's transferor [or directly to the depositary bank under subsection (2) of Section 4–212] (*see note to Section 4–212*) after learning that the item has not been paid or accepted, as the case may be; and

(c) settling for an item when the bank receives final settlement; and

(d) making or providing for any necessary protest; and

(e) notifying its transferor of any loss or delay in transit within a reasonable time after discovery thereof.

(2) A collecting bank taking proper action before its midnight deadline following receipt of an item, notice or payment acts seasonably; taking proper action within a reasonably longer time may be seasonable but the bank has the burden of so establishing.

(3) Subject to subsection (1)(a), a bank is not liable for the insolvency, neglect, misconduct, mistake or default of another bank or person or for loss or destruction of an item in transit or in the possession of others.

Official Comment

Prior Uniform Statutory Provision: None; but see Sections 5 and 6, American Bankers Association Bank Collection Code.

Purposes:

1. Subsection (1) states the basic responsibilities of a collecting bank. Of course, under Section 1–203 a collecting bank is subject to the standard requirement of good faith. By subsection (1) it must also use ordinary care in the exercise of its basic collection tasks. By Section 4–103(1) neither requirement may be disclaimed.

2. If the bank makes presentment itself, subsection 1(a) requires ordinary care with respect both to the time and manner of presentment. (Sections 3–503, 3–504, 4–210.) If it forwards the item to be presented the subsection requires ordinary care with respect to routing (Section 4–204), and also in the selection of intermediary banks or other agents.

3. Subsection (1) describes *types* of basic action with respect to which a collecting bank must use ordinary care. Subsection (2) deals with the *time* for taking action. It first prescribes the general standard for seasonable action, namely, for items received on Monday, proper action (such as forwarding or presenting) on Monday or Tuesday is seasonable. Although under current "production line" operations banks customarily move items along on regular schedules substantially briefer than two days, the subsection states an outside time within which a bank may know it has acted seasonably. To provide flexibility from this standard norm, the subsection further states that action within a reasonably longer time may be seasonable but the bank has the burden of proof. In the case of time items, action after the midnight deadline, but sufficiently in advance of maturity for proper presentation, is a clear example of a "reasonably longer time" that is seasonable. The standard of requiring action not later than Tuesday in the case of Monday items is also subject to possibilities of variation under the general provisions of Section 4–103, or under the special provisions regarding time of receipt of items (Section 4–107), and regarding delays (Section 4–108). This subsection (2) deals only with collecting banks. The time limits applicable to payor banks appear in Sections 4–301 and 4–302.

4. At common law the so-called New York collection rule subjected the initial collecting bank to liability for the actions of subsequent banks in the collection chain; the so-called Massachusetts rule was that each bank, subject to the duty of selecting proper intermediaries, was liable only for its own negligence. Subsection (3) adopts the Massachusetts rule. But since this is stated to be subject to subsection (1)(a) a collecting bank remains responsible for using ordinary care in selecting properly qualified intermediary banks and agents and in giving proper instructions to them.

Cross References:

Sections 1-203, 4-103, 4-107, 4-108, 4-301, and 4-302.

Definitional Cross References:

"Collecting bank". Section 4-105.
"Depositary bank". Section 4-105.
"Documentary draft". Section 4-104.
"Item". Section 4-104.
"Midnight deadline". Section 4-104.
"Presentment". Article 3, Part 5.
"Protest". Section 3-509.

§ 4-203. Effect of Instructions.

Subject to the provisions of Article 3 concerning conversion of instruments (Section 3-419) and the provisions of both Article 3 and this Article concerning restrictive indorsements only a collecting bank's transferor can give instructions which affect the bank or constitute notice to it and a collecting bank is not liable to prior parties for any action taken pursuant to such instructions or in accordance with any agreement with its transferor.

Official Comment

Prior Uniform Statutory Provision: None; but see Section 2 of the American Bankers Association Bank Collection Code.

Purposes:

This Section adopts a "chain of command" theory which renders it unnecessary for an intermediary or collecting bank to determine whether its transferor is "authorized" to give the instructions. Equally the bank is not put on notice of any "revocation of authority" or "lack of authority" by notice received from any other person. The desirability of speed in the collection process and the fact that, by reason of advances made, the transferor may have the paramount interest in the item requires the rule.

The Section is made subject to the provisions of Article 3 concerning conversion of instruments (Section 3-419) and other provisions of Article 3 and this Article concerning restrictive indorsements (Sections 3-205, 3-206, 3-419, 3-603, 4-205). Of course instructions from or an agreement with its transferor does not relieve a collecting bank of its general obligation to exercise good faith and ordinary care. See Section 4-103(1). If in any particular case a bank has exercised good faith and ordinary care and is relieved of responsibility by reason of instructions of or an agreement with its transferor, the owner of the item may still have a remedy for loss against the transferor (another bank) if such transferor has given wrongful instructions.

The rules of the Section are applied only to collecting banks. Payor banks always have the problem of making proper payment of an item; whether such payment is proper should be based upon all of the rules of Articles 3 and 4 and all of the facts of any particular case, and should not be dependent exclusively upon instructions from or an agreement with a person presenting the item.

Cross References:

Sections 3-205, 3-206, 3-419, 3-603, 4-103(1) and 4-205.

Definitional Cross References:

"Collecting bank". Section 4-105.
"Restrictive indorsement". Section 3-205.

§ 4-204. Methods of Sending and Presenting; Sending Direct to Payor Bank.

(1) A collecting bank must send items by reasonably prompt method taking into consideration any relevant instructions, the nature of the item, the number of such items on hand, and the cost of collection involved and the method generally used by it or others to present such items.

(2) A collecting bank may send

(a) any item direct to the payor bank;

(b) any item to any non-bank payor if authorized by its transferor; and

(c) any item other than documentary drafts to any non-bank payor, if authorized by Federal Reserve regulation or operating letter, clearing house rule or the like.

(3) Presentment may be made by a presenting bank at a place where the payor bank has requested that presentment be made.

As amended in 1962.

Official Comment

Prior Uniform Statutory Provision: None; but see Section 6, American Bankers Association Bank Collection Code.

Purposes:

1. Subsection (1) prescribes the general standards applicable to proper sending or forwarding of items. Because of the many types of methods available and the desirability of preserving flexibility any attempt to prescribe limited or precise methods is avoided.

2. Subsection (2)(a) codifies the practice of direct mail, express, messenger or like presentment to payor banks. The practice is now country-wide and is justified by the need for speed, the general responsibility of banks, Federal Deposit Insurance protection and other reasons.

3. Full approval of the practice of direct sending is limited to cases where a bank is a payor. Where non-bank drawees or payors may be of unknown responsibility, substantial risks may be attached to placing in their hands the instruments calling for payments from them. This is obviously so in the case of documentary drafts. However, in some cities practices have long existed under clearing house procedures to forward certain types of items to certain non-bank payors. Examples include insurance loss drafts drawn by field agents on home offices. For the purpose of leaving the door open to legitimate practices of this kind, subsection (2)(c) affirmatively approves direct sending of any item other than documentary drafts to any non-bank payor, if authorized by Federal Reserve regulation or operating letter, clearing house rule or the like.

On the other hand subsection (2)(b) approves sending any item direct to a non-bank payor if authorized by a collecting bank's transferor. This permits special instructions or agreements out of the norm and is consistent with the "chain of command" theory of Section 4-203. However, if a transferor other than the owner of the item, e.g., a prior collecting bank, authorizes a direct sending to a non-bank payor, such transferor assumes responsibility for the propriety or impropriety of such authorization.

4. Section 3-504 states how presentment is made and subsection (2) of that Section affirmatively approves three spe-

cific methods by which presentment may be made. The methods so specified are permissive and do not foreclose other possible methods. However, in view of the substantial increase in recent years of presentment at centralized bookkeeping centers and electronic processing centers maintained or used by payor banks, many of which are at locations other than the banks themselves, subsection (3) specifically approves presentment by a presenting bank at any place requested by the payor bank. [This paragraph was added in 1962].

Cross References:

Sections 3–504, 4–501 and 4–502.

Definitional Cross References:

"Collecting bank". Section 4–105.
"Documentary draft". Section 4–104.
"Item". Section 4–104.
"Payor bank". Section 4–105.
"Presenting bank". Section 4–105.

§ 4–205. Supplying Missing Indorsement; No Notice from Prior Indorsement.

(1) A depositary bank which has taken an item for collection may supply any indorsement of the customer which is necessary to title unless the item contains the words "payee's indorsement required" or the like. In the absence of such a requirement a statement placed on the item by the depositary bank to the effect that the item was deposited by a customer or credited to his account is effective as the customer's indorsement.

(2) An intermediary bank, or payor bank which is not a depositary bank, is neither given notice nor otherwise affected by a restrictive indorsement of any person except the bank's immediate transferor.

Official Comment

Prior Uniform Statutory Provision: None.

Purposes:

1. Subsection (1) is designed to speed up collections by eliminating any necessity to return to a non-bank depositor any items he may have failed to indorse.

2. For the purpose of permitting items to move rapidly through banking channels, intermediary banks and payor banks which are not also depositary banks are permitted to ignore restrictive indorsements of any person except the bank's immediate transferor. However, depositary banks may not so ignore restrictive indorsements. If an owner of an item indorses it "for deposit" or "for collection" he usually does so in the belief such indorsement will guard against further negotiation of the item to a holder in due course by a finder or a thief. This belief is reasonably justified if at least one bank in any chain of banks collecting the item has a responsibility to act consistently with the indorsement.

Cross References:

Sections 3–205, 3–206, 3–419, 3–603 and 4–203.

Definitional Cross References:

"Collecting bank." Section 4–105.
"Customer." Section 4–104.
"Depositary bank". Section 4–105.
"Intermediary bank." Section 4–105.
"Item." Section 4–104.
"Payor bank." Section 4–105.
"Restrictive indorsement." Section 3–205.

§ 4–206. Transfer Between Banks.

Any agreed method which identifies the transferor bank is sufficient for the item's further transfer to another bank.

Official Comment

Prior Uniform Statutory Provision: None.

Purposes:

This section is designed to permit the simplest possible form of transfer from one bank to another, once an item gets in the bank collection chain, provided only identity of the transferor bank is preserved. This is important for tracing purposes and if recourse is necessary. However, since the responsibilities of the various banks appear in the Article it becomes unnecessary to have liability or responsibility depend on more formal indorsements. Simplicity in the form of transfer is conducive to speed. Where the transfer is between banks this section takes the place of the more formal requirements of Section 3-202.

Cross References:

Sections 3-201, 3-202.

Definitional Cross References:

"Bank". Section 1-201.
"Item". Section 4-104.

§ 4-207. Warranties of Customer and Collecting Bank on Transfer or Presentment of Items; Time for Claims.

(1) Each customer or collecting bank who obtains payment or acceptance of an item and each prior customer and collecting bank warrants to the payor bank or other payor who in good faith pays or accepts the item that

(a) he has a good title to the item or is authorized to obtain payment or acceptance on behalf of one who has a good title; and

(b) he has no knowledge that the signature of the maker or drawer is unauthorized, except that this warranty is not given by any customer or collecting bank that is a holder in due course and acts in good faith

(i) to a maker with respect to the maker's own signature; or

(ii) to a drawer with respect to the drawer's own signature, whether or not the drawer is also the drawee; or

(iii) to an acceptor of an item if the holder in due course took the item after the acceptance or obtained the acceptance without knowledge that the drawer's signature was unauthorized; and

(c) the item has not been materially altered, except that this warranty is not given by any customer or collecting bank that is a holder in due course and acts in good faith

(i) to the maker of a note; or

(ii) to the drawer of a draft whether or not the drawer is also the drawee; or

(iii) to the acceptor of an item with respect to an alteration made prior to the acceptance if the holder in due course took the item after the acceptance, even though the acceptance provided "payable as originally drawn" or equivalent terms; or

(iv) to the acceptor of an item with respect to an alteration made after the acceptance.

(2) Each customer and collecting bank who transfers an item and receives a settlement or other consideration for it warrants to his transferee and to any subsequent collecting bank who takes the item in good faith that

(a) he has a good title to the item or is authorized to obtain payment or acceptance on behalf of one who has a good title and the transfer is otherwise rightful; and

(b) all signatures are genuine or authorized; and

(c) the item has not been materially altered; and

(d) no defense of any party is good against him; and

(e) he has no knowledge of any insolvency proceeding instituted with respect to the maker or acceptor or the drawer of an unaccepted item.

In addition each customer and collecting bank so transferring an item and receiving a settlement or other consideration engages that upon dishonor and any necessary notice of dishonor and protest he will take up the item.

(3) The warranties and the engagement to honor set forth in the two preceding subsections arise notwithstanding the absence of indorsement or words of guaranty or warranty in the transfer or presentment and a collecting bank remains liable for their breach despite remittance to its transferor. Damages for breach of such warranties or engagement to honor shall not exceed the consideration received by the customer or collecting bank responsible plus finance charges and expenses related to the item, if any.

(4) Unless a claim for breach of warranty under this section is made within a reasonable time after the person claiming learns of the breach, the person liable is discharged to the extent of any loss caused by the delay in making claim.

Official Comment

Prior Uniform Statutory Provision: None; but see American Bankers Association Bank Collection Code, Section 4.

Purposes:

1. Subject to certain exceptions peculiar to the bank collection process and except that they apply only to customers and collecting banks, the warranties and engagements to honor in this section are identical in substance with those provided in the Article on Commercial Paper (Article 3). See Sections 3-414, 3-417. For a more complete explanation of the purposes of these warranties and engagements see the Comments to Sections 3-414 and 3-417.

2. In addition to imposing upon customers and collecting banks the warranties and engagements imposed by the original Sections 65 and 66 of the Uniform Negotiable Instruments Law and those of Sections 3-414 and 3-417 of Article 3, with some variations, this Section 4-207 is intended to give the effect presently obtained in bank collections by the words "prior indorsements guaranteed" in collection transfers and presentments between banks. The warranties and engagements arise automatically as a part of the bank collection process. Receipt of a settlement or other consideration by a customer or collecting bank is a requirement but any settlement is sufficient regardless of whether the settlement is concurrent with the transfer, as in the case of a cash item, or delayed, as in the case of a non-cash straight collection item. Further, the warranties and engagements run with the item with the result that a collecting bank may sue a remote prior collecting bank or a remote customer and thus avoid multiplicity of suits. This section is also intended to make it clear that the so-called equitable defense of "payment over" does not apply to a collecting bank and that no statute of frauds provision will defeat recovery. Subsections (2) and (3) indicate that these results are

intended notwithstanding the absence of indorsement or words of guarantee or warranty in a transfer or presentment. Consequently, if for purposes of simplification or the speeding up of the bank collection process, banks desire to cut down the length or size of indorsements (Section 4-206), they may do so and the standard warranties and engagements to honor still apply.

3. With respect to the exceptions to the warranties in favor of a holder in due course specified in sub-paragraphs (b) and (c) of subsection (1), collecting banks usually have holder in due course status (Sections 4-208, 4-209). However, if in any case there is a holder in due course but a subsequent collecting bank does not have holder in due course status (e.g., in a straight non-cash collection where no settlement of any kind is made until the bank itself receives final settlement) the bank still has the benefit of the exceptions (if it acts in good faith) under the shelter provisions of Section 3-201. It is to be noted that these shelter provisions, by virtue of successive transfers, benefit not only the immediate transferee from a holder in due course but also subsequent transferees.

4. In this section as in Section 3-417, the (a), (b) and (c) warranties to transferees and collecting banks under subsection (2) are in general similar to the (a), (b) and (c) warranties to payors under subsection (1); but the warranties to payors are less inclusive because of exceptions reflecting the rule of Price v. Neal, 3 Burr. 1354 (1762), and related principles. See Comment to Section 3-417. Thus collecting banks are given not only all the warranties given to payors by subsection (1), without those exceptions, but also the (d) and (e) warranties of subsection (2).

5. The last sentence of subsection (3) provides that damages for breach of warranties or the engagement to honor shall not exceed the consideration received by the customer or collecting bank responsible "plus finance charges and expenses related to the item, if any". The "expenses" referred to in this phrase may be ordinary collecting expenses and in appropriate cases could also include such expenses as attorneys fees. "Finance charges" are also referred to because in some cases interest or a finance charge is charged by the collecting bank for the time that the bank's advance on the item is outstanding prior to receipt of proceeds of collection. An example of this type of case would be where a bank undertakes a foreign collection in South America or Europe and makes an advance on the item at the time of receipt but may not receive proceeds of the foreign collection for three months or more.

Cross References:

Sections 3-201, 3-414, 3-417, 3-418, 4-206, 4-208, 4-209 and 4-406.

Definitional Cross References:

"Collecting bank". Section 4-105.
"Customer". Section 4-104.
"Draft". Section 3-104.
"Genuine". Section 1-201.
"Good faith". Section 1-201.
"Holder". Section 1-201.
"Holder in due course". Section 3-302.
"Insolvency proceedings". Section 1-201.
"Item". Section 4-104.
"Party". Section 1-201.
"Payor bank". Section 4-105.
"Person". Section 1-201.
"Presentment". Section 3-504.
"Protest". Section 3-509.
"Unauthorized signature". Section 1-201.

§ 4-208. Security Interest of Collecting Bank in Items, Accompanying Documents and Proceeds.

(1) A bank has a security interest in an item and any accompanying documents or the proceeds of either

(a) in case of an item deposited in an account to the extent to which credit given for the item has been withdrawn or applied;

(b) in case of an item for which it has given credit available for withdrawal as of right, to the extent of the credit given whether or not the credit is drawn upon and whether or not there is a right of charge-back; or

(c) if it makes an advance on or against the item.

(2) When credit which has been given for several items received at one time or pursuant to a single agreement is withdrawn or applied in part the security interest remains upon all the items, any accompanying documents or the proceeds of either. For the purpose of this section, credits first given are first withdrawn.

(3) Receipt by a collecting bank of a final settlement for an item is a realization on its security interest in the item, accompanying documents and proceeds. To the extent and so long as the bank does not receive final settlement for the item or give up possession of the item or accompanying documents for purposes other than collection, the security interest continues and is subject to the provisions of Article 9 except that

(a) no security agreement is necessary to make the security interest enforceable (subsection (1)(a) of Section 9-203); and

(b) no filing is required to perfect the security interest; and

(c) the security interest has priority over conflicting perfected security interests in the item, accompanying documents or proceeds.

Official Comment

Prior Uniform Statutory Provision: None; but see American Bankers Association Bank Collection Code, Section 2.

Purposes:

1. Subsection (1) states a rational rule for the interest of a bank in an item. The customer of the depositary bank is normally the owner of the item and the several collecting banks are his agents (Section 4-201). A collecting agent may properly make advances on the security of paper held by him for collection, and when he does acquires at common law a possessory lien for his advances. Subsection (1) applies an analogous principle to a bank in the collection chain which extends credit on items in the course of collection. The bank has a security interest to the extent stated in this section. To the extent of its security interest it is a holder for value (Sections 3-303, 4-209) and a holder in due course if it satisfies the other requirements for that status (Section 3-302). Subsection (1) does not derogate from the banker's general common-law lien or right of set-off against indebtedness owing in deposit accounts. See Section 1-103. Rather subsection (1) specifically implements and extends the principle as a part of the bank collection process.

2. Subsection (2) spreads the security interest of the bank over all items in a single deposit or received under a single agreement and a single giving of credit. It also adopts the "first-in, first-out" rule.

3. Collection statistics establish that in excess of ninety-nine per cent of items handled for collection are in fact collected. The first sentence of subsection (3) reflects the fact that in such normal case the bank's security interest is self-liquidating. The remainder of the subsection correlates the security interest with the provisions of Article 9, particularly for use in the cases of non-collection where the security interest may be important.

Cross References:

Sections 3-302, 3-303, 4-201, 4-209, 9-203(1)(b) and 9-302.

Definitional Cross References:

"Account". Section 4-104.
"Agreement". Section 1-201.
"Bank". Section 1-201.
"Item". Section 4-104.
"Security interest". Section 1-201.
"Settlement". Section 4-104.

§ 4-209. When Bank Gives Value for Purposes of Holder in Due Course.

For purposes of determining its status as a holder in due course, the bank has given value to the extent that it has a security interest in an item provided that the bank otherwise complies with the requirements of Section 3-302 on what constitutes a holder in due course.

Official Comment

Prior Uniform Statutory Provision: Negotiable Instruments Law, Section 27.

Purpose:

The section completes the thought of the previous section and makes clear that a security interest in an item is "value" for the purpose of determining the holder's status as a holder in due course. The provision is in accord with the prior law (N.I.L. Section 27) and with Article 3 (Section 3-303). The section does not prescribe a security interest under Section 4-208 as a test of "value" generally because the meaning of "value" under other Articles is adequately defined in Section 1-201.

Cross References:

Sections 1-201, 3-302, 3-303 and 4-208.

Definitional Cross References:

"Bank". Section 1-201.
"Holder in due course". Section 3-302.
"Item". Section 4-104.
"Security interest". Section 1-201.

§ 4-210. Presentment by Notice of Item Not Payable by, Through or at a Bank; Liability of Secondary Parties.

(1) Unless otherwise instructed, a collecting bank may present an item not payable by, through or at a bank by sending to the party to accept or pay a written notice that the bank holds the item for acceptance or payment. The notice must be sent in time to be received on or before the day when presentment is due and the bank must meet any requirement of the party to accept or pay under Section 3-505 by the close of the bank's next banking day after it knows of the requirement.

(2) Where presentment is made by notice and neither honor nor request for compliance with a requirement under Section 3-505 is received by the close of business on the day after maturity or in the case of demand items by the close of business on the third banking day after notice was sent, the presenting bank may treat the item as dishonored and charge any secondary party by sending him notice of the facts.

Official Comment

Prior Uniform Statutory Provision: None.

Purposes:

1. This section codifies a practice extensively followed in presentation of trade acceptances and documentary and other

drafts drawn on non-bank payors. It imposes a duty on the payor to respond to the notice of the item if the item is not to be considered dishonored. Notice of such a dishonor charges parties secondarily liable. Presentment under this Section is good presentment under Article 3. See Section 3-504(5).

2. A drawee not receiving notice is not, of course, liable to the drawer for wrongful dishonor.

3. A bank so presenting an instrument must be sufficiently close to the drawee to be able to exhibit the instrument on the day it is requested to do so or the next business day at the latest.

Cross References:

Sections 3-501 through 3-508, 4-501 and 4-502.

Definitional Cross References:

"Acceptance". Section 3-410.
"Banking day". Section 4-104.
"Collecting bank". Section 4-105.
"Item". Section 4-104.
"Party". Section 1-201.
"Presentment". Section 3-504.
"Secondary party". Section 3-102.
"Send". Section 1-201.

§ 4-211. Media of Remittance; Provisional and Final Settlement in Remittance Cases.

(1) A collecting bank may take in settlement of an item

(a) a check of the remitting bank or of another bank on any bank except the remitting bank; or

(b) a cashier's check or similar primary obligation of a remitting bank which is a member of or clears through a member of the same clearing house or group as the collecting bank; or

(c) appropriate authority to charge an account of the remitting bank or of another bank with the collecting bank; or

(d) if the item is drawn upon or payable by a person other than a bank, a cashier's check, certified check or other bank check or obligation.

(2) If before its midnight deadline the collecting bank properly dishonors a remittance check or authorization to charge on itself or presents or forwards for collection a remittance instrument of or on another bank which is of a kind approved by subsection (1) or has not been authorized by it, the collecting bank is not liable to prior parties in the event of the dishonor of such check, instrument or authorization.

(3) A settlement for an item by means of a remittance instrument or authorization to charge is or becomes a final settlement as to both the person making and the person receiving the settlement

(a) if the remittance instrument or authorization to charge is of a kind approved by subsection (1) or has not been authorized by the person receiving the settlement and in either case the person receiving the settlement acts seasonably before its midnight deadline in presenting, forwarding for collection or paying the instrument or authorization,—at the time the remittance instrument or authorization is finally paid by the payor by which it is payable;

(b) if the person receiving the settlement has authorized remittance by a non-bank check or obligation or by a cashier's check or similar primary obligation of or a check upon the payor or other remitting bank which is not of a kind approved by subsection (1)(b),—at the time of the receipt of such remittance check or obligation; or

(c) if in a case not covered by sub-paragraphs (a) or (b) the person receiving the settlement fails to seasonably present, forward for collection, pay or return a remittance instrument or authorization to it to charge before its midnight deadline,—at such midnight deadline.

Official Comment

Prior Uniform Statutory Provision: None; but see Sections 9 and 10, American Bankers Association Bank Collection Code.

Purposes:

1. Subsection (1) states various types of remittance instruments and authorities to charge which may be received by a collecting bank in a settlement for an item, without the collecting bank being responsible if such form of remittance is not itself paid. The action of the collecting bank in receiving these provisional forms of remittance is approved and the risk that they are not paid is placed on the owner of the item, and not on the collecting bank. Justification for these results lies in the fact that with the tremendous volume of items collected it is simply not mechanically feasible to remit or pay in money or other forms of technical "legal tender". Since it is not feasible for banks to perform their collection functions except with the use of these provisional remittances, they should not be penalized for acting in the only way they can act.

2. The first approved form of provisional remittance having these results is a check of the remitting bank or of another bank on any bank except the remitting bank (subsection (1)(a)). A check on the remitting bank itself is not approved because this would merely be substituting for the original item another item on the same payor.

3. A cashier's check or similar primary obligation of the remitting bank which is a member of or clears through a member of the same clearing house or group as the collecting bank is approved by subsection (1)(b) because this is just as speedy and effective a means of settlement through a clearing house as any other type of instrument or a check on another bank. On the other hand such cashier's checks or primary obligations are not approved for use, at the owner's risk, outside a single clearing house or clearing area because when so used they do not constitute a means of final settlement but merely substitute one item on the remitting bank for another one on the same bank. To the remitting bank they may have benefit in maintaining "float" or having the use of money even though drawn against, but this is not looked upon as sound practice.

4. Subsection (1)(d) recognizes and approves the general and consistent practice of collecting banks to accept cashier's checks, certified checks or other bank checks or obligations as a proper means of remittance from non-bank payors, with the owner of the original item carrying the risk of non-payment of these bank instruments rather than the collecting bank, to the extent there is any risk. Here again this rule and practice is justified by the fact that payment in money for all practical purposes is no longer feasible and consequently is not used except in rare instances. Subsection (1)(d) recognizes the standard medium that is used.

5. This section does not purport to deal with all kinds of settlements for items. It does not purport to deal with settlements for "cash items" (described in Comments to Section 4-212), settlements merely by debits and credits in accounts between banks (Section 4-213) or settlements through clearing houses. The section is limited to those situations where a collecting or payor bank or a non-bank payor receives an item and ac-

counts for it by "remitting" or "sending back" something for the item, usually some form of a remittance instrument, order or authorization. Some specific rules are needed for remittance cases because of time required to process the remittance instrument.

Failure to mention in subsection (1) entries in accounts between banks and clearing house settlements carries no implication of impropriety of these types of provisional or final settlement. Approval of these means of settlement is evidenced by the definition of "settle" in Section 4–104(j), provision for charge-back and refund in Section 4–212, and provisions regarding settlements becoming final (Section 4–213). Further, the specific listing in subsection (1) of certain usual types of remittances does not imply that all other types of remittances are improper (Section 4–103(4)).

6. Subsection (2) provides that if a remittance is one of the kinds approved by subsection (1) and the collecting bank receiving the item acts seasonably in handling it before the bank's midnight deadline, the bank is not liable to prior parties in the event of dishonor. The subsection also provides for an additional situation. If without any authorization whatsoever the payor or remitting bank or person remits with an improper remittance instrument, the collecting bank should not be penalized where it is without fault. Nevertheless, the owner of the item may not be served if the collecting bank rejects the improper instrument. In many cases the best course would be to collect the instrument as rapidly as possible. Subsection (2) provides that if this is done the collecting bank is not responsible in the event of dishonor.

7. Subsection (3) complements subsections (1) and (2) by providing when a settlement by means of a remittance instrument or authorization to charge becomes final. Subparagraph (a) provides that in situations specified in subsection (2) the settlement becomes final at the time the remittance instrument or authorization is finally paid by the payor by which it is payable. The standards determining this final payment are those prescribed in Section 4–213. Conversely, under subparagraph (b) if the person receiving the settlement has authorized remittance by certain specified media not approved by subsection (1) the settlement becomes final at the time of receipt of such check or obligation. In this event the person receiving the settlement assumes the risk that the remittance instrument is not itself paid. A prior course of dealing of receiving unapproved forms of remittances from the payor or remitting person in question would be the equivalent of an authorization and effective as such. Subparagraph (c) provides for most, if not all, remaining remittance situations. Here settlement becomes final at the midnight deadline of the person receiving the remittance.

Subsection (3) provides that the times of final settlement prescribed apply both to the person making and the person receiving the settlement. Further, by use of the term "person", these rules also apply to non-bank payors of items and non-bank customers for whom items are being collected, as well as to collecting and payor banks.

8. When settlement is by credit in an account with another bank Section 4–213 controls.

Cross Reference:

Section 4–213.

Definitional Cross References:

"Account". Section 4–104.
"Bank". Section 1–201.
"Clearing house". Section 4–104.
"Collecting bank". Section 4–105.
"Item". Section 4–104.
"Midnight deadline". Section 4–104.
"Money". Section 1–201.
"Payor bank." Section 4–105.
"Person". Section 1–201.
"Remitting bank". Section 4–105.
"Settle". Section 4–104.

§ 4–212. Right of Charge-Back or Refund.

(1) If a collecting bank has made provisional settlement with its customer for an item and itself fails by reason of dishonor, suspension of payments by a bank or otherwise to receive a settlement for the item which is or becomes final, the bank may revoke the settlement given by it, charge back the amount of any credit given for the item to its customer's account or obtain refund from its customer whether or not it is able to return the items if by its midnight deadline or within a longer reasonable time after it learns the facts it returns the item or sends notification of the facts. These rights to revoke, charge-back and obtain refund terminate if and when a settlement for the item received by the bank is or becomes final (subsection (3) of Section 4–211 and subsections (2) and (3) of Section 4–213).

[(2) Within the time and manner prescribed by this section and Section 4–301, an intermediary or payor bank, as the case may be, may return an unpaid item directly to the depositary bank and may send for collection a draft on the depositary bank and obtain reimbursement. In such case, if the depositary bank has received provisional settlement for the item, it must reimburse the bank drawing the draft and any provisional credits for the item between banks shall become and remain final.]

Note: *Direct returns is recognized as an innovation that is not yet established bank practice, and therefore, Paragraph 2 has been bracketed. Some lawyers have doubts whether it should be included in legislation or left to development by agreement.*

(3) A depositary bank which is also the payor may charge-back the amount of an item to its customer's account or obtain refund in accordance with the section governing return of an item received by a payor bank for credit on its books. (Section 4–301).

(4) The right to charge-back is not affected by

(a) prior use of the credit given for the item; or

(b) failure by any bank to exercise ordinary care with respect to the item but any bank so failing remains liable.

(5) A failure to charge-back or claim refund does not affect other rights of the bank against the customer or any other party.

(6) If credit is given in dollars as the equivalent of the value of an item payable in a foreign currency the dollar amount of any charge-back or refund shall be calculated on the basis of the buying sight rate for the foreign currency prevailing on the day when the person entitled to the charge-back or refund learns that it will not receive payment in ordinary course.

Official Comment

Prior Uniform Statutory Provision: None; but see Sections 2 and 11, American Bankers Association Bank Collection Code.

Purposes:

1. Under current bank practice, in a major portion of cases banks make provisional settlement for items when they are first received and then await subsequent determination of whether the item will be finally paid. This is the principal charac-

teristic of what are referred to in banking parlance as "cash items". Statistically, this practice of settling provisionally first and then awaiting final payment is justified because more than ninety-nine per cent of such cash items are finally paid, with the result that in this great preponderance of cases it becomes unnecessary for the banks making the provisional settlements to make any further entries. In due course the provisional settlements become final simply with the lapse of time. However, in those cases where the item being collected is not finally paid or where for various reasons the bank making the provisional settlement does not itself receive final payment, under the American Bankers Association Bank Collection Code, under Federal Reserve Regulations and operating letters and under various types of agreements between banks and between customers and banks, provision is made for the reversal of the provisional settlements, charge-back of provisional credits and the right to obtain refund. Subsection (1) codifies and simplifies the statement of these rights.

2. Various causes of a bank not receiving final payment, with the resulting right of charge-back or refund, are stated or suggested in subsection (1). These include dishonor of the original item; dishonor of a remittance instrument given for it; reversal of a provisional credit for the item; suspension of payments by another bank. The causes stated are illustrative; the right of charge-back or refund is stated to exist whether the failure to receive final payment in ordinary course arises through one of them "or otherwise".

3. The right of charge-back or refund exists if a collecting bank has made a provisional settlement for an item with its customer but terminates if and when a settlement received by the bank for the item is or becomes final. If the bank fails to receive such a final settlement the right of charge-back or refund must be exercised promptly after the bank learns the facts. The right exists (if so promptly exercised) whether or not the bank is able to return the item.

4. Subsection (2) is an affirmative provision for so-called "direct returns". This is a new practice that is currently in the process of developing in a few sections of the country. Its purpose is to speed up the return of unpaid items by avoiding handling by one or more intermediate banks. The subsection is bracketed because the practice is not yet well established and some bankers and bank lawyers would prefer to let the practice develop by agreement. The contention is made that substantive rights between banks may be affected, e.g. available set-offs, but proponents contend advantages of direct returns outweigh possible detriments. However, if the subsection were omitted, the election to use direct returns would be on the depositary bank and it would probably be necessary for that bank to specifically authorize direct returns with each outgoing letter. This is a cumbersome way of meeting the problem. If the subsection is retained the payor bank, unless it has been specifically directed otherwise, will have the right to make the decision whether it will return an unpaid item directly. Since the subsection is permissive and its inclusion tends toward greater flexibility, its retention is recommended.

5. The rule of subsection (4) relating to charge-back (as distinguished from claim for refund) applies irrespective of the cause of the nonpayment, and of the person ultimately liable for nonpayment. Thus charge-back is permitted even where nonpayment results from the depositary bank's own negligence. Any other rule would result in litigation based upon a claim for wrongful dishonor of other checks of the customer, with potential damages far in excess of the amount of the item. Any other rule would require a bank to determine difficult questions of fact. The customer's protection is found in the general obligation of good faith (Sections 1-203 and 4-103). If bad faith is established the customer's recovery "includes other damages, if any, suffered by the party as a proximate consequence" (Section 4-103(5); see also Section 4-402).

6. It is clear that the charge-back does not relieve the bank from any liability for failure to exercise ordinary care in handling the item. The measure of damages for such failure is stated in Section 4-103(5).

7. Subsection (6) states a rule fixing the time for determining the rate of exchange if there is a charge-back or refund of a credit given in dollars for an item payable in a foreign currency. Compare Section 3-107(2). Fixing such a rule is desirable to avoid disputes. If in any case the parties wish to fix a different time for determining the rate of exchange, they may do so by agreement.

Cross References:

Sections 1-203, 3-107, 4-103, 4-211(3), 4-213(2) and (3), 4-402.

Definitional Cross References:

"Account". Section 4-104.
"Collecting bank". Section 4-105.
"Customer". Section 4-104.
"Depositary bank". Section 4-105.
"Intermediary bank". Section 4-105.
"Item". Section 4-104.
"Midnight deadline". Section 4-104.
"Payor bank". Section 4-105.
"Send". Section 1-201.
"Settlement". Section 4-104.
"Suspension of payment". Section 4-104.

§ 4-213. Final Payment of Item by Payor Bank; When Provisional Debits and Credits Become Final; When Certain Credits Become Available for Withdrawal.

(1) An item is finally paid by a payor bank when the bank has done any of the following, whichever happens first:

(a) paid the item in cash; or

(b) settled for the item without reserving a right to revoke the settlement and without having such right under statute, clearing house rule or agreement; or

(c) completed the process of posting the item to the indicated account of the drawer, maker or other person to be charged therewith; or

(d) made a provisional settlement for the item and failed to revoke the settlement in the time and manner permitted by statute, clearing house rule or agreement.

Upon a final payment under subparagraphs (b), (c) or (d) the payor bank shall be accountable for the amount of the item.

(2) If provisional settlement for an item between the presenting and payor banks is made through a clearing house or by debits or credits in an account between them, then to the extent that provisional debits or credits for the item are entered in accounts between the presenting and payor banks or between the presenting and successive prior collecting banks seriatim, they become final upon final payment of the item by the payor bank.

(3) If a collecting bank receives a settlement for an item which is or becomes final (subsection (3) of Section 4-211, subsection (2) of Section 4-213) the bank is accountable to its customer for the amount of the item and any provisional credit given for the item in an account with its customer becomes final.

(4) Subject to any right of the bank to apply the credit to an obligation of the customer, credit given by a bank for an item in an account with its customer becomes available for withdrawal as of right

(a) in any case where the bank has received a provisional settlement for the item,—when such settlement becomes final and the bank has had a reasonable time to learn that the settlement is final;

(b) in any case where the bank is both a depositary bank and a payor bank and the item is finally paid,—at the opening of the bank's second banking day following receipt of the item.

(5) A deposit of money in a bank is final when made but, subject to any right of the bank to apply the deposit to an obligation of the customer, the deposit becomes available for withdrawal as of right at the opening of the bank's next banking day following receipt of the deposit.

Official Comment

Prior Uniform Statutory Provision: None; but see Section 11, American Bankers Association Bank Collection Code.

Purposes:

1. By the definition and use of the term "settle" (Section 4–104(j)) this Article recognizes that various debits or credits, remittances, settlements or payments given for an item may be either provisional or final, that settlements sometimes are provisional and sometimes are final and sometimes are provisional for awhile but later become final. Subsection (1) of Section 4–213 defines when settlement for an item or other action with respect to it constitutes final payment.

Final payment of an item is important for a number of reasons. It is one of several factors determining the relative priorities between items and notices, stop-orders, legal process and set-offs (Section 4–303). It is the "end of the line" in the collection process and the "turn around" point commencing the return flow of proceeds. It is the point at which many provisional settlements become final. See Section 4–213(2). Final payment of an item by the payor bank fixes preferential rights under Section 4–214(1) and (2).

2. If an item being collected moves through several states, e.g., is deposited for collection in California, moves through two or three California banks to the Federal Reserve Bank of San Francisco, to the Federal Reserve Bank of Boston, to a payor bank in Maine, the collection process involves the eastward journey of the item from California to Maine and the westward journey of the proceeds from Maine to California. Subsection (1) adopts the basic policy that final payment occurs at some point in the processing of the item by the payor bank. This policy recognizes that final payment does not take place, in such hypothetical case, on the journey of the item eastward. It also adopts the view that neither does final payment occur on the journey westward because what in fact is journeying westward are *proceeds* of the item. Because the true tests of final payment are the same in all cases and to avoid the confusion resulting from variable standards, the rule basing final payment exclusively on action of the payor bank is not affected by whether payment is made by a remittance draft or whether such draft is itself paid. Consequently, subsection (1) rejects those cases which base time of payment of the item in remittance cases on whether the remittance draft was *accepted* by the presenting bank; Page v. Holmes-Darst Coal Co., 269 Mich. 159, 256 N.W. 840 (1934); Tobiason v. First State Bank of Ashby, 173 Minn. 533, 217 N.W. 934 (1928); Bohlig v. First Nat. Bank in Wadena, 233 Minn. 523, 48 N.W.2d 445 (1951); Dewey v. Margolis & Brooks, 195 N.C. 307, 142 S.E. 22 (1928); Texas Electric Service Co. v. Clark, 47 S.W.2d 483 (Tex.Civ.App.1932); cf. Ellis Way Drug Co. v. McLean, 176 Miss. 830, 170 So. 288 (1936); 2 Paton's Digest 1332; or whether the remittance draft was itself *paid*; Cleve v. Craven Chemical

Co., 18 F.2d 711 (4th Cir. 1927); Holdingford Milling Co. v. Hillman Farmers' Co-operative Creamery, 181 Minn. 212, 231 N.W. 928 (1930); or upon an election of a collecting bank under Section 11 of the American Bankers Association Bank Collection Code; United States Pipe & Foundry Co. v. City of Hornell, 146 Misc. 812, 263 N.Y.S. 89 (1933); Jones v. Board of Education, 242 App.Div. 17, 272 N.Y.S. 5 (1934); Matter of State Bank of Binghamton, 156 Misc. 353, 281 N.Y.S. 706 (1935); cf. Malcolm, Inc. v. Burlington City Loan & Trust Co., 115 N.J.Eq. 227, 170 A. 32 (1934). Of course, the time of payment of the remittance draft will be governed by subsection (1) but payment or nonpayment of the remittance draft will not change the time of payment of the original item.

3. In fixing the point of time within the payor bank when an item is finally paid, subsection (1) recognizes and is framed on the basis that in a payor bank an item goes through a series of processes before its handling is completed. The item is received first from the clearing house or over the counter or through the mail. When received over the counter, the bank may receipt for it in some way by making a notation in the customer's passbook or by receipting a duplicate deposit slip. After the initial receipt the item moves to the sorting and proving departments. When sorted and proved it may be photographed. Still later it moves to the bookkeeping department where it is examined for form and signature and compared against the ledger account of the customer to whom it is to be charged. If it is in good form and there are funds to cover it, it is posted to the drawer's account, either immediately or at a later time. If paid, it is so marked and filed with other items of the same customer. This process may take either a few hours or substantially all of the day of receipt and of the next banking day.

Within this period of processing by the payor bank subsection (1) first recognizes two types of overt external acts constituting final payment. Traditionally and under various decisions payment in cash of an item by a payor bank has been considered final payment. Chambers v. Miller, 13 C.B.N.S. 125 (Eng.1862); Fidelity & Casualty Co. of New York v. Planenscheck, 200 Wis. 304, 309, 227 N.W. 387, 389, 71 A.L.R. 331 (1929); see Bellevue Bank of Allen Kimberly & Co. v. Security Nat. Bank of Sioux City, 168 Iowa 707, 712, 150 N.W. 1076, 1077 (1915); 1 Paton's Digest 1066. Subsection (1)(a) first recognizes and provides that payment of an item in cash by a payor bank is final payment.

4. Section 4-104(j) defines "settle" as meaning "to pay in cash, by clearing house settlement, in a charge or credit or by remittance, or otherwise as instructed. A settlement may be either provisional or final;" Subsection (1)(b) of Section 4-213 provides that an item is finally paid by a payor bank when the bank has "settled for the item without reserving a right to revoke the settlement and without having such right under statute, clearing house rule or agreement". Subsection (1)(b) provides in effect that if the payor bank finally settles for an item this constitutes final payment of the item. The subsection operates if nothing has occurred and no situation exists making the settlement provisional. If at the time of settlement the payor bank reserves a right to revoke the settlement, the settlement is provisional. In the alternative, if under statute, clearing house rule or agreement, a right of revocation of the settlement exists the settlement is provisional. Conversely, if there is an absence of a reservation of the right to revoke and also an absence of a right to revoke under statute, clearing house rule or agreement, the settlement is final and such final settlement constitutes final payment of the item.

A primary example of a statutory right on the part of the payor bank to revoke a settlement is the right to revoke conferred by Section 4-301. The underlying theory and reason for deferred posting statutes (Section 4-301) is to require a settlement on the date of receipt of an item but to keep that settlement provisional with the right to revoke prior to the midnight deadline. In any case where Section 4-301 is applicable, any settlement by the payor bank is provisional solely by virtue of the statute, subsection (1)(b) of Section 4-213 does not operate and such provisional settlement does not constitute final payment of the item.

A second important example of a right to revoke a settlement is that arising under clearing house rules. It is very common for clearing house rules to provide that items exchanged and settled for in a clearing, (e.g., before 10:00 a.m. on Monday) may be returned and the settlements revoked up to but not later than 2:00 p.m. on the same day (Monday) or under deferred posting at some hour on the next business day (e.g., 2:00 p.m. Tuesday). Under this type of rule the Monday morning settlement is provisional and being provisional does not constitute a final payment of the item.

An example of a reservation of a right to revoke a settlement is where the payor bank is also the depositary bank and has signed a receipt or duplicate deposit ticket or has made an entry in a passbook acknowledging receipt, for credit to the account of A, of a check drawn on it by B. If the receipt, deposit ticket, passbook or other agreement with A is to the effect that any credit so entered is provisional and may be revoked pending the time required by the payor bank to process the item to determine if it is in good form and there are funds to cover it, such reservation or agreement keeps the receipt or credit provisional and avoids it being either final settlement or final payment.

In other ways the payor bank may keep settlements provisional: by general or special agreement with the presenting party or bank; by simple reservation at the time the settlement is made; or otherwise. Thus a payor bank (except in the case of statutory provisions) has control whether a settlement made by it is provisional or final, by participating in general agreements or clearing house rules or by special agreement or reservation. If it fails to keep a settlement provisional and if no applicable statute keeps the settlement provisional, its settlement is final and, unless the item had previously been paid by one of the other methods prescribed in subsection (1), such final settlement constitutes final payment. In this manner payor banks may without difficulty avoid the effect of such cases as: Cohen v. First Nat. Bank of Nogales, 22 Ariz. 394, 400, 198 P. 122, 124, 15 A.L.R. 701 (1921); Briviesca v. Coronado, 19 Cal.2d 244, 120 P.2d 649 (1941); White Brokerage Co. v. Cooperman, 207 Minn. 239, 290 N.W. 790 (1940); Scotts Bluff County v. First Nat. Bank of Gering, 115 Neb. 273, 212 N.W. 617 (1927); Provident Savings Bank & Trust Co. v. Hildebrand, 49 Ohio App. 207, 196 N.E. 790, 791 (1934); Schaer v. First Nat. Bank of Brenham, 132 Tex. 499, 124 S.W.2d 108 (1939) (bill of exchange); Union State Bank of Lancaster v. Peoples State Bank of Lancaster, 192 Wis. 28, 33, 211 N.W. 931, 933 (1927); 1 Paton's Digest 1067.

5. If a payor bank has not previously paid an item in cash or finally settled for it, certain internal acts or procedures will produce final payment of the item. Exclusive of the external acts of payment in cash or final settlement, the key point at which the decision of the bank to pay or dishonor is made is when the bookkeeper for the drawer's account determines or verifies that the check is in good form and that there are sufficient funds in the drawer's account to cover it. Previous steps in the processing of an item are preliminary to this vital step and in no way indicate a decision to pay. However, a more tangible measuring point is desirable than a mere examination of the account of the person to be charged. The mechanical step that usually indicates that the examination has been completed and the decision to pay has been made is the posting of the item to the account to be charged. Therefore, subsection (1)(c) adopts as the third measuring point the completion of the process of posting. The phrase "completed the process of posting" is used rather than simple "posting" because under current machine operations posting is a process and something more than simply making entries on the customer's ledger. Subsection (1) follows

fairly closely the New York statute, 37 McKinney's Consolidated Laws of New York, Negotiable Instruments, Art. 19-A, Sec. 350-b as amended by L.1950, C. 153, Sec. 1. However, subsections (1)(a) and (b) furnish more precise rules for determining "final settlement" by the payor bank than does the New York statute in using the term "irrevocable credit", the definition of which is not helpful.

6. Subsection (1)(d) covers the situation where the payor bank makes a provisional settlement for an item, which settlement becomes final at a later time by reason of the failure of the payor bank to revoke it in the time and manner permitted by statute, clearing house rule or agreement. An example of this type of situation is the clearing house settlement referred to in Comment 4. In the illustration there given if the time limit for the return of items received in the Monday morning clearing is 2:00 p.m. on Tuesday and the provisional settlement has not been revoked at that time in a manner permitted by the clearing house rules, the provisional settlement made on Monday morning becomes final at 2:00 p.m. on Tuesday. Subsection (1)(d) provides specifically that in this situation the item is finally paid at 2:00 p.m. Tuesday. If on the other hand a payor bank receives an item in the mail on Monday and makes some provisional settlement for the item on Monday, it has until midnight on Tuesday to return the item or give notice and revoke any settlement under Section 4-301. In this situation subsection (1)(d) of Section 4-213 provides that if the provisional settlement made on Monday is not revoked before midnight on Tuesday as permitted by Section 4-301, the item is finally paid at midnight on Tuesday even if the process of posting the item to the account of the drawer has not been completed at that time.

7. Subsection (1) provides that an item is finally paid by the payor bank when any one of the four events set forth in subparagraphs (a), (b), (c) and (d) have occurred, whichever happens first, and then provides that upon a final payment under subparagraphs (b), (c) or (d) the payor bank shall be accountable for the amount of the item. It is not made accountable if it has paid the item in cash because such payment is itself a sufficient accounting. The term "accountable" is used as imposing a duty to account, which duty is met if and when a settlement for the item satisfactorily clears. The fact that determination of the time of final payment is based exclusively upon action of the payor bank is not detrimental to the interests of owners of items or collecting banks because of the general obligations of payors to honor or dishonor and the time limits for action imposed by Sections 4-301 and 4-302.

8. Subsection (2) states the countrywide usage that when the item is finally paid by the payor bank under subsection (1) this final payment automatically without further action "firms up" other provisional settlements made for it. However, the subsection makes clear that this "firming up" occurs only where the settlement between the presenting and payor banks was made either through a clearing house or by debits and credits in accounts between them. It does not take place where the payor bank remits for the item with some form of remittance instrument. Further, the "firming up" continues only to the extent that provisional debits and credits are entered seriatim in accounts between banks which are successive to the presenting bank. The automatic "firming up" is broken at any time that any collecting bank remits for the item with a remittance draft, because final payment to the remittee then usually depends upon final payment of the remittance draft.

9. Subsection (3) states the general rule that if a collecting bank receives settlement for an item which is or becomes final, the bank is accountable to its customer for the amount of the item. One means of accounting is to remit to its customer the amount it has received on the item. If previously it gave to its customer a provisional credit for the item in an account its receipt of final settlement for the item "firms up" this provisional credit and makes it final. When

this credit given by it so becomes final, in the usual case its agency status terminates and it becomes a debtor to its customer for the amount of the item. See Section 4-201(1). If the accounting is by a remittance instrument or authorization to charge further time will usually be required to complete its accounting (Section 4-211).

10. Subsection (4) states when certain credits given by a bank to its customer become available for withdrawal as of right. Subsection (4)(a) deals with the situation where a bank has given a credit (usually provisional) for an item to its customer and in turn has received a provisional settlement for the item from an intermediary or payor bank to which it has forwarded the item. In this situation before the provisional credit entered by the collecting bank in the account of its customer becomes available for withdrawal as of right, it is not only necessary that the provisional settlement received by the bank for the item becomes final but also that the collecting bank has a reasonable time to learn that this is so. Hence, subsection (4)(a) imposes both of these conditions. If the provisional settlement received is a provisional debit or credit in an account with the intermediary or payor bank or a remittance instrument on some bank other than the collecting bank itself, the collecting bank will usually learn that this debit or credit is final or that the remittance instrument has been paid merely by not learning the opposite within a reasonable time. How much time is "reasonable" for these purposes will of course depend on the distance the item has to travel and the number of banks through which it must pass (having in mind not only travel time by regular lines of transmission but also the successive midnight deadlines of the several banks) and other pertinent facts. Also, if the provisional settlement received is some form of a remittance instrument or authorization to charge, the "reasonable" time depends on the identity and location of the payor of the remittance instrument, the means for clearing such instrument and other pertinent facts.

11. Subsection (4)(b) deals with the situation of a bank which is both a depositary bank and a payor bank. The subsection recognizes that where A and B are both customers of a depositary-payor bank and A deposits B's check on the depositary-payor in A's account on Monday, time must be allowed to permit the check under the deferred posting rules of Section 4-301 to reach the bookkeeper for B's account at some time on Tuesday, and if there are insufficient funds in B's account to reverse or charge back the provisional credit in A's account. Consequently this provisional credit in A's account does not become available for withdrawal as of right until the opening of business on Wednesday. If it is determined on Tuesday that there are insufficient funds in B's account to pay the check the credit to A's account can be reversed on Tuesday. On the other hand if the item is in fact paid on Tuesday, the rule of subsection (4)(b) is desirable to avoid uncertainty and possible disputes between the bank and its customer as to exactly what hour within the day the credit is available.

12. Subsection (5) recognizes that even when A makes a deposit of cash in his account on Monday it takes some period of time to record that cash deposit and communicate it to A's bookkeeper (the bookkeeper handling A's account) so that A's bookkeeper has a record of it when she considers whether there are available funds to pay A's check. Where as indicated in Comment 5 A's bookkeeper is the particular employee in the bank to determine, in most cases and subject to supervisory control, whether the item may be paid, the effectiveness of a deposit of cash as a basis for paying a check must of necessity rest upon when the record of that deposit reaches such bookkeeper rather than when it passes through the teller's window. Consequently, although the bank is charged with responsibility for cash deposited from the moment it is received on Monday the cash is not effective as a basis for paying checks until the opening of business on Tuesday.

Cross References:

Sections 3-418, 4-107, 4-201, 4-211, 4-212, 4-214, 4-301, 4-302, and 4-303.

Definitional Cross References:

"Account". Section 4-104.
"Agreement". Section 1-201.
"Banking day". Section 4-104.
"Clearing house". Section 4-104.
"Collecting bank". Section 4-105.
"Customer". Section 4-104.
"Depositary bank". Section 4-105.
"Item". Section 4-104.
"Money". Section 1-201.
"Notice". Section 1-201.
"Payor bank". Section 4-105.
"Presenting bank". Section 4-105.
"Settlement". Section 4-104.

§ 4-214. Insolvency and Preference.

(1) Any item in or coming into the possession of a payor or collecting bank which suspends payment and which item is not finally paid shall be returned by the receiver, trustee or agent in charge of the closed bank to the presenting bank or the closed bank's customer.

(2) If a payor bank finally pays an item and suspends payments without making a settlement for the item with its customer or the presenting bank which settlement is or becomes final, the owner of the item has a preferred claim against the payor bank.

(3) If a payor bank gives or a collecting bank gives or receives a provisional settlement for an item and thereafter suspends payments, the suspension does not prevent or interfere with the settlement becoming final if such finality occurs automatically upon the lapse of certain time or the happening of certain events (subsection (3) of Section 4-211, subsections (1)(d), (2) and (3) of Section 4-213).

(4) If a collecting bank receives from subsequent parties settlement for an item which settlement is or becomes final and suspends payments without making a settlement for the item with its customer which is or becomes final, the owner of the item has a preferred claim against such collecting bank.

Official Comment

Prior Uniform Statutory Provision: None; but see Section 13, American Bankers Association Bank Collection Code.

Purposes:

1. The underlying purpose of the provisions of this section is not to confer upon banks, holders of items or anyone else preferential positions in the event of bank failures over general depositors or any other creditors of the failed banks. The purpose is to fix as definitely as possible the cut-off point of time for the completion or cessation of the collection process in the case of items that happen to be in such process at the time a particular bank suspends payments. It must be remembered that in bank collections as a whole and in the handling of items by an individual bank, items go through a whole series of processes. It must also be remembered that at any particular point of time a particular bank (at least one of any size) is functioning as a depositary bank for some items, as an intermediary bank for others, as a presenting bank for still others and as a payor bank for still others, and that when it suspends payments it will have close to its normal load of items working through its various processes. For the convenience of receivers, owners of items, banks, and in fact substantially everyone concerned, it is recognized that at the particular moment of time that a bank suspends payment, a certain portion of the items being handled by it have progressed far enough in the

bank collection process that it is preferable to permit them to continue the remaining distance, rather than to send them back and reverse the many entries that have been made or the steps that have been taken with respect to them. Therefore, having this background and these purposes in mind, the section states what items must be turned backward at the moment suspension intervenes and what items have progressed far enough that the collection process with respect to them continues, with the resulting necessary statement of rights of various parties flowing from this prescription of the cut-off time.

2. The rules stated are similar to those stated in the American Bankers Association Bank Collection Code, but with the abandonment of any theory of trust. Although for practical purposes Federal Deposit Insurance affects materially the result of bank failures on holders of items and banks, no attempt is made to vary the rules of the section by reason of such insurance.

3. It is recognized that in view of Jennings v. United States Fidelity & Guaranty Co., 294 U.S. 216, 55 S.Ct. 394, 79 L.Ed. 869, 99 A.L.R. 1248 (1935), amendment of the National Bank Act would be necessary to have this section apply to national banks. But there is no reason why it should not apply to others. See Section 1-108.

Cross References:

Sections 1-108, 4-211(3) and 4-213.

Definitional Cross References:

"Collecting bank". Section 4-105.
"Customer". Section 4-104.
"Item". Section 4-104.
"Payor bank". Section 4-105.
"Presenting bank". Section 4-105.
"Settlement". Section 4-104.
"Suspends payment". Section 4-104.

PART 3

COLLECTION OF ITEMS: PAYOR BANKS

§ 4-301. Deferred Posting; Recovery of Payment by Return of Items; Time of Dishonor.

(1) Where an authorized settlement for a demand item (other than a documentary draft) received by a payor bank otherwise than for immediate payment over the counter has been made before midnight of the banking day of receipt the payor bank may revoke the settlement and recover any payment if before it has made final payment (subsection (1) of Section 4-213) and before its midnight deadline it

(a) returns the item; or

(b) sends written notice of dishonor or nonpayment if the item is held for protest or is otherwise unavailable for return.

(2) If a demand item is received by a payor bank for credit on its books it may return such item or send notice of dishonor and may revoke any credit given or recover the amount thereof withdrawn by its customer, if it acts within the time limit and in the manner specified in the preceding subsection.

(3) Unless previous notice of dishonor has been sent an item is dishonored at the time when for purposes of dishonor it is returned or notice sent in accordance with this section.

(4) An item is returned:

(a) as to an item received through a clearing house, when it is delivered to the presenting or last collecting bank or to the clearing house or is sent or delivered in accordance with its rules; or

(b) in all other cases, when it is sent or delivered to the bank's customer or transferor or pursuant to his instructions.

Official Comment

Prior Uniform Statutory Provision: None; but see American Bankers Association Model Deferred Posting Statute.

Purposes:

1. Deferred posting and delayed returns is that practice whereby a payor bank sorts and proves items received by it on the day they are received, e.g. Monday, but does not post the items to the customer's account or return "not good" items until the next day, e.g. Tuesday. The practice typifies "production line" methods currently used in bank collection and is based upon the necessity of an even flow of items through payor banks on a day by day basis in a manner which can be handled evenly by employee personnel without abnormal peak load periods, night work, and other practices objectionable to personnel. Since World War II statutes authorizing deferred posting and delayed returns have been passed in almost all of the forty-eight states. This section codifies the content of these statutes and approves the practice.

2. The time limits for action imposed by Subsection (1) are adopted by Subsection (2) for cases where the payor bank is also the depositary bank, but in this case the requirement of a settlement on the day of receipt is omitted.

3. Subsection (3) fixes a base point from which to measure the time within which notice of dishonor must be given. See Section 3-508.

4. Subsection (4) leaves banks free to agree upon the manner of returning items but establishes a precise time when an item is "returned". For definition of "sent" as used in subsections (a) and (b) see Section 1-201(38).

5. Obviously the section assumes that the item has not been "finally paid" under Section 4-213(1). If it has been, this section has no operation.

Cross References:

Sections 3-508, 4-213, 4-302.

Definitional Cross References:

"Banking day". Section 4-104.
"Clearing house". Section 4-104.
"Collecting bank". Section 4-105.
"Customer". Section 4-104.
"Documentary draft". Section 4-104.
"Item". Section 4-104.
"Midnight deadline". Section 4-104.
"Notice of dishonor". Section 3-508.
"Payor bank". Section 4-105.
"Presenting bank". Section 4-105.
"Sent". Section 1-201(38).
"Settlement". Section 4-104.

§ 4-302. Payor Bank's Responsibility for Late Return of Item.

In the absence of a valid defense such as breach of a presentment warranty (subsection (1) of Section 4-207), settlement effected or the like, if an item is presented on and received by a payor bank the bank is accountable for the amount of

(a) a demand item other than a documentary draft whether properly payable or not if the bank, in any case where it is not also the depositary bank, retains the item beyond midnight of the banking day of receipt without settling for it or, regardless of whether it is also the depositary bank, does not pay or return the item or send notice of dishonor until after its midnight deadline; or

(b) any other properly payable item unless within the time allowed for acceptance or payment of that item the bank either accepts or pays the item or returns it and accompanying documents.

Official Comment

Prior Uniform Statutory Provision: None; but see American Bankers Association Model Deferred Posting Statute.

Purposes:

Under Section 4–301, time limits are prescribed within which a payor bank must take action if it receives an item payable by it. Section 4–302 states the rights of the customer if the payor bank fails to take the action required within the time limits prescribed.

Cross Reference:

Section 4–301.

Definitional Cross References:

"Acceptance". Section 3–410.
"Banking day". Section 4–104.
"Customer". Section 4–104.
"Depositary bank". Section 4–105.
"Documentary draft". Section 4–104.
"Item". Section 4–104.
"Midnight deadline". Section 4–104.
"Notice of dishonor". Section 3–508.
"Payor bank". Section 4–105.
"Properly payable". Section 4–104.
"Settle". Section 4–104.

§ 4–303. When Items Subject to Notice, Stop-Order, Legal Process or Setoff; Order in Which Items May Be Charged or Certified.

(1) Any knowledge, notice or stop-order received by, legal process served upon or setoff exercised by a payor bank, whether or not effective under other rules of law to terminate, suspend or modify the bank's right or duty to pay an item or to charge its customer's account for the item, comes too late to so terminate, suspend or modify such right or duty if the knowledge, notice, stop-order or legal process is received or served and a reasonable time for the bank to act thereon expires or the setoff is exercised after the bank has done any of the following:

(a) accepted or certified the item;

(b) paid the item in cash;

(c) settled for the item without reserving a right to revoke the settlement and without having such right under statute, clearing house rule or agreement;

(d) completed the process of posting the item to the indicated account of the drawer, maker or other person to be charged therewith or otherwise has evidenced by examination of such indicated account and by action its decision to pay the item; or

(e) become accountable for the amount of the item under subsection (1)(d) of Section 4–213 and Section 4–302 dealing with the payor bank's responsibility for late return of items.

(2) Subject to the provisions of subsection (1) items may be accepted, paid, certified or charged to the indicated account of its customer in any order convenient to the bank.

Official Comment

Prior Uniform Statutory Provision: None.

Purposes:

1. The comments to Section 4–213 describe the process through which an item passes in the payor bank. Prior to this

process or at any time while it is going on, the payor bank may receive knowledge or a legal notice affecting the item, such as knowledge or a notice that the drawer has filed a petition in bankruptcy or made an assignment for the benefit of creditors; may receive an order of the drawer stopping payment on the item; may have served on it an attachment of the account of the drawer; or the bank itself may exercise a right of setoff against the drawer's account. Each of these events affects the account of the drawer and may eliminate or freeze all or part of whatever balance is available to pay the item. Subsection (1) states the rule for determining the relative priorities between these various legal events and the item.

2. The rule is that if any one of several things has been done to the item or if it has reached any one of several stages in its processing at the time the knowledge, notice, stop-order or legal process is received or served and a reasonable time for the bank to act thereon expires or the setoff is exercised, the knowledge, notice, stop-order, legal process or setoff comes too late, the item has priority and a charge to the customer's account may be made and is effective. Certain of the tests determining the priority status of the item are the same as for final payment under Section 4-213(1), but additional tests apply in the context of the present section. The first event mentioned, namely, acceptance, means formal acceptance as that term is used and defined in Section 3-410. Certification is the type of certification defined in Section 3-411. Payment of the item in cash under Section 4-213(1)(a), final settlement for the item under Section 4-213(1)(b) and completion of the process of posting under Section 4-213(1)(c) all constitute final payment of the item and confer priority. After a cash payment, final settlement or the completion of the process of posting, any knowledge, notice, stop-order, legal process or setoff comes too late and cannot interfere with either the payment of the item or a charge to the customer's account based upon such payment.

3. The sixth event conferring priority is stated by the language "or otherwise has evidenced by examination of such indicated account and by action its decision to pay the item." This general "omnibus" language is necessary to pick up other possible types of action impossible to specify particularly but where the bank has examined the account to see if there are sufficient funds and has taken some action indicating an intention to pay. An example is what has sometimes been called "sight posting" where the bookkeeper examines the account and makes a decision to pay but postpones posting. The clause should be interpreted in the light of Nineteenth Ward Bank v. First Nat. Bank of South Weymouth, 184 Mass. 49, 67 N.E. 670 (1903). It is not intended to refer to various preliminary acts in no way close to a true decision of the bank to pay the item, such as receipt of the item over the counter for deposit, entry of a provisional credit in a passbook, or the making of a provisional settlement for the item through the clearing house, by entries in accounts, remittance or otherwise. All actions of this type are provisional and none of them evidences the bank's decision to pay the item. In this Section as in Section 4-213 reasoning such as appears in Cohen v. First Nat. Bank of Nogales, 22 Ariz. 394, 400, 198 P. 122, 124, 15 A.L.R. 701 (1921); Briviesca v. Coronado, 19 Cal.2d 244, 120 P.2d 649 (1941); White Brokerage Co. v. Cooperman, 207 Minn. 239, 290 N.W. 790 (1940); Scotts Bluff County v. First Nat. Bank of Gering, 115 Neb. 273, 212 N.W. 617, 618 (1927); Provident Savings Bank & Trust Co. v. Hildebrand, 49 Ohio App. 207, 196 N.E. 790, 791 (1934); Schaer v. First Nat. Bank of Brenham, 132 Tex. 499, 124 S.W.2d 108 (1939) (bill of exchange); Union State Bank of Lancaster v. People's State Bank of Lancaster, 192 Wis. 28, 33, 211 N.W. 931, 933 (1927); 1 Paton's Digest 1067, is rejected.

4. The seventh and last event conferring priority for an item and a charge to the customer's account based upon the item is stated by the language "become

accountable for the amount of the item under subsection (1)(d) of Section 4-213 and Section 4-302 dealing with the payor bank's responsibility for late return of items". Under Section 4-213(1)(d) if a payor bank makes a provisional settlement for an item and fails to revoke the settlement in the time and manner permitted by statute, clearing house rule or agreement, such combination of events constitutes final payment of the item. Under Section 4-302 a payor bank may also become accountable for the amount of an item in certain other situations even though there has been no provisional settlement for the item or such action as constitutes final payment under Section 4-213(1). Expiration of the deadlines under Sections 4-213(1)(d) or 4-302 with resulting accountability by the payor bank for the amount of the item, establish priority of the item over notices, stop-orders, legal process or setoff.

5. In the case of knowledge, notice, stop-orders and legal process the effective time for determining whether they were received too late to affect the payment of an item and a charge to the customer's account by reason of such payment, is receipt plus a reasonable time for the bank to act on any of these communications. Usually a relatively short time is required to communicate to the bookkeeping department advice of one of these events but certainly some time is necessary. Compare Sections 1-201(27) and 4-403. In the case of setoff the effective time is when the setoff is actually made.

6. As between one item and another no priority rule is stated, other than the convenience of the bank. This rule is justified because of the impossibility of stating a rule that would be fair in all cases, having in mind the almost infinite number of combinations of large and small checks in relation to the available balance on hand in the drawer's account; the possible methods of receipt; and other difficulties. Further, where the drawer has drawn all the checks, he should have funds available to meet all of them and has no basis for urging one should be paid before another; and the holders have no direct right against the payor bank in any event, unless of course, the bank has accepted, certified or finally paid a particular item, or has become liable for it under Section 4-302. Under subsection (2) the bank obviously has the right to pay items for which it is itself liable ahead of those for which it is not.

Cross References:

Sections 3-410, 3-411, 4-213(1), 4-301, and 4-302.

Definitional Cross References:

"Accepted". Section 3-410.
"Account". Section 4-104.
"Agreement". Section 1-201.
"Certified". Section 3-411.
"Clearing house". Section 4-104.
"Customer". Section 4-104.
"Item". Section 4-104.
"Notice". Section 1-201.
"Payor bank". Section 4-105.
"Settle". Section 4-104.

PART 4

RELATIONSHIP BETWEEN PAYOR BANK AND ITS CUSTOMER

§ 4-401. When Bank May Charge Customer's Account.

(1) As against its customer, a bank may charge against his account any item which is otherwise properly payable from that account even though the charge creates an overdraft.

(2) A bank which in good faith makes payment to a holder may charge the indicated account of its customer according to

(a) the original tenor of his altered item; or

(b) the tenor of his completed item, even though the bank knows the item has been completed unless the bank has notice that the completion was improper.

Official Comment

Prior Uniform Statutory Provision: None.

Purposes:

1. It is fundamental that upon proper payment of a draft the drawee may charge the account of the drawer. This is true even though the draft is an overdraft since the draft itself authorizes the payment for the drawer's account and carries an implied promise to reimburse the drawee.

2. Subsection (2) parallels the provision which protects a holder in due course against discharge by reason of alteration and permits him to enforce the instrument according to its original tenor. Section 3-407(3). It adopts the rule of cases extending the same protection to a drawee who pays in good faith. The subsection also follows the policy of Sections 3-115 and 3-407(3) by protecting the drawee who pays a completed instrument in good faith according to the instrument as completed.

Cross References:

Sections 3-115 and 3-407.

Definitional Cross References:

"Account". Section 4-104.
"Bank". Section 1-201.
"Customer". Section 4-104.
"Good faith". Section 1-201.
"Holder". Section 1-201.
"Item". Section 4-104.
"Properly payable". Section 4-104.

§ 4-402. Bank's Liability to Customer for Wrongful Dishonor.

A payor bank is liable to its customer for damages proximately caused by the wrongful dishonor of an item. When the dishonor occurs through mistake liability is limited to actual damages proved. If so proximately caused and proved damages may include damages for an arrest or prosecution of the customer or other consequential damages. Whether any consequential damages are proximately caused by the wrongful dishonor is a question of fact to be determined in each case.

Official Comment

Prior Uniform Statutory Provision: None.

Purposes:

1. This section is new to the Uniform Laws, although similar statutory provisions are in existence in twenty-three jurisdictions.

2. The liability of the drawee for dishonor has sometimes been stated as one for breach of contract, sometimes as for negligence or other breach of a tort duty, and sometimes as for defamation. This section does not attempt to specify a theory. "Wrongful dishonor" excludes any permitted or justified dishonor, as where the drawer has no credit extended by the drawee, or where the draft lacks a necessary indorsement or is not properly presented.

3. This section rejects decisions which have held that where the dishonored item has been drawn by a merchant, trader or fiduciary he is defamed in his business, trade or profession by a reflection on his credit and hence that substantial damages may be awarded on the basis of defamation "per se" without proof that damage has occurred. The merchant, trader and fiduciary are placed on the same footing as any other drawer and in all cases of dishonor by mistake damages

recoverable are limited to those actually proved.

4. Wrongful dishonor is different from "failure to exercise ordinary care in handling an item", and the measure of damages is that stated in this section, not that stated in Section 4-103(5).

5. The fourth sentence of the section rejects decisions holding that as a matter of law the dishonor of a check is not the "proximate cause" of the arrest and prosecution of the customer, and leaves to determination in each case as a question of fact whether the dishonor is or may be the "proximate cause".

Definitional Cross References:

"Bank". Section 1-201.
"Customer". Section 4-104.
"Item". Section 4-104.

§ 4-403. Customer's Right to Stop Payment; Burden of Proof of Loss.

(1) A customer may by order to his bank stop payment of any item payable for his account but the order must be received at such time and in such manner as to afford the bank a reasonable opportunity to act on it prior to any action by the bank with respect to the item described in Section 4-303.

(2) An oral order is binding upon the bank only for fourteen calendar days unless confirmed in writing within that period. A written order is effective for only six months unless renewed in writing.

(3) The burden of establishing the fact and amount of loss resulting from the payment of an item contrary to a binding stop payment order is on the customer.

Official Comment

Prior Uniform Statutory Provision: None.

Purposes:

1. This section is new. It is intended to replace separate statutes in twenty-nine states which regulate stop-payment orders.

2. The position taken by this section is that stopping payment is a service which depositors expect and are entitled to receive from banks notwithstanding its difficulty, inconvenience and expense. The inevitable occasional losses through failure to stop should be borne by the banks as a cost of the business of banking.

3. Subsection (1) follows the decisions holding that a payee or indorsee has no right to stop payment. This is consistent with the provision governing payment or satisfaction. See Section 3-603. The sole exception to this rule is found in Section 4-405 on payment after notice of death, by which any person claiming an interest in the account can stop payment.

4. Payment is commonly stopped only on checks; but the right to stop payment is not limited to checks, and extends to any item payable by any bank. Where the maker of a note payable at a bank is in a position analogous to that of a drawer (Section 3-121) he may stop payment of the note. By analogy the rule extends to drawees other than banks.

5. There is no right to stop payment after certification of a check or other acceptance of a draft, and this is true no matter who procures the certification. See Sections 3-411 and 4-303. The acceptance is the drawee's own engagement to pay, and he is not required to impair his credit by refusing payment for the convenience of the drawer.

6. Normally a direction to stop payment is first given by telephone. Notwithstanding statutes which require a written order, banks customarily accept such directions, and have been held to

waive the writing. Subsection (2) is intended to protect both parties by making the oral direction effective for only a short time during which the drawer must confirm it in writing, and by eliminating thereafter any claim of waiver by acceptance of the oral direction.

7. The existing statutes all specify a time limit after which any direction to stop payment becomes ineffective unless it is renewed in writing; and the majority of them have specified six months. The purpose of the provision is, of course, to facilitate stopping payment by clearing the records of the drawee of accumulated unrevoked stop orders, as where the drawer has found a lost instrument or has settled his controversy with the payee, but has failed to notify the drawee. The last sentence of subsection (2), together with the second clause in Section 4–404, rejects the reasoning of such cases as Goldberg v. Manufacturers Trust Company, 199 Misc. 167, 102 N.Y.S.2d 144 (1951).

8. A payment in violation of an effective direction to stop payment is an improper payment, even though it is made by mistake or inadvertence. Any agreement to the contrary is invalid under Section 4–103(1) if in paying the item over the stop payment order the bank has failed to exercise ordinary care. The drawee is, however, entitled to subrogation to prevent unjust enrichment (Section 4–407); retains common-law defenses, e.g., that by conduct in recognizing the payment the customer has ratified the bank's action in paying over a stop payment order (Section 1–103); and retains common-law rights, e.g., to recover money paid under a mistake (Section 1–103) in cases where the payment is not made final by Section 3–418. It has sometimes been said that payment cannot be stopped against a holder in due course, but the statement is inaccurate. The payment can be stopped but the drawer remains liable on the instrument to the holder in due course (Sections 3–305, 3–413) and the drawee, if he pays, becomes subrogated to the rights of the holder in due course against the drawer. Section 4–407. Any defenses available against a holder in due course remain available to the drawer, but other defenses are cut off to the same extent as if the holder himself were bringing the action.

Cross References:

Point 3: Sections 3–603(1), 4–405.
Point 4: Section 3–121.
Point 5: Sections 3–411 and 4–303.
Point 8: Sections 3–305, 3–413, 3–418, 4–103 and 4–407.

Definitional Cross References:

"Account". Section 4–104.
"Bank". Section 1–201.
"Burden of establishing". Section 1–201.
"Customer". Section 4–104.
"Item". Section 4–104.
"Send". Section 1–201.

§ 4–404. Bank Not Obligated to Pay Check More Than Six Months Old.

A bank is under no obligation to a customer having a checking account to pay a check, other than a certified check, which is presented more than six months after its date, but it may charge its customer's account for a payment made thereafter in good faith.

Official Comment

Prior Uniform Statutory Provision: None.

Purposes:

This section incorporates a type of statute adopted in twenty-six jurisdictions. The time limit is set at six months because banking and commercial practice regards a check outstanding for longer than that period as stale, and a bank will normally not pay such a check without consulting the depositor. It is therefore not required to do so, but is given the option to pay because it may be in a position to know, as in the case of dividend checks, that the drawer wants payment made.

Certified checks are excluded from the section because they are the primary obligation of the certifying bank (Sections 3-411 and 3-413), which obligation runs direct to the holder of the check. The customer's account was charged when the check was certified.

Cross References:

Sections 3-411 and 3-413.

Definitional Cross References:

"Account". Section 4-104.
"Bank". Section 1-201.
"Check". Section 3-104.
"Customer". Section 4-104.
"Good faith". Section 1-201.
"Present". Section 3-504.

§ 4-405. Death or Incompetence of Customer.

(1) A payor or collecting bank's authority to accept, pay or collect an item or to account for proceeds of its collection if otherwise effective is not rendered ineffective by incompetence of a customer of either bank existing at the time the item is issued or its collection is undertaken if the bank does not know of an adjudication of incompetence. Neither death nor incompetence of a customer revokes such authority to accept, pay, collect or account until the bank knows of the fact of death or of an adjudication of incompetence and has reasonable opportunity to act on it.

(2) Even with knowledge a bank may for 10 days after the date of death pay or certify checks drawn on or prior to that date unless ordered to stop payment by a person claiming an interest in the account.

Official Comment

Prior Uniform Statutory Provision: None.

Purposes:

1. This section is new, although similar statutory provisions are in existence in seven states.

2. Subsection (1) follows existing decisions which hold that a drawee (payor) bank is not liable for the payment of a check before it has notice of the death or incompetence of the drawer. The justice and necessity of the rule are obvious. A check is an order to pay which the bank must obey under penalty of possible liability for dishonor. Further, with the tremendous volume of items handled any rule which required banks to verify the continued life and competency of drawers would be completely unworkable.

One or both of these same reasons apply to other phases of the bank collection and payment process and the rule is made wide enough to apply to these other phases. It applies to all kinds of "items"; to "customers" who own items as well as "customers" who draw or make them; to the function of collecting items as well as the function of accepting or paying them; to the carrying out of instructions to account for proceeds even though these may involve transfers to third parties; to depositary and intermediary banks as well as payor banks; and to incompetency existing at the time of the issuance of an item or the commencement of the collection or payment process as well as to incompetency occurring thereafter. Further, the requirement of actual knowledge makes inapplicable the rule of some cases that an adjudication of incompetency is constructive notice to all the world because obviously it is as impossible for banks to keep posted on such adjudications (in the absence of actual knowledge) as it is to keep posted as to death of immediate or remote customers.

3. Subsection (2) provides a limited period after death during which a bank may continue to pay checks (as distinguished from other items) even though it has notice. The purpose of the provision, as of the existing statutes, is to permit holders of checks drawn and issued shortly before death to cash them without the necessity of filing a claim in probate. The justification is that such checks normally are given in immediate payment of an obligation, that there is almost never any reason why they should not be paid, and that filing in probate is a useless formality, burdensome to the holder, the executor, the court and the bank.

This section does not prevent an executor or administrator from recovering the payment from the holder of the check. It is not intended to affect the validity of any gift causa mortis or other transfer in contemplation of death, but merely to relieve the bank of liability for the payment.

4. Any surviving relative, creditor or other person who claims an interest in the account may give a direction to the bank not to pay checks, or not to pay a particular check. Such notice has the same effect as a direction to stop payment. The bank has no responsibility to determine the validity of the claim or even whether it is "colorable". But obviously anyone who has an interest in the estate, including the person named as executor in a will, even if the will has not yet been admitted to probate, is entitled to claim an interest in the account.

Definitional Cross References:

"Accept". Section 3-410.
"Bank". Section 1-201.
"Certify". Section 3-411.
"Check". Section 3-104.
"Customer". Section 4-104.
"Depositary bank". Section 4-105.
"Item". Section 4-104.
"Payor bank". Section 4-105.

§ 4-406. Customer's Duty to Discover and Report Unauthorized Signature or Alteration.

(1) When a bank sends to its customer a statement of account accompanied by items paid in good faith in support of the debit entries or holds the statement and items pursuant to a request or instructions of its customer or otherwise in a reasonable manner makes the statement and items available to the customer, the customer must exercise reasonable care and promptness to examine the statement and items to discover his unauthorized signature or any alteration on an item and must notify the bank promptly after discovery thereof.

(2) If the bank establishes that the customer failed with respect to an item to comply with the duties imposed on the customer by subsection (1) the customer is precluded from asserting against the bank

(a) his unauthorized signature or any alteration on the item if the bank also establishes that it suffered a loss by reason of such failure; and

(b) an unauthorized signature or alteration by the same wrongdoer on any other item paid in good faith by the bank after the first item and statement was available to the customer for a reasonable period not exceeding fourteen calendar days and before the bank receives notification from the customer of any such unauthorized signature or alteration.

(3) The preclusion under subsection (2) does not apply if the customer establishes lack of ordinary care on the part of the bank in paying the item(s).

(4) Without regard to care or lack of care of either the customer or the bank a customer who does not within one year from the time the statement

and items are made available to the customer (subsection (1)) discover and report his unauthorized signature or any alteration on the face or back of the item or does not within 3 years from that time discover and report any unauthorized indorsement is precluded from asserting against the bank such unauthorized signature or indorsement or such alteration.

(5) If under this section a payor bank has a valid defense against a claim of a customer upon or resulting from payment of an item and waives or fails upon request to assert the defense the bank may not assert against any collecting bank or other prior party presenting or transferring the item a claim based upon the unauthorized signature or alteration giving rise to the customer's claim.

Official Comment

Prior Uniform Statutory Provision: None.

Purposes:

1. This section is new to Uniform Laws. It is to replace statutes in forty jurisdictions dealing with the general subject of a depositor's duty to discover and report forgeries and alterations. In these statutes there is substantial variation in rules prescribed as to the following matters: application of the statute to unauthorized signatures, raised checks or altered checks; inclusion of special provisions with respect to fictitious payees; periods of time prescribed for termination of right of customer to assert claims against bank; time when limitation period begins to run; restriction of rights of customer stated in terms of liability for loss, preclusion of rights or limitations on time in which suits may be brought.

2. Subsection (1) states the general duty of a customer to exercise reasonable care and promptness to examine his bank statements and items to discover his unauthorized signature or any alteration and to promptly notify the bank if he discovers an unauthorized signature or alteration. This duty becomes operative when the bank does any one of three things with respect to the statement of account and supporting items paid in good faith. The first action is the sending of the statement and items to the customer. The sending may be either by mailing or any other action within the definition of "send" (Section 1–201). The second action is the holding of such statement and items available for the customer pursuant to a request for instructions of the customer. The third action is stated as "or otherwise in a reasonable manner makes the statement and items available to the customer." Such wider residual language is desirable to cover unusual situations. An example might be where the bank knows a customer has left a former address but does not know any new address to which to send the statement or item or to obtain instructions from the customer. The third residual type of action, however, must be "reasonable" and any court has the power to determine that a particular action or practice of a bank, other than sending statements and items or holding them pursuant to instructions, is not reasonable.

3. Subsection (2) states the effect of a failure of a customer to comply with subsection (1). The first effect stated in subparagraph (a) is that he is precluded from asserting against the bank his unauthorized signature and alteration if the bank establishes that it suffered a loss by reason of the customer's failure. The bank has the burden of establishing that it suffered some loss.

Under subparagraph (b) if, after the first item and statement becomes available plus a reasonable period not exceeding fourteen calendar days, the bank pays in good faith any other item on which there is an unauthorized signature or alteration by the same wrongdoer, which payment is prior to receipt by the bank of notification of such unauthorized signature or alteration on the first item, the customer is precluded from asserting the additional unauthorized signature or alteration. This rule follows substantial case law that payment of an additional item or items bearing an unauthorized signature or alteration by the same wrongdoer is a loss suffered by the bank traceable to the customer's failure to exercise reasonable care in examining his statement and notifying the bank of objections to it. One of the most serious consequences of failure of the customer to comply with the requirements of subsection (1) is the opportunity presented to the wrongdoer to repeat his misdeeds. Conversely, one of the best ways to keep down losses in this type of situation is for the customer to promptly examine his statement and notify the bank of an unauthorized signature or alteration so that the bank will be alerted to stop paying further items. Hence, the rule of subparagraph (b) is prescribed and to avoid dispute a specific time limit for action by the customer is designated, namely fourteen calendar days.

4. The two effects on the customer of his failure to comply with subsection (1) (subparagraphs (a) and (b) of subsection (2)) are stated in terms of preclusion from asserting a claim against the bank. However, these two effects occur only if the customer has failed to exercise reasonable care and promptness in examining his statement and items and notifying the bank and as to this question of fact the burden is upon the bank to establish such failure. Further, even if the bank succeeds in establishing that the customer has failed to exercise ordinary care, if in turn the customer succeeds in establishing that the bank failed to exercise ordinary care in paying the item(s) the preclusion rule does not apply. This distribution of the burden of establishing between the customer and the bank provides reasonable equality of treatment and requires each person asserting the negligence to establish such negligence rather than requiring either person to establish that his entire course of conduct constituted ordinary care.

5. Whether the preclusion rule of subsection (2) operates or does not operate depends upon determinations as to ordinary care of the customer and possibly of the bank. However, subsection (4) places an absolute time limit on the right of a customer to make claim for payment of altered or forged paper without regard to care or lack of care of either the customer or the bank. In the case of alteration or the unauthorized signature of the customer himself the absolute time limit is one year. In the case of unauthorized indorsements it is three years. This recognizes that there is little excuse for a customer not detecting an alteration of his own check or a forgery of his own signature. However, he does not know the signatures of indorsers and may be delayed in learning that indorsements are forged. The three year absolute time limit on the discovery of forged indorsements should be ample, because in the great preponderance of cases the customer will learn of the forged indorsements within this time and if in any exceptional case he does not, the balance in favor of a mechanical termination of the liability of the bank outweighs what few residuary risks the customer may still have. In thirteen of the existing statutes there are limitations on the liability of a bank for payment of items bearing forged indorsements which limitation periods range from thirty days to two years. In the remaining twenty-seven no provision is made for forged indorsements.

6. Nothing in this section is intended to affect any decision holding that a customer who has notice of something wrong with an indorsement must exercise reasonable care to investigate and to notify the bank. It should be noted that under the rules relating to impostors and signatures in the name of the payee (Section 3-405) certain forged indorsements on which the bank has paid the item in good faith may be treated as effective notwithstanding such discovery and notice. If the alteration or forgery results from the drawer's negligence the drawee who pays

in good faith is also protected. Section 3–406.

7. The forty existing statutes on the subject as well as Section 4–406 evidence a public policy in favor of imposing on customers the duty of prompt examination of their bank statements and the notification of banks of forgeries and alterations and in favor of reasonable time limitations on the responsibility of banks for payment of forged or altered items. In two New York cases, however, it has been held that a payor bank may waive defenses of the kind prescribed by the section and ignore the public policy indicated by these defenses and recover the full amount of a forged or altered item from a collecting bank. Fallick v. Amalgamated Bank of New York, 232 App.Div. 127, 249 N.Y.S. 238 (1st Dep't 1931); National Surety Corp. v. Federal Reserve Bank of New York, 188 Misc. 207, 70 N.Y.S.2d 636 (1946), affirmed without opinion 188 Misc. 213, 70 N.Y.S.2d 642 (1946). Subsection (5) is intended to reject the holding of these and like cases. Although the principle of subsection (5) might well be applied to other types of claims of customers against banks and defenses to these claims, the rule of the subsection is limited to defenses of a payor bank under this section. No present need is known to give the rule wider effect.

Cross References:

Sections 3–404, 3–405, 3–406, 3–407, 3–417 and 4–207.

Definitional Cross References:

"Alteration". Section 3–407.
"Bank". Section 1–201.
"Collecting bank". Section 4–105.
"Customer". Section 4–104.
"Good faith". Section 1–201.
"Indorsement". Section 3–204.
"Item". Section 4–104.
"Payor bank". Section 4–105.
"Send". Section 1–201.
"Unauthorized signature". Section 1–201.

§ 4–407. Payor Bank's Right to Subrogation on Improper Payment.

If a payor bank has paid an item over the stop payment order of the drawer or maker or otherwise under circumstances giving a basis for objection by the drawer or maker, to prevent unjust enrichment and only to the extent necessary to prevent loss to the bank by reason of its payment of the item, the payor bank shall be subrogated to the rights

(a) of any holder in due course on the item against the drawer or maker; and

(b) of the payee or any other holder of the item against the drawer or maker either on the item or under the transaction out of which the item arose; and

(c) of the drawer or maker against the payee or any other holder of the item with respect to the transaction out of which the item arose.

Official Comment

Prior Uniform Statutory Provision: None.

Purposes:

1. Section 4–403 states that a stop payment order is binding on a bank. If a bank pays an item over such a stop order it is prima facie liable, but under subsection (3) of 4–403 the burden of establishing the fact and amount of loss from such payment is on the customer. A defense frequently interposed by a bank in an action against it for wrongful payment over a stop-order is that the drawer or maker suffered no loss because he would

have been liable to a holder in due course in any event. On this argument some cases have held that payment cannot be stopped against a holder in due course. Payment can be stopped, but if it is, the drawer or maker is liable and the sound rule is that the bank is subrogated to the rights of the holder in due course. The preamble and subsection (a) of this section state this rule.

2. Subsection (b) also subrogates the bank to the rights of the payee or other holder against the drawer or maker either on the item or under the transaction out of which it arose. It may well be that the payee is not a holder in due course but still has good rights against the drawer. These may be on the check but also may not be as, for example, where the drawer buys goods from the payee and the goods are partially defective so that the payee is not entitled to the full price, but the goods are still worth a portion of the contract price. If the drawer retains the goods he is obligated to pay a part of the agreed price. If the bank has paid the check it should be subrogated to this claim of the payee against the drawer.

3. Subsection (c) subrogates the bank to the rights of the drawer or maker against the payee or other holder with respect to the transaction out of which the item arose. If, for example, the payee was a fraudulent salesman inducing the drawer to issue his check for defective securities, and the bank pays the check over a stop order but reimburses the drawer for such payment, the bank should have a basis for getting the money back from the fraudulent salesman.

4. The limitations of the preamble prevent the bank itself from getting any double recovery or benefits out of its subrogation rights conferred by the section.

5. The spelling out of the affirmative rights of the bank in this section does not destroy other existing rights (Section 1-103). Among others these may include the defense of a payor bank that by conduct in recognizing the payment a customer has ratified the bank's action in paying in disregard of a stop payment order or rights to recover money paid under a mistake.

Cross Reference:

Section 4-403.

Definitional Cross References:

"Holder". Section 1-201.

"Holder in due course". Section 3-302.

"Item". Section 4-104.

"Payor bank". Section 4-105.

PART 5

COLLECTION OF DOCUMENTARY DRAFTS

§ 4-501. Handling of Documentary Drafts; Duty to Send for Presentment and to Notify Customer of Dishonor.

A bank which takes a documentary draft for collection must present or send the draft and accompanying documents for presentment and upon learning that the draft has not been paid or accepted in due course must seasonably notify its customer of such fact even though it may have discounted or bought the draft or extended credit available for withdrawal as of right.

Official Comment

Prior Uniform Statutory Provision: None.

Purposes:

To state the duty of a bank handling a documentary draft for a customer. "Documentary draft" is defined in Section 4-104. Notice that the duty stated exists even when the bank has bought the draft.

This is because to the customer the draft normally represents an underlying commercial transaction, and if that is not going through as planned he should know it promptly.

Cross References:

In Article 4: Sections 4-201, 4-202, 4-203, 4-204 and 4-210.

In Article 5: Sections 5-110, 5-111, 5-112 and 5-113.

Definitional Cross References:

"Documentary draft". Sections 4-104, 5-103.

§ 4-502. Presentment of "On Arrival" Drafts.

When a draft or the relevant instructions require presentment "on arrival", "when goods arrive" or the like, the collecting bank need not present until in its judgment a reasonable time for arrival of the goods has expired. Refusal to pay or accept because the goods have not arrived is not dishonor; the bank must notify its transferor of such refusal but need not present the draft again until it is instructed to do so or learns of the arrival of the goods.

Official Comment

Prior Uniform Statutory Provision: None.

Purposes:

The section is designed to establish a definite rule for "on arrival" drafts. The term includes not only drafts drawn payable "on arrival" but also drafts forwarded with instructions to present "on arrival". The term refers to the arrival of the relevant goods. Unless a bank has actual knowledge of the arrival of the goods, as for example, when it is the "notify" party on the bill of lading, the section only requires the exercise of such judgment in estimating time as a bank may be expected to have. Commonly the buyer-drawee will want the goods and will therefore call for the documents and take up the draft when they do arrive.

Cross References:

In Article 4: Sections 4-202 and 4-203.
In Article 5: Section 5-112.

Definitional Cross References:

"Collecting bank". Section 4-105.

§ 4-503. Responsibility of Presenting Bank for Documents and Goods; Report of Reasons for Dishonor; Referee in Case of Need.

Unless otherwise instructed and except as provided in Article 5 a bank presenting a documentary draft

(a) must deliver the documents to the drawee on acceptance of the draft if it is payable more than three days after presentment; otherwise, only on payment; and

(b) upon dishonor, either in the case of presentment for acceptance or presentment for payment, may seek and follow instructions from any referee in case of need designated in the draft or if the presenting bank does not choose to utilize his services it must use diligence and good faith to ascertain the reason for dishonor, must notify its transferor of the dishonor and of the results of its effort to ascertain the reasons therefor and must request instructions.

But the presenting bank is under no obligation with respect to goods represented by the documents except to follow any reasonable instructions seasonably received; it has a right to reimbursement for any expense incurred in following instructions and to prepayment of or indemnity for such expenses.

Official Comment

Prior Uniform Statutory Provision: Section 131(3), Uniform Negotiable Instruments Law.

Changes: Completely rewritten and enlarged.

Purposes:

1. To state the rules governing, in the absence of instructions, the duty of the presenting bank in case either of honor or of dishonor of a documentary draft. The section should be read in connection with Section 2-514 on when documents are deliverable on acceptance, when on payment.

2. If the draft is drawn under a letter of credit, Article 5 controls. See Sections 5-109 through 5-114.

Cross References:

Point 1. Section 2-514; see also Section 4-504.

Point 2. Article 5, especially Sections 5-109 through 5-114.

Definitional Cross References:

"Documentary draft". Sections 4-104, 5-103.

"Presenting bank". Section 4-105.

§ 4-504. Privilege of Presenting Bank to Deal With Goods; Security Interest for Expenses.

(1) A presenting bank which, following the dishonor of a documentary draft, has seasonably requested instructions but does not receive them within a reasonable time may store, sell, or otherwise deal with the goods in any reasonable manner.

(2) For its reasonable expenses incurred by action under subsection (1) the presenting bank has a lien upon the goods or their proceeds, which may be foreclosed in the same manner as an unpaid seller's lien.

Official Comment

Prior Uniform Statutory Provision: None.

Purposes:

To give the presenting bank, after dishonor, a privilege to deal with the goods in any commercially reasonable manner pending instructions from its transferor and, if still unable to communicate with its principal after a reasonable time, a right to realize its expenditures as if foreclosing on an unpaid seller's lien (Section 2-706). The provision includes situations in which storage of goods or other action becomes commercially necessary pending receipt of any requested instructions, even if the requested instructions are later received.

The "reasonable manner" referred to means one reasonable in the light of business factors and the judgment of a business man.

Cross References:

Sections 4-503 and 2-706.

Definitional Cross References:

"Presenting bank". Section 4-105.

"Documentary draft". Sections 4-104, 5-103.

APPENDIX XI

1994 AMENDMENTS TO UNIFORM COMMERCIAL CODE

As Approved by the National Conference of Commissioners on Uniform State Laws

July 31, 1994

Amendment 1

Section 1–201 of the Act is corrected to read:

§ 1–201. General Definitions.

Subject to additional definitions contained in the subsequent Articles of this Act which are applicable to specific Articles or Parts thereof, and unless the context otherwise requires, in this Act:

(1) "Action" in the sense of a judicial proceeding includes recoupment, counterclaim, set-off, suit in equity and any other proceedings in which rights are determined.

(2) "Aggrieved party" means a party entitled to resort to a remedy.

(3) "Agreement" means the bargain of the parties in fact as found in their language or by implication from other circumstances including course of dealing or usage of trade or course of performance as provided in this Act (Sections 1–205 ~~and~~, 2–208, and 2A–207). Whether an agreement has legal consequences is determined by the provisions of this Act, if applicable; otherwise by the law of contracts (Section 1–103). (Compare "Contract".)

(4) "Bank" means any person engaged in the business of banking.

(5) "Bearer" means the person in possession of an instrument, document of title, or certificated security payable to bearer or indorsed in blank.

(6) "Bill of lading" means a document evidencing the receipt of goods for shipment issued by a person engaged in the business of transporting or forwarding goods, and includes an airbill. "Airbill" means a document serving for air transportation as a bill of lading does for marine or rail transportation, and includes an air consignment note or air waybill.

(7) "Branch" includes a separately incorporated foreign branch of a bank.

(8) "Burden of establishing" a fact means the burden of persuading the triers of fact that the existence of the fact is more probable than its non-existence.

(9) "Buyer in ordinary course of business" means a person who in good faith and without knowledge that the sale to him is in violation of the ownership rights or security interest of a third party in the goods buys in

ordinary course from a person in the business of selling goods of that kind but does not include a pawnbroker. All persons who sell minerals or the like (including oil and gas) at wellhead or minehead shall be deemed to be persons in the business of selling goods of that kind. "Buying" may be for cash or by exchange of other property or on secured or unsecured credit and includes receiving goods or documents of title under a pre-existing contract for sale but does not include a transfer in bulk or as security for or in total or partial satisfaction of a money debt.

(10) "Conspicuous": A term or clause is conspicuous when it is so written that a reasonable person against whom it is to operate ought to have noticed it. A printed heading in capitals (as: Non-Negotiable Bill of Lading) is conspicuous. Language in the body of a form is "conspicuous" if it is in larger or other contrasting type or color. But in a telegram any stated term is "conspicuous". Whether a term or clause is "conspicuous" or not is for decision by the court.

(11) "Contract" means the total legal obligation which results from the parties' agreement as affected by this Act and any other applicable rules of law. (Compare "Agreement".)

(12) "Creditor" includes a general creditor, a secured creditor, a lien creditor and any representative of creditors, including an assignee for the benefit of creditors, a trustee in bankruptcy, a receiver in equity and an executor or administrator of an insolvent debtor's or assignor's estate.

(13) "Defendant" includes a person in the position of defendant in a cross-action or counterclaim.

(14) "Delivery" with respect to instruments, documents of title, chattel paper, or certificated securities means voluntary transfer of possession.

(15) "Document of title" includes bill of lading, dock warrant, dock receipt, warehouse receipt or order for the delivery of goods, and also any other document which in the regular course of business or financing is treated as adequately evidencing that the person in possession of it is entitled to receive, hold and dispose of the document and the goods it covers. To be a document of title a document must purport to be issued by or addressed to a bailee and purport to cover goods in the bailee's possession which are either identified or are fungible portions of an identified mass.

(16) "Fault" means wrongful act, omission or breach.

(17) "Fungible" with respect to goods or securities means goods or securities of which any unit is, by nature or usage of trade, the equivalent of any other like unit. Goods which are not fungible shall be deemed fungible for the purposes of this Act to the extent that under a particular agreement or document unlike units are treated as equivalents.

(18) "Genuine" means free of forgery or counterfeiting.

(19) "Good faith" means honesty in fact in the conduct or transaction concerned.

(20) "Holder," with respect to a negotiable instrument, means the person in possession if the instrument is payable to bearer or, in the case of an instrument payable to an identified person, if the identified person is in

possession. "Holder" with respect to a document of title means the person in possession if the goods are deliverable to bearer or to the order of the person in possession.

(21) To "honor" is to pay or to accept and pay, or where a credit so engages to purchase or discount a draft complying with the terms of the credit.

(22) "Insolvency proceedings" includes any assignment for the benefit of creditors or other proceedings intended to liquidate or rehabilitate the estate of the person involved.

(23) A person is "insolvent" who either has ceased to pay his debts in the ordinary course of business or cannot pay his debts as they become due or is insolvent within the meaning of the federal bankruptcy law.

(24) "Money" means a medium of exchange authorized or adopted by a domestic or foreign government and includes a monetary unit of account established by an intergovernmental organization or by agreement between two or more nations.

(25) A person has "notice" of a fact when

(a) he has actual knowledge of it; or

(b) he has received a notice or notification of it; or

(c) from all the facts and circumstances known to him at the time in question he has reason to know that it exists.

A person "knows" or has "knowledge" of a fact when he has actual knowledge of it. "Discover" or "learn" or a word or phrase of similar import refers to knowledge rather than to reason to know. The time and circumstances under which a notice or notification may cease to be effective are not determined by this Act.

(26) A person "notifies" or "gives" a notice or notification to another by taking such steps as may be reasonably required to inform the other in ordinary course whether or not such other actually comes to know of it. A person "receives" a notice or notification when

(a) it comes to his attention; or

(b) it is duly delivered at the place of business through which the contract was made or at any other place held out by him as the place for receipt of such communications.

(27) Notice, knowledge or a notice or notification received by an organization is effective for a particular transaction from the time when it is brought to the attention of the individual conducting that transaction, and in any event from the time when it would have been brought to his attention if the organization had exercised due diligence. An organization exercises due diligence if it maintains reasonable routines for communicating significant information to the person conducting the transaction and there is reasonable compliance with the routines. Due diligence does not require an individual acting for the organization to communicate information unless such communication is part of his regular duties or unless he has reason to know of the

transaction and that the transaction would be materially affected by the information.

(28) "Organization" includes a corporation, government or governmental subdivision or agency, business trust, estate, trust, partnership or association, two or more persons having a joint or common interest, or any other legal or commercial entity.

(29) "Party", as distinct from "third party", means a person who has engaged in a transaction or made an agreement within this Act.

(30) "Person" includes an individual or an organization (See Section 1–102).

(31) "Presumption" or "presumed" means that the trier of fact must find the existence of the fact presumed unless and until evidence is introduced which would support a finding of its non-existence.

(32) "Purchase" includes taking by sale, discount, negotiation, mortgage, pledge, lien, issue or re-issue, gift or any other voluntary transaction creating an interest in property.

(33) "Purchaser" means a person who takes by purchase.

(34) "Remedy" means any remedial right to which an aggrieved party is entitled with or without resort to a tribunal.

(35) "Representative" includes an agent, an officer of a corporation or association, and a trustee, executor or administrator of an estate, or any other person empowered to act for another.

(36) "Rights" includes remedies.

(37) "Security interest" means an interest in personal property or fixtures which secures payment or performance of an obligation. The retention or reservation of title by a seller of goods notwithstanding shipment or delivery to the buyer (Section 2–401) is limited in effect to a reservation of a "security interest". The term also includes any interest of a buyer of accounts or chattel paper which is subject to Article 9. The special property interest of a buyer of goods on identification of those goods to a contract for sale under Section 2–401 is not a "security interest", but a buyer may also acquire a "security interest" by complying with Article 9. Unless a consignment is intended as security, reservation of title thereunder is not a "security interest", but a consignment in any event is subject to the provisions on consignment sales (Section 2–326).

Whether a transaction creates a lease or security interest is determined by the facts of each case; however, a transaction creates a security interest if the consideration the lessee is to pay the lessor for the right to possession and use of the goods is an obligation for the term of the lease not subject to termination by the lessee, and

(a) the original term of the lease is equal to or greater than the remaining economic life of the goods,

(b) the lessee is bound to renew the lease for the remaining economic life of the goods or is bound to become the owner of the goods,

(c) the lessee has an option to renew the lease for the remaining economic life of the goods for no additional consideration or nominal additional consideration upon compliance with the lease agreement, or

(d) the lessee has an option to become the owner of the goods for no additional consideration or nominal additional consideration upon compliance with the lease agreement.

A transaction does not create a security interest merely because it provides that

(a) the present value of the consideration the lessee is obligated to pay the lessor for the right to possession and use of the goods is substantially equal to or is greater than the fair market value of the goods at the time the lease is entered into,

(b) the lessee assumes risk of loss of the goods, or agrees to pay taxes, insurance, filing, recording, or registration fees, or service or maintenance costs with respect to the goods,

(c) the lessee has an option to renew the lease or to become the owner of the goods,

(d) the lessee has an option to renew the lease for a fixed rent that is equal to or greater than the reasonably predictable fair market rent for the use of the goods for the term of the renewal at the time the option is to be performed, or

(e) the lessee has an option to become the owner of the goods for a fixed price that is equal to or greater than the reasonably predictable fair market value of the goods at the time the option is to be performed.

For purposes of this subsection (37):

(x) Additional consideration is not nominal if (i) when the option to renew the lease is granted to the lessee the rent is stated to be the fair market rent for the use of the goods for the term of the renewal determined at the time the option is to be performed, or (ii) when the option to become the owner of the goods is granted to the lessee the price is stated to be the fair market value of the goods determined at the time the option is to be performed. Additional consideration is nominal if it is less than the lessee's reasonably predictable cost of performing under the lease agreement if the option is not exercised;

(y) "Reasonably predictable" and "remaining economic life of the goods" are to be determined with reference to the facts and circumstances at the time the transaction is entered into; and

(z) "Present value" means the amount as of a date certain of one or more sums payable in the future, discounted to the date certain. The discount is determined by the interest rate specified by the parties if the rate is not manifestly unreasonable at the time the transaction is entered into; otherwise, the discount is determined by a commercially reasonable rate that takes into account the facts and circumstances of each case at the time the transaction was entered into.

(38) "Send" in connection with any writing or notice means to deposit in the mail or deliver for transmission by any other usual means of communication with postage or cost of transmission provided for and properly addressed and in the case of an instrument to an address specified thereon or otherwise agreed, or if there be none to any address reasonable under the circumstances. The receipt of any writing or notice within the time at which it would have arrived if properly sent has the effect of a proper sending.

(39) "Signed" includes any symbol executed or adopted by a party with present intention to authenticate a writing.

(40) "Surety" includes guarantor.

(41) "Telegram" includes a message transmitted by radio, teletype, cable, any mechanical method of transmission, or the like.

(42) "Term" means that portion of an agreement which relates to a particular matter.

(43) "Unauthorized" signature means one made without actual, implied, or apparent authority and includes a forgery.

(44) "Value". Except as otherwise provided with respect to negotiable instruments and bank collections (Sections 3–303, ~~4–208~~ 4–210, and ~~4–209~~ 4–211) a person gives "value" for rights if he acquires them

(a) in return for a binding commitment to extend credit or for the extension of immediately available credit whether or not drawn upon and whether or not a charge-back is provided for in the event of difficulties in collection; or

(b) as security for or in total or partial satisfaction of a pre-existing claim; or

(c) by accepting delivery pursuant to a pre-existing contract for purchase; or

(d) generally, in return for any consideration sufficient to support a simple contract.

(45) "Warehouse receipt" means a receipt issued by a person engaged in the business of storing goods for hire.

(46) "Written" or "writing" includes printing, typewriting or any other intentional reduction to tangible form.

Amendment 2

Section 2–103 of the Act is corrected to read:

§ 2–103. Definitions and Index of Definitions.

(1) In this Article unless the context otherwise requires

(a) "Buyer" means a person who buys or contracts to buy goods.

(b) "Good faith" in the case of a merchant means honesty in fact and the observance of reasonable commercial standards of fair dealing in the trade.

(c) "Receipt" of goods means taking physical possession of them.

(d) "Seller" means a person who sells or contracts to sell goods.

(2) Other definitions applying to this Article or to specified Parts thereof, and the sections in which they appear are:

"Acceptance". Section 2–606.

"Banker's credit". Section 2–325.

"Between merchants". Section 2–104.

"Cancellation". Section 2–106(4).

"Commercial unit". Section 2–105.

"Confirmed credit". Section 2–325.

"Conforming to contract". Section 2–106.

"Contract for sale". Section 2–106.

"Cover". Section 2–712.

"Entrusting". Section 2–403.

"Financing agency". Section 2–104.

"Future goods". Section 2–105.

"Goods". Section 2–105.

"Identification". Section 2–501.

"Installment contract". Section 2–612.

"Letter of Credit". Section 2–325.

"Lot". Section 2–105.

"Merchant". Section 2–104.

"Overseas". Section 2–323.

"Person in position of seller". Section 2–707.

"Present sale". Section 2–106.

"Sale". Section 2–106.

"Sale on approval". Section 2–326.

"Sale or return". Section 2–326.

"Termination". Section 2–106.

(3) The following definitions in other Articles apply to this Article:

"Check". Section 3–104.

"Consignee". Section 7–102.

"Consignor". Section 7–102.

"Consumer goods". Section 9–109.

"Dishonor". Section ~~3–507~~ 3–502.

"Draft". Section 3–104.

(4) In addition Article 1 contains general definitions and principles of construction and interpretation applicable throughout this Article.

Amendment 3

Section 2–511 of the Act is corrected to read:

§ 2–511. Tender of Payment By Buyer; Payment By Check.

(1) Unless otherwise agreed tender of payment is a condition to the seller's duty to tender and complete any delivery.

(2) Tender of payment is sufficient when made by any means or in any manner current in the ordinary course of business unless the seller demands payment in legal tender and gives any extension of time reasonably necessary to procure it.

(3) Subject to the provisions of this Act on the effect of an instrument on an obligation (Section ~~3–802~~ 3–310), payment by check is conditional and is defeated as between the parties by dishonor of the check on due presentment.

Amendment 4

Section 5–103 of the Act is corrected to read:

§ 5–103. Definitions.

(1) In this Article unless the context otherwise requires

(a) "Credit" or "letter of credit" means an engagement by a bank or other person made at the request of a customer and of a kind within the scope of this Article (Section 5–102) that the issuer will honor drafts or other demands for payment upon compliance with the conditions specified in the credit. A credit may be either revocable or irrevocable. The engagement may be either an agreement to honor or a statement that the bank or other person is authorized to honor.

(b) A "documentary draft" or a "documentary demand for payment" is one honor of which is conditioned upon the presentation of a document or documents. "Document" means any paper including document of title, security, invoice, certificate, notice of default and the like.

(c) An "issuer" is a bank or other person issuing a credit.

(d) A "beneficiary" of a credit is a person who is entitled under its terms to draw or demand payment.

(e) An "advising bank" is a bank which gives notification of the issuance of a credit by another bank.

(f) A "confirming bank" is a bank which engages either that it will itself honor a credit already issued by another bank or that such a credit will be honored by the issuer or a third bank.

(g) A "customer" is a buyer or other person who causes an issuer to issue a credit. The term also includes a bank which procures issuance or confirmation on behalf of that bank's customer.

(2) Other definitions applying to this Article and the sections in which they appear are:

"Notation Credit". Section 5–108.

"Presenter". Section 5–112(3).

(3) Definitions in other Articles applying to this Article and the sections in which they appear are:

"Accept" or "Acceptance". Section ~~3–410~~ 3–409.

"Contract for sale". Section 2–106.

"Draft". Section 3–104.

"Holder in due course". Section 3–302.

"Midnight deadline". Section 4–104.

"Security". Section 8–102.

(4) In addition, Article 1 contains general definitions and principles of construction and interpretation applicable throughout this Article.

Amendment 5

Section 9–203 of the Act is corrected to read:

§ 9–203. Attachment and Enforceability of Security Interest; Proceeds; Formal Requisites.

(1) Subject to the provisions of Section ~~4–208~~ 4–210 on the security interest of a collecting bank, Section 8–321 on security interests in securities and Section 9–113 on a security interest arising under the ~~Article~~ Articles on Sales and Leases, a security interest is not enforceable against the debtor or third parties with respect to the collateral and does not attach unless:

(a) the collateral is in the possession of the secured party pursuant to agreement, or the debtor has signed a security agreement which contains a description of the collateral and in addition, when the security interest covers crops growing or to be grown or timber to be cut, a description of the land concerned;

(b) value has been given; and

(c) the debtor has rights in the collateral.

(2) A security interest attaches when it becomes enforceable against the debtor with respect to the collateral. Attachment occurs as soon as all of the events specified in subsection (1) have taken place unless explicit agreement postpones the time of attaching.

(3) Unless otherwise agreed a security agreement gives the secured party the rights to proceeds provided by Section 9–306.

(4) A transaction, although subject to this Article, is also subject to _______ *, and in the case of conflict between the provisions of this Article and any such statute, the provisions of such statute control. Failure to comply with any applicable statute has only the effect which is specified therein.

Note: *At * in subsection (4) insert reference to any local statute regulating small loans, retail installment sales and the like.*

The foregoing subsection (4) is designed to make it clear that certain transactions, although subject to this Article, must also comply with other applicable legislation.

This Article is designed to regulate all the "security" aspects of transactions within its scope. There is, however, much regulatory legislation, particularly in the consumer field, which supplements this Article and should not be repealed by its enactment. Examples are small loan acts, retail installment selling acts and the like. Such acts may provide for licensing and rate regulation and may prescribe particular forms of contract. Such provisions should remain in force despite the enactment of this Article. On the other hand if a retail installment selling act contains provisions on filing, rights on default, etc., such provisions should be repealed as inconsistent with this Article except that inconsistent provisions as to deficiencies, penalties, etc., in the Uniform Consumer Credit Code and other recent related legislation should remain because those statutes were drafted after the substantial enactment of the Article and with the intention of modifying certain provisions of this Article as to consumer credit.

Amendment 6

Section 9–206 of the Act is corrected to read:

§ 9–206. Agreement Not to Assert Defenses Against Assignee; Modification of Sales Warranties Where Security Agreement Exists.

(1) Subject to any statute or decision which establishes a different rule for buyers or lessees of consumer goods, an agreement by a buyer or lessee that he will not assert against an assignee any claim or defense which he may have against the seller or lessor is enforceable by an assignee who takes his assignment for value, in good faith and without notice of a claim or defense, except as to defenses of a type which may be asserted against a holder in due course of a negotiable instrument under the Article on ~~Commercial Paper~~ Negotiable Instruments (Article 3). A buyer who as part of one transaction signs both a negotiable instrument and a security agreement makes such an agreement.

(2) When a seller retains a purchase money security interest in goods the Article on Sales (Article 2) governs the sale and any disclaimer, limitation or modification of the seller's warranties.

Amendment 7

Section 9–302 of the Act is corrected to read:

§ 9-302. When Filing is Required to Perfect Security Interest; Security Interests to Which Filing Provisions of This Article Do Not Apply.

(1) A financing statement must be filed to perfect all security interests except the following:

(a) a security interest in collateral in possession of the secured party under Section 9-305;

(b) a security interest temporarily perfected in instruments or documents without delivery under Section 9-304 or in proceeds for a 10 day period under Section 9-306;

(c) a security interest created by an assignment of a beneficial interest in a trust or a decedent's estate;

(d) a purchase money security interest in consumer goods; but filing is required for a motor vehicle required to be registered; and fixture filing is required for priority over conflicting interests in fixtures to the extent provided in Section 9-313;

(e) an assignment of accounts which does not alone or in conjunction with other assignments to the same assignee transfer a significant part of the outstanding accounts of the assignor;

(f) a security interest of a collecting bank (Section ~~4-208~~ 4-210) or in securities (Section 8-321) or arising under the ~~Article~~ Articles on Sales and Leases (see Section 9-113) or covered in subsection (3) of this section;

(g) an assignment for the benefit of all the creditors of the transferor, and subsequent transfers by the assignee thereunder.

(2) If a secured party assigns a perfected security interest, no filing under this Article is required in order to continue the perfected status of the security interest against creditors of and transferees from the original debtor.

(3) The filing of a financing statement otherwise required by this Article is not necessary or effective to perfect a security interest in property subject to

(a) a statute or treaty of the United States which provides for a national or international registration or a national or international certificate of title or which specifies a place of filing different from that specified in this Article for filing of the security interest; or

(b) the following statutes of this state; [list any certificate of title statute covering automobiles, trailers, mobile homes, boats, farm tractors, or the like, and any central filing statute *.]; but during any period in which collateral is inventory held for sale by a person who is in the business of selling goods of that kind, the filing provisions of this Article (Part 4) apply to a security interest in that collateral created by him as debtor; or

(c) a certificate of title statute of another jurisdiction under the law of which indication of a security interest on the certificate is required as a condition of perfection (subsection (2) of Section 9-103).

(4) Compliance with a statute or treaty described in subsection (3) is equivalent to the filing of a financing statement under this Article, and a security interest in property subject to the statute or treaty can be perfected only by compliance therewith except as provided in Section 9–103 on multiple state transactions. Duration and renewal of perfection of a security interest perfected by compliance with the statute or treaty are governed by the provisions of the statute or treaty; in other respects the security interest is subject to this Article.

* **Note:** *It is recommended that the provisions of certificate of title acts for perfection of security interests by notation on the certificates should be amended to exclude coverage of inventory held for sale.*

Amendment 8

Section 9–312 of the Act is corrected to read:

§ 9–312. Priorities Among Conflicting Security Interests in the Same Collateral.

(1) The rules of priority stated in other sections of this Part and in the following sections shall govern when applicable: Section ~~4–208~~ 4–210 with respect to the security interests of collecting banks in items being collected, accompanying documents and proceeds; Section 9–103 on security interests related to other jurisdictions; Section 9–114 on consignments.

(2) A perfected security interest in crops for new value given to enable the debtor to produce the crops during the production season and given not more than three months before the crops become growing crops by planting or otherwise takes priority over an earlier perfected security interest to the extent that such earlier interest secures obligations due more than six months before the crops become growing crops by planting or otherwise, even though the person giving new value had knowledge of the earlier security interest.

(3) A perfected purchase money security interest in inventory has priority over a conflicting security interest in the same inventory and also has priority in identifiable cash proceeds received on or before the delivery of the inventory to a buyer if

(a) the purchase money security interest is perfected at the time the debtor receives possession of the inventory; and

(b) the purchase money secured party gives notification in writing to the holder of the conflicting security interest if the holder had filed a financing statement covering the same types of inventory (i) before the date of the filing made by the purchase money secured party, or (ii) before the beginning of the 21 day period where the purchase money security interest is temporarily perfected without filing or possession (subsection (5) of Section 9–304); and

(c) the holder of the conflicting security interest receives the notification within five years before the debtor receives possession of the inventory; and

(d) the notification states that the person giving the notice has or expects to acquire a purchase money security interest in inventory of the debtor, describing such inventory by item or type.

(4) A purchase money security interest in collateral other than inventory has priority over a conflicting security interest in the same collateral or its proceeds if the purchase money security interest is perfected at the time the debtor receives possession of the collateral or within ten days thereafter.

(5) In all cases not governed by other rules stated in this section (including cases of purchase money security interests which do not qualify for the special priorities set forth in subsections (3) and (4) of this section), priority between conflicting security interests in the same collateral shall be determined according to the following rules:

(a) Conflicting security interests rank according to priority in time of filing or perfection. Priority dates from the time a filing is first made covering the collateral or the time the security interest is first perfected, whichever is earlier, provided that there is no period thereafter when there is neither filing nor perfection.

(b) So long as conflicting security interests are unperfected, the first to attach has priority.

(6) For the purposes of subsection (5) a date of filing or perfection as to collateral is also a date of filing or perfection as to proceeds.

(7) If future advances are made while a security interest is perfected by filing, the taking of possession, or under Section 8-321 on securities, the security interest has the same priority for the purposes of subsection (5) with respect to the future advances as it does with respect to the first advance. If a commitment is made before or while the security interest is so perfected, the security interest has the same priority with respect to advances made pursuant thereto. In other cases a perfected security interest has priority from the date the advance is made.

APPENDIX XII

1994 AND 1995 AMENDMENTS TO ARTICLES 1, 3, 4, 5, 9, AND 10 CONFORMING TO 1994 REVISION OF ARTICLE 8

CONFORMING AMENDMENTS TO ARTICLE 9

[Changes from present law are shown by underscore and ~~strikeout~~.]

§ 9–103. Perfection of Security Interest in Multiple State Transactions.

. . .

(6) ~~Uncertificated securities~~ Investment property.

~~The law (including the conflict of laws rules) of the jurisdiction of organization of the issuer governs the perfection and the effect of perfection or non-perfection of a security interest in uncertificated securities.~~

(a) This subsection applies to investment property.

(b) Except as otherwise provided in paragraph (f), during the time that a security certificate is located in a jurisdiction, perfection of a security interest, the effect of perfection or non-perfection, and the priority of a security interest in the certificated security represented thereby are governed by the local law of that jurisdiction.

(c) Except as otherwise provided in paragraph (f), perfection of a security interest, the effect of perfection or non-perfection, and the priority of a security interest in an uncertificated security are governed by the local law of the issuer's jurisdiction as specified in Section 8–110(d).

(d) Except as otherwise provided in paragraph (f), perfection of a security interest, the effect of perfection or non-perfection, and the priority of a security interest in a security entitlement or securities account are governed by the local law of the securities intermediary's jurisdiction as specified in Section 8–110(e).

(e) Except as otherwise provided in paragraph (f), perfection of a security interest, the effect of perfection or non-perfection, and the priority of a security interest in a commodity contract or commodity account are governed by the local law of the commodity intermediary's jurisdiction. The following rules determine a "commodity intermediary's jurisdiction" for purposes of this paragraph:

(i) If an agreement between the commodity intermediary and commodity customer specifies that it is governed by the law of a particular jurisdiction, that jurisdiction is the commodity intermediary's jurisdiction.

(ii) If an agreement between the commodity intermediary and commodity customer does not specify the governing law as provided in subparagraph (i), but expressly specifies that the commodity account is maintained at an office in a particular jurisdiction, that jurisdiction is the commodity intermediary's jurisdiction.

(iii) If an agreement between the commodity intermediary and commodity customer does not specify a jurisdiction as provided in subparagraphs (i) or (ii), the commodity intermediary's jurisdiction is the jurisdiction in which is located the office identified in an account statement as the office serving the commodity customer's account.

(iv) If an agreement between the commodity intermediary and commodity customer does not specify a jurisdiction as provided in subparagraphs (i) or (ii) and an account statement does not identify an office serving the commodity customer's account as provided in subparagraph (iii), the commodity intermediary's jurisdiction is the jurisdiction in which is located the chief executive office of the commodity intermediary.

(f) Perfection of a security interest by filing, automatic perfection of a security interest in investment property granted by a broker or securities intermediary, and automatic perfection of a security interest in a commodity contract or commodity account granted by a commodity intermediary are governed by the local law of the jurisdiction in which the debtor is located.

Official Comment

. . .

The term "at wellhead" is intended to encompass arrangements based on sale of the product as soon as it issues from the ground and is measured, without technical distinctions as to whether title passes at the "Christmas tree" or the far side of a gathering tank or at some other point. The term "at minehead" is a comparable concept.

9. Subsection (6) of Section 9-103 specifies choice of law rules for perfection of security interests in investment property. Paragraph (b) covers security interests in certificated securities. Paragraph (c) covers security interests in uncertificated securities. Paragraph (d) covers security interests in security entitlements and securities accounts. Paragraph (e) covers security interests in commodity contracts and commodity accounts. The approach of each of these paragraphs is essentially the same. They identify the jurisdiction's law that governs questions of perfection and priority on the basis of the same principles that are used in Article 8 to determine other questions concerning that form of investment property. Thus, for certificated securities, the law of the jurisdiction where the certificate is located governs. Cf. Section 8-110(c). For uncertificated securities, the law of the issuer's jurisdiction governs. Cf. Section 8-110(a). For security entitlements and securities accounts, the law of the securities intermediary's jurisdiction governs. Cf. Section 8-110(b). For commodity contracts and commodity accounts, the law of the commodity intermediary's jurisdiction governs. Since commodity contracts and commodity accounts are not governed by Article 8, paragraph (e) contains rules that specify the commodity intermediary's jurisdiction. These are analogous to the rules in Section 8-110(e) specifying a securities intermediary's jurisdiction.

Under this subsection, if litigation about perfection or priority arises in this State, the relevant choice of law rule of paragraphs (b) through (e) may point to the law of this State or to the law of another State. If the litigation were in a tribunal of a jurisdiction that has not enacted this section, it would follow its own choice of law rules. The choice of law rules prescribed here by statute conform to generally accepted principles of choice of law. The simplicity and clarity in the choice of law rules, coupled with the explicit recognition that the parties to some securities transactions may agree on a governing law, are intended to assure that there will be one clear choice of law regardless of forum.

Paragraph (f) adapts the general choice of law principles of this subsection to cases where a secured party claims perfection on the basis of filing, or by virtue of the automatic perfection rules in Section 9-115(4)(c) and (d). In such a case, the law of the debtor's jurisdiction determines whether the requirements for that form of perfection have been satisfied. The rules in Section 9-103(3) on the debtor's location ~~*can be looked to in applying subsection (f)*~~ *and effect of change of location apply to cases governed by paragraph (f)**. The main reason for the paragraph (f) rule is to specify the proper filing office. Under the substantive rules of this Act, a security interest in investment property perfected only by filing is enforceable against the debtor or lien creditors, but not against most other claimants. See Sections 9-115(5) and (6), 8-105(e), 8-303, and 8-502. Because the choice of law rules in this section may, in some circumstances, have the effect of directing a court in a jurisdiction that has adopted this Act to look to the law of another jurisdiction, it is possible that the jurisdiction so specified will be one that has not adopted rules concerning the effect of filing as a method of perfection for investment property. In such cases, or other circumstances where the governing substantive law is not this Act, the effect of filing on the rights of other parties should be interpreted in light of the role of that form of perfection under this Act; that is, the rights of a secured party in investment property as determined under this Act perfected only by filing against another secured party or any other person who purchases or otherwise deals with the investment property should be interpreted to be no greater than the rights of that secured party under this Act. **Amendments in italics approved by the Permanent Editorial Board for Uniform Commercial Code November 4, 1995.*

The following examples illustrate these rules:

Example 1. A customer residing in New Jersey maintains a securities account with Able & Co. The agreement between the customer and Able specifies that it is governed by Pennsylvania law. Through the account the customer holds securities of a Massachusetts corporation, which Able holds through a clearing corporation located in New York. The customer obtains a margin loan from Able. Subsection (6)(d) provides that Pennsylvania law—the law of the securities intermediary's jurisdiction—governs perfection and priority of the security interest.

Example 2. A customer residing in New Jersey maintains a securities account with Able & Co. The agreement between the customer and Able specifies that it is governed by Pennsylvania law. Through the account the customer holds securities of a Massachusetts corporation, which Able holds through a clearing corporation located in New York. The customer obtains a loan from a lender located in Illinois. The lender takes a security interest and perfects by obtaining an agreement among the debtor, itself, and Able, which satisfies the requirement of Section 8-106(d)(2) to give the lender control.

Subsection (6)(d) provides that Pennsylvania law—the law of the securities intermediary's jurisdiction—governs perfection and priority of the security interest.

Example 3. A customer residing in New Jersey maintains a securities account with Able & Co. The agreement between the customer and Able specifies that it is governed by Pennsylvania law. Through the account, the customer holds securities of a Massachusetts corporation, which Able holds through a clearing corporation located in New York. The customer borrows from SP1, and SP1 files a financing statement in New Jersey. Later, the customer obtains a loan from SP2. SP2 takes a security interest and perfects by obtaining an agreement among the debtor, itself, and Able, which satisfies the requirement of Section 8-106(d)(2) to give the SP2 control. Subsection (6)(f) provides that perfection of SP1's security interest by filing is governed by the location of the debtor, so the filing in New Jersey was appropriate—assuming New Jersey has adopted the revisions of Article 9 permitting perfection of security interests in investment property by filing. Subsection (6)(d), however, provides that Pennsylvania law—the law of the securities intermediary's jurisdiction—governs all other questions of perfection and priority. Thus, Pennsylvania law governs perfection of SP2's security interest, and Pennsylvania law also governs the priority of the security interests of SP1 and SP2.

. . .

§ 9-105. Definitions and Index of Definitions.

(1) In this Article unless the context otherwise requires:

. . .

(h) "Goods" includes all things which are movable at the time the security interest attaches or which are fixtures (Section 9-313), but does not include money, documents, instruments, investment property, commodity contracts, accounts, chattel paper, general intangibles, or minerals or the like (including oil and gas) before extraction. "Goods" also includes standing timber which is to be cut and removed under a conveyance or contract for sale, the unborn young of animals, and growing crops;

(i) "Instrument" means a negotiable instrument (defined in Section 3-104), ~~or a certificated security (defined in Section 8-102)~~ or any other writing which evidences a right to the payment of money and is not itself a security agreement or lease and is of a type which is in ordinary course of business transferred by delivery with any necessary indorsement or assignment. The term does not include investment property;

(2) Other definitions applying to this Article and the sections in which they appear are:

"Account".	Section 9-106.
"Attach".	Section 9-203.
"Commodity contract".	Section 9-115.
"Commodity customer".	Section 9-115.
"Commodity intermediary".	Section 9-115.
"Construction mortgage".	Section 9-313(1).

"Consumer goods".	Section 9–109(1).
"Control".	Section 9–115.
"Equipment".	Section 9–109(2).
"Farm products".	Section 9–109(3).
"Fixture".	Section 9–313(1).
"Fixture filing".	Section 9–313(1).
"General intangibles".	Section 9–106.
"Inventory".	Section 9–109(4)
"Investment property".	Section 9–115.
"Lien creditor".	Section 9–301(3).
"Proceeds".	Section 9–306(1).
"Purchase money security interest".	Section 9–107.
"United States".	Section 9–103.

(3) The following definitions in other Articles apply to this Article:

"Broker".	Section 8–102.
"Certified security".	Section 8–102.
"Check".	Section 3–104.
"Clearing corporation".	Section 8–102.
"Contract for sale".	Section 2–106.
"Control".	Section 8–106.
"Delivery".	Section 8–301.
"Entitlement holder".	Section 8–102.
"Financial asset".	Section 8–102.
"Holder in due course".	Section 3–302.
"Note".	Section 3–104.
"Sale".	Section 2–106.
"Securities intermediary".	Section 8–102.
"Security".	Section 8–102.
"Security certificate".	Section 8–102.
"Security entitlement".	Section 8–102.
"Uncertificated security".	Section 8–102.

. . .

Official Comment

. . .

"Instrument": the term as defined in paragraph (1)(i) includes not only negotiable instruments ~~and certificated securities~~ but also any other intangibles evidenced by writings which are in ordinary course of business transferred by delivery. As in the case of chattel paper "delivery" is only the minimum stated and may be accompanied by other steps. *Amendment approved by the Permanent Editorial Board for Uniform Commercial Code November 4, 1995.*

. . .

§ 9–106. Definitions: "Account"; "General Intangibles."

"Account" means any right to payment for goods sold or leased or for services rendered which is not evidenced by an instrument or chattel paper, whether or not it has been earned by performance. "General intangibles" means any personal property (including things in action) other than goods, accounts, chattel paper, documents, instruments, investment property, and money. All rights to payment earned or unearned under a charter or other contract involving the use or hire of a vessel and all rights incident to the charter or contract are accounts.

§ 9-115. Investment Property.

(1) In this Article:

(a) "Commodity account" means an account maintained by a commodity intermediary in which a commodity contract is carried for a commodity customer.

(b) "Commodity contract" means a commodity futures contract, an option on a commodity futures contract, a commodity option, or other contract that, in each case, is:

(i) traded on or subject to the rules of a board of trade that has been designated as a contract market for such a contract pursuant to the federal commodities laws; or

(ii) traded on a foreign commodity board of trade, exchange, or market, and is carried on the books of a commodity intermediary for a commodity customer.

(c) "Commodity customer" means a person for whom a commodity intermediary carries a commodity contract on its books.

(d) "Commodity intermediary" means:

(i) a person who is registered as a futures commission merchant under the federal commodities laws; or

(ii) a person who in the ordinary course of its business provides clearance or settlement services for a board of trade that has been designated as a contract market pursuant to the federal commodities laws.

(e) "Control" with respect to a certificated security, uncertificated security, or security entitlement has the meaning specified in Section 8-106. A secured party has control over a commodity contract if by agreement among the commodity customer, the commodity intermediary, and the secured party, the commodity intermediary has agreed that it will apply any value distributed on account of the commodity contract as directed by the secured party without further consent by the commodity customer. If a commodity customer grants a security interest in a commodity contract to its own commodity intermediary, the commodity intermediary as secured party has control. A secured party has control over a securities account or commodity account if the secured party has control over all security entitlements or commodity contracts carried in the securities account or commodity account.

(f) "Investment property" means:

(i) a security, whether certificated or uncertificated;
(ii) a security entitlement;
(iii) a securities account;
(iv) a commodity contract; or
(v) a commodity account.

(2) Attachment or perfection of a security interest in a securities account is also attachment or perfection of a security interest in all security entitlements carried in the securities account. Attachment or perfection of a security interest in a commodity account is also attachment or perfection of a security interest in all commodity contracts carried in the commodity account.

(3) A description of collateral in a security agreement or financing statement is sufficient to create or perfect a security interest in a certificated security, uncertificated security, security entitlement, securities account, commodity contract, or commodity account whether it describes the collateral by those terms, or as investment property, or by description of the underlying security, financial asset, or commodity contract. A description of investment property collateral in a security agreement or financing statement is sufficient if it identifies the collateral by specific listing, by category, by quantity, by a computational or allocational formula or procedure, or by any other method, if the identity of the collateral is objectively determinable.

(4) Perfection of a security interest in investment property is governed by the following rules:

(a) A security interest in investment property may be perfected by control.

(b) Except as otherwise provided in paragraphs (c) and (d), a security interest in investment property may be perfected by filing.

(c) If the debtor is a broker or securities intermediary a security interest in investment property is perfected when it attaches. The filing of a financing statement with respect to a security interest in investment property granted by a broker or securities intermediary has no effect for purposes of perfection or priority with respect to that security interest.

(d) If a debtor is a commodity, intermediary, a security interest in a commodity contract or a commodity account is perfected when it attaches. The filing of a financing statement with respect to a security interest in a commodity contract or a commodity account granted by a commodity intermediary has no effect for purposes of perfection or priority with respect to that security interest.

(5) Priority between conflicting security interests in the same investment property is governed by the following rules:

(a) A security interest of a secured party who has control over investment property has priority over a security interest of a secured party who does not have control over the investment property.

(b) Except as otherwise provided in paragraphs (c) and (d), conflicting security interests of secured parties each of whom has control rank equally.

(c) Except as otherwise agreed by the securities intermediary, a security interest in a security entitlement or a securities account granted to the debtor's own securities intermediary has priority over any security interest granted by the debtor to another secured party.

(d) Except as otherwise agreed by the commodity intermediary, a security interest in a commodity contract or a commodity account granted to the debtor's own commodity intermediary has priority over any security interest granted by the debtor to another secured party.

(e) Conflicting security interests granted by a broker, a securities intermediary, or a commodity intermediary which are perfected without control rank equally.

(f) In all other cases, priority between conflicting security interests in investment property is governed by Section 9–312(5), (6), and (7). Section 9–312(4) does not apply to investment property.

(6) If a security certificate in registered form is delivered to a secured party pursuant to agreement, a written security agreement is not required for attachment or enforceability of the security interest, delivery suffices for perfection of the security interest, and the security interest has priority over a conflicting security interest perfected by means other than control, even if a necessary indorsement is lacking.

Official Comment

1. Overview. This section sets out the principal rules on security interests in investment property. Investment property, defined in subsection (1)(f) is a new term for a category of collateral that includes securities, whether held directly or through intermediaries, and commodity futures. The term investment property is used in Article 9 as one of the general categories of collateral, such as goods or instruments. Investment property is excluded from the definitions of goods, instruments, and general intangibles. See Sections 9–105(1)(h), 9–105(1)(i), and 9–106.

This section is added as part of the revision of Article 8 on investment securities. It relies in part on terms and concepts defined in Revised Article 8. For an overview of Revised Article 8, see the Prefatory Note to that Article. Prior to the 1978 amendments to Article 8, the rules on security interests in securities were included in Article 9. The 1978 amendments moved the key rules to Article 8. The revision of Article 8 returns these matters to Article 9. In order to avoid disruption of section numbering, the new rules on security interests in investment property are collected in this section, rather than being distributed among the various sections of Article 9 dealing with corresponding issues for other categories of collateral. On matters not covered by rules set out in this section, security interests in investment property are governed by the general rules in other sections of this Article.

The distinction between the direct and indirect holding systems plays an important role in the rules on security interests in securities. Consider two investors, X and Y, each of whom owns 1000 shares of XYZ Co. common stock. X has a certificate representing 1000 shares and is registered on the books maintained by XYZ Co.'s transfer agent as the holder of record of those 1000 shares. X has a direct relationship with the issuer, and receives dividends, distributions, and proxies directly from the issuer. In Revised Article 8 terminology, X has a direct claim to a "certificated security." If X wishes to use the investment position as collateral for a loan, X would grant the lender a security interest in the "certificated security." The Article 9 rules for such transactions are explained in Comment 2. XYZ Co. might not issue certificates, but register investors such as X directly on its stockholder books. In that case, X's interest would be an "uncertificated security." The Article 9 rules for uncertificated securities are explained in Comment 3. By contrast to these direct relationships, Y holds the securities through an account with Y's broker. Y does not have a certificate and is not registered on XYZ Co.'s stock books as a holder of record. Rather, Y holds the securities through a chain of securities intermediaries. Under Revised Article 8, Y's interest in XYZ common stock is described as a "securities entitlement." If Y wishes to use the investment position as collateral for a loan, Y would grant the lender a security interest in the "securities entitlement." The Article 9 rules for security entitlements are explained in Comment 4.

A commercial setting in which security interests in investment property play a most economically significant role is the "wholesale" level, that is, finance of securities firms and security interests that support the extension of credit in the settlement system. Comments 6 and 7 deal with these transactions. The rules on security interests in investment property also apply to commodity futures. Comment 8 deals with these transactions.

The rules on security interests in investment property are based on the concept of "control," defined in Sections 8–106 and 9–115(1)(e). If the secured party has control the security interest can attach even without a written security agreement. See Section 9–203. A security interest in investment property can also be created by a written security agreement pursuant to Section 9–203. Security interests in investment property can be perfected by control. See subsection (4)(a). Although other methods of perfection are also permitted, the basic priority rule, set out in subsection (5)(a), is that a secured party who obtains control has priority over a secured party who relies on some other method of perfection. The control priority rule is explained in Comment 5.

2. Security interests in certificated securities. A security interest in a certificated security can be created by conferring control on the secured party. Section 8–106 provides that a secured party has control of a certificated security if the certificate has been delivered, see Section 8–301, and any necessary indorsement has been supplied. Section 9–203 provides that a security interest can attach, even without a written security agreement, if the secured party has control. Section 9–115(4)(a) provides that control is a permissible method of perfection.

A security interest in a certificated security can also be created by a written security agreement pursuant to Section 9–203, and can be perfected by filing, see subsection (4)(b). (The perfection by filing rule does not apply if the debtor is a broker or securities intermediary.) However, a security interest perfected only by filing is subordinate to a conflicting security interest perfected by control. See subsection (5)(a) and Comment 5. Also, perfection by filing would not give the secured party protection against other types of adverse claims, since the Article 8 adverse claim cut-off rules require control. See Section 8–510.

Section 9–115(6) deals with cases where a secured party has taken possession of an unindorsed security certificate in registered form. It provides that even though the indorsement is lacking, delivery of the certificate to the secured party suffices for attachment and perfection of the security interest in the certificated security. It also provides that such a possessory security interest has priority over a conflicting non-control security interest, such as a security interest perfected by filing. However, without the indorsement the secured party would not get the other protections against adverse claims that flow from obtaining control. See Section 8-510.

3. Security interests in uncertificated securities. The rules on security interests in uncertificated securities apply only where the debtor is the direct holder of an uncertificated security. For example, mutual funds typically do not issue certificates, but the beneficial owners of mutual funds shares commonly are the direct holders of the shares, whose interests are recorded on the books of the issuer. If such an investor grants a security interest in the mutual funds shares, the rules in this section on security interests in uncertificated securities apply. These rules are not germane to situations where a debtor holds securities through a securities intermediary. Security interests in positions held through securities intermediaries are governed by the rules on security entitlements and securities accounts, not the rules on uncertificated securities.

A security interest in an uncertificated security can be perfected either by control or by filing. See subsection (4)(a) and (b). (The filing rule does not apply if the debtor is itself a broker or securities intermediary.) Priority disputes among conflicting security interests in an uncertificated security are governed by subsection (5). Under subsection (5)(a), a secured party who obtains control has priority over a secured party who does not have control. Thus, although filing is a permissible method of perfection, a secured party who perfects by filing takes the risk that the debtor has granted or will grant a security interest in the same property to another party who obtains control. See Comment 5.

The requirements for control with respect to uncertificated securities are set out in Section 8-106(c). There are two possibilities. First, a secured party has control if the uncertificated security is transferred from debtor to secured party on the books of the issuer. See Sections 8-106(c)(1) (control by "delivery") and 8-301(b) (defining "delivery" of uncertificated security). So far as the issuer is concerned, the secured party is the registered owner entitled to all rights of ownership, though as between the debtor and secured party the debtor remains the owner and the secured party holds its interest as secured party. Second, a secured party has control over an uncertificated security if the issuer agrees that it will comply with "instructions" originated by the secured party without further consent by the registered owner. See Section 8-106(c)(2). If the debtor, secured party, and issuer agree that the secured party has the right to direct the issuer to dispose of the security without further action by the debtor, the secured party has control even though the debtor remains listed as the registered owner and continues to receive dividends and distributions. Note, though, that there is no statutory requirement that issuers of uncertificated securities offer such arrangements.

4. Security interests in security entitlements and securities accounts. This section establishes a structure for creating security interests in securities and other financial assets that a debtor holds through an account with a securities intermediary. Under Revised Article 8, the interest of a person who holds securities through a securities account with a broker or other securities intermediary is described as a security entitlement. Thus, the Article 9 rules governing the use of that person's investment position as collateral are the rules for security entitlements and securities accounts, not the rules for certificated securities or uncertificated securities.

Attachment of security interests in security entitlements and securities accounts is governed by Section 9-203 and subsections (2) and (3) of this section. Unless the secured party has control, a written security agreement is necessary for attachment. For purposes of description of the collateral in a security agreement, it is not essential that the precise Article 8 terminology be used. See subsection (3). For example, if a debtor who holds 1000 shares of XYZ Co. common stock through a securities account signs a security agreement which describes the collateral as "1000 shares of XYZ Co. common stock," that description is sufficient, even though the debtor's interest would be described under Revised Article 8 as a "security entitlement" to 1000 shares of XYZ Co. common stock.

The Article 8 term security entitlement also covers the interest of a person in a "financial asset," if the person holds that financial asset through a securities account. "Financial asset" is a broader term than "security." See Section 8-102(a)(9). For example, a bankers' acceptance is an Article 3 negotiable instrument and hence an instrument under Section 9-105(1)(i). If a person who holds a bankers' acceptance directly wishes to grant a security interest in it, the Article 9 rules for instruments apply. However, if a person holds a bankers' acceptance through a securities account, the person has a security entitlement to the bankers' acceptance. If the person wishes to grant a security interest in the security entitlement to the bankers' acceptance, the Article 9 rules for investment property apply.

Subsection (1)(f)(iii) provides that the term investment property also includes "securities account." This is intended to facilitate transactions in which a debtor wishes to grant a security interest in all of the investment positions held through a particular account rather than in particular positions carried in the account. Just as a debtor may grant a security interest either in specifically listed items of equipment or in all of the debtor's equipment, so too a debtor who holds securities or other financial assets through a securities account may grant a security interest either in specifically listed security entitlements or in all of the security entitlements held through that account. Referring to the collateral as the securities account is a simple way of describing all of the security entitlements carried in the account. Section 9-115(2) provides that attachment or perfection of a security interest in a securities account is also attachment or perfection of a security interest in all security entitlements carried in the securities account. A security interest in a securities account would also include all other rights of the debtor against the securities intermediary arising out of the securities account. For example, a security interest in a securities account would include credit balances due to the debtor from the securities intermediary, whether or not they are proceeds of a security entitlement.

A security interest in a security entitlement or securities account can be perfected either by control or by filing. See subsections (4)(a) and (4)(b). (The filing rule does not apply if the debtor is itself a broker or securities intermediary.) Priority disputes among conflicting security interests in a security entitlement or securities account are governed by subsection (5). The basic rule of subsection (5)(a) is that a secured party who obtains control has priority over a secured party who does not have control. Thus, although filing is a permissible method of perfection, a secured party who perfects by filing takes the risk that the debtor has granted or will grant a security interest in the same property to another party who obtains control. See Comment 5.

The requirements for control with respect to security entitlements and securities accounts are set out in Sections 8-106(d) and 9-115(1)(e). There are two possibilities. First, Section 8-106(d)(1) provides that a secured party has control over a security entitlement if the secured party becomes the entitlement holder, that is, the position is transferred from debtor to secured party on the books of a securities intermediary. See Examples 1 and 2 in Comment 4 to Section 8-106. Second, Section 8-106(d)(2) provides that a secured party has control over a security entitlement if the securities intermediary agrees that it will comply with entitlement orders originated by the secured party without further consent by the debtor. See Example 3 in Comment 4 to Section 8-106. If the debtor, secured party, and issuer agree that the secured party has the right to direct the securities intermediary to dispose of the collateral without further action by the debtor, the secured party has control even though the debtor remains listed as the entitlement holder and continues to receive dividends and distributions. The secured party can obtain control even though the debtor is also allowed to continue to trade. See Section 8-106(f) and Comment 7 thereto. The three-party control agreement device is based on arrangements that have already developed in the securities business. Even under prior law, some securities brokers developed standard forms of such agreements. Note though that, as is the case with respect to issuers of uncertificated securities, there is no statutory requirement that securities intermediaries offer such control agreement arrangements.

Subsection (1)(e) provides that a secured party has control over a securities account if it has control over all security entitlements carried in the account. Thus, the rules in Section 8-106(d) on control with respect to security entitlements determine whether a secured party has control over a securities account. Control with respect to a securities account is defined in terms of obtaining control over the security entitlements simply for drafting convenience. Of course, an agreement that provides that the securities intermediary will honor instructions from the secured party concerning a securities account described as such is sufficient since such an agreement necessarily implies that the secured party has control over all security entitlements carried in the account.

If a customer borrows from its own securities intermediary, e.g., to purchase securities "on margin" or for other purposes, and grants a security interest to its intermediary, the intermediary has control. See Section 8-106(e). A securities firm could also provide control financing arrangements to its customers through a different legal entity than the securities intermediary itself, e.g., the securities trading, custody, and credit services might be provided by different corporate entities within the financial services firm's "family." So long as the agreement with the customer provides that the entity providing the custodial function (the "securities intermediary") will act on instructions received from entity providing the credit, the credit entity has control.

5. Priority Rules. Subsection (5) specifies the priority rules for conflicting security interests in the same investment property. Subsection (5)(a) states the most important general rule—that a secured party who obtains control has priority over a secured party who does not obtain control. The other priority rules, in subsections (5)(b) through (5)(e), deal with relatively unusual circumstances not covered by the control priority rule. Subsection (5)(f) provides that the general priority rules of Section 9-312 apply to cases not covered by the specific rules in subsection (5). The principal application of this residual rule is that the usual first in time of filing rule applies to conflicting security interests that are perfected only by filing. Because the control priority rule of subsection (5)(a) provides for the ordinary cases in which persons purchase securities on margin credit from their brokers, there is no need for special rules for purchase money security interests. Accordingly, subsection (5)(f) provides that the purchase money priority rule of Section 9-312(4) does not apply to investment property.

The following examples illustrate the basic priority rules of this section:

Example 1. Debtor borrows from Alpha and grants Alpha a security interest in a variety of collateral, including all of Debtor's investment property. At that time Debtor owns 1000 shares of XYZ Co. stock for which Debtor has a certificate. Alpha perfects by filing. Later, Debtor borrows from Beta and grants Beta a security interest in the 1000 shares of XYZ Co. stock. Debtor delivers the certificate, properly indorsed, to Beta. Alpha and Beta both have perfected security interests in the XYZ Co. stock. Beta has control, see Section 8-106(b)(1), and hence has priority over Alpha.

Example 2. Debtor borrows from Alpha and grants Alpha a security interest in a variety of collateral, including all of Debtor's investment property. At that time Debtor owns 1000 shares of XYZ Co. stock, held through a securities account with Able & Co. Alpha perfects by filing. Later, Debtor borrows from Beta and grants Beta a security interest in the 1000 shares of XYZ Co. stock. Debtor instructs Able to have the 1000 shares transferred through the clearing corporation to Custodian Bank, to be credited to Beta's account with Custodian Bank. Alpha and Beta both have perfected security interests in the XYZ Co. stock. Beta has control, see Section 8–106(d)(1), and hence has priority over Alpha.

Example 3. Debtor borrows from Alpha and grants Alpha a security interest in a variety of collateral, including all of Debtor's investment property. At that time Debtor owns 1000 shares of XYZ Co. stock, which is held through a securities account with Able & Co. Alpha perfects by filing. Later, Debtor borrows from Beta and grants Beta a security interest in the 1000 shares of XYZ Co. stock. Debtor, Able, and Beta enter into an agreement under which Debtor will continue to receive dividends and distributions, and will continue to have the right to direct dispositions, but Beta will also have the right to direct dispositions and receive the proceeds. Alpha and Beta both have perfected security interests in the XYZ Co. stock. Beta has control, see Section 8–106(d)(2), and hence has priority over Alpha.

Example 4. Debtor borrows from Alpha and grants Alpha a security interest in a variety of collateral, including all of Debtor's investment property. At that time Debtor owns 1000 shares of XYZ Co. stock, held through a securities account with Able & Co. Alpha perfects by filing. Debtor's agreement with Able & Co. provides that Able has a security interest in all securities carried in the account as security for any obligations of Debtor to Able. Debtor incurs obligations to Able and later defaults on the obligations to Alpha and Able. Able has control by virtue of the rule of Section 8–106(e) that if a customer grants a security interest to its own intermediary, the intermediary has control. Since Alpha does not have control, Able has priority over Alpha under the general control priority rule of subsection (5)(a).

Example 5. Debtor holds securities through a securities account with Able & Co. Debtor's agreement with Able & Co. provides that Able has a security interest in all securities carried in the account as security for any obligations of Debtor to Able. Debtor borrows from Beta and grants Beta a security interest in 1000 shares of XYZ Co. stock carried in the account. Debtor, Able, and Beta enter into an agreement under which Debtor will continue to receive dividends and distributions and will continue to have the right to direct dispositions, but Beta will also have the right to direct dispositions and receive the proceeds. Debtor incurs obligations to Able and later defaults on the obligations to Beta and Able. Both Beta and Able have control, so the general control priority rule of subsection (5)(a) does not apply. Compare Example 4. Subsection (5)(c) provides that a security interest held by a securities intermediary in positions of its own customer has priority over a conflicting security interest of an external lender, so Able has priority over Beta. (Subsection (5)(d) has a parallel rule for commodities intermediaries.) The agreement among Able, Beta, and Debtor could, of course, determine the relative priority of the security interests of Able and Beta, see Section 9–316, but the fact that the intermediary has agreed to act on the instructions of a secured party such as Beta does not itself imply any agreement by the intermediary to subordinate.

The control priority rule does not turn on either temporal sequence or awareness of conflicting security interests. Rather, it is a structural rule, based on the principle that a lender should be able to rely on the collateral without question if the lender has taken the necessary steps to assure itself that it is in a position where it can foreclose on the collateral without further action by the debtor. The control priority rule is necessary because the perfection rules provide considerable flexibility in structuring secured financing arrangements. For example, at the "retail" level, a secured lender to an investor who wants the full measure of protection can obtain control, but the creditor may be willing to accept the greater measure of risk that follows from perfection by filing. Similarly, at the "wholesale" level, a lender to securities firms can leave the collateral with the debtor and obtain a perfected security interest under the automatic perfection rule of subsection (4)(c), but a lender who wants to be entirely sure of its position will want to obtain control. The control priority rule of subsection (5)(a) is an essential part of this system of flexibility. It is feasible to provide more than one method of perfecting secured transactions only if the rules ensure that those who take the necessary steps to obtain the full measure of protection do not run the risk of subordination to those who have not taken such steps. A secured party who is unwilling to run the risk that the debtor has granted or will grant a conflicting control security interest should not make a loan without obtaining control of the collateral.

As applied to the retail level, the control priority rule means that a secured party who obtains control has priority over a conflicting security interest perfected by filing without regard to inquiry into whether the control secured party was aware of the filed security interest. Prior to enactment of this section, Article 9 did not permit perfection of security interests in securities by filing. Accordingly, parties who deal in securities have never developed a practice of searching the UCC files before conducting securities transactions. Although filing is now a permissible method of perfection, in order to avoid disruption of existing practices in this business it is necessary to give perfection by filing a different and more limited effect for securities than for some other forms of collateral. The priority rules are not based on the assumption that parties who perfect by the usual method of obtaining control will search the files. Quite the contrary, the control priority rule is intended to ensure that secured parties who do obtain control are entirely unaffected by filings. To state the point another way, perfection by filing is intended to affect only general creditors or other secured creditors who rely on filing. The rule that a security interest perfected by filing can be primed by a control security interest, without regard to awareness, is a consequence of the system of perfection and priority rules for investment property. These rules are designed to take account of the circumstances of the securities markets, where filing is not given the same effect as for some other forms of property. No implication is made about the effect of filing with respect to security interests in other forms of property, nor about other Article 9 rules, e.g., Section 9-308, which govern the circumstances in which security interests in other forms of property perfected by filing can be primed by subsequent perfected security interests.

6. Secured finance of securities firms. Modernization of the commercial law rules governing secured finance of securities dealers and security interest arrangements in the clearance and settlement system is essential to the safe and efficient functioning of the securities markets.

Secured financing arrangements for securities firms are currently implemented in various ways. In some circumstances lenders may require that the transactions be structured as "hard pledges," where the securities are transferred on the books of a clearing corporation from the debtor's account to the lender's account or to a special pledge account for the lender where they cannot be disposed of without the specific consent of the lender. In other circumstances, lenders are content with so-called "agreement to pledge" or "agreement to deliver" arrangements, where the debtor retains the positions in its own account, but reflects on its books that the positions have been hypothecated and promises that the securities will be transferred to the secured party's account on demand.

The perfection and priority rules of this section are designed to facilitate current secured financing arrangements for securities firms as well as to provide sufficient flexibility to accommodate new arrangements that develop in the future. Hard pledge arrangements are covered by the concept of control. If the lender obtains control, the security interest is perfected and has priority over a conflicting non-control security interest. For examples of control arrangements in this setting see Examples 4 through 8 in Comment 4 to Section 8–106. The secured party can obtain control even though the debtor retains the right to trade or otherwise dispose of the collateral. See Section 8–106(f) and Examples 7 and 8 in Comment 4 to Section 8–106.

Non-control secured financing arrangements for securities firms are covered by the automatic perfection rule of subsection (4)(c). Under prior law, agreement to pledge arrangements could be implemented under a provision that a security interest in securities given for net value under a written security agreement was perfected without filing or possession for a period of 21 days. Although the security interests were temporary in legal theory, the financing arrangements could, in practice, be continued indefinitely by rolling over the loans at least every 21 days. Accordingly, a knowledgeable creditor of a securities firm realizes that the firm's securities may be subject to security interests that are not discoverable from any public records. The perfection rule of subsection (4)(c) makes it unnecessary to engage in the purely formal practice of rolling over these arrangements every 21 days.

Priority questions concerning security interests granted by brokers and securities intermediaries are governed by the general control priority rule of subsection (5)(a), as supplemented by the special rules set out in subsections (b), (c), and (e). In cases not covered by the control priority rule, conflicting security interests rank equally. The following examples illustrate the priority rules as applied to this setting. (In all cases it is assumed that the debtor retains sufficient other securities to satisfy all customers' claims. This section deals with the relative rights of secured lenders to a securities firm. Disputes between a secured lender and the firm's own customers are governed by Section 8–511.)

Example 6. Able & Co., a securities dealer, enters into financing arrangements with two lenders, Alpha Bank and Beta Bank. In each case the agreements provide that the lender will have a security interest in the securities identified on lists provided to the lender on a daily basis, that the debtor will deliver the securities to the lender on demand, and that the debtor will not list as collateral any securities which the debtor has pledged to any other lender. Upon Able's insolvency it is discovered that Able has listed the same securities on the collateral lists provided to both Alpha and Beta. Alpha and Beta both have perfected security interests under the automatic perfection rule of subsection (4)(c). Neither Alpha nor Beta has control. Subsection (5)(e) provides that the security interests of Alpha and Beta rank equally, because each of them has a non-control security interest granted by a securities firm. They share pro-rata.

Example 7. Able enters into financing arrangements with Alpha Bank and Beta Bank as in Example 6. At some point, however, Beta decides that it is unwilling to continue to provide financing on a non-control basis. Able directs the clearing corporation where it holds its principal inventory of securities to move specified securities into Beta's account. Upon Able's insolvency it is discovered that a list of collateral provided to Alpha includes securities that had been moved to Beta's account. Both Alpha and Beta have perfected security interests; Alpha under the automatic perfection rule of subsection (4)(c), and Beta under that rule and also the subsection (4)(a) control perfection rule. Beta has control but Alpha does not. Beta has priority over Alpha under subsection (5)(a).

Example 8. Able & Co. carries its principal inventory of securities through Clearing Corporation, which offers a "shared control" facility whereby a participant securities firm can enter into an arrangement with a lender under which the securities firm will retain the power to trade and otherwise direct dispositions of securities carried in its account, but Clearing Corporation agrees that, at any time the lender so directs, Clearing Corporation will transfer any securities from the firm's account to the lender's account or otherwise dispose of them as directed by the lender. Able enters into financing arrangements with two lenders, Alpha and Beta, each of which obtains such a control agreement from Clearing Corporation. The agreement with each lender provides that Able will designate specific securities as collateral on lists provided to the lender on a daily or other periodic basis, and that it will not pledge the same securities to different lenders. Upon Able's insolvency, it is discovered that Able has listed the same securities on the collateral lists provided to both Alpha and Beta. Both Alpha and Beta have control over the disputed securities. They share pro rata under subsection (5)(b).

7. Secured financing arrangement in the settlement system. Under the rules or agreements governing the relationship between a clearing corporation and its participants, the clearing corporation may have a security interest in securities that the participants have deposited with the clearing corporation pursuant to guaranty fund arrangements or in securities that are in the process of delivery to or from a participant's account in the settlement process. The control rules protect the clearing corporation's rights as secured party in such arrangements, since the clearing corporation would have control over the collateral under the Section 8-106 rules. The control rules also protect the rights of "upper-tier" intermediaries that are not themselves clearing corporations. For example, if a securities dealer carries its inventory through a clearing bank that provides both custodial and credit services, the clearing bank as secured party would have control and hence be assured of perfection and priority over any potential conflicting security interests granted by the securities dealer.

In some circumstances, a clearing corporation may be the debtor in a secured financing arrangement. For example, a clearing corporation that settles delivery-versus-payment transactions among its participants on a net, same-day basis relies on timely payments from all participants with net obligations due to the system. If a participant that is a net debtor were to default on its payment obligation, the clearing corporation would not receive some of the funds needed to settle with participants that are net creditors to the system. To complete end-of-day settlement after a payment default by a participant, a clearing corporation that settles on a net, same-day basis may need to draw on credit lines and pledge securities of the defaulting participant or other securities pledged by participants in the clearing corporation to secure such drawings. The clearing corporation may be the top tier securities intermediary for the securities pledged, so that it would not be practical for the lender to obtain control. Even where the clearing corporation holds some types of securities through other intermediaries, however, the clearing corporation is unlikely to be able to complete the arrangements necessary to convey "control" over the securities to be pledged in time to complete settlement in a timely manner. However, the term "securities intermediary" is defined in Section 8-102(a)(14) to include clearing corporations. Thus, the perfection rule of subsection (4)(c) applies to security interests in investment property granted by clearing corporations.

In secured financing arrangements for clearing corporations and other securities intermediaries, it is sometimes necessary to specify that a secured lender will have a security interest in a certain bundle of securities that, after all the calculations necessary to complete a processing cycle are completed, turn out to be appropriate and available for pledge. At the time the security interest attaches, the necessary computations may not have been completed, though the information that ultimately will determine what positions are to be pledged has been entered. Accordingly, subsection (3) provides that the description of collateral in a security agreement may identify the collateral by means of a computational or allocational formula.

8. Security interests in commodity futures. Section 9-115 establishes rules on security interests in commodity contracts and commodity accounts that are, in general, parallel to the rules on security interests in security entitlements and securities accounts. Note, though, that commodity contracts are not "securities" or "financial assets" under Article 8. See Section 8-103(f). Thus, the relationship between commodity intermediaries and commodity customers is not governed by the indirect holding system rules of Part 5 of Article 8. For securities, the UCC establishes rules in Article 9 on security interests, and rules in Article 8 on the rights of transferees, including secured parties, on such matters as the rights of a transferee if the transfer was itself wrongful so that another party has an adverse claim. For commodity contracts, Article 9 establishes rules on security interests, but questions of the sort dealt with in Article 8 for securities are left to other law.

Subsection (1) contains the definitions of the terms used in substantive rules on security interests in commodity contracts and commodity accounts. The key term "commodity contract" is defined in subsection (1)(b). Section 8-103(f) provides that a commodity contract, as defined in Section 9-115, is not a security or a financial asset. The result is that the indirect holding system rules in Revised Article 8 Part 5 do not apply to anything that falls within the definition of commodity contract in this section. The indirect holding system rules of Article 8, however, are intended to be sufficiently flexible that they can be applied to new developments in the securities and financial markets, where that is appropriate. Accordingly, the "commodity contract" definition in this section is narrowly drafted to ensure that it does not operate as an obstacle to the application of the new Article 8 indirect holding system rules to new products. The term commodity contract covers those contracts that are traded on or subject to the rules of a designated contract market, and foreign commodity contracts that are carried on the books of American commodity intermediaries. The effect of this definition is that the category of commodity contracts that are excluded from Article 8 but governed by Article 9 is essentially the same as the category of contracts that fall within the exclusive regulatory jurisdiction of the federal Commodities Futures Trading Commission.

Commodity contracts are rather different from securities or other financial assets. A person who enters into a commodity futures contract is not buying an asset having a certain value and holding it in anticipation of increase in value. Rather the person is entering into a contract to buy or sell a commodity at set price for delivery at a future time. That contract may become advantageous or disadvantageous as the price of the commodity fluctuates during the term of the contract. The rules of the commodity exchanges require that the contracts be marked to market on a daily basis, that is the customer pays or receives any increment attributable to that day's price change. Because commodity customers may incur obligations on their contracts, they are required to provide collateral at the outset, known as "original margin," and may be required to provide additional amounts, known as "variation margin," during the term of the contract.

The most likely setting in which a person would want to take a security interest in a commodity contract is where a lender who is advancing funds to finance an inventory of a physical commodity requires the borrower to enter into a commodity contract as a hedge against the risk of decline in the value of the commodity. The lender will want to take a security interest in both the commodity itself and the hedging commodity contract. Typically, such arrangements are structured as security interests in the entire commodity account in which the borrower carries the hedging contracts, rather than in individual contracts. Section 9–115 provides a simple mechanism for implementation of such arrangements, either by granting a security interest in the commodity account, or in particular commodity contracts carried in the account. The security interest can be perfected by filing or by control. Under subsection (1)(e) the secured party can obtain control over a commodity contract or commodity account by obtaining an agreement among the commodity customer, the secured party, and the commodity intermediary in which the commodity intermediary agrees to apply any value distributed as directed by the secured party. This provides a clear and certain legal framework for practices that have already developed in the industry.

One important effect of including commodity contracts and commodity accounts in the new Article 9 rules is to provide a clearer legal structure for the analysis of the rights of commodity clearing organizations against their participants and futures commission merchants against their customers. The rules and agreements of commodity clearing organizations generally provide that the clearing organization has the right to liquidate any participant's positions in order to satisfy obligations of the participant to the clearing corporation. Similarly, agreements between futures commission merchants and their customers generally provide that the futures commission merchant has the right to liquidate a customer's positions in order to satisfy obligations of the customer to the futures commission merchant. Section 9–115 treats these rights as security interests and applies to them the same priority rules that apply to the somewhat analogous relationships between securities clearing corporations or securities intermediaries and their participants or customers. Subsection (1)(e) provides that the commodity intermediary has control, and therefore the security interest is perfected under subsection (4)(a). Subsection (5)(d) provides that the security interest of a commodity clearing organization in its participant's commodity contracts has priority over any security interest granted by the participant to a third-party lender. Similarly, an FCM's security interest would have priority over any security interest granted by its customer to a third-party lender.

The main property that a commodity intermediary holds as collateral for the obligations that the commodity customer may incur under its commodity contracts is not other commodity contracts carried by the customer but the other property that the customer has posted as margin. Typically, this property will be securities. The commodity intermediary's security interest in such securities is governed by the rules of this section on security interests in securities, not the rules on security interests in commodity contracts or commodity accounts.

Although there are significant analytic and regulatory differences between commodities and securities, the development of commodity contracts on financial products in the past few decades has resulted in a system in which the commodity markets and security markets are closely linked. The Section 9–115 rules on security interests in commodity contracts and commodity accounts provide a structure that may be essential in times of stress in the financial markets. Suppose, for example that a firm has a position in a securities market that is hedged by a position in a commodity market, so that payments that the firm is obligated to make with respect to the securities position will be covered by the receipt of funds from the commodity position. Depending upon the settlement cycles of the different markets, it is possible that the firm could find itself in a position where it is obligated to make the payment with respect to the securities position before it receives the matching funds from the commodity position. If cross-margining arrangements have not been developed between the two markets, the firm may need to borrow funds temporarily to make the earlier payment. The Section 9–115 rules would facilitate the use of positions in one market as collateral for loans needed to cover obligations in the other market.

9. Relation to other law. Section 1–103 provides that "unless displaced by particular provisions of this Act, the principles of law and equity . . . shall supplement its provisions." There may be circumstances in which a secured party's action in acquiring a security interest that has priority under this section constitutes conduct that is wrongful under other law. Though the possibility of such resort to other law may provide an appropriate "escape valve" for cases of egregious conduct, care must be taken to ensure that this does not impair the certainty and predictability of the priority rules. Whether a court may appropriately look to other law to impose liability upon or estop a party from asserting its Article 9 priority depends on an assessment of the party's conduct under the standards established by such other law as well as a determination of whether the particular application of such other law is displaced by the UCC.

Some circumstances in which other law is clearly displaced by the UCC rules are readily identifiable. Common law "first in time, first in right" principles, or correlative tort liability rules such as common law conversion principles under which a purchaser may incur liability to a party with a prior property interest without regard to awareness of that claim, are necessarily displaced by the priority rules set out in this section since these rules determine the relative ranking of security interests in investment property. So too, Article 8 provides protections against adverse claims to certain purchasers of interests in investment property. In circumstances where a secured party not only has priority under Section 9–115, but also qualifies for protection against adverse claims under Section 8–303, 8–502, or 8–510, resort to other law would be precluded.

In determining whether it is appropriate in a particular case to look to other law, account must also be taken of the policies that underlie the commercial law rules on securities markets and security interests in securities. A principal objective of the revision of Article 8 and corresponding provisions of Article 9 is to ensure that secured financing transactions can be implemented on a simple, timely, and certain basis. One of the circumstances that led to the revision was the concern that uncertainty in the application of the rules on secured transactions involving securities and other financial assets could contribute to systemic risk by impairing the ability of financial institutions to provide liquidity to the markets in times of stress. The control priority rule is designed to provide a clear and certain rule to ensure that lenders who have taken the necessary steps to establish control do not face a risk of subordination to other lenders who have not done so.

The control priority rule does not turn on an inquiry into the state of a party's awareness of potential conflicting claims because a rule under which a party's rights depended on that sort of after the fact inquiry could introduce an unacceptable measure of uncertainty. If an inquiry into awareness could provide a complete and satisfactory resolution of the problem in all cases, the priority rule of this section would have incorporated that test. The fact that it does not necessarily means that resort to other law based solely on that factor is precluded, though the question whether a control secured party induced or encouraged its financing arrangement with actual knowledge that the debtor would be violating the rights of another secured party may, in some circumstances, appropriately be treated as a factor in determining whether the control party's action is the kind of egregious conduct for which resort to other law is appropriate.

Definitional Cross References:

"Broker". Section 8-102(a)(3).
"Certificated security". Section 8-102(a)(4).
"Collateral". Section 9-105(1)(c).
"Control". Section 8-106.
"Debtor". Section 9-105(1)(d).
"Delivery". Section 8-301.
"Entitlement holder". Section 8-102(a)(7).
"Secured party". Section 9-105(1)(m).
"Securities account". Section 8-501.
"Securities intermediary". Section 8-102(a)(14).
"Security". Section 8-102(a)(15).
"Security agreement". Section 9-105(1)(*l*).
"Security certificate". Section 8-102(a)(16).
"Security entitlement". Section 8-102(a)(17).
"Security interest". Section 1-201(37).
"Uncertificated security". Section 8-102(a)(18).

§ 9-116. SECURITY INTEREST ARISING IN PURCHASE OR DELIVERY OF FINANCIAL ASSET.

(1) If a person buys a financial asset through a securities intermediary in a transaction in which the buyer is obligated to pay the purchase price to the securities intermediary at the time of the purchase, and the securities intermediary credits the financial asset to the buyer's securities account before the buyer pays the securities intermediary, the securities intermediary has a security interest in the buyer's security entitlement securing the buyer's obligation to pay. A security agreement is not required for attachment or enforceability of the security interest, and the security interest is automatically perfected.

(2) If a certificated security, or other financial asset represented by a writing which in the ordinary course of business is transferred by delivery with any necessary indorsement or assignment is delivered pursuant to an agreement between persons in the business of dealing with such securities or financial assets and the agreement calls for delivery versus payment, the person delivering the certificate or other financial asset has a security interest in the certificated security or other financial asset securing the seller's right to receive payment. A security agreement is not required for attachment or enforceability of the security interest, and the security interest is automatically perfected.

Official Comment

1. This section establishes two special rules concerning security interests in investment property in order to provide certainty in the securities settlement system.

2. Depending upon a securities intermediary's arrangements with its entitlement holders, the securities intermediary may treat the entitlement holder as entitled to the securities in question before the entitlement holder has actually made payment for them. For example, many brokers permit retail customers to pay for securities by check. The broker may not receive final payment of the check until several days after the broker has credited the customer's securities account for the securities. Thus, the customer will have acquired a security entitlement prior to payment. Subsection (1) provides that in such circumstances the securities intermediary has a security interest in the entitlement holder's security entitlement as security for the payment obligation. This is a codification and adaptation to

the indirect holding system of the so-called "broker's lien," which has long been recognized in existing law. See Restatement of Security § 12. An intermediary who has a security interest under this section will have control by virtue of Section 8–106(e). The security interest has priority over conflicting security interests granted by the entitlement holder, under Section 9–115(5)(a) and (c).

3. Subsection (2) specifies the rights of persons who deliver certificated securities or other financial assets in physical form, such as money market instruments, if the agreed payment is not received. In the typical arrangement for settlement of physical securities, the seller's securities custodian will deliver the physical certificates to the buyer's securities custodian and receive a time-stamped delivery receipt. The buyer's securities custodian will examine the certificate to ensure that it is in good order, and that the delivery matches a trade in which the buyer has instructed the seller to deliver to that custodian. If all is in order, the receiving custodian will settle with the delivering custodian through whatever funds settlement system has been agreed upon or is used by custom and usage in that market. The understanding of the trade, however, is that the delivery is conditioned upon payment, so that if payment is not made for any reason, the security will be returned to the deliverer. Subsection (2) is intended to clarify the rights of persons making deliveries in such circumstances. It specifies that the person making delivery has a security interest in the securities or other financial assets, securing the right to receive payment. No security agreement is required for attachment, and no filing or other action is required for perfection.

Definitional Cross References:

"Certificated security". Section 8–102(a)(4).

"Financial asset". Section 8–102(a)(9).

"Securities account". Section 8–501.

"Securities intermediary". Section 8–102(a)(14).

"Security agreement". Section 9–105(1)(*l*).

"Security entitlement". Section 8–102(a)(17).

"Security interest". Section 1–201(37).

§ 9–203. Attachment and Enforceability of Security Interest; Proceeds; Formal Requisites.

(1) Subject to the provisions of Section 4–208 on the security interest of a collecting bank, ~~Section 8–321 on security interests in securities~~ Sections 9–115 and 9–116 on security interests in investment property, and Section 9–113 on a security interest arising under the Article on Sales, a security interest is not enforceable against the debtor or third parties with respect to the collateral and does not attach unless:

(a) the collateral is in the possession of the secured party pursuant to agreement, the collateral is investment property and the secured party has control pursuant to agreement, or the debtor has signed a security agreement which contains a description of the collateral and in addition, when the security interest covers crops growing or to be grown or timber to be cut, a description of the land concerned;

(b) value has been given; and

(c) the debtor has rights in the collateral.

. . .

§ 9–207. Rights and Duties When Collateral is in Secured Party's Possession.

. . .

Official Comment

. . .

3. The right of a secured party holding instruments or documents to have them indorsed or transferred to him or his order is dealt with in the relevant sections of Articles 3 (Commercial Paper), 7 (Warehouse Receipts, Bills of Lading and Other Documents) and 8 (Investment Securities). (Sections 3–201, 7–506, ~~8–307~~ 8–304(d).) *Amendments approved by the Permanent Editorial Board for Uniform Commercial Code November 4, 1995.*

. . .

Cross References:

Point 1: Section 1–102(3).

Point 3: Sections 3–201, 7–506 and ~~8–307~~ 8–304(d). *Amendments approved by the Permanent Editorial Board for Uniform Commercial Code November 4, 1995.*

Point 4: Section 9–501(2) and Part 5.

§ 9–301. Persons Who Take Priority Over Unperfected Security Interests; Rights of "Lien Creditor."

(1) Except as otherwise provided in subsection (2), an unperfected security interest is subordinate to the rights of

. . .

(d) in the case of accounts, ~~and~~ general intangibles, and investment property, a person who is not a secured party and who is a transferee to the extent that he gives value without knowledge of the security interest and before it is perfected.

. . .

§ 9–302. When Filing is Required to Perfect Security Interest; Security Interests to Which Filing Provisions of This Article Do Not Apply.

(1) A financing statement must be filed to perfect all security interests except the following:

. . .

(b) a security interest temporarily perfected in instruments, certificated securities, or documents without delivery under Section 9–304 or in proceeds for a 10 day period under Section 9–306;

. . .

(f) a security interest of a collecting bank (Section 4-208) ~~or in securities (Section 8-321)~~ or arising under the Article on Sales (see Section 9-113) or covered in subsection (3) of this section;

(g) an assignment for the benefit of all the creditors of the transferor, and subsequent transfers by the assignee thereunder~~.~~;

(h) a security interest in investment property which is perfected without filing under Section 9-115 or Section 9-116.

. . .

§ 9-303. When Security Interest Is Perfected; Continuity of Perfection.

(1) A security interest is perfected when it has attached and when all of the applicable steps required for perfection have been taken. Such steps are specified in Sections 9-115, 9-302, 9-304, 9-305 and 9-306. If such steps are taken before the security interest attaches, it is perfected at the time when it attaches.

. . .

§ 9-304. Perfection of Security Interest in Instruments, Documents, and Goods Covered by Documents; Perfection by Permissive Filing; Temporary Perfection Without Filing or Transfer of Possession.

(1) A security interest in chattel paper or negotiable documents may be perfected by filing. A security interest in money or instruments (other than ~~certificated securities or~~ instruments which constitute part of chattel paper) can be perfected only by the secured party's taking possession, except as provided in subsections (4) and (5) of this section and subsections (2) and (3) of Section 9-306 on proceeds.

. . .

(4) A security interest in instruments ~~(other than certificated securities)~~, certificated securities, or negotiable documents is perfected without filing or the taking of possession for a period of 21 days from the time it attaches to the extent that it arises for new value given under a written security agreement.

(5) A security interest remains perfected for a period of 21 days without filing where a secured party having a perfected security interest in an instrument ~~(other than a certificated security)~~, a certificated security, a negotiable document, or goods in possession of a bailee other than one who has issued a negotiable document therefor

. . .

(b) delivers the instrument or certificated security to the debtor for the purpose of ultimate sale or exchange or of presentation, collection, renewal, or registration of transfer.

. . .

§ 9-305. When Possession by Secured Party Perfects Security Interest Without Filing.

A security interest in letters of credit and advices of credit (subsection (2)(a) of Section 5-116), goods, instruments ~~(other than certificated securities)~~, money, negotiable documents, or chattel paper may be perfected by the secured party's taking possession of the collateral. If such collateral other than goods covered by a negotiable document is held by a bailee, the secured party is deemed to have possession from the time the bailee receives notification of the secured party's interest. A security interest is perfected by possession from the time possession is taken without a relation back and continues only so long as possession is retained, unless otherwise specified in this Article. The security interest may be otherwise perfected as provided in this Article before or after the period of possession by the secured party.

. . .

Official Comment

. . .

1. As under the common law of pledge, no filing is required by this Article to perfect a security interest where the secured party has possession of the collateral. Compare Section 9-302(1)(a). This section permits a security interest to be perfected by transfer of possession only when the collateral is goods, instruments ~~(other than certificated securities, which are governed by Section 8-321)~~, documents or chattel paper: that is to say, accounts and general intangibles are excluded. As to perfection of security interests in certificated securities by possession, see the general rules on perfection of security interests in investment property in Section 9-115(4) and the special rule in Section 9-115(6) dealing with cases where a secured party takes possession of a security certificate in registered form without obtaining an indorsement. See Section 5-116 for the special case of assignments of letters and advices of credit. A security interest in accounts and general intangibles—property not ordinarily represented by any writing whose delivery operates to transfer the claim—may under this Article be perfected only by filing, and this rule would not be affected by the fact that a security agreement or other writing described the assignment of such collateral as a "pledge". Section 9-302(1)(e) exempts from filing certain assignments of accounts which are out of the ordinary course of financing: such exempted assignments are perfected when they attach under Section 9-303(1); they do not fall within this section. *Amendments approved by the Permanent Editorial Board for Uniform Commercial Code November 4, 1995.*

. . .

§ 9-306. "Proceeds"; Secured Party's Rights on Disposition of Collateral.

(1) "Proceeds" includes whatever is received upon the sale, exchange, collection, or other disposition of collateral or proceeds. Insurance payable by reason of loss or damage to the collateral is proceeds, except to the extent that it is payable to a person other than a party to the security agreement. Any payments or distributions made with respect to investment property collateral are proceeds. Money, checks, deposit accounts, and the like, are "cash proceeds". All other proceeds are "non-cash proceeds".

. . .

(3) The security interest in proceeds is a continuously perfected security interest if the interest in the original collateral was perfected but it ceases to be a perfected security interest and becomes unperfected ten days after receipt of the proceeds by the debtor unless

(a) a filed financing statement covers the original collateral and the proceeds are collateral in which a security interest may be perfected by filing in the office or offices where the financing statement has been filed and, if the proceeds are acquired with cash proceeds, the description of collateral in the financing statement indicates the types of property constituting the proceeds; or

(b) a filed financing statement covers the original collateral and the proceeds are identifiable cash proceeds; ~~or~~

(c) the original collateral was investment property and the proceeds are identifiable cash proceeds; or

~~(c)~~(d) the security interest in the proceeds is perfected before the expiration of the ten day period.

Except as provided in this section, a security interest in proceeds can be perfected only by the methods or under the circumstances permitted in this Article for original collateral of the same type.

. . .

§ 9–309. Protection of Purchasers of Instruments, Documents, and Securities.

Nothing in this Article limits the rights of a holder in due course of a negotiable instrument (Section 3–302) or a holder to whom a negotiable document of title has been duly negotiated (Section 7–501) or a ~~bona fide~~ protected purchaser of a security (Section ~~8–302~~ 8–303) and such holders or purchasers take priority over an earlier security interest even though perfected. Filing under this Article does not constitute notice of the security interest to such holders or purchasers.

§ 9–312. Priorities Among Conflicting Security Interests in the Same Collateral.

(1) The rules of priority stated in other sections of this Part, and in the following sections shall govern when applicable: Section ~~4–208~~ 4–210 with respect to the security interests of collecting banks in items being collected, accompanying documents and proceeds; Section 9–103 on security interests related to other jurisdictions; Section 9–114 on consignments; Section 9–115 on security interests in investment property.

. . .

(7) If future advances are made while a security interest is perfected by filing, the taking of possession, or under Section ~~8–321 on securities~~ 9–115 or Section 9–116 on investment property, the security interest has the same priority for the purposes of subsection (5) or Section 9–115(5) with respect to the future advances as it does with respect to the first advance. If a commitment is made before or while the security interest is so perfected, the

security interest has the same priority with respect to advances made pursuant thereto. In other cases a perfected security interest has priority from the date the advance is made.

Conforming Amendments to Articles 1, 3, 4, 5, and 10

[Changes from present law are shown by underscore and ~~strikeout~~.]

§ 1–105. Territorial Application of the Act; Parties' Power to Choose Applicable Law.

. . .

(2) Where one of the following provisions of this Act specifies the applicable law, that provision governs and a contrary agreement is effective only to the extent permitted by the law (including the conflict of laws rules) so specified:

. . .

Applicability of the Article on Investment Securities. Section ~~8–106~~ 8–110

. . .

§ 1–201. General Definitions.

. . .

Official Comment

17. "Fungible". See Sections 5, 6 and 76, Uniform Sales Act; Section 58, Uniform Warehouse Receipts Act. Fungibility of goods "by agreement" has been added for clarity and accuracy. ~~As to securities, see Section 8–107 and Comment.~~ *Amendment approved by the Permanent Editorial Board for Uniform Commercial Code November 4, 1995.*

. . .

§ 1–206. Statute of Frauds For Kinds of Personal Property Not Otherwise Covered.

. . .

(2) Subsection (1) of this section does not apply to contracts for the sale of goods (Section 2–201) nor of securities (Section ~~8–319~~ 8–113) nor to security agreements (Section 9–203).

Official Comment

Purposes: To fill the gap left by the Statute of Frauds provisions for goods (Section 2–201)~~, securities (Section 8–319),~~ and security interests (Section 9–

203). As to securities, see Section 8–113. The Uniform Sales Act covered the sale of "choses in action"; the principal gap relates to sale of the "general intangibles" defined in Article 9 (Section 9–106) and to transactions excluded from Article 9 by Section 9–104. Typical are the sale of bilateral contracts, royalty rights or the like. The informality normal to such transactions is recognized by lifting the limit for oral transactions to $5,000. In such transactions there is often no standard of practice by which to judge, and values can rise or drop without warning; troubling abuses are avoided when the dollar limit is exceeded by requiring that the subject-matter be reasonably identified in a signed writing which indicates that a contract for sale has been made at a defined or stated price. *Amendments approved by the Permanent Editorial Board for Uniform Commercial Code November 4, 1995.*

. . .

§ 1–209. Subordinated Obligations.

. . .

Official Comment

. . .

4. The enforcement of subordination agreements is largely left to supplementary principles under Section 1–103. If the subordinated debt is evidenced by ~~an investment security, Section 8–202(1)~~ a certificated security, Section 8–202(a) authorizes enforcement against purchasers on terms stated or referred to on the security certificate. If the fact of subordination is noted on a negotiable instrument, a holder under Sections 3–302 and 3–306 is subject to the term because notice precludes him from taking free of the subordination. Sections 3–302(3)(a), 3–306 and 8–317 severely limit the rights of levying creditors of a subordinated creditor in such cases. *Amendments approved by the Permanent Editorial Board for Uniform Commercial Code November 4, 1995.*

. . .

§ 3–102. Subject Matter.

. . .

Official Comment

. . .

2. The reference in former Section 3–103(1) to "documents of title" is omitted as superfluous because these documents contain no promise to pay money. The definition of "payment order" in Section 4A–103(a)(1)(iii) excludes drafts which are governed by Article 3. Section 3–102(a) makes clear that a payment order governed by Article 4A is not governed by Article 3. Thus, Article 3 and Article 4A are mutually exclusive.

Article 8 states in ~~Section 8–102(1)(c)~~ Section 8–103(d) that "A writing that is a ~~certificated~~ security certificate is governed by this Article and not by Article 3, even though it also meets the requirements of that Article." Section 3–102(a) conforms to this provision. With respect to some promises or orders to pay money, there may be a question whether the promise or order is an instrument under Section 3–104(a) or a certificated security under ~~Section 8-102(1)(a)~~ Section 8-102(a)(4) and (15). Whether a writing is covered by Article 3 or Article 8 has important consequences. Among other things, under Section 8-207, the issuer of a certificated security may treat the registered owner as the owner for all purposes until the presentment for registration of a transfer. The issuer of a negotiable instrument, on the other hand, may discharge its obligation to pay the instrument only by paying a person entitled to enforce under Section 3-301. There are also important consequences to an indorser. An indorser of a security does not undertake the issuer's obligation or make any warranty that the issuer will honor the underlying obligation, while an indorser of a negotiable instrument becomes secondarily liable on the underlying obligation. *Amendments approved by the Permanent Editorial Board for Uniform Commercial Code November 4, 1995.*

Ordinarily the distinction between instruments and certificated securities in non-bearer form should be relatively clear. A certificated security under Article 8 must be in registered form (~~Section 8-102(1)(a)(i)~~ Section 8-102(a)(13)) so that it can be registered on the issuer's records. By contrast, registration plays no part in Article 3. The distinction between an instrument and a certificated security in bearer form may be somewhat more difficult and will generally lie in the economic functions of the two writings. Ordinarily, negotiable instruments under Article 3 will be separate and distinct instruments, while certificated securities under Article 8 will be either one of a class or series or by their terms divisible into a class or series (~~Section 8-102(1)(a)(iii)~~ Section 8-102(a)(15)(ii)). Thus, a promissory note in bearer form could come under either Article 3 if it were simply an individual note, or under Article 8 if it were one of a series of notes or divisible into a series. An additional distinction is whether the instrument is of the type commonly dealt in on securities exchanges or markets or commonly recognized as a medium for investment (~~Section 8-102(1)(a)(ii)~~ Section 8-102(a)(15)(iii)). Thus, a check written in bearer form (i.e., a check made payable to "cash") would not be a certificated security within Article 8 of the Uniform Commercial Code. *Amendments approved by the Permanent Editorial Board for Uniform Commercial Code November 4, 1995.*

Occasionally, a particular writing may fit the definition of both a negotiable instrument under Article 3 and of an investment security under Article 8. In such cases, the instrument is subject exclusively to the requirements of Article 8. ~~Section 8-102(1)(c)~~ Section 8-103(d) and Section 3-102(a). *Amendments approved by the Permanent Editorial Board for Uniform Commercial Code November 4, 1995.*

. . .

§ 4-102. Applicability.

Official Comment

1. The rules of Article 3 governing negotiable instruments, their transfer, and the contracts of the parties thereto apply to the items collected through banking channels wherever no specific provision is found in this Article. In the case of conflict, this Article governs. See Section 3-102(b).

Bonds and like instruments constituting investment securities under Article 8 may also be handled by banks for collection purposes. Various sections of Article 8 prescribe rules of transfer some of which (see ~~Sections 8-304 and 8-306~~ Sections 8-108 and 8-304) may conflict with provisions of this Article (Sections 4-205, 4-207, and 4-208). In the case of conflict, Article 8 governs. *Amendments approved by the Permanent Editorial Board for Uniform Commercial Code November 4, 1995.*

. . .

§ 4–104. Definitions and Index of Definitions.

(a) In this Article, unless the context otherwise requires:

. . .

(6) "Documentary draft" means a draft to be presented for acceptance or payment if specified documents, certificated securities (Section 8–102) or instructions for uncertificated securities (Section ~~8–308~~ 8–102), or other certificates, statements, or the like are to be received by the drawee or other payor before acceptance or payment of the draft;

. . .

§ 5–114. Issuer's Duty and Privilege to Honor; Right to Reimbursement.

. . .

(2) Unless otherwise agreed where documents appear on their face to comply with the terms of a credit but a required document does not in fact conform to the warranties made on negotiation or transfer of a document of title (Section 7–507) or of a certificated security (Section ~~8–306~~ 8–108) or is forged or fraudulent or there is fraud in the transaction:

. . .

§ 10–104. Laws Not Repealed.

[(1)] The Article on Documents of Title (Article 7) does not repeal or modify any laws prescribing the form or contents of documents of title or the services or facilities to be afforded by bailees, or otherwise regulating bailees' businesses in respects not specifically dealt with herein; but the fact that such laws are violated does not affect the status of a document of title which otherwise complies with the definition of a document of title (Section 1–201).

~~[(2) This Act does not repeal ______________________________*, cited as the Uniform Act for the Simplification of Fiduciary Security Transfers, and if in any respect there is any inconsistency between that Act and the Article of this Act on investment securities (Article 8) the provisions of the former Act shall control.]~~

~~Note: *At * in subsection (2) insert the statutory reference to the Uniform Act for the Simplification of Fiduciary Security Transfers if such Act has previously been enacted. If it has not been enacted, omit subsection (2).*~~

Official Comment

This section subordinates the Article of this Act on Documents of Title (Article 7) to the more specialized regulations of particular classes of bailees under other legislation and international treaties. Particularly, the provisions of that Article are superseded by applicable inconsistent provisions regarding the obligation of carriers and the limitation of their liability found in federal legislation dealing with transportation by water (including the Harter Act, Act of February 13, 1893, 27 Stat. 445, and the Carriage of Goods by Sea Act, Act of April 16, 1936, 49 Stat. 1207); the Warsaw Convention on International Air Transportation, 49 Stat. 3000, and Section 20(11) of the Interstate Commerce Act, Act of February 20, 1887, 24 Stat. 386, as amended. The Documents of Title provisions of this Act supplement such legislation largely in matters other than obligation of the bailee, e.g., form and effects of negotiation, procedure in the case of lost documents, effect of overissue, possibility of rapid transmission.

~~Doubts have been expressed whether Article 8 provides as complete protection on transfers of securities by fiduciaries as the Uniform Act for the Simplification of Fiduciary Security Transfers. The Editorial Board entirely favors the policy of simplifying fiduciary security transfers and believes that Article 8 soundly implements this policy. However, since the shorter Simplification Act has been so widely enacted and has been working satisfactorily, the Editorial Board recommends that it be retained [As amended in 1962].~~

Cross Reference:

Section 7–103.

APPENDIX XIII

PRE–REVISION (1994) ARTICLE 8

Set forth below are the Text and Official Comments of Article 8 as they existed prior to revision in 1994.

ARTICLE 8

INVESTMENT SECURITIES

PART 1. SHORT TITLE AND GENERAL MATTERS

PART 2. ISSUE—ISSUER

PART 3. TRANSFER

PART 1

SHORT TITLE AND GENERAL MATTERS

§ 8–101. Short Title.

This Article shall be known and may be cited as Uniform Commercial Code—Investment Securities.

Official Comment

Purposes:

This Article sets forth certain rights and duties of the issuers of and the parties that deal with investment securities, both certificated and uncertificated. Unlike a corporation code, it does not set forth general rules defining property rights that accrue to holders of securities. And unlike a Blue Sky statute it does not set forth specific requirements for disclosing to the public the nature of the property interest that is the security. Rather it sets forth rules relative to the transfer of the rights that constitute securities and to the establishment of those rights against the issuer and other parties.

As is true with respect to all other Articles of the Code, parties may by agreement create rights and duties between themselves that vary from those set forth in this Article. Section 1–102(3). But prejudice to the rights of those not party to the agreement is limited by Code provisions (*e.g.*, Sections 8–313 and 8–321) as well as by general legal principles that supplement the Code. See Section 1–103 and Comment 2 to Section 1–102.

This Article does not purport to determine whether a particular issue of securities should be represented by certificates, in whole or in part. That determination is left to the parties involved, subject to federal and state law.

§ 8–102. Definitions and Index of Definitions.

(1) In this Article, unless the context otherwise requires:

(a) A "certificated security" is a share, participation, or other interest in property of or an enterprise of the issuer or an obligation of the issuer which is

(i) represented by an instrument issued in bearer or registered form;

(ii) of a type commonly dealt in on securities exchanges or markets or commonly recognized in any area in which it is issued or dealt in as a medium for investment; and

(iii) either one of a class or series or by its terms divisible into a class or series of shares, participations, interests, or obligations.

(b) An "uncertificated security" is a share, participation, or other interest in property or an enterprise of the issuer or an obligation of the issuer which is

(i) not represented by an instrument and the transfer of which is registered upon books maintained for that purpose by or on behalf of the issuer;

(ii) of a type commonly dealt in on securities exchanges or markets; and

(iii) either one of a class or series or by its terms divisible into a class or series of shares, participations, interests, or obligations.

(c) A "security" is either a certificated or an uncertificated security. If a security is certificated, the terms "security" and "certificated security" may mean either the intangible interest, the instrument representing that interest, or both, as the context requires. A writing that is a certificated security is governed by this Article and not by Article 3, even though it also meets the requirements of that Article. This Article does not apply to money. If a certificated security has been retained by or surrendered to the issuer or its transfer agent for reasons other than registration of transfer, other temporary purpose, payment, exchange, or acquisition by the issuer, that security shall be treated as an uncertificated security for purposes of this Article.

(d) A certificated security is in "registered form" if

(i) it specifies a person entitled to the security or the rights it represents; and

(ii) its transfer may be registered upon books maintained for that purpose by or on behalf of the issuer, or the security so states.

(e) A certificated security is in "bearer form" if it runs to bearer according to its terms and not by reason of any indorsement.

(2) A "subsequent purchaser" is a person who takes other than by original issue.

(3) A "clearing corporation" is a corporation registered as a "clearing agency" under the federal securities laws or a corporation:

(a) at least 90 percent of whose capital stock is held by or for one or more organizations, none of which, other than a national securities exchange or association, holds in excess of 20 percent of the capital stock of the corporation, and each of which is

(i) subject to supervision or regulation pursuant to the provisions of federal or state banking laws or state insurance laws,

(ii) a broker or dealer or investment company registered under the federal securities laws, or

(iii) a national securities exchange or association registered under the federal securities laws; and

(b) any remaining capital stock of which is held by individuals who have purchased it at or prior to the time of their taking office as directors of the corporation and who have purchased only so much of the capital stock as is necessary to permit them to qualify as directors.

(4) A "custodian bank" is a bank or trust company that is supervised and examined by state or federal authority having supervision over banks and is acting as custodian for a clearing corporation.

(5) Other definitions applying to this Article or to specified Parts thereof and the sections in which they appear are:

"Adverse claim".	Section 8-302.
"Bona fide purchaser".	Section 8-302.
"Broker".	Section 8-303.
"Debtor".	Section 9-105.
"Financial intermediary".	Section 8-313.
"Guarantee of the signature".	Section 8-402.
"Initial transaction statement".	Section 8-408.
"Instruction".	Section 8-308.
"Intermediary bank".	Section 4-105.
"Issuer".	Section 8-201.
"Overissue".	Section 8-104.
"Secured Party".	Section 9-105.
"Security Agreement".	Section 9-105.

(6) In addition, Article 1 contains general definitions and principles of construction and interpretation applicable throughout this Article.

As amended in 1962, 1973 and 1977.

Official Comment

Prior Uniform Statutory Provision: None.

Purposes:

1. This is Article 8's definitional Section. It is supplemented generally by the definitions in Article 1 and in particular matters is supplemented by definitions in other Articles. Subsection (5) enumerates several important supplementary definitions and their locations in the Code.

2. Subsection (1) defines "security," the basic term of this section. Paragraphs (a) and (b) respectively define "certificated security" and "uncertificated security," and paragraph (c) states that the term "security" comprises both. These definitions are functional rather than formal. At the core is the notion

that a security is a share or participation in an enterprise or an obligation that is of a type commonly traded in organized markets for such interests or is commonly recognized as a medium for investment. The ambit of the definition will change as "securities" trading practices evolve to include or exclude new property interests. It is believed that the definition will cover anything which securities markets, including not only the organized exchanges but as well the "over-the-counter" markets, are likely to regard as suitable for trading. For example, transferable warrants evidencing rights to subscribe for shares in a corporation will normally be "certificated securities" within the definition, since they (a) are issued in bearer or registered form, (b) are of a type commonly dealt in on securities markets, (c) constitute a class or series of instruments, and (d) evidence an obligation of the issuer, namely the obligation to honor the warrant upon its due exercise and issue shares accordingly.

Notice that the definition of uncertificated security does not include the phrase "or commonly recognized in any area in which it is issued or dealt in as a medium for investment." Since there is no requirement of representation by an instrument, a great many interests that might be regarded as media for investment would be classified as securities under the umbrella of the omitted phrase. For example, interests such as bank checking and savings accounts are intended to be excluded from the definition because they are not commonly traded; but since those accounts are commonly recognized as media for investment, the omitted language might bring them within the scope of the definition.

Interests such as the stock of closely-held corporations, although they are not actually traded upon securities exchanges, are intended to be included within the definitions of both certificated and uncertificated securities by the inclusion of interests "of a type" commonly traded in those markets. See paragraphs (1)(a)(ii) and (1)(b)(ii).

The second sentence of (1)(c) is intended to eliminate confusion arising from the fact that certificated securities are alternatively viewed as the actual pieces of paper and the interests they represent. The final sentence of (1)(c) is to recognize that an issuer that nominally issues certificated securities but does not normally send the certificates to the owners is functionally identical to the issuer of uncertificated securities and should be guided by the same rules.

3. The consequence of determining that an interest is a "security" is that this Article will provide the relative rights of issuers, owners, purchasers and creditors as to transfer of rights, notice of claims, registration of interests, etc. This definition has no bearing upon whether an interest is a "security" for purposes of federal securities laws. By the same token the definitions of "securities" for purposes of those laws has no bearing upon whether an interest is a security within the definition of this Article.

4. A certificated security is a negotiable instrument (Section 8-105) but is nonetheless governed by this Article rather than by Article 3. A critical distinction between certificated securities and other negotiable instruments is that one indorsing a security does not undertake the issuer's obligation or make any warranty that the issuer will honor the underlying obligation. One indorsing other negotiable instruments becomes secondarily liable on the underlying obligation.

5. The definition of "clearing corporation" in subsection (3) reflects the fact that a 1975 amendment to the Securities Exchange Act provides for registration of "clearing agencies" with the Securities and Exchange Commission.

Cross Reference:

Section 3-103.

Definitional Cross References:

"Bearer". Section 1-201.
"Issuer". Section 8-201.
"Money". Section 1-201.
"Person". Section 1-201.
"Rights". Section 1-201.

"Term". Section 1-201.
"Writing". Section 1-201.

§ 8-103. Issuer's Lien.

A lien upon a security in favor of an issuer thereof is valid against a purchaser only if:

(a) the security is certificated and the right of the issuer to the lien is noted conspicuously thereon; or

(b) the security is uncertificated and a notation of the right of the issuer to the lien is contained in the initial transaction statement sent to the purchaser or, if his interest is transferred to him other than by registration of transfer, pledge, or release, the initial transaction statement sent to the registered owner or the registered pledgee.

As amended in 1977.

Official Comment

Prior Uniform Statutory Provision: Section 15, Uniform Stock Transfer Act.

Purposes:

1. The rule of Section 15 of the Uniform Stock Transfer Act is made applicable to all securities covered by the Article. An analogous rule as to restrictions on transfer imposed by the issuer appears at Section 8-204. Compare also Section 8-202. This section differs from those two sections in that the purchaser's knowledge of the issuer's claim is irrelevant.

"Noted" makes clear that the text of the lien provisions need not be set forth in full. However, this would not override a provision of an applicable corporation code requiring statement *in haec verba*.

2. The purchaser of an uncertificated security is charged with notice of all provisions in the initial transaction statement, whether or not it is sent to him personally. Similarly, one who takes a certificated security is charged with notice of all provisions noted on the certificate whether or not he actually receives the certificate. When a purchaser takes a security under circumstances in which no initial transaction statement is sent to him by the issuer and no certificated security is delivered to him, he must look to the person to whom a transfer or pledge of the uncertificated security has been registered or the person in possession of the certificated security for the appropriate notice or absence thereof. If the purchaser is not notified of a lien he may have a right of action for breach of transfer warranties. See Section 8-306. Compare Section 8-202 and its Comment 1.

Cross References:

Sections 8-202 and 8-204.

Definitional Cross References:

"Certificated Security". Section 8-102.
"Conspicuous". Section 1-201.
"Initial Transaction Statement". Section 8-408.
"Issuer". Section 8-201.
"Purchaser". Section 1-201.
"Security". Section 8-102.
"Uncertificated Security". Section 8-102.

§ 8-104. Effect of Overissue; "Overissue".

(1) The provisions of this Article which validate a security or compel its issue or reissue do not apply to the extent that validation, issue, or reissue would result in overissue; but if:

(a) an identical security which does not constitute an overissue is reasonably available for purchase, the person entitled to issue or validation may compel the issuer to purchase the security for him and either to deliver a certificated security or to register the transfer of an uncertificated security to him, against surrender of any certificated security he holds; or

(b) a security is not so available for purchase, the person entitled to issue or validation may recover from the issuer the price he or the last purchaser for value paid for it with interest from the date of his demand.

(2) "Overissue" means the issue of securities in excess of the amount the issuer has corporate power to issue.

As amended in 1977.

Official Comment

Prior Uniform Statutory Provision: None.

Purposes:

1. Deeply embedded in corporation law is the conception that "corporate power" to issue securities stems from the statute, either general or special, under which the corporation is organized. Corporation codes universally require that the charter or articles of incorporation state, at least as to capital shares, maximum limits in terms of number of shares or total dollar capital. Historically, special incorporation statutes are similarly drawn and sometimes similarly limit the face amount of authorized debt securities. The theory is that issue of securities in excess of the authorized amounts is prohibited. See, for example, McWilliams v. Geddes & Moss Undertaking Co., 169 So. 894 (1936, La.); Crawford v. Twin City Oil Co., 216 Ala. 216, 113 So. 61 (1927); New York and New Haven R.R. Co. v. Schuyler, 34 N.Y. 30 (1865). This conception persists despite modern corporation codes under which, by action of directors and stockholders, additional shares can be authorized by charter amendment and thereafter issued. This section does not give a person entitled to validation, issue or reissue of a security, the right to compel amendment of the charter to authorize additional shares. Therefore, in a case where issue of an additional security would require charter amendment, the plaintiff is limited to the two alternate remedies set forth in paragraphs (a) and (b) of subsection (1).

2. Where an identical security is reasonably available for purchase, whether because traded on an organized market, or because one or more security owners may be willing to sell at a not unreasonable price, the issuer, although unable to issue additional shares, will be able to purchase them and may be compelled to follow that procedure. West v. Tintic Standard Mining Co., 71 Utah 158, 263 P. 490, 56 A.L.R. 1190 (1928).

Paragraph (1)(a) gives the issuer the choice to transfer either a certificated or an uncertificated security. As a practical matter the issuer will have the choice only when the securities of the issue involved are partly certificated and partly uncertificated; and in those circumstances section 8-407 gives the owner (or registered pledgee) the right to choose the form of the security. Thus the issuer likely will transfer a security of the form requested by the person entitled to the security.

3. The right to recover damages from an issuer who has permitted an overissue to occur is well settled. New York and New Haven R.R. Co. v. Schuyler, 34 N.Y. 30 (1865). The measure of such damages, however, has been open to question, some courts basing them upon the value of stock at the time registration is refused; some upon the value at the time of trial; and some upon the highest value between the time of refusal and the time

of trial. Allen v. South Boston Railroad, 150 Mass. 200, 22 N.E. 917, 5 L.R.A. 716, 15 Am.St.Rep. 185 (1889); Commercial Bank v. Kortright, 22 Wend. (N.Y.) 348 (1839). The purchase price of the security to the last purchaser who gave value for it is here adopted as being the fairest means of reducing the possibility of speculation by the purchaser. Interest may be recovered as the best available measure of compensation for delay.

4. This section modifies and controls the rules otherwise laid down in this Article as to the validation and issue of securities. The particular sections so modified are listed in the cross-references.

Cross References:

Point 4: See Sections 8-202, 8-205, 8-206, 8-208, 8-311 and Part 4 of this Article.

Definitional Cross References:

"Certificated Security". Section 8-102.
"Issuer". Section 8-201.
"Security". Section 8-102.
"Uncertificated Security". Section 8-102.
"Value". Section 1-201.

§ 8-105. Certificated Securities Negotiable; Statements and Instructions Not Negotiable; Presumptions.

(1) Certificated securities governed by this Article are negotiable instruments.

(2) Statements (Section 8-408), notices, or the like, sent by the issuer of uncertificated securities and instructions (Section 8-308) are neither negotiable instruments nor certificated securities.

(3) In any action on a security:

(a) unless specifically denied in the pleadings, each signature on a certificated security, in a necessary indorsement, on an initial transaction statement, or on an instruction, is admitted;

(b) if the effectiveness of a signature is put in issue, the burden of establishing it is on the party claiming under the signature, but the signature is presumed to be genuine or authorized;

(c) if signatures on a certificated security are admitted or established, production of the security entitles a holder to recover on it unless the defendant establishes a defense or a defect going to the validity of the security;

(d) if signatures on an initial transaction statement are admitted or established, the facts stated in the statement are presumed to be true as of the time of its issuance; and

(e) after it is shown that a defense or defect exists, the plaintiff has the burden of establishing that he or some person under whom he claims is a person against whom the defense or defect is ineffective (Section 8-202).

As amended in 1977.

Official Comment

Prior Uniform Statutory Provision: None.

Purposes:

1. Although certificated securities are negotiable instruments, this Article and not Article 3 provides the rights and

duties relative to such instruments. See Sections 8-102(1)(c) and 3-103(1). But in subsection (3) of this section the particular rules stated in Section 3-307 for the negotiable instruments governed by Article 3 are adapted to certificated securities. Further, those rules are adopted with respect to signatures on initial transaction statements, although subsection (2) makes clear that such statements are not negotiable instruments.

2. Paragraph (3)(d) makes clear that the effect of establishing the validity of signatures on an initial transaction statement is to create a presumption that the facts stated therein were true as of the time it was issued. The issuer is free to show that later events—e.g., a subsequent transfer—changed the stated facts.

3. "Any action on a security" includes any action or proceeding brought against the issuer to enforce a right or interest that is part of the security—e.g., to collect principal or interest or a dividend, or to establish a right to vote or to receive a new security under an exchange offer or plan of reorganization.

Cross References:

Section 3-103, 3-307, 8-202, 8-301.

Definitional Cross References:

"Certificated Security". Section 8-102.
"Initial Transaction Statement". Section 8-408.
"Instruction". Section 8-308.
"Security". Section 8-102.
"Uncertificated Security". Section 8-102.

§ 8-106. Applicability.

The law (including the conflict of laws rules) of the jurisdiction of organization of the issuer governs the validity of a security, the effectiveness of registration by the issuer, and the rights and duties of the issuer with respect to:

(a) registration of transfer of a certificated security;

(b) registration of transfer, pledge, or release of an uncertificated security; and

(c) sending of statements of uncertificated securities.

As amended in 1977.

Official Comment

Prior Uniform Statutory Provision: None.

Purposes:

1. This section states a special rule for conflicts of laws relating to certain matters covered by this Article. Except as provided in this section, the generally applicable conflicts rules stated in Section 1-105 apply to Article 8.

2. Generally speaking, this section makes the law, including the conflict of laws rules, of the jurisdiction in which the issuer is organized applicable to determine the rights and obligations of the issuer with respect to security. Further, the *effectiveness* of registration by the issuer is to be governed by the law of the jurisdiction in which the issuer is organized. Thus whenever an uncertificated security is transferred through registration on the issuer's records, Section 8-313(1)(b), this section provides the choice of law rule as to the effectiveness of the registration to effect the transfer. Similarly, the effectiveness of a registration on the issuer's records to create and perfect a security interest in uncertificated securities (see Section 8-321) is within the ambit of this section.

It is significant that this section makes applicable the conflict of laws rules as well as the substantive law of the jurisdiction in which the issuer is organized. Because of this provision many matters related to the registration of transfer—for example, the appointment of a guardian for an incompetent person and the existence of agency relations—may be governed by the substantive law of a jurisdiction other than that in which the issuer is organized.

Any transfer of securities that is not effected through registration on the issuer's records is subject to the law provided by general choice of law rules. Transfers (including pledges) of certificated securities are not effected by registration on the issuer's records, and thus are subject to general choice of law rules. Similarly, some transfers of uncertificated securities are not covered by this section. See Section 8-313(1)(d) and (f)-(j).

Cross References:

Sections 1-105 and 8-202 and Part 4 of this Article.

Definitional Cross References:

"Certificated Security". Section 8-102.
"Issuer". Section 8-201.
"Security". Section 8-102.
"Uncertificated Security". Section 8-102.

§ 8-107. Securities Transferable; Action for Price.

(1) Unless otherwise agreed and subject to any applicable law or regulation respecting short sales, a person obligated to transfer securities may transfer any certificated security of the specified issue in bearer form or registered in the name of the transferee, or indorsed to him or in blank, or he may transfer an equivalent uncertificated security to the transferee or a person designated by the transferee.

(2) If the buyer fails to pay the price as it comes due under a contract of sale, the seller may recover the price of:

(a) certificated securities accepted by the buyer;

(b) uncertificated securities that have been transferred to the buyer or a person designated by the buyer; and

(c) other securities if efforts at their resale would be unduly burdensome or if there is no readily available market for their resale.

As amended in 1977.

Official Comment

Prior Uniform Statutory Provision: None.

Purposes:

1. The rights and interests that constitute securities of the same issue are "fungible". Section 1-201(17). This is true of both certificated and uncertificated securities. Subsection (1) states the generally accepted legal consequences of such fungibility. "Unless otherwise agreed", the seller, bailee, broker or other "person obligated to transfer securities" need not transfer any specific instrument, but may select (e.g., from "a fungible bulk" (Section 8-312(2)) any security of the proper issue, in bearer form or appropriately registered or indorsed, or may transfer an uncertificated security of the same issue.

Rules of the organized markets limiting the forms in which securities are transferable in transactions on such markets are matters "otherwise agreed". Cases such as Parsons v. Martin, 77 Mass. (11 Gray) 111 (1858) and Rumery v. Brooks, 205 App.Div. 283, 199 N.Y.Supp. 517 (1st Dept. 1923), holding a broker liable for conversion if he registers transfer of a customer's securities held in "cash account" out of the customer's name or tenders on demand for delivery a different though equivalent security, are rejected. However, this Act does not enlarge the rights of a broker as to such securities so as to permit him without the customer's consent to pledge them for his own indebtedness, as he may properly do with securities held in a "margin account" to the extent he has acquired a lien for advances. The distinction is carefully preserved in statute (e.g., N.Y.Penal Law § 956) and case law. In re Mills, 125 App.Div. 730, 110 N.Y.Supp. 314 (1st Dept. 1908).

2. Subsection (2) is designed to follow the dictum in Agar v. Orda, 264 N.Y. 248, 190 N.E. 479 (1934) in this context. Paragraph (c) is applicable where for example (i) the securities are those of a "closely-held" corporation not dealt in on any organized market; or (ii) because of the necessity for compliance with the registration requirements of the Securities Act of 1933 or other regulatory provisions or procedures prior to offering the particular securities on the market substantial delay and expense would be involved. The approval of these particular remedies does not constitute disapproval of other remedies that may exist under other rules of law. Section 1-103.

Cross References:

Sections 1-103; 2-708; 2-709; 8-313; 8-319.

Definitional Cross References:

"Action". Section 1-201.
"Certificated Security". Section 8-102.
"Contract". Section 1-201.
"Person". Section 1-201.
"Security". Section 8-102.
"Uncertificated Security". Section 8-102.

§ 8-108. Registration of Pledge and Release of Uncertificated Securities.

A security interest in an uncertificated security may be evidenced by the registration of pledge to the secured party or a person designated by him. There can be no more than one registered pledge of an uncertificated security at any time. The registered owner of an uncertificated security is the person in whose name the security is registered, even if the security is subject to a registered pledge. The rights of a registered pledgee of an uncertificated security under this Article are terminated by the registration of release.

As added in 1977.

Official Comment

Prior Uniform Statutory Provision: None.

Purposes:

This section introduces the concept of the registered pledge of uncertificated securities. The term "pledge" is used, notwithstanding the absence of physical delivery, because it reflects common terminology employed in connection with security interests in investment securities. Note that the same term has been used in Section 8-320 to describe the security interest created by book entry made by a securities depository. The rights of a registered pledgee, set forth in other sections (particularly Section 8-207), are intended to resemble, as closely as possible, the rights of the pledgee of a certificated security who retains possession of the pledged security without re-registration. Although the registration of pledge requires communication to the issuer, no details of the security agreement between the debtor and the secured party need be disclosed.

There is no provision for the registration of more than one pledge at a time. This limits the burden on issuers and insulates them from problems of conflicting priorities and the like. The registration of pledge is only one among several methods of creating security interests under Section 8-313(1), and other methods can be effectively employed to create security interests junior to that of the registered pledgee or even first security interests if, for some reason, the use of the registered pledge mechanism is inadvisable. See Section 8–321, which deals comprehensively with security interests and incorporates the transfer rules of Section 8–313(1) by reference.

The third sentence makes it clear that the registered owner, and not the registered pledgee, is the person in whose name an uncertificated security is registered as, for example, to determine how an unsecured creditor may reach his debtor's interest under Section 8–317(2). The registration of release, in effect, nullifies the registration of pledge, and is functionally equivalent to the redelivery of a pledged certificated security to the pledgor.

Cross References:

Sections 8–207; 8–321; 8–401.

Definitional Cross References:

"Secured Party". Section 9–105.
"Security". Section 8–102.
"Security Interest". Section 1–201.
"Uncertificated Security". Section 8–102.

PART 2

ISSUE—ISSUER

§ 8–201. "Issuer."

(1) With respect to obligations on or defenses to a security, "issuer" includes a person who:

(a) places or authorizes the placing of his name on a certificated security (otherwise than as authenticating trustee, registrar, transfer agent, or the like) to evidence that it represents a share, participation, or other interest in his property or in an enterprise, or to evidence his duty to perform an obligation represented by the certificated security;

(b) creates shares, participations, or other interests in his property or in an enterprise or undertakes obligations, which shares, participations, interests, or obligations are uncertificated securities;

(c) directly or indirectly creates fractional interests in his rights or property, which fractional interests are represented by certificated securities; or

(d) becomes responsible for or in place of any other person described as an issuer in this section.

(2) With respect to obligations on or defenses to a security, a guarantor is an issuer to the extent of his guaranty, whether or not his obligation is noted on a certificated security or on statements of uncertificated securities sent pursuant to Section 8–408.

(3) With respect to registration of transfer, pledge, or release (Part 4 of this Article), "issuer" means a person on whose behalf transfer books are maintained.

As amended in 1977.

Official Comment

Prior Uniform Statutory Provision: Sections 29, 60, 61 and 62, Uniform Negotiable Instruments Law.

Purposes:

1. Part 2 of Article 8 describes the rights and duties of an "issuer" of a security. It is generally understood that an "issuer" is the one who creates the property interest that is a "security" and who thereby incurs obligations to purchasers of that interest. This section provides the criteria for determining whether a person has incurred the obligations—and gained the rights—given to an issuer in this Article. Numerous rights and obligations arise from sources other than Article 8. This section does not determine whether a person is an "issuer" for purposes of those sources of law.

2. Paragraph (1)(a) makes a person an "issuer" for purposes of this Article if he authorizes the placing of his name on a certificate intending that it should be a certificated security (Section 8-102(1)(a)). This paragraph bears a close relationship to Section 8-102(1)(a), which describes the property interests that may constitute a "certificated security." The latter section describes those interests in terms of rights against "the issuer," while this section defines issuer in terms of authorizing the placing of a name on a "certificated security." The effect is to add to the definition of "certificated security" the requirement that it bear the authorized name of the person creating the property interests. Thus, if a certificate bears the *unauthorized* name of the purported issuer, the purported issuer is not an "issuer" within this Article; and the certificate is not a "certificated security." See Section 8-202(3) and its Comment 4. Section 8-205 describes the circumstances in which the purported issuer will be treated as if he were a true "issuer" despite the absence of his authorized signature.

3. Read in conjunction with the definition of "uncertificated security" in Section 8-102(1)(b), paragraph (1)(b) makes a person an "issuer" if he creates, and maintains books for the registration of ownership of, property interests that fit within the definition of an uncertificated security.

4. Subsection (2) distinguishes the obligations of a guarantor as issuer from those of the principal obligor. However, it does not exempt the guarantor from the impact of subsection (4) of Section 8-202. Whether or not the obligation of the guarantor is noted on the security or initial transaction statement (Section 8-408(4)) is immaterial. Typically, guarantors are parent corporations, or stand in some similar relationship to the principal obligor. If that relationship existed at the time the security originally was issued, the guaranty probably would be noted on the security or initial transaction statement. However, if the relationship arose afterward—e.g., through a purchase of stock or properties, or through merger or consolidation—probably the notation would not be made. Nonetheless, the owner of the security is entitled to the benefit of the obligation of the guarantor.

5. Subsection (3) narrows the definition of "issuer" for purposes of Part 4 of this Article (registration of transfer). It is supplemented by Section 8-406.

Cross References:

Points 1, 2, and 3: Sections 8-102, 8-202 and 8-205.

Point 4: Section 8-202.

Point 5: Part 4 of this Article.

Definitional Cross References:

"Certificated Security". Section 8-102.
"Person". Section 1-201.
"Rights". Section 1-201.
"Security". Section 8-102.
"Uncertificated Security". Section 8-102.

§ 8-202. Issuer's Responsibility and Defenses; Notice of Defect or Defense.

(1) Even against a purchaser for value and without notice, the terms of a security include:

(a) if the security is certificated, those stated on the security;

(b) if the security is uncertificated, those contained in the initial transaction statement sent to such purchaser or, if his interest is transferred to him other than by registration of transfer, pledge, or release, the initial transaction statement sent to the registered owner or registered pledgee; and

(c) those made part of the security by reference, on the certificated security or in the initial transaction statement, to another instrument, indenture, or document or to a constitution, statute, ordinance, rule, regulation, order or the like, to the extent that the terms referred to do not conflict with the terms stated on the certificated security or contained in the statement. A reference under this paragraph does not of itself charge a purchaser for value with notice of a defect going to the validity of the security, even though the certificated security or statement expressly states that a person accepting it admits notice.

(2) A certificated security in the hands of a purchaser for value or an uncertificated security as to which an initial transaction statement has been sent to a purchaser for value, other than a security issued by a government or governmental agency or unit, even though issued with a defect going to its validity, is valid with respect to the purchaser if he is without notice of the particular defect unless the defect involves a violation of constitutional provisions, in which case the security is valid with respect to a subsequent purchaser for value and without notice of the defect. This subsection applies to an issuer that is a government or governmental agency or unit only if either there has been substantial compliance with the legal requirements governing the issue or the issuer has received a substantial consideration for the issue as a whole or for the particular security and a stated purpose of the issue is one for which the issuer has power to borrow money or issue the security.

(3) Except as provided in the case of certain unauthorized signatures (Section 8-205), lack of genuineness of a certificated security or an initial transaction statement is a complete defense, even against a purchaser for value and without notice.

(4) All other defenses of the issuer of a certificated or uncertificated security, including nondelivery and conditional delivery of a certificated security, are ineffective against a purchaser for value who has taken without notice of the particular defense.

(5) Nothing in this section shall be construed to affect the right of a party to a "when, as and if issued" or a "when distributed" contract to cancel the contract in the event of a material change in the character of the security that

is the subject of the contract or in the plan or arrangement pursuant to which the security is to be issued or distributed.

As amended in 1977.

Official Comment

Prior Uniform Statutory Provisions: Sections 16, 23, 28, 56, 57, 60, 61, 62, Uniform Negotiable Instruments Law.

Purposes:

1. A purchaser must have some method of learning the terms of the security he is purchasing. The printing on the certificate or on the initial transaction statement ("ITS") is designed to notify the purchaser of those terms. If he purchases without examining the certificate or ITS, he does so at his peril, since he is charged with notice of terms stated thereon.

Some methods of transferring a security do not involve the actual delivery of a certificate or the sending of an ITS to the actual purchaser. See Section 8-313(1)(c)-(j). The situations in which these methods of transfer will be used can be divided into two categories—those in which an intermediary takes a transfer for his principal and those in which a bailee "holding" a security effects a transfer by receiving notice of, or sending acknowledgement of, the purchase. In either type of situation the purchaser will be charged with notice of all terms stated on the certificate if the security is certificated or, if the security is uncertificated, with notice of all terms stated in the ITS sent to the registered owner or registered pledgee. For example, suppose that Customer purchases an uncertificated security that is already registered in the name of his broker. Customer is content to allow the security to remain registered in Broker's name, so that Customer never receives an ITS. Customer is charged with notice of the terms stated on the ITS sent to Broker when Broker became the registered owner. Or suppose that Purchaser buys a certificated security and the transfer is effected not by delivering the certificate but by having Bailee, who holds the security, acknowledge that he holds for Purchaser. Purchaser is charged with notice of the terms written on the certificate.

It is apparent that in these situations a purchaser must rely upon the intermediary or bailee who "holds" the security for him.

2. Subsection (1)(c) states, in accordance with the prevailing case law, the right of the issuer (who prepares the text of the security or statement) to include terms incorporated by adequate reference to an extrinsic source, so long as the terms so incorporated do not conflict with the stated terms. Thus the standard practice of referring in a bond or debenture to the trust indenture under which it is issued without spelling out its necessarily complex and lengthy provisions is approved. Every stock certificate or ITS will refer in some manner to the charter or articles of incorporation of the issuer. At least where there is more than one class of stock authorized, applicable corporation codes specifically require a statement or summary as to preferences, voting powers and the like. References to constitutions, statutes, ordinances, rules, regulations or orders are not so common except in the obligations of governments or governmental agencies or units; but where appropriate they fit into the rule here stated.

Following the basic principles of the Negotiable Instruments Law the cases have generally held that an issuer is estopped from denying representations made in the text of a security. Delaware-New Jersey Ferry Co. v. Leeds, 21 Del.Ch. 279, 186 A. 913 (1936). Nor is a defect in form or the invalidity of a security normally available to the issuer as a defense. Bonini v. Family Theatre Corporation, 327 Pa. 273, 194 A. 498 (1937); First National Bank of Fairbanks v. Alaska Airmotive, 119 F.2d 267 (C.C.A.Alaska 1941).

This general rule of estoppel is here adopted in favor of purchasers, with the exception noted above.

3. The last sentence of subsection (1) and all of subsection (2) embody the concept that it is the duty of the issuer, not of the purchaser, to make sure that the security complies with the law governing its issue. The last sentence of subsection (1) makes clear that the issuer cannot, by incorporating a reference to a statute or other document, charge the purchaser with notice of the security's invalidity. Subsection (2) gives to a purchaser for value without notice of the defect the right to enforce the security against the issuer despite the presence of a defect that otherwise would render the security invalid. This right accrues to a purchaser regardless of whether the security has been transferred to him through physical delivery of a certificate (Section 8-313(1)(a)), through registration of transfer or pledge of an uncertificated security (Section 8-313(1)(b)), or through some other method in which he receives no certificate or initial transaction statement. (Section 8-313(1)(c)-(j)). There are three circumstances in which a purchaser does not gain such rights: first, if the defect involves a violation of constitutional provisions, these rights accrue only to a subsequent purchaser (Section 8-102(2)). This Article leaves to the law of each particular state the rights of a purchaser on original issue of a security with a constitutional defect. No negative implication is intended by the explicit grant of rights to a subsequent purchaser.

Second, governmental issuers are distinguished in subsection (2) from other issuers as a matter of public policy, and additional safeguards are imposed before governmental issues are validated. Governmental issuers are estopped from asserting defenses only if there has been substantial compliance with the legal requirements governing the issue or if substantial consideration has been received and a stated purpose of the issue is one for which the issuer has power to borrow money or issue the security. The purpose of the substantial compliance requirement is to make certain that a mere technicality as, e.g., in the manner of publishing election notices, shall not be a ground for depriving an innocent purchaser of his rights in the security. The policy is here adopted of such cases as Tommie v. City of Gadsden, 229 Ala. 521, 158 So. 763 (1935), in which minor discrepancies in the form of the election ballot used were overlooked and the bonds were declared valid since there had been substantial compliance with the statute.

A long and well established line of Federal cases recognizes the principle of estoppel in favor of bona fide purchasers where municipalities issue bonds containing recitals of compliance with governing constitutional and statutory provisions, made by the municipal authorities entrusted with determining such compliance. Chaffee County v. Potter, 142 U.S. 355, 12 S.Ct. 216, 35 L.Ed. 1040 (1892); Oregon v. Jennings, 119 U.S. 74, 7 S.Ct. 124, 30 L.Ed. 323 (1886); Gunnison County Commissioners v. Rollins, 173 U.S. 255, 19 S.Ct. 390, 43 L.Ed. 689 (1898). This rule has been qualified, however, by requiring that the municipality have power to issue the security. Anthony v. County of Jasper, 101 U.S. 693, 25 L.Ed. 1005 (1879); Town of South Ottawa v. Perkins, 94 U.S. 260, 24 L.Ed. 154 (1876). This section follows the case law trend, simplifying the rule by setting up two conditions for an estoppel against a governmental issuer: (1) substantial consideration given, and (2) power in the issuer to borrow money or issue the security for the stated purpose. As a practical matter the problem of policing governmental issuers has been alleviated by the present practice of requiring legal opinions as to the validity of the issue. The bulk of the case law on this point is more than 50 years old and it may be assumed that the question now seldom arises.

Section 8-104, regarding overissue, provides the third exception to the rule that an innocent purchase for value takes a valid security despite the presence of a defect that would otherwise give rise to invalidity. See that section and its comment for further explanation.

4. Subsection (3) is in effect a definitional provision. The person purported to have issued a certificated security is not an "issuer", and the certificate is not a "certificated security", unless that person actually took the actions that constitute issue. See Sections 8–102(1)(a) and 8–201(1). Similarly, a statement purportedly sent by an issuer is not an "initial transaction statement" if it was not actually sent by the issuer (Section 8–408(4), (1), (2) and (3)). Section 8–205 is a caveat to both of these general rules.

5. Subsection (4) gives the general rule that defenses of the issuer are ineffective against a purchaser for value without notice of the defense. Notice to the purchaser may come from sources other than a notation on a certificate or an initial transaction statement. Compare Section 8–103 with respect to an issuer's lien.

6. Subsection (5) is included to make clear that this section does not affect the presently recognized right of either party to a "when, as and if" or "when distributed" contract to cancel the contract on substantial change.

Cross References:

Point 1: Section 8–313.

Point 2: Sections 1–201, 8–103, 8–203, 8–204.

Point 3: Sections 1–201, 8–102 and 8–104.

Point 4: Sections 8–102, 8–201 and 8–205.

Point 5: Section 8–103.

See Sections 8–104, 8–203, 8–205, and 8–206.

Definitional Cross References:

"Certificated Security". Section 8–102.
"Delivery". Section 1–201.
"Genuine". Section 1–201.
"Initial Transaction Statement". Section 8–408.
"Issuer". Section 8–201.
"Money". Section 1–201.
"Notice". Section 1–201.
"Person". Section 1–201.
"Purchaser". Section 1–201.
"Security". Section 8–102.
"Subsequent Purchaser". Section 8–102.
"Term". Section 1–201.
"Unauthorized Signature". Section 1–201.
"Uncertificated Security". Section 8–102.
"Value". Section 1–201.

§ 8–203. Staleness as Notice of Defects or Defenses.

(1) After an act or event creating a right to immediate performance of the principal obligation represented by a certificated security or that sets a date on or after which the security is to be presented or surrendered for redemption or exchange, a purchaser is charged with notice of any defect in its issue or defense of the issuer if:

(a) the act or event is one requiring the payment of money, the delivery of certificated securities, the registration of transfer of uncertificated securities, or any of these on presentation or surrender of the certificated security, the funds or securities are available on the date set for payment or exchange, and he takes the security more than one year after that date; and

(b) the act or event is not covered by paragraph (a) and he takes the security more than 2 years after the date set for surrender or presentation or the date on which performance became due.

(2) A call that has been revoked is not within subsection (1).

As amended in 1977.

Official Comment

Prior Uniform Statutory Provision: Sections 52(2), 53, Uniform Negotiable Instruments Law.

Purposes:

1. The problem of matured or called securities is here dealt with in terms of the effect of such events in giving notice of the issuer's defenses and not in terms of "negotiability". The substance of this section applies only to certificated securities because such securities may be transferred to a purchaser by delivery after they have matured, been called or become redeemable or exchangeable. It is contemplated that uncertificated securities which have matured or been called will merely be cancelled on the books of the issuer and the proceeds sent to the registered owner or registered pledgee, as the case may be. Uncertificated securities which have become redeemable or exchangeable, at the option of the owner, may be transferred to a purchaser, but the transfer is effectuated only by registration of transfer, thus necessitating communication with the issuer. If defects or defenses in such securities exist, the issuer will necessarily have the opportunity to bring them to the attention of the purchaser in the initial transaction statement sent to him.

2. The fact that a certificated security is in circulation long after it has been called for redemption or exchange must give rise to the question in a purchaser's mind as to why it has not been surrendered. After the lapse of a reasonable period of time he can no longer claim that he had "no reason to know" of any defects or irregularities in its issue. Where funds are available for the redemption of the security it is normally turned in more promptly and a shorter time is set as the "reasonable period", subsection (1)(a), than is set where funds are not available.

It is true that defaulted certificated securities are frequently traded on financial markets in the same manner as unmatured and undefaulted instruments and a purchaser might not be placed upon notice of irregularity by the mere fact of default. An issuer, however, should at some point be placed in a position to determine definitely its liability on an invalid or improper issue, and for this purpose a security under this section becomes "stale" two years after the default. But notice that a different rule applies when the question is notice not of issuer's defenses but of claims of ownership. Section 8-305 and comment.

3. Nothing in this section is designed to extend the life of preferred stocks called for redemption as "shares of stock" beyond the redemption date. After such a call, the security represents only a right to the funds set aside for redemption.

Cross References:

Sections 8-104, 8-202 and 8-305.

Definitional Cross References:

"Certificated Security". Section 8-102.
"Delivery". Section 1-201.
"Issuer". Section 8-201.
"Money". Section 1-201.
"Notice". Section 1-201.
"Purchaser". Section 1-201.
"Right". Section 1-201.
"Security". Section 8-102.
"Uncertificated Security". Section 8-102.

§ 8-204. Effect of Issuer's Restrictions on Transfer.

A restriction on transfer of a security imposed by the issuer, even if otherwise lawful, is ineffective against any person without actual knowledge of it unless:

(a) the security is certificated and the restriction is noted conspicuously thereon; or

(b) the security is uncertificated and a notation of the restriction is contained in the initial transaction statement sent to the person or, if his interest is transferred to him other than by registration of transfer, pledge, or release, the initial transaction statement sent to the registered owner or the registered pledgee.

As amended in 1977.

Official Comment

Prior Uniform Statutory Provision: Section 15, Uniform Stock Transfer Act.

Purposes:

1. Use of the words "noted" and "notation" is intended to make clear that the restriction need not be set forth in full text. See Allen v. Biltmore Tissue Corporation, 2 N.Y.2d 534, 141 N.E.2d 812 (1957).

2. Securities traded on financial markets are generally assumed to be free of adverse claims (Section 8-302). That assumption should not be lightly negated. Therefore, a strict rule as to notice of a restriction on transfer is here imposed. The issuer can protect itself by noting the restriction on the certificate or initial transaction statement. Refusal by an issuer to register a transfer on the basis of an unnoted restriction constitutes a conversion and the issuer can be compelled to register the transfer under the policy of Part 4 of this Article. Hulse v. Consolidated Quicksilver Mining Corporation, 65 Idaho 768, 154 P.2d 149 (1944); Mancini v. Patrizi, 110 Cal.App. 42, 293 P. 828 (1930). Conversely, the issuer to whom a certificated security with proper notation of a restriction is presented thereby receives timely notification of an adverse claim and is under a duty to inquire (Section 8-403).

A purchaser with actual knowledge of an unnoted restriction certainly has notice of an adverse claim (Section 8-304 and Comment). In that situation this section adopts the reasoning of Baumohl v. Goldstein, 95 N.J.Eq. 597, 124 A. 118 (1924), and Tomoser v. Kamphausen, 307 N.Y. 797, 121 N.E.2d 622 (1954), rejecting the contrary holding of such cases as Costello v. Farrell, 234 Minn. 453, 48 N.W.2d 557, 29 A.L.R.2d 890 (1951).

3. A transferee who purchases securities in organized financial markets often may neither take physical delivery of a certificated security nor have an uncertificated security registered in his name. See Section 8-313(1)(c) through (j). Under those circumstances the transferee may have no occasion to examine the writing on the certificate or the initial transaction statement. Nonetheless the transferee is charged with notice of restrictions noted on the certificate or on the initial transaction statement sent to the registered owner or registered pledgee. See Section 8-202(1) and Comment 1 thereto.

4. Most jurisdictions recognize the right of issuers to impose restrictions giving either the issuer itself or other stockholders the option to purchase the security at an ascertained price before it is offered to third parties. Vannucci v. Peduni, 217 Cal. 138, 17 P.2d 706 (1932); People ex rel. Rudaitis v. Galskis, 233 Ill.App. 414 (1924); Bloomingdale v. Bloomingdale, 107 Misc. 646, 177 N.Y.S. 873 (1919). This is the type of restriction contemplated by the present section. Mere notation on the certificate or initial transaction statement cannot, of course, validate an otherwise unlawful restriction. The present section in no way alters the prevailing case law which recognizes free alienability as an inherent attribute of securities and holds invalid unreasonable restraints on alienation such as those requiring consents of directors without establishing criteria for the granting or withholding of such consents and those giving the directors an option of purchase at a price to be fixed in their sole discretion. Howe v. Roberts, 209 Ala. 80, 95 So. 344 (1923); People ex rel. Malcom v. Lake Sand Corporation, 251 Ill.App. 499 (1929); Morris v. Hussong Dyeing Machine Co., 81 N.J.Eq. 256, 86 A. 1026 (1913); New England Trust Co.

v. Abbott, 162 Mass. 148, 38 N.E. 432, 27 L.R.A. 271 (1894).

No interference is intended with the common practice of closing books for proper corporate purposes.

5. Cooperative associations and ventures, as well as private clubs are generally considered an exception to the rules against restrictions on transfer as unreasonable restraints on alienation and are permitted for example to require the consents of governing bodies such as a board of directors. Penthouse Properties, Inc. v. 1158 Fifth Avenue, Inc., 256 App.Div. 685, 11 N.Y.S.2d 417 (1939).

Historically restrictions on transfer were most commonly imposed by so-called "closely-held" issuers (including cooperatives and the like) in an attempt to restrict control if not total membership to a homogeneous security holder group. They have been increasingly resorted to by issuers with publicly held securities seeking to police enforcement of the registration requirements of the Securities Act of 1933 against persons purchasing their securities in a transaction exempt from those requirements (e.g., one "not involving any public offering" [Securities Act of 1933, Section 4(2)]) or against persons in a "control" relationship to the issuer. [See Securities Act of 1933, Section 2(11) and Rule 405 of the Rules and Regulations of the Securities and Exchange Commission under that Act.] Particularly in the latter context in which notation of the restriction on all affected certificates or initial transaction statements may not be practical, the issuer enforces it by notifying the holders of such certificates and refusing requests to register transfer out of the name of the "controlling person" either for purposes of sale or for delivery after sale, relying on the stated exception as to a person "with actual knowledge" of the restriction.

6. This section deals only with restrictions imposed by the issuer and restrictions imposed by statute are not affected. See Quiner v. Marblehead Social Co., 10 Mass. 476 (1813); Madison Bank v. Price, 79 Kan. 289, 100 P. 280 (1909); Healey v. Steele Center Creamery Ass'n, 115 Minn. 451, 133 N.W. 69 (1911). Nor does it deal with private agreements between stockholders containing restrictive covenants as to the sale of the security as in In re Consolidated Factors Corporation, 46 F.2d 561 (S.D.N.Y.1931).

7. An analogous provision concerning issuer's liens appears at Section 8-103.

Cross References:

Point 7: Section 8-103.
See Part 4 of this Article.

Definitional Cross References:

"Certificated Security". Section 8-102.
"Conspicuous". Section 1-201.
"Initial Transaction Statement". Section 8-408.
"Issuer". Section 8-201.
"Knowledge". Section 1-201.
"Person". Section 1-201.
"Security". Section 8-102.
"Uncertificated Security". Section 8-102.

§ 8-205. Effect of Unauthorized Signature on Certificated Security or Initial Transaction Statement.

An unauthorized signature placed on a certificated security prior to or in the course of issue or placed on an initial transaction statement is ineffective, but the signature is effective in favor of a purchaser for value of the certificated security or a purchaser for value of an uncertificated security to whom the initial transaction statement has been sent, if the purchaser is without notice of the lack of authority and the signing has been done by:

(a) an authenticating trustee, registrar, transfer agent, or other person entrusted by the issuer with the signing of the security, of similar securities, or of initial transaction statements or the immediate preparation for signing of any of them; or

(b) an employee of the issuer, or of any of the foregoing, entrusted with responsible handling of the security or initial transaction statement.

As amended in 1977.

Official Comment

Prior Uniform Statutory Provision: Section 23, Uniform Negotiable Instruments Law.

Purposes:

1. In current practice the problem of forged or unauthorized signatures arises most frequently where an employee of the issuer, transfer agent or registrar has access to securities which he is required to prepare for issue by affixing the corporate seal or by adding a signature necessary for issue. This section is based upon the issuer's duty to avoid the negligent entrusting of securities to such persons. Issuers have long been held responsible for signatures placed upon securities by parties whom they have held out to the public as authorized to prepare such securities. See Fifth Avenue Bank of New York v. The Forty-Second Street & Grand Street Ferry Railroad Co., 137 N.Y. 231, 33 N.E. 378, 19 L.R.A. 331, 33 Am.St.Rep. 712 (1893); Jarvis v. Manhattan Beach Co., 148 N.Y. 652, 43 N.E. 68, 31 L.R.A. 776, 51 Am.St.Rep. 727 (1896). The "apparent authority" concept of some of the case-law, however, is here extended and this section expressly rejects the technical distinction, made by courts reluctant to recognize forged signatures, between cases where the forger signs a signature he is authorized to sign under proper circumstances and those in which he signs a signature he is never authorized to sign. Citizens' & Southern National Bank v. Trust Co. of Georgia, 50 Ga.App. 681, 179 S.E. 278 (1935). Normally the purchaser is not in a position to determine which signature a forger, entrusted with the preparation of securities, has "apparent authority" to sign and which he has not. The issuer, on the other hand, can protect itself against such fraud by the careful selection and bonding of agents and employees, or by action over against transfer agents and registrars who in turn may bond their personnel.

2. It is contemplated that purchasers of uncertificated securities will rely on initial transaction statements (ITS's) sent to them, much as purchasers of certificated securities rely on certificates. The issuer's signature is thus required to ensure genuineness of the ITS. Section 8-408(4). In this regard the principal difference between certificates and ITS's is that only the one to whom the ITS is sent can safely rely on it, whereas a certificated security is a negotiable instrument and may be relied upon by transferees other than the original purchaser. The issuer's responsibility for unauthorized signatures otherwise is the same in both instances.

A transferee of an uncertificated security may be protected indirectly by this section despite the fact that he has not received the ITS. If his transferor received an ITS and was protected by this section, Section 8-301(1) gives those rights to the transferee.

3. The issuer cannot be held liable for the honesty of employees not entrusted, directly or indirectly, with the signing, preparation, or responsible handling of similar securities or similar ITS's and whose possible commission of forgery it has no reason to anticipate. The result in such cases as Hudson Trust Co. v. American Linseed Co., 232 N.Y. 350, 134 N.E. 178 (1922), and Dollar Savings Fund & Trust Co. v. Pittsburgh Plate Glass Co., 213 Pa. 307, 62 A. 916, 5 Ann.Cas. 248 (1906) is here adopted.

4. This section is not concerned with forged or unauthorized indorsements (Section 8-311), but only with unauthorized signatures of issuers, transfer agents, etc., placed upon certificated securities or initial transaction statements during the course of their issue. The protection here stated is available to all purchasers for value without notice and not merely to subsequent purchasers.

Cross References:

Point 4: Section 8-311.
See Section 8-202(3).

Definitional Cross References:

"Certificated Security". Section 8-102.
"Initial Transaction Statement". Section 8-408.
"Issuer". Section 8-201.
"Notice". Section 1-201.
"Person". Section 1-201.
"Purchaser". Section 1-201.
"Security". Section 8-102.
"Sign". Section 1-201.
"Unauthorized Signature". Section 1-201.
"Uncertificated Security". Section 8-102.
"Value". Section 1-201.

§ 8-206. Completion or Alteration of Certificated Security or Initial Transaction Statement.

(1) If a certificated security contains the signatures necessary to its issue or transfer but is incomplete in any other respect:

(a) any person may complete it by filling in the blanks as authorized; and

(b) even though the blanks are incorrectly filled in, the security as completed is enforceable by a purchaser who took it for value and without notice of the incorrectness.

(2) A complete certificated security that has been improperly altered, even though fraudulently, remains enforceable, but only according to its original terms.

(3) If an initial transaction statement contains the signatures necessary to its validity, but is incomplete in any other respect:

(a) any person may complete it by filling in the blanks as authorized; and

(b) even though the blanks are incorrectly filled in, the statement as completed is effective in favor of the person to whom it is sent if he purchased the security referred to therein for value and without notice of the incorrectness.

(4) A complete initial transaction statement that has been improperly altered, even though fraudulently, is effective in favor of a purchaser to whom it has been sent, but only according to its original terms.

As amended in 1977.

Official Comment

Prior Uniform Statutory Provision: Sections 14, 15 and 124, Uniform Negotiable Instruments Law; Section 16, Uniform Stock Transfer Act.

Purposes:

1. The problem of forged or unauthorized signatures necessary for the issue or transfer of a security or for the authentication of an initial transaction statement is not involved here, and a person in possession of a blank certificate or of a writing that would be an initial transaction statement if it were properly signed is not, by this section, given authority to fill in blanks with such signatures.

2. Completion of blanks left in a transfer instruction is dealt with elsewhere (Section 8-308(5)). Blanks left upon authentication of an initial transaction statement or upon issue of a certificated security are the only ones dealt

with here, and a purchaser for value without notice is protected. A purchaser is not in a good position to determine whether blanks were completed by the issuer or by some person not authorized to complete them. On the other hand the issuer can protect itself by not placing its signature on the writing until the blanks are completed or, if it does sign before all blanks are completed, by carefully selecting the agents and employees to whom it entrusts the writing after authentication. With respect to a certificated security or an initial transaction statement that is completed by the issuer but later is altered, the issuer has done everything it can to protect the purchaser and thus is not charged with the terms as altered. However, it is charged according to the original terms, since it is not thereby prejudiced.

If the completion or alteration is obviously irregular, the purchaser may be charged with notice. See Section 1-201(25).

3. Only the purchaser who physically takes the certificate or receives the initial transaction statement is directly protected. However, a transferee may receive protection indirectly through Section 8-301(1).

4. The protection granted a purchaser for value without notice under this section is modified to the extent that an overissue may result where an incorrect amount is inserted into a blank (Section 8-104).

Cross References:

Point 2: Sections 1-201, 8-302 and 8-308. Point 3: Section 8-301. Point 4: Section 8-104. See Sections 8-205 and 8-311.

Definitional Cross References:

"Certificated Security". Section 8-102.
"Initial Transaction Statement". Section 8-408.
"Notice". Section 1-201.
"Person". Section 1-201.
"Purchaser". Section 1-201.
"Security". Section 8-102.
"Term". Section 1-201.
"Uncertificated Security". Section 8-102.
"Value". Section 1-201.

§ 8-207. Rights and Duties of Issuer With Respect to Registered Owners and Registered Pledgees.

(1) Prior to due presentment for registration of transfer of a certificated security in registered form, the issuer or indenture trustee may treat the registered owner as the person exclusively entitled to vote, to receive notifications, and otherwise to exercise all the rights and powers of an owner.

(2) Subject to the provisions of subsections (3), (4), and (6), the issuer or indenture trustee may treat the registered owner of an uncertificated security as the person exclusively entitled to vote, to receive notifications, and otherwise to exercise all the rights and powers of an owner.

(3) The registered owner of an uncertificated security that is subject to a registered pledge is not entitled to registration of transfer prior to the due presentment to the issuer of a release instruction. The exercise of conversion rights with respect to a convertible uncertificated security is a transfer within the meaning of this section.

(4) Upon due presentment of a transfer instruction from the registered pledgee of an uncertificated security, the issuer shall:

(a) register the transfer of the security to the new owner free of pledge, if the instruction specifies a new owner (who may be the registered pledgee) and does not specify a pledgee;

(b) register the transfer of the security to the new owner subject to the interest of the existing pledgee, if the instruction specifies a new owner and the existing pledgee; or

(c) register the release of the security from the existing pledge and register the pledge of the security to the other pledgee, if the instruction specifies the existing owner and another pledgee.

(5) Continuity of perfection of a security interest is not broken by registration of transfer under subsection (4)(b) or by registration of release and pledge under subsection (4)(c), if the security interest is assigned.

(6) If an uncertificated security is subject to a registered pledge:

(a) any uncertificated securities issued in exchange for or distributed with respect to the pledged security shall be registered subject to the pledge;

(b) any certificated securities issued in exchange for or distributed with respect to the pledged security shall be delivered to the registered pledgee; and

(c) any money paid in exchange for or in redemption of part or all of the security shall be paid to the registered pledgee.

(7) Nothing in this Article shall be construed to affect the liability of the registered owner of a security for calls, assessments, or the like.

As amended in 1977.

Official Comment

Prior Uniform Statutory Provision: Section 3, Uniform Stock Transfer Act.

Purposes:

1. Subsection (1) states the issuer's right to treat the registered owner of a certificated security as the person entitled to exercise all the rights of an owner. This right of the issuer is limited by the provisions of Part 4 of this article—once there has been due presentation for registration of transfer, the issuer has a duty to register ownership in the name of the transferee. Section 8–401. Thus its right to treat the old registered owner as exclusively entitled to the rights of ownership must cease.

The issuer may, under this section, make distributions of money or securities to the registered owners of certificated securities without requiring further proof of ownership, provided that such distributions are distributable to the owners of all securities of the same issue and the terms of the security do not require its surrender as a condition of payment or exchange. Any such distribution shall constitute a defense against a claim for the same distribution by a person, even if that person is in possession of the security and is a bona fide purchaser of the security. See PEB Commentary No. 4, dated March 10, 1990 [Appendix V, infra].

Subsection (2) states a parallel rule for uncertificated securities, with the important exception that the rights of the registered owner are curtailed when the uncertificated security is subject to a registered pledge. See Section 8–108. Thus, subsection (3) denies the registered owner the power to order transfer of an uncertificated security subject to a registered pledge until the pledge has been released by order of the pledgee. See Section 8–308(4) and (7)(b).

Subsection (4) establishes the right of the registered pledgee to control the transfer of an uncertificated security subject to his pledge. The three paragraphs of subsection (4) illustrate the mechanics for three common transactions: (a) the outright transfer of the security, free of the pledge; (b) the transfer of registered ownership, subject to the pledge; and (c) the transfer of the pledgee's interest without disturbing the registered ownership. These transactions are not intended to be exclusive. For example, the transfer of a pledged uncertificated security to a new owner subject to the interest of a new pledgee might be accomplished in several ways. There could be a release of his interest by the old pledgee followed by a transfer of registered ownership from the old owner to the new owner and a pledge from the new owner to the new pledgee. Or, if the respective pledgees wished to maintain complete control over the security, the old pledgee could order a transfer of his interest to the new pledgee under paragraph (c) and the new pledgee could then order the transfer of registered ownership from the old owner to the new owner under paragraph (b). Still other combinations are possible, depending on the positions of the parties.

Subsection (6) insures that stock dividends or splits issued with respect to a pledged uncertificated security and securities or money distributed or paid in exchange for a pledged uncertificated security will remain within the control of the registered pledgee. This result cannot be extended to pledges of certificated securities because the issuer will normally be unaware of the pledgee's rights unless the pledgee has caused a transfer to be registered.

2. The rule of such cases as Turnbull v. Longacre Bank, 249 N.Y. 159, 163 N.E. 135 (1928), which held the issuer liable for paying out dividends to the record holder after the transferee had given notice of the transfer and demanded that a new certificate be issued to him, is left unchanged. However, such cases as Morrison v. Gulf Oil Corporation, 189 Miss. 212, 196 So. 247 (1940), holding that Section 3 of the Uniform Stock Transfer Act did not change the common law as to the issuer's liability for dealing with the record holder after mere notice of a pledge, are expressly rejected. Mere notice is not enough under this section to impose upon the issuer the duty of dealing with the pledgee although it may constitute notice to the issuer of a claim of ownership under Part 4.

Subsections (1) and (2) are permissive and do not require that the issuer deal exclusively with the registered owner. It is free to require proof of ownership before paying out dividends or the like if it chooses to. Barbato v. Breeze Corporation, 128 N.J.L. 309, 26 A.2d 53 (1942).

3. This section does not operate to determine who is finally entitled to exercise voting and other rights or to receive payments and distributions. The parties are still free to incorporate their own arrangements as to these matters in seller-purchaser agreements which will be definitive as between them.

4. No change in existing state laws as to the liability of registered owners for calls and assessments is here intended; nor is anything in this section designed to estop a record holder from denying ownership when assessments are levied if he is otherwise entitled to do so under state law. See State ex rel. Squire v. Murfey, Blosson & Co., 131 Ohio St. 289, 2 N.E.2d 866 (1936); Willing v. Delaplaine, 23 F.Supp. 579 (1937).

5. No interference is intended with the common practice of closing the transfer books or taking a record date for dividend, voting and other purposes, as provided for in by-laws, charters and statutes.

Cross References:

Section 8–108 and Part 4 of this Article.

Definitional Cross References:

"Certificated Security". Section 8–102.
"Instruction". Section 8–308.
"Issuer". Section 8–201.
"Money". Section 1–201.
"Notification". Section 1–201.
"Person". Section 1–201.
"Registered Form". Section 8–102.
"Right". Section 1–201.
"Security". Section 8–102.

"Security Interest". Section 9-105.
"Uncertificated Security". Section 8-102.

§ 8-208. Effect of Signature of Authenticating Trustee, Registrar, or Transfer Agent.

(1) A person placing his signature upon a certificated security or an initial transaction statement as authenticating trustee, registrar, transfer agent, or the like, warrants to a purchaser for value of the certificated security or a purchaser for value of an uncertificated security to whom the initial transaction statement has been sent, if the purchaser is without notice of the particular defect, that:

(a) the certificated security or initial transaction statement is genuine;

(b) his own participation in the issue or registration of the transfer, pledge, or release of the security is within his capacity and within the scope of the authority received by him from the issuer; and

(c) he has reasonable grounds to believe the security is in the form and within the amount the issuer is authorized to issue.

(2) Unless otherwise agreed, a person by so placing his signature does not assume responsibility for the validity of the security in other respects.

As amended in 1962 and 1977.

Official Comment

Prior Uniform Statutory Provision: None.

Purposes:

1. The warranties here stated express the current understanding and prevailing case law as to the effect of the signatures of authenticating trustees, transfer agents, and registrars. See Jarvis v. Manhattan Beach Co., 148 N.Y. 652, 43 N.E. 68, 31 L.R.A. 776, 51 Am.St.Rep. 727 (1896). Although it has generally been regarded as the particular obligation of the transfer agent to determine whether securities are in proper form as provided by the by-laws and Articles of Incorporation, neither a registrar nor an authenticating trustee should properly place a signature upon a certificate or transaction statement without determining whether it is at least regular on its face. The obligations of these parties in this respect have therefore been made explicit in terms of due care. See Feldmeier v. Mortgage Securities, Inc., 34 Cal.App.2d 201, 93 P.2d 593 (1939).

2. Those cases which hold that an authenticating trustee is not liable for any defect in the mortgage or property which secures the bond or for any fraudulent misrepresentations made by the issuer are not here affected since these matters do not involve the genuineness or proper form of the security. Ainsa v. Mercantile Trust Co., 174 Cal. 504, 163 P. 898 (1917); Tschetinian v. City Trust Co., 186 N.Y. 432, 79 N.E. 401 (1906); Davidge v. Guardian Trust Co. of New York, 203 N.Y. 331, 96 N.E. 751 (1911).

3. The charter or an applicable statute may affect the capacity of a bank or other corporation undertaking to act as an authenticating trustee, registrar or transfer agent. See, for example, the Federal Reserve Act (U.S.C.A., Title 12, Banks and Banking, Section 248) under which the Board of Governors of the Federal Reserve Bank is authorized to grant special permits to National Banks permitting them to act as trustees. Such corporations are therefore held to certify as to

their legal capacity to act as well as to their authority.

4. Authenticating trustees, registrars and transfer agents have normally been held liable for an issue in excess of the authorized amount. Jarvis v. Manhattan Beach Co., supra; Mullen v. Eastern Trust & Banking Co., 108 Me. 498, 81 A. 948 (1911). In imposing upon these parties a duty of due care with respect to the amount they are authorized to help issue, this section does not necessarily validate the security, but merely holds persons responsible for the excess issue liable in damages for any loss suffered by the purchaser.

5. Aside from questions of genuineness and excess issue these parties are not held to certify as to the validity of the security unless they specifically undertake to do so. The case law which has recognized a unique responsibility on the transfer agent's part to testify as to the validity of any security which it countersigns is rejected.

6. This provision does not prevent a transfer agent or issuer from agreeing with a registrar of stock to protect the registrar in respect of the genuineness and proper form of a certificated security or initial transaction statement signed by the issuer or the transfer agent or both. Nor does it interfere with proper indemnity arrangements between the issuer and trustees, transfer agents, registrars and the like.

7. An unauthorized signature is a signature for purposes of this section if and only if it is made effective by Section 8-205.

Cross References:

Sections 8-102, 8-205 and 8-406.

Definitional Cross References:

"Agreed". Section 1-201.
"Certificated Security". Section 8-102.
"Genuine". Section 1-201.
"Initial Transaction Statement". Section 8-408.
"Issuer". Section 8-201.
"Notice". Section 1-201.
"Person". Section 1-201.
"Purchaser". Section 1-201.
"Security". Section 8-102.
"Uncertificated Security". Section 8-102.
"Value". Section 1-201.

PART 3

TRANSFER

§ 8-301. Rights Acquired by Purchaser.

(1) Upon transfer of a security to a purchaser (Section 8-313), the purchaser acquires the rights in the security which his transferor had or had actual authority to convey unless the purchaser's rights are limited by Section 8-302(4).

(2) A transferee of a limited interest acquires rights only to the extent of the interest transferred. The creation or release of a security interest in a security is the transfer of a limited interest in that security.

As amended in 1977.

Official Comment

Prior Uniform Statutory Provision: Section 58, Uniform Negotiable Instruments Law.

Purposes:

1. The concept of transfer is defined only by example (Section 8-313), but it clearly involves the passing of rights in the security from one party to another. Subsection (1) states the "shelter" provi-

sion of the Negotiable Instruments Law—upon transfer of the security a purchaser acquires the rights his transferor had. There are at least three exceptions to this basic rule, two of which limit the purchaser's rights and one of which expands them. First, subsection (1) explicitly makes its rule subject to Section 8-302(4), which prevents certain transferees from being freed of the taint of earlier fraud or notice. The second exception, stated in subsection (2), is that there may be a transfer explicitly limited to an interest less than the transferor's entire interest. Finally Section 8-302 provides that a bona fide purchaser takes certain rights of his own account, regardless of the rights his transferor had.

2. Transfers by operation of law are not intended to be covered by this Article. For example, transfers from decedent to administrator, from ward to guardian, and from bankrupt to trustee in bankruptcy are governed by other law as to both the time they occur and the substance of the transfer. Subsequent delivery and registration on the issuer's records merely confirm what has already happened.

Cross References:

Sections 3-201 and 8-321.

Definitional Cross References:

"Purchaser". Section 1-201.
"Rights". Section 1-201.
"Security". Section 8-102.
"Security Interest". Section 1-201.

§ 8-302. "Bona Fide Purchaser"; "Adverse Claim"; Title Acquired by Bona Fide Purchaser.

(1) A "bona fide purchaser" is a purchaser for value in good faith and without notice of any adverse claim:

(a) who takes delivery of a certificated security in bearer form or in registered form, issued or indorsed to him or in blank;

(b) to whom the transfer, pledge, or release of an uncertificated security is registered on the books of the issuer; or

(c) to whom a security is transferred under the provisions of paragraph (c), (d)(i), or (g) of Section 8-313(1).

(2) "Adverse claim" includes a claim that a transfer was or would be wrongful or that a particular adverse person is the owner of or has an interest in the security.

(3) A bona fide purchaser in addition to acquiring the rights of a purchaser (Section 8-301) also acquires his interest in the security free of any adverse claim.

(4) Notwithstanding Section 8-301(1), the transferee of a particular certificated security who has been a party to any fraud or illegality affecting the security, or who as a prior holder of that certificated security had notice of an adverse claim, cannot improve his position by taking from a bona fide purchaser.

As amended in 1977.

Official Comment

Prior Uniform Statutory Provision: Sections 52, 57, 58 and 59, Uniform Negotiable Instruments Law; Section 7, Uniform Stock Transfer Act.

Purposes:

1. Any purchaser for value of a security without notice of a particular defect may take free of the issuer's defense based on that defect, but only a purchaser taking by a formally perfect transfer, for value and without notice of any adverse claim, may take free of adverse claims. The "bona fide purchaser" here dealt with is the person taking free of adverse claims. His rights against the issuer are determined by Part 2 of this Article and his rights to registration are determined by Part 4.

2. Not every form of transfer can confer upon the purchaser the status of bona fide purchaser. In particular, transfers effected through the acknowledgement of a bailee who is not a financial intermediary or through the acknowledgement of a financial intermediary who holds for the transferee a proportionate interest in a fungible bulk do not confer bona fide purchaser status. However, the transferee can acquire all the rights of a bona fide purchaser through the "shelter" provisions of Section 8-301(1) if the transferor had those rights.

3. Protection is extended to bona fide purchasers of all investment securities, whether such securities were considered negotiable or non-negotiable under the prior law. This is the result sought by many cases which have resolved doubts in favor of negotiability despite terms in bonds which militated against their negotiability under the provisions of the Negotiable Instruments Law. See Paxton v. Miller, 102 Ind.App. 511, 200 N.E. 87 (1936); Scott v. Platt, 171 Or. 379, 135 P.2d 769 (1943). Such cases as U.S. Gypsum v. Faroll, 296 Ill.App. 47, 15 N.E.2d 888 (1938), protecting bona fide purchasers of stock certificates under the provisions of the Stock Transfer Act are adopted and approved.

4. An adverse claim may be either legal or equitable, e.g., that the claimant is the beneficial owner of a security, though not the legal owner of it, or that it has been or is proposed to be transferred in breach of trust or a valid restriction on transfer (See Section 8-204 and Comment). Note that there may be claims of ownership that are not "adverse"—e.g., the claim of a principal against his agent including that of a customer against his broker (Section 8-303). The agent's knowledge of his principal's claim thus cannot defeat the agent's right to be a bona fide purchaser under this section.

5. Subsection (4) provides an exception to the "shelter" provisions of Section 8-301(1), but applies only to a transferee of a certificated security who as a prior holder of the particular security had notice of adverse claims or who has been a party to fraud or illegality affecting the particular security.

Cross References:

Sections 3-302 and 8-301. Point 4: Section 8-204 and its comment.

Definitional Cross References:

"Bearer Form". Section 8-102.
"Certificated Security". Section 8-102.
"Delivery". Section 1-201.
"Good Faith". Section 1-201.
"Holder". Section 1-201.
"Indorsed". Section 8-308.
"Notice". Section 1-201.
"Person". Section 1-201.
"Purchaser". Section 1-201.
"Registered Form". Section 8-102.
"Security". Section 8-102.
"Uncertificated Security". Section 8-102.
"Value". Section 1-201.

§ 8-303. "Broker."

"Broker" means a person engaged for all or part of his time in the business of buying and selling securities, who in the transaction concerned acts for, buys a security from, or sells a security to, a customer. Nothing in this Article determines the capacity in which a person acts for purposes of any other statute or rule to which the person is subject.

Official Comment

Prior Uniform Statutory Provision: None.

Purposes:

This section defines "broker" for purposes of this Article in terms of function in the particular transaction. The term is applicable to the person performing the function. The differentiation under the Securities Exchange Act of 1934 between "broker" and "dealer" is of no significance under this Article. This and similar distinctions are preserved for other purposes by the last sentence of the section.

Definitional Cross References:

"Person". Section 1-201.
"Security". Section 8-102.

§ 8-304. Notice to Purchaser of Adverse Claims.

(1) A purchaser (including a broker for the seller or buyer, but excluding an intermediary bank) of a certificated security is charged with notice of adverse claims if:

(a) the security, whether in bearer or registered form, has been indorsed "for collection" or "for surrender" or for some other purpose not involving transfer; or

(b) the security is in bearer form and has on it an unambiguous statement that it is the property of a person other than the transferor. The mere writing of a name on a security is not such a statement.

(2) A purchaser (including a broker for the seller or buyer, but excluding an intermediary bank) to whom the transfer, pledge, or release of an uncertificated security is registered is charged with notice of adverse claims as to which the issuer has a duty under Section 8-403(4) at the time of registration and which are noted in the initial transaction statement sent to the purchaser or, if his interest is transferred to him other than by registration of transfer, pledge, or release, the initial transaction statement sent to the registered owner or the registered pledgee.

(3) The fact that the purchaser (including a broker for the seller or buyer) of a certificated or uncertificated security has notice that the security is held for a third person or is registered in the name of or indorsed by a fiduciary does not create a duty of inquiry into the rightfulness of the transfer or constitute constructive notice of adverse claims. However, if the purchaser (excluding an intermediary bank) has knowledge that the proceeds are being used or that the transaction is for the individual benefit of the fiduciary or otherwise in breach of duty, the purchaser is charged with notice of adverse claims.

As amended in 1977.

Official Comment

Prior Uniform Statutory Provision: Sections 37, 56, Uniform Negotiable Instruments Law.

Purposes:

1. Section 8-302 defines "bona fide purchaser" in terms of three distinct elements, "value", "good faith", and lack of "notice of any adverse claim". This section deals only with notice and presents specific situations in which a purchaser is

charged with notice of adverse claims as a matter of law. The listing is not exhaustive and does not exclude other situations in which the trier of the facts may determine that similar notice has been given. For example, receipt of notification that the particular security has been lost or stolen raises the question of notice "forgotten" in good faith. Kentucky Rock Asphalt v. Mazza's Admr., 264 Ky. 158, 94 S.W.2d 316 (1936); Graham v. White-Phillips Co., 296 U.S. 27, 56 S.Ct. 21, 80 L.Ed. 20, 102 A.L.R. 24 (1935) but cf., First National Bank of Odessa v. Fazzari, 10 N.Y.2d 394, 179 N.E.2d 493 (1961). Also suspicious characteristics of the transaction may give a purchaser (particularly a commercially sophisticated purchaser such as a broker) "reason to know". U.S. Fidelity & Guaranty Co. v. Goetz, 285 N.Y. 74, 32 N.E.2d 798 (1941); Morris v. Muir, 111 Misc. 739, 180 N.Y.S. 913 (1920).

2. Subsection (1)(a) refers to situations in which a certificated security indorsed "for collection" or "for surrender" is being offered for transfer and follows in effect Section 37 of the Negotiable Instruments Law, which provides that subsequent indorsees acquire only the title of the first indorsee under a restrictive indorsement.

3. A purchaser of an uncertificated security is charged with notice of adverse claims noted in the initial transaction statement. If the security is transferred to him other than by registration on the issuer's records, he is charged with notice of claims noted in the statement sent to the registered owner (or to the registered pledgee if his rights were transferred by notice to or acknowledgement from a registered pledgee).

Situations may arise in which the issuer receives notice of an adverse claim after registration of transfer, pledge or release but before the initial transaction statement is prepared and sent. The issuer ought not to note those claims on the statement. See Section 8–408(1)(d), (2)(d) and (3)(d). If the issuer should mistakenly note such a claim, subsection (2) does not charge the purchaser with notice.

4. In subsection (3) some situations involving purchase from one described or identifiable as a fiduciary are explicitly provided for, again imposing an objective standard, while leaving the door open to other circumstances which may constitute notice of adverse claims. Mere notice of the existence of the fiduciary relation is not enough in itself to prevent bona fide purchase, and the purchaser is free to take the security on the assumption that the fiduciary is acting properly. The fact that the security may be transferred to the individual account of the fiduciary or that the proceeds of the transaction are paid into that account in cash would not be sufficient to charge the purchaser with notice of potential breach of fiduciary obligation but as in State Bank of Binghamton v. Bache, 162 Misc. 128, 293 N.Y.S. 667 (1937) knowledge that the proceeds are being applied to the personal indebtedness of the fiduciary will charge the purchaser with such notice.

5. The notice here involved is to purchasers. A broker acting as such (Section 8–303) is treated in this section as a purchaser though he may not be a purchaser under the definitions of that term (Section 1–201(33)). On the other hand, a bank, stock-broker or other intermediary who, in the particular transaction acts purely in that capacity, is not a purchaser. Cf. subsections (3) and (4) of Section 8–306 and Comments 3 and 4 to that Section. Subsection (3) follows the policy of Section 4 of the Uniform Fiduciaries Act and of Section 3–304(2) with respect to commercial paper. Compare Section 7(a) of the Uniform Act for Simplification of Fiduciary Security Transfers.

The fact that the broker is expressly mentioned in this section carries no negative implication in other sections in which merely the word "purchaser" is used.

An issuer is not a purchaser. Its duty of inquiry is set forth in Part 4.

Cross References:

Point 5: Part 4 of this Article. See Sections 8–104, 8–302, 8–305 and 8–308.

Definitional Cross References:

"Adverse Claim". Section 8-302.
"Bearer Form". Section 8-102.
"Broker". Section 8-303.
"Certificated Security". Section 8-102.
"Indorsed". Section 8-308.
"Initial Transaction Statement". Section 8-408.
"Intermediary Bank". Section 4-105.
"Issuer". Section 8-201.
"Notice". Section 1-201.
"Person". Section 1-201.
"Purchaser". Section 1-201.
"Registered Form". Section 8-102.
"Security". Section 8-102.
"Uncertificated Security". Section 8-102.
"Writing". Section 1-201.

§ 8-305. Staleness as Notice of Adverse Claims.

An act or event that creates a right to immediate performance of the principal obligation represented by a certificated security or sets a date on or after which a certificated security is to be presented or surrendered for redemption or exchange does not itself constitute any notice of adverse claims except in the case of a transfer:

(a) after one year from any date set for presentment or surrender for redemption or exchange; or

(b) after 6 months from any date set for payment of money against presentation or surrender of the security if funds are available for payment on that date.

As amended in 1977.

Official Comment

Prior Uniform Statutory Provision: Sections 52(2), 53, Uniform Negotiable Instruments Law.

Purposes:

1. The fact of "staleness" is viewed as notice of certain defects after the lapse of stated periods, but the maturity of the security does not operate automatically to affect holders' rights. The periods of time here stated are shorter than those appearing in the provisions of this Article on staleness as notice of defects or defenses (Section 8-203) since a purchaser who takes a security after funds or other securities are available for its redemption has more reason to suspect claims of ownership than issuer's defenses. An owner will normally turn in his security rather than transfer it at such a time.

Of itself, a default never constitutes notice of a possible adverse claim. To provide otherwise would not tend to drive defaulted securities home and would serve only to disrupt current financial markets where many defaulted securities are actively traded.

2. The owner is provided with a means of protecting himself while his security is being sent in for redemption or exchange. He may endorse it "for collection" or "for surrender," and this constitutes notice of his claims (Section 8-304). The present section does not come into operation unless the time period here stated has elapsed.

3. Unpaid or overdue coupons attached to a bond do not bring it within the operation of this section, although under some circumstances they may give the purchaser "reason to know" of claims of ownership. Georgia Granite R. Co. v. Miller, 144 Ga. 665, 87 S.E. 897 (1916).

4. This section has been made expressly applicable to certificated securities only, since the transfer of an uncertificated security normally will involve communication with the issuer and a consequent opportunity for the issuer to give the transferee effective notice of adverse claims.

Cross References:

Point 1: Section 8–203. Point 2: Section 8–304. See Section 8–103.

Definitional Cross References:

"Adverse Claim". Section 8–302.
"Certificated Security". Section 8–102.
"Money". Section 1–201.
"Notice". Section 1–201.
"Purchase". Section 1–201.
"Right". Section 1–201.
"Security". Section 8–102.

§ 8–306. Warranties on Presentment and Transfer of Certificated Securities; Warranties of Originators of Instructions.

(1) A person who presents a certificated security for registration of transfer or for payment or exchange warrants to the issuer that he is entitled to the registration, payment, or exchange. But, a purchaser for value and without notice of adverse claims who receives a new, reissued, or re-registered certificated security on registration of transfer or receives an initial transaction statement confirming the registration of transfer of an equivalent uncertificated security to him warrants only that he has no knowledge of any unauthorized signature (Section 8–311) in a necessary indorsement.

(2) A person by transferring a certificated security to a purchaser for value warrants only that:

(a) his transfer is effective and rightful;

(b) the security is genuine and has not been materially altered; and

(c) he knows of no fact which might impair the validity of the security.

(3) If a certificated security is delivered by an intermediary known to be entrusted with delivery of the security on behalf of another or with collection of a draft or other claim against delivery, the intermediary by delivery warrants only his own good faith and authority, even though he has purchased or made advances against the claim to be collected against the delivery.

(4) A pledgee or other holder for security who redelivers a certificated security received, or after payment and on order of the debtor delivers that security to a third person, makes only the warranties of an intermediary under subsection (3).

(5) A person who originates an instruction warrants to the issuer that:

(a) he is an appropriate person to originate the instruction; and

(b) at the time the instruction is presented to the issuer he will be entitled to the registration of transfer, pledge, or release.

(6) A person who originates an instruction warrants to any person specially guaranteeing his signature (subsection 8–312(3)) that:

(a) he is an appropriate person to originate the instruction; and

(b) at the time the instruction is presented to the issuer

(i) he will be entitled to the registration of transfer, pledge, or release; and

(ii) the transfer, pledge, or release requested in the instruction will be registered by the issuer free from all liens, security interests, restrictions, and claims other than those specified in the instruction.

(7) A person who originates an instruction warrants to a purchaser for value and to any person guaranteeing the instruction (Section 8–312(6)) that:

(a) he is an appropriate person to originate the instruction;

(b) the uncertificated security referred to therein is valid; and

(c) at the time the instruction is presented to the issuer

(i) the transferor will be entitled to the registration of transfer, pledge, or release;

(ii) the transfer, pledge, or release requested in the instruction will be registered by the issuer free from all liens, security interests, restrictions, and claims other than those specified in the instruction; and

(iii) the requested transfer, pledge, or release will be rightful.

(8) If a secured party is the registered pledgee or the registered owner of an uncertificated security, a person who originates an instruction of release or transfer to the debtor or, after payment and on order of the debtor, a transfer instruction to a third person, warrants to the debtor or the third person only that he is an appropriate person to originate the instruction and, at the time the instruction is presented to the issuer, the transferor will be entitled to the registration of release or transfer. If a transfer instruction to a third person who is a purchaser for value is originated on order of the debtor, the debtor makes to the purchaser the warranties of paragraphs (b), (c)(ii) and (c)(iii) of subsection (7).

(9) A person who transfers an uncertificated security to a purchaser for value and does not originate an instruction in connection with the transfer warrants only that:

(a) his transfer is effective and rightful; and

(b) the uncertificated security is valid.

(10) A broker gives to his customer and to the issuer and a purchaser the applicable warranties provided in this section and has the rights and privileges of a purchaser under this section. The warranties of and in favor of the broker, acting as an agent are in addition to applicable warranties given by and in favor of his customer.

As amended in 1962 and 1977.

Official Comment

Prior Uniform Statutory Provision: Sections 65, 66, 67, 69, Uniform Negotiable Instruments Law; Sections 11, 12, Uniform Stock Transfer Act.

Purposes:

1. The warranties with respect to certificated securities have been recognized by the prevailing case law as well as by the prior Acts cited. See Boston Tow Boat Co. v. Medford Nat. Bank, 232 Mass. 38, 121 N.E. 491 (1919); Burtch v. Child, Hulswit & Co., 207 Mich. 205, 174 N.W. 170 (1919).

Usual estoppel principles apply with respect to transfers of both certificated and uncertificated securities whenever the purchaser has knowledge of the defect, and these warranties will not be effective in such a case. In addition, under Section 1-102(3) these provisions apply only "unless otherwise agreed" and the parties are free to enter into any express agreement they desire where both are aware of possible defects.

2. The second sentence of subsection (1) limits the warranties made by a bona fide purchaser whose presentation of a certificated security is defective in some way but who nonetheless is given a reissued certificated security or an initial transaction statement confirming the transfer of an uncertificated security to him. The effect is to deny the issuer a remedy against such a person unless at the time of presentment the person had knowledge of an unauthorized signature in a necessary indorsement. The issuer can protect itself by refusing to make the transfer or, if it registers the transfer before it discovers the defect, by pursuing its remedy against a signature guarantor.

3. Subsection (3) and (4) are designed to eliminate all substantive warranties in the case of deliveries of certificated securities by intermediaries and pledgees. Such parties deal primarily with the draft or other claim and, having no access to direct knowledge about the security, they cannot be held to warrant its genuineness or validity. Subsection (8) similarly limits the warranties given by a secured party (or its agent) originating an instruction at the behest of the debtor.

4. The so-called "stock-broker" normally functions as a broker (see definition of "broker", Section 8-303) and on a few occasions another institution such as a bank may function as a broker—e.g. for a standard broker's commission or similar compensation. In those situations the warranties, rights and privileges of the broker are spelled out in subsection (10). Nevertheless either the so-called "stock-broker" or the bank can qualify for the protection given by subsections (3) and (4) to an "intermediary" where in the particular transaction it does not function as a broker—e.g. when it transfers securities on a customer's instructions, either without charge or for a nominal handling charge.

5. Subsection (5) establishes the rights of the issuer against one who originates an instruction (Section 8-308(4)) that is fraudulent or otherwise improper. The issuer's loss—which necessitates the remedy—arises only if the issuer registers the requested transfer, pledge or release and is subjected to liability for improper registration. See Section 8-404(3).

6. Subsection (6) sets forth the warranties made by the instruction originator to a person specially guaranteeing his signature. These warranties mirror those made by the special signature guarantor.

7. Subsection (7) sets forth the warranties made to a purchaser for value by one who originates an instruction. These warranties are quite similar to those made by one transferring a certificated security, subsection (2), the principal difference being the absolute warranty of validity. If upon receipt of the instruction the issuer should dispute the validity of the security, it seems proper to place the burden of proving validity upon the transferor. Because the guarantor of an instruction makes an absolute warranty of rightfulness, Section 8-312(6), he is given the benefit of a similar warranty from the originator in subsection (7).

Cross References:

See Sections 1-102(3), 8-103, 8-301, 8-311 and 8-405.

Definitional Cross References:

"Adverse Claim". Section 8-302.
"Appropriate Person". Section 8-308.
"Broker". Section 8-303.
"Certificated Security". Section 8-102.
"Debtor". Section 9-105.
"Delivery". Section 1-201.
"Genuine". Section 1-201.
"Good Faith". Section 1-201.
"Indorsement". Section 8-308.
"Initial Transaction Statement". Section 8-408.

"Instruction". Section 8-308.
"Issuer". Section 8-201.
"Knowledge". Section 1-201.
"Notice". Section 1-201.
"Person". Section 1-201.
"Purchase". Section 1-201.
"Purchaser". Section 1-201.
"Secured Party". Section 9-105.
"Security". Section 8-102.
"Security Interest". Section 1-201.
"Unauthorized Signature". Section 1-201.
"Uncertificated Security". Section 8-102.
"Value". Section 1-201.

§ 8-307. Effect of Delivery Without Indorsement; Right to Compel Indorsement.

If a certificated security in registered form has been delivered to a purchaser without a necessary indorsement he may become a bona fide purchaser only as of the time the indorsement is supplied; but against the transferor, the transfer is complete upon delivery and the purchaser has a specifically enforceable right to have any necessary indorsement supplied.

As amended in 1977.

Official Comment

Prior Uniform Statutory Provision: Section 49, Uniform Negotiable Instruments Law; Section 9, Uniform Stock Transfer Act.

Purposes:

1. As between the parties the transfer of a certificated security is made complete upon delivery, but the transferee cannot become a bona fide purchaser of the security until indorsement is made. The indorsement does not operate retroactively, and notice may intervene between delivery and indorsement so as to prevent the transferee from becoming a bona fide purchaser. This Article rejects such cases as Bethea v. Floyd, 177 S.C. 521, 181 S.E. 721 (1935), certiorari denied 296 U.S. 622, 56 S.Ct. 143, 80 L.Ed. 442, holding that the indorsement of a note delivered prior to maturity but indorsed thereafter took effect as of the date of delivery to permit the purchaser to become a holder in due course. Although a purchaser taking without a necessary indorsement may be subject to claims of ownership, any issuer's defense of which he had no notice at the time of delivery will be cut off, since the provisions of this Article protect all purchasers for value without notice (Section 8-202).

2. The transferee's right to compel an indorsement where a certificated security has been delivered with intent to transfer is recognized in the case law and the Article of this Act on Documents of Title. See Coats v. Guaranty Bank & Trust Co., 170 La. 871, 129 So. 513 (1930), and Section 7-506 of this Act.

3. A proper indorsement is one of the requisites of transfer which a purchaser of a certificated security has a right to obtain (Section 8-316). A purchaser may not only compel an indorsement under that section but may also recover for any reasonable expense incurred by the transferor's failure to respond to the demand for an indorsement.

Cross References:

Point 1: Section 8-202. Point 2: Section 7-506.

Point 3: Section 8-316. See Sections 8-302, 8-308 and 8-309.

Definitional Cross References:

"Bona Fide Purchaser". Section 8-302.
"Certificated Security". Section 8-102.
"Delivery". Section 1-201.
"Indorsement". Section 8-308.
"Purchaser". Section 1-201.
"Registered Form". Section 8-102.
"Right". Section 1-201.

§ 8-308. Indorsements; Instructions.

(1) An indorsement of a certificated security in registered form is made when an appropriate person signs on it or on a separate document an assignment or transfer of the security or a power to assign or transfer it or his signature is written without more upon the back of the security.

(2) An indorsement may be in blank or special. An indorsement in blank includes an indorsement to bearer. A special indorsement specifies to whom the security is to be transferred, or who has power to transfer it. A holder may convert a blank indorsement into a special indorsement.

(3) An indorsement purporting to be only of part of a certificated security representing units intended by the issuer to be separately transferable is effective to the extent of the indorsement.

(4) An "instruction" is an order to the issuer of an uncertificated security requesting that the transfer, pledge, or release from pledge of the uncertificated security specified therein be registered.

(5) An instruction originated by an appropriate person is:

(a) a writing signed by an appropriate person; or

(b) a communication to the issuer in any form agreed upon in a writing signed by the issuer and an appropriate person.

If an instruction has been originated by an appropriate person but is incomplete in any other respect, any person may complete it as authorized and the issuer may rely on it as completed even though it has been completed incorrectly.

(6) "An appropriate person" in subsection (1) means the person specified by the certificated security or by special indorsement to be entitled to the security.

(7) "An appropriate person" in subsection (5) means:

(a) for an instruction to transfer or pledge an uncertificated security which is then not subject to a registered pledge, the registered owner; or

(b) for an instruction to transfer or release an uncertificated security which is then subject to a registered pledge, the registered pledgee.

(8) In addition to the persons designated in subsections (6) and (7), "an appropriate person" in subsections (1) and (5) includes:

(a) if the person designated is described as a fiduciary but is no longer serving in the described capacity, either that person or his successor;

(b) if the persons designated are described as more than one person as fiduciaries and one or more are no longer serving in the described capacity, the remaining fiduciary or fiduciaries, whether or not a successor has been appointed or qualified;

(c) if the person designated is an individual and is without capacity to act by virtue of death, incompetence, infancy, or otherwise, his executor, administrator, guardian, or like fiduciary;

(d) if the persons designated are described as more than one person as tenants by the entirety or with right of survivorship and by reason of death all cannot sign, the survivor or survivors;

(e) a person having power to sign under applicable law or controlling instrument; and

(f) to the extent that the person designated or any of the foregoing persons may act through an agent, his authorized agent.

(9) Unless otherwise agreed, the indorser of a certificated security by his indorsement or the originator of an instruction by his origination assumes no obligation that the security will be honored by the issuer but only the obligations provided in Section 8–306.

(10) Whether the person signing is appropriate is determined as of the date of signing and an indorsement made by or an instruction originated by him does not become unauthorized for the purposes of this Article by virtue of any subsequent change of circumstances.

(11) Failure of a fiduciary to comply with a controlling instrument or with the law of the state having jurisdiction of the fiduciary relationship, including any law requiring the fiduciary to obtain court approval of the transfer, pledge, or release, does not render his indorsement or an instruction originated by him unauthorized for the purposes of this Article.

As amended in 1962 and 1977.

Official Comment

Prior Uniform Statutory Provision: Sections 31 through 37, 64 through 69, Uniform Negotiable Instruments Law; Section 20, Uniform Stock Transfer Act.

Purposes:

1. The simplified method of indorsing certificated securities set forth in the Uniform Stock Transfer Act is continued in subsections (1) and (2). Although more than one special indorsement on a given certificated security is here made possible, the desire for dividends or interest, as the case may be, should operate to bring the security home for registration of transfer within a reasonable period of time. The usual form of assignment which appears in the back of a stock certificate or in a separate "power" may be filled up either in the form of an assignment, a power of attorney to transfer, or both. If it is not filled up at all but merely signed, the indorsement is in blank; if filled up either as an assignment or as a power of attorney to transfer, the indorsement is special.

2. Subsection (3) recognizes, in contradistinction to the rule under the Uniform Negotiable Instruments Law, the validity of a "partial" indorsement of a certificated security—e.g., as to fifty shares of the one hundred represented by a single certificate. The rights of a transferee under a partial indorsement to the status of a bona fide purchaser are left to the case law.

3. Subsections (4) and (5) together indicate that an instruction is an order from an "appropriate person" (subsection (7)) to the issuer demanding registration of some form of transfer of an uncertificated security. Functionally, presentation of an instruction is quite similar to the presentation of an indorsed certificate for re-registration. The instruction may be in the form of a writing signed by an appropriate person or in any other form agreed upon in writing by the issuer and an appropriate person. Allowing non-written forms of instructions will permit the development and employment of

means of transmitting instructions electronically.

When a person originates an instruction in which he leaves a blank and the blank later is completed, subsection (5) gives the issuer the same rights it would have had against the originating person had that person completed the blank himself. This is true regardless of whether the person completing the instruction had authority to complete it. Compare Section 8–206 and its Comment, dealing with blanks left upon issue.

4. Subsections (6) and (7) give basic rules for determining who is an appropriate person to indorse a certificated security or to originate a transfer instruction for an uncertificated security. Subsection (8) defines the various situations in which persons other than those designated in subsections (6) and (7) will also be "appropriate persons." The provisions are not mutually exclusive; for example, the same certificated security may be effectively indorsed either by the registered owner under subsection (6) or by his agent under (8)(f). Paragraph (8)(a) is made explicitly alternative to make it clear that there is no conflict with paragraph (3)(a) of Section 8–403, permitting the issuer to rely on the continued power of a fiduciary to act where he is the registered owner and the issuer has not received written notice to the contrary. Similar protection is given to other persons dealing with the security. See also the Comment to Section 8–404.

Paragraphs (e) and (f) in particular are comprehensive. For example, where a "small estate statute" permits a widow to transfer a decedent's securities without administration proceedings, she would be "a person having power to sign under applicable law." Similarly, in the usual partnership case, the signature of a partner would be that of "a person having power to sign under ... [a] ... controlling instrument."

Indorsement or origination by "an appropriate person" is included in the scope of the guarantee of signature (Section 8–312). It is prerequisite to the issuer's duty to register a transfer (Section 8–401) and to his exoneration from liability for improper registration (Section 8–404).

5. Subsection (9) makes clear that the indorser of a certificated security and the originator of an instruction do not warrant that the issuer will honor the underlying obligation. In view of the nature of investment securities and the circumstances under which they are normally transferred, a transferor cannot be held to warrant as to the issuer's actions. As a transferor he, of course, remains liable for breach of the warranties set forth in this Article (Section 8–306).

6. Subsection (10) of this section makes the indorsement or instruction speak as of the date of signing. Section 8–312 on guaranty of signature and Section 8–402 on assurance that indorsements and instructions are effective apply the same reasoning. Thus, the signatures on a security indorsed by A during his lifetime or on behalf of X corporation by Y as president during his incumbency do not become "unauthorized" (Section 8–311) because A dies or Y is replaced as president by Z. Authority to deliver a certificated security and thus to complete the transfer is not covered by this section. Subsection (11) supplements Section 8–403(3)(b) by making it clear that certain matters go to rightfulness of the transfer rather than to the validity of the indorsement or instruction. An example is the failure of a duly appointed guardian to obtain a required court approval of the transfer. Such a guardian is an "appropriate person" under paragraph (8)(c) of this section, and his indorsement may be effective even though, e.g., a required court order is not obtained.

Cross References:

Point 1: Section 8–306. Point 4: Section 8–312 and Part 4 of this Article.

Point 6: Sections 8–301, 8–302, 8–307, 8–309 and 8–312.

Definitional Cross References:

"Bearer". Section 1–201.

"Certificated Security". Section 8–102.

"Holder". Section 1–201.

"Honor". Section 1-201.
"Issuer". Section 8-201.
"Person". Section 1-201.
"Registered Form". Section 8-102.
"Security". Section 8-102.
"Sign". Section 1-201.
"Uncertificated Security". Section 8-102.
"Writing". Section 1-201.
"Written". Section 1-201.

§ 8-309. Effect of Indorsement Without Delivery.

An indorsement of a certificated security, whether special or in blank, does not constitute a transfer until delivery of the certificated security on which it appears or, if the indorsement is on a separate document, until delivery of both the document and the certificated security.

As amended in 1977.

Official Comment

Prior Uniform Statutory Provision: Section 30, Uniform Negotiable Instruments Law; Sections 1, 10, Uniform Stock Transfer Act.

Purposes:

1. There must be a voluntary parting with control in order to effect a valid transfer of a certificated security as between the parties. Levey v. Nason, 279 Mass. 268, 181 N.E. 193 (1932), and National Surety Co. v. Indemnity Insurance Co. of North America, 237 App.Div. 485, 261 N.Y.S. 605 (1933).

2. The provision in Section 10 of the Uniform Stock Transfer Act that an attempted transfer without delivery amounts to a promise to transfer is here omitted. Even under the prior Act the effect of such a promise was left to the applicable law of contracts, and this Article by making no reference to such situations intends to achieve a similar result.

With respect to delivery there is no counterpart to Section 8-307 on right to compel indorsement, such as is envisaged in Johnson v. Johnson, 300 Mass. 24, 13 N.E.2d 788 (1938), where the transferee under a written assignment was given the right to compel a transfer of the certificate.

Cross References:

Point 2: Section 8-307. See Sections 8-202(4) and 8-313.

Definitional Cross References:

"Certificated Security". Section 8-102.
"Delivery". Section 1-201.
"Indorsement". Section 8-308.

§ 8-310. Indorsement of Certificated Security in Bearer Form.

An indorsement of a certificated security in bearer form may give notice of adverse claims (Section 8-304) but does not otherwise affect any right to registration the holder possesses.

As amended in 1977.

Official Comment

Prior Uniform Statutory Provision: Section 40, Uniform Negotiable Instruments Law.

Purposes:

1. The concept of indorsement applies only to registered certificated securities, and a purported indorsement of bearer paper is normally of no effect.

An indorsement "for collection," "for surrender" or the like, charges a purchaser with notice of adverse claims (Section 8-304(1)(a)) but does not operate beyond this to interfere with any right the holder may otherwise possess to have the security registered in his name.

2. The provisions of Section 40 of the Negotiable Instruments Law as to the liability of special indorsers of bearer instruments have no applicability here since this Article negates the liability of indorsers as such upon the issuer's obligation (Section 8-308(9)).

Cross References:

Sections 8-304 and 8-308.

Definitional Cross References:

"Adverse Claims". Section 8-302.
"Bearer Form". Section 8-102.
"Certificated Security". Section 8-102.
"Holder". Section 1-201.
"Indorsement". Section 8-308.
"Notice". Section 1-201.
"Right". Section 1-201.

§ 8-311. Effect of Unauthorized Indorsement or Instruction.

Unless the owner or pledgee has ratified an unauthorized indorsement or instruction or is otherwise precluded from asserting its ineffectiveness:

(a) he may assert its ineffectiveness against the issuer or any purchaser, other than a purchaser for value and without notice of adverse claims, who has in good faith received a new, reissued, or re-registered certificated security on registration of transfer or received an initial transaction statement confirming the registration of transfer, pledge, or release of an equivalent uncertificated security to him; and

(b) an issuer who registers the transfer of a certificated security upon the unauthorized indorsement or who registers the transfer, pledge, or release of an uncertificated security upon the unauthorized instruction is subject to liability for improper registration (Section 8-404).

As amended in 1977.

Official Comment

Prior Uniform Statutory Provision: Section 23, Uniform Negotiable Instruments Law.

Purposes:

1. Most present day security purchases are made through brokers. The purchaser who normally receives and sees only a certificated security registered in his own name or an initial transaction statement addressed to him cannot realistically be held to have notice of or to have relied upon a forged or unauthorized indorsement on the original security transferred or upon the unauthorized instruction. A good faith purchaser who has received an initial transaction statement or a new, reissued or re-registered certificate is therefore protected. Compare Telegraph Co. v. Davenport, 97 U.S. 369, 24 L.Ed. 1047 (1878). That line of cases which has refused to apply this rule where the new security is still in the hands of the party to whom it was issued is expressly rejected. See Weniger v. Success Mining Co., 227 F. 548 (C.C.A.Utah 1915); Hambleton v. Central Ohio R.R. Co., 44 Md. 551 (1876).

2. The original owner of a security which has been transferred on the basis of a forged indorsement or instruction is protected by the issuer's liability for wrongful registration of transfer (Section 8-404). The issuer's duty to issue a similar security to the owner unless an overissue would result is made explicit in Part 4 of this Article, as is his obligation to purchase available securities on the open market for transfer to the owner where overissue is involved (see Section 8-104). Compare Prince v. Childs Co., 23 F.2d 605 (1928); West v. Tintic Standard Min-

ing Co., 71 Utah 158, 263 P. 490, 56 A.L.R. 1190 (1928). The issuer's recourse is against the forger and the guarantor of the latter's signature, if any. But since the issuer has a right to require a guarantee of signature, a bona fide purchaser presenting the certificated security or instruction to the issuer should not be held liable on any implied warranty of title theory unless he knew of the forgery (Section 8-306).

3. A bond which has been registered as to principal and subsequently is returned to bearer form is, at that point, a "new security" within the meaning of this Section.

Cross References:

Point 2: Sections 8-104, 8-306(1), 8-312 and Part 4 of this Article.

Definitional Cross References:

"Adverse Claim". Section 8-302.
"Certificated Security". Section 8-102.
"Good Faith". Section 1-201.
"Initial Transaction Statement". Section 8-408.
"Instruction". Section 8-308.
"Issuer". Section 8-201.
"Notice". Section 1-201.
"Purchaser". Section 1-201.
"Uncertificated Security". Section 8-102.
"Value". Section 1-201.

§ 8-312. Effect of Guaranteeing Signature, Indorsement or Instruction.

(1) Any person guaranteeing a signature of an indorser of a certificated security warrants that at the time of signing:

(a) the signature was genuine;

(b) the signer was an appropriate person to indorse (Section 8-308); and

(c) the signer had legal capacity to sign.

(2) Any person guaranteeing a signature of the originator of an instruction warrants that at the time of signing:

(a) the signature was genuine;

(b) the signer was an appropriate person to originate the instruction (Section 8-308) if the person specified in the instruction as the registered owner or registered pledgee of the uncertificated security was, in fact, the registered owner or registered pledgee of the security, as to which fact the signature guarantor makes no warranty;

(c) the signer had legal capacity to sign; and

(d) the taxpayer identification number, if any, appearing on the instruction as that of the registered owner or registered pledgee was the taxpayer identification number of the signer or of the owner or pledgee for whom the signer was acting.

(3) Any person specially guaranteeing the signature of the originator of an instruction makes not only the warranties of a signature guarantor (subsection (2)) but also warrants that at the time the instruction is presented to the issuer:

(a) the person specified in the instruction as the registered owner or registered pledgee of the uncertificated security will be the registered owner or registered pledgee; and

(b) the transfer, pledge, or release of the uncertificated security requested in the instruction will be registered by the issuer free from all liens, security interests, restrictions, and claims other than those specified in the instruction.

(4) The guarantor under subsections (1) and (2) or the special guarantor under subsection (3) does not otherwise warrant the rightfulness of the particular transfer, pledge, or release.

(5) Any person guaranteeing an indorsement of a certificated security makes not only the warranties of a signature guarantor under subsection (1) but also warrants the rightfulness of the particular transfer in all respects.

(6) Any person guaranteeing an instruction requesting the transfer, pledge, or release of an uncertificated security makes not only the warranties of a special signature guarantor under subsection (3) but also warrants the rightfulness of the particular transfer, pledge, or release in all respects.

(7) No issuer may require a special guarantee of signature (subsection (3)), a guarantee of indorsement (subsection (5)), or a guarantee of instruction (subsection (6)) as a condition to registration of transfer, pledge, or release.

(8) The foregoing warranties are made to any person taking or dealing with the security in reliance on the guarantee, and the guarantor is liable to the person for any loss resulting from breach of the warranties.

As amended in 1977.

Official Comment

Prior Uniform Statutory Provision: None.

Purposes:

1. In subsection (1) the commonly accepted liability of the guarantor of the signature of the indorser of a certificated security, which includes a warranty of the authority of the signer to sign for the holder as well as of the capacity of the signer to sign, is made express so that issuers and their agents may have a clear understanding of the extent to which they may rely upon such guarantees.

2. Consistent with the coordinate provisions of Sections 8–308, 8–401 and 8–404, this Section provides that a signature guarantor warrants as to facts "at the time of signing."

3. Subsection (2) sets forth the warranties that can reasonably be expected from the guarantor of the signature of the originator of an instruction, who, though familiar with the signer, does not have before him any evidence that the purported owner or pledgee is, in fact, the owner or pledgee of the subject uncertificated security. This is in contrast to the position of the person guaranteeing a signature on a certificate who can see a certificate in the signer's possession in the name of or indorsed to the signer or in blank. Thus, the warranty of appropriateness in clause (b) is expressly conditioned on the actual registration's conforming to that represented by the originator. If the signer purports to be the owner or pledgee, the guarantor under clause (b), warrants only his identity. If, however, the signer is acting in a representative capacity, the guarantor warrants both his identity and his authority to act for the purported owner or pledgee. The additional warranty of clause (d) as to the taxpayer identification number is intended to prevent error or fraud resulting from identical or similar names. The warranties of subsection (2) are intended to provide satisfactory assurance to the issuer who needs no warranty as to the facts of registration because he can ascertain those facts from his own records.

4. Subsection (3) sets forth a "special guarantee of signature" under which the

guarantor additionally warrants both registered ownership or pledge and freedom from undisclosed defects of record. The guarantor of the signature of an indorser of a certificated security effectively makes these warranties to a purchaser for value on the evidence of a clean certificate issued in the name of the indorser, indorsed to the indorser or indorsed in blank. By specially guaranteeing under subsection (3), the guarantor warrants that the instruction will, when presented to the issuer, result in the requested registration free from defects not specified. It is contemplated that the special guarantee of signature will be used principally in brokerage transactions where the broker will be specially guaranteeing the signature on an instruction originated by his own customer. The broker's risk will be no greater than that of a broker who executes the sale of a security for his customer without the absolute assurance that his customer will deliver a clean certificate at settlement.

5. Subsection (4) makes clear that the warranties of a person guaranteeing a signature are limited to those specified in this section and do not include a general warranty of rightfulness. On the other hand subsections (5) and (6) make clear that a person guaranteeing an indorsement or an instruction does warrant that the transfer is rightful in all respects.

6. Subsection (7) makes clear what can be inferred from the combination of Sections 8–401 and 8–402, that the issuer may not require as a condition to transfer a guarantee of the indorsement or instruction nor may it require a special signature guarantee. But the voluntary furnishing of such a guarantee and its acceptance by the issuer may save the time and expense of an inquiry into possible adverse claims (cf. Section 8–403).

7. Subsection (8) is expressly designed to encourage issuers and their agents to rely upon signature guarantees and to avoid needless waste of time and duplication of effort in ascertaining the facts so guaranteed.

Cross References:

Point 1: Section 8–308. See Part 4 of this Article.

Definitional Cross References:

"Appropriate Person". Section 8–308.
"Certificated Security". Section 8–102.
"Genuine". Section 1–201.
"Indorsement". Section 8–308.
"Instruction". Section 8–308.
"Issuer". Section 8–201.
"Person". Section 1–201.
"Security". Section 8–102.
"Security Interest". Section 1–201.
"Sign". Section 1–201.
"Uncertificated Security". Section 8–102.

§ 8–313. When Transfer to Purchaser Occurs; Financial Intermediary as Bona Fide Purchaser; "Financial Intermediary".

(1) Transfer of a security or a limited interest (including a security interest) therein to a purchaser occurs only:

(a) at the time he or a person designated by him acquires possession of a certificated security;

(b) at the time the transfer, pledge, or release of an uncertificated security is registered to him or a person designated by him;

(c) at the time his financial intermediary acquires possession of a certificated security specially indorsed to or issued in the name of the purchaser;

(d) at the time a financial intermediary, not a clearing corporation, sends him confirmation of the purchase and also by book entry or otherwise identifies as belonging to the purchaser

(i) a specific certificated security in the financial intermediary's possession;

(ii) a quantity of securities that constitute or are part of a fungible bulk of certificated securities in the financial intermediary's possession or of uncertificated securities registered in the name of the financial intermediary; or

(iii) a quantity of securities that constitute or are part of a fungible bulk of securities shown on the account of the financial intermediary on the books of another financial intermediary;

(e) with respect to an identified certificated security to be delivered while still in the possession of a third person, not a financial intermediary, at the time that person acknowledges that he holds for the purchaser;

(f) with respect to a specific uncertificated security the pledge or transfer of which has been registered to a third person, not a financial intermediary, at the time that person acknowledges that he holds for the purchaser;

(g) at the time appropriate entries to the account of the purchaser or a person designated by him on the books of a clearing corporation are made under Section 8–320;

(h) with respect to the transfer of a security interest where the debtor has signed a security agreement containing a description of the security, at the time a written notification, which, in the case of the creation of the security interest, is signed by the debtor (which may be a copy of the security agreement) or which, in the case of the release or assignment of the security interest created pursuant to this paragraph, is signed by the secured party, is received by

(i) a financial intermediary on whose books the interest of the transferor in the security appears;

(ii) a third person, not a financial intermediary, in possession of the security, if it is certificated;

(iii) a third person, not a financial intermediary, who is the registered owner of the security, if it is uncertificated and not subject to a registered pledge; or

(iv) a third person, not a financial intermediary, who is the registered pledgee of the security, if it is uncertificated and subject to a registered pledge;

(i) with respect to the transfer of a security interest where the transferor has signed a security agreement containing a description of the security, at the time new value is given by the secured party; or

(j) with respect to the transfer of a security interest where the secured party is a financial intermediary and the security has already been transferred to the financial intermediary under paragraphs (a), (b), (c), (d), or (g), at the time the transferor has signed a security agreement containing a description of the security and value is given by the secured party.

(2) The purchaser is the owner of a security held for him by a financial intermediary, but cannot be a bona fide purchaser of a security so held except in the circumstances specified in paragraphs (c), (d)(i), and (g) of subsection (1). If a security so held is part of a fungible bulk, as in the circumstances

specified in paragraphs (d)(ii) and (d)(iii) of subsection (1), the purchaser is the owner of a proportionate property interest in the fungible bulk.

(3) Notice of an adverse claim received by the financial intermediary or by the purchaser after the financial intermediary takes delivery of a certificated security as a holder for value or after the transfer, pledge, or release of an uncertificated security has been registered free of the claim to a financial intermediary who has given value is not effective either as to the financial intermediary or as to the purchaser. However, as between the financial intermediary and the purchaser the purchaser may demand transfer of an equivalent security as to which no notice of adverse claim has been received.

(4) A "financial intermediary" is a bank, broker, clearing corporation, or other person (or the nominee of any of them) which in the ordinary course of its business maintains security accounts for its customers and is acting in that capacity. A financial intermediary may have a security interest in securities held in account for its customer.

As amended in 1962 and 1977.

Official Comment

Prior Uniform Statutory Provision: Section 191, Uniform Negotiable Instruments Law; Section 22, Uniform Stock Transfer Act.

Purposes:

1. Subsection (1) lists the various methods by which legal rights in a security may be transferred from one person to another. Subsection (1) is expressly made applicable to limited interests, including security interests, as well as to entire interests. Compare Section 8-301(2). The word "only" in the first sentence is intended to provide that the methods of transfer listed are exclusive and that compliance with one of them is essential to a valid transfer. Transfers by operation of law are excepted because they are not transfers to a "purchaser".

2. This section is intended to bring the law of securities transfers into line with modern security trading practices and to allow for future development of those practices. It is recognized that most transfers are not effected through physical delivery of a certificate from seller to buyer, but rather through adjustments in balances of the parties' accounts with various intermediaries. Whether each intermediary has physical possession of a certificate to match every security it "holds" in its customer accounts is of no importance. So long as the intermediary exercises ultimate control, the securities may equally well take the form of an account with a securities depository, with another intermediary or with a transfer agent.

Thus a "financial intermediary," which as defined in subsection (4) must be a person that as part of its ordinary business "maintains security accounts" for its customers, must control the disposition of securities pursuant to its customers' orders but may exercise its control in any of a number of forms—e.g. maintaining possession of certificated securities, being registered owner or registered pledgee of uncertificated securities, or having its own account with another financial intermediary. The important factor is that the intermediary must "hold" securities in an account for the customer. Notice that one who is a professional agent for holding securities accounts is not a financial intermediary with respect to any particular transaction in which it is not holding securities in an account for its customer. For example, a bank may as part of its business hold securities in accounts for its customers and therefore hold as a financial intermediary with respect to those accounts; but if it takes a pledge of securities not held in account for the borrower to secure a loan, it is not a financial intermediary with respect to the securities pledged, since it holds the securities for its *own* account rather than for a customer. On the other hand, a broker is a financial intermediary with respect to a margin account, since even though it has a personal interest in the securities, it holds securities in an account for a customer.

3. Paragraphs (a) and (b) of subsection (1) describe the most basic forms of transfer for certificated and uncertificated securities respectively. Paragraph (d) is the basic provision for transfers effected through entries in the records of a financial intermediary. For a valid transfer to be effected there must be both an entry made in the records and a confirmation sent to the purchaser. Confirmation is required to ensure that evidence exists to prove that the securities are held by the intermediary in a customer account rather than for its own account. This provision is important principally with regard to potential insolvency of an intermediary. So long as the financial intermediary holds the securities in an account, the *form* in which it "holds" the securities makes no difference to the effectuation of a transfer. The form does, however, make a difference as to whether the purchaser can become a bona fide purchaser. See subsection (2) and Section 8-302(1)(c).

Paragraphs (e) and (f) of subsection (1) provide for transfers of certificated and uncertificated securities held by a "third person" who is not a financial intermediary. Acknowledgement by that person that he holds for the purchaser is the only condition to the transfer. Requiring acknowledgement forces the transferee to have the arrangement made explicit.

Paragraph (g) sets forth the requirements for a transfer of a security held by a clearing corporation. The transfer occurs when the appropriate entries are made. No confirmation is required, since the fact that a clearing corporation holds no securities for its own account eliminates the possibility that customers' securities might be intermingled with securities owned by the clearing corporation.

Paragraphs (h), (i) and (j) relate only to transfers of security interests. Paragraph (h) is analogous to Section 9-305, which provides the rule for perfecting a security interest in property in the possession of a bailee. Paragraph (h) makes explicit that if the transferor's interest is in an account with a financial intermediary, that intermediary is the proper person to receive notice of the transfer regardless of whether it has physical possession or registration in its own name or whether it has securities in an account with another intermediary. The notification to the "bailee" must be written and must be signed by the debtor or by the secured party, according to whether the security interest is being created or released. The transfer is also conditioned upon the existence of a written security agreement signed by the debtor and adequately identifying the security. This requirement is included in paragraph (h) because Section 8-321, which sets forth the requirements for creation and perfection of security interests, gives no formality requirements other than the existence of a valid transfer.

Paragraph (i) is similar to Section 9-304(4). Read in conjunction with Section 8-321, it provides for "automatic" perfection for 21 days after new value is given with respect to a security interest as to which the debtor has signed a security agreement.

Paragraph (j) also deals only with the creation of security interests. In conjunction with Section 8-321, it provides that a financial intermediary that already controls disposition of a security may take a perfected security interest by giving value and having the debtor sign a security agreement.

4. Subsection (2) sets forth the principle that a purchaser is the owner of any security "held for him"—i.e. controlled pursuant to his instructions—by a financial intermediary. For example, a purchaser owns the securities in his custody account with a bank or his margin ac-

count with a broker. However, unless specific securities are separately identified as belonging to the purchaser, he cannot become a bona fide purchaser. A bona fide purchaser takes particular securities free of all claims and defenses. If bona fide purchaser status were given to those whose securities are held as part of a fungible bulk, there would be a possibility of inconsistent claims between two or more bona fide purchasers, since if the bulk should prove to be smaller than was expected, the claim of one or both must be compromised. An exception is made with respect to securities held by clearing corporations, since the fact that those entities hold *only* for customer accounts makes the chance of inconsistent claims small. Securities held by intermediaries pursuant to paragraphs (c) and (d)(i) of subsection (1) are identifiable as belonging to a particular customer, and the customer therefore can be a bona fide purchaser. Those customers that are not bona fide purchasers own a proportionate property interest in the bulk of securities of that nature held by the intermediary. Thus the group of customers together own the entire bulk, and in the event of insolvency of the intermediary they would as a group be secured to the extent the bulk covered their ownership claims. If the bulk were insufficient to provide each customer his full claim, each would share ratably.

5. Subsection (3) provides protection to both financial intermediary and customer whenever notice of an adverse claim is received after the intermediary takes delivery of a certificated security as a holder for value or after the transfer, pledge or release of an uncertificated security has been registered free of the claim to a financial intermediary. It also states the principle that as between the intermediary and its customer, the latter is entitled to a "clean" security, i.e. one as to which no notice of adverse claim has been received. Isham v. Post, 141 N.Y. 100, 35 N.E. 1084, 23 L.R.A. 90 (1894), which permitted a broker acting as agent to deliver to his customer a security as to which a claim of forgery was made after its receipt by the broker, is rejected. An intermediary is in the business of handling securities. It is better equipped to clear up any questions of genuineness or adverse claim, and even though it acts in whole or in part as agent for its customer, it is not permitted to pass such problems on to its customer. However if the problem arises because of the customer's own act or omission to act, he is estopped to rely on it as a basis for rejecting the security. Section 1-103.

Cross References:

Sections 8-301, 8-302, 8-314, 8-315, 8-320, 8-321, 9-304(4) and 9-305.

Definitional Cross References:

"Adverse Claim". Section 8-302.
"Bona Fide Purchaser". Section 8-302.
"Certificated Security". Section 8-102.
"Clearing Corporation". Section 8-102.
"Debtor". Section 9-105.
"Delivery". Section 1-201.
"Fungible". Section 1-201.
"Holder". Section 1-201.
"Indorsed". Section 8-308.
"Notice". Section 1-201.
"Notification". Section 1-201.
"Person". Section 1-201.
"Purchase". Section 1-201.
"Purchaser". Section 1-201.
"Secured Party". Section 9-105.
"Security". Section 8-102.
"Security Agreement". Section 9-105.
"Security Interest". Section 1-201.
"Send". Section 1-201.
"Signed". Section 1-201.
"Uncertificated Security". Section 8-102.
"Value". Section 1-201.

§ 8-314. Duty to Transfer, When Completed.

(1) Unless otherwise agreed, if a sale of a security is made on an exchange or otherwise through brokers:

(a) the selling customer fulfills his duty to transfer at the time he:

(i) places a certificated security in the possession of the selling broker or a person designated by the broker;

(ii) causes an uncertificated security to be registered in the name of the selling broker or a person designated by the broker;

(iii) if requested, causes an acknowledgment to be made to the selling broker that a certificated or uncertificated security is held for the broker; or

(iv) places in the possession of the selling broker or of a person designated by the broker a transfer instruction for an uncertificated security, providing the issuer does not refuse to register the requested transfer if the instruction is presented to the issuer for registration within 30 days thereafter; and

(b) the selling broker, including a correspondent broker acting for a selling customer, fulfills his duty to transfer at the time he:

(i) places a certificated security in the possession of the buying broker or a person designated by the buying broker;

(ii) causes an uncertificated security to be registered in the name of the buying broker or a person designated by the buying broker;

(iii) places in the possession of the buying broker or of a person designated by the buying broker a transfer instruction for an uncertificated security, providing the issuer does not refuse to register the requested transfer if the instruction is presented to the issuer for registration within 30 days thereafter; or

(iv) effects clearance of the sale in accordance with the rules of the exchange on which the transaction took place.

(2) Except as provided in this section or unless otherwise agreed, a transferor's duty to transfer a security under a contract of purchase is not fulfilled until he:

(a) places a certificated security in form to be negotiated by the purchaser in the possession of the purchaser or of a person designated by the purchaser;

(b) causes an uncertificated security to be registered in the name of the purchaser or a person designated by the purchaser; or

(c) if the purchaser requests, causes an acknowledgment to be made to the purchaser that a certificated or uncertificated security is held for the purchaser.

(3) Unless made on an exchange, a sale to a broker purchasing for his own account is within subsection (2) and not within subsection (1).

As amended in 1977.

Official Comment

Prior Uniform Statutory Provision: None.

Purposes:

1. This section, together with the section on warranties to the purchaser (Section 8-306) and the section on transfer to the purchaser (Section 8-313), states the

rights and duties of the parties involved in the transfer of a security from the original transferor to the ultimate purchaser. Particular emphasis has been placed upon transactions on organized exchanges or through brokers or dealers since they account for the great bulk of security sales. Normally the sale of a security on such an exchange or through brokers involves at least three intermediate transactions, and perhaps more, depending upon the number of correspondent brokers concerned. Rarely is the same security transferred through the entire transaction, and the duty of each intermediate party in the chain of transfer must therefore be stated. The increased use of clearing houses is also recognized—in subparagraph (1)(b)(iv) a selling broker is specifically permitted to make delivery by clearing the sale through such a clearing agency.

2. Subparagraphs (1)(a)(i), (1)(a)(ii), (1)(b)(i) and (1)(b)(ii) set forth the basic methods of fulfilling the duty to transfer in exchange transactions. The selling customer can fulfill his duty by physically delivering a certificated security to the selling broker or by effecting the transfer of an uncertificated security to him on the records of the issuer. Similarly the selling broker can satisfy its duty to transfer to the buying broker by delivering a certificate or causing registration of an uncertificated security. Further, with respect to exchange transactions subparagraphs (a)(iv) and (b)(iii) of subsection (1) provide that the duty to transfer can be conditionally satisfied by the delivery of an instruction. Such delivery does not constitute complete performance if the instruction is timely presented for registration and the issuer refuses to comply with its request. The burden of timely presentment is placed on the recipient of the instruction and it is not intended that instructions so given will circulate in the manner in which certificated securities now commonly circulate by indorsement. It is contemplated that this method of performance will be commonly employed in transactions settled through brokers, with, in many cases, the selling broker specially guaranteeing the signature of the originator of the instruction pursuant to Section 8-312(3).

3. Under subsection (2), absent agreement, one transferring a security to a purchaser in a transaction not consummated on an exchange or through brokers must either make physical delivery of a certificated security or cause the registration of transfer of an uncertificated security. Further, at the request of the purchaser he can satisfy his duty by causing acknowledgement to be given to the purchaser by a third person who controls the security (Section 8-313(1)(d) and (e)). He cannot, for example, just put a certificated security in transit and impose the risk of loss upon the recipient; nor can he fulfill his duty by delivering to the purchaser a transfer instruction.

4. Subsection (3) covers the situation in which one in business as a broker is, in the particular transaction, his own customer. When he buys or sells for a customer other than himself, whether as agent or as principal, he is a "broker" under this Article (Section 8-303) and the transaction is within subsection (1) of this section.

Cross References:

Sections 8-303, 8-306 and 8-313.

Definitional Cross References:

"Agreed". Section 1-201.
"Broker". Section 8-303.
"Certificated Security". Section 8-102.
"Contract". Section 1-201.
"Instruction". Section 8-308.
"Issuer". Section 8-201.
"Person". Section 1-201.
"Purchase". Section 1-201.
"Purchaser". Section 1-201.
"Security". Section 8-102.
"Uncertificated Security". Section 8-102.

§ 8-315. Action Against Transferee Based Upon Wrongful Transfer.

(1) Any person against whom the transfer of a security is wrongful for any reason, including his incapacity, as against anyone except a bona fide purchaser, may:

(a) reclaim possession of the certificated security wrongfully transferred;

(b) obtain possession of any new certificated security representing all or part of the same rights;

(c) compel the origination of an instruction to transfer to him or a person designated by him an uncertificated security constituting all or part of the same rights; or

(d) have damages.

(2) If the transfer is wrongful because of an unauthorized indorsement of a certificated security, the owner may also reclaim or obtain possession of the security or a new certificated security, even from a bona fide purchaser, if the ineffectiveness of the purported indorsement can be asserted against him under the provisions of this Article on unauthorized indorsements (Section 8-311).

(3) The right to obtain or reclaim possession of a certificated security or to compel the origination of a transfer instruction may be specifically enforced and the transfer of a certificated or uncertificated security enjoined and a certificated security impounded pending the litigation.

As amended in 1977.

Official Comment

Prior Uniform Statutory Provision: Section 7, Uniform Stock Transfer Act.

Purposes:

1. This Section grants to all owners of securities—certificated or uncertificated—a remedy for wrongful transfer. The general rule permitting an owner to reclaim possession of a certificated security wrongfully transferred is continued in paragraph (1)(a). Also, the owner of either a certificated or uncertificated security that has been wrongfully transferred may obtain a certificated security representing the same rights or may compel the origination of an effective transfer instruction for an uncertificated security comprising the same rights. Finally, the owner may have damages.

An exception is made, as in the prior law, in favor of bona fide purchasers. However, where the transfer is based upon a forged or unauthorized indorsement the exception operates in favor only of a good faith purchaser who is protected by Section 8-311. See that section and the comments thereto.

2. This section is not intended to exclude any rights an owner may have to damages for conversion under the case law. But see Section 8-318, which protects innocent brokers and other agents and bailees from liability for conversion.

Cross References:

Sections 8-302, 8-311 and 8-318.

Definitional Cross References:

"Action". Section 1-201.

"Bona Fide Purchaser". Section 8-302.

"Certificated Security". Section 8-102.

"Indorsement". Section 8-308.

"Instruction". Section 8-308.

"Person". Section 1-201.

"Right". Section 1-201.

"Security". Section 8-102.
"Unauthorized Indorsement". Section 1-201.
"Uncertificated Security". Section 8-102.

§ 8-316. Purchaser's Right to Requisites for Registration of Transfer, Pledge, or Release on Books.

Unless otherwise agreed, the transferor of a certificated security or the transferor, pledgor, or pledgee of an uncertificated security on due demand must supply his purchaser with any proof of his authority to transfer, pledge, or release or with any other requisite necessary to obtain registration of the transfer, pledge, or release of the security; but if the transfer, pledge, or release is not for value, a transferor, pledgor, or pledgee need not do so unless the purchaser furnishes the necessary expenses. Failure within a reasonable time to comply with a demand made gives the purchaser the right to reject or rescind the transfer, pledge, or release.

As amended in 1977.

Official Comment

Prior Uniform Statutory Provision: None.

Purposes:

1. The registration of the transfer of a security is a matter of vital importance to a purchaser and he is here provided with the means of obtaining such formal requirements for registration as signature guarantees, proof of authority, transfer tax stamps and the like. The transferor is the one in a position to supply most conveniently whatever documentation may be requisite for registration of transfer, and his duty to do so upon demand within a reasonable time is here stated affirmatively. But if the transfer is not for value the transferee should pay expenses. For these purposes a release from pledge by a secured party to a debtor is a transfer for value.

2. If the transferor's duty is not performed the transferee may reject or rescind the contract to transfer, pledge or release. He is not bound to do so—he may prefer his action for damages for breach of contract. If an essential item is peculiarly within the province of the transferor so that he is the only one who can obtain it, the purchaser may specifically enforce his right. Compare Section 8-307.

Cross References:

Section 8-307.

Definitional Cross References:

"Certificated Security". Section 8-102.
"Purchaser". Section 1-201.
"Reasonable Time". Section 1-204.
"Right". Section 1-201.
"Security". Section 8-102.
"Uncertificated Security". Section 8-102.
"Value". Section 1-201.

§ 8-317. Creditors' Rights.

(1) Subject to the exceptions in subsections (3) and (4), no attachment or levy upon a certificated security or any share or other interest represented thereby which is outstanding is valid until the security is actually seized by the officer making the attachment or levy, but a certificated security which has been surrendered to the issuer may be reached by a creditor by legal process at the issuer's chief executive office in the United States.

(2) An uncertificated security registered in the name of the debtor may not be reached by a creditor except by legal process at the issuer's chief executive office in the United States.

(3) The interest of a debtor in a certificated security that is in the possession of a secured party not a financial intermediary or in an uncertificated security registered in the name of a secured party not a financial intermediary (or in the name of a nominee of the secured party) may be reached by a creditor by legal process upon the secured party.

(4) The interest of a debtor in a certificated security that is in the possession of or registered in the name of a financial intermediary or in an uncertificated security registered in the name of a financial intermediary may be reached by a creditor by legal process upon the financial intermediary on whose books the interest of the debtor appears.

(5) Unless otherwise provided by law, a creditor's lien upon the interest of a debtor in a security obtained pursuant to subsection (3) or (4) is not a restraint on the transfer of the security, free of the lien, to a third party for new value; but in the event of a transfer, the lien applies to the proceeds of the transfer in the hands of the secured party or financial intermediary, subject to any claims having priority.

(6) A creditor whose debtor is the owner of a security is entitled to aid from courts of appropriate jurisdiction, by injunction or otherwise, in reaching the security or in satisfying the claim by means allowed at law or in equity in regard to property that cannot readily be reached by ordinary legal process.

As amended in 1977.

Official Comment

Prior Uniform Statutory Provision: Sections 13, 14, Uniform Stock Transfer Act.

Purposes:

1. In dealing with certificated securities the instrument itself is the vital thing, and therefore a valid levy cannot be made unless all possibility of the security's wrongfully finding its way into a transferee's hands has been removed. This can be accomplished only when the security is in the possession of a public officer, the issuer, or an independent third party. A debtor who has been enjoined can still transfer the security in contempt of court. See Overlock v. Jerome-Portland Copper Mining Co., 29 Ariz. 560, 243 P. 400 (1926). Therefore, although injunctive relief is provided in subsection (6) so that creditors may use this method to gain control of the security, the security itself must be reached to constitute a proper levy whenever the debtor has possession. The method used in Hodes v. Hodes, 176 Or. 102, 155 P.2d 564 (1945), where the Oregon court enjoined the transfer of a security in a safe deposit box in the state of Washington, directing a copy of the writ to be served upon the issuer, although not operative as an effective levy, is a method of reaching the security approved by the section.

2. Whenever the security is not in the form of a negotiable instrument in the debtor's possession, an effective levy can be made by serving process upon the person controlling transfer. Thus subsection (2) provides that when the security is uncertificated and registered in the debtor's name—or, what in effect is the same situation, whenever a certificated security is in the issuer's possession (Section 8-102(1)(c))—levy can be made only by serving process upon the issuer. The most logical place to serve the issuer would be the place where the transfer records are maintained, but that location might be difficult to identify, especially when the separate elements of a computer network might be situated in different places. The chief executive office is selected as the appropriate place by analogy

to Section 9-103(3)(d). See Comment 5(c) to that section.

This section indicates only how attachment is to be made, not when it is legally justified. For that reason there is no conflict between this section and Shaffer v. Heitner, 433 U.S. 186, 97 S.Ct. 2569, 53 L.Ed.2d 683 (1977).

3. An attachment filed at the issuer's office against certificated securities is ineffective unless the security itself has been surrendered to the issuer. The case law holdings that priority in time of transfer or attachment governed the validity of the levy are rejected under this Article as under the Stock Transfer Act. See for example, National Bank of the Pacific v. Western Pac. R. Co., 157 Cal. 573, 108 P. 676, 27 L.R.A.,N.S., 987, 21 Ann.Cas. 1391 (1910).

4. Subsection (3) provides that when a security, either certificated or uncertificated, is controlled by a secured party, an effective lien can be established by service on the secured party. This section does not attempt to provide for rights as between the creditor and the secured party, as, for example, whether or when the secured party must liquidate the security.

Subsection (4) recognizes that securities are frequently held in account for customers by banks or brokers and that such securities may be registered not only in the name of the debtor but, more commonly, in street or other nominee name. Additionally, in such cases, the securities may have been commingled, repledged or deposited so that no particular security could be identified as that of the debtor. The subsection provides that the debtor's account can be reached by process upon the entity upon whose books the interest of the debtor appears. This appears to be the most effective way of preventing the transfer of the debtor's interest and thus protecting the creditor. It is only that entity that is aware of the debtor's interest, irrespective of where the securities are located or in what name they happen to be registered.

Subsection (5) expressly provides that securities in which the debtor's interest is reached pursuant to subsections (3) or (4) may be transferred for new value, free of the creditor's lien, but also provided that when and if they are transferred, the lien will be transferred to the proceeds. Nothing in subsection (5) is intended to validate any transfer that would otherwise constitute a fraudulent conveyance. Furthermore, subsection (5) is expressly subject to the procedural laws of the states, and no attempt has been made to prescribe the consequences of obtaining such a lien or the procedures for its enforcement.

5. Particular terms to describe creditor's process have been avoided in this section. This section is not intended to have any effect on the availability of garnishment or similar third-party process as a pre-judgment or post-judgment remedy. Cf. Sniadach v. Family Finance Corp., 395 U.S. 337, 23 L.Ed.2d 349, 89 S.Ct. 1820 (1969); Fuentes v. Shevin, 407 U.S. 67, 32 L.Ed.2d 556, 92 S.Ct. 1983 (1972); Mitchell v. W. T. Grant Co., 416 U.S. 600, 40 L.Ed.2d 406, 94 S.Ct. 1895 (1974). Such matters are a proper concern of the procedural rules of the states, subject, of course, to constitutional limitations.

6. This section deals with the problems of attaching or levying creditors. It does not apply in cases where a governmental agency, for reasons of public safety or the like, seeks to confiscate securities. See, for example, the situation in Silesian American Corp. v. Clark, 332 U.S. 469, 68 S.Ct. 179, 92 L.Ed. 81 (1947), upon which this section has no bearing.

Definitional Cross References:

"Certificated Security". Section 8-102.
"Creditor". Section 1-201.
"Debtor". Section 9-105.
"Financial Intermediary". Section 8-313.
"Issuer". Section 8-201.
"Secured Party". Section 9-105.
"Security". Section 8-102.
"Uncertificated Security". Section 8-102.
"Value". Section 1-201.

§ 8–318. No Conversion by Good Faith Conduct.

An agent or bailee who in good faith (including observance of reasonable commercial standards if he is in the business of buying, selling, or otherwise dealing with securities) has received certificated securities and sold, pledged, or delivered them or has sold or caused the transfer or pledge of uncertificated securities over which he had control according to the instructions of his principal, is not liable for conversion or for participation in breach of fiduciary duty although the principal had no right so to deal with the securities.

As amended in 1977.

Official Comment

Prior Uniform Statutory Provision: None.

Purposes:

This Section negates the liability of agents, including brokers, and of bailees for innocent conversion or participation in breach of fiduciary duty. Gruntal v. National Surety Co., 254 N.Y. 468, 173 N.E. 682 (1930) is followed. Compare Section 7(a) of the Uniform Act for Simplification of Fiduciary Security Transfers.

Notice that the concept of good faith includes the objective element of observing reasonable commercial standards when the agent or bailee is in the business of dealing with securities.

Cross Reference:

Section 7–404.

Definitional Cross References:

"Certificated Security". Section 8–102.
"Delivery". Section 1–201.
"Good Faith". Section 1–201.
"Security". Section 8–102.
"Uncertificated Security". Section 8–102.

§ 8–319. Statute of Frauds.

A contract for the sale of securities is not enforceable by way of action or defense unless:

(a) there is some writing signed by the party against whom enforcement is sought or by his authorized agent or broker, sufficient to indicate that a contract has been made for sale of a stated quantity of described securities at a defined or stated price;

(b) delivery of a certificated security or transfer instruction has been accepted, or transfer of an uncertificated security has been registered and the transferee has failed to send written objection to the issuer within 10 days after receipt of the initial transaction statement confirming the registration, or payment has been made, but the contract is enforceable under this provision only to the extent of the delivery, registration, or payment;

(c) within a reasonable time a writing in confirmation of the sale or purchase and sufficient against the sender under paragraph (a) has been received by the party against whom enforcement is sought and he has failed to send written objection to its contents within 10 days after its receipt; or

(d) the party against whom enforcement is sought admits in his pleading, testimony, or otherwise in court that a contract was made for the sale of a stated quantity of described securities at a defined or stated price.

As amended in 1977.

Official Comment

Prior Uniform Statutory Provision: Section 4, Uniform Sales Act (which was based on Section 17 of the statute of 29 Charles II).

Purposes:

1. This Section is intended to conform the statute of frauds provisions with regard to securities to the policy of the like provisions in Article 2 (Section 2-201). The chief difference is that this Section requires that quantity and price be specified.

2. What will be sufficient specification will vary with the circumstances. Where the transaction is on an exchange or an over-the-counter market where daily quotations of the security are available "100 shares X. Corp. comm. at market" should suffice. If there is no readily available standard to interpret "at market" there is no "defined or stated price."

3. Paragraph (b) sets forth several actions which, if taken by a transferee, constitute manifestation of intent to purchase. The person receiving an initial transaction statement is given a period of 10 days to object, since there is no overt manifestation of intent. While acceptance of delivery of a certificate or instruction is seen as an overt manifestation so that there is no grace period, in practice there will often be a question as to what constitutes acceptance by an organization. Failure to object to delivery within a reasonable period will be a factor to consider. Making payment is a more definite indication of intent.

4. Paragraph (c) is particularly important in the relationship of broker (Section 8-303) and customer. Normally a great volume of such business is done over the telephone. Orders are executed almost immediately and confirmed on the same or the next business day, usually on standard forms which as to the broker more than meet the minimal requirements of paragraph (a). It is reasonable to require the customer to raise his objection, if any, within ten days after the confirmation has been received (Section 1-201).

Cross Reference:

Section 2-201.

Definitional Cross References:

"Action". Section 1-201.
"Broker". Section 8-303.
"Certificated Security". Section 8-102.
"Contract". Section 1-201.
"Delivery". Section 1-201.
"Initial Transaction Statement". Section 8-408.
"Instruction". Section 8-308.
"Issuer". Section 8-201.
"Party". Section 1-201.
"Purchase". Section 1-201.
"Reasonable Time". Section 1-204.
"Security". Section 8-102.
"Send". Section 1-201.
"Signed". Section 1-201.
"Uncertificated Security". Section 8-102.
"Writing". Section 1-201.

§ 8-320. Transfer or Pledge Within Central Depository System.

(1) In addition to other methods, a transfer, pledge, or release of a security or any interest therein may be effected by the making of appropriate entries on the books of a clearing corporation reducing the account of the transferor, pledgor, or pledgee and increasing the account of the transferee, pledgee, or pledgor by the amount of the obligation or the number of shares or rights transferred, pledged, or released, if the security is shown on the account of a transferor, pledgor, or pledgee on the books of the clearing corporation; is subject to the control of the clearing corporation; and

(a) if certificated,

(i) is in the custody of the clearing corporation, another clearing corporation, a custodian bank, or a nominee of any of them; and

(ii) is in bearer form or indorsed in blank by an appropriate person or registered in the name of the clearing corporation, a custodian bank, or a nominee of any of them; or

(b) if uncertificated, is registered in the name of the clearing corporation, another clearing corporation, a custodian bank, or a nominee of any of them.

(2) Under this section entries may be made with respect to like securities or interests therein as a part of a fungible bulk and may refer merely to a quantity of a particular security without reference to the name of the registered owner, certificate or bond number, or the like, and, in appropriate cases, may be on a net basis taking into account other transfers, pledges, or releases of the same security.

(3) A transfer under this section is effective (Section 8–313) and the purchaser acquires the rights of the transferor (Section 8–301). A pledge or release under this section is the transfer of a limited interest. If a pledge or the creation of a security interest is intended, the security interest is perfected at the time when both value is given by the pledgee and the appropriate entries are made (Section 8–321). A transferee or pledgee under this section may be a bona fide purchaser (Section 8–302).

(4) A transfer or pledge under this section is not a registration of transfer under Part 4.

(5) That entries made on the books of the clearing corporation as provided in subsection (1) are not appropriate does not affect the validity or effect of the entries or the liabilities or obligations of the clearing corporation to any person adversely affected thereby.

As added in 1962 and amended in 1977.

Official Comment

Prior Uniform Statutory Provision: None.

Purposes:

1. Consistent with the underlying purposes and policies of this Act "to permit the continued expansion of commercial practices through custom, usage and agreement of the parties"—subsection (2)(b) of Section 1–102—this Section expressly authorizes a newly developing and commercially useful method of transferring or pledging securities on the organized securities markets, particularly among brokers and banks but not necessarily so limited. A clearing corporation is a special kind of financial intermediary. It holds securities on deposit from brokers, banks and other financial institutions, and clears trades among its depositors by making entries on its records. This section sets forth rules for determining when such entries are effective to constitute a transfer (Section 8–313(1)(g)).

The basic requirements, outlined in subsection (1), are that the security ultimately be subject to the control of the clearing corporation making the entries and that the security be in a form that would allow the clearing corporation (or a person acting subject to its orders) to have a new security registered in the name of, and transferred to, a purchaser. The latter requirement is specified in some detail. A certificated security must be in the custody of either the clearing corporation making the entries, another clearing corporation, a custodian bank or nominee; and it must be either in bearer form, registered in the name of the clearing corporation (or of one of the clearing corporations if there are more than one involved), or else indorsed so that the clearing corporation (or one of them) could obtain registration of a transfer from the issuer. (The phrase "registered in the name of the clearing corporation" in subparagraph (1)(a)(ii) should be interpreted liberally so as to include restrictive indorsements and also to include registration or indorsement to either of the clearing corporations.) An uncertificated security must be registered in the name of a clearing corporation, a custodian bank or a nominee.

The requirement that the security be subject to the control of the clearing corporation means that if a certificated security is in the custody of, or an uncertificated security is registered in the name of, another clearing corporation or a custodian bank, the clearing corporation on whose records the entries in question are made must have the right to give orders to that person as to how and when to dispose of the security. That right may be an indirect one—for example, a security is subject to the control of Clearing Corporation A if the security is certificated and has been deposited in A's account with Clearing Corporation B, which in turn has deposited the security in its account with C, which may be either another clearing corporation or a custodian bank. Clearing Corporation A can give orders to B which in turn can give orders to C.

2. Subsection (2) makes clear that securities of the same issue may be treated as fungible interests, and that entries may be merely debits and credits to the accounts of the participants.

3. Subsection (4) makes clear that transfer, pledge or release under this Section does not affect the registration of ownership or pledge on the issuer's records.

Subsection (5) states that the entries made pursuant to this Section are effective to transfer the subject securities regardless of the fact that the entries were not appropriate. A person wronged by an inappropriate transfer may pursue his remedies against the transferee and against the clearing corporation. The nature of the rights between the clearing corporation and its participants is left to private contract and case law. See Section 8-315 as to actions against the transferee.

Cross References:

Sections 1-102(2)(b), 8-301, 8-302, 8-313, 8-315 and 8-321.

Definitional Cross References:

"Appropriate Person". Section 8-308.
"Bearer Form". Section 8-102.
"Bona Fide Purchaser". Section 8-302.
"Certificated Security". Section 8-102.
"Clearing Corporation". Section 8-102.
"Custodian Bank". Section 8-102.
"Fungible". Section 1-201.
"Indorsed". Section 8-308.
"Person". Section 1-201.
"Purchaser". Section 1-201.
"Rights". Section 1-201.
"Security". Section 8-102.
"Security Interest". Section 1-201.
"Uncertificated Security". Section 8-102.
"Value". Section 1-201.

§ 8-321. Enforceability, Attachment, Perfection and Termination of Security Interests.

(1) A security interest in a security is enforceable and can attach only if it is transferred to the secured party or a person designated by him pursuant to a provision of Section 8-313(1).

(2) A security interest so transferred pursuant to agreement by a transferor who has rights in the security to a transferee who has given value is a perfected security interest, but a security interest that has been transferred solely under paragraph (i) of Section 8-313(1) becomes unperfected after 21 days unless, within that time, the requirements for transfer under any other provision of Section 8-313(1) are satisfied.

(3) A security interest in a security is subject to the provisions of Article 9, but:

(a) no filing is required to perfect the security interest; and

(b) no written security agreement signed by the debtor is necessary to make the security interest enforceable, except as provided in paragraph (h), (i), or (j) of Section 8-313(1). The secured party has the rights and duties provided under Section 9-207, to the extent they are applicable, whether or not the security is certificated, and, if certificated, whether or not it is in his possession.

(4) Unless otherwise agreed, a security interest in a security is terminated by transfer to the debtor or a person designated by him pursuant to a provision of Section 8-313(1). If a security is thus transferred, the security interest, if not terminated, becomes unperfected unless the security is certificated and is delivered to the debtor for the purpose of ultimate sale or exchange or presentation, collection, renewal, or registration of transfer. In that case, the security interest becomes unperfected after 21 days unless, within that time, the security (or securities for which it has been exchanged) is transferred to the secured party or a person designated by him pursuant to a provision of Section 8-313(1).

As added in 1977.

Official Comment

Prior Uniform Statutory Provision: None.

Purposes:

1. This section is intended to govern the creation, perfection and termination of security interests in all securities, certificated and uncertificated. Subsection (1) requires an effective transfer under Section 8-313(1) as formal evidence of the security interest. The requirement that there be formal evidence of the creation of a security interest in collateral other than securities can be satisfied by having the debtor sign a security agreement or by having the secured party take possession of the collateral. Section 9-203. Transfers pursuant to paragraphs (a)-(g) of Section 8-313(1) all involve either delivery to the secured party or else some other specific event that is the functional equivalent of delivery. Transfers pursuant to paragraphs (h)-(j) do not involve any event that serves that function, but they require a security agreement signed by the debtor.

2. Subsection (1) provides that when value has been given and the debtor has rights in the collateral, an appropriate transfer will result not only in an enforceable security interest but also in one that is perfected. Under this section, an unperfected security interest in a security cannot be created. A security interest created by transfer under Section 8-313(1)(i), however, may become unperfected if, within 21 days, the requirements of another method of effective transfer are not satisfied.

3. Subsection (3) expressly makes a security interest in securities subject to

the provisions of Article 9 except those provisions dealing with the creation and perfection of security interests. Those matters are governed by this section. In addition, the provisions of Section 9–207, which govern the rights and duties of the pledgee of a certificated security, are extended, to the extent they are applicable, to all secured parties, whether or not the possession of a certificated security is involved. Thus, in the absence of agreement to the contrary, the secured party, who might be the registered owner of an uncertificated security, would have the duty to remit dividends he received to the debtor or to apply them in reduction of the obligation under Section 9–207(2)(c).

4. Subsection (4) provides that a security interest is terminated by retransfer to the debtor unless the parties otherwise agree. Even when the parties agree that the security interest is to continue, it will become unperfected unless there is delivery of a certificated security for the limited purposes described in the second sentence. Compare Section 9–304(5) and (6).

Cross References:

Sections 8–313 and 9–203. See generally Article 9.

Definitional Cross References:

"Certificated Security". Section 8–102.
"Debtor". Section 9–105.
"Person". Section 1–201.
"Rights". Section 1–201.
"Secured Party". Section 9–105.
"Security". Section 8–102.
"Security Agreement". Section 9–105.
"Security Interest". Section 1–201.
"Signed". Section 1–201.
"Value". Section 1–201.

PART 4

REGISTRATION

§ 8–401. Duty of Issuer to Register Transfer, Pledge, or Release.

(1) If a certificated security in registered form is presented to the issuer with a request to register transfer or an instruction is presented to the issuer with a request to register transfer, pledge, or release, the issuer shall register the transfer, pledge, or release as requested if:

(a) the security is indorsed or the instruction was originated by the appropriate person or persons (Section 8–308);

(b) reasonable assurance is given that those indorsements or instructions are genuine and effective (Section 8–402);

(c) the issuer has no duty as to adverse claims or has discharged the duty (Section 8–403);

(d) any applicable law relating to the collection of taxes has been complied with; and

(e) the transfer, pledge, or release is in fact rightful or is to a bona fide purchaser.

(2) If an issuer is under a duty to register a transfer, pledge, or release of a security, the issuer is also liable to the person presenting a certificated security or an instruction for registration or his principal for loss resulting from any unreasonable delay in registration or from failure or refusal to register the transfer, pledge, or release.

As amended in 1977.

Official Comment

Prior Uniform Statutory Provision: None.

Purposes:

1. Section 8–201(3) defines "issuer" as used in this Part 4 as the person on whose behalf transfer books are maintained. Transfer agents, registrars or the like have rights and duties under this Part within the scope of their respective functions, similar to those of the issuer (Section 8–406).

2. There is a substantial and heterogeneous body of case law as to the issuer's duty to register a transfer and as to his liability for improper registration, e.g., on an unauthorized signature (Section 8–311), or where the indorsement is not that of an appropriate person (Section 8–308), and generally under circumstances where the issuer is deemed to have had notice of an adverse claim (Section 8–302) and thus of the possible wrongfulness of the transfer.

In general this section and those which follow it continue the well-settled rules found in the case law as to duty to register and as to liability for improper registration on an unauthorized signature, or where the indorsement is not that of an appropriate person. They also extend the application of those rules to uncertificated securities.

In all other areas, the issuer's potential liability for wrongful registration of transfer has been substantially reduced. The rules found in the case law are drastically modified in furtherance of a considered policy to speed up the registration process by narrowing the field in which the issuer historically has first sought to assure itself that it cannot be held to be one notice of an adverse claim, and, failing that assurance, has imposed rigorous requirements of proof that there is no possible impropriety.

3. This section states the basic duty of the issuer to register transfers. It states that a duty exists, but only if certain preconditions exist. If any of the preconditions do not exist, there is no duty to register transfer. If the indorsement on a security is a forgery, there is no duty. If the instruction to transfer an uncertificated security is not originated by an appropriate person, there is no duty. If there has not been compliance with applicable tax laws, there is no duty. If the security is properly indorsed but nevertheless the transfer is in fact wrongful, there is no duty unless the transfer is to a bona fide purchaser (and the other preconditions exist). Cf. Kaiser-Frazer Corp. v. Otis & Co., 195 F.2d 838 (2d Cir. 1952), certiorari denied 73 S.Ct. 89, 344 U.S. 856, 97 L.Ed. 664.

This section does not constitute a mandate that all preconditions must be met before the issuer registers a transfer. If it so desires, the issuer can waive the reasonable assurances specified in paragraph (b). If it has confidence in the responsibility of the persons requesting transfer, it can ignore questions of compliance with tax laws. If it has no duty to inquire into or otherwise recognize adverse claims, it can and it should register transfer without inquiry as to the rightfulness of a transfer.

Sections 8–402 and 8–403 are the sections dealing with the specific rules as to assurances and duty to inquire.

4. By subsection (2) the person entitled to registration may not only compel it but may hold the issuer liable in damages for unreasonable delay.

5. See Section 8–404 as to the issuer's liability for wrongful registration of transfer.

Cross References:

Point 1: Sections 8–201(3) and 8–406.
Point 2: Sections 8–204, 8–301, 8–308 and 8–311.

Definitional Cross References:

"Adverse Claim". Section 8–302.
"Appropriate Person". Section 8–308.
"Bona Fide Purchaser". Section 8–302.
"Certificated Security". Section 8–102.

"Genuine". Section 1–201.
"Indorsement". Section 8–308.
"Instruction". Section 8–308.
"Issuer". Section 8–201.
"Person". Section 1–201.
"Registered Form". Section 8–102.
"Security". Section 8–102.

§ 8–402. Assurance That Indorsements and Instructions Are Effective.

(1) The issuer may require the following assurance that each necessary indorsement of a certificated security or each instruction (Section 8–308) is genuine and effective:

(a) in all cases, a guarantee of the signature (Section 8–312(1) or (2)) of the person indorsing a certificated security or originating an instruction including, in the case of an instruction, a warranty of the taxpayer identification number or, in the absence thereof, other reasonable assurance of identity;

(b) if the indorsement is made or the instruction is originated by an agent, appropriate assurance of authority to sign;

(c) if the indorsement is made or the instruction is originated by a fiduciary, appropriate evidence of appointment or incumbency;

(d) if there is more than one fiduciary, reasonable assurance that all who are required to sign have done so; and

(e) if the indorsement is made or the instruction is originated by a person not covered by any of the foregoing, assurance appropriate to the case corresponding as nearly as may be to the foregoing.

(2) A "guarantee of the signature" in subsection (1) means a guarantee signed by or on behalf of a person reasonably believed by the issuer to be responsible. The issuer may adopt standards with respect to responsibility if they are not manifestly unreasonable.

(3) "Appropriate evidence of appointment or incumbency" in subsection (1) means:

(a) in the case of a fiduciary appointed or qualified by a court, a certificate issued by or under the direction or supervision of that court or an officer thereof and dated within 60 days before the date of presentation for transfer, pledge, or release; or

(b) in any other case, a copy of a document showing the appointment or a certificate issued by or on behalf of a person reasonably believed by the issuer to be responsible or, in the absence of that document or certificate, other evidence reasonably deemed by the issuer to be appropriate. The issuer may adopt standards with respect to the evidence if they are not manifestly unreasonable. The issuer is not charged with notice of the contents of any document obtained pursuant to this paragraph (b) except to the extent that the contents relate directly to the appointment or incumbency.

(4) The issuer may elect to require reasonable assurance beyond that specified in this section, but if it does so and, for a purpose other than that specified in subsection (3)(b), both requires and obtains a copy of a will, trust, indenture, articles of co-partnership, by-laws, or other controlling instrument,

it is charged with notice of all matters contained therein affecting the transfer, pledge, or release.

As amended in 1977.

Official Comment

Prior Uniform Statutory Provision: None.

Purposes:

1. As is noted in the Comment to Section 8-401, the issuer is absolutely liable for wrongful registration of transfer when the signature of the indorser is unauthorized or is not that of an appropriate person or when an instruction is not originated by an appropriate person. The issuer is entitled to require such assurance as is reasonable under the circumstances that all necessary indorsements are effective, and thus to minimize its risk. This section establishes the requirements the issuer may make in terms of documentation which, except in the rarest of instances, should be easily furnished. If a demand for further assurance is reasonable under the circumstances, subsection (4) applies.

2. Under subsection (1)(a) the issuer may require in all cases a guarantee of signature (Section 8-312). When an instruction is presented the issuer always may require either a warranty of taxpayer identification number or some other reasonable assurance as to the identity of the originator. Subsection (2) allows the issuer to require that the person making these guarantees be one reasonably believed to be responsible, and the issuer may adopt standards of responsibility which are not manifestly unreasonable. In this aspect this section approves the practice of the organized securities markets.

3. This section, by paragraphs (b) through (e) of subsection (1), permits the issuer to seek confirmation of the effectiveness of the indorsement or instruction. The permitted methods act as a double check on matters which are within the warranties of the guarantor of signature. See Section 8-312. In addition, to some extent they act also as a check on the right to transfer (i.e. to deliver the indorsed certificated security or to transmit an instruction). Thus, an agent may be required to submit his power of attorney, a corporation to submit a certified resolution evidencing the authority of its signing officer to sign, an executor or administrator to submit the usual "short-form certificate", etc. But failure of a fiduciary to obtain court approval of the transfer or to comply with other requirements does not make his signature unauthorized. Section 8-308(11). Hence court orders and other controlling instruments are omitted from subsection (1).

Subsection (1)(c) authorizes the issuer to require "appropriate evidence" of appointment or incumbency, and subsection (3) indicates what evidence will be "appropriate". In the case of a fiduciary appointed or qualified by a court that evidence will be a court certificate dated within sixty days before the date of presentation. Where the fiduciary is not appointed or qualified by a court, as in the case of a successor trustee, subsection (3)(b) applies. Compare Section 4 of the Uniform Act for Simplification of Fiduciary Security Transfers. If the security is registered in the name of the fiduciary, the issuer may under Section 8-403(3)(a) assume without inquiry that the fiduciary status continues until written notice to the contrary is received. Hence no evidence of appointment or incumbency is needed unless such a notice has been received. Compare Section 2 of the Uniform Act for Simplification of Fiduciary Security Transfers.

Where subsection (3)(b) applies, the issuer may require a copy of a trust instrument or other document showing the appointment, or it may require the certificate of a responsible person. In the absence of such a document or certificate, it may require other appropriate evidence. If a document is obtained solely as "appropriate evidence of appointment or incumbency" under subsection (3)(b), the issuer is not charged with notice of its contents except to the extent that the contents relate directly to the appointment or incumbency. But if the document is obtained for any other purpose, the issuer may be charged under subsection (4). See Point 6 below.

4. There are many other types of situations where, under the case law, the issuer would be deemed to have notice of possible adverse claims, and therefore would register transfer at its peril. Typical are: knowledge that the registered owner is dead, the fact that he is described or identifiable as a fiduciary, etc. Perhaps the most ubiquitous is where a will, trust indenture or other controlling instrument is on file with the issuer or transfer agent for some other purpose (e.g., in the banking as distinct from the corporate agency department of a trust company), but, unless specifically asked for, would not come to the attention of the officers responsible for the registration of security transfers. Here, under the cases, there is an area of liability based upon notice of possible adverse claims affecting the right to deliver the security, an area to which the warranties of the guarantor of signature specifically do not extend. See Section 8-312(4). Also, it is the area in which in the past issuers and their agents, fearing possible lawsuits based upon unauthorized transfers by fiduciaries and the like, have made it a practice to demand complete and convincing evidence that the transfer is proper in all of its aspects. Sections 8-403 and 8-404 strictly circumscribe the issuer's liability in such cases, and this section therefore makes no provisions for assurances to cover them.

5. Circumstances may indicate that a necessary signature was unauthorized or was not that of an appropriate person. Such circumstances would be ignored at risk of absolute liability, and to minimize that risk the issuer may properly exercise the option given by subsection (4) to require assurance beyond that specified in subsection (1). On the other hand, the facts at hand may reflect only on the rightfulness of the transfer. Such facts do not operate, as they did under prior law, automatically to create a duty of inquiry, unless there is timely notification of the existence of an adverse claim. See Section 8-403(1) and (4). If there is a duty of inquiry under Section 8-403, the issuer may follow the procedure provided in Section 8-403(2) or (5), or it may discharge the duty of inquiry as to a certificated security "by any reasonable means". The same is true if the issuer's overriding duty to conduct its functions in good faith (Section 1-203) comes into play—e.g., where the certificated security is indorsed or the instruction is originated by a person known to the employee handling the transaction for the issuer to be wanted by the police.

6. Specifically to implement the policy of this Act to discourage issuers from requiring excessive documentation, subsection (4) provides that if the issuer elects to require additional documentation for any purpose other than to obtain "appropriate evidence of appointment or incumbency" under subsection (3)(b) and both requires and obtains a copy of a will, trust, indenture, articles of co-partnership, by-laws or other controlling instrument, it is charged with notice of all matters contained therein affecting the transfer. It follows that an instrument voluntarily submitted, without having been "required" by the issuer, may be returned without examination.

But if the issuer has no duty to inquire and demands more than reasonable assurance that the instruction or the necessary indorsements are genuine and effective, the presenter of the instruction or the certificated security may refuse the demand and sue for improper refusal to register. Section 8-401.

Cross References:

Point 1: Sections 8-308 and 8-311.
Point 2: Section 8-312.
Point 3: Sections 8-308 and 8-312.
Point 4: Sections 8-312, 8-403 and 8-404.
Point 5: Sections 1-203 and 8-403.

Point 6: Section 8–401.

Definitional Cross References:

"Adverse Claim". Section 8–302.
"Certificated Security". Section 8–102.
"Genuine". Section 1–201.
"Indorsement". Section 8–308.
"Instruction". Section 8–308.
"Issuer". Section 8–201.
"Notice". Section 1–201.
"Person". Section 1–201.
"Signed". Section 1–201.

§ 8–403. Issuer's Duty as to Adverse Claims.

(1) An issuer to whom a certificated security is presented for registration shall inquire into adverse claims if:

(a) a written notification of an adverse claim is received at a time and in a manner affording the issuer a reasonable opportunity to act on it prior to the issuance of a new, reissued, or re-registered certificated security, and the notification identifies the claimant, the registered owner, and the issue of which the security is a part, and provides an address for communications directed to the claimant; or

(b) the issuer is charged with notice of an adverse claim from a controlling instrument it has elected to require under Section 8–402(4).

(2) The issuer may discharge any duty of inquiry by any reasonable means, including notifying an adverse claimant by registered or certified mail at the address furnished by him or, if there be no such address, at his residence or regular place of business that the certificated security has been presented for registration of transfer by a named person, and that the transfer will be registered unless within 30 days from the date of mailing the notification, either:

(a) an appropriate restraining order, injunction, or other process issues from a court of competent jurisdiction; or

(b) there is filed with the issuer an indemnity bond, sufficient in the issuer's judgment to protect the issuer and any transfer agent, registrar, or other agent of the issuer involved from any loss it or they may suffer by complying with the adverse claim.

(3) Unless an issuer is charged with notice of an adverse claim from a controlling instrument which it has elected to require under Section 8–402(4) or receives notification of an adverse claim under subsection (1), if a certificated security presented for registration is indorsed by the appropriate person or persons the issuer is under no duty to inquire into adverse claims. In particular:

(a) an issuer registering a certificated security in the name of a person who is a fiduciary or who is described as a fiduciary is not bound to inquire into the existence, extent, or correct description of the fiduciary relationship; and thereafter the issuer may assume without inquiry that the newly registered owner continues to be the fiduciary until the issuer receives written notice that the fiduciary is no longer acting as such with respect to the particular security;

(b) an issuer registering transfer on an indorsement by a fiduciary is not bound to inquire whether the transfer is made in compliance with a controlling instrument or with the law of the state having jurisdiction of the fiduciary relationship, including any law requiring the fiduciary to obtain court approval of the transfer; and

(c) the issuer is not charged with notice of the contents of any court record or file or other recorded or unrecorded document even though the document is in its possession and even though the transfer is made on the indorsement of a fiduciary to the fiduciary himself or to his nominee.

(4) An issuer is under no duty as to adverse claims with respect to an uncertificated security except:

(a) claims embodied in a restraining order, injunction, or other legal process served upon the issuer if the process was served at a time and in a manner affording the issuer a reasonable opportunity to act on it in accordance with the requirements of subsection (5);

(b) claims of which the issuer has received a written notification from the registered owner or the registered pledgee if the notification was received at a time and in a manner affording the issuer a reasonable opportunity to act on it in accordance with the requirements of subsection (5);

(c) claims (including restrictions on transfer not imposed by the issuer) to which the registration of transfer to the present registered owner was subject and were so noted in the initial transaction statement sent to him; and

(d) claims as to which an issuer is charged with notice from a controlling instrument it has elected to require under Section 8–402(4).

(5) If the issuer of an uncertificated security is under a duty as to an adverse claim, he discharges that duty by:

(a) including a notation of the claim in any statements sent with respect to the security under Sections 8–408(3), (6), and (7); and

(b) refusing to register the transfer or pledge of the security unless the nature of the claim does not preclude transfer or pledge subject thereto.

(6) If the transfer or pledge of the security is registered subject to an adverse claim, a notation of the claim must be included in the initial transaction statement and all subsequent statements sent to the transferee and pledgee under Section 8–408.

(7) Notwithstanding subsections (4) and (5), if an uncertificated security was subject to a registered pledge at the time the issuer first came under a duty as to a particular adverse claim, the issuer has no duty as to that claim if transfer of the security is requested by the registered pledgee or an appropriate person acting for the registered pledgee unless:

(a) the claim was embodied in legal process which expressly provides otherwise;

(b) the claim was asserted in a written notification from the registered pledgee;

(c) the claim was one as to which the issuer was charged with notice from a controlling instrument it required under Section 8–402(4) in connection with the pledgee's request for transfer; or

(d) the transfer requested is to the registered owner.

As amended in 1977.

Official Comment

Prior Uniform Statutory Provision: Section 3, Uniform Fiduciaries Act.

Purposes:

1. In consonance with the general policy of this Part 4 (See the Comments to Sections 8–401 and 8–402), and subject always to the overriding duty of good faith in the performance of its functions (Section 1–203) this section limits the issuer's duty as to adverse claims to the specific situations stated in subsections (1) as to certificated securities and (4) as to uncertificated securities.

Paragraph (a) of subsection (1) is the ordinary "stop transfer" notice commonly resorted to by the owner of a lost or stolen certificated security or in a situation where breach of trust, disregard of a valid restriction on transfer, or other improper action is feared to have occurred or to be about to occur.

Notification under paragraph (a) of subsection (1) must be "written" (Section 1–201(46)) and must be "received" (Section 1–201(26)) "at a time and in a manner which affords the issuer a reasonable opportunity to act on it prior to the issuance of a new, reissued or re-registered security." Cf. Section 1–201(27). Its contents must be such as to make reasonably clear who makes the claim and with respect to what security, and where communications may be addressed to him. Compare Section 5(a) of the Uniform Act for Simplification of Fiduciary Security Transfers.

A notification once so received is easily keyed to the appropriate records. Therefore, no defense of "forgotten notice", possibly relevant on the issue of bona fide purchase as to bearer form securities, is available under this section.

As to paragraph (b) see the Comment to Section 8–402.

2. With respect to certificated securities subsection (2) does not limit the issuer to any specific method of discharging a duty of inquiry. It may use "any reasonable means" including the procedure spelled out in the subsection. That procedure, based on a New York statute respecting adverse claims to bank deposits and on commercial practice, should be effective in the large majority of cases to protect the rights of all interested parties and relieve the issuer of further responsibility. No delay during the thirty day period will be "unreasonable" under Section 8–401(2).

3. Subsection (3) is the converse of subsection (1) and spells out some specific situations in which under prior law a duty to inquire existed or may have existed. Compare Sections 2 and 3 of the Uniform Act for Simplification of Fiduciary Security Transfers. As to the effect of subsection (3)(a) on the effectiveness of an indorsement, see the Comment to Section 8–404.

4. Transfer of uncertificated securities does not take place until registration, so that any mandated delay seriously impairs an owner's ability to sell or pledge his security. Since a prudent purchaser may not pay unless he receives a clean initial transaction statement, the effect of a rule giving the issuer a duty to inquire any time it received any written notice of an adverse claim, however, frivolous, would be disastrous. Because of this important difference between certificated and uncertificated securities, there are separate provisions as to duty to inquire. Subsections (4), (5), (6) and (7) apply only to uncertificated securities, and are intended to accommodate the interests of

owners, purchasers, issuers and adverse claimants.

Subsection (4) states that an issuer has no duty as to adverse claims except in four described situations. Mere written notifications result in a duty only when they come from existing owners and pledgees and are analogous to stop payment orders on checks. There is a duty as to claims to which the security was subject when it was purchased by the present owner, a situation with which the owner is already familiar. There is a duty as to claims arising from the issuer's request for documentation under Section 8–402.

The significant difference of subsection (4) from subsection (1) is that claims asserted by third parties, in order to impose a duty on the issuer, must be supported by legal process. This will constitute assurance that the claim is not merely frivolous and that its assertion is more than harassment. In most cases the owner will have been notified and have had the opportunity to be heard. While claims thus asserted may ultimately be adjudged invalid, the owner will not be tied up by a bare written communication from the claimant. On the other hand, while a more substantial burden is imposed on the claimant, there is a channel through which he can assert his claim before the rights of a bona fide purchaser intervene.

If the claimant sues the owner in a court that has no jurisdiction over the issuer and an injunction is issued against the owner forbidding him to transfer the security, the issuer has a duty under paragraph (4)(a) if it receives an authenticated copy of the order. Even though in that situation the order is not directed to the issuer, it is "legal process served upon the issuer" for purposes of paragraph (4)(a). There is sufficient guarantee that the complaint is not frivolous. Further, the issuer might breach its duty to act in good faith if it registered a transfer in spite of such clear evidence of impropriety.

5. Once it is established that the claim imposes a duty on the issuer, notations of the claim must be contained in all statements sent with respect to the security, and registration of transfer or pledge must be refused unless the nature of the claim is consistent with transfer or pledge subject to the claim. When transfer or pledge is registered subject to the claim, subsection (6) requires that the claim be noted in all statements sent to the transferee or pledgee.

Subsection (7) deals with the situation in which an uncertificated security is already subject to a registered pledge when the issuer first learns of an adverse claim as to which it has a duty. In that event, the registered pledgee who became such without notice of the claim may be a bona fide purchaser with the right to transfer the security free of the claim. That right cannot be curtailed by the claim of a third party (including the registered owner) unless legal process embodying the claim expressly deals with the pledgee's interest. There is obviously no curtailment of the pledgee's right when the claim is asserted by the pledgee himself. It should be curtailed if the pledgee's right to obtain registration of transfer is called into question by a controlling instrument which the issuer elects to require before acting on the pledgee's request. Since the transfer to the registered owner is the equivalent of a release of the pledge, such a transfer does not terminate the issuer's duty as to the claim.

Cross References:

Sections 1–203, 8–304, 8–401, 8–402, 8–404, 8–405 and 8–408.

Definitional Cross References:

"Adverse Claim". Section 8–302.
"Appropriate Person". Section 8–308.
"Certificated Security". Section 8–102.
"Indorsement". Section 8–308.
"Initial Transaction Statement". Section 8–408.
"Issuer". Section 8–201.
"Notice". Section 1–201.
"Notification". Section 1–201.
"Person". Section 1–201.
"Security". Section 8–102.
"Uncertificated Security". Section 8–102.
"Written". Section 1–201.

§ 8-404. Liability and Non-liability for Registration.

(1) Except as provided in any law relating to the collection of taxes, the issuer is not liable to the owner, pledgee, or any other person suffering loss as a result of the registration of a transfer, pledge, or release of a security if:

(a) there were on or with a certificated security the necessary indorsements or the issuer had received an instruction originated by an appropriate person (Section 8-308); and

(b) the issuer had no duty as to adverse claims or has discharged the duty (Section 8-403).

(2) If an issuer has registered a transfer of a certificated security to a person not entitled to it, the issuer on demand shall deliver a like security to the true owner unless:

(a) the registration was pursuant to subsection (1);

(b) the owner is precluded from asserting any claim for registering the transfer under Section 8-405(1); or

(c) the delivery would result in overissue, in which case the issuer's liability is governed by Section 8-104.

(3) If an issuer has improperly registered a transfer, pledge, or release of an uncertificated security, the issuer on demand from the injured party shall restore the records as to the injured party to the condition that would have obtained if the improper registration had not been made unless:

(a) the registration was pursuant to subsection (1); or

(b) the registration would result in overissue, in which case the issuer's liability is governed by Section 8-104.

As amended in 1977.

Official Comment

Prior Uniform Statutory Provision: None.

Purposes:

1. This section states the basic exonerative policy of this Article where there is no duty to inquire into adverse claims and the certificated security is appropriately indorsed or the issuer receives an instruction from an appropriate person.

Note that under subsection (1)(a) exoneration depends on whether or not the necessary indorsements were in fact on or with the security. The issuer cannot, for example, defend a suit based on its having registered a transfer on a forged indorsement on the ground that it received the assurances listed in Section 8-402 and was under no duty to go further. It has that option under Section 8-402(4).

Note, however, that this Act excludes from the category of "unauthorized indorsement" (Section 8-311) certain situations that might have been included in that category under prior law—e.g., where there has been a change of circumstances subsequent to the signature (subsection (10) of Section 8-308), and where the signature is that of a fiduciary who has failed to obtain court approval of the transfer (subsection (11) of Section 8-308). Similarly, when an issuer acts on the assumption permitted by subsection (3)(a) of Section 8-403, that a fiduciary registered owner continues to act as such, the "necessary indorsement" under subsection (1)(a) of this section is that of the registered owner under Section 8-308(8)(a), even though a successor has in fact been appointed. In these and other cases, where the question is one affecting only the rightfulness of the transfer, the issuer need only establish that it had no duty under Section 8-403 to inquire into adverse claims or that it has discharged any such duty.

2. The registered owner's right to receive a new security where the issuer has wrongfully registered a transfer is established, but the cases have also recognized his right to elect between an equitable action to compel issue of a new security and an action for damages. Cf. Casper v. Kalt-Zimmers Mfg. Co., 159 Wis. 517, 149 N.W. 754 (1914). Such election of remedies is no longer available. The true owner of a certificated security is now required to take a new security except where an overissue would result and a similar security is not reasonably available for purchase. See Section 8-104. The true owner of an uncertificated security is entitled and required to take restoration of the records to their proper state, with a similar exception for overissue.

Nothing in subsections (2) and (3) is intended to deny the owner the right to choose the form of his security whenever the issuer maintains securities of the same issue in both certificated and uncertificated form (Section 8-407).

Cross References:

Point 1: Sections 8-308, 8-402 and 8-403.

Point 2: Sections 8-104, 8-405 and 8-407.

Definitional Cross References:

"Adverse Claim". Section 8-302.
"Appropriate Person". Section 8-308.
"Certificated Security". Section 8-102.
"Deliver". Section 1-201.
"Indorsement". Section 8-308.
"Instruction". Section 8-308.
"Issuer". Section 8-201.
"Overissue". Section 8-104.
"Party". Section 1-201.
"Person". Section 1-201.
"Security". Section 8-102.
"Uncertificated Security". Section 8-102.

§ 8-405. Lost, Destroyed, and Stolen Certificated Securities.

(1) If a certificated security has been lost, apparently destroyed, or wrongfully taken, and the owner fails to notify the issuer of that fact within a reasonable time after he has notice of it and the issuer registers a transfer of the security before receiving notification, the owner is precluded from asserting against the issuer any claim for registering the transfer under Section 8-404 or any claim to a new security under this section.

(2) If the owner of a certificated security claims that the security has been lost, destroyed, or wrongfully taken, the issuer shall issue a new certificated security or, at the option of the issuer, an equivalent uncertificated security in place of the original security if the owner:

(a) so requests before the issuer has notice that the security has been acquired by a bona fide purchaser;

(b) files with the issuer a sufficient indemnity bond; and

(c) satisfies any other reasonable requirements imposed by the issuer.

(3) If, after the issue of a new certificated or uncertificated security, a bona fide purchaser of the original certificated security presents it for registration of transfer, the issuer shall register the transfer unless registration would result in overissue, in which event the issuer's liability is governed by Section 8-104. In addition to any rights on the indemnity bond, the issuer

may recover the new certificated security from the person to whom it was issued or any person taking under him except a bona fide purchaser or may cancel the uncertificated security unless a bona fide purchaser or any person taking under a bona fide purchaser is then the registered owner or registered pledgee thereof.

As amended in 1977.

Official Comment

Prior Uniform Statutory Provision: Section 17, Uniform Stock Transfer Act.

Purposes:

1. By failing to notify the issuer within a reasonable time after he knows or has reason to know of the loss or theft of his certificated security, the owner is estopped from asserting the ineffectiveness of a forged or unauthorized indorsement and the wrongfulness of the registration of the transfer. Compare Section 8-311. If the lost security was indorsed by the owner, then the registration of the transfer was not wrongful under Section 8-404 unless notice had been given to the issuer.

2. The long standing corporate practice of voluntarily issuing new certificated securities to replace lost, destroyed or stolen ones is now incorporated into law. Where reasonable requirements are satisfied and a sufficient indemnity bond supplied, a court order is no longer necessary but, of course, the court may compel a recalcitrant issuer to take action.

Subsection (2) gives the issuer the alternative of issuing an uncertificated security rather than a new certificated security. This alternative will exist only when the particular issue is partly certificated and partly uncertificated; and as a practical matter the ultimate choice will belong to the owner (Section 8-407). Compare Section 8-104 and its Comment.

3. Where an "original" certificated security has reached the hands of a bona fide purchaser, the registered owner—who was in the best position to prevent the loss, destruction or theft of his security—is now deprived of the new security issued to him as a replacement. If the security is certificated, the issuer has a right to recover it; and if the security is uncertificated, the issuer may simply cancel the registration. This changes the prior law under which the original security was ineffective after the issue of a replacement except insofar as it might represent an action for damages in the hands of a bona fide purchaser. Keller v. Eureka Brick Mach. Mfg. Co., 43 Mo.App. 84, 11 L.R.A. 472 (1890). Where both the original and the new security have reached bona fide purchasers the issuer is now required to honor both securities unless an overissue would result and the security is not reasonably available for purchase. See Section 8-104. In the latter case alone, the bona fide purchaser of the original security is relegated to an action for damages. In either case, the issuer itself may recover on the indemnity bond.

Cross References:

Sections 8-104, 8-311, 8-312, 8-402, 8-403, 8-404 and 8-407.

Definitional Cross References:

"Bona Fide Purchaser". Section 8-302.

"Certificated Security". Section 8-102.

"Issuer". Section 8-201.

"Notice". Section 1-201.

"Notify". Section 1-201.

"Overissue". Section 8-104.

"Person". Section 1-201.

"Reasonable Time". Section 1-204.

"Rights". Section 1-201.

"Security". Section 8-102.

"Uncertificated Security". Section 8-102.

§ 8–406. Duty of Authenticating Trustee, Transfer Agent, or Registrar.

(1) If a person acts as authenticating trustee, transfer agent, registrar, or other agent for an issuer in the registration of transfers of its certificated securities or in the registration of transfers, pledges, and releases of its uncertificated securities, in the issue of new securities, or in the cancellation of surrendered securities:

(a) he is under a duty to the issuer to exercise good faith and due diligence in performing his functions; and

(b) with regard to the particular functions he performs, he has the same obligation to the holder or owner of a certificated security or to the owner or pledgee of an uncertificated security and has the same rights and privileges as the issuer has in regard to those functions.

(2) Notice to an authenticating trustee, transfer agent, registrar or other agent is notice to the issuer with respect to the functions performed by the agent.

As amended in 1977.

Official Comment

Prior Uniform Statutory Provision: None.

Purposes:

1. Transfer agents, registrars and the like are here expressly held liable to both the issuer and the owner for wrongful refusal to register a transfer as well as wrongful registration of a transfer in any case within the scope of their respective functions where the issuer would itself be liable. Those cases which have regarded these parties solely as agents of the issuer and have therefore refused to recognize their liability to the owner for mere nonfeasance, i.e., refusal to register a transfer, are now rejected. Hulse v. Consolidated Quicksilver Mining Corp., 65 Idaho 768, 154 P.2d 149 (1944); Nicholson v. Morgan, 119 Misc. 309, 196 N.Y.Supp. 147 (1922); Lewis v. Hargadine-McKittrick Dry Goods Co., 305 Mo. 396, 274 S.W. 1041 (1924).

2. The practice frequently followed by authenticating trustees of issuing certificates of indebtedness rather than authenticating duplicate certificates where securities have been lost or stolen now becomes obsolete in view of the provisions of the preceding section of this Article, which makes express provision for the issue of substitute securities. It can no longer be considered a breach of trust or lack of due diligence for trustees to authenticate new securities (or initial transaction statements). Cf. Switzerland General Ins. Co. v. N.Y.C. & H.R.R.Co., 152 App.Div. 70, 136 N.Y.S. 726 (1912).

3. "Good faith and due diligence" require the use of reasonable care and the observance of "reasonable" commercial standards, and preclude arbitrary, capricious, over-cautious and supertechnical objections and requirements. See Powers v. Universal Film Mfg. Co., 162 App.Div. 806, 148 N.Y.S. 114 (1914). Compliance with the provisions of this Article as to the documents which an issuer may properly require before registering a transfer in cases where there has been no notice of adverse claims (Section 8–402) constitutes due diligence on the part of these agents, and by insisting upon more they could incur liability for wrongful refusal to register a transfer.

Cross References:

Point 3: Sections 3–401, 8–402, 8–403 and 8–404. See Sections 1–201, 8–207, 8–208, 8–312, 8–401, 8–402, 8–403, 8–405, 8–407 and 8–408.

Definitional Cross References:

"Certificated Security". Section 8-102.
"Good Faith". Section 1-201.
"Holder". Section 1-201.
"Issuer". Section 8-201.
"Notice". Section 1-201.
"Person". Section 1-201.
"Security". Section 8-102.
"Uncertificated Security". Section 8-102.

§ 8-407. Exchangeability of Securities.

(1) No issuer is subject to the requirements of this section unless it regularly maintains a system for issuing the class of securities involved under which both certificated and uncertificated securities are regularly issued to the category of owners, which includes the person in whose name the new security is to be registered.

(2) Upon surrender of a certificated security with all necessary indorsements and presentation of a written request by the person surrendering the security, the issuer, if he has no duty as to adverse claims or has discharged the duty (Section 8-403), shall issue to the person or a person designated by him an equivalent uncertificated security subject to all liens, restrictions, and claims that were noted on the certificated security.

(3) Upon receipt of a transfer instruction originated by an appropriate person who so requests, the issuer of an uncertificated security shall cancel the uncertificated security and issue an equivalent certificated security on which must be noted conspicuously any liens and restrictions of the issuer and any adverse claims (as to which the issuer has a duty under Section 8-403(4)) to which the uncertificated security was subject. The certificated security shall be registered in the name of and delivered to:

(a) the registered owner, if the uncertificated security was not subject to a registered pledge; or

(b) the registered pledgee, if the uncertificated security was subject to a registered pledge.

As added in 1977.

Official Comment

Prior Uniform Statutory Provision: None.

Purposes:

This section deals with the right of the holder of a certificated security to exchange it for an equivalent uncertificated security and the right of the registered owner or registered pledgee of an uncertificated security to obtain a certificated security in exchange for it. This section is applicable only in those situations where both certificated and uncertificated securities exist within the same issue and either form is available to the particular owner. Subsection (1) so limits its applicability.

Neither this nor any other section of this Article is intended to mandate the establishment or continuance of a dual system of registration. It is contemplated that some issuers may provide for both forms of securities on a more or less indefinite basis. Issuers of existing issues which are necessarily wholly certificated may make uncertificated securities available with the intention to phase out the certificated securities over a period of time. Some issuers, if permitted by relevant law, may restrict the availability of uncertificated securities to particular categories of owners, e.g., brokers, banks and institutions.

Subsection (2) provides the mechanism for the holder of a certificated security to surrender it to the issuer and have an equivalent uncertificated security issued in exchange. Subsection (3) provides an analogous mechanism for the registered owner of an unencumbered uncertificated security or the registered pledgee of an otherwise unencumbered uncertificated security to obtain equivalent certificated securities from the issuer. Since Section 8-403 treats adverse claims with respect to certificated securities differently from adverse claims with respect to uncertificated securities, subsection (2) requires the issuer to honor the request only if it has no duty as to adverse claims. If it honored the request despite the presence of such a duty, the adverse claimant's right to block transfer might be modified. For example, if the issuer of a certificated security had received written notice from the claimant, it would be under a duty to inquire and to delay registration of transfer pending the results of the inquiry. However, if it issued an uncertificated security in place of the certificate, then it would no longer be under a duty (Section 8-403(4)(b)) and would register transfer to a bona fide purchaser without including any notation of the claim (Section 8-403(5)).

On the other hand, if the issuer is under a duty as to adverse claims with respect to an uncertificated security it will also be under a similar duty with respect to a certificated security issued to represent the same interest. Compare subsections (1) and (4) of Section 8-403. Potential purchasers will be unable to purchase free of the claim, since they will be given notice through notation on the certificate. See Sections 8-304, 8-202 and 1-201(25).

Cross References:

Sections 8-104, 8-403 and 8-405.

Definitional Cross References:

"Adverse Claim". Section 8-302.
"Appropriate Person". Section 8-308.
"Certificated Security". Section 8-102.
"Conspicuous". Section 1-201.
"Delivery". Section 1-201.
"Indorsement". Section 8-308.
"Instruction". Section 8-308.
"Issuer". Section 8-201.
"Person". Section 1-201.
"Security". Section 8-102.
"Uncertificated Security". Section 8-102.
"Written". Section 1-201.

§ 8-408. Statements of Uncertificated Securities.

(1) Within 2 business days after the transfer of an uncertificated security has been registered, the issuer shall send to the new registered owner and, if the security has been transferred subject to a registered pledge, to the registered pledgee a written statement containing:

(a) a description of the issue of which the uncertificated security is a part;

(b) the number of shares or units transferred;

(c) the name and address and any taxpayer identification number of the new registered owner and, if the security has been transferred subject to a registered pledge, the name and address and any taxpayer identification number of the registered pledgee;

(d) a notation of any liens and restrictions of the issuer and any adverse claims (as to which the issuer has a duty under Section 8-403(4)) to which the uncertificated security is or may be subject at the time of registration or a statement that there are none of those liens, restrictions, or adverse claims; and

(e) the date the transfer was registered.

(2) Within 2 business days after the pledge of an uncertificated security has been registered, the issuer shall send to the registered owner and the registered pledgee a written statement containing:

(a) a description of the issue of which the uncertificated security is a part;

(b) the number of shares or units pledged;

(c) the name and address and any taxpayer identification number of the registered owner and the registered pledgee;

(d) a notation of any liens and restrictions of the issuer and any adverse claims (as to which the issuer has a duty under Section 8–403(4)) to which the uncertificated security is or may be subject at the time of registration or a statement that there are none of those liens, restrictions, or adverse claims; and

(e) the date the pledge was registered.

(3) Within 2 business days after the release from pledge of an uncertificated security has been registered, the issuer shall send to the registered owner and the pledgee whose interest was released a written statement containing:

(a) a description of the issue of which the uncertificated security is a part;

(b) the number of shares or units released from pledge;

(c) the name and address and any taxpayer identification number of the registered owner and the pledgee whose interest was released;

(d) a notation of any liens and restrictions of the issuer and any adverse claims (as to which the issuer has a duty under Section 8–403(4)) to which the uncertificated security is or may be subject at the time of registration or a statement that there are none of those liens, restrictions, or adverse claims; and

(e) the date the release was registered.

(4) An "initial transaction statement" is the statement sent to:

(a) the new registered owner and, if applicable, to the registered pledgee pursuant to subsection (1);

(b) the registered pledgee pursuant to subsection (2); or

(c) the registered owner pursuant to subsection (3).

Each initial transaction statement shall be signed by or on behalf of the issuer and must be identified as "Initial Transaction Statement".

(5) Within 2 business days after the transfer of an uncertificated security has been registered, the issuer shall send to the former registered owner and the former registered pledgee, if any, a written statement containing:

(a) a description of the issue of which the uncertificated security is a part;

(b) the number of shares or units transferred;

(c) the name and address and any taxpayer identification number of the former registered owner and of any former registered pledgee; and

(d) the date the transfer was registered.

(6) At periodic intervals no less frequent than annually and at any time upon the reasonable written request of the registered owner, the issuer shall send to the registered owner of each uncertificated security a dated written statement containing:

(a) a description of the issue of which the uncertificated security is a part;

(b) the name and address and any taxpayer identification number of the registered owner;

(c) the number of shares or units of the uncertificated security registered in the name of the registered owner on the date of the statement;

(d) the name and address and any taxpayer identification number of any registered pledgee and the number of shares or units subject to the pledge; and

(e) a notation of any liens and restrictions of the issuer and any adverse claims (as to which the issuer has a duty under Section 8–403(4)) to which the uncertificated security is or may be subject or a statement that there are none of those liens, restrictions, or adverse claims.

(7) At periodic intervals no less frequent than annually and at any time upon the reasonable written request of the registered pledgee, the issuer shall send to the registered pledgee of each uncertificated security a dated written statement containing:

(a) a description of the issue of which the uncertificated security is a part;

(b) the name and address and any taxpayer identification number of the registered owner;

(c) the name and address and any taxpayer identification number of the registered pledgee;

(d) the number of shares or units subject to the pledge; and

(e) a notation of any liens and restrictions of the issuer and any adverse claims (as to which the issuer has a duty under Section 8–403(4)) to which the uncertificated security is or may be subject or a statement that there are none of those liens, restrictions, or adverse claims.

(8) If the issuer sends the statements described in subsections (6) and (7) at periodic intervals no less frequent than quarterly, the issuer is not obliged to send additional statements upon request unless the owner or pledgee requesting them pays to the issuer the reasonable cost of furnishing them.

(9) Each statement sent pursuant to this section must bear a conspicuous legend reading substantially as follows: "This statement is merely a record of the rights of the addressee as of the time of its issuance. Delivery of this statement, of itself, confers no rights on the recipient. This statement is neither a negotiable instrument nor a security."

As added in 1977.

Official Comment

Prior Uniform Statutory Provision: None.

Purposes:

1. This section obliges the issuer of uncertificated securities to send certain statements. The required statements are of two types. Transaction statements, required by subsections (1), (2), (3) and (5) are analogous to debit and credit advices and the periodic statements can be reconciled from them. Periodic statements, required by subsections (6) and (7) are analogous to bank statements and will advise owners and pledgees of their positions at given points in time.

The transaction statements, which are mandated upon the registration of transfer, pledge or release, must be sent within two days after the relevant registration, but it is contemplated that such statements will be prepared virtually simultaneously with the actual registration and sent immediately thereafter. They are intended to serve two functions. They are notice to the transferor—(the owner in the case of transfer or pledge, the pledgee in the case of release from pledge, and both the owner and the pledgee in the case of transfer subject to a pledge, transfer of the pledge interest alone or simultaneous transfer and release from pledge)—that his interest has been altered. In the event of fraudulent, unauthorized or otherwise improper registration, the transaction statement will serve as notice that timely action should be taken.

More importantly, these statements are notice to the transferee (new owner in the case of a transfer, pledgee in the case of a pledge, present owner in the case of a release) that the increase of his interest has, in fact, been registered. Furthermore, since all statements except those required by subsection (5) must include a notation of defects or an express statement that there are none, these statements will give the transferee the assurance equivalent to that afforded by a "clean" certificated security and create an estoppel against the issuer. Since registration is the critical step in the transfer of rights, the issuer's transaction statement should include, and the purchaser who receives the statement should be charged with notice of, only those claims, liens and restrictions existing at the time of registration. Compare Section 8-304(2).

It is contemplated that transferees will and should be able to rely on these statements and, in many cases, will not part with their consideration until they receive them. To ensure that the statements will have the desired effect of establishing rights for the transferee against the issuer, subsection (4) requires that the copy of each transaction statement sent to the transferee, called an "initial transaction statement," be signed. Note that Section 1-201(39) does not require a manual signature for compliance with this requirement. Compare also Sections 8-103(b), 8-105(3)(d), 8-202, 8-204(b), 8-205, 8-206, 8-208, 8-304, 8-311, 8-319 and 8-403 for the effects of initial transaction statements.

2. Whenever the issuer registers a transfer of the pledge interest alone, subsections (2) and (3) read together require the issuer to send transaction statements to both the registered owner and the former registered pledgee as well as to the new registered pledgee. Compare Section 8-207(4) and its Comment 1.

3. The frequency of one year, with which periodic statements must be sent to owners and pledgees, is intended to be a minimum requirement for all issuers, including closely held corporations. Owners and pledgees are entitled to request additional statements of position at any time. It is contemplated, however, that publicly held issuers will adopt the practice of sending quarterly statements conforming to the common practice of sending quarterly reports and dividend

checks. For those that do, subsection (8) eliminates the obligation to furnish additional statements of position on request unless the issuer is reimbursed for the additional cost.

4. Subsection (9) requires that a conspicuous legend be borne by each statement as a protection against unjustified reliance on statements of uncertificated securities by persons who might deal with them. Except for this requirement and the requirement of subsection (4) that the words "Initial Transaction Statement" be included, the form of the statements required by this section is not prescribed. Perhaps the forms now used by the transfer agents of mutual funds to confirm acquisitions, dispositions, reinvestment of dividends, periodic liquidations and statements of position will serve as a model.

Cross References:

Point 1: Sections 8–103, 8–105, 8–202, 8–204, 8–205, 8–206, 8–208 and 8–304.

Point 2: Section 8–207.

Definitional Cross References:

"Adverse Claim". Section 8–302.
"Conspicuous". Section 1–201.
"Delivery". Section 1–201.
"Issuer". Section 8–201.
"Rights". Section 1–201.
"Security". Section 8–102.
"Send". Section 1–201.
"Signed". Section 1–201.
"Uncertificated Security". Section 8–102.
"Written". Section 1–201.

APPENDIX XIV

1995 AMENDMENTS TO ARTICLES 1, 2, AND 9 CONFORMING TO REVISED ARTICLE 5

CONFORMING AND MISCELLANEOUS AMENDMENTS TO ARTICLE 1

[Changes from present law are shown by underscore and ~~strikeout~~.]

§ 1–105. Territorial Application of the Act; Parties' Power to Choose Applicable Law.

. . .

(2) Where one of the following provisions of this [Act] specifies the applicable law, that provision governs and a contrary agreement is effective only to the extent permitted by the law (including the conflict of laws rules) so specified:

. . .

Governing law in the Article on Funds Transfers. Section 4A–507.

Letters of Credit. Section 5–116.

Bulk sales subject to the Article on Bulk Sales. Section 6–103.

. . .

CONFORMING AND MISCELLANEOUS AMENDMENTS TO ARTICLE 2

§ 2–512. Payment by Buyer Before Inspection.

. . .

(b) despite tender of the required documents the circumstances would justify injunction against honor under ~~the provisions of~~ this Act (Section ~~5–114~~ 5–109(b)).

. . .

COMPLEMENTARY AMENDMENTS TO ARTICLE 9

§ 9–103. Perfection of Security Interest in Multiple State Transactions.

(1) Documents, instruments, letters of credit, and ordinary goods.

(a) This subsection applies to documents, ~~and~~ instruments, rights to proceeds of written letters of credit, and ~~to~~ goods other than those covered by a certificate of title described in subsection (2), mobile goods described in subsection (3), and minerals described in subsection (5).

. . .

§ 9–104. Transactions Excluded From Article.

This Article does not apply

. . .

(*l*) to a transfer of an interest in any deposit account (subsection (1) of Section 9–105), except as provided with respect to proceeds (Section 9–306) and priorities in proceeds (Section 9–312); or

(m) to a transfer of an interest in a letter of credit other than the rights to proceeds of a written letter of credit.

Official Comment

. . .

[ ]

§ 9–105. Definitions and Index of Definitions.

. . .

(3) The following definitions in other Articles apply to this Article:

. . .

"Letter of credit". Section 5–102.

. . .

"Proceeds of a letter of credit". Section 5–114(a).

§ 9–106. Definitions: "Account"; "General Intangibles."

"Account" means any right to payment for goods sold or leased or for services rendered which is not evidenced by an instrument or chattel paper, whether or not it has been earned by performance. "General intangibles" means any personal property (including things in action) other than goods, accounts, chattel paper, documents, instruments, investment property, rights to proceeds of written letters of credit, and money. All rights to payment earned or unearned under a charter or other contract involving the use or hire of a vessel and all rights incident to the charter or contract are accounts.

§ 9–304. Perfection of Security Interest in Instruments, Documents, Proceeds of a Written Letter of Credit, and Goods Covered by Documents; Perfection by Permissive Filing; Temporary Perfection Without Filing or Transfer of Possession.

(1) A security interest in chattel paper or negotiable documents may be perfected by filing. A security interest in the rights to proceeds of a written

letter of credit can be perfected only by the secured party's taking possession of the letter of credit. A security interest in money or instruments (other than instruments which constitute part of chattel paper) can be perfected only by the secured party's taking possession, except as provided in subsections (4) and (5) of this section and subsections (2) and (3) of Section 9-306 on proceeds.

. . .

(6) . . .

Special Legislative Note: *As Sections 9-304 and 9-305 appear in the Official Text of the Conforming Amendments to Revised Article 5 (1995), they incorporate the amendments made to these sections in 1994, when Revised Article 8 was promulgated. If Revised Article 5 with Conforming Amendments, as promulgated in 1995, is adopted by any State before Revised Article 8 with Conforming Amendments of 1994 is adopted, the 1990 text for Sections 9-304 and 9-305 should be used as a basis for amendment, as follows:*

SECTION 9-304. PERFECTION OF SECURITY INTEREST IN INSTRUMENTS, DOCUMENTS, PROCEEDS OF A WRITTEN LETTER OF CREDIT, AND GOODS COVERED BY DOCUMENTS; PERFECTION BY PERMISSIVE FILING; TEMPORARY PERFECTION WITHOUT FILING OR TRANSFER OF POSSESSION.

(1) A security interest in chattel paper or negotiable documents may be perfected by filing. A security interest in the rights to proceeds of a written letter of credit can be perfected only by the secured party's taking possession of the letter of credit. A security interest in money or instruments (other than certificated securities or instruments which constitute part of chattel paper) can be perfected only by the secured party's taking possession, except as provided in subsections (4) and (5) of this section and subsections (2) and (3) of Section 9-306 on proceeds.

. . .

SECTION 9-305. WHEN POSSESSION BY SECURED PARTY PERFECTS SECURITY INTEREST WITHOUT FILING. *A security interest in ~~letters of credit and advices of credit (subsection (2)(a) of Section 5-116),~~ goods, instruments (other than certificated securities), money, negotiable documents, or chattel paper may be perfected by the security party's taking possession of the collateral. A security interest in the right to proceeds of a written letter of credit may be perfected by the secured party's taking possession of the letter of credit. If such collateral other than goods covered by a negotiable document is held by a bailee, the secured party is* *deemed to have possession from the time the bailee receives notification of the secured party's interest. A security interest is perfected by possession from the time possession is taken without a relation back and continues only so long as possession is retained, unless otherwise specified in this Article. The security interest may be otherwise perfected as provided in this Article before or after the period of possession by the secured party.*

Official Comment

. . .

§ 9-305. When Possession by Secured Party Perfects Security Interest Without Filing.

A security interest in ~~letters of credit and advices of credit (subsection (2)(a) of Section 5-116),~~ goods, instruments, money, negotiable documents, or chattel paper may be perfected by the secured party's taking possession of the collateral. A security interest in the right to proceeds of a written letter of credit may be perfected by the secured party's taking possession of the letter of credit. If such collateral other than goods covered by a negotiable document is held by a bailee, the secured party is deemed to have possession from the time the bailee receives notification of the secured party's interest. A security interest is perfected by possession from the time possession is taken without a relation back and continues only so long as possession is retained, unless otherwise specified in this Article. The security interest may be otherwise perfected as provided in this Article before or after the period of possession by the secured party.

Special Legislative Note: *See Special Legislative Note, Section 9-304.*

Official Comment

. . .

1. As under the common law of pledge, no filing is required by this Article to perfect a security interest where the secured party has possession of the collateral. Compare Section 9-302(1)(a). This section permits a security interest to be perfected by transfer of possession only when the collateral is goods, rights to proceeds of letters of credit (if written), instruments ~~*(other than certificated securities, which are governed by Section 8-321)*~~*, documents or chattel paper: that is to say, accounts and general intangibles are excluded. *As to perfection of security interests in certificated securities by possession, see the general rules on perfection of security interests in investment property in Section 9-115(4) and the special rule in Section 9-115(6) dealing with cases where a secured party takes possession of a security certificate in registered form without obtaining an indorsement.** ~~See Section 5-116 for the special case of assignments of letters and advices of credit.~~ A security interest in accounts and general intangibles—property not ordinarily represented by any writing whose delivery operates to transfer the claim—may under this Article be perfected only by filing, and this rule would not be affected by the fact that a security agreement or other writing described the assignment of such col-

lateral as a "pledge". Section 9-302(1)(e) exempts from filing certain assignments of accounts which are out of the ordinary course of financing: such exempted assignments are perfected when they attach under Section 9-303(1); they do not fall within this section. **Amendments in italics approved by the Permanent Editorial Board for Uniform Commercial Code November 4, 1995.*

. . .

APPENDIX XV

PRE–REVISION ARTICLE 5

Set forth below are the Text and Official Comments of Article 5 as they existed prior to revision in 1995.

ARTICLE 5

LETTERS OF CREDIT

Section

---

§ 5–101. Short Title.

This Article shall be known and may be cited as Uniform Commercial Code—Letters of Credit.

Official Comment

Letters of credit have been known and used for many years, in both international and domestic transactions, and in many forms; but except for a few provisions, like Section 135 of the Negotiable Instruments Law, they have not been the subject of statutory enactment, and the law concerning them has been developed in the cases.

This provision of the Negotiable Instruments Law is no longer in the Code. See the contrary rule in Section 3–410 on the definition of acceptance. The other source of law respecting letters of credit is the law of contracts with occasional unfortunate excursions into the law of guaranty. This Article is intended within its limited scope (see Comment to Section 5-102) to set an independent theoretical frame for the further development of letters of credit.

Cross References:

Sections 5-102, 5-103 and 3-410.

§ 5-102. Scope.

(1) This Article applies

(a) to a credit issued by a bank if the credit requires a documentary draft or a documentary demand for payment; and

(b) to a credit issued by a person other than a bank if the credit requires that the draft or demand for payment be accompanied by a document of title; and

(c) to a credit issued by a bank or other person if the credit is not within subparagraphs (a) or (b) but conspicuously states that it is a letter of credit or is conspicuously so entitled.

(2) Unless the engagement meets the requirements of subsection (1), this Article does not apply to engagements to make advances or to honor drafts or demands for payment, to authorities to pay or purchase, to guarantees or to general agreements.

(3) This Article deals with some but not all of the rules and concepts of letters of credit as such rules or concepts have developed prior to this act or may hereafter develop. The fact that this Article states a rule does not by itself require, imply or negate application of the same or a converse rule to a situation not provided for or to a person not specified by this Article.

Official Comment

Prior Uniform Statutory Provision: None.

Purposes:

To define the transactions to which this Article applies and to indicate that the rules stated are not intended to be exhaustive of the law applicable to letters of credit.

1. Although letters of credit are commonly thought of as being issued by banks and private bankers, other financing institutions can and do enter into transactions which fit the traditional concept of letters of credit. This is particularly true when the financing institution at the request of a buyer of goods promises the seller of the goods that it will pay or accept drafts or demands for payment on either the buyer or itself if the drafts are accompanied by documents of title covering the goods involved in the sales contract. Banks and private bankers also issue money credits which do not require documents of title to be presented as one of the conditions of honor. So far as these institutions are concerned the accompanying papers can range from a certification that certain building contracts have been performed in whole or in part or a notice that goods have been sent or a notice of default of some kind into the more traditional document of title. Subsection (1) attempts to make clear that automatic application of this Article to the transaction in question depends upon the nature of the issuer. Paragraph (1)(a) is applicable to banks and states that whenever the promise to honor is conditioned on presentation of any piece of paper, the transaction is within this Article whereas paragraph (1)(b) makes automatic application of the Article to transactions involving issuers other than

banks dependent upon the requirement of a document of title.

Since banks issue "clean" as well as "documentary" credits and since other persons may desire to bring transactions involving papers other than documents of title within the coverage of this Article, paragraph (1)(c) permits the issuer to do so by conspicuous notation that the paper is a letter of credit. Whether a transaction falls within the mandatory or the permissive paragraphs of subsection (1) is also of importance on the question of payment of funds held by an issuer at the time of its insolvency (See Section 5-117).

Subsection (2) states the negative of the rules of applicability of subsection (1) for greater clarity but is not intended to either enlarge or limit the tests of applicability there laid down.

2. Subsection (3) recognizes that in the present state of the law and variety of practices as to letters of credit, no statute can effectively or wisely codify all the possible law of letters of credit without stultifying further development of this useful financing device. The more important areas not covered by this Article revolve around the question of when documents in fact and in law do or do not comply with the terms of the credit. In addition such minor matters as the absence of expiration dates and the effect of extending shipment but not expiration dates are also left untouched for future adjudication. The rules embodied in the Article can be viewed as those expressing the fundamental theories underlying letters of credit. For this reason the second sentence of subsection (3) makes explicit the court's power to apply a particular rule by analogy to cases not within its terms, or to refrain from doing so. Under Section 1-102(1) such application is to follow the canon of liberal interpretation to promote underlying purposes and policies. Since the law of letters of credit is still developing, conscious use of that canon and attention to fundamental theory by the court are peculiarly appropriate.

Cross Reference:

Section 1-102.

Definitional Cross References:

"Agreement". Section 1-201.
"Bank". Section 1-201.
"Conspicuous". Section 1-201.
"Credit". Section 5-103.
"Documentary draft". Section 5-103.
"Document of title". Section 1-201.
"Draft". Section 3-104.
"Honor". Section 1-201.
"Person". Section 1-201.

§ 5-103. Definitions.

(1) In this Article unless the context otherwise requires

(a) "Credit" or "letter of credit" means an engagement by a bank or other person made at the request of a customer and of a kind within the scope of this Article (Section 5-102) that the issuer will honor drafts or other demands for payment upon compliance with the conditions specified in the credit. A credit may be either revocable or irrevocable. The engagement may be either an agreement to honor or a statement that the bank or other person is authorized to honor.

(b) A "documentary draft" or a "documentary demand for payment" is one honor of which is conditioned upon the presentation of a document or documents. "Document" means any paper including document of title, security, invoice, certificate, notice of default and the like.

(c) An "issuer" is a bank or other person issuing a credit.

(d) A "beneficiary" of a credit is a person who is entitled under its terms to draw or demand payment.

(e) An "advising bank" is a bank which gives notification of the issuance of a credit by another bank.

(f) A "confirming bank" is a bank which engages either that it will itself honor a credit already issued by another bank or that such a credit will be honored by the issuer or a third bank.

(g) A "customer" is a buyer or other person who causes an issuer to issue a credit. The term also includes a bank which procures issuance or confirmation on behalf of that bank's customer.

(2) Other definitions applying to this Article and the sections in which they appear are:

"Notation Credit".	Section 5-108.
"Presenter".	Section 5-112(3).

(3) Definitions in other Articles applying to this Article and the sections in which they appear are:

"Accept" or "Acceptance".	Section 3-409.
"Contract for sale".	Section 2-106.
"Draft".	Section 3-104.
"Holder in due course".	Section 3-302.
"Midnight deadline".	Section 4-104.
"Security".	Section 8-102.

(4) In addition, Article 1 contains general definitions and principles of construction and interpretation applicable throughout this Article.

As amended in 1994.

See Appendix XI for material relating to changes made in text in 1994.

Official Comment

Prior Uniform Statutory Provision: None.

Purposes:

To define terms used in this Article.

1. Paragraph (a) of subsection (1) in defining a "credit" or "letter of credit" sets forth the requirement that the engagement of the bank or other person to honor drafts or other demands for payment be at the request of another and involve a transaction falling within the scope of this Article (Section 5-102). It then makes clear that the "engagement" may be by way of agreement, that is, a promise to honor, or by way of an authority to honor, thus including within the definition of letter of credit, papers called "authorities to purchase or pay". The definition also makes clear that the engagement may be either revocable or irrevocable, the legal consequences of which are spelled out in Section 5-106 on the time and effect of establishment of a credit. Neither the definition nor any other section of this Article deals with the issue of when a credit, not clearly labelled as either revocable or irrevocable falls within the one or the other category although the Code settles this issue with respect to the sales contract (Section 2-325). This issue so far as it affects an issuer under this Article is intentionally left to the courts for decision in the light of the facts and general law (Section 1-103) with due regard to the general provisions of the Code in Article 1 particularly Section 1-

205 on course of dealing and usage of trade.

2. Paragraph (b) is intended to show that the word "document" is far broader than "document of title" for the purposes of this Article. This is of special importance with respect to the application of the Article to banks under Section 5–102(1)(a) and differs from the definition of "document" in Article 9 on secured transactions which is there limited to documents of title. See Section 9–105(1)(e).

3. The legal relations between the issuer (1)(c) and the beneficiary (1)(d) and between the issuer and the customer (1)(g) are spelled out in other sections of this Article. The legal relations between the customer and the beneficiary turn on the underlying transaction between them: if that transaction be one of sale of goods, their rights depend upon Article 2; if the transaction involves the sale of investment securities, Article 8 will be applicable; if the transaction involves the transfer of commercial paper, Article 3 will be applicable; if documents of title are transferred, Article 7 will be applicable; and if the transaction is intended to create a security interest, Article 9 will apply. The issuer is not a guarantor of the performance of these underlying transactions. See Section 5–109.

4. The definition of customer in subsection (1)(g) is explicitly made to include a bank which is acting for its customer, so that a particular transaction may well involve a metropolitan issuing bank and two customers, one of whom is the ultimate customer as, e.g., the buyer of goods and the other of whom is the buyer's local bank which has requested the metropolitan bank to issue the credit.

5. The definitions of "advising" and "confirming" banks in subsection (1)(e) and (f) do not include a statement of their legal consequences. These are set out primarily in Section 5–107 on advice of credit; confirmation; error in statement.

Cross References:

Point 1: Sections 5–102, 5–106, 1–103, 1–205, 2–325 and Article 1.

Point 2: Sections 5–102, 1–201 and 9–105.

Point 3: Articles 2, 3, 7, 8 and 9; Section 5–109.

Point 5: Section 5–107.

Definitional Cross References:

"Agreement". Section 1–201.
"Bank". Section 1–201.
"Document of title". Section 1–201.
"Gives notification". Section 1–201.
"Honor". Section 1–201.
"Person". Section 1–201.

§ 5–104. Formal Requirements; Signing.

(1) Except as otherwise required in subsection (1)(c) of Section 5–102 on scope, no particular form of phrasing is required for a credit. A credit must be in writing and signed by the issuer and a confirmation must be in writing and signed by the confirming bank. A modification of the terms of a credit or confirmation must be signed by the issuer or confirming bank.

(2) A telegram may be a sufficient signed writing if it identifies its sender by an authorized authentication. The authentication may be in code and the authorized naming of the issuer in an advice of credit is a sufficient signing.

Official Comment

Prior Uniform Statutory Provision: None.

Purposes:

1. Subsection (1) is to make clear that, except for the statement or title required by Section 5–102(1)(c) to bring certain transactions within the scope of this Article, no particular form need be followed; it is sufficient that the credit is in writing and signed by the issuer. The subsection also states that any modification is subject to the same requirements of signing

and writing. Compare Section 2-209(3) on sale of goods. Questions of mistake, waiver or estoppel are left to supplementary principles of law. See Section 1-103.

2. Subsection (2), although perhaps unnecessary in view of the definition of "signed" in Section 1-201, is inserted here to make certain that code and authorized naming of an issuer is a sufficient signing. These forms of signing are so customary that their explicit inclusion is useful to eliminate all controversy on the point.

Cross References:

Point 1: Sections 5-102, 2-209, and 1-103.

Point 2: Section 1-201.

Definitional Cross References:

"Confirming bank". Section 5-103.
"Credit". Section 5-103.
"Issuer". Section 5-103.
"Signed". Section 1-201.
"Telegram". Section 1-201.
"Term". Section 1-201.
"Writing". Section 1-201.

§ 5-105. Consideration.

No consideration is necessary to establish a credit or to enlarge or otherwise modify its terms.

Official Comment

Prior Uniform Statutory Provision: None.

Purposes:

It is not to be expected that a financial institution will engage its credit without some form of expected remuneration. But it is not expected that the beneficiary will know what the issuer's remuneration was, or whether in fact there was any identifiable remuneration in a given case. And it would be extraordinarily difficult for the beneficiary to *prove* the issuer's remuneration. This section dispenses with such proof.

Definitional Cross References:

"Credit". Section 5-103.
"Terms". Section 1-201.

§ 5-106. Time and Effect of Establishment of Credit.

(1) Unless otherwise agreed a credit is established

(a) as regards the customer as soon as a letter of credit is sent to him or the letter of credit or an authorized written advice of its issuance is sent to the beneficiary; and

(b) as regards the beneficiary when he receives a letter of credit or an authorized written advice of its issuance.

(2) Unless otherwise agreed once an irrevocable credit is established as regards the customer it can be modified or revoked only with the consent of the customer and once it is established as regards the beneficiary it can be modified or revoked only with his consent.

(3) Unless otherwise agreed after a revocable credit is established it may be modified or revoked by the issuer without notice to or consent from the customer or beneficiary.

(4) Notwithstanding any modification or revocation of a revocable credit any person authorized to honor or negotiate under the terms of the original credit is entitled to reimbursement for or honor of any draft or demand for payment duly honored or negotiated before receipt of notice of the modifica-

tion or revocation and the issuer in turn is entitled to reimbursement from its customer.

Official Comment

Prior Uniform Statutory Provision: None.

Purposes:

To define when a letter of credit is established in relation to the customer and the beneficiary, and to set forth for both irrevocable and revocable credits the legal consequences of the fact of establishment.

1. The primary purpose of determining the time of establishment of an irrevocable credit is to determine the point at which the issuer is no longer free to take unilateral action with respect to the cancellation of the credit or modification of its terms. So far as the customer is concerned this point of time is reached when the issuer "sends" (as that term is defined in Section 1–201) the credit or when its authorized agent, the advising bank, sends the advice of the credit to the beneficiary. Since the sending is pursuant to an agreement between the issuer and the customer, it is the issuer's performance of the first stage of the contract and under Section 5–107(4) the risk of transmission is on the customer. The beneficiary, however, cannot rely upon the credit until and unless he receives it. His right to protest to the issuer in the event of cancellation or modification, therefore, turns on receipt. Nothing in this section affects the beneficiary's right to protest the improper nature of the credit or its cancellation (i.e., its non-receipt) as against the customer, who will normally have agreed to have a letter of credit issued in favor of the beneficiary under some underlying contract. See, e.g., Section 2–325(1) on buyer's failure to seasonably furnish an agreed letter of credit pursuant to a sales contract.

2. So far as a revocable letter of credit is concerned, the rules stated in subsections (3) and (4) are intended to show that so far as the customer or beneficiary are concerned establishment of such a credit has no legal significance unless the parties provide otherwise in their contracts with the issuer. The primary significance of the establishment of a revocable letter of credit is the obligation it imposes upon the issuer to innocent third parties who have negotiated or honored drafts drawn under the credit before receiving notice of its cancellation or change. The purpose of this rule is to further the movement of goods which the underlying transaction typically envisages and to preserve the solidity of American credits. As a necessary consequence of the imposition of this duty upon the issuer, a duty of reimbursement of the issuer is placed upon the customer by explicit mention here even though it would fall within the general duty of reimbursement imposed by Section 5–114(3).

Cross References:

Point 1: Sections 5–107, 2–325.
Point 2: Section 5–114.

Definitional Cross References:

"Beneficiary". Section 5–103.
"Credit". Section 5–103.
"Customer". Section 5–103.
"Draft". Section 3–104.
"Honor". Section 1–201.
"Issuer". Section 5–103.
"Notice". Section 1–201.
"Person". Section 1–201.
"Receive notice". Section 1–201.
"Send". Section 1–201.
"Written". Section 1–201.

§ 5–107. Advice of Credit; Confirmation; Error in Statement of Terms.

(1) Unless otherwise specified an advising bank by advising a credit issued by another bank does not assume any obligation to honor drafts drawn or demands for payment made under the credit but it does assume obligation for the accuracy of its own statement.

(2) A confirming bank by confirming a credit becomes directly obligated on the credit to the extent of its confirmation as though it were its issuer and acquires the rights of an issuer.

(3) Even though an advising bank incorrectly advises the terms of a credit it has been authorized to advise the credit is established as against the issuer to the extent of its original terms.

(4) Unless otherwise specified the customer bears as against the issuer all risks of transmission and reasonable translation or interpretation of any message relating to a credit.

Official Comment

Prior Uniform Statutory Provision: None.

Purposes:

1. An "advising bank" is defined in Section 5–103. Subsection (1) of this section states its obligations to transmit accurately but not to honor drafts. The advice may of course not be accurate. The advising bank is responsible for its own error; under subsection (3), however, the issuer is bound to honor only in accordance with the original terms of the credit.

2. A "confirming bank" is defined in Section 5–103. Subsection (2) of this section states its obligations and rights. The obligation, to the extent of the confirmation, is that of an issuer and so too is the right of reimbursement. The most important aspect of this rule is that a beneficiary who has received a confirmed credit has the independent engagements of both the issuer and the confirming bank. A confirming bank may of course be an advising bank so far as the issuer's engagement is concerned but this is rarely of importance because its own engagement if the terms be improperly advised will be to honor in accordance with those terms.

3. Subsection (4) distributes the risks, as between customer and issuer, of errors in transmission and translation by placing them on the customer in the absence of specific agreement to the contrary. See also Section 5–109(1)(b).

Cross References:

Sections 5–103 and 5–109.

Definitional Cross References:

"Advising bank". Section 5–103.
"Bank". Section 1–201.
"Confirming bank". Section 5–103.
"Credit". Section 5–103.
"Customer". Section 5–103.
"Draft". Section 3–104.
"Honor". Section 1–201.
"Issuer". Section 5–103.

§ 5–108. "Notation Credit"; Exhaustion of Credit.

(1) A credit which specifies that any person purchasing or paying drafts drawn or demands for payment made under it must note the amount of the draft or demand on the letter or advice of credit is a "notation credit".

(2) Under a notation credit

(a) a person paying the beneficiary or purchasing a draft or demand for payment from him acquires a right to honor only if the appropriate notation is made and by transferring or forwarding for honor the documents under the credit such a person warrants to the issuer that the notation has been made; and

(b) unless the credit or a signed statement that an appropriate notation has been made accompanies the draft or demand for payment the issuer may delay honor until evidence of notation has been procured which is satisfactory to it but its obligation and that of its customer continue for a reasonable time not exceeding thirty days to obtain such evidence.

(3) If the credit is not a notation credit

(a) the issuer may honor complying drafts or demands for payment presented to it in the order in which they are presented and is discharged pro tanto by honor of any such draft or demand;

(b) as between competing good faith purchasers of complying drafts or demands the person first purchasing has priority over a subsequent purchaser even though the later purchased draft or demand has been first honored.

Official Comment

Prior Uniform Statutory Provision: None.

Purposes:

1. Practice has varied in regard to requiring notation on a letter of credit of the drafts drawn thereunder, and dispute has been rife for more than a century over the effect of failure by a purchaser to make such notations when they are required. The confusion has been due to a failure to distinguish two different types of credit and the different results which flow from each.

Under subsection (3), if an issuer chooses to issue a credit not requiring notation or if the credit is available in portions (see Section 5–110) without requirement of notation the issuer avoids all troubles attendant on any purchaser's failure to make notations, but he also imperils the utility of the credit to a beneficiary by reason of its possible exhaustion before any particular purchaser may have discounted drafts under it, so that there may be no market at all for such drafts. Yet this way of operation becomes useful and desirable at least whenever the credit is "domiciled," i.e., when it is explicitly made available only through one particular named correspondent, who will have his own records of prior drafts.

Subsection (3) expressly protects the issuer under such a credit (almost exactly as in the case of drafts drawn in a set under Section 3–801) in regard to any drafts which he honors in good faith, even though they are in the hands of a party who as against some other purchaser of drafts is not entitled to their proceeds. Similarly, in the last sentence, the rights of successive good faith purchasers are regulated as with drafts in a set.

2. Under subsection (2), on the other hand, the notation machinery is made available where the credit provides for notation in accordance with subsection (1). This is useful particularly where the credit is intended (as a traveler's letter would be) for roving use, but the responsibility is put upon the purchaser to make the appropriate notation on pain of reimbursing the issuer for any loss occasioned by the failure. The provision in regard to delay of honor while evidence of notation is being procured is novel in the law, but is believed to be a necessary addition first, to protect the issuer, and second, to educate purchasers.

Subsection (2)(a) avoids a difficult question of conflict of laws by making the obligation to note a condition of the credit itself, governed, therefore, by the law which controls the issue of the credit.

Cross References:

Sections 3–801 and 5–110.

Definitional Cross References:

"Beneficiary". Section 5–103.
"Credit". Section 5–103.
"Customer". Section 5–103.

"Document". Section 5-103.
"Draft". Section 3-104.
"Good faith". Section 1-201.
"Honor". Section 1-201.
"Issuer". Section 5-103.
"Person". Section 1-201.
"Purchase". Section 1-201.
"Purchaser". Section 1-201.
"Rights". Section 1-201.
"Signed". Section 1-201.

§ 5-109. Issuer's Obligation to Its Customer.

(1) An issuer's obligation to its customer includes good faith and observance of any general banking usage but unless otherwise agreed does not include liability or responsibility

(a) for performance of the underlying contract for sale or other transaction between the customer and the beneficiary; or

(b) for any act or omission of any person other than itself or its own branch or for loss or destruction of a draft, demand or document in transit or in the possession of others; or

(c) based on knowledge or lack of knowledge of any usage of any particular trade.

(2) An issuer must examine documents with care so as to ascertain that on their face they appear to comply with the terms of the credit but unless otherwise agreed assumes no liability or responsibility for the genuineness, falsification or effect of any document which appears on such examination to be regular on its face.

(3) A non-bank issuer is not bound by any banking usage of which it has no knowledge.

Official Comment

Prior Uniform Statutory Provision: None.

Purposes:

1. The extent of the issuer's obligation to its customer is based upon the agreement between the two. Like all agreements within the Code, that agreement is the bargain of the parties in fact as defined in Section 1-201(3) and includes the obligation of good faith imposed by Section 1-203 and the observance of any course of dealing or usage of trade made applicable by Section 1-205. Subsection (1) of this section states, as a particular application of those general rules, the issuer's standard obligation of good faith and observance of general banking usage. Disclaimer of the obligation of good faith is governed by Section 1-102(3); conflict between express terms and a usage otherwise applicable is governed by Section 1-205(4).

Subsection (1) also clarifies the areas over which the issuer assumes no liability or responsibility except as the agreement of the parties may indicate the contrary. Paragraph (a) rests on the assumptions that the issuer has had no control over the making of the underlying contract or over the selection of the beneficiary, and that the issuer receives compensation for a payment service rather than for a guaranty of performance. The customer will normally have direct recourse against the beneficiary if performance fails, whereas the issuer will have such recourse only by assignment of or in a proper case subrogation to the rights of the customer.

Paragraph (b) also rests in part on the assumption that the issuer has not selected the other persons who may be involved in the transaction. Even though this assumption fails, however, as where the issuer selects the advising bank, the customer by entering the underlying transaction has assumed the risks inherent in it, including the risk of loss or destruction of the papers involved. The allocation of such risks between the parties to the underlying transaction is a proper subject for agreement between them, and the small charge for the issuance of a letter of credit ordinarily indicates that the issuer assumes minimum risks as against its customer. For comparable reasons Section 5-107(4) puts risks of transmission and translation upon the customer.

Paragraph (c) again emphasizes that normally an issuer performs a banking and not a trade function. This paragraph makes an exception to Section 1-205(3), giving effect to usages of which the parties "are or should be aware." The comparable provision for non-bank issuers in subsection (3) of this section is limited to unknown banking usages and is thus merely a definition of a particular type of case not included by the words "should be aware" in Section 1-205(3).

2. Subsection (2) states the basic obligation of the issuer to examine with care the documents required under the credit. Under Section 1-102(3) this obligation cannot be disclaimed but standards of performance can be determined by agreement if not manifestly unreasonable. There are not infrequent cases in which both parties understand that peculiar circumstances make any check-up on some particular type of document impossible and it is agreed that the issuer may take it "as presented"—so, e.g., export licenses in politically disturbed conditions, or "shipping documents" when no document in standard or regular form can be procured. These agreements will be controlling provided they are not manifestly unreasonable.

The purpose of the examination is to determine whether the documents appear regular on their face. The fact that the documents may be false or fraudulent or lacking in legal effect is not one for which the issuer is bound to examine. His duty is limited to apparent regularity on the face of the documents. The duties, privileges and rights of an issuer who has received documents which are regular on their face but are in fact improper because forged or fraudulent are dealt with in Section 5-114.

Cross References:

Point 1: Sections 1-102, 1-201, 1-203, 1-205, 5-107.

Point 2: Sections 1-102, 5-114.

Definitional Cross References:

"Bank". Section 1-201.
"Beneficiary". Section 5-103.
"Branch". Section 1-201.
"Contract". Section 1-201.
"Contract for sale". Section 2-106.
"Credit". Section 5-103.
"Customer". Section 5-103.
"Document". Section 5-103.
"Draft". Section 3-104.
"Genuine". Section 1-201.
"Good faith". Section 1-201.
"Issuer". Section 5-103.
"Knowledge". Section 1-201.
"Person". Section 1-201.
"Term". Section 1-201.

§ 5-110. Availability of Credit in Portions; Presenter's Reservation of Lien or Claim.

(1) Unless otherwise specified a credit may be used in portions in the discretion of the beneficiary.

(2) Unless otherwise specified a person by presenting a documentary draft or demand for payment under a credit relinquishes upon its honor all claims to the documents and a person by transferring such draft or demand or causing such presentment authorizes such relinquishment. An explicit reservation of claim makes the draft or demand non-complying.

Official Comment

Prior Uniform Statutory Provision: None.

Purposes:

1. The beneficiary may desire to draw more than one draft under the credit, each draft accompanied, for instance, by documents evidencing a single shipment under the underlying sales contract. Subsection (1) makes clear that unless otherwise specified he may do so. Of course, if he does, each draft and its accompanying documents must satisfy the terms of the credit and their total must not exceed its amount. See comment to Section 5–108(3) on exhaustion of a credit on the rule governing the situation in which the total drafts drawn do total more than the maximum amount of the credit.

2. The entire purpose of the usual letter of credit transaction, from the customer's point of view, is to induce the beneficiary to deliver to him through the issuer the documents described in the credit. The buying customer wants the goods, and arranges the transaction in order to get the documents controlling the goods. Therefore, upon honor of the draft, the documents must be delivered free of claims even though the letter of credit is not for the full invoice price and any reservation of claim makes the draft non-complying. A beneficiary who wishes to prevent such delivery must do so by agreement with the customer in the underlying contract and must treat the failure to provide a sufficient letter of credit as a breach of that contract (Section 2–325). So far as the issuer's duty to honor is concerned, the terms of the letter of credit are controlling and the rule of subsection (2) is applicable.

Cross References:

Point 1: Section 5–108.
Point 2: Sections 2–325, 5–114.

Definitional Cross References:

"Beneficiary". Section 5–103.
"Credit". Section 5–103.
"Documentary draft". Section 5–103.
"Document". Section 5–103.
"Draft". Section 3–104.
"Honor". Section 1–201.
"Person". Section 1–201.

§ 5–111. Warranties on Transfer and Presentment.

(1) Unless otherwise agreed the beneficiary by transferring or presenting a documentary draft or demand for payment warrants to all interested parties that the necessary conditions of the credit have been complied with. This is in addition to any warranties arising under Articles 3, 4, 7 and 8.

(2) Unless otherwise agreed a negotiating, advising, confirming, collecting or issuing bank presenting or transferring a draft or demand for payment under a credit warrants only the matters warranted by a collecting bank under Article 4 and any such bank transferring a document warrants only the matters warranted by an intermediary under Articles 7 and 8.

Official Comment

Prior Uniform Statutory Provision: None.

Purpose:

The purpose of this section is to state the peculiar warranty of performance made by a beneficiary and to make clear the intermediary character of the persons moving the documents from the beneficiary to the customer. The beneficiary's warranty of compliance with the conditions of the credit in subsection (1) is expressly extended to all interested parties unless agreed to the contrary. So far as the draft or the relevant documents are concerned, the beneficiary's warranties are usually those of an ordinary transferor or indorser for value although varying circumstances may alter this. The usual warranties of an intermediary, listed in subsection (2), are primarily its own good faith and authority. See also Comment to Section 5-114(2).

Cross References:

Sections 3-417, 4-207, 7-507, 7-508, 8-306.

Definitional Cross References:

"Advising bank". Section 5-103.
"Bank". Section 1-201.
"Beneficiary". Section 5-103.
"Collecting bank". Section 4-105.
"Confirming bank". Section 5-103.
"Credit". Section 5-103.
"Documentary draft". Section 5-103.
"Draft". Section 3-104.
"Party". Section 1-201.

§ 5-112. Time Allowed for Honor or Rejection; Withholding Honor or Rejection by Consent; "Presenter".

(1) A bank to which a documentary draft or demand for payment is presented under a credit may without dishonor of the draft, demand or credit

(a) defer honor until the close of the third banking day following receipt of the documents; and

(b) further defer honor if the presenter has expressly or impliedly consented thereto.

Failure to honor within the time here specified constitutes dishonor of the draft or demand and of the credit [except as otherwise provided in subsection (4) of Section 5-114 on conditional payment].

Note: *The bracketed language in the last sentence of subsection (1) should be included only if the optional provisions of Section 5-114(4) and (5) are included.*

(2) Upon dishonor the bank may unless otherwise instructed fulfill its duty to return the draft or demand and the documents by holding them at the disposal of the presenter and sending him an advice to that effect.

(3) "Presenter" means any person presenting a draft or demand for payment for honor under a credit even though that person is a confirming bank or other correspondent which is acting under an issuer's authorization.

Official Comment

Prior Uniform Statutory Provision: None.

Purposes:

1. A bank called on to honor drafts under a credit must examine the accompanying documents with care. See Section 5-109(2). That may take time. Subsection (1) of this section therefore allows a longer period than in the case of ordinary drafts (Section 3-506) for the decision. The language in the postamble to subsection (1) particularizes for letters of credit the general rule on what constitutes dishonor for negotiable instruments (Section 3-507) and makes it clear that not only the draft but the credit is dishonored. If the particular draft is for a portion of the credit only, its wrongful dishonor is anticipatory repudiation of the entire credit and the beneficiary may proceed under Section 5-115(2) as well as 5-115(1).

2. Many letters of credit involve transactions in international trade and include as required documents the documents of title controlling the possession of goods on their way to the place of issuance of the credit. The ordinary rule requiring physical return of dishonored documenta-

ry drafts (Section 4–302) would therefore frequently work commercial hardship on the mercantile parties to the transaction; resale of the goods might be more difficult if the controlling documents of title were not available at the place of arrival of the goods. Subsection (2) therefore expressly permits the issuer to retain the documents as bailee for the presenter if it advises the presenter of its retention for that purpose. Compare Sections 4–202(1)(b), 4–503 and 4–504 on the duties of presenting banks.

3. The definition of "presenter" is to make clear that the term may include a bank which has rights in the documentary draft or which is in one sense the agent of the issuer. Such a bank may nevertheless give consent under subsection (1), and the advice authorized in subsection (2) may be sent to it.

4. Insofar as the banks involved may also be depositary, collecting or paying banks, Article 4 is applicable. Article 3 applies to the extent that a negotiable instrument is involved.

Cross References:

Point 1: Sections 3–506, 3–507, 5–109, 5–114 and 5–115.

Point 2: Sections 4–202, 4–302, 4–503 and 4–504.

Point 4: Articles 3 and 4.

Definitional Cross References:

"Bank". Section 1–201.
"Confirming bank". Section 5–103.
"Credit". Section 5–103.
"Documentary draft". Section 5–103.
"Draft". Section 3–104.
"Honor". Section 1–201.
"Issuer". Section 5–103.
"Send". Section 1–201.

§ 5–113. Indemnities.

(1) A bank seeking to obtain (whether for itself or another) honor, negotiation or reimbursement under a credit may give an indemnity to induce such honor, negotiation or reimbursement.

(2) An indemnity agreement inducing honor, negotiation or reimbursement

(a) unless otherwise explicitly agreed applies to defects in the documents but not in the goods; and

(b) unless a longer time is explicitly agreed expires at the end of ten business days following receipt of the documents by the ultimate customer unless notice of objection is sent before such expiration date. The ultimate customer may send notice of objection to the person from whom he received the documents and any bank receiving such notice is under a duty to send notice to its transferor before its midnight deadline.

Official Comment

Prior Uniform Statutory Provision: None.

Purposes:

1. A draft and accompanying documents may almost comply with the terms of the credit, but fail in some particular. The issuer is then not obligated to honor the draft, but it may be willing to do so if properly indemnified against the particular defect. Subsection (1) makes clear that it is proper for a bank seeking payment, acceptance, negotiation or reimbursement under the credit to give such indemnities, and that doing so is a proper part of the business of banking and therefore not ultra vires.

2. Subsection (2)(a) limits the agreed indemnity to defects in the documents, since under Section 5–109(1)(a) the issuer is ordinarily not responsible for perfor-

mance of the underlying transaction. The parties are free to agree further on the scope of the indemnity, but the agreement must be explicit, since an indemnity against defects in the goods would be most unusual.

3. Subsection (2)(b) makes it clear that the indemnity in the absence of explicit agreement for a longer time continues for ten days after the receipt of the document by the ultimate customer, i.e., the customer who is a party to the underlying transaction. This ten day period may not be shortened. If the customer fails to send notice of objection within the period, he loses his right to object and the need for the indemnity disappears. Compare Section 2-605(2). Thus indemnitors are free of the possibility of unknown long-continuing contingent liability, a danger under existing law.

4. The question whether a particular banking usage may require honor of documentary drafts accompanied by indemnities for particular defects goes to the meaning of the terms of the credit and is beyond the scope of this section. See, e.g., Dixon, Irmaos & Cia, Ltda., v. Chase Nat. Bank of City of New York, 144 F.2d 759 (2d Cir., 1944). If by virtue of indemnities and usage the credit is complied with, the rights of the customer rest on the implications of the usage rather than on breach of the issuer's duty under this Article. Even so, the policy of this section and its terms require notice before the expiration date.

Cross References:

Point 2: Section 5-109.
Point 3: Section 2-605.
Point 4: Section 1-205.

Definitional Cross References:

"Bank". Section 1-201.
"Credit". Section 5-103.
"Customer". Section 5-103.
"Documents". Section 5-103.
"Honor". Section 1-201.
"Midnight deadline". Section 4-104.
"Person". Section 1-201.
"Send". Section 1-201.

§ 5-114. Issuer's Duty and Privilege to Honor; Right to Reimbursement.

(1) An issuer must honor a draft or demand for payment which complies with the terms of the relevant credit regardless of whether the goods or documents conform to the underlying contract for sale or other contract between the customer and the beneficiary. The issuer is not excused from honor of such a draft or demand by reason of an additional general term that all documents must be satisfactory to the issuer, but an issuer may require that specified documents must be satisfactory to it.

(2) Unless otherwise agreed when documents appear on their face to comply with the terms of a credit but a required document does not in fact conform to the warranties made on negotiation or transfer of a document of title (Section 7-507) or of a certificated security (Section 8-108) or is forged or fraudulent or there is fraud in the transaction:

(a) the issuer must honor the draft or demand for payment if honor is demanded by a negotiating bank or other holder of the draft or demand which has taken the draft or demand under the credit and under circumstances which would make it a holder in due course (Section 3-302) and in an appropriate case would make it a person to whom a document of title has been duly negotiated (Section 7-502) or a bona fide purchaser of a certificated security (Section 8-302); and

(b) in all other cases as against its customer, an issuer acting in good faith may honor the draft or demand for payment despite notification from the customer of fraud, forgery or other defect not apparent on the face of the documents but a court of appropriate jurisdiction may enjoin such honor.

(3) Unless otherwise agreed an issuer which has duly honored a draft or demand for payment is entitled to immediate reimbursement of any payment made under the credit and to be put in effectively available funds not later than the day before maturity of any acceptance made under the credit.

[(4) When a credit provides for payment by the issuer on receipt of notice that the required documents are in the possession of a correspondent or other agent of the issuer

(a) any payment made on receipt of such notice is conditional; and

(b) the issuer may reject documents which do not comply with the credit if it does so within three banking days following its receipt of the documents; and

(c) in the event of such rejection, the issuer is entitled by charge back or otherwise to return of the payment made.]

[(5) In the case covered by subsection (4) failure to reject documents within the time specified in sub-paragraph (b) constitutes acceptance of the documents and makes the payment final in favor of the beneficiary.]

Note: *Subsections (4) and (5) are bracketed as optional. If they are included the bracketed language in the last sentence of Section 5–112(1) should also be included.*

As amended in 1977 and 1994.

See Appendix XII for material relating to changes made in text in 1994.

Official Comment

Prior Uniform Statutory Provision: None.

Purposes:

To define the areas in which the issuer must honor drafts or demands for payment under a credit and those in which he has an option to do so and to make explicit the customer's duty of reimbursement.

1. The letter of credit is essentially a contract between the issuer and the beneficiary and is recognized by this Article as independent of the underlying contract between the customer and the beneficiary (See Section 5–109 and Comment thereto). In view of this independent nature of the letter of credit engagement, the issuer is under a duty to honor the drafts or demands for payment which in fact comply with the terms of the credit without reference to their compliance with the terms of the underlying contract. This is stated in subsection (1). Attempts by the issuer to reserve a right to dishonor by including a clause that all documents must be satisfactory to itself are declared invalid as essentially repugnant to an irrevocable letter of credit. Such a reservation can be made by issuing a revocable credit. See Section 5–106. Particular documents, such as bills of lading or inspection or weight certificates can, of course, be required to be satisfactory to the issuer. The duty of the issuer to honor where there is factual compliance with the terms of the credit is also independent of any instructions from its customer once the credit has been issued and received by the beneficiary. See Section 5–106.

2. Documents, however, may appear regular on their face and apparently conforming to the credit whereas in fact they are forged or fraudulent or in other respects non-conforming to the warranties which arise under other Articles of the Code on their transfer or negotiation. Since the issuer's duties to its customer are limited to examination of the documents with care (Section 5–109) and since it is important to preserve both the independent character of the issuer's engagement and the reasonable reliance on that engagement of persons dealing with papers regular on their face and in apparent compliance with the terms of the credit, subsection (2)(a) includes as an area in which the issuer's duty to honor exists cases in which persons have acted in a manner which would make them the equivalent of holders in due course under Article 3 or, where relevant, persons to whom documents have been duly negotiated under Article 7 or bona fide purchasers of certificated securities under Article 8. The risk of the original bad-faith action of the beneficiary is thus thrown upon the customer who selected him rather than upon innocent third parties or the issuer. So, too, is the risk of fraud in the transaction placed upon the customer.

When, however, no innocent third parties as defined in subsection (a) are involved the issuer is no longer under a duty to honor; but since these matters frequently involve situations in which the determination of the fact of the non-conformance may be difficult or time-consuming, the issuer if he acts in good faith is given the privilege of honoring the draft as against its customer, that is to say, with a right of reimbursement against him. The issuer may, however, refuse honor. In the event of honor, an action by the customer against the beneficiary will lie by virtue of either the underlying contract or Section 5–111(1) of this Article. In the event of dishonor, if the presenter is a person who has parted with value, he also may recover against the beneficiary under Section 5–111(1).

3. Subsection (3) represents the standard form for reimbursement. The words "duly honored" include not only situations where the issuer has honored because it was his duty to do so but also where he was privileged to do so as in subsection (2)(b) or has done so as under Section 5–106(4).

4. Optional subsections (4) and (5) are for the purpose of clarifying a situation which has arisen under the currency restrictions of a few nations and in which payment is required to be made under the credit before opportunity exists to examine the documents. The Article resolves this situation by making clear that the payment is conditional in nature and may be reversed by subsequent timely discovery of defects in the documents.

Cross References:

Point 1: Sections 5–106 and 5–109.
Point 2: Sections 5–106, 5–109, 5–111 and Articles 3, 7 and 8.
Point 3: Section 5–106.

Definitional Cross References:

"Bank". Section 1–201.
"Beneficiary". Section 5–103.
"Contract". Section 1–201.
"Contract for sale". Section 2–106.
"Credit". Section 5–103.
"Customer". Section 5–103.
"Document". Section 5–103.
"Document of title". Section 1–201.
"Draft". Section 3–104.
"Good faith". Section 1–201.
"Holder". Section 1–201.
"Honor". Section 1–201.
"Issuer". Section 5–103.
"Notification". Section 1–201.
"Receives notice". Section 1–201.
"Security". Section 8–102.
"Term". Section 1–201.

§ 5–115. Remedy for Improper Dishonor or Anticipatory Repudiation.

(1) When an issuer wrongfully dishonors a draft or demand for payment presented under a credit the person entitled to honor has with respect to any

documents the rights of a person in the position of a seller (Section 2-707) and may recover from the issuer the face amount of the draft or demand together with incidental damages under Section 2-710 on seller's incidental damages and interest but less any amount realized by resale or other use or disposition of the subject matter of the transaction. In the event no resale or other utilization is made the documents, goods or other subject matter involved in the transaction must be turned over to the issuer on payment of judgment.

(2) When an issuer wrongfully cancels or otherwise repudiates a credit before presentment of a draft or demand for payment drawn under it the beneficiary has the rights of a seller after anticipatory repudiation by the buyer under Section 2-610 if he learns of the repudiation in time reasonably to avoid procurement of the required documents. Otherwise the beneficiary has an immediate right of action for wrongful dishonor.

Official Comment

Prior Uniform Statutory Provision: None.

Purposes:

1. Subsection (1) states the rights of a person entitled to honor, both with respect to any documents and against the issuer, when there is wrongful dishonor. Whether dishonor is wrongful and whether a particular person is entitled to honor depend on the terms of the credit and on the provisions of this Article, particularly Section 5-114 on the issuer's duty to honor and Section 5-116 on transfer and assignment.

2. Subsection (2) states the rights of the beneficiary upon repudiation of the credit, both against the issuer and with respect to any documents or goods. Note that wrongful dishonor of a draft for a portion of the credit is dishonor of the credit under Section 5-112(1), and makes applicable subsection (2) of this section as well as subsection (1).

3. Both subsections are limited to irrevocable credits. Since under Section 5-106(3) revocable credits may be modified or revoked without notice to the customer or the beneficiary, rights against the issuer like those here provided can hardly arise under them. The rights of innocent third persons under revocable credits are governed by Section 5-106(4) rather than by this section.

Cross References:

Point 1: Sections 2-707, 2-710, 5-114 and 5-116.

Point 2: Sections 2-610, 2-611, 2-703 through 2-706, and 5-112.

Point 3: Section 5-106.

Definitional Cross References:

"Action". Section 1-201.
"Beneficiary". Section 5-103.
"Credit". Section 5-103.
"Document". Section 5-103.
"Draft". Section 3-104.
"Issuer". Section 5-103.
"Person". Section 1-201.
"Rights". Section 2-201.

§ 5-116. Transfer and Assignment.

(1) The right to draw under a credit can be transferred or assigned only when the credit is expressly designated as transferable or assignable.

(2) Even though the credit specifically states that it is nontransferable or nonassignable the beneficiary may before performance of the conditions of the credit assign his right to proceeds. Such an assignment is an assignment of an account under Article 9 on Second Transactions and is governed by that Article except that

(a) the assignment is ineffective until the letter of credit or advice of credit is delivered to the assignee which delivery constitutes perfection of the security interest under Article 9; and

(b) the issuer may honor drafts or demands for payment drawn under the credit until it receives a notification of the assignment signed by the beneficiary which reasonably identifies the credit involved in the assignment and contains a request to pay the assignee; and

(c) after what reasonably appears to be such a notification has been received the issuer may without dishonor refuse to accept or pay even to a person otherwise entitled to honor until the letter of credit or advice of credit is exhibited to the issuer.

(3) Except where the beneficiary has effectively assigned his right to draw or his right to proceeds, nothing in this section limits his right to transfer or negotiate drafts or demands drawn under the credit.

As amended in 1972.

Official Comment

Prior Uniform Statutory Provision: None.

Purposes:

1. The situation involved is typified by that of an exporter who has made a contract for sale with a foreign buyer and is beneficiary of a letter of credit initiated by the buyer, especially where the subject matter involves goods still to be manufactured. The exporter is frequently in need of the wherewithal not only to finance payment to his supplier but to assure the latter against cancellation of the order during the process of manufacture. For this purpose assignment of the exporter's rights under the letter of credit is frequently desirable.

Since, however, there is general confusion of thought as to the meaning of "assignment or transfer of a credit," the law remains uncertain. If "assignment of the credit" includes delegation of performance of the conditions under the credit then the initiating customer, who in many cases has put his faith in performance or supervision of performance by a beneficiary of established reputation, may be deprived of real and intended security. See Comment to Section 2-210 on the comparable situation as to the sales contract. On the other hand, all "negotiation credits" involve a transfer of the rights of the beneficiary by way of negotiations of the draft and such transfer involves no important loss of the initiating party's intended safety. Meanwhile, the exceedingly useful institution of "back to back" credits, in which an American bank issues a credit with the exporter as the initiating customer and the exporter's supplier as the beneficiary, is dangerous for the banker unless he can secure in advance an effective assignment from the exporter of the latter's rights under the initial credit issued on behalf of his foreign buyer. Against this background, the section is drawn.

2. Subsection (1) requires the beneficiary's signature on drafts drawn under the credit unless it is expressly designated as assignable or transferable. If it is so designated, the normal rules of assignment apply and both the right to draw and the performance of the beneficiary can be transferred, subject to the beneficiary's continuing liability, if any, for the nature of the performance.

3. Subsection (2) makes clear that to safeguard among other things the letter of credit "back to back" practice, the assignability of proceeds in advance of performance cannot be prohibited in advance of performance. In this respect the letter of credit is treated like any other

contract calling for money to be earned. See Section 9–318 generally and Section 2–210 as to sales contracts. But the special nature of the letter of credit as evidence of the right to proceeds is recognized by the additional requirement of delivery of the letter to the assignee as a condition precedent to the perfection of the assignment. Similarly, the fact that letters of credit normally require presentation of drafts or demands for payment which are drawn under it and that as a result notice of assignment of proceeds can exist simultaneously with a draft payable by order or indorsement to either the beneficiary or another third person leads to the necessity for permitting an issuer to protect itself against double payment by requiring exhibition of the letter or advice of credit.

4. Subsection (3) makes clear that the section has no application to the normal case of negotiation of a draft or the transfer of a demand for payment unless effective assignment under the section has taken place.

Cross References:

Point 1: Section 2–210.

Point 3: Sections 2–210 and 9–318 and Article 9.

Definitional Cross References:

"Accept". Section 3–410.
"Account". Section 9–106.
"Beneficiary". Section 5–103.
"Credit". Section 5–103.
"Draft". Section 3–104.
"Honor". Section 1–201.
"Issuer". Section 5–103.
"Receive notification". Section 1–201.

§ 5–117. Insolvency of Bank Holding Funds for Documentary Credit.

(1) Where an issuer or an advising or confirming bank or a bank which has for a customer procured issuance of a credit by another bank becomes insolvent before final payment under the credit and the credit is one to which this Article is made applicable by paragraphs (a) or (b) of Section 5–102(1) on scope, the receipt or allocation of funds or collateral to secure or meet obligations under the credit shall have the following results:

(a) to the extent of any funds or collateral turned over after or before the insolvency as indemnity against or specifically for the purpose of payment of drafts or demands for payment drawn under the designated credit, the drafts or demands are entitled to payment in preference over depositors or other general creditors of the issuer or bank; and

(b) on expiration of the credit or surrender of the beneficiary's rights under it unused any person who has given such funds or collateral is similarly entitled to return thereof; and

(c) a charge to a general or current account with a bank if specifically consented to for the purpose of indemnity against or payment of drafts or demands for payment drawn under the designated credit falls under the same rules as if the funds had been drawn out in cash and then turned over with specific instructions.

(2) After honor or reimbursement under this section the customer or other person for whose account the insolvent bank has acted is entitled to receive the documents involved.

Official Comment

Prior Uniform Statutory Provision: None.

Purposes:

A bank which issues a letter of credit acts as a principal, not as agent for its customer, and engages its own credit. But the resulting liability is not like that to its depositors, and the security and indemnity furnished by the customer against it and the documents which it receives on honor of complying drafts are not like its own investments.

The typical letter of credit transaction facilitates the movement of goods. The bank's credit is engaged, but it expects to be put in funds by its customer before it makes disbursements, or to be reimbursed immediately afterwards. And everybody understands that the documents received upon honor of complying drafts are to be turned over to the customer at once when he makes reimbursement or signs trust receipts. Only the bank's commission, if the transaction is completed, will enter the bank's general assets and join the other backing of its deposit liabilities.

It is therefore proper, when insolvency occurs before the letter of credit transaction is completed, to regard both the outstanding liabilities, the security held and funds provided to indemnify against those liabilities, and the related drafts and documents, as separate from deposit liabilities and from general assets, and to deal with them as separate. To do so carries out the original purpose, which is to facilitate the underlying mercantile transaction, and does no wrong to the bank's depositors and other general creditors.

This section states appropriate rules to carry out these principles. The section is limited to transactions under Section 5-102(1)(a) and (b) to prevent abuse in situations where the commercial purpose of facilitating the movement of goods, securities or the like may be lacking.

Cross Reference:

Compare Section 4–214, and the Comment thereto.

Definitional Cross References:

"Advising Bank". Section 5–103.
"Bank". Section 1–201.
"Beneficiary". Section 5–103.
"Confirming Bank". Section 5–103.
"Credit". Section 5–103.
"Customer". Section 5–103.
"Document". Section 5–103.
"Draft". Section 3–104.
"Honor". Section 1–201.
"Insolvent". Section 1–201.
"Issuer". Section 5–103.
"Person". Section 1–201.

INDEX TO
UNIFORM COMMERCIAL CODE

References are to sections

†